KITTO'S
DAILY BIBLE
ILLUSTRATIONS

KITTO'S DAILY BIBLE ILLUSTRATIONS

Studies of Key Characters and
Problem Passages in the Scriptures

by
JOHN KITTO

Volume One: GENESIS - ESTHER

KREGEL PUBLICATIONS
Grand Rapids, Michigan 49501

Kitto's Daily Bible Illustrations by John Kitto.
Copyright © 1981 by Kregel Publications, a division of Kregel, Inc. All rights reserved.

Library of Congress Cataloging in Publication Data
Kitto, John, 1804-1854.
  Kitto's Daily Bible Illustrations.

  Reprint of the 1901 ed. published by W. Collins,
London.
  Includes indexes.
  1. Bible—History of Biblical events.
2. Family—Prayer-books and devotions—
English.   3. Devotional calendars.   I. Title.
BS635.K54   1981   220.6   80-8069
ISBN 0-8254-3026-9   AACR 1

Printed in the United States of America

CONTENTS
(Volume One)

LIFE OF JOHN KITTO

DAILY BIBLE ILLUSTRATIONS

CONTENTS

ILLUSTRATIONS

(Volume One)

SCRIPTURE REFERENCES

As the Contents of the Volumes follow the order of the Scripture History, and can thus be readily referred to, only such passages are inserted in the following Index as are out of their natural order, or are incidentally illustrated.

GENESIS

Reference	Vol.	Page
Chap. i. Ver. 1,	i.	151
i. 7,	i.	156
i. 9,	i.	157
i. 26,	i.	163
iii. 15,	i.	173
iv. 7,	i.	188
iv. 24,	i.	486
iv. 25,	ii.	131
v. 29,	ii.	131
vi. 6,	i.	511
vi. 9,	ii.	24
vii. 4,	i.	486
ix. 3,	i.	166
ix. 4,	i.	344
ix. 6,	i.	164
x. 7,	ii.	35
x. 13, 14,	i.	565
x. 17,	ii.	307
x. 23,	ii.	20
x. 28,	ii.	35
xi. 1,	i.	229
xi. 7,	i.	230
xii. 5,	ii.	723
xii. 7,	i.	478
xii. 7, 8,	i.	868
xii. 16,	ii.	19
xiii. 5,	i.	240
xiii. 6,	i.	238
xiii. 10,	i.	262
xiii. 14, 15,	i.	478
xiii. 17,	i.	478
xiii. 18,	i.	270
xiv. 16,	ii.	723
xv. 2,	i.	372
xv. 13-16,	i.	478
xv. 15,	i.	287
xv. 18,	i.	330
xvi. 12,	ii.	75
xvii. 12,	i.	248
xviii. 4,	i.	240, 345
xviii. 4-8,	i.	240
xviii. 17,	ii.	102
xxi. 6,	i.	256
xxi. 16,	i.	928
xxi. 31,	i.	485
xxi. 33,	i.	240
xxi. 33,	i.	868
xxii. 2, 4,	i.	868
xxii. 3,	ii.	35
xxii. 14,	i.	373
xxii. 21,	ii.	20
xxiv. 67,	i.	240
xxv. 3,	ii.	35
xxviii. 18, 22,	ii.	311
xxix. 14, 15,	i.	255
xxix. 15,	ii.	723
Chap. xxxi. Ver. 33,.	i.	240
xxxi. 34, 35,	i.	240
xxxi. 39,	ii.	398
xxxi. 47, 48,	i.	506
xxxi. 54,	i.	868
xxxii. 30,	ii.	510
xxxii. 32,	i.	615
xxxiii. 17,	i.	239
xxxiii. 19,	ii.	129
xxxvi. 28,	ii.	20
xxxviii,	i.	593
xxxix. 14,	i.	347
xl. 15,	i.	313, 347
xli. 8,	i.	310
xli. 12,	i.	347
xli. 14,	i.	317
xli. 45,	i.	312
xli. 48,	i.	503
xlii. 15,	ii.	724
xlii. 23,	i.	265
xliii. 3,	ii.	724
xliii. 32,	i.	347
xlv. 22,	i.	333
xlvii. 23,	i.	248
xlix, 3, 4,	i.	286
xlix. 27,	i.	575
l. 10,	i.	486

EXODUS

Reference	Vol.	Page
i. 10,	i.	347
i. 16,	i.	347
ii. 5-7,	i.	316
iii. 18,	i.	347
v. 7-16,	i.	359
v. 12,	i.	359
vii. 5,	i.	373
vii. 17,	i.	373
viii. 22,	i.	379
viii. 26,	i.	334
xii. 9, 10,	i.	391
xii. 38,	i.	431
xiii. 18,	i.	395
xiv. 2,	i.	890
xiv. 6, 7,	i.	397
xvi. 31,	i.	407
xix. 12,	i.	622
xx. 4,	i.	829
xxii. 13,	ii.	398
xxii. 30,	i.	486
xxv. 18-22,	i.	830
xxvi. 31-37,	i.	240
xxix. 37,	i.	486
xxx. 11-16,	ii.	591
xxx. 12,	i.	327
xxxiv. 13,	i.	269, 868
xxxiv. 16,	i.	998
Chap. xxxv. Ver. 26,	i.	240
xxxvi. 8, 19, 34,	i.	622
xxxviii. 8,	i.	828

LEVITICUS

Reference	Vol.	Page
iv. 32-35,	ii.	517
vii. 26, 27,	i.	344
x.,	i.	425
xi. 5,	ii.	173
xiii.,	ii.	44
xiii. 44-46,	ii.	47
xvi. 8,	i.	491
xvi. 22,	ii.	226
xvii. 10, 12, 13,	ii.	740
xviii. 24, 25,	i.	479
xix. 28,	i.	909
xix. 33, 34,	ii.	740
xx. 2-5,	i.	272
xxi. 5,	ii.	41
xxiii. 42,	i.	239

NUMBERS

Reference	Vol.	Page
i. 49,	i.	327
iv. 4-15,	i.	620
vi.,	i.	548
vii. 3-9,	i.	620
xi. 4,	i.	431
xi. 8,	i.	407
xi. 32,	i.	407
xii. 1,	i.	364
xii. 10,	ii.	44
xii. 14,	ii.	47
xiii. 1,	i.	499
xx. 5,	i.	322
xxii. 21,	ii.	35
xxii. 22,	ii.	34
xxiii. 19,	i.	512
xxiii. 29,	i.	486
xxiv. 4, 16,	ii.	216
xxiv. 17,	ii.	473
xxv.,	ii.	788
xxx. 6-8,	i.	600
xxxii. 32,	i.	355
xxxiv. 5,	i.	330
xxxiv. 11,	ii.	751
xxxiv. 14,	i.	355

DEUTERONOMY

Reference	Vol.	Page
i. 21, 22,	i.	499
i. 22,	i.	439
ii. 6,	i.	453
ii. 9,	i.	457
Chap. iii.,	i.	453
iii. 11,	i.	455
iii. 25,	i.	355
iv. 2,	ii.	215
vii. 3,	i.	998
vii. 5,	i.	868
vii. 5,	ii.	311
vii. 22,	i.	550
viii. 15,	i.	452
ix. i, 2,	i.	442
xi. 13-15,	ii.	316
xii. 2, 3,	i.	868
xii. 3,	ii.	311
xii. 13,	i.	269
xii. 30, 31,	i.	479
xiii. 1,	ii.	215
xiv. 1,	ii.	41
xiv. 7,	ii.	173
xv. 23,	i.	344
xvi. 21,	i.	868
xvii. 14,	i.	650
xvii. 14-20,	i.	647
xvii. 15,	ii.	553
xvii. 16,	i.	238
xviii. 18, 19,	ii.	215
xix. 3,	i.	653
xx. 10-14,	i.	476
xx. 15-17,	i.	477
xx. 19, 20,	ii.	319
xxi. 17,	i.	286
xxi. 22, 23,	i.	326
xxii. 23, 24,	ii.	439
xxiv. 1,	ii.	439
xxiv. 16,	i.	968
xxv. 4,	i.	591
xxv. 5-10,	i.	595
xxv. 17, 18,	i.	409
xxviii. 53-57,	i.	950
xxix. 11,	i.	431
xxxii. 2,	i.	930
xxxii. 11, 12,	i.	588
xxxii. 13,	i.	551
xxxii. 29,	ii.	334
xxxii. 30, 37,	ii.	311
xxxiii. 17,	ii.	113
xxxiv.,	i.	468

JOSHUA

Reference	Vol.	Page
ii. 9-11,	i.	400
iii. 15,	i.	489
iv. 5-9,	ii.	311
iv. 6, 7,	i.	505
v. 1,	i.	475
ix. 24,	i.	477
x.,	i.	243
x. 4, 5,	i.	657

FOREWORD

This outstanding series of studies by the renowned John Kitto merits the widest circulation among preachers and students of the Word of God.

Dr. Kitto's famous *Pictorial Bible* and these studies, entitled *Daily Bible Illustrations,* were standard works in the last century, receiving the highest commendation from such evangelical leaders as C.H. Spurgeon.

Spurgeon said of them: "Of course, gentlemen, you will economize rigidly until you have accumulated funds to purchase *Kitto's Pictorial Bible*. You need to take that goodly freight on board before you launch upon the sea of married life.... Add to this ... *Kitto's Daily Bible Illustrations*. They are not exactly a commentary, but what marvellous exposition you have there! You have reading more interesting than any novel that was ever written and as instructive as the heaviest theology."

Perhaps the reason that Kitto has not been reprinted until now is due to his somewhat dated archaeological information. Naturally enough, more recent excavations have shed much new light in that field. However, to not have this work available for that reason would be to lose the unique value of his brilliant scholarship.

Dr. Kitto was, beyond any shadow of doubt, a genius: in the writing of magnificent character studies, the reconstruction of confusing Biblical events, and the unravelling of problem passages. As he proceeds through the Bible, his mind seems to home naturally on the deep and perplexing events and statements. Where so many commentaries disappoint, Dr. Kitto excels himself.

He maintains an exceptional level of original thought and comment; so that even in the treatment of familiar passages, something new, significant and challenging will almost always be suggested.

These studies will repeatedly lift the reader's thoughts above the level of the obvious, and somehow convey a breath of reality to the narrative. If the cliche *he has the power to make dry bones live* may be fairly used of an author, then it must be applied to Dr. Kitto.

These notes were originally intended for use as daily Bible reading notes by those quite advanced in the spiritual pathway. They quickly gained acceptance as a standard commentary of a particularly novel character. Generations of preachers have found them a great aid and provocation to lively thought for many situational and problem passages.

Just occasionally, Kitto's rare mind runs slightly away from his solid orthodoxy, and, in this edition, the editor is never slow to say so.

Seldom is so much fresh material to be found in pages which are so easy to read: so freely flowing in style. May this series of studies be once again a great help to the Lord's messengers, and, indeed, to all who are hungry for companion materials to assist their regular Bible study.

"Spurgeon's" Metropolitan Tabernacle, London

PETER MASTERS, LITT. D.

LIFE OF JOHN KITTO

1

BIRTH AND BOYHOOD

JOHN KITTO, the eldest son of John Kitto and Elizabeth Picken, was born at Plymouth on the 4th of December, 1804. So small and sickly was the infant, that but a few hours of life were expected for it. Though nursed with uncommon tenderness and assiduity, it was long before the child was able to walk. This original feebleness was never surmounted. His stature was considerably below the average height, and his limbs were defective in vigour; while a headache, recurring at longer or shorter intervals, accompanied him from his cradle to his grave. As this constitutional frailty unfitted him, to a large extent, for the society of other boys, and debarred him from their sports, it must have prevented, or at least greatly retarded, a healthful physical development. Bodily exercise was his grand necessity all his days, but he never relished it, and, indeed, never took it, till he had partially paid the penalty of neglect. Distaste for it may have originated in his incapacity to run and riot with his childish comrades; but it clung to him, and grew upon him as he advanced in years—nay, led him, when charged by his physician to walk so many miles a day, and when his life depended on punctual compliance, to seek, by various shifts and pleasantries, to lessen the amount of his pedestrian regimen.

If a boy that has not sufficient strength and hardihood to keep pace with his fellows in their boisterous pastimes, should be often seen with his book behind a hedge, or on a sunny slope, or found quietly seated in his own corner of the domestic hearth, it would naturally be concluded that he had been well educated; that since he reads so much, volumes are freely at his disposal; that he meets with parental encouragement; that no misery preys upon his heart; and that there is no undue demand for labour upon his youthful sinews. But Kitto's condition was exactly the reverse. He was not sent to school till he was eight years of age; the majority of his books were begged or borrowed, by continuous and untiring effort; his home was a scene of misery and degradation; and, by the time he was twelve years old, the dwarfed skeleton was yoked to the heavy drudgery of a mason's labourer.

It is scarcely possible to estimate the amount of evil influences that were thrown around Kitto from his childhood. His parents, both in humble life, had married young—the bridegroom, a mason by trade, and doing business on his own account, being in his twentieth year, and the bride in her eighteenth. But, alas! the gay "morning, with gold the hills adorning," was speedily overcast, and there closed in a dark and stormy afternoon. The young husband and father soon fell into intemperance, and his heart and home became a wreck. Character was not only lost, but the love of a good reputation died away within him. He was, as his son has said, of "the class of men whom prosperity ruins," and from being a master, he sank into a servant. The curse of poverty fell upon his family, for what he earned he consumed upon his lusts. Swiftly pursuing his wreckless and downward career, he found himself more than once in "durance vile," and at length, and at a later period, a more serious misdemeanour threatened such consequences, that his poor boy writes, in the bitterness of his soul—"What will they now say of Kitto, the felon's son?"[*] To snatch the delicate child out of his wretchedness, he was transferred, in his fourth year, to his grandmother's poor garret. She, "dear old woman," nursed him with more than a mother's tenderness, and her he regarded with inexpressible affection. She, too, had been blighted by

---

[*] It may be added, that Kitto's uncle, who had got a superior education, fell a victim to intemperance, as well as his father. The uncle had some local fame as an engineer, having "constructed the Upper Road across the Laira marshes from Plymouth towards Exeter, and embanked a great portion of this road from the tide."—*Lost Senses*, p. 7. Both brothers had come from their native parish of Gwennap, in Cornwall, to Plymouth, attracted by the high rate of wages. Mrs. Picken, with her two daughters, Mary and Elizabeth, lived in the same street with them, and the result was, that the two Kittos courted and married the two sisters about the same period. Kitto, in his Workhouse Journal, fills some pages with the sad story of his uncle, who was at length so reduced that he wrought on the Hoe as a pauper, and he concludes by saying, "Drunkenness is the bane of our family, and the name of Kitto is synonymous with drunkard."

intemperance.   Her second husband, John Picken, though usually reckoned a sober man, had gone from Plymouth to Bigbury, a distance of thirteen miles, and spent the evening to a late hour with friends in the alehouse; so that, as he was riding home somewhat intoxicated, his horse trotted into a pond, and its rider falling from its back, was drowned in his helplessness. Kitto's mother was born a month after the melancholy event.   "Alas!" says her son, on a comparison of his grandmother's and mother's fate—"My mother has the sad pre-eminence in misery.   For the shadow which had fallen upon her birth gathered over her wedded life in more terrible gloom.   Intemperance had made her a posthumous child, and now it made her an unhappy wife, and a broken-hearted mother.   Menial offices of the lowest form she was at length glad to do, working, as she once tells her boy, " from five in the morning to ten in the evening," that she might have something to put into the mouth of her babes.

From his fourth to his eighth year, though Kitto enjoyed a partial asylum with his grandmother, who "pinched herself to support" him, yet he got no schooling.   True, he enjoyed another kind of education, perhaps as essential to his welfare.   He strolled through the fields and lanes with his venerated relative, and gathered the flowers and plucked the fruits, which grew around him in wild luxuriance, his grandmother deftly using her staff to hook down the clusters of nuts and berries which were beyond his reach.   At other times they turned their course to the sea-beach, and both were nerved by the breezes, which carried the surf to the feet of the aged pilgrim and her tiny charge.   As they returned from these frequent and happy excursions, she usually supplied him liberally "with gingerbread, plums, apples, or sugar-stick," her indifference to the sweetness of the last article often filling his young imagination with great amazement.*

At the age of eight Kitto was sent to school, and he remained, for various periods, and at various places of tuition, during the next three years.   The congenital malady of headache was perpetually attacking him, and destroying the punctuality of his attendance.   But there was another reason for his irregularity.   His grandmother was too poor to pay the requisite fees, and his father either would not, or could not, spare a few pence for the purpose; so that when the fees could be saved from the ale-cup, the boy attended school, and when not, he stayed at home.†   Perhaps this circumstance may account for the changes made in the schools he was

* The record of his abode with his grandmother is given at full length in a letter by Kitto, dated Bagdad, June 25, 1832 —an interesting piece of autobiography, from which our knowledge of this portion of his life is derived, so that the source of the subsequent quotations needs not be again referred to.
† Letter addressed to Sir Walter Scott, found among his papers.

sent to; for he was "placed, for short and interrupted periods, at the schools of Messrs. Winston, Stephens, Treeby, and Goss."*   Probably, at first, he lost as much in these forced recesses as he had gained in the previous weeks of attendance.   Still there must have been great carelessness on the part of his parents, "for they might have availed themselves of the opportunities which the many charity schools of the town afforded, for the instruction of poor boys in elementary knowledge."†   But such neglect was inevitable—the father still drank, and the mother was obliged to go out and char.   Kitto did not gain a great deal by this desultory schooling; his early attainments not extending further "than reading, writing, and an imperfect use of figures."   The first specimens of writing which we have, about four years after this date, are legible, but by no means very elegant; and as the occasional blunders in spelling and syntax in the same papers indicate, his English acquired at school was not to be measured by a very high standard.   His "granny" once boasted that he was the best scholar in Plymouth; but he blushed at the unmerited honour, and rejected it, adding, however, as her apology, " she did it ignorantly, but affectionately."

But his real, as distinct from his formal, education began under his grandmother's roof.   The little fellow, seated quietly at her knee, was, for his amusement and occupation, taught by her to sew; and such was his assiduity, that he exulted in having done the greater portion of a " gay patchwork" for her bed, besides having finished "quilts and kettle-holders enough for two generations."   His fingers might, indeed, soon fall out of practice with needle and scissors, but he was unconsciously training to that retired and patient industry which characterized his subsequent life of seclusion and silence.   Then, too, from his grandmother's lips, he came first to know the current lore of ghosts, hobgoblins, fairies, and witches; and a lively shoemaker, named Roberts, who dwelt in the same tenement, added his contribution of nursery literature, and repeated, with awl and cord in hand, the tales of *Bluebeard* and *Cinderella, Jack the Giantkiller,* and *Beauty and the Beast.*   "Assuredly," says Kitto, in 1832, " never have I since felt so much respect and admiration of any man's talents and extent of information as those of poor Roberts."   The young listener was charmed.   By and bye, he found out that such wondrous stories were not mere traditions, to be heard only from the lips of his grandmother and the cordwainer, but that they might be actually seen in print, in Mrs. Barnicle's shop-window, ay, and be had for a copper trifle.   "This information," he says, "first inclined me to reading."   He was at once induced to buy them, as often as he could afford the small expense. The passion grew upon him, and every spare penny

* Preface to his first publication.   † *Ibid.*

went for the purpose. He willingly denied himself the dainties which his doting grandam would have provided for him—no confections so witching as a picture-book, and no fruit so sweet as a nursery-rhyme. His desire of reading was indicated by his growing love of quietness, and by his decreasing relish for amusements out of doors, while it was nursed by the zealous watchings of his relative, who, when he was permitted to go out for a brief period to play, soon interrupted him by her loud call from the garret window, of "Johnny, Johnny!"—a sound, he pathetically adds, more than twenty years afterwards, "which, notwithstanding my deafness, rings in my ears at this moment." It was surely a kind Providence which was so disciplining him, that the work of his subsequent life did not necessitate a sudden and violent change of habit. He was thus, at a very early period, thrown much upon himself and upon books for his amusement, a proof, as he was wont to argue, that his love of literature was certainly not created, though it was ripened and confirmed, by his subsequent deafness. The books in his grandmother's possession were speedily explored—" a *Family Bible*, with plenty of engravings; a *Prayer-book; Bunyan's Pilgrim; and Gulliver's Travels.*" " The two last I soon devoured," says he, "and so much did I admire them, that, to increase their attractions, I decorated all the engravings with the indigo my grandmother used in washing, using a feather for a brush. Some one at last gave me a fourpenny box of colours, and between that and my books, I was so much interested at home, that I retained little inclination for play; and when my grandmother observed this, she did all in her power to encourage those studious habits, by borrowing for me books of her neighbours." All the books in the street passed speedily through his hands. Prior to his twelfth year, he had got into a new world, and he was at first bewildered by its variety. Nothing would satisfy him but book upon book. The voracious student was not at all backward in maintaining a supply by pen or tongue. His first efforts at composition were written to the kind and obliging mistress of a neighbouring charity school, and were either requests for the loan of a volume, or apologies for putting the lender to so much trouble. " Many of the old neighbours," he says, "will remember what a plague I was to them in this respect." In fact, if he heard of a book being within reach, he pestered everybody about him till he got it. What he calls his "first literary effort," was at this time also achieved by him, and he has thought it of such importance, as to place it on record himself. Nay, when looked at in the light of his subsequent career, it might be regarded as a propitious omen. The following is his amusing account of the transaction :—

" My cousin came one day with a penny in his hand,

declaring his intention to buy a book with it. I was just then sadly in want of a penny to make up fourpence, with which to purchase the history of King Peppin (not Pepin), so I inquired whether he bought a book for the pictures or the story? ' The story, to be sure.' I then said, that in that case, I would, for his penny, write him both a larger and a better story than he could get in print for the same sum, and that he might be still further a gainer, I would paint him a picture at the beginning, and he knew there were no painted pictures in penny books. He expressed the satisfaction he should feel in my doing so, and sat down quietly on the stool to note my operations. When I had done, I certainly thought my cousin's penny pretty well earned; and as, at reading the paper and viewing the picture, he was of the same opinion, no one else had any right to complain of the bargain. I believe this was the first penny I ever earned. I happened to recollect this circumstance when last at Plymouth, and felt a wish to peruse this paper, if still in existence; but my poor cousin, though he remembered the circumstance, had quite forgotten both the paper and its contents, unless that it was 'something about what was done in England at the time when wild men lived in it'—even this was farther than my own recollection extended."

As the boy occasionally sauntered through the streets, and had so much time on his hand, he read all the play bills posted on the walls; and though he had never read or seen a play, he resolved to get up one—the " price of admission being, ladies eight pins, gentlemen ten." Dresses were prepared, such as ribbons and sashes, caps and feathers, and the play was acted; the value of the pins collected amounted to three halfpence. The drama was a tragedy, so sweeping in its mimic massacre, that only one little actress remained alive at the end; and the audience, consisting of fifteen boys and girls, were perfectly satisfied with the performance. The whole affair was sufficiently childish, though Kitto was disposed to make his share—the play bill and the plot—a proof of his literary progress.

It is plain, from these statements, that Kitto's early love of reading was no whim, or mere childish curiosity, but that there was a craving for information awakened within him. He rose gradually, even in his boyhood, to a more select and useful class of books. The cousin referred to, and for whom the booklet was extemporized, was as fond of books as Kitto, and could far more easily procure them; but his love of reading soon passed away from him, and in his manhood he scarce turned the leaf of anything, "save a jest-book or a song." With him, literary relish was only a variety of juvenile caprice, and the ball and the book might, at any moment, change places in his fancy; whereas in Kitto's case, the thirst for knowledge had really been excited, and, no matter how often baffled, it was never to be repressed. He enjoyed, at the same time, some religious education, and could answer a few questions from the Church Catechism. He also attended church so often, as to have caught the manner of Dr. Hawker the vicar, and be able to imitate it, to his grandmother's vexation, when he read the Bible to her. Yet no serious impression seems to have been made upon him: "After," says he, "I had studied the engravings, and read so much of the text as seemed to explain these, I felt then no disposition to study the Bible further." There was much in it to interest him, had he chosen to read it—many scenes and stories that might have fascinated him both in the Old and New Testament; but the time had not yet come when he was to find it a refuge to the weary, and a balm to the smitten in heart, and when its illustration was to form the daily business of his life.

But the sky was gradually lowering around him. His grandmother ceased, in 1814, to have any separate means of support, while age and disease were leaving their traces upon her. Reduced to poverty and attacked by paralysis, she was forced to go to live with her youngest daughter. Under his father's roof again, Kitto soon felt the saddening change. The boy must do something for his maintenance, and, in the spring of the year 1815, he was sent as a species of apprentice to a barber's shop. "Old Wigmore," as his facetious underling records, "had practised on board a ship-of-war, and related adventures which rivalled Baron Manchausen;" had a face so "sour," that it sickened one to look at it, and "which was beside all over red by drinking spirituous liquors."* While in Wigmore's service, he learned only so much of his art, as to be able to shave. For want of better occupation, he seems to have practised so frequently upon himself, as, by the age of sixteen, to have induced a growth of no ordinary thickness on his upper lip, while by the repeated application of the scissors to his eye-brows, they acquired also a similar premature "bushiness." But, from this occupation, he was summarily dismissed. His master's stock-in-trade, or at least his best razors, were put under Kitto's charge, and taken home by him every night. One morning, as he came up to the shop, with the precious implements of his calling under his arm, a woman in front of the unopened place of business, professed to be anxiously waiting for Wigmore, and that no time might be lost, she induced Kitto to leave his parcel with her, and run and call his master. As might have been anticipated, she was off before Kitto returned, and the surly old fellow discharged the little craftsman on suspicion of his being an accomplice of the thief. Kitto keenly felt the imputation, for his mere simplicity was branded as

* Workhouse Journal.

knavery. And thus ended his first and curious engagement.

What, then, was the boy to do, but occasionally put on a smock-frock, and go out and assist his father? He did so, both in town and country—the grieved witness and reporter of his parent's profligacy. When left at leisure at any time, he usually took to wandering in the fields, and among the rocks. He felt himself growing out of harmony with his home and the world around him. As his mind opened, he became more and more conscious of his unhappy lot. He confesses that he first "knew what happiness was, by his own exclusion from it." He pined for solitude with book in hand—

"Away, away, from men and towns,
To the wild woods and the downs;
To the silent wilderness
Where the soul need not repress
Its moaning, lest it should not find
An echo in another's mind."

In fact, morbid imaginations began at this time to gather upon him. Having picked up a dog's head, which had been long bleached on the sands, he at once determined to make it a sort of symbolical memento, and having given it a more ghastly appearance, by reddening its jaws, and replenishing its eyeholes and mouth with artificial orbs and tongue, he hung up the grotesque teraphim at the foot of his bed. He had long sought in vain for a human skull, that he might place it in the same position. The abode of his father was old and tall, and John's dormitory, in the very apex of it, was of small dimensions, seven feet by four. It was ventilated by an aperture that admitted the wind, and could not exclude the rain, and was furnished with a rickety table, framed originally to stand on three feet, but now sustaining itself with difficulty on two. This dark oak table was an old heirloom, and highly prized even in its decrepitude. The bed was in keeping with the table, and was by turns a seat and a couch, according as the strange inmate of the den wished to work or sleep. A chest was there, too, having its appropriate uses, with a box of smaller dimensions, holding pebbles and shells, and the other contents of his museum, and which was fastened with a string, passing through a huge and rusty padlock— "a satire on security." The walls were spattered with such prints as he could afford to buy, and such drawings as he was able to execute. Here was his library of a dozen volumes, having among them a Bible "imprinted by Barker in the days of Queen Elizabeth," and here he continued, so far as his intermittent toil allowed, his habits of miscellaneous reading. His spirit was gladdened, amidst all his oppressions and wrongs, by such literary vigils. He made indexes to his books, and even then he delighted to hang over the lines of Young and Spenser. We can easily imagine the sorrow of his grandmother, at the changed condition and shrouded prospects of her favourite. Perhaps she regarded his position in life as fixed, and suspected that, if his strength at all permitted, he would naturally follow his father's occupation. Who, at that moment, could have gainsaid such a prediction? But Providence interposed, and suddenly changed the entire current of events.

On the 13th of February 1817, the elder Kitto was engaged in repairing the roof of a house in Batter Street, Plymouth. His slim and ragged son was, about half-past four in the afternoon, engaged in carrying up a load of slates, and, when in the act of stepping from the top of the ladder to the roof, he lost his footing and fell, a distance of thirty-five feet, into the court beneath. There he lay insensible, bleeding profusely at mouth and nose. On being lifted, about five minutes after, consciousness returned for an instant, and he could not divine why he came there, or why so many people were staring at him. For more than a week, he continued in prostrate insensibility; for four months, he was obliged to keep his bed, and he did not entirely recover his strength till other four months had also elapsed. But the accident had deprived him wholly of the faculty of hearing. What injury was done to the organ was never ascertained, and no possible form of treatment could remove it. He was subjected to every variety of surgical torment and experiment, but all in vain. The action of the auditory nerve was completely paralysed, perhaps, as has been surmised, from the entire internal apparatus being gorged with blood. The sense was not simply dulled, it was extinguished. He became deaf, not comparatively, as if he could hear only a little, and that even with extreme pain and difficulty, but absolutely, for he could not hear at all. The base of the skull had also sustained some fracture beyond the reach of detection or reparation—a sad supplement to his constitutional headache.

In after years, Kitto often reflected upon the accident, and he virtually assigns no less than three causes for it. His first account of it in his Workhouse Journal (1820), enters into no such details, and the probability is, that the reasons ultimately urged, had really little to do with the matter, but are rather the suggestions of an inquisitive and introspective mind, which tried to connect the fall with some previous mental associations, through which he might have been thrown off his guard. The phenomenon has happened too often to be one of mystery. Any one may stumble, after he has often mounted a ladder, under a heavy burden—much more a feeble boy like John Kitto, who never enjoyed great power of limb or firmness of step. It does not need any analysis of his previous thoughts to account for his mistake. He had climbed repeatedly

with a portion of mortar and slates during the day; and familiarity with the pathway may have induced a momentary carelessness. Or the frequent ascent may have so wearied his sinews, that when he had reached the summit of the ladder, and a different muscular action was required, he had not the complete control of them. Or his knee-joints, stiffened with the short and hard jerk of so many steps up and down, repeated for so many hours, may not have stretched so far as he imagined, when he attempted to throw his foot on the eaves. In one account, he refers to the anticipation of a wonderful book, which had been promised him by the town-crier for that evening; and in another, to the prospect of a smock-frock, on which his grandmother had been a long time working, and which he greatly needed, for he was in tatters, "out at elbows, out at shoulders, out at breast, out all over;" and, lastly, he seems to impute the accident to the *post mortem* examination of a young sailor's body, going on in one of the rooms of the house on which his father was employed, the effect of which he had happened to notice, as he was ascending the ladder, in the form of bloody water spouting from the gutter. Were the last the true version, there would have been a physical source of unsteadiness—vertigo or momentary faintness, which, however, he does not affirm, but speaks simply of a "shock;" whereas the two former reasons adduced by him, could only have produced absence of mind. Besides, the third hypothesis would supersede the other suspected causes, which are purely mental, and which, moreover, had been just as powerful during the whole day, as at the fatal moment. All the three could not well co-exist, and the circumstance of a *post mortem* dissection could hardly affect so deeply the nerves of one who had long tried, in various ways, to get the skull of a human skeleton, for the guardian symbol of his couch.

On being carried home, the stunned youth lay in a trance of nearly a fortnight. At length he wakened up "as from a night's sleep," and perceived that it was two hours later than his usual time of rising, but he could not even move in bed. Many an hour he spent in "trying to piece together his broken recollections," so as to comprehend his position. How he learned that he had become deaf, is thus particularly related by himself. There was profound silence in the room in which the pathetic scene took place, and alas! that silence reigned around him ever afterwards.

"I was very slow in learning that my hearing was entirely gone. The unusual stillness of all things was grateful to me in my utter exhaustion; and if, in this half-awakened state, a thought of the matter entered my mind, I ascribed it to the unusual care and success of my friends in preserving silence around me. I saw them talking, indeed, to one another, and thought that, out of regard to my feeble condition, they spoke in whispers, because I heard them not. The truth was revealed to me in consequence of my solicitude about the book which had so much interested me on the day of my fall. It had, it seems, been reclaimed by the good old man, who had lent it to me, and who doubtless concluded that I should have no more need of books in this life. He was wrong, for there has been nothing in this life which I have needed more. I asked for this book with much earnestness, and was answered by signs, which I could not comprehend. 'Why do you not speak?' I cried; 'Pray, let me have the book." This seemed to create some confusion; and at length some one, more clever than the rest, hit upon the happy expedient of writing upon a slate, that the book had been reclaimed by the owner, and that I could not, in my weak state, be allowed to read. 'But,' I said in great astonishment, 'Why do you write to me? why not speak? speak! speak!" Those who stood around the bed exchanged significant looks of concern, and the writer soon displayed upon his slate the awful words—'YOU ARE DEAF.' "*

A more complete case of isolation can hardly be imagined. Had it not been for the boy's previous acquaintance with books, into what misery would he not have fallen? How many, with such an infirmity, without education, and in his rank of life, taunted as useless, and tormented as semi-maniacs, would have sunk into objects of pity or contempt, would have fallen into the dregs of society, and disappeared in a nameless tomb—in the pauper's or stranger's corner of the graveyard! Had there not been a powerful principle within him, nursed and sustained by his eagerness for reading, he might, as has been the case with not a few in his social position and with his defect, have become sullen and discontented, out of harmony with himself, and in antagonism with all around him—first a burden and then a pest. His own idea was, that "such trials and deprivations have been generally found to paralyse exertion, and reduce the mind to idiocy, inducing a mere oblivion of thought and feeling."

What circumstances, then, could be so discouraging as those of Kitto—a poor deaf boy, with none to care for him, none to guide him, or stimulate him to healthful mental exercise? Such an inmate of such a home —how helpless and how hopeless! He was able to do little for himself before, and he could certainly do less now. The father might gain a penny from his son's toils once, but now he left him wholly to his own vagaries. His grandmother's resources were exhausted too, and not a farthing to buy a book came into his possession. He resorted, therefore, to what he has

graphically called, a "Poor Student's Ways and Means." He went down to Sutton Pool,* where the "fishing trawlers" and small coasters discharged their cargoes, and, wading among its black and fetid ooze and mire at low water, he groped, along with other boys, for pieces of rope, iron, and other nautical fragments. Some of his comrades could gather as much in a day, as amounted, when sold, to threepence; but Kitto was never very nimble in his movements, and his weekly profits only swelled up once to fourpence. But he happened, on one occasion, to tread on a broken bottle, and such a wound put an immediate end to this form of industry. Then he turned to his box of paints, and bethought him of artistic employment, wondering, all the while, at the vulgarity of his previous occupation. Having laid out his capital sum of twopence on paper, he set about a series of paintings—human heads, houses, flowers, birds, and trees. Grotesque they were, according to his own account—"faces all profiles, and all looking the same way;" birds sufficiently weighty to "bow to the dust" the branches on which they were awkwardly perched; and flowers, "generally in pots," with a "centre in all cases yellow, and with any number of petals." But in describing this handicraft, he subjoins, with a simple honesty, "Thus far I can *now* smile, but no further. I cannot smile when I recollect the intense excitement with which I applied myself to my new labours, and the glorious vision of coppers and reputation which attended my progress. How knew I but, in process of time, my pictures might be pasted on the walls or over the mantelpieces of most of the rooms in the lane where I lived! This was the extent of my ambition; for I do aver that I did never, even in thought, aspire to the dignity of being framed. The boyish ambition that might thus be acquired among my compeers, was, however, a perfectly secondary object; that which I wanted was money." But his pictures were painted for sale, and not for criticism; and being arranged in all their glory, in his mother's window, he sat down behind it, and anxiously awaited customers. Few were attracted, for few passed the court, and fewer came in to buy. Yet, the average weekly income of the artist from this source, was about twopence-halfpenny. Then he resolved to have a "standing" in Plymouth Fair, and wrought hard to provide his stall with an adequate supply of goods. The character of his wares attracted many spectators, and it was probably for his comfort that he could not hear their remarks. Their staring curiosity annoyed him, but he gained a larger sum of money by this public sale, than he had ever before possessed. Certain labels in the windows of the lanes and outskirts of the town, had long been an eyesore to

* *Lost Senses—Deafness.* By John Kitto, D.D., pp. 11, 12.

* The details are given by Kitto in two papers in the fourth volume of the *Penny Magazine*, pp. 218 and 227.

him. The spelling and writing were equally wretched —"Logins for singel men," "Rooms to leet enquair withing." He prepared neat and accurate substitutes, and took many a long and weary journey to dispose of his productions. Occasionally he succeeded, but as often he failed from bashfulness. The boy's infirmity sometimes secured him sympathy, and sometimes led to a testy rebuff; and his inability to talk about his articles made his customers, in one place, kind and generous, and in another, brief and surly in their dealings with him.

The money gained from employment so precarious, was spent on books. Attachment to study might well have been chilled in a stripling who seemed to himself the most forlorn and helpless of human beings. Yet he read and pondered, frequented Mrs. Bulley's circulating library, and contrived to plod his way through numerous volumes—many, indeed, of an inferior class, but others of a higher stamp and excellence. Still he loved to stroll into the country, or recline among the shelving crags with the surge beating at his feet, and to create for himself, through his reading and reverie, a temporary Elysium. There was a stillness around him, unbroken even by his own footfall. Wearied out after a day's solitary wandering, heart-sick at the misery and privation of his home, with bitter memories of the past, and dreary anticipations of the future, his only refuge was with his books, and in his little attic, where many a tedious hour was beguiled, and where the growing consciousness of intellectual strength could not but frequently cheer and sustain him. He used, at this time, and after being sent to the workhouse, to go to Devonport, once almost every fortnight, to visit a bookstall in the market. He feasted among the volumes, and the keeper not only did not disturb him, but gave him books at the cheapest rate, in exchange for the few pence he had scraped together.* This man he reckoned a prince in generosity, and a perfect contrast to a "sour old woman," and a "surly little man," by whom two other stalls were kept, and who did not relish the sight of so "shabby a fellow" handling their literary wares. And he naively adds, " I had another more logical mode of reasoning on the matter, which settled it in my mind beyond any possibility of dispute, that my friend of Devonport market, and others of his kind in general, were, and must be, the happiest men in the world. If, I used to say, they sell the books, they are happy in the money they get; but if they do not sell them, they are happy in the books they retain."† This period has been described by Kitto himself in the following eloquent terms:—

" For many years I had no views towards literature

* Old Aubrey, the antiquary, says of Hobbes, " He took great delight to go to the bookbinders' and stationers' shops, and lye gaping on mapps."
† Letter to George Harvey, Esq., January 19, 1827.

beyond the instruction and solace of my own mind; and under these views, and in the absence of other mental stimulants, the pursuit of it eventually became a passion, which devoured all others. I take no merit for the industry and application with which I pursued this object, nor for the ingenious contrivances by which I sought to shorten the hours of needful rest, that I might have the more time for making myself acquainted with the minds of other men. The reward was great and immediate; and I was only preferring the gratification which seemed to me the highest. Nevertheless, now that I am, in fact, another being, having but slight connection, excepting in so far as ' the child is father to the man,' with my former self; now that much has become a business which was then simply a joy; and now that I am gotten old in experiences, if not in years, it does somewhat move me to look back upon that poor and deaf boy, in his utter loneliness, devoting himself to objects in which none around him could sympathize, and to pursuits which none could even understand. The eagerness with which he sought books, and the devoted attention with which he read them, was simply an unaccountable fancy in their view; and the hours which he strove to gain for writing that which was destined for no other eyes than his own, was no more than an innocent folly, good for keeping him quiet and out of harm's way, but of no possible use on earth. This want of the encouragement which sympathy and appreciation give, and which cultivated friends are so anxious to bestow on the studious application of their young people, I now count among the sorest trials of that day; and it serves me now as a measure for the intensity of my devotement to such objects, that I felt so much encouragement within, as not to need or care much for the sympathies and encouragements which are, in ordinary circumstances, held of so much importance. I undervalue them not; on the contrary, an undefinable craving was often felt for sympathy and appreciation in pursuits so dear to me; but to want this was one of the disqualifications of my condition, quite as much so as my deafness itself; and in the same degree in which I submitted to my deafness as a dispensation of Providence towards me, did I submit to this as its necessary consequence. It was, however, one of the peculiarities of my condition, that I was then, as I ever have been, too much shut up. With the same dispositions and habits, without being deaf, it would have been easy to have found companions who would have understood me, and sympathized with my love for books and study, my progress in which might also have been much advanced by such intercommunication. As it was, the shyness and reserve which the deaf usually exhibit, gave increased effect to the physical disqualification; and precluded me from seeking, and kept me from incidentally finding, beyond the narrow sphere in which I moved, the sympathies which were not found in it. As time passed, my mind became filled with ideas and sentiments, and with various knowledges of things new and old, all of which were as the things of another world to those among whom my lot was cast. The conviction of this completed my isolation; and eventually all my human interests were concentrated in these points, to get books, and, as they were mostly borrowed, to preserve the most valuable points in their contents, either by extracts, or by a distinct intention to impress them on the memory. When I went forth, I counted the hours till I might return to the only pursuits in which I could take interest; and when free to return, how swiftly I fled to immure myself in that little sanctuary, which I had been permitted to appropriate, in one of those rare nooks only afforded by such old Elizabethan houses as that in which my relatives then abode.*

This condition, so well depicted, did not last long. It was a cold gleam of sunshine in the last hour of a wintry day. Nor was it wholly beneficial to Kitto. He was becoming too much the lord of himself, for he seems to have been gratified in all his caprices that did not involve pecuniary outlay. The sympathy so naturally felt for him by his relations, inclined them to fondle and humour him. Nay, the child, author and artist, was in danger of being admired as a prodigy. But a severe and curative probation was before him. About the end of the year 1818, his grandmother was obliged to leave Plymouth, in order to reside at Brixton. The darling grandchild could not accompany her, and he was left alone with his parents, and entirely dependent on them. Ah! then did he suffer. His father was unreformed: vice had turned his heart into a stone; and he was insensible alike to his own disgrace, the degradation of his wife, and the cries of his young ones for bread. It was certainly no merit of his that his famishing children preserved their honesty, and did not stray into those courses toward which temptation is ever pointing so many in quest of food and raiment. For months was the boy a pitiable spectacle—pinched with hunger, shivering in rags, and crawling about with exposed and bleeding feet. A picture of more abject wretchedness could not be found, than this deaf and puny starveling. Every prospect was closed upon him, and to screen him from "cold, and hunger, and nakedness," he was, on the 15th of November 1819, admitted into the Plymouth Workhouse.† The sorrow and want of his home had been

* Lost Senses.—Deafness, pp. 76-78.

† This workhouse, originally founded in 1630, was called the "Hospital of the Poors' Portion." A new one has now been erected in a different part of the town. The old building still stands, however, in its comparative desolation, as when we saw it in the beginning of last year. It had been tenanted a short time before by about fifty Emancipadoes from Cuba—negroes who had purchased their freedom, and who

long notorious; the neighbourhood was scandalised at his daily and hopeless privations; charity was roused at length to interfere without regard to his wishes and feelings; and, therefore, as the last and unwelcome resource, he was seized and sent to the common receptacle of aged and juvenile pauperism and wretchedness.

2

THE WORKHOUSE

Some stratagem was necessary to secure the lad's entrance into the workhouse, for he was wild and shy; and when he learned that he was in virtual captivity, his sorrow was without bounds. But the wayward and defiant pauper submitted, in course of time, to the salutary curb; and he was in need of it, for he had long moved simply as it pleased him, and acted under no law but that of his own moods, which brooked neither challenge nor control. Not only were the order and discipline of the workhouse of essential service to him, but his fellowship with the other boys was also of immense advantage. It revealed to him various aspects of human nature, and tended to soften such misanthropic asperities as solitude is apt to produce. It gave employment also to his pen, and his facility of composition eventually drew attention to him. He had been going down the valley of humiliation, and the workhouse was the lowest step but one in the descent. For there was still another, and a deeper one; but it was the last, and the next step beyond it commenced the up-hill journey. Kitto's desultory life, prior to his entry into the workhouse, would never have brought him into observation; but now his power was more concentrated, and he gradually came into closer contact with the benevolent Governor and the Board of Guardians. If he felt acuter misery, he had also acquired a keener power of telling it; and such a power in such a narrator, could not but excite surprise. If he had to make complaints, his fearless utterance usually secured redress; and if he was obliged to enter into self-vindication, the cleverness of his advocacy was at least as conspicuous as the rectitude of his conduct.

Mr. Roberts, who was governor of the workhouse at the time of his admission, treated him kindly, and permitted him some indulgences, even so far as sleeping at home; and Mr. Burnard, his successor, was Kitto's kind friend and sympathizing correspondent through

were on their way to Lagos and Abeokuta. Our friend Dr. Tregelles and his lady, with others, were very attentive to them. Services in Spanish were held with them every Lord's Day, as well as many meetings during the week. The old workhouse seemed alive again with its sable inmates, and the Christian efforts did not appear to be without fruit.

his whole eventful career. The youth was set to learn the making of list-shoes, under Mr. Anderson, the beadle, and he grew, in no long time, to be a proficient in the business. Probably his friends were happy that now he might be able at least to maintain himself, and that there was something between him and abject penury. Within a year of his entering the workhouse, he began to keep a journal, and this curious and extraordinary document* is the best record of this portion of his life and progress. For this purpose, therefore, we shall freely employ it.

It might perhaps be supposed that a lad, brought up as John Kitto had been, in comparative pauperism, should be a stranger to delicacy of feeling. It might be imagined that the hardship of his condition could not but blunt any mental refinement, and that therefore now, within the walls of a workhouse, he had more than ordinary reason for contentment among boys of his own years and class. What is thus surmised might be true of many, perhaps of the majority, in Kitto's circumstances; but it was certainly not true of him. He was painfully conscious of his degradation. In spite of all he suffered, he never sank into callousness. What he might have been ever stood out to him in sad contrast to what he was, and his present condition was out of all harmony with his ideal prospects. He felt, and he keenly felt, so that in his Journal, when he becomes sentimental or sketchy at any time, or describes what enjoyments he coveted, or what anticipations feasted him, he suddenly and testily checks himself, and cries, "But what has a workhouse boy to do with feelings?" or, "The word pauper sticks in my throat."

The interesting quarto is styled, "Journal and Memorandum, from August 12, 1820, by John Kitto, jun." The motto on the title-page might have been ascribed to undue self-appreciation, had it not been vindicated by his subsequent career—

"Full many a gem of purest ray serene,
    The dark unfathomed caves of ocean bear,
Full many a flower is born to blush unseen,
    And waste its sweetness on the desert air."

The volume is, "with reverence, inscribed to the memory of Cecilia Picken, my Grandmother, and the dearest friend I ever had," etc. It was an odd thing for a pauper boy to think of such a project as keeping a diary. It shows, at least, that his mind was stirring, and that he was resolved to exercise himself in observation and in composition. When was a journal compiled in such circumstances—amidst such physical and social disadvantages—by a deaf boy in a poorhouse, of

* Kitto mentions, in a letter to Mr. Burnard, from Bagdad, that he had found some of his early papers, which had escaped the flames to which, some time previously, he had committed his early MSS. The papers thus accidentally preserved, seem to have been the Workhouse Journal.

whom no higher estimate was formed, than that he might be a passable shoemaker, and for whom no loftier wish was entertained than that he might be able to maintain himself by his craft, and without being an expense to the community! Compassion was felt for him, but no hopes were cherished about him. Men blamed the father and pitied the child, and then thought no more of him, but as the victim of complicated and repeated misfortunes.

As to his motive in writing it, he says, that as he had no time to finish his drawings, and they did not sell when finished, and as he could not command a sufficient quantity of books, so he thought that writing was a good substitute, both for painting and reading. He adds, too, that he adopted the plan of a journal as a useful thing—as something to instruct others years hence (if he should be spared), in the misfortunes and sorrows of his early years, while he admits that there may be a little bit of human vanity in the resolution. But the journal has realized its purpose. What, in fact, would the record of his early life be without it?

The following is his description of himself—racy and rather picturesque, though several features of the external portraiture were subsequently modified or toned down by the higher physical culture which he afterwards enjoyed:—

"Yesterday I completed my sixteenth year of age, and I shall take this opportunity of describing, to the best of my ability, my person, in which description I will be no egotist. I am four feet eight inches high; and, to begin with my head, my hair is stiff and coarse, of a dark brown colour, almost black; my head is very large, and, I believe, has a tolerable good lining of brain within. My eyes are brown and large, and are the least exceptionable part of my person; my forehead is high, my eyebrows bushy; my nose is large, mouth very big, teeth well enough, skin of my face coarse; my limbs are not ill-shaped; my legs are *well*-shaped, except at their ends they have rather too long a foot; when clean, my hands are very good; my upper lip is *graced*, or rather disgraced (as in these degenerate days the premature down of manhood is reckoned a disgrace!—how unlike the grave and wise Chinese, who envy us fortunate English nothing but our beards) with a beard."

There was indeed something peculiar in his appearance:—

"*March* 30.—I observe that my decorated lip exposes me to observation, and that when I walk along the streets, all men, women, and children, do me the honour to stare me in the face. I got leave to come out this afternoon, and shaved myself with my father's razor." In a fragmentary autobiography, dated June 26, 1823, he writes,—"My manners are awkward and clownish. I am short in stature, stoop much in walking, and walk as though I feared I should fall at every step, with my hands almost always, when I walk, in my pockets."

" *October* 7.—When I go any where, I am almost afraid to meet any of my own sex; there is, it seems, something about me that exposes me to observation, and makes me stared at; and I find, by experience, that the best way to come off well, is not to avert the face, but to look unconcerned, stare at them in return, and assume an impudent look. What a world is this, in which modest bashfulness is contemned, and impudence caressed!"

His deafness, "laboured asthmatic breathing," and apparent powerlessness, often made him the butt of the other boys in the hospital, and he was obliged to make sudden and smart reprisals.

" *October* 12.—When afterward, in the evening, Torr was making faces at me again in the court-yard, I could bear it no longer, but gave him such a blow as made him fall down. You cannot imagine, Madam,* how this seeming trifle provoked me.

" *October* 22.—I to-day experienced the truth of the maxim, that *meanness* is a medal, the reverse of which is *insolence*. When I was waiting under the porch till Mr. Burnard should pass by, to ask leave to come out, one of the blue-coat boys, named Peters, kept making faces at me. At first I treated his foolery with the contempt it deserved, by taking no notice of it. But at last he provoked me so far, by attempting to pull my nose, that (though no boxer, and not over courageous) I gave him a blow on the forehead, with such good will, as made him reel to the opposite wall, and brought the water into his eyes. When I had done so, I fully expected a return of the favour, but he, so far from resenting it, desisted from his foolery, and soon sneaked off."

" *March* 21.—At eight o'clock, as we were going to prayers, Rowe gave me an unprovoked blow on the back, and ran away. I pursued him, and hemmed him into a corner, when, finding he could not escape, he placed himself in a pugilistic attitude; but a few blows made him stoop to defend his ears, and at the same time to pick up a bone and a large cinder to throw at me. While I was disarming him of those missile weapons, I was attacked in the rear by ten or twelve boys, who delight in mischief. Having disarmed Rowe, I turned against my new opponents, and, discharging a bone at one, and a cinder at another, and some blows among the rest, put them all to flight."

Sometimes, when bad boys were flogged, Kitto was selected to hold their legs, probably because, from his inability to hear their cries, he was under no temptation to slacken his grasp. The next extract is a reflection, in his own style, upon his early disaster.

* The diary often addresses some ideal personage.

" *October* 9.—I found, on coming to my senses, that I had just been bled, and that by my fall I had lost my hearing, and from that time to this there has

> 'Not to me returned
> The sound of voice responsive, no feast divine
> Of reason, the "flow of soul," nor sports
> Of wit fantastic : from the cheerful speech
> Of men cut off, and intercourse of thought
> And wisdom.' *

I did not entirely recover my strength till eight months after, four of which I kept my bed from weakness, during which time I had leeches applied to my temples and under my ears, also an issue on my neck, besides taking plenty of nauseous physic—all to no purpose as to my deafness, for I do not expect to hear any more. Ever since, after dark or sunset, and in a great measure in the day, I have always had an irregular uneven pace and a labouring gait, and after dark I stagger like a drunken man. Thus, you see, no sooner had youthful fancy begun to sport in the fairy fields of hope, than all my hopes anticipated, and present pleasures and happiness, were, by this one stroke, destroyed. O! ye millions, who enjoy the blessing of which I am deprived, how little do ye know how to appreciate its enjoyment! Man is of such a fickle nature, that he ever slights the pleasures he has, to sigh for those he has not. However, I will attempt to give you an idea of my deprivation. Fair lady, how should you like to forego the incense of flattery (so gratifying to female vanity) offered you by the admiring throng? I believe, my Lord, you would regret being deprived of the fulsome adulation offered you daily by abject (pardon me, my Lord) sycophants. Sir, who are you? What are those who extol you to the skies? You are a wonder, I must own—a rich poet. Yet, remember it is not to your poetical or personal merit they pay homage, but to your wealth you owe it; nor forget that such men as those who flatter you, could suffer, unmoved, an Otway, a Chatterton, and many others, to die 'unpitied'—I had almost added, 'unknown'—the former of want, and the latter of ——; but let me not withdraw the veil benevolence has thrown over his memory. Should you, Sir, like to be deprived of this degrading flattery? Ye men of genius, and of wit! Ye patriots and statesmen! Ye men of worth and wisdom! Ye chaste maids and engaging matrons! And ye men of social minds! Should you like to be

> 'From the cheerful speech
> Of men cut off, and intercourse of thought
> And wisdom?'

If not, guess my situation, now I am grown somewhat misanthropic, with no consolation but my books and my granny."

* Imitated from Milton, by Miss Palmer.

He had passed through the fire, and the smell of singeing was upon him. But he never sank into

> "A grief without a pang, void, dark, and drear,
> A stifled, drowsy, unimpassioned grief,
> Which finds no natural outlet, no relief
> In word, or sigh, or tear."

Strange it is to find the editor of the *Pictorial Bible* thus recording of himself :—

"I was to-day most wrongfully accused of cutting off the tip of a cat's tail. They did not know me who thought me capable of such an act of wanton cruelty.

"*June* 2.—I am making my own shoes.

"*June* 9.—I have finished my shoes—they are tolerably strong and neat.

"*August* 14.—I was set to close bits of leather.

"*August* 15.—Said bits of leather that I had closed, were approved of, and I was sent to close a pair of women's shoes, which were also approved of.

"*August* 16.—I was most unaccountably taken from what I had just begun to learn, to go to my old work (making of list shoes), in which I am perfect as it is possible to be. S—— who, without being acquainted with the structure of a list shoe, dictates to us who are, without any authority but that of being a man (a very little one too), and bids us, under pain of the stirrup, make a pair of shoes per diem, which is particularly hard on me, who, besides doing my own work, am obliged to teach the rest.

"*November* 14.—I forgot to mention that, on Monday, I had been a year in the workhouse, during which time I have made seventy-eight pairs of list shoes, besides mending many others, and have received, as a premium, one penny per week.

"*November* 20.—Set to tapping leather shoes to-day."

In striking contrast with these revelations about list and leather, tapping and closing, waxing and sewing, occurs the following entry, which proves that the mind of the pauper shoemaker was not only busy, but stretching far above and beyond the walls of the workhouse:—

"I burnt a tale of which I had written several sheets (quarto), which I called 'The Probationary Trial,' but which did not, so far as I wrote, please me."

The discipline of the workhouse was occasionally administered in profusion, and on a somewhat miscellaneous principle. He records that, on one occasion, having finished his shoes, and when he was waiting for the soles of others to be cut out, he began to '*write a copy*' for Kelly, and had only written one letter, when the beadle came in, and "gravely gave us a stirrupping all round"—idleness being the alleged ground of the castigation.

Amongst the most interesting entries in the Journal, are those relating to his grandmother, who had nursed and watched him with more than maternal fondness and self-denial, and whom he regarded with more than filial affection. On the first page occurs the following entry, which we copy as it stands :—

"1819.—Granny has been absent in Dock this 2 days. Tho' but for so short a period I severely feel her absence. If I feel it so acutely now, how shall I bear the final separation when she shall be gone to that 'undiscovered country from whose bourn no traveller returns?' She cannot be expected to live many years longer, for now she is more than seventy years of age. O, Almighty Power, spare yet a few years my granny —the protector of my infancy, and the . . . I cannot express my gratitude. It is useless to attempt it."

His interviews with this relative are the epochs of his life. He carefully notes her gifts to him, is rejoiced when she is pleased, and sadly dismayed when he hears of her being in a "fine taking" about any domestic occurrence. After numerous incidental allusions, he writes :—

"*April* 16.—Granny is worse again. She seems almost unconscious of everything; yet she knows me, for she held out her hand to me when I was going.

"*April* 17.—She does not know me!—She is speechless. Aunt tells me that the surgeon has given her over—that—she is dying.

"*April* 18.—She is dead.

This was the sensitive and affectionate boy's first great sorrow.

"*April* 20, *Good Friday.*—Being now a little recovered from the first shock, I have, after several attempts, summoned courage to detail particulars. On Wednesday evening, when I came out [from the workhouse], I trod softly up stairs lest I should disturb her repose. Useless precaution! Aunt met me at the head of the stairs, in tears. I entered;—a white sheet over the bed met my view. She was dead! Think you I wept! I did not weep! Tears are for lesser sorrows ; my sensations were too powerful for tears to relieve me. The sluices of my eyes were dried! My brain was on fire! Yet I did not weep. Call me not a monster because I did not weep. I have not wept these four years : but I remember I *have*, when a boy, wept for childish sorrows. Then why do I not weep for this great affliction? Is not this a contradiction? Am I hard of heart? God forbid that tears should be the test, for I felt—I felt insupportable agony.

"Even to an indifferent person the sight of a dead person awakens melancholy reflections ; but when that person is connected by the nearest ties—oh, then— when I saw the corpse—when I saw that those eyes which had often watched my slumbers, and cast on me looks of affection and love, were closed in sleep eternal! —those lips which often had prest mine, which often had opened to soothe me, tell me tales, and form my infant mind, are pale and motionless for ever!—

when I saw that those hands which had led, caressed, and fed me, were for ever stiff and motionless—when I saw all this, and felt that it was for *ever*, guess my feelings, for I cannot describe them. Born to be the sport of fortune, to find sorrow where I hoped for bliss, and to be a mark for the giddy and the gay to shoot at—what I felt at the deprivation of my almost only friend, the reader can better conceive than I can describe. Yet that moment will ever be present to my recollection to the latest period of my existence. Gone for ever! that is the word of agonizing poignancy. Yet not for ever—a few short years at most, and I *may* hope to meet her again—there is my consolation. Joyful meeting! yet a little while to bear this

> 'Fond restless dream which idiots hug,
> Nay, wise men flatter with the name of *Life*,'

and we may meet again. Already I anticipate the moment when, putting off this frail garb of mortality, and putting on the robe of immortality, of celestial brightness and splendour, in the presence of our God we may meet again;—meet again, never to part;—never again to be subject to the frail laws of mortality—to be above the reach of sorrow, temptation, or sickness—to know nought but happiness—celestial happiness and heaven! Accursed be the atheist who seeks to deprive man of his noblest privilege—of his hopes of immortality—of a motive to do good, and degrade him to a level with the beast which browses on the grass of the fields. What were man without this hope? I knelt and prayed for her departed spirit to *Him* in whose hands are life and death, and that He would endue us with resignation to His decrees, for we know that *He* had a right to the life which *He* gave.* Her countenance is not in the least distorted, but calm and placid, like one asleep.

"*April 23, Easter Monday.*—The day before yesterday being the day prior to my grandmother's funeral, and not being certain that I should be able to come out early enough to be present, as it would take place at nine o'clock, I determined to take what might eventually be a last view of the revered remains. I raised the cloth—it was dusk—the features were so composed that I was for a few moments deceived, and thought it *sleep*. I pressed my lips to her forehead; it was cold as monumental marble!—cold for ever! A thousand recollections rushed upon me, of her tenderness and affectionate kindness to me. She, who was now inanimate before me, was, a short time since, full of life and motion; on me her eye then beamed with tenderness, and affection dwelt in each look. When I

---

* This language is only, in Kitto's case, the vehement expression of attachment and sorrow. It meant little more than an earnest hope that his grandmother had gone to heavenly glory.

was sick, she had watched my feverish pillow, and was my nurse; when I was a babe, she had fondled, caressed, and cherished me; in short, she had been more than a mother to me. And this friend, this mother, I never was to behold again. A thousand bitterly pleasing instances of her kindness to me occurred to my recollection, and I found a kind of melancholy pleasure in recalling them to remembrance. I gazed on each well known feature. I kissed her clay cold cheek and pallid lips. I remembered how often my childish whims had vexed her. I remembered how I had sometimes disobeyed her earnest and just commands. I mentally ejaculated,

> 'O that she would but come again!
> I think I'd vex her so no more.'

Fruitless wish! Will the grim tyrant death give up his prey? Will the emancipated soul return to its dreary prison? Ought I to wish it? 'No!' said reason; 'No!' said religion: such a convincing 'No!' they uttered, that I blushed for the wish. Shall I, a frail mortal, wish that undone which my *Maker* has done, and by implication censure His decrees? If (as we may hope) she be happy, will she not grieve to see us repining at her bliss? I will try to be resigned. I thought of all this; but yet I did not weep; for 'twas not a *tear*—my eyes water sometimes; I did not weep; it certainly was not a tear that fell from my eyes as I leant over the open coffin, but it was probably caused by my looking stedfastly at one object. I continued bending over the coffin till darkness hid the features entirely from my sight, and then tore myself away."

Who could surmise that these paragraphs, so fluent and correct, so vivid and tender, were written within the walls of a workhouse, by a deaf and disabled stripling, almost uneducated, wholly unpractised in composition, and seated, in pauper livery, on a tripod from morning till night, working at a list shoe on his lap?

"*April 24.*—About a quarter past eight on Easter Sunday, my father went to Mr. Burnard, and got leave for me to come out. Crape was put round my hat. . . How unable are the trappings of woe to express the sorrow doubly felt within! I looked once more and for the last time on the corpse, once more and for the last time pressed her cold lips, and then she was shut from my view for ever! I felt a something at my heart that moment, which baffles description. I felt as though I could have freely given my life to prolong hers a few years. What! had I viewed for the last time her who was my only benefactor, parent, and friend, and was I never to see her more? 'No!' whispered doubt; 'Yes!' said faith; and she was right. . . At the appointed time we walked in 'sad array' behind the coffin—first, Uncle John and

Aunt Mary. . . . There were about forty persons present : the service was read by Dr. Hawker's curate; the coffin was deposited in the grave and covered with earth. . . . The moment in which the coffin which contains the remains of a beloved relative, is hid from our sight, is, perhaps, a moment of greater agony than at their demise, for *then* we have still the melancholy consolation of contemplating the features of the beloved object; but when that sad and gloomy comfort is taken from us, the feelings of our loss occur with accumulated force; we consider what, a short time since, the contents of the coffin *were*, and what, in a short time, they *will be;* we consider that, in our turn, we shall be conveyed to a similar, if not to the same place, and in our turn be wept over with transient tears, and soon be forgotten. I thought the man almost guilty of sacrilege, and could have beaten him, who threw the earth so unconcernedly on her remains. 'Why does he not weep?' I internally asked. 'Why does not every human being join with me in lamenting her loss?' But I shall not attempt to describe my feelings; they were such, that the moment when I stood on the brink of the grave, eagerly looking on the coffin till the earth concealed it, I shall never forget till the hand that writes this shall be as hers, and the heart that inspires it shall cease to beat. When we came home I felt a kind of faintness coming over me, and if Aunt Mary had not timely rubbed my temples with cold water, I should have fainted. Grandmother is buried on the left hand side of the aisle, opposite the steeple, near the church door (Charles' Church), beneath the headstone erected to the memory of her grand-children."

Still Kitto could freely criticise the perfunctory manner in which he thought the funeral service had been gone through. But the next entry reveals the lacerated state of his heart, and opens up a glimpse of his unhappy home.

"*April* 27.—In consequence of the loss of this revered relative, I already begin to feel a vacuum in my heart, which it is impossible to describe. Who shall supply her place? Nature points to my mother.

While she (grandmother) lived, I had no cause to regret the want of kindness in any other person. But now, alas! she is gone, and I feel myself an isolated being, unloving and unloved; for whom this world, young as I am, has few charms. . . . .

"When I return from the restraint of the workhouse, the rooms look desolate, for she is not there. She who greeted me with looks and smiles of affection is not there! She who prepared my tea, and rejoiced if she had some little delicacy to offer me, is not there! She who chode me if I left her even a short time, is not there! In short, she who loved me, is not there! Who shall supply her place? My mother, or my aunt? My mother! it must be so, it shall be so.

To do her justice, she has been very kind to me since the sad event, and so has aunt. Yes, mother has been very kind. She knows, amongst other things, that my grandmother's death would deprive me of the means of getting almost the only thing I value—*books:* therefore, with great kindness and consideration, my father wrote, by her direction I suppose, 'I will give you the money to get the books.' 'Indeed,' I said, 'but do you know how much it will come to?' 'No.' 'Why, you know,' I said, 'I have got a penny per week at the workhouse, and I change my books (two vols. small, or one large vol.) three times a week, and pay a penny each time; that penny will pay but for one of those changes.' Father wrote, 'You shall never want twopence the week.' Was not this kind? very kind, I think. I shall have no occasion to put their kindness in this last instance to the test as yet; but will this kindness last? Will they not, when they think the edge of my grief is blunted, relapse into their former indifference? I expressed this doubt to my mother. She assured me of her continued kindness, and that she would see this last act of it duly performed. I would have said, but did not—O, my mother! representive of the dear friend I have lost, would that I were certain that this kindness would continue; would that I were certain that your present kindness would never cease, and that while I am in need of your aid, you will continue to accord it to me; and then, when manhood shall have nerved my arm, and age have enfeebled *yours*, and you will need the aid of your children, how happy shall I be, and how shall I exult to be able to step forward and say, 'My father, and my mother! while I was yet a boy and needed your help, you granted it me; then, O my parents, how I longed for opportunity to show my gratitude! The time is come, and now you need it; as you once offered me your aid, so now I offer you mine, henceforth let all mine be yours.' . . I think I could love my mother almost as well as I did love my grandmother." And in his mother's old and infirm days he did verify his wish.

"*June* 10.—I have been to aunt's; was received kindly; before I came away uncle wrote, 'You must come out here as often as you can, for it was the dying request of your grandmother that *we* should be kind to *you.*' And did she think of *me!* to the last anxious for me—interested even in death for my welfare! and making friends for me! My only friend! my revered benefactor! my dearest grandmother! in death didst thou think of *me!* Oh that I had been present! Yet, no, I could not have borne it. Father! receive her soul into Thy mercy, and guide my steps in the intricate paths of human life, beset as it is with thorns and briars, with temptations and sorrows : and if it be Thy pleasure that I should drink the cup of human misery and affliction to the very dregs—even then, Lord, in the midst of all, grant me strength that I may not swerve from Thy will, nor murmur at Thy decrees; for well I know that whatsoever Thou doest is just and right, and that, though Thy commandments teach me to resist the dominion of my senses, they, in the end, lead to the eternal mansions of the blessed. I humbly pray Thee, my God, that there I may at last arrive, through Jesus Christ, and there meet her who has gone before me."

He had sad doubts that the affection now shown by some of his nearest relatives would soon cool, and he felt that then he should be desolate indeed. Thus he sobs—"Why do I feel? why dare I think? Am I not a workhouse boy? My father, if you could but imagine what, through your means, I suffer, you would—Begone pen, or I shall go mad."

Whatever appealed to Kitto's eye gratified him; and among his ocular amusements, the "shows" at Plymouth fair occupied a prominent place. A fair was great or small, in his boyish estimation, in proportion to the number and splendour of such exhibitions. What he saw he describes in his journal with picturesque minuteness: the transparencies and pictures; an "ill looking pock-marked dwarf," or a giantess so plump and fleshy as to "make the mouth of an anatomist water." The various devices and blazonries, stars and fireworks, first on the conclusion of Queen Caroline's trial, and then at the King's coronation, were a special treat to him. But his deafness occasionally filled his soul with sad regrets. The constables had on one occasion collected into the workhouse all the unfortunate women of the town. Kitto gazed on the scene with melancholy, and moralized upon the lost creatures "covered with shame, abandoned by friends, shunned by acquaintances, and thrown on the wide world—insulted with reproach, denied the privilege of penitence, cut off from hope, impelled by indigence, and maddened by despair." After service, "one of the best gentlemen in Plymouth addressed them, so that many of them wept, as well as five-sixths of all the people in the room. Even I," he adds, "had almost wept from sympathy." In recording this, there came upon him at once the overpowering sense of his own desolation. And he writes, October 15, in touching moans :—"Yet I alone was insensible to the inspiration that flowed from his lips. To all, insensible! Devotion! oratory! music! and eloquence! To all of ye alike insensible!"

In a similar cheerless spirit he soliloquizes :—

". . . I should be inconsolable under my great misfortune, were it not for the conviction, that it is for wise purposes the Almighty Power has thought proper to chastise me with the rod of affliction. And dare I, a worm, the creature of His will, to repine at His behests? Besides, He has declared, 'Those whom I

love I rebuke and chasten.' But whither do I wander? Dare I to think that an accident was His infliction? Dare I to hope that the Omniscient will deign, when I pray, to attend to my supplications? I dare not— 'twere presumption—'twere almost impiety—to think *He* would incline His ear to such a one as *me—me*, of all my species created the inferior—*me*, whom each eye views with contempt—who am mocked, buffeted, and despised. And why am I thus treated with contumely? Because I am—unfortunate! And does misfortune render me inferior in Thy eyes, O my God? No, for Thou hast said, Thou art no respecter of persons. Thou hearest alike the king on his throne, and the beggar on his dunghill. Though man treats me with contumely, Thou wilt not be less merciful. Pardon my doubt, which had dared to prescribe limits to Thy mercy, and endue me with resignation to kiss the salutary rod with which Thou (I dare almost say it) chastisest me. . . . I fear I am deplorably ignorant in religious matters."

The language employed in the preceding and succeeding paragraphs is scarcely that of a quiet resignation, but rather of a stubborn acquiescence. The youth who had suffered such degradation from a father's intemperance as now to be a pensioner on a public charity, and who had, by a mysterious Providence, been suddenly bereft of a precious faculty, succumbed, indeed, to his lot, but at first with seeming reluctance, and with a strange curiosity to "cast the measure of uncertain evils."

"1821, *January* 1.—Welcome 1821! Though thy greeting is but rough (uncommonly cold), boding a year of as great events as thy predecessor, I pray God that, as I am conscious I have but ill performed my duty as an accountable being the preceding year, and that my lot in life is but low, He will deign to look on the most humble of His creatures, and blot out of the book of His remembrance the sins I have committed heretofore; to endue me with fortitude to bear with resignation whatsoever misfortunes may yet assail me, and to enable me to resist temptation, the allurements of vice, and even my own thoughts when they lead to ill; and to enable me, if it be His pleasure, to drink the cup of misfortune to the very dregs without repining; and, finally, through all my life to make me bear in mind that this life is but a probationary trial, to fit us for a greater and a better state hereafter."

Kitto's powers of composition were in the meanwhile improving, and he criticises public characters in a free and independent style. The first sentence of the following description is felicitous. It was inserted in his diary on learning the Queen's acquittal. Many glowing sentences were written at the period: the eloquent declamation and satire of Brougham and Denman thrilled the nation; but the hearty and stirring tribute of the obscure workhouse cobbler has never been printed before.

"*November* 14.—Bells ringing, flags flying, and almost every person rejoicing, on the occasion of innocence and the Queen being triumphant; for the bill of pains and penalties was withdrawn on Saturday, November 10th, by the Earl of Liverpool, from the House of Peers. The day on which the Queen was victorious over slander and revenge will ever claim a distinguished place in the annals of this country—a day on which slander, perjury, and guilt were vanquished by innocence and truth. This trial has been such a one continued scene of iniquity as has not been equalled since the time of the Tudors (except in the instance of Charles I. and Louis XVI.) Last week has shown these are not such days as those unenlightened days in which the tyrannic Henry swayed despotically the symbol of mercy—those days when Britons could tamely see an innocent Queen (Anne Boleyn) led to the scaffold on a pretended charge of adultery. No! Such days are over; and now the generous character of Britain will not suffer an unprotected female to be persecuted with impunity. Not unprotected neither! She cannot be called unprotected who has the hearts of two-thirds of all Britain warmed with enthusiasm in her cause; and experience has shown that their hearts are no despicable protection. The conclusion of this iniquitous transaction has overwhelmed the enemies of the Queen with shame and confusion. Greater part of Britain will be illuminated in the course of the week—Plymouth on Wednesday.

"16*th*.—Plymouth was illuminated last night."

The next excerpt, in a different strain, is a meditation on the death of Napoleon. It betokens the interest taken in public matters by the young recluse, who never "saw a newspaper to read till he was nearly twenty years of age."

"*July* 6.—Learned that Napoleon Buonaparte died on the 6th of May, of a cancer in his stomach. He was ill forty days. I doubt not but that the public journals, newspapers, etc., have detailed all the particulars of his exit from the theatre of the world, in which he has shown as a meteor—a meteor of destructive influence; and I shall only give a few observations on his character, according to my idea of it.* That he had talents, no man who has attentively considered his conduct and character can doubt; but such talents! He was an innate tyrant—he introduced himself to notice by his eminence in adulation and cruelty. That he was a cruel man, his conduct has always shown. Witness the dreadful Bridge of Lodi, the massacre of

* The page is adorned with a portrait of Napoleon, done in glaring colours, and looking rather fierce, and is said by Kitto to be copied from a plate in Barre's *Rise, Progress, etc., of Buonaparte's Empire.*

Jaffa, and the poisoning his own sick soldiers. He was more than suspected as the murderer of the Duke d'Enghien. I consider him as a man who, from the earliest period of public life, was resolved to let no considerations of honour, religion, humanity, or any other consideration, to interfere with his advancement. Nor did they interfere. He certainly had not always thoughts of obtaining the sovereign power; but his ambition for sovereignty arose from circumstances, step by step. After the abolition of royalty and nobility, and the declaration of equality, he was resolved to admit of no superior. That he was ungrateful, may be seen by his treatment of his former patron. One or two centuries hence, and even now—if we knew not its reality—it would be considered as an improbable fiction, belonging to the ages of romance, that a man of obscure origin should thus become the ruler of nearly all Europe—thus realize the visions of Don Quixote, and reward his Sanchos with kingdoms at his pleasure —thus spread desolation, fire, and sword, where nought but peace was known before;* that a man—a simple man—an unsupported man, should thus make princes crouch at his footstool, and should have his will obeyed as a law. How many thousands of widows and orphans has he not made? A lesser villain would have been hanged for the thousandth part of his crimes; yet he has his admirers. Notwithstanding what has been said by many to the contrary, I allow him the meed of personal courage, and that he was grateful when he could gain nothing by being the contrary. He was an hypocrite and an infidel; for he has different times been of almost all religions, Mohammedan included. He was generous by starts—condescending when Emperor—irritable, hasty, insolent, and choleric. It will not be considered as the less extraordinary part of his story, that, in the end, he was unfortunate—obliged to abdicate his throne, and was twice banished; but, above all, that this man—this Napoleon Buonaparte—died in his bed of a cancer, while the great and the good Henry died by the hand of an assassin, and the meek Louis died on a scaffold!! On the whole, it may be said of Buonaparte, that he was a glorious villain!!"†

And yet, amidst all the youth's dejection, there were forereachings of spirit, anxious anticipations, the picturings of possible propitious circumstances. His highest

* Switzerland.
† It would seem that Kitto had been reading a well known passage in Milton, one of his favourite poets:—

" Might only shall be admired,
And valour and heroic virtue called;
To overcome in battle and subdue
Nations, and bring home spoils with infinite
Manslaughter, shall be held the highest pitch
Of human glory, and for glory done
Of triumph, to be styled great conquerors,
Patrons of mankind, gods, and sons of gods.
Destroyers rightlier called, and plagues of men."

ambition at this time was to have a stationer's shop and a circulating library, with twelve or fourteen shillings a week. His anxious question was, " When I am out, how shall I earn a livelihood?" Shoemaking could yield but a slender remuneration; and as he had been taught to make coarse shoes alone, he could only expect small wages. Yet he thought that he might travel, and that some kind gentleman might take him, even though it were in the humble capacity of a servant, " to tread classic Italy, fantastic Gaul, proud Spain, and phlegmatic Batavia"—nay, " to visit Asia, and the ground consecrated by the steps of the Saviour." This odd anticipation of Asiatic travel was wondrously realized, for a " kind gentleman" did afterwards take him to the banks of the Tigris.

The long and heavy affliction of Kitto had brought him under religious impressions. He had felt the Divine chastening, and stooped to it. It was a necessity to which he was obliged to yield, and, as he could not better himself, he bowed, though he sometimes fretted.

" O nature," he exclaims, " why didst thou create me with such feelings as these," which spring from " superiority of genius?" " Why didst thou give such a mind to one in my condition? Why, O Heaven, didst thou enclose my proud soul within so rough a casket? Yet pardon my murmurs. Kind Heaven! endue me with resignation to Thy will."

But a quieter emotion gradually acquired the ascendency within him, and he strove to feel that it was the hand of God his Father which had placed him beyond the reach of sound or echo. His knowledge of the Bible began to produce its quickening results, and spirit was infused into the forms of religion. He wished earnestly to be confirmed, and made the necessary application. He was found to be deficient, when first examined, in some portion of the Catechism; but he adds, " I learnt the Catechism perfect," and he was then approved by Mr. Lampen, the officiating minister of St. Andrews. Yet at the first occasion on which he attended, he was not confirmed; the bishop, and " the man with the gold lace cloak," with the crowds about him, divided his attention, while his want of hearing prevented him from understanding and following the order of the ceremonial.

Mr. Nugent, teacher of one of the schools in the hospital, began at this time to pay special attention to him, wrote out some theological questions for him to answer, and promised to be his friend. Mr. Burnard's interest was also increased by reading certain papers of Kitto's, suggesting a plan of judicature among the boys. He proposed to the thoughtful projector, a short time afterwards, to write lectures to be read to them, " respecting their duty in the house, and their future conduct." This proposal agreeably surprised

Kitto, and he could not contain himself: " You can scarcely imagine, my friend, how this letter delighted me, and set me a walking up and down the court with uncommon quickness, eagerly talking to myself. Take a bit of my soliloquy: 'What! I, John Kitto, to write lectures to be read to the boys! Mr. Burnard seems to think me competent to it too!' rubbing my hands with great glee." The youth was filled with gratitude to both these gentlemen, formally adding Mr. Nugent to the list of his benefactors, and saying, in the fulness of his heart, of Mr. Burnard, " I wish, I wish his life was in danger, and I could risk my own to save him. That won't do either—too much danger for him." This feature of Kitto's character grew with his growth, and in his last work he lays down the true doctrine: " He who most clearly sees God as the source of his blessings, is the man who will be most grateful to the agents through whom these blessings come to him.* Kitto, on one occasion, hints that he did not like to see Mr. Burnard whipping the boys, for it was so unlike his generous nature.

The boys used to teaze Kitto a good deal, when the eye of their superiors was withdrawn, till his patience was at length exhausted, and he made a formal complaint to Mr. Burnard. The " frisky letter," as one of the accused styled it, was at once acknowledged, and his tormentors were severely cautioned as to their misconduct, and prohibited from indulging any longer in such wanton cruelty and sport.

He was becoming, as we have said, more and more anxious about his religious duties. He speaks, under date of October 12, of its being one of the inconveniences of the workhouse, that he was not able to kneel when prayers were publicly read, but resolves to begin on that day to pray " with himself" in the morning, " inclining one knee against a chest" which was under the window.

Kitto's dealings with his father are much to his credit. We give two extracts, the first a specimen of humour, and the second of integrity:—

" *February* 17, 1821.—The week before last, father wrote on the table with chalk, 'you never gave me anything to drink yet.' I went, gravely, and emptied out a cup of water, and gave it to him, and said, 'There—drink.' He blushed deep at this pun, and said no more about it."

" *October* 7.—Father wrote a paper as follows, and wanted me to give it to Mr. Burnard:—'Sir, I should be much obliged to you if you will be so good as to give a ticket for a shirt, as I am out of work.—Jn. Kitto.' 'Father, thou sayest the thing that is not— you are not out of work.'—'You must give this paper to Mr. Burnard.' 'Are you out of work, father?'— 'No.' Then, do you think that I will deceive my

* *Daily Bible Illustrations* Vol. 1, p. 335.

benefactor, and permit you to say, through me, that you are? I will not give it to him.' So I said, and so I did. . . . I am inclined to think that I was right. My duty to my parents shall never interfere with that to God."

Though Kitto felt the restraint of the workhouse, he had become reconciled to it. He was at times, indeed, anxious to quit it, and at other times willing to remain when liberty was offered him. His father on one occasion held out some hopes to him, and, though he refused at first to leave, yet he soon altered his mind, and became very desirous to get out. But his father had changed his purpose, if ever he had seriously entertained it, and the lad was sorely disappointed. The father put forward a variety of objections, but the excited son rebutted them all in succession. "Liberty," he cries, "was my idol—liberty, not idleness. If it were not for the bounty of the kind Mr. Burnard, the workhouse would be insupportable. Methinks when I am out of the house, I breathe almost another air. . . . Like the wolf in the fable, I would rather starve at liberty than grow fat under restraint." Believing that his father was only "seeking causes" against his getting out, he waxes warm, and tells him, "There is no fear of my starving in the midst of plenty—I know how to prevent hunger. The Hottentots subsist a long time on nothing but a little gum; they also, when hungry, tie a tight ligature round them. Cannot I do so too? Or, if you can get no pay, take me out without, and then I will sell my books, and pawn my neckerchiefs, by which I shall be able to raise about twelve shillings, and with that I will make the tour of England. The hedges furnish blackberries, nuts, sloes, etc., and the fields turnips—a hay rick or barn will be an excellent bed. I will take pen, ink, and paper with me, and note down my observations as I go—a kind of sentimental tour, not so much a description of places as of men and manners, adventures and feelings. Finally, me and father said much more." The debate was resumed a couple of months afterwards, and Kitto still thought himself ill used, his father having raised "false hopes" within him. He admits, that, in displaying such pertinacity, he was in the wrong; "for, upon the whole," he writes, "I am not dissatisfied with my present condition." But he drew up what he calls "articles of capitulation," and presented them to his parents, insisting that his father, when he agreed to any of them, should write "granted" opposite to it, while his mother was to make a cross to signify her assent. The principal heads were—that he should be taken out on the 1st of April 1822, or sooner if he was maltreated; that his boxes and papers were not to be rummaged at home; that he was not to be interrupted in his studies; and that, if he died, his body was not to be taken from the workhouse to the grave, but first carried home, and thence conveyed to the place of interment, "in New Churchyard, beside granny." The last of the stipulations reveals his suspicions, for it is, "that you be kind to me." To all these articles the parents agreed. The curious document thus solemnly concludes :—" We, the undersigned, do hereby promise to abide by what we have in the above promised to perform, and if we in the least tittle infringe it, we do consent that John Kitto, junior, shall do as he has said; as witness our hands this sixth day of August, in the year of our Lord one thousand eight hundred and twenty-one. On the part of John Kitto, junior,

" JOHN KITTO, Jun.

" On the part of J. and E. Kitto, seniors,

" JN. KITTO.

" + ELIZABETH KITTO, her mark."

He adds, however, that by this formal arrangement he " gained nothing more than before." But he was soon released in a manner, and with a result, that he little anticipated.

It was quite common with the guardians of the poorhouse to apprentice the boys under their care to tradesmen in the town. They were anxious, as Mr. Burnard expresses it, that Kitto should " learn a trade, so that he might be able to support himself without parish relief."* This was a kind and considerate motive on their part. It was, in fact, the only design which they could legitimately entertain. That the lad should not be a burden to society or to them, that he should be able to maintain himself by honest handicraft, that at least he should not return to them and be a pensioner on their bounty—was the loftiest purpose they could form for him. Therefore Anderson, the beadle, taught him shoemaking, and he made great progress. To perfect him in his trade, he was then indentured, on the 8th November 1821, to one John Bowden, who had selected him for his proficiency, and in spite of his infirmity. He was to remain under this engagement till he was twenty-one years of age, and he was now about seventeen. The guardians probably congratulated themselves that they had done their duty to their ward, John Kitto, and that they had fitted him to be a useful member of society. They had got him capricious and wayward, and now they turned him out a quiet and thoughtful youth, who had shown some mental power, was inordinately fond of reading, and had subjected himself to an excellent moral discipline. Probably they lamented, at the same time, that his deafness would exclude all rational hopes of elevation and progress.

By this time, as we have seen, Kitto had subdued his spirit to the routine and degradation of a poorhouse life. He was even comparatively contented

* Letter to Mrs. Kitto, written after Dr. Kitto's death.

among his pursuits and associates. And yet, though he had found such an appreciation of his talents as might have ministered to his youthful vanity, and not a few indulgences were given him, still he seems sometimes to have regarded the hospital as a species of Bastile, and he rejoiced in the idea of quitting it. He was periodically anxious to be gone; grumbled that his father had not kept his word and taken him out; nay, he threatened again and again to run away, though he usually laughed to himself at such a clumsy mode of exit and escape. The first offer to remove did not tempt him, for it presented, in fact, few inducements; so that he hesitated, but afterwards consented. And then the idea of finally quitting such a domicile filled his spirit with exultation, and, with a flourish of his pen—not elegant, indeed, but expressive—he writes :—

❦ EPOCHA. ❦ .

"I am no longer a workhouse boy—I am an apprentice." He felt that he had risen a step in society, that he had ceased to wear the badge of serfdom, and that he was once more master of himself, save in so far as he was bound by the terms of his indenture. What we have said is quite consistent with his indifference when the proposal was originally made. He said "No" to Bowden's first invitation; but some of the boys, "aside," held out the inducement "of food, clothes, money, and freedom;" "I pleaded deafness." "I do not care," he replied to repeated questions, "I would as soon stay as go." Some time was spent in negotiations, and at last his coy reluctance was overcome. He never was easily induced to change his habits, and this inflexibility of nature did, for the moment, almost conquer his oft expressed desire to get out of confinement. His own exclamation, however, leaves no doubt of his rapture—"I am no longer a workhouse boy !" The going home at night, the possession of his evenings for himself, the power of reading in his own garret without molestation, the dropping of the poorhouse uniform, food in plenty, and good clothes—these formed an irresistible temptation. "Therefore, on Friday 2," he records, "I gave a paper to Mr. Burnard expressing that desire, and soliciting his aid to my being apprenticed."

The only objection to Kitto's leaving the workhouse was made by Anderson, and that was because the hospital could not afford to dispense with his services, since he was the only boy perfect in the making of list shoes. Nay, Anderson afterwards wished to get him back for the same reason, but Bowden was too shrewd and selfish to part with him.

Kitto had, during his residence, become attached to many things about the workhouse ; and, in the prospect of quitting it, he relates—" So I went and took a

farewell look of the bed on which I used to sleep, the tripod on which I had sat so many hours, and the prayer-room. I shook hands, in idea, with the pump, the conduit at which I washed, the tree against which I leaned, nay, the very stones on which I walked. . . I then took a final leave of the hospital, and we went to Mr. Bowden's house again, when I was aproned and seated, and set to rip off the old tap of a boot."

But the hopes of the buoyant apprentice were soon and terribly blasted. His next year's journal opens in a tone of hopeless anguish. He had been delivered into the hand of a brutal tyrant—one who hoped that the infirmity of his apprentice would disable him from making any complaint, and prevent him from obtaining any redress. Bowden's previous apprentice had also been deaf, and we cannot suppose that his treatment differed from that suffered by his successor. But the poor creature had not a tongue to tell, nor a pen to reveal his woes. Bowden, on looking round the busy inmates of the hospital, selected John Kitto, not simply because he discerned him to be the best workman in it, but because he imagined that his deafness, like that of his predecessor, might enable his master to work him beyond right, and punish him without limit, and yet run no risk of being himself detected and exposed. A speechless apprentice he had found to be a helpless victim, who could neither murmur under exhaustion, nor appeal against stripes. The six months of his apprenticeship with Bowden formed the most miserable period of Kitto's existence. He groans mournfully indeed :—

"January 19.—O misery, art thou to be my only portion! Father of mercy, forgive me if I wish I had never been born. O that I were dead, if death were an annihilation of being ; but as it is not, teach me to endure life; enjoy it I never can. In short, mine is a severe master, rather cruel." The retrospect of two months is sad as he gives it. Bowden threw a shoe at his head, because he had made a wry stitch, struck him again and again—now a blow on the ear, and now a slap on the face. He wept at this unkind usage. "I did all in my power to suppress my inclination to weep, till I was almost suffocated : tears of bitter anguish and futile indignation fell upon my work and blinded my eyes. I sobbed convulsively. I was half mad with myself for suffering him to see how much I was affected. Fool that I was! O that I were again in the workhouse!

December 12.—My head ached, and yet they kept me to work till six o'clock, when they let me come away. I could eat nothing."

"January 14.—He threw the pipe in my face, which I had accidentally broken ; it hit me on the temple, and narrowly missed my eye."

"January 16.—I held the thread too short; instead of

telling me to hold it longer, he struck me on the hand with the hammer (the iron part). Mother can bear witness that it is much swelled; not to mention many more indignities I have received—many, many more; again, this morning, I have wept. What's the matter with my eyes!"

" I here leave off this Journal till some other change, or extraordinary misfortune, takes place!"

Such is the melancholy end of the Workhouse Journal.

He did not know what awful thing was to happen him, for he had been tossed about like a ball, and he could not predict where next he should either alight or rebound. He could not bear up. He had already suffered much. He had felt in former days the pang of hunger and the cold of nakedness. But now he was oppressed, overwrought, and maltreated,—for sixteen and often eighteen hours of the twenty-four, did his master force him to drudge, and all the while strike and buffet him without mercy. Workhouse boys have few to look after them, and fewer still to interfere for them. And why should Kitto be any exception? The slavery could not be endured. He had been all the while devoting his spare hours to mental labour—and even this luxury was at length denied him. To keep himself awake for study, he had to torture himself by several cunning appliances. He was willing to have wrought twelve hours so to have some time for reading, thankful to snatch a brief period for sleep. But to toil from six in the morning to ten at night left him so exhausted, that only by a painful effort could a little ·space be given to reading and thought. This tyranny preyed upon his mind, such castigations galled him, the long hours of labour, and the short intervals left for study, oppressed and fretted him. His nervous system was shattered, trains of morbid reasoning usurped supremacy over him, conscience was perverted by sophistical ingenuities, and his spirit, weary and worn out, looked to suicide as its last and justifiable refuge. The crisis came; but, as in the case of Cowper, a watchful Providence interposed, and Kitto lived. In the volume of essays which he published on leaving the workhouse, there are two papers on suicide. In the first, the sin is set in its true light; in the second, it is described more leniently, and much in the way in which, in the period of his misery and gloom, he had gradually brought himself to contemplate it. In illustration of his remarks, he gives, under the assumed name of William Wanley, a portion of his own biography, detailing his dark sensations, how he formed the purpose of self-destruction, justified it, and resolved to carry it out. But the attempt failed. The valuable life, which was about to fall a sacrifice to wretchedness and despair, was preserved for higher ends, and did work them out, till God's time came for its final release.

The Life and History of Wanley were his own, and he formally identifies them. He tells Mr. Woollcombe, some years afterwards (December 1825), that " his mind was darker and more wretched than anything he had ever read of "—that " the letter of Wanley was no posterior fabrication, no picture of imagined anguish, but emanated from a warm and loving heart, every vein and fibre of which seemed lacerated with misery too highly for the highest powers of language to express." In sending the Essay and Letter of Wanley to Mr. Woollcombe, prior to their being printed, he wrote this admission :—

" *January* 8, 1824.—You will experience no difficulty in discovering the identity of Wanley. Though he is happier, very much happier, now than at any period during the last half of his life, all his endeavours cannot prevent the occurrence of that melancholy which predominated once so absolutely over him. . . The event which I have narrated is one which he now contemplates with grief, and on which he looks back with the greatest repentance." In a brief sketch of his early life, written just before he left the workhouse, he confesses more explicitly—" The life of misery I led reduced me to such a state of despair, that I twice attempted my liberation from his [Bowden's] tyranny by a means that I now shudder to think of."

The complaints of Bowden's apprentice against his master became at length the subject of judicial investigation. The trial was adjourned in the first instance, and one of those times of " despair," to which Kitto refers in the previous sentence, happened in this interval of suspense, when, misunderstanding the forms of procedure, he believed that he had been formally condemned to be sent back to undergo, without hope or respite, Bowden's cruel and lawless oppression. But at length he obtained redress. The instrument of his slavery, " with its formidable appendage of seals and signatures," was cancelled, after his case had been fully heard before the magistrates, with whose sanction he had been originally indentured. In his appeal to them Kitto acquitted himself to admiration. He wrote so fluently and so correctly as to astonish the bench. His pen delivered him from bondage, and gave him the consciousness of possessing an undeveloped power. He became aware that he could not only think, but express his thoughts—that he could not only feel, but give fitting language to his emotions. The gentlemen, who tried the case, wondered, questioned, sympathized, applauded, and set him at liberty, but did not trouble themselves much more about him. They must have thought him a bold and bright little fellow, who was armed with a rare power of self-defence, and would not be easily put down; but, while they delivered him from the tyrant, they took no steps to improve his condition. They had only a very partial acquaintance with him, and probably judged that the workhouse was his happiest asylum.

Thus Kitto returned to the hospital, and was set down again to his former occupation, to be perfected in it—still for the avowed purpose of enabling him to earn an honest livelihood. He received many minor privileges, for which he was thankful. Bright visions of the future began, however, to cheer him. He thought himself destined to something. What might he not do? Might he not write or compose a work? Be it in poetry or in prose, might it not immortalize his name? What should hinder the achievement? Might not every obstacle be surmounted, and John Kitto become an author known to fame? Thanks to Bowden's outrage. It stung him into life. He began to criticise some things he had written, and pronounce them trash,—the first sign of growing taste and judgment. He had proposed a higher standard for himself, and now laboured to come up to it. His reading had enabled him to judge of style, and had supplied him with many illustrations. His awakened power longed for exertion, but he knew not as yet where to find the proper field for it.

The experiences of this period are thus delineated by him :—" I had learned that knowledge is power ; and not only was it power, but safety. As nearly as the matter can now be traced, the progress of my ideas appears to have been this—Firstly, that I was not altogether so helpless as I had seemed ; secondly, that, notwithstanding my afflicted state, I might realise much comfort in the condition of life in which I had been placed ; thirdly, that I might even raise myself out of that condition into one of less privation; fourthly, that it was not impossible for me to place my own among honourable names, by proving that no privation formed an insuperable bar to useful labour and self-advancement. . . . To do what no one under the same combination of afflictive circumstances ever did, soon then ceased to be the limit of my ambition." *

But he must, in the meantime, learn his craft, to please Mr. Burnard and commend himself to the guardians. He and they, however, were fast diverging in purpose. They thought of him as a shoemaker ; he pictured himself as an author. They saw him on " the tripod ;" he beheld himself at a desk. They strove to give him the ability of making a shoe ; he dreamed of the power of producing a book. But immediate duty must be attended to, and Kitto passed more months in the workhouse. Again and again did he enjoy his solitary walks—a favourite scene of recreation being the Hoe, a magnificent parade, with the sea and breakwater before it, the ships and docks on one side of it, and, to the right, the classic groves and shady retreats of Mount-Edgecumbe.

* *Lost Senses—Deafness*, pp. 82, 83.

The style of his correspondence at this epoch indicates higher moral health, and a more refined taste. The cloud was passing away, and his mind was possessing itself " in patience." His fevered brow was cooler, and the dew had fallen on his parched heart. He knew not what was before him, but he was becoming equal to anything that might occur. Though he was conscious of talent, there was no inflation of pride, for he was resolved to refuse no offer that might promise to be of advantage. He knew that only step by step could he reach the summit ; nor did he seem to be devoured by eagerness for elevation. Probably, however, he was disappointed that nothing further was done for him. But he had awakened interest on his behalf—such interest as sufficed, when a project was started for his benefit, to crown it with success. His case was matter of wide notoriety ; yet no one stepped forward to lend a helping hand to the deaf and lonely aspirant.

But Mr. Harvey came at length to the rescue. This famed mathematician and man of science had observed Kitto's demeanour in a bookseller's shop, and anxiously inquired about him. Learning his history and circumstances, his benevolent heart knew no rest till he had interested others on Kitto's behalf, and induced them to contribute something, either money or stationery, to the studious youth's assistance. Mr. Nettleton also, of the *Plymouth Weekly Journal*, inserted some of his compositions in that paper. So that Kitto became known, was more and more asked after, and a deeper anxiety being excited, a few friends issued a joint circular on his behalf, the language of which shows the favourable impression which his character and talents had created. The following is the circular referred to :—

" The attention of the public has lately been drawn, by some Essays published in the *Plymouth Weekly Journal*, to the very extraordinary talents of John Kitto, who is now a pauper in the Plymouth workhouse. He is about eighteen years of age, and has been nearly four years in the workhouse, to which he was reduced by the inability of his parents to maintain him, after his having lost his hearing by a fall from a house in Batter Street, where he was employed as an attendant on the masons. This loss of hearing has been accompanied with other bodily infirmities ; but he has been thus so entirely thrown on the resources of his mind, that he has cultivated his intellectual faculties with singular success, and gives promise of making very considerable attainments. An inquiry into his conduct and general character has proved most satisfactory to the undersigned, who are thus led to believe that he must greatly interest those who feel for the difficulties under which virtue and talents labour when they have to struggle with poverty and misfortune. He has of late been employed as a shoe-maker in the workhouse, and in that capacity he has given proofs of great skill and industry; but it seems desirable that he should be placed in a situation more consistent with his feelings and abilities, and to which his deafness might not render him incompetent. It has been suggested that, as a temporary measure, application should be made to the Committee of the Plymouth Public Library, to employ him as a Sub-Librarian; and that a sum might be raised, by small subscriptions, to enable him to obtain board and lodging in some decent family, until something permanently advantageous should be suggested. In the meantime, although he could not be in the receipt of a salary, he would have opportunities of improving himself, and would be enabled to direct the powers of his mind to those pursuits in which he is so well qualified to excel, and in which, perhaps, the world may find his useful-ness, and he himself a merciful and abundant com-pensation for all his deprivations. Great reliance may be placed on his industrious habits, and it is confidently believed that small contributions from several indivi-duals would enable him to get over the chief impedi-ments to success in a way for which he seems so peculiarly well qualified. The undersigned, who have carefully examined into his character and acquire-ments, are anxious to give the strongest testimony in his behalf; and will receive, with great pleasure, any contributions, pledging themselves to use the utmost discretion in their power in the application of any money that may be thus intrusted to their management.—JOHN HAWKER, HENRY WOOLLCOMBE,* WILLIAM EASTLAKE, THOMAS STEWART, JOHN TING-COMBE, GEORGE HARVEY, ROBERT LAMPEN.—*Plymouth, 26th June,* 1823."

This modest narrative and appeal were successful, and the governor and guardians of the workhouse subscribed five pounds to the fund. On the 17th of July, the following entry is found in the workhouse Minutes:—"John Kitto discharged, 1823, July 17. Taken out under the patronage of the literati of the town." Kitto was then boarded with Mr. Burnard, and had his time at his own disposal, with the privilege of using the public library. A great point was thus gained for him. He was released from manual labour, and had all his hours for reading and mental improve-ment. He must have been aware that efforts were making for him; and this knowledge, acting on a sanguine temperament, seems to have originated and moulded the following dream, as he calls it, and which,

* Mr. Woollcombe, whose early and continued attentions to Kitto were as stimulating as they were kind, was the founder of the Plymouth Institution, a promoter of literature and the arts, and connected with all the philanthropic movements and societies of the neighbourhood. He was a highly respectable solicitor, and an alderman of the borough, in which he had great and merited influence.

though probably a waking reverie, is very remarkable as a true presentiment—a correct delineation of his subsequent career. It is dated three days prior to his discharge, and occurs in a letter to Mr. Tracy:—

"Methought (this is the established language of dreamers, I believe) I was exactly in the same situa-tion in which I really was before I slept, and indulging the same reflections, when there suddenly appeared before me a being of more than mortal beauty. He was taller than the sons of men, and his eye beamed with celestial fire; a robe of azure hue, and far richer than the finest silk, enfolded his form, a starry zone of glittering gems encircled his waist, and in his hand he bore a rod of silver.

"He touched me with his rod, and gently bending over me, he said, 'Child of mortality, I am the Angel Zared, and am sent to teach thee wisdom. Every man on his outset in life proposes to himself something as the end and reward of his labours, his wishes, and his hopes; some are ambitious of honour, some of glory, and some of riches. Of what art thou ambitious, and what are the highest objects of thy earthly hopes?'

"I was astonished at the visit and the words of the angel, and replied not to his demand.

"'Thou canst not readily find, O child of the earth, words to express the scenes which thy fancy has drawn. It matters not; I know thy wishes, and will give thee possession of the state that is the highest of which thou art ambitious.'

He touched me with his rod, and my form expanded into manhood: again he touched and then left me. On looking around me, I found myself seated in a room, two of the walls of which were entirely concealed by books, of which I felt myself conscious of being the owner. On the table lay letters addressed to me from distant parts of the Island, from the Continent, and from the New World: and conspicuously on the chimney-piece were placed several volumes, of which I was conscious that I was the author, and was also sensible that the house wherein I was, was mine, and all that was in it. I went forth into the street. Ridicule no longer pointed her finger at me; many whom I met appeared to know and esteem me, and I felt conscious that I possessed many sincere and disin-terested friends. I met a blind fiddler, and placing my hand instinctively in my pocket, I found that it lacked not money. I returned, and exclaimed, as I took Cæsar's *Commentaries,* in their original language, from the shelf, 'Now at last I am happy!' but before I had concluded the word, the Angel Zared again appeared before me, and touching me with his silver rod, restored me to the state in which he found me.

"I felt a momentary sensation of disappointment and regret at the transition, till the angel spoke to me, and said,—

" ' Listen to my words, O child of mortality, while I withdraw, as far as I am permitted, the veil of thy future destiny. Thou has been afflicted with misfortune, and taught in the school of adversity. Think not that HE who made thee, and me also, regards with displeasure those whom He purifies by sorrows, or that those are His peculiar favourites who are permitted by Him to enjoy the good things of this world. Whenever thou findest thyself inclined to murmur at the dispensations of Providence, recollect that others, greater, better, and wiser than thou art, have suffered also,—have suffered more than thou hast, or ever wilt suffer.

" ' The time approaches when thou shalt attract the notice of thy superiors, who shall place within thy reach the means of acquiring that knowledge for which thou thirstest. They will transplant thee into a soil fit for thee, and if thou attendest well to the cultivation of thy intellectual and moral faculties, thou mayest perhaps become a permanent occupant of a station like that which I have permitted thee to enjoy for a moment. I say, *perhaps*, for only HE knows, in whose breast is hid the fate of worlds, whether thou art to live beyond the day on which I visit thee; but of this I am permitted to assure thee, that the period of thy sojourn on earth will not be, at the furthest, very many years.

" ' Be not, O son of earth, dejected, if thou again meetest with disappointments and misfortunes; neither suffer prosperity too highly to elate thee; and in every situation, and in every moment of thy life, remember that thou art mortal, and that there is a God and a hereafter. So live, that thou mayest not fear death, at whatever moment he may approach thee; and if thus thou livest, thou wilt have lived indeed ——.' Zared perhaps would have spoken longer; but a book falling from the shelf upon my head, I awoke, and, as honest John Bunyan says, behold it was a dream !"

One might say to such a wondrous dreamer—

" Thy life lies spread before thee as a sheet
    Of music, written by some gifted hand,
    Unsounded yet: to longing, listening hearts,
    Translate its small mysterious silent notes
    Into full thrilling chords of life and power."

He was now afraid of being overrated, and to show that he was not unduly lifted up by his good fortune, we may quote what he says to Mr. Harvey:—

June 15, 1823.—" I sometimes doubt the efficacy of any trifling abilities I possess to retain that patronage with which you honour me. I have not mentioned my unattractive person or clownish manners as likely to operate in the least with a gentleman of your good sense to my disfavour." Or again, he writes to the same correspondent, September 30, of the same year —" I apprehend that you are not disappointed on discovering that I am not one of those meteors

which sometimes emerge from darkness, and illumine the hemisphere of science with their blaze. On two subjects I am not indifferent. I wish to be known in the world. I wish to get myself a name, and to be esteemed by the wise, the learned, and the good. But even this wish is inferior to that which I have to extend my knowledge, and to compensate, by literary acquirements, for the deprivation under which I labour." On June 23, he chides Mr. Burnard, for having altered his style of address to the pauper boy who had risen in rank :—" Will you permit me to find fault with the address, 'Mr. John Kitto?'—how cold and formal ! From any other person I might not object to it, but from *you*, my earliest and best friend, it must not be. Call me, I entreat you again, plain John Kitto, or, if possible, by some more affectionate appellation." His hopes were not yet very high, and this is his humble solace—" I am perfect in my trade; and should circumstances send me back to the workhouse, I hope in Mr. Burnard for all his former kindness and attention."

Kitto's mind was at this time specially sensitive, and somewhat irritable. There was the prospect of relief, but it might not be realized; the blessing of elevation was close upon his grasp, but yet not within it. A few of his Essays had appeared in the papers, and some people suspected that he had been assisted in their composition. On this point he was exceedingly tender, as the following letter to Mr. Burnard indicates :—

" *July* 22—*Public Library.*

" SIR,—I am not happy: I am very uneasy—more than uneasy, or I should not now write to you. Pardon me, sir, if I write incoherently, for I address you under the impulse of feelings that have recently been wounded to the quick. Those gentlemen were in the right who foretold that I should meet with disappointments. I went down stairs to read last evening, when it grew dark. I had not been there long before a gentleman came in, who, after having read a few minutes, asked me whether I could hear loud sounds? My answer to this, and other interrogations much more disagreeable, were perused with so evident an intention of finding fault, that it mortified me in the extreme. The pencil was slowly traced beneath the lines; each word was weighed in the scale of grammatical nicety, and one was found to be improper. I observed, in answer to one of his questions, that I had not, till within these few days, begun to study grammar, and that I did not think it fair that I should be judged by rules with which I was unacquainted. He replied, ' You are in the right, I believe; but how came you to write so correctly in the Essays in the newspaper? Did any one correct them for you?' I leave you to judge, sir, whether this was a proper question for a gentleman, and a stranger, to make. I replied in the negative, adding, that 'I repeatedly transcribed them, improving and correcting them each time, till I thought them sufficiently accurate. In the two first Essays, however, the editor corrected some errors in punctuation, and he prefixed the quotation from Anon. to my Essay on Home; but, in the Essay on Contemplation, he, at my request, made no correction or alteration whatever, further than adding three lines from Shakspere to it as a motto.' Yet I believe that Essay is the best. Do you not think so too, sir? . . . It was very evident, by his triumphant exhibition of a grammatical error and other circumstances, that he was, beforehand, determined to find fault, and that he departed with a very contemptuous opinion of me and my abilities. Whatever was his intention, it is certain that he has made me very uneasy, and greatly discouraged me; for, undoubtedly, 'the scoff of pride' is not celebrated for its powers of stimulation."

At this juncture, and while his plans of life were still uncertain, a proposal was made to publish a volume of his Essays. But he scrupled at the censorship of his friends, and wished the papers to be left wholly to his own taste and selection. He had no objection that Mr. Lampen should read and revise them, provided that he himself might finally bestow upon them "additional corrections and improvements." But before the volume was published another change had taken place in his social position, and he had mounted another step upwards.

His time, meanwhile, being fully his own, was principally spent in the Public Library, and he was not less miserly in the distribution of it than formerly. He devised various means of economising it, such as forming a diagram of method, marked with different colours; lamented that of late he had been in bed full seven hours, while six were quite sufficient; resolved against heavy dinners; would like a little ale, but would prefer a small quantity of wine to his frugal and solitary meal, and so hoped to be able to read or write, with little interruption, from nine in the morning till five in the afternoon. Conscientiously did he occupy his leisure. While he was free to choose any line of study, he decidedly preferred literature to science. Opening his mind to Mr. Harvey (June 1st), he declares of Natural Philosophy, "I have no desire to make any particular branch of it my study. As I have but few hours in the day at my own disposal, and when I attain to manhood am likely to have still fewer, it would be absurd in me to hope to succeed (even if I had the inclination) in such branches of philosophical and scientific research, as geometry, chemistry, electricity, and others equally abstruse, which are calculated only for men of great talents, and those who have been blessed with a liberal education." "Mine," he explains to Mr. Wooll-

combe (Sept. 25), "is a mind not adapted to scientific pursuits. *Man*, I have repeatedly said, and that which relates directly to him, shall be the chief subjects of my research. Let chemists analyse the elements in their alembics, but let me analyse the passions, the powers, and the pursuits of man in the alembic of the mind." Accordingly he gave himself to reading chiefly in metaphysics. "The novels, the poems, and the periodicals slept quietly on the shelves." History, also, occupied a portion of his time, and he retained through life his liking for it. But the metaphysical theories with which he came in contact, ultimately perplexed him, and he abandoned the pursuit. Yet, before he laid it aside, he had gathered from it "some useful knowledge, acquired some useful habits, and drawn some useful conclusions." His mind liked to store itself with information, rather than penetrate into profound questions, or range among subtile hypotheses. His intellectual nature was not fitted to deal with such subjects, and his metaphysical studies were pursued, not for the love of mental science, but for the sake of general knowledge. Instinctively he valued the palpable more than the abstruse, and immediate utility outweighed, in his estimate, every form of speculation. He was, indeed, in danger of being injured by the desultory nature of his exercises, for when any mental pursuit ceased to delight him, he was at once inclined to abandon it. He did not relish mathematics, for he "pursued the steps to the demonstration without pleasure or curiosity." He resolved to go through Euclid, but was easily seduced from the task; and at length confessed that whenever he ventured over the Asses' Bridge, he usually "fell into the water."

But he thought of "beginning Latin," and of "possessing the Greek language also." Though he had been, and was still, so voracious a reader, he knew that the mere perusal of books was not to be identified with intellectual improvement. He puts the case strongly :—
"Were it possible for one man to read all the books which have been printed, from Caxton to Bensley, that man might still be a blockhead. For reading the thoughts of other men will not in itself enable us to think justly ourselves, any more than the wearing of a Chancellor's wig would endue us with the legal knowledge of a Lord High Chancellor." *

He had not been long boarded with Mr. Burnard, when his constitutional monitor spoke to him, as it afterwards did, periodically, till his death. In a letter to Mr. Harvey, August 13, he laments :—
"Since Tuesday night I have experienced more illness than within an equal space of time since my fall. Sickness is well calculated to produce wise reflections and conclusions in the mind. In the fervour of my hopes, and in the anticipation of future attainments

* *Essays*, p. 209.

and subsequent usefulness, I had almost forgotten that it was in the power of death to prevent their fulfilment.

"You may, perhaps, sir, also say, that my trifling illness does not justify an anticipation of early dissolution. On such a subject no one can speak with certainty; yet I may be permitted to say, that I believe my demise will be at no distant period; and, indeed, I think that, at no other time, it could be more eligible than now. Were my decease to take place at present, sympathy might shed a tear over my grave, and I might be lamented by the benevolent, the pious, and the learned, as one who, had he lived, might have been a useful member of society. In after life I may be exposed to criminal temptations, which I may not have power to resist. I may form ties which it would be agony to tear asunder; and I may have miseries to endure of which I have now no conception, all of which my demise *now* would prevent. I imagine you pause here, and take up your pen to ask me, "Are you then tired of life, and do you wish for death?" Oh no, sir, I wish to know, and to communicate my knowledge. I would live, could I command it, till time shall have 'covered my head with hoary honours. I would live till I had learned how to die with a well grounded hope of future bliss. The reasons above alluded to are by no means such as to make death desirable. It would be absurd to wish for death in order to avert evils, the occurrence of which is no more than probable. However, the frequent thoughts of death will certainly render his approach less terrible when he ultimately arrives. "Considered abstractedly from the probability of my early dissolution, I think my future prospects very invigorating indeed. Henceforth I shall not look too anxiously on the future, but rely on that Great Being who has been so merciful to me, and hope that He will enable me to be happy in any condition which I may be called to occupy." *

With all his high prospects, a feeling of gloom occasionally stole over him—the shadow of his earlier sensations. To such despondency he makes frequent allusion. He was tormented by fears, and he wisely advised himself to take long walks, and unbend his mind, by partaking of any harmless amusements.† But, with all his dark tendencies, his gratitude was great. When he looked on what he had been, felt what he had become, and hoped what he might yet be, his spirit was filled with thankfulness; and he describes his emotions, in a letter, published in his earliest volume:—

TO MR. WILDE.

"*Plymouth Public Library, Oct. 16, 1823.*

"DEAR SIR,—With much pleasure I avail myself of the first opportunity of returning my grateful acknow-

* *Essays*, p. 30.   † *Essays*, p. 48.

ledgments for the attention you have shown to my accommodation and comfort in the library; and, at the same time, of saying something about myself. When I recollect (and can I ever forget?) how miserable I once was; how I was exposed to ignominy, to insult, neglect, and oppression, my joy is great to have escaped such evils, and my heart expands with gratitude towards those disinterested individuals who have rescued me from them.

"In the most enthusiastic of my reveries, I never imagined that I should ever be as I am now, or that I should attract that attention which has been, and is directed towards me. I wrote; I endeavoured to acquire knowledge, because my deafness had divested me of all relish for common amusements, because I could find no other enjoyment or occupation equally interesting, and because the employment of my few leisure hours and moments gave me the satisfactory consciousness of spending my time well, without having the most distant idea that this occupation of my leisure would lead to the beneficial results to which it has led.

"An unprepossessing exterior, and deportment somewhat singular, made me to be persecuted and despised by my equals and superiors in age, who knew me no further than as they saw me, or thought me a being not far removed from idiocy. Misery, sir, had rather quickened than blunted the native sensibilities of my heart; and great as my sufferings were, I probably felt them more acutely than many others would have done in the same circumstances.

"Amidst all these troubles, however, my thirst for knowledge was not destroyed. My closet was my only refuge, and a book, when I could procure it, my only consoler; for there were none to enter into my feelings or sympathise with me, and by deafness I was cut off from social intercourse with every human being.

"Thus unhappy as I was, if you can form an idea of my situation, you can also conceive the satisfaction which I felt when I suddenly became an object of attention and commiseration to those who have assisted to rescue me from the state in which they found me, and placed me in that which I now occupy. I, the lowly being who, a few days before, was unnoticed and unknown, now became an object of curiosity and wonder to persons who would never have become acquainted with my existence, or have heard my name mentioned, if some trifling circumstances, which I should denominate *accidents*, if I had not been accustomed to trace the finger of an overruling Providence in many of those events which the irreligious, the ignorant, and the careless, call by the name of *chances*, had not introduced me to the notice of those who have made me known to others.

" It must be evident, however, that this is not my final destination; and I feel no other anxiety or uneasiness than as it respects futurity. The vast ocean of human life lies before me, and my only wish is that my little bark may in future escape those dangers by which it was once once assailed, and that it may proceed in peace and comfort, undisturbed by the blasts of adversity, till it ultimately rest in the quiet haven of the grave."

One can scarce wonder at the following wish, expressed by such a child of misfortune and poverty, who had never handled a piece of money of any value. It occurs in a Journal that dates from February 19, 1824, to April 3:—

"I have some time been desirous of consulting my kind and zealous friend, Colonel Hawker, on the propriety of my desiring to have at Whitsuntide and Christmas, or any other two periods of the year, a sovereign, but I have been loath to mention it to him, for he has lately, and indeed always, been so attentive to my wishes, that I am unwilling again to make so great a claim on his consideration. I do not think Mr. Woollcombe or Mr. Lampen would make much if any objection to it; but perhaps Mr. Hawker might, and I am not willing to make a proposal which there is any probability of his rejecting, for if he disapproves of it, I shall not mention it to any other person. I should not be so reluctant, if it were not for the great increase which has been kindly and spontaneously made to my weekly stipend. Well, and what do you want with twenty shillings twice a-year? Why, as to that, it is partly a wish of having what I never had before, for I *never* touched a note in my life, nor a piece of gold coin, but once, which was ten years ago, when I was permitted to hold a seven-shilling-piece in my hand for a few seconds. I wish also to have a small sum always at hand, to answer any particular want which may occur. I should also, with part of it, purchase some old books, and thus gradually increase my little store. With half of it, ten shillings, I have no doubt of being able to purchase, at my old acquaintances, ten or twelve volumes of books. I could also supply myself with some minor articles of clothing out of it, and thus prevent the necessity of too frequent applications to Mr. Hawker and the other gentlemen on that account."

Amidst all this anxiety for himself, his wants, and prospects, it is pleasant to find Kitto " looking on the things of others." His favourite subjects of composition had been, and still were, childhood and affliction.* He wrote of the former with a kind of melancholy pleasure, and of the latter in a tone of earnest commiseration. His life had been a companionship with grief, and such an experience taught him to enter readily into the trials of "brethren in tribulation." Sickness had often visited him, and death had once "come nigh unto him;" nay, had laid in the tomb his aged and beloved grandparent. He had often craved for sympathy toward himself, and therefore he was forward to express his condolence with those who sorrowed, and mingle his tears with those who wept. He records in his Journal the death of Mr. Burnard's son, and adds, under a twinge of despondency, "I consider his fate as enviable; and nothing but the consciousness that it is my duty to support the life which my Creator gave, prevents me from being absolutely weary of my existence, and anxious to quit it." But he who had called himself "John, the Comfortless," essayed to comfort the bereaved mother :—

"*April* 29, 1824.

"DEAR MADAM,—That at the present moment I write to you with reluctance on the subject you suggested, I must candidly acknowledge. At an earlier period it would have been more proper than now, and I should at such a period have written, had I not been deterred by the reasons I mentioned to you. The natural effect of time is to soften that grief which every afflictive occurrence inspires; I should therefore have deemed it a duty to avoid the mention of any circumstances likely to revive that intensity of sorrow which time must necessarily in some measure have ameliorated, had you not expressed a willingness to receive any communication on the subject I might make. That your son should be lamented by you, is natural—perfectly natural. Robert was a son of whom any parent might be proud; and had he lived, and enjoyed health, there could be no doubt of his proving a blessing to all connected with him, and an honour to human nature, if, as nobody denies, human nature can be adorned by piety, talent, and virtue. These are just causes for the sorrow you felt and continue to experience; but I cannot persuade myself that any causes can justify unjust repinings, overstrained lamentations, and rebellious murmurings at the dispensations of that Almighty Providence which never acts but for the good of its creatures. Let it not be imagined that I suppose you feel in this manner. Far from it? you feel only a just and natural grief. But if I indeed thought so, I would say so. Recollect the state in which he spent the last year of his life, and say whether you should have preferred to have had him live for years in this state of mental and bodily anguish? for, doubtless, independent of his personal sufferings, he endured much in being cut off from nearly all the gratifications and enjoyments which render life desirable. Do you believe him happy? Undoubtedly. Well, then, is it kind to repine at his happiness?

---

* A series of brief essays on "Childhood," were addressed by him to Mr. Woollcombe, and many of his earlier compositions take the form of letters or addresses to the afflicted.

Supposing, and there is no absurdity in the supposition, that his immortal part be conscious of your actions, can it be thought that his felicity receives any increase from seeing the relatives whom he loved, lament as those who have no hope, and murmur at the dispensations of that Gracious Being who has mercifully seen fit thus early to reward his virtues, by taking him from a state of anguish to one of unutterable felicity? Far from it: on the contrary, I conceive this consciousness, if it be indeed possessed by disembodied spirits, to be the only alloy of which their present happiness is capable; and, therefore, if it were possible that any being should have rejoiced in the death of your son, that being would be in reality less his enemy than you who thus bewail his loss. Loss! Who has lost? What is lost? Has *he* lost anything? Yes, he lost mortality, he has lost pain, he has lost all the miseries of human life—these are his losses; but he has in compensation for these losses, gained—but his gains I will not attempt to enumerate, for only a disembodied spirit can describe those pleasures, which only a disembodied spirit can enjoy. And you, have you lost anything? No, nothing has been *lost ;* your son has gone a journey, and you know that he is happy, eminently happy, in the country which he inhabits. You know also that a great many years cannot elapse before you will be sent for to the same happy regions, where you will dwell *for ever* with him, without fear of further separation. But supposing for a moment that *you* had *lost* anything by the demise of your son, you are certain that *he* has gained; and could you in that case be so selfish as to repine at your own individual loss, when the same cause has rendered your child so supremely happy? If you could, it would not be acting the part of a mother and friend. Such, my dear madam, are some of the reflections which I would have suggested to your consideration, if I had supposed that in your instance they had been requisite. As my own sentiments respecting death are pretty well known, I shall not now intrude on you any longer than to assure you that I am, yours most respectfully,

"John Kitto

"To Mrs. Burnard"

Kitto's continued and prayerful study of the Bible, with the assistance of the best Commentaries which he could procure, was greatly blessed, for there seems to have been all this while the steady growth of religious principle within him.

"*April 2.*—I am in a state which I cannot exactly describe. I become every day more sensible of my own neglect of the duties due to the Almighty, and of my offences against His commandments. I have not that due sense of His mercy, His love, and His benevolence, which I ought to have. I do not form a proper estimate of the vanity of human life, and the contemptible nature of human pursuits, compared with those of a spiritual order. I have not that overwhelming sense of my own religious and moral criminality which I ought to possess, nor have I that effectual and lively faith in Jesus Christ without which everything else is of no value. It is true that I believe Jesus Christ to be the Son of God, that He existed with the Father from all eternity, and that it is only through His atoning blood that we can hope for mercy and forgiveness: I believe all this; but this *theoretical* faith I feel to be utterly insufficient, unattended by practical results, and these practical results I do not experience. There is an internal monitor within me, independent of the written words of inspiration, which makes me fully assured that of myself I can do nothing —that my own efforts are contemptible—and that through a Mediator, and a Mediator only, I can hope for salvation. That Mediator is Jesus Christ; through Him I may obtain mercy and pardon, and His righteous blood can wash away my sins. But I do not feel myself sufficiently grateful to Him, having sufficient faith in Him, sufficiently desirous of living only for Him and to Him, or feel Him absolutely necessary to me. Should I not pray for all this? I have—I have —but I cannot pray as I ought to pray. I cannot draw nigh to God in spirit and in truth. I do not approach him with a humble and contrite spirit, and with that awful veneration which I ought to experience. The busy thoughts of the world and literary subjects intrude, and call off my attention from the solemn occupation in which I am engaged, and thus I rise from my knees more guilty than when I began to kneel. O my God! Enable me distinctly to discern the path in which I should walk, and give me strength to pursue it."

He reveals also to Mr. Burnard, April 9, the nature of the emotions which gave birth to such sentiments, "My uneasiness is not the cause, but the effect of the humiliating sense under which I labour, of my own moral and religious imperfections." "It originates in a lately awakened sense of my unworthiness. I am afraid that mine is a cold theoretic belief, rather than an effectual and saving faith."

This anxiety of soul quickened him, taught him from experience the value of prayer as a means of relief, and led him to read the Scriptures with still greater relish and constancy. The idea of becoming a missionary struck a chord in his bosom. When he heard the question thrown out, "Might not Kitto become a useful missionary, if he studied with effect the only book of sound principles and perfect science ever written?" he caught at the suggestion, and nobly expressed himself on the character and aims of the missionary enterprise, in a letter to Mr. Flindell on the subject.* Nay more, he was on fire at the thought of becoming a minister. In his Diary, March 31, we note this meditation—

"*Apropos* of Kirk White—I learn that his deafness was one of the reasons which induced him to relinquish the study of the law for the clerical profession. Till I had learnt this, I had understood that a defect of hearing was an insurmountable bar to entering into holy orders. Were it possible, O my God! that I could become a minister of Thy word; that I could be permitted to point out to erring sinners the paths of peace and salvation, what more could I desire of Thee? If an ardent zeal for the salvation of souls, if an unshaken belief in the faith promulgated by Jesus Christ and His apostles, if a fervent attachment to the Scriptures, and if a deep sense of the *natural* depravity of human nature, are qualifications for the ministry, then I am so qualified. How truly happy should I be in some retired and obscure curacy, where I should have no other business but the delightful one of instructing others in their duty to God and their fellow-men, and in which I should have sufficient leisure to read, to study, and to write!"

GATE OF THE HOSPITAL OF THE POORS' PORTION

* *Essays and Letters,* p. 49

3

EXETER

WHILE his mind was in this propitious state, Kitto was introduced to Mr. Groves, a dentist, residing at Exeter. Mr. Harvey had hinted at a University education for him, and believed that he had sufficient interest to obtain a fellowship. But Kitto's other friends would not entertain such a proposal. He was, therefore, left free to form an engagement with Mr. Groves, who had heard something of his history, and had judged favourably of him, from having seen one of his letters to Mr. Flindell, editor of the *Western Luminary*. Mr. Groves offered to instruct Kitto in his profession, to board him, and give him for his services, £15 the first, and £20 the second year, with prospect of higher remuneration. Kitto accepted the offer, and this engagement was the turning point in his career. It deepened and sealed his piety, and ultimately led him to the East, in preparation for the great work of his life. He had already written a paper on the Antinomianism of Dr. Hawker, which shows some familiarity with Scripture, though not a very distinct conception of some portions and aspects of the scheme of grace. But the example of Mr. Groves quite electrified him, and every fibre of his heart vibrated under the living impression. A vital and decided change passed over him,—the result of long preparation and prayer.

His mind had been always susceptible of religious impression, but it had not yet quickened into life. The blade had shot up, but there now began to appear the "full corn in the ear." He had put on record, before he left the hospital, a specimen of his prayers, in a style of no ordinary magnificence—a specimen which becomes a moral and intellectual wonder, when we consider the upbringing and the circumstances of him who wrote it—a boy, rendered totally deaf by an accident, suffered to grow up uneducated, made a pauper by his father's vices, and now learning an humble trade in a workhouse:—

"MORNING PRAYER

"King of the Universe! I, an atom of that universe, dare humbly pray Thee to incline Thy ear, while at Thy footstool I confess that I am a wretched sinner; that I have broken Thy laws, and Thy commandments I have trodden under my feet; that I have slighted Thee, my Maker; that I have not done my duty to Thee, my neighbour, or myself; that I have deserved nothing at Thy hands but Thy displeasure. I have wasted the precious moments which Thou gavest me to improve. I have murmured at Thy decrees, because Thou, in Thy mercy, wast pleased to afflict me, and because Thou gavest me to drink of the cup of affliction. I have not loved Thee as Thou oughtest to be loved. I have suffered impure desires and evil passions to influence my actions. In short, O Lord, I am a miserable self-convicted sinner. I have deserved Thy wrath and fearful indignation; and I do not remember one good action that ever I did, which makes me know that Thou alone canst save me. Therefore, Almighty God, overburdened as I am with sin, I dare humbly sue Thee to pardon my sins; remember not against me my iniquities, but blot them from the book of Thy remembrance, and erase them from the tablets of Thy memory. Hear me, O God, when I cry to Thee for that mercy I do not deserve. Give me, most merciful Father, the gifts of Thy grace. Give me repentance, for, without Thy aid, I cannot repent of my sins nor abide by my purpose of leading a new life; without Thy aid I cannot know myself. Give me, Eternal King, faith, that no doubts may obtrude themselves, that I may believe in Jesus Christ, and keep Thy law. Do Thou also grant unto me, O Lord, content, that I may be satisfied with whatever situation in life it be Thy pleasure to assign me, and that I may be convinced that whatsoever Thou doest is for my benefit; and that I may thank Thee even for the rod with which Thou dost chastise me.

"I most humbly entreat Thee, Omniscient God, to grant me strength to resist the allurements of sin, Satan, my own flesh, and mine own thoughts, that I may not give way to temptation, but resist it. Take from my breast, O Lord, this heart—harder than adamant, black with impurity, and stubborn—and, O Lord, substitute in its place a heart purified in the blood of Jesus.

"Inspire Thou those under whom I am placed with kindness unto me, and give me, O Lord, power to please them. Shed over me Thy grace, and reveal Thyself unto me, through Jesus Christ, in whom alone we can know Thee, and that I may become a new being, casting off all evil habits and unholy feelings, and conduct myself as beseemeth a being whom Thou hast redeemed. Guide Thou my steps in the way which, though to mortal eye it is rough and unpleasant to the sense, leads to everlasting life. And do Thou, Almighty power, give me strength to avoid the road which appears to abound with unalloyed pleasure, but which leads to eternal death.

"If it be Thy pleasure to give me hereafter affluence, grant that I may not abuse Thy bounty; if poverty, grant that I may not murmur;—but I pray Thee, O Lord, grant me not riches nor poverty—yet not my will, but Thine always be done, for Thou knowest what is for my benefit better than myself.

"Bless, O God, my benefactors, relatives, and friends. Teach me how to pray unto Thee, in spirit and in truth.

"Grant me, O Lord, I humbly entreat Thee, grace that I may so conduct myself here on earth, that when it is Thy pleasure to take me hence, I may die with the conviction that my sins are pardoned, and that at the last I may be able to exclaim, 'O death! where is thy sting? O grave! where is thy victory?'

"Lord! be merciful to me, a sinner, and grant that I may be one of that happy number to whom it shall be said, 'Well done, good and faithful servant, enter thou into the joy of thy Lord.' I ask from Thee not, O Lord, worldly blessings. I ask of Thee neither fame, nor riches, nor honours; but, Lord, I ask of Thee a pure and contrite spirit. I ask of Thee patience, to bear with resignation whatsoever afflictions Thou art pleased to send me.

"I thank Thee, O Father, for the manifold favours I have received from Thee. I thank thee for life, health, friends, connections. I thank Thee that Thou hast forebore hitherto to punish me as my sins have deserved. I thank Thee for all the good I have enjoyed, or may enjoy hereafter; particularly for the protection Thou hast afforded me heretofore, especially in the past night; and I humbly pray Thee to continue my Protector through the coming day, and grant that at the end thereof, I may look back on a well spent day. These, and all other favours, which are for my good, I pray Thee grant in the name of Thy beloved Son, Jesus Christ, Who loved our souls so well, that He took upon Himself our sinful nature, bled for our sins, bore Thy anger in our stead, and suffered death for our iniquities, and Who taught us, in the perfect form of words, to say, 'Our Father which art in heaven,' etc.

"The above is not all that I pray for, only a brief view of the principal heads. What say you to it, dear Harry? Not worthy the Being to whom it is addressed?"

But in Exeter a great spiritual advance had been made, experience had ripened, and he discloses himself to Mr. Burnard, June 1824:—

. . . "When I look back, I am surprised at the very great change which has taken place in my views since I came hither—a change which I had never anticipated—a change which clearly convicts me, in many former instances of my life, of folly and impropriety—and a change which, I hope, will ultimately, under Divine teaching, make me wise unto salvation, and enable me to become a Christian, and an useful member of society. To what is this change to be imputed? Perhaps to a more exclusive contemplation of Divine things, to a more attentive study of the Word of Life, to abstraction from many temporal things which at Plymouth too deeply interested me and engrossed my thoughts, to my intercourse with Mr. Groves; but chiefly, I conclude, to the grace of God, who has at length permitted that 'day-spring from on high' to arise, for the *appearance of which I have long prayed*, and which, when fully risen, will enable me to behold the beauty of holiness in all its glory and perfection, and by the strengthening influence of the Holy Spirit, to pursue that light which will then be revealed more completely than at present."

Again, writing to the same correspondent, in September, he reverently marks his first sacramental enjoyment:—

"Since I wrote last, I have for the first time partaken of the Communion, and the day in which I did so was one of the most pleasant in my life—most particularly was it distinguished by that absorbing and sublime devotional feeling which it is my most earnest desire may ultimately become the continual feeling of my daily life, repelling worldly affections and earthly wishes, and making me perpetually act and think from the simple motive of love to our Divine Master.

. . . "You must be sensible, from the tone of my letters to yourself and those which you may have seen of mine to other persons—that the John Kitto you will see, is rather a different person from the John Kitto you have seen; and I am sure you will rejoice with me when you understand that this is not a mere alteration of the external manners or appearance, but an alteration most deeply felt in the heart, and entering into every feeling, every passion of the mind, insomuch that I should now be disgusted with much in which I once delighted, and many things are now most pleasant and delightful, which once were indifferent to me."

Kitto got on well with Groves, as his Diary shows:—

"*May* 19.—Troubles of Latin.—Surely this inaptitude must lower me in Mr. Groves' estimation.

"*May* 22.—Mr. G. desired to know if I was happy in my situation with him. I replied 'that it was beyond my anticipations, and equalled my wishes.' It would be ungrateful were I to express myself dissatisfied with his disinterested and zealous endeavours to promote my happiness and comfort. He added, 'That it would be a subject of great regret, if any consideration should induce me to wish to leave the bosom of a family, to every member of which I was an object of interest and attachment.'"

During his residence at Exeter, Kitto corresponded regularly with his Plymouth friends, upon a variety of themes, and treats, for example, in a series of letters, the topic of capital punishments. Subjects seem to have been proposed to him from time to time; and his style, through exercise, acquired considerable freedom and energy. He was in the habit of distributing tracts in Exeter, and he was often pained by the scenes of profligacy which he witnessed—such as

"fellows emerging from a beer-house, and fighting in the street." "My dear sir, my heart is quite sick when I contemplate such scenes of brutal violence. Reflecting on this state of things, it is the duty of every one whom the Holy Ghost has enlightened, whatever his rank or degree may be, to devote himself exclusively to the service of his Master, and to aid His great cause to the utmost stretch of his power. . . . Now, my dear sir, of what I have said I would make personal application, and addressing the Master, say, Behold me, then, my Father! I offer myself, and all that Thou hast made me, to Thee. Send me where Thou wilt, do with me what Thou wilt, and require my services as Thou mayest, I thank Thee that Thou hast made me willing to obey Thy summons; and, Eternal God, so prosper me, as by Thy grace I seek, above all things, Thy glory and Thy honour."*

The portion of his Diary which describes his sojourn at Exeter, concludes with the following prayer:—

"Almighty and ever living God, who madest all things, and lovest all that Thou hast made, deign to incline Thine ear to the prayer of a sinner, who thus humbly, at Thy footstool, entreats of Thee, not this world's goods, or its pleasures, or its honours, but that portion of Thy grace, that infusion of Thy Spirit which maketh wise unto salvation. Grant me these, Righteous Father, and nothing more do I entreat of Thee, for in these all lesser blessings are included. If it be Thy good pleasure that I should drink to the dregs that bitter cup of adversity, of which I have already drunk so largely, proportion my strength to the trials which Thou givest me to undergo; make me submit, in humble acquiescence, to Thy chastening rod, and make me, in circumstances of apparent sorrow, to exclaim, 'Father, if it be Thy pleasure, take this cup from me; nevertheless, not my will, but Thine be done.' But if, on the other hand, Thou bestowest upon me those things which men so highly seek and desire, O grant that they may have no injurious effect; that they may not draw my heart from its hold on Thee, and that I may feel myself nothing more than the steward of Thy bounties, and the deputed dispenser to the poor, the unhappy, and the destitute, of a portion of those blessings which Thou mayest give to myself, or rather which Thou hast deigned to give me in trust. If what I have asked be for my good, grant it, O father, for the sake of Jesus Christ.—Amen."

That Kitto had surrendered the "fortress of his silence," prior to the time he left Plymouth, is evident from some statements in what he calls his "Private Diary." Who his "little flame" was, we know not, except by name. He was always fond of female society—he loved sisterhood. An impression had

---

* Letter to Mr. Burnard, 24th March, 1825.

been made upon him, which cost him no little pain, when with "many terrible conflicts" he sacrificed it on what he believed to be the shrine of duty, and in obedience to the warnings of Mr. Groves.

"*April* 24.—Visited H. this evening; communicated as much as I thought necessary of my Exonian destination. She did not seem much more pleased with it than with the more superb University plan, an insight into which I gave her. Well, whatever happens, God preserve her, and make her happy, and while she is so, I can never myself be completely miserable."

We have given the previous extract, simply to show that, while so many painful circumstances had conspired to make Kitto solitary and dull, and force him into a lonely and self-devouring asceticism, he had neither sunk into moroseness, nor avenged himself by a scornful misanthropy. He could not exclaim, "man delights not me, nor woman neither," for, to his benefactors of the one sex he was sincerely grateful, as his letters testify, and there was one in the other sex who had power to attach him, and charm him out of his solitude, and of whom he says, after the correspondence had been broken off,—"she clings to my heart with a force almost irresistible." He had pleaded, and that powerfully, for this attachment, against the remonstrances of Mr. Burnard. This susceptibility of a first love shows that his heart had not been utterly wrecked by his bitter experiences. He had been saved from himself even when a hard and dry incrustation seemed sometimes to be gathering about him. "Nay," he says in his volume of *Essays*, published soon after (p. 85), "marriage is in general the principal component part of a happy home." In an Essay on Beauty (p. 102), he declares, "I am an enthusiastic admirer of personal beauty. Expression is to beauty what the soul is to the body. I now repeat, I am an enthusiastic admirer of female loveliness. . . . Mental charms in a woman will give pleasure and excite admiration, when the attractions of beauty and youth exist no longer.". .

About this time, in the beginning or spring of 1825, the volume of Kitto's *Letters and Essays* just referred to, was published.* Neither title-page nor preface has any date. The duodecimo, of 210 pages, was patronised by above 400 subscribers. It is premised that the volume does not "consist of papers composed expressly for publication. They are selections from letters which he wrote in the workhouse, and essays with which he exercised his fondness for literary occupations, and they were chosen from the mass of his writings, rather to give an impression of the character of his mind and talent, than as conveying any particularly striking or original views of the subjects of which

it treats. . . . The volume is now offered to the public in the hope that it may justify the attention that has been paid to the merits of this deserving young man, and that it may be the means of affording him encouragement in the pursuit of that line of conduct by which he now gratifies his friends."

It may be well to pause for a moment over Kitto's earliest production, as the index and fruit of his mental progress; and as many of its sections are autobiographical, we may find confirmation of the statements we have already made, and learn how, in the dawn of his release, he regarded his previous hardships, what trains of reflection they suggested, what circles of emotions they produced, what lessons he extracted from them, and what share they had in directing and moulding his subsequent career.

And first, there was realized, to some extent, another and early dream of Kitto, which he has given in his Workhouse Journal, with considerable picturesqueness and power. He represents himself as being in a book-shop, "and well dressed"—a sly hit at the poorhouse uniform. He is surveying on the counter his own journal in a published form, when a family entered the shop—a sage father, "a flauntily dressed elderly lady, with their son and daughter, both dressed as a dandy and dandyzette." The young coxcomb laughed outright as he took up the volume. "When asked what excited him, he read the title-page of my unfortunate book—'Journal and Memoranda of a Man with Four Senses, by John Kitto, Shoemaker, Pauper,' etc. 'Was there ever such a thing heard,' continued he, 'as for a pauper! a shoemaker! to write anything proper for the perusal of a man of sense!' adjusting the ribband of his quizzing-glass, with the air of a person well satisfied with his own sense. 'No, certainly,' said his mother, 'and I would wager a guinea that it may be classed among the Methodistical jargon which the authors are pleased to call Journals, and of which so much has been obtruded on the public.' 'I, too, would wager a guinea,' said the young lady, that in this bantling of *wax* there are no tender embarrassments—no ghosts—no tears of sensibility—nor any duels—for nothing but the most gross vulgarity can be expected from this son of the awl.'— 'Yes, indeed! was ever such extravagance heard of, as for a shoemaker, an occupation found only among the very dregs of the vulgar, to pretend to write a book? I should not now wonder, 'pon my honour, if the barber should favour us with a treatise on beards —the sign-dauber with a history of painting—or even the catgut-scraper with a history of music,' concluded the young gentleman, with a loud and long 'He! he! he!' at his own wit; 'for,' added he 'they may as readily do it as a pauper write a Journal.' The grave looking old gentleman, who had attentively listened to all

* *Essays and Letters*, by John Kitto, with a Short Memoir of the Author. Plymouth.

that had been said, advanced towards the rest and said, 'Ladies and young man, I must dissent from what all of you have said' (an angry and satirical 'indeed!' proceeded from all three at the same time).—The old gentleman, not noticing this interruption, proceeded—'Particularly with regard to what has been said about the incapability of mechanics. For, from my own experience, I can assure you that I have met with genius, probity, and honour, in many instances, among what you are pleased to call the dregs of the people. I have always looked upon an honest mechanic, though even a shoemaker, as a much more useful member of society than he who, blessed with affluence, holds time a burden—who lives merely to circulate that which would make hundreds happy, and who spends every hour, every day, in what is falsely called pleasure, and who lives for not one of the ends of his creation; who, so far from improving that *time* which every hour shortens, thinks himself happy when he has hit on an idea to kill that time of which he is not certain of a moment's continuance. But the best way to convince you of your error is to give you examples of genius amongst the lower classes. I will mention but a few names of the many that occur; as, for instance, R. Bloomfield, Burns, Chatterton, G. Morland, Savage, Lloyd, Otway, and Shakspere. I scarce need have told any but you that most of these were poets—very celebrated poets, and more particularly that Bloomfield was a shoemaker—the fourth was one of our best English painters—and yet none of these were bred in affluence, nor were their talents cultivated by education. But with regard to the book, the merits of which you have decided without opening its pages, I have read it, and though written by a pauper, it does not sink *much* below mediocrity—the misfortune of the author renders it in some measure interesting; the language is simple, the orthography not very incorrect; it has some humour; learning cannot be expected; yet the author is not ignorant, and he seems an honest youth, with sentiments much above his condition. Upon the whole, it is better than could be expected from one of his years and situation; and if it does no good, it will have the negative merit of doing no harm, and it shall be placed in my library.'"

He who could so express himself was on the high way to write a book, and leave behind him the "flannel jacket and leathern apron"—the badge of poverty and St. Crispin, and must soon cease to be "shoemaker and pauper."

The volume bears witness to his multifarious reading. One wonders how he had found time to run through so many books, and read them so carefully as to be able to make such frequent and pertinent allusions to them. The amount of his reading would not have dishonoured a university student; nay, few of them lay in such a stock of general information. In metaphysics, intelligent and distinctive reference is made to Malebranche and Hume, Reid and Stewart, Berkeley and Des Cartes, Locke and Stillingfleet. Lord Bacon and Madame de Stael are familiarly quoted. In an essay on Sublimity, where he refers to the fine arts, he contrasts the Tuscan and Doric orders of architecture with the Gothic, especially as seen in Westminster Abbey, and in the ruins of Tintern and Glastonbury; tells what the pencil of Salvator Rosa achieved, and what Gainsborough could effect; assigns their respective positions to Titian and Raphael; then passes on to sculpture, criticising the Apollo Belvidere, the group of the Laocoon, and the Choragic monument of Lysicrates. His papers, entitled "Rabnah and Abdallah," are rather happy imitations of the once famous Jewish apologues of Hawksworth and Johnson, and many of the "desultory reflections," which conclude the volume, are terse, pointed, and memorable. Kitto denies imitation in style, but many of his first compositions controvert the statement. He fell unconsciously into such imitations. What he had been reading deeply interested him, and left its impress on his next composition, while inability to hear his own sentences prevented him from detecting the similiarity. Does not the following sentence sound like a piece of a Saturday *Spectator ?*—

"When we consider the numberless claims that the Deity has to our gratitude, our adoration, and our love—what a great Friend, a merciful Father, and a bounteous Benefactor He has been to us, and that on Him depends everything we value and desire—the coldness with which we sometimes perform our religious duties appears to me truly strange and unaccountable."

Would not the following pass for a portion of the *Rambler ?*—

"It were well, perhaps, if the wealthy and the prosperous could have a periodical fit of misfortune, which, independent of its other uses, would give them an opportunity of discovering who were their real and who their pretended friends."

There occurs also, in the Workhouse Journal, a pretty good imitation of Sterne, in an account of a real occurrence. Kitto describes a poor fellow who, from a double amputation, shuffled along on his knees, but did not beg. A marine, passing him, poured the whole contents of his pocket into the maimed man's hand, went away, and wiped his eyes, as if he thought a tear disgraceful. "Thou wast wrong, generous soldier! That tear, that action did thee more honour in my eyes than if thou hadst slain with thine own hand thousands of thy fellow-men, and wert therefore called a hero! Thou, noble veteran! wast more charitable and more praiseworthy than a rich man, if he had given fifty pounds. Thou gavest thy little all. In the perils of war, and temptations of peace, God be with thee, generous marine!" Kitto was fond of Shakspere, and specially fond of Spenser; and his proneness to form allegories, and shape his fancies into dreams, arose probably from this last predilection.

His deafness laid him under the necessity of writing. The thoughts of his heart struggled for utterance; and what could not be spoken, must at least be written. Had he been able to converse freely, his feelings would have sooner expended themselves, and when afterwards committed to writing, would have lost somewhat of that intensity which characterised them. But his emotion, unwasted by oral expression, appears on paper with undiluted strength. Even his ordinary thoughts, pent up within him, and turned over again and again, and examined on all sides, in prolonged and undisturbed reflection, assumed a mature fulness and symmetry when his pen gave a deliberate and final utterance to them. This record of his inner history is striking and characteristic :—" I never was a *lad !* From the time of my fall, deprived of many external sources of occupation, I have been accustomed to *think*, to find sources of occupation within myself ; to think deeply ; think as I read, as I worked, or as I walked. Even in my sleep I dreamt ; the addresses, letters, sermons, puns, bon-mots, and tales, I have composed in idea, would, if committed to paper, fill a folio. While other lads were employed with trifles, I thought as a man, felt as a man, and acted as a man." Yet the appetite for human intercourse led him again and again to write as if addressing another party in an ideal dialogue ; and the same yearning for social speech prompted him to write formal letters to himself, specimens of which are inserted in this published collection. The solitary boy created an imaginary companionship. Some of his letters and papers, illustrative of previous parts of his life, have been spoken of already, such as his letter to Mr. Flindell on the Moral Dignity of a Missionary, and his essay on Suicide. There is, in fine, an excellent paper in the volume, suggested by a passage in Bishop Hall's " Balm of Gilead," which unfolds much of his inner thoughts. In harmony with what the good bishop has said, he delivers his own experience :—

" Next in pre-eminence in the list of misfortunes, after blindness, comes deafness. To me the whole world is dumb, since I am deaf to it. No more the music of the human voice shall charm. All around, below, and above me, is solitary silence—ever-during silence—stillness unbroken. Words of advice, of comfort, of instruction, or reproof, to me convey no knowledge, nor make me wiser, better, or more happy. For me the feathered warblers tune their little throats in vain! To me the violin or the harp gives no music;

the deep-toned bell and the pealing organ, no sound. Behold the people crowd to the house of God, to hear the preacher display the riches of redeeming love ; but if I go I hear not his words, which to me alone are profitless; I hear not his voice, which only to me is mute. I am now a mere cipher among men—of no value, importance, or estimation. My door is shut, and ever barred against the entrance of knowledge ; and in no capacity can I hope to be a useful member of the community. Liable to continual mistakes and mortification—cut off from social communication— incapable of receiving pleasure from many of the impulses of sympathy, and of enjoying congenial intercourse—a being completely solitary and desolate, life would be robbed of all its sweets did there not exist some

' Motives for consolation.'

Some of these consolations are mentioned by the pious prelate:—' Had it pleased God to shut up both senses from thy birth, thy estate had been utterly disconsolate : neither had there been any access for comfort to thy soul ; and if He had done so to thee in thy riper age, there had been no way for thee but to live on thy former store : but now that He hath vouchsafed to leave the one passage open, it behoves thee to supply the one by the other, and to let in those helps by the window which are denied entrance by the door.'" Kitto then proceeds with his comment :—" An anonymous author tells us that ' The way to be happy, is to look down on those who suffer, and not up to those who shine in the world.' This I hold to be an excellent maxim, and, to be consistent with it, though I cannot look much lower than myself, instead of lamenting the loss of my hearing, I will rejoice that I am not blind. I thank Thee, O my Father ! that Thou didst rather close the doors than the windows of knowledge and delight ; and that, having barred the doors, Thou didst not also darken the windows. If I were both blind and deaf, in what a wretched situation should I be ! If both the windows and doors were shut, whereat could knowledge enter ? It has been my earnest endeavour, since my fall, to ' supply the one sense by the other,' and to give entrance at the window to as much information as I could possibly obtain. If I could not read, how deplorable would be my condition ; and I earnestly entreat all who may chance to read this, of whatever condition, sex, or degree, that they will not be backward in lending me *books ;* for if they attentively reflect on my situation, they will perceive that no other sources of information, knowledge, or instruction, and, I might add, of amusement, are left open to me than those which books afford. Without books, I should quickly become an ignorant and senseless being, unloving and unloved, if I am not so already. I apprehend that I have sometimes offended my acquaintance, by the importunity with which I have solicited the loan of books. But if I had a house full of books myself, and knew any person to whom they would be so necessary as to me, and who would make so good a use of them as I do, I would not stay to be entreated, nor scruple to lend any, or all of them, in succession, to such a person. What earthly pleasure can equal that of reading a good book? O dearest tomes! Princely and august folio! Sublime quarto! Elegant octavo! Charming duodecimo! Most ardently do I admire your beauties. To obtain ye, and to call ye mine, I would work day and night; and to possess ye, I would forbid myself all sensual joys. . . . . The Almighty afflicts but to bless. Notwithstanding that His judgments often seem harsh and severe to those who are afflicted, they are in reality just and merciful. It is mercy in Him when He sends us one evil to preserve us from some greater and more serious ill. How do I know but that God permitted my deafness, as an instrument through which I might be saved from some far worse evil, which He foreknew would have happened to me if I had continued possessed of my hearing. But be that as it may, while I regret the loss of a valuable sense, can I ever forget to thank Thee, O my Father, that, when I fell, I did not lose my reason or life instead of my hearing? Never!" *

Such, then, was Kitto in his twentieth year—an unfortunate and feeble stripling, who had sunk into poverty and wretchedness, nay, had fallen so low as to dwell in a workhouse to acquire a trade, and thus become, as the guardians thought, provided for. Now, through his talents and character, he has emerged into a position of respectability, has turned his busy reading to good account, is the author of a handsome volume, patronised by many of the clergy, and by peers and peeresses of the realm, and is talked about as a kind of prodigy. The Hospital of the Poor's Portion is proud of him, and he is in the way of higher preferment, though as yet his friends discern not his ultimate career, nor does he himself foresee the rugged and devious path by which he must reach the great labour of his life. Yet he hints to Mr. Burnard that he is in high hopes of prospective authorship. "If my days be lengthened, nothing is more likely than that I shall publish again; but never will I publish, unless it be something far more worthy of attention than this; but I question whether my next publication, however superior to this it may be, will be equally well supported." Right, and yet wrong. His next publication was both vastly superior and far better supported. But he did not as yet even dream of it, for it was the *Pictorial Bible*, with which his

* This Essay is dated Plymouth Workhouse, Feb. 16, 1823.

name has become identified, nor was he then trained and equipped for such an undertaking.

A fortunate change speedily took place in Kitto's condition. Mr. Groves had been for some time contemplating the work of a missionary for himself, and had kept terms at Trinity College, Dublin, to prepare for episcopal ordination. As, therefore, his residence in Exeter could not be of long continuance, he was anxious to secure some settled mode of subsistence for his assistant. Several plans were proposed, to enable him, if he should abide by his vocation as a dentist, to practise either in Plymouth or the metropolis. But a wise Providence had otherwise determined. Mr. Groves had learned that the presses at several stations of the Church Missionary Society were in need of hearty workmen, and, knowing the devotedness of Kitto's spirit, and his vast admiration of evangelical labour, he proposed that he should take part as a printer in the great missionary enterprise. Kitto caught at the proposal, and thus addressed Mr. Woollcombe :—

" Exeter, June, 1825

"SIR,—To you and my other friends I feel it necessary to write, before the recurrence of the periods respectively assigned, in order to communicate a circumstance, for which you are more prepared than any of the other gentlemen to whom I am about to write. From something which passed when I had the honour of waiting on you whilst I was at Plymouth, in November last, you are, I presume, sir, sufficiently aware of the high interest which I felt in relation to the general subject of missions. And, indeed, from a letter written before I had the least idea of coming hither, it will probably have appeared that my mind was early impressed with a sense of the great privileges and importance of the missionary character. Will not these circumstances, sir, have operated on your mind as preparatives for the intelligence, that I hope myself to be permitted to occupy the high station of a labourer in the vast field of missionary exertion? That is the intelligence I write to communicate. And, requesting to be allowed to suppose, for a moment, the existence of a common feeling in relation to *one great object* between us, I may be allowed to anticipate your sympathy in the gratification which I derive from having enlisted under the banners of The Church Missionary Society. Attached as I am to the soft domestic charities of life, and open as my prospects of being permitted to enjoy them were, it cannot be necessary that I should inform you, sir, that nothing but a deep sense of the duty which I owed to him who has been so very good and merciful to me, and an ardent desire to contribute the humble offering of my individual exertions to the great, the noble cause, of assisting to dispel that darkness which is so deeply to be deplored, could have induced the offer of my services to that Institution. At a time like this, which may not improperly be considered a *crisis* in every point of view in which it can be contemplated, I think it very essential that every Christian should assist the mighty energies now in active operation, by the practice of that absolute and exclusive self-devotion to the service of the Almighty, the principles of which the Scriptures so strongly inculcate and enforce. Hence I rejoice in an occasion of practically demonstrating the *reality* of that willingness, which I have not been backward in professing, to appropriate myself, and every talent which God has committed to my trust, to the cause of Him from whom all things are derived, and whose right they therefore are. To do this is my honour, the highest honour I can attain—my privilege, my duty; and to it every rational consideration suggested to my mind—every *proper* feeling of my heart— irresistibly impels me, in spite of a certain degree of reluctance which I have naturally experienced at the idea of entering on a career of high moral responsibility and active exertion. Instead of these general statements and reflections, it will, perhaps, sir, be more necessary that I should enumerate the leading features of the circumstances under which I live. It having been discovered that the Church Missionary Society was in want of printers in various of its stations, the idea occurred to Mr. Groves that I might be very useful in such a capacity, and that I seemed peculiarly adapted for such a situation. When I had properly considered the suggestion, I eagerly entered into the idea it contained. Being satisfied, then, that this must be a most *useful* sphere of action, it of course became my duty to labour in it. Mr. G. therefore wrote to Mr. Bickersteth, the secretary, offering my services to the Society. No answer was immediately received, but Mr. Groves received an intimation from a third person, which induced him to go to London. He was there enabled to put the affair in a more desirable chain of operation than it had previously been; but the question was reserved for the decision of the Committee, which was held the week before last. On Friday evening information was received that the Committee did not consider my deafness as any material impediment to my usefulness as a printer at one of the Society's stations. They wish me, therefore, to come to London, where I am to be instructed in the business by Mr. Watts, their printer. Printers are much needed in Calcutta, Malta, and several other places; and if I go out under the Society, my employment will be to superintend the operations of the natives in the printing establishments. I know nothing, sir, in which I could be more useful than this; and to be useful is the only object, if I had any preference at all, for which I should wish to live. Even in a temporal

point of view, if my mind had even adverted to such a consideration, this would be no undesirable provision, as the Society takes care of its labourers in cases of inability arising from sickness, age, or any other cause equally unavoidable with these. Certainly I do not, sir, expect that, either in London, or on any of the Continents, I shall not have many trials and difficulties to support; but I hope and believe that He who has hitherto been with me will give strength and patience sufficient for me in *all* the varied circumstances of action and of being to which He may see fit to call me.—I remain, Sir, your greatly obliged and obedient servant,

"J. KITTO"

Kitto was accepted by the Board in London, Mr. Groves making a liberal offer of fifty pounds a year, for two years, towards the defraying of his expenses. In July 1825 he took up his residence at the Missionary College in Islington, and was assigned to the care of Mr. Watts to learn printing. What trades he had passed through already—barber, shoemaker, dentist, and now a printer! The last, however, was viewed by him in a spiritual aspect. He was qualifying, as he imagined, for the purpose of circulating the Bible and religious books. The work was, therefore, to his liking. He had thought of various projects before he left Mr. Burnard's, and suggested to Mr. Harvey* " that active measures should be taken to procure me some situation, before the money be exhausted, which you have with so much trouble collected." . . . . "Food and clothing are my only objects." He had at that time a strong desire to be attached to some gentleman's country residence, as he was willing to work for his maintenance in any humble capacity, provided all his time was not occupied, but some of it left for his own literary pursuits. He had a strong aversion to either editorial or subordinate connection with a newspaper, but would not have demurred to being "connected with Mr. Drew and the *Imperial Magazine*." Other schemes were afterwards started in his fertile ingenuity, but none of them were adopted. Such a place as that which he had so recently held under Mr. Groves had never once been thought of, and his position in Islington as a printer, in connection with the Church Missionary Society, was as remote from his usual anticipations. The calculations of his own prudence had all been defeated, and he could not but feel that, as a ward of Providence, his steps had been under the leading of a kind and invisible Hand. The unschooled cobbler of the Plymouth Workhouse was now an honoured inmate of Islington College.

* Library, September 30, 1823.

4

ISLINGTON

KITTO was highly gratified with the attention shown him by all the persons connected with the Institution at Islington, and he speaks very decidedly of the piety and zeal of the eighteen students resident in the house. He tells his friends in Plymouth of a great meeting, Lord Gambier in the chair, when fifteen missionaries received parting addresses. It was "the most grand and impressive occurrence" he had ever beheld, and, he adds, "a finer delivery than that of some of those speeches I never *witnessed*." In Mr. Watt's printing office he learned first to set Greek types, and he enjoyed much "delightful contemplation while working at his Greek cases." Then he tried Persic on Henry Martyn's translation of the New Testament. This manual labour was fatiguing, but still he gave himself to reading. He enjoyed what he called "pocket reading"—that is, taking one of his volumes and reading it as he walked to and from the place of business, and at every spare moment he could snatch during the day. The reader will remember how the boy, either in rags or in the dress of the workhouse, prowled about the bookstalls in Plymouth and Devonport, and poured over their miscellaneous and tattered contents. Now, when he had come to London, this passion met with an ampler gratification. He revelled in the luxury, and philosophised upon its superior delights. The paradox which he maintains is evidently a relic of his early vagrant life. He rejoiced in his perambulations, and seemed to prefer such half hours of literary license to undisturbed and sedentary study. "Bookstalls," he writes, in high glee, to Mr. Harvey,* "are very numerous in and about the town; bookstalls, the least of which will not admit any comparison with any provincial bookstall I have ever seen; and if I had formerly lived here, I might have had many hours of comfortable reading every day, merely by going from one bookstall to another, and spending half an hour or so at each; and by the time I might have visited the last in my circuit, I should have been long enough absent from that with which I had begun, to venture thither again, and so on, circuit after circuit. Now, if this state of things be compared with what I have already mentioned to have been the case in Devon, the advantages of a residence in London, to a person of literary habits, is sufficiently obvious in the instance I have selected. Few, on this plan, would be able to boast a larger library than myself. The advantages of such a library are obvious also. *First*, No money is paid for the privilege. *Secondly*, The usual effects of sedentary occupation are prevented, as the student is

* Islington, January 19, 1827.

obliged to stand while reading, and to walk both before and after. *Thirdly*, The opportunity of studying human character is one of peculiar importance; for the character of the book-man or book-woman, when they form the accompaniment of the stall, which happily is not always the case in London, is a subject of such essential importance to ourselves, that we study them with an anxiety the most intense, and penetration can never be more strongly excited by circumstances than in such an instance. And, *Fourthly*, there are peculiar benefits attending this mode of reading. When we have books in abundance of our own, or have them in any way at our own disposal, we are apt to neglect them, knowing we can read them at any time we please; and when we do read them, we are apt to do it cursorily, knowing that we can turn to them again whenever we wish to do so. But at the bookstall we read for our lives. We know that no time is to be wasted. We know that it is not likely we shall ever see the book again. Stolen reading, too, is sweetest; and, upon the whole, there is probably nothing we ever read which is so impressed on the memory, and so treasured up in the mind, as that which is read at the bookstall. This is easily accounted for. We know that the only future benefit we can derive from the volume, is that which the memory may afford; and hence the effort of the mind is strong to retain that which it has taken in. The person likely to avail himself of such a system, has also so little else to read, that the little he does thus read is the more easily retained. *The best readers are not those who read most.* I read a great deal in the Plymouth library, but I remember less of that than of what I had previously read at my friend's bookstall, and in the windows of booksellers' shops. A person who has many books of his own, or who can get books to read without difficulty, will never understand the advantages of bookstalls as I have related them, because he will want that intense and powerful stimulus which the bookless student possesses."

In the meantime, his eye had not been idle, nor was his heart seared. The pain he had suffered in relinquishing his early attachment did not prevent him from forming another. His heart yearned for affection. He was continually striving, as he tells us, "to win the affection of children, and was often disappointed in their caprices and fickleness." Three months after coming to Islington, he had seen a lady at church, who invited him to the joint use of her hymn-book, and he had been pleased by her appearance.* He could tell nothing about her. Neither her name nor residence was known to him: nor does he seem to have

* The incidents are given by himself, somewhat minutely, in a paper entituled *A Memorial of Two Years and a Half of the Life of J. K.*

made any anxious inquiry about them. But one of
his periodical illnesses overtook him. He had been
leeched on the temples, and during his convalescence
he went out and walked one afternoon in Barnsbury
Park. As he was returning to the college, he happened to enter a shop and engage in conversation with
the lady who kept it, and who was a "respectable and
serious looking woman." The talk was about Sunday
schools, and "she supported her part of the discourse
on a slate." She invited her customer into the parlour, which was "hung round with prints of eminent
ministers, framed and glazed." She showed him the
prize-books which her children, six in all, had got at
a neighbouring Sabbath seminary, and he naturally
wished to see the family. The reply was, that they
were all at school but one, and when that one obeyed
the maternal summons to appear, Kitto was agreeably
surprised to recognize in her the object of his previous
admiration. She did not, however recollect him. A
courtship naturally began, and proceeded, on successive visits, to his great satisfaction. A matrimonial
union was ultimately agreed on. Mr. Groves did not
now attempt to reason down his passion, but approved
of the project; and Mr. Bickersteth, the secretary,
gave also his formal consent. He lost no time in informing Mr. Burnard of his choice, for "he who has
rejoiced in my joy, and sympathised in my distress,
will assuredly rejoice with me in this; and great will
be my pleasure, my dear sir, in introducing to you
no common character—a Christian wife, a Christian
daughter, a Christian woman." Marriage was no new
idea to him. Even when he was the immediate pro-
tegè of charitable friends in Plymouth, and before
any door was opened to him, he avows, if he should
get a curacy—"Then I shall marry, and shall enjoy
domestic comfort and my favourite pursuits at the
same time."

Kitto's spirit glowed into poetry when it felt the
"new sense," or laboured under the "madness" which
he ascribes to his love, and he sent the following
meditation to Mr. Burnard. The prelude is—"My
dear Sir,—Though you know that John Kitto is no
poet, still I hope that, at a leisure minute, this may
give you pleasure :—

A REVERIE ON MARRIAGE

COMPOSED WHILE SITTING TO A PORTRAIT PAINTER

FULL many a man has sunk to rest
With social kind affections blest—
A heart to cherish and enjoy
The tender, soft connubial tie.

And yet these men have seldom known
The social happiness *of home;*
But, served by menial hands and rude,
Have mourned in cheerless solitude.

Say, such be I, then. Shall I sigh,
And sunken and dejected die,
Because to human joy unknown,
Gently to soothe me there is none?

None to sympathise in glee,
And, when I weep, to weep with me;
None to ease life's weary load,
And walk with me the narrow road;

None near me in the trying hour,
Soft balm into my wounds to pour;
None in pain to hold my head;
None to mourn me when I'm dead.

.   .   .   .   .

His hand shall soothe me when in pain;
That hand can make me whole again.
In death my God will still be nigh;
Yes; He'll be with me when I die.

Domestic sweets—the social band—
Are doubtless present; but the hand,
Which them and other blessings lends,
Can give a bliss that never ends.

Why, then, should I complain and moan,
As one quite cheerless and alone?
When, having God, in Him I've all
We justly happiness can call.

Human delights, I ask them not;
Be Thou the guardian of my lot;
And give a heart to count but loss
All, all things for the Christian Cross.

Give, Lord, a heart of warm desire,
Touch it with coals of living fire,
And kindle there a radiant flame
To burn for ever to Thy name.

And Thou, O Man of Galilee,
Who bled and agonized for me,
Through the strength that's only Thine,
Be victory and triumph mine.

December 30, 1825."

The lines that succeed were addressed to the object
of his devoted attachment. It is now the betrayal of
no secret, that if Hannah were substituted for Mary,
the poem would stand as originally composed. Kitto
himself published it in the *Lost Senses*, with the
fictitious name :—

"In silence I have walked full long
    Adown life's narrow, thorny vale,
Deaf to the melody of song,
    And all music to me mute,
        From the organ's rolling peal
        To the gay burst or mournful wail
Of harp, and psaltery, and lute.
Heaven's dread answer I have heard
    In thunder to old ocean's roar,
As while the elements conferred,
    Their voices shook the rock-bound shore :—
I've listened to the murmuring streams,
Which lulled my spirit into dreams;

Bright hopes, and fair imaginings;
But false as all that fancy flings
Upon a page, where pain and strife
Make up the history of life:
And so, beneath o'ershadowing trees,
I've heard leaves rustle in the breeze,
Which brought me the melodious tale
Of the all vocal nightingale,
Or else the cushat's coo of pride,
O'er his own new-mated bride.
Yes: I have heard thee—Nature, thee—
In all thy thousand voices speak,
Which *now* are silent all to me.
Ah, when shall this long silence break,
And all thy tides of gladness roll
In their full torrent on my soul!

But as the snows which long have lain
On the cold tops of Lebanon,
Melt in the glances of the sun,
And, with wild rush, into the plain
Haste down, with blessings in their train:
So, Mary, gilded by thine eye,
Griefs melt away, and fall in streams
Of hope into the land of dreams,
And life's inanities pass by
Unheeded, without tear or sigh.

True, that the human voice divine
Falls not on this cold sense of mine;
And that brisk commercing of thought
Which brings home rich returns, all fraught
With ripe ideas—points of view
Varied, and beautiful, and new,
Is lost, is dead, in this lone state,
Where feelings sicken, thoughts stagnate,
And good and evil knowledge grows
Unguided and unpruned, and throws
Too often a dull sickening shade,
Like that by trees of Java made
O'er hopes and o'er desires which might
Have lived in glory and delight,
Blessed and blessing others, till
The gaspings of this life were still.

But Mary, when I look on thee,
All things beside neglected lie:
There is deep eloquence to me
In the bright sparkle of thine eye.
How sweetly can their beaming roll
Volumes of meaning to my soul,
How long—how vainly all—might words
Express what one quick glance affords.
So spirits talk, perhaps, when they
Their feelings and their thoughts convey,
Till heart to heart, and soul to soul,
Is in one moment opened all.

Mary, one sparkle of thine eye
I'd not exchange for all the gems
That shine in kingly diadems,
Or spices of rich Araby.
My heart would count th' refined gold,
Which Eastern kings have left untold,
But as a begger's price, to buy
One sparkle of my Mary's eye."

. . . . . .

What Kitto had already avowed, was still true of him—"I cannot accuse myself of having wasted or misemployed a moment of my time since I left the workhouse." All his hours were carefully spent. The frugal youth usually had for his dinner, on the days he did not fast, a roll and a sausage, which he bought at a shop in the vicinity of Temple Bar. From a brief journal, in which he wrote occasionally during his residence at Islington, we learn some other particulars of interest.

"*April* 4, 1826.—At the outset I had best make such an arrangement of my time, and form such resolutions, as I have, for a considerable time, had in contemplation, and I pray God that if it be for His glory, I may be enabled to adhere to this arrangement and keep these resolutions. I am sure that it is more than I should be able to do in any strength of my own.

" WORK

" 1. When business is regular, I purpose to leave Islington for town before breakfast, and leave the office directly after tea.

" 2. Stay at home every alternate Wednesday, and the forenoon of the other Wednesday—when not practicable, the earliest opportunity occurring subsequently.

" HOME

" 3. When at home from any cause, to spend the morning in writing till dinner. After dinner call on Miss A.,* and spend the evening as occasion may require—reading if possible."

He then specifies the days of the week, with their peculiar duties. Thus, as a sample:—

" *Wednesday*.—I have for some time observed this as a day of abstinence and humiliation. But finding that it is very injurious to my head to go without breakfast, I hardly think myself justified in abstaining from it. I shall therefore take breakfast, and content myself with the omission of dinner and tea." It may be added, that Friday was observed, like Wednesday, as a fast-day.

" HOURS OF REST

" My hours of rest have been very irregular since I left Mr. Groves. Sometimes I have gone to bed early—sometimes late, but generally very late, so late that I have not thought it worth while to put off my clothes, but have lain down in them, and on an average I have seldom risen earlier than six. I propose, therefore, to go to bed from eleven to half-past, and to endeavour to get into the habit of rising at five. Thus I allow one-fourth of my time, six hours, for sleep, rather more than I can afford.

* The visits to Miss A. are set down as very frequent, almost daily, occurrences.

"Scriptures

"My method has been to divide my Bible into four parts—from Genesis to Job, from Psalms to Malachi, from Matthew to Acts, from Romans to Revelation; and it has been my general rule to read in two of these parts, one of the Old and one of the New Testament, daily, in alternation, so that if I read in the historical part of the New Testament on one day, I read on the same day in the didactic and prophetic part of the Old; and if I read on another day in the epistolary part of the New Testament, I the same day read in the historical part of the Old. I have found this method more useful and pleasant than any other, and therefore I shall continue to pursue it.

"I appropriate the first half-hour after rising to my Bible, that is, till half-past five, when I am dressed by five, and another half hour in the evening is to be employed in the same way. . . The Bible will be read of course at other times, particularly on Sundays.

"Devotions

"The half-hour succeeding those appropriated to the Scriptures, I propose to apply to the purpose of prayer, prefaced generally by the reading of a few hymns; and I have thought it would be very desirable to apportion the different objects which intercessory prayer should embrace on the different days of the week—a plan which I consider as presenting many advantages and great facilities for the due discharge of this important duty. I adopt, therfore, the following arrangement:—

SUNDAY.   *Morning.*—For clergymen, and ministers, and their congregations—a blessing on the preached Gospel.

,,   *One o'clock.*—At this time, on the two first, or when there are five in the month, the three first Sundays in the month, my dear H—— and myself will be engaged in simultaneous prayer for each other.

,,   *Evening.*—Church of England, and the Christian Churches in general—a catholic spirit among the different denominations.

MONDAY.   *Morning.*—England and its authorities.
,,   *Evening.*—The States called Christian.
TUESDAY.   *Morning.*—Religious Societies.
,,   *Evening.*—Children—Sunday Schools.
WEDNESDAY.   *Morning.*—Parents and Relatives.
,,   *Evening.*—Friends and Enemies.
THURSDAY.   *Morning.*—Jews.
,,   *Evening.*—Turks, Infidels, and Heretics.
FRIDAY.   *Morning.*—Missionary Societies and Missions.
,,   *Evening.*—Simultaneous Prayer.
SATURDAY.   *Morning.*—Missionaries and Students.
,,   *Evening.*—Outpouring of the Holy Spirit on ALL flesh."

A few disclosures from his Diary at this period, will throw light on several interesting points of his experience and character:—

"10.—On the sixth I was so very ill when I came home, that I was obliged to lie down immediately, and the next morning continued so unwell, that Mr. Yates thought it necessary to send for the medical gentleman who attends the house. He directed that twelve or fourteen ounces of blood should be taken from the back of my neck, by cupping, and furnished me with some medicines. I have not been to town since, but I think I feel better to-day than I have done since Thursday. I have often, during this time, experienced excruciating pains in the head and breast. But I do not repine. I have no cause to do so. I feel and am persuaded that it is sent me for good and not evil, and most truly can I, from experience, say that those periods of indisposition to which I am subjected, have been, and are, visits of mercy, seasons of refreshing to me, from the presence of the Lord. The retirement of a sick chamber, too, is pleasant to me, if only from the contrast with the bustling nature of general engagements. Here I can commune with my own heart—here I can read, and write, and pray, and, when pained and weary, can lie down in my bed unmolested, and unseen by any but by Him whose presence I seem almost sensibly to enjoy. Oh may these seasons be more and more sanctified to me! May my Master, my crucified Master, appear thus to me more and more the fairest among ten thousand, and altogether lovely! May I more and more enter into the *chambers of imagery* in my own mind, and be more and more strengthened by the Holy Spirit, in tearing down and demolishing every idol, whatsoever it be, which has there exalted itself against the knowledge and the love of God my Saviour.

"12.—I am better to-day than I have been since taken ill; and if I do not go to town this week, hope I shall not be detained longer. I have experienced much kind attention from Miss Hart. She has done everything to meet my wishes and render me comfortable, and the very servants, too, have laid me under much obligation, by their uniform manifestations of every little kindness that they may have had it in their power to exhibit. That it is the same with many of my dear fellow-servants, it is superfluous to say. All are very kind to me: thus, for instance:—Brown has come to my room every evening, to dress my neck while it needed dressing, and my dear Marsh has called up frequently to see me. When I came, I anticipated that I should be quite among strangers, and was prepared to find it so. But my kind and gracious Master has ordered things otherwise for me than I had expected. I feel that I am among brethren and friends, and that there are several within these walls who feel a most affectionate regard for me. What cause, then, have not I for thankfulness and gratitude to Him who thus far has made crooked places straight, and rough places plain before me? Oh that this cold heart were more alive and open to all those thankful emotions and impressions which such a continued course of mercy and loving-kindness from my heavenly Father should communicate!

"15.—Hoping my health would allow me to return to the discharge of my regular duties on Monday, I determined to terminate my keeping at home by a long walk and tract distribution. After breakfast, therefore, I stored my pockets with about eighty tracts, an equal number of handbills, and some fifteen little handbooks. This, with my Testament, pocket-book, and the last number of the 'Register,' completely filled my pockets. I walked out about four miles from Islington, and returned by another road. I distributed tracts chiefly in returning, as my walk out was in a very retired direction—a road in which I had never been before. I have seldom had a more pleasing excursion than this. The weather was beautiful, and my mind had attained to that exquisite tone of feeling and of thought, of which it is indeed susceptible, but which it is so unfrequently permitted to enjoy. Under a different modification of feeling, I might possibly have contemplated all the objects I beheld, without experiencing that interest they have now communicated; or without deriving any improvement from them. But before I went, my heart was prepared to respond to the language of the Psalmist, and to say, 'Thou, even Thou, art Lord alone. Thou hast made heaven, the Heaven of heavens, with all their host, and all things that are therein; and Thou preservest them all, and the host of heaven worshippeth Thee. O Lord, how manifold are Thy works! in wisdom Thou hast made them all! The earth is full of Thy riches.' And hence I was interested—hence I was instructed and improved. My walk out, as I have said, was retired. It was one also in which I had never before walked. It lay sometimes on the bank of the canal, sometimes beneath the shade of trees, sometimes through fields and pleasant lanes, and at others, over steep hills, from which I had extended and beautiful views before me, and could distinctly discern objects which lay at a very great distance from me. My Testament was a most valuable companion to me, and did not leave my hand till I turned my face towards Islington again, and began to distribute tracts in good earnest. While I soared with the eagle-minded John, or rather with the Divine Master whose words he records, the various objects spread around me, and the blue skies above my head, seemed softly to speak to me a sweeter and more exalted language than that which the natural man can

hear. The spirit seemed to enjoy a freedom it never had before—to breathe an air it never before imbibed —and, for a short and fleeting moment, to experience the foretaste of another world's enjoyments, in holding communion with beings of a higher world; yea, with Him who, of all beings and all worlds, is the Cause and the Creator! I think that God, the Holy Ghost, has been graciously pleased more to enlighten my understanding in reference to many things in His sacred Word, which had not appeared to me before, than in any equal period of time within my recollection. Oh! it is most pleasant to feel and know that the self-same hand which wrote the beautiful and splendid volume of nature, wrote also the far more precious book of Revelation for us; that the High and Holy One, who called into being and arranged—

'The pomp of groves, and garniture of fields,
And all the dread magnificence of heaven,'

is not an abstract quality—an awful, unknown something,—but the very same Friend, Guide, and Father, who in mercy and in love has revealed Himself in Christ Jesus—the very same whose loving-kindness and whose truth has followed us through all the devious and intricate paths of our pilgrimage, and has brought us hitherto, and who Himself has promised that He will be with us still—that He will never leave us nor forsake us, but bear and carry us even to the end. I am fully aware that a man, not duly impressed with a sense of the amazing value of the Christian verity, may yet be capable of contemplating the sublimities and beauties of nature, with exalted emotions of wonder and delight. But he cannot have the interest and kind of property in them which a Christian has—he cannot recognize in them the hand of his best and dearest Friend—he cannot, oh, he cannot experience that undefined and inexpressible emotion with which the Christian philosopher can look below, around, above him, and, laying his hand upon his breast, can say, 'My Father made them all.' I had a very pleasing success in the distribution of my tracts —and I pray my dear Master to let His blessing rest on the seed which I have thus been enabled to sow by the way-side. I am looked up to as an authority on tract matters here."

It happened that there was not in the printing-office a sufficiency of Persic types, and Kitto, unwisely using his own discretion, sometimes stayed at home all day, and occasionally left the office before the appointed hour. These absences began to be marked, and to form the subject of suspicious comment. Kitto hastened to explain, but his explanation was not reckoned wholly satisfactory. He vindicates himself to Mr. Watts thus:—

"SIR,—I am sorry to be obliged again to intrude on you, but I feel it necessary to mention distinctly that, although I recollect to have said *once* that I did not think *setting up pie* was a useful employment of my time, or much calculated to promote my knowledge of the business, yet, I added, what your informant has seen proper to omit, 'That if I could obtain nothing better I should do that of course.' I *never* did object to anything else, nor to this more than once. On this subject, however, I hope I shall be pardoned for saying that I think now as I did then. . . As you are pleased to refer to your apprentices, I would just remark that it seems to me, that as I have so much to acquire in a period so much more limited than theirs, the same system of instruction cannot well apply to both. . . .

"In reference to the irregular attendance you mention, I must be contented with what I said yesterday, that it arose from insufficient employment. I have generally gone to the office every day, even when I expected to find no work. I have waited there, a longer or shorter period, frequently the best part of the day, and if I could get nothing to do, have returned home. I wish to state distinctly *now*, since I have been misunderstood before, that regular attendance may be expected from me when I have regular work."

But the truth is, that Kitto and the Committee did not understand one another. He was never fond of control, and could scarce endure it in Exeter, where he laments, "I am less a free agent than formerly." He wished very much to be master of his time, conscious that he ever made a due and diligent improvement of it. The Committee thought that he was neglecting the main point for which they had engaged him, and that he was slighting the business for which they had hired him. The terms of agreement must have been somewhat loosely made, and Kitto's deafness prevented him from entering into any minute enquiries or stipulations; for, certainly, had he known that he was expected to give up his entire time to mechanical labour, foregoing his precious and coveted hours of reading, he would rather have remained at Exeter, and cut the "tusks of certain foreign animals" into the semblance of human teeth. His belief was, that he was bound to learn to print, but, bound in a higher sense, to prepare for writing something that might be printed. He aspired to be at least a translator. Authorship for men's spiritual good was his aim; and every other vocation was, in his opinion, to occupy a subordinate place. The Committee, on the other hand, not knowing what was in him, and not, perhaps, fully acquainted with his habits and his ambition, resolved that he should simply be a printer, and that the setting of types should be the one present employment, and the ultimate business of his life, at least in connection with their Society. On being challenged, he made an honest confession, telling how he thought and felt,

praying not to be judged harshly, narrating his early experiences and hardships, and how the love of books grew so strongly upon him.

"I should have been, perhaps, much gratified if my immediate duty to the Society could have been more identified with those habits and pursuits, or rather, that they be brought to bear more immediately upon that duty than it appears they can, in the line of employment now chalked out for me. As it is, however, I am very desirous of being informed whether it be indeed, as seems to be intimated, required of me that I should relinquish these pursuits *altogether*. If it be, I am sorry to say, that I cannot think myself called upon or justified in making any promise to that effect. As the Society could devise no line of service for me which would harmonise more fully with the peculiar bent and tone of my mind, is it therefore necessary that this should be wholly merged in the other? I do myself think not. I cannot believe, although I have tried to believe it, although I have earnestly prayed that the Lord's thoughts for me, and my own thoughts for myself, might coincide, and although I know that a gift to the service of the Lord's house, would not be estimated according to its intrinsic value, but according to the spirit in which it might be offered, yet I cannot believe that it is designed by Him, whose dispensations towards me have been so strongly marked, that the maximum of my service should depend upon that degree of manual exertion which another—a mere printer—might perform much better and more efficiently than myself."[*]

He was then distinctly told what was expected from him, and that he could not be sent abroad "till his altered conduct should show his cordial compliance with such regulations." This resolution unduly pressed the matter to a crisis; no sympathy was shown him; there was no appreciation of his peculiarities; nothing would be accepted but formal and unreserved submission. Aye or no—select the alternative at once, and abide by it. Kitto was irritated, and resigned his situation.

His friends were exceedingly angry at him, and some of his Plymouth patrons were prepared to cast him off. He was inundated with counsels, and cut to the quick by harsher words and rebukes. But he met with special sympathy from the students, whom he delighted to greet as "brethren and friends." On the second anniversary of the Institution, he had delivered an address to them, and they had tendered him their hearty thanks by a unanimous and unprecedented vote. Now he sold his books to them, and wrote them a farewell address, which winds up as follows:—

"I am permitted to remain a short time at the

* Letter to the Rev. J. N. Pearson, President of the Missionary College—December, 1826.

Institution, till I have arranged matters for my departure to the place whither He, who has led others through the wilderness before, may lead me. I leave you, and I do most truly lament that I leave you in a manner so very different from any that I had foreseen or anticipated. Brethren, suffer me to hope that I shall be followed by your prayers. Permit me to believe that you will not consider the bond to be quite broken which bound me up together with you. Forbid it not, that I still look upon myself as a fellow-labourer with you; indeed, that I still shall hold the sickle of the reaper, to gather in the harvest of God, although I no longer have a reaper's name."

At this period, when so much was at stake, and he must find some employment for himself to live by, he applied to the London Missionary Society; but his deafness was held to be a barrier to his usefulness as a foreign evangelist.

That Kitto was conscious of no such breach of contract as was laid to his charge, may be learned from some incidental expressions in his letters. He had written to Mr. Woollcombe in June—"I scarcely recollect the time when I have read so little as I do now, certainly never since I left the workhouse."

But he soon regretted the hasty step he had taken, and to Mr. Burnard he poured out his spirit:—

"I have essayed my own will and my own way, and I have found that will and that way to be bitter. I have therefore endeavoured to return to His way and His will for me. I have thrown myself upon Him again. I have said to Him, 'Thou seest I fall except Thou help me. I cannot walk by myself. I will no longer try to do so. Lead me and guide me.' I am satisfied that I sinned in relinquishing my connection with the Church Missionary Society. I did not, however, sin with my eyes open. It was the sin of blindness. I do not wish to extenuate. Most of my friends have been offended, chiefly because I gave up a good temporal provision. But that was not my sin, nor was it the real ground on which others should have been angry with me. It was the proud heart, the lofty mind. My offence had been chiefly spiritual, intellectual; chiefly against God, at least more against Him than against man."

In the journal to which we have referred, he also put down these words of mingled bitterness and hope:—

"*February* 29, 1827.—What am I now? What have I been doing? I awake as from a dream. In what difficulties am I not involved? Friends dropping away from me on every side, and stripped thus by degrees of human consolation, comfort, hope. Hope, yet I have hope—hope not fallacious and delusive, because it is built on the Rock Christ. How desolate now do all things earthly seem to me! I look around;

all things seem dark, and black, and gloomy—and what were I, could I look nowhere but around me! I look to Thee, O my God! I wait for Thee more than they that wait for the morning. Arise, arise, O light! and shine upon me, and enlighten the darkness of my way. I have dealt very treacherously against Thee from my youth up. Yet Thou wert long-suffering, and barest with me, and lo? Thou hast brought me hitherto, and now wilt Thou leave me—now? Thou wilt not. Thou hast promised that Thou wilt not, O my God! Look down upon me in pity, and let not the enemy triumph over me! Whom have I but Thee —to whom can I look but Thee? O, then, teach me to look to Thee indeed, to lean upon Thee indeed, to the end of my journey. I go forth, O my Lord, into the wilderness of this world, and know not whither I go. Thou art my hope. Go with me—lead me— guide me. Direct my steps and my wanderings by Thy Providence. Watch over me for good; and when I have finished my appointed course, receive me to Thy bosom to live, and there be cherished for ever. Do not leave me; I throw myself upon Thee for guidance and protection; and when I am far away from those charities and ties with which men do surround themselves—when I have no home to shelter me, no pillow on which to lay my head, be Thou my Shelter, my Refuge; and when my wanderings are finished, do Thou plant me where I may grow, and live, and die to Thy glory—where I may be fruitful as the vine, verdant as the fir, strong as the cedar."

Kitto, four years afterwards, added a note to this extract:—

"*March* 21, 1831.—When I wrote the above, I recollect it was my intention to set out on foot and travel in England, till I should find some way or other of subsistence. How little experience, how little knowledge of the world I had then! I was as a child in every respect. Most likely it would have ended in my being sent to the House of Correction as a vagrant. . . . That prayer is better than I thought would be in my heart at *that* time. The Lord's dealings with me have been wonderful from a child." It is probable that the example of Goldsmith suggested this desire to wander through the country—a desire which had already been keenly expressed by him when he was in the workhouse.

Mr. Groves, the Rev. Mr. Hatchard of Plymouth, and other friends, interfered for him, and the Society restored him to his place. But he gave a rash pledge, to abandon literary pursuits—a pledge which, unless his intellectual nature had been changed, he could not redeem. He praises Mr. Hatchard highly, and Mr. Groves very highly, for the pains they had taken to secure his reinstatement. He contrasts Mr. Groves with others of his friends, whose coldness had keenly wounded him. "He did not say, like others, 'Lie in the bed of your own making;' but, though himself the most aggrieved, has come forth repeatedly to my help."

It was deemed advisable that Kitto should be sent forthwith to a foreign station, and Malta was selected as his field of labour. When he was in suspense as to the decision of the Committee, we find him urging not only his own anxiety, but also that of another, as a reason why he should like to have speedy intelligence. He says to Mr. Groves, "for *her* account, it is therefore my hope to find that the matter is to be decided, or will be soon." It was resolved, however, that he should go to Malta alone, but that the bans should be proclaimed prior to his departure. This preliminary step was taken, and Kitto expected to be followed in a few months by his betrothed.

It may be added, in conclusion, that, during his residence at Islington, and when he was worried so much about his own affairs, which at one time looked dismal, he busied himself in various efforts to find a comfortable situation for a young man, who had recently married Betsy, his eldest and favourite sister. This brother-in-law had come to London in quest of employment, but failed to find it. Kitto notes some of the counsels and comforts which he set before him at one of their interviews, and concludes:—

"I spoke of the nature of trials and adversities, the blessed purposes they were calculated to answer; on trust in God, and casting all our care upon Him, knowing that He careth for us; on seeking first the kingdom of God, and His righteousness, and having all other things necessary to us. I adverted to my own case. I had once nothing. The bread I ate, the water I drank, was bitter; and that bitter bread and water was procured with trouble and difficulty. I had not sought then the kingdom of God and His righteousness; but since I have been enabled to do so —since I have sought, in the first place, objects of pre-eminent and absorbing importance—the living water which cometh down from Heaven, the bread which perisheth, and the raiment which waxeth old, have been added to me, and I have lacked nothing. I recommended the seeking of this above all things, and could assure him that, if he did so, He who arrays the lilies of the field, and feeds the fowls of the air when they cry, would not fail to take care of him, to feed and clothe him and his also. I went on, at considerable length, in the same strain. I was heard with attention, but not, I fear, with interest. Indeed, I have seen so little out of myself of the Holy Spirit's operations in softening the hardness of the human heart, and I contemplate that heart as so deplorable, and everything but hopelessly bad, and disinclined to the things of God, that I labour under very great dis-

couragement in speaking and acting, and exert myself, in either way, less from the hope of being instrumental in bringing a blessing to those whom I address, than from the conviction that it is my duty to declare the truth of God on such occasions, and speak and act for Him."

Kitto left England on the 20th June 1827, rejoicing in the work that lay before him, and hoping that the bride he had left behind would soon come out to Malta and be his wife—the ornament and joy of his home. The "Wilberforce" (Captain Denck) was detained for some time at Torbay by contrary winds, and Kitto had the satisfaction of feeling that the last land he set his foot on was that of his native county of Devon.

5

MALTA

KITTO's mind had, for some time, been steadily under the power of a motive to which it was originally a comparative stranger. The desire of usefulness had supplanted or outgrown the mere love of fame. He craved to be known, in the first instance, and "get himself a name;" but now his soul was bent on imparting benefit to his fellow-creatures. In a letter to Mr. Pearson of the Missionary College, he confesses, "*Fame* was the idol I was taught to bow down too and worship. I hope that in reference to myself it is on the throne no longer, and that I have no other wish on this point than that my light may so shine before men that they may glorify my Father who is in heaven." Let us listen for a moment to his deeper self-analysis, made at a period of subsequent and leisurely meditation:—

"It has often occurred to me that the stimulant which the desire of fame offers is specially adapted to one's youth, in which it is indeed most entirely in operation, and that it has been providentially given to that period of life to supply the absence of the more sedate stimulants which advancing life introduces. Rightly understood, it is then an incentive to good and a curb to evil, which, in the spring-time, are so much needed, for he who, in his sanguine youth, hopes that the world will hereafter take notice of his course, will not be unsolicitous to keep his garments clean.

"The desire to be honourably known among men— the craving for approbation—the wish to do something which might preserve one's memory from the oblivion of the grave—and the reluctance to hurry on through this short life and disappear along with the infinite multitudes who

'Grow up and perish as the summer fly,
   Herds without name—no more remembered:—'

these things savour, seemingly, of that 'love of fame' of which so much has been said or sung. I cannot say that this, as a motive to exertion and to perseverance in the course which I had taken, did not find a way to my mind.

"I have confessed that self-advancement eventually became one of the objects which I contemplated as the possible result of my exertions. Very few of my readers will complain of this; but considering the generally sacred character of my pursuits, which, I will venture to say, have been, however tremblingly, directed not less to the glory of God than to the use of man, some will be disposed to ask, whether self-advancement is a legitimate object of exertion; and whether it was not rather my duty to have been content in the station to which it had pleased God to call me. Now, by 'self-advancement,' I mean melioration of the evils of my condition; and no one can object to that without affirming that it was my duty to lie still, to be content and happy, under the unmitigated calamities of the condition to which I had been reduced. I believe that *this* was not required of me. I am persuaded that the state of life to which the Almighty calls every man is that for which he is fitted, and to which he may be able to rise by the just and honourable use of any and every talent which has been confided to him. In *that* station let him be content, and not waste his heart in aiming at things beyond his reach. I have read the Bible ill, if this be not its meaning. Saint Paul enjoins the Christian slaves to be content in their stations; and yet he tells them, that 'if they be made free, *to use it rather.*' Was ever any slave in so hard a bondage, bondage so hopeless as that into which deafness brought me? and if I might by exertions not degrading but elevating be free, should I not 'use it rather?' Let the answer be found in the contrast between the uselessness of my first condition, and the usefulness of that to which I have now attained." *

It was with the view of taking an active and honourable part in what he reckoned the highest function of redeemed humanity, that Kitto left Islington. He felt that he was going out to Malta to labour in Christ's cause, for the Master had said to him, "Son, go work to-day in My vineyard," and he gladly, and to the best of his ability, obeyed the charge.

The institution at Malta had for its object to supply tracts to the Church missionaries, in Greek, Arabic, Maltese, and Italian. It had three presses, and employed six individuals. Mr. Jowett and Mr. Schlienz were the principal labourers, accomplished, scholarly, and devoted. Of Mr. Jowett, Kitto says, "He is second to none; or if second to any, only to Mr. Groves; and Mr. Schlienz works, in another way, far

* *Lost Senses—Deafness*, pp. 84, 87.

harder than we printers do, for he preaches, and that frequently, twice on Sunday." Though there was not a bookseller's shop in the island, the Romish clergy were their principal opponents, and the circulation of tracts was forbidden by sacerdotal authority. But the works of the missionary press at Malta were largely circulated in other countries. Kitto rejoiced that, in sailing to join such an institution, he was assuming, though in an humble form, the coveted character and position of an evangelist.

But his sojourn in Malta was, in Scottish religious phrase, a "crook in his lot." The voyage to the Mediterranean was, however, of lasting service to him. His deafness had been accompanied by a growing reluctance to speak, and indisposition to use his vocal organs had almost produced inability.

"When I first went to the Mediterranean, the companions of my outward voyage were Dr. Korck, a German physician, who had lately taken orders in the Anglican Church, and Mr. Jadownicky, a converted Polish Jew, lately arrived from America, where he had been completing his Christian education. These well informed and kind hearted men, being always with me, soon perceived how the matter really stood; and, after much reasoning with me on the matter, they entered into a conspiracy, in which the captain of the ship joined, not to understand a word I said, otherwise than orally, throughout the voyage. In this they persevered to a marvel; and as I had much to ask, since I had not before been at sea, I made very great progress with my tongue during the six weeks' voyage, and, by the time we reached our destination, had almost overcome the habit of clutching a pen or pencil, to answer every question that was asked me. From this time I usually expressed myself orally to those whom I knew, in the ordinary intercourse of life; but when my communication required many words, it was usually conveyed in writing. This also I at length dropped, and strangers only were addressed in writing. Finally, I ventured to accost even strangers with the tongue; and it was only when not understood that I resorted to the pen. At first, strangers could rarely understand me without much difficulty; but, under the improvement which practice gave, my voice was so much bettered, that the instances in which it was not readily understood, gradually diminished, and, at the present day, I rarely find even a foreigner to whom my language is not clear." *

The gain to Kitto from this voyage, therefore, was immense; and he felt under no little obligation to his kind and earnest friends, who broke his pernicious habit, and won him back to the use of speech. The voyage was pleasant to him, for he was a stranger to sea-sickness. He felt, indeed, what sometimes terrifies

* *Lost Senses—Deafness*, pp. 20, 21.

or distresses a landsman, the instability of cabin furniture and dinner equipage from the blowing of smart breezes ; and while he had made up his mind to such annoyances, and could smile at them, yet he liked an occasional calm, and rejoiced over "the capture of two fine turtles." His letters to his friends, Woollcombe, Harvey, Lampen, and Burnard, contain such details as, in his opinion, would be most relished respectively by each of his correspondents.

He states generally, that his mind was no stranger to those emotions which men so often feel on leaving their native shores—that a "feeling of desolateness," had occasionally come over him, but that he felt each evening "Whose presence was with him," and he hoped that such feelings "threw him more upon God."

His first sensations, off the coast of Portugal, are detailed to Mr. Woollcombe, July 10 :—

"I fetched my bolster from the cabin, and arranged a bed for myself on the tafferel, by laying Mr. Jadownicky's thick cloak along, to lie upon, and then wrapping myself in my own cloak and fur cap, to defend me from the dew. I remember walking about the deck, or sometimes leaning on the gangway, till between twelve and one o'clock, when, feeling sleepy, I retired to my new bed, and lay there, so that I could look the moon in the face till I fell asleep. An accident awoke me about a quarter past two, and then I got up and walked about for nearly an hour, went to bed again, and slept till a few minutes before sunrise, which of course is considerably later here than in England. The sun rose with great splendour from behind the Lusitanian Mountains, but I have seen far more gorgeous risings of the sun than this, from the Hoe, at Plymouth, and from the Catdown. Both the risings and settings of the sun do not seem such slow and majestic affairs as in England; and, indeed, I understand that the farther we advance to the south, the shorter is the morning and evening twilight, and the less time the sun takes in rising and setting. I have just enquired at the captain, and find that, as I suspected, the mountains adjoining the Rock of Lisbon are those of Cintra, of which Lord Byron speaks, in the fourteenth stanza of the first Canto of *Childe Harold* :—

'Cintra's mountains greet them on their way.'

And, indeed, it was to us, as to him, a pleasant greeting, after having been, for so many days, out of sight of anything like land."

The good ship "Wilberforce," with a "gilt effigy" of the senator at her prow, entered at length the straits of Gibraltar ; and as Kitto looked alternately on the African and European land, so close on each other, many trains of meditation passed through his mind. He reached Malta in safety on the 30th of July, entering the harbour of La Valetta in the evening, and disembarking next morning. The accommodation provided for him was not of the best description, for he slept several weeks on the floor, and some time elapsed ere he enjoyed the luxury of a chair and a table. At length he got two rooms, a study and within it a bedroom—"the highest in a high house"—but abounding in windows, which commanded a fine marine prospect. He had also a bookcase, with a good collection on its shelves. But who will wonder at his confession, that of an impatient bridegroom—"My heart was in England, and my mind continually travelled thither?" He set to work with ardour, and especially occupied himself with Asiatic types ; nay, he spontaneously entered, at the same time, upon Arabic studies. The literary departments were filled by the clerical missionaries, and the translators were natives of the countries into whose languages they were rendering Christian books and tracts. From half-past seven till half-past four was he occupied every day in the printing office. He liked his work ; and he rejoiced in its prospective results. He declares, in his letters, how happy he was that his connection with the Society had been renewed.

"It is easy," he says to Mr. Burnard, November 13, "to *talk* about missionary service when we are at home, or even when we are preparing at home for personal service in the cause, and yet understand very little of what it really is. In this, as in other things, an ounce of experimental knowledge is worth a pound of speculation or conjecture. . . . Believe me, it is not my wish to magnify any sacrifice I may have been enabled to make, far from it. I only mention this that I might say how 'the consolations of Christ' do abound in these situations, notwithstanding the difficulties and sacrifices with which they must be obtained. In my own case, I feel that my most ordinary employments, even my daily occupations, are, with the blessing of God's Spirit, calculated to be the means of great usefulness to the Christian cause. This is what few, but those in our situation, can say of their most *ordinary* duties."

Kitto saw the carnival, with all its puerile follies, which he alleges were on the decline—not more than a fourth part of the people wearing masks, and the maskers being prohibited from tossing sugar balls at the unmasked, or in any way molesting them. "Sweetmeats, generally small comfits, were thrown about in great abundance, chiefly by English and Russian officers, who had small bags full, which they frequently replenished at the stalls. These were generally thrown into the coaches, in the faces of the ladies, who commonly returned the compliment with zeal, and often were the first to give it."

The Committee in London, by one of their minutes,

dated March 20th, 1827, on re-admitting Kitto to their employment, and sending him to Malta, gave a conditional sanction to his marriage, "on the understanding that, at a future period, should he conduct himself to Mr. Jowett's satisfaction, H. A., to whom he is under matrimonial engagements, may join him at that place, with a view to their marriage." But the lady of his heart, whom Kitto had left behind him in England, proved faithless to her engagement. He was disposed to blame the Committee at home for being careless about forwarding his correspondence. "I have now," he says, "been absent from England for something more than eight months, and have not, in all that time, had one letter from Miss A.; and therefore I feel assured that several successive letters have been left with the Society, on the understanding that they would be sent out. If the separation, for a short time, between us, to which I was unwillingly induced to assent, was at all necessary, this surely is not also necessary. This surely might have been spared." He did not know what to think about her whom he calls his "ladye faire"—"she whom I had trusted before all earthly beings—she who was dearer to me than all other things my heart ever knew or cherished."

His suspicions, at the end of these eight weary months, were at last confirmed, by the intelligence that she had deserted him, and had been married to another person. His hopes were in a moment dashed to the ground, and his heart was oppressed with sad and bitter thoughts. He had loved intensely, and was in daily expectation of being married. He was ever picturing the comforts of home, when she should fill it and grace it; but, alas! she had plighted her troth to another. On receiving the tidings, he went at once into his room, shut the door upon him, and did not leave it for more than two days, not even for his meals. During that dark period no one saw him. The servant became alarmed, and told Mr. Jowett. Knocking was in vain; but a ladder was got, that the servant might, by means of it, see in above the door, and ascertain whether Kitto were dead. On his friends looking into the chamber, he was discovered sitting on his disconsolate and solitary hearth, with his head bent on his knee. The intelligence grieved him beyond any former affliction which he had been called upon to suffer. "My spirit is bowed down indeed." "I am alone," he says to one correspondent, "but what else I am I cannot tell." "I often found myself," he says to another friend, "engaged in the repetition of two lines, which I must have picked up somewhere at a former period—

'No more, no more, oh never more on me
The freshness of the heart shall fall like dew.'

". . . I know I can never again confide as I have confided. . . . I have read over what I have written. It is not all good. There is an unhealthy spirit in it. True, my own spirit is diseased, for it has been deeply wounded, and the wound is not yet healed. May Almighty God give me the spirit of health and strength—give me a sound mind—bind up again that which is broken—heal that which is wounded! He can, I doubt not; that He will, I am willing to hope and believe. In outward nature He revives again in the spring that which the winter seems to wither away. Does God take care for plants, for trees, for flowers, and shall He not take care for me? Shall not I revive again also? I will hope that I may, and, believe me, I do endeavour to cast myself and all my cares and troubles upon Him in whom I have never vainly trusted, by whom my confidence and trust have never been betrayed. I trust He will make good to me all these evils; and that they may be made instrumental in drawing me still nearer to our crucified Lord, who can give me *here* comfort, strength, things in my spirit, far better than all I can now lose, than all that can be taken away from me; and who can give me hereafter 'quiet and enduring chambers' in His Father's house, where none of the things that now trouble and distract me, can vex me further."

To his mother he thus unbosoms himself:—

"*March* 7, 1828.

"MY DEAR MOTHER,—I write this letter to you in very great sorrow of heart. I received news yesterday from the Society, which has given me a blow that it will be very long before I shall recover. It was this —that H—— A—— is married to some person in England! Oh, my mother, you cannot imagine what this has made me suffer! I had expected that she would soon come to me, and hoped that we should be very comfortable and happy together in this place— when all my hopes and happiness in this life were at once destroyed by this intelligence. I hardly know how to believe it. But it was the Secretaries of the Society themselves who wrote to tell it to Mr. Jowett, and they would not have written it had they not been quite certain about it. They wrote very kindly, and assured me of their sympathy and prayers, and my friends here have also been very considerate and kind on this occasion to me. But the kindness of man can do little for such a wound as this. I am very unwell, my dear mother, and my spirit is quite broken up. It is a very severe trial to me, and I should quite sink under it, if the Lord were not graciously with me, to support and strengthen me, under the heavy burden I have to bear. I hope it will be sanctified to me, as my other trials have been. I wish you were with me now, that I might talk with you; for I am desolate indeed, and my cup of sorrow is very full. The Lord is with me, however, and puts a little peace into my heart, else I could not live. Indeed, I do not care to live at all. I have had nothing to make me love life. My life has been quite full of disappointment and sorrow, and I shall be very, very glad, when my labours are ended, and I am permitted to go to my home in heaven—to that quiet rest from all these troubles, which the Lord has prepared there for His people."

His mother replied in a letter which has the genuine maternal stamp upon it. Indignation at the lady's conduct, and sympathy with her son, struggle alike for utterance. She tells him that God, for some wise purpose, had not designed her for him, and, descending from this altitude, she affectionately advises him to walk a good deal, take plenty of exercise, and converse pleasantly and often with his associates.

In a letter to the lady's cousin, he sends the following message :—

"*Malta, March* 7, 1828

" . . . Tell her that I have no wish to reproach her. God can bear me witness, that I have desired her happiness above all things ; and although she has wounded me so deeply, and made me desolate indeed, I shall rejoice if she prove to be happy in her new situation. But I doubt whether she will. They who can sport so with the happiness of others, are seldom happy themselves. They may seem to be so for a season, but, in the end, they are not. Their happiness passes away like a dream. Believe me, it is my prayer that hers may be lasting. But mine would not in her situation. I do not think I could rest quietly upon my pillow if I had served her, or any other person, as she has served me. To murder the peace of another is the worst of all murders ; and she has murdered mine. I think, however, that I can forgive her, and I pray God to forgive her also."

We do not know all the reasons which induced the lady to withdraw her pledge to Kitto. We find, in his Islington Journal, in an incidental record of his most secret thoughts, the following complaint :—

" Went to Hannah before coming to the Institution. I do not really know what to think about her. That she loves me I have very great reason to believe ; yet, on this supposition, and knowing that she is *not* naturally volatile, I have felt much at a loss to account for a degree of inattention to me when at her house, which has very frequently distressed my feelings much, very much indeed. The most trivial and unimportant circumstance has the power of diverting her attention from me, even though I should be speaking of something which may seem to me peculiarly interesting ; and I have seen her chatting and laughing, for a long time occasionally, without seeming to be in the least conscious that such a being as John Kitto was present. I am very foolish to mind such things, yet I cannot help minding them—lovers are very foolish beings. . . . That she is faultless, I am not obliged, by the most ardent affection, to believe. . . . If she do not experience that warmth for me which I do for her, that surely cannot be imputed to her as a *fault*—it is my *misfortune*."

We should be inclined to lay no great stress on this lover's lamentation, for Kitto was very sensitive in society ; and, from his deafness and isolation, was apt to think himself slighted. He never ascribes to her any alteration of affection, but says, some years afterwards, that her conduct " admitted of much extenuation, owing to the awkward predicament in which the Society had placed them both." We have learned, on good authority, that Kitto's letters from Malta were studiously kept back from the lady ; that she was taught to believe that he had forgotten her ; that it was under the pressure of maternal authority that the match was broken off ; and that the instability of his connection with the Society was a topic principally insisted on. What Kitto calls the " deep repentance " of the lady's death-bed, was the result of her coming too late to a knowledge of these painful circumstances.

The result was, that a severe illness overtook him. His heart had been crushed, and his health now failed. In fact, he was fast sinking into that morbid state which had oppressed his early years. He felt as if he had been cut off from the world, and as if some curse had fallen upon him. He had suffered much already for sins not his own—had been the inmate of a workhouse, had lost one of his senses, had been twice misjudged, as he thought, by his Committee—and " all these things were against him." Was he never to enjoy the sunshine ? Was a sudden eclipse for ever cruelly to interpose ? Providence had been mysterious in its actings towards him, and was man, in addition, continually to thwart him ? His spirit sank under such reflections, and sickness preyed upon him. " I became dangerously ill," he tells Mr. Frere, " and we all thought that my cares and my afflictions, my miscalculations and my errors, would now at last be terminated. It pleased God, nevertheless, that I should be again restored."* Such was his lassitude, even when recovering, that he had no heart for his duties ; nay, his physical strength was not equal to the task. A peculiar weakness of his ankles, which he had felt ever since his fall, and more than once described and lamented, disabled him from standing at a case ten hours a-day. He began to perceive that he was not giving satisfaction to his superiors. He had rashly bound himself to relinquish literary pursuits. But his own explanation seems to have been— that literary pursuits and literary relaxation were different things—that he might safely indulge the latter without devoting himself, heart and soul, to the

_____
* Letter to the Right Hon. J. H. Frere. Malta, Dec. 4, 1828.

former. Though, therefore, he spent his hours of leisure in reading and meditation, he did not think that he had broken his pledge. The Committee, however, judged that the way in which he passed his evenings, did not leave him sufficient time for exercise and sleep; and that, in consequence, he must come to his employment under them, with a jaded mind and an exhausted frame. Mr. Jowett, when about to leave Malta for England, had told him so; and Mr. Bickersteth, the Secretary, sent him a lecture on the "Sacrifice of Self-will and Self-gratification." The Committee gave it as their opinion that his "habits of mind were likely to disqualify him for that steady and persevering discharge of his duties, which they considered as indispensably requisite." "It is clear," writes the unflinching Secretary, "that the Society cannot continue in its service those who will not devote themselves to their engagements." Kitto had been under espionage in Malta, for his previous breach with the Society had been only partially healed. He was, in fact, on trial, though he was not aware of it, and, perhaps, no one put him on his guard. He accordingly thought himself unjustly used, and affirmed that he had kept his pledge, —that his general hour of retiring to rest was eleven o'clock, and that if he remained out of bed longer at any time, it was because painful feelings would have scared sleep away, had he lain down to woo it. He adds, with some degree both of tartness and truth— "If I had employed an equal portion of my evenings lolling on the sofa and smoking my pipe, it seems all would have been well—no blame would have been imputed to me." It was allowed that, when in the office, he was faithful to his work as a compositor, but it was surmised that his studies out of it must unfit him, to some extent, for its manual labours. The Committee and he were both in error. He had made too large a promise, and they were too exacting and dictatorial as to his performance of it. An expression of sympathy would have done more to accomplish their end, than the stern declaration of authority. He might have been led to more exercise and earlier hours, but he could not be forced to them. Kindness might have moved him, but rigour only confirmed him. He was not to be concussed into what he deemed a species of helotry. The Committee were resolved to keep him to his place, for he had already offended, and a second misdemeanour could not be tolerated. They would not put up with insubordination on the part of such a servant, and the unconscious Kitto was, therefore, warned, rebuked, and virtually dismissed. We cannot blame the Society so deeply as some have done, though, certainly, according to their own premises, if they acted toward the misguided lad in equity, they showed him but small lenience. If he was "out of the way" they exhibited but slender "compassion" for

the invalid at once fevered in body and bruised in heart.

Kitto's residence of eighteen months in Malta was nearly lost time to him, and it was the most miserable portion of his maturer life. He had been disappointed where he had "garnered up his heart." He had tried to please his employers, and had failed. His views in life were darkened. He had hoped to rise to a position of honour on the missionary staff, but he had been sharply severed from it. And what, then, should he do? What would his former patrons say of him now? Would they not disown him, and reckon their confidence in him misplaced? In what "line of things" could he promise himself success? No wonder his spirit preyed upon itself, for even Mr. Groves did not, in this instance, justify him. In this forlorn and unhappy condition, and with the horizon lowering all around him, Kitto embarked for England, on the 12th of January 1829,* in the "Maria," Captain Tregarthen. The ship was first detained for a while in port, and was also long on her voyage. When she was off the Lizard, Kitto composed a letter for Mr. Harvey, which might be sent to Plymouth in some fishing-boat. His object was to assure his Plymouth friends of his safety. He was the only cabin passenger, and the voyage had improved his health. He is thankful that his detention in Malta enabled him to get a resolution of the Society, in which they promise to "make it their business to assist me in the best way of doing well for myself. . . . . God make me very thankful and grateful to Himself first." On the voyage out, Kitto had been in raptures as he gazed upon the mountains of Granada, and he thought that the eyes of another coming after him would admire them too. But, on his return, the magnificent scenery made no impression on him, for "his heart was too hard and cold to care two pins for all the snowy mountains in the universe."

Before Kitto set sail, he had proposed to Mr. Frere to write at length a history of the island. † Concerning another literary composition, relating to missions and Scripture, we find among his papers the following prayer:—

"ON COMMENCING MY BOOK

"Almighty God! without Whom nothing is good, nothing is holy, without Whom all my best designs are vain, I pray Thee bless this undertaking to Thine own glory and the blessing of many. To me, also,

---

* In the *Missionary Register* for January, 1829, it is simply stated, that "Mr. Kitto's health has suffered much; and on this, and on some other accounts, he is about to retire from the Society's service." In the printed Report for 1828-29, it is mentioned, quite as vaguely, that "Mr. Kitto, on account of his want of health, and other circumstances, has relinquished his connection with the Society."

† Letter to Mr. Frere, just before leaving Malta, in which he signifies his wish to lay his case before the king—his early misfortunes and his literary desires.

may it be sanctified. Grant that I be not led astray by the poor lust of literary honour and distinction. Fill my heart with Thyself, and out of the fulness of my heart may I be enabled to speak to others in the book which now, with this promise, and by Thy grace, I purpose to write and to send forth into the world."

In the prospect of leaving Malta, he composed a farewell in verse. Though not certainly of a high order, it was written with some care; and it is rather quaintly topographical and minutely antiquarian in its allusions. Place after place is saluted, and its ancient history glanced at. Copious notes in prose illustrate the poem and conclude the paper. It opens thus:—

> " Dear isle, farewell ! I had not thought
>   To find so soon my bark afloat—
>   So soon to have again to spell
>   That short but painful word, farewell !
>   Less had I thought, with much regret,
>   To speak that word to thee. . .
>   Farewell, then, Malta; yet, once more,
>   Why linger my feet on thy shore ?
>   To thee, a few months since, I came
>   With heart in love, and hopes in flame,
>   Trusting to find in thee a rest,
>   In others blessing being blest.
>
>   .   .   .
>
>   But now I leave thee.   Soon England
>   I tread upon thy smoother strand ;
>   Yet, sooth to say, I little care ;
>   For what have I to bless me there ?
>   The hopes, which once around me flourished,
>   Have faded all away and perished.
>   So, then, can I be anxious whether
>   I dwell in this clime or another ?
>   No; regions all alike we call
>   When misery we find in all.
>   England to greet I shall not grieve,
>   Nor Malta do I gladly leave."

On his arrival in London, Kitto met with Mr. Groves, who was about to embark on his mission to the East. His faith had not been shaken in his former apprentice, and he proposed that the cast-off printer should accompany him. Before coming to a decision, the forlorn adventurer went down to Plymouth, and there he resolved not to go out with his benefactor. He said " No " most firmly to the very proposal which moulded his subsequent life, and raised him to his ultimate position of usefulness and honour. But a mysterious Providence brought him suddenly to another decision, and he then hastened to be gone. Meanwhile his sojourn in Plymouth was far from being comfortable. Many who had helped him in former days, refused further assistance, and taunted him with his repeated breaches with the Missionary Committee, as a proof that he was proud and intractable. Conscious of his integrity, and disdaining to volunteer such a minute and lengthened explanation as might be construed into an apology, or interpreted as a confession, he seems sometimes to have

wrapped himself in dignified reserve, and thus offended another class of his friends. The case did appear suspicious; and many seem to have thought that their high opinion of his talents had been unwarranted, as being the dictate of sympathy rather than of judgment, that they had erred also in their estimate of his character, that his promotion had turned his head, and that a self-willed obstinacy, or a hasty temper, was evidently the fatal bar to his advancement. Now that he was again flung upon them, they resolved that he should be left to his unaided resources; for, if he were determined to throw away such auspicious opportunities as he had already enjoyed, they concluded that their money, influence, and advice, would be grievously mis-spent.

Kitto, in a letter to Mr. Harvey, as far back as 1823, mentions an unknown gentleman who had made him a present of *Butler's Analogy*, and warned him that, when he ceased to be a novelty, then would come the great test of his abilities. Kitto mused, and acquiesced so far—" When novelty has ceased, and curiosity has evaporated, and after I have had my hopes raised by the transient attention shown me, I shall be neglected, laid upon the shelf, and forgotten." Was he now doomed to realize his own prophecy ? In his moments of melancholy, he looked upon himself as one " marked out for pain, trouble, and bitterness, to whom expectation is delusive, and all hope vain." He seemed, in short, to embody the poet's description:—

> " I am all alone, and the visions that play
>   Round life's young days have passed away,
>   And the songs are hushed that gladness sings,
>   And the hopes that I cherished have made them wings,
>   And the light of my heart is dimmed and gone,
>   And I sit in sorrow, and all alone."

He was galled excessively by this procedure on the part of so many of his friends; and the following paragraph is, perhaps, the only instance in his whole correspondence of something like a querulous and ungrateful spirit. It was in the worst of testy moods that he wrote it, and the fact of his being so misjudged and frowned upon is his apology. It occurs in a letter to Mr. Lampen:—

"Plymouth, April 6, 1829.

" . . . I lament to have perceived that those gentlemen of Plymouth, to whom I most naturally look at this juncture, are less willing than I had hoped and expected, to afford me the advantage of their powerful influence, in obtaining for myself a future provision. I certainly did not expect much assistance of any sort; but whilst my expectations were not of a pecuniary nature, I thought there might be a readiness to exert so cheap a thing as *influence* on my behalf. It appears that I have been mistaken in this, as in many other things. I regret to have seen, that the friends to whom I am so much indebted for the kind intentions on which they have at former periods acted towards me, seem now to be apprehensive lest I should again become burdensome to them. *They* know best whether I have been so or not. If I have, I am sorry for it; but it will be borne in mind, that so far as I may have been so, it was not I who threw this burden on them, but *they* who voluntarily, unsought of by me, and with kindness which can never be forgotten, took it on themselves. They did so, perhaps mistakenly, perhaps on hasty impressions. I do not know. It is not for me to judge. But I had been happier, perhaps, if they had not done so; and now I cannot again be happy, as I have been, or as I might have been."

He still wished to justify the measure of kindness which he had received, and which he frankly acknowledges in the previous sentences; and as the Society had not only given him a quarter's salary, but voted him £30 to enable him to find some remunerative situation, he resolved to set up a stationer's shop or circulating library, at Moricetown, in the vicinity of Plymouth. "The gentlemen of Plymouth," he says somewhat caustically, "have studiously proved to me that I am fit for nothing—for no regular employment, for none of the common businesses of life; and, indeed, I do not myself know what regular employment there is, to say nothing of my deafness, the duties of which the present state of my health would allow me to fulfil. What, then, remains for me but *this?*

But his funds were soon exhausted. "He drank to the dregs again the cup of misfortune and poverty." He became anew what he once called himself, *J. Lackpenny,* and was obliged to pawn his watch and other articles, as he confesses in a brief note to Mr. Harvey, where he states a plan of redeeming them—that plan being to proceed to London, and draw the thirty pounds which the Society had kindly set apart for him. The bookselling project, about whose expenditure and income he made many grand calculations, and all upon the side of profit, came to nothing, or rather was superseded by a note from the indefatigable Mr. Groves, in which he offered him a situation in Teignmouth. John Synge, Esq., of Glanmor Castle, County Wicklow, who had been residing for some time with his family in Teignmouth, was busy in printing, at his own private press, "some little works in Hebrew and Greek," and wished to engage a practical assistant. Mr. Groves, knowing the rock on which Kitto had split, wisely advised him that Mr. Synge's object was "*simply printing,*" italicising the words, and asked his determination. Kitto, warned by many, and by Mr. Groves himself, that his mercantile enterprise would be a failure, at once agreed to the offer, and pledged himself to enter into Mr. Synge's employment on the 1st June.

Man proposes, but God disposes. In the month of May Kitto went up to London, to make preparatory arrangements; chiefly to see Mr. Groves, and take a long farewell of his kind and considerate guardian, who was on the eve of departure for Persia. But while he was in London on this errand, the lady who had disappointed him and married another, died—and died, as he affirms, "under mysterious circumstances, which seemed in a striking manner to connect her demise with her conduct towards me and my return to England." What he had learned of her bitter remorse in her last illness, induced him to go and look on her corpse; and the spectacle excited such a terrible train of thought in his mind, that when Mr. Groves asked him a second time to accompany him to the East, he returned an immediate and affirmative reply. "Will you come?" said Groves. "Yes," said Kitto—question and answer alike remarkable for conciseness and practical aim. Anything to afford relief to his spirit, Kitto would have grasped at. He longed vehemently to be away—

"From the wreck of hopes so scattered,
Tempest shattered,
Floating waste and desolate."

In a letter to Mr. Harvey from Bagdad, Sept. 25, 1831, he explains this period:—"I returned from Malta with a desire not to leave England again. But I left Plymouth in great bitterness of feeling, which, combined with some heart-rending scenes of death and sorrow I had to pass through at Islington, rendered odious to me the only two places in England in which I had any interest." In the short space of three days Kitto prepared himself to go, renouncing without scruple a good situation, but gratified at the field of prospective usefulness which was so suddenly presented to him.

As we have already recorded, the workhouse boy had, nine years before, said in his Journal, "I have even thought of plans to enable me to visit Asia and the ground consecrated by the steps of the Saviour. Even *now,* notwithstanding my deafness, it would not be impracticable, if some kind gentleman, on his travels, would permit me to be his (though not expert) faithful servant. After all, I fear it is a vain scheme, never to be realised." And yet it was realised, and that far beyond expectation, for he went out in the immediate character of tutor to the two little boys of Mr. Groves. The mission of Mr. Groves was certainly peculiar in its origin and complexion, and as strange was his selection of a deaf and self-taught tutor for his children. But such an appointment proved that, whatever others thought of Kitto, Mr. Groves had not lost faith in him; neither in the reality of his talent, nor the genuineness of his piety; neither in his honesty of purpose, nor in his sincere desire to give the utmost satisfaction to those above him, by his conscientious discharge of duty. Nor was he so ill qualified for the responsible situation as one might imagine. He was now in his twenty-fifth year, and his acquirements, the result of such continuous labours and vigils, were highly creditable to him. True, indeed, as he confesses, he had to learn some branches, in order to teach. But he instructed his pupils in Hebrew, Scripture, theology, history, geography, writing, arithmetic, and English composition, and surmounted, by devices of his own, the disability of his deafness. Again had he risen—lately a printer, now an educator—another step upward and onward to his destiny. Thus the cloud was lifting, though he knew it not; and the next four years of his life, spent in travel and eastern residence, originated those Biblical works which have immortalized his name. "Darkness" was made "light before him," though he but dimly perceived its dawn; and "crooked things straight," though, from his angle of observation, he could scarcely measure the change. His journal of travel to Bagdad is very full, but much of it presents no topics of biographical interest or of characteristic detail; and we shall, therefore, make use only of such sections as either afford a glimpse into his inner life, or present some striking observation or amusing incident, or show how his mind was fascinated by oriental scenery and manners, and thus prepared to illustrate Holy Scripture.

6

JOURNEY TO THE EAST

MR. GROVES, who had already taken Kitto to Exeter, and who now engaged him to travel, was a man of marked peculiarity. He had latterly, and before leaving Dublin University, joined in such extra-ecclesiastical meetings for sacramental fellowship and prayer as characterize the religious party now commonly known by the name of Plymouth Brethren. He abandoned a lucrative profession in order to become a missionary, and made no stipulation for maintenance when he went abroad, but relied solely on the voluntary aid of Christian friends, and "on what his Master inclined the hearts of his brethren to furnish." His notions of self-dedication were acted out by him with rigid fidelity. He was a "good man," and "full of faith." His labours in Persia did not by any means produce the anticipated fruits; but his subsequent toils in India were largely blessed. He was one of those men who exercise an immediate and deep personal influence upon others. Mr. Müller of Bristol, a

near relative of Mr. Groves, and the originator and promoter of that marvellous orphan-house on Ashley Down, says, in his interesting *Narrative*, that the example of Brother Groves both excited and cheered him in his prolonged and arduous efforts—efforts which, sustained by no visible machinery, but resting solely on "faith in God as to temporal things," have realized £77,990, and which actually received in one year no less a sum than £15,000. Mr. Groves being himself in earnest, had strong force of character, and made his imperious will the law to all around him. So that various estimates were formed of him by those who came in contact, and those who came into collision with him; by those who beheld his actions at a distance, and by those who were immediately under his control. Whatever he felt to be duty, no matter how he made the discovery, he would do it at all hazards, and every one in his sphere was expected to bend to his convictions. These convictions sometimes bordered on fanaticism. On one occasion, in Exeter, when the mind of Mrs. Groves was in doubt as to a critical point of duty, she proposed that "Kitto should search out the mind of the Lord from the New Testament, and say what he thought." "The result" of this oracular inquiry Mr. Groves laments, "was, as might be expected, seeing Kitto had no interest in the question;" that is, Kitto's decision was contrary to that of Mr. Groves himself, and he would not be bound by it. In various parts of his journal, he avows his belief that miracles might be still expected by the Church; nay, he argues, "that as miracles were designed for unbelievers, and not for the Church, we must expect to see them arise among missionaries to the heathen." Might they not, therefore, be expected in his own position? Now, if one gift more than another was needed and coveted by him, it was the Pentecostal gift of Tongues; and yet we find him again and again lamenting the fatiguing labour gone through, and the precious time spent in acquiring a new and eastern language, the pursuit of which "disordered his soul greatly."

He relates, in his second journal, published in 1832, that when Mr. Newman * was sick, and "at the worst, and they had given up all hopes of him, they anointed him with oil, according to James v. 14, and prayed over him, and the Lord had mercy on them; yea, and on me also, and restored him. It seems to me truly scriptural." But his unguarded notions were sometimes sharply corrected; for, when the plague did enter

* Professor Newman, now of University College, London, who, in a fit of devotedness, joined Mr. Groves at Bagdad, but whose early creed, springing to a large extent out of a strange facility of impression from men and books, has gradually been abandoned by him to the awful point of abjuring the teaching, challenging the character, and impeaching the life and honesty of Jesus Christ.—See *Phases of Faith*, etc., chap. vii. Fourth edition.

his dwelling, take away his wife, and prostrate himself, he slowly admits that he did not expect such a visitation, but rather thought he had been secured against it, and that his "error arose from considering the temporal promises of the 91st Psalm as legitimate objects of faith."

On being asked by Mr. Burnard as to some points in Mr. Groves' Christian character, Kitto replied from Exeter, after he had been a short time in his employment, "Mr. Groves is not a Methodist, a Calvinist, a Lutheran, or a Papist. What, then, is he? A Deist, a Unitarian, an Antinomian? No. He is one of those rather singular characters—a Bible Christian, and a disciple of the meek and lowly Jesus; not nominally, but practically and really such. A man so devotedly, so fervently attached to the Scriptures, I never knew before." Of his benignant influence on Kitto we have already spoken, and his young friend, though he could not agree with him ultimately in many of his peculiar views, never ceased to regard him with esteem and affection.

The company that embarked with Mr. Groves consisted of seven persons. Those immediately connected with him were his wife and sister, Miss Taylor, his two boys, and Kitto. The "Osprey," a vessel of forty-five tons, and belonging to the Royal Yacht Club, conveyed them, free of expense, to St. Petersburg; and its owner, Mr. Puget, along with Mr. Parnell, now Lord Congleton, accompanied them to the Russian capital. We can afford space for only a few sketches of the journey. Kitto wrote copious letters about some parts of it, and kept as copious journals of other parts of it. He was ever writing, that being of necessity his principal and almost only method of giving utterance to his thoughts. Most of us are fond of detailing what our impressions are in scenes of novelty. Kitto's method of record was not by the use of his tongue, but by the tracery of his pen; and some of these papers were composed with a view to subsequent publication. Indeed, he often meditated a book of travels; but the fruits of his journeys assumed a different form.

Mr. Groves and his friends sailed from Gravesend on the 12th June, 1829, and, after encountering a heavy storm in the Cattegat, cast anchor before the village of Wedbeck, in the vicinity of Copenhagen, on the 20th of the same month. The yacht had sustained some damage in the gale, and underwent the necessary repairs at the Danish capital. During almost the whole voyage, the "Osprey's" people had worship on deck morning and evening. The first notice of Kitto in Mr. Groves' journal is under date, Sunday, June 14:—"K—— is not quite well, complaining of headache."[*] The second is Monday, June 22:—"K——'s

connection with the dear little boys is most promising, and leads us to feel assured that he is really sent us by the Lord for that very end, and others important to the mission. He seems happy, and, I trust, is so, which comforts us greatly." [*] The next allusion is still more characteristic. July 1:—"I feel the expediency of forming a more regular plan with K—— about the little boys. May the Lord, in His great goodness, lead us to adopt a wise one, in the spirit of Christian wisdom! I perceive that K—— has a deep sense of neglect, or apparent want of respect. May all things be so ordered, that he may not feel this! I feel his heart is worth winning even on natural grounds, for he has affections that are strong and true; but on spiritual grounds it is our duty, and may it be felt by us also to be our privilege." [†]

The party stayed for some days at Wedbeck with the British Charge d'Affaires, and then sailed for St. Petersburg. Prevailing light winds made the voyage longer than was anticipated. At Cronstadt, Kitto saw a portion of the Russian fleet, and, after the Thames, never beheld such a forest of masts. The "Osprey" was brought up the river nearly to the city, and then her passengers went ashore in a boat. A pilot had been hired for the difficult navigation; and this transaction set Kitto on thinking of Peter the Great, who often conducted vessels from Cronstadt, and uniformly demanded the usual wages. After three weeks' sailing, Kitto was glad to set his foot on land, and to "lie down on a quiet bed;" but the pilot in the channel, and the scenes in England which had so grated on his spirit as to impel him to travel, were wrought into a dream, which he relates in impressive style:—

"Methought—you see I begin in the orthodox style —methought the scene was the same as that of the preceding day, only sublimed in the alembic of dreams. Rocks tremendous and awful, and dangerous shallows, were there, which the charts do not exhibit; and the city in the distance, to which we were approaching, seemed more glorious than Petersburg by far; more glorious than the cities of Arabian tales; than the hundred-gated Thebes, Nineveh, or Babylon. Rivers of peace—bowers of repose—and palaces, and walls, and gates refulgent with diamond and gold, in magnificent perspective, were laid out there. Amidst these rocks and shallows, not knowing which way to take with safety, we lay to, and made signals for a pilot. One came off in a boat from the shore. He was the Great Peter himself. He had clouted shoes, and, excepting the band and hat, was dressed much like the peasants I had seen at Cronstadt. He seized the helm; issued his orders as pilot with dignity; and guided the vessel with the air of one who was fully confident that he could bring her, through all the difficulties by which we were surrounded, to the desired haven.

" I gazed on this extraordinary character with interest and emotion; but a change suddenly came over the spirit of my dream; a mist arose, which concealed the pilot from me. The mist dissipated, and the autocrat was no longer at the helm. His place was suplied by a tender and delicate woman—by H——— A——— herself. (I like to dream, but I would cease to dream for ever, rather than dream once more of her. Once she had made my waking dreams very happy, but now—Well ! you know it all.) She was attired in the white vestments of a bride—which were also the vestments of her grave. There was nothing warm or vital in her appearance. She gave impulse to the helm indeed; but her eyes were fixed on the deck, and, though open, there was no motion in them. I was not surprised. People are not generally surprised in dreams. I tried to speak, but I could not; to move, but I could not. My first impulse was to haste and take the helm from her hand. She had made shipwreck of my heart and its best feelings once before —and should she again guide the helm ? No. But I could not carry this conviction into effect. I sat down in desperate idolatry, and gazed upon her. Do what thou wilt;—let me live—let me die—let me arrive in safety, or let the deep swallow me up.

" Once more the mist arose, and veiled one whom I had loved 'not wisely, but too well.' When it expanded, the helm was in the hand of the Master Himself. There was nothing terrible in the appearance. He was as in the days of His sojourning among men —meek, lowly, and kind. Yet I trembled. But He said to me, 'Fear not, for I am with thee.' Then I thought, What should I fear, if Thou art with me ? and I ceased to be afraid. Oh ! how happy I was then. I had no doubt. This was the Pilot who never yet made shipwreck of aught that He ever guided; and our safety now was assured. Happy he, the vessel of whose hopes and whose desires Thou steerest, O Lord.

" This was my dream. An interpretation occurs to me; but as I should like to compare notes with you on the subject, I shall expect to receive your interpretation in the first letter you send me after this comes to hand."

Really, as to the interpretation, it is not very difficult. The dream, as any one may perceive, was but a reproduction of past sensations and agonies, cast into naval imagery by the recent passage through the shoals and intricacies, islands and lighthouses, of Cronstadt Channel. Ben Jonson sang—

" And phantasie, I tell you, has dreams that have wings,
   And dreams that have honey, and dreams that have stings;
   Dreams of the maker, and dreams of the teller;
   Dreams of the kitchen, and dreams of the cellar."

It requires not a soothsayer to tell under what class the preceding vision of the night should be placed. Kitto, it may be said in passing, had considerable faith in dreams, and, as his papers show, he again and again philosophised on their character and predictive power.*

During Kitto's stay at the northern Russian capital, many Christian friends showed him attention. He makes grateful mention of Mr. Knill and of Miss Kilham, a lady who was patronised by Prince Galitzin and the imperial family, in her excellent educational institution. In writing to Miss Hypatia Harvey, from Bagdad, October 17, 1831, he thus records his reminiscences of this lady :—

" Did you never hear of *Mrs. Hannah Kilham*, the Quaker lady, who has made so many voyages to Africa, with the view of benefiting the poor negroes ? If not, the history of her most benevolent labours is worth inquiry. The lady I speak of is her daughter, who walks in the steps of her noble mother most entirely, and who has resided some years in Russia, promoting the work of female education, and superintending a

* The phenomenon of dreaming has often engaged, and as often eluded, the researches of physiologists and metaphysicians. It is, however, in a different style that Kitto dwells upon it, and the following is a specimen of his lucubrations on the subject:—"My own conclusion is, that there is a prophetic principle in the soul, by which, with proper attention, our future path in life may be distinctly enough marked out. What is this principle—whence does it arise ? These, and such questions as these, cannot be more easily answered than the questions, What is mind itself—whence does it proceed— what are its principles ? . . . I should rather think that there are three species of dreams, quite distinct from each other. *First,* Such as arise from repletion, from recent impressions, or from intoxication and the use of drugs, as opium. These are the 'reasonable soul run mad.' These are the most common dreams, and they are in general so gross, physical, and empty, that they have brought discredit on dreams altogether. These are the vagabonds, swindlers, and pickpockets in the society of dreams; but why should the whole society be counted disreputable for their sakes ? *Second—* Dreams which seem to proceed from the immediate influence of a supernatural agent. I am sufficiently aware that this will be called fanatical. Be it so. I am inquiring after truth, and I will take it under whatever form it appears to me. Reason, Scripture, and experience teach, that there are dreams proceeding from such influence on the mind in sleep. *Third* —Under a third class may be arranged dreams which are prospective, future, and prophetic. Of these there is less distinct knowledge. There is no room for mystical interpretation in them. They picture out exactly the persons who shall be seen, and the circumstances which shall occur, but they seem unmeaning, because they have no relation to any previous experience, and are therefore not recognized as having any personal relationship to ourselves, till the persons are seen and the circumstances occur. I do not suppose these dreams at all peculiar to myself. Most people must have had dreams, which, in the same manner, exhibit in regular concatenation the history of their lives and their connections in life; but, in the intervening period, the bustle and hurry of daily circumstances, obliterate them from the mind, and prevent that recognition which might be otherwise obtained. . . . In conclusion, I think this general inference may fairly be deduced, that there are powers and principles in the soul hitherto hidden and unthought of, but which it is possible to discover, define, and apply to practical uses."—[From a long paper, the title of which has been lost.]

school of Russian females, half of whom were slaves. I saw them. They were fine girls. So far as female education is at all an object of attention in Russia, French and dancing are its primary objects. Miss Kilham's institution has nothing to do with these studies. They are taught to read their native language; to write—cipher—sew, and, in general, the affairs of domestic life; to qualify them for useful wives—mothers—servants; and, above all, to teach them their duty to God and man, which is done in a way beautifully simple and impressive. This is a sort of model school, and is, I hope, the germ of a most valuable system of education for the lower classes of females in Russia. Miss Kilham, with nothing outwardly on which the eye of man rests with pleasure, has that superior beauty of *"the king's daughter, all glorious within"* (Psalm xlv.), which, being combined with infinite humility, and a manner unassuming, quiet, and unostentatious, conciliates the affection of many who do, and the respect of those who do not, understand the high principles on which her mind and character are formed. For myself, I count it among the best fruits of my travel, to have formed so inestimable a friendship."

Kitto formed no high idea of the Russian people, or of their government: "Their calendar is unreformed, the peculiar costume remains; the knout remains; slavery remains; ignorance remains." "There is little show of literature. The booksellers' shops are few, and those few about as well furnished as the bookstalls of London. Upon the whole, the exterior of Russian society is repulsive, notwithstanding the gloss, which the courtesy and politeness natural to all classes of the Russians throw upon it. The air of military despotism—the strut of office which meets you at every turn, and the abject worship which inferiors render to their superiors, are most disgusting. Government! government! There is nothing to be done or said without government. Government must control all your movements. Government would know the secrets of your chamber. With a feeling of much personal kindness to Russians as individual men, I detest such a system of minute rule and legislation."

"The mass of the people are much more superstitious than I had expected; in this respect, there seems little to choose between this and a Popish country. But superstition is here of a less imposing character. Very pitiful pictures are placed about the city, before some of which lamps are continually burning, and which the people salute in passing, crossing themselves repeatedly and bowing. Statues are no objects of aversion in the Russian Church, and, though pictures are more frequent, I have seen the same homage paid to statues and to figures in alto and basso relievo. This species of idolatry is more common than I ever saw it in Malta, and if religion were measured by it, the Russians might be pronounced a very religious people. But this is all their religion. Their mode of crossing is considered heterodox by the Romish Church. I do not understand the difference; but I remember that at a grand religious procession at Malta, when a company of Russian sailors stood crossing and bowing after their fashion to every banner, statue, picture, and cross that passed by, they were grossly derided by the Catholic worshippers. Poor fellows! why, in all the boasted improvements of their nation, has it not been endeavoured to teach them that 'God is a Spirit, and they that worship Him, must worship Him in spirit and in truth.' From this species of homage, men in the employ of government seem to consider themselves exempt. I never saw it rendered by a soldier; and I do not recollect to have seen one man of the crowds who pour out from the admiralty, at eight o'clock in the evening, stop to cross himself at a famous crossing place near."

Miss Groves was prevented by sickness from proceeding on the journey, but her brother was joined here by Mr. Bathie, and Mrs. Taylor and her suite, who had preceded him by way of Lubeck.* The company left St. Petersburg on Thursday, the 16th of July, and arrived at Moscow on the 24th—a city which Kitto regarded as the most pleasant he had ever been in. On his first night's journey, he saw some fires, round which gipsies, as he fancied, were encamped. To show his prevailing thoughts at this time, we subjoin his reflection:—"Is the conversion of gipsies impossible? If not, why, having them at our doors in England, have they been so much neglected there? Their former hardy and vagrant habits would admirably prepare them for some departments of missionary service. Most likely a gipsy missionary would ramble with peculiar pleasure in Cabool, Beloochistan, Bokhara, and Khorassan." Still he was not very sure of his own ultimate position with Mr. Groves; for he uses such language as this—"As a Christian, I do not know if I may say, Missionary." He went three times to inspect the Kremlin. "There are others," he writes, "to measure columns, to paint scenery, and to describe churches and palaces; to them I leave it." He has given no description of Moscow. Somewhere he speaks of his intention of doing it, but confesses that, after leaving the city, he found that his impressions were not distinct enough to warrant an account of that

* Mrs. Taylor was an Armenian lady, the wife of Major Taylor, British resident at Bagdad. She had been staying for some time in England, and was returning to her husband. Mr. Bathie was a young Scotchman that Mr. Groves had met in Ireland, and induced to join his mission.

strangely fated capital, which one of its own poets
thus addresses :—

> " Proud city ! sovereign mother thou
> Of all Sclavonian cities now !
> Work of seven ages !—beauty once
> And glory were around thee spread ;
> Toil-gathered riches blest thy sons,
> And splendid temples crown'd thy head ;
> Our monarchs in thy bosom lie
> With sainted dust that cannot die !
> Farewell ! farewell ! thy children's hands
> Have seized the all-destroying bands,
> To whelm in ashes all thy pride !
> Blaze ! Blaze ! thy guilt in flames be lost ;
> And heaven and earth be satisfied
> With thee, the nation's holocaust !
> The foe of peace shall find in thee
> The ruined tomb of victory."*

Mr. Groves' caravan left Moscow on the 28th July,†
and reached Astrachan on the 15th of August—a
distance of 1,401 versts, or about a thousand miles.
Kitto, in his Journal, makes the usual remarks of
travellers, and instinctively compares the scenery
through which he was passing, with the landscapes of
his own country. The ordinary incidents occur : a
landau sticking in the sand, and crowds gathering
around the strangers, while Mrs. Taylor's negro servant
was absolutely mobbed. "I believe all our heads
ache : mine does." In the churchyard of Ekinnouskoy,
he witnessed a scene which prompted him not only to
record his emotion, but to cluster around it a host of
fancies and reflections :—

"As I passed through it, on my return from the
river, I observed over a grave on which the grass had
not yet grown, a group which affected me strongly.
There was one very aged woman kneeling, with her
head on the grave; another middle-aged woman kneeling also, with her lips to the consecrated earth ; and
there were three sweet children, the eldest of whom,
a girl, lay flat alongside the grave.

"It was easy to guess the story :—a son lay there,
the prop of his mother's age—a husband, taken in his
prime from the wife of his youth—a father, a beloved
one, the support of his children, their protector, their
guide, their friend. He lies there, in whom all this
combination of beautiful relations was bound—all dissolved now, and broken, and lost.

"I looked on at a distance, for I had no mind to
disturb the sorrow of which I partook. How universal
the true feelings of nature ! I was surprised to meet
here such an exhibition of those feelings ; but why
surprised ? True, they were poor—they were rude,
and slaves, perhaps ; but had they not spirits, like me,

* Bowring—Russian Anthology.
† In Mr. Groves' Journal (1857) it is said that he and his
party did not leave Moscow till Monday, August 9. But on a
following page, Sunday, August 9, is spoken of as a period
when they were far on their journey

to feel and suffer ; had they hearts less warm, feelings
less acute, than mine ? I was ashamed of my surprise.

"Death, thought I, is a terrible thing after all that
philosophers have said, and written, and acted—
terrible to the dead, terrible to the living. It was
intended to be terrible ; and I do not admire the
philosophy which exhibits death as an object of contempt. It is not contemptible. Is it not terrible to
close the eye for ever on the happy vales and ancient
mountains ? Is it not terrible to hear no more the
voices which have been our music ? to mingle no more
in the dear relations which, with all their burdens, are
so pleasant ? Oh, it is terrible—very terrible to die !
And then, as to all the fine sayings about the independence of the spirit on the body, and that the body, not
being part of ourselves, we should think only of the
better half—it is all cant and rigmarole. It is part of
ourselves—an essential part ; and if it were not, why
does our holy religion teach that these scattered
elements shall be collected once more, be once more
married to their former companion. If the body be
not part of ourselves, why would not rather the
unessential part be left to corruption and the grave ?
Then, is it not terrible to feel that *that* part of ourselves, with which all our pleasures, our feelings, our
hopes, have been identified, must, in a day or two,
become a ' kneaded clod ? '

"And still more terrible it is to hang over the dead.
To wonder, in the midst of our sorrows, by what
marvellous process could thus become cold—cold—
cold—that warm, ardent, sentient being, which, but a
little while ago, was one of ourselves—went with us
to and fro—talked with us, felt with us, and loved us.
Indeed, I could never look upon the dead with the
conviction that there was nothing vital left—no sense,
no apprehension, in that which lay before me. Could
I have realized this conviction, I should have gone mad
long ago.

"But were there no bright side to this picture, man
were, indeed, most miserable. I believe the Bible,
without doubt or reservation, and though I find nothing
there to tell me that death is not terrible, I find there
much consolation in the article of death. There is
nothing to inculcate indifference to it, but much to
strengthen under its infliction. That combination of
soul and body, which, separate from all mysticism and
metaphysical distinction, is properly and truly ourselves,
and out of which no idea of distinct personality can
exist, has undergone no endless dissolution. The spirit
waits a happier union, in a happier place, where He
that sits upon the throne shall dwell among His
redeemed. In anticipation of this happy union, we
may venture to meet him, whom even Scripture calls
' the king of terrors,' undismayed. And with these
bright prospects before us, there may be even moments

in which, feeling the dissolution of these elements a necessary preliminary to full enjoyment, we may eagerly look forward to that hour—

'When this material
Shall have vanished like a cloud.'

But, perhaps, the permanent realization of this feeling would not be either happy or wise. It does very well in poetry, but nowhere else.

"As the poor people were returning home, I contrived to slip a small donation into the hand of one of the children, and as I could not speak their language, I contented myself with praying that God would be more than son, husband, father, to them. In another half hour our carriage rolled away from Ekinnouskoy."

The Moravian settlement of Sarepta was also visited, and found to be no longer a missionary station, but simply a colony of artificers. Melons were sold at one copec each. As the travellers approached Astrachan, Dr. Glen met them, and during their brief sojourn in that city, showed them no little kindness. He was then in connection with the Scottish Missionary Society, and was engaged in translating the Old Testament into Persian, having at this period proceeded as far as Ezekiel. Many years afterwards, Kitto refers to this visit in the following glowing terms :—

"It was, in 1829, the privilege of the present writer to witness something of the progress of this great work. He was then one of a large party which found themselves, for several days, the inmates of Dr. Glen's primitive missionary establishment at Astrachan, and beheld, with admiration, the quiet way in which this good man, absorbed in his task, pursued his wonted course, undiverted for one hour by the engagements or excitement which the arrival of so large a body of Christian friends from home might have been expected to create. At his appointed hour he withdrew, and was to be seen no more until the labour of his day had ended. Yet this was made consistent with the most cordial hospitality, and the utmost attention to, and consideration for his visitors. We were reminded, by application, of the words of Nehemiah—' I am doing a great work, so that I cannot come down: why should the work cease, whilst I leave it, and come down to you?'—Neh. vi. 3."*

According to Kitto's Journal, they left Astrachan on Monday, August 25, and yet he dates the following Thursday as the 27th.† The routine and monotony of

* *The Court and People of Persia*, by John Kitto, D.D. London : Religious Tract Society, 1848. Dr. Glen, while engaged, in connection with the United Presbyterian Church, in circulating his own Persian version, and that of Henry Martyn, died suddenly at Tehran, January, 1849.

† In the Memoir of Mr. Groves, it is stated that they left it on the 23rd, which would be a Saturday,—not a very likely day for Mr. Groves to take his departure on. Mr. Groves also thought very highly of Mr. Glen, and speaks of "the kindness and Christian love which had been manifested by the dear Glens."

travel, one day so like another, seem to have made both Groves and Kitto somewhat oblivious of the Calendar. Under the last date, and at Koumskaia, he went to sleep on a cart, with some straw under him, and a saddle for a pillow. The hardness of this primitive couch did not prevent him from both ruminating on and dreaming of "the dear objects which, desolate as he was, he had left behind him." In the morning he became the subject of close inspection, and condescended, in his humour, to give the curious on-lookers a proof of his skill in the earliest craft he had learned.

"I was awakened by the efforts of a Tartar to withdraw the saddle, which was wanted, from under my head. He endeavoured to do it with a polite cautiousness, not always met with among more civilized people, but it awoke me, nevertheless. As I lay a few moments longer, to yawn and stretch myself, some other Tartars gathered round the cart. They were most inquisitive. They examined the texture of the camlet cloak on which I lay, and of my trousers, which were of the same material, with peculiar minuteness. I amused myself and them by an exhibition of the articles I had about me. My pocket-book, lined with green silk, and containing a pair of scissors, knife, with two blades, and tweezers, was an object of peculiar attention, and one Tartar must needs have some of his mustaches clipped with the scissors. The same man wanted to shave off the scanty hair on his face and chin with the penknife, till I explained to him its use, by cutting my pencil with it. Of this and the case containing it, their admiration was boundless, greater, I think, than at any other article I produced, and the case with which I protruded the pencil and drew it in, occasioned nothing short of amazement. The one whose mustaches had been clipped, lifted up his hands with wonder, and I verily believe he began to doubt whether there might not be greater and wiser people than Tartars. I suffered him to take the pencil, and instructed him how to draw it in and out. He soon understood it, and I think his admiration was greater of the simple principle on which it acted, and accompanied with more pleasure, than it had been before. I have observed, on this and other occasions, that even the savage mind admires more that which it can understand than that which it cannot. The principle of the pocket compass I could not make this interesting man understand, further than that, though the needle was movable, and did actually move, the magnetized point always settled so as to turn to the same point of the horizon. This seemed to be contemplated with more awe than admiration, and none were so anxious to touch this, as the other articles. My English knife, with three blades, one of them large, was completely admired, for though they did not seem to have seen

one before, its utility was at once understood. My
watch was an object of curiosity, but not of peculiar
admiration, as they seem to have seen watches before.
With my large clasp knife, the man before mentioned
wished to withdraw and shave himself, promising to
bring it back again. I had no doubt that he would
return it, but whilst I explained to him that it would
not do so, I promised to shave him myself. I then
produced my dressing-case to dress myself. The whole
process was watched with intense interest by the same
congregation. Every article of the case was examined
in detail, with more or less admiration, but the brush,
I think, had the largest portion. I unscrewed the top,
and made them expect something was to come out.
Every eye was fixed to see what, and when the brush
came, every hand was lifted up in amazement. When
I had done, the man anxiously reminded me of my
promise. So, seating him on the axle of a cart, and
telling him to keep his head still, I shaved him. After
this was done, no man ever strutted more in the dignity
of a chin newly shaven. I had cut a pimple which
bled a little. On this I put a bit of court plaster; of
the black patch, which he considered ornamental, he
was infinitely proud.

"One article struck me as peculiar. It was shaped
more like one of the vulgar circular horn lanterns than
anything I can remember, moving on a pivot inserted
through the centre. It was formed of hard dark wood,
well carved, considering by whom it was wrought—
chiefly Calmuc-Tartaric characters. On my requesting
to know its use, an old man took off his cap, and, with
much gravity pulled a string, which made it revolve on
its axis, pointing his hand upwards at the same time.
This brought to my mind the praying machines of
which I had read; this was doubtless one. I inquired
if anything were inside, and received a negative reply.
The same old man, who seems the patriarch of the
camp, produced a copy of the Evangelists in Calmuc-
Tartaric. It had been well read and thumbed, and
some leaves were wanting. He valued it so highly,
as scarcely to trust it out of his own hands. He afterwards brought it up, and our Persian friend assured us
he read it fluently. Indeed, I could perceive, by signs
which he used in speaking, that he was explaining one
of the miracles of Christ. May we not hope, that this
book has been, or may be, a means of directing their
views to the true object of devotion, and to the true
salvation by Jesus Christ? He says he got it from
Petersburg."

Beyond the Terek, they fell in with a large party,
having a military escort. Kitto, for a great part of
the dusty journey, kept up on foot with the procession,
and at night had "a memorable fit of the headache."
He slept on the roof of the stable; but the lightning and
rain were a sad discomfort, and he went into the house,
at Mr. Groves' suggestion. At Ardoon, an officer who
had been wounded at Waterloo, and attended by an
English surgeon, was very attentive to them, and a
sentinel was placed over their carriages, robbers being
daring and rife.

"The next day (Tuesday) we woke at beat of drum.
About noon we stopped at a place called Archom. The
remainder of the stage was whiled away by amusing
conversation, which was interrupted by our arrival at
Kophkai. Its Church, with some good white houses,
gives it a pretty effect in the distance, which is sadly
lessened on a nearer approach. We were quartered in
a tolerable cottage; and the knowledge that we should
pay for our accommodation, procured also the use of a
room in the next cottage, for some of the ladies to sleep
in. The woman of the cottage, on this occasion, made
a very pretty display of some clothing, in the English
style, which she had. She really made, *pro tempore*,
a very tolerable Englishwoman. In my various travels,
I have found men vary very much in their national
characteristics; but women are so much the same in
all countries, that they are only distinguished by language and feature. With this view, when a friend
has married, I seldom enquire what countrywoman he
has married, as all essential knowledge is sufficiently
implied in the significant and comprehensive designation, '*woman.*'"

At length they came to the grand pass of the Caucasian mountains; the valley narrow, and the road in
part cut out of the rock. Betweens Lars and Dariel,
they threaded their way through the narrowest defile.

"We were very much struck by the tremendous
precipices on either hand, and with the scene of wild
and savage magnificence presented to us. The rapid
motion of the Terek, dashing and foaming along the
base of the right hand precipices, was admirably in
unison, and must have been more so to those whose
ears are not closed to the music of nature. Here, and
on many other occasions during our Caucasian journey,
the inquiry spontaneously arose—Who can paint like
nature? Can imagination? The negative reply could
not fail to be very decisive."

The Calmuc tents at Dariel resembled English pig-
sties. From Kobi they climbed up several sharp
ascents to the Mountain of the Cross—the monument
of a Russian victory. On descending, Mrs. Taylor's
carriage upset, the drag-chain having given way, and
the horses darting down the hill at their highest speed.
Providentially the carriage was empty at the time.
Then they came to the most "fearful pass of all the
Caucasus"—a narrow defile, rich and wooded heights
overhanging it on all sides.

"The view was the most splendid I ever saw, or my
imagination ever pictured. The snow-capped mountains
behind—the water falling in beautiful white cascades

down the gullies—the finely wooded mountain before us, contrasted with the grassy mountains behind and the snowy ones beyond—the valley below, with a village and farm on either side of the Aragvi, diminished in the distance—the castle, surrounded with firs on the high projecting hill of basaltic rock, which stretched out its bold, nearly circular form, on the other side of the valley—the shepherds watching their snow-white flocks on the sides of the mountains—all, among other little details, combining to compose a scene, such as, having seen once, I will never expect to see again in any other place. At Kashaur we arrived about six in the evening, having been twelve hours in accomplishing a stage of as many English miles. It is situated in a cultivated valley, amongst a considerable number of native farms and villages."

While Kitto's eye and imagination revelled in the picturesque so lavishly strewed round about him, we cannot suppose him insensible to the higher and holier influences which such scenery and travel are so fitted to produce. No doubt, his soul often retired into itself, or rose in rapture to the gates of heaven. Though, from his "maimed sense," he could not literally enjoy many of the sensational experiences depicted by the poet of *The Christian Year*, yet he could, and we believe did, often and easily realize them. Nature spoke to "reason's ear," and he listened, understood, and was comforted.

" Where is thy favoured haunt, eternal Voice,
   The region of Thy choice,
Where, undisturbed by sin and earth, the soul
   Owns Thy entire control?
'Tis on the mountain summit, dark and high,
   When storms are hurrying by;
'Tis 'mid the strong foundations of the earth,
   Where torrents have their birth.

" No sounds of worldly toil ascending there
   Mar the full burst of prayer;
Lone nature feels that she may freely breathe,
   And round us and beneath
Are heard her sacred tones: the fitful sweep
   Of winds across the steep,
Through wither'd bents—romantic note and clear,
   Meet for a hermit's ear.

" The wheeling kite's wild solitary cry,
   And, scarcely heard so high,
The dashing waters, when the air is still,
   From many a torrent rill
That winds unseen beneath the shaggy fell
   Track'd by the blue mist well;
Such sounds as make deep silence in the heart,
   For thought to do her part.

.   .   .   .

" There lies thy cross; beneath it meekly bow;
   It fits thy stature now:
Who scornful pass it with averted eye,
   'Twill crush them by and bye.

" Raise thy repining eyes, and take true measure
   Of thine eternal treasure,
The Father of Thy Lord can grudge thee nought,
   The world for thee was bought:
And as this landscape broad,—hill, field, and sky,—
   All centre in thine eye,
So all God does, if rightly understood,
   Shall work thy final good."

The exit from the Caucasus was as beautiful and romantic as the entrance, though the descent was difficult. They passed several stations or villages, in one of which was a church dedicated to St. Ahithophel—perhaps the patron saint of Russian diplomacy. Opposite a place called Ananour, Kitted saw a blasted tree, and at once, as was his wont, thought of himself:—

" Just opposite, or rather below this place, I observed what I never observed before, a tree rent asunder by lightning—the half which had fallen was withered and dried up, but that which stood, though burnt also, spread forth its leaves as if nothing were the matter. I thought this something of a phenomenon. In physical nature it may occur, but rarely does it happen in our moral nature that he whose better half of being—his fresh and pleasant hopes—has been dried up, can himself, though standing, put forth his green leaves and fruits again."

" I omitted to mention in its place that, early this morning, I had expressed the pleasure I should feel in seeing a white thorn,—as a truly English shrub which I did not remember to have seen since we left our own country. The wish had hardly been expressed half an hour, when a white thorn actually occurred, and afterwards continued to be of frequent occurrence. The thorn seems to me to be to England what the thistle is to Scotland, and the shamrock to Ireland. I do not know why the rose should be the national plant. It is more properly that of Persia and other countries, where the 'Gardens of Gul' bloom far more beautifully than in our own isle; and roses, and thistles, and all, have thorns. We like nothing which has not a thorn of some sort or other, although these may not always be so palpable as in roses and thistles."

Teflis was seen at a considerable distance before the travellers reached it, and this first view of it did not raise great expectations. For thirteen nights before they reached it, the party had not had their clothes off. Teflis was found to be a disagreeable place; but there was some relief in intercourse with a curious colony of German settlers. The observant traveller says of the other sex:—

" I have been rather disappointed in the Georgian ladies. To say nothing of their dreadful eyes and eye-brows, which last are too remote from the eye and from each other, indicating a character volatile, easily moved, and little enterprising, but withal open, warm, and of quick sensibilities; their foreheads recede too much; their noses enormous; teeth and mouth good, and often the chin; but the nether part of the face is so much wider than the upper, as to give a character of bluffness to the whole, which is quite unpleasing. Their figures are, in general, large and awkward, and their hands and feet great clumsy things indeed. *Expression* is not to be looked for in a Georgian face. I never saw it in one."

At Teflis the mode of conveyance was changed. The carriages were parted with, and German waggons without springs substituted. The new vehicles distressed their intimates by their terrible jolting, and it was some time before they became accustomed to the motion. On the road toward Shusha Kitto found some brambles, and remembered, in a moment, his grandmother's excursions with him when he was a child.

"Brambles begin to be frequent this stage, and at the place where we stopped, there was almost a thicket of them, interspersed with trees and shrubs. Being the season for blackberries, they afforded an agreeable regale to some of us. I have always relished this humble but pleasant fruit; and although I have been in the countries of the fig-tree and the vine, I continue to like it. I remember how often, when a boy, I wandered far in search of them. Sometimes I found none,—sometimes I did; and when I did, my hands were lacerated and my clothes torn. How much is this like many parts of my subsequent experience! How many things have I wandered after which I have found, and which were sweet to me, but there were briars and thorns in them and with them, which tore my hands and my feet, and rent my very heart asunder!"

Annafield, a colony of German Millennarians, was passed, and at another, called Helmsdorf, they spent the Sabbath. "We here first," he says, " observed Persian women in the streets, walking about, muffled up in their long striped veils."

"The people had heard of us before we came, and we experienced a kind and hearty reception. There is a freemasonry in Christianity, by which Christians, in all places, are known to each other, and sympathize with each other, without the intervention of human language. The people have, in this country, found a refuge from the persecutions to which they were subjected in their own country. Every man here sits, literally, under his own vine, and under his own fig-tree, and there are none to make him afraid. How far this peaceable state of things may have had the effect of subduing their ardent expectations of the second advent, I have yet to learn. During the late war with Persia, the people of this village were despoiled of some of their little property by the Persians, but no other harm was done. The Russian

Government is very tolerant to all denominations whilst they continue in the profession of their fathers, but it looks with an evil eye on all conversions from one denomination to another, unless to the Greek Church."

On their arrival at Shusha they met with a most ardent reception from the German missionaries. On the 29th of September they left this town, and Herr Zaremba, one of the missionaries, accompanied them to the Araxes, the river that here separates Russia from Persia, and had his horse stolen from him during the journey. Mr. Pfander also joined them for the purpose of going to Bagdad. In seven days they reached Tabreez. On the last stage of the journey, Kitto's horse threw him; but as he had lost his cap the day before, and now wore a turban, its thick folds saved his skull from being crushed by the fall. "Yes, my mother," he writes in reference to this escape, "God has not done with me yet; I have more yet to do in this world, and more to suffer." At Tabreez, Mohammed Ali Khan, a Mohammedan married to an English lady, gave them accommodation. But their own countrymen, of whom there was a considerable number at Tabreez, had heard of the fanatical character of the strangers, and were not prepared to welcome them. Here the party was lessened in number. Mr. Nisbet, of the East India Company's Service, married Miss Taylor, and as some compensation to Mr. Groves for the loss of one of his assistants, the bridegroom gave him a handsome pecuniary subscription.

Miss Taylor's marriage must have confirmed Kitto in the views which he had already expressed. For in one of his letters from St. Petersburg, composed a very few weeks previously, he discusses the question, whether unmarried ladies should go to the East as missionaries; and he is hostile to the idea, because so many of them fall away from missionary labour by accepting the offer of a husband. It is different, he admits, in other portions of the world, but in the East there are peculiar temptations. "I always thought that the energy of the Christian principle of action was never more strongly exemplified than when a tender and delicate woman goes out to 'the wilderness and solitary place,' with no other arm than that of her God, without a husband's arm to lean upon for support, and without a husband's wing to protect her." But after taking exception to single females coming out to the East, since, being brought into contact often with men from their own country, they listen to matrimonial overtures, and cause the "adversary to speak reproachfully of missionary motive," he adds, "I except Quaker ladies, because they would be less tempted by such overtures, and I believe them less temptable. Their independent character, their masculine understanding, their deliberate energy, give them great power and intensity in the pursuit of those objects they understand and feel distinctly."

At Tabreez, Kitto met with Mr., now Sir John M'Neill, and the meeting was to the lonely and eager inquirer of immense benefit. Sir John's kindly manners overcame the young man's modesty, and drew him into conversation. He found him very intelligent, and having the "utmost avidity for information;" and especially did he gratify him with some illustrations of Biblical customs, which his own experience in the East had made familiar to himself. Kitto's mind was evidently occupying itself a little with such ideas, but Sir John gave it new impulse and ardour, and he referred the inquisitive student to Morier's *Second Journey through Persia*. The reader cannot but mark with peculiar interest those conversations of such a stranger with Kitto at this time; for, in fact, they touched and awoke a latent power, which, after years of development and training, gave its possessor his merit and his fame. To the results of Sir John M'Neill's sympathizing and suggestive interviews with Kitto, we shall soon have occasion again to refer.

After the cavalcade left Tabreez, it came into Koordistan. The ferocious character of the inhabitants was at once apparent, daggers being drawn on the slightest provocation. When the Mehmandar * of the party had shown his usual tyranny to the people of the first village they entered, they at once resented it —brandished their weapons, and let loose their dogs, while even the old women thumped the travellers with clubs. Similar scenes occurred from time to time. They left Bannah, and reached Suleimaniyah over the most frightful roads they had seen. On November 30, they crossed the last and formidable pass, amidst agitation and alarm about robbers, and the people appeared to be more wretched than the Koords.† A month was spent in the journey between Tabreez and Bagdad, and they reached the latter city on the morning of Sunday, the 6th December, 1829, about six months after their departure from Gravesend. According to Mr. Groves, the journey of three thousand miles from St. Petersburg to Bagdad, cost about £38

* Kitto defines the Mehmandar as "a person who has great powers, and whose duty it is to provide accommodation for us." Mr. Morier gives a more terse and telling description: "He acts at once as commissary, guard, and guide, and also very much as Tissaphernes, who, in conducting the ten thousand Greeks through Persia, besides providing markets for them, was also a watch upon them, and a reporter to the king of all their actions."—*Second Journey through Persia, etc.*, p. 46. London, 1818.

† Perhaps the only instance of humour in Mr. Groves' first Journal occurs where he says of one of those Koords—"If this man be a specimen of the general state of clothing among these banditti, it would be difficult for a missionary to go clad, however simply, without at least, in this respect, furnishing an object of temptation."—Pp. 109, 110.

for each person of his party, including the expense of living and travelling. Kitto writes:—

"On taking a mental review of this journey, I feel there is great cause to thank God for His many mercies towards us, and His gracious protection of us from many apparent and real evils. I do most truly believe in the doctrine of a *particular* providence, and I shall feel happy in the assurance that you do so. It is a doctrine from which I have, in the course of my life, derived much consolation and support, and I would not for a great deal, relinquish the satisfaction it is so capable of affording.

"We have been till now the guests of Major Taylor, the Resident, and live, and shall live, in a house connected with his. He is a man of much talent, and is very kind to us, being also fully disposed to assist our undertakings. He is of much authority here, and the Residency is a sanctuary. It is contemplated that Bagdad should be the head-quarters of the mission, whilst its members itinerate about in the surrounding countries. I have no locomotive talents, and shall probably be a fixture here, writing books and tracts, and bringing up the little boys."

Bagdad was once renowned over all the East. The "Old man" says of it, to Thalaba,—

"It is a noble city that we seek;
Thou wilt behold magnificent palaces,
And lofty obelisks, and high-domed mosques,
And rich bazaars, whither from all the world
Industrious merchants meet and market there
The world's collected wealth."

But now it had fallen far from its high estate. Literature had decayed in the once famous capital of Haroun-al-Raschid, and it was said that a perfect copy of the *Arabian Nights Entertainments* could not be found in a place that figures so conspicuously on its merry pages. It has often been besieged and pillaged by various armies. Though built on the Tigris, the Euphrates is distant from it only a six hours' march, and its surplus waters during an inundation are here discharged into the Tigris by means of the canal of Isa. Mr. Groves selected this city as the commencement of his mission, but left it in 1833 for India, where he laboured in various schemes of benevolent enterprise during the remainder of his life. Failing health obliged him to return home in 1852, and he died in peace and hope at Bristol, May 20th of the following year.

It may be mentioned in passing, that, as the following letter indicates, Kitto identified himself with Mr. Groves' mission, though he was not formally engaged in evangelical work.

"*Bagdad, April* 30, 1830.

". . . We are now settled in a house of our own, in the Christian quarter of the city, in which we have room for an Armenian school, which is this day opened, and which we hope it may please God to bless to His own glory, and the benefit of that highly interesting people, who have hitherto been so much neglected in missionary operations. We have thought it most expedient to begin with an Armenian school, as the Mohammedans here are very jealous, and this jealousy will be less provoked in the first instance by an Armenian school than an Arabic one; but we hope before long to have that also. We anticipate less opposition from the natives than from the Catholic Bishop of Babylon. But he has thus far contented himself with forbidding his people to send us their children. From his flock, however, we meet with attention and kindness, and some of them have offered to send their children, provided we would teach them English.

". . . You will be glad to hear that, though we are here, in the head-quarters of Islamism, we are subject to no personal molestation. A rude boy may call us ' dogs,' as we pass the streets, but this rarely occurs, and this is all at present. There are many circumstances, however, which lead us to feel that we hold our lives on a very uncertain tenure, in a place where a man's head can hardly be considered as safe as his hat in England.

". . . I have an undertaking in hand of a laborious character, which was suggested to me by Mr. Groves himself. It is to combine, in one view, our own observations with those of various travellers and authors, to form a view of the sects and denominations of Asia and of Asiatic countries, for missionary purposes, rejecting all information but such as may be thought useful to a missionary."

Kitto's residence in Bagdad was monotonous—the daily teaching of the boys, the solitary walk on the housetop, and the writing of letters and journals. But his observant eye noted much, and he has recorded many of his observations. Of the houses he says :—

"I will just mention, en passant, that the roofs of our houses, though not gardens, clearly illustrate the gardened roofs of Babylon. The internal aspect of the upper rooms is that of an arch, supported on pilasters, these rest on an abutment, which runs round the middle of the room, and form very convenient recesses for books, etc. Sometimes, however, the ceiling is flat, and then the beams are occasionally seen, unless otherwise covered with ornamental wood work. In both cases, the actual roof is supported by great beams, over which mats are laid, on which earth or clay, three or four feet deep, is heaped. This lies tolerably firm, and I have not known an instance in which rain water penetrated. There seems no reason at all why, if the people wished it, or understood it, or it were to their taste, proper earths being used, gardens might not be formed on these terraces. They, however, prefer, perhaps wisely, to reserve them as bed-rooms for summer. Rains would not much interfere with such an arrangement. It never, or very rarely, falls, but in winter, and then not in large quantities; and I do not see that, in this respect, there is any difference between this place and Babylon. Such roofs would not do at Malta, where, from its insular situation, there is a good deal of rain. In that island, therefore, they spread the terraces with a composition, which hardens almost to the solidity of stone, and in which, I believe, lava from Sicily is a principal ingredient. In more rainy places hereabouts, where they use the same roofs, they seem obliged to *roll* their roofs after every rain, to give them consistence. At Suleimaniyah, which, being among the mountains, is rainy, I saw, after a shower, many persons drawing stone rollers over the roofs—this I never saw here." Again,—"The houses here swarm with vermin; mosquitoes all the year round, but most in summer. They are, however, not so abundant as in Malta, and in the country between Volga and the mountains. Fleas swarm, even in the most cleanly houses, for a month or six weeks about the commencement of summer; but we are not made aware of their existence for the rest of the year. During that season, even English ladies are not ashamed to complain of them. Scorpions are not numerous in the houses. On removing some clothes from an open recess in the wall one day, I found one—the first I had ever seen—and not being sufficiently acquainted with verminology to recognize it, I felt no alarm; but, not liking its appearance, I brushed it out with my hand, and crushed it under my foot. Of rats and mice there are plenty."

He describes the streets in no flattering terms :—

"The state of the streets after rain is such as would disgrace the worst village in England. The causeways, where there are any, are about a foot wide, and in as bad a state as the road—a level of three feet it is impossible to find, and the mud is ankle deep. The pedestrians either wear great buskins of red leather over their usual slippers, or else go barefoot on such occasions—the last most generally—men, women, and all, holding up their clothes higher than is quite decent —that is, the poor women, for others either do not go out at all, or wear the great boots aforesaid. I have often thought that the state of government is indicated by the state of the streets. In all the countries I have been in, subseqent experience has confirmed the impression thus first obtained. Pavements are bad, or none at all, where the government is bad. In Russia, I have not seen a regularly paved street out of Petersburg and Moscow. In Georgia, still worse; and in Persia and Turkey, worst of all. Pavements bad in Spain and Portugal — in England, very good.

Verily, the principles of a government may be read in the dust of the ground. I saw one woman, having a sort of clogs on her naked feet, raised high, and fastened over the instep by a band of leather, like a print in Calmet. I never saw it before. There is nothing here like the system of mutual accommodation and civility in street-walking which we find in England. None give the wall, not even the poorest, nor turn aside at your approach, but expect you to step off the causeway, such as it is, into the muddiest mud."

Nor has he forgotten to tell us of the social habits and common occupations :—

"The people may be considered to have but one regular meal, which is supper, at or a little after sunset. This is generally a *pillau*, that is, mutton or fowls, with rice. The poor seldom get animal food; bread, dates, and fruit, are their chief provisions. Mutton is the principal animal food used. Beef is little esteemed, and wild buffaloes' and camels' flesh is mostly eaten by the poor. The Christians can procure pork without much difficulty—we do; wild hogs are common among the reeds down the river. A Mohammedan considers it a defilement to touch a pig; yet a Moslem water-carrier, who serves the house with water, brought a small live hog the other day as a *present*, for which, however, he expected in return its full value. The venison is very good; we get it sometimes, though not so often as pork. The wild gazelle is found about the river, and I think the flesh superior to any I have tasted. Coffee is drunk continually by those who can afford it, but only regularly in the morning. The poor seldom get it. Coffee, as made in England, is brown water; here it is *coffee;* as they make it and take it without milk or sugar, all its delicious *aroma* is preserved. It is handed round in small cups of delicate china, in cases of silver or even gold, to prevent scalding the fingers. Each cup contains about a table-spoonful, the contents as black as ink, but as they are the very essence of a considerable quantity of coffee, I have felt more refreshed after such a small cup, than after a pint of the washy stuff dispensed in the London coffee-houses.

"*February* 12.—I have been, at times this week, considering, with some amusement, the operations of the native carpenters. They uniformly work squatted on the ground, which a European carpenter would consider no very convenient posture. Work benches are things quite unknown in this country. Thus, in planing a plank, as a tableboard, they sit down cross-legged upon it, and having planed the space before them, change their position, and perform the same operation on the space themselves had before occupied. Of course they ride upon the board, from the impulse of the plane, to some distance from the place where the board lay when they commenced; but when they change their position to plane the other portion, they ride back again! They make much use of their toe in holding their work. I am not aware that they have chisels, hatchets, or gimblets; the adze performs by far the greatest portion of their work. Holes they drill with a bow. They have saws, of course, but the teeth are indented in quite the reverse position to ours; they, therefore, are obliged to use the strongest exertion, not in pushing the saw from them, as with us, but in pulling it to them. Of this instrument they make, comparatively, but little use. They have much more idea of reducing the wood on which they labour to the required dimensions, by hewing with the adze, than by sawing. I believe a carpenter, working from sunrise to sunset, earns about sixpence sterling, which, considering the price of provisions, is about nine shillings a week; and considering the little work they do, this is no inadequate recompense. A good deal of their time is spent in smoking, which, as their pipes are long (a long stick inserted into an earthen bowl), prevents them from working and smoking too; sometimes, however, when they are pressed, they will take out the earthen bowl, which has a short stem, and smoke while they work.

"Most of the Mohammedans of this city, being of Arabian descent, wear beards. The Osmanlees wear simply mustaches. These are the only general rules. The rest of the people wear beards or mustaches indifferently, according to their fancy, but I think mustaches are most general among the Christians, though they often wear beards. Jews have more generally beards, though often mustaches. As you seldom see a head in these countries uncovered, it is not easy to know whether they are shaved or not; but from those I have happened to see uncovered, I conclude they are not completely shaven—about half so, that is to say, about half the space between the ear and the crown is shaven quite round, leaving a semicircle of hair on the top, where the hair is suffered to grow thick. This is commonly enough dyed red; but beards are not dyed of this colour so frequently as in Persia. Occasionally, however, it is done, and a most disgusting and sometimes ludicrous effect it has. A northern eye, which is accustomed to see the natural red, is not for a moment deceived by the imposture, even so far as the colour is abstractly considered, as it has none of the glossy hue of the natural red hair; and, accustomed as we are to associate this colour with a fair complexion, a red beard on a dark face seems to be a monstrous anomaly. Moreover it frequently happens, from the neglect of the proprietor of the red beard, that the part which has grown out since the operation, is of the original colour—black, grizzled, or venerable white, whilst all the rest is red, presenting, from the contrast of colours, a most curious and truly laughable appearance.

"My barber, a tall Osmanlee, with a white turban, is the gravest barber, certainly, under whose hands I ever sat. He bends his tall figure over me with infinite solemnity, and proceeds slowly and deliberately at his work, taking, I think, half an hour to cut my hair, inflicting martyrdom upon me, and causing me to feel most acutely the excision of every particular hair."

He thus describes the opinions of the people:—

"Here (speaking more particularly of Bagdad and its neighbourhood) the English are much better known than any other Franks, partly from the frequent intercourse with India, and the presence of many who have resided there many years, and partly from the highly respectable and respected Residents the East India Company has had here. Of the power, the wealth, the integrity, and justice of the English, they have very exalted ideas. Defective as the system of our Indian administration is, according to our English notions, the Asiatic, who can compare it only with Asiatic systems, has a better idea of it; and I am sure you will be gratified to learn that those who come here, after having resided there, generally eulogise so highly the comparative impartiality, justice, and liberality of the English administration in India, and the security of person and property they enjoyed under its protection, that there seems a general wish among the mercantile and other more intelligent classes, that the English would take Bagdad into their hands, and they calculate with satisfaction the possibilities that such an event may occur one day or other. Like most other foreigners, perhaps brother Jonathan only excepted, they seem to think Englishmen are made of gold. It puzzles me sometimes, when men, not ill informed for Asiatics, occasionally inquire if England is as large as Bagdad, how they can suppose the land able to contain all the gold they think Englishmen derive from it. The Russians, though nearer neighbours, are *here* less distinctly known; they seem to be regarded with much the same sort of feeling, as I regarded, and, I suppose, we have all regarded, when children—the Ogres, the fee-faw-fum men of nursery tales."

That Kitto, the deaf pauper boy, should find himself so far from home as Bagdad, must have sometimes surprised him. When he thought of himself as a little ragged urchin, running wild about the streets, or pictured his seat of lowly and solitary toil in the Hospital—

"As one past hope, abandoned,
    And by himself given over"—

then, indeed, he must have felt that it was a watchful and mysterious Providence which had guided his steps by a tardy and circuitous route from Plymouth, through Exeter, Islington, and Malta, to the "City of a hundred mosques." In this spirit he writes to Mr. Burnard, February 25, 1830:—

"MY DEAR MR. BURNARD, . . . Here I am, in this city of enchantment and wonder, the renowned seat of an empire which stretched its gigantic arms from the Indus to the Mediterranean, and the great scene of Arabian tale and romance. I am quite amazed to think, when I think of it all, how different the actual scenes and circumstances of my life have been from any I could previously have anticipated for myself, or others for me. At one time I had no idea but that I should spend my days in the obscurities of my humble vocation, and then, when this view was altered, it seemed so much the tendency of my deafness to make me a fixture in some chimney corner, that I should quite as soon, perhaps sooner, have thought of crossing the rivers of the moon as the Neva, the Volga, the Terek, Araxes, or the Tigris. But here, in spite of a thousand anti-locomotive habits and dispositions, and ten thousand fireside attachments, I have been wandering about the world by a way I have not known, and in which I had not intended to walk; and, as I am now situated, I see no end to my wanderings on this side of that bright city to which, I trust, notwithstanding my weakness, my sin, my evil, I belong, and to which I hasten, forgetting many things which are behind, and pressing forward to them that are before. So true it is, that 'a man's heart deviseth his way; but the Lord directeth his steps.' None have had cause to feel this more strongly than myself; and, with my past experience, I am almost tired of devising anything at all, but am inclined to sit down quietly and take whatever it pleases God to send me, whether it appear to me good or evil, pleasant or painful. I know you are not a predestinarian; it has been the tendency of many circumstances in my life to make me one; but I do not tell you whether I am one or not. . . .

"I have at present tolerable health and spirits. I find myself upon the whole very congenially situated, and I am not aware that I have at any time regretted the determinations which have a second time brought me abroad. I thank God for that faithful and tried friend, with whom I am now again connected more closely and naturally than before, and whose unexampled, and persevering, and untired kindness to me, I am happy to be able in some poor measure to repay, by undertaking, among my other employments, the education of his sons. May I thus be enabled, in my humble way, to acknowledge, though I can never adequately return, the many obligations he has at different times laid me under!"

Kitto's language at this period betokens, not only that he had felt the purification of sorrow, but that, apart from the growth of religious principle, his own observation and experience, stimulated by travel and enlarged by intercourse, had taught him the great truth unfolded by Spenser, his beloved bard—

"It is the mind that maketh good or ill,
　That maketh wretch or happie, rich or poore;
For some that hath abundance at his will,
　Hath not enough, but wants in greater store;
And other that hath little, asks no more,
But in that little is both rich and wise,
　For wisdom is most riches; fooles, therefore,
They are which fortunes do by vowes devize,
Since each unto himself his life may fortunize."

Presence of mind, trust in God, calmness of heart, self-denial, and unrepining adaptation as well to sudden evils as to expected trials, had been gradually acquiring strength within him. Very soon were they all put into requisition, so that, while their genuineness was tested, their power was at the same time developed, in the midst of pestilence, flood, famine, and siege.

7

RESIDENCE IN BAGDAD

By the month of April, the Pashalic of Bagdad was in agitation. The Pasha was out of favour with the Porte, and the Arabs were at war, both among themselves and with him. Several messengers had been sent from Constantinople for his head, but none of them had ever returned to report his success. In August, between twenty and thirty thousand Arabs encamped close upon the city; but Daoud Pasha prudently made peace with them, and for the present they dispersed. The plot, however, was thickening, which ended in a siege. Meanwhile, the plague had reached Kerkook. It had already devasted Tabreez in the previous year, and now it came slowly and surely down upon Bagdad. Who could watch the stealthy approach of the foe that " walketh in darkness," without feeling either anxiety for himself, or deep commiseration for the helpless victims fluttering and trembling on all sides of him? Kitto says:*—

". . . But you will wish to know how we are personally affected in the prospect of plague and siege. I am sure Mr. Groves feels no personal anxiety on this subject. While he laments the misery which the people have in prospect, he is fully persuaded (and I endeavour to get the same feeling, and do, *in limine*, concur with him) that we shall be safe; or if we are visited by the pestilence or the sword, it will be for some wise and useful purpose. He thinks it would be a very poor return for the protection we received from Almighty Providence during our long and perilous journey, particularly in the mountains of Koordistan,

* Letter to Mr. Woollcombe, Bagdad, February 19, 1831.

were we, in the prospect of new dangers, to distrust that care by which we have hitherto been preserved. The Resident, with his usual kindness, has offered him accommodation, during either the plague or the siege, or both, in the Residency. In the latter case, I know he is at present averse to accept the protection of armed men, which we should there have, for, besides his servants and retainers, the Major has a guard of thirty sepoys; but whether this repugnance extends also to the case of the plague, I have not yet asked him, and cannot do so at the moment. I think, on his principles, it would. Now, for myself, I am afraid that I think more precaution consistent with reliance on the Providence of God than he does. However, I am ashamed to feel any anxiety, which no one about me feels, and, in fact, I do not feel much; but what I may feel when the crisis arrives, I do not calculate upon. I hope to have within me all adequate support from above; and, at the worst, or that which would be thought the worst, I trust I have prospects of good beyond the grave, and life has not been altogether so pleasant a thing to me, to give an interest of much intensity to a question which, at most, involves no more than its possible loss. . . . I often think of the Library, and the first happy, very happy days of new life I spent there. The outward face of every book *then* there, and the inward contents of many, with the feelings and impressions with which they were perused, seem before me now. Many later things, and books more lately read, I do not so well remember."

At length, in March 1831, the plague was officially declared to be in the city. Seven thousand perished in the first fortnight of the awful visitation, the population being probably about 75,000; so that 500 persons seem to have died in a day. The malady whetted its edge and widened its circle of operation, so that in April some days witnessed from 1,000 to 1,500 deaths. In two months, 50,000 are supposed to have been cut down. Nearer and nearer it came— entered the English Residency—took off some persons attached to Mr. Groves' household—and seized Mrs. Groves on the 7th of May. After a week's suffering, she died on the 14th. Kitto was deeply distressed by such a stroke. He kept the boys in his own room, and shared with the women the nursing of the baby.

When this melancholy bereavement threatened Mr. Groves, Kitto again appears in his journal, thus :—

" Poor nature is bowed very, very low, when I look at my dear boys and little babe, and see only poor little Kitto to be left for their care for hundreds of miles around. . . . Dear little Kitto, I feel for his situation with all my heart. . . . Poor dear Kitto and the little boys are now become the sole nurses of the dear baby by day and by night.

" *May* 12.—Up to this day I am well, thank God;

but, seeing the ways of the Lord are so marvellous, I have arranged all my little concerns, and put them into the hands of dear Kitto. But poor Kitto is so little able to provide even for himself."*

The awful scene is described by Kitto in the following terms :—

"Mrs. Groves was interred a few hours after her decease, and the things she had used were burned. It went very sharply to my heart, to see the corpse of so good a friend brought out, wound up in the way of the country, in a sheet, without a coffin, and laid on a sort of grating made of palm branches, which was fastened on horseback with cords, by two strange men, who took it away for interment with little ceremony. No one followed her beloved remains to the grave, no funeral rites were performed there—indeed, we know not the spot of her interment—but our hearts followed her, not to the grave, but to the throne of the heavenly King, where she appears certainly not the least brilliant gem among the jewels of His kingdom.†

"My dear little pupils bore the news better than I expected, after the first impression. Indeed, if we did not know the character of a child's mind, and the transient tone of its impressions, this event seemed to visit them much more lightly than I could wish. But there is so little—I have myself felt it bitterly—*so very little strong and permanent feeling among men and women*, that I know not what right we have to expect it from children.

"Mr. Groves himself also bore it much better than, from the extent of his affection to his departed wife, and her apparent importance to his happiness and comfort, I should have expected. However, there were circumstances to make this dispensation particularly mysterious to him. . . . Since she came here, she had experienced a peace and joy in Christ which she had not before known, and her faith was remarkably strong and implicit ; so that her husband was led to cherish the idea, that the Lord was ripening her for usefulness, and to strengthen his hands in the work of the Lord. How short-sighted are the best of men, when they leave the proper sphere of faith in forming definite expectations for the future, beyond the

general persuasion, that all things shall 'work together for good' to the children of God. I know many other instances of similar miscalculation. When we see the children of God become more strongly built up in Christ, and more visibly grown and strengthened, and fructified in Him, we have concluded them to be ripening for great usefulness in the Church, while, in fact (as in this case), they were all the while ripening for the garner in heaven, which we perceive when they are actually gathered in.

". . . If it be one property of faith to believe *all* mysteries, and receive them, it is not in the abstruse points of theology that the difficulty lies—such as the Trinity, Freewill, etc.—but to believe and receive such great mysteries as this, that the stroke which separates us from the desire of our eyes, the companion of our way, the beloved of our youth, and lays the garden of our earthly hope a bare and desolate thing, is intended in kindness, and to work final good. Yet nothing is more certain than this great mystery. This we shall, in such cases, understand ere long—and this, they who are taken, understand already, and adore, and wonder that there is so much of mercy and love in that which they once thought grievous and hard. I, too, my dear Marsh, have had losses, more personally my own than this, to sustain ; and I have felt it useful, at such times, to think of the feelings and points of view in which the liberated spirit probably saw the dispensation I mourned under ; or, in other words, to borrow the eye of the other world with which to look on the calamities of this.

". . . I confess to you, I did not say a syllable to Mr. Groves on the subject of this visitation for nearly two days after it occurred, because I did not know what I could say. To many other men I should have had a great deal to say; but I rather look to him, to profit by his words and example, than expect I could be of any use. Till, therefore, he spoke himself about it, I was content that he could see and feel how deeply I sympathised in the loss he had sustained." Again :—

"Whilst the plague was in the house, the chief object of my anxiety was Mr. Groves. I was indeed persuaded he would be spared, yet I could not but feel the possibility of his being taken ; and when I considered how much he had been exposed to the contagion, it seemed he could hardly escape without a miracle. I have sat for hours watching him, with an anxiety which I cannot describe, and which unfitted me for reading or study of any kind. On the Monday following Mrs. Groves' death, he seemed poorly in the morning, and at dinner took his meal apart, which he had not done the preceding day. In the afternoon he arose from his couch, and came, with rather a tottering gait towards me, and said, 'Have a firm and steadfast

* Journal, London, 1856, pp. 132, 137.
† "Dead bodies were often tossed into the streets, and devoured by the lean and hungry dogs." "He did much, then, who took the dead of his household to the river, and threw them in." In a stable-yard, close to Kitto's dwelling, nearly a hundred graves were opened and filled in the course of a day and a half. "It was a frightful thing to see the uncoffined dead brought on barrows, or on the backs of asses, and laid upon the ground till the graves were ready for them." "Rich persons took the precaution of buying their own winding-sheets, and the monopolist, who sold them at prodigious prices, did not long enjoy the fruits of his greed. Little orphans were running through the streets crying in despair for their father and mother ; and grandsires were sometimes left alone without a single surviving relative."—*See Kitto, in Penny Magazine for 1833, p. 458.*

heart towards God, and be sure He does all things well: I feel the same symptoms coming upon me as my dear wife mentioned. It is the earnest desire of my heart to be where she is, but for the sake of the dear little ones, I thought it might be better to stay. But He knows best.' I said something, with tears, as to the consolation I had felt in all these calamities, in the hope he would be spared. He said, 'The Lord does wondrously.' He then gave me some instructions in the event of anything having happened to Major Taylor, as the plague had been carried from hence to Bassorah, recommending me to write to England to his friends for money immediately, and to Aleppo, and to wait here until I got answers. His only thought, he said, was for the children and me; yet he was quite sure the Lord would care for us, for His holy name's sake. The next day he was much better, and now seems quite well. There is no doubt, however, that it was really an attack of the plague, as the Worshabet's* attack, which occurred two days after, began with exactly the same symptoms, and which, therefore, no doubt, might have been fatal, but for the great mercy of God to the poor children and myself."

Kitto himself escaped, but he knew not how soon he might be prostrated, and, at this critical moment, he addressed a farewell letter (May 1831) to his mother, from which we present a lengthy extract :—

". . . So far as I consider myself a dying man, I am led to review my life a little. It has been a striking one, abounding in mercies, and also in troubles; and also in the elements of happiness : and yet my life, as a whole, has been unhappy ; and, perhaps, this is one reason why I the less regret the prospect of its termination. How little would my grandmother have thought, or how little should I have thought myself, ten years ago, that I should have thus been led about the world to die in Irak Arabia. I am glad now that I am not married. When I put myself in dear Mr. Groves' present case, and think what I should feel in his situation, supposing that he has the plague himself, and knowing that his beloved wife has—apprehending, also, that he shall have to leave three little orphans in a strange city, under the care of a deaf man,—when I think of this, I am afraid I could not bear it as he does, and I thank God I am not so tried. Yet, if I were, perhaps *He* would strengthen me, as He does Mr. Groves, to bear all He might lay upon me. How easy it is, in comparison, for me to die ! As to me, it seems of little consequence to any whether I die or live ; but as to Mr. Groves, it seems of much consequence to many, and to his own family, at least, that he should

* A Worshabet, or Wartabiet, is an Armenian priest and teacher; a Moolah has usually some connection with a mosque; an Imaum is a higher spiritual head ; and a Moonshee is an amanuensis or interpreter. Mr. Groves was taught Arabic by an Imaum.

live. For myself, I only say, 'Do with me as Thou wilt, only make Thy will mine.' In case of my death, you will, my dear mother, perhaps, feel it as a little trial—if so, may that and every other trial be blessed to you, in bringing you nearer to Jesus Christ, who became Himself a man of sorrows and acquainted with grief, for our sake. That will be a blessed thing, whatever it be, which brings us nearer to Him, and carries you more frequently to your Bible. As for myself, I have nothing to boast of ; no ground of consolation in the prospect of death, but in the free mercy of Christ. I have been a very great sinner—though not habitually indulging in external sin; but my besetting sins have been *within*, sins of the mind; I doubt if my heart were ever truly converted to God, till after I was at Plymouth the last time.

"My dearest mother, I hope you will earnestly seek after the salvation of God. I hope you will attend at Mr. Hatchard's regularly. I know no minister at Plymouth who is so well acquainted with the way of life. Above all, do not neglect the Bible and private prayer.

"God bless you, my dear father, and put your *heart*, or keep it if it be there, in that true way which your *head* knows so well. Dear Betsy, dear Mary Ann, dear William, believe me that I love you all very tenderly, and would do anything I could have done for your welfare, whether spiritual or temporal. I hope you may all walk with Christ through the wilderness of this world, that by and bye you may join your elder brother in that house not made with hands eternal in the heavens, whither he goes before you. Take care of our parents. Think how much we owe them; you must do the more for them, now that Johnny can no longer share this pleasure with you. I had hoped to see you again, but God knew better than I what was good. I have a great many things I could say, but I have no room, and my head aches bitterly.

"My dear brother Tucker, as a legacy, I give you an article I highly value, my sister Betsy. It is the best thing, next my parents, belonging to me, and I hope you will regard it for my sake. God bless you both, and make you still more happy together than you have been. I would kiss little Jack Hickerthrift, if I could, but as I cannot, I hereby send him word that he must be a good boy. Tell him that his uncle John prays the Great King in heaven to bless him, and that uncle John wants him to learn the way to come and gather flowers with him in the gardens of Paradise.

"And now, my dearest father and mother, believe how sincerely I have ever been and am, till I put on my new being, and *then* too, perhaps, your affectionate son,

"J. KITTO."

Kitto must have suffered not a few privations during this forced confinement, but he bore them all with patience, and at some of them he could smile :—

"After describing so much calamity, on a grand scale, it is a little awkward to descend to minor inconveniences. You would, however, have been surprised to see your friend performing, at least in his own apartment, the usual duties of housemaid, such as sweeping the floor, making the bed, and keeping things generally in order. But at the beginning of the plague, the Jew who did our errands left for Bassorah, and the man-servant, who was much terrified at the plague, for Mosul; then only the two women remained, one of whom had enough to do in nursing the baby, and the other in cooking; and when the latter died, we had not only all our own things to do, but also to nurse the baby, whilst the nurse performed some of the duties of the deceased servant. Thus, also, no washing could be done—not at home, because water and hands were both wanted; not without, on account of the plague. Our stock of linen was, however, sufficient to prevent much annoyance from this cause, except the occasional necessity of washing a handkerchief or so for ourselves.

"Among these grievances, I should not, perhaps, mention, in my own case, that of being unsupplied with snuff. When the plague began, I was an inveterate snuff-taker. I, however, did not approve the habit in which I indulged, and had often thought of breaking it off; but the craving of the nasal organ was so intense, when its supplies were suspended, that I forgot all the arguments against the practice. I therefore was led to determine to make it a matter of compulsion. So, when the plague began, having enough of the titillating dust to last three weeks, I resolved to lay in no further supply. When that was exhausted, no further supply could be had, and, as I had foreseen, my appetite bitterly repented this determination, while my conscience approved it. So, after I had taken every grain that was to be found, in any hole or corner of box, shelf, or wrapper, I was obliged to sit down without, and, after a few uneasy days, my appetite was reconciled to its want, and, long before the plague was over, I had ceased to desire an article which seemed, two months before, to have assumed the character of an absolute necessary. There are many habits with which it is no of use to reason. They will not be talked down or argued down; they must be compelled; and however lightly some may think of the exertion necessary to overcome a habit apparently so insignificant, I venture to believe, that the degree of fortitude which a man must exert in overcoming or resisting such a habit as opium-eating, snuff-taking, or tobacco-smoking, would gain him a high name, if applied to some public or prominent object. But mankind have not learned to estimate *mind* by its own measure, but by its modes of exhibition."

But misfortunes did not come singly. The river overflowed its banks to an extent "without recorded or traditional example," and on the night of April 27th threw down seven thousand houses, and fifteen thousand people, the majority of them already stricken with the malady, lost their lives. Hosts of fugitives from the doomed city were caught by the waters and prevented from escaping. Many of them died, and some gained the heights, on which, though spared by the plague, they perished of want. The house in which Kitto dwelt was exposed to the danger :—

"The house we live in is, perhaps, as strong as any in Bagdad. The waters have not flowed into our street, though they were only kept out at one end by an accidental elevation of the ground. The water, however, soon found its way into the *Sardaubs*, where it now stands to the depth of nine feet, and though now stationary, has nearly attained the level of the court-yard. Mr. Groves, while dressing in the morning, in the room which he and Mrs. G. had usually occupied, observed some dust fall down from a crack in the wall, and at last it occurred to him to remove from the room his things, which mostly lay there. All were employed in this business except myself, (who held the baby), and it had been finished but a quarter of an hour, when the arch which supported the room gave way, and the floor of earth and brick fell into the water with a horrid crash. Blessed be the Hand that supported the arch till such precious lives were withdrawn from the danger! A few evenings after, as I was sitting in my room, I felt the house shake, and was almost suffocated by a cloud of dust, and, rushing out, found, as soon as the dust had settled a little, that the wall of the same room, which had separated it from another, had fallen, and with it a great portion of the roof or terrace of the house, which it helped to support; and when, after the dust had subsided, one stood on the housetop and looked down into the very cellars from thence, and saw a confused mass of earth, bricks, great beams, and water, it was affecting to think of the Divine goodness which had been exhibited in these transactions; for, in this last instance, also, the servant, with the baby in her arms, had but a few minutes before been in the room, which the fallen wall divided from that of the floor which had already fallen."

The reflecting journalist adverts to the proximate causes of these terrific scenes of plague and mortality :—

"*Bagdad, July 3, 1831*

"We have not, I think, to seek for the cause of the terrible character it assumed, in anything inherent in the plague : we may, then, inquire what collateral causes gave it this destructive character. The answer is, *the inundation*. In these countries people have no other resource than to run away when the plague appears. In the present case, however, this common resource was precluded by the inundation, as if the Agent of Destruction acted with design (and did he not?) in unbinding the rivers, that the waters might confine his victims, as in a prison, awaiting execution. Now, within the walls of Bagdad, there is not much room to spare. It is not a widely spaced town, and, of course, in such a case, the danger is greater in proportion, as the population, being thus confined, are more exposed to the chance of contact, and the miasmatic corpuscles are more condensed, longer held in suspension, and more slowly dissipated in the purer air; and not only, it appears, will the smaller mass of air be more strongly impregnated by the greater quantity of miasma, but the air will be, on the same account, additionally loaded by the foul effluvia of a crowded population, as well as from the decomposition of animal substances left in the streets, including, in our own case, bodies unburied, as well, perhaps, as the thousands buried within the walls, slightly under ground, in which the miasma of the plague will not readily dissolve. And to these causes may be added, the probable generation of bad air by the action of the sun on the waters, which so widely surrounded the city—all circumstances concurring to give a peculiarly noxious character to the pestilential miasma in this case. And when the full operation of all these proximate circumstances was effected, by the destruction of such a great number of houses by the eruption of the waters, which obliged the survivors to crowd together, thirty or forty in a house in the uninundated parts, the wonder, physically speaking, seems to be, not that five out of seven have died, but that the remaining two escaped." *

The horrors of a siege followed the havoc of plague and flood. After various feints on the part of Daoud Pasha, the Arab Pashas of Mosul and Aleppo advanced against him. They had been waiting at Mosul till the pestilence and the waters should subside. Robbers

---

* It may be added, that the heat at Bagdad is sometimes so excessive, that the birds sit on the palm trees gasping for air. At the time referred to, in consequence of the inundation, the inhabitants could not retire into the sardaubs or sardebs—subterranean apartments, where the atmosphere is several degrees cooler than in the higher rooms of the house. Various devices of funnels and chimneys are employed to send a current of air down into the apartments of a Persian house, as in the allusion in "Lalla Rookh:"—

"If Zephyrs come, so light they come,
  Nor leaf is stirred, nor wave is driven;
The wind-tower on the Emir's dome
  Can hardly win a breath from heaven."

The embankments of the river are now made more secure, for a few years since the water rose 22½ feet, considerably higher than in 1831, and yet no damage was done.

took the advantage, and began to plunder the city; entered Mr. Groves' dwelling, in their lawlessness, firing a shot through the door; but a civil answer and some money, about a pound sterling, pacified them. The Georgian defenders of the reigning Pasha having fallen before the plague, no resistance could be offered to the invaders. The Pasha was taken prisoner, and Kitto saw him carried past the door under a strong guard. Yet the crafty governor contrived to re-establish his authority for a season at Bagdad, and held the uncertain reins of power till September; the Pasha of Mosul, who had taken his place, being, in the interval, condemned and put to death. Such a daring act could not be pardoned, and the Pasha of Aleppo finally gathered his forces for a regular blockade. The city, knowing the insecurity of its ruler, was full of disorder, and on the night of the 28th of August, the house of Mr. Groves was broken into and partially plundered. The loss fell heavily on him who could not hear the robbers' intrusion, and he thus recounts it :—

"*August 29*, Monday.—I was surprised this morning, on arising and coming down from the roof of the house, where, like other people, we sleep in summer, to find some of the contents of my clothes-box scattered about in the adjoining room and the verandah. My first idea was that thieves had visited us; but the servant-maid, who had risen just before, and, on observing the same had gone to ascertain that the door was safe, as no other means of access to the house occurred to her, was looking on with some terror, being afraid to touch the things which lay here and there, in the persuasion that the devil had been busy about them; for here they assign the same paltry and mischievous employment to the Prince of Darkness as in enlightened England.

"We soon ascertained, however, that, whether men or devils, they had not left us empty-handed, and that they had obtained access by wresting out the wooden framework of a window, in a neglected room, which looked into that same yard where so many of the dead were buried during the plague, and which, though high up in the wall, they had probably ascended without a ladder (a ladder is here a ponderous pair of steps), the people here being expert in climbing, from their habit of clambering up high date trees. Now, we had no idea that thieves, though we expected them, would come otherwise than openly and forcibly by day; or else that the house was impregnable against silent robbery; hence our doors were all unlocked, and the robbery was so silently managed, that neither we, nor the man-servant, who slept on the same floor with the rooms robbed, and quite opposite to them, knew anything of it. I say *we*, though, as far as *hearing* goes, they might have pulled the house down for me. Yet I was not undisturbed, for I dreamt of seeing a man hung outside Newgate, probably at the very time the robbery was going on, illustrating the peculiarity of my dreams, which I have before had occasion to consider.

"On examination, it was found that their principal depredations were committed on poor me. They seem to have visited the rooms in the order of march; from the first they took bread, but omitted to take the silver spoons, which lay there quite exposed. It is plain that they had no light with them; and as the room was dark, not admitting the beams of the moon, the spoons escaped their notice. In the next room, that of the little boys, they found nothing to their purpose; and in the next, which is an open room, between mine and theirs, there was nothing to steal.

"The next room was mine. The contents of my box (chiefly of the things in actual wear, for what was not so I had, some weeks before, put away in a secret place) they seem to have taken out to the moonlight to see what was most worth taking; hence the things in the adjoining open room and the verandah. All my clean shirts, about a dozen, they took, leaving only two coarse ones; also my hose, sheets, pillow-cases, towels, handkerchiefs, and some flannel articles. The last loss is irreparable, as also that of shirts, which no one now in Bagdad knows how to make. There was one little parcel also, which I had made up the preceding day, and intended to *bury* on this, and which contained some little articles belonging to my lost one. This they opened, and, taking thence some small valued trinkets of silver and gold, left the other articles strewed about. That they had left any of the contents of this dear parcel I thank them, whilst my heart quarrelled with them for having taken that which they did. A bundle, containing old rags, etc., they also took, and another, containing Persian and other worsted hose, together with a quantity of linen cloth. This was the extent of their depredations, on me; my money was hid away; and, happily, they did not look farther than my box, else they would have found razors and other cutlery, the loss of which would have been irreparable here. I think, indeed, they took alarm when they had done examining my box; and hence had no leisure to examine the room fully, or the next, that of Mr. Groves. They went there, indeed, and brought out some of his clothes to the light; but they stole nothing, nor seemed to have examined more than one box, though the others contained property much more valuable than they could find with me. For several hours we thought that I had been the only loser, but it was found then, that from another room they had taken two fine Persian carpet rugs, worth about £6. Mine, however, is the greater loss, consisting of various articles of use, and some of that adventitious value, which things derive from having belonged to friends now in heaven. If there were an Englishwoman, a wife, or a sister here, such losses as these I mention would not signify, but one feels it, in present circumstances, a little vexatious; and then one is more vexed to think that such things should have the power of vexing at all. My books, which I value most, will not tempt them—my money, and more valuable things, are concealed among the ruins of the fallen arches and roofs, and of that which remains they have taken that which pleased them best; so really there is some comfort in having been robbed; and, to be a little more serious, I trust I may say that I am enabled to take 'joyfully the spoiling' of my goods, knowing of better goods in possession and prospect, which man did not give to me, and cannot take from me."

The siege was continued with all its usual fruits, and the Pasha was reduced to the last extremity; the population in the town proving as dangerous to him as the beleaguering foe beyond it walls. Kitto's quaint observations are tinged with sadness.

"*September* 11.—The siege has now been going on for several months. In such circumstances, my deafness is no small benefit to me. I am not disturbed by the noise of artillery and musketry, and of other commotions around; and I do not, except sometimes through Mr. Groves, hear the reports which are so heart-sickening. Upon the whole, if not told, I should hardly know what was going on, as I do not go out of doors, and life passes with me as it was wont, were it not that we are now straitened in several articles of provisions to which we have been accustomed; and if, when I walk in the cool of the evening on the house-top, I did not perceive the flash of mortars, cannons, and muskets, and observe the ascent and fall of bombs. The besieging party regularly begin to bombard the city about three quarters of an hour after sunset, when, in this country, it is dark, though it would not be so in England so shortly after the sun had set. If not for the feeling of their being destructive, the flight of the bombs so high, and their frequent explosion in the air, would have a very fine effect. Most of them do burst in the air. We have to be thankful that we are so near the middle of the city, where the bombs do not often fall; yet one did fall on the top of a house not far from ours, and, by its explosion, killed three persons who slept there. But, upon the whole, I have not understood that their bombs have done much harm to the city or people; and, altogether, it seems the city has much better and more artillery than the enemy. We often pick up musket balls in the court and on the terrace. The enemy seems to be straitened for metal. The balls, both for cannon and musket, are often of *clay*,—the application of which to such a purpose is quite a new thing to me. Such balls, however, have quite force enough to kill a man, it seems; though that they have made a breach I have not yet learned. I know not what stronger evidence we could have of the misery of man, and the ruined state of the world, than what we have seen and heard in Bagdad in the course of the year 1831. In Europe particularly in England, the world is presented under so many disguises, and in features so externally attractive, that it requires no ordinary discernment to perceive the utter worthlessness, vanity, and hopelessness of all it can offer. She is here naked, and the heart sickens at the deformity which sin has made in her once excellent form of character; and in the depth of its abhorrence and disgust at all it looks on, is tempted to cry, perhaps too impatiently, 'O that I had wings like a dove, for then would I fly away and be at rest.' May all we have felt and suffered be made useful to our spirits! And I think it cannot fail to be so. We have known and seen what can never be forgotten, and which, while we remember, we cannot easily fall into the error, which most do, of mistaking earth for heaven; and in its legitimate effects on our minds, must lead us to feel as strangers and sojourners in it more strongly than we have ever done."

The Pasha, to raise funds, sold his dagger, studded with diamonds, and the jewels of his wives. The roofs of the bazaars were torn down and sold for fuel, and a drunken rabble did as it pleased with property and life. Provisions had risen in price, and there were all the horrors of a famine. The favourite pigeons of Kitto's pupils had to be killed, and the goats on which the motherless baby depended for milk could not be spared. On September 15th, Daoud Pasha fled, and he of Aleppo prepared to take possession. As in Samaria in the days of Elisha, the aspect of things suddenly changed, and, as Groves states, "wheat, that sold on Wednesday for 250 piastres, sold on Thursday for 40, and other things in proportion." After five months' close confinement in the house, from pestilence, inundation, and blockade, Kitto ventured out, and the appalling spectacle deeply affected him. The old Hebrew sovereign was, in the day of Divine anger, offered his choice among God's "sore judgments"— dearth, sword, and pestilence—and he humbly and wisely replied, "Let me now fall into the hand of the Lord;" but Bagdad suffered from all these scourges, either simultaneously or in rapid succession. While the angel of death might be seen standing over the city with his drawn sword, the Tigris was collecting its furious torrent among the hills, and the "hand of man" was mailing itself to join in the devastation,— the camp fires of the Arabs gleaming in the distance. The combined results of this resistless agency, acting on a crowded, perverse, fatalistic, and misgoverned city, cannot be easily imagined, and Kitto's narrative is not by any means overcharged:—

"October 1.—I went out this afternoon for the first time these five months, in order to get myself a book or two from Major Taylor's library, to which I under-

stood there was still access, notwithstanding his absence. The contrast between the aspect of the streets now, and when I was last in them, was very striking, and greater than I expected to find, after the accession of strangers which the place has received, and the distance of the plague. The streets I had to pass through are among the most populous of the city; but I doubt if I met more than fifteen persons in going and returning, except in one part of the way which lay through the bazaar. This desolation was very affecting, when its cause struck the mind; when it occurred to one's thoughts, that of the busy and anxious population which went through the streets a few months back in their many-hued and multiform array, plotting and scheming for years to come, three-fourths now lay buried beneath the soil they then trod. I looked round for the accustomed faces which, from frequent passing, had become familiar, but they were all gone. Most I meet now seem to be strangers. The former frequenters of the streets were, at last, accustomed generally to our European dresses, and ceased to stare much at us; but those I meet now eye me with the wondering gaze of strangers, and such, indeed, their dress betrays many of them to be. All the time I have been in Bagdad before, I think I never saw a real Turkish dress, except on Captain Chesney, a traveller, who assumed it; but now, many of the persons I meet have that dress, which, though a nearer approximation to ours than the long flowing attire of the Arabians, is far less gratifying to a European taste; and the simple red cap, without a folding around, which the common Turks wear, has an unpleasant effect, compared with the striking and stately head-dresses which all, except the poorer Jews, delighted to wear; these often contented themselves with a little coloured handkerchief twisted round the red cap, which, however, was better than nothing. The red cap, though it forms a pleasing part of the proper head-dress, is a contemptible thing of itself. In Greece, however, and the Western Arabic Provinces, it is often worn alone, —here, never till now, the Bagdadians being most rigid turbanites; a predilection which does credit to their taste, for, after having seen almost every variety of masculine head-dress, I venture to pronounce that none are more graceful, imposing, or useful, perhaps, in a hot country. The shops also in the bazaar, or leading to it, were nearly all closed, to as large an extent as in England on a Sunday. Often, I do not think more than one was open. The men who used to sit there cross-legged, with their stores around them, and smoking their pipes, are all dead. How terrible, how very terrible, these things are to a European, and, of all Europeans, to an English mind!

"I was surprised, also, to see the number of houses which had been thrown down by the inundation. I had thought that the consequences of that calamity had been confined to one part of the city; but here I saw houses fallen, and others partly fallen, among those which remained entire. Some had simply their fronts fallen, whilst the rest remained entire, exposing to view the best and well decorated apartments of many houses. Nothing can present a more striking contrast than the gloomy outside to the gay, and even splendid interior, of the houses in Bagdad. Many of the internal decorations seem in very good taste, however little of it the Turks exhibit in other respects. It is usual to report these people as wanting in taste. I know not on what this imputation is founded, except in the difference of their taste from ours. As to dress, I venture to think our European dresses exquisitely absurd, and can excuse my Arabic friends for thinking so; but what European ever thought the Arabian, the Albanian, or the Persian dress absurd? And, in building, I know no structure more effective, more finely proportioned, and delicately turned, than the minars I see around me. If they make no display of taste or skill in their houses or palaces externally, the reasons are pretty well known; but when we come *within*, I will say with confidence that, in the cities of Turkey and Persia, and particularly Bagdad—though I know this is not by any means the finest, or one of the finest, cities—there is a *greater proportion* of houses, elaborately finished and tastefully ornamented within, than in any cities in Europe, not excepting Italy, where such processes are confined to the palaces. Of this assertion, the gracefully arched ceiling of the room I write in is a proof and illustration. It is true, the style of embellishment is different generally from ours, except as in this room, which is a Gothic chapel in miniature. The common style, however, is more light and gay, more of both, indeed, than at the first glance would be thought very compatible with the apparently sombre and heavy genius of the Turks. Yet, I don't know, either. The tame Arabs, who form the basis of the population, are far enough from anything that is sombre and heavy. As I looked around, from the top of Major Taylor's house, the city seemed in a great measure laid open, from the falling down of garden and other walls, and I did not, in any one instance, perceive that the least attempt was making to build up that which was fallen. Indeed, I doubt very much if the city will ever regain its former footing, low as that was compared with its ancient fame."

These weary and eventful months taught Kitto many a salutary lesson, and deepened within him a spirit of calm resignation. The crisis had again and again brought him face to face with death. The firmness of Mr. Groves, under the trying circumstances, was not lost upon him. There must have been "great searchings of heart" until unwavering confidence in God was established in his soul: "Thou wilt keep him in perfect peace whose mind is stayed on Thee." In October, Mr. Groves had an attack of typhus fever, and Kitto again felt no ordinary responsibility. But he persevered and fainted not, committing all to Him who has a Father's heart to pity, and a Father's arm to guard and bless.

On recovering, Mr. Groves contemplated a journey to Aleppo, to confer with some friends there. The design, however, was immediately abandoned. But towards the beginning of next year, the monotony of Kitto's sojourn at Bagdad was varied by an unexpected trip down the Tigris, in company with Sir John M'Neill, who was on his way to Bushire, to another political post. Kitto had suffered much in body and mind during the five months of disaster and evil tidings; but no sooner did he meet Sir John M'Neill again, than the ruling passion revived, and he recurred to the old topics of conversation at Tabreez,—the illustration of the Bible through Oriental manners and legislation. It had by this time become a subject of settled study, and he was desirous above all things of increasing his acquaintance with it.

The party sailed down the river in a species of barge, and not, as is often done, on rafts resting on inflated skins.* Kitto, never very sure in his footing, fell into the water the first day, and having, as might have been anticipated, a load of books in his pockets, he sank at once to the bottom. But he playfully adds:—"I fortunately pulled a Persian groom of Mr. M'Neill's *in* with me, in return for which he had the good nature to pull me *out*. This was a transaction which the light-hearted Iranee always thought of afterwards when he saw me, and never thought of without "roars of laughter," as they say in the House of Commons' reports; and this, at last, to my no small annoyance, as my perception became too obtuse to perceive where the joke lay which amused him so highly."

On one occasion Kitto strayed from the party, and when the boat was about to sail, he could not be found. To shout to him or fire a shot was needless. Sir John M'Neill started in pursuit, and commenced naturally to call after him, ere he recollected that he was only wasting his breath. "After a sharp run," he says, "I came up with him, but as he could not hear my approach, he was completely taken by surprise, and when

---

* These inflated skins are still used for navigation, as they have been for many ages past. Kitto refers to Herodotus and Xenophon as having mentioned them, or at least, he says, Major Taylor so translated Herodotus. But in the passage probably referred to, I. 194, the historian speaks simply of hides stretched on ribs of willow, and calls such vessels, πάντα σκύτινα—"wholly of leather." Xenophon, however, in his *Anabasis*, 1-5, 10, speaks of skins stuffed with hay being employed in the construction of rafts. Layard describes the building of those referred to by Kitto.—*Nineveh*, Vol. II. p. 96.

I seized him by the collar of his coat, supposing himself in the hands of some Arab robber, he turned on me a face of such agony, that, ludicrous as the circumstances were, I could hardly laugh." * On another occasion, during night, or rather towards morning, the party was attacked by some Arabs, and shots were exchanged, "without injury to any of the fleet," though Kitto supposed, from their yelling, after a volley had been fired at them, that some of the invaders had been wounded. "The cries of the women," he mentions, "were very conspicuous on this occasion, and indeed they are always active participators in such affrays. This I was about to mention as a peculiar disgrace to the 'womankind' of this country, but I have just read the account of the Bristol riots † in the *Courier*."

At Zechigyah, Major Taylor met them with the information that the pestilence was raging at Bassorah, and that Mr. M'Neill's appointment at Bushire had been cancelled. They had no alternative but to return to Bagdad, and be again shut up during a second threatened visitation of the plague. Kitto felt more anxiety about this second exposure to the malady than about the first. Of the kindness of Sir John M'Neill and of the Resident, he speaks in the highest terms. He kept, as he describes it, a "terribly copious journal" of this brief voyage. "Mr. Groves himself has written a very good journal. . . . I find, on comparing our journals, that my attention has been directed to many things with interest, which Mr. Groves did not at all observe, or did not think it worth while to mention. Moreover. I have been by far the most *minute* observer of the two, as is, indeed, natural for a *little* man to be. . . . In England, the notes I have been in the habit of making, and shall make during our future journeys, if it pleases God to prolong my life, will afford me, I hope, interesting materials for communications to my friends; though I am not ignorant that the ideal value the mind gives to what comes from afar, would make the same facts and observations, which I may then relate, of much greater interest, if they came from Bagdad, in letters smoked and dried, like a neat's tongue, and stabbed through and through, as I suppose mine are." ‡

Kitto's Journal, chiefly scrolled in pencil, is certainly minute and topographical, though there is not much in it of special interest, beyond an account of the banks

of the river, the scenery within view, the ruins and villages passed, the interviews with the Arabs, and some scattered remarks on their character and condition. On returning to Bagdad, the family were shut up in Major Taylor's house, the plague having broken out, but not with the severity of the preceding year. The city, however, was so deserted, that the very women walked through the streets unveiled.

By midsummer, Kitto's thoughts were turned toward England. He felt that he was becoming of less and less service to Mr. Groves. Mr. Newman, who had recently come out to Bagdad, was doing the work of a tutor, and Kitto was not permitted to exercise any of the functions of a missionary. But the object of his journey to the East had been served, though he was not himself aware of it. His mind had been storing itself with the knowledge of Oriental customs, laws, and other peculiarities, and he had seen the importance of these for the illustration of Scripture. The first awakening of his attention to this point was the critical moment of his life, and it is recorded in his Journal under date August 3, 1829.

"The different modes of raising water in Russia may not be unworthy of notice, particularly as one of them seems to illustrate a passage of Holy Writ. I do not know what mode obtained, till about half-way between Petersburg and Moscow; but there, a very long pole serves the purpose, which is balanced from a beam, placed over the well, by the bucket at one end and a block of wood at the other. The weight of the bucket causes it to descend, when a strong exertion of manual strength is applied, and in the same manner to ascend when strongly pulled, by the assistance of the balance at the other end. A large number of these poles, stretching out their long arms, form very curious and conspicuous objects in Russian scenery. The other mode of raising water is by means of a wheel, from six to eight feet in circumference, which, being turned round in one direction, carries the bucket down to the depth requisite to fill it, and then brings it up again. It depends, in a great measure, on the weight of the bucket and balance, but I have tried very few of these wheels which I could turn with ease. As it is a very simple plan, it is also a very ancient one most likely, and I agree with Dr. Henderson in thinking it sufficiently illustrates 'the wheel broken at the cistern,' in Eccles. xii. 6. In some places pumps are used, but I have not much recollection of having seen a windlass."

The next instance occurred at Teflis, where he saw the oxen treading out the corn; and the third is mentioned as having struck him at Shusha:—

"Two women were there, occupied in baking bread. The elder of these made me understand, by signs, that the whole establishment, including the threshing-floor

---

* Communication from Sir John M'Neill to Mr. Ryland. *Memoirs of Dr. Kitto*, second edition, p. 351.
† These riots, unparalleled in the modern history of England, occurred in the last week of October, 1831. The bishop's palace, the prisons, the excise office, and nigh fifty private dwellings were set fire to, and some hundreds of individuals were killed or wounded. The disturbances arose in connection with some procedure of Sir Charles Wetherell, the recorder of the city, who was exceedingly unpopular, from his hostility to the Reform Bill.
‡ Precautions used by the post-office with regard to letters from infected countries.

adjoining, belonged to her. The baking process is very simple, and I am inclined to suppose it, from the rapidity of the work and coincidence of circumstances, to be the scriptural method of baking cakes. A convex plate of iron is supported on three stones. Under this a fire is kindled, and the dough, spread out into very thin cakes, is placed upon it. Each cake is dressed in a minute or two. Cakes are thus made more or less thin. At Shusha, where I write, they are our common bread. The cakes are as thin as brown wrapping paper, and more flexible, and, as is well known, the Persians use them for napkins at table, and then eat them. They are really very palatable. The nature of the process renders turning necessary, which reminds one of the passage, ' Ephraim is a cake not turned.'"—Hosea vii. 8.

In Bagdad he alludes to another point:—

"When you look at the higher class of buildings, you have an idea of their solidity, which is by no means correct. You see walls three or four feet thick, but they are merely loosely faced with bricks, and the rest is filled up with dust and rubbish. They are, in short, entirely adapted to a climate where it seldom rains. In an inundation of the river, even when the streets are not flooded, the cool cellars already mentioned, lying below the then level of the water, are soon filled, and, in a few days, sap the foundations of the arches which support the rooms above, which then fall in. How easily, then, are such buildings swept away when exposed to the full tide of waters, and how much more, the habitations of the poor, who, as in Job's time, ' dwell in houses of clay.'"

Before coming to Tabreez his attention had been pointedly turned to this subject, for he speaks of a person clad in a certain costume as resembling " one of the prints in Calmet's *Dictionary*." At length his mind became full of it, and he seized on information wherever he could procure it. His interviews with Sir John M'Neill, at Tabreez and Bagdad, and in the brief voyage on the Tigris, were exciting and beneficial to him, and powerfully contributed to give his mind that tendency which ultimately carried him to the great work of his life. Kitto was very sensible of Sir John's kindness, felt at home in his company, and was thankful for the varied information which he was so frank in communicating. Great credit is due to him for the sympathy he felt with the little deaf querist, for the pains he took with him, for his appreciation of his talents and acquirements in spite of numerous drawbacks, and for his readiness in at once gratifying his curiosity, and stimulating his mind to future and deeper inquiry.

Kitto was now ready to come back to England, though he knew not what spheres of labour might be opened to him. What he should do on his return was an object of great anxiety, and the subject had been repeatedly talked of with Mr. Groves and Major Taylor. "At Mr. Groves' desire," he writes to Mr. Lampen,* "I have opened to him my views and feelings, and he has entered into them with greater kindness and consideration than I have been accustomed to even from him." Still, Mr. Groves thought that he was becoming low in his aims—that mere literature was a sinking of the missionary character, which he had so decidedly preferred. He lamented over such defection, and suspected that his nine years' connection with Kitto had produced little or no spiritual fruit. Another tutorship was out of the question, for no one would be likely to employ him, and his deafness would be held to be an insuperable barrier. Not hearing the conversations of his pupils, he could not check any froward word or unguarded expression, and was, therefore, incapacitated for one special function of the office. Kitto makes this admission himself, adding, however, "it seems, upon the whole, the least repugnant to my habits of the things I have hitherto tried." But he was rarely troubled with doubts of his fitness, when any end was to be gained, and his mind turned to periodical literature and an editorship. He was wishful that such a situation, in the first instance at least, might be found for him about his native town.

"If Plymouth has its Roscoe, I will hasten to wipe his shoes. Meanwhile I have a most exaggerated notion of the influence of a newspaper, if the editor of a well supported print, keeping this object steadily in view, might not, in this respect, be of some use. A magazine might do more in the end; but a magazine does not seem the thing to *begin* with. There seems no spirit for so spirited a thing, as, otherwise, I think I could lay my finger on the names of several persons who, among them, might construct a very able periodical. . . . When I was at Plymouth, poets seemed as thick as blackberries. Besides four known ones, I remember a lady sent me a poetical invitation to dinner, and an artizan wrote a very tolerable acrostic on my poor name. Prose writers are not so common, unless it be taken for granted that a good poet must also necessarily be a good prose writer, which I doubt.

"As to my own competency for this same editorship, there is not a single *if* or *but* in Mr. Groves and Major Taylor's admission of it. You will see, by my letter to Mr. Harvey, what spirits they have put me into by their saying, that they have now *no doubt* that I shall be able to get a comfortable living in some of the departments of literary employment. This admission from them seemed the slow and tardy recompense for all my retired, unencouraged, uncheered, and often *opposed* exertions in the improvement of my own

* Bagdad, April 6, 1832.

mind. I shall, perhaps, surprise you by declaring that, excepting the year in the Library, and excepting that I have had greater facilities in procuring books, my opportunities for study have been fewer since I left the workhouse than while in it. I have had less time from my stated employments. Even now, for instance, I write this nearer to one than twelve at night, when every one else has been three hours in bed; by day I have no time. My employments, indeed, are more pleasant to me than before, but they do not inform my mind. If I were asked, whether, in my secret mind, I think myself equal to such an employment, I, who never pretended to more humility than sixpence would cover, would answer instantly, *I do.* And now, at this period, I think I may venture to mention a bit of a secret. My simple love of knowledge, and habits of attachment to pursuits which I venture to call *literary*, would, I think, have failed under the discouragements I have met with, but the admixture of another feeling urged me on. Then, I know perfectly well, that many thought you and my other earliest friends not justified in their original kindness to me, by any actual possession or future promise I held out. What is more, I soon began to think so too myself. But I thought then, and think to this day, that all the fine stories we hear about *natural ability*, etc., etc., are mere rigmarole, and that every man may, according to his *opportunities and industry*, render himself almost anything he wishes to become. I proposed it, therefore, as an object to myself, to make such attainments—to possess myself of such qualifications as might justify my friends to themselves and others, for their early kindness, and the mode of its exhibition. I think that, small as my opportunities, upon the whole, have been, I can now do this, and shall hereafter be able to do it better; for I should grieve to think that every day will not be with me a day of some improvement, till the last of my existence—an existence which I should desire to be prolonged to that period when the faculties of improvement must fall into 'the sear, the yellow leaf.' I am now near thirty, a period at which it is surely high time for a man to enter upon his plans of life—to endeavour to get into that path in which he desires and intends to walk; and no one can be more deeply sensible than myself, of the danger of postponing, from year to year, such designs, till postponement becomes a habit—till no strength or vigour remains for enterprise—for the effort necessary to carry those designs into effect. If, therefore, it be my lot to spend the remaining period of my existence in the class of employments I desire, and which are now admitted to be best for me, it is certainly high time to make the effort, and encounter the risk necessary; and I think my mind is now wound up, to make every possible effort necessary

before I can be led to relinquish these designs; and if, at last, I must do so, the relinquishment will then probably be final. That I have no 'small certainties' in *other* things, will, perhaps, at this juncture, be an advantage to me. I have long been in the habit, according to a suggestion of Lord Bacon, of noting down the idea of any paper or work which occurred to me. Among the mass of such ideas, there are enough which my mature judgment would approve, to occupy, in their accomplishment, a longer life than I wish mine to be; and new ideas are continually occurring, so that a dearth of matter is the thing which I shall at any time least dread.

"What reception I am likely to meet with on my return, I cannot tell. I shall need encouragement from my friends, but, I confess, there are some at whose hands I do not very sanguinely expect it; and this misgiving arises from circumstances which occurred when I was in England last. However, I hope the best; for I can see no reason why I should not be kindly welcomed to my native land once more. I return under no imputation of blame, under no suspicion of having merged my duty in my own inclinations. If I had any *duty* that required my stay here, it was the tuition of Mr. Groves' sons. I always contemplated to return when this duty should be fulfilled, and now, accordingly, I am retired from it and left disengaged; the rather, as Mr. Groves himself admits, that my deafness precludes me from any occupation that can be called *missionary;* and, I confess, I see not how any one, free from the obligations of detaining duties, could prefer to live in this miserable land. Thus, clear from any just ground of censure in returning, and with a mind improved, I trust, by travel, and stored with images it had not before, I do apprehend I shall occupy a much more advantageous position in returning this time than the last."*

"I thank God," he had already written to Mr. Lampen,† "with all my heart, that I have been able to give satisfaction to somebody, particularly when it is one whose satisfaction circumstances have taught me to rate at no common value."

There was, as his repeated language implies, one impression which Kitto wished most especially to make on his friends, in the prospect of his return to England, and that was, that he came back with no imputation of blame, and under no suspicion of having merged his "duty in his own inclinations." He remembered the crisis in Islington, when he renounced his connection with the Missionary Society, and he had not forgotten the emotions which preyed upon him when he returned from Malta, or the cold reception he met with on his last visit to Plymouth. Now, his anxiety was to let it

* Letter to Mr. Woollcombe, Bagdad, July 21, 1832.
† Bagdad, April 6, 1832.

be known that no such misunderstandings or objections had prompted him to leave Bagdad. He knew what he had suffered already, and he was careful to warn all his correspondents that he was not dismissed from any dissatisfaction with him, and that he had not sullenly thrown up his situation, but that the object of his engagement being accomplished, he was at liberty to come home, there being no further prospects for him in the East. And thus he opens his mind to Miss Puget—an intimate friend of Mr. Groves—on September 8, 1832:—

"My return is not so difficult to account for, or so unpleasant to think of, as it assuredly would have been, if I could have allowed myself to think, or if I had been allowed to think, that I had any *missionary* business here. But as it was admitted on all hands that I had none, and as the only thing I could regard as an imperative and detaining duty, was the charge of the dear little boys which devolved upon me, so when Mr. Groves contemplated taking them to England, I had no idea of returning again from thence. This intention of Mr. Groves first suggested the idea of return; and when that intention was altered, in consequence of letters from the friends at Aleppo, who have now so happily joined us, purposing to take the dear little fellows under their charge, the question of my return remained as it was—since *they* (the boys) would then be so very much better provided for in the matter of their instruction than was in my power. A letter I received from Mr. Newman, about the same time, on the subject of my [Missionary] Gazetter, expressed his impression, that things of that nature had much better be done in England than here, from the difficulty and delay in obtaining the necessary books; and as things of that nature are the only things in which I could hope to be even indirectly useful to the missionary cause, my way, upon the whole, seemed clear enough to return. I am sure Mr. Groves, if he mentions the subject to you, will say it does not arise from any misunderstanding or unkind feeling in any sense, and I am equally sure his prayers and good wishes will follow me home. It will, therefore, appear to you, and other friends who may have felt some interest about me, in consequence of my connection with Mr. Groves, that my return does not imply that I have turned back from the class of feelings which led me into missionary connections, or that I have relinquished any principle my heart ever held. I shall ever count the day happy in which I came, for, I hope, I have been enabled to learn much which before I either knew not at all, or very imperfectly. . . . However, I have no desire to magnify my attainments, my feelings, my character, my motives; and if any think badly of my return, let it be so. If I have gained anything more of the true riches than I brought out, may the praise be the Great

Giver's, who has forced upon my heart, in hard and bitter ways—truths, lessons, gifts, which, but for its hardness, might have been sent gently down upon it, 'like rain on the mown grass.' The man does not live, who thinks, or can think, so low of me, as I do think myself low in all high things."

Kitto had become aware, at a very early point of his career, that his letters were freely handed about by his friends as literary curiosities. His knowledge of this publicity naturally prompted him to give them more of a general than of a personal interest. The influence of this motive remained with him; and, therefore, many of his letters to his Plymouth friends indulge in dissertation, and are a species of colloquial essay, wanting that inimitable charm which belongs to those of Cowper. But the following epistle is a remarkable exception—the affectionate unbaring of a son's distressed heart to his mother. It reveals some of his secret griefs and fears in connection with one whose vice had brought shame upon his child even in its tender years. As he thought that he might get employment in Plymouth or the west of England, he was anxious to pave the way for his future peace by such a preliminary statement :—

"Bagdad, Sept. 2, 1832

"MY DEAREST MOTHER,—. . . . It was my earnest desire to be able to live at Plymouth; but since I got your letter, I feel this desire much weakened; for it seems to me I am not likely to find much comfort in living where father is. Vexation and trouble is only likely to arise from my connection with him. My poor father! God knows how gladly I would do all which might be in my power to help him, if he were disposed to lead a quiet and sober life; but as it is, if I did not know the mighty power of God, I should be altogether without hope for him, and I do not see, even if it be in my power, what it will be possible to do with him. I think I can only hold myself ready to help him in sickness; but while he is well, leave him to himself, unless it pleases God to work a change in his heart. I never trusted to his religious-looking letters, while he talked of his *misfortunes* and sufferings, instead of speaking as a repentant *sinner*—as one who mourned deeply before God over his own pitiable state,—a state to which he was brought, not by *misfortune*, but by *sin*. He has not been an *unfortunate* man. The Kittos have been very fortunate men. God put many blessings in their hands, and they were in a fair way of living with their families in respectability and peace. But they threw His gifts from them, and both John and William, and Dick too, not only ruined themselves, but brought poverty, misery, and shame on their families also. Yet they call themselves *unfortunate* men! I most earnestly desire my dear father's welfare, and I would do anything to promote it; and notwithstanding the shame he has brought and will bring yet, I fear, upon me and the rest of his family, I have no harsh or unkind feeling towards him; but whilst he goes on thus, and continues in health, I have made up my mind that he shall never touch a farthing of my money, however the Lord may prosper my own undertakings. The Lord has enabled me thus far to make my way through all my *misfortunes* (for mine have been real ones) and difficulties, and I trust He will continue to do so; but I shall never feel it my duty to let the money I may hardly and honestly earn be spent in public-houses. This is my resolution, which, the Lord helping me, I will keep, let people say what they will; but still holding myself in readiness to help him when any real calamity or distress falls upon him, and even then I shall endeavour to benefit him without trusting him with money. With yourself, my dearest mother, the case is very different indeed. I am sure you will believe there is nothing I will not do for you which may be in my power; and as you are now alone, it will be the easier to manage. I hope I shall be enabled to be both a husband and son to you. Wherever I live, it will be my desire to get an apartment, and have you to live with me to manage things for me, and I have no doubt we shall live very happily and comfortably together. But when I come home, and have found out what I shall be able to do for myself, I shall be able to see more distinctly the course which had better be taken. That I shall be able to obtain a decent provision in some way or other, neither Mr. Groves nor I doubt, though I may find at first some difficulty. . . . Billy's account of the doings at the King's coronation amused me. The 'most splendid arches' he mentions, I hope to see when I come to Plymouth, unless the children have eaten away all the gingerbread they were made of. That the dear fellow is in the way of doing for himself, and getting his livelihood by an honest trade, is a great comfort to my heart, for I have had many anxieties about him. Now they are over, and God grant I may never have to hear of anything to make me ashamed of him, as I have been of many other of my relatives. I think I never shall. I pray God bless him, and guide him in all that is good and right and honest all his life. I only remember him as a boy, but suppose he has got a beard by this time. I hope he will take great care in the choice of his companions. Much of his happiness or misery in this life, if not in the other, may depend on his choice of company. I hope he does not think of marrying yet. One piece of advice I may now give him, which is, never to get a bird till he has a cage to put it in. I have waited for my cage till the season for catching birds is over. I hope now to get a cage soon; but you, my mother, are the bird for my cage, and you shall sing me there all your old songs over again. Give my love to Billy, Betsy, Mary Ann, Tucker, Aunt Mary, and all my friends, and remember me kindly to Mr. and Mrs. Burnard.—My dearest mother, I am, your very affectionate son,

"J. KITTO"

His connection with Mr. Groves had been of signal benefit to Kitto, and it was now about to be terminated. In the private notes of Mr. Groves to him, there is much plain speaking, and no doubt it was occasionally needful. Many faults, which resulted from defective training, had to be rectified, and Mr. Groves did speak to him with fidelity, if not always with tenderness. He could not bear what he thought Kitto's self-sufficiency, though that self-sufficiency referred not to spiritual matters, but to the ordinary business of life. Nor had he patience with his continuous anxiety to rise, since himself had voluntarily descended, and left all for Christ's sake. One ambitious peculiarity in his character he saw and rebuked, to wit, that any situation he had obtained was usually held merely as a stepping stone to another, and that the duties of the first were sometimes overlooked in preparation for the next. During their residence at Bagdad, Kitto gave him satisfaction in regard to his boys, and Mr. Groves often alludes to it. But it could scarcely be supposed that persons of temperaments so different, as were Mr. Groves and the teacher of his boys, could be at one on all points. Correspondence by written documents must also have often been very unsatisfactory, for what is written is written, and it wants those numerous and indefinable modifications which tone or countenance might give it. An epithet has a distinctness on paper which it might not convey when spoken. Kitto's notes to Mr. Groves did sometimes so irritate him, that on one occasion he replies —"You cannot forget the expression contained in your last letter to me during the last time we had any misunderstanding; if you have, I never can; though I have not, relative to it, the slightest unkind feeling." The fact is, that Kitto was beginning to despond again, and to reckon any longer residence in Bagdad as so much lost time; and he wished Mr. Groves to carve out some new path for him. Mr. Groves, however, refused to interfere, for he was afraid that his decision would not be in harmony with Kitto's own views. Both men, indeed, were akin in mental constitution. Mr. Groves was of a nature that would maintain its own course, and in this respect his tutor closely resembled him. He was a reserved man, too, living much in his thoughts, and among his own griefs and disappointments; and the deafness of his younger friend naturally tended to lessen the amount of communication between them. In a letter written a short period after Kitto left him, he confesses*—"I cannot tell you how I lament over my own folly, in not discharging my Christian service to you, and leaving all results to God. Had I so done, instead of living years with you, without confidence or affection, I might have had you given me of the God of grace, to have comforted me in my sorrows, and it might never have come to a separation." He then commends to him his fellow-traveller, Mr. Newman, of whom he says—"I love him as my soul, for the faithfulness and truth which the God of grace has given him."† Kitto, on his part, complained that Mr. Groves sometimes made arrangements, "without thinking it necessary in the least to consult him;" and he adds, in his Journal, about the beginning of 1832—"I am persuaded no one can live happily with Mr. Groves *in a dependent situation*. . . . I am willing to suppose the fault is in myself, as no doubt partly it is. Yet, I doubt not, he might live happily with *friends and equals;* and from my inmost soul do I honour and love him, while I feel most intensely (and the more fully, since I am not singular), the extreme difficulty of living with him happily in a *dependent* character. Yet it is still good for me to be with him now, and thus far certainly." On the 19th of September 1832, Kitto, in company with Mr. Newman, left Bagdad for England.

8

RETURN FROM THE EAST

THE homeward route of Kitto and Newman was to Trebizond, and thence by the Black Sea to Constantinople. In prospect of going to Aleppo at the beginning of the year, Kitto had prepared a Journal, and composed a preface, in which he enters somewhat into the philosophy of journalism, and makes the just remark —"that to travel usefully, one must carry information with him, and the information obtained will be in exact proportion to the weight of information carried." At that period he did not care much about going home, his reason being—"I do not yet feel qualified to enter on the path of action and life I contemplate there." But his opinion had changed in a few months, and he accordingly bade adieu to Bagdad, "accompanied into the open country by Mr. Groves and the other dear friends, where we took leave of them with tears." The journey was on horseback, in eastern style, the animal carrying all necessary equipments, and its rider, who had again cultivated a mustache, dressed in a dark cap of Persian lambskin, a Turkish gown, and an Arabian

black cloak—presenting rather a grotesque spectacle. He soon felt what thirst was, and yet, though his throat was parched, he passed the river Dialah, but was afraid to dismount, lest he should not manage to climb up to his horse's back again. His "bones ached miserably," and his face and hands were scorched and blistered with the sun. The travellers soon joined a caravan of some size—"200 mules, 100 asses, and 50 horses." The native Christians of the party were kept at a distance by the haughty Mohammedans. About a week after his departure, he records, with evident satisfaction, that a messenger brought him "memorials from all the dear little boys."

He was obliged to have recourse to various shifts for comfort :—

"I also found this day the use of cording my trowsers tight round my legs, drawing a pair of long English hose over these, and over the feet of these placing a pair of Persian worsted socks, which are inserted into a pair of red Turkish shoes with peaked toes. For want of some precautions of this kind last time, my legs were much excoriated. As for the shoes, they are much too large, and thus, also, require to be filled up. When I complained to the man of their capacity, he said they would hold six pair of stockings besides my feet, and six pair of stockings I should find it necessary to use when I got among the mountains."

He notes carefully the villages through which they passed, and the caravanserais at which they halted; but one day's journey very much resembled another —mosques, tombs, ruins, and water-courses. One Mohammedan gentleman was very kind to him, and did everything but eat with him and take a pinch out of his box. How they ate with those who would eat with them is thus portrayed to the life :—

"The men tucked up their sleeves as if going to slay a sheep. We did the same; and water having been poured on our hands—each man's handkerchief serving him for a towel—we fell to with our fingers, having been supplied with part of a cake of bread each. This we introduced into the stew, taking up as much with it as we could. For the rice, N. and I were accommodated with a wooden spoon, one for both. We were made very welcome, and ate a hearty supper, which concluded with bread and cheese. After supper we washed again with *soap*. Upon the whole, the Oriental mode of feeding seems much more disgusting in theory than in practice. People may have felt disgust in hearing the process described, but few, I apprehend, in seeing the thing practised."

The nights were spent by the travellers as best they might, though Kitto sometimes complains of his fellows —one man's foot poking him in the ribs, and another claiming more than half his pillows, which were merely portions of his horse's furniture. They were occasionally taken for Russians, and sometimes for Georgians. The Mohammedan gentleman referred to knew them to be English, but thought England and India the same country. The encampment was usually well watched at night, each man sleeping with his weapon by his side; for the thieves would have made no scruple to steal the bed on which the sleepers reposed—nay, now and then succeeded in similar daring attempts. Kitto prudently put away his watch, "lest," as he owns, "its display should get me robbed." He and his companion did not carry arms, and the people imagined that they had no property but books—"a very safe conclusion for us, as it may save us from pillage." One person seemed greatly taken with his companion :—

"This man seemed so much pleased with Mr. Newman, that he told me by signs he was a good man, but I—imitating my stoop and other infirmities—I was a little, crooked, deaf, dumb, good-for-nothing fellow, an opinion to which I nodded assent; but afterwards, when I had given him a pinch of snuff—the first Mohammedan in the caravan who has accepted it—he signified that I was good also, at which I smiled, but shook my head in dissent. I see in Mr. N.'s glass that I really cut a curious figure now. To say nothing of my beard, the skin of my face, neck, and hands hangs in tatters about me, the sun having burnt it up. Whether my new skin will be sun-proof I cannot tell, but I hope so."

He complains, with some show of justice :—

"I do not ride at all comfortably. The men are very impertinent, perhaps the more from our being unarmed. Sometimes they strike my mule behind, which makes him start forward so suddenly as almost to unseat me, not seldom getting entangled among the back horses, or crushing against some one who may be before. One man, whom we crushed slightly, drew his scimitar, and held it close up to my throat; a joke perhaps, but a joke they would not take with an armed man."

An occasional squabble diversified the scene :—

"Soon after, a grand dispute arose between some of our caravan men and the Persians of the village, in which this young man most hastily mingled. There were most loud language, vehement gestures, pushes, pulls, and some few knocks on both sides. In the heat of the fray, the Seid came down briskly, and acted as arbitrator and pacificator, speaking vehemently also— an advocate, it seems, on the side of the party he took, which was that of the caravan men. Both sides seem to look on a Seid as a very fitting umpire and judge, a character which I did not before know at times devolved upon them. We exerted ourselves a great deal; and one of the most violent disputants, a respectable Turk, he laid hold of by the shoulders, and pushed him away, following him in that manner. The

occasion of the dispute was the attempt of the Persian Governor of the village to extort a tax on some bags of dates imported by our caravan. This exaction was resisted, and finally not paid by our people. Before we lay down, Mr. N. conversed with me about pronunciation and metre. He thinks I speak better than could be expected in one deaf so long; but, among other faults, he endeavoured this evening to teach me to enunciate the final *L* distinctly. When initial, he says I can do it well enough. I am afraid, however, that in this case the best theoretical instruction will have little influence on my practice. Mr. N. conjectures that we are about 2,000 feet above the level of the sea, and that a mountain, the remotest of three ridges lying not very distant, is about 2,000 above our present level."

" *Thursday*, 27.—I have, since I became a traveller, some occasion to regret my ignorance of botany and geology. Perhaps I shall begin these studies in England. Study also is vanity! We learn many things we think we may have a use for, but never find that use; and in the use of life we discover we have left many things unlearnt, which we set about acquiring when the occasion of their use is past, and will not return.

"Mr. N. relates, that I am a great object of interest to the people of the places we have passed through. I can, upon the whole, readily apprehend that a people who have, like the Persians, an exquisite sense of the ridiculous, must find something exquisitely exciting to that sense in our many oddities, as talking on the fingers, etc. Their impression of the ridiculous is, in this case, however, apparently softened to a milder feeling, by the consideration, that the oddest of these circumstances arises from a misfortune—my deafness. As it is, I suspect that they will frequently, in time to come, relate among their odd and curious recollections what they saw of *Numa* (Mr. Newman), as they call him, and poor me. Be it so. I shall have also something to say of them. It seems they take us for spies."

They reached Kermanshah on the 30th of the month —"the first great stage of the journey." Kitto gives this month—September—thirty-one days in his Journal, writing down *Sunday* as the 31st, but corrects himself by calling Monday, October 2. "The city made but a poor appearance." Kitto went out to see the sights, and surveyed the bazaar with some attention.

"In eastern towns, life can be best studied in the bazaars. The artizans seem very industrious. Several seemed to feel it irksome to have their labour interrupted by serving a customer. I went through all the bazaar, in all its parts, as well for the purpose just stated as to make purchases. Notwithstanding my Turkish dress, which is common enough here, they seemed easily to detect that I was not a Turk or Persian.

Several accosted me, to whom I replied in English, feeling it much better than to make signs. In the latter case they laugh ; in the former they turn quietly away, finding they could not understand. I should wonder if they did, for not many Englishmen understand me till accustomed to my manner of speech.* But when I wanted to deal, I signified plainly that I was deaf, and managed the matter by signs. . . .

"Snuff-boxes are here, but no snuff. Wherever I enquired, and made the sign of taking a pinch, they produced spices and perfumes ; and when I showed the small quantity I had left, they thought I wanted to sell it ; others, that I wished to get it scented. At last one old man, after groping about in a box, found a small quantity in a paper, for which he charged me so highly, that I must at this rate make my present stock serve till we get to Europe, small though it be."

Impertinent queries were often showered upon the foreign pilgrims. Mr. Newman parried them as best he could, and Kitto was often annoyed by such teasing investigations.

"I have now regularly adopted the plan of conversing in English when accosted in a way I either do not like, or do not wish to reply to in the more intelligible way of signs. So, to-day, when I went to fetch a jug of water, I was accosted by half-a-dozen men, whose countenances seemed to me impertinently curious ; so I replied something as Benjamin Franklin to his American landlord, — My name is John Kitto of England ; I am from Bagdad, and going to England, at which I hope soon to arrive, by way of Tehran ! They seemed wonderfully edified by this communication, and then, as I observed, seeming to repeat the words 'Bagdad' and 'Tehran,' ceased to molest me with any more questions."

Kitto reached Hamadan on the 5th of October, and visited the bazaars, as was his wont, but did not go to the so-called Tomb of Esther, because he could ill afford the present usually paid to the sacred edifice. Before he left the city, he relates—

"Last night I was amused by dreams of home— England, I should say ; for I am not one of those who have a home in any land to go to. One of the most

* The following is Sir John M'Neill's description of his voice : —"It is pitched in a far deeper bass tone than is natural to men who have their hearing. There is in it a certain contraction of the throat, analogous to wheezing ; and, altogether, it is eminently *guttural*. It may be suspected that this is attributable to the fact, that his deafness came on in boyhood, before the voice had assumed its masculine depth. The transition having taken place without the guidance of the ear, was made at random, and without any pains bestowed upon it by those who could hear and correct it. His pronunciation is generally accurate enough as regards all such words as young boys are likely to be familiar with, and as to others which closely follow their analogy, but is naturally defective in respect to words of later acquirement. In spite of the too great guttural action, his articulation of every English consonant and vowel, considered in isolation, is perfect."—*Lost Senses—Deafness*, p. 22.

pleasant exhibited me as finding at an old book-stall a copy of a book I read in my boyhood, and of which I have often sought a copy in vain. May I find it indeed, and if I dream, may I find there all my waking and sleeping dreams tell me of ; but this my not over sanguine mind often questions. Well, I have equally weighed, I trust, the results of both success and disappointment, and have a mind prepared to look either quietly in the face."

Sometimes, on the journey toward Tehran, Kitto was the caterer for the party :—

"Mr. N. was of opinion that I, even I, poor Pilgarlick, was a better marketer than Kerian. He is of opinion that my dress and Oriental countenance impose so far upon them, that, though they perceive I am a foreigner, they do not suspect me for a Frank ; and my deafness preventing questions, they, unless I tell them I talk English, suppose I am dumb also—all which readily accounts for my peculiarities without supposing me a Frank, or exposing me to exorbitant charges. My being deaf, and perhaps, in their view, dumb, i. e., a mute, and it may be a dwarf to boot, facilitates my entrance into their houses, which would not be allowed to any other stranger than one under some physical incapacity, which, in their view, is calculated to preclude harm, or which they are accustomed to consider as removing reserve. I therefore volunteered, with these qualifications, to go in quest of fruit to the village."

They reached Tehran, the present capital of Persia, on the 14th of October. So Kitto's Journal intimates ; but he calls it the 13th, in a letter to Mr. Woolcombe. They were at once kindly received by the Elchee or ambassador, Captain Campbell. Kitto was joked by the ambassador and by Sir John M'Neill upon his sun-burnt and hirsute appearance, his beard being nearly of a month's growth. No sooner was he in Sir John's company again, than he set to his old work. "I have given him," says the restless inquirer, "a paper of queries, which he has promised to answer me, and which will much extend my little stock of information." And he gratefully acknowledges, before he left Tehran—"Mr. M'Neill has given me satisfactory answers to my twenty queries, and has promised to do the same to seven more I have proposed to him." Various incidents of his stay in Tehran may be grouped together.

"Yesterday I was chiefly employed in writing to my friends at Bagdad. After breakfast, I noted the English servants congregating with their Prayer-books and Bibles ; and soon after, Mr. M'N. called me into the dining-room where all the English were assembled, to whom Captain M'Donald read the prayers and lessons for the day. I confess I entered into much of the service with great satisfaction, after having been so long precluded from services in which I could not, from my deafness, have any actual participation. I feel very comfortable here, after the fatigues and privations of the journey. A journey is like life—an alternation of repose and labour, of progression and rest, of good and evil. The pleasure now of having English faces around us, and to me still more of faces I knew before, is a satisfaction which, in the route pointed out, we cannot easily expect again to experience. . . They are all here very kind to me, and put to shame my proud doubt of whether I ought to come when not *by name* invited in the letter sent by the Gholam, and my proud question, whether they would admit poor Pilgarlick to their table or not. I meant the Elchee, for I had before been a guest at Mr. M'Neill's. However, having been freely entertained, both at the Resident's in Bagdad, and the Elchee's in Tehran, I hope to have my foolish thought on that foolish subject at rest in time to come—satisfied that, if I have not yet found a place in general society, I shall one day do so. I shall! I shall!"

Kitto and Newman were both taken ill at Tehran, and in Mr. M'Neill's absence. Kitto's malady was supposed to be the ague.

"The friends here, and Dr. Daoud Khan, the Shah's physician, were disposed to set it down for the ague, which I did not myself think it was; and they adduced as a proof, the shaking of my right foot, which proof I overthrew by the assurance that my grandmother, my mother, and myself, had shaken our right feet all our lives long, under the pressure of mental or bodily pain. I myself had more confidence in Captain M'Donald, nephew of the late Elchee, than in the Shah's physician; and, indeed, the kindness and care which this gentleman manifested towards us, and the trouble he took, have left on my heart an impression not easily to be effaced. At length, in the height of our malady, Captain Burnes, a gentleman who had come from India on an exploratory tour, saw us in bed, and pronounced our case *bilious fever*; and without more ado, or consulting the doctor, he went away for a barber, who bled Mr. N.; but my bleeding, much against the wish of this warmhearted and decisive man, was postponed out of regard to the Khan, who had expressed a particular opinion on the subject. When he came, however, he agreed to my being bled in the evening, though he assured me I "had no symptom to be bled." Accordingly, in the evening, an old barber with a red beard came; and, strapping up my arm with a leathern thong, produced a rude-pointed instrument, and performed the operation with no small dexterity. From that time we both grew better, and now the only thing we want is *strength*. This we now seem gathering, and I

trust we shall soon be on the road again. I thought, not once nor twice, that my journey would end at Tehran; but it has pleased God otherwise, and I do thank Him for it—for though I trust I am enabled to look at death as quietly as most men, yet there are times when death seems a very terrible thing. Miserably wet and wearisome seems the journey before us; but after this sickness, the spirit seems as it would go forth mad as a March hare, rejoicing in all things it can find under the open heaven.

"Our arrival at this place, and kind reception, were very reviving after the privations and fatigues to which we had been exposed during the journey; nor, for my own part, was I at all insensible to the good cheer which the Elchee's table supplied to me, who had been living so long on nothing but bread and fruits. The party, we found, consisted of the Elchee, 'one of that numerous division of the human species,' to quote the author of *Adam Blair*, 'answering to the name of Captain Campbell,' a remarkably handsome gentleman, with black bushy mustaches, meeting his equally black and bushy whiskers—a conjunction which has a very imposing effect; Mr. M'Neill, our old friend with whom we voyaged on the Tigris, a gentleman of much oriental and occidental knowledge, and who has supplied me with a good deal of information on points of which I desired to be informed. *He*, I suspect, is the spirit of the Mission, though not, nominally, its head. Then there is Captain M'Donald, the nephew of the late Sir John M'Donald, and whose kindness and attention to us during our illness, I have already had occasion to mention. All these are remarkably fine men, and, perhaps, if such were an object, few could be selected calculated to give a people who judge so much by externals as the Persians, a better impression of our countrymen. There are also the ladies of the Elchee and Mr. M'Neill, both fine women, and after so long an exclusion from the society of Englishwomen, it was very pleasant to look upon their faces. Mrs. M'N. is the sister of Professor Wilson, otherwise Christopher North, the editor of *Blackwood's Magazine*. With this lady I have enjoyed more conversation, on the whole, than with any other member of the party, having known her before on the Tigris. She contemplates that I may turn my travels to account in the end. This I do not at present know, nor to what account I could turn them. I regret more and more every day that we came at this season of the year. I hate winter altogether, and I hate travelling in winter more than I hate winter itself. All that I may see between I would gladly forego, to be set down quietly in England at once. My desire to be there becomes hourly more intense; and whilst I am not blind to the difficulties I may meet with, and entertain no vast expectations, the spirit with which I do anticipate obtaining, in some way or other, a decent subsistence and a settled home, has not yet failed me, and I trust will not while I need its support. It is wonderful to me what a staid and sober old fellow I find myself becoming, and I am sure you would wonder too, if you could see my little plans of *life* (not *literature*) as they are chalked out in my mind."

Of Mrs., now Lady M'Neill, Kitto formed a very high and just estimate:—

"On Friday I went to their house, and looked at her books. On showing me *Adam Blair*, she mentioned its being written by Mr. Lockhart. I remarked, it seemed of the same class with the *Lights and Shadows of Scottish Life;* to which she assented, and added, that the latter work was written by her brother. I then had an opportunity of stating that it was not till the preceding day I knew her relationship to Professor Wilson, at which she seemed surprised. She showed me her brother's poems; and I regretted I had not time to read more than a few passages of *The City of the Plague*, a subject on which I feel interested, from having been in the midst of the city of a plague more horrible than that of London. I was pleased to obtain *Adam Blair*, and a volume of *Blackwood* to amuse my frequent comparative idleness."

His mind, recovering from the lassitude of an exhausting sickness, was in doubt, as it often was, as to the future and its results.

"*November* 1.—Where shall we go now! I do not know. Travelling, wearisome and irksome though it be, seems paradise when compared with the miseries of a sick bed. O England, pray God I may soon be set down in thee, and walk in thee again! Oh! oh! I wish with all my heart I could plump into London at once!"

On Monday, the 4th November, the travellers left Tehran for Tabreez. The route had all the novelties and all the usual discomforts. Kitto's busy pen narrates somewhat jocosely:—

"N. tells me that, from the habit of talking to me, spelling each word on his fingers, he finds himself spelling the words in which he thinks; and when he repeats to himself a passage of Scripture, he generally spells it through. I expressed a hope that he would not spell audibly in company in England. . . I am fully persuaded that N. thinks his talk on his fingers audible to me; he often talks to me when my back is towards him, and admits he has often been discouraged, after having been telling me some long story, to find that I have not been observing him." Yet Kitto hints that his companion sometimes complained of the fatigue and irksomeness of talking so much and so often to him on the fingers. It must, indeed, have been no easy task to be speaking in this form every minute to one so curious to know all that was passing,

and so prone to put crowds of questions about anything or everything that either came into his head, or happened to arrest his attention.

Tabreez was reached on the 23d of November. Mr. Nisbet, who, as narrated on a previous page, had married Miss Taylor, received the travellers with abundant hospitality, and his lady and he had, with praiseworthy consideration, fitted up a room in their house called the "Missionaries' Room," perhaps in imitation of the prophet's chamber in the dwelling of the Shunammite. Mr. Newman here left Kitto, and proceeded overland to Constantinople. Kitto, however, consoled himself for his friend's departure as any one that knew him would have anticipated:—"Doubtless, I shall be more *independent* without him; notwithstanding his peculiarities, I love him, and find the prospect of going without him more painful than I would have thought." But at this place he unexpectedly got a new companion, with whom his own subsequent history was strangely bound up, and about whom his first notice is:—

"Mr. Shepherd I have just seen, and, to my surprise, find him an Indo-Briton—nothing the worse for that, however. I am led to expect that we have no principle in common, but that his obliging disposition will prevent our coming into collision on any point."

It may be added that Mr. Shepherd had been attached to the Persian Political Mission, and was now returning to England to enter into business, and with the prospect of marrying a lady in London, to whom he had been for a considerable period engaged

On the first of December the new associates left Tabreez. The weather, being exceedingly cold and frosty, caused them no small discomfort, but Kitto several times eulogises Mr. Shepherd as a travelling companion.

His own birth-day came round, and he moralised—

'*Wednesday, Dec.* 4.—My birth-day! Are there any who remember to-day that it is my birth-day? I know not, but hardly think so. Before my next I must be something that now I am not; but what, time must disclose. I know not by what it has been distinguished more than my feeling, for the first time, seriously about my cough. It is now nearly three weeks since I took the cold that brought it on, and, according to the usual process of my colds, it ought to have gone long since. I apprehend its ending in consumption; and what that ends in every one knows. I was a fool to slight it so far as not to apply to Dr. Cormick about it. If it lasts to Stamboul, I hope the physician of the Embassy will do something for me. On the whole I have felt this a very uncomfortable day, both as to health and travel."

On the sixth of the month, Kitto obtained the first view of Ararat, and revelled in the spectacle. "Its grandeur surpasses all description. I made my neck ache in turning my head to look at it, till I felt it was firmly fixed in my mind's eye. . . Great Ararat is of irregular shape, and its top has not that appearance of unsullied white which I have seen in points of inferior elevation. It has a black and white appearance, the hollows being full of snow, whilst the more prominent parts appear in dark contrast. Its blunt and irregular appearance is strikingly different from the regular and pointed cone of Demavend. My feelings, as I rode beside these solitary mountains, were more excited, or rather impressed, than I have at any former time during this journey experienced.

" . . . Close by Diadin flows a small stream of beautiful clear water, shallow and easily stepped over. This is the *Euphrates*. I stood astride it a moment, and then passed over. I was never before so near the source of a mighty and famous river ; and my thoughts were many, and to me interesting, though, perhaps, to others they would seem commonplace enough. The water seems to me more pleasant than any I have ever tasted, and I have drunk a great deal of it. It is something to have seen Ararat and the Euphrates in one day ! At the fountain there were the maidens of the village drawing water in vessels of truly classical form."

What a glorious eyeful for one day—the Euphrates and Ararat !

At the monastery of Utch Kilissa, Kitto's spirit was stirred within him at the gross superstitions which met his view.

" I have said the body of the church is a cross, with two side aisles, or which may be considered as divided into three compartments in breadth, by the square pillars, or rather congeries of pillars, which support the arches. Of these three, the eastern, of course, includes the altar. It is laid with carpets, and hung with pictures ; while the altar itself, in a recess, with a curtain before it, which was withdrawn for us, is adorned with a small picture of the Virgin and Child. I felt disgusted with this tawdry, childish array, the more so, as contrasted with the simplicity of the naked walls of the church itself. We were permitted to enter this most holy precinct, and I felt some interest in examining the pictures, most miserable daubs, the execution of which would disgrace a country sign in England. Of Scripture subjects, I recognized but two, the Crucifixion and the Ascension ; the rest were portraits of saints, monks, and bishops, with historical and legendary subjects. Of the legends, I recognized George and the Dragon, and that of the miraculous picture of the handkerchief with which Christ wiped His face, and which a king holds in his hands. One of the principal pictures represents Gregory baptizing: the converts kneel in grand procession ; a king foremost, with his crown at the saint's feet, behind whom are men, bearded black and brown, and women, among whom is a queen. Above, on a cloud supported by little cherubs, sit the Father and the Son, the last with a circular, and the first with a triangular glory, which is black or brown. The Holy Ghost, in the form of a dove, also with a transparent glory, is between them, and held as it were by both, which describes, I suppose, their belief in the equal procession of the Holy Ghost from the Father and the Son. Another represents a jolly-looking angel standing on a dead body, apparently of a king, and holding a little child, or, to speak from the picture, a fairy, in his left hand, whilst his right holds a drawn sword, which appears to have done fearful execution. In the upper corner stands the Devil, with his European tail and horns, and black complexion, and goatish extremities. He appears in the act of tearing some papers, which angels are snatching from him. One is in the act of doing this, while another is flying away with the paper preserved. What this means, I know not."

On the 18th of December Kitto arrived at Erzeroum, the chief town of Armenia, where he was kindly received by M. Zohrab, the vice-consul, who had been educated in England.

" *December* 21.—M. Zohrab was one morning asking me about the Breakwater,* understanding I was a native of Plymouth. I could tell him some things, but not about measures of length, depth, breadth, etc. He inquired, good-humouredly, how it was that I was so imperfectly acquainted with so noble an undertaking at my native place, and was yet so anxious to collect information everywhere abroad; 'but so,' said he, 'it always is.' I replied that, while residing at Plymouth, I was a boy; and unless for a short visit or two, I had not been there for ten years. 'A difficult question very well retorted,' he replied, and then related the following anecdote:—As a Turk was quietly smoking his pipe in the presence of an Englishman, he asked how many times he might fill his pipe from an *oke* of tobacco; the Briton, after some consideration, said 'four hundred.' Soon after the Turk saw the Englishman writing very quickly, and said, 'Since you could answer the question that had no connection with your own habits, you will doubtless find it easier to answer another that has. How many sheets of paper will you fill with an oke of ink ?' 'Really,' said the Englishman, 'I cannot tell; you ask a puzzling question.'

* The Breakwater at Plymouth, about which the vice-consul inquired at Kitto, is at low water a mile long. It is forty-five feet broad at the top, and two feet, in some places 3 feet, above the high water of spring-tides. 3,500,000 tons of stones have been employed in its formation; many of those in the original mass, flung into the sea, being from a ton to ten tons in weight. The expense to the present time has been about a million and a half sterling.

"*Dec.* 21, *Saturday.*—We ate, at dinner yesterday, a fish from the Euphrates, near Erzeroum, not unlike a herring in size and taste. Fish is somewhat of a rarity to me since I left England, except at Astrachan, where I ate plenty of sturgeon, which, I think, among the best fish I ever tasted. Since leaving Bagdad, I only got fish at the Elchee's table. Somewhat of a grievance this to a decided *Ichthyophagist.*

"It is agreed, in consideration of Mr. Shepherd's state, helpless from rheumatic pains, that we will go in the kind of litter called *cajavas,* which hang, like panniers, on the mule's back, but are high and arched, and covered with felt. The prospect of such a comfortable mode of journeying makes me more willing to set out. They are short, so that one cannot lie down, but may recline or sit upright, and sleep, or perhaps read; this is the way in which women and invalids commonly travel.

"*Dec.* 27.—Still at Erzeroum. We were to have gone to-day, but it was found that the litters wanted some improvement, and the carpenter was sick, and another, who promised to come in the evening, did not. Now, however, they are at it; yet, to-morrow being Friday, we shall not be able to go, as the Moslems do not begin a journey on that day. . . . I feel more and more every day that it will never do for me to mix in company. At the best, a deaf man must always cut an awkward figure in it; and, from the peculiarity of his situation, he will find it difficult to preserve to himself that consideration to which he thinks himself entitled. It is manifest to me that I can only comfortably mingle in society when I have a right to make myself a place in gentlemanly society; in all other a deaf man must suffer much. May I be enabled to establish my claim to such a place. My stay here has been for the benefit of my correspondents. The want of books, and anything to do, has driven me to write to them largely; and now that I have written all my writing, read all my reading, mended all my mending, and bought all my buyings, it is high time for us to go. I shall be glad enough altogether when we get off, as I am equally weary of vulgarity on the one hand, and of the consequential condescensions of patronage on the other. I am tired to death of everything now, myself included. . .

"*Dec.* 30, *Sunday.*—The muleteer, with whom we have stood some days engaged, refuses to go, on the ground that he cannot get lading for all his horses. However, another set of less respectable looking men came with him, with whom we have engaged, and we are still, it seems, to go to-morrow. Our litters look very comfortable, being lined with thick felt within, and covered with it without. Only they look too *high*,

not less than four and a half feet, I think, and I am in fear of their capsizing, which would be a fearful job in any of the terrible mountain passes of which Mr. S. speaks. . . . I am also afraid I shall see little during this journey, thus shut up; but, in fact, what did I see but snow during the last part of our pilgrimage. However, I shall endeavour to see all that is to be seen, which is not much, unless some fine scenery, which the snow will, at this season of the year, have much marred.

"*Dec.* 31, *Monday.*—Rose in high spirits for the journey. We were somewhat startled this morning to receive a bill of fifteen ducats, for necessaries during our stay, and in preparation for the journey, and more so to find among the items, a charge of more than £1 for firing, and another charge for porter *drunk at the table of our host.* The men were a long time getting our things ready for departure, and, at one time, they came to declare the impossibility of the horse carrying the cages. This arose, however, from their inexpertness in adapting the vehicle to the back of the horse, and, it seems, their ignorance of it altogether; for, from the crowd assembled in the street, to look at them, and partly perhaps at us, I inferred this mode of conveyance not to be common in these parts. Indeed, except at Teflis, I do not recollect such another exhibition of curiosity as was manifested on this occasion. At last, about one o'clock, we got fairly into these machines. It was then found, as I suspected, that Mr. S., though himself a light man, far outweighed me, and that it was necessary to adjust the balance. This was done by the men tying their horse-bags, etc., to my side of the litter. I had myself with me, in the litter, a pair of little saddle-bags containing books, etc. At last this was adjusted too, and on we went. I found the cage much smaller than I expected; within, about four feet high, three and a half feet long, and two wide. Its narrowness prevented me from sitting in the most convenient posture, cross legged—most convenient, not only from its occupying the smallest space of any posture, but also from keeping the feet warm, which I found no easy matter as it was. However, I wore boots, which, even under other circumstances, would have prevented my sitting cross-legged. Another inconvenience is, that we ride backward, and the door being before us (open if you please), you have no view of what is ahead of you, and you come upon everything, and everything comes upon you, unexpectedly. The convenience, however, is very great. First, being lined with thick felt within and without, it is warm comparatively, and I felt the convenience very sensibly, when contrasted with the frozen beards and mustachios of those without, who were also exposed to the snow and sleet which fell about through the ride. And though the motion, under certain paces of the horse, was inconvenient, lumping one's head about, yet, on the whole, it was not worse than that of a coach on an English road; indeed, shutting the eyes, one might also fancy oneself in a coach. Lastly, the comparative *repose* of such a mode of riding is a very important circumstance, reclining or sitting being assuredly a more convenient posture than sitting astride. If one be dozing, also, he may indulge the propensity if he can, without the fear of a fall. . . With the power of seeing fully behind, and through a hole on one side, I do not expect to lose much as to seeing. In consequence of this riding with the face to the tail of the horse, seeing nothing but the caravan, the servant who rode behind us, and the tail of our own horse, when he frisked it about, Erzeroum was fully in sight till the usual evening mist arose, and first obscured and then concealed the view. . . In the *muhaffy* I was soon settled so cosily and snugly, that it was some time before I could make up my mind to exert myself so far as to take a pinch of snuff; and when I had made up my mind, I found myself so confined, that it was with much trouble I got at the snuff-box, and then, from the motion of the cage, it was no easy matter to take one pinch without spilling half-a-dozen ; hence I was obliged to wait my opportunity of momentary pauses, and actually succeeded in taking no less than three pinches. I had also purposed to amuse myself by reading, but for this, also, it was a good while before I got heart, and then I found it, from the same cause, impossible to read. This I had anticipated, and, therefore, looking out those passages in Spenser which I had marked as memorable, I proceeded to de-cipher a line now and then, and learn it by heart. At this rate I hope to have stored my mind with some pleasing, beautiful, and striking images, by the time we reach Trebizond. This, with my snuff-box, and compass to mark the direction of the road, will amuse the time well enough. To-day, the road W.N.W., sometimes due W. . . . How full Spenser is of beautiful images, fine sentiments, and striking pas-sages! It is a pity he is so little known but by name. I shall not think my time unemployed in endeavouring to know him intimately. This few do, because to do so is a work of labour ; yet there is enough of the beautiful and pleasing, even on his surface, richly to reward those who will not think it worth their trouble to cultivate an intimate acquaintance with him. Where, in all poetry, is anything more lovely than the lay which some one chanted in the Bower of Bliss—evil as its object was ? I am anxious to see what Todd * has done with him. It is one of the first books which I shall inquire after. If I am not satisfied, I may possibly, though most unequal, attempt something

* The allusion seems to be to Archdeacon Todd's edition of Spenser, eight volumes, 8vo. 1805.

myself, less elaborate, but more illustrative, than I expect to find in that commentator. If Shakspere has found work for a thousand and one commentators, surely there is enough in Spenser for two. Spenser is the only poet I have a wish to deal with in a literary way. A slighting word of Spenser and his Faery Queen goes to my heart."

In January 1833, Kitto passed the village of Gun-nish-Khora, and, from the nature of the road, was obliged to pursue his journey on horseback, entering Trebizond on the 11th of the same month. And he thus describes the prospect :—

" On ascending the difficult mountain behind Trebi-zond, we had a full view of the Black Sea, extending boundlessly in front, but rather bounded by Cape Vona on the left, and Cape Kereli on the right. Being accustomed to look upon the sea with delight from a child, and viewing it now as the termination of the more arduous part of our journey, I can hardly describe the emotion with which I gazed on the great blue expanse before me."

He made his usual visit to all the public places, enjoying the company of the consul and his partner, and lamenting, however, this drawback, that " there were no ladies." He witnessed the absurd ceremony of " blessing the water," the archbishop who performed it having been " a woman's tailor formerly ;" " hypocrisy and roguery " being, in one of his friends' estimation, " the only talents necessary to an archbishop more than a tailor."

" We, however, saw the archbishop stand forth, and lifting up his hands, throw a cross, as far as he could, into the water, and, after a short interval, another. There were two men swimming about in the water with there drawers on, this very cold morning, and when the cross was thrown, there was a competition between them who should get it ; he who got it threw it farther into the sea than the bishop had been able. Then the procession left the rock and proceeded to the church, to which we did not follow them. I am not aware that any particular blessing is expected to come to the waters from this ceremony. The Black Sea looked neither the blacker nor whiter for it ; nor, in the expectation of less rough seas after the ceremony, do we felicitate ourselves that our voyage has not taken place before it. To use an expression of the consul, nothing but drunkenness comes of it."

Kitto did not sail from Trebizond till the first of March, and before he left it he had prepared himself for enjoying the voyage to Stamboul, by reading the Argonautics of Apollonius Rhodius, in Fawkes' trans-lation.* The assistance got from reading such a version of such an original, must have been of very little

* London: J. Dodsley, in Pall Mall. 1780.

service, for the poem is noted for its mere mediocrity,[*] and is full to excess of mythological episodes, and very sparing and indistinct in its topical allusions. The fabulous voyage of the Argonauts to possess themselves of the " golden fleece," presents no lists of places like a descriptive chart, save in a very few instances, and can by no means give such aid and interest to the traveller as the *Lord of the Isles* does to any one sailing up the Sound of Mull. The poem is in imitation of the Homeric verse, but at an immeasurable distance, though a few lines here and there have some fire and power. On board, Kitto amused himself in studying the character of the motley group of his fellow-passengers, in reading Spenser, and in identifying scenes of actual or legendary interest on the shore. After a brief voyage, the ship entered the Bosphorus on the evening of the 7th. When Kitto got up next morning, the scene entranced him.

" When I first came on deck in the morning, a scene was presented which I had often heard described, but of which description had conveyed to me no adequate idea. It seemed as if Europe, at the point where Asia looks upon her, had put on all her garments of beauty, and Asia had made herself pleasant to her eyes in return. He who has not seen Stamboul may be said to want a sense—a feeling of the beautiful, which no other object can convey. . . . The shipping in the harbour are much more numerous than I had been led to expect—I suppose not less than a hundred merchant vessels. In this enumeration of the objects presented to view, I must not omit the numerous canoe-shaped boats, having low beaks, scudding about on the water. They are very neat, ornamented with much carving, and without any water in the bottom, as is common in English boats; they are admirably adapted to easy and rapid progress, but easily overset, being very narrow, and having little depth in the water. The house of Leander is no very classical object, notwithstanding its name. It stands on a low rock between Constantinople and Scutari, but nearest the latter, and looks like a mosque or chapel, gaily painted and enclosed by a low battlemented wall. Such were some of the objects which drew my attention; but a panoramic exhibition only could convey a clear notion of the glorious and beautiful whole. It was not simply the object, as it lay before me, which interested, but the geographical, the political, the historical interest connected with it, and which the more interested me, from my previously

studying in Gibbon the account of the last days of the Greek empire, which enabled me to trace out the scenes of that most interesting contest, though I suppose the city presents a very different aspect now from what it did in the time of the Eastern empire."

The American missionaries, Dwight and Goodell,[*] received him very kindly. With Mr. Goodell he had been acquainted in Malta, and here, too, he met Mr. Schauffler and his old friend Mr. Hullock. His Journal is full of remarks suggested by the kindness of the missionary family. But his fellow-traveller, Mr. Shepherd, was confined by sickness at Pera. During Kitto's stay in Constantinople, as he rambled about the city and suburbs, two rather amusing incidents befell him, in consequence of his want of hearing. First his umbrella got him into danger :—

" Arriving at Constantinople, from countries farther to the East, and having learnt to regard the umbrella as a mark of high distinction, I was much astonished to find it in very common use there in rainy weather. I should imagine that the example of the Europeans, established in the suburb of Pera, brought it into use, and much opposition to the innovation was not to be expected from the present reforming Sultan. However, I had soon occasion to learn that traces still remained of the distinction, so usually throughout the East associated with that article. I resided principally at Orta Khoi, a village on the Bosphorus, about three miles above Constantinople; and having urgent occasion, one wet day, to go down to Pera, I set out, umbrella in hand. On arriving at the waterside, none of the boats that usually ply between the village and the Golden Horn remained, and I was therefore under the necessity of walking all the way along the road, behind the row of buildings that face the Bosphorus. One of these buildings is a favourite palace of the Sultan, in which he was then residing. As I approached the gate of this mansion, with my umbrella over my head, I observed that one of the sentinels stationed there accosted me in a commanding manner; but not comprehending what he said, I went on. Upon which the soldier ran towards me with his fixed bayonet levelled, and without any indication of a friendly intention towards my person. That I took it safely that day to the great city, was probably owing to the good nature of a Turk, who was walking close behind me at the moment, and who, on observing the advance of the soldier upon me, snatched my umbrella with violence from my hand, and thrust me forward, partially inter-

---

* Æquali quadam mediocritate. Quintilian. *Instit. Orat.* Lib. x. i. One of the most spirited portions of the poem is the description of Prometheus chained to the rock of the Caucasus, the eagle that preyed upon his vitals first wheeling, with heavy oar-like pinions, round the ship, then rushing up to his prey, and again, when gorged, sailing slowly down the side of the mountain.

* Dr. Goodell is known by his version of the Armeno-Turkish Scriptures; Mr. Schauffler by his Spanish-Hebrew Bible; Mr. Dwight, by *Researches in Armenia*, 1833. Kitto was also acquainted with Dr. Eli Smith, who was subsequently the companion and philological coadjutor of Dr. Robinson in his travels, and recently died, while engaged in a most admirable Arabic translation of the Old Testament.

posing himself between me and the assailant, who then returned to his station, and allowed me to proceed in peace. The friendly Turk, in returning my umbrella, endeavoured to explain a fact, which I afterwards ascertained more distinctly, that it was incumbent on every one to take down his umbrella in passing the actual residence of the Sultan. I had, indeed, observed, with some surprise, that persons walking before me had lowered their umbrellas as they approached the palace, and again elevated them when they had passed, notwithstanding the heavy rain; but without imagining that this was a matter of obligation. Now that my attention was directed to the circumstance, I failed not to observe, on subsequent occasions, that persons passing on the Bosphorus in boats never omitted to take down their umbrellas as they approached in front of the mansion, which "the brother of the sun and moon" honoured with his presence.*
The other jeopardy was more formidable:—

"I was detained in Pera longer than I expected; and darkness had set in by the time the wherry in which I returned reached Orta Khoi. After I had paid the fare, and was walking up the beach, the boatmen followed, and endeavoured to impress something upon me, with much emphasis of manner, but without disrespect. My impression was, that they wanted to exact more than their fare; and as I knew that I had given the right sum, I, with John Bullish hatred at imposition, buckled up my mind against giving one para more. Presently the contest between us brought over some Nizam soldiers from the guard-house, who took the same side with the boatmen; for, when I attempted to make my way on, they refused to allow me to proceed. Here I was in a regular dilemma, and was beginning to suspect that there was something more than the fare in question; when a Turk, of apparently high authority, came up, and, after a few words had been exchanged between him and the soldier, I was suffered to proceed. As I went on, up the principal street of the village, I was greatly startled to perceive a heavy earthen vessel, which had fallen with great force from above, dashed in pieces on the pavement at my feet. Presently such vessels descended, thick as hail, as I passed along, and were broken to shreds on every side of me. It is a marvel how I escaped having my brains dashed out; but I got off with only a smart blow between the shoulders. A rain of cats and dogs is a thing of which we have some knowledge; but a rain of potter's vessels was very much beyond the limits of European experience. On reaching the hospitable roof which was then my shelter, I learned that this was the night which the Armenians, by whom the place was chiefly inhabited, devoted to the expurgation of their houses from evil

* *Penny Magazine*, vol. iv., p. 480.

spirits, which act they accompanied or testified by throwing earthen vessels out of their windows, with certain cries, which served as warnings to the passengers: but that the streets were, notwithstanding, still so dangerous, that scarcely any one ventured out while the operation was in progress. From not hearing these cries, my danger was of course twofold, and my escape seemed something more than remarkable: and I must confess, that I was of the same opinion, when the next morning disclosed the vast quantities of broken pottery with which the streets were strewed. It seems probable that the adventure on the beach had originated in the kind wish of the boatmen and soldiers to prevent me from exposing myself to this danger. But there was also a regulation preventing any one from being on the streets at night without a lantern; and the intention may possibly have been to enforce this observance, especially as a lantern would this night have been a safeguard to me, by apprising the pot-breakers of my presence in the street."*

On the 14th of April Kitto set sail for England, having parted from his missionary friends at Orta Khoi, with regret; feeling, as he confesses, "miserable and irritable, and with few prospects of happiness before him." So sunken was he in heart, that, unlike himself, he was disposed to repress the caresses of a little dog that fawned upon him. But his kinder nature triumphed.

"I thought better, and caressed him, poor fellow! I wished myself in his place; bowed down by a load of cares, as I felt, and felt how gladly I would have changed mine for any animate or inanimate condition —a tree, to grow in the blest sunshine, and bear my fruit; a dog, to frisk about, and know no care; anything but what I was. But there was no condition I so much envied as that of the missionaries, particularly Dwight, married, having children—his blest Madonna-like wife—his useful, respectable, quiet, and happy life, and his happier feelings, with heaven here and heaven hereafter. . . . Kind people! God bless them abundantly, for all their kindness to one ready to perish. It tore my heart to part with them, more than the hearts of others were torn, though I saw they were affected, and tears were in the eyes of some; mine flowed. Dwight vexed me by saying his little boy would not be able to hold me long in remembrance. I would not that anything I love should forget me. They kindly gave me memorials of their regard, which I hold above all price."

Ere he left he kissed the little ones all round; and Messrs. Goodell, Dwight, and Hullock, accompanied Newman and Kitto to the beach; the first-named gentleman going on board and dining with them. Mr. Shepherd, whose strength had been exhausted

* *Lost Senses—Deafness*, pp. 120, 121.

by the long journey, and by severe and protracted rheumatism, was carried to the vessel " on a kind of wheelbarrow." When the captain joined them, he saluted Kitto with nautical freedom, told him " how highly he regarded him, and that he looked quite a different person in his European dress." " I replied," says Kitto, " that I believed I was much the same for all that. He said he believed so too. As he thought well of me before, doubtless this was intended for a compliment. I confess I did not feel it as such. He also told Mr. Shepherd, that if he did not get better I should take his sweetheart. I told him that my heart was too sour to be sweetened even by a sweetheart; and that, at all events, the lady would prefer Shepherd sick to Kitto well." The captain's blunt humour was ominous, though no one at the time gave any thought to his prediction. Certainly not Kitto, for he heaves a sigh and adds, " Now then, ' once more upon the waters,' God speed us ! I confess that I have a fancy running about in my head for several days, that I shall never land in England." The captain told his passengers some exaggerated stories about pirates, which so greatly frightened the harmless Kitto, that he jots down in his Journal, " If a skirmish arises and any one is killed, I think it will be myself, and I never cared less about such a result." The dark sensations of an earlier period were returning, for he was coming home without any cheering anticipations of literary employment and reward. But reading and conversation with Mr. Newman beguiled the weary hours on the billow. " I am," he records, " annoyed by the short tacks in traversing the Hellespont. Soon after I fix myself in the sun, the new tack puts me under the shadow of the sails, and obliges me to shift my position. I love the sunshine, and whatever man may deny of the world's sunshine, of God's man cannot deprive the poorest and the humblest."

The Journal of the voyage to London is filled with reports of Mr. Newman's sayings and criticisms, not forgetting the ordinary incidents of weather and sailing, and the capture on one occasion of three turtles —" a glorious day's sport." The vessel passed near to Malta, the scene of his former painful residence; yet he says, " I should feel less pleasure in reaching London than in touching at Valetta. In the last place I have many friends; in the former few indeed, if any. God bless them for all their kindness to me while I remained among them. A beautiful sunshiny day, notwithstanding the high wind. I wonder how it is that Sunday is generally the sunniest day in the week, in every country I have been in, and every sea I have been on."

The vessel skirted the Spanish shore, and by the middle of May the snowy mountains of Granada appeared in sight. But the spectacle, like everything else at this period, only tended to depress him, by recalling previous emotions, and he writes as if in bitterness :—

" They are the same as when I first saw them ; but oh ! how changed am I, and all things in my retrospections of the past, and my hopes of the future. When I first beheld them, they were the first high, the first snowy mountains I had seen, and my heart was open entirely to their beauty. I have seen others since, more high, more beautiful, more grand ; and they now interest more, from the recollection of what I formerly felt than what I feel now. When I saw them first, I thought, too, that other eyes than mine would soon look upon them and admire, but those eyes never saw them, and are now shut up in the darkness of the grave, and left my own only open to see the desolation of all my hopes and blessings."

The captain, mate, and some of the crew, pleased Kitto immensely by their literary taste—their anxious perusal of Shakspere, and particularly of Spenser.

" May 28.—I was interested yesterday, and on former occasions, to see one of the sailors engaged in reading one of the cheap editions of Shakspere, which belongs to himself. I perceived that the last time he was reading *All's Well that Ends Well.* Verily, it is something to talk of, when our common mariners find pleasure in such books as Shakspere and the Faery Queen. My edition of the latter is in two volumes, and I can hardly keep one for my own use, so anxious is every one to read in it. The mate has read both volumes once through, and yet snatches up a volume whenever I lay it down on deck. The captain has got through the first, and now begins the second. The same man who reads Shakspere borrowed the second volume of me, which, when he had done, I lent him the first; but the captain, who wished to read it, made him give it back again. I am really afraid, in dispensing the loan of my Spenser, of giving offence, by my partiality. Now the first volume is vacant, the captain having done with it, yet I am rather afraid of giving it back to the man from whom it was taken, lest I should offend the mate. I trust my Spenser will not generate a mutiny."

On June 2, the cliffs of England were hailed, but " only *pro forma* " by Kitto, and " with no very impetuous emotions :"—

" June 4.—Close by land ; two miles perhaps. We saw a white cliff, which, said the mate, was Beachy Head, with Hastings beyond; but which turned out to be the Culver Cliff of the Isle of Wight, so that we are actually gone a good way back with the current since I went to bed. Lovely England ! who can view thy beautiful shores, and think of what they enclose, and what thou art, and what thou mightest be, without being proud that he is an Englishman ? I cannot, and would not. And, albeit my heart has gathered sterner stuff around it than it once had, it cannot but feel deeply and strongly in looking on these shores once more, that I had not hoped to see so soon."

Still later, and when the shores of England were smiling before him, he inserts in his Journal :—" How happy should I be now, were it not for the uncertainty that hangs over my future prospects." Then nerving himself, he subjoins, in pithy terms :—" God help me : the struggle—a death struggle—comes."

The coasts of Sussex and Kent interested him :—

" Oh, when I look thus intently on the verdant fields, velvet greens, fine trees, and pleasant villages of my own land, the beauties and excellencies of all others fade before me, and I say to myself, what I have often said, ' Who that can live *in* England, would live *out* of it ?' I return to the land I have loved, and I see few possible inducements before me to make me leave it again. I have already wandered more than nine hundred and ninety men in a thousand, and am content to think I have wandered enough ; but if it be not so, let me for the future wander from one of her own pleasant scenes to another, and from one of her bright cities to another.

" Passing Dungeness, with its conspicuous high red lighthouse, and a place which does not seem more than a village to a spectator from the sea, and Hythe and Folkestone, we came to *Shakspere's Cliff*, below the town of Dover. It is probably a unique circumstance that a place should be called after the name of a poet who had described it. Dover Castle is a very fine object ; as fine as any of the Turkish castles on the Bosphorus and Dardanelles, and finer."

The ship, being laden with silk, was obliged to lie under the law of quarantine in Stangate Creek. Mr. Shepherd had gradually sunk during the voyage ; and though he was immediately and kindly taken into the physician's own vessel for better treatment, he died on the evening after his removal. Kitto had been charged by him, in the prospect of his death, with some tender messages, tokens, and farewells to the lady to whom he had been engaged, and whom he was coming home to wed. He sets down, in his minute record, that there came to the doctor's ship, at Mr. Shepherd's decease, the father and brother of Miss F., his intended bride. The elder of the two was a " venerable gentleman ;" and the latter he thus sketches :—
" I recognized the younger as the brother of poor Shepherd's betrothed from his resemblance to the portrait which S. had of the lady. I did not," he quietly concludes, " introduce myself to them, but when relieved from quarantine shall do so, in compliance with the wishes to that effect expressed by poor S." How he discharged this melancholy task, and with what romantic result, will be seen in the sequel.

It was on Friday, June 12, 1829, that Kitto left Gravesend for the East, and four years all but a day after—that is, on June 11, 1833—Mr. Shepherd's funeral took place. The body, enclosed in " a coffin without a plate, and with pieces of rope for handles," was taken on shore by the sailors, and buried close to the water's edge, the other two vessels in quarantine, the " Nymph " and the " Leander," wearing their colours half-mast high, while the doctor's servant read a portion of the burial service. The piece of ground selected for interment had its *uses* indicated by what the captain called " *wooden tombstones*," there being only two of them, and both dated 1832. One is tempted to ask if the captain now remembered his prediction, made when his ship was weighing anchor at Constantinople ? The outburst of his hilarity may have been forgotten by himself, but as it rose to the memory of John Kitto, he imagined and pondered.

By the end of June the vessel was dismissed from quarantine, and Kitto once more rejoiced in being at home in England. His sensations at this period were afterwards touchingly portrayed by himself :—

" Only those who have spent years in distant lands can tell the yearning of the heart for one's native country—the craving, increasing in intensity as time passes, to return to its loved shores—to live there a few more years before life closes, and at last to die in our own nest.

' 'Tis distance lends enchantment to the view.'

Distance of either place or time lends this enchantment to the view which the mind takes of the far-off or long forsaken home ; and not less to the returned exile than to the man long sick, when he ' breathes and walks again '—

' The common sun, the air, the skies,
To him are opening paradise.'

But the feeling is more enduring ; for if one is at length privileged to return to his own land, he finds that land has acquired an interest in his eyes which age cannot wither nor use exhaust. This is not speculation, but experience ; for the writer can declare that, after some years of absence in the far-off lands of the morning, with little thought or intention of ever returning, and after the first agonizing rapture of greeting once more his natal soil had subsided, he has not ceased, during nineteen years, to feel it as a joy and a privilege, which has in its measure been a balm to many sorrows, to dwell in this land ; and he has experienced a constant intensity of enjoyment in the mere fact of existence in it, which had not formerly been imagined, and which only the facts of privation and comparison can enable one thoroughly to realize."*

* *Daily Bible Illustrations* Vol. 2, p. 330.

He narrates to Mr. Woollcombe * his first experiences on returning :—

"My poor mother will have it to be a miracle that I have at last returned in safety. I would not say so; but, believing in a special Providence, as I think you do, I do feel that I owe my life to its protection under all the varieties of danger to which I have been exposed since I left my native land. I desire to be enabled, by my future life, to express the thankfulness I ought to feel for the most undeserved mercies which I have received. I will only just mention, that the first event which happened within a quarter of an hour after my landing, was to have my pocket picked of a silk pocket-handkerchief."

He also tells this correspondent how, as the result of his eastern life, he felt amazed at first on seeing women walking unveiled, and averted his eyes when a lady passed; but archly adds, "this is nearly off already, and I run into the other extreme, of looking at every one that passes; and, verily, in walking from Barnsbury Park to the turnpike gate, I see more lovely countenances than in all the four years of my second absence, and in all my wanderings from Dan to Beersheba."

His residence in an eastern climate had somewhat darkened his face:—

"Those who do not know me often take me for a foreigner, and to this mistake, perhaps, my complexion, browned by the various suns of the East, not a little conduces." †

Somewhat later he writes to Lady M'Neill, at Tehran :—

"I had understood that the world had been turned upside down while I had been out of it in the East; but when I came back, no other tokens of change were at once visible to the naked eye, than new churches, bridges, and streets; and of the Reform Bill itself, no other indication was immediately apparent besides "Reform" inns, coffee-houses, coaches, and shaving-shops. In whatever else the people of all classes differ, in one thing they all agree, that the times are bad. I am sure I believe so; for ever since I can remember, I never heard any one say that they were good; and I question if the Wandering Jew himself, in all the ages he has lived, and all the countries he has travelled, ever once heard that they were. Maybe some simple lads and lasses, during some hours of their wedding-day, may have thought so: but even they soon found out that the times were bad—as bad as they could be, and worse than they ever were."

Toward the beginning of July, as if by a fascination which he could not resist, he had established himself in lodgings at Islington. The era of preparation was

over, and that of active labour was about to commence. He had little doubt of being able to secure a maintenance if any engagement should be open to him. It mattered not to him what toil it should cost, for he had braced himself

"To scorn delights and live laborious days."

He had already advised his friends in Plymouth of his return, asking their assistance in securing for him some remunerative employment, and Mr. Lampen and Mr. Woollcombe at once responded to the earnest appeal of the returned wanderer.

9

LONDON—FIRST LITERARY ENGAGEMENTS—PICTORIAL BIBLE

AND what had Kitto gained by those travels, from which he was now resting?

At an early period in his career, and when he was dreaming of the future, rather than earnestly training himself for it, he had freely expressed his opinion as to the theoretic advantages of travel. He hoped to visit the continent and some "interesting parts of the island," in company with some person who would not think him an incumbrance. "Important advantage would accrue to me from travel," he remarks, "viz., it will enable me to write, with the confidence of personal observation, of the characters and natural and artificial productions of other parts of Britain and Europe." * This was but a modest desire, for he had then only a limited object in view. Any one who had seen him a few months before he made this statement, within the walls of the workhouse, and plying his trade with undisturbed assiduity, would have thought him as firmly fixed to Plymouth for life, as the limpets to the rocks on its shores. He never travelled, indeed, as he originally contemplated, for he passed through various foreign countries, not to see them, but only to reach a distant point beyond them. He never was a traveller in the same sense in which Robinson and Livingstone are travellers—men who make a journey with an avowed and definite geographical purpose. He sailed and rode to the East in order to get to Bagdad, and he rode and sailed to the West in order to get to London. But his experiences of travelling cooled his earlier ardour. Though he prized the results, he did not relish the process of obtaining them. "To have travelled is a very fine thing, but it is not a very fine thing to travel"—is his language to Mr. Harvey. † Three months afterwards

* Upper John Street, Islington, July 8, 1833.
† "Deaf Traveller, I."—Penny Magazine, Vol. II., p. 310.

* Letter to Mr. Harvey, Public Library, Plymouth, August 7, 1823.
† Bagdad, September 25, 1831.

he declares to Mr. Burnard * more emphatically :— "I hate action, I hate travel, unless, indeed, I must travel; and by and bye I must." Yet, on his progress homeward, he makes another revelation to Mr. Woollcombe :—" As to travelling, it will be borne in mind, that I am not travelling as a traveller; and in the way I have travelled, I never would travel, except on business, again. If I do not marry, it by no means appears to me that I may not travel again. But my ideas of future travel are vague and remote, and at all events will in a great measure depend, in their consequences, on the direction given to the current of my life on reaching England." †

Though a dark hour sometimes passed over him, as toward the end of his residence in Bagdad, the moral influence of his travels was certainly healthful. His own acknowledgment in his Journal, under March 12, 1831, is—

"I assured Mr. Pfander that, though there were some circumstances that did not quite satisfy me in coming abroad, I rejoiced, upon the whole, in having done so; for this one reason among others, that my love of mankind has been more extended than under any other circumstances it probably would have been. When I left England, I had a general disgust, if not contempt, toward mankind, fully including myself; I despised men for being what I thought they were, and I hated myself for being like them. My personal associations, even with religious people, had not been happy, nor had much tended to raise my respect and love for their character. But the many truly excellent and amiable individuals I have become acquainted with since I left England, have brought round my feeling to a more healthy tone."

Kitto had also made no little intellectual gain by his journeyings and residence in the East. The extracts from his Letters and Journals, which fill so much of the three preceding chapters, sufficiently attest his powers of observation and his habits of reflection. Whatever he saw interested him; whatever befell him excited inquiry. His eye was ever busy, and was never "satisfied with seeing;" nay, it had acquired a special dexterity in taking in a large panorama, and photographing an indelible image of it on the memory. Customs and habits so different from those of England arrested his attention, and led him to study humanity under "new aspects of society and forms of life." His mind was enlarged, and his stock of information greatly increased. " Facts and images" were laid up, and he distinctly knew "some things which the untravelled can only conceive."‡ In spite of his deafness, he had made himself acquainted with all he wished to know.

Indeed, the appetite of his youth retained its eagerness in his maturer years, for he thus limns himself in a miniature portrait of his boyhood.

"At a very early period of life, and in the midst of untoward circumstances, and of occupations which left me the least possible leisure, I was a diligent collector of all the odds and ends of knowledge that fell in my way. I read all the bills that were posted on dead walls and empty houses. I studied all the title-pages and open leaves that appeared in the windows of booksellers' shops; joyfully hailing the day when the windows of a particular shop were cleaned, and a change of books and pictures introduced. Sometimes, also, when I was allowed a little leisure, I brushed myself up as smart as possible, and ventured so far on the respectability of my appearance as to make the tour of the book-stalls, pausing at each; and, after dallying a little "about it and about it," taking up some humble looking volume, and devouring so much as was possible of the information it afforded, with the utmost intensity of appetite, and all the excitement that attends a stolen enjoyment. In process of time, I knew well the state of every bookstall, and could tell at a glance what books had been sold, and what additions had been made since my last visit; and many severer troubles in my subsequent life have made my heart ache less than sometimes to find a book gone, from which I had calculated on gleaning more information on a second occasion than my first spell at it had enabled me to obtain. I knew perfectly the dispositions of every proprietor of a stall in the three towns of Plymouth, Devonport, and Stonehouse, and could tell to a minute how long I might dabble at his books before he would look sour; and in process of time, most of the stall-men, on their part, became habituated to me, and came to regard me as a tolerated nuisance, or as one of the customary inconveniences incident to the trade."*

What the youth had been, the man was still, but the curious boy had become the inquisitive traveller; gratifying the same desires on a larger scale, and with proportionate results. He had "laid up in store against the time to come," and that time was now at hand. He had also been qualifying himself for literary labour, for his pen had not been idle at Bagdad. He tells Mr. Harvey, 25th September 1831, that he was "preparing an account of the cities, towns, etc., between the Mediteranean and the Indus, which claim the attention of a missionary," and that, for this purpose, he was in correspondence with missionaries in Armenia and Syria, having, at the same time, collected nearly all the information which Major Taylor's library could supply, and being also in daily expectation of books from England. Hosts of Essays, Tales,

* Bagdad, December, 1831.
† Tehran, October 30, 1832.
‡ Letter to Mr. Woollcombe, Bagdad, December 15, 1831.

* *Penny Magazine*, Vol. IV., p. 171.

Dialogues, Disquisitions, Allegories, and Sketches, had also been thrown off by him.* Shut out from human intercourse, he was necessitated to give shape to his ideas, and body forth his imaginings, so that by the time he returned to England, he had acquired great facility of composition, and found it a comparatively easy matter to give expression to his teeming thoughts and reminiscences.

On being settled down in London, Kitto, as in time past, displayed uncommon ingenuity in devising plans for himself, though, as was usual with him, he was apt to overlook their feasibility. What appeared most plausible to his own mind, sometimes failed to commend itself to the judgment of others. But if one scheme failed, he had no hesitation in proposing or adopting another. Anything rather than rely on bounty, or be abandoned to total idleness. "Language would fail to describe all the anxieties I felt on my return about a temporal provision. Many dear plans of my own were in a short time blown to atoms, and I was sinking down into despondency."† But he was, sooner than he expected, relieved from his distress, and he entered at once on that career which grew in brightness as it extended in usefulness, till the gloom of the sepulchre was suddenly thrown over it.

Through the influence of his friends, Kitto was brought under the notice of the Society for the Diffusion of Useful Knowledge, of which Lord Brougham, then Lord Chancellor, was president, Sir Henry Parnell, and afterwards Lord John Russell, vice-president, with a large committee of high and honoured names in London and throughout the provinces. In July, Mr. Woollcombe gave him a note of introduction to Mr. Coates, the secretary, recommending him for employment. On the 18th of that month, he waited on Mr. Coates, and handed him a written proposal to give a brief account of his travels, in the shape of weekly numbers, like the *Penny Magazine*, or of volumes in the Library of Entertaining Knowledge. Mr. Coates told him that the latter alternative could not be adopted, but referred him to Mr. Charles Knight, the editor and publisher of these popular serials. On the 19th he wrote to Mr. Knight, stating

his willingness to make up papers from his Journals for the *Penny Magazine*, and on the 20th he had a personal interview. After the exchange of a few letters, and the presentation of a few approved specimens of his composition, he became a regular contributor to the *Penny Magazine*—a rich collection of miscellanies, read, it was supposed, by a million of people in England, besides being reprinted in America, and translated into French, German, and Dutch.

The rate of remuneration was a guinea and a half per page, but he was limited to two or three columns weekly. His first two contributions appeared in the same number for the 10th of August—one a collection of Arabian proverbs, and the other a paper introductory to his travels. Its title is "The Deaf Traveller," and it is headed with the following editorial explanation :— " We have much pleasure in placing before our readers the first of a series of papers which, we think, will be found highly interesting, not only from their intrinsic merit, but from the peculiar circumstances of the writer. These circumstances he has described in the following introductory account of himself. We have only to add, that the writer has been introduced to the notice of the Society by a valuable member of one of the local committees, who is fully aware of his singular history." Some interest attaches to this paper as the first-born of so many successors in many walks of literature. Kitto gives in it a succinct account of his previous life. " There are circumstances in my condition which would exonerate me from censure, had I nothing at all to say, or less than I really have. It is not yet a month since I returned to my native shores. I made a pause at the first book-shop, and the *Penny Magazine* attracted my gaze. . . . Some of the papers I had purchased at the shop I skimmed over on my way home, cutting open the leaves with my forefinger for want of a knife ; and before I reached my lodgings I felt that I should like to have to do with some of these publications, particularly the *Penny Magazine*, in which I felt an especial interest.* . . . I have certainly in the course of my life been in very remarkable and interesting situations, but I remember few more interesting than that in which I am now placed, whilst talking to a million of people about myself." Referring to his past days, he makes this further disclosure :—"Though, with a painful effort, I *could* speak, I seldom uttered five words in the course of a week for several years. I always said the little I had to say in writing, and I know not whether it be not to this circumstance I owe that habit of composition which now enables me to address the readers of the *Penny Magazine*. . . .

* The following are the titles of some of his compositions, which range over a great variety of topics—"The Seals of the Kaliphs;" "On the Mendicant Orders;" "The Astrologer;" "Caligraphy;" "Mahomet Ali Khan;" "The Principle;" "Maria Bell;" "The Modern Student;" "Ancient Student;" "Sights and Insights;" the "Silver Spoon;" "The Chrystal;" "The Angel of the Ruby;" "Hot-Cross Buns;" "Recollections and Collections about Malta;" "Language;" "On a Future State of Being;" "Chosrou;" "Plague of Bagdad;" "Childhood;" "Hubert and Eleanora;" "The Stars;" "Geographical Queries;" "Lella;" "Bastan;" "London in 2417;" the "Young Astrologer;" "Blindness;" "Persia;" "Farewell to Malta," a Poem; "Lylan;" "Hebrew names of God," &c., &c.

† Letter to Lady M'Neill, Tehran. London, August 12, 1833.

* On his return from Malta in 1829, the first place he stopped at was a bookshop, but his eye fell on the following title-page, " A Treatise on the Art of Tying the Cravat."

I have endeavoured to keep one object steadily in view —the acquirement of such information and general knowledge as I found open to me in the midst of much occupation, and of difficulties which, though so considerably different from those of my earlier life, have often been very great."

He was now fairly harnessed for work, and began to reap the fruit of his toils and travels, his consistent behaviour, and his honest perseverance. Writing from Bagdad to Mr. Woollcombe, July 21, 1832, he expressed his gratitude, and gave as the reason : "For you have waited so patiently and so long to see whether the wild and rude plant you assisted to transplant and water, would at last become fruitful." His introduction, through the same friend, to the Useful Knowledge Society, had now produced at least promising first-fruits. His contributions being so acceptable, and his month of virtual probation being successfully passed, Mr. Knight offered him a general engagement at a salary which Kitto thankfully accepted, saying, "the terms offered would be sufficient, not only for my present, but for my prospective wants." What occurred during the interview which led to this arrangement, is artlessly told by himself.

"Mr. Knight said, 'I am perfectly satisfied with what you have done, and only fear you may feel such employment dull ; but I trust its usefulness will in time make it pleasant to you.' I also spoke on the subject of my independent contributions to the *Penny Magazine*, as The Deaf Traveller, etc. You have perceived that my papers have been few and far between ; and as I thought this might be from fear of tiring the readers, by the frequent recurrence of the same subject, I expressed the satisfaction I should feel in being permitted to fill up with other subjects the intervals between the various papers of The Deaf Traveller. Mr. Knight said he would be glad if I did so ; but the reason The Deaf Traveller had not come in more frequently, was the fear that I had not exactly hit his meaning in preparing the papers. I had better take some one subject, and bring my collected information to bear upon it, rather than carry the readers on from stage to stage, as in a book of travels. 'I do not say, don't write a book,' Mr. Knight remarked, 'for that is a different matter, but don't write a book for the *Penny Magazine*.' I am now preparing the papers on this principle."

Kitto was also to take a certain charge of the *Penny Cyclopædia*, suggesting new words or additions, looking through German, French, and Italian books of reference, and answering letters of contributors. He was somewhat dismayed by the prospect, but Mr. Knight very kindly encouraged him, and told him, that "his zeal would overcome all difficulties." This task necessitated his personal attendance for seven hours

daily in Ludgate Street. "I sit," he boasts to Mr. Harvey,[*] "in Mr. Knight's room, with plenty of books about me, and more below. Whatever spare time the *Penny Magazine* does not require is spent in perfecting my knowledge of French and Italian, and in acquiring German." Though he entered on his labours with some anxiety, he was soon enabled to go through them with credit. No one knew better than Mr. Knight what contributions were adapted to such periodical literature as that which he was issuing, and Kitto was therefore under a kind and able monitor. Mr. Knight gently checked his strong propensity to dwell on a subject, and work it out to a disproportionate length.[†] Kitto was now as busy as he could desire, doing whatever was required of him—abridging, compiling, translating, as well as composing original articles. The *Penny Magazine* was largely indebted to his pen, and the *Penny Cyclopædia* to his care. His pecuniary income was considerable, and had every appearance of steadiness and increase. He had climbed long and bravely, and he was now but a few steps from the summit.

When the vessel which had brought him from Constantinople was casting anchor in Stangate Creek, he concluded a section of his Journal with this racy soliloquy :—"Give me a little house, a little wife, a little child, and a little money in England, and I will seek no more, and wander no more."

In a few days after, this aspiration assumed a practical aspect, and in a manner quite as peculiar and striking as had been the previous steps of his life. Bitter disappointment with a bride who had deserted him, wedded another, and then died in sorrow and remorse, sent him to the East; and now, when he had returned, the mysterious hand of death brought him into connection with the betrothed of a fellow-passenger, who had sickened on the journey, and expired within sight of the shores of England. For Mr. Shepherd, who had died when the vessel was lying in quarantine, had charged Kitto with several bequests and memorials for Miss Fenwick, the lady to whom he had been long engaged. Mr. Newman and Kitto made their first visit together to express their condolence—the former relating to the lady all the painful circumstances, while, according to her own description, Kitto "sat all the time mute, the very image of sympathy." Such an interview did not suffice for Kitto, for he had private matters, both of Mr. Shepherd's and of his own, to talk about. The whole circumstances of the drama, so touching and so strange, had impressed Kitto very deeply, and disposed him to forecast

* August 18, 1833.
† Thus, at a later period, the *Cyclopædia of Biblical Literature*, and the *Daily Readings*, grew to double the size originally agreed on.

"whereunto this would grow." For attachment was springing out of the melancholy adventure; and he had learned to love her,

> ". . . Though her thoughts are straying
> To one who sleeps the dreamless sleep
> Of death; though midst her sighs are playing
> The hopes o'er which her visions weep."

Again he called upon her, and again, and found her, as he describes the result of his interviews to his friend, Lady M'Neill, to be "a very interesting person, with much information and more understanding. The loss she takes more sadly than I should have expected, and, of course, she will henceforth 'wither on the virgin thorn for ever.' So she thinks—not I, knowing, as I do, that no intense feeling can be lasting, or any resolutions permanent, which are formed under their influence. I believe our minds are wisely and well thus constituted. I remember the time when I had firmly made up my mind to die an old bachelor, but now, if I find any one who will have me, nothing is further from my intention."

He knew by the time he wrote these words that there was one not averse to him, nay, that he had found one who was willing to have him. My "sympathy," he says to Mr. Lampen, in reference to his first errand, "made my company pleasant to her; and though I did not for some time think of her in any particular way, she won upon me by her modes of thinking, her correct feeling, and strong and accomplished mind. She was ultimately led to think that she might find happiness with me." The wooing— the success of which he owed to some extent to his innate persistence—had all but accomplished its object, when he felt that it behoved him to try to learn the probable amount, and especially to ascertain the certainty of his future income. There was only one way of coming to a satisfactory conclusion on the delicate subject, and that was by sounding his employer. Accordingly, on the 13th of September, he wrote a confidential letter to Mr. Knight, freely stating his position, and his anxiety to be assured about his prospects of work and pay. The main question was thus put—"Whether my engagement with you is one which *you* wish me to retain? . . . I should say, there is nothing I desire more than to remain." Mr. Knight returned a satisfactory answer, and Kitto's heart was rejoiced beyond measure. Every impediment was thus easily removed, and the charge of imprudence could not be urged against the step which he was about to take. What he had so intensely longed for—a hearth and home of his own—was now to be attained. The cup had been dashed from his lips before, but again it was filled to overflowing. The happy day was at length fixed, and accordingly, on the 21st of September, and at Christ's Church,

Newgate Street, was solemnized the marriage of John Kitto and Annabella Fenwick. The church was under repairs at the time, and the workmen being obliged to suspend their noisy operations during the ceremony, became its amused spectators. The bridegroom afforded them some merriment which they were scarcely able to conceal, for more than once, from his deafness, he got before the officiating clergyman, and had to be recalled to the actual duty which the course of the service devolved upon him. The day of his marriage was the famous St. Matthew's day, and as the civic dignitaries of London were on their annual visit of ceremony to Christ's Hospital "next door," there was no small stir in the neighbourhood. The bridegroom wondered much at the bustle, especially at the Lord Mayor's "fine coach" waiting without, but could not at the time divine the reason. Yet the lively scene was not forgotten, and many years afterwards he referred to it on occasion of the admission of one of his boys to the great educational institution, jocularly remarking, that the time, place, and circumstances of their father's marriage seemed to give them some claim upon it.

This new connection added unspeakably to Kitto's happiness, and contributed in no ordinary degree to his usefulness. At the termination of the honeymoon, he rejoices to proclaim, "she now thinks she has found happiness, and I hope to give her no cause to think otherwise. I have now a fireside of my own to sit down by, and on the other side is my wife darning stockings." But she was not allowed to keep long by such domestic employment, for her time, during some years, was largely occupied in gathering literary materials for her busy husband. She daily visited the British Museum with him; and each, in that ample repository, pursued a separate path, he plying his immediate task, and she amassing materials for other meditated productions. She was the lion's provider, and was obliged to cater liberally among all sorts of authors, living and dead; for, as his den was a scene of uncommon voracity, his daily prey required a skilful and diligent purveyor.

If the previous pages indicate that Kitto was alive to female charms, other portions of his writings show his high appreciation of the sex, on which he has pronounced many noble and graceful eulogies. He has recorded his sentiments more than once, and that towards the last years of his life. For example, the history of Samson suggests to him, that "reliance upon the tenderness and truth of woman's nature is not in itself a bad quality; nay, it is a fine, manly, and heroic quality—and we may be allowed to regret that Samson fell into hands which rendered it a snare, a danger, and a death to him." [*]

[*] *Daily Bible Illustrations* Vol. 1, p. 554.

Or, again, he has thrown out this striking sentiment :—

"But not to dwell further on particular instances, it may be well worth our while to note one great matter that deserves to be mentioned to their praise, and to be kept in everlasting remembrance. We have read of men once held in high esteem, who became apostates —Demas, Alexander, Philetus, and others; but never, by name, in all the New Testament, of a woman who had once been reckoned among the saints. This is great honour. But not only have women been thus honoured with extraordinary gifts; they have been otherwise favoured with special marks of attention from the Lord. To whom but unto women did Christ first appear after His resurrection? Of what act did He ever so speak as to render it everlastingly memorable, save that woman's, who poured upon His feet her alabaster box of precious ointment; and to whom He promised that, wherever, in the whole world, His Gospel should be preached, there should her work of faith be held in remembrance?" *

Or, still further, in vindication of Job's wife, and against the opinions which some commentators have formed of her words, translated in the English version, "Curse God and die," he protests right cheerily :—

"It was telling him that death was his best friend; that it was better for him to die than to live a life like this. Such a life was a continual death; and it were better to die at once than to die daily. Now, as many ladies are among our readers, we will at once ask them, if this is a true or probable explanation? We will feel assured that they will at once say it is not; that this is not the language which any true-hearted wife would hold to her afflicted husband, and that the advice is not 'wholesome,' as this explanation supposes. It is the ingenious speculation of dry old scholars, shut up among their books, and not of men knowing anything about the hearts of wives." †

Kitto's work with Mr. Knight was somewhat multifarious, but he was pleased with it. For a time, indeed, he walked "fearfully and tremblingly," but he gradually gained confidence and courage. Toward the close of this eventful year, on December 9, 1833, he gives some recital of his experience to Mr. Woollcombe.

"52 St. John's Road, Islington.

". . . With me things have gone on as smoothly as I could reasonably expect. . . I have to bring into admissible form the contributions of correspondents, whose letters I also answer. In this last employment I have great occasion to feel how much I owe to your kind recommendation, as I have often to write for Mr. Knight, declining offers of assistance, which I cannot

* *Daily Bible Illustrations* Vol. 1, p. 579.
† Ibid., Vol. 2, p. 49.

sometimes help thinking, would be more efficient than my own. I am happy to hope that I have not altogether discredited your recommendation, and I trust that I shall not. I find my employments so very congenial, and my facilities in them increase so rapidly, that I think often that I have at last been enabled, through your kindness, to find my proper place and level. . . There is a letter of Mr. Groves in the *Record* newspaper of last Thursday. I am sorry to say that no letter from him has yet come into my hands. I have been poorly lately."

The next year, 1834, was passed in similar industry, his remuneration being £18 a month. Still, as his work grew familiar to him, he contemplated some other and future tasks; nay, as labours multiplied upon him he "sang in his heart." At length more than half the Magazine was of his preparing, and he avers, with some exultation, "all the papers I write now are printed." Books for children held a prominent place in his projected authorship, of which *Uncle Oliver's Travels in Persia* is a favourable specimen. His articles being printed anonymously, he was saved from the imputation of inordinately thirsting for a name. He was all the while acquiring practice for higher achievements, for he was training himself to harmonise compactness with detail. The brief and uniform limits of the Magazine constrained him to proportion the space he occupied to the differential value of his topics. The hardest lesson he had to learn was that of literary perspective, and he never thoroughly mastered it; nay, he almost complains, that "the readers of the *Penny Magazine* are so accustomed to condensation, that they cannot bear details."

During this year was born his eldest child, Annabella Shireen—the second name being a reminiscence of his Persian travels. She was a source of new joy to him, and he had a thousand happy ways of delighting and amusing her in her infancy. When the little lady gave any sign of being gratified, he would at once turn to her mother and say (with what a tone !) "Does she make a noise? Pray tell me what kind of noise it makes." The tear starts in the eye on reading these touching words. He complains seldom, but ah ! he utters a deep and mournful sigh as he thinks of "children's voices, and the sweet peculiarities of infantile speech," and then points to his daily sorrow and privation as he sat among his darlings, being doomed "to *see* their blessed lips in motion, and to *hear* them not."

The materials to be employed in Biblical illustration had for a period been stored up in Kitto's mind; but as yet no outlet had been found for them. He had, however, some notion of their value, and of their adaptation to general purposes. But his plans had been overruled. Yet the germ of the *Pictorial Bible*

lies in the following statement :—"I am to undertake
the description of remarkable things and customs in
foreign countries, beginning with those in which I
have actually travelled.   It was the very thing I
wanted to do when I first came home."   This idea,
which was still uppermost, only received a special
direction when the *Pictorial Bible* was edited.   The
light which would have been scattered on a variety of
points, grew brighter and steadier by its concentration
on Scripture.   At a later epoch, after he had acquired
"celebrity," and when "black mail" was freely levied
upon him, though not to the extent he sometimes imagined, he indicated the peculiar source of his superiority and power by the avowal, "Nothing in fine
saves me from being smothered by my own children,
but the certainty of *actual knowledge* which my residence and travels in the East confer." *   This "actual
knowledge" was his tower of strength.   For the description of a veritable eye-witness differs usually from
that of a mere compiler, as much as a green garland
from a faded chaplet.   He who has seen the animal
killed and cooked by one continuous process, and has
partaken himself of the feast, diving into the pillau
of rice or barley with his naked hand, and fetching up
his morsel, can paint the festive scene with a few vivid
touches, as he illustrates Abraham's hospitality, or
give an edge to Solomon's proverb about the slothful
man's hiding his hand in the dish, that is, not using his
three fingers, as is generally done, but so filling his
whole palm at once, and loading it, as to save such
repeated motion.†   The flesh of animals is in the East
more a luxury than an article of daily food, and men
are cautioned in Scripture against being "riotous
eaters" of it.   The Arab, as often as he can, does feed
himself to satiety, but the spectator can add his own
humorous touch :—

"We have often had occasion to witness a meal of
meat indulged in under such circumstances, to a degree
of inconceivable intemperance, and enjoyed with a
degree of hilarity very much like that which attends
the consumption of strong drink in our northern
climates.   We have the Arabs more especially, but
not exclusively, in view; for it is in connection with
this people that the present expression, "riotous eaters
of flesh," has been brought most forcibly to our mind,
on beholding the strong and irrepressible satisfaction
with which a party of them would receive the present
of a live sheep, and on witnessing the haste with
which it was slaughtered and dressed, the voracity
with which it was devoured, and the high glee, not
unattended with dance and song, which seasoned the
feast.   We are almost afraid to say how much an un-

restricted Arab will eat when an opportunity is given.
It is commonly considered that an Arab can dispose of
the entire quarter of a sheep without inconvenience;
and we have certainly seen half-a-dozen of them pick
the bones of a large sheep very clean."*

The rider who has carried at his saddle the skin
filled with water or wine, or the guest who has been
cognisant of the Persian fashion of debauch, which
begins at sunrise, or before it, can give point to an
exposition either of the trick of the Gibeonites, or of
the prophet's denunciation, "Woe unto them that rise
up early in the morning, that they may follow strong
drink."   The invalid who has been unfortunately under
the hands of Oriental physicians, can speak from experience of their thirst for bleeding their patients with a
dull lancet, or a knife rudely made into the shape of
one, or of their fondness for the actual cautery with a
common iron nail, or a piece of wire."

The "publicans" of the New Testament, or officers
of inland revenue, were specially detested.   Why?
Let Kitto's experience declare :—

"It has not been our lot to be acquainted with any
country, the inhabitants of which are so alive to their
obligations to the State, as to receive with pleasure
and regard with respect the collectors of the revenue,
under whatever name they may come, whether tax-
gatherers, rate-collectors, excisemen, customhouse officers, or tollmen.   The popular dislike to this class of
public servants has always existed everywhere: and
in an eminent degree it has always existed, and does
exist, in the East, where the antipathy to anything
like a regular and periodical exaction for government
objects, goes far beyond the dogged churlishness, with
which the drilled nations of the West meet the more
complicated demands upon them.   This may, among
other causes, be owing to the fact, that the eastern
tax-gatherer feels quite at liberty to use his stick freely
upon the person of a tardy, inadequate, or too reluctant tax-payer."†

Speaking of the erroneous application of western
forms and ideas to eastern usages, and that in reference to the scene of the Saviour's birth, so inaccurately
handled by poets and painters, the pilgrim can affirm
from observation :—

"The explanation we give of this incident is founded
upon actual observation, made while ourselves, more
than once, were constrained to lodge in the stable,
because there was 'no room in the inn;' and was, in
fact, suggested in a place that led us to say, 'In such
a stable as this was Jesus born; here might have been
an excellent retreat for the Virgin; here she would be
completely screened from observation at the time it
was needed ; and here, in this very "manger," she

---

* Letter to Mr. Oliphant, October 30, 1851.
† The allusion is based upon a peculiar interpretation of
Proverbs 26:15.

* *Daily Bible Illustrations* Vol. 2, p. 169.
† Ibid., Vol. 2, p. 553.

might have found no unsuitable cot for her first-born son.' " *

The student who, one afternoon at Bagdad, had been startled from his book by a sudden obscuration of the sky, as if the sun had been eclipsed, and had ascertained the cause to be a cloud of locusts, black from its very thickness, and covering the city "like a pall," could not fail to be picturesque in his comment on the first and second chapters of Joel.

As to the character and effect of eastern salutations, one who had often made and returned them, with all their picturesque formality, is warranted to say :—

"The servile demeanour of the poor in this country is hateful to every well ordered mind. It has grown out of circumstances which there has been too little effort to resist; and we may go to the East to learn how the poor may be treated with courtesy, and be continually reminded, in every passing form of speech, of their natural and religious brotherhood, without being thereby encouraged to disrespect or insubordination, but with the effect of a cheerful and willing character being thereby imparted to obedience." †

The gaze that had frequently wandered over Asiatic fields, entitled the expositor to show the immense loss which the foxes let loose by Samson did to the harvest —thus :—

"The reader must recollect that the cultivated lands are not separated by hedgerows into fields as with us, but are laid out in one vast expanse, the different properties in which are distinguished by certain landmarks, known to the owners, but not usually obvious to a stranger. Thus, as the time of harvest approaches, the standing corn is often seen to extend as far as the eye can reach, in one vast unbroken spread of waving corn. Hence the flames, once kindled, would spread without check till all the corn of the locality was consumed; and we are further to remember, that there were fifty pairs let off, doubtless in different parts." ‡

The oratory at Philippi was by the river side, and the sojourner in remote Russia can quote an apposite illustration :—

"It is rare at the present time to witness worship by a number of persons under such circumstances, as they usually find other means for ablution; but it happened to us, that the first act of Moslem worship we ever witnessed, was thus performed. This was nearly a quarter of a century ago, in the Caucasian mountains, at a time when many Turkish prisoners of war were kept there by the Russians. Bodies of these were conducted, at the hours of prayer, under a guard of soldiers, to any open place traversed by a river, near the military stations, and after performing their ablutions at the stream, they prostrated themselves upon the green sward, and went through the several acts of their remarkably demonstrative worship." *

But not to multiply examples. Almost every one is aware how unlike an Oriental dwelling is to one among ourselves. But the wayfarer who has lived in both, can give a striking picture of the difference, and invest it, too, with an architectural interest.

"The probability is, that the majority of the houses of Nineveh, like those of many eastern cities of the present day, consisted but of one storey, spread therefore over a large extent of ground. We have always observed the Orientals to be exceedingly adverse to ascending stairs; and where ground is not an object, as it seldom is, they consider it absurd to build habitations in which they must be continually going up stairs and down, when they are at liberty to spread out their dwellings over the ground as widely as they like. Hence the accommodation which we secure by piling storey upon storey, they think they realize with much more advantage, by placing these storeys separately upon the ground, connecting them by doors, galleries, courts, and passages. This is their idea of comfort, and we must confess to being considerably of their opinion. The result is, however, that the house of an eastern gentleman in a town will generally occupy four or five times as much ground as that of an Englishman in the corresponding condition of life." †

These extracts are only a specimen of that full and exact illustration which one can adduce who "testifies what he has seen." Though they are taken from Dr. Kitto's last work, they show what stores he had at command for his earliest Biblical exposition. Sir John M'Neill gave him, when he met him at Tabreez, a peculiar illustration of the territorial meaning wrapt up in the phrase, "Jacob digged a well," by informing him, that in Persia the law enacted, that he who digs a well in the desert, is entitled to all the land which it will irrigate. Morier's *Second Journey through Persia*, also recommended to him by the same authority, contains numerous elucidations of customs and sayings in the Old Testament, some of them ambiguous, indeed, and others based on misconception, but the majority of them singularly perspicuous and happy, and many of them verified by the deaf yet sharp-eyed wanderer himself. It is true, indeed, that Kitto did not travel in Palestine ; but the East has an unvarying type among its Shemite races, and especially among those of the Syro-Arabian dialects. Manners are in

---

* *Daily Bible Illustrations* Vol. 2, p. 448.
† Ibid., Vol. 1, p. 586. **Dr. Kitto might have noticed that our own common forms of salutation had once a religious significance. Adieu, is a commendation to God ; and Good b'ye, is God be with thee.**
‡ Ibid., Vol. 1, p. 555.

* *Daily Bible Illustrations* Vol. 2, p. 809.
† Ibid., Vol. 2, p. 403.

many things the same on the banks of the Tigris as on those of the Jordan—the same among the children of Elam as among the children of Eber. What are often called Jewish customs are, apart from religion, not confined to Abraham's progeny through Isaac, but belong equally to his descendants through Ishmael. Dr. Ashael Grant forgot this truth in one part of his argument, when he endeavoured to prove that the Nestorian Christians are the remains of the Ten Tribes, from certain customs and ceremonies which, so far from being distinctive of Israel, are common to all the provinces of Western Asia.*

While Kitto wrought heartily on the *Penny Magazine* and other periodicals, he had not yet found his appropriate function. Still he was but a common literateur, and in that "line of things" would scarcely ever have been known beyond the immediate circle in which he moved. But when the hour came the man was ready. Exploring his dim and uncertain way towards his right sphere, he had been frequently and partially baffled, though he was constantly nearing it.

"The cygnet finds the water, but the man
Is born in ignorance of his element,
And feels out blind at first."

At this juncture, the active and enterprising mind of Mr. Knight, suggested the idea of an annotated Bible, and he thought that his man of all work was well qualified to write that portion of the notes which related to Oriental manners and life, and which his travels might help him to furnish. The plan at once rivetted Kitto's attention as something peculiarly fitted for him, and in which he could excel. He prepared a specimen, with which Mr. Knight was so pleased, that he resolved to gratify Kitto's earnest solicitations, and intrust him with the execution of the entire work. This decision was a wise one on the part of the publisher, and a happy one for the editor. Kitto thankfully owned Mr. Knight's kindness, as one "qualified beyond most men to judge of another's fitness," and he eulogizes his "generous confidence in intrusting to my untried hands a great and noble task, which others would have deemed to need the influence of some great name in literature."

This new experiment brought him at once into the field which he had been long preparing to occupy, and for the occupation of which much of his previous training and travels had really qualified him. Prior to that objective preparation which his eastern journey had given him, and along with it, there had been another and a superior discipline. The Bible had become to him the Book of Life. Before his fall from the house-top, he had regarded the Bible "as a book especially appointed to be read on Sundays," and had

not "ventured to look into it on any other day. It seemed a sort of profanation to handle the Sacred Book with work-day fingers." But, as he lay on that bed of slow convalescence, the exhaustion of his slender literary resources drove him to it, and then he read it, "quite through, Apocrypha and all." His studies from this period took a marked direction towards Theology. Works of a religious kind were found and devoured by him, such as Foxe's Martyrs, Josephus, Hervey's Meditations, Bunyan, Drelincourt, Baxter's Saint's Rest, Sturm's Reflections, and Watts' World to Come. In course of time, indeed, he extended his reading to a more miscellaneous class of books, and especially in the public library did he give himself to Metaphysics; yet he hints, that "amidst all this, the theological bias given by my earlier reading and associations remained."* But it was at Exeter that the "day-spring" for which he had long prayed arose upon him. Up to that time the Bible, he confesses, had been "a sealed book" to him, for the "instructing influences of the Holy Spirit did not attend" his reading of it, and he did not come to it "with the humble and teachable spirit of a little child." Now, and for some years, the inspired Word had been the food of his soul —the daily theme of that devout and earnest meditation which, "comparing spiritual things with spiritual," makes "wise unto salvation through faith which is in Christ Jesus."† So that, when in due time, he came to illustrate Scripture, he did it in the right spirit, and never forgot the divinity of the volume on whose pages he was lavishing so many literary and pictorial illustrations. Spiritual qualifications guarded and hallowed scholastic equipment.

The work, commencing in the end of 1835, was published in monthly parts, and completed in May 1838. During its progress Kitto "received £250 a-year, and when it was finished he was presented with an additional sum, which seemed to him a little fortune." ‡

The *Pictorial Bible* rose at once into high popularity. It was his first work in that department, and it led the way to all his subsequent productions. No sooner had he entered on this form of labour than—

"Almost thence his nature was subdued
To that it worked in, like the dyer's hand."

Little, indeed, had been previously done in this neglected province of illustration. There had been huge commentaries, and good ones too—the quaint and pithy Henry, the solid and judicious Scott, and the more erudite and ambitious volumes of Patrick, Lowth, Whitby, and Adam Clarke. These authors, however, had, to a great extent, treated Scripture in

---

* *The Nestorians; or, the Lost Tribes.* By Ashael Grant, M.D., chap. xviii. London, 1841.

* *Lost Senses—Deafness*, p. 14.   † Ibid., p. 16.
‡ Article "Kitto," in *Knight's English Cyclopædia*—Biography. Vol. III.

one aspect. But the Bible, like the Redeemer whom it reveals, has two sides of view—divine and human. The former had been principally thought of by earlier expositors. They regarded more the truth of Scripture than the mode in which it had been conveyed. Their attention was given rather to the sound of the trumpet, than to the shape of the instrument, or the music of the peal. They busied themselves more with what history said, than with the style of recital; more with what the ritual taught, than with the scenes and ceremonies of the pageant itself; more with what poetry had sung, than with the lyre, drapery, and attitude of the Hebrew muse; more with what prophecy revealed, than with the allusions and colouring of its oracles. So that, with all the important service which they rendered, they had left a wide field unoccupied. For the Bible, though a Divine revelation, is also a human composition; and though "given by inspiration," it is essentially an Asiatic or Oriental book—the product of Hebrew mind, and laden with the riches of Hebrew imagination.

Various illustrations of manners and customs had been already collected, such as the treatises of Harmer, Burder, and Paxton; the travels of Sandy, Purchas, Maundrell, Shaw, Niebuhr, and Burckhardt, were not unknown; and every scholar was acquainted with such writers on antiquities, geography, and natural history, as Bochart, Reland, D'Herbelot, Pococke, Celsius, Forskal, Harris, Jennings, Jahn, and Roberts. Many of the more prominent features of the eastern world had also been distinctly apprehended. It was perfectly well understood that houses in the East had flat roofs, that the so-called bottles were of skin, and that sheep followed the shepherd, and were not gathered or driven by dogs. But Dr. Kitto's merit lay, not so much in discovery as in application. He brought the public mind into vivid contact with Oriental scenery and life, by moulding them into the form of a continuous commentary on the Old and New Testaments. His readers are so initiated, that they are placed under the eastern sky, with its bright days and starry nights; and are so privileged that they may gaze on the glory of Lebanon, the beauty of Carmel, and the rugged sublimity of Sinai; throw the net with the fishermen on the Lake of Galilee; raise the "shout" of the vintage on the slopes of Eshcol; recline by the "still waters" with the shepherd, when the "pastures are clothed with flocks;" work and sing with the reaper when the "valleys are covered over with corn;" go up at the great festivals to "the testimony of Israel," with "the tribes of the Lord;" or march with the accoutred yeomen of the land, to fight for hearth and altar against Moab or Philistia, Ammon or Syria, the foes of the old theocracy. The *Pictorial Bible* gave glow and reality to ancient scenes and customs, and threw a wondrous light on what is external, or Oriental, in the drapery of Scripture.

Striking and appropriate illustration is borrowed from the Egyptian monuments. Witsius and others had laboured hard to disprove any religious connection between Israel and Egypt. Their arguments were, however, more of a theological than of an artistic and antiquarian nature, and there is no doubt that Marsham and Spencer carried their opposite speculations to an unwarranted extent. But it is natural to suppose that no small portion of Hebrew custom and art was learned in Egypt, so famed for its "wisdom." Therefore the figures on the monuments, so various in their allusions, and portraying so much both of the religious and common life of the nation, are a fertile source of illustration for the Pentateuch—the law and the history of the chosen people, just after it had migrated from the shores of the Nile. And thus, in the notes and woodcuts you have Egypt everywhere—its wheat and its bulrushes, its flax and its frogs, its gods and its mummies, its priests and its ark, its feasts and its funerals—all of them verifying and explaining the Mosaic annals and legislation. The same felicity is displayed in the references to Oriental usage, which is so brought before the reader with pen and pencil that he lives in it. Distinctness is given to his conceptions, for every intelligent reader of scenes, travels, battles, and manners, must form a mental picture to himself as he proceeds, and Kitto sets before him the exact similitude, copies from Nature both to be "seen and read." Some of the curious and difficult points of Hebrew jurisprudence are well illustrated by apposite examples and analogies, some of them better than those which Michaelis has collected. We need not allude to the many engravings taken from Petra, Persia, and Babylon, and so profusely scattered through the exposition of the prophetical books. The introductions prefixed to the various sections, though brief and unpretending, are full of good sense, and convey useful information.

We need not wonder, therefore, at the immediate popularity of the *Pictorial Bible*. It was a new idea successfully carried out. It brought down to the people what had lain on the shelves of students, or been stored away in the treasures of the British Museum. It gave an impulse to this species of biblical study, familiarised the ordinary readers of Scripture with its geography and antiquities, and showed that research, no matter how far or in what direction it was carried, served to confirm the truth, authenticate the history, develop the beauty, and promote a fresher and fuller understanding of the Book of God. It was at first objected that the comment wanted the evangelical element; but the author's purpose must be kept in view, and as he professed to deal with neither exegesis nor theology, he must be judged by the aim which he sought to realise.

What are called "Illustrations from the Old Masters," are usually of little value. Nay, they often mislead. Those of them, for instance, which are found even in the first volume of the *Pictorial Bible* are of this nature. In the one which forms the frontispiece, the artist has paid no attention to Egyptian features, dress, or custom. In the plate representing Laban's covenant with his son-in-law, Jacob is pictured as still a young man, whereas he could not have been far from threescore years and ten. But it was the special superiority of the *Pictorial Bible* that it discarded such fanciful illustrations, except as mere occasional ornament, and that it figured actual animals, plants, garments, and scenes, so as to give to the reader's eye the zoology, botany, costume, geography, and ethnography of Scripture. Many objectionable plates in the first edition were excluded from the fourth, for they were often inaccurate as exponents of history, and imperfect as representations of manners and dress. The first edition, completed in 1838, formed three large imperial octavo volumes, and from the stereotype plates of it various large impressions were taken.

The book was published anonymously. Its reception not only gratified Kitto immensely, but decided what was to be the labour of his subsequent years. For the reviews were very favourable. One of them spoke of the *men* employed in the publication "as fully competent to their anxious undertaking;" and the *one* man who did the entire work, secretly and heartily enjoyed the plural reference. The approbation of the public was not only a reward to him for his toils and anxiety, but he took it as the index of Providence pointing out what he now rightly regarded as the work to which he had been called, and for which so many years of study and travel, and growing religious faith, had so admirably disciplined him. The "almost unprecedented favour" with which the book was received, was therefore owing to its real worth, and not to any fame of its author—for his name was concealed—nor to any sympathy with the workhouse boy, who had wandered from Plymouth to Bagdad, and plodded his way back again to London. Kitto could not but record his high satisfaction with the result—"The degree of attention with which my labours have been favoured, has not arisen out of any sympathies for, or had reference to, my peculiar condition, for my greatest and most successful labour was placed before the public without any name; and although the author's name has been attached to later works, it has not been accompanied by any information concerning the circumstances which have now been described. As, therefore, the public has had no materials on which to form a sympathising, and therefore partial, estimate of my

services, and has yet received them with signal favour, I may venture to regard the object which I had proposed to myself as in some sort achieved. And since it is at length permitted me to feel that I have passed the danger of being mixed up with the toe-writers and the learned pigs of literature, I have now the greater freedom in reporting my real condition." *

He stated also to Professor Robinson of New York,† then in London, that "through incidental notices and allusions in periodical publications, the public had got some notice of his history," but that even then (1840) he was not extensively known as the Editor of the *Pictorial Bible*. Not that there had been any studious concealment, but, he declares, "it has rather been my wish that I should not seem to owe any part of the success I might attain as an author to the sympathies which my sufficiently singular personal history might be likely to produce." Indeed, he affirms, more unreservedly, and with some degree of warmth, that at an early period he had found little encouragement from others, even from those who ultimately favoured him with their notice; that when he spoke of literature, he had been kindly pointed away to other means of occupation and usefulness; that his literary predilections had usually obtained no encouragement, but had rather been opposed as an unreasonable infatuation; and that therefore he had "determined, at whatever risk, to act upon his own soul-felt conclusions, and to stand by the truth or fall by the error of ineradicable convictions." ‡ So completely unknown was he in Scotland, that when we first heard that the *Pictorial Bible* was edited by "John Kitto," we thought that the brief and uncommon name must surely be a *nom de plume*.

In a fragmentary Journal, July 4, 1837, we find this characteristic paragraph:—

"Newman writes me,—'I have taken in the *Pictorial Bible*. Parnell tells me that you were the editor. I said, perhaps of the later portions. Is it true that you were the editor of the Pentateuch part?' Bah! I answered, rather shortly, yes,—and did not altogether omit the opportunity of slightly girding at the discouragements I had received, and the calamities which were foretold me from my adherence to my literary predilections; to which adherence I owe all the benefits I now enjoy. I said just enough to let him see that I did feel something of triumph, to have it thus established that I was right in my obstinacy. These old college folks, I fancy, cannot like the successes of parvenus, self-educated men like myself."

In short, though Kitto rejoiced in doing all manner of service for the *Penny Magazine*, and other useful and popular periodicals, he felt, for the first time, that

---

* *Lost Senses—Deafness*, p. 83.   † September 28, 1840.
‡ *Lost Senses—Deafness*, p. 90.

he was in his true element when he commenced his studies for the *Pictorial Bible.* His benefactors, in their kindness, had assigned him different forms of labour, from the making of shoes to the setting of Persic types, from the teasing of oakum to the manufacture of artificial teeth, and in all of them he did his best, but in none of them was he contented. Each was but a resting place—his heart still said, Excelsior! and he arose and climbed again. Various spheres of work were opened up to him, but he could not find a home at Plymouth or Exeter, Malta or Bagdad, when Providence at length set him down in Ludgate Hill, and yoked him to the great business of his life. And then he felt that he had been slowly training for his high vocation, and that what had disabled him for the physical toils under which his soft sinews had first bent, had but set him apart to higher and more exhausting labours. Then, too, he learned that no phase of his life had been without its advantages—that his love of lore now enabled him to pay his tribute of veneration to the Book of books, and that his journey to the Tigris yielded fruits to be afterwards reaped on the Thames. And thus he waxed "strong in faith, giving glory to God."

During the progress of this first and great labour he tells Mr. Knight, in the fulness of his heart—

"I cannot begin any observations respecting the *Pictorial Bible*, without stating how highly I have been gratified and interested in the occupation it has afforded. It has been of infinite advantage as an exercise to my own mind. It has afforded me an opportunity of bringing nearly all my resources into play; my old Biblical studies, the observations of travel, and even the very miscellaneous character of my reading, have all been highly useful to me in this undertaking. The venerable character of the work on which I have laboured, the responsibility of annotation, and the extent in which such labour is likely to have influence, are also circumstances which have greatly gratified, in a very definite manner, that desire of usefulness which has, I may say, been a strong principle of action with me, and which owes its origin, I think, to the desire I was early led to entertain of finding whether the most adverse circumstances (including the privation of intellectual nourishment) must necessarily operate in excluding me from the hope of filling a useful place in society. The question was, whether I should hang a dead weight upon society, or take a place among its active men. I have struggled for the latter alternative, and it will be a proud thing for me if I am enabled to realise it. I venture to hope that I shall: and to *you* I am, in the most eminent degree, indebted, for the opportunities, assistance, and encouragement you have always afforded me in my endeavours after this object."

Sir John M'Neill and Mr. Knight were, each in his time and place, of essential service to Kitto; the one in the East had greatly and opportunely helped to store his mind, and the other in London devised the plan which brought out his knowledge into popular and practical form. The one encouraged him to gather the ore, and, after its fusion, the other shaped the mould, and there "came out" the *Pictorial Bible.* During the years in which it was in process of publication, his toil was incessant, though he was never far ahead of the press; so that he complained of the time lost by going in search of books, especially to the British Museum, and wished a few serviceable volumes to be procured for himself. Matters connected with the work, over and above the writing of the notes, took up, he affirms, "a fourth of his time, and more than half of his anxiety." And he ends his request with the memorable declaration, "The Museum day is but *six* hours long, whereas mine is sixteen.

It may be added, that the *Pictorial Bible* was reprinted in four quarto volumes, in 1838, but not stereotyped; that in 1840 the notes and some of the illustrations, without the text, were published in five small octavos; and that in 1847 was commenced what may be called the standard edition, completed in 1849, in four volumes imperial octavo. Kitto bestowed special pains upon this edition, and "received upwards of £600 for his labour."[*] Not only did it excel its predecessors in better paper, larger page, choicer woodcuts, and more tasteful printing, but it possessed other and higher improvements. The editor, who was best qualified to speak of it, for he knew the labour it had cost him, says himself:—

"The final results appear in a considerable body of fresh matter, exhibited in some thousands of new notes, and in additions to and improvements of a large number of the notes contained in the original work. Space for this has been provided by an actual increase of the letterpress, by the omission of one class of woodcuts, by the careful excision from the original work of such matters as might, it was judged, be spared, not only without loss but with advantage, and by the pruning and condensation of many notes which remain without essential alteration. The effect of all this may be seen in the fact that, in the Pentateuch alone, besides introductions occupying several pages, between four and five hundred new notes have been introduced without the sacrifice of any valuable matter contained in the original work, and with the addition of a large number of really illustrative engravings, which did not appear in that publication.

"The general result may be thus stated: that the matter of the original work has undergone a most careful and elaborate revision; that nothing of inter-

---

[*] Article "Kitto," in *Knight's English Cyclopædia.*

est or value in the original work is wanting in the new edition; and that large additions have been made, equal altogether to above one-third of the whole work, of the same kinds of useful information which have secured for the *Pictorial Bible* the high consideration with which it has been favoured."*

In this edition, there was prefixed to each book a list of commentators upon it, and the editor regarded this as a "new feature." Certainly it was; but he adds, "A complete list is scarcely possible." His lists are fuller than any we have seen extending to all the various books of Scripture; but we have met with much fuller lists on separate books. He has omitted, especially in the New Testament, several good expositors, both on the Gospels and Epistles. Some that he has put in his lists are mere curiosities; but it was impossible for him to assign their several value to books which he had never seen, and their respective merits to authors whom he had never consulted. There is this benefit, however, that "even the thoughtful general reader may find some matter for suggestive meditation in these lists. They will enable him to see what are the books which have been chiefly attractive for separate exposition; he will perceive how much more attention has, until of late years, been given to the separate consideration of particular sacred books abroad, than in this country; and he may trace the periods in which this department of biblical literature was most cultivated."†

It is stated in the preface to Dr. Chalmers' *Daily Scripture Readings*, that what he called his "Biblical Library," consisted of the *Pictorial Bible*, a Concordance, Poole's *Synopsis*, Henry's *Commentary*, and Robinson's *Researches in Palestine*. In another place, Dr. Chalmers says to his grandson:—"Perhaps when I am mouldering in my coffin, the eye of my dear Tommy may light upon this paper; and it is possible that his recollection may accord with my fervent anticipations of the effect that his delight in the *Pictorial Bible* may have, in endearing still more to him the holy Word of God."

The labour of the last three years had been so incessant, that Kitto had no time to fill much space in his diary. Twelve months elapse between some of the entries. But a few scattered notes of some interest occur:—

"*June* 20, 1837.—This day the king died, and this day I put the last hand to the second volume of the *Pictorial Bible*. *Mem.*—I am, it would seem, a dab at presentiments. At the beginning of the year, I

* *Journal of Sacred Literature*, Vol. IV., 1849, pp. 162-165.
† The stereotype plates of this last and improved edition belong now to the Messrs. Chambers of Edinburgh, who have issued an elegant reprint, with useful and interesting appendices to the first three volumes, by a qualified contributor, referring to books of research not published in 1848.

had a presentiment that the king would die this year. Mentioned it at the time to Bell (Mrs. Kitto), who recollects it. Would I had been a false prophet! Who is not sorry that the king is dead? I am sure I am.

"*Same day.*—Very anxious about baby—indeed miserable. A lump on her head. Doctor says she has no bone on the left side of her head, and showed Bell, in the skull of a dead child, the very bone which the living one wanted. A case of great ultimate danger, probably fatal. She has good health now; and it is awful to see the dear little thing crawling about, laughing, and affecting to address me on her fingers, and to know that the sentence of death is upon her. I have not often—never—been more distressed; for I do love the dear little article most entirely."

"*June* 21.—Sent her to Sir Astley Cooper. After a very slight examination, he said that the bump contained extravasated blood, probably arising from a fall; doubtless, the fearful fall she received about two or three months back; nothing could be done but rub it with vinegar. No danger whatever. When told about the *bone*, he said 'Pho! Then you may tell the medical man, from me, whoever he is, that he is mistaken.' Now, blessed be Sir Astley Cooper! I receive the dear little creature as one given me back from the grave. May she live a thousand years! Bless her little eyes!"

The humour which the next excerpt contains was native to him, as the reader must have frequently perceived in the course of the narrative:—

"*June* 30.—Was much amused by the piscatory propensities of the juvenile cockneys about the New River, which are well worth an extended notice; *e. g.*, one boy, with a basket, rod, line of black worsted, and bent pin, proceeding, with great importance, riverward, between two other boys, proud of being parties in the affair, and dying with envy at the luck of their companion, and the dignity to which he had attained. Some respectable looking boobies, approaching manhood, groping the poor river with very complete and costly apparatus. Others of all sorts, returning fishless home, their blank looks admirably contrasted with the animation and glad expectation of those proceeding river-ward. Coming home by the green, met with a capital practical satire on this—at the butcher's, a boy about four, infected with the piscatory mania, was fishing out of the window into the road with one of his father's flesh-hooks."

Mr. Groves paid a visit to England, on his return from India, in 1835; and though Kitto and he had parted in the manner already described, yet they rejoiced to see one another in their native land. Kitto tells Mr. Woollcombe (April 12), "Your letter conveyed to me the first impression that Mr. Groves was in England. I heard nothing further of him until, on returning from Mr. Knight's to dinner, about a month since, I found he had called in my absence, and left word that he was about to start for the Continent, but should be in Chancery Lane till four o'clock (it was then three), if I could call upon him there. I did so, and had the greatest satisfaction in seeing him once more." Two months afterwards, June 10th, he informs Mr. Lampen—

"I have had the pleasure of seeing Mr. Groves several times since his return to this country, and I was gratified to learn that he had an opportunity of seeing you at Plymouth. I confess to you that there are many of his views in which I do not concur nearly so much as I seemed to myself to do, while I was under that strong personal influence, which I think he exerts over those who are in near connection with him, through the warmth and energy which, more than any man I ever knew, he throws into his opinions. Whether the difference between *now* and *then*, in my mode of considering the subjects to which my attention, while with him, was so forcibly drawn, results from a more dispassionate and uninfluenced view of the same subjects, or merely from the greater ascendancy of worldly influences in my mind, I cannot venture to determine. I fear Mr. Groves might be disposed to consider the latter the most probable account; while *you*, perhaps, might be willing to allow the former cause as sufficient to produce the effect."

10
VISIT TO PLYMOUTH—
BIBLICAL AND LITERARY LABORS—
SOCIAL, DOMESTIC AFFAIRS

AFTER the *Pictorial Bible* was completed, Kitto and his family paid a friendly visit to Plymouth, and were received in a manner which must have been highly gratifying to him. How different his condition now from that in which he had visited his birth-place on his arrival from Malta! Then, appearances, to say the least of it, were against him; now realities were for him. He had achieved celebrity; and every friend who had ever given him a kind word might greet him as a man of note, and claim an interest in his success. Many must have reversed their previous opinion, and perhaps affirmed that, after all, they had uniformly believed, and had indeed so predicted, that John Kitto would make a figure. Some of humbler rank might remember the deaf and ragged boy, who had devoured so many books; or the poor and pitied youth, who had drudged so contentedly in the workhouse. We wonder whether Mr. Bowden, whose tyranny had brought the

smart youngster into notice, lived to see or hear of the editor of the *Pictorial Bible*.

Kitto tells one friend that he often "mused on his inner history," but his outer life also presented many topics of reflection. As, therefore, he walked through Plymouth, and visited Seven Stars Lane, the place of his birth, or surveyed the grim walls of the hospital, or shook hands with some one whose friendly countenance he might not recognize, he must have wondered at the changes in his history; his memory must have suddenly leapt back to days gone by, and brought them into immediate contrast with present scenes and enjoyments. Once it was night—poverty, rags, hunger, toil, and loneliness without a home : now the day had dawned—competence, study, fame, and usefulness, with a smiling and a growing household. He was designedly taking his own picture when he grouped and arranged the opposite elements of such an experience as the following :—

"Afflictions and trials are often allowed to accumulate, one after another, without rest or pause for a certain time, until a point of such accumulated wretchedness is reached, that it seems as if the last point to which even human endurance can stretch— the utmost pitch to which even heavenly sustainments can uphold this earthly essence, has been attained, and that it needs but one atom more added to the agglomerated burden of these troubles to break the spirit on which it has been piled up. Then, at what seems to us the last moment, He who knoweth our frame, and remembereth that we are dust—He who will never suffer us to be tempted beyond what we are able to bear—appears as a deliverer. With His strong hand He lifts the burden from the shoulder, and casts it afar off; tenderly does He anoint and bind up the deep sores it has worn in the flesh, and pour in the oil and the wine; and graciously does He lead us forth into the fresh and green pastures, where we may lie down at ease under the warm sunshine of His countenance, till all the frightful past becomes as a half-remembered dream—a tale that is told." *

After a sojourn of three weeks in Plymouth, Kitto returned to his daily toils. "Uncle Oliver," † on which he had been long working, was published during the year. The devotion of so much of his time to the *Pictorial Bible* had greatly retarded its completion. The book is a description of Persian scenery, with an account of plants, animals, villages, houses, habits, markets, domestic customs, and religion. Uncle Oliver is an old gentleman who has travelled in Persia, and who doles out his information night after night to

* *Daily Bible Illustrations* Vol. 1, p. 726.
† *Uncle Oliver's Travels in Persia*, giving a complete picture of Eastern manners, customs, arts, sciences, and history, adapted to the capacity of youth, in the manner of Peter Parley. Illustrated with twenty-four woodcuts. 2 vols., 18mo.

two nephews and a niece, while Mr. Dillon, tutor to the two boys, vouchsafes occasional explanations. Uncle Oliver has, of course, almost all the talk to himself, the boys and girl putting in a word only at intervals; but his descriptions are simple, and, being those of an eye-witness, they are interesting and well adapted to the young. The style is professedly in "the manner of Peter Parley." It does not seem to have excited much sensation on its appearance, nor did its author seemingly care much about it.

Kitto's next great work, after the *Pictorial Bible*, was *The Pictorial History of Palestine and the Holy Land, including a complete History of the Jews.* Nine months were spent in laborious preparation— "collecting books, examining authorities, and digesting materials." The want of books was still felt by him, for many of those he coveted were of an exorbitant price. He had, however, been fortunate in gaining some valuable tomes, many of which had once been in Mr. Heber's collection, "containing Travels and Descriptions of Palestine," extending from the fifteenth century to the present time. But he experienced great difficulty in getting authentic information as to the natural history of the country. "The work," he says to Lieutenant-Colonel Smith, "is, therefore, in this part, one of original research sufficiently laborious and difficult." The first volume, with a considerable portion of the second, contains the national history of the Jews, commencing with the patriarchs, descending through the times of the Old Testament, filling up the interval between the Restoration and the birth of Christ, and concluding with the capture of Jerusalem and the ultimate dispersion. The physical history occupies by no means so large a space, and was, perhaps, curtailed, to keep the work within certain fixed dimensions. He opens this section with a brief sketch of various writers on the subject—beginning with that storehouse, the *Hierozoicon* of Bochart; glancing at the *Arboretum Biblicum* of Ursinus, and the *Hierophyticon* of Hiller; eulogising, as it deserves, the *Hierobotanicon* of Olaus Celsius, the patron of Linnæus,—not forgetting, at the same time, Paxton, Harris, Calmet, and Taylor; and describing some strange and valueless peculiarities in the engravings which so profusely embellish the *Physica Sacra* of the Swiss physician Scheuchzer. The very full list of travellers is arranged, to some extent, according to the countries to which they belonged—those being specially referred to who have added to our stock of information on the natural history of the Holy Land. He next discusses, under separate heads, mountains, geology, valleys, lakes, and rivers, history of the months, and zoology,—the animals being arranged according to the order of Cuvier's *Règne Animal.*

The *Pictorial History of Palestine and the Holy Land*

never reached the popularity of the *Pictorial Bible*, and probably has never been fully appreciated. It seemed to be supposed that the mass of its information had already been anticipated in its predecessor. The supposition is so far correct in reference to the Bible history, and that has always formed the special object of interest. Many of the illustrations also are repeated from the previous work. Nor do general readers care to find Sacred Narrative done into other words —recomposed in another style, which, as it mingles up illustration and paraphrase, and is broken by explanatory references, wants the simplicity and terseness of the inspired original. The book, however, contains much that is valuable, and, of course, treats of portions of Jewish history which are not found in Scripture. Nine months of incessant and conscientious preparation for the task could not be without some proportionate fruit.

The part which contains the physical history is deficient in arrangement. To describe all the hills and rivers collectively and in separate sections may make up good dissertations, but it fails to give the reader a full and correct notion of geography—that is, of the features and character of the country as they really present themselves. It would have been better to have constructed an ideal pilgrimage through the land, bringing out scene after scene as they actually occur. The imaginary tour might have begun in the peninsula of Sinai and advanced northward, or it might have followed the poet's order, and commenced its survey where

> "Hoar Lebanon! majestic to the winds,
> Chief of a hundred hills, his summit rears
> Unshrouded; thence by Jordan south,
> Whate'er the desert's yellow arms embrace—
> Rich Gilead, Idumea's palmy plain,
> And Judah's olive hills; thence on to those
> Cliff-guarded eyries, desert bound, whose height
> Mocked the proud eagles of rapacious Rome—
> The famed Petræan citadels—till, last,
> Rise the lone peaks, by Heaven's own glory crowned,
> Sinai on Horeb piled."

Such a method, while it would have imparted more variety and interest, would have also taken away from the work its detached and miscellaneous appearance. One prefers to see Palestine as it is, rather than to have it dislocated into fragments: one of these built up of all its mountains, and another overflowing with all its waters. The same objection partly applies to the history of the months, arranged after Buhle and Walch. That portion is replete with useful facts, but of such a kind, that the reader would never think of consulting the section for them. The author pleads for his arrangement, that by it the largest information might be thrown into the smallest space. True. The argument is good for those who may read through the *Economical Calendar*, as Charles Taylor calls his translation of Buhle; but it is forgotten that many a one buys such a book for reference, and that its value is in proportion to the facility with which he finds at once what he wants. Who, without some previous knowledge, would search for almonds under January, or hennah under May—sycamores under August, or agricultural operations under October? Had Kitto, with his subsequent experience, handled the work for a second edition, he would have turned out almost a new production. Having been paid for this work "according to the highest scale of literary remuneration," and having laboured on it so long and diligently, he was greatly disappointed at its slow sale, and thus explains himself to Mr. Knight—May 28, 1840 :—

" . . . I was deeply disappointed to learn that the success of the *Pictorial Palestine* is so much below your expectations. I feel assured in my mind that it deserves to succeed, and will still hope that it may afford an adequate remuneration to you, when it comes to be sold in a completed form. If I have misgivings, they arise from the fact, that the work will not be completed to the extent which was promised. . . It is quite true that the Scriptural narrative was too diffuse at the beginning, arising partly from the difficulty of calculation, and partly from my wish to bring out characteristic customs and ideas. . . . I am, on the whole, well satisfied that, as it will stand, the *Pictorial Palestine* will do no discredit to the editor of the *Pictorial Bible*. It is, in fact, a much superior work, though, as it happens, it would seem to be less adapted to attract attention 'in the market of literature.' I know nothing that could mortify me more than to hear you say that the *Physical History* would not sell by itself. It is a pocket question to me; for most of the time spent by me in preparation, before the work went to press, was occupied in forming collections for this very portion. With the other portion, by which I gain as much, and which will be more profitable to you, I could have gone to press at once, and furnished a part month by month. It seems possible to make books *too good* for the great world : and if so, you can neither afford to publish nor I to write good things that will not sell."

Thus will authors complacently misjudge the comparative merits of their productions. Yet he admits that Professor Robinson of New York, then in London, had pointed out several inaccuracies in the plates of some of the most beautiful of the landscapes ; and it is plain, from a tedious correspondence, that there was considerable misunderstanding between publisher and author about the size and proportions of the work. He had also expressed distrust of Professor Robinson's view as to the scene of the passage through the Red Sea,* stating, in his usual tone of unqualified firmness,

that the traveller could scarcely be unbiassed in his judgment, and would see nothing to disturb his 'foregone conclusions,' as he had previously published the same opinion in an American periodical. Professor Robinson then wrote him, calmly denying the imputation,* and Kitto replied † in a long letter, conveying his full appreciation of the traveller's successes, and his hearty thanks for the unparalleled service he had rendered to biblical geography. Many points, too, on which Kitto gives a decided judgment, such as the identification of Sinai, are yet unsettled—points on which Lepsius, Ritter, Robinson, Stanley, Stewart, and others well qualified to judge, are by no means agreed, and further research is still indispensable to a just conclusion.

The question may now be naturally asked, how did Kitto find leisure to get through those multifarious employments—how did he so divide and occupy his hours as to bring so much labour within the limits of human capability? His plans necessitated no ordinary industry, and twelve hours were not sufficient for his day. From early life he had taught himself to be a miser in the use of every moment, and he was so disciplined as to content himself with a very small amount of sleep. His quiet and retiring habits, formed before his marriage, were not altered by it. He would still sit at breakfast with a book in his hand, as if he had forgotten that he had ceased to be a bachelor. At tea, however, he made it a point to offer compensation for the morning's monopoly; by reading aloud to his wife, but the deep and unvarying bass of his guttural tones, prolonged for hours, often set "his sole auditor" asleep. So innocent was he in his own opinion, that, when gently spoken to as to his persistence in the practice, he could not at first understand what possible cause of complaint he had given. He had imagined that what had so interested himself as to induce him to try his vocal organs upon it, could not fail to interest his wife. But the practice, he admits, "brought to light new and previously unknown talents in him." "Were I again in Persia," he merrily exclaims, "it would be in my power to realise a handsome income by the exercise of a gift, which is only there well appreciated. It throws into the shade all the boasted wonders of the mesmeric trance, to behold the gradual subsidence of my victim under the sleep-compelling influences of my voice, in spite of all her superhuman struggles to avert the inevitable doom !" ‡ In many ways did Mrs. Kitto feel at first those strange peculiarities which his habits and labours had created or fostered ; for while he coveted

---

* *Pictorial History of Palestine*, Vol. I., p. 189.

* Letter to Mr. Kitto—Regent Square, London, October 12, 1840.
† October 19, 1840.
‡ *Lost Senses—Deafness*, p. 28.

the seclusion of a hermit for his work, he had the intense relish of a husband for domestic and social enjoyment. Indeed, his wife had to undergo a willing process of assimilation, and soon became not only so reconciled to his modes of life, but so much at one with him in admiration of his abilities, and in sympathy with all his pursuits, as to be able herself to put on proud record that, "during the twenty-one years of our married life, I may say, in perfect truth, that ten hours have not been spent separate from him in visiting." His toil was incessant, and many a day his only walk was from his study to his parlour, and from his parlour to his study. To overtake his many tasks, he began to sit up during night, but soon abandoned such a dangerous method, for nature would assert its claims, and he insensibly dropped asleep before midnight among his books and papers. Suddenly starting from slumber, he would resume his pen, and by the third watch of the morning would be found eager and busy at his allotted duty. His lamp, however, did not always shade its flame, when he nodded, and more than once there was the risk of a conflagration. Then he betook himself to a far better and healthier plan, that of early rising—the alarum-clock employed for the purpose first rousing his partner, who could hear it, and she touching him. A bell, which could be rung by the watchman, was next substituted for the alarum; but still he must have depended on the faithful ears of another, and his wife was often obliged, sorely against her will, to wake him from a slumber which his exhausted frame so much required. Getting up at the first summons, usually at four, he at one period repaired directly to his study, prepared himself a cup of tea by means of a spirit lamp, and then sat down and laboured till the hour of breakfast. After breakfast a few turns were occasionally taken in his garden, and having dressed, he went to his workroom, and remained till he was called to dinner at one. The writing of letters, the correcting of proofs, and other miscellaneous duties, occupied him till tea at five; then he returned to his desk, writing till toward ten, and reading till eleven. This was a work day of sixteen hours, and of incessant application. All the socialities of out-door life were completely set aside. His wife was enlisted in his service, and so well did she drill herself, that, so far from being a cypher, as she at first thought, he used jocularly to call her his "hodman." She never allowed him to be checked or interrupted in his labours by any domestic hindrances; so that no visitor ever found him, like Melancthon, Hooker, and Thomas Scott, holding a book in one hand, and rocking the cradle with the other. So essential did she become to him, that he could never bear her absence from home. Her activity blended so admirably with his sedentary habits,

that he delighted in his own humorous image, "What with my centripetal and her centrifugal force, we move in a very harmonious orbit."

When he was employed in Mr. Knight's office, he commonly went and came with book in hand, for the noise around could cause him no distraction. Then and afterwards he ran no little risk in the streets of London. His load of books in his pockets had nearly drowned him in the Tigris; and the volume on which he pored amid the crowded thoroughfares of the metropolis, frequently brought him into jeopardy of life and limb. And even when he had no book to fill his eye and occupy his attention, he sometimes saw the people staring as if at some novelty, and could not divine what or who it was, till a whip laid smartly across his shoulders, told him that himself in imminent peril had been the unconscious object of curiosity and alarm. At other times the excited gestures of a policeman warned him to look behind, just as the hot breath of a horse blew into his face, and its uplifted hoof was about to tread him to the ground. But he was mercifully preserved; and the coarse epithets of cab drivers and waggoners, and the more sympathising badinage of orange women, as the one cursed, or the other commiserated his stupidity, were all happily lost upon him.

While his daily toils left him little leisure, he yet delighted to relax for a brief period with his children. He took them, as soon as they were able, to assist him in his gardening operations, and they were delighted at the symbols of approbation, whenever they received them. Rejoicing in their little joys, he partook of their gambols, and each, on its birth-day, was sure to receive an appropriate present. But while they enjoyed themselves to the utmost in their pastimes, and could range their home without restraint, to one room they were debarred access. The library was a sacred place; and if they did cross the awful threshold, they were solemnly interdicted from touching anything in it. They must have often looked on its litter with curious wonder—its piles of letters and bundles of papers—books shut and open huddled together on the table, and volumes as large as themselves strewed in heaps on the floor. Shireen was at length allowed the high and envied privilege of occasionally touching some of the papers, and arranging a few of the books. But she was bound in her procedure by a strict and formal stipulation, to all the articles of which she promised a rigid adherence. The formidable document ran as follows:—

"Plan, Programme, Protocol, Synopsis, and Conspectus, for clearing Dr. Kitto's Table:—

"1. Make one pile of religious books. 2. Another of books not religious. 3. Another of letters. 4. Another of written papers other than letters. 5.

Another of printed papers. 6. Put these piles upon the floor. 7. The table being now clear, dust, scrub, rub, and scour the table till you sweat; and when you have sweated half a gallon, give over, and put the piles upon the table, leaving to Dr. K. the final distribution.—Signed, sealed, and delivered, this 28th day of May, in the year of our Lord 1852.

"*Witness*, HOLOFERNES PIPS. ✠ JOHN KITTO."

His home, in short, with all its monotonous and incessant toil, was to him a source of perpetual delight. His previous life had prepared him to relish it. He who had so often been a guest under others' roofs, and so long "a stranger in a strange land," felt his own hearth and household to be an unspeakable pleasure. We have been with him in the height of his fame, and when his family were round him. How heartily he was one with them! He was a happy and playful father, and his young ones were full of innocent freedom in his presence, each anxious to say a word to him—that is, to present it in visible form to the paternal eye—even the infant imitating in its own way, and with "infinite seriousness," the finger-talk going on so busily round about it, and crowing in ecstasy at its success in obtaining a nod or a smile. "It was quite a treat," says one of his visitors,* "to see him out of his study, especially at family devotion, conducted with so much solemnity by your dear husband, surrounded by his little family. The dear little one, too, brought in for its morning kiss by his aged mother, and then herself receiving the same token of affection. I think I have never seen so much love and reverence manifested by children for a father—indeed, all was love and harmony; and that *look* of affection (over his glasses) so often bestowed on them, impressed my mind more deeply than words could have done, that he tenderly loved them." Again and again had he intimated, in his Journals and Letters, his desire to provide for his mother, who had seen so much of the shady side of life; and now, in the evening of her days, she was an honoured inmate of his dwelling; and so much was she bound up in him and his family, that when his failing health obliged him to go to Germany, and leave her behind, she was so grieved and stunned by the separation, that she seldom spoke afterward, but sunk into a melancholy which continued till her death at the end of last year.†

His children, all of whom had acute ears, and tongues of rattling eloquence, were each of them, as they grew up, at a loss for a time to understand their father's infirmity. They could not comprehend why a word or a call should not at once tell upon him as upon their mother. They were unable to divine why, at

their cry of "Papa," he did not lift his head from a book, or lay down his pen for a moment; while the cry of "Mamma" brought her at once to their side, no matter in what business she might happen to be engaged. From mere imitation, they began the finger-talk before they could speak, and resorted to it when other infantine signals failed. "If the little creatures are so placed as to be unable to engage my attention by touching me, they call me, and on finding that also unavailing, blow to me; and if that also fails, stamp upon the floor; and when they have, by one or other of these methods, attracted my eyes, begin their pretty talk upon the fingers. One of the least patient of them used to stamp and cry herself into a vast rage in the vain effort to engage my attention. It is very singular that these practices should have been taken up by all of them in succession, like natural instincts, without having learned them from one another." *

His modes of recreation were, at this period, like himself, somewhat peculiar. It was not exercise he coveted, but rather a ride in an omnibus, and a walk home afterwards. The flowers in Covent Garden in summer, and the glory of the shops in winter, greatly delighted him. But scarcely more than once a week could he afford such an indulgence. "If I failed," such is his own record, "to secure this recreation, from press of editorial or other literary business, during the early portion of the week, I seldom missed it on Saturday night. This was because, as an observer of character, I took much interest in seeing the working people abroad with their wives, laying out the money which their week's labour had produced; and in witnessing the activity which this circumstance gave to many streets, and inspecting the commodities there exposed for sale in the open air. I felt that I could enter with interest into the feelings of the various parties pausing, hesitating, or purchasing, at the various shops and stalls, materials for the hiss of universal fry, which on Saturday night ascends from fifty thousand hearths, or for the scarcely more enjoyed bake of the Sunday dinner. It was something to be able to enter into these matters, and to follow a hundred of these parties home, to assist in blowing the fire, to turn out before the eyes of the bigger children the treasures of the basket, to pacify the young ones, now all alive in bed, with an apple or other nicety, to watch the spit and sputter and hubbub of the frying pan, and at length to share its steaming contents with all. What a multitudinous host of beggars are then abroad, whom one sees not at any other time! Their faith in their own class—always willing, but then only able to assist them—their assurance of the warm sympathies of those who have dominion over Saturday night, more than in the cold charities, or colder

* Mrs. Hullock, in a letter to Mrs. Kitto—Plainfield, Massachusetts, Nov. 5, 1855.
† 1856.

* *Lost Senses—Deafness*, p. 98.

uncharities, of gentlefolks who have rule over the rest of the week, are the influences which that night may draw forth into the streets, from their wretched nooks, hundreds of miserable creatures, who, but for the gleams of sympathy and kindness which, on that one evening, shine upon their hearts, would, perhaps cast themselves down in helpless despair to curse God and die. Then, also, the music is all abroad. Barrel-organs we have at all times; but on Saturday nights bands of fine instruments are about in all directions, as well as songsters and solitary fiddlers. This is not without enjoyment to me. I like to stand a few paces aloof from a party of Saturday night people gathered round the musicians. I watch the impression it makes upon them. I sympathize in their attention, and by identifying myself with them, derive real enjoyment from the music through them, and drop my dole into the plate with as much cheerfulness as if the whole concourse of sweet sounds had rushed into my own ears." *

She who had the best experience of his social qualities has thus described them :—

"I desire to give some idea of my dear husband's habits with friends, but I find the task somewhat difficult. No one who ever saw that noble brow, and that eye lighted up with intelligence, could doubt his social powers. That bright thoughts were ever passing within, might be inferred from the glowing expression of his features, even when unuttered by the lips. In ordinary company he was far from comfortable, and could only take refuge in a book. Most of his friends, though they might enjoy hearing him talk—that is, the few who could understand him, had themselves so little to say, or were so discouraged by the slow process of finger-talk, and the still more cumbrous resource of pen and paper, that they seldom or never made the effort to speak. Thus he was generally left to himself reading, or while watching an opportunity to speak, perhaps incurring the mortification of finding that he had interrupted some one. When he met with literary characters, or men of real information, he kept them continually writing, often catching, with his quick eye, the meaning of their answers before they were fully written. He had one friend who was capable of keeping him in a state of continued excitement. Though I could execute the finger-talk with great rapidity, I could never read it; so that I could only guess at what had been said by other persons from the tenor of my husband's remarks. I was always aware when the company was irksome to him. Husbands are not clever at hiding their feelings from their wives; and I could easily discern his, which often made me quite as miserable as himself. I felt that he ought not to be made to feel his infirmity, which was always the case

* Lost Senses—Deafness, p. 153.

when he was out of his library. We therefore mutually agreed, that the reception of friends was not suited to our condition, and learned to live alone. But there was one dear family of children, whose growing intelligence he had watched from their infancy, on his visits to their parents. Them he delighted to visit, or to be visited by. They had all been drawn to him in love during their childhood, and had learned to talk on their fingers, and could as freely ask and reply to questions as any of his own family. He always kept these young people in full talk, and, while in his company, there was no reprieve for their poor fingers. Sometimes he insisted on their playing on the piano the Battle of Prague, and he sat with his fingers placed on the sounding-board, seeming to derive pleasure from the vibrations he felt. His entire helplessness in all matters extraneous to his library, rendered him quite dependent on me; whilst I felt it a privilege thus to guard and keep in quiet one whose time was devoted to such noble ends. But the cares of a large family quite destroyed, of late years, the close union of the early period, and I may say, quite separated us, except at meal-times; for it rendered such exactions of labour necessary on his part that he had no spare time—but of this he never complained. He would say, 'My work is my pleasure also, and, if it please God to give me strength, I have only to work a little harder.'"

Of the *Christian Traveller*, a periodical publication which Kitto had thought of for fifteen years, and which was now commenced, he formed the highest expectations—" a work devoted to a cause for which the public gives half a million a year out of its pocket," must, he argued, " be received with favour." The object of the papers was to give sketches of the missionary enterprise in various parts of the world. He was anxious, for several reasons, to do all the work himself, as he rightly thought that the editing of what he did not himself compose would take up very much of his valuable time, and if he should ask for contributions, he shuddered to " think of the showers of twaddle by which he should be inundated!" He felt that he was competent to the task, for he could now do before breakfast what he should once have considered a good day's work; and one personal reason for the undertaking is honestly stated by himself. It was not simply that he wished to get all the credit, but this,—" I have to build up the provisions for my family from the foundations, and under any possible contingency, there is not one on earth from whom those that God has given to me can expect a crust of other bread than such as I may be enabled to provide for them."

Only three parts of the periodical were published, when it was stopped by the pecuniary embarrassment of Mr. Knight's publishing house. Kitto, so suddenly severed from remunerating labour, was soon reduced to straits. He had been able to earn only a little more than daily bread by hard exertion ; and when occupation could not be found, difficulties at once enveloped him, and so grew upon him, that he was obliged to sell his house at a considerable loss, leave London, and remove to Woking in Surrey.* Fits of his early melancholy sometimes recurred ; and no wonder—a wife and four children were now dependent on him.

His own explanation is, " in 1841, the only publishing house with which, up to that time, I had been connected, fell into difficulties, and was obliged to bring to an abrupt close an engagement with me, which had promised a fair income for some years. I thus became out of employment at a time when the general difficulties of the trade for a long time indisposed booksellers to enter upon new undertakings, At first I lived upon the little I had saved ; then upon the sale of my books, helped out by a little credit for the necessaries of life to a large family." At a later period, he states more fully to Mr. Groves, that between the ending of one task and beginning of another, he had no employment for twelve months, and that he had made an arrangement to pay what he owed by instalments in three years. " This," he adds in 1848, " has been done to the uttermost farthing."

But during such domestic eclipses, he could conceal his own discomfort, and charm away that of others with a little touch of gaiety. On one occasion, when the more solid portion of the family dinner depended on the sale of some books, which necessity had compelled him to part with, and when she who had gone on the melancholy errand returned without having converted the volumes into money, he surveyed first his children's faces of anxiety and disappointment, and then, moving towards the window, exclaimed, " Well, we must look at the butcher's shop opposite to get the right relish for our bread."

Let it then be understood, that Kitto's straits arose, not from inadequate compensation, but from want of employment. Had he enjoyed constant work, he would have lived in comfort. His books were not of a nature to bring him or his publishers very large profits, yet they had an excellent circulation. They could not, like the works of Dickens, realize a magnificent revenue, but they would have insured him a sufficient income. His great helplessness lay in the precariousness of his means. His torment was not a surplus, but a want of work. " Leave to toil," was his prayer, for he knew that abundant fruit would follow. " There

* A few pages of what he calls *Village Memoranda* have been preserved, but they contain nothing of note. "I begin to perceive," he says, "how people in the country can appear as grandees on an income which would barely enable them to support the appearance of respectability in London."

are ten thousand things in the world that I fear more than work," he says; and he might have added, " What I dread above all things is the want of work." He states to his friend, Mr. Tracy, * " The position which I have attained is not without its anxieties. I see, for instance, a large family growing around me, and entirely dependent upon the labours of my pen, which, *in the line I have chosen,* are much more productive of honours than emoluments." Lest a want of economy, or some other folly, should be laid to his charge, he explains, a month afterwards, to the same friend—" I heard, last week, that there is a general impression in the city of my being a very rich man. I accept this as an acknowledgment, that one whose works have been so well received by the public *ought* to be so. So I might have been, probably, if I had commenced my career with any capital to enable me to retain the copyright of my own works." This statement speaks for itself. He could never command property in his books, but was obliged to compose them for daily support, so that, when the work was finished, the salary ceased. He never was able to finish a work, and then sell it. He simply presented his plan, made his bargain, and was paid in proportion as the work advanced. But the possession of literary property was still his hope, though he never could manage to secure it. Accordingly, two years afterwards, in offering to Mr. Oliphant the *Daily Bible Illustrations,* he declares, " It was my wish to undertake this intended set of books on my own account, but circumstances have arisen to render it more expedient to pursue, at least for a time, the plan upon which all my works have hitherto been produced, viz., *by making arrangements for them, before I get to work seriously upon them.*" But we have been anticipating.

Previously to his removal from London to a rural retreat, his anxious mind had been devising many forms of literary industry. Not a few prospectuses were penned by him, and sent abroad in various directions. He proposed to the Religious Tract Society to write for them either a Biblical Cyclopædia or a Life of Christ, entering at length into an explanation of his views ; but the Society do not seem to have entertained the offer. The project of a new Cyclopædia of Biblical Literature, sent to Messrs. Black of Edinburgh, engaged their attention; and they entered into a correspondence with him, the issue of which was the publication, in the first place, of a *History of Palestine, from the Patriarchal Age to the Present Time,* 12mo, pp. 378, Edinburgh, 1843. This was a brief school history ; and while it put a little into the author's pocket, it added nothing to his fame. Some months elapsed before the Cyclopædia could appear—months in which his household suffered the pinch and pressure of want. The *Thoughts*

* Woking, Jan. 20, 1847.

among Flowers * was published in 1843, by the Religious Tract Society. The little volume shows the author's love of flowers, and how he could moralise among them, and indicates what snatches of poetry lay in the stores of his memory. The reflections are occasionally far fetched, and are not the natural scent of the blossoms, but rather a borrowed fragrance. Between 1841 and 1843, he prepared for Mr. Fisher the letterpress of the *Gallery of Scripture Engravings*, in three volumes quarto. The letterpress is simply to explain the engravings, and, except as a show-book, the volumes are of no great utility. In 1845 he prepared for Mr. Knight *The Pictorial Sunday Book, with 1,300 engravings, and an appendix on the Geography of the Holy Land.* † This volume was in folio, and a portion of it was published separately, under the title of the *Pictorial History of our Saviour.* "The publication," it is stated in the preface, "now submitted to Christian families, is intended to present, at the very cheapest rate, a series of engravings illustrative of the Bible history, the prophecies, the psalms, the life of our Saviour, and the Acts of the Apostles, exhibiting the scenes of the great events recorded in Scripture, the customs of the Jews, the natural history of the Holy Land, and the antiquities which throw a light upon the Sacred Writings. With these are united some of the more striking and impressive compositions of the great painters, and original designs. These pictorial illustrations are connected with a course of Sunday reading, which, avoiding all matters of controversy, endeavours to present, in the most instructive and engaging form, a body of Scriptural narrative and explanation." There is nothing new in the volume—it is but a classified re-exhibition of plates and wood-cuts employed in previous publications of various kinds, both secular and biblical, with pages of letterpress between. The physical geography annexed is a reprint, with a few changes, of the similar portion of the *Pictorial History of Palestine.* Yet, apart from its immediate value in relation to Scripture, and that value is not great, the volume contains such a number and variety of engravings, both from nature, the Egyptian monuments, and the masters of all schools and countries, that it is an amusing and informing production, and was certainly of marvellous cheapness at its first appearance.

In the meantime the *Cyclopædia of Biblical Literature*, published by the Messrs. Black of Edinburgh, had been commenced. The idea was his own, and he had much correspondence about the details of the plan. In the multitude of opinions proposed to him, he held in the main to his own original view, but was obliged to depart from his first resolution to do the whole work

* 32mo, p. 156.
† Charles Knight & Co., 1845.

himself. He knew what had been achieved in this department, and what remained to be done. Nor was he confined to British assistance in the enterprise—he laid his hands also on several German contributors. The book, as it proceeded, grew to a size not originally contemplated,—a circumstance not unusual with its editor. But the allotment of articles to respective writers was a responsible task, and it needed some tact to get the contributions in time from his numerous assistants. Swarms of suggestions poured in upon him as the publication went on, and he sometimes felt that the multitude of counsellors endangered safety. Objections, too, were started, and there was ground for some of them. He replies, in his own portion of the preface, "that he felt that he could not find forty independent thinkers, among whom there should be no visible diversities of sentiment;" observes that "it did not become him to dictate to them the views they were to take of the subjects intrusted to them;" and confesses that some of them exhibit opinions in which he is not able to concur, though he regards them as not less competent than himself to arrive at just conclusions. He claims, however, and that justly, that the book be judged not by particular articles, but by its general character; and he adds, that his "physical privation," placing him in complete isolation from many external influences, "had enabled him to realise more extensive co-operation in this undertaking, than under any pastoral or official connection with any religious denomination he could expect to have obtained." "The work owes its origin to the editor's conviction of the existence of a great body of untouched materials applicable to such a purpose, which the activity of modern research and the labours of modern criticism have accumulated, and which lay invitingly ready for the use of those who might know how to avail themselves of such resources." The book was at once felt to meet a want of the age. Nothing of a like nature existed in the English language. Previous dictionaries were defective both in scholarship and materials. Calmet had been done into English, and overlaid with learned fancies; while Winer could not bear translation at all. Other works of less pretension were also in circulation. But Dr. Kitto had concluded an enterprise which embraced the ripest scholarship, and took in the most recent researches. The *Cyclopædia*, therefore, rose at once to a lofty position, and, as we have elsewhere said, "can be excelled only by itself in a new and corrected edition." It is beyond our present business to offer any criticism on the unequal merits of the various articles, written by so many contributors. Only, we may say, that Dr. Kitto did not appear to full advantage as an editor. Though his own religious views were fixed, yet his catholicity of temper unfitted him for doing the harder work, and pronouncing the sterner decisions of the editorial chair. He received a thousand pounds as editor, and more than double that sum was expended on contributions and illustrations. We regret that he was not spared to superintend a second edition, for he was well aware that a second edition would require to be, in many respects, a new book.

When the great work was at length brought nigh to its termination, and its toils and dangers were past, we find its indefatigable editor relaxing, and recording thus,—

"*July* 13, 1845.—Put the last hand to the regular work of the B. C. ; that is, did the last article in Z that was upon my list. A day to be remembered on many accounts besides.

"*July* 14.—Cleared my table of the books that have lain on it for three years—placed them on the shelves, not long to slumber there perhaps."

On the title-page of the *Biblical Cyclopædia*, when published in two volumes, the editor's name stands no longer in naked simplicity. It is now John Kitto, D.D., F.S.A.—a very different addition from that which he assumed in his early dream of authorship. It was then "John Kitto, shoemaker, pauper, etc.," the inmate of a workhouse ; but now, it is John Kitto, Doctor of Divinity, Fellow of the Society of Antiquaries—a double elevation to which he had never aspired in his wildest reveries. To be a missionary, sometimes appeared to him a probable occurrence—to be a clergyman, was scarce within the range of possibility ; but now he had received a theological title, and was the first, and we suppose the only English layman, who ever possessed such an honour. In 1844, the University of Giessen, through his friend Professor Credner, sent him the diploma of Doctor of Divinity. And had he not earned it by his literary works?—the works of a man who had passed through such a boyhood of privation and suffering, and had spent such a youth of desultory and unsatisfactory pursuits. Among Kitto's papers there are preserved two documents, that stand out in startling contrast : the one his indenture to Bowden, the shoemaker, somewhat ragged and torn, with its many "seals and signatures ;" and the other his diploma from the University of Giessen. They mark the two opposite poles of his life. In 1845, Dr. Kitto became a fellow of the Royal Society of Antiquaries, and this body honoured themselves in thus honouring him. We have occasionally seen the epithet "reverend" prefixed to his name. The error arose, no doubt, from the idea that a theological title implies a clerical status. But degrees are simply academical, not ecclesiastical distinctions. In Germany, as Dr. Kitto explains, they are sometimes conferred on scholars who are not "in orders," as very recently on the Chevalier Bunsen ; and in such a case,

if one, who has already obtained the title of Doctor of Divinity, "desires to undertake the pastoral office, he is ordained without the examinations which all others must undergo." "Thus Tholuck was Doctor of Divinity and Professor of Theology before his ordination to the ministry, which consequently took place without the usual examinations."*

In 1845 Dr. Kitto made two contributions to Mr. Knight's *Weekly Volume.* Both are named the "Lost Senses ;" the first part having the special title "Deafness," and the second "Blindness." The first is a charming little book—in fact, an autobiography—a revelation of his life and history, as they were modified or developed by his deafness. "His condition," he admits, "is not new ; but that it has never hitherto been described, may be owing to the fact, that a morning of life, subject to such crushing calamity, has seldom, if ever, been followed by a day of such self-culture." He was a D.D. when he penned these words. In this brief volume he first traces the growth of his mind with great distinctness, and shows clearly under what awful disadvantages he laboured. The books in common circulation in his young days were far inferior to those now produced ; but he had triumphed over such a drawback. After his deafness he became more and more loath to speak, till his friends, during his voyage to Malta, forced him : and through life he used no superfluous terms—"avoiding all remarks about the weather, all expletives, adjuncts, complimentary phrases," and even terms of endearment ; so much so, that one of his boys was startled when his father, for the first time, called him "*dear.*" There is a chapter of great interest on "percussions." The loudest thunder-storm was perfectly inaudible to him, though once, a peal having shaken the house, he supposed it was the servant moving the table in an adjoining room. He could not hear the throb or music of a set of bells ; but when he was placed in contact with the tower in which they were ranged, he was conscious of a dull percussion overhead, as if blows had been hitting the wall above him. The great clock of St. Paul's struck when he happened once to be examining it with a friend, and the sensation was that of heavy blows upon the fabric on which he stood, communicated to his feet, and diffused over his body. When a cannon was fired near him, he heard no sound, but felt as if a fist, covered with a boxing-glove, had knocked him on the head. The drawing of furniture, slapping of doors, or falling of books upon the floor, produced a vibration that often distressed him, though he could not determine precisely whence the disturbance proceeded. A knock at the street door he could not hear, but the shutting of it, affecting the entire edifice, was "painfully distinct." The lightest

* *Daily Bible Illustrations* Vol. 2, p. 701.

footfall upon the floor of his room would sometimes rouse him from sleep. He *felt* the sound of vehicles in Fleet Street only when they were on the same side of the pavement, and opposite to him, but this "sense of sound" did not affect him in the house. When the points of his finger nails rested on the board over which the wires of a piano are stretched, he could make out the higher notes, in such a stormy piece of music as the *Battle of Prague.* In corroboration of what he has said in the *Lost Senses,* we may add another of his subsequent experiences. He witnessed, from the apartments of the Society of Antiquaries, in Somerset House, the great procession of the Duke of Wellington's funeral. But he says, "Not the shadow of a sound, or the faintest vibration, struck upon the paralysed organ from the great military bands that passed below, though a person, I have been in the habit of supposing as deaf as myself, told me he could not only distinguish the sound, but follow the notes with considerable distinctness." *

Yet there were some compensations. He had developed within himself a keen sense of the beautiful, and a passionate love for it. He could not bear what was ugly. He loved to gaze on the moon "walking in brightness;" and "high mountains were a feeling." "The slaughtering of a tree affects me more sensibly than that of an animal." He was fond of colours, and, when a boy, knew every print in every window of Plymouth by heart. He travelled over every countenance distinctly within his view, as a florist would inspect a bed of tulips, and often performed the same experiment upon character as he walked from St. Paul's to Charing Cross, or from the top of Tottenham Court Road to the Post-office. He hated to sit in twilight. Dr. Kitto then paints some of those disqualifications which deafness produces, and how he rose above the trials of his earlier years; how the craving to be honourably known grew upon him, and how this was refined into a passion to be useful. He felt that deafness, while it aided the amount of work done, had many drawbacks; for it prevented explanation, retarded business, and the making of bargains. This defect had more than once annoyed him in his transactions and literary covenants. "Men of business have a feeling that affairs can be transacted much better by personal interview than writing. In fact, there is no concealing it, that the deaf man is likely to be regarded as a bore. Sensitively alive to this danger, he will perhaps depart, leaving his business unfinished." "The deaf man," he repeats, "is confined to the solid bones, the dry bread, the hard wood, the substantial fibre of life, and gets but little of the grace, the emotion, the gilding, and the flowers, which are to be found precisely in those small things which are 'not worth' reporting on the fingers."

* Letter to Mr. Oliphant, Nov. 20, 1852.

He has a very playful chapter on the shifts to which deaf people resort to catch the talk of a general company, and how they are usually far behind in their enjoyment of clever and witty sayings, beginning to smile at one piece of humour, while those around them are concluding their laughter over another which has superseded it. He might have added, that the epithet "absurd" has its origin and meaning from the common misappropriateness in time or subject of a deaf man's answer. Strange to say, he was six years deaf before he knew that there was any mode of communication by means of the fingers.

Dr. Kitto then enters at some length into the philosophy of teaching deaf mutes, and diverges into an account of some famous institutions for their education. He used to attend public meetings at Exeter Hall, and the most animated speakers pleased him most. When the audience "broke into loud cheers," he became keenly alive to his privation. In the House of Commons he was more amused than awestruck — was shocked by the want of solemnity; and he says, "My far too entire sense of the ridiculous almost overcame me, when the very remarkable sergeant-at-arms shouldered his mace, with the air of a musketeer, and escorted up to the table two masters in Chancery, who brought down a bill from the Lords, and who, in retiring, walked backwards the whole length of the floor, stopping at regulated intervals in their retrogressive move, to bow very low to the Chair." Towards the conclusion of the book, Kitto hazards a conjecture as to the origin and signification of his name. The English would have it to be Cato, the Spaniards Quito, the Italians Chetto. Himself gives it a Phœnician source, Κιττώ in Dioscorides meaning a species of cassia, pronounced in Hebrew קיץ, and he avows that the Phœnicians, in their early intercourse for tin in Cornwall, probably planted the name in that southern province. The likelihood is, that it is simply a miner's contraction of an older and longer Cornish name. The Cornish and Celtic are closely allied; the epithet ciotach, in Irish, means "left-handed," and this Celtic term is not unknown in a more Anglicised form. The reader will remember Colkitto as the epithet of the royalist chieftain Macdonnell in Milton's eleventh sonnet. The original spelling Kittoe, is also so far fatal to the eastern derivation. Cato or Catto is a common name in Aberdeenshire, and may be only our northern Doric form of the English word. This small autobiography is Kitto's record of his first difficulties and subsequent progress, of his physical disability and its results—a record made at a period when he was able to take a patient survey of his inner life and its outer course.

The second volume, *Blindness,* has not the charm of the former, chiefly because it does not contain the results of self-analysis and experience. It describes many cases of blindness, and shows what high excellence in various departments of art and science the blind have attained. For the roll of the blind includes many illustrious names, far more than that of the deaf mutes. The deprivation is, in fact, less than that of hearing, for the want of hearing necessitates the want of language. Among blind poets, we have Homer and Milton, and at a great distance Blacklock, who was also a clergyman; Euler and Saunderson, among mathematicians; and Huber among naturalists. Many have been musicians; and Handel was blind in the last years of his life. Lieutenant Holman, blind from his twenty-fifth year, had travelled round the world, being at one time sent out of Russia as a spy; and in 1834 he published his travels, in four volumes. James Wilson was the blind biographer of the blind. Dr. Kitto adduces many instances of persons whose touch was a kind of second sight—who could distinguish colours by smell or touch—or who were able to comprehend locality in a marvellous degree, such as Tom Wilson of Dumfries, not only an ingenious mechanic, but one who often was seen, on a Saturday evening, conducting a "groggy neighbour" home to his wife and children. We ourselves knew as remarkable a case as any that Dr. Kitto has mentioned—that of Blind Alick of Stirling, who, as he twirled his key in his hand, would repeat the words of any portion of Scripture, if you simply named its chapter and verse, and who, if you recited any passage, would, in a moment and as easily, tell you the chapter and verse where it occurred. We heard, in our boyhood, of a Blind tailor, too, in the same town, who was famous for his taste and accuracy in sewing tartan dresses, distinguishing the various colours by the sense of touch. Dr. Kitto dwells with special tenderness on the sad condition of those who are at once blind and deaf and dumb, creatures in perfect isolation; the most remarkable cases being those of James Mitchell, in the north of Scotland,* and the well known Laura Bridgman of America. In fact, Laura Bridgman is the most awful example on record—totally blind, deaf, and dumb, with no power of smell, and almost none of taste. Touch alone remains; and her education is a surprising instance of ingenuity and perseverance.†

* We saw James Mitchell at Nairn last summer (1857.) He is certainly a strange creature; yet contrives to walk about, feeling on all sides of him, and has great pleasure in ascertaining, in his own way, the progress of any new buildings in the town.

† The following incident in the history of Laura Bridgman, her first interview with her mother after eighteen months' absence in the Institution, is one of the most touching ever recorded in any language:—

"The mother stood some time, gazing with overflowing eyes upon her unfortunate child, who, all unconscious of her presence, was playing about the room. Presently Laura ran against her, and at once began feeling her hands, examining

The volume, however, notwithstanding its interesting statements, never did, and never could, obtain the popularity of its predecessor.

Between 1846 and 1849 Dr. Kitto composed, for the Tract Society's Monthly volume, *Ancient and Modern Jerusalem*, two parts; *the Court and People of Persia*, two parts; and the *Tartar Tribes*. These little books, when not dealing in extracts from accredited authors, are very interesting, and put into plain language and brief compass, the result of former researches and previous publications. *The Tabernacle and its Furniture* was published in a thin quarto in 1849, and is well worth reading.

By the time that the *Cyclopædia* was nearly concluded, Dr. Kitto had fallen again into pecuniary diffi-

her dress, and trying to find out if she knew her; but not succeeding in this, she turned away as from a stranger, and the poor woman could not conceal the pang she felt that her beloved child did not know her. She then gave Laura a string of beads which she used to wear at home, which were recognized by the child at once, who, with much joy, put them around her neck, and sought me eagerly, to say she understood the string was from her home. The mother now tried to caress her, but poor Laura repelled her, preferring to be with her acquaintances. Another article from home was now given her, and she began to look much interested. She examined the stranger much closer, and gave me to understand she knew that she came from Hanover; she even endured her caresses, but would leave her with indifference at the slightest signal. The distress of the mother was now painful to behold; for, although she had feared that she should not be recognized, the painful reality of being treated with cold indifference by a darling child, was too much for a woman's nature to bear. After a while, on the mother taking hold of her again, a vague idea seemed to flit across Laura's mind that this could not be a stranger! She therefore felt her hands very eagerly, while her countenance assumed an expression of intense interest; she became very pale, and then suddenly red. Hope seemed struggling with doubt and anxiety, and never were contending emotions more strongly depicted upon the human face. At this moment of painful uncertainty, the mother drew her close to her side, and kissed her fondly; when at once the truth flashed upon the child, and all mistrust and anxiety disappeared from her face, as, with an expression of exceeding joy, she eagerly nestled to the bosom of her parent, and yielded to her fond embraces. After this, the beads were all unheeded, the playthings which were offered to her were utterly disregarded; her playmates, for whom but a moment before she gladly left the stranger, now vainly strove to pull her from her mother, and though she yielded her usual instantaneous obedience to any signal to follow me, it was evidently with painful reluctance. She clung close to me, as if bewildered and fearful; and when, after a moment, I took her to her mother, she sprang to her arms and clung to her with eager joy. The subsequent parting between them showed alike the affection, the intelligence, and the resolution of the child. Laura accompanied her mother to the door, clinging close to her all the way, until they arrived at the threshold, where she paused and felt around to ascertain who was near her. Perceiving the matron, of whom she is very fond, she grasped her with one hand, holding on convulsively to her mother with the other; and thus she stood for a moment. Then she dropped her mother's hand, put her handkerchief to her eyes, and turning round, clung, sobbing, to the matron, while her mother departed with emotions as deep as those of her child."
—The preceding description is by Dr. Howe, her teacher.

Another very remarkable instance of the pursuit of knowledge under difficulties, will be found in a volume called—*The Rifle, Axe, and Saddlebags*. By William Henry Milburn, the Blind Preacher. Reprinted from the American edition, with a Preface by the Rev. Thomas Binney. London: S. Low & Son, 1857.

culties, which preyed upon him for some years to come. He could not readily find employment of a kind to support him, and his sources of income were scanty and precarious. The composition of the small works we have referred to, was of little value in money. The new edition of the *Pictorial Bible* took up more time than he expected, and for what he called "surplus time" he obtained no remuneration. His friends, however, stood forward to assist him, and His Royal Highness the Prince Consort was a generous contributor.

At this period he projected the *Journal of Sacred Literature.* His object was noble, but the circulation never repaid him for toil and effort. The prospectus was of considerable size, and embraced a great variety of topics. The editor represents that there are many excellent religious periodicals, and much valuable matter locked up in them, but they are little read save by adherents of the ecclesiastical bodies to which they belong as organs. Very much more is equally lost in languages which few general readers know, and not many scholars understand. His inference is, that there is, therefore, an undoubted want of "a publication which, being established on a wider basis, should not be regarded as the organ of any one religious denomination, or of any one country; but should be the means of enabling different denominations and different countries to impart to one another whatever they know, which is likely to advance the general interests of biblical literature." There is truth in this statement, but much is taken for granted. Denominational predilections, though certainly weaker in this branch of sacred learning than any other, are not wholly without antagonistic influence. The editor adds:—" It will also appear that the current thological literature of this country, and especially its religious periodical literature, is too exclusively formed out of materials arising among ourselves, and in our own language. We have the apostolical assurance, that 'they who measure themselves by themselves, and compare themselves among themselves, are not wise;' and yet, for nearly two hundred years, we have done little else. There were of old 'giants' of biblical literature in our land, who, in their lifetime, kept up a profitable intercourse with the scholars of the Continent, and whose names are even now cited with respect by eminent foreign writers, who have but little acquaintance with our more modern labours in sacred literature. We therefore want a publication which shall keep us acquainted with all that is sound and valuable in the labours of biblical scholars of the European Continent and of North America, and in whose pages such of them as now live may interchange the results of their researches with our own writers.

"All these wants, and more than these, it is the object of the present publication to satisfy; and those who are apt to discern 'the signs of the times,' are strongly sensible that the time is come in which the demand for such a work is most urgent, and in which it may, with the greatest advantage, be produced."

"The editor was induced to think of this publication by the frequent representations, to the above effect, which he has been in the habit of receiving from various quarters; and already the private notification of his intention to venture on the undertaking has excited much interest both in this country and abroad. It is only, indeed, in consequence of the extensive literary co-operation which he was enabled to organise for the purposes of another publication (*The Cyclopædia of Biblical Literature*), that he has been induced to think seriously of this work in the form which it bears in the present prospectus: but with the like, and even more extensive co-operation, applicable to the existing undertaking, he finds no reason to distrust his means of producing a publication adequate to the supply of the wants which have been indicated."

Nobody will question Dr. Kitto's desire to promote biblical scholarship, but he regarded the working of the machine as too easy a matter. He forgot that many persons had not his promptitude in pouring forth the ripened results of their research and judgment; that it is one thing to induce a scholar to write an article for the *Cyclopædia*—a work of permanent value, and quite another thing to prevail upon him to send an elaborate contribution to a periodical, the interest of which too often passes away with the current number. The conspectus, as first published, embraces a wide range—Original Essays on Biblical History, Geography, Natural History, Antiquities, Biography, Bibliography, with Reviews, Notices, and Quarterly Lists of New Publications, Expository Passages, Philological Essays, Ecclesiastical History, Translations and Reprints, Oriental Literature, Correspondence and Intelligence. Dr. Kitto thought that his previous success secured a basis of prosperity to his new undertaking. "Every writer," he tells us, "does, in the course of time, gather around him a public who understand him better, and sympathise with him more than the rest of the world. Such a public, consisting chiefly of the possessors of his former publications, the editor of the *Journal of Sacred Literature* may venture to suppose that he, after many long years of well accepted labour, has brought around him; and though the present publication is of much wider range than any of his former productions, singly taken, and a proportionate increase of readers may be expected for it, he naturally looks to his old friends as the chief and most earnest supporters of an undertaking, to which the matured plans and the most cherished hopes of usefulness are now irrevocably committed, and in connection with which he has assumed responsibilities more anxious than he ever before ventured to incur."

Dr. Kitto, in forming such an estimate, evidently forgot to distinguish between scientific and popular literature. Thousands of the readers of the *Pictorial Bible*, who were delighted and benefitted with the work, set no value whatever on biblical criticism or Oriental literature; and many of those who purchased the *Cyclopædia*, did so because, from its compacted form and its learned treasures, it could be easily and profitably consulted. When they opened it, they could turn at once to the article they wanted. Whereas, in subscribing for a periodical, they did not know what they might get to read, or what peculiar subjects or texts might be handled. The notes of the *Pictorial Bible*, if scattered through the volumes of a *Quarterly Review*, would never have attracted hosts of readers— their charm lay in being so compendious, and in being found so readily in connection with the text of the Sacred Volume.

Dr. Kitto sadly miscalculated when he thought of finding so large a circle of subscribers to his *Journal*. The very prospectus warned away hundreds who had rejoiced in his previous labours, and who might wish him success in a path in which they had neither inclination nor ability to follow him. Yet who cannot sympathise with the editor when he thus winds up his address?—"If it tends to advance the glory of God by promoting the better understanding of His word and His ways, if it contributes in any useful degree to the advancement of sacred literature in this country, and if, by the sympathies of common labour, and by the development of common interests, it becomes a uniting tie among all those to whom those objects are dear, then may God bestow His blessing upon it, that it may prosper; but if it does none of these things, it is useless, it is not wanted: let it perish." The objects sought are noble, and it will be a happy day for the various churches when they can be reached; when sanctified scholarship shall have lost all sectarian bias; and when ministers of the Gospel shall seek their mental nutriment in biblical science, and be active in its advancement. At present, however, a Review, if it maintains its scientific character, must address itself to a select circle even of clerical readers, and can rarely have a large and compensating circulation. A better period is commencing. Erudition is rising above denominational influence, and assuming a true catholicism both in commentaries and in higher forms of periodical literature. Still, it must be admitted, that while a religious journal, in order to succeed, must have its party to appeal to, and fall back upon for support, Dr. Kitto failed, for other reasons, to realise his own purpose. In his delicacy toward his allies, no small amount of inferior matter was introduced by

him, and contributions were subjected to no rigid scrutiny, either as to sentiment or erudition. What may be a very instructive paper for a popular magazine, may be wholly out of place in a journal of biblical science. It should be explained, however, that Dr. Kitto felt fettered in rejecting or altering articles, from being almost solely dependent on the voluntary assistance of his friends, since the profits of the publication did not admit of the usual honorarium. In his letters to Mr. Blackader, publisher of the second series of the *Journal*, and one who, from his literary and biblical tastes and acquirements, ably seconded the exertions of the editor, he alludes now and again to his being so hampered by the want of funds, that only a very few of his contributors received any pecuniary recognition. His hope was, that his "friends would aid him for the sake of the good cause till better times came round. This has been the answer of some who have stood by me in all my struggles, but it is not to be expected from all." [*] His heart, however, was set upon his *Journal*, and he laboured anxiously for it. His notes to the publisher show his continuous anxiety about all points connected with it—advertisements as well as papers, postages as well as contributions. He strove to offend nobody in any way, and was sadly perplexed on falling into a dilemma, either when some one complained of delay in the insertion of an article, or a book was sent him with a request or virtual stipulation that the critique might be favourable, or two of his friends happened to forward a contribution on the same subject, or wished to review the same volume. There seemed to be a nervousness in all this business, quite unlike his usual firmness and composure. But the *Journal*, neither in its first nor second series, came up to his own idea; and, though it improved in several aspects, it never took that high place which his name and fame were expected to give it. The first number appeared on the first of January 1848; and, after anxiously watching over it for several years, till eleven volumes had been printed, he was obliged to give it up. But he made some stipulations as to its future character. Though sorrowing to take leave of it, he wished it still to retain its original impress, and thus wrote:—" I have secured effectual guarantees that it shall be always conducted on the essential principles on which it was founded—that it shall retain its comprehensive and catholic character—that it shall be orthodox—and that it shall not be sectarian." [†] It did not at first "pay print and paper." "I hope the best," he wrote to Mr. Tracy. . . . "I have little misgiving,—less now, indeed, than ever;"—but this was in November 1847. "The *Journal* is getting up nearly to one thousand copies," writes he to the same friend in March 1848.

* Letter to Mr. Blackader, Oct. 7, 1852.
† Ibid., Aug. 11, 1853.

What disappointment he must have felt! His plan had not succeeded; his anticipations were blasted. He should have begun with a large reserve fund, which might have been easily raised for the purpose, and not involved his own means and the bread of his family in the undertaking. Other and onerous duties pressed upon him, his health had also given way, and in 1853 he reluctantly handed over the *Journal* to Dr. Burgess, its present able and indefatigable editor.

Dr. Kitto had now lived some years at Woking; but he felt that while such a rural residence might enable him to economise, it was exceedingly inconvenient for his literary pursuits. Accordingly, in March 1849, he returned to London, and took up his abode first at 21 High Street, Camden-town, removing the following year to 1 Great Camden Street, where he remained till his final departure for Germany, in August 1854.

11

DAILY BIBLE ILLUSTRATIONS
LAST DAYS—DEATH

Dr. Kitto had so often felt his way toward employment, that he knew somewhat of the tastes of each publisher, and the characteristic wares of each publishing house. To the enterprising publishers of the *Encyclopædia Britannica* he addressed the project of a *Biblical Cyclopædia;* and to the Messrs. Oliphant of Edinburgh, so well known for their issue of many practical religious books fitted for general circulation and enjoying it, he sent, in June 1849, a long letter, out of which sprang, in a brief period, his last work— the *Daily Bible Illustrations.* The plan which he sketched himself was different from that ultimately adopted. In his delineation of it, he premises that "he primarily looked to an extended measure of usefulness in that which seemed to have become his proper vocation." "The general title I purpose to be that of *Bible Evenings;* and as I incline to think that the book of Ruth affords an appropriate theme for the first portion, the full title of the volume we commence with would be—*Bible Evenings—the History of Ruth Conversationally explained and illustrated,* by J. K., &c.; or perhaps, *Conversations on the History of Ruth* would be as well for the second title. The attraction in subjects of this sort is known to be very great; but it is my hope to enhance this attraction by the manner of treatment. It is meant that the interlocutors shall be, not *sticks* but *characters,* and that the progress shall be enlivened and diversified by such scenes, incidents, and circumstances, as might naturally arise among such persons. The leading idea is, that a family in the middle educated class, devotes two evenings in the week to conversations on the Bible. Of the persons,

one may be a biblical scholar, supposed to be able to explain everything that is not assigned to the other characters; another will be a traveller, who has seen everything, and been everywhere, and who is, therefore, able to supply a lively description of places and products, and to point out the analogous manners, customs, and ideas of the *Modern* East; a third may suggest practical improvements; and by so doing, he will give the key note to one more, who has a wonderful memory for all kinds of ancient and modern anecdotes, which appear to him to illustrate or bear upon the principles developed, or the conduct followed; and there may be another yet, apt to remember or to fabricate all kinds of poetry and snatches of verse, having some kind of connection with the matter in hand. All this is to be produced, not in the stiff A B C style of interlocution, but with all the animating turns and incidents of natural conversation.

"The result, as I conceive, would be a most instructive and entertaining book, for which there could not fail to be a large demand. The elements of success, in such undertakings as this, have been most carefully considered, and the work will be expressly formed to embrace them all. It is not designed to be ostensibly a book for children, but care will be taken that there shall be nothing beyond the range of intelligent young people of ordinary education; and the volume would, without doubt, be seen to be well suited to them, and would be largely used in presents to them."

The sketch is ingenious, and such a colloquy would have been interesting; but it would have been very difficult to execute the plan, so as to give each scene a living and natural aspect, apportion his remarks to each speaker with natural propriety, and prevent the whole from becoming an artificial and tiresome set of little discourses. The true dramatic presentation cannot be elaborated by effort. Dr. Kitto had a vigorous imagination; but such a work would have taxed his powers to the utmost in forecasting the various dialogues, and giving to every character its harmonious utterance. Indeed, *Uncle Oliver* is a failure, so far as dramatic ease and fitness are concerned. The scheme adopted was far better. It cost him less labour, was far more natural, and it has been eminently acceptable. Mr. Oliphant suggested a series of papers for every day in the year, each paper being on a separate topic, and the whole of them, in order, forming volumes of consecutive reading and comment. Dr. Kitto acquiesced in the plan, for it was not new to him, having been one of his multitudinous projects, which he purposed to call *Bible Readings for every day in the year,* or else the *Daily Scripture Reader.* The Sunday papers were to be on themes in unison with the sacred day, and the treatment of them was to be in harmony. Dr. Kitto's own mind was growing in spirituality, and he preferred to write these last papers himself, rightly refusing some assistance which had been offered to him. "I shall be glad," is his argument to the publisher, "of the opportunity of refreshing my mind by some spiritual writing; and, besides, I am partial to this kind of writing, and have had considerable experience in it, though the general tendency of my undertakings has been to drive me out of it."

He entered upon his work in a spirit that could not fail to ensure success:—

"Since I wrote last, I have been enabled to look more closely into our new enterprise, and I cannot but say that the more I grapple it as a practical matter, the better I like it. I feel that the task which thus devolves on me is one which I shall execute with real zest and pleasure. I see that the execution of the design affords a fair opportunity of *usefulness*, which has always been a consideration with me, while it presents me with an occasion, not always to be found, of producing an agreeable and popular book. This encourages me; for, although I have produced books of the class, I began to dread getting too much entangled in books heavy with scholarship and the solidities of knowledge. I therefore enter upon this work with the determination that I will, and with the conviction that I can, produce a book which shall be read—and this not by being superficial, but by exhibiting, in an attractive manner, all the information that can be fitly produced, and the best of all such thoughts as my meditations may suggest." Again, and after having succeeded, he states, in one of his prefaces, that his object had been "to make the new familiar, and to make the familiar new."

The first volume was produced a few days after the stipulated period; and he confidently says to the publisher, "I never put a book out of my hands, of the success of which I have felt so sure as this." And his confidence was fully justified. He pledged himself to punctuality in the publication of the volumes; and gave as his ground, "that his working day was of twice the usual length, from 4 A.M. to 9 P.M., with little interruption." His first work each morning was the paper for the day, though he felt such continuous labour to be occasionally a "hard job." The volumes were to be published quarterly. The first volume, *The Antediluvians and Patriarchs*, is dated December 1849, and takes in the first three months of the year; the second, *Moses and the Judges*, is dated April 1850, and is meant for April, May, and June. In the preface to this volume, the author avows his thankfulness "for the warm favour with which the first volume was received," and feels himself encouraged to "hope for a blessing upon his labours in the direction which has now been given to them." The third volume, for the months July August, and September, brought Dr.

Kitto to his usual explanation, that the limits originally fixed for the work were too small, and that his plan must not be "crushed in the attempt to force the substantial matter of two volumes into one." Half the volume is occupied with the Life of David, and this portion is of great interest. The King of Israel is portrayed truthfully, without any attempt to palliate his sins, or tone down the darker traits of his character; yet how unlike he appears to the picture of him in Bayle, or to that in the article "David" in Kitto's own *Cyclopædia*. In fact, we have always been charmed by the papers on David; so much is brought out incidentally, and so many of the secret links of his court and policy are unfolded, by a reference often to a single clause of the inspired history; so just an appreciation of Joab and the other notable men about him is interwoven, and there is so striking an estimate both of his weakness and of his strength, of his sins and of his sorrows, of the raptures and the tears of his lyrical muse. "David," he says, "was always great in affliction." The bird which once rose to heights unattained before by mortal wing, filling the air with its joyful songs, now lies with maimed wing upon the ground, pouring forth its doleful cries to God." The volume which completes the year is named *Solomon and the Kings*—the characters of principal interest in it being the wise monarch and the prophet Elijah.

The publication of this last volume had been retarded four or five months by subordinate engagements. He completed a work for Mr. Bohn, named *Scripture Lands Described in a Series of Historical, Geographical, and Topographical Sketches*. London, 1850. These sketches are simply a memoir to accompany and explain a beautiful biblical atlas of twenty-four maps, and are "not wholly a reproduction of materials previously used by the same writer," but contain the results of recent researches, though not to any large extent. There is, however, a very full and useful index, exhibiting the ancient and modern names of scriptural places, with their latitude and longitude, and other important information, in a tabular form. This excellent volume forms one of Bohn's *Illustrated Library*, and is, like others in the same series, handsomely got up. The other productions, which occupied a portion of Kitto's time, was a book which had been written two years before for the Tract Society, but the printing of which had been delayed for want of requisite illustrations. *The Land of Promise* is a re-exhibition of a great deal that he had said before, though in form and arrangement it differs much from *Scripture Lands*, and one special object of it was to describe every place or site of interest "*as it now appears.*"

At a personal interview between Mr. Oliphant and Dr. Kitto in London, in 1850, the second series of

Daily Bible Illustrations was virtually agreed on, and in September of the same year, the publisher had suggested the dedication of the work to the Queen, when it should be completed. Kitto at first objected, inasmuch as such dedications are " usually prefixed to works which cannot stand alone, and a royal dedication has come to be almost considered as a sign of intrinsic weakness. There seems, also, to my mind, in this case, a sense of disproportion, like mounting Great Tom of Oxford on a village church. One would think this distinction would better suit some great work, such as I may hope hereafter to produce. Yet, on the other hand, this is not absolutely a small work as to size, nor, if I may believe half that I read in the notices you send me, is it altogether unimportant or valueless in its contents. It is not unlikely that it might interest her Majesty more than any work I have yet produced. Upon the whole, perhaps, I should rather like it, if it can be shown to be a proper thing to do ; and I do see one point very clearly, that if the pension should be granted, it would be a very proper and graceful thing for me to take the *first* opportunity that subsequently offers, of thus expressing my grateful acknowledgments. Nothing can be clearer than that. Then, again, if this benefit should not be realised in October, such a dedication might advance the matter somewhat; but of this I am not able to judge. It is well to wait, to see what October brings forth."

The allusions in these last sentences lead us to state, that it had been deemed advisable by Dr. Kitto's friends to make a united and hearty effort to obtain a grant for him from the Civil List. Memorials and letters were forwarded to the Prime Minister from all religious parties in the kingdom, including peers, bishops, clergy, civilians, and literary and theological professors. The application was at length successful ; and on the 17th of December, Lord John Russell conveyed the brief but gratifying intimation, " the Queen has directed that a grant of £100 a-year should be made to you from her Majesty's Civil List, on account of your useful and meritorious literary works."

By February in the following year, Dr. Kitto had got permission to inscribe his volumes to her Majesty, and he was somewhat at a loss to know in what words to frame the dedication. Nor was he sure whether it might not be necessary for him to go to court, adding —" I may take it into my head to go after all, especially if I can get hold of some one to help me through it." He would have presented his volumes in person, if it had been deemed necessary ; still, such an appearance would have been a trial to one of " his nervous retiredness of temper," and who had abstained from all public assemblies. " It may be," he consoles himself, " that the feeling which thus holds me prisoner is but a protective instinct, guarding me from the circumstances which might press *too painfully* upon me the consciousness of my condition." On the 24th June, the four volumes, with a copy of the *Lost Senses*, handsomely bound, were sent to Colonel Phipps, at Buckingham Palace, who acknowledged the receipt of them —adding besides, " I have not failed to present these books to her Majesty the Queen, by whom they have been very graciously accepted."

Before Dr. Kitto had finished the first series, and at the beginning of 1851, there were decided indications of approaching cerebral debility. The pain in the back of his head, which he had often felt before, had become too intense to allow of mental toil. He was compelled to moderate his labour and shorten his hours. Rising at four or five in the morning was totally out of the question. To stoop his head to write created excruciating agony. He had vomited blood annually for a long period, but not during the last two years; and the cessation of this self-relieving process may have burdened his brain. But the hemorrhage returned in the crisis, and a medical friend having bled him copiously besides, the neuralgia abated. These warnings were so far slighted by him, that he did not adopt decided measures to maintain his health and prolong his working powers. It was in this weakened state that he wrought upon the *Evening Series*, the first volume of which was published in December 1851, and the last in January 1854—more than double the time that was fixed on for the production of the *Morning Series*.

We need not characterise at length the *Evening Series*, which is quite equal to the *Morning Series*. The first volume was *Job and the Poetical Books*—to wit, Psalms, Proverbs, Ecclesiastes, and the Song of Songs—and has " more of a literary cast" than any of its predecessors. The second volume, *Isaiah and the Prophets*, is rather miscellaneous in its nature—giving some prominence to the person and exploits of Cyrus, as well as the local fulfilment of prophecy, and containing a digest of the results of those researches which Botta and Layard had prosecuted at Nineveh. The third is the *Life and Death of Our Lord*, and the last is the *Apostles and the Early Church*. The *Life of Christ* is presented synoptically, and therefore the various chapters are closely connected ; while the sketch of the Apostles inweaves the historical intimations contained in the Epistles.

This work, to the eight volumes of which we have so briefly alluded, has obtained, as it merits, a wide popularity. The topics are selected with admirable skill, and are usually founded on some striking scene or novel adventure, some fact or sentiment, some attractive feature of character, or remarkable incident in eastern life and enterprise. Thus, in the first volume, you pass from the simplicity of the tent to the bravery of the camp, from the fire on the hearth to the flame of the altar ; and whether the paper be on a marriage or a funeral, a sacrifice or a scene of revelry, whether the theme be Abel's death, Lamech's polygamy, Jubal's harp, Enoch's piety, Noah's ark, Sarah's veil, Hagar's flight, Lot's escape, Jacob's pillar, Joseph's bondage, or Pharaoh's signet, each is told with a charming simplicity, surrounded with numerous and beautiful illustrations, and interspersed or closed with pointed and just reflections. Dr. Kitto throws light, throughout the series, on many obscure allusions, says many tender and many startling things, opens his heart to the reader, as he unfolds the stores of his learning—all his utterances being in harmony with his avowed design, to make this work "really interesting as a reading book to the family circle, for which it is primarily intended." It is not easy to characterise the volumes ; and the author seems to have felt this difficulty himself, when he says, in the preface to the second of them, this work is "not a history—not a commentary—not a book of critical and antiquarian research—not one of popular illustration, nor of practical reflection—but it is something of all these." He admits that "it would have been easy to have written a more learned work ;" but he carefully avoided the "forms and processes of scholarship" on the one hand, and, on the other hand, he made no pretension of "writing down" to any class of readers. He aimed "to put the whole into brisker language than is needful in heavier works." "I am amused," he says, as the work was proceeding, "to see what a hankering there is among the noticers, that I should make these papers 'practical,' &c.—that is, turn them into little sermons. This would be to spoil the thing altogether. It would be, to abstain from my own line, in which, from peculiar circumstances, studies, tastes, and travels, I can do better than many others, to attempt that of which there is already a superabundance, and which thousands could execute as well as, or better than myself. This tone of remark is, however, natural for those who do not sufficiently consider my peculiar vocation. I do, however, try to give a religious turn to matters where I have a fair opportunity of doing so ; and, upon the whole, this is probably the most religious work I have yet written." The papers are each independent and complete—a parable for the day, or a meditation for the night. The interest never flags, dry detail is avoided, and the themes for the Lord's Day are in exquisite keeping with its sacred character. These eight volumes are, in fact, the cream of all that Dr. Kitto had previously written. There is a special charm about them, and a vein of serious instruction runs through them. A rich and racy humour now and then shines out, not indeed so frequent as in Matthew Henry, nor so salient and picturesque as in Thomas Fuller. Nothing like a morbid spiritualism

is found in them—it is open-faced godliness. They are suggestive, too, in their nature ; many things are placed 'in a novel light, and many of the remarks made are so new, and yet so much in point, that you wonder they never struck you before. Difficulties are honestly met, and are never set aside by any rationalising process. The author has availed himself of all his former labours, as if "anxious to disburden his full soul" of its treasures. He writes, too, with earnestness and living power ; and the results of his travels, experience, and research suffer no deterioration from being moulded anew in the fire of a devout soul, and set in the frame work of an ingenious and healthful piety.

In the autumn of 1852, Dr. Kitto was again and more seriously endangered. The pain was more intense and alarming, and he could no longer fight against it. Medical advice was resorted to, and he was enjoined to do less work and take more exercise. At least two hours a-day was he enjoined to walk in the open air. But he complains, September 7, to his publisher, of such consumption of time :—

"I have not got well so rapidly as I expected, and am still under active medical treatment. The last week was nearly a blank for practical purposes, and the anxiety thus occasioned has probably retarded my recovery. I am, however, gathering strength, and am undoubtedly better. The excruciating pains are less violent, and I can venture to sit longer at my desk without bringing them on. Thus, I am beginning to return to my usual habits, although, for the present, on a reduced scale as to time. The new habit of *walking* has been so seriously impressed upon me, that I hope to cultivate it as a matter of duty. The want of a *definite* object is the difficulty : care for one's health seems too vague an inducement for a practice so adverse to one's habits, and, in its immediate aspect, a serious loss of precious time. I suppose, however, that some one or other will always be dragging me out now, and Mrs. Kitto will probably look to it, as the doctor has enjoined her to turn me out daily, and not to let me in again till my time is up. I felicitated myself at first, that he only stated how long I was to walk, not how *fast*, or how much, so that, as I thought, I might manage to make the business entertaining, by sauntering about among the book-stalls; but the doctor is now too sharp for me, and talks of six miles a-day. Think of that for a man who has almost lost the power of putting one leg before another ! However, seeing that there are so many little ones whose immediate welfare seems to have been made dependent upon my existence, and that I have set before me many labours which I should be loath to leave unexecuted, I hope to be enabled to adapt myself to this new condition of affairs. It may be the Lord's method of strengthening and preserving me for such work as He means me to do. In this point of view, the death of one whom I knew, Mr. Porter of the Board of Trade, 'from want of exercise'—a cause I never before saw assigned in an obituary notice—has made considerable impression on my mind."

Certainly the death of Mr. Porter, and from such a cause, should have checked his exhausting industry; yet, when we think of the numerous family supported by his daily labours—a family of five sons and five daughters—we must not judge him harshly. Still his disease was of such a nature, that it was not to be tampered with; for the organ attacked was his only implement of labour and source of income. Weakness or injury to it would sadly diminish the supplies, or stop them altogether. He was visited with another relapse ere September expired, in which the head-pains were continuous. On his being cupped, and on the application of other means, he revived, and, by the constant exercise to which he had been forced, his "too solid flesh" was somewhat "melted off." He could well spare some. Mrs. Hullock, an old Malta friend, who had accidentally discovered him through means of *The Lost Senses*, was surprised, on visiting him, to see "the little *slender* man become so great in *person* and name." He was very thankful for recruited strength, and in October was tolerably well, but complaining of the *immediate* loss of time which his daily walk occasioned. He should have remembered that Milton, one of the poets of his earliest admiration, used to walk daily after dinner in his garden, three and four hours at a time. Even the Exhibition in 1851 had small enticements for him. Fleet Street and the Strand were greater to him than the Crystal Palace, but he did not very often frequent them. Occasionally he sauntered down Oxford Street, Regent Street, the Strand, and Holborn, "looking for bargains and curious things at the bookshops;" and even this lounging was better than no recreation at all. He, however, did visit the great Exhibition, and saw it at its close; and though the noise made not the least impression upon him, "the scene was striking—even to grandeur." But he sighs and says, "I certainly do not feel that I lost a day, but my work did." This perpetual toil was fast wearing him out, and still he grudged the slightest relaxation. Yet one is glad to find that, on September 30, being the last of his boys' Michaelmas holidays, he went with them "a-nutting to Epping Forest," "not sorry to have so good an excuse for a run." He found relief at this period from Pulvermacher's hydro-electric chain, which threw a "sensible continuous current of electric fluid through the part affected."

Anxious to have some stable means of support, when the *Daily Bible Illustrations* should be concluded, he was induced to edit a weekly religious periodical—*Sunday Reading for Christian Families.** It did not succeed, and, after three months, was abandoned, though it deserved a better fate. The capital papers which its editor wrote for it, were not sufficient to ensure its success. Though warned that the project would be a failure, he was resolved to try, and the trial satisfied him. Thus he delivers himself :—"The case is this—For many years I have been desirous of finding a fixed basis of occupation and usefulness in the conduct of a periodical publication, which, by affording me a salary, would make regular and determinate a portion of the income I require, leaving me comparatively free for the book-work, which would be needful to complete that income, and relieving me from the perils of an entire dependence thereon."†

But his malady soon returned in still more awful violence. The electric chain in which he had so fondly trusted could not charm the pain away; and, while he was in this state of prostration, he was visited with another trial. His youngest child, Henry Austin, died. This was the first entrance of death into his dwelling; and every parent knows the pang of a first bereavement. Aye, though it be an infant that is taken away when yet unable to prattle, the new sorrow pierces and lacerates the parental heart. Kitto's softened spirit bowed to the chastisement. He loved his children dearly, and never, with all his solitary study and toil, "hid his face from his own flesh."

This little child had wound itself round his heart. His earliest intimation to Mr. Oliphant is (April 12) :—

"This is the first letter I have written for a week, and the first time I have taken up my pen for any purpose since Saturday. There has been much besides my ill health : a beloved child of mine has been dying, and now it lies here dead. God took it from us on Monday morning, and while I bow in submission to this stroke, knowing it is from my Father's hand, my heart is very sore. During the years that I have had a home of my own, death has not been permitted to enter, and its presence is, from its strangeness, the more grim and terrible. During that long time, I have indeed been tried with many griefs; but *this* form of trial, the hardest of all to bear, has been spared to me. Now, this also has come, and finds my heart very weak. May the Lord strengthen it for me, and enable me in due time to learn what lesson it is that He means to teach me by this new stroke of His rod !"

The Rev. Dr. Brown of Edinburgh, whose wide sympathies extend to every "companion in tribulation," sent him one of his useful and solacing little books—*Comfortable Words for Christian Parents bereaved of Little Children.* "It touched him much." Mrs. Kitto

* London : Needham, 1853.
† Letter to Mr. Blackader, March 3, 1853.

also felt that it fulfilled the promise in its title, and as its balm dropped into her heart, she did not refuse to be comforted. The father was thankful for the "seasonable memorial," and in his own way tells how dear this babe had become from its very weaknesses, and how the only land he possessed had been purchased for a burial-place—a sacred spot with a precious deposit:—

"It was but a little child, thirteen months old. He was from the first difficult to rear, and required the constant care of his mother; and this brought his infancy, with its numerous little ways, more under my own notice than that of any other of the children; and the great solicitude with which he had needed to be watched over and prayed for, endeared him greatly to us. At length all difficulty seemed to be overcome, and he waxed fair and strong, and his mother ventured to trust him partially from her own constant care. Then he caught cold, and after a few weeks of suffering, heart-rending to witness, he died. His mother, with many tears, reproaches herself, that if she had never trusted him from her own care, but had continued to nurse him in her own arms, he would yet have lived. It is difficult to realise the idea that, nevertheless, he has not fallen without the will of God. It is hard to learn, but she is learning it, and so am I, and I feel that all real comfort, under a trial like this, must be rooted in that conviction. I am now become, for the first time, the owner of a grave—all the land in this wide world that I possess. This afternoon I shall be constrained to consign to it the remains—still beautiful in death—of this dear little child, into whose bright eyes I have for so many months been daily looking for matter of hope or fear. May the Lord strengthen in the hour now near, and make realities to my own heart the comforts I have sometimes endeavoured to impart to others!"

Those comforts which he had dispensed to other mourners, had been no mere commonplaces, no trite courtesies, no empty or unavailing regrets. He did not only throw his flower on the sepulchral urn, but he touched and stayed the bleeding heart with his "bundle of myrrh." "When," he writes in reference to the death of the widow of Zarephath's only son, "we behold that a child so dear—

. . "Like a flower crusht with a blast is dead,
And ere full time hangs down his smiling head,"

how many sweet interests in life, how many hopes for the time to come, go down to the dust with him! The purest and most heart-felt enjoyment which life offers to a mother in the society of her little child, is cut off for ever. The hope, the mother's hope, of great and good things to come from this her son, is lost for her. 'The live coal that was left,' and which she had reckoned that time would raise to a cheerful flame, to warm her home, and to preserve and illustrate the name and memory of his dead father, is gone

out—is quenched in darkness. The arms which so often clung caressingly around her, and whose future strength promised to be as a staff to her old age, are stiff in death. The eyes which glistened so lovingly when she came near, now know her not. The little tongue, whose guileless prattle had made the long days of her bereavement short, is now silent as that of the 'mute dove.' Alas! alas! that it should ever be a mother's lot to close in death the eyes of one whose pious duty, if spared, should be in future years to press down her own eyelids. This is one of the great mysteries of life, to be solved only thoroughly, only fully to our satisfaction, in that day when, passing ourselves the gates of light, we behold all our lost ones gather around our feet."*

Thus his afflictions were multiplying, for the process of refinement was to be severe, because it was not to be long. He who "sits as a purifier," gave special intensity to the "refiner's fire," as its action was not to be of continued duration. Beautifully had the mourner expressed himself already as to the results of discipline:—

"It is only by the grafting of our will into His that we can bear much fruit—any fruit; and no branch was ever yet grafted without being cut to the quick. In what He allows us, or in what He takes from us, in His dealings with us, or in His action upon us through others, the same object is always kept in view, of teaching us our dependence upon Him; and it is well with us—very well, then *only* well—when our will so works with His, that in all we see, or hear, or enjoy, or suffer, we strive to realise for ourselves that which He strives to teach—to see His will, and to have no will but his." †

At this period of sorrow he became worse himself, and found no relief from any of his previous appliances. The late Dr. Golding Bird was then consulted, who, refusing at first to entertain the case of a deaf patient, as it consumed so much of his valuable time, no sooner learned who the applicant was, than, in characteristic terms, he expressed the warmest interest in him, and afterwards received his fortnightly visits with the greatest cordiality, refusing, at the same time, the customary fees. He said to the sufferer, "If you mean to live, you must work less, and take more exercise." But, at the expiry of a few months, he declared Dr. Kitto incurable, because the intractable patient had systematically counterworked his physician's skill and prescriptions. His brain wanted rest. Dr. Bird had tried to subdue the cerebral irritation; but Dr. Kitto persisted in thinking and writing, and nullifying all his medical adviser's kindness and efforts. It was pressed upon him, that he must cease from labour for a period; but he replied, "No; I must finish the work for which I have had the money, and if I knew I should die with the pen in my hand, I will go on as

* *Daily Bible Illustrations* Vol. 1, p. 899. † Ibid., p. 943.

long as the Lord permits." So that he virtually sealed his own doom. In August he went down to Ramsgate, and though "he spent much of his time in the open air, his head became rather worse than better." To induce him to prolong his stay, a box of books was sent for ; but "the books spoiled the holiday, and the holiday spoiled the books." His general health was, however, materially improved, and so little apprehensive was he of any serious ailment clinging to him, that he amused himself with projecting a plan of travel in Egypt and Palestine, "*mainly* for the purpose of biblical illustration," which might be produced after his return "in the shape of, perhaps, two 8vo volumes." But he came back to London "in *one* respect, not sensibly better ;" and believing that, nevertheless, some "salutary influence" had been received, he resolved to "run about as much as time and circumstances would allow." It was at this period that, as already stated, he resigned the *Journal of Sacred Literature* into the hands of Dr. Burgess. But his hours of study were greatly curtailed, and his labours on his closing work greatly abridged. He was forbidden to rise at four or five in the morning, as he had done for fifteen years, and enjoined to walk in the forenoon, "one of the prime portions of his time." These and similar explanations he made to his Edinburgh publisher, confessing "his fretting anxiety at his inability not to get on faster." He had decided, at all hazards, to finish the book on hand ; and had for it and other pressing labours been tempted to neglect Dr. Bird's keen and honest warnings.

It would be wrong, however, to suppose that the *Daily Bible Illustrations*, though professedly his main work, were either the heaviest or most exhausting element of his labours. It was his anxiety about his other engagements that fretted and fatigued him. He took too much in hand, and, in his haste to keep all his appointments, he overtasked himself. What he had been doing for Bohn's Library and for the Tract Society, his new enterprise in connection with the Sunday Reading for families, and his uneasy feelings and unrelaxing tension of soul about his *Journal*—this combination of effort and vigilance was far more damaging to him than any study or writing necessary for the *Daily Bible Illustrations*. The series of chapters required for this work cost him little labour in comparison, many of them being subjective in their nature —the welling out of his own spontaneous reflections, and the others which exhibit research, being upon topics long familiar to him, and on which he had already delivered his thoughts. Though the *Daily Bible Illustrations* were, at this time, his largest, they were,

on the whole, his easiest work, for he had ceased to compose a paper a day, and the toil had become a pleasure to him, as well as oftentimes a relief to his burdened spirit. Nor did he die, as he had protested, with the pen in his hand, and his labour unfinished. The angel of death calmly waited for him till he had laid it down.

He carried out his resolve as to the eighth volume of the *Daily Bible Illustrations*,* amidst much weakness and delay, and at length concluded his task. His wife and he together blessed God when the last sentence was written, and felt that they had abundant and pressing reason to "offer thanksgiving." This closing composition of a closing life has for its subject the Catacombs at Rome, and the striking picture of early Christianity furnished by them. And his last words are, "In these solemn recesses we meet with 'none but Christ.' It is the unobscured light of His countenance, as of the sun shining in its strength, that irradiates the gloom of these solitudes. He is the Alpha, the Omega, of all around. All is of Him—

' HIM FIRST, HIM LAST, HIM MIDST, HIM WITHOUT END.' "

It was in the frame of mind indicated by these glowing words, that he gave thanks to Him who had guarded and blessed him in his last great labour upon earth, and had carried him to its termination, though sickness and sorrow had often threatened interruption.

And the work was not finished a day too soon. The last day of regular toil was succeeded by the first day of his final illness ; for next morning, as he attempted to rise, he felt a strange powerlessness, and said, in sad and hurried tones, to his wife, "O Bell ! I am numb all down my side." The effects of this stroke of paralysis continued for a considerable period, yet he gave what time he could afford to the revision of the *Biblical Cyclopædia* for a new edition. This work being stereotyped, the corrections could not be very many, though some of them were very important. Nor did he go over a large portion of the book, for the malady soon returned in a more intense and alarming shape. On the morning of the 4th of February, he was seized with a fit, which lasted till he was bled by Dr. Tunaley, his medical attendant. Consciousness was quite restored, but violent and agonising headache, the result of congestion of the brain, still remained. That rest which he had been so unwilling to take, was now forced upon him by extreme debility. He was worn out by continuous and unrelieved labour. Still, Dr. Bird had thought and said that a year's rest might yet restore him. The farmer allows his field to lie fallow, and he believes that he loses nothing by a year's unproductiveness. But the powerless and moneyless author had, in the meantime, his household to support, and without work there was no income, save the small pension from her Majesty. Mrs. Kitto consulted Mr. Oliphant, and

---

*Formerly published in 8 volumes by Wm. Oliphants in 1893, now issued in 1981 by Kregel Publications, Grand Rapids, Michigan, complete and unabridged in two volumes.

a plan was proposed to raise such a sum as might secure the overdone labourer two years' release. But before the idea was wrought out, he was seized again, and more severely; so that a larger and more permanent form of assistance was projected. Committees for the purpose were formed in London and in Scotland, presided over respectively by John Labouchere, Esq., a generous philanthropist in the metropolis, and by his old and valued friend, Sir John M'Neill. Sir John took the chair at a meeting in Edinburgh, and delivered, in his opening address, a just and eulogistic criticism on Dr. Kitto's biblical labours. When the plan was brought into operation, contributions were received not only from admirers at home, but from New York, Nova Scotia, and South Australia. The final result did not, however, come up to expectation, the sum received being only £1,800.* Had the particulars of Dr. Kitto's early life been extensively known—his hardships and privations, his fortitude and triumphs—much more, we believe, would have been promptly contributed.

For many weeks, Dr. Kitto was utterly prostrated; but he was in no small degree gratified by the public interest shown in his behalf. It was not, however, till the month of June, that he was able to pen a note, though he had made several attempts; and he wrote, on the 20th of that month, to Mr. Oliphant, under great depression and feebleness :—

"At the present time, my head is, upon the whole, considerably better, and I have, on most days, intervals of comparative ease; but, at best, it is exceedingly tender, and any little movement or effort brings on *acute* pain. I am led out now and then by Mrs. Kitto, or one of the elder children, for a short crawl; but I generally return in great distress, the movement, however gentle, having disturbed my head, and the lower limbs being still very feeble, from the effects of the repeated seizures, though the more obviously distressing results of these seizures have most materially abated. I rejoice to learn, that my medical adviser is of opinion that, in the state to which I have been brought by diet and medical treatment, there is little probability of further attacks of this nature. Still, however, the original slight numbness along the whole left side, which I was, if I remember rightly, describing to you in the letter I left unfinished, and which was forwarded to you after the dreadful attack of the 4th of February—this has remained all through, though less sensibly felt at some times than at others. The doctor is, however, persuaded that this also will be displaced, under a change of air. This change has been retarded by various circumstances, with which you are ac-

quainted; and now, lastly, by my wife's illness, which added much to my other distresses. But, through the Lord's mercy, she seems much better to-day, though far from well; and I entertain the hope, that the change, when it does take place, will re-establish her health, which has been much shaken of late.

"I cannot write more now; but I cannot close this, my first and necessarily short letter, without expressing how deeply I have been affected by the kind interest which, under these most trying circumstances, you have manifested on my behalf, and the zealous exertions you have made to ameliorate the evils of this condition. God has been very gracious to me, not only in keeping my heart from sinking in the evil day, but in raising up many friends to testify their effectual sympathy for me and mine. This is most cheering; and, if it should please Him to remove the cloud which now hangs over my tabernacle, I shall hope to be enabled to evince my gratitude by more entire devotement to that service in which alone perfect freedom is found—in actual labour, if that be possible, or, if not, in patient waiting for Him."

Labour, indeed, was denied him, and "patient waiting" was henceforth to be his duty. "Wait" had been his motto,—"only wait, only believe" had been his shield against despondency. In these seasons of trial, the Master had been saying to him, "I come quickly;" and his response was, "Amen, even so come."

A journey to the Continent, which had been meditated for some time, was postponed for the purpose of trying the benefit of further medical skill in London. The experiment, alas! did not succeed. His daughter Shireen had gone down to Edinburgh, on her way out to Canada; but failing health obliged her to return to London. Her father, in this dark hour, writes in July to the same correspondent :—

"Shireen returned from Edinburgh on Saturday, without much exhaustion. Her return was a mixed pain and pleasure to me—pain, that her meritorious hopes and endeavours should be frustrated, and pleasure, to be reunited to one who had seemed lost to us. Under all, I thank God, however—and it is much to be thankful for—that I have been enabled to rest in the full and satisfying persuasion, that all things will assuredly work together for good, *vital* good to myself, and to those whom God has given me. I have no ground to expect—I never have expected, that the Lord should establish on my behalf an exemption from all trouble; but I believe and know that all must be for *eventual* good, though it may be by ways I should not prefer, or by ways that I might even wish to avoid. I am very unable to express the sense I entertain of the munificent kindness and delicate consideration which you have evinced towards me, both before and since this present emergency and trial. The *last* in-

---

* Of this sum, there remains about £1,200, which has been invested in the names of Trustees for the benefit of Dr. Kitto's widow and family.

stance is peculiarly gratifying to me, and will occupy a pleasant place in my recollections of this time."

The next letter has some faint scintillations of his former humour :—

"*July* 31. . . . It seems that we are to go on Wednesday se'nnight, and that in a day or two we leave this house, in which I had thought I had made my life's nest, for furnished lodgings, as a preparatory step, having let the house. Changes so radical have become hard to me; but the Lord's will be done, and I think that I seek only to know what His will is. At Shireen's supplication, I sat to the sun for my portrait on Saturday. Till I saw it, I had no idea how grand I look; it seems the concentrated essence of twenty aldermen and ten bishops, all in one. Mrs. K. sat also; but, womanlike, she spoke in the very crisis of the operation, and so spoiled the likeness. I amused myself much with the idea, that the sun, who has hitherto lived like a gentleman, is now obliged to work for his living."

As originally contemplated, Dr. Kitto left for Germany on the 9th of August, with his wife and seven of his children, the other two remaining for the sake of their education in England, one of whom had in 1850, to his father's great delight, received a presentation to Christ's Hospital, through the influence of his old friend Mr. Tracy. They were accompanied by a sympathising friend, the Rev. Cornelius Hart, incumbent of Old St. Pancras. Landing at Rotterdam, the party proceeded up the Rhine by Mayence and Mannheim, and thence to Stuttgart. There Dr. Kitto became greatly worse again, and Dr. Ludwig, the king's physician, was brought to him. On his visit, he repeated what the medical men had said in London, and the certainty of speedy dissolution seems, from this time, to have become a conviction with Dr. Kitto. A dream, as at the beginning of his life, pictured out his waking thoughts, and he saw, in sleep, his wife a widow and his children fatherless. The telling of this sad vision next morning filled his eyes with tears, for he believed that the presentiment would soon be realised. Stuttgart was found to be very hot, and the invalid next took up his residence at Cannstatt on the Necker. The mineral waters at this place are much resorted to, but Dr. Kitto found from them no great benefit.

The "beginning of the end" had arrived. First his youngest child, Henry Harlowe, aged ten months, was taken from him on the 21st of September. The infant had been always delicate. "His mother spent the days and nights in walking to and fro with him, for so only would he be quiet, shedding many tears over her once beautiful baby, now so wasted, and so soon to be taken from her. For me, I could only spend my hours in prayer to God, that He would be gracious to her and me, and spare us, if it were possible, this heavy stroke of His hand. Indeed, I felt emboldened

to pray with great importunity for the life of this child. I ventured to ask it as a token for good, as an encouragement to my faith; and I promised to receive it back as a trust and a gift—a double gift, from the womb and from the grave—and as such (should my life be spared), to watch his steps with daily solicitude, and give my best time and earnest endeavours to the task of bringing him up for the Lord, in the ways of holiness. I allow myself to think this prayer was heard and accepted. Certain it is, that at at his next visit the doctor began to express hopes, and the child has since been reviving, and although still very feeble, he is now so much better, that even my poor Rachel refuses not to be comforted.

"I have written this by short instalments; my head has been easier during the two nights which have intervened since I began it. . . .

"*P.S.*—*Sept.* 22.—I was mistaken. Our dear child was taken from us yesterday—Henry Harlowe Kitto, aged ten months. Our hearts are very sore. May He who does not afflict willingly, strengthen us to bear this new grief; but these are the things I find it hardest to bear, and the most difficult to understand. My poor wife suffers greatly, for her heart was strongly set on this child. Please ask Dr. Brown if he will write to her."*

Dr. Brown did not and could not refuse such an appeal. Nay, such an appeal was not required to elicit his sympathies, and bring out his genial words of comfort.

But the shadow of death was settling down on his household in thicker gloom. His first-born, unable to proceed to Canada, as she intended, had returned to London in declining health; and her removal to Germany, with its change of air, had effected no improvement on her. The watchful eye of her father saw her real condition, and it smote him to the heart.

"I have yet to grieve that I am obliged to report less favourably of our dear Shireen; she seems gradually sinking under her disease; and although there is perhaps no *immediate* danger, the hope of her ultimate recovery is very faint. It is sad to a parent's heart to see one so promising—his first-born—laid thus low, and I trust that the prayers of my friends will not be wanting to strengthen ours on her behalf."†

Her disease was a complicated form of dropsy; and when the little Henry died, she was confined to bed from extreme debility, and never again rose from it. During the last twelve days of her life, her father seldom left her bedside, but strengthened and comforted the dying girl, though his own condition and her weakness made the necessary finger talk very exhausting to both. Her eldest brother John was summoned from England, but before he could reach Cannstatt, his sister had expired. Her mother tells the sad tale:—

"We had both been desirous that she should feel

* Letter to Mr. Oliphant, Cannstatt, Sept. 18, 1854.   † Ibid.

that her change was near, but how were we to tell her? I felt I could not. Her dear father read and talked to her, and gave some gentle hints that the doctors would not be answerable for the results, and indeed, that they thought it a critical case. Whilst we were hesitating thus to communicate with her, the Lord Himself showed His intentions towards her. One morning, as I was attending to her, she said, 'Mamma, I dreamt last night that the dean of the place came and told me I was only to live a fortnight.' I took advantage of the opportunity as well as I was able, and said to her, 'Well, my dear, the Lord speaks in various ways, and perhaps this is His message to you.' 'Yes,' she said, 'I think it is, for certainly I cannot live long thus.' After that she became quite resigned and composed, and daily talked very sweetly on the subject of her decease, both with her dear father and myself. She died exactly at the end of the fortnight, as her dream had told her."

Her spirit had been gradually ripened for the great change, and the evident preparation for it gave her father unspeakable joy in the midst of his distress. After her decease, he writes to Mr. Oliphant:—

"*Cannstatt, Oct.* 18, 1854

"It has pleased God to withdraw from us the bodily presence of our dear daughter Shireen, our first-born thus following in just three weeks our last-born to the tomb. I blessed God in the midst of my distress for allowing me the comfort of finding that she not only submitted to the Divine appointment concerning her, but accepted it with a cheerful spirit, and was enabled to move on, day by day, consciously nearing the unseen world with an unshaken countenance, strong in the assured belief that to depart and to be with Christ was far better for her than aught which life could have in store. I thanked God with all my heart for this high grace granted to her; and while our affections have been deeply smitten by the loss of one so dear and so highly gifted, we refuse not the comfort which the contemplation of a death so serene and cheerful is calculated to afford to those who know that hopeless sorrow is a sin."

His sensations at this period of bereavement were such as himself had already portrayed, though he knew not then how soon the case described was, in God's mysterious providence, to be his own. As he bent over the corpse of his lovely and accomplished daughter, his first-born and joy, did he not remember what he had once said with such truth and tenderness?

"With this instance in view [that of the Prince Abijah], we can find the parallels of lives, full of hope and promise, prematurely taken, and that in mercy, as we can judge, to those who depart. The heavenly Husbandman often gathers for His garner the fruit that early ripens, without suffering it to hang needlessly long, beaten by storms, upon the tree. Oh, how often, as many a grieved heart can tell, do the Lord's best beloved die betimes—taken from the evil to come; while the unripe, the evil, the injurious, live long for mischief to themselves and others! Roses and lilies wither far sooner than thorns and thistles."[*]

The corpse, being that of a young and unmarried woman, was, according to the custom of the country, crowned with a wreath of myrtle blossoms, and the father was moved to tears at the spectacle. His deep sorrow had not as yet ventured to express itself in words. It was a double trial in a land of strangers,—himself expecting soon to be joined to both his children, and anxious to have a place secured for his own grave, by the side of that of Shireen.

"The circumstances of this great loss, following so soon upon the other, awakened much sympathy among the kind-hearted Germans, and the myrtle-crowned corpse was followed to the tomb by a large train of spontaneous mourners, composed *mostly* of persons unknown to us, and who are not likely to be known. I was not among them; for although I had seen her die, the doctor and our friends here prevailed upon me to abstain from attending her to the grave. But neither the bier nor the tomb is here invested with the dismal incidents and ideas which prevail in England. All is here made significant of cheerful hope, as among the early Christians. All the symbols and inscriptions in the churchyard are of this character, and the yard itself is called 'peace-yard' (*Friedhof*), a sense which is probably local, as I find it not in dictionaries. I forbear to tell you of the many things this dear child was to do for me, and with me, 'when she got well;' and I am not yet strong enough to dwell upon the close affinities of mind and character, and the ever ready and quick apprehension on her part, which drew her very near to me, and rendered my intercourse with her a delight. But all this is over. Year after year, week after week, I am bereaved of my children; and other trials—frustrated purposes, loss of health, loss of means, expatriation from the land I love—all these, though heavy, seem light in comparison. God help me —and I assuredly know and believe that, even with this large addition to my afflictions, He *does* and will help me, and that His help is sufficient for me in all things.

"My head has suffered considerably from these trials, which necessarily involved the suspension of my usual exercise. But my poor wife, in addition to these wounds, to her maternal affections, has had great personal fatigues and nights of watching to undergo; and these together have left her in a state of much disturbed health, from which I trust that rest may restore her. She and I, with our son, have been this day to visit the grave of our two children (for they allowed the little one to be taken up and deposited with his

[*] *Daily Bible Illustrations* Vol. 1, p. 866.

sister), and we found it overspread with very beautiful garlands—free-will offerings of the good people here."

Dr. Kitto's last letter but one has a peculiar interest attaching to it. Mr. Davis, once a publisher in London, but latterly a very prosperous settler in South Australia, having seen, in a London newspaper, some account of the benevolent exertions making for Dr. Kitto, generously transmitted a subscription; and to him, as an acknowledgment in return, was sent the following note, so ripe in Christian feeling and hope :—

"Cannstatt, Wurtemberg, Oct. 27, 1854.

"Dear Sir,—Mr. Oliphant has forwarded to me your kind letter, with its enclosure, and I beg you to accept my earnest thanks for both. In the midst of the trials which have been sent me, and by which I am laid aside from the labours in which I took much delight, I have been greatly comforted and encouraged by the strong interest for me which has been expressed by many who have known me only by those labours, and which has been evinced in warm and hearty endeavours to ameliorate the relievable evils of the condition to which I am reduced. Of these kind voices, none have reached me from so distant a quarter, nor have any been more encouraging than yours. To know that any of my writings which I have been enabled to produce have been useful, under the circumstances you indicate, in the land most distant from our own, is a satisfaction very dear to my heart; and the accompanying expressions of kind sympathy towards me will not be the less precious to me, as coming from one whose name is familiar to my remembrance, from its presence on the titles of many publications which I used to see in former times.

"The refreshment of your very friendly communication comes most seasonably to me; for, in the short time since I have been in this place—for benefit of health and economy of living—my cup has been filled very high, in the loss of my eldest daughter and youngest son, whom, within three short weeks, I have laid in one grave. But though heart-smitten, I have not been allowed to sorrow as having no hope; and I begin to perceive that, by these variously afflictive dispensations, my Lord is calling me 'up hither' to the higher room in which He sits, that I may see more of His grace, and that I may more clearly understand the inner mysteries of His kingdom. What more awaits me, I guess not. But the Lord's will be done.—I am, dear sir, with affectionate regards, most truly yours,

"John Kitto."

On the same day, Dr. Kitto wrote his last letter to his friend and publisher. It breathes a spirit of deep composure; for the writer was now, as himself says of David, "past all danger, for he knew he was to die." "We are still more sorrowful; but, not being 'forsaken,' we try to gather strength from the belief, that

He whose love has been so often proved, would not willingly lay upon us one stroke more than is needed for our essential welfare, and for the final welfare of those whom He has taken. My dear wife was greatly cheered by Dr. Brown's most kind and considerate letter. I may mention that, upon our first loss here, we read his *Comfortable Words* all through together (that is, I read it to her), and were indeed greatly comforted by it. We, more than once, exclaimed with Mr. Sherman, 'God bless John Brown for writing this book!'"[*]

The time had now come when he "must die." His work was over, and he was calmly waiting to be called up. He was neither impatient to depart nor anxious to remain, for, by God's grace, he was enabled to say "My times are in Thy hand." The last weeks of his life were spent in quiet meditation; and as soon as Shireen was buried, he selected as his favourite chamber the room in which she had died, whom he was so soon to follow. He was soothed by looking "on the same scenes she had last looked on." His spirit must have often pondered on the strange path by which Providence had led him—a ragged boy, toiling beyond his strength, till a terrible calamity disabled him—a miserable stripling, forced into an almshouse—an apprentice to an ingenious form of surgical art—a printer on a Mediterranean isle—a stranger in a far-off city of the plague—a literary workman in the metropolis—a famed illustrator of Scripture —and now a worn-out invalid, about to enter upon his final rest and reward. Thoughts, too deep for utterance, and too sacred for publicity, must have often sprung from such a retrospect. He had survived an accident all but fatal; had outlived his own purpose to die; had stood unscathed when thousands fell before the "burning pestilence" on all sides of him; and now he understood the reason why Divine benignity had uniformly spared him. The dreams of his youth had been more than realised, for—

"Dreams grow realities to earnest men."

But he had been informed long ago, by the Angel Zared, that "the period of his sojourn on earth would not be, at the farthest, very many years." Of this ideal warning he had been reminded by the alarming illnesses which had so often seized him, and which had proved themselves to be seated beyond the power of dislodgment in that vital organ, which, though it had been so materially injured in early life, had still, by the forced abundance of its fruits, provided food and raiment for him and his. For many years of

---

[*] Mr. Sherman said so in a letter of sympathy to the Rev. Dr. M'Farlane of Glasgow, prefacing the benediction by these words:—"If you have not seen his sweet book, read it; if you have, read it again."—See Dr. M'Farlane's touching and consolatory little work, *Why Weepest Thou?* pp. 74, 75. London: Nisbet.

his earlier manhood, there had been little to attach him to life. Then he felt himself to be all but useless, and he was to a great extent dependent on others. But the latter portion of his career had been signally successful; and, in the midst of his fame and usefulness, these premonitions of decease gathered thickly around him. The idea that he had fallen into a second state of dependence and uselessness, deeply affected him; yet he repined not; and, though he might wonder at the mysterious dispensation, he strove to profit by it. Two mornings before he died, he said, among other things, to his wife—" Somehow I begin to feel a sad distaste of life. I am now in a useless state, with little hope, that I can see, of ever being useful again." He added, " I, who have all my life been in the habit of referring everything to God, naturally sit and ask myself what all these things mean, and endeavour, if possible, to find out what His mind towards me is; and, unless it be to draw me to Himself, I confess I am at a loss."

His conclusion was just, and it was consoling too, as his experience had told him; for, since to-morrow was to be his last day on earth, there had been special kindness in weaning him from life, and filling him with the consciousness, that every step towards and along the " dark valley " was a step nearer glory and God. She who had so deep an interest in it, has herself described that solemn scene, which left her a widow and her children fatherless :—

" In the evening he read to me Thackeray's *Lecture on Goldsmith*, and said, that was the right spirit in which to view literature, and expressed how much more happily and respectably he had spent his life in that pursuit than he could have done in any other occupation. He sat reading till eleven o'clock, and seemed quite pleased that I had been able to rest so long listening to him. He then retired for the night. About three o'clock in the morning, I was awakened by his step in the room. I immediately sprang up, and inquired what was the matter. He said, ' Unless I can be sick, I feel I shall be very ill.' I applied some remedies, which had the desired effect, and wished to send for Dr. Burckhardt, his medical attendant, but he would not allow me, saying, ' it would pass off.' I did not feel any particular alarm, and he went again to bed, and slept till about seven, when I inquired how he was. He said he felt better, and asked for his *sauerwasser*. He then rose and dressed himself, but said he would defer the more laborious process of shaving and washing till he had taken his breakfast. He sat at the table with the children and myself. As soon as they had gone to school, he said, ' Well, after all, I think I must have a very strong constitution to stand what I have gone through. I never felt so conscious as last night of the approach of a fit, and had I not been sick I am sure I should have had one.'

Then, making two or three circles with his finger, to signify giddiness, he added, almost in the same breath, ' Look sharp, Bell!' I saw he was greatly affected, and caught hold of him, calling loudly to the servants, whom I hurried off to fetch Dr. Burckhardt, and our kind friend Mr. Hirsch, who had shown himself throughout most anxious to render every assistance in his power. Dear Kitto, seeing I was greatly agitated, waved his hand gently up and down, signifying to me to be composed. His chest heaved violently, and continued doing so at intervals of about half an hour. Between the paroxysms, he kept trying his eyes, his fingers, and his tongue, and said, ' My impression is I shall die.' Medicine was given, but it could not be retained. He sat on his chair, with his feet in a mustard bath, and leeches on his temples, and, after an interval of some hours, he was bled in the foot. There seemed, however, no signs of amendment. About two o'clock in the day he was removed to bed. But the chest kept constantly heaving, and the head was swollen, and the face very red. Stertorous breathing commenced, and it became very difficult to understand him; all told too plainly that, in a few hours, we should be left desolate. In the early part of the evening he said, ' I am being choked. Is it death?' I spoke with my fingers, but I saw that he could not make out what I said. I then, with my head, signified that it was. He added, ' Pray God to take me soon.' These were his last words. He continued for some hours in this agony, which no human power could alleviate. Mr. Hirsch, and other kind friends, offered to sit with us during the night, but all help of man was vain. Towards five o'clock, the convulsive struggle became too agonising to witness, and Dr. Burckhardt, who had been sent for, insisted upon my retiring, and would not suffer me again to return. I never saw him afterwards. About seven o'clock I was told that all was over, and that my beloved husband had entered into the rest prepared for the people of God."

Yes, rest had been prescribed for him by physicians, and urged upon him by friends, and he had gone to Cannstatt in search of it; but on the morning of the 25th of November, he passed into that repose which the brave and the true enjoy, through the merits and mediation of the Exalted Redeemer.

" Spirit ! thy labour is o'er !
Thy term of probation is run :
Thy steps are now bound for the untrodden shore,
And the joy of immortals begun.

" Spirit ! look not on the strife
Or the pleasures of earth with regret—
Pause not on the threshold of limitless life,
To mourn for the day that is set.

" Spirit ! no fetters can bind,
No troubles have power to molest :
There the worn out like thee—the weary shall find
A haven, a mansion of rest.

" Spirit ! how bright is the road
For which thou art now on the wing !
Thy home it will be with thy Saviour and God,
The loud hallelujah to sing."

The funeral, according to German usage, took place two days after his death. Dr. Gleissberg the dean officiated, and the service began and concluded with praise and prayer. A sketch of Dr. Kitto's life and labours was also given, and followed up with such impressive lessons as the scene suggested. The English residents, and a large concourse of the native population, followed to their resting place the remains of the illustrious stranger, whose brief abode among them had been checkered with such trials. To be buried at Plymouth, "in New Churchyard, beside Granny," was his boyish prayer, but he sleeps with his two children in the cemetery of Cannstatt; and a handsome monument, erected by the publisher of his last work, marks and adorns the hallowed spot. The monogram, surrounded by a chaplet and winged with palm leaves, which is carved on the upper part of the stone, is taken from a slab in the Roman catacombs, and was the print selected by him for the concluding paper of his *Daily Bible Illustrations,* and appropriately symbolises his own warfare and his victory—ay, more than victory—through Christ.

The monument, with its inscription, is here presented:—

In Memoriam

IOANNIS KITTO, D.D., ANGLI,

INGENIO, DOCTRINA, PIETATE CLARISSIMI,
QUI ETSI MULTIS FORTUNÆ IMPEDIMENTIS OBSTRICTUS,
ATQUE JAM PUER CASU CAPTUS FUIT AURIBUS,
TAMEN LEGENDO ET PEREGRINANDO
MAGNAM VARIAMQUE SIBI CUMULAVIT ERUDITIONEM,
QUAM PERMULTIS LIBRIS,
IMPRIMIS SCRIPTURAS SACRAS ILLUSTRANTIBUS,
EXPOSUIT.

STUDIIS CONFECTUS IN GERMANIAM SE CONTULIT
UT VALETUDINEM DEBILITATAM RESTAURARET,
IBIQUE VITAM SEMPITERNAM IN CHRISTO INVENIT.

NATUS PLYMOUTHIÆ DIE IV MENS. DECEMB. AN. MDCCCIV,
MORTUUS EST CANNSTADIÆ DIE XXV MENS. NOVEMB.
AN. MDCCCLIV.

ANNABELLA SHIREEN, FILIA EJUS PRIMOGENITA, MORTEM OBIIT
XIII OCTOB. MDCCCLIV, ANNO ÆTATIS VICESIMO PRIMO;
HENRICUS HARLOWE, FILIUS NATU MINIMUS, XXI SEPTEMB.
EJUSDEM ANNI, VIX DECEM. MENSES NATUS.

THE CHURCHYARD AT CANNSTATT, THE BURYING PLACE OF DR. KITTO

12

REVIEW OF CHARACTER AND CAREER

MANY authors are remembered, not for their lives, but for their works. Their personality is lost, and they are known by what they have achieved, not by what they have been—

> " Not myself, but the truth that in life I have spoken;
> Not myself, but the seed that in life I have sown,
> Shall pass on to ages, all about me forgotten,
> Save the words I have written, the deeds I have done."

But this silent separation of the author from his works cannot happen in the case of Dr. Kitto, whose name is now immortally associated with biblical study and literature. For the measure of his success is not more amazing in its amount than in the means by which he reached it. His life is as instructive as are his labours; and the two combined, present an unequalled picture of triumph over obstacles which have been very rarely so surmounted, and over circumstances which few have ventured to encounter, and which fewer still have mastered to such advantage. He did not merely neutralise the adverse position of his earlier years, but he wrung from it the lessons and habits which slowly built up his fame, as they prepared him for his ultimate achievements. Truly has he realised the riddle of Samson—"Out of the eater came forth meat, and out of the strong came forth sweetness." What a contrast between the deaf and pauper boy of 1819, wheedled into a workhouse to keep him from "hunger and fasting, cold and nakedness," and the John Kitto of 1854, Doctor of Divinity though a layman, member of the Society of Antiquaries, Editor of the *Pictorial Bible*, and the *Cyclopædia of Biblical Literature*, and author of the *Daily Bible Illustrations*! The interval between the two extremes was long, and sometimes very gloomy: yet he bore bravely up, with earnest resolution and strong faith in God, often murmuring to himself—

> " Be still, sad heart! and cease repining,
> Behind the clouds the sun is shining."

We have already characterised, in the preceding pages, those numerous literary and biblical productions which occupied the last twenty years of Dr. Kitto's life. Suffice it now to say of them generally, that they work principally on the outer aspects of Scripture, and seldom touch the deeper difficulties that lie beneath. Such labours have, however, their own value; for, though they do not interpret, they may conduct to the interpretation. They break the husk, though they do not bring out the kernel. Many of the topical descriptions so lavishly given in the quartos of Conybeare and Howson, contribute not a whit to a just exposition;

but they wonderfully freshen our conceptions of the toil and travels of the great apostle. On the other hand, Smith's expository description of Paul's voyage[*] is true to the life; the nautical language—ropes, anchors, sails—is dexterously unravelled; the positions of the labouring ship, day after day, are laid down with a seaman's precision; and the wreck and the scene of it are delineated with such fulness and accuracy, that at once he sketches a picture and completes an exegesis.

Sometimes Dr. Kitto's illustrations are too ingenious, and sometimes, though rarely, they are beside the mark. Thus, in the *Pictorial Bible*, and in the *Daily Bible Illustrations*, he holds up Ephron the Hittite as utterly supple and dishonest in his transactions with Abraham, about the cave of Macphelah, and denies him all generosity, if not integrity—a mode of representation unwarranted by the narrative, and which errs in interpreting the ancient and simple manners of Canaan by the ingenious flatteries and lying courtesies of modern Persia. In writing under Acts xix. 2, of the question which, properly rendered, is, "Did ye receive the Holy Ghost when ye believed?" and of the answer, "We did not so much as hear whether there be any Holy Ghost," he understands the language as referring to the existence or person of the Spirit: whereas the context makes it obvious that it is to the gift, or rather the extraordinary endowments of the Spirit, that the querist and his twelve respondents refer—for when they were baptised, "the Holy Ghost came on them, and they spake with tongues and prophesied." In his remarks upon the rapid increase of Israel in Egypt, he declares—"After all the learned and sagacious talk about the laws of population and of human increase, there is really no law of increase in any population but the will of God." No one doubts this great truth, yet surely the will of God neither acts without law nor by miracle, but according to certain physiological principles, which may be detected and explained. Under Ezekiel xiii. 10, 11, he has a curious dissertation on "cob-walls"—a species of rude buildings formed of mud, and found in the south-west of England. But he jumps at once to the conclusion, that the process had been carried, like his own name, from Phœnicia to Devonshire, from Canaan to Cornwall. But the same methods of clay masonry are found in Scotland and elsewhere, and need not be traced to any other origin than poverty and necessity. Mr. Urquhart and he are puzzled much about the syllable "cob," which certainly has a variety of meanings in compounded forms, and they regard "cobweb" as meaning the wall and the web; whereas the first syllable in *cob*web is simply the last of the early name of the insect, called

[*] *The Voyage and Shipwreck of St. Paul*, etc. By James Smith, Esq. of Jordanhill, F.R.S. London, 1848.

attercop still in Denmark, and in many parts of Scotland and England.

The late Hugh Miller, an immortal example of the successful pursuit of science under difficulties, which to the majority of men would have been insuperable, has, in his last work, *The Testimony of the Rocks*, taken Dr. Kitto as the exponent of the popular view of the universality of the Noachic deluge. In our opinion, his direct refutation of Dr. Kitto fails on some points, turning the edge of the weapon without breaking it, and is greatly inferior in cogency and conclusiveness to the positive and very striking argument for his own hypothesis. Another recent author has taken up and rebuked both Dr. Kitto and ourselves upon a point on which he possesses practical skill and experience.* The matter in dispute is the demolition of the golden calf by Moses. The conjecture may be untenable, that Moses dissolved the calf in some chemical fluid, and mixed the nauseous potion with the water which he compelled the Israelites to drink, though certainly a solvent sufficient for the purpose might easily be fixed upon, and might be known to Egyptian chemistry. The words of Moses are, " he burned it in the fire, and ground it to powder, and strewed it upon the water" —" he stamped it and ground it very small, even until it was small as dust." The text implies that the " burning " in the fire was not fusion, as our opponent supposes, for surely burning is not melting, but some unknown process that prepared the metal for being " stamped " and then " ground " to powder—a process which Mr. Napier, though he meditated a book on *The Chemistry of the Bible*, has certainly not discovered, but has been obliged to leave unexplained.

Dr. Kitto's life was one of heroic daring and perseverance. With a dissipated father and a broken-hearted mother, afflicted with a deafness which a sad accident had brought upon him, left pretty much to himself, and prone to wander about the fields, or lie among the rocks, the lad might have grown up to lead a vagabond life, without settled aim or occupation. But the waif, tossed about on the billows, and in danger of being carried out to sea, was floated into the haven of the old Plymouth workhouse. And what was to be done with him there? In kindness, the overseer set him to shoemaking, and probably his relations thought him now provided for during life, and reckoned the use of awl and pincers a fitting occupation for a jobbing mason's disabled apprentice. And had it not been for

The Ancient Workers and Artificers in Metal, from References in the Old Testament and other Ancient Writings. By James Napier, F.C.S. 1856. This interesting and informing little work loses much of its value to the student, because, with the exception of quotations from Scripture, it does not note the sources of its extracts. It is, besides, far more profuse about modern than ancient metallurgy, and ingeniously misinterprets several passages of the Bible, by giving them a chemical allusion rather than a popular sense.

his mental elasticity, he would certainly have been a poor labourer all his days. By and bye he is leased out to a brutal tyrant, who made the poor boy so utterly wretched, that he cherished to familiarity the idea of suicide. He " tried hard to be happy, but it would not do," and at length he longed

" to be hurled
Anywhere, anywhere, out of the world."

Ah! little did Mr. Bowden know, when he was so cruelly cuffing his helpless drudge, and dashing a tobacco pipe or a shoe in his face, that the object of his contumely was faithfully committing to record, in his Journal, the whole of the brutal procedure, to be turned up thirty years afterwards to the gaze and reprobation of the world. The indenture must be cancelled, and the magistrates mercifully sent him back to the almshouse : but he did not sink into apathy, nor did his spirit prey upon itself, and become the nursery or the victim of dark and vengeful passions. Many, alas! in more propitious circumstances than his, have yielded to such temptation. Byron's lameness was an evil incomparably less than Kitto's deafness, and yet it so soured his Lordship's temper, that he could not endure an unwitting allusion to his halt. It could be borne that his mother called him a brat, but that she called him " a lame brat," was ever a plague spot on his memory. Shut out from intercourse with society, Kitto never learned to hate it— cheerless and homeless, a butt to the wilder boys, sometimes pitied and sometimes slighted, he maintained a calm and firm temper ; and, at length, he could speak and write of his infirmity with the analytical precision of a physiologist, and the quiet resignation of a child of God, to whom all things " work together for good." It was, indeed, a rough training to which he had been subjected. But it was not without its benefits; for though he was not what he has himself called a " mother bred youth," yet a good deal of his earliest days would have badly " fitted him to endure the sharp air and gusty winds of practical life." " The *hardening* of such a character is the most distressing moral process to which life is subject. Tender to touch as the mimosa, morbidly sensitive to every influence from without, even the kindness of *men* seems rough, while neglect wounds and unkindness kills. Apt to see offence where love is meant, mortified to be no longer the *first* object of thought and solicitude to all around, —such a young man, in his first adventure from home, cannot possibly find any society in which his self-esteem will not be deeply wounded." * The distinctness of this picture shows that it was a sketch of himself, and the reminiscence is as sore as if the wounds had scarcely been healed.

And that terrible fall was a prime means of his

* *Daily Bible Illustrations* Vol. 2, p. 774.

elevation. But for this accident, the Cornish miner's grandson might have been a decent tradesman, superior to his class in intelligence and moral worth, an active member of a Mechanics' Institute, or a leading spirit in the committee of a public library. Men might have said, that the younger Kitto had retrieved the good name which his father had lost. The boy had always a fondness for books; but his deafness, shutting him out of the world, forced him, by an irresistible instinct, to hold converse with himself and others upon paper. There was in him a yearning for interchange of thought, and therefore, as he had few friends, he wrote letters to himself, and communed with himself through his " Journal." Had he been born a deaf mute, the same result and tendency would not have been so strongly felt. But twelve years of boy life, formed an experience not easily forgotten. Through that mysterious and instinctive necessity which exists between thoughts and language, what he had been accustomed to put into words, he longed to put into words still. As he could not hear his own words, so he compensated himself with seeing them, and the eye became the natural substitute for the ear. In the meanwhile, his spirit was sustained by such nutriment and solace; and literature, of the humblest sort, was a welcome luxury. The native vigour of his mind achieved for him a good self-education. Kind friends noticed him, and took him out of the Workhouse—" O happy hour!"* But few of them guessed what was in him. They could not see what fire was in the flint, for it had not been struck. He was at this period not unlike Beattie's Minstrel, the object of most opposite opinions—

" Silent when glad—affectionate, though shy;
And now his look was most demurely sad;
And now he laughed aloud, yet none knew why;
The neighbours stared and sighed, and blessed the lad;
Some deemed him wondrous wise, and some believed him mad. "

He was, in fact, not fully aware of his own capabilities, and, step by step, was he unconsciously led on to celebrity and usefulness. Had there not been a deeper power in him than was surmised, he might have remained in charge of book shelves in Plymouth or in Exeter—might, perhaps, have written a few miscellanies, or done work for some of the London publishers. But he would have come short of that high excellence to which he ultimately attained—an excellence, based as much on the nature of his studies as on the success with which they were pursued. As he has said in one of his Journals, " Talent is common, but the art of unfolding talent is not so common. Those whom we call men of talent had, perhaps, ten thousand contemporaries of equal talent, but who had not equal art and facility in unfolding the gifts they possessed."

His romantic connection with Mr. Groves was the turning point of his life. It opened up a new path of labour in connection with the Church of England Missionary Society. Manual toil it was, but it awoke novel ideas and prospects. At length his journey to Bagdad fulfilled one of his first dreams, and revealed to his quick eye the very dress and manners of early times. He saw the East, and soon learned to perceive what biblical illustrations might be gleaned from it. The seeds of piety had been sown in his heart by his kind and loving grandmother, but they were quickened by the conversation and example of Mr. Groves; so that, when the time came, he took to biblical work as a congenial task, and therefore he rose in it to signal eminence. Again, his deafness aided him. It threw him ever on his own mental resources; led him to retire into his own heart, and commune with his Maker; and gave his mind that special liking for Scripture, and all about it, which fitted him so well to illustrate it. The mere love of fame, so natural to youth, gradually subsided, though the natural desire of appreciation still remained. " I did," he avows, " earnestly desire to leave to the age beyond some record of my past existence, and thereby establish a point of communication between my own mind and the unborn generations." * He has recorded his obligation to a member of the Society of Friends, who showed him great kindness when few thought of him, and especially impressed upon him this idea, " that it was the duty of every rational creature to devote whatever talents God had given him to useful purposes."† The counsel took effect, and, as " a word spoken in season," aided in producing large results.

Had Dr. Kitto been born in such affluence as to receive a good education, and to have been enabled to live among books, and occasionally to compose a biblical paper for amusement, he would have been regarded as a literary phenomenon. Had he done even a tithe of what he has done, without any such disadvantages as he had to contend with, he would still have been entitled to no little thanks. But he had to fight for life as well as for learning, had to work sore and hard for food and raiment, while slowly acquiring the elements of knowledge. His question was not what shall I eat, but how shall I get it—not what shall I put on, but how shall I contrive to provide it. Such a conflict might have absorbed all his energies, but the battle for bread only hardened him for the struggle after knowledge. The late Duke of Sussex possessed a magnificent biblical library, comprising many thousand volumes, and he could occasionally talk of better versions and happier renderings. Many gentlemen who have similar tastes, and are not without extensive information in the literature of Scripture, can propose various readings, and defend ingenious translations. But study is to these dilettanti a matter of luxury and pastime, and rarely

* Letter to Mr. Harvey, July 20, 1823.

* *Lost Senses—Deafness*, p. 89.   † Ibid., p. 91.

do they produce much of permanent merit or utility. Kitto, on the other hand, had to educate himself while wearied out with manual toil. He had to gather his library with the fragments of his scanty earnings, the crumbs that fell from his frugal table—had, in fact, both to create his instruments, and teach himself how to use them. He had to collect the clay and glean the straw; and not only has he made the bricks, but he has built them into structures, stored with richer treasures than were Pithom and Raamses.

There can be little doubt that Dr. Kitto's infirmity increased his natural love of books. His own account is, "Whatever acquirements I have been able to make, have been built up in solitude upon the foundation of the taste for and habit of reading, which I had acquired at an early age, *before* I had lost my hearing. How it would have fared with me had not this taste been previously formed, I am afraid to conjecture."[*] Books became his companions. He did not simply handle them, he fondled them. A book was a thing of life and fellowship to him. It spoke to his heart in frank companionship. What a wistful eye he cast on some favourite lying on a bookstall, when he painfully knew the purchase to be beyond his means! He seemed to feel that the book instinctively understood his yearning towards it, and sympathised with him. Day by day, as he passed the spot, the book and he exchanged lovers' glances; and this coquetry would last for months. When speaking of Kirjath-Sepher, as meaning "Book-city," and therefore probably having some library within it, he says, with true zest, "By the dear love we bear to books, which place within our grasp the thought and knowledge of all ages and of all climes, we exult in this inevitable conclusion." Referring to the *Pictorial Bible*, he tells Mr. Knight, "Never was there any commentary that required more help from books, and yet perhaps no work of the kind was ever undertaken by a person with a more scanty library. It was my peculiar disadvantage to have no books at all when I came to England. I had a very decent collection for a person in my circumstances; but I have never heard of it since I left it at Bagdad, to be sent home by way of India."[†] Books, however, were gradually accumulated by him at no small expense, till he could boast of a library "three thousand five hundred strong."

The books common in his younger days were of a far inferior class to those in circulation in his riper years, and were also considerably dearer in price. "To bring this home," he calculates, "let us see how I might now employ a weekly sixpence, which in those times would only have furnished me with about thirty-two loosely printed octavo pages, sixteen of quarto, or eight of folio, being a portion of a work to be completed in

from thirty to a hundred numbers, and perhaps containing a cut in every fourth number. The same sum would now enable me to obtain regularly the *Penny Magazine*, one number; the *Penny Cyclopædia*, two numbers; the *Saturday Magazine*, one number; and *Chambers' Edinburgh Journal*, one number; leaving me, besides, an overplus of a weekly halfpenny, which, at the end of the month, would more than enable me to obtain *Chambers' Information for the People*. Thus, for my weekly sixpence, I should have five distinct publications, containing a large body of interesting information, and comprehending about eight times the quantity of printed matter which my sixpence would formerly have purchased. Besides this, instead of one engraving for every third or fourth sixpence which I expended, I should now have from eight to twelve neat and instructive cuts included with my printed matter; and, at the end of the year, I should be the possessor of six large volumes, containing altogether upwards of 2,000 closely printed pages, and comprehending from 400 to 500 engravings."[*]

Few men have made better use of books than Dr. Kitto. All his productions teem with the results of his multifarious reading. Not that he multiplies extracts unnecessarily, either with slovenly profusion or with the parade of learning; for his selections tell at once upon the case in hand, and in their aptness lies their force. So appropriate are many of them, so exactly do they hit the precise point, that one is apt to compare him to the left-handed warriors of Benjamin, who could "sling at an hairbreadth and not miss." The awful stillness in which he lived, gave him special facility in consulting books, and his undisturbed attention enabled him to turn all that he read to the best advantage.

His deafness gave also peculiar power to his eye,—

"For oft when one sense is suppressed,
    It but retires into the rest."

This ocular discipline was, indeed, a natural necessity. But it imparts a vividness to his descriptions. He excels in word-painting. He tells you what he has seen so distinctly, that you see it too. Every scene that he beheld seemed to be photographed on his memory. Even when, as he quaintly describes it, he *saw* without *looking*, he could trust implicitly to his impressions. He adduces in proof, that his wife and he went to Woking to look out for a house, and that, when they began to talk about it afterwards—the day, indeed, before taking possession of it—she, who had been on a second visit to it, affirmed that the front was of plaster, while he maintained that it was "good red brick." He had merely seen, and not looked; but he was correct. "I confess," he adds, "that I allowed myself to exult at this, as it was a very strong proof

* Letter to Mr. Oliphant, March 30, 1850.
    † Letter to Mr. Knight, Feb. 22, 1837.

* *Penny Magazine*, Vol. IV., p. 228.

of the *distinctness* of the faculty of minute observation." He had been in the habit of noting whatever he observed. At Bagdad, objects of natural history interested him; and his accounts, in his Journal, of the form, habits, and doings of certain species of wasps and spiders, have not a little of the quaint and amusing minuteness of Gilbert White of Selborne. In consequence of this faculty, one of his paragraphs is often equal to an engraving or a panoramic picture. The effect is the same, whether he describe a tree or a mob, a landscape or a portion of dress. His style is eminently pictorial, and by a few masterly strokes, he paints what he has set before you. In this power he resembles another, who has raised himself to imperishable renown in physical science. When the late Hugh Miller figures in words a fossil fish, its jaw, or fin, or general shape; or describes the attitude in which it was found, the species of rock in which it was imbedded, or the scene in which the discovery took place, his reader comprehends the object or place as clearly as if he beheld it, and the pencil is felt to be almost a superfluous aid.

Dr. Kitto's eye was one peculiar source of enjoyment to him. It drank in a rich and unfailing pleasure from the landscape. He loved, therefore, to traverse the Hoe at Plymouth, to saunter on the baraccas or high terraces at Malta, and to gaze around him as he lounged on the housetop at Bagdad. A flower or tree was a special delight; nature, in all her visible forms, enchanted him. He liked to see the old trees swinging their great boughs in the storm, and "to *fancy the sound*." He could well comprehend the seductions of grove worship, from the sensation which he experienced among "the endless fir woods of northern Europe, the magnificent plane trees of Media, and the splendid palm groves of the Tigris." His study was usually selected, not so much for his convenience, as that it might enable "his view to rest upon trees, whenever his eyes were raised from the book he read or the paper on which he wrote."* He could describe, with astonishing vividness, not only what he looked on, but also any imaginary scene which appealed to the vision. What he saw in his mind's eye, he could tell as clearly, and with the same effect, as what he saw with those large and lustrous orbs. "I can live again," he assures us, "at will, in the midst of any scenes or circumstances by which I have been once surrounded. By a voluntary act of mind, I can in a moment conjure up the whole of any one out of the innumerable scenes, in which the slightest interest has been at any time felt by me. If I wish to realise a scene, or to conjure up the view of a place, it comes before me, peopled with the very persons I saw in it."† Paintings delighted him; but

he could not endure such glaring improprieties as painters of Scripture scenes too often commit—"the Prodigal Son in trunk breeches, and king Joash as a half-naked mulatto;" or, we might add, the Jewish high-priest, in full pontifical costume, immolating Jephthah's daughter; blind Bartimeus with a violin on his arm; or the angelic choir over the common of Bethlehem, chanting with a music-book spread out on the clouds before them. His eye had also a special quickness, and its informing glance told him what question you were about to propose. The writer was struck with this peculiarity when he met with Dr. Kitto. The moment he saw you looking at anything, he divined at once what you meant to ask, or what had attracted your attention. He read the thought as unerringly as if he had heard the question. Long practice had produced a facility, which had all the promptness and sureness of an instinct. The vigour, in short, of many of his descriptive passages, is owing to the use which he was forced to make of his vision, to supply, as far as possible, the service of the organ which had been so utterly destroyed.

Yet there is no question that this defect told upon his composition in another form. His sentences sometimes want rhythm, the clauses are occasionally rugged, and his manuscripts exhibit a word or an epithet recurring in contiguous members of the same sentence. He had lost so far the feeling of sound, and his eyesight could not guide him. His poetry exhibits this aural defect of "halting, hopping feet;" and he admits that he could not recognize or rectify it, and that he had always a misgiving on the subject. The effect of such verbal repetition could be learned only from reading, for though he might read aloud himself, he heard no syllable. A strange mystery—to use what were sounds to others, but none to himself; to speak, with what tones he could not tell; and to articulate, with what results he could only faintly remember or dimly imagine. He was sensible of this defect, and sought sometimes to prove his MSS. by fancying the effect of reading them. Still he had sensations which appeared like those of sound. Perceiving, on one occasion, that I did not fully comprehend his deep guttural speech, he said at once, "*I feel* that I am not in good voice to-day." "I have often," he assures us, "calculated that above two-thirds of my vocabulary consist of words which I never heard pronounced." The words of his first vocabulary he continued to pronounce as he had done in boyhood, and he could not get over the provincial pronunciation of *tay* for *tea*, though he was perfectly aware of the error. Uneducated people are apt to write words according to their sounds; but he was liable to pronounce words as they are written, and as he generally brought out all the syllables, German strangers, having some acquaintance with English, usually understood him better than his own countrymen.*

But while we ascribe so much to the disaster which befel him, we must not forget his extraordinary diligence and perseverance. What he did, he did with his might. It was not a feat, and done with it, but patient and protracted industry. He did not spring to his prey like the lion, but he performed his daily task like the ox. He did his work with considerable ease, but he was always at his work. He was either fishing or mending his nets, either composing or preparing for composition. From his earliest days he could not be idle; his repose was in activity—not unlike the swallow, which feeds and rests on the wing. He wrote to Mr. Woollcombe, in 1827 :—"I have no peculiar talent; I do not want it; it would do me more harm than good. I only think that I have a certain degree of industry, which, *applied to its proper object*, may make me an instrument of usefulness—of greater usefulness, perhaps, than *mere talent* can enable any man to effect." He declares also to the same friend from Bagdad :— "All the fine stories we hear about *natural ability* are mere *rigmarole;* every man may, according to his opportunities and industry, render himself almost anything he wishes to become." At a later period, in 1841, he asserts to Mr. Knight, "I am quite sensible that I am in a condition to undertake what others would shrink from. I am fitted, by a variety of circumstances, for hard work. From my predilection for study and composition, it is not easy for work to become labour to me."

Though under the pressure of a calamity which would have broken the fortitude of many, he resolved, not so much to be famous as to be useful.; and, though numerous providences seemed conspiring to thwart him, he boldly acted out his resolution. He often felt exhausted, and sometimes dispirited, on the rugged and up-hill path. But though "faint" he was still "pursuing." Every time he fell, he rose with renewed vigour. His stout heart and indomitable perseverance carried him through. "Perhaps," said he toward the end of his career, "few men are more contented than I am. I have attained the object of youthful aspiration—I am satisfied with the position I have gained, and which I feel to be *mine*—I have to work, but, unlike very many men, my work is what I would do for pleasure, though I were not obliged to do it." † Will any one blame him for feeling that he had achieved something, and done good service to his age? After the traveller has climbed the hill, may he not, as he gazes on the scenery beneath him, contrast his present elevation with the humbler position which he occupied at starting? We remember

* *Lost Senses—Deafness*, pp. 23, 24.
† From a journal of some of his more remarkable sayings, kept by his eldest daughter.

how amused and gratified he was, when we took a venerable friend, the Rev. Dr. Beattie of Glasgow, with us to see him, and who paid him, through Mrs. Kitto, such a compliment as this :—"Madam, I am disappointed in your husband's appearance exceedingly. I had thought, from the amount of information he possesses, that he must be double the age he is, and, from the quantity of labour he has gone through, that he must possess twice the physical vigour." Yet, in spite of many temptations which naturally sprang out of his singular career, he maintained his humility as deeply as when he said, in 1832, to Mr. Woollcombe, "I know perfectly well that many thought you and my earliest friends not justified in their original kindness toward me. What is more, I soon began to think so too myself." But he had won his position by toil, in season and out of season, toil such as no constitution could long sustain. "The working day of the Museum," he wrote to Mr. Knight, "is six hours—mine is sixteen hours." What physical frame could long bear up under such continuous strain and pressure? "A merciful man regardeth the life of his beast;" and Dr. Kitto's soul should have had compassion on its "earthen vessel," and not worn it to death.

It is true that, in his latter years, there were great demands upon him. The cares of a numerous family summoned his pen into perpetual motion. He told me, when I saw him during the period of the Great Exhibition, that he had not been across his threshold for about six weeks. It was a manful struggle which he maintained in order to support a wife and ten children, by his literary labours. Such toils are not the most remunerating—very unlike the lighter works of fiction, which often draw a princely revenue. "They are of the world, therefore the world heareth them;" but treatises like those of Dr. Kitto, though they bear upon the highest interests of mankind, neither awaken the curiosity, nor gratify the relish, of the common circle of readers. They are set aside as serious productions, to be read perhaps by and bye, but when or where the unwelcome study may be forced upon him, their rejector does not know. There seems every reason to believe that Kitto's head had sustained some serious internal injury, and there was, therefore, all the more need that every precaution should be taken that labour should not deepen into drudgery, and that, along with intervals of entire relaxation, the amount of study should be meted out with rigid regard to constitutional capability of endurance. The bow should have often been unbended, that the cord might not be speedily snapped, or become so flaccid as to be useless. Less work—longer work, should have been the motto of his life. His memory began to fail under those attacks which so prostrated him—first the memory of names, and then the scraps of poetry which had been so abundantly stored up, "leaked out." He was to some extent aware of this danger. "It may not," he is obliged to confess, "be always prudent or safe for a man to be constantly on the stretch, doing all he can." Yet with this conviction, we find him, during his residence at Woking, say to Mr. Tracy, "I fancy that I must soon trundle into town, notwithstanding the disinclination to motion which results from the corpulency engendered by my sedentary habits, which are so rooted that I can seldom bring myself to move beyond my garden once in three or four weeks." This reluctance to physical exercise had always made travelling a species of self-denial, even though he had enjoyed such benefit from it. "I would not," he says to Mr. Burnard from Bagdad, "give five *para* to see the finest city in the universe, unless I could see *without going to see.*"

It is somewhat remarkable that one is able to trace in Kitto's early boyhood the visible germs of those tastes and habits by which he was afterwards distinguished. Few lives are moulded by merely accidental circumstances. Childhood often supplies the key to the interpretation of ripened character. The soul has its "seed in itself," and its growth is the result of a thousand invisible influences. Kitto's mind contained within it a strong formative principle, which was fostered and strengthened by causes apparently the most unpromising and disastrous that can well be imagined. His love of books was almost an infant passion. A cordwainer's recitation of juvenile stories set him to buy them. He tasted, and his thirst was never quenched. Mrs. Barnicle's shop-window became the scene of daily and intense gaze and wonderment, finding, however, a more formidable rival in a book-stall in the market. The boy begged or borrowed volumes wherever he could find them. The money that other youths threw away on sweetmeats, he cheerfully spent on books. This book-love resisted every temptation—even that most tempting of luxuries to older palates, the clotted cream of Devonshire. And the passion was a lasting one. In his Workhouse Journal, he stated his highest ambition to be, to gain a livelihood by means of a circulating library. A very short period before his death, he said to a friend, who declared his relish for the country, because it afforded hunting, fishing, and shooting—"I like hunting too, but in London; I hunt books—*they* are my game."

Not only so, but one who reads the story of his boyhood, may discover in it the foreshadow of his authorship; nay, the special form of literature which he should prefer was thus early indicated. Copies of the *Pilgrim* and *Gulliver's Travels* with illustrations, had been very attractive to him, and he daubed all the engravings with his mother's washing indigo. The story book he wrote on one occasion for his cousin, was decorated by a *pictorial* embellishment. Boys usually like pictures, and often amuse themselves with drawing. Kitto, however, not only painted, but he did it with energy, and to good practical purpose. Pictorial works were his subsequent masterpiece. His early shifts were also, as it were, typical of his later forms of industrious ingenuity. He wanted a penny, and he bargained to write a book to his cousin for it. Really, what else did he do during his life?—he still wanted a penny, and he still bargained to write a book for it. If he wished anything, he was seldom baffled in obtaining it. The deaf boy, unfit to work, and abandoned to himself, used to wade at low-water in Sutton-pool, to fish out pieces of rope or scraps of iron. Treading on a broken bottle, he was laid up; and then he resorted to painting, having expended twopence on paper to set himself up in business. When the first method of exposing his wares had lost its novelty, he next erected a stall at Plymouth Fair, and threw open to the public gaze his Art exhibition. Then he fell upon the device of printing labels, and was so engaged when, to keep him from utter misery, he was lodged in the "Hospital of the Poor's Portion." It was much the same with him afterwards. If one thing failed, he tried another: the conclusion of one labour was the beginning of another—either shoeing peoples' feet in Plymouth or repairing their mouths in Exeter; setting types in Malta or nursing and tutoring little children in Bagdad; writing for the *Penny Magazine* at Islington, editing the *Cyclopædia* at Woking or completing the cycle with the *Daily Bible Illustrations* at Camden Town. His letters to myself teemed with projects to occupy him when this last work should be concluded; and they were all more or less connected with Eastern life or biblical illustration. His industry was unceasing—from the period when his thrifty grandame taught her quiet and delicate charge to sew patchwork and kettle-holders, to the period when he felt the week by far too short to turn out in it the expected and necessary amount of copy. He liked to have his hands full, and they were sometimes too full; it puzzled him what to do first, though the indispensable "penny" had often summarily to settle the question.

> "Thus from its nature will the tannen grow,
>   Loftiest on loftiest and least sheltered rocks,
>   Rooted in barrenness, where naught below
>   Of soil supports it 'gainst the Alpine shocks
>   Of eddying streams; yet springs the trunk, and mocks
>   The howling tempest, till its giant frame
>   Is worthy of the mountains from whose blocks
>   Of rude bleak granite into life it came
> And grew a giant tree: this life has proved the same."

His literary projects were truly multifarious. In prospect of finishing one work, he generally sketched a score of successors. Before the *Daily Bible Illustrations* were concluded, he had in view a Bible for the young, with three volumes on Joseph, Ruth, and

Esther, for the purpose of expounding at length the customs and institutions of the patriarchal age, the daily rural life of the Hebrew nation, and the connection of the exiled people with the court and kingdom of Persia. He proposed also a series of great dictionaries —I. One of Ecclesiastical History, including not only sects, dogmas, ceremonies and usages, but ecclesiastical geography and chronology, antiquities and liturgies ; II. Dictionary of Christian Biography, containing fathers, martyrs, heretics, missionaries, popes, and divines; III. British History and Biography of the Nineteenth Century. The first two works, had they been combined with the materials of the *Cyclopædia of Biblical Literature,* would have formed a work not unlike the great German work in course of publication—the *Real-Encylopædie,* edited by Professor Herzog, with the assistance of a numerous circle of famous scholars and critics. Kitto's gigantic plans of literary labours seem to be equalled only by those of Antoine Court de Gebelin, one of the illustrious French Protestants who lived and suffered under Louis XIV.—one who not only read with astonishing voracity on all subjects, and who might be seen with the *Complutensian Polyglott* on one side of him, and a *Treatise on Mathematical Infinitudes* on the other, but who sketched a prodigious repository, in twenty or thirty volumes, to be called the Primitive World Analysed and Compared with the Modern. The first volume was to deal in Eastern allegories, the generating principle of the ancient religions ; the second in universal grammar; the third in the natural history of speech ; the fourth in the history of the Calendar, etc. etc. ; the three next being etymological dictionaries of the French, Latin, and Greek languages. "Why, it would take twenty men to do all that," interrupted an astonished auditor, as he listened to a partial detail of the plan up to the tenth volume. "Twenty men, you say ? " replied the smiling projector, "I begin to be reassured ; Mons. d'Alembert asserted that it would require forty." * Dr. Kitto equalled De Gebelin in laying out plans, and, like him, thought of executing them too by unaided effort.

Though Kitto, in his youth, had seasons of melancholy, yet he was buoyed up by sanguine anticipations. "The question was," he says to Mr. Knight (1837), "whether I should hang a dead weight on society, or take a place among its active men. I have struggled for the latter alternative." Even when he was seated on Mr. Burnard's tripod, he displayed an innate vitality, and lived in the ideal regions of his own creation. Occasionally he pictured to himself what he might, by God's grace, become ; and he laboured hard to realise his picture. He looked to the future, and lived in it.

* See *The Priest and the Huguenot,* by Bungener, p. 215. Edinburgh : Nelson and Sons, 1854.

"I slept and dreamed that life was beauty ;
I woke and found that life was duty :
Was then thy dream an idle lie?
Toil on, sad soul, courageously !
And thou shalt find thy dream to be
A noon-day light and strength to thee."

Indeed, he revealed his own secret, when he said to a friend, in 1853—"If you dreamed, you should not have awoke ; you should have striven to make your dreams realities. The very act of dreaming these aspirations and desires, shows that we possess the power to make them so." He never wholly renounced faith in dreams, though his own recorded ones may be traced to an active imagination giving sphere and form to its waking thoughts and fancies. He dreamed, and then he dared. Nothing was too arduous for him. " I am," says he in his *Eastern Journal,* "not myself a believer in impossibilities." When he lived at Woking, and wished to have some means of livelihood of a more permanent and regular kind than literary labour could secure, he had serious thoughts of applying for the wardenship or secretaryship of a new cemetery to be established in his vicinity. The writer remembers how he wished him to make interest with one of the directors, and especially what plans and contrivances he proposed to ward off the objection about his deafness, and to meet the auricular demands which such an office would necessarily bring upon him.

The reader is not to suppose from these statements that Kitto was a mere bookworm—a dry creature speckled with dust, and living in the congenial brotherhood of moths. He was a recluse from necessity, not from choice. He valued society, and keenly felt the loss of being, as he has phrased it, " shut out from good men's feasts." He did not condemn festivities, though he could not join in them ; nay, he expressly vindicates them, as "one whose infirmity frees him from all misconception" on the subject. In his Workhouse Journal the boy records that. on a visit to his aunt, she regaled him with " a baked pig's ear," and the man was never an ascetic skeleton. Many who deem themselves the victims of circumstances, too often think that they owe society nothing but a grudge, and they make war on the world. But Kitto yearned for brotherhood, ay, and sisterhood too. He loved " children, especially girls." When in Exeter, he encouraged the girls to whom he gave tracts, and whom he otherwise laboured to instruct, to indite short essays and letters to him ; and, as his Journal shows, he wrote them earnest, faithful, and beautiful replies. His heart was in no risk of ossification. Benevolence was a distinguishing feature in his nature. One of his last acts, before leaving London for Germany, was to take some wine and a few confections to a poor invalid, incarcerated for debt, whom he had often before relieved, even when in pressing straits himself.   This prisoner was the son of Mrs. Barnicle, whose little books had enraptured him, and who had been kind to him in his boyhood.   Out of tenpence which he gained when toiling as a shoemaker's serf in 1821, he records that he gave "a halfpenny each to five little children"—a large proportion, for he expended only double the sum for paper and books, the idols of his soul.   He was fond of his native country, and what he had seen abroad but endeared it to him the more.   The account of what he suffered from the savage to whom he was given out as an apprentice, reveals also the depth of his emotion.   There was no stoicism, real or affected, with him.   He did not morosely retire into himself, though he was forced to spend so much time by himself.   When she whom he had wooed and won broke her plighted troth, his letters referring to this sad disappointment reveal a crushed spirit overflowing with tenderness, moaning under an agony which refused to be comforted, and so smitten, as to be anxious to travel out of view into a dark and solitary future.*   He felt that this condition of mind was morbid and "unhealthy," and he prayed God to revive him.   And when the wound was healed, and time had brought him one who has proved a help-meet in so many respects, no one more enjoyed his home.   His trials had taught him that "if we are wise, the fruit comes after the blossom has departed, and that, although less pleasant to the eye than the blossom, is much more useful." †

So far, then, from being, as some might imagine from his history and labours, an inkstained recluse or a living mummy, Kitto was a man both of heart and humour.   He enjoyed a good story, and could also tell one.   So unexpectedly did his wit break out, that it lost nothing by his apparent gravity.   When a friend quoted the lines of Pope as the motto of his desires—

> " Give me again a hollow tree,
>   A crust of bread, and liberty,"

he archly replied—" I would rather have a good dinner and a comfortable library."   After he had felt what it was to be tried and crossed, he composed a specimen of a new Lexicon, to be called Love's Dictionary, with illustrations in prose and verse.   Three examples may suffice :—ADHERENCE—a word well known to the ancients, practical meaning now forgotten ; ADVICE—that which those who are in love never take ; ACHE—indispensable in the idiosyncrasy of a lover's heart, etc.

The eloquence of the following paragraph is equalled only by its pleasantry :—" I have had but an indifferent taste for anything which travel offered (mountains and trees excepted), save man, and the circumstances by which he is surrounded ; and even ruins

have been interesting to me, chiefly as circumstances belonging to men of a past age, and I have cared for them only as I could read man in them.   Oh, how it has delighted me to take a man, distinguished from his brother man by a thousand outward circumstances, which make him appear, at the first view, almost as another creature—and after knocking off his strange hat, his kullan, or his turban—after helping him off with his broadcloths, his furs, or his muslins—after clipping his beard, his pigtail, or his long hair—after stripping away his white, black, brown, red, or yellow skin—to come at last to the very man, the very son of Adam, and to recognize, by one 'touch of nature,' one tear, one laugh, one sigh, one upward or downward look—the same old, universal heart—the same emotions, feelings, passions, which have animated every human bosom, from the equator to the poles, ever since that day in which the first of men was sent forth from Paradise." *

He was fond of poetry, and occasionally wrote it himself.   A fine conception or a glowing image afforded him intense pleasure.   He had met with the following verse from Longfellow, as a motto, in some book he had been reading—

> " Art is long, and life is fleeting,
>   And our hearts, though strong and brave,
>   Still, like muffled drums, are beating
>   Funeral marches to the grave."

He committed the lines at once to memory, and advised his eldest daughter to do the same.   "I would," added he, " give £50 to be the author of that verse.   He has done something for the world; he has given it a fine and beautiful idea."   A quaint humour, as we have already said, peeps out occasionally in his writings, and often in the *Daily Bible Illustrations.*   "Lamech had his troubles, as a man with two wives was likely to have, and always has had."   " When Jacob kissed his fair cousin, he lifted up his voice and wept. . . . . Had the faults of Jacob been greater than they were, we could forgive them for these tears."   " Laban's daughter was a match for her father, even in his own line."   " In dreams, we not only see, but *hear.*"   " A razor is itself a good thing, especially if it be a good one"—a reminiscence of the earliest craft which he was sent to learn.   Describing the frontal ornament of the women of Lebanon, he affirms, that the horn, from its height and weight, "needs as many forestays and backstays to keep it in position as the mainmast of a seventy-four." †   In reference to Solomon's prayer for wisdom, he avers, that "if twelve men were taken, whether from our colleges, or our streets, or our church doors, not more than one would say, as the Hebrew king said, "Give me wisdom," most of them would

* See page 53.
† Letter to Rev. F. F. Tracy.   June 1847.

* *Lost Senses—Deafness*, pp. 150, 151.
† *Daily Bible Illustrations* Vol. 2, p. 83.

think themselves as wise as Solomon. It has not occurred to us in all our life, not now scant of days, though, alas! scant in accomplished purposes, to have met with one man who avowed any lack of wisdom, or who therefore would have made the choice of Solomon, had that choice been offered to him." *

He went once up to the gallery at the top of the dome of St. Paul's, and was exceedingly nervous in ascending, and especially in descending; but he accounts for his fears by saying, " My old experience in falling may have had some effect in producing this trepidation." † The attempt to explain away the miracle of the manna, by referring it to the gum of the Tamarisk falling round the camp six days, and intermitting the seventh day, is, says he, "much harder of belief than the simple and naked miracle— much harder than it would be to believe that hot rolls fell every morning from the skies upon the camp of Israel." Referring to a kind of rough and ready water cure, applied to persons under fever in the East, he writes, with considerable naiveté—" We have ourselves received exactly this treatment, under the orders of a native physician, in a fever that seemed likely to be fatal, and we certainly recovered—though, whether by reason of this treatment, or in spite of it, we know not." In the sublime contest between Elijah on the one hand, and the hundreds of Baal's priests on the other, the conclusion agreed to was, "the god that answereth by fire, let him be God." The commentator argues that the Baalite priests could not, with a good grace, refuse to abide by such an ordeal, seeing that " Baal was none other than the sun, whence it should have been very much in his line thus to supply them with the fire which they wanted for his service." According to his own account, he was four feet eight in stature when a lad of sixteen—and certainly he never attained a much greater altitude. He is hard upon Samuel for admiring Saul on account of his being a head taller than any of the people, and he is rather satirical in the sentence which follows :—" Even we want not experience of this in the involuntary respect with which tallness of stature and powerful physical endowments are regarded among ourselves by the uncultivated—and, indeed, by persons not wholly uncultivated, if we may judge from the not unfrequent sarcasms which we may meet with in the most ' respectable' monthly, weekly, and daily publications, upon the shortness, by yard measure, of some of the most eminent and highly gifted public men of this and a neighbouring country." He is witty on the ponderous folios of Caryl upon Job—a book so awfully large, that a clergyman's son, on going to India, left his father reading it, and found him by no means near the end

* *Daily Bible Illustrations* Vol. 1, p. 811.
† *Lost Senses*-Deafness p. 66.

of it when he returned. " Life in sheep," said he on one occasion, " is merely salt to keep them fresh, till they are wanted for eating." Describing the unearthly sort of noise he made when speaking in the open air, he represents people as starting and staring in astonishment; and adds, that, in the Burlington Arcade, " the preternatural rumble of the voice is heard afar, and the wonder really is, that all the busy inmates of that industrious hive flock not forth from their cells to learn what calamity threatens their flimsy habitations."

Allusions to himself are sometimes found in the *Daily Bible Illustrations*, and his loss is incidentally mentioned. Still he felt it, even in his resignation:— "Very cheerless was the lot that seemed to be before him." Describing the peacocks imported by Solomon's fleet, he says of the original name, that it is probably imitated from the cry; and, as if he had ventured too far, he adds, " but we do not know, for *we* never *heard* it." Illustrating the phrase, "the wheel broken at the cistern," he introduces a machine which might be referred to by the royal sage—one which was at work every morning in front of a house he had dwelt in on the banks of the Tigris; and he adds, as if painfully reminded of his " slain sense," it is *said* to produce a creaking disagreeable noise." In alluding to Zacharias as struck dumb, he at once puts in, as if it were an extraordinary alleviation of the judgment, but "he was not deaf." As if the sentiment did deeply gratify him, he announces: —" Some of the most eminent men of ancient times were subject to infirmities—Moses had a stammering tongue, Jacob was lame, Isaac was blind—yet they were not the less chiefs of the chosen race, and accepted of God." And we might venture to say, that the terseness of the following sentence has its edge from the pangs of boyish experience:—" The sight of the pottage was pleasant, and the odour overpoweringly tempting to a man ravenously hungry." Esau knew that, if he did not get it, he must wait some time—" an age to a famishing man." Such remarks might be indefinitely extended. The samples which we have given tend at least to show, that Dr. Kitto was of no peevish or misanthropic nature, but was kind, social, frank, and generous—attached to domestic comfort, and well fitted to enjoy it. His hours in his parlour were as pleasant as those in his study : and when you saw him of an afternoon, with the festive cup in his hand, so happy and so much at ease, you could not have thought that that hand had held a pen for eight or ten hours previous to your pleasant interview.

It would be excess of eulogy to say, that Dr. Kitto was a paragon of scholarship, though certainly his attainments were extraordinary in proportion to his opportunities. He had as much knowledge of Hebrew;

Greek, Latin, and the modern tongues, as sufficed for his purpose. His English style is pleasant, and, on the whole, correct. Occasionally, it has a tendency to diffuseness, and it has many sudden changes, as if the writer were holding a conversation with himself. He thought, however, that his style was "rather sententious than conversationally fluent," a style for which, in reading, he avows a decided preference. As his mind was somewhat poetical, many pathetic and beautiful fancies adorn his compositions. The reader is never at a loss for his meaning; whether you agree with him or not, you always understand him. He wrote with great ease—an ease not always consistent with vigour. Sheridan's remark, that "easy writing makes hard reading," does not, however, apply to him. His references to books and authorities are unusually accurate, and quite trustworthy.*

His mind was sagacious and well balanced, and he had one faculty in a very high degree—that of constant appropriation. Naturalists tell us, that though the zoophytes are fixed to one spot, yet they are for ever tossing their arms about them, and drawing in to themselves whatever minute nutriment floats within their reach. It was so with Dr. Kitto. He was well aware that there wrought within him "a strong faculty of mental association, which enabled him to discover illustrative analogies where few would perceive them, and thus gain constant accession of materials not commonly thought of or usually available." "Recognition, recollection, and research," were his "threefold cord." In his *Daily Bible Illustrations*, there are many facts taken, not only from the class of works usually referred to, but also from current literature—from books he happened to read in the course of his labours. Not only have we Benjamin of Tudela, but we have also Beldam and Bartlett; verification is brought from Holinshed, and likewise from Lord Claud Hamilton; contribution is levied from Sir Charles Napier, the Indian commander, and from Emerson Tennent, the governor of Ceylon; Napoleon III. and Abd-el-Kader, the prince and the exile, are both pressed into his service; Marco Polo and Mayhew are alike at his command; the *Fair Maid of Perth* and the Arabian

* But even "good Homer" occasionally nodded. An amusing instance of oversight occurred in the paper on "God's Retributions," in the first edition of the *Bible Illustrations*. Wishing to show that the Romish Church still maintains its ancient persecuting principles, he inserted a quotation, very pat to his purpose, from a recent pamphlet, purporting to be written "by the Bishop of Bantry," and having much the appearance of a genuine Roman Catholic document. On his attention being called to it, and the pamphlet placed in his hands, with the intimation, "not by the Bishop of Bantry, but of *Banter*—the thing is a *jeu d'esprit*"—leaning his cheek on his hand, as was his wont, he looked amazed for a moment or two, and then, as he turned over a few pages, its true nature flashed upon his mind, and he burst into a hearty laugh, exclaiming, "Well, this is the first time I ever fell into such an absurd mistake."

romance of *Antar* do him equal service; the "school at the end of the street" gives one example, and the temple palace of Karnak affords another; "our own house" is put in contrast with "the old lady in Threadneedle Street," and her nightly "guard of bearskin capped grenadiers;" sculptured slabs from Koyunjik at Nineveh figure by the side of sepulchral tablets from the catacombs at Rome; extracts are given from such passing publications as *Notes and Queries*, and the *Missionary Record of the United Presbyterian Church*; *Sanchoniatho* stands at the one extreme of reference, and the *Times* newspaper at the other. The same faculty was in active exercise, even to his latest days. When he was at Cannstatt, and smitten by bereavements, he loved to study the processes of the vintage going on around him, which, he says, "have made clearer to me many of the allusions of Scripture on the subject—all being here conducted in a primitive style." But he concludes, in mournful tone—" I find myself unable to enter into these matters with the eager zest of former days." Yes, his work was over. He needed not to be detained by the cutting of the clusters, and the treading of them in the press, for he was so soon to drink of the fruit of the vine new in his Father's kingdom.

Sentiments both beautiful and striking sparkle in his pages. Had space permitted, we might have quoted the long eulogy which he has pronounced on Moses—"the greatest of woman born, with the exception of One only, and that One more than man." Or we might have referred to the admirable summing up of the character of Joshua—"an Asiatic conqueror, without personal ambition, without any desire of aggrandisement." Or we might have selected, for illustration, the concluding paper on the book of Esther, in which he refutes and tosses away the frivolous objection against this old historical fragment—that the name of God does not occur in it.

In fine, what point and truth are there not in the following paragraph?—

"There are many who pride themselves on their deep 'knowledge of human nature,'—that is, being interpreted, on their keen appreciation of the dark things and the foul things of the human heart. The Lord preserve us from too much of this knowledge! He who has none of it is little better than a fool, and he who has most of it is much worse than a man. For we usually find among men the highest degree of this knowledge united to the lowest degree of appreciation of—a moral incapacity of apprehending—a total inability of feeling, that which, through the grace of God, is divine and spiritual, and therefore good and holy, in the soul of man. . . . The most perfect master of this learning is Satan, and he is at once the most consummate example, and the most egregious dupe of that ignorance. It were difficult to find the man in whose soul some faint glimmering of faith in God or man does not linger. But Satan has none. He is the most finished pattern of knowledge without faith. This is his character : HE HAS NO FAITH. This is his weakness and his shame. In this possession and in this want, he has reached heights and depths impossible to man."*

The power of religious principle was the mainstay of Dr. Kitto's life. The reader will not have forgotten the sublime prayer which he wrote after his introduction to the workhouse, nor his great desire to be confirmed at the bishop's visitation. Early impressions were deepened by the Divine Spirit; and the Bible, which had been a sealed book, was then read by the guidance of a new sense, and welcomed with the aspirations of a new heart. The ardour of Mr. Groves communicated fresh impulse, and the terrible visitations which crowded upon him at Bagdad—plague, famine, inundation, and blockade—threw him, unreservedly, into the arms of his heavenly Father. From Exeter he wrote, in 1824, to Mr. Harvey :—"I did think of religion *now* and *then*, but I did not make it the constant subject of my thoughts." In 1834, he said to the Rev. Mr. Lampen :—"I never talked about religion less than I do now, but there is much about religion which I never felt so decidedly and deeply." His faith in God ever helped him on. Rescued from any crisis, he "thanked God, and took courage." Assured that God had work for him, he never wholly lost the assurance that He would bring him to that work in the right place, and at the right time. He had long studied the Bible, for itself and its spiritual benefits, and not with any view to its public illustration. It had been to him the Book of Life before it became a text for pictorial comment. He had searched the Scriptures, and discovered the Christ which they reveal, ere he invited others to ascend the hills or traverse the valleys, mark the manners or investigate the antiquities, of the Lands of the Morning. "On coming home," he humbly and thankfully states to Mr. Tracy, in 1847, "I was enabled to lay all that I had during long years of silent study acquired, and all that I had gathered together in foreign parts, upon God's altar; and I sometimes venture to think, that He has been pleased to accept and honour even that humble offering." He had a firm faith in the plenary inspiration of the Bible, and he knew full well that mere truthfulness in those Oriental allusions, which he was so happy in illustrating, is not, of itself, as many have erroneously supposed, any proof of a Divine origin. Agreement with the "form and pressure of the age" around it is demanded of any production, and the want of it in Scripture would certainly be fatal to

* *Daily Bible Illustrations* Vol. 2, p. 34.

any higher claim. But historical veracity is not identical with canonical authority, though essential to its evidence.

His trust in God was unwavering :—"There is One," he solemnly writes, "higher than the highest, whose honour is not to be the second or the third, but the FIRST matter for consideration." It was very natural in him, who referred all things to God, to ask, on a review of the "sad passages" of David's life, "How is it that we hear no more of David's asking counsel of the Lord?" And he nobly records :—"Thirty years ago, before 'the Lord caused me to wander from my father's house,' and from my native place, I put my mark upon this passage in Isaiah, 'I am the Lord : they shall not be ashamed that wait on Me.' Of the many books I now possess, the Bible that bears this mark is the only one that belonged to me at that time. It now lies before me; and I find that, although the hair which was then dark as night, has meanwhile become 'a sable silvered,' the ink which marked this text has grown into intensity of blackness as the time advanced, corresponding with, and, in fact, recording the growing intensity of the conviction, that 'they shall not be ashamed that wait for Thee.' I believed it then, but I know it now; and I can write *Probatum est*, with my whole heart, over against the symbol, which that mark is to me, of my ancient faith. 'They shall not be ashamed that wait for Me.' Looking back through the long period which has passed since I set my mark to these words —a portion of human life, which forms the best and brightest, as well as the most trying and conflicting in all men's experience—it is a joy to be able to say, 'I have waited for Thee, and have not been ashamed. Under many perilous circumstances, in many most trying scenes, amidst faintings within and fears without, and under sorrows that rend the heart, and troubles that crush it down, I have waited for Thee; and, lo! I stand this day as one not ashamed.'"*

During a period of great straits, in 1848, he penned these words to a friend : †—"My sensations have become less acute, not because my burden is less heavy, but because I have become more accustomed to its weight. . . . It has not yet pleased God to relieve me from the great present distress, in which I have been so long plunged; yet I still wait day by day for this help, believing that He will not suffer one who has been enabled to trust so much in Him to be ultimately confounded. I shall learn one day the lesson He designs to teach me; and I know that, when the lesson I am to learn has reached my heart, He will stay His hand. My heart had fainted long since unless I had believed in that fatherly care, which

* *Daily Bible Illustrations* Vol. 2, p. 304.
† Rev. Mr. Lewis.

has never yet failed me, and never will. None but those who have been tried in the furnace of affliction can tell or conceive the bitterness—greater than the bitterness of death—of the trials which one day after another brings to me, and under which I sit still in a depressed and sorrowful, but not in a despairing spirit. I have hope, but it is 'hope deferred.' "

We present only another illustration, the sentiment of which has its source in his own domestic experience, and the number of his "olive plants : "—" There are tens of thousands among us, who would by no means be thankful for such an intimation as that which the angel of God brought to Manoah and his wife. How is this? Alas, for our faith! which will not trust God to pay for the board and lodging of all the little ones He has committed to our charge to bring up for Him. Good old Quarles, who was himself the father of eighteen children, enters feelingly into this matter:—

> "Shall we repine,
> Great God, to foster any babe of Thine !
> But 'tis the charge we fear; our stock's but small :
> If heaven, with children, send us wherewithal
> To stop their craving stomachs, *then* we care not.
> Great God !
> How hast Thou crackt Thy credit, that we dare not
> Trust Thee for bread ? How is't we dare not venture
> To keep Thy babes, unless Thou please to enter
> In bond for payment ? Art Thou grown so poor,
> To leave Thy famished infants at our door,
> And not allow them food ? Canst Thou supply
> Thy empty ravens, and let Thy children die ?" *

The last days of his life were clouded, as we have narrated, by successive family bereavements. In that land of strangers whither he had gone to die, his youngest child, and then his eldest one, the lovely and bright-eyed Shireen, preceded him to the tomb. The trial shook him with intense agony. But though he mourned, he did not murmur—looking to Him who "healeth the broken in heart," and wipes away the tears of the bereaved. There pressed upon him, too, the consciousness of physical disability ; and the sad thought, that, at the end ·as at the beginning of his life, he was dependent on the bounty of others. He cannot, indeed, be classified among the *infanti perduti* —authors noted for misfortune and sorrow. His works, as he says, had a steady, though not always an immediate sale ; but his calamity lay in failing health and occasional want of employment. He was, however, no exception to Sir Edward Bulwer Lytton's statement—"For the author there is nothing but his pen, till that and life are worn to the stump."

Dr. Kitto was in connection with the Church of England, but he was a man of catholic spirit. He was won't to say that he belonged to the Church Universal, meaning that he had no sectarian leanings, and that he was not, and could not be, a constant and visible worshipper in any sanctuary. But he punctually attended

the Episcopal Church on communion Sabbaths, for this reason, among others of high moment, that with his prayer-book "he could follow the service." He thought, too, that this absence of ecclesiastical bias tended to recommend his writings to all classes of the community. The example of Mr. Groves was not in this respect lost upon him. "Talk," said this worthy man, " of loving me, while I agree with them. Give me men that will love me, when I differ from them and contradict them." * Every Christian was a brother to Dr. Kitto, and he loved the image of the Master wherever he saw it. On parting with Mr. Pfander at Bagdad, he sets down this meditation in his Journal : —" The personal separation of Christians, even in this life, is less complete than that of other people. There is a spiritual intercourse which still subsists when their bodies are widely separated. There is also the feeling of being children of one common Father, who Himself sees and loves all *His*, whilst they are unseen to one another ; and who thus, so to speak, becomes a medium of intercourse with their spirits, which all centre in Him. *Him* whom I love, they love also ; *Him* to whom they look every day, I also look to daily, and I see them in Him ; and He who talks to my heart, talks with theirs also. No ! thus members of one body, we cannot be completely separated." Nay, he had a strong desire to serve the Lord in what he justly reckoned the highest form of earthly service, that of an Evangelist to a heathen country. His want of hearing, indeed, disqualified him ; but, even with this drawback, he felt the handling of types to be a sacred duty, from its connection with Bible circulation, and he looked on his journey to the East in the light of a missionary tour.

Dr. Kitto's life was marked by gratitude to all his friends and patrons, and he rejoiced to make prompt and cordial declaration. His early epistles are full of his thanks; and, in his last letter, referring to the public subscription in process of being raised for him, he writes : "I am deeply thankful for what has been already done, and for the most kind attentions of which, under these circumstances, I have become the object." † This dying testimony at Cannstatt, is only the echo of his first acknowledgments in the Plymouth Workhouse. Mr. Tracy, at the time one of the surgeons of the Public Dispensary, visited the boy who had fallen, and " his sympathetic and good-natured face" being the first that met the poor patient's gaze on a momentary return to consciousness, was never effaced from his recollection. "Are you Mr. Tracy?" scribbled the little cobbler on a slate, as that gentleman was afterwards passing through the wards of the Almshouse, for the questioner was anxious to recognize and

---

* *Daily Bible Illustrations* Vol. 1, p. 560.

* Newman's *Phases of Faith*, p. 37. Fourth Edition.
† Letter to Mr. Oliphant, Cannstatt, Oct. 27, 1854.

honour him. In 1847 he wrote to him:—"Thirty
years ago—Is it possible that it is thirty years ago?—
I lay before you as one dead." "Ten years after, I
saw you in London. I went and returned, and now
we meet again."

The only objection which can be brought against
our statement is, that Dr. Kitto does not, in any of
his works, make allusion to Mr. Groves: not only in
places where he refers to his journey to the East, but
even in the *Lost Senses*, where many of the changing
pursuits of his life are described. We believe that
Mr. Groves himself, on visiting Kitto in London,
asked why his name had never been mentioned by
him in any of his writings, and that Kitto replied,
that the silence was in accordance with his own peremptory request before the separation at Bagdad. Mr.
Groves then made some explanation as to the meaning
and purpose of his injunction, to the effect that it was
not intended to forbid all mention of him, but only
the mention of him in connection with his religious
history and mission. This awkward misconception, if
it were one on the part of the deaf author, is but
another example of the loss sustained through his infirmity—which prevented, as we have said more than
once, all supplemental talk with him; and, indeed, he
confesses in a note to Mr. Blackader, that he "had
always an unfortunate turn for taking people at their
word." This same tendency led him to express his
own opinions in a bold and unmodified style. We
have referred to the foregone conclusion which he
ascribed to Professor Robinson;* and he asserts with
equal bluntness of Sir Gardner Wilkinson, in reference
to the question of human sacrifice in Egypt, that,
throughout his work, "he keeps the subject as much
as possible out of view, for a very pardonable unwillingness to bring forward into broad light a matter so
disparaging to the civilisation of a people whom he
has made it the business of his life to comprehend,
and, from the influence of that devotedness to a single
object, to extol and magnify."†

Dr. Kitto was, at the same time, of an honest and
independent nature. Though he had been so much
patronised, he had never learned to cringe. In July
1823, he began thus to Mr. Woollcombe:—"I commence my letter with telling you, that I have ever been
accustomed to write my opinions with freedom, and
that I should deem myself unworthy of your patronage
if I could be so base as to sacrifice my intellectual and
moral independence at the shrine of interest. Much
of my future welfare depends, I believe, on you; yet,
were I certain that you were my only friend, and that
on you rested my every hope of earthly comfort, I

would not seek the way to your continued favour by
endeavouring to accommodate my opinions to yours."
What the lad, who had just thrown off the workhouse
livery, said so firmly, the man continued to assert and
exemplify. He was too self-reliant to be servile. All
he sought was opportunity to put forth his energies.
He was noted for his uniform candour and truthfulness, and for his kindness to all his correspondents and
coadjutors. He had no jealousies of others, and he
loved to encourage promising talent. Perhaps, from
his peculiar situation, he might imagine slights where
none were intended; and that persistency which made
him what he was, must have sometimes assumed, in
the view of others, the character of obstinacy.

In whatever aspect we view him, he is a wonder.
It is a wonder that he rose in life at all; a wonder
that he acquired so much, and that he wrote so much
is yet a higher wonder. Many have excelled him in the
amount of acquisition, but few in the patience and
bravery which he displayed in laying up his stock of
knowledge, in the perfect mastery he had over it, and
in the freedom and facility with which he dispensed it
in Magazine, Review, or Treatise. Most certainly he
hit upon the moral of his life when he couched it in
these vigorous terms:*—"I perhaps have as much
right as any man that lives, to bear witness, that there
is no one one so low but that he may rise; no condition
so cast down as to be really hopeless; and no privation
which need, of itself, shut out any man from the paths
of honourable exertion, or from the hope of usefulness
in life. I have sometimes thought that it was possibly
my mission to affirm and establish these great truths."
We do not mean to place him among those men, of
whom the Italian poet sings—

"Natura il fece, e poi ruppe la stampa;"

"Nature made him, and then broke the die;" but, take
him all in all, he was a rare phenomenon—an honour
also to his age and country. He struggled manfully,
and gained the victory; nay, out of his misfortune he
constructed the steps of his advancement. Neither
poverty, nor deafness, nor hard usage, nor ominous
warnings, nor sudden checks, nor unpropitious com-
mencements, nor abandoned schemes, chilled the ardour
of his sacred ambition. He lived not to a long age,
but he had not lived in vain; and when death at
length came, it was but the Master saying, as of old, to
the deaf one, "Ephphatha—be opened!" and his spirit,
which had so long dwelt in distressing silence, burst
away to join the hymning myriads whose song is—

"Louder than the thunder's roar,
Or the fullness of the sea
When it breaks upon the shore."

---

* Page 111.
† *Pictorial History of Palestine*, Vol. I., p. 584.

* *Lost Senses—Deafness*, p. 73.

PUBLISHER'S PREFACE

This new edition of *Kitto's Daily Bible Illustrations* in two volumes contains all of the material found on the original eight-volume and the subsequent two-volume edition.

This classic work was produced as a scholarly, daily guide to the Scriptures covering morning and evening devotionals indicated by the week number and the day of the week above each topic. When reprinting, it was thought advisable to remove the daily designations in the interest of facilitating its wider use.

Since the original work was written, important discoveries have been made in the geography and antiquities of Eastern lands. Biblical criticism and interpretation have also made considerable advances. It has been the object of the editor to introduce the leading results of modern research into this edition, insofar as they are embraced in the original design of the author. He has done so by notes, which are separate from the text, being appended in smaller type. When edited by Dr. J.L. Porter, this is indicated with the letter "P" and when by Dr. John Stoughton, a letter "S" follows the editor's notes.

The publisher is delighted to offer Kitto's rare notes and solid orthodoxy for the Lord's messengers and those who are hungry for companion study aids. A list of Scripture references is available on unnumbered pages in the front of volume one of this work. In volume two you will find an exhaustive index of subjects and an index of authors quoted and referred to. *Kitto's Daily Bible Illustrations* should once again become a standard tool for devotional and Bible study use.

DAILY BIBLE ILLUSTRATIONS

(Volume One)

GOD THE CREATOR

Genesis 1:1

WHEN we open the Sacred Volume, the first aspect in which God is seen to present himself to us is that of the Creator of the world. In the fulness of that knowledge which has become our heritage since He, who "at sundry times and in divers manners spake in times past unto the fathers by the prophets, hath in these last days spoken unto us by his Son" (Heb. i. 1), very few of us can appreciate the entire force and importance of this disclosure. The doctrine which it teaches is to us so elementary, that it requires some knowledge and some thought to grasp the whole of its significance. Yet it is very important. We know not, indeed, any fact which so distinctly brings out the full extent of our privileges as this—that a doctrine so great, so solemn, so awful in old time; which was clearly known only to the chosen people; and which, if guessed at, or inherited remotely by the thoughtful men of other nations, was set forth only in dark hints, or muttered faintly to a privileged few under the shades of night, with fearful ceremonies, in caverns, and in solitary groves;—that this great ancient secret has become in our days so common a possession, that we scarcely heed its value, any more than we do that of the air, in which, notwithstanding, our life lies.

Yes, this great doctrine, written as it were upon the posts of our doors, and proclaimed upon our house-tops, is among the truths which many kings and priests and wise men of old groped after darkly, if haply they might find it, and found it not; and desired to see, but saw it not. But blessed are our eyes, for they see, and our ears for they hear—not only this, but the deeper and more hidden mysteries which even the angels of God, who shouted together for joy at the formation of our world, desire to look into!

When we behold the highest intellects of ancient Greece perplexed by the inquiry, whether the world in its present state existed from eternity, or whether the whole of this goodly fabric was not at some time formed by a fortuitous combination of pre-existing materials; and when we see that the highest pitch to which human thought could reach, was that of the one or two who taught that, although the substantive matter of the world was eternal, it was moulded by an intelligent Deity into the form it bears; we then begin to appreciate the clearness, if not the importance, of the belief which the ancient Hebrews received from the first sentence of Holy Writ: "In the beginning God created the heaven and the earth;" and which at once placed the mind of the humblest peasant among them, high in divine knowledge above the most enlightened of the ancient heathen.

Even in our own day, those whose lot it is to dwell in the lands where pagan darkness reigns, can tell with what wonder and delight the youth in the schools hail the mighty doctrine which this verse discloses. To them, who had deemed it natural to believe that the world was self-created, and had no intelligent author,[1] it is a great and astounding revelation—it lets in a flood of light upon the mind, to know, that, "in the beginning God created the heaven and the earth." But it is not needful for us to explore the darkness of ancient or modern paganism, to know the importance of this doctrine. It is written with

[1] "The world appears to have been self-created, as it was natural at all times that the world should be self-created, and perish by itself. . . . It does not appear that this world has been created by any one."—Upham's *Buddhist Tracts*.

a sunbeam in the Old Testament; and it is well that we strive, for our profit, to realize that vivid impression concerning it, which has perhaps been too much deadened by our familiarity from child-hood with the sacred record which sets it forth. We all know that the Hebrew polity and doctrine were full of shadows, which were fulfilled in Christ; and that the ultimate object of the separ-ation of the seed of Abraham from among the nations, was to prepare the way for the coming of the Messiah. Yet we also know, that one immediate and manifest object of that polity was to uphold this great doctrine of the creation of the world by one independent and almighty Being; and that it might never pass out of mind, one day in seven was set apart for its commemor-ation. Hence Hebrew poetry and prophecy abound in allusions to this great truth, and the whole Scripture is replete with acknowledgments of this central fact; while remote allusions, even darkly hinting at it, though sought with care in the ancient pagan writers, have been found with difficulty.

Now, that to which God saw fit to give such prominence under the old law, must not be alto-gether forgotten by us; or, although acknow-ledged as a matter of course, be excluded prac-tically from our meditations and our devotions. Yet how seldom do we adore God as the Creator, in which capacity He saw fit to present himself so conspicuously to His elder children! Nor is this the doctrine of the Old Testament only; it is also the doctrine of the New. Indeed, the New sets it before us in fresh and endearing relations. It shows to us that He by whom the world was made, was no other than He who, in a later age, came down in sorrow and suffering to redeem that world from its pollutions, and to repair the ruin which sin had caused in His own fair work. The creation belongs no less to the New Testament than to the Old. The Gospel *connects* creation and redemption—the Creator and the Redeemer. They are one; and we shall do well to regard them, not separately, but to-gether. In the beginning of the Old Testament, the Son of God is by us recognized in the Creator; in the close of the same, His approach as a Redeemer is announced. In the beginning of the New Testament, the Son of God has come as the Saviour of the world; in the close of the same, another coming, for which creation groaneth, is announced; and happy are they who can from the heart hail that announcement in the words of the Evangelist: "Even so, come, Lord Jesus; come quickly."

The truth embodied in Gen. i. 1 is one of the most ennobling ever revealed to man; and the farther human research reaches, the more ennobling it becomes. It gives us views of divine wisdom, power, and love, which nothing else could give. We look up to the heavens; they are thickly studded with stars. Having reached the limits of vision, we take the telescope, and by its aid penetrate into space farther than figures can express or the mind conceive. The whole is filled with worlds. God created them every one. From the heavens we turn to the earth. We see air, and sea, and soil, teeming with life in endless variety. Reaching the limits of human vision here too, we take the microscope, and lo! countless as are the orbs of heaven, countless are the minute organisations revealed to our wondering gaze. God created them every one. What a wondrous conception does this give of His power!

Then in the heavens we see unceasing motion, endless evolutions—all working in most perfect harmony. Here is wisdom with power. In the world of life, again, we see perfect harmony combined with the most delicate and beautiful adaptations—the eye to light, the ear to sound, the nerves to touch, external nature in its various and varying forms to the tastes and aspirations of the mind within. We see, moreover, providential arrangements for supplying the multitudinous wants of these multitudinous creatures. God is the author of all. And here infinite love is linked with wisdom infinite, and the two with power.

The power, wisdom, and love of the one only great First Cause—the living God—is the Grand lesson of this passage. How ennobling to contemplate such a Being, and especially fondly, lovingly to contemplate Him as *our* God, OUR FATHER!

"These are thy glorious works, Parent of Good—
Almighty! Thine this universal frame,
Thus wondrous fair! Thyself how wondrous, then!
Unspeakable! Who sitt'st above these heavens,
To us invisible, or dimly seen
In these thy lowest works; yet these declare
Thy goodness beyond thought, and pow'r divine."—MILTON.

P.

CHAOS—GEOLOGICAL DISCOVERIES

Genesis 1:2

IN the first verse of Genesis we are assured of this grand truth, unknown to ages and to genera-tions, that the visible heavens and the earth did not exist from all eternity, nor arise from accidental combinations of pre-existing matter; they had their beginning from God. *Wherever* that beginning was in time, or *whatever* it was in form, that beginning was God's creative act. This is the great truth concerning the creation which the Scriptures design to teach; and no other information is afforded, no details are given, but such as tend to establish and bear upon this doctrine. Yet these details constitute the information which God has given us concerning the origin of ourselves, and of the world which we inhabit. These are questions of great interest to us. There are indeed questions of higher interest—those which concern our future destinies; yet *these* questions belong to subjects respecting which the mind craves for knowledge; and all the information here afforded has therefore, in its every word, been explored, examined, and discussed with the most sedulous anxiety, and the most minute and critical attention.

In past days, men, receiving the record as from God, knowing that only He who made the world could have supplied the information given concerning its origin, and having no idea that any other sources of knowledge could exist on matters belonging to the time before men lived, were content simply to explore the meaning of the sacred record; and when they found a conclusion in which they could rest, they were satisfied. The conclusion in which men did generally rest was this: that the creation of the world, in its crude state, immediately preceded the work of the six days; and that the earth was, in the first instance, brought into that state of watery unorganized chaos which was immediately afterwards reduced into order.

But, in these latter days, men have found in the bowels of the earth, and in the sides of its mountains and its raven cliffs, new facts, new circumstances, which, as they conceived, went to show that the world had, under various modifications, existed thousands of ages before the creation of man, or at least before the comparatively recent date to which the record ascribes man's origin.

The pious man was alarmed at this, as adverse to those impressions respecting the creation in which he had grown up; and in his earnest but short-sighted zeal, he repelled the new science with abhorrence, as an unholy thing, and shut his eyes to the solid facts which it produced. And, on the other side, the scoffer laughed, and exulted in a new weapon against the truth and authority of the divine word. These things have passed away. A new generation has grown up.

And now certain facts in the science of the earth are seen to be indisputable, whatever doubt lies upon the various theories, successively pushing out each other, which have been founded on them. And yet God reigns; and yet the Bible is true; and yet the sacred record is not only unshaken in the war of theories, but stands firm—firmer than ever—strengthened by the very facts which once seemed to threaten its overthrow,—a pillar of central truth, to which all those facts gravitate, and by the measure of their adhesion to which, their worth is tested.

Men began to separate the theories from the facts. The facts poured in from all parts of the world. The disclosures were not reasonings, nor conjectures, nor hypotheses; they were facts of the least mistakeable kind—disentrenched remains of ancient generations of the earth—remains tangible, visible, certain, and reconcilable with no hypothesis which allows no more ancient date to the earth than the commencement of the week which closed in the creation of man.

Then the wise, the men well instructed in the things of God, began to consider. They began to see in these things a new law of God, a new disclosure of God's work and will, written in the stony tablets of the earth. They saw that truth is one; and that if these things were truths respecting God's work, they could not be at variance with the truths disclosed to Moses in times of old. The record was then more carefully examined, and enough was found to dispose the most careful men to hail the new science as, in its facts, not an opponent, but an auxiliary, of inspired truth; as a new commentary, left entombed for ages, but now at last brought to light, to show forth the hitherto hidden meaning of one portion of the sacred word.

At first there was an inclination to suppose that the days of creation were not natural days, but long intervals of time, answering to the successive developments which had been found in the strata of the earth. But this was not quite satisfactory to any. On the one side the theologian felt that some force was put upon the plain construction of the Mosaic narrative; while, on the other, the geologist was not content with the most liberal concession which could under this interpretation be afforded to him, nor could he make the order of the divine operations during the six days coincide with the succession of phenomena which the bowels of the earth disclosed.

The inspired record was then again examined with still closer attention; and it then appeared to many that that sacred course of authentic information does afford an interval which may have been of any duration that the researches of the earth-explorers may exact. It is said that, "in the beginning God created the heaven and the earth;" that is, that the material of the world was not eternal, as some had dreamed, but was in its beginning, however remote, the work of God. The object of this revelation, then, being simply to record for man's instruction how the earth assumed its present goodly frame, and acquired its present inhabitants, nothing is said of its intermediate condition, in which it may have lain during long ages; but the inspired writer goes on to state that, previous to its existing organization, it lay, and had probably for a long time lain, "without form, and void," a dark and empty confusion; and that this was of a watery nature, is shown by the immediately following text, which states that, "the Spirit of God moved upon the face of *the waters.*"

That such an interval, which the discoveries of our own generation so nobly prove and illustrate, occurs in the sacred text, is not, however, an absolutely new discovery; nor has it altogether been extorted from the volume of inspiration by the demands of the new science. Ages before such discoveries were thought of, or such demands were made, it was conceived by several of the ancient fathers that a long period of time existed between the "beginning" of the creation and the beginning of the six days. No startling novelty is therefore offered in an interpretation which finds in the Mosaic narrative an interval of time defined by no limit, and allowing full scope for all the succession of operations which modern science has brought to light. Whatever *facts* are recorded in the book of God, the volume of the earth confirms; and for the other facts, unrecorded in Scripture, which are written in his stony volume, a sufficient interval of silence and of time is afforded.

Do there remain difficulties? Let us have patience. Let us wait. The Mosaic narrative is still not without difficulties, which it doubtless remains for future time and advancing discoveries to clear up. We do not know that we as yet thoroughly understand the sacred record, that we have as yet fathomed all its depths. But we do know that geological science is not yet perfected; we know that it is continually advancing by new facts, by which previous views are often considerably modified. And we do know that the more this science—the science of creation—has advanced, the more that it has become a truth, the more the apparent discrepancies between its facts and the teachings of the Mosaic record have diminished. Let us be taught by this experience. Let us rest assured that it will be thus even to the end.

Thus the wonderful book of God is never a thing of the past. It is ever in advance of us and of our science, and of the labours of our most ardent students and our highest intellects. The facts which are drawn forth, as time rolls on, from the firmament of heaven, from the bowels of the earth, and from the depths of the sea, are always found to be, *in their ultimate results,* in accordance with the sacred book, and serve to evolve the inner meanings, which were not suited to earlier times, and which antecedent ages and generations were therefore unable to discover.

It is often alleged that the facts of science are opposed to the statements of Bible history. So far is this from being the case, that science has of late proved a noble handmaid to sound biblical interpretation. Truths which have lain concealed in the language of the Bible for well nigh four thousand years, have recently been brought to light by an advancing science. It was not the object of the Author of the Bible to teach men science, nor was it his object to forestall or anticipate scientific discovery; but it was his object so to frame the record, that on every point in which it touches scientific subjects, it should be perfectly consistent with all that ever can be known. This is one grand feature of the Bible, which distinguishes it from all human books. Whenever any new scientific truth, fully established, *seems* to run counter to a biblical statement, we may rest assured our interpretation of the written word is defective. The Bible rightly interpreted, and scientific truth fully established, must always be in harmony. The most advanced scholar only stands as yet on the threshold of the temple of science. He has got only a limited and dim view of the interior. So, too, the most accomplished student of the Bible is still very far from having arrived at a full knowledge of all the sublime truths embodied in that book.

It is the duty of each—of the man of science and the theologian—patiently to explore and reverently to inquire, rather than vaguely to theorize, or boldly to dogmatize.

P.

THE FIRST LIGHT

Genesis 1:3

"AND God said, *Let there be light: and there was light*." Striking and magnificent as these words are in the current version, their native force is much weakened by dilution. Here are eight words to translate four of the original. The Hebrew expressed in English characters, is YEHI AOR ; VAYEHI AOR,—the letters being exactly alike in the two clauses, with the sole exception of the letter prefixed to the third word to express *and*. The Latin version expresses these grand words with almost the force and brevity of the original—"sit lux, et lux fuit." The Greek version of the Septuagint is not equal in either of these qualities to the original or to the Latin ; and yet it was from this version that the critic Longinus derived the impression—a heathen's impression—of their surpassing majesty. And let us not say that our own language is incapable of expressing the sacred text more concisely: "And God said, 'Light! be ;' and light was," would perhaps be as good a version as any language could produce. But in truth this wonderful sublimity lies not merely, nor principally, in the *words*, but in the grand *idea*—the idea of the instant succession of light upon the utterance of the Almighty word. This was more striking to a heathen than to ourselves. The Scripture has furnished our minds from our infancy with conceptions of Almightiness, and made us familiar with many wonderful manifestations of divine power ; and hence these magnificent views impress our minds with less force than that with which they smote the thoughts of such of the heathen as became acquainted with them, to whom the idea which they presented was altogether new. Yet even we, though familiar with the idea, and regarding the passage as a mode of expressing a fact not strange to our minds, cannot help pausing upon it, and regarding it as the most magnificent passage to be found embodied in the language of men.

We must not here overlook Milton's amplification of this text :—

> " Let there be light, said God ; and forthwith light
> Ethereal, first of things, quintessence pure,
> Sprung from the deep ; and from her native east
> To journey through the aery gloom began,
> Sphered in a radiant cloud, for yet the sun
> Was not : she in a cloudy tabernacle
> Sojourned the while."

And so an elder poet, Du Bartas, as translated by Sylvester :—

> " No sooner said He, Be there light ! but, lo,
> The formless lump to perfect form 'gan grow.
> All hail, pure Light ! bright, sacred and excelling,
> Sorrow and care, darkness and dread dispelling,—
> God's eldest daughter : Oh, how thou art full
> Of grace and goodness ! Oh, how beautiful ! "

The greatest apparent difficulty in the history of the creation, arises from the production of light on the first day ; whereas, in the sequel of the narrative, the creation of the sun and moon seems to be ascribed to the fourth day. Geology, which was at first regarded as increasing the difficulties of a solution, may now claim the credit of having pointed out the true sense in which these intimations are to be received. If we admit that the earth existed, and was replenished with successions of animal and vegetable life, before the whole was reduced to that chaotic confusion in which we find it before the work of reorganization commenced, we must allow also that the light of the sun shone upon it in those more ancient times. It appears by the fossil remains of those creatures which then walked the earth, but whose races were extinguished before man appeared, that they were furnished with eyes as perfect and wonderful in their structure as those of our present animals, and these eyes would, without light, have been useless ; and the vegetable productions which are always found in connection with these animals, could not without light have flourished. Besides, the changes of day and night, which are described as existing before the fourth day, could not have existed without the sun, seeing that they depend upon the earth's relation to that luminary. Geology concurs with Scripture in declaring the existence of the watery chaos previously to the era in which man and his contemporary animals received their being. The earth then existed as the wreck of an anterior creation, with all its previous and interim geological arrangements and fossil remains ; but strangely convulsed and fractured, submerged in water and enshrouded in darkness. Thus it lay, probably for an immense period : life was extinct ; but matter continued subject to the same laws with which it had been originally endowed. The same attraction, the same repulsion, the same combination of forces, which, by the will of God, have ever been inherent in it, still existed. The sun, then, acting by its usual laws upon so vast a body of waters, gradually, in the continuous lapse of ages, drew up a prodigious mass of dense and dark vapours, which, held suspended in the atmosphere, threw a pall of blackest night around the globe. All things beneath it became invisible, and no ray of light could pierce the thick canopy of darkness. Layer upon layer, in almost infinite succession of closely packed and darkling clouds, filled the atmosphere, and absorbed every particle of light long before it could reach the surface of the earth; and in the fullest extent was the language of Scripture justified, that "darkness was upon the face of the deep."

But when God saw fit, in the fulness of time, to commence the new creation, and prepare the desolate earth for the abode of man, this dense barrier, which shut out the light, began at His high word to disperse, precipitate, or break up, and to let in light upon the waters. It was not likely to be, nor was it necessary to be, a sudden change from the depth of utter darkness to the blaze of sunny day, but the letting in of light without sunshine, the source of this light—the body of the sun—not becoming visible until the fourth day, when its full glory was disclosed, and when once more its beams shone through the purged atmosphere upon mountains and valleys, and upon seas and rivers, as of old.

A critical examination of the order and grammatical structure of the Hebrew original throws some light on this part of creation's work. It is thus seen that *the earth*, as distinct from the heavens, is now the object before the writer's mind. He tells us what was its state, how it was acted upon, and what effects followed. "The earth had become shapeless and waste,"—so the words may be translated. Water completely covered it; "and darkness was upon the surface of the waters." It is not said that there was absolute darkness in the universe, or in the higher heavens, but *upon the surface* of the waters that covered the earth. The cause of the darkness is not stated. The sacred writer records facts as a historian; he leaves it to man to account for them. Philosophy can assign a probable cause for the darkness.

Observe the next step in the record: "The Spirit of God was hovering over [or hovered over] the surface of the waters." The Divine Spirit was thus operating in the region or stratum of the darkness. How He operated is not stated; but we may suppose that He was in some powerful though mysterious manner preparing for the great event which followed: "Then said God, Let light be; and light was."

The thoughtful reader will observe the analogy between the production of light in the old or physical creation and

in the new or spiritual. The Apostle Paul brings it out with great beauty and power : "God, who commanded the light to shine out of darkness, hath shined in our hearts, to give the light of the knowledge of the glory of God in the face of Jesus Christ."

P.

THE FIRMAMENT—LAND AND WATER

Genesis 1:6-8

WE are told that on the second day of creation, "*God made the firmament*" (Gen. i. 7). The primary meaning of the Hebrew word rendered "firmament" is *expansion, out-stretching, attenuation, elasticity,* which are the very properties of our atmosphere. But the word used by the Greek translators, together with the long prevalent notion, that the material heavens formed a solid hemispheric arch, shining and pellucid, in which the stars were set, led subsequent translators to render the word by *firmament.* This word, as well as the Greek (στερεωμα), is, however, admissible, if by solidity is meant no more than that the fluid atmosphere has density or consistence sufficient to sustain the waters above it.

It is thus easy to apprehend what is meant by the sacred historian, when he tells us that this *firmament* "divided the waters which were under the firmament from the waters which were above the firmament." One portion of the dense watery shroud which had invested the surface of the earth, consisting of the lighter particles thereof, was exhaled, rarified, and carried up into clouds, remaining suspended in the upper regions of ether; the remaining and heavier portion, being condensed, was at the same time forced down by the action of gravity, and merged into the waters that covered the earth. The expanse left void by their separation is the expanse or firmament which formed the work of the second day. It is perhaps not correct to say, as some do, that our atmosphere now first existed. The pall of dense vapour which is supposed to have previously invested the earth, implies the existence of an atmosphere. But it now first, at this time, existed as a *separating* expanse; and now, divested of the gross murky particles with which it was charged, it became transparent and respirable, the medium of light and of life to the surface of the earth. Let us not fail to note the historical mindfulness with which the expanse is described as separating the waters from the waters. We, describing it *now*, should speak differently; we should say that it lay between, or separated, the clouds and the *earth*. But the historian speaks as things would have appeared to a spectator of the time of the creation. A portion of the heavy, watery vapour had flown into the upper regions, and rested there in dense clouds, which still obscured the sun; while below, the whole earth was still covered with water, for the dry land had not yet appeared. Thus we see the exquisite propriety with which the firmament is said to have divided "the waters from the waters."

We have now a purer and a clearer sky; but still our earth is drenched with water, and inept for production. The water must be partly removed; and confined within proper bounds; and this is the work of the THIRD day of creation. "And God said, Let the waters be gathered together into one place; and let the dry land appear." The historian adds, "And it was so;" but he gives us no details of the operation. We are apt to pass over this great incident of the hexæmeron more lightly, or with less observation, than its relative importance demands. It is, however, easy, with our advanced knowledge, to conceive that this act of creative power must, to be thus immediate, have been attended by a tremendous convulsion of the exterior of the globe, upheaving certain portions of the land, and perhaps depressing others (though the elevation of some portions is sufficient to give depression to the rest), thereby leaving vast hollows, into which the waters diffused over the earth's surface receded, and within which they were confined. It is not impossible that many of the irregular and broken appearances, and traces of violent action which the surface of the earth exhibits, may be in part ascribed to this great event, to the agency of which the present condition of the earth's crust in the distribution of land and water must in a great degree be referred. Most sublimely does Milton describe the immediate effect of the divine command which the third day heard:—

"Immediately the mountains huge appear
    Emergent, and their broad bare backs upheave
    Into the clouds; their tops ascend the sky:
    So high as heaved the tumid hills, so low
    Down sunk a hollow bottom broad and deep,

Capacious bed of waters: Thither they
    Hasted with glad precipitance, uprolled,
    As drops on dust, conglobing from the dry;
    Part rise in crystal wall, or ridge direct,
    For haste: such flight the great command imprest
    On the swift floods. As armies at the call
    Of trumpet (for of armies thou hast heard)
    Troop to their standard, so the watery throng,
    Wave rolling after wave, where way they found:
    If steep, with torrent rapture; if through plain,
    Soft ebbing: nor withstood them rock or hill,
    But they, or underground, or circuit wide,
    With serpent error wandering, found their way,
    And on the washy ooze deep channels wore."

Nor in reference to this may be forgotten the noble words of the Psalmist, although it is not certain whether they allude to this event or to the subsidence of the waters after the deluge—perhaps it is to both: "Thou coveredst it [the earth] with the deep as with a garment: the waters stood above the mountains. At thy rebuke they fled; at the noise of thy thunder they hasted away. They go up by the mountains; they go down by the valleys unto the place which thou hast founded for them. Thou hast set a bound that they may not pass over; that they turn not again to cover the earth." Ps. civ. 6-9.

The waters having thus retired to their receptacles, and left a portion of the chaotic mass so dry as to be fit for vegetation,—behold this earth suddenly, at the divine word, clothed with verdure, and replenished with all sorts of herbs and trees, with inherent powers to reproduce themselves, and to continue their propagation to the end of time. Most beautifully and simply is this great work of creative power expressed in the sacred record. Poetry comes not near it. Yet the noblest poetical account of these operations which we possess, that of Milton, is here peculiarly fine, and may be quoted.

"He scarce had said, when the bare earth, till then
    Desert and bare, unsightly, unadorned,
    Brought forth the tender grass, whose verdure clad
    Her universal face with pleasant green;
    Then herbs of every leaf, that sudden flowered,
    Opening their various colours, and made gay
    Her bosom, smelling sweet; and, these scarce blown,
    Forth flourished thick the clustering vine, forth crept
    The swelling gourd, upstood the corny reed
    Embattled in her field, and th' humble shrub,
    And bush with frizzled hair implicit. Last
    Rose, as in a dance, the stately trees, and spread
    Their branches, hung with copious fruit, or gemmed
    Their blossoms: with high woods the hills were crowned;

With tufts the valleys, and each fountain side ;
With borders long the rivers : that earth now
Seemed like to heaven." [1]

It is a very strong argument against the theory
which assigns long ages to the "days" of Scripture, that the rays of the sun did not shine upon
the earth until the fourth day; for if each "day"
were a thousand or six thousand years, as some
suppose, the vegetation of the world would have
been left without that direct light and heat of
the sun, which are essential to most forms of
vegetable existence. It is clear that the plants
to which the voice of God had given life, could
not have matured their products, or maintained
their being, had not the solar action been very
shortly after produced. We have in this, indeed,
a reason for the admission of the solar influence
next after the creation of the green herb. Without the solar light and heat, an interval of time,
equal only to the existence of the plant whose
duration is the briefest, would have extinguished
that plant from the new creation. It would have
served no purpose. It would have been created
in vain.

The divine work on the second day was not necessarily
a new creation. It may have been, and probably was,
only a new arrangement by Almighty power of elements
already in existence. Some change effected in that black
mantle of vapour that encircled the earth, dissipated the
vapour, raising up the dark clouds to higher regions, and
diffusing a stratum of purer air over the surface of the
watery waste. Such a stratum—such an atmosphere, in
fact, as that now around us—may have existed at some
antecedent age, but may have been temporarily disturbed
by a great geological convulsion. The wondrous effects of
such convulsions on the strata of the earth's crust, and the
vapours on the earth's surface, are only now beginning to
be observed.

The way in which the dry land was made to appear, and
the waters to flow together, is a favourite subject for speculation among biblical commentators. All such speculations are vain ; in unskilful hands they are dangerous.
The silence of Scripture is often suggestive, and nowhere
more so than here. It is rash speculation which usually
brings the sacred interpreter into collision with the man of
science, and not unfrequently gives a temporary triumph
to the infidel. Let us not attempt on such topics to be
wise beyond what is written.   **P.**

[1] In this, as in other parts of his description of the work
of creation, Milton owes much to Du Bartas, whose curious
work, in the excellent translation of John Sylvester (time
of James I.), scarcely deserves the neglect into which it has
fallen. But Milton's hand turns to gold whatever it
touches ; and here we have set before us, with wonderful
skill, the essence of many pages of Du Bartas.

In reference to Dr. Kitto's remark, I would say, it is no
doubt interesting to read Milton's *Paradise Lost*, in connection with the first Chapter of Genesis :—and also to
turn to such a curious work as that of Du Bartas ; but not
for one moment must we lose sight of the vast difference
between the two authors on the one side, and the Divine
historian on the other. The former give us mere imaginations, often beautiful, but sometimes, scientifically considered, untrue : the latter presents simple unadorned
statements on the authority of the Holy Spirit, not at
variance with ascertained facts.

S.

THE GREAT LIGHTS

Genesis 1:16-18

WHAT now is wanting to complete the scene of
inanimate nature ? The mountains lift their
heads to heaven. The valleys lie in soft repose,
traversed by rivers and by streams, which seem,
in the various motions of their course, to give the
only idea of *life* the earth is yet able to afford.
The waters have retired to their ocean beds.
The scene is invested with all the glories and all
the beauties of vegetable life. What more is
wanting? More light—by the full manifestation
of those bright luminaries which had, optically
speaking, been hitherto veiled in mist, which
their rays had not yet been able to dissipate and
rarify into a pure azure sky. The light which
had previously appeared is probably more intelligible to ourselves than even to the inhabitants
of the East, who have but little, if any, twilight,
and whose sun is seldom obscured from view.
But we, with our long twilights, and with mists
which sometimes constrain us to kindle lights at
noon-day, can easily apprehend the kind of light
which prevailed before the misty pall was at the
divine word drawn aside, and disclosed the moon,
"walking in brightness" through the high heaven
among the starry host ; and when morning came,
the sun, shedding a full blaze of light and glory,
from the beautiful blue sky, upon all the work
which God's hand had wrought.

The sun and moon were not, of course, simultaneously, but successively, disclosed ; and we
place the moon first, because the fourth day in
which both appeared was, like the other days,
composed of the night with the *following* day.
If the sun had first appeared, the day would have
closed when the sun set, and then the appearance

of the moon on the following night would have belonged to another day. But seeing that they appeared both on the fourth day, and that the days are reckoned from evening to evening, and not from morning to morning, we may be sure that it was the moon whose rays first shone on the new earth. If man had then existed upon the earth, the appearance of the "pale regent of the night" would have prepared his mind and his eye for the glory of that "greater light" which the ensuing day was to disclose.

But although man was not, it is ever to be borne in mind that all these changes are throughout described as they would have presented themselves to his eye had he then existed. To a spectator on the earth's surface, these luminaries would have appeared as if then first called into being—then first created. Indeed they may, according to Scripture usage, be said to have been "made;" because they then first began to be visible in the exercise of their natural office with respect to the earth. It may be observed that the word "made" is not the same in the Hebrew as that translated "created." It is a term frequently employed in Scripture to signify "constituted, appointed, set for a particular purpose or use." Thus it is said "that God *made* Joseph a father to Pharaoh;" "*made* him lord of Egypt;" "*made* the Jordan a border between the tribes;" "*made* David the head of the heathen;" and so in numerous other examples. A critic, whose learning claims the respect which cannot be always allowed to his opinions, says, with regard to the clause "Let there be lights in the firmament," etc., "The words 'Let there be,' are in my conception equivalent to 'Let there appear;' and if I had allowed myself the freedom which some modern translators have taken, I should thus have rendered the verse: "Let the luminaries which are in the expanse of the heavens, be for the purpose of illuminating the earth," etc. Let it be borne in mind that this author (Dr. Geddes) wrote before science had established a necessity for the pre-existence of the heavenly bodies. "Thus, therefore," as it has been well remarked, "as the rainbow was *made* or constituted a sign, though it might have existed before, so the sun, moon, and stars may be said to have been made or set as lights in the firmament on the fourth day, though actually called into existence on the first, or previously. The same result had indeed been really effected by the same means during the previous three days and nights; but these luminaries were henceforth, by their rising and setting, to be the visible means of producing the separation or succession." [1]

It may be, and has been, objected to this view, that it assigns no specific work of creation to the fourth day—the operation of which is reduced to the clearing away of the mist, clouds, and vapours, and thereby rendering the atmosphere clear and serene; while the same terms are employed which are admitted to apply in other instances, in the same chapter, to the higher acts of creative power. But it is to be considered, that the principle of life and action which was at first infused into the mass, would still be exerting its energies. The work of creation would be ever advancing towards completeness, on the fourth day as on former days, until the hosts of heaven broke into view from behind the vanishing veil of clouds and mistiness. Appearing for the first time, and of course as new creations, they would be described as such in the same phraseology that had been formerly used. Besides, as already hinted, the principal point in the mind of the sacred writer, is the purpose which they were destined to serve in this world, as organized for the habitation and rise of man. It is not so much, therefore, their creation on the fourth day, as the use to which they were to be put, on which he insists. It is by no means then necessary to understand the sacred writer as asserting the creation of the heavenly bodies on that day, but only their development on that day as adapted to the purposes intended, their creation having previously taken place.

It will be observed that there are two great stages or divisions of God's creative work. The first occupied the three first days, the second the three last; and there is a remarkable parallelism between them. The same order is observed, and the same objects are successively acted upon in each. Thus, the first stage begins with the diffusion of light in the darkness; then the atmosphere is made, and the waters collected; and finally the dry land is formed. The second stage begins by the calling forth of the great lights of heaven; then the air and waters are filled with life; and finally the dry land is peopled with animals. It may be said that the first stage was one of preparation, the second one of occupation.

P.

[1] Bush *On Genesis.* This has become nearly the general sentiment of theologians with reference to the subject.

CREATION OF FISHES AND BIRDS

Genesis 1:20-22

THE earth has now become a delightful abode, but it is entirely without inhabitants. Two days more shall people it with animals; and the water itself, which has hitherto been the obstacle of production, shall be first of all rendered productive. God said, "Let the waters bring forth abundantly the moving creatures that hath life, and fowl that may fly above the earth in the open firmament of heaven." And the effect of this creative word is recorded with some variations, which it may be well to note. "And God created great whales, and every living creature that moveth, which the waters brought forth abundantly, after their kind, and every winged fowl after his kind."

In connection with the remark offered yesterday as to the use of the word *made*, as distinguished from that of the word *created*, the reader will not fail to observe that now again, when the statement has reference to a direct calling into existence of that which did not previously in any form exist, the latter word is again employed.

Milton scarcely anywhere, in so narrow a compass, indicates his profound knowledge of biblical lore, as in the version he has given of the first clause of the divine mandate, uttered on the fifth day of creation:—

> "Let the waters generate
> Reptile with spawn abundant."

He knew that the word translated "moving creature," was not "moving," or "creeping" (as elsewhere rendered), but "rapidly multiplying," or "swarming creatures,"—in short, that it meant all kinds of living creatures, inhabiting the waters, which are oviparous and remarkable for fecundity, as we know is eminently the case with the finny tribes. In other passages of Scripture it is applied even to the smaller land animals and reptiles noted for their swarming abundance. The word translated "moving creature," is, in fact, the noun of the very verb which, in the same verse, is rendered "to bring forth abundantly." Thus we see that the existence of immense numbers of these creatures,—the astonishing fecundity with which they were

endowed,—is the prevalent idea of this description. Indeed, there is no phrase in human language in which, both by noun and verb, this idea could be more forcibly expressed than in the Hebrew original. And yet all language fails to convey an idea of the amazing extent of that "abundance" in bringing forth, with which these creatures were endowed on the day of their creation. This is, of course, more remarkable in some species than in others, and is most obvious to our notice in the immense shoals of herrings, pilchards, and mackerel, upon our own shores. Many other species are probably equally prolific; but not being of gregarious habits, are not seen together in such vast numbers, and are in consequence less easily taken." But any one who attempts to estimate the number of eggs in the roes of various kinds of fish, may form some faint conception of the degree in which the sea generates "reptiles with spawn abundant." The old microscopist, Leuwenhoek, gave estimates which the mind could scarcely grasp. The greater accuracy of modern research has somewhat moderated his statements; but enough remains to fill the mind with astonishment. Thus the roe of a codfish has been found to contain nine millions of eggs; of a flounder, nearly a million and a half; of a mackerel, half a million; of tenches, three hundred and fifty thousand; of the carp, from one to six hundred thousand; of the roach and sole, a hundred thousand; of herrings, perches, and smelts, twenty and thirty thousand; lobsters, from seven to twenty thousand; shrimps and prawns, above three thousand. In fact, scarcely a month passes in which the reader may not gather from the commonest sources some facts showing the enormous productiveness of fish. At one time, we are told that a hundred thousand mackerel are in the season brought weekly to the London fish-market (Billingsgate); at another time, we hear that herrings or pilchards have been caught so abundantly, as to have no market value except as manure, for which purpose they are carted away in tens and hundreds of thousands by the farmers near the coast. Look, then, at the sprats, the white bait, the shrimps, and consider what hetacombs of these minute existences are sacrificed to help the dinner of a Dives, or to form the supper of a Lazarus.

Nor, if we look at the text, does this function of bringing forth abundantly apply only to the inmates of the waters, but is extended to the inhabitants of the air. And how truly! Look at the countless number—millions on millions—of the eggs of one species of birds only, that are consumed in the London market, and consider that nearly all these might, in the course of nature, become birds, did not man interfere; and hence form some idea of the marvellous productiveness of the feathered tribes. Still more, the vast shoals of fish have a most exact parallel in the immense flocks of some kinds of birds. The passenger pigeon of North America has been seen in flocks a mile broad, that took four hours in passing, at the rate of a mile a minute; and which have been reckoned, on these data, to contain about two thousand and a quarter millions of birds. So Captain Flinders, in that remarkable voyage, one of the bird-facts in which a poet of our own day has immortalized,[1] saw a flock of petrels, three hundred yards or more broad, and fifty to eighty yards deep, flying as compactly as their wings could move, and that took an hour and a half in passing, at the rate of thirty miles an hour. This immense body was reckoned to comprise a hundred and fifty millions of birds. So, in the Antarctic regions, the ground is sometimes covered, to the extent of two or three miles, with millions of that strange bird, the penguin; and when the purple gracule of America assembles for migration, a congregated multitude of many hundred thousands is at once present to the view.

A modern writer, in a work which embodies a vast variety of curious, but not well digested nor always accurate facts, well remarks on this subject:[2]—"The quantity of individuals of the various bird genera which are at any one time, and at all times, existing in our world, surpasses not only our usual supposition, but even all power of human numeration, at least as to any real distinct conception of the amount; for we can only pen down the words, millions, billions, trillions, quadrillions, and such other augmentative terms, in which all actual comprehension soon becomes lost in mere verbal sounds."

Thus has been fulfilled, in these creatures, the great command, which became to them the law of their being: "Be fruitful, and multiply, and fill the waters of the seas, and let fowl multiply in the earth."

[1] James Montgomery, in his *Pelican Island.*
[2] Sharon Turner, in his *Sacred History of the World.*

In the midst of this account of the world's creation, one is reminded of modern inquiries into the relation which the Mosaic narrative bears to mythological legends. They have been carefully considered in Lücken's *Traditions of the Human Race, or the Primitive Revelation of God among the Heathen.* Münster, 1856. The heathen cosmogonies are similar. We have *chaos;* this chaos developing itself in the great world egg; this world egg producing man: man, so produced, constituting a microcosm, in which the life of nature begins, and things separate, to multiply in several divisions. Primitive generating existence is imagined under the form of some huge animal. Yet, in these myths, there appear recognitions of some Divinity presiding over the mundane changes. It is not all self-evolution. Moreover, a world comes first, and man afterwards; yet man precedes animals, and, so, while there is some faint resemblance in these cosmogonies to the book of Genesis, there is a wide difference. Matter is clearly distinguishable in the latter. Matter is confounded with Spirit in the former. Matter is coherent with God in the predominantly pantheistic systems of emanation. In some, matter emanates from the Divinity; in others, Divinity emanates from the world or chaos. Sometimes the relation between the two is hostile: sometimes there is a peaceful parallelism. The comparison of the two kinds of representation, the biblical and the mythical, decidedly supports the superiority and Divinity of the Mosaic accounts. "If the Mosaic cosmogony was derived from the heathen, as is contended, how very strange it is, and counter to what takes place in all similar derivations, that the Hebrew mind (a very gross mind, they say), should have taken it, in this impure and monstrously confused state, and refined it back to that chaste and sublime consistency which the Bible narrative, whatever may be thought of its absolute truth, may so justly claim."—Professor T. Lewis, LL.D., in *Lange's Commentary* (Clarke), I. 181.

·S.

CREATION OF LAND ANIMALS

Genesis 1:24-25

THE waters are now inhabited; the air is peopled; and terrestrial animals alone are wanting. Accordingly, when the morning of the sixth day dawned, God is described in the sacred record as resuming His creative work, in the words: "Let the earth bring forth the living creature after its kind, cattle and creeping thing, and beast of the earth after its kind."

From the variety of the terms employed, something like a classification of the various inhabitants of the earth is evidently here intended. Yet it is remarkable that perhaps not one English reader in ten thousand has any distinct idea of the division denoted by these various terms, plainly meant to be distinctive. Few have spent a thought on the subject, or have taken the trouble to inquire; the great body of readers resting content in the knowledge that the several terms taken collectively must designate the various creatures by which the earth is inhabited.

The term "living creature," seems to be a *collective* designation of the animals which are there indicated according to their kind.

Under the term of "cattle" are included the ruminant herbivora, generally gregarious and capable of domestication. To call them "tame" or "domestic" at the time of their creation, as some do, would be absurd, seeing that their domestication was future; but this is the class of animals in which are included most of the species which, in the prescient providence of the Creator, were designed for the more immediate use and service of the coming man, and which were therefore endued with habits suited to their intended connection with him. But although this class comprehends all the animals essentially of a gentle nature and susceptible of domestication, it does not include all animals which are now regarded as tame or domestic; for there are some, such as the cat and the dog, whose domestication is of very ancient date, which were not originally natives of the more pacific genera, but are specimens of the wild tamed into the gentle.

Next, not in order of enumeration but in the order of nature and character, we come to the "beasts of the earth," which are the carnivora or beasts of prey in their various kinds. The name by which they are designated comes from a word signifying "life" or "living," and is well suited to the vivacious, active, and vigorous character which they display in comparison with the animals which crop the herb of the field. But were these animals indeed wild and fierce at their creation, and were their appetites even then such as to demand the immediate destruction, for their use, of the life which God had just given to other creatures? This is a hard question. The organization of these animals, their teeth, their feet, their intestines, are all adapted to a carnivorous and predatory existence; and it may be thought that the life of other animals must from the beginning have been necessary to their subsistence. Yet the mind revolts from the idea of the new creation being at once disfigured by scenes of slaughter and death, before the sin of Adam had brought woe into the world. We know that many of these animals, perhaps all,

can be brought to subsist on vegetable products, as man himself can subsist wholly on flesh, or wholly on vegetables, as he chooses; and the intimations in Genesis, so far as they go, are in accordance with the more pleasing and attractive opinion, that although these animals were in their organization adapted to what was to become their final condition, yet their fierceness was held in check; and that, although more active in their movements, they were not more agressive than other animals. This is the opinion of the poets; and it is pleasant to be of their opinion whenever we can. The prophetic intimations favour this interpretation; for that the beasts of prey shall be divested of their fierceness is a prominent feature in their descriptions of the final restoration of the earth to its originally paradisaical condition. This hint our poets have not been slow to take.

> "The lion and the libbard and the bear
> Graze with the fearless flocks. All bask at noon
> Together, or all gambol in the shade
> Of the same grove, or drink one common stream.
> Antipathies are none. No foe to man
> Lurks in the serpent now: the mother sees,
> And smiles to see, her infant's playful hand
> Stretched forth to dally with the crested worm,
> To stroke his azure neck, or to receive
> The lambent homage of his arrowy tongue.
> All creatures worship man; and all mankind
> One Lord, One Father."—COWPER.

Old Du Bartas answers, under the same views, this difficult question:

> "Lord, if so be Thou for mankind didst rear
> This rich round mansion (glorious everywhere),
> Alas! why didst Thou on this day create
> These harmful beasts, which but exasperate
> Our thorny life?
>   'Pardon, good God, pardon me;' 'twas our pride,
> Not Thou, that troubled our first happy tide.
> Before that Adam did revolt from Thee,
> And (curious) tasted of the sacred tree,
> He lived King in Eden, and his brow
> Was never blankt with pallid fear, as now:
> The fiercest beast would, at his word or beck,
> Bend to his yoke their self-obedient neck."

Under the remaining class, rendered by "creeping thing" (in Hebrew REMES), we have not only the minor quadrupeds that seem to creep rather than walk, and such as creep on many feet, but all that glide along the surface of the soil—the serpents, annelides, &c. The idea throughout this classification is that of *creeping*. In the Arabic language, the same word as the Hebrew is applied to long, luxuriant grass, that seems to *creep* over the ground; and in this sense it is still used in some parts of Scotland, in its original form, *Ramsh.*

A fact is here broadly stated which scientific research has since fully demonstrated, namely, that the real origin of species is the direct act of the Creator. Each species was called into being by an immediate exercise of Almighty power. The theory of development is as much opposed to the sacred record as it is to natural law.

Another point may be here noticed. Each species of animals has its own instincts or natural propensities. There is no ground for assuming that these instincts were so changed by the fall of man as that animals originally formed to subsist on vegetable food were rendered carnivorous, and made to prey upon others. The structure of the teeth, claws, and stomach must in that case have undergone an entire change. In fact, the very division which in this passage is made of animals into wild and domestic, would not, under such circumstances, have been strictly applicable. Nor can we legitimately appeal to the statement of the prophets in confirmation of any such theory. Their language is to be understood metaphorically when they speak of "the lion eating straw like the ox," etc.

It is further remarkable, that the order of creation in this chapter is a natural order. "Cuvier decided," says Hugh Miller, "that, in the natural division, fishes should be placed at the bottom of the scale, reptiles next in place, birds next, then the irrational mammals, and man at the head of all." So it is here. And this too appears to be the geological order in the strata of the earth's crust.   **P.**

In the light of the latest scientific discoveries, it has been justly observed, that the phenomena under the earth's surface correspond with the succession as described in this chapter. A period of comparative gloom, with more vapour and more carbonic acid in the atmosphere—then of greater light, of vegetation, of marine animals and huge reptiles, of birds, of beasts, and lastly of men. The Testimony of the Rocks thus far confirms the testimony of the Book of Genesis. "The chief difference, if any, of the two witnesses would seem to be, that the Rocks speak of (1) marine plants, (2) marine animals, (3) land plants, (4) land animals in their successive developments; whereas Moses speaks of (1) plants, (2) marine animals, (3) land animals—a difference not amounting to diversity. As physiology must have been nearly, and geology wholly unknown to the Semetic nations of antiquity, such a general correspondence of sacred history with modern science is surely more striking and important than any apparent difference in details." Whilst we should never forget that the Bible is given, not to teach us science, but to teach us religion, it is impossible for thoughtful people to neglect watching the points of contact between the two. There must be no contradiction of palpable facts on the one hand, and no violence done to the written book on the other; but while each department of divine teaching is left to speak for itself, it tends to confirm our faith in both, to recognize such accordance as that just pointed out, contrasting as it does with the gross contradictions of sacred writ by the Hindoo cosmogony. "The only important resemblance of any ancient cosmogony with the Scriptural account, is to be found in the Persian or Zoastrian; which is most naturally accounted for, first, by the fact that the Persians, of all people except the Hebrews, were the most likely to have retained the memory of primitive traditions; and secondly, that Zoroaster was probably brought into contact with the Hebrews, and perhaps with the prophet Daniel, in the court of Darius, and may have learned much from such association."—*Speaker's Commentary*, vol. I.

In a valuable geological treatise just published (*The Dawn of Life*, by J. W. Dawson, LL.D., 1875), it is remarked "No one probably believes that animal life has been an eternal succession of like forms of being. We are familiar with the idea that in some way it was introduced; and most men now know, either from the testimony of Genesis or geology, or both, that the lower forms of animal life were introduced first, and that these first living creatures had their birth in the waters, which are still the prolific maker of things innumerable. Further, there is a general impression, that it would be the most appropriate way, that the great procession of animal existence should commence with the humblest types known to us, and should march on, in successive bands, of gradually increasing dignity and power, till man himself brings up the rear." The author states—"After long and patient research there still remained a large residuum of the oldest rocks, destitute of all traces of living beings, and designated by the hopeless name Azoic;" and in the work just mentioned he describes signs of the "Dawn of Life," to be found in certain Canadian rocks, at the base of the old Azoic formations, called *Laurentian*, from their situation near the St. Lawrence Valley. This order accords with the Mosaic account.

S.

THE IMAGE OF GOD

Genesis 1:26-27

THE great work of creation now approaches its close:—

" Now heaven in all her glory shone, and rolled
    Her motions, as the great first Mover's hand
    First wheeled their course : earth in her rich attire
    Consummate lovely smiled ; air, water, earth,
    By fowl, fish, beast, was flown, was swum, was walked,
    Frequent ; and of the sixth day yet remained ;
    There wanted yet the master-work, the end
    Of all yet done."—*Milton.*

In approaching to the creation of man, the sacred narrative assumes a more solemn air, and more dignified style : "And God said, Let Us make man in our image, after our likeness ; and let them have dominion over the fish of the sea, and over the fowl of the air, and over all the earth." And it is added: "So God created man in his own image; in the image of God created He him."

It is impossible to read this account of the origin of our first parents, and not to acknowledge that it conveys an intimation of some eminent distinction, which has been conferred exclusively upon the human race. "We are indeed," says a fine writer on this subject,[1] "the beings of a day; incapable of counting on a single hour as our own; uncertain whether we shall be permitted to carry our slightest purpose into execution; exposed to a thousand perils; and liable to be diverted from our holiest and most steadfast resolution by the sudden gust of passion, or the unexpected temptation; but still, though weak and frail, we are invested with the highest dignity which can be bestowed upon any creature, for there is some portion of our nature which bears the impress of the image of the Creator."

It is said that he still bears this image; for although some have urged, that whatever was intended by it must have been lost at the fall, we agree with this writer in thinking that there is Scripture evidence to the contrary. The Almighty, addressing Noah after the deluge, and uttering this solemn denunciation against murder, says, "Whoso sheddeth man's blood, by man shall his blood be shed; *for in the image of God made He man*."[2] The reason here urged for respecting the life of man, could have been of no conceivable force had the image of God been wholly and irrecoverably forfeited by Adam's transgression. In what, then, did this image, by which man is made like to his Maker, consist?

The old and still too common idea, that it is to be found in the linaments and erect figure of man, although taken up by the poets and orators, and hence invested with images and illustrations by which its actual offensiveness is hidden, is painfully revolting to one who is enabled to realize a distinct conception of the great fact that "God is a Spirit."

Does this image then lie in the "dominion" which is given to man over the inferior creatures? Some think that it does, and have written largely on that view; but if we examine with care the text on which that notion is founded,[3] we shall see that the dominion is a power which belongs to man because he bears the image of God, and does not in itself constitute that image.

Does it then lie in that immortality which is denied to all lower creatures, and which, indeed, invests man with a dignity which might certainly, under particular points of view, be regarded as the image of God? Even this would be still an incomplete image. The immortality of God is an eternity of past and future; ours, of the future only. But above all, consider that Satan and his angels are also inheritors of an immortal being; and it will not surely be urged that the language in which the Scripture describes the nature of Adam is applicable to them, as it must be if mere immortality constituted the image of God.

A more prevailing theory is, that it lies in man's intellect—his powers of reason, of thought, of invention, by which he is made only a little lower than the angels. Proud sinners that we are, to be thus ever prating about our intellect, the efforts of our genius, the wonders of our invention, the grasp of our thought! We forget that the devil and his angels have more of all this than we possess, and that, so far from giving *them* the image of God, it probably only accelerated their departure from Him. Reason is a fine thing; but let us not think too much of it. God does not. We know of a surety—we know on the authority of His word—that all the proud and high things of man's intellect, are of infinitely less value in His sight than the humblest aspiration after mercy and truth—than the heart uttered groans of a contrite spirit. Besides, there is no real likeness between the reason of man and the Uncreated Intellect. God does not labour in thought. All truth, all knowledge, is intuitive to Him—is part of His own essence. Where, then, is the likeness in this?

Since, therefore, the image of God is not to be sought in the perfection of man's body, nor of his mind as the seat of the intellect, this holy endowment can only be found in his soul, the seat of his moral faculties. It must be a living energy in the human breast, reflecting the likeness of the God who made us. Surely, therefore, it is evinced in the capacity of resembling Him in moral attributes; of being holy as He is holy; of loving Him with something of that love wherewith He first loved us. This is plainly intimated in the words of the apostle, where he speaks of "putting off the old man with his deeds, and of putting on the new man, which is renewed in

---

[1] Rev. William Harness, *Sermons on the Image of God in Man.* 1841.

[2] Genesis 9:3.   [3] Genesis 1:26.

knowledge *after the image* of Him that created him."[1] So, also, when he speaks to the Ephesians of "putting on the new man, which after God is created in righteousness and true holiness."[2] Nothing can be clearer than these two passages, taken together ; both of which, indeed, have a most distinct reference to the very text of Genesis by which this inquiry has been excited.

It is therefore in the capacity for, or in the possession of, true "knowledge," "righteousness," and "holiness," that the image of God is found ; and seeing that all these faculties have their root in love,—love to God, a feeling of God's love to us, the love of God in the soul,—it is in LOVE that the image of God is perfected ; and he is most like God, sets forth most of God's image, who loveth most. There can be no doubt about this. To bear the image of God is to be like Him in that attribute in which He is chiefly presented to our view, and is related to us ; and that is love. The book of God's hand in the natural world, and the book of His Spirit in the Scriptures, concur in setting forth His love in creation and in providence ; while the latter discloses to us the special wonders of His love in redemption. "Love is of God," says the beloved disciple ; "and every one that loveth is born of God, and knoweth God : FOR GOD IS LOVE. In this was manifested the love of God towards us, because that God sent his only-begotten Son into the world, that we might live through him. . . . Beloved, if God so loved us, we ought also to love one another."[3]

If, then, "God is love," to love Him, and to love mankind,—because they bear His image in being endowed with the capacity for the same love of Him,—is to be like God—to bear that image of Him in which Adam was created. Not faintly did our Lord Himself indicate this view, when He told the hopeful scribe, that the essence of all the law and the prophets was comprised in the two great commandments, "Thou shalt LOVE the Lord thy God with *all* thy heart, with *all* thy soul, and with *all* thy mind ;" and in this other, "Thou shalt LOVE thy neighbour as thyself."[4] Let us therefore desire to bear more and more of God's image, by having more of that love in our hearts which is the fulfilling of the law. Few men loved more than David. It was in this that he was the man "after God's own heart"—that

is, after God's image. Yet he was continually aspiring to higher degrees of conformity to the divine excellence. "I shall be satisfied," he says, "when I awake with thy likeness" (Ps. xvii. 15). Let this also be our desire and prayer. May we be satisfied with nothing less !

As indicated above, the Apostle Paul furnishes the true key to the meaning of the statement, that "God created man in his own image." Man, the last and greatest of the Creator's works, stands out in striking contrast from all the other creatures in two aspects—*intellectually* and *morally*. To the former Paul refers in Col. iii. 10, when he states that it is a renewal in *knowledge* which restores man to the lost image of his Maker ; while to the *moral* or ethical he refers in Eph. iv. 24, "That ye put on the new man, which after God is created in righteousness and holiness of truth." We err if we confine our view of the divine image in Adam to either the one department or the other. Both intellectually and morally that divine image was enstamped upon him. The intellectual stands first, and is the basis of the ethical. Man's intellect fits him for rational observation, for logical comparison, for scientific research ; but above all, it fits him for the acquisition of the highest and best knowledge, the knowledge of the being, nature, and attributes of God. When the intellect is thus exercised, the ethical powers are brought into full operation. God, fully known in all the wonders of His power, love, and grace, is the grand—indeed, the only effectual—stimulant to a life of holiness. **P.**

Before leaving the subject of Divine creation, it is well to remember "God inspired Moses and the prophets to write as they have written. They were not to tell men that the first thing to be learnt was, how to be rich ; or how to be strong ; nor even how to be happy : but that the first thing to be learnt was, that God created the heaven and the earth."

The first chapter of Genesis should be read in connection with the first chapter of St. John's Gospel, and the first chapter of St. Paul's Epistle to the Colossians—"In the beginning was the Word, and the Word was with God, and the Word was God. The same was in the beginning with God. All things were made by him ; and without him was not anything made that was made. In him was life ; and the life was the light of men." "Who is the image of the invisible God, the firstborn of every creature : for by him were all things created, that are in heaven, and that are in earth, visible and invisible, whether they be thrones, or dominions, or principalities, or powers : all things were created by him, and for him : and he is before all things, and by him all things consist."

"Blessed is he who believes that—who believes that the same person who was born in a stable ; had not where to lay His head ; went about healing the sick, and binding up the broken heart ; suffered under Pontius Pilate ; was crucified, dead, and buried, and rose again the third day, and ascended into heaven,—ascended thither that He might fulfil all things ; and is none other than the Lord of the

---

[1] Colossians 3:9,10.
[2] Ephesians 4:24.
[3] 1 John 4:7-11.
[4] Matthew 22:35-40.

earth ; and of men the Creator, the Teacher, the Saviour, the Guide, the King, the Judge of all the world." We are justified in using such language, believing, as we do, that Jesus Christ was God manifest in the flesh. Without deifying his humanity, we devoutly recognize the Word that was God, as tabernacling with us in human nature, so as to be God and man in one person ; and it adds immensely to the joy of contemplating creation, with its various scenes of beauty and glory, when we see the shadow of the adorable Saviour falling over all, as Maker, Upholder, and Lord. " I am in the kingdom of the babe of Bethlehem. He put me here. And He put this world here likewise, and that is enough for me. He created all I see or can see —I care little how, provided that *He* created it ; for then I am sure it must be very good."—C. Kingsley's *Gospel of the Pentateuch.* **S.**

FOOD OF PRIMEVAL MAN

Genesis 1:29-30

WHEN God informs the newly created man that He assigns to him for meat "every herb bearing seed, and every tree in the which is the fruit of a tree yielding seed," it seems impossible to resist the conclusion, that this is designed to point out to him the kind of food intended for his use, and that what was not so pointed out, was not designed to be food for him. To contend that the specification of herbs, grain, and fruits can in any way comprehend the use of the flesh of animals, seems altogether monstrous ; and it may be safely affirmed, that the flesh of animals is the last thing a man would think of eating, who has been told that his food is to consist of vegetables. It seems clear to us that animal food—even to this day but sparingly used in the East, and in some Eastern countries held in abhorrence—was not intended to be the food of man, at least in his original condition. Instinctively we recognize the fitness that it should not have been so. We know not what were the divine intentions with respect to the state of man in case he had not fallen ; but it is reasonable to assume that this rule respecting food would have continued in operation, and that his climate, and other circumstances, would not have been such as to create the need of, or appetite for, the flesh of animals. This appetite is after all, to a great extent, the effect of climatic influences ; and it was probably not until mankind had spread into climes far distant from their first seat, that they began to transgress this rule of food ; for we

agree with those who think that the distinction of clean and unclean beasts, at the time of the flood, implies the *previous* use of animal food, From the permission to use such food, expressly granted to Noah after the deluge, it may be thought that he and other righteous persons had abstained therefrom in obedience to the paradisaical law ; or at least that they had been troubled with doubts on the subject, and were hence favoured with the express permission to use the flesh of beasts. It is even more than possible, that the constitution of the earth underwent such changes at the deluge, as rendered meat, more than before, suitable for the food of man. In any case, it appears to us that the words then uttered contain a distinct reference to the original grant, and an extension of it : " Every moving thing that liveth shall be meat for you ; *even as the green herb have I given you all things* " (Gen. ix. 3). And if, as the language most clearly implies, the extension was now first made, and was necessary to satisfy the conscience of a righteous man, it is manifest that animal food could only, before the flood, have been eaten by those whose transgressions brought that awful judgment upon the world.

From this it seems clear, that whatever we say as to the period between the fall and the deluge, vegetable food only was allowed to man, or used by him in his first estate. The poets, therefore, are here again right in regarding vegetables alone as

> "The food of man,
> While yet he lived in innocence, and told
> A length of golden years, unfleshed in blood,
> A stranger to the savage arts of life,
> Death, rapine, carnage, surfeit, and disease ;
> The lord, and not the tyrant, of the world."
> *Thomson.*

This abstinence from animal food is in fact preserved in the traditions of all nations, as one of the characteristics of their golden age— the age of innocence. Some have thought that the restriction was designed for a temporary purpose, in order that there might be no check to the increase of the newly created races ; but if so, it would have been equally necessary after the deluge, when only the few animals that had been saved in the ark remained alive.

It is not at all necessary to enter into the old and somewhat entertaining question as to the comparative merits of vegetable and animal diet. As it is certain that but little of the latter is used in warm countries, whereas large quantities are consumed in colder regions; and as we can observe in our own experience, that the inclination for flesh meat is less active in summer than in winter,—the matter seems to be, in the result, chiefly one of climate—men residing in the colder latitudes requiring a stronger nutriment than vegetables supply, to make up for the greater waste of animal heat. Be this as it may, there cannot be in the practice anything essentially wrong, or it would not have been expressly permitted by God himself after the deluge.

The objections as to the cruelty of the practice sound well in poetry, but will not bear the test of reason. Myriads of animals have been called into being, and cared for and well fed by man,—have been allowed the full enjoyment of the happiest period of animal life,—that would not have existed at all, or could not have been maintained in existence, had they not been needful to him. What would be the result for the advantage of the domesticated animals were they not thus needful to man? Most of the land now left for pasturage would be brought under culture; and the animals not being needed, and therefore not being worth the cost of rearing, would not be allowed to increase; or they would be destroyed, like young cats, at their birth; or being left to themselves, they would starve, or become the prey of ravenous beasts.

Even in the article of death, the animals are not losers. Sickness and decay, softened by many tender circumstances to the human creature, are horrible, involving as they do death by starvation, to animals constrained in a state of nature to seek their own food; and the other alternative, death from beasts of prey, is accompanied by circumstances of dread, horror, and pain, in the pursuit, the struggle, and the torturing laceration, which are unknown under the hands of the butcher, who suddenly and once for all attacks the seat of life.

Doubtless there is more real humanity in the system which allows ten thousand animals to enjoy their youth, than in that which would, in proportion, only permit *one* to live, to exist to old age, and to die of slow decay. Of the fifty millions, or thereabout, of sheep in these islands, how many would have known existence, were mutton not an article of food.

ADAM IN EDEN

Genesis 2:8

THE sacred narrative informs us that the newly created man was placed in a garden, in the eastern part of a land called Eden. The land of Eden was in a well watered, fertile, and pleasant country; and the best and choicest part of that land, planted as a paradise or garden, was to be the abode of the first man. Let not the reader be troubled. We intend not to inquire into the site of Eden. It may be doubted whether the changes wrought on the face of the earth at the deluge, have not placed the spot beyond discovery or recognition. But we are sure that it was a most pleasant place—pleasanter, without doubt, than any the world has since beheld. Here, probably, all that was sublime and gentle in the scenery of the whole earth was exhibited in pattern, and all that could delight the uncorrupted tastes of the new man, with all that could excite the earnest inquiries of his mind, were spread out before him. He had labour to employ his attention, without wearying him; and he had time, leisure, for his highest pursuits—those connected with the knowledge, which he eagerly desired to possess, of God, His will, and His works. There was no disharmony in nature to pain his soul. The birds sang sweetly to him as he walked, or wrought, or rested; and the beasts gambolled playfully around their master. He was endowed with a rational and immortal spirit; he was holy, and therefore happy; and he enjoyed sensible intercourse with God, and probably with angels. What a state of blessedness was this! To men embued with the spirit of the fall, to whom the excitements of conflict and conquest are necessary, and who will not be happy unless they can " ride in the whirlwind, and direct the storm," the paradise of Eden may seem insipid, and the loss of it no great privation, merely as a condition of life. But to those to whom the strifes of men are hateful; who faint beneath the cares of life; who are cut off from sun and air by the necessities of daily toil; or who groan under the burden of their sins,—the repose, the rest, the happiness of Eden, glorified by the presence of God, appears beyond all measure inviting, and well may they cry, " O Adam, what hast thou done, to lose for thy children so fair a heritage!" Yet even such may be of good cheer; for the second Adam has found for them a fairer home, and a more blessed inheritance.

There has been much speculation respecting the condition of Adam in regard to knowledge. All accounts necessarily assign to him the utmost physical perfection of man's nature. But in the view of some he was merely a naked savage, who had all things to acquire by experience. This theory has not been held from any intended disrespect to the father of mankind; but because it was an old opinion, that knowledge, intelligence, and the arts of civilisation, were progressively acquired in the first ages; and it was therefore necessary that the progenitor of the race should be in a state of ignorance, as it could not but be supposed that he would impart such knowledge as he possessed to his descendants. On the other hand, there are those who urge that Adam, instructed of God, must have been possessed of all knowledge of which the mind of man is capable, and have been deeply skilled in all the sciences and arts of civilisation.

That both extremes are wrong, we have no doubt. Adam was at his creation not a child; he was a man, in the vigour of physical and mental life. There is no need of placing any limit to his powers of thought, of reasoning, of comparison, of imagination. He was taught of God, and not left to gather, by slow experience, all that he wanted to know. If Adam could talk at all, and we know that he could, language must have been supernaturally imparted to him. He had no means of acquiring it but from God. From the same source he must have derived the knowledge he possessed of the properties of the animate and inanimate objects around him. He had the employment assigned him of keeping and dressing the garden; and this involves the knowledge of many operations, and of many properties of plants, which, although they may be in our day possessed by one man, are nevertheless the result of ages of experience. The commonest gardener who works for us, brings to his labour the progressive knowledge of many generations. If Adam had gone to work without previous instruction, or without being on the instant inspired (as was probably the case) with the knowledge of what was proper to be done in every new circumstance, he would soon have made sad ravages, even in the garden of Eden.

To cultivate a garden implies the use of tools. These must either have been supplied to him, or he must have been endowed with the skill, and with the knowledge of materials, necessary to enable him to make them for this purpose.

Again, that he was endowed with the knowledge of the common and more conspicuous qualities of animals, is evident from his being able to give appropriate names to the creatures brought under his notice. This was probably suggested to him, with the force of an intuitive perception, at the moment that his attention was directed to the species; for it would have required much and long continued observation to have done this without the aid of implanted perceptions.

But it does not, on the other hand, seem to us at all necessary to suppose that Adam was endowed with any other knowledge than was suited to the condition in which he was placed, and needful to the full enjoyment of its advantages. That he was learned in all science, and skilled in all art, there seems no reason to believe. Some make him greater than all his sons in astronomy, in zoology, in botany, in chemistry; and as well versed as they in the social and constructive arts. If this were necessary for him, we find no difficulty in believing that it would have been imparted to him; but as we cannot see that it was necessary, or that it belonged to his condition, we conceive that no such knowledge was in his possession. As much as the happiness of his condition required was given; and whatever else he might require in his state of innocence, would doubtless, in like manner, be imparted. But in the altered circumstances which eventually arose, and to which the law of Eden could not be applicable, men were left to the slower teaching of experience and observation for their advance in knowledge and the arts.

In one thing the state of Adam in Eden must have been far different from that of which we have any conception. All the past, which comes to us so fruitful in teachings and experiences, laden with vast stores of accumulated facts and knowledges, and rich in the memories of young joys and parental tendernesses,—this was a blank to him. This alone must have made a serious difference between his state and ours; a difference so great, that it is scarcely possible for us to realize to our minds all the mysteries of his existence. It is as a *difference* solely that we point it out. We know not that the first of men was, even in this respect, under any *disadvantage*. He had no *need* of antecedents. God was all to him—his past, his present, his future.

Much has been written about the geographical position of Paradise. Hales in his *Chronology* (I. 316), remarks, "It has been sought for in every quarter of the globe. Widely different are the sites assigned to it by ancient and modern geographers: *Armenia, Babylonia, Syria, Palestine, Ethiopia, Tartary, Hindustan*, and *China*." Calvin, Huet, Bochart, and others, believed the river described in Gen. ii. 10-14, to have been : in the north, the united streams of the Tigris and Euphrates ; and in the south, Gihon the eastern and Pison the western channels, by which the waters branch out below Bassora before falling into the ocean. This, perhaps, is the least objectionable solution, and is adopted by the best modern commentators. It is that most favourably regarded by Dr. Harold Browne, Bishop of Winchester, in the *Speaker's Commentary*, I. 40. It is said, in the *Bible Educator* (Vol. 1. 153), after noticing geographical and allegorical views of this subject, " We might adopt a middle view, that, while Eden is, perhaps, significant of a condition, or a quality, rather than of a place ; yet, that the garden of pleasure, described by the Book of Genesis, connected as it is with the definite and well known geographical names of the Euphrates and Tigris, can hardly be other than a definite area, unknown, indeed, to us, and probably undiscoverable, but certainly in the east, and agreeing, in general, with what appears to have been the starting point of the history of the human race." **S.**

ADAM NAMING THE LIVING CREATURES

Genesis 2:19-20

IN the progress of the sacred narrative we are told that God said that it was "not good for man to be alone," and declared his intention of making a suitable companion, or " help meet for him ;" but instead of proceeding with the account of this creation, the record proceeds to a very different matter. " And out of the ground the Lord God formed every beast of the field, and every fowl of the air, and brought them unto Adam, to see what he would call them ; and whatsoever Adam called every living creature, that was the name thereof." What has this to do with the providing of an help meet for the first of men ? The narrative proceeds : " And Adam gave names to all the cattle, and to the fowl of the air, and to every beast of the field ; but "—and here comes the secret—" but for Adam there was not found an help meet for him." It was therefore evidently the design of the benevolent Creator to enhance, in the view of the man, the value of the gift He was about to bestow upon him, by showing him that the existing races of animated nature, abounding as they did in elegant and beautiful species, did not afford any creature suited to be his companion, or to satisfy the yearning of his heart for the fellowship of an equal being. Nothing was better calculated to realize this impression than to bring the various animal existences under the notice of Adam, and at the same time to endow him with that perception of their several qualities and natures, which is implied in his being able to give them distinctive and appropriate names. It is very possible that, being as yet ignorant of the divine intention, Adam considered that he was expected to find out for himself a meet companion among these creatures. So Milton understood it, in a very remarkable passage, in which he seems to ascribe the power of reasoning to brutes. God is represented as saying to Adam,—

"Is not the earth
With various living creatures, and the air
Replenished, and all these at thy command,
To come and play before thee ? Knowest thou not
Their language and their ways ? *They also know
And reason not contemptibly.* With these
Find pastime, and bear rule ; thy realm is large.
So spake the Universal Lord, *and seemed
So ordering.*"

In previously describing the names of the cattle, Milton takes the same view as we do, that the knowledge involved in that act was conveyed by instant and supernatural enlightenment.

"Each bird and beast behold
Approaching two and two : these cowering low,
With blandishment : each bird stooped on his wing.
I named them as they passed, and understood
Their nature ; *with such knowledge God endued
My sudden apprehension ;* but in these
I found not what methought I wanted still."

Of course, modern rationalizing philosophy has found something in this remarkable statement on which to hang its cavils. It has been ascertained, it is urged, that animals are adapted exclusively to the regions which they inhabit, and that it would be contrary to their nature, and zoologically impossible, for them to leave their own climates, and to assemble in one place. It is certain that, if this did take place, as is assumed, it was a supernatural impulse which urged them to travel to one point; and we should think that no believer in the existence and power of God can doubt the possibility of such an impulse being imparted, whether he believes that it *was* given or not. Is that impossible to God, which is possible even to man, who can show us, in any of his large cities, animals brought together from all the climates of the earth, from the Equator to the Arctic circles? But again, how do we know that various climates did exist before the deluge? There is good reason to think, that before that time the temperature of the earth was everywhere more equable than it has been since; and hence the animals would have no inducement to classify themselves into their climates, nor any difficulty in passing from one part of the world to any other part.

But again, was there any necessity for this migration of the animals of different climes to Eden? On what ground is it assumed thus quietly that animals were created in their different climates? Why might they not be created in the same locality in which man received his existence, afterwards dispersing themselves, as his own race did, to the several parts of the earth? If the climate before the deluge was equable, there could be no difficulty in this dispersion from a common centre; and if there *were* then various climates, the animals would gradually wander till they came to the region best suited to their natures, and there remain. It is only necessary to suppose that the creation took place in a medium climate, such as all animals could at least bear till they found their congenial abodes. This is not altogether hypothesis; for it is the same course of dispersion, from a common centre, which, as we know, did take place after the deluge, and which may therefore well have taken place after the creation.

In fact, instead of being embarrassed by the difficulty of the subject, we are apt to be confused by the variety of the explanations which occur to our thoughts, and any one of which will furnish a satisfactory solution of all that has been indicated as "hard to be understood" in the Scripture narrative of the circumstances.

If the animals were dispersed before this over the world, the sacred text does not impose upon us any inevitable necessity of providing for their migration to Eden, although we have done so.

The text may be very well understood to refer to the animals in or near Eden. The Hebrew word rendered by "all" (*kol*), is not always understood in the largest sense of universality, but often of many, or of a large part; and that it is in this instance to be received with some limitation, is evident from the fishes not being specified. Supposing all the animals already dispersed, it is obvious that it was not necessary that such as were wholly unsuited to engage Adam's attention for the object in view, should be brought from their several localities for the purpose. Or if they were assembled in one place previously to their dispersion, it would be equally needless that his attention should be engaged by animals which he was not likely ever to see again, and which exhibited no qualities to suggest even a possible suitableness for the purpose immediately in view.

We see no reason to suppose that more than a single pair of any species, as of man, were in the first instance created, in which case, and supposing that they dispersed as they multiplied, the land of Eden must at the first have been like a vast zoological garden—such a garden as man never formed, seeing that it contained the primeval representations of *every* species. In this must that land have differed from all other lands, which have since contained many individuals of a few of the multitudinous species of animals upon the earth, instead of a few individuals of all the different species.

As these various creatures doubtless presented themselves to the notice of Adam in pairs, he must the more deeply have been convinced of his own isolated condition. All these creatures had suitable companions, and he had none: each of them was already provided with a mate, and could be no help meet for him.

The point indicated in the last paragraph opens the way, as I believe, to a full understanding of verses 18-20. God's gracious intention to provide a suitable companion for man is first expressed. Man himself was not yet fully conscious of his want. He felt his solitary condition the less, because of his close communion with God. But to bring it fully before his mind, God caused the whole animal kingdom to pass in review before him. They appear to have passed in pairs, "the male and his female," as they sprung fresh from the Creator's hands. In an instant, by divine intuition, Adam saw their natures and propensities; and as he distinguished and named them, he observed that there was none solitary like himself, and that such companionship as they enjoyed was absolutely necessary, not only to their happiness, but to the full development of God's designs regarding them. Perceiving this, he became conscious of his own wants; his soul yearned for "an help meet"—a sharer of his thoughts, his joys, and his purposes. Thus was he prepared for the gift which God was about so wondrously to bestow.

When these points are overlooked, the connection between verses eighteen and nineteen appears abrupt and unnatural; but when they are kept in view, the whole narrative exhibits perfect and beautiful order.

P.

EVE

Genesis 2:21-24

ADAM was not long left by his indulgent Creator to that feeling of disappointment which he must have experienced when he realized the conviction that there was not among the creatures of the earth one suited to be his companion. As he one day awoke from a deep sleep which the Lord had caused to fall upon him, he saw before him a creature whom he at once recognized as the being his heart had sought,—the being wonderfully suited by her bodily frame and mental constitution to fill up the sole void, the only want, of his happy existence. Whence came she? Adam knew; for when he saw her he said, "This is now bone of my bone and flesh of my flesh: she shall be called Woman, because she was taken out of man." It is therefore probable that the "deep sleep" was supernatural, or a kind of trance, in which he had been conscious, although without pain, but rather perhaps with rapture, of the whole process of her formation. This is the idea generally entertained by the Jewish writers, and by the old Christian fathers, and it has been adopted and beautifully brought out by Milton:—

"Mine eyes He closed, but open left the cell
Of fancy, my internal sight; by which
Abstract, as in a trance, methought I saw,
Though sleeping, where I lay, and saw the shape
Still glorious before whom awake I stood;
Who stooping opened my left side, and took
From thence a rib, with cordial spirits warm,
And life-blood streaming fresh; wide was the wound
But suddenly with flesh filled up and healed:
The rib He formed and fashioned with His hands;
Under His forming hands a creature grew,
Man-like, but different sex; so lovely fair,
That what seemed fair in all the world, seemed now
Mean, or in her summed up, in her contained
And in her looks; which from that time infused
Sweetness into my heart, unfelt before."

This is in close conformity with the Mosaic description of our first mother's origin, which, however, it amplifies by the addition of circumstances. He says the rib was taken from the left side, probably for the poetical association of that part being nearer the heart; but the Jewish Targumist makes it the right side, and says that it was from an odd or thirteenth rib on that side.

Many have been offended at this account of woman's origin, being unable to make out, or unwilling to receive, the circumstances as related. Some have rejected it altogether. With such we have nothing to do. To us the Bible is the Word of God; and these pages are designed for the use of those who receive it as such; so that we are relieved from the necessity of discussing the cavils of unbelievers, though willing to notice the difficulties which occasionally embarrass the sincere inquirer. This is perhaps one of the passages which do present such difficulties, whence some very well meaning people have been disposed to regard the whole recital as an allegory. But we must not be too ready to admit of allegories, lest we give the enemy occasion to turn into allegory, or *myth*, as they call it now, whatever he does not wish to be plainly understood. Besides, if we take this to be allegorical, what is there in this history of creation that we are to take as real? If we admit the allegorical in one place, how can we shut it out in others, where we would less readily allow it? Who is then to distinguish between the allegorical and the real?

There seems to us no more difficulty in taking this part of the history of creation literally, than in so understanding many other parts of it; and sooner than allow an entrance for the dangers which attend the admission, that one portion of the same narrative is real and another part allegorical, we should be inclined to allow the whole history of the creation to be an allegory. You might then allege that this, from the remote antiquity and peculiar nature of the transaction, needed to be veiled in allegory; but if you admit the account to be substantially literal, and yet admit of allegorical incidents therein, you preclude yourself from denying that there may be allegorical incidents in other and later portions of Scripture which you desire to be throughout literally understood. In this case, is there any greater difficulty in taking literally the creation of woman, than the creation of man? Adam was made of the dust of the ground. Why? Had it not been quite as well that he should at once have started into being at the divine word, without any intermediate process like this? It is a sufficient answer, that God thought fit it should be otherwise; probably because, all modes being equal to Him, He chose that which might impress upon man a moral lesson, even by the physical fact of his origin: a lesson important to repress pride, even in the unfallen man; but which became terribly emphatic when, after the fall, man heard the awful words, "Dust thou art, and unto dust thou shalt return!"

If we admit this to be sufficient in the case of man's creation, why not in that of woman? Whether there was some peculiar organization in Adam (such as an additional rib), in order to provide for the formation of woman, or whether God substituted another rib for the one He had taken, it is not very important for us to know; but it is most important to understand that He to whom all modes are the same, chose one which should serve vividly to impress upon the minds of man and woman their *peculiarly* intimate relation to each other. Among other creatures, there was no natural connection between the pairs in the very act of their creation. In them the sexes were created independently of each other. But in man the union was to be of peculiar significance and solemnity; it was even to set forth, as by a symbol, the union between Christ and his church. The fact of the woman's derivation from man—a part of himself, separated, to be in another form reunited to him, was calculated to originate an especial tenderness in their nuptial state, and to indicate its indissoluble character. See how beautifully St. Paul works out these ideas; and understanding, as he manifestly does, the account of woman's origin as given in Genesis to be literal, *his* inspired authority ought to be conclusive on the matter: "So ought men to love their wives as their own bodies: he that loveth his wife loveth himself. For no man ever yet hated his own flesh; but nourisheth and cherisheth it, even as the Lord the church: for we are members of his body, of his flesh, and of his bones." Eph. v. 28-30. Surely, to teach such lessons as these was a sufficient reason for the mode of woman's creation. She was to be created in some mode or other, and however created, in *that* creation the miracle consisted. The mere

mode was a lesser matter, and might be determined by circumstances *comparatively* unimportant; and indeed, when the world was new, it might have been difficult for the most astute of those who take it upon them to question the ways of God, to discover any circumstance more important for determining the mode of operation than those by which, in this case, it appears to have been influenced.

There is another idea embodied in this narrative, and intended to be shadowed forth in the singular mode of the woman's creation. Man, when alone, is incomplete. There is a felt want in his mind, and in his bodily conformation, unsupplied; there are divine purposes, moral as well as physical, which he cannot accomplish. That completeness which God graciously designed for the consummation of man's happiness, is effected by the marriage union. The necessity for it is in the sacred record indicated by the fact that the woman was made of a part of the man. "Therefore,"—on this account, because woman was taken out of the man, and forms part of him,—"Therefore shall a man leave his father and his mother, and shall cleave unto his wife." Close and dear as is the relationship between parent and child, closer and dearer far is that between husband and wife. "They twain shall be *one flesh*." Their entire natures must be made one by the feeling of love. There is, or ought to be, unity of spirit, unity of thought, and unity of purpose; for "they are no more twain, but one flesh."—See Mark x. 8; Eph. v. 28, 29.

P.

THE SERPENT

Genesis 3:1

In the sad history of the Fall, there is scarcely any one incident which more exercises our thoughts than the nature of the creature by whose baneful suggestions man's ruin was brought to pass.

The sacred record in the third chapter of Genesis says plainly enough that it was a "serpent," described as being "more subtile than any beast of the field;" and the final curse also indicates the serpentine condition—"Upon thy belly shalt thou go, and dust shalt thou eat all the days of thy life."

Hence some have regarded the tempter as a serpent, and nothing more. This opinion has many more advocates than the reader might suppose; or rather it *has* had them, for there are few who *now* entertain this opinion. To the question,

How could a mere serpent tempt Eve? it is answered, that the temptation lay in the repeated use by the serpent of the forbidden fruit in her presence, without any of the apparent effects upon him which she had been taught to dread. The influence of this example, and the thoughts that hence arose in her mind, are then represented, agreeably to the genius of Oriental and figurative language, in the form of a conversation. The great objection to this is, that the figurative style alleged to be employed here is adverse to the literal tone and character of the whole narrative; and what is far more conclusive, that another agent is clearly pointed out in the New Testament, and may, by the light thus afforded, be discovered even in the original account.

That agent is the devil, or Satan; and the general opinion is, that he employed, or actuated, the serpent as his instrument. Thus the latter appears to reason and to speak; the woman converses with him; and she is led, by the artful representations which the devil enables him to make, to break the divine law. No mere animal could have taken the part this serpent did. But it may be doubted whether Eve knew this. It is possible that the intuitive perception of the qualities of animals which Adam possessed was not shared by Eve, but was to be imparted to her by him; and it is highly probable that he had not yet communicated to her all the knowledge of this kind which had been acquired by him before she had existence. It is far from unlikely that the knowledge of this fact was among the considerations which induced Satan to apply his seductions, through the serpent, to the woman rather than to the man. As she was continually making new discoveries in the animal creation, she would be little surprised in at length finding one creature that could speak and even reason. Or supposing she did know the animals could not do either, it seems to us possible that the serpent, by eating the fruit in her sight, may have led her to conclude that his superior gifts were owing to his having partaken of this sovereign food. This supposition is quite in harmony with the general drift of the fatal argument. The curse pronounced upon the deceiver is plainly addressed to an intelligent agent, designedly guilty of an enormous crime; and would have been unmeaning and unworthy of the divine character, if addressed to a mere animal, which, in following the instincts of its nature, had unconsciously raised seductive thoughts in the mind of the woman.

That the phraseology of the curse is, however, in its outer sense, applied to the condition of the serpent, while in its inner meaning it is terribly significant to the intelligent agent, seems to us very clearly to show that the serpent was really, and not figuratively, employed in this awful transaction. The more closely the language of the curse is examined, the more its real purport, as addressed to the intelligent agent of the temptation, under forms of speech adapted to the serpentine condition, will be obvious. The closing portion of it, " I will put enmity between thee and the woman, and between thy seed and her seed: it [he] shall bruise thy head, and thou shalt bruise his heel," could have no significance with reference merely to the serpent; but to the real tempter it was of awful importance. They were words to shake hell, and to fill the archfiend with consternation. It is not at all likely that the fallen pair understood these words nearly so well as *he* did. Yet even to them it must have appeared that it promised some great and crowning triumph to " the seed of the woman," and perhaps a recovery from the Fall, after the enemy had seemed for a time to triumph over him, and to " bruise his heel." But its meaning is probably better known by us than it was either by the first pair, or at that time even by Satan himself. We can see that it was the first Gospel promise, foretelling the sufferings of Christ and His final triumph over the Evil One—His victory in our behalf, by means of suffering.

There is, however, another explanation which supposes that there was no serpent at all engaged in this transaction; but that Satan acted without any such instrument, being himself *called* the serpent, by way of contempt, and with reference to his insidious nature, just as our Lord calls Herod a fox. This title is certainly applied to him in the New Testament; but it seems to us that the choice made by him of the instrumentality of the serpent in this transaction, and the curse pronounced upon him in the person of that creature, sufficiently explain his being so named in the later Scriptures.

But there arises the further question: If Satan did not use the instrumentality of the serpent, how did he act? Did he appear at all, or in what likeness did he appear? Some think that he did not make any visible appearance, and that the temptation was in the way of suggestion in the mind of Eve. But for the fact that a personal presence is expressed in the curse, and that this presence *was*, as we think, embodied in a serpent, we should deem this a reasonable explanation. We see no harm in it, except that we cannot think it true. Some, however, who agree so far as to hold that "serpent" is merely a term to designate the great enemy of man, yet contend for his personal appearance, and consider that appearance to have been as an "angel of light." This seems to have been founded on the text, 2 Cor. xi. 13, 14, where Paul says, "For such are false apostles, deceitful workers, transforming themselves into the apostles of Christ. And no marvel; for Satan himself is transformed into an angel of light." It seems very doubtful whether this passage at all refers to the history of this temptation; and even if it does, it admits of being applied to the serpent, for some species of these animals are very beautiful, and one gifted with speech and reason must have seemed as engaging an object as creation could well supply.

But for the presence of a serpent being too clearly set forth in the narrative to be evaded, many minds might rest with pleasure in the explanation to which we have just referred. There is every reason to think that the walks of the first pair in Eden were cheered by the society of angelic visitants; and the appearance of Satan as one of these to Eve, might seem a most reasonable and probable form of the temptation. But it is not likely that the Almighty would allow them to have the excuse of so plausible and overpowering a temptation as this. At any rate, here is the serpent in the third chapter of Genesis. We cannot but see a serpent there. It may have been a very fine serpent—a very plausible serpent,—but still a serpent, we conceive, it must have been.

One important point may be noted here. The original temptation to sin did not come from God. Then, as now, it could be affirmed, "Let no one when tempted say, I am tempted from God; for God is unversed in things evil, and *He* tempteth no man." James i. 13 (in the Greek). God is not the author of sin. Nor did the temptation originate in man himself. Man was created holy. Everything as it came forth from the Creator's hand was good. The evil sprung from without—from another being, animated by another principle. The origin of evil, therefore, concerns first and mainly the apostasy of the devil. The apostasy of Adam resulted from it. Of the nature and cause of the

devil's apostasy nothing has been revealed. These truths are embodied in our Lord's remarkable accusation of the Pharisees: "Ye are of your father the devil, and the lusts of your father ye will do. He was a murderer *from the beginning*, and abode not in the truth, because there is no truth in him. When he speaketh a lie, he speaketh of *his own; for he is a liar, and the father of it.*" John viii. 44.   **P.**

WESTERN TRADITIONS OF

THE SERPENT AND THE FALL

SEEING that all mankind are descended from the pair who were tempted to disobedience under the enticements of the serpent, and whose disobedience

"Brought death into the world, and all our woe,"

we should expect to find throughout the world variously corrupted traditions of that event. The subject is a large one, and we may but touch upon it here. But the fact that such traditions do exist, and that all the main circumstances as related by Moses may be recognized in them, is of material importance. The variations are not greater than might be expected to arise in the course of ages, among different nations, in different regions, under different degrees of cultivation, and within different systems of religious corruption. Indeed, taking these differences into account, the substantial agreement among them, in the essential facts is wonderful, and can in no other way be accounted for than by the *literal* truth of the history of this event which the Scripture has given to us, and by the belief that, as Moses affirms, all the races of men have a common origin. It ought to have some influence upon our judgment as to the actual instrumentality of a serpent, to find how that animal figures in these accounts. In this and other points, had the relation we possess been merely a Hebrew allegory, it would have been difficult to see how the traditions of the remote and ancient nations came to be in substantial agreement with that narrative. But all becomes plain everywhere, if we regard that account not only as true but as *literally* true; for then the facts, as stated, must have been known to those who survived the deluge, and would be borne by their descendants to the various regions into which they dispersed.

Let us glance very cursorily at some of the most remarkable of these traditions.

According to the simple legend of Hesiod's *Works and Days*, the ancient Greeks supposed that man originally lived wifeless and ignorant, but innocent and happy. Prometheus, however, steals fire from heaven, and teaches man its use. The incensed Jupiter threatens vengeance. He orders Vulcan to form a woman of clay, on whom the gods bestow every grace and beauty, but at the same time they fill her heart with vanity and cunning, and all violent devices. This woman, Pandora, Jove presents to Epimetheus, who accepts the gift and marries her, notwithstanding the dissuasions of Prometheus, his brother. From that moment disease and evil of all sorts become the lot of men. Here there is much substantive coincidence. In both accounts, the unlawful thirst of forbidden knowledge (in this account represented by *fire*, and in our account by the *tree*) is the great offence, and in both the woman is the instrument by which the evil is introduced.

We have before us the whole history of this transaction in an engraving[1] from an ancient bas-relief; and what is most remarkable, there are two groups at each extremity of the tablet, offering, as it were, a Biblical key to the whole scene. On the one hand are a man and woman standing naked under a tree: the woman in a drooping

BAS-RELIEF ANALAGOUS TO ADAM AND EVE

and disconsolate posture; the man with one hand raised to the tree, and the other directed towards the woman. It is such a picture that a child would at once say, "That is Adam and Eve!" At the other extremity is a sedate and august figure, seated upon a rock, and strangling the serpent with his outstretched hand.

In the history of the sacred persons of heathen mythology, many remarkable allusions to the same circumstances may be found; and they are the more noticeable for the intimations they afford, that the ancient promise of ultimate victory over the old serpent was not forgotten

[1] See Creuzer's *Symbolik.* Pl. 158.

by mankind. Thus Apollo is represented as the son of the supreme God. Out of love to mankind he destroyed the serpent Python, by shooting him with an arrow. After his victory the conqueror underwent a lustration in the Vale of Tempe. Here also he was crowned with laurel, and, according to some, with that mysterious fruit, the gathering of which had proved the source of all evil, and occasioned the necessity for the defeat of the serpent. All this he is said to have undergone out of love to mankind.

So, of the garden of the Hesperides, we read that, being situated at the extreme limit of the then known Africa, it was said to have been shut in by Atlas on every side by lofty mountains, on account of an ancient oracle that a son of the Deity would at a certain time arrive, open a way of access thither, and carry off the golden apples which hung on a mysterious tree in the midst of the garden. Having procured access to the garden, and having destroyed the watchful serpent that kept the tree, the hero gathered the apples. Here we have a strange mixture of the external and internal incidents of Paradise; the ideas of the primeval people, viewing from without the Eden from which they were excluded, and coveting its golden fruits, being mixed up with those which belong properly to the Fall, the serpent, and the tree of life, or the tree of knowledge— for in these old traditions the trees are not so well distinguished as in the Mosaic account. In this legend of Hercules, the idea seems to be that the access to the tree of life is impossible, till the Son of God opens the way, and overcomes the serpent by whom that access is prevented. It deserves remark, that in most of these accounts of the dragon or serpent, which the heathen regarded as the source of evil, and which could be vanquished only by the Son of God in human form, he is called Typhon or Python, a word which signifies "to over-persuade, to deceive." Now this very name Pitho, or Python, designates the great deceiver of mankind. When the damsel at Philippi is said to have been possessed by "a spirit of divination," it is called in the original "a spirit of Python" (Acts xvi. 16); manifestly showing that the pagan Python was and could be no other than "that old serpent called the devil and Satan, which deceiveth the whole world." Rev. xii. 9.

In engravings from gems and other ancient remains, many representations of this event may be found. In all of them the Python is a serpent, and in all of them he is wreathed around the fruit-laden tree, exactly as modern painters represent him in their pictures of Eve's temptation. But we find variations in the pictorial, as well as in the written legend. In some the fruit is gathered for the hero by one of the Hesperides, while another lulls the watchfulness of the serpent; but in others the hero takes the fruit by force, while the serpent covers his head in submission. In one, a very remarkable bas-relief representing this scene, the serpent hangs unwreathed and drooping on the tree, while Hercules deals one more tremendous blow to end the strife. We are to recollect that the worship of Hercules, and the traditions connected with it, were avowedly derived from the East, and that the place where he was held

HERCULES AND THE SERPENT

in highest honour was Tyre. Let it also be remembered that Hercules is represented as the mortal son of the supreme God, and was attacked even in his cradle by two large serpents, which he destroyed.

Still more of Hercules. At Cadiz, which was originally a Phœnician colony, there was a pleasant garden consecrated by mystic rites and ceremonies to idolatrous worship. In the midst of it were two very remarkable trees, which grew out of the tomb of another of the monsters (*Geryon*) whom Hercules overthrew. One of these was of a mixed nature, and it was affirmed of it that it distilled drops of blood. This seems to point to the tree of life, the living tree. Near this, upon an islet in a small lake, was a temple in which Hercules was worshipped under the name of *Soter*, or the Saviour. From this sacred enclosure all women were driven away, as their sex was looked upon as the cause of all calamity and mischief. The whole temple was moreover guarded by lions and a flaming fire, which turned every way to forbid the approach of the unholy and the profane. Within the sacred enclosure was also an altar dedicated to Old Age, and those who attended it are mentioned as the only persons who sang pæans in honour of death. Near this were three other altars, dedicated to Poverty, Hard Labour, and to Hercules the Saviour. Here,

surely, are too many coincidences to have been the result of accident.

Again, in the rites of Bacchus, who was worshipped as the first planter of trees and cultivator of gardens, the god is represented naked, drawn in a car by leopards, lions, and other beasts of prey, in manifest allusion to the primitive state of man, and the harmlessness of the wildest animals in that golden age. The persons who took part in the ceremony bore serpents in their hands, and waved them, shouting "Eva! Eva!" with frantic screams. When it is recollected that in the eastern pronunciation the name of Eve is always given in two syllables, there is little question that these orgies had some reference to the circumstances of Paradise.

There were other sacred enclosures of the same nature, but without pausing to describe them, let us notice that traditions of the same kind are embodied with still more remarkable distinctness, in the theology of the remoter north. Thor is represented, in the Edda, as the first-born of the principal divinity; and is exhibited as a middle deity—a mediator between God and man. He is said to have wrestled with death, and in the struggle to have been brought upon his knees; to have bruised the head of the great serpent with his mace, and in his final engagement with the monster to have beaten him to the earth and slain him. The victory, however, costs the life of the mediator-god; for, recoiling back nine steps, he falls dead upon the spot, suffocated with the flood of venom which the serpent vomits forth upon him.

What shall we say to these things? This: that the nations embodied in these traditions their remembrances of Paradise, of the Fall, and of the promised Salvation. In respect to the past, they are tolerably distinct; but they become vague, uncertain, and conflicting, when they darkly set forth their ideas respecting the promised Deliverer, who was to bruise the serpent's head, and respecting the nature of that deliverance which he was to accomplish.

Innumerable questions may be mooted respecting the first condition of Adam and Eve. Diversity of opinion may be expected, but it will be generally allowed that the progenitors of our race came into existence possessed of a physical, intellectual, emotional, and moral nature, such as lies at the basis of all experience and history, and that they were placed at once in a conscious relation to the rest of the universe, and to that adorable ONE in whom they lived and moved and had their being. To them, in the possession of such a nature, a *Divine Revelation* was made. The fact lies on the surface of the narrative, and it is so reasonable and so necessary for the explanation of the after condition of mankind, that it is wonderful how any one can object to it. "Indeed," says Archbishop Whately, "even independently of the Bible History, without taking into account anything that we read in that, we might draw the same conclusion from what is matter of actual experience, and, as it were, before our eyes at this day. For it appears that mere savages, if left to themselves, without any instruction, never did, and never can, civilize themselves; and consequently the first of the human race that did acquire any degree of civilization, since they could not have had instruction from other men, must have had a superhuman instructor. But for such an instructor mankind would have been savages at this day. The mere fact that civilized men do exist is enough to prove, even to a person who never heard of the Bible, that at some time or other men must have been taught something by some superior being: in other words, that there must have been a Revelation." Whether or not, without the Bible, men would have come to such a conclusion, is a question we do not undertake to decide; but we feel the force of the Archbishop's argument as to the necessity of divine help for instructing men in the arts of life, and so far adopt what he says as corroborating the fact of an early Revelation.—*Lessons on Religious Worship*, p. 9.   **S.**

THE VOICE OF GOD

Genesis 3:8

THERE is something inexpressibly affecting in the circumstances of the first interview of the fallen pair with their kind Lord after their sin. As recorded in the simple and touching words of the sacred writer, the circumstances are of deep interest in themselves, and every word abounds in matter for edifying thought.

When the guilty pair "heard the voice of the Lord God, walking in the garden in the cool of the day," they went and "hid themselves from the presence of the Lord God among the trees of the garden." That they thus foolishly hoped to hide themselves from Him whose presence fills heaven and earth, clearly shows the kind and condescending manner in which He had hitherto revealed Himself to them, and had held intercourse with them. As a child hides himself from the father he has offended, so did they hide themselves from Him. It was a "voice" they heard. It is clear that the tones of that voice had been to them always tones of kindness and love. There is no reason to suppose that, as it

now fell upon their ear, that voice was less kind than it had been; for the Lord had not chosen to appear to know their crime but from their own acknowledgment. It was the consciousness of sin that made all the difference,—that made the presence most terrible which had hitherto been hailed by them with reverent joy and filial confidence. Sin did in them as it does in all their descendants,—create a cold and cheerless distance between the heart and God. And certainly their condition was very awful. *We,* under our strongest experiences of sin as alienating the soul from God, know that there is a way of escape, a way of reconciliation, a way of hope. But this Adam knew not. He knew not, as we do, how it is possible that where "sin hath abounded, grace" may "MUCH MORE abound." The case must in his eyes have appeared most hopeless; and he could have expected nothing less than the death which He who cannot lie had declared to be the penalty of transgression.

But let us listen. What excuse does the poor man allege for hiding himself? "I heard thy voice in the garden and I was afraid, because I was naked." Ah! not only naked, but poor and miserable, and blind. He knew that: and we, in virtue of our sad heritage from him, know that also—keenly know it, are deeply conscious of it, at some time of our lives. What, then, is our course? To hide ourselves, like Adam, from God's presence, *because* we are naked? Nay, rather, for that very reason, to hasten to Him. It was only when the naked prodigal cast himself at his father's feet, saying, "Father, I am no more worthy to be called thy son!" that the father said, "Bring forth the best robe, and put it on him." It is to the naked He says, "I counsel thee to buy of *me* white raiment, that thou mayest be clothed, that the shame of thy nakedness do not appear." It is only when we know that we are naked, that we shall desire to appear before God, in order that we then may receive of Him the wedding garment, in which alone we can stand before Him, find in his house a mansion, and become the guests of His table.

In answer to Adam's declaration of his nakedness, the Lord demands—"Who told thee that thou wast naked?" Adam knew not that this very consciousness betrayed him. A new faculty had come into play. He found that he had a judge within him, of whose presence, when all things smiled, he had not been conscious. Not, indeed, that he himself was well aware of its active presence; but the power within him was at work, and moved him as it listed. Not that he had yet a tender or an instructed conscience; but conscience was there; had awaked to sleep no more. A new and terrible taskmaster held the scourge over him.

> "Conscience, what art thou? Thou tremendous power,
> That dost inhabit us without out leave,
> And art within ourselves another self,—
> A master-self, that loves to domineer,
> And treat the monarch frankly as the slave."—*Young*.

Conscience performed its part. It made the fallen pair miserable in the knowledge of sin. It filled them with shame and dread. It could do no more, and this was much. It is well that the conscience be tender and watchful, that it smite and torment us, and that it allow us no rest, when we sin against God. But the right effect has been missed unless we are thus driven *to* God, not *from* Him, as was Adam; unless our souls are filled with grief, as a child is distressed at having offended a loving father, more than by the fear of punishment; and unless we cast ourselves in deep contrition at his feet, confessing that our only hope is in his pity and in his love.

This was not the case with our first parents. Though they know and feel that they have sinned, they are far from contrite. They will not humble themselves. Adam even insults the Creator. He reflects upon God himself: "The woman whom *Thou gavest* to be with me, she gave me of the tree, and I did eat." Alas, wretched Adam, how many of thy sons are like thee in this! However, let us not forget that any of them, in acting thus under the sense of sin, are less to be excused than Adam. To us all the mysteries of God's love in Christ are unveiled—are written before our eyes as with a sunbeam. We *know* that love to be boundless, and that we offend most deeply in distrusting its extent. Adam knew not this; and hence, were excuse to be found for his distrust of God, it might seem to be found here: although we may well say that the natural instincts of a child should have guided him better, and would have done so, had not the subtle venom of sin entered his very heart. It is by this conduct that he evinces the dreadful nature of his fall, which would have been less manifest had his behaviour been more becoming. It may be that this hardness and impenitence of heart prevented any more distinct intimation of the divine purpose than was afforded; and that it was thus obscurely veiled under a curse upon the serpent, whom they supposed to be, and were still suffered to regard as, the tempter. Let us not forget that the terms of that dark utterance were designed for the first pair, and were suited to their minds; and we may then more clearly apprehend the reason why the obscurity which now tries our understandings was suffered to remain over the transaction. Look at their state of mind, and consider whether, when Adam was casting his crime upon Eve, and Eve upon the serpent, it would have been well to apprise them more clearly what that serpent was. In this frame of mind it is certain they would have regarded the higher quality of the tempter as a palliation of the guilt of their overthrow, and a diminution of its shame. Alas! Adam is one of us; he is our father; his enemy is also ours, and that enemy employs to-day, and will employ to-morrow, against us, the same tools with which he wrought so effectually six thousand years ago.

The result of sin was twofold—shame and fear. There was a consciousness of degradation in the offenders in each other's presence, giving rise to shame; and there was a consciousness of guilt in the presence of God, giving rise to fear. It is instructive to trace to their source these new and bitter feelings.

The moment they had eaten, "the eyes of them both were opened, and they knew that they were naked." The change that took place was inward, not outward. It was this: the previously pure and natural desires were transformed by sin into impure and burning passions. The robe of innocence which before covered them was now stripped rudely off. The carnal mind was uncovered, the carnal propensities were developed, and an overpowering sense of shame made them have recourse to external clothing.

More painful still was the sense of fear. God was wont, in gracious condescension, to walk and commune with them in the garden. He took delight both in the abode and in the companionship of his new creatures. With what intense longing must they have looked for his approach! With what joy must they have hailed the music of his voice! But now all is changed. That voice rings like a knell in their guilty hearts. Conscience-stricken, fear-stricken, they vainly strive to hide themselves from his presence. They had in a moment lost all confidence in Him as a Father, all love to Him as a Benefactor, all delight in communion with Him as Friend and Guide. And it was still the sense of nakedness that caused it. "I was afraid, because I was naked." His soul was naked now, with all its guilt, with all its passions, with all its pride and rebellion. Adam was fearfully conscious that his whole moral deformity was "naked and open" to the eye of God.   P.

EASTERN TRADITIONS
OF THE FALL

THE Eastern traditions of Paradise and of the Fall are less distinct than those of the West, with regard to the leading external facts; but the doctrine itself is more clearly announced, is more broadly recognized as an article of belief; and the influences by which the downfall of man was brought about are more clearly indicated. This fact produces the impression that there is *greater* conformity with the Scripture narrative in the Eastern than in the Western legends; although the former take comparatively· small notice of the serpent, the woman, and the fruit. The Western legends, in fact, dwell upon the *details* and incidents, which are *generalized* in the Oriental systems.

According to the Chinese, man in his original condition was obedient to the heavens, and his state was one of innocence and happiness. There was no disease, no death; he was good and wise by *instinct;* he was all spirit. But the inordinate thirst of knowledge, according to one authority, or, according to others, flattery, or the temptation of the woman, was the ruin of mankind. Man held no more power over himself; lust and passion gained ascendency over him, and he lost his moral pre-eminence. All beasts and birds and reptiles now waged war against him; and, as he acquired science, all creatures became his enemies.[1] Thus the original state of man is described as being nearly the same as we find it in the Hebrew records, and his downfall is ascribed to the same motives.

The traditions of the Lamaic faith give a length of days to the first of men, which throws the longevity of the Mosaic antediluvians quite into the shade—not less than 60,000 years. They were holy men, invisibly nourished, and possessing the power of ascending at pleasure to the skies. In an evil hour the earth produced a kind of manna—a honey-sweet substance: a glutton ate of it, and seduced the rest of mankind to follow his example. From that time man lost his happiness and innocence; his body became gross; his commerce with the skies was past; his days were shortened; and his stature no longer at-

tained its former gigantic proportions. In time, the manna failed, and man resorted by degrees to food more and more gross; and at last all virtue fled the world, and wickedness prevailed. Eventually the spontaneous increase of the earth no longer sufficed, and man began with labour and sorrow to till the ground.[1]

Very similar, in some respects, to this is the Buddhist doctrine as held by the Cingalese. After the rising of the world from the waste of waters, some souls who had ended their lives in heaven descended upon the earth. They were without parts or passions; and reflecting from themselves sufficient light without the sun or moon, they were much delighted with their new situation. After a time these heavenly creatures became so much inflated with pride, and debased by lust, that they were changed into human beings of both sexes; and their resplendent properties having departed from them, they lived long in darkness, until at last the sun, moon, and stars shone forth. Their food was the sweet clay of the earth; but on account of their avarice in accumulating vast quantities for their pleasure, it was rendered insipid for their punishment. After this they resorted to other kinds of food, which, one after another, they lost by the same means; their nature still degenerating, and their wickedness increasing, till they were at length driven to till the ground for subsistence.[2]

In the Hindu mythology the references to the Fall become even more distinct. The facts narrated uniformly correspond, and the consequences are equally tremendous with those of the Mosaic account. In this mythology the king of the evil assoors or demons is called "the king of the serpents," of which poisonous reptiles, folded together in horrible contortions, their hell is formed. What is very remarkable is, that the name of the serpent monarch is *Naga,* and he is the prince of the Nagis or Nacigs; in which Sanscrit appellation we plainly trace the Hebrew NACHASH, which is the very word for the particular serpentine tempter, and, in general, for all the serpents throughout the Old Testament.[3]

The testimony of the Vishnu Purana—for a translation of which the public is indebted to Professor Horace Wilson—is still more to the

---

[1] *Memoires Chinoises,* vol. i. 107; De Guigues, *Chou-king: Diss. Prelim.*

[1] Pallas, *Travels,* i. 334, etc.
[2] Upham's *Buddhist Tracts,* pp. 16, 156; Joinville in *Asiatic Researches,* vii. 438.
[3] Maurice's *Hindustan,* ii. 346; Moor's *Hindu Pantheon.*

purpose: "The beings who were created by Brama were at first endowed with righteousness and perfect faith; they abode wherever they pleased, unchecked by any impediment; their hearts were free from guile; they were pure, made free from soil by the observance of the sacred institutes. In their sanctified minds Hari dwelt; and they were filled with perfect wisdom, wherewith they contemplated the glory of Vishnu. After a time, that portion of Hari which has been described as one with Kala ('time'), infused into created beings sin,—as yet feeble, though formidable,—and passion, and the like. The impediment of the soul's liberation—the seed of iniquity—arose from darkness and desire. The innate perfectness of human nature was then no more evolved. All the perfections were impaired, and these becoming feeble, sin gained strength, and mortals became subject to pain."

Even this is somewhat too general; but let us look to the history of Krishna. He was one of

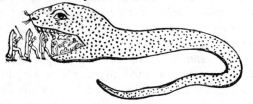

GREAT SERPENT, KALI NAGA

the incarnations of the Almighty in human shape. He had a fearful conflict with the great serpent, *Kali Naga*, who had poisoned the waters of the river, and thereby spread death and destruction around. Yet some of the representations seem to exhibit the people as walking very deliberately into the very jaws of the devouring monster. Krishna, casting an eye of divine compassion upon the multitudes of dead which lay before him, attacked the mighty serpent, which soon twisted its enormous folds around his body; but Krishna took hold of the serpent's heads, one after another, and

TRIUMPH OF KRISHNA OVER THE SERPENT

set his foot upon them. The monster struggled in vain, and, after expending all his poison, found

himself totally overwhelmed. This triumph of Krishna is a favourite subject of Hindu paintings;—in whose history mythologists discover the analogy to Hercules and to Apollo, but altogether overlook, or touch but lightly on, its bearing upon the history of the Fall and the promise of a Deliverer.

More distinct than all this is the doctrine of the ancient Persians, who seem in this, as in many other points, to have made nearer approaches to the truth than any of the ancient nations. Their doctrine, very briefly stated after the Zendavesta, is this: The world itself was created during five successive periods, and in a sixth, man himself received his being. After his production, man enjoyed a period of innocence and happiness in an elevated region which the Deity (Ormuzd) had assigned him. But it was necessary to his existence in this state, that he should be "humble of heart, and humbly obey the divine ordinances; pure he must be of thought, pure of word, pure of deed." And for a time the first pair were thus holy and happy. They said, "It is Ormuzd who hath given us the water, the earth, and the trees, and the stars, and the moon, and the sun, and all things pure." But at last Ahriman, the evil one, appeared, and beat down their good dispositions; and under the influence of his glozing lies, they began to ascribe their blessings to him. "Thus Ahriman deceived them, and even to the end will seek to deceive." Emboldened by this success, Ahriman the liar presented himself again, and brought with him fruit, of which they ate: and in that instant, of a hundred excellences which they possessed, all but one departed from them, and they became subject to misery and death. The legend proceeds to state how they went on finding inventions and acquiring arts, but becoming more and more under the influence of the evil one—clearly alluding by this to the fruit of the tree of knowledge of good and evil. Another form of the legend compresses the same leading ideas into the brief myth: that Ahriman, after having dared to visit heaven, descended to the earth, and, approaching the man in the form of a serpent, poisoned him with his venom, so that he died. From that time the world fell into confusion; the enemy of all good appeared everywhere, mixing himself with everything, and sought to do mischief both above and below.

If we put these two legends together, regarding

them not as two accounts, but as one differently told, we have an account of the Fall remarkably conformable to that of Moses. Of all the old traditions, it is the only one in which the intervention of the devil is distinctly recognized. Other legends have the serpent, but here alone in that serpent the evil one is seen. It is remarkable that the intervention of the woman is not distinctly recognized in any of these Eastern traditions, though it is implied in some of them. Does this singular omission arise from the low position held by women in the East, which rendered unpalatable, that view of her relation to man in Paradise, which the fact of his yielding to her temptation would suggest? In the account last noticed, the fact, though not expressed, is implied in the additional statement, that upon the Fall, discord arose between the man and the woman, so that they lived apart for fifty years.

MAN
AFTER THE FALL

WHO is there among us that would not give twenty of the best volumes from his shelves, for twenty lines which should acquaint him with the condition of our first parents during the first years after the Fall, and their expulsion from Paradise? This knowledge is withheld from us; yet, from what does transpire, some inferences may be deduced, and some reasonable conjectures offered.

A question of deep interest is, Whether they repented of their crime, and humbled themselves before Him whom they had so deeply offended? From all that appears up to the time when judgment was pronounced, they were in a state of mind which God could not regard with pleasure, and which would have left little hope for their welfare in this world, or in the world to come, if they had continued in it. We therefore seize with eagerness every hint, however slight, which will allow us to hope that their hearts were touched and softened, by their being dealt with much more leniently than they could have ventured to hope. Death was indeed brought into the world, and woe; but death was not immediately inflicted, and it was divested of many of its terrors; and the woe, though awful, was attended with mitigating circumstances and

prospects of deliverance. They might have been swept from off the face of the earth. But to what purpose? Should man's sin render the work of God of none effect? No; this race should still replenish the earth with intelligent inhabitants, fit to bear rule over all other creatures,—punished, indeed, and degraded, but not consumed; cast down, but not destroyed. We are apt to regard the scene as one merely of punishment; but it was one of mercy also—of great mercy, of far greater mercy than Adam and Eve had any right or reason to expect. We therefore willingly embrace the opinion, that they did humble themselves under the mighty hand of God; and that the same hand which provided for the comfort of their now shivering frames, by covering them with the skins of beasts in lieu of the rudely intertwisted leaves with which they had, in the first instance, covered their naked bodies, did also soothe their grief, and send comfort into their souls. This is the general belief of the Oriental writers, who furnish ample accounts of the remorse and lamentations of the first man. The Jewish writers enter into the same view, and even go so far as to ascribe to Adam the authorship of the twenty-second Psalm. We see no reason to concur in that opinion; but it must be admitted that the particular Psalm has been selected with judgment. The poets are entirely on the same side. Thus Milton makes Adam, after some discourse (not all pleasant) with Eve, conclude thus:—

> "We need not fear
> To pass commodiously this life, sustained
> By Him with many comforts, till we end
> In dust, our final rest and native home.
> What better can we do, than, to the place
> Repairing where He judged us, prostrate fall
> Before Him reverent; and there confess
> Humbly our faults, and pardon beg; with tears
> Watering the ground, and with our sighs the air
> Frequenting, sent from hearts contrite, in sign
> Of sorrow unfeigned, and humiliation meek:
> Undoubtedly He will relent, and turn
> From His displeasure; in whose look serene,
> When angry most He seemed, and most severe,
> What else but favour, grace, and mercy shone?"

Probably more than a hundred and twenty years of the life of Adam and Eve pass without record in the sacred narrative, save what relates to the history of Cain and Abel. These sons seem to have been born soon after the expulsion from Eden; and as Seth, who was born when Adam was a hundred and thirty years old, received his name in commemoration of the then recent death of Abel, we cannot suppose the interval much less than a hundred and twenty-five years, even allowing for some time in Eden before the Fall. A period fruitful in experiences this must have been in the life of the first pair. Adam was to till the ground from which he was taken; and as he had previously dressed and kept the garden of Eden, he had a knowledge of the processes and implements necessary to this culture. He had also, as we apprehend, much knowledge of various kinds, brought with him from Eden, and was far from being the mere "noble savage" which some fancy him to have been. Still, in his new condition, with a sterner soil, a less genial climate, and less pacific animal subjects, Adam would have many wants in food, clothing, and habitation, of which he had no experience in Eden; and it is our impression, that instead of being now, as before, inspired with all the knowledge necessary to his condition, he was left much to his own resources, to build up a mass of knowledge acquired by experience upon the basis of his attainments in Eden. In this, no doubt, he made great progress; for although no longer gifted with the very enviable faculty of acquiring knowledge by intuition, there is no reason to question that his intellectual powers were strong and active, and that, with the advantage of his education in Paradise, they would readily suggest to him the uses of things, and the means by which the results he desired might be achieved. We do not know of any writer who has endeavoured to fill up this blank in the history of Adam more fully and pleasingly than the old French poet Du Bartas, whose work we have more than once had occasion to quote.

He thinks that at first Adam must have had rather hard work to get a living.

> " Ere yet the trees, with thousand fruits, yfraught,
>   In formal chequers were not fairly brought;
>   The pear and apple lived dwarf-like there,
>   With oaks and ashes shadowed everywhere.
>   And yet, alas! their meanest simple cheer,
>   Our wretched parents bought full hard and dear.
>   To get a plum sometimes poor Adam rushes,
>   With thousand wounds, among a thousand bushes.
>   If they desire a medlar for their food,
>   They must go seek it through a fearful wood;
>   Or a brown mulberry, then the rugged bramble
>   With a thousand scratches doth their skin bescramble."

They are then described as hoarding up nuts for their subsistence during the winter.

With regard to their clothing, Du Bartas conveniently chooses to forget that they had dresses of skin by the special providence of God, that he may have the poetical satisfaction of decking them out with leaves, which he does most fancifully. While Adam is foraging for food, Eve also collects all the fine feathers that fall in her way:—

> " And then with wax the smaller plums she sears,
>   And sews the greater with a white horse hairs:
>   (For they as yet did serve her in the stead
>   Of hemp, and tow, and flax, and silk, and thread :)
>   And thereof makes a medley coat, so rare
>   That it resembles Nature's mantle fair,
>   When in the sun, in pomp all glistering,
>   She seems with smiles to woo the gaudy spring."

This splendid dress she works secretly, and when it is completed presents it to her husband; and is abundantly rewarded by his applause and admiration, and by the magnificence of his appearance when he puts it on. This is a very fine fancy.

The approaching winter, with its frosts, creates the need of warmer clothing; and this the poet provides by making Adam meet with a flock of sheep, whose comfortable raiment suggests to him the feasibility and fitness of appropriating the fleece to his own use, which he does (we are sorry to say) by knocking the fairest of them down, and flaying it with a fish bone.

Then, as to their dwelling:—

> " A vaulted rock, a hollow tree, a cave,
>   Were the first buildings that them shelter gave."

But finding the one to be too moist, the other too narrow, and the third " over cold," a more commodious habitation was designed:—

> " Within a wood they choose
>   Sixteen fair trees that never leaves do lose,
>   Whose equal front in quadran form prospected,
>   As if of purpose Nature them erected;
>   Their shady boughs first bow they tenderly,
>   Then interbraid and bind them curiously:
>   That one would think who had this arbour seen,
>   'T had been true ceiling painted over green."

From this they are eventually led to the construction of a still better habitation, a framework of dry boughs, walled with straw-compacted mud, and the poet leaves them somewhat comfortably lodged.

There is one statement in the sacred record calculated to throw some light upon the feelings, and thus upon the conduct and life, of man after the Fall. Our author, usually so thoughtful and observant, seems in a great measure to have overlooked it. It is the PROMISE.

Apparently only a very short time—perhaps an hour or two—elapsed between the sin and God's visit. Brief as the time was, it must have been one of terrible suffering. God came, and with the very words of the entailed curse, He mixed a promise. To guilty, despairing man this promise was light in darkness, life from the dead. It must have kindled every spark of gratitude in his soul. He had just broken the divine command; but that gracious Being whose love he had outraged, now reveals new purposes of love infinitely transcending all experienced before. We know not how much of the divine plan of salvation Adam was made to comprehend; but I doubt not he knew the great leading fact embodied in the promised seed of the woman. This glorious truth, this wondrous purpose of grace, revealed at such a time, must have constrained man to humblest penitence, to child-like submission, and to earnest devotion to God's service. Sin had not obtained such complete mastery as to quench the impulses of gratitude; and we may well believe the mercy which prompted at such a time the promise of a Deliverer, would bring it home with saving power to Adam's soul.

The joys of Paradise closed thus abruptly in midnight darkness; but upon that darkness speedily dawned the cheering morn of the Gospel day.　　　　**P.**

The words of promise were: " I will put enmity between thee and the woman, and between thy seed and her seed; it shall bruise thy head, and thou shalt bruise his heel." These words, read in the light of the Gospel, are found to contain a wonderful depth of meaning: in them may be discovered a prophecy of the battle of good with evil ever since—in them we may recognize folded up, the blessed after-promises of salvation through a Messiah—"the seed of the woman"—and a final victory achieved by him over the Evil One; but the exact meaning which the words at first conveyed, it is impossible to ascertain; however, there can be no doubt they would inspire religious encouragement and hope.

　　　　S.

CAIN AND ABEL

Genesis 4:1-2

It was natural that Eve should exult greatly when a man-child was born unto her. At this day, when the earth is full of people, and the relations of mother and child are well understood before they are actually experienced, which of all Eve's daughters does not find her heart leap with joy when her first-born son enters the world! How much more would this be the case with Eve! The whole matter was beyond the range of her experience and her ideas. It was all new, all wonderful to her. The child then ushered into life, was not only her first-born, but the first child that had been born into the world, the first child that she had ever seen, the first infant that ever smiled in gladness or wept in grief. It was natural that she should therefore have attached the utmost importance to this event. That she did so, we know from the name she bestowed upon the child—Cain, which means an *acquisition* or *possession,* "because," she said, " I have acquired a man from the Lord." This pious recognition of the agency of the Lord in providing her with so great a blessing, is one of the circumstances which indicate that the first pair were brought to a right state of feeling after their fall and banishment. There are some who would translate the words by " I have gotten a man, the Lord," implying that she supposed this to be the promised seed, who was to bruise the serpent's head, and avowing her belief in His divinity by calling Him Jehovah (the Lord); but this notion will scarcely bear examination, and it assumes a measure of religious knowledge which there is no evidence that Eve possessed. That she expected some great eventual blessing from that promise, and that she regarded the birth of her first-born son as a pledge of its accomplishment, is probable, and may well have formed part of her joy. If, as some suppose, this child was not bestowed until some time had passed after the loss of Eden, the first pair may have doubted whether any children would be given to them, or in what manner the promise was to be fulfilled. In that case many prayers must have been offered for this blessing; and when it came at last, well might Eve, in the fulness of her heart, cry that at length " she had obtained a man-child from Jehovah."

The first of mothers, the first woman who ever dandled a babe upon her knee, or nourished it from her breast, would, however, soon learn that her new relation was not without its anxieties and trials, and that it involved duties peculiarly onerous to one who had never known childhood herself, but had at once burst into fulness of life. All her experience must have been founded upon what she had observed in animals, whose young became in a very short time active, frolicsome, and entertaining; and this would little prepare her to expect the long and helpless infancy of her new-born child, with the restraints which that infancy imposed, and the sedulous attention which it exacted;—in all of which she, the sole woman upon the earth, had none of that aid from others which her daughters have always been able to obtain.

It is quite as probable from these causes as from any others that have been suggested, that the birth of the next son was not hailed with the same exultation—that the mother bestowed upon him no name of gladness, but one (Abel, *vanity*) indicating the vain and uncertain character of human expectations. As this name happened to correspond to the unhappy fate of this son, some have thought that it must have been given after his death; but this is altogether unlikely, since that of Cain, his brother, was manifestly bestowed at his birth : and it is easy to conceive that life had already, by the time Abel was born, become to the first pair what it has been since to all their descendants—so replete with troubles and disappointed hopes, as renders a name of sorrow always appropriate.

As the lads grew up, distinctive walks in life were chosen by them, or were assigned to them by their father, doubtless in conformity with their tastes and habits of body and mind. Cain became a tiller of the ground, and Abel a keeper of sheep. The fact is valuable. It shows that the first men were not in that rude condition into which some branches of their descendants fell. The distinction of pursuits belongs to a certain state of civilisation. The savage man has but one pursuit, or each man follows equally all the pursuits that collectively make up his form of life. But here the two first-born of men took up different and distinct pursuits, and doubtless applied all the inventive force of their minds to the improvement of their respective arts.

The tillage of the ground began in Eden, and had been carried on after the fall by the father of mankind. When Cain began to employ himself in agriculture, it had no doubt been brought into an advanced condition in many of its principal processes; and if Cain possessed any of the inventive ingenuity which distinguished his descendants, it must have improved materially under his hands. Were it not that there is reason to fear that Cain's sin and fall had root in an inordinate appreciation of the results of his skill and toil, it would be pleasant to think of the delight and pride with which the strong young man would lay before his parents larger and more luscious fruits, finer and more juicy roots, and fuller ears of corn,—the product and reward of his care,—than *he* had ever seen in a state of nature, or than

had met *their* view since that ever remembered day when the cherubim waved their flaming swords between them and Paradise.

Adam had brought no small knowledge of animals from Eden, and this, imparted to Abel, must have availed him much in the commencement of his pursuit as a keeper of sheep. He does not appear, however, to have gone further than the domestication of sheep, and perhaps of dogs, as the guardians of his flock. The domestication of the larger cattle appears to have been the unaided invention of a later age. The charge of a flock has always been regarded as a more contemplative and gentle pursuit than any other, and more favourable to holy and prayerful thought. Many other pursuits, even agriculture, require the mind and hand to be intent upon the actual labour which they involve; whereas, the care of a flock affords leisure for meditation. It is in conformity with this experience, that the more gentle and thoughtful character is usually, in our minds, ascribed to Abel, and the more abrupt and active to Cain; somewhat analogous to the difference between Jacob and his brother Esau; and the subsequent facts of their history are in accordance with this impression.

EARLY POPULATION

THERE are two prevalent notions connected with the date of the death of Abel, both of which are doubtless wrong. One is, that Cain and Abel were both young men, some twenty or thirty years of age. But we have shown reasons for believing that they were not less than a hundred and twenty-five years of age when that dreadful event took place. But it is yet true that they were young. When the life of man reached to nearly a thousand years, an age like this was youthful.

The other is, that besides their parents, Cain and Abel were the only persons in the world, or at most, that there were besides merely their wives, and perhaps a few young children of theirs. But the fact that so many years had passed, would alone render improbable what might have seemed likely under the notion that but a few years had elapsed. It is quite incredible that the pair, destined to replenish the earth, and who had children after that calamity, should have been without any in the long interval. Those whom we do know are named only because there was something remarkable to record of them; but that there were others, not named, is certain, from the facts which imply that there were other people in the earth at the time. We know that there were daughters; and the fact that their existence only incidentally transpires, expresses the probability of a similar silence respecting other children. Cain, we know, was married, which was probably the case also with Abel. They must, therefore, from the necessity of the case, have had sisters, with whom they contracted marriage, although neither their names nor the fact of their birth are recorded. One would have liked to possess some information respecting these first daughters of Eve. There is an old tradition, that Cain and Abel had respectively twin-sisters, and that the twin of Cain became the bride of Abel, and the twin of Abel the bride of Cain. She who was born with Cain is, in Arabian tradition, called Achima, and she born with Abel, Lebuda; but the oriental Christians know them as Azrun and Ovain.[1] We have seen a calculation in Saurin's *Dissertations*, which makes it out that at the time of the death of Abel (which the writer supposes to have been in the year of the world 128), there might have been 32,768 persons, descended from eight children of Cain and Abel, born before the year 25; and that adding other subsequent children of Cain and Abel, their children's children, there might then have been 421,164 men descended from them, without reckoning women and children. But there is always some flaw in these round calculations. In this case it is forgotten that the antediluvians do not appear to have had children so early. In the antediluvian genealogy, none of the persons named has a son before he is sixty-five, and some not till far past a hundred years of age. This implies that the period of childhood and adolescence was protracted in proportion to the duration of life, and renders it probable that the old patriarchal fathers were in appearance and constitution as young at sixty or sixty-five, as our youth are at sixteen or seventeen. Still, even according to this rule, Cain and Abel may have had a considerable number of children and grand-

[1] D'Herbelot, Art. *Cabil.*

children at the time indicated; and allowing for other possible children of Adam and Eve, there must have been at the time a considerable number of persons in the world—quite sufficient to account for Cain's dread of being slain for the murder of Abel; and also for his building a city soon after his migration from the paternal roof.

Let us counsel the reader to be content with such broad facts as assure us that, according to the intimations in Genesis, there may well have been a considerable number of persons in the region around Eden at the death of Abel, and a large population in the world before the Deluge. For exact arithmetical calculations there is no basis. The law of population itself is fluctuating, and is affected by a thousand circumstances which such calculations cannot embrace. Thus it is certain that, if the population had gone on since the Deluge in the ratio which certain calculations assume or endeavour to establish, the world could not by this time have contained the inhabitants thus provided for it, and we should have been standing in layers three or four deep upon each other's heads.

Having thus been led into the question of early population, we cannot but say how little reliance ought to be placed on such calculations as those of Bishop Cumberland, and in later days of Mr. Malthus, as to the rate of increase in population. The former learned calculator, reckoning the population after the flood, quietly assumes that every child born shall live forty years at least, and that every young man and woman shall marry when twenty years of age, and shall become the parents of twenty children in the next twenty years; and this is supposed to be universal; not one is allowed to die until his task is accomplished.[1] All this is in opposition to known facts, as shown in the history of the patriarchs. If we may build upon the genealogy in the tenth chapter of Genesis, the allowance of children to a family seems not to have been materially greater than at present; and we know that Abraham's father had but three sons, one of whom died prematurely; that Abraham had no children till he was past eighty; that Isaac did not marry till he was about forty years old, and had but two sons; and that Jacob and Esau also (although they had more children) were above forty when they married. In view of facts like these, which occur in every age,—and in the

[1] Cumberland's *Essay on Populousness.*

recollection of the wars, pestilences, and famines with which God scourges the pride of man,—we cannot but assent to the remarks of a writer who had occasion to consider this matter closely.[1]

"The increase of mankind seems to be, in an especial manner, kept by the Almighty under His own immediate sovereign disposal, and so mysteriously, that we cannot calculate, nor even guess at, the probable produce of any marriage, under whatever circumstances of rank, wealth, health, age, or climate. The most healthy of every class in life are very often barren; while we constantly see a numerous offspring from sickly, diseased, or even deformed parents. Uncertainty of this kind does not exist as to the lower orders of the creation; as to their increase, we are allowed to calculate and speculate with tolerable exactness. This utter uncertainty as to the very root of population, involves the whole subject, more or less, in its consequences; and with all our labours and tables, however useful and convenient we may find them for the present purposes of life, no sooner do we attempt to open vistas into futurity than we find ourselves on ground forbidden to the children of men."

Thus, for the last ten years, we have been estimating the increase of the population of these islands at a thousand a day; and most dismal apprehensions were entertained by many as to the consequence that might be expected to result, at no distant time, from over-population within a territory bounded by the ocean. But now (1851) we learn that, instead of a thousand a day, the increase has been only a thousand a week; and that in the part of the realm that seemed most threatened with over-population, there has been no increase at all, but a most fearful diminution. This forcibly teaches the futility of paper calculations of increase in population. If we err so egregiously in matters before our own eyes, what faith can be claimed for calculations going back to the early ages of the world?

These reflections are connected with an important inquiry, which at the present day attracts the attention of scientific men :—How did civilization originate? Was primeval man a savage? Did he gradually work his way out of barbarism into a civilized condition? One of the latest and most learned writers on the subject remarks :— "To us it seems that, so far as the voice of history speaks at all, it is in favour of a primitive race of men, not indeed

[1] Crosthwaite's *Synchronology*, p. 247.

equipped with all the arts and appliances of our modern civilization, but substantially civilized, possessing language, thought, intelligence, conscious of a Divine Being, quick to form the conception of tools, and to frame them as it needed them, early developing many of the useful and elegant arts, and only sinking by degrees and under peculiar circumstances, into the savage condition."

The writer then adduces in proof the narrative of Genesis ; observing that, " no savages are this simple pair, but clever, intelligent, quick to execute, able to sew themselves coats" (Gen. iii. 7), "and able to enjoy converse with God and each other." What follows is adduced in evidence of incipient civilization. We meet with "a tiller of the ground," and "a keeper of sheep" (Gen. iv. 2) ; of one who builded a city (iv. 17) ; of those who made tents (iv. 20), and invented musical instruments ; of those who smelted copper and iron (iv. 22), and fashioned tools of industry and weapons of war. All this indicates the existence of at least rudimentary civilization at the earliest period of human history. Such is the account given in one of the earliest historical records that has come down to us—a record whose historical value is not diminished by the fact that, according to the general belief of the Jewish and Christian worlds, it is inspired."

With the general view thus presented, accords the traditions of ancient races. They point back to "a golden age." In the Zendavesta, we are told of a time when there was "neither overbearing nor mean-spiritedness, neither stupidity nor violence, neither poverty nor deceit, neither puniness nor deformity, neither huge teeth nor bodies beyond the usual measure." There were odoriferous trees, golden pillars, and ambrosial feasts. The Chinese speak of "a first heaven," and "an age of innocence ;" the Mexicans of a "golden age ;" the Peruvians of "the children of the sun ;" and the Greeks, through Hesiod, of "a golden race."

"Leaving the regions of mythical poetry, and treading the ground of history, we find, in the earliest records of Egypt and Babylonia, not memories of rudeness and barbarism, but of arts and habits, manners and customs, which denote intelligence, invention, and culture."

What is taught in the Book of Genesis respecting the early condition of mankind, is confirmed by the results of modern scientific inquiry on the subject.[1]

S.

***

OFFERINGS OF CAIN AND ABEL

Genesis 4:3-7

WE are informed that, "in process of time, Cain brought of the fruit of the ground an offering to the Lord. And Abel, he also brought of the firstlings of his flock, and of the fat thereof."

[1] Papers "On Civilization," by Rawlinson, in the *Leisure Hour*. 1876.

If the record stopped here, this proceeding would doubtless meet our approbation as exceedingly suitable and becoming. What could be more proper than that Cain, who was a cultivator, should bring his fruits; or, that Abel, who was a shepherd, should bring his sheep,—each offering being perfectly appropriate to the condition and pursuits of the offerer?

But let us read on: "And the Lord had respect unto Abel and to his offering; but unto Cain and to his offering He had not respect." This sets us to inquire, Where lay the root of offence in Cain's offering, and of acceptance in Abel's? Was the offering of Cain in itself objectionable, or was the offence in the mind and temper of the offerer? We must turn to the New Testament for more light on this matter. The author of the Epistle to the Hebrews tells us that it was "by faith" that "Abel offered unto God a more excellent sacrifice than Cain;"[1] and another apostle, evidently alluding to this offering, plainly states that Cain's works were evil, and his brother's righteous.[2] Cain had therefore in this matter an untoward disposition, and displayed a lack of faith. But was this want of faith shown in the nature of the offering itself, or in the frame of mind with which it was presented? Whatsoever in the things of God is not of faith, is sin; and, beyond question, Abel himself might have sinned by the deficiency of faith, even in offering a proper oblation. We are led to think, however, that God had appointed a certain manner of approach to Him; and that to approach Him in another manner than this was offensive and rebellious.

What first strikes us is the remarkable fact of the existence of sacrifice at this early period, so soon after the Fall. This implies further communications of God's will to man than we have as yet been distinctly acquainted with. The usage of sacrifice—the idea that the life-blood of an animal could be an acceptable offering to God —could hardly have arisen in this early and unbloody age without a special intimation of some kind from heaven. It is so repugnant to all the notions that we associate with that age, that the idea of its human origin at once strikes the mind as a moral impossibility. If, then, this rite has been so early inculcated,—it would seem immediately after the Fall,—some idea of its meaning must have been afforded, that it might

[1] Hebrews 11:4.   [2] 1 John 3:12.

seem reasonable and proper—that it might become an expression of faith among a simple-minded people. If any explanation of its purport were supplied, it could only be this: that man was a sinner; that without shedding of blood there was no remission of sin; and that although the blood of animals could not take away sin, yet men could thereby declare their guiltiness before God, and express their faith and hope in the atonement thereafter to be offered by "the Lamb slain from the foundation of the world." We know that this was the purport of the sacrifices under the law of Moses; and as these sacrifices were the same as those which had previously existed, both had no doubt the same meaning attached to them. Now, the need of this form of faith was not peculiar to the keepers of sheep; it has been practised by men of all kinds of occupation in all ages. With this clue, we may therefore be able to detect the causes of the ill reception which Cain's offering found.

Was it not that he declined to enter into the spirit of the sacrificial institution; and while willing to bring a thank-offering in testimony of the Lord's goodness, refused to offer that acknowledgment of sin, and to express his sense of that need of atonement by blood, which the animal sacrifice declared? If we contend that the offence of Cain lay at all in the difference of his offering from that of Abel, we cannot see any other satisfactory explanation than that which this supposition affords. This explanation does not, indeed, as some allege, necessarily grow out of the mere difference; for although we must ever maintain that sacrifice had a divine origin, designed to set forth the atonement by the death of Christ, yet, having found existence, it was not always offered in that high meaning, but was often simply a thank-offering. As a thank-offering, the offering of Cain might have been as acceptable as that of Abel. If, therefore, we lay any stress upon the difference,—and it is impossible to avoid doing so,—we must allow that the time when the offering was made,—"at the end of days," for such is the meaning of the words rendered "in process of time,"—was some day commemorative perhaps of the Fall; or it may have been a Sabbath, on which a sacrifice of atonement was expected and usually rendered. That Cain refused to render this service, but brought his vegetable products, in which he may be presumed to have taken much pride,—as if an acknowledgment of the

Lord's goodness in the bounties of nature was all that could be claimed from him,—seems to meet all the difficulties of the case, and to correspond to all the New Testament allusions thereto.

But how did the Lord testify His approval of Abel's offering, and His rejection of Cain's? The mode most in accordance with Scripture examples is, that the accepted offering was consumed by supernatural fire. It may be that in those primitive times, when the intercourse of God with man seems to have been still more immediate than it afterwards became, this sign of acceptance was always afforded, and perhaps this instance was the first in which it had been withheld. This would intimate that Cain had previously, under the influence of his father, made proper offerings, and now ventured upon a new and a wrong thing. If, as some suppose, and as the narrative seems to imply, the first family still remained in the neighbourhood of Eden, in presence of "the flaming sword," or sword-like flame, which precluded all return to that happy seat, it is by no means unlikely that this flame was regarded as the Shekinah, or symbol of the divine presence, like the "glory of the Lord" in after times; and that the flame was darted therefrom to consume the accepted offering. There are many facts in the corruptions of paganism which seem to owe their origin to the altered circumstances of man's condition on the outside of Eden, but in presence of the sacred symbols, the cherubim and the flaming sword, by which it was shut in.

There does not seem to us anything to indicate that this was the first occasion on which offerings were made by Cain and Abel. Considering the length of time which had now elapsed since the Fall, all probability is against that notion. There must, therefore, have been something new—some innovation on the part of Cain—to account for the higher favour with which Abel's offering was received. It was probably an act of rebellion, the rising of a proud and haughty spirit against an act of humiliation and contrition for sin. The deep displeasure evinced by Cain shows that this was no common matter, and that some strong principle was involved. That it was of the nature which has been suggested, will be placed beyond question, if we receive an interpretation of the Lord's remonstrance, which has strong claims to consideration. In the common version, God says to Cain, "Why art thou wroth? and

why is thy countenance fallen? If thou doest well, shalt thou not be accepted? and if thou doest not well, *sin lieth at the door.*" This rendering of the last clause has the advantage of a popular idiom in the English language, which gives it an adventitious force and signification. In the marginal reading of some editions of our English Bible, it has, instead of "sin," "the punishment of sin;" but the Hebrew word means in many places a sin-offering, that is, an animal victim; and that being understood here, the words will admit, and we incline to think that they require, a signification which may be thus paraphrastically expressed: "If thou doest not well, lo, there now lieth at thy very door a lamb, by offering which for thy sin thou mayest acceptably express thy contrition and obtain forgiveness." This sense is not so new as some think it; it has now obtained the sanction of many sound scholars and theologians; and it appears to settle the question involved in this offering, in conformity with the view of the subject which has seemed to us the most probable.

The words of the Apostle Paul form the best and safest comment on this difficult passage: "*By faith* Abel offered unto God *a more excellent* sacrifice than Cain." This shows, first, that there was an internal moral distinction in the minds of the offerers. Abel had faith; Cain had not. Faith being "the substance of things hoped for," must have reference to a promise; and *the* promise on which the faith of God's people rested was that of the Messiah. But, secondly, Abel's sacrifice is described as "more excellent" than Cain's. There was, therefore, also a distinction in the offerings. Abel's was a slain beast, prefiguring the great sacrifice of Christ on which his faith was grounded. Cain's was a mere thank-offering—an acknowledgment of temporal favours, without any recognition of human guilt or of the atonement destined to take it away. Cain, it would seem, was a cold rationalist; Abel was a faithful and devoted Christian.   **P.**

"By the circumstance of the apostacy, the religion of the species was entirely changed. While in paradise, it was the direct and simple effusion of gratitude, arising from the bosom of innocent intelligence. It was the instinctive exertion of unimpaired intellect, and the spontaneous effort of holy feeling, employed in the contemplation and devoted to the service of the supreme nature. There was no barrier then between earth and heaven. There was no interposing obstruction between man and God. There was no darkness investing the Divinity, to excite in his creatures perplexity and terror. He could feel no fear whose bosom was burdened with no guilt. And while God saw upon His works the same loveliness as when He pronounced them good, He had no reason to withdraw His complacency, or to retire into the depths of His everlasting dwelling-place. As soon, however, as humanity had sinned, and the ratification of its punishment was pronounced, this seems to have been demanded by the Majesty of the Eternal. He established, indeed, a covenant of grace, but then He withdrew in a manner from the scene of pollution, and enclosed Himself within the precincts of that unseen world 'where nothing that defileth' is permitted to approach. It comported not with the dignity of the Supreme to maintain as before familiar intercourse, or even treat *directly* with the apostate. Henceforth, he was commanded to come with the significant expressions of extrinsic dependence. His religion became completely altered from what it was at first. It consisted of other acts and other feelings. Instead of being nothing more than the simple gratitude of innocence, and the glowing adoration of virtue, it was the service of a creature conscious of crime, exposed to punishment, pleading for forgiveness, confiding in mercy, and saved by mediation."—Binney *On the Practical Power of Faith*, p. 40.

S.

DEATH OF ABEL

Genesis 4:8

FROM the position which the account of the death of Abel occupies, immediately after the narrative of the sacrifice, it has always been considered that the murder of his brother by Cain, arose out of the envy and ill feeling which the Lord's preference of Abel's offering engendered. This seems to us probable; but unless the circumstance had a natural and obvious connection, the allocation would not make this clear, seeing that in this most concise and rapid narrative, events closely joined to each other in description, are often separated by intervals of many years.

It would seem, however, that there was some short interval during which Cain nourished his wrath in his heart, and awaited an opportunity of testifying his resentment, without allowing his brother to perceive how deeply he was moved. One day he invited Abel in a friendly manner to walk abroad with him into the fields, as they had no doubt been used to do. The original as it stands—"And Cain said to (not talked with) Abel his brother," has no immediate grammatical connection with what follows, and in some of the Hebrew copies a blank space is left after these words, as if something had been omitted. This blank is filled up in the Samaritan copy and in the Septuagint version, so that in

them the text reads : " And Cain said to Abel his brother, Let us go forth into the field. And it came to pass when they were in the field, that Cain rose up against Abel his brother and slew him." Whether Cain premeditated this result when he invited his brother to walk with him, or whether it was suggested during the walk, when something that passed between him and Abel might kindle Cain's smouldering passions into a consuming flame, can never be known. The most natural and probable supposition is, that although he did intend evil, he had not contemplated the death of his brother ; but, as too often happens among men, the excitement of his ungoverned passions carried him far beyond his purpose, and ceased not until his brother lay dead at his feet. It may be even doubtful whether Cain intended or expected to slay his brother when " he lifted his hand against him." Such an intention implies far more than that phrase would express at this day. To us the idea of human death is familiar. Scarce a month passes in which some one whom we knew,—scarce a year in which some one whom we loved,—is not cut down ; and from day to day our ears are filled with reports of the death of man from violence, accident, or crime. But it was not thus when Abel died. The death of man was not yet numbered among human experiences. The eye had not yet seen, and therefore the heart could scarcely yet conceive, that most awful sight—a human corpse. That Cain should have premeditated Abel's death, is, therefore, scarcely to be imagined. If he did, it must have been like an invention to him. He knew indeed that man was to die ; and he had seen animals dead. But it is open to question whether he even supposed man liable to death by violence. Considering man's higher nature and endowments, and in the absence of all experience of the matter, it seems more than probable that Cain could scarcely have supposed that the life of man might be as easily extinguished as that of an animal,—and indeed more easily than that of most of the inferior creatures.

It is remarkable that Oriental tradition, which is always ready with inventions to supply the deficiency of knowledge, ascribes the death of Abel to the direct instigation of Satan. Cain was, according to the Moslem legend, filled with envy and hatred towards his brother, but *did not know* how he might destroy his life. But one day Iblis (Satan) placed himself in Cain's way, as he walked with Abel in the fields, and seizing a stone, shattered therewith the head of an approaching wolf; Cain followed his example, and with a large stone struck his brother's forehead till he fell lifeless to the ground. [1]

The Jewish tradition recognizes the intervention of a dispute between the brothers; and this is in itself probable, though we may well question whether it was at all of the character which is supposed. Cain and Abel, says this tradition, divided the world between them, the one to have the movable and the other the immovable things thereof. Upon this there arose a quarrel between them. Abel said to his brother, "Take off the clothes thou wearest, for they are part of the movables, and belong to me;" whereupon Cain said to Abel, "Avaunt! get thee up into the air, for the earth on which thou treadest is mine." And there arose a conflict between them, in which Abel was slain. [2] This is simply puerile; and the Jerusalem Targum has a better legend,—that Cain denied with warmth the doctrine of eternal life, of a just judge, and of a judgment to come; but that Abel affirmed and vindicated these points; whereupon his brother rose upon him and slew him. We may rely upon it, that had the legendist, who makes these high doctrines the subject of dispute, himself understood the great doctrine of atonement, as expressed in the act of sacrifice, he would have made *that* the subject of their discussion.

We are not told what became of Abel's body. Yet the first human death necessitated the discovery of some mode for the disposal of the corpse. This must have been a serious difficulty. No animals bury their dead; one species eats up the dead of another. But this mode of disposing of the dead revolts the feelings of an intelligent being. The mere idea of this must have been most shocking to the persons who stood before the first human corpse. It seems to us, that the first and most natural impulse must have been to protect the corpse from that common lot, by concealing it from the beasts of prey. Or if this did not in the first instance occur, the progress of decomposition would soon awaken the other natural desire of placing the remains of the dead out of sight. This might be done, either by depositing the body in a cavern and closing up the entrance; by heaping stones or earth over the body; or by digging a grave in which it might be laid. All these are natural suggestions, in which different forms of sepulture have originated; and it is hard to say which was most probably followed. It may further be asked, Was the body buried by the murderer or by the parents? Poets, who delight in picturing human emotion of the deepest class, adopt the notion that the body was found by the father, and laid by him in the grave. Oriental tradition takes another view. It states that Satan, having tempted Cain to slay his brother, changed himself into a raven, and having slain another raven, dug a hole in the earth with his bill, and laying the dead one into it, covered it with the earth he had dug up. Cain did the same with his brother. As for Adam, he long remained in ignorance of what had become of his beloved son; but one day his ploughshare struck against an obstruction in the field, and opening the ground, he discovered the still distinguishable remains of his lost Abel. It is beautifully added, that "it was not until he thus fully learned what had befallen Abel, that he resigned himself to the will of God, and was comforted." This, the current Moslem tradition, is founded on a Jewish one, which states that "Cain was not aware of the Lord's knowledge of hidden things; he therefore buried Abel, and met the inquiry, 'Where is Abel thy brother?' by the bold question, 'Am I my brother's keeper?'" It certainly does seem to us, that both the inquiry and the answer become more emphatic on the supposition that Cain had actually concealed the body of his murdered brother.

There is, however, another Hebrew legend,—not without beauty,—which agrees better with the poets, and in which the Moslem raven appears: "The dog which had watched Abel's flocks, guarded also his corpse, protecting it against beasts and birds of prey. Adam and Eve sat beside it, and wept, not knowing what to do. But a raven, whose friend had died, said, I will go and teach Adam what he must do with his son! It dug a grave, and laid the dead raven in it. When Adam saw this, he said to Eve, Let us do the same with our child! The Lord rewarded the raven, and no one is therefore allowed to harm their young; they have food in abundance, and their cry for rain is always heard."

[1] Weil's *Biblical Legends;* D'Herbelot, Art. *Cabil.*
[2] *Midrash,* 11; Tr. *Amudeh Sheva.*

PRESENCE OF THE LORD

Genesis 4:10-16

ACCORDING to the Scripture record, Cain, judged of God for his awful crime, is banished, and wanders forth into the country eastward of the land of Eden, in which it thus appears that the primeval family had hitherto sojourned. There is something more in this than meets the ear. Was this banishment after all a heavy punishment? Cain thought so, and he could well judge. The *land* of Eden was not the *garden* of Eden, and though probably a fertile spot, there were doubtless other spots on earth as fair as that. He was banished from what had been till now his home; and we may admit, that this was a greater punishment to the first-born man, than it has been to any since. Of the world that lay beyond that central spot, he had no knowledge. There are but small portions of the earth with the condition of which we are unacquainted. The experience of innumerable travellers by land and sea is in our hands, to tell us what we may expect in any region to which we may go. But none had brought to the family in the land of Eden the good or evil report of the world beyond; and, as the unknown is generally terrible, Cain may have conceived the outer world to be little better than a desolate waste.

But there was something more than this that made Cain feel his punishment to be greater than he could bear. He knew what that was, and he himself states it: "From thy face I shall be hid." It does not seem to us that this refers to the internal consciousness of God's favour and protection, which he now felt that he should no longer possess. Cain could not be so ignorant as not to know that this did not depend upon place, for it was within himself. He might have lacked this as much in staying as in going; and yet he speaks of it as that of which his departure would deprive him. We can only understand that he refers to some sensible and local manifestation of God's presence, by which that spot was glorified, and from which distance would remove him. Having reached thus far, we are at no loss to find this manifestation in the sword-like flame, between the cherubim that kept the way of the tree of life. This we know was at the east end of the *garden* of Eden, and the garden itself was in the

eastern part of the *land* of Eden. If, therefore, the first family remained in presence of the splendour and of the cherubim, they were on the east side of Eden, and one going directly therefrom would proceed eastward. And a corroboration of this view is afforded by the fact, that Cain is described as proceeding eastward when he "went out from the presence of the Lord." Genesis iv. 16.

When it is borne in mind that the Mosaic law was to a great extent a renewal of ancient patriarchal usages which had in the course of time become corrupted or obscured, we derive a strong confirmation of this view from the fact, that under that law the presence of God was manifested among his people in the supernatural radiance, or Shekinah, which rested over the ark, between the cherubim; and as, in the land of Eden, we in like manner find the radiance and the cherubim, it is quite natural and allowable to suppose, that these objects occupied relatively the same position in the one sacred dispensation as in the other. This was, then, we may infer, the symbol of the "presence of the Lord" from which Cain went forth; and from it probably issued the voice which then pronounced his doom, and which had before graciously reasoned with him. In this Presence worship was rendered, and sacrifices were offered; and from it the signs of the Divine complacency or displeasure were afforded. That Cain regretted the withdrawment of any spiritual privileges in being cast forth from the presence of the Lord, looking to his character, may be doubted. But having grown up before it, he had no idea of life apart from it, and he probably regarded it as essential to his safety and temporal well-being. His mind was gross; and it may be questioned whether he could realize the idea of a spiritual presence apart from the symbol. This is indicated in his attempt to conceal his crime from God, when asked what had become of his brother; and it has more than once occurred to us, that this fact is explained and illustrated by the supposition, that the murder was perpetrated in some spot where intervening objects—rocks or trees—hid the radiance from his view; and to which, therefore, he ventured to imagine that the Divine cognizance, embodied in that radiance, could not extend.

What state of mind Cain carried with him into his banishment, is not recorded in the sacred narrative, and cannot with certainty be known. That he repented of the murder of his brother,—that a horror-stricken conscience attended him all his life long,—that

"He found, where'er he roamed, uncheered, unblest,
    No pause from suffering, and from toil no rest,"

is probable, and may indeed be regarded as part of the doom denounced against him. But that he truly repented,—that there was any vital change in that evil of the heart which led to his sin, and entailed this punishment,—there is no evidence to show. Indeed, the evidence inclines the other way; for, if he had clearly seen, and thenceforth eschewed, the evil which had slain his peace, he could not but have brought up his children in the nurture and admonition of the Lord. But instead of that, we find his descendants busy for the present life, its schemes and interests,—strong in arts and arms,—but also "inventors of evil things," filling the earth with violence, and urging on that deepening stream of corruption which eventually drowned the world.

Yet let us not ascribe all the evil of the old world to the race of Cain, nor cast any needless stigma upon the great fathers of useful arts who are named as of his race. It was not until the times just before the flood that the corruption became universal; and then it was not confined to the seed of Cain, but extended to all but one small family of the race of the righteous Seth, not to speak of the descendants, probably numerous, of the other sons and daughters whom the Scripture assigns to Adam. We may hope that, in the earlier ages, there were many, even in Cain's race, who lived and died in the fear of God. The family of Cain was, however, the first that went forth from the presence of the Lord, and was thereby withdrawn from the paternal influence and instruction, as well as from the accustomed means of worship and incitements to obedience. The ordinary experience of life enables us to see that corruption and crime would *soonest* arise among such a people, and might from them extend to the other races of mankind.

The traditions and opinions of the Jews respecting the further career of Cain, as held at and about the time of our Saviour, are embodied in the statement furnished by Josephus,[1] who alleges that Cain, so far from amending his life after his sentence, plunged into deeper evils, and went on from crime to crime,—abandoning himself to his lusts, and to all kinds of outrage, without regard to common justice. The wicked became his companions, and he enriched himself by rapine and violence. By the invention of weights and measures, he corrupted the simplicity and plain-dealing of former times, and exchanged the innocency of the primitive generosity and openness, by new contrivances of human policy and suspicious craft. He was the first who invaded the common rights of mankind by bounds and enclosures; and the first who built a city, and fortified and peopled it. Although much of this is absurd, and seems based on that ancient superstition which identifies great knowledge with great wickedness, it indicates the current of ancient opinion respecting the after career of Cain; and that opinion was probably correct enough in its substantial purport, however absurdly illustrated.

———

One or two other points of importance are suggested by this melancholy narrative. The first part of Cain's sentence was, "Now art thou cursed from the earth;" and he appears to interpret this as signifying, "Thou hast driven me out this day from the face of the earth." He does not mean the whole world, but that part of it which had been stained by his crime, that part which was his home, and was alone inhabited by man. Cain was thus banished from the society of his brethren. He was a reckless, dangerous man; already a murderer; and his presence could not therefore be tolerated. He was henceforth to be a lonely, despised, and dreaded outcast. Can we wonder that he should say, "My punishment is greater than I can bear?"

Another part of the curse was, "When thou tillest the ground, it shall not henceforth yield unto thee her strength." He would get only an imperfect return for his labour. Cain was "a tiller of the ground," and this curse would therefore come upon him with double force. He was a worldly man, glorying apparently in the ample fruit of his skilful toil, and congratulating himself perhaps, as many still do, that, though he could not enjoy the favour of Heaven, his worldly prospects would not thereby suffer. But the Lord taught him, and through him mankind, a solemn lesson. The crimes of men, when they become an outrage so to speak, upon humanity, bring down the curse of Heaven upon human labour, upon the soil tilled, and even upon the whole country which guilt pollutes. History proves that the curse of Cain in this respect was not an isolated one. Sodom and Gomorrah, Nineveh and Babylon, Egypt and Palestine, all afford instances of retributive justice of a similar kind.

P.

[1] *Complete Works of Josephus*
Kregel Publications, *Antiq.*, i, 2, 2, p. 27.

DISCOVERY OF FIRE

THE Scripture, although it does notice various important inventions, has no record of the discovery of fire. Yet the sacred history affords some facts by which the investigation of the subject may be materially assisted.

There seems a general impression that fire was not known until after the Fall. It never seems to have entered any one's mind that there could be need of fire in Eden. The happy temperature must have prevented the need of fire for warmth; and no one has ever supposed that the first pair had any other food in paradise than fruits in their natural state.

The fire which guarded Eden shows the *presence* of fire, but does not indicate that man had yet learned how to reduce that fierce element to his service. Nor is this proved even by the existence of sacrifice; for it has already been supposed possible that accepted offerings were consumed by supernatural fire—perhaps from that which guarded the approach to paradise. All we can say with certainty is, that the use of fire must have been discovered before Tubal-Cain became "an instructor of every artificer in brass and iron."

We have, however, little doubt that the use of fire was, if not known in Eden, discovered soon after the Fall. In this we have both the traditionists and the poets on our side; and on a subject of this kind it is pleasant to listen to their statements.

We notice that the Moslem traditions regard the use of fire as a supernatural revelation, and indeed hold that most of the primary arts of life were taught to Adam by angels. This was the case even with fire. We are told that Gabriel instructed Adam and Eve how to make bread; and when an oven had been prepared under his direction, he fetched fire from hell with which to heat it. The angel, however, had the precaution to *wash* this fire seventy times in the sea, as otherwise it would have burnt up the earth, and all that it contained.

Old Du Bartas handles this subject with remarkable ingenuity and poetical fancy. He relates that, on some occasion, the winds blowing through the grove, drove the trees against each other, till two of them caught fire by the concussion. Adam, who witnessed this, fled with terror when he saw the ruddy flame arise from the copse, which was soon all on fire. The flame pursued him till a naked plain arrested its progress. Recovering his courage, Adam turned back, and observed with interest that cheerful glow which the heat imparted to his frame, and the speed with which it dried his damp clothing. Amid the cold of the ensuing winter, Adam often thought with regret of this, and, since this fire was not again kindled among the trees, tried a thousand ways to achieve its reproduction.

> "While (elsewhere musing) one day he sate down
> Upon a steep rock's craggy-forked crown,
> A foaming beast come toward him he spies,
> Within whose head stood burning coals for eyes;
> Then suddenly with boisterous arms he throws
> A knobby flint, that hummeth as it goes;
> Hence flies the beast, th' ill-aimed flint-shaft grounding
> Against the rock, and on it oft rebounding
> Shivers to cinders, whence there issued
> Small sparks of fire, no sooner born than dead.
>   This happy chance made Adam leap for glee:
> And quickly calling his cold company,
> In his left hand a shining flint he locks,
> Which with another in his right he knocks
> So up and down, that from the coldest stone
> At every stroke small fiery sparkles shone.
> Then with the dry leaves of a withered bay,
> The which together handsomely they lay,
> They take the falling fire, which like a sun
> Shines clear and smokeless in the leaf begun."

Nor is the mother of mankind without some part in the operation. Here is quite a picture:

> "Eve, kneeling down, with hand her head sustaining,
> And on the low ground with her elbow leaning,
> Blows with her mouth; and with her gentle blowing
> Stirs up the heat, that from the dry leaves glowing
> Kindles the reed, and then that hollow kix
> First fires the small, and they the greater sticks."

Thus the poet, in the exuberance of his imagination, provides us with two modes in which the use of fire might have been discovered; and yet the two modes are skilfully connected, because if Adam had not experienced the use in the first instance, he would not have cared for the hint which the second afforded.

The friction of dry wood seems to be the mode most usually indicated as the probable source of the discovery. It is thus stated in the Phœnician annals, as preserved by Sanchoniatho, though they refer the invention to the *third* generation. Genus (Cain), the son of Protogenus (Adam) and Eon (Eve), begets mortal children, whose names are Phos, Phor, and Phlox (light, fire, and flame). "These found out the way of producing fire by rubbing two pieces of wood against each other, and taught men the use thereof." In fact this mode is that to which the Greeks also and the Chinese ascribed the origin of fire; and the process has been noticed as actually in use among various savage nations.

Nature, however, offers other processes of combustion, which might have suggested the modes of obtaining fire, and perhaps have disclosed some of its uses. Lightning not unfrequently kindles fires on earth; and to incidents of this sort the discovery of fire was ascribed by the ancient Egyptians. Spontaneous combustion is often also produced by the fermentation of certain substances heaped together, as we too often hear is the case with stacks of hay. Then, without speaking of volcanoes, we find natural fires in various places from the ignition of gases, or from some combustible quality of the soil. Woods have also been kindled by the eruption of subterraneous fires.

Yet man might know fire as an element long before he thought that it might be rendered of some use; and the ancient accounts have scarcely exaggerated the importance or difficulty of the discovery. This is indicated by the fact that various nations have been found, to whom the use of fire was altogether unknown. This was the case with the inhabitants of the Philippine and the Canary Isles at their first discovery; and also with various tribes in Africa and America, who consequently fed on raw flesh. The inhabitants of the Mariana Isles, discovered in 1521, had not the least idea of fire. When they first saw it, as introduced by Magellan's people, they regarded it as a species of animal which fed upon wood. The first who approached were burnt, which inspired great fear of the terrible creature that could thus painfully wound with its strong breath. A volume—and one of no common interest—might be written on the origin, the history, the traditions, the powers, and the uses of fire, which was of old worshipped in many nations as a god.

THE FIRST CITY

Genesis 4:17

UNTIL Noah was instructed to build an ark, there is not in the sacred record any invention in art or handicraft ascribed to any who were not of the family of Cain. This is remarkable. Look at the two lists of the descendants of Cain and of Seth respectively. In the former are simply names, interrupted by a snatch of old verse, by the account of some equivocal proceedings of Lamech, and by a hint concerning the inventors of arts. In the genealogy of the line of Seth, the *persons* acquire distinct individuality. Not only are the names given, but it is stated how old they were when favoured with a son, how long they lived after, and what was the sum of their age. These facts give the list the utmost importance as a chronological document, and it is only from it that we have our knowledge of the time which has passed since man's creation, and of the duration of the interval between the Creation and the Deluge. The interruptions in the list have no respect to inventions or any such matters, but have reference to the religious character or religious hopes of the individuals. The Cainite list is of the earth, earthy; the Sethite list has a savour of heaven, and yet is of the highest secular interest, being in fact the basis of chronology and history.

It is no doubt in a great degree from the facts of this record, transmitted through the survivors of the Deluge, that most of the traditions of mankind ascribe the great inventions in art to evil men. It may be that the decay of higher interests directed all force of mind in the Cainite race into the channel of invention and discovery, for the aggrandisement of this life, and led them unconsciously to furnish a fresh illustration of the truth learnt even in Eden, that

"The tree of knowledge is not that of life."

The only fact we learn of Cain himself after his exile is, "that he built a city and called it after the name of his son Enoch." In considering this fact, we must not forget the important evidence it affords, that houses were earlier than tents, towns than encampments, and the settled than the nomade life; and in correspondence with it, the origin of the tent-dwelling life is afterwards ascribed to a period long subsequent

—the sixth generation from Cain. This is not the course which an inventor would take in recording the progress of mankind, nor is it in accordance with the hypothesis of those who contend that man advanced progressively out of the savage state. By such theorists, tents covered with the skins of beasts are regarded as being of earlier date than houses—a prior stage in human civilisation. But in the true record, the first-born man builds a city, and the tent comes later by more than a thousand years.

We must not, however, allow ourselves to form any magnificent ideas of Cain's city. We have no reason to suppose that it was more than a collection of low cottages or hovels, each consisting probably of a wooden frame wattled with reeds or twigs, and plastered with mud; or the more likely supposition is, that the houses were substantially constructed with layers of dried mud successively deposited—a very ancient and still common mode of building in the East. The latter mode of construction may at the first view seem less likely than the former to be of early date. But it is in reality, if simplicity be required, much more simple, the operations being fewer, and scarcely any other implements being needed than the hands and the feet. It may also be noted that clay and mud are the first building materials which are mentioned in Scripture, if the book of Job be entitled to that ancient date which is generally claimed for it.[1] It is possible that an Irish mud-cabin forms no inadequate representative of the buildings of Cain's city. But the term implies the existence, scarcely perhaps of a wall, but of a fence, to protect the domestic animals from the depredations of beasts of prey, if not from the incursions of human enemies. This may also have been formed of mud, as many town walls are still so made in the East. It may even have been constructed of loose stones, if stones were found in the locality; but it may quite as probably have been a hedge of briars or of the thorny cactus, of which fences are still constructed in the East, these being found to be not only impervious to beasts of prey, but to form a sufficient protection from the sudden incursions of predatory hordes. Jericho is at this day so defended, and many places on the coast of Palestine are hedged in with the prickly pear. In fact, a thinly-dressed or half-naked people have much dread of strong thorny plants which

[1] Job 4:19; compare 24:16.

tear the flesh; and this gives to such plants an adaptation for defence of which we, with our thick clothing, can scarcely form a conception.

The Hebrew word here translated "city" signifies "a fortified place," as distinguished from an open village or camp. Probably the towns at the agricultural stations of some tribes of Bedawîn in Nejd would give the best idea of this first city. They consist of rude dwellings, grouped close together, and encircled by a strong rough wall of stones or sun-dried bricks. This defence is intended to preserve the flocks and herds from wild beasts, and to secure stores of grain and other property against the attacks of robbers. Cain's "fenced city" thus indicates a feeling of insecurity and fear. It also perhaps indicates that worldliness of mind, that proud idea of self-dependence previously manifested, as contradistinguished from a confiding trust in God's providence. He resolved, as it would seem, to be his own protector.

The literal translation of the passage ought not to be overlooked. It is, "He was building a city;" he had commenced but he had not finished it. We know not how long he was occupied with the work, nor how long it was after the Fall when he began to build; nor what was the size of the city. When these facts are kept in mind, the statement as it now stands in our English Bible will cease to surprise the thoughtful reader.

The name given to both his son and the city may perhaps indicate some little shade of change in the feelings of Cain toward God. *Enoch* signifies "consecration." May not this intimate, that having learned from sad experience the value of the divine blessing, he attempted by a formal and nominal dedication of his son and his city to God, to secure that blessing?

P.

LAMECH

Genesis 4:19-24

IN going through the list of Cain's descendants, we find nothing to arrest our attention till we come to Lamech, who was the fifth in descent from Cain, and who must have lived about the same time with the Enoch of Seth's line, or somewhat above six hundred years from the Creation.[1] This Lamech seems to have been a very remarkable person; and out of seven verses devoted to the posterity of Cain, six are occupied by the sayings and doings of himself and his two sons.

[1] This is according to the common or shorter chronology, which, as that in general use, we feel bound to follow in a work of this kind, although strongly persuaded, with most scholars, that the longer chronology, as preserved in the Septuagint version, is the most correct.

Reserving the sons for separate notice, let us give our present attention to Lamech. The record concerning him is singular, striking, and abrupt. It comprises poetry, rhetoric, and history; and yet, although it suggests much, and sets the mind to work, there is little in it to satisfy the curiosity it excites.

First, we are informed that Lamech had *two* wives, called Adah and Zillah—beautiful names, and the first female names that occur since Eve. Why is this fact so pointedly mentioned, unless to intimate that the practice of having more than one wife was a new thing, and among the inventions of the house of Cain? This is the general sentiment of antiquity; and the early Christian writers who have occasion to allude to the matter, agree with Tertullian in regarding Lamech as the first man who reversed the order of nature and of creation, by taking two wives unto himself.

Adah bore to Lamech two sons, Jabal and Jubal, and by Zillah he had one, named Tubal-Cain—all famous inventors, of whom there will be more to say anon. " And the sister of Tubal-Cain was Naamah." This is all we hear of *her*. It is remarkable that her name should be found at all in a record in which the names of so few women are preserved; and it is still more remarkable, that it is given without any circumstances to indicate the cause of its insertion. The name means *fair*, or *beautiful*. Was her beauty her distinction? Did that beauty produce effects by which great families were united or broken? Beauty has, within the compass of historical time, moved the world. Did it in her person shake the old world also? Her brothers were the great fathers of social arts. Was her fame of the same sort as theirs? Some ascribe to her the invention of spinning and weaving; and others, who find in her brother the Vulcan of the Greeks, recognize in her Minerva, who had among her names that of Nemanoun.[1] But all this is bald conjecture. Her name was Naamah; her father was Lamech; her mother Zillah; her brother Tubal-Cain: she lived; she died. This is all we know of her. To what she owed her fame—a fame of five thousand years—must remain inscrutable. As one finds among the ruins of time some old gray monument, too important and distinguished to have been constructed for a person of mean note, but discovers thereon only a NAME,

[1] Plutarch, *De Iside et Osiride.*

which the rust of ages has left unconsumed, so it is with Lamech's illustrious daughter.

Lamech had his troubles, as a man with two wives was likely to have, and always has had; but whether or not his troubles grew directly out of his polygamy, is not clearly disclosed. We know them only through an address which he makes to his two wives. The subject-matter of this address is hard to be understood; but there can be no mistake as to its form, which embodies the parallelisms and other characteristics of Hebrew poesy. This is the most ancient piece of poetry in the world; the only fragment of verse that has come to us from the ages before the Flood. Is its production intended, by an actual specimen, to indicate that, as one of his sons was the father of music, so he was the father of poetry? At any rate, the actual utterance of verse by the father shows that, as we might expect, poetry was invented before music. Perhaps the former even originated the latter. What more probable than that the first efforts of the tuneful Jubal were made in giving the sweet voice of music to his father's harmonious numbers?

The lines have been variously translated. We give them thus:

> " Adah and Zillah, hear my voice!
>   Wives of Lamech, receive my speech!
> If I slew a man to my wounding,
>   And a young man to my hurt;
> If Cain was avenged seven times,
>   Then Lamech seventy times seven."

This is not very plain as to the meaning, but we can only imitate the admitted obscurity of the original. To what do these words refer? Almost every possible sense which they can by any translation or interpretation be construed to bear, has been assigned to them by different commentators. The Jewish tradition preserved in the *Midrash* is founded upon the mention of Cain, and upon the interpretation (which the best Jewish interpreters allow to be unfounded) that the promise to Cain was not that vengeance should be exacted sevenfold upon any one that slew him, but that vengeance should not be taken until the seventh generation, which generation Lamech, as being the seventh from Adam in the line of Cain, represented. The story runs that Lamech, being blind (to account for his not seeing "the mark" upon Cain), slew his ancestor with a dart or arrow, under the direction of his son Tubal-Cain, who took the movements made by Cain lurking in the woods for those of some beast. But when the truth was seen, Lamech, in his horror at the deed, slew the son whose misdirection had brought this crime upon his soul. His son was thus "the young man" to whom the verse refers. Now, it is true that it was not promised to Cain that he should never be slain; but that if he were slain, sevenfold vengeance should be exacted for him. But for the rest, it is not likely that blind men went a hunting even before the Deluge; and the story has other improbabilities too obvious to need indication. No more need be said.

Josephus did not receive this tradition, if it existed in his time. He gives a favourable turn to the whole matter, observing that Lamech, who saw as far as any man into the course and method of divine justice, felt great concern in the prospect of that judgment which he apprehended to hang over his family for the murder of Abel, and under the force of that apprehension spoke of the matter to his wives. It is on this hint that Shuckford, followed by others, appears to have founded his view of these verses. He thinks that the death of Abel had occasioned a complete alienation between the family of Seth and that of Cain; that the latter, although living apart, were kept in constant apprehension that a bloody vengeance would some day be exacted; but that Lamech, when he came to be the head of a people, sought to reason them out of their apprehensions by the argument contained in his words, which are understood to mean: If sevenfold vengeance were denounced upon the slayer of Cain, who murdered his own brother, there must surely be a far sorer punishment for those who may attempt to destroy any of us on the same account. The fault of this is, that it is too vague and hypothetical, and has not a sufficiently pointed application to the words of the text.

It is an ingenious thought of some, that the wives of Lamech took alarm at the invention of more formidable weapons than had hitherto been seen by Tubal-Cain, and fancied that they might be some day employed against his life; but that he here comforts them by the assurance that, as he had never shed the blood of man, no one had an interest in destroying him.

On the other hand, many have thought that Lamech had slain not only one, but two ("a man" and "a young man"); and that, considering how Cain had enhanced his crime and pun-

ishment by obdurate concealment, he here openly avows his offence, and contritely confesses himself a greater sinner than Cain.

Our own impression, coinciding with that of Lowth, is, that Lamech had slain in self-defence some man by whom he had been assaulted and wounded. His wives would apprehend the exaction of blood revenge by the friends of the man who had been slain, on which he puts his justifiable homicide on the proper footing, by contrasting it with the murder committed by Cain, and urges that the difference of the offence rendered the danger of vengeance in his case but small. If the life of Cain were protected by the penalty of sevenfold vengeance, surely his by seventy times seven.

Another translation of the words of Lamech is as follows :—

" Adah and Zillah! hear my voice;
Ye wives of Lamech! give ear unto my speech:
For a man had I slain for smiting me,
And a youth for wounding me:
Surely seven fold shall Cain be avenged,
But Lamech seventy and seven."

It is regarded by Herder as a song of exultation on the invention of the sword of Tubal-Cain as an efficient means of defence. Another and similar view is this :—"Amid the violence of the times, especially among the descendants of Cain, Lamech comforts his wives with the assurance that, with the aid of the bronze and iron instruments now in his hands, he could kill any one who injured him (I slay, or would slay, a man for wounding me), and that, if it had been promised to Cain, that he should be avenged seven fold, there was power in the hands of Lamech's family to avenge seventy-seven fold." "All persons will agree in the remark of Bishop Kidder, that the occasion of the poem not being revealed, no man can be expected to determine the full sense of it." By some, these verses by Lamech, pointing to revenge, are compared with v. 29 of the following chapter—"He called his name Noah, saying, this same shall comfort us concerning our work and toil of our hands, because of the ground which the Lord hath cursed." Another Lamech was the speaker in this instance— Lamech descended from Seth,—and what he says contrasts with the words of Lamech descended from Cain. The one is a fighter, the other a peaceful worker. The Cain-Lamech finds comfort in weapons of war; the Seth-Lamech in the toils of husbandry."—Smith's *Dictionary of the Bible,* Art. Lamech. *Speaker's Com., in loco,* Vol. I., 58. Lange *Com.,* Genesis, 261.

S.

JABEL AND JUBAL

Genesis 4:20-21

ONE of the sons of Lamech by Adah was Jabal. "He," we are told, "was the father of such as dwell in tents, and of such as have cattle." This is a very important fact. It shows that man had existed thirteen centuries upon the earth before the origin of the nomade life, to which a large proportion of mankind have since been addicted. There had been shepherds before, and sheep had before this been kept; but it was not until the time of Jabal that pasturage was organised into a distinct form of social existence. By him men were led to extend their care to larger animals than sheep; they were also taught to cast off the restraints which the habit of living in towns and villages imposed, and to betake themselves wholly to the pastures, dwelling in portable habitations, and removing from place to place for the convenience of pasturage. This is a mode of life frequently brought under our notice in the Scriptures, being essentially that of the patriarchs whose history occupies the greater portion of the book of Genesis. The circumstance, therefore, will come frequently under our notice, and will not need here any anticipatory description.

Jabal had a brother named Jubal, and "he was the father of all such as handle the harp and the organ." Had, then, the world been for above a thousand years without music, till Jubal appeared? Perhaps not. Man could scarcely for so long a time have been without some efforts to produce musical sounds; and the birds could scarcely for so many ages have poured forth their melodious throats to him, without some attempts at imitation. But hitherto, probably, all their attempts had been vocal, until Jubal discovered that instruments might be contrived to give vent to musical sounds of greater compass and power. We may conceive that he had many anxious thoughts, many abortive trials, until perseverance conquered—as it always does—and he had brought his "harp and organ" to perfection. The "harp" was something of that sort which we call a lyre, and the form and character of which are better known to us from sculptures, paintings, and medals, as well as from poetical descriptions, than from actual knowledge, the instrument being virtually extinct. And let not "the organ" of Jubal perplex us with large ideas of pipes, and keys, and bellows. It was nothing more than a simple "mouth organ"—a bundle of reeds, a Pandean pipe, that is, such a pipe as the god Pan is seen to blow in ancient sculptures, and such as is often enough to this day witnessed in our street exhibitions.

Jubal has been, of course, a favourite with the poets, who strive to render due honour to the great promoter, if not the originator of the sister art. Du Bartas, to whom we always refer with pleasure, very fancifully supposes that the idea of instruments for producing musical notes may have been suggested to Jubal by the regulated strokes of the hammer upon the anvil of his Vulcanian brother, and his companions:

> "Thereon he harps, and ponders in his mind,
> And glad and fain some instrument would find
> That in accord these discords might renew,
> And th' iron anvil's rattling sound ensue,
> And iterate the beating hammer's noise
> In milder notes, and with a sweeter voice."

Accident, such as only occurs to the thoughtful and the observant, who know how to take the hints which nature offers to all but the slow of understanding, enabled the son of Lamech to realise his hopes:

> "It chanced that, passing by a pond, he found,
> An open tortoise lying on the ground,
> Within the which there nothing else remain'd
> Save three dry sinews in the shell stiff-strain'd;
> This empty house Jubal doth gladly bear,
> Strikes on those strings, and lends attentive ear;
> And by this mould frames the melodious lute,
> That makes woods hearken, and the winds be mute,
> The hills to dance, the heavens to retrograde,
> Lions be tame, and tempests quickly vade."

Nor does he stop here:

> "This art, still waxing, sweetly marrieth
> His prancing fingers to his warbling breath:
> More little tongues to 's charm-care lute he brings,
> More instruments he makes: no echo rings
> 'Mid rocky concaves of the babbling vales,
> And bubbling rivers roll'd with gentle gales,
> But wiry cymbals, rebeckes sinew twined,
> Sweet virginals, and cornet's curl'd wind."

So a poet of our own day—whose very name is a word of honour—James Montgomery, in his *World before the Flood*, renders due homage to Jubal, though he finds no place for Jabal or Tubal-Cain. There is a touching and beautiful conception with reference to him, which we should be reluctant to omit noticing:

"Jubal, the prince of Song (in youth unknown),
Retired to commune with his heart alone:
For still he nursed it like a secret thought,
Long-cherish'd, and to late perfection wrought;
And still with cunning hand and curious ear,
Enrich'd, ennobled, and enlarged its sphere,
Till he had compass'd, in that magic round,
A soul of harmony, a heaven of sound."

He sings to his instrument of God, of man, and of creation. The song is given: then, couched before him, like a lion watching for its prey, he beheld a strange apparition:

"An awful form, that through the gloom appear'd,
Half-brute, half-human, whose terrific beard,
And hoary flakes of long dishevell'd hair,
Like eagle's plumage ruffled by the air,
Veil'd a sad wreck of grandeur and of grace."

Who was this? It was Cain, who had seven years since gone mad under the stings of conscience:

"Jubal knew
His kindred looks, and tremblingly withdrew:
He, darting like the blaze of sudden fire,
Leap'd o'er the space between, and grasp'd the lyre:
Sooner with life the struggling bard would part;
And ere the fiend could tear it from his heart,
He hurl'd his hand with one tremendous stroke
O'er all the strings; whence in a whirlwind broke
Such tones of terror, dissonance, despair,
As till that hour had never jarr'd in air.
Astonish'd into marble at the shock,
Backward stood Cain, unconscious as a rock,
Cold, breathless, motionless through all his frame.
But soon his visage quicken'd into flame,
When Jubal's hand the crashing jargon changed
To melting harmony, and nimbly ranged
From chord to chord, ascending sweet and clear,
Then rolling down in thunder on the ear;
With power the pulse of anguish to restrain,
And charm the evil spirit from the brain."

It had this effect upon Cain, who exhibits signs of returning consciousness and intellect:

"Jubal with eager hope beheld the chase
Of strange emotions hurrying o'er his face,
And waked his noblest numbers to control
The tide and tempest of the maniac's soul:
Through many a maze of melody they flew,
They rose like incense, they distill'd like dew;
Pour'd through the sufferer's breast delicious balm,
And soothed remembrance till remorse grew calm;
Till Cain forsook the solitary wild,
Led by the minstrel like a weaned child."

From that time, the lyre of Jubal was to Cain what in later ages the harp of David was to Saul:

"The lyre of Jubal with divinest art,
Repell'd the demon and revived his heart."

And thus the poet concludes:

"Thus music's empire in the soul began:
The first-born poet ruled the first-born man."

The permanent occupation of nomad shepherds probably arose from necessity. The race of men, multiplying with great rapidity, soon filled the rich agricultural plains of the Euphrates and Tigris. Bordering upon them was the vast desert of Arabia, fit only for pasturage. Its lack of water and scanty herbage made migration necessary. Each tribe or family was forced to send away from its limited agricultural settlement a company of shepherds to tend and feed the flocks and herds on the distant pasture grounds, just as the Arab tribes of Nejd do to this day. These shepherds could not return at night to their villages. Some kind of shelter was needed. It must be portable; thus *tents* were invented.

The tents were in all likelihood like those still in use among the nomads of Arabia. They could not be more simple. A large oblong web of black haircloth; two or three rude poles set erect to support it in the centre; the two ends and one side fastened down by pegs of wood or iron; the remaining side open. Such is the *beit-shâr* ("hair-house") of the modern Bedawy, and such, doubtless, was the tent invented by Jabal.

The names applied in our English version to the first musical instruments are inappropriate. Our "harp" is large and complicated, and our "organ" still more so. The word rendered "harp" (*kinnûr*) signifies merely a "stringed instrument." It is not extinct in the East, as Dr. Kitto supposes. A very small instrument, something in the form of a guitar, but with only a single string, is now in common use among the Arabian nomads. It is called *kamanjeh*, and is played with a bow. I saw it for the first time when prisoner in an Arab tent near Palmyra. It has a sweet plaintive sound, and is the only form of stringed instrument I ever met with among the Bedawîn. There can be little doubt that it is identical with the old biblical *kinnûr*.

The "organ" was a "flute" or "pipe." The Hebrew word is derived from a root which signifies "to blow." The Arabs have still the flute, and delight in its music. They make it themselves, and it is rude and simple. A common reed is taken, cut the required length, holes are burned in it, a mouth-piece is fitted on, and the instrument is complete.

P.

____

TUBAL—CAIN

Genesis 4:22

THE son of Lamech by Zillah supported well the renown of his family for discoveries in the arts. His name was Tubal-Cain. He was "an instructor of every artificer in brass and iron." For "brass" read "copper;" brass being a factitious metal, of certainly much later invention. Was, then, the use of metals wholly unknown to men during the eight or nine centuries of not savage life which had passed since Adam received his being? Perhaps not. It is hard to conceive that extensive agricultural operations could have been carried on, that cities could have been built, or the useful and elegant arts brought into use, without this knowledge. We can, indeed, conceive that the use of iron does not date from an earlier period than this. That metal is hard to find, and difficult to bring into the state which fits it for use. It is usually the last of the metals to be brought into man's service; and nations which have possessed all the other metals have wanted iron. This is not the case with copper. It is often found on or near the surface in its metallic state: it is soft, and easily wrought; and nations whose instruments were only of this metal have been known to execute great works, and to attain an advanced state of civilisation. All antiquity, indeed, vouches for the remotely ancient (but not earliest) discovery of iron; but all antiquity also affirms, that although iron was known, the difficulty of the first operations in rendering it available greatly restricted its use, and a large number of implements, utensils, and weapons, which we should expect to have been of iron wherever that metal was known, are found to have been nevertheless of copper. On the other hand, it must be admitted, that the ancients being obliged to rely so much upon copper, laboured diligently in overcoming the inconvenience which its natural softness could not but occasion. By certain amalgamations and manipulations, they seem to have succeeded in imparting to copper some of the hardness of iron; and it is certain that, with their tools of this material, they were able to perform operations which we cannot execute without instruments of iron. It is probable that the ancients possessed some secret in hardening copper, which has been lost since the more general use of iron threw it out of use for such purposes.

Not to pursue this theme further at this time, we may remark that copper is here placed before iron, and that, taking all things into account, the probability is that Tubal-Cain's improvements were more in copper than in iron. The text itself seems to intimate that great and important discoveries in the working of metals were made by him, rather than that he was the first to apply them to any use. He is not, like his brothers Jabal and Jubal, called "the father," or originator, of the art he taught, but an "instructor" of those that wrought in it. So strong is our impression

respecting the earlier use of copper, and the comparatively limited employment of iron, that we would almost venture to conjecture that Tubal-Cain's researches in metallurgy, which led him to great *improvements* in the working of copper, also led him to the *discovery* of iron. Du Bartas, who, in his poem on *The Handicrafts*, has exercised much ingenuity upon the origin of inventions, appears to have felt great difficulty in accounting for the discovery of iron, and seems to have found it only possible to do so by supposing that it had been seen in a state of fusion, and afterwards hardening as it cooled, in the operations of nature:

> "While through the forest Tubal (with his yew
> And ready quiver) did a boar pursue,
> A burning mountain from its fiery vein
> An iron river rolls along the plain:
> The witty huntsman, musing, thither hies,
> And of the wonder deeply 'gan devise.
> And first perceiving that this scalding metal,
> Becoming cold, in any shape would settle,
> And grown so hard, that with its sharpen'd side
> The firmest substance it would soon divide,
> He cast a hundred plots, and ere he parts,
> He moulds the groundwork of a hundred arts."

After describing Tubal-Cain's successful working out of the idea thus suggested, the poet breaks forth into an eulogium upon this metal, which, if merited in his time, may now be uttered with tenfold emphasis:

> "Happy device! we might as well want all
> The elements as this hard mineral.
> This to the ploughman for great uses serves;
> This for the builder wood and marble carves;
> This arms our bodies against adverse force;
> This clothes our backs; this rules the unruly horse;
> This makes us dry-shod dance in Neptune's hall;
> This brightens gold; this conquers self and all;
> Fifth element, of instruments the haft,
> The tool of tools, the hand of handicraft."

Certain it is, that whatever was the precise nature and extent of Tubal-Cain's inventions in metallurgy, they were of such great use and service to mankind as rendered him famous in his day, and attached honourable distinction to his name in all succeeding generations, so that there is scarcely any ancient nation which has not preserved some traditional notices of his character and improvements. There is even reason to think that he was eventually worshipped by various ancient nations, and under names which, however different, signify an "artificer in fire." In the name and character of Vulcan, the blacksmith-god of the Greeks and Romans, it requires no great penetration to discover the Tubal-Cain of Genesis. Omitting the *Tu*, which was likely to be regarded as a prefix, and making the exceedingly familiar change of the *b* into *v*, you have Vulcain or Vulcan. This, and other analogies of a like nature, might tempt us into investigations from which we must at present refrain.

It is also worthy of note, that the Mosaic narrative is not the only ancient record which ascribes the invention or improvement of metallurgy to this seventh generation of mankind. Thus, the Phœnician annalist, Sanchoniatho, says of this generation: " Of these [the leaders of the preceding generation] were begotten two brothers, who discovered iron and the forging thereof." He says that one of these was called Chrysor, "who is the same with Hephæstos"—both names derived from "fire." The Hindu records—the Puranas—furnish no facts, but only names. Yet the names are significant, and in this seventh generation the name is Sumarti, a word which signifies a fiery meteor; and in this we have the brothers of the Phœnician annalist designated by terms which signify "heating" and "hammering."

Gen. iv. 22 might be more correctly translated thus : " And Zillah, she also bare Tubal-Cain, a forger (or hammerer) of every instrument of brass and iron." The allusion appears to be rather to the peculiar department of labour which Tubal-Cain took up, than to any original discoveries in metallurgy. He was probably an agriculturist, and was able, from his skill in working metals, to improve the necessary instruments. Arms may also have been manufactured by him.

Division of labour is here remarkable, as showing a high degree of civilisation. Art, manufacture, and pastoral life, were now distinct pursuits. Lamech's was a gifted household. It embraced a poet, a musician, a skilled artificer, and the originator of a new system of sheep and cattle farming. The daughter, too, from her beauty and accomplishments, as the name *Naamah* appears to indicate, was deemed worthy of mention by the sacred historian.

P.

ARTS BEFORE THE FLOOD

It seems very clear to us that the antediluvians, commencing with the knowledge imparted to Adam before his fall, and acquired by him subse-quently, made high improvements in the arts, and attained to a state of considerable civilisation. If this be true, there is consequently no foundation for the notion of man's gradual progress from the savage to the civilised condition. Indeed, how any one who believes in the sacred origin of the book of Genesis can take that view, is inconceivable. According to that account, the various nations of the world are descended from the men who survived the Deluge, and who were certainly not an uncivilised family. They built a large and capacious vessel, and their doing this implies the possession of tools suited to so great a work. They were also skilled in agriculture. Noah betook himself to the culture of the ground as soon as he quitted the ark, from which we gather that he was not a stranger to husbandry ; and the successful management of so many animals that were committed to his care in the ark, implies much knowledge of cattle. All this we know ; and knowing this, it is not too much to suppose that the various members of this family possessed all the arts which existed before the Deluge, and of which we have already taken some notice. Indeed, there is evidence of this in the great undertakings of their descendants, previous to their dispersion into nations and languages.

But it will be asked, if this were the original condition of mankind, how came so many forms of savage life to exist ? How is it that some of the commonest social arts are unknown to many nations—that there are those to whom (as already shown) the use of fire is unknown, and that many are in their entire condition but a few degrees above the beasts that perish ? Is it possible that these are descended from civilised ancestors, have lost much that their primeval fathers knew, and have retrograded rather than advanced in the scale of civilisation ? Painful as it may be to those who uphold the doctrine of human progress, the affirmative is, we apprehend, not only probable, but certain ; and might be illustrated by a cloud of examples in which nations have gone back in civilisation, and have lost arts which were in former times known.

A very sensible and thoughtful writer[1] has expressed this fact in a way perfectly in accordance with the view we have long entertained. " The first men were not wandering and ignorant

[1] Robert Forsyth, in *Observations on the Book of Genesis*, p. 47.

savages, although those who wandered from the parent stock and ceased to have any connection with it, generally fell into a state of barbarism and ignorance, as in Africa, America, and the Asiatic and other isles. Science, arts, and civilisation were confined to those who maintained their connection with the central stock of the first men, or departed in numbers sufficient to enable them to exercise and carry along with them the subdivisions of art and labour necessary to civilised life." Besides, many of the separated parties, in the course of their migrations, arrived at regions in which, from the difference of products, of climate, and of the physical circumstances of the country, some of the arts cultivated by the original families were no longer needed, and would therefore cease to be cultivated, and be in a few generations forgotten.

The arts of useful life, which were lost in the process of dispersion, are known to have been recovered in the course of time, either by re-invention, under the same conditions as those in which they were first discovered, or by renewed intercourse with those branches of the human family which still retained possession of them. The latter process is indicated by the numerous traditions of various ancient nations, who traced the origin of their arts and civilisation to some stranger who came to them from the sea, and imparted instruction to them. And as to the former process, it is clear that families which lost the arts belonging to their original condition, when that condition became changed, often recovered them, when, by the lapse of time, the population had so increased, and other circumstances had so arisen, as to create the need for them. Hence we find the invention of various arts claimed by different nations, which could not, since the original dispersion, have had communication with each other.

Upon the whole, it seems to us that the civilisation and knowledge in art of the antediluvians, and of the postdiluvians up to the dispersion, have been greatly underrated, by our views having been too much directed to the progressive civilisation of particular branches of the human race, which had greatly degenerated from ancient knowledge. Indeed, when we consider the advantages which length of days afforded to the earliest generations of mankind, giving to one man in his own person the accumulated knowledge and experience of a a thousand years, it

seems difficult to over estimate the advancement that may have been made, and the knowledge in art that may have been acquired. We think much of the advantages we possess in books, which give to us the knowledge of the past. But the advantages of the antediluvians were greater. There are few books of more than two or three centuries old from which we derive any knowledge, in the material arts at least, of any avail to us; but *then* fathers could impart, by the living voice, and by the living practice, the knowledge of a thousand years, to sons who might build up the experience of another thousand years upon that large foundation. If man had gone on to this time, adding at the same rate to the knowledge possessed by the antediluvians, it is inconceivable what progress he might have made: if, indeed, we had only steadily improved upon the knowledge possessed by the ancient Assyrians, Egyptians, Babylonians, and Phœnicians, or even upon that of the Greeks and Romans, it is impossible to say to what height of knowledge the world might by this time have attained. But God has put limits to human progress, lest man should be exalted above measure. The shortening of human life, the confusion of tongues, and the consequent dispersion, did in primeval times the work which has since been accomplished by less direct agencies, which have successively said to man in the highest state of his advancement, "Hitherto shalt thou come, but no further; and here shall thy proud mind be stayed."

Thus it has come to pass, that one nation after another has become highly civilised; then it has fallen, the arts which it possessed having been lost or discontinued; dark ages follow: then arise other nations, gradually recovering these old arts, and adding, it may be, some new ones; but not more, perhaps, than serve to counterbalance the old ones that have *not* been recovered. We too much overrate the present, because we know it better than the past. But ancient histories, and monuments older than history, disclose to us that there were, two, three, and four thousand years ago, nations scarcely less advanced in material civilisation, and in the arts of social life, than ourselves; who certainly possessed arts that we do not, and were able to execute works which we cannot surpass, and even some which we cannot equal—sufficient to counterbalance our possession of arts which they had not acquired, and our execution of works which they had not imagined.

It has been proved that many, and it may turn out that more, of our inventions and improvements are but revivals of old things. This was felt twenty-eight centuries ago, by one who knew the primeval history as well as we do, if not better; and there is deep truth in the words of the Preacher: "The thing that hath been is that which shall be; and that which is done is that which shall be done, and there is no new thing under the sun."

From such catastrophes as have from time to time thrown back the tide of human advancement, and prevented man from fully gathering the fruit of the tree of knowledge, for which his soul has hungered ever since the Fall, we think ourselves exempt by means of the printing press, which has embalmed our inventions and discoveries beyond the possibility of loss. It may be so : but let us grant that whatever advantage in this respect we possess, was enjoyed more abundantly by the primeval fathers, by reason of the length of their lives ; so that it is morally impossible but that their material condition should have been one of high and progressive advancement during the period which is now under our survey.

In further corroboration of the argument, that the recent invention of many arts, and the savage condition of many nations, are not adverse to the conclusion that the fathers of mankind were not a barbarous but a cultivated people, let us listen to the hypothesis built by Plato upon natural and thoughtful reasoning from known facts. He admits that men, in these ancient times, possessed cities, laws, and arts ; but desolations coming in the shape of inundations, epidemics, malaria, and the like, those that escaped betook themselves to the mountains, and kept sheep. Most of the arts and sciences which were formerly common, were then more and more disused and forgotten among them. But mankind afterwards multiplying, they descended into the valleys ; and by degrees, mutual conversation, the necessities of their condition, and the due consideration of things, gradually revived among them the arts which had been lost by long intermission.

Sir Matthew Hale, who, in his profound work on the *Primitive Origination of Mankind*, incidentally touches on this subject, says : " We are not to conclude every new appearance of an art or science is the first production of it ; but, as they say of the river Tigris and some others, they sink into the ground, and keep a subterranean course, it may be for forty or fifty miles, and then break out above ground again, which is not so much a new river as the continuation and reappearance of the old : so many times it falls out with arts and sciences, though they have their non-appearance for some ages, and then seem first to discover themselves where before they were not known, it is not so much the first production of the art, as a transition, or at least a restitution, of what was either before in another, or in the same country or people : and thus also some tell us that guns and printing, though but lately discovered in Europe, were of far ancienter use in China."

ENOCH WALKED WITH GOD

Genesis 5:22

THE fifth chapter of Genesis is chiefly a list of names and ages,—a geneaology that seems at the first view to offer little to engage the peculiar interest of the devout mind. But let us not be discouraged. Let us examine it closely. Lo! we are well rewarded. Here, hid among these names, is a sentence more precious than gold: "Enoch walked with God; and he was not, for God took him." How this came to pass we know not, and we need not care to know. We know that God graciously removed him from the evil to come, and we know why : " he walked with God." Well, then, what is this walking with God ? Was this a peculiar privilege of the antediluvian saints ? We read but of two who " walked with God," and these were both born before the Flood. Enoch, he walked with God, and God took him; Noah, he walked with God, and God did *not* take him, but preserved him *in* the world when all but himself and his family perished, and made him the second father of mankind. To be visited with such distinguished honour is surely a high privilege. Who is there among us that will not covet it, strive after it; and mourn for it, if it should prove to be among the honours of a past condition ?

But let us not mourn. This privilege is indeed ours : it is as open to us as it was to the fathers before the flood; and it is at this day as highly considered by God, as it was in times of old.

And do not our hearts burn within us to know this? Do we not instantly resolve to gird our pilgrim loins, and walk with God for the rest of life's rough and troubled way? Alas! too many of us have small care about it. Too many of us hear with but languid interest, with but half concealed indifference, that it may be our privilege to walk with God, as truly as Enoch walked, as truly as Noah walked, with Him.

And is it an easy matter to walk with God? Alas! nothing of the spiritual life is easy to the proud natural heart of man; but when the Spirit of God has made that heart soft, to walk with God is an easy and a pleasant thing; and to tread the rough paths of the world by His side, and under His protection and upholding grace, becomes the highest and most cherished privilege of our pilgrim state.

And what, then, is it to walk with God? If thou art a father, take thy little son by the hand, and walk forth with him upon the breezy hills. As that little child walks with thee, so do thou walk with God. That child loves thee now. The world—the cold and cruel world—has not yet come between his heart and thine, and it may be hoped that it never will. His love *now* is the purest and most beautiful he will ever feel, or thou wilt ever receive. Cherish it well; and as that child walks *lovingly* with thee, so do thou walk lovingly with God.

But he walks *humbly* also. He looks up to thee as the greatest and the wisest man in the world; and in *his* world thou art such. He has not seen thee subject to the proud man's contumely; he has not witnessed thy visage become pale under "the cold charities of man to man;" he comprehends not the foolishness of thy wisest things. He only knows thee in thy strength, where thou art lawgiver and king, and where thy master is far away. Thus conscious of thy greatness, and unconscious of thy littleness, he walks *humbly* with thee; and thus humbly as he walks, do thou walk with him whose strength is real, for it can bear even the burden of thy sins; whose wisdom is real, for even thy foolishness cannot perplex it.

And thy little son has faith in thee; he walks *confidingly* with thee. The way may be long, and rough, and trying; but he knows that if he wearies, his father can carry him through in his arms. The way may to his thought be dangerous; he deems that there may be evil beasts in the wood, or evil men by the road. But he fears not. He feels that his father's strong arm is between him and all danger, and he believes that no harm can befall him by his father's side. How happy is he, how free, how joyous in his trust in thee! The trials that perplex thy life are unfelt by him. The griefs that rend thy heart touch him but lightly. Thou bearest all his burden. His life's welfare rests upon thy going in and thy coming out; and he knows it not. He needs not know it. He feels with unmisgiving faith that thou art his shield, and rests in gleeful peace behind that broad protection which shuts out all care and thought of the rough world from his view. Thus *confidingly* as thy son walks with thee, walk thou with God. Believe that

"Thou art as much his care, as if, beside,
No man nor angel lived in heaven or earth."

Believe of Christ, that,

"On thee and thine, thy warfare and thine end,
Even in His hour of agony He thought."

And believe that, if thou walkest trustingly, lovingly, and humbly with God—even as thy son walks with thee—thou walkest with Him as Enoch walked, and shalt not fail of as high a recompense.

There is no way of walking with God but as a little child. To the world we may offer a bold and resolute front; for there is much to try us, much to battle with there. But to God we can only turn with childlike trust and affection, crying to Him in the firm persuasion of His love to us, in reliance upon His power, and in the humbleness of our hearts, "My Father, Thou art the guide of my youth!"

Furthermore, to walk with God as Enoch walked, is under all circumstances to realize His presence with us. When Moses asked of the Lord, "Show me thy way"—meaning the way by which the Lord would have him to go through the toilsome wilderness—what was the answer? Did He describe the way to Moses? No; but He told Him something far better: "My presence shall go with thee, and I will give thee rest." What needed Moses to know more of the way than this? In all his walk and travel, God would be ever present with him to guide all his steps—the light before him, the shade at his right hand. This was enough for Moses; and it is enough for us in our no less perilous journey through the waste howling wilderness. If we walk with God, if we enjoy His presence in all our way, it is well with us—we are safe, we have rest. All men walk not alike with God. Some

"Leap exulting, like the bounding roe,"

in the joy of their hearts and the fulness of their grace. Others move on with strong but staid and steady pace; and some walk lamely, and struggle on with pain and labour: but they all walk; and if they keep God's presence with them, they are all safe, for they all walk with God.

Is not this in fact the test of one's walk with God? To walk with God, is to walk as in God's presence. If, therefore, the feeling that He is ever present with thee, that His eye is always upon thy heart, be a trouble and not a joy to thee, a terror and not a hope, there is ground for fear that thou hast not yet attained to the blessedness of walking with God as Enoch walked, and as the saints in all ages have walked with Him.

Enoch's biography, though so simple and so brief, is most suggestive to the thoughtful and critical reader. " He walked with God," literally " with *the* God." The Hebrew name *Elohim* here occurs for the first time with the article. This appears to imply that other gods had been set up, that idolatry prevailed. Amid this prevailing idolatry Enoch worshipped the God of heaven. Amid wide-spread wickedness he walked in faith and holiness, manifesting in life and character the wondrous power and ennobling principles of true religion.

The result of this was twofold. *First,* "he walked with God;" consequently God was with him. There was close communion. Something of that cheering fellowship Adam enjoyed in Paradise, Enoch realized now. *Second,* "he was not, for God took him." In the Hebrew the meaning is indefinite; but the translation of the Septuagint explains it, and as the explanation is adopted by Paul in Heb. xi. 5, it must be true: "He was not found, for God translated him." God took him to Himself, because his life and his labours on earth were no longer useful. Men had become so hardened, that Enoch's holiness was probably made the occasion of contumely and ridicule. God took him to heaven, as He afterwards took Abraham to Canaan, in order to free him from temptation, and from the influences of wicked relatives and associates.

It is a remarkable fact, that the story of Enoch is embodied, in one form or another, in the legends of most ancient nations. Classic writers tell of the translation of Ganymede. The chronicles of Mexico state that four of the progenitors of man were removed to heaven. The Mohammedans also have their Enoch.

The apocryphal book of Enoch is one of the most interesting uninspired works which have come down to us.

P.

ANTEDELUVIAN NAMES

Genesis 4:17,18; 5:3-32

IT is observed by Dr. Chalmers,[1] that he had "met with no remarks upon the similarity of names between the two families of Cain and Seth. Enos, Enoch; Irad, Jared; Mehujael, Mahalaleel; Methusael, Methusalem; and at length both pedigrees terminate in Lamech."

The real reason why no one has made remarks upon this similarity is, that it does not exist. The apparent resemblance is merely an incident of transcription. In the original they are, with one or two exceptions, wholly different in *signification*, and considerably more different in *form* than as they appear in our English Bibles.

The subject is, however, curious and important, and well deserves attention.

It is clear, from the reasons assigned for the names which Eve gave to her sons, and from that which the Sethite Lamech gave to his son Noah, that these names are all significant, and that they expressed the views and hopes with respect to their children, of those by whom these names were imposed. Many of them are holy and good names, and some of them contain the sacred name of God; and seeing that *such* names occur in the line of Cain as well as in that of Seth, it may be questioned whether the opinion (founded chiefly on a doubtful interpretation respecting the "sons of God," and "daughters of men"), that Cain's race were all unholy and evil minded people, is founded in truth. It may indeed be urged, that for some unknown reason the Cainites borrowed such names from the race of Seth. But in the first place, only two of the names are at all identical, and these occur much earlier in the line of Cain than in that of Seth; for it is to be remembered that the line of Cain is carried down not more than seven generations, for the apparent purpose of introducing Lamech and his famous sons. But the line of Seth is carried down ten generations, connecting the generations before and after the Flood. Although, therefore, Lamech is the penultimate name in the Cainite series, and the ante-penultimate in the Sethite, the Cainite Lamech must have been born two or three hundred years before the Lamech of Seth's line.

[1] *Posthumous Works; Daily Scripture Readings,* in loc.

The first of the analogies indicated by Dr. Chalmers does not exist. The names Enoch and Enos are altogether different both in orthography and in the meaning of the four Hebrew letters composing each of these names. This would have been obvious even in the transcription, had the former been given more exactly, as Chanoch, the difference between which and Enos is at once perceived. There is no resemblance but in the two middle letters, NO. But although Seth does not give to his son the same name, nor even a similar one, to that which Cain's son had before received, that name does yet appear in Seth's line as possessed by the man who "walked with God."

The further consideration of these names is of some interest, especially if they help us to some information respecting the hopes or fears of the race of Cain. Respecting the race of Seth, we have such distinct information of another kind, as renders any that may be derived from this source of less importance.

Cain, then, called the son first born to him after his expulsion by the name of Enoch, which means *dedicated*. The value of this name depends upon the nature of the dedication. When we meet with the same name in a later age, as that of the man whom God permitted to escape from the world without tasting of death, we readily understand that his pious parents dedicated him to God when they set that name upon him. Have we a right to give it a different meaning in the case of the son of Cain? May we not rather be permitted to regard it as the expression of his wish or hope, that his son might be a wiser and a holier man than the father had been?

The next name in the Cainite line is Irad—similar to, but not the same as, that of Jared in the line of Seth. The latter name means simply a *descent;* but the former combines therewith the word for a town, and seems to be rightly explained by Jerome (who undertook to interpret, but not always correctly, the names of Scripture) to mean a *low-lying* or *descending city*. It may suggest that even as Cain built a city, and called it after the name of his son Enoch, so Enoch built a town on a lower site, or on the declivity of a hill, and gave to his son a name descriptive of its situation.

In the next generation the Cainite name is Mehujael. This is a touching and sorrowful name. It sounds like the groan of a broken spirit. It means *smitten of God*. Whatever gave occasion to it, whatever calamity, whatever grief, it acknowledges the hand of God, and expresses none of that obduracy and hardihood in evil which we are apt to ascribe to all the sons of Cain. The Sethite name of Mahalaleel, which Dr. Chalmers couples with it, is altogether different. Leaving out the final syllable (*el*), which expresses God, there is (in the original) but one letter alike in the two, and the meaning (*praise of God*) is also wholly dissimilar.

The next name in the Cainite line, Methusael, has a deeper significance than any we have yet reached. It means, *a man of God*. Such a name in the leading line of Cain—even more directly religious than any name to be found in the line of Seth—is deeply suggestive of better things in that line than we have been accustomed to seek therein. We have no right to assign any other interpretation to it than we should give if it were found in the line of Seth; and we think those critics are greatly to be blamed for unfairness, who, in their determination to find nothing good among the Cainites, suggest that the name of God, in this and in the last name, bears some reference to a profane use of that name in magical superstitions. We may add that Methusael has no analogy or resemblance to Methuselah, which Dr. Chalmers couples with it. The latter appellative has not even the name of God in it. The signification of it is, a *man of the dart*—a name of entirely secular meaning, in whatever circumstances it may have originated.

The next name among the Cainites is that of Lamech, to whom already one of our Readings has been appropriated.[1] It means *humbled*, and is a good name for any man to bear, though we cannot even guess at the precise circumstances in which it originated. It is the same as that borne in the Sethite line by the father of Noah, being the only real analogy of the several supposed by Dr. Chalmers, and one of the two instances of similarity that actually exist.[2]

Among the names at which we have glanced, all seem to be proper and becoming. Among these names, all that are not humble are holy,

---

[1] *Daily Bible Illustrations* Vol. 1, pp. 195-199.

[2] The other is that of the two Enochs, which escapes Dr. C., who rather dwells upon the similarity (which does not exist) between the Enos of the one line and the Enoch of the other. We cannot comprehend how these remarkable oversights arose.

with the exception of one (Irad), which bears an indifferent local sense. Out of five names, two contain the name of God; whereas, out of eight names in the longer line of Seth, only one contains that name. We find not among these names one that is arrogant, boastful, or defiant—such as our notions respecting this family might lead us to expect. All are just the reverse, and are such as would not have disgraced the line of Seth. This is assuredly a point worthy of notice, with respect to an age in which names were facts and expressed sentiments.

This is touchingly shown in the case of the name which the Sethite Lamech imposed upon his son: "And he called his name Noah (comfort, rest), saying, This shall comfort us concerning our work and toil of our hands, because of the ground which the Lord hath cursed" (Gen. v. 29): by which it would appear that men still retained a lively recollection of what they had heard from Adam and Eve respecting the blessedness of Eden, and were conscious of the contrast which the outer earth presented. If men lived entirely on vegetable produce at this time, they must have consumed the more of it, and the labour exacted in the culture of the soil must have been the greater in proportion; and now, when the population had so largely increased, it must have become the more onerous. Therefore Lamech, exhausted and fatigued by the labour he is forced to bestow upon the soil which the Lord has cursed, rejoices that a son is born to him who may share his labours, comfort him when he is worn out, and provide for him when he is old and feeble.

LONGEVITY OF THE ANTEDILUVIANS

Genesis 5

There has been much speculation respecting the longevity of the antediluvians. Out of nine men whose ages are recorded, one reached to nearly a thousand (969) years; and with the anomalous exception of Noah's father, who was cut off prematurely at the age of 777, the lowest of the nine reached 895 years. The average of life, reckoned upon the whole nine, is 912 years; and upon the eight, when the anomalous example has been omitted, 929 years.

In the midst of the reflections which this marvellous length of days awakens, the mind is led to dwell with reverent admiration upon the wisdom of God in making this remarkable and temporary provision for the increase of the human race. It had been as easy for His infinite power to have, in the beginning, created many pairs of human beings as to create one, and by that means to have ensured the more rapid peopling of the earth. But it was His gracious purpose to make of one blood all the nations of men that dwell upon the face of the earth, that the tie of brotherhood might the more intimately subsist among them by their derivation from the same ancestors; and that the peopling of the world might not be retarded by this limitation, He gives an immense duration to the lives of the primeval generations, whereby the population of the earth goes on as rapidly as if He had in the first place given existence to twelve or fifteen pairs of human beings. Thus, before the Flood, parents survived to see several generations of their children, and might in their lifetime behold thousands of their descendants.

We have already intimated our belief that no materials exist for any exact calculation of the population of the antediluvian world, seeing that there may have been then, as there always have been since, some disturbing or counteracting forces by which the laws of geometrical increase are in part neutralized. Nevertheless, making the largest allowance for the possible operation of such disturbances, it may seem a moderate calculation to assume, that where the deaths were so few in proportion to the births, and where the circumstances were probably at least as favourable to the natural development of the population as they are in America at this moment, the world was, at the time of the Deluge, scarcely less populous than at present. This is only allowing for the population before the Deluge a rate of increase twofold greater than it has been since, although the duration of life rendered the advantages for increase manifoldly greater. The brevity of the historical narrative, and the fewness of the generations which cover the space of time, tend to prevent us from realising with distinctness the great duration of the period between the Creation and the Flood. We forget that it exceeds by more than four hundred years the length of the period from the birth of Christ to this day—that is, according to the longer or Septuagint computation, which is generally regarded by chronologers as the most correct; but even the shorter computation makes the period not quite two centuries less than the time since the birth of our Lord—a vast period of time, during which the whole face of Europe and of a large part of Asia has been changed, and nations have grown to greatness which were at its commencement scarcely known by name. The nearly equal period before the Deluge, we are too apt to regard as a fixed point; the recorded facts concerning it being so few, as to make "the antediluvians" form, as it were, but a single idea in the mind. But it was a period of great increase of population—of large improvement in the arts—of terrible conflicts—of gigantic crimes —of extraordinary virtues—of miraculous interpositions—all of which are dimly hinted at in the divine record. Through the whole runs the great fact of the longevity of the generations before the Flood, which connected by a small number of living links the extremities of this long period of time, and which must have produced conditions of human experience materially different from those which our brief space of existence enables us to realise.

The importance of this consideration, in thinking of the arts and sciences of this period, has already been hinted at. Touching on this theme, it is well remarked by Mr. Forsyth: "A man of talent in those days, commencing with all the knowledge communicated to Adam, and directing his attention to any art, such as the cultivation of corn, and the taming and breeding of animals, the working of metals, the art of music, the manufacture of cloths, etc., could afford to employ five or six hundred years in his favourite occupation, or in his favourite experiments. In that time he might make more progress than a succession of men can now do in a succession of ages, because each can only afford a dozen or two of years to his favourite pursuit, and then leaves the unfinished task, not perhaps to be immediately taken up by a successor. This accounts for the rapid progress of the arts in the antedeluvian world." [1]

It seems to us that the purpose of God in replenishing the earth, sufficiently accounts for the primeval longevity of man; and to find an adequate reason for it, is the only difficulty it offers. Whether, in case the sins of mankind

[1] *Observations on Genesis*, p. 47.

had not brought on the purgation of the Deluge, man's life would have continued of the same duration; whether the physical circumstances of the earth were more favourable to length of life before that event than they afterwards became, —are points that cannot now be ascertained: but if the effect of longevity upon the increase of population be considered, we should think that the duration of life must in any case have been shortened, or else the world, which is not yet fully peopled, would long ere this have been crowded with a more dense population than it could have maintained. It is possible that the duration of man's life, and the resulting increase of population, have, in the depths of the divine wisdom, been adjusted with reference to the duration of the present state of the world, so that the world shall not over-swarm with people before "the time of the end."

Some have imagined that the years in which the antediluvians' lives are stated were shorter than ours—that, in fact, they were lunar months. This involves the question in greater difficulties than are removed by it; and, above all, it would make the duration of the world shorter than even historical evidence allows.

In fact, the longevity of the primeval generations is corroborated by many ancient traditions. Josephus could appeal to them. After stating the particulars in conformity with the Mosaic account, he says: "I have, for witnesses to what I have said, all who have written antiquities both among the Greeks and barbarians; for even Manetho, who wrote the Egyptian history, and Berosus, who collected the Chaldean monuments, and Moochus and Hestiæus, and, besides these, Hieronymus the Egyptian, and those who composed the Phœnician history, assent to what I here say: Hesiod also, and Hecatæus, Hellanicus and Acusilaus, and, besides these, Ephorus and Nicolaus, relate that the ancients lived a thousand years." [1]

This appeal shows, that such accounts were actually possessed, although most of them have been lost to us; and being possessed, they must either have come down as traditions from remote times, or have been derived from the books of Moses at a very ancient period; supplying, in the latter alternative, a piece of evidence for the antiquity of those books. Tradition is, however, the most probable source; for we find the same

[1] *Antiquities*, i. 3, § 9. Page 29.

accounts of primeval longevity in the records of China and Hindustan. Extending not beyond the Flood, the Chinese annals give to the eight generations following Noah, nearly the same duration as the Hebrew historian; and Hoang-tee, who reigned in China seven hundred and thirty years after the Flood, is described as remarking the gradual decline of the term of human life, and as inquiring how it came to pass that the lives of the ancients were so long, and the life of man so short in the age in which he lived. The institutes of Menu, also, state that in the first ages (after the Flood) the life of man extended to four hundred years.

Kalisch's remarks on the primeval longevity of man, and its gradual diminution, are perhaps as satisfactory as any which it is now possible to make: "Man was originally intended for an immortal existence: sin brought death upon him; every progress in the career of sin caused a new reduction in the years of his life: toil increased, and the years were again curtailed; the greater the interval which separated man from the happy days of Paradise, the shorter grew his life, till it was at last contracted to its present narrow limits. . . . The unbounded strength with which the nature of man was originally furnished, and which made unending life a physical possibility, gradually exhausted itself; the next generation inherited but a part of the paternal vigour; the heroic forms and iron limbs of the ancestors were thus imperceptibly weakened, till they reached that transitory condition, the origin of which is by the Bible ascribed to the sin of man." (*Commentary on Genesis*, p. 159.)

The effect of the length of human life upon the history of those early ages ought not to be overlooked. From the lips of Adam Lamech doubtless heard the narrative of creation and the fall; and he was able personally to communicate them to Shem, and Shem to Abraham. Then, again, the story of the ark and the flood, Noah could tell to Terah, the father of Abraham.

And if we believe, as I think we have reason to do, that God at the beginning taught man to write as well as to speak, then those venerable documents contained in the first four chapters of Genesis may have been penned by Adam, and by him put into the hands of Lamech. Noah next wrote the history of his own times; Abraham, Jacob, and Joseph followed with their autobiographies, and sketches of patriarchal life; and the whole documents were finally embodied by Moses, under the infallible guidance of the Divine Spirit, in the book of Genesis.

It may be interesting to note that Lamech was contemporary with Adam 56 years, with Noah 595, and with Shem 93. Shem was 50 years contemporary with Isaac, and Isaac about 20 years with Joseph.

P.

THE SONS OF GOD

Genesis 6:2

WE are informed, in the beginning of the sixth chapter of Genesis, that when men began to multiply on the face of the earth, "the sons of God saw the daughters of men that they were fair; and they took them wives of all which they chose." And again: "There were giants (*nephilim*) on the earth in those days; and also after that, when the sons of God came in unto the daughters of men, and they bare children to them, the same became mighty men, which were of old, men of renown." It is to be regretted that a passage which, were it correctly understood, might be found to throw considerable light upon this obscure period, is in itself very difficult to comprehend. One broad fact, which is perhaps the only one that it is really important for us to know, stands out, however, with sufficient distinctness—that much evil, much irreligion, apostasy, violence, and wrongdoing, resulted from incongruous unions between two classes, distinguished as "the sons of God" and the "daughters of men," the intercourse between whom produced a race not properly belonging to or recognized by either; and who, placed beyond the pale of society, like bastards in the Middle Ages, had recourse to brute force and violence to provide for their wants and appetites.

The question at once presents itself, What were the two classes whose union produced the powerful and mighty race which acquired such bad eminence in the primeval world?

The first impression of many readers will perhaps be, that the "sons of God" were angels, and "the daughters of men" human females; and this view of the subject has been entertained by many, both in ancient and modern times.

But against this it is urged, there is neither marrying nor giving in marriage among the inhabitants of heaven, with whose spiritual nature earthly pleasures are incompatible. An ancient theologian, who warmly disputes this view, produces the texts, Gen. vi. 3, "My Spirit shall not always strive *with man, for that he also is flesh;*" and ver. 5, "God saw that the wickedness of *man* was great;" and ver. 13, "The end of *all flesh* is come before me," in order to show that the offenders were not angels, but men. "If they were angels," he asks, "how shall we reconcile it with the justice of God to drown mankind for the incontinence of those spirits that had done them so great an injury?"[1] We like not these precarious speculations respecting the justice of God; but it must be allowed there is much force in these objections.

If these "sons of God" are not angels, what then are they? One set of expositors, observing that in the Old Testament the children of Israel are sometimes called "the children of the Lord," and the Moabites the people of Chemosh, and strange women "the daughters of a strange god,"[2] conclude that the expression "sons of God" is but a figurative expression for the worshippers of God, the Sethites, who are thus placed in opposition to those who worshipped no God whatever ("the daughters of men"), the descendants of Cain. Another body of commentators, however, look to the genius and idiom of the Hebrew language for an explanation. They call to mind that a great rushing wind is called "a wind of God;" a lofty mountain, "a mountain of God;" kings and mighty men, "sons of God;" and they urge that the words which are translated "sons of God" should be rendered "sons of the mighty;"[3] and that the passage then means, that the antediluvian chiefs and nobles took wives of all the handsome inferior women that they chose.

In regard to this last explanation it may suffice to observe, that no such stigma as is here assumed is attached in the Bible to the marriages of exalted men with women of inferior rank and position; nor does it consist with the ideas and usages of the East, where the great are not held to disgrace themselves, if they do sometimes honour the poor by taking their wives from among them.

We are thus led to consider the other interpretation, which makes the "sons of God" to mean the pious descendants of Seth, who are assumed to have been seduced into alliances with the women of the corrupted race of Cain, "the daughters of men," from which the usual consequences of such ill assorted unions ensued. The distinction between the righteous and the

unrighteous was no longer maintained, and in a generation or two was entirely lost; and the tide of general corruption advanced, until, when "God looked upon the earth, behold it was corrupt: for all flesh had corrupted his way upon the earth."

This explanation has the great merit of being perfectly comprehensible; for it quite consists with every-day experience, that when the people of God cease to regard themselves as a separate people, forbidden to touch the unclean thing, but go out into the world and willingly place themselves under its debasing influences, and bind themselves in its unholy ties, their downfall is an assured thing.

It is an interesting observation of one of the best of the Jewish commentators,[1] that of Seth only it is said, that Adam, who was created after the image of God, "begat a son in his own likeness, after his image;" an expression not applied either to Cain or Abel. Hence he infers that the descendants of Seth are called "sons of God," after whose resemblance—that is, in the highest perfection their nature admitted—they were created; while the descendants of Cain are called "sons of men," as an inferior race.

Another more recent Jewish writer[2] extends this to an interpretation nearly meeting that which Christian expositors usually give, but differing in some particulars from it. "Mankind appear at that time to have been divided," he says, "into two classes; the one, those first in descent from Adam and Eve, and their children, who were possessed of physical and mental perfections, and acknowledged the Lord according to the instruction of their first parents, and are therefore called sons or children of God; and the second class, the remoter descendants of the first parents, who were inferior to their progenitors in physical and mental powers, knew not the Lord, and therefore are called sons or children of men." This is a very noticeable view of the passage, and seems to meet more perfectly than any other the physical as well as the spiritual conditions of the case. It seems to us that nothing can be clearer, than that the sacred text means to state that the class called "sons of God" were of a race not only spiritually but physically superior to that from which they took wives. This explanation assumes that there was a gradual degeneracy in the physical qualities of man after

[1] Theodoret. *Quæst.* in Gen., p. 40.

[2] Deuteronomy 14:1; Numbers 21:29; Malachi 2:11.

[3] So actually rendered in De Sola's recent Jewish translation of Genesis.

[1] Aben Ezra.   [2] Mendelssohn.

the Fall, as well as in his spiritual state. In this period, when, from the length of man's life, many generations were contemporary with each other, it is quite probable that men of the older and mightier generations might be won over to contract alliances with women of the later and feebler generations. The physical degeneracy of strength and stature, which they might lament or scorn in the men, might seem to form an attraction and a beauty in the women, and might indeed constitute their seducing power. It is admitted that they were surpassingly fair in the sight of these "sons of God;" and this implies some difference between these women and those to whom they were accustomed, which it is otherwise difficult to account for. A life of nearly a thousand years' duration allowed of intermarriages between different generations, without the same objections from great discrepancy of age as the shortness of man's present life occasions. The explanation here given has the further advantage of supplying an answer to the difficulty which has been felt from the apparent intimation in the sacred text, that a mightier race of men grew out of these unions than those of the generation immediately preceding: for if the fact of physical degeneracy be assumed, it follows that the immediate progeny of these elder generations would, according to the common analogies of life, be more powerful men than would arise from intermarriages between persons on both sides of the best generation.

We have thus wrought out the view suggested in the extract we have given, because it appears, in some respects, to meet the difficulties which, on the one hand, disincline us to suppose "the sons of God" were merely men of the same generation; and which, on the other, make one afraid to say that they were angels. It has, however, been suggested that a clear and important meaning would be brought out of the passage, if it were shown to point, as is not impossible, to the rise of polygamy—a grievous departure from the original domestic constitution—to its introduction by persons of power and wealth, and to the influence which this abomination had on the rapid deterioration of the race, which at last drew down the judgments of Heaven. That polygamy was included in this evil, whatever else it might be, seems obvious from the expression, "they took *wives of all which they chose.*"

Whatever explanation we receive or reject, we shall not be far wrong in concluding that "the sons of God," in our text, were great and good men—true worshippers of God, whose liking for the fair daughters of the world shook their own stedfastness, involved their descendants in apostasy, and brought eventual ruin upon the world.

The difficulties of this passage, which have troubled commentators so much, arise, I believe, from attempts to isolate the words, and then to explain them by apparently similar expressions taken from other books of Scripture. The difficulties disappear when we interpret the narrative in its natural connection, keeping clearly before us the scope of the context. The scope may be embodied in the following propositions : 1. The human family is traced down through two distinct lines ; the line of the outcast Cain, and that of the elect Seth. 2. Seth was recognized by his parents as a special gift from God (iv. 25) ; and according to Oriental idiom, he was therefore *a son of God*. Cain, on the other hand, "went out from the presence of God" (iv. 16). His aspirations were all human : and according to the same idiom, he was *a son of man*. 3. In the line of Seth the worship of God was kept up. His *fatherhood*, so to speak, was acknowledged (iv. 26; v. 24). In the line of Cain, God's paternal care and government appear to have been almost wholly ignored. 4. "The daughters of men were fair." The name *Naamah* ("beautiful"), borne by Lamech's daughter (iv. 22), may throw light upon this. 5. These marriages took place when men "had begun to multiply." Before that time the two lines were widely separated. Now they were brought geographically near each other, and mutual intercourse was established. 6. The words translated "they took them wives" express the *marriage relation* established by God at creation.

All these facts tend to show that the "sons of God" must mean the descendants of Seth ; and "the daughters of men" the descendants of Cain.

The fourth verse has also been misinterpreted, and this has served still more to increase the difficulty. "The giants" (*nephilim*), mentioned in the first clause, existed before these marriages, and are quite distinct from the "mighty men (*gibborim*) and men of renown" who were the children of the union. There is no evidence that in physical stature the latter were greater than the ordinary race of men then existing.

P.

THE ARK

Genesis 6:14-16

WAS the ark built by Noah the first example of naval architecture ? did the art of the shipwright take its origin in this remarkable structure? We think not. It is scarcely credible that man had been so long upon the earth without discovering some means of floating upon the rivers and the seas. Are we to think so low of the state of the arts among the antediluvians—with all the peculiar advantages they enjoyed—as to suppose that they had not discovered an art known in modern times to the most savage and barbarous nations? Indeed, the instructions given to Noah for the making of the ark are so general as to imply that they were addressed to one who knew how to work out the details. These instructions do not enable us to define the form of the vessel, or to have more than a very obscure notion of its arrangements. This is because we lack the previous knowledge which Noah and those who wrought with him possessed, and which enabled them with these instructions to produce the intended fabric.

It is remarkable that the Phœnician annals ascribe the origin of the ark to the fifth generation—just in the middle period between the Creation and the Deluge. According to that account, the discovery took place in this manner: "Usous having taken a fallen tree and broken off its boughs, was the first who dared to venture on the sea."

Let us look to the description: " Make thee an ark of gopher wood." This is generally understood of the cypress-tree. " Chambers shalt thou make in the ark:" these chambers were doubtless cells or stalls for the different kinds of animals; and it appears from what ensues that these cells were arranged in three stories. " And pitch it within and without with pitch "—probably bitumen, the substance of all others best adapted to exclude the water. " And thus shalt thou make it: the length of the ark three hundred cubits, the breadth of it fifty cubits, and the height of it thirty cubits." These dimensions will presently be noticed. " A transparency shalt thou make to the ark;" not " a window," but what should serve as the means of admitting light, and at the same time excluding the water. Had the antediluvians the knowledge of glass? The word may, however, mean translucency merely, and not necessarily transparency. It does, however, indicate something *shining*. The words of the next sentence but one, defining that the doorway was in the side of the ark, indicate that the translucency, or series of windows, was at the top; and it was indeed needful that it should be very high, to prevent the waves from

breaking in. " And to a cubit shalt thou reduce it at the top," is a difficult phrase. We are not sure that we understand it; but it seems to mean that the roof, in which the translucency was set, sloped to a ridge of about a cubit wide. " And the doorway of the ark shalt thou place in the side thereof." This clearly shows that it was not a decked vessel. The door must have been of some size to admit the larger animals, for whose ingress it was mainly intended. The door was no doubt above the highest draught-mark of the ark, and the animals ascended to it probably by a sloping embankment. A door in the side is not more difficult to understand than the portholes in the sides of our vessels. Yet the sacred writer is aware of the apparent danger of a large door in the side, and therefore satisfactorily relieves our anxiety, by informing us that "the Lord shut him in:" and in all ages, he whom the Lord shuts in is safe indeed. " With lower, second, and third stories shalt thou make it;" which shows that no space in this vast fabric was wasted; but every cubit of its enormous area, from floor to ceiling, was laid out in receptacles for the various animals. In all probability, the larger animals were kept in the lower floor, and the birds in the upper.

Such is the description of the ark. Of its shape nothing is said. But we have the dimensions. Taking the cubit at the usual estimate,[1] these give it the length of five hundred and forty-seven feet two inches; the width of ninety-one feet two inches; and the height of fifty-four feet eight inches. This is nearly three times the size of the largest British man-of-war; and to make a vessel of these colossal proportions—a floating world—must clearly have required no small amount of practical as well as scientific knowledge.

The proportions simply as stated suggest the idea of an immense oblong box or chest, and many have thought that this was its actual shape. They consider, it seems to us rightly, that the ark was not framed for any other purpose than to *float* safely, and to keep steady upon the waters. It had not necessarily to make any progress from point to point; it may be doubtful if it had even to contend with strong winds or

[1] That is, 21·888 inches. We adopt it merely to avoid the incidental discussion of a large subject; but we think the reader may very safely, in his current computations of Scripture measures, regard the cubit as half a yard.

heavy waves; and if, at the worst, it were at times driven before the wind, acting upon the vast surface it presented, no great harm could come of this, as by striking against shores or rocks, seeing that all the world was under the water.

The form, therefore, usually given to the ark by painters, who have in view its *progress* through the waters, is probably erroneous, and is framed to meet conditions which did not actually exist. That figure is, indeed, in itself preposterous, and contrary to all the rules of naval architecture. We see nothing to prevent us from conceiving that the ark was shaped something like a house, secured upon a strong raft-like floor. It is right, however, to observe, that the "ark of the covenant," which was certainly a chest, affords no ideas which can aid our apprehension of the structure of Noah's ark. The words are altogether different in the original; the one being TEBAH, and the other ARUN.

Whatever be our ideas as to the *form* of the ark, there is no question that its *dimensions* were well adapted to the object in view. There were formerly some experiments made, in Holland and Denmark, with vessels having the same proportions of parts. About 250 years ago, in particular, a Dutch merchant, named Peter Jansen, caused a vessel to be built for him in the same proportions as (but of smaller dimensions than) Noah's ark. It was a hundred and twenty feet long, twenty broad, and twelve deep. Jansen happened to be a Mennonite; and while his work was in progress, it was regarded as the enterprise of a fanatical visionary, and he was exposed to quite as much sport and derision as Noah himself could have encountered. But it was afterwards found that a vessel like this was well suited to commerce in times of peace, as it would take in a third part more lading than any other vessel, without requiring a greater number of hands. Accordingly, the name of Navis Noachica was by some given to this kind of vessel. The account of this matter is preserved in a letter written to Petrus Reinerus, who married the daughter of the person who built this vessel, on the supposed model of Noah's ark, for Jansen, which is to be found in one or two old books on Noah's ark. In one of these works, the author, Reyher,[1] states that the like experiment had been made in his own country; and

[1] In his *Mathesis Mosaica*.

affirms that the kind of vessels called *Fleuten*, or "Floats," have almost the very same proportions as those of the ark.

THE DELUGE

Genesis 7

GOD, who in the midst of judgment remembers mercy, gave the old world ample space for repentance. A hundred and twenty years was the time during which the appointed judgment was suspended. And here we may point out the incidental corroboration this affords to the duration which the record ascribes to human life before the Flood. All other circumstances which do transpire are proportioned to that fact. A hundred and twenty years would have been too long, according to the present duration of life: for many who were not born when the judgment was first denounced, would have died before it was accomplished; and so long a delay of judgment would have weakened the force of the denunciation, and would have allowed most people to view it as a thing not to happen in their time, which, therefore, they would but lightly regard. But a hundred and twenty years were little more than the eighth of the average duration of antediluvian life; and, in respect of warning, were not more to that generation than nine years would be to us. It was therefore an interval just long enough for effective warning, without being so long as to allow any man that lived to deem that he might neglect that warning without danger.

Noah himself seems to have been the instrument of making this warning known, and of preaching repentance. St. Peter calls him "a preacher of righteousness;"[1] from which, as well as from the probability of the case, we gather that he laboured diligently to make known the purpose of God, and to exhort that untoward generation to flee from the wrath to come. But the construction of the ark was in itself a warning the most impressive. It evinced the sincerity of Noah's conviction that the judgment he declared really impended over mankind; and as its vast proportions slowly rose before the eyes of

[1] 2 Peter 2:5.

men, the rumour of this immense and strange undertaking must have spread far and wide, not unaccompanied with the report of the reasons which the builder gave for its construction. Thus "the long-suffering of God waited in the days of Noah, while the ark was a preparing."[1] Did it wait in vain? We cannot wholly say that. In the interval of a hundred and twenty years many must have died, among whom there may have been some who were suitably impressed by the threatened judgments of an offended God.

But we know that of those that were alive just before the flood came, there were none that took these things to heart. Our Saviour Himself, in a few awful words, describes their condition: "In the days that were before the flood, they were eating and drinking, marrying and giving in marriage, until the day that Noah entered into the ark, and knew not—UNTIL THE FLOOD CAME AND TOOK THEM ALL AWAY."[2] We see too much around us to be greatly astonished at this. We see at this day how few there are in the world, on whom the prospect of a judgment to come makes any serious impression; and we are assured by our Lord Himself, that as it was in the days before the Flood, so shall it be in the day when the Son of man cometh.

There was a pause of seven days after Noah had entered the ark, before the flood of waters came. How awful that pause! Were there any who were *then* smitten with fear—any on whom the striking spectacle of the animals passing into the ark, and the Noachic family last of all entering, and all being then shut securely in, made any salutary impression? Our Saviour says that they were obdurate until the day that Noah entered into the ark; were they *all* obdurate the day after—the seven days after? We cannot know. If any one *then* bethought himself of the evil of his way, and his heart turned to God, it was well for him, well for his soul; but it was too late for this world—the door of the ark was shut.

Even then the judgment was not instant. The fountains of the great deep were broken up, and the rain fell not in drops, but in cataracts; yet it was not immediately that the lower levels were filled. Thus it was forty days before the ark floated, and a hundred and fifty days before the waters rose to their highest point, which was twenty-seven feet above the loftiest mountains. Thus were the various tribes of creatures driven, day by day, from one resource to another, until none was left. The men, who hoped that the waters would soon subside, or whose retreat from their towns and villages was cut off by the surrounding flood, may be conceived to have retreated to the towers and the trees, watching with horror the gradual rise of the waters, and dropping off, one by one, in fatigue and want, from the extremest boughs into the encroaching flood, even before it reached them. For those who retreated to the high lands, there was reserved even a more terrible lot than for those whom the waters soonest slew. Thousands who had succeeded in reaching the mountains, must have perished with hunger even before the flood swept off the miserable remnant of their number. With them, how soon did the joy of escape to a station of fancied safety, give place to the consciousness that they were without food, or the means of obtaining any, upon the mountains, and that they must speedily perish there unless the waters soon subsided? But they did not subside. They rose; and in their rise narrowed day by day the area of possible existence. The young and tender died; the aged died; men in their prime died; till at last, some sole survivor, who had seen all the dear companions of his prime perish before his eyes, stood alone upon the mountain, and rushed to meet the flood in his frenzy, or sunk into it in the listlessness of his despair.

The horrors of this most fearful judgment that the world has ever yet seen, are imperfectly realized, if we think of it, as we usually do, as a sudden visitation. It was slow—dreadfully slow; and during the months in which the waters rose, the scenes of agony and despair which one day after another presented in different quarters, are such as strike terror into the heart, and sickness into the soul, of him who suffers his mind to dwell upon them, and to picture forth the horrible details. The eye shrinks from the backward view of the righteous judgment of God; and the ear vibrates with torture at the cries of children, at the sobs of women, at the groans of men and at—

> "The bubbling cry
> Of some strong swimmer in his agony."

---

[1] 1 Peter 3:20.   [2] Matthew 24:38,39.

EXTENT OF THE DELUGE

Genesis 7:19

It has been much urged of late, that the deluge was not universal, but was confined to a particular region which man inhabited. It may be admitted freely, that seeing the object of the flood was to drown mankind, there was no need that it should extend beyond the region of man's habitation. But this theory necessarily assigns to the world before the Flood a lower population, and a more limited extension of it, than we are prepared to concede. Our reasons for believing the world to have had a large and extended population before the Flood have already been given. Let us now add, that when we consider how widely the population descended from Noah had increased and spread, within a period after the Flood greatly shorter than that which elapsed between the Creation and the Deluge, with advantages very far below those which the antediluvians possessed, it is simply incredible that mankind should at the time of the Deluge have been confined within the limits required.

It appears to us, that a plain man sitting down to read the Scripture account of the deluge would have no doubt of its universality; and although our interest lies not in reasoning upon the greater or less probabilities of the case, but in ascertaining what the word of God means to teach us, it is gratifying to believe that the greater amount of even human probability is in concurrence with this more obvious meaning of Scripture. As to that meaning, what limitation can we assign to such a phrase as this: " All the high hills that were UNDER THE WHOLE HEAVEN were covered?" If the phrase here had been " upon the face of the whole earth," we should have been told that " the whole earth " had sometimes the meaning of " the whole land; " but, as if designedly to obviate such a limitation of meaning, we have here the largest phrase of universality which the language of man affords —" under the whole heaven."

Furthermore, if the deluge were local, what was the need of taking birds into the ark, and among them birds so widely diffused as the raven and the dove? A deluge which could overspread the region which *these* birds could inhabit, could hardly have been less than uni-versal. If the deluge were local, and all the birds of these kinds in that district perished— though we should think they might have fled to the uninundated regions—it would have been useless to encumber the ark with them, seeing that the birds of the same species which survived in the lands not overflowed, would speedily replenish the inundated tract as soon as the waters subsided. It is altogether a most remarkable circumstance, that of the creatures which were contained in the ark, those only are *named* whose existence upon earth would not have been affected by any deluge of limited range. And if the waters of the deluge rose fifteen cubits above all the mountains of the countries which the raven and the dove inhabit, the level must have been high enough to give universality to the flood.

We yield our judgment to what appears to us to be the force of these considerations with reference to the meaning of Scripture. Apart from these reasons, we should have been inclined to regard the deluge as partial, though extensive; for it must be allowed, that the doctrine of the flood's universality has on its side considerable difficulties, which, however, do not seem to us insuperable. We believe, further, that when once the real meaning of the Scripture is ascertained, we shall have gained the standard of truth as to these great facts; and all true science will then be found to be reconcilable with its statements, if not confirmatory of them.

The subject is a large one, and we may not here discuss or even state it fully. But there is one branch of it possessing great and peculiar interest, to which some attention may be given. We mean the traditions of the deluge which have been found to exist among all nations.

It used to be urged, that the universality of these traditions proved the universality of the deluge. But it must be allowed that they prove nothing, either way, on the subject. Those who have taken such great and laudable pains in collecting the traditions of tribes and nations deponing to the fact of an overwhelming deluge in the days of their remote ancestors, and who have inferred from the existence of such traditions in every quarter of the globe, that the deluge had belonged to every region in which such traditions were found, appear to have overlooked the important circumstance, that as all men sprang from Noah, their traditions are to be traced to their origin, and that they would naturally carry these traditions to any region in which they might afterwards settle. Commentators have erroneously reasoned as if the traditions had originated in the various regions in which every diversity of the human species has been found. Dr. J. Pye Smith and other able advocates of a partial deluge, successfully remove this stumbling-block from their path. But it is clear that although the argument for a general deluge loses this support, that for the partial deluge gains nothing by it.

These traditions are, however, important, as showing two things in corroboration of the Scriptural account. They show that there was, as Scripture affirms, a flood by which all mankind, except one righteous family, were destroyed; and they prove, in further conformity with the Scripture record, that all the existing tribes and nations of mankind are descended from that one family which survived the flood. In this point of view they are of high interest; and we shall presently consider some of the more remarkable coincidences which they offer. It will be seen in them, that, as was natural, the tradition of every settled nation makes its own land and its own mountains the scene of these circumstances—the traditions of a settled people being always localized. On that ground alone the traditions of a nomad people, as the Hebrews were with respect to localities, would be entitled to preference, even had they no higher claims. Such nations had no local, but only family attachments; and hence, while every other tradition makes the ark rest upon some high mountain in the land where that tradition reigns, the Hebrew account assigns the ark to a mountain far away from any land with which that people were connected, and which it is not at all probable that any of them had, in the time of Moses, ever beheld.

———

That the sacred writer intended to convey the idea that the deluge was universal, I think no man who reads the whole narrative critically, apart from all preconceived theories, would venture to deny. We read that the flood was intended "to destroy all flesh, wherein is the breath of life, from under heaven" (vi. 17); that by divine command there went into the ark "of clean beasts, and of beasts that are not clean, and of fowls, and of everything that creepeth upon the earth, they went in two and two, the male and its female (vii. 8, 9), to keep them alive" (vi. 20); that "the waters prevailed exceedingly upon the earth, and all

the high hills that were under the whole heaven were covered" (vii. 19); that "all flesh died that moved upon the earth, both of fowl, and of cattle, and of beast, and of every creeping thing that creepeth upon the earth, and every man" (vii. 21).

These statements, so clear and so emphatic, admit of no other acceptation than a universal deluge. True, some geologists affirm that a universal deluge could not have taken place within the period of man's abode upon the earth. All scientific men, however, are not agreed upon this point. To me it seems absolutely impossible for any man to ascertain the effects which a temporary flood would produce upon the earth, with such minuteness as to be able to affirm positively whether it had taken place within a given period or not.   P.

———

"The question, Was the deluge universal? has long divided those who believe that it was historically true, and that it is correctly related by Moses. The most literal interpretation of the language, especially of the words, Gen. vii. 19, 'All the high hills that were under the whole heaven were covered,' would lead to the conviction that it must have been universal. Yet it is certain that many who accept implicitly the historical truth of the narrative, believe the inundation to have been partial. Of such we may distinguish two classes of writers—1st, Those who think that all the then living race of man was destroyed; but that those regions of the earth not then inhabited by man were unaffected by the flood; 2nd, Those who believe that the flood swept away only that portion of mankind with which the sacred narrative is chiefly concerned, and which had become corrupted and vitiated by the promiscuous marriages mentioned in ch. vi. 1, 2.

"In order to place ourselves in a fair position for judging of these questions, it may be well to consider the nature of the narrative, and the common use of language among the Hebrews. And if we do so carefully, we shall surely be led to conclude that the deluge is described as from the point of view of an eye-witness. It has been so much our wont to look on all the early portions of Genesis as a direct revelation from God to Moses, that we rather consider the picture to be drawn, if we may speak so, as from the point of view of the Omnipotent. Yet, even if we are right in esteeming all as a simply direct revelation, it may be that the revelation was given in prophetic vision, and that Moses wrote, not merely what he had heard, but also, and rather, what he had seen." "Now, just so is the deluge described in Genesis. It is pictured as it would have presented itself to the eyes of Noah and his family. Moreover, on the principle just mentioned, it is in the highest degree probable that the description is really that which was given by one of such eye-witnesses."

"If this be the true explanation of the narrative, we may then more readily see how the question of the universality of the deluge stands. The words used may certainly mean that the deluge was universal, that it overwhelmed not only all the inhabited parts of Asia, but also Europe, Africa, and America, Australia, New Zealand, and Oceania; most, if not all, of which islands and continents were probably then without human inhabitants. Yet, if only the inhabited world was inundated, and all its inhabitants destroyed, the effect would have been the same to Noah, and would, most likely, have been described in the same words. The purpose of God was to sweep away the sinful race of Adam. That purpose would have been effected by a deluge which covered the whole of that portion of the globe which may be called the cradle of the human race. The words of the narrative are perhaps no stronger than would have been naturally used to describe such a catastrophe."

"The most serious difficulty in conceiving of a flood universal (not only to the world inhabited by man, but to the whole surface of the globe), is in the history of the distribution of the animal kingdom. For example, the animals now living in South America and in New Zealand are of the same type as the fossil animals which lived and died there before the creation of man. Is it conceivable that all should have been gathered together from their original habitats into the ark of Noah, and have been afterwards redistributed to their respective homes? The difficulty, however, vanishes entirely if the sacred narrative relates only a submersion of the human race, and of its then dwelling place, a sense of that narrative, which exact criticism shows to be possible, perhaps even the most probable, irrespective of all questions of natural science."
—*Speaker's Commentary*, Vol. I., Part I., 75-77.

S.

"GOD REMEMBERED NOAH"

Genesis 8:1

CONSIDER the condition of Noah and his family in the ark, with numerous beasts, some of them of savage natures. Five months had he been pent up from the sweet freedom of nature, and the fresh products of the ground. Five months had the waters gone on increasing, with no prospect of abatement, although long since, as far as he could see, the object of the flood had been accomplished, and mankind had perished from the face of the earth. How long was this to go on? When might he hope for release? Since the Lord had shut him in, he had received no communication from Him. Had he no misgivings? Noah was a man like ourselves, though good and holy; and his faith was greatly tried. It scarcely detracts from the glory of that faith, to suppose that there were moments in which he feared that God had forgotten him.

But "God remembered Noah," and his covenant with him. The Lord had never forgotten him; and although He gave no sensible token of His presence, He had never been absent from His servant. Speaking after the manner of men, the Lord is said to remember him whom He had at no time forgotten, when the time had come that He should *manifest* his knowledge of him, His kindness for him, and His watchful care over him.

> "Strange to our ears the church-bells of our home,
> The fragrance of our old paternal fields
> May be forgotten; and the time may come,
> When the babe's kiss no sense of pleasure yields
> Even to the doting mother; but thine own
> Thou never canst forget nor leave alone."

Let not the fact that "God remembered Noah" pass unregarded as a matter of no concern or profit to us. Let us see, further, that Noah was not alone remembered; but He also remembered "every living thing, and all the cattle that was with him in the ark." Not the smallest creature in that large ark was forgotten by Him. "Are not two sparrows sold for a farthing?" asked our Saviour; "and not one of them," He added, "is forgotten before God."

How many are they, to whom the consideration of these facts suggests needful and profitable reflections? How many are they, who, "shut in" upon themselves, and shut out from the world, by privation, poverty, or pain, are tempted to think that the Lord has forgotten them, because He has not yet moved for their deliverance? Daily have they cried to Him, and asked a token for good—some sign that they are still the objects of His care, that they are still unforgotten by Him, even if the time for their deliverance has not yet come. The world has left them. They know that by and bye, when the morning light again shines, the Dariuses of the world will come to ask them, "Hath the God whom thou servest continually been able to save thee out of the mouth of the lions?" And they burn with desire to be enabled, not less for God's glory than for their own comfort, to return the proper answer—that when man had forsaken them, and left them to pass the long and weary night alone, the Lord had taken them up, and made them more than conquerors over toil, and pain, and care.

But they have not yet this comfort. To task the care and thought of others for us, is hard; for in this age, man, like Martha of old, is "careful and troubled about many things." The world is a hard taskmaster to one who devotes himself to its affairs, and but seldom

> "Leaves him leisure to be good."

Besides the complications of our social system,

the hardness which the intense world-worship of the age engenders, tends more and more to narrow the circle of human sympathies and affections; and we are fallen upon times in which man heeds but little, or heeds but briefly, the sorrow that does not touch the bones and marrow of his own house. How often, therefore, do we meet, away in solitary corners, those whom the world has forsaken, and who sit there waiting for God to appear in their behalf! Their hope from man has ceased. They have tried the world, and have sorrowfully learned the value of its promises and hopes. They now, therefore, rest wholly upon God. They know His power. They call to remembrance His loving-kindness of old. They have not forgotten the days of the right hand of the Most High. Many a time have they been brought low, and He has helped them. But He does not come at their call. He does not hasten at their prayers. Then grows the thought: Has He also forgotten them? is He also weary of them? will not even He come to their help? "O thou afflicted, tossed with tempest, and not comforted," be of good cheer: He hath not forgotten thee: He is nigh, intimately nigh:

"He sees thy wants, allays thy fears,
    And counts and treasures up thy tears."

Behold, He has graven thee upon the palms of His hands; behold, thou hast His seal upon thy forehead; behold, He shall yet lay thy stones with fair colours, and thy foundations with sapphires. O thou of little faith, wherefore didst thou doubt? But so it is: we are creatures of sense. We will not believe that God is nigh, unless we see Him; that He has not forgotten us, unless He is continually affording some strong sign of His remembrance. Yet are His presence and carefulness not less truly shown in the silent watchings of His love, and when He stretches forth His hand to pluck the brand from the burning. Still He often condescends to our infirmity, remembering that we are but dust, and grants to us the sign our feeble faith requires. To Noah, the assurance that He who never forgets, "remembered" him, was conveyed to him by the wind that blew over the waters, and before which they assuaged.

There was a prophet of old who knew more of the ways of God than most men. He was led to expect the manifestation of God's presence. There arose a mighty wind that brake the rocks in pieces; and after the wind there was an earthquake, and after the earthquake a fire. To all this the prophet stood motionless. But after that, "a still small" voice was heard; and then the man, whom the wind, the earthquake, and the fire had not moved, "wrapped his face in his mantle, and went out;" for he knew that God was there. Alas, how few are they who would not rather expect the presence of God in the wind, in the earthquake, or in the fire, than in the still small voice!

Let us not, therefore, be in haste to think ourselves forgotten of God, or think less of the insensible than the sensible tokens of His remembrance of us. An anecdote will point our meaning.

A minister was once speaking to a brother clergyman of his gratitude for a merciful deliverance he had just experienced.

"As I was riding here to-day," said he, "my horse stumbled, and came near throwing me from a bridge, where the fall would have killed me; but I escaped unhurt."

"And I can tell you something more than that," said the other; "as I rode here to-day, my horse did not stumble at all."

TRADITIONS OF THE DELUGE

IT is difficult to condense within the limits which are here appropriated to it, the substance of the traditions which are found among various nations with reference to the flood. We shall, however, attempt to state the leading points of coincidence, and shall at the close indicate to the reader the sources from which more extended information may be obtained. In going thus cursorily through the subject, it will not fail to be noticed, that in proportion as we recede from the Ararat of Armenia, the traditions become less distinct, and more mixed up with extraneous matters; and this seems to us a strong argument in favour of the general conclusion that this was the mountain on which the ark rested, and therefore the cradle of the human race—the centre from which mankind diverged into all lands, as population increased after the deluge.

The Chaldeans believed that during the reign of Xisuthrus, the *tenth* king of Babylon (corresponding with the tenth generation of mankind, in which it really happened), the deluge thus took place: The god Chronus appeared to this Xisuthrus in a vision, and warned him that on

NOAH GOETH FORTH FROM THE ARK

the fifteenth day of the month Dæsius there would be a flood, by which mankind would be destroyed. He therefore enjoined him to build a vessel, and take with him into it his friends and relations; and to convey on board everything necessary to sustain life, together with all the different animals, both birds and quadrupeds, and to trust himself fearlessly to the deep. In obedience to these directions, Xisuthrus built a vessel five stadia (about three-quarters of a mile) in length, and two in breadth; into which he put everything he had prepared, and last of all went into it himself, with his wife, children, and friends. After the flood had been upon the earth, and was in time abated, Xisuthrus sent out birds from the vessel, which, finding no food or place for rest, returned to him. After some days he sent them forth again, and they came back with their feet tinged with mud. Subsequently he made a third trial with them, and they returned no more, by which he judged that the surface of the earth had appeared above the waters. He therefore made an opening in the vessel, and on looking out found that it was stranded upon a mountain which he afterwards found to be in the land of Armenia.[1]

The tradition of a general deluge was also preserved among the ancient Persians. The subject is only widely alluded to in the Zendavesta;

[1] This tradition in full may be found in Cory's *Ancient Fragments*, from Syncellus and Eusebius.

but among the ancient books of the Parsees (who inherit the worship and ideas of the ancient Persians) is one[1] which states that the world having been corrupted by Ahriman, the evil one, it was thought necessary to bring over the world a universal flood of waters, that all impurity might be washed away. Accordingly the rain came down in drops as large as the head of a bull, until the earth was wholly covered with water to the height of a man, and all the khan-fathers (the creatures of the evil one) perished. The waters then gradually subsided, and first the mountains and then the plains appeared once more. In this tradition there is the remarkable deficiency of a family preserved in an ark, which we find in even remoter regions. But it is stated that after the flood there was a new creation of men and animals.

It is usually alleged that the Egyptians had no tradition of the deluge. But this is not correct. We have the means of knowing that they were acquainted with the doctrine of a general deluge, though the details of their belief have not been transmitted to us. The Egyptian historian, Manetho, as quoted by Syncellus and Eusebius, speaks of certain inscribed pillars which were set up by the Thoth, the first Hermes, and the inscriptions on which were, *after the deluge*, transcribed into books. Plato also stated in his *Timæus*, that having questioned a certain Egyptian priest on the subject, he was informed that the gods, wishing to purify the earth by water, overwhelmed it by a deluge. On this occasion certain shepherds and herdsmen were saved upon the tops of the mountains, but those who dwelt in towns were swept away by the rising waters. It might be doubted whether this statement applied to the general deluge, were it not that the religion of the ancient Egyptians abounds in Noachic memorials, which fix the true purport of such statements; and it is also true, that men in later ages became disposed to localize in their various nations the general traditions of the deluge.

The famous tradition of Deucalion's deluge, as preserved among the Greeks, has the closest coincidence with that of Noah, so that the accounts which we possess seem to read like amplified reports of the record in Genesis. Philo, the Alexandrian Jew, who was well acquainted

[1] The Boun-dehesch, of which there is a translation by Anquetil du Perron, the translator of the Zendavesta.

with both sacred and pagan literature, plainly affirms that Deucalion was Noah; and of this there can be no question. We have two accounts of this deluge: one by Lucian and another by Ovid. The latter is the more poetical and the fuller in descriptive details, but the former is the more consistently accordant with the Mosaic details *throughout*. The great variation is, that Ovid does not provide for the safety of any animals, and Lucian does. The substance of the account given by Lucian is this: There was another race of men before the present, which owes its origin to Deucalion. The first race of men were a fierce and haughty people, who committed most heinous iniquities. On account of this a horrible calamity came over them. All at once the waters burst forth from all parts of the earth, and floods of rain came down from above, till the earth was covered with water, and all mankind perished. Deucalion alone was preserved, on account of his piety and uprightness, for the propagation of a new race. He had a very large chest, in which he packed his wives and children, and last of all went in himself. Just as he was entering, there came running to him all kinds of wild beasts and creeping things, *pair-wise*. He took them all in; and Jupiter instilled into them such peaceful dispositions, that they did him no harm, but lived in the most peaceful accord together, and were thus preserved in the chest as in a ship so long as the flood lasted.

The chief variation in Ovid's description of the same deluge is, that Deucalion and his wife (not wives and children, nor animals) escape the flood in a small skiff, which is stranded upon Mount Parnassus. But in his account the incidents are finely brought out, and the divine intervention more strongly indicated. Strikingly does the poet represent the unbounded riot of the ocean covering the hills, and the strange waves dashing on the mountain-tops, and the birds falling into the water from fatigue, because there was nothing left on which they could alight to rest their wings.[1] He does not, indeed, specify the exact duration of the flood at its height; yet he supposes that it lasted long, because he makes hunger, from the absence of

all food, destroy all those whom the water spared: namely, such as, availing themselves of rafts or boats, contrived to float above the flood, but being taken unprepared for such a voyage, necessarily died of famine.[1] This is indeed a very satisfactory solution of the only objection of apparent weight that could have been urged against the reasons we have adduced for the strong persuasion, that vessels for floating upon the water existed among the antediluvians before the ark of Noah was constructed.

Proceeding to more remoter regions, we find in the far East substantially the same traditions. The earliest sacred books of China contain frequent, although not very precise, notices of the deluge. The waters are represented as covering the hills on every side, and overtopping the mountains, and reaching even unto heaven; and the people as struck with terror, and perishing.[2]

In India the traditions are more copious. In ancient time the god Vishnu appeared to the sun-born monarch Satyavrata in the form of a fish, and said: "In seven days all creatures that have offended me shall be destroyed by a deluge; but thou shalt be preserved in a capacious vessel miraculously formed. Take, therefore, all kinds of medicinal herbs and esculent grains for food, and, together with the seven holy men, your respective wives, and pairs of all animals, enter the ark without fear." Satyavrata conformed himself to these directions, and after seven days the floods descended and drowned the world.[3]

Going now to the extreme West, we observe, with surprise, that the traditions of the deluge exist among all the various tribes and nations of the American continent, where, from the great remoteness, we should expect to find but faint traces of that event. The Mexicans had traditions of a flood that had destroyed all animals with the exception of one man and his wife, who escaped in the hollow trunk of an *ahahuete* or cypress (gopher) tree. The children born numerously to them after the subsidence of the waters were dumb, until they received the gift of speech from a dove, which came and perched itself upon a lofty tree.

---

[1] " Quæsitisque diu terris, ubi sidere detur,
   In mare lassatis volucris vaga decidit alis.
   Obruerat tumulos immensa licentia ponti,
   Pulsabantque novi montana cacumina fluctus."
                                   Ovid, *Metam.*, i. 307.

[1] " Maxima pars undâ rapitur: quibus undâ pepercit,
   Illos longa domant inopi jejunia victu."
                                   Ovid, *Metam.*, i. 311.
He had before spoken (*ibid.* 294) of some sailing over the tops of the houses, and rowing where they used to plough.
[2] Sir William Jones, in *Asiatic Researches*, ii. 376.
[3] Sir William Jones, in *Asiatic Researches*, ii. 116, 117; see also i. 230.

There are Mexican paintings of this event extant, in which Coxcox, the Noah of the Mexicans, and his wife Xochiquetzal, are seated in the trunk of a tree covered with leaves, and floating amid the waters,[1] while the goddess of water, called Matalcueje, or Chalchiuhege, pours down her floods upon the earth. In the different representations of this scene, men appear swimming and

THE MEXICAN NOAH AND HIS WIFE

perishing in the waters, and birds are seen fluttering and dying upon the surface, where they have fallen exhausted.

The following seems to have a mixed reference to the fall and to the deluge. It is part of an allegorical painting, the whole of which may be found in plate 15 of Humboldt's *Vues des Cordilleras*. A serpent cut asunder, but still living, is

MEXICAN ALLEGORY OF THE FALL AND DELUGE

seen shut up in a tank full of water, from the midst of which a plant arises. To the left is a woman crowned with a garland, probably the voluptuous Tlamezquimille; while to the right is seen a man shut up in a kind of jar. In the part we have not copied, a personage is represented to

[1] Humboldt's *Vues des Cordilleras*, pl. 26, pp. 206, 207; also Herrera to the same effect.

whose victorious arm the miserable condition of the serpent is to be ascribed. The allegory thus pictured has reference, Humboldt says, to the serpent which poisoned the water, the source of all organic life; to the victory over him, like that of Krishna over the dragon Kaliya; to the seduction of the world, and to its purification by water. In this we cannot fail to see the deluge, and more exact enquiry into the tradition would probably furnish still more striking Scripture analogies.

The Mechoachans, a people contiguous to the Mexicans, believed that mankind, becoming forgetful of their origin and their duty, were punished by a universal deluge, from which the priest Tezpi, and his wife and children, were alone preserved. He shut himself up in a large chest of wood, into which he put all kinds of animals and useful seeds. When the Great Spirit ordered the waters to subside, Tezpi sent out a bird called aura,[1] which finding food in dead carcases, returned not; then several other birds, till at length the humming bird returned with a branch in his beak.[2]

In North America there are more or less obscured traditions of the deluge among most of the tribes. The most distinct is perhaps that among some of the lake tribes, who hold that the father of all their tribes originally dwelt towards the setting sun, where, being warned in a dream that a flood was coming, he built a raft, on which he preserved his own family and the whole of the animal world. The raft drifted for many months upon the waters, till at length a new earth was made, and man and the animals placed upon it.[3] The traditions of Peru, of Terra Firma, of the Guancas, of the Cubans, and many others, might be mentioned, but they all resemble some of those which have been cited. The Brazilians had a very peculiar tradition of a deluge, which grew out of a quarrel between two brothers, and which rose till the earth was entirely covered. All mankind were destroyed except these two and their wives, who were saved by climbing to the tops of the mountains.

Is it credible, or even possible, that such

[1] The zopilote, a species of vulture (*Vultur aura*), an American substitution for the raven.

[2] Humboldt's *Researches*, ii. 65; Clavigero, *Hist. Mex.*, i. 204; Herrera, *Hist. Mex.; Hist. Gen. des Voyages*, xviii. 590.

[3] Thatcher's *Indian Traits*, ii. 148, 149.

numerous and wide-spread traditions, embodying so many pointed coincidences, and in which the ark and the dove so frequently appear, could have been founded on merely local deluges; and not rather on that from which the second father of all mankind was saved?[1]

MONUMENTS OF THE DELUGE

OUR attention was yesterday given to the consideration of the direct traditions of the deluge, as existing among all or nearly all the nations of mankind. But there is another kind of tradition, not less significant and impressive, which commemorated the same great event in names, and buildings, and ceremonies; and by means of which the memorials of the deluge were wrought into the entire structure of heathenism.

We cannot undertake to present to the reader a tithe of the copious information which exists on this subject; but it may be in our power to indicate its general purport.

It appears, then, to be very certain that the prominent features of the life and character of Noah are incorporated with the history and attributes of many of the deities worshipped in the heathen world. As it is not our intention to occupy our space with a branch of the subject which has been so often discussed as this, we shall be content to point out the names of Osiris, Bacchus, Saturn, Uranus, Deucalion, Minos, Janus, and the northern Bore; and leave it to the reader to explore the points of resemblance for himself, the materials being easy of access.

In looking to the mere external monuments of the deluge, it is a curious confirmation of the

---

[1] The reader who is disposed to pursue this inquiry, will find ample information in the works named below:— Bryant's *Analysis of Ancient Mythology*; Faber's *Origin of Pagan Idolatry*, and *Mysteries of the Cabiri*; Catcott *On the Deluge*; Harcourt's *Doctrine of the Deluge*. The traditions are also stated in portions or chapters of Sharon Turner's *Sacred History of the World*; by Professor Hitchcock in the *American Biblical Repository* for 1836; and more fully in Smith's *Sacred Annals*. Bochart in his *Phaleg* also collects some of the traditions. The interest of the subject is far from adequately represented by the brief indications we are here enabled to afford.

view which identifies the Egyptian Osiris with Noah, to find that the most famous temple of this god was at Theba (Thebes), or rather that the temple itself was so called, and the city was thus named from it. Now THEBA is, as we have

EGYPTIAN SHRINE OF THE ARK

already shown, the very name of the ark, by which it may appear that the temple itself was meant to represent the ark in which Osiris was shut up by Typhon, and cast upon the waters. With this should be connected the boat-like shrine, which appears to have been the most sacred object in most of the Egyptian temples, and which has an obvious connection with this tradition.

The same kind of memorial is to be observed in other countries, where some kind of ark or ship was introduced in the mysteries, and carried about in procession upon the sacred festivals. In

WOMAN WITH ARK

a series of pictures, representing ceremonies in honour of Bacchus, found in the lava-whelmed city of Herculaneum, appears what may be supposed with some probability to indicate the form which the ancients supposed the ark to bear; and which agrees well enough with the idea we have been led to entertain of it. A woman is carrying upon her shoulder a box, having a projecting roof, and at the end a door. Being carried in a commemorative procession, it is clearly a sacred Theba or ark. Its door at the side, and projecting roof, declare that it was not a mere chest; while the absence of the usual characteristics, and the occasion of its use, show that it is not a model house or a votive offering.

More striking still, as a direct memorial of the deluge, is the famous Apamæan medal. It was struck during the reign of Philip the Elder, at the town of Apamea in Phrygia. The city is known to have been formerly called Kibotos, or "the ark;" and it is also known that the coins of cities in that age exhibited some leading point in their mythological history. The medal in question represents a kind of square vessel floating in the water. Through an opening in it are seen two persons, a man and a woman, the latter wearing a veil. Upon the upper verge of this chest or ark is perched a bird, and over against it is another, which seems to flutter with its wings, and bears a branch, with which it approaches the ark. Before the vessel is a man following a woman, who, by their attitude, seem to have just quitted it, and to have got upon the dry land. These are doubtless the same pair shown in a different action. Whatever doubt might be entertained as to the purport of this representation, seems to be removed by the letters engraved upon the ark itself, beneath the persons enclosed therein. These represent the word ΝΩΕ, Noe—being the very name

APAMÆAN ARKITE MEDAL

of Noah in its Greek form—which form is the one it bears in the New Testament. This is a most surprising circumstance; not the representation, for we have others nearly as distinct, but that the very name of Noah should have been so long preserved among the heathen, in nearly its original form.

There seems to be little doubt that the sacred mountains which we find in various lands, are commemorative of the mountain on which the ark rested, and which was venerated as the spot of ground, once isolated among the waters, to which the nations of mankind may all trace their origin. We find such sacred mountains not only in America, but in Polynesia, Africa, India, and Arabia. The "high places" on which the Jews were wont to offer their worship, appear to have had the same reference. So strong was the veneration for the holy mount, that those who in the course of their dispersion came to extensive and unbroken plains, erected enormous masses of building, designed to represent or symbolize the mountain from which their fathers had gone forth. Hence, probably, the pyramids of Egypt; and hence, with still stronger probability, the tall masses of broken masonry that still appear in the Babylonian plains, whether or not the tower of Babel is to be reckoned among the number.

It was a natural consequence of this veneration for mountains, by which they were thus appropriated to purposes of religion, that imitations of them in miniature should be constructed to answer the same purpose, with the advantage of greater convenience. Hence arose those sacred heaps of earth or stones, in valleys as well as on heights, denominated by the Hebrews Bamoth, by the Greeks Bomoi, and by the British Cairns.

CAIRN.

Kern or Karn signifies, in Arabic, the top of a mountain higher than the rest. They could only therefore be so called mystically and emblematically, when they were constructed, as they frequently were, on plains. In fact, they were more needed in level tracts of country by those who wished to have sacred places, and to continue the rites to which they had been accustomed among the mountains. Having no natural hills to which they could resort, they were under the necessity of making miniature imitations of them near the places of their residence; and then it may be supposed that every tribe, and almost every distinguished family, would have an oratory, or place of worship, of its own. The vast number of them which appear in such situations, needs no other explanation. They are mostly of a conical shape, unless in such situations or of such materials as to have been worn down by the weather; and the most perfect of those which have in different countries fallen under our own notice, bear considerable resemblance to the summit of Ararat,—the whole figure of which is deeply impressed upon our memory, having had it constantly in view for many days. They are found everywhere in the old world, and are scarcely less frequent in the new,—not less than three thousand of them having been counted in North America alone, the smallest of which are twenty feet high. It has been thought that the circles of stones, commonly called druidical circles, have the same reference. The circle marks the limits of the space enclosed to represent the diluvian mountain, while the larger stone in the centre indicates the summit itself. In some cases, these stones actually do encircle a mound, upon the top of which the central stone is placed, or some other stone erection,—such as cromlechs.

kistvaens, or shapeless rocks, the separate diluvian or arkite[1] import of which we may now consider.

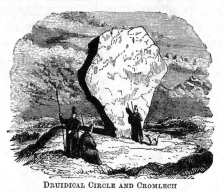

DRUIDICAL CIRCLE AND CROMLECH

Cromlechs, as most of our readers know, are composed of a large flat stone, supported in a horizontal position by others that stand upright. They are generally placed on elevated grounds; sometimes on the natural soil; sometimes on the top of cairns, or artificial mounts; sometimes within a circle of upright stones. The kistvaen, or "stone-chest," as the name means, differs only from the cromlech by the upright stones being broader, so as to leave the covered space less open—enclosing it, in fact, like a chest. These are much rarer than cromlechs. The most perfect specimen in this country (Kits Coty House,

KITS COTY HOUSE

near Aylesford, in Kent) is of oblong figure, the back stone being the broadest, and it is open in front. But in examples of similar structures which are found in Palestine, on the east of the Jordan, the front is also closed by a large stone, in which there is a door. In all cases they are of rough unhewn stones; and the whole are kept in form by the great weight of the covering

[1] A word used to denote the various forms of worship or veneration connected with the traditions and monuments of the ark and the deluge.

stone. The kistvaens have been often supposed to be tombs; but this is disproved by their interior length being less than that of a man. The general belief is, that they were designed to represent the ark of Noah, and we regret that space does not allow us to produce the reasons which are supposed to establish that opinion. Cromlechs have been conceived to be altars by some who admit the kistvaens to have been arkite memorials. But many of them are, from their form and height, so utterly unsuited to the purposes of an altar, that it is much safer to regard them as a somewhat different mode of representing the ark. Both were not only monuments, but instruments of ritual service. In the ark, mankind passed, as it were, from the old sinful world to a new world, which was as yet unpolluted by sin. Hence, in process of time, when the traditions of the deluge became mixed up with human inventions, the ark was regarded as a symbol of purification from sin. It is on record that devotees, remaining cramped up in the purposely narrowed bounds of these stone arks for a period of time, supposed to represent that of Noah's confinement, came forth expurgated from the taints of their former condition. We think it might be shown, that commencing with those that were most close and narrow, the devotees progressed through a series of these arkite enclosures, till at last they *passed merely through* some one of those that were more open, to signify their final passage out of their old into their new condition.

There seems some evidence to show that the isolated hollow towers which are found in various parts of the world are, in like manner, symbols of the mount and the ark, and that a sojourn within their narrow bounds, followed by the passage out, was regarded as an act of purgation, if not of regeneration. The round towers of Ireland have received many worse explanations. Natural caverns have in many lands been esteemed sacred under the same ideas. In all these cases, under all these varieties of circumstances, it appears that the sojourn in the ark was regarded as a state of death to the old man; and the coming out through the door of the ark a passage to a new life in a regenerated condition. The ancients, stumbling among the dark mountains, sought thus to express their obscure traditions, and obscurer hopes, in matters which have, through God's mercy, become noontide facts to us.

The immense number of "High Places" in Palestine and Syria is calculated to strike the observant traveller with astonishment. Traces of them are seen on the top of almost every hill and mountain, and on the summits of most of the tells that stud the great plains. Whatever may have led to the selection of such conspicuous spots for sanctuaries at first, there can be no doubt that at a more recent period they were chiefly consecrated to Baal, or sun-worship.

One of the most remarkable of these primeval high places I discovered, in the year 1852, on the very summit of Mount Hermon, at an elevation of about 10,000 feet. The apex of the mountain is a mass of limestone from fifteen to twenty yards in diameter, and rising some twenty feet above the ground around it. In the crown of this rock is a large artificial pit, or excavation, the sides of which bear the marks of fire. It was manifestly the place in which the Baal-fire was lighted of old. Round the rock is a circlet of massive stones, ranged in order like the Druid rings of Britain; and on one side are the ruins of a small temple of more recent date. A fragment of an inscription shows that it was of Greek origin, probably built during the age of Seleucidæ.

This great high place appears to have been already celebrated in the time of Moses, and gave to the mountain a name twice applied to it in Scripture, *Baal-Hermon* (Judg. iii. 3; 1 Chron. v. 23). The latest notice I have been able to discover of it is in the writings of Jerome, at the close of the fourth century.[1]

ARARAT

Genesis 8:4

THE mountain which the general consent of western Asia and of Europe regards as the Ararat on which the Ark rested, is the mountain of Ara Dagh, in Armenia. One would think there should be no question as to the identity of Ararat, seeing that the texts of later Scripture, in which the name occurs,[1] appear plainly to refer to Armenia, and in that country there is no mountain comparable to this. It is in all respects a most noble mountain—the finest, perhaps, in the world, and well worthy of the distinction assigned to it as the cradle of the human race, and of the place which it holds in the monumental history and the religion of the world. He whose mind is imbued with such conclusions as were yesterday exhibited, and regards this as the source and centre of the stone religion and stone history of the world, must look upon it with an interest greatly enhanced by all the considerations which

MOUNT ARARAT

that view of it opens. When our own eyes first beheld the "dread magnificence" of Ararat, we had already seen the loftiest and most remarkable mountains of the old world; but yet the effect of the view of *this* mountain was new and surprising. The reason appeared to be this—

[1] See Porter's *Damascus*, ii. 294.

most of the loftiest mountains of the world are but peaks of the uppermost ridge of mountain

[1] 2 Kings xix. 37; Isa. xxxvii. 38; Jer. li. 27. Ararat occurs nowhere as the name of a *mountain*, but of a country or district among "the mountains" of which the ark rested; and Ararat, or Ararad, is affirmed to have been the name of one of the ancient provinces of Armenia.

chains. It is these, perhaps, only that are visible in the distance; and by the time you come near enough to look directly up to the summit, your ascent, however gradual, has been such that you are surprised at the small apparent height of the peak above you. We recollect to have experienced this effect very sensibly on reaching, after a long ascent, the village of Kasbek, at the foot of the highest peak of the same name in the Caucasus. The snowy height seemed so small, that one could scarcely believe this to be the same mountain which had been visible a hundred miles off, shining gloriously among the clouds of the morning; and it required an effort of recollection, upon all the ascending way we had for many days passed, to apprehend how high indeed it was.

Now Ararat is not by any means in actual altitude so high as the Caucasian summit; yet the view of it is far more grand and impressive. The reason is, that it is not merely a summit of a ridge; it is a whole and perfect mountain. Whether it be seen distant or near, the whole of its noble proportions, from the level of the plain to the summit, covered with snow even in the height of summer, are taken in at one view. It is, in fact, the culminating point, the gigantic corner-stone, of the ranges of mountains which bound the three great empires of Russia, Turkey, and Persia. Never had nations a more noble boundary; nor is there perhaps another object on earth, which, from its mere natural aspect, would seem so worthy to be regarded as a monument of the greatest event in the world's history, the bridge between the antediluvian and the postdiluvian worlds. "Nothing," as Mr. Morier well remarks, "can be more beautiful than its shape, more awful than its height: all the surrounding mountains sink into insignificance when compared with it; it is perfect in all its parts; no hard, rugged features, no unnatural prominences; everything is in harmony, and all combine to render it one of the sublimest objects in nature." The valley from which it rises is that of the river Aras, the ancient Araxes. The rise of the mountain from its broad base is gradual, till it reaches the region of perpetual snow, which is somewhat more than one-third below the summit, when its shape becomes more conical and steep. The cone is surmounted with a crown of ice, which glitters in the sun with peculiar brightness, and becomes the cynosure of the traveller's eye for many days. This peak is, however, not alone in all its glory. It has near to, and arising from, the same broad base, "another self,"—alike most nearly, but lower and smaller in all its proportions; although, if not overlooked by its tall neighbour, it would be reckoned among high mountains. Hence, perhaps, it is that the sacred text speaks of the "mountains of Ararat," rather than of a single mountain.

The taller summit of Ararat is 17,325 feet above the level of the sea, and 14,406 feet above the level of the plain; the lesser summit is 13,093 feet above the sea, and 10,174 feet above the plain. Many attempts were made in former times to attain the summit, access to which the native Armenians believe to be supernaturally interdicted; yet with strange incongruity they sell to pilgrims relics from the wood of the ark, which is still believed to lie upon the summit. It was not till 1829 that a successful attempt[1] was made by Professor Parrot, a German, acting under Russian auspices. Twice was he repelled by the snowy crest; but in the third attempt he succeeded, and stood upon the mountain of the ark! He found himself on a slightly convex and nearly cruciform surface, about two hundred paces in circuit, which at the margin declined rather steeply on all sides. This was the silver crest of Ararat, composed of eternal ice, unbroken by a rock or stone. In the extensive view around, only the chief masses could, on account of the great distances, be plainly distinguished. The whole valley of the Araxes was covered with a gray mist, through which the towns of Erivan and Sardarabad appeared as dark spots no larger than the hand. To the east-south-east was the lesser Ararat, whose head, as viewed from this higher point, did not appear like a cone, as it does from the plain, but like the top of a square truncated pyramid, with larger and smaller

[1] The success of this attempt has, however, been much questioned, and was stoutly denied by all persons in the neighbourhood of the mountain when we were there in 1832. A Russian traveller, M. Automonoff, is, however, said to have ascended Ararat in 1834, and is stated to have found the large cross set up by Parrot, nearly covered with snow. The summit of the mountain is understood to have been also nearly reached by Colonel Stoddart, who perished in Bokhara. There seems to be, therefore, no real ground for questioning the veracity of Professor Parrot, who appears to have been well entitled to the high eulogium pronounced upon him by Humboldt, that "he was constantly guided by the love of truth."

rocky elevations at the edges and in the middle. In that case it must have presented much the appearance of a druidical circle, with its central object; and this is a curious fact, when taken in connection with the notion which some entertain, that the ark in fact rested on the lesser Ararat; as it is not easy to see how the inmates of the ark, including heavy cattle, could have descended from the higher summit.

The party spent three-quarters of an hour on the mountain-top, and then, after planting an oaken cross thereon, descended. In going down, "it was a glorious sight to behold the dark shadows which the mountains on the west cast upon the plain, and then the profound darkness which covered all the valleys, and which rose gradually higher and higher on the side of Ararat, whose icy summit was still illuminated by the beams of the setting sun."

It remains to be added, that Ararat has since been the scene of a fearful visitation, which in a few moments changed the entire face of the country. This was a dreadful earthquake, which commenced in June 1840, and continued at intervals till September in the same year. As the most destructive shock occurred in the day-time, the loss of life did not exceed fifty; but the destruction of property was great, and traces of the calamity will be borne down to future ages in the fissures and landslips of the district. Even the aged mountain did not escape. Vast masses of rock, ice, and snow were detached from the summit and lateral points of the mountain, and thrown, "with hideous ruin and combustion down," at a single bound, into the valley of Akhori, where the fragments lie to this day, scattered over an extent of several miles.

THE DISPERSION

Genesis 10

THAT all the tribes and nations of mankind have a common origin is the doctrine of Scripture; and that doctrine has been abundantly confirmed by the most learned and able researches into the physical history of man. This being the case, it is impossible to account satisfactorily for the great and essential diversity of language that exists, but by a miracle. The sacred record does account for that diversity, and accounts for it by miracle. It even acquaints us with the circumstances which rendered that miracle necessary to secure a great and important end.

It seems that as mankind increased in the land in which the ark rested after the flood, a principle began to manifest itself among them, wholly adverse to the divine intentions. It was the will of God that the fair regions of the earth should not be left unoccupied, during the many ages which must have elapsed before mankind could reach them, under the slow process of certain portions of the surplus population being successively driven out from the common centre by the pressure of their wants. All the scriptural intimations sustain the explanation to this effect given by Josephus, that they were required to send forth colonies to people the earth; and there can be no doubt that the divine intention in this matter was fully known to the leaders of the people. It was certain that mankind would eventually spread itself out over the different parts of the world. But it is clearly intimated in Scripture, that they were intended to disperse themselves according to their families, that is, in a regular and orderly manner; whereas if they remained together until their wants compelled them to spread forth, only the needy outcasts and desperate characters would go out, and thus a confused mixture of all the families, for as yet they all spoke the same language. By keeping together, also, the population of the world would not increase so rapidly as it would do by this dispersion. Nothing is more clearly established, than that population increases far more rapidly in new countries, where the resources of the land are without limit, than in old ones, where men keep together in masses, whose numbers press closely upon the means of subsistence. These family colonies, if they had gone forth, as they were eventually *compelled* to do, would have become the nucleus of a rapidly growing population in the lands to which they went. There is a very old tradition, that when the population had considerably increased, Noah, who lived long enough after the flood to witness that increase, was commanded to give the needful directions for their migration, dividing the world, as it were, among them. That something of this kind formed the divine plan with respect to the dispersion of men, is shown by the fact, that it was what actually took place when the obstinacy of men, in refusing to follow the course indicated, rendered coercion necessary; for it is evident that the compulsion eventually laid upon them was for no other purpose than to constrain them to take the very course which they had, without compulsion declined to follow.

Well, then, we perceive the several families of Noah's descendants perversely keeping together, leaving many fair regions of the world without inhabitants. Eventually, we find that the population of the still united families had extended itself so far as the land watered by the Tigris and Euphrates, and had come, whether by succession, or consent, or violence, under the chieftainship of "a bold, bad man," of the name of Nimrod. Concerning the *possible* character of this man much has been written; but we really know nothing more than that he was a strong, forceful, and unscrupulous character, a leader of men in his generation, and the first founder of the Assyro-Babylonian empire, which, however small in its beginning, was destined, ages after, to overshadow the nations.

Having come thus far, and finding nothing beyond them to the south and west but inhospitable deserts, they may easily have supposed that their extension had already reached the bounds of the habitable earth; and that to disperse in order to explore those seemingly uninhabitable regions, would be to peril their existence. These apprehensions coincided with the policy of their leader, whose ambition seems to have aimed at nothing less than the rule over mankind, which could only be secured by keeping the families of Noah together. They therefore, perhaps at his suggestion, concluded to make their stand against further dispersion, in the fertile land and by the abundant rivers to which they had come. But coming, as they did, from a land of mountains, and from the sacred shade of Ararat, into a flat plain, seemingly as boundless as the sea; and observing that in this plain—the unexplored extent of which must have been greatly exaggerated in their minds—any marked object, such as a tree, could be seen from a great distance, they concluded to set up a lofty tower, which might at once, as a common centre, be to them what the mountain of the ark had been, and would at the same time declare their purpose not to disperse; and by affording a signal landmark from afar, protect them, as they thought, from being lost or accidentally dispersed in the illimitable plain. In this we may recognize the natural actions of men who, having these objects in view, find themselves for the first time without those landmarks and objects of distant recognition which mountains afford.

So they set about building a city, and therein "a tower whose top should reach unto heaven." They used for this purpose the materials still employed in the same country, where there is no

BIRS NIMROD, BABYLON

stone, and where the dryness of the climate prevents the need of burnt bricks. They constructed their works of sun-dried masses of mud, cemented and strengthened with the bitumen which is abundantly produced in the same region. Two mighty heaps are found on the desolate site of Babylon, formed of the foundations and fallen superstructure of great ancient works thus constructed; and it is thought by some that one of these (either the Mujelibe or the Birs Nimroud) may present the foundations of the very building which those men undertook, but were prevented from completing, although in later ages it may have formed the basis of the tower which counted among the wonders of the ancient world.

" He who sitteth in the heavens " derided this foolish attempt to frustrate His counsels. Hitherto they had all spoken the language of the antediluvians, and of their father Noah, This, indeed, had alone rendered possible the union which they were so anxious to preserve. But God " confounded their language," so that they could no longer understand each other; and they were not only constrained to abandon their work, but their continuance together became no longer convenient or practicable. As the researches of the most learned philologers have appeared to show that the languages of men may be traced to three principal roots, it is enough to suppose that the result was the formation of two new languages, which, with that already existing, would give one to each of the families of Noah; thus constraining their separation, their dispersion, and the fulfilment of their destinies. But if any one think this number of languages inadequate to the proper distribution of mankind, we contend not. It is quite possible that each of these three stems of language might have run into branch dialects, unintelligible to those by whom the other dialects were spoken. A very limited degree of experience suffices to show how unintelligible the different dialects of the same language may become to all but those who use them. Du Bartas, whom we formerly had occasion to quote, gives a graphic and curious account of the immediate effect of the confusion of tongues upon the operations of the builders of Babel:—

" Bring me, quoth one, a trowel, quickly, quick;
One brings him up a hammer : Hew this brick
(Another bids), and then they cleave a tree :
Make fast this rope; and then they let it flee.

One calls for planks; another mortar lacks.
They bear the first a stone; the last an axe.
One would have spikes; and him a spade they give :
Another asks a saw, and gets a sieve;
Thus crossly-crost, they prate and pant in vain :
What one hath made, another mars again."

The Scripture narrative of the confusion of tongues, and the consequent dispersion of men, has become a subject of special interest in the present age. Scientific investigation has been directed with singular diligence and zeal to two subjects—the origin of language, and the origin of man. Darwin's book on *The Origin of Species,* however wild in some of its theories, has done good service in this respect, that it has established on an immovable basis the common origin of mankind. The very first step back in his line of proof shows that all the families of the earth are of one blood; for if the races of the human family are of one species, it follows that they have one origin.

The researches of philologists are no less striking in the testimony they bear, sometimes when it is far from welcome, to the truth of Scripture. It is now ascertained that there are just *three great families* of languages—the Aryan, the Semitic, and the Turanian. In the formation of words and in grammatical structure, these three are widely distinct; whereas there is a very striking similarity in these respects between the different branches of each family. The analogy between the different branches is such as would seem to indicate a natural process of formation and divergence. The most careful researches would also seem to indicate that all the three families radiated primarily from some one point in Central Asia.

Another most remarkable fact has been clearly brought out by Max Müller, in his admirable work on *The Science of Language.* It is this. While the three great families are characterized by wide distinctions in form and structure—distinctions which natural causes cannot fully account for—there is at the same time such an amount of similarity in the leading roots of all three as would indicate something like a common origin. Müller says, " It is possible even now to point out radicals which, under various changes and disguises, have been current in these three branches ever since their first separation;" and again, " Nothing necessitates the admission of different beginnings for the formal elements of the Turanian, Semitic, and Aryan branches of speech."[1]

Does not this tend to illustrate the Scripture narrative of the confusion of tongues? The elements of language still remained with men; the leading root-words which embodied their primary thoughts and perceptions were still retained in the memory; but a miraculous confusion in formation, in structure, and in pronunciation, was effected by divine agency, so that the speech of one family became unintelligible to another. This is most beautifully brought out by a critical examination of the Hebrew text. The literal translation of Gen. xi. 1 is as follows :—" The whole earth was *of one lip,* and of *one stock of words."* These expressions are not synonymous.

[1] *Lectures on the Science of Language,* p. 342, 1st series.

The latter indicates the material of language—its radical words. The former denotes the manner of utterance, the laws of inflection, derivation, and construction. Then in ver. 7, God says, "Let us go down *and confound their lip,* that they may not understand one another's *lip.*" From this we learn that the elements of language—the roots, or stock of words—were not changed; but that the laws of inflection and derivation, and the mode of pronunciation, were confounded.

Thus it is that minute scientific research and accurate Scripture interpretation lead to the same result.

P.

ABRAHAM

Genesis 11:27-29; 12:1-5

AFTER the flood, the sacred narrative rapidly conducts us to the· man, the history of whose descendants—their sins, their sorrows, their excellences, their rewards, and their punishments—forms the great theme of the remainder of the Old Testament. It seems that, in ten generations after the flood, mankind had again corrupted their way, and had fallen very far into forgetfulness of God. Yet God would not again destroy the earth for man's sake. The purpose of the Most High was to choose a man, and in him a family and a nation, to be his witness upon the earth, and the repository of ancient truths, and of Messianic hopes, until the fulness of redeeming time should come.

The person on whom this choice fell was Abraham,[1] the son of Terah, of the line of Shem, whose native place was "Ur of the Chaldees." Besides Abraham, Terah had two sons, Nahor and Haran. Haran, though named last in the sacred text, was plainly the eldest, as was Abraham the youngest, of the three, although for dignity named first; for the father was 70 years old when the first of his sons was born, but he was 130 years old at the birth of Abraham, seeing that his son was 75 years old when his father died at the age of 205. Haram, however, died prematurely "before his father;" and from the emphasis with which this is mentioned, it seems to have been in that age a most extraordinary thing for a man to be

[1] Or rather Abram, as he was at first named ; but we find it convenient to give him throughout the name he subsequently acquired, and by which he is generally known.

cut off in his prime. He left two daughters, named Sarah[1] and Milcah. The former became the wife of Abraham, the latter of his brother Nahor. The son, whose name was Lot, became famous from the connection of his history with that of Abraham. The great seniority of Haran is shown in the fact that his daughter Sarah, who became Abraham's wife, was but ten years younger than Abraham, and his son Lot seems to have been about the same age as the patriarch.

In "Ur of the Chaldees" the word of God came to Abraham, when he was seventy years old, saying, "Get thee out of thy country, and from thy kindred, and come into the land which I shall show thee." Acts vii. 3. The country to which he was to go was not then indicated : he was simply required to detach himself from all the ties of kindred and country, and proceed in a direction to be shown. This was a hard command; but Abraham obeyed it, and forthwith quitted his native land. His father and brother were, however, willing to go with him. But they halted on the way at Haran, in Mesopotamia, from some unknown cause, till the death of Terah, when the command to Abraham was renewed, and the country to which he was to proceed was clearly indicated. This was the land of Canaan, destined to become the possession of this man's descendants. It may be conjectured that the divine intention was to isolate Abraham and his seed completely, by removing him to a strange land : it did not consist with that purpose that he should thus be accompanied by his family into Canaan; but out of regard to his filial affection, Abraham was graciously permitted to remain at Haran, and lay his father's head in the tomb, before any further indication as to the course of his journey was afforded.

It is painful to state, that there can be no doubt that the family of Terah was involved in the general idolatry of the age and country. This is expressly affirmed in Josh. xxiv. 2 : "Your fathers dwelt on the other side of the flood (the Euphrates) in old time, even Terah the father of Abraham and the father of Nahor ; and they served other Gods." It is even asserted by Epiphanius and others, that Abraham's father and grandfather were makers of idolatrous images. Bishop Newton and others question whether men had descended so low in idolatry

[1] Or rather Sarai, as she was named at first ; but we shall call her throughout by her later name.

at this time as to employ images in their worship. But we do not feel so clear on this point, knowing that Laban, belonging to this age, and a member of this family, had images (the teraphim) which he called "his gods," and which were at least used for divination, if not for worship.

Ancient story and tradition undertake to fill up the blank in the early history of Abraham, by informing us of his search after the true God, his discovery of the impotence of idolatry, and his persecution for righteousness' sake. It happens that the name of the place from which Abraham came (Ur) means "fire," on which simple fact is doubtless built the legend of his being cast into the fire by Nimrod (!) and miraculously delivered therefrom.

Nevertheless, seeing that Abraham must have already known the God who required him to quit for his sake all that he held dear, and whom he even to that extent obeyed; and seeing that he had acquired this knowledge while the member of an idolatrous family, he had doubtless meditated much on these things, and had been favoured with special communications by that God who intended to make his name great, and to render him a blessing to many nations.

A specimen or two of the early researches after truth, which Oriental or Jewish tradition ascribes to Abraham, may not be unpleasant to the reader. The Jewish legend is this: Terah was an idolater; and as he went one day on a journey, he appointed Abraham to sell his idols in his stead. As often as a purchaser came, Abraham inquired his age; and when he replied, "I am fifty or sixty years old," he said, "Woe to the man of sixty who would worship the work of a day!"—so that the purchaser went away ashamed.

One day a woman came with a bowl of fine flour, and said, "Set it before them." But he took a staff and broke all the idols in pieces, and put the staff into the hands of the largest of them. When his father returned, he inquired, "Who hath done this?" Abraham said, "Why should I deny it? There was a woman here with a bowl of fine flour, and she directed me to set it before them. When I did so, every one of them would have eaten first; then arose the tallest and demolished them with his staff." Terah said, "What fable art thou telling me? have they any understanding?"

Abraham replied, "Do thy ears hear what thy lips utter?"

Whereupon Terah took him and delivered him to Nimrod, who said to Abraham, "Let us worship the fire."

"Rather the water that quenches the fire."

"Well, the water."

"Rather the cloud which carries the water."

"Well, the cloud."

"Rather the wind which scatters the cloud."

"Well, the wind."

"Rather man, for he endures the wind."

"Thou art a babbler," said the king; "I worship the fire, and will cast thee into it. Can the God whom thou adorest deliver thee thence?" Abraham was then cast into the burning fiery furnace, but was saved by the power of the Lord.

The Mohammedans have also large traditions on the same subject, from mixed Jewish and old Arabian sources. They enter largely into the contest between Abraham and Nimrod, of which we can only give the outline.

Nimrod, forewarned of danger from the birth of a boy, commanded all the male children born at that time to be slain. Abraham was however preserved, and nourished secretly by his mother in a cave, but was sustained far more by miraculous food. There he grew and flourished. On stepping out the first time beyond the cave, he saw a beautiful star, and said, "That is my god, who has given me meat and drink in the cave." But soon the moon arose in full splendour, and made the star look dim. Then he said, "That is not my god, I will worship the moon." But when, towards morning, the moon waxed pale and the sun appeared, he acknowledged the latter for his god, until he also sank below the horizon. He then asked his mother, "Who is my god?" and she replied, "It is I."

"And who is thy god?" he inquired further.

"Thy father."

"And who is my father's god?"

"Nimrod?"

"And Nimrod's god?"

But his mother had by this time got to the end of her resources; so she struck him on the face, and bade him be silent. He was silent; but he thought within himself, "I will acknowledge no other God than He who created heaven and earth, and all that is in them."

Then follows the affair of his destroying the idols, nearly as already given, his being brought before Nimrod, and condemned to the flames. A month was the pile in preparation, and every one who contributed wood to it thought that he did his god service. "The women," it is said, "were especially active. They washed, or did other work for hire, and with their earnings bought wood wherewith to burn the blasphemer." Nimrod, after one more effort to convince Abraham of his own title to divine honours, consigned him to the fire. But God made the flames cool around him. They seemed to burn, but had lost all their warmth. Seven days was his faith tried in the fire; "and," it is beautifully said, "these seven days Abraham, in later times, frequently called the most precious of his life."

UR OF THE CHALDEES.—One of the most important results of recent geographical research has been the discovery of the site and ruins of this ancient city, and of inscribed records on bricks and cylinders, *dating back to the time of Abraham*. The ruins, which now bear the name *Mugheir*, lie about six miles west of the river Euphrates, opposite its junction with Shat-el-Hie, and midway between Babylon and the Persian Gulf. They consist of a circlet of mounds, half a mile in diameter, dotting a vast marshy plain. The name Mugheir is specially given to a building which stands near the north end of the mounds. It is constructed of large bricks, and from their being cemented with bitumen originates the modern appellation Mugheir ("bitumened"). It consists of two massive stories; the lower measuring 198 feet in length, by 133 in breadth, and 27 in height. It is faced with red bricks; but the interior, which is solid, is composed of sun-dried bricks. On one of the bricks an inscription was found, which explains the origin and object of the building: "Orchamus, king of *Ur*, is he who has built this temple of the moon-god."

From his examination of the numerous brick and cylinder inscriptions of Mugheir, Sir Henry Rawlinson regards this as one of the earliest sites colonized in this country. These records bear the names of a series of kings from Urukh, B.C. 2230, to Nabonidas, B.C. 540. Among others is that of *Chedorlaomer* who, with his associates, in the time of Abraham, captured and pillaged Sodom, Gen. xiv. 1. The name Ur, found on many of the bricks and cylinders of Mugheir, proves its identity with "Ur of the Chaldees;" and Sir Henry Rawlinson also discovered that one district of Ur was called *Ibra*, from which he supposes Abraham to have set out for Canaan, and from it came the word *Hebrew*, ever since a name for the Jewish race. The brick and cylinder inscriptions of Mugheir are invaluable, as confirming the authenticity and illustrating the history of the Bible.[1] Many of them are now in the British Museum.   P.

URFAH, SUPPOSED UR OF THE CHALDEES

SARAH IN EGYPT
ROYAL RIGHTS OVER WOMEN

Genesis 12:10-20

ABRAHAM had not been long in Canaan before a severe famine in that land constrained him to withdraw into Egypt. The scarcity, as usual in that country, was doubtless occasioned by a season of drought; and the exemption of Egypt, then and in after ages, from a visitation which afflicted all the neighbouring countries, must be ascribed to the fact, that its productiveness depends not upon rains, but upon the periodical

[1] See an outline of the discoveries at Ur in Kitto's *Cyclopædia of Biblical Literature*, 3d. ed., Art. UR.

overflowings of its river. It was doubtless owing to the same physical advantages that Egypt had already become the place of a wealthy if not of a great nation, and the seat of an organized kingly government and of a luxurious court. The intimation of these facts, which we owe to the mention of Abraham's visit to that country, is abundantly confirmed by its own authentic monuments.

But now a new and strange matter comes to light. Abraham, who had dwelt without fear in the thinly peopled land of Canaan, whose unappropriated lands were still open to nomad pastors, and which seems to have been subject to a number of petty princes or chiefs, not singly more powerful than himself, became alarmed for his safety in going down to Egypt; and the cause of his fear enables us to see that women had already fallen to that low place—valuable only as the property of man—which she has ever since occupied among the settled nations of the East.

Abraham knew that his wife was very beautiful, and his judgment in that respect is confirmed by the dangers into which more than once she was brought by her comeliness. Some persons have ventured to make themselves merry with the idea of Sarah's dangerous beauty at the mature age of sixty-five, and again, much later, when she was ninety years old. Such sneerers forget Ninon de l'Enclos; they forget also Madame de Valentinis, of whom Brantome declares, that at the age of seventy her countenance was as beautiful, as fresh, and as engaging, as if she had been but thirty years old. But it is not necessary to suppose that Sarah was the De l'Enclos or De Valentinis of her age. The life of man was still twice its present length; and according to that, a woman sixty, or even ninety, years old, was still in the prime of life. We are also to remember that Sarah was childless, and had therefore been exempt from that wearing down which the bearing and nutrition of children are said to produce. Nor is it to be forgotten, that she came from a region where the women have fresh and clear complexions, which was likely to be a rare endowment and singular attraction in the eyes of the dusky inhabitants of Egypt, who, if their own monuments do not belie them, were a copper coloured and not remarkably handsome race.

The apprehension of Abraham was no less than that he should be put to death by some of the great ones in Egypt, who might desire to obtain possession of his wife. This apprehension appears to indicate that he knew there was such a respect for the conjugal tie, as would prevent the hand of power from taking his wife by violence from him; and it was more to be feared that they would dissolve that tie, by making her a widow. This is illustrated by the existing practice of the East, where, although the sovereign may take possession of the sisters or daughters of a subject at his pleasure, and without being regarded as having committed an unseemly act of power; to take a man's wife from him against his will, would be such an outrage as even the oriental habit of submission to despotic sovereignty would not long endure.

In this emergency the faith of Abraham failed him, and he resorted to an unworthy expedient, which the occasion may palliate, but cannot justify. He desired his wife to declare that she was his sister. Now it is true that she was the daughter of his half-brother Haran; a relationship which might, according to eastern usage, be properly so described, even as Abraham himself elsewhere calls his nephew Lot his "brother." But the declaration was intended to be taken as a denial that she was his wife, and it was so taken; and it cannot therefore be regarded otherwise than as an equivocation unbecoming the high character of the patriarch. The Jewish writers themselves, who are naturally very anxious to vindicate the character of their great ancestor, do not generally rest their defence on this ground. They allege that he went down into Egypt without authority from God; and that, thinking he had no special claim to the divine protection out of the land of Canaan, in which he had been commanded to sojourn, he was, by the influence of this doubt, led to expedients of human policy and prudence. From this, if true, an important lesson might be drawn; but it is merely a conjecture, founded upon the absence of any intimation that Abraham received express permission to take this important step.

Abraham had not misapprehended the character of the Egyptian court. The arrival of such a large camp as that of himself and Lot, could not but excite attention. "The princes of Pharaoh saw" Sarah, "and commended her before Pharaoh; and the woman was taken into Pharaoh's house." "Of how large a picture," says a recent writer, "may these be faint outlines! The princes of Egypt are struck by the beauty of Sarah : but they are courtiers ; they know no passion but that of gain ; they feel no desire but that of standing well with their king ; and to his presence they hurry. They tell him of the fair stranger ; they speak of her with the warmth of lovers ; their words burn, though their hearts be cold; they are poets in her praise, and the devoted slaves of their sovereign. And what is their object ? what their motive ? They seek to supplant some favourite sultana, or to supply her loss ; to give to a Maintenon the place of a Montespan, or to find a Barry for a Pompadour, and thus to work their way to court honours, court favours, and court pensions. In these princes of Pharaoh we may see the prototypes of the titled valets of the Fourteenth and Fifteenth Louis ; and in this short verse the character of the court memoirs of the seventeenth century."

What thus happened was clearly beyond the calculations of Abraham. He had feared that some powerful and lawless noble might be attracted by the beauty of Sarah, and endeavour to get rid of him if it were known that she was his wife; but he calculated that, if she passed for his sister, any such person would make proposals to him for her; and he probably reckoned that he might temporize with the suitor, on questions of dower and other matters, until the famine ceased. But if he could have foreseen that the king himself would have sought her, he would have known it to be safer that she should appear as his wife than as his sister. The king, in his high public capacity, would hardly have dared to outrage public opinion, by rending a wife from the bosom of her husband. But a sister he might, as public opinion went, take without offence, without the consciousness of wrong-doing, and without the parties having any right to complain. We see this more clearly still in the later but nearly parallel case of Abimelech, king of Gerar, who, although he must certainly have taken Sarah away, under the same apprehension, without seeking the consent of either party, is acknowledged to have done this " in the integrity of his heart, and the innocency of his hands." Awful it is to think that such grievous infractions of personal liberty, and encroachments upon the dignity and delicacy of women, should, even in this early age, have come to be regarded as a public right. It is probable, however, that Pharaoh felt he had unduly stretched his power in dealing thus with a great pastoral chief, who was no subject of his, and had only come to sojourn for a short time in his land. And this consciousness may account for his princely munificence to Abraham, whom he treated well for his sister's sake, bestowing upon him a large abundance of property suited to his condition—sheep, oxen, asses, camels, and slaves.

But although Abraham, by his resort to human policy, had made too light of God's protection, that God had not forgotten His servant, nor left him to the consequences of his own acts. The house of the Egyptian king was smitten with a disease which made him see that he was under a divine judgment. His inquiries probably led Sarah to disclose that she was Abraham's wife ; and on learning this fact, he forthwith sent for him, and the words which he uttered must have been felt by the patriarch as a strong rebuke : "What is this that thou hast done unto me ? Why didst thou not tell me that she is thy wife ? Why saidst thou, She is my sister ? so I might have taken her to me to wife : now therefore behold thy wife, take her, and go thy way." And in fact he was hurried out of the country, with all belonging to him ; the king being apparently fearful that it should transpire among his own people that he had, even unwittingly, taken away a man's wife from him.

Among the Egyptian papyri, in the British Museum, is one called the *Papyrus d'Orbiney*, a fac-simile of which has been published. "It contains nineteen pages of hieratic writing, remarkably clear and legible ; the style is simple, and presents fewer difficulties than any similar document." It furnishes a curious story—said to be the earliest fiction in existence—relative to one of the Pharaohs, who, informed by his brother of the beauty of a certain woman, sent two armies to murder her husband, and to bring her off as a prize for his own harem. The incidents described are of the wildest description, but the sketch given of Egyptian manners and customs is very graphic, and apparently truthful; the period of the story and its composition being the reign of Rameses II., a king of the nineteenth dynasty. This, according to the best schemes of Egyptian chronology, is later than the time of Abram, and cannot be a contemporary record of anything referring to the patriarch ; but it affords, at least in some degree, an instance of that kind of interference with matrimonial rights, which Abram feared might occur when he went down to Egypt. And this part of the patriarchal history is illustrated by what is found in a papyrus, preserved at Berlin, belonging to the twelfth dynasty. The wife and children of a foreigner are described as becoming the property of the king, even as Sarai was seized and conveyed to the royal palace. Though such related incidents are no historical proofs of what happened to Abram, they indicate that occurrences of the kind were not unknown to the Egyptians. Moreover, in the sepulchral monuments at Beni-Hassan, pertaining to the reign of Osirtasin II., a king of the twelfth dynasty, contemporary, according to some modern Egyptian scholars, with the founder of the Hebrew race, there is a picture of a nomad chief, with his family and dependants, seeking protection from an Egyptian sovereign. The name of the chief is Absha, which some, without sufficient reason, have endeavoured to identify with Abram. Others, again, have thought that they could discover in the figures depicted, Israel and his sons with their wives, entering the land when Joseph was governor. Indeed, in some books, the picture has been copied with the title "Arrival of Jacob's Family in Egypt." But though this idea must be given up, the scene remains as a truthful representation of intercourse between foreigners and the monarch and court on the Nile banks, of refuge sought on the one side, and hospitality afforded on the other. For further information on these interesting points, see Wilkinson's *Ancient Egyptians*, II. 296 ; Speaker's *Commentary*, I. 217, 445 ; *Bible Educator*, I. 103.

S.

GOD'S PURPOSES AND MAN'S DEVICES

IF we look closely into that portion of Abraham's history which has lately engaged our attention, we shall find much matter for profitable thought therein.

It is among the sayings of the wisest of men, " There are many devices in a man's heart; nevertheless the counsel of the Lord, that shall stand;" Prov. xix. 21. Not only Scripture history, but the history of the world, is full of evidences of this serious and important truth; it is written as with a sunbeam throughout creation, and in the whole state of man. Yet there is scarcely any truth which we so habitually forget or overlook. It is well, therefore, that we should suffer our minds to dwell upon every circumstance in our experience or our reading, and especially in our reading of God's word, which may serve to impress so great a fact in man's history—so great a fact in the history of every one of us—as this, upon our remembrance. We have had before us a circumstance of this character: for it seems that Abraham, acting without sufficient reference to the will of God, which he might have ascertained, chalked out for himself what must have

seemed to him a very sagacious and politic course of proceeding. But this course of conduct not only did not produce the effect he contemplated and desired, but was attended by the very results which he most dreaded and most laboured to avert. Nothing of all that had been devised remained unshaken, save the counsel of God.

Thus, in the first place, by leaving the land of Canaan for Egypt, the patriarch expected that he might abide there in tranquillity until the period of the famine had passed away. But the result was far otherwise. He was compelled to quit Egypt after a very short stay, and to return to the famine-stricken land, where God—"whose eye is upon them that fear Him, upon them that hope in His mercy, to deliver their soul from death, and to keep them alive in famine " (Ps. xxxiii. 18, 19)—sustained him and his numerous household in ease and plenty.

Again, the evil which Abraham apprehended with respect to Sarah did indeed happen, but it was brought about by the very means he had taken to avert it ; and there is every reason to suppose that, had he from the first boldly declared that she was his wife, relying upon the protection of God, nothing of the kind would have taken place. As it was, this very device of passing her off for his sister, which was designed to secure his safe sojourn amid the plenty of Egypt, became the very instrument for compelling his return to the dearth of Canaan.

Now, let us not whisper to our own hearts, that we are in this, at least, wiser than Abraham. Alas ! it is not so. There are few of us whose wisest things are wiser than the foolishness of Abraham. Do we not every day speculate with confidence upon the results of this or of that undertaking or course of action ? Do we not every day calculate, with little misgiving, that this or that course of proceeding towards another, or with reference to particular circumstances, can hardly fail to produce the effect we have in view? But does it produce that effect ? Seldom more so than in the case of Abraham. There are few, if any, whose course of action in any particular matter has led to the very results which they had in view, or has yielded all the fruit they expected to gather from it. There are few, if any, whose prosperity, whose comfort, whose safety, has grown out of their own carefully planned and deliberated measures; few, if any, who do not know that their advantages have proceeded from circumstances which they never had in view, which formed no part of their own plans, and over which their own course of action had no conceivable influence. Many of us may have been enabled to do something wiser, greater, better than ever entered our minds; but this result has been brought about perhaps in a way contrary to what our judgment or will originally proposed, and through the overruling providence of Him, "of whom, and through whom, and to whom are all things."

What shall we say to these things? There is nothing better than that a man should live in the feeling that it is not in his purpose, but the purpose of God, that must stand sure. He may have plans and designs—indeed the business of life cannot well go on without them; but he must know that God is not bound by his plans, and is under no obligation to bestow his prospering blessing upon his designs. God has a plan of his own for every one of us. If our plans agree with with His, well—He may bless them; but if not, He will either make them promote the purpose which He intends, and which we did not intend, or will try our faith by blasting our cherished plans altogether—that He may bless us in His own way, and lead us to safety, to usefulness, to success, by paths that we know not of, and by ways that never did enter, nor could enter, our minds. Let us not, therefore, be discouraged, if our plans do not answer our wishes—if everything turns wrong upon our hands. We know that He is not unkind; we know that He does not forget us; and we have reason to hope that He only brings our own small plans and devices to nought because He has something of His own— something larger, something better in store for us. How many are there to whom God had not spoken comfortably until He lured them into the wilderness, where the soul, withdrawn from amid the ruins of its broken plans and frustrated hopes, is now alone with Him, sees Him alone, leans on Him only!

Oh for the blessedness of that man who has been enabled to realize the most entire conviction—and that not as a theory, but as a practical truth—that God doeth all things well, and that His work is perfect! The grinding and low cares of this life have no place with him. He knows that all his affairs are guided by One who cannot err—that he is watched over for good by One who is never weary. Human friends may weary of him, and shake him off, if he becomes troublesome by his wants; but he heeds this little —his God invites, solicits, is gratified, by the entireness of his dependence, and the full and undivided burden of his cares. Strange it is, that we are so slow to claim the rights thus given to us, and which we ought to regard as inestimable privileges. How few are they, known to any of us, who do truly realize the many precious promises and gracious invitations to do that which can alone make this life tolerable! How few are they who realize experimentally the declaration of the prophet, "O Lord, *I know* that the way of man is not in himself; it is not in man that walketh to direct his steps!"[1] Or this: "Except the Lord build the house, they labour in vain that build it; except the Lord keep the city, the watchman waketh but in vain. It is in vain for you to rise up early, to sit up late, to eat the bread of sorrows; for so He giveth His beloved sleep."[2]

May God give to us that sleep, that perfect rest amid all the labours, turmoils, and cares of life, which only His beloved can know, because they only have unreserved confidence in Him, and can trust their bodies no less than their souls to his care!

PATRIARCHAL WEALTH

Genesis 12:16; 13:2

IT is well that we should entertain some distinct ideas respecting the real condition of the patriarchal fathers as to wealth and power. The history dwells so little on these matters, that it requires some experience of the corresponding condition of life, as it still subsists in the East, to apprehend the force of the few intimations which do incidentally transpire.

There are probably few readers who conceive further of Abraham's establishment, than that it consisted of one, or at most two or three tents, with some half-a-dozen servants, and flocks of sheep and other cattle feeding around. Now this is altogether wrong. His encampment must have formed, so to speak, quite a village of tents, with inhabitants equal to the population of a large village or a small town. Great numbers

[1] Jeremiah 10:23.   [2] Psalms 127:1,2.

of women and children were to be seen there, and some old men; but not many men in their prime, these being for the most part away, from a few to many miles off, with the flocks, of which there was probably less display immediately around the tents than the lowest of the common estimates of Abraham's station would assume.

We are told that Abraham was "very rich," and it is stated of what his riches consisted; but we are not told of the amount of these riches which he possessed. However, by putting circumstances together, we may arrive at some notions not far from the truth.

We have the strong fact to begin with, that Abraham was treated by the native princes and chieftains of the land as "a mighty prince," an equal, if not a superior, to themselves. Then we learn that his house-born slaves, able to bear arms and to make a rapid march, followed by a daring enterprise, were not less than three hundred and eighteen. A body of such men can be furnished only by a population four times its own number, including women and children. We cannot therefore reckon the patriarch's camp as containing less than 1,272 souls; and this number of people could not well have been accommodated in so few as a hundred tents.

Now as to the cattle. One of the most tangible statements we can find, is of the wealth of the same sort which, in or about the same age, rendered Job "the greatest of all the men of the east;" making some allowance for the fact that Job was not exactly a nomad shepherd, but cultivated the ground also, and had a fixed residence. His wealth consisted of 7,000 sheep, 3,000 camels, 1,000 (500 yoke of) oxen, and 500 asses. Now it appears to us, that the wealth of a camp whose chief numbered above a thousand dependants, could not well have been less. Let us, however, test this by another computation. Jacob, when he was returning to Canaan with the pastoral wealth he had gained during his twenty years' sojourn in Padan-aram, set apart a selection from his stock of animals wherewith to placate his offended brother. Now, as we know the number of the animals in this costly offering, we should have something to go by if we could tell what proportion this present bore to the whole of his possessions. Was it a tenth, the proportion which Abraham thought a fit offering to a king? We think it was probably

more, because Esau feared to impoverish his brother by taking so much from him, and was only prevailed upon to do so, by Jacob's declaring that he had still enough. Take it, then, at one-fifth. Now it is hardly to be supposed that the wealth which Jacob had been able to acquire by his twenty years' service in Mesopotamia, was at all comparable to that which had been formed by Abraham in the course of more than thrice the time, on the basis of a large inheritance, and enhanced by his acquisitions in Egypt; and still less to the same property as increased during a long lapse of years by Isaac; and least of all to the property which was formed when Jacob's own separate acquisitions were added to the paternal stock. Let us therefore make what, under the circumstances, is a very moderate calculation—let us assume that Jacob's offering to Esau was one-fifth of his substance, and that Jacob's whole substance was equal to one-third of the patriarchal property of the same kind in Canaan. Under this view, the first column in the subjoined table shows Jacob's offering to Esau; the second column gives that amount quintupled; the third exhibits the latter amount trebled; and the fourth column shows Job's property of the same kinds, for the sake of comparison:—

	Esau.	Jacob.	Patriarch.	Job.
Goats, ...	220	1100	3300	—
Sheep, ...	220	1100	3300	7000
Camels and Colts,	60	300	900	3000
Oxen, ...	50	250	750	1000
Asses and Foals, .	30	150	450	500

These calculations appear to us to be corroborated by their near coincidence with the account of Job's wealth. The only serious difference is in camels, and that is very great. The difference as to sheep is more apparent than real; for although Job has twice the number of sheep which is assigned to the patriarchal family, he has no goats; and the patriarchal goats and sheep together form a number only 400 less than the 7,000 sheep of Job.

The chief difference is caused by either the extraordinary abundance of camels in the account of Job's wealth, or the extraordinary deficiency of these animals in the stock of Jacob. We have counted the foals in the estimate of the latter, and yet the number is small in proportion to that of other animals. Upon the whole, we incline to think that Jacob, coming from Mesopotamia, where to this day camels are few in comparison with those possessed in and on the borders of Arabia, had not the usual proportion of these animals, and that, with respect to them, the estimate formed on the basis of his present to his brother, does not adequately represent the wealth of the patriarchs in Canaan. There is every probability that the number possessed by them was as large in proportion to their other cattle as in the case of Job.

It cannot fail to strike the attention of the most cursory reader, that horses, which form so important a part of the modern Bedouin's possessions, are altogether absent in the statements of the same kinds of wealth belonging to Abraham, Jacob, and Job. It is scarcely possible that the animal should have been unknown to them. In fact, although Job did not possess horses, his book contains the most magnificent description of a war-horse that has ever been given; Job xxxix. 19-25. Again, although there is no mention of horses among the animals which Abraham received from the king of Egypt, this cannot well have been owing to the want of them in that country; for they are found in the most ancient sculptures, and are in this very book mentioned as present in the funeral procession of Jacob from Egypt to the land of Canaan. The truth probably is, that horses were in these early ages used entirely for warlike purposes, and that the powerful patriarchs were averse to the responsibility attached to the use or possession of such animals, especially in a country like Canaan, to which the employment of horses, even for war, does not seem to have at this time extended. This view of the exclusively warlike character of the horse in early times, throws some light upon the injunction in the law against the use of horses; Deut. xvii. 16.

I find from conversation with thoughtful men in this country upon the scriptural accounts of patriarchal life, that it is not unusual to suppose that the numbers of the flocks and herds as given by the sacred writers are either exaggerated, or else that they have been in some way tampered with. That Job really possessed 7,000 sheep and 3,000 camels, or that 50,000 camels and 250,000 sheep could have been taken by the Israelites from the Ishmaelitish tribes (1 Chron. v. 21), is thought incredible. My personal knowledge of the wealth of many of the great desert tribes would have convinced me, had I required any such proof, that the Bible narratives are in this respect, as in all others, literally true. In the spring of 1857, I was for two days among the Wulid Ali Bedawîn.

They had more than three hundred tents; and I estimated the number of their camels at from thirty to forty thousand. When travelling to Palmyra in 1851, I passed through several subdivisions of the Sebâ tribe. Their flocks and herds were spread over the plains far as the eye could see. I was told that it was no uncommon thing for the camels to cover the pasture grounds to a distance of a day's journey from the tents. On one occasion I was partly witness to a successful Arab raid upon the flocks of Hums and Hamath, in the valley of the Orontes, in which they were said to have captured no less than *thirty thousand* sheep and goats.

These facts illustrate some of those stirring incidents of patriarchal life recorded in Scripture. They show, too, how natural was the statement of the sacred writer in regard to Abraham and Lot—"The land was not able to bear them, that they might dwell together: for their substance was great, so that *they could not* dwell together;" Gen. xiii. 6.

P.

THE TENT

Genesis 13:3

It is an interesting fact, which we have already had occasion to notice,[1] that the house was earlier than the tent, and the settled than the migratory condition of life. No sooner, however, did man betake himself to that mode of life which obliged him to move often from place to place in search of pasturage, than he found it necessary to devise some kind of portable habitation. It would be interesting to trace, were it possible, the stages by which tents reached the form and texture which they have now for many ages retained in South-western Asia. The limitation to this region is necessary; for the quality of these portable habitations depends very much upon the climate, and other local circumstances of the country in which they are found. It is by no means probable, that the tents invented by Jabal before the Deluge were in all respects the same as those which formed the encampment of the patriarchs in the land of Canaan—even apart from the question, whether the climate of the region in which Jabal wandered was not materially different from that in which Abraham sojourned.

Thus, in well wooded countries, temporary habitations are often, in various parts of the world, formed of the interwoven branches of trees, constructed so rapidly, and with so little

[1] *Daily Bible Illustrations* Vol. 1, pp. 194-195.

cost of labour, as to be abandoned without regret when the station is quitted; and if a return is made thereto, new dwellings are formed in the same manner, while the dry materials of the previous encampment, left formerly on the spot, then become useful as fuel. It is by no means clear that the patriarchs did not resort to this plan, perhaps as an agreeable change, when the nature of the country allowed. What else was the "house" that Jacob dwelt in for a time on his return from Mesopotamia?[1] It is even likely that the Israelites, during their forty years' wandering, did not live wholly in tents. In the annual commemoration of their pilgrimage in the feast of tabernacles, they lived, not in tents, but in booths made of green boughs.[2] This would have been very inappropriate, had not such habitations been in partial use by the Israelites during the time of their sojourning; for a tent would have been in many respects better suited for commemorative purposes, as a family that once possessed it could retain it many years for that service. A tent is, however, a better habitation than a booth; and since, in every large encampment, as in a large village or town, there must have been some indigent persons, it is likely that these possessed no tents, but constructed for themselves, at each removal, temporary habitations of such materials as could be found on the spot, and these would frequently be booths of green branches.

In some parts of the East, as among the Hindus, the tents or huts are of bamboo or osier reeds, and easily portable. We have ourselves seen the encampments of Arabian and Kurdish tribes wholly formed of reeds; but this is chiefly on the banks of rivers, where such materials are easily obtained.

Portable habitations may even be rendered suitable to the exigencies of severe climates. Thus, the Samoede constructs a somewhat warm habitation with the bark of trees, sewed together and covered over with skins. This is, however, a later invention, when men got into climates where they found that the tent of skin alone was an insufficient protection from the severity of the cold.

Perhaps the most perfect and convenient habitation of this class, at least of all the different kinds with which we have ourselves had occasion

[1] Genesis 33:17.
[2] Leviticus 23:42; Nehemiah 8:14-17.

to become acquainted, is that of the Kalmuk Tartar. It owes its completeness, probably, to its being required to afford shelter not only from the heat in summer, but from somewhat severe cold in winter. These tents consist of a number of parts, which are easily put together and taken to pieces. They are round, with a funnel-shaped

KALMUK TARTAR TENTS

roof, and blunt at the top. The framework is composed of willow laths about an inch thick, perforated where they cross, and fastened with leathern thongs. Six or eight pieces of lattice-work, when fastened together with woollen bands, compose a circular wall not quite the height of a man. The doorway is inserted separately in its own frame, and consists of two small folding valves. From this lower framework proceed a number of poles on every side, meeting in a common centre above, where they are intercepted by a sort of hoop having holes in which their extremities are inserted. Over these poles a few woollen girths are passed crosswise, and attached to the framework below. The whole of the skeleton is then covered over with coarse, porous, unfulled felts, of considerable size, secured by woollen girths and bands.

Seeing that this kind of habitation originated in the pastoral life, we incline to think that the original tents were covered with skins—the skins of sheep or goats, at first probably with the wool or hair on, but eventually the skin alone, separated from the hair, and, in time, prepared with various leys and earths, so as to resist the influences of heat and wet. When men became hunters—for the pastoral preceded the hunting life—they for the most part retained this form of tent, with this difference, that it was covered with the skins of the beasts of their pursuit, instead of those they tended. Hence the tent or wigwam of the North American Indian is covered with the skins of bisons, instead of the skins of sheep. This is almost the sole difference. There is a trace of this use of skins for the

NORTH AMERICAN INDIAN WIGWAMS

covering of tents in the Pentateuch; for one of the coverings of the splendid tabernacle constructed in the wilderness, was of "rams' skins dyed red." Why "dyed red?" Doubtless the skins were prepared with some red ochreous matter, which would have the effect of throwing off the rain, thereby protecting the more costly inner coverings.

At the present day, and as far back as historical intimations extend, the tents of south-western Asia have been of wool or goats' hair, usually dyed black, if not naturally of that colour, or else in broad stripes of black and white. They are, in fact, of cloth, woven in the camp by the women, from the produce of the flocks. Such, without doubt, are most of the tents mentioned in Scripture. The women in the wilderness spun and wove goats' hair coverings for the tabernacle;[1] and in Solomon's Song,[2] black is the colour ascribed to Arabian tents.

Still, it is not very clear whether the patriarchal tents were of skin, or felt, or cloth. As tents of skin were the earliest, the continued use of skin coverings, together with those of woven cloth in the tents of the wilderness, may be thought to imply that the latter were a com-

ARABIAN TENT

paratively recent invention, seeing that it had not yet wholly driven out the older usage. Nevertheless, we incline to think that the patri-

[1] Exodus 35:26. [2] Song of Solomon 1:5.

archal tents were much the same as those which we now find among the Arabian tribes. These are mostly of an oblong shape, and eight or nine feet high in the middle. They vary in size, and have, accordingly, a greater or lesser number of poles to support them—from three to nine. If the sheikh or emir is a person of much consequence, he may have three or four tents for his own purposes,—one for himself, one for his wives, one for his immediate servants, and one for the entertainment of strangers. It is more usual, however, for one very large tent to be divided into two or more apartments by curtains; and this is the model followed in the holy tabernacle.[1] The patriarchal tents were probably not of the largest class. We find that the principal members of the family had each a separate tent—as Sarah, Leah, Rachel, and the maid-servants.[2] That they consisted of but one apartment, seems probable from the fact, that the camel furniture in the same chamber with the sick Rachel excited no suspicion;[3] and that single apartment, except perhaps in the rainy season, may have been used for sleeping merely, as Abraham at Mamre received and entertained the three strangers outside his tent.[4] Yet these tents, whatever their size or quality, were considered valuable, for "tents" are mentioned among the possessions of Lot.[5]

As the whole camp belonged to the patriarch, and consisted of persons for whom he was bound to provide, these were all doubtless accommodated in the tents. But it is not so in ordinary encampments, which usually include many who are too poor to have any tent. Such contrive to shelter themselves from the inclemencies of the weather by a piece of cloth stretched out upon poles, or by retiring to the cavities of the rocks. This was also the case in the patriarchal age; for Job describes the poor as "embracing the rock for want of shelter."[6] Trees have become too scarce in those regions to afford booths to such persons now; but as the shade of trees is very agreeable in a very warm climate, the Bedouins, like the patriarchs, are at great pains to find out shaded situations for their encampments. Abraham's tent at Mamre was under a tree,[7] and at Beersheba in a grove.[8]

[1] Exodus 26:31-37.
[2] Genesis 24:67; 31:33.
[3] Genesis 31:34,35.
[4] Genesis 18:4-8.
[5] Genesis 13:5.
[6] Job 24:8.
[7] Genesis 18:4.
[8] Genesis 21:33.

THE FIRST WAR

Genesis 14

THE fourteenth chapter of Genesis is of deep interest to the student of ancient usages. It contains a brief and rapid, but suggestive history, not indeed of the first war, but of the first war of which any record has been transmitted to us. The history itself implies the existence of previous wars; and the manner in which this war is conducted, evinces that men had already gained much experience in the art of afflicting and destroying their fellows.

It appears that certain kings from beyond the region of the Tigris and Euphrates, whether independent or acting under some great power is uncertain, had at a former period invaded the country formed by, and extending along the east side of the valley of the Jordan, and of the hollow valley called the Arabah, which at the present day reaches from the Dead Sea to the eastern arm of the Red Sea. It is difficult to account for their confining their operations to this line, and making no attempt upon the comparatively rich country *west* of the Jordan, without assuming that the object was to obtain the possession or the command of a line of country which was at once a natural frontier westward, and an important military and commercial route. If this power at the same time held possession of Egypt, as some suppose, and constituted the intrusive dynasty known in history as the Hyksos, or shepherd kings, the necessity of keeping open this line of communication with that country must be obvious.

Whatever were the precise objects of the expedition, or the nature of the power brought into action, it was successful, and all the tribes and nations upon this line were brought into subjection.

Under this subjection they continued for twelve years, when they ventured to throw off this foreign yoke. They were in due time called to account for this. It was in the thirteenth year of their subjection that they rebelled: and in the fourteenth their former conquerors reappeared in the north, and pursuing their victorious march southward along the western border of the valley, from the sources of the Jordan to the Red Sea, returned northward along the country west of the Arabah,[1] subduing the tribes by which that district was inhabited. Approaching still farther north, they descended into the valley, purposing to reduce the towns in the enclosed plain, which now forms the basin of the Dead Sea, but which was then beautifully fertile and well inhabited. The principal towns were five: Sodom, Gomorrah, Admah, Zeboiim, and Zoar. In the first of these Abraham's nephew, Lot, had his abode; for soon after their return from Egypt, the great increase of their substance, and the consequent quarrels of their shepherds about rights of water and pasturage, had constrained them to separate. One would think that the invading force was not large, for the inhabitants of these towns and neighbouring villages determined to give it battle, although returning victorious and laden with the spoil of conquered places.

The conflict was soon, however, decided in favour of the invaders. The beaten citizens of the Pentapolis fled before them, and many of them lost their lives in the " slime pits " which were at that day visible, and which still, under the deep waters, throw up their asphaltum. The conquerors then plundered the towns, and crossing the plain, passed out of it on the east side laden with spoil, and followed by a train of captives destined for bondage. Among the captives was Lot, and his substance was among the spoil.

Abraham was no farther off than Mamre, near Hebron; and yet, as the invaders had carefully avoided trespassing on the proper land of Canaan, to which the vale of Siddim (as it was called) was not regarded as belonging, the transaction does not seem to have engaged his attention till one of the fugitives brought him the intelligence. No sooner did the patriarch learn that Lot was among the captives, than he at once decided to pursue the conquerors, and rescue his nephew from their hands.

For this purpose he armed as many of his slaves as were fit for the service. They were three hundred and eighteen, and were exclusively such as had belonged to him from their birth ("born in his own house"), as he could better rely upon their zeal and devotedness than on the slaves who had been presented to him (as in Egypt), or had been "bought with his money." Considering the distance from Hebron, the pur-

[1] The prevalent name of the broad valley which extends from the Dead Sea to the eastern arm of the Red Sea.

suit probably occupied three days, as the enemy were not overtaken till they reached the sources of the Jordan. Here they lay for the night, free from all suspicion of danger, weary probably with the rapid march they had made, and burdened with spoils and captives. Abraham's manner of dealing with a force doubtless much greater than his own, was similar to that of Gideon in a later age, who, indeed, may very possibly have taken the hint from this memorable action of his great progenitor. In the darkness of the night he divided his force, and directed an assault to be made upon the secure and sleeping host, at once on different sides, probably with great outcries. The enemy, confused by so unexpected an attack, which must have led them to entertain most exaggerated ideas of the assailants' force, soon fell into disorder and fled, hotly pursued by the victors, who did not give over the pursuit until they had reached the neighbourhood of Damascus. All the spoil that had been taken away was thus recovered; and of all the persons, not a woman or a little child was lost.

Night attacks of this nature are still common in the East, and are generally successful, if the assailants can so contrive that the enemy shall have no intimation of their intention. The movements are usually so timed, that the assailants arrive on the ground late at night, or rather towards morning, when it is certain that the men of the camp, against which the expedition is aimed, are in their deepest sleep. Such operations are also much facilitated by the great and extraordinary neglect of keeping watch at night, which is still the characteristic of eastern military or predatory operations, and of which there are most remarkable examples in Scripture.

By the usage of the East, all the spoil that had been recovered belonged to him by whom it had been recaptured, while the persons who had been rescued returned to their former condition. Accordingly, the kings of the plundered towns, who met their deliverer on his returning march, proposed to Abraham, through the king of Sodom, that he should retain the goods, and return the persons to them. But the truly great patriarch, whose disinterestedness in this respect can only be appreciated by those who have studied the class of sentiments which belong to the condition of life in which he moved, declared that not a particle of all this vast spoil should remain with him; and to preclude all remonstrance, he said

that he had already taken a most solemn oath to that effect: "I have lifted up mine hand (in the act of taking an oath) to the most high God, the possessor of heaven and earth, that I will not take from a thread even to a shoe latchet, and that I will not take anything that is thine." And why not? what was the special motive that influenced him? It was the becoming spirit of independence. He did not conceal it. It was, he said, "Lest thou shouldst say, 'I have made Abraham rich.'" This he could not endure, at least not from strangers with whom his relations were not peculiarly amicable, whose character was indeed objectionable, and whom he had served merely for the sake of Lot.

This transaction must, however, have greatly enhanced the credit and influence of Abraham in the land of his sojourning; and it doubtless materially contributed to procure for him that respect and consideration with which we subsequently find him treated by the native chiefs and princes of the country.

A few points in this chapter are worthy of more special note in these days, as showing the minute historical and geographical knowledge of the sacred writer. It seems highly probable that the narrative was originally written by Abraham, for he was personally acquainted both with that region of Central Asia from which the invaders came, and with the country which they ravaged.

A few years ago, Mr. Loftus exhumed from the desolate mounds which now mark the site of Ur of the Chaldees, an inscribed tablet containing a list of the rulers of Chaldæa; and in that list is the name of *Chedorlaomer*, one of the four kings here mentioned.

The route of the invading force is traced with singular exactness of detail. They first attacked the "Rephaims in Ashteroth Karnaim," situated among the mountains of Bashan; then they marched southward upon the Zuzims and Emims, who inhabited the high table land east of the Dead Sea; they next proceeded to Mount Seir (Edom), amid whose wild ravines the Horites originally dwelt; then turning westward, they crossed the great valley of Arabah into the wilderness of Paran. This was the utmost range of the expedition. Wheeling round, they reached the fountain of Kadesh, which at that period appears to have been regarded as both a sanctuary and an oracle.[1] Here they probably rested for a time. Setting out again, they swept the country of the Amalekites, which lay along the southern declivity of the Judæan mountains. Then they marched northward, and defiling through the ravines of the wilderness of Judah, attacked Engedi, which, from its palm groves, was anciently called Hazezon-Tamar. They were now on the borders of the rich plain of Sodom.

[1] The name *Kadesh* signifies "holy place;" and *En-Mishpat* means "fountain of judgment," or of "the oracle."

The inhabitants seeing their danger, made a united effort to oppose the invaders. They were defeated; their cities were captured; and the conquerors, laden with booty, retired slowly up the Jordan valley.

Abraham was encamped at Hebron. A fugitive carried to him the intelligence, probably on the evening of the day of the conflict. He would require a day to collect his "trained servants," and at least four to reach Dan, where he overtook the retreating host. He attacked them at night. And he must have followed them during the whole of that night and the next day; for we are told that he "pursued them unto Hobah, which is upon the left hand (or north) of Damascus," and which is nearly fifty miles from Dan, on the other side of Anti-Lebanon.

It is a remarkable fact, that one of the most ancient sanctuaries around Damascus is about three miles *north* of the city, and is called *Makâm Ibrahîm*, "the Station of Abraham." The story goes that here the patriarch worshipped God on turning back after his great victory.

P.

KINGS AND KINGDOMS— MELCHIZEDEK

Genesis 14:18-20

SEVERAL kings of Canaan are mentioned in the fourteenth chapter of Genesis. We must not allow ourselves to entertain any large ideas of their power and greatness. In the area of the present Dead Sea alone, which, if it was not even then occupied by a lake, as some suppose it to have been, did not exceed some of our smaller English counties in extent, there were no fewer than five "kings;" and at even a considerably later period there were thirty-one in that portion of the small country of Canaan which Joshua was enabled to conquer. The fact clearly is, that each of these kings was no other than the head man, sheikh, or chief, of some considerable town and the district belonging thereto. They seem to have been independent of each other in the management of their own affairs; but, as in the case of the kings of the plain, the princes of a particular district appear to have combined in such matters as were of general concernment to them all. Whether, with respect to such outside affairs, they allowed a sort of superiority to one of their number—say the chief of the most important town in the locality—cannot with certainty be stated. But we think that this was the case; not only because it is seen that

this is the course which small tribes or communities are led by experience to regard as the best in times of war and trouble, but because there appears, even in this narrative, some faint indication that the king of Sodom was, during this transaction, regarded as the leader of the five kings of the plain. We know also, that at the later period to which we have just referred, and in the same neighbourhood, one of five "kings" of this description assumed the leadership of the others in a time of danger, and directed the movements of their united force: Josh. x. Such power was probably only temporary, for we find that under analogous circumstances, among the Syro-Arabian tribes, great and jealous care is taken to exact the entire abdication, on the return of peace, of all the authority of leadership conceded, for the common good, in time of war and trouble. It is, indeed, highly probable that the eventual formation of larger dominions, originated in the successful attempts of such leaders to retain permanently the power thus temporarily entrusted to them.

It may be stated that, even at the present day, the same and the neighbouring countries offer some tolerable analogies to the state of things indicated. Every town and village has its sheikh, by whom almost all its concerns are managed, with the aid and counsel of the other principal inhabitants. If the country is not in a well organized state, this personage makes war with other towns, and enters into alliance with the wandering tribes that frequent the neighbourhood; and on him devolves the duty of entertaining strangers. He is accountable to the general government; but he is rarely interfered with, so long as he provides the taxes due from his place, and so long as the inhabitants make no complaint against him. Suppose this sheikh independent, instead of subject to a general government, and we have in him, as it seems to us, one whose situation very nearly corresponds to that of the kings of Canaan. In fact, except in the Syro-Arabian provinces of the Turkish empire, these chiefs are called *sultans;* and we can well remember the surprise which the large ideas attached to this title, as appropriated by us to the grand seignior, created, when we *first* heard its application to a rough old man, nowise distinguishable in manner, appearance, dress, or mode of living, from the other inhabitants of the place. Now, here is a perfectly analogous instance to

the scriptural one, of the same title being applied
to the chief of a village, and the lord of an empire. Our own small island once formed many
kingdoms; but the kings of the heptarchy were,
in regard to extent of dominion, mighty sovereigns compared with the ancient kings of
Canaan.

A disorganised society falls back into the same
state as an unorganised society; and when the
general government is weak, the local chiefs become almost or wholly independent. Hence we
read, in William of Tyre, that, during the Crusades, when king Bohemund laid siege to Arsur,
"several kings" came down from the mountains
of Samaria to the plain of Antipatris, bringing
with them bread and wine, and dried figs and
raisins. These "kings" were doubtless such as
we have described, and such as the ancient kings
of Canaan were.

This incident is in itself strikingly analogous
to what happened to Abraham; for we are told
that Melchizedek, king of Salem, "brought forth
bread and wine" to him, on his victorious return
from the slaughter of the kings. The simple fact
of the similarity, not only of the act, but of the
refreshments offered, is the best answer to the
opinion advanced by some of the old Romanists,
and lately also by other writers, that "the bread
and wine" were emblematic of the eucharistic
elements. Figs and raisins were probably also
included in the one case as in the other; for, in
the language of Scripture, "bread and wine," as
the chief articles of meat and drink, represent all
kinds of food.

Melchizedek, who brought these presents to
Abraham as his troops arrived at or passed near
his town, is a remarkable person in Scripture.
It is said that "he was priest of the most high
God," and he bestowed a solemn blessing upon
Abraham in the name of "the most high God,
possessor of heaven and earth;" and, which is
more extraordinary, Abraham gave to him "tithes
(or a tenth) of all." Who was this Melchizedek,
who is honoured with such high titles, and whom
Abraham treats with such respect? The question is a large one, upon which volumes have
been written. The union, in his person, of the
royal and sacerdotal characters, excites no surprise, as this was usual in ancient times. The
Jews generally think that he was Shem, for their
short chronology of the period would allow him
to have lived down to this time. But without

now questioning that chronology, it may be
asked, how came Shem to be living and reigning
here, among people of the Canaanitish race? and
if it were Shem, how is it that Abraham, who
had now been a considerable time in the land,
had no previous intercourse with his venerable
ancestor? Besides, why should Moses speak of
Shem by another name than that by which he
had previously described that personage? and if
he were known to be Shem, how could Paul say
that his parentage was unknown, Heb. viii. 3,
seeing that we are very well acquainted with the
genealogy of Shem? The probability seems to
be, as Josephus indicates, that Melchizedek was
a Canaanitish prince, belonging to the older long
lived generation, who maintained the knowledge
and worship of the true God, which, indeed, does
not seem to have been, up to this time, so generally lost in Canaan as in the land from which
Abraham came; for we find no traces of idolatry
existing among the inhabitants at this period,
and we know from Scripture that the iniquity
of the Canaanites was not full until four hundred
years later. The difference of their religious
training, while they adored the same God, is
perhaps shown in the fact, that while to Abraham
God is known as Jehovah, or simply as Elohim,
with Melchizedek he is the "most high God, the
possessor of heaven and earth;" and it is not a
little remarkable, that Abraham himself adopts
the same title, for that once only, when naming
God in the presence of Melchizedek, or rather
combining it with his own more usual designation
of the Almighty: "I have lifted up my hand to
Jehovah, the most high God, the possessor of
heaven and earth."

There is, and must always remain, great obscurity upon the history of Melchizedek, and
upon some important points in Abraham's intercourse with him. It seems to us far from
improbable that Moses, writing under divine
direction, was withheld from furnishing further
information respecting Melchizedek, that he might
thus be rendered a more efficient type of Christ
in his priestly office; and that sacred writers in
later ages might find the means of illustrating,
from what is known, and more from what is not
known, of Melchizedek, this important feature in
the official character of the Divine Redeemer.[1]

Some of our readers will have heard, that the
Salem of which Melchizedek was king was no

[1] See Psalms 110:4 and Hebrews 7:6,10.

other than Jerusalem. But we see no proof of this. It seems far more likely that Salem was some town between the lake of Gennesareth and the Dead Sea, as was formerly understood. Jerusalem is indeed called Salem in Ps. lxxvi. 2; but this, probably, is no more than a poetical contraction. All the circumstances of the history are in favour of a more northern position. The interview between these illustrious personages took place in "the valley of Shaveh, which is the king's dale;" and we are referred to the parallel text (2 Sam. xviii. 18): "Absalom had reared up for himself a pillar, which is in the king's dale." But this passage throws no light on the geographical position of the "king's dale;" and to assume that it is near Jerusalem, is to beg the only point in question.

THE COVENANT

Genesis 15

ABRAHAM is rich; Abraham is prosperous; Abraham is victorious; Abraham is great; Abraham has won an illustrious name, and has entitled himself to a nation's admiration and gratitude.

But as we know that in the life of man, that in our own life, the moments of our highest exaltation are often followed by those of our deepest humiliation and heaviness; as we know that the thorn in the flesh is seldom wanting to prevent man from being exalted above measure; it is no surprise to us that the next thing we learn of the patriarch, after all this glory, is, that he is exceedingly cast down, and greatly in need of special encouragements from God.

This case is not difficult to understand. Abraham, a man of peaceful tastes and habits, had been roused to an unwonted course of action; but now, as he walks in the solitude of his own tents, and all the recent excitement has passed away, there is a strong reaction. Human regrets and fears press him down, and solemn and earnest thoughts overwhelm him. How does he know that the defeated kings, having been overcome by surprise, may not return in overpowering force, and exact a bloody price for the victory he has won? Then, what is his reward for all the toil and labour he has undergone? Lot, whose alienated heart he had probably hoped to win by

so great a service, is still as far from him as ever. For the sake of the fat pastures and well-watered lands of Sodom, he is content still to dwell among men, whom he must by this time have known from experience to be "sinners before the Lord exceedingly."

In the midst of these thoughts, the voice of God falls upon his ear: "Fear not, Abraham, I am thy shield, and thy exceeding great reward;" or rather, "thy reward shall be exceeding great." These great words, so well suited to refresh and strengthen a troubled and weary spirit, failed not of their effect upon Abraham. Still, the nothingness of human greatness pressed heavily upon his heart. It was true that he had all this greatness, this honour, this wealth. But what did it avail him? He was among strangers; the attachment of his only relative within some hundreds of miles, he had failed to win; he was approaching life's farthest verge, and he still was childless. Soon his accumulated wealth would pass into other hands; and, no son having been given him to transmit his name and race to future days, his memory would utterly perish from the earth. Under the influence of these feelings he said, "*What* wilt Thou give me?" As much as to say, "Thou hast already given me in abundance all thy outer blessings; and what can more of the same avail, seeing I go childless, and the steward of my house is this Eliezer of Damascus?" This he afterwards explains by saying, "Lo, one born in mine house is mine heir." This was an old and attached house-born slave, in whom he had confidence, and who, in the absence and alienation of all natural ties, would become the possessor of his substance. But although this man was worthy, and although his tried faithfulness was a comfort and a blessing, he was not a son; and his heirship could give the patriarch none of those hopes and interests in the great future which he had been led to expect.

But God told him plainly, that not Eliezer, not any stranger, but a son of his own, should be his heir. It was night; and he was drawn forth into the fields, and bade to look upon the stars, and to count them if he could,—for as countless as they, should his posterity become. The sight of the heavenly host may not have been without influence in convincing him, that what God had promised He was able to perform. He lost all doubt and fear. He and his wife were both old; both had reached that time of life at which men and women were wont to see their grown-up sons and daughters around them, and to dandle their children's children upon their knees. But Abraham "staggered not at the promise of God." There were difficulties, to human judgment insuperable; but they were to him as dust in the balance against the promise of God. He believed with all his heart that it would be as God had said. This was Abraham's faith. It was no milk-and-water faith. It was strong faith—faith to live by. He believed; and God counted that belief to him for righteousness.

To reward this faith, the Lord condescended to renew, in the most solemn manner, his other promise,—which was to give to Abraham's descendants the possession of that land in which he was himself a pilgrim and a stranger. Abraham immediately asks, "Whereby shall I know that I shall inherit it?" This has seemed to many a sad lapse from the strong faith he had just indicated. But we do not so view it. He saw the land already containing a large population, which must be greatly increased in number long before his posterity could be increased into a nation fit to possess this heritage; and like Mary, at the salutation of the angels, he asks not, "*Can* this thing be?"—he knew that it could—but "*How* shall this thing be?" Chrysostom, in his homily on this place, seems to have hit the sense rightly. He paraphrases the words thus: "I firmly believe that what Thou hast promised shall come to pass, and therefore I ask no questions from distrust. But I should be glad to be favoured with some such token or anticipation of it as may strongly affect my senses, and raise and strengthen my weak and feeble apprehensions of this great matter."

The way in which the Lord chose to meet his wish, is, in all respects, remarkable. He entered into a formal ritual covenant with him, after the manner of men. It was the most solemn of all forms of ratifying a treaty or covenant among divers ancient nations, and among others of the Chaldeans (as may be seen from Jer. xxxiv. 18), to divide the carcase of a victim, as butchers divide a sheep, into two equal parts lengthwise; these were placed opposite to each other, and the covenanting parties entering at the opposite extremities of the passage thus formed, met in the middle, and there took the oath. Accordingly, Abraham was directed thus to divide and lay out a heifer, a she-goat, a ram, a turtle-

dove, and a young pigeon. These he watched, to protect them from birds of prey, and to wait the expected manifestation. As the sun was going down, the great and darksome horror, and the partial unconsciousness—unconsciousness of his clayey burden—that fell upon him, disclosed to Abraham that God was sensibly near. He heard a voice declaring to him the destiny of his sons for four generations, after which they should come triumphant from bondage to take possession of that land. The voice ceased; the darkness deepened; and, lo! a flaming fire in the midst of what seemed like the smoke of a furnace, passed between the pieces. This was the well known symbol of the divine presence; and thus was the covenant ratified by the most solemn sanction known in ancient times among men.

To estimate the full effect of this awful solemnity upon the mind of Abraham, it should be borne in mind what deep importance was, in ancient times, attached to oaths and covenants in almost all nations, even those which, in the ordinary intercourse of life, were by no means remarkable for truthfulness. The judicial legislation of the East does at this day recognize a false oath as a moral impossibility; and hence, among some of the most mendacious peoples in the world, an accusation on oath is held to be true, in the absence of other testimony, unless the accused will consent to purge himself by a counter oath. Even in ancient Greece, where a lie was a small matter, to distrust an oath seems to have been regarded as a high crime. The same sentiment is indicated in the special judgments from heaven, which were expected to await the breaker of treaties, or the man who had sworn falsely. So, in the *Iliad*, when the truce has been broken by the act of Pandarus, Agamemnon comforts his wounded brother thus:—

> "The foe
> Hath trodden under foot his sacred oath,
> And stained it with thy blood. But not in vain
> The truce was ratified, the blood of lambs
> Poured forth, libation made, and right hands joined
> In holy confidence. The wrath of Jove
> May sleep, but will not always; they shall pay
> Dear penalty."—*Cowper.*

And farther on he says to the Greeks:—

> "Jove will not prosper traitors. Them who first
> Transgressed the truce the vultures shall devour:
> And we, their city taken, shall their wives
> Lead captive."

We may compare with this the more Oriental

notion expressed in the *Institutes of Menu:*— "He whom the blazing fire burns not, whom the water forces not up, or who meets with no speedy misfortune, must be held veracious in his testimony on oath." This implies that God is so sure to punish him who has no regard for his oath, that the absence of punishment is an evidence of truthfulness.

SLAVES

In the history of Abraham, the existence of slavery, that is, the actual right of property which one man holds over another, meets us at every turn; and subsequently, throughout the Scripture, it frequently comes under our notice as a large and important fact in the history and condition of nations.

As, in the history of Abraham, we may recognize almost every species of slavery that existed in later ages, the system must, in his time, have been of long standing. Whether it existed before the deluge or not, cannot be certainly known; but the probability is that it did, for the same causes existed before that event, that produced it within so short a time afterwards. The men who, before the flood, filled the earth with violence and with crime, were not likely to leave unattempted this encroachment upon human rights. The knowledge of the existence of this practice before the flood, would facilitate and hasten its reproduction after that event.

Abraham himself possessed many slaves: indeed, there is no reason to doubt that his encampment was wholly composed of such persons—male slaves, with their wives and families; all equally the property of their lord, but becoming such under different circumstances, which practically produced some difference in the estimation in which they were held, if not in the treatment which they received from their master.

The first were house-born slaves, that is, slaves born the property of their master, being the children of all the other kinds of slaves previously possessed. We are told that we ought to view these matters in the same light as the ancients and the orientals. We see not the necessity of this. We may view the conduct of

men by the light of their age and country; and we may judge leniently of practices respecting which we have ourselves been very slow and very late in coming to a right judgment. But having now, at last, in the nineteenth century of Christ, come to that right judgment, there is no reason why we should not, and every reason why we should, exercise it in judging of ancient things. So judging, the presence of house-born slaves seems to be the most revolting particular in the whole system. We can understand that a man might forfeit his personal liberty by crime or by misfortune; but that his children, and his children's children, should to all generations be involved in the same doom, merely because they are his descendants, and without any taint derived from him, is indeed horrible, and seems the most atrocious invention that ever entered into the minds of men. Most things of this nature are, however, worse in principle than they appear to be in practice. The house-born slaves, whose condition seems at the first view the most degraded, are in fact the most privileged, trusted, and favoured. Their services are the lightest and most confidential; they are nearest the person of their master; growing up under his eye, they learn to regard him in some sort as their father; and taking into view the extent of paternal authority in the East, and the respectful distance at which children are kept, the demeanour of the house-born slave towards his master is, in its combination of deference and attachment, scarcely distinguishable from that of his own children. Except in the utmost extremity of evil fortune, no man will part with a slave of this class. It is counted disgraceful to sell him. And although theoretically this bondage is eternal, it very seldom lasts for two generations. It is very usual for a master to bequeath liberty to all his house-born slaves at his death. He frequently bestows freedom upon some of them in his lifetime, if they will accept it, or if he finds an occasion of thereby advancing their welfare. An accomplished and faithful slave often receives the hand of his master's daughter, and thus becomes a free member of his family.[1]

An instance of this occurs in 1 Chronicles 2:34,35,—and that, too, with reference to one who was not, it would seem, a house-born but an acquired slave. "Sheshan had no sons, but daughters; and Sheshan had a servant, an Egyptian, whose name was Jarha. And Sheshan gave his daughter to Jarha his servant to wife."

Not seldom the master, if childless, adopts a slave of this class for his son, and brings him up as such; or at his death leaves all his possessions to one of them who has obtained the highest place in his favour, or whose attachment has been the most tried. In the case of Abraham, we see it is only the house-born slaves that he arms for the pursuit of the five kings; and in the event of his dying childless, he clearly indicates the intention of making his house-born slave Eliezer his heir. He had probably acquired many slaves of this sort by inheritance; and a portion were the progeny of these and of his other slaves.

Some of his slaves Abraham held by right of purchase. They were "bought with his money," Gen. xvii. 12. There seems, indeed, to have been a regular traffic in the persons of men. We have an instance of this in the case of Joseph. When the unnatural brethren were deliberating upon taking away his life, the approach of a company of travelling merchants on their way to Egypt suggested to them the idea of selling him for a slave. The proposal was made, and the transaction completed, without any apparent emotion of surprise, or any nice inquiry into the right of disposal. Had the dealers been in the habit of paying any heed to circumstances, or to the representations and complaints of the persons offered to them for sale, they would not have purchased Joseph for a slave. We are not, however, to suppose that Abraham had any concern in acts of this questionable nature. Such slaves passed from hand to hand; and doubtless Abraham's purchased slaves were acquired not at first hand, but in the market—perhaps in Egypt, which, from the earliest historical time, was a great mart for slaves.

Many of Abraham's slaves were, however, presented to him. Of these, we know that he received some from the king of Egypt: Hagar may have been one of the number, for she is called "an Egyptian." Was she so called because she was acquired in that country, or because she was a native Egyptian? If the latter, how did she become a slave in her own country? And how came a native Egyptian to be given or sold to a foreigner like Abraham? There seems a difficulty in this; and also one still greater in the fact (as appears by the case of Jarha, just noticed) that the Israelites could hold Egyptians as slaves, even in Egypt. As natives of the country in which they were slaves, these could not have been captives taken in war, who formed by far the greater proportion of slaves in all times. In early wars, a captured enemy was regarded as having forfeited his life, and was accordingly put to death; until it was found more advantageous to preserve his life for the sake of his labour, or for the sake of the money that might be obtained from those to whom his services might be useful. This, which was in the first instance the effect of wars, eventually produced wars; for the captives were thus rendered so profitable, that wars were often made, and aggressive expeditions undertaken, for the sake of the captives and spoil, as is at this day the case in Africa.

Again, the paternal authority in ancient times was such, that the father possessed the most absolute power over the life and condition of his children. It was, and still is in some countries, optional with him from the first, whether the child shall live or not. If he suffered it to live, he had a perfect right, under any exigency that might arise, of casting forth, of selling, or even of slaying his child. Many were sold, especially in times of famine, when the parent, being no longer able to find food for them, would consider that he rendered them a kindness by selling them, and all his rights in them, to those who were able to provide for them. This occurs in our own day. We have with our own eyes beheld parents, in "the straitness of the famine and want of all things," offering their children for sale in the streets, and asking but the veriest trifle for them.

Then, in countries where there is no legal provision for the poor, a man will often, in time of scarcity, or under some pressing want, sell himself, for the purpose of obtaining food or money. This slavery was sometimes for a limited time, as in the case of Jacob, who served Laban fourteen years for his two daughters; and in that case this condition approaches that of our servants. But it is oftener absolute, as in the case of the Egyptians who sold themselves for bread to their king.[1]

Then, again, creditors had the right of seizing the children of a debtor, and himself also, and of selling them in payment of his debts. The children were, indeed, liable to be sold for the debts of the parent even after his death, as we find by

[1] Genesis 47:23.

the case of the widow who complained to Elisha that, being unable to pay the debts of her deceased husband, the merciless creditor threatened to take her two sons for bondmen.[1] With this, other cases, in Neh. v. 1-5 and Matt. xviii. 25, may be compared.

Men were also enslaved as a punishment for their crimes. But in general, except in Egypt, where human labour was much in demand for public works, this was confined to cases in which restitution for a wrong might thus be made. In other cases, the punishments of crimes were, in old times, generally corporeal,—death, mutilations, tortures, stripes,—as is still the case in the East.

We thus see that persons might become slaves even in their own country. And in view of the instances of Egyptians being slaves to foreigners, to which we have referred, it is very possible that the law of Moses aimed at the correction of this sort of grievance, when it forbade that a native Israelite should be sold to a foreigner out of his own country. In his country a stranger might be his master, although in that case his friends, or other Israelites, had the right of redeeming him out of that alien servitude.

From the character of Abraham, as well as from the generally mild tone of eastern slavery, we must conclude that all his slaves were treated not only with justice and humanity, but with paternal kindness and consideration; and, in many cases, there being brought into his family must have been a great blessing to them, as the means of bringing them to an acquaintance with God. Living in times when slavery was the usual form of servitude, and knowing that by themselves the power was humanely and conscientiously exercised, even the patriarchs would be slow to perceive the evil principle that lurked in this absolute power of man over man, and would fall into the practice, as affording the *only* mode in which the services they needed could be obtained.

FAITH OF ABRAHAM

Genesis 15:6

" He believed in the Lord, and he counted it to him for righteousness." It is very important for

[1] 2 Kings 4:1.

us to understand rightly what was the nature of that faith in Abraham which God "counted to him for righteousness." That faith does not belong to things that have passed away. Abraham exercised it, and it was counted to him for righteousness, before he was under the covenant of circumcision. Although there be different degrees of faith, they are but different measures of the same thing. The faith that justifies (which is what is meant by its being counted for righteousness) is that faith which saves; and saving faith has ever been the same in its nature, and has always had one object. This is placed beyond a doubt by the fact that Saint Paul more than once sets before Christians the faith of Abraham as the model for their own. In the patriarch, therefore, we have an example of that faith which is needful to ourselves; and it thus the more behoves us that this example should not be misapprehended.

No man with whose history we are acquainted has ever shown stronger faith than Abraham. He is called to abandon his friends and country, and he obeys: "he went forth, not knowing whither he went." God promises to him a son, and he believes, although he is already old, and the accomplishment is many long years delayed. God promises that his posterity shall be as the sand that is by the sea-shore innumerable; and he believes, although he is childless. God tells him that the land in which he is a stranger shall be the heritage of his children; and he believes, although he sees not *how* so great an event can be brought to pass. The promised son is born, and grows up, when he is commanded to slay him in sacrifice; and he forthwith proceeds to obey that commandment, although he regarded that son as the medium of all the blessings promised to him and his. What more do we require than this? Is not this sufficient to constitute the faith which justified and saved his soul? Alas! no. Abraham himself knew this very well. All this does not constitute the faith which the Gospel requires of us, and which we are assured is the same faith that Abraham held. From all that appears in the facts stated, the faith of Abraham consisted in his belief that it was God who spoke to him, and that whatever God promised He was able to perform. His strong acts of obedience were proportioned to the strength of his belief. But is this saving faith? We find many who exhibit strong trust in God's providence and care, and who exhibit much energy in acts of obedience to his commandments, but who do not and cannot claim to have received the anointing from the Holy One. There are many such, not even nominally Christians. They are good men and true in their order; but their order is not in Christ, and they are none of His. Even the faith that can remove mountains is not in itself the faith that saves and justifies; and it is to be feared that many who have had *that* faith alone will utterly perish. We write these words with awe; for they form a sentence of condemnation against many from whom the heart cannot withhold its love.

Seeing, then, that Abraham had saving faith, and that this faith is not inevitably connected with such acts as those which his history sets before us, why is not its real nature and object more clearly pointed out to us? It *is* clearly pointed out, although *not* in the history. The sacred volume comes to us as a whole, and the information not given in one part of it is generally to be found in another. The gospels and the epistles clearly tell us wherein lay that faith of Abraham which was counted to him for righteousness. If it be asked, why this is not set forth in the history itself? it may as well be asked, why the doctrine of redemption is not as clearly set forth in the Pentateuch as in the prophecies of Isaiah? It is indeed as fully set forth, now that we can read with anointed eyes the types and symbols under which it was at once veiled and expressed. It was not the purpose of God that the mysteries of His kingdom should be fully unveiled until the fulness of time was come. He gave more and more, stronger and stronger light, dispersing gradually the morning shades, until we reached the noontide splendours of that day in which Christ rose from the dead. All was then known.

What, then, is this essential faith, which, according to the testimony of Christ and his apostles, Abraham possessed, and through which alone he could be justified—justified, not as *being* righteous, but as being "*counted* righteous" before God? We will give the answer from the able but neglected book of a clear-minded writer.[1] "Faith is a grace wrought in the soul of a sinner by the Holy Spirit, whereby, being emptied of all opinionative thoughts of his own righteous-

[1] *A Practical Treatise of Saving Faith.* By Abraham Taylor. 1730. It is remarkable, however, that this writer does not once allude to the case of Abraham.

ness, strength, and fulness, he is enabled to look to Christ, to betake himself to Him as his only Saviour, to receive Him, to rest and rely upon Him for the remission of his sins, for a righteousness to justify him in the sight of God, for strength to enable him to perform duty, to follow after holiness, and to encounter spiritual enemies; and for eternal life, when his work of faith and labour of love are ended, and when he comes to finish with joy his course. This is the Scripture notion of saving faith: and it has God for its fundamental and principal object, as He is a God of truth reconciled to sinners; but it has Christ for its immediate object, for it is only by His mediation that a sinner can come to God."

Had Abraham this faith? There can be no question of it. There can be no question that he was enabled to find in the divine promises made to him far more than met his ear. He had a spiritual perception of their purport, and apprehended through them a hope of heaven, and an interest in its blessedness. As this can be only realized through Christ, this alone would be evidence that his faith had reference to the promised Messiah. But we are not left to any conjecture in this matter. Our Lord himself says: "Abraham longed to see my day: and he saw it, and was glad." John viii. 56.

This means that Abraham earnestly desired to have a distinct conception, a clear representation, of the work of the Messiah—his promised seed, in whom all the families of the earth were to be blessed; and that this privilege was in a special manner afforded to him, and filled his heart with gladness. In Christ, therefore, and in His great redeeming work, his faith centred. This was, in his view, the ultimate object of all the promises he received; and while he did look forward to a numerous posterity through Isaac, he was also permitted to behold in faith the far larger heritage which should accrue to him through that great Son,—the heirs of his faith, the inheritors of the blessings belonging to his spiritual seed, numerous as the stars, and not less glorious.

These are not fancies. As the words of our Lord disclose to us the nature of Abraham's faith, so the words of the apostle indicate the sense we have given, as that in which our Lord's words are to be understood. Saint Paul, in the fourth chapter of Romans, treats largely of the nature of Abraham's faith, showing that the promises made to the patriarch had, besides their natural meaning, a spiritual one which he fully understood. He shows that Israel had no exclusive inheritance in the promises made to Abraham, that he should be "the father of many nations," and the "heir of the world:" and whether the large views which we are thus led to take of these promises and facts were opened to the patriarch or not, there is every reason, from the declaration of our Saviour, to conclude that his faith did embrace these spiritual views of the Messiah and His work to which reference has been made, and that in the degree of light imparted to him, his faith was the same in its essence as our own.

In his epistle to the church in Galatia, the same apostle returns to a subject obviously full of interest to him. He declares plainly, that the Gospel—nothing less than the Gospel—was preached to Abraham, when it was declared to him that in him all nations should be blessed. "So, then," he adds, "they that be of faith are blessed with faithful Abraham."

It must be admitted, that on the surface of the narrative, the expectations and the hopes of Abraham are temporal, and the promises also. It is refreshing to be enabled thus, by the aid of the later Scriptures, to penetrate to their inner meaning, and find that they were not merely such. Through faith, his views, like our own, extended beyond the grave, and rested not short of heaven. His portion was not in this world. He was thus well content to dwell in a strange country, without any abiding place, because, as the same apostle assures us, "he looked" not in this world, but in the world to come, "for a city which *hath foundations*, whose builder and maker is God." Heb. xi. 10. Truly and beautifully applicable to him, as was designed, are the lines of the poet:—

> "No foot of land do I possess;
>   No cottage in this wilderness;
>   A poor wayfaring man.
>   I lodge a while in tents below,
>   Or gladly wander to and fro,
>   Till I my Canaan gain.
>   Nothing on earth I call my own,
>   A stranger to the world unknown,
>   I all their goods despise;
>   I trample on their whole delight,
>   And seek a city out of sight,
>   A city in the skies."

HAGAR

Genesis 16

IT is worthy of note that Abraham's wife had female slaves of her own, or at least one such, over whom the master had little if any power. This is still the case in the East, with respect to all such slaves as by gift, or purchase, or dower, are the actual property of the mistress. Where, indeed, there is only domestic female slavery, the mistress assumes the entire control of the female slaves bought by the master for the service of his house; but where such slaves are employed in out-door service, such as the tending of cattle, the power of the mistress is limited to those engaged in domestic service, while the others are under the more direct control of the master. This statement may serve to illustrate the relative conditions of the female slaves in the camp of Abraham, who were probably numerous.

One of these women, named Hagar, was Sarah's own slave, apparently in the highest sense, as having been presented to her, or bought by her. As this woman is called an Egyptian, and was the personal attendant of Sarah, there may be reason to suppose, as was formerly remarked, that Hagar had been given to her as an attendant by the king of Egypt, while she was detained in his house. When the monarch gave her "brother" men-servants and maid-servants for her sake, he was not likely to leave Sarah without some such tokens of his consideration.

Abraham had no doubt acquainted Sarah with the various promises from the Lord which had been made to him. But she was less disposed than he to await God's own time and mode of accomplishing the purpose He had declared. A most notable device entered her mind, which seems strange to us, but which was probably in conformity with then existing customs, such as still subsist in India and in China. She proposed that Abraham should take her maid as a kind of secondary wife, so that if any children came from this union, they might, as the children of her handwoman, be accounted hers. There was nothing in this that could have appeared wrong to Abraham, though to us it wears an unpleasant aspect, and, in any case, he ought to have waited in faith for the fulfilment of the high promise he had received. It, however, claims to be noticed, that although Abraham had received the assurance of a son, he had not yet been told that Sarah was to be that son's mother; and he may have supposed that the course which was taken was in full accordance with the divine intention. It is clear that Sarah herself had altogether abandoned the hope of giving birth to a child, and that it was at her urgency Abraham consented, probably against his better judgment, to become a party to this expedient. It is indeed remarkable, that of the three patriarchs, the two who gave their sanction to the practice of polygamy, did so, not of their own free will, but were driven into it by the contrivances of others.

The evil of this measure soon appeared in its effects. It was not long before it was evident that Hagar would become the mother of a child. The prospects which this condition opened so worked upon her mind, so exalted her in her own sight, that Sarah no longer received from her that respect to which she had been accustomed. Every indication of this sort would appear in the darkest colours to the naturally jealous mind of Sarah, who, if we do not misjudge her, by the reaction not seldom seen in human character, regarded with dislike the woman who had been made the instrument of her own designs, as soon as it appeared that she would shortly enjoy the advantage, so long denied to herself, of becoming the happy mother of a child. It is far from improbable that the whole transaction became hateful in her eyes, when its objects appeared likely to be fulfilled. She now assailed her husband with the language of recrimination and censure, as if he had been faulty in the matter, and laid at his door all the blame of a transaction which was entirely of her own devising. To pacify her, Abraham, who manifestly abhorred domestic strife, and generally avoided it by letting Sarah have her own way, told her, "Behold, thy maid is in thy hand: do to her as it pleaseth thee." This she could have done without his permission formerly, while Hagar was simply her own slave; but the woman had now acquired a new character, which, although it did not take her wholly out of Sarah's power, precluded the latter from disposing of her without his consent. But his words restored to her all her original power over her handmaid, and divested him of all right of interfering, even should her conduct towards Hagar be utterly averse to

his own inclinations and wishes. It does not appear that Abraham had any knowledge of these dissensions in the interior of the women's tent, till he was made acquainted with them by Sarah; and being informed by her, in her own way, of the assumptions of Hagar, and being asked whether he was inclined to support her in her pretensions, it does not seem to us unnatural, that he should decide the matter in favour of her who had been hitherto the sole companion of his life, and the repository of all his hopes and fears, and who was entitled, by the double tie of consanguinity and marriage, to all consideration and kindness from him. It was, therefore, doubtless under a strong impression of duty to her that, even at the risk of losing his child, he admitted her full authority over her own slave. He hoped, perhaps, that her jealousy would be allayed, and Hagar's growing arrogance repressed, by this strong measure—a measure which certainly does, under all explanation, seem unduly harsh towards Hagar, or, at least, not duly considerate for her, seeing that he thus divested himself of all power of interfering for her protection under any treatment she might receive. It is necessary to keep this fact in view, as it accounts for his subsequent passiveness. The reader may remember the incident in ancient Persian history, that when Amestris asked her husband Xerxes to give her the wife of his brother, the king, obliged by custom, consented. He foresaw the treatment which awaited his sister-in-law; but having placed her at his wife's disposal, he took no precautions to avert the cruelty of Amestris, which was worse than barbarous. The story may be found in the ninth book of Herodotus.

So Sarah now uses her power so unsparingly, that Hagar abandons all her high prospects and aspirings, and determines to seek relief in flight. She withdrew into the southern wilderness, probably intending to find her way to Egypt. But one day, as she rested by a well of water, the angel of God found her there, and conveyed to her the comforting assurance that she was not forsaken. He told her to return to her mistress, and behave with submission to her; and to encourage her obedience, he proceeded to disclose the destinies of her unborn child. "Thou shalt bear a son, and shalt call his name Ishmael, because the Lord hath heard thy affliction. And he will be a wild man; his hand will be against every man, and every man's hand against him;

and he shall dwell in the presence of all his brethren."

HAGAR AND ISHMAEL CAST FORTH.

It was no doubt well understood by her that this character was designed to describe not merely the individual, but the race to spring from him. Taken in that point of view, it is a most extraordinary prediction. The character which it describes was too common in an unsettled age to excite special attention. What is remarkable in the prediction is, that this, in the case of Ishmael, was to remain, as it ever has done in the persons of his Arabian descendants, the character of a race. Other nations have changed their habits of life, and not one retains its original character. The sole exception is in the descendants of this man, in accordance with a prediction published at a time when no human knowledge could foresee, nor any human power ensure, the certainty of its fulfilment. The wilderness life, which is incident only to a certain stage of man's social history, has become permanent with them; and, although they have been compacted and embodied as a nation for more than three thousand years, they have resisted those changes of habits which it is the effect of civil union so long continued to induce. Still, as we shall have ample occasion to show, does the Ishmaelite exhibit in his manner of life the characteristics impressed upon him by the words spoken to the runaway bond-woman in the wilderness of Shur. Nor is this all: his race was always to remain in the possession of the land originally acquired; for so the expression, that he should dwell in the presence of all his brethren, is usually interpreted. And how wonderfully true has this been of the Arabian! While other nations and tribes have again and again changed their habitations, or have become subject to strangers in their own lands, the Arabians have always occupied the same country. "They have roved like the moving sands of their deserts; but their race has been rooted while the individual wandered. That race has neither been dissipated by conquest, nor lost by migration, nor confounded with the blood of other countries. They have continued to dwell in the presence of all their brethren, a distinct nation, wearing, upon the whole, the same features and aspects which prophecy first impressed upon them."[1]

One great division of the Arab nation has in every age preserved the memory of its descent from Hagar; and for more than two thousand years it bore the distinguishing appellation of *Hagarite* (1 Chron. v. 10, 19). Indeed, the name of Sarah's Egyptian maid is not yet extinct in the Arabian peninsula.

Every event in the long history of the Arabs, from the time when Ishmael "became an archer, and dwelt in the wilderness," down to the present day, may be regarded as alike an illustration and fulfilment of the remarkable prediction in this chapter: "He will be a wild ass man; his hand against every man, and every man's hand against him; and he shall dwell before (or in the presence of) all his brethren." The grand characteristic of the race is delineated in the first clause. Like the wild ass, the Arabs glory in freedom; they are impatient of all restraint; they are untameable. They are never stationary, but roam at will from pasture to pasture, and from fountain to fountain.

The second clause is a graphic sketch, in outline, of their history. Every nation, tribe, and individual, that has ventured to approach their border, or penetrate their desert home, has realized the truth of the declaration, "His hand will be against every man." The Israelites of old realized it when their fields were desolated by the locust-like swarms of the "children of the East." The Romans realized it when their legions were driven back in disgrace from the Arabian deserts, and when they were compelled to protect their eastern frontier by a line of fortresses. The whole world realized it when the fierce followers of the false prophet issued from their desert home, and swept like a tornado over the fairest kingdoms of Asia, Africa, and Europe. The Turks now realize it in those raids of the Bedawîn, which are gradually laying waste the fertile plains of Syria and Mesopotamia.

The last clause requires no comment. One has only to read history to see how the Arab has ever dwelt "in the presence of all his brethren." None have ever subdued him. None have driven him from his home. None have been able to curb his free roving spirit. In the proudest periods of Jewish, Assyrian, Persian, Greek, Roman, Tartar, and Osmanli dominion, the Arabs have maintained their place and position in their presence.　　P.

[1] Davison, *Discourses on Prophecy*, p. 493.

PASTORAL HOSPITALITIES

Genesis 18

THERE is, perhaps, no chapter of Genesis which brings so vividly before us the actual circumstances of patriarchal life, as the eighteenth. One might muse over it for hours with untiring interest, and volumes might be written upon the text which it offers.

The aged patriarch is sitting in his tent door in the heat of the day. There, while shaded from the sun by the tree beneath which his tent is pitched, he may receive refreshment from the cooling breeze which plays around him. He is absorbed in thought. His eyes are fixed upon the ground, as he muses probably on the destinies of his race, on God's covenant with him, and on the qualities which his son Ishmael, by this time a grown-up boy, begins to develop. Suddenly he is aware that three strangers—wayfaring men —have approached near to him unobserved. He starts from his seat, and hastens to meet them. He bows himself very low before the one who seems to be the chief among them; he asks no questions, but presses upon them the hospitalities of his tent. They accept them as freely as they are offered. They seat themselves beneath the tree, and while water is brought to refresh their travel-stained feet, the patriarch hastens to tell his wife to bake bread upon the hearth; then he speeds to the herds, and singles out the fatted calf. With his own hand he prepares the feast; with his own hand he sets it before them; and, as becomes his place, he stands by them under the tree, ready to minister to their wants, while they do eat his butter, his milk, his bread, and his meat.

How beautiful this hospitality; how grandly courteous this demeanour! It strikes us the more strongly from its contrast to our own usages. A man of the existing pastoral tribes, or even of the rural districts of the East, would simply see the truthfulness of the picture, and would recognize usages in all respects similar to his own.

In every Arabian encampment, the sheikh or chief regards it as at once his privilege and his duty to entertain strangers. All who come are freely received, usually in a tent set apart for the purpose. Luxuries are never indulged in except on some festivals, or on the arrival of a stranger; and it is only on such occasions that animal food is ever eaten, even by the possessors of numerous flocks and herds. Nor is it every stranger that is treated with animal food. For a common guest bread is baked, and served up with the *ayesh* (or flour made up with sour milk, and boiled) which forms the standing daily fare of the people. If the guest be of some consideration, coffee is prepared for him, and *behatta* (or bread with melted butter). It is only for a person of some apparent rank that a kid or a lamb is killed. When this occurs, the lamb is boiled with *burgoul* (a sort of malted corn) and milk, and served up in a large wooden dish, around the edge of which the meat is placed. As there is no means of obtaining a joint of meat but by slaughtering an animal, the whole of which must be consumed, the people of the camp get what the strangers do not eat, and therefore fare the better for such visits. We thus see the reason why it is always stated in Scripture that the lamb, the kid, or fatted calf, is killed for the entertainment of strangers, or on any occasion of high rejoicing.

ARAB ENCAMPMENT

It should be remarked that no questions are asked; but after the stranger has dwelt in the tent three days and four hours, he is expected to state his name, his tribe, and his business; and if his stay appears likely to be prolonged, he is reasonably expected to take part in the duties of the camp. It was thus that Jacob in the first month of his stay with Laban, which he certainly did not mean to be of such long duration as it proved, was enabled to evince the importance and value of his services in performing the duties of those who have flocks and herds. Gen. xxix. 14, 15.

As to the washing of the feet of the travellers, we know not that this custom exists in the desert, where water is scarce and precious; nor, perhaps, did it exist there even in patriarchal times. But it is still found where water is plentiful. In India, it is considered a necessary part of hospitality to wash the feet and ankles of the weary traveller, and this service is usually performed by servants. Even in Palestine, this interesting custom is not extinct. Thus, when Dr. Robinson and his party arrived at Ramleh, they repaired to the abode of a wealthy Arab, whose second son, in the absence of his father, did the honours of the place. Soon after they had arrived, says Dr. Robinson, "our youthful host proposed, in the genuine style of ancient oriental hospitality, that a servant should wash our feet. This took me by surprise, as I was not aware that the custom still existed here. Nor does it indeed towards foreigners, though quite common among the natives. We gladly accepted the proposal, both for the refreshment and the scriptural illustration. A female Arabian slave accordingly brought water, which she poured upon our feet over a large shallow basin of tinned copper; kneeling before us, and rubbing our feet with her hands, and wiping them with a napkin. It was among the gratifying minor incidents of our whole journey." It seems to us that the *comparative* decay of the custom arises from the fact that travellers now seldom journey on foot, but ride on horses or camels. Where foot travelling is still usual, so is the washing of feet.

Nothing that has been used at one meal is kept for another in the East, but no more is prepared than the meal or the day requires. The climate would not indeed allow any other practice. Thus it is that there is always new preparation, even to the baking of bread, when a friend or stranger arrives; and hence the coming of a stranger, considerable enough to have an animal slaughtered for him, especially if a sheep or camel (for Arabs have no oxen), is a most acceptable matter to the camp, however burdensome to the sheikh. But the sheikh himself is glad to show his hospitality on any proper occasion. A reputation for hospitality is scarcely inferior to that of military prowess in the East. It gives influence and distinction; and Arabian chiefs have on this account been known to perform such acts of prodigal hospitality as excite our astonishment. Such facts evince the diffusion of this quality among a people; for very few will care thus to waste their own substance, unless they know that there are others who will do the same. Yet this hospitality is scarcely reckoned a virtue in the East; so much as the want of it is regarded as a vice, if not as a crime.

The reader is probably a little astonished to see the great and wealthy Abraham so forward in doing himself what so many of his slaves might as well have done, while with her own hands Sarah bakes the cakes upon the hearth. But so it is now. A Bedouin sheikh, who may be the master of five hundred horses, does not disdain to saddle and bridle his own, or to give him his feed of barley and chopped straw. In his tent, the wife makes the coffee, bakes the bread, and superintends the dressings of the victuals; while his daughters and kinswomen wash the clothes, spin and weave the wool, and go with pitchers on their heads, and veils on their faces, to draw water from the fountain.

We are apt to ascribe much of the peculiar respectfulness of Abraham to his perception of the high quality of his guests. But there is no sign that he did perceive it, until it was made known by themselves; and all the marks of obeisance and respect are such as are still common in the East. Even the deference shown by him in *standing* by while his guests partook of his food, without presuming to take part with them, has been more than once witnessed by ourselves in eastern lands. We have noticed instances in which, when the host was a man of rank and consequence, he has brought in, with his own hands, some principal dish, and remained standing, or in attendance, during the whole meal, directing the operations of the servants in removing and in laying on. It is rude to take notice of this, or to press him to share the meal, because, although he may comply, it lays him under a kind of necessity of committing what he feels to be an indecorum. No one can, however, take him for a servant: the deference of the real servants to him, the authority with which he directs their proceedings, the manner in which the guests receive his attentions, and the tone in which they speak to him, clearly enough indicate what he is. Although painful to the feelings of Europeans, when it first comes under their notice, it is a beautiful and significant act of humility and deference, most gracefully becoming in an oriental. Among us, so different is the mould in which our habits are cast, it would be difficult to prevent a similar usage from becoming ridiculous, although we apprehend that something analogous might be produced from among our old customs.

LOT IN SODOM—INTERCESSION

Genesis 18,19

THE strangers whom Abraham entertained became known to him before they went on their way. He whom the patriarch had instinctively recognized as their chief, soon disclosed himself as no other than the Lord, and is, indeed, distinctly named in the sequel as JEHOVAH, and the others are in the event seen to be angels. This disclosure was made by the manner in which the Lord began to speak to Abraham respecting his promised son: and now, for the first time, he learned with certainty that this child of promise was not Ishmael, but was to be the son of Sarah; and further, that this child of promise should be born very soon. Sarah, who overheard this declaration as she stood within the tent, laughed in her heart, as at a thing impossible to credit. But the Lord heard that silent doubt, and taxed her with it; ending with the unanswerable question: "Is anything too hard for the Lord?" Abraham, on a like occasion, had himself laughed, and was not rebuked. But the difference of feeling in this matter between him and his wife, is shown by the circumstance, that he forthwith prostrated himself before the Lord; whereas Sarah, when charged with her laughter, denied that she had laughed at all. The circumstance affords the reason for the name Isaac, which was given to the son; for the meaning of that name is *laughter*.[1]

The custom of the East required Abraham to escort his guests a little on their way; and as he proceeds, the Lord makes known to him that a dreadful visitation impends over Sodom and the other cities of the plain, for their awful iniquities. Abraham avails himself of this previous intimation to plead for those cities. If there had been but the very few righteous persons that he supposed might be found in Sodom, the place would have been spared, at his desire, for their sake; and it had been well for them that they had such an intercessor. How well, then, for us, who have *always* an intercessor at God's right hand on our behalf! We have heard much about the efficacy of prayer, and many pious minds have been exercised as to the degree in which they may venture to pray in respect of temporal things. But there can be no question with respect to intercession. If any one has doubts on that subject, we know no better solution than is to be found in this intercession of Abraham. In the tenderness of his heart, and in his firm conviction that God does not willingly stretch forth his right arm in wrath over a guilty world, he ventures to come with boldness before the throne of grace. Let us take the intended lesson from his example, and come, as we are invited, with boldness before God in prayer, that we may obtain mercy for ourselves and others, and find grace to help in time of need. Abraham at first thought it probable that there might be sixty righteous men in Sodom, and he prayed that the place might be spared for their sake. This the Lord freely granted. The patriarch then had a misgiving that there might not be so many; and he ventured, with great humility, to make successive intercessions for the reduction of their number, until at last he thought he had ensured the safety of the place, when the Lord had graciously promised to spare the town, if but *ten* righteous men were to be found therein. How little do the men of this world know the extent of even their worldly obligations to the righteous! How often has the Lord spared great cities from plague, pestilence, and famine, from earthquake, fire, and sword, for the sake of the

---

[1] The word "smile" does not occur in Scripture: that is, the Hebrew has no separate word to express smiling; but we who have should not always translate the original by "laughter." Smiling is no doubt in many instances in-tended, and there are some texts in which the sense would be much improved by the substitution. See the following: Genesis 21:6; Job 5:22; 29:24; Psalms 2:4; Ecclesiastes 3:4. We suppose that Abraham in the one instance, and Sarah in the other, merely smiled. Indeed, what else can it be "to laugh *in the heart?*"

little sanctuary He had therein, among those to whom His name was dear! They may be passed unregarded by, in the market and in the street; but they are the salt, they are the leaven, that keeps the mass from corruption. They are His own now, and they shall shine forth more eminently His in the day when He maketh up His jewels; it is for them that a blessing rests upon the place where iniquity abounds, and it is for their sake that the curse and ruin are averted from it. In the belief that the duty and privilege of intercession is too much neglected among Christians, we do earnestly recommend this case of Abraham's intercession for Sodom to the consideration of the reader. It shows that the Lord is very pitiful and of great mercy; and it demonstrates that intercession has power with Him, and can prevail.

Abraham could not have been unmindful of Lot, who was in Sodom. The more the reader thinks of Lot, the more difficult his case seems to us. From all that appears in the history, there was nothing very lovely in his character; for even his being eventually saved, was more for Abraham's sake than for his own. He appears, from the history, to have been a weak and selfish character. On the return from Egypt, he seems to have taken part with his herdsmen in their quarrels with those of Abraham; and when at length the latter proposes a separation for the sake of peace, and leaves him the choice of situation, he has not the grace to decline the generous offer of his elder and uncle, but grasps it eagerly, and adopts for his home the fat pastures of Sodom, although he well knows that the men in that quarter are the most wicked in the land. At first he did not intend, however, to mix with the citizens, but to live in his tent. But it is dangerous to palter with duty, or to venture too near the strongholds of sin. Even as the moth careers merrily and thoughtlessly around the flame, and at last is overcome by the fascination, and plunges therein to its ruin, so Lot, ere long, has left his tent, and has got a house in Sodom. There he forms family ties; there his daughters marry; and he gradually gets more and more entangled. So strong is that entanglement, that even his capture and rescue by Abraham do not suffice to break the chains which the world has cast around him. He goes back to Sodom, and tarries there; and it would appear that this was under circumstances which inflicted much pain upon Abraham, and probably offended him greatly. It is else difficult to see how, in looking to the possibility of dying childless, he refused to regard Lot as his heir.

One of Lot's measures, or suggestions, when the angels who went to destroy Sodom were with him, seems to show that although still a good man, his moral sense had been somewhat weakened by daily intercourse with the ungodly people with whom he had fixed his home; and his reluctance to leave Sodom, and the enormities into which his too easy nature was led, after his escape to the mountains, are facts of the same purport, and speak with trumpet-tongue of the danger of this intercourse with sinners. No good can ever come from such intercourse—in his day or in ours; and let none of us, as he perhaps did, rely too much on his own strength; for who can daily touch pitch without being defiled? If Lot had been altogether right-minded, not the finest pastures of the world, not all the conveniences and apparent advantages for the settlement of his daughters which a residence in the town presented, would have induced him to go or to stay there. Rather would he have fled the place. Rather would he have plunged at once into the desert. There was nothing to prevent him; for he was not, like his uncle, under any command to remain in the land of Canaan.

For all that appears in the history, we might have strong fears of this man's state. But St. Peter calls him "just Lot," and says, that while in Sodom, "that righteous man, dwelling among them, in seeing and hearing, vexed his righteous soul from day to day, with the unlawful deeds and filthy conversation of the wicked." This relieves us, by showing that his character was still *substantially* true. But it does not altogether clear him from these imputations. It shows that he had good feelings and perceptions; but was a feeble-spirited man, lacking the strength to act on his own convictions. He was content to mourn over the guilt he saw; and would rather passively sit down amid the certainties of danger, and the probabilities of judgment, than rouse himself to one great and energetic effort to be free, and, at whatever sacrifice, to depart from the tainted and abominable place.

Let us profit from the example, which is less different than it may seem from the experience of many of us. Still there are Sodoms; and still there are Lots who think that, with a religious profession, they may live in the world, and pursue its profits and its pleasures without danger. Let them beware. They are in great peril. If we be indeed God's people, let us come out of the world, and touch not the unclean thing—remembering that the Church of God is not mixed up in the world, and to be left undistinguishable from it; but is, indeed,

> " A people walled around,
> Chosen, and made peculiar ground;
> A little spot enclosed by grace
> Out of the world's wide wilderness."

PILLAR OF SALT

Genesis 19:26

ONE of the most remarkable incidents in the history of the destruction of the Cities of the Plain is, that the wife of Lot, looking and probably lingering behind, " became a pillar of salt."

The explanation of this which is now usually current is that of Bishop Patrick. The reader has, no doubt, seen it in many varied forms of phraseology, and we may therefore present it in the words of the author. The Bishop thinks, then, " that some of that storm which overwhelmed her country, overtook her; and falling upon her, as she stood staring about, and minded not her way or guide, suddenly wrapt her body in a sheet of nitro-sulphurous matter; which congealing into a crust as hard as stone, made her appear, they say, a pillar of salt, her body being, as it were, candied in it." This explanation is, however, older than Patrick, though he may be regarded as having made it current in this country; for this view of the subject had been before entertained by many Jewish and Christian writers.

We have no explanation to offer that seems to us better suited to meet the recorded circumstances. From the nature of the case, and from the peculiarly bituminous and saline character of the locality, through which this phenomenon was produced, we must not expect to discover many parallel instances which might be quoted in illustration. Accordingly, we find that the illustrative parallels which have been diligently sought by old commentators, have rarely any real bearing on the subject, being for the most part accounts of persons frozen to death, and long preserved in that condition uncorrupted, in the boreal regions; or else of persons first suffocated and then petrified by the mineral vapours of the caves in which they were hid; or otherwise of persons " turned to stone," and found, generations after, standing in the postures wherein they found their death. The only instance which we have met with that seems appropriate, and which rests on the authority of a contemporary of fair credit, is related by Aventinus, who states that in his time, about fifty country people, with their cows and calves, were, in Carinthia, destroyed by strong and suffocating saline exhalations which arose out of the earth immediately upon the earthquake of 1348. They were by this reduced to saline statues or pillars, like Lot's wife, and the historian tells us that they had been seen by himself and the chancellor of Austria.[1]

It is to be noticed, that the word translated a " pillar," does not express any particular form, but denotes any fixed standing object. The probability seems to be, however, that by the rapid cooling of the nitro-sulphurous crust, which enveloped the woman, she became fixed in a standing position, which might become a nucleus for more of the same materials, leaving an object of considerable bulk, widest at the base, but probably of no considerable height.

It would scarcely seem that such a saline body was likely to be of long duration in a very humid climate, subject in winter to heavy rains and the action of water-courses. If God designed that it should be preserved as a monument of the transaction, there is no difficulty in supposing that it was so. But this does not appear to have been the case. There is no allusion to any such monument as still subsisting in the whole Scripture; and the usual formula " unto this day," by which the sacred writers in the history of great transactions usually indicate the continuance, to their own time, of ancient monuments and names, is in this instance omitted. Besides, the whole appearance of the district, and of the lake which now covers the vale of Siddim, is, to this day, a most grand

[1] *Annal. Bavar.*, lib. 7.

and standing monument of the whole of that dreadful judgment of which the death of Lot's wife was one incident; and of the woman herself, the record in the book of Genesis is itself the most striking and ineffaceable memorial.

Nevertheless, when men acquainted with this history found in the neighbourhood something like a pillar, or some erect figure composed of salt, they immediately concluded that they had found the pillar into which Lot's wife was turned. Some necessity was felt to account for its preservation for so many ages; and while, on the one hand, it was alleged that it was preserved by the miraculous reproduction of the wasted parts, on the other, it was held sufficient to suppose that all waste was naturally repaired by the deposits of the dense exhalations with which the air was impregnated.

The first notice of its supposed existence is in the apocryphal Book of Wisdom, written in the first or second century before Christ. Speaking of the destruction of the Cities of the Plain, the writer says: "Of whose wickedness even to this day the waste land that smoketh is a testimony, and plants bearing fruit that never come to ripeness: *and a standing pillar of salt is a monument of an unbelieving soul.*" Wisd. x. 7. This shows clearly enough the opinion prevailing among the Jews in the time of the writer of the Book of Wisdom.

Josephus declares that it was standing in his time, and that he had seen it with his own eyes. This must be taken to show that he had seen a pillar of salt by the Dead Sea, and that he believed it to be the one into which Lot's wife was changed; but we have no evidence which can satisfy us that his impression was correct. Any actual transmitted *knowledge* of such a monument must have been broken during the sojourn in Egypt for some generations; and ever afterwards, and indeed always, the monument, if it still existed, lay in a quarter away from all travelled routes, and but rarely visited by Jews, even when Palestine was fully peopled. Clement of Rome, a Christian contemporary of Josephus, also states in one of his epistles, that the pillar of Lot's wife was still in existence; and Irenæus, in the next century, repeats the statement, with the addition of a hypothesis as to how it came to last so long with all its parts entire.

The statement of Jewish rabbis and Christian fathers is to the same effect; but as they merely repeat these earlier statements, little is really added to the weight of testimony. At length travellers began to inquire after this remarkable monument. The success of their inquiries may enlighten us as to the origin of the earlier accounts; and may well suggest that the natives of the region and the neighbouring shepherds have in all instances imposed upon the credulity of travellers, by following their usual practice of answering leading questions in accordance with the supposed wish of the inquirer, and even by pointing out any object that could be made to pass for what the traveller sought. We have been at some pains to make, for our own satisfaction, a collection of instances; and we find that hardly any two of them agree as to the locality in which the mysterious pillar was shown to them, or in which they were assured that it existed. Some meet with it on the east side of the lake, others on the west side; some near the northern extremity, others at the southern; some find it upon a rock, or cliff, or slope, others upon the beach, or in the water, or under the water. In proportion as inquiry has become more exact, our accounts of this pillar have been fewer; and most of the best travellers who have been in this quarter for the last two hundred years, have left the subject altogether unnoticed.

The researches of the recent American expedition to the Dead Sea, have thrown new and interesting light upon the matter. The course of their survey could hardly fail to bring under notice every marked object upon either shore; and one they did find, an obviously natural formation, which—or others in former times like which—might readily be taken by persons unaccustomed to weigh circumstances with the precision we are now accustomed to exact, for the pillar of Lot's wife.

Among the salt mountains of Usdum,[1] on the *west* side of the kind of bay which forms the southern extremity of the Dead Sea, the party beheld, to their great astonishment, while boating along the shore, a lofty round pillar, standing apparently detached from the general mass, at the head of a deep, narrow, and abrupt chasm. They landed, and proceeded towards this object over a beach of soft slimy mud, encrusted with salt, and, at a short distance from the water, covered with saline fragments and flakes of bitumen. The pillar was found to be of solid

[1] An apparent transposition of Sodom.

salt, capped with carbonate of lime, *cylindrical in front and pyramidal behind*. The upper or

PILLAR OF SALT AT USDUM.

rounded part is about forty feet high, resting upon a kind of oval pedestal or mound, from forty to sixty feet above the level of the sea. It slightly decreases in size upwards, crumbles at the top, and is one entire mass of crystallization. It is not isolated, though it appears so in front. A prop or buttress connects it with the mountain behind, and the whole is covered with debris of a light stone colour. It is added, by the narrator of the expedition, that " its peculiar shape is, doubtless, owing to the action of the winter rains."

It had previously been heard from the Arabs that such a pillar was to be found somewhere upon the shores of the sea; but their reports in all other matters had proved so unsatisfactory, that little attention had been paid to them in this instance. Lieut. Lynch, the officer in command of the expedition, and who has written the account of its discoveries, does not suppose he here found the pillar of Lot's wife, nor does it appear that even the Arabs supposed it to be such; but it is very properly pointed out that it was probably a pillar of this sort, produced by the action of water upon one of the masses of rock salt, which abound toward the southern extremity of the Dead Sea, that the ancient writers had in view, and which they supposed to be that into which Lot's wife was turned. We are by this instance enabled to see the

natural process by which such pillars are formed. It seems to us that the real pillar of Lot's wife must have been on the opposite side of the lake, for the fugitives were proceeding to Zoar, which lay in that direction. And it must not escape our notice, that the unhappy woman appears to have been overtaken by her death in the plain; whereas this pillar stands upon a hill from forty to sixty feet above the beach, with loftier mountains immediately behind. The pillar itself also is forty feet high, which we should suppose to be considerably taller than either Lot or his wife. Yet all these circumstances would, in ages of less exact observation, have had no weight, and this very pillar would assuredly have been pronounced as being beyond all doubt or question, the " monument of an unbelieving soul."

DEAD SEA DIFFICULTIES

Genesis 19

IT is probably the general impression among the readers of Scripture, that the vale, or enclosed plain, now covered by the waters of the Dead Sea, was formerly dry land, and formed, as a whole, the fertile vale, " well-watered everywhere," which Lot sought for its rich pastures. On looking more closely, however, a difficulty is seen in this which may at the first view elude our notice. It is clear that the Jordan must always have come into this vale as it does at present; and the general impression doubtless is, that it was then traversed by that stream, which contributed greatly to its beauty and productiveness; besides which there are other lesser streams— lesser, but still considerable, especially in winter —which must then, as now, have entered the same basin, adding their waters to the Jordan.

This, altogether, forms a very large body of water, continually passing into the vale; and the question was, What became of it after having passed through this enclosed plain, before there was a lake to receive it? There appeared no satisfactory solution. It was seen that it could not have gone off westward or south-westward to the Mediterranean, on account of the height of the intervening district; and the same objection appeared to apply to its progress to the Red Sea.

Some thought it might have been absorbed in irrigation; but the water would have been far more than sufficient to irrigate a greatly larger area than that of the vale, had every inch of it

THE DEAD SEA

been under cultivation; and that it was far from being wholly under cultivation is shown by the fact, that Lot repaired to this vale with his large flocks and herds for pasturage. It was then thought by some that the river must have had a subterraneous outlet to the Mediterranean; and although this was objectionable, as a purely gratuitous hypothesis, there appeared no other mode of surmounting this very serious difficulty.

So the question rested, until the researches of Burckhardt in this region, in the year 1816, brought to light the very important and interesting fact, that a broad valley, like the bed of a river, extends along the foot of the mountains of Seir, all the way from the Dead Sea to the eastern arm of the Red Sea, anciently known as the Ælanitic Gulf, and now as the Gulf of Akaka. We had thus at once provided for us a most satisfactory solution of the difficulty. What could seem more plain and evident than that, previously to the formation—in that day when the Lord over-threw Sodom—of the lake now called the Dead Sea, the river Jordan, enhanced by tributary streams, made its way down this valley to the Red Sea?

Having ourselves personally felt a deep interest in this question, and having so long rested in this as a most satisfactory and beautifully simple elucidation of a great geographical problem, it was with real disappointment, and with something not unlike grief, that at a later period we felt that this explanation must be given up, in the face of the serious difficulty which a more recent explorer brought against it. This was Dr. Robinson of New York, who, in his *Biblical Researches*, urged that the Jordan could never have flowed down the valley in question, seeing there is not a descent in that valley towards the Red Sea, but an *ascent* from the lake to it; and that, in fact, the waters of this vale (called the Arabah) do, in the northern part, direct their course *towards* the Dead Sea, and not from it. This discovery, while it throws a great and apparently insurmountable obstacle in the way of the previous hypothesis, enabled Dr. Robinson to dispose of the waters of the Jordan, by leading him to conclude that a lake, receiving the waters of the south as well as of the north, did always exist in the plain; but it was supposed that the waters were, before the destruction of Sodom, sweet and wholesome, and that the lake was of less extent than it afterwards became. In fact, it seems to be assumed that the increase was formed by the submersion of that comparatively small portion (about one-fifth of the whole), which now forms the southern extremity or bay of the lake, separated therefrom partly even now by a peninsula.

With this we were obliged to be content, though far from being satisfied, as there still remained some considerable difficulties. It had always been felt that the whole basin of the Dead Sea was but a small area for the dominion of the five kings; but now they were driven into a mere corner of the space previously allowed them. All the five cities must have been in this contracted area. They were at least considerable cities for that age; and could not have been much nearer each other than is usually the case at the present day with the towns of thinly peopled countries. Within this space, their very gardens and orchards (which commonly extend to a considerable distance around even small towns in the East) must have touched each other, without a provision for arable fields. How, then, was there so much free pasture that Lot removed into the plain with all his herds to enjoy it? Again, it is clear that in Genesis xiii. 10, the plain to which Lot went is called "the plain of the Jordan," implying that the Jordan flowed through it; whereas, if a lake had been previously there, that lake lay between him and the Jordan, seeing that he must have been in the land at the southern extremity of it. Again, it is said that the land to which Lot went, this "plain of the Jordan," was "well watered everywhere before the Lord destroyed Sodom; even as the garden of the Lord, like the land of Egypt, as thou comest unto Zoar," or rather, "as far as unto Zoar" (the southernmost of the five cities). "Well watered," indicates a river, not a lake. The comparison to Egypt and its Nile has the same force. How, then, could the whole district, from north to south, be like the garden of the Lord, if three-fourths of the entire surface were covered by the waters of a lake?

In view of these difficulties in the new theory, we longed to find our way back to the perfect satisfaction and comfort of the anterior hypothesis. And we rejoice to say that this seems to have been found, or at least indicated, by the late American expedition to the Dead Sea. The narrator of the expedition (which explored this lake as well as the Jordan in all its parts) considers the inference from the Scripture account to be, that this entire chasm was a plain *sunk* and "*overwhelmed*" by the wrath of God; and this view he considers to be borne out by the extraordinary character of the soundings obtained. From these it was seen that the bottom of the lake consists of *two* submerged plains, an elevated and a depressed one. The former, which is merely the southern bay, is at an average of thirteen feet below the water. The other, or northern part, forming the great body of the lake, lies fully thirteen hundred feet below the surface. Through this largest and deepest portion, *in a line corresponding with the bed of the Jordan*, runs a ravine, which again seems to correspond with the Wady-el-Jeib, or ravine within a ravine, at the south end of the Dead Sea. The obvious inference from this is, that the channel of the Jordan through this plain, with the plain itself through which it flowed, *sank down*, leaving the ancient bed of the river through the middle still distinguishable. Thus, of course, would be formed a deep basin to receive and retain, with a sufficient expansion for their passing away by evaporation, the waters which previously passed onwards through the plain. This depression seems to have been not wholly confined to the present bed of the Dead Sea, which was formerly but an expanded part of the valley of the Jordan, but to have extended its influence certainly to the higher or northern, and probably to the lower or southern portion of the Jordan's bed. The narrator says: "Between the Jabbok [1] and the sea, we unexpectedly found a sudden break-down in the bed of the Jordan. If there be a similar break-down in the water courses to the *south* of the sea, accompanied with the like volcanic characters, there can scarcely be a doubt that the whole Ghor (or valley of the Jordan, including the Dead Sea) has sunk from some extraordinary convulsion, preceded probably by an eruption of fire, and a general conflagration of the bitumen which abounded in the plain."

Apart from all other considerations, it is indeed difficult to account for the most wonderful depression of the bed of the Dead Sea to the depth now ascertained, without a convulsion thus extensive and terrible, and all the signs of which are still exhibited on the spot. As it satisfactorily answers all the objections which we have indicated, it best agrees with the scriptural statement; and here, therefore, also, as in all other cases, the more precise and certain our discoveries become, the more they are found to be in unison with the scriptural accounts.

Many collateral corroborations of this conclusion are set forth by Lieut. Lynch in his book. [2] Of these there is but one we can here mention, which

[1] The Jabbok enters the Jordan about thirty miles, in a direct line, above the Dead Sea.

[2] *Narrative of the United States' Expedition to the River Jordan and the Dead Sea.* 1849. To this work we are indebted for the plan of the Dead Sea given in the opposite page, and which is copied with no other alteration than the reduction of fathoms to feet for the soundings.

is, that the mountains around the sea are older than the sea itself; or, in other words, that their relative levels have not always been the same as

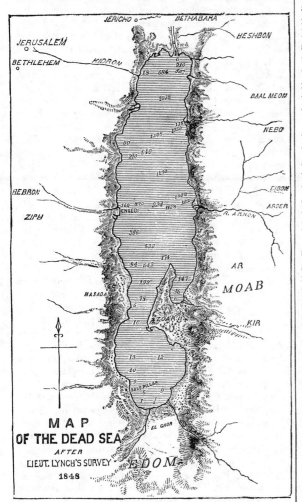

MAP
OF THE DEAD SEA
AFTER
LIEUT. LYNCH'S SURVEY
1848

they are now,—a most important fact, and one which is easily ascertained by such as are skilled in geological phenomena.

The writer concludes his account with these important words: "We entered upon the sea with conflicting opinions. One of the party was skeptical,[1] and another, I think, a professed unbeliever of the Mosaic account. After twenty-two days' close investigation, if I am not mistaken, we were unanimous in the conviction of the truth of the scriptural account of the destruction of the Cities of the Plain."

[1] So the Americans invariably spell "sceptical;" and the alteration is an improvement in the eyes of those who regard the analogy of language.

The view here advocated by Dr. Kitto cannot be reconciled with the results of recent scientific research in the Jordan valley. The whole valley, from the lake of Merom to the borders of Edom, is below the level of the ocean; and its physical conformation is such that it is manifest no sensible depression has taken place in it within the historic period. There is not a single trace of any convulsion so extensive and terrible as Dr. Kitto supposes. As this subject is both interesting and important, it may be well to sum up here the principal results of scientific research, and to indicate the light they throw on the formation of the Jordan valley, the origin of the Dead Sea, and the destruction of the cities of the plain.

1. The most careful examination has demonstrated that the formation of the great valley of the Jordan was coeval with that of the mountain ranges on each side, and long antecedent to historic times. It has demonstrated, further, that the valley was at some remote period filled with water up to the level of the ocean, and that the water gradually decreased, leaving a number of shore-lines along the sides to indicate its level at different periods. All these shore-lines are of a pre-historic age.

2. The Dead Sea is divided into two parts by the peninsula of Lisân. The northern forms a distinct basin of very great depth, which appears to have existed in its present form and extent long anterior to Abraham. The southern part is shallow, only a few feet; and, in many places, only a few inches of water, covering a flat, slimy plain. Sulphur springs exist along its shores; pure sulphur is strewn in layers and detached fragments over the surrounding plains; and masses of bitumen are from time to time thrown up from its bottom.

3. Along the south-western shore is a range of salt hills, seven miles long, called to this day *The Ridge of Sodom*.

4. In a valley, at the northern end of this ridge, Mr. Tristram recently made a most interesting discovery. The sides of the valley are cliffs of limestone, showing here and there on their surface traces of post-tertiary marl. "But since the marl has been washed out, there has been a second filling in of an extraordinary character, which is only now in course of denudation. There are exposed on the sides of the wady large masses of bitumen mingled with gravel. These overlie a thick stratum of sulphur, which again overlies a thicker stratum of sand, so strongly impregnated with sulphur, that it yields powerful fumes on being sprinkled over a hot coal. The layer of sulphurous sand is generally evenly distributed on the old limestone base, the sulphur evenly above it, and the bitumen in variable masses. In every way it differs from the ordinary mode of deposit of these substances as we have seen them elsewhere. Again, the bitumen, unlike that which we pick up on the sea-shore, is strongly impregnated with sulphur, and yields an overpowering sulphurous odour. Above all, *it is calcined, and bears the marks of having been subjected to extreme heat*."[1]

We may now venture to compare these results of scientific research with the Bible narrative.

There can be no doubt that the destruction of the cities of the plain was miraculous. The Lord rained upon them a shower of ignited sulphur. The vale of Siddim, we are told, was filled with bitumen pits. Bitumen is inflam-

[1] *The Land of Israel*, p. 354.

mable; and when ignited by the fiery shower, the pits and the whole plain, which was filled with them, would burn fiercely. Does not all this appear to be most strikingly illustrated by the discoveries of Mr. Tristram? His remarks deserve careful consideration: "So far as I can understand this deposit, if there be any physical evidence left of the catastrophe which destroyed Sodom and Gomorrah, we have it here. The whole appearance points to a shower of hot sulphur and an eruption of bitumen upon it, which would naturally be calcined and impregnated by its fumes; and this at a geological period quite subsequent to all the diluvial and alluvial action, of which we have such abundant evidence. The catastrophe must have been since the formation of the wady, since the deposition of the marl, and while the water was at its present level; therefore probably during the historic period."

The sacred writer states that the vale of Siddim became the Salt Sea, or was submerged (xiv. 3). The destruction of the plain and the cities was effected by fire. But this is not inconsistent with a subsequent inundation of the site. The whole southern part of the lake is, as has been stated, a muddy flat, covered with a few feet of water. This was once a fertile plain, and abundantly irrigated by numerous streams, which still flow in from the south and east. Suppose that vale to have sunk a few feet, or the water of the lake above to have risen a few feet, after the miraculous conflagration. Either supposition would accord with the biblical narrative, and would not be without a parallel in the history of countries exposed to earthquakes.

P.

To these remarks I add the following :—

I. The region is by no means of the character such as used to be described. Mr. Grove, in his article on the Salt Sea, in Dr. Smith's *Dictionary of the Bible*, gives a long list of plants, in addition to those mentioned by Dr. Hooker, in his article on Palestine. Mr. Tristram, in his *Land of Israel*, besides describing many species which he discovered, tells us how, as he rode along the shores, he could not resist the temptation to leave his horse and fill both arms with bundles of strange plants, in luxuriant bloom. The natural history of the neighbourhood is rich. Kingfishers stalk along the shores. The sportsman brings down wild duck and teal, sandpipers, Norfolk plovers, and large Greek partridges. Thrushes hop amongst the acacias; chiff-chaffs and blackheaded warblers, resort to the rills; wheatears are plentiful on the cliffs; and pretty little blackstarts may be obtained in any number. Mr. Tristram states, "I collected 118 species of birds, several of them new to science, on the shores of the lake, or swimming or flying over its waters. The cane brakes and oases which fringe it are the homes of about 40 species of mammalia, several of them animals never before brought to England; and innumerable tropical or semi-tropical plants, of Indian or African affinities, perfume the atmosphere."

II. Mr. Grove, who with great skill masses together the results of various observations, in reference to the geology of the district, states generally, that we are not sufficiently informed as to the manner in which the chasm of the Jordan and its lakes were produced; but present appearances, so far from proving that within the historic period the valley was dry, and then covered with water, plainly show just the contrary; the terraces and aqueous deposits pointing to the existence of a much wider and deeper body of water formerly than at present.

III. As to the exact level of the Dead Sea, that is now satisfactorily ascertained by Captain Wilson's Survey. On the 12th of March, 1865, the depression was found to be 1,292 feet below the level of the Mediterranean; but at some periods of the year, it rises two feet six inches higher. He also learned, from inquiry among the Bedouins, that during the early summer, the level is lower by at least six feet. The party who accompanied me to the Dead Sea, that same year, tested the buoyancy of the water. They floated more easily than I was able to do; but we all found ourselves very uncomfortable afterwards, as though we had been rubbed with soap or oil.

IV. The situation of the cities, until a recent period, was supposed to be at the south end of the lake. There Kitto locates them. The idea was founded on local traditions; the occurrence of names like Sodom and Gomorrah; the existence of a salt mountain; and the imagined situation of Zoar. Another opinion is now gaining ground. The argument as to the position of Zoar is demolished by the fact that it is sixteen miles distant from the traditionary site of Sodom. The similarity of names is not to be trusted when unsupported by other circumstances. The salt mountain can go for nothing in the matter. On the other hand, the testimony of Scripture points to a site on the north of the present lake. In Genesis xiii. 10-13, Abraham and Lot are represented as standing between Bethel and Ai—and there they see "all the plain of Jordan, that it was well watered everywhere, before the Lord destroyed Sodom and Gomorrah, even as the garden of the Lord, like the land of Egypt, as thou comest unto Zoar." The conditions of this narrative are met not at the *south* end, but the *north* end of the lake. The narrative implies that the cities were amidst the well watered gardens which Abraham and Lot saw from the height where they stood; but if the landscape was at the south end, they would not have been visible from that point of view. Besides, if Lot journeyed *east* (Gen. xiii. 11) to reach Sodom, Sodom could not have been lying far to the south. Again, we are told (Gen xix. 28), that Abraham, from Mamre, "looked toward Sodom and Gomorrah, and toward all the land of the plain, and beheld, and, lo, the smoke of the country went up as the smoke of a furnace." From a height near Hebron, a cloud of smoke to the north of the lake would be seen more easily than a cloud from the south.

V. The cities are not said to be submerged, but overgrown with grass (Deut. xxix. 23); and uninhabited (Is. xiii. 20); and covered with nettles, and salt pits (Zeph. ii. 9). In the Apocrypha, the spot is described as bearing fruit that never comes to ripeness, and as lying in clods of pitch and heaps of ashes (Wisd. x. 7; 2 Esd. ii. 9). These notes of desolation correspond with the tract of country to the north of the Dead Sea.

S.

SARAH'S VEIL

Genesis 20:16

THE destruction of Sodom, the shock of which must have been felt even in the camp of Abraham, and the effects of which he went out to view from the hills on the following morning, could not but make a deep impression upon the mind of the patriarch, who had hoped that his earnest intercession would suffice to arrest the overthrow. It was probably, however, not long before he learned that Lot had escaped; for when he heard that Zoar had been spared, he would naturally send one of his servants thither for intelligence. But as Zoar was on the other side of the scene of this fearful visitation, which, with the consternation created by the calamity, would probably for some days prevent intercourse, it is likely that Lot had left Zoar, and withdrawn to the mountains before Abraham's messenger could arrive; for it is clear that his alarm prevented him from making any stay in that place. This may explain what has seemed to many a difficulty — that even this calamity did not bring these near relatives together.

It was probably owing to the confusion into which the country was thrown by this awful judgment, that Abraham soon after removed his encampment to a more distant place than he had visited since his return from Egypt. This was in the territories of Gerar, towards the Mediterranean. The people here were, even thus early, Philistines, and had a king named Abimelech. Here the very same thing took place with respect to Sarah as had happened in Egypt; and she was delivered from the danger by the same means. Indeed, there is much similarity in the state of things generally in this country, and especially in the condition of regal power, to that which existed in Egypt at the time of Abraham's journey thither; and if the people who then ruled in Lower Egypt were, as there is reason to think, the intrusive dynasty of conquering strangers known to history as the Hyksos or Shepherd kings,[1] there is abundant reason to infer that the

Philistines were, in their origin, a branch of the same race which had extended itself in this direction. We find in both countries a more orderly regal government than existed among the princes of Canaan. On entering both, Abraham was led to deny his wife, from fear of the regal power. In both, he communicated directly with the kings; both monarchs knew and feared, in a certain sense, the name of the Lord; both spoke the language of Abraham (which the native Egyptians did not, Gen. xlii. 23); both exercised the same rights over women, and both made use of them in the case of Sarah. The differences arise chiefly from the character of the men; and Abimelech is the more interesting individual of the two. He indeed, like Pharaoh, loads Abraham with gifts of slaves, oxen, and sheep, in atonement for his unknowing injustice; he does not, however, send the patriarch away, but says with princely courtesy, "Behold my land is before thee; dwell where it pleaseth thee!"

His remonstrance with Abraham is also dignified and becoming; and the neat sarcasm, too complimentary to wound, with which he closes that remonstrance, is highly worthy of attention. In our Bible it is read thus,—it is to Sarah he speaks,—"Behold, I have given thy *brother* a thousand pieces of silver; behold, he is to thee a covering of the eyes, unto all that are with thee, and with all other." Thus, adds the sacred historian, "she was reproved." It must be confessed that this does not read very intelligibly. It is generally agreed that the words rendered "a covering for the eyes," or "eye-covering," denote a veil: and it appears to us that Abimelech means to say, that having given this money, she might procure therewith a veil—such as, according to the custom of towns, might hide her fatal beauty; or such as might indicate her wifehood, that she may not again be taken for an unmarried woman. It is under this view that a learned German translator thus renders the text: "Behold, I have given thy brother a thousand shekels of silver; with it buy thee a veil, and wear it before all that are with thee, and before all other, so that thou mayest be distinguished." The words undoubtedly denote an "eye-covering;" and we

tians, on account of the memories of that race from whose tyrannies they had been lately delivered. In Joseph's time all is Egyptian, implying that the native race of kings had then recovered its power, and had expelled the intruders.

think it has not been clearly explained how this should come to denote a veil. It is, as it seems to us, because there is a kind of veil or head wrapper used in the East, which does not cover

EASTERN VEIL OR HEAD WRAPPER

the eyes, but leaves exposed so much of the face as lies between the forehead and the mouth; and it was not this kind of veil, but one which should cover the face wholly, and therefore the eyes also, that Sarah was counselled to wear.

In further explanation, it is to be observed that, even at the present day, unmarried females among the pastoral tribes do not wear any kind of veil. The married women do *partially* veil the face by means of a kerchief, passed around the head, with the ends drawn round the neck, and covering the lower part of the face below the mouth. In towns, the face is wholly covered; and this custom is so far adopted among the tribes which lie near large towns, and have much intercourse with them, that the men compel their women to appear veiled before strangers. Now, if these usages anciently existed, as there is every reason to suppose, Sarah, when passing as Abraham's sister, must have gone unveiled, when seen at all. As a married woman, she would have worn the head dress which covered part of the face; but now Abimelech counsels her, not only to do that—not only to assume the veil proper to her order, but, while near the town, to shade her dangerous attractions altogether, even to the extent of covering her eyes with the kind of veils worn by the women of towns. Thus understood, the words of Abimelech afford a very fine example of a compliment wrapped up in a good humoured reproof.

It has been urged against this interpretation, that the sum named is too large for the purpose.

We do not, however, know the precise value of these pieces of silver. But the whole amount could not have been very considerable; and the higher class of veils are at this day very expensive. But granting that it were more than the occasion required, there is surely an obtuse literality in exacting that the money should have so precise a relation to the object indicated by the king. How often do we see a sum of money presented, which is suggested in a gay or off-hand manner to be for the purchase of a nosegay or a ribbon, although sufficient for a much larger and more costly appropriation. In our own case this is regarded as a graceful under-valuation of the offering; and why not so in the case of Abimelech?

There is a wedding custom among the Bedouins, which strongly illustrates the distinction made by the veil between a married and unmarried woman. The custom has not come under our own cognizance, but it rests on the high authority of Burckhardt, who states "that the bride is taken to her father's tent by her young men, who there place her in the women's apartment; and one of the bridegroom's relatives immediately throws over her an abba or man's cloak, completely enveloping her head, and exclaims, 'None shall cover thee but such a one!'" This also brings to mind poor Ruth's supplication to Boaz, that he would take her matrimonially under his protection: "Spread thy skirt over thine handmaid."

It appears from all this, that the use of the veil as a covering for the face of women had already come into use in towns, but was not employed any more than at present among the pastoral tribes; nor does it appear to have been at any time in *general* use as a covering for the face among the Hebrew women.

Mr. Forsyth, in his excellent *Observations on Genesis*, is clearly wrong in supposing, from the facts stated, that veils were *not* yet in use; but he rightly accounts for the origin of the practice: "It appears to have been introduced in consequence of the want of regular government, or the mismanagement of the country. A man who had a beautiful wife or daughter, desired her to cover herself with a veil, lest she should be coveted and carried off by violence. The veil was thus a mark of beauty, or that the wearer was in danger on account of her good looks. Hence women of more ordinary features were led to covet it, that they too might get credit for beauty; and so the veil became fashionable: all women used it, and use it to this day in these countries. It never was in general use in Europe, where polygamy did not exist; and the free and bolder spirit of the people rendered such proceedings dangerous on the part of the chiefs."

"GOD OPENED HER EYES"

Genesis 21:19

WHEN Sarah at length gave birth to a son, the event doubtless diffused a general gladness throughout the camp of Abraham. Yet the joy was not universal. Hagar, the bond-woman, beheld with sorrow of heart the frustration of the hopes she had cherished respecting her son as the future heir of Abraham. This feeling strengthened into jealousy and dislike, which she seems to have imparted to Ishmael, who was about twelve years old at the birth of Isaac. Sarah also, on her part, was by the birth of a son of her own, freed from the considerations which had probably hitherto restrained and regulated her conduct towards them. Nor is it difficult to account for this; for from one so much the senior of Isaac as Ishmael, and of a resolute and intractable character, she might reasonably apprehend some danger to the heritage, and even to the person, of her son, in case Abraham should depart from life during his nonage. Such feelings on both sides came to an explosion on the occasion of a public festival, held three years after the birth of Isaac, to celebrate his weaning. The hostility and rancour of Hagar and her son were so undisguisedly manifested on this occasion, that Sarah cast off all restraint, and insisted with Abraham that both mother and son should be forthwith sent away. But the "thing was very grievous in Abraham's sight, because of his son." It is not said because of Hagar, for it will be remembered that he had given up all right of control over her to Sarah; but it might be questioned whether she had the right to demand that his son should be expelled from the camp; and there seems a probability that on this point he would have resisted his wife's behest, had he been wholly left to himself. But he was not left to himself.

The word of God came to him, assuring him that this demand of Sarah, harsh as it seemed, was in conformity with the divine purposes concerning his sons, and would be eventually best for both of them. It is indeed not difficult to see that much strife and danger must have arisen from the continued presence of Hagar and Ishmael in the camp. Once assured of the will of God, the patriarch no longer hesitated. He "rose up early in the morning," and, after providing them with such refreshments as they were likely to need on the journey, he sent them away.

So they went forth, and wandered in the wilderness of Beersheba. Hagar, in the blindness of her sorrow, seems to have lost her way; and the water which she had in a skin-bottle was spent long before she came to any well, or to the tents where hospitality would have been extended to her. The young Ishmael, unused to hardship and weariness, was the first to break down. He could go no farther, and seemed likely to die of thirst in that hot wilderness. His mother, who had hitherto sustained his fainting steps, at length laid him down under the shelter of a shrub, and withdrew a little way off, that the sight of her irrepressible grief might not disturb his dying slumbers. "She sat down over against him, and lifted up her voice and wept." Did she cry to God? He had before met her in that very wilderness, and had spoken comfortably to her, and she might think that He would not forsake her now. There is not, it must be confessed, any sign that she remembered this; and too often in our extremest need do we, like her, forget what most it behoves us to remember. But if she had forgotten God, He had not forgotten her. In that moment of her deepest despair, when she sat most forlorn and bereft of hope, a voice which she had reason to remember, called to her with paternal tenderness, "What aileth thee, Hagar? Fear not." There was a gentle rebuke in this. Had she but faith in the promises made to her of old respecting the future destinies of her son, she might have known and felt that she had nothing to fear for him. She was then encouraged to rouse herself from this crippling despair, and bestow upon the lad the soothing attentions of her motherly love; and the promise that he should yet become "a great nation" was emphatically renewed.

At that moment "GOD OPENED HER EYES, and she saw a well of water." All care, all trouble, was now over. She hastened to fill her skin-bottle, and brought drink to her son, to whom that refreshment soon imparted new life and strength.

To the piously thoughtful mind, there is much that suggests serious reflection in the closing incident. The well was there all the time; its refreshing waters were all the time within her reach; but she saw them not until "the Lord opened her eyes." So with us, it is our blindness that is the cause of all our grief. And our blindness is proportioned to our unbelief. It has been most truly said, that

"Unbelief is blind;"

but it is more than blind, it is blindness. What avails it to the blind man who is hungry, that food is close before him? he sees it not. What profit to him, when worn with long travel, that there is a resting-place by the wayside at his right hand? he sees it not; and being unseen, it is the same to him as if it were a thousand miles off. What boots it to him, that when dangers surround him, and he fears to set one foot before another in dread of stumbling upon "the dark mountains," a guide who never misleads is walking before him; and that a strong arm that will not suffer a hair of the head to perish, is stretched out over him, to guard him from all peril? Alas! he is blind. All these things are as if they were not, to him. He is athirst and hungry, not because there is not abundance of meat and drink, but because he sees not his father's storehouses and barns; because he considers not that his Father's cattle are upon a thousand hills; and because his world-shaded eyes behold not the fountains of living waters which spring up throughout his Father's land, to quench all thirst, and to refresh all weariness. He feels ready to perish because of the long and weary way; not because there is not rest, but because he sees not the beckoning hand, because he hears not the hailing voice, "Come unto me, all ye that labour and are heavy laden, and I will give you REST!" not because there is no safe path among the sands of the desert, but because the guide is not seen, and the voice is unheard that cries, "*This* is the way; walk ye in it!" He lives in terror of soul for the dangers around him; not because there is no safety, no deliverer, no tower of hope, but because these things are hidden from weak and unbelieving eyes. The fortress of our strength is to such eyes invisible, although it rises gloriously upon the hills, strong in bulwarks, and beautiful with banners. But men pass tremblingly on, not seeing the glorious citadel. They are blind, and they are also deaf; for they hear not the strong but silvery voice that rings clearly through all the valleys, "Turn ye to the stronghold, ye prisoners of hope."

May God open our eyes, and keep them open! Ah! what sights should we behold; what assurance against all the trial, and doubt, and fear that sadden life, should we possess, were our eyes anointed with spiritual eye-salve, that we might see! Should we not, with Hagar, behold wells of refreshing water in the wilderness? Should we not, with Jacob, see the angels of God ascending and descending on errands of mercy to mankind? Should we not, like the servant of Elisha, behold the hosts of heaven engaged for our defence? Should we not, if we could look up steadfastly to heaven, like Stephen, see the glory of God, and Jesus standing at His right hand? And were our eyes thoroughly opened, as faith can open them, might we not view, as distinctly as did the disciple "whom Jesus loved," "that great city, the holy Jerusalem," in which not only the "abominable," but "the *fearful* and the *unbelieving*," can have no part?

A cursory perusal of the narrative of Hagar's expulsion from the household of Abraham is calculated to leave a somewhat painful impression upon the mind. One feels inclined, on first thoughts, to say that Abraham's conduct was unnatural, and even cruel, considering the relationship in which she stood to him. A fuller consideration of the whole circumstances, however, effectually removes such hasty conclusions and misconceptions. The immediate cause of Hagar's expulsion was her own and her son's misconduct. On a festive occasion, when every member of Abraham's family ought to have rejoiced with him and Sarah, Ishmael attempted to make Isaac an object of laughter and mockery. Both he and Hagar, his mother, must have known that Isaac was the child of divine promise—that he was, in fact, a special gift from God; and therefore this insolent mockery was all the more unseemly and inexcusable. It would appear, besides, that Ishmael assumed something of a threatening attitude. Sarah's remark, "The son of this bond-woman shall not be heir with my son," implies that Ishmael had threatened to keep his old position in Abraham's house, even though it should be by violence. If this was the case, then the peace and safety of the family demanded his expulsion. It ought to be remembered that Ishmael was no mere child now. He was nearly seventeen years old. His fierce and restless character, as predicted by the angel of the Lord (chap. xvi. 12), had ere this begun to be developed. Further, it must not be supposed that Abraham sent away Hagar and his son altogether unprovided for into the wilderness, or, as some suppose, to find their way to her people in Egypt. It is much more likely that he gave them directions to go to some outlying section of his own people ; and that his purpose was to assign Ishmael a fitting portion, and to let him begin life for himself. The skin of water and the bread he gave Hagar were enough to meet their wants until they should reach the place appointed. In journeying, however, they lost their way. God appears to have ordered it thus, that He might show them their sin, and humble their proud spirits. He waited till all natural hope was past—till the fiery youth had laid him down to die—till the ambitious mother had given way to despair; and then He demonstrated to both His watchful care and providence, and He saved them by a miracle.

P.

THE GROVE

Genesis 21:33

In the history of Abraham's descendants, the use of groves is continually represented as objectionable and idolatrous ; and we find that, on entering the land of Canaan, they were particularly enjoined to cut down the groves of the inhabitants, or to burn them with fire. It is named among the most serious offences of the kings of Israel, and some of those of Judah, that they planted groves, or did not cut down the groves ;[1] and those kings by whom groves were destroyed are greatly applauded.[2]

Yet we see Abraham planting a grove at Beersheba, where his camp had for some time been established, and which became afterwards one of the chief stations of his tribe. What can be more natural, it may be asked, than that a man should plant a grove for shade and refreshment near his camp? Yet it is not so. Planting trees is among the very last objects that a pastoral chief would think of, had he no further views. And, indeed, it is expressly stated that he *had* a religious object. "Abraham planted a grove in Beersheba, and called there on the name of the Lord, the everlasting God." How, then, did that which was harmless or laudable in Abraham become a crime to his descendants? The answer is not difficult to find.

[1] Exodus 34:13; Deuteronomy 12:13; 1 Kings 14:15.
[2] 2 Kings 18:4; 23:14; 2 Chronicles 14:3; 17:6; 19:3; 31:1; 34:3.

We must regard Abraham not as an isolated individual, but as the chief and master of many hundred persons, who worshipped God with him by sacrifice and prayer. They must have met together for these acts of worship, which, doubtless, the patriarch himself conducted. One tent could not have contained them all; but a grove of trees would afford all the shade and shelter required. Hence, when men had no fixed abodes, or afterwards, when they had not yet learned how to construct edifices large enough for many persons to join them in an act of worship, groves of trees became their temples—the first temples of mankind. It was also, it would seem, regarded as becomingly reverent, that the altar appropriated to sacrificial worship should not stand out among the common objects of the wayside, but should be decently veiled from careless notice by a screen of trees.

This seems obvious and natural, and is alone sufficient to account for the use of groves in worship. But as things rapidly tended to corruption in those early ages, the worship in groves became idolatrous, and ideas came to be connected with them which were in the eyes of God abominable. It was with them as with the brazen serpent, which in the first instance was preserved as a monument of a memorable transaction, but which, when it began to be looked to by the people with idolatrous eyes, was very properly destroyed by the good king Hezekiah (2 Kings xviii. 4). So the worship in groves was not in itself blameable. It was even usefully solemnizing ; and it appears to have involved a recollection of Eden, to which it would be difficult to ascribe any other than a salutary influence. But when gross idols arose around, and the groves were considered proper to their worship, it behoved God to make a distinction between His worship and theirs, and to show that He had no fellowship with the powers of darkness. Therefore, groves were forbidden to be planted near His sanctuary or altar, and those which had been polluted by idol-worship were to be destroyed. Let it also be recollected that it was in the highest degree important to check among the Israelites the universal tendency to multiply gods, and to localize them, which would have unfitted them for that testimony to the divine unity which it was their special calling to bear, and for which they had been set apart among the nations. It was therefore strictly enjoined that there should be in their land but one altar, and one place of ritual service. Had groves and altars been allowed to be set up in every place that men thought proper, it is not difficult to see that a separate and distinct god would soon have been assigned to every shrine; and the great doctrine, to uphold which Israel was made a nation, would in no long time have been utterly lost, so far as their agency in its conservation was concerned. Nothing but a stringent and absolute interdiction could have met the danger. Looking at the subject in this view we find ample reasons not only for the prohibition of groves near the altar of God, but for their general suppression throughout the land. With regard to the former interdiction, it may be added that the existence of a grove near the sanctuary might not only have seemed to assimilate the Lord to the idols of neighbouring lands, but might have tended to bring down His worship to a level with theirs. Nothing is more notorious than the shameful orgies that were celebrated in these sacred groves; and it might well be feared that the presence of a grove would soon bring around the sanctuary a crowd of idle devotees, coming, not to worship, but to enjoy themselves, and where the leafy screen and the cool and pleasant shade would soon allure to all kinds of licentious freedom. The many allusions to the subject in Scripture show how general and how ancient was this addiction to worship in groves; and the difficulty with which the Israelites were kept from it appears throughout the sacred history. Indeed, so common was the practice, that the geographer Strabo, who lived in the century before Christ, states that in his time "all sacred places, even where no trees were to be seen, were called groves."

That this practice probably originated in the traditions of the garden of Eden, in reference to the tree of life and the tree of knowledge, we have had a former occasion of indicating,[1] and some remarkable corroborations of this were then pointed out. From the nature of the case, the analogies of this kind are to be sought in the actual practices of the heathen, and not in the short allusions, mostly prohibitive, of Scripture. There is, indeed, one text which has been thought to bear strongly on this view. It is in Isa. lxvi. 17: "They that sanctify themselves and purify themselves in the gardens, behind one *tree* in the

[1] *Daily Bible Illustrations* Vol. 1, pp. 174-177.

midst." But the text will not bear this stress. The very word ("tree") which is most important to this view is not in the original, but is supplied; and the "one in the midst" does not appear to be a *tree* but a *person*, behind whom the other worshippers in the grove arranged themselves, while their worship was conducted by him. It is still the usual practice in the worship of eastern nations for a person to set himself in advance of the others, as a sort of fugleman, whose acts and motions are imitated by the others. In this, as in many other cases, support for particular views has often been sought in texts which are seen to have a wholly different meaning when they come to be rightly understood.

It claims to be noticed, that although Beersheba is the only one of Abraham's stations in Canaan where he is said to have planted a grove, yet there is evidence that there were trees at two of the three other stations which he frequented in that land. His first station on entering the land was near Shechem, under or hard by some great and famous tree, or collection of trees, for the

ABRAHAM'S TREE NEAR HEBRON

place called the *plain* of Moreh means properly the terebinth tree (or grove) of Moreh; and there is evidence to show that this spot was regarded as a place peculiarly appropriate to the worship of God. To this source, indeed, may be traced the figure which Shechem makes in the sacerdotal history of the Old Testament; probably long after the original terebinth grove in the neighbourhood had ceased to exist, and when any attention to the place as a grove would have been against the law.

Then again at Mamre, by Hebron, the presence of a grove is clearly indicated. In Gen. xiii. 18, it is said, "Abram removed his tent, and came and dwelt in the plain of Mamre." The word translated "the plain" is plural; and accordingly in xviii. 1 we read, "The Lord appeared unto him in the plains of Mamre." The plural would be awkward if the word really meant *plains;* but it means *trees,*—the same as at Moreh, that is, terebinth trees, though some think oaks. In fact, immediately after, we read that the patriarch invited his guests to rest "under the tree;" that is, as we may conceive, the nearest, and probably the most conspicuous, beside which his tent was pitched. In fact, the tree of Abraham at this place is historically famous; and on the spot there is still a most noble tree, locally regarded as representing that beneath which the angels were entertained by the patriarch.

Abraham's oak, as it is called, stands a short distance from Hebron. I rode to it through the valley of Eschol, rich in barley fields, studded with budding fig-trees and quinces in bloom, and innumerable fine streams, including numerous old stocks of the vines, successors, no doubt, of those which produced the enormous and goodly clusters borne back to the camp of Israel by the Jewish spies. The oak is a lofty and wide-spreading tree, twenty-two feet in girth—on the whole, the noblest son of the forest I saw in Palestine; but, of course, not the identical oak under which Abraham pitched his tent and received the angel visitors; for that oak grew more to the east, at Mamre, where now only a miserable olive or two can be found.

S.

HEROIC FAITH

Genesis 22

It is well remarked by an old writer, "that the labours or trials of Abraham's faith would afford a very fruitful subject for a philosophical and theological essay upon the nature and powers of heroic faith."[1]

Of this "heroic faith," Abraham's unflinching obedience, when the Lord saw fit to subject it to a great and fierce trial, by exacting from him the sacrifice of the son of so many promises and hopes as Isaac, is a most signal example. The world's history presents nothing like it. The instances which have been sometimes cited as parallel, will not stand comparison with it. The Lord's own

[1] Parker, in his *Bibliotheca Biblica*, a valuable work, published anonymously, in 5 vols., 4to, in 1720.

estimate of its importance and value is shown in the crowning recompense of His high approval and blessing,—a blessing the most full, emphatic, and solemn ever pronounced by God upon man.

Isaac, the heir of the promises, has grown up to be a young man, probably not less than twenty years of age; and the father rests happy in his tents, blessed with the favour of God, and beholding in this his son the accomplishment of all his hopes. Suddenly the command comes: "Take now thy son, thine only son Isaac, whom thou lovest, and get thee into the land of Moriah, and offer him there for a burnt-offering upon one of the mountains which I will tell thee of." Every word was fitted to rend his heart, and did doubtless rend it. And what did he say? Nothing. We may conceive much that he might have said —that *we* might have said in the like case. But Abraham *said* nothing: he *did* as he was commanded. He was not only obedient, but he was prompt and forethoughtful in his obedience. There might be no suitable materials for the intended sacrifice at the spot to which he was going: he therefore prepares everything before he sets out; even the wood to form the fire which is to consume his son, he prepares and takes with him. Abraham appears to be anxious that there shall be on his part no sign of reluctant, lingering delay. "Early in the morning" he rises, and saddles his ass for the journey; and with his son, and attended by two servants, speeds on his way.

Two days they journeyed, and on the third Abraham lifted up his eyes, and beheld the place afar off. This place was "a mountain" in "the land of Moriah;" and Moriah being, as we know, the name of one of the hills of Jerusalem, there can be little or no question that it was in or near the site of the future city; and seeing that so long a journey to this particular spot was not likely to have been ordered without a special object, it is far from improbable that the place which was indicated for the scene of this transaction, was the very same on which, at a later day, a father greater than Abraham offered up a Son more illustrious than Isaac.

Here the servants were bidden to wait; and the father and son went on: the son bearing on his strong shoulders the wood which was to consume him; and the father having in one hand the fire with which the wood was to be enkindled, and the knife with which the son he loved was to be slain. But where was the victim? Abraham knew, but Isaac did not, and naturally asked his father the question; and the answer was: "My son, God will provide himself a lamb for a burnt-offering." This would seem to intimate that he expected some such substitution as actually took place; and we do know, that so assured was he that God would faithfully perform the promises to which the life of Isaac was essential, that, although he knew not how, he was satisfied that his son could not be eventually lost to him. As it cannot be doubted that he was fully determined to carry out his obedience, even to the extent of sacrificing his son, he must, as the apostle intimates, have expected that God would even raise him from the dead, rather than that His promises should be of no effect. He was prepared to believe anything rather than that God could be unfaithful to His plighted word. They arrive at the spot; the altar is made; the wood is laid on; and Isaac is bound, and laid upon the altar. The father's hand is uplifted, to fall upon the life of his son; but it falls not. The stroke is stayed by a quick and sudden word from heaven—"Abraham, Abraham! Lay not thine hand upon the lad, neither

ABRAHAM'S SACRIFICE

do thou anything unto him: for now I know that thou fearest God, seeing thou hast not withheld thy son, thine only son, from me." With fingers tremblingly glad did the father then unbind his son; and both united—their bosoms swelling with unutterable joy—in offering up the victim which the Lord *had* provided—a ram caught by the horns in a thicket hard by. Then

came down the great and rewarding words: "BY MYSELF HAVE I SWORN, saith the Lord; for because thou hast done this thing, and hast not withheld thy son, thine only son; that in blessing I will bless thee, and in multiplying I will multiply thy seed as the stars of the heaven, and as the sand which is upon the sea-shore; and thy seed shall possess the gate of his enemies: and in thy seed shall all the nations of the earth be blessed; because thou hast obeyed my voice." Nor, perhaps, was this all his reward. It is supposed by many that it was on this occasion that Abraham saw the day of Christ, and was glad;[1] his eyes being opened to behold the purposes of God, in that great and solemn act of atoning sacrifice through his well-beloved Son, which this transaction might very well typify or represent. If Abraham was thus instructed, as the words of our Lord permit us to suppose, there seems no other occasion in the whole history of the patriarch on which the revelation was so likely to be afforded. The obvious preparation for the disclosure, in his being directed to go to the very neighbourhood where our Lord suffered, seems to point to this conclusion; while there are reasons not difficult to assign, why the sacred historian may not have been authorized to make known the precise nature of the communication which made the heart of Abraham glad.

The prevalence of child-sacrifice in the ancient pagan world is known to the reader. It is indeed frequently indicated in Scripture, and it certainly existed in Canaan and the neighbouring countries in the time of Moses.[2] Hence arises the question, whether or not it was known before the time of Abraham. Some think that it was; and that hence the demand did not strike him with the astonishment which it would have produced, had the offering up of a son been previously unheard of. He would then also have felt that it became not him to withhold from the Lord the costly offering which the idolators offered to their gods, in the earnestness of their zeal to yield up that which they valued most. But, on the other hand, it is urged by some, that all the sacrifices of this sort among the heathen had their origin in mistaken inferences from this act of Abraham. It is difficult to decide this question; nor is it of much importance to do so. But even supposing that child sacrifice did not previously exist, it is difficult

[1] John 8:56.   [2] Leviticus 20:2-5.

to imagine that it could originate in the interrupted sacrifice of Isaac. A sacrifice so silently resolved upon, so unostentatiously prepared for, and the execution of which was so solemnly and so strikingly prevented, was but little calculated to induce other nations, even neighbouring nations, to imitate it and adopt it into their rites. It seems to have been far better suited to discourage such sacrifices than to originate or encourage them.

Many parallels from ancient history and poetry to this remarkable transaction have been produced. The most striking is that of Agamemnon in offering, or rather in consenting to offer, his daughter Iphigenia at the demand of the oracle. But this transaction altogether lacks the simple virtue and "heroic faith" of Abraham's behaviour. Agamemnon was a "king of men," and a mighty warrior; but in true heroic force of character he is not to be named with Abraham. Agamemnon is quite unmanned by grief and distraction, whereas Abraham is perfectly composed and equable; he is not only fixed and resolved in his obedience, but prompt and ready in all the needful preparations. Agamemnon, sorely against his will, complying with the demand of the oracle, hides his face with his mantle, that he may not see the last moments of his daughter; but Abraham, in obedience to the demand upon his faith and duty, wields with his own hand the weapon which is to take his child's life away. Again, the Grecian king seems to have been moved to compliance by the fear of provoking or discouraging his subjects and soldiers, and by that means of incurring failure or disgrace in all the objects of glory, ambition, or revenge, involved in the war in which he was embarked. But Abraham had no country to win or lose, no objects of human ambition to fulfil. His one object was to obey God, regardless of men's opinions. The only human opinion in which he had concern was that of his own house, which would probably have condemned him, and made his entire life bitter, had the deed been consummated. Further, the sacrifice of Iphigenia was public; in the presence of a host of armed men; of generous hearted soldiers, from whose compassion the father might have hoped a rescue when things came to the worst: for he must have often seen that other interests, views, and passions, are overruled and brought to nought by some sudden gush of human pity. But Abraham's proceedings were altogether private. Not even the servants were allowed to behold the deed, nor was even Isaac himself acquainted with the purpose till he came to the very place where he was to die. Besides, Agamemnon probably had other children; Abraham essentially but this one. Agamemnon's wife was not barren, and probably not old; Abraham's was both. Neither this one, nor any other of the hero's children, were sent to him as earnests or pledges of extraordinary promises or blessings, much less of such high and glorious privileges as appeared to be bound up in the life of the son thus doomed to die. Thus the comparison fails at every point, except that of human tenderness, and not perhaps in that; for Abraham loved Isaac very dearly, and never did he love him more than in that moment when his hand was lifted up to smite him down.

Let it not escape our notice, that Isaac himself was a willing victim. There can be no question, that in the last awful moments, Abraham communicated the truth to his son, and that he consented to yield obedience to the command of God and the authority of his father. This is implied in the fact of his consenting to be bound : for he was grown to strength and manhood ; and if he had but thought fit to struggle for his life, we cannot doubt that he might easily, without violence, have escaped from his father's hands and fled away. Much may be allowed for the absolute authority of a parent in those ages, even to life and death, over his own son ; but still, to the young, life is very sweet; and but for the high sense of duty to God, which such a son was likely to acquire from such a father, Isaac would not have been so passive in this transaction.

The mountain to which Abraham was directed, is here identified with Moriah at Jerusalem. To this view, assent is given by Dr. Harold Browne, in the *Speaker's Commentary*, and by Lange in his work *On Genesis*. But De Wette, Bleek, and Tuch amongst the Germans ; and Dr. Stanley and Mr. Grove, amongst English scholars, understand *Moreh* near Nablous to be the place. Mr. Grove (Smith's *Dictionary*) argues that Jerusalem lies out of the path of patriarchs, and has no part in the history of Israel till the establishment of the Monarchy. "The towers of Jerusalem," says Stanley, "are, indeed, seen from the ridge of Mar Elias, at the distance of three miles, but there is no elevation, nothing corresponding to the 'place afar of,' to which Abraham 'lifted up his eyes.'" (Stanley's *Sinai and Palestine*, 249). Moriah, the

Hill of the Temple, is not visible till the traveller is close upon it. If Salem was Jerusalem, and there stood Moriah, then the sacrifice could not have been appointed in a desolate place, but under the very walls of the royal city of Melchizedek. On the other hand, Moreh, attached to the town of Shechem, was a place well known to Abraham, being the spot of Abram's first residence in Palestine. Robinson reckons it a journey of twenty and a half hours from Beersheba to Jerusalem, and thirty-five hours from Beersheba to Shechem. When I was in the Holy Land, and travelled between the two points, it seemed to me quite possible to come within sight of *Moreh* on the third day. The argument of Mr. Grove, that Jerusalem lies out of the paths of the patriarch might be met by reference to Gen. xiv. 17, 18. Melchizedek, king of Salem or Jerusalem, met Abram in the valley of Shaveh, which is the king's dale, thought to be near Jerusalem. But the identification of Salem and Jerusalem is not certain ; and, if so, this would impair another of Mr. Grove's arguments. On the whole, I should say the question is not decided *clearly* either way.

S.

THE SEPULCHRE

Genesis 23

THE twenty-third chapter of Genesis is one of the shortest in the book; yet it is so full of circumstances illustrative of primitive customs and ideas, that every verse in it might form a sufficient theme for one of our Daily Illustrations. We must, however, be content to point out the general tendency and result of these circumstances.

The chapter relates the death of Sarah, and the negotiations of Abraham with the people of the land for a burial-place. Sarah died at the encampment at Mamre, near Hebron, at the age of one hundred and twenty-seven years. It is remarkable, that Sarah is the only woman whose complete age, death, and burial, are mentioned in Scripture. This was done, no doubt, to confer special honour on the mother of the Hebrew race; but it was also necessary, not only to form a proper introduction to the ensuing relation of the purchase of a hereditary burial-place, but to inform us that it was vouchsafed to her to live thirty-seven years after having brought forth Isaac at the age of ninety, and to see him grown up to man's estate.

We first see Abraham mourning for his dead. He leaves his own tent, and goes to that of Sarah, and sits upon the ground before the corpse, mourning, and not only mourning, but weeping for her. Some here interpose the remark, that the Hebrew mourning was for seven days, implying that Abraham sat for so many days before the corpse. This is absurd. However long the mourning, the burial of the dead has always taken place very soon in the East, seldom later than the day after dissolution. It was therefore with the freshness of his grief still upon him, that Abraham had to consider how his dead should be buried out of his sight. This is a question which is seldom in the East left to be considered in these awful moments. But Abraham was a stranger in Canaan, and had not acquired the possession of so much as a sepulchre in the land destined to be his heritage. This possession he had now, in this trying hour, to seek; for both propriety and feeling required that the wife of Abraham and the mother of Isaac should not be placed in any but a separate and appropriated family sepulchre, well secured from future application to any other use.

There was in a field near Hebron, a cave, which, from its name of Machpelah, appears to have been double; and on this Abraham had set his mind. It belonged to a person of wealth and distinction among the Hethites (or Hittites), who then occupied Hebron. The most obvious course would, according to our own usages, have been to go to this person and ask him to sell his cave. But our ability to do this with safety, arises from the perfection of the legal securities which may pass privately between man and man. In ancient times no security was felt, especially in matters connected with the sale and transfer of land, but in publicity and the presence of witnesses. Hence we see, throughout the Scripture, that all transactions of this nature are conducted in public, and usually in the gate of the city.

In the absence of buildings devoted to public business, and perhaps at first in the want of such paramount authority in any one magistrate or elder, as justified him in expecting the attendance of the others at his own house, the town gate was the most natural and obvious place of concourse. Here a sufficiency of witnesses to every transaction could be obtained; here the men whose evidence was required could attend with the least hindrance, as they passed morning and evening to and from their fields and their labour; and here, at such times, the parties whose presence was especially needed could be called, as they passed by, without any need of an apparitor. We see an instance of this in the book of Ruth. Boaz goes to the gate; and when the person whom he requires passes by, he calls to him, " Ho, such a one! turn aside, sit down here." Ruth iv. 1.

HEBRON, WITH THE CAVE OF MACHPELAH

So now, having this object in view, Abraham proceeds to the gate of the town, at the time when he knew the elders of the place would be there assembled. He was received with attention and respect; and on stating his wish to obtain possession of a burying-place, the answer was: " Hear us, my lord: thou art a mighty prince among us; in the choice of our sepulchres bury thy dead." They did not seem to understand that he wanted to have a sepulchre appropriated to his exclusive use, and supposed that they met his wishes by thus offering him permission to deposit the body of Sarah in any of their own tombs. But this, although a very handsome offer, according to the notions of the East, did not meet the views of Abraham. He, however, courteously acknowledged their civility, by rising from his seat and bowing to the people of the land.

He wanted the cave of Machpelah, and he saw the owner present; but, being apparently doubtful whether a person in such good circumstances would be willing wholly to alienate a part of his possessions, he does not propose the matter to him directly, but requests the elders that they will intercede with Ephron, that he may sell the cave to him for its full value in silver. Ephron, who, even if he had been so inclined, could not decently refuse a request thus tendered by such a man as Abraham, appears, nevertheless, in the eyes of those whom experience has taught to see through the outward shows of eastern character, to have been determined to make the best bargain he could, consistently with the necessity of preserving the appearance of liberality and deference. Abraham wanted only " the cave at the end of the field;" but Ephron, while professing, three times in one sentence, to make the whole a free gift to Abraham, takes care to intimate that he will be expected to take not only the cave, but the field in which it stood, probably in the feeling that the value of the field to himself would be deteriorated by the presence in it of a sepulchre belonging to another. But Abraham understands this show of boundless generosity very well; and he could not but know that the acquisition would cost him dear, if he consented to accept it as a present, and lay himself under the obligation of meeting the future expectations of Ephron as to a suitable return of the favour. Besides, the dignified independence of the man who refused to allow the king of Sodom the shadow of a ground for saying that he had made Abraham rich, would assuredly prevent him in any case from accepting a favour of this sort from any inhabitant of Canaan. He rose, and bowed himself once more, not to Ephron, but to "the people of the land." But his words were addressed to Ephron; and without objecting to the inclusion of the field in the bargain, he insisted on paying the full price for the whole property.

Nothing now remained but for Ephron to name the value, which he does with all the polite artifice of a modern oriental; for his words virtually amount to this: "Why should friends and wealthy men like us use many words about a piece of land worth only four hundred shekels of silver?[1] Bury thy dead, and thou canst pay me this trifle hereafter." But having got him to name his price, Abraham at once paid down the money in the presence of the witnesses, Ephron's own countrymen; thus securing the purchase beyond all question.

In the record of this concluding part of the transaction, we are told that "Abraham *weighed* to Ephron . . . four hundred shekels of silver, current money with the merchant." In these few words several important facts meet our notice: that silver had become the standard of value and the medium of exchange; but not yet perhaps absolutely to the exclusion of other but less perfect mediums, for Abraham clearly states (as in the original) his intention to pay the full in *silver*, as an advantage to the party of whom he makes the purchase. That which silver had thus already become, it remains throughout the Scripture; for gold was never in ancient times more than a costly commodity, not the standard of value; and, indeed, it is not such at this day in scarcely any country but our own. Other countries may have some small proportion of coins in gold, but the bulk of the currency is in silver, and silver only is the standard of value.

The next point that engages our notice is, that the silver was *weighed*. How does this consist with its being "current money with the merchant?" If it were current money, what need of its being weighed? That it was weighed at all, would suggest to most minds that it was not coined money; and various considerations would seem to show that it was not. Among these circumstances we do not, however, count the absence of any central authority—in Canaan, for instance—whose stamp should give authenticity to the coin; because if such a power existed anywhere, in Assyria or in Egypt, the coins of that power would doubtless circulate beyond the limits of its own territory, just as Spanish dollars are at this day current over nearly all the world. The probabilities are that the silver was cast into forms convenient for commercial interchanges; and these, receiving some mark or stamp which

[1] About fifty pounds.

showed that the metal was of the commercial standard of purity, became current money with the merchant, the quantity being still determined by weighing. It is even possible that the mere shape of these pieces of silver was taken to determine the purity of the metal; and that shape may have been in rings, which appears from the monuments to have been the earliest form of money among the ancient Egyptians.

EGYPTIAN RING MONEY

But although it seems to us probable that money was not in this early age properly coined, the fact of the silver being weighed is by no means conclusive evidence against its being so. At this day coined money is weighed in all the markets of the East; and even among ourselves, when any of our readers has had occasion to receive a sum in gold at the Bank of England, he will have had the sovereigns weighed out to him in bulk. In the latter case this is merely to save time, counting being a much slower process than weighing. But a saving of time is the last thing ever thought of in the East; and the weighing there of coined money is to secure that the pieces shall be of just weight. This point is admirably illustrated in an anecdote given by Mr. Forsyth. "Before the time of Lord Cornwallis, the silver rupee, for example, in Bengal, was of considerable thickness, and bore a stamp on each side; but it was not stamped, or, as it is called, 'milled' around the edges. Hence it could be easily pared or cut in the edges, so that the ordinary rupees were not all of one weight, in consequence of fraudulent operations on them. The stamp showed the purity of the metal, so as to render it current coin; but not being milled or stamped around the edges, it was necessary to weigh it, in order to ascertain that the proper weight in silver was delivered. Lord Cornwallis, when Governor General, put an end to this inconvenient kind of money, by establishing a mint at Calcutta, in which *thin* pieces milled round the edges were coined, in order to ascertain, as with us, *both* the quality and quantity of the coin, and so to supersede the necessity of weighing the money." We doubt if this simple contrivance has even yet, in the East, extended beyond India. Some of the most valuable eastern coins, in gold and silver, that we were a few years ago in the habit of seeing daily, had scarcely any edge at all, but exhibited irregular masses of metal around the border, dropping beyond the margin of the impression made by the die, in such excrescent shapes, as absolutely to suggest the idea of clipping, as an improvement to the figure of the coin.

The cave of Machpelah, in which Sarah was buried, exists to this day. It is the oldest known sepulchre; and from the time when Abraham wept by its open mouth, over the body of his wife, it has ever been held in the highest veneration. The Jews enclosed it within a splendid mausoleum; the Christians built a church over it; and the Mohammedans converted the church into a mosque. The three sects have thus united in honouring the patriarch's tomb with almost equal devotedness.

The town of Hebron lies in the narrow vale of Eshcol. On the eastern hill side, over it, tower the massive walls of Abraham's tomb. It overtops all the houses, and forms the one distinguishing feature of Hebron. The building is an open quadrangle two hundred feet long, one hundred and fifteen wide, and fifty high. It is constructed of colossal stones, beautifully hewn in the Jewish style, and reminding one of those in the foundation of the temple wall. This external shell is the mausoleum mentioned by Josephus, and was probably built in the age of Solomon. Within the enclosure is an elevated platform occupying the whole area, partly artificial, but mainly composed of a crown of limestone rock. At its south end is the mosque, originally a church. In this building are little shrines or chapels, enclosed with railings, similar to those which surround the royal tombs in Westminster Abbey. They contain respectively the tombs of Abraham and Sarah, Isaac and Rebecca, Jacob and Leah. Each so-called tomb consists of a coffin-like structure, built up of marble, and hung with embroidered palls. These are not, of course, the real tombs, but merely monuments in honour of the illustrious dead, who lie in the ancient cave beneath the platform. The cave itself is not now open to visitors; even the Prince of Wales could not obtain admission. Indeed, the guardians affirm that no man ever enters it. However this may be, one thing is certain—the burial place of the patriarchs is beneath this venerable structure, and has been guarded with the utmost jealousy from the earliest ages. It is not only quite possible, but highly probable,

that some remains of them, especially of the embalmed body of Jacob, still lie in the tomb. There is something at once solemn and exciting in the thought that our minds are led up by an uninterrupted and independent local tradition to the very time when Scripture history records, with such simplicity, and yet with such graphic power, the death and burial of the great heads of the Jewish nation. The cave of Machpelah is thus a connecting link between the patriarchal age and our own times.

P.

The mosque over the cave of Machpelah is an object of great attraction. When I was at Hebron, I examined the exterior. There are two flights of steps on the south side, and I would have given much for permission to ascend; but permission was impossible. The inhabitants of the town are most fanatical, and guard the shrine with extraordinary care; only two parties have been permitted to explore the chamber—the Prince of Wales, with his attendants, formed one; Mr. Fergusson, and those who accompanied him, another. A Mussulman told us no one since the Prince had entered the precincts. Whether Fergusson's visit was so secret that the people were not aware of it, or whether they simply wished to conceal the fact, I cannot say.

It is interesting to read Dr. Stanley's description:—

"I now proceed to describe the tombs of the patriarchs, premising always that these tombs, like all those in Mussulman mosques, and indeed like most tombs in Christian churches, do not profess to be the actual places of sepulture, but are merely monuments or cenotaphs in honour of the dead who lie beneath. Each is enclosed within a separate chapel or shrine, closed with gates or railings similar to those which surround or enclose the private chapels or royal tombs in Westminster Abbey. The two first of these shrines or chapels are contained in the inner portico or narthex, before the entrance into the actual building of the mosque. In the recess on the right is the shrine of Abraham, in the recess on the left that of Sarah, each guarded by silver gates. The shrine of Sarah we were requested not to enter, as being that of a woman. A pall lay over it. The shrine of Abraham, after a momentary hesitation, was thrown open. The guardians groaned aloud. But their chief turned to us with the remark, 'The princes of any other nation should have passed over my dead body sooner than enter. But to the eldest son of the Queen of England we are willing to accord even this privilege.' He stepped in before us, and offered an ejaculatory prayer to the dead patriarch, 'O friend of God, forgive this intrusion!' We then entered. The chamber is cased in marble. The so-called tomb consists of a coffin-like structure, about six feet high, built up of plastered stone or marble, and hung with three carpets, green embroidered with gold. They are said to have been presented by Mohammed II. the conqueror of Constantinople, Selim I. the conqueror of Egypt, and the late Sultan, Abdul Mejid. Fictitious as the actual structure was, it was impossible not to feel a thrill of emotion at standing on such a spot—an emotion enhanced by the rare occasion which had opened the gates of that consecrated place, as the guardian of the mosque kept repeating to us, as we stood round the tomb, 'to no one less than the representative of England.'

"Within the area of the church or mosque were shown the tombs of Isaac and Rebekah. They are placed under separate chapels, in the walls of which are windows, and of which the gates are grated, not with silver, but iron bars. Their situation, planted as they are in the body of the mosque, may indicate their Christian origin. In almost all Mussulman sanctuaries, the tombs of distinguished persons are placed, not in the centre of the building, but in the corners. To Rebekah's tomb the same decorous rule of the exclusion of male visitors naturally applied as in the case of Sarah's. But on requesting to see the tomb of Isaac, we were entreated not to enter; and on asking, with some surprise, why an objection which had been conceded for Abraham should be raised in the case of his far less eminent son, were answered that the difference lay in the characters of the two patriarchs— Abraham was full of loving-kindness; he had withstood even the resolution of God against Sodom and Gomorrah; he was goodness itself, and would overlook any affront. But Isaac was proverbially jealous, and it was exceedingly dangerous to exasperate him. When Ibrahim Pasha (as conqueror of Palestine) had endeavoured to enter, he had been driven out by Isaac, and fell back as if thunder-struck. The chapel, in fact, contains nothing of interest; but I mention this story both for the sake of the singular sentiment which it expresses, and also because it well illustrates the peculiar feeling which has tended to preserve the sanctity of the place—an awe, amounting to terror, of the great personages who lay beneath, and who would, it was supposed, be sensitive to any disrespect shown to their graves, and revenge it accordingly. The shrines of Jacob and Leah were shown in recesses corresponding to those of Abraham and Sarah, but in a separate cloister, opposite the entrance of the mosque. Against Leah's tomb, as seen through the iron gate, two green banners reclined, the origin and meaning of which was unknown. They are placed in the pulpit on Fridays. The gates of Jacob's tomb were opened without difficulty, though with a deep groan from the bystanders. · There was some good painted glass in one of the windows. The structure was of the same kind as that in the shrine of Abraham, but with carpets of a coarser texture. Else it calls for no special remark."—Stanley's *Sermons in the East,* 154.

S.

THE JOURNEY

Genesis 24:1-10

THE marriage of Isaac is the first of which we have any particulars in Scripture. Yet, instead of being short and meagre, as all the illustrations of social manners are in the most ancient histories of every other nation, this, which is the earliest, is also the fullest marriage narrative that the large volume of Scripture contains. One of the longest chapters in Genesis is devoted wholly to it. The narration is beautifully simple, and, like all the other social narratives of the book, is invested in the fullest degree with that indescribable charm of *naturalness,* which to every rightly constituted mind speaks more clearly for the authenticity of the book in which they are found, than whole volumes of argumentative evidences. The manners described are wholly different from ours; yet they have throughout, in even the smallest incidents, that obvious and coherent truthfulness, which is invariably recognized even by those who may not be thoroughly informed that the same system of manners and usages still subsists in the East.

The first thing that strikes us is the great and absorbing anxiety of Abraham that his son should not marry among the native women of Canaan, or among any but his own family, away in Mesopotamia. This is usually ascribed to his wish to keep the blood of the chosen seed, from which the Messiah was to come, from foreign intermixture. This may have had some weight in *his* estimation, perhaps, but it was of little real consequence, as we find women of alien blood among the ancestresses of the Lord Jesus; and, singular as the fact may appear, the names of none but such alien females do find place in His genealogy as given by Matthew. Without, however, overlooking this, we have a plainer and more satisfactory explanation in the general anxiety which we find existing among the Arabs at this day, that marriages should run in the same tribe or family; and that among them, as among the Jews, a man is held to have a right prior to all others to the hand of his cousin.

As Abraham cannot undertake this matter in person, and as he probably considered himself precluded from allowing the heir of the promises to return even temporarily to the land of his nativity, he was obliged to confide the business to the hands of the chief servant and steward of his household, identified by some with Eliezer of Damascus, whom we have previously seen as the person looked upon by Abraham as his heir before the birth of Ishmael. The patriarch had the highest confidence in this man's fidelity; he trusted all his substance into his hands; yet, on an occasion so momentous, he brings him solemnly under the obligation of an oath to execute faithfully the mission entrusted to him. The danger that Abraham apprehended was, lest this person, to save himself the fatigue and trouble of so long a journey, should bring a woman from some nearer and more accessible quarter, and introduce her as having been brought from the family of Padan-aram. It is difficult to see that Abraham could have apprehended anything else; and that he apprehended this—that such an imposition was regarded as possible—implies that such a woman would not, from any obvious circumstances in her appearance, manners, or speech, be at once detected; and it therefore shows that there could have been no very essential difference in these respects between the women of the remoter and the nearer country.

The servant is worthy of such a master as Abraham. He is conscientiously anxious to understand the nature of his enterprise, before he swears to carry it out. He suggests the possibility that the woman may not be willing to follow him. What does Abraham answer to this? Does he tell him to set forth the wealth and power of his master, to dwell upon the glorious promises of which Isaac was the heir, to expatiate upon the dignity and influence which will belong to her as the lady of this noble camp? Nothing of the kind occurs to his thoughts. "The Lord," said he, "before whom I walk, will send his angel with thee, and prosper thy way." What glorious freedom from all anxiety and care about events is there in such a thought as that! How happy are they who can enjoy—as all may that will—such blessed repose! This conviction and assurance inspirited the servant. He at once took the oath, and hastened his preparations for the journey.

At a future day the grandson of Abraham took the same journey on foot, and crossed the Jordan with a simple staff in his hand, Gen. xxxii. 10; but the servant of Abraham takes with him not less than ten camels. These, with the necessary attendance, would give the mission a respectable appearance in the eyes of the intended bride and her relatives, and stand in evidence of the wealth of Abraham. The animals would also carry the provisions required by the ambassador and his men for the journey, with the presents intended for the bride and her friends; and the number, doubtless, included the dromedaries to bring her and her suite, and two or three spare camels—of which a proportion is required in every considerable journey, to provide for the contingency of any of them falling lame or dying, or being lost or stolen.

CAMELS CAPARISONED FOR A JOURNEY

It will be observed, that this is the first historical notice of actual riding upon camels. These animals are so useful for other purposes than riding, that their mere presence in the patriarchal flocks would not alone assure us that they were employed for this purpose. But the information respecting this journey leaves us satisfied that the camel had already come to be engaged in those services of transport and of travel for which it is to this day used. To these it is well adapted by a physical constitution which gives it extraordinary power in resisting thirst, which enables it to endure much fatigue with little sustenance, and which renders the scant herbage of the desert its choicest food; and by the possession of a foot specially adapted, in the wise providence of God, for traversing the sandy wastes and arid tracts which, but for its aid, would be impassible. The journey which Abraham's servant took was not, however, through a *sandy* desert; but over a region which for the most part, where not green, consists of hard gravelly ground, for which, even better than for soft sand, the foot of the camel is adapted. This journey is one which is usually performed on horseback, and would in this instance probably have been so, had the horse been at this time brought into use for such common purposes.

Having been led to mention the camel thus particularly, we may notice that with all the frequent reference to the animal in Scripture, and with all the existing evidence of its great usefulness, there is not a word in its commendation throughout the sacred volume, which is not sparing in the praise of many other animals, seemingly less useful. There is a reason for this. If the matter be looked at, it is seen that all the most glowing eulogiums on the camel come from those who know it least, and who transfer, unconsciously, perhaps, the impression created by its great usefulness to its temper and character. But it is only in the descriptions of western travellers that the camel bears the same character of a

"Patient, honest, guileless animal,"

which the poet ascribes to the ox. But, alas! the camel, although it may be reasonably honest, is anything but patient or guileless. On the contrary, of all the animals which have been domesticated for higher purposes than to serve mankind merely as food, the camel is, past all doubt, the most churlish, irascible, revengeful, and self-willed. We have heard of strong attach-

ments between man and all other domestic animals, but never between a man and his camel. Of all the creatures promoted to be man's com-

THE APPEARANCE OF THE CAMEL WHEN CRYING

panion in travel and in rest, no one so unloving and unloved as the camel exists. Its very countenance, which the inexperienced call patient, is the very impersonation of malice and ill nature—even when its eyes are not kindled up into active spite, and when its mouth does not quiver with burning rage. Even among themselves quarrels are frequent; and he who

CAMELS FIGHTING

has been summoned by their sharp and bitter cries to witness a camel fight, will not easily forget the scene.

It is by the sheer force of important services that the camel has won his way into man's esteem, in spite of the evil qualities of his nature.

A MARRIAGE

Genesis 24

THE visit of Abraham's servant to Padan-aram is interesting and important, not only in its incidents, but from introducing us to an acquaintance with the stationary branch of Abraham's family, and with a phase of life and manners somewhat different from that which the Hebrew patriarch led. This family does not dwell in tents, but has a fixed abode in a town of some importance. Yet all its habits are essentially pastoral; some of the flocks and herds being kept near home, but the greater part being sent out, under the care of shepherds, to distant pastures, according to the exigencies of the season. It is nearly the condition of existence to which Lot came when he had settled himself in the town of Sodom, and has much resemblance to the form of life exhibited in the book of Job. Whatever other arguments there may be against the early date usually ascribed to that book, the one derived from the fact that Job had a fixed abode has therefore no weight, seeing that others, contemporaries and relatives of Abraham, dwelt in towns without abandoning the pastoral life.

The family, it should be remembered, is that of Nahor, the brother of Abraham and Haran. Nahor had eight sons by his wife Milcah, the daughter of his deceased brother Haran. One of these sons was Bethuel, who had a son called Laban and a daughter named Rebekah. Thus, through the late period of life at which Abraham became the father of Isaac, the branch of the family in Haran has gained one generation in advance of the emigrated branch. Indeed, as Nahor was considerably the elder brother of Abraham, it seems likely that his son Bethuel was not much younger than Abraham himself; for at this time he appears to have been a very old man, who, although named as living, leaves everything to the direction and management of his son.

The family has clearly become among the first, if not the very first, in the town of Haran; and Abraham's servant could doubtless have proceeded to the house at once to declare his errand, if he had so pleased. But having arrived at the place, he first sought an interval for deliberation and for prayer. His camels needed water; and having come to the well outside the town, he made them kneel down, in their posture of rest. The well was probably secured; but if not, and if he had the power, it would have been a great offence to the people of the place to take the water before they came to draw it for their own use, and without their permission. Observing the evening shades begin to fall, he knew that some would soon be there to draw water. So he sat down meanwhile to consider how he might best execute the commission with which he had been entrusted. He concluded to leave the direction of the matter in the hands of God. He prayed, therefore, that among the many damsels of the place who would shortly come for water, the one who should respond in the mode he indicated to his application for drink, should be the lady intended for his master's son. It is remarkable that he did not fix the sign upon the one who should first offer her services, but upon the one who should first willingly grant the service asked of her. In this he proceeds warily, conceiving, it would seem, that the maid shows no maidenly spirit who, unasked, tenders so slight a service as a drink of water *at the well* to an apparently wealthy stranger; and deeming, perhaps, that attentions so paid might be an excuse for curiosity, and an evidence rather of officious forwardness than of an obliging disposition. In so plain a matter as that which lay before him, it may be doubted whether this man was altogether right in thus appointing a sign to God; nor should we be wise to follow the example. There are peculiar circumstances in this case, however, which might well make a servant shrink from the responsibility of proceeding entirely upon his own judgment in choosing a wife for his master's son; and God, for Abraham's sake, accepted the sign, and made it indicate the right person—the very same, so far as appears, who would have been obtained had he gone straight to Bethuel's house.

If such a mission were at all possible under our own system of manners, it would certainly not be among the girls gathered round the village pump that the messenger would expect to find a match in all respects suitable for the son of his wealthy and well-born master. But in that age, when, as now in the same countries, the young females of the most honourable families discharged the commonest domestic offices, and took peculiar pleasure in the fetching of water from the well outside the town, from its enabling them to meet their companions, the servant knew that the young females whom he might shortly expect to see at that place must include the very class from which his choice was to be made.

He had scarcely formed his resolution and uttered his prayer, when a very beautiful young damsel was seen advancing to the well, with her pitcher on her shoulder. The women now usually carry their water vessels on their heads, in western as well as in eastern Asia; but in India it is the privilege of females of high caste to carry their vessels on the shoulders; and if this should have been the case in the times which now engage our attention, the fact would be curious and interesting. As is frequently the case in the East, when the water does not lie deep in the well, there was here no apparatus for drawing up the water; but some steps led down to it, and those who came thither went down and filled their vessels. As the damsel he had noted came up with her full pitcher on her shoulder, the servant of Abraham ran to meet her, and said, "Let me *sip*,[1] I pray thee, a little water out of thy pitcher." But she said promptly and kindly, "*Drink* [not *sip*], my lord;" and she hasted to let down her pitcher upon her hand, that he might quench his thirst. Had she stopped there, she had not become one of those who "did build the house of Israel." But he had no sooner finished, than, of her free and open-hearted bounty, she added, "I will draw for thy camels also, until they have done drinking;" and without awaiting the man's answer, she proceeded to execute her intention. Now, it is easy to offer that which costs us nothing. But this truly well bred lady offers her trouble, her labour, to oblige a stranger. And, indeed, it was no slight labour to go up and down these steps, bearing each time a pitcher of water, which she emptied into the trough (frequently still found near such wells), until the camels had received enough. This was the very sign Eliezer had appointed; and one more proper for his purpose—more becoming— could scarcely have been devised.

The man was astonished that the matter had turned out so circumstantially as he had wished; but still, until he learned who the damsel was, he feared to think he had so soon been fully prosperous. However, as an acknowledgment of the attention he had received, and as an intro- duction to the inquiries he was about to make, the steward presented to her a nose-ring of gold— such as is still worn by the women of Arabia— which, it is remarkable to observe, is among the ornaments presented to a bride on her betrothal. Nor was this all; for he also gave two golden

[1] Sip, and not "drink," is the meaning of the original word.

bracelets, of much higher value than the nose- jewel. Such ornaments are still very generally

NOSE JEWELS

used in the East, not on extraordinary occasions, but for everyday wear. Indeed, ornaments of this kind are, as fixed property, highly valued, and are much more sought after than articles of mere dress. It is not unusual to see a woman, clad comparatively in rags, but adorned with bracelets, anklets, nose-rings, and other orna- ments worth many rich dresses. The bracelets are seldom of gold; more frequently they are of silver; sometimes of amber or coral; while

ANCIENT EGYPTIAN ARMLETS

poor women content themselves with bracelets of silvered steel, of copper, or of brass. Several pairs are frequently worn on the arms at the same time, and it is not uncommon for the space between the wrist and elbow to be almost covered with them. The most ancient specimens are flat, as in the monuments of Egypt; but those now generally in use are round and bulky, like manacles, but are for the most part hollow, and therefore not heavy in proportion to their bulk. The bracelets presented by the servant to Rebekah appear to have weighed about five ounces of gold, and could not therefore have been worth less than twenty pounds, exclusive of the nose-ring, the value of which cannot be well estimated.

The servant then ventured to ask the maiden whose daughter she was, and whether there was room in her father's house for him and his people to pass the night. With a glad heart he learned that she was the daughter of the son of his master's brother; and the damsel failed not to inform him that there was ample room for his entertainment, and abundance of " straw and provender " for the camels. On this, the man saw that the Lord had indeed prospered him, and his first most becoming act was to bow down his head and prostrate himself before the Lord God of his master Abraham, who had led him in the right way to the house of his master's kinsman. This he said aloud, as is usual throughout the East; and no sooner had the maiden, whose name was Rebekah, caught the purport of his words, than she sped off to make them known at home.

On hearing this, her brother Laban repaired to the well, where Abraham's servant still remained with the camels. Laban addressed him with the cordial words: " Come in, thou blessed of the Lord; wherefore standest thou without? for I have prepared the house, and a place for the camels." So he followed Laban, and having seen the camels ungirded and fed, and his own feet and those of the men having been refreshed with water, he was pressed to eat; but, mindful of the service on which he came, he declined to taste food until he had told his errand and had received his answer. He recited all the circumstances from the commencement, and clearly indicated his opinion that Rebekah was the damsel destined of God to become his young master's wife. Bethuel and Laban were of the same opinion, and their answer expressed that conviction. "The thing proceedeth from the Lord: we cannot speak unto thee bad or good. Behold, Rebekah is before thee. Take her, and go; and let her be the wife of thy master's son, as the Lord hath spoken."

On hearing this, the pious servant again bent himself in thankfulness before the Lord, who had thus brought his mission to a successful close. Many precious things, " jewels of gold, and jewels of silver, and raiment," he brought forth from his treasures, and presented to Rebekah, and to her brother and mother—the latter being probably of the nature of the dowry usually given for a daughter. With hearts at ease, the servant and his men feasted themselves well that night; but next morning he declined to make any longer stay, and was at length suffered to depart, with Rebekah and her maidens mounted on camels.

It was an anxious moment to both the servant and Rebekah, when, as they approached the end of their journey, Isaac was beheld in the distance. He had, in accordance with his quiet and contemplative character, gone " out to meditate in the field at eventide;" but when he looked up, and saw the camels coming, he hastened to meet them. Seeing him approaching, Rebekah put on her veil, which females

WOMEN MOUNTED ON CAMELS

usually assume in the presence of a stranger; but on hearing the servant say, "It is my master," she alighted from her camel, in testimony of that respect which is still marked by the same action in the East. Having heard the particulars of the journey from the servant, Isaac conducted his fair cousin to the vacant tent of his mother, thereby installing her as the lady of the camp. She thus became his wife, and in her love he found comfort for the loss of his mother, which until now he had not for three years ceased to mourn.

THE BIRTHRIGHT

Genesis 25:19-34

THE attentive and thoughtful reader of Scripture has many gratifications which escape him whose reading is but cursory. Thus, the consideration of dates and ages is wholly overlooked by readers of the easy class; but these are carefully noted by the true student, who derives from them much interesting information. Let us see, for instance, how this applies here. Abraham survived Sarah thirty-eight years. Isaac was thirty-seven years old when his mother died; and as he was forty years old when he married Rebekah, we learn that the camp of Abraham remained three years without a mistress. Again, Isaac was sixty years of age before his sons Esau and Jacob were born. Thus for more than twenty years the heir of the promises remained childless; and Abraham, but for his faith, must have been sorely tried by this second long protraction of the hope he most cherished. This is, among the trials of his faith, not recorded, and only discoverable by the comparison of dates. Again, as Abraham's death is recorded before the birth of Isaac's sons is mentioned, nine readers out of ten probably consider that Abraham was dead before his grandsons were born. But by looking at his age when he died, and comparing it with the age of Isaac when his sons entered the world, we see that Abraham not only waited twenty years before his grandsons were born, but actually lived to see them seventeen or eighteen years old; so that it is almost beyond a doubt that Jacob and Esau had, and certain that they might have had, much intercourse with their venerable grandfather.

Whether the elder of the two profited much by this advantage, does not appear; but it is probable that Jacob, the younger, owed much of his strong faith in the Lord's providence to the example and instructions of the patriarch.

Although distinguished as elder and younger, the two lads were in fact twins, Esau having simply been the first to enter the world in the same birth. Yet, if the distinctions of elder and younger are of importance for social or other privileges, a few moments' priority is as good as a priority of years. It is remarkable, however, how little value seems to be attached to these distinctions in the counsels of God. In fact, it is observable how very frequently, in cases of preference and selection, the choice falls upon the younger sons. The righteous Abel is the younger son of Adam; Abraham is the younger son of Terah; Jacob is the younger son of Isaac; Joseph is the youngest but one of Jacob's twelve sons; the favoured Ephraim is the younger of Joseph's sons; Moses is the younger of Amram's sons; David is the youngest of Jesse's sons; and Solomon is among the youngest of the sons of David.

The intended preference of the younger over the elder—of Jacob over Esau—was disclosed to the mother before the children saw the light, and was probably the source of the special regard in which she always held that son, while the feelings of the father inclined as strongly to his first-born.

The character of each of the two men as they grew up is very strongly distinguished, following remarkably the difference observed in their persons even at the birth. The elder was rough, ruddy, and hairy—a description which implies the possession of great bodily strength, and a temperament which would incline him to exciting and hazardous pursuits. The juvenile appearance of Jacob is not described, but the silence of the historian on this point implies that he was the reverse of his brother—smooth, tender, and infantine. As they grew up, the difference of character was shown in their pursuits. The peaceful occupations and interests of pastoral life, which suited well the quiet temper of Jacob, became hateful to his more ardent brother, who gave his days to the chase, the excitement and violent exertions of which supplied the kind of rough stimulant which his impulsive temper required, and the bodily exercise which his strong and active frame demanded.

The character of Jacob will come often enough under our notice in the course of the ensuing days; but that of Esau, which will less require our attention, may be indicated in the words of a very able American writer: "Esau, it would seem, belonged to the class of rough, sensual natures; men who, acting under the influence of present impulse, have no steadiness of character. They are distinguished by an imposing directness of conduct, the very opposite to anything deceitful or cunning. They have feeling and kindness; they readily forget an injury, and cherish no malice. These amiable qualities are associated, however, with levity, sensuality, and passion, leading to acts of violence, as circumstances may prompt."[1]

This man, returning one day unsuccessful, weary, and famishing from his hunting, saw Jacob preparing a most savoury mess of red looking pottage. It was made of those red lentiles which at the present day form a dish highly relished in Syria and in Egypt. Esau knew not its name, for his rough, roving life left him but little knowledge of domestic cookery. But the sight of it was pleasant, and the odour overpoweringly tempting to a man ravenously hungry. He cried impatiently, "Give me some of that red—that red!" So rarely is it the case that any choice cookery is seen among those who dwell in tents, that it may be well understood that the mess was as valuable in the eyes of Jacob as it was inviting in those of his brother. Still Jacob was not personally a selfish man in small matters, though in large objects he sometimes sought, not by the most direct policy, the means by which his interests might be advanced; and we may therefore believe that he would not have grudged the loss of his choice meal had it not occurred to him that the occasion might be employed for securing an object he had much at heart. Truly he must have had no very exalted opinion of his brother's sense or self-control, when he made to him the extraordinary proposal of exchanging this mess of pottage with him for his birthright. But he knew the man; he knew him to be one of those to whom the present is all, and on whom the remote and the ideal make no impression.

The result does more honour to Jacob's pene-

[1] Dr. Samuel H. Turner, in his *Notes on Genesis*. Here, however, he much follows a German writer of high repute, named Dreschler.

tration than to his brotherly love. Esau closed with the proposal, "Behold," said he, with an hunter's exaggeration, "behold, I am at the point to die; and what profit shall this birthright do to me?" The full effect of this declaration has not been well understood by those unacquainted with the East. We are apt to think he might have taken some bread and cold meat—anything in the way to refresh himself and stay his appetite till a more substantial meal should be got ready. And hence the whole burden of his declaration is made to rest on his special fancy for Jacob's red pottage. Now, it is true that he liked the pottage; but it would seem that his great desire for it arose from its being the only food to be obtained by him with which to appease the rage of hunger. We have already explained (p. 255) that there is never anything ready in eastern tents, and scarcely in houses, for a sudden demand; all has to be prepared, if a demand arises between the times of meals. Hence Esau knew that unless he obtained this pottage he should have to wait some time—an age to a famishing man—until some food was prepared for him, or until the next meal-time came round. Probably, as Esau was returned from hunting, this was the last meal of the day; and as it had been expected that, as usual, he would provide for himself from the game he shot, no preparation had been made for him; so that unless he obtained Jacob's supper, or endured the delay of preparing another for himself at an unseasonable hour, he would get no food until the morning. This was enough to act upon the mind of a man who lived so much for the present, and had so little value for his birthright as Esau. He consented, and, at Jacob's demand, confirmed the transfer of his birthright by an oath.

It is impossible to approve of Jacob's conduct in this matter. It was sinister and unfraternal; and it was more; it was unfaithful. He knew that all he sought had been promised to him by One of whose faithfulness in all His promises he must often have heard from his grandfather. It was, therefore, his duty to leave the accomplishment to Him in His own time, without seeking to aid by paltry underhand schemes the purposes of God. But we must view the character of Jacob in its progress of development and formation. It is our fault that we view men at all times as one; whereas there is often as little resemblance between the same man in youth and in mature age as there is between any two indi-viduals who pass along the road. So the Jacob of advanced life—taught of God at Bethel, Mahanaim, and Peniel—matured by experiences, and tried by sorrows, is found to be a different man in many respects from the Jacob dwelling in his father's tents, and under the influence and training of a sharp and unscrupulous mother.

But what was this birthright which Jacob so greatly coveted, and which his brother so lightly esteemed? The ordinary privilege of the first-born consisted in precedence over the other brothers, and in a double share of the paternal estate.[1] To this some add, upon doubtful reason-ing, the privilege of the priesthood. But the early Jewish writers, who naturally felt much interest in the subject, and were well able to in-vestigate it, think that the privilege which Jacob desired and obtained had nothing to do with present secular advantages, but had reference to that heritage of the promises made to Abraham which was supposed to go to the eldest born. They appeal to facts which are decidedly in their favour. "As to power and authority," says one of these writers (Abarbanel), "Jacob never exer-cised any over Esau, but, on the contrary, humbly and submissively addresses him as *my lord,* and styles himself Esau's *servant.* (Gen. xxxii. 5.) And as to the double portion of Isaac's property, so far from obtaining it, Jacob not only declares, *with my staff I passed over this Jordan,* but sur-renders a considerable portion of his own pro-perty in the shape of a gift to Esau." In fact, Esau, who "despised his birthright," received his possessions earlier than Jacob; and he founded a nation, without subjecting his progeny to any disgrace, like that which the Israelites sustained in Egypt.

To be the heir of the promise—to acquire pos-session of Canaan—to be associated with God in Abraham's covenant, and, under it, to be the in-strument of imparting a blessing to all the earth —were matters on which Jacob's thoughts were fixed. It was not his own personal worldly advantage to which he looked, but the future welfare—temporal, spiritual, and eternal—of his progeny; and inasmuch as the man who is in-spired by exalted hopes and purposes—he who holds "large discourse, looking before and after" —is more entitled to our respect than the impul-sive, sensuous creature who says, "Let us eat and

[1] Genesis 49:3,4; Deuteronomy 21:17; 1 Chronicles 5:1,2.

drink, for to-morrow we die," we cannot even in this transaction, rightly understood, hold Jacob in light esteem, however deeply we may deplore and censure the unkind and ungenerous manner in which he acquired a human claim to that which had been his, by divine right, before his birth.

The prophetic answer of the Lord to Rebekah's prayer, uttered in the agony of her grief and pain, is deserving of special note. It is one of those brief but comprehensive and graphic delineations of national character, and sketches of national history, which we meet with so frequently in the early books of the Bible. A struggle is commenced before birth, which is continued not only through the whole lives of the twin brothers, but throughout the whole history of the nations that sprang from them: "Two nations are in thy womb, and two manner of people shall be separated from thy bowels; and the one people shall be stronger than the other people; and the elder shall serve the younger." The unnatural struggles between Jacob and Esau about the birthright and the paternal blessing, were renewed by their descendants at the very commencement of their national existence, and carried on without intermission for nearly eighteen centuries. "When the Israelites, in their wanderings from Egypt to Canaan, had reached the territory of the Edomites, they asked in vain for permission to pass through their territory, though they promised to abstain from every act of violence, to pay for all the wants they might require, and to perform their journey on the ordinary public road. Not only was their request haughtily rejected, but a strong army of the Edom-ites marched out to oppose them. Their enmity grew with the advancing generations; wars were almost continually carried on between both nations; the Edomites were alternately subjected and free; till, in the time of the de-struction of the first temple, they displayed the most in-veterate hatred and the most ungenerous jealousy." (Kalisch *On Gen.*) With deep feeling and holy indignation is this crowning act of national hatred recorded by the Psalmist, who laments as a captive by the rivers of Babylon: "Re-member, O Lord, the children of Edom in the day of Jerusalem; who said, Raze it, raze it, even to the founda-tion thereof." (Ps. cxxxvii. 7.)

P.

"GATHERED TO HIS PEOPLE"

Genesis 25:8

SUCH a chapter as the twenty-fifth of Genesis, composed in great part of names, is apt to be passed through too rapidly by unstudious readers. Yet even the most lax attention will be fastened by such a verse as the 8th: "Then Abraham gave up the ghost, and died in a good old age, an old man, and full of years; and was gathered to his people." Here is a remarkable collection of epithets applicable to death and burial, every one of which is well worthy of consideration, and may suggest some profitable thoughts.

By "giving up the ghost," we now understand giving up his spirit, as by "ghost" we usually suppose "spirit" to be meant. We doubt if the translators intended it to bear this sense; and apprehend that they rather meant it to express the giving up the breath of life, or *breathing out* one's life, which is the true meaning. It is there simply equivalent to the modern and usual phrase, "he expired." The term is thought by Jewish writers to express death by old age only, without previous sickness or pain. This is the kind of death which results from the natural dissolution of the body, when the radical heat and moisture by degrees dry up and wear away. Such a kind of death was that *Euthanasia*, that good and easy departure which was greatly desired by the ancients, and which was indeed desirable when old age was really venerated, and treated with solicitude and respect,—with far more of both than we fear it finds under the influences and activities of modern civilisation. This kind of death, this gentle sliding out of life, had been promised to Abraham as a blessing: "Thou shalt go to thy fathers in peace; thou shalt be buried in a good old age." Gen. xv. 15. And we are now informed that this took place, to show that there was no point, however comparatively inconsiderable, in which the promises of God were left unfulfilled. The conviction which Abraham, in life and in death, was enabled to realize of the Lord's faithfulness to His promises, must have been the source of his highest joys and deepest consolations. And it may be so to us. We have still better hopes and promises from God than those that were given to Abraham; and we shall be happy here, or miserable, in proportion to the intensity with which we are enabled to realize the conviction, that "all the promises of God in Him (Christ) are yea, and in Him amen."

But Abraham is also said to have "died in a good old age." Not only in old age, but in a *good* old age. The old age which the sacred writer calls good, is very different from the sad, broken, fretful, and weary old age of which these later generations seem to furnish more examples than were dreamt of in old time, which invariably

speak of old age as a good and a blessing. But this old age is good, because healthful, sound, long in coming, leaving the senses still in perfection, and free from that peevishness and moroseness which make old age unpleasant in and to so many. We are sorry to record an observation we have made, that age seems to be generally more sound, vigorous, and cheerful in eastern than in western lands, in which old age has almost ceased to be regarded as a blessing. Perhaps it is *not* altogether such under the New Testament dispensation, as it was under the Old, which looked far more to this life and its blessings than we are now authorised to do. He who is enabled to know that he belongs to Christ, has little inducement to wish for a prolonged stay in this house of his pilgrimage. To depart and to be with Christ—to take possession of the mansion prepared for him in his Father's house—and to join his kindred in heaven, who, as life advances, become more numerous than those who remain on earth—will seem to him a distinction well exchanged for length of days.

He was "an old man." He was a hundred and seventy-five years of age. His great-grandfather had reached to two hundred and thirty years, and his father to two hundred and five years; yet so rapidly was the time of man's life diminishing, that although Abraham died at a comparatively early age, he was an old man among his contemporaries. Fallen as was the duration of life, his years passed by a hundred the ordinary limit at which human life has now stood for many ages. He had seen the years which few of our people survive, before he entered the land of Canaan, and one hundred years he had passed in that land.

Abraham was, however, not only old; he was "full of years." The word "years" is not in the original; and the word rendered "full" is to be satisfied, satiated, or filled, and is often in Scripture applied to a person having had enough of food or of drink. It may, therefore, here well signify that Abraham had lived as long as he desired; had finished the business of life; and was quite willing to die. He was satisfied with life; he had had enough of it, and stood with girded loins, ready to depart.

Finally, "he was gathered to his people,"—a striking phrase, over which the mind lingers. What, however, does it really mean? It is commonly interpreted as applying to burial—to sleeping in the grave with one's kindred and friends. But this is not the sense here, it would seem. *His* people were not here, nor was he here buried with them. Sarah was the only one belonging to him that had died in this land, and with her he was buried. What, then, can this gathering to his people mean, but that his soul was gathered to theirs? The phrase is certainly more appropriate to the soul than to the body; for the body is gathered to corruption, but the soul to glory and blessedness. It is usual to say that in the Pentateuch there are no indications of a life to come. Is not this one such indication? The usual form of the expression is, "to be gathered to one's fathers;" yet in other instances, as in this, it is applied to those who could not be said to be gathered to their fathers in the grave. It is also spoken of as a blessing to those who were so gathered. It must, therefore, it would seem, imply not only their continued existence, but their existence in a state of blessedness. In other words, those to whom Abraham, Isaac, Jacob, and others, were gathered or assembled at death, must be some then really existing; for to those that had no form of being, there could be no such gathering. It appears, therefore, that there could hardly be any plain foundation for the phrase, if well examined, but in the belief that the fathers, to whom they were at the death of the body assembled, had *then* a real existence. It is really of some importance to obtain even this piece of evidence in support of the existence of a belief in the immortality, or even in the survivance, of the soul, of which it has been strongly denied by many that the books of Moses bear any testimony.

So, then, it is seen that these patriarchal fathers had the same desire, and the same hope, of being gathered at death to all they had in past times venerated, loved, and lost, that we have. Indeed, it stands to reason that they should have had it. The condition of any people would seem scarcely tolerable without it.

> "The seasons, as they fly,
> Snatch from us in their course, year after year,
>   Some sweet connection, some endearing tie.
> The parent ever honoured, ever dear,
>   Claims from the filial breast the pious sigh;
> A brother's urn demands the filial tear,
>   And gentle sorrows gush from friendship's eye.
> To day we frolic in the rosy bloom
> Of jocund youth ; to-morrow knells us to the tomb."

These things were the same in old time as now ; and is it credible that men who then walked with God, and were honoured with direct communications from Him, were left in the dark on matters so essential to their comfort?—that when they followed their dead ones to the tomb, they could not say that they should ever again behold them; and that in due time—in a time not long to any—they should themselves be gathered to the great assembly of those who died once, and are yet alive for evermore? Did David, when in a later day he said of his lost child, "I shall go to him, but he will not return to me," speak of the grave only, or of something beyond the grave? Let the heart answer.

THE BLESSING

Genesis 27

It is surprising how little we know of Isaac, in comparison with his father and his son. He makes no stir in the world—no noise; he excites no emotion. We only catch glimpses of him now and then, sufficient to enable us to recognize him as a dutiful son to his father, a loving son to his mother, an affectionate and even uxorious husband, a partial father, and a pious but weak old man. He seldom speaks. He wants force of character, and soon subsides into an instrument in the hands of others, who use him for their own purposes. It is the destiny of such to be acted upon, rather than to act upon others. So we never meet with Isaac in positive and decisive action, but commonly find him in some instrumental position or other. He seems to have also been of a weakly constitution. We read of infirmity or illness in none of the other patriarchs till they came to their death-beds; but at an age far short of that which his father, and even his son attained, we find him blind and feeble, confined to his bed, and expecting to die.

By far the most important and most fully recorded incident of his life occurs while he is in this condition ; and as thus the fullest picture of him is given,

> " In age and feebleness extreme,"

we perhaps derive therefrom an impression of his character different from that which might have been entertained, had we been permitted to behold him as distinctly in the prime and vigour of his days. One would be ready to suppose that the quiet and home-staying Jacob was more likely to be a favourite with such a father than the rough, boisterous, and rambling Esau. But we often observe that persons manifest the greatest liking for those whose character and habits are least similar to their own. Esau, and not Jacob, was the favourite of Isaac. Believing death to be near, he privately desired this beloved son to procure him by his hunting, some food, such as he was especially fond of, that after partaking of it he might bestow on him the paternal benediction. This is overheard by Rebekah, whose skilful cunning contrives to pass off Jacob upon him for Esau ; and thus the blind old patriarch is led to believe that he is invoking blessings upon his elder son, when it is in fact the younger whom he addresses. The details of this scene of unprincipled deception—the more shocking from such advantage being taken of the infirmities of a father—are familiar to the reader ; and we may gladly be spared following the particulars which the Scripture necessarily, for the coherence of the narrative, relates. By sparing ourselves this pain and regret, we obtain room for a few observations on some remarkable circumstances in the narrative.

It is the mother who suggests the device, and who, in fact, seeks to ease the alarm of Jacob's conscience by taking all the consequences upon herself. It is quite possible that she thought she was doing a duty. Knowing that the blessing Isaac was about to bestow on Esau belonged, in the purposes of God, to Jacob, and was his also as a portion of his purchased birthright, she might easily conceive that she was preventing a wrong—was only doing evil that good might come. It was " a pious fraud ;" and when we consider how dubious great authorities, favoured with all the light of Christian doctrine and morality, have been on the subject of such frauds, we need not too greatly wonder that Rebekah and Jacob failed to see the path of right and duty clearly. It appears to us that Rebekah felt all to be right—both means and end ; and that Jacob thought the end to be right, but was staggered at the means, until his mother succeeded in soothing, if not in extinguishing, his alarms. Jacob was, however, not a child. He was full forty years of age, and very well capable of exercising an independent judgment in a matter which concerned him so nearly. All the responsibility of the transaction cannot be shifted to the mother, willing as she was to take it upon herself.

Rebekah, with two kids, prepares for Isaac " savoury meat," intended to be passed upon him—and which does pass upon him—for the very same that he loved, and desired as the produce of Esau's hunting. How is it that he, the possessor of numerous flocks, should depend upon his son's hunting for a feast which might thus easily be prepared to his liking with his own kids ? And what kind of game might that be, for which the flesh of a kid could be taken ? In answer to this, it suffices to refer to a former statement—that an animal from the flocks or herds is rarely killed and eaten, save to entertain a stranger ; and that the possessor of untold herds and flocks would deem it unheard-of extravagance to slay an animal to supply a meal for himself. Hence the Israelites, with all their cattle, when they were in the wilderness, groaned for the taste of flesh, and had to be supplied with game by miracle. Particular objection is also felt to the slaughter of young animals, regard being had to the value to which they will grow if suffered to live. In fact, this is regarded among pastoral people in the same point of view as that in which living upon capital is regarded in this commercial country. Thus a stray wild animal, or bit of game, is as highly prized and as eagerly sought after by them as by any people. It may thus appear possible that Isaac, at a hundred years old, scarcely knew the taste of kid's flesh ; or if he did, the flesh of a kid is not unlike that of a young gazelle, and, prepared in the way that both are usually dressed in the East, might easily be taken for one.

Esau must have been a formidably hairy person ; for, that Jacob may pass for Esau in case Isaac should feel him, the skins of the kids are placed by Rebekah upon his hands and " the *smooth* of his neck." If he were thus equipped to resemble Esau's smoothness, what must Esau's roughness have been ? The smooth of his neck, however, means the part not covered by the beard. There is no doubt that Esau's hairiness was very extraordinary, he being, even at birth, described as if invested all over with a hairy garment. There is, however, perhaps no animal whose skin might be so easily taken for that of a very hairy man as the skin of a kid. It is well known that the long silky hair of the Angora goat was used among the Romans as an artificial succedaneum for human hair. Wigs made of Angora goats' hair are mentioned by the Roman satirist Martial. Besides, it is to be borne in mind, that the senses of Isaac appear to have become obtuse with age, which had produced the failure of his sight.

It is an interesting fact, that Jacob was clad in a dress of Esau's, which, notwithstanding that he had several wives, and therefore a home of his own, his mother had in her charge. The object seems to have been that the fresh smell, which the garments had imbibed from the herbs of the field, might assist the deception. Isaac expressly alludes to it: "Behold, the smell of my son is as the smell of a field which the Lord hath blessed." Some think the garments were perfumed; but if so, this could not have been distinctive of Esau. Others apprehend that the odour was that peculiar one which the dress of a hunter contracts, from his handling the skins and furs of animals. But it is surely enough to suppose, that the fragrance of Esau's garments proceeded from the herbs and flowers of the field, his constant abode. Ancient writers concur with modern travellers in speaking with delight of the aromatic odours of the Syro-Arabian meadows and plains. The natural odours of Lebanon are frequently mentioned in the Sacred Scriptures.

It is remarkably true that every scene of deception, however well planned and artistically managed, fails in some point or other. The ordinary reading or experience of every one will supply examples of this. So, in the present instance, while Rebekah and Jacob had so carefully disguised the outward man of the latter, the necessity of disguising the voice had been wholly overlooked. This single oversight had nearly exploded the entire plot. The suspicions of Isaac were violently awakened at hearing a voice which he recognized as that of Jacob speaking in the person of Esau. At the first sound of that voice he asks, "Who art thou, my son?" and still not satisfied with the assurance, "I am Esau, thy first-born," he says, "Come near, I pray thee, that I may feel thee, my son, whether thou be my very son Esau or not." An alarming moment was that for the deceiver—a moment of agony, almost a sufficient punishment for his crime, when his father passed his hands over him.

"The voice," said the old man, "is the voice of Jacob, but the hands are the hands of Esau." But he was satisfied: the feel of the hands and

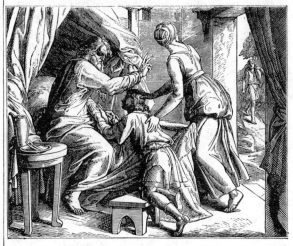

JACOB OBTAINING THE BLESSING OF ISAAC

fresh smell of the raiment prevailed over the misgiving which the voice had awakened; and the much desired blessing was bestowed.

It is interesting to note how the leading characteristics of the two nations, the Israelites and Edomites, were typified in the characters and acts of Jacob and Esau. Jacob in early life, and even up to a ripe manhood, exhibited only too frequently that low trickery and unscrupulous effort to advance his own interest, "which, even to a proverb, we call in scorn *Jewish*." Dean Stanley has sketched these features with his wonted vividness and skill : "Who does not feel at times his indignation swell against the younger brother? 'Is he not rightly named Jacob, for he hath supplanted me these two times?' He entraps his brother, he deceives his father, he makes a bargain even in his prayer ; in his dealings with Laban ; in his meeting with Esau, he still calculates and contrives, he distrusts his neighbours ; he regards with prudential indifference the insult to his daughter, and the cruelty of his sons. . . . In Jacob, we see the timid, cautious watchfulness that we know so well, though under darker colours, through our great masters of fiction,—in Shylock of Venice and Isaac of York."[1] It was not until God had sanctified that cunning, plotting, worldly spirit, by long years of toil and hardship, by repeated exposures to imminent peril, and by heart-rending domestic affliction, that the nobler qualities of a great mind, and the higher feelings of a large heart, began to be fully developed. Then, under divine guidance and through divine power, *Jacob* the "supplanter" was at last transformed into *Israel* "the prince of God." And as Stanley says : "In the nobler side of his career do we trace the germs of the unbroken endurance, the undying resolution, which keeps the nation alive even in its present outcast condition, and which was the basis,

[1] *Lectures on the Jewish Church*, p. 53.

in its brighter days, of the heroic zeal, long-suffering, and hope of Moses, of David, of Jeremiah, of the Maccabees, of the twelve Jewish apostles, and the first martyr Stephen."

The character of Esau was a complete counterpart to that of his brother. He was rash and thoughtless in act. Whenever any present gratification or personal indulgence was to be obtained, he eagerly grasped it, caring nothing for consequences. Free, generous, and unsuspicious by nature, he was at the same time wild, reckless, and bloodthirsty when passion was roused. He had neither stedfastness of purpose nor loftiness of principle to guide or control his erratic spirit. In all these respects he was a type of that restless, daring nation that took up its abode amid the fastnesses of Edom, and became for centuries Israel's bitterest foe. Josephus gives their character in a single sentence: "A turbulent and unruly race, always hovering on the verge of revolution, always rejoicing in changes, roused to arms by the slightest motion of flattery, rushing to battle as if they were going to a feast."

P.

BETHEL

Genesis 28

WHO is this solitary traveller striding on from the way of the southern wilderness? His loins are firmly girded; a strong staff assists his steps; and he has nought else with him, unless it be that his small wallet contains a little oil, some bread, and a few hard dates. This is no common man. Mighty destinies hang around his head. A special and peculiar providence watches over him. Angels bend from their starry heavens to look upon him. It is Jacob, the son of the wealthy Isaac—the undoubted heir of glorious promises—the chosen and beloved of God. And how is it thus with him? The servant of Abraham travelled this way before, bent on the same journey, with ten laden camels and many men. Could not even one camel, one ass, one servant, be spared for Isaac's son? Alas! he flees for his life, and must leave no track behind him. Hence he goes alone, stealthily, and poor. He flees from a deeply wronged brother, whose wrath threatens nothing less than his life, as soon as he shall no longer be restrained by the dread of breaking his father's heart. He is going to Padan-aram, to spend a few weeks with Laban, until his brother's anger has passed away; and he is not without hope of finding a wife there, as his father had done before. Alas, he little knows what lies before him, nor how many long years shall pass before he sees again his father's house; and little

did his mother think, when she bade him farewell, that her eyes should never again rest upon the son she so deeply loved, and for whose sake she had burdened her soul. Both were punished.

The traveller, as the shades of evening lengthen, comes to "a certain place," and there he resolves to spend the night. He unbinds his girdle; he anoints his joints with oil; he takes a little of his hard fare; he drinks water from the stream. Now he craves rest. But how shall he sleep? That is easy; he selects a stone for his pillow, and his bed is made. His thoughts had been troubled. Looking at the consequences that had flowed from his proceedings, he could not but doubt whether he had acted well or wisely, or whether he had any title to expect the blessing and care of Abraham's God. But that God had not forgotten him; and it was at this moment, when he was alone with his own heart, that the Lord saw fit to commence the course of teachings and encouragements which ended but with his life, and by which he profited well. It does not appear that Jacob had hitherto received any communications from God; and he who was eventually destined to enjoy awfully near approaches to the divine presence, must first be taught in vision. He dreams on that hard stone. He sees a ladder extended from earth to heaven, and thereon the angels of God are passing up and down. He is thus taught that he is not alone, but is regarded with attention by the very angels of heaven, who employ themselves in his concerns. Some interpret it to signify God's care of the world and its affairs. We interpret it to signify God's care of Jacob and his affairs. The top of the ladder was in heaven, but its foot rested on the spot where he, the son of Isaac, lay. That he might be at no loss to collect the purport of his dream, God himself appeared above all, and he heard His voice. Yes, God spoke to him, and made Himself known as "the Lord God of Abraham his father, and the God of Isaac." He then proceeded to give him the words of the covenant, and to acknowledge him as the true heir of the promises. Nor was his personal welfare below God's thought. "Behold, I am with thee," He said; "I will keep thee in all places whither thou goest, and will bring thee again into this land; for I will not leave thee, until I have done that which I have spoken to thee of."

Jacob awoke deeply awed, "How dreadful," he said, " is this place! this is none other but the house of God, and this is the gate of heaven." His first act brings to our notice a new and remarkable custom. He takes the stone which had served him for a pillow, and sets it up as a monument, and pours some of his oil upon the top of it. This was an act of consecration. It showed that the spot was to be considered holy. Setting up the stone merely was the natural act of one wishing to identify the spot when he should come that way again. But the pouring out of oil was at least a formal and devout acknowledgment of the fact commemorated, if it did not, as we think it did, set apart the spot as one hereafter to receive an altar, and to become a place for sacrifices. In doing this, he called the place by a new name. It had been called Luz, but he named it Bethel—the house of God; and it is remarkable that the consecrated stones, which in following ages we find among the ancients, bear the analagous name of Baitulia. It would lead us too far to inquire how this analogy arose. The custom does not appear to have been a new one, when this first recorded instance of it occurred in Jacob's history. It is known, by the testimony of various writers, that it was a very ancient custom among the Phœnicians, the Greeks, and the Romans, to set up stones as memorials of remarkable events or places, and to pour oil, or wine, or blood thereon, as a consecrating libation. In the East the custom is not yet extinct. The object of Jacob is further shown by the vow to which he at the same time gave utterance; "If God will be with me, and keep me on this way that I am going, and will give me bread to eat, and raiment to put on, so that I return again to my father's house in peace, and the Lord will be my God; then this stone which I have placed for a monument shall become God's house; and of all that Thou shalt give me, I will surely tithe it unto Thee." We have adopted in this place Dr. Raphall's Jewish translation. Here we see that, in conformity with the results of careful criticism, the most essential point of the vow is divested of the unseemly conditional character which the authorized translation gives to it. "If God will be with me, . . . then shall the Lord be my God," etc., which is always read with pain, and mars the effect of this beautiful and impressive vow. The single Hebrew letter as a prefix, which is translated by "then," is more generally rendered by "and," and ought to have been so given in this place.

It is worthy of notice how moderate Jacob's wishes are for himself—how low is the personal ambition of the man who had dared so much for the great future. All that he asks is to be suplied with what is absolutely and indispensably necessary; food, however hardly earned, so that it sustain life; clothing, however coarse, so that it but cover his nakedness. He is ready to submit to every privation and suffering, so that he may be sure that he shall eventually return in peace to his father's house. What a chapter is this, for those who go forth even in our own day to battle with the world!

The Lord did for Jacob far more than he ventured to ask; and Jacob on his part, redeemed his vow when he repaired to the place, after his removal from Shechem, and built an altar there. The words he then used are remarkable: "Let us rise and go up to Bethel, and I will make there an altar unto God, who answered me in the day of my distress, and was with me in the way that I went." The spot thus consecrated was afterwards further distinguished as, for a time, the seat of the ark of the covenant and of the tabernacle; and it was one of the places in which Samuel held his circuit court as the judge of Israel.[1]

As to the tenth, which Jacob vowed to give, we can have no doubt that he kept his vow; but how, we know not. There was never any establishment for worship at Bethel in Jacob's time that required this appropriation, and we find not any person to whom he could give the tenth, as Abraham did to Melchizedek. That instance, however, shows that it was an ancient oriental custom, with which Jacob promises compliance. We are inclined very much to approve the suggestion of an eminent Jewish commentator (Aben Ezra), who interprets the words to mean, "I will bestow it on whosoever is worthy to receive it for the glory of God," and that consequently Jacob redeemed his vow by appropriating the tenth of all his increase to works of charity and beneficence. That "he who giveth unto the poor lendeth unto the Lord," is a truth known as early as the time of Jacob at least.

The history of Bethel is sad but instructive. It was one of the very earliest sanctuaries of "The Land of Promise." Beside it Abraham built an altar, and called upon the name of the Lord (Gen. xii. 8; xiii. 3, 4). But it was

[1] Judges 20:26,27; compare 1 Samuel 7:16; 10:3.

Jacob's glorious vision which rendered it pre-eminently "holy ground." Awaking, he exclaimed, "Surely the Lord is in this place. . . . How dreadful is this place! this is none other but the house of God, and this is the gate of heaven." It was God's house, because, resting there, God was with him, and gave him the greatest and best of all promises. It was the gate of heaven, because there, from heaven's open portal, ministering angels "ascended and descended." Four centuries later, Bethel became the seat of one of Israel's great national councils, under the rule of the Judges. But almost the first public act of the wily rebel Jeroboam, "who made Israel to sin," was to set up at Bethel a golden calf. Taking advantage of the popular reverence for the ancient sanctuary of Abraham and Jacob, he made it the sanctuary of his new kingdom, thereby hoping to wean the people's thoughts from Jerusalem (1 Kings xii. 32). The spot consecrated by divine presence and promise was thus polluted. The honoured name *Bethel*, "House of God," was by divine inspiration changed to *Beth-aven*, "House of Idols" (Hos. iv. 15; x. 5, 8); and its final and terrible doom was pronounced by Amos, "*Seek not Bethel, for Bethel shall come to nought*" (v. 5). Its desolate ruins, strewn in heaps over the hill-top, and its rifled tombs in the valleys and cliffs around, are silent witnesses of the truth of Scripture, and of the literal fulfilment of the prophetic curse.

P.

HARAN

Genesis 29

CHEERED by the vision at Bethel, Jacob went on his way rejoicing. The refreshment of his spirits quickened his steps, and gave vigour to his tread. This natural effect of a gladdened heart is lost in the translation, which merely tells us that he "went on his journey;" but the original (as in the margin) states that "he lifted up his feet," which in eastern language still signifies to walk quickly, to reach out, to be in good earnest, not to hesitate. Probably the heaviness of his heart, on quitting his father's tents, and separating himself from his mother's love, had up to this point made his steps reluctant and slow; but now the knowledge that God is with him in the way that he goes, and has promised to bless him, makes him press forward with new hope and strength —with more thought of what lies before him, and with less of what he had left behind.

On his arrival at Haran, the incidents are exceedingly similar to those which took place when Abraham's servant went to seek a wife for Isaac. The servant, however, when he came to the well outside the town, had camels, attendants, and stores of precious things; but the son stands by the same well alone, and empty of all things but his claims and his hopes. Jacob also tarries by the well, till the damsel destined to become his spouse appears; but she comes not, like Rebekah, to fetch water for domestic use from the well, but to water the home flock of her father Laban, which is under her care. Here also, Jacob, as became his youth and appearance, waits not to receive the notice of the maiden, as did the steward of Abraham, but hastens to show her manly and becoming attention, by rolling away the stone which covered the well's mouth, and by watering the flock for her. He knows who she is; for as she approached, the shepherds at the well had told him that this was Laban's daughter Rachel. There was much to awaken strong emotion: the damsel was the daughter of "his *mother's brother;*" the sheep were "the sheep of his *mother's brother.*" It is not without purpose that his mother is thus produced before us. It apprises us that his mother was present to Jacob's mind. He pictured to himself, that just as that maiden appeared there before him, so, in that very place, had his mother appeared before Abraham's servant some sixty years previously; and that now he was among the scenes of *her* youth, of which he had often heard her speak. We can therefore well understand how, when he kissed his fair cousin, and told her who he was, "he lifted up his voice and wept." This is a fine touch of nature; and had the faults of Jacob been much greater than they were, we could forgive them for those tears. We begin to feel that there is truth in this man, of whom we have not yet seen much that is praiseworthy. Our hearts begin to go with him. We begin to like him. His future career begins to interest us.

Notwithstanding the selfish and ungenerous character which Laban evinces in the sequel, his conduct on the arrival of Jacob was by no means wanting in that hospitality and warm affection for kindred which even at the present day distinguish the eastern people. He no sooner heard from his daughter that his sister's son was out by the well, than "he *ran* to meet him, and embraced him, and kissed him, and brought him to his house." Some commentators have striven to make out interested influences even from the first in the conduct of this man. But no selfish man is invariably selfish—no mean spirited man always mean. We may therefore suppose that Laban was properly affected by the arrival of his sister's son, by whom he might hear tidings of her welfare, without allowing himself to be influenced by Jacob's humble and destitute appearance, or by his obvious inability to offer those rich presents which might be expected from Isaac's son. When he heard Jacob's story, he simply remarked, "Surely thou art my bone and my flesh;" as much as to say, "Although thou comest empty-handed, and hast no immediate resources, yet thou art my near relative, dear for my sister's sake, and art truly welcome here."

During the month which followed his arrival, Jacob made himself so very useful in the business of the flock, and showed so much skill in the management of cattle, that Laban began to think of establishing an abiding interest in his services. We must confess that there is much in the narrative of this twenty-ninth chapter which we can only explain on the supposition that Jacob had during this month heard from home, through some channel or other—perhaps by a caravan— that there, circumstances were not likely to admit of his return so soon as had been expected; that Esau was still so implacable, that he could not prudently either return or claim any separate settlement for himself out of the paternal estate; and that his father's health had been so far re-established, as to afford no likelihood that his death would, for a good while to come, make any change in the posture of affairs. When, also, we consider that the patriarchal wealth was not in money, but in cattle; and that even money existed only in the form of precious metal, difficult and dangerous to transport in bulk,—we may understand, that if Jacob did hear this, he would have inferred that he had little aid to expect from home, and that he had only to do the best he could for himself in Padan-aram, until, after the lapse of some years, circumstances should admit of his return.

It was probably the arrival of news of some such tendency, that induced Laban to make him an offer to engage his services at an adequate remuneration. On this, he offered to serve his uncle seven years for the hand of his daughter Rachel, whom by this time he tenderly loved. That he made an offer to pledge his services for so long a time, shows that, from some cause or other, he had by this time abandoned the hope with which he left Beersheba, of any speedy return to his own home. This period of service was to be in lieu of the remuneration, or, as it is now plainly called, the *price*, which a father has always in the East been entitled to expect for his daughter, and which, indeed, it would be discreditable in a husband not to pay in some shape or other. Personal servitude to the father is still, in some parts of the East, including to this day Palestine, the mode in which this price is paid by young men who have no other means of providing what the parent has a right to expect; and seven or eight years of such servitude, during which the man receives only food and clothing, are still regarded as but a fair remuneration for the daughter of a person of any consideration. It appears to us that this arrangement was not so absolute in its condition of servitude, but that, had circumstances arisen to alter Jacob's position, and to afford him the means of direct payment, he might so have redeemed from Laban any portion of his term of years that might then remain unexpired.

By an infamous trick, when the time came that Jacob should receive his wife, an elder daughter of Laban, named Leah, was substituted by the father. This was apparently done in the calculation that Jacob loved Rachel too well thus to part with her, and that he would offer another term of his valuable services to obtain her also. So it came to pass. He offered another seven years for Rachel; and thus only, on the hard terms of fourteen years' service, could he obtain the bride whom he desired to possess. Yet he thought her not too dearly purchased by this long service; and he seems to have felt an honest pride in being thus enabled to show the depth of the love he bore to her.

It is remarkable how much against his will, and against his eventual peace, Jacob, who would have been content and happy with Rachel only, was absolutely driven, by the force of circumstances, to take not only two wives, but four. Having got the wrong wife in the first instance, he could only obtain the right one by taking her as an addition to the first. Then, as the beloved one proved childless, he could not refuse her importunities to take her handmaid Bilhah, as Abraham had taken Hagar, that she might through her obtain children, and be put on an equality with her fruitful sister and rival, Leah.

Having done this, and the plan having produced the desired results, he could not in justice refuse Leah the same advantage, and was obliged to take her handmaid Zilpah in like manner. Thus Jacob became encumbered with four wives at once, all through his first disappointment, by the culpable contrivance of Laban. With respect to these handmaids, it should be observed that they were slaves whom Laban had presented to his daughters, as their own peculiar property, at the time of their marriage, and who were entirely at their disposal, and free from the control of the husband. Such handmaidens had before been given to Rebekah, and had accompanied her to the land of Canaan. We meet with these dotal servants frequently in the ancient and modern East, and even among the classical ancients. Their condition, indeed, among the Greeks and Romans, seems to have been in all respects similar to that in which it here appears. Many curious instances might be collected from the dramatic poets in particular. Take one or two as examples. In his *Iphigenia in Aulis*, the tragic poet Euripides represents Clytemnestra as preparing all things for her daughter's marriage, and she says: "I, as the bride-leader, am present; let therefore the dotal maids, whom as part of the dowry I bring, go forth out of the chariots," &c. And again, in the same tragedy, the queen thus says to one of her confidants, "I know you to be an old servant in my family." "And know you not," her servant answers, "that king Agamemnon received me as part of your dowry," or, "as one of your dotal servants?"

Again, king Phalaris, in one of his epistles, gives orders for four of such dotal maidens to be sent, for the service of the bride at a marriage he had appointed. In the *Asinaria* of Plautus, also, one of the characters, old Demænetus, is told by his slave that his wife had brought him such a dotal servant as had more in his hands than even he himself had. Furthermore, Cato, writing to enforce the Lex Voconia, produces the case of a rich lady who had brought a great fortune to her husband, but had reserved to herself part of the estate, out of which she lent a considerable sum to her husband. But some difference arising between them, she ordered her dotal and reserved servant to go and demand of her husband all that he had borrowed of her, and unless he paid it, to commence a suit against him for it. On which case it is remarked by Aulus Gellius, that as none of her husband's servants could be commanded by her in this affair, she was obliged to make this her exempted and reserved slave to be her solicitor for the money, he not having been given away by her, but retained by the marriage contract under her sole and separate jurisdiction.

By these instances, we see that the dotal servants of the wife, whether male or female, were at her entire disposal, and that the husband, apart from her, had not the slightest authority or control over them. This is still the case throughout the East, as we could show by many instances, if space allowed.

THE FLOCK

Genesis 30

WHEN we reflect upon Rebekah's conduct in the mode of obtaining Isaac's blessing for Jacob; when we consider Jacob's own proceedings in securing the birthright and the blessing; when we regard Laban's scandalous deceit in respect of Jacob's marriage, in which his daughter Leah took part; and when we look to the various proceedings of the two sisters as rival wives, with the theft of her father's images by Rachel, and her readiness at lying and deception to conceal that theft,—we have, taken altogether, about as full an amount of immorality and lack of truthfulness as it would be easy to find in any one family. How is this? We fear that we cannot withhold our concurrence from the opinion of Dr. Chalmers, who, in his pain at the apparently low moral sense of even persons entitled on many grounds to respect, more than once alludes to the matter. "We cannot help thinking," he says, "that this family of Haran must have been a wily, politic, deceitful set. Laban was characterized by it all over; Rebekah had her full share; and we can detect no small spice of it in their descendants—as in Jacob on the one hand, and Rachel on the other. There seems to have been a very unformed *morale* among them."

Previously, in regard to Abraham's deception in Egypt, recorded without any animadversion on the evil of it, he remarks: "Though morality is in the abstract unchangeable, it looks as if in the concrete there was a progressive morality from one era to another—an accommodation to the earlier and ruder periods of humanity—distinctly intimated by our Saviour when he tells of polygamy being allowed before the times of the Gospel, because of the hardness of their hearts." He adds: "It is worthy of remark, that there is no example, as far as I can recollect, of any deception or imperfect morality of any sort being recorded of Christian disciples in the New Testament without a prompt and decided condemnation." And again, in reference to Jacob's dealing with the cattle of Laban, Dr. Chalmers remarks: "Altogether, our notion is very much confirmed with regard to the low standard of virtue in those days; not that we have a higher morality, but a higher rule of morality, than in the patriarchal ages of the world. 'You have heard that it was said'—not done, but said—'by them of old time; but I say unto you,' etc. They had a worse system of virtue in those days, even though at present we should fall short of them in practice. They had an inferior schooling to what we now have—a dimmer moral light—whether they were before or behind us in actual observances."

All this is admirably just and true, and our readers cannot do better than carry these ideas with them, in considering the doubtful conduct of some personages in the early Scriptural history. With regard to Jacob's bargain with Laban, which he was enabled by his superior craft to turn to such advantage as greatly to enrich himself from the produce of Laban's flock, we have been accustomed to regard it as entitled to serious reprehension. But, on further consideration, we incline to think that the transaction admits of an interpretation which, without leaving the conduct of Jacob altogether free from reproach, may render it doubtful whether he be liable to *all* the blame which on this account has been laid at his door. We are indebted for the outlines of this view to the Hebrew commentators whose observations on the subject have been collected in the Commentary on Genesis published in 1844 by the Jewish ministers, De Sola, Lindenthal, and Raphall; but it is right to state that even among Jewish expositors there are some who take quite as unfavourable a view of Jacob's conduct in this affair as any Christian interpreters have ever done. We shall give in a connected statement this view, which, in the above mentioned work is presented in detached notes.

The fourteen years during which Jacob had agreed to serve Laban for his two daughters expired about the time that Rachel—who had so long been childless—gave birth to a son named Joseph. As soon as mother and child were sufficiently strong to undertake so long and fatiguing a journey, Jacob asserts his right, and declares his wish to return to Canaan. The happy return to his native land, which had been promised to him at Bethel, was the end and aim of all Jacob's hopes and wishes; and the Jews have an opinion or tradition that Rebekah about this time fulfilled her promise of sending for him as soon as he could return with safety—Gen. xxvii. 45—which made him the more desirous of returning. As anticipated, Laban received this intimation with much disturbance. He knew well the value of Jacob's services; and now that he can no longer command, he bends himself to entreaty and acknowledgment: "I pray thee, if I have found favour in thine eyes, tarry; for I have learned by experience that the Lord hath blessed me for thy sake." He also said, "Appoint me thy wages, and I will give it."

In this proposition, Jacob sees the means of securing an independent provision for his family; for now, after fourteen years' service, he has no wealth but four wives and twelve children. It was usual in that age, and is still usual in the East, for those to whom the charge of a flock is entrusted, to obtain their recompense from the produce or increase of the flock; and Jacob founds his proposal for the remuneration of his future services on that basis.

Sheep are generally altogether white in the East, and goats wholly black. Sheep of the latter colour are very scarce, but some of a dark red are found. Such as are parti-coloured are very rare indeed—far rarer than even with us. Jacob proposed that all the parti-coloured young hereafter born in the flock entrusted to his charge should be his perquisite, after all the present lambs and kids thus marked had been removed, and placed under separate care. Thus far it would seem that Jacob relied on the blessing of God upon the natural increase of the animals thus distinguished, under the condition, to his own disadvantage, that the parti-coloured young should be removed. Laban consented to this arrangement. But the very day that it was completed, he caused to be separated from the flock not only the parti-coloured young of the sheep and goats, as Jacob contemplated, but all, whether old or young, that had any variation of colour in them; and placing the small flock thus composed under the charge of his sons, he directed that it should be removed three days' journey apart from the large flock that Jacob fed. This is alleged to have been a clear infraction of the agreement, since Jacob had only consented to the reduction of his probabilities of large gains by the removal of the parti-coloured *young*, but required the old rams and ewes so marked to remain in the flock, as without this there was little human probability of his reaping any benefit from the contract. The proportion of spotted or parti-coloured animals born in an oriental flock is usually very small; and by removing the few spotted rams and ewes, the proportion was reduced to nothing. This first great deviation of Laban from the original terms of the agreement compelled Jacob, it is urged, to abandon the fair and regular course which he at first contemplated, but of which Laban deprived him by removing the rams and ewes.

The measure he did resort to was to act upon the imagination of the animals, by placing parti-coloured rods before their eyes, so as to induce the production of parti-coloured young. It was quite successful. The question is, whether, at the time he entered into his contract, he knew that he possessed the means of turning it to his advantage, to an extent which Laban could not foresee, and would not have allowed. If he did, and if he entered into the contract with this intention, his conduct deserves the worst things that have been said of it. But it is assumed by one class of vindicators, that it was one part of the agreement between Laban and Jacob, that the latter was to be at liberty to employ any means in his power of increasing his own remuneration, and that Laban consented to these terms in the conviction that no artificial means could be available for producing such a result as Jacob eventually succeeded in obtaining.

But others, without insisting upon any such understanding, urge that Laban's removal of the rams and ewes was such an infringement of the treaty as, by depriving Jacob of any hope of remuneration by ordinary means, reduced him to the necessity either of using reprisals, or of submitting a second time to be the dupe of his unprincipled uncle. He was then driven to the expedients suggested by his intimate knowledge —acquired by long and intelligent experience in pastoral pursuits—of the nature, instincts, and susceptibilities of the animals under his care. But although this knowledge might have led him to conjecture that the means which occurred to him might be effectual, yet, as the experiment had never been tried, it was at the best a very hazardous one, which he could not in the first instance have contemplated, and which he did not employ until Laban's selfishness and injustice left him no other choice. The conclusion drawn from this view of the case is, that "although Jacob's conduct on this occasion may not be praiseworthy, it does not merit the harsh interpretation with which it has been assailed."

It must be admitted, that there is sufficient in this explanation to permit us to regard the case as doubtful. But allowing Jacob all the benefit of the doubt, and all the advantage of this explanation, it may be asked, how the injustice of Laban rendered his case so hopeless as to drive him to this questionable expedient. His refuge from Laban was with God, who had *promised* to make his way prosperous. It is to be feared that in this case, as in that of the blessing, Jacob was but too prone to find expedients for *helping* God to accomplish his own purposes. Then, again, if all the rest were right, or at least not blameable, what shall we say to the eager greed which urged him so to manage his proceedings, by subjecting only the strong ones to the operation from which he was to reap advantage, that all the strong animals became his, and all the weak ones Laban's? This is revolting; and we do wrong, if, out of respect to the character of a man whom the sacred Scripture represents to us with all the light and shade of natural character, we suffer our young ones to receive the impression that right and wrong are matters of conventional interpretation, and not clear and certain facts, to be known and read of all men. Our rising generation must not thus learn the lessons which the Bible was given to teach. We love Jacob with all his faults; we love him more as he grows older. But it is better that Jacob's character should suffer, than that any of these little ones should perish, through any unwise attempts to prove that his wrong was right.

It is one distinguishing characteristic of Scripture history, that it narrates all acts and events, good and bad, with equal fulness and truth. It never excuses a crime, it never palliates a fault, and it never glosses over a failing. It exhibits the noblest and best of men with all their weaknesses and sins; to teach us that human perfection is but a dream of worldly philosophy, and that as from Christ alone we can obtain pardon of sin, so to Christ alone we must look for a perfect pattern of virtue. When the Spirit of God, speaking in Scripture, does not palliate or excuse the faults and crimes of patriarchs, prophets, and apostles, we should not attempt to do so. We weaken the cause of divine truth by such attempts; and we manifest at the same time an entire misunderstanding of the object of Scripture history. The biographic sketches of the Bible were intended as life-lessons for us, to show that lies and deception, immorality and crime, entail sorrow and suffering on earth, while they peril the immortal soul; and above all, to show the absolute necessity, in the case of every man, of divine teaching, guidance, and sanctifying and saving grace.

P.

THE DEPARTURE

Genesis 31

THE increase of Jacob's substance was in sheep and goats; yet we are told that at the end of the six years—that is, of twenty years in all—he had "much cattle, bondmen and bondwomen, camels and asses." How were these obtained? Some have found a difficulty in this, which we are unable to perceive. Obviously he sold part of his increase in sheep and goats, and bought other property with the proceeds. He has now enough. He has provided for his household, and the wish to return home revives, and is strengthened by circumstances.

The substance of the thirty-first chapter of Genesis is composed of a statement of—

Jacob's reasons for departing.

His wives' reasons for concurring with him.

And Laban's reasons for opposing his departure.

Jacob's reasons are imparted to his wives, whom, for greater privacy, he summons to the fields for the purpose of conferring with them together, as they lived separately. Here it is worthy of notice, that the two secondary wives are not consulted in the matter. This is a mark of their inferior condition. There is no distinction made in any way between the sons of these women and those of Leah and Rachel, though the mothers are thus unfavourably distinguished. The reason is, that the sons of Bilhah and Zilpah,

the handmaids, have been adopted by Rachel and Leah as their own, and have been recognized by Jacob as his sons. This removes all distinction between them, but does not render their mothers equal to Jacob's free wives.

Jacob's reasons were, that God had commanded him to return; that he had been very badly treated by Laban, whom to the best of his power he had faithfully served; and that now the increase of wealth which God had given to him was viewed with jealous eyes by Laban and his family.

The wives' reasons lay, first, in their assent to Jacob's own reasons. But, besides this, they had special reasons of their own. They had clearly, they said, nothing to expect from their father, who treated them as strangers, belonging to Jacob rather than to himself. And furthermore, by bartering them for Jacob's services, he had appropriated all the advantages to himself; for if he had been paid for them in goods or money, custom would have required him to employ some part of it in gifts to them, which in the course taken was avoided, whereby they were left without the separate means to which they were by their rank in life entitled.

Having obtained the concurrence of his wives, Jacob delayed not his departure. He had reason to fear that Laban would attempt to detain him or his property by force; and he therefore stole away secretly, while Laban was engaged, three days' journey off, in shearing his sheep. The

JACOB DEPARTING FROM LABAN

women and children were mounted on camels, and soon the whole of the flocks and herds and people were on the march for the land of Canaan. Jacob might have hoped that the circumstance that he had six days' start would discourage Laban from attempting a pursuit. But if so, he was mistaken. Laban, travelling without encumbrance, might yet hope to overtake, before reaching the Jordan, a large and impeded caravan, going slowly, and making short stages, on account of the young cattle, the women, and the children. And, in fact, Laban did overtake them on the wrong side of the Jordan, among the mountains of Gilead. It might have gone ill with Jacob, for Laban had his kinsmen with him; but God had not forsaken Jacob, and Laban was warned in a dream to do him no harm. He did not, however, avoid the interview with Jacob. That interview is exceedingly characteristic. When Laban came up, Jacob had encamped in Gilead; and Laban having encamped in sight, went over to the camp of Jacob. It is remarkable that Laban, in his complaint, says not a word about the property; but having been prevented from taking the course which he had contemplated, he makes the offence rest upon the unfriendly distrust evinced by this secret departure. He complains that his daughters had been carried away like captives taken with the sword. And again, he had not been suffered to kiss his daughters, before what was meant to be a final separation. The poor man is full of his daughters; for whom, according to their own account, he has no real regard at all. Let him, however, have the credit of the feeling he claims. It is a hard thing for a man to part with his children for ever, even though he may have slighted them while they were near. The sluggish depths of even the worldly heart are stirred by such an occurrence; old paternal memories revive, and the fatherly sympathies awaken in their force. We shall, on these grounds, always be most safe in according to every one that degree of paternal affection which he exhibits or claims under such circumstances.

Once more: " Wherefore didst thou abscond secretly, and steal away from me, and didst not tell me, that I might have sent thee away with mirth and with songs, with tabret, and with harp?" This is interesting. The harp, or lyre, has before been mentioned as among the instruments invented by Jubal; but this is the first mention of the " tabret." The original word is *toph*, meaning a kind of hand-drum or tambourine.

The same instrument is at this day known by the corresponding name *doff* in Syria, Egypt, and

ANCIENT TABRETS

Arabia. This, with other instruments of music, together with songs and cries, is still used when a person of any note sets out upon a long journey in the East. The "songs" were probably such vocal sounds as are still used in the East on the like occasions by the women, to express joy, exultation, or any not decidedly mournful emotion. This is the *Ziraleet*, which consists of the words *lillé, lillé, lillé*, repeated as often as the person can utter them in one breath; and being uttered very rapidly in a shrill tone, the sound is heard to a great distance. It is preceded, on such occasions as this, and on some other occasions, by a stanza of four lines, recited by a single voice, expressive of thanks to God for benefits received, or of supplications or good wishes. These are usually extempore, and therefore the more precisely appropriate to the occasion and the circumstances.

Furthermore, and to clench all the rest, Laban makes the astounding charge that Jacob had stolen—his gods! It is clear that Laban knew and acknowledged the Lord, but with the worship of Him he had mixed certain strange gods, or at least certain superstitious images, such as elsewhere occur in Scripture under the name of *teraphim*, and which appear to have borne the human figure, and to have been used chiefly for purposes of divination. Josephus says, with probability, but with reference to a different matter, that it was the custom of the Mesopotamians to have all the idols they worshipped in their own houses, and to take these with them on their journeys. Aware of the possibility that these images might have been taken, Jacob, although shocked at the charge, did not venture to assert positively that they were not in the camp; but he gives Laban leave to seek for them, and declares that he may put to death any one in whose possession they may be found. Alas! he little thinks that it is his beloved Rachel who has them. She had stolen them before her departure; for what purpose is not clear, but it is to be feared that she did so for superstitious uses. Had Jacob known where they were, he would have trembled when he saw Laban, in his search, enter Rachel's tent. But he need not have feared. Laban's daughter was a

TERAPHIM

match for her father, even in his own line, and fairly outwitted him. She had these images under "the camel's furniture," upon which she sat in the tent; and professing to be too ill to rise to pay her proper respect to him, by standing in his presence, he hurriedly and considerately abstained from insisting upon her rising that he might examine her seat. What this "camel's furniture" was, has been questioned. Some think it was the small tent or cradle which is shown in p. 283; but these are only used on the camel's back, and never for seats. We see no reason to alter the opinion we have had other occasions of expressing: that it was the camel's pack-saddle, which is peculiarly appropriate to the purpose of a seat, or rather of a cushion, against which a person seated on the floor may lean. These saddles, commonly made of wood, are high; and the concavity, usually filled by the convex back of the camel, would have formed a good hiding-place for the images. If any object to this, that the saddles are not usually removed from the camels' backs at the end of a day's journey, when the traveller is to resume his course on the morrow, it may still be suggested that the teraphim might have been con-

cealed by Rachel under the *hesar*, which consists of carpets, cloaks, cloths, and the like, heaped upon the saddle to form a comfortable seat for such women as do not ride in the cradle. These things are always taken off at the end of the day's journey, and form a kind of mattress in the tent upon which a person may sit or lie down. Between these parts of the camel's furniture the alternative seems to lie.

When Laban returned from the last tent unsuccessful, Jacob at length spoke out. He spoke like a man of sense and spirit, and his words were words of weight. He demanded with warmth why he had been so hotly pursued. He set forth his services and sufferings; and he declared his conviction, that "unless the God of my father, the God of Abraham, and the Revered One of Isaac, had been with me, surely thou hadst now sent me away empty. God hath seen my affliction, and the labour of my hands, and rebuked thee yesternight."

Laban did not, could not, directly reply. He said vaguely, that all Jacob had, all the substance spread upon the hills before him, was virtually his; but insinuated that he waived his claim to it, in consideration of his daughters and grandchildren. He proposed that there should be a covenant of peace between them, and that a monument should be set up in testimony of the transaction. Jacob, as he had done at Bethel, set up a stone as his memorial, while Laban and his friends piled up a heap of stones. The covenant proposed by Laban, and consented to by Jacob, was, that seeing (as he alleged) the property was his, it should not be allowed to be shared by others, by Jacob's taking any wives besides his daughters; and that they were neither of them to pass the boundaries defined by these memorials for harm to the other. In this point of view these became boundary monuments, analogous to others of the like kind found in various countries. Witness that mentioned in the treaty of peace between England and Scotland, as recited by Hollinshed: "That Malcolm shall enjoy that part of Northumberland that lieth betwixt Tweed, Cumberland, and Stainmore, and do homage to the kinge of England for the same. In the midst of Stainmore there shall be a crosse set up, with the king of England's image on the one side, and the king of Scotland's on the other, to signify that one is on his march to England, and the other to Scotland. The crosse was called the Roi-crosse, that is, the crosse of the kings." The intention of the cross, and the pains taken to defend it, seem, as Sir Walter Scott remarks,[1] to indicate that it was intended to be a landmark of importance. In this case the two images represented the two contracting parties, shown, by a different kind of memorials, in the transactions between Jacob and Laban.

An interesting controversy has recently sprung up regarding the real site of Haran. Until within the last few years no one appears to have doubted that it was identical with Harrân in Mesopotamia. Dr. Beke, however, a learned Orientalist, has started the theory that the Mesopotamia or Padan-aram mentioned in the story of Jacob, lay in the plain of Damascus, between the Abana and Pharpar; that Haran, the city of Nahor, is represented by the modern village of Harrân-el-Awamîd, discovered and described a few years ago by the writer of this note;[2] and that "the river" which Jacob passed over on his flight to Canaan was not the Euphrates, but the Pharpar. His principal argument is the distance of Harrân of Mesopotamia from Gilead (300 miles), and the alleged impossibility of Laban accomplishing it in seven days. Dr. Beke's arguments are not sufficient to disturb the opinion which has hitherto prevailed. It is quite possible for men on swift dromedaries to ride even more than 300 miles in seven days; and it is at the same time possible, and seems probable, that both Laban and Jacob may have started from a point much nearer Gilead than the town of Haran. Their pastoral habits often led them far away from home. At the time of Jacob's flight, Laban was three days' journey distant shearing his sheep.

P.

THE FIRST PRAYER

Genesis 32

THE natural curiosity which we experience to know what Esau had been doing during the twenty years of Jacob's absence, is in part gratified. Still it is merely a glimpse of him and his condition that we obtain. He resided chiefly among the mountains of Seir, which were then occupied by the Horites; and by the power which he acquired through the gathering around him of persons of like bold and hardy character and habits, eventually strengthened by the pastoral wealth which he received on the death of

[1] In *Rokeby*.
[2] Porter's *Five Years in Damascus*, i. 376.

his father, his children were enabled to establish a paramount influence in the country, and to become its sovereigns. Even at the time of Jacob's return, Esau's power had become very great; for when he received a submissive and most respectful message from Jacob, making known his return, he was able to command the services of four hundred men, at whose head he set forth to meet his brother.

What his intentions were in taking this step he did not disclose to the messengers. They might be friendly; for, according to the custom of the East, the respect shown to a person is in proportion to the extent and splendour of the train sent forth to meet him. But Jacob feared, and had reason to fear, that his design might be hostile, although it does not often happen that men of Esau's impulsive temper retain their anger for twenty years. But the angels of the Lord encamp round about those that fear Him: and Jacob had been encouraged by a vision, in which he beheld the protecting angels, in two hosts, at Mahanaim. Still, his heart was moved by the intelligence which his messengers brought; and as a measure of precaution, he divided his people and flocks into two companies—the one to be in advance of the other, that if the foremost were smitten by his brother, the other, containing the women and the children, might be able to escape. What more · could he do? He prayed. This prayer is the first on record; for the intercession of Abraham for Sodom was more of the nature of a remonstrance or argument, and Eliezer's utterance at Haran rather a proposal than a prayer. Many prayers had been offered before the time of Jacob, but this is the first of which we have any account; and since the most ancient remaining example of any human act or thought is deemed worthy of peculiar notice and consideration, the first human prayer that has reached us is entitled to attention. It is short, emphatic, comprehensive, and strictly appropriate to the exigency: "O God of my father Abraham, and God of my father Isaac, the Lord who saidst unto me, 'Return unto thy country and to thy kindred, and I will deal well with thee;' I am not worthy of the least of all the mercies, and of all the truth, which Thou hast showed unto Thy servant: for with my staff I passed over this Jordan, and now I am become two bands. Deliver me, I pray Thee, from the hand of my brother, from the hand of

Esau: for I fear him, lest he will come and smite me, and the mother with the children."

It does not seem that there could be a finer model for a special prayer than this, the most ancient of all. He first claims his interest in the broad covenant with Abraham and Isaac—just as we might, and indeed ought, to set forth our interest in mercies covenanted to us in Christ; then he urges the covenant of personal mercies and promises; then he humbles himself into nothing before God, confessing with most affecting emphasis his utter unworthiness of the blessings that have been showered upon him, yet venturing notwithstanding to hope for deliverance from the danger that lay before him. His prayer was heard. Mysterious encouragements were given him that very night, when he remained alone, after he had sent his people over the river Jabbok. An Unknown Traveller engaged, as it were, in a struggle with him, in the course of which it seems that the Stranger did not disclose His spiritual nature, but allowed His opponent to seem the stronger of the two, until at length He put forth an atom of His shrouded strength, and by a simple touch caused the sinew of Jacob's thigh to shrink. Then, knowing that his conflict was not with flesh, Jacob yet retained his hold, and, with the strong importunity and boldness of conquering faith, cried, "I will not let Thee go, except Thou bless me." And he *was* blessed. And not only so; but he received a new name—the name of ISRAEL—intended to denote his power with God, and therefore to assure him and his against any cause of dread from the power of man.

The whole scene, which some do not hesitate to regard as the most important event in the life of Jacob, seems so like the spiritual struggles which take place in the experience of men at the present day, that some have doubted whether there is more in this than the representation of mental thought and conflict under the figure of bodily action; while others have supposed that Jacob, having remained behind, wrapped himself up in his mantle and slept, then undergoing in vision the conflict which is described. There is not, in the nature of things, any intrinsic objection to this, for we read in Genesis of divers communications being made to man in visions; but we shall not always be safe in regarding that as a vision which Scripture records as a fact. The circumstance, too, that Scripture records

some things as visions, and others as facts, renders it the more difficult to regard as a vision that which the text describes as a fact. If we admit this, it must become uncertain what is visionary and what is true, unless we contend that a vision is not less true than a fact. And it may be so; yet in the case of a fact we can ourselves judge of it; whereas in a vision the judgment of another, in the interpretation of that vision, is interposed between us and the simple truth. Besides, in those ages, God taught mankind by more sensible manifestations and representative actions than are now, with our fuller light, required; and it seems to us that we are precluded from regarding this as a vision, by the circumstance, that when Jacob resumed his journey, he actually "halted upon his thigh" where the angel had touched him,—a physical fact, physically commemorated by the Israelites to this day, in their abstinence from the particular part of the animals they eat, which answers to "the sinew that shrank" in the thigh of Jacob. Men do not become lame in visionary conflicts. With the greater or lesser probability of real and of visionary conflicts we have nothing to do. We are to see what it really is that Scripture teaches or communicates. Rightly apprehended, the circumstance, whether a vision or a fact, is full of matter to awaken thought, and to afford encouragement. Let those who wish to see how it may be applied, and what sweetness may be extracted from it, read Charles Wesley's noble hymn, beginning—

> "Come, O Thou Traveller unknown,
>   Whom still I hold, but cannot see!
> My company before is gone,
>   And I am left alone with Thee:
> With Thee all night I mean to stay,
> And wrestle till the break of day."

And ending thus:

> "Contented now, upon my thigh
>   I halt till life's short journey end;
> All helplessness, all weakness, I
>   On Thee alone for strength depend;
> Nor have I power from Thee to move—
> Thy nature and thy name is Love."

This encouragement to rely upon the divine protection did not seem to Jacob to require any alteration of the arrangement he had previously made, with the view of propitiating his brother. This consisted of the noble present from his own flocks and herds, which he proposed to send on in advance in different droves, the leaders of which were instructed severally to declare, when questioned by Esau, that "these be thy servant Jacob's: it is a present unto my lord Esau; and, behold, he also is behind us." This is the first direct case of making presents, as distinguished from gifts, from a superior or equal, which we find in the Scripture,—a custom which we often meet with afterwards; and the case is in entire conformity with the existing usages of the East. No one dreams there of approaching a superior without a present; and the respect and consideration he means to evince are estimated by the value of his offering, due regard being had to his circumstances. In this case it was not only a mark of attention, but an acknowledgment of inferiority.

After all this preparation, it was still a trying moment when the two brothers, the cautious Jacob and the rough but warm-hearted Esau, came in sight of each other after so long separation. Jacob, who was probably riding, dismounted when Esau appeared, and adopted the form of advance which a subject uses in approaching a prince in the East. He stopped, at intervals, seven times, to bow very low—"bowed himself to the ground"—as he advanced. The seventh pause, the seventh bow, brought him very near to his brother. They saw each other face to face once more; and although " a brother offended is harder to be won than a strong city," Esau was won. He yielded to his heart's impulse, and rushed forward to give the embrace of a brother to his father's son: " He ran to meet him, and embraced him, and fell upon his neck and kissed him; and they wept."

As nobody could be spectator of this mysterious conflict, it seems most reasonable to regard the narrative as resting on the authority of the Patriarch himself, who would not be likely to conceal from his family an occurrence so full of instruction and comfort. He would relate the wonderful circumstances as they appeared to him at the moment. We have here, I apprehend, the impression made on his own mind; and the physical effect would serve to show, as remarked already, the *real*, as opposed to any mere visionary nature, of the Divine manifestation. The physical and the spiritual are wondrously interlinked in the Divine universe; but it is admonitory to remember that in this transaction the physical phenomenon is a sign of weakness, not of strength.

S.

BENONI

Genesis 35:18

OF Jacob's twelve sons, all but the youngest were born in Padan-aram. The youngest, the only one native to the land of promise, was also the child of his well beloved Rachel, whose earnest and not always reasonable craving for children had rendered much of her husband's life uncomfortable. At length her desires were gratified. She had one son in her own country. That was Joseph. And now, when Jacob was on the way from Bethel to join his father at Mamre, just before coming to Bethlehem, another was given to her. But this blessing was won at a costly price. She died in giving him birth. In her dying agony she gave her child the name of BENONI, "the son of my sorrow;" but Jacob changed this name to Benjamin, "son of the right hand."

Thus Jacob lost, soonest of all, and while she was still young, the wife he loved most, and probably the only one to whom he felt bound by any other tie than that of duty. That loss, and the deep pang it gave, he remembered well; it was always present with him to his dying day. Witness that touching incident in his last discourse with Joseph—the abrupt transition of ideas with which, while discoursing of other

RACHEL'S GRAVE

matters, he suddenly and sorrowfully remarks: "As for me, when I came from Padan, Rachel died by me in the land of Canaan, in the way, when yet there was but a little way to come unto Ephrath; and I buried her there, in the way to Ephrath."

How is it that the favourite of Heaven should thus suffer? Except David—also highly favoured of God—and scarcely excepting him, there is no man in all the Scriptures so deeply tried in his affections as Jacob. That which he most loves, on which his heart is most fixed, is constantly torn from him, and more than once he has occasion to ask,

"Could not the grave forget thee, and lay low
Some less majestic, less beloved head?"

First he lost Rachel, whom he loved so, that his seven long years of service for her "seemed to him but a few days for the love he bore to her." Then the son of the lost Rachel twines himself around his heart, and that son is also suddenly reft from him. He sees his bloody robe; he believes him torn of beasts; and when his sons and daughters rise to comfort him, he refuses to be comforted, and he says, "For I will go down to the grave, unto my son, mourning." Next, his Benjamin, the sole remaining relect of that beloved wife, is demanded from him, and he gives him up in the strong fear that he shall see his face no more. He resists long in this instance: "My son shall not go down with you, for his brother is dead, and he is left alone; if mischief befall him in the way in which ye go, then shall ye bring down my grey hairs with sorrow to the grave." But stern necessity compels. He yields him up; he suffers him to depart with the sad words, which strike the ear like a groan, "If I be bereaved, I am bereaved." (Gen. xlii. 38; xliii. 14.)

It was therefore in his most treasured affections—in the things that touch the heart most nearly—that it was the lot of Jacob to be tried. We all have our trials—one after this manner, another after that. That was *his* trial. And it is the hardest to bear. What is the wrath of man; what is the loss of substance, of comfort, of health, compared with such trial, such loss as this? The deceitfulness of Laban was hard, but Jacob had a spirit that rose above it, that trod it down, that turned it to good. The fierce threats of Esau were terrible; but his heart was in God's hand: he might relent, he did relent. But the grave knows no relenting; the dead come back no more. All other loss is remediable; but this can never be repaired, while the heart lives to

suffer. Besides. as in this case, it is the most loved that is soonest lost. Too strong earthly love, and even love not all earthly, seems to blight its object. It is burnt up suddenly, as by the very warmth of our affections, or it wastes silently away before their glowing heat.

But *why* was the man chosen of God, even in his mother's womb, thus tried where he would feel most severely? It might be for the very reason that this *was* the point in which he would feel most acutely, and in which, therefore, he might be most effectually corrected. He needed correction. There was much in him, as in all of us, which was of the earth earthy, and which needed sharp fires to burn it out; and *this* was the fire in which God tried him, because it would best purify him. Even the inordinateness of his affections needed correction. He was one of those men whose affections are not expansive, but concentrative. There were many objects—wives and children—with claims upon his affection; but he must have some *one* object to love preeminently, while the rest were less regarded. First there was Rachel, then Joseph, then Benjamin. But this inordinateness of special affection is often a snare to the soul. It borders on idolatry. It sets a rival on God's throne, and establishes a conflicting interest between earth and heaven. This must not be. It is dangerous and soul-destroying; and therefore often does God, out of mere kindness and pity, take away the desire of our eyes with a stroke. The wit of man can find no other reason than this most sufficient one, why it is that the objects we cherish most are soonest lost.

Again, we may observe in this the necessity of submitting our desires to God. Rachel made her own life and her husband's unhappy, by her deep anxiety for children. Well, she has children, and she dies. Had children still been withheld from her, she might have lived many years, enjoying the society of him whose love was to her better than ten sons. How often thus are we judged and punished by the gratification of our choice desires! We are not content to rely upon the Lord's judgment of what is best for us. We weary Him with complaints as to what He sends, or what He withholds, till at last He says, "They are given to idols; let them alone." Our wish is granted, and we perish, or find that we have won only sorrow or shame.

Happy they who, in the midst of such afflictions, from the loss of friends by death or circumstances, can say, with chastened hearts:

> " As for my friends, they are not lost :
> The several vessels of thy fleet,
> Though parted now, by tempest tost,
> Shall safely in the haven meet."—*Baxter.*

No one can fail to be much struck by the deep significance of the change of the child's name from Benoni to Benjamin. Having regard to the significance of these names, the fact is wonderfully suggestive. There are few whom it will not remind how often that which came as a grief remains as a joy and a blessing; how often, within their own experience, the son of their sorrow has become the son of their right hand. It had been something to change the name for one of neutral meaning, that it might not remain as a memorial of grief; but it is more when it is changed into a name of strength—a name of gladness and of power. We have known the cases of men greatly bowed down by some affliction, which threatened to make life a blank and a burden to them; but God enabled them to endure. God gave him strength, and in that strength they rose triumphant over privation, and pain, and care. Their very sorrow they seized, and made it an instrument of power. Their cross, when manfully taken up, became a sword in their hands, with which they went forth conquering and to conquer; and the thorny crown became a diadem of glory and beauty upon their brows. These are the Jacobs whose Benonis became their Benjamins.

MOVEMENTS

Genesis 35

THERE is some difficulty in understanding the movements of Jacob on his return to Canaan. When he parted with Esau, he expressed an intention of following him at his leisure to Mount Seir; but this intention he did not at that time execute. Seeing how sorely he had longed after his father's house, we expect him to go forthwith to his father; but this was by no means the case. And, considering the vow he had made at Bethel, we suppose that he will hasten to fulfil it when he returns in peace; but this he does not do. He goes to the valley of Shechem, where, so far as we can learn, he had never been before. He had doubtless a reason. We may recollect that this was the place of Abraham's first encampment when he entered the land of Canaan; it was the place in that land where God first appeared to him; and the place, too, of the first altar that he built. Here also was the tree, the trees, or the grove of Moreh; and, putting all these venerable recollections together, it may not be difficult to discern the reasons which led Jacob to turn his steps in this direction, like the grandfather, the promises made to whom he inherited, and in whose paths he desired to tread. It may appear that the tree, with the altar, combined with these recollections, made this a sacred place; and how much it was honoured in after times, we know. This spot was doubtless included in "the field" which Jacob at this time bought of the people of the land, and which he afterwards bequeathed, as "one portion above his brethren," to Joseph, whose bones, brought up from Egypt, were buried there. Abraham had not needed to purchase this spot; and the land being then more more thinly peopled, the place was not appropriated. But when Jacob arrived here, one hundred and twenty years after, the population had become less sparse. A town had been built in the valley; and a spot like this, in the near neighbourhood of the town, could no longer be secured as an exclusive possession, but by distinct purchase from the inhabitants.

To Bethel Jacob did not proceed, until he received the divine command to do so. This was after his sons had made their names odious in the neighbourhood, and their longer stay unsafe, by the cruel revenge which they took upon the people of the town, for the dishonour which the son of the emir had inflicted upon their sister Dinah.

We are startled at the terms of the order which Jacob issued to his camp, in announcing his intention to proceed to Bethel, that he might " build there an altar unto God, who answered him in the day of his distress." It was in these words: " Put away the strange gods that are among you; and be clean, and change your garments." What strange gods were these ? We know, but did Jacob know, that Rachel had her father's images, which he called his " gods ? " and did he know, or suppose, that similar superstitious objects had been brought by others from beyond the Euphrates? We are reluctant to think that Jacob would tolerate such things through a period of some duration, and that he only now thought of putting them away. There-

NABLOUS, THE ANCIENT SHECHEM

fore we are inclined to suppose that these "strange gods" were idolatrous and superstitious objects, of which his sons had, as he knew, just before got possession when they pillaged the town of Shechem—valuable for the materials of which they were composed, but which Jacob feared might in the end prove dangerous.

The part of the injunction which directs the people to purify themselves, and to put on clean vestures, is remarkable, as the first example of the personal cleanness which was afterwards regarded as essential to a becoming appearance before God in worship,—a salutary observance, which became a matter of ceremonial regulation under Moses, but which, like many other observances of the law, had its origin in earlier times.

In obeying this injunction, we learn that they gave to Jacob not only "all the strange gods which were in their hands," but "all their ear-rings which were in their ears." This is the first mention of ear-rings in Scripture, for the "ear-ring" which was given to Rebekah was in reality a nose-jewel. We may be surprised to find these included here among the idolatrous objects. This was probably on account of their bearing the form of idolatrous images, and of their being used as superstitious symbols, or at least as amulets or charms. But in whose ears were they? It is scarcely credible that Jacob

had allowed his people to wear these things, which he now saw to be objectionable, before his eyes every day. We incline, therefore, to the opinion of the best Jewish interpreters, that these ear-rings had been taken from the ears of the slain and the captive Shechemites, and were now required to be given up, notwithstanding their value. In the time of Moses we find ear-rings among the spoil won from the Midianites; and it is generally supposed that they had been taken from the bodies of the slain, and were therefore worn by men. This may have been the case, as it may be collected from ancient monuments that ear-rings were in early times much worn by men of various nations; yet in this instance, as in the case of the Shechemites, there were numerous female captives, from whose ears, quite as probably as from those of the slain men, the pendants

EAR-RINGS FROM ANCIENT SCULPTURES

might have been taken. Ear-rings are not now worn by the men of Western or Mohammedan

Asia, doubtless by reason of the sumptuary law of their religion, which forbids the use of gold and silver ornaments to men. Through the operation of this law, of comparatively recent origin, the existing practice in the lands of the Bible contributes no adequate illustration to the subject, which is better understood from ancient examples, collected as in the foregoing engraving, from ancient Egyptian monuments.

The use of ear-rings as amulets or charms, formed into idolatrous or astrological symbols, seems to have been carried by the Phœnicians into Africa, where it remained among Christians in the time of Augustine, who speaks of them with detestation.[1]

Jacob's disposal of all these things is somewhat remarkable. He "hid them under the oak which was by Shechem," which was, without any reasonable doubt, the very oak, or rather tere-binth-tree, at Moreh, which we had occasion formerly to notice;[2] and the very same, standing by the sanctuary of God, beneath which, in a later day, a stone was set up by Joshua in testimony of Israel's covenant with God.[3]

At Bethel Jacob performed his vow by building an altar. He does not seem to have made a very long stay in the place; but before he left it, a remarkable incident occurred, namely, the death of Deborah, the nurse of his mother Rebekah. In the East, as among the classical ancients, the nurse still remains attached to the family of the children she has nourished, and follows the fortunes of the child who has been the special object of her charge, being regarded with a consideration scarcely less than that of a mother. Thus Deborah had accompanied Rebekah when she left her home to become the bride of Isaac; and we are somewhat surprised to find her now in the camp of Jacob. We may entertain the reader by mentioning a few of the conjectures that have been brought to bear on the subject; for there is scarcely a single historical point which the Scripture has left in doubt, that has not become a subject of numerous conjectural explanations. A very favourite opinion among the Jews is, that Rebekah had sent Deborah to Padan-aram to invite Jacob to return, according to her promise that she would send to fetch him home. But women are not now, nor do we suppose that they ever were, employed on such

missions in the East. Some, however, conjecture that as Jacob had many small children, his mother had sent him her old nurse to assist his wives. Others are more disposed to imagine that Jacob, before he finally settled with all his family at Hebron, had paid a temporary visit to his father, on which occasion Deborah had returned with him to live with his wives, who were her countrywomen. But another opinion is, that Deborah had, after Rebekah's marriage, returned to her own country, and now intended to avail herself of the opportunity to see once more her old mistress. This, however, is contrary to eastern customs. Besides, Rebekah appears to have been by this time dead; and if we may add a conjecture of our own to these, it would be, that Deborah had on that event received permission either to return home, or else to join Jacob's camp after his arrival in the land of Canaan. It is not to be supposed but that some intercourse, by interchange of communications and messages, was kept up between Isaac and his son, although the fact is not particularly mentioned. The estimation in which this aged and attached dependant was held, is shown incidentally in the striking fact that the tree under which she was buried at Bethel was called "the oak of weeping," on account of the great mourning which was made for her.

It was shortly after this, and from this place, that Jacob at length journeyed southward to join his father; Rachel dying on the way, under the circumstances which yesterday engaged our attention.

It is extremely interesting for the Bible student to be able to trace the footsteps of the patriarchs in all their wanderings over Bible lands. When one reads the sacred narratives on the spot where they were written, they assume the freshness and vividness of life pictures. Jacob parted from his brother amid the verdant oak forests which then clothed, as they still clothe, the picturesque banks of the Jabbok. Though the meeting had been to outward appearance so cordial, there was a lurking suspicion in Jacob's mind, increased no doubt by the formidable retinue of Esau. Jacob promised to follow his brother leisurely to Seir; but no sooner was Esau's back turned than he struck off westward, and crossed the Jordan. Amid the abundant pastures and flowing streams of Succoth he rested after his long desert journey. The next stage was up one of the wild mountain glens to Shalem, a city of Shechem. It retains its ancient name in the Arabic form *Salem*, and lies a few miles east of Nabulus (Shechem). There Jacob pitched his tent before the city, in one of the richest upland plains of Central

---

[1] In his Second Book, *De Doctrina Christiana*.
[2] See Vol. 1, pp. 269-271.   [3] Joshua 24:26.

Palestine; and in the end bought the plain of the old Shechemites. The well he dug to water his flocks, and the tomb of his son Joseph, whose embalmed body was buried in "the parcel of ground" more than three centuries later (Josh. xxiv. 32), mark to this day the patriarch's first possession in the land of promise. From

RIVER JABBOK

Shechem he went to Bethel, travelling southward, first through the picturesque glens of Ephraim, and then over the rocky mountains of Benjamin. Bethel became once more to him "a house of God." From thence we can follow his footsteps southward, past the heights of Gibeah and the fortress of Jebus. Bethlehem at length came into view, perched on its rocky ridge, overlooking the wilderness where David in after years kept his father's sheep. Ere he reached it, however, the long caravan was arrested; and the voice of mourning was heard among the mountains. When "there was but a little way to come to Ephrath," Rachel died, and was buried in the way to Ephrath, which is "Bethlehem;" and her sepulchre is as well known, and almost as much honoured, this day, as it was in the time of Moses.

P.

DREAMS

Genesis 37:5-10

IT is difficult to avoid distinguishing an object of peculiar affection by some marks of special favour. It may not be always possible for a parent to avoid loving some one of his children more than the others; and elder children are usually tolerant of the special tenderness commonly shown to their younger brothers or sisters, seeing that it is demanded by their comparatively helpless condition. But a wise father will not, after his younger children pass the age of privileged infancy, allow this feeling to appear. He will not suffer it to influence his conduct in any serious way; and still less will he invest his attachment with invidious distinctions. Joseph was dear to Jacob for his mother's sake; and he was also dear, apparently, for his engaging qualities, his intelligence, and his personal beauty. This might be: but to distinguish his favourite by a finer, richer, and more showy dress—"a coat of many colours"—was unwise and foolish. It was even dangerous in a family composed, like his, of children by different mothers, whose small jealousies and spites against each other were assumed and shared in some degree by their sons.

This might, however, have passed. But the lad began to have dreams of distinction and honour, confirmatory of the pre-eminence with which his father's partiality had seemed to invest him. He not only dreamed, but told his dream—and that, probably, not without some degree of juvenile exultation. These dreams, like all others to which a representative significance is attached in Scripture, were symbolical; but the symbols were, even at the first view, more easily intelligible than the dreams of Pharaoh's servants, of Pharaoh himself, of Nebuchadnezzar, and of Peter, and even, perhaps, than that of Jacob at Bethel. The brethren were binding sheaves in the field, when their sheaves bowed down to his sheaf, or fell to the ground, while his remained erect. Another dream was more remarkable still : the sun, the moon, and the *eleven* stars did obeisance to him. Even Jacob, who easily interpreted this to mean himself, his wife, and his eleven other sons, was not altogether pleased ; and as for the brothers, these dreams strengthened into positive hatred the dislike with which Joseph was already regarded.

In our day, or rather among ourselves, such dreams would be but little considered, and we are therefore the more struck by the serious attention with which they were in ancient times regarded. Which is right—our long neglect of dreams, or the strong attention which they received in former days, and do still receive among many nations ? There can be no question respecting the dreams of Scripture. They were certainly pre-figurative—they were true, they were important, and the attention they received was most proper. There can be no doubt of this: the question, therefore, really is, Whether dreams have ceased to be significant—whether this door of intercourse with the invisible and the future has been closed ? The view of dreams set forth in Scripture, and which pervades the sacred books, is, that God does sometimes make known His will to man, and disclose His purpose, in dreams: " God speaketh once, yea twice, yet man perceiveth it not. In a dream, in a vision of the night, when deep sleep falleth upon men, in slumberings upon the bed; then He openeth the ears of men, and sealeth their instruction, that He may withdraw man from his purpose, and hide pride from man." (Job xxxiii. 14-17.) So also the prophet Joel, quoted by Peter on the great day of Pentecost, regards dreams as a form of prophetic intimation: " Your sons and your daughters shall prophesy ; and your young men shall see visions, and your old men shall dream dreams." [1] The question is, whether these things have ceased ? It may be so : miracles have ceased ; prophecy has closed ; why may not significant dreams also have ceased ? They may; but have they ? Few of the dreams of Scripture, scarcely any, have reference to spiritual matters ; and some of them are of no importance but to the

[1] Joel 2:28; Acts 2: 16,17.

dreamers themselves, affecting them only as individuals. We cannot, therefore, say that they would be discontinued for spiritual reasons; and still less can we say that the state of man requires them less now than of old. If we believe there is a spiritual world, why should we be eager to shut up almost the only door of intercourse with it ? The state of man may often require intimations more distinct than can be conveyed by *impressions* upon the mind. These more distinct intimations can only be conveyed by words or signs; but oral communications have ceased. The voice of God is not now heard in our gardens, or upon our mountains; but a most fitting mode of symbolical or pictorial intimation is left, when the world is shut out, the bodily senses are dormant, and the mind alone is awake, and is capable of receiving any impression that may be made upon it. We can not only see, but hear. There is nothing that man can learn in his waking state which may not be imparted to him in a dream. It seems probable, or more than probable, that " God" still " speaketh once, yea twice," in dreams, yet man " perceiveth it not." It may be that the circumstances of our high civilisation are unfavourable to such perceptions. "A dream," says the wise man, " cometh through much business." [1] By multiplying our ideas, by increasing the objects which engage our interest and attention, our modern civilisation has so extended the materials of mental association, and so awakened the activity of the mind, that ordinary dreams are probably much more numerous than in older and simpler states of society, and the impressions they make consequently become more faint. The late rising and the number of hours devoted to rest among us, are also favourable to the increase of dreams ; whereas men leading a less wildering waking life sleep regularly and shortly, but soundly, and, rising early in the morning, have comparatively few dreams. It is well known that dreams seldom arise during sound sleep: and all the sleep of men of simple oriental habits is sound. Hence dreams, being more numerous and less vivid, make less impression on the mind, and those among them that may be really significant become less heeded. Nevertheless, history, biography, and the experience of most of us, supply not a few modern instances, in which dreams have been most important for warning, for guidance, or for the

[1] Ecclesiastes 5:3.

detection of crime. Those of the last class are not perhaps the most frequent in themselves; but they are most generally and authentically known, as their evidence is necessarily produced in the investigation of the case. Yet even in these cases there has seemed a general disposition to underrate their importance, for which we feel unable to account, but from the general disposition among the men of the world to discountenance the idea of a particular providence. This idea is necessarily involved in the belief that God speaks to man in dreams; and this very reason, which renders the belief distasteful to the world, should recommend it to the earnest consideration of those to whom that doctrine is dear. Many of our readers will remember a case which filled the newspapers some years ago. One point in it, which was only produced because it was historically necessary to complete the case, engaged our attention greatly at the time. A young woman was murdered in a barn, and buried under the floor. She was thought by all who concerned themselves about her to be still alive in another place; and the murder remained not only undiscovered, but unsuspected at the time, when the young woman's mother was warned *repeatedly* in a dream to search the barn. She did so; the murder was thus discovered, and the murderer (Corder) condemned and executed. Now, from what other cause than a supernatural action upon the mind of the mother could this dream have been produced? But men *would not* perceive or acknowledge this. The counsel on both sides, the judge, the jury, the reporters, the editors,—all with one consent pushed this most prominent feature of the case aside. It did not elicit one serious reflection, one pious remark. It was to them only a dream. To us it was the finger of Providence; it was the voice of God responding to the cry of innocent blood.

Other cases, perhaps more striking, might be produced, to show that God has not ceased to speak to man in dreams, whether he will perceive it or not; and that Pilate's wife's message to her husband, " Have thou nothing to do with that just man, for I have suffered many things this day in a dream because of him,"[1] and Paul's seeing in a dream a man of Macedonia entreating him for help,[2] are not the last examples of such communications to mankind.

---

[1] Matthew 27:19.   [2] Acts 26:9.

It would be curious to trace the idea of dreams entertained by different nations. We have scriptural evidence that, among the Egyptians and Babylonians, dreams were most seriously regarded, and the task of interpreting them entrusted to a distinct and learned profession.[1] Great importance was attached to dreams among the Persians; and it is reported that Cyrus was cast forth at his birth, because a dream of his mother was interpreted to promise him universal empire. In the *Chouking* of the Chinese, it is in dreams that the sovereign of heaven makes his will known to the sovereign of the earth. In Homer, dreams came from Jove; and by both Greeks and Romans it was believed that in the solitude of caves, and groves, and temples, the gods appeared in dreams, and deigned to answer in dreams their votaries. Among the Hindus, dreams give a colouring to the whole business of life. Men and women take long journeys, perform arduous penances, and go through expensive ceremonies, from no other cause than a dream. Among the North American Indians, *all* dreams are of importance, but some are of mysterious fatality to the dreamer; so intimately connected with his well-being, and even his existence, that to obtain their fulfilment becomes the one object of his thought, and the aim of all his endeavours. Among the Moslems good dreams are held to be from God, and bad from the devil. Good dreams were held by Mahommed to be one of the parts of prophecy. He is reported in one of the traditions to have said: " A good dream is from God's favour, and a false dream is from the devil. Therefore, when any of you dreams of what he likes, he must not tell it to any one but a friend; but when you see anything you dislike, you must seek protection with God from its evil, and from the wickedness of the devil, and spit three times over your left shoulder, and not tell the dream to any one; then, verily, it never will do you any harm." The injunction not to tell bad dreams is curious. Perhaps there was a similar feeling of old; for Pharaoh's butler and baker seem to have been both reluctant to tell their dreams. The point is particularly insisted upon by Mohammed: we read, " A man once câme to the prophet, and said, 'I dreamed my head was cut off.' Then his Majesty laughed, and said, 'When the devil plays with any one of you in his sleep, do not mention it.'" In another place he denounces nothing less

---

[1] Genesis 41:8; Daniel 2:2; 4:7.

than hell-fire against those who, to serve a purpose, invent and relate a dream they have not had.[1]

EGYPTIAN SLAVERY

Genesis 39

It smites the heart with pity to behold the change which reduces the young Joseph, beloved and cherished of his father, and honoured by him with enviable distinctions, to the condition of a slave in Egypt.

Sent by his father to inquire after the welfare of his brothers, who were away with the flocks, they knew him afar off by his coat of many colours, and proceeded to plot not only against his welfare, but his very life; regardless not only of the bond of brotherhood between them, but of the anguish of soul which they knew that the deed contemplated by them would inflict upon their father. At the suggestion of Reuben, they do, however, shrink from actually murdering him on the spot, but cast him into one of the cisterns which still abound in Palestine, and which are generally dry in summer, and left him there to perish. The providential passage of a caravan of Arabian merchants, going down to the great market of Egypt, with their camels

JOSEPH IS SOLD BY HIS BRETHREN

laden with the drugs and spices which have always found a ready sale in that country,

[1] *Mischat ul Masabih*, book xxi. ch. 4, part 1.

suggested an equally secure and more profitable mode of disposing of him, by selling him to these merchants for a slave. This would also burden their consciences less; for, bad as they were, reflection made them shrink from the commission of more crime than appeared to them needful to ensure their object. The bargain was soon completed; for, as their purpose was only to get rid of an obnoxious brother, they set no high price upon him, and the merchants had him for twenty pieces of silver; not so much as three pounds, if the pieces were, as is generally supposed, equal to shekels of silver.

The Ishmaelite merchants knew that they carried the youth to a good market; for Egypt has always, from that day to this, remained the seat of a great mart for slaves. We have but little knowledge of the ancient condition of slaves in that country. Those who were captives of war seem, indeed, to have been badly treated; and, like the Israelites eventually, had hard task-work imposed upon them, under the superintendence of men who plied the stick freely when not satisfied. But the case of domestic slaves, bought with money, seems to have been very different, and in most respects similar to that of the same class at the present day in the same country. Some facts, therefore, in illustration of their present condition, may be suitably introduced here, as tending to throw light on the position which Joseph occupied. It is to be observed, however, that white slaves, male or female, are comparatively rare in Egypt at the present day; and the statements refer chiefly to the deep-brown coloured slaves from the country of the Gallas, and negro slaves from Eastern Africa. Whiteness of complexion, though making a difference less regarded in the East than with us, does better the condition of a slave, because white slaves have, from the influences of civilisation, become more scarce and valuable; but as they were formerly as common in those countries as black ones are now, and perhaps more common, the condition of the white slave in ancient times was probably not materially different from that of the coloured one at present.

It may be doubted, from the instance before us, whether a regular slave trade existed then as at present. In other words, we cannot collect that it was then a regular business for men to go into a country for the express purpose of buying up slaves, and conducting them in gangs to the place where they were to be sold. The probability is, that the collecting of slaves was an incident of general traffic, rather than a distinct pursuit.

Joseph was about seventeen years of age. This was a good age for his value as a slave. If anything, a better price would probably have been obtained for him had he been younger : for there is a general feeling in both Egypt and Arabia, that little dependence can be placed upon slaves that have not been brought up in the family ; and hence there is a great reluctance to the purchasing of grown-up slaves for domestic purposes. Such as are above the age of fifteen do not, at this day, bring much more than the price that was given for Joseph ; and they are bought chiefly by the Bedouins, who employ them as shepherds.

The slave dealers are said to pay great attention to the breed or origin of the slaves, experience having taught them that there is little variety of character among individuals of the same nation. This may be so with respect to the nations from which slaves are now usually procured, which have but a few simple ideas and pursuits ; for it would seem that individuality of character among persons of the same nation is in some degree the result of the various circumstances and influences which civilization produces. But it may be that this discrimination of the slave dealers has regard to little more than the few leading points of habit and temper which constitute what is called national character.

It may be noted that the Mohammedan inhabitants of these countries change the names of the slaves who come into their possession, unless they have already acquired a name from a previous master. The name of Joseph was eventually changed for an Egyptian name ;[1] as those of Daniel and his companions were changed for Babylonish names.[2]

As the dealer is afraid lest the condition of his slave, and consequently his marketable value, should be deteriorated, he usually treats him well during the journey, and while he remains in his possession. They usually call him *Abouy* (Hebrew *Abi*), " my father," and are seldom beaten, are well fed, spoken to in a kind manner, and not overworked. This, however, is less from humanity than with a view to prevent them from pining, or

from attempting to abscond. Those, however, who are grown up, or whose disposition has not been tried, or cannot be depended upon, are kept closely confined, well watched, and often chained. On the journey, slaves of this sort are tied to a long pole, one end of which is fastened to a camel's saddle, and the other, which is forked, is passed on each side of the slave's neck, and tied behind with a strong cord, so as to prevent him from drawing out his head. In addition to this, the right hand is also fastened to the pole, at a short distance from the head, thus leaving only the legs and left arm at liberty. In this manner he marches the whole day behind the camel ; at night he is taken from the pole and put in irons.

There are few families in Egypt that do not possess one or two slaves. In that country, as well as in Arabia, it is rarely the case that a slave remains in a respectable family for a number of years without being made free ; and then he is either married to a female slave of the house, or remains voluntarily as a servant, and receives wages. It is thought a mean action to sell a slave after he has been long resident in a family ; though, before he comes into the possession of the master who retains him, he usually passes through several hands. Male slaves are, for the most part, treated like children of the family, and always better than free servants. Female slaves are not so well off, as they suffer from the jealousy of their mistresses. If a slave behave ill, he is degraded from domestic service, and sent into the country to labour in his master's fields.

A slave brought up in the house, like Eliezer of Damascus,[1] at least in Southern Egypt and the lands beyond, thinks himself superior to every other person in it except the master. He is admitted to all the family councils ; he is allowed to trade or to engage in any business, on his own account ; and he may, in fact, do just as he pleases, provided he prove himself a bold fellow, who may be relied upon as ready and able, in case of emergency, to wield a sword in defence of his master.

If a slave kill a free man, his master is obliged to pay the price of blood, otherwise his own family becomes exposed to the retaliation of the relations of the deceased ; for the death of a slave is not considered an adequate atonement for the blood of a free man.

---

[1] Genesis 41:45.   [2] Daniel 1:7.

[1] See Vol. 1, pp. 247-249.

In Arabia and Egypt, the law gives the slaves one great advantage against the harsh conduct of a master. If they are discontented, and decidedly determined not to remain with him, they have a right to insist upon being sent to the public slave market to be re-sold. They must make this demand in the presence of witnesses, and if persevered in, it must be granted.

In connection with the abduction of Joseph, which he himself describes as his being "stolen away out of the land of the Hebrews," Gen. xl. 15, it may be observed, that it is not at this day in Egypt regarded as a crime to be punished by the judges, to steal a free-born child, but it is such to steal a slave. The reason is, that the latter is property, and the former is not.

In this land of Egypt, Joseph was no doubt taken to be sold in the slave market of the metropolitan city, where he was purchased by Potiphar, one of the king of Egypt's officers.

Jacob was residing at Abraham's favourite camping ground, in "the valley of Hebron" (Gen. xxxvii. 14), when he sent Joseph on the eventful mission to his brethren. They had gone to feed their flocks on Jacob's property at Shechem. Joseph followed them; but on reaching the plain, his brethren had proceeded northward to Dothan. It is a singular fact that this place, though now deserted, still retains its ancient name; and beside its ruins are large cisterns, from which in all probability it took its name, (*Dothan*, "The two wells.") It is situated in a little upland plain encompassed by swelling hills; and the envious shepherds, grouped apparently round the wells, could see their young brother approaching, and form their plans for his destruction ere he came up to them. On reaching them, he was seized and thrown into one of the dry cisterns. The great ancient highway from northern Gilead to Gaza and Egypt runs through the valley of Dothan. While Joseph's fate hung in the balance, the company of Ishmaelite merchants were seen travelling along it, with spices and "balm of Gilead" for the Egyptian market. Joseph was drawn up out of the pit and sold to them. It was a cruel and unnatural deed. The mind revolts from it. But God in His infinite wisdom and mercy, overruled it in the end for the salvation even of its brutal perpetrators.

P.

CAPTAIN OF THE GUARD

Genesis 39:1

IF the reader look to the marginal reading of his English Bible, he will see that the office of Joseph's master, which is described in the text as that of "captain of the guard," is indicated as being literally "chief of the slaughter-men;" a dreadful and sanguinary title, calculated to give an unpleasant idea of the nature of Joseph's employments. We are afraid to say how much has been written upon the simple question, What was the real character of the office thus described? If this personage was "chief of the slaughter-men," what did his men slaughter—men or beasts? The title is certainly very equivocal, and its meaning is only to be gathered from analogical researches. The inquiry is not only interesting in itself, as showing under what circumstances Joseph spent many years of his life, but as bringing some curious old customs under our view.

The Greek translation of the Old Testament (the Septuagint) having been made in Egypt, is thought to have a peculiar value in the elucidation of the passages of Scripture which relate to that country. The title which these translators give him is *Archimagiros*. Now as to the *magiri*, of whom he is here said to be chief, they are found to have been of two sorts—those who provided the meat, and those who prepared or dressed at home the meat thus provided. The standing of the latter was much higher and more honourable than of the former; and if Joseph's master belonged to this class, he would be master-cook, or intendant of the royal kitchen, an officer of no mean importance in ancient times. In the curious work of Athenæus, of which we trust the English reader will not much longer lack a translation, a person of this class is introduced as enforcing the consideration due to his place and station, by urging that he had served Seleucus, king of Syria, in the quality of clerk of the kitchen. Hence some have supposed that the Seventy intended to represent Potiphar either as having the chief direction or prefecture of the royal kitchen, or else as presiding over all the inferior officers and men who belonged to the king's slaughter-house. But it is now generally conceived that this was not the office of Potiphar; nor is it now universally supposed that the Seventy meant by the term they employed to allege that it was such.

It is seen, from the intimations respecting the nature of his office, that Potiphar was really, as he is styled in the text of the authorized version, the "captain of the guard,"—that is, of the military force employed in the service of the court. Why such an officer should be called "chief of the slaughter-men," or "executioners," must be explained by a reference to the fact, that in ancient times all penal inflictions adjudged by the king—from scourging to death—were executed by the soldiers forming the royal guard, under the orders of their chief. In his house was also the prison, in which accused persons were confined till their cases should be determined; and this military custody was a high and responsible function, belonging only to an officer of the highest rank. There are several incidents in Scripture which throw light upon the nature and functions of this office.

The prophet Micaiah, having displeased king Ahab by his boldness, is sent to Amon, the governor of the city, and to Joash, the king's son, to be put under confinement;[1] showing that Amon's post and authority in the matter was co-ordinate with that of the prince-royal; and from this it appears that the administration of the military custody was a very distinguishing trust of honour and power, which the nearest branches of the royal family did not regard as beneath them. Jehu's commission to the fourscore men, called the "guard and the captains," for slaying the worshippers of Baal,[2] gave them the same kind of authority and commission that we have in view as possessed by the guard. A more striking instance we have in Solomon's sending the illustrious Benaiah, the chief captain of the guard, to put to death Joab, Adonijah, and Shimei.[3] Nebuzaradan, who held this post under the king of Babylon, actually commanded the army by which the temple and city of Jerusalem were destroyed.[4] In Herod's massacre of the infants at Bethlehem, a body of military men, probably of the royal guard, was engaged. Of the same class was the executioner sent by Herod the tetrarch to behead John the Baptist in prison;[5] as well as those who were employed in imprisoning, scourging, and putting to death our Lord and His apostles.[6]

Many instances to the same effect might be produced from the profane historians; and from all this it clearly enough appears, that the administration of the penal law, in all its forms, belonged to military men, and in particular to the guard immediately about the person of the king, whose commander might therefore well be called the chief of the executioners. The custom no doubt arose from the judicial and executive powers possessed by the kings, whereby they were in the constant habit of ordering the infliction of summary and capital punishments, for the execution of which the military guard, always present, were the most efficient and the readiest instruments. Besides, men whose trade lay in the shedding of blood, always seemed the fittest, by their acquired indifference to human suffering, to be the agents of corporeal punishments; and in ancient times, as still in the East, nearly all punishments were corporeal, and therefore barbarous in the view of modern and European civilisation, although, by summary inflictions, all the difficult and complicated questions respecting imprisonment and transportation, which perplex the minds of modern statesmen, were avoided. However, between beheadings, cutting off feet, hands, noses, and ears, plucking out tongues and eyes, and inflicting the bastinado, the men of the royal ancient guards had enough of savage work to go through, and were subjected to a kind of hardening discipline, which scarcely prepares us for the apparently mild and forbearing character which Potiphar exhibits.

What was Joseph's first employment we do not exactly know, further than that it was about the house, not away in the fields. The Orientals, who are greatly taken with the history of Joseph, and repeat it in tale and song, with ample embellishments and numerous variations, give us to understand that Potiphar, who was childless, bought the Hebrew lad with the intention of adopting him for a son, and that he was employed in the garden, where he had a separate lodge for his abode. This is probably because, with their present habits, which are much less free with regard to women than were those of the ancient Egyptians, of whom they know nothing, they find themselves unable to account in any other way for the evidently easy access to his mistress which he enjoyed. This mistress makes no mean figure in the Eastern poems founded on this history, in which she bears the name of Zuleekah; and concerning her many particulars are recorded, which are quite new to plain readers of the Bible.

[1] 1 Kings 22:26,27. [2] 2 Kings 10:24,25.
[3] 1 Kings 2. [4] 2 Kings 25.
[5] Mark 6:27.
[6] Matthew 26,27; Acts 12:6; 16:27; 22:24; 27:1; 28:16.

It is interesting to observe to what consideration a purchased slave might in a short time rise in ancient Egypt. Joseph must soon, although still so young, have evinced to his master those engaging qualities, and that high intelligence in the conduct of affairs, which marked his illustrious career. Potiphar learned to like him, and to repose the utmost confidence in him, eventually making him steward of his household, and leaving all his affairs in his hands. This was the Lord's doing; for it was in consequence of its being seen that everything prospered to which Joseph put his hand that he obtained advancement and consideration. If he had begun to despair in his affliction of the fulfilment of those hopes which his dreams had awakened, this must have strengthened his heart, by giving him the assurance that he was not forgotten. There is nothing in the East that tends more to a man's advancement than the opinion that he is one in whose hands all business prospers; hence the emphasis with which it is declared, that his master discerned Joseph to be "a prosperous man;" or, in the more homely but not less exact language of the elder versions, "The Lord was with Joseph, and he was a luckie felowe;"[1] or, as another, "became a luckie man."[2] The reputation of being "lucky," arising from the observation that matters habitually go right in a man's hands, will in the East, and perhaps in the West, make any man's fortune, apart from any considerations of goodness or rectitude; but when, as in the case of Joseph, this reputation is enjoyed by one of irreproachable manners and unsuspected conduct, the claim to consideration becomes invincible. Potiphar had some reason to think the purchase of that Hebrew slave the best bargain he ever made.

EGYPTIAN CRIMES AND PUNISHMENT

THE Apostle Paul lays down a beautiful law for the conduct of servants, that they are to discharge their duties to their masters on earth as in the view of their Master in heaven, "with good will doing service as to the Lord, and not to men." (Eph. vi. 6, 7.) No man ever more faithfully

[1] Rogers' Version. [2] Bishops' Bible.

exemplified this rule of conduct than Joseph. So, when his mistress tempts him to sin, he shrinks from the idea of thus returning the kindness and confidence of his master; but his still more absorbing thought is, "How can I do this great wickedness, and sin against God?" Here we have the secret of his admirable conduct, his integrity, his virtue, and, by consequence, of his prosperity, and of the blessing of God attending all his steps. The world, as usually happens, was content to know him as a "luckie felowe;" but all his "luck," his "good fortune," his prosperity, his high advancement, was the effect of a certain cause. He lived as under the eye of God; and he discharged his duties and regulated his conduct with the feeling that there was One above whose approbation was of more importance to him than that of all the world. Such a man could not but prosper. Still it is hard to be misunderstood—hard to rest under injurious imputations in the minds of those who have laden us with favours, and whom we respect and love. It is hard for the innocent to bear this; but it would be harder to bear it if not innocent. Joseph, when cast into prison by his offended master, on the accusation of a revengeful woman, was no doubt deeply pained; but he would, and doubtless did, take comfort in the thought that his father's God knew him to be a good and faithful servant, and would not fail in due time to vindicate his righteousness.

It is not, however, our intention to dwell on the *incidents* of this or any other part of Joseph's story, seeing that no repetition of them that we ever saw preserves half the force of the original narrative. We shall be content to illustrate some remarkable or obscure points of it, and to gather up the indications of Egyptian usages which it affords.

In the narrative of Joseph's temptation, what strikes one as greatly different from modern Egyptian usage, is the free access which Joseph and the other men-servants had to their mistress. This surprises the eastern reader of the narrative, but to us it seems natural, being much in accordance with our own customs. Now, this circumstance, so adverse to Oriental notions, is remarkably in accordance with what we know of the ancient Egyptians, and supplies one of the many incidents found in the history of Joseph to confirm the verity of the sacred record. Indeed, this history must be regarded as the most remarkable and interesting account of the ancient Egyptians that we possess, and in fact, if we except, perhaps, some of their own monuments, the only account of so ancient date which has come down to us.

It is, then, admitted, on the evidence of the ancient historians, confirmed by the history of Joseph, and by that of the monuments, that the women in Egypt were indulged with greater privileges than in any other country; and this we may certainly accept as an evidence of their higher civilisation. The Greek historians seem, indeed, to ascribe a certain superiority in Egypt to the women over the men; but this does not seem to have been true, although the statement may be accounted for, by considering the impression which the polite and formal obeisance of man's strength before women's weakness and delicacy—such as exists also in modern Europe— would make upon Greek travellers, whose usages were very different. It is just as if an Oriental should infer, from the deferential attention which females receive from men under our social system, that women here rule over men, and should deem his discovery confirmed by the fact that a lady reigns over the land. The same phenomena might indeed, even to this extent, be witnessed in Egypt, where the royal authority and supreme direction of affairs were entrusted without reserve to women. Even the mistakes into which the ancient writers fell, in viewing the customs of the Egyptians regarding females, from their being precisely similar to those into which an Oriental would fall respecting those of civilised Europe, serve to show us where the truth lay. That the wife of Potiphar was enabled from day to day to converse with Joseph, and that the male servants of the household could come before her at her call, is a fact as astonishing to an Oriental as anything he would witness in our own customs. It shows that the ladies of Egypt enjoyed quite a European measure of freedom at home. Nor, probably, were they subject to modern oriental restraints abroad. On this point there are few facts; but at a later period, we find the king's daughter walking down to the river, with her maidens, with such freedom and unreserve as allowed of her being accosted by a stranger. (Ex. ii. 5-7.)

At some of the public festivals it is known that women were expected to attend, not alone, like the Moslem women at a mosque, but in company with their husbands and relations. Josephus indeed states that it was on an occasion of this kind, when it was the custom for women to go to the public solemnity, "that the wife of Potiphar, having pleaded ill health, in order to be allowed to stay at home, was excused from attending, and availed herself of the absence of her husband, to make her last and deliberate assault upon the virtue of Joseph."

In this instance, also, it is seen that the Egyptian, although a person of high office and manifest wealth, has no more than one wife. We are informed by Diodorus that the Egyptians were not restricted to any number of wives. But it would appear from the testimony of Herodotus, that it was nevertheless customary to take but one; and the numerous scenes in the ancient mural paintings, illustrative of their domestic life, confirm the testimony that a plurality of wives was exceedingly rare. So it is also among the Mohammedans of the present day, who, although allowed by their law to take four wives without sin, very rarely have more than one. Such was, and indeed is now, the case among the Hebrews themselves, who are not by their law restricted in this respect, but among whom a plurality has been and is the rare exception, and not the rule.

Some people have wondered that, when Potiphar listened to his wife's accusations, he did not at once put Joseph to death, seeing that he had power to do so, as the offender was his own slave, and the offence a capital crime. It has been urged, indeed, that Potiphar had a twofold right over Joseph's life, not only as his slave, but as being captain of the guard, which is thought by some to have given him an absolute power of life and death over all his own servants, and all connected with the court. The latter is a great mistake. The sovereign alone, and those invested with delegated sovereign power as governors of provinces, have ever had such power in the Egyptian, or have it in any oriental court. All cases but such as the sovereign himself decides— and his power is absolute in his own court, and over his own household—must go before the courts of justice. If, therefore, Potiphar had wished to inflict death upon Joseph, he could only have done it by bringing the matter before the king, or before the judges; and as an officer of the court, the former would probably have been his alternative. Then, as to putting him to death as a slave, that was not allowed by the laws of Egypt,—just laws for the most part,—which, while they sanctioned slavery, prohibited the master from putting his slave to death. Furthermore, notwithstanding the assertion too often made, that the crime of adultery was punished with death among all ancient nations, it was not so punished by the Egyptians. The punishment of the woman was to have her nose cut off, and of the man to receive a thousand stripes. If indeed it were proved that violence was used towards a free woman, the man was subject to a cruel and inhuman punishment, but still he was not put to death.

These facts help us to understand the conduct of Potiphar, and show us why, when Joseph was charged with this dreadful crime, his master did not slay him, or subject him to any immediate punishment, beyond casting him into the prison in his own house, in which persons accused of crimes within the verge of the court were detained until their cases could be investigated.

He *could not* put him to death; and thus is explained what some have been unable to account for, but by supposing that Potiphar did not really believe the charge brought against Joseph by his wife. But the Scripture expressly says that he did believe her; for it states that "his wrath was kindled" by her recital, and that it was in consequence of this kindling of his wrath that he cast Joseph into prison. This was, in fact, all that he could do, unless, perhaps, he had caused him to be beaten, which at the time might scarcely seem to him an adequate punishment. He reserved him for something worse. But as he detained him so long in confinement without bringing the matter to an investigation and punishment, which it was only possible for him to do in consequence of his position as master of the prison, it would seem that on cooler reflection he had some misgivings on the subject, or felt reluctant to make the affair a matter of public scandal, and was therefore well content that Joseph should remain in prison, especially when he found that even there he had made himself useful, and that he could be there kept in a quiet manner, out of the way of his wife.

THE ROUND HOUSE

Genesis 39:20

THE prison into which Joseph was cast, and which was undoubtedly within the premises of his master, is called in the text by a term which signifies the "house of roundness," or "the round-house." It is a curious fact, that the temporary prisons of the constable or police, in which persons are detained until their cases can be investigated by the magistrates, were formerly called "round-houses" throughout our own country, now exchanged for the more recent name of "police-station." It is difficult to see how this name became appropriated to such structures, unless from the originally round form of the prison. In the present case, the term might, with reference to existing usages, be thought to imply an edifice, or portion of the official mansion, mostly subterranean, of which the roof or vault, rising immediately from the surface of the ground, was round, or shaped like an inverted bowl. That it was of this nature has been inferred from its being called, in chap. xli. 14, the "dungeon." Such dungeons are still, under similar circumstances, used in the East; and they have commonly an aperture at the top by which some light and air are admitted, and through which the prisoners are let down. All this may have been applicable to the prison of Joseph, with the exception of the subterranean character, which was hardly possible in Egypt; and also, perhaps as to the roundness of the roof, for we have no evidence that the ancient Egyptians possessed the art of constructing vaulted roofs. It is quite sufficient to suppose that Joseph's prison was some part of the captain of the guard's premises convenient for this use, though not perhaps built expressly for it, although, as the Egyptians more than any other ancient people had buildings for distinctive uses, we cannot venture to infer too strongly from modern Oriental usages, the absence among them of buildings properly constructed for the confinement of prisoners. Such, or any other places of detention, are always within the premises of the chief of the guard, or of the magistrate. In Persia, for instance, every magistrate invested with a charge of criminal judicature generally engages the services of certain persons to act as guards or constables. He commonly prefers such as have been in the service of his predecessor, and have therefore experience in their business. He does not pay them. On the contrary, they render him a considerable annual rent, in consideration of the profit which they contrive to draw from their employment. To these persons the officer or magistrate assigns a suite of apartments, consisting of three or four chambers in the outer part of his mansion. Here they detain such criminals as come into their custody. The doors of the chambers are kept shut; but, like other doors of the country, they have little strength, and might be burst open with the foot. Yet, from the construction of eastern buildings, little anxiety is felt about the escape of the prisoners, nor are any unusual precautions taken to prevent it; the porter, always at the outer gate of the house, being the only fixed jailor. The custody is secure enough, and the prisoners are quite as uncomfortable as they could be in any public prison. They are not allowed to see any persons but those who have them in charge; and the chambers, besides being often crowded, are purposely left in a filthy and unwholesome condition, that the prisoners may be induced to purchase, at a high price, the enjoyment of the air, and the privilege of some addition to their comfort. If any one is detected in an attempt to escape, he is punished on the spot by a great number of blows with a stick, inflicted by the sole order of the jailor, or the chief of the men who have charge of the prison. To him, or to these men, the prisoners are entirely left by the magistrate, who troubles himself no further about them, the person who has them in charge acting just as he likes towards them, his sole responsibility being to produce them when required. Hence we see the importance to Joseph of his having gained the good-will of "the keeper of the prison," whom, for want of a clear perception of the nature of a practice so different from our own, some have regarded as no other than Potiphar himself, in whose house the prison was.

It is thus by no means an advantage to prisoners that there are no public prisons, which can only exist where imprisonment is a punishment, and not simply a means of detention. In Joseph's case, through his being the slave of the officer who had the prison in his house, the detention was long enough to have the effect of a punishment; and he might probably have been kept in

confinement any length of time his master had seen fit, had not the Lord prepared a way for his deliverance.

It would seem that he was at first harshly treated. The Psalmist says of him, "Whose feet they hurt with fetters: he was laid in iron," Ps. cv. 18. This treatment was probably under the first wrath of the master; but however painful while it lasted, it was not of long duration. It can scarcely be questioned that the keeper of the prison was previously well acquainted with Joseph, who had long acted as sole manager of his master's household. He was probably also, sooner than Potiphar himself, convinced of Joseph's innocence; for he was not subject to the same influence which led that personage to credit the story his wife had told him; and previous intimations of the character and designs of this woman had probably come to his notice, which the husband himself would be the last to learn. Joseph also, as a slave, possessing nothing but what depended on the favour of a master who had become his enemy, was not of the class whose circumstances could offer to the governor of the prison, any gainful inducements to harsh or extortionate conduct. Nothing was to be gained by using him ill; while a man of his tried abilities might be, in many respects, useful even in a prison if properly treated. It speaks well for Joseph, that in the position of command in which he had been placed, and which is one usually distinguished by the insolence of those who fill it, he had made, not enemies, but friends. Had it been otherwise—had an ill feeling been excited against him in his former office, there would have been little disposition in the prison to trust him and to treat him with consideration. But we must not forget that this was the Lord's doing. It was He who "gave him favour in the sight of the keeper of the prison."

The prison was, however, not that of an ordinary magistrate: it was that of the captain of the guard; and in it the court prisoners were confined. The office of keeper was therefore one of most serious responsibility. Yet, great as that responsibility was, the keeper, in the fulness of his reliance upon Joseph's integrity and good conduct, soon committed the whole management of the affairs of the prison into his hands: "and whatsoever they did there, he was the doer of it;" or rather, perhaps, "he directed it to be done." With how many strange facts of courtly life he must then have become acquainted! for doubtless, among those who abode for a time in this place, were many persons high in rank and office, from whose complaints or statements much knowledge might be gathered, calculated to be of great use to him in the future career which the providence of God had marked out for him, and for which, therefore, this imprisonment was no bad training. By this means he must have eventually come to the court possessed of not a little information respecting the state of parties—if there were such things as parties in those days—and the standing and character of the leading men in the king's service. We know that the great personages who found their way to this prison did converse freely with Joseph; and, as political reserve is a thing utterly unknown in the East, it is beyond doubt that he learned much from them, not only respecting themselves and their own affairs, but respecting many other persons of weight and influence, who never themselves came under the care of the keeper of the prison.

The chief butler and the chief baker (or rather cook) of the king of Egypt were among those who were brought to the prison while Joseph had the management of it. These were very high officers, especially the former. We had occasion, two days ago, to indicate the importance of the office held by the latter. That of chief butler was not less important, and it has retained its distinction much later than the other, even in western courts. The noble family of Butler in this country, which formerly held the now extinct dukedom of Ormond, owes its foundation to a person who exercised this office at court, and, we believe, possessed a hereditary claim to it. We have even a scriptural instance in the case of Nehemiah, who was cup-bearer to the Persian king, and was manifestly a person of high consequence, as indicated not only by his receiving the appointment of governor of Judea, but by the immense wealth which enabled him to sustain at his own cost for several years the charges of that expensive office. So also Rabshakeh, one of the chief generals of the Assyrian host, was, as his name imports, *chief cup-bearer* to his king.

"REMEMBER ME WHEN IT SHALL BE WELL WITH THEE"

Genesis 40:14

SOME have thought, as will be shown in tomorrow's paper, that Joseph's anxiety to find a place in the remembrance of the chief butler, when he should become prosperous, is not altogether free from objection. It must be confessed that his words have a worldly sound. But since God generally works by means, and did so work in a signal manner throughout the history of Joseph, it may be thought that he was right in taking such means as appeared to him proper for effecting his deliverance; nor is it needful to suppose that he thereby abandoned his trust in God. His conduct on this occasion may, however, be written here as one of those instances of human weakness, from which the history of no one of the patriarchs is wholly free. We incline to this view. Joseph desires the influence of this man, to speak on his behalf to the king; which does not look as if it was then

CUP-BEARERS

strongly present to his mind, that he had direct access to a greater King than Pharaoh, who, he had full reason to suppose, had a special regard for him, and would not suffer a hair of his head to perish. If this be a correct view of the case, we are not, nevertheless, to be hard upon Joseph; but the fact should be pointed out, lest that which may be regarded as a temporary failure of his faith should be hastily deemed a rule of conduct. The strongest faith has at times wavered; and if in this instance Joseph's faith was for a moment shaken, it may be said in his behalf, that very few, perhaps none, have lived, whose faith would not under the same circumstances have been shaken far more. It was a trying moment, when he had to tell this man, who had been but a short time a prisoner, that in three days he would go forth from his dungeon, and be restored to light and honour; and to feel that for himself, who had lain in bonds so much longer, there was no such prospect. Ask any one who has been shut up in the prison-house, whether at any time the sense of bondage is so strong and painful, and the craving for liberty so intense, as at that moment when a fellow-prisoner goes forth to freedom. It was under the influence of this strong and natural feeling that the captive Joseph spoke.

But, again, although God works by means, it is by means of His own choosing. There is not one point more clearly taught by the history of Joseph than this. Human plans and contrivances, human calculations of probabilities, come to nought, or, if attended with any effect, that effect is altogether different from what was intended—is even adverse to it. But God, in His own time, is seen moving the hearts of men, and turning their devices to accomplish His own high purposes; and even the fierce and proud wrath of man is constrained to glorify His providence and grace.

Without, however, inquiring further, whether Joseph was right or wrong in bespeaking the interest of the great man whom the Lord had given him an opportunity of obliging, let us see how exactly the words he employs are such as form the general rule of conduct in the world: "Remember me when it shall be well with thee." Are not these the words which, although not uttered in the streets and high places, are muttered in the world's universal heart? Is there any one of our readers who can look around him—who can look at home—without being able to instance this insatiate craving to be remembered, thought of, favourably considered by those who stand well with the world? What anxiety to hold a place in their esteem! How proud to claim the honour of their acquaintance! What a struggle to obtain their notice! What labour to win their interest! How highly prized, how boasted of, how exaggerated, their slightest attentions! Have they expectations?—what trouble to bespeak their remembrance when it shall be well with them! Are they prosperous?—how eager to know them, now it is well with them! Have they wealth?—how ready to bow down and worship, to lick the very feet of the golden god? Have they rank?—what solicitude to obtain some notice; how inordinately a nod, a smile, a word, is prized! Oh, this terrible world-worship, which defiles the very church of God, and which eats as doth a canker the soul of man! Will it stand the fire which is appointed to burn up all the hay, the wood, and the stubble of the universe?

When did we ever hear of people anxious for the remembrance of those on whom the world has frowned, or whom it has not favoured? How rarely is it said—if it ever be said—"Remember me when it shall be *ill* with thee!" Yet the remembrances of the afflicted and cast-down are of infinitely more real value for this world, and for the world to come, than all the recognitions of the prosperous and the powerful, which men prize so highly. Is not the prayer of the poor and the afflicted swiftly heard in heaven? Is not their blessing powerful for good to him who is honoured with it? Indeed, if we knew how dear that prayer, how precious that blessing, is in the sight of God; if we lived less for this world and more for the world hereafter, the beck of nobles and the smile of kings would seem most worthless in the comparison.

This is a matter on which it cannot be said that the Scripture utters any uncertain sound. Yet, how few are they who plainly and from the heart act in the spirit of this text! "If there come unto your assembly a man with a gold ring, in goodly apparel, and there come in also a poor man in vile raiment, and ye have respect to him that weareth the gay clothing, and say unto him, Sit thou here, in a good place, and say to the poor, Stand thou there, or sit here under my footstool: are ye not then partial in yourselves, and are become judges of evil thoughts? Hearken, my beloved brethren, Hath not God chosen the poor of this world, rich in faith, and heirs of the kingdom, which He hath promised to them that love Him? But ye have despised the poor." (James ii. 2-6.) Never was anything more plainly expressed than this; and it forms part of that high law which God in the fulness of His mercy has given for a lamp unto our feet. Yet never was there anything uttered or written more habitually neglected—and not only neglected, but contravened—than this; and that by us—by those who, by their covenant with God, undertake to make it the rule of their conduct. And let us be plain. We have among us the ark of God, and we do enjoy most peculiar and valuable spiritual privileges among the nations of the earth. Yet, speaking as having ourselves seen no small part of the wide world, we solemnly declare our conviction that there is not upon earth any Christian people—and certainly there is not any heathen or Moslem people—who are so pitiably as ourselves absorbed in the worship of the world—its greatness, its wealth, its splendour; who so flagrantly "*despise* the poor," and so little cherish their attachment or value their blessing,—a blessing which brings down not only more of spiritual refreshment, but more of temporal advantage than all that the interest or power of the great can give.

Nor is this all. We learn that, in the sequel, the butler "did not" in his prosperity "remember Joseph, but forgat him." No doubt he had promised all that Joseph asked; but he forgat it all. He did not simply *neglect*, he *forgat*; the matter did not seem worthy of a place in his remembrance. All this while poor Joseph sat in his prison, expecting from day to day to receive some token of his illustrious friend's remembrance and intercession. Hour after hour did he watch for the messenger of deliverance; but no deliverance came. He invented excuses for the great man,—a thousand things, he would think, might have prevented him from at first acting in his case. He was doubtless absorbed in the congratulations of his friends, on his coming out of prison. Arrears of business had accumulated in his department, which required all his attention. Many things had gone wrong in his absence, which his time was occupied in adjusting. No doubt he was watching for a favourable opportunity of mentioning his prison friend to the king. How many hours of anxious thought were thus spent in speculating upon the possible movements in his behalf of the man who all the time did not move at all; who all the time did not remember—not even remember—Joseph, but forgat him! Long was it before the poor prisoner could allow a doubt to cross his mind respecting the cup-bearer's solicitude in his behalf. Bitter was the first doubt that rose—bitterer the fears that followed—bitterest the conviction, which came slowly and last of all, that he was altogether neglected and forgotten.

Does our wrath rise against this butler? Let us refrain. This is not an Egyptian custom. It is not an ancient usage of four thousand years ago. It is the way of the world in all climes and ages. It belongs to ourselves and to our fathers. It is a thing of yesterday and to-day. It is part of the cruel system of man's hardness against man; which serves, as much as anything else—and perhaps more than anything else that is not of a spiritual nature—to demonstrate the terrible Scripture doctrine of man's fall from his first estate, and the corruption of his heart. As sure as the low, the afflicted, and the poor, are anxious for a place in the remembrance of the high, the prosperous, and the rich, so sure are the latter to neglect and to forget them. The wrong is mutual; too much is expected on one side—too anxiously expected; and too little is done on the other. These two things fret the great sore of life, and leave the heart of man without rest, but in God. And this is well. Here is the good out of all this evil.

THE BUTLER'S DREAM

Genesis 40:1-13

THE profession of the two court officers, who came under Joseph's charge in the prison, has suggested the notion that the offence of which they were suspected was an attempt to poison the king their master. There is positively no other foundation for this than the nature of their employments. This, however, makes it a sufficiently obvious conjecture; and it is in some degree corroborated by the severe punishment—no less than that of death—to which the one eventually found to be guilty was subjected; for the Egyptians were by no means given to inflict that punishment hastily, or for light offences.

It is always curious to see how an oriental imagination *supplies* the details which the Scripture does not furnish. The Mohammedan account of this matter is, that a foreign king, then at war with Egypt, sent an ambassador, ostensibly for the purpose of negotiating a peace, but in reality to seek the means of slaying the Egyptian sovereign. A woman of his own country, living in Egypt, whom he consulted, advised him that the best course of proceeding was to bribe either the chief cook or the chief butler to poison his master. The ambassador therefore made the acquaintance of both; but finding the chief cook the more tractable, he cultivated a closer intimacy with him, until he succeeded at last, by means of a few talents of gold, in gaining him over to his purpose. He then prepared for his departure, but previously visited his countrywoman, with the view of communicating to her the chief cook's promise. But as she was not alone, he could merely say that he had every reason to be gratified with his success. These words of the ambassador soon reached the ears of the king; and as they could not be referred to his ostensible mission, since the negotiation for peace had come to nothing, a secret of some kind was suspected. The woman was led before the king, and subjected to torture, till she confessed all she knew; but as she could not say which of the two was guilty, the king commanded both the chief cook and the chief butler to be cast into prison, until it should be ascertained which of them had taken this crime upon him.

The observations on dreams which we made a few days since, relieve us from any necessity of remarking largely upon those with which these two persons were visited, while they lay in the prison. Joseph noticed that they looked unusually sad and depressed one morning, and found that it was on account of dreams which had troubled their minds during sleep. If people allowed all dreams to trouble them, life would be miserable; but it would seem that in this case they were disturbed because the dreams were so connected and coherent, and had respectively such relation to their different employments, as to show that they were not the mere wanderings of a disordered imagination. This may indeed be one rule for distinguishing a significant from a worthless dream.

The butler's dream involves some points of interest. He saw a vine with three branches, which, while he looked at it, went through the processes of budding, of blossoming, and of producing ripe grapes. These grapes he took in his hand, and pressed the juice into the king's wine-cup, which he then presented, as in times of old. Some have pretended to doubt whether the vine was formerly cultivated, or even grown, in Egypt; but the frequent notice of it, and of Egyptian wine, in the sculptures, and the authority of ancient writers, sufficiently answer these objectors, and confirm the intimations of the butler's dream. Indeed, the regrets of the Israelites at having left the vines of Egypt (Num. xx. 5) prove them to have been very abundant, since even people in the condition of slaves could procure the fruit. In the mural paintings at Thebes at Beni-Hassan, and at the Pyramids, some of which are supposed to be as ancient as the time of Joseph, there are representations of vineyards and vine arbours; of the ripe clusters being protected by boys from birds, which they frighten away with the sling and by the sound of their voice; of the gathered clusters being carefully deposited in deep wicker baskets, which men carried either on the head or shoulders to the wine-press; but which, when intended for eating, were deposited, like other fruits, in flat open baskets, and covered over with leaves. It might be inferred from the text before us, that only the crude juice of grapes was drunk, mixed perhaps with water, as a kind of sherbet. This may have been the case in the present instance; for if the dream is to be on this point literally and not symbolically taken, the drink offered to Pharaoh by his butler was not wine, but sherbet. But that this was the sole form in which the juice of the grape was used in Egypt, is disproved not only by the ancient accounts, which describe the qualities of the wines of Egypt, but most abundantly by the ancient paintings and sculptures, in which all the processes of wine-making, and even the effects of wine upon men and women, are most curiously and accurately represented. The chief mode of making the wine was, as afterwards among the Hebrews, by treading with the feet in the wine-press; but sometimes the wine-press was simply a bag, into which the grapes were put and squeezed, by means of two poles turning in contrary directions, or by one pole when the bag was fixed in a frame; a vase being placed below to receive the falling juice. The twisted bags were perhaps used to subject the grapes to

EGYPTIAN WINE-PRESS

a further and more stringent pressure, after being taken from the foot-press. After fermentation, the juice was dipped out of the vats, and placed in large jars, or amphoræ; after standing in which for a time, the jars were closed with a lid resembling an inverted saucer, covered with liquid clay, pitch, gypsum, or other composition, which was stamped with a seal. They were then removed from the wine-house, and placed upright in the cellar. We specify these processes, not merely because they are Egyptian, but also because they appear to be in all respects the same as those in use among the Hebrews, to which there are frequent allusions in the poetical books of Scripture.[1]

Joseph, speaking, as he declared, by the inspiration of God, pronounced the three branches to mean three days, and affirmed that within three days the king would restore the butler to his post. He took the opportunity of bespeaking the kind remembrance of the butler; and implored that, when restored to his office near the king, he would make mention of his case, which he describes with great tact and delicacy, so as to

[1] The reader who feels interest in the matter may find ample information in Wilkinson's *Ancient Egyptians*, ii. 142-169.

set forth his grievance without compromising any of those who had been the instruments of his affliction. It was necessary indeed that he should vindicate his innocence, lest the butler, deeming his slavery and imprisonment the just punishment of his crimes, should decline to interfere in his behalf. He says, first, that he was stolen away from the land of the Hebrews—that is to say, that he was of a class superior to that from which slaves were usually taken, and had been kidnapped; but he studiously avoids accusing his brethren of the theft, and much less the Arabs who had sold him to Potiphar. Again, he declares that he had "done nothing for which they should put him into this dungeon;" but refrains from mentioning the criminal conduct of his mistress, which had caused his incarceration, or the selfish policy of his master in detaining him there, although he must by this time have been almost certain of his innocence. This reluctance to throw blame on others is an amiable trait in the character of Joseph, well worthy of imitation. It had important results in this case; for it may be much questioned whether the king would have been, in a later day, so favourably disposed to Joseph's brethren, had their former misconduct towards him come to his knowledge.

Neither the Jewish nor Mohammedan writers are quite satisfied that Joseph was right in thus anxiously imploring the kind offices of the butler. They consider that he ought to have left the matter of his deliverance entirely in God's hands, without this anxiety to secure a human interest and influence. It was, besides, wholly abortive; for although he did eventually obtain his deliverance through the butler's mention of him at court, that personage had meanwhile wholly neglected his request; and when the butler did think of him, it was not in consequence of his request. The Jewish tradition affirms that Joseph remained yet two years in prison, because he had asked the butler to remember him. The Moslem tradition, which had previously stated that God had changed Joseph's cell into a pleasant and cheerful abode, by causing a fountain to spring up in the midst thereof, and by making a tree grow at his door to afford him shade and refreshing fruit, now declares that, on his making this request to the butler, his tree withered, and his fountain dried up, "because, instead of trusting in Allah, he had relied upon the help of a feeble man." This is a fable of course, but it lacks not a moral.

THE CHIEF BAKER'S DREAM

Genesis 40:16-19

THE chief baker's dream is no less remarkable than that of the butler.

He dreamed that he was carrying upon his head three wicker baskets. In the uppermost basket were various kinds of baked meats for the king's table; but as he went along, the birds of the air came and ate them out of the basket. Taking this to be a representation of circumstances with which this man was familiar in life, it offers some points which deserve to be noticed.

We observe, first, that the meats were carried not in wooden trays, as would be the case with us, but in baskets. This agrees with the indication which the ancient Egyptian monuments afford of the varied and extensive applications of basket work, natural in a country where wood was scarce, but on the banks of whose river reeds and rushes abounded. Indeed, there are actual specimens of such baskets in the British Museum; and the representation of some of them in the annexed cut, furnishes a very favourable idea of the basket work of these ancient times. Some of them are worked ornamentally with colours (figs. 3, 5). Of these specimens, fig. 5 is perhaps

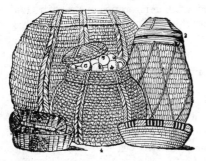

ANCIENT EGYPTIAN BASKETS

the only one suited to the purpose which the dream indicates. But although we have preferred these from the interest attached to them as actual specimens, the Egyptian paintings and sculptures show a much larger variety of all kinds of baskets, many of them flat and broad, and therefore well suited to this use. The stronger and larger sorts of these baskets seem to be made of the mid-rib of the palm frond,

as is still the case in the palm countries of the East, and the finer sorts of the leaves of the same. Not unfrequently they are of rushes; but not so often of reeds. This is still the case not only in Egypt, but in regions of similar physical constitution, such as the lower Euphrates and Tigris, where also the palm tree is plentiful; and, in its frond rib and leaflets, furnishes the chief material for different kinds of baskets.

CARRYING TRAY ON THE HEAD

Then the baker had three baskets, one upon another, and all carried upon his head. We are told what was in the upper basket, but not what was in the two underneath. The contents of the upper basket are no doubt stated, because that only was exposed to the depredations of the birds. The other baskets, however, probably contained dressed meats of the same kind as the uppermost for Pharaoh's table. As to their being carried upon the head, there might seem to be no need of any illustration of this; for the inhabitants of our own towns may see bakers pass every day with their baked meats upon their heads on trays; and it is obvious that they could not conveniently carry more than one dish in any other way. In this way they can carry many dishes in a perfectly horizontal position, without any other care than to keep the tray steady, which those who are used to this mode of bearing burdens can do without difficulty. It is certainly the best and least laborious mode of carriage for anything that *can* be so carried; and on going to the East, one is at first surprised to observe how habitually this is preferred to every other mode of bearing a burden. Even women generally carry their pitchers of water upon their heads, although, from the shape of the vessels, this would seem peculiarly difficult. It has, indeed, been thought, that the eastern damsels owe their peculiarly erect and graceful carriage to the habit formed by the necessity of holding the head erect and steady in carrying their water vessels.

It was the same among the ancient Egyptians, with whom, as we discover from the monuments, this mode was preferred to every other, when the nature of the burden rendered it available. We may, however, be surprised to see that the chief baker carries not a single basket, but three baskets upon his head at once. One would think that one basket of baked meats would be a sufficient burden: and yet we have seen burdens quite as great as the three baskets could possibly be, carried freely upon the head. Nor need we go to the East for illustrations of this. Scarcely a day passes in the season in which we do not see, going by on the other side of the road in which we dwell, men and women with baskets of flowers upon their heads. The weight of them, or rather of the mould and the pots, is very considerable—much greater, in fact, than the spectator might imagine. This we have had occasion to know, from having been in the habit of receiving the like baskets full of plants from the florists. Yet such baskets as we could scarcely lift from the ground, and singly far heavier, doubtless, than the three baskets of the Egyptian baker, were borne along by these people without apparent oppression: although we remember that a man lately urged us to purchase some of his plants, on the ground that he was anxious to lighten his too heavy burden.

How is it that the baker was carrying the king of Egypt's dinner through the open air, without, as it seems, a covering to protect the dishes from birds and insects? We should not relish this here; and much less would it seem desirable in a country where the air swarms with winged vermin, always ready to fall upon whatever has the appearance or the odour of being eatable. We can only explain this, by supposing that the Egyptians were not so particular in these matters as we are; and by stating, that in all the eastern houses in which we have ourselves lived, the kitchen is on the side of the court opposite to that which contains the principal apartments, so that the dishes have to be carried across the court to the dining-room. There can be no doubt that this was the case in Pharaoh's palace.

As to the birds, that which seems a strange incident to us, is a very common one in such countries as Egypt, where the air teems with animal life. It may be doubted whether, in this case, the birds were kites, which make nothing of carrying off large joints wholesale, or lesser birds, which were content to pick away what they could not carry off. We incline to the former supposition, as we observe from the mural paintings, that the Egyptians had not much taste for made dishes, but had their tables supplied chiefly with joints and large birds (such as geese) dressed whole, and very convenient, therefore, for kites to carry off. Their doing this is a matter of constant occurrence, and it is still a common complaint that such a man has lost his dinner from its having been seized and carried off by a kite as he bore it upon his head, or even in his hands, in the open air. Those who have read the *Thousand and One Nights*—and who has not?—will remember some instances of this. There is, for example, the case of Cogia Hassan Alhabbal, which is no doubt such as the writer of the tale knew to have often occurred. "I went to the shambles, and bought something for supper. As I was carrying the meat I had bought home in my hand, a famished kite flew upon me, and would have taken away my meat if I had not held it very fast; but the faster I held the meat the more the bird struggled to get it, drawing me sometimes on one side, sometimes on another, but would not quit the prize, till unfortunately, in my efforts, my turban fell to the ground; the kite immediately let go his hold, and seizing the turban before I could pick it up, flew away with it." Two friends to whom he told this felt no surprise at the attack on the meat, but were astonished that the bird made off with the turban. One said, "What have kites to do with turbans? They only seek for something to satisfy their hunger." But the other thought even this part of the affair probable, and "told a great many as surprising stories of kites, some of which he affirmed that he knew to be true."

THE BIRTHDAY

Genesis 40:20

In Egypt, the birth-days of the kings were celebrated with great pomp. They were looked upon as holy. No business was done upon them; and all classes indulged in festivities suitable to the occasion. Every Egyptian attached much importance to the day, and even to the hour, of his birth; and it is probable that, as in Persia, each individual kept his birth-day with great rejoicings, welcoming his friends with all the amusements of society, and a more than usual profusion of the delicacies of the table.[1]

Such a day, the birth-day of the king, came round at the end of the three days to which Joseph had limited the fulfilment of Pharaoh's imprisoned officers' dreams. We are told that on that day "Pharaoh made a feast to all his servants," and the absence on that occasion of two so eminent as these could not fail to be much noticed. Besides, the very nature of the festivities of that day was well calculated to remind the king of the absence of those whose services had usually contributed much to the enjoyment of them. He determined to inquire at once into their case, and the result was as Joseph had predicted—that the butler was restored to his office, and the baker was put to death.

Some speculation has been founded upon the *mode* in which this functionary was executed. Joseph, in his interpretation of the dream, says: "Within three days shall Pharaoh lift up thy head from off thee, and shall hang thee on a tree; and the birds shall eat thy flesh from off thee." Sir J. G. Wilkinson infers from this, that hanging was in use among the Egyptians as a capital punishment. But this is a mistake. Everywhere in the Old Testament, except in the book of Esther (the scene of which is in Persia), hanging means the gibbeting of the body, after death has been inflicted by the sword or other means. Of proper hanging—that is, death by suspension —as a punishment, we find no instance but in the case of Haman, and in the Persian decree in Ezra.[2] The case of Judas in the New Testament was one of suicide.[3] The text just quoted suggests decapitation, and the subsequent gibbeting

[1] Wilkinson's *Ancient Egyptians*, ii. 45.
[2] Ezra 6:11; Esther 7:9,10.   [3] Matthew 27:5.

of the body on a tree. The striking incident of the birds eating away the flesh, indicates the nature of the "hanging up" intended. We cannot but feel some surprise that Sir J. G. Wilkinson infers from the instance before us, not only that hanging was a capital punishment, but that gibbeting was *not* practised. If the object is merely to deprive of life by hanging, the body does not remain long enough for the flesh to be eaten by birds; and if it be left sufficiently long for that, it is gibbeting, whatever the mode of death may have been. It is clear that the mind of the chief baker was familiar with the idea of bodies thus exposed to be devoured by birds of prey. It was probably in the fear lest their acquaintance with this frightful practice in Egypt should lead the Israelites to adopt it, that they were expressly forbidden by the law to expose bodies in this manner longer than till the sunset of the day of execution.[1] This regulation evinces a degree of humanity, and of regard for public decency, unexampled in any ancient code of laws, and which modern civilization, even under Christian influences, has been slow to imitate. In this country itself, which is apt to boast of its distinguished humanity and enlightenment, it is within the memory of men—and of not old men either —that the land was disfigured with these fatal trees, with the bodies of murderers left to corruption upon them. It is not clear even that this kind of "hanging" after death, as mentioned in Scripture, denotes suspension by cords. It means simply any kind of suspension; and the only thing of the sort that we can recollect to have seen represented in ancient painting or sculpture,

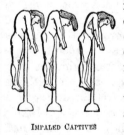

IMPALED CAPTIVES

is among the recently discovered Nineveh sculptures, one of which shows three dead men *stuck* under the ribs upon the sharpened tops of as many poles driven into the ground; their heads and arms hanging down in a manner very painful to behold.

Before quitting the transactions of this day, we may direct attention to what seems a slight, but is really a very significant, variation in the interpretation, and consequent accomplishment, of the dreams. To the butler Joseph says, Pharaoh shall "lift up thy head;" and to the baker, "shall lift up thy head *from off thee*." The first

[1] Deuteronomy 21:22,23.

of these phrases occurs also (in the original) in Ex. xxx. 12, and Num. i. 49, in the sense of numbering; and in this sense it agrees well with the words used in describing the fulfilment; "he lifted up the head of the chief butler and of the chief baker in the midst of his servants." It might, then, be translated literally, "shall take thy poll;" that is, in recounting his officers, Pharaoh shall remember thee, and as it follows, shall restore thee to thy station.[1] To the same phrase in the interpretation of the baker's dream, a different meaning is given by the addition of the words (or rather word, for it is but one in Hebrew) "from off thee"—signifying, shall put thee to death, and that probably, but not certainly, by beheading.

This may suggest that the kings of Egypt revised the lists of their court officers on their birth-days, and that the appointments were nominally annual, though in most cases actually during pleasure. It may still require explanation how such a phrase as "lifting up the head" came to denote an enumeration. We meet with an explanation of Junius Piscator's in Parker's *Bibliotheca Biblica*, which has at least the merit of being curious and ingenious. "The ancients, in keeping their reckonings or accounts of time, as days, months, years, and their lists of domestic officers and services, made use of tables with holes bored in them, in which they placed a sort of pegs or nails with broad heads, exhibiting their particulars, whether numbers or names, or whatever it was. These nails or pegs the Jews called *heads;* and the sockets of these heads they called *bases.* The meaning, therefore, of *lifting up the head* is, that Pharaoh should take up the peg that had the butler's name on the top of it, read it, and will *restore him*, that is, his peg, into its place, there to stand good."

On the other hand, there are those who dismiss all these views, and teach that the phrase "to lift up the head" in the chapter before us, is elliptical for the full expression "to lift up thy head out of prison," such places of confinement being, it is alleged, usually under ground. And here we are directed to 2 Kings xxv. 27, where the words occur in reference to the king of Babylon and his captive, the king of Judah, whom he released from a long imprisonment. Here the idea of taking the poll would seem to be inadmissible; and it is most probable that it there-

[1] See Turner's *Notes to Genesis*, p. 340.

fore denotes removal from prison, and restoration to liberty. Such is the explanation which a great authority[1] gives. But he has overlooked the simple fact, that Egypt, being simply the valley of a river, by whose waters the land is periodically inundated, is the very last country in which phrases derived from *subterraneous* constructions could exist. All is above ground in Egypt, and necessarily so, as any constructions below the ground would be constantly full of water. The Egyptians were too intent upon contrivances for keeping their land above water, to dream of going below ground for any purpose whatever. From this, in a very considerable degree, arises the peculiar character of Egyptian buildings and architecture. Even Babylon, to which the explanation also refers, was in this respect considerably like Egypt. We cannot therefore receive this explanation.

THE RIVER NILE

Genesis 41:1

WE have had the dreams of Joseph, the dream of the chief butler, and the dream of the chief baker, and now the time is come for the king himself to dream. The dream is altogether a state dream, and the dreamer dreams it officially, as the head of the state. Given to any other person, it would have wanted its due weight, and would have secured less attention. It was all of God. The time was come for Him to show Himself for the thousands of Egypt, for the tens of Israel, and for the slave in the prison house. There were, in fact, two dreams following each other, in which, although the symbols are varied, the purport is so obviously the same, as to command attention among a people not accustomed to suffer even dreams of apparent significance to pass heedlessly by.

In both dreams the king stood by the river Nile. In the first dream, he saw come up out of the water seven thriving kine, which fed upon the reed-grass beside the river. Presently came up also seven starving kine, which stood near to the others on the river's brink, and soon devoured them up. In the second dream, seven full ears

[1] Gesenius, in his *Hebrew Lexicon*.

of corn, rank and good, came up upon one stalk; but soon seven parched and withered ears came up after them, and devoured, or absorbed, all the rich and exuberant ears.

There are some points in this that demand attention. The most prominent object in both dreams is the river. The king is by the river; all takes place on the brink of the river; and both the fat and the lean kine come up from the stream. Every one knows that the existence of Egypt depends upon the river. There is little or no rain. But for the river, which periodically overflows the lands, and renders them fit for culture, and fertilizes them by its deposits, the whole country would be a barren, sandy, and uninhabitable desert. A few feet more or less in the rise of the river at the appointed time, makes all the difference between "a good Nile" and "a bad Nile"—between abundance and starvation. Hence the deep attention and profound anxiety with which everything connected with the river is regarded.

VIEW ON THE NILE

These facts have been so often recorded in prose, that we are glad to be able to report them here in the language of a recent poetical traveller:[1]—

"Scarce with more certain order waves the sun
　His matin banners in the eastern sky,
　Than at the reckoned period are begun
　The operations of fertility;
　Through the long swamp, thy bosom swelling high
　Expands between the sandy mountain chains,
　The walls of Libya and of Araby,
　Till, in the active virtue it contains,
The desert bases sink, and rise prolific plains.

"See through the naked length no blade of grass,
　No animate sign, relieves the dismal strand,
　Such it might seem our orb's first substance was,
　Ere touched by God with generative hand;
　Yet at one step we reach the teeming land
　Lying fresh-green beneath the scorching sun,
　As succulent, as if at His command
　It held all rains that fall, all brooks that run,
And this, O generous Nile! is thy vast benison."

　　[1] R. Monckton Milnes, in his *Palm Leaves.*

Seeing that the Egyptians owed so much to this stream, and that their prosperity and very existence depended on it, the poet thinks it no wonder

"That gratitude of old to worship grew,
　That as a living god thou wert addrest,
　And to itself the immediate agent drew
To one creative power the feelings only due."

To this he adds in a note: "In the oldest form of Egyptian theology of which we have cogniz-ance, the Nile is a god. . . . The Egyptian theologians also imagined divisions in heaven similar to those of the earth, and could conceive no paradise without a celestial Nile." To the lines—

"For in thy title, and in nature's truth,
　Thou art, and makest, Egypt,"

a note is also appended, in which the writer truly remarks that "the 'Egypt' of Homer is the river, not the country; all the other Greek names of Egypt are derived from the Nile. Its Coptic name was Phairo—hence probably Pharaoh. In somewhat of the same sense is India derived from the Indus."

It is far from unlikely that the king supposed himself in his dream visiting the Nile, in discharge of some of the duties connected with the idolatrous worship rendered to that stream. There were many such. The most important was the Niloa, an annual festival for invoking the blessings of the inundation. This was one of the principal of the Egyptian festivals. It took place about the summer solstice, when the river began to rise ; and the anxiety with which the people looked forward to a plentiful inundation induced them to celebrate it with more than usual honour. It is stated that the rites of this solemnity were deemed of so much importance by the Egyptians, that unless they were performed at the proper season, and in a becoming manner, by the persons appointed to the duty, they felt persuaded that the Nile would refuse to rise and inundate the land. Their full belief in the efficacy of the ceremony secured its annual performance on a grand scale. Men and women assembled from all parts of the country in the towns of their respective nomes, or shires ; grand festivities were proclaimed, and all the enjoyments of the table were united with the

priests through the villages, in solemn procession, that all might appear to be honoured by his presence and aid, while invoking the blessings he was about to confer.[1] If the dreams of Pharoah followed the day of such a solemnity as this—as seems to us highly probable—they could not fail to be regarded as peculiarly significant and important.

The modern inhabitants of Egypt, being for the most part Mohammedans, do not now worship the Nile after this fashion ; but, after their own manner, they do still look upon it with great veneration ; and whatever be the place of their sojourning, the natives of the Nile still speak of its waters with the most enthusiastic regard. The poet we have lately cited finely touches on this :

" And now, in Egypt's late degraded day,
  A venerating love attends thee still ;
  And the poor Fellah,[2] from thee torn away,
  Feels a strange yearning his rude bosom fill.
  Like the remembered show of lake and hill,
  That wrings the Switzer's soul, though fortune smile,
  Thy image haunts him, uncontrolled by will,
  And wealth or war in vain the heart beguile,
That clings to its mud hut and palms beside the Nile."

In fact, a peculiarly luscious, refreshing, and nutritive quality is ascribed by the natives to the waters of the Nile : and it is almost affecting to hear the expressions of intense longing with which a native who has been any time away from Egypt speaks of the Nile water. One would think that it was at once meat, and drink, and medicine to them.

DRAWING WATER FROM THE NILE

In one of the tales of the *Thousand and One Nights*, some merchants of Mosul, who had seen much of the eastern world in their time, are represented as speaking of the wonders they had seen in their various travels. " Say what you will," said one, " the man who has not seen Egypt has

solemnity of a holy festival. Music, dances, and appropriate hymns, marked the respect which they felt for the deity ; and a wooden statue of the tutelary deity of the river was carried by the

not seen the greatest rarity of the world. . . . If you speak of the Nile, where is there

[1] See Wilkinson's *Ancient Egyptians*, ii. 293.
[2] Peasant.

a more wonderful river? What water was ever lighter or more delicious? The very slime it carries along in its overflowing fattens the fields, which produce a thousand times more than other countries that are cultivated with the greatest labour. Observe what a poet said of the Nile, when he was obliged to depart from Egypt: 'Your Nile loads you with blessings every day. It is for you only that it comes from distant lands. Alas! in departing from you, my tears will flow as abundantly as its waters. You are to continue in the enjoyment of its sweetnesses, while I am constrained to forego them against my will.'"[1]

It is a singular fact that the word *Nile*, now in such common use, never occurs either in the Hebrew or English Bible. Though it is probably of eastern origin, it cannot be traced beyond the early Greek writers. It is supposed to be allied to the Sanscrit word *Nilah*, "black," and to be descriptive of the dark colour of the water. The Egyptian name of the river in the time of Moses appears to have been *Yeor*, which he generally uses in the Pentateuch. It signifies, in the old Egyptian language, "river." The Nile being the great and the only river of Egypt, *Yeor* came to be used as a proper name for the Nile, and is so employed by all the sacred writers except Daniel. Unfortunately it has been rendered as an appellative by the translators of our Bible, so that we read Pharaoh "stood by *the river*," when it ought to be "by *the Yeor*." The passage in Ex. i. 22 should be read, "Every son that is born ye shall cast into *the Yeor*."

In that remarkable passage in which the boundaries of the land given in covenant promise to Abraham are described, the Nile is termed "the river of Egypt:" "Unto thy seed have I given this land, from the river of Egypt unto the great river, the river Euphrates."[2] The phrase "river of Egypt," however, is not exclusively employed in the English Bible in reference to the Nile. Where it is the translation of the Hebrew *Nakhal Mitzraim*, it means Wady el-Arish, a valley and winter stream on the northern border of Egypt.[3] The Nile is also called *Shihor* (or *Sihor*) by the sacred writers. Thus it is said, "So David gathered all Israel together from *Shihor of Egypt* even unto the entering of Hemath;"[4] and Jeremiah exclaims, "What hast thou to do in the way of Egypt, to drink the waters of *Sihor?*"[5] Isaiah also, in describing the glory of Tyre, says, "And by great waters, *the sowing of Sihor*, the harvest of *Yeor*, is her revenue."[6] Tyre, with the whole of Phœnicia, drew its supplies of corn mainly from Egypt.

[1] The tale of the *Jewish Physician*. Lane's translation has merely the skeleton of the passage, which is preserved more fully in the old translation.
[2] Genesis 25:18.
[3] As in Numbers 34:5; Joshua 15:4,47; 1 Kings 8:65, etc.

[4] 1 Chronicles 13:5. [5] Jeremiah 2:18. [6] Isaiah 23:3.

Shihor is a descriptive name, signifying "the black," and is thus equivalent to *Nile*.

The Nile is the longest river in the world; but its vast importance cannot even be estimated by its magnitude. Without the Nile Egypt would be a desert; by it the country is made one of the most productive on earth. The periodical inundations of the Nile have attracted the attention of men in all ages. Year after year, at the summer solstice, it begins to rise, and goes on steadily increasing, until at the vernal equinox it has attained an elevation, at Cairo, of some twenty-six feet above its lowest level. Its waters now inundate the whole of the low plains along its banks, irrigating the soil, leaving a rich deposit of alluvium, and thus making the country most productive. As there is no rain in Egypt, should the Nile not attain a sufficient height to overflow its banks—should it rise only twenty instead of twenty-six feet, a failure of the whole crop of Egypt would be the result. Such failures do occasionally occur. The long continued drought which withers up the herbage of neighbouring countries, prevents the rain from falling on the mountains of Central Africa, and consequently the sources of the Nile are greatly diminished, and the river does not attain a sufficient height to irrigate the parched soil. Arab historians mention two such catastrophes in the eleventh and twelfth centuries. The first lasted for seven years; and the record given by Abd el-Latif[1] of its fearful effects enables us to understand the cry of the people to Joseph: "Give us bread, for why should we die in thy presence? Buy us and our land for bread." And also their thankfulness at a later period: "Thou hast saved our lives; let us find grace in the sight of my lord, and we will be Pharaoh's slaves." It is also a well known fact, that when the Nile rises a few feet above its usual elevation, a season of extraordinary fruitfulness follows. Thus the "seven years of plenty" were no doubt occasioned.

                                                   P.

THE ROYAL DREAMS

Genesis 41:1-36

YESTERDAY we pointed out the considerations suggested by the presence of the Nile in the king of Egypt's dreams. There are some other matters in these remarkable visions which will this day demand our attention. If the incidents of the dreams were, as we have supposed, substantially such as might be witnessed in actual life, although not in exactly the same combinations, it may seem a strange circumstance that cattle should appear to come up out of the river. That they should appear to do so, was needful to give the symbols their proper connection and significance. But for that purpose it would have

[1] *Relation de l'Egypte*, ii.

been sufficient that the animals should come up out of the river's bed; and cattle which had been down to the water to drink, might every day be seen coming up as it were from the river itself—that is, from its bed. But if any will contend for a more literal analogy, it is sufficient to state that buffaloes, a variety of the ox well known anciently in Egypt, delight to stand in the water in hot countries, and seem to be almost amphibious. These animals, male and female, will remain for hours in the water, with all their bodies immersed except the head; and the most broad and rapid rivers are swum by them with great ease. The sight of horned cattle coming up actually out of a river is therefore by no means an incident of rare occurrence. The animals were in the present instance kine; not oxen for labour, but cows for milk—well suited, therefore, to a symbolical representation of plenty.

It is said in the common version that the animals "fed in a meadow;" a better translation would be, "on the reed grass." The word so translated is apparently an Egyptian one—ACHU; and a considerable amount of learned investigation has been bestowed upon it. It may be questioned that the meaning of the term has even yet been ascertained. Professor Royle seems doubtful that any specific plant is intended, but supposes that, if such be the case, it is perhaps one of the edible species of scirpus or cyperus; "or it may be a true grass—some species of panicum, for instance, which form excellent pasture in warm countries, and several of which grow luxuriantly in the neighbourhood of water." This learned botanist adds: "But it is well known to all acquainted with warm countries subject to excessive drought, that the only pasturage to which cattle can resort is a green strip of different grasses, with some sedges, which runs along the banks of rivers, or of pieces of water, varying more or less in breadth, according to the height of the bank, that is, the distance of water from the surface. Cattle emerging from rivers, which they may often be seen doing in hot countries, would naturally go to such green herbage as intimated in this passage of Genesis."[1]

All was natural enough thus far; and so likewise it is, that when the lean kine came up also, and found that there was nothing left for them to eat, they should stand beside the others, without attempting to seek nutriment in the now

[1] Art. "Achu," in *Cyclopædia of Biblical Literature.*

close-cropped and parched ground. But it was altogether unnatural and most surprising that the lean kine should, even in the extremity of their hunger, fall upon their obese fellows. Such things, however, happen in dreams. But it is not at all wonderful that a circumstance so extraordinary shocked and startled the royal dreamer, and awoke him from his sleep.

The seven ears of corn on one stalk, in the second dream, was not, as some suppose, an extraordinary or unnatural circumstance; the wonder lay in the extraordinary fulness of each of the seven ears, and in the recurrence of the number seven. There is a species of bearded wheat, not only now and anciently grown in Egypt, but supposed to be native to that country, and hence known by the name of "Egyptian wheat," otherwise "many spiked wheat." It is allied to the summer or spring wheat,[1] but the spike is four

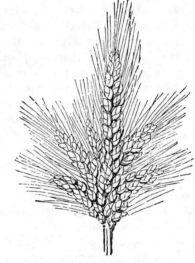

EGYPTIAN WHEAT

times as large, and a hand in length, formed of spikelets, in two rows, from nine to ten in number,—the lower ones shorter, and the upper larger and more erect. If this, as is probable, were the species seen by the king in his dream, the circumstance to strike him was, that all the spikelets or ears were large and full, which is not ordinarily the case, and that the number of them was seven, which is by no means a usual number of spikelets or ears in this variety of wheat.

It is not easy to see how, even in a dream, the seven lean ears of corn could eat up the full ones. Therefore, although the Hebrew word is the

[1] *Triticum æstivum.* Linn.

same in both cases, our translators have in this instance wisely adopted the more general term of "devoured." In horticulture, we continually see one plant consumed by another being planted too near it, and so exhausting its nourishment; and this, we should suppose was the kind of devouring witnessed by the king in his dream, only with greater rapidity, and with more immediate results, than is ever seen in nature.

The dream, on the whole, has some analogy to that of the Roman knight in Tacitus, who beheld the emperor (Claudius) crowned with a wisp of straw, with the stalks bent backward or downward, which was understood to prefigure a scarcity.

There was certainly enough in these dreams to trouble the mind of Pharaoh. As with the egg of Columbus, the dreams seem so easy to understand, now that we have Joseph's interpretation before us, that we are inclined to wonder, not that the court interpreters and wise men could not explain them, but that they were so simple as to miss the interpretation. It is probable that they got astray from the plain and obvious signification, in seeking after one more remote, by the rules and calculations of their art—a case not very uncommon. The Jewish Rabbins amuse themselves with speculations in this matter, and tell us that the interpretation which the wise men reached by the rules of their art was, that Pharaoh's seven daughters (for that number they make him to have had) were to die, and that seven others should be born to him in their stead. But this, as may be supposed, was not at all satisfactory to their lord; for the new daughters would, according to the dream, have been but an indifferent compensation for the others. It is more likely that, as Josephus apprehends, they continued silent, and did not even pretend to offer an explanation. If we consider the dream so plain that an interpretation of some kind would at least be offered, it must be answered that the minds of the Egyptian interpreters were probably for the moment so confounded, that the whole matter appeared as a dense mystery to them; the Lord having purposed, in the sovereignty of His will, and for the designs of His providence, to give the honour of the interpretation to Joseph, and make it the means of that high advancement which he had, even in boyhood, been led to expect. It must be admitted to speak well for the integrity of the Egyptian "wise men," that they did not, so far as appears, attempt to satisfy the mind of the king by some invention which might seem to explain his dreams. False as their art was, they believed it a truth, and would not act at all when its rules afforded them no result on which they could rely.

EGYPTIAN CLEANLINESS

Genesis 41:14

ALTHOUGH it is easy enough to account for the chief butler's forgetfulness of Joseph, on the common principles which operate among men, we cannot but recognize the providence of God in preventing the *accident* of his remembrance until the time when his recollection could not fail to be attended with results of great importance. The whole matter had been doubtless appointed for the hour which was at length come. For this Joseph had been cast into prison; for this he became known to the chief butler there; for this that person and his companion had their dreams, that, by the interpretation of them, Joseph might impress a fact concerning himself upon the chief butler's mind, which, although for a time forgotten, he would not fail to remember in the important hour when his royal master should be perplexed by the want of an interpreter for his dreams. In that hour he *did* remember the Hebrew youth, and spoke to his master of the circumstance which had occurred in the prison. On hearing this, the king sent in great haste to have Joseph brought from the prison. Yet, urgent as was the occasion, care was taken that he should "shave himself and change his raiment," before he was introduced to the presence of the king. In the ancient courts, no one could enter the royal presence in a slovenly or offensive garb or appearance. See another instance of this at the Persian court, in Esther iv. 2. This seems so natural to us, as an instinct of natural etiquette, that we are apt to overlook some of the illustrative points connected with the incident. These things are now little heeded in the East, except at formal audiences, and at such highly ceremonial courts as those of Persia and China. A man called or admitted in so great an emergency, would be introduced much as he had been found.

Another matter requires notice. In any country mentioned in the Bible, excepting only Egypt, dressing the beard or the hair, instead of shaving, would have been the kind of preparation required. But in Egypt, and in Egypt only, a man put himself into decent condition by an operation which, in any other country, would have been ignominious. But this is one of the minute touches by which the exact historical truth of the narrative is established; for the testimony of all antiquity, as well as the sculptured and pictured monuments, concurs with this intimation, in describing the Egyptians as a shaven people. It is mentioned by Herodotus among the distinguishing peculiarities of the Egyptians, that they were commonly shaven, but in mourning allowed their beards to grow. This agrees with the sculptures, as well as with the present text. "So particular, indeed, were they on this point, that to have neglected it was a subject of reproach and ridicule; and whenever they intended to convey the idea of a man of low condition or slovenly person, the artist represented him with a beard. It is amusing to find that their love of caricature was not confined to the lower orders, but extended even to the king; and the negligent habits of Remeses VII. are indicated in his tomb at Thebes by the appearance of his chin, blackened by a beard of two or three days' growth. But it is likewise given as a test of hardships undergone in a severe campaign; and the warlike character of Remeses the Great is pointed out in the same manner.[1]

The Egyptians did not, like the Romans of a later age, confine the privilege of shaving to free-born citizens, and compel slaves to wear their beards and hair long, as a badge of servitude. Foreigners brought to Egypt as slaves had usually beards on their arrival in the country; but as soon as they came into the service of this civilised people, they were obliged to follow the cleanly habits of their masters: their beards and heads were deprived of hair, and they adopted a cap.

Among this people the priests shaved not only the beard, but the head; and others, if they did not, like them, and like the modern Orientals, shave the head with a razor, were accustomed to wear the hair very short. The abundant and

[1] Wilkinson's *Ancient Egyptians*, iii. 357.

long hair which sometimes covers the heads of the figures on the monuments, seems to have

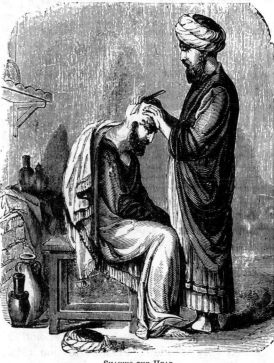

SHAVING THE HEAD

been false, like our wigs. Indeed, actual specimens of such wigs have been found, and may be seen in museums of Egyptian antiquities. This practice respecting the hair and beard is known to have been regarded by the neighbouring nations, and especially by the Asiatics, as peculiar to the Egyptians.

Wilkinson, in connection with this subject, remarks that "barbers may be considered as the offspring of civilisation." So many will continue to think; although, according to that view, the increasingly hirsute appearance of modern Europe, since this was said, might argue a backward stride towards barbarism.

The extreme personal cleanliness of the ancient Egyptians is indicated not only in the shaving of Joseph, but in his change of raiment; and perhaps also, as Wilkinson imagines, in "the changes of raiment" which Joseph gave to his brethren when they set out to fetch their father and families to Egypt. (Gen. xlv. 22.) The attention which the priests, in particular, paid to this matter, is noticed by ancient authors. But it was not confined to their order. "Every Egyptian prided himself," says Wilkinson, "on the encouragement of habits which it was considered a disgrace to neglect. We can therefore readily account for the disgust they felt in seeing the squalid appearance and unrefined habits of their Asiatic neighbours, whose long beards were often the subject of ridicule to the Egyptian soldier; and for their abhorrence of the bearded and long haired Greeks, which was so great, that, according to Herodotus, 'no Egyptian of either sex would on any account kiss the lips of a Greek, make use of his knife, his spit and cauldron, or taste the meat of an animal which had been slaughtered by his hand.'"

But although the beards and long hair of the Greeks may have contributed to this result, it is not, as Wilkinson seems here to imply, stated by the historian that this was the proximate cause of their abhorrence. This rather arose from their treatment of cows, which the Egyptians, out of regard to Isis, "worshipped with a more profound reverence than any other cattle;" and they held the Greek mouth to be defiled by the eating, the knife by the cutting, and the crock by the boiling of the flesh of kine. Hence the apprehension of the Israelites in a later day, that they should be stoned if they sacrificed "the abomination (idol) of the Egyptians before their eyes." (Ex. viii. 26.)

This imputed uncleanness of those who eat forbidden food, and those who use their utensils, exists at the present day in the East, both among Moslems and heathen. Among many examples of this that occur to us, we give one of very recent occurrence. It is from Lieutenant Lynch's account of his expedition to the Dead Sea :—

"In the evening some of the tribe of Ta'amirah came in, a little more robust, but scarcely better clad, than the Raschayideh. They were warm and hungry, from walking a long distance to meet us. They had no food, and I directed some cooked rice to be given to them. They had seated themselves round the pot, and were greedily about to devour it, when one of them suggested, that perhaps pork had been cooked in the same vessel. They rose, therefore, in a body, and came to the cook to satisfy their scruple. I never saw disappointment more strongly pictured in the human countenance, than when told that the vessel had often been used for that purpose. Although nearly famished, they would not touch the rice, and we could give them nothing else."

Such facts as these have no unimportant bearing upon the scruples of the Egyptians to eat with the Hebrews, the inferences to be deduced from which will soon require our separate attention.

GOD IN ALL

Genesis 41:51-52

IT is well worthy of our special notice, that every circumstance in the prosperity and glorious estate to which Joseph is now advanced, is as it were confronted with some other circumstance in his former adverse and calamitous condition. His brethren despised and hated him, and subjected him to most injurious treatment; but now the king of Egypt and his princes delight to honour him, and advance him to high place among themselves. His exile is turned into exultation. All the slavish work of his hands is now exchanged for the royal signet on his finger. The coat of many colours, torn by violence from him, and defiled with blood—the garment left in the hand of the adulteress—are exchanged for vestures of fine linen from a king's hand. For irons on his feet, he has now a chain of gold about his neck. Formerly he ministered to prisoners, now to a monarch. The splendour of the king's second chariot succeeds to the darkness of his dungeon. There was a time when he was trampled upon; but now the nation is called to bend the knee before him. He was scarcely known by name before, but now the king bestows a name of honour upon him. And now he who fled with horror from the solicitations of another man's wife, is made happy in a union with a noble consort of his own. How did all these circumstances affect him? In old time, men expressed their feelings in the names they bestowed upon their children. Now Joseph had two sons, and the names he gave to them embody the sentiments which he desired to connect with these transactions, and to form standing memorials of them.

The first son he called MANASSEH, which means *forgetting;* or it may, as a substantive, be rendered *forgetfulness.* And why? "For God, said he, hath made me to forget all my toil, and all my father's house." It is a beautiful and interesting circumstance in the history of Joseph, that he has God ever before his eyes

When tempted to sin, his cry is, "How can I do this great wickedness, and sin against God?" When the court officers in prison were troubled by their dreams, he said, "Do not interpretations belong to God?" When the king tells him that he had heard of his skill in the interpretation of dreams, he is anxious to turn the credit from himself to God: "It is not in *me;* GOD shall give Pharaoh an answer of peace." When the purport of the royal dreams becomes clear to him, he again sees God in them: "God hath showed Pharaoh what He is about to do." "The thing is established by God; and God will shortly bring it to pass." So, when he discloses himself to his brethren, and they are overwhelmed with shame and compunction, he says, "Be not grieved, nor angry with yourselves that ye sold me hither; for God did send me before you to preserve life;" and "God sent me before you, to preserve you a posterity in the earth, and to save your lives by a great deliverance. So it was not ye that sent me hither, but God." Again, in the message sent to his father, "God hath made me lord of all Egypt." Also, in the address to his brethren after the death of his father, "Ye thought evil against me, but God meant it for good." At last, he dies in the conviction that "God will surely visit you, and bring you out of this land;" and so assured is he of this, that he takes an oath of them that they will carry his bones with them to the land of their future possession. It is this constant reference to God in all things, before all things, and for all things, that forms the real characteristic of Joseph's history, and is the true secret of all his glory and success. So here, in the name of his first-born son, he erects what he means to be, and what he knows will be, an imperishable monument of his conviction that it is God who has made him to forget all his misery, and all his father's house.

Now, it is the infirmity of our flesh that we look too much to the immediate instruments of our blessings, and forget God in them, or content ourselves with a cold and formal acknowledgment. It is well for us when, like Joseph, we are able—or rather when we are enabled—to make the consciousness of God's presence and intervention in all our affairs a vital principle of action—a law of life unto ourselves. Nor shall we be therefore the less grateful to the instruments of our mercies. Far otherwise. For he who most clearly sees God as the source of all his blessings, is the man who will be most grateful to the agents through whom these blessings come to him.

Joseph's mention of the fact, in giving his son the name of Manasseh, shows the sense in which he is to be understood as having forgotten his toil and his father's house. It does not mean that these things were obliterated from his mind, for the very act is one of remembrance. It was, in fact, his duty and privilege to remember them; for his impressions of the divine goodness would have become weak had he forgotten the evils from which he had been delivered. But in one sense he had forgotten the misery of his former state. He did not allow the memory of it to embitter his present advantages. He cherished no resentful remembrances against those who had been the instruments of his affliction. The memory of his troubles was comparatively lost in the happiness that had now succeeded. So also in what he says of his father's house. His subsequent conduct shows that he had a most lively recollection of his father, and of all the tenderness which had been showered upon his early years. Neither had he ceased to remember the cruel treatment of his brethren; but he ceased to lay it to heart: all that was painful in the remembrances of the past was expelled from his mind. It was with him as with the captives of Babylon. "When the Lord turned again the captivity of Zion, we were like them that dream. Then was our mouth filled with laughter, and our tongue with singing; then said they among the heathen, The Lord hath done great things for them. The Lord *hath* done great things for us, whereof we are glad." (Ps. cxxvi. 1-3.)

So shall it be with us one day; but not yet, not here. When the Lord shall turn the captivity of our Zion; when the church militant has become the church triumphant—when a King greater than Pharaoh shall put in our hands victorious palms, and array us in more glorious vestments than Joseph wore—then shall we also forget, or remember as a dream, the toil through which we have passed, and all the afflictions of our earthly house.

To his other son Joseph gave the name of EPHRAIM, which means *fruitfulness,* for which he gives the strong reason, "For God hath made me to be fruitful in the land of my affliction," in that very land in which he had endured so

much trouble and disgrace. No man had ever
more occasion than Joseph to know the fruitfulness of affliction; and his history is a striking
manifestation of what we have all more or less
occasion to experience—that God, in the dispensations of His providence and grace, cuts even to
the quick the branches of the vine that He wills
to bear much fruit. We shall search history, we
shall consult the knowledge and experience of
others, or such as our own lives may have supplied, in vain for any instance of much fruit for
God or for man having been yielded by unafflicted
men; and, in general, the ingathering of useful
fruits has been proportioned to the intensity of
the affliction—short of crushing the soul. May
God give it to all of us to be fruitful in the land
of our affliction, always remembering that there
are better lands beyond, and better days to come!

It must strike the thoughtful reader of Genesis, that the
character of Joseph conforms more closely to that high
standard of moral consistency, uprightness, and truth,
which Christianity places before us, than that of any of the
other patriarchs. He had not, perhaps, the deep, all conquering faith which Abraham showed on Mount Moriah;
but neither had he that timidity and distrust which betrayed both Abraham and Isaac into the meanness of
deception and lies. He had not, perhaps, Jacob's wondrous
power of prayer,—a power that carried him, in seasons of
imminent peril, into the very presence of God, aud gained
for him at Peniel the proud title of *Israel;* but neither had
he the deceit, and trickery, and worldliness, which make
our hearts sometimes swell with indignation as we read the
early life of his father. For single acts of transcendent
faith, Abraham is far first among men; but for stedfast
principle, unfaltering truthfulness, and uniform devotion to
God, Joseph stands pre-eminent. His father's unwise partiality did not spoil him; the evil example of his brothers
did not lead him astray. Though his brothers hated him,
he seems to have been unconscious of it, thinking doubtless,
that their hearts were as honest and as guileless as his
own. When removed to a new sphere, and placed in new
circumstances, new and still nobler characteristics manifested themselves. His trust in God was never shaken by
adversity and wrong. He never gave way to gloomy and
enervating despondency. He made the best use of his
time and talents in every position in which he was placed,
—in slavery, in prison, and in the court of Pharaoh. His
high moral principle made him sacrifice position, and even
risk life, rather than yield to temptation. And in everything that happened he saw the hand of God,—in the
sorest trials, and in the highest honours; and he submitted
willingly and cheerfully. When he attained to all but unlimited power, and received the highest honours an earthly
monarch could bestow, he showed no pride. He used his
power with equal tact, wisdom, and generosity. His administrative skill in bringing a great nation safe through a

terrible crisis, was only equalled by the noble generosity
with which he treated those who had sold him into slavery.
When circumstances put them completely in his power, he
acted with such consummate wisdom, considering the times
and the men, that their base cruelty to a helpless little
brother was brought home with terrible force to their
consciences; and yet there was no harshness, no vindictive-
ness. Watchful care and tenderest affection were shown in
everything. And when at length he made himself known
to them, and they stood in his presence overwhelmed with
shame and fear, he carefully concealed their shame from
strangers, and with his own lips framed their excuse:
"Now, therefore, be not grieved, nor angry with yourselves, that ye sold me thither; for God did send me
before you to preserve life."

In the history of Joseph we have one of the noblest and
most instructive life lessons of Scripture. It is only excelled by that embodied in the life of our Lord Himself.

P.

JOSEPH'S HONORS

Genesis 41:13-43

THE advancement of Joseph to the highest place
in the realm of Egypt which a subject could hold,
in consequence of his interpretation of the king's
dreams, and of the sagacious counsel which he
founded thereon, is far more surprising to us than
it would be to an Oriental. When we consider
that he was a prisoner and a slave at the time he
came into the presence of the king, and that he
departed from that presence the second man in
the kingdom, the transition is so vast, that with us
it appears too much at variance with probability
to be tolerated, even in a romance. In the East,
however, it is otherwise; and an advancement so
great and so abrupt is still, although not common,
of occasional occurrence, so as that instances more
or less analogous would, in reading this history,
occur to every eastern mind. But although the
advancement in this way of a person of low station, even of a slave, as Joseph was, may still be
witnessed, it is certainly not often so quick and
so abrupt, simply because the opportunity of
distinguishing himself by some act of valour or
wisdom, which may justify such advancement,
is, in the nature of things, not often afforded to
any man. But the Scripture itself supplies a
parallel instance in the case of Mordecai at the
Persian court, twelve centuries later than this
occurrence. Indeed, the circumstances, and still

more the ceremonies of investiture, are so singularly analogous, that the reader may with great interest and advantage compare the forty-first chapter of Genesis with the sixth chapter of Esther.

Before proceeding to notice the circumstances of the investiture, it may be well to state, that Joseph's high and sudden promotion arose not merely from the conviction of his wisdom, and of the singular political sagacity and administrative judgment which his counsel indicated, but from the belief that he enjoyed the special favour of God, and was therefore likely to prosper in whatever he undertook. What deity it was that thus favoured him, none were probably very solicitous to inquire. It was enough that it was the powerful God who was able to impart to the king important warnings, and to afford His servant the interpretation which the most renowned of the wise men of Egypt had been unable to furnish. This is clearly indicated in the words of the king: "Can we find such a one as this is, a man in whom the spirit of God is?" and again, in his words to Joseph: "Forasmuch as God hath showed thee all this, there is none so discreet and wise as thou art." This was a great thing for the king to say to a foreigner; for Egypt was so famous of old time for its knowledge and learning, that the wisest in other lands thought it not beneath them to repair thither in search of wisdom.

In looking into the terms of this appointment to high office, we see that the authority conferred is of the most absolute kind that even an ancient eastern king could bestow. It made him, in fact, vizier of Egypt, or what in Europe is termed "prime minister." "At thy word," said the king, "shall all my people be ruled: only in the throne will I be greater than thou." And again, "See, I have set thee over all the land of Egypt." The utmost authority the king could give was indeed necessary to enable Joseph to carry out with effect the large and comprehensive scheme that he had projected. The fact is, however, of great interest, as showing that the practical administrative functions of royalty were, even at this early period of the world's history, entrusted to a chief minister.

The first ceremonial act of the king, in conferring this high honour, is very significant. "He took off his ring from his hand, and put it upon Joseph's hand,"—a circumstance which suggests

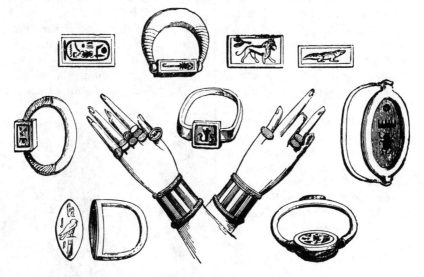

SIGNET RINGS OF ANCIENT EGYPT

to one of our elder commentators,[1] that the "honours conferred upon Joseph partly resembled those of a Lord Privy Seal with us." The ring was no doubt the signet of sovereignty with which the royal acts were to be sealed, and

[1] Parker, in *Bibliotheca Biblica*.

which rendered them authentic and authoritative. It empowered the person who held it to enforce his measures by the royal authority, he remaining responsible to the sovereign for the manner in which he used the high powers thus entrusted to him. In modern European states, the royal signet is used only under the direction of the sovereign or his council; but in the ancient East the possession of the royal signet, which was equivalent to the sign-manual with us, gave to him who held it a power only less than sovereign, in that it was a responsible authority, which might at any time be taken away. The ring, doubtless, contained the name or insignia of the king; and we are not to imagine that it was, as with us, employed in sealing with wax. Nothing of that sort can be used in so warm a climate as that of Egypt. It must have been employed in impressing the royal name *with ink* upon the documents to which it was applied. In this employment of the signet ring, the thick ink, which resembles that used by printers, is rubbed over the whole surface, so that the body of the impression therefrom is black, while the engraved characters are blank, or white. We are well acquainted with the signet and other rings of the ancient Egyptians, as many specimens have been found. They are usually of gold. The form of the scarabæus, or sacred beetle, was that usually preferred for this purpose. In some cases the stone, flat on both faces, turned on pins, like many of our seals at the present day; and the ring itself was bound round at each end, where it was inserted into the stone with gold wire. Sir J. G. Wilkinson states, that one of the largest signets he had ever seen was in the possession of a French gentleman at Cairo, which contained twenty pounds' worth of gold. "It consisted of a massive ring, half an inch in its largest diameter, having an oblong plinth, on which the devices were engraved, one inch long, six-tenths in its greatest, and four-tenths in its smallest breadth. On one face was the name of a king, the successor of Amunoph III., who lived about B.C. 1460;[1] on the other a lion, with the legend, "lord of strength," referring to the monarch: on one side a scorpion, on the other a crocodile. Here we have an undoubted specimen of a royal signet, little more than two centuries posterior to the time under consideration.

Joseph was next "arrayed in vestures of fine linen," which was not only a high distinction, as coming from the king—thereby constituting it a dress of honour, still conferred as a mark of high favour by the sovereigns of the East—but denoted the eminent station to which he was exalted, as

[1] Not long after the death of Joshua.

it appears that dresses of this fine fabric were only allowed to be worn by persons of the highest rank and distinction in Egypt. We shall not here inquire whether the word rendered "fine linen" really does denote linen or cotton. The general impression seems to be, that cotton was not so early known, even in Egypt, and that therefore the alternative chosen by our translators is correct. It is certain that the more delicate textures of the Egyptian loom were costly and highly prized. An unfavourable impression has been formed of the Egyptian cloths, from the comparatively coarse texture of the specimens in which the mummies are enfolded, and which have been ascertained to be commonly, if not universally, of linen. But it would not, at the present day, be considered right to seek the finest specimens of textile manufactures among the vestments of the dead, and we know not that the case was formerly different. Among the Egyptians, it is very possible that the finer cloths were regarded as unsuited to form any part of the cerements in which the dead were enveloped. Nevertheless, some very fine and delicate specimens have been occasionally found; and in the paintings which represent the dresses of the living, it is seen from their transparency and from their folds, that they were, among the higher ranks of people, of very fine and delicate texture. Sir J. G. Wilkinson declares that he has in his possession actual specimens of Egyptian "fine linen, the quality of which fully justifies all the praises of antiquity, and excites equal

EGYPTIAN DRESSES

admiration at the present day, being to the touch comparable to silk, and not inferior in texture to our finest cambric."

The dress of persons of rank in Egypt consisted of a kind of apron or kilt, sometimes simply bound round the loins and lapping over in front, but generally secured by a girdle, or by a sort of sash, tied in front in a bow or knot. It was sometimes folded over, with a centre-piece falling down in front, beneath the part where it overlapped: over this was worn a loose upper robe of the "fine linen," with full sleeves, secured by a girdle around the loins. Or else the dress consisted of the mere apron, and a shirt with short close sleeves, over which was thrown a loose robe, leaving the right arm exposed. The dress of the king himself seems to have differed only in the apron and head-dress, which were of peculiar form, and belonged exclusively to his rank as king.[1]

Besides these vestures, Pharaoh put a chain of gold around the neck of Jacob's son. In reference to this mark of distinction, the existing monuments of Egypt afford us abundant information. In the tombs at Beni-Hassan many slaves are represented, each of whom has in his hand something that belongs to the dress or ornaments of his master. The first carries one of the necklaces with which the neck and breast of persons of high rank are generally adorned. Over it stands, "necklace of gold." At the same place there is also a similar representation, in another tomb, of a noble Egyptian. By the *form* of the necklace, the distinction of individuals with regard to rank and dignity was probably denoted. Men of the common order seldom wear such ornaments, while the pictures of the kings and of the great are constantly adorned with them.[2]

In fact, the use of gold chains among ourselves, as marks of civic, judicial, knightly, and courtly honours, leaves little need for remote or foreign illustration of the subject. It seems to us highly probable that, among the articles of dress with which Joseph was invested, we are to seek in the necklace and the signet-ring the special insignia by which the high office to which he was appointed might be recognized.

It was necessary that his recognition should be public, and that it should therefore be openly proclaimed throughout the city. We ensure adequate publicity by announcements in the *Gazette.*

But the Egyptians, with all their wonderful advances in civilisation, possessed no such valuable organ of publicity; and therefore the general expedient of a public parade and proclamation through the streets became necessary, —an expedient still kept up partially in our own court, and in our civic ceremonies, though no longer exacted by the conditions in which it originated. This was also done at the court of Persia, in the case of Mordecai. (Esther vi. 8-11.) In the procession of Mordecai, however, the object of honour appeared on horseback—on the king's own horse ; but in Egypt, where men rode rather in chariots than on horseback, Joseph appears in the second state chariot of the realm. The Egyptian chariots were a species of gig, drawn by two horses. They were of light and elegant construction. On grand occasions the horses were decked with fancy ornaments; a rich striped or chequered housing, trimmed with a broad border, and large pendent tassels, covered the whole body; and two or more feathers, inserted in lions' heads, or some other device of gold, formed a crest upon the summit of the head-stall. But this display was confined to the chariot of the monarch or high military chiefs. And as Joseph rode in the monarch's chariot, the horses were no doubt thus decorated.

In this high state was Joseph paraded through the chief streets of the royal city, while the heralds that went before him cried ABRECH!— an Egyptian word, the meaning of which is not well known. The English version renders it by " Bow the knee !" some by " Bow the head!" while others, of no mean authority, apprehend that it proclaimed him to be " A native Egyptian!" notwithstanding his foreign extraction. At all events, that he should be publicly recognized as a naturalized subject, must, however effected, have been a consideration of no small weight with a people so jealous of foreigners as the Egyptians.

In connection with the history of Joseph, it is interesting to form a *general idea* of the civilization of Egypt. At that period villages and towns studded the Nile banks; large massive temples stood there, such as are represented in our museums, with colossal figures, rigidly calm, their hands resting on their knees, guarding the entrances; and a grand stern sphinx looked down on the people, as one sees near Geezeh. Fancy all this, with slaves at work; merchants engaged in traffic; soldiers at drill; processions marching along the highway; pleasure and dissipation

---

[1] Wilkinson's *Ancient Egyptians,* iii. 119, 347-351 ; *Cyclop. of Biblical Literature,* Art. "Sesh."

[2] Hengstenberg's *Egypt and the Books of Moses,* pp. 31, 32. American edition.

flaunting without shame; and the people dressed in costumes such as are depicted on ancient Egyptian monuments; and you have Egypt in the days of Joseph. Profane history bears witness to the country as a strip of wonderful fertility; and its appearance at the present day in spring, so green and fresh, so promising of plenteous recompense to the tiller's and the reaper's toil, corroborates the evidence.

Egyptian antiquities, as we find from Kitto's *Illustrations*, shed abundance of light on the state of the land in the days of Joseph; but the difficulty of identifying Bible narratives with *particular* Egyptian localities remains insuperable. There is, however, one exception, in the case of the marriage of Joseph with the daughter of Potipherah, priest or prince of On—On being identical with Heliopolis. Two miles from Cairo there exists a well known obelisk, said to belong to the reign of Osirtasin I., head of the twelfth dynasty, dating B.C. about 2000. If so, the obelisk must have been there in the days of Joseph; this had a startling effect on my mind as I gazed upon it.

"Obelisks were employed in Egypt from the earliest times, and dwarf examples were planted before the doors of sepulchres at a moderate computation of 4,000 years ago. They formed a part of the sepulchre, standing before its door. They were made of a single piece of stone, and at a later period, and for public buildings, granite appears to have been preferred. They are squared columns, tapering slightly from the base to the apex, and the proportions of the base are one-tenth of the height of the shaft up to the base of the pyramidion or pyramidal top."—*The Times*, Feb. 1877.

S.

THE CORN POLICY

Genesis 41:34-36, 47-57; 47:13-26

THE policy which Joseph recommended to the Egyptian king, and which he carried into effect when invested with the requisite power, well deserves our attention.

During the seven years of plenty, Joseph caused one-fifth of all the produce of every district to be hoarded up in its towns—every town containing, in immense granaries, the redundant produce of its district. The proportion is remarkable. It might seem inadequate, seeing that this fifth part of the produce of each year of plenty was to sustain the whole population during a year of famine. But when we consider the exuberant production of corn in that country, as evinced by the enormous export of grain which continued even to later times, when Egypt was the granary of Italy, it may readily be apprehended, that one-fifth of the produce of a

remarkably fertile year might be made to suffice for consumption during one year of scarcity. It is somewhat of a question how the crown acquired possession of this corn. Some think that the whole produce was taken up by the government, in order to ensure the economical use of it, and that it was then doled out to the people during even the abundant years. Others understand that merely a certain calculable surplus was taken and stored up; and there are those who deem it probable, by the light of subsequent events, that the produce-tax of one-tenth, usually paid to ancient governments, was at this time doubled, and made one-fifth, which constituted the surplus treasured up for future years. As this was afterwards *sold* to the people, some infer that the corn was bought up by the crown; and to account for the ability of the court to meet the outlay needful for the purchase of such countless stores of food, it is remarked, that this might be done at comparatively small cost in a time of abundance. This is true; and the prospect of a gainful return would encourage this outlay, besides that the king could not but be influenced by the desire to preserve his people. It may be hard to say what was the precise nature of the transaction. We must confess that we have not that conviction of the freedom and generosity of the Egyptian government which some have derived from the glowing descriptions of Diodorus Siculus. All the facts known to us which bear upon the subject seem to indicate a government of the most absolute character. The most despotic king the East ever yet produced could not speak a language more unreservedly absolute than that which the Egyptian king uses in bestowing upon Joseph his high commission: "I am Pharaoh; and without thee shall no man lift up his hand or foot in all the land of Egypt." However, looking at the course which affairs take under such exigencies, we consider the probability to be that either the people were serfs to the crown, for which they cultivated the land, and that hence the government took as of right all the produce they did not require for their subsistence, or else that the ancient, like the modern government of the country, claimed, and in this instance exercised, the right of purchasing, *at its own price*, as much as it required of the produce of the land, leaving sufficient for the sustenance of the producers. The mere existence of such a right is sufficiently hard; but we must judge these matters by the light of other days and of other lands than our own. The Orientals have never troubled themselves much about abstract rights. It is the harsh or mild exercise of powers, whether these powers be formally recognized or not, which they chiefly regard; and they seldom question any power a monarch thinks fit to assume, so long as its application does not press insupportably upon the individual. In the present case, it is quite probable that the extreme importance and urgency of the occasion was regarded as justifying the utmost exertion of the royal power, without greater regard for private rights—if any such rights were recognized—than we usually find among eastern nations. The mission of Joseph was to provide for the famine; and this he was bound to do in conformity with the existing ideas and institutions of the nation, with which a residence of thirteen years must have made him well acquainted, without embarrassing his operations by raising new questions of government and political right.

The case may have been somewhat different when the years of famine came, and all the food of the land was in his hands; food which would, without his care, have disappeared during the years of plenty, and thus the people have been left to remediless starvation. The nation then lay at his feet; and seeing that a man will give all that he hath for his life, he had the power of acting as seemed good in his eyes. Whether he had regard mainly to the advantage of the people, or to that of the crown, whose servant he was, may be a question with us; but it was probably no question with him, in whose view the advantage of the king and that of the people were doubtless one. After the deep study which the principles of government and of political economy have of late years received, and in the absence of those crude notions of unbounded state profusion which people were wont to admire, but which are now seen to form in their results a curse to any people, the conduct of Joseph in this trying position may be considered with advantage.

The state had corn in abundance, and the people had no food. What was the state to do? However people might talk fifty years ago, as if it were the duty of the state to open its stores and feed the people during all these years without cost, few thinking men would now take this to be the wisest course. It was the duty of the state to see that none should perish from want, while there was food in the land; but it was not the duty of the state—it would not have been wise or prudent—it would even have been mischievous, to supply corn without cost to those who had the means of paying for it in money or in money's worth. This is now so well understood, that, during the recent famine in the sister country, our own government taxed its ingenuity to find means, that those who had nothing but their labour to sell, should give that labour in exchange for the food which the care of the state provided. The whole care and solicitude of the government was to avoid the appearance, and as far as possible the reality, of *giving* of its mere bounty the food for which it had ransacked the world. No doubt, the men who spent their days in mending, or in seeming to mend, the roads, would have been better pleased had the food been given them without this cost; but the wise thought differently. And if so much danger was in this case apprehended, from the precedent of feeding a people gratuitously for a few months, how much greater would have been the danger of doing this during the seven long years of famine in Egypt! It is not too much to say, that seventy times seven years would scarcely have enabled the nation to recover from the shock which its character and its industry would, during these seven years, have sustained. So far, then, is Joseph's plan of *selling*, instead of *giving*, the corn to the people, from being a matter of reprehension, that we ought to be astonished at a course of proceeding which anticipated the discoveries of the nineteenth century of Christ; and at the strength of mind which enabled the minister of the Egyptian crown to forego the vulgar popularity which profuse but unreasoning bounty can always secure. We have ourselves had, at intervals, frequent occasion to examine the conduct of Joseph in this transaction very closely; and we must acknowledge that the more we have examined it, and the better we have understood it, the more laudable, the more wise, and the more free from objection, it has appeared. And we have reached this judgment quite independently; for we are by no means bound to conclude that all that Joseph did in this matter was right. The Scripture, as usual, records the proceedings without passing any judgment upon them; and considering the influences by which he was surrounded, and the age and the circumstances in which he lived, it would be surprising indeed to find all his proceedings conformable to modern European notions of political justice. It would be enough to find that his measures were such as would in his own age be considered just and wise; and if in any point, as in the one we have noticed, his ideas were in advance of his age, he is entitled to the greater credit; for we cannot rightly expect more from him than the spirit of his own age demanded.

Let us now indicate briefly the true character of the transaction, without pausing to discuss the merits of every step in the operation.

When the famine commenced, Joseph opened the stores and began to sell the corn not only to the Egyptians, but to such foreigners as came for it; and that foreigners did come from all the neighbouring lands to Egypt to purchase corn, shows that it was not offered at an exorbitant or monopoly price to the Egyptians. The foreigners clearly came in the hope of sharing in the benefits enjoyed by the people of Egypt, by purchasing corn at the price it was sold for in that land. At first the payments for corn were made with money; but this at length became exhausted; and as, from the universal character of the visitation, there were none to give money for other property, Joseph consented, on the application of the people, to take property in exchange for corn. They began with their cattle. As they had not the means of feeding their live stock, and they must have been anxious that their horses, flocks, herds, etc., should be in hands that could preserve them from perishing with hunger; and as the number must have been greatly diminished during the previous period of famine, we need not be surprised to learn that this resource lasted but one year, at the close of which all the cattle in Egypt had passed into the possession of the crown. What resource then remained? These were not times for lending or borrowing—for putting the evil day far off—for any of the common resources by which men seek to avert present evil. The questions before men then were questions of life and death. They came to Joseph, and, showing that they had nothing left but their persons and their lands, they offered both as the price of their subsistence during the remainder of the famine, including seed-corn for the time when the operations of agriculture might be resumed. This offer was accepted by Joseph. He did not make the proposal. It was one that he would

perhaps have hesitated to make; but when it was made by the people, and even pressed upon him, he yielded to their urgency, and, without nicely inquiring into the extent of their meaning, accepted it in the same large terms as offered; the particular limitation being then in his hands, and the liberal construction of these terms being well calculated to bring credit to his master.

However, the offer as made is not to be understood under the popular acceptation of buying and selling, the application of such an idea to this transaction being calculated to mislead the judgment; as Joseph's phrase, in speaking to them, "I have bought you this day, and your land, for Pharaoh," tends to excite a feeling to the disadvantage of his character, which rests on insufficient grounds. It means little more than "acquired," just as anciently, and indeed at the present day, in the East, a wife is said to be "bought," and the money that passes between the husband and her father is called the "price." This is far from implying that she has become a slave. So in the present case, although the people relinquish their lands, they do not expect to cease to occupy or cultivate them. They are indeed anxious that the land shall not be desolate; and one of their stipulations is for seed-corn, all of which would have been idle and useless had they become mere slaves or serfs. Had the land under their offer become absolutely that of the king, they had little reason to care about it. He would know how to care for his own land; and they might safely leave to him the providing of seed-corn for its culture. And so, had the condition into which they came been that of slaves, he would have been bound to care for them; and it could to them matter but little whether the land lay desolate or not. What they did expect was clearly that they should henceforth become tenants of the crown, instead of free proprietors. This they call being "servants," a term which merely implies that they were under obligations short of absolute freedom. There is no word in Scripture answering to "tenant." The tenant is called the "servant" of the proprietor; and according to this phraseology our own tenant farmers would be called servants, seeing that they cultivate lands not their own, and are bound to render to the landlord a large proportion of the value of the produce as rent. Although, therefore, Joseph's language, "I have *bought you* this day, you and your lands, for Pharaoh," must sound harsh to us, it is well to understand that the true signification of what he says is this: "Having this day acquired for Pharaoh certain rights over you and your lands, I shall now proceed to inform you to what extent these rights will hereafter be enforced." He then states, in accordance with the explanation we have given, that they were to remain in occupation of the lands of which the king had become by their cession the proprietor, and that they were to pay one-fifth of the produce as rent to the sovereign as their landlord, in lieu of all other imposts and charges whatever. When we consider that, in all probability, a tenth at least had always been paid to defray the expenses of government, the real *addition* is ten per cent, making the entire charge twenty per cent. This is certainly a heavy impost; but it is as nothing in comparison with what is paid for rent in almost any country in Europe at the present day; and still less will it bear comparison with the *combined* charges of rent and taxation which this rent charge in Egypt appears to us to represent. It is somewhat remarkable, that amid the vicissitudes to which that country has been subject, the compact between the ruler and his subjects entered into by Joseph has always subsisted there in principle. To this day, the fellah, or peasant, in Egypt cultivates the land for his sovereign, and receives a portion of the produce for his own wants. But amid the grasping exactions of our own age, and the harsh oppressions to which he is subject by the government and its officers, he has much reason to regret that the moderation of Joseph does not actuate its present rulers.[1] Mr. Lane, in his excellent book on the modern Egyptians, declares with emphasis that "it could scarcely be possible for them to suffer more and live."

[1] In Burckhardt's curious book of *Arabic Proverbs*, there is a calculation of the cost and produce of the culture of seventeen acres in Egypt. It may be thus summarily stated in piastres:—

Total produce,	.	.	.	1802
Total expense,	.	.	.	993½
Clear produce,	.	.		808½
Government taxes,	.	.	.	493
Remainder in return for cultivation,				315½

This shows that the taxes alone levied by the modern government amount to about sixty per cent of the clear produce of the farm.

The point of view from which we derive our estimate of Joseph's proceedings must be the age in which he lived. It is, therefore, well that we have the means of knowing how it was regarded, not merely by his contemporaries generally, but by the people themselves, whose harsh treatment some writers have affected to bewail. Let it be remembered that the proposal was their own; and that when Joseph had accepted their offer, under a more liberal construction than they had perhaps expected, their language was not that of complaint, but of warm and admiring gratitude: "Thou hast saved our lives!"

It deserves further to be noted, that although, in accepting the offer, Joseph uses the same broad terms in which it had been tendered, yet, when the law in which he embodied the results of this transaction is given, nothing is said about the *persons:* only the lands are specified, the edict itself liberally and gracefully waiving the point which was most liable to abuse, but which had formed part of the bargain. If it was to be enforced, or if it had any significance beyond what we have ascribed to it, this edict is the very place in which to seek it; but the edict only says that the fifth part of the produce was to be the king's, without one word of personal servitude, or of persons in any way.

THE ENTERTAINMENT

Genesis 43:16-34

AMONG the foreigners who came to buy corn in Egypt, were the brethren of Joseph—all of them except his full brother Benjamin, who was especially dear to his father as his youngest son, and (as Jacob supposed) the only surviving child of his beloved Rachel. Joseph knew them; but they could not discern in this Egyptian grandee, who seemed to have all power in his hands, the brother they had sold for a slave. He forbore to disclose himself; and, pretending to take them for spies, he drew from them full information respecting his father's house. The absence of Benjamin, however, alarmed him; and fearing that he also had suffered foul treatment from them, he detained Simeon as a hostage, and enjoined the others not again to appear before him without their youngest brother.

When the sons of Jacob came the second time to Egypt to purchase corn, they naturally went to the public office, where the business connected with the distribution of grain was transacted under the superintendence of Joseph. He had, no doubt, been long expecting their return, and he had no difficulty in guessing that the stranger who now appeared among them was his own brother—the son of [his mother. He, however, restrained all present emotion, and directed " the ruler of his house" to take them home, and to " slay and make ready " a suitable entertainment for so many guests, as he meant that they should dine with him at noon.

There are in this some intimations that deserve attention. One is, that even in the metropolitan city animals were slaughtered at home, instead of the meat being purchased in the market. This seems hard to understand. In a village or small town, we might explain it by supposing that, there being no demand sufficient to carry off, so promptly as a warm climate requires, any animal that might be killed for sale, none were so killed; but every one who wished for a joint of meat had to slay an animal in order to obtain it. This we have often witnessed; but it can hardly apply to a great city. Yet even in a very large city, we have known a gentleman who wished to give an English entertainment obliged to purchase an ox, and have it slain on his own premises. This was simply because beef was not usually eaten by the people, and was therefore not to be found in the market of even a large town. We should have been almost inclined to think that Joseph was minded to give his brethren an entertainment different from that which the markets of Egypt would supply, but such as they had known in Canaan, were it not that the fact of cattle being killed in the premises where an entertainment is given, is proved to have been usual by the subsisting monuments of Egypt. The cause of this remarkable circumstance, which seems to imply that what we call butcher's meat was not be had at shops or markets, remains to be found. We have representations of poulterers' shops; but whenever we find the slaying of quadrupeds for food, it is in a private house. It may be that, as there is indeed reason to believe, poultry, fish, and vegetables formed the chief food of the people, and that flesh meat was seldom used but at entertainments, which created a demand so uncertain and irregular, as to deter any tradesman from attempting to supply it in a land where meat will not keep longer than a few hours. It may be also that they desired the blood for their culinary operations. It is clear that it was received in vessels for this purpose; and it is probably with reference to this Egyptian practice that the use of blood was by the law forbidden to the Israelites.[1]

From all the representations that exist, it is, then, seen to have been the custom in Egypt, in conformity with the incidental intimation of the fact here given, to take the animal into a courtyard near the house; to tie its four legs together, and then to throw it upon the ground. In this position it was held by one or more persons, while the butcher, sharpening his broad knife upon a steel attached to his apron, proceeded to cut the throat, as nearly as possible, from one ear to the other, sometimes continuing the opening downward along the throat. The head was then taken off, and was usually given away to some poor person, unless there were foreigners to whom it could be sold. They next proceeded to flay the animal, beginning with the head and the neck; and the carcase being then cut up, the joints were taken in trays to the kitchen, where the cook seems to have at once commenced his operations upon them. This last fact is indeed implied in the narrative before us, as the meat that was to be eaten at noon had still to be killed in the forenoon when Joseph gave this order. This mode of dressing meat before the warmth of life has altogether passed from it, is almost necessary in a hot climate. This is partly shown in the practice of our own butchers, who, in winter, kill their animals several days before they cut up the carcases, but in summer kill only the day before, or even the same morning. These matters are determined by habit and climate; and the Orientals, under such influences, think as hardly of our practice as we can do of theirs; for they regard with disgust and abhorrence the length of time meat is kept by Europeans before it is cooked. In their view it is no better than carrion. One consequence is, however, that meat dressed so soon after killing requires to be completely overdone in order to be tender; and from this arise

---

[1] Leviticus 7:26,27; Deuteronomy 15:23 The prohibition was, however, also of earlier date, although thus renewed. See Genesis 9:4.

some of the most peculiar forms of eastern cookery.[1]

It is stated that, on their arrival at the house, Joseph's brethren had water brought with which to wash their feet. This custom we have already had occasion to notice.[2] Yet it is known from ancient writers, that the Egyptians washed their

WASHING HANDS

hands before dinner; but the washing of the feet was probably confined to those who desired it, or who had come from a journey. There are indeed no representations of these operations in any of the ancient Egyptian paintings; but ewers, not unlike those used at the present day, are represented, with the basins belonging to them, in the paintings of a Theban tomb. It is certain that basins were kept for the purpose of washing the hands and feet of the guests, and that in the houses of the rich they were of gold. Herodotus mentions a gold basin belonging to Amasis, which he and the guests who dined with him used for washing their feet. But it is probable that those who lived near their host were expected to perform their ablutions before they left home, and this perhaps accounts for no representations of the process being shown in the paintings.

It will also be observed that the dining hour was noon,—an hour which, although in many respects inconvenient, as coming in the midst of the day's labour, has singularly maintained its place as that in which the great mass of people

in most nations take their principal meal. It is probable, however, that, like the Romans, they also ate a substantial supper in the evening, as is still the custom in the East.

The table used by the ancient Egyptians was very similar to that which is in use at the present day in Egypt. This is a small stool supporting a round tray, on which the dishes are placed. These tables were sometimes brought in and removed with the dishes upon them. Occasionally each guest had a table to himself. From the mention of persons sitting in rows, according to rank, it has been supposed by some that the tables were of a long figure. This, Wilkinson thinks, may sometimes have been the case in Egypt, even during the Pharaonic period, since the brethren of Joseph sat before him, " the first-born according to his birthright, and the youngest according to his youth," Joseph himself eating alone at another table. We quite agree, however, with this writer in regarding it as by no means certain that the table was in this instance long, or in any way different from their usual round table, since people might even then be seated according to their rank, and the similar modern Egyptian table is not without its post of honour and fixed gradation of rank.

The brethren are represented as *sitting* at table. Hengstenberg, in his clever book on *Egypt and the Books of Moses*, notes here a variation from the patriarchal practice of reclin-

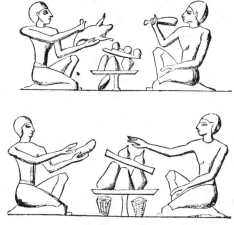

EGYPTIANS AT MEAT

ing. We have some doubt whether the text to which he refers—Gen. xviii. 4, " rest yourselves " will bear the stress he lays upon it. But it is certain from the monuments that the Egyptians

---

[1] Those of our readers who desire to acquaint themselves further with the details of Egyptian culinary operations, should consult Wilkinson's *Ancient Egyptians*, ii. 364-406.

[2] See Vol. 1, pp. 254-255.

did, as here represented, *sit* at meals. All the modes of sitting upon the ground now in use in the East—cross-legged, crouching, and upon the heels—may be found in the paintings and sculptures. But the Egyptians also sat on chairs and stools. In the paintings representing meals, we sometimes see the guests sitting on low stools, or else upon the ground; but we notice that one peculiar mode of sitting upon the ground is invariably adopted as best suited to give command of the table at dinner. The person kneels on one knee, and sits back upon the heel of the same leg, while the sole of the other foot is planted on the ground, and the leg correspondingly raised.

Although Benjamin, as the youngest, has the lowest place assigned to him, Joseph shows him the special favour of sending to his table messes five times as large as any of the others receive. To present choice morsels with the hand to those at the same table, and to send dishes from his own table to that of any other person (always understanding that every two or three have a separate tray and table), is still the highest and most flattering distinction which an eastern host can show to the guest whom he delights to honour. And this was doubtless the nature of the attention which Joseph showed to his mother's son. This disproportion of five to one must, however, have been very astonishing to the other brothers, and even to the Egyptians, if, as Herodotus tells us, the distinction in such cases to the kings themselves at public feasts and banquets was no more than a double mess. Agesilaus, when in Egypt, used to have a double portion brought to him— one for himself, and the other to bestow on whomsoever he felt inclined to confer a mark of his favour. Other instances of the kind are frequent in antiquity. Although in Europe, at least in modern times, the delicacy of the parts we give at table is more considered than the quantity, yet the traditions of these two customs are essentially the same. Indeed, the antiquity and curiosity of many of the intimations which bear on so small a matter, may warn us to count nothing little that illustrates the prevalence and descent of ancient usages.

THE SHEPHERD KINGS

Genesis 43:32

THE declaration that to "eat with the Hebrews was an abomination to the Egyptians," opens questions of considerable interest, which have not failed to engage the attention of the scholars of this and former generations. One obvious cause has already been suggested,[1] in the fact, that by the Hebrews and other pastoral tribes, the cow, which was almost the only animal *generally* worshipped in Egypt (the worship of most others being local), was offered in sacrifices, and the flesh eaten without scruple.

But there was yet another, and perhaps a deeper reason,—the previous occupation of Egypt by a pastoral race, who had committed great cruelties during their occupation of the country. The precise date of this invasion has not been, and perhaps never will be, ascertained. But we are strongly disposed to agree with Sir J. G. Wilkinson and others, in thinking that "the already existing prejudice against shepherds, when the Hebrews arrived in the country, plainly shows that their invasion happened previous to that event."[2] This is the view which the writer may claim to have always taken; and although it has of late years been most formidably opposed by some continental writers, there still seems to him no other theory that is so probable in itself, and certainly none which so well harmonizes with *all* the scriptural intimations. We cannot here trace that view so fully as might be wished; but the leading points of it are these: That the intrusive dynasty, called the Hyksos, or "shepherd kings," were in Egypt at the time of Abraham's visit to that land; that they had recently been expelled when Joseph attained to honour in that country; and that the Pharaoh of his history was a native Egyptian prince. Hence Joseph, appearing as an Egyptian, spoke to his brethren by an interpreter; hence the dislike of the Egyptians to eat with a pastoral people; hence the fact that the fertile pastoral district of Goshen happened to be then vacant for appropriation to the Israelites; for, according to the history of that invasion, this was the very district in which the Hyksos made their last

[1] See Vol. 1, pp. 332-334.

[2] Ancient Egyptians, 2. 16.

stand, and in which they for a good while maintained themselves after their expulsion from the rest of Egypt. The king of a later age, who " knew not Joseph," and who oppressed the Israelites, had, according to this view, no connection with this change, but was the first of a dynasty from Upper Egypt, who united the crowns of the upper and lower countries, which before his time were held apart, and who had little knowledge of the services, or care for the family of Joseph, but looked upon them as a branch of the great pastoral race from which Egypt had formerly suffered so much, and which it had still reason to regard with apprehension.

The other view assumes a later date for the incumbency of the shepherd kings. It holds that they were in the height of their power in Egypt in the time of Joseph, and that the change which eventually took place in the treatment of the Israelites settled in Goshen, arose from the expulsion of the intrusive dynasty, and the succession of the native sovereign, who would naturally regard the Israelites as merely a branch of the same obnoxious race. Although we cannot receive this view, we have no desire to underrate the learning and ability with which it has been supported. It has, however, this fault, that we cannot reconcile it so well as we can the other with the facts of Scripture, and that it does not satisfactorily meet any one of the requisites which we have described as originally recommending the earlier date to our preference.

As the English reader has not had much opportunity of becoming acquainted with the grounds on which the later date is advocated, the leading points may be stated for his information. Since, however, the statements of this view by different writers vary in circumstances, we shall chiefly follow that of a German writer by whom it has been most ably advocated.[1]

On the assumption, then, that the king who knew not Joseph was the first native king who reigned after the expulsion of the shepherds, who had dominated over the country for 260 years, it is held that the shepherds were Shemites, descended probably from Eber, and allied to the Israelites in spirit, language, and occupation, which very circumstance would make the latter hateful to the Egyptians. This agrees with the apprehensions of Pharaoh, that the Israelites, who had become exceedingly numerous, might avail themselves of the occasion of a war to leave the country, and increase the number of hostile neighbours.[1]

The settlement of the Israelites in Egypt must, if this view be correct, have taken place soon after the commencement of that dynasty. This is deemed to be corroborated by the narrative of Joseph, which supposes the reader to be acquainted with Egyptian history. In the first place, the term Hebrew is applied, without immediate reference to Israel,[2] whose family was small, to the whole body of the shepherd people, who were much hated by the Egyptians. This agrees, it is urged, with the opinion that they had conquered the country, and that the ruling monarchs were selected from their number, and forced upon the people, by whom they were held in detestation, though they did accommodate themselves to Egyptian usages.

It is next urged, that it was only under a foreign dynasty in such circumstances that Joseph could have been raised to distinction. Hence the cup-bearer mentions him as a Hebrew youth, able to interpret dreams ; and hence the king, of the same stock originally, determined to send for him, as the Egyptian wise men gave him no satisfaction. The advice of Joseph was gladly taken, because the king perceived immediately that the establishment and independence of the people would be promoted by it. To have a Hebrew in his service as administrator of the kingdom, would be agreeable to his dependants ; and his foes, the priests, were conciliated by being exempted from civil burdens, and secured in their revenues. And although he conferred the right of citizenship on Joseph, giving him an Egyptian name, and bringing about his marriage with the daughter of a priest of the sun, yet he did not venture to violate the feelings of the people, and Joseph did not sit at the same table with the Egyptian lords, because they would not eat with the shepherd race.

Again, when Joseph's brethren came to Egypt they undoubtedly recognized him as a Hebrew,

[1] Jost, in his *General History of the Israelitish People* (*Allgemeine Geschichte des Israelitischen Volks*). It is also advocated by Heeren, in his *Historical Researches* (*Ideen, etc.*); and by M. D. J. M. Henry, in his *Pharaonic Egypt* (*L'Egypte Pharaonique*).

[1] Exodus 1:10.
[2] Genesis 39:14; 40:15; 41:12; 43:32; Exodus 1:16; 3:18.

for his story must have been generally known; but it never occurred to them that he was their brother whom they had sold, for there were certainly many Hebrews in the land, and some of them men of distinction. He confirmed their error by employing an interpreter. It is only on this supposition that he could affect to regard his ten brethren as spies; for while the shepherd race held the power, it is very conceivable that their jealousy should be excited by the apprehension of further inroads from the same stock. Such a feigned charge, preferred by a governor acting under the authority of a really Egyptian family, would be altogether inexplicable.

Lastly, it is stated that Pharaoh was pleased with the account of Joseph's family. But were he an Egyptian, would he have allowed such men, hateful to his people, to settle in Egypt? On the contrary, if he himself were of the same stock, his own satisfaction and that of his courtiers is what might be expected from the characteristic hospitality of the race. Thus the Israelites were connected with the government, but hated by the Egyptian people. The remains of Jacob were embalmed, and, agreeably to his last will, committed to his own sepulchre, accompanied by many Egyptian lords,—solemnities which it is not to be supposed that the enemies of the shepherd race would have allowed. The place in Canaan where the mourning ceremonies of the funeral were performed, was called by the inhabitants Abel Mizraim (mourning of the Egyptians), not necessarily because they were really Egyptians, but because they came from Egypt, and the ceremonies were conducted in the manner of that country.

That among these various suggestions there are none of any weight, it would be too much to say; but we grievously miscalculate the penetration of our readers, if they will not be able of themselves to disprove most of these arguments, on the basis of the indications we have already afforded. It will not fail to be seen that the state of feeling which, according to all but such as adopt this view, arose out of the long and oppressive occupation of the land by the shepherds, is throughout quietly assumed not only to have existed, but to have been manifested even at court, *during* the period of their sovereignty, and indeed at a period which must have been very soon after its commencement. It will also be perceived that even the most probable of

the facts adduced become more probable still under the explanation that the court of Egypt in the time of Joseph was native Egyptian, the intrusive pastoral dynasty having been then expelled. Even the circumstance that Joseph affected to take his brethren for spies, which is triumphantly alleged to be inexplicable under a native dynasty, is, in fact, more easily explained under the hypothesis that such a dynasty reigned; for if the shepherds had been at a recent date driven out of the country, it was quite natural that a careful watch should be kept over persons of the same order entering the land, who might be suspected of some attempt that might be made by the expelled pastoral tribes to recover the power they had lost. It may also be remarked, that the assertion that Joseph and his family, though favoured by the court, were hated by the people, is not only unsupported by Scripture, but is at variance with the general tendency of its intimations. Look, for instance, at Deut. xxiii. 7, "Thou shalt not abhor an Egyptian, because thou wast a stranger in his land," a passage which is justly held by Hengstenberg to imply that the Israelites received in some respects better treatment from individuals of the Egyptians than from the state; so that the Israelites had cause for grateful regard to them in return, since the phrase "because thou wast a stranger in his land" is not a sufficient reason for the command, "Thou shalt not abhor an Egyptian," unless it means that the Egyptians performed the offices of hospitality to the Israelites, and earned for themselves the claim of reciprocity.

It seems to us that the disposition to assign the later date to the shepherd dynasty of Egypt has arisen from the wish to account in what might seem the most satisfactory manner for the change of policy which took place when a dynasty, comparatively insensible to the ancient services of Joseph, came into power in Lower Egypt. But this is sufficiently accounted for by the succession of a king from the upper country, who had previously reigned in the distant province of Thebes, and who would be naturally inclined to look upon the Hebrews with the same distrust and contempt with which foreigners, and especially pastoral foreigners, were usually treated by the Egyptians. Accordingly it is at this time, sixty years after the death of Joseph, that Wilkinson, in his Tables, fixes the accession of the Theban dynasty in the person of Amosis, whom he with reason regards as "the new king who knew not Joseph."

There is one point, incidentally produced, as to the origin of the shepherds, which may require a word of notice. The notion that the term Hebrews applies to the whole body of the shepherd people, including the Israelites, is now maintained by great authorities. If the name Hebrew be derived from Eber, as seems to be generally understood, there is no reason that it should not be applicable to other descendants of Eber besides the family of Abraham. The strongest passage for this interpretation is that in which Joseph says he was stolen from " the land of the Hebrews," which, it is urged, is scarcely applicable to the single family of Jacob. It may be allowed that there is a difficulty; but the difficulty is as great the other way, as it is by no means easy to see in what sense the land of Canaan, then in great part a settled country, could in this wider sense be called " a land of pastoral tribes;" and as far as appears, Abraham's family was the only one of Shemitic origin in the land. Still, this objection has much to recommend it, although the proof is less satisfactory than might be desired. Some evidence may yet be found to settle this difficult question; but while the opinions of intelligent and learned men differ so greatly, it must be held that the materials for a positive conclusion do not exist. Wilkinson at first held that the Hyksos were from Assyria, but now or lately regards them as a Scythian tribe. Some bring them even from India, others find them in the Berbers of Africa, and many seek them in the neighbouring pastoral tribes of Shemitic origin. Perhaps the last view is the safest to entertain, till a more positive conclusion can be reached.

The history and chronology of Egypt have received much elucidation since the period when the foregoing remarks were written. Though all obscurity is very far from being dispelled, some negative conclusions at least have been reached by the most distinguished Egyptian archæologists, and this is one—that the age of the shepherd kings was not before the time of Joseph. That he went down to Egypt during the dynasty of the *Hyksos*, as these kings are called, is an old opinion, and is still supported by ingenuity and learning; and it is supposed that the existence of a Shepherd Dynasty at that period best explains the extraordinary circumstance of a foreigner belonging to a nomadic tribe, rich in flocks and herds, being raised to high office in the Egyptian State. But it leaves this insuperable difficulty, that when Joseph was at the zenith of his power, shepherds

are said to have been "an abomination to the Egyptians." Dr. Kitto cites that passage in support of his own theory, but that theory is inadmissible on grounds stated by modern scholars. In a long and learned disquisition *On the Bearings of Egyptian History upon the Pentateuch*, by Canon Cook, these grounds of objection are stated; and he comes to the conclusion that the Pharaoh under whom Joseph was prime minister can best be identified with Amenemha III., one of the twelfth dynasty, which included seven Pharaohs and a queen regnant, and covered a period including Abraham and Joseph. How far that whole position is tenable we leave undecided; but he alleges good reasons for believing, at least, that Amenemha III. is the Pharaoh of Joseph; and between the twelfth dynasty and that of the *Hyksos*, there came a thirteenth. The Hyksos are now reckoned as forming the thirteenth and following dynasties, down to the seventeenth. It is remarkable that in an inscription belonging to the twelfth dynasty, in the time of a king before Amenemha III., there was a ruler under him of whom it is said, " he injured no little child, he oppressed no widow: he detained for his own purpose no fisherman: took from his work no shepherd: no overseer's men were taken. There was no beggar in his days: no one starved in his time. When years of famine occurred, he ploughed all the lands of the district producing abundant food. No one was starved in it; he treated the widow as a woman with a husband to protect her." Some have supposed all this must refer to Joseph, but the supposition cannot be maintained; yet the passage shows, that there could be under the twelfth dynasty such an officer of state as Joseph was: and from another papyrus of the same period, it appears that a foreigner could be preferred to such a position (*Canon Cook, Speaker's Commentary*, I., 446, 451). This disposes of the objection that the episode of Joseph is improbable in the reign of any native prince who maintained his own national polity and religion.

S.

DIVINING CUPS

Genesis 44

WHEN Joseph, in pursuance of his plan of dealing with his brethren, directed his steward to put his silver cup into the sack of Benjamin, and then when they had departed to pursue and charge them with the theft, his object probably was to ascertain the state of their feeling towards Benjamin, and whether they extended to him— the only other child of his mother—the dislike which had led them to contemplate his own death, and which had induced them actually to sell him for a slave. If the state of their feeling were not right towards Benjamin, they would doubtless leave him in the hands of the steward and make their way home; but if they were true men, they would not abandon him to his fate, but would make every effort to save him from that slavery, the penalty of his assumed offence, to which they had so readily consigned his brother. Nobly did they stand the test. They rent their clothes in grief, and returned with their brother to plead for mercy before the

JOSEPH MAKING HIMSELF KNOWN TO HIS BRETHREN

austere governor of Egypt. The result of Judah's noble and manly appeal, which moved Joseph to tears, is well known. What would have been the result had they given way in this trial, may be easily conjectured. Joseph, having possession of his beloved brother, would doubtless have disclosed himself to him, and have provided well for him in Egypt. But it is very doubtful if he would have cared any further for his recreant brothers; and the migration of the whole family into Egypt would not, humanly speaking, have taken place. But doubtless even in that case, on learning from Benjamin the difficulty with which the aged Jacob had consented to his departure with the others, and the serious consequences which his not returning might be expected to produce, Joseph would have found means of communicating to his father the intelligence that *both* the sons of his beloved Rachel were alive and prosperous in Egypt.

But what strikes the reader most, perhaps, in the account of this transaction, and what seems more to need explanation than almost any other point in the narrative, is that, to enhance the importance and value of the cup, and to deepen the enormity of the offence, the steward is in-

structed to declare that this was the cup whereby his lord practised divination; and personally when they come once before Joseph, he turns to

EGYPTIAN WINE CUPS

this point himself in the stern question: "Wot ye not that such a man as I would certainly divine?" As we believe this rendering to convey the correct meaning, we shall not trouble the reader with an account of the various interpretations the words have received. It is a well established fact that the ancient Egyptians had a kind of divination which the Greeks distinguished by the name of cup-divination; and it is remarkable that, in the translation of the Old Testament into Greek by the Seventy, the word *kondu* is employed, and it is observable that the sacred chalice of the Hindu priests is to this day called *kundi*.

However, we should do wrong to suppose that Joseph really practised divination, from his instructing his steward to make the charge in this form. We, with our high Christian standard of truthfulness, cannot altogether approve of his using this pretence; but it is in keeping with the whole transaction, which was a feint throughout. Joseph was supporting the character of an Egyptian of rank; and as it was believed that such a person would daily consult his divining cup for the good or evil auguries of the day, the prompt detection of the alleged thief would be the more readily accounted for.

Now, in explanation of this practice of divination by cups, we learn from ancient authorities, that prognostics were drawn from the figures reflected by the rays of light in the clear water which the cup or basin contained. Another, perhaps a less ancient, mode of divination is said to be this: small pieces of gold or silver leaf, or thin plate, were thrown into the cup, intermingled with precious stones, on which certain characters were engraved. Then the inquirer repeated certain forms of adjuration, and invoked his gods. The answer was variously given. Sometimes a voice was heard; sometimes certain of the signs engraven on the stones were seen reflected in the water; and sometimes the image of the person respecting whom inquiry was made appeared therein. This mode of divination is said to have been common to the ancient Egyptians, Assyrians, and Chaldeans.

It was also known among the Persians. Nothing is more famous in their history than the cup of Jemsheed. In digging the foundation of the city of Istakhar (Persepolis), a turquoise vase or cup was found during his reign, capable of containing a quart of liquor. The valuable properties of the cup were soon ascertained; it was called Jemsheed, or vase of the sun; and many suppose that from the possession of this valuable article the monarch took his name. It seems to us more likely that the story is an invention, to account for so remarkable a name as that which the monarch bore. Nevertheless, it is certain that cups or vases named Jem or Giam[1] are famous for their occult qualities. The Orientals make this sort of vase of all kinds of metal, as well as of glass or crystal. They are of various forms, but all make some approach to a spherical figure. They are called not only cups, but mirrors, and celestial globes. The idea connected with them is, that when consulted with proper ceremonies, the matter concerning which any information may be desired is pictorially represented. The cup of Jemsheed was of this sort, and Alexander the Great had another of the kind, by means of which an exact knowledge of all mundane affairs was acquired; nor were the secrets of the supernatural world hidden from their view.

We recognize the same notion among the Greeks in Homer's description of the cup of Nestor. From the East it travelled westward; and the "crystals" with which those conversant with the occult literature of the sixteenth and

seventeenth centuries are well acquainted, were no other than such vases or globes—were the same as the oriental divining cups; and the information sought from them was exactly the same, and was obtained, or alleged to be obtained, in the same manner. This sort of utensil is well described by Spenser. It was made by Merlin, and was given by him to king Ryence for his protection. The king's daughter, Britomart, finds it in her father's closet, and obtains therein a view of a matter which concerns her nearly.

" It vertue had to show in perfect sight
    Whatever thing was in the world contaynd,
    Betwixt the lowest earth and heven's hight,
    So that it to the looker appertaynd :
    Whatever foe had wrought or frend had faynd,
    Therein discovered was, ne ought mote pas,
    Ne ought in secret from the same remaynd ;
    Forthy it round and hollow-shaped was,
Like to the world itselfe, and seemd a world of glas."[1]

Even at the present time, something of the kind—that is to say, the occult or superstitious use of vases or cups—may be found in several countries. Its continued existence in Egypt is shown by a remarkable passage in Norden's Travels. When this author and his companions had arrived at Derri, the most remote extremity of Egypt, or rather in Nubia, where they were able to deliver themselves from a perilous position only through great presence of mind, they sent one of their company to a malicious and powerful Arab to threaten him. He answered them, "I know what sort of people you are. I have consulted my cup, and found in it that you are from a people of whom one of our prophets has said, 'There will come Franks under every kind of pretence to spy out the land. They will bring hither a great multitude of their countrymen to conquer the country and destroy all the people.'"

But we find the divining cup even in the South Seas. At Tongataboo, one of the Friendly Islands, Captain Cook bestowed upon the king a pewter plate which he had been observed particularly to notice. He received the gift with undisguised satisfaction, and remarked that, whenever he had occasion to go to any of the other islands, he would leave this plate behind him at Tongataboo, as a sort of representative in his absence, that the people might render to it the same obeisance as to himself in person. On being asked what he had usually employed for this purpose before this plate came into his possession,

[1] This is the orthography of D'Herbelot, from whose *Bibliotheque Orientale* (arts. " Giam" and " Giamshid") the particulars in this paragraph are chiefly taken.

[1] *Faery Queene*, iii. 2, 19.

"we had the satisfaction of hearing from him," says the Captain, "that this singular honour had hitherto been conferred upon the wooden bowl in which he washed his hands. Another extra-ordinary use to which the king meant to apply the plate in lieu of his wooden bowl was, it seems, to discover a thief. He said that, when anything was stolen, and the thief could not be found out, the people were all assembled together before him, when he washed his hands in water in this vessel; after which it was cleaned, and then the whole multitude advanced, one after another, and touched it in the same manner that they touch his foot when they pay him obeisance. If the guilty person touched it, he died imme-ately upon the spot, not by violence, but by the hand of Providence; and if any one refused to touch it, his refusal was a clear proof that he was the culprit."

JACOB'S OBSEQUIES

Genesis 50

"Now let me die, since I have seen thy face, be-cause thou art yet alive," were the words which Jacob uttered when he wept upon the neck of the governor of Egypt, and knew that he embraced his long-lost son. He did not, however, then die, though a joy not greater than his has brought many men to their graves. At the close of a life of many sore trials, he spent some happy years in the land of Goshen, of which Joseph had got the grant to him and his for a residence. Seven-teen years had passed when "the time drew near that Israel must die." He knew it, and called his sons together; and while they stood around, he gathered strength to bestow upon them his inspired blessing, prophetic of what should befall them and their tribes in future days. When he had finished, he gathered up his feet in his bed, and died. Joseph was there; and it devolved on him to close his dead father's eyes.

What follows, in the account of the obsequies of the patriarch, comprises various particulars which well deserve attention, from their bearing upon the usages of Egypt, and as showing the writer's true acquaintance with that country.

In the first place, we learn that "Joseph com-manded his servants the physicians to embalm his father." In speaking of almost any other country, one physician would have been thought sufficient for even so great a man as Joseph; but this was peculiarly appropriate to Egypt. What Herodotus says of the healing art among the Egyptians is here in point: "The medical practice among them is divided as follows: each physician is for one kind of sickness, and no more; and all places are crowded with physicians; for there are physicians for the eye, physicians for the head, physicians for the teeth, physicians for the stomach, and for internal disease."[1]

It ought not, therefore, to appear strange that Joseph had a considerable number of family physicians. "Every great family, as well as every city, must, as Herodotus expresses it, have swarmed with the faculty. A body of these domestics would now appear an extravagant piece of state, even in a first minister. But then we see it could not be otherwise, where each distem-per had its proper physician."[2] The Egyptian physicians were renowned in ancient times. Cy-rus had a physician sent to him from Egypt; and Darius[3] always had Egyptian physicians with him.

Something of the kind seems to grow up in every highly advanced nation. We have our-selves oculists, aurists, dentists, etc.; and although the general body of physicians and surgeons pro-fess to attend to all diseases, many of them rest their fame upon their peculiar study of certain classes of maladies.

The embalming is here performed by the ser-vants of Joseph, the physicians. But according to the accounts of classical authors, the embalmers were a hereditary and organized class of men in Egypt, among whom different duties were assigned to different persons. If, however, a proper dis-tinction of time be observed, there is here no contradiction. It is natural to suppose that the entire operation was in earlier times performed by those to whom a knowledge of the secret pro-cess was communicated. But afterwards, when the embalming was executed more according to the rules of art, a distinct class of operators gradually arose.[4]

The antiquity of the custom of embalming the dead in Egypt is well known. Mummies have

[1] Herodotus, ii. 84.
[2] Warburton's *Divine Legation*, iv. 3, 83.
[3] Herodotus, iii. 1, 129.
[4] Hengstenberg, *Egypt and the Books of Moses*, p. 71.

been found with the names of the earliest Egyptian kings. Various reasons have been given for the practice. An eminent French physician, celebrated for the extent of his knowledge, and for the zeal with which he has often confronted death in the pursuit of science, Dr. Pariset, attributes the origin of embalming to the care which was taken to prevent the bodies of the dead from undergoing putrefaction, which in a country like Egypt would often give birth to pestilence. To this he ascribes the absence, anciently, of the plague in Egypt, of which it has since become the headquarters. But this seems to be

MUMMY.

a pure conjecture; and it has not the advantage of any support from fact. If the Egyptians did embalm the bodies of the human species, and of the animals accounted sacred, they buried the remains of others, and that, too, at so little depth below the surface, that in burying the carcases of oxen, the horns were allowed to appear above the ground.[1] The plague, the first appearance of which cannot be traced back farther than to the fifth century before our era, desolated all Egypt at that time, before it passed into Greece, although the practice of embalming was then in full activity. It is clear, also, that the ancients ascribed to the scourge no such origin; for Strabo speaks of the pestilential maladies of Egypt as being caused by the exhalations from the marshes of the Delta.

[1] Herodotus, ii. 41.

It may also be remarked, that the religious ideas attached to the preservation of the human body are by no means peculiar to the Egyptians. That which may be conceded to them is the practice of a more costly and elaborate embalmment than was known among other nations. There is, indeed, scarcely any part of the world in which traces. of this usage have not been found.[1] The mode adopted by the Egyptians in the preservation of the body belongs to, and expresses the nature of, the soil which they inhabited, and was different from that of the Ethiopians from among whom it is now generally supposed that they came. The land produces no resinous trees; but natron is found in great abundance. This, therefore, was the material principally employed by them, in place of the vegetable resins in use among most other nations. The use of natron seems to have been universal during the earliest times; but the knowledge of foreign aromatics introduced more lately a kind of luxury into the embalmments of the rich and great, while the bulk of the people were disposed of by the more simple process,—inequality of *rank* being thus manifested even in the tomb.

It is stated in the text, that "forty days were fulfilled for him; for so are fulfilled the days of those who are embalmed." This is rather obscure; and we think that the Jewish translators of Genesis have understood it rightly by rendering —"And they [that is, the physicians] finished it for him in forty days, for this completed the days of embalming." The number of days here mentioned as required for embalming agrees with some codices of Diodorus, though Herodotus speaks of seventy days as required for the more expensive and durable process of embalming. But this account has reference only to the method followed at Thebes, while the text speaks of that employed at Memphis; and modern research has demonstrated that the mummies of Thebes greatly excel those of Memphis, and must therefore have required greater care and longer time in the preparation. It is moreover probable that the corpse of the patriarch was simply so embalmed as to stand the journey to Canaan, and did not pass through the process of making a mummy, as described by Herodotus; though that of Joseph himself, of whose embalmment we read farther

[1] See a curious collection of examples in Henry's *L'Egypte Pharaonique*, i. 328, 329.

on, doubtless was prepared in the most perfect manner then known.

The Egyptians mourned for the father of their vizier during seventy days. This included, doubtless, the forty days of embalming. The family mourning continued until after the body had been deposited in the sepulchre; and at the place of sepulture, the Egyptians joined in the grand and final act of lamentation. The classical writers give full details respecting the solemn mournings of the Egyptians for the dead, especially for those of high rank. The demonstrations of grief were of the most clamorous and violent kind; and the representations on the monuments confirm the information of the historians. "When a man died in a house—that is, if one of rank—all the females of his family, covering their faces with mud, and leaving the body in the house, ran through the streets, girded up, and striking their bare breasts, with loud lamentations. All their female relations joined them. The men beat their breasts in like manner, and girded up their dress." Diodorous gives substantially the same account, but adds, that they went about the streets in this manner until the body was buried; that they abstained from all pleasant and ordinary food, and also neglected their persons, and appeared in sordid raiment. Many of these ceremonies of mourning have been inherited by the modern Egyptians.

MOURNING BEFORE A MUMMY

The embalmment of the body prevented the need of haste in the actual interment. It was not, therefore, until the seventy days of general mourning had expired, that Joseph applied for permission to carry the body of his father for burial to the land of Canaan, alleging that Jacob had on his deathbed made him swear to do so. The king's answer, "Go up and bury thy father, as he made thee swear," gives us reason to suspect that but for this oath he would have hesitated to allow Joseph to depart. On this the Jewish

annotator, Dr. M. J. Raphall, remarks: "Jacob's foresight, prudence, and worldly wisdom appear unimpaired, when he is at the brink of the grave. He knows that the jealousy with which foreigners are regarded in Egypt, is strongly against their quitting the country after they have once been permitted to reside in it, and that communication with or return to Canaan might be considered particularly objectionable. He therefore exacts from Joseph an oath, which he knows the religious feelings and scruples of the Egyptians will not call upon him to violate. Thus Jacob not only secures his end, but Joseph stands exonerated from all blame, as the circumstance which compels him to solicit leave of absence is so solemn and so sacred, that it places him above all suspicion."

This must have been a very grand funeral procession—moving to a country which was distant three hundred miles—such a burial indeed as the world has seldom seen. There were not only the family of Israel, and not only the officers of the court, "the servants of Pharaoh," but "the elders of Egypt," or the grandees of the empire. There were also chariots and horsemen, so that, including the attendants taken with them by so many high persons, the camp was very great, as the text itself states. The terms would seem to suggest that the party was strong in a military point of view. There is a tradition among the Jews that Joseph contemplated the possibility of an attack from the family of Esau, which also claimed the cave of Machpelah; and that it actually came to a battle between the two parties, in which Joseph was victorious. Even in the present age, so rich a caravan could not pass through those countries without an armed escort, sufficiently strong to protect it against the predatory attacks of the desert Arabs. The object of the sacred historian is, however, simply to indicate the grandeur and magnificence of Jacob's obsequies, which indeed seem to be without a parallel in history.

"What hitherto has most affected me in the comparison," says Parker, "was indeed the noble obsequies of Marcellus, as Virgil has described them. But how do even these, with all the parade of poetry about them, fall short of the plain and simple narrative before us! Let the Campus Martius be as honourable among the Romans as they please. Let the honours there paid to that heroic youth, whom Augustus had adopted for his heir, be tenfold superior to what at the best they were. What parallel can there be between the procession and magnificence of both? What are the six hundred beds, for which the Roman solemnities on this occasion were so famous, in comparison with that national itinerant multitude, which swelled like a flood and moved like a river—to all Pharaoh's servants; to the elders of his house; and all the elders of the land of Egypt; all the house of Joseph and his brethren, and his father's house, the chariots and horsemen, and the whole retinue, conducting their solemn sorrows for near three hundred miles into a distant country? [1]

Two points in this interesting narrative require some further explanation. *First*, The embalming of Jacob; and *second*, The route taken by the funeral procession to Machpelah.

The Hebrew words may be thus rendered literally: "And they fulfilled for him forty days, for so they fulfil the days of the embalmed; and the Egyptians mourned for him seventy days." There were several modes of embalming; but it seems, from the length of time occupied, that the most expensive was in this case adopted; and the cost must have been about £250. The brain and intestines were first removed; then the body was filled with sweet spices, profusely anointed, sewed up, and steeped in natron for a considerable number of days. It was afterwards taken out, washed, perfumed, and finally wrapped up in bandages of linen covered with gum. By this long and laborious process the features were admirably preserved, and time effected little change upon them. Some of the mummies recently brought from the tombs of Egypt are so perfect, that could their friends see them now, they would have little difficulty in identifying them. We have reason to believe that the remains of the patriarchs have never been disturbed since they were laid in the cave of Machpelah, and consequently the embalmed body of Jacob may be there perfect to this day.

A strange mistake has been made regarding the route of the funeral procession from Egypt to Hebron. It originated in the statement: "They came to the threshing-floor of Atad, *which is beyond Jordan*." "Beyond Jordan" is the usual designation for the east side, and it is supposed to have that meaning here. Even such an accomplished geographer as Dean Stanley says, "They came not by the direct road which the patriarchs had hitherto traversed on the way to Egypt by El-Arish, but round the long circuit by which Moses afterwards led their descendants, till they arrived at the banks of the Jordan." [2] This would have been a most remarkable route for a procession composed of "all the servants of Pharaoh, the elders of his house, and all the elders of the land of Egypt." It would have been utterly impracticable, besides, for horses and chariots. The direct road from Memphis to Hebron is about two hundred and sixty miles; but the route indi-

[1] *Bibliotheca Biblica*, i. 977.   [2] *Jewish Church*, i. 74.

cated by Stanley would be at least seven hundred. The expression "beyond Jordan" evidently signifies the west side. Just as Moses prayed, when standing on the east side of the river, "Let me go over and see the good land *that is beyond Jordan*;" so, writing the narrative of Jacob's burial from the same point of view, he employs the same expression in the same sense (cf. Deut. iii. 25; Num. xxxii. 32; xxxiv. 14). We conclude, therefore, that the funeral procession journeyed direct across the desert of El-Tih to Hebron.

P.

THE CHOSEN PEOPLE

A NEW scene now opens to us. Between the books of Genesis and Exodus there is a considerable chasm, corresponding to the interval between the time of Joseph and that of Moses. At the remoter edge of this chasm, the Israelites, few in number, are seen peaceably seated among the good things of Egypt, in the land of Goshen; flourishing under the protection of a government grateful for the eminent services of Joseph. At the nearer edge we find the nation increased to a mighty host, but groaning under the oppressions of a government that "knew not Joseph."

But the purposes of God are ripening. And now that we enter upon a period in which the great doctrines of eternal truth—lost to the world, or smothered beneath the burden of man's inventions—are to be seen embodied in the institutions and muniments of one of the smallest of the nations, let us for a moment glance at a few of the questions which exercise the thoughts of those, who look closely at this condition of the world's affairs.

We have already had more than one occasion, in the course of these Daily Illustrations, to intimate that the object of the revelation made to Moses was to put the Jewish people in possession of a pure religion, and to place them in a condition to maintain it amid the corruptions of the earth, and eventually to become the instruments of communicating it, under more complete developments, to the rest of the world. It may be asked, and it has been asked, Why should so desirable a revelation, of the truths of which the whole idolatrous world stood so much in need, be limited to a single nation, and that a nation politically so unimportant? To this it may in the first place be answered, that to have a pure worship of God ascend but from one corner of the earth, seems even to human reason to be an object in all respects well worthy of the Divine wisdom, and in itself suitable to be accomplished. But when such questions are asked, we are always too much in the habit of thinking only of man's apparent advantage, as if there were nothing else to be taken into account. We are always measuring, not only earth, but heaven, by the standard of our own very scant knowledge, and of our own very limited ideas ; forgetting, or remembering but faintly, and expressing very delicately, as if only to round a period or to fill up a sentence, the great and solemn fact, that there is One higher than the highest, whose honour is not to be the second or the third, but the FIRST matter for consideration. If we look to this, we may see that the question of man's greater or less benefit is not always to be the first, and still less the sole object in every consideration of divine things : and although we, for ourselves, hold that man's most essential well-being has been marvellously made consistent with the highest glory to God's great name, it yet behoves us to consider whether *that* is not worthy of being an independent object—an adequate and sufficient object in itself ; and whether, as such, it might not most worthily be consulted by His worship not being allowed to be wholly banished from the earth.

But it is further asked, Why this revelation should have been communicated to the Jews alone, while other nations were not allowed to partake of its benefits ? Now, to this we have no right to expect an answer, further than as one may be furnished by observation of the whole course of divine providence. We might quite as well ask, why one nation enjoys a finer climate than another ? why among men there are native differences of talent and disposition ? why one man is made to live under a government which oppresses his mind, and another under social influences which give all his faculties free scope and excitement ? Why one man's religious interests are made from the first to flourish under the fostering influence of parental care, while another is exposed from infancy to every kind of moral contamination ? The question respecting the abstract justice of such inequalities, may or may not be one hard to answer ; but such as it is, it relates to the whole acknow-

ledged course of the divine administration of the world's affairs, and cannot therefore, with any propriety, be made a ground of distrust as to the divine origin or essential fitness of the Mosaic dispensation. It applies quite as much to Christianity as it does to Judaism ; and not more to either than it does to the endless variety of human fortunes and conditions.

This being the ordinary course of the divine government, which carries its final adjustments by the scale of justice and truth into a world yet future, where all apparent inequalities are to be settled and explained, it would have been a deviation from that course had not one part of the world, and one people, been in this instance and for this purpose preferred before another ; and, had the preference fallen on some other nation than the Jews, the same question would still have remained to be asked. The selection of that nation in particular, may or may not have been arbitrary. The later Scriptures, to discourage the conceit of the Jews on account of the peculiar honour put upon them, seem to urge that it was at least so far arbitrary, that it was for no peculiar and distinctive merit of their own that they were chosen ; yet the same Scriptures admit the privilege of their descent from the covenant fathers as a ground of distinction, which therefore merely carries this question farther back, to seek the grounds on which Abraham became the root of that covenant. Still, even if there were nothing (though there may have been something undiscoverable by us) in the capacities, character, conditions, and relations of this particular people, to account for the honour put upon them, we certainly are not historically acquainted with any other people better entitled to it on any conceivable ground of claim ; and it ought to satisfy the mind to know, that even if the Hebrews had no special fitness for this high destination, we know not of any nation which had more, or which could exhibit any preferable claims. Either way, there is nothing to excite surprise in our inability to see distinctly what it was that determined the divine preference of this nation ; nor does this raise any presumption against the fact, that such a preference was actually exercised.

It may also be observed that, in point of fact, the selection of one nation was not in this instance an exclusion of the rest of mankind. Other men, to whom the knowledge of this religion might come, were at liberty to adopt it if so inclined, and special provision was made for their admission to all the privileges of the chosen race; and we find, in both the early and later history of this nation, that proselytes from divers nations did in fact receive the religion, and came to stand in relation to it on the same footing as the descendants of Israel. But still further: the Mosaic institution, while it sternly refused on its own part to mingle with the various systems which corrupted the world, and strove to keep altogether aloof from them, was so far from excluding, in any conceivable sense, the mass of mankind from its benefits, that it was expressly designed to be ultimately for the benefit of all mankind, by being an introduction to Christianity—by preparing the way for a system which, in their existing state of culture, the nations could not have been made to embrace, without stronger compulsion than, in His dealings with the nations, God has ever yet seen fit to exercise. Men were then universally bigoted to idolatry; and to reclaim them eventually to better views, the fittest way for God to adopt—seeing that He always works by means—was to reclaim first a portion of mankind, by subjecting them to a minute and detailed discipline, only capable of being administered to a small community. Such was the system organized under the agency of Moses, a system well adapted to train one community to the profession of religious truth, which, when they were established in it, they would be fit instruments of communicating in an extended and spiritualized form to the world.

Far be it from us to think that God is bound to give us an account of any of His matters, or to make the path which He takes plain to our understandings. Many things there are that He has not seen fit to disclose clearly to us; and many there are that we have not the capacity of understanding, because they belong to another and a higher realm of thought and spirit than that of which we are for the present citizens. With respect to both, we may be content to feel that what we know not now, we shall know hereafter. It is nevertheless pleasant to be enabled to understand the reasons of His high dealings with the sons of men; and in *this* branch of spiritual knowledge, there is little that He has seen fit to withhold from us that may not be discovered in the careful consideration and comparison of His word, and of His past doings in the government of the world. In general, the reason why we do not see, is oftener because we are blind, than because it is dark.

Another question will probably be suggested to the thoughtful reader by the chasm in sacred history between Genesis and Exodus. Not a word is said of either the Israelites or Egyptians from the death of Joseph till the birth of Moses, a period of at least eighty years. Why is this? A wider examination of the Pentateuch occasions still more surprise. The book of Genesis embraces the history of about 3,400 years, while the four following books are taken up with the history of only forty years. Again, Genesis has fifty chapters. Of these, thirty-nine are occupied with the biographies of three men; while the remaining eleven contain a narrative extending over fully three thousand years. This peculiarity of Biblical history is not sufficiently considered; and the important conclusions to which it leads are not, I fear, generally known.

The sacred penmen are not mere historians. It was not their object to write history, or to become the biographers even of great and good men. They had a nobler work to do. They were the commissioned revealers of divine truth. Truth was unfolded not at once, but gradually, as men required it. God in His infinite wisdom did not see fit to develop a great system of abstract doctrines and laws. He made His revelation progressive; adapting each new ordinance, doctrine, and precept, to the circumstances of His people in successive ages. Hence the Bible was made to assume a historical form. It contains, however, not a political but a religious history; not a history of the world, but of those men and nations in the world who were the immediate recipients of revealed truth. The sacred writers, under the guidance of the Holy Spirit, selected for notice those, and those only, to whom God gave revelations, or who formed connecting links in the historical scheme of divine grace. And, still further, only such incidents even in their lives are recorded, as are calculated to show God's dealings with them, and through them with His church. Hence Scripture history, from a political point of view, is incomplete and fragmentary; but from a religious point of view, it is perfect.

Another aspect of the historical sketches in the Pentateuch ought not to be overlooked. They are typical as well as historical. All the leading personages whose histories are recorded were types of Christ and His church, designed of God to exhibit to the ancient Israelites the person, offices, and work of the promised Messiah. All the rites of the patriarchal and Mosaic economies were likewise types of our Lord and His kingdom. The most remarkable events and things also described in the Pentateuch were typical—such as the tree of life, the deluge and ark, Jacob's ladder, the Egyptian bondage, the smitten rock, and the brazen serpent. Looking at Old Testament history in this light, it becomes invested with a new interest. It is the shadow, of which the Gospel is the substance; it is the bud, of which the Gospel is the full-blown flower.[1]

P.

----

[1] See Porter's *Pentateuch and the Gospels.*

THE HARD BONDAGE

Exodus 1

WHEN we examine the numerous facts and incidents pictorially registered in the monuments of Egypt, and understand that some of them can be traced up to the time of Moses, the question naturally arises, Whether we may not hope to find among them some record of the events, so important in Egyptian history, connected with the residence of the Israelites in the land of Egypt, and their departure from it? As the principal and most ancient monuments of this kind are in Upper Egypt, we should not look for any memorials of that portion of public history with which the name of Joseph is connected in our minds, because that history belongs to Lower Egypt, which was not then, as we apprehend, under the same crown as the upper country. Neither should we expect to find any record of the remarkable circumstances connected with the plagues of Egypt and the exode of the Israelites; for, although the upper and lower countries were then under one crown, and although such events as the death of the first-born, and the overthrow in the Red Sea, were of sufficient national importance for such commemoration, we do not find that nations, and certainly not the Egyptians, manifest any readiness to perpetuate their own dishonour. But if there be any circumstance in the history of Israel's sojourn in the country which tends to exalt the power and glory of Egypt, of *that* we might not unreasonably expect to find some trace on the monuments.

Accordingly, the only representation which has been supposed by the students of Egyptian antiquity to bear any reference to the Israelites, exhibits them in the state of oppression and humiliation, when it became the policy of the new dynasty from Upper Egypt, "which knew not Joseph" and his services, to depress the Hebrew population, and reduce them to a servile condition, by making "their lives bitter with hard bondage, in mortar, and in brick, and in all manner of service in the field."

This representation, which has been regarded with great interest by scholars and travellers, is found painted on the walls of a tomb at Thebes. A copy and explanation of it were first furnished by the distinguished Italian professor, Rosellini,

in his great work on the monuments of Egypt. His account of it is headed, "Explanation of a picture representing the Hebrews as they were engaged in making brick." In this picture, some

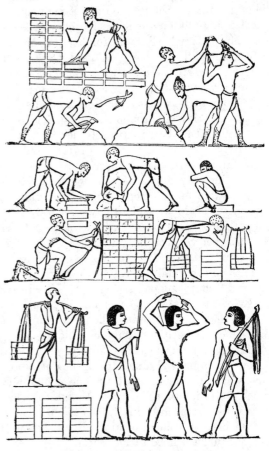

HEBREWS MAKING BRICKS, FROM TOMB AT THEBES

of the labourers are employed in transporting the clay in vessels; some in working it up with the straw; others are taking the bricks out of the moulds and setting them in rows to dry; while others, by means of a yoke upon their shoulders, from which ropes are suspended at each end, are seen carrying away the bricks already dried. Among the supposed Hebrews, four Egyptians, very distinguishable by their figure and colour, are noticed. Two of them, one sitting and the other standing, carry a stick in their hand, superintending the labourers, and seemingly ready to fall upon two other Egyptians, who are represented as sharing the labours of the supposed Hebrews.

This scene does certainly illustrate in all points the labours of the Israelites; for we are told, not only that they wrought in the making of bricks —which was a government work in Egypt, and bricks bearing the royal stamp have been found —but that the king "set over them taskmasters to afflict them with their burdens;" and that "all the service wherein they made them serve was with rigour." We also know that the bricks made by the Hebrews were compacted like these with straw; for at a later period we are told that the crown would not allow them the straw with which to compact their bricks, but left them to provide it for themselves, without the tale of bricks previously exacted being at all diminished: "And the taskmasters hasted them, saying, Fulfil your works, your daily tasks, as when there was straw." The straw was used to compact the mass of clay, and not, as some have supposed, to burn the bricks. These being only dried in the sun, which suffices in a dry climate, the straw, which would be destroyed were the bricks burned, remains perfect and undiscoloured in bricks nearly 4,000 years old. That the sticks of the taskmasters were no idle insignia of authority, is shown by the complaints of the Israelites: "There is no straw given unto thy servants, and they say to us, Make bricks; and, behold thy servants are beaten." (See the whole passage, Exod. v. 7-16.)

The picture is found at Thebes, in the tomb of a person called Roscherê. The question hence arises, How, if it represents the labours of the Hebrews, it came to be there, and in the tomb of this person? It is answered that Roscherê was a high officer of the king, being overseer of the public buildings, and consequently having charge of all the works undertaken by the crown. In the tomb are found other objects of a like nature: two colossal statues, a sphinx, and even the labourers who hewed the stone-works which he by virtue of his office had caused to be made in his lifetime. This great officer, being entombed at Thebes, any important labour in any part of the kingdom would naturally be represented there, for the kingdom was one, and the whole department seems to have been under his control; and it is now admitted that the inscription does not so expressly declare as was at first imagined, that the bricks were made for a building *at Thebes*. But even were this the case, the difficulty is not insuperable. It is true that the Israelites during their bondage occupied their ancient home (so far as the men were allowed to enjoy a home) in Goshen, which was far distant from Thebes; but we know of nothing, either in Scripture or elsewhere, which would confine their labours to Goshen. On the contrary, when they were ordered, in this very business of brick-making, to find straw for themselves, we are constrained to suppose that they were at work for the royal monopolist of this manufacture in all parts of Egypt; for in Exod. v. 12, we read, "So the people were scattered abroad *throughout all the land of Egypt*." This certainly does not convey the idea that they were making bricks in Goshen only. There is indeed reason, from other testimony, to suppose that the usage in the working of the Israelites was to send them out in gangs, or classes, under overseers, for a considerable time, making these gangs successively relieve each other; and there can therefore be no objection to the opinion, that some of these gangs may have been sent even so far as Thebes, for the sake of their work at the place where there was most demand for it. We may be certain that no considerations of humanity were likely to prevent this among such a people as the Egyptians. Indeed, it was evidently for the interest of the Egyptian oppressors, who alleged the *numbers* of the Israelites as the ground of their apprehensions, to scatter them in small bodies over all Egypt, as far as might be practicable.

Upon the whole, therefore, although it is not alleged that anything like positive certainty can be attained, there is nothing to render improbable the conclusion to which the complexion and peculiar physiognomy of the workmen, and the age of the monument, would lead, that these brickmakers were Israelites, and that they are represented in the act of executing the very labours which the Scripture commemorates. The complexion is such as the Egyptian artists usually give to the natives of Syria. The dress might have afforded some further and interesting evidence, as the artists were very particular in preserving the details of costume; for the figures are represented as unclad, save for the short trowsers or apron which they wear at their labour. It may be doubted, however, whether, after such long residence in Egypt—which was indeed the native country of all the Israelites of that age—they had preserved the style of dress which the single family of Jacob brought with it from Canaan. It is far more likely that they had by this time conformed, in this respect, to the habits of the country, which were better suited to the climate than any costume their ancestors could have brought from the less fervid climate of Syria. This also meets partly the objection which has been made to the want of beards in these figures. They are not to be regarded as strangers come recently to Egypt with all their foreign usages about them, but as tribes long settled in the country, many of the customs of which they had necessarily adopted. They may to some extent have adopted the Egyptian habit of shaving the beard, or such of them as were in government employment may have been constrained to do so. We have already [1] had occasion to notice that the Egyptians compelled their servants, of whatever nation, to shave their beards. In this representation, however, all the figures are not beardless. Upon the whole, we see no reason why the reader should deny himself the satisfaction of believing, that in this scene he contemplates a representation, by Egyptian artists, of the very scene which the sacred books describe. [2]

THE ADOPTION OF MOSES

Exodus 2:10

WHILE Israel lay under long and heavy oppression in Egypt, the man appointed to be the deliverer was born, and was undergoing the training requisite for the office he was destined to bear. This man was MOSES. The circumstances attending his deliverance by the king's daughter, are doubtless familiar to the reader. We shall therefore rather call attention to another matter of no small interest, concerning which we are left comparatively in the dark. This is the youth of Moses. We know that he was nursed by his own mother—not known to

[1] See Vol. 1, pp. 332-334.

[2] This subject is fully discussed by Rosellini, as above quoted by Sir J. G. W. Wilkinson, in his *Ancient Egyptians;* by Hengstenberg, in his *Egypt and the Books of Moses;* by Osburn, in *Egypt's Testimony;* and recently by an American writer, Dr. Hawks, in his work on the *Monuments of Egypt.*

be such—and that, when he was of a proper age, he was brought to Pharaoh's daughter, "and he

THE FINDING OF MOSES

became her son." This is all that we are told. The next verse resumes the history when he is forty years of age, and we know nothing of his circumstances and demeanour during that long period. It does appear, however, that he had spent this time among the Egyptians, and not with the Israelites; for we are told that he *then* (as if for the first time) "went out unto his brethren, and looked upon their burdens." It is respecting this interval that we would inquire.

That he became "the son" of the king's daughter, or that he was adopted by her, suffices to indicate the general course of his early condition and training. It must not, however, lead us to suppose that, as some fancy, he by this adoption became the heir of the crown. It is indeed very true that there was no Salic law in Egypt, and it was quite possible that the princess, who is said to have been named Thermuthis, might, in failure of male heirs, have succeeded to the throne. But it does not appear that there was any probable want of male heirs to the crown; and it is likely that, although the *adoption* of a foreign child of a race hated by the Egyptians may have sufficed to render him the heir to her private estate, it yet conferred upon him no political standing with reference to the crown. We cannot, however, speak with confidence on this point,—Indian history having recently afforded some striking evidence of the full equality, in the East, of adoptive with natural rights.

It has seemed to some a difficulty that so inveterate a persecutor of the Hebrews as this Pharaoh should consent to the adoption by his daughter of one of the very children he had doomed to destruction. We think it a sufficient answer that the crusade against the male children was probably over long before the time that the child was brought home and adopted by Thermuthis. Some, however, conjecture that the princess, though married, was childless, and was hence led to adopt the Hebrew infant, whom she imposed upon her father as her own son.

One short verse in Stephen's address to the Jewish council is our only further source of authentic information; and so far as it goes, it is in conformity with the traditionary accounts of the youth of Moses which have been transmitted to us, and may, therefore, to a certain extent, seem to authenticate them. The words are: "Moses was learned in all the wisdom of the Egyptians, and was mighty in words and in deeds." This certainly implies that he received the most learned and accomplished education which the world could then perhaps afford, and was put in possession, under the ablest teachers, of all the highly extolled, and anciently much desired, wisdom of the Egyptians. It also intimates that he was enabled to distinguish himself in some remarkable manner, both by "words," and by "deeds."

Now, the Jewish traditions which stand on record in Josephus and in the Midrash, are to this effect:—

It is clearly stated in Scripture that Moses was a very beautiful child. His comeliness was such, Josephus says, as to excite the pleasant surprise of all who beheld him. It frequently happened, he alleges, that those who met him as he was carried along the road, were obliged to turn again to gaze after the child; while those who were at work by the wayside left what they were about, and stood long in motionless admiration to behold him, so engaging were the charms of his infant countenance. Nor was his understanding less remarkably developed. It was much in advance of his years; and when he was taught, he manifested a quickness of apprehension quite unusual at his age; while the manliness of his conduct and demeanour bore promise of the greatness of his mature age.

Josephus and other Jewish writers, allege that the king's daughter having adopted Moses, introduced him to her father as one who was to become his successor, in case she were not blessed with children of her own. She is made to say: "I have brought up a child who is of a heavenly form, and of a generous mind; and as I have received him in a wonderful manner from the bounty of the river, I have thought proper to adopt him for my son, and the heir of thy kingdom." On this, the story runs on, the king took the child in his arms, and caressed him. In a pleasant way he took off his diadem and put it upon the child's head; but he threw it to the ground in a seemingly childish passion, and trod it beneath his feet. On this the monarch looked grave, discerning in this boyish act an evil presage for Egypt. This was confirmed by the sacred scribe then present, who declared that this child was born for disaster to the kingdom, and counselled that he should be forthwith slain. But Thermuthis prevented this, by hastily removing the boy; and even the king was not hasty in following such harsh counsel: "God Himself, whose providence protected Moses, inclining the king to spare him."

The Jewish and Moslem legends embellish this comparatively plain statement by informing us that the king commanded two bowls, one filled with Shoham stones (rubies), and the other with burning coals, to be brought; by means of which it would be seen whether the child had acted thoughtlessly or from reflection. If he seized the flaming coals, he should live; but if he took the glittering gems, he should die. This was done, and the child, endued with manly understanding, was about to grasp a handful of the gems; but God, watchful over his life, sent an angel, who invisibly, and against the child's will, directed his hand into the burning coals, and even caused him to put one into his mouth. By this Pharaoh was reassured, and apologized to Thermuthis; but Moses, it is added, was burned in the tongue, and was a stammerer from that day. This last incident is introduced to account for what Moses says of himself, Exod. iv. 10: "I am slow of speech, and of a slow tongue."

If the words which the Jewish historian subjoins to this statement may be regarded as supplying authentic information, they are very important, as showing—what we cannot learn from any other source—the point of view in which the position of Moses was regarded by the Hebrews on the one hand, and by the Egyptians on the other. "He was therefore educated with great care. The Hebrews depended on him, and were of hope that great things for their advantage would be done by him. But the Egyptians had doubts of what might arise from such bringing up. Yet because, if Moses had been destroyed, there was no one, either akin to or adopted by the royal family, likely to be of greater advantage to them, and who had any pretensions to the crown by oracular predictions,[1] they spared his life."

Amidst all this, one thing is very certain, that Moses was brought up as the son of the king's daughter. In regard to the ends which, in the providence of God, were secured by his being brought up in the royal palace, it may be observed that, according to the common course of things, no one, either Hebrew or Egyptian, but the king's own daughter would have been likely to dare to undertake, in the first instance, the responsibility of preserving a child devoted by the royal decree to destruction; nor was it possible, humanly speaking, that he should by any other means, in the existing condition of this people, have obtained the high education and training which he thus secured. By means of this princely education, he became a person most accomplished in his temper, demeanour, and intellect; he was also trained in that largeness of view and generosity of spirit which are supposed to result from such relations, and which qualified him to sustain with dignity and authority the offices of ruler of a people and general of armies, which eventually devolved upon him. This education, also,—involving, as it must have done, an intimacy with the highest science and philosophy of the Egyptian sages, was well calculated to secure for him the attention and respect of the Egyptians when he stood forth to demand justice for an oppressed race.

History proves that whenever God has a great work to be done in His church or in the world, He raises up a great agent to do it. Men of transcendent genius and special training have always appeared, on great emergencies, to carry out grand schemes of reform and deliverance.

[1] This alludes to an alleged previous prediction of the same sacred scribe who has just been mentioned. Before the birth of Moses, he had foretold that about this time there should be born to the Israelites one who, if he were suffered to live, would lower the power of Egypt, exalt the Israelites, and win for himself a glorious name.

The Scripture student can point to the familiar examples of Abraham, Moses, Samuel, David, Ezra, and Paul. Among Old Testament heroes, Moses is *facile princeps*. His genius was of the very highest order—profound, comprehensive, ready, practical. His education was in all respects the best then attainable. In addition to instruction in the simple and pure faith of the patriarchs, he was learned in all the wisdom of the Egyptians, then the most enlightened nation in the world; he was for many years under the practical teaching of the sage and prudent priest of Midian; while over and above all, he was in direct intercourse with Jehovah. Thus endowed and thus trained, Moses was able to grasp the most sublime truths; he was able to understand and develop a moral and political code which has formed the basis of all that is just and pure in the laws of modern nations; and he was able to lead a great nation safely through a series of struggles, privations, and appalling dangers, such as the world has never witnessed.

It is well to employ all the results of scientific research, and all the resources of scholastic learning, in the illustration of Scripture doctrine, and in the fuller delineation of Scripture characters. But I do not like the plan of mixing up mere silly legends with the grand historic facts of the Bible. Instead of shedding additional light upon them, it mars their beauty and strips them of their noble simplicity. I infinitely prefer that the few graphic sketches of Moses' birth and training, given in the Pentateuch by himself, and in the New Testament by Luke (Acts vii. 20-31), and Paul (Heb. xi. 23-28), should be placed before the mind of the Christian student alone, rather than that they should be combined with apocryphal and incredible stories culled from Jewish and heathen writers. I believe that thus we would be in a position to form a far juster and nobler estimate of his character and his work.

P.

EARLY DEEDS OF MOSES

WE know historically that Moses was "mighty in words and in deeds," *after* he received his commission to deliver Israel. But the declaration of Stephen clearly intimates that this was the case *before* he was forty years of age—before he visited the Israelites,—and therefore while he was still at the Egyptian court, and was still regarded as the son of Pharaoh's daughter. The information furnished by Josephus and other Jewish writers is, doubtless, such as was current at the time when Stephen uttered these words, which must be regarded as referring to facts held to be true by all those who heard him, and recognized as being at least substantially true by this reference to them. Indeed, it is not easy to see how, in the position which he occupied, Moses could be "mighty in deeds" but by rendering important public services—and those probably of a military kind—to the Egyptian crown and people. We are therefore somewhat inclined to take the Jewish accounts, and especially that of Josephus, as substantially true; and consequently as supplying an interesting *connection* of the several parts of the history of Moses. The Scripture, having only the object of setting forth those portions of his history which bore directly on his high mission, as connected with the Israelites, relates most briefly all that portion of his life which preceded his call in Horeb; and it altogether omits, or leaves to common sources of information, his life among the Egyptians. It may be added, that the account given by Josephus bears all the internal marks of authentic history, from whatever source the particulars may have been derived.

According to this account, the land of Egypt was invaded by the Ethiopians, who at first contemplated only an inroad for the sake of spoil. But having defeated the Egyptians in battle, and perceiving that the conquest of the country would be a less difficult enterprise than they had imagined, they ceased not until they had overrun the land—one city after another yielding to them, even to the walls of Memphis and to the sea.

The Egyptians, in the desperateness of their affairs, consulted their oracles, which were constrained by God to declare that their deliverance could only be effected through Moses. On this the king prevailed upon him to take the command of the army; and it seems to be inferred, as is indeed in itself probable, that the Hebrews acted with the Egyptians under his orders. We find the Jewish historian indicating the difference in the views with which this appointment was regarded by the Hebrews and Egyptians respectively. "The sacred scribes of both nations were glad." Those of the Egyptians, relying upon the oracle, hoped that the nation would be delivered by him, but trusted, that in the course of the inevitable conflict, he might by some management be slain. The Hebrews, on the other hand, calculated that under Moses, as a victorious general, they might take their departure with a high hand out of Egypt.

The course followed by Moses was to take the enemy unawares. Therefore, instead of march-

ing along the river, he conducted his forces inland, through a region which none would expect him to traverse, on account of the multitudes of fierce and venomous serpents with which it was infested. Moses, however, met this difficulty by an ingenious stratagem. He caused a large number of crates to be provided, in which were enclosed a multitude of that serpent-slaying bird, the ibis, formerly so abundant in Egypt,

THE IBIS

where it received sacred honours for its useful services to mankind. As, therefore, the army reached the land of the serpents, the birds were let loose, and cleared the way for the safe advance of the troops. Different readers will estimate differently the probability of this story. Those who have read the *Stratagems of War*, by Polyænus, will have found there accounts of contrivances quite as remarkable. This does not appear to us to offer any great difficulty. The ibis being a tame bird, might be secured in almost any number required for such a purpose; and both sacred and secular history evince that whole districts bordering on Egypt were grievously infested by serpents, so numerous as to form a very serious obstruction to the progress of armies. Being thus enabled to come upon the Ethiopians unexpectedly, and so to take them unprepared, they were soon routed and driven out of Egypt, pursued by the victorious army. The fugitive host at last threw itself into Saba, a royal city of Ethiopia, rendered impregnable by strong ramparts and surrounding waters, which in a later age received the name of Meroe. While the Egyptian army lay idle before this place, unable to bring the Ethiopians to battle, Moses unconsciously won the affection of the Ethiopian king's daughter, Tharbis, who had beheld his person, and witnessed his valiant exploits from the walls. She caused a proposal to be made to him, through the most faithful of her servants, that he should make her his wife; which he promised to do if she procured the surrender of the city. No sooner was this agreement made than it took effect. The city surrendered; Moses made the Ethiopian princess his wife; and having returned thanks to God, led the Egyptians back to their own land.[1]

The latter incidents of this account are remarkable. Josephus, who gives this notice of the acquisition by Moses of an Ethiopian wife, says nothing in the sequel of his history of the variance between Moses on the one hand, and his brother and sister on the other, on account of an Ethiopian wife that he had. (Num. xii. 1.) It is clear, therefore, that neither he nor his authorities devised this marriage to account for that variance. It is a fact which is not to him of any historical use. But the Scripture itself does record the misunderstanding between Moses and his relatives respecting an Ethiopian wife, without stating how he came to be united to her. This perfectly undesigned coincidence between the Scripture narrative and the Jewish historical tradition, does therefore give a material corroboration to the latter. Nor is this the only instance in which the silence of the one account is supplied by the declarations of the other.

All our readers have felt some difficulty in realizing to their own minds the circumstances under which Moses, who had just before been described as "the son of Pharaoh's daughter," appeared among his countrymen in Goshen apparently as an unattended and powerless man. If we turn to Josephus, we at first seem to get no satisfaction, as he omits this visit altogether, and makes Moses withdraw at once from the Egyptian court to the land of Midian. But it is yet possible to connect the reasons which he gives for that withdrawal with the actual visit to the Israelites. The historian states, that the renown which Moses acquired in this expedition made him seem more dangerous in high quarters, and roused the fears and the envy of the king. Plots were laid against his life; and, being daily pressed by the sacred scribes,

[1] See Josephus Antiq., ii. 10, pp. 57-58.

the king had nearly assented to his being quietly disposed of. Hearing of all this, Moses withdrew secretly from the court. Josephus says he retired to the land of Midian; but we know that he went first to visit his nation in Goshen. He perhaps expected to find concealment among them, until he could prevail upon them to follow him out of Egypt. That this was his object is clearly indicated by Stephen, who says, "he supposed his brethren would have understood that God by his hand would deliver them; but they understood not." If the Jewish historian is to be regarded as a sufficient authority for believing that they had been prepared to regard him as a leader and deliverer, when he appeared as a victorious general against the Ethiopians, we can perceive the grounds of the expectation with which he went among them; neither is it difficult to understand the views upon which they now declined to place themselves in revolt under the guidance of one who, at a time when circumstances were more favourable—when their hosts were in embattled array under his orders, and ready, in the ardour of triumph and invincible might, to follow where he listed—had refused to respond to their wishes. The reason of Moses' conduct under this view would be plain. He had in the first instance been the trusted servant of the Egyptians, and could not betray the high charge committed to him; but the base return he had experienced, left him at liberty to act without any reference to the ties of obligation and of public trust. He threw up his connection with the Egyptian court; he refused any longer to be regarded as the son of Pharaoh's daughter, and went to cast in his lot with the people of his fathers, whose sad condition engaged his sympathy, and whose great heritage of promises and hopes had more charm for him than all the riches, the honours, the power, and the wisdom of Egypt. But the time was not fully come; and the Israelites refused to recognize in the powerless fugitive, clad only in his inherent greatness, the leader they would have hailed with shouts as the commander of armies and the son of Pharaoh's daughter.

It is thus, as we apprehend, that the Jewish accounts may be made to supply the silence of Scripture, and that the details may be woven into one consistent and harmonious whole.

MOSES IN MIDIAN

Exodus 2:15-22

WHEN Moses repaired to the land of Goshen, we may be sure that the movements of one who, according to the most authentic accounts, must have been a person of great consequence, could not fail to be regarded with solicitude at the Egyptian court; and considering the jealousy his position excited, and the fears his national ties engendered, it is more than merely probable that his doom was left to be decided by any marked indication he might furnish of his feelings and intentions. Such an indication, his slaying an Egyptian, for the protection of an oppressed Israelite, soon afforded; and it was one that could not be mistaken by the court. It manifested a sympathy for the oppressed Hebrews, and an abhorrence of their oppressors, which in such a man could not but be regarded as dangerous. It was, therefore, probably far more on this account than for the mere homicide, that the king no sooner heard of this fact than he sought his life. If any weight is to be attached to the account yesterday produced from Josephus, it is open to us to infer that this circumstance, as used by the enemies of Moses, wrung from the king that consent to his death which had hitherto been refused. Indeed, Moses so well knew what he had to expect, that he no sooner became aware that his deed had transpired, than he fled for his life, and rested not until he came to the land of Midian, which lay upon the eastern arm of the Red Sea.

His introduction to the connections he formed in that place, and to the life he led there, is strikingly illustrative of the usages among pastoral people, and reminds one of Jacob's transaction with Rachel at the well of Haran. In this case, Moses came to a well belonging to a place in the land of Midian. While he sat there to rest and refresh himself, the seven daughters of Jethro, the "priest," or "prince of Midian,"[1] came to water their father's flock. They drew the water,

[1] The original Hebrew word has both meanings, and it is uncertain which of them is here the correct one—perhaps both—as the offices were generally united in ancient times. It is best to regard Jethro as a sort of emir or sheikh, exercising for his people the sacrificial duties which constituted priesthood.

and filled with it the troughs from which the sheep drank. All this time the stranger, known by his garb to be from Egypt, and regarded as an Egyptian, sat by, without proffering his aid, as Jacob had done to Rachel. But presently, when certain shepherds came with their cattle, and drove away the women and their flock, taking for their own use the water they had drawn, the stranger, whose hatred of oppression and high-handed wrong had been already shown, even unto death, rose in his might, and with strong words, if not with blows, scared away these churlish shepherds, and helped the damsels to water their flock. We see in this, as in other instances, a trait of the character of Moses. He does not think of rendering, nor does his courtesy lead him to proffer, services where they are not actually required. The sense of DUTY is always needed to *compel* him: but when thus compelled—when his aid or his services are really wanted, who so zealous, who so strong, who so regardless of self as he? We see this characteristic pervading the history of Moses. We see it here. He sat quietly by, until he had a duty to perform; until his blood was quickened even to tingling by the tyranny of the strong; and then he became as another man—active, powerful, valiant, polite, laborious: whatever faculty or power God had given him, whatever gift or talent he had acquired, nay, the whole man was instantly at the service of duty, the moment it became clear to him. If we look closely to his career, we shall see that this was the sort of person—the very man—that was required for the great duties which were hereafter to devolve upon him.

But we must not quit the well. Our minds linger over the scene which took place there as one of the most picturesque and interesting of the numerous indications of Eastern manners and habits which the Pentateuch affords. The immense value of water; the labour of raising it; the disputes arising from conflicting claims to preference in watering—all are points which, at this day as of old, produce transactions precisely analogous to those which the books of Moses have recorded. We could quote many examples from Eastern books. A striking one occurs in an old Arabian romance, written more than a thousand years ago, in which the customs of the pastoral tribes are most vividly depicted. The Daji mentioned in it is the head or managing slave of the king's eldest son; and the anecdote altogether is an apt illustration of the water tyrannies practised in the Arabian wilds.

"One day the poor men, the widows, and the orphans met together, and were driving their camels and their flocks to drink, and were all standing by the water side. Daji came up, and stopped them all, and took possession of the water for his master's cattle. Just then, an old woman, belonging to the tribe of Abs, came up, and accosted him in a suppliant manner, saying: 'Be so good, Master Daji, as to let my cattle drink. They are all the property I possess, and I live by their milk. Pity my flock; have compassion upon me; grant my request, and let them drink.' But he paid no attention to her supplication, and abused her roughly. She was greatly distressed and shrunk back. Then came another old woman, and addressed him: 'Oh, Master Daji, I am a poor, weak, old woman, as you see! Time has dealt hardly with me; it has aimed its arrows at me, and its daily and nightly calamities have destroyed all my men. I have lost my children, and my husband; and since then I have been in great distress. These sheep are all that I possess; let them drink, for I live on the milk that they produce. Pity my forlorn estate. I have no one to tend them; therefore grant my supplication, and of thy kindness let them drink.' But in this case the brutal slave, so far from granting this humble request, smote the woman to the ground." When the then untried young hero Antar witnessed this, he, Moses-like, felt his choler roused; he struck the ruffian, and engaged in a conflict with him, which ceased not until the oppressor lay dead at his feet.

It seems that Jethro's daughters were subject to the kind of molestation from which they were in this instance delivered by Moses; for when, on their return home, their father expressed his surprise at their being so early, their answer implies that they had been this time freed from a customary hindrance: "An Egyptian delivered us out of the hand of the shepherds, and also drew water enough for us, and watered the flock." It seems difficult to understand how the daughters of one who held the station of emir or priest, should have been subject to such oppression. It may be that the shepherds were Bedouins, who at this season came up with their flocks to this neighbourhood; and, being stronger than the ordinary inhabi-

tants, paid little respect to their rights of water. The Mohammedan writers suppose that Jethro (whom they call Shuib) was a worshipper of the true God, living, like Abraham in Canaan, and Lot in Sodom, among idolaters who hated him, and who lost no opportunity of testifying their dislike, and of doing him harm. It is difficult to say which has the greater probability; but either supposition will very well account for the readiness with which Jethro and his family eventually abandoned this settlement, and went with the Israelites into Palestine. That they *there* retained the habit of dwelling in tents (Judg. iv. 11), when the Israelites themselves inhabited houses, shows that they were tent-dwellers in Midian; and not such as, like Laban in Haran, and Job in the land of Uz, abode in houses, while retaining the essential habits of pastoral life.

It is usually understood among us, that the service thus rendered by Moses to Jethro was the cause of the hospitable treatment he received from that person. A nice perception of oriental ideas of hospitality will, however, teach us that it was merely the proximate cause, in so far as it led the daughters to mention the fact that there was a stranger needing hospitality; but we apprehend that, had no such service been rendered, his treatment would have been the same. The eastern writers, looking at the matter from their own point of view, so explain it; clothing, as usual, their ideas in the form of an addition to the narrative. "Moses," say they, "consumed with hunger, did not touch the refreshments which were set before him; and when Shuib inquired why he rejected his hospitality, he replied, 'I am not of those who accept a reward for any good deed that I have done.' 'Neither,' replied Shuib, 'am I of those who show hospitality only to their benefactors. My house is open to every stranger; and as such, not as the protector of my daughters, thou mayest accept my invitation.' Moses then ate until he was satisfied.'

It was probably in consequence of the communications he then made to his entertainer—letting him see that his journey had no definite object, and that he sought nothing but a safe and obscure home—that Jethro proposed to him to remain there and take charge of his sheep, which would prevent the recurrence of such unpleasant adventures as had that day been witnessed at the well.

The circumstances are very similar to those of Jacob at Haran. The eastern writers make that resemblance greater even than it appears in the sacred narrative; for he is by them supposed to have served eight or ten years for his host's daughter, Zipporah. As he certainly espoused the maiden, the supposition is not unlikely, seeing that the "price" of a wife in the East is always exacted in some shape or other; and it does not appear that Moses had aught but his time and services to give. Jethro was but little likely, in the case of a stranger, to dispense with the payment which Laban exacted from his own nephew.

Where was the "land of Midian?" The question is not so easily answered as it might at first sight appear. The Midianites are met with on the eastern frontier of Palestine, and on the northern border of Egypt. Both land and people took their name from one of Abraham's sons by Keturah. (Gen. xxv. 2.) It is plain that the country inhabited by Jethro, when Moses went to him, and then called "the land of Midian," was in the Peninsula of Sinai. It was while watching his flock on the side of Horeb, that he saw the glory of the Lord in the burning bush. It would appear, however, from a comparison of the several incidental notices of Jethro in the Pentateuch, that the Peninsula of Sinai was not his settled place of abode. When Israel was encamped at Horeb, Jethro brought thither Moses' wife and two sons; and, after a brief stay, "he went his way into his own land." (Exod. xviii. 1-3, 27; Num. x. 29.) The Midianites were nomads, roaming over a wide region, but, like most Arab tribes, having one permanent nucleus. This nucleus was specially their home; it was the "land of their kindred;" yet they also claimed the whole region in which they pastured their flocks as their own. The nucleus of the Midianites was somewhere on the eastern border of Edom, but their pasture grounds extended probably as far as Bashan on the north and the Red Sea on the south. Hence Horeb was said to be in the land of Midian (Exod. ii. 15; iii. 1); while it is also said that Jethro left the camp of Israel at Horeb, "and went his way into his own land," that is, to the chief seat of his tribe on the east of Edom. The Midianites were accustomed to lead their flocks and herds over the whole of that region which the Israelites afterwards traversed: the choice pastures, fountains, and wells were all known to them. This throws light on Moses' urgent request to his father-in-law: "Leave us not, I pray thee; forasmuch as thou knowest how we are to encamp in the wilderness, and thou mayest be to us instead of eyes." (Num. x. 31.)[1]

P.

[1] See Kitto's *Cyclopædia of Biblical Literature*, last edition, *s. v.* Midian.

THE CALL

Exodus 3

FORTY years were spent by Moses in the land of Midian. This is an important period in the life of any man; and to Moses, who reached the age of one hundred and twenty years, it was the middle period of life—the period of strongest action, of sternest realities, of most resolute purposes. Yet to him it was the period of least apparent action, during which he lived in seclusion and quiet, preferring to such scenes as he was once familiar with the humble duties of pastoral life. He married; he had two sons; he led his flock to the pastures and the waters. These few facts form, as far as he is concerned, the history of that period of life which is to other men the time of the most energetic action. The common course of life was to him reversed. Without relying too much upon the traditional history which makes the first of the three periods of forty years each, into which his life may be divided, one of high and heroic action, it may be observed that the last period, which is one of repose to most men, was to him the most undoubtedly active in all his existence; and the days of his quiet repose and secluded rest did in his case precede instead of following the days of his labour.

Yet during these years he was in all probability happier than at any other period; happier than when in Egypt, as the son of Pharaoh's daughter, he received the homage of servile crowds, while his heart yearned sore after his father's house, and he knew himself to be the object of secret dislike and envy to those who bowed before him; happier than when in later life the burden of Israel lay upon him, and he felt that burden most hard to bear. At least, thus we may think; but the consciousness of high responsibilities and of solemn duties, although it may seem to involve mental disquietude, and to be attended with great labour, has to many, and probably had to Moses, satisfactions more than commensurate with the enjoyments of secluded life and humble vocations. Moses, perhaps, knew not this; and his seclusion was so pleasant to him, that the idea of quitting it to encounter the storms and high tasks of active life was most alarming to him, when first presented to his mind.

It is, however, only by comparison with what afterwards devolved upon him, that the life of Moses during these forty years may be called obscure or easy.

"How various his employments, whom the world
    Calls idle!"—*Cowper.*

The duties of pastoral and domestic existence, though they involve not the labours and responsibilities of him who stands out to take a part in the public life of nations, are still sufficient to occupy, not unpleasantly or uselessly, the time and attention of any man of moderate desires and simple tastes. It is a life, moreover, that affords much leisure for thought and meditation, and hence the distinction which men of pastoral habits have on many occasions acquired. The two greatest men in the Old Testament, Moses and David, were both called from following the sheep to be the leaders of God's flock—His Israel. There is nothing improbable in the supposition that Moses employed a portion of the leisure, which in this state of life fell to him, in composing some of those admirable books which he has transmitted to the church, and which will form a most inestimable portion of its heritage to the end of time. It is almost the general opinion of the church that the book of Genesis was, during this period of repose, written by him; and those who hold him to be the author of the book of Job, think that it is to this time of his quiet sojourn in Midian that its composition should be assigned. Indeed, the book is throughout impregnated with the ideas and usages of the kind of life which he during this period led. But there are many who doubt whether that book was the production of Moses. This is a question we have not here to discuss; but if the book was written by him, *this* is the period of his existence to which we should be disposed to fix its composition.

How Moses enjoyed the kind of life he led, and how little he desired to quit it for a wider and grander field of labour, is shown by the manner in which he received the call to proceed to Egypt for the deliverance of Israel. He had led his flock to the green pastures which were to be found in the valleys and beneath the barren declivities of the Sinai mountains, when his eyes were attracted by a remarkable phenomenon. He beheld a bush in flames, and although, as he watched, it burned fiercely, it remained unconsumed. This was truly a "great sight;" but as he went near to inspect it with closer attention, a Voice from the bush commanded him to show the common mark of oriental respect to a superior presence, or holy spot, by taking off his sandals, and standing barefoot—for the place on which he stood was holy ground. He then knew that the Lord's presence was manifested there; for it is His presence that maketh holy. He obeyed; and stood wondering, no doubt, what manner of communication awaited him. He might, however, have seen, in that moment's thought, that the bush burning, yet unconsumed, was an apt and striking symbol of the Israelites in Egypt, of whom it is said, that the more they were afflicted the more they grew. The communication was emphatic and solemn. The speaker announced Himself as the God of Abraham, of Isaac, and of Jacob. He declared that He had beheld with divine compassion the miseries of His people; and that the time, the long appointed time, for their deliverance was come. All this was well. It doubtless made the heart of Moses glad. But the closing words filled him with consternation, for it declared that he was to go back to Egypt, to present himself before the king then reigning, and to demand for Israel leave to depart. This filled him with unfeigned astonishment. "Who am I, that I should go unto Pharaoh, and that I should bring forth the children of Israel out of Egypt?" The answer was undeniable and sufficient—"I will be with thee." Still Moses was not satisfied. The difficulties of the enterprise—his own supposed unfitness for it—his reluctance to plunge into the conflicts he foresaw,—all crowded upon his thoughts, and made his heart sad. One objection after another that he produced was condescendingly removed; yet, when he had nothing further to urge in the way of specific objection, he rolled the whole mass of reluctant feeling into one strong groan for release from so fearful a task: "O my Lord, send, I pray Thee, by the hand of him whom Thou wilt send." But he was the man appointed for that task; for this he had been born; for this preserved; for this trained; and there was no escape for him. God knew his fitness better than Moses knew it himself, and the command imposed upon him an imperative obligation.

An interesting writer thus remarks upon the reluctance of Moses to accept the most important office—the deliverance of an oppressed nation—

ever offered to man:—"Many causes may be assigned for this reluctance. Moses had reconciled his mind to his condition, with which he was contented. He knew too well the court of Egypt, to have any desire to return to it, especially with a hostile purpose. He had no wish to become the chief of a multitude of miserable slaves, not fit for war, and not trained to submission under a mild and equitable government. He saw no means of supporting such a multitude in a march across the desert of Palestine, even if they should escape the hostility of the Egyptians; and no probability that at the head of such invaders he could conquer Palestine. But, above all, Moses had no adequate faith in his Employer, the speaker from the burning bush. That Employer might possess all power; but could Moses rely on being able, at all times of his need, to command the exercise of that power? It is clear that this distrust was at the bottom of the extreme reluctance shown by Moses to accept of the commission to rescue the Israelites; for, afterwards, when he found himself supported and backed by that Being under whom he acted, his proceedings were prompt, and his courage and zeal never failed."[1] The fact is, that there is a great difference, as an incentive to enterprise, between the general and the particular promises of God. There may be some promises, the fulfilment of which depends upon certain conditions, and there are others to which no condition is annexed. To be the messenger of the former is indeed a glorious ministry, but it is also humbling and dangerous. He upon whom God confers it, may live in perpetual fear of promising something in God's name without effect, because they to whom the promise is made may be wanting in some of the conditions required of them. But nothing can dishearten a man to whom a commission of the second kind has been given, because the infallibility of the event strengthens him against all the obstacles he meets with in his way. Moses seems to have been afraid that the unbelief of the Israelites might in the end prove a bar to their deliverance; and it is against this fear that God encourages him, and condescendingly points out facts to satisfy him that the result is determined in his counsels, independently of all events and all conditions. He not only promises,

[1] Forsyth: *Observations on the Books of Genesis and Exodus*, pp. 88, 89.

He foretells; He particularizes the nicest and minutest circumstances; He not only acquaints him that the people shall be delivered, but indicates the exact place—the very mountain before which he stood—where they shall pay their homage to their Deliverer, after their deliverance has been accomplished. This detail becomes to him a token of the certainty of the event, and then at length he is satisfied.

"The place whereon thou standest is holy ground," were words addressed to Moses at the burning bush. If we could identify the spot, we certainly should feel that its associations gave it a singularly sacred character. A chapel is shown in the convent of St. Catherine, at Sinai, built by the empress Helena, said to cover the "ground" on which grew the bush, at once symbolic of the Divine presence, and of Israel's destiny—"burning with fire yet unconsumed." No authority can be attached to the tradition, and where the bush stood it is impossible to determine. It is worthy of note, as an indication of the writer's acquaintance with the natural history of the desert, that not the palm, but the acacia (*seneh*), still to be seen in the neighbourhood, is represented as the subject of the miraculous appearance. (*Student's Old Test. Hist.*, 107.) It is one of the convent legends, that from the *Gebel ed Deir*, a mountain height of the great range, a sunbeam darts once a year into the chapel, lighting up the scene of the Mosaic wonder. When Dr. Stanley ascended *Gebel ed Deir*, he found it, he tells us, of all spots of the kind, "the best suited for the feeding of Jethro's flocks in the seclusion of the mountain." (*Sinai and Palestine*, 76.) There a deep cleft opens upon the convent, through which light may at a certain time fall on the chapel—a circumstance which accounts for the legend. The solitude of the spot is very awful, and well illustrates the accompaniments of the divine sign, in the sweeping valleys and the soaring hills, which must have surrounded Moses, when the call came to him from heaven.

Keble, in the *Christian Year*, thus describes what the appointed Leader of Israel witnessed:—

> "Far seen across the sandy wild,
>   Where like a solitary child,
>   He thoughtless roam'd and free,
>   One towering thorn was wrapt in flame—
>   Bright without blaze it went and came;
>   Who would not turn to see?

> "Along the mountain ledges green,
>   The scattered sheep at will may glean
>   The Desert's spicy stores;
>   The while, with undivided heart,
>   The shepherd talks with God apart,
>   And, as he talks, adores."

THE DEMAND

Exodus 5

THE state of Egypt had so far changed during the long interval of forty years since he fled the country, that Moses knew that he incurred no personal danger in making his appearance. All those were dead who had sought his life, or to whom he had been an object of dislike or envy; and if they had been still alive, there was nothing in his existing position to awaken their ancient and bygone resentments. It must not be supposed that, when he reappeared in Egypt, it was forgotten who and what he had been, or that he made any concealment of it. His very name, so peculiar and distinctive, and his connection with his brother Aaron, who accompanied him as his spokesman, must have suggested the fact. It is probable that it was the knowledge of his former connection with the court, which procured him more ready access to the king, and enabled him to speak to that haughty personage with greater freedom, and to win from him more attention than any other Israelite could have secured. The knowledge of his thorough Egyptian education may also have obtained for him more respect than might have been shown to any one who could not boast a privilege which they so highly appreciated. He was in their view an educated man, while all the other Israelites were probably little more in their sight than an uneducated rabble, being ignorant of that which was to them education. In all countries *education* is held to consist in the knowledge of certain things, and he who knows not these is held to be uneducated, whatever else he may know.

There were therefore no difficulties in the way of Moses but such as resulted from the nature of his mission; and he appeared under advantages which no other Israelite could claim. Nevertheless, the enterprise upon which he had entered must have seemed hopeless to him, had it not been for the strong assurances with which he had been favoured. The reception which his application obtained at the Egyptian court was calculated to discourage a less assured spirit. He preferred his request in this simple and mitigated form: "Thus saith Jehovah, the God of Israel, Let my people go, that they may hold a feast unto me in the wilderness." The king's answer is short, and terribly decisive: "Who is Jehovah, that I should obey His voice to let Israel go? I know not Jehovah, neither will I let Israel go." We are not to infer from this that Pharaoh was an atheist. Atheism was not the religion of Egypt —which had gods all too many—but the king knew not the name of Jehovah as a god; and regarding Him as the special and particular God of the Hebrews, he saw nothing in their condition to convince him that this God possessed such power as to make it imperative upon him to obey. It therefore behoved the Lord, through the agency of His commissioned servant, to set forth His power in the eyes of the Egyptians, and convince them that the demand came from One whose high behests were not to be despised. Thus He might show them the vanity of the idols in which they trusted, and vindicate the honour of His own great name.

This is the *argument* of the great transactions which followed. It amounted to a contest for power between the idols of Egypt and the God of Israel. The result would show with whom the power and the glory lay; and the name of the Lord, which they knew not, and which they had despised, would be magnified in the sight of the Egyptians. The king did not deny the existence of Jehovah, or that He had authorized such a demand as Moses made in His name; but regarding Him as the national God of the Hebrews only, he considered that Egypt had stronger gods of its own, who would not fail to protect him from whatever anger the God of the Israelites might evince at the neglect of a mandate so contrary to the interests of the nation which claimed *their* guardianship. We see much of this reasoning among idolaters in the sacred Scriptures—as in the case of the Philistines, who supposed that their god Dagon had prevailed over Jehovah when the ark was taken;[1] and as in the case of the Syrians, who fancied that they had been beaten because the God of Israel was a god of the hills, whereas theirs were gods of the valleys.[2] In both these cases, as in the present, the honour of Jehovah was engaged to protect His high name from such disparagement.

Now it appears that during the long time Moses had been away, although individuals had been changed, the policy of the Egyptian court towards the Israelites had remained unaltered.

[1] 1 Samuel 4:7-5:2.   [2] 1 Kings 20:23,28.

They were kept under the same condition of oppression and degradation as at the birth of Moses. They indeed retained the occupation of the territory originally assigned them; and within that territory possessed the rights of private property in flocks and herds, and in the products of the ground, although, doubtless, all were subject to heavy taxation. The grievance was, that a large number were required to be constantly supplied to labour, for little more than their food, upon the public works—in the making of bricks, in the building of cities, and in the culture of the ground. They probably served a few months at a time in alternating gangs; and the intensity of the oppression must have consisted in the excessive hardships to which the persons actually out on the service were exposed, the increased labour which devolved on those at home, in consequence of the high proportion of the hands required by the government, and in the liability of the whole to serve in their turn. They were drawn, probably, something after the manner of the militia with us—all being liable, but such as could afford it procuring substitutes instead of serving in person. The number required in proportion to the population was probably such that all were required for actual service in due rotation, excepting those who were exempted by age or infirmity, such as even the Egyptians would exempt on account of their social standing in the offices they exercised, and such as had wealth enough to pay for exemption.

In the dispensations of the Lord's providence, it often happens that the afflictions of His people become the most grievous when the day of their deliverance draws nigh, as the darkest hour is that which precedes the break of morning. So it was now. The king affected to regard this application as a mark of disaffection, created by too much leisure and too little work, and he directed new burdens to be laid upon them. The form in which the increased burden was imposed is remarkable. Hitherto they had been supplied with the materials of their principal labour of brick-making—the clay and the straw; but it was now directed that the straw should be withheld, and yet that the exacted tale of bricks should be in no wise diminished. This was hard. It was impossible to make bricks without straw; and the time consumed in collecting it would not allow the tale of bricks to be provided within the

appointed time. This difficulty increased; for in proportion as the straw they could provide was diminished, they had to go to greater distances to gather the stubble of the fields instead. This implies that they had used up the chopped straw which had been reserved as food for their cattle, and had now to gather, with much toil and loss of time, the stubble of the distant fields, which, although useless for any other purpose, might serve as straw in the making of bricks. The story of their wrongs was thus carried throughout the land; and there is reason to suppose that the sympathies of the Egyptians as a body were engaged on their behalf, and that the proceedings of the government were not generally approved.

The result was, that the taskmasters, who were responsible to the government for the production of the bricks, reprimanded, and even beat, the Hebrew overseers, who were accountable to them. The beating is a striking incident, characteristic of the people; for one needs only to look into a book of Egyptian antiquities, to see how freely the stick was administered to people of all ages, and of either sex, among the Egyptians. In fact, from the evidence which this people have themselves left to the world in their monuments, it would seem as if Egypt was, as much as China or Persia at the present day, ruled by the rod. The overseers were at length urged to carry their complaints to the king, supposing, perhaps, that this rigour had been imposed upon them by the taskmasters without his consent. But if this were their impression, they were soon undeceived. The stern answer was, " Ye are idle, ye are idle: therefore ye say, Let us go and do sacrifice to Jehovah. Go therefore now and work."

Thus the intended deliverer of Israel was led to experience the lot which often befalls good men in the best of causes. Their interference only aggravates for the time the evil they hoped to remove; and they themselves become odious to the people whose hopes they have excited, and who ascribe the increase of their burdens to their blind and blundering zeal. So it was now. The people were indignant at the interposition which, however well intended, had produced results so disastrous; and hard as their condition had been before Moses came among them, they now looked back upon it with regret, as a state of comparative ease, and considered that, as they emphatically declared, the brothers had put a sword into the hand of the government to slay them.   Moses himself was greatly distressed, and complained to the Lord, " Why is it that Thou hast sent me?" The answer reassured him. " Now shalt thou see what I will do to Pharaoh," began the response, and it went on with promises of high deliverance and special favour. Moses went to make known this encouragement to the people; but—and the observation is impressingly suggestive—" they hearkened not unto Moses, for anguish of spirit and for cruel bondage."

JEHOVAH

Exodus 6:3

In the Lord's encouraging words to Moses, we find this remarkable declaration: "I appeared unto Abraham, unto Isaac, and unto Jacob, by the name of God Almighty (El Shaddai), but by my name JEHOVAH was I not known to them." This declaration is calculated to surprise the reader, who, by a slight exertion of memory, will recollect occasions on which that name is so used in the history of the very patriarchs named, as to imply that it *was* known to them. Nevertheless these words are true, and the only difficulty is in apprehending the sense in which they are to be understood. There are two explanations, each of which has so much probability in its favour, that by regarding either as tenable, we find ourselves rather embarrassed between the choice of two sufficient explanations, than at a loss to find any explanation. This proves to be often the case when we come to examine closely the alleged difficulties of Scripture. It will be found to be so in most of the cases of this nature to which we may have to call attention; and the relief afforded in these instances by the more earnest consideration of the subject, will be extended to other cases which may not come under our notice; for, if explanations can be given in some few remarkable examples, it will justly be dèemed that other cases of the like nature are equally free from insuperable difficulty.

It is held by some, that the words in question are to be taken in their most strict and literal sense, and that it is consequently affirmed, that the ineffable name of Jehovah was altogether unknown to the ancient patriarchs, and was first revealed to Moses at the burning bush, where, when he asked the name which he should announce to Israel, God declared Himself by the sacred designation, " I am that I am," which is of precisely the same origin and import with " Jehovah;" and then said of the name JEHOVAH, " *This* is my name for ever, and this is my memorial unto all generations." The advocates of this opinion are not unaware of the objection to their view, derivable from the presence of the name in the book of Genesis; but they urge that there is no evidence that the book of Genesis was written until after the divine appearance to Moses at Horeb, where this great name was first revealed; and the mere fact of making use of the name in that book, is no sufficient proof that the name was known to those of whom he writes, any more than the mention of a place called " Dan," in the time of Abraham (Gen. xiv. 14), proves that the place, which we know was at that time called " Laish," was then known by that name. It is further urged, that since Moses wrote both for his own age and for the ages to come, it was highly proper that, in writing the history of the Hebrew nation from the earliest period, he should use, by anticipation, that peculiar name by which the Most High was known to them as their God—the very same God who brought them out of Egypt, and who, just before that event, had made the name known to them as that by which he would especially be called, in memory of that great event.

Still, there are passages in which the patriarchs are represented as expressly addressing the Lord by this very title of Jehovah. We have an instance of this in Gen. xv. 2, where Abraham says, Lord GOD [1] (*Adonai*-JEHOVAH), what wilt Thou give me ?" It is supposed, according to this view, that such passages are corrupted in the original text, and that later transcribers have substituted " Jehovah " for " Elohim," or " Adonai," which Moses probably wrote. In further support of this opinion, it is urged that, had the name been already known before it was disclosed to Moses at Horeb, and had it been the common appellation of the God of the patriarchs, the question of Moses, " Behold, when I come unto the children

[1] Here the word JEHOVAH, usually translated by LORD, is rendered GOD, because Adonai, which is usually rendered by "Lord," is joined to it. It would have been much better to have put it as " Lord JEHOVAH."

of Israel, and shall say unto them, The God of your fathers hath sent me unto you; and they shall say to me, What is His name? what shall I say unto them?" (Exod. iii. 13), would have been needless, for God had before told him that He was the God of his fathers—the God of Abraham, the God of Isaac, and the God of Jacob. It is hence clear that Moses knew not that He had any particular name, and that this name JEHOVAH was now for the first time announced as that by which He would be known as the covenant God of the Israelites.

But there are those who rather understand the words of this declaration as implying, not that the literal name JEHOVAH was unknown to the patriarchs, but that its true, full, and complete import had not been disclosed to them; whereas henceforward the chosen people would come to understand it practically, experimentally, devoutly, in all its deep meaning and significance. Now, it is to be understood that the name JEHOVAH denotes not only God's eternal existence, but His unchangeable truth and almighty power, which give life to His promises by the actual performance of them. The fathers believed in the things that were promised. They "were persuaded of them, and embraced them, and confessed that they were strangers and pilgrims on the earth;" but they did not experimentally know them in their actual accomplishment. But now the time was come for the doing of that which had been decreed and promised, and the name Jehovah should no longer be known to them, as to the fathers, in its dead letter, but in its living and realized truth. Accordingly, in the words which immediately follow, and which may be regarded as explanatory of this declaration, the Lord proceeds to pledge himself to the immediate and complete fulfilment of his ancient promises. In corroboration of this view, we are referred to divers passages in which God is said to make Himself "known" under this august designation of Jehovah, by bringing to pass the grand predicted events of His providence.[1]

[1] These are examples: "And the Egyptians shall know that I am JEHOVAH, when I stretch forth my hand upon Egypt."—Exodus 7:5. "In this shalt thou know that I am JEHOVAH: behold, I will strike with the rod that is in mine hand upon the rivers, and they shall be turned to blood."—Exodus 7:17. "And they shall know that I am the LORD (JEHOVAH), when I shall have executed judgments in her, and shall be sanctified in her."—Ezekiel 28:22.

It is hence contended, that the words in the place before us are to be understood not as an absolute but as a comparative negative; for that the literal name "Jehovah" was known to the ancient fathers is undeniable, from the various passages in which the name occurs, and especially from Gen. xxii. 14, "And Abraham called the name of that place Jehovah-Jireh," a text which it is absolutely impossible to reconcile with the hypothesis of corruption or of anticipatory use, which the other interpretation alleges. It must be admitted that such comparative modes of speech are not unfrequent in Scripture. A remarkable instance, stronger than the one here contended for, may be found in Jer. vii. 22, 23: "I spake not unto your fathers, nor commanded them in the day that I brought them out of the land of Egypt, concerning burnt-offerings or sacrifices: But this thing commanded I them, saying, Obey my voice, and I will be your God, and ye shall be my people." Now, it is certain that such commandments regarding ritual service were given at the time of Israel's deliverance; but what the prophet means to say by this strong mode of statement is, that in the commandments which were enjoined far more importance was attached to moral than to ritual obligations.

The reader has now the principal explanations of this important and certainly difficult text before him, and will be enabled to judge for himself which of the two is the more probable. Our own view is, that the interpretation in this, as in other cases, is the most correct, which takes the text of Genesis as it stands, and requires no supposition of alteration by transcribers, or of an anticipatory but not strictly correct use of the sacred name in that portion of Scripture. In judging between various interpretations, that is most probably the right one which agrees best with the sacred text as we now have it in our hands. The alterations of transcribers, especially in regard to proper names, are possible, and have in some cases been proven; but we must not assume their existence while any other explanation, which dispenses with this necessity, is possible.

The most plausible form of the objection against the antiquity and unity of the book of Genesis has not been mentioned by Dr. Kitto. As it has of late been urged by Colenso and others with great force and learning, and as it is in part founded on Exod. vi. 3, it cannot well be overlooked in this place. It is affirmed that the book of Genesis is a compilation, of which an ancient document forms the basis. To this document the name *Elohistic* is given, from the fact that in it the Divine Being is uniformly called *Elohim*. It is affirmed that it must have been written previous to Moses' alleged interview with God at Horeb, as described in Exod. iii. To this document another is said to have been added as a supplement; the latter being termed *Jehovistic*, because God is in it called *Jehovah*. And it is affirmed that the Jehovistic document must have been written after the time when, as represented in Exod. iii. 14, the name *Jehovah* was first revealed. Such is the fundamental principle of what is called the *document hypothesis;* but in its development sceptical critics have differed as widely from each other as from the plain historical truth.

I admit that there are traces of distinct documents in Genesis. The English reader can discover them by glancing at the following passages: Genesis i. 1; ii. 4; v. 1; vi. 1; vi. 9; vii. 1; x. 1, &c. I admit that they exhibit some slight differences in style; and that in some of them God is called exclusively *Elohim*, while in others the name *Jehovah*, or the compound *Jehovah-Elohim*, is given to Him. I deny, however, that these facts warrant us in concluding, either (*first*) that the book of Genesis as it now stands was of a comparatively late date, or (*second*) that Moses was not its author. Is it not reasonable, and is it not in accordance with analogy, to suppose that Moses, in writing his history, embodied, under divine direction, authentic and inspired documents handed down to him from the patriarchs? I deny also that the statement in Exod. vi. 3 was intended to convey the idea that the name Jehovah was previously unknown. It may be well, as the subject is of great importance, to explain this point more fully than Dr. Kitto has done.

The name *Jehovah* signifies, according to its etymology, "the eternal, self-existent, immutable God." But we can form no idea of abstract immutability. Hence this name is chiefly used in connection with promises and historical development. It is intended to assure man that what God is, He was—what He said, He will do. Hence the appropriateness of that name as given to Moses at Sinai. (Exod. iii. 14.) The very name conveyed the assurance that the God of Abraham was the *same* God still to His people; that what He promised to Abraham He would now perform. This explains Exod. vi. 3, "I am *Jehovah;* and I appeared unto Abraham, unto Isaac, and unto Jacob, by the name *God Almighty;* but by my name JEHOVAH was I not known to them." This does not mean that the name Jehovah was entirely unknown to the patriarchs, but that the full development of the name's meaning had not been exhibited to them. The glorious attribute of *immutability* was not yet displayed in connection with promises between whose announcement and fulfilment a long and almost hopeless interval had elapsed. To the patriarchs God was especially exhibited as *El-Shaddai*, "God Almighty," providing for and protecting them. To the Israelites at the Exodus He was exhibited as *Jehovah*, "The Immutable," fulfilling all His promises after a lapse of five centuries. In Mal. iii. 6 we read, "I am *Jehovah*, I change not;" in which it may be noted that the attribute of *immutability* is embodied in the name, and

that it is connected with the promise of the Messiah, in the fulfilment of which that attribute was most wonderfully exemplified.

P.

THE CONTEST

Exodus 7:1-14

THE contest has now begun. Its object is to impress upon the mind of Pharaoh the conviction that the God of the Hebrews—the Jehovah whom he "knew not," and to whom he refused obedience—was one whose power was far too great to be safely defied,—so great, that his own gods could afford him no protection from it. In proportion to his obstinacy, the manifestations of divine power must become more terrible, until at last the severity of the judgment shall wring from him the consent, so long withheld, to the departure of the Israelites—the glory of the Lord having, in the process of working this result, been magnified in the sight of all Egypt. From the nature of the case, the conflict could only be one of miracles; which also, from the nature of the case, must increasingly become miracles of judgment. These miracles Moses and Aaron were commissioned to execute. It would then be naturally expected by the king, that the servants of his own gods would perform the like mighty works, in order to show that their gods were not less powerful and efficient than the God of the Hebrews. The conflict was precisely of the same nature as that between Elijah and the priests of Baal, except that the latter were unable, from the circumstances by which they were surrounded, or from their ignorance of the high secrets in art for which the Egyptian priests were always famous, even to simulate the miracle they vainly called upon their god to execute. The conflict was here between the might of the Lord and the "wisdom" of Egypt. The triumphant result accomplished the twofold object of compelling the king to acquiesce in the demand made in the name of Jehovah, and of assuring the minds of the wavering and timid Israelites, that they might safely entrust themselves to the guidance of Moses, at whose word these wonders were wrought. Some are apt to wonder that Pharaoh's heart was so very hard, as that he was not by the result rendered a worshipper of Jehovah, nor indeed awakened to any distrust of the existence of the gods he served. But this was not the effect intended to be produced. He looked not upon these things as those who do know that there is but one God—that One who by Moses and Aaron spoke to him ; but he regarded the matter as a polytheist, who believed that he had gods of his own, as the Hebrews had theirs. The ultimate effect of the failure of the Egyptian magicians, would be to convince him, either that the God of the Hebrews was more powerful than he had at first supposed, or, which is more probable, that he had incurred the displeasure of his own gods—that they refused to interfere— and that it was *their* will that the Israelites should depart. We may hence conceive that he held out so long and so obstinately, in the hope that his own gods would at last relent, and put forth in the behalf of their worshippers the power which he still believed them to possess. That this *was* the effect produced on his mind, is shown by the fact that, after he had been compelled to consent to their departure by the most awful judgment ever inflicted upon a nation, he no sooner heard that the Israelites had made what appeared to be a false step in the direction of their march, than he concluded that his own gods had at length begun to move in his behalf, and hastened to pursue them—to his own undoing. If the conviction of the supreme power of Jehovah had been wrought before he consented to the departure of the Hebrews, this step would hardly have been taken.

In examining the miracles which constituted the memorable " plagues" of Egypt, we are placed at some disadvantage from our still imperfect knowledge of the mythology of the Egyptians. We can see in one or two cases, that the inflictions were such as to bring disgrace on the gods of Egypt, and we may believe that the others bore in some way not only upon the material comfort, but the religious ideas, of the people. From the want of this knowledge, much of the intended effect of these miracles is lost to our apprehensions, as we are only able to regard them in their material relations, which to the Egyptians themselves were probably not the most significant part of them. Had the accounts been given more in detail, this obscurity would not exist; but details were unnecessary for the information of contemporaries, and the want of them, it is likely, would

long continue to be supplied by the reports which went down from father to son.

It is not our intention to investigate fully all these miracles, but we shall point out some considerations in connection with each of them, that appear likely to interest the readers of these *Daily Illustrations*.

Moses and Aaron presented themselves before the king, who seems to have required them to produce some sign by which their mission might be authenticated. Aaron then, by divine direction, threw down his staff, and it immediately became a serpent. This was a sign well suited to the understanding of an Egyptian king, considering the extent to which serpents figured among the symbols and objects of his faith. He, however, sent for his wise men and sorcerers ; and now the contest between the Jewish leaders and the court of Egypt fairly began. The "wise men" threw down their staves in like manner, and they also became serpents. How was this accom-

NAJA HAJE, THE ROD-SERPENT OF EGYPT

plished? The question recurs as to the subsequent performances. Some think that, by the power of the evil one, these acts were really performed as represented, while others hold that they were feats of legerdemain, or produced by great skill in the natural sciences. The latter is our own belief. Thus, in the present case, the taming of serpents so as to conceal them about the person, and substitute them, by a sudden movement, for something held in the hand, is well known to be in the East, at the present day, one of the most common arts of jugglery. This, we should say, was what was done in the instance before us. The mere appearance of the transformation of a rod into a serpent by an adroit and rapid concealment of the one, and production of the other, is certainly an illusion fully within the compass of the art of modern serpent charmers, and may be conceived by any as a delusion which may be practised upon the senses. There is, in fact, a serpent in Egypt, which, by a particular pressure upon the neck, known to the serpent charmers, becomes so intensely inflated as to be quite rigid and motionless—not unlike a staff. It may in that state be held out horizontally, without bend or flexure; but, on being again touched in a particular manner, it recovers from its trance, and returns to the state in which it was before. May not this serpent have been employed by those Egyptians? In this case, the difference between the real and the pretended miracle lies here, that while the real serpents of the wise men assumed the appearance of rods, the real rod of Aaron became a real serpent; and, when both were opposed in a state of animated existence, that the rod devoured the real living animals, thus conquering the great typical representation of the protecting divinity of Egypt.

It is obvious that these men had opportunity for preparation. It is to be presumed that, in summoning them to the king's presence, they were informed of what had been done, and of what they would be expected to do. But something happened that they were not prepared for, and that could not enter into their calculations. They were consequently baffled. "Aaron's rod swallowed up their rods," and we do not read that they either attempted to prevent this, or to follow it by an imitation. By this, and by the serpent reverting to a rod when Aaron took hold of it, it was shown that the power which he exercised was unspeakably superior in its nature to theirs, and that it was far above all delusive art. Even serpents do not naturally devour each other; neither, were that the case, could one serpent devour many; and, from the very nature of the circumstances, the act of one serpent eating others could not have been a delusion. The feeding of serpents is always a slow operation; and in this instance it was watched by most keen and suspicious eyes. Had the serpent of Aaron merely become a rod again, this also they might have imitated, either by jugglery, or by availing themselves of the natural qualities of the serpent, to which we have referred; but the ultimate swallowing of their serpents by that of Aaron placed the transaction out of the reach of their experience, and beyond the resources of their art.

THE BLOOD AND THE FROGS

Exodus 7:15-8:15

THE transaction of Moses and Aaron with the wise men of Egypt, seems to have made no impression upon the king favourable to the claim of the Israelites, although it may have satisfied him that Moses and Aaron were no common men, and were invested with extraordinary powers. Some have thought that he regarded them merely as skilful conjurors; but if, as was doubtless the case, he believed his own magicians to act by the power of the gods, it is far more probable that he regarded the brothers as acting by the power of *their* God. If, however, as we believe, the magicians were themselves impostors, producing by art effects which they ascribed to the power of their idols, it is quite likely that *they* supposed Moses and Aaron to be merely more skilful adepts than themselves, until at length effects were produced so evidently, even in their view, beyond the simulations of human science, as to draw from them the memorable confession, "*This* is the finger of God."

The future acts were to be of judgment, since that which was merely demonstrative had been disregarded. Considering the estimation in which the river Nile was held by the Egyptians, who regarded it as a god, it is not without meaning that the first judgment smote that god, and rendered its most pleasant and salubrious waters noisome and pestiferous. Aaron, acting as usual for his brother, "lifted up his rod, and smote the waters that were in the river, in the sight of Pharaoh, and in the sight of his servants; and all the waters that were in the river were turned into blood. And the fish that was in the river died; and the Egyptians could not drink of the river; and there was blood throughout all the land of Egypt." We do not suppose that there was actual blood, but that the water became red as blood, and acquired such properties as not only destroyed the fish, but caused the Egyptians to loathe to drink from that stream which they, not without reason, regarded as affording the most delicious water in the world. Nothing was better calculated to humble the pride of Egypt. However, the magicians tried to produce the same result, and so far succeeded as to assist the king in hardening his heart against conviction. One would think that they might much better have evinced their power by removing the plagues, than by attempting to increase them by their imitation. But this they could not do; and it better suited their policy to produce, on a small scale, something that looked like the real miracle. Did we not know the extent to which confidence in persons blinds the eyes to their actions, it might seem amazing that the king found any satisfaction in their simulated operations; for they must necessarily have been on a small scale in comparison with the mighty deeds of the Hebrew brothers, whose interposition he was in every instance compelled to implore for the removal of the plague. That the imitations of the Egyptian magicians were on a small scale, and, although marvels to antiquity, were quite within the limits of modern science, is clear in every instance. In the present case, it is distinctly stated that this blood-like water filled the river, and consequently all the canals connected with it. This, indeed, is expressly declared, for the "streams" mentioned besides the Nile could be no other than these canals, seeing that Egypt has no other river than the Nile. This is further shown by the fact that the people could only obtain water fit for any use by digging for it. Now, the immense scale on which this miracle was performed, rendered any delusive imitation of it on the same large scale absolutely impossible, and indeed precluded even the attempt of any such imitation. The mass of waters being already changed, all that the wise men could have to practise their impostures upon was a limited quantity obtained by digging along the river's bank. That they were able—with the preparation they could easily make, in consequence of Moses and Aaron having threatened the act beforehand—with a small quantity of water so obtained and produced, perhaps in a vessel, to exhibit by means of some red infusion, a very humble copy of what had been done, is a circumstance which ought to occasion no surprise. Any chemist could do the same thing at this day.

In fact, we historically know that the ancients had the means of so dealing with colourless liquids, that they should shortly, on exposure to the air or light, assume the appearance of blood, or of other colours desired. A striking instance is that of Marcos, the leader of one of those sects which, in the earlier ages of the church,

endeavoured to amalgamate with their doctrines peculiar dogmas and rites of imitation. On one occasion he filled wine cups of transparent glass with colourless wine: during his prayer the fluid in one of these cups became *blood-red;* in another, purple; and in a third, an azure blue.[1] At a later period, a well might be seen in an Egyptian church, the waters of which, whenever they were placed in a lamp, became of a sanguine colour.[2]

The continued obstinacy of the king caused God to send upon him and his people the plague of frogs. These by no means agreeable

EGYPTIAN FROGS

animals came up at the command of Aaron from the river, "and covered the land of Egypt." They were everywhere: in the king's house, in his bed-chamber, in the houses of his servants, upon the persons of his people, in his very ovens and kneading-troughs, so that his very food was tainted with their abominable presence. The fact that these noxious vermin were thus prompted to forego their natural habits, and instead of confining themselves to the waters and moist soils, to spread over the country and make their way into the driest and most frequented places, indicates the countless numbers in which they came forth; and this is still further confirmed by the

[1] Epiphan. *Contra Haeres,* i. 24.
[2] Macrizi, cited by Quatremere in *Mem. sur l'Egypte,* i. 419.

immense heaps of their carcases which eventually corrupted the land. There is always an abundance of frogs in the Nile and its marshes; and here the miracle seems to have consisted in their quitting in swarms, at the appointed hour, the localities best suited to their nature, and extending themselves in all directions. An active Dutch imagination might work out for itself the probable details of such a visitation, and has done so in fact, in the highly singular prints of a work in four folio volumes, which lies before us.[1] Here one may see the people—men, women, and children—contending with besom and staff, with fire and torch, against the monstrous nuisance. The frogs are seen upon everything of food, which people bear along, and women cast them forth in dense masses from their water vessels and their tubs. Some flee before them, some dance them under foot. Dogs seem inclined to contend with them, but flee astonished when the frogs spring strongly against them. But the storks and cranes are fluttering with gladness, and hold a mighty feast among themselves amid the general confusion and dismay.

Here the same remark applies as was made before. We are told that the magicians produced in some way the same apparent results; but it is clear that the most they could do, under the circumstances, when in the precincts of Pharaoh's court they pretended to copy the act of Moses, was to practise their imitation on a small space of ground, artificially cleared of the presence of the offensive reptiles for this very purpose. What they were undertaking to produce, already existed in noxious abundance all around them. What they proposed to bring in, was with difficulty kept out; and under these circumstances, it is ascribing very little indeed to their knowledge of *pharmacy* (the phrase of the Septuagint), to suppose that they were able to use some substance to attract into the vacant space some specimens of an animal whose instincts and habits could not but be well known to them.

In this case, also, a creature held in honour by the Egyptians was made the instrument of their affliction, and they were compelled to regard it with disgust and horror. In the Egyptian mythology the frog was an emblem of man in embryo. There were also a frog-headed god and goddess —the former supposed to be a form of Pthah, the creative power. The importance attached

[1] *Mosaize Historie der Hebreuwse Kerke.* Amsterdam, 1700.

to the frog in some parts of Egypt is shown by its being embalmed and honoured with sepulture in the tombs of Thebes.

Under the plague of blood, pure water might still be obtained, though with cost and labour; but from this plague of frogs there was no respite nor relief. In their houses, in their beds, at their tables, the Egyptians were incessantly infested by these hateful intruders; and whatever numbers of them were destroyed only infected the air by their stench, while their places were filled up by fresh numbers, so that the very lives of the people became a weariness to them. No longer able to endure this, the king humbled himself to the brothers so far as to promise that, if they would intercede for the removal of the frogs, he would comply with their demand. This is a striking acknowledgment of the power by which he was afflicted, and may have been wrung from him to silence the gainsayers of later ages. To render the character of the visitation still more conclusively manifest, Moses allowed the king himself to appoint the time when the frogs should be removed. He named the morrow. It may be asked why he did not urge the instant removal of so great a nuisance. He probably thought that some time was needed for the intercession of Moses and Aaron with their God; or perhaps he cherished a latent hope that the frogs might meanwhile take their departure, and that he might thus obtain some ground for distrust and disobedience. But it was not so. At the hour appointed, and not before, the frogs died away in all the places where they were found. Had they been simply driven off to the waters whence they came, it might have been urged that they had come and withdrawn in obedience to some natural instinct; but their sudden destruction closed the door to that age and to this against such attempts to weaken the force of the miracle.

GNATS AND BEETLES

Exodus 8:16-32

THE third plague which the continued obduracy of Pharaoh brought upon the land was of *gnats;* for such seems to be the true meaning of the word which the authorized version renders by "lice." It, however, suffices to know, that some small and noxious insect was intended. Aaron in this case was directed to take his rod and "smite the dust of the land;" and forthwith "all the dust of the land became gnats throughout the land of Egypt." The terrible nature of this immense production of gnats can only be truly appreciated by those who know the degree in which the *ordinary* presence of these creatures tends in the East to embitter life. But another reason than this probably dictated the choice of this form of infliction. We find that even the magicians were baffled by it, and were obliged to acknowledge the hand of God in it; and it was probably to constrain this result that this minute instrument of torture was fixed upon. It is very striking that the acknowledgment, not extorted by the blood-like waters nor by the visitation of frogs, was constrained by a creature so small and insignificant. But not in this instance only has God, in the dispensations of His providence, made use of the things that are despised to bring down the pride of the high and honourable. It was such a visitation as, from the nature of things, the Egyptian magicians were unable to simulate. We can ourselves detect where their difficulty lay; and the fact of their failure in the first case that presented real difficulty, clearly shows that all their doings were tricks and contrivances, and not, as some have fancied, real miracles wrought by the aid of demons.

On this occasion, for the first time, we do not read of any summons being sent to the wise men, or of any kind of warning being given to them, so that now they had no longer the advantage of preparation in carrying on their frauds. Further, if they were to proceed as before, in an imitation of Aaron's work, the size of the insect which they were to appear to produce, in some space cleared for the purpose, was such that, to discern it, the eye of the spectator would have to be brought close to the scene of their operations, thus increasing greatly the difficulty of deluding the sense. Under these circumstances, after an attempt designed to sustain the appearance of confidence on their part in the arts which they professed, the wise men were fain to give up the contest, and to aver that there was superhuman power at work. "*This*," said they, "is the finger of God;" or perhaps more correctly, "of the gods," for the word is plural, and the use of it by polytheists gives it here a plural signification. After this admission they never ventured to renew the contest, and they probably rejoiced in being thus released from the necessity of exposing their credit to great danger, and their arts to detection, in the continuance of the struggle.

In the next plague the divine agency became more distinctly visible, so as to show that it was not only the work of the "gods," but of the very God of the Hebrews, in whose name Moses and Aaron acted and spoke. This was a most important circumstance, leaving the obduracy of the king altogether without excuse. It mattered comparatively little by what agent a fact so momentous was evinced. Indeed, there is more difficulty in deciding what animal was made use of in this plague, than in settling almost any question relating to the other plagues; nor, perhaps, will the point be ever satisfactorily determined. The word is, in our authorized version, translated "swarms *of flies*," the word "flies" being in italics to show that it is not in the original. In the description of this plague by the Psalmist, the same Hebrew word (AROB) is translated "divers sorts of flies." (Ps. lxxviii. 45.) The word is generally supposed to signify a mixture of some kind or other. By the Jewish writers it is generally supposed to denote "a mixed multitude of noisome creatures," or a swarm of different wild beasts. That they were not flies seems to be clear from the passage just referred to in the Psalms, in which they are said to have "devoured" the Egyptians—which term seems unsuited to flies; while in the very text which denounces and describes the judgment the ground is said to be full of them, or covered by them—a term certainly inapplicable to flying insects. It appears, however, from the manner in which the visitation is described in Exod. viii. 21, 22, that some particular *species* of creature must be designated; and, upon the whole, although no certainty is attainable, we retain the impression which we long ago had occasion to express,[1] that the creature designated is no other than the Egyptian beetle. All the indications agree therewith, and it was a most fitting instrument for the humiliation of the Egyptians, seeing that this creature, which most persons regard with dislike, was held in high honour and worship among that singular people, and the figure con-

[1] *Pictorial Bible*, note on Exodus 8:22.

tinually occurs in their monuments; it was, in fact, a sacred creature, and a most prominent one with them. "A great portion of Egypt," Pliny says, "worships the Scarabæus (Egyptian or sacred beetle) as one of the gods of the country; a curious reason for which is given by Apion, as an excuse for the religious rites of his nation—that in the insect there is some resemblance to the operations of the sun." In fact, the beetle was an emblem of the sun, to which deity it was peculiarly sacred; and it is often represented as in a boat, with extended wings, holding in its claws the globe of the sun, or elevated in the firmament as a type of that luminary in the meridian. Figures of other deities are often seen praying to it when in this character. It was also an emblem of Pthah, or the creative power; it was, moreover, a symbol of the world; and it is frequently figured as an astronomical sign, and in connection with funeral rites. In some one or other of the various acceptations in which it was honoured, its figure was engraved on seals, was cut on stone as a separate object, and was used in all kinds of ornaments, particularly rings and necklaces. Some of the largest of these carved figures frequently had a prayer or legend connected with the dead engraved on them; and a winged beetle was generally placed upon the bodies that were embalmed according to the most expensive process. The beetle was not only venerated when alive, but was embalmed after death, and some have been found in that state at Thebes. Considerable ingenuity has been exercised in order to discover the real sacred beetle of Egypt, and to ascertain to what extent other species may have partaken of the honours paid to that one. These questions do not require discussion here. It may suffice to observe, that the species usually represented appears to be the *Scarabæus sacer* of Linnæus, which is still very common in every part of Egypt.[1] It is about the size of the common beetle, and its general colour is also black; but it is distinguished by a broad white band upon the anterior margin of its oval corselet. Perhaps the most remarkable, and certainly the most gigantic, of the ancient Egyptian representations of the sacred beetle is that in the British Museum, carved out of a block of greenish coloured granite.

The exhibition of these venerated vermin as their tormentors—invading them in their most

[1] Wilkinson's *Ancient Egyptians*, v. 256, 257.

EGYPTIAN SACRED BEETLE

land was corrupted" by their immense numbers —must have been painful and humiliating to the Egyptians, who had no choice but to crush under foot, to sweep away from their houses and streets, and to regard with loathing, in the aggregate, creatures that separately they adored. It may be feared, indeed, that this had little salutary effect upon them. But the Lord thus won for His great name glory over the Egyptians and their idols; and the results which they witnessed could not fail to strengthen the faith of the Israelites in the God of their fathers, and to teach them that there was none with Him, nor any like Him. This must, in after time, have been impressed upon all their recollections by these marvellous transactions; and as there is reason to apprehend that they had contracted during their long stay in Egypt some reverence for the idols of that country, and too much intimacy with its system of worship, the immediate lesson which was taught them, through the humiliation of the Egyptians and their gods, was of very great importance.

The word translated "lice" in our English version, and "gnats" by Dr. Kitto, is only used in the description of this plague. Its etymology is unknown. It is probably of Egyptian origin. Hence the difficulty of ascertaining its exact signification. Its equivalent in the Septuagint is σκνῖφες, which may either signify "fleas" or "gnats." Philo describes the insect thus: "It is of very small size, yet exceedingly annoying; for not only does it injure the surface, causing intolerable and protracted itching, but it also penetrates the nostrils and ears. It flies into the eyes and injures the pupils, unless one takes great care.[1] This description would seem to be especially applicable to a little insect well known in Egypt and Syria as the "sand fly." It is much smaller than the mosquito, and its sting is more irritating.

P.

[1] *Life of Moses*, i. 19.

MURRAIN AND PESTILENCE

Exodus 9

THE peculiar nature of the fourth plague, and the intensity of the evil, brought Pharaoh into great perplexity. On the one hand, neither he nor his people could any longer endure this affliction; and on the other, he had no disposition to allow the Israelites to depart. He therefore struck out a compromise, or half-way measure, by which he hoped to surmount the difficulty. He sent for the Hebrew brothers, and told them that they might go and sacrifice to their God, but that they must do it in the land of Egypt. This, however, Moses declined, on the ground that the hatred and even violence of the Egyptians would be excited, were they—as must be the case—to offer in sacrifice the very animals that they venerated. This is the usual interpretation of the words of Moses : " Shall we sacrifice the abomination of the Egyptians before their eyes, and will they not stone us ? " But a very acute and learned writer [1] has thrown some doubt on this. He argues that the designation " abomination " is not appropriated to the consecrated animals. " This indicates that the animals the Israelites slaughtered were not too good, but too bad for offerings." To this it may be answered, that the term " abomination " *is* applied in Scripture to objects of idolatrous worship. Thus in 1 Kings xi. 5, 7, Milcom is called " the abomination " of the Ammonites, and Chemosh " the abomination " of the Moabites ; and in 2 Kings xxiii. 13, Ashtoreth is called " the abomination of the Zidonians." The other objection is of more force. This is, that " the animals which were commonly taken among the Israelites for offerings, were also among the Egyptians not sacred. The only one of the other animals generally considered as sacred—the cow —was also among the Israelites, except in the case of Num. xix., which is entirely by itself, not offered. The animals most commonly sacrificed—oxen—were also both sacrificed and eaten by the Egyptians." This author therefore considers that the offence of the Israelites would rather be, that they then at least—that is, before the delivery of the law, if not after—

[1] Hengstenberg, in his *Egypt and the Books of Moses.*

omitted the inquiries respecting the cleanness of animals, which was attended to with the greatest strictness among the Egyptians. *Their* particularity in this respect astonished the ancient Greeks, who record the matter with wonder. Of oxen, only a red one could be offered, and a single black hair rendered it unclean. They also placed dependence on a multitude of marks besides this ; the tongue, the tail, etc., were accurately examined. Each victim was, after a prescribed examination in confirmation of its fitness, to be sealed on the horns ; and to offer an unsealed ox was a crime punished with death.

Although we allow due weight to these circumstances, it can scarcely be supposed that the Egyptians were likely to trouble themselves with the consideration whether the animals which the Israelites offered to a God avowedly *unknown* to them, were clean or not. Besides, although the cow only was universally sacred among the Egyptians, oxen and sheep and goats —animals offered by the Israelites—were sacred in different parts of Egypt, the inhabitants of which could not endure the sacrifice of the animals they venerated ; and this was in fact often a matter of serious contention among the Egyptians themselves. Besides, it is not true that oxen were most commonly offered by the Israelites. Before the giving of the law, there is no instance of the sacrifice of an ox ; and, after that period, oxen were only offered on great occasions, and as free-will offerings on high

HAWK

festivals. Sheep and goats were the common sacrifices ; and we know that the goat, if not the sheep, was sacred in that part of Egypt in which the royal court was held. How little the Egyptians would be inclined to tolerate the destruction of the sacred animals within the districts in which they were worshipped, is shown by one of our author's own quotations from Herodotus, who states that, "if any person kill one of these animals intentionally, he expiates his crime by death; if unintentionally, he must pay the fine which the priest imposes. But whoever kills an ibis or a hawk, whether intentionally or not, must die." Upon the whole, therefore, the more current view of the subject is that with which we must recommend the reader to rest satisfied.

But in connection with the objection urged by Moses for insisting upon his original demand, a question will occur to the reader, which, we are sensible, must for some time have been present to his mind. What did Moses mean by asking for permission to take a three days' journey into the wilderness? Did he intend to return if the permission were granted? Was not the king justified in suspecting that they never would come back if this permission were obtained? We must avow that these are hard questions. In the first place, however, we are to recollect that Moses knew—having been so assured by God Himself—that the king would not yield even to this reasonable request; and that thus the burden of the refusal would lie upon him, with all its consequences. Still Moses must have been prepared for the contingency of a compliance with the request he made. Was he then insincere in making that request? had he such unavowed intentions as warranted the king's suspicions? No doubt he did mean to sacrifice unto the Lord at the distance of three days' journey. But was that all? Are we to suspect the great leader of Israel of the same kind of *suppressio veri* as that into which Abraham himself fell when he visited this land? We think not. There appears to us no authority for supposing that any disingenuousness was intended to be practised in the original request. Had the proposal been assented to by Pharaoh, it is to be presumed that Moses would have led the people back in accordance with the implied engagement. In their once retiring together into the wilderness to sacrifice, a useful precedent would, as an able American writer[1] remarks,

[1] Dr. Palfrey, in his *Academical Lectures on the Jewish*

have been established, and an important step taken towards ultimate liberation and nationality.

The objection of Moses extorted from the king a reluctant consent to their going into the wilderness; "only," he stipulated, "ye shall not go very far away." This seems to render it quite clear that he did suppose they meant to avail themselves of the occasion of making their escape. The stipulation of itself does, however, indicate that the king meant to keep his word; but, as is too commonly the case, when the calamity which wrung this promise from him had ceased, he manifested no readiness to perform it.

This brought on the fifth plague, which smote the Egyptians by the loss of their cattle; mortal disease appearing among the flocks and herds, but sparing those of the Israelites. It is said that "all the cattle of Egypt died;" but this was not literally the case, as we find them subsequently still possessed of cattle. The meaning is that there was death among all the cattle of Egypt—no kind was spared. A slight incident indicates the impression made by this on the king's mind. Not satisfied with the reports which he received as to the exemption of the cattle of the Israelites, he sent competent witnesses to the district occupied by them to ascertain the fact. The result must have satisfied him that the hand of God was in this matter; but no permanent good was produced upon his obdurate mind, for he still refused to let Israel go. This persistence against such an accumulation of calls, warnings, and judgments, became at every step a sin of increasing magnitude, and called for increasing severity and solemnity of punishment. The next time, therefore, the plague went home to the *persons* of the Egyptians themselves, and touched their skin and their flesh, in the form of ulcerous eruptions, from which none escaped. And for a token that it was by the power exerted through them that the plague was sent, Moses and Aaron, in the presence of the king, took the ashes of a furnace in their hand, and flung them wide into the air, declaring that they should "become small dust in all the land of Egypt;" that is, the

Scriptures and Antiquities,—a work from many of the conclusions in which we seriously dissent, but which embodies much original and instructive thought, and much careful research, marred occasionally by imperfect study of oriental geography and eastern usages. We owe much help to this work in the early portion of the present volume.

pestilence which this sign was intended visibly to connect with the agency of Moses, would be as extensive as if this sign were exhibited throughout the realm, instead of in the royal presence alone. The action is very remarkable, and is not without existing parallel in the East. Mr. Roberts, in his *Oriental Illustrations* relates that, "when the magicians pronounce an imprecation on an individual, a village, or a country, they take the ashes of cows' dung (that is, from a common fire) and *throw them into the air*, saying to the objects of their displeasure, Such a sickness, or such a curse, shall surely come upon you.

STORM AND LOCUSTS

Exodus 9:22 - 10:15

THE next plague which the obduracy of the king brought upon the land of Egypt, was a fearful storm of thunder, lightning, rain, and hail. Such a storm, terrible in any country, would be peculiarly awful in Egypt, where these natural phenomena are comparatively unknown. We say comparatively; for it is not correct to say, as some to magnify the miracle have said, that Egypt knows not rain nor hail. It was of the same essential character as the other plagues—an intense production, at an appointed time, of phenomena not unknown to the country; and there is no more reason for contending that rain and hail are naturally unknown, than that frogs were unknown before that day in which swarms of them overspread the land. Indeed, the Scriptural statement that this storm was "such as hath not been in Egypt since the foundation thereof, even until now," clearly intimates that storms of inferior power had before been known, and that this was unexampled only in degree. The scene is in Lower Egypt. In that part, and especially towards the Mediterranean, rain is not uncommon in January, February, and March; hail is not unknown, though rare; and thunder is sometimes heard. Farther south, towards Cairo and through Middle Egypt, these phenomena are still more rarely witnessed; and in Upper Egypt hail is unknown, and rain is a rare phenomenon. A storm in which these elements were combined

with prodigious power—the rain in floods, hailstones of prodigious size and force, thunder in awful crashes, and lightning that ran like fire along the ground—must have been a most astonishing and dreadful spectacle to the Egyptians. Nor was the terror all. The actual calamities inflicted were most serious. Those who, despite the warning, left their cattle abroad in the fields, saw them stricken dead by the hailstones, which also smote every bush, and broke every tree of the field. It is well worthy of notice, as one of the numerous incidents which evince the authenticity of the narrative—facts and circumstances being adduced which show the writer's familiar knowledge of Egypt, and which could not have been stated by a fabricator—that the time when this occurred is included within the period during which alone the cattle are turned out to graze in Egypt. This is in the months of January, February, March, and April. In these months only can green food be found, and during the rest of the year the animals are supplied with dry fodder. It was about the middle of this period that the recorded event occurred, and agreeably to this the cattle are described as abroad in the fields. At any other period of the year, this incident would have been inappropriate and untrue.

Again, we are told: "The flax and the barley were smitten, for the barley was in the ear, and the flax was bolled. But the wheat and the rye were not smitten, for they were not grown up." This is one of those texts which have a bearing on the authenticity of the composition in which they appear, the more satisfactory on account of their unobtrusive character. The fact here mentioned is not of the sort which tradition would be at all likely to preserve, or an historian of any subsequent age to introduce. But in an eyewitness of the scene, excited as his mind was by its whole aspect, it was natural to record such particulars. It would have been unaccountable in a writer otherwise circumstanced. The peculiar nature of the climate and physical constitution of Egypt produces particular conditions with respect to these products, which do not apply to the neighbouring countries; and it is this fact which renders such indications peculiarly valuable and important. Flax and barley are there nearly ripe when wheat and spelt are yet green. Barley is especially important in Egypt. It there comes to maturity about a month earlier than wheat, and its harvest is peculiarly abundant. Barley and flax are generally ripe in March, wheat and spelt in April—the two latter coming to maturity about the same time. In the land of Canaan, the season for the ingathering of all these products is from a month to six weeks later.

Under the influence of this most serious calamity, and under the unusual terrors of "mighty thunderings and hail," the king was strong in his expressions of contrition and of good resolutions for the future. "I have sinned," he said, "and I and my people are wicked. Entreat the Lord (for it is enough) that there be no more mighty thunderings and hail, and I will let you go, and ye shall stay no longer." But Moses knew him better than he knew himself, and placed no faith in this transient manifestation of right feeling. Yet he complied with his wish. He went out beyond the city and spread his arms abroad unto the Lord, and forthwith "the thunder and the hail ceased, and the rain was not poured upon the earth."

Finding that the king was regardless of his promise, Moses was commissioned to go again before him, and threaten that an army of locusts should to-morrow invade the land, and consume all that had escaped the hail. Swarms of this devouring insect had often before scourged the land, but this was to be beyond all former precedent; and their number, size, and voracity would be such that they should render the very ground invisible, and consume every green thing. The wheat and spelt which had escaped the ravages of the hail, would now be swept away by the locusts, and whatever trees retained their foliage were now to be stripped bare. The idea of such a calamity appalled the minds of the Egyptian courtiers, whose property had already greatly suffered, and who had by this time learned that the threatenings of the Lord through Moses failed not in any one point of their accomplishment. They ventured to interfere. They said, "How long shall this man be a snare unto us? let the men go, that they may serve Jehovah their God: knowest thou not yet that Egypt is destroyed?" These words were not without weight with the king. He could not but infer that if his own courtiers and counsellors were of this opinion, he was no longer sustained by the concurrence of his people in the resistance which he was still disposed to offer to the demand of the Hebrews.

He could not but see that they now lamented his obstinacy, and were disposed to consider that, as the least of many evils, and in order

"To gather breath in many miseries,"

it were better that the request of the Israelites should be complied with. Perceiving this to be the feeling of his court and people, Pharaoh shrank from the responsibility of opposing himself single-handed to it: he resolved so far to meet their wishes, as to show a disposition to let the Hebrews depart, on what might appear to be reasonable terms—so as at least to exonerate himself from the odium of unreflecting resistance. He therefore sent to call Moses and Aaron back; and although he must already have well understood their wishes, he asked who they were whose departure they desired. The answer was plainly, "All,"—not a living soul was to be left behind; all—young and old, sons and daughters, flocks and herds. This bold and uncompromising answer was too much for the proud king. Highly exasperated, he commanded them to be driven from his presence, intimating that the men might go, but the women and children must be left behind as hostages. But a rod was held over him more terrible than the sword of kings. That rod was

THE LOCUST

lifted up, and the locusts came. Has the reader ever seen a locust? They are common enough in entomological collections. If not, a grasshopper will very well represent it,—a locust being, in fact, a sort of grasshopper. Hard it is to think, that this not very formidable looking, and far from unpleasant creature, should be so terribly destructive. But it is the incredible immensity of their numbers, and the aggregate result of the intense and rapid voracity of every one of them, which render even this small creature one of the most terrible of the plagues with which God scourges the earth. We, in our happy exemption from such an evil, can but imperfectly apprehend its force; for words cannot adequately represent it. We have ourselves seen the mid-day light darkened to evening shades as their myriads passed, layer above layer, overhead, for more than half an hour. We have seen the ground covered with them for miles around, without a visible interstice; and we have seen districts which were as the garden of Eden before them, left behind them as a desolate wilderness. Other travellers furnish points more illustrative of this plague than such as have fallen within our own experience, as it is but rarely that they alight upon a house or on towns in the entire body; although a flock cannot pass without a number of stragglers alighting upon the housetops and the trees, which would be thought considerable but for the presence of the immense host that passes on. To show the intensity of this visitation in countries bordering on Egypt, we give a few passages from a large statement on the subject, as regards Abyssinia, which may be found in a valuable collection of travels, published in 1625.[1] It is translated from an account of the proceedings of the Portuguese missionaries in the dominions of Prester John or Prete Janni. " In this country, and in all the dominions of Prete Janni, is a very great and horrible plague, which is an innumerable company of locusts, which eat and consume all the corn and trees; and the number of them is so great, as it is incredible; and with their multitude they cover the earth, and fill the air in such wise, that it is a hard matter to be able to see the sun. And again, I say it is an incredible thing to him that hath not seen it. And if the damage which they do were general through all the provinces and realms of Prete Janni, they would perish with famine, and it would be impossible to inhabit the same. But one year they destroy one province, and in another some other. Sometimes in two or three of these provinces, and wherever they go, the country remaineth more ruinate and destroyed than if it had been set on fire. . . . . Oftentimes we heard say, Such a country, or such a realm, is destroyed with locusts. While we abode in the town of Barua, we saw the sign of the sun and the shadow of the earth,[2] which was

all yellow, whereat the people were half dead for sorrow. The next day the number of these vermin which came was incredible, which to our judgment covered four-and-twenty miles in compass, according to what we were informed afterwards."

In a journey subsequently: " We travelled five days' journey through places wholly waste and destroyed, wherein millet had been sown, which had stalks as great as those we set in our vineyards, and we saw them all broken and beaten down as if a tempest had been there; and this the locusts did. The trees were without leaves, and the bark of them was all devoured; and no grass was there to be seen, for they had eaten up all things; and if we had not been warned and advised to carry victual with us, we and our cattle had perished. This country was all covered with locusts without wings; and they told us these were the seed of them which had eaten up all, and that as soon as their wings were grown they would seek after the old ones. The number of them was so great that I shall not speak of it, because I shall not be believed; but this I will say, that I saw men, women, and children sit as forlorn and dead among the locusts; and I said unto them, Why stand ye as dead men, and will not slay these vermin, to be avenged of the mischief which their fathers and mothers have done unto you, seeing that those which you shall kill will never more be able to do you harm? They answered that they had not the heart to resist the plague which God sent upon them for their sins. And all the people of this country departed. We found the ways full of men and women, travelling on foot, with their children in their arms and upon their heads, going into other countries where they might find food, which was a pitiful thing to behold."

These incidents form an emphatic commentary upon the text before us: " They covered the face of the whole earth, so that the land was darkened; and they did eat every herb of the land, and all the fruit of the trees which the hail had left; and there remained not any green thing in the trees or in the herbs of the field through all the land of Egypt."

The subject is well suited for poetry; but we remember no poet who has dealt with it except Southey, whose clear and vivid descriptions of oriental matters must excite the wonder of those who recollect that he never visited the East:

---

[1] Purchas, *his Pilgrimes*, pt. ii., pp. 1046-1048.
[2] This is explained by what the writer had before said, that the approach of the locusts was known the day beforehand by the yellow tinge of the heavens, " and the ground becometh yellow through the light which reverberateth from their wings, whereupon the people became suddenly as dead men, saying, 'We are undone, for the locusts come!'"

"Then Moath pointed where a cloud
        Of locusts, from the desolated fields
        Of Syria, wing'd their way.
    'Lo, how created things
        Obey the written doom.'

"Onward they came, a dark continuous cloud
        Of congregated myriads numberless;
    The rushing of whose wings was as the sound
        Of some broad river, headlong in its course,
    Plunged from a mountain summit; or the roar
        Of a wild ocean in the autumnal storm,
    Shattering its billows on a shore of rocks.
    Onward they came, the winds impelled them on;
        Their work was done, their path of ruin past,
        Their graves were ready in the wilderness."

The locust is unquestionably the most terrible scourge of eastern lands. It is impossible to convey any full idea of the appearance of a locust flight, or of the ravages they commit. I had an opportunity of witnessing their devastations on one occasion. I was in Damascus at the time. For three successive days the bright Syrian sun was dimmed by the living cloud. The heat was intense. The air was quite still; but there was a strange, deep, penetrating sound, like that of a strong breeze sweeping through a forest. A peculiar and unpleasant odour was felt. The locusts were flying northward, many of them close to the ground. They struck against windows, walls, trees, and houses like hailstones. Thousands fell on the flat roof of my house, and in the open court. It was impossible even to keep the rooms free, for at open doors and windows they came in like snowdrift. Those that fell never rose again. They covered terraces and pavements so thickly, that nothing could be seen but the living, crawling mass. They eat up every green thing—flowers, foliage, and even the more tender stalks of young plants. It was a melancholy, it was a terrible sight. A few days before, all was fresh, and green, and beautiful; now all was bare, and black, and desolate. I had occasion to ride to a village some thirty miles distant on one of the days. The roads and fields were covered with locusts, in some places to the depth of two or three inches. My horse killed dozens of them at every step. The fountains, streams, and wells were almost choked up with them. My arms soon became quite weary by vain attempts to keep them off my person. They were on my back, on my head, in my beard, in my pockets—on and in every place, in short, where they could light, or into which they could crawl.

In a few days the cloud had passed over, and those on the ground had died. The stench of the festering masses then became almost intolerable. The whole air was poisoned with it. After that painful experience I was able to understand the horrors of "the plague of locusts."

                                                                P.

I can testify from my own experience to facts of the kind here recorded. During the spring of 1865, when I was in the East, a frightful visitation of locusts occurred in Palestine. We first met with them in Philistia, but it was in crossing the Plain of Esdraelon that we found them most numerous. They came over us like a dark yellow cloud, and numbers of them fell on the ground. We thought of the expression, in reference to the Midianites, who encamped in that very neighbourhood, "like grasshoppers for multitude." (Judges vii. 12.) As we rode on we found heaps of them lying by the wayside; and in villages and towns afterwards noticed them piled up in large quantities.

If I remember rightly, rewards were offered for the destruction of these noxious insects.

There are locusts of different kinds. As many as nine are enumerated by Mr. Tristram, in his *Natural Hist. of the Bible*, 308-313.

"As in the visitation of Egypt, so now it is found that the only means of deliverance from the plague is when a strong wind drives them into the sea; and even then, as mentioned by Joel, their dead bodies taint the air and induce pestilence. This was the experience of 1865 (the year just referred to), as well as the record of Hasselquist more than a century ago," p. 315.

I may add that I once saw an enormous swarm of insects of the moth kind, lying several inches thick in drifts, on the bridge at Heidelberg.

                                                                S.

DARKNESS AND DEATH OF FIRSTBORN

Exodus 10:21-29; 11; 12:29-30

Now at length Pharaoh sends in haste for the Hebrew brothers, and we are prepared to conclude that he can hold out no longer, and is ready to allow of the departure of the Israelites. But, alas! he cannot give himself up unreservedly to the stern necessities of his position. His language is indeed as strong as might be desired—"I have sinned against Jehovah your God, and against you;" but when the locusts were, at the word of Moses, carried off to sea by "a mighty strong west wind," he was still inexorable, and refused to let them go. Then came darkness—thick darkness, "darkness that might be felt"—for the space of three days, over one of the sunniest lands in the world. The Hebrew word which expresses this darkness is the same which describes that "darkness" which covered the deep at the time of the creation; and, like that darkness, this probably consisted of thick clammy fogs of vapours and exhalations, so condensed that they might almost be perceived by the organs of touch. Considering that the sun was among the chief deities of Egypt, and that there *any* obscuration of the sky in the day-time is of most unusual occurrence, the consternation with which the people were seized at this infliction may easily be conceived. The darkness occasioned by the locusts was nothing compared to this. *That* was an obscuration—*this* was "a horror of thick darkness."

It is said that "they saw not one another, neither rose any one from his place for three days." This probably means, that the heavy and humid state of the atmosphere rendered any kind of artificial light useless; and that every one was, during these awful days, prevented from leaving home to attend upon his usual business. The old Dutch artist to whom we lately had occasion to allude, has depicted this plague with considerable effect and force. He allows us, through the darkness which envelops his engraving, to discern the shadows of men stumbling along the way, running against each other, groping in vain to find their doors, coming full butt against monuments, and falling over steps. Here and there are men with lamps; but they radiate no light—they are small white specks, and the men hold them close down to the ground to find their path: others, in some instances, are seen to be holding on behind to avail themselves of the guidance of the persons thus painfully and fearfully seeking the pathway. Meanwhile, in the distance, lies the favoured land of Goshen under a flood of light, contrasting well with the Egyptian darkness. Until we saw this print, we had no idea that darkness could be pictorially represented.

This visitation again compelled the king to send for Moses and Aaron. Nevertheless, he is still bent on compromise. He will now permit the children to go, but the flocks must be left behind: he must still have some pledge for the return of the Israelites, by the retention of their property. This Moses meets by a plain and blunt refusal: "Our cattle also shall go with us; there shall not a hoof be left behind." He assigned the very sufficient reason, that from the flocks and herds the offerings must be made, and it could not be known what would be needed till they came to the appointed place. Pharaoh doubtless thought that he made a reasonable and moderate proposal; and the high-toned refusal of Moses strengthened his suspicions, and roused his indignation to the uttermost. "Get thee from me," he said, "take heed to thyself,

see my face no more: for in that day thou seest my face, thou shalt die." Moses accordingly left the presence with the ominous words, "Thou hast spoken well; I will see thy face again no more."

The contest is now over, and Moses is directed to prepare for the last awful infliction—the crowning stroke—which shall compel the king to let the oppressed go free; nay, to urge and command their immediate departure. This was to be no less than the sudden death, in one night —in one hour—at one fell swoop, of all the first-born of Egypt, "from the first-born of Pharaoh that sitteth upon his throne, even unto the first-born of the maid-servant that is behind the mill; and all the first-born of cattle."

The mind needs here to pause to contemplate the length, the breadth, the depth, the fulness, of this terrible doom. This is one of the great matters that cannot be taken in at one impression. The mind must dwell on it—must rest on the details—must penetrate to the homes and hearts of the Egyptian people—must follow the course of this infliction from the throned Pharaoh to the poor bondwoman drudging behind the mill. This is not difficult. Here is no question of Egyptian antiquities or of peculiar customs. After all, the Egyptians were men of like passions as we are, and were subject to the same griefs and emotions, the same trials and struggles, by which we are affected. Even the obdurate Pharaoh had somewhere a heart; and even he was once a little child, who sucked from a mother's bosom the milk of human kindness— who was horrified when he first looked upon death—who wept when he first saw blood—and who hated, once, wrong-doing and oppression. The "great cry" which arose at midnight, when every house was roused to witness the dying agonies of its first-born, was not different from that which would have been heard at the present day, had such a calamity befallen in London, New York, or Pekin. The heart—the human heart—was smitten and felt then, as it would under the like circumstances be smitten and as it would feel now. It was a dreadful stroke. It was a blow that wounded where the heart was most susceptible. "The pride, the hope, the joy of every family was taken from it. The bitterness of grief in fathers and mothers for their first-born is proverbial. Here, in every house, were Egyptian parents "weeping for their children, because they were not." It was a woe without remedy or alleviation. He that is sick may be restored. A body emaciated or ulcerated, maimed or enfeebled, may recover soundness and strength; but what kindly process can re-animate the breathless clay, and give back to the arms of mourning affection an only son—a first-born—smitten with death? Hope, the last refuge and remedy under other evils, was here to be cut up by the roots. Again, the blow was to be struck at midnight, when none could see the hand that inflicted it, and most were reposing in quiet sleep. Had this sleep been silently and insensibly exchanged for the sleep of death, the circumstances would have been less overwhelmingly awful. But it was not to be so. Although for three days and three nights previously they had been enveloped in thick darkness, and none had risen up from their places; yet now they were to be roused from their beds, to render what fruitless aid they could to their expiring children, and to mourn over their slain."[1] All this misery was, as the same writer remarks, crowned by the keen reflection, that *it might have been prevented*. "How would they now condemn their desperate madness, in provoking a power which had so often and so forcibly warned them of their danger! If Pharaoh were not past feeling, how dreadful must have been the pangs which he felt in the thought, that after attempting to destroy by unheard of cruelties an innocent and helpless race of strangers, he had now ruined his own country by his obstinate perseverance in impiety and folly!" All the first-born, from the man in the vigour of manhood to the infant that had just been born, died in that one hour of night. The stay, the comfort, the delight of every family, was annihilated by a single stroke. Truly this was a pity and a grief. But let it not escape our notice, that in this there is a direct but mysterious retribution—delayed, but sure. The time was, when, by the order of this government, all the new-born male infants of Israel were slain by the hand of man—rent pitilessly from the mother's breast, and cast ruthlessly into the waters. And this was not the first-born only, but all—all that drew the breath of life. But now the hour is come, and Israel is in like sort signally avenged; and we may add this to a thousand instances, which prove that no public wrong, and especially no wrong against the truth

[1] Bush, *Notes on Exodus*, i. 133.

of natural feeling, no savage wrong, ever fails of retribution. Scripture is full of incidents that prove it, and so is history.

Still there are some who will, with the light amid which we are privileged to live, be shocked at the general nature of this awful judgment. It may be urged, Pharaoh and his courtiers—those who had most notoriously sanctioned his miserable policy—might be thus punished; but why the whole of the Egyptians, many of whom had individually no part or voice in the matter? The answer must be, that in the common course of Providence, it is in the nature of national sins to draw down national judgments. The sin of holding in slavery the Israelites, of destroying the innocent liberty of a free people, who had trusted themselves to their hospitality, was a crime of no common magnitude, and is chargeable upon the Egyptian nation as well as upon their monarch. He must have been countenanced and encouraged in it by their concurrence. It was a national sin, which, as far as justice was concerned, it was as fit that the Judge of all the earth should punish by some miraculous work, as by some merely providential infliction.

"And there shall be a great cry throughout all the land of Egypt, such as there was none like it, nor shall be like it any more." The full significance of these words can only be understood by those who have witnessed a death-scene in a Syrian or Egyptian family. It is totally different from anything we ever see in this country. The nearest approach to it, perhaps, is the *keen* which may still be heard in some of the remote districts of Ireland. We are all familiar with the tears and sobs of the bereaved, and even with the bitter, despairing cry of a mother over her dead child. But in the East grief is expressed in a different way. The moment life is extinct, the whole female members of the household gather round the body, rend their clothes, throw dust or ashes on their heads, beat their bare bosoms, and then raise their voices in a long, united, piercing wail that rings through the whole neighbourhood. Again and again it is repeated. Many a time, during the stillness of an Eastern night, have I been roused from sleep by that well known and thrilling death-cry. When we consider that in every house throughout Egypt the first-born was dead; that death came to each victim at the same moment—in the deep silence of the midnight hour; that from every house in city, village, and rural district, that wild wail rose until the whole land was filled with it, we may then form some faint idea of that "great cry—such as there was none like it, nor shall be like it any more."

P.

CHRIST OUR PASSOVER

Exodus 12

WE apprehend that there are very few Christian readers of the twelfth chapter of Exodus who will have any difficulty in supposing that the ordinance there described was designed to set forth, as by a type or prophetic symbol, the death and atonement of the Lord Jesus. If they should hesitate, the New Testament itself makes this clear, by its numerous references to the paschal ordinance, as foreshadowing the various incidents of our Lord's death and sufferings. Indeed, the more one studies the *Old* Testament, with no other desire than to build himself up in the faith, and to know the mind of God, the more intense, we apprehend, will the conviction become that the old law had in itself the Gospel, veiled purposely in shadows and symbols, which the wise, the taught of God, might penetrate and comprehend; but which were hidden from the many, until that day in which the veil was rent, and

FEAST OF THE PASSOVER

the broad light—the light of full accomplishment —was let in upon all the mysteries of God.

This was most eminently true of the grandest ordinance of the Mosaic dispensation, the feast of the Passover—all the types in which were accomplished, all the Gospel in which was preached to

the world, in that day when "Christ our passover was sacrificed for us." It was surely no undesigned circumstance that the two events were made, even with respect to time, to coincide; and that the Jews celebrated the passover, and consummated all its types, by bringing to his death, *on the same day,* "the Lamb slain from the foundation of the world."[1]

The victim itself was to be a lamb, the most gentle and innocent of all God's creatures, and therefore the most fitting emblem of "the Lamb of God, that taketh away the sins of the world."

It was to be a lamb of the first year, without blemish. Had it borne the mark of the slightest deformity, or even deficiency, it would have been a forbidden sacrifice, and a victim unfit to represent Him of whom it is said, "We are redeemed by the precious blood of Christ, as of a lamb without blemish and without spot."

The lamb was to be set apart four days before it was slain, not only to mark the previous designation of Christ to be a sacrifice, but perhaps also, as some have suggested, to foreshow that He should, during the last four days of His life, be examined at different tribunals, to ascertain whether there was the smallest flaw in His character, that so His bitterest enemies might be constrained to confess His innocence, and thereby unwittingly to declare that He was fit to be a sacrifice for the sins of the whole world.

The lamb of the passover was to be eaten with unleavened bread and bitter herbs. The herbs were no doubt primarily meant to awaken the remembrance of the bitter bondage to which the Israelites had been subject in Egypt; but besides this, they were apparently designed to show the necessity of penitence for sin, and to

[1] The Jewish day extends from sunset to sunset, not, as with us, from midnight to midnight. The *night* on which the passover was eaten, and the *day* following, on which Jesus was crucified, formed, therefore, the same DAY.

shadow forth the hardships and trials that await the Lord's pilgrims in the journey to the Canaan of their rest. And it is doubtless as impossible spiritually to partake of Jesus Christ, as the paschal lamb of our salvation, without abiding godly sorrow for sin, and without a sacred resolve to take up the cross and bear it cheerfully in all the trials of life, as it is to bring light out of darkness. Equally impossible is it to partake savingly of the mercies of the Son of God, while the leaven of any iniquity is indulged and cherished within the heart.

That not a bone of the paschal lamb was to be broken, may seem in its first signification merely to be one among the many circumstances illustrative of the haste with which the Israelites partook of the feast at its first institution. But it seems also to signify, that what has once been offered to God ought not to be unnecessarily disfigured or mangled. The blood must be shed, for that was the seal of the covenant; the flesh might be eaten, for that was given for the sustentation of life; but the bones, forming no part either of food or sacrifice, were to be left in their original state until consumed in the morning by fire, with such of the flesh as might then remain. But without doubt there was an ulterior allusion in this commandment respecting the paschal lamb. We read of our Lord, in the account of His crucifixion, that "when the soldiers came to Jesus and saw that He was dead already, they brake not His legs;" and that the evangelist regarded this as a fulfilment of this part of the passover institution is clear, for he adds, "For these things were done that the Scripture should be fulfilled, 'A bone of Him shall not be broken.'" It would thus appear that a special providence watched over the crucifixion of our Saviour, to secure His sacred person from fracture, and thus to bring about the fulfilment of the typical prediction.

Under this view, the sprinkling of the blood of the slain lamb upon the door-posts as a sign of safety to those within, is highly important and interesting. The Lord pledged Himself, that when He saw the blood upon the lintel, the destroying plague should pass by and not come near. So with us, the Israel of God is composed of creatures by nature fallen, and exposed to wrath even as others. In themselves they do not deserve, they have no claim to, exemption from the doom which hangs over a guilty world; and they are as much in the pathway of the divine anger as the dwellers in Goshen would have been, had they been unmarked for safety. But the oblation has been offered for them—the Lamb is slain; and they are sprinkled with His blood, sealed by His Spirit, and may now claim the heritage of His covenant. It is very important to observe that the blood of the paschal lamb did not save the Israelites by being *shed*, but by being *sprinkled*. In the same manner, it is not the blood of Christ as shed on Calvary, but as sprinkled on the soul, that saves us from the wrath to come.

We have indicated a few leading correspondences between the type and the antitype of the passover observances. Many more may be found in some commentaries—in others too many; for while the general purport of the ordinance, in its typical reference, is placed by the Scripture itself beyond all question, it must be admitted that the parallel has been pressed by many into more minute and fanciful analogies than the subject will bear, or than the Spirit of God appears to have intended. What place to give to the following we scarcely know, and we introduce it as a remarkable fact, without meaning to press upon the analogy as the writer does. That writer is the very learned Dr. Gill, whose Exposition presses more strongly than any other in our language upon the typical import of the Old Testament ordinances. The passage forms the substance of his note on the direction that the paschal lamb is not to be " sodden at all with water, but roasted with fire." " The manner of roasting, according to the Jewish canons, was this : They bring a spit made of the wood of the pomegranate, and thrust it into its mouth quite through it; they do not roast the passover lamb on an iron spit or an iron grate. Maimonides is a little more particular and exact in his account. In answer to the question, How do they roast it? he replies : 'They transfix it through the middle of the mouth to its extremities with a wooden spit; and they hang it in the midst of the furnace with the fire below.' Thus, then, it was not turned upon a spit, according to our mode of roasting, but was suspended on a hook and roasted by the fire beneath ; and so was the more exact figure of Christ suspended on the cross, and enduring the fire of divine wrath. And Justin Martyr is still more particular, who was by birth a Samaritan,[1] and well versed in Jewish affairs.

[1] Justin was a native of Samaria, but was not of the Samaritan sect.

He, even in conversing with Trypho the Jew, who could have contradicted him had he said what was wrong, says, the lamb was roasted in the form of a cross. One spit, he says, went through the lower parts of the head, and again another across the shoulders, to which the hands (or rather fore-legs) of the lamb were fastened or hanged, and so was a very lively emblem of Christ crucified."

Whatever may be thought of such details, the great truths shadowed forth by this remarkable ordinance must be allowed to form no unimportant part of that education and training, whereby the "law was our schoolmaster to bring us unto Christ."

FOURTEENTH OF NISAN

Exodus 12

THE night of the fourteenth day of the month Nisan—that night of grief to the Egyptians—was a night of earnest waiting, of solemn preparation, for the Israelites. Before that night came, they had received instructions for observing it in that form in which it was to become to all generations a yearly commemorative festival of their deliverance. Like the great Christian solemnity of the Lord's Supper, it was thus instituted previous to the actual occurrence of the momentous event, the memory of which it was designed to keep alive in coming ages. Intended to be the great national festival of the Israelites, "the passover" commemorated not only the deliverance wrought for them by their Almighty Protector, but their introduction into an independent national existence; and the solemnities with which it was to be observed were directed to be such as should call up vividly to the mind the remembrance of that event. As each house had its own special deliverance from the calamity which carried wailing into the houses of Egypt, so there was to be in each a domestic celebration. As, in the night of the emancipation, no Israelitish house that had been marked with the blood of the slain lamb had been invaded by death, so the sprinkling of the lamb's blood on the door-post of every Hebrew dwelling was to make through all time a part of the commemoration. As the people had hurried forth from the land of bondage, so they were to meet around the table of this festival in the attitude of haste; their sandals bound upon their feet, their girdles tightened on their loins, and their staves in their hands, as if ready for the toils of travel. They were for the same reason to throw away the bones of the lamb, without, as usual, breaking them to taste the marrow; and they were to eat unleavened cakes in remembrance of the urgent circumstances which, on that memorable night, had not permitted their fathers to eat bread prepared in the usual manner. Other regulations[1] appear to have been framed to prevent idolatrous observances from creeping in among the ceremonies of a time so exciting. And to make the season in all respects august, it was ordained that the month in which it occurred, should in all future time be reckoned the first of the national religious year. From this time, accordingly, in ecclesiastical computation, the year began in the month Nisan, otherwise Abib (March-April), while the civil year continued to be reckoned, as it had been, from Tishri (September-October).

Such, in substance, were the directions given to the Israelites in anticipation of this memorable night, and which they so duly observed, that they were in the very act of their commemorative feast at the moment when the midnight cry for the slain of Egypt arose. The Israelites had been directed to remain that night within their own doors, both to ensure that their families should be collected when the moment of departure came, and, perhaps, as Dr. Palfrey suggests, to prevent the Egyptians from attaching to the people any suspicion of personal agency in the impending desolation. Further, to impress it upon their minds with the utmost distinctness, that Jehovah could and would protect an obedient people, and to give to the ceremonies of the commemorative rite the liveliest power over the imaginations of the coming generations who were to observe it, the people were directed to put a mark—a mark of blood—the blood of the slain lamb (an authentic figure of Christ's ransoming blood) upon their dwellings; and were assured that all of them who should perform that first act of allegiance, God would recognize as His own, so that while ruin was

[1] Such as those in Exodus 12:9,10. They are so regarded by Maimonides and other Jewish writers.

raging all around them, it should enter no portal distinguished by that sign.[2]

In further preparation for their departure from the Egyptian territory, which was now about to take place, the Israelites received a direction from Moses, which has been made the subject of much misconception and causeless complaint. Moses is made, by our translation, to say to the people, under the divine direction, "Let every man borrow of his neighbour, and every woman of her neighbour, jewels of silver and jewels of gold." Here, by the use of the word "borrow," meaning to ask and receive under a pledge of repayment, is conveyed an implication of the Hebrews being directed to act dishonestly. But this idea is entirely without foundation in the language of the original narrative. The word in Hebrew is an exceedingly common one, and means simply "to ask;" and, as Kennicott remarks, "should any one here contend for rendering it by "borrow," let him try to render it so in Psalm cxxii. 6, 'O borrow the peace of Jerusalem!'" It is better and more just to preserve here the ordinary sense of the word, and the interpretation of it in that sense will not be difficult. We may understand that the Israelites were directed to ask and reclaim, before their migration, such portions of their own property as they might have lent to their neighbours; or to ask that the payment of what might be due to them might be made in light and valuable articles, suitable for convenient carriage in the approaching journey. Or even if they were directed to ask gifts of such as, from motives of friendship, might be disposed to bestow some token of good-will at parting, still there is no recommendation of discreditable conduct. At all events, no such idea as that of borrowing, out of which the whole question grows, is involved in the original word.

Nevertheless, if any one likes to stand out for

[2] Voyaging up the Nile, the Rev. F. A. Strauss arrived at Manfalut during the day commencing the great Moslem festival: "Into whatever house we looked, the inhabitants seemed busy in the preparation of the lamb. A woman came out from one habitation with a basin containing the blood of the slain lamb, which she first sprinkled with her hand on the door-posts, and then poured the remainder on the door; forcibly reminding us of the sprinkling of the blood of the passover lamb on Israel's departure from Egypt. But no further connection could we trace between them."—*Sinai and Golgotha*, p. 63. This, it will be observed, is a Mohammedan—not a Jewish—custom in Egypt. That it has some reference to the Jewish institution we doubt not, but the process of transmission is uncertain.

this word—borrowing—even that may be explained without implying the slur upon the character of the Israelites which it has been thought to convey. When this transaction took place, there is no reason to suppose that the Israelites knew that they were not to return to Egypt, although they certainly did expect some present advantage, and ultimate deliverance, from the step to be taken. It may be even questioned whether this was known until that decisive moment on the third day of their departure, when they were directed "to turn and encamp before Pi-hahiroth, between Migdol and the sea" (Exod. xiv. 2,) whereby Pharaoh first gained the assurance that the people had fled. It may be doubted whether Moses himself had any assurance until then. The strongest fact to show that he had, is, that the bones of Joseph were taken away; but rightly apprehended, this may imply no more than that he felt doubtful whether they might return, or be directed to pursue their journey after they had actually departed; and while there was in this matter the least uncertainty, it would be felt to be right that the remains of Joseph should be removed, lest there should be no opportunity of returning for them. Besides, the oath which Joseph had required of them was absolute, that they should take his bones with them when they departed; and in that strict regard for the letter of an oath, for which they were honourably distinguished among the nations, the elders of Israel would feel bound to carry his corpse with them, seeing they were literally about to quit the land, even though they might be persuaded that they would have to bring it back again.

This being the case, it would be in entire conformity with the customs of the East, that they should borrow of their wealthy Egyptian neighbours, "jewels of silver and jewels of gold," with which to adorn themselves during this their high festival—the only one they had been for generations afforded an opportunity of commemorating. If the custom of personal adornment on such occasions existed—and it did exist—we may be certain that the Israelites would desire to appear in the utmost splendour of ornament they could command. It is in the blood of the nation; and no one who lives in a place where two Jews can be found, will need any evidence how desirable the ornaments of "jewels of silver and jewels of gold" are in their esteem. At this day, when the Orientals go to their sacred festivals, they always put on their best jewels. Not to appear before the gods in this manner, they consider, would be disgraceful to themselves and displeasing to the deities. A person whose clothes or jewels are indifferent, will *borrow* of his richer neighbours; and Roberts assures us, that nothing is more common than to see poor people standing before the temple, or engaged in sacred ceremonies, well adorned with jewels. The almost pauper bride or bridegroom at a marriage may often be seen decked with gems of the most costly kind, which have been *borrowed* for the occasion. The knowledge, therefore, that the Israelites were going to hold a feast in honour of that God whose power the Egyptians had by this time abundant reason to know, would be a strong inducement to them to lend the valuables that might be required, as they themselves were accustomed at their sacred festivals to wear such things (as we know from their monuments), and also, doubtless, to lend them to one another. This, on the hypothesis of borrowing—which, however, for the reasons stated, we do not entertain—may still account for the great readiness with which, as the sacred narrative assures us, the Egyptians responded to the parting request of the Israelites.

ON, OR HELIOPOLIS

Before leaving Egypt, in connection with Moses, it is interesting to remark, that one of its monuments has been

presented by the Khedive to this country. It has long been lying at Alexandria, near Cleopatra's Needle, having been brought there from Heliopolis, where it stood before the temple of the rising and setting sun.

"It is to the period of Egypt's splendour, the summit of its power, and the reign of Thothmes III., the powerful monarch and conquerer, that the fallen obelisk of Alexandria belongs, and it was one of the triumphal columns raised by that monarch to record his victories over Asia and Ethiopia. The central line of hieroglyphs on each side the original dedication, contains the name and titles of the monarch, and records that it was erected to the god Ra, or the Rising Sun, and to Tum, or the Setting Sun, on the occasion of the Festival of Thirty Years at On, or Heliopolis. It is probably one of the obelisks for which Thothmes appointed a daily offering of bread and beer, as if it were a statue or living being, to be ever worshipped. The inscription states that it was capped with gold, but, of course, it has been stripped of that ornamental portion. How or when it fell is unknown; probably the effects of an earthquake, or the undermining of the soil by the sea, to which it lies so near, may have caused it to fall."— *The Times*, Feb., 1877.

S.

THE DEPARTURE

Exodus 12:29-39

AMPLE reason had Egypt to mourn that the obduracy of its rulers had drawn down upon it a judgment such as had not been known since that day in which God brought down a flood of waters to destroy the earth. We cannot sufficiently dwell on the fact that a judgment not less severe than this had been, by this obduracy, rendered *necessary* to produce the intended result. Let us think not only of the judgments of God, but of His mercy and forbearance. The Egyptians had from the first deserved the utmost severity of judgment for the most atrocious deeds of which a nation, as such, is capable. They were guilty of reducing a free and generous people not only to political, but to personal bondage, and of murdering the children to prevent the increase of the race. Yet when the appointed time of deliverance came, God did not at once bare the arm of vindictive justice against this people. He acted forbearingly and leniently with them; and had they in time relented, and agreed to relax the iron yoke which they had laid upon Israel's neck, all had been well, and their great wrong would have passed unpunished. Let us wonder at the forbearance and long-suffering of God, no less than at the awful severity of His justice. The hand of man, armed with irresistible might, would not thus long have forborne to inflict the consummating horror—would not so long have endured these repeated evasions and breaches of promise—would not so long have tried, by successive steps, with *how little* of compulsory judgment they might be induced to let the oppressed go free. And even terrible as this last infliction —the death of the first-born—was, it was not one jot more than was necessary to produce the result; for, after all this, there was yet one more relapse to hardness of heart—yet one more act of bold defiance which rendered another exterminating sweep of God's fiery sword necessary.

The immediate effect, however, of the death of the first-born, was exactly such as had been calculated. It was a signal act of faith, when an entire nation stood in the dead of the night awake, ready for a journey, in the conviction that a certain judgment was to be inflicted by the hand of Heaven; and that this infliction would infallibly ensure their departure from the house of bondage. In that conviction much labour had been undergone, and large preparations completed; for we may conceive that it was no light matter for so vast a body of people, with all their flocks and herds, and with numerous women and children, to have perfected their arrangements for a sudden departure without confusion or disorder. That all this had been done, and that every direction of Moses and Aaron was implicitly followed, amply proves that the judgments of the Lord upon the Egyptians, and the exemption of the Israelites from the plagues which had been showered upon the land, had not failed of their effect in bringing up to the proper pitch of faith, confidence, and resolution, a people whose spirits had naturally and excusably become enfeebled by the slow poison of slavery.

They waited not long, nor vainly. Moses had declared, when he last quitted the presence of Pharaoh, that he would see his face no more; but he foretold the time was near when "all these thy servants shall come down unto me, and bow down themselves unto me, saying, Get thee out, and all the people that follow thee." And so it soon came to pass. When the stroke had fallen, the people were terrified to think of the dangers to which the detention of the Israelites exposed them. In the apprehension that the visitation that rent their hearts might be the precursor of one more dreadful, which would sweep off all the population in a mass, they became urgent for the instant departure of the Hebrews; and, for all that appears, would have driven them out by force had they evinced the least disposition for delay. It is clear that the people were wrought up to such a frame of mind, that it would have been as much as the king's crown was worth for him to attempt to detain the Hebrews one moment longer. But it does not seem that even he was now so inclined. That very night he sent to Moses and Aaron an urgent command to do at once all that they had so long and vainly sought his consent to: "Rise up, and get you forth from among my people, both ye and the children of Israel; and go, serve Jehovah as ye have said." Nor is this all. We remember how stoutly he before held out for the retention of the flocks. But now his imperial pride is so effectually humbled, that he hastens to remove any idea of reservation or evasion which his past conduct might awaken; and he therefore quickly adds, "Also take your flocks and your herds, as ye have said, and be gone." Still more extraordinary: he was desirous not to part from them in anger; he craved to be allowed to feel that he was no longer under the ban and exposed to the wrath of the great and terrible God—terrible to him— whose hand had abased him so low. Therefore his last words were, "And bless me also." Is it then to come to this, that he who declared that he knew not Jehovah, and would not obey His voice, is at length constrained to crave the blessing of His servant, that the anger he has so daringly invoked may no longer hang over his head?

So now there is nothing to impede the free course of the Israelites, and forth they march. "Such an emigration as this," as a recent writer well remarks,[1] "the world never saw. On the lowest computation, the entire multitude must have been above two millions, and in all

[1] Smith's *Sacred Annals*, ii. 47. London, 1850.

probability the number exceeded three millions. Is the magnitude of this movement usually apprehended? Do we think of the emigration of the Israelites from Egypt as of the emigration of a number of families twice as numerous as the population of the principality of Wales, or considerably more than the whole population of the British Metropolis (in 1841), with all

AN ORIENTAL MIGRATION

their goods, utensils, property, and cattle? The collecting together of so immense a multitude, the arranging of the order of their march, the provision of the requisite food for even a few days, must, under the circumstances, have been utterly impossible, unless a very special and overruling Providence had graciously interfered to obviate the difficulties of the case. To the most superficial observer it must be evident that no man, or number of men, having nothing but human resources, could have ventured to undertake this journey. Scarcely any wonder wrought by divine power in Egypt appears greater than this emigration of a nation, when fairly and fully considered."

It is said, in the authorised version, that they went up out of Egypt "harnessed" (Exod. xiii. 18), which means fully equipped for war or for a journey, in which latter sense only it is now used. This is obviously the sense here intended by the translators. The marginal reading is "by five in a rank;" but although there is, in the original Hebrew word, an obscure reference to the number five, the word probably means, as the translators in their textual rendering understood, that they went out in an orderly manner, fully equipped for the journey, as we indeed know was the fact.

It is possible they may have marched in *five* large divisions, and hence the choice of this particular word; but that it meant "five in a rank" could only be fancied by those who had no just conception of the number of the people. At this rate, if we allow the ranks of only the 600,000 men fit to bear arms to have been three feet asunder, they would have formed a procession sixty miles in length, and the van would almost have reached the Red Sea before the rear had left the land of Goshen; and if we add to these the remainder of the host, the line would have extended, by the direct route from Egypt, quite into the limits of the land of Canaan. This fact is stated, not only to correct an erroneous impression, but to assist the reader to a tangible idea of the vastness of that body of people which Moses led out of Egypt, and which the Lord sustained in the wilderness for forty years.

The computation of the number of the Israelites is formed in this way:—Our information is, that the efficient men in the Hebrew host amounted to 600,000. Now, it is known that the number of males too young and too old for military service, is at *least*, in every average population, equal to that of efficient men.[1] This raises the

[1] Strictly, the number of males under twenty is about

number to 1,200,000 males of all ages; and, as this number is to be doubled for the females of all ages, the whole amounts to 2,400,000; or we may safely say two millions and a half, especially if we take account of the "mixed multitude" who, we are told, went out with the Israelites. These we take to have been native Egyptian vagrants and convicts, and foreign captives, whom community of suffering had brought into contact with the Israelites, and who, with or without their consent, quitted the country along with them. They were like the camp followers of an army; which, in the case of an eastern army, are often as numerous as the soldiers themselves. That they were numerous, is historically known. It is quite safe to calculate, that they raised the whole number from somewhere about two and a half to three millions; but this number is not calculable like that of the Hebrews, which, on the data given, we feel assured must have been about 2,400,000 or 2,500,000. The presence of this "mixed multitude" proved a great inconvenience and danger to the Israelites, not only from their being foremost in all discontent and rebellion, but from their keeping idolatrous tendencies alive in the camp. If they did eventually conform to the outward observances of Hebrew worship, it is clear that the bulk of them were in fact idolaters, absorbed in the mere externals of their condition, and having no real share in the hope or faith of Israel.

One of the leading arguments of Dr. Colenso against the historic credibility of the Pentateuch is founded on the view which Dr. Kitto here takes of the Exodus. He represents the Israelites as *all* assembling at Rameses on the passover night—men and women, sick and infirm, women in childbirth, and young infants. From every part of a large district they were brought together at a moment's notice, with their flocks, herds, and movable property. Then, having been marshalled by Moses, they set forth in one dense column. Colenso, after describing the scene in his own graphic style, says, "I do not hesitate to declare this statement to be utterly incredible and impossible."

In reply to this and similar objections, which have become very popular of late, I ask, Does the sacred narrative warrant Colenso's description? Does it state, or does it imply, that the people *all* assembled at Rameses, with

equal to that over twenty. Allowing that the age of military service commences under twenty, the number thus gained to the class of efficient males is counterbalanced by the number too old for military service, so that the duplication is good either way.

their flocks, herds, and baggage? It would seem, from a careful study of the whole, that the flocks, herds, and mixed multitude did not assemble at Rameses at all, and did not even follow the line of route taken by Moses. The people had been long preparing for the journey. A system of communication was established, by which Moses was able to convey his orders with great rapidity to every part of Goshen. The flocks and herds were doubtless away on the open plains near the eastern frontier. Most of the people, being shepherds, were necessarily semi-nomads, and had their wives and children with their flocks. Moses and the leading men of the nation, with those who had been engaged in labour by Egyptian taskmasters, had assembled at Rameses, and they marched out in order. But the others would naturally take a more northerly course: passing round the head of the Gulf of Suez, and leading the flocks through the best pasture lands. It is worthy of note, that the cattle are not mentioned at the passage of the Red Sea, nor at Marah, nor at Elim. The migration of a modern tribe of Bedawin will best illustrate the exodus. The chiefs and main body of armed men keep close together; while the flocks and their attendants roam far and wide.

It will be observed, that by many modern critics the divine element is entirely ignored in the exodus. It is judged of as a simple case of migration, in direct opposition to what is repeatedly and emphatically affirmed by the sacred historian. The power of the Lord was directly exercised in every stage. We know not how far it extended; how it strengthened the weak, healed the sick, or directed the movements of the whole host. We do know, however, that it was exercised. Without it the exodus would have been impossible.

P.

THE RED SEA

Exodus 14

THE expiration of three days from their departure was a critical time for the Israelites. It will be remembered that their application to the king was, that they might go three days' journey into the wilderness, there to worship their God. It is clear, therefore, that to have continued their march any farther, would have indicated the intention *not* to return, which the suspicions of Pharaoh had imputed to them. By this time they were near the head of the Red Sea; and here they received the direction, at that time mysterious, to turn southward, and put themselves in such a position between the mountains which border the sea on the west, and the sea itself, as would completely shut them in and stay their farther progress, unless they could pass over the sea in front, or return through a valley behind them into the heart of Egypt. This command must have astonished the Israelites themselves not a little; but they were assured that there was an ulterior design of Providence in this direction, and they obeyed, nobly obeyed, although it must have seemed to them that by this step they placed themselves at the mercy of the Egyptians, should their enemies be induced to follow them. It is no objection to this movement, but, on the contrary, its highest recommendation, and the best proof of its divine prescription, that it is one which no human leader would have directed. It was taken for this very purpose, that a yet more signal display might be furnished of the Lord's power, in the discomfiture of the Egyptians, and in the deliverance of Israel not only from present danger, but from the fears of Egyptian vengeance, by which they would otherwise have been haunted continually during their long sojourn in the wilderness. To the Egyptians, who by their scouts took care to watch the movements of the Hebrew host, their proceeding in this direction must have seemed the height of suicidal infatuation; and no sooner did the king hear of it, than, concluding that they were forsaken by the God who had hitherto been their shield, and whose power he had full cause to know, he resolved to take advantage of such egregious folly, and pursue them with all the forces at his immediate disposal. This shows that, notwithstanding the humbled language he had used in allowing the Israelites to take their departure, his heart was still essentially unsoftened; and now that the opportunity seemed to offer of regaining the mastery, of avenging the disgrace and loss he had sustained, he prepared for action against the fugitive host. The loss of so large a body of useful slaves must have been severely felt by the Egyptians; and probably, therefore, his primary object was to drive them back through the valley of Bedea. He knew that, from the position in which they had placed themselves, as well as from their enfeebled character, they were unfit of themselves to resist a comparatively small disciplined force, and he might therefore hope to compel them to return without a struggle; or if not, what then? They were at his mercy: he could drive them forward into the sea, for there was no retreat. Blindly obdurate as this king of Egypt was, we can hardly suppose that he would

have ventured to take this step, had he not conceived that the God of the Israelites had forsaken them, or that his own gods had now at length bestirred themselves in the cause of Egypt. But how could the former impression be consistent with the visible demonstration of the divine presence, as shown in the pillar of cloud, which became one of fire by night, and moved on before the Hebrew host, marking out the path it was to take? He could not have been ignorant of this appearance, which his scouts would not fail to report to him. But it is not likely that they, viewing it at a distance, were acquainted with its real nature. At the present day, in great caravans, such as that of the annual pilgrimage of the Mohammedans to Mecca, a large cresset containing fire is borne aloft before the moving host, the smoke of which by day, and the fire by night, serve the purpose of an ensign or waymark for the people, the most conspicuous, and therefore the most useful, that can be devised. The king probably thought the pillar of cloud something of this nature,

FIRE-ENSIGN OF GREAT CARAVAN TO MECCA

and was therefore not deterred by its presence from his enterprise.

To the student of Egyptian antiquities there is something of deep interest in the two verses (Exod. xiv. 6, 7) which describe the force of the Egyptians: "He made ready his chariot, and took his people with him; and he took six hundred chosen chariots, and all the chariots of Egypt, and captains over every one of them." Here the pursuing force is described as composed entirely of chariots. This is entirely in conformity with the existing testimony of the monuments, which exhibit no kind of military force but war-chariots and infantry—no cavalry properly so called, that is, warriors on horseback. But few horsemen are represented on the monuments, and these are not Egyptians but foreigners. In a hot pursuit like this, the infantry could, from the nature of the case, take no part; and there being no mounted cavalry, the matter was left entirely to the chariot-warriors. It is true that in verses eighteenth and twenty-sixth we read of "chariots and horsemen," and in twenty-third of "horses, chariots, and horsemen;" but it has been shown grammatically that the "horses" are those of the chariots, and the "horsemen" (properly "riders") those who rode in them. Indeed, it appears from the narrative that only chariots were involved in the result. The war chariots of the Egyptians

ANCIENT EGYPTIAN WAR CHARIOTS

were of very light construction, and drawn by two horses. They mostly carried two persons, one of whom managed the horses, while the other plied his weapons of war; but sometimes the warrior stood alone in his chariot, the reins being lashed around his body. They must have been expert riders to discharge arrows standing in a chariot, with the horses in full gallop, while the horses were to be guided by the movements of the body. But it is likely that the reins, which at the first view appear as a hindrance, actually afforded some support to the body in this position.

That the king was able to commence the pursuit so promptly implies the existence under the Egyptian government of a standing force, which is attested by all ancient writers to have been the case from the earliest times in Egypt. The number seems small. The six hundred were, however, the "chosen chariots," that is, those of the royal guard; and besides these there were "all the chariots of Egypt," that is all the available chariots, which doubtless formed a numerous force. Now this kind of force was always, until a late period of their history, regarded with awe and terror by the Israelites; and no sooner did it appear on this occasion than they began to

murmur against Moses and Aaron for having brought them into such a case, and indeed for having brought them out of Egypt at all, only to perish in the wilderness. If left to themselves, they would in all probability have yielded to the Egyptians, and have submitted to be driven back like cattle before the chariots of Egypt. The idea of resistance does not seem to have entered their minds, notwithstanding the enormous superiority of their number, under the highest calculation that can possibly be given to the pursuing force. There may be more reason than appears for this. They were probably unarmed. The Egyptians did not, as the modern Orientals do, wear arms, except on actual military service. On this account, and also perhaps from their position as bondmen, the Israelites probably did not possess any, or, if they did, would not, in the face of customary usage, have been likely to assume them in what was professedly a peaceful expedition.

They were with difficulty pacified by assurances of a divine deliverance; and the Egyptians, satisfied that they had secured their prey, and that it was impossible for them to escape, were in no haste to assail them. They were themselves also probably wearied with their rapid march. They therefore encamped for the night —for it was towards evening when they arrived— purposing, no doubt, to give effect to their intentions in the morning. The Israelites were also in their encampment, awaiting the result with trembling anxiety; when, to their amazement, the pillar of cloud which was in front of them moved round in silent and stately majesty through the air, and took its station in their rear, between them and the Egyptians. Nor was this all: for whereas formerly it had been a pillar of cloud by day and of flame by night, it was now both at once. To the Egyptians it remained a pillar of cloud still; but to the Israelites it became, as usual at night, a pillar of flame. The effect was, that the Egyptians were in darkness, while the Israelites had abundance of light, and that the two hosts were hidden from the view of each other; for the opacity of the cloud towards the Egyptians would prevent them from seeing what took place among the Israelites.

And what was it that took place? Moses, at the command of God, lifted up his rod upon the waters, and forthwith a strong east wind began to blow, dividing the waters, and making a pathway through the deep. Encouraged by the light which they enjoyed, and by the marvellous interposition of God in their favour, the Israelites ventured into the miraculous channel thus opened, and began their march to the other side, the waters being as a wall to them on the right hand and on the left.

It was not until the morning, when the rear of the Israelites had nearly reached the other side, that the Egyptians became aware of what had taken place. Advancing then, and finding the camp of Israel deserted, they hurried on by the road which Israel had evidently taken. It is not clear that the Egyptians knew or thought that they were following the Hebrews into the bed of the sea. Considering the darkness, additional to that of night, which had come between the pursuers and the pursued, it is not probable that they had any clear perception of the course in which they were moving, and least of all that they were travelling in the bared bed of the divided waters. They could hear the noise of the flying host before them, and could see confusedly a little way about their feet; but in all likelihood they were little able to distinguish the localities around them, and may even have thought that they were pursuing the Israelites up the valley of Bedea, on their return to Egypt. But by the time day broke they became aware of their position; and fearful for them did the discovery prove. They were already far advanced in the miraculous road; and the east wind ceasing towards morning, the waters piled up by its agency began to return. But the bottom, along which they were marching, had also been poached by the previous march of the people and cattle of the Israelites; and finding a heavy sea returning on them from the west, the king's army thought it high time to retreat. But it was too late. They were embarrassed by the state of the ground; and before they could extricate themselves from their dangerous position, the waters returned and covered them all— consummating, by one fearful stroke, the deliverance of Israel and the overthrow of the Egyptians.

TRIUMPH

Exodus 15

THE destruction of the Egyptian host in the depths of the Red Sea, was in every respect an event of the utmost importance to the Israelites.

It ensured their safety. Suppose that they had not in the first instance been pursued, and that consequently this judgment had not befallen the Egyptians. It would, in that case, have been possible at any time for the king of Egypt to pursue them; and the dread of his doing so, during their long sojourn in the wilderness, must for many years have troubled their minds, and prevented them from enjoying the confidence of safety, unless they looked with more assurance to the certainty of the divine protection than they were disposed to do. But now this source of apprehension was quieted for ever. The death of the king, and the destruction of his forces, must have greatly crippled the resources of his successor, and may well have prevented him, had he been so inclined, from pursuing an object which had brought so much disgrace and ruin upon the nation. But the probability is, that he had no inclination to follow the policy which had been maintained chiefly by the personal obstinacy of the late king. Indeed, it is not unlikely that the frequent talk of the Israelites, subsequently, of returning to Egypt, may have arisen from the conviction that the state of affairs was so materially altered in that country by this great event, that they might do so without danger of the old oppression being renewed; and they may possibly have even thought, that in the confusion which would attend this calamitious blow upon Egypt, they might stand a fair chance of gaining the upper hand in that country, as the shepherd kings had done before.

Another result of the overthrow would be that they would acquire possession of great and valuable spoil, especially in weapons and armour, which they greatly needed. The flower of Pharaoh's army, the chivalry of Egypt, lay dead upon the shore of the Red Sea, and offered to the Israelites a most valuable and easily acquired booty, such as has rarely fallen to the lot of any people. This must have formed a very material contribution to the wealth which the Hebrews are known to have possessed in the wilderness.

This signal display of the divine power for their protection had also a most important influence upon the future history of the nation, and this by the impression produced both upon their own minds, and upon the minds of the neighbouring nations. As to themselves, we cannot question that this marvellous interposition must have had a material effect in impressing them with a conviction of the Lord's goodness and power. Their tendency to distrust and unbelief must have been greatly checked by it; and although that tendency now and then broke out in acts of discontent and rebellion, nothing can more clearly show that a strong and salutary impression was produced, than the prominent manner in which this event is set forth, and the pointed way in which it is referred to, in all the subsequent literature of the people, and especially in the Psalms of David. Every nation has some one prominent point of history which it regards with special interest, and allusions to which occur more frequently than to any other, in the songs of the poets and the glowing words of orators; and to the Hebrews the passage of the Red Sea, and the overthrow of Pharaoh and his splendid host, was this one point of fixed regard, which it would not have been, but through the impression originally produced on the national mind. Later ages cannot create any enthusiasm with regard to a past event, which was not experienced at the time when it was a new and living fact.

No less conspicuous was the effect produced upon the neighbouring nations. It had much influence in protecting the Israelites from hostilities, and in facilitating their future progress, by inspiring a salutary dread of the God by whom they were so manifestly protected. It is clear that they, at least, who had the best opportunities of knowing the facts, never in the least doubted that this event was a most stupendous miracle; and it is only as such that it could have produced upon them the effect which is recorded. Forty years after, kings trembled on their thrones when they thought of it; and it had even more remarkably taken a distinct place in the minds of the common people—of those who had no concern with public affairs. Thus does Rahab, a woman of the small town of Jericho, speak at the same date to the Hebrew spies: "I know that the Lord hath given you the land, and that your terror is fallen upon us, and that all the inhabitants of the land faint because of you. For we have heard how the Lord dried up the water of the Red Sea for you, when ye came out of Egypt. And as soon as we had heard these things, our hearts did melt, neither did there remain any more courage in any man because of you."[1] Even three hundred years after the miracle, when the ark of God was brought into the camp of Israel, the Philistines were terrified by the recollection of this then ancient event, and cried, "Woe unto us! who shall deliver us out of the hand of these mighty Gods, that smote the Egyptians with all the plagues in the wilderness?"[2] An impression thus strong and durable could not but contribute very materially to the safety of the Israelites in the wilderness, and to their ultimate conquest of the Promised Land.

A recent writer[3] has forcibly directed attention to the manner in which the people rejoiced at their deliverance, as not only illustrating the orderly state of the multitude, but evincing their intellectual and moral culture, and we may avail ourselves of some of his remarks. It is to be noted that they had escaped from evils as weighty in aggravated affliction, and as humiliating and debasing in their effects, as had ever pressed upon any people. Yet how did these men manifest their joy, after having suddenly obtained a great accession of wealth through the destruction of their tyrant foes, and when they felt themselves restored to perfect freedom? Much as the statement implies, it may be safely answered that they did it in a manner worthy of the great occasion. Moses composed a thanksgiving ode, which the ten thousands of Israel, both men and women, united in singing, as they exulted in their new-born freedom on the shores of the Red Sea. In this noble piece of poetry, full of sublime thoughts, breathing deeply pious and grateful feeling, and replete with enlarged views of the consequences that might be expected to result from this glorious deliverance, we have an expression of the mind of the Hebrew public on this great occasion. As the ode was adapted for

[1] Joshua 2:9-11.　　[2] 1 Samuel 4:8.
[3] *Sacred Annals*, by George Smith, F.S.A., ii. 67.

alternate recitation, not only did the men of Israel shout forth their joy in sacred strains, but the women also, led on by Miriam, and accompanying their voices with the sound of the timbrel and the motions of the dance, swelled the chorus of thanksgiving, and re-echoed to the skies the bold *refrain*, "Sing ye to the Lord, for He hath triumphed gloriously: the horse and his rider hath He thrown into the sea." "Where, in all history, do we find a great national deliverance so appropriately acknowledged? Let this public action be tested by her highest standard in regard to elevated religious devotion, striking intellectual dignity, eloquent and cultivated, and then let those who speak of these Hebrews as a horde of semi-savages, tell us what great public act, in the best ages of Greece and Rome, will bear comparison with this grateful conduct of the redeemed Israelites."

DANCE WITH TIMBRELS

Our readers are no doubt aware that there is a dispute as to the locality where the passage of the Red Sea took place. We have not here entered into the question. No certainty can be obtained on this subject; but we have always entertained the impression that they came out at or near the place called Ain Mûsa (Fountain of Moses). The sea is here about eight miles across, and the station is about twelve miles from the extremity of the gulf at Suez. A few shrubs and stunted palms are here nourished by the brackish waters of six or eight shallow pools, which appear to be scooped out in the dark hard earth deposited from the water itself. This deposit has, in the course of three or four thousand years, acquired considerable elevation, so that the waters are above the level of the grounds around. Some of the shallow wells are evidently recent, others are more ancient. From none of them does the water run freely; but the ground around is kept moist, and the scanty vegetation affords some

WELLS OF MOSES

relief and contrast to the neighbouring desolation.

Why do these fountains, it may be asked, bear the name of Moses? Were they digged by him?

Did the hosts of Israel assemble around them after the passage of the Red Sea; or have they merely attracted the great lawgiver's name, which tradition has connected with almost every prominent point between Egypt and Sinai? It is not at all probable that the present pits were dug by Moses; but from the nature of the ground in which they are sunk, it is likely that they mark an important watering station for the Bedouins from time immemorial. It is also evident that they once occupied a lower level, which has been raised by constant deposition from the waters. This gradual elevation has diminished the quantity of water, and rendered it more brackish. It is reasonable, therefore, to conclude, that anciently the waters were sweet and abundant. And if the conclusion be correct, that the Israelites emerged from the bed of the Red Sea at no great distance southward from these wells, and that nearly a month afterwards they had advanced scarcely fifty miles towards Sinai, we may infer that they rested for some time in the neighbourhood of the miraculous passage. Yet we do not hear of their wanting any water until they had commenced their marches in the wilderness of Shur, where, having

to the north, there is much probability that they remained for some time encamped around them.

As to the question—Where did Moses lead Israel through the Red Sea? an approximate answer may be offered. There can be no doubt that the Gulf of Suez once extended farther north than it does now. All appearances lead to that conclusion; and, therefore, the miracle *may* have occurred in some part of the arm of the sea long since dried up. An attentive examination of the narrative by Moses points to some position higher than the present water line. It is said (Ex. xiii. 20-22; xiv. 1-4) the Israelites "took their journey from Succoth, and encamped in Etham, in the edge of the wilderness. And the Lord went before them by day in a pillar of a cloud, to lead them the way; and by night in a pillar of fire, to give them light; to go by day and night: He took not away the pillar of the cloud by day, nor the pillar of fire by night, from before the people. And the Lord spake unto Moses, saying, Speak unto the children of Israel, that they turn and encamp before Pi-hahiroth, between Migdol and the sea, over against Baal-zephon: before it shall ye encamp by the sea. For Pharaoh will say of the children of Israel, They are entangled in the land, the wilderness hath shut them in. And I will harden Pharaoh's heart, that he shall follow after them; and I will be honoured upon Pharaoh, and upon all his host; that the Egyptians may know that I am the Lord. And they did so."

Succoth is a word meaning *booths*, and probably refers to a temporary encampment. The other names seem to relate to well known towns and towers, which have left no vestiges; and the prepositions "*by*," "*before*," "*beside*," and "*over against*," are very indefinite. *Migdol*, however, must surely be the town or tower called by the Greeks *Magdolon*, situated to the north of the present gulf; and it is equally clear that *Etham* must have been to the northeast of the same gulf, for *Etham* is described as "in the edge of the wilderness" (Numb. xxxiii. 6): and this wilderness, on the edge of which *Etham* stood, which seems to have taken its name from such contiguity, is the same wilderness, which goes by the name of *Shur*. Now, the Israelites came to the edge of the *Etham* wilderness

PILGRIM'S POOL, SUCCOTH

proceeded for three days without finding any, they began to complain; and as there is no present indication of water in this vicinity, except at these wells, and at the fountain of Naba, half-an-hour

before they crossed the sea; and again into this wilderness they entered when they had crossed. Consequently it would appear, that the wilderness ran north and south of the east shore, and somewhere east of the spot where Suez stands. On the other hand, *Pi-hahiroth* seems to have been to the south-west of *Etham*, because it was visited by the people before they crossed the water from the western shore. It is also said, that at *Etham* they were commanded *to turn* and encamp before *Pi-hahiroth* (Ex. xiv. 2); and, again (Numb. xxxiii. 7), we are told that "they removed from *Etham, and turned* again unto *Pi-hahiroth*." Their route was to *Succoth*, then to *Etham*, as if they were going directly to Canaan; then they turned back, and went to other places which seem to have been lying south-west, and thence they crossed the gulf. The most satisfactory conclusion is, that their wanderings were to the north of Suez. When they left Egypt, it was anticipated that Pharaoh would say, "They are entangled in the land, the wilderness hath shut them in." The place where he thought they would be entangled was *Pi-hahiroth*, near the sea. Some scholars say the word signifies "the mouth of mountain gorges;" but others say that the word has nothing to do with mountains, but refers to a country abounding in sedges and pools, and such a country continues to exist round the northern end of the Gulf of Suez.

Wherever the passage took place, it was miraculous, yet the miracle was connected with the operation of natural laws. "And Moses stretched out his hand over the sea; and the Lord caused the sea to go back by a strong east wind all that night, and made the sea dry land, and the waters were divided." (Ex. xiv. 21.)

S.

THIRST

Exodus 15:23-27

WHEN the Lord appeared to Moses in Horeb, in the bush that burned without being consumed, it was indicated that the Israelites, after their deliverance, should render homage to God in that very place. Accordingly, when they quitted the spot where they had crossed the Red Sea, they took their course in that direction along its shores. Three days they marched without finding any water. We do not, with some, suppose, that during all this time they were without water. This was impossible. They must have brought water in their leathern bottles with them from the last station. But this time having passed without an opportunity of replenishing their vessels, the supply was at length exhausted, and they began to suffer fearfully from thirst. Let us not think lightly of their distress. Thirst is a cruel thing; and it is known to be such even in a humid clime, where the sensation is rarely and lightly experienced, and is very easily removed. But amid the hot sandy waste, under a burning sky, without any means of relief, the suffering is horrible. There is nothing like it. If we reflect that this vast host of men, women, and children, with numerous herds of cattle, had to travel over the sandy waste mostly on foot, with the burning sun over their heads, we may be able to form some faint and inadequate idea of their condition. But if we endeavour to picture to ourselves the circumstances of their case, and the unmistakeable signs of suffering and misery which it presented, we shall have a more distinct apprehension of their wretched condition. They plod moodily and heavily on, no man speaking to his fellow. Many cannot speak if they would. Their tongues are parched and rough, and cling to the roofs of their mouths; their lips are black and shrivelled; and their eyeballs are red with heat, and sometimes a dimness comes over them, which makes them stagger with faintness. There is not one in all that multitude who probably would not have given all he possessed in the world, who would not have parted with a limb or have given up his life, for one cool draught of water. And this was suffered by a people who had been used to drink without stint of the finest water in the world.

But lo! their misery, they think, is past. In the distance they behold trees and bushes clad in refreshing green, and they know there must be water near. With glad looks and quickened steps they push joyously on.

> " For sure through that green meadow flows
> The living stream! And lo! their famished beast
> Sees the restoring sight!
> Hope gives his feeble limbs a sudden strength,
> He hurries on!"—*Thalaba.*

What a rush to the water! what eagerness to gulp the refreshing flood! But whence that universal groan, and horror, and despair? The water is bitter—so bitter as to be loathsome even to their intense agony of thirst. Pity them; but judge not them too severely, if, in that awful moment of disappointed hope, with the waters of Marah before their faces and the waters of the Nile before their thoughts, they did murmur, they did complain that they had been brought from unfailing waters to perish in that thirsty desolation. They should have trusted in God. They had been rescued from more imminent danger; and it was no arm of flesh, but the sacred pillar of cloud, which had indicated their way and brought them to that place. They should have prayed to their Divine Protector to supply their wants, as He was well able to do; and although there is much in the real misery they suffered to extenuate *this* offence, their forgetfulness and neglect were most blameworthy. Yet, in consideration of their sufferings, God Himself excused them in this more readily than man has done. It will be seen in the sacred record that He dealt tenderly with them. He did not, as on other occasions, when they sinned in like manner without the like excuse, reprove them; but when Moses cried to Him for help, He, in the tenderness of His great pity, at once healed the waters, and made them sweet and salutary. Yet here, as usual, He wrought by means. He showed Moses a tree, and directed him to cast it into the spring, and immediately the bitterness departed from the waters. Some travellers have innocently sought in this quarter for some tree or shrub, possessing the natural quality of healing such unwholesome waters; but they have found none. The natives know nothing of the kind. As well might they have sought near Jericho for the kind of salt with which Elisha healed the bad waters of the fountain there.[1] The tree never existed, the mere immersion of whose branches could naturally correct the bad qualities of so much water as was needed to quench the thirst of so large a host.

The sites of both Marah and Elim appear to have been identified,—the former in Ain Howarah, a fountain about thirty-three miles to the south of Ain Mûsa. The site is marked by two lone palm trees, or rather bushes, in the distance, and a nearer approach discloses some ghurkud[2] shrubs. The fountain is a shallow pit, seldom holding more than a hundred gallons of water. The well is scooped out at the top of a broad flat mound, formed by a whitish substance deposited by the water in the course of many centuries. It is probable that, when the Israelites arrived here, the hill had scarcely begun to form, and of course the waters were at a much lower level. The waters were also, doubtless, more abundant; for the Scripture narrative does not indicate that there was any want of water in the neighbourhood, but only that it was bitter, whence the place received the name of Marah. The quality of the water, as well as the quantity, has probably been somewhat changed in the course of

[1] 2 Kings 2:20-22.   [2] *Peganum Retusum.*

ages. The Arabs, however, regard it as the worst water along the coast, and only drink it when it is impossible to obtain any other. The camels do not refuse it; and if anciently its qualities were the same as they now are, its loathsomeness to the thirsty Israelites can only be explained by its being the first decidedly bad water which had been encountered by a people accustomed to the sweet waters of the Nile. Water which, even at this day, the rough-tasted Arabs shun, must have been detestable to the Israelites. Its qualities, perhaps, vary with the time of the year, being worst in the driest season. We thus account for the somewhat varying statements of travellers. Its taste is, however, unpleasant, saltish, and somewhat bitter. One compares it to a weak solution of Epsom salts, and another intimates that the effects are similar. It is to be hoped that some future traveller will secure a bottle of it for analysation.

The next station, Elim, with its palm trees, is identified with Wady Ghurundel, about six miles south of Marah. This is a considerable valley, filled with wild tamarisks and other bushes, and also with some small trees, among which are palms. This spot seems like "green pastures," compared with the desolate and sterile tracts which the traveller has passed since quitting the neighbourhood of the Nile. Wholesome and sweet water is found here, by scooping out the sand to the depth of two or three feet. The fountain itself, lying up the valley out of the direct route to Sinai, had not been visited by travellers until Mr. Bartlett determined to find it out for himself; and he had not proceeded for more than half-an-hour before he reached the principal spring. It wells out at the foot of a sandstone rock, forming a small pool of refreshing water, bordered by sedges, and looks highly refreshing after Ain Mûsa and Hawarah. "There was even—delightful sight!—a little grass, and birds were hopping about enjoying the rare luxury. The water trickling off pursues its way some distance down the valley, forming a reedy marsh, interspersed with thickets of bushes and dwarf palm trees, and a considerable quantity of tamarisks and other shrubs; and as there are also considerable masses of similar vegetation above this point, there are probably several other springs which nourish it. Altogether it was a reviving sight in the thirsty desert; and I saw no spot which could so well correspond with the wells and palm trees of Elim through the entire route to Wady Feiran."[1]

The character of the country through which the Israelites passed after crossing the Red Sea, favours the view advanced in a preceding note, that only a part of the people, forming what might be called the headquarters of the host, marched in a body with Moses. Their numbers cannot now be ascertained; but if we take modern Arab tribes as a guide, they probably did not amount to more than one-tenth of the whole.

The route after the passage of the Red Sea must have been along the shore towards the south-east. Here is an undulating plain, averaging some ten miles in breadth, shut in on the land side by a mountain range, which rises bare, precipitous, and uniform, like a cyclopean wall: It is bleak and barren, partly covered with white gravel, partly with drifting sand. Skilful shepherds, like the Israelites, would never have led their flocks along such a route. The scanty supplies of water at Marah and Elim, even though they may have been ten times more copious then than now, could not have supplied the wants of two millions of people, with their vast flocks and herds. They would be sufficient, however, for the body of men who marched with Moses. I feel convinced that the others, with the sheep and cattle, were spread far and wide over the country.

It may be, and has been, objected to this view, that, if spread over a wide district, the flocks must have been exposed to the depredations of hostile tribes, and must in consequence have been constantly guarded by armed men. The promises of God, frequently repeated and miraculously fulfilled, form a sufficient answer to such objections. God said expressly, "I will send my fear before thee. . . . And I will make all thine enemies turn their backs unto thee." (Exod. xxiii. 27; see also Num. xxii. 2-4; Deut. ii. 24, 25.) And in the song of Moses, the effect of the stupendous miracle of the Red Sea is thus prophetically described:—" The people shall hear, and be afraid; sorrow shall take hold on the inhabitants of Palestina. Then the dukes of Edom shall be amazed; the mighty men of Moab, trembling shall take hold upon them: all the inhabitants of Canaan shall melt away. Fear and dread shall fall upon them." (Exod. xv. 14-16.) Under such circumstances, the flocks of the Israelites might roam in perfect safety over the whole country, from the borders of Egypt to Canaan.

P.

HUNGER

Exodus 16

THE people were still to be taught the great lesson of trust in God—implicit trust—which

[1] Bartlett's *Forty Days' Wanderings in the Desert*, 33, 34. See also Laborde, and the American travellers, Doctors Robinson, Olin, and Durbin.

was most essential to qualify them for the great work to which they had been appointed. Without this, every step in their "march of mystery" through the wilderness had been a stumble and a disaster, and their conflict with the embattled host of Canaan a defeat and an overthrow.

In one point their faith was sorely tried. We have seeen it tried in thirst; we next behold it tried in hunger. A military man, who has witnessed the difficulty of providing a regular supply of victuals, even in a peopled country, for a large body of men, whether by purchase or by enforced contribution, can better than any other person appreciate the faith required from Moses, when he undertook to lead into "the waste howling wilderness," where no provisions existed, or could be obtained by force or purchase, a people whose number exceeded threefold the largest army which the ambition or pride of man ever brought together. We have often had occasion to reflect upon this fact, and have always returned to it with new and increased astonishment at the "largeness of heart" which it is possible for God to bestow on man, in that He gave such marvellous capacity of faith to Moses, as enabled him to believe that the immense host which he had led from amid the fatness of Egypt, would, by the power of God's bountiful right hand, be sustained in comfort in the wilderness. He acted not blindly. He knew well what he was doing. He had spent forty of the best years of his life in that very region; and he knew better than any the absence there of any appreciable resources for the support of such a multitude. He was quite sure, when he led them forth, that without a miracle, inconceivable in its extent and continuous in its duration, the whole multitude must perish, after he and his had probably been sacrificed to the disappointment and rage of the people, who would inevitably conclude that they had been beguiled to their ruin. It seems to us that this is second to no act of faith which the sacred history relates.

It was soon put to a severe test. In about a month after their leaving Egypt, they came to the next important encampment after Elim, in the wilderness of Sin. By this time the provisions they had brought with them from Egypt appear to have been wholly exhausted; and as, during the whole of this period, they had found little or no food in the country through which they had passed, nor saw the prospect of any in the still wilder region that lay before them, they began to speculate on the impossibility of finding subsistence for their myriads under such circumstances. The more they considered it, the more gloomy their views became. They thought of their wives and little ones, and their hearts failed them. For their sake probably, more than for their own, they began to lament that they had committed themselves to this wild adventure, and to regret that they had left the abundance of Egypt. It is the nature of man to underrate past evils, and to overrate past advantages, in comparison with the present. So now, the Israelites thought much of the plenty of Egypt, while its slavery and its toil faded from their view; and they were keenly alive to the privations of their present position, while regardless of the manly freedom they had attained, and of the high hopes that lay before them. In fact, they thought too much. They were not required to think, but only to believe. They were suffered to endure this distress, that their faith might be tried and educated. It had been as easy for God to anticipate and prevent their wants, as to satisfy them when they were expressed. But so He deals not with the children to whom He is teaching the great lessons of His school. A man, it seems, limits his duty to the *feeding* of his slaves; but he tries, he trains, he disciplines his children—and God dealt with them as with His children.

Although, as we have said, these thoughts were natural, they are not on that account to be excused. After what they had seen, no persons could be less excusable than they for distrust or lack of faith. Had they reflected, as they ought to have done, they should have thought of what the Lord's high hand had marvellously wrought on their behalf, and from that experience have gathered hope and confidence.

The real wants of this people have probably been underrated through the supposition that they might, if they had thought proper, have lived upon their apparently numerous flocks and herds. But we have already had occasion to observe that a pastoral people do not live upon the flesh of their flocks and herds, but upon the produce of them, and only slay their cattle for food on high or hospitable occasions; and besides, were the case otherwise, we are to recollect that their flocks and herds were not the common property of all, but were undoubtedly the private

property of a comparatively small number of persons, the great body of the people being destitute of even this resource. And supposing, as an extreme case, that the owners of these flocks and herds had given them up to the wants of the multitude, the supply, however large, could not have lasted long, nor would such provision alone have been wholesome to a people who had been so much used to vegetable as well as animal food in Egypt. The cry was therefore for both bread and meat; and they looked back with regret upon the time when in that rich land they not only " sat by the flesh-pots," but when they " did eat bread to their full." A miraculous supply of both was promised to them, not without a mild reproof for their murmurings and distrust, which, as Moses justly warned them, although ostensibly levelled at himself and his brother, were really directed against the Lord, who had made them His peculiar care.

The promised flesh came in the shape of a vast flock of quails, which, being wearied probably

THE QUAIL

with a long flight, flew so low that they were easily taken in immense numbers by the hand. This bird, of the gallinaceous kind, is something like a partridge. The larger species is of the size of the turtle dove, and is still found abundantly in the spring in the deserts of Arabia Petræa, and the wilderness bordering Palestine and Egypt, coming up at that time from the countries of the Arabian Gulf. The miraculous ordination here, therefore, was that they came at the appointed time, that they passed directly over the Hebrew camp, and that they there flew so low as to be easily taken. They were taken in such numbers as to serve not only for the present, but for some time to come. But how were they to be preserved for future use? The Israelites knew how that was to be accomplished. It is known that the Egyptians, from among whom they came, lived much upon wild fowl as well as upon tame. The latter could be killed as they were wanted, but the former, being only occasionally caught in large numbers, required to be preserved for future use. This was done by drying them in the sun, and perhaps slightly salting them; and in the Egyptian monuments there are actual representations of

ANCIENT EGYPTIAN POULTERERS

birds, slit like fish, and laid out to dry. Great numbers of various birds, and among them quails, are still, in the season of passage, caught in Lower Egypt, especially towards the sea, and are efficiently, though somewhat rudely, preserved. The manner of doing it now is by stripping off the feathers with the skin, and then burying them in the hot sand for a short time, by which process the moisture is absorbed, and the flesh preserved from corruption. One of these modes, most probably the former, was followed by the Israelites on another like occasion, and doubtless on this "they spread them all abroad for themselves round about the camp."[1]

The very next morning the face of the ground around the camp was seen to be covered with "a small round thing, as small as the hoar-frost on the ground." The people did not comprehend it, and asked one another, "What is this?"—the Hebrew of which being MAN-HU, caused the name of MANNA to be given to it. Moses was able to answer the question. He told them that *this* was the substance which, in the place of bread, God destined for their substantial food—their

staff of life. It was, he told them, to fall every morning, except on the Sabbath-day; but on the day preceding, a double quantity would fall, as a supply for the two days. On other days none was to be left until the morning; and when some avaricious or distrustful persons gathered more than the day's consumption required, they found that "it bred worms and stank." Was it not, therefore, a miraculous circumstance that although it would not ordinarily keep for more than one day, the double supply gathered on the sixth day was good for two days? We incline to that opinion, the rather as it appears to be corroborated analogically by the fact that a vessel filled with this very manna, which dissolved in the heat of the sun if left upon the ground, and which corrupted if preserved in the shade, was retained as a memorial of this transaction to future generations. Nevertheless, this matter is open to the remark that Moses directs them to boil or to bake on the previous day what was required for the consumption of the Sabbath; and although this may be, and is usually, understood to denote that this was to prevent the customary operations of dressing it on the Sabbath-day, yet it may signify that they usually ate it undressed, as gathered, while that which they collected the day before the Sabbath was directed to be cooked *in order to its preservation*. There is some corroboration to this view in the fact that the people seem to have used it in *both* ways, from the manner in which the taste of it, as eaten raw, and as taken dressed, is distinguished. Eaten as gathered, it tasted like cakes made of meal and honey; but when dressed, it acquired the taste of fresh oil, a flavour highly agreeable to the Israelites.[1] In shape it was like coriander seed, but in colour it was white. In Num. xi. 8 the people are said to have usually prepared it by first grinding it in a mill, or pounding it in a mortar, and then baking it in, or rather on, pans, into cakes. This primitive mode of baking is still used in the East, and consists of baking the dough upon a plate of metal, propped horizontally at a proper height, and heated by a small fire underneath. This is a peculiarly desert mode of baking cakes, the whole of which we, in recollection of this passage, have often watched with much stronger interest than the mere desire of allaying our hunger with the bread thus prepared could inspire.

There is a kind of tree or shrub, a species of

Numbers 11:32. The particulars of this second supply are more circumstantially related. We have, therefore, taken some of the details to illustrate the first supply, that the reader may have in one view all the facts belonging to this miraculous provision.

[1] Compare Exodus 16:31; Numbers 11:8.

tamarisk, found in this and other regions, which yields at certain times, and in small quantities, a kind of gum, to which the name of manna has been given, in the belief that it really was, or that it resembled the manna by which the Israelites were fed. If any human infatuation could surprise a thoughtful and observant mind —and especially if any folly of those who deem themselves wiser than their Bible could astonish— it might excite strong wonder to see grave and reverend men set forth the strange proposition that two or three millions of people were fed from day to day, during forty years, with this very substance. A very small quantity—and that only at a particular time of the year, which is not the time when the manna first fell—is now afforded by all the trees of the Sinai peninsula; and it would be safe to say, that if all the trees of this kind, then or now growing in the world, had been assembled in this part of Arabia Petræa, and had covered it wholly, they would not have yielded a tithe of the quantity of gum required for the subsistence of so vast a multitude. Indeed, it remains to be proved, that it would be at all salutary or nutritive as an article of constant and substantial food. To us, this explanation, which attempts to attenuate or extinguish the miracle, by supposing this natural product to have been at all times and in all places sufficient —to have fallen regularly around the camp in all its removals, and to have been regularly intermitted on the seventh day—is much harder of belief than the simple and naked miracle, much harder than it would be to believe that hot rolls fell every morning from the skies upon the camp of Israel. A miracle we can understand, however difficult of comprehension; but that which attempts to elucidate a miracle on natural grounds, must make no demands upon our faith—must be full and satisfactory—must be consistent and coherent in all its parts.

A grand miracle of healing came after these miracles of supply. Moses lifted up the serpent in the wilderness, to heal the people wounded with bites of reptiles, as of fire, and in doing that prefigured the wondrous redemption of our souls by the lifting up of the blessed Saviour on the cross. All these wonders were evidences of the presence and power of God. They were the credentials of Moses. They clothed his person and office with a grandeur, calculated deeply to impress such a race as were those, whom God sent him to lead, and teach, and save.

But beyond their evidential force, the miracles had a typical and representative value. A typical value, inasmuch as they illustrated higher, purer, nobler blessings; supplies for the soul, the bread and water of eternal life, guidance and protection for the soul, God's revelation of His mind and will through His glorious word, healing and salvation for the soul, the exodus from the bondage of sin, and the cure of the devil's bite. But, in addition, the miracles had a representative value, thus: ordinary was indicated by the extraordinary. God's special dispensations were intended to indicate and illustrate His common dispensations.

S.

THE UPLIFTED HANDS

Exodus 17:8-16

THE Sinai peninsula was not wholly uninhabited when the hosts of Israel came up into it out of the sea. There was a tribe of Amalekites which had here its headquarters, and seems to have led a life somewhat analogous to that of the Bedouins who still inhabit the same region, except that the former appear to have paid some attention to agriculture, and did not perhaps live wholly in tents. There are traces of buildings and of ancient culture in Wady Feiran (Paran), one of the fertile valleys of the lower Sinai, through which lies the main approach to the upper region. These are ascribed by local and ancient Arabian traditions to the Amalekites; and without laying much, if any, stress on this, it must be admitted that the spot is well chosen for the abode of this people with reference to the history before us.

Hitherto, from all that appears in history, we might suppose the Israelites to be alone in the wilderness. But we now see that their proceedings were closely watched by dangerous eyes, which did not behold with indifference the sudden inroad of so vast a host into these formerly quiet solitudes. The great wealth with which they were laden, and their valuable possessions in flocks and herds, must have excited the eager cupidity of this people, if they were at all like the modern Arabs of the desert. They knew that numbers did not constitute strength; and the composition of this host must have rendered it obvious to them, that they were not likely to prove very formidable enemies in an encounter. One would think, however, that the recent miracles wrought by the hand of God in behalf of the Israelites would have been likely to deter the Amalekites from any attempt to molest a people so protected and so favoured. But after the examples we have seen in Egypt of the *hardness* of unbelief, we are not prepared to expect much from the forbearance of the Amalekites. And, in fact, they did attack the Israelites on their march to, or halt at, Rephidim. In Exodus it is simply written, "Then came Amalek, and fought with Israel in Rephidim." But in Deut. xxv. 17, 18, further particulars are given: " Remember what Amalek did unto thee by the way, when ye were come forth out of Egypt; how he met thee by the way, and smote the hindmost of thee, even all that were feeble behind thee, when thou wast faint and weary; and he feared not God." The last clause is emphatically added, because such an invasion of the chosen people, under these circumstances, was a virtual defiance of the power which had so lately destroyed the Egyptians. This, with the treacherous and unmanly character of the first assault, may account for the deep resentment which was afterwards expressed against this people, and for the doom of eventual destruction which went forth against them. Upon the whole, it would seem that there were two assaults—one upon the feeble rear when the host was on the march, the result of which encouraged the Amalekites to suppose themselves quite able to meet its full strength, and they therefore marched against Israel when encamped at Rephidim. Certainly, the fact that the rear of the Israelitish host was " smitten," might lead their antagonists to suppose that they were not invulnerable, nor so protected as to preclude the hope of conquest, and would thus encourage them to more daring proceedings.

When the Amalekites appeared in force, and manifested their intention to engage the Israelites, Moses, reserving to himself a more important post, directed Joshua—a young man personally attached to him, and who had probably already evinced the courage and conduct proper to a commander —to choose out a number of men from the general body, and give the enemy battle on the morrow. And what did Moses purpose to do himself ?—" I will stand on the top of the hill, with the rod of God in my hand." And so it was done. Joshua led forth his men to the field : and Moses mounted the hill accompanied by Aaron his brother, and by Hur, who is supposed to have been his brother-in-law. Here Moses stood, and held up his hand on high, with the wonder-working rod therein.

it was no doubt held up, in the first instance, as a kind of banner or signal, to be seen by the warring host below, and designed to operate as a continual incentive to their valour and prowess while engaged in the contest; and the sight of this symbol and instrument of the power which had worked so wondrously on their behalf, could not fail to nerve their arms with new vigour every time their eyes were turned towards it. Yet it needed but little reflection to assure them that, as is very manifest, there was no inherent virtue in the rod to produce this effect; and that it derived all its efficacy from the divine appointment, as a visible symbol of that unseen succour and strength which God was pleased to minister to His militant servants fighting His battle, and maintaining the high glory of His name.

Moses was eminently an intercessor with God for the people committed to his charge; and there can be no question that, in connection with these external and symbolical actions, fervent prayer for the divine aid was offered; the uplifting of the rod being thus merely an accompaniment of the earnest intercessions which breathed from the lips and hearts of the venerable men upon the mountain. And even if this were not the case, the circumstances and the result are strikingly analogous to those of intercessory prayer, and suggestive of them.

It was soon seen, that while the hand of Moses was uplifted, Israel prevailed over Amalek; but when the prophet's hand was no longer raised, Amalek was stronger than Israel. Perceiving that Moses could not longer maintain a standing posture, his friends took a stone and put it under him for a seat; and that his hands might no longer fail, they placed themselves one on each side of him, and sustained his hands until the victory of Israel was achieved. In performing this office, we are not to suppose that both his hands were held up on either side at the same time; for in that case the hands of Aaron and Hur would soon have become as weary as those of Moses had been. The main object of sustaining his arms was, that the rod might be held up. This he doubtless shifted at times from one hand to the other; and then Aaron and Hur upholding each the hand which was next to him, successively relieved both him and each other.

The view of the prayerful tenor of this action is not new; it is more or less hinted at by every commentator on Scripture, though it has been less made the subject of pulpit illustration than might have been expected. It is the one taken by the Jews themselves, in whose Targums we read, that "when Moses held up his hands *in prayer*, the house of Israel prevailed; and when he let down his hands *from prayer*, the house of Amalek prevailed."

Let us then observe, that we notice here grouped together that hallowed combination of agencies which ought never to be separated—the dependence upon Heaven, with the use of appointed means. The rod in the hand of Moses, and the sword in that of Joshua; the embattled host in the valley below, and the praying hand in the mount above—all were necessary in the divine economy to the victory of Israel over his foes. So must it be in our conflict with the Amalek which lies ambushed within, to hinder our progress to the mount of God. We may expect no manifestation of the Lord's power, no interference of His goodness, but as the result of a blessing upon our own zealous conflict with temptation. "Prayer without active duty is mockery of God. He who entreats deliverance from the onset and power of evil, yet never makes an effort in his own behalf, nor strives against the sin that wars within him, draws nigh to God with his lips, but is wholly estranged from the fervour of that supplication that issues from the depths of the heart."[1] Yet it was intended to be taught, and was most effectually taught, by this example, that the uplifted hand of Moses contributed more to the safety of the Israelites than their own hands—his rod more than their weapons of war; and, accordingly, their success fluctuates as he raises up or lets down his hands. In like manner will the Christian warfare be attended with little success, unless it be waged in the practice of unceasing earnest prayer. It will never be known on this side the Lord's second coming, how much His cause, and the work of individual salvation, have been advanced by the "effectual fervent prayer" of righteous men. And it is surely a cheering reflection, in the heat and burden of the day of battle, that, while we are contending below, faithful servants of God have ascended the hill of spiritual prayer, and are imploring blessings upon our efforts.

It is greatly our desire that we could express, with all the emphasis of our own convictions, our sense of the importance and value of that

[1] Buddicom's *Christian Exodus*, p. 366.

precious intercessory prayer which the example before us illustrates. It is, we fear, a duty too much neglected, or too languidly performed,—a privilege not well understood, or too seldom claimed. How few are they who will be able on their death-beds to declare, with a late man of God,[1] "that the duty of intercession for others is the one in which they have less failed than in any other!" All duty has its reward; and there is none in which the reward is more delightful than this. There is nothing which so pleasantly realizes the beautiful idea of "the communion of saints." There is scarcely anything that more enriches the Christian than the circulation of this holy commerce, than the comfort of believing, that while we are praying for our Christian friends, we are also reaping the full benefit of their prayers for us.

If we look carefully at the passages of the Pentateuch which illustrate the sentiments and character of Moses, we shall find that there was perhaps no one who felt the importance of this duty, or practised it with more persevering and vehement energy, than this man of God. On one occasion he "fell down before the Lord forty days and forty nights" in behalf of Israel, showing how deeply convinced he was of the importance of earnest and continued intercession for their welfare. Indeed, this strikes us in the history of others of the Old Testament saints; and we call to mind the remarkable words of Samuel in the like case, "As for me, God forbid that I should sin against the Lord in ceasing to pray for you," implying that this was regarded by him as a regular and imperative obligation of religion.

And if we are tempted at any time to faint in the discharge of this duty, or to find too little enjoyment in the exercise of this privilege, let us take to ourselves all the encouragement derivable from the assured knowledge, that He who marshals the consecrated hosts, leads them to battle, and fights in their behalf, sustains another office equally important. He has ascended to the summit of the everlasting hills, and is there employed in prevalent intercession for their success; and we may well be consoled with the assurance that a greater than Moses is mediating for us in the mount above, and that His hand is never weary, His love never faint, His voice never silent.

[1] Rev. Thomas Scott. See *Memoir* by his Son.

REPHIDIM

Exodus 17:1-7

NOTHING particular is recorded of the onward march of the Israelites till they reached a place called Rephidim, which appears to be just one

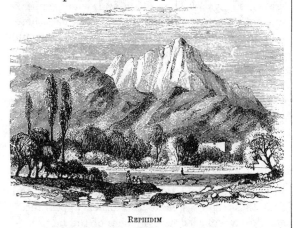

REPHIDIM

day's journey short of their destination, which was the base of the central mountains of Sinai. Their entrance into this mountain wilderness is generally supposed to have been through the Wady Feiran, a broad valley which is overspread with vegetation and tamarisk trees, or occupied with gardens and date plantations. It is now much frequented by the Bedouins for pasturage. Rephidim is supposed to have been at the extremity of this valley, which has now assumed the name of esh-Sheikh, where it enters by a narrow gorge into the high granite cliffs of the central region. We may suppose, then, that it was somewhere in this vicinity that the Israelites encamped at Rephidim. Here they again wanted water; their murmurings were now more violent, and their conduct more outrageous, than at Marah. We had then some sympathy for them, and were inclined to plead some extenuating circumstances in their behalf. But we have not a word to say for them now. Their misbehaviour is most flagrant; and the harshest judgment cannot estimate their offence too severely. They had lately seen their wants relieved in a similar emergency; and at this very time they were receiving, every morning, from heaven their daily bread. Yet so strangely unreasonable was their spirit, that they reproached Moses for having brought them out of Egypt, to kill them

and their children and their cattle with thirst; and their violence of manner was such as led Moses to cry unto the Lord, saying, "What shall I do unto this people? they be almost ready to stone me." Alas! it had come to this already. Already—in one little month—were the ransomed people prepared to deal thus with their deliverer, all whose toil and thought were spent for their advantage. Thus soon did they justify the prescient reluctance with which he had abandoned for these responsibilities the safe and quiet life he loved so well. It seems to have been in order that Moses might not be plunged in deeper discouragement, that the Lord forbore to declare His own displeasure. He simply indicated the mode in which He meant to provide for their wants. There was something remarkable in this. The people were to remain in the camp. But Moses himself, attended by the elders of Israel, and having in his hand the rod with which he had smitten the Nile to change its sweet waters into blood, was to proceed onward to Horeb. There he was to smite a rock, from which a copious stream of waters should flow out, to furnish the people with a suitable supply.

It is usually, but erroneously, supposed that the miracle was wrought at, or close by, the encampment. But if this had been the case, the Israelites, in their parched condition, would doubtless have gladly accompanied their leader on his mission. The account of the selection of the elders, and of their going to Horeb, implies that there was some considerable distance to go. This is also implied in the words that follow, "And Moses did so in the sight of the elders of Israel,"—clearly in their sight only, as witnesses, and not in that of the people also, as would have been the case had the place been near. If the camp at Rephidim were at the spot indicated, it was a good day's journey from Sinai, and so situated that a stream of water flowing from Horeb would run directly to it. The waters of the rock thus smitten, flowing in a downward stream through the valleys, are doubtless those alluded to in the other passages by which this interpretation is corroborated. So, in a later day, Moses says: "I took your sin, the calf which ye had made, and burnt it with fire, and ground it very small, even till it was as small as dust; and I cast the dust thereof into the brook *that descended out of the mount*." The water may have flowed to the Israelites when encamped at Rephidim, at the distance of miles from the rock, as the winter torrents do now through the valleys of Arabia Petræa. The language of the psalmist would also lead us to conclude that this was actually the case: "He clave the rocks in the wilderness, and gave them drink as out of the great depths. He brought streams also out of the rock, and caused waters to run down like rivers." "The rock, too," as Dr. Wilson thinks, "may have been smitten at such a height, and at a place bearing such relation to the Sinaitic valleys, as to furnish in this way supplies of water to the Israelites during the first of their journeyings 'from Horeb by way of Mount Seir, unto Kadesh-barnea.' (Deut. i. 2.) On this supposition new light is cast on the figurative language of the apostle, when he speaks of the 'rock following' the Israelites," meaning the streams from the rock. "On this supposition, also, we see why the rock should have been smitten to yield a large supply to flow to a distance, even though springs and rills might have been found pre-existent in Sinai." [1]

It must be admitted that, bearing these considerations in view, the remarkable rock in Sinai which tradition regards as the one which Moses smote, is at least well chosen in regard to its

THE ROCK OF MOSES

situation, whatever opinion we may form of the truth of that tradition, which it seems to be the disposition of late travellers to regard with more

[1] Lands of the Bible, i. 233-235.

respect than was formerly entertained. It is an isolated mass of granite, nearly twenty feet square and high, with its base concealed in the earth—we are left to conjecture to what depth. In the face of the rock are a number of horizontal fissures, at unequal distances from each other; some near the top, and others at a little distance from the surface of the ground. An American traveller says: "The colour and whole appearance of the rock are such that, if seen elsewhere, and disconnected from all traditions, no one would hesitate to believe that they had been produced by water flowing from these fissures. I think it would be extremely difficult to form these fissures or produce these appearances by art. It is not less difficult to believe that a natural fountain should flow at the height of a dozen feet out of the face of an isolated rock. Believing as I do, that the water was brought out of a rock belonging to this mountain, I can see nothing incredible in the opinion that this is the identical rock, and that these fissures, and the other appearances, should be regarded as evidences of the fact." [1]

A still later American traveller [2] declares, that he visited the spot with the settled conviction that "the legend with regard to the rock was but a fable," and that the fissures had been wrought by art to give it an apparent sanction. But he confesses, notwithstanding his scepticism on this point, "This stone made more impression upon me than any natural object claiming to attest a miracle ever did." He adds, "Had any enlightened geologist, utterly ignorant of the miracle of Moses, passed up this ravine, and seen the rock as it now is, he would have declared—though the position of the stone and the present condition of the country around should have opposed any such impression—that strong and long continued fountains of water had once poured their gurgling currents

[1] Dr. Olin, Travels in the East, i. 417.
[2] Dr. Durbin, Observations on the East, i. 149.

from it and over it. He could not waver in his belief for a moment, so natural and so perfect are the indications. I examined it thoroughly; and if it be a forgery, I am satisfied, for my own part, that a greater than Michael Angelo designed and executed it. I cannot differ from Shaw's opinion, that 'neither art nor chance could by any means be concerned in the contrivance of these holes, which formed so many fountains.' The more I gazed upon the irregular mouth-like chasms in the rock, the more I found my skepticism shaken; and at last I could not help asking myself, whether it was not a very natural solution of the matter, that this was indeed the rock which Moses struck, that from it the waters 'gushed forth,' and poured their streams down Wady Leja to Wady esh-Sheikh, and along it to Rephedim, where Israel was encamped, perishing with thirst?"

Whether or not this were the particular rock which sent forth its streams when smitten by the rod of Moses—which, after all, it is of little importance for us to know—there can be little doubt that, from the nature of the case, it was somewhere in this upper region, to which Israel afterwards made a day's journey, and where they remained encamped for nearly a year. Had not this been the case, another miracle would have been required to furnish water for the camp in Sinai; but the fountain being placed at the head of the valley in Horeb, it formed a source of supply to the people during the whole of their stay in the vicinity, if not after they had taken their departure.

The route of the Israelites from Sin to Rephidim appears to have been through Wady Feirân. It was a long journey, with two intervening stages, Dophkah and Alush (Num. xxxiii. 13, 14). Yet there is no complaint of want of water. This may be accounted for by the fact that in Wady Feirân is one of the largest fountains in the whole Peninsula. Wady esh-Sheikh falls into Feirân after sweeping round northwards in a semicircle from the base of Mount Sinai. It forms the only practicable approach from the westward to that mountain. Rephidim must have been in Wady esh-Sheikh. When going to it from Feirân the Israelites marched nearly due north. At Rephidim there was no water, and they murmured, Moses was commanded "to go on before" with the elders, and to smite "the rock in Horeb." The rock must have been some distance from the camp at Rephidim; and yet not so far as to prevent the people going thither for a supply of water. It could scarcely have been more than three miles distant. The wady runs on to the very foot

of Sinai, a broad open valley, shut in by magnificent ranges of granite cliffs.

The attack of the Amalekites appears to have followed immediately the miracle of the smitten rock; and as it was begun by an assault upon the rear of the Israelites,—upon "all that were feeble behind thee, when thou wast faint and weary" (Deut. xxv. 18),—it would seem probable that it took place when the able-bodied men had gone forward with Moses and the elders to procure water. This throws new light upon the incident. The people were taken by surprise, and the Amalekites gained a temporary advantage. On the following day, however, the Israelitish warriors were marshalled under Joshua, and the enemy routed.

It is usual to connect the Amalekites with Feirân, and to represent the battle as a brave attempt on their part to defend the paradise of their desert home. Dr. Kitto in part adopts this view. But it is without any satisfactory evidence. The home of the Amalekites was away upon the borders of Palestine; and it is questionable whether they had ever any possessions among the mountains of Sinai. Why, then, did they attack the Israelites? It would seem that they knew of the intention of the people to invade Canaan. They were watching their movements. When they saw them encamp at Rephidim, they feared that they were about to advance northward. Consequently they embraced what they deemed a favourable opportunity, swept down through the passes from the northern plateau, and attacked them in the rear, thinking thus to destroy them by one bold stroke.

P.

With regard to the rock in the Wâdy Leja, Mr. Palmer, the distinguished traveller, who scientifically explored the wilderness, in connection with the Ordnance Survey, in 1868-9, remarks that "there are sundry niches or fissures, in this stone, which are construed by the credulous into twelve mouths, whence, they say, that water gushed forth to supply the twelve tribes. Monkish legend, founded on a too literal interpretation of a passage in St. Paul, supposes that this rock followed the children of Israel throughout the whole of their wanderings, and continued to furnish them with water." (*The Desert of the Exodus*, i. 120.) Mr. Palmer afterwards describes the Wâdy Feirân as "a large and comparatively fertile tract, with a palm-grove which extends, notwithstanding the late destructive flood, for miles along the valley." (P. 158.) My own recollections of it, as it was twelve years ago, would lead me to speak of its park-like scenery as very beautiful, and, for the desert, very rich. There the battle with Amalek occurred. The desert tribes collected in the neighbourhood would seek to defend the wells and streams against the Israelites, who would naturally wish to take possession of them. Hence the want of water experienced by the latter. It was not because there was no fountain or stream, but because they could not approach them on account of the Amalekites. "The miracle of striking the rock released them from this difficulty; and, as we are told, immediately afterwards 'then came Amalek, and fought with Israel in Rephidim.' (Ex. xvii. 8.) But it is a significant fact," Mr. Palmer goes on to say, "that in Wâdy Feirân, immediately before the part of the valley where the fertility commences, I discovered a rock, which Arab tradition regards as the site of the miracle. This rock, which has never before been noticed by travellers, is called *Hesy el Khattâtîn*, and is surrounded by small heaps of pebbles, placed upon every available stone in the immediate neighbourhood; these are accounted for as follows: When the children of Israel sat down by the miraculous stream, and rested after their thirst was quenched, they amused themselves by throwing pebbles upon the surrounding pieces of rock. This has passed into a custom, which the Arabs of the present day keep up in memory of the event." (P. 159.) The objection to the identification of Rephidim with a spot in the Wâdy Feirân, is the distance of it from Jebel Mûsa, regarding that as the Mosaic Sinai. But though the distance would be too great to be crossed by a multitude with laden camels in a single day, it may be crossed by a few travellers without baggage in that time, for I did it myself. Our party started from Wâdy Feirân early in the morning, and ascended the Nagb Hawa, and so reached the convent by moonlight, about seven or eight o'clock, leaving the heavy baggage to be carried round by camels through the Wâdy es Sheikh. They reached the convent next day. Mr. Palmer says, "Captain Wilson and myself being desirous, on one occasion, of pushing on to Jebel Mûsa by a certain day, actually adopted this expedient." (P. 161.)

S.

SINAI

Exodus 19

WE must now conduct our readers to Sinai itself, to which sacred mount the next move brought the Israelites. We will accept the guidance of a very intelligent traveller, in taking the first view of this renowned mountain. It is only necessary first to premise, that it belongs to the high central group of the Sinai mountains; and seeing that the name of Horeb seems to be given convertibly to the mount on which the law was delivered, we agree with those who take Horeb to be the general name for the entire group of mountains, and Sinai for the particular summit. The traveller we take for our guide is Dr. Durbin; but it is right to point out that the Israelites are regarded as having approached the plain in front of the mountain, by a somewhat more circuitous and more practicable route than that of the traveller. The results, however, are the same. "For two hours we ascended the wild, narrow pass, enclosed between stupendous granite cliffs, whose debris encumbered the defile, often rendering the passage difficult and dangerous. Escaping from the pass,

we crossed the head of a basin-like plain, which declined to the south-west, and, ascending gradually, gloomy precipitous mountain masses rose to view on either hand, with detached snow beds[1] lying in their clefts. The caravan moved slowly, and apparently with a more solemn measured tread; the Bedouins became more serious and silent, and looked steadily before them, as if to catch the first glimpse of some revered object. The space before us gradually expanded, when suddenly Tualeb,[2] pointing to a black perpendicular cliff, whose two riven and rugged summits rose some 1,200 or 1,500 feet directly in front of us, exclaimed 'Jebel Musa!'[3] How shall I describe the effect of that announcement? Not a word was spoken by Moslem or Christian; but slowly and silently we advanced into the still expanding plain, our eyes immovably fixed on the frowning precipices of the stern and desolate mountain. We were doubtless on the plain where Israel encamped at the giving of the law, and that grand and gloomy height before us was Sinai, on which God descended in fire, and the whole mountain was enveloped in smoke, and shook under the tread of the Almighty, while His presence was proclaimed by the long loud peals of repeated thunder, above which the blast of the trumpet was heard waxing louder and louder, and reverberating amid the stern and gloomy heights around, and then God spake with Moses. 'And all the people removed, and stood afar off, and trembled when they saw the thunderings and lightnings, and thick darkness where God was; and said unto Moses, Speak thou unto us; but let not God speak with us, lest we die.'[4] We all seemed to ourselves to be present at this terrible scene, and would have marched directly up to the mount of God had not Tualeb recalled us to ourselves, by pointing to the convent far up in the deep ravine between Horeb and Jebel Deir."[5]

It is easily conceivable, and the history seems to require it, that the Israelites approached this place by a more convenient route, if any existed, than that which unencumbered travellers prefer. It is therefore usually understood, that instead of going through the narrow and difficult mountain passes and ravines, which indeed would have been scarcely possible then, they, on leaving the Wady

[1] This is accounted for by the time of the year—February.
[2] The Arab guide.   [3] Mount of Moses.
[4] Exodus 20.   [5] *Observations on the East*, i. 132-134.

Feiran, swept round to Mount Horeb by the comparatively broad valley of Wady esh-Sheikh. The author of *Forty Days in the Desert* is one of the most recent travellers who have passed *that way*, and we must not refuse the reader the pleasure of his company. His description is, however, somewhat marred by the preconceived notion that the Mount of God was to be sought in another quarter.

" From the descriptions of the pass which I had read, I expected unusual grandeur in the scenery, as well as great difficulty in the ascent; but after our clamber up the terrific precipices of the Serbal,[1] those which were in this desolate ravine appeared very insignificant, while the zig-zag pathway built up with stones seemed comparatively like a broad and easy turnpike-road, which we surmounted with little effort.[2] Not so, how-

VALLEY AND CONVENT OF SINAI

ever, did the camels; their piteous cries filled the air, and echoed wildly in the recesses of the shattered cliffs. Catching, as we mounted higher and higher, the still freshening breeze from the cool regions above, we felt equal to anything. . . . The narrow valley widened gradually into a high, dreary, undulating plain, hemmed in by still drearier mountains, which upreared their dark, shattered, thunder-stricken peaks higher and higher on each side as we advanced; while right before us, closing up the plain and shutting it in, towered sheer from its level an awful range of precipices, which seemed to bar our farther progress through this region of desolate sublimity. As we still advanced a narrow glen opened up between them, running deeper into the heart of the solitude; and at some distance up this, half lost between walls of naked rock, peeped out the high wall of the convent, and the dark verdure of its garden, looking, as some one has well described it, like the end of the world."

The plain of er-Rahah, into which both routes thus lead, is regarded by Dr. Robinson, and by most other travellers after him, as the camping ground of the Israelites. Its extent is still further increased by lateral valleys, receding from the plain itself, between the foot of the first range of mountains and that of the grand central mass of crags,—the left one being the Wady esh-Sheikh, of very considerable extent; the right, a smaller recess,—these making together a very extensive open space, supposed until lately to be the only one existing in this high central region which could at all meet the necessities of the case, but still such as a military man, accustomed to estimate the ground which a large army requires for

[1] Another of the Sinaitic mountains, which some have regarded as the Sinai of Scripture.

[2] This facility is, however, an argument in favour of this route for the Israelites; but, as the author remarks, the route must have presented great difficulties before the construction of the road.

encampment, would perhaps hardly consider sufficient for the immense host of Israel.

It so happens, however, that the identification of this plain as the site of the Hebrew encampment required a change of view as to the summit on which the law was delivered; for the mountain which had hitherto been regarded as the scene of that solemn event is not visible from this plain, and therefore could not be seen by the host assembled there, the view of its summit being intercepted by a nearer mountain.

The reader must clearly understand that Horeb, taken in the largest sense, is an oblong mountain, about three miles in length, all around the base of which sweeps a deep, irregular, and narrow defile, as if the Almighty Himself had set bounds around it as holy ground. Even the mountains round about, which seem thrown together in wild confusion, are cut off from any communication with the Mount of God. At the southern extremity of this oblong edge rises a summit, in lofty and stern grandeur, to the height of about 7,500 feet above the level of the sea; and this is the Jebel Mûsa which tradition regards as the Sinai of Scripture, the mount where the law was delivered. The only ground on which its claim to this distinction—which it seems entitled to by its surpassing grandeur—has been questioned, is, that it is not visible from the plain which has been fixed upon as the camping ground of the Israelites. Most of those who have on this ground questioned its identity, have done so with avowed reluctance, seeing how fully in all other respects the mountain corresponds to the ideas one has previously formed of the Mount of God. But finding no help, they repair to the other extremity of the oblong mount, and discover there another pinnacle, which, although lower than Jebel Mûsa, boldly confronts the plain of the encampment, and is visible from all parts of it. It bears the name of Sufsafeh, and is the "Horeb" of the traditions which give to the two grand summits the distinctive names of Horeb and Sinai. Though inferior to the southern summit, it is not wanting in grandeur and magnificence, and it is of very difficult access, though some have contrived with no small risk to reach the summit. Dr. Durbin, who went to it directly from the summit of Jebel Mûsa, says, "No one who has not seen them can conceive the ruggedness of these vast piles of granite rocks, rent into chasms, rounded

into small summits, or splintered into countless peaks, all in the wildest confusion, as they appear to the eye of an observer from any of the heights. But when we did arrive at the summit of es-Sufsafeh, and cast our eyes over the wide plain, we were more than repaid for all our toil. One glance was enough. We were satisfied that here, and here only, could the wondrous displays of Sinai have been visible to the assembled host of Israel; that here the Lord spoke with Moses: that here was the mount that trembled and smoked in the presence of its manifested Creator! We gazed for some time in silence; and when we spoke, it was with a reverence that even the most thoughtless of our company could not shake off. I read on the very spot, with what feelings I need not say, the passage in Exodus which relates the wonders of which this mountain was the theatre. We *felt* its truth, and could almost see the lightnings, and hear the thunders, and the 'trumpet waxing loud.'"

SINAI DIFFICULTIES

WE heartily sympathize in the disappointment some readers will feel in learning that the conclusions exhibited yesterday, in favour of Sufsafeh as "the Mount of God," and of the plain er-Rahah as the camping ground of the Israelites, are not, after all, so irrefragable as some of the travellers we have cited assume. But the geographical inquirer must inure himself to such disappointments. There are several points in Scripture geography in which we ourselves have had to change our opinion two or three times within the last fifteen years; a position that seemed strong and invincible on the evidence before us having appeared, in the progress of discovery and of more certain information, to be no longer tenable. In such cases, after carefully examining all the new information, and taking the possibilities of further evidence into account, we have repeatedly been constrained to give up our most cherished conclusions in favour of some new opinion which came before us with invincible evidence. This we have done not unreluctantly, not without much groaning of mind, but still in reasonably cheerful obedience to the claims of truth. This is a useful process. And it is not without encouragement, for it has sometimes happened that the latest and surest discoveries have permitted us to return with rejoicing hearts, and almost with exulting shouts, to our first love, to the very view of the matter which we adopted or wrought out when our thought and labour were first engaged in the investigation. An instance of this has been seen in "Dead Sea Difficulties;"[1] and something of the same sort occurs with regard to the Sinai mountain.

The view set forth yesterday is that which has been currently entertained since Dr. Robinson's admirable *Biblical Researches in Palestine* were published—now about ten years ago; and it is likely to retain its hold on the public mind for some years to come. People will not be ready to give it up until the evidence for some other alternative assumes a very positive character. Indeed, we are inclined to suspend our own judgment; for, notwithstanding the frequency with which this region has been visited, it does not appear to us that some parts of it have as yet been adequately explored.

It has been seen that the old determination was in favour of Jebel Mûsa, the tallest and southernmost summit of the mass of mountains which in Scripture seems to have borne the name of Horeb. Its rejection, and the selection of the lower summit at the northern extremity of the ridge, were, as we have seen, founded on the impression that there was no open space before it and in sight of it where the Israelites could have encamped. A great number of travellers are quite positive on this point. Language cannot be more strong than their declarations. Yet it now appears, on evidence quite as strong, that there is, at the southern base of Jebel Mûsa, the old Sinai, a level valley, affording even more and better ground for encampment than that in front of the northern cliffs.

The question was raised in America, to which it properly belongs. The great geographer of the day, Dr. Carl Ritter of Berlin, in a letter to Dr. Robinson, which was printed, pointed out that a geographical commentary on Exodus and Numbers, by Laborde,[2] had now for the first time established the existence of the plain of Wady

[1] See Vol. 1, pp. 260-264.

[2] *Commentaire Geographique sur l'Exode et les Nombres.* Paris, 1841.

es-Seba'îyeh, *at the southern base* of Sinai, and had thus furnished an important point for the elucidation of the giving of the law. This induced a scholar and artist (Mr. M. K. Kellog), who had visited Sinai in 1844, to give the public some extracts from the journal he kept at that time, by which *this* view is strongly corroborated. It also accounts for the mistake of previous travellers, by showing that, *by the path usually taken*, this important valley is shut out from view by the spurs of the mountains. The traveller's narrative is longer than we can introduce here, but the substance of it we can give.

On the 6th of March 1844, the traveller remained behind at the convent, while his companions went to explore Mount St. Catherine; but some time after their departure with the guides, he took a little Arab boy with him to carry his sketch book and water bottle, and walked up Wady Shu'eib until he came to the

1 Horeb.	5 Rock of Moses.
2 Sufsafeh.	6 Plain er-Rahah.
3 Jebel Mûsa (Sinai).	7 Plain Seba'îyeh.
4 Jebel Katerin.	8 Wady esh-Sheikh.

GROUND PLAN OF THE SINAITIC MOUNTAINS

little mountain of the Cross (*Neja*), which almost shuts up the passage into Wady Seba'îyeh, and where he had for the first time a view of the southern face of Sinai. Here opened an extended picture of the mountains lying to the south of the Sinai range, for he was now some three hundred feet above the adjacent valleys.[1]

After much difficulty, the traveller succeeded in climbing over immense masses of granite to the side of the mountain of the Cross, which he ascended above five hundred feet on its south-western face, in order to obtain a good view of the peak of Sinai, which he was anxious to sketch. "Here, close at my right, arose almost perpendicularly the holy mountain; its shattered pyramidal peak towering above me some four-teen hundred feet, of a brownish tint, presenting vertical strata of granite which threw off the glittering rays of the morning sun. Clinging to its base was a range of sharp, upheaving crags, from one to two hundred feet in height, which formed an almost impassable barrier to the mountain itself from the valley adjoining. These crags were separated from the mountain by a deep and narrow gorge, yet they must be con-sidered as forming the projecting base of Sinai.

"Directly in front of me was a level valley, stretching onward to the south for three or four miles, and enclosed on the east, west, and south by low mountains of various altitudes, all much less, however, than that of Sinai. This valley passed behind the mountain of the Cross to my left and out of view, so that I could not calculate its northern extent from where I stood. The whole scene was one of inexpressible grandeur and solemnity."

On returning to the convent, the traveller's friends, on seeing his sketch-book, remarked that there was no such plain as he had there repre-sented. On being assured that he had copied what was before him, 'they laughed, and remarked that none but a painter's imagination could have seen the plain in question; for they had passed entirely around the mountain that day, and could assert *positively* that there was no such plain.' Nevertheless, one of the friends was prevailed upon to see for himself; for the next day was spent in this very valley, the existence of which had been so stoutly denied; and it was clearly seen that, by the route taken the previous day, it had not been brought into view,—a point very intelligible to those who are conversant with mountain scenery. We have then a fuller de-scription of the plain. It spreads out directly in

front of the mountain, 'level, clean, and broad, going on to the south, with varied widths, for about three miles, on gently ascending ground, where it passes between two sloping hills, and enters another wady which descends beyond, from which it is probable that Sinai may yet be clearly seen. On the east, this plain of Seba'îyeh is bounded by mountains, having long sloping bases, and covered with wild thyme and other herbs, affording good tenting ground immediately fronting Sinai, which forms, as it were, a grand pyramidal pulpit to the magnificent amphitheatre below. The width of the plain, immediately in front of Sinai, is about sixteen hundred feet; farther south the width is much increased, so that on an average the plain may be considered as being nearly one-third of a mile wide, and its length, *in view of Mount Sinai*, between five and six miles. The good tenting ground on the mountain would give much more space for the multitude on the great occasion for which they were assembled. This estimate does not include that part of the plain which stretches to the north, and Wady esh-Sheikh, from which the peak of Sinai is not visible, for this space would contain three or four times the number of people which Seba'îyeh would hold."

By all this it would appear, that those who in old times looked upon Jebel Mûsa as the Mount of God, were by no means so blind to circum-stances and probabilities as travellers in their own imperfect information have imagined; and now that it has been shown that the want of a camp-ing ground, which alone created the desire to give a different locality to Sinai, does not exist, there appears no reason why the despised mountain should not have its ancient and crowning glory restored to it. It is probable that no stronger instance has ever occurred tending to show the necessity that there is for observing the utmost caution, and for being furnished with the most unequivocal data, in disturbing established con-clusions in matters of this nature, which may have been founded on circumstances actually existing, though hidden from us.

Sinai is one of the most interesting spots on earth. Every reader of the wonderful narrative recorded in the Pentateuch will naturally be anxious to know whether recent researches have at all contributed to clear away the difficulties regarding its true site. Dr. Kitto has stated very fairly two theories, and he appears to have

---

[1] A neighbouring ridge to that of Horeb, and the highest in the whole region.

been in doubt as to which was preferable. I think it well, therefore, to give my own view, and the leading arguments upon which it rests.

It is important to keep before the mind the very clear statements and incidental notices of Sinai given by the sacred writer, and minutely to compare these with local topography.

The Israelites "departed from Rephidim, came into the wilderness of Sinai, . . . and *camped before the mount*" (Exod. xix. 1, 2). The base of the mount in front of the camp appears to have been so sharply defined, that barriers were put up to prevent any of the people from approaching rashly or inadvertently to "touch the mount" (ver. 12). The top of the mount was in full view from the camp, so that when the Lord "came down" upon it, the thick cloud in which His glory was shrouded was "in sight of all the people" (vers. 11, 16). While Moses was receiving the law on the summit of Sinai, "the thunderings and lightnings, and the voice of the trumpet," were so near the camp, that the people in terror "*removed and stood afar off*," yet still remained in sight of the mount (xx. 18; xxiv. 17).

In these notices there are implied three specifications, which must all be present in any spot answering to the true Sinai. 1. A mountain summit overlooking the place where the people were encamped. 2. Space sufficient, adjacent to the mountain, for so large a multitude to stand and behold the phenomena on the summit, and even, when afraid, to remove afar off and still be in sight. 3. The relation between this space where the people stood, and the base of the mountain, must be such that they could approach and stand at "the nether part of the mount;" that they could also touch it; and that bounds could be set round it.

There is one peak, and one only, in the Peninsula, which seems to agree with all these requirements: it is *Ras es-Sufsafeh*, "the peak of the willow," so called from a willow tree which grows in one of its clefts. Its summit is very clearly defined, rising high above the peaks around it. In front it descends in broken crags of naked granite to the plain of Râhah. It commands the whole extent of this plain, which is above two miles long, and ranges from one-third to two-thirds of a mile in breadth. From the summit the eye can follow the windings of the plain as it runs away among the mountains in the distance. The level expanse of Wady esh-Sheikh, which joins Râhah, is clearly seen opening out on the right; while opposite it on the left is another section of plain forming a recess in the mountains. From near the summit a wild ravine runs down the front of the peak, conveying a winter torrent into Râhah. Up this ravine the ascent may be made from the plain.

I feel convinced that Sufsâfeh is the true Sinai, "the mount of the Lord." Every requirement of the sacred narrative is supplied, and every incident illustrated, by the features of the surrounding district. Here is a plain sufficient to contain the Israelitish camp, and so close to the mountain's base, that barriers could be erected, and would be needed, to keep back the heedless and rash from touching it. Here is a peak where the clouds that enshrined the glory of the Lord would be seen by the vast multitude, even when in fear they would withdraw to a distance. From this peak the thunderings would resound

with terrific effect through the plain. When descending, Moses could also hear the songs and shouts of the infatuated people as they danced round the golden calf. In "the brook that descends out of the mount" (Deut. ix. 21), through the ravine into the plain of Râhah, he could cast the dust of the destroyed idol. In fact, the mountain, the plain, the stream, and the whole surrounding topography, correspond in every respect with the historical account given by Moses.[1]

P.

As to the claims of Gebel Mousa in connection with the Wâdy Sebâyeh, we must refer to Dr. Stanley. "The only point which now remained," he says, "was to explore the Wâdy Sebâyeh on the other side, and ascertain whether its appearance, and its relation to Gebel Mousa from below, was more suitable than it had seemed from above. This I did on the afternoon of the third day, and I came to the conclusion, that it could only be taken for the place if none other existed. It is rough, uneven, narrow. The only advantage which it has is, that the peak from a few points of view rises in a more commanding form than the Râs Sasâfeh. But the mountain never descends upon the plain. No! If we are to have a mountain without a wide amphitheatre at its base, let us have Serbâl; but if otherwise, I am sure that if the monks of Justinian had fixed the traditional scene on the Râs Sasâfeh, no one would for an instant have doubted that this only could be the spot. . . . Considering the almost total absence of such conjunctions of plain and mountain in this region, it is a really important evidence to the truth of the narrative that one such conjunction can be found, and that within the neighbourhood of the traditional Sinai." Two confirmatory circumstances are mentioned by the same author. First, in coming down from Sasâfeh to Er Râheh, one might catch such a sudden view as is attributed to Moses when, drawing nigh to the camp, he threw down the tables of stone "beneath the mount." (*Sinai and Palestine*, p. 74.) And, next, there is a brook—the brook of the Wâdy Leja—which issues into the Wâdy Râheh, which coincides with the brook into which Moses cast the fragments of the golden calf—"the brook that came down out of the mount." Without any hesitation we give it as our opinion, that the delivery by the law to the people by Moses occurred on Sasâfeh, commanding the plain of Er Râheh. But, we may add, it seems highly probable that Gebel Mousa, the loftier peak of the range to the south of Sasâfeh, was also connected with the revelation of the law, as the point where Moses held communion with the Lord God.

I venture to add the result of my own experience and observation.

I ascended Gebel Mousa, under the guidance of one of the brethren, who pointed out the chapels of the Virgin and of Elijah, which form stages in the ascent. The view from the summit of Gebel Mousa is vast, varied, magnifi-

[1] For fuller information on this interesting subject, the reader is referred to the writer's articles, "Sinai" and "Wandering," in the last edition of Kitto's *Cyclopædia of Bib. Lit.*

cent—a perfect wilderness of peaks and chasms, as if the Pacific Ocean had been drained, and all the coral reefs and gulfs had been left bare. To the south-west is Mount Catherine, and other noble peaks, with glimpses of wâdys to the south-east. Nothing, however, of the plain of Er Râheh can be seen from that point. It is completely shut out by the peak of Sasâfeh, which is most conspicuous looking toward the north. The peak of Sasâfeh I did not ascend, but some of my companions did; and they confirmed the descriptions of it by Robinson and others. The precipice sweeps down to the edge of the plain of Râheh; and up to its sides the multitudes might have come and touched it, but for the divine prohibition. The plain, from the summit of Sasâfeh, appears, as it does wherever it is looked at, a spacious amphitheatre, just fitted to be the gathering-place of the tribes, where they could conveniently assemble to witness the delivery of God's law.

There is one prominent circumstance recorded in the divine narrative of the transaction, which mainly determines my judgment as to the site where it occurred. "There Israel camped before the mount." (Ex. xix. 2.) The Lord said He would "come down in the sight of all the people upon Mount Sinai." (Ex. xix. 11.) Bounds were to be set to the people round about, that they might not touch the mount. (Ex. xix. 23.) "Moses brought forth the people out of the camp to meet with God, and they stood at the nether part of the mount." (Ex. xix. 17.) "And all the people saw the thunderings, and the lightnings, and the noise of the trumpet, and the mountain smoking; and when the people saw it, they removed, and stood afar off." (Ex. xx. 18.) From all this it plainly appears, that, close to the mountain of the law—indeed, at its very foot—there was a plain; a space so large as not only to admit of the people encamping within it, but of their moving from one point of it to another, so as not to lose sight of the peak on which the great and miraculous wonder was displayed. The two indispensable conditions, then, in reference to any spot claiming to be the scene of the delivery of the law are, a mountain rising boldly and abruptly from a plain, and a plain so vast as to provide room for the gathering of the hosts, and for their retirement from the roots of the great mountain without losing sight of its summit. These conditions are met in the peak of Sasâfeh and in the plain Er Râheh, and nowhere else.

It may be as well to say, that *Sasâfeh* and *Sufsâfeh* are only different ways of spelling the same Arabic name. *Gebel Mousa* is sometimes spelt *Jebel Mûsa*.

S.

THE GOLDEN CALF

Exodus 32:1-6

THE Hebrews remained at their station in Horeb a few days more than eleven months. During this time the theocracy was fully established; Jehovah Himself was constituted their sovereign; His law, as such, was promulgated in dread solemnity from the mount, and committed to them as written by the finger of God on the two tables of stone; their government was duly organized; their national laws and institutions were established, to separate them from all other nations as the future depositaries of the oracles of God; the tabernacle was set up for the house or palace of their King Jehovah, who visibly dwelt among them in the glory that rested above the ark; and the regular service of His royal court, by priests and Levites, was established. In the same interval of time, they were severely rebuked for their defection from their God and King in the worship of the golden calf; the sanctions of the law were solemnly repeated; the people were numbered and mustered for war; the order of encamping, breaking up, and marching, was accurately settled; and the whole constitution of the state was completed.

Of all these transactions the space to which we are limited allows us only to notice particularly the sin of Israel in the matter of their setting up and worshipping the golden calf, during the protracted absence of Moses on the mount, while holding his high intercourse with God. We do this the rather, seeing that the transaction has been much misunderstood. Some, conceiving that it amounted to a renunciation of the God who had brought them out of Egypt, and whom they had solemnly accepted as their King, have used this as a handle for discrediting the miracles which attended that deliverance. It is argued in effect, that it is morally impossible that a people who had witnessed such great miracles should so soon have called the being and sovereignty of God in question; therefore, it is concluded, no such miracles were witnessed by them—none such were performed. The plain answer to this is, that the Israelites did not deny their God or question His being—they transgressed, not the first commandment, but the second. They made an image after the imagination of their own hearts, or rather after the notion they had imbibed in Egypt, to represent or symbolize the Lord, debasing "their Glory to the similitude of an ox that eateth grass." This simple view of the matter renders all the obscure parts of the history, as commonly understood, very easy of explanation.

Moses had been away in the mountain no less than six weeks, when the people began to give vent to their uneasiness at the absence of the leader to whom they looked to give effect to their new institutions, and to lead them out of the wilderness into their promised heritage. Impelled by these feelings, they presented themselves in a tumultuous manner to Aaron, with a proposal which, however deplorable, conveys no intimation of a wish to renounce the authority of Moses, or to abandon their fealty to their Divine King. They said in effect, "Since Moses, who undertook to be our leader, and to whom, if he were present, we should address ourselves, delays his return so long, make thou for us an image, through which we may address our worship to the God whom we have taken for our guide." In estimating the force and purport of this application, it should be recollected that the tabernacle and the ritual worship were not yet established, nor the ark with its hovering cherubim established in the sanctuary; so that they had not then the visible symbols and forms of service which they afterwards possessed, and the need of which *to them*, this very application strikingly manifests. In fact, Moses was, at the very time, receiving instructions in the mount regarding the mode in which a form of visible service was to be established among them; ignorant of which, and yet craving something of the kind, they were resolved to set up a form of service and symbols for themselves, although they were still willing that the brother and representative of Moses should give effect to their desire. We shall fail to apprehend aright the reason for these things being recorded, if we do not see in all this a clear indication of the peculiar fitness, for a people like the Israelites, of the material and sensible forms of worship, which were conceded to them. Nor can this tendency in them be estimated fairly, unless we recollect that there was not then in the world any people who could, more than they, understand or be satisfied with a worship purely spiritual.

The proposal was, however, a clear infraction of the second commandment; and Aaron at least could not be ignorant of this, though, from his conduct in the matter, it may be doubted whether even he was fully sensible of the criminality of their request. His conduct now lacked the simple firm-handed rectitude and singleness of purpose which we find in Moses, and shows how wisely God had chosen, between these

brothers, the one who should be the leader of His people, while yet employing the other for such service as *his* more showy gifts and capacities qualified him to render. Aaron seems to have temporized from the fear that his opposition might urge the people to cast off the authority they were still willing to recognize; or the manner in which he met the proposal may be regarded as having been dictated by policy, and conceived in the hope that if he could not, by interposing the force of selfish motives, arrest the progress of the scheme, he might delay its accomplishment until Moses should return, and by his authority stay further proceedings. It required from them a sacrifice which he might hope they would not be very ready to make, and which could not, at all events be accomplished without some expense of time. "Break off," he said, "the golden ear-rings, which are in the ears of your wives, of your sons, and of your daughters, and bring them unto me." He had underrated the earnestness of the people, if he supposed their ardour was to be thus chilled. In a very little time the required ear-rings were produced, and Aaron found himself involved in an implied engagement from which he had not the courage to recede; and he proceeded to cause a symbolical representation of the Almighty to be made in the form to which they had been used

EGYPTIAN SACRED CALF

in Egypt, where the most honoured of the gods was worshipped under the similitude of a bull. As to the form, called in contempt a "calf," there cannot be a doubt that it was that of the Egyptian god Apis, or the corresponding Mnevis of Lower Egypt, primarily represented by a living bull, and by various images of that bull dispersed throughout the land. An image must have some form or other; and while the familiarity of this symbol in Egypt would suggest it most readily to the mind, it is certain, that whatever symbol had been chosen, the same question might still have been raised, Why this symbol rather than another?—and probably we should not, with regard to any other, have found so obvious an explanation.

Much question has been raised as to the mode in which this image was executed. In the text we read, "He received them at their hands, and fashioned it with a graving tool, after he had made it a molten calf." The *simplest* view of this is, that this idol was a solid molten image, moulded, cast, and afterwards touched up with the graving tool, in the ordinary style of finishing. To this idea it is admitted that no objection can be brought, either from the particular recital of the circumstances, or from the general state of art at the time. The great quantity of precious metal requisite on this plan, and uselessly consumed, or else the very small size of the idol, presents the only ground for suspecting its correctness. It would, however, have been only a higher step in mechanical practice, and by no means beyond the existing resources of the art, while it is equally consistent with the sacred text to suppose that the image was a perfect molten work, cast hollow, and consequently modelled with more dexterity. But there is another class of opinions in this matter, proceeding upon the view that the idolatrous work in question was one of *laminated* art. In such a case, the inner substance must have been formed of some soft

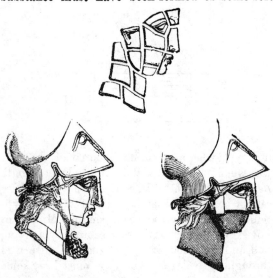

LAMINATED SCULPTURES

and easily carved material, as wax in miniature, and clay or wood in large figures. The case, or

framework, being thus quickly finished, could be rapidly covered over with thin plates of the external coating, which, in the instance before us, was of gold. These *laminæ* either overlapped at the edges, or were fitted into each other. The facility with which such a work could be executed suits the exigency in question, while the beauty and utility of similar artistic operations, are abundantly proved by the earlier works of the Greeks, and by the wonderful chryselephantine sculptures of Phidias. Of the archaic specimens of this art, we still possess such information as seems clearly to demonstrate that to this species of art belonged the sculpture of Aaron. Pausanias describes a statue of Jupiter by Learchus —the most ancient then known, having been executed in the eighth century before our era— formed of plates of brass hammered round, and fastened by rivets, with a "case" or "foundation" of wood, exactly as the calf in the wilderness is supposed to have been constructed. Of this character are all the most ancient metallic statues, and to this description of sculpture all the accounts of the art to be found in Homer refer. A head of Osiris, with the internal wooden nucleus still subsisting within the metal coating, has been published among the antiquities of the Dilettante Society; and other examples of the similar application of ivory exist. Thus the earliest classic records lead us up to Egyptian practice—for to Egypt all concede the parentage of ancient art— and thence we easily obtain the most probable idea of the true nature of Aaron's performance— "Israel's molten god."[1]

The people received the image with gladness, and hailed it as the symbol of the God who had brought them out of the land of Egypt,—a clear indication that they did not intend it to represent any other god.[2] When Aaron witnessed the enthusiasm with which the image was received by the people, he knew that they would not brook delay in celebrating the rites of worship before it; and, therefore, still bent on directing the ser-

[1] Dr. Memes on *Fine Art among the Jews*, in the *Journal of Sacred Literature*, vol. iii. pp. 69, 70.

[2] The authorized version does indeed convey the impression that it did: "These be thy *gods*, O Israel, that brought thee up out of the land of Egypt!" But the word rendered "gods" is simply the name of God in its usual plural form *Elohim*, and translated "God," except when supposed by the translators to apply to idols, as here. The mere fact, however, that the image itself was but one, shows that the plural is here very improperly employed.

vice to the true object of worship, he caused an altar to be set up before the image, and proclaimed throughout the camp that the morrow was to be regarded as a feast to Jehovah. The people rose the next morning early—such was their eagerness—to celebrate that feast before their new bauble, after the fashion in which such feasts were held by idolaters. Profusely did they offer the flesh of their cattle, and the wine of drink-offering; and then, as was the custom, they sat down to feast upon the remainder of that which had been offered. When they had feasted, and their senses were excited by wine, they rose to the dances, and games, and wanton sports, which then formed, and do still form, the mode in which the rites of some (not all) idols were celebrated. This was probably among the things that Aaron dreaded, but could not prevent, after his temporizing conduct had given a sort of sanction to their proceedings. How much more becoming, had he from the first raised his voice on high against their device, which *he* knew, however they may have glossed it over, to be in direct contradiction to the commandment which had but lately been given in an audible utterance from amidst the terrors of Sinai. It is true, they might have slain him. The probability, however, seems to be that they would not have gone so far. But what if they had? Moses would have perished—we can feel sure of that—rather than have moved one inch in this evil way. And they who undertake to lead a people into new ways of truth and righteousness—as Aaron did, equally with Moses—should be at all times ready to give their life's blood to evince the earnestness of their purpose, and to show forth their own conviction of the supreme importance of the objects which they set before the people. No man is truly great who has not before him great objects, for which he would think it worth his while to die. Nevertheless, it is true that the *real* martyr spirit is rare in every age. It was rare in that age—it is rare in this.

JUDGMENT

Exodus 32:7-35

WHERE was Moses all the time that these abominations were perpetrated in the camp? He was

in the mount with God, receiving his ordinances; when suddenly the divine voice said to him, "Get thee down; for *thy* people, whom *thou* broughtest out of the land of Egypt, have corrupted themselves: they have turned aside quickly out of the way which I commanded them." He was then told wherein they had sinned; and the Lord threatened to abandon this stiff-necked people to their doom, and to make Moses himself the heir of the promises. Some have asked, What would then have become of the promises of God made to the fathers? The answer is, that the proposition had its purpose, and God knew that the contingency would not arise. The promises were at one time bound up in the life of Isaac, whom nevertheless his father was commanded to immolate. No one imagines, that at any part of that transaction it was actually the divine intention to allow that sacrifice to be consummated; yet no one denies on that account the fitness of the proposal as the means of trying and illustrating the patriarch's faith. So now this proposal had two obvious effects, both of them salutary and important; namely, to afford the Hebrew leader an occasion of manifesting his disinterestedness, and to benefit the people, by exciting their alarm at the possible desertion of their Almighty Friend, and the forfeiture of the privileges they had deemed so secure. But, suppose Moses had accepted the proposal?—We have no right to ask what would have been the consequences, had everything taken place that did not. But if it had been so, God's promises to the patriarchs had still been fulfilled; for Moses was a son of Abraham, of Isaac, and of Jacob, and in him and his the promises might have been fulfilled. Where is the difficulty?

But this prospect had no charms for Moses. It filled him with consternation and grief. His earnest and humble expostulation evinced that regard for the honour of God's name, which seems to have been always the master feeling in his mind. Aware of the point of view in which the Egyptians and the neighbouring nations regarded the recent conflict, as one testing the power of the God in whom Israel trusted, he urged, "Wherefore should the Egyptians say, For mischief did He bring them out, to slay them in the mountains, and to consume them from the face of the earth?" This was a thought the heart of Moses could not endure. But he rested not there: he pleaded the ancient promises to the patriarchs, especially as regarded the multitude of their race; for that increase must be long postponed, if he and his were substituted for the existing thousands in Israel.

His prayer prevailed; and, speaking after the manner of men, the Lord is said to have repented of the evil which He had thought to do unto His people.

Moses then went down. On the way he joined Joshua, who had been left below the clouded top of the mountain, and had remained waiting patiently for his master. Together they descended; Moses bearing in his hands the stone tablets on which the substance of the moral law, as embodied in the ten commandments, was written by the hand of God. As they proceeded, the air bore to their ears the distant sounds of the joyful shouts of the people in their jubilation before their golden idol.

Joshua, all whose instincts were martial, thought of nothing but a hostile assault upon the encampment. Like Job's war horse, he smelleth the battle afar off. "There is a noise of war," said he, "in the camp." This is one of those small, delicate touches, which mark a historian drawing from fact—recording from nature. But Moses was not so deceived. He said, "It is not the voice of them that shout for mastery, neither is it the voice of them that cry for being overcome; but the voice of them that sing do I hear."

And so it proved. Their continued descent brought them in full view of the camp; and there were the chosen people seen giving themselves up to bacchanalian revelries, and dancing around the idol they had formed. At that awful sight, Moses, who, with all his gentleness and patience, could endure nothing that brought dishonour upon the Lord of hosts, was moved with holy indignation; and, casting from his hands the precious tablets that he bore, he brake them to pieces beneath his feet. Nor was this act without signification. This people had but lately entered into high and solemn covenant with Jehovah: He to be their God and King, and they to be His people and subjects. The tables of stone contained, as it were, on the part of God, the terms of the agreement, and formed a pledge that He would on His part fulfil all that He had promised. That covenant they had, in a most essential matter, broken and cast to the winds; and by that act, all their expectations from Him were destroyed and broken, as a matter of bonded and covenanted right. Moses, by casting the tables from him, and breaking them in their sight, adopted the most proper and significant mode of representing his view of the transaction.

Consider well the moral courage of Moses. He was but one man. Yet he ventured, armed only with the terrors of holy wrath, to confront that inebriate host, and the conscience-stricken crowd shrank before him; and not a hand was lifted up in resistance, when he strode straight up to their idol, cast it to the ground, and utterly destroyed it before their eyes.

This destruction of the golden calf is particularly described, and demands a moment's attention: " He took the calf which they had made, and burnt it in the fire, and ground it to powder, and strawed it upon the water, and made the children of Israel drink of it." Many years after, in describing the transaction to a new generation, Moses says: "I took your sin, the calf which ye had made, and burnt it with fire, and stamped it, and ground it very small, even until it was as small as dust; and I cast the dust thereof into the brook that descended out of the mount." Much inquiry has been founded on this. A French writer,[1] dwells on the difficulty of the operation, known to be such by all who work in metals. He argues from it the advancement in chemical art of the Egyptians, from whom he thinks Moses must have acquired the secret. "The heads of commentators," he says, "have been much perplexed to know how Moses burnt and reduced the gold to powder. Many have offered vain and improbable conjectures; but an experienced chemist has removed every difficulty upon the subject, and has suggested this simple process: In the place of nitro-muriatic acid (the aqua regia of the alchymists) which we employ, the Hebrew legislator used natron, which is common in the East. What follows respecting his making the Israelites drink this powder, proves that he was perfectly acquainted with the whole effect of the operation. He wished to increase the punishment of their disobedience, and nothing could have been more suitable; for gold, reduced and made into a draught in the manner I have mentioned, has a most disagreeable taste."

This is very ingenious and interesting. It proceeds, however, upon the supposition that the

[1] Goguet in his *Origine des Lois*.

image was of solid gold, or at least wholly of gold. But if, as we have supposed, the nucleus was of wood, covered with plates of metal, we may then dispense with all this elaborate process, the application of which, under the circumstances, appears to us very difficult, and obtain another explanation much more directly in unison with the sacred record. The fire would, of course, calcine the wood, and reduce that to powder; and from the residue the plates of metal might easily be beaten or hammered out (as the "stamping" implies) very thin, and from that form reduced to fine dust, which, with the ashes of the wood, might be easily cast upon the water. Or, if the scientific appliances were at all necessary, they would be much more effectually and immediately operative in rendering friable the plates of metal than a solid or dense mass of gold. In regard to the drinking, the people were thus made to express the same contempt for it as the Egyptians would have done in eating any of their animal-gods; and it was, in this view, at the same time a punishment for their sin and a humiliation to their idol. But it is not, after all, clear that they were constrained to drink it as a designed punishment; for it may have resulted, as an inevitable incident, from the fragments being cast into the stream descending from the mount which supplied drink to the camp.

It then devolved upon Moses to execute judgment upon the chief offenders. When he stood in the gate calling those who were on the Lord's side to gather to him, the Levites came. At his command they took their swords and passed through the camp, smiting all those, to the number of three thousand, whose appearance evinced the active part they had taken in these idolatrous orgies.

Then Moses returned to the mount; and let us heed well the words he uttered: "Oh, this people have sinned a great sin, and have made them gods of gold. Yet now, if Thou wilt forgive their sin——: and if not, blot me, I pray Thee, out of Thy book which Thou hast written." What a glorious

abruption is this! How beautiful! how grand! We know nothing like to it in literature. Overpowered with emotion at the mere idea of the sin of Israel remaining unforgiven, he cannot finish the sentence; and after a pause of overwhelming feeling, he declares that in that case it were better for him to die than to live, and prays that it may be so. It was usual to keep a genealogical registry of living persons. When any one died, his name was blotted out. God, in this and similar expressions in Scripture, is supposed to keep such a book—the book of the living; and to be blotted from it was to die.

―――

STRANGE FIRE—MOURNING

Leviticus 10

AMONG the incidents of Sinai which may be regarded as historical, is one which intimately concerned the family of Aaron. It occurred after he and his sons had been set apart to the priesthood, and—the tabernacle having been

ALTAR OF INCENSE

erected—the system of ritual worship was in full operation. Aaron had four sons, Nadab, Abihu, Eleazar, and Ithamar, who had daily duties to discharge at the tabernacle. The two former, as the elder, enjoyed special consideration, and they had been with their father and Moses in the sacred mount, which had not been the case with their brothers. Among the priestly services was that of offering the precious incense upon the golden altar within the tabernacle, at the very time that the daily sacrifice was being consumed upon the brazen altar in the court without. At the time the ritual service had been inaugurated, the fire of the great altar was kindled from heaven; and it was made an ordinance that this holy fire should always be kept up and preserved, and that this, and this alone, was to be used in all the sacred services. The priests who offered incense had therefore to fill their censers with fire from the great altar when they went into the tabernacle to burn incense. It was in this matter that Nadab and Abihu sinned. Treating this ordinance as of no importance, thinking to themselves that common fire would burn their incense quite as well as the other; or, perhaps, as there is reason to fear, having been led into a mistake or neglect by inebriety, they filled their censers with " strange fire," unhallowed fire, not from the altar, and ventured to bring it into the tabernacle. The altar on which they were to lay it stood before the veil or curtain which separated the outer chamber from that inner one in which lay the ark of God, and over which, " between the cherubim," shone that divine and burning radiance usually called the " glory of the Lord," but properly distinguished by the Hebrew

ARK OF THE COVENANT

term Shekinah. No sooner did they enter the place with their strange fire, than a penetrating flash shot forth from the symbol of the sacred presence and laid them dead. The effect was like that of lightning; for the fire which " de-

voured " their lives left their sacred vestments unconsumed.

This was an awful thing. Was it not terribly severe ? We must answer that it was NECESSARY. At any time the offence would have been very grievous; but at this time, when the ritual service was so newly established, and just coming into regular operation, such an infraction of it by the very persons whose official charge it was to maintain its sacredness, demanded a most rigid punishment, even a miraculous interposition, to protect the sacred service, and indeed the whole law, from that disesteem on the part of the people which might naturally have resulted from it, if it had been passed over without the severest notice.

And what did Aaron say to this—the afflicted father, who saw the two eldest of his sons taken from him at one stroke ? He said nothing. "HE HELD HIS PEACE." Never did that eloquent tongue utter words so cogent or so beautiful as was his silence then. It reminds us of him who said, "I was dumb, I opened not my mouth; because THOU didst it." This simply natural and touching circumstance raises Aaron in our esteem. We view his veiled sorrows with the respect which the most clamorous grief might vainly claim; and we feel more than ever disposed to extenuate the weakness which belonged to some parts of his career.

The occasion gave Moses the opportunity of enforcing upon the father and brothers, and in them, upon all future high priests and priests, the obligations of public duty as limiting the indulgence of private feeling. Eleazar and Ithamar, consecrated as they were to the divine service, were not to adopt the usual signs of lamentation, nor so much as to suspend the offices in which the calamity found them engaged. This was obviously insisted upon, lest a relaxation of the precision of the ritual on any account, at this early period, before habit had made it familiar, should be looked upon as a dispensation for future negligence. To the deeper feelings of the bereaved father some allowance was shown. The goat of the sin-offering, instead of being partly consumed, and partly reserved for use, to be eaten by the priests as directed, had been wholly consumed on the altar, perhaps because the grief of the bereaved family not allowing them to assemble for a repast, they knew no better way of disposing of it. Moses remonstrated with Eleazar and Ithamar on this negligence; but Aaron said, that after what had befallen him he had no heart for feasting, and he could not think that such a service would be demanded or accepted by the Lord; and we are told that " when Moses heard that, he was content."

The prohibition laid upon the priests in reference to the customary signs of mourning, because the vows of the Lord were upon them, shows us what were the ceremonies or expressions of mourning in use among the Israelites. The words are: " Uncover not your heads, neither rend your clothes." The book of Leviticus contains further regulations on the same subject. In the twenty-first chapter, first five verses, the priests are forbidden to contract the defilement involved in mourning, except for their nearest kindred; and the high priest not even for them, not even for his father, or mother, or child, or brother, or sister. The acts prohibited are thus specified: " They shall not make baldness upon their head, neither shall they shave off the corner of their beard, nor make any cuttings in their flesh." The priests might rend their garments; not, we apprehend, their sacerdotal vestments, but their ordinary raiment; but the high priest might not do even this; and the priests, though so far allowed to appear as mourners, might not do so to the extent of disfiguring their persons in any manner.

It is remarkable that the book of Job, usually considered as produced in the same age as the Pentateuch, embodies notices of nearly all the ancient and subsisting practices of eastern mourning. Two of those here indicated are produced in one verse. The patriarch, when informed of the death of his children, as the climax of his trials, " arose, rent his mantle, shaved his head, and fell upon the ground and worshipped." [1] Other early instances are those of Reuben rending his clothes, when he found not Joseph in the pit; [2] and of Jacob also doing this when he understood that his beloved son was killed. [3] This is certainly not the least significant or impressive of the acts of mourning in the demonstrative grief of the East. It is, in a certain degree, a natural impulse, and, as such, has kept its ground, while many merely conventional tokens of sorrow have passed away. It is to be recollected that by such means the ancient as well as modern Orientals, including the Jews, sought to obtain

the result which we ourselves achieve by a distinctive dress. They had no mourning dress, and therefore denoted their condition by rent clothes, by lack of ornaments, and even by personal disfigurements.

It is somewhat remarkable that there is in Scripture no indication that any of the people, except the priests and military men, wore any covering upon their heads. It would therefore seem at the first view, that the clause forbidding them to " uncover their heads" in mourning, signifies that they were not to lay aside the turbans peculiar to their office. That this was included in the prohibition is very likely. But it must also mean more; for if they were not to forego this covering of the head, much less might they cut or shave away their hair, as, from the instance cited from Job, and from others that will occur to the reader, appears to have been customary. Shaving the head is now common throughout Western Asia, as it was among the ancient Egyptians; and it has hence, as an act of mourning, become extinct. This may seem to us too deliberate an act to be a natural expression of mourning. But eastern grief, though demonstrative, is deliberate; besides that, the word does not necessarily mean shaving with a razor, but may denote any mode of cropping or shearing the hair with knife or scissors. However, there is not really more of formal deliberation in having the head shaven even with a razor, than in being measured for a suit of mourning clothes. The directions in reference to what is to be avoided, may be seen in the apocryphal book of Baruch,[1] where the mourning practices of heathen priests are indicated: " Their priests sit in their temples, with their clothes rent, and their heads and beards shaven, and have nothing upon their heads; and they roar and cry before their gods, as men do at the feast when one is dead." This passage, in fact, recognizes these acts as common customs of mourning among the Jews; but the writer is, as a Jew, surprised at their being exhibited by priests. Compare it with the following words of Jeremiah:[2] " There came from Shechem, from Shiloh, and from Samaria, four-score men having their heads shaven and their clothes rent, and having cut themselves," &c. This was in token of affliction.

Much curious speculation has been applied to " the corner of the beard," which it is forbidden

[1] Job 1:20.   [2] Genesis 37:29.   [3] Genesis 37:34.

[1] Baruch 6:31,32.   [2] Jeremiah 41:5.

to "shave off." Some take it to mean that it is the beard as a whole which the mourning priest is forbidden to disfigure in mourning. It seems rather, however, to signify that the Israelites were not to destroy the whiskers or upper extremities of their beards. This implies, that although they were so recently from Egypt, they did allow their beards to grow ordinarily, contrary to the practice of the Egyptians, from whom they were thus distinguished. On the other hand, it appears from the representations of Syrian and Arabian foreigners, which are to be found upon the monuments of the Egyptian people, that some of these nations did trim away the whiskers, while they allowed the beard to grow. The annexed engraving is a collection of

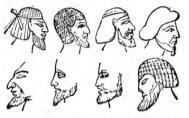

MODES OF WEARING THE BEARD

such heads, showing the different modes of wearing the beard which these monuments exhibit; and it is seen that in most of them the whiskers or the corners of the beard are shaved away.

The text in question would therefore intimate that the practice of the Israelites in preserving the "corners of their beards," distinguished them also from these nations, and that that distinction was not to be destroyed even in the act of mourning.

The slashing of the flesh with knives or lancets in the transport of grief or enthusiasm, still

EASTERN DEVOTEE, WITH CUTTINGS OF THE FLESH.

occurs often enough in the East; but it is not now a regular custom of mourning, though it may be found as such among some American tribes. Herodotus states that it was not an Egyptian custom, but affirms that it was a Syrian

one; and in this he is confirmed by the remarkable case of the priests of Baal, who "cut themselves, *after their manner*, with knives and lancets, till the blood gushed out upon them." [1] From this statement it is easy to see how many regulations, apparently of small consequence, must have operated to *distinguish* the Israelites from the various nations among whom they were placed, and thus have tended towards the maintenance of their existence as a separate people. As an act of mourning, the cutting of the flesh seems to have been retained by the Israelites, [2] it having been seemingly understood as forbidden only to the priests, in whom it might have been regarded as a religious act, and might so lead to the notion, that the sight of human suffering was pleasing to God, or might tend, even when self-inflicted, to excite His compassion or move His purposes. In this sense the custom is not extinct among the devotees of the Pagan or Moslem East. In the latter there are—fewer now indeed than formerly—certain calendars or dervises, who treat themselves after the fashion of the man in the prefixed engraving, copied from an old Dutch book of travels in Palestine. He has iron spikes thrust through the muscles of his arm, a scimitar stuck through the fleshy part of his side, and a feather inserted into a cut in his forehead.

———

HOBAB

Numbers 10:29-32

SEEING that Israel in the wilderness is to be regarded as a type of the church of God in its pilgrim state, and Canaan of that rest which remaineth for the people of God, the devout mind cannot but reflect with peculiar interest upon the striking words which Moses addressed to his brother-in-law Hobab, to induce him to cast in his lot with the chosen people: " We are journeying unto the place of which the Lord said, I will give it you: come thou with us, and we will do thee good; for the Lord hath spoken good concerning Israel." Every word of this deserves most attentive consideration, and is in the highest degree suggestive of comfortable and encouraging thought. We feel that we are in the

[1] 1 Kings 28:28.   [2] Jeremiah 16:6; 48:37.

place of Hobab—that to us is this invitation given —that to us are these inducements held out. It is one of a thousand passages in the Pentateuch which open the heart and set the mind to work in such a manner as might convince us—if only by that "intuition" of which we now-a-days hear so much—that the law was indeed, in more ways than one, "a shadow of good things to come."

Moses first states where Israel is going, and whither he invites Hobab to go. On what ground does Moses rest the assurance that Hobab may have a home in that land? He does not point to the numbers and the strength of Israel, nor expatiate upon their resolution to conquer the land flowing with milk and honey. He gives a better ground of confidence: he says that the Lord *hath promised* to give it. That is all. And it is highly honourable to Hobab, that Moses felt he would be, as he ought to be, satisfied with this reason. He *was* satisfied, for he went; and although the thirty-nine years of wandering which followed were unexpectedly interposed between him and the fulfilment of his expectation, and might seem to cancel the engagement, he persevered to the last, and entered with Israel the promised land, in which we find his descendants settled. (Judg. iv. 11.)

The case is, to the letter, parallel with our own. The same considerations are presented to ourselves. Our hope has no other tenure than that of Hobab. It is not by any works or worthiness of theirs that we feel our Canaan opened to those with whom we have cast in our lot. But God hath said He will give it to them. If our expectation had any other foundation than this promise, anxious and terrible would be our wilderness way. If it rested with ourselves only, there is not a day of our pilgrimage which would not leave us in peril of losing that heritage; but now we can rest secure, rest in perfect peace under the shadow of the covenant, knowing that the promised land is secured, by every pledge that the God of love can give, to all upon whom, in token of their citizenship, Christ has written His new name. Let us not, therefore, be more distrustful than Hobab. Let us believe with him, that although the way to that land, through this "waste howling wilderness," be winding and trying—though it be much longer than we thought —and may tempt us sometimes, in the language of hope deferred, to cry, "How long, O Lord, how

long?" yet it is safe; it is really short: and when we stand on the brink of our Jordan, and are about to pass into our promised land, the way which the Lord our God hath led us these forty years will be seen to have been not wanting in precious remembrances, nor destitute of wilderness privileges. We shall know that the cloudy pillar has been our guide, that we have been fed on manna, that we have drunk of the smitten rock; that with us has been the tabernacle, with us the ark, and that amid all our cares and trials, the glory of the Lord has remained fixed upon the mercy-seat.

With this assurance before him, Moses cordially invites Hobab to come. He does not appeal to Hobab's kindness, to his good feeling, to his friendship. He takes higher ground. He speaks as one who has rich inducements to offer. He tells Hobab to come for his own sake: "Come thou with us, for we will do thee good." Moses was not a beggar to receive boons, but a prince— "a prince of God"—to bestow them. He offers the inducement of good, great good, to the man whom he invites to accompany him—one near to him, one whose society he had daily enjoyed while he abode in the tents of Midian, and whose interests were therefore no doubt very dear to him. The Jewish lawgiver would not have deceived him on any account, nor have held out expectations the fulfilment of which he doubted. For this good Hobab had not, strictly speaking, to wait for forty years. He realized much of it even in the wilderness, more of it probably than he could have enjoyed among his own people and in his own land. It was good, it did him good, to be among a people who lived under God's special covenant, to the privileges of which he was no doubt admitted. There were those around him with whom he might daily take sweet counsel in the things of God. That was good. He had opportunities unattainable elsewhere of *realizing* the presence of God among His people. That was good—that was a precious privilege to him. The air he breathed, the sights he beheld every day, the sounds he heard, all had God in them—all were full of God. And that was very good for him; it tended, all tended, to build up his faith, to cheer his heart, to keep him from being "discouraged because of the way." We need not apply this. It *is* applied even by the terms in which it is expressed. It is far better to be a doorkeeper in the house of God than to dwell in the tents of wickedness; and in the conviction of the high privileges which belong to their condition, the people of God may freely and confidently say to those who go with them that it shall be good for them, good for them in the wilderness, and good for them in the promised land.

We have the same ground of confidence and the same authority that Moses had. We have no other: "For the Lord hath spoken good concerning Israel." What is there of possible good which the Lord hath not spoken concerning His people? all of which, by the pledge of His sacred word, is theirs now, and theirs hereafter. You may open the book of God at Genesis, and turn it over to Revelation, finding in every one of its leaves some precious promise of good, some high encouragement, some holy hope. Yet even this fails to convey the sum of all the blessings and privileges which belong of right to those who have been enabled to choose their " better part " with the people of God. Now God, to be heard of man, must speak in language that man can understand; and human language fails to express, human thought to grasp, the large amount, the unutterable, inconceivable sum of all the blessedness which is theirs, and shall be theirs for ever. It is written, " Eye hath not seen, nor ear heard, neither have entered into the heart of man, the things which God hath prepared for them that love Him.[1] Yet it is added, that God hath revealed them to us by His Spirit—that Spirit which beareth witness with our spirits that we are the children of God, and as such are entitled to all the blessings of His house and of His kingdom. When enriched with these privileges, no more are we aliens from the commonwealth of Israel, and strangers to the covenant of promise; no more strangers and foreigners, but fellow-citizens with the saints and of the household of God.[2] From this household will God withhold no good thing;[3] and every member of it shall " dwell on high; his place of defence shall be the munitions of rocks; bread shall be given him, his water shall be sure. His eyes shall see the King in His beauty; they shall behold the land that is very far off."[4] We shall then *have right* to that tree of life,[5] which was protected from the grasp of man when he fell, by the glittering swords of the cherubim. In view

of these things well may we cry, " Oh how great is Thy goodness, which Thou hast laid up for them that fear Thee; which Thou hast wrought for them that trust in Thee before the sons of men!"[1]

There is a difficulty connected with the name Hobab, which must force itself on the attention of the thoughtful reader. It may be stated as follows : Was Hobab Moses' brother-in-law, as Dr. Kitto states, and therefore the son of Raguel ? Or was he Moses' father-in-law, as is stated in Judg. iv. 11, and therefore identical with Raguel ?

It is well to note that Raguel and Reuel are only different English forms of the same Hebrew name (Exod. ii. 18; Num. x. 29); and further, that Jethro was another name of the same person (Exod. ii. 18; iii. 1).

In Num. x. 29, we read, "And Moses said unto Hobab, the son of Raguel the Midianite, Moses' father-in-law," etc. It is plain from this that Raguel was Hobab's father ; but the construction is such, that the clause "Moses' father-in-law " may either be referred to Raguel or to Hobab. At first sight it seems more natural to apply it to the former ; yet, on closer examination, I am inclined to think it applies to Hobab, who had not only another name—Jethro—but was also called by his father's name, Raguel. In this way the passage is at once harmonized with Judg. iv. 11, where Hobab is distinctly said to be the father-in-law of Moses.

Some maintain, however, with Dr. Kitto, that Hobab was the son of Moses' father-in-law. They argue that the sacred narrative requires this, for it is said in Exod. xviii. 27, that "Moses let his father-in-law depart, and he went his way into his own land ;" whereas Hobab appears certainly to have accompanied the Israelites into Palestine (Num. x. 31; Judg. i. 16; iv. 11). I do not attach much weight to this, for Jethro may have returned to his son-in-law, and yielded to his persuasions, as indeed is stated in Num. x. 30, 31. It is also said that the Hebrew word translated father-in-law in Judg. iv. 10, may signify any relation by marriage, and consequently may mean that Hobab was Moses' *brother-in-law*. I admit that it might have that meaning ; but a comparison of Exod. iii. 1, with chap. ii. 18 and xviii. 1, shows that the specific meaning father-in-law is attached to it. I conclude, therefore, that Raguel, Jethro, and Hobab were just different names of the same individual, and that he was the father of Moses' wife.

P.

THE SON OF SHELOMITH

Leviticus 24

THERE was another sad matter that occurred before the Israelites quitted their encampment in Sinai.

We should very imperfectly realize to our minds the idea of the great Hebrew camp, if we

---

[1] 1 Corinthians 2:9. [2] Ephesians 2:12,19.
[3] Psalms 84:11. [4] Isaiah 33:16,17.
[5] Revelation 22:14.

[1] Psalms 31:19.

ignored the existence in it of a large body of Egyptian people. To their presence, their character, and the evil nature of the influence they exerted, we have more than once alluded. That they were of the lowest order of the people, in a nation where castes were distinctly marked, will be obvious from the consideration that they could have had no other apparent object in leaving with the Israelites than to better their condition; and those whose condition could be bettered, in human calculation, by following into the wilderness the liberated bondmen of Egypt, could have had no comfortable homes in their own country. The manner in which the books of Moses mention them, confirms abundantly this impression. In Exod. xii. 38, those who went up with the Israelites are described as "a great rabble," for such is the literal import of the Hebrew phrase. In the grosser discontents and base repinings of the host, it was, as might be expected from a people of this low condition, "the mixed multitude" who took the lead, Num. xi. 4; and in Deut. xxix. 11, the members of this great body, the strangers of the camp, seem to be described as having in the course of time subsided into the condition of servants to the Hebrew host: "Thy stranger that is in thy camp, from the hewer of thy wood to the drawer of thy water."

If there is any one who asks whether it be possible that the wealthy, powerful, and luxurious Egypt contained any people so low and miserable as to be willing to cast in their lot with the wanderers of Israel, we need but look at home for an answer. In our own case, a nation, perhaps the most powerful in the world, probably the most luxurious, and certainly the most wealthy, exhibits a greater amount of abject poverty, of utter destitution, than any other nation of the world can show, excepting perhaps only China, which is also a very wealthy, luxurious, and powerful nation. And if we not only see this, but see tens of thousands of our naturally home-loving people driven from our golden shores year by year in search of bread, let us not wonder that there were among the Egyptians a multitude of people willing and glad to quit their country with the Hebrews, in the knowledge that for them any change must be for the better, because it *could not* be for the worse. But we do not want analogies to prove that Egypt afforded a sufficiency of people in this low condition. We have facts.

History concurs with the monuments in placing before us the most marked and manifest distinctions of society, resulting in part, no doubt, from the institution of castes, such as we find in India, although, as we have seen, that institution is not *necessary* to account for it. "A part of the people," says Hengstenberg,[1] "appear to have been in the deep degradation that now presses upon the Fellahs. According to Herodotus, the caste of swine herds, a native tribe, was unclean and despised in Egypt. All intercourse with the rest of the inhabitants, even entrance into a temple, was forbidden, and they were as much despised as the Pariahs in India. The contempt in which they were held was not certainly the consequence of their occupation, but their occupation of the disdain which was felt for them." But full light falls upon the notices of the Pentateuch, through the painting in Thebes representing the making of bricks, to which we have already had occasion to refer. There, whether the labourers be Israelites or not, they are certainly foreigners, in an enslaved and despised condition; and among them we see native Egyptians reduced to the same condition, and sharing their labours and their stripes. In fact, so much were a certain class of Egyptians connected with the Israelites even in Egypt, that intermarriages were contracted between them; and in the chapter before us we have the case of a young man whose father was an Egyptian, but whose mother was a woman of Israel, named Shelomith, of the tribe of Dan. As this person was old enough to engage in a personal conflict with a man of Israel, the union between his mother and his Egyptian father must have been accomplished at least eighteen or twenty years before, in the time of the hard bondage. No doubt there were many persons of *this class* in the camp; and from the mixed influence under which they were brought up, we may easily believe that, although probably recognized as members of the commonwealth of Israel, and occupying a higher position than persons of wholly alien parentage, they were, as a class, the most unsteady and dangerous persons in the camp. It is precisely such a person whom we should suspect to be more apt than any "Hebrew of the Hebrews" to treat with irreverence the sacred name of Jehovah. And this was the case. The young man, in the course of his quarrel, dared to utter words of blasphemy against that holy name. In

[1] *Egypt and the Books of Moses*, p. 83.

the authorized version it is written that he "blasphemed the name *of the Lord,* and cursed." The words in italics are supplied, and do not exist in the original, where it is, "blasphemed the NAME, and cursed." Perhaps it had better been left so, for there can be no doubt as to what is meant by "the Name;" and the intentional and reverent abstinence of the sacred writer from giving the name itself in this place, seems more strikingly and emphatically to paint the frightful profanity of the man who dared to use it blasphemously. It would seem as if he shrank from the idea of connecting that great name with the thought of its having been profaned. It is not impossible that this example may have had weight with the Jews in originating the practice which is known to have existed among them from a very early period, of regarding themselves as prohibited from uttering the name JEHOVAH except on sacred and solemn occasions, and scarcely on these; for it is well known that even in reading the Scriptures in Hebrew, they always pronounce the word *Adonai,* Lord, when they come to the word JEHOVAH. This practice our own translators have imitated, so far as generally to write the word LORD (in capitals) where the original has JEHOVAH. The recent Jewish translators of Genesis into English give a singular instance of avoidance in the only case in which it is preserved in that book by our translators, and where it seems to be indispensably required. This is in chap. xxii. 14; "Abraham called the name of that place JEHOVAH-JIREH;" where the Jewish translators have, "Abraham called the name of that place ADONAY-YER'EH." Frequently, indeed, the Hebrews did, and do, use the word *hash-shem,* "the Name," for "JEHOVAH." Ancient evidence of the custom of thus alluding to the Deity, without mentioning His name, has been found upon the marbles of Palmyra, among whose inscriptions we find such as these: "To the blessed NAME be fear for ever;" "To the blessed NAME, for ever good and merciful, be fear;" "To the blessed NAME for ever be fear," etc. This may remind one of a still earlier instance than the present of the direct mention of the sacred name being avoided, or rather expressed by periphrasis: this was when "Jacob sware by the Fear (rather by the Revered One) of his father Isaac." (Gen. xxxi. 53.)

It is recorded that there have been nations which had no law against parricide, because they would not that the law should recognize the possibility that a crime of such enormity could be committed. So in the present case, no law against this unparalleled offence had been given; and therefore the Hebrew magistrates, sensible of the deep enormity of the offence, but not able to measure the degree of punishment, and aware that a precedent was now to be established which would be followed in time to come, proceeded with becoming solemnity and deliberation. Nothing further was done in the matter than to detain the man in custody, "that the mind of the Lord might be showed them." This was soon known — having been ascertained, probably, by the means now regularly appointed — from the Shekinah, between the cherubim. The divine utterance from the supreme Judge and Sovereign of the nation was, "Bring him forth that hath cursed without the camp, and let all that heard him lay their hands upon his head, and let all the congregation stone him;" and a law was given that this should hereafter be the doom of every one, whether a native Israelite or a stranger dwelling in the land, who blasphemed the name of JEHOVAH.

As the presence of the Lord among His people rendered the camp of Israel holy, the execution within its bounds of one who had rendered himself so abominable and accursed was not to be endured; and hence the direction that he should be stoned without the camp. Thus also our Lord, who was brought to death on a false charge of blasphemy, was executed without the gate; and thus likewise Stephen, who suffered on the same charge, was "cast out of the city," and there stoned.

As to the witnesses laying their hands upon his head, this was a significant act by which those who had heard the blasphemy bore testimony to his being fully convicted, and declared that his blood rested upon his own head, and that they and the congregation of Israel were by his death freed from the stain of so great a crime. The Jewish commentators say that this ceremony only took place in the case of those convicted of blasphemy; and they are probably right, as we read of no other examples of the kind in the canonical Scriptures; and the apocryphal book of Susanna, which does contain an instance in a narrative of the punishment of a different crime, is of too little authority, even in regard to Jewish customs, to be cited for the disproof of this assertion.

The Jews made another law for themselves, that every one who heard the name of God blasphemed should rend his clothes. According to this, the high priest before whom our Lord was brought rent his garments when he heard what he chose to regard as blasphemy; not, of course, the sacerdotal garments·which he wore in the temple (for that would have been a high crime, it being expressly forbidden to rend them even in utmost grief), but those which he wore on ordinary occasions, or which belonged to him in his judicial or civil capacity.

The Jews did not err in declaring that they had a law by which the blasphemer ought to be put to death; their crime was that, in order to compass the death of Jesus, they accused Him unjustly, and against all evidence, of this offence —it being the very one which they knew to be the best calculated to excite the rage of the people against Him, and to lead them to think that they did God service by putting Him to death.

MURMURINGS

Numbers 11

WHEN all the purposes of Israel's sojourn among the Sinai mountains had been accomplished, the signal for their departure was given. This was on the twentieth day of the second month of the second year of their departure from Egypt. It was wisely ordered by the providence which watched over Israel, that Moses was relieved from all responsibility with respect to times of removal and places of encampment, by the whole matter being visibly ordered by an authority which none could gainsay. Whenever the appointed time of removal came, the pillar of cloud, usually stationary, was seen to move. It arose, and then the direction it took indicated the course they were to follow; and the spot where it again settled pointed out the place of encampment. Thus miraculously guided, the tribes, moving in an orderly and appointed manner, proceeded for three days, till they came to the wilderness of Paran, and there they were directed to pitch their tents.

At this place the people began to murmur, from what cause we are not told, but probably at the hardships and fatigues of their march in the desert. The indulgence allowed to their weakness on their departure from Egypt, is no longer conceded to them after the training and organization they had undergone, and after the further opportunities afforded them of understanding their relation to the Lord, and of knowing His care, His bounty, His power, and His judgments. All murmurings before they came to Sinai were passed over, or merely rebuked; all murmuring and rebellion after Sinai bring down punishment and doom. They have now a law; they know what it exacts from them, and by that law they must be judged. So in this case, the fire of the Lord came, and "consumed them that were in the uttermost parts of the camp." Any fire sent by the Lord is a fire of the Lord. Some think it was a fire wholly supernatural; others that it was lightning; others that it was the simoom, or hot wind of the desert; while some reduce it to a burning of the dry brushwood of the desert, which extended to and fired the tents on the outskirts of the camp. Any of these means might have been a fit instrument of judgment in the Lord's hand, and the judgment was recognized as His punishment of their sin. The name of Taberah, or *the burning*, was given to the spot in sorrowful commemoration of the event.

As the Israelites encamped in a most orderly manner, according to their tribes, those in the uttermost parts of the camp must surely have been the mixed multitude which we have had former occasion to notice. How little they profited by this correction is seen by the fact of a new and more serious murmuring which arose among them at the very next station, and which spread rapidly among the tribes. There it is expressly said to have been "the mixed multitude" among whom this arose. The term hardly conveys the contemptuous force of the original. They have formerly been called "a rabble;" they are now called the A-SAF-SUF, the force of which can perhaps only be conveyed by such strictly analogous terms as riff-raff or tag-rag. This term, however, is applied rather to denote their moral and social disorganization, than their low estate in this world's possessions; for poverty, low birth, destitution, are in themselves never mentioned with disrespect or contumely in the books of Moses.

And what can be supposed to ail them now? There is not now any lack of food or water for them. No: but they are become dainty. They have taken a surfeit of the manna—their soul loathes "this light food," as they slightingly call it, and they long for the fish, the flesh, the vegetables, they had eaten in Egypt. We fear that there are many who in fact sympathize with them, though formally obliged to condemn conduct which the Scripture deems so culpable. But let us consider that all their wants were provided for day by day, without their care, thought, or labour, and that the poorest of them had as much wholesome food as he could eat without cost; whereas what they had in Egypt, which would have been less wholesome in the life they now led, had been the purchase of their stripes and hard toil. Let us remember that this manna, which they had already come to contemn, was highly nutritive and wholesome food, as nearly as possible analogous to what forms the staff of life, be it rice or corn, to the present inhabitants of the desert, who rarely taste meat or vegetables, and are but too happy if they can get enough of their customary food. But more than all, let us consider that at this time they were actually on their march to the Promised Land, and had reason to suppose that, in a few months at most, they would be in possession of all their hearts could wish; and besides that, as free men, with heads erect in all the dignity and honour of independence, they ought, even if their present position had been quite as bad as they seem to have supposed—if the manna, instead of being "bread from heaven," had been quite unwholesome and unpalatable—to have cheerfully borne all, in consideration of the circumstances in which they were placed, of the prospect of speedy relief, and of the high hopes which lay before them. Taking all these things into account, we shall be the better able to understand the deep displeasure this conduct awakened in their divine King, and the intense grief and indignation which Moses himself expressed. In fact, Moses must by this time have begun to suspect, that this generation, fresh from Egypt, and enfeebled in soul by its bondage, was hardly fit for the vocation to which it had been called. It was probably in consequence of some such thought, that his own language became unusually desponding and distrustful, and that, for the time, his strong spirit fainted under the burdens that lay upon him. Hear the language of his grief and despair: "Have I conceived all this people? Have I begotten them,

that Thou shouldst say unto me, Carry them in thy bosom, as a nursing father beareth the sucking child, unto the land that Thou swarest unto their fathers?" How apt the similitude! they *were* indeed as sucking children, looking to him as dependently, and as regardless of his position or resources, for food, and raising the like clamours if it were not given. But he proceeds: "Whence should *I* have flesh to give unto all this people? for they weep unto me, saying, Give us flesh, that we may eat. I am not able to bear all this people alone, because it is too heavy for me. And if Thou deal thus with me, kill me, I pray Thee, out of hand, if I have found favour in Thy sight; and let me not see my wretchedness." And this is Moses. Alas for the strength of man! What is it but weakness at the best? Still, we do not see that he yet distrusts God; but he is becoming hopeless of any good from this people. He sees that they are, in all but physical condition, children; and he feels that it is not in him to raise them to the sentiments and views of men. God can provide for their real wants; but what avails it? Nothing will satisfy them long.

The Lord had great pity on His fainting servant; and as he appeared to be breaking down under the labours which the government of a nation so recently organized imposed upon him, the aid was given to him of seventy elders, on whom was bestowed, in a public manifestation at the tabernacle, a portion of that spirit which dwelt abundantly in him. Nor was this all. The much-coveted flesh was promised—flesh not for one day only, nor for two, nor for five, nor for ten, nor for twenty, but even for a whole month. This intimation startled even the faith of Moses. "The people among whom I am," he said, "are six hundred thousand footmen: and Thou hast said, I will give them flesh. Shall the flocks and the herds be slain for them to suffice them?"

The answer was by another question, full of suggestion and rebuke to him: "Is the Lord's hand waxed short?"

The words of Moses are, however, well worthy the consideration of those—and there are some such—who speculate upon the possibility of the Israelites being supplied with food in that wilderness, otherwise than by miracle. The leader himself clearly knew and felt the impossibility of maintaining so large a multitude for merely a short time, in that region, even with the sacrifice of their own flocks and herds. One would think that those who never travel beyond their own firesides might, in this day of general information, contrive to realize this idea; even though it should be less forcibly impressed upon their minds than upon the minds of those who have traversed the same or similar regions. The difficulty is still greater than appears in the sacred volume; for there we read only of the natural difficulty of supplying the people with food, with no mention of the difficulty of finding pasture for their flocks and herds, if these were numerous in proportion to the usual extent of such possessions among a pastoral people. It is indeed possible that their wealth of this kind was much less than is usually supposed, having declined during the later years of their sojourn in Egypt, occupied as they were in bond-labour, and in the culture of the ground.

On these points we must suffer a very intelligent American traveller to speak: " No reflection forced itself upon me so often or so urgently as the utter and universal inaptitude of this country for the sustenance of animal life. It really seems to possess no element favourable to human existence besides a pure atmosphere; and no appearances favour the supposition that it was ever essentially better. I am filled with wonder that so many travellers should task their ingenuity to get clear of the miracles which, according to the narrative of Moses, were wrought to facilitate the journey of that vast unwieldy host, when it is demonstrable that they could not have subsisted three days in this desert without supernatural resources. The extensive region, through which we were twelve days in passing on dromedaries, is, and ever must have been, incapable of affording food sufficient to support even a few thousand, or a few hundred, people for a month in the year. There is no corn-land nor pasturage, no game nor roots, hardly any birds or insects, and the scanty supply of water is loathsome to the taste, promoting rather than appeasing thirst. What could the two millions of Israel have eaten without the miracles of the manna and the quails? How could they have escaped destruction by drought but for the healing of the waters of Marah? . . . One of the chief difficulties I met with in the narrative of Moses, is that of accounting for the subsisting of the numerous herds and flocks that belonged to the retreating host. We hear of no miraculous provision for

their support: and it seems incredible that they could have subsisted upon the scanty verdure afforded by the flinty soil of the desert, after making all possible allowance for its deterioration by the physical changes of three thousand years. They were probably much less numerous than we are accustomed to suppose, from the very general and indefinite language used in the Bible upon the subject; and they were undoubtedly dispersed over the whole region lying between the long range of mountains now known as Jebel Raha and Jebel Tih on the east, and the Red Sea on the west.[1]"

The promised supply of flesh was provided, as formerly, by immense flocks of quails that poured into the camp, being brought up from the direction of the sea by a strong wind; and the people stood up all that day and night, and the following day, and secured an ample provision. But although their request was granted, the flesh, greedily collected and devoured ravenously, "was still between their teeth," when a great pestilence broke out among them, in token of the divine displeasure; and large numbers of them—it is not said how many—died, and from their being buried there, the place took the name of Kibroth-hattaavah, "the graves of lust." They were thus taught the wisdom of leaving the supply of their wants to the will of Him who watched over them with paternal care, and who knew what was best for them in all the circumstances of their condition. It is very possible that the inordinate indulgence in animal food, after long abstinence therefrom, became the instrument of their punishment; for it is known that dangerous and often fatal maladies are frequently thus produced. Some have thought that the quails themselves might at this time be "out of season," and therefore unwholesome, forgetting that a supply of the same food at the same season the preceding year had not been followed by any ill effects. But at that time they had been too recently from Egypt to be injuriously affected by it as a change of food.

The difficulty felt by commentators regarding the flocks and herds of the Israelites arises mainly from a misconception as to their mode of travel. It is generally taken for granted that they marched in one vast and dense column, something like a modern army. Had such a mode of travel been adopted, nothing short of a continuous miracle could have supplied the flocks, herds, and people with food

[1] Dr. Olin, *Travels in the East*, i. 382.

and water. But no eastern tribe ever travels in this way. I have often seen Arab tribes migrating. Their numbers were small in comparison with the Israelites; and yet their flocks, herds, and shepherds with their families, often covered a region thirty miles in breadth. So the Israelites travelled on leaving Egypt. The route of the main body under Moses is traced. The stations where they encamped are enumerated. They travelled very slowly, stopping for several days at a time. The whole distance from Rameses to Sinai is not 200 miles, and yet it occupied a month and a half. During all this time the flocks and herds were roaming far and wide, having been led to the best pastures and the most copious fountains. They and the people appear to have been brought together for the first time around Sinai.

Another cause of difficulty is ignorance of the features and resources of the Peninsula. Western travellers, comparing it with their own lands, pronounce it utterly barren. Such was Olin's idea, as quoted by Dr. Kitto. It is quite erroneous. The country, even after eighteen centuries and more of neglect and desolation, affords sufficient pasture for very large flocks of goats, sheep, and camels. It is not a desert. It is a pastoral region. During the rainy season it is covered with a sparse vegetation; and there are some spots which almost rival the green meadows of England. The remains of large towns and villages dot its surface. In the torrent beds, now dry, but cut deeply through the gravelly soil, and in the blasted trunks of old trees which here and there linger along the glens and hill-sides, we see evidences of a bygone age, when rain was more abundant, and forests covered, in part at least, the great plateau of et-Tîh. Though the hand of the improvident Arab has long been engaged in the work of destruction, though trees have been cut down, buildings ruined, fields neglected, wells filled up, yet the traces of ancient industry, and of a comparatively numerous population, have not been wholly obliterated. Field enclosures are seen in many places; wells of living water exist; and thickets of tamarisks extend for miles along the moist beds of some of the deeper valleys. The region, too, is of vast extent. Its superficial area exceeds 15,000 square miles. I conclude, therefore, that the Israelitish shepherds could have had little difficulty in finding both pasture and water for their flocks.

P.

The desert of Tîh is the desert of the wanderings, and the route of the Israelites, after leaving Gebel Músa, must have been towards the sea, not through the heart of the desert, for we hear Moses saying, "Shall the flocks and the herds be slain for them, to suffice them? or shall all the fish of the sea be gathered together for them to suffice them?" (Num. xi. 22.) "There went forth a wind from the Lord, and brought quails from the sea." (Num. xi. 31.) These words, which relate to the march of the tribes after leaving Sinai, point clearly to the coast—the shores of the Gulf of Akaba. Much of their history during thirty-eight years remains enveloped in mystery. Where they went, and what they did, the Divine narrative does not inform us. Kadesh appears to have been their principal and longest place of encampment; and, by the name, we conclude is meant, a region, rather than some one definite spot.

"They would," remarks Mr. Palmer, in his *Desert of the Exodus*, p. 517, "have free access to the Sinaitic peninsula, especially to the north-east corner of it. This country, although of no considerable extent, supports, even at the present day, a large Bedawîn population; and there is no difficulty in supposing, that at a time when we know it must have been more fertile, it was capable of supporting even so large a host as that of the Israelites. Their flocks and herds would afford them ample means of subsistence, as do those of the Arabs of the present day, whom they undoubtedly resembled in their mode of life."

Dr. Olin's idea, quoted by Dr. Kitto, is quite erroneous; and is contradicted by the testimony of recent travellers. Wherever water is utilized, the desert even now, by careful cultivation, can be rendered productive. I was much struck with two instances of this—first, near Mokatteb, where Major Macdonald established himself in a Robinson Crusoe like dwelling, in order to collect turquoises. He cultivated a patch of ground by damming up and preserving water, so as to produce a good supply of vegetables, of which, in the enjoyment of his hospitality, our party plentifully partook; and next, in the convent garden at Sinai, where the monks raise excellent crops of useful produce, including fruit. The wilderness of old probably had many oases like Wâdy Feiran; trees were in parts plentiful, and pasturage sufficient to feed numerous flocks and herds.

We must never, on the one hand, lose sight of the supply of manna by the hand of God in an extraordinary way; nor, on the other, overlook supplies yielded by the ordinary dispensations of His bountiful providence. In Numbers xxxi. 22, reference is made to the possession of gold, silver, brass, iron, tin, and lead; and again to jewels of gold, chains, bracelets, rings, ear-rings, and tablets (v. 50). In Deut. ii. 7, Moses speaks of a blessing on the people's industry; and in the verse before that, he tells them they were to *buy* meat for money, and water for money. Thus, it appears, that they had the precious metals, and the means of purchasing provisions; and that they laboured with their hands,—so that their condition must have been different from that supposed by the writer quoted in Dr. Kitto's illustration. It is a great mistake to multiply miracles, when the sacred narrative clearly describes means of support, such as the Almighty affords in His ordinary and bountiful providence.

S.

AARON AND MIRIAM

Numbers 12

THE twelfth chapter of Numbers is full of painful matter, and offers some points of difficulty.

The substance of it is a misunderstanding between Moses on the one hand, and his brother and sister on the other, clearly indicative of low and very unexpected jealousy on their part at the authority exercised and the powers assumed by Moses. One may fancy that Aaron, who had seen not long ago, his two eldest and most favoured sons perish before his eyes, would still be too broken-hearted, too much bowed down by the weight of grief, to find room in his mind for such matters. But it is not so. This way is the way of man's life. It is with him even as with the cedar, whose great branches bend down in winter, as it would seem, almost to breaking, beneath their load of snow ; but day by day a morsel drops off, or melts insensibly away, and so they slowly rise, until at last, by one vigorous bound, each branch throws off its hoary trouble, and grows and looks green again.

Hitherto Moses seems to have had the cordial support of his own family. But one cannot help thinking that Aaron's mind had become somewhat too elated by the very distinguished position to which he and his had been raised. Self-esteem keeps a man's mind so much awake to his own real or supposed claims, that he is almost certain to have present to his own mind whatever views of the importance and dignity of his station can have occurred to the minds of others. Now it is obvious to us, and it can scarcely have escaped the notice of Aaron himself, that the position assigned to him in the commonwealth was in some respects superior to that of Moses. The function of Moses was temporary, and would pass away with his life ; whereas Aaron's was permanent in himself and his heirs, and would leave him and them the foremost and most important persons in the state. He might not therefore always regard with patience the degree in which the full development of his own high office was superseded by the existing authority of Moses. No doubt he remembered he was the elder brother; and we know that men seldom consider any advancement to be beyond their merits and their claims : it is more than probable that he overlooked the fact that the place he had attained was, as far as we can see, given to him entirely on account of his brother, and from consideration of the part he had been allowed, for that brother's sake, to bear in the deliverance of Israel. That he was discontented is certain ; that he made no secret of that discontent is clear; and that it had its principal source in the jealousy entertained of the powers exercised by Moses is plainly stated. " It is a hard thing," says Bishop Hall, " for a man willingly and gladly to see his equals lifted over his head. Nothing will more try a man's temper than questions of emulation." And he adds well, " That man hath true light who can be content to be a candle before the sun of others."

We are sorry to see Miriam also engaged in this murmuring. For *her* a somewhat different ground of discontent may be expected; and it is to her that we are disposed to ascribe that part of the dissatisfaction which rests upon the marriage of Moses with " an Ethiopian woman." There is a difficulty in understanding this. Some suppose that it refers to the Ethiopian princess whom Moses had espoused, according to the Jewish traditions to which we formerly referred,[1] before he originally left Egypt, and who now rejoins him in the wilderness. Others, chiefly old commentators, fancy that Moses actually married a new wife at this time, and that she was an Ethiopian, which some suppose to mean actually a black woman, who in their hands becomes a type of the Gentile Church. But it is safest to adhere to *known* facts. The facts we do know are, that Moses had a wife called Zipporah, the daughter of Jethro; that during the encampment in Sinai she had been brought by her father and brother to Moses; and that the brother, Hobab, had been prevailed upon to accompany the Israelites, to whom his knowledge of the country might be useful. Now if we can show that this woman might with propriety be called an Ethiopian, a perfectly satisfactory explanation grows out of this circumstance. And we can show this. The name translated " Ethiopian " is " Cushite," from Cush, the son of Ham. This name is applied in Scripture not only to Africa, but to Arabia, which is explained by the descendants of Cush having left their name in certain regions in which, on their migration from the common centre, they tarried some time prior to their final passage into Africa. Or a body of them may have remained a long time in Arabia, before they eventually passed over to join the main stock of their people (if ever they did), for the descent of many of the more ancient Arabian tribes has been by no means very clearly deduced, and some of them may have been of Cushite origin. The land in which Jethro dwelt may indeed have been at this very time occupied mainly by such tribes, to whom belonged the hostile shepherds who wronged Jethro's daughters at the well. But it

[1] See Vol. 1. pp. 362-364.

suffices that they were once in this region and left their name in it, to understand that Zipporah may have been called a Cushite, not as being herself of the children of Cush, but as belonging to a country which had received from them its name. This explanation is not new. In fact, it is the one that is now current, and we object not to receive it, although there *is* a difficulty which has escaped all those by whom it has been urged; and that is, that the Israelites, whose ideas were more tribal than territorial, especially at this time, ere they possessed a country of their own, usually denominated any people whose origin they knew, rather from their descent than from the country in which they lived.

But admitting the existence of any sense in which Jethro's daughter could be called an Ethiopian, it is obvious that her arrival might be very unwelcome to Miriam, who would find herself unpleasantly superseded in the position which, as the sister of both Moses and Aaron, she had hitherto held as a mother in Israel, and chief lady in the camp. The wife of Moses would at least share, if not engross, the deference and attention which had hitherto belonged to his sister alone. The high consideration with which Jethro had been treated on his visit to the camp; the improvements in the dispensation of justice which had been made through his wise suggestions; and the influential position now taken by his son Hobab, who was to remain with them, may have been distasteful to Aaron in his present temper, as dividing the power and authority which he wished to retain in the Levitical priesthood, and which his recollection of the concentration of power in the hands of the Egyptian priesthood might lead him to regard as properly belonging to his office. Thus we see that Aaron and Miriam might, under somewhat different influences, make common cause in their discontent at the connection in marriage which Moses had formed.

But there was one who guarded the honour of Moses too well for him to be afflicted at the hard speeches even of a sister and a brother. It is emphatically remarked, that "the Lord heard it." They were all three—the two brothers and the sister—suddenly summoned before the door of the tabernacle. To that door the pillar of cloud visibly moved, and the voice of the Lord spoke to the culprits from it, in words well suited to fill their hearts with shame. They claimed equal powers; they were prophets no less than he; and by them also had the Lord spoken. But what said the Lord Himself? To others, however highly favoured, He had disclosed His will only in visions and dreams: " But my servant Moses is not so, who is faithful in all mine house. With him will I speak mouth to mouth, even apparently, and not in dark speeches; and the similitude of the Lord shall he behold. WHEREFORE THEN WERE YE NOT AFRAID to speak against my servant Moses?" The sign of His glorious presence was then withdrawn; and the proof of His anger was seen in the fact that Miriam had become a leper. This was a peculiar and striking judgment. There had been special regulations regarding the treatment of those infected with the leprous taint, under which it became the duty of the priest himself to judge of its existence, and pronounce the doom of exclusion from the camp. It is therefore not without a significance, sometimes overlooked, remarked that " Aaron *looked upon* Miriam, and, behold, she was leprous!" This fact made him the very person to pronounce the sentence upon the sharer of his sin. Indeed, he may not at the moment have known but that Miriam saw the same signs of the disease in him that he saw in her, and that he also had been smitten with leprosy. Hence his intercession was for both, and he very humbly confessed that they had both been in this matter sinful and foolish. The woman, whose tongue had before been so free in animadversion upon her brother's conduct and character, was now mute with horror. She who had been so high, whose views were so aspiring, was now to be cast forth as an unclean thing from the camp, and live separate, she knew not for how long, for the disease seldom passed away soon, and was often never eradicated. Yet pity was shown her; and though she might not be spared this humiliation, the period of her exclusion was limited to the seven days which those once afflicted with leprosy were required to pass before they could be re-admitted. It would now be Aaron's duty to visit her without the camp. If the symptoms of the complaint had not disappeared during that period, there would be no help for her. She must be reduced to the condition of confirmed lepers. These not only dwelt without the camp, but they had also even there the responsibility of taking care that clean persons should not come near enough to them in their walks to be rendered ceremonially unclean by contact with them. The eye of the stranger would be able to distinguish them by the badge they were constrained to wear upon their faces, by their uncovered heads, and by their sordid raiment. And that the ear might supply the information which the eye might not readily take up, they were bound to cry out, "Unclean! unclean!" whenever they saw a stranger approach.

But if she were then free from this loathsome affliction, and declared to be such on the authority of the priest, ceremonial acts of lustration and sacrifice would enable her to return to the camp, and join once more in the intercourse of common life. When this did take place—after the people had remained at this station a whole week on her account—Miriam came back to the tents, humbled no doubt in her own eyes, but strengthened in her soul by the correction she had received. The best proof of the efficacy of that correction is, that we hear no more of her until her death.

THE GOOD REPORT

Numbers 13

At length the Israelites are found upon the southern border of the promised land, high in hope of soon realizing the blessing of the land "flowing with milk and honey" which had been promised to their fathers, and which would be doubly precious in their eyes from their having encountered the hardships of the wilderness.

From this point twelve men, one from each tribe, were sent out to explore the country, and to report their observations on its advantages, and capacities for defence against the intended invasion. In the earlier narrative of Exodus, Moses is described as taking this measure; but from the parallel place in the later narrative (Deut. i. 22), it appears that it was on the motion of the people that he did so. This relieves us from some uneasiness, as we can conceive that a measure which he would not himself have suggested, might be such as he could not refuse to sanction when proposed by the people for their own satisfaction.

But, indeed, this step, though natural enough in men left to the resources of human prudence, was in *them* but feebleness of faith. God had told them that Canaan was a land flowing with milk and honey, and they had therefore no need to distrust its advantages. God had promised to give the land to them, and it was needless for them to ascertain the strength of the inhabitants —as if *their* strength could render the performance of the promise difficult, or their weakness make it easy to Him. It is profoundly remarked by Bishop Hall on this very case, "That which the Lord moves unto prospers; but that which we move Him to first seldom succeedeth."

Forty days did they spend in the search, and forty years—a year for a day—of toilsome wanderings did that search cost them, connected as it was from beginning to end with distrust and unbelief. They traversed the country in its whole length, even unto Hamath; probably not in a body, but in parties of two or three. That they were able to do this unsuspected and unmolested would seem to show that their language was the same as that spoken in Canaan, or not materially different from it. Their general personal appearance must have been similar— there could have been nothing to suggest to the Canaanites that they were foreigners; for had it been known that they belonged to the Hebrew host assembled in the southern frontier, they would hardly have returned with their lives.

Generally, the business of a spy is in western armies entrusted to inferior persons; but it was not so among the Hebrews, with whom, as with the Greeks of Homer, its very responsible duties were assigned to persons of consideration, the weight of whose character would give authority to their reports. So, in this instance, men of some importance in their several tribes were chosen for this task. Their names are given, but among them there are only two of historical importance, and these are Caleb for Judah, and Joshua for Ephraim. The high position of these two men indicates the quality of the others.

It was the season of vintage and fruitage; probably they set out early in September, and returned about the middle of October. When they did return, the multitude gazed with eager and admiring eyes on the luscious fruits which they brought as specimens of the country's produce—figs, pomegranates, grapes—kinds which indeed they might have seen in Egypt, but where, the climate not being congenial to them, they attain no great perfection. Especially did a vast

THE RETURN OF THE SPIES FROM CANAAN

cluster of grapes from the valley of Eshcol excite their admiration. It had been borne between two on a pole, partly by reason of its great size, and in part to protect it from being bruised. The statement about this vine cluster has excited the astonishment of many, and even the incredulity of some. They have inferred, unwisely, that the cluster or bunch was so large that it needed two men to sustain its weight; whereas the text indicates no more than that it was of such a size that it could not conveniently be conveyed in any

GRAPES OF PALESTINE

other way uninjured. The statement says nothing as to the size of the grapes, but of the cluster. To produce large grapes is not the distinction of good vines, as the largest grapes are seldom the best; nevertheless, while Palestine has varieties of the vine, the grapes of which are small and

luscious, there are others whose grapes are large enough to draw expressions of wonder from even the inhabitants of European vine countries. Laborde has given a figure, in the natural proportions of some that he saw; and this corroborates the assertion of an Italian traveller, that the grapes were often as large as plums.

But; in conformity with the text before us, the size and richness of the *clusters* of the grapes in many parts of Palestine excite more astonishment than even the size and richness of the grapes. An Italian traveller[1] avers, that in different parts of Syria he saw clusters that would be a sufficient burden for one man. A German traveller[2] declares, with some solemnity of assertion, that in the mountains of Israel he had seen and eaten from vine-clusters that were half an ell long, and the grapes of which were equal to two finger-joints in length. A very intelligent French traveller[3] is still more particular. He declares that one who had seen the vine only in the vine countries of France and Italy, could form no just conception of the size to which the clusters attain in Syria. He had himself seen clusters weighing ten or twelve pounds; and he had reason to believe that in the Archipelago clusters of thirty or forty pounds were not uncommon. A still older traveller of the same nation[4] tells us that, travelling near Bethlehem, he found himself in a delightful valley, replete with rose-trees and aromatic plants, and planted with vines. This was that which tradition regards as the valley of Eshcol, from which the spies obtained their cluster. Not being there in the season, he did not see the fruit himself; but he was assured that clusters of ten and twelve pounds were not seldom gathered from these vines. We share the doubt, however, that this was the vale of Eshcol, which seems rather to have been near to Hebron. It was in this neighbourhood that Nau saw the large vine-clusters of which he makes mention. In this quarter the hill-sides are still thickly planted with vineyards, the vines of which are laden with large clusters of delicious grapes. It is beyond a doubt, that the cluster in question was gathered in the south of Palestine; for as the spies had seen these grapes in their outward way, it would have been absurd for them to gather any but at the last available point towards their own encampment. As striking an instance as any

[1] Mariti.   [2] Neitzschutz.
[3] Nau.   [4] Doubdan.

that we have quoted, has occurred in our own country, in regard to the produce of a *Syrian* vine at Welbeck, the seat of the Duke of Portland. A bunch from this vine was sent, in 1819, as a present to the Marquis of Buckingham, which weighed nineteen pounds. It was conveyed to its destination, more than twenty miles distant, on a staff, by four labourers, two of whom bore it in rotation; thus affording a striking illustration of the means adopted by the explorers in transporting the Eshcol cluster. The greatest diameter of this Welbeck cluster was nineteen inches and a half; its circumference four feet and a half; and its length nearly twenty-three inches.

This display of rich fruit formed of itself a most emphatically good report of the land, as to natural advantages and productiveness; and the explorers confirmed it by their words. They spoke, indeed, as men who needed to say but little, with the material evidence they were enabled to produce: "Surely it floweth with milk and honey; and THIS IS THE FRUIT OF IT." But does the land indeed deserve all the praise anciently bestowed upon its productiveness? Many, looking at that land now, have been disposed to doubt this; and are even inclined to suspect that the explorers, fresh from the sterility of the desert, might unintentionally exaggerate the advantages of a land not even then remarkably fertile. But it should be remembered, that although they had spent above a year in the desert, they had not yet forgotten—they remembered but too well—the fertile banks of the Nile. That Palestine is not now a land flowing with milk and honey—that its general aspect does not correspond with the glowing descriptions left us of its fertility and abundance—is most certain. But there are manifold indications that its former state was very different; and there is nothing in its present condition which cannot be accounted for by long continued neglect of tillage, resulting from the scantiness of the population. It is possible, indeed, that some parts of the land, once fertile, are now irreclaimable. The entire destruction of the wood that once covered the mountains, and the utter neglect of the terraces that supported the soil on steep declivities, have given full scope to the rains, which have left many tracts of bare rock where formerly were vineyards and corn fields. It is likely, too, that the disappearance of trees from the higher grounds, where they invited and arrested the passing clouds, may have diminished the quantity of rain, and so have exposed the whole country in a greater degree to the evils of drought, and doomed some particular tracts to absolute sterility. But, apart from this, the most competent observers have declared that they do not recognize any permanent or invincible causes of barrenness, or any physical obstacles in the way of restoring the land to its pristine fertility.

Mr. Tristram, in his *Natural History of the Bible* (p. 404), speaks of Eshcol, or Grape Valley, a little to the south of Hebron, as still clad with vines, and the grapes as the largest and finest in Palestine. After repeating what is said above, that clusters weighing ten or twelve pounds have been gathered, he adds, that with care and judicious thinning, bunches weighing twenty pounds may be obtained from good vines. When I was riding through the valley twelve years ago, I noticed innumerable vine-stocks, successors, no doubt, of those which yielded the goodly clusters in the days of Joshua. It was spring, and the neighbourhood was rich in barley fields, and studded with budding fig-trees and blooming quinces; whilst the tangled honeysuckles and wild flowers so encumbered the path, that the white arab on which I rode sometimes found it difficult to make his way.

S.

THE EVIL REPORT

Numbers 13:28-33; 14

THE good report which the explorers brought to the camp of Israel respecting the land of promise, confirmed by the actual presence of its splendid fruits, must have warmed the hearts of the people, and awakened an eager desire to possess a country so rich and beautiful. But the rising delight was suddenly cast down by the further report of the spies, that, desirable as the land was for a possession, its acquisition was impracticable; so warlike, numerous, and powerful were the inhabitants, and so well secured in their strongholds. But let us hear their words: "Nevertheless the people be strong that dwell in the land, and the cities are walled, and very great: and, moreover, we saw the children of Anak there." This is their most moderate and prepared account. But when, observing the dismay with which this statement filled the people, Caleb (with whom Joshua concurred) attempted to soothe the multitude by saying, "Let us go up at once, and possess it; for we are well able to overcome it," the other explorers contradicted him, and enforced their previous account by truly oriental exaggerations: "We be not able to go up against the people; for they are stronger than we. . . . . The land, through which we have gone to search it, is a land that eateth up the inhabitants thereof; and all the people that we saw in it are men of a great stature. And there we saw the giants, the sons of Anak, which come of the giants : and we were in our own sight as grasshoppers, and so we were in their sight." Allowing for the figures, not intended to be literally understood, but only to convey a strong impression, this account was correct enough ; and the evil report of the spies consisted not in rendering this account, but in rendering it in such a manner as to discourage the people, by leading them to draw the inference that the invasion of such a land, defended by such inhabitants, was sure to end in defeat. They forgot that, to Him who had dried up the Red Sea before them, and smitten Egypt with all His plagues, the high walls of the Canaanites, and their tall stature, could be no obstacles to the performance of His solemn promise of putting that land in their possession. So Caleb does not deny the facts ; but, valiant in faith, combats the inference drawn from them. That the facts were correct is affirmed by the best of all authorities, that of Moses himself. Many years after, when a new and more promising generation was about to enter the land, he says to them, " Thou art to pass over Jordan this day, to go in to possess nations greater and mightier than thyself, cities great, and fenced up to heaven ; a people great and tall, the children of the Anakim."[1] This, indeed, is an adoption of the precise words used by the spies, as reported orally by himself, to the same audience, in a preceding chapter.[2] Elsewhere, in the course of the same address or discourse, which constitutes the book of Deuteronomy, Moses describes other old gigantic tribes by a reference to the known stature of the sons of Anak. Thus, in the second chapter, the Emim and the Zam-zummim are respectively described as "a people great, many, and tall as the Anakim." In the prophecy of Amos[3] there is a reference to the Amorites, nearly as strong, for the purposes of comparison, as that of the explorers in describing

the Anakim: "Yet destroyed I the Amorite before them, whose height was like the height of the cedars, and who was strong as the oaks." We are to consider that the Hebrews had known no other towns than those in the level country of Egypt, where, although many cities were doubtless walled, the walls would make but a faint impression upon their minds. In Canaan, however, the principal towns and fortresses were upon the summits and declivities of such hills and mountains as they had never before seen inhabited, and, as *looked up to* from lower ground, could not fail to convey to their minds the notion of impregnable strength. And this impression would be the stronger, if, as there is reason to conclude, the walls of the principal towns were of stone ; whereas those of Egypt were of brick, and perhaps of brick only dried in the sun. European readers can scarcely conceive the formidable character which a strong wall presented in the ages before artillery existed, and before engines of war were known. The long duration of ancient sieges, even with the advantage of the best military engines which ancient art could invent, may suggest what must have been the case before such engines were known. A single piece of artillery would have probably breached in one day—or the Roman engines in a week— the Trojan city, which it took the Greeks ten years to reduce, and that only by stratagem at last.

As to the giants, if we be asked whether the race of men were in early times taller than at present, we must answer frankly that we do not know. No facts in favour of that conclusion have been found. All the facts in history, and art, and human discovery, are against, rather than for, that notion, and tend to show that the stature of men in general has not been greater than at present, within any period to which any kinds of monuments extend. What may be said to be, at the first view, the most striking argument in its support, is the impression that the stature of men in the olden time may have borne some proportion to the duration of their lives. But the supposition rests on an analogy which has no foundation in nature, for it is not seen that long-lived animals are generally larger than short-lived ones; and if the conjecture had all the force that could be assigned to it, it would not account for the Canaanites, or any tribes of them, being taller than the Israelites or than the

Deuteronomy 9:1,2. [2] Deuteronomy 1:28. [3] Amos 2:9.

Egyptians, who were their contemporaries; seeing that among them all, the average duration of life, for aught that appears, was the same.

But if we are asked whether there might not be gigantic races, which, however originated, increased and multiplied? we answer, Yes,—because the Scripture affirms it in the case before us, and in other cases; and because the facts of human experience are in favour of it. We see that stature is somewhat influenced by climate, and that men are taller generally in moist and temperate climes than in those which are very hot, or very cold, or very dry; and it is on record, that tall parents have tall children born to them; and if they cared, by their intermarriages, to preserve the distinction, they might keep up a race of giants; but not generally caring for this, the stature of their descendants dwindles, sooner or later, down to the common standard. Such races the Anakim, and others mentioned in Scripture, seem to have been. In this case their descent from a single giant, of the name of Anak, is repeatedly recorded. This race seems to have been rather numerous at the time under notice, but in the course of the four following centuries had declined so much, probably by intermarriages with persons of common stature, that only a few individuals remained, and they were all destroyed by David and his worthies. As Goliath, whom David slew, was of this race, his stature, which may be taken at about nine feet, is a good measure by which to estimate that of the Anakim, whose appearance so alarmed the Israelites. It is clear that the explorers only mean to describe these, and perhaps one or two other races, as of extraordinary stature: for in their first statement they carefully distinguish the Anakim as those whose appearance alarmed them; and although, in the second statement, they generalize the special instance into the designation of "the inhabitants," they still indicate that it was the Anakim whose appearance had filled them with dismay. All that we can safely gather from these facts is, that the ancients, accustomed to venerate the appearance or reality of physical dignity and prowess, were careful to perpetuate and multiply the distinctions of this kind that from time to time arose in every land. Hence the races of giants of which we read in ancient history, and of which some existed in Palestine.

The multitude manifested the most intense and degrading consternation at this report. Caleb and Joshua, who strove to excite them to more worthy thoughts, and to rekindle their faith in their Almighty Deliverer's arm, had well nigh been stoned for their zeal. The people actually wept at the condition in which they were placed; they deplored that they had ever quitted Egypt, and they talked of appointing a new leader to conduct them back to that country. To what lengths they might have proceeded, had not their course been arrested, cannot be known; but there is nothing too preposterous to be supposed possible, had they been left to themselves. The Lord, however, interposed. He declared to Moses His anger, and threatened to destroy them with pestilence, and make of Moses himself a great nation. But the generous leader most earnestly and prevailingly interceded for them, and their doom was respited. They were indeed to perish in the wilderness, but not yet: forty years were the adults to wander; they were gradually to die out, and never to see or enter the promised land, until they—cowardly, distrustful, unenterprising, and enfeebled by long bondage—should be succeeded by their sons, trained up under the institutions God had given them, moulded under them into a nation, and strengthened into manly character under the freedom which had been so triumphantly won for them.

It has been mentioned, by way of objection, that to the Lord it must have been known from the first, that the people were morally and physically incapacitated for this great enterprise, the taking possession of Canaan, and that it was highly expedient, so to speak, that it should devolve upon a new and worthier generation, educated in the freedom of the wilderness, and under the noble institutions of Sinai. There can be only one answer—God did know it. Why, then, was this not brought to pass by their simple detention for that time in the desert, without its being thus made to appear to be the punishment of their pusillanimity? The answer is, Because it *was* such; yet had they proved equal to the occasion, the enterprise had not been withheld from them. And furthermore, it was *necessary* that their unfitness should be made manifest to themselves, or at least that a sufficient and unanswerable reason should be given for their detention in the wilderness until their institutions were consolidated. Had the Israelites been

detained, year after year, at a distance from
Palestine, and the delay been in no way explained, there would have been no answer for
Moses to give to the remonstrances of their discontent. Now, as often as they manifested impatience, he had an answer with which to seal
their lips—they had shown themselves unequal
to the task which they wished to hasten. Had
their want of preparation been assigned as the
reason of the delay, still had there been no
notorious fact to appeal to in proof of that want,
its reality might have been denied, and the argument would have lost its force. Submission to
this arrangement was now their only course—
their only wisdom.

CONSPIRACY

Numbers 16

THE most formidable conspiracy which was ever
formed against the authority of Moses and Aaron,
took place soon after the doom of forty years'
wandering had been pronounced. It was precisely at such a time—if at one time more than
another—that we might expect to hear of plots
and conspiracies among the people. It must be
remembered, that the arrangement of the sacred
and political administration was still recent. It
could not have been organized without exciting
disappointment and dissatisfaction on the part of
some, who considered their claim as good as that
of the men who were preferred to them; and
there had not yet been time for the habit of subordination to assuage their discontent, and lead
their retainers and partisans to a quiet acquiescence in the established order of things. On the
other hand, the people were depressed and uneasy,
and in a fit condition to be tampered with by
factious leaders. Mortified as they must have
been by the recollection of their late unworthy
conduct, and goaded by the thought of having
been condemned in consequence to renounce for
life the hope of occupying their long promised
home, the time must have been favourable for
engaging them in a rebellious movement. They
would now, if ever, be ready to lend an open ear
to the assurance, that under the auspices of other
leaders than those who had lately denounced

against them a humiliating sentence, they might
be able forthwith to prosecute an enterprise on
which their hearts had been so strongly set.

The circumstances of the time being thus so
favourable for the ringleaders, the conspiracy
which comes before us was formed by the very
persons who might be expected to move in it.
The sacred writer does not, indeed, evince any
solicitude to set forth the motives of the parties
engaged; but his plain recital, and the names and
circumstances which he sets down, give us a clear
insight into the nature of the case.

We perceive two interests at work—one against
the sacerdotal, and the other against the political,
power and pre-eminence; and we find the two
coalescing to produce the objects sought by both.
We do not discover that they desired to disturb
the institutions as established; but they aspired
to take to themselves the power which these institutions gave to others.

Previously to its separation for sacerdotal services, the tribe of Levi, like the other tribes, was
governed as to its internal matters, and as to the
part it should take in general matters, by the
patriarchal chief or emir, called in Scripture the
prince of the tribe, who seems to have been the
representative of the eldest branch of the tribe—
the one, in short, who was to be regarded as the
heir of the founder. Now, to this ruling branch
Moses and Aaron did not belong; and the representative of that elder branch would find himself
deprived of his special and peculiar powers under
the new institutions which made the high priest
the virtual head of the tribe, and would see himself and his connections merged in the general
Levitical body; the priesthood, which had become the part of Aaron in the tribe, being given
to another family. Korah was a Kohathite, descended from a brother of the progenitor of
Aaron, probably an elder son of the common
ancestor; and the feeling seems to have been
that the priesthood should, by right of birth, have
belonged to his family, and by consequence that
he should have been high priest. This point of
his personal ambition was not indeed obtruded at
the first view, but seems to have been sagaciously
kept back by him, in the knowledge that if he
succeeded in establishing the claims of his family
to become the priestly house, the other result
would follow of course. Indeed, he set himself
forth as the champion of the whole Levitical
body, less asserting the claims of his own family

than contesting the invidious distinction conferred on Aaron's family over the whole tribe. He was aware that if this family were deposed, it would soon become necessary to appropriate another to the particular service, and that then the claims of his own family would be paramount; for the grounds on which that of Aaron had been deposed would leave room for no other claim than that hereditary one which he and his family could advance. We are thus enabled to sound the depths of this plot as to the part which certain of the Levitical body took in it.

Some of the same grounds which led the eldest family of Levi to claim the rights which were conceived to belong to it in that tribe, would exist also in leading the chiefs of the eldest tribe, that of Reuben, to murmur at the *practical* deposition of that tribe from its natural birthright, which had indeed been announced long ago by the dying Jacob, but which was now for the first time enforced as a reality and an accomplished fact. Inasmuch as the chiefs of the tribes represented the patriarchal power which the sons of Jacob during their lifetime exercised over the tribes which sprang from them, the chief of the eldest tribe represented not only the founder of the particular tribe, but the common founder of all the tribes whose heir he was. This gave him some general right not only of counsel and control over all the tribes, but of taking a certain initiatory part in measures of common concernment to the whole nation; and in his person, more than that of any other man, was found the tie which bound the tribes together. Certain rights of precedence also belonged to him; and the performance of priestly acts—that is, of taking the leading part in acts of public worship by sacrifice or otherwise—had always been considered as no mean part of the birthright of the eldest born. But in forming the arrangements of the new government, the tribe of Reuben was altogether overlooked, and its pride must have been much wounded, considering how highly the rank of primogeniture was valued, by the precedence assigned to the tribe of Judah in all the encampments used on the march; and this, perhaps, galled it more sorely than the absorption of all sacerdotal office and influence, as well as of considerable political power, by the Levitical tribe. Hence we are not surprised to find that such of the leaders as were not of the tribe of Levi were of that of Reuben. Their names were Dathan, Abiram, and On; and the manner in which the Levitical conspirators kept their own private claims as much as possible in the background— generalizing them to the utmost—may strongly suggest to the mind that this was done to keep their Reubenite allies in good humour, by not strongly putting forward their own claims to the exercise of a function which these allies considered as belonging of right to the first-born. In fact, no one can look closely into this transaction without perceiving that the Levitical conspirators were playing a deep game, in which not only the people generally, but their own Reubenite friends, were little more than the tools with which they sought to work out their own objects; and that, in fact, they had ulterior objects of special advantage, which they did not, and dared not, then openly avow, or even disclose to their companions. There may perhaps be ground to suppose that the Reubenites suspected something of this; for although we find On's name among the leading conspirators, it does not appear when the names are repeated in the subsequent proceedings, and in the final judgment; and this may suggest that he became suspicious and dissatisfied, and hence seceded from the conspiracy in good time.

It deserves to be noticed that, in a camp which must have covered an extent of many miles, the situation of the two parties in relation to one another when encamped, was such as to afford them all facilities for exciting one another's passions and for maturing the plot. The allotted place of the tents of Reuben was on the south side of the central area in which the tabernacle stood; and between them and the tabernacle was the encampment of the Kohathites—the division of the Levitical family to which Korah belonged. Our judgment of historical incidents must often be materially influenced by small circumstances like this, which are apt to escape common notice.

Considering the nature of this conspiracy, the objects at which it aimed, and the importance of the men engaged in it, it was in the highest degree necessary that it should not only be frustrated, but brought to nothing by some such signal and terrible judgment as should effectually repress the tendency to such baleful manifestations of private ambition and popular discontent, and afford the infant state the protection needful to prevent its welfare from being subject to perpetual hazards, machinations, and broils.

On hearing the charges daringly brought

against his conduct and designs by the conspirators, Moses fell on his face before the Lord;
and having obtained the requisite directions, he
appointed the next day for the trial of this great
matter. They complained of the usurpation of
the priesthood; but to show whether this appointment had been of man or of God, let them
come to the tabernacle and perform the priestly
function of offering incense, and the Lord would
make it known who were the objects of His choice.
Accordingly, on the next day, "Korah and his
company" appeared at the tabernacle. Moses
also sent for the Reubenite leaders; and although
they returned an insolent refusal to attend,
their curiosity to witness the result induced them
to come out and stand in the doors of their
tents, where they could command a perfect
view of the proceedings. Moses then arose
awful from his supplicating knees, and directed
the people to stand clear of the tents of Dathan
and Abiram; and the habit of obedience to the
voice of their great leader caused his command
to be followed, though from the manner of
encampment these persons must, for the most
part, have been their friends and neighbours.
The man of God then spoke: "Hereby ye shall
know that the Lord hath sent me to do all these
works. If these men die the common death of
all men, or if they be visited after the visitation
of all men, then the Lord hath not sent me. But
if the Lord make a new thing, and the earth
open her mouth, and swallow them up, with all
that appertain unto them, then ye shall understand that these men have provoked the Lord."
From the beginning of the world unto this day,
no man ever made so bold and noble an assertion
of divine approval, or subjected his claims in the
presence of a nation to a test so immediate and
so infallible. But the response to this dread
appeal was not for a moment delayed. The
earth did open; and Dathan and Abiram—they,
their tents, and all they had—went down, and
the earth closed over them: they were seen no
more. At the same moment a fire went forth
from the presence of the Lord, and smote down
with instant death the men with their censers at
the door of the tabernacle—in number two
hundred and fifty. Thus both branches of
the great conspiracy were at once extinguished
by a judgment most signal, immediate, and
miraculous.

SIN OF MOSES

Numbers 20

THIRTY-EIGHT years did the Israelites wander in
the wilderness, during which nothing of their
history is recorded. This fact is favourable,
seeing that it shows that nothing of serious
importance had occurred to affect their condition,
or to disturb the training of the rising generation in the institutions under which the nation
was designed to live.

So is it well for our soul's history when there
is little of secular incident or worldly adventure
to record of us. The peace that passeth all un-
standing, which those who are in Christ enjoy,
affords but little material for the historian or
biographer. It is passed by in the human records
of life; but it is that part of our history which is
written with adamantine pen in the registers of
heaven.

During this long time, all but a few of those
who were above twenty years old at the commencement of that period had died off, according
to the sentence pronounced upon that generation;
and all of these few but the two faithful spies,
Caleb and Joshua, seem to have been removed
before entering the promised land. Though this
does not strike the mind so strongly as if the
doom pronounced upon the extinct generation at
Kadesh had been suddenly executed, it was, after
all, fully as remarkable, and nothing less than
a very special dispensation of providence. In
ordinary course, a very considerable proportion
of those who were at that time between twenty
and thirty-five or forty years of age, would have
been alive at the expiration of the period, forming the elders of the nation. But these being,
with those of still more advanced years, cut off,
this remarkable consequence followed, that (with
two exceptions) there were none in the camp
above sixty years of age; in other words, there
were no aged men in it, no elders, none unfit by
reason of age to bear arms in active warfare.
Thus, therefore, the new Israel were not only
better trained, morally, for the great work before
them, but were physically more equal to it; the
host being encumbered with no useless numbers,
but, on the contrary, every man being fit to stand
up as a soldier, and take part in the enterprise
assigned to the chosen people.

Considering the extraordinary shortening of the life of man during this period, it is remarkable that there had been no greater decrease of the population than to the extent of 1,820. Looking at the rapid increase which had taken place in their numbers in Egypt, we may conceive that there would have been a considerable addition to the population while in the wilderness, notwithstanding the shortening of the time of life. But very many lives were lost in the repeated rebellions of the people; and the same reasons did not exist in the divine intention, if we may reverently judge of it, for promoting their advance in numbers at this time. There were obvious reasons for their being greatly and rapidly multiplied in Egypt. But the same reasons did not exist for their further increase at this time. They were already almost unmanageably numerous, whether we regard the conditions of their abode in the desert, or their intended conquest of Canaan. Seeing that they were to *occupy* the country as well as to subdue it, their numbers were barely sufficient for *that* purpose; but for the operations of the conquest itself, and all the movements connected with it, the number could not well have been larger, humanly speaking, without occasioning embarrassment, and leading to confusion and disaster.

After all the learned and sagacious talk about the laws of population and of human increase, there is really no law of increase in any population but the will of God. The same ratio of increase was never for any length of time maintained among any people. If it be His will that a people shall become numerous, they rapidly increase; if it be His purpose that they shall be "minished and brought low," it is done. Let us not measure our prosperity by these things. In the fat bondage of Egypt, the Israelites increased; but their spirits waxed feeble and poor. In the bare freedom of the wilderness, their numbers diminished; but their souls gathered more strength, their hearts became more firm: even their bodies were dignified by the hardness they were called to endure, for there was not one feeble or diseased among all their tribes.

During these years of wandering, the Israelites must have led a purely Bedouin life—under the institutions of their law—moving from place to place according to the exigencies of the season and the wants of the flocks and herds—often probably returning to the same place in the course of their peregrination. At some places they probably encamped a long while—for months together. The determination of this matter was not, however, left to themselves, seeing that the movements of the cloudy pillar appointed their stations and directed their course.

If we try to realize the nature of their desert life, this cloudy pillar must become a conspicuous object in our view. It prevented all consultation, speculation, or debate, on what is now a fertile subject among the few topics of desert discourse —the propriety of moving the camp, and the choice of the next station. The Israelites felt their volition in this matter taken altogether away. They had only to look at the pillar of cloud; and it must have been the cynosure of every eye in the camp—the first object they looked to in the morning, and the last at night. The young, easily tired and fond of change, would look to it with eager hope, that it would move soon; the old, fond of rest and indisposed to change, would regard it with some apprehension of its moving sooner than they wished; and when it did move, what stir in the camp—what excitement in those who first caught the sight— what eager running from tent to tent to tell the news, without waiting till the trumpet of preparation sounded!

How many, with whom this life has gone hard, and who find themselves entangled among the thorns and briers, or endangered in the sands of the wilderness, would rejoice in such guidance, in such relief from the peril of choosing their own path among many paths which seem all equally to repel by their danger, or equally to invite by their promise! And, blessed be God, we are supplied with help no less effectual; but we will not learn to receive it in humble faith. We have the pillar of cloud in the word of God, which, although it contain things "hard to be understood," is nevertheless a lamp unto our feet; and we want not the pillar of fire in the Spirit of God, which, although it burn up the hay, the straw, the stubble of our souls, is a sure guide for us into all true and holy things.

We see that in the course of the thirty-eight years which passed, between their leaving Kadesh-Barnea and their return thither, there was a great and important change in the constitution of the Hebrew host. Yet it must be confessed that their proceedings on their arrival at that place afford no very favourable indication of this fact.

Much distress was here experienced from want of water, and the people expressed their discontent in language nearly as violent and unreasonable as their fathers, under the like distress, had used at Rephidim. Moses does not seem to have been at all prepared to expect such conduct from this generation; and not only was his concern very great, but he appears to have been more excited and irritated than on any former occasion. The relief was afforded in the same way as at Rephidim, by the smiting of a rock. This time, however, it was done in the presence of the assembled people, to whom Moses addressed some words before the rock was smitten by his rod: "Hear now, ye rebels! must we fetch you water out of this rock?" on which he struck the rock not once, but twice—this is particularly mentioned —and thereupon an abundant and refreshing stream gushed forth. These particulars are of peculiar interest, as it appears that both Moses and Aaron sinned in this matter, so as to compromise the honour of God in the sight of the people; and they were, on that account, subject to the sentence of exclusion from the promised land. This seems a hard doom for them; but it was important that the people should see that even their great and honoured leaders, who had given forth the Lord's sentence of exclusion from Canaan against their fathers, were, in the equity of the divine judgment, which knows no respect of persons, subject to the very same doom, when they in like manner sinned. But what was the sin? This is not clearly stated, and the subject is one respecting which different opinions have been entertained. The Lord Himself says it was "because ye believed me not, to sanctify me in the eyes of the children of Israel." In what this distrust was shown is not clear. It might have been in the heart only; but it is stated to have been rendered obvious to the Israelites themselves. The Psalmist, in saying that on this occasion Moses "spake unadvisedly with his lips," seems to refer the offence to the words he uttered.

Upon closely inspecting the narrative, we find various circumstances on which the imputation might rest, and which, taken together or separately, may have constituted the offence. It is true that Moses only appears in them, whereas Aaron also shares the blame. But Aaron was present, and, considering the office he bore, sanctioned by his silence whatever was wrong in the proceedings of Moses. On such an occasion as this, it behoved him to speak, if a wrong against the Lord's honour were committed. First, we take notice of the immoderate and unbecoming anger which Moses expresses; then his speaking to the people, when his orders were only to speak to the rock; then his smiting it at all, when he should only have spoken to it; his smiting it *twice* in the heat and flame of anger; and his smiting it with the rod, taken, "from before the Lord" in the tabernacle, this being no other than the rod which had blossoms, buds, and almonds, and which was therefore wholly unfit for striking, and which might be injured thereby, although its preservation was probably the reason why he was ordered not to strike, but to speak. Then, from his having been said to have spoken "unadvisedly," it may be doubted whether he ought to have spoken at all to the people, having no authority to do so: whereas he not only spoke, but spoke vehemently to them, in words involving more than one distrustful implication. It has been even thought that the words, "must WE fetch you water out of this rock?" are a dangerous assumption of the credit of the miracle; and although we dare not suppose that Moses had any such meaning, it must be allowed, if the emphasis claimed for the personal pronoun be conceded, that the words might be easily so misapprehended by a generation which had not the same acquaintance as their fathers with the spirit in which the earlier miracles were executed. An eminent scholar,[1] following the Jewish commentators, has suggested that the particular fault may have been that Moses expressed his resentment at the Israelites that their murmuring had occasioned another rock to be opened, which he regarded as portending a new and long stay in the wilderness, at a time when he and Aaron were expecting to be permitted to conduct them into the promised land. And indeed, when we consider the long period which had been passed in waiting for this consummation, it is very conceivable that there may have been a deep anxiety in the minds of the two brothers, lest any fresh misconduct on the part of the people should occasion the term of wandering to be still further prolonged.

[1] Lightfoot, on *Harmony of the Old Testament, sub* 2553 A.M. Ness, in his *History and Mystery of the Old and New Testaments*, 1690, repeats this with approval (without giving the authority).

All these particulars are sufficiently suggestive and significant. But it is possible that we have to look for an explanation not so much in any one or two of them, as in that general air of impatience and petulance, and that want of calm dignity and placid confidence in God, which betrayed itself in their acts and language, as these are described to us, and very possibly in other particulars of their conduct which are not recorded.

MOUNT HOR

Numbers 20:22-29

WHEN the Hebrew host was last at Kadesh, it had clearly been intended that their passage into the land of Canaan should be by the south. We now find, however, that this course is abandoned, and that it is intended to make the entrance from the east above the head of the Dead Sea. The reason for this change is not given, and some have conjectured that it arose from the nature of the country, or from the character of the inhabitants. But these reasons would have been equally operative against their first approach in that quarter; and the face of the country could have presented no obstacles comparable to the obstacle which the river Jordan offered to an approach on the east. It is our strong conviction that the reason of the change was, that the faith of the new generation might be strengthened by a miracle as signal as any that their fathers knew, and calculated to facilitate their intended conquest, by striking dismay into the hearts of the inhabitants.

In accordance with this intention, Moses sent ambassadors to the king of Edom, soliciting permission to pass through his territory, which was necessary to enable him to get into the country east of the Dead Sea and the Jordan. The message was highly conciliatory. The king was reminded of the relationship between the two nations; he was informed of their deliverance from Egypt; and he was told that they were on the way to the land which the Lord had promised them for a possession. To relieve him from any apprehensions, from the passage of so large a host through his territory, he was assured that the Israelites had no hostile intentions, and would not in any way molest the inhabitants. They would only " pass through on their feet," and would pay for whatever they required; even the water they would not drink without paying for it. This is a stipulation which would not be thought of with us; but it was of very great importance in a country where the inhabitants depend, during the greater part of the year, upon the water which may be collected in the season when rain falls. The king returned a very churlish answer, not only refusing a passage through his country, but threatening to oppose them by force of arms if they made the attempt. This they were not allowed to do; on the contrary, they were enjoined to respect the fraternal tie which the Edomitish king was so little disposed to acknowledge. They were therefore to retrace their steps to the head of the eastern gulf of the Red Sea, where the land of Edom ended, and passing round the extremity of the chain of mountains which constituted the chief part of that realm, put themselves on the eastern border of that territory, and so proceed northward to the region east of the Dead Sea. A reference to any map of this district will show that the mountains of Edom extended along the eastern side of that broad valley (the Arabah) which lies between the Dead Sea and the Gulf of Akabah. It seems to have been down this valley that they proceeded on their retrogressive movement. On the way they encamped at Mosera, which appears to have been at or near the present Wady Musa, in which lie the ruins of Petra, the city whose marvellous excavations have only within the present century been brought to light, and have since formed the theme of many able pencils and eloquent pens. The encampment must, we apprehend, have been in the neighbourhood of the mouth of this valley, and in presence of Mount Hor.

This mountain is of great scriptural interest; for, arrived at this spot, Aaron, in obedience to his recent doom, was commanded to go up to this mount and die. He was to be accompanied by his brother and his eldest son, who were to divest him of his priestly robes, to receive his dying sigh, and to deposit his remains safely in this high place. The spot was probably selected not only to impress the Israelites with the solemnity of the occasion, but to enable the dying pontiff to give one last look over the camp of Israel, surrounding in goodly rows the tabernacle of God; to survey the scene of his long pilgrimage; and to catch a distant glimpse of the utmost borders of the promised land, before stepping across the boundary between this world and the world to come. There is no doubt whatever about the mountain which was the scene of this transaction. Even local tradition has preserved the memory of the event: the mountain itself bears the name of Aaron (Harun); and upon the top an old Moslem tomb stands to his honour, which is much visited by Mohammedan pilgrims, few of whom quit the place without sacrificing a sheep in honour of the Hebrew saint.

Mount Hor juts out in a singular manner, like an advanced post of the mountains of Edom; and from its isolated peak the eye plunges down the rugged ribs of the mountain itself, into a maze of

MOUNT HOR

fathomless defiles, which, advancing for some miles from the great central range, or backbone of the country, and sinking gradually from the Wady el-Arabah, from the ancient territory of Edom, well styled in Scripture a "nest in the rocks"—a natural fortification, enclosing narrow valleys of difficult access, some of which are seen from this exalted post. Of this wilderness of craggy summits, some are sharp and jagged, without footing even for a gazelle; others are buttressed and built up as if by art, in huge square piles rising from a narrow table-land; while the great central range from which they project is quite dissimilar in appearance, being rounded and smooth, and covered with fine pasturage, proverbially excellent. To the west, in the view from the summit of this mountain, lies the valley of el-Arabah, like the bed of a vast river, encumbered with shoals of sand, and sprinkled over with stunted shrubs; beyond expands the desert in which Israel wandered for thirty-eight years, until every individual of the host perished; to the north are seen the mountains of the promised land, upon which, doubtless, Aaron cast his last look when he died; to the south the Arabah stretches away to the Red Sea, where Israel turned eastward, and thence northward "to compass the land of Edom;" to the east a magnificent range of yellowish mountains bounds the view, between which and the mountains on which we stand once lay nestled among the rocks the fair city of Petra. "So strongly marked are the features of this region, and so preserved by their sublime unchanging barrenness, that when we behold at once the defiles of Edom, the frontier hills of Palestine, the Arabah, and, far stretched out to the westward, the great sepulchral wilderness, the lapse of ages is forgotten, and those touching and solemn events rise up before the mind with an almost startling reality."[1]

The building upon the top of the mountain,

[1] Bartlett, *Forty Days in the Desert.* See also Robinson, Wilson, Durbin, Irby, and Mangles, etc. The *first* description of the spot by Burckhardt is still worth consulting.

called the Tomb of Aaron, and doubtless either upon or close to the spot where he died and was buried, differs little in appearance from the tombs of sheikhs in the principal villages of Egypt, and perhaps does not date farther back than many of these. It seems to have been constructed on the site of another and a much better edifice, whose foundation walls are visible amid the rubbish, a part of whose beautiful mosaic pavement may be seen in the floor of the present tomb, and the sections of whose columns are worked into its walls, while a beautifully carved piece of pure white marble crowns the rude dome. The interior contains nothing but a small square tomb, about four feet high, constructed with the fragments of the former more costly building. On it, as votive offerings deposited by pilgrims, lie a few white and red rags, and above it hang some tattered garments and ostrich eggs. The panel at one end contains a long Arabic inscription. This is the visible tomb of the great high priest, but the grave is in a vault below. Lighting a torch, one may descend into the vault by a flight of three steps, and stand before a niche cut in the living rock, and once defended by beautiful brass doors of open work, which now hang suspended by cords instead of turning on hinges. This subterranean apartment is small, filled with rubbish, begrimed with the smoke of flambeaux, and altogether of a most forbidding aspect. It would seem to have been a small subterranean chapel; and no one will of course entertain the notion that it was excavated by Moses and Eleazar when they buried the high priest of Israel here.

The second visit of the Israelites to Kadesh appears to have been prolonged like the first. It was signalized also by some solemn incidents. The first of these was the death of Moses' sister, thus simply recorded: "And the people abode in Kadesh ; and Miriam died there, and was buried there" (Num. xx. 1). Another murmuring of the people followed because the supply of water failed. The "sacred spring" was not sufficient for the wants of such a multitude. God therefore commanded Moses to smite one of the neighbouring cliffs with his rod: "And the water came out abundantly, and the congregation drank, and their beasts" (ver. 11). This last clause is important. It proves that the flocks and herds had survived the forty years' wandering, and had been brought together at Kadesh probably in the prospect of an immediate entrance into Canaan. The Israelites appear to have hoped that the Edomites would permit them to pass direct through their territory, and thus reach the eastern bank of the Jordan without a long and painful march through the great desert of Arabia. In this they were disappointed.

It does seem strange, that when the Israelites were upon the southern frontier of Palestine, they did not enter the country at that point. I am inclined to assign a reason for this different from that suggested by Dr. Kitto. The approach of the people, and the gathering of such a vast multitude at Kadesh, had attracted the attention of the warlike tribes that inhabited the southern mountains, who would naturally form an alliance with the Amalekites of the Negeb, and the Philistines of the western plain. These tribes had apparently assembled in force to defend the difficult passes that lead up from Kadesh into Palestine. This view is substantiated by the fact that, as soon as the Israelites turned back from Kadesh, they were attacked in the rear by the Canaanites (Num. xxi. 1-3 ; xxxiii. 40). In order to penetrate Palestine at a point thought to be impracticable, and thus to give the Israelites an easy victory, God led them to the eastern frontier, and opened up a way through the waters of the Jordan.

P.

FIERY SERPENTS

Numbers 21

In pursuing the course which had been marked out for them, the Hebrew host traversed southward the arid, hot, and sandy Arabah, and passing by the head of the eastern gulf of the Red Sea, gained the equally desolate region constituting the desert *east* of the mountains of Edom. By this time "the soul of the people was much discouraged because of the way." This is not, perhaps, surprising; for after having been permitted to reach the borders of the promised land, and to look up the green valleys of Edom, they had been sent back to take another long journey through the worst parts of the desert, on which they fully supposed that they had turned their backs for ever. It is possible, also, that the absence of any interposition to enforce for them a short cut through the territory of Edom, had shaken their confidence in the certainty of the divine aid in taking possession of the land of Canaan. All this might have been the case; but their complaints took the gross form of murmurings at the scarcity of water, and of expressions of disgust at the manna. On this occasion it is not flesh they long for, but bread: "There is no bread, neither is there any water : and our soul loatheth this light food." We see in this that the people, confined to one kind of diet for nearly forty years, had been looking forward with eager expectation to the change of food which might be expected when they entered a peopled country; and the postponement of an expectation so eagerly entertained, must have materially enhanced the disappointment which the renewal of the journey occasioned. Even the short delay of some anticipated good on the very point of being realized, is a disappointment far deeper than one of larger actual amount, when the fruition is not near. Still, something better might have been expected from a people trained and tried as they had been; and as they seem to have been emboldened by the impunity of the murmurings at Kadesh-Barnea, it became necessary to remind them sharply of their covenanted duty. So "the Lord sent fiery serpents among the people, and they bit the people, and much people of Israel died." In another place we are informed that the wilderness in which they had sojourned abounded in venomous creatures. It is called in Deut. viii. 15, "The great and terrible wilderness, wherein were fiery serpents, and scorpions, and drought." Yet we never hear of their being bitten or killed by them till now. From this we infer that they had been marvellously protected hitherto from this as from other dangers of the way; but the protection which they had experienced being now withdrawn, the serpents—in this part of the desert unusually numerous—had their poisonous jaws unbound, and smote them at their will. The testimony of travellers respecting the frequency of serpents in these parts is very remarkable. The ancient historians tell us that the people who inhabited the maritime parts of the Red Sea were subject, among other strange distempers, to one in which the flesh of their legs and arms bred little snakes or serpents, which, eating through the skin, thrust out their heads through the orifices; but as soon as touched, retired again into the flesh, and in this manner occasioned most violent and dangerous inflammations.[1] It is added, that this was a disorder peculiar to this region, and not known in any other parts of the world—perhaps not then known; but it seems not dissimilar to the disease now occasioned in Africa by the "Guinea worm."

At a point on the shore, a little below the extremity of the eastern gulf of the Red Sea, and therefore not far from the place where the Israelites met with this visitation, Burckhardt

[1] Agatharcides in Plutarch, *Sympos.*, i. 9.

found the sandy shore of a bay, bearing everywhere the impression of the passage of serpents, crossing each other in many directions; and the bodies of some of them could not, from the tracks they left, have been less than two inches in diameter. The traveller continues: "Ayd told me that the serpents were very common in these parts; that the fishermen were much afraid of them, and extinguished their fires in the evening, before they went to sleep, because the light was known to attract them." He further observes: "As serpents are so numerous on this side, they are probably not deficient towards the head of the gulf on its opposite shore, where it appears the Israelites passed when they journeyed from Mount Hor, by the way of the Red Sea, to compass the land of Edom, and where the Lord sent fiery serpents among them."

It was also in the region near the head of the Red Sea, and more directly in the track of the Israelites, that Laborde relates an incident which occurred in his camp. "The night passed over quietly, and the cold of the morning had warned us to rise, when we found beneath the carpet which formed our bed, a large scorpion of a yellow colour, and three inches in length.[1] When he was detected he endeavoured to effect his escape, though not with sufficient rapidity to ensure his safety; but our Arabs did not wish that he should be killed. . . . The Alaouins told us that scorpions and serpents abound in this part of the desert." After alluding to the circumstance before us, this writer adds; "The fact thus recorded in Scripture is fully confirmed by the Arabs, as well as by the vast numbers of these reptiles (serpents) which we found two leagues to the east of this place, on our return to Akabah."

It is much to be regretted that no one has taken the trouble to ascertain the species of these serpents. This might have helped to settle the question, What is meant by the epithet "fiery" applied to them? Was it from their colour, or from the burning inflammation which their bites produced? Perhaps from both. The fact that the representative serpent was made of brass, may at least suggest that the natural serpents were of a burnished, glaring, or yellow appearance.

Under this infliction the people were speedily brought to a sense of their error, and very humbly

[1] This is hardly "large" for a scorpion, if the tail be included. We have ourselves found some, under similar circumstances, nearly twice as long.

confessed that they had sinned,—"for we have spoken against the Lord, and against thee." On this the Lord directed Moses to make a brazen serpent, and set it upon a pole, that every bitten Hebrew who looked upon it might be healed. This was no doubt designed to render the cure a result of faith; for no one who doubted the sufficiency, as appointed by God, of a means so apparently inadequate, would look to this representative serpent, and he would consequently, from his lack of faith, die of the poison in his veins. It is this that rendered the brazen serpent so lively a type or symbol of our Lord, who appropriated it to himself in the memorable words, " As Moses lifted up the serpent in the wilderness, even so must the Son of man be lifted up; that whosoever believeth in him should not perish, but have eternal life."[1] In the serpent being made of brass, the Jews take notice of a miracle in a miracle—in that of God's healing against the common course and order of nature—for brass they allege (with some Christian interpreters) to be hurtful to those who have been bitten by serpents. This they compare with the bitter wood making the water sweet at Marah. A very learned writer,[2] whom others have followed, thinks that this great transaction led to the heathen god of healing, Æsculapius, being usually represented with a serpent by him, or holding a rod with a serpent twisted round it; to his being worshipped in the form of a serpent; and to his being enrolled among the stars under the person and name of Ophiuchus. We are ourselves inclined to refer this to still earlier notions of the serpent, derived from primeval traditions, which we know to have overspread the earth. But if we might suppose that the knowledge of this circumstance had reached the heathen, and had spread among them, there is nothing more strange in their making the serpent an object of worship, than that the Israelites themselves should in a later age have been disposed to render sacred honours to this very serpent of brass, which had been preserved in the holy place as a memorial of this judgment and deliverance.[3]

The desert of Arabia, east of Edom, was the scene of the last wanderings of the Israelites. It is a vast table-land extending from the mountain range of Edom to the horizon, without tree or shrub, streamlet or fountain. The surface is either bare limestone rock, or white gravel mixed with flints, or drifting sand. The very Arabs fear it. For days together the daring traveller who ventures to cross it must hasten onward; and should the supply of water which he is obliged to carry with him fail, all hope is gone. Wallin, one of the very few who traversed it, says ; "It is a tract the most desolate and sterile I ever saw. Its irregular surface is, instead of vegetation, covered with small stones, which shining sometimes in a dark, swarthy, sometimes in a bright white colour, reflect the rays of the sun in a manner most injurious to the eyes."[1] Mr. Palgrave, who crossed it more recently, almost in the track of Wallin, also gives a fearful description of it.[2] It is far more desolate and terrible than any part of the region west of the Arabah. All their previous experience of desert life and travel had not prepared the Israelites for the privations and horrors of " this great and terrible wilderness." From the knowledge we now possess of that barren waterless waste, we can fully understand the words of the sacred historian, and the bitter complaints of the suffering people : " And the soul of the people was much discouraged because of the way. And the people spake against God, and against Moses, Wherefore have ye brought us up out of Egypt to die in the wilderness ? for there is no bread, neither is there any water."

P.

KING OG'S BEDSTEAD

Numbers 21:33-35; Deuteronomy 3

IT may be observed, that the wants which had driven the Israelites into murmuring and rebellion, had on former occasions been supplied by miracle. We read of no such supply in the case of the murmuring for water and bread which had occasioned the plague of serpents. Yet they *were* supplied with all they needed. It shows the use and importance of comparing scripture with scripture, that quite an incidental and nonhistorical passage in another book [3] apprizes us of the fact, that the northward journey along the eastern frontier of Edom, which had threatened so many terrors, was relieved by the friendly disposition of the Edomites on that frontier, who readily brought out their stores, to sell them for money to the advancing host, to whom the bread, the meat, the fruits, the water thus obtained, must have formed, after their long confinement to desert fare, a most agreeable and refreshing

---

[1] John 3:14,15.
[2] Huet, in *Demonstr. Evangel.*, Propos. 4, c. 8, sec. 6.
[3] See 2 Kings 18:4.

[1] *Journal of the R. Geog. Soc.*, xxiv. p. 135.
[2] *Travels in Arabia*, i.   [3] Deuteronomy 2:6.

antepast of their future enjoyments. It is remarkable that, at the present day, the inhabitants
of the only inhabited village now on this frontier
supply in the same manner with refreshments
the great pilgrim caravan on its yearly march
from Damascus to Mecca. This place is called
Tayfle, supposed to be the Punon which is named
among the stations at which the Israelites rested,
probably by reason of the facilities of obtaining
supplies which this place then, as now, afforded.
In a short time after they had encamped, the
people would bring out all they had to sell, and
the scene would become that of a market or a
fair. At present, the profit derived from the
large quantity of provisions they are enabled
once in the year to sell to the caravan, forms the
basis of their prosperity, and enables them to
cultivate the ground with advantage. How
delighted must the drouthy Israelites have been
to encamp among the ninety and nine[1] streams
and rivulets of Tayfle; to behold the plantations
of fruit trees, which were probably then even
more extensive than at present; and to eat the
fruits they yielded! Even now, apples, apricots,
figs, pomegranates, and olive and peach trees of a
large species, are here cultivated in great numbers.

belonged to the Moabites, who had been driven
into the narrow southern tract on the east of the
Dead Sea, between the brook Zered and the
river Arnon, by the Amorites, who had dispossessed them of a much finer and larger country
to the north of that river. The Amorites, who
had thus established themselves in the country
east of the Jordan, seem to have been a colony
sent forth by the same nation in Canaan. Probably the great increase of their numbers had
rendered their possessions in the west country
too narrow for them, and had induced a proportion of the most daring of them to seek, under
warlike leaders, new settlements in the eastern
region, then inhabited by less ancient and powerful nations than those which divided the land of
Canaan, and not allied to them by the ties of
consanguinity and ancient neighbourhood, which
bound together the inhabitants of Canaan. The
Amorites were among the nations whose territories were promised to the Israelites; yet it is
clear that Moses did not consider that this applied
to any but their ancient territories in the proper
Canaan west of the river, and that he did not at
all contemplate any acquisitions on the east
of the Jordan. Israel had been expresly forbidden to enter into any treaty or compact with
the people of Canaan;
yet Moses sent to ask the
permission of Sihon, the
king of these eastern
Amorites, to pass through
his territory, with the
same offer that had been
made to Edom, of leav-
ing the inhabitants un-
molested, and of purchas-
ing all the victuals re-
quired on their march;
and he asks it as leave
to pass "to the land
which the Lord our God
hath given us"—clearly
distinguishing   the
western country as that
alone to which their

VIEW IN THE LAND OF MOAB

Advancing northwards, the Hebrew host, on
crossing the brook Zered, which enters the Dead
Sea near the southern end, ended their long
pilgrimage in the wilderness, and entered into a
cultivated and settled country. That country

attention was directed. Sihon, however, not
only refused this request, but did what the
king of Edom had only threatened—came out
in arms against them. The conflict, which it
then became impossible to avoid, was thus by no
means of Moses' seeking, nor was its result

[1] So the Arabs express their large number.

contemplated by him. That result was, that Sihon was utterly defeated; and the Israelites, quite beyond their calculations, found themselves in possession of a fine country, full of towns and villages. What was of more immediate importance to them, they had secured a free passage to the Jordan, and, if left unmolested, they would have sought no further warfare or conquest on the east of the river. But Og, the king of Bashan, whose territories lay to the north of those of which Sihon had been dispossessed, by no means relished the presence of his new neighbours, and burned to avenge the overthrow of his friends and allies. Although, therefore, he had no immediate interest in the matter, seeing that the Israelites had nothing to ask of him, he collected his forces and marched to give them battle. He was in his turn defeated and slain, and thus Israel became possessed of two kingdoms, whose united territories extended from the river Arnon to the roots of Lebanon, forming one of the finest countries in the world, well wooded, and full of rich pastures. Thus the Israelites began their career of conquest by acquiring a valuable possession over and above what had been promised to them; and by this their faith must have been much encouraged.

But there is more to be said of king Og. He was the last member of an old gigantic race, which had long held sway on this side of the river. It is in Deut. iii. 11 that we read more of him: "Only Og remained of the remnant of the giants; behold, his bedstead was a bedstead of iron: is it not in Rabbath of the children of Ammon; nine cubits was the length thereof, and four cubits the breadth thereof, after the cubit of a man." This length we take to be thirteen and a half feet, at the rate of half a yard to a cubit. But a man's bedstead is usually larger than himself, yet not so much larger but that it may be taken as affording some indication of his stature. It is so intended in the text, which clearly shows that, then as now, bedsteads were not much longer than the person who lay in them. If, therefore, the bedstead were thirteen and a half feet, the man may have been about ten or eleven feet high—a very great stature—higher than that of Goliath, but not incredible or unexampled. We have, however, already engaged the reader's attention sufficiently on this subject, and shall not return to it here. The moderate estimates of Scripture, in all these matters, in which the eastern imagination is most prone to exaggerate, may be judged from the circumstantial rabbinical traditions respecting him. They regard him as "a remnant of the giants" who lived before the flood, and as the only one who survived the general destruction. There are two accounts of the manner of his preservation: one, that he was tall enough to walk by the side of the ark through the water; and the other, that he rode astride on the top of the Noachic vessel, receiving from the inmates a daily supply of victuals. During the time he was thus their guest, he consumed a thousand oxen, and the same number of every sort of game. It is also alleged that he afterwards became the servant of Abraham, under the name of Eliezer. His stature, according to these accounts, throws into the shade all the imaginations of Gulliver and Sinbad. According to one account, the soles of his feet were forty miles long; and Moses, though himself of gigantic stature, and armed with a spear of proportionate length, could smite him no higher than the ankle. One time, while in Abraham's service, on being scolded by his master, fear shook a tooth out of his head. This Abraham took, and make himself a bedstead of it, on which he lay and slept. Other authorities equally credible, however, assure us that it was not a bed that the patriarch made of Og's tooth, but a chair, on which he sat as long as he lived.

As to the bedstead, concerning which much speculation has been excited, we have some remarks to offer. Many, having but a rough knowledge of the East, have imagined that there are no bedsteads save couches or divans running along the whole side of a room, and having therefore no reference to the stature of the person

BEDSTEAD MADE OF THE PALM-FROND

lying on them. This is a great mistake. We have ourselves slept constantly on a bedstead of the form and construction here represented, which is not only in common use at the present day in

Egypt and Arabia, but is of very ancient date, being represented in the mural paintings of Egypt. It is made of the mid-rib of the palm-frond, and was probably so made formerly in Palestine and Syria, where the palm tree was more common than at present, although now it is more generally made of boards in these countries. For sleeping on the house-top during summer, this bedstead is in very general use. We conceive the bedstead of king Og was of this sort. But such bedsteads are incapable of resisting any undue weight without being disjointed and bent awry; and this would dictate the necessity of making the one destined to sustain the vast bulk of Og, rather with bars of iron than with palm sticks. All such bedsteads bear the same proportion to the human stature that our own do, affording a sufficient reason for its dimensions being given, to indicate the tallness of this gigantic king.

Our own not unfrequent use of iron bedsteads, divests the fact of Og's bedstead being so framed of all strangeness. In the warm climates of the East, bedsteads of metal seem to have been more in use anciently than at present, for the purpose of excluding the insects that are disposed to harbour in those of wood. Heathen writers notice bedsteads of gold and silver. Herodotus and Diodorus Siculus describe beds and tables of these metals, which they observed in eastern temples.[1] Such beds are, in the book of Esther,[2] ascribed to the Persians; and accordingly, a bed of gold was found by Alexander the Great in the tomb of Cyrus.[3] Sardanapalus caused a hundred and fifty beds of gold, and as many tables of the same metal, to be burned with him.[4] The Parthian monarchs ordinarily slept on beds of gold, and this was counted a special privilege of their estate.[5] At the time of the Trojan war, Agamemnon had several beds of brass.[6] Both Livy and St. Augustine affirm that the Romans brought beds of brass from Asia to Rome, after the wars they had in that part of the world.[7] It is related by Thucydides, that when the Thebans had de-

stroyed the city of Platea, they took away many beds of brass and iron, which they found there, and consecrated them to Juno.[1] These are sufficient instances of the ancient usage; but most of them show that such beds or bedsteads were not in common use, but belonged to princes and persons of distinction.

From the remotest historic age down to our own day, there has been something of mystery and strange wild interest connected with the old kingdom of Bashan. In the raid of the Arab chiefs of Mesopotamia into Palestine, we read that the *Rephaim* in Ashteroth-Karnaim bore the first brunt of the invasion. The *Rephaim* were, as the name signifies, "giants"—men of stature, beside whom the Jewish spies were as grasshoppers (Num. xiii. 33). They were the aborigines of Bashan, and probably of the greater part of Canaan. Most of them died out or were exterminated at a very early period; but a few remarkable specimens of the race existed at and long after the Exodus. Among these were Og, king of Bashan; and Goliath, Sippai, and Lahmi, the formidable foes of the Israelites in the time of David. It is remarkable that traditionary memorials of these primeval giants are found even now in almost every part of Syria; such as the tomb of Abel at Damascus, *thirty feet* long; that of Seth in Anti-Lebanon, about the same size; and that of Noah in Lebanon, which measures no less than *seventy yards*. It is still more remarkable that the cities built and occupied by these primeval giants exist to this day in Bashan. I have traversed their streets; I have opened the doors of their houses; I have slept peacefully in their long deserted halls.

The conquest of Bashan, begun under the leadership of Moses, was completed by Jair, one of the most distinguished chiefs of Manasseh. In narrating his achievements, the sacred historian brings out another remarkable fact connected with the kingdom of Bashan. In Argob, one of its provinces, Jair captured no less than *sixty great cities*, "fenced with high walls, gates, and bars; besides unwalled towns a great many" (Deut. iii. 4-14). Such a statement seems all but incredible. Often, when reading the passage, I used to think that some strange statistical mystery hung over it; for how could a province measuring not more than thirty miles by twenty support such a number of fortified cities? But incredible as it appeared, *I have seen* that it is literally true. The cities are there to this day. Some of them retain their ancient Bible names. The boundaries of Argob are as clearly defined as those of our own island home. These cities of Bashan contain probably the very oldest specimens of domestic architecture in the world.[2]

P.

[1] Herod., i. 181. Diodor., vi. 10.　　[2] Esther 1:6.
[3] Arrian de *Expedit. Alex.*, lib. 6.
[4] Ctesias apud Athenæum, 50. 12.
[5] Josephus, *Antiq.*, xx. 3. page 47.
[6] Thersites apud Athenæum, xiii. 11.
[7] Liv. 50. 39. August. de *Civit. Dei*, iii 21.

[1] Thucydides, l. 3.
[2] For a full account of Bashan and its interesting ruins, the reader is referred to Porter's *Giant Cities of Bashan*.

MALEDICTION

Numbers 22

THE overthrow of the Amorites opened the way for the march of the Israelites to the "plains of Moab," where they remained encamped during all the subsequent transactions which took place, until they passed the Jordan into the promised land.

These plains are formed by a narrow strip of land, scarcely two leagues in breadth, lying along the eastern bank of the Jordan, opposite to the plains of Jericho. The Dead Sea lies to the south of it, Mount Pisgah on the south-east, and the mountains on the east; and towards the north, losing its specific name, this plain continues as "the valley of the Jordan," even to the Lake of Tiberias. This plain, with that of Jericho on the opposite side, form together, in fact, an expansion of the valley of the Jordan. This side comprised part of the territory which had formerly been taken by the Amorites from Moab: but, as usual in such cases, it still retained the name of the previous possessors. The Moabites, who, driven from the valley, now occupied the mountains along which the Israelites passed before they entered the valley of the Jordan, were "sore afraid of the people, because they were many." They did not, however, venture to impede their course, and the Israelites passed peaceably by their territory, purchasing food for sustenance, with money. (Deut. ii. 28, 29.) They did not go through it, but kept along the outermost eastern border, until only the territory of the Amorites interposed between them and the Jordan; and through that territory, now become their own, they march to their destination. It is very certain that the Moabites had no good feeling towards the Israelites. Probably when they first looked down from the mountains upon the long train of the wanderers from the desert, they regarded them as going on to certain ruin from their own redoubted conquerers, the Amorites; but when they beheld the busy encampment firmly established in their own ancient territory, and the northern kings utterly overthrown, their alarm became very great. They had no real cause for distrust or fear; for the Israelites had been forbidden to distress the Moabites, or to contend with them, as they were to retain their domains in consideration of their descent from Lot. (Deut. ii. 9.)

"Willing to wound, but yet afraid to strike," the Moabites felt that it would be in vain to contend with them, while they so manifestly enjoyed the blessing and protection of a mighty God. But they did think that it might be possible to withdraw or neutralize the force of that advantage, by laying upon them the heavy ban of some powerful magician; and by having them thus rendered weak as other men, they might be assailed with every prospect of success. It must have been a great recommendation of the design to them, that the result would enable them to recover the territory which had once been theirs, but which the Israelites now held by right of conquest from the Amorites. Indeed, could the Israelites be exterminated or driven back into the desert, the children of Lot might well calculate on not only recovering what they had lost, but on adding the rich lands of Argob and Bashan, which the Israelites had won from Og, to their former territories; and they would thus, with some allied tribes of Abrahamic origin, become the sole possessors of the whole country east of the Jordan.

That the Moabites apprehended that the Hebrew host, large as were its numbers, might be overcome if once divested of the divine protection, seems to evince that even they perceived wherein its great strength lay, and that, apart therefrom, its intrinsic force was by no means formidable.

Their procedure, in seeking to lay the armies of Israel under a curse, that their own arms might be successful against them, is a strange notion to us. But it is not so in the East. Even at the present day, the pagan orientals, in their wars, have always their magicians with them to curse their enemies, and to mutter incantations for their ruin. Sometimes they secretly convey a potent charm among the opposing troops, to ensure their destruction. In our own war with the Burmese, the generals of that nation had several magicians with them, who were much engaged in cursing our troops; but as they did not succeed, a number of witches were brought for the same purpose. We may indeed trace it as a very ancient opinion among all people, that the maledictions and the blessings, the charms, the incantations, and the devotements of men who were believed to be inspired by a superior spirit, good or evil, had the most marked effects, not only upon individuals, but upon regions and entire nations, and even upon cattle and upon the fruits of the field. Not seldom they sought by strong enchantments to evoke the tutelary divinities of their enemies' cities, desiring thus to deprive them of what was regarded as their chief defence. Hence the proper name of many great cities was preserved as a state secret, that no enemy might be able to make use of it in their invocations. The names by which cities were ordinarily known —as, for instance, Troy, Carthage, Rome—were not the true and secret names of these places. Rome was called Valentia—a name known as hers by very few persons; and Valerius Soranus was severely punished for having disclosed it.[1] The heathens had, indeed, certain solemn invocations, by means of which they devoted their enemies to certain divinities, or rather to malignant and dangerous demons. The following is the formula of one of these imprecations, as preserved by Macrobius:[2] "Dis-Pater, or Jupiter, if it better please thee to be called by that name—or by whatever name thou mayest be invoked—I conjure thee to pour upon this army (or this town) the spirit of terror and trepidation. Deprive of their sight all those who shall aim their strokes at us, our armies, or our troops. Spread darkness over our enemies, over their cities, their fields, their forces. Look upon them as accursed. Bring them under the most rigorous conditions to which any armies have ever been obliged to submit. Thus do I devote them; and I and those whom I represent, the nation and the army engaged in this war, stand for witnesses. If this doom be accomplished, I promise a sacrifice of three black sheep to thee, O Earth, mother of all things, and to thee, great Jupiter."

BALAAM

Numbers 22

SOMEWHERE among the high lands of Mesopotamia, upon the Euphrates, eighteen or twenty

[1] Plin. *Hist. Nat.*, iii. 5; xxviii. 2; Solin., cap. 2; Plut., *Problem* vi.   [2] *Saturnal*, iii. 9.

days distant from the plains of Moab, was a place called Pethor, where abode a diviner named Balaam (more correctly Bileam), whose fame was widely spread through all this region. It had

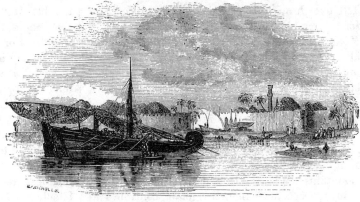

VIEW ON THE EUPHRATES

even reached the land of Moab, whose king— Balak—resolved, notwithstanding the distance, to secure his services, at whatever cost, in laying a curse upon the host of Israel. He accordingly sent to him ambassadors, with the rich "rewards of divination" in their hands. Arrived upon the banks of the Euphrates, the messengers presented themselves before the soothsayer, and declared their errand, closing with the strong expression of their master's confidence: "For I *know* that he whom thou blessest is blessed, and he whom thou cursest is cursed." This declaration, in connection with the attending circumstances, clearly shows that Balaam was deemed to possess very peculiar qualifications for the task he was invited to undertake, and for rendering the curse efficient. This is further shown by the fact, that among the herd of soothsayers he alone is desired, he alone is deemed equal to the occasion. Keeping in mind the points brought under notice yesterday, it may not be difficult to discover the nature of his qualifications. It has been seen that, for the purpose of efficient invocation, it was always deemed necessary that the diviner should know the god, and his true name, who presided over the destinies of the people upon whom he was required to act. This knowledge of Jehovah, who was regarded as the national God of the Hebrews, Balaam was supposed to possess; and this must in those days have been a very rare qualification indeed, and one that constituted his peculiar fitness for the office which the king of Moab now wished to devolve upon him. How he came to be supposed to possess this knowledge, it is not difficult to understand. Distant as the region of the Euphrates was, there was much communication between it and the country east of the Jordan and Dead Sea. There are ulterior indications that Balaam was personally known among the Midianites, and had connections among them; and as we learn from the very verse (the fourth) preceding that in which Balaam is first mentioned, that the king of Moab had been in communication with the Midianites, it is highly probable that he obtained his information concerning him from them. In the list of Edomitish kings given in Gen. xxxvi. 31-43, there is notice that one Saul of Rehoboth upon the Euphrates became king of Edom. It is likely that, if not recently, yet at some time during the forty years since Israel left Egypt, this remarkable man had been in these parts, where, as we know, the mysterious march of this people had struck all the neighbouring nations with astonishment. Such being the case, the wonders of Egypt, of the Red Sea, and of the wilderness, must have been a frequent and untiring subject of conversation in society, and must often have been discussed in his presence. It is certain that, on such occasions, all that was marvellous in their career was ascribed to the power of their God; and it is probable that Balaam had then, more than once, been heard to speak of their God, as better known to him than to those with whom he spoke. Or we may reverse the line of indication, and suppose that persons from these realms visiting the place where Balaam abode, had discoursed of these matters, and had heard him so speak. It comes to the same result either way. As his peculiar fitness arose from his intimacy with affairs of the Hebrews, and his knowledge of their God, the fact of that fitness could only be known through his own declarations, heard in such a way as to become notorious in the land.

Now the question arises, Was this knowledge a reality or a pretence? If we take the narrative in its plain meaning—and that is the meaning in which we think that all historical Scripture should be taken—there can be no doubt that Balaam actually had this knowledge, that he not only held the truth, or much of truth, though he held it in unrighteousness, but that God did, in subservience to His own high purposes, actually communicate with him. Any other explanation,

however ingenious, is but a continuous and painful distortion of the whole narrative, which revolts the understanding more than do even the strong facts which it tries to mitigate, in deference to the tastes and tendencies of the age. Besides this, the deep attention that Balaam had given (and was doubtless known to have given) to the affairs of the Hebrews, and his acquaintance with their early history, their existing condition, and their future hopes, are shown in the noble prophecy which he was eventually constrained to utter.

How he became possessed of the knowledge he held—and held with so little advantage to his own soul—is a question that looks more difficult than it is. May he not have owed something to such remains of the patriarchal religion as still existed in Mesopotamia when Jacob was there, and which his residence for twenty years in that quarter may have contributed to maintain? But the only supposition which accounts *fully* for the knowledge which Balaam possessed of Jehovah, whom He generally mentions by that high and peculiar name, is the one which adds to whatever knowledge he possessed from other sources, that which he owed to the Israelites themselves. The way in which this knowledge might be acquired is clear. There could not but be many reports concerning the Israelites during their forty years' wandering in the desert. With a mind awake to everything which concerned his profession, he would be naturally attracted by the reports of the deliverance effected by the Lord for this people who had come out of Egypt, and whose parentage could not be unknown to him. He had surely heard of the passage of the Red Sea, of the waters of Meribah, of the miracle of the brazen serpent; and, as in the case of Simon Magus, a new source of celebrity and of emolument seemed to open up before him, most enticing to his besetting sins. He then, we may conceive, adopted Jehovah as his God, and named himself Jehovah's prophet. Nor, it may be, was this wholly with views of worldly advantage. It is quite possible, as a learned writer supposes,[1] that there was a mixture of a higher order of sentiments, a sense of the wants of his moral nature, which led him to seek Jehovah, and laid

[1] Dr. Hengstenberg, of whose ingenious and learned disquisition on this subject there is an excellent translation by Mr. J. E. Ryland of Northampton, under the title of *History of Balaam and his Prophecies.*

the foundation of his intercourse with Him. This is all the more probable, as we feel bound to understand that the Lord did, in the accomplishment of His own great purposes, vouchsafe unto him special manifestations of the divine will.

According to the view which we take of Balaam's character, it is not so peculiar as it seems. Separated from the external accidents of time, of country, and position, we may go into the streets, and find a Balaam in every third man we meet. He belonged to that still numerous class who theoretically know God, and who actually do fear Him, but whose love and fear of God are not the regulating and governing principles of their minds. They are convinced, but not converted. They can prize and strongly desire the privileges of God's elect; they long to "die the death of the righteous," but are unwilling to live their life. They would serve God, but they must serve mammon also; and in the strife between the two contending influences, their lives are made bitter, and their death is perilous.

Speaking of this man, an able and pious writer[1] says: "It would be vain to assert, in opposition to the whole course of his history, that he had no acquaintance with the character, the will, and the dealing of Jehovah. It is indeed certain that he was a diviner, and a pretender to those magical arts and incantations so common in his age and country. But, with these abatements, he possessed, from whatever source derived, knowledge of a higher and nobler character, which, improved to its legitimate end, would have gifted him with distinction immeasurably transcending every dream of worldly avarice, or all the wealth and power which the king of Moab could bestow. Unreal as his divinations and sorceries were, he had communications from the God of heaven which might have made him wise unto salvation, and a diffusive blessing to all around him. But, alas! the illumination of the mind is by no means necessarily associated with the conversion of the heart. There are many who know God, yet glorify Him not as God, by a sanctified use of their attainments to His honour. He only knows God aright whose will and affections are overruled to obey Him. 'The fear of the Lord is the beginning of wisdom. A good understanding have all they that do His commandments.' He

[1] Rev. R. P. Buddicom, *Christian Exodus*, ii. 213.

whose knowledge of divine truth is merely theoretical, resembles the ill assorted image of Nebuchadnezzar, whose head was of fine gold, but his feet part of iron and part of clay."

"We are expressly told that the persons to whom God sends strong delusion that they should believe a lie, are those who love not the truth, but have pleasure in unrighteousness; whereas, on the other hand, our Lord assures us, that if any man will do His will, he shall know of the doctrine whether it be of God or no. There is no doubt that the fact is so; that men of honest and fair minds have a very clear and sound judgment in all points of practice, whilst insincere men, endowed perhaps with much higher abilities by nature, become absolutely blinded and weak, when they come to determine questions of duty. Nor is it to be doubted that this law of God's providence is a just and wise one; inasmuch as it enables persons of inferior understandings to correct their deficiencies by the goodness of their hearts, while it deprives the wicked man of the benefits of those talents which he is abusing. It is not without great reason that the Scripture so often recommends purity and singleness of heart, and threatens the double-minded. Few men, comparatively speaking, will make up their minds to do evil at any rate; and the number of those who wish to serve mammon only, is perhaps even smaller than that of those who wish to serve God only. The great mass of mankind are undone by a vain endeavour to serve at once both God and mammon; to their consciences they hold out the quieting language of Balaam. 'If Balak would give me his house full of silver and gold, I cannot go beyond the commandment of the Lord to say less or more;' while to their appetites they whisper at the same time, 'Tarry ye here awhile, that I may know what the Lord will say to me more.' Then it is that the voice of the Lord, which they pretended to wait for, does indeed lead them to their ruin. For their conscience is God's voice speaking within them; and this, when dishonestly applied to, becomes a false guide, disguising the guilt of our conduct, or encouraging us to hope that the mercy of God will grant it forgiveness. It permits us to do things for which God's anger will surely be kindled; and although we should make answer that we did no more than we believed to be right, yet we shall be reminded that they who killed Christ's servants, thought that they were doing God service; but that this their blindness rather aggravated their sin than lessened it; for it was a proof, as Christ Himself declares, that they had neither known His Father nor Him. Man indeed may not be able to judge of the heart of man, nor can we pretend to say that our neighbour's ignorance in many points is not an innocent ignorance, rather than a blindness sent by God, as an earnest of His future condemnation. But, though we may not judge of one another, yet He who judges us all, can see through every corner of our souls, can separate insincerity from truth, and can well perceive the weakness of those excuses, which to human eyes might appear fair and reasonable. 'Lord, I will follow thee whithersoever thou goest, but suffer me first to go and bury my father,' was a speech that could have conveyed no just suspicion to any man that heard it; but He to whom all hearts were open, knowing that the desire to follow Him was a mere pretence, cut down his hypocrisy, with calling on him to follow Him, 'and let the dead bury their dead.'" [1]

S.

BALAAM'S ASS

Numbers 22:6-35

HAVING yesterday considered the character of Balaam, we shall to-day be the better able to understand his conduct.

As he could not but have been aware that the people he was called upon by the ambassadors of Moab to curse were the peculiar objects of Jehovah's care, a plain and decisive refusal to entertain the proposal made to him was the only course open to a righteous man. But Balaam was not a righteous man. The rewards of divination were before him, and acted strongly upon his covetous mind; while, on the other hand, he feared to incur the divine displeasure. He therefore, between the two influences, parleyed with the temptation. He desired the messengers to lodge with him that night, and in the morning he would bring them word what Jehovah would have him do. That night God did commune with him, probably in a dream or vision, and in answer to his statement of the errand of the messengers, told him with a distinctness which left his future conduct without excuse, "Thou shalt not go with them. Thou shalt not curse the people, for they are blessed." Balaam accordingly arose in the morning and sent away the messengers. But in doing this he contrives to qualify the prohibition in such a manner as to intimate how willingly he would have gone, but that he was under the necessity of submitting to the command of God. "Jehovah refuseth to give me leave to go with you." He wished to go; he would have run greedily for reward; and, restrained as he was by a servile fear of the Most High, he could not frame his lips to that positive denial which might have preserved him from further solicitation. The grounds on which his desire to go was based—his ambition and his love of gain—seem to have been manifest to the elders

[1] Arnold's *Sermons*, pp. 59-62.

of Moab; and in accordance with their impression, the king, their master, was induced by their report to send a more urgent application, by a more splendid and influential embassage—"princes more and more honourable," with power to offer boundless rewards, all that his heart could wish.

When the new messengers arrived at Pethor, they stated their sovereign's message: "Let nothing, I pray thee, hinder thee from coming unto me; for I will promote thee unto very great honour, and I will do whatsoever thou sayest unto me; come, therefore, I pray thee, curse me this people." Balaam's answer was worthy of a prophet of the Lord, but only shows that his perception of duty was clear enough to leave him without excuse: "If Balak would give me his house full of silver and gold, I cannot go beyond the word of Jehovah my God, to do less or more." Then why not at once dismiss the messengers? He already knew the mind of God, and he ought to have known that "God is not a man, that He should lie; nor the son of man, that He should repent." Instead of that, he says, "Now therefore, I pray you, tarry ye also here this night, that I may know what the Lord will say unto me more." What "*more?*" Did Balaam fashion to himself a god after his own heart, and imagine that he also was to be moved from his declared purpose by the gifts and promises of Balak? Could he mean to insult God by his importunities? Did he hope to extort from Him, out of regard to his own worldliness, permission to bring a curse upon an entire nation which, as was well known, had been so long the object of His covenant care? Even such was what Peter well calls "the *madness* of the prophet." To rebuke it, the Lord says to him, "Go; but yet the word which I shall say unto thee, that shalt thou do." Here his going in the abstract is not forbidden, but his going in order to curse. How are we to reconcile this with the Lord's being angry with him because he went? Because He who knew his heart saw that he did go in order to curse. His only inducement to go was the rewards which he hoped to win from Balak, and he knew that these could only be obtained by doing what he desired. To go, therefore, without the hope and desire of cursing, would have been useless. Had he also declared plainly to the messengers the full meaning of the communications he had received, and the conditions under which he went, there is little likelihood that they would have pressed for his attendance.

As it was, "Balaam rose in the morning and saddled his ass, and went with the princes of Moab." We have seen the high rank of Balaam argued from his riding upon an ass. But although princes and judges rode upon asses in those days, all were not princes and judges who rode on asses. As far as appears, there was no other animal, except the camel, yet used in these parts for riding; and, no doubt, differences of breed and colour determined the value of the animal, and indicated the quality of the rider. The asses of that region generally are still much larger and finer animals than those we are in the habit of seeing, and some of the breeds are very handsome beasts indeed. We know that "white asses" were then (as is still the case in the East) highly prized, as are white elephants in India, and were preferred by persons of high station. Such, probably, was the one on which Balaam rode.

That Balaam *saddled* his ass, must not lead us to suppose that there were in these days any proper saddle. This is a far later invention, even for riding on horseback, and is not even now in the East generally used in riding on asses. On this subject we have the negative evidence of sculptures. In Egypt, indeed, there are no equestrian sculptures at all except those which represent riding in chariots. Classical sculpture has no saddles or saddle-cloths. We used to think that the earliest saddles were to be seen in the sculptures of the Sassanian dynasty at Shahpur in Persia; but the following passage would take them back to the last age of the Assyrian empire: "In the earliest sculptures (at Nineveh) the horses, except such as are led behind the king's chariot, are unprovided with cloths or saddles. The rider is seated on the naked back of the animal. At a later period, however, a kind of pad appears to have been introduced; and in a sculpture at Kouyunjik was represented a high saddle, not unlike that now in use in the East."[1]

The saddling of asses mentioned in Scripture probably consisted merely in placing upon their backs such thick cloths or mats as we see in some of the asses represented in the Egyptian paintings, as copied in the annexed engraving. Something of the same kind, or pieces of rag, felt,

[1] Layard's *Nineveh*, ii. 357.

carpet, or cloth, are still in general use; although a kind of pad is now frequently to be seen upon asses in the large towns of Egypt, Syria, and Arabia, especially among those let out for hire. Such town asses have also bridles, and sometimes

EGYPTIAN ASSES SADDLED

stirrups, none of which, any more than the pad, do we remember to have noticed on asses upon actual journeys; and we have known of asses being used continuously on journeys quite as long as that which Balaam now undertook, and that by persons whose position in life quite enabled them to ride a horse or mule had they so chosen. It would not be at all extraordinary, even now, that a person, expecting to be laden with riches and honours, should ride upon an ass, still less in an age and country where no other mode of conveyance, except that of riding upon camels, appears to have been known.

Well, Balaam set forth with the princes of Moab, attended by two servants of his own. After a while the Moabites seem to have gone on before; for when the subsequent transactions occurred, the presence of the servants alone is indicated. In the East the roads are like bridle paths across commons; and even through cultivated grounds they are wholly unenclosed, except where they pass through gardens and plantations in the neighbourhood of towns. Now, as Balaam rode contentedly along, he little knew that the angel of the Lord had gone forth for an adversary to oppose his progress. Balaam saw him not. But the ass beheld him standing in the way with a drawn sword in his hand, and she turned aside out of the path, wide into the fields through which it passed. The prophet forced her back by blows into the road. But presently they came to a place where a digression from the road was not possible, seeing that it was confined by vineyard walls on the right hand and on the left. This shows that they were approaching a town or village, and suggests that the Moabite lords had gone on to prepare a place for the diviner's reception. In this narrow way the ass again saw the angel; and being no longer able to swerve into the field, or to turn back (the two servants being behind), she forced herself up against the wall, and crushed the foot of her master. At this Balaam was wroth, and again smote his beast, which then moved on, the angel having for the moment disappeared. But a little farther on, where the road was narrower still, the ass once more beheld the angel, and in the excess of her alarm fell to the ground under her master. On this Balaam smote her still more severely with his staff. Then, lo, a wonder! the ass spoke as with a man's voice, expostulating with him against this harsh treatment: " What have I done to thee, that thou hast smitten me these three times ?" A common author would have paused here to describe the astonishment felt by Balaam at hearing his ass speak; but it is a fine and truthful trait of the sacred writer, that he represents the prophet as too much overcome by his wrath to notice the extraordinary character of this fact. Instead of this, he at once answered the ass, as if her utterance had been the most common circumstance in the world. He said quite naturally, " Because thou hast mocked me: I would there were a sword in my hand; for now would I kill thee." The ass replied, in effect, " Hast thou not always ridden upon me ? and have I ever been wont to be restive and obstinate ?" implying that it must be supposed she had not now acted so contrary to her habits without strong reason. Balaam was constrained to acknowledge the truth of this appeal, and at that moment the real cause of the animal's unusual behaviour became evident. Until now the soothsayer had seen nothing to prevent the ass from proceeding on her way; but his eyes were now opened, and he beheld the angel, before whom he bowed himself reverently.

How is this most remarkable transaction to be understood ? Some have been inclined to think that it took place in a trance or vision, and that

although the circumstances were realities to Balaam, they were so to him only : in short, that they were open not to his external sense, but to his internal perception. This is implied in his eyes being said to be opened when he saw the angel. For, doubtless, his external sense was open before ; and what remained to be opened was the internal perception, which is inoperative without spiritual quickening. In proof of this view, it may be pleaded that the transaction was not obvious to the sense of the servants of Balaam who were with him. We see no objection to this view in itself, for it merely brings it into the same class of revelations as that which met Paul on his journey to Damascus, which is expressly said to have been distinct to *his* sense only, the words which passed being audible to him alone : the rest heard only what seemed to them the rolling of distant thunder, while the light that struck him blind by its intensity upon his quickened sense, had upon them no such effect, for they saw it only as a " great light." This explanation, however, which assumes that the circumstance did really occur, though perceptible to Balaam only, is different from that which regards it as a mere dream, which had no existence but in his imagination, and different also from that which regards all the circumstances as literal. Those who take the last of these views have much to urge in favour of it. Besides the usual objections to the introduction of a vision without intimation in a historical narrative, there is the assertion of St. Peter, that " the dumb ass, speaking with a man's voice, rebuked the madness of the prophet." Moreover, what seems to us the strongest objection to any other than a literal view—and one which has escaped the notice of commentators—is this : We are told not only what Balaam did see, whether literally or not, but also what he did *not* see. The angel was present, had changed his position, and had alarmed the ass no less than three times, before Balaam was aware of his presence. *Not* seeing is a mere negation of perception ; and Balaam, even in a vision, could not dream that he did *not* see the angel. If there were a vision, there was therefore something literal before the vision commenced. Why do we wish for a vision ? Not, surely, for the sake of avoiding the actual appearance of the angel, for such appearances we have had on former occasions. Is it to avoid the speaking of the ass ? But if there were a vision, the words "the Lord opened his eyes" must be taken to mark when that vision commenced. Then, if at all, he was thrown into a different state. But then the ass had *already* spoken. Besides, we do not suppose that the ass thought or reasoned, though there is perhaps nothing beyond the sense or comprehension of an ass in the words which were uttered; nor that the animal had any intention or volition in the utterance of these words. Words appropriate to the rebuking of the prophet were made to flow from the mouth of the ass, without any intention or consciousness on the part of the poor beast.

Balaam now confessed his error to the angel, and offered to return home. But the answer is: "Go with the men; only the word that I shall speak unto thee, that shalt thou speak." From this it is evident, that this man had gone with an eager anxiety to win the rewards offered to him; and the purpose of this manifestation was not to prevent the journey, but to impress it upon his mind, that he was to speak only that which should be given him to declare by Jehovah, and to make him feel the peril of transgression.

GOD AND MAMMON

Numbers 23, 24

WHO are these two men upon the mountains that overlook the camp of Israel? The one who gazes with rapt attention upon the scene is the prophet of Pethor; the other, who with eager solicitude points out all the circumstances of the scene, is the king of Moab, who has brought him from "the mountains of the east," that he may pronounce his curse upon the people whom the Lord has blessed. Oh, vain man! to think that the power which but yesterday was not sufficient to slay an ass, would to-day be able to ruin a great people. But see! the prophet seems affected. Perhaps one of his better moments is come—the moment in which the proud mind of the flesh, and the power of worldliness, relax their strong gripe upon the heart, and allow the better feelings of the soul, prisoned in its dark chambers, to rush forth for one moment into the glad sunshine and the pleasant air. He sees the goodly array of the chosen people, "like lign aloes which

the Lord hath planted, and like cedar trees beside the waters;" he beholds in the midst of them the glorious tabernacle of the Lord; and he views the magnificent pillar of cloud spread over them as a shield for their defence against his maledictions. He sees more: again his eyes are opened and his view extends into the great future, in which he beholds their victories over the enemies of the Most High, and is even allowed a glimpse of the remote "Star of Jacob;" nor is he perhaps left wholly ignorant of its deep significance. He could not be altogether unmoved. Struck with a solemn conviction of the peculiar privileges and mercies of this people, and contrasting them with the dim consciousness of his own condition, he cries out, "How goodly are thy tents, O Jacob! and thy tabernacles, O Israel! Let me die the death of the righteous, and let my last end be like his!"

This is not a strange thing. It is not beyond the ordinary experience of the soul's life. How often is it seen that transgressors are checked for a moment by the voice of conscience; and on comparing their condition with that of the Lord's servants, are compelled to echo the words of the worldly-minded prophet! Perhaps the offender never lived who has not at times sighed for a share in the mercies and blessings, in life and in death, of the righteous, and who has not, in the gush of temporary feeling, been ready to cry out, "Bless me, even me also, O my Father." (Gen. xxvii. 38.)

But such temporary aspirations soon pass away, and leave no trace behind. Balaam could wish at this time to have his dying portion with the righteous; yet that wish had no abiding influence upon his conduct. The present, the gains and honours of the world, were still the subjects of his thoughts, and to win them the great object of his solicitude. Therefore his "end" was far from that. In the tents of Midian, where he lingered, or to which he returned to claim the rewards of unrighteousness, his sun went down in blood, leaving a name that has become a byword in the world.

It is a fearful thought, that a man may have "his eyes open" as wide as Balaam's were, and see as distinctly as he "the vision of the Almighty," and yet perish in practical unbelief; for that belief avails only for condemnation which is not operative upon the heart, and allows a man still to have his portion with the world.

Yet it is possible that Balaam, with his high doctrinal knowledge and his clear vision of God, thought himself safe. We see such things daily. There are thousands now who cherish the ruinous delusion, that they may walk after their own devices, live to themselves only, and dishonour the Lord that bought them, and yet have their portion with those who have devoted themselves in holy faith to the service of religion, who have denied themselves, and have lived to the glory of their Redeemer. This fatal delusion may continue to deepen and enlarge around such men; it may even withstand that influence of the truths which a dying hour usually brings home to the soul; and the self-deceiver may depart, whispering peace, peace, to his soul, when there is no peace. But darkness flies not before the rising sun so speedily and so surely, as error and self-deceit will be scattered before the glory of that light which will issue from the effulgence of the throne set up in the day of judgment. Of such our Lord Himself says, "Many shall say unto Me in that day, Lord, Lord, have we not prophesied in Thy name, and in Thy name cast out devils, and in Thy name done many wonderful works? And then will I profess unto them, I never knew you; depart from me, ye that work iniquity."

It is a significant indication of Balaam's state, that his sacrifices to the Lord were offered upon the high places of Baal. While conscious of a divided spirit—with mammon, the spirit of the world, reigning, though not undisturbedly, in his heart—it must have seemed a small matter that Baal's high places were appropriated for the nonce to the worship of Jehovah; but to him were applicable the words which a truer and sterner prophet addressed to men of like temper: "How long halt ye between two opinions? If the Lord be God, follow him; but if Baal, then follow him."[1] And still more the words of our Lord: "No man can serve two masters. . . . Ye cannot serve God and mammon."[2] Not but that a man may in the literal sense serve two masters; although, however, he serve two, it is to one only that his heart can be devoted. To which master Balaam was devoted, we need not tell. "He was," as an old writer[3] remarks, "one of those unstable men

whom the apostle calls 'double-minded,'[1] an ambidexter in religion, like Redwald, King of the East Saxons (the first that was baptized), who (as Camden relates) had in the same church one altar for the Christian religion and another for sacrificing to devils; and a loaf of the same leaven was our resolute Rufus, that painted God on one side of his shield, and the devil on the other, with this desperate inscription, *In utrumque paratus*—'I am ready for either—catch that catch can.' Or this was such a sinful mixture as was that worship of those mongrels[2] who 'feared God, and feared him not,' that is *rightly*; for they feared Him only for His lions that He sent to slay them, not truly, nor totally, for God will not part stakes with the devil at any hand."

One cannot help thinking with delight of the quiet security in which Israel rested in their tents, while all these machinations were going on against them. So shall it be with all who truly love and serve God. No weapon that is formed against them shall prosper. Their minds may rest in perfect peace, being stayed upon Him. They did not even suspect the mischief which Balaam and Balak were plotting against them, but which the Almighty threw back upon the inventors. The victory was gained for them before they knew of their danger, and their salvation was wholly of the Lord. "Who is he that will harm you, if ye be followers of that which is good?"[3] "The angel of the Lord encampeth round about them that fear Him, and delivereth them."[4] The enemy cannot do them violence—the sons of wickedness cannot approach or hurt them. "Happy is that people that is in such a case; yea, happy is that people whose God is the Lord."[5]

Compelled, notwithstanding the urgency of the king, to suppress the curse that filled his mouth; compelled by the strong power upon him even to bless where he desired to curse, Balaam was constrained to quit Moab under the strong displeasure of the king at his obstinacy, and without the honours and rewards for which he had perilled his soul. His advice, however, led to a war between the Israelites and Midianites, among whom he withdrew; and in that war he perished.[6]

---

[1] 1 Kings 18:21.   [2] Matthew 6:24.
[3] Christopher Ness, *History and Mystery*, vol. i. Appendix, p. 88.

[1] James 1:6-8.   [4] Psalms 34:7.
[2] 2 Kings 17:28-34.   [5] Psalms 144:15.
[3] 1 Peter 3:13.   [6] Numbers 31:8.

THE MIDIANITES

Numbers 25, 31

AMONG the people who knew and discussed the events which befell the Israelites since their migration from Egypt, it must have been notorious that there had been signal punishments inflicted upon them for breaches of fealty to their King. Pondering this in his mind, the infernal sagacity of Balaam led him to conclude, that if they could but be seduced from their allegiance to their Divine King, the protection which rendered them invincible would be withdrawn, and they would be easily subdued by their enemies. This discovery he made known to the king of Moab before his departure; and it illustrates the character of the man, that he could form this device, and counsel the king to act upon it, just after his mouth had poured forth, even by constraint, eloquent blessings upon the people whose ruin he now devises. And all this was purely gratuitous; for his business with Moab was ended. He could not curse Israel; and he had incurred the anger, rather than secured the honours, of the king of Moab. He seems to have retired among the neighbouring people of Midian, close allies with Moab, until he should behold the results of the course which he had suggested, and in which he seems to have induced the Midianites to co-operate. However dissatisfied with the result of their sending for him, the Moabites were still too deeply impressed with the notion of his superhuman sagacity, not to pay the most heedful attention to his advice. This was in effect that the women should be rendered instrumental in seducing the Israelites to take part in the obscene rites of Baal-Peor. It is not to be supposed that they recognized distinctly the grounds on which this course would expose the Hebrew host to the displeasure of their God. They thought that Jehovah was no doubt a true God, as the God of the Hebrews; and they acknowledged that, as His acts had shown, He was a mighty God. But Baal-Peor they held to be no less true as their own god; and whatever wrath Jehovah might manifest against His people would not, to their understanding, be because He claimed exclusive and universal worship, but because of His jealousy that His own people should incline to render the worship to a rival god, which He alone had a right to claim from them.

The policy followed was but too successful. As the Hebrews lay encamped in the plains of Moab, unsuspicious of the bad feeling of the Moabites and Midianites towards them, an intercourse gradually, and seemingly in due course, sprang up between the kindred nations. The daughters of Moab and Midian came to visit the women of Israel, and thus fell under the notice of the men. The men of Israel, also, new to a peopled country, and strange to a friendly intercourse with strangers, amused themselves and gratified their curiosity by visiting the towns and villages in the vicinity. This intercourse was perilous for them. Dazzled and bewildered by magnificent and seductive appliances of vice, to which in their simple wandering life *they* had been all unused, although their fathers had seen the like things in Egypt, they were prevailed upon by the idolaters of Moab and Midian to take part in the riotous and lustful orgies of their gods. It does not appear to us that they meant to abjure their faith in Jehovah, or so much as adopted a belief in Baal-Peor along with it. What they did was to participate in the licentious acts by which his votaries professed to honour him. "They joined themselves to Baal-Peor"—rather, "bound themselves with his badge;" for it was the custom in ancient times, as it is now in all pagan countries, for every idol to have some specific badge, or ensign, by which his votaries were known. As formerly by an insubordination which threatened the permanency of the state, so now, by practices which outraged the great principle and object of its institution, they created a necessity for a severe and exemplary visitation of the divine displeasure. No miracle for this purpose was, however, needed. The corruption was not general, and the faithful were sufficient to enforce the decisions of the Sovereign Judge against the offenders. The men of rank and authority, "the heads of the people," who had lent the sanction of their example to this abomination, were ordered to be put to death. The direction to "hang them up against the sun," does not mean that they were to be put to death by hanging, but that after they had been slain by the sword or by stoning, their bodies should be exposed to public view until sun-down. This awful task being accomplished, Moses gave the word that the different judges dispersed among the tribes should execute the Lord's judgment upon all the offenders within their jurisdiction. It is probable they were easily known by their badges. This was done; and there fell on that day, under the sword of justice, no fewer than twenty-four thousand men.

While these things were being done, and while the people were mourning before the tabernacle, an act of high-handed daring, in one of the chiefs of Simeon, in conducting publicly to his tent one of the "fair idolatresses," by whom all this mischief had been caused, so kindled the zealous wrath and indignation of Phinehas, the son of the high priest, that he followed them, and transfixed both the man and woman with a javelin, at one stroke. For this he was commended. He but executed the judgment which had been passed on such offenders; and in this case, at such a time, and under such circumstances, the crime was trebly flagrant. He needs no excuse, for he had his commission; but if he did need excuse, God, as Bishop Hall well remarks, "pardons the errors of our fervency, rather than the indifferences of our lukewarmness."

At a later period, Moses was ordered to wage a war against the Midianites, whose devices had caused this danger and loss to Israel. He accordingly detached a force of twelve thousand men, one thousand from each tribe, who attacked some of the cities of this people, put to death a portion of its male population, and returned with numerous prisoners (women and children), and a large booty in beeves, asses, and sheep.

Among the causes which justify war, none is more unanimously asserted by political writers, than one attempt on the part of one community against the civil institutions, and so against the integrity and internal peace, of another. The Hebrews had therefore an undoubted right, even apart from the divine command, to attack the people of Midian, who had treacherously endeavoured to withdraw them from their allegiance, and thus to unsettle the foundations of all their union, prosperity, and peace, and prepare them to become an easy conquest for their own arms.

Now, if it be right to wage war at all, it is not only right to wage it in such a manner as shall accomplish its object, but it would be wrong to wage it in any other manner. War is, in its very nature, the infliction of suffering in order to an ulterior good; and the infliction of any degree of suffering is unjustifiable, unless so far as it may tend to this result. If, therefore, in the prosecution of a war, the measures adopted are of such lenity as to be insufficient to produce the end in view, namely, protection for the present and security for the future, the mitigated evil then becomes uncompensated by any ulterior good. It is then a causeless and unjustifiable evil; it is not mercy, but cruelty and crime. This principle is clear, and is theoretically acknowledged; yet when any application of it, however wise and just, tends to severities which we are not accustomed to regard as belonging to the necessities of the case, our feelings are naturally shocked. Yet the principle continues to operate, and is acknowledged in all our warfare, although, with the progress of civilization, it has come to be understood in civilized communities that inflictions formerly resorted to shall be forborne. But in their conflicts with barbarous nations, who have no such understanding, they are accustomed to adopt harsher measures; and this for the simple and sound reason, that the object would not otherwise be gained, and that if they were to allow a war to be to their adversaries a less evil than these adversaries were in the habit of expecting it to prove, such a self-prostrating lenity would tend to a speedy reverse of the contest; for among such nations lenity is ascribed to weakness, and not to the pride of conscious strength. Severity, in short, is beneficent, when it is suited to guard against the necessity of its own repetition; and how much or how little is adequate to that end, is a question to be determined by reference to some existing state of society. The Israelites conducted their warfares on the principles generally recognized in their time; and to have done so on any other or milder principle, against such enemies as they had to contend with, would have been ruinous and suicidal. Thus only could it be effectual; and war not intended to be effectual should not be waged at all. It is confidently hoped and believed, that the time is coming, is near at hand, when war, as now conducted by ourselves—when any war, will be looked back upon with the same feelings of disgust and horror, as those with which we now regard the conflicts of the nations beyond the Mediterranean three-and-thirty centuries ago.

These remarks are appropriate to the war usages which are about to come under our notice; and they are especially appropriate to the present occasion, as the circumstances of this war with the Midianites have been exposed to much animadversion. It is certain that the Israelites gave no quarter to the men. It was not the custom of the age to do so, except perhaps among the Egyptians and other civilized nations, which had much use for the labour of slaves. Nevertheless, the words "they slew all the males" do not mean that they exterminated all the men of the nation, as some have thought, but only that they slew all who withstood them; for the nation itself subsisted in considerable strength, and was able in a few generations to bring the Israelites themselves under subjection.

A more difficult point is the command of Moses, that the adult females and the male children among the prisoners should be put to death. Pained as we are by the recital of such horrors, and glad as we feel that such usages have passed away from the practices of war, a close examination will enable us to see that the principles which have been laid down supply an adequate excuse for a course which Moses himself must have regarded as distressing. His course was designed to act *in terrorem*, with a view to future security. It is clear that he had no satisfaction in the task. On the contrary he appears to have been strongly excited when he beheld the array of prisoners, and to have uttered a rebuke which shows that he would far rather that whatever severity needed to be exercised should have been finished in the furious haste of onset, than that it should thus be left for execution in cold blood. As it was, however, the prisoners were upon his hands, and he had to dispose of them as the recent hazards and the present condition of the state demanded, in an age when the necessities of the world's government involved the use of a much harsher instrumentality than is now requisite. Taking these considerations with us, it may be asked, What was to be done with these prisoners? Should they be sent home unharmed, or should they be welcomed on an equal footing to the hospitality of Israel? Then, if the views already stated are sound, the war ought not to have been undertaken. This follows, even without insisting upon the circumstance, that had the latter alternative been adopted, the youthful sons of the Midianitish warriors would soon have grown up to be a sword in the bosom of the still feeble state, and possibly to compel the hazards and hardships of another conflict. Then, with respect to the adult females, it is to be considered that

it was their wicked instrumentality which had led Israel to sin, and had given occasion to the recent war; and, on the other hand, the danger to be apprehended from them, if they were allowed again to try their seductive arts upon the Israelites, had just been proved to be such as the infant state could by no means tolerate.

Keeping in view, therefore, the time and country in which Moses lived, and the circumstances by which he was surrounded, it will be a bold thing for any one to say, that as a man entrusted with the welfare of a nation he acted wrongly. That he acted only from a strong sense of duty, every one who has studied his character must know; and who among us, in these altered times, is better able than he was to judge of what his duty exacted? But if in this case he did err, in judging that the stern obligations of political duty allowed him to show no pity on more than one class of his prisoners, let him alone bear the blame of the deed. He appears to have acted upon his own judgment, and does not, as usual, adduce the command of the Lord for the course which was taken.

MOSES' CHARACTER AND DEATH

Deuteronomy 34

THE day approached when Moses must die. The people for whom he had so long cared, and whom he had so anxiously led, were now ready to enter the promised land; but he was forbidden to go in with them. His work was done; his great task was accomplished; and it only remained for him to render up his life.

Yet it was fit that, before this venerable servant of God laid down his charge, he should see that part of it which could be transmitted deposited in proper hands, that he might die in the comfortable assurance that the great work he had undertaken might be vigorously prosecuted after his decease. Ever since the fatal day of Meribah, the prophet knew that he was doomed to die, without setting the sole of his foot upon the land which was to form the heritage of his people. But now he receives a distinct intimation, similar to that which had been given to his brother, that the appointed time was come; and, like him, he is directed to ascend the neighbouring mountain, there to render up his life. Observe how he receives this intimation. What is the foremost thought in his mind? Nothing that concerns himself—no regret of his own; all his thought is for the welfare of the people: "Let Jehovah, the God of the spirits of all flesh, set a man over the congregation, who may go out before them, and who may go in before them, and who may lead them out, and who may bring them in; that the congregation of the Lord be not as sheep which have no shepherd." Here is the same loftiness of spirit, rising above every thought of self—the same zeal for the honour of God—the same devoted concern for the welfare of the people, which had hitherto marked his whole career. "We may wade through folios of history and biography, narrating the mighty deeds of warriors, statesmen, and professed patriots, before we find another case equal to it in interest."[1]

The suit of Moses was heard; and Joshua, who had already had opportunities of distinguishing himself by his faithfulness and his courage, was appointed to be solemnly inaugurated at the tabernacle as the future leader of the Hebrew host. Nothing then remained for Moses to do, but to pour out his heart before the people in lofty odes and eloquent blessings. Then he retired to the appointed mountain, that he might before his death survey the goodly land in which the people were to establish that noble commonwealth which he had so laboriously organized.

This was the only privilege allowed him, when, in the most touching language, he deplored, at the time when his sentence was first pronounced, this exclusion from the consummation of his hopes: "I pray Thee, let me go over and see the good land that is beyond Jordan, that goodly mountain, and Lebanon."[2] Who can tell the eagerness of the glance which he now threw westward, and southward, and northward, over the magnificent country that opened to his view? Tracing with his eye the course of the Jordan upon his right hand, he beheld the hills of Gilead, and the rich fields of northern Canaan bounded in the remote distance by the dim and shadowy Lebanon. Upon his left, below where the Jordan is lost in the Dead Sea, the vast and varied territory, afterwards of Judah, detained his view, until it was lost in the haze of the southward deserts. At his feet, upon the other side of the Jordan, he beheld Jericho amid its palm trees;

[1] Smith's *Sacred Annals*, ii. 104. [2] Deuteronomy 3:25.

and, traversing the hills and plains of Benjamin and Ephraim, his undimmed eye[1] might perhaps discover the utmost limit formed by the clouds which rise from the waters of the Mediterranean Sea. Upon this scene his eye closed; and in the recesses of the mountain, out of the sight of the host, in a hollow of the hilly region where he died, his corpse was deposited. Had the spot been known, it would without question have become first the goal of pious pilgrimages, and then perhaps, by the apotheosis of one so venerated, a scene of idolatrous worship. It is in harmony with the self-renouncing spirit which his whole life displayed, that means were taken to prevent the place of his last rest from being visited by the coming generations, which would have such good cause to revere and bless his name.

Here we leave him. But we quit with reluctance the man whose career and character, as connected with, and developed in, a large and important part of Scripture, have engaged so much of our attention. The various incidents which have passed under our notice, and the principles of action we have had occasion to examine, leave us but little need for expatiating upon the character of one whom all must regard as the greatest of woman-born—with the exception of ONE only, and that One more than man. As the mind tries, however, to rest upon the prominent points of the character which his career evinces, we find ourselves unexpectedly baffled. All the great men of sacred as well as of profane history, possessed some prominent virtue or quality, which stood out in bolder relief than their other excellences. We think of the faith of Abraham, of the conscientiousness of Joseph, of the contrition of David, of the generosity of Jonathan, of the zeal of Elijah; but what do we regard as the dominant quality of Moses? It is not to be found. The mind is perplexed in the attempt to fix on any. It is not firmness, it is not perseverance, it is not disinterestedness, it is not patriotism, it is not confidence in God, it is not meekness, it is not humility, it is not forgetfulness of self, that forms his distinguishing characteristic. It is not any ONE of these. It is ALL of them. His virtues, his graces, were all equal to each other; and it was their beautifully harmonious operation and development which constituted his noble

[1] "His eye was not dim, nor his natural force abated."

and all but perfect character. This was the greatness of Moses—this was the glory of his character. It is a kind of character rare in any man; and in no man, historically known, has it been so completely manifested. The exigencies of even those great affairs which engaged his thought, did not, and could not, call forth on any *one* occasion, *all* the high qualities with which he was gifted. It is rarely possible to see more than one high endowment in action at the same time. But we find Moses equal to every occasion: he is never lacking in the virtue which the occasion requires him to exercise; and by this we know that he possessed them all. When we reflect that Moses possessed all the learning of his age, and that he wanted none of the talents which constitute human greatness—knowing, as we do, that such endowments are not invariably accompanied by high character and noble sentiments—we honour his humility more than his glory; and, above all, we venerate that divine wisdom which raised up this extraordinary man, and called him forth at the moment when the world had need of him.

The scene of the death of Moses must be regarded as one of the most interesting spots in the East. The mountain he was to ascend is spoken of twice as Pisgah; twice as Abarim; and twice as Nebo. A line of heights, or crests, seem to be intended; and it is difficult to identify that on which the lawgiver expired. The true position of Mount Nebo was a desideratum to Dr. Robinson. He himself did not explore the neighbourhood. The most recent, and the fullest information on the subject, is furnished by the Rev. A. E. Northey, in his *Expedition to the East of Jordan*, Palestine Exploration Statements, 1872, p. 62. He ascended *Jebel Jabud*, 2,700 feet high, situated near the north-eastern shore of the Dead Sea, overlooking the Plain of Moab and the Jordan Valley. He describes the view as magnificent in every direction. Proceeding thence, he pitched in the *Wady Hesbân*, then passed *Ain Suderah* and *Wady Suderah;* and, after mounting steadily three hours, reached the height called *Jebel Nebba*, pointed out as the true Nebo. *Ayun Mousa* lies to the north. The view seems to have been a little disappointing. Another hour farther south would have taken him to the highest point of the range, but this he did not reach. At all events, he ascended *Jebel Nebba*, an achievement greatly desired. The view, he says, is a glorious one, whatever the drawbacks; and the exact spot he visited may be identified by one special characteristic. "The field, or hog's back, through which we passed on turning westward from the road in order to reach the summit, is full of deep holes—traps for falls to unwary travellers' horses." He speaks of the *El Belka*, an adjacent plateau, consisting of immense rolling plains of corn like those of Gaza.

How interesting to ascend in imagination this famous mountain height, and to picture the scene which spread out under the eyes of Moses. There, beyond the dark salt lake, are the mountains to be called after Judah, who is one day to hide Bethlehem within those folds, and to bear Jerusalem upon that brow. Yonder is Jordan, as a line dividing the land in two, on the farther side—and there stand the hills which Ephraim and Manasseh are to possess, with Gerazim and Gilboa, destined to throw their shadows over bloody battles and over holy scenes. And north, by the river source, are the summits of a range in Naphtali, which runs up into the bolder peaks of Lebanon, to form a distant background to the sea of Galilee, hereafter to witness miracles of healing, and to flash with a light which the people sitting in darkness shall behold. And the land of Gilead unto Dan borders the hither side of Jordan, while eastward are the deserts from which now Moses turns away his eyes, as from that with which he has no more to do. And the land before him, he sees as it is to be. The goodly sight of the camp just under him, where he has parted for ever with the pilgrim people, is goodlier to him than it was to Balaam. He sees all with keener vision, purer thoughts. He is come to die. And it seems scarcely an imagination to picture the sun, which rose on Balaam, going down, as Moses there ends his long life journey—"the fair hills of Judah and the soft plains and banks of the Jordan, purple in the evening light as with the blood of redemption, and fading in their distant fulness into mysteries of promise and of love."

We cannot resist the pleasant temptation to insert the following well known lines :—

> " By Nebo's lonely mountain
> On this side Jordan's wave,
> In a vale in the land of Moab
> There lies a lonely grave.
> And no man knows the sepulchre,
> And no man saw it e'er,
> For the angels of God upturned the sod
> And laid the dead man there.

> " That was the grandest funeral
> That ever past on earth.
> And no man heard the trampling,
> Or saw the train go forth.
> Noiselessly as the daylight
> Comes back when night is done,
> And the crimson streak on ocean's cheek
> Grows into the great sun.

> " Noiselessly as the spring time,
> Her crown of verdure weaves—
> And all the trees on all the hills
> Open their thousand leaves.
> So, without sound of music,
> Or voice of them that wept,
> Silently down from the mountain's crown,
> The great procession swept.

> " This was the truest warrior
> That ever buckled sword—
> This the most gifted poet
> That ever breathed a word—

And never earth's philosopher
Traced with his golden pen,
On the deathless page, truth half so sage,
As he wrote down for men.

" And had he not high honour?
The hillside for a pall—
To be in state, while angels wait
With stars for tapers tall,—
And the dark rock-pines, like tossing plumes,
Over his bier to wave ;
And God's own hand, in that lonely land,
To lay him in the grave.

" In that strange grave, without a name,
Whence his uncoffined clay
Shall break again, O wondrous thought !
Before the Judgment Day,—
And stand with glory wrapt around
On the hills he never trod,
And speak of the strife that won our life
With the Incarnate Son of God.

" O lonely grave in Moab's land !
O dark Beth-peor's hill !
Speak to these curious hearts of ours,
And teach them to be still.
God hath His mysteries of grace,
Ways that we cannot tell ;
He hides them deep, like the hidden sleep,
Of him He loved so well."

S.

ESPIALS

Joshua 2

It must have been evident to Joshua, that the large and strong city of Jericho, which lay embosomed among its palm trees on the other side of the river, must be the first object of his operations on entering the land of Canaan. Very much depended upon the result of this initiatory step. Jericho was, for that age, a strongly walled town ; and we have already had occasion to observe, that the Israelites were considerably afraid of walled towns—though such as lay in plains, like this Jericho, were doubtless less formidable to them than such as were stationed upon the hills. It was obviously desirable, therefore, that, before commencing operations, they should endeavour to receive such information as might tend to their encouragement in this great enterprise. We cannot indeed question that the Hebrew host had been put in good heart by its

victories on the east of the Jordan; but still they probably entertained, from the traditions of the spies, most exaggerated notions of the power of the proper nations of Canaan, and they very

JERICHO

probably supposed those whom they had overcome on the east of the river to be less mighty than the ancient nations on the west. It was evidently under the influence of such considerations, and less for his own information than to give confidence to the people, that Joshua concluded to despatch two men on the delicate and dangerous task of entering the city, and bringing back a report of its condition. The expedition is full of curious and interesting indications of eastern manners and usages, some of which well deserve to engage our attention.

Although it is likely that considerable vigilance was exercised in the presence of an enemy separated from the city by little more than the breadth of the river, yet the two spies succeeded in getting into the town. As there was no friend in the place to receive them, and as it might have been dangerous to go at once to a public khan or caravanserai, they went to lodge at the house of a woman named Rahab. They had not been there long, before an alarming intimation reached them, that their presence, not only in the town, but in that very house, was known, and that their errand was also more than suspected : for messengers came from the king of Jericho requiring the woman to produce them. In modern Europe, the officers of the government would have entered the house without wasting the precious time in parley. But formerly, as now, in the East, the privacy of a woman was respected, even to a degree that might be called superstitious; and no one will enter the house in which she lives, or the part of the house she occupies, until her consent has been obtained, if indeed such consent be ever demanded. In this case it was not asked. Rahab was required not to let the messengers in, but to bring out the foreigners she harboured. The keen-witted woman, gathering, from what the messengers said, who her guests were, at once determined to save them: for, from a consideration of the wonders which the Lord had wrought for Israel, her confidence in their ultimate success was so strong, that she concluded to take advantage of this opportunity, by laying the men under such obligations as would ensure the safety of herself and her friends. She withdrew from the window, whence probably she had heard the messengers for a moment; and hurrying the spies to the flat roof of the house, she hid them under the stalks of flax which had been laid out there to dry, probably informing them at the moment, that the king's messengers were at the door inquiring for them. In this we see what has not hitherto appeared, that the houses were at that time, as they still are, flat or terraced; and' that the flat roof formed then, as now, an important part of the economy of oriental life. This is the place where, in the cool of the day, the fresh air is breathed by a people who never walk out expressly for air or exercise. Here they sleep during the nights of summer, when the interior apartments are too hot and sultry for refreshing repose, and when the coolness then enjoyed enables the constitution to bear up against the heat of the day. These were especially important matters in the almost tropical climate of the plain of Jericho. Here, also, such things as require to be dried by the heat of the sun are laid out in a situation which effectually protects them from depredation, or even notice, and at the same time exposes them in the completest manner to the action of the solar heat.

The woman then returned to the messengers, and assured them that, although the two men had come to her house, they had not tarried till then. In the dusk, just before the time for shutting the town gate, they had departed. Whither they went she knew not; but they had gone so recently, that she thought they would be overtaken if vigorously pursued. The men believed her; for not only could there be no perceivable reason to them why she should seek to shelter such deadly foes, but the falsehood was ingeniously framed to deceive: for nothing could be more natural than that the men should take their departure at the time she indicated, when the shades of evening would allow them to pass out without any close inspection. Some have thought from this instance that gates were shut only in time of war, or when danger was apprehended from a foe; but it appears to us that gates were then, as at present in the East, always closed in the evening and opened in the morning, it being necessary at all times to guard against the night incursions of plunderers and beasts of prey. Not only are gates in the East habitually thus shut in the evening—generally, as in the case before us, when it becomes dusk—but so rigidly is the keeping them closed enforced, that the guards themselves usually cannot open them to admit any persons without a special order from the governor of the place, which is not often obtained, unless by persons of some consideration. Hence it not seldom happens, even in winter, that persons arriving too late are obliged to spend all the night outside the walls; and the apprehension of being shut out of the place to which they are going, makes all travellers push on briskly towards the close of day.

But what is to be said of Rahab's being so ready with a lie—declaring that the men were gone when they were really in the house? That sense of truthfulness, which is the growth of Christian culture, is shocked at an untruth so circumstantial; and we cannot allow the motive which influenced her to have been a justification of her conduct, seeing that it is forbidden to do evil that good may come. It has been urged, that by her act she took part with the Israelites, and that what would have been done by them in regard to their enemies might be done by her; it being lawful to deceive an enemy in war, as was often done by good men among the Israelites. Without discussing this closely, and contenting ourselves with simply observing, that the mere fact that the state of warfare renders "lawful" many practices which the Christian religion condemns, is one of the strongest arguments against war, we pass on to observe, that among the ancient heathen, as among those which still remain in the world, lying was scarcely regarded even as a venial error, much less as a crime. There was no *principle* of truthfulness; and although men generally spoke truth where there was no benefit to gain or evil to avert by telling an untruth, as without this the common intercourse of social life could not be carried on, yet the slightest inducement was sufficient to drive them to the resort of a lie. An oath was obligatory, and for the most part a man might be believed as to what he affirmed on oath; a mere word, however, was but lightly regarded. It is observed by missionaries among the heathen, that so weak is the feeling of obligation as to the observance of strict veracity, that even apparently sincere converts have the greatest difficulty in freeing themselves from the habit of equivocation, and need continual watching and admonition in that respect. It is among the most important of the many *social* advantages which Christianity has conferred upon mankind, that to its teaching we owe the feeling—prevalent among all Christian nations—that a falsehood is a disgrace and a sin; and that a man is bound, religiously and morally, no less by his word than by his oath.

All this was unknown, however, to poor Rahab, who, having been brought up among a people so unprincipled as the Canaanites, had probably never heard that there was the least harm in lying, much less when an apparently good end was to be answered by it. These considerations may be fairly urged in extenuation of Rahab's falsehood. God Himself claims from us according to what we have, and not according to what we have not. In us, who have opportunities of better knowledge, untruthfulness must be judged by a different standard here and hereafter.

When all was safe, Rahab went to the men, who now left their hiding-place. She told them that the people of the land were stricken with terror at the presence and known designs of the Hebrew host, having fully heard of all the marvellous deeds which had been wrought in their behalf. She was perfectly assured that by the might of their God they must prevail; and in that confidence she exacted a pledge of safety for herself and for hers in consideration of the aid she had afforded. This was readily given by the men. She was to tie a scarlet cord, which they gave her, to a particular window of her house. This was to enable them to recognize the house;

and they pledged themselves for the safety of all who might be in that house when the city should be taken. We have little doubt that the sign was chosen by the spies with some reference to their own passover solemnity, when the doorposts were sprinkled with blood, to denote that the destroying angel passed by the doors so marked when the first-born of Egypt were slain.

Meanwhile the gates had been shut after the pursuers had gone, and they were probably guarded with unusual care, to prevent the escape of the spies, should they still be in the city. But the house of Rahab being situated upon the town wall, at a distance from the gate, she was enabled to let them down by a cord from one of the windows, in the very same manner as that in which

ESCAPE FROM A WINDOW

Paul made his escape from Damascus. (2 Cor. xi. 33). They made their way to the wild mountains which border the plain of Jericho, as Rahab had advised; and when the pursuit after them had cooled, they returned to the camp. They felt they had discharged their mission; for the intelligence they brought as to the alarm of the Canaanites was in the highest degree encouraging to the people.

THE PASSAGE

Joshua 3

DURING great part of the year the waters of the Jordan are so low, that the river is fordable in many places. But in spring and early summer, or in "all the time of harvest," the river is in flood. It then "overflows all its banks," and is a strong and rapid stream. It had probably been supposed by the Israelites themselves, and expected by their enemies, that the host would ford the river when the stream was low. This operation might, we believe, have been practicable, though certainly not very convenient to a large and encumbered host; and might have held out to the Canaanites the hope of an advantage in meeting them on the other side. Nevertheless, we see that in taking a course which necessitated the passage of the Jordan, the same consequences were not involved as when they took a step

ANCIENT BRIDGE OVER THE JORDAN

which left them no other way of progress or escape than the passage by miracle through the depths of the Red Sea. The step was not at all inexplicable, or even strange, in this instance. They might either wait till the river fell, or, as the whole country along the eastern bank of the stream was by this time in their possession, they might march northward, and either cross the

lessened stream at the spot where, being in the common and ancient caravan track, there was probably a bridge, as now; or by a still farther progress, they might pass towards the source, where the river, there a brook, offers no obstacle even at the time of flood. All the indications must have seemed to the Canaanite in favour of the former alternative, for the Israelites evinced no sign of moving northward; and besides, it would have been foolish to undertake a long and toilsome march to attain an object which might in a few weeks be realized by remaining where they were. If we inquire into the reason why the course of proceeding northward to a point of the river always fordable was not taken, the answer is, that it was intended, in the divine wisdom, that their entrance into the promised land should be effected in such a manner as essentially to promote the object in view. It was also designed that the southern part of the country should be first subdued. The same reasons, in addition to these, which prevented them from being allowed to enter the land by the southern frontier, were still more cogent against their entrance on the north.

The Canaanites thus, no doubt, felt secure by the intervention of the full stream of the Jordan, from any immediate incursion of the Israelites. There was, meanwhile, a solemn pause. The doomed nations on the one side, and the commissioned exterminators on the other, were separated by an interval, impassable for the present, which scarcely exceeded that of a wide street.

But one morning a strange movement is observed in the Hebrew camp. The tents are struck—the tabernacle is taken down and packed up for removal—the standards advance—and the tribes dispose themselves in their usual marching order. This must have been altogether unintelligible to the people on the other side. Do the Israelites, after all, mean to take the northern route?

May they not have been ordered to go round the Dead Sea, and enter the land on the south? Perhaps their hearts fail them—perhaps they have heard of some mighty host coming down from the north, and they are retiring once more into the desert, which has been so long their home. Who knows but that they may have got some news from Egypt which encourages them to think that they have the chance of a better home in that country than Canaan offers? Any cause, any possible course, might be imagined by those who witnessed the movement, except the truth. But the truth soon appeared. "The ark of the covenant of the Lord of the whole earth," borne by the priests, is seen moving down in solemn state towards the river, followed at a becoming distance by the vanguard of the Hebrew host. What will they do? Is it some great lustration of the people, some solemn baptism, about to be performed upon the river's brink? No. The priests, bearing their holy burden, march on, without perceptible shrinking of the flesh, without start or pause—into the river. But, lo! no sooner does the first foot touch the stream than the waters part—they stop in full career—and a way is opened for the Lord's people to pass through! The ark moves on, and rests in the mid-channel, and there stands between the heaped-up waters and the people, who, strong in faith, pass on below without halt or fear.

From the description, it would seem that the waters below the point at which the priests' feet touched the stream, ran off to the Dead Sea, while those above stood still—waited, until the Israelites passed over. When all were safe on the other side, the priests also, with the ark, went up out of the channel, and instantly, as they came out from it, the imprisoned waters, like a strong steed relieved from the restraining hold of a masterhand, bounded forward in their course, and rushed in a mighty torrent to the sea.

This seems to us even a more signal miracle than the passage of the Red Sea; and it appears as if expressly framed not only to effect its own objects, but to relieve the other from all naturalistic interpretations. In connection with the Red Sea passage, we hear travellers and scholars talk learnedly about east winds, and tides, and shallows, so that, whether intentionally or not, the fact, as a demonstration of divine power, is explained away or attenuated. But nothing of this is possible in the case of the pas-

sage of the Jordan. The fact must be taken as it stands. It was a miracle, or it was nothing. There has not been, and there cannot be, any explanation of it on natural grounds. And if, therefore, men are obliged to admit this, it becomes scarcely worth their while to tamper with the Red Sea miracle, unless they would deny the authority of the narrative altogether.

But what was the use of this miracle? As it seems that the Hebrews could have entered the land without crossing the Jordan at all; and as, a little earlier or a little later in the season, or somewhere higher up, they could have crossed the Jordan without a miracle, what need was there for this gratuitous display of that divine power which is said to be never vainly nor idly exerted? We have not far to seek for an answer. In the first verse of the fifth chapter, the reason for the miracle is shown in the result which is produced: "And it came to pass, when all the kings of the Amorites, which were on the side of Jordan westward, and all the kings of the Canaanites, which were by the sea, heard that the Lord had dried up the waters of Jordan from before the children of Israel, until we were passed over, that their heart melted; neither was there spirit in them any more, because of the children of Israel." To produce this impression was, beyond question, the primary object of the miracle. We can ourselves, in some measure, judge of the importance of this impression being made upon the minds of the people with whom the Israelites were about to commence a terrible warfare; but any military man will be able to tell us, with great intensity of conviction, that for the purposes of the war, such an impression upon the mind of any enemy, however produced, is equal in value to a succession of victories; for it is seldom until an enemy has been repeatedly beaten, that he can be brought into that state of enfeebling discouragement which this verse describes.

A brief description of the Jordan will illustrate the narrative of the miraculous passage of that river by the Israelites. The most remarkable feature of the Jordan is, that throughout nearly its entire course it is below the level of the sea. Its valley is a huge fissure in the earth's crust, which has at the lake of Galilee a depth of about 700, and at the Dead Sea 1,300 feet below the Mediterranean. The section of the river lying between these two lakes is the Jordan of Scripture. The valley through which it flows is a long low plain, running in a straight line from north to south, between steep mountain ridges; the eastern ridge rising fully 5,000 feet above the river's bed, and the western about 3,000. The width of the plain at its northern end is six miles; but it gradually expands to twelve at Jericho.

Down the centre of the plain winds a ravine varying from an eighth of a mile to half a mile in breadth, and from 40 to 150 feet in depth. Through this the Jordan runs in a tortuous course. The river has thus two distinct lines of banks: the lower confining the stream, and from five to ten feet high; the upper, at a distance from the channel, forming the sides of the ravine. The river averages about forty yards in breadth. The current is very rapid; and though the depth is not great, the fords are few and difficult. In fact, there is not a single point at which such a host as the Israelites could have passed with ease, or even safety, at any season of the year.

Near the Dead Sea the plain of the Jordan attains its greatest breadth. The mountain ranges on each side are higher, more rugged, and more desolate. The river winds through its centre between two sets of banks. The lower banks which usually confine the water are soft clay, fringed with jungles of canes, willows, and tamarisks. Beyond these lie strips of meadow, dotted with tamarisk shrubs, and shut in by the high white banks of the ravine.

It was harvest time—the beginning of April—when the Israelites crossed. The rain was still falling in the mountains, and the snows of Hermon were melting, so that the river was made to "overflow all its banks," or, as the Hebrew signifies, it was *full up to all its banks*—that is, not merely up to the banks of the stream itself, but up to the banks of the ravine; covering wholly or partly the low strips of meadow on each side, and thus rendering the fords impassable. The opening of a passage through the Jordan at such a season was a stupendous miracle, well calculated to strike terror into the hearts of the Canaanites. Had it been late in summer, it might have been thought that natural causes operated; but in harvest the finger of God was manifest to all.

P.

HEBREW RIGHT TO CANAAN
WHAT IT WAS NOT

SOME of our readers have been tired by the questions—What right had the Israelites to Canaan, a country already occupied? What right had they to disturb the inhabitants in the peaceable possession of it? What right to wage a war of extermination against nations who had never given them any offence? These questions are in certain points of view difficult. We have, however, in these Daily Readings, rather sought than evaded difficult questions, in the wish to put the reader in possession of the best way of disposing of them; and therefore we turn to the questions now asked, notwithstanding the difficulties which they appear to present. It will probably be found that these difficulties lie not so much in the questions themselves, as in the considerations with which they have become invested.

Without attempting to state all the explanations which have been offered—for the purpose, as it seems to us, of turning the edge of the real difficulties—we can only notice the two or three which have acquired most prevalency, and in one or other of which inquirers have been generally advised to rest.

It is urged by many, that in point of fact the Israelites were *not* commanded to exterminate the Canaanites without exception. They were, on the contrary, it is said, to offer terms of peace to all the Canaanitish cities, and only in the event of the rejection of this offer were the inhabitants to be destroyed. Whatever cities accepted the proposals became the vassals of Israel; a lot which, according to the mild laws of servitude among that people, was by no means intolerable. In proof of the correctness of this opinion, we are referred to Deut. xx. 10-14.[1] It is very singular that so pleasant a theory should have been built upon this passage; for we have only to read on to find its incorrectness, and to see that this was the law for foreign warfare, that is, for warfare with countries not within the limits of Canaan, and therefore not included among the doomed nations: "Thus shalt thou do unto all the cities which are *very far off from thee*, which are not of the cities of these nations;" that is, of the very nations the treatment of which by the Israelites is now under question. And if this does not suffice, let us read on: "But of the cities of these people, which the Lord thy God

[1] "When thou comest nigh unto a city to fight against it, then proclaim peace unto it. And it shall be, if it make thee answer of peace, and open unto thee, then it shall be, that all the people that is found therein shall be tributaries unto thee, and they shall serve thee. And if it will make no peace with thee, but will make war against thee, then thou shalt besiege it: And when the Lord thy God hath delivered it into thine hands, thou shalt smite every male thereof with the edge of the sword: But the women, and the little ones, and the cattle, and all that is in the city, even all the spoil thereof, shalt thou take unto thyself: and thou shalt eat the spoil of thine enemies, which the Lord thy God hath given thee."

hath given thee for an inheritance, thou shalt save alive nothing that breatheth; but thou shalt utterly destroy them, as the Lord thy God hath commanded thee."[1] One would think that nothing could be plainer than this. But if we want further evidence, there is the case of the Gibeonites, who, under the pretence of coming from a far country, stole a peace from the Hebrews, knowing well that no peace would have been granted had they been known for Canaanites. And that theirs was no erroneous impression, is shown by the demeanour of the Israelites when the truth became known to them.[2]

There are other views which, while admitting the plain character of the war, as the Scripture describes it, deem it to require more justification than the word of God directly supplies. According to one of these views, Palestine was originally, and from time immemorial, a land of Hebrew shepherds; and the Israelites, who had never surrendered their rights, required it again of the Canaanites as unlawful possessors. Under this view, the Canaanites were not the original occupants, but coming up from the countries of the Red Sea, they gradually spread into Canaan, establishing commercial towns and factories, taking possession by degrees of the country, and superseding the former inhabitants. Who were they? This is not clearly stated. But the country is supposed to have been originally peopled by Eber or Heber, from beyond the Euphrates, from whom all the Hebrews, including the Israelites, derived their name,[3] and who held it in pastoral occupation. Abraham is regarded as having been his heir or representative, although his migration was of later date, not having taken place until the Canaanites had gained ground in the land. In this view, it is not without significance that it seems to be made a matter of complaint in Gen. xii. 6, that the Canaanites were then in the land—seemingly as if their encroachments had rendered the land too narrow for the flocks and herds of the patriarchs. Bearing in mind that, among other incidental corroborations, the land of Canaan is called, in Gen. xl. 15, "the land of the Hebrews," this view is entitled to much consideration. To still more attention is that modification of it entitled, which does not deny that the Canaanites originally settled in

this country, but urges that they had not taken possession of the whole. The pasture lands lay open for those who wished to appropriate them. This was done by the ancestors of the Israelites. During their sojourn in Egypt, the Canaanites unlawfully occupied them. After leaving Egypt, the Israelites again asserted their claims; and since the Canaanites would not acknowledge them, the Israelites took possession of part of the country by virtue of their ancient occupancy of it, and of the other part by right of conquest. Now, this matter of territorial and pastoral right in the East is one of which we may claim to know something; and we think that some have gone too far in denying that the Hebrews could acquire any rights of the kind here demanded for them. A pastoral tribe has a right to appropriate to its own exclusive use lands not occupied by any other pastoral tribe which has digged wells therein; nor by any settled people by whom it has within any recent period been put under cultivation. The feeling is, that no one has a right to lands which he cannot use. We have no doubt, therefore, that the Israelites established a right to the possession of certain unoccupied lands in Canaan, in which they not only digged wells, but grew corn and planted trees, as at Beersheba. Those who oppose this view, by urging that the Hebrews *purchased* sepulchres and lands of the Canaanites for money, and therefore had no right but to lands thus acquired and secured, do greatly err. The lands thus bought were such as other persons before them had appropriated, and to which, therefore, they could only by purchase acquire a legal and permanent right. But again, the Eastern territorial law does not recognize the right of any persons to lands acquired in the way indicated longer than they are able to keep them in occupancy. Since the land is God's gift to man and beast, they would count it sinful to exclude it from use, and suffer it to lie idle and unappropriated, out of regard to the abstract and conventional rights of parties who, though they were the first to take possession, have been away one, two, or three centuries. Whatever pastoral, or even agricultural, rights they had acquired, would long ago have been foreclosed by their absence. If they had themselves laid any stress upon such rights, we should have heard of it. But, indeed, it were absurd to think of three millions of people claiming the right to settle in the small pasture

---

[1] Deuteronomy 20:15-17.   [2] Joshua 9:24.
[3] See Vol. 1, pp. 346-349.

grounds which, some generations back, had sufficed for as many hundreds. Such a claim would simply have been a ridiculous and insulting pretext for conquest. But no such claim was urged by the Israelites. They took far higher ground.

HEBREW RIGHT TO CANAAN
WHAT IT WAS

ALTHOUGH it is not to be denied that some of the considerations advanced yesterday, as urged by various parties to prove the human claims of the Israelites to the land of Canaan, would be of considerable weight in the absence of any other grounds advanced in the sacred books, they lose all their importance in the presence of the repeated and clear declarations in Scripture of the point of view in which the whole matter is to be regarded. We may or may not like the view thus stated. That is not the question. Is any clear ground of claim stated or not? That is the real question. If any ground be stated, that and no other is the view which we are bound to adopt and to defend. To set aside the view presented to the Israelites themselves, and on which they acted, in order to seek out others not once presented to *their* minds, nor once alluded to in Scripture, may be very ingenious, very satisfactory to our own understandings, but is, in fact, tantamount to a denial, in so far as this matter is concerned, of the truth and authority of the record which is the only source of our information.

We therefore recur to the old and authentic belief in this matter, seeing that it rests entirely on the scriptural declarations. It is certainly none the worse for being the received opinion of the church from the most ancient times; whereas the others are but the speculations of a few learned individuals.

In the first place, be it observed, that the possession of Canaan by the Israelites is constantly set forth as a free gift of the divine favour, by which all ideas of human right are completely excluded. This is clearly stated in the original promise to Abraham, made immediately upon his entering the land, and before any human rights could have been acquired by

him: "Unto thy seed will I give this land;[1] and again, soon after, "Lift up now thine eyes, and look from the place where thou art, northward, and southward, and eastward, and westward; for all the land which thou seest, to thee will I give it, and to thy seed for ever."[2] And that this was not limited to the land in actual occupation by his flocks and herds, to which alone Abraham could acquire any kind of human right, is shown by what immediately follows: "Arise, walk through the land, in the length of it, and in the breadth of it; for I will give it unto thee."[3] These passages appear so conclusive in showing that the land was entirely the free and absolute gift from God to His people, of that to which they had no sort of human claim, that it seems needless to cite the numerous passages in the Pentateuch by which that view is corroborated. In fact, no other view is presented. The uniform tenor not only of the Pentateuch, but of the whole Scripture, is in conformity with these original intimations.

But while, on the one hand, the donation of this land to the Israelites was an act of the Lord's free favour, the denial of it to the Canaanites was no less an act of His retributive justice —of such justice as it behoved the moral Governor of the world to administer against a people laden with iniquity. Gen. xv. 13-16 is a passage which proves this clearly.[4] Abraham is there informed that, before his posterity would receive that goodly heritage, a long period of four hundred years must elapse, great part of which would be spent by them under oppression, in a land which was not theirs. Eventually they should be brought forth with great substance; and in the "fourth generation[5] they shall come hither again." Why is their return so long deferred? Why not until the fourth generation? Hear the reason:

[1] Genesis 12:7.   [2] Genesis 13:14,15.
[3] Genesis 13:17.
[4] "And He said unto Abram, Know of a surety that thy seed shall be a stranger in a land that is not theirs, and shall serve them; and they shall afflict them four hundred years: And also that nation whom they shall serve will I judge; and afterward shall they come out with great substance. And thou shalt go to thy fathers in peace; thou shalt be buried in a good old age. But in the fourth generation they shall come hither again: for the iniquity of the Amorites is not yet full."
[5] This period is variously computed. Most probably it denotes the fourth generation from the entrance of the Israelites into Egypt.

"For the iniquity of the Amorites[1] is not yet full."

These last words are important for more than one reason. First, they exclude all human right of the Hebrews to Palestine; for if such a right had existed, why, for its being enforced, should the filling up of the iniquity of the Amorites be required? Secondly, if the cause why Abraham's descendants were not now, but after a long interval, to obtain possession of the promised land, was, that the iniquity of the Amorites was not yet full, it is thereby equally intimated that this filling up of their iniquity would justify, if not demand, the divine judgment, which under existing circumstances would have been unjust—in the same way as God, before He destroyed Sodom and Gomorrah by His immediate decree, first of all permitted the abandoned depravity of the inhabitants most notoriously to manifest itself.

When the time was fully come, the Canaanites became a doomed people—doomed to expulsion or extermination by the Israelites, to whom was committed the sword of judgment, and who were the destined inheritors of the land of which the Canaanites had by that time proved themselves unworthy. This solemn doom is expressed in the Hebrew by a peculiar word (CHEREM), which is always applied to such devotement to destruction in vindication of the divine justice; and this is the term constantly applied to the Canaanites, as to a people who, by their enormities, had dishonoured the moral government of God, and were therefore to be constrained, by the judgment inflicted upon them, to glorify that government, and thereby to set forth the great truth, that there is a pure and holy Ruler of the nations.

Then, again, the Israelites, favoured as they were for their fathers' sake, were apprised that even they held the land by no other tenure than that which the Canaanites were to be destroyed for infringing. Over and over again were they warned, that if they fell into the same dreadful transgressions for which the Canaanites had been cast out, they would subject themselves to the same doom—be like them destroyed—like them cast out of the good land which they had defiled. We are not left altogether in the dark as to the nature of the abominations which pervaded the land, and which cried to God to show Himself as one abhorring iniquity, and to prove that the world was not left fatherless of His care. In one place, the sacred text, after enumerating various cases of unchastity and impiety of the vilest kind, goes on to say, "Defile not yourselves in any of these things, for in all these things the nations are defiled which I cast out before you. And the land is defiled; therefore I do visit the iniquity of the land upon it, and the land itself vomiteth out her inhabitants."[1] In another place, the Israelites are solemnly warned against imitating the conduct of their predecessors, lest they incur the same penalties: Take heed to thyself that thou be not snared by following them. Thou shalt not do so unto the Lord thy God; for EVERY ABOMINATION TO THE LORD WHICH HE HATETH have they done unto their gods; for even their sons and their daughters have they burnt in the fire to their gods."[2] What more emphatic testimony can be required than this?

This is the view of the case set forth in the Scripture, and the grounds on which it rests appear sufficient and satisfactory in themselves, although we are not prepared to affirm that there may not have been other reasons with which the Israelites were not made acquainted. But if those produced are sufficient, there is no need to seek for any more. It seems to us that the most serious objection to this view of the case, lies in the alleged danger that a nation should take upon itself to judge of another, and act towards it as the Israelites did to the Canaanites. But there is no such danger. The Israelites did not act upon their own judgment, but upon the distinct commission which they received, and which was attested by the miracles which attended their career. The passage through the Red Sea and through the Jordan,—the miraculous overthrow of the walls of the city of Jericho, the first to which they laid siege,—the hailstones at Gibeon, which, without touching the Israelites, slew more of their enemies than the sword,—and the remarkable phenomenon in the heavens, likened to the standing still of the sun and the moon,—were all so many proofs of their commission, and of the authority by which they acted. That authority and commission were attested by the belief of the very enemies against whom they warred, and who were very far from thinking that they

---

[1] That is, of the Canaanites generally—one of the principal nations being put for the whole, to avoid a long enumeration.

[1] Leviticus 18:24,25.　　[2] Deuteronomy 12:30,31.

had mistaken a fancy of their own for a divine commission. They found it all too real.[1]

On the point discussed in the lessons of to-day and yesterday, we should be careful to take the high scriptural ground, and never to deviate from it. To indulge in theories, or to suppose or invent other reasons for God's actions than those set forth in His Word, is not only vain but it is dangerous. By extending unduly our lines of defence, we weaken them, and thereby imperil the great citadel of truth.

God is Sovereign of the universe. He has a right to dispose of any part of it as He will. God is also infinitely just. He governs His kingdom in strictest accordance with justice. To punish the guilty is a just act. The Canaanites were guilty. By a long continued course of rebellion and abominable crime, they had become not only altogether corrupt, but absolutely hopeless. Their iniquity became full. Then God drove them out to make room for His own people.

A great truth is sometimes either forgotten or ignored by the sentimental school of philosophers, that "the punishment of the wicked is as indispensable a part of moral government as the reward of the good." The remarks of Kalisch on this subject are admirable: "If we survey the biblical system with regard to this subject, we are surprised by its grandeur and comprehensiveness. The Canaanites themselves were not the original inhabitants of the land; they settled there after having destroyed most of the earlier tribes—the Rephaim, the Emim, the Anakim, and others. They had therefore had a personal experience of how God punishes wantonness and impiety; but they were not warned by it: they gradually fell into the same vices and crimes; and they were doomed to suffer the same extreme judgment. But whilst the measure of their iniquity was filling, God reared in a foreign land the future occupants of their abodes: the degeneracy of the Canaanites kept pace with the increase and development of the Israelites. However great and awful the former might have been, the God of mercy protracted and delayed long the day of judgment; and however glorious Abraham's merit was, on account of which his descendants were destined to possess Canaan, the God of justice did not accelerate their deliverance from the oppression in Egypt, which they had deserved by their faithlessness. The Israelites, regenerated by their trials in the desert, were the instruments of chastisement to the Canaanites; as, later, the Assyrians and Babylonians, though unconscious of their office and mission, were used as the rod of destruction against the Israelites. This is the only view in which the occupation of Palestine by the Hebrews can be regarded according to the biblical allusions."[2]

P.

[1] On the subject of this Day, there is a large and able article by Hengstenberg, excellently translated in a volume of his *Dissertations on the Pentateuch*, by Mr. J. E. Ryland of Northampton. This Dissertation has to a considerable extent formed the framework of our consideration of the matter.

[2] On Genesis 15:16.

OLD CORN

Joshua 5

IT is a very remarkable circumstance, that during all the sojourn of the Israelites in the wilderness, two of the prominent institutions of their law were entirely neglected. These were the rite of circumcision and the ordinance of the passover. The former had, it seems, been entirely dispensed with, perhaps in accommodation to their pilgrim state; and the latter had been observed twice only since its institution—once in Egypt, and once in Sinai. Now, however, that they had entered the Promised Land, and were no longer in the pilgrim state, the reasons which had prevented the celebration of these observances, whatever they were, no longer existed; and their first care, on establishing the camp at Gilgal, was to impress themselves with the sign of the covenant by circumcision. Then followed the passover, celebrated, no doubt, with peculiar solemnity, from its being a new observance to most of the existing generation, and from its following so immediately the rite of the covenant.

It will be remembered, that the time when the Jordan overflowed its banks was the time of harvest; and it was at this time that the river had been crossed. Indeed, the passover corresponded with the commencement of the barley harvest; and on "the morrow after the Sabbath" they were required (Lev. xxiii. 10, 11) to wave a sheaf of the first-fruits before the Lord as an offering, after which they were allowed to gather in and use the rest. Now, in conformity with this, we are told that "they did eat of the old corn of the land on the morrow after the passover, unleavened cakes and parched corn on the self-same day." It was necessary to eat unleavened bread during the passover; and in this case it was made of the old corn of the land—such, no doubt, as had been found stored up in the defenceless villages from which the inhabitants had fled when the Hebrew host appeared in the plain. The parched corn was corn of the new harvest, burnt in the ear, the fire at the same time consuming those parts that cannot be eaten, and parching the edible grain. This was like the "parched corn" which Boaz handed to Ruth at the meal eaten in the harvest field. Corn thus parched is still much relished in Palestine, and is regarded as something of a delicacy peculiar to that season of the year; for it is new corn only that is parched. This must have been an interesting day to the Israelites; for probably more

HARVEST IN PALESTINE

than two-thirds of the people—that is, all not above forty years of age—had never eaten bread before in all their lives. It is true they had manna, and the manna was probably better than bread; but bread was a change, and therefore delightful to them.

On the next morning, the manna, which had not (except on the Sabbaths) ceased a single day to fall for forty years, was no more found around the camp. This discontinuance of the supply by which the people had been so long sustained, no less marks the signal providence of God, than the original grant of it, and its long continuance. It came not one day before it was needed, and it was continued not one day longer than was really required by the wants of the people. This strikingly showed the Lord's care, and evinced the miraculous nature of the supply. Such indications as this of the Lord's presence and power, were little less than visible manifestations of Deity.

The life of the believer does not lack similar experiences. In tracing his life back through its varied scenes, how plainly can he see that, however his heart may at times have failed him, his Lord has, under all circumstances, cared for him, even in the matters which belong to his daily bread. He can see that one resource has not failed him until another has been ready to open.

Sometimes he has been supplied as by miracle; help was raised up for him, he knew not how, except that it was the Lord's doing, and it was marvellous in his eyes. But then, as soon as he had learned the great lesson of child-like dependence upon his Father's care, and had realized the assurance contained in the words, "I will never leave thee, nor forsake thee," the extraordinary sources ceased, and ordinary ones, sufficient for all his wants, were opened. Oh, what tranquillity of mind, what blessedness of rest, may be realized—what slavish fears, what harassing anxieties, may be avoided—if we will only let such experience have its perfect work, by inducing us to cast all our care upon Him who careth for us, leaving Him to determine what we shall lose and what retain, in the firm conviction that He will decide well for us—better for us, than we, who often know not what we ask, and who can never determine with certainty what may be eventually good for us, could decide for ourselves.

Again, "the manna ceased on the morrow after they had eaten of the old corn of the land; neither did the children of Israel eat manna any more; but they did eat of the fruit of the land of Canaan that year." Thus extraordinary resources fail, when the common course of God's providence becomes equal to the necessities of His church. To have continued both together—to have had the old store of natural food and the manna—would have been a needless profusion of the divine bounty, a waste of goodness and power such as we do not discover in the ordinary operations of the Lord's providence. Had the manna been in the first instance bestowed in the midst of plenty, it would have been viewed as no very striking interposition of Providence, nor would it have been very thankfully received; so now, had it been continued amid the fulness of Canaan, it would have grown into disesteem, and have been regarded rather as an ordinary production of nature, than as a special display of the riches of the divine goodness. If the people wantonly disparaged the manna, even in the time of their necessity, when they had no other food; if even then what was easily obtained was lightly prized—how much more would they have contemned it in a land flowing with milk and honey? God will not be too prodigal of His favours; He will not so lavishly expend them as to allow them to be scorned as superfluous things. The manna ceased, never to be renewed again. It was no longer needed. To have continued the supply, or even to have afforded it in the exigencies of occasional scarcity, would have bred indolent and luxurious habits in the people. It would have been ruinous to their industry and to the cultivation of the ground; for men will not adequately labour in cultivating the soil, when it is not necessary to their subsistence and their safety. What can no longer serve the purpose of its bestowment, may well be dispensed with. The Lord best knows how long and in what measure His supplies will be needed; and will regulate His dispensations accordingly. Many things—good things—have ceased, never to be renewed to us; but we have not found that there has been in this case any reason to complain. We have been no losers. Other blessings have been given in the place of those taken away, which have rendered their continuance or renewal needless. It may be that the things taken from us—the things of our first love, the things of our glowing youth, the things of our golden prime—were sweeter than those that remain to us, and we regret their loss. But if we consider closely, we shall find that, although these things were proper and becoming in those former states, and although we had blessings then which we have not now, yet we have others now that we had not then; and that we now enjoy, in ripened fruits and corn of old store, advantages which become the condition to which we have attained, and which strengthen our souls and fit us for usefulness as well, perhaps better, than the sweet and tender manna with which we were nourished when the dews of our youth were fresh upon us.

The question may be asked, How did the Israelites, who amounted to at least two millions, obtain sufficient corn in the comparatively narrow valley of the Jordan to supply their wants? It will be remembered that they had just returned from the conquest of Moab, Gilead, and Bashan, —a territory equal in extent to the land of Canaan west of the Jordan, and much richer. Bashan is to this day the granary of a large section of Palestine. The people of the East have always been accustomed to store away their grain, after each harvest, in immense subterranean magazines. These the Israelites no doubt opened, and appropriated their contents. The oxen, asses, and other beasts of burden, they had taken from the Midianites, with those captured during the campaign against Sihon and Og, afforded sufficient and ready means of transport. In fact, the whole stores of the very richest section of the country were at once opened up to the Lord's people.

P.

FALL OF JERICHO

Joshua 6

THE Israelites commenced their military operations in Canaan in a very extraordinary manner. No city was ever besieged or conquered after the mode which they were in this instance directed to adopt. But there were reasons. It was highly important that the Israelites should succeed in this enterprise, to them a difficult one, because their failure would embolden the enemy and discourage themselves; and yet, on the other hand, there was great danger that, in the event of success in the use of ordinary means, their deeply seated presumption might induce them to cry, in total forgetfulness of the Lord of hosts, "Our sword, and the might of our arm, have gotten us the victory." It was therefore the Lord's purpose to ensure to them the victory, and yet to do this in such a manner as should exclude all high notions, and leave to Himself the undivided glory. The whole army was to march around the city once daily for six days together. They were to be preceded by the ark, before which were to march seven priests, bearing "seven trumpets of rams' horns." These trumpets were the same that were used in the sacerdotal services, and particularly in proclaiming the jubilee. It has been disputed whether they were made of the horns of rams, or merely in the shape of such horns. In favour of the latter opinion it may be remarked, that with us a well known musical instrument of brass is called a "horn," from its shape; and another "a serpent," for the same reason. One reason urged for supposing this to have been the case is, that no one ever heard of trumpets made of rams' horns, which seem unsuited for the production of musical sounds. But this is somewhat hastily affirmed. We cannot indeed call to mind an instance of a ram's horn trumpet, but we can of a goat's; and in Syria, as well as in Greece, the horns of the common breeds of rams and goats are very similar. Dr. E. D. Clarke relates that, when at Corinth, he saw "an Arcadian pipe, on which a shepherd was playing in the streets. It was perfectly Pandean, consisting simply of *a goat's horn*, with five holes for the fingers, and a small aperture at the end for the mouth. It was extremely difficult to produce any sound whatever from this small instrument; but the shepherd made the air resound with its shrill notes." It is probable that instruments of this sort were at first the horns of animals, and retained the original names when they came to be made of metal in the same shape.

Every day the Israelites, having accomplished their march, returned to the camp without any apparent result from their strange procedure, which must have been most amazing to the people of the beleagured city. We do not, with some, think that the proceeding was likely to awaken their mirth; it is more likely that it made a solemn impression upon their minds, as the host, preceded by that which was regarded with awe as the symbol of the presence of the God of Israel, marched firmly on, silent, save the stately tramp of their numerous feet, and the sound from the sacred trumpets. The people of Jericho had seen and heard too much already of the great results connected with the seemingly strange proceedings of the Israelites, to find much diversion in a measure which, whatever its exact meaning might prove, was clearly levelled against their city.

But why this delay? The six days' operations, so far as can be seen, contributed nothing to the result, which might as well have been accomplished the first day. So men judge. So, perhaps, many among the Israelites themselves judged; for men, at least men in large bodies, are ever prone to precipitate measures; but God moves deliberately, and He would have His people abide in patient faith His time. "He that believeth shall not make haste." In the present case, the time seems to have been lengthened out to afford opportunity for a continual exercise of the faith and patience of the people, and also to impress the more deeply upon both the besieged and the besiegers, the supernatural power by which the result was to be accomplished. The delay also allowed time for the news of this extraordinary proceeding to spread through all the country around; and the result was no doubt watched for with intense solicitude and curiosity by the princes of Canaan, upon whom it must have made a deep impression when it actually occurred.

The seventh day was the great day. On that day the city was compassed not once, but seven times; and on the completion of the seventh circuit, the priests blew a long blast, on hearing which the army, as previously instructed, raised a mighty shout, and the wall of the city fell down flat, affording free and open access to the besiegers.

THE WALLS OF JERICHO FALL DOWN

The faith of the people was throughout rigorously tried and exercised in this matter, not only in the daily march and by the delay, but in their implicit obedience to the directions they received, the precise object of which they do not appear to have then seen. For, even as the people do not seem to have been informed how they were to cross the Jordan until they came to the river's brink, so now Joshua seems to have forborne disclosing to them how they were to become masters of the city until they had compassed it six times, or until he gave the final command, "Shout; for the Lord hath given you the city." Their implicit obedience, therefore, in this case, is worthy of all commendation, and gives us a favourable impression of the spirit by which the new generation was animated. Indeed, the author of the Epistle to the Hebrews bears distinct and strong testimony on this subject: "By faith the walls of Jericho fell down, after they had been compassed about seven days," (Heb. xi. 30.)

The fact that the Hebrew host made the circuit of the city seven times on the seventh day, proves that the town could not have been very large. It proves also that the whole host could not, as some have fancied, have been engaged in this operation. As the fighting men alone amounted to 600,000, and the mass of the people could not well have been less than two millions more, it is obviously impossible that this could have been the case. There can be little doubt that only a select body of men, sufficient for the occasion, was employed. This was the most obvious course of proceeding; and, besides, it was this method which was followed in other cases, as in the wars with the Amalekites and the Midianites, and subsequently in the siege of Ai. It was therefore probably followed in all other cases, although the fact is not particularly mentioned. Indeed, in the subsequent operations, it appears clear that the great body of the people remained encamped at Gilgal, until some progress had been made in the conquest of the country, the men-at-arms serving in turns in the different expeditions. No occasion appears to have arisen on which they could all be employed at once.

It may be well to point out, that the siege of Jericho had commenced in due form before this remarkable course was taken. We are told that "Jericho was straitly shut up because of the children of Israel: none went out and none came in." In fact, they had commenced a blockade; and but that they were supernaturally helped, they would probably have wasted months before the town, until they had starved it into a surrender. This was the usual course of ancient sieges, and is still the common course in many parts of the East. Thus it is recorded, that when the Mahrattas intend to besiege a town, they generally encamp around the walls; and having by that means deprived the garrison of all external means of assistance, the besieging army waits with patience, sometimes for several years, until the garrison is starved into a capitulation.[1] From such protracted operations the Israelites could in this case scarcely have been spared by less than a miracle.

[1] Forbes's *Oriental Memoirs*, ii. 63.

THE NUMBER SEVEN

Joshua 6:3-6

THE most cursory reader cannot fail to be struck by the prevalence and continual recurrence of the number *seven* in the sacred Scriptures. It is very true that in many instances it is, as a number of completeness or perfection, used in an indefinite sense—an indeterminate number being expressed by a determinate one, just as we say *ten* or a *dozen*—but in the majority of instances the actual number of seven is expressed by it. Indeed, it may well be considered that the adoption of this number, in that indeterminate sense which is expressed by our phrase "a good many," as distinguished from a few on the one hand, and from a large number on the other, must have grown out of the frequency of its use in the determinate sense, and out of the ideas of perfection and completeness in this number in which that determinate use originated.

We find this remarkable regard for the number seven not among the Hebrews only, but among all ancient peoples. It pervades all ancient literature, and is found among all nations. It seems to us impossible that this universal regard for the number seven, evinced in every possible way, could have originated in other than primeval facts and ideas common to all the races of man. It seems to us that the one great fact in which all this originated is the work of creation in seven days—six days, so to speak, of labour, and the seventh of rest from completed work. The knowledge of this fact was once common to all mankind; and however it may have been eventually lost sight of among many of the nations into which they became divided, the institutions and ideas which the fact impressed while it was generally known would remain among these nations. This universal regard for the number must have existed before the races, which trace their common origin to Adam, were dispersed abroad. But it is difficult to understand how the knowledge of a fact anterior to and beyond the scope of human observation and experience, could of itself make this deep and abiding impression. We do not find it so. It is not the abstract knowledge of a great fact which establishes universal usages and makes ineffaceable impressions; but it is by iteration, by frequency, by the idea being kept continually before the mind. Although, therefore, we make no question that the peculiar distinction assigned by all nations to the number seven had its origin in the seventh day of completed creation, we are persuaded that this fact alone, without some institution which kept it constantly before the mind, and made it part of life's pulsation, could not have been operative to the extent we witness. Such an institution is the Sabbath—an institution designed to commemorate the creation, and abundantly adequate, but not more than adequate, by its recurrence at short intervals, to produce a regard, so diffused and permanent, for the number seven. This is to us one strong proof that this institution of the seventh day rest did from the earliest times exist, and was not, as some have supposed, a merely Jewish institution. If the seventh day Sabbath was observed from the time of man's creation, an observance which made so large a part in his life adequately accounts for all those phenomena in regard to the number seven which we witness. But if that institution had no existence, we are completely at a loss on the subject—we have nothing to say—nothing to conjecture.

Allowing, then, that the Sabbath originated in Paradise, the revival of the sabbatic institution among the Hebrews, and the distinctness with which the doctrine of creation was presented to their minds, after many other nations had lost sight of it, sufficiently explain the more prevalent regard for the number seven, and the familiar use of it, which we find among them. And this regard for that number was not among them a matter of mere habit—not a vain superstition; it was in many respects a matter of prescribed observance, with the apparent intention of strengthening the impression with regard to the creation which the sabbatic institution itself was framed to produce.

These remarks are suggested by the very remarkable manner in which the number seven is produced in the account of the siege of Jericho. The city was to be compassed on seven successive days, and on the seventh day seven times; and the procession was to be headed by seven priests, bearing the seven trumpets of rams' horns. The progress during the six days, and the twofold production of the number seven on the seventh day, when, on the completion of the seventh circuit, the work was accomplished,

seem to involve a very distinct reference to the period of creation, and thence to seven as the number of completion—of perfect consummation. Seven was, in fact, in some sort a sacred number, whence the solemnity of an oath is enhanced by connection therewith. Indeed, in the Hebrew language, as in the Sanscrit, the words for "an oath" and for "seven" are the same. In the former language SHEBA has that twofold meaning: hence the question, whether the name Beer-sheeba, where Abraham and Abimelech confirmed their covenant by a solemn oath, means "the well of the oath," or "the well of seven," or "seven wells." If in this remarkable instance we dispense with the allusion in the name to the number seven, that number is still present; for before the oath was uttered, Abraham set apart *seven* ewe lambs in so marked a manner as to attract the inquiries of the king, to whom the patriarch answered, "These seven ewe lambs shalt thou take at my hand, that they may be a witness unto me that I have digged this well." From this it appears that there was but one well, and seven lambs were set apart, not as one for each of seven wells, but because seven was a number appropriate to the solemnity of the occasion. We may therefore understand the name as the "well of the seven," that is, of the seven lambs which confirmed the oath, or the "well of the oath," from the oath itself, "because there they sware, both of them." It seems to us that the two sevens merge into each other, and that both are included in the single denomination. This connection is not peculiar to the Hebrews. We find it among the ancient Arabians, of whom we learn, that when men pledge their faith by oath to each other, blood drawn from an incision near the mid-finger of the contracting parties, was sprinkled upon seven stones, placed between them; and while this was done, they called upon their gods.[1] So, among the gifts with which Agamemnon proposed to seal a covenant of peace with Achilles, we find

"Seven tripods unsullied yet with fire;"[2]

and farther on, seven female captives, skilled in domestic arts, the latter especially intended as an atonement-offering to the wrathful hero, for *one* of whom he had been deprived. Even at the present day, the number seven is curiously regarded in Germany in matters of evi-

[1] Herodotus, iii. 8.　　　[2] *Iliad*, ix. 122.

dence.[1] Nor is the number unknown to ourselves in matters of land and legal obligation, as in the term of seven years for the duration of Parliaments, for coming of age (thrice seven), for leases of houses, for apprenticeships, for the transportation of criminals, and other matters of the kind.

In some of the sacrifices of Scripture we find also a prominent reference to the number seven. So Balaam erects seven altars, and offers a bullock and a ram on every altar.[2] So, when Asa reformed his kingdom and renewed the national covenant with God, seven hundred bullocks and seven thousand sheep were offered unto the Lord at Jerusalem;[3] and on a like occasion, King Hezekiah offered seven bullocks, seven rams, seven lambs, and seven he-goats, as a sin-offering for his kingdom.[4] Here the reference to a fixed idea respecting the special fitness of the number seven is remarkably produced. Apart from that, he might have chosen twelve, as representing the tribes comprising the house of Israel, or two, if he had regard only to his own kingdom. But the large ideas connected with the number seven, and the veneration in which that number was held, caused it to be regarded as the more appropriate and significant—the general fitness of that number overpowering the special fitness of twelve or of two.

We may trace this connection further. The altar itself, at its original establishment, was to be consecrated for seven days, to render it most holy.[5] A young animal was not held to be fit for sacrifice until it had remained seven days with its dam,[6] and so likewise the male child among the Hebrews was, after seven days—that is, on the eighth day, consecrated to the Lord by circumcision. These instances seem designed to indicate that nothing was considered perfect until the number seven had been completed. On the same basis we find that number involved in all the rites of uncleanness and purification. Whoever became defiled by various kinds of uncleanness, from the living or from the dead, or from leprosy and other diseases, was required to spend seven days before his state of ceremonial purity could be recovered. As seven days was the period of uncleanness for contact with a corpse,

so also was seven days the period of mourning for the dead.[1] The number seven was in other respects connected with the idea of purification; or rather, as we apprehend throughout, of six as a process, and seven as the consummation. So the Syrian leper was directed to dip seven times in Jordan; and it was no doubt at the seventh plunge that his leprosy departed from him.[2]

With uncleanness and with sorrow is connected the idea of punishment, and in this also the number seven is reproduced. So the memorable words of Lamech: "If Cain shall be avenged sevenfold, surely Lamech seventy and seven."[3] And it is scarcely needful to remind the reader of the seven days of impending judgment at the deluge;[4] of the seven Canaanitish nations consigned to the sword of Israel; of the death of David's child on the seventh day;[5] of the choice offered to him between seven years' famine and three days' pestilence;[6] of Pharoah's seven lean kine, and seven stunted ears, as signs of seven years of famine; of the Lord's delivering the Israelites into the hands of Midian seven years, in punishment for their sins;[7] of the seven "times" or years that passed over the Babylonish king in his bestial state.[8] Look also at the seven apocalyptic plagues;[9] the seven troubles named by Job;[10] and the seven things displeasing to God specified by the wise man.[11]

In fact, time and space fail us to point out the most remarkable alone of the allusions to this number which are contained in the Scriptures; much less can we enumerate the parallels which may be found among the ideas and usages of ancient and modern nations. We must, however, call to mind the seven years' release of bondmen under the law, and the seven times seven years' general release of mortgaged lands. Then there are the seven locks of Samson in which his great strength lay; the ten times seven years of the Babylonish exile; the seven branches of the golden candlestick; and in the Apocalypse, the seven golden candlesticks, the seven churches, the seven stars, the seven seals, the seven trumpets, the seven vials, the beast with seven heads, the seven mountains, the seven kings, and the seven angels.

[1] Grimm, *Rechtsalterthum*, pp. 807, 858.
[2] Numbers 23:29.   [3] 2 Chronicles 15:11.
[4] 2 Chronicles 29:21.   [5] Exodus 29:37;
[6] Exodus 22:30.   2 Chronicles 7:9.

[1] Genesis 50:10; 1 Samuel 31:13; 1 Chronicles 10:12
[2] 2 Kings 5:10,14.   [7] Judges 6:1.
[3] Genesis 4:24.   [8] Daniel 4:32.
[4] Genesis 7:4.   [9] Revelation 15:1, 21:9.
[5] 2 Samuel 12:18.   [10] Job 5:19.
[6] 2 Samuel 24:13.   [11] Proverbs 6:16-19.

THE RIVER JORDAN

THE prominence given to the Jordan in the sacred books, and the many stirring associations which connect themselves with that famous stream, awaken the desire to know something of its natural features. This desire we are now enabled to gratify with more advantage than at any former period; for the portion of the river which is alone of any Scriptural interest, and which until lately was known at only two or three points, has now been explored through its whole length. This portion extends between the Lake of Tiberias and the Dead Sea; and the explorer is Lieutenant Lynch of the American navy, who at his own request was sent by the Government with a party of picked men and with proper boats on this particular and very interesting service. This was in 1848. It is true that, in the preceding year, the whole of this portion of the river had been explored by one of our own officers, Lieutenant Molyneux, of H.M.S. "Spartan." But the river was too low to enable him to pass down in his boat from the one lake to the other, as the Americans did. It was carried partly on a camel, and this officer made his journey by land. Besides, even if he had passed down the stream in the boat, the public would not have reaped the benefit, for his untimely death prevented the results of his observations from being imparted to the world. The notes which he left were in cypher, and not therefore readily available; and their value is now, indeed, superseded by our acquaintance with the more complete exploration by Lieutenant Lynch and his companions.

The boats provided in America for this service were of metal—one of copper and the other of galvanized iron. These were mounted on trucks, and drawn by camels from the sea-shore across the country to the Lake of Tiberias. Here the only native boat upon that once frequented lake was taken into the service of the party, and the three proceeded together to thread the whole course of the lower Jordan to the Dead Sea.

There was, in fact, an important geographical problem to be solved. It had been ascertained that the Dead Sea was more than a thousand feet below the level of the Lake of Tiberias; and as the distance between the two was but sixty miles,

this would give a fall of about seventeen feet per mile—greater, it was then thought, than any river in the world exhibited. The Mohawk river in America was held to be the one of greatest fall, and that averages not more than four or five feet to the mile; but it is *now* known that the Sacramento in California has a fall of two thousand feet in twenty miles, or an average of one hundred feet to a mile. It was then, however, thought that such a fall as it seemed necessary to suppose in the case of the Jordan, from the difference of level between the two lakes which it connected, was without example; and as its course was presumed to be tolerably straight, and as it was not known to contain any rapids, an error in the calculation of the difference of level between the two lakes was more than suspected. This problem it was left for Lieutenant Lynch to set at rest. In the first place the river is full of rapids. The boats plunged down no less than twenty-seven very threatening ones, besides a great number of lesser magnitude; and then, although the direct distance does, as stated, not exceed sixty miles, the course of the river is made at least two hundred miles by the exceedingly tortuous course of its stream. This reduces the fall to not more than six feet in the mile, for which the numerous rapids in the river sufficiently account.

The descent by the river occupied no less than a week. So great were the difficulties caused by the rapids, that in two days not more than twelve miles were accomplished; and on the third day the wooden boat brought down from the Sea of Galilee was abandoned on account of her shattered condition. None but metal boats could have stood the severe work of this passage. It was, nevertheless, made at the time of flood—at the same season that the Israelites passed the river—which, although the most unfavourable without boats, should be the most favourable with them. In fact, it is stated that a few weeks earlier or later the passage down the river in boats would, as in the case of Lieutenant Molyneux, have been impracticable, from the want of sufficient water to carry them over the rapids.

The wide and deeply depressed plain or valley (Ghor) through which the river flows, is generally barren, treeless, and verdureless; and the mountains, or rather cliffs and slopes of the river uplands, present for the most part a wild and cheerless aspect. We have no generalized description of the river; but the following condensed account, which applies to the central part, may be taken as sufficiently indicating the general character of the whole:—

" The mountains towards the west rose up like islands from the sea, with the billows heaving at their bases. Deep-rooted in the plain, the bases of the mountains heaved the garment of earth away, and rose abruptly in naked pyramidal crags, each scar and fissure as plainly distinct as if we were within reach, and yet we were hours away; the laminations of their strata resembling the leaves of some gigantic volume, wherein is written by the hand of God the history of the changes He has wrought. The plain that sloped away from the bases of the hills was broken into ridges and multitudinous cone-like mounds,[1] resembling tumultuous water at the meeting of two adverse tides; and presented a wild and chequered tract of land, with spots of vegetation flourishing upon the frontiers of irreclaimable sterility. A low, pale, and yellow ridge of conical hills marked the termination of the higher terrace, beneath which swept gently this lower plain with a similar undulating surface,

THE RIVER JORDAN

half redeemed from barrenness by sparse verdure and thistle covered hillocks. Still lower was the valley of the Jordan—the sacred river! its banks fringed with perpetual verdure, winding in a

thousand graceful mazes; the pathway cheered with songs of birds, and its own clear voice of gushing minstrelsy; its course a bright line in this cheerless waste. Yet, beautiful as it is, it is only rendered so by contrast with the harsh calcined earth around." [1]

The waters of the Jordan are described as being clear and transparent, except in the immediate vicinity of the rapids and falls; and numerous fishes are seen in its deep and steady course. There is no trace of the lions and bears which once were found in the thicket; but the tracks of a leopard [2] were observed, and several wild boars were noticed.

On approaching the Dead Sea, the mountains on either hand recede, or rather, the cleft which forms the valley of the Jordan widens, having a broad plain traversed by the river, the portion on the west being called " the plain of Jericho," and that on the east the " plains of Moab." It was here that the Israelites crossed; and here, probably, that Jesus was baptized of John, when multitudes resorted to his baptism. In that belief, and in the persuasion that the same spot was the scene of both events, a pilgrim host comes yearly from Jerusalem at Easter to bathe in the Jordan. This part of the river has therefore been the most visited, and is the best known. The American expedition adds nothing to the information previously possessed respecting this portion of the river. The lofty mountains that bound the valley of the Jordan on both sides continue to bear the same essential characteristics which have been already indicated. Those to the west are the more precipitous; while the eastern, rising by a gradual slope, attain to nearly double their elevation. The plain generally is bare of

[1] This effect is seen in the engraving at p. 260, of these Daily Illustrations.

[1] Lynch's *Narrative of the Expedition to the Dead Sea and the Jordan*, pp. 232, 233.

[2] They say "a tiger," ignorant that Palestine never had tigers.

vegetation; but about a mile from the river a meagre sprinkling of shrubs begins to appear, giving the plain here much the appearance of the more verdant parts of the Arabian desert. Half a mile farther we descend to a lower stage of the plain, into what may be properly regarded as the outermost channel of the river. This is separated from the higher level by a bank of marl or clay, from thirty to forty feet in height, generally precipitous, but cut through in many places by channels, formed perhaps by the passage of the water that falls in the rainy season upon the upper plain. The plain along the base of this high bank is covered with mud, but clay predominates towards the river, on approaching which one is soon involved in a jungle of luxuriant shrubs and low tangled bushes. The immediate banks of the river are covered with a low luxuriant forest of willows, oleanders, tamarisks, and canes. The highest of the trees do not attain an elevation of more than thirty or forty feet, and few of them are more than five or six inches in diameter. The willow is held in high estimation by the pilgrims, who prefer it for staves, which they dip in the river, and preserve as sacred memorials. It is this part of the channel, this lower terrace, covered towards the stream with jungle, which is overflowed with water when the river is in flood. Hence the Scripture alludes to the wild beasts, driven from their retreats in the thickets by "the swellings" of the Jordan.[1] The inundation does not now, nor is there any probability that it ever did, extend beyond the wooded verge of this lower terrace. Just beyond this narrow fertile tract the ground rises several feet, and the region extending thence to the high bank is quite too elevated to allow of the supposition of its being inundated by the overflowing of the river. It exhibits no traces of such inundation; and although the river is usually visited at the season of flood in the spring, no traveller has ever seen the waters extend beyond the narrow verge already described. The language of the text, "Jordan overfloweth all his banks all the time of harvest,"[2] does not necessarily imply an inundation of greater extent than this.

In its proper channel, when the bed is full but not overflowed, the river is in this part from thirty-five to forty yards wide. The stream sweeps along with a rapid turbid current. The water is discoloured, and of a clayey hue, not

[1] Jeremiah 49:19.　　　[2] Joshua 3:15.

unlike that of the Nile, and although muddy, is pleasant to the taste. It has the appearance of being deep; but we do not know that the depth has been ascertained. Persons entering the stream are soon out of their depth, and are borne rapidly towards the Dead Sea by the current.

It will from these particulars be seen, that although only relatively and historically an important river, the Jordan still verifies abundantly all the statements made in reference to it by the sacred writers. It still "overfloweth all its banks in harvest;" and a miracle would be no less necessary now than in the days of Joshua to enable an immense multitude of men, women, and children, and flocks and herds, unprovided with boats, to pass it at that season.

Note.—For some additional information on the Jordan, see the Editor's note on pp. 475-476.

P.

The River Jordan has been fully traced from its sources down to the sea of Galilee by Mr. M'Gregor, in his famous canoe. Its three main original streams unite at the foot of a small mound named *Tell Sheikh Yusuf*, near Banias, at the foot of Hermon. We remember being struck with the scenery in that neighbourhood as resembling somewhat certain landscapes in South Wales, while buffaloes were standing knee deep in the water, at the hour of noon, like the cattle which in the same manner cool themselves on a summer's day in our northern clime. The river afterwards turns and twists, running swiftly between lofty banks, and then spreading out into wide lagoons, and afterwards dividing itself into six channels, till lost in "a tangled maze of bushes eight feet high," along which not even a reed raft can make its way. Through a mass of papyrus the stream struggles into Lake Huleh, "the waters of Merom." Then the river proceeds with a gentle current to the Bridges of Jacob's daughters, without any fall or cascade, and at length enters the Sea of Galilee.

The river between that sea and the Dead Sea was explored in 1847 by Lieutenant Molyneux, R.N., and in 1848 by Lieutenant Lynch, U.S.N. In 1868 Captain Warren, R.E., made a journey up the western banks, and in 1873-74 Lieutenant Conder surveyed the country for the Palestine Exploration Fund. The river takes a decided southerly course, but on its way meanders in countless little twists and bends, which greatly increase the distance. The Ghor, or valley, sinks lower and lower, shut in by the Judean and Samaritan hills on one side, and the mountains of Gilead on the other. Here and there are pleasant spots on the banks, especially at the ford near Jericho, with overhanging trees, familiar to all travellers who visit the Holy Land.

From the Hasbeya source to the Dead Sea the direct distance is 120 miles, increased by the windings 100 per cent. The Hasbeya source is 1,700 feet above the Mediterranean, and the Dead Sea is 1,300 feet below it.

S.

THE ACCURSED THING

Joshua 7

THE city of Jericho was decreed, even before it was taken, to be wholly an accursed thing, or rather a thing *devoted to destruction,* according to the explanation lately given[1] of the meaning of the Hebrew word CHEREM. Not only the city itself, but everything that it contained, was to be consumed—all, except the articles of precious metal, which could not well be destroyed, and the devotement of which to the Lord was therefore to take the form of an appropriation thereof to the service of the sanctuary.

It has seemed to some rather a severe exaction, that the soldiers should have been forbidden, under the severest penalties, from appropriating to themselves the least benefit from the spoil of this wealthy city. But there may be seen many reasons for it. The principal seems to have been to impress upon them in the most lively manner, the fact that the conquest of the city was not in any respect due to the power of their arms, and that therefore they had no right to any portion of the spoil. Nothing was so well calculated as this privation to remind them to whom alone this important conquest was due. It was also a prudential measure. On the one hand, it tried the obedience of the people—and, all things considered, it is certainly a wonderful instance of the religious and military discipline of the troops, that an order of this stringent nature was so well obeyed—while, on the other hand, it would have been inexpedient to allow the soldiers at the outset to glut themselves with the spoils of a rich city, whereby they would have been more disposed for luxury and idleness than for the severe labours which lay before them in the martial conquest of Canaan. The city had also been won without the exhausting toils or feats of valour which might seem to demand such recompense. It may be added, that it has been at all times usual in military operations to deal severely with the first town taken by storm, the garrison of which has held out to the last, in order to strike such a dread into the people as may facilitate further conquest, or induce submission in order to avoid a similar doom. Upon the whole, Jericho was to be regarded as the first-fruits of conquest, and

[1] See Vol. 1 pp. 478–480.

as such was to be offered up to the Lord as a burnt-offering.

Joshua meant that the city should stand in its ruined condition as a monument of this transaction. He therefore pronounced this solemn adjuration: "Cursed be the man before the Lord that riseth up and buildeth this city Jericho: he shall lay the foundation thereof in his first-born, and in his youngest son shall he set up the gates of it." No one was bold enough to defy this doom until the ungodly reign of king Ahab, when one Hiel of Bethel rebuilt the city; and in him that doom was accomplished. His eldest son died when he commenced the work by laying the foundation; other sons during the progress of the work; and the last of all, the youngest, perished when he completed his undertaking by setting up the gates. (1 Kings xvi. 34.) This course, of making a monument of a conquered and destroyed city or building, by solemnly interdicting the restoration thereof, has not a few parallels in ancient history. Thus, the Romans made a decree full of execration against any who should dare at any future time to rebuild Carthage,[1] which had been their rival in empire, and the situation of which was so advantageous as to create the fear that it might be restored. Similar imprecations were pronounced by Agamemnon against such as should rebuild Troy, and by Crœsus against those who should restore Sidene, "according to ancient custom," says Strabo, by whom the fact is reported.[2]

The other prohibition respecting the spoil was transgressed by one man only; but this single transgression infringed the covenant of devotement, and brought disaster upon the army of Israel in the next operation, which was directed against the town of Ai. As a military man, Joshua was deeply and painfully sensible of the injurious effects of such a stain upon the hitherto irresistible arms of the Israelites. He and the elders of Israel, with rent clothes, and dust upon their heads, lay prostrate before the ark till eventide. In reply to the words in which the hero expressed his dejection and dismay—perhaps more of both than we should have expected from him—he was informed of what had taken place, and was told that Israel could not prosper while "the accursed thing" remained among them. He was then instructed in the steps to be taken for

[1] Zonar. *Annal.,* lib. ix. 409.
[2] *Geograph.,* lib. ix. 13.

the discovery of the offender. God could at once have named him to Joshua, but this was not in accordance with the usual course of His providence. Yet as the offence had been without human witness, it was necessary to resort to an extraordinary process. This was the lot, conducted in the same manner as that by which, in a later age, Saul was chosen king. First the lot selected the tribe, then the family, then the household, then the individual. The exact process followed in casting the lot is not known, nor is the matter of much importance; but we incline to the opinion of those who conceive that tickets, marked with the names of the twelve tribes, were put into an urn, and the lot fell upon the one that was taken out; that then they cast as many tickets as there were ancestral families, or clans, in the tribe whose name was drawn; then as many as there were households in that family; and lastly, as many as there were heads in that household. However this may be, it is certain that the lot, for the decision of uncertain, and the discovery of hidden things, was much employed by the Jews,[1] and was highly esteemed by them.[2] Its use among the pagans is shown in Jonah i. 7. That it was lawful, is clearly shown by its being used in other cases by divine appointment,[3] and more than all by its having been apparently resorted to by the apostles to fill the vacancy in their number.[4] The pagan superstitions, which eventually became intermingled with the practice, and the evil purposes to which it was applied, rendered it so dangerous and criminal, that it was discountenanced by the church, and fell into disuse. It is very possible that this expedient was resorted to in the present case, partly to afford the culprit an opportunity of staying the proceedings by a repentant avowal of his crime. There would have been some show of penitence in this, but nothing of the kind occurred; and some obduracy and unbelief seem to be indicated in his remaining silent to the last, as if to take the chances of any error in the appointed process of detection. He could only escape by a wrong indication of the lot. And if he were willing to assume the possibility of such an error in the sacred lot, he must also have been willing that some other person should suffer for the crime he had committed.

By the process directed, the tribe taken was that of Judah, the family that of the Zarhites, the household that of Zabdi. That household was then brought, man by man, and Achan the son of Carmi was taken. This person, on being spoken to by Joshua, verified the indication of the lot by confessing his crime. He said, "When I saw among the spoils a goodly Babylonish garment, and two hundred shekels of silver, and a wedge of gold, then I coveted them and took them; and, behold, they are hid in the earth, in the midst of my tent, and the silver under them." In the place which he pointed out, all those articles were accordingly found. They were things of value, and well suited to tempt such a man as Achan. The ingot of gold, somewhat in the shape of a tongue (not a wedge), must have been worth, at the present value of gold, about ninety-six pounds, and the silver about eight pounds. The "goodly Babylonish garment" awakens some interest. Bochart,[1] with his usual erudition, proves by authorities that robes of various colours were made at Babylon, adorned with coloured patterns in the style of Turkey carpets, very shining, rich, and much sought after in all the eastern world. The Babylonians had the credit of inventing this sort of work, made in the loom with the needle, and of several colours. Their money value was very great even at a comparatively late period; and judging from the other plunder of Achan, he coveted the article more for what he might get for it than for its beauty. He could not use it without detection, and therefore must have designed to turn it into money when opportunity offered. We know not that any one has been able to describe a Babylonish robe of this sort from actual representation of it. But in all probability it differed little, if anything, from the equally prized robes of their Assyrian neighbours, of which the newly discovered monuments have enabled Mr. Layard to furnish a description; indeed, from the vague manner in which the term "Babylonish" was applied to what was brought from the countries bordering on the east of the Euphrates or Tigris, we lean to the opinion that what Achan calls a Babylonish garment may have been an Assyrian one. "The Assyrians were celebrated," says Layard, "for the magnificence and luxury of their apparel. 'The Assyrian garments' became almost a proverb, and having first been borrowed by the

---

[1] 1 Samuel 10:20,21; 14:40-42.   [2] Proverbs 18:18.
[3] Leviticus 16:8; 1 Chronicles 24:5,7. [4] Acts 1:24-26.

[1] *Phaleg.*, i. 6.

Persians, descended at a later time even to the Romans. The robes, as portrayed in the sculptures, confirm the traditions of their beauty and costliness. The dress of the king consisted of a long flowing garment, descending to the ankles, and elaborately embroidered, and edged with fringes and tassels. It was confined at the waist by a girdle, to which were attached cords with large tassels, falling down almost to the feet. Over this robe a second, nearly of the same length, but open in front, appears to have been thrown. It was also embroidered and edged with tassels."[1] This agrees very well with the description which Herodotus gives of the dress of the Babylonians.

After the confession which Achan had made, there was but one course of dealing with one who had troubled Israel, and brought so deep a stain upon its honour, and disgrace upon its arms. He was stoned, and the corpse was consumed by fire along with the accursed things, and with all that belonged to him.

In the 8th chapter of Joshua, after describing the capture of the city of Ai, the historian relates how the law was read in the presence of the assembled people, in the valley at the foot of Ebal. "And all Israel, and their elders and officers, and their judges, stood on this side the Ark and on that side before the priests the Levites, which bare the Ark of the Covenant of the Lord, as well the stranger, as he that was born among them ; half of them over against Mount Gerizim, and half of them over against Mount Ebal ; as Moses the servant of the Lord had commanded before, that they should bless the people of Israel. And afterward he read all the words of the law, the blessings and cursings, according to all that is written in the book of the law. There was not a word of all that Moses commanded, which Joshua read not before all the Congregation of Israel, with the women and the little ones, and the strangers that were conversant among them." There is a natural amphitheatre near the eastern end of the vale of Nablous, which was probably the scene of this interesting solemnity, of which a description is given in the *Statements of the Palestine Exploration Fund*, 1873, p. 70. "It is hardly too much to say that there is no other place in Palestine so suitable for the assembly of an immense body of men within the limits to which a human voice could reach, and where, at the same time, each individual would be able to see what was being done. The recesses in the two mountains, which form the amphitheatre, are exactly opposite to each other, and the limestone strata running up to the very summits in a succession of ledges present the appearance of a series of regular benches."

"Two questions have been raised in connection with the reading of the law—the possibility of hearing it read, and the possibility of assembling the twelve tribes on the ground

[1] *Nineveh and its Remains*, ii. 319.

at the same time. Of the first there can be no doubt." "During the excavations on Mount Gerizim the Arab workmen were on more than one occasion heard conversing with men passing along the valley below." With regard to the second point, "without making a minute contoured plan of the mountain sides, it is not possible to form a correct estimate of the exact number of persons who could be assembled within the amphitheatre. There are, however, few localities which afford so large an amount of standing ground on the same area."

S.

THE CRAFT OF THE GIBEONITES

Joshua 9

IN the ninth chapter of Joshua we have a very singular illustration of the terror which the wonderful success of the Hebrew arms inspired.

There was an important city called Gibeon, a few miles to the north of Jerusalem, the inhabitants of which, expecting that their turn would

GIBEON

speedily come, and despairing of being able to hold out against the invincible host, resolved to try to escape the doom which hung over them. In ordinary cases, they would have thought of submission to the invading force. But they knew that the submission of no Canaanite city would be accepted. Coupling this with the knowledge that the Hebrews were not forbidden to enter into treaty with, and accept the submission of, distant nations, they resolved to save their lives at least, by beguiling the invaders into a treaty of alliance with them, by inducing them to believe that they belonged to a far country.

For this purpose they would send to the camp of Israel an embassy, invested with every circumstance tending to confirm the intended delusion, by affording every indication of their having made a long and weary journey. Let us examine for a moment the nature of their equipment, and look to the articles of which it was composed. These we find to be the same which are still required for a journey in the East.

First, "*they took old sacks upon their asses.*" What were the sacks used for? Interpreters seem at a loss with regard to these "sacks," having no clear notion of their use. It appears to us that they were the same as the large bags, usually of hair, in which the Orientals pack up for convenient transport on the backs of animals, all the baggage and commodities required for the journey, excepting only water-bags and large kettles. Beds, boxes, provisions, pots, packages of goods,—all are carried in such bags, slung over the back of the animal, one hanging at each side. Being a good deal knocked about and exposed to the weather, these saddle-bags, as one might call them but for their size, suffer in a long journey;

EGYPTIAN WINE BOTTLES

and hence the Gibeonites took old bags, to convey the impression that a long journey had been made.

The *wine bottles* which they took with them are also said to have been "old and rent, and bound up." At present in Western Asia we do not meet with wine-bottles, but only water-bottles, wine being interdicted by the Moslem law, and therefore, although enough used, not being publicly carried about; and in the farther pagan East, the vine does not grow, and neither wine nor wine-bottles are used. The bottles were of leather, or rather of skins, like those in which

water is now, and was indeed formerly, carried about. Classical antiquity has afforded many representations of these wine-skins, for the use of them was by no means confined to the East.

ANTIQUE WINE SKINS

At the present day the same kind of bottles are used for keeping as well as for conveying wine in Spain and in the Christian country of Georgia beyond the Caucasus, where, at the city of Teflis, we beheld them for the first time. In that city we found at once every example of the ancient wine-bottles of skin to which there are so many allusions in Scripture. This, indeed, we imagine to be the native country of the vine; for here only have we beheld it growing wild in the thickets beside the rivers, affording small but very pleasant grapes. The people here have no casks, but preserve their wine in earthen jars and leathern bottles. The latter are made of the skins of goats, oxen, and buffaloes, turned inside out, clipped with the scissors, washed, and rubbed over with warm mineral tar or naphtha. The openings are closed with a sort of wooden bung, except at the feet, where they are only tied up with a cord. The wine is drawn at one of the feet, merely by opening or closing the noose. It is a very strange and whimsical sight in the eyes of a stranger, to behold oxen and buffalo-skins full of wine lying in the wine-booth or about the streets, with their legs stretched up. These skins, however, are very convenient for home use or for carriage; for they may be found of all sizes, some very small, the skins of young kids holding only a few of our bottles. It is thus seen how *such* bottles might be "rent," and the rents mended temporarily by being "tied up;" and the nature of the bottles explains the caution of our Saviour against putting new wine into old bottles, lest the bottles should be burst by the wine.

In further confirmation of the designed delusion, their "*shoes were old and clouted.*" For "shoes" read "sandals," such being in most cases denoted by the word translated "shoes" in the authorized version. Now, although little more than soles of some kind fastened to the foot by thongs, the sandals might need clouting or patching, as may be seen by the figures of ancient Egyptian sandals, to which those used in Syria were probably similar, unless, from the greater roughness of the country, we may suppose them to have been of stouter make and materials. Of such we have not only figures in sculpture and painting, but actual specimens in cabinets of

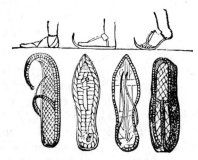

ANCIENT EGYPTIAN SANDALS

Egyptian antiquities. They are seen to vary somewhat in form. Those worn by the upper classes and by females were usually pointed and turned up at the toes, like skates, and indeed like the eastern slippers of the present day. They are mostly made of a sort of woven or interlaced work of palm leaves and papyrus stalks, or other similar materials, and sometimes of leather, and they were frequently lined with cloth. In Syria they were probably more exclusively of hide. They were seldom mended, being of so little value that they could be easily renewed when the worse for wear. We have seen a man make himself a new pair out of a piece of skin in a few minutes, for sandals are not wholly disused in the East. The mere fact that articles so easily renewed were patched in this instance, was well calculated to suggest the idea of a long journey, in which the convenience of purchasing new ones, or materials for making them had not been found; for which reason they had been obliged to make their old ones serve by patching. It was a singular thing to see sandals clouted at all, and only a journey could explain the fact.

The *garments* of these pretended ambassadors were also old. It behoves ambassadors in the East to do credit to their master, and show be-

coming respect to those to whom they are sent, by making a clean and decent, or even a splendid appearance. This was so essential, that their appearance with old and travel-stained clothes could only, upon any common principle, be explained by the assigned reason, that they had come direct from a long journey; implying also, that as the place to which they came was a camp and not a town, they had not found an opportunity of repairing the damage to their attire which the journey had occasioned.

Lastly, their *bread*, which they affirmed to have been hot from the oven when they left their home, had become "dry and mouldy" by the length of their journey. This translation conveys a somewhat erroneous impression. The Hebrew word translated "mouldy" is the same which is rendered by "cracknels" in 1 Kings xiv. 3. This word denotes a kind of crisp cake. The original term (*nikuddim*) would seem, from its etymology, to denote something spotted or sprinkled over; and it is supposed, from the old Jewish explanations, to denote a kind of biscuit, or a small and hard-baked cake, calculated to keep (for a journey or other purpose) by reason of its excessive hardness and freedom from moisture; or perhaps by being *twice* baked, as the word *bis-cuit* expresses. Not only are such hard cakes or biscuits still used in the East, but they are, like all biscuits, punctured to render them more hard, and sometimes also they are sprinkled with seeds—*either* of which circumstances sufficiently meets the etymology of the word. The ordinary bread, baked in thin cakes, like pancakes, is not made to keep more than a day or two, a fresh supply being baked daily. If kept longer it dries up, and becomes at last excessively hard—harder than any biscuit that we ever knew. It was this kind of common bread that the Gibeonites produced, and they indicated its hardness—"*hard as biscuits*"—in evidence of the length of the journey they had taken.

The device of these Gibeonites was managed very skilfully. The evidence thus furnished seemed to the Israelites so strong, that although aware of the danger of being imposed upon, they entered into a covenant of peace, and bound themselves by the oath of their elders to its observance. A few days after, the error into which they had been led was discovered. The people were then indignant at the conduct of their leaders in this business, knowing that they could have guarded themselves from all mistake by consulting the divine oracle. This especially ought they to have done in regard to the first treaty of any kind into which, as a people, they had entered. This came of trusting too much to appearances, of leaning too much to their own understandings, and fancying that it was impossible to mistake such plain evidence as the guileful Gibeonites produced. We do not, however, suppose that the people of Israel had that thirst for blood which some have ascribed to them on account of the displeasure they expressed on this occasion. It is far more likely that they regretted being thus deprived of the spoil of one of the richest cities in the neighbourhood; and they may not have been without apprehension that such an infraction of the law given them respecting the conquest of the land might not be unvisited by some tokens of their Divine King's displeasure. Such, however, was the respect felt by all the Israelites for the oath which had been taken, that no one supposed there was any other course now to be followed than to spare the lives and respect the property of the Gibeonites; yet, to punish their deception, it was directed that they should henceforth be devoted to the service of the tabernacle, and be employed in the servile and laborious offices of hewing the wood and drawing the water required in the sacred offices, from which the Israelites themselves were thenceforth relieved. It is not to be supposed that the whole, or the greater part of them, were thus employed at once. A certain number of them performed it in rotation, while remaining in possession of their city and of their goods.

JOSHUA'S MIRACLE

Joshua 10

A CONSEQUENCE that could hardly have been foreseen resulted from the league which had been formed with the Gibeonites. It seems that Gibeon belonged to a confederacy of southern states, in which the small kingdom of Jerusalem took the lead. We assume that these states were independent of each other, but that one of the number was regarded as entitled to take the precedence in matters of common interest. These states regarded with high displeasure the defection of the Gibeonites from the common cause. To them it wore the aspect of treachery to the patriotic cause of the defence of the country against the invasion, and they could not but see that the transaction was calculated to damp the spirits of the people. It was therefore concluded by the confederates, on the call of Adoni-zedek, king of Jerusalem, to bring them to severe punishment for the step they had taken. This was no less than to march against Gibeon with their whole united force,—a display of strength needed not only by the relative power of the Gibeonites, but by the probability of their being aided by the Israelites. In fact, no sooner did the Gibeonites see the united host encamped before their walls, than they sent to demand the help of Joshua. This was readily granted. Notwithstanding the fraudulent manner in which the compact had been obtained, the Israelites shrank not from the duties which it imposed. Besides, their sacred oath had been pledged before the Lord; and to slight the obligation which it imposed, would have been a dishonour to that name in the eyes of the heathen. Joshua, therefore, with a large body of picked men, departed from the camp at Gilgal to raise the siege.

This was, in a military point of view, the most important action in which the Israelites had yet been engaged. It was to be a conflict in the open field between the army of Israel and the greatest force which the powers of southern Canaan could bring into action. The result could not but have the most important effects upon the Canaanites on the one hand, and upon the Israelites on the other. Joshua was well aware of the serious responsibilities which rested upon this transaction; and it may be that he regarded them not without some anxiety. To relieve him, the gracious promise of victory was given to him before he set out; and thenceforth he suffered not his mind to rest upon the apparent insufficiency of his comparatively untrained force to contend with the disciplined troops and glorious chivalry of Canaan, but reposed in the faith that what God had promised He was able to perform. Yet he did not therefore neglect any human means of securing the results which he desired, but took all the measures which might become a general who supposed that all depended upon his skill and the valour of his troops. He made a forced march all night from the camp of Gilgal to Gibeon, and seems to have fallen at once upon the allied force by which that city was invested. Inspired with terror at so fierce and sudden an assault, their strength was broken, and they fled.

The interest of this great day lay not in the battle, but in the pursuit. It was in every way most essential that the victory should be effectual, which would be by no means the case if the fugitives were allowed the opportunity of rallying their scattered forces, or of making their way back to the strongholds from which they had issued. And the Lord helped the Israelites. There came down a tremendous fall of hailstones —or such hail as is known only in the East, whereby great numbers of the fugitives were stricken down—more than had fallen by the sword at Gibeon. Bearing in mind the havoc which had been committed by the hailstones in Egypt, and recollecting the immense size of the stones of hail in the East, we can scarcely be surprised that this effect should have been produced. This was doubtless an extraordinary storm, and the hailstones of size unusual even in that country; or, perhaps, wholly of the largest size of hailstones known in Syria. But let us hear what is said of ordinary hailstones. "Hail falls most commonly in the latter part of spring in very heavy storms, and the hailstones are often of most enormous size. I have seen some that measured two inches in diameter; but sometimes irregularly shaped pieces are found among them, weighing above twenty drams."[1] Sometimes there are such storms of hail as work ravages fully equal to those of the Egyptian plague, and by no means inadequate to the result described in the case before us. There was such a storm at Constantinople in 1831. Many of the hailstones, or rather masses of ice, weighed from half a pound to above a pound, and in their fall appeared as large as the swell of a large water decanter. Under this tremendous fall the roofs of houses were beaten in, trees were stripped of their leaves and branches, many persons who could not soon enough find shelter were killed, animals were slain, and limbs were broken. In fact, none who know the tremendous power which the hailstones of the East sometimes exhibit, will question, as some have questioned,

[1] Russell, *Natural History of Aleppo*, i. 71.

the possibility that *any* hail should produce the effect described. That a fall of hail thus severe and extraordinary, though not unexampled, occurred at this precise time, could only have been, as it is said to have been, of the Lord's doing, which is also shown in its partial character; for the fugitives were alone visited by it, while the pursuers, who could not have been at any great distance behind, suffered nothing.

Still the pursuit continued; and as the day began to decline, the fugitives hoped that the approaching shades of night would give them safety, and enable them to reach their strong towns undisturbed, if not to collect their scattered forces in the field. Joshua on his part regarded the decline of the sun towards the horizon with concern, fearing that the approach of night, by compelling him to abandon the pursuit, would leave his victory incomplete, and the power of the enemy less entirely broken than he desired. Aware of the immense importance of the results which this victory, if completed, must produce, he longed for a few hours more of day. Then the thought was suggested to him —"Is anything too hard for the Lord?" and strong in the faith which that consideration inspired, he cried aloud, "Sun, stand thou still

VALLEY OF AJALON.

upon Gibeon; and thou, moon, in the valley of Ajalon." And the Lord heard him, for "the sun stood still, and the moon stayed, until the people had avenged themselves upon their enemies." But the sun does not revolve around the earth, but the earth around the sun. This is true. But when the greatest philosophers of this age in their popular discourses, no less than the common people, speak of the sun's rising and setting, we can have no ground for cavil at the mode in which Joshua expressed his wish that the day might be prolonged. That was all he meant; and his object could only *apparently* be attained in the way he indicated. There is no reason to suppose that Joshua had any better knowledge of the system of the universe than was generally possessed at that time. But if he had been a very Newton, he would have been mad to express himself in any other language than this. If he had expressed himself with philosophical precision, his language would have perplexed the understandings of men far more than three thousand years, than they have done in the three hundred years since the truth of the world's system has been known.

But, admitting the propriety of the expression, it will be asked *how* this miraculous fact was brought to pass? To this we answer plainly, we do not know. It is not necessary to know. The day was prolonged for all the essential purposes which Joshua had in view, when his strong faith impelled him to utter these great words. But after what manner this was affected must be open to conjecture, until the time to come discloses the knowledges that are hidden in its womb.

It has been supposed by some that the motion of the earth upon its axis was for the time arrested. This, no doubt, would effect the result intended. But it would—without an additional and equally stupendous exertion of almighty power—have produced other and very tremendous effects upon the whole earth. The natural consequence of such a sudden check to the earth's motion would have been, by means of the atmosphere, to crush at once all animal and vegetable existence, to level with the ground the loftiest and most massive structures, and, in fact, to sweep the whole surface of the globe as with the besom of destruction. God might have prevented this. But while there is a mode of producing the effect which Joshua desired, which does not naturally involve such consequences, it may be best, in the present state of our knowledge, to suppose that it was so effected. It answers all the conditions of the question, while it implies a most stupendous exhibition of the power of the Almighty in that day when " He hearkened to the voice of a man," to suppose that the *light* of the then setting sun

was supernaturally prolonged, through the operation of the same laws of refraction and reflection, by which the sun's disc is ordinarily seen above the horizon some time after he has really sunk below it. He who created the heavenly luminaries, and established the laws which transmit their light, could at this time have so altered the medium through which the sun's rays passed, as to render it visible above the horizon long after it must, under ordinary circumstances, have disappeared. This, to the apprehension of the Israelites, would have all the effect of staying the career of the sun; and to ours, that of arresting the earth's revolution on its axis; and this is all that the sacred text requires—all that Joshua required—all that we need require.

In no part of Palestine was I so deeply impressed with the minute accuracy of the details of the Scripture narrative, than when riding over the scene of Joshua's great victory. With perfect ease, I was able to trace the line of his advance into the upland plain of Gibeon ; then the field, by the fountain, where, according to Josephus, he fell suddenly upon the Canaanite host as it lay encamped before the embattled heights of Gibeon ; then each stage in the headlong flight and pursuit.

Gibeon stands on a low circular hill having steep sides and a flat top, and around it lies an undulating plain some four or five miles in diameter. About a quarter of a mile west of the town there is a sharp ascent from the plain to a broad ridge. Up this the Amorites fled after the first terrible assault ; and the Israelites " chased them along the way that *goeth up* to Beth-horon" (Josh. x. 10). From the top of the ridge a long and rugged descent leads to Beth-horon, which is seen in front crowning a projecting shoulder of the mountain. The nature of the ground favoured the fugitives ; but " as they fled from before Israel, and were in the *going down to Beth-horon*, the Lord cast down great stones from heaven upon them." Joshua led the van of his troops. He saw that the victory was complete, but yet that night must eventually save the Amorites from total destruction, and enable a large body of them to escape to their cities through the valley of Ajalon, at the foot of the pass down which they were now rushing. Then, standing on some commanding rock in the sight of the whole people, in the fulness of faith and in the ardour of enthusiasm, Joshua gave utterance to that wondrous prayer-prophecy : " Sun, stand thou still upon Gibeon ; and thou, moon, in the valley of Ajalon." The sun stood still, and the Israelites rushed onward in pursuit down the pass of Beth-horon, down the valley of Ajalon, along the plain of Philistia, until at length the flower of the Amorite army was slain, and the five kings were captured in the cave of Makkedah, where they vainly attempted to hide themselves.

P.

CALEB

Joshua 14:6-12

THE distribution of the southern land which had been conquered, although some strong cities in it remained unsubdued, was attended with one interesting incident. The allotment to Judah brought forward the pious old Caleb, one of the twelve spies who explored the land forty and five years before, and whose concurrence with Joshua in an encouraging report not only exempted them from the doom which befell the other spies, but made them the sole survivors of that generation. This is the very man whom we should wish to come forward to tell us his experience and his impressions; and we hail his address with all the satisfaction with which it seems to have been received by Joshua and the elders among whom he sat. The strain of familiarity which he adopts in addressing his old companion and friend, is exceedingly natural and becoming: "Thou knowest the thing that the Lord said unto Moses, concerning me and thee, in Kadesh-barnea. Forty years old was I when Moses, the servant of the Lord, sent me from Kadesh-barnea to espy out the land: and I brought him word again as it was in mine heart." We may pause a moment to note these words. From all that appears, the motion to search the land was made by the Israelites, and only conceded by Moses; and the appointment of the spies seems to have been by each tribe, one for itself. Indeed, the appointment of them by Moses in the name of the Lord might have seemed invidious. Why, then, does Caleb imply that the Lord sent him? There is but one answer. Whatever a man undertakes with the desire to serve God, and executes so as to obtain His approval, is a work of the Lord, a work on which he was sent—to which he was appointed. Again, he would consider that circumstances were overruled, in the Lord's providence, to lead to the appointment of himself among the twelve, that the truth might not be left without witnesses. When he perceived that, according to his wish, he had done the Lord's work, he could not but look beyond the external circumstances of his appointment—to the inner guidance and supreme direction which, through the outward form of man's appointment and choice, ordered and

directed the whole matter. He may have been aware of circumstances which at the time rendered it as likely, or more likely, that another should have been appointed by the tribe of Judah to this service; but that the choice fell on himself, would, when he came to look at the result, seem a special ordination of Providence, and doubtless it was such.

Well, then, on what plan and policy did he undertake this charge? Did he go with the purpose of framing his report according to the desires of Moses, and according to what he presupposed to be the mind of the Lord? Not so. He had no plan—he had no purpose but that of telling the plain and simple truth: "I brought him word again, as it was in mine heart." Therefore, that his testimony, coming from the simple impulses of his heart—of a right judgment, was well-pleasing to God, shows that his heart was right with God; and that he had formed true conceptions of His character, His designs, and His covenant relations to Israel. The other spies spoke no less, we may suppose, from their hearts, than he did from his. But their hearts were *not* right with God—they were filled with fear and unbelief; and although they did speak the truth as it appeared to them, they spoke wrongly and falsely, because there was a disharmony between their spirits and the Spirit of God. A good understanding have all they that seek God—all they that love Him; and they can venture to speak all that is in their hearts, knowing under what influence their judgments have been formed. This was the case, as we apprehend, with Caleb.

He adds: "Nevertheless, my brethren that went up with me made the heart of the people melt; but I wholly followed the Lord my God." In this all his secret, all his distinction, lay. He wholly followed the Lord—he had no reserve, no secondary objects, no low fears, no regard to human influence or man's opinions. He wholly followed the Lord. And he had his reward, as those who follow the Lord wholly always have. Let us hear what that in his case was.

"And Moses sware on that day, Surely the land whereon thy feet have trodden shall be thine inheritance, and thy children's for ever, because thou hast wholly followed the Lord my God." Such was the promise; and now, after forty-five years, when the companions of his prime have perished around him, he is alive and strong to claim its fulfilment: "And now, behold, the Lord hath kept me alive." It was the Lord who did everything for him. He does not exult in the strength of his constitution, on which time had made so slight an impression. It was the Lord who had kept him alive, when in the ordinary course of things he would have been dead; and it was in spite of the tendencies of nature to decay and dissolution, that he now stood among the living in so much health and strength. His present existence, under all the circumstances, was a kind of resurrection from the dead. Therefore he glories in it—this old man—twenty years older than the oldest (except Joshua) in his nation: he glories in it as a thing of God. "The Lord has kept me alive these forty and five years, even since the Lord spake this word to Moses, while the children of Israel wandered in the wilderness; and now, lo, I am this day fourscore and five years old. And yet I am as strong this day as I was in the day that Moses sent me: as my strength was then, even so is my strength now, for war, both to go out and to come in." By this he not only glorifies God, who had so preserved him, and who was the strength as well as the length of his days, but intimates to Joshua that the grant of his application for the inheritance which Moses promised to him, and which was still in the hands of the Canaanites, would not be throwing away a portion upon a weak old man, unequal to the task of either taking or retaining it. On the contrary, if, as was the case, it were to be taken from the hands of giants—for it was Hebron, where the sons of Anak were seen—and would require the utmost prowess, energy, and nerve of the youthful warrior, he was still able to put it forth; and he was not afraid, at eighty-five, to cope with the same power which he would readily have encountered at forty. Yet, after all, he does not too implicitly rely upon the prowess of his green old age. His confidence lies elsewhere. Let us hear him; "Now therefore give me this mountain, whereof the Lord spake in that day: for thou heardest in that day how the Anakims were there, and that the cities were great and fenced; *if so be the Lord will be with me, then I shall be able to drive them out,* as the Lord said." Notwithstanding his consciousness of strength even in age, he does not venture to think himself equal to this great enterprise, unless the Lord were with him.

But there is one point to which an interesting writer directs attention,[1] and which deserves especial notice. It is that the inheritance was "a mountain that he had himself seen, and that must have been present to his mind's eye during the whole forty years of wandering. He had seen the mountain when a spy, and notwithstanding all that unbelief did object, believed it would become his, now forty-five years before possession. This singular felicity was the reward of his singular piety. No doubt the thought often proved sweet to his mind, and made his future inheritance so present to view as to give rest in wandering, and make him feel rich while as yet he had nothing. The believer in Jesus, though he has not yet seen it with his eye, may claim a part in the portion of his people, and with much satisfaction leave to his covenant God what that part shall be. Oh to pass through time with general but lively impressions of that fairer inheritance mercy has entailed upon the faithful, that when the time of the promise shall draw near, and we are ready to enter into rest, we may be able to put in an humble claim, and say to Him who is the divider of His people's portion, 'Give me this mountain, whereof the Lord spake in that day.' Sweet is it to come to a period that fills the mind with the expectation of long promised blessings, when just about to receive what the Lord, many years since, has spoken of concerning His people—to realize in old age what has been their hope in youth, and has been their support and solace in the pilgrimage of a lengthened life."

The explanation of Dr. Kitto does not entirely remove the difficulty which meets us in critically comparing the several passages relating to the sending of the spies. In Num. xiii. 1, we read, "The Lord spake unto Moses, saying, Send thou men, that they may search the land of Canaan: . . . of every tribe of their fathers shall ye send a man. . . . And Moses, by the commandment of the Lord, sent them from the wilderness of Paran. . . . These are the names of the men which Moses sent to spy out the land." But in Deut. i. 21, 22, an apparently different version of the story is given. Moses said to the people, when at Kadesh, "Go up now and possess the land. . . . Fear not, neither be discouraged. And ye came near unto me every one of you, and said, We will send men before us, and they shall search us out the land." With the former narrative the words of Caleb in Josh. xiv. 7 agree: "Forty

[1] *The Church in Canaan.* By William Seaton. London, Holdsworth; Edinburgh, W. Oliphant. 1823. Vol. i. pp. 199, 200.

years old was I when Moses the servant of the Lord sent me from Kadesh-barnea to espy out the land."

The real difficulty lies in this, that in Numbers and Joshua the sending of the spies appears to have been the act of the Lord through Moses; whereas in Deuteronomy it appears to have been the act of the people. Both accounts are strictly true, and the reconciliation is simple. When the Israelites were ordered to enter Canaan from Kadesh, they were afraid. They appear to have dreaded some great unknown difficulties. The idea of sending spies then suggested itself to them, that through them they might get direct and authentic information regarding both the Canaanites and their country. Though prompted by unbelief, God mercifully yielded to the suggestion, and commanded Moses to select and send the men. This solution is at once simple and satisfactory.

It ought not to be forgotten, in reading Bible history, that the sacred writers never intended to give a full narrative of events in all their phases and details. Their object was higher and holier than that of the mere historian. It was to reveal God's will to man, and to exhibit the method of God's dealings with man in some of the great affairs of life. Whatever subserved these ends was recorded; all else was passed over.

P.

THE BOOK CITY

Joshua 15:15

One of the towns taken by the Israelites in the course of their war for the conquest of Canaan was KIRJATH-SEPHER. It is historically famous as the strong city, for the capture of which Caleb, in whose lot it lay, held forth the hand of his daughter Achsah as the prize, which prize was won by his gallant nephew Othniel, afterwards a judge in Israel. But a still higher interest, not very obvious to the general reader, lurks in this city, and that merely in its name. KIRJATH-SEPHER means "the Book-City."

To those who like to look back into ancient things, this name, found at a date so remote, excites the most intense curiosity, and suggests a thousand questions. While scholars are disputing whether any literature, or any but the scantiest, existed at a date so ancient, we come quietly upon a great fact lurking in a name. We read here in this name, not only of a book, but of a book-city, a city distinguished in some way or other for its connection with literature. It is difficult to conceive that it was so called for any other reason than because it was either eminent for books or archives, or for its being the resort

of men who were conversant with literature, such, whatever it was, as existed in that age. In some sort, then, it was a place of literature. Was it a place of libraries, of archives, of academies? Either alternative implies the presence of such literature as the age afforded among the Canaanites, and at least proves that they were not an illiterate people. The Targum calls the place Kirjath-arche, or the city of the archives, in which were laid up the public records of the Canaanites. This is not unlikely. We know that there were in a later age special cities in which the archives of kingdoms were deposited, and it might be particularly desirable in a dominion of small states like those of Canaan, that the public records, in which all had an interest, should be deposited in one place.

This Kirjath-sepher is, again, undoubtedly the same which is farther on called Kirjath-sannah (ver. 49). This *Sannah* means, in Arabic and in the old Phœnician or Canaanitish dialect, law, doctrine, manner of life, and is applied by the Moslems to the secondary law of the Koran, answering to the Jewish Mishnah. The Greek translators render it by the "city of letters." It seems, therefore, that the one name denotes the general character of the town as a city of books, and the other the nature of these books, or the objects to which they tended, which were indeed the objects of all ancient literature.

Think as we will, reason as we will, it remains clear, that if there was a city called the Book-city, there must have been in it books of some kind or other. By the dear love we bear to books, which place within our grasp the thought and knowledge of all ages and of all climes, we exult in this inevitable conclusion. Let us not, however, form any large ideas of the collections of books which the Book-city contained. The mere fact that a city was distinguished by its very name for the possession of books, implies that books were then rare. It is not for qualities or possessions common, but rare, that cities or persons acquire a name. There was no Bodleian or Advocates' Library, no British Museum; a small closet or a box might perhaps contain all the manuscripts which the Book-city possessed. But whatever their quality or number, they were precious in the eyes of the Canaanites; and in ours this bundle of books and their appreciation of its value do them far more honour than all their chariots of iron. What a treasure they would have been to us now! What stores of ancient knowledge they would have opened! What light would have been thrown upon many dark matters, all the more important from their connection with the early history of our sacred books! We should have been able to read them had they been preserved, and their value to us would have been beyond all price. We can feel this—we see this at a glance. How much more, then, would this have been the case had the books which comprise our Bible been lost, though known to have once existed! How we should have grieved over that loss! How sensible we should be of their unutterable value; how intensely we should appreciate the privilege of being acquainted with the high knowledge they comprise! But we have these books in our hands; all the treasures of human and spiritual knowledge which they contain lie as an open page in the hands of our very children; here are books as old, and books far more precious, than any that the Book-city of the Canaanites contained. Some are sensible of their value; some devote all their days to the study of them; and to many every word of the sacred volume which contains them is more precious than gold. But these are few in number compared with the thousands by whom this volume, so accessible to all, and so worthy of all our regard, is neglected like any common thing, or to whom it is as a sealed book. In the contemplation of this far richer possession, we may soothe our regrets at the loss of the library of Kirjath-sepher.

But, after all, what did become of these books? When Caleb acquired the city, did he preserve or destroy them? It does not seem to us likely that he would treat with much respect books which, however precious they might be to us in our day, for the illustration of ancient history and ethnography, would in his eyes exhibit much that was profane and abominable. The whole had probably the flavour of idolatry, and much must have had reference to the superstitious rites and acts to which the Canaanites were addicted; and these things, however interesting they may be as materials of antiquarian investigation into matters long since extinct, are received differently as living and actual things. At the present day a nobleman will give large sums for a collection of the very broadsides and chap-books with which, at the time of their publication, one or two centuries ago, a gentleman would have

scorned to soil his fingers. Besides, the collection very probably included records and covenants respecting the ancient arrangements of estates and territories, which a conquering people could have no interest in preserving, but had a very obvious interest in destroying. So it is by no means unlikely that old Caleb threw the entire bundle of books that formed the library of Kirjath-sepher into the fire. We may the rather think so, as, although the name of Kirjath-sepher is a perfectly intelligible one in Hebrew, the conqueror evidently regarded it with no favour; for he hastened to change its name to Debir, by which it was afterwards known. Yet we should not like to lay much stress on this; for even the new name seems to have some analogy to the old reputation of the place. Debir means a "word," or "oracle," and is applied to that most secret and separated part of the temple—the holy of holies—in which the ark of God was placed, and where His oracles were delivered from between the cherubim. It is, therefore, not unlikely that this, equally with the old name, although in another form, communicates the fact that Debir had been some sacred place or seat of learning among the Canaanites, and the repository of their books and records. It is indeed quite possible that it was not without some regard to the old reputation of the place, as a seat of ancient learning, that at a later day it was made a city of the priests. The town appears to have lain a few miles to the west of Hebron, but no trace of it has yet been discovered.

SURVEYING

Joshua 18

THE war which commenced with the defeat of the confederate kings ceased not until the whole of the south country had been subdued by the Israelites. This portion of the land was assigned by lot to the tribes of Judah and Ephraim, and the unprovided half-tribe of Manasseh. The withdrawment of three populous tribes to take possession of their allotments, must have caused a sensible diminution of the numbers encamped around the tabernacle at Gilgal, and have made it inconvenient as a place of resort to those who were becoming settled at a distance. It hence became advisable to remove the tabernacle to a more central position. The spot selected—probably by divine appointment—was Shiloh, in the territory of Ephraim, to the north of Bethel. The spot, if correctly identified by Dr. Robinson with the present Seilun, is surrounded by hills, with an opening by a narrow valley into a plain on the south. After this there was a considerable interval of time during which little or nothing was done by the unprovided tribes to gain possession of the rest of the country. The cause of this "slackness" is not stated. But as the portion allotted to Judah was soon found to be too large, and that assigned to Ephraim too small, the probability is, that they were unwilling to make the imperfect survey, on which that appropriation had been founded, the basis of a further distribution. At least, this may have been made an excuse by the people for their own slothfulness in a matter of so much importance. At present they did not feel that there was any need to bestir themselves in the matter. They were enriched by the spoils of the country already won, and enjoyed abundance from the stores laid up for the use of the former inhabitants. They were thus living at ease in the midst of their brethren, while the lands which remained to be divided were remote from the station around which they were clustered; and if they went to take possession of them, they must break up their present connections, disperse their flocks and herds, change their habits of life, convey their families to strange places, and undergo new hardships and trials. Besides, the unappropriated districts were well filled with warlike Canaanites, who were disposed to leave the Israelites unmolested at present, but who could not be expelled without great exertion and peril. So they sat still, contented with things as they were, and disposed to let the future take care for itself.

But Joshua at length came forward to rouse them from this state of mind. He urged them no longer to delay taking possession of their heritage; and that there might be no excuse, he ordained that there should be a new and more systematic survey of the country in its entire extent. Hitherto the distribution had only extended to the land actually possessed. But now the whole was to be first surveyed, and then distributed, without regard to the present state of its occupancy; and the several tribes would naturally be stimulated to exertion by the heritage appropriated to their possession being placed in this distinct form before them. Three men from each of the unprovided tribes, twenty-one in all, were to go through the length and breadth of the land, to take proper note of the particulars, and to divide the whole into seven parts, the special appropriation of which among the tribes was afterwards to be determined by lot. When we look in the map to the unequal extent of the allotments made on the basis of this survey, we may presume that the interpretation which Josephus puts upon their instructions is correct. According to him, they were to take careful note of the relative advantages of the several districts; and as it often happened, especially in Palestine, that one acre of a particular sort of land was of equal value with a thousand other acres, they were to make the division under the careful consideration of these circumstances.

This was an arduous and difficult operation. To be of any value, it must have been a scientific survey; and that it was such, is shown by the minute description of the boundaries of the several portions, as assigned to the tribes by lot. In fact, this seems to us the most interesting scientific operation recorded in the early Scripture, and indeed the only one of the kind of which very ancient history has left any record. It is out of all sight the earliest example of land surveying of which we have any knowledge; and that it was undertaken in the circumstances, shows that there was more of scientific knowledge among the Israelites at this time than they have usually credit for, and that they were by no means so rude a people as some have conceived.

Josephus says that the survey occupied seven months; and to be so particular and accurate as it was, it could not well have been done in less time. We are told that "the men passed through the land, and described it by cities, into seven parts, in a book." For "book" read "tablet," and understand a kind of map or chart, accompanied perhaps by a written description of the leading features of the country. What a treasure beyond price would a copy of this map and of these notes be to us now! But the substance of the latter is probably embodied in the description of the boundaries of the tribes, which is eventually furnished, and which was doubtless taken from these materials.

The explorers must have been acquainted with geometry, or rather, perhaps, as Josephus says, some geometricians were sent with the responsible explorers, whose skill ensured a correct statement and an accurate division of the land. This knowledge had doubtless been acquired in Egypt, to which country all ancient authorities concur in ascribing the origin of land surveying and geometry. It took rise from the peculiar exigencies of that country, in the continual necessity that there was for adjusting the claims of persons with regard to the limits of lands, under the changes annually produced by the inundation of the Nile. It is reasonable to suppose that much litigation arose between neighbours respecting the limits of their unenclosed fields; and the fall of a portion of the bank, carried away by the stream during the inundation of the Nile, frequently made great alterations in the extent of the land near the river-side. We therefore readily perceive the necessity which arose for determining the quantity which belonged to each individual, whether to settle disputes with a neighbour or to determine the tax due to the government. It is indeed difficult to ascertain when this science of land mensuration commenced in Egypt; but there is evidence that it was already a well established science in that country before the age of Sesostris (to which Herodotus ascribes the invention), and even in and before the age of Joseph.

The measure in question was of a larger nature, and involves no less the observations proper to geography than the demonstrations which belong to geometry. Here again we are referred to Egypt. Not as unimportant, but as beside our object, we can afford to neglect the traditions which assign to the Egyptians, in the most remote ages, a knowledge of geography such as no other nation possessed, and which, among the writings ascribed to the first Thoth or Hermes, find one of cosmography, including the chorography of Egypt, and a description of the course of the Nile. We are content with the intimations of Scripture, which indicate the existence of this knowledge, in making known to us the fact that Egypt was already divided into provinces, or nomes, in the time of Joseph, which he visited in succession, to take such measures as the particular resources of each province might afford against the impending famine.[1] We wish some one would collect all the

intimations of ancient geographical knowledge which exist in the early Scriptures. Such a person will not get beyond the second chapter of Genesis without finding matter for admiration in the geographical particularity with which the site of Paradise is described. It has all the characters of a geographical description. It was situated in the land of Eden, towards the east. A river went out of it, which became divided into four branches. The course of each of these branches is described, and the countries watered by it are named. Even the several and more remarkable productions of one of these countries are mentioned in a very special manner. The historian not only says that the land of Havilah afforded gold, but adds that the gold of that land was very pure. There also, he continues, were found the bdellium and the onyx. It is impossible to read these details without perceiving that geographical science and description had made much progress before the age of Moses, and that there might well be Israelites qualified to furnish a satisfactory topographical survey and description of the land of Canaan.

THE ALTAR OF THE REUBENITES

Joshua 22

WE have sometimes wondered that no traveller in Palestine has ever thought of looking for the great monumental altar which was erected near the Jordan by the men of Reuben, Gad, and Manasseh, on their return to their own land. As it was " a great altar to see to," that is, a very conspicuous object from afar, and was produced by the united labour of no small army of men, it was in all probability a vast heap or mound of earth and stones ; and as such constructions last for ages, and this was intended to endure to future generations, it is by no means unlikely that it is still in existence. That it has not been recognized, is probably owing to its having become in the course of ages covered with mould and overgrown with shrubs, so as to be scarcely distinguishable to the inexperienced from a natural hillock. But

[1] Genesis 41:48, where " the field (or district) round about every city" is believed to mean the province or nome of which every such city was the local capital, like our county towns.

its form and position would probably suggest its true character to those who have had opportunities of observing such monuments, or tumuli, in other countries; and careful excavations in it might lead to some curious conclusions.

The occasion of the erection of this altar is very remarkable, and in the highest degree honourable to all the parties concerned.

It will be remembered that the tribes of Reuben and Gad, with the half-tribe of Manasseh, had received their inheritance beyond the Jordan, on the express condition of sending their warriors to assist their brethren in the conquest of Canaan. They very faithfully and honourably performed this engagement. We do not suppose that they were for so many years, seven at least, without seeing their families or visiting their homes. That would have been an absurd and needless self-denial. They doubtless went home while the camp lay in winter quarters; and they could, moreover, seeing how short the distance was between them, go home on leave, when particular domestic circumstances required their presence. Still they must have been truly glad when Joshua called them before him, and after commending their conduct, and reminding them of their duties, dismissed them, with his blessing, finally to their homes.

They had not been long gone when it· was whispered tremblingly among the people at Shiloh, that these men had no sooner crossed the river to their own country, than they had set up a great altar on the cliffs overhanging the eastern border of the Jordan, visible from afar. Well, where was the harm? There was, in fact, room for much suspicion of danger in this act, which, however free from evil intention, was not remarkable for discretion under all the circumstances, seeing especially that a previous explanation had not been given. The harm was, that the law, to repress all danger of that plurality of worship which was the bane of all ancient religions, as well as to preserve the unity of the tribes, had decreed that there should be but one altar—that at the tabernacle—for all the people. The act of the returning warriors was therefore open to the suspicion that they meant, if not to adopt another worship, at least to set up another and an independent establishment for worship, on their own side the Jordan, which, besides the obvious tendency to idolatry, could not fail in the event to destroy the connection by which the tribes

were linked together. The obligation of *all* the Israelites to resort three times in the year for worship to the sole altar of the people, was admirably suited to retain them as one people, by continually keeping before their minds their common origin and common obligations; but if a separate establishment were allowed to exist on the other side the Jordan, there could be no difficulty in divining that they would cease to put themselves to the trouble of visiting the parent establishment in Canaan, and would in no long time come to regard themselves as a separate people.

This was precisely the view of the case which struck the minds of the people; and those who heard it in the several places of their abode, seriously and sadly buckled on their arms, and repaired to Shiloh for orders, resolved, if so commanded, to call to a severe account for their disloyalty, the brethren with whom side by side they had lately fought in the battles of Canaan. Their holy jealousy on this occasion for the glory of God, and for the honour of the institutions He had given them, is most becoming, and gives us a favourable opinion of the character of this generation. The sequel bears out this impression. The task which lay before them, though clear, was painful; and they resolved, in the meekness of wisdom, not to proceed hastily, or without proper inquiry, in a matter of such deep importance. True, the facts seemed scarcely capable of other than one interpretation: still, it was just possible that they might be mistaken; and, at all events, they would not have it laid to their charge that they had condemned their brethren unheard. They resolved to send a deputation to inquire into the affair, and to remonstrate with the transjordanic warriors. Phinehas, the son of the high priest, and with him ten of the great family chiefs, one from each tribe, were chosen for this important office. They were thus persons of great weight of character and approved discretion, entitled by their high position to demand an explanation, and less likely than younger men to have their judgments warped or compromised by the hasty impulses of passion.

The delegates proceeded on their mission, and on their arrival in Gilead stated the grounds of complaint, prefaced by the impressive words which they were fully authorized to use—"Thus saith the whole congregation of the Lord."

On hearing to what constructions they had

laid themselves open, and how the transaction had been viewed, the two and a half tribes were overwhelmed with astonishment and grief; and with becoming warmth, amounting to horror, disclaimed the injurious imputation, and declared the views on which they had really acted. They commenced by invoking God Himself to witness the innocency of their intentions. The form in which they did this is the most emphatic that language can express, and such as can scarcely be represented in a translation. There are three principal names of God in Hebrew—El, Elohim, Jehovah—and all the three are used together by them, and repeated twice. "El, Elohim, Jehovah —El, Elohim, Jehovah,"—He knoweth, &c. If translated at all, it might be perhaps thus:— "Almighty God, Elohim, Jehovah," etc.; for the first term involves the idea of might or strength.

The two and a half tribes proceeded to declare, that their object was in all respects the very reverse of that imputed to them. Instead of meaning a separation, they had set up their altar as a monument to future ages of the connection between the tribes divided by the river; so that if, at any time to come, their descendants should attempt to cast off the connection and assert their own independence, or if the Israelites should hereafter attempt to disown their union, and declare that the people beyond the river had "no part in the Lord," this monument might be pointed to in evidence of the fact. Some have thought from this, that the altar set up had an actual resemblance to the altar of burnt-offerings at the tabernacle. That could not be the case, for the altar there was of brass; but as it is said to have been after the same pattern, there was no doubt a general resemblance to that altar in the structure, which was of heaped earth and stones, and of vastly larger proportions. Its general purpose, as explained, was the same as that of all such erections. Its presence would excite inquiry; this would produce the history of the circumstances in which it originated, and the purpose for which it was established, the knowledge of which would be thus transmitted to future ages, and kept alive in all generations. To this a resemblance of some sort is not at all necessary. If the Monument in London were

entirely without sculptures and inscriptions to denote its object, still that object would not be forgotten, so long as a people lived around its base. The child would not be able to see so remarkable an object without asking his father what it meant; and the answer which he received he would in a later day give to his own son, when asked the same question. We have a remarkable example of this in the case of the stones taken out of the bed of the Jordan, and set up at Gilgal: "That this may be *a sign* among you, that when your children shall ask their fathers in time to come, What mean ye by these stones? then ye shall answer them, That the waters of Jordan were cut off before the ark of the covenant of the Lord; and these stones shall be for a memorial to the children of Israel for ever." (Josh. iv. 6, 7.) The object, and probably the construction, of this

MEMORIAL STONES

monument set up by the tribes in the present case, was almost precisely similar to that, and, to refer to another case, to the heap which Jacob and Laban set up as a memorial of the covenant between them. That heap was, in fact, in this same land of Gilead, probably not far from the altar now set up, the establishment of which may indeed have been suggested by the older monument. This seems to be indicated also by the name they gave to the altar, and the terms in which they described it. They "called the altar Ed (a witness), for it shall be a witness between us that Jehovah is God." Compare this with the other case: "Laban called it Jegar-sahadutha; but Jacob called it Galeed"—both names meaning "the heap of witness;" and then the reason, "This heap is a witness between me and thee this day."[1] Joshua himself, at a later day, gave his sanction to this kind of memorial. After the people had, at his instance, renewed their covenant with God, he "took a stone, and set it up under an oak that was by the sanctuary of the Lord. And Joshua said to all the people, Behold this stone shall be a witness unto us; *for it hath heard* all the words of the Lord which He spake unto us: it shall be therefore a witness unto you, lest ye deny your God."[2] This is a fine idea, going into the region of high poetic conception. The stone would become an enduring monument of that which it had *heard*, when the men who also heard it had descended to the tomb. This invests the stone with a living presence, such as that which the mind insensibly gives to some old rock or tree upon the site of great deeds, of which it stands the sole existing witness. The consciousness of this was present to the mind of the warrior who told his troops, "that forty centuries looked down upon their exploits from the pyramids of Egypt."

The great monumental altar erected near the Jordan by the men of Reuben, since the above illustration was written, has been looked for and found. The identification is, with much probability, produced in the quarterly *Statements of the Palestine Exploration Fund*, 1874, p. 241.

It is observed by Lieut. Conder, to whom we are indebted for the identification, that the altar must have been near the direct route of the Reubenites from Shiloh to the land of Gilead and Bashan ; it must have been erected on the west side of the Jordan, for the correct reading of Josh. xxii. verse 11, is, "at the boundary of Canaan, by the Gelilloth of Jordan, at the place where the Israelites crossed the river;" it must have occupied a conspicuous position, and it must have been no ordinary kind of work. There is one, and only one, spot in Palestine, which fulfils these requirements—the *Kurn Surtabeh*, a culminating summit of an almost isolated hill which closes in the broader part of the Jordan valley to the north. From the summit the whole valley is spread out like a map. On the south lie the black groves round Elisha's fountain, the sharp peaks and the blue ranges round the Dead Sea ; and on the east a mountain wall stretches away north. At the base, 2,000 feet below, lies a green plain, gay with flowers. The cone or summit is difficult of approach, and when reached presents an oblong area of about 30 by 100 yards, enclosed by a wall of fine hewn blocks. It stands above the Damieh Ford of the Jordan, and beside the direct route from Shiloh on the western side of the river. It is remarkably conspicuous to travellers in all directions, and on the summit are the remains of a large monument. In addition to other proofs of

[1] Genesis 31:47,48.   [2] Joshua 24:26,27.

identification, is one derived from the name of a valley in the neighbourhood to the north—*Tal'at Abu'Ayd*—"The ascent of the Father of Ayd." The Arabic "*Ayd*" and the Hebrew "*Ed*" are as nearly as possible identical. From the ordinary camping ground at Jericho this peak is visible.

S.

JOSHUA

Joshua 23-24

AFTER a long career of victorious warfare, followed by an old age of comparative repose, during which, upon his estate at Timnath-Serah, in the mountains of Ephraim, he was permitted to enjoy the blessings of the land he had conquered, Joshua consciously drew near to the term of his earthly existence, and, like Moses, determined to give to the assembled Israelites the advantage of his parting counsels. The tribes were convened at Shechem, where the tabernacle seems at this time to have been, and where on a former occasion, between the mountains of Ebal and Gerizim, they had entered into covenant with God. Nothing can be conceived more impressive or more sublime, than the circumstances of this last public interview of the aged leader with the people whom he had put in possession of the goodly land of Canaan, and who had so often followed him in his victorious path. In the midst of the elders, the chiefs, and the magistrates of Israel ; surrounded by a respectful people, formerly bondsmen of Pharaoh, but now in possession of a rich and beautiful country, and the sole survivors of an untoward generation,—their illustrious and venerable commander, the oldest man in all their nation, spoke to them as to his sons. And of what did he speak ? He was a soldier, and his career had been essentially military ; but he spoke to them, not of conquest —the sound of the trumpet and the gleam of the sword cannot be recognized in his address— but of the holiness and the obedience which become the people chosen of God. It is such a discourse as a patriarch might have given upon his death-bed, or a prophet might have uttered from the valley of vision. He called to mind the benefits which, age after age, had been showered upon the race of Abraham; he humbly summed up the victories to which he had himself led them, in a single allusion; and concluded with the impressive words, "Choose ye this day whom ye will serve; but as for me and my house, we will serve the Lord." The entire

JOSHUA'S LAST CHARGE TO ISRAEL.

people, with one voice, responded to this call by loud and hearty declarations of their determined faithfulness to their covenant with God; and the aged Joshua, after he had written these words in the book of the law deposited in the ark, set up a stone under a tree that grew near the tabernacle, as a memorial of this renewal of the covenant. His work, both of war and of peace, was then done, he could now lay down his head and die in thankful peace. So he died, and was buried in his own grounds at Timnath-Serah.

The character of Joshua is not only one of the finest in Scripture history, but one of the most remarkable that the world ever saw. There is scarcely any other great conqueror, and certainly no Asiatic conqueror, like him—without personal ambition, without any desire of aggrandisement. His whole heart was in the highest degree PATRIOTIC, under a system which required patriotism to take the form of religious obedience. In the distant view, the personal and even the public character of this man is overshadowed by the very greatness of the events and circumstances in which he is placed. The events are greater than the man, and engage the attention more; and hence individually he appears with less *éclat*, and attracts less attention, than an inferior man among events of less importance. This, when rightly viewed, is not a dishonour to him, but a

glory; for it shows how accurately he measured, and how truly he understood, his right position. A lesser man, in all the attributes of true greatness, would have been seen and heard more; but it is the magnanimous character of real greatness to shroud the power it exercises. Littleness is more demonstrative; greatness is quiet in the calm repose of conscious strength and influence.

Looking more closely, we appreciate the character of Joshua better. We see that it is only his essential *fitness* for the place he filled, for the great work which devolved upon him, that prevents him from being more seen. We then behold in him a rare combination of the highest qualities of the statesman and the warrior. We see that he is quite equal to every emergency under which he has to act, and that he puts forth just that degree of power—just that degree of the qualities suited to the occasion which may be required—no more, for that would be vainly demonstrative; no less, for that would be incompetency. If his gifts were less brilliant than those of Moses, they were such as befitted *his* successor; and few men have lived to whom it would not be high praise to say, that they were capable of succeeding such a man as Moses with credit. We find Joshua valiant without temerity, and active without precipitation. No care, no advantage, no duty is neglected by him. In the passage of the Jordan, in the judgment of Achan, in the siege of Ai, he forgot nothing which might tend to deepen the impression which the miracle produced—nothing which might render the justice of the doom manifest—nothing by which the victory might be ensured. The generation which he led was better and wiser than that which came forth from Egypt, and yielded to him a more willing obedience than Moses had obtained from their fathers. Towards the enemy alone was his countenance terrible; for, regarding himself as the minister of the divine anathemas against a guilty people, he executed his awful commission with no shrinking hand, but at the same time with calmness and without fury. His piety is, however, gentle, while his faith is impregnable, and his confidence in God unshaken.

In short, no man that ever lived could win a higher or more honourable character than that given to this great man by the sacred writer who records his death, and whose words form a striking epitaph upon the hero, and the most appropriate memorial of his career: "And it came to pass, after these things, that Joshua the son of Nun, THE SERVANT OF THE LORD, died, being a hundred and ten years old."

THUMBS AND GREAT TOES

Judges 1:1-7

ONE is shocked to learn that, when the Israelites had taken captive Adoni-bezek the king of Jerusalem, they cut off his thumbs and his great toes. The man who has studied the war usages of ancient times, cannot indeed feel much surprise at any instance of barbarity or savageness of which he reads, although the distress of his feelings may be as great as that of the person to whom such things are new. For the reasons already stated, it was not to be supposed that the Hebrews would carry on warfare more mildly than their neighbours; yet it must be admitted that this treatment of a captive king is, at the first view, regarded with pain, and with something like abhorrence. But let us wait a little. Let us read a few lines more of the record. How did this king himself regard this treatment? How did it affect his mind? Did he fill the air with outcries at this cruel indignity, and call down upon his conquerors the curses of all his gods? Did he fold his arms in calm dignity upon his breast, and submit his outraged majesty to the insults of a barbarous people? Nothing of the kind! He was humble, he was contrite. He regarded himself as an offender brought to justice, and confessed that he richly deserved the doom inflicted upon him. Hear his words: "Threescore and ten kings, having their thumbs and their great toes cut off, gathered their meat under my table. As I have done, so God hath requited me." Do the Hebrews after this need any excuse? Why, the man they thus roughly handled is himself their apologist and vindicator. So far from taking pleasure in such barbarities, it was precisely to express their abhorrence of them, as exercised by him, that they had subjected him to the very same treatment, that he might learn there is a God that judgeth in the earth. And he did learn it. Nothing can be more shocking

than the scene this wicked king depicts. Seventy kings, not only thus mutilated, but reduced to a condition worse than slavery—their misery paraded at the conqueror's court—and instead of sitting at his table, constrained to gather their food like dogs below it! This helps us to some insight of the state of the country under the native princes, whom the Israelites were commissioned to expel. Conceive what must have been the state of the people among whom such a scene could exist—what wars had been waged, what cruel ravages committed, before these seventy kings, however small their territories, became reduced to this condition; and behold in this a specimen of the fashion in which war was conducted, and the treatment to which the conquered were exposed. Those are certainly very much in the wrong who picture to themselves the Canaanites as "a happy family," disturbed in their peaceful homes by Hebrew barbarians from the wilderness. Behold how happy, behold how peaceful they were!

It may not be clear to some of our readers what may have been the special object of this form of mutilation. We have read, often enough, of various kinds of mutilation inflicted upon prisoners of war, but this kind is new to us. It is still, however, not less significant than blinding and other modes of privation adopted in such cases. The object was, in the first place, to disable the kings from taking part in war, without so impairing any of their faculties or functions as to deaden or lessen the sense of suffering and humiliation. This incapacitation was a great matter, when kings were expected to lead their armies in person, and to take an active part in the conflict. It is clear that no man deprived of his thumbs could handle any weapon, and that one destitute of the great toes could not have that firmness of tread in walking, racing, and climbing, which was essential to a military chief, particularly among a people who went barefoot, or who at least wore only such feet-coverings as permitted the full natural action of the toes, among which the great toes are of the highest importance. We almost think that this privation must have operated as a disqualification for any future restoration to the throne, and was intended so to operate. There can be no doubt, that when the Israelites proceeded with their miserable captive to his city of Jerusalem, they restored to their liberty the seventy kings whom they had thus avenged, and with whom they had in this uncouth manner expressed their sympathy. Nor can there be any doubt, that when the seventy discrowned princes beheld their old oppressor thus brought low, they rose from the dust to greet him, crying, "Art thou also become like unto us, thou that didst weaken the nations, thou that madest the land to tremble?" A mutilation like that which the threescore and ten had survived, was not likely to be in itself mortal; and it was therefore more probably from humbled pride than of his wounds, that Adoni-bezek died at Jerusalem.

It is observable, that in the Hebrew the great toe is called the thumb of the foot, and hence the phrase here is, "the thumbs of the hands and feet." This is the case in other oriental and in some European languages. In the Hindoo the thumb is called "sevia viril," the great finger of the hand, and the large toe is named the great finger of the foot. Mr. Roberts, in his curious *Oriental Illustrations*, states that this punishment was in ancient times very common in India, and was inflicted principally upon those who had committed some flagrant offence with the hands or with the feet. Thus, those convicted of forgery or of numerous thefts, had their thumbs cut off. The practice is now extinct, but the memory of it still exists, as it is now one of the bugbears of the nursery and of domestic life: "If you steal any more, I will cut off your thumbs;" "Let me find out the thief, and I will soon have his thumbs," and the like.

It is not expressly stated by the sacred historian that the punishment inflicted on Adoni-bezek was inflicted in obedience to a divine command. From the whole scope of the passage, however, we may infer that it was. Some have stigmatized his treatment as an act of wanton and barbarous cruelty, such as could never have been ordered or authorized by a just and holy God. In reply to such sentimental criticism, it is enough to observe, that the justice of that law which demands that "whoso sheddeth man's blood, by man shall his blood be shed," is acknowledged by all civilized nations. If, therefore, wanton and deliberate murder is justly punished by death, may not wanton and deliberate mutilation be justly punished by mutilation? The same principle runs through both. This too is the law of God as revealed in the Pentateuch. "Thou shalt give life for life, eye for eye, tooth for tooth, hand for hand, foot for foot, burning for burning, stripe for stripe" (Exod. xxi. 23-25). And again, "If a man cause a blemish in his neighbour; as he hath done, so shall it be done to him" (Lev. xxiv. 19). It must be kept in mind that in those ages there was no systematic mode of confining and punishing criminals such as we now have. Our present system is more in accordance with modern ideas. But it is very questionable whether the penal code is improved; whether that now in force is better adapted for the preservation of life and property, and for the suppression of crime, than the summary punishments enjoined in the Mosaic law.

P.

GOVERNMENT

Judges 2

ATTENTION has oftener than once, in the course of these papers, been called to the fact, that before the time of Moses the Hebrew tribes had been severally governed patriarchally by their own chiefs, and under them by the heads of the great families or clans into which the tribes were divided; and then, again, by the heads of houses. This internal organization appears to have been regarded as sufficient for all common purposes of government, for it still existed under Moses and Joshua, and in the times of the judges and the kings. There are exact parallels to it still subsisting among the Arabian and Tartar tribes. The alteration made by the law did not consist in the abrogation of this institution, but in the establishment of a general government over all, through which the tribes might be bound more effectually together as one nation. This general government centred in the person of Jehovah Himself, who condescended to become, in a special sense, their sovereign, and dwelt among them in a sensible and living presence in the tabernacle. To Him, through His high priest, they were to refer in all great matters that concerned the interests of religion and the welfare of the nation—in all, in fact, that lay beyond the scope of those functions which the tribal chiefs exercised. To Him, while they sacrificed to Him as their God, they rendered tribute as to their king, as a rent to the sovereign proprietor of the land which He alone had given to them, and which belonged to them only in grant from Him; and to maintain the vitality of their allegiance, they were bound to repair three times in the year to render suit and service to Him as their king, in the place where He sat on His throne "between the cherubim," and held His court in the tabernacle.

Under the government thus established, the functions of Moses, and after him of Joshua, were extraordinary, and altogether temporary. Moses was to bring the nation forth out of the house of bondage, and to organize its institutions in the wilderness; Joshua was to conduct them into the land of Canaan, and to give it to them for a possession. To fulfil such special missions, these men were invested with extraordinary powers, which gave them a sort of place between the heads of tribes on the one hand, and the Divine King, whose commissioned servants they were, and for whom they acted, on the other. They were themselves most anxious to keep before the minds of the people this character of their office, and this feature of their position, by taking no step of the least consequence without reference to the Lord's will, and by acting on all occasions as ministers of His will, ascertained in the appointed way.

It will therefore appear, that those who marvel that Joshua did not, like Moses, appoint a successor, and who are disposed to ascribe to that omission the disorders that ensued in the commonwealth, do utterly misconceive the true nature of the case. Moses appointed Joshua to succeed him, or rather to carry out the work he had left unfinished, not of his own mere will, but by the divine command. If any successor to Joshua had been needed, he would have been commanded to appoint one; and without such a command, this was not to be expected from him. The truth is, that the functions of Moses, and after him, of Joshua, formed one grand initiatory operation, which was completed by the latter, and the completion of which left the Hebrew state on its proper and permanent foundations,—a theocracy, with the Lord at its head, as the Divine King, abiding among them in His tabernacle; with the high priest as the medium of intercourse with Him, and the official interpreter of His will; and with the heads of tribes, of families, and of houses, as the instruments of local government. It is by our losing sight of the presence of this latter feature of the constitution, that all the difficulty arises. But its importance and general sufficiency may in some degree be illustrated from our own municipal institutions, which are found to be sufficient, under the general operation of the laws, for all local purposes throughout the land, leaving but little occasion for reference to the general government, except when something

goes seriously wrong—when some calamity has occurred—or when some large improvements are contemplated.

The object of this institution obviously was, to keep the nation in a state of direct dependence upon the providence and care of the Divine King, who had condescended to become in this special manner their sovereign, and the head of their polity. The intervention of any vicegerent, under whatever name, would materially have impaired, if not destroyed, the directness and the essential purposes of this government; for it is in man's nature, and especially was it in the Hebrew nature, to look away from the unseen to the seen; and with a visible and human vicegerent, invested with the the external attributes of power and government, the invisible King would have soon become, as to the *practical* recognition of His government, a mere abstraction, a name, a ceremony.

We are not to inquire whether this was in itself the most perfect form of political government. It was a special and peculiar government, adapted to a peculiar people, and framed for the accomplishment of peculiar ends; and being appointed by God Himself as adapted to that people, and suited to these ends, it was the most perfect for them, without being *necessarily* on that account the best for, or indeed possible to, any other people. But it may be, and it has been asked—If this were the best government for the Hebrews, how comes it to pass that they did not thrive under it? The answer is plain: The proper result, which would have led them to prosperity and power, was frustrated by their own disloyalty and disobedience. They allowed themselves to be seduced into the very connections with the remaining Canaanites, which had been most solemnly interdicted; they mixed with them in marriage, in traffic, in social intercourse, and eventually in the solemnities of their superstitious worship. They then became alienated from their Divine King, and forgot or neglected the invaluable privileges to which they were entitled under His government. How, then, was that government to be carried on? Were the terrors of the divine power to be incessantly manifested, to restrain them forcibly from yielding to their vicious and idolatrous propensities? Such is not the method of the divine government; and it would indeed have been contrary to the very idea and use of a moral governor. Was He, then, to abandon them altogether to the influence of their own corrupt tendencies, which would soon have plunged them into remediless idolatry, and thus have defeated all the purposes for which they had been set apart among the nations? If neither of these courses could be taken, there only remained that course which the Lord's providence actually took in dealing with this people. When any portion of the nation—any section of the tribes—became so far gone in idolatry as to adopt the public worship of other gods, the Lord withdrew His protection from them. Then, forsaken of their strength, they soon fell under subjection to some neighbouring state, and had to endure exactions and oppressions of intensity proportioned to their offences. This position, so grievous to a conquering people, generally brought them in time to their senses. They humbled themselves before their offended Sovereign; and, mindful of His old deliverances, they implored Him to appear once more in their behalf. And He heard them. The fit man was found and appointed to act as the Lord's vicegerent for the occasion. Under his conduct the desired deliverance was effected, and the Lord's providence and sovereignty were magnified. The deliverer, after he had, in the Lord's might, broken the foreign yoke from their necks, continued to act upon the commission he had received, and exercised such authority over that portion of the nation which had needed his services, as enabled him to maintain them in their allegiance to Jehovah during his lifetime. Nor did the influence of his exertions always disappear with his own life, and that of the generation to whom this experience of judgment and mercy had been given. The Lord enforced the authority of His law, by thus visibly controlling the nation, and proportioning their prosperity and adversity to the degree of obedience which they yielded to it; and they were hence led to look immediately to Him for protection, without interposing any permanent human authority, on which they might be apt too exclusively to depend, and thus forget their Divine King.

Although it must be admitted that the Israelites did not, during the period under consideration, maintain the position which belonged to them, and which they would have held, had they proved worthy of it, yet it may appear that the impression of their prevalent misconduct and unfaithfulness during that period,—or, as some view it, of the insufficiency of the government under which they were placed—goes considerably beyond the facts of the case. By a superficial observer, as Dr. Graves well remarks,[1] " the whole period under the judges may easily be mistaken for an unbroken series of idolatries and crimes, from his not observing that the lapses which incurred punishment, and the divine deliverances which attended repentance, are related so fully, as to occupy almost the whole narrative; while periods when, under the government of the judges, the people followed God, and the land enjoyed peace, are passed over in a single verse, as productive of no event which required a particular detail." This writer enters into a calculation, by which it appears that, out of the 450 years under the judges (without including the forty years' government of Eli), there were not less than 377 years, during which the authority of the law of Moses was acknowledged in Israel. Of the state of things which existed during this period, a charming picture, incomparable in the hearty piety and the pure and simple manners which it exhibits, is to be found in the book of Ruth, on which we forbear to expatiate, only because its indications must soon engage our full attention.

THE REPENTANCE OF GOD

Judges 2:18

GOD is oftener than once described in Scripture as repenting of something that He had done. In the text before us it is said, when His people had been allowed to fall under the oppression of their enemies to punish them for their sins, and they at length turned to Him, the Lord repented because of their groanings, and raised them up a deliverer. An equally strong case is that of the antediluvians, whose crimes were such that it is said the Lord repented that He had made man upon the earth.[2] So He "repents" of having made Saul king;[3] He repents of the evil He had said He would bring upon the Ninevites;[4] and in various places

[1] *Lectures on the Pentateuch.*
[2] Genesis 6:6.   [3] 1 Samuel 15:35.   [4] Jonah 3:10.

He is described as "repenting"[1] of the evil He
had thought to do, on certain occasions, and did
it not. In fact, that God should thus "repent for
his servants," seems to have been promised to the
Israelites by Moses in Deut. xxxii. 36. Yet it is
very remarkable that in one of the strongest of
these examples, that of Saul, the very same
chapter which contains one of the most signal
instances of repentance ascribed to God, contains
also the strongest declaration that He never
repents. In 1 Sam. xv. 11, the Lord says, "It
repenteth me that I have set up Saul to be king,
for he is turned back from following me." In
the 29th verse we read, "The Strength of Israel
will not lie nor repent; for He is not a man, that
He should repent." Even the Pentateuch, which
affords some of the strongest instances of this
mode of expression, declares, "God is not a man,
that He should lie; nor the son of man, that He
should repent."[2]

How are we to understand these things? Is
there anomaly or contradiction here? By no
means. Whatever the Scriptures positively assert
of the character of God is to be taken plainly as
it stands—it is part of the Scripture doctrine of
His being and His attributes; but when, in the
description of God's part in human history, certain
sentiments are ascribed to Him, seemingly inconsistent with those more general and abstract
characters of the Divine Being, we are to understand that these expressions are used in accommodation to our modes of thought. Man cannot
well comprehend anything beyond the range of
his own intellectual or sentient experience,—the
utmost stretch of his mind cannot grasp the vast
idea of God's nature and infinite perfections;
and it is in the knowledge of this that He, in
His great condescension, and with a view to His
conduct being made intelligible to man's understanding, has allowed Himself to be set before
him as moved by the feelings and passions which
man himself experiences. In so far as we are
enabled to realize, by the later light of the Gospel,
some faint notions of the perfections of the divine
nature, the more are we struck by the unutterable love, the tender consideration, the infinite
condescension, which for man's good allowed, in
ages of unrefined intellect, these humanized representations of Himself to be set before men. The
height of this condescension was reached when,

[1] 2 Samuel 24:16; 1 Chronicles 21:15;
Jeremiah 26:3,13,19.
[2] Numbers 23:19.

in the depths of the divine wisdom, a plan was
devised, perfect for man's salvation, which required Him to assume the very nature of man,
and as a man to live and suffer.

What, then, does the "repenting" of God really
mean? It is clear that we are not to ascribe to
God's immutable mind the fickleness of human
purposes, or to suppose that He on any of the
occasions specified really repented, or was grieved,
or disappointed. This is not possible to God,
with whom there is no variableness nor shadow
of turning. (James i. 17.) These and similar
expressions are taken from what passes among
men when they undergo change of purpose, or
are disappointed in their expectations and endeavours. As a potter, on finding that a vessel on
which he has spent his utmost care does not
answer his purpose, regrets his labour, and casts
the worthless object out of sight; so, at the
Deluge, for instance, God is represented, in
accommodation to our feeble apprehensions, as
repenting and being grieved at heart that He had
bestowed upon man so much labour in vain. In
the same manner also, as a man, when he repents,
changes his course of procedure, God, when He
changes His procedure, is said to repent, seeing
that such change would be in man the result of
repentance. Yet there is here a change, not, as
in man, of the will or purpose, but of the work
or procedure only. Repentance in man is the
changing of his will as well as of his work;
repentance in God is the change of the work
only, and not of the will, which in Him is incapable of change. Seeing that there is no mistake
in His counsels, no disappointment of His purposes, no frustration of His expectations, God
can never change His will, though He may will
to change His work. The decrees and purposes of
God stand like mountains of brass. (Zech. vi. 1.)
Always immutable, God is incapable of the frailty
or fickleness which belongs to man's nature and
experience. So also, in that singular phrase
where, on account of the wickedness that brought
on the Deluge, God is said not only to repent,
but to be "grieved at His heart," the very phrase,
emphatic as it sounds to our human experience,
indicates the real sense in which such expressions
are to be understood. In strict propriety of
speech, God has neither heart nor grief. He is
a most pure Spirit—an uncompounded Being, far
above the influence of human passion. He is
impassible; and it were at variance with His

infinite perfection that anything should grieve or work repentance in Him. The cause is in all these cases put by metonymy for the effect.

It has often occurred to us, that all these expressions whereby God is presented to the mind as invested with human parts and passions, involve a sort of looking forward to that period in which they would all become appropriate, by our being permitted to view God in Christ, who has carried the real experiences of our nature into the very heavens, where He sits, not as one who cannot be touched with the feeling of our infirmities, but as one who has been tempted like as we are, yet remained without sin. Had God been, in the Old Testament, set before the mind wholly in the abstract qualities of His being, there would have been a lack of unity in the mode in which He is presented to the apprehension of the heart (we say not of the *mind*) under the two dispensations. But the Lord, knowing from the beginning the aspect in which He would be eventually revealed to the church in Christ, permitted beforehand these humanized indications of Himself, that there might be under both dispensations that oneness of feeling in regard to Him, which enables the most enlightened servant of Christ to make the language of ancient David his own when he thinks and speaks of God.

I think the exact meaning of those passages in which the repentance of God is spoken of, has scarcely been caught by Dr. Kitto, and a very questionable view seems to be advanced in the statement that God " is impassible."

Human language was intended for human beings, to embody and to convey their thoughts, and to describe their acts. It is adapted to the capacity of man. But man is unable fully to comprehend the character, attributes, and acts of God; and human language, therefore, cannot fully express them. All knowledge of God must be communicated by words originally designed to express what concerns humanity. But these words are used and must be interpreted analogically. When, for example, affections, passions, and sufferings are in Scripture ascribed to God, in language which can only in its ordinary sense be applicable to man, the language must be interpreted in a way altogether different from what it would be if applied to man. We learn this from Scripture itself, which affords us incidentally sound canons of interpretation. While it tells us that God " repents," that He is " angry," that He taketh " vengeance ;" while it speaks of " the hand of God," and " the eye of God," and the " throne of God," it also tells us that God is invisible, spiritual, and absolutely free from all human passions and mutations. We can form no clear conception of pure spirit or of absolute unchangeableness. When we speak of spirit, it must be in

language adapted to material constitutions ; when we think of spirit, our thoughts are moulded according to what partakes of humanity ; and when the Eternal Spirit reveals to us His nature, acts, or attributes, it must necessarily be through the medium of words which have a *direct* material signification. Consequently, such expressions as the repentance of God, His jealousy, anger, grief, vengeance, while they do not convey, as they would if applied to man, any idea of materialism, or weakness, or mutability ; yet they are at the same time intended to show that the God of the Bible is not impassible, that He is not a cold abstraction, but a being of the most exquisite feelings, and of the tenderest sympathies, and who is deeply interested in humanity. Man was created in God's image. To that image he must be again restored ere he can enter heaven. The regenerate soul, therefore, is to some extent a reflection of the divine image. The graces which adorn and the affections which animate it, are reflections of the divine attributes. Our Lord was "the brightness of the Father's glory, and the express image of His person ;" and He, in connection with wisdom and power infinite, manifested a love and a tenderness, and also an abhorrence of sin, such as the world never witnessed.

P.

SUBJECTION

Judges 3:1-17

THE first subjugation under which the Israelites fell was to a foreign prince named Chusanrishathaim, king of Mesopotamia. As early as the time of Abraham, we see princes from the Euphrates undertaking expeditions and making conquests in this quarter, and the present is another instance of the same kind. It is much to be regretted that we have not more full information respecting the regions beyond the river at this early time, that we might more perfectly understand the nature of the relations which subsisted between their people and those of the countries towards the Jordan. There are hints here and there in the early Scriptures, of a degree of connection, peaceful sometimes, and sometimes warlike, that we have no means of tracing or understanding. Indeed, as our most ancient history takes little or no notice of any other nations than those of Egypt, Arabia, Canaan, and Israel, we almost grow up in the notion that these nations formed the world in those days. We know these only; and it is with something of surprise that we occasionally catch a glimpse of other and more remote nations, great and strong. What was the nature of the oppression

to which this conqueror subjected the Israelites, is not very clear. There is no reason,
however, to suppose that he remained in occupation of the land; but he more probably exacted
heavy and oppressive tributes, which they were
constrained to pay under the penalty of another
devastating visit from his armies, and by which
the wealth of the nation was drained, and the
people kept in a state of poverty and wretchedness.

Eight years did the Israelites remain under
Chusan-rishathaim, and then, on their repentance,
they found a deliverer in Othniel, that gallant
son of Kenaz, whose exploit, which won him the
hand of Caleb's daughter, we have already had
occasion to notice. Under him the land enjoyed
rest for forty years. Then the people, after
Othniel's death, again fell into sin, and for that
sin were delivered into the hands of the Moabites.
This was a more terrible judgment than the
other. The dominion of a near neighbour, whose
resources are close at hand, is always more fearful than that of a stranger, the centre of whose
power is far off. In this case we may also
presume that something remained of the old
animosity which induced a king of Moab to hire
the Chaldean soothsayer to lay a curse upon the
Israelites, with a view to their overthrow.
Baulked then, the Moabites are now successful.
The Protector who would not suffer even the
impotent curse of Balaam to light upon His
people's head, has now withdrawn His interposing hand, and left them to their own resources,
and they are lost. Now Moab may vent at will
the gathered envy, hatred, and malice of sixty
years.

We feel some interest in knowing what became
of the tribes beyond the Jordan. Nothing is said
of them. One is ready to suppose that they must
have interfered to prevent this motion on the
part of the Moabites. But it seems likely that
they were previously subdued, as it is scarcely
credible that the Moabites would not desire first
to recover their own ancient possessions beyond
the Jordan, before carrying their aggressions into
the country west of the river.

The king of the Moabites at this time was
Eglon, described as "a very fat man." Of all the
numerous personages brought under our notice in
the Scriptures, this is the only one distinguished
as being "fat." This seems to imply the rarity
of this bodily characteristic. Corpulency is
indeed very rare in Western Asia among men.
Few instances of it occurred in our own somewhat extensive observation, and still fewer of
persons who might be called stout from largeness
of build. Probably, however, the obesity of
Eglon would not have been noticed, but from
the fact afterwards mentioned, that when he met
his death, the dagger thrust into his body could
not be again drawn out, from the fat closing
over it.

This conqueror made his subjugation of Israel
the more oppressive, by his actually remaining in
the land with a military force to hold the people
in awe. He retained in his actual possession the
plain of Jericho, which, as formerly described,
forms, when viewed geographically, part of the
same plain as that of Moab on the other side of
the river. He remained there for the facility of
communication which he thus had with his native
territory, whether as regarded the obtaining of
prompt reinforcements from thence, or his retreating thither in case of emergency. His
retaining the command of the fords of the Jordan
would also enable him to prevent the tribes
beyond the river from affording any succour to
their oppressed brethren, if they were in a condition to render any. We can see that, although
he desired to secure his supremacy by remaining
in the land, and maintaining a force there,
sufficient as it seemed to repress all attempts
to resist or shake off the authority he had
established, he was prudent enough not to venture into the mountainous interior of the land,
and so afford the Israelites an opportunity of
cutting off his communication with his own
country.

The presence of a foreign prince, ruling over
them in the plain of Jericho, ever present and
watchful, could not but form a far more harassing oppression than that to which they had
been previously subject. But the aggravation of
a second offence required this heavier punishment.
This state of things lasted eighteen years, during
which the dominion of Moab acquired something
like the character of an established authority,
from the quiet submission of the Israelites. The
grievance on the part of the latter lay, we may
suppose, in the heavy tribute demanded by their
masters, and in the lawless conduct of the occupying force towards the conquered people. The
tribute of the tribes held under the yoke seems
to have been carried periodically to the Moabitish

king in the plain of Jericho, at "the city of palm trees," a name that once belonged to Jericho, but which seems now to have been appropriated by some other town that had arisen in another part of this palmy plain. From the description we have of the manner in which this tribute was on one occasion presented, the various matters of which it was composed appear to have been borne by a great number of persons, who, marching in orderly procession, successively laid down their valuable burdens before the king. This is in perfect conformity with modern eastern manners. Tributes, the products of provinces, the gifts periodically or occasionally tendered to a sovereign, are always presented in great state, and with much solicitude to enhance the apparent extent of the offering. Four or five men or horses are laden with what might most easily be carried by one; and jewels, trinkets, and other articles of value, which one tray might very well hold, are displayed in ten or fifteen. So it was also in ancient times, as we find by the sculptures of Persia and the paintings of Egypt, in which interesting exhibitions of such processions of tribute-bearers are found. In the latter we see the various offerings received by the king on his throne, then borne away to the stores, and duly registered by the proper officers.

EHUD AND EGLON

Judges 3:18-30

It is remarkable, that although the name "Benjamin" signifies "the son of the *right* hand," yet, from some cause or other, multitudes of persons belonging to this tribe were *left*-handed. This is one of the most curious examples of that sort of discrepancy between names and characters, which has often given occasion to amusing remark. In the original Hebrew this contrast is more distinctly noted than in the translation, seeing that the word rendered "left-handed" signifies "short," or "obstructed in the *right* hand." This being the true meaning, it is erroneous to suppose, as some have done, that the seven hundred left-handed men of Benjamin (mentioned in Judg. xx. 16), every one of whom could sling stones at a hair and not miss, were

ambidexters—that is, who were not literally *left*-handed, but could use *both* hands equally well—the left hand no less than the right. Yet this is the impression which both the Septuagint and the Vulgate translations convey. It is much that men whose right hands are torpid (which is the elegant translation of the Syriac in this csse) should be able to use the left hand with the same advantage with which men commonly use the right; but it is more—it is a bold and noble triumph over infirmity, turning it into a gain—when men, as in this case, cultivate the powers of the wrong member to the extent of making their left-handed operations more skilful than the right-handed deeds of other men.

One of this body of left-handed Benjamites was Ehud, the second judge of Israel. He seems to have been a man of consequence in his tribe before he rose to this distinction, for he was the person appointed on one occasion to command the party which bore the tributes of Israel to king Eglon, at the city of palm trees. It is well to note that this city of palm trees, with the whole plain of Jericho, was in the lot of Benjamin; that tribe must therefore have been, more particularly than the others, aggrieved by the Moabitish oppression. The Benjamites paid tribute like the other tribes; but, besides, they had the conquering power in the midst of them, reigning in part of their territory, and they were therefore continually subject to the annoyances, insults, and special exactions which the presence of an occupying soldiery, and of a greedy and insolent court, never fails in the East to impose upon a conquered country. It was natural, therefore, that the Benjamites should have been the first to move against this oppression, and that the deliverer should have been a chief man of this tribe. The animus of personal hatred, which was thus engendered, also helps to account for the unscrupulous measure which Ehud adopted in giving the first blow to the oppressor.

Having delivered his present in the way which we yesterday described, Ehud withdrew, and accompanied his men so far as the "quarries that were by Gilgal," on the way homeward. There is, perhaps, some point intended in this mention of the "quarries." The verb from which the word so translated comes, means "to cut out," or "to carve as a sculptor;" and hence some have supposed that it was a place of graven images, which the Moabites had set up in the sacred land; and, connecting this with the fact that Gilgal had long been the place of the Hebrew encampment, when they first entered the land, and where the twelve memorial stones, taken out of the bed of the Jordan, had been placed, it has been conjectured that the Moabitish idols had been set up in a spot thus memorable, and in some degree hallowed, in studied contempt of the religion and worship of the Israelites. The more the reader considers the peculiar estimation in which, from historical and religious associations, this spot was regarded by the Israelites, and the more he studies the peculiar modes in which the ancient heathens expressed their triumph over a fallen foe, and over *his gods*, the more reason there may be to see some probability in this seemingly fanciful conclusion. Recollecting how the Philistines triumphed by sending the ark of the Lord to the temple of their Dagon, nothing can be more likely than that, if the Moabites regarded the place as a sacred one of the Hebrews, and looked upon the stones as religious monuments of theirs, they would inflict upon them the insult of setting up their own idols in this very spot.

The ensuing actions of Ehud may therefore appear to have been stimulated, or his wavering purpose strengthened, by the view of this profanation. We at least know that, on arriving at this place, he turned again, and went immediately into the presence of Eglon. Having been there just before, on an errand so agreeable to the king and those about him, he would find easy access, on pretence of having some forgotten part of his mission to discharge. Such, indeed, was Ehud's pretence. He had, he said, "a secret errand" to deliver. On this the king commanded his attendants to withdraw, and he remained alone with the avenger. Ehud appeared to be unarmed. It was probably a rule that no one, and especially no Israelite, should appear armed in the presence of the king; but this man had a long two-edged dagger girded upon his *right* thigh, under his raiment. Such weapons were usually worn of course upon the left thigh, to be drawn by the right hand; but Ehud being left-handed, was enabled to wear it, for efficient use, upon a part of his person where its presence would not be suspected. He was aware of the danger of giving an alarm; and his anxiety therefore was, as Josephus alleges, to find the opportunity of giving one fatal stroke, that the king might perish without cry or struggle. This could not be achieved while Eglon remained seated; therefore, drawing near at the same time, and to make him rise, he said, "I have a message from God unto thee." On this the king, heathen as he was, rose to receive such a message with becoming respect, and that instant the dagger of Ehud was buried in his bowels. So terrible was the stroke, that the haft went in after the blade, and could not be withdrawn. Leaving it there, Ehud "went forth through the porch, and shut the doors of the parlour upon him, and locked them."

It had previously been noticed that the king "was sitting in a summer parlour, which he had for himself alone." The term "summer parlour" scarcely conveys the full sense of the original. The marginal reading, "parlour of cooling," is nearer. Of the two words employed, one denotes that the room was an *upper chamber*, and the other, that it was constructed for the purpose of *coolness*, a provision which must have been very needful in the almost torrid climate of the plain of Jericho. The fact is interesting merely as a point relating to antiquities, that measures were in this early age adopted for promoting coolness in certain parts of the house during the heat of summer. Taking into account the peculiarly warm climate of the plain of Jericho, we may conceive that the provision made was probably such as we find in the corresponding climates of the valley of the Nile, and the plains of the Tigris and Euphrates. These methods were two-fold.

There is first, then, in most good houses a chamber in the upper part of the house, often thrown considerably apart from the general mass of building, in order to secure the principal object of its appropriation. This is, that at the end opposite the entrance there shall be a large oriel or projecting window, occupying the entire end of the room, thrown forward and overlooking the most open situation that can be commanded, whether it be a street, a river, or a garden. The recess formed by the window is raised a foot or so above the general level of the room, and is fitted with cushions, where the master of the house reposes during the heat of the day, refreshed by the air which is admitted through the fine lattice-work of wood, which is so close as to exclude the glaring light and the heat, as well as to prevent the interior from being seen from without, while the person from within can command a perfect view through the interstices. There can be no question about the antiquity of such arrangements; for such a window, thus latticed, is expressly mentioned in Judg. v. 28, where Sisera's mother and her ladies are described as watching through the lattice for the return of his chariot. All the arrangements of this room are adapted to promote coolness, and to form a pleasant and refreshing retreat during the heat of the day. These sitting apartments are sometimes seen thrown quite across the street, joining the houses on either side, forming a pleasing variety to the architecture, particularly when seen, as they often are, half-shaded by the leaves of the palm tree that overshadows them from the court within.

Another mode of promoting coolness in this and other rooms is by means of the *mulquf*, or wind-conductor. This is a construction rising above the roof, and open to the wind, so that a constant stream of cool air passes down into the apartments below. In the region of the Tigris

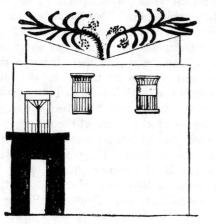

HOUSE WITH WIND-CONDUCTOR

these constructions, always open to the prevailing winds of the locality, are substantially built with bricks covered with plaster, and present the appearance of low towers or chimneys; but in the region of the Nile they form a kind of shed or dome, consisting of a strong framework, to which several planks of wood are nailed, according to the height and breadth proposed; and if required to be of cheaper materials, the place of planks is supplied by reeds or mats covered with stucco, and protected and supported by wooden rafters. That this arrangement is by no means of modern date—that it is, at least, as ancient as the time of

Eglon—is shown by its being distinctly exhibited in the ancient tomb-paintings, wherein the early domestic arrangements of the Egyptians are exhibited. Indeed, the ancient inhabitants of Egypt seem to have had this arrangement in greater perfection than the modern, as their wind-conductors, like those of Chaldea at the present time, were adapted to catch the wind from different directions, whereas those now in use are only open to the north-west.

The retiredness of these "cool parlours," and the use to which they were appropriated, are shown by the fact that the servants of Eglon, although aware that Ehud had departed, and surprised at the time which had elapsed without their being called, did not venture to intrude upon their master's privacy. They supposed he was taking his afternoon's sleep; but when at length the unusual lapse of time roused their alarm, and they entered the apartment, they found their master dead on the floor, long since dead, with the dagger of Ehud in his bowels. The consternation which this deed inspired was not lessened when they soon found Israel in arms. Ehud, escaping to the mountains, had blown the trumpet of revolt, crying "Follow after me; for the Lord hath delivered your enemies the Moabites into your hands." Following him they hastened to seize the fords of the Jordan; so that when the Moabites awoke from the stupor which the loss of their king inspired, they found themselves hemmed in by eager enemies, without a leader, and the retreat to their own country cut off. Under these circumstances they seem to have been too much dispirited to make any vigorous stand; they were slain by thousands; not one of them escaped; and Israel once more was free.

Such deeds as that of Ehud, when prompted, as his was, by patriotism, have won the praise of men, as in the case of Brutus and others. We cannot praise his achievement, nor sympathize with it, attended as it was by circumstances of barbarity and deceit. Some allowance may be made for the views, different from ours, but into which human nature is still prone to relapse, of the obligations or rights of patriotic enthusiasm. But since space does not allow us to discuss the subject fully, we can only say that God has often, in the history of the world, as in the instance of Jehu, made the wrath and cruelty of man to praise Him, and to accomplish His decreed purposes.

It is probable that the oppression practised by the Mesopotamian princes and the Moabites on the Israelites was similar to that to which the settled inhabitants of Eastern Palestine are now exposed at the hands of the great desert tribes. These tribes are nomads. They spend the winter months amid the uplands of Nejd, or along the banks of the Euphrates. With early spring they approach Palestine. Like locusts they invade the land, eating up all before them. Those who live on the exposed border must give black-mail, or else their flocks and crops will be swept away together. Most of the villages east of the Jordan, and even many on its western side, pay annually a large tribute to the Arabian freebooters. It is not unusual for a section of a nomad tribe to settle down with their flocks and herds for months together in a region where water and pasture are abundant, and the resident inhabitants completely under control. On such occasions the ravages committed are terrible. I have seen the plateau of Jaulân, on the east side of the Sea of Tiberias, covered with the flocks and herds of the Anezeh; and I have seen another large tribe encamped on the plain of Esdraelon, levying tribute from all the villages on its borders.

P.

THE HUSBANDMEN

Judges 3:31

The Philistines were not among the nations devoted to the sword of Israel. They were not in fact Canaanites; but foreigners, who had at an early period possessed themselves of a portion of the Canaanitish territory. They were there, as we formerly saw, so early as the time of the Hebrew patriarchs. The fact of their exemption shows for what reason it is that this warlike people have not hitherto appeared upon the scene of the Hebrew history, in which they were destined eventually to make a conspicuous figure. They were not molested by the Israelites, and therefore they do not seem to have cared whether the territories to which they did not themselves advance any claim were possessed by the Israelites or by the Canaanites. Indeed, the nations of Canaan themselves, considering the wonders which the Lord had wrought for Israel, would not probably have attacked the Israelites until put upon their defence; and the Philistines not being so put upon their defence, may well have been restrained by what they saw and heard from interfering with a people so signally favoured of heaven. We see also how their distinct origin, and their appearance in the land as an originally hostile race, prevented such alliances between them and the Canaanitish tribes as might have brought them into conflict with the Hebrews. In time, however, as their power and population increased, they began to manifest a disposition to repel the Israelites from their frontier, if not to bring such as bordered on it into subjection. Much of the original terror with which the Israelites were regarded must by this time have been abated, if only from the consideration that this favoured people had already been twice in a state of subjection—the second time to no greater a people than the Moabites, who seem to have found ten thousand men sufficient to keep in subjection the very tribes, the southern ones, against whom the Philistines themselves desired to act.

They appear as the next disturbers of Israel—and that merely in the south, after all the tribes had enjoyed eighty years' peace since the yoke of Moab had been cut off by the dagger of Ehud. There had been probably before this some small operations and petty bickerings, which the sacred historian has not recorded. In the narrative they appear with startling abruptness, in the territory probably of either Judah or Dan. They are espied by the husbandmen at work in the fields, who, under the conduct of one Shamgar, gather together and give them battle with their agricultural implements, having no time to provide themselves with better; and the grim Philistines, struck with terror from God, are amazed at this sample of the spirit of the nation, speedily took to flight, and left six hundred of their number dead on the field. This recital gives what we conceive to be the correct interpretation of the single verse of Scripture which records this exploit: "And after him [Ehud] was Shamgar the son of Anath, which slew of the Philistines six hundred men with an ox-goad." This seems to make it the deed of Shamgar alone; but as one man would find it somewhat heavy work to slay six hundred men with an ox-goad, even if they stood still for the purpose, we presume that, as is often the case in all history, the exploit of Shamgar and the rustics whom he got hastily together is, for conciseness, ascribed to the single arm and weapon of the leader. Still, some of the exploits of Samson in a later age come up to this; and it is impossible to affirm positively that this is not the more correct interpretation.

We do not know that our own agriculture supplies any implement so well suited for being used as a weapon of war as the ox-goad of Palestine. This may be seen by the description given of the instrument by Maundrell, who was the first to apply his actual observation to the illustration of this passage of Scripture. He says: "The country people are now everywhere at plough in the fields, in order to sow cotton. It was observable, that in ploughing they used goads of extraordinary size. Upon measuring of several, I found them eight feet long, and at the bigger end eight inches in circumference. They were armed at the lesser end with a sharp prickle for driving the oxen, at the other end with a small spade or paddle of iron, strong and massy, for cleansing the plough from the clay that encumbered it in working. May we not from hence conjecture, that it was with such a goad as one of these that Shamgar made that prodigious slaughter related of him? I am confident that, whoever shall see one of these instruments, will judge it to be not less fit, perhaps fitter, than a sword for such an execution. Goads of this sort I always saw used hereabouts, and also in Syria; and the reason is, that the same single person both drives the oxen and manages the plough, which makes it necessary to use such a goad as

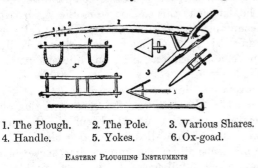

1. The Plough.   2. The Pole.   3. Various Shares.
4. Handle.   5. Yokes.   6. Ox-goad.

EASTERN PLOUGHING INSTRUMENTS

is above described, to avoid the encumbrance of two instruments." This implement also engaged the attention of Buckingham, who, in describing his journey from Tyre to Acre, remarks of the ploughing which he witnessed: "Oxen were yoked in pairs, and the plough was small and of simple construction, so that it was necessary for two to follow in the same furrow, as they invariably did. The husbandman, holding the plough with one hand, by a handle like that of a walking crutch, bore in the other a goad of seven or eight feet in length, armed with a sharp point of iron at one end, and at the other with a plate of the same metal shaped like a calking chisel. One attendant only was necessary for each plough,

as he who guided it with one hand spurred the oxen with the point of the goad, and cleansed the earth from the ploughshare by its spaded heel with the other."

PLOUGHING WITH ONE-HANDED PLOUGH

The above cuts, which show all the implements which in Syria are employed in ploughing, will render these details more clear. It claims to be noticed that some versions, such as the Septuagint and the Vulgate, make the instrument employed by Shamgar to have been the culter of his plough. We do not believe this to be a correct interpretation of the original, and most of our readers will smile at it as an absurdity. Yet it is not quite so absurd as it appears. This may be seen by the engraving, which shows that the hollow piece of pointed iron, which arms the point of the wooden ploughshare, might easily be taken off, and when fitted to a staff as a handle, would become a formidable weapon of war. It was no doubt this easy adaptation of agricultural implements to warlike purposes, coupled with a keen remembrance of Shamgar's ox-goad, which led the Philistines, when they had the upper hand in a later age, not only to disarm the Israelites, but even to deprive them of the means of sharpening their instruments of husbandry: "But all the Israelites went down to the Philistines to sharpen every man his share, and his culter, and his axe, and his mattock. Yet they had a file for the mattocks, and for the culters, and for the forks, and for the axes, *and to sharpen the goads.*" (1 Sam. xiii. 20, 21.)

I once saw a goad in the hand of a Druse ploughman, on the mountains of Bashan, which as a weapon of war would be far more effective in the hands of a strong man than nine-tenths of the spears in use among the modern Bedawîn. The shaft was ten feet long, and made of an oak sapling; the goad appeared to be an old spearhead, very sharp, and firmly fastened. On examining it, and expressing some surprise at its size and strength, the Druse remarked with a smile, "It is for the Arabs as well as the oxen." Probably the Israelites on the Philistine border were accustomed, like the Druses of Bashan, to use their implements of husbandry as weapons of war.

P.

THE OPPRESSED LAND

Judges 5:6-10

THE victory of Shamgar over the Philistines seems, as we have remarked, to have occurred eighty years after that of Ehud over Moab. In the history nothing is said of the condition of the country and people during the period which intervened between the exploit of Shamgar, and the oppression of the northern Canaanites under Jabin, king of Hazor. Indeed, of the state of the people during that period, which lasted twenty years, no information is furnished. But in the noble song of Deborah there is a statement applicable to the whole period, which is a most graphic and interesting indication of the condition of an oppressed people in the East. It deserves to be considered well. We confine ourselves to some preliminary particulars now; the song itself will in a day or two claim our notice.

It may be premised, that in introducing this description, Deborah speaks of a judge called Jael, not named in the history itself. Shamgar is supposed to have died in the same year in which he performed that great exploit for which alone he is remembered. The brevity of the Scripture notice of him, without any reference to the time of his rule, confirms the intimation of Josephus to that effect. Jael probably judged Israel in the interval between Shamgar's death and the commencement of the northern tyranny; but it is impossible to speculate safely upon the circumstances which have left the mere existence of his government to be gathered from two words in an ancient poem.

The poetess says, that in the days of Shamgar and of Jael, and, by implication, in the years that followed, "the ways lay desert, and travellers went by winding bypaths."[1] This is a very striking and natural circumstance. The people were so much subjected to violence and insults upon the common and frequented roads,—smitten plundered, stripped, and perhaps often slain,— that they gradually abandoned the high roads altogether, and stole from place to place by obscure and unfrequented routes. The same idea is expressed in a much later age by the prophet Isaiah: "The highways lie waste, the wayfaring man ceaseth."[1] This indeed heightens the picture; for not only, as in the former case, do people travel by unfrequented paths, when constrained to leave their own towns, but travelling itself becomes greatly diminished, and almost ceases, people leaving their homes as little as possible, and only on occasions of the extremest urgency. We have ourselves known in the East, in unsettled times, persons afraid to stir, for months together, beyond their towns and villages, and for still longer periods travelling wholly abandoned, or undertaken only in large and well armed bodies. In point of fact, this was the general state of Palestine even until our own time, before a somewhat more orderly state of things was established in Syria by Mohammed Ali, when travelling became comparatively safe. The danger in this case is from the Arab tribes occupying the open country, who greatly endangered, by their aggressions upon travellers, the communications between different parts of the land.

Another circumstance is, that "the villages ceased."[2] Villages are the characteristics of a settled country. In unsettled countries the people are collected in walled towns, at wide distances from each other, the intervening space being unrelieved by villages. In times of trouble, the rural population, subject as they are to continual annoyance and plundering, against which they have no defence, gradually withdraw into the nearest towns with their movables, leaving the villages deserted, and abandoning all cultivation but such as can be carried on within reach of the towns. Thus, therefore, not only the villages, but the peasantry ceased, as a necessary consequence, in countries thus troubled. Hence

the *American Biblical Repository* for 1831, to the notes accompanying which we are also under obligation.

[1] Isaiah 33:8.

[2] Here we adopt the common version, not being satisfied with the reasons Dr. Robinson advances for translating "the leaders ceased."

[1] The quotations, when not from the authorized version, are from the admirable translation of Dr. E. Robinson, in

Luther was indirectly right in translating the word by "peasants" (*Bauren*).

But there was not safety even in towns, for "war was then in the gates;" which doubtless has reference to the hostile incursions in which the cities of Israel were surprised and plundered by their watchful and daring foes. We may find a specimen of this in a later age, in the case of Ziklag, which, during the brief absence of David, was surprised, fired, the women and children carried away captive,—no doubt to be sold for slaves,—and all the property taken for spoil by the Amalekites. That the benefits of peaceful life and regular government were not enjoyed, is still further indicated by the fact, that the gates were the places where the magistrates administered justice, and where the public business of the community was transacted. But the continual incursions of the enemy deprived the magistrate of his dignity, and the people of the benefit of government. There being no peace to him that went out or him that came in, the stated administration of justice must have been grievously interrupted in such times.

We are next told that "a shield or spear was not found among forty thousand in Israel." The shield and spear were the principal weapons of ancient warfare, and here stand for weapons of all kinds. The inference is, that they had been disarmed by their enemies,—an obvious policy, much used in ancient times, and which we had yesterday occasion to notice. A round number —forty thousand—is used for an indefinite one, to express the idea that the people were altogether without arms. This destitution of arms may account for the small number which eventually came forward to strike for the deliverance of Israel, and the general reluctance to appear in the field which the song of Deborah indicates. Some have thought that the passage, by this poetical form of expression, only declares the reluctance of the Israelites to take arms; and they point to the fact, that the ten thousand who actually took the field must have had arms. To this it may be answered, that no search for arms is ever so effectual but that some are concealed, so as to appear in the hands of their owners when occasion for their use is found. Besides, we do not know with what weapons Barak's warriors fought. Shamgar's husbandmen had defeated the Philistines with ox-goads.

In the sequel there is a beautiful apostrophe to certain classes of the people—from the highest to the lowest—calling upon them to exult in their deliverance from danger. The verse in the common version is "Speak ye, that ride on white asses, ye that sit in judgment, and walk by the way." Robinson's is—

> "Ye who ride upon white asses,
> Ye who recline upon splendid carpets,
> And ye who walk the streets,
> Prepare a song."

We had occasion not long ago[1] to remark on the use of asses for riding, and on the distinction of riding on white asses. At the present day in the East, no man of the least note moves a few yards from his own door but on the back of some animal; and where horses are in very general use, men of grave judicial functions or religious character affect to ride on asses and mules, as if appearing on horseback scarcely befitted their character. When, however, the ass was the only beast which was mounted, the riding of these animals could not have been indicative of condition or character. The distinction of judicial dignity therefore lay in the riding on *white* asses. Asses of this colour, being scarce, are costly; and hence to possess one is still a mark of easy circumstances.

White asses are very uncommon in Europe, and rare in Syria and Egypt; but they are not absolutely so scarce as some report. In Arabia, and the towns on its frontiers, they are often seen. In Bagdad, for instance, one of the things that must strike a stranger is the number of white asses. There is thus quite a fashion for asses of this colour; and we can scarcely meet a person of respectability, man or woman, who is not mounted on one of these valued quadrupeds, except perhaps men of the more warlike classes, who despise anything under the grade of an Arab steed. Most persons belonging to the learned and sacred professions prefer the meeker animal, and so do all the ladies; so that the number in use is very great. These asses are, we believe, of a peculiar breed, and fetch very high prices, from forty to fifty pounds sterling (a very important sum there) being no unusual price for one of large size, good blood, and fine paces. They are richly caparisoned, and they all have their nostrils slit, which is believed to make them longer winded. As to the "judges" riding these asses, the term may signify nobles, princes, magnates—the first

[1] See Vol. 1, pp. 461-464.

class of the people, and not merely magistrates, as distinct from these. We read farther on, that thirty sons of Jair, who judged (or ruled) Israel, and the seventy sons and nephews of Abdon, who also judged Israel, "rode upon asses' colts" (Judg. x. 4; xii. 14), which seems to be mentioned as a circumstance proper to their rank. It may be inferred from this, that the first class of the people had during the oppression been prevented from riding about, as in former times, upon their white asses; but now that the oppression was over, they might ride forth in honour and safety, amid the salutations of those who passed them on the way.

The next class are "those who sit in judgment," which, if the previous clause be understood of judges merely, would be a mere description of the same class by another phrase; but not so, if that be understood of the chiefs and nobles, and this of the magistrates. We take this to be the case; for to *sit* is the proper characteristic of this class, as to *ride* is of the other. The phrase is, however, one hard to be understood. Robinson takes it, as we see, to mean, "those who recline on splendid carpets:" and there is reason and authority for this interpretation. The word, however, should be taken for anything extended out to sit upon, whether a carpet or not; and if the Hebrews, like the modern Orientals, sat upon the ground, or upon low divans or couches, these were doubtless carpets, or something serving the same purpose. Those who so sit are the opulent, the persons in good circumstances, but not in high authority; and therefore here particularly distinguished, on the one hand, from the nobles who ride, and on the other, from the poor who walk. From the general sense of the word, even thus understood, it supplies no evidence for the antiquity of carpets, properly so called, but only of something spread out to sit upon. At such a time opulent persons could not, amid prevailing troubles, with their lives and property in jeopardy every hour, enjoy the ease which their condition in life allowed; but when the time of oppression was passed, they could recline securely, without starting in alarm at every sound, expecting to learn that the destroyer was at the gates.

Even the poor people walking by the way are called upon to rejoice that their dangers are also ended. If "the way" means the roads beyond the town, it is explained by what has been already stated in regard to the insecurity of the roads. If it means the streets, it implies the presence of their enemies in the very towns; and there were many in which the Israelites and Canaanites lived together. The latter, formerly tributaries, would now gain the upper hand in these towns; and to appear, even in the streets, would be unsafe. The disposition of the Orientals to inflict wanton and cruel wrong in such cases, upon those they pass in the streets, must be witnessed to be understood. We have known cases of poor and inoffensive persons being wantonly maimed and wounded in passing along the streets; and even of females being assaulted, and the ornaments of their ears and noses violently rent from them. By the indication of their various classes, the sacred poetess describes the condition of the whole nation, and calls upon it as a whole to rejoice in its deliverance.

A MOTHER IN ISRAEL

Judges 4:4-5, 5:7

UNDER the circumstances described yesterday, Israel was not destitute of a judge; and that judge was a woman, the only woman who ever held that high office, if office it may be called, it being rather a function or position. In this instance also, as in some others, the post was not, as was generally the case, acquired by some warlike exploit tending to the deliverance of Israel, but seems to have grown out of the respect and honour which were paid to Deborah as one taught of God, and eminent for her sagacity, her wisdom, and her high utterances. This led to her being much consulted and referred to, and to the eventual establishment of a recognized influence and status, which made her virtually the judge of the nation. She calls herself "a mother in Israel," which is, in fact, the most striking and emphatic description of her position which could be given.

She is called "Deborah the prophetess." The name Deborah means a bee, forming one of a class of names, such as are derived from material objects, not uncommon in Scripture. Thus we find Rachel, a lamb; Chasidah, a stork; Hadessah (Esther), a myrtle; Tamar, a palm tree; Caleb, a dog; Nehushta, a serpent; Irad, a wild ass;

Achbar, a mouse; Agabus, a locust; Cephas, a rock or stone; and many others. Nor are such names unknown to us. Thus we have Margaret, a pearl; Agnes, a lamb; Phillis, a green bough; Penelope, a species of bird (turkey-pheasant?); Rose; Giles, a little goat; Lionel, a little lion, etc. Then, still more analogously, there are our surnames, in which almost every material object is represented.

Of Deborah, an old writer quaintly remarks, that she was indeed a bee, having honey for the friends and a sting for the enemies of Israel. Then she was a "prophetess." The words "prophet" and "prophetess" are of very extensive and somewhat ambiguous signification in Scripture, being sometimes applied to persons extraordinarily endowed by God with the power of foretelling future events, or of working miracles, or of chanting or singing forth the praises of God under supernatural influence, and sometimes to those who were remarkably instructed in divine knowledge by the immediate inspiration of the Spirit of God, and therefore appointed to act as interpreters of His will. The reader will easily call to mind personages in Scripture who belong to these different classes, but who are all equally called "prophets." To which class does Deborah the prophetess belong? It seems to us, that in her, as in some others, two or more of these different sorts of prophecy were united. The last formed, probably, the foundation of her credit, and led the people to resort to her for guidance. But that she was also a prophetess in the sense of a foreteller of things to come, is shown by the assurance of victory she gave to Barak, and more clearly by her prediction that the commander of the enemy's forces would fall by a woman's hand; while the high poetic inspiration, which is sometimes called prophecy, is not more clearly evinced in any portion of Scripture than in that most noble ode, in which Deborah celebrates the praise of the Lord for the victory of Israel over king Jabin's host. Of that hymn, which we find in the fifth chapter of Judges, it is impossible to speak in language adequate to the peculiar merits and beauties which render it one of the most illustrious examples of early Hebrew poesy. Even in a translation, which in a composition like this can be but a pale reflection of the original, its strong claims to our highest admiration are obvious to every reader. It abounds in traits, some of which we specified

yesterday, of the age in which it was written and the circumstances in which it originated, and is full of warmth and animation. The natural gradation and progress are more observed in this than in most other sacred songs, while the solemn and unexpected, though not abrupt close—"So let all thine enemies perish, O Lord!"—may be indicated as being, in the connection in which it stands, unsurpassed by anything of the kind that was ever written. "Her strains are bold, varied, and sublime; she is everywhere full of abrupt and impassioned appeals and personifications; she bursts away from earth to heaven, and again returns to human things. She touches now upon the present, now dwells upon the past, and closes at length with the grand promise and results of all prophecy, and of all the dealings of God's providence, that the wicked shall be overthrown, while the righteous shall ever triumph in Jehovah's name."[1]

There is, as Dr. Chalmers well remarks, "a beautiful and antique simplicity" in the description of Deborah's dwelling, under a remarkable and noted tree, still known as "the palm tree of Deborah" at the time the book of Judges was written. The situation of this palm tree is particularly pointed out, "between Ramah and Bethel, in Mount Ephraim." But whether this is designed to intimate that her settled habitation was in this place, or that it was the spot in the open air, shaded by the tree, to which she repaired for hearing the applications that were made to her, it may not be quite easy to determine.

It is worthy of notice, that Deborah is stated to have been a married woman, and probably, from her calling herself "a mother in Israel," she was somewhat advanced in years. She is described as the wife of Lapidoth. Much curious consideration has been bestowed upon this name. It is in the feminine plural in Hebrew, whence some have doubted whether it can be a man's name at all. But those who thus doubt have not agreed what "Lapidoth" shall be. Some take it to be the name of a place, and apprehend the phrase to mean that Deborah was "a woman of Lapidoth;" while others look to the signification of the name, which is "lamps," and therefrom infer that she was "a woman of lamps," supposed to mean one who made wicks for the lamps of the tabernacle! Again, others, looking

[1] Dr. Robinson, in *Biblical Repository* for 1831, p. 569.

to the metaphorical sense of the word, which has the material sense of "lamps," consider that we should translate the phrase into a "woman of lights, illuminations, or splendours," that is to say, an enlightened woman; and we should be disposed to incline to this, did we see any good reason for questioning the common interpretation. The only objection has no solid foundation, seeing that there are other instances of men's names with the feminine plural termination, such as Shelomith, in 1 Chron. xxiii. 9; Meremoth, in Ezra viii. 33; and Mikloth, in 1 Chron. xxvii. 4.

Deborah's position in this respect reminds one of another "mother in Israel"—"Huldah the prophetess, the wife of Shallum." (2 Kings xxii. 14.) As the Hebrew word for wife may apply either to one who has been or is married, it may be, however, as some suppose, that Deborah was at this time a widow; and that the husband, although named, does not in any way appear, and that she seems to have an independent existence, are circumstances in favour of that conclusion; for under the ancient as well as under the modern notions and institutions and ideas of the East, the separate individuality of a married woman is rarely apparent to the world. It has also been thought by some that Barak was the son of Deborah; but for this we are unable to see any evidence. It is a pure conjecture, which nothing in the history requires, and nothing sustains.

JAEL AND SISERA

Judges 4:6-22

IN the time of Joshua the most powerful of the Canaanitish sovereigns ruling in the northern part of the land was Jabin, whose seat was in the strong city of Hazor, not far to the north of the lake Merom. This city was taken and destroyed by Joshua, about one hundred and fifty years before the date of Barak's conquest, after a most decisive victory over Jabin and the northern princes confederate with him. Jabin seems to have been a common name of the princes of Hazor, like Pharaoh in Egypt, and Abimelech among the Philistines; for we now find the city and the realm restored, and a mighty king called

Jabin again reigning there. This Jabin was evidently the greatest of the princes known to the Israelites. The indications are, indeed, those of a very formidable and well organized military power for that age. We are with marked emphasis informed that this king possessed "nine hundred chariots of iron," that is, probably, chariots armed with iron hooks and scythes, which committed cruel execution upon the adverse army, against which they were forcibly

CHARIOT ARMED WITH SCYTHES

driven. Such means of assault would not now be regarded as very formidable, or inspire much alarm; and were eventually found to create so much confusion among those who used them, that they were discontinued among all nations in which war became a science. But they were much dreaded by those who were not acquainted with them, and were formidable against the ancient means of defence and mode of fighting. Especially were they dreadful to the Israelites, who were peculiarly apprehensive of chariot warfare of all kinds, and more than all of these "chariots of iron." It is highly probable that the possession of these chariots, by the mere terror which they inspired, and the idea of formidable strength they conveyed, rendered the subjection of the Israelites an easy task to king Jabin, who held them in severe bondage for twenty years. To the same terror may also be ascribed the utter prostration and discouragement under which the tribes fell, so that it became exceedingly difficult to rouse them from their despondency, and induce them to take the field against the oppressor. From the gratitude which Deborah evinces towards the people for the effort which they finally made, we are warranted in concluding that she had long endeavoured in vain to instigate them to this step. At length she sent for Barak the son of Abinoam, from Kedesh, a city of Naphtali, on a mountain not far from Hazor, and made known to him the will of God, that he should undertake an enterprise for the deliverance of his country. But such was his disheartened state of feeling, and at the same time such his confidence in the superior character and authority of Deborah, that he consents to go only on condition that she shall accompany him. To this she at length consented, not without a gentle rebuke for the faintness of his faith. They then repaired together to Kedesh, and collected there

MOUNT TABOR.

in the immediate vicinity of Hazor ten thousand men. There was deep wisdom in thus first seeking support in the very quarter where the tyranny of Jabin was most strongly felt. Many would have supposed it better to have raised a revolt in a distant quarter of the land. But so judged not Deborah. Even here, this comparatively small force was got together not without difficulty; and with it Barak marched southward and encamped on Mount Tabor, this being the first instance in which that celebrated mountain is historically mentioned in Scripture.

Hitherto we have seen the kings leading their armies in person, and owing, indeed, their power to their military skill. The Philistines in the

time of Abraham had a " captain of the host," or commander-in-chief, separately from the king. But this is the only instance before the present of a custom which afterwards became very general. Jabin was not wont to lead his troops to the field in person, the command of the army being committed to a far renowned general named Sisera, who was stationed at Harosheth, and who was obviously a person of high dignity and authority in the state. This great commander, on learning that the Israelites had taken to arms under Barak, gathered a formidable army, and with his nine hundred chariots of iron moved southward, encamping in the plain of Esdraelon. Then Deborah, who was with the Hebrew forces, said to Barak, in words stirring as a trumpet's blast, " Up; for this is the day in which the Lord hath delivered Sisera into thy hands. *Is not the Lord gone out before thee ?* " Inspirited by these noble words, which conveyed to him the assurance of victory, Barak no longer thought —if he had ever thought —of maintaining the post which he had chosen, with all its advantages, upon a mountain inaccessible to the iron chariots of the enemy, but courageously went down with his far inferior force into the plain, thus giving every possible advantage to Sisera, and thereby enhancing the glory of that victory which, in the strength of the Lord's might, he expected to win. The bold and unexpected charge of Barak seems to have been made instrumental in the Lord's hand in inspiring the enemy with a supernatural panic, a dread of spirit, which soon threw men, horses, and chariots into wild disorder, so that they fell quickly under the keen edge of the Hebrew sword, and soon sought safety in flight. It was thus " the Lord that discomfited Sisera, and all his chariots, and all his host, with the edge of the sword before Barak." In Deborah's triumphal song we are told that " the stars in their courses fought against Sisera." This has probably been rightly explained in the description of the battle which Josephus has given. He says, that when they got to close action, there came down from heaven a great storm, with a vast quantity of rain and hail, and the wind blew the rain in the faces of the Canaanites, and so darkened their eyes that their slings and arrows were of no advantage to them; nor would the sharp coldness of the air permit the soldiers to use their swords, while the storm did not so seriously incommode the Israelites, as it came upon their backs. This account as to the great rain is confirmed by the further statement, that numbers of the fugitives were drowned in the river Kishon,—a stream of no consideration in ordinary weather, but liable to be swollen into a wide and deep flood by heavy rains.

The great Sisera himself, that invincible commander, was among the fugitives; and what was more, he lighted down from his chariot and fled on foot. He might indeed have fled more swiftly in his chariot, but the chariot would have been a marked and conspicuous object of pursuit or arrest, and would have exposed him to be recognized, and taken or slain; whereas on foot he might hope to get beyond danger undiscovered. It may remind one of Bonaparte's quitting his chariot, on the escape from the field of Waterloo, only, however, to be taken by the pursuers, while he continued his flight on horseback.

In his flight, Sisera came to the encampment of Heber the Kenite, who was of the descendants of that portion of the family of Jethro which had accompanied the Israelites into Palestine. He had some time before quitted the main body of the tribe, and had settled his camp away northward in this part of the land, still leading the ancient nomad life of his people. Recollecting that there was no hostility between his sovereign and this tribe—but forgetting, as Matthew Henry remarks, "that although they did not themselves suffer from Jabin's power, they heartily sympathized with God's Israel that did,"—Sisera bethought him of claiming from this tribe of Arabian habits, the *dakheel* or protection, which is rarely sought in vain, and which, when once granted, is never dishonoured. The chief himself was absent; but his wife Jael, who seems to have known the person of the fugitive warrior, waited not to be asked. She went out to meet him, and invited him into her own tent, the sanctity of which he knew

well that no pursuer would dare to violate; for the tent, or part of a tent or house, occupied by the women, is, as its very name (*haram*, sacred) implies, so protected from all intrusion of men by public opinion, that to enter it forcibly or uninvited, would be to inflict such a disgrace and insult upon the whole tribe, as to exact undying vengeance and bloodful hatred. Knowing this, Sisera entered with confidence; but to render assurance doubly sure, he asked for drink, not only because he was thirsty, but because he knew that, among these people, to give a person drink is to give a pledge of protection, even with life, against all danger and wrong. Jael readily granted this favour: she did more than he asked. He asked for water, she gave him sour milk,—a drink much used in the East, and very wholesome and refreshing. Fully assured, he then desired to take some rest, which he much needed; and she covered him up, and left him to sleep. He had requested her to stand by the door, and to answer in the negative in case any one passed by and asked if a man were in the tent. It does not appear that Jael promised to commit an offence held so venial in this "not at home" age; but she certainly left him to infer that she would do as he desired.

We are strongly inclined to think that up to this time the woman had been sincere in her Arab faith, and fully intended to protect Sisera. But his quiet sleep gave her time to think. She saw the great oppressor of a kindred people lie helpless as a child before her. She began to reflect how easily that strong life might be struck out—even a woman's arm might do it. Then, what safety to Israel lay in that deed! what glory to herself as the deliverer! what gratitude for so great a service from a people now triumphant, and who would, it might be feared, become full of anger if they ever learned, as they were likely to do, that while they had been seeking their great enemy, he had all the while been safely sheltered in the tent of Jael! Strange thoughts wrought in her mind; until at last, to avert the anger of Israel, and to win their favour, became her only care. The means were not wanting. She seized one of the long nails which fasten the tent cords to the ground, and with this in one hand, and a mallet in the other, she approached the sleeping chief. She applied the point of the nail to his temple—she smote; and knowing the doom that lay in that stroke, she smote with such force that the nail passed through, and pinioned his head to the ground.

The deed was done—a deed for ages to wonder at; and soon after this woman had to invite another man into her tent. This man was Barak himself, who came that way still in pursuit of Sisera. Without waiting to be asked questions, she said, "Come, and I will show thee the man whom thou seekest." The conqueror accordingly entered, and there beheld the redoubted warrior, the scourge of Israel, dead, with the nail still in his temples, dishonoured by death from a woman's hand, and happy only in that he died ignorant of that deep disgrace.

Hazor, the home of Jabin, and afterwards of Barak, was situated on the hills of Napthali. It lay to the south of Kedesh, not far from the waters of Merom. A rocky spot, called *Khuraibeh*, has been pointed out by Dr. Robinson as the probable site; but the identity is questioned, and the only certainty is, that it stood not far off *Kedes*, a place well known to Eastern travellers. The region is altogether exceedingly pleasant, consisting of streams, olive groves, corn fields, and rich alluvial plains, yielding lentils and barley. Mulberries and vines grow in the neighbourhood; and writing home from Meis-el-Jebel, close by, I remarked: "At the door of my tent I can look upon a landscape which one might mistake for an English park, being a smooth sweep of grass, dotted over with trees." At *Kedes* are some most curious remains, consisting of large stone buildings, formed of plain blocks of marble. They are in a line, and seem as if they once formed the side of a street. There are also spacious sepulchres, and large double sarcophagi, ornamented with leaves and conventional patterns. It is difficult to assign a date to these ruins, but they can scarcely be earlier than the period of Roman dominion; they clearly indicate the existence then of a numerous population in the vicinity. Most likely they are successors of buildings which rose over those beautiful hills in the days of Barak, and witnessed the scenes described in the book of Judges.

Kedes was the birthplace of Barak, and he was dwelling here when inspired by the songs of the prophetess Deborah. Here were gathered round him the warriors of Zebulun and Napthali, and hence he marched to Tabor. And Heber, the Kenite, "pitched his tent *at the terebinths* of Zaanaim, which is by Kedesh." Sisera, on foot, from the defeat at Kishon, fled to the Kenites, and sought shelter in that tent, of which Jael lifted up the curtain and showed Barak the corpse of his enemy lying on the ground, with the nail driven into his temples. "The black tents of the Turkmân and Kurds, strangers like the Kenites," says Dr. Porter, "may still be seen pitched among the oaks and terebinths that encompass the little plain of Kedesh, proving that, after the lapse of more than 3,000 years, the state of society in the country is but little changed." The remark is correct, no doubt, respecting the nomadic tribes, but anciently the existence of large towns or cities must have given the region in some respects a different appearance from that which it wears now.

S.

THE SUN-LIKE COURSE

Judges 5:31

IN reading the fifth chapter of Judges, we have always found occasion to pause upon the final clause of the song of Deborah. We quote the whole sentence, but the latter portion of it alone arrests our present attention: "So let all Thine enemies perish, O Lord: but let them that love Him be as the sun when he goeth forth in his might." This comparison of those that love the Lord to the sun going forth in his might, strikes every one as being a bold figure; but few stop to consider in what sense the progress of those who love the Lord—that is, of believers—may be compared to that of the sun.

The comparison, we see, is not merely to the sun, but to its *going*—its course. There is a very parallel passage in Prov. iv. 18: "The path of the just is as the shining light, that shineth more and more unto the perfect day." There is this difference, that the comparison of believers to light necessarily ceases at the high noon, when the light is perfect; whereas the comparison to the sun itself contemplates the whole of the believer's course, from the rejoicing rising in the morning to the glorious setting in the evening. The Scripture is full of images and expressions which, like this, describe the believer's life as one of progress—progress in knowledge, holiness, and grace. The Psalmist compares the course of the sun to a race: "The sun, which is as a bridegroom coming out of his chamber, and rejoiceth as a strong man to run a race" (Ps. xix. 5); and in like manner, this our Christian course is repeatedly in the New Testament compared to a race, which has for its goal and object "eternal life." There is in the life thus characterized—this inner life—no standing still, no rest in present attainments, or degrees of progress; we must go on, growing into greater conformity to the divine image, until that day when our race is run, and we awake *satisfied* with His likeness. The fruit that does not go on to ripen, rots or falls to the ground; and this our present life is but a ripening of the soul for the life to come. Let us not, therefore, rest satisfied with any present experience in the divine life, however precious; let us go on, continually on, in earnest prayer for the ripening influences of God's Spirit upon our souls; in shunning whatever may stain the white robe—the wedding garment, which has been given to us; in seeking whatever things are lovely, true, and of good report; and in cherishing every holy thought, every sacred purpose, every pious impression. To whatever we have reached in this our course, let us not think we have already atttained, or are already perfect. He who was not behind the very chiefest of the apostles in grace and knowledge, thought not so of himself. "Brethren," he writes to the Philippians (iii. 13–15), "I count not myself to have apprehended: but this one thing I do, forgetting those things that are behind, and reaching forth unto those that are before, I press towards the mark for the prize of the high calling of God in Christ Jesus." He adds, "Let us therefore, as many as be perfect, be like-minded." Let us mark well these words. Perfection, then, does not consist in having reached some high point where we can sit still, resting in what has been already attained; but in the most earnest vigour of pursuit, of race-like, of sun-like *progress.* He says not, "Let the imperfect," but, "Let the perfect, be thus minded." That is, minded as he describes himself to be; minded to press eagerly onward to lay hold on eternal life.

It is not necessary, perhaps, that this course should be always *visible,* even to our own eyes, much less to the eyes of others. Nay, it is not perhaps necessary that the soul itself should be exactly conscious of it. The Spirit of God casts the seed into the ground, and it grows by night and day we know not how, bearing first the blade, then the ear, and then the full corn in the ear. It may be with the soul, even as with the youthful body, which grows from day to day, making great progress, and undergoing most important changes; and yet we know it not, are by no means conscious of all the gradations of this progress, and become sensible of it only when we find that our old clothes have become too strait for us, or when we try to realize the idea of what we were a few years ago.

It may often happen that, in the confusion which the world and the evil one try to raise

around us, our sense of perception becomes obscured, and it may appear to ourselves that we have made no progress, or are even going backward, have lost ground in spiritual things. This often tries the soul. It is a grief, and we must bear it. Yet let us strive to be of good cheer. If we know that God has given to our souls a movement in the right direction, and feel that we have striven to avoid whatever might impede, and have sought whatever might expedite our course; if we are sure that "God, who commanded the light to shine out of darkness, hath *shined in our hearts,* to give the light of the knowledge of the glory of God, in the face of Jesus Christ,"—let us not be too greatly cast down, even though the path of our onward course may not be so obviously clear to our own eyes as we might wish. If we have the treasure of this knowledge, that we are in Christ, let us remember that we hold this treasure in earthen vessels, that the excellency of the power may be of God, but not of us; and, therefore, although we may be troubled on every side, yet let us not be distressed; though perplexed, let us not be in despair; though persecuted, let us feel that we are not forsaken; though cast down, let us know that we shall not be destroyed. It may be

"Through danger's path and sorrow's gloom"

that we march in our heavenward course, but let us be content to feel that we do march; and if we feel it not, let us cling but the more closely to Christ, from whom our safety and our strength come. There may be actual progress, although to consciousness it be scarcely discernible. Here also the parallel of the sun's course holds good. How often is he hid by clouds from our view for hours together! We see not his progress, we cannot find his place in the heavens; yet he has steadily pursued his course behind the clouds that hide him from our view—not less steadily nor less speedily than if his glorious career had been all day visible to us; and at the appointed hour, no less on the gloomy than on the cheerful day, he reaches with unfailing certainty his bourne. Besides, his course, which figures forth our own, cannot be always hidden from our observation. We know that the sun is there, and that he pursues his way behind the clouds that hide his face. We know that these clouds abide not there for ever—that they abide not long. In a certain sense the words of the poet are in this case beautifully applicable, and to every human or infernal enemy of the Christian's sun-like course they might well be spoken:

"Fond impious man, think'st thou yon sanguine cloud,
  Raised by thy breath, has quench'd the orb of day?
To-morrow he repairs the golden flood,
  And warms the nations with redoubled ray."—*Gray*.

NOMAD AGRESSIONS

Judges 6:1-6

THE next oppression under which the Israelites fell for their sins, after forty years of rest, well deserves our consideration, involving, as it does, a form of calamitous visitation still but too well known in settled countries bordered by tribes of nomad habits, always on the watch for any signs of weakness which may embolden them to enter the land.

The old enemies of Israel, the Midianites, had, in the course of two hundred years, recovered strength. Living on the borders, between cultivated countries and the desert, between settled nations and Arabian tribes, they were marked by the habits of both. Their semi-nomad character was indicated, at the time of their overthrow by Gideon, when "the ornaments that were about their camels' necks" formed no mean portion of the spoil. They now began to move against the Hebrews. The remembrance of Israel's ancient might made them feel, probably, that they were not strong enough to act by themselves; besides which, they might apprehend that the engagement of their forces in a distant expedition would tempt the neighbouring tribes to ravage their own land. They therefore engaged these tribes to unite with them in an undertaking so congenial to their habits, and so promising of the kind of spoil they most desired. The presence of these tribes, among whom were the most ancient and inveterate enemies of Israel, the Amalekites, gave, by the predominance of their numbers in the united host, an entirely Bedouin character to the expedition.

It does not appear that there was any general action in opposition to them, when they came up with their flocks and herds to devour the land. Their numbers seem to have been too enormously great, to allow the thought of opposition to this dreadful incursion to be entertained. It is emphatically stated that "they came up like locusts,"—an image which conveys a lively idea of both their countless numbers and their cruel ravages. Like locusts, "they destroyed the increase of the earth; and left no sustenance for Israel, neither sheep, nor ox, nor ass." They came up, doubtless, as is now the custom, at the commencement of summer, before the time of the harvest—which they gathered, or appropriated to their own use, after the peasants had cut it down—and remained till after the season of autumnal fruits, which they in like manner appropriated, their flocks and herds meanwhile consuming all the herbage of the land. To this would be added severe exactions in money from the people, and the violent seizure of whatever seemed good in their eyes. At the present day, something of the same state of things prevails in the different parts of Syria, and particularly in the country beyond the Jordan, once occupied by the people of Moab, and by the tribes of Reuben and Gad. One cannot take up a book relating to that region, without being able to gather from it abundant facts in illustration of Israel's oppression under the Midianites. We shall produce some of these presently; but let us go on now to observe, that in consequence of these things—the peasantry finding it useless to sow what they may not reap—the culture of the ground is in a few years abandoned, whence arises the utmost extremity of want. They consider, however, that since they must want, it is as well to want without as with the expenditure of their strength upon the culture from which they are allowed no benefit; and they may also hope that the spoiler will soon desist from that degree of violence which destroys the source of his own gains. Their only resource is then to abandon their homes, and repair to the mountains, if in them they can find or make habitable retreats, however wretched, in the caves and dens. With such retreats Palestine is abundantly provided; and we read, accordingly, that "because of the Midianites the children of Israel made them the dens that are in the mountains, and the caves and strongholds." In general, when the Arab tribes suspect that things are coming to this extremity, and in order not to cut off thereby their own resources, they agree to accept a kind of annual ransom for the harvest, which is generally very heavy, and aggravated by extraordinary extortion and violence,—care being taken that while the exaction shall not be so oppressive as to compel the abandonment of cultivation, nothing beyond a scanty and miserable subsistence shall be allowed. The Midianites had overstepped this limit, and had caused the cultivation to be given up, except in some remote places, and had thus driven the people to their retreats in the mountains; who probably returned to their homes in the winter, when the enemy had for the time retreated to his deserts. But had this domination continued, the Arab tribes, having grown into the habit of periodically occupying this rich land, would have found it their interest so far to relax the rigour of their oppression, as to enable the people to resume the cultivation, of which they were to reap the substantial benefits.

It is, with good reason, supposed that it was during the scarcity occasioned by this abandonment of cultivation, that Elimelech and his family withdrew into the land of Moab; and that to the discontinuance of the oppression and the return of plenty, we are to refer the return of his widow and her daughter-in-law Ruth to the land of Israel.

We now give a few notes from travellers in illustration of the state of oppression which has been indicated :—

We may begin with the latest—Lieutenant Lynch, the commander of the American expedition for the exploration of the Dead Sea. The party made a trip to Kerak, a place of historical celebrity, about twelve miles to the east of ·the southern extremity of the Dead Sea, the main body of the inhabitants of which are Christians. The writer repeats the information he obtained from Abd'Allah, the Christian sheikh of the town : "They are kept in subjection by the Muslim Arabs, living mostly in huts outside the town. He stated that they are in every manner imposed upon. If a Muslim [Arab] comes into the town, instead of going to the house of another Muslim, he quarters himself upon a Christian, and appropriates the best of everything; that Christian families have been two days together without food—all that they had having been consumed by their self-invited guests. If a Muslim sheikh buys a horse for so many sheep, he makes the Christians contribute till the number be made up. Their property, he said, is seized at will, without there being any one to whom to appeal ; and remonstrance on their part

only makes it worse. Already a great many have been driven away, poverty alone keeping the remainder. . . . . The locusts and the sirocco have for the last seven years blasted their fields, and nearly all spared by them has been swept away by the Muslims."[1]

So Burckhardt, in speaking of the Bedouins of the Hauran, beyond the Jordan, says that they are of two classes—those who are resident, and those who visit it in the spring and summer only. "By resident I do not mean that they have fixed habitations, but that their wanderings are confined to the Hauran, or some particular districts of it." But besides these, "in May the whole Hauran is covered with swarms of wanderers from the desert, who remain there till September. They come for a twofold purpose—water and pasturage for the summer, and a supply of corn for the winter. The oppressions of the government on the one hand, and of these Bedouins on the other, have reduced the fellah (cultivator) to a state little better than that of the wandering Arabs. Few individuals die in the same village where they were born. Families are continually moving from one place to another. In the first year of their new settlement, the sheikh acts with moderation towards them ; but his vexations being in a few years insupportable, they fly to some other place, where they have heard that their brethren are better treated, but they soon find that the same system prevails over the whole country. This continued wandering is one of the principal reasons why no village of the Hauran has either orchards, or fruit trees, or gardens for the growth of vegetables. 'Shall we sow for strangers,' was the answer of a fellah to whom I once spoke on the subject."[2] All these tribes, whether resident or visitant, consider themselves entitled to certain tributes from all the villages, in consideration of which they abstain from touching the harvest of the village, and from driving off its cattle and camels when they meet them in the way. The amount of this tribute is continually increasing, for the Arab sheikh is not always contented with the quantity of corn he received the preceding year, but asks something additional as a present, which soon becomes a part of his accustomed dues. Besides this, depredations are often committed beyond the possibility of redress.[3]

[1] *Narrative of the Expedition to the Dead Sea*, p. 362.
[2] *Travels in Syria*, pp. 306-308.   [3] Ibid., 301, 302.

GIDEON

Judges 6:11-23

NOTHING can more graphically illustrate the circumstances which distinguished the Midianite oppression from others to which Israel had been subject than the operations which we find under the hand of the next deliverer of Israel, when the Lord was pleased to call him to his great work.

We see a young man of Ophrah in Manasseh, west of the Jordan, engaged in "threshing wheat by the wine-press, to hide it from the Midianites." How it was thus to be hidden from the Midianites does not strike the reader unversed in the customs of the East. It may here be observed that corn is usually threshed near the field where it is grown, on an open area prepared and levelled for the purpose. The wine-press would necessarily be at a good distance among the vineyards, and would be on many accounts the least likely place in which any one would suspect the threshing of corn to be carried on. The time was come when the culture of the ground was for the most part abandoned; and the little corn that was therefore raised in a few places was guarded with the more care on the one hand, and sought for with the more avidity on the other. Further, corn was usually threshed by oxen, either by simple treading—as seems to have been generally the case in scriptural times—or by their drawing over it a rude apparatus of logs, by which the grain was crushed out and the straw broken; only smaller seeds were beaten out by the flail. (Isa. xxviii. 27.) Yet in this case, not only was the corn threshed at the wine-press, but it was done, not by the usual treading of oxen, but by the flail. This does not appear in the translation. But it does in the original, where the word translated "threshed" indicates not only the fact, but the mode of threshing. Why was this? Clearly for the sake of silence. The lowing of the oxen in so unusual a place might betray the thresher. But surely a flail makes noise enough? Yes, with us; but in the East no wooden floor resounds beneath the stroke of the flail. The regular threshing floor even is of trodden earth merely, and the place by the wine-press was no doubt merely a smooth and clean spot of ground.

The sudden appearance of a stranger to Gideon under these circumstances, must, in the first instance, have given him much alarm. An unexpected witness of what one wishes to conceal is always startling. The first words of the stranger must, however, have reassured him: "The Lord is with thee, thou mighty man of valour!" One would think from this, that Gideon had already found the opportunity of distinguishing himself by some well known display of high courage or personal prowess. The words "the Lord is with thee" are not at variance with this, for they were but the ordinary form of salutation in religious and truthful times, as one may see by the same salutation being given, in the very same generation, by Boaz to his reapers. (Ruth ii. 4.) However, the place was idolatrous, and a high seat of Baal's worship. The name of Jehovah was seldom heard, therefore; and hence this once ordinary salutation sounded strangely in Gideon's ears. Being strange, it struck him with a degree of emphasis and force such as the words always possessed, but which are not so readily recognized in phrases of daily and familiar occurrence. His mind grasped the full significance of the phrase, which in other days had passed with feebler impression upon his ear. They seemed like a cruel irony to him. The nation had forsaken Jehovah; and being therefore, for the time, forsaken of Him, they came to confound cause and effect, and to trace their misery to His absence as a protector, rather than to their sins, by which that absence had been occasioned. Trace this in Gideon's answer: "O my Lord, if Jehovah be with us, why then is all this befallen us? and where be all His miracles which our fathers told us of?" The stranger did not argue the matter with him. He looked earnestly upon him, and in the words of authority and power said, "Go in this thy might, and thou shalt save Israel from the hand of the Midianites. Have not *I* sent thee?" What a disclosure was in that "*I*!"

Gideon understood it partly; but although he no longer dared question that Israel might be saved, he, under views yet clouded, still, like Moses of old, demurred at the felt insufficiency of the instrument, whose fitness his modesty led him to underrate. "O my Lord, wherewith shall *I* save Israel? Behold, my family is poor in Manasseh, and *I* am the least in my father's house." Here there is another sort of "*I*"—the mortal and the immortal EGO confronted with each other. The immortal and the omnipotent

is then more distinctly and authoritatively disclosed, bearing down, as it should do, the weakness of the mortal: "Surely *I* will be with thee,
and thou shalt smite the Midianites as one man."
What did the matters of such great concernment
to him—the position of his family in Manasseh,
and his own position in his family—signify then?
How small the whole matter seems in presence of
that grandly simple assurance, "*I* will be with
thee!" Still Gideon's ideas were so much bewildered, through the corruptions of the times—
which had introduced so much that was false, as
to render the presence of the true difficult to
recognize by the spiritual sense—that he was not
yet free from misgivings, and desired some sign,
some work of supernatural power, by which his
faith might be relieved from the hesitancy under
which he still laboured. And He who denied
any other sign than that of Jonah to a hypocritical
age, refused not to the sincere man the sign which
was required to strengthen his faith for the great
work he was called to undertake.

But before he ventured to prefer his request,
Gideon besought leave to offer the "present"
which usage exacted of one who made a request,
to which he had no right, of a superior, and such
also as the hospitable usages of the East required
him to offer to any stranger who came to him.
Abraham, in a similar situation, had asked permission previously—and the reason in both cases
was the same—that the knowledge of an intention, which it required some time to execute,
might induce the stranger to wait until it could
be performed. In this case the stranger must
have waited at least an hour, while Gideon made
ready the meal which he brought forth. It was,
however, such as might be most readily prepared,
and such as, in substance, forms the meal usually
presented in the like circumstances. A kid was
dressed, and thin cakes of unleavened bread were
baked for the occasion. This unleavened bread
was more quickly got ready than any other,
which was probably the reason for the form of
bread chosen.

There is some noticeable particularity in the
account of the presentation of the meat. "The
flesh he put in a basket, and he put the broth in
a pot, and brought it out unto him under the
oak." The Orientals do not use broth in which
meat has been boiled as soup, as we do. But
they do use stews, such as the "pottage" for which
Esau sold his birthright; and such as the sons of

the prophets were preparing when they put into
it by mistake some poisonous herb. In this way
we apprehend part of the kid was prepared, and
this was the part brought in the pot. While this
was in preparation over the fire, the other part
had been cut up into slips, and roasted before the
fire upon skewers, in which way meat is very
rapidly dressed in the East into what is called
kaboobs, which for extemporizing a meal stands in
the same place as chops and steaks with us, only
that the pieces are very much smaller. This,
we apprehend, was what was brought in the basket.
Some have thought that this was *intended* as
a meat-offering to a Divine Being, and not as
a meal to be eaten, and have remarked that the
ingredients were the same as in a meat-offering.
True; because a meat-offering *was* a meal, composed of such ingredients as were in use for a meal:
hence the resemblance. The interpretation has
arisen probably from what subsequently occurred;
but we apprehend that Gideon meant to show
his respect and attention in the usual way, without thus looking farther. The basket and the
pot together were simply modes of preparation
suggestive of a meal more than of an offering.
Into an offering, however, and that by fire, the
heavenly stranger turned it, by directing Gideon
to place the food on the top of a rock that was
near. He then touched it with the end of his
staff, and forthwith fire arose out of the rock and
consumed it all. This marvellous sight engaged
the amazed attention of Gideon; and when he
turned, the stranger had disappeared. That
the result had not been expected by him, and
that he had not been fully aware of the character of his guest, is clear, from the amazement with which he now realized the conviction
that he had spoken with one from heaven.
"Alas, O Lord God!" he cried, "for because I
have seen an angel of the Lord face to face."
This was founded on the old and very prevalent
notion, that no one could behold a visitor from
heaven and live; or that the appearance of such
was a sign of approaching death. Nor was this
notion unsanctioned by the Lord's declaration to
Moses: "There shall no man see me, and live!"
But that had regard to the beholding the fulness
of His glory, and not to those manifestations which,
in condescension to man's weakness, He might
choose to make of himself. In this case Gideon was
relieved of his fears; for the Lord said to him,
"Peace be unto thee; fear not: thou shalt not die."

In connection with the foregoing remarks, it is interesting to read the following passages from Lieutenant Conder's Report in the *Statements of the Exploration Fund*, 1874, p. 182. "The nomadic hordes of the Midianites had, like the modern Beni Suggar and Ghazawíyeh Arabs, come up the broad and fertile valley of Jezreel, and their encampment lay, as the black Arab tents do now in spring, at the foot of the hill Morah (Nebi Dahy), opposite to the high limestone knoll on which Jezreel (Zer'ain) stands. As on

JEZREEL

the first night of our camping at Sulem (Shunem), when six horsemen and fifteen foot of the Bedouin came down on the village and retreated, after stealing a horse and a cow, followed by the fellahîn with shouts and a dropping fire, so in Gideon's time the settled Jewish inhabitants assembled to drive back the marauders. The well Harod, where occurred the trial which separated 300 men of endurance from the worthless rabble, was, no doubt, the 'Ain Jalúd, a fine spring at the foot of Gilboa, issuing blue and clear from a cavern, and forming a pool with rushy banks and a pebbly bottom more than 100 yards in length. The water is sweet, and there is ample space for the gathering of a great number of men. It has, however, like most of the neighbouring springs, a slightly sulphurous taste, and a soft deep mud covers the middle of the basin below the surface. The graphic description of the midnight attack, when, no doubt concealed by the folds of the rolling ground, the 300 crept down to the Midianite camp 'in the valley beneath,' and burst on the sleeping host with a sudden flicker of the concealed lamps, can be most readily realized on the spot. The immediate flight of the nomadic horde is most easily traced on the map. 'The host fled to Beth-shittah in Zererath, and to the border of Abel-meholah' (vii. 22), a course directly down the main road to Jordan and to Beisan. Beth-shittah may perhaps be identified with the modern village of Shatta, and Abelmea (as it was called in Jerome's time) with Wady Maleh. Zererath would appear to be a district name, and is generally connected with the Zerthan and Zeretan of other passages of the Old Testament. It is known to have been 'below Jezreel,' and near Beisan. I think, therefore, we can scarce doubt that the name still exists in the Arabic, 'Ain Zahrah' and

Tullúl Zahrah, three miles west of Beisan. Thus the immediate pursuit drove the enemy some ten or fifteen miles towards the Jordan banks. A systematic advance immediately followed. Messengers went south two days' journey to Mount Ephraim, and the Jews descended to the lower fords of Jordan at Bethbarah, which has been supposed identical with the Bethabara of the New Testament, and which was in all probability situate at the traditional site—the pilgrims' bathing-place near Kasr el Yehúd, east of Jericho. Meantime Gideon, having cleared the Bethshan valley of the Midianites, crossed by the fords near Succoth, at its southern extremity (the modern Makhathet Abu Sús), and continued the pursuit along the east bank of the Jordan. The Midianites were thus entirely cut off. They appear (or at least some part of the host) to have followed the right bank southwards towards Midian, intending, no doubt, to cross near Jericho. But they were here met by the men of Ephraim, and their leaders Oreb and Zeeb, executed on that side of Jordan, their heads being subsequently carried to Gideon, 'on the other side.'"

S.

BAAL

Judges 6:24-32

WE now become acquainted, as it were incidentally, with the lamentable fact, that the worship of the gods of the heathen was freely practised in Israel, and that among the very family from which Gideon the appointed deliverer was chosen. We have been told this in general terms before; but now we have it presented to us through the medium of a scene in idolatrous Israel, by which we are enabled to realize a more distinct conception of the actual state of affairs, and of the depth of corruption by which such severe corrections had been rendered necessary.

The very night after the divine appearance, a message came to Gideon, well calculated to test his faith and the extent of his obedience. He is commanded to throw down the altar of Baal that his father had, and to cut down "the grove" that was by it. The altar, it seems, although belonging to Gideon's father, whose name was Joash, as being in his grounds, was destined for the common service of the town. But for the part which he eventually took, one would suppose that Joash was a prime leader, if not the actual priest, of this idolatry; and it is not clear from the part he did take that he was not. Under new influences, or the excitement of other circumstances, and especially under the constraining power of divine grace, the most active promoters of a cause or an invention often become its most vehement opponents. Having thrown down the altar and cut down the grove, Gideon was to build an altar to Jehovah, and offer sacrifice thereon. For the sacrifice he was to take his "father's bullock, even the second bullock of seven years old." This expression about the second bullock has somewhat puzzled commentators. It seems to us probable, that as the Midianites took away all the cattle of the Israelites that they could lay their hands on, Joash had very few left, the second of which, in point of age, Gideon is directed to offer for sacrifice. Why one, however, of seven years of age?—one three years old being by the law declared the most fit for sacrifice. Perhaps there was some reference in this to the seven years during which the oppression of the Israelites had lasted; or it may be, that of the few cattle of Joash, the second, although seven years old, was the youngest over three years.

Gideon could not but be well aware of the danger of the task thus imposed upon him. To a man of weaker faith it would have seemed like tempting certain destruction; but he wavered not. He had a command, and was determined to obey it. His only solicitude was to do this effectually; and therefore, not from fear, but in order that he might not be prevented, he, aided by his servants, executed his commission in the night.

The next morning, when the inhabitants of the place came to render their customary service at Baal's altar, lo! his altar was demolished; the trees that grew around it were cut down; and conspicuous upon the rock at some distance appeared the altar which Gideon had erected to Jehovah, with the marks thereon of a recent offering. Seeing that the mode of constructing an altar to the Lord is laid down in the law, it is probable that they could at once perceive that this altar was dedicated to Jehovah. This fact may have been more likely to moderate than to strengthen their wrath; for, much as they had neglected their Lord, they had not come to hate Him or to reject Him; but they had transgressed in rendering to other gods, which indeed were no gods, the worship due to Him only. Rather, perhaps, they cherished a vague reverence for the establishment at Shiloh, and still regarded as their true paternal God Him who was there served with offerings and

sacrifices; but had come to think they wanted *also* a local god and a local service, in honour of some god whose claims they fancied might not interfere with His. But they soon found this local worship to fill their thoughts and minds; and while Baal had at Ophrah all the real and practical worship that was offered, their own true God, in His distant holy habitation, was removed more and more from them, away in the cold regions of dim abstraction.

To the first blank amazement with which this devastation was regarded, followed eager and angry inquiry as to the perpetrator of the deed. It soon transpired that this had been the work of no other than Gideon; and instantly a hundred clamorous voices cried to Joash: "Bring forth thy son, that he may die." Parental affection, strengthened perhaps by some internal convictions that his son must have acted with sufficient authority, and that he was right, at once prompted Joash to stem or divert the torrent of barbarous wrath. It may be even that the son, aware of what was likely to come, had, before this time arrived, apprised his father of what had taken place, and of the commission he had received; and had thus prepared and engaged him to interpose his authority and influence for his protection. There was no reason why Gideon should not do this, and every reason for his being likely to do it. Be this as it may, Joash executed his part with consummate ability and address. The argument of his brief oration amounted to this: "Do nothing rashly against my son. If Baal be really a god, he will know how to avenge this affront; but if he be not a god, then it is they who plead for him, and not my son, who deserve to die." This reasoning was sufficiently cogent. It put Gideon in the position of one standing forward, not to excuse, but to vindicate his act, and to defy the utmost wrath of the god he had treated with so much contempt. What could they say to this? They knew that Jehovah had often vindicated His own honour by manifest and signal judgments; and no reason could be urged why Baal, if he were a god, should not do the same. They perhaps looked on in expectation that Gideon would have been smitten down dead. But nothing followed; and the people dispersed with thoughtful faces to their houses.

As to Baal, whose worship had been adopted from their heathen neighbours by this people, it has been rightly observed, that the word means "lord," and is therefore in a certain sense applicable to any of the different gods worshipped in this part of the world, and is in fact so applied in Scripture. But, on the other hand, it seems to be generally agreed, that when the word has the definite article in the original language (not preserved in translation), a particular idol is meant,—namely, the one worshipped by the Phœnicians of Tyre and Sidon, whose worship spread with the power and influence of that people, and was at its height in Israel after the marriage of king Ahab with the king of Tyre's daughter, continuing only in Judah during the usurpation of Athaliah. The Baal in this passage has the definite article, and therefore according to the rule, denotes this Phœnician idol. He is not here first mentioned. We have him before in Judg. ii. 13, where the addiction to his worship throughout the period of the judges is clearly stated: "They forsook the Lord, and served Baal and Ashtaroth." The latter was clearly a Phœnician idol also, and the name is not subject to the same large interpretation as Baal. Their being joined together, strengthens the reference of the one, as of the other, to a Phœnician idol. It is generally agreed, that under Baal the power of the sun was personified, and under Ashtaroth that of the moon. Some of the rites with which both were worshipped, together or separately, we shall have some future occasions of noticing. Baal had temples and images, as well as altars and groves; but in this case we read only of the elementary apparatus of his worship—the altar and the grove. In time, if not checked, the images would have appeared, and the temples have been erected.

Baal was the chief deity worshipped by the people of Canaan before the Israelitish conquest. The name signifies "Lord," but in the sense of "possessor" rather than "ruler." It is probably identical with the later Babylonian *Bel*.

It would seem, from the name of one of their kings, that the worship of Baal was adopted by the Edomites at a very early period. (Gen. xxxvi. 38.) It was firmly established in Moab at the time of the Exodus; and towards the close of the forty years' wandering, the Israelites were first seduced to it by the wily counsels of Balaam. (Num. xxv. 3; xxxi. 16.) On entering Canaan, they found the sanctuaries of Baal on the top of almost every hill and mountain. The summit of Hermon appears to have been one of the chief of these "High-places." (Judg. iii. 3.)

The existence of so many sanctuaries in the country, the superstitious veneration with which the old inhabitants regarded them, and the example of the wealthy and influential Phœnicians, induced the Israelites to engage from time to time in the worship of the idol. Though frequently and severely punished for it, they still clung to it with a strange and fatal pertinacity, until at length, under the infamous Jezebel, it became the established worship of the northern kingdom.

The worship of Baal was attended with rites at once barbarous and grossly immoral. The priests danced round the altars with frantic shouts, tearing their hair, and cutting themselves with knives. (1 Kings xviii. 26-28.) Human sacrifices were not unfrequent; young men and children being burned upon the altars. (Jer. xix. 5.) The licentious rites sometimes practised are sufficiently indicated by the narrative of Num. xxv.

The origin of the worship of Baal would seem to be indicated by the name. With the original idea of "possessor of all things," that of *productive power* came naturally to be associated; and this power was represented by the *sun*. Hence Baal and the sun were often identified.

P.

TESTS

Judges 6:33-40, 7:1-15

AT the proper moment the Spirit of the Lord "clothed"[1] Gideon, and he knew that the time for him to work for the deliverance was come; and he felt within him a heart equal to the enterprise to which he was called. He caused the trumpet to be blown for volunteers. The Abi-ezrites, the men of his own clan, were the first to join him; and this is highly creditable both to his character and to theirs. The northern tribes alone were summoned to the war; which is to be noted, seeing that the midland tribes, especially Ephraim, were greatly affronted at being overlooked.

Having thus gathered what seemed to him an adequate number of troops, Gideon wished for a sign—perhaps the same he had formerly been prevented from proposing by the sudden disappearance of the angel. He now, however, required it; not, perhaps, so much for the confirmation of his own faith, as to authenticate his commission in the eyes of the strangers who had responded to his call. Yet, taking into account the weakness of human nature, it is not incredible,

[1] Such is the real meaning of the word rendered "came upon."

that although clothed with the Spirit of the Lord, and after all the evidence he had received, his own faith needed some further strengthening in presence of the countless hosts of Midian overspreading the vast plain of Esdraelon. The sign he made choice of was remarkable, and well calculated to make an impression upon the minds of his followers. The tenor of the request is expressed in such a manner as would have been offensive to any man of spirit, who had given solemn assurances to another; but the Lord is very merciful, very long-suffering,—more of both than man,—and Gideon's request was granted without a rebuke. Perhaps, also, the terms employed are to be regarded as not so much the emanation of his own feeling, as his mode of stating the case for the understanding of his people. "If Thou wilt save Israel by my hand, and do as Thou hast said, behold, I will put a fleece of wool on the floor; and if the dew be on the fleece only, and if it be dry upon all the earth beside, then shall I know that Thou wilt save Israel by my hand, as Thou hast said." This is an experiment natural enough to occur to a man of few and simple ideas, and these connected chiefly with agriculture and cattle. That it is such as would not be at all likely to be thought of by the inhabitants of towns, only proves its natural truth.

The thing came to pass as Gideon had desired; "for he rose up early in the morning, and thrust the fleece together, and wrung the dew out of the fleece, a bowl full of water." It is remarkable that the correlative part of the miracle is not mentioned—that the ground about the fleece was quite dry; but this is implied. Gideon, for further assurance, and with a becoming apology for his presumption, ventured to ask that the miracle might now be reversed—this time the fleece to be dry, and the ground wet with dew. This, of the two, was the stronger proof of supernatural interposition, seeing that it is a property of wool to absorb whatever dew may fall; and its dryness, when the ground about was wet with dew, was altogether a miraculous thing. The dew itself was not preternatural, we should think; but only the mode of its exhibition. Dews fall in Palestine, as we know from Scripture and from travel. It depends much upon locality, however; the dews being heavy in the high lands, but scarcely perceptible in the low and even plains. In travelling in some parts of Western Asia, we

found the difference remarkable, as affected by high or low lying situations. In the former we have often found cloaks of sheep-skin, exposed to the open air, as heavy with dew as if they had been dipped in water; in the latter we have slept all night upon the house-tops, without finding in the morning any trace of dew upon the bed clothes. Dew would seem to be not naturally abundant, at least at the time of the year at which the event took place, in the neighbourhood where Gideon was favoured with this sign; for the quantity of dew on the fleece, in the first sign, is pointed out as a most extraordinary circumstance.

Immediately upon receiving the assurance he desired, Gideon marched with his men to the nearer neighbourhood of the enemy's camp. If he had any remaining misgiving, it probably was that his warriors were too few to cope with the myriads of Midian.[1] How much, therefore, must he have been astonished to receive the intimation that they were *too* many! And why too many? "Lest Israel vaunt themselves, saying, Mine own hand hath saved me." The enforcement was therefore required of the very remarkable law of Moses, which was admirably calculated to secure the presence of none but efficient and courageous men in an army, while apparently diminishing its strength. This consisted in the making of a proclamation, that whoever was fearful and fainthearted might withdraw to his home. Considering that all of Gideon's army were volunteers, it speaks much for the impression which the nearer approach to the host of Midian had produced, that more than two-thirds of his army withdrew. Twenty and two thousand went away, and only ten thousand remained. We cannot but suppose that Gideon was regarding this result with amazement and concern, when he was told that they were still too many, and that another experiment for reducing their number must be made. The mode of reduction adopted in this instance was very singular. The whole army was to be taken down to the water, and every one that "lapped the water with his tongue, as a dog lappeth," was to be set apart from those who bowed down on their knees to drink. Some difficulty has been found in identifying the first of these processes. The explanation which we

[1] 135,000 *at least* of "men that drew sword," not to speak of others, with women and children. See Judges 8:10.

give is founded upon our own observation of the different modes in which men drink in haste when coming to a stream on a journey, without being provided with vessels wherewith to raise the water to their mouths. It is to be observed that this class is further described as "the number of those that lapped, putting their hand to their mouth." The chief distinction between them and the others is, that they did not bow down on their knees to bring their mouths near the water, and luxuriate in a more leisurely draught. They continued standing, stooping so far only as to be able to reach the water with their hands, the hollow of which they filled, and then brought it rapidly to the mouth, jerking in the refreshing contents. The motion, compared to a dog's lapping, cannot apply to the tongue, first, because the human tongue is not framed for lapping; and secondly, because if so, it would be an action belonging rather to those who brought their faces down to the water, than to those who stood upon their feet. Supposing lapping with the tongue at all a possible action to a man, it would certainly not be resorted to by one who had succeeded in bringing a handful of water so far as his mouth. It would have been a needless, if not silly, delay in quenching his thirst. The motion expressed by " lapping," must therefore apply to the hand, the rapid motion of which, between the water and the mouth, might be not unaptly compared to the rapid projection and retraction of a dog's tongue in lapping. This last action, if taken, as is apparently meant, for an indication of character, would denote men of rapid and impulsive action, too earnest in the work before them to endure to satisfy their animal wants with the leisurely action of men at ease: a few hasty handfuls of water were all that the impatience of their spirit, in the great interests before them, allowed them to take. These were the men to save Israel. They were but three hundred in number; and all the rest of the ten thousand were, to their great amazement, sent away, and Gideon remained alone with his small band of men.

Gideon had asked signs of God, and had been forgiven; and now, again, God gives him other signs calculated to strengthen his faith, beautifully illustrating the divine consideration for the frailty and feebleness of man—"for that he also is flesh." First, there was the sign which pointed out to him the men on whom he might rely; and as their number was but small, he has another sign to show him, that even this small force is sufficient. He receives an intimation that he is to go down by night to the very camp of the Midianites; and, for his encouragement, he is allowed to take with him Phurah, his armour-bearer. So the two stole down to the camp in the darkness of the night. It was too dark to see anything, and the chief may have been perplexed to know wherefore he had been sent. He had been sent to hear, not to see. Presently he heard one of the outposts speaking to his fellow respecting a dream that had troubled him that night, remarkable enough to awaken his attention, and suggest to him that it was no common dream, though he knew not how to discover its purport. He dreamed that as the host lay there encamped, a cake of barley meal rolled down from the hills, and smote the tent against which it came with such violence, that it fell down. Josephus says it was the royal tent, which is not unlikely; for the word rendered "tent," with the definite article, which the original has, means the fairest and strongest tent. The man to whom the dreamer told his dream readily undertook to interpret it. The barley cake, he said, was the sword of Gideon; "for into his hand hath God delivered Midian and all the host." This was enough for Gideon. It was of no importance to him whether the interpretation was correct or not: one thing was true and certain, that the Midianites were afraid of him, and themselves believed not only in the possibility, but the probability, the certainty, of their own overthrow. In that conviction of theirs, the victory was already his.

It is curious that the man should have seen in the humble cake of barley meal a symbol of Gideon. It was, however, an apt and recognizable symbol of the condition of the Israelites, whose representative he was to be considered. Hear Volney as to the condition of Syria in our own times under the like state of things : " From all these causes we may easily imagine how miserable must be the condition of the peasants. They are everywhere reduced *to a little flat cake of barley*, or doura; to onions, lentils, and water." [1]

[1] *Travels in Egypt and Syria*, ii. 412.

THE STRATAGEM

Judges 7:16; 8:17

AMONG all the stratagems in ancient military history, which abounds in them—in the entire volume of instances collected by Polyænus—we find none so remarkable as that to which Gideon resorted, or having the slightest resemblance to it. The device strongly manifests that faculty of inventiveness which appears to have been a prominent feature in Gideon's character. We see this not only here, but in the matter of the fleece, and in some other incidents of his after career, such as his punishment of the men of Succoth, and in the dangerously novel use to which he applied his portion of the spoil. The Lord, who employs those faculties in man which may best promote the purposes of His will, seems to have wrought with, and stimulated the inventiveness of Gideon. Thus, in the trial of the men by the drinking of water, there was a contrivance after his own heart; and the gratification which it afforded to his imagination, could not have but inclined him with the less reluctance to acquiesce in the result which it determined.

GIDEON'S VICTORY

Never, surely, before or since, did a general lead three hundred men against a hundred and thirty-five thousand, with only a trumpet in one hand, and a pitcher containing a lighted torch in the other. His object, however, was not to fight them, but to frighten them, or rather to raise into a panic the fears which he knew that they already entertained. He divided the men into three equal bodies, each of which, in the darkness of the night, silently approached the enemy's camp in a different quarter. At a given signal they all threw down their pitchers, with a loud crash, raised their torches on high, blew their trumpets, and shouted, "The sword of the Lord, and of Gideon." The soldier had interpreted the barley cake to be no other than "the sword of Gideon." The hero adopts that as his war-cry; but with becoming piety, he avoids even in a war-cry to claim the glory for his own sword, by introducing the name of the Lord. As the enemy dreaded *his* name, he could not withhold that; but he added another name, the awful name of JEHOVAH, which the remembrance of ancient judgments rendered still more terrible to them. The result of this fearful din on all sides, with the sudden glare of torches upon the margin of the camp, had precisely the effect which Gideon had calculated. In being thus suddenly awakened from their sleep, it seemed to the Midianites that they were surrounded on all sides by enemies who had perhaps come from distant parts in aid of Gideon; the crash of the pitchers seemed to them as the noise of chariots; so many trumpets must imply the presence of a vast host; the glare of light must have led to the impression that the camp had been already set on fire in different parts. In the terror and the confusion, they therefore fell foul of one another, and fought and slew as an enemy every one whom they encountered. To estimate this effect, it is to be rembered that the camp must have extended for many miles, and that the light of the torches must have appeared as a distant glare, but not an enlightening blaze, to all but those on the outskirts of the camp. And even if they had given light, which they could not, to all the host, there were not such distinctions of dress between the parts of the variously composed host, or between them and the enemy, as might enable them in the confusion to distinguish friend from foe. There was thus a frightful slaughter without the Israelites striking a blow. Then followed a tumultuous flight; but by this time the country was roused, and the fugitives found enemies at every turn. The men who had been sent away the day before, probably also rendered good service this day upon the flying host. They were still out in arms, for it is not likely that many of them had yet reached their homes, or had indeed hastened to withdraw from the neighbourhood; for they were not of the number which had claimed exemption on the ground of being "faint-hearted." The passes of the Jordan were also seized at the request of Gideon by the Ephraim-ites, who, although offended at not having been at first called into action, forbore not to obey, for the public good, the man by whom they deemed themselves slighted. Thus it came to pass, that of all the vast host not more than fifteen thous-and were able to make good their escape to the land beyond the Jordan, under the conduct of two of their princes, Zebah and Zalmunna. Gideon was not minded that even these should escape; and he crossed after them, being joined in this pursuit by the Ephraimites, who brought him the heads of two kings—Oreb and Zeeb—of the allied host, whom they had slain. They could not, however, refrain from complaining warmly of the manner in which they—proud as they were, and important as they deemed them-selves—had been overlooked at the outset. The incident is worth noticing, as marking an early indication of the pretensions of this great tribe to a leading place in the nation. Had the move-ment commenced in the great rival tribe of Judah, or had the leader been any other than of their own kindred tribe of Manasseh, they would not perhaps have been so easily pacified by the soft answer with which Gideon turned away their wrath. He knew the arrogant temper of this tribe, and soothed their wounded vanity by magnifying their exploits in comparison with his own.

The pursuit beyond the Jordan reveals an important fact, that a lack of sympathy had already grown up between the tribes separated by that river. For when Gideon applied at two towns on his way for refreshment for his weary troop, he was refused by both with insult. He stayed not to argue or punish, but threatened what he would do on his return. Still displaying his ingenious inventiveness, he does not, like a warrior of one idea, threaten to destroy them, or to burn their cities; but he tells the men of Succoth that he will humble their chief men with the scourge, and that with a new kind of scourge—"the thorns and briers of the wilder-ness." The offence of the men of Penuel was precisely the same, but he does not threaten to scourge *them*. No; he will "break down this tower"—the tower which was the strength and ornament of the place, and in which they trusted. He performed both threatenings to the letter, and perhaps something beyond, when he returned soon after victorious, with the two kings as prisoners. He not only pulled down the tower of Penuel, but "slew the men of the city;" and it is not clear that he did not subject the men of Succoth to the same doom, after having dealt with them according to his threat. He might have done it, indeed, in the execution of his threat; for there was an ancient punishment, in which death was inflicted by laying the naked bodies of the offenders under a heap of thorns, briers, and prickly bushes, and then drawing over them threshing-sledges, and other heavy imple-ments of husbandry. A remark in connection with this subject which we made some years ago, has often since been quoted: "In northern nations, where the body is completely covered, the idea of such punishment with thorns on the naked person seems a far fetched device; but in the East, where the clothing leaves much more of the person exposed, and where, in consequence, men are constantly lacerating their skins in pass-ing through thickets, the idea of such laceration is always kept present to the mind, either by the actual experience of the suffering, or by the con-stant observation of it. Thus, tearing the flesh with thorns comes to be a familiar idea of penal infliction, and as such, is still popularly mentioned in the East as among the punishments which evil-doers deserve, or will obtain, not only in this life, but in the life to come."[1]

The scene of this memorable victory was the valley of Jezreel, an arm of the great plain of Esdraelon, extending down eastward, between the parallel ranges of Morah and Gilboa, to the Jordan. It was on the same battle-field that Saul and Jonathan afterwards fell. The Midianites and their allies, with their vast flocks and herds, lay along the northern side of the valley, at the base of Moreh; probably covering the whole district between the towns of Shunem and Bethshean. The little army of Gideon occupied the heights of Gilboa, above the well known fountain, now called Ain Jalûd, nearly two miles east of the ruins of Jezreel. The fountain is copious—in fact, one of the best in the district. Its waters gush up among the rocky roots of Gilboa, forming a large pond, and then wind down the rich vale towards Bethshean.

In the spring of 1857 I witnessed at this fountain a

[1] *Pictorial Bible*, on Judges 8:16.

gathering of Bedawy tribes, not unlike that of the Midianites, under a noted chief Akeil Agha. The day before, they had attacked, defeated, and plundered a camp of Kurdish horse in the pay of Government. Now they "lay along in the valley, like grasshoppers for multitude." I almost felt, as I looked on the wild faces, and warlike array, and heaps of plunder, as if sacred history had been realized. There were Beni Sukhr sheikhs from beyond Jordan, with beautiful horses and long tufted spears; there were chiefs from the south, mounted on dromedaries with gay trappings, and ornaments of silver round their necks (Judg. viii. 21); there was Akeil himself, and two or three other leaders grouped round him, in scarlet robes, tinted deeper here and there with spots of blood, fit representatives of Oreb and Zeeb, the "raven" and the "wolf." The dress, the trappings, the habits, and the wars of the Bedawîn, are just what they were thirty centuries ago.

P.

A KING

Judges 9

THE history of the Israelites exhibits one peculiarity which does not seem to have been duly noticed. Nothing is more frequent in both ancient and modern history, than the real or alleged ingratitude of the people to those who have rendered them signal services. The histories of Greece and Rome teem with instances of this, which will present themselves to the mind of every reader; and the modern histories of the nations with which we are best acquainted—our own not excepted—are not wanting in them. But this is exceedingly rare among the Israelites. There may be some touches of the kind in the histories of Moses, Samuel, and David; but any ungrateful feeling towards them was only temporary,—the permanent feeling towards them was good and proper; and the final estimation of these personages by their nation manifests a high appreciation of their character and motives, and an intense recognition of their services. In fact, *all* the great names of their history are to this day held by them in more intense respect than we find to be the case among any other people. We almost think that the disposition of the Hebrews lay all the other way, and that they were more inclined to error on the side of man-worship than of man-neglect. In the time of the judges, by one great service, a man—from whatever rank in life—so secured the gratitude and

respect of the people, that he remained in power as their governor all the rest of his life, however long that life might be. In the case of Gideon they went farther. The service rendered by him, in delivering them from so grievous an oppression, was in their view so eminent, that they were not only willing and desirous that he should be their governor during life, but were anxious that the government should be made hereditary in his family; in short, that he should be their sovereign, and should transmit his power to his descendants. This was a most extraordinary proposal. It shows that the Israelites had already begun to crave for a human monarchical government, and that they imperfectly understood or did not adequately prize the advantages they enjoyed under their peculiar constitution, which brought them into so near a relation to their Divine King. To his great honour—far more to his honour than even his victory over the Midianites—the patriotic virtue of Gideon was not moved by this great temptation. He was mindful of what they had forgotten; and to the invitation, "Rule thou over us, both thou, and thy son, and thy son's son also," his prompt answer, in the true spirit of the theocracy, was, "I will not rule over you, neither shall my son rule over you: the Lord shall rule over you." Considering that the love of power is one of the strongest passions in man, and that Gideon was the father of a large family of promising sons, whose advancement might seem a reasonable object of paternal solicitude, this refusal, solely on principle, to become the first monarch of the Hebrew state, deserves to be ranked with the most illustrious examples of patriotic self-denial which history has recorded.

Unhappily, all of his sons—and he had many —were not like-minded with their father. There was one of them, the son of his concubine, or secondary wife, who, on the death of Gideon, many years after this, determined to grasp the distinction which his father had declined. His mother was a woman of Shechem; and through the connections of her family, his influence was very strong in that quarter. He repaired thither on the death of his father, and, opening his design to his mother's family, urged them to prevail upon the people of the place to give him the kingdom. He assumed that some of his brethren would govern, notwithstanding Gideon's disclaimer on their behalf; indeed, he assumed that *all* of them would govern. Whether this was, as we suspect, an imputation devised by himself to advance his own objects, or whether it was founded upon some resolution among Gideon's sons as to the division of power among, or the common administration of power by, themselves, it is impossible to say. The argument, however, was, " Whether it be better for you, either that all the sons of Jerubbaal,[1] which are threescore and ten persons, reign over you, or that one reign over you?" Anticipating the answer to this plain proposition, which, as usual in such cases, presumed no other object than the public good, he proceeded to insinuate that *he* should be the one person so distinguished. This intimation was conveyed with astute indirectness—" Remember *I* am your bone and your flesh." These words were not spoken in vain. Local and family ties are all prevailing in the East; and the hearts of the men of Shechem inclined to follow Abimelech, for they said, " He is our brother." Being so inclined, they were not likely to be restrained by regard for the considerations which withheld Gideon from accepting the throne; for we find, in fact, that idolatry had gained ground in this and probably in other places during the lifetime of that judge. There was here a " house of Baal-berith," which, if it mean a temple, as it probably does, is the first of which there is any mention in Scripture—in fact, the first on record. Temples must therefore have existed among the heathen nations of Canaan before this date, or they would not have been thus early imitated by the idolatrous Israelites. Not very long after we find other instances of temples, also called " houses," among the Philistines. Out of the treasures accumulated in this house from the offerings of the votaries, the people of Shechem, after having chosen Abimelech king, supplied him with money, which enabled him to attach a considerable number of loose and idle vagabonds to his person and service, by whose aid he was enabled to assume some of the state and exercise some of the power of a king.

It will occur to the reader to ask, What right the people of Shechem had to nominate a king by their sole authority? In the first place, it must be remembered that the land had formerly been governed by a number of petty kings, ruling over some strong town and its immediate district

[1] A name acquired by Gideon, as stated in Judges 6:32.

and dependent villages; and it is likely that the Shechemites claimed no more than to appoint Abimelech as such a king over themselves, assuming that they, for themselves, whatever might be the view of others, had a right to choose a king to reign over them. Besides, Shechem was one of the chief towns of the tribe of Ephraim; and that proud and powerful tribe always claimed to take the leading part in public affairs, if not to determine the course of the other tribes—except, perhaps, of those connected with the tribe of Judah in the south. It was under the influence of this desire for supremacy that the revolt against the house of David was organized in that tribe, and resulted in the establishment of the separate kingdom for the ten tribes, in which kingdom Ephraim had the chief influence. Indeed, that establishment of a separate monarchy was eventually accomplished at this very place where Abimelech is now declared king. Taking all this into account, it may seem reasonable to conclude that the Shechemites had the support of the tribe in this transaction, or might at least reckon with reasonable confidence upon its not being withheld. Then, again, a king chosen at Shechem, and supported by this powerful tribe, might reasonably calculate that the other tribes would soon give in their adhesion, seeing that in the time of his father their monarchical predilection had been so strongly manifested.

Abimelech was certainly a king. He is called such by one who had reason to hate him; and his government is called a reign. He, therefore, was the first king in Israel, though it is usual to give Saul that distinction. He was inaugurated with some considerable ceremony, "by the plain of the pillar that was in Shechem,"—or rather, as in the original, by the "oak of the pillar,"—which, we strongly incline to think, alludes to the tree near which Joshua erected a pillar, as a witness of the covenant renewed between God and Israel. We need not be amazed that worshippers of Baal-berith should seek the sanction of so venerable an association; for, as we have already had occasion to remark, their idolatry did not consist in an absolute rejection of Jehovah and His law, but in the adoption of other gods beside Him, resulting in the neglect of His worship and ordinances. This inauguration at a pillar in some sacred place became afterwards part of the regular ceremonial of what we should call a coronation; for we read that the young king Joash stood by a pillar in the court of the temple at his solemn inauguration by the high priest Jehoiada. (2 Kings xi. 14).

After all, it does not appear that Abimelech was able greatly to extend his kingdom; for, after three years, we find him besieging towns not very distant from Shechem, that refused to submit to his authority. In one such siege he met death; for, as he advanced to set fire to the gate, a woman cast down upon him the upper mill-stone (called "the rider," because it is made to revolve upon the lower one). Finding himself mortally wounded, he got his armour-bearer to run him through with his sword, lest it should be said that *a woman slew him*. This has been curiously, but perhaps needlessly, illustrated as a peculiar point of ancient military honour. But we apprehend that an officer of our own, or any other army of modern Europe, would quite as little relish, as did the ancients, the idea of its being said of him that he died by a woman's hand, although he might not resort to the same means of evading so great a stain upon his heroic fame.[1]

* * *

A PARABLE

Judges 9:7-15

It seems to us very probable, that one cause of the ill success of Abimelech's attempt to establish a kingdom, lay in the general abhorrence of the deed which he committed when he had secured the adhesion of the men of Shechem. Attended by the unprincipled men whom he had attached to his person, he went down to the abode of his father's family at Ophrah, and there put to death all his brethren, the sons of Gideon, probably by beheading, "upon one stone." There is, however, some danger of measuring by our own feelings—and therefore of over estimating—the impression

such a deed was likely to make upon an ancient oriental people. The fact that Abimelech did commit this barbarous and unnatural atrocity, seems to show that the policy, which has had numerous later examples in the East, had already become usual in the kingdoms around Palestine, from which it was adopted by Abimelech. This policy aims to secure the throne to the person who ascends it by destroying all his brothers, that the people, if discontented, may be deterred from dethroning or slaying their king by the feeling that there is no one of the royal race to be preferred. This was, for centuries, the regular policy of the Ottoman court, and has only been abandoned within the memory of man. It was also, from a far earlier date, the policy of the Persian court, until it was found that the object might be attained by destroying the eyes, instead of taking the life, of all the sons of the king but the one who reigned. It is on record that all the sons of Futteh Ali Shah, whose reign terminated only in 1834, grew up in the belief that their eyes would be taken from them on the death of their father. There is a touching incident of one of the boys being seen by an English lady walking about the harem blindfold, in order, as he said, that he might know how to walk when blind, as he knew that his sight would be taken from him when the king his father should die.

One young son of Gideon—indeed, the youngest—did, however, escape the massacre. His name was Jotham. One would think that he would have gone and hid himself in the remotest part of the land, striving to keep even his existence a secret from his bloodthirsty brother. But, with the astonishing hardihood which we sometimes witness in men in his circumstances, he no sooner heard that the elders of Shechem were going to make Abimelech king, than he determined to take a very extraordinary part in the ceremony. At the time when they were assembled in the valley to inaugurate their chosen king, a voice was heard calling to them from Mount Gerizim. They looked up! and, behold, it was Jotham, standing boldly out upon a cliff of the mountain, and inviting their attention to his words: "Hearken unto me, ye men of Shechem, that God may hearken unto you." Instead of the eager remonstrance or warm protest which they probably expected, he gave them a *fable*— the most ancient in history, and, in all respects, the first specimen of this kind of composition.

---

[1] "As we returned into the town (Ceuta), a stone, nearly of the size of a man's head, was shown to us, by which the skull of the Portuguese commander who first entered the place, was, like that of Pyrrhus, broken by a woman from a tower. A Moorish sovereign who was so wounded despatched himself, like Abimelech, with his own sword, to cover his disgrace."—Urquhart's *Pillars of Hercules*, 1850, i. 96.

It is seven hundred years older than Æsop, the most ancient heathen name in parabolic literature; and it cannot be denied, that it is at least equal to anything which that great fabulist produced. As in most works of this description the earliest are the best, we may be prepared to admit that Jotham's parable, though the oldest that has been preserved, is a perfect specimen of its kind, and in every respect a model for this species of composition.

The trees, he said, went forth to choose a king. First, they went to the olive tree, but the olive tree refused to leave its fatness to go to be promoted over the trees; then they went to the fig tree, which in like manner declined to quit its sweetness; the vine refused also to leave its gladdening wine; and the trees, in their despair, went to the bramble, which considered the matter sagely, and consented to reign on conditions which the rich olive or the fruitful vine would not have exacted: " If in truth ye anoint me king over you, then come and put your trust in my shadow; and if not, let fire come out of the bramble, and devour the cedars of Lebanon." The terse and biting application of this parable to Abimelech is obvious, and was made by Jotham himself ere he fled. There are other applications of it which we may very well make for our own profit.

The reluctance of the trees generally to desert the useful station in which they were planted and fixed, to move to and fro (as the word rendered " promoted " signifies), and to reign over trees, is a wholesome lesson to us of contentment in the stations and lines of private usefulness we respectively fill, without an eager grasping after public honour and authority, attended with responsibilities, which we may not be very well able to discharge, and with cares in which we are untried. It is often the case that these, from their engrossing nature, and from the public notice they involve, cannot be discharged without much neglect of private affairs, and the sacrifice of much ease and comfort, amounting to an abandonment of the fatness, the sweetness, and the wine of life—of all that renders our existence really useful to others, and really happy to ourselves. Happiness is *suitableness;* and he who abandons the means of usefulness which have grown with his growth in the sphere in which he moves, for untried, and therefore probably unsuitable, responsibilities and powers is likely to pierce himself through with many sorrows,

and forego all that has blessed his past existence. It is well to note, that the trees considered that the promotion offered to them involved the abandonment of all that was proper to them, and that constituted their usefulness. In this age and country, men have not the offer of crowns; but in this age and country, more perhaps than in any other, there is an extensive craving after public honours and powers—political, municipal, ecclesiastical, commercial—which renders these considerations far from inappropriate. In the state, in the city, in the church, in the club, in the company, and even in the workshop and the school, there is a general seeking after the power and dominion involved in the idea of " reigning," which is justly open to the caution contained in this parable. There are, indeed, legitimate objects of the highest ambition, and of the most exalted aspirations. Crowns and kingdoms lie beneath the feet of him who pursues with steady pace his high career towards the city of the Great King, where he knows there is laid up for him a crown of glory that fadeth not away, a crown of righteousness which the Lord, the righteous Judge, will bestow upon all that love His appearing.

Consider also the eagerness of the bramble to accept the honours which the nobler trees declined, and the arrogant pretensions which it connected with its acceptance of them. By this we may learn, as Jotham intended to teach, that they are men of an inferior order of capacity and usefulness, to whom these earthly distinctions are most precious, and by whom they are most earnestly coveted. A good man may accept honours and powers, which have occurred to him as the result of his high labours and eminent services. Were it otherwise, the power which man exercises over man would be in the hands only of the worthless. But to seek the honours themselves, to make them the direct object of ambition and of thought, or even to accept them without the right which high services confer, is low, is mean, is brambleish. Now a bramble is not only one of the most useless of plants, but it is offensive by its thorns, so that silly sheep which accept the shelter to which it invites them, escape not without leaving some of their fleece behind. So also, from its very worthlessness, it is much used in the East for the light fuel which in such climates is alone required. Yet, as such, it may kindle a flame which may prostrate the very cedars of Lebanon. Hence it is not the highest of men, the lofty and the gifted, who crave for dominion over their fellows, and invite them to put their trust in their shadow; but the low, the unworthy, and the hurtful, who take what they cannot use, and offer what they cannot give. The bramble Abimelech was the only one in the line of the judges who attained to greatness without any public services; and yet he claimed higher honours and powers, in his mere unworthiness, than the greatest of those judges ever exercised or would have accepted. There have been, and there are, many such Abimelechs; and generally, in all their insatiate cravings after power, the arrogance of the pretension is proportioned to the scantiness of the desert.

JEPHTHAH

Judges 11

THE next defection of the Israelites into idolatry was very grievous. The tribes in the different districts seem to have adopted the worship of the nearest heathen nations on their borders. For this they were subjected to a twofold oppression; for while the Philistines afflicted the south, the Ammonites oppressed the tribes beyond the Jordan, and at length crossed over, and extended their incursions into the country west of the river. The deliverer at this time was of Gilead. His name was Jephthah,—a man who, having, as the son of a concubine, been, upon the death of his father, cast forth upon the world, had put himself at the head of a set of brave but lawless men, who led the life of freebooters, making incursions into the territories of the bordering nations, and living upon the spoil thus acquired. This kind of life was such as David led during his wanderings, and was far from being accounted discreditable in those times, nor is it indeed at present so deemed in the East. Although the nation generally had long been addicted to idolatry, which, with his own wild habits of life, must have left Jephthah's notions very imperfect and confused as to many points of duty and legal obligation, there is no doubt that he had a true zeal for the Lord, and a sincere faith in the sufficiency of His protection. His mode of life necessitated many daring exploits, and gave him such opportunities of manifesting his courage and

abilities, as no other person in that age possessed; and hence it was natural that, when the people had resolved to strike for their deliverance, and felt the want of an experienced leader, they should have applied to Jephthah to take the command against the Ammonites. After some demur he consented, and was completely successful in his great enterprise; and Israel once more was free. The great point of interest in this transaction is that which resulted from the rash vow made by this commander when he set out to lead his host against the children of Ammon. He then "vowed a vow unto the Lord, and said, If Thou wilt without fail deliver the children of Ammon into my hands, then shall it be, that whatsoever cometh forth of the doors of my house to meet me, when I return in peace from the children of Ammon, shall surely be the Lord's, and I will offer it up for a burnt-offering."

The terms of this vow seem to us altogether such as to show the extremely limited nature of the knowledge which Jephthah possessed as to the law of Moses, and especially of its regulations concerning vows. Throughout, it savours far more of the superstition which might be expected from the long night of sin and sorrow through which Israel had passed, than of the correct religious faith of one who had been nourished with the marrow of the covenant. The idea of bargaining with God in this manner for His assistance is offensive to the rightly nurtured mind, and has a heathenish savour, such things being exceedingly common under every pagan system. Almost every important undertaking was accompanied among them with similar vows of offerings and sacrifices to some god, to bribe him, as it were, to give the undertaking the advantage of his assistance. An instance of this has been given in p. 458 of this volume. Upon the whole, one who has closely studied the character of the times, and the circumstances of the man, will readily perceive that Jephthah might think to propitiate Jehovah, even to the extent of a human sacrifice, by presenting such an offering as was sometimes made, in great emergencies, by the heathen. Among the doomed nations of Canaan, as well as among the surviving nations around, human sacrifices were far from uncommon; it being held that what was most valuable and precious in the sight of man, that which was dearest to him, that which it would cost him most to part with, was the most fitting expression of his zeal for the gods, the fullest possible manifestation of his devotion and gratitude. No doubt the law declared such sacrifices to be abominable to God; but it is easy to conceive that such a man as Jephthah, living in the time he did, was far better acquainted with the leading facts of the history of his people than with the details of the law. Of the former he evinces much knowledge in his answer to the remonstrance of the Ammonites. Men of the class of minds and capacities to which he belonged readily possess themselves of broad facts, but heed little the details of such laws as are not embodied in tangible institutions. In that age the law would be little taught or studied; and although the tabernacle institutions may have remained in outward operation at Shiloh, we cannot suppose that what was neglected on the west side of the Jordan was not far more neglected in the east. Few of the people resident there had probably ever been at the tabernacle on the yearly festivals, or had access to such instructions as the priests and Levites might have been able to afford. Knowledge of these matters, from private intercourse with those who were acquainted with the law, could not have gone far in that corrupt generation; and in such a time, not many, probably, beyond the Jordan had even *heard* the law read once in seven years at the feast of tabernacles. It may therefore be quite possible that Jephthah was wholly ignorant that such sacrifices were unlawful, while his recollection of facts may have helped him to a very erroneous conclusion in the matter, from Abraham's intended sacrifice of Isaac by divine command.

We say this, because we cannot resist the conviction that Jephthah, when he uttered his vow, did contemplate the possibility that the sacrifice which he would be called to offer might be the sacrifice of a human life. Look at the terms of his oath. What could he suppose would come out of the doors of his house *for the purpose* of meeting him, but a human being? He did not keep sheep or oxen in his house; nor do *they* come forth to meet their returning owners. A dog might do so; but the Israelites did not keep dogs in their houses. In his house he had many human beings, servants, slaves, followers—no relations, for he was the son of a harlot, and his father's connections had cast him off. Yet there was one, a daughter—the only child he had; and although he may have contemplated the mere possibility that she might be the one that would come out to meet him, he could not nullify the supposed virtue of his vow, by formally excepting from its operation her who was dearest of all to him.

Yet, when the moment of trial came—when, as he drew nigh his house, his daughter appeared, leading the damsels, who with timbrels and with dances greeted the triumphant return of her now glorious father,—the hero shrank beneath the blow. "Alas, my daughter," he cried, "thou hast brought me very low; for I have opened my mouth unto the Lord, and I cannot go back." We cannot but sympathize in his grief, while we deplore his ignorance. The very words he uses now, show in a degree that he had contemplated from the first the possibility of such a sacrifice, not knowing it to be unlawful; for had the vow, as uttered, involved a result forbidden by God, and therefore sinful, so far from being obliged to perform his vow—so far from being restrained from going back, he would, notwithstanding his vow, have been obliged not to perform it. The original sin of making such a vow, which might lead to unlawful consequences, was great; but that sin, instead of being diminished, would be aggravated, by his performing the unlawful act. That his daughter did not know that such a vow had been made, is another proof that we have rightly interpreted its tenor. To have made it known to her, or to any of his household, would have been to make it a mockery, with the possibility of a human sacrifice in view; but had an animal sacrifice only been in his thoughts, there is no reason why he should not have made it known: indeed, there was every reason why he should do so, for these things were usually declared openly, for the encouragement of the troops.

When, therefore, we are told that "Jephthah did with his daughter according to his vow," we, in full recollection of all the ingenious explanations which have been produced, and which we regret that our space does not allow us to examine, see no alternative but to conclude, although we would gladly avail ourselves of any fair ground of escape from that conclusion, that he offered her up in sacrifice. This is the sense conveyed by the ancient versions, and by the text of our own. It is also the statement of Josephus, though he is prone to extenuate or suppress that which he holds to be not for the honour of his nation;

while, at the same time, he considers it as a deplorably mistaken and unlawful act. We may sympathize in the wish of vindicating the memory of one of the heroes of Scripture history from such gross ignorance, resulting in so foul a crime; still we feel bound to take the narrative in its plain and simple meaning, which is that taken at the first view, and apart from all note and comment, by any reader of the original narrative, as well as by that very correct translation of it which our own version supplies. The considerations at which we have hinted may tend to diminish our surprise, though not our grief, by showing how the very mistaken view under which Jephthah acted, is not at all incredible in the age in which he lived, and under the circumstances in which he was placed. Let not the reader, however, take up the absurd fancy of the painters, that this deed was perpetrated by the high priest at the altar of God. The high priest would have known his duty better. All our surprise is, that whatever may have been the alienation between the tribes on the opposite sides of the Jordan, he did not send, or go to prevent, by such little authority as he had left, so dreadful a consummation. We have, however, a reason for this also. The Ephraimites, in whose tribe the tabernacle was, had actually at this time come to blows with Jephthah, through the offence they had, as in the time of Gideon, conceived, at not having been summoned to take part in the war with Ammon. This would tend to cut off all communication between the opposite sides of the river for the time; and while the high priest would be less likely on this account to hear of the matter, he would be the less able, if he did hear of it, to interfere with any advantage. The awful sacrifice was doubtless made on some one of the old altars, or perhaps on a new one, in Gilead. But we can pursue the consequences of the case no farther, being most glad to draw a veil over the possible circumstances of the last scene, when perhaps the father's own hand struck down the life that was dearer to him than his own.

I cannot by any means agree with Dr. Kitto in his interpretation of this difficult and much controverted passage. The structure of the Hebrew text does not require such an interpretation as he gives, and there are incidental expressions in the narrative which, in my opinion, are decidedly opposed to it. I think it right, therefore, to give a full exposition of the text.

The record of Jephthah's vow in ver. 31 may be thus translated : " *That which* (or, *he who*) *cometh to meet me out of the doors of my house,* when I return in peace from the children of Ammon, *shall belong to the Lord,* (or, *and*) *I will offer it for a burnt offering* (or, *a whole-offering*)." The Hebrew word translated *and* in the English version is the same which is translated *or* in the Tenth Commandment (Deut. v. 21) ; and also in the passage, " He that curseth his father *or* his mother" (Exod. xxi. 17). The context must decide whether it is to be taken as a *conjunctive* or a *disjunctive*. If taken in the latter sense here, all difficulty is removed ; for then the last clause is opposed to, and not explanatory of, the one before it. The meaning of the vow would then be, if that which meets me be a thing fit for a burnt-offering, it shall be made one ; but if it be fit for the service of God, it shall be consecrated to Him.

Some affirm, however, that the Hebrew particle must here be taken as conjunctive and explanatory, and not as disjunctive. Even admitting this—which I do not, however—the passage may be satisfactorily explained. The word rendered " burnt-offering" does not necessarily involve the idea of burning, but simply that of "going up" upon the altar, or of *complete surrender and dedication to the Lord.* The word is used to signify a " whole-offering," as distinguished from the other sacrifices, of which only a part was given to the Lord. When a virgin is said to be so offered, she was set apart as *a spiritual whole-offering,* belonging henceforth entirely to the Lord. Either of these interpretations will remove the difficulty.

I shall now point out those incidental phrases in the sacred narrative which show that Jephthah did not, and never intended to offer up his daughter as a burnt-offering.

Every Hebrew scholar will see that the very grammatical form of the vow shows that Jephthah must, at any rate, have had the possibility of some human being coming to meet him in his mind. He could not have been so ignorant—no Jew could have been—as not to know that human sacrifices were prohibited in the law under pain of death, as an utter abomination in the sight of the Lord. He shows in his treaty with the Ammonites that he was well versed in Jewish history ; and besides, it is expressly stated that "the Spirit of the Lord came upon" him, to fit him specially for this great mission. Under such circumstances, he never could have made a vow involving human sacrifice.

But again, the terms in which the sacred writer records the fulfilment of the vow lead to the same conclusion. The entreaty of his daughter, that he would give her two months *to lament her virginity* upon the mountains with her friends, is surely out of all keeping with the supposition that she was to be put to death. To mourn her virginity does not mean to mourn because she was to die a sacrifice, but because she was to live and abide a virgin. It would seem reasonable enough to ask for a two months' reprieve ; but that she should only think of bewailing her virginity, when a terrible death was before her, is contrary alike to natural feeling and common sense. Then observe the statement made by the historian after he relates that Jephthah " did with her according to his vow which he had vowed :" "*And she knew no man.*" Is this in harmony with the supposition of a sacrificial death? This clause would add nothing to the description in that case, since it was already known she was a virgin. The words get their full and proper sense only when connected with the preceding clause, and when taken as describing what she did in fulfilment of the vow. The father fulfilled his vow upon her, through the fact that she knew no man, but dedicated herself to the Lord, a spiritual offering, in a life-long chastity.

In this interpretation there is no wresting of the words of Scripture. There is a preservation of the full and literal sense. There is more, as I believe: there is attention given to the whole scope of the narrative, and to those incidental yet expressive statements which must guide the interpreter to the real meaning.

P.

Without entering into the controversy between Dr. Porter and Dr. Kitto on this subject, it may be stated that the current of opinion, on the part of the best biblical critics, has of late been in favour of the latter. Dr. Alexander, in his edition of Kitto's *Cyclopædia* (art. Jephthah), presents the arguments on the other side; but Dr. Stanley, in his *Lectures on the Jewish Church*, the Rev. W. T. Bullock, in Dr. Smith's *Dictionary* (art. Jephthah), and Lord A. Hervey, Bishop of Bath and Wells, in *The Speaker's Commentary* (Vol. ii. 184), take a similar view to that of Dr. Kitto. He says, on Judges xi. 31, if the words "*shall surely be the Lord's*" stood alone, Jephthah's vow might be understood as Hannah's. But the words which follow "and I will offer it (Heb., *him*), for a burnt offering" preclude any idea but that of a human sacrifice. "This need not however surprise us, when we recollect his Syrian birth and long residence in a Syrian city, where such fierce rites were probably common. The Syrians and Phœnicians were conspicuous among the ancient heathen nations for human sacrifices."

S.

THE NAZARITE

Judges 13

THERE is no judge in Israel whose history is so fully related as that of Samson. It occupies four of the twenty-one chapters which compose the book of Judges. It is full of striking and marvellous incidents, arising from the great physical strength and the great moral weakness of the hero, mixed up with a prevailing and childlike trust in the Lord, in which lies all of greatness that belongs to his character. The history, in its main features, is familiar to all our readers from childhood. We need not, therefore, occupy our shortening space in the recapitulation of it, but may select for observation the facts which seem to us suitable for remark in these Daily Readings.

Samson's history commences before his birth. He is introduced with great pomp, which awakens expectations scarcely satisfied by the ultimate facts and real results of his career. This may not strike us at first, the events being so far uncommon as to appear great by their very singularity. But closely considered, there are none of his feats, or all of them together, of nearly so much importance as the simple victories of Barak, Gideon, or Jephthah. This, we think, can only be accounted for by his great destinies having been marred by his vices and indiscretions, which incapacitated him from acting efficiently as the leader of the people, by rendering it impossible for them to trust in him, though he displayed the most astonishing acts of individual prowess that the world ever witnessed. Some have blamed the Israelites for not placing themselves under his guidance and crushing the Philistines, who were in his time their oppressors. But it seems to us that they were completely justified in withholding their confidence from him. A mere slave of the senses like him, who could repeatedly sacrifice or endanger the most important interests to a woman's sigh, was not one into whose hands the elders and warriors of Israel could entrust their lives and fortunes. Had he wrought out the possibilities of his destiny, and had his character been equal to his gifts, there is no knowing to what greatness he might have attained; but as it was, he left a name which is at once a miracle and a byword, a glory and a shame.

Of persons whose births were solemnly announced beforehand by angels, there are but two in the Old Testament, and Samson was one of them. This was a great and splendid distinction. In both instances the mothers were barren women, and had abandoned the hope of children, which circumstance greatly enhanced to both the importance of the communication. In the case of Isaac, the announcement was made to Abraham in the hearing of Sarah; in the case of Samson, it was made to the woman in the absence of her husband. The man to whose wife the angel came, was of Zorah, in the tribe of Dan, a place close upon the borders of the Philistine territory. His name was Manoah. We do not know that the appearance of an angel is anywhere in the historical Scriptures described with so much particularity as in this account. The wife herself, in describing him to her husband, says: "A man of God came unto me, and his countenance was like the countenance of an angel of God, very terrible: but I asked him not whence he was, neither told he me his name." By this it appears that she took him in the first instance for a prophet sent from God, yet entertained the suspicion that he might be something more than human. A favourite old poet well describes the heavenly seen through the earthly, which must have given rise to this impression—

> "In his face
> Terror and sweetness laboured for the place.
> Sometimes his sun-bright eyes would shine so fierce,
> As if their pointed beams would even pierce
> The soul, and strike the amaz'd beholder dead:
> Sometimes their glory would disperse and spread
> More easy flame, and like the star that stood
> O'er Bethl'em, promise and portend some good;
> Mixt was his bright aspect, as if his breath
> Had equal errands both of life and death:
> Glory and mildness seemed to contend
> In his fair eyes."[1]

Again, in relating the same to Manoah, the woman says:

> "Appeared before mine eyes
> A man of God: his habit and his guise
> Were such as holy prophets used to wear;
> But in his dreadful looks there did appear
> Something that made me tremble; in his eye
> Mildness was mixt with awful majesty."

The angel, not yet fully known to be such, both foretold the birth of a son, and gave directions as to the manner of his upbringing, seeing that he was to be "a Nazarite unto God from the womb." His vocation as one to deliver, or rather, "to begin to deliver," Israel from the Philistines, was indicated.

The law of Nazariteship is laid down in the books of Moses;[2] but this is the first instance we have of its practical application. The Nazarite (or separated one) was to be considered as in a special manner separated from ordinary life to religious purposes; and his condition, as consecrated to the service, worship, and honour of God, was to be manifested by certain personal peculiarities and acts of self-denial. The chief personal peculiarity consisted in the hair being suffered to grow during the whole period, even for life; and the chief self-denial in abstinence from wine and all strong drink. The obligation against the drinking of wine was secured from

evasion, by the fruit of the vine being forbidden in every shape, from the stones to the husk. This was a very mild asceticism, unlike what we now witness in the Pagan East, and even in Christian Europe. A Nazarite might eat, and drink, and marry, and possess, and mingle in society; and his condition, as under vows to the Lord, was marked only by a becoming peculiarity, and by a wholesome abstinence. He was also to take special care to keep himself from ceremonial pollution, particularly from such as was involved by contact with a dead body. He was not to make himself unclean by touching the corpse of even a relative. But if he did contract accidental defilement, he was to shave his head; and counting as lost all the time of his separation which had previously passed, he was to begin anew. The obligation was usually undertaken for a limited time, but sometimes for the remainder of life. It might be imposed by parents upon their children, even before their birth, as in the case of Samuel; and in this case of Samson, as well as in that of John the Baptist, the condition was imposed, before birth, by divine appointment. In these cases there was of course no discharge from the obligations of the vow, as there might be when it was voluntarily undertaken, and for a limited time.

Although Samson was obviously made a Nazarite to indicate his being specially set apart to serve the Lord by the endowments bestowed upon him, yet there was a peculiar fitness in the vow being imposed upon one who was to be so gifted with the utmost perfection of physical strength. His bushy locks were a sign and symbol of his extraordinary strength, inasmuch as men possess them more abundantly than women, and strong men more abundantly than weak. Wine and strong drink also impair the strength and clearness of the intellect. The retention of the hair, therefore, and the abstinence from vinous drinks, expressed the highest perfection of body and mind—the full possession of all his powers and capacities in the individual. This had an analogical conformity with the law, which required that animals offered to the Lord in sacrifice should be free from all blemish and defect.

It is worthy of note, that when Manoah received from his wife this information, he fully believed that the angel's promise should be fulfilled. Every one else to whom such a promise was ever made,

---

[1] Quarles: *History of Samson.*   [2] See Numbers 6.

whether by prophet or angel, received it with distrust. Abraham and Sarah "laughed;" the Shunammite woman said to Elisha, "Nay, my lord, do not lie unto thine handmaid;" and the father of John the Baptist, although a priest, and addressed by an angel under the most solemn circumstances, said, "Whereby shall I know this?" and was struck dumb for his unbelief; even the Virgin Mary said, "How shall this thing be?" But Manoah, the only one who received no direct intimation from angel or prophet, had no hesitation in believing that what had been promised to his wife would come to pass. He was, however, not without fear that she might not clearly have apprehended the directions given to her; and therefore he implored the Lord that another interview with "the man of God" might be afforded. His suit was granted. The angel came again, when he was absent in the field. But his wife ran for him, and to him the seeming prophet repeated the instructions already given to the woman. Perfectly satisfied, Manoah proposed to offer the usual hospitality to the stranger, requesting him to tarry until a kid could be got ready for his entertainment. The stranger agreed to remain, but suggested that the kid should be rather presented as a burnt-offering to the Lord. During the delay, Manoah entered into conversation with the stranger, and among other things ventured to ask his name, with the view, as he said, of rendering him becoming honour when his prediction should be fulfilled—probably by spreading the fact abroad, and also by presenting him with some proper token of acknowledgment. But the angel answered, "Wherefore askest thou after my name, seeing it is secret?" By this time Manoah may have suspected the heavenly nature of his guest, and all doubt was removed when the kid was presented; for the angel then disappeared, ascending upward in the flame and smoke of the offering.

THE LION

Judges 14:1-10

AFTER Moses, the only eminent persons of the Old Testament whom we are permitted to know from their birth, are Samson, Samuel, and Solomon. Of these, the early life of Samuel is the best known. Of that of Samson we only know—and it is much to know—that "the child grew, and the Lord blessed him." By this, having his destination in view, we may understand that the Lord gave evident proofs that the child was under His peculiar protection; and by the gifts He bestowed, gave sign that He was preparing him for something great and extraordinary. We should have liked to possess a few details of his boyhood. He whose manhood was so remarkable, could not pass an undistinguished boyhood among his playmates in the streets of Zorah. How that long-haired, lion-like boy, must have been looked up to among his young companions! What sweets of power he enjoyed! For there is no admiration in the world, no reverence, comparable to that with which a set of boys will look up to supreme bodily prowess in any one of their companions; no authority so despotic as that which he may, if he wills it, exercise; no subjects are there so willing and devoted in their obedience as those who receive his command. The homage which all covet, is by no man of full age received in so large and unreserved measure, as that which such a boy receives.

It is worthy of note, that when Samson grew up, all the attachments which he successively formed were to females of the Philistines—the power that held southern Israel in bondage. No daughter of his own people appears to have engaged his attention at any time. There was, as intimated, a providence in this, that therefrom might result circumstances which should bring him into collision with the Philistines, disgraceful and disastrous to them. Samson's first attachment to a young woman of Timnath was highly distasteful to his parents. This, however, must have been solely on the ground that a marriage into a foreign and idolatrous nation was adverse to the principles of the law and the feelings of the people; for this was not one of the Canaanitish nations, marriages into which were absolutely interdicted. As the Israelites had been much in the habit of contracting such alliances notwithstanding this prohibition, a marriage with a Philistine woman must have seemed no very heinous offence; and although the parents of Samson did somewhat demur to the match, and did suggest that he had better seek a wife among the daughters of his own people, they were easily prevailed upon, not only to give way to their son's inclination, but to go down to Timnath and make the proposal to the damsel's family in due form. Some commentators, unacquainted with the customs of the East, assume that the parents went down to see how they liked the young woman who had won their son's regard, and whose consent had been by him already obtained. This would have been in the highest degree indecorous. They went to make the proposal, and to arrange the conditions with the parents of the damsel; all these matters being settled by the parents, or through some confidential retainer, before the young pair had any near access to each other.

A singular adventure happened in the way down. Samson had digressed from the road into the vineyards, "probably to eat grapes," Matthew Henry supposes, forgetting that the fruit of the vine was forbidden in any form; but Quarles more poetically conjectures, that he had stept aside

"To gain the pleasure of a lonely thought,"

when a young lion came and roared against him. By "a young lion" is meant not a young whelp, for which the Hebrew has quite a different word; but a young lion arrived at the fulness of its growth, and therefore more full of animal spirits and vigour than at a later age, and consequently a more dangerous enemy to encounter. A lion, in presence of prey or of an enemy, roars at the time when it springs; and Samson therefore became aware of the presence of this fierce

SAMSON KILLETH A LION

adversary in the very moment of onset. But the weaponless hero received the strong beast

with his sinewy arms, and "rent him as he would have rent a kid," leaving the carcase upon the ground. He then rejoined his parents, and said nothing of what had happened, which is certainly a singular instance of discretion, modesty, and self-control, the more so when we consider that it is not at all in the East considered unseemly for a man to speak vauntingly of his own exploits.

This is the first instance which occurs of the presence of lions in Palestine; but the frequent allusions to them by the sacred writers, and the familiar acquaintance with their habits evinced by them, as well as the variety of names by which the various circumstances of the lion's growth and age are distinguished, show how common, in former times, in Syria, was this noble animal, now not found nearer in Asia than the banks of the Euphrates, and there very rarely. Its presence, indeed, is shown by historical incidents, such as David's combat with a lion in defence of his flock;[1] the slaughter of a lion in a pit on a snowy day by one of David's worthies;[2] the destruction of the disobedient prophet by a lion;[3] the notice of the lions being driven up, by the swellings of the river, from the thickets of the Jordan;[4] and the remarkable instance of their rapid increase, and the ravages committed by them, when the land became thinly occupied, through the slaughter and departure of the Israelites.[5] This strikingly illustrates the reason given why the Lord would not all at once drive out the Canaanites before the Israelites, when they entered the promised land: "Lest the beasts of the field should increase upon them."[6] If in the latter period, much more in the earlier, must lions have been included. The lion lives to above fifty years; and, consequently, having annual litters of from three to five cubs, they increase very rapidly, when the sparseness of the population of any country in which they are found leaves them comparatively unmolested.

European readers will expect that Samson would marry the damsel of his choice, and take her home with him. Not so. The contract of betrothal was then to be entered into; and it was, and is still, a custom among the Jews, and one probably of the Philistines, for an interval

[1] 1 Samuel 17:34.   [2] 2 Samuel 23:20: 1 Chronicles 11:22.
[3] 1 Kings 13:24.   [4] Jeremiah 49:19.
[5] 2 Kings 17:25, 26.   [6] Deuteronomy 7:22.

of some months, commonly not less than a year, to elapse between the betrothal and the marriage.

It was after some such interval that Samson went down once more to Timnath, to celebrate the nuptials. On the way his curiosity prompted him to turn aside to see whether any traces existed of the lion he had some months before slain. To his astonishment he found the dead carcase replete with life:

> " His wond'ring ear
> Perceived a murmuring voice : discerning not
> From whence that strange confusion was, or what.
> He stays his steps and hearkens. Still the voice
> Presents his ear with a continued noise.
> At length his gently moving feet apply
> Their paces to the carcase, where his eye
> Discerns a swarm of bees, whose laden thighs
> Reposed their burdens, and the painful prize
> Of their sweet labours, in the hollow chest
> Of the dead lion, whose unbowell'd breast
> Became their plenteous storehouse."—*Quarles.*

It has seemed to many, judging from what happens to the dead body of a beast in our own climate, scarcely credible that so sensitively clean and neat a creature as a bee should establish itself in so offensive a domicile. The answer is —that it was *not* offensive. In the East, vultures and insects, particularly numerous swarms of ants, which abound in vineyards, will in an astonishingly short time clean completely out all the soft parts of any carcase, leaving the skeleton entire, covered by its integuments; for the flesh having been *picked out*, the skin would not be rent and destroyed. This would happen rather in the country than in a town, where the dogs would not be likely to leave the outer form of the animal in this state. The circumstances are therefore entirely appropriate to the situation in which they occurred. All the softer parts being thus removed, the bones and skin will rapidly be deprived of all their moisture by the heat of the sun; and the skeleton, covered over with the dry parchment into which the skin has been turned, becomes a sweet and very convenient habitation in which a swarm of bees would be very likely to settle, especially in a secluded spot, among the shrub-like vines. In the East, bees establish themselves in situations little thought of by us: many wild swarms, being left to find homes for themselves, fix in any hollow which seems to

them suited to their wants; often in the clefts of the rock, whence the mention of "honey out of the rock;"[1] often in trees, whence the mention of the dropping of the honey-comb,—a singular instance of which we have in the case of Jonathan, who found honey dropping from the trees to the ground, in his way through a forest.[2]

In the present case, Samson took some of the honey-comb, and gave part of the honey to his parents when he rejoined them, without telling them how it had been obtained. The whole of the affair of the lion is mentioned in the sacred narrative, not merely as an exploit, but on account of the circumstances which grew out of it. Samson doubtless performed many mighty feats which are not recorded; those only being mentioned which directly influenced the current of his history, and brought him more or less into collision with the Philistines. No one would have thought that out of this slaughter of the lion, and the finding a swarm of bees in the skin-enveloped carcase, occurring as it did while the hero was engaged in forming amicable relations with the Philistines, occasion for the exertion of his destroying energies against the oppressors of Israel would have arisen. But so it came to pass. The most unlikely agents—lions, bees, honey-combs—may become the instruments of accomplishing the purposes of God, and of leading or driving man to his appointed task, when he thinks not of it.

Hugh Miller relates the following singular story, which may be regarded as in some measure illustrating Samson's discovery of the swarm of bees in the carcase of the lion: —" A party of boys had stormed a humble-bees' nest on the side of the old chapel-brae, and digging inwards along the narrow winding earth passage, they at length came to a grinning human skull, and saw the bees issuing thick from out a round hole at its base—the *foramen magnum.* The wise little workers had actually formed their nest within the hollow of the head, once occupied by the busy brain ; and their spoilers, more scrupulous than Samson of old, who seems to have enjoyed the meat brought out of the eater, and the sweetness extracted from the strong, left in very great consternation their honey all to themselves."[3]

P.

[1] Deuteronomy 32:13.   [2] 1 Samuel 14:25-27.
[3] *My Schools and Schoolmasters,* p. 69.

THE RIDDLE

Judges 14:10-19

THE account of Samson's marriage feast is given with unusual detail, and we are thus enabled to distinguish some of the ancient marriage customs of Palestine, most of which were such as still exist in the East. As the law of Moses did not affect any customs of this sort, nor establish any special set of usages for the Hebrews, it is not probable that their practices in this matter differed from those of their neighbours. In the present case, Samson celebrating his marriage as a stranger in a Philistine town, and leaving the particulars to be managed by the Philistines, doubtless followed the customs of the place; and that most of these customs can, at later or earlier periods, be discovered among the Hebrews themselves, shows the essential identity of their matrimonial usages.

First, then, we are informed that "Samson made there a feast; *for so used the young men to do.*" Such feasts are still celebrated throughout the East, during which all kinds of merriment prevail. This feast, as we learn farther on, lasted for *seven* days; exactly the same period as the feast with which, six hundred years before, Jacob celebrated his successive marriages. Considering that Samson was a stranger at Timnath, his feast was no doubt held at the house of a Philistine acquaintance. The common reader may suppose that the feast was held at the house of the bride's father after the nuptial ceremonies. But this would have been contrary to all the ideas of the East. There would be indeed a feast there; but it was the feast of the bride, her female relations, and her fair companions. The sexes do not eat together in the East, and did not feast together even among the Jews, although in matters that concern women we find among them more liberal and less unsocial usages than now prevail among the Orientals. On such occasions they did not, and do not now, feast in the same house, unless under circumstances that render this unavoidable. Some would fancy that this separation of the sexes renders such feasts more decorous than they might be otherwise. We apprehend not. Men are apt to be indecorous when unrestrained by the presence of women; and in every nation those feasts are always the most proper and becoming in which females take part. This is in favour of our own usages, in the balance between the East and the West.

It was usual that the bridegroom should have a certain number of companions, who were always with him at his service during the period of the feast, and who exerted themselves to promote the good humour and hilarity of the entertainment. These are in the New Testament called the "friends of the bridegroom," and the "children of the bride-chamber."[1] One of these, usually an intimate friend of the bridegroom, and distinguished for his social qualities, and by his capacity for keeping the guests at their ease, and for his tact in repressing disorderly conduct, presided over the whole, and managed all the business that grew out of the protracted entertainment, that the bridegroom might be left free from all the distracting cares which are apt to beset the man who gives a feast. This important bridal officer is called, in the account of the marriage at Cana, "the governor of the feast;" and in the Baptist's discourse to his disciples, "the friend of the bridegroom," that rejoices to hear the bridegroom's voice.

Such "companions" and such a "friend" were not wanting at the marriage feast of Samson. Of the former there were no fewer than thirty; and as he was a stranger in the place, the choice of them was left much to the Philistines. Looking at the subsequent conduct of these men, there is probably an intended emphasis in its being stated "*When they saw him*, they brought thirty companions to be with him." We may perhaps gather, that when they observed the stature, form, countenance, and demeanour of the strong Hebrew, they thought him a man to be watched; and therefore, under the show of enabling him to give his feast with the customary honour and observance, really stationed these young men as spies and guards upon his person. Israel was in bondage; and an Israelite who exhibited a resolute bearing, joined to formidable powers, was likely to be closely observed. They would have watched Samson still more closely had they been aware of his exploit with the lion which he had hitherto most studiously concealed.

Among the amusements common at such festivals, was that of proposing riddles, the non-solution of which involved some kind of forfeit,

[1] Matthew 9:15; John 3:29.

and the solution a reward. They were particularly common among the Greeks, who were wont to call riddles, contrived to puzzle and perplex, by the significant name of "banquet riddles," or "cup questions." This was altogether a very favourite exercise of ingenuity among the ancients; and perhaps, taking into account the ingenuity required to devise them, and to discover their significance, with the faculties they keep in pleasant exercise, and the small surprises they involve, this species of wit has fallen into undeserved neglect among our sources of social entertainment. There may, however, be something in the fact, that our festal entertainments are so comparatively short, as to need fewer and less varied sources of ingenuity to prevent them from becoming a weariness. If we held feasts of seven days long, without the admixture of female society, we should betake ourselves to riddles and other resources of the sort for beguiling the long hours; and, as it is, the numerous people among us who cannot get through the brief space of our own entertainments without having recourse to cards, have small reason to regard the riddles of the ancient feasts with disrespect.

This kind of sport had been going on probably for some time, and Samson had perhaps been somewhat chafed by some defeats in this play of wit; when he at length declared, that he would now in his turn put forth a riddle, the terms being, that if they—that is, any one of the thirty —could make it out, he would forfeit to them thirty dresses of a superior description, that is, one to each; but if they could not solve it, each of them should forfeit a dress of the same kind to him. Thus the hero set himself and his riddle as it were against the whole body of his companions. If the riddle were not solved, each of them lost but one dress; if it were solved, he, singly, had to provide thirty. The advantages were on their side; but it suited Samson's humour that it should be so. In these, as in other matters, he liked to have the odds against him. It is possible, however, that he might not have made so unequal a bargain, had he not felt assured in his mind, that it passed the wit of man to find out the riddle he meant to propose, seeing that it was founded on his recent discovery of honey in the carcase of the lion, with which he was quite sure that none but himself could be acquainted. It was indeed soluble; but it depended upon a combination of incidents of very rare occurrence,

which was not likely to present itself to any one's mind. It was—

> "Out of the devourer came forth meat;
> Out of the strong came forth sweetness."

The antithesis is, in the first clause of this riddle, clear enough, but scarcely so in the second, seeing that the opposite of sweetness is not strength, but sharpness or bitterness. It is satisfactory, therefore, to find, that in the original the word for "bitter" is occasionally used for "strong" and "sharp," or "sour" for both. Hence some translators have, "Out of the bitter (or else *sour*) came forth sweetness." A word thus equivocal required to be used: for if a word distinctly denoting ferocity had been employed, a stronger clue to the meaning would have been given than the proposer meant to furnish.

No sooner was the riddle proposed, than every mind rushed to seize the meaning; but the nearer they approached, the more misty it appeared—the more it eluded the grasp of their understandings. After trying it in every possible way, they concluded that the attempt to reach its meaning was hopeless. Yet they were not willing to incur so great a forfeit, and still less to own that they were defeated, even in the play of wit, by this rough and long-haired Hebrew stranger. Whether they had, in their daily festal intercourse, discovered Samson's weak point—the yieldingness in a woman's hand of him whom man could not subdue—or whether their bow was shot at a venture, cannot be said. But they concluded to persuade the bride to extract the secret out of her husband. The argument they used with her was none of the gentlest. They simply threatened to "burn her and her father's house with fire," unless she got them out of this difficulty. But men do not resort to threats, even in the East, with a lady, until arguments have failed; it is therefore but just to this young woman, to draw the inference that she had in the first instance indignantly refused the treacherous task they sought to impose upon her, so that they were driven to this savage threat, by which they at length prevailed.

The first attempt upon Samson was somewhat sternly met: "Behold, I have not told it to my father nor my mother, and shall I tell it unto thee?" We perhaps do not see quite so much cogency in this argument as an Oriental does. But to him, *especially* while he is still young and newly married, his parents are first in his confidence, and his wife only second. Polygamy, and the facility of divorce together, have no doubt something to do with this; but so it is.

The poet Quarles—for he *was* a poet, and that of no mean order—works up the scene between Samson and his bride with great effect and poetic fire. He makes the chorus plead extenuatingly for her—

> "May not her tears prevail? Alas! thy strife
> Is but for wagers; hers, poor soul, for life."

Her tears did prevail: the strong Samson could never stand out against a woman's tears. We blame him not for giving way on this occasion, or we should not do so, but that we see in this the same fatal facility of temper which eventually led him to

> "Give up his fort of silence to a woman,"

in matters of solemn and sacred obligation. Few would, any more than Samson, have held out in this matter of the riddle, though the woman's importunity must have looked suspicious to a less open mind than his. The experience which he now obtained, rendered subsequent transgression under the like influences the less excusable. He seems to have been one of those unsuspecting beings, who cannot allow themselves to suppose that a woman is capable of treachery or harm, or that a fair face can hide a black or selfish heart. This reliance upon the tenderness and truth of woman's nature is not in itself a bad quality—nay, it is a fine, manly, and heroic quality—and we may be allowed to regret that Samson fell into hands which rendered it a snare, a danger, and a death to him.

When, at the appointed time, the companions, in whose sure defeat he was grimly exulting in his thoughts, came boldly before him and interpreted his riddle in the questions, "What is sweeter than honey? what is stronger than a lion?" Samson saw at once that he had been betrayed. But he scorned to complain. Having bitterly remarked, "If ye had not ploughed with my heifer, ye had not found out my riddle," he proceeded to find the means of paying his forfeit, which he resolved should be at the expense of the Philistines. He therefore went down to the Philistine town of Askelon, and smote thirty persons whom he found in the neighbourhood, and returning to Timnath, deposited their raiment in redemption of his forfeit. The great odds of one man against thirty relieves this procedure from some of the odium it excites as done against the people of a town which had given him no offence; but it still can only be excused by the supposition that he felt himself acting in his proper vocation as the commissioned avenger of Israel upon the Philistines generally,—a commission he was but too apt to forget, when not acted upon by the external stimulus of a personal grievance.

THE FOXES

Judges 15:1-7

SAMSON did not see his wife on his return to Timnath from Askelon, but went straight home to Zorah, when he had paid his forfeit. This is usually attributed simply to his resentment. But pondering lately, with deep admiration, upon the masterly picture which the chief of the poets has drawn of the self-consciousness of impulsive ferocity in Achilles, which renders him solicitous to prevent the aged Priam from saying or doing anything to provoke his terrible wrath, and cast him loose from his little self-control, it struck us that Samson feared to see his wife for the same reason, lest he should be tempted by her presence, while the sense of his great wrong was still warm within him, to commit some outrage upon her, if he trusted himself into her presence.

The very singular vengeance which he took upon the Philistines, when he found, after a while, that his wife had been, in his absence, given away in marriage, to the very man who had acted as his "friend" at the wedding feast, has engaged much attention. The fields were white for harvest, and Samson determined to set this harvest on fire. As his aggressive movements upon the Philistines seem to have been commissioned even before his birth, we cannot say anything against this part of his conduct. But any other man who did this would deserve to be hanged. BREAD is in our eyes, as in that of the Orientals, so precious a gift of God—the staff of man's life—that it looks like a sacrilegious offence deliberately to waste and destroy it. We must confess that we never read this fact without horror, too forgetful, perhaps, of the commission under which the hero acted, to do to the Philistines all the harm in his power.

He caught, probably by the help of others, no fewer than three hundred foxes—animals which to this day abound in the same region. These, at the time he had chosen, he tied tail to tail, fixing a slow firebrand, likely to be kindled into flame by the air in rapid motion, between each pair of tails. Being then let loose, the alarmed animals naturally sought shelter among the standing corn, and soon set it in a blaze in every direction.

Some difficulties have been started with regard to this account. As to the number of foxes collected, it is admitted that in this there was no insuperable difficulty. But it is asked, Why foxes at all? Could it not have been done better without any foxes? We answer: The tendency of foxes to run to cover when in trouble, rendered them peculiarly suited to this service. Dogs, for instance, would in the like case scour the open roads, and not run to shelter among corn. Still it is asked, Why should the foxes be tied tail to tail? They would surely then attempt to run in opposite directions, and so not run at all. The answer is, that the bushy tail of the fox rendered it well qualified for this service. Any brand tied to the tail of one only, would drag on the ground and be extinguished, whereas between two it would be sustained at tension by their mutual exertions. Besides, a single fox, with a brand at its tail, would, in its alarm, have run to its hole, which was rendered impossible by two being attached together, not only because they would have different retreats, but because the same hole could not be entered by both. As to their pulling in opposite directions, we wish the experiment were tried. In this, and in many other matters, people write large dissertations to prove or disprove points which might be determined in five minutes by a simple experiment. Now it has been our rare chance to see two dogs similarly entangled; and we noticed that, instead of persisting in the attempt to run off in opposite directions, they soon turned round, on finding that endeavour useless, and went away side by side with considerable speed. Now foxes have not the reputation of being duller than dogs; we have no doubt that they would, and that Samson's foxes did, hit upon the same device, in the execution of which the length of their tails would give them much advantage; while the same length of tail, by enabling them to run more apart, would render their operation with the brands the more destructive. Still it must be supposed that, even thus, they would so thwart each other in running, as, by occasional pauses, to give the fullest effect to the intentions of the destroyer. It will appear, therefore, upon the whole, that Samson did not adopt a senseless or ill considered means of effecting the object he had in view.

To estimate the full effect of the destruction thus produced, the reader must recollect that the cultivated lands are not separated by hedgerows into fields as with us, but are laid out in one vast expanse, the different properties in which are distinguished by certain landmarks known to the owners, but not usually obvious to a stranger. Thus, as the time of harvest approaches, the standing corn is often seen to extend as far as the eye can reach, in one vast unbroken spread of waving corn. Hence the flames, once kindled, would spread without check till all the corn of the locality was consumed; and we are further to remember that there were three hundred foxes, forming a hundred and fifty pairs, let off, doubtless, in different parts. The operation seems, however, to have been confined to the neighbourhood of Timnath, the whole harvest of which for the year was destroyed. The flames would cease when they reached the limits of local culture, for at the time of harvest the herbage in Palestine is not in that parched state which would enable it to transmit the fire to distant fields; and we should suppose that the brands with which the foxes were furnished would die out before they could carry them any considerable distance.

The Philistines were at no loss to discover that this was the work of an incendiary. Indeed, the mode in which it was effected may very probably have been rendered obvious to them, by some of the foxes having been found nearly disabled, or dead, with their tails scorched, and the remains of the brand between them. Their inquiries would disclose the occasion of this mischief; and on learning that it had been produced by Samson's indignation at the treatment he had received from his wife, her father, and his own "friend," the popular feeling found vent in setting their house on fire and burning them to death therein. Thus the miserable woman found in the end that death, the mere threat of which by the bridesmen had caused her to sin so deeply against the faith she owed her husband. We see also that the Timnathites themselves were made to suffer by the very agency which they had invoked for the purpose of drawing Samson's secret from his wife.

The hero does not seem to have considered himself bound by this to abstain from further aggressions upon the Philistines; for he probably thought, as we do, that this was not so much designed to be an act of justice to himself, as an outbreak of popular fury, of which he would himself have been the object had he been within reach. He soon after, therefore, found an opportunity of assailing a large body of Philistines. The occasion is not stated; but his assault was perhaps provoked by an attempt to seize his person, which was by this time well known to the Philistines. We are told, that on this occasion "he smote them hip and thigh with a great slaughter." This phrase of *hip and thigh* seems to have been one of those proverbial expressions which exist in every language, and the *precise* signification of which eludes detection when it has passed out of living use. Many such expressions, now obsolete, engage incessant inquiry in our periodicals as to their real purport; and many still exist in popular use, which will be inscrutable should the English ever become a dead language. Lexicons and grammars avail little for their solution. The phrase is literally "leg upon thigh." One learned interpreter[1] makes this to mean, that he cut them in pieces in such sort, that their limbs, their legs and thighs, were scattered and heaped promiscuously together. This is too literal, and wants point. If that were the meaning, "leg upon arm" would have been more significant; and in fights of this sort arms are more frequently lopped off than legs, and would therefore have been more obvious to notice in a popular phrase. Others take it to be a phrase equivalent to "horse and foot," seeing that the riders sit on their hips, and the latter are on their legs. But it is forgotten that men do not appear to have yet in this country ridden on horseback, and even in fight they rode in chariots; and besides, in fight men did not sit in chariots, but stood in them. One further explanation, which we may adduce, is the quaint one of Christopher Ness: "Thereupon he falls pell-mell (as we may say) upon them, and *smote them hip and thigh*,—a proverbial expression, denoting that he laid upon them with his heavy hands

[1] Gesenius, in his *Thesaurus*.

and lusty legs, cuffing and kicking them, so that he not only knocked to the ground all that felt his fatal blows and spurns, but also he lamed them by putting their hips and thighs out of joint, so rendering them incapable of any military employ against Israel, which peradventure was the only design of Samson in this present expedition; and although we read *with a great slaughter*, yet the Hebrew may be read *with a great stroke*, and possibly his blows were mortal unto some: his mauling them with his hands and punching them with his feet (for he had no weapon in his hand) might give passport (as we say) to a few, yet at this time he aimed only to maim and lame them, so as to render them useless for war."[1]

THE JAW-BONE   THE GATE

Judges 15:9-20; 16:3

THE fact that the people of Judah, in whose tribe Samson afterwards found a retreat in a cleft or cavern of some unknown rock then called Etam, actually delivered him up bound at the demand of the Philistines, and the anxiety they felt and expressed lest these proud heathen should take offence at their harbouring their own great champion, shows how completely the nation had lost heart and spirit. Some allowance may be made for the fact that Samson was not in his native tribe; and that, as before remarked, there was much in his character to repress that confidence in his leadership, without which they could not hopefully have marched out under him against the Philistines, as seems to have been the only alternative. Still, it makes one shudder to hear the hero stipulating with the elders of Judah before he consents to be bound, that they shall not themselves "fall upon him," that is, kill him, but deliver him to the Philistines. To this he made them swear; and to their rebukes, that his proceedings had exposed them to the wrath of their masters, he gave answer, "As they did unto me, so have I done unto them." How the Philistines exulted when they saw the redoubted champion brought down from the rock towards their camp, bound with

[1] *History and Mystery*, ii. 148.

strong new cords! With a most savage shout of vengeful triumph they made the valley ring as he approached. The noise of that shout was to him the signal for action. He rent his strong bands from off his wrists with as much ease as if they had been "flax burnt in the fire." A rope or cord of flax or hemp that has been burnt in the fire retains its form when taken out; but it has no strength, it is a mere cinder, which falls to pieces at the slightest touch: such, in point of strength, became the cords with which the hero was bound. But he had no weapon. Casting his eyes rapidly around, he espied upon the ground the "new jaw-bone of an ass," which he forthwith seized, and with it flew upon the Philistines. It is not without reason mentioned that the jaw-bone was "new;" for in that state it was better suited to his purpose, being not only heavier, but less liable to be broken by the fierce blows he dealt. With this strange weapon he ceased not to deal his terrible strokes, until "a thousand" men lay dead upon the field. It is not necessary to suppose that the number was exactly a thousand. A large round number is used to express a large uncertain quantity, or to denote the greatness of the exploit; just as the damsels of Israel ascribed the slaughter of " tens of thousands " to David, when, for all that appears, he had slain not more than one person—but that one was Goliath!

This exploit drew a short triumphal pæan from the victor himself; it being by no means un-usual in the East for a man to celebrate his own exploits.

" With the jaw-bone of an ass, heaps upon heaps ;
With the jaw-bone of an ass have I slain a thousand men !"

There is in the original an effect which is lost in the translation. It is an elegant play upon the words—a paronomasia, founded upon the identity of the Hebrew word for an *ass* and for a *heap*, whereby the Philistines are represented as fall-ing as tamely as asses.[1]

Samson then cast away the jaw-bone; and, justly thinking the exploit worthy of commemo-ration, purposed that the place should be called Ramath-lehi (hill of the jaw-bone), or, for short-ness, Lehi (the jaw-bone). Being then sore athirst from the heat, and from his superhuman

[1] The reader may catch this effect even by the eye, in the first clause,

Bilechi ha-chamor chamor chamorathayim.

exertions, he cried to God for help. It is a strong presumption in favour of the genuineness and active vitality of his faith that he did so. Not many would have had such strong persuasion of the Lord's providential care as would lead them to cry to Him for water to supply their personal wants in the like exigency. This, therefore, is one of the incidents which enabled the author of the Epistle to the Hebrews to put the name of Samson among the heroes of the faith. The in-cident shows what manner of man, essentially, he was, and indicates the kind of spirit in which his great operations were conducted.

The Lord heard him, and suddenly a spring burst out from a cleft in the hill, to which he had just given the name of Lehi, or the " Jaw-bone." It is very unfortunate that our translators have perplexed the passage by *translating* the proper name, thereby making it appear as if the spring arose out of the jaw-bone of the ass, which he had cast away from him. For this there is not the least foundation in the original. Indeed, this is clear from what follows, for it is said of the fountain thus created, that it "is in Lehi unto this day;" but if the spring arose from the "jaw-bone," we ought to retain the word here, and in-stead of saying, that it was " in Lehi unto this day," say that it was " in the jaw-bone unto this day." But the translator saw the absurdity of this, and therefore retained as a proper name the very word which he had *translated* before.

It is immediately after this that we are told " Samson judged Israel in the days of the Philis-tines twenty years ;" and as we see no signs of his being recognized as a judge in Israel before the late events, it may probably have been after them that a sort of authority was conceded to him, on account of his services in holding the Philistines in check, in those south-western parts of the land which suffered most from their op-pression. It was "in the time of the Philistines," for their general domination still subsisted during his lifetime, and was not entirely subverted till the time of David.

From the statement of the duration of his government being interposed at this place, it was probably several years after that his next exploit occurred. In the interval he had, no doubt, per-formed many illustrious deeds, tending to hold the oppressors in check, and to keep alive in their minds their dread and hatred towards him. The next exploit, however, at whatever interval it occurred, shows that Samson was still the same man in his strength and in his weakness. Indeed, his weakness becomes more and more manifest. Hitherto, though unwise and indiscreet, there has been nothing to allege against his personal purity; but the remaining transactions of his life were stained with vice.

It looks like astonishing and needless hardihood in Samson, that he should have trusted himself in Gaza, the strongest and wealthiest of the Philistine cities. However, such a man as he was not likely to weigh nicely the question of safety; and as this southernmost city of the Philistines lay somewhat remote from the main scene of his past exploits and of his usual residence, he might suppose that he could pass in the crowd of that busy commercial town unrecognized. In fact, he did enter and wander about the town unmolested, but perhaps not unsuspected. His life-long growth of hair pointed him out for a Hebrew and a Nazarite, which, with his stalwart figure, might well suggest that this was Samson, but for the utter unlikelihood that Samson would venture there. It is possible that he might have been also seen by some from Timnath and Askelon, who were better acquainted with his person. At all events, it was soon whispered about Gaza that Samson was in the town. The lion was then at last caged, they thought; and as they knew not where to find him, they set a strong force at the gate to destroy him when he should attempt to make his egress in the morning; for the gates being now shut for the night, they had no thought that he would attempt to depart till then.

But where was Samson during all the commotion which the knowledge of his presence could not but occasion? Alas! in the house of a harlot, by whose beauty he had suffered himself to be ensnared as he passed carelessly along. He was not, however, so absorbed in gross enjoyments, as to be altogether unwatchful. At midnight he seems to have found cause to suspect what was going on without. Perhaps, as Quarles supposes,

> "He heard a whisp'ring, and the trampling feet
> Of people passing in the silent street."

He then arose and went forth, making his way straight for the gate. Whether the guards, not expecting him till the morning, were asleep or unwatchful, or whether they were terrified at

his unexpected appearance, is not stated, but he does not at any rate seem to have been opposed. He might now, we should think, have kicked open the gate if he had liked; but instead of that, and in strong and insulting derision at the attempt to restrain him by bolts and bars, he lifted it off with all its ponderous appendages, by sheer force of arm, and bore it away upon his shoulders to a considerable distance on the road towards Hebron. When they afterwards came to take it back, the number of men required to restore it to its place, must have impressed upon them a very lively conviction of the vast strength with which the hero was endued.

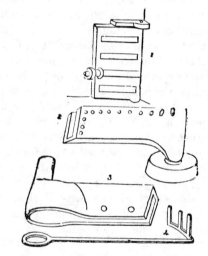

1. Ancient Egyptian door.   2, 3. Bronze pins for doors.
2. Pin and socket.   4. Key.

But a word remains to be said of the gates. Mr. Urquhart, in his recent work,[1] speaking of Moorish buildings, and their analogy to those of ancient and modern Asia, observes: "They have such gates as Samson carried from Gaza, or Lord Ellenborough sent for to Cabul, and are traced on the sepulchre of the kings at Jerusalem. They do not fit into the wall, but lie against it. They are not shaped to the arch; they close, but rectangularly and folding. They cover it as the hurdle did the orifice of the rush mosques I saw along the lake. There is no hinge, but the joints of the doors descend into a socket in the stone, and in like manner the door is secured above in a projecting bracket of wood. In the smallest buildings it is colossal." This kind of door is still used in Egypt; and its antiquity

[1] *Pillars of Hercules.*   London, 1850.   Vol. ii. p. 259.

there is evinced by the monuments. It is also used in Syria, and in the countries of the Tigris and Euphrates. All the doors, large and small, of the several houses in which we have lived in the East, were of this construction. There is no difficulty, but in the *weight* of the larger doors, in lifting them out of their sockets; and the feat of Samson consisted in thus lifting out both the valves at once—for they were barred together—of the heavy town gate, and carrying them away.

When at Gaza a few years ago, I was examining a large heap of ruins, apparently the remains of a tower of the ancient city wall. While intent on exploration, an old Mohammedan came up and entered into conversation. Thinking he might perhaps be able to throw some light on the massive ruins, I asked their name, and what the building had originally been. He replied at once, " This is Samson's Gate ;" and he pointed out the line of the old street, and a portion of the colossal foundations of the wall. He also directed my attention to a *makam*, or " sanctuary," beside the gateway, which he said contained the tomb of Samson. On asking my friend, who was unusually polite and communicative, how far Samson had carried the city gates, he pointed to a hill some two miles distant, and said he had deposited them on its summit.

There was something deeply interesting in thus finding traditions of the life and exploits of the Hebrew warrior still lingering on the old scenes, among a people of another race and another faith, after the lapse of three thousand years.

P.

Coming upon Gaza by the Nukhl route, crossing the hill to the south of that ancient place, all at once a landscape bursts on the sight, never to be forgotten. The four districts of the city, like a group of picturesque Oriental villages, adorned with mosques and minarets, are nestled amidst olive groves and fruit gardens, bordered by gigantic hedges of prickly pear. And away towards the blue waters of the Mediterranean, looming in the western distance, spread rich breadths of park-like scenery, reminding one of England. Above three thousand years have changed somewhat the architecture of the country, and witnessed vast political and religious revolutions ; but the natural features of the regions do not now materially differ from what they were in the days of Samson. The modern city has, in some respects, taken the place of the old one. It is larger and more populous than Jerusalem. It can boast of an extensive soap manufactory, and it is a good market for corn. Various trades are plied in its streets, and its bazaars are well furnished with goods. Corn fields encircle its precincts, and the sound of the millstone, as when Samson was grinding in the prison, may still be heard within its houses. The place carries back our thoughts to ancient times, and the manners and customs of the people illustrate Scripture ; but the old Gaza has disappeared. There is an identity of name, a continuity of history ; but, as we learn from Jerome, scarcely a vestige of more ancient Gaza remained in his day, and the new town was built on a different site from the old one. The sand has long encroached upon the neighbourhood, and wave after wave has rolled up from the Mediterranean, so that, looking from an eminence, it is as if an immense snow-storm had fallen on the fields and drifted over the gardens. Under that sand, hewn stones, as of ancient buildings, have been discovered, and pottery and marble may be seen in the hollows. Walls, fragments of buildings, and remains of foundations still exist, indicating the existence of the former Gaza as distinguished from the present.

The tragical fate of the great Hebrew hero is one of the chief memories lingering around the city, and a curiously travestied version of his death, in the form of a Mohammedan legend, is still given to travellers. Two prostrate columns, one fractured in the middle, are pointed out, in a pathway leading up to the Governor's house. " Once on a time," said the people to our dragoman, as we passed by the columns, " there was a good Mussulman, very strong, who fought with the infidels (Christians), and at last pulled a large temple down in which they were assembled, and they were crushed beneath the ruins." The hill on the south-east, looking towards Hebron, cannot fail to be recognized as that up which the stalwart champion carried the city gates ; and on one of the mornings of our stay outside the walls, we were roused at an early hour by a procession of Mohammedans, with flags and music, on their way to the hill, there to pray for the blessing of rain. The corn fields now, all along the cultivated track of the Shephelah, are just such fields as Samson entered when he tied the foxes or jackals tail to tail, and grimly watched his own " facetious outrage," as the creatures ran amongst the standing grain, and kindled it into a blaze, while the firebrands frighted them into mad haste. Vineyards there, like those of Timnath and Sorek, still bear fruit, and the names of villages are identified with meanings which recall " the lions" and " the bees," or hornets, as well as " the foxes," or jackals, of the mighty man.

S.

RETROSPECT

IN the rapid survey we have thus far taken of certain points in the remarkable career of Samson, we have not been able to refer to the topics of profitable reflection which it suggests. This day they may very properly engage our attention.

It may occur to us, that in Scripture it is almost always to barren women that angels and prophets are sent to announce the promise of a distinguished son. Why is this ? There are several reasons. First, that the child may be more manifestly the gift of God. All children are the gift of God—although, unhappily, we do not always so receive them. But it is important to mark this fact, by special arrangements, which shall make it conspicuously obvious in the case of those to whom a peculiarly high function or vocation is assigned. God also desires His highest gifts to be appreciated; and therefore, in these cases, the gift of a son is bestowed on those who, from long privation and disappointment, know how to prize it most. Besides, God is very pitiful —He likes to visit with some surpassing joy the afflicted soul; and to a Hebrew woman there was no affliction comparable to that of being sonless. It might be safely predicated of any woman of Israel, if she had already many sons, that the gift of another would still be great joy to her: how much more, then, to her who had none! But again, how is it—owing to what vice in our social system, or in ourselves, does it happen,— that there are among us tens of thousands, to whom the promise of children would be a sorrow and a trouble, rather than a comfort and a joy? There are tens of thousands among us, who would be by no means thankful for such an intimation as that which the angel of God brought to Manoah and his wife. How is this? Alas for our faith! which will not trust God to pay us well for the board and lodging of all the little ones He has committed to our charge to bring up for Him. Good old Quarles, who was himself the father of eighteen children, enters feelingly into this matter:

> "Shall we repine,
> Great God, to foster any babe of thine?
> But 'tis the charge we fear; our stock's but small:
> If Heaven, with children, send us wherewithal
> To stop their craving stomachs, *then* we care not.
> Great God!
> How hast Thou crackt thy credit, that we dare not
> Trust Thee for bread? How is't we dare not venture
> To keep thy babes, unless Thou please to enter
> In bond for payment? Art Thou grown so poor,
> To leave thy famished infants at our door,
> And not allow them food? Canst Thou supply
> Thy empty ravens, and let thy children die?"

The idea of Manoah and others, that they should perish because they had "seen the face of God," or of an angel of God—this horror and dread of soul at the presence of a heavenly nature—we may take as a very affecting illustration of the Fall, showing that we are the true sons of that father who, when he had sinned, no longer dared to look upon God, but hid himself among the trees, because "he was afraid" when he heard the "voice of the Lord God walking in the garden:"

> "O whither shall poor mortals flee
> For comfort? If they see thy face, they die;
> And if thy life-restoring count'nance give
> Thy presence from us, then we cannot live.
> On what foundation shall our hopes rely,
> See we thy face, or see it not, we die."—*Quarles.*

When Cain raised the lamentable cry, "From thy face I shall be hid,"[1] he had a strong, if not an effectual, sense of this penalty of sin. Well is it for us if we are of those who are even now permitted to behold "the glory of God in the face of Jesus Christ;"[2] and are privileged to realize the assured conviction, that although we can see but as through a glass darkly now, the time is near when we shall see face to face, and know also even as we are known. (1 Cor. xiii. 12.)

Most commentators are apt to think that Samson somewhat infringed the strictness of his Nazarite vow of ceremonial purity, by taking the honey found in "the foul and putrid carcase of a dead beast," but we have shown that the remains of the lion were perfectly clean and wholesome; and it is forgotten that it was not the dead body of a beast, but the corpse of a human being, that imparted defilement under the law of Moses. Had it been otherwise, a man could not have eaten his dinner without defilement. Nevertheless the pious inferences founded on this misconception are correct and beautiful. So Bishop Hall: "Good may not be refused, because the means are accidentally evil. Honey is honey still, though in a dead lion. Those are less wise and more scrupulous than Samson, who abhor the graces of God because they find them in an ill vessel. It is a weak neglect not to take the honey, because we hate the lion. *God's children have a right to their Father's blessings, wheresoever they find them.*"

Most of the old writers are very sharp upon Samson and his Timnite wife—upon her for beguiling him, and upon him for yielding to her entreaties. Christopher Ness quaintly remarks that, since his first experiment with Adam and Eve, "Satan hath broken many a man's head with his own rib." Bishop Hall sorrowfully observes, that "Adam the perfectest man, Samson the strongest man, Solomon the wisest man, were

[1] Genesis 4:14.   [2] 2 Corinthians 4:6.

betrayed with the flattery of their helpers. As there is no comfort comparable to a faithful yoke-fellow, so woe be to him that is matched with a Philistine."

Quarles leads us to a still more practical conclusion. After contemplating the perils of a man's life between open foes and bosom entice-ments, he bursts out into the fine prayer:

> " Lord, clarifie mine eyes, that I may know
> Things that are good, from what is good in show;
> And give me wisdom, that my heart may learn
> The difference of thy favours, and discern
> What's truly good, from what is good in part;
> *With Martha's trouble, give me Mary's heart.*"

Without entering into the frequent inquiry of old writers, in how far Samson may in some things have been a type of Christ, it is pleasant when in these histories we find any circumstance or any expression which wings the thoughts irre-sistibly to Him. There is a very striking inci-dent of this kind in the surrender of Samson bound to the Philistines by the men of Judah. Who is there that is not by this reminded of Jesus delivered up bound to the Romans, that He may die? But the difference of the result in the two cases is very marked, and magnifies the glory of our Divine Saviour. Samson submits to be bound by his own countrymen, knowing that he should, by the power given to him, victoriously free himself; Jesus that He might die, yielding Himself up a sacrifice for sin.

Both were victorious—Jesus by dying, Samson by inflicting death. It was not that the Lord's hand was so shortened, that He who had saved others could not save Himself. He had far mightier power for His own deliverance than Samson had. One word, one wish, would have brought twelve legions of angels from the Father to His rescue; but how then had the world been saved? That thought made Him more than conqueror over all the malice of His enemies, over all the agonies of the cross, over all the terrors of the grave.

> " O Thou that art
> The Samson of our souls! how can the heart
> Of man give thanks enough, that does not know
> How much his death-redeemed soul doth owe
> To thy dear merits!"—*Quarles.*

Pursuing this line of thought and comparison, Bishop Hall, with reference to Samson's unaided victory, observes: " It is no marvel if he were thus admirably strong and victorious, whose bodily strength God meant to make a type of the spiritual power of Christ. And, behold, as the three thousand of Judah stood still gazing, with their weapons in their hands, while Samson alone subdued the Philistines; so did men and angels stand looking upon the glorious achieve-ments of the Son of God, who might justly say, 'I have trod the wine-press alone.'"

THE BEGUILEMENT

Judges 16:4-18

As Samson judged Israel twenty years, and as these twenty years could not well have com-menced before that great action, in which he singly smote the Philistines in the presence of the magnates of Judah, by whom he had been delivered up, the remaining scenes of his life belong to the close of that period, when one should suppose he could not well be under, and was probably somewhat above, forty years of age. He is therefore now no longer young; but he is the same man—as strong as ever, and as weak as ever. "The princes of the Philistines knew already where Samson's weak-ness lay, though not his strength."[1] His strength was so manifestly superhuman, that it was clear to them, that any ordinary means taken to destroy him must prove abortive. This admis-sion on their part, incidentally indicated, is very important, and ought alone to satisfy those who incline to think that Samson was merely a very strong man. It shows that he was much more than this—that he was, for special purposes, endowed with powers far above any that natur-ally belong to the strongest of the sons of men.

With the convictions which they entertained, the object of the Philistines was to discover wherein lay his great strength—whether it con-sisted in the possession of any charm or amulet, the loss of which would divest him of his super-natural powers, and leave him nothing more than a strong man. We do not read of any king among the Philistines till the time of David, and then only at Gath. Yet in the days of Abraham they had a king. At this time, each of the five great cities, Ashdod, Gaza, Askelon, Gath, and

[1] Bishop Hall, *Contemplations*, x. 5.

Ekron, seems to have formed, with its dependencies, a separate state, presided over by its own Seren,[1] but united to each other, by their common origin and interests, for general purposes. All these *Seranim*[2] now made common cause against Samson. It was useless to bring armies into the field against an individual, and such an individual; but they were determined to support each other in the attempt to crush him, and to share among them whatever expense and trouble the attempt might involve. So they lay watchful for any advantage which the proceedings of the Hebrew champion might offer. The careless hero was not long in affording them all the advantage they could have desired. They heard that he had become devoted to a woman named Delilah, inhabiting the vale of Sorek. The history does not say that she was a harlot, like the woman of Gaza; but neither is she called his wife; and had she been such, she would have been taken to his own house, and we should not find him visiting at hers. Nothing could have occurred more opportunely for the Philistine Seranim. They repaired to her, or sent to her in one of the intervals of Samson's visits, and offered her a large bribe to entice from him the secret of his strength. The sum was eleven hundred pieces of silver from each of the five. The pieces were probably shekels, in which case the whole sum amounted to more than six hundred pounds of our money, a sum not inconsiderable even now, and a very large one for that age and country.

In reading the record of this enticement, we should bear in mind that the facts are related with extreme brevity. In the conversations between Samson and the woman, results only are stated: the final purport only is given, without any notice of the little artifices of conversation and dalliance, the watching for favourable moments and natural turns of thought and incident, which disguised the wickedness of the design, and gave a seeming indirectness to the woman's attempts to get possession of his secret. The various attempts on her part to betray the confidence she supposed Samson had reposed in her, are so related, also, as to appear to have followed in rapid succession. But the form of scriptural narrative does not require us to sup-

pose this was necessarily the case; and that it was so, is against the probable truth of circumstances and natural analogies. It is far more likely that these attempts were made at different visits of Samson to the vale of Sorek, when a sufficient interval had passed to blunt the keenness of any suspicions that may have been awakened in his mind. Simple-minded and confiding as Samson was, he was not altogether so silly as an unintelligent mode of reading the narrative may make him appear.

Samson very clearly indicated his consciousness of what became him, by the siege he stood before his great trust was surrendered. He did this after a manner of his own, however; and his conduct is less becoming than formerly with his wife at Timnath. Her he told plainly that he could not disclose his secret, although that was one of small importance in comparison. But to Delilah he seems incapable of giving a distinct refusal. He shrinks from the importunity to which it would expose him; and therefore he tries to amuse her by one invention after another, which, but for the immediate test to which she subjected them—that is, if she had been, as he supposed, sincere—might have passed off with her for the real secret.

First, he told her that if he were bound with seven green withes which had never been dried, then he should become weak as another man, and unable to rend them asunder. This is interesting, as showing that ropes of crude vegetable fibre were in use among the Hebrews of that age, as they are now in many countries, composed of such things as vine-tendrils, the tough fibres of trees, pliable twisted rods, osiers, hazels, and the like. Such ropes are strong enough; although less compact, and of greater bulk in proportion to their strength, than those of spun flax or hemp. The strength of such ropes may be estimated from the fact, that the legs of wild elephants and buffaloes are usually bound with them, when newly caught, in India; and it is rarely indeed that they give way to the force of the most powerful animals that the whole creation can supply. Such ropes are strongest, and least liable to break, when green, that is, when newly made; but we suppose that it was not on this account that Samson was led to name them, but because of some occult relation to his own strength which they might be supposed to bear. Not doubting that she should

---

[1] A *peculiar* title, rendered by "lord" and "prince" in the authorized version, and probably denoting a chief or magistrate.

[2] The title only occurs thus in the plural.

now win her reward, the faithless woman then bound him, probably while he slept, with the green ropes, which the Philistines very gladly provided. She then roused him with the words, "The Philistines be upon thee, Samson." This was no vain alarm. They were there, probably in an adjoining room, and were to rush in on a preconcerted signal, if it should be found that he was properly secured. But Samson sprang up, and rent the green ropes from his arms like burnt tow. The Philistine liers in wait, finding this to be the case, probably did not show themselves; and the woman was thus enabled to pass the matter off as a fond attempt to test his truthfulness. This supposition, that the Philistines did not show themselves, and that Samson was not aware of their presence, relieves the transactions from much of their apparent difficulty, and explains the fact that Samson could still go on dallying with the danger. The authorized translation unreasonably places the liers in wait in the *same chamber;* but this needlessly perplexes the subject, and has no warrant in the original, which signifies that "the liers in wait sat for her in an inner chamber."

The second time, when he seemed to yield to her importunites, he told her that new twisted or spun ropes would do, showing that such ropes were known, although those of crude vegetable material had not yet gone out of use. Flax, we know, was before this time an article of culture in both Egypt and Palestine; and with this, such ropes seem to have been made. Hemp was probably also cultivated, although the fact is not so distinctly mentioned in the sacred books. The result in this instance was precisely the same as before.

In the next invention by which Samson tried to amuse the importunity of Delilah, he approached dangerously near to his great secret. His infatuation was like that of the moth, approaching gradually nearer and nearer to the flame which destroys it at last. This device was suggested by the presence of the small loom in which the women of those days wove their household stuffs, —a kind of industry from which it would seem that females even of Delilah's stamp did not hold themselves exempt. These looms, as shown in Egyptian sculptures, and as still subsisting in the East, are very simple, and comparatively light, and must by no means be confounded with the ponderous apparatus of our own hand-loom weavers. Samson told her, that if the long locks of his hair were woven in with the web, he would become as powerless as any other man. This was done; and to make the matter more certain, the guileful woman actually fastened the web, with the hair thus woven in it, with a strong pin or nail to the wall or to the floor. But this availed not; for when the alarm was given, although he could not disengage his hair from the web, he rose and went forth, dragging the weaving frame, the web and the pin—the whole apparatus—after him by his hair.

At length, worn out by the woman's importunities, who protested that his repeated deceptions, and his obstinacy in refusing to gratify her curiosity with the knowledge of a secret, of little consequence to her but for the love she bore to him, contradicted his professions of regard for her; and, above all, seeing there was nothing in the past to give *him* that knowledge of her treachery which *we* possess, he yielded: "he told her all that was in his heart." His hair, he informed her, was the sign and seal of his consecrated condition from birth, by which alone he held all his superhuman strength. To take off his hair would be to cut him off from that consecrated state, and to divest him of the powers he held in virtue of it. He would then "be like any other man;" not necessarily a weak man, but not stronger than any man of his thews and sinews might be expected to be. The woman saw, from the earnestness of his manner, that this time he had not deceived her. One might think she would have been moved from her fell purpose by this strong proof of his regard for her; but no: the use she made of it was to revive the faith, which had ere this been shaken, of the Philistine Seranim, as to the success of their scheme, by causing such strong assurance of success to be conveyed to them, that they hurried down with the money for which she had sold Samson into their hand. The terms of the message would almost imply that they had given up the enterprise, at least in this form, and had determined to be fooled no more as they had been: "Come up *this once,* for he hath showed me all his heart."

THE SECRET

Judges 16:19-21

THE last scene in the history of Samson is a drama in itself, and, as such, has been taken by Milton as the basis of his "Samson Agonistes," —perhaps the grandest dramatic poem, after the ancient model, that our language contains. It is not, however, in its historical developments that we have to regard it. For this, space would fail us. We have to seek in it those indications of character and manners, to the explanation of which our task is limited.

The woman of the valley of Sorek having possessed herself of Samson's secret, and all her arrangements for turning it to account having been perfected, she delayed not the consummation of her crime. In the heat of the day, probably, when men in the East take a short repose, she made the hero sleep with his head upon her lap. This is still not unusual in the East in the case of a full-grown son or a husband. The women sit cross-legged upon the carpet or mat; and the man, having laid himself down, pillows his head upon her lap, and she gently taps, strokes, sings, and soothes him to sleep. Samson being safe asleep, a man was introduced, who soon deprived him of his invincible locks. This man was probably a barber. The business of eastern barbers lies in shaving the head rather than the beard; and they do it so skillfully and gently, that, so far from a sleeping man being awakened, a waking man is lulled to sleep under the operation. Considering the great mass of hair of which Samson had to be deprived, he would probably have been roused by inexperienced hands, which may be the reason why Delilah herself did not operate upon the recumbent Nazarite, as painters falsely represent that she did. In that operation his strength passed from him. No mighty heaving of the strong man's frame, no convulsive sob, disclosed the fact. He still slept on, unconscious that he had indeed "become as other men," which was *to him* a degradation and a scorn. He had to be roused as usual; and this time it was not to him a false alarm, as it had on previous occasions seemed. He arose. The altered appearance he presented —his vast head, once clouded with those terrible locks, now shorn to the skin—must have been very striking. But he was not conscious of it; and none else had time to consider it then. The Philistines *were* upon him. The signal was given, and they now appeared indeed; and Samson, struck with horror and remorse at finding he had indeed "become weak as other men," was soon overpowered by them.

> "Even as a dove, whose wings are clipt for flying,
> Flutters her idle stumps, and still relying
> Upon her wonted refuge, strives in vain
> To quit her life from danger, and attain
> The freedom of her air-dividing plumes ;
> She struggles often, and she oft presumes
> To take the sanctuary of the open fields ;
> But, finding that her hopes are vain, she yields ;
> Even so poor Samson," etc.—*Quarles.*

Poor indeed! Behold him! That is he, trudging wearily along upon the way to Gaza, whose gates he not long since bore away triumphantly upon his shoulders. His once strong arms are bound with cords, which yesterday one wrench of his wrists would have broken like a thread; and the escort, now sufficient, would yesterday have fled at the mere lifting of his hand. His glorious locks are left behind, trodden in dust; and his head, once shrouded by them from the light, is now exposed and bare to the sun's pitiless rays. See his firm and vigorous tramp exchanged for a stumbling, feeble, and uncertain trail. Alas, he is blind—newly blind! and experience has not yet taught him how to walk without the guidance of his sight. The first thing the Philistines did, when they had secured him, was to disable him past hope, by extinguishing the light of those eyes whose fierce glare had so often struck terror into their souls. In this they did not even wait till the destination should be reached, but blinded him on the spot, to preclude all hope of rescue or escape. Perhaps but for the possession of this resource for securing him and rendering him helpless, they would have put him to death; but they thus were enabled to keep him alive, in order to magnify their triumph. This is the first instance of blinding which occurs in Scripture; and it is an apt illustration of the principle on which this doom has been inflicted—less as a judicial punishment and formal infliction, than as a mode of incapacitating a dangerous person from further power or harm, without taking his life. In this point of view we had occasion but a few days ago to remark upon it.[1] Besides, the instances were very few in which it was desired

[1] See Vol. 1, pp. 542-544.

to detain persons in permanent custody; and there being consequently no regular prisons, a private infliction of this nature was resorted to, not only to lessen the chances of escape, but to render the man harmless if escape should be effected. In this guise the prisoner was led to Gaza—the strong Samson, helpless, bowed down, and blind. Those who know the sort of treatment a great captive receives in the East, and the savage insults to which he is exposed, may apprehend the sort of reception which the fallen hero found at Gaza, and the commotion his arrival excited.

On his arrival, the cords which had bound him on the journey were exchanged for "fetters of brass." In modern times, the possession of strong prisons enables us to dispense with chains and fetters; but in the absence of regular jails, the incarcerated are, for the most part, chained or fettered for greater security. The emphasis here lies in Samson's being put in bands of *metal*, instead of thongs and cords, like other prisoners. That his fetters were of *brass*, or rather copper, is not remarkable; for that metal was more common than iron, and was used for numerous purposes to which iron is now applied. Not only chains and fetters, but instruments of labour, culinary vessels, knives, axes, and almost every kind of utensil for which metal is desired, were made of this metal. The Psalmist speaks of "binding kings with chains, and nobles with fetters of brass;"[1] and in a much later age, the last king of David's royal line was treated much like Samson: "his eyes were put out, and he was laden with fetters of brass."[2] In the monuments of Egypt and Nineveh, prisoners are represented as bound with fetters and manacles, obviously of metal. Layard says that the latter were of *iron*.

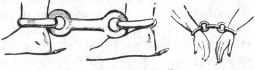

FETTERS AND MANACLES FROM NINEVEH

We doubt this; and as the figures are sculptures, not coloured paintings, there is no evidence to prove that they were not of brass. Samson was destined not merely to be detained as a captive, but to be treated with ignominy as a slave; and yet such a slave as was of too great importance, if only as a monument, to be allowed to pass into

[1] Psalms 199:8. [2] 2 Kings 25:7.

private hands. He was hence to be regarded as a public slave—the worst of all conditions into which a man can be brought. That is the condition not only of a slave, but of a slave in a state of punishment. It was the custom anciently, and it is so still, in countries where slavery exists, for slaves who had committed any serious fault to be shut up in chains. An ancient writer (Apuleius) has given a striking picture of these unhappy men in their sad abode. They were, he says, quite livid with bruises; and all their skin showed deep traces of the cuts of the lashes which had been inflicted on them. Many were only partly covered with some scanty piece of sordid raiment; others were wholly naked, save as to the parts which all men seek to cover; and all were so ill clad that their scarred flesh was everywhere visible; while their faces showed marks impressed in the flesh, not only as a punishment for their offences, but as a means of recognition. As to the "prison-house," this is the first time we have read of a prison since Joseph's imprisonment in Egypt. Indeed, it is surprising to note how many things come under observation among the Philistines which we had already occasion to observe in that country, did we not know that the Scripture itself deduces their origin from Egypt—at least their proximate origin as regards Palestine. (Gen. x. 13, 14.) The prison-house was, in all probability, such as existed there, and one in which the inadequacy of the building was made good by the greater stringency of personal restraint.

THE AVENGEMENT

Judges 16:21-31

THE Orientals have too few prisoners—imprisonment not being a *judicial* punishment—to make it worth their while to think of turning their labour to account. Yet, in the case of those whom they wished deeply to humble or grievously to punish, the inconsistency of allowing them to remain in idleness could not fail to be seen. Therefore some species of labour was occasionally devised. In the whole of Scripture, however, Samson's is the only case which occurs of imprisonment with hard labour; and this fact shows the aggravated and unusual humiliation to which he was subjected by the hatred of the Philistines. He was set to "grind in the prison-house." This, while it may show that consider-able natural strength—the strength of a strong man—remained to him, evinces less the desire of the Philistines to turn his strength to account, than to inflict upon him indignity and humili-ation. In itself, grinding was very suitable for prison labour, being performed by a hand-mill, the upper stone of which, called "the rider" by the Hebrews, was made to revolve upon the other by strength of hand. Being usually per-formed by females, the Philistines, studious of insult, regarded it as well suited to disgrace a man, and especially such a man as Samson had been; while, by providing stones of sufficient size and weight, the work might be made labor-ious even for him. The humiliating character of

HAND-MILL

this labour is shown by the allusions to it in Scripture, as a disgrace which the Chaldeans would inflict upon such of their Hebrew captives as they meant to chastise and degrade.[1] The Romans condemned to work in the public mills of the city those who were convicted of crimes not worthy of death. The mill-stones in common use in the East are seldom more than a few inches above two feet in diameter, though we have sometimes seen them larger. They are cir-

[1] Isaiah 47:2; Lamentations 5:13.

cular and flat. The upper stone is made to turn upon the other by means of a handle of wood, which is inserted into it, and by means of which two women, seated opposite to each other, are able to keep it in rotatory motion without exces-sive labour. The grain falls upon the surface of the lower stone by means of a trough or hollow in the middle of the upper one, the circular movement of which spreads it over the lower one, where it is crushed and reduced to meal. This meal, escaping at the edges of the mill, is received upon a board or cloth, and is then collected for use. It is a general prejudice in the East, whether well or ill founded, that the meal ground by the hand-mill has a much better flavour than that ground by mills worked either by wind or water.

Among a pastoral people, the preparation of milk answers in some degree to the grinding of corn among an agricultural people. We have therefore been much struck by the description which Herodotus gives of blinded slaves being among the Scythians employed in this labour. He says: "The Scythians drink milk; and all the slaves who attend to the business of milking are deprived of sight. Two slaves are employed together; for while one milks the mare, the other, by tubes formed of bone, causes an inflation of the udder. This process, as they think, increases the quantity of milk. When they have obtained the milk, they pour it into deep hollow bowls. The blind slaves are then stationed around these bowls, and give a whirling motion to the milk. That which swims on the surface they re-move, deeming it the choicest part, while that which subsides is accounted of less value. It is for performing this opera-tion that the Scythians put out the eyes of all the prisoners they take in war."[1] By this he probably means, that they would not be able to execute this whirling work unless blinded, which is likely. Although other nations may not have put out the eyes of captives to enable them the better to perform those rotatory labours, it may have seemed one of the few kinds of labour which the blind were qualified to perform even better than those who could see. There is noth-

[1] Herodotus, iv. 2.

ing in grinding corn with the hand-mill that requires attention which a man deprived of sight cannot give; while he has this advantage, that his head is not fatigued by the rotatory action which he gives to the upper stone. We ourselves employ blind horses, or blindfold those that can see, when we employ them in rotatory labour.

In his captivity the hair of Samson "began to grow again," as might be expected; and it is implied that his strength grew with it, and with it his remorse for the sin and weakness—for the weakness of the strong is sin—which had brought all this calamity upon him. The loss of his hair had deprived him of strength, only because it took him out of that condition of Nazariteship with which his strength was inseparably connected; so that, from the return of his strength with the growth of his hair, we can only understand that he repented, and renewed voluntarily the vows of devotement which had been imposed upon him before his birth, and which he had so miserably broken. This important fact the Philistines probably did not know, nor would it consist with his object to disclose it to them. They knew that he was still a strong man; but they knew not that his more than human strength was returning to him.

A day at length came—delayed, perhaps, on account of the needful preparation for so grand an occasion, or because it was reserved so that it might fall at the time of some periodical festival; but that it was delayed, appears from the growth of Samson's hair—when the Philistines held a high feast and sacrifice to Dagon their god, in the belief that he had delivered Samson, their enemy, into their hand. It is likely that there was a great resort of Philistines from all parts on this great occasion; and the importance that was generally attached to the fact that they held him so completely in their power, is evinced by the exultation and thankfulness they manifested when they beheld him. "They praised their god, for they said, Our god hath delivered into our hands our enemy, and the destroyer of our country, who slew many of us." These cries must have struck upon Samson's heart. He now saw, with deep intensity of shame and sorrow, how the name of the Lord had been dishonoured through his misconduct, seeing that they ascribed to their own god that triumph over the covenanted servant of Jehovah, which they owed only to his own folly and sin. He knew, that in the

view of the Philistines the triumph over him was equivalent to a triumph of their god over the God whose servant he professed himself to be, whose protection he claimed, and whose people he in some sort represented. Yet out of this despair he gathered hope. He was aware that Jehovah was a jealous God, and that He knew well how to vindicate the honour of His own great name. The question was now put upon a different ground. It was no longer a matter between Samson and the Philistines, but between Jehovah and Dagon; and he might venture to think that, fallen as he was, he might yet hope for the divine assistance in any effort which occasion might present, to strike one great blow in discharge of his mission as THE DESTROYER, seeing that thereby he would vindicate the superiority of the Lord over the miserable idol which the Philistines worshipped as their god. The opportunity he desired was offered, and in such a shape as to confirm his purpose, by his being compelled to be present at their odious triumph, and by being himself the object of their keen taunts and bitter scorn.

After the sacrifice, there was, as usual, much feasting, amid the exhilaration produced by which, there was a proposal to "call for Samson, that he may make us sport." He was accordingly brought from the house used as a prison, and set in the enclosed area of the building, the roofs and galleries of which were thronged with men and women, seemingly those of the highest quality, for "all the lords of the Philistines were there." What "sport" he was expected to make is not clear; but he did make it. Some think that he was merely there that he might be seen by this great assembly, and become the object of their mockeries and insults; but others conceive that he was required to exhibit some feats of strength for their amusement—of strength still great, though no longer supposed by them to be formidable. We do not see any reason why both opinions may not be right; but that the last was at all events included, we incline to think, from the consideration that in the East athletic sports and feats of strength in the area of the palace form a conspicuous part of the entertainments at high festivals; and because it was evidently under the excuse of weariness, after he had "made them sport," that he desired to lean against the pillars, which supported the superstructure of the building upon that side of the area to which he had been withdrawn for rest. Having thus secured possession of the two middle pillars on which chiefly the house stood, Samson felt that the hour of great and terrible "vengeance for his two eyes" was come. Holding them with his hands, he breathed a prayer to the Lord, to help him but this once; and then with the cry, "Let me die with the Philistines," he bowed himself with all his might, the pillars gave way, and the house fell upon him and upon all the people —three thousand in number—that were there. Thus, as the sacred historian remarks, "the dead which he slew at his death, were more than they which he slew in his life."

SAMSON'S DEATH

Some difficulty has been felt in understanding how the whole building, and a large building too, could be supposed to rest upon two pillars. But this is not what is affirmed; for that Samson took hold of the *two middle pillars*, implies that there were other pillars which contributed to the support of the building; though, if the two middle ones, on which the others depended, or with which they were connected, gave way, the connection and dependence of the whole arrangement would be destroyed, and the other pillars would be unable of themselves to support the superstructure. As most of the explanations which have been offered—including, we must confess, some that we ourselves have given— overlook the fact that there were more pillars than the two—and the supposition that there were but two creates the difficulty—we might pause here, without providing for the stricter exigency. But it is not difficult to provide even

for that. In very many eastern buildings, the whole centre of the principal side of the enclosed area (towards which all parts of the general building front) is made to rest upon one or two pillars, so that their removal would most certainly involve the downfall of that part; and from the connection of the parts, this would involve the overthrow of the whole range of building on that side at least. And if this be the obvious result in ordinary cases, much more certain would it be here, when the roof, and no doubt the galleries, if any, looking towards the court, were crowded with people, whose weight must have created so great a strain and pressure, that the withdrawal of any single prop must bring the whole to the ground in an instant. If the reader examine the figures of oriental buildings with a view to an explanation, he may not be able to find any one which meets in all respects his ideas of what sort of building that overthrown by Samson must have been; but he will find many—not in other respects answering to his idea—which will abundantly satisfy him on the only point in question, how a building might be pulled down by the support of one or two pillars being withdrawn. For the rest, under the change of religion, and in the absence of such festivities as were connected with paganism, such buildings —except mosques and royal palaces—as would accommodate three thousand persons on their roofs and galleries are not found in the East. Some think that this was a temple; but although it is probable that the Philistines had temples, as we meet with them not very long after, when the ark of God was taken, we doubt if festivals like these were celebrated in the temple courts, or if such multitudes assembled on their roofs; and we feel quite sure, that if Dagon and his temple had been included in the overthrow, a circumstance of so much importance would not have been passed unrecorded. It may have been a sort of palace, but scarcely a royal one, as the Philistines had no king, and the chief magistrate of the small separate state of Gaza was not likely to reside in any very extensive or magnificent palace. It is probable that it was a large building, in which public business was transacted, assemblies held, and feats and games celebrated, constructed probably on the general plan of dwelling-houses, but with special accommodation for spectators on the galleries and roofs. Even in the large structures framed for some of these purposes by the Romans, illustrations of the fact before us might be found. Pliny speaks of two theatres built at Rome by Caius Curio, which were large enough to contain the whole Roman people, but were so constructed as to depend each upon one hinge or pivot.[1] And in Tacitus we read of a disaster caused by the fall of an amphitheatre, very similar to this in which Samson was concerned.[2]

The border land between the mountains of Israel and the broad plain of Philistia was the chief scene of Samson's exploits. During my residence in the East I explored it with great care, and I was never more impressed with the peculiar adaptation of the physical features of the country to the romantic details of the sacred story. The mountains descend to the plain in a series of steep rocky declivities, divided by narrow winding ravines. Along the banks we see terraces like steps of stairs, and braes bristling with rocks, whose jagged tops shoot up over thickets of thorny shrubs and dwarf oaks; while here and there a naked cliff of gray limestone raises up its bold front over the green corn field that rests peacefully at its base. Never was there a fitter scene for border raids. Samson knew every inch of the ground from childhood; for, on the very summit of a ridge which shoots far out into the plain, stood, and still stands, his native village, Zorah.

Stanley has traced with a master's hand the connection between the Bible narrative and the features of the country: "There is no portion of the sacred story more stamped with a peculiar local colour. Unlike the heroes of Grecian, Celtic, or Teutonic romance, whose deeds are scattered over the whole country or the whole continent where they lived, the deeds of Samson are confined to that little corner of Palestine in which was pent up the fragment of the tribe to which he belonged. He is the one champion of Dan. To him, if to any one, must be the reference in the blessing of Jacob, 'Dan shall judge his people as one of the tribes of Israel.' In his biting wit and cunning ambuscades, which baffled the horses and chariots of Philistia, must probably be seen 'the serpent by the way, the adder in the path, that biteth the horse's heels, so that his rider shall fall backwards.'

"Amongst his fathers' tombs, and amidst the recollections of his fathers' exploits, 'the Spirit of Jehovah began to move him,'—to strike, as the expression implies, on his rough nature as a drum or a cymbal, till it resounded like a gong through his native hills.

"Then began what were literally his 'descents' of love and war upon the plain of Philistia from Zorah on the hills above. The vines on the slopes of these hills, the vineyards of Timnath and of Sorek, were famous throughout Palestine. It was probably amongst these, as the maidens whom the Benjamites surprised among the vineyards of Shiloh, that he met both his earliest and his latest love. The names of the surrounding villages bear traces of the wild animals whom he encountered, and used as instruments of his great exploits: Sebaoth ('the lionesses'), Shaalbim ('the jackals or foxes'), Zorah ('the hornets'). The

corn fields of Philistia, then as now interspersed with olive groves, then also with vineyards, lay stretched in one unbroken expanse before him, to invite his facetious outrage. Once he wandered beyond the territory of his own tribe and that of his enemies, but it was only into the neighbouring hills of Judah. In some deep cleft, such as doubtless could easily be found in the limestone hills around the Vale of Etam, he took refuge. The Philistines then, as afterwards in David's time, had planted a garrison in the neighbourhood. The lion of Judah was cowed by their presence. 'Knowest thou not the Philistines are rulers over us?' Out of the cleft he emerges, and sweeps them away with the rude weapon that first comes to hand. The spring and the rock which witnessed the deed, though now lost, were long pointed out as memorials of the history. The scene of his death is the great temple of the fish god at Gaza, in the extremity of the Philistine district. But his grave was in the same spot which had nourished his first youthful hopes, . . . 'between Zorah and Eshtaol, in the burial-place of Manoah his father.'"[1]

P.

THE LEVITE

Judges 17-18

THE last five chapters of the book of Judges form a sort of appendix, relating incidents which, in their chronological place, would stand nearer to the commencement than the close of the book. The incidents are of a very different complexion; but they are very important, from the distinct impression they enable us to realize of the loose condition of society during the anarchical period which intervened between the death of "the elders who outlived Joshua" and the government of Othniel. To that period it is generally conceived that these events should both be referred; and we acquiesce in the conclusion, without feeling it necessary here to state the grounds on which it seems to us probable. We turn rather to note the information which may be gleaned from these transactions.

There was an old woman dwelling with her married or widowed son,[2] Micah, in Mount Ephraim, who one day missed a treasure of eleven hundred pieces of silver, probably the savings of her life, which she had carefully laid up. Her imprecations upon the thief were so

---

[1] *Hist. Nat.*, xxvi. 15.   [2] *Annals*, vi. 62.

[1] *Lectures on Jewish Church*, i. 368.

[2] He had grown-up sons, and must therefore have been the one or the other. That the woman was advanced in years, is proved by her grandsons being of adult age.

awful, that her son, who had really taken the money, fearing lest some of that dreadful thing, a mother's curse, might unknowingly alight on his head, informed her that it was he who had removed her silver. In him this, under the circumstances, was a comparatively light offence, the money being what he supposed must soon come to him by inheritance. His mother did not therefore reproach him, but rather blessed him; and proceeded to explain, that her anxiety in the matter had proceeded from the special destination which she had made of the money, and which, she supposed, would not be less advantageous to him than the inheritance of it. She had "wholly dedicated it to Jehovah;" and she now invited him to take the money and give effect to her intention. He, however, preferred to leave the money in her hands, while he wrought with her in carrying out the design. This was no less than to set up a small establishment like that at the tabernacle, the service of which appears to have been at this time much neglected, and the access to it, from the troubled state of the country, difficult. Micah and his mother seem to have thought, that the restriction to one place of ceremonial worship respected only sacrifice; and that, while he abstained from setting up an altar for offerings of blood, he should not only be committing no offence, but doing a laudable action, and one which would be acceptable to God, by setting up a place for His service by prayer, and perhaps by bloodless offerings.

So he soon had what he conceived to be "a house of God."[1] He had a chamber, it would seem, set apart for this service; and in it was a priest's dress ("an ephod"), and "a graven image and a molten image." For "image," some read indefinitely "thing," which the original will admit; and they suppose that imitations of the sacred utensils, or of some of them, are intended, such as the candlestick, etc. Whether so or not, there were certainly images, for "teraphim" are presently mentioned. As these teraphim occur in Scripture in somewhat diversified applications, some of which bore a resemblance to the human figure,[2] we incline to the supposition that they were designed to represent the cherubim in the tabernacle.

Micah was now a happy man. His chapel was intended not only for the advantage of his household, but to form a centre of worship and prayer to the neighbourhood. There was nothing idolatrous in it, so far as the intention of Micah was concerned, who deemed that it was doing God service, being unable to discover the *tendencies* to idolatry which placed it among forbidden things. One feels a kind of sympathy for this obviously sincere man, while deploring his grievous and dangerous error of judgment.

There was one want. There was the framework of a little ecclesiastical settlement; but the animating spirit in an officiating minister was wanting. A patriarch would have been content to suppose that he might becomingly lead the devotions of his household; but the idea of a distinct priesthood being by this time established, nothing would satisfy Micah but the presence of some one specially set apart for the service of his house of prayer. Not being able, however, to get a priest, or even a Levite, he remembered that the Levitical tribe were taken into the Lord's service in lieu of the first-born of all the tribes, and therefore he set apart his own son, probably his first-born, for this duty.

Though he adopted this resource, Micah was aware that this was not altogether correct, and desired to have a Levite for his officiating minister. He was not long unsatisfied. One day a wandering Levite called at his house, either from having heard as he passed of the establishment there, or to claim the hospitality usually shown to strangers, and which the law particularly enjoined to be shown to the Levites. His name was Jonathan, and he belonged to Bethlehem in Judah. This, at the outset, seems an irregularity, for the Levites had cities of their own among the different tribes, and Bethlehem was not a Levitical city. But it would seem that, in times of confusion like this, the regulation was not much heeded; and the Levites, or a considerable proportion of them, were dispersed over the land, as necessity, convenience, or private connections suggested. Indeed, seeing that in their towns they derived their subsistence from the provision made for them by the law, and that they were not, like the men of other tribes, landowners, they would be obliged, in unsettled times, when the payment of the dues on which

---

[1] "A house of gods" in the authorized version; but it is more agreeable to the circumstances that the plural form should here, as usual, be understood in the singular sense.

[2] As, for instance, the image or teraph which Michal put in David's bed, and passed off for himself, sick.

they depended was neglected, or became insufficient for the whole body, to leave their towns and go to other places in search of a maintenance. This would be especially the case with the younger Levites; and, indeed, the Jewish writers intimate with sufficient clearness, that even in good times—and perhaps as a characteristic of good times—the Levites went much about the country as teachers of the law and educators,—these functions being really the same, for education among the Hebrews consisted primarily of instruction in the law, and the capacity of reading it. The function of the priesthood was to offer sacrifices, not to teach; the function of the Levites, besides assisting the priests in the lower departments of their duty, was to teach, and not to sacrifice. They were the teachers of the law; and, although not stated in Scripture, there is reason, from the mere probability of the case, to believe that the Jewish writers are not wrong in affirming that zealous Levites dispersed themselves about the country, and went from place to place, tarrying wherever their services seemed to be required, in discharge of this important branch of their functions. The subject is interesting, but is too large for incidental discussion here; and therefore we pass it, with the remark that, seeing the function of a Levite was to teach—seeing he exercised no trade or profession, it must have been only as a teacher, an educator of a people, a guide in religious matters, that a Levite could seek employment; and when, therefore, we find one travelling in search of an opening for his services, this implies that such openings were to be found, and that in various localities a demand for such services existed.

This was the case with our Levite. He told Micah that he was in search of a place where he might settle: "I go to sojourn where I may find a place." On hearing this, Micah gladly seized the opportunity of completing, as he conceived, his establishment, by engaging this Levite for his minister. This person seems to have been no more conscious of the gross irregularity of the proceeding than Micah himself, who, in the joy of his heart, exclaimed, "Now I know that Jehovah will bless me, seeing that I have a Levite to be my priest." Alas for him, if he had no other hope of a blessing than this!

The terms on which Micah engaged the services of this young Levite are remarkable. "I will give thee ten shekels of silver by the year, and a suit of apparel, and thy victuals." We are startled at the smallness of the sum, which does not exceed five-and-twenty shillings at the present value of silver. But the worth of the money with regard to the cost of commodities, by which the real value is determined, must have been much greater, relatively, in that age and country. Even at the present day, money is, in that relation, of three or four times the value in Syria that it bears with us—that is, it will go three or four times as far in the purchase of necessaries; and Burckhardt informs us that, thirty years ago, about six pounds by the year was all the income which the Bishop of Kerak [1] derived from his see; it is probably not so much at present, as his see is certainly in a less flourishing condition. We are also to consider, that in a simple age, and in a country then without commerce, a young man was held to have little occasion for expense, when provided with clothing and food. Micah evidently made what he conceived to be a liberal offer; and as the Levite himself received it as such, we have no reason to consider that it was otherwise. The *suit* of apparel does not, as our use of the word implies, consist of a single dress, but a complete set of apparel; including, probably, an ordinary dress, and another to use in the services of the office he had undertaken.

The engagement, however, was not so splendid but that the Levite, somewhat too eagerly for any strong sense of gratitude to his patron, accepted an offer to exercise the same functions for that division of the tribe of Dan, which passed this way in going to find a new settlement in the north—at Laish, afterwards called Dan; and there is reason to apprehend that he did not very eagerly protest against the abstraction by the strong-handed Danites of the whole paraphernalia of Micah's establishment, on which a little fortune had been expended. Micah was absent at the time; but he soon discovered his loss, and pursued the party with the people of the neighbourhood, who were equally interested in the support of his establishment. They found, however, that the Danites were too strong for them, and reluctantly returned, after Micah had received a rough hint as to the danger he incurred by not putting up quietly with his loss. It may be hoped that the loss was his eventual gain. But the original of this remarkable establishment, as well as the eagerness of the Danites to appropri-

[1] Mentioned before at p. 530.

ate it to themselves, is very painfully demonstrative of the loose notions of the age; and it is of importance, as supplying the link in the downward progress to that direct idolatry into which the nation not long after generally fell. In the leading narrative the transition seems very abrupt. But there were intermediate corruptions and degeneracies, and here their nature is sufficiently indicated.

THE OFFENCE

Judges 19

In the last three chapters of the book of Judges, we have another illustration of the disorders that prevailed in the same period to which the transaction considered yesterday has been referred. That transaction evinces the religious disorder and uncertainty into which that age had fallen. The one now before us equally illustrates the social disorders of the time, while it instructs us that the theocratical institutions had fallen into irregular action even at headquarters. But besides, and indeed probably as its main object, it serves to account for the great diminution of importance which the warlike tribe of Benjamin underwent, and the small figure it makes (except for its dependence on, and in connection with, Judah) in the subsequent history of the nation. In both transactions a Levite occupies a conspicuous place. In this case the name of the Levite is not given; but it seems noticeable that his abode was in the same quarter, "on the side of Mount Ephraim," where Micah, not long before or after, had set up his very questionable establishment, and that the woman who is painfully engaged in the transaction belonged to the very town of Bethlehem-judah, from which the other Levite came. That woman was his "concubine,"—a name of more odious import now than even at the time when it was used by our translators. The original word (*pilgash*) has no ill sense in Scripture; and it ought not to be represented by a word which expresses an infamous condition. In the Scripture it denotes the condition of a secondary wife—such as Hagar, and the two handmaids of Leah and Rachel, to whom several of the twelve tribes traced their origin. The wives of this class differed from

those of the first chiefly in being not so well connected, and in being taken from an inferior condition of life—often captives—that is, slaves promoted thus to the side of their master. The marriage was contracted with fewer ceremonies and legal obligations than that with a wife of the first class; nor did the husband enter into any contract to endow them, or to make their children his heirs. They were, however, as much entitled to sustentation, raiment, and matrimonial rights as the other wives, and their position was in no respect discreditable. Their children might share the paternal heritage, if the father so appointed; and in any case they were entitled to a portion of his goods, according to circumstances. These two ranks of wives were not only allowed by the law of Moses, but a man might take as many of either as he thought good, or considered himself able to maintain. This, however, was practically a sufficient limitation; so that, among the Hebrews, as is still the case in the East, a man is seldom seen to have more than one or two wives, except among the princes and magnates of the land. All the incidental allusions in Scripture to matrimonial life assume that a man has but one wife; and in all the post-patriarchal history of the Bible, the only man below the rank of a ruler or prince who is *recorded* to have had even two wives, is the father of Samuel, and in that case a reason is furnished in the fact that one of the wives was childless.

Well, this Levite of Mount Ephraim had a "concubine wife;" and she proved unfaithful to him, and went home to her father at Bethlehem. By the law, both classes of wives were equally obliged to be faithful to their husband; but whether, in case of infidelity, the second class was liable to the same capital punishment as the first, is not determined. But if found guilty, after full proof, the husband was obliged to divorce her for ever from him, if not to prosecute her for adultery. It was therefore altogether an irregular and unseemly thing—however it may bespeak his affection—that, after four months of separation, he resolved to go in search of her, and bring her back to his home. He accordingly went to Bethlehem "to speak friendly to her," or, as the original has it, "to speak to her heart;" that is, to conciliate her affection, to rekindle her tenderness, to whisper forgiveness to her, and to implore her to return to the home she had left desolate. He had, perhaps, heard that she was penitent; for the phrase often denotes the giving of comfort to one who is in sorrow. He was so confident of the result, that, in addition to the ass he rode, he took another with him to bring her back. He had also a servant with him, to drive the asses from behind. He might, perhaps, have dispensed with this for himself, but a servant must be in attendance to drive the ass that a woman rides.

The woman's father was glad indeed to see his son-in-law arrive on such an errand, which promised a much less painful result of this distressing affair than he could have supposed probable. The satisfaction was such, that he detained him for three days as a guest; and even on the fourth day, when the Levite fully proposed to set out on his return, he was delayed so late in the day by the kind urgencies of his entertainer, that he was constrained to tarry over another night. The next morning he arose with the firm purpose of not losing another day, but was prevailed upon reluctantly to stay till the afternoon was far advanced, when he was entreated to remain another night; but fixed in his purpose, he set forth, late as it was. All the painful results grew out of this detention and late outsetting, and may help, if every day did not supply lessons enough, to teach us the danger and weakness of allowing our better judgment to be overcome by even the kind importunities of others.

Owing to the late hour of the departure, the travellers had got no farther than Jebus (afterwards Jerusalem), which was but six miles from Bethlehem, when, as there was a woman of the party, it became necessary to seek a place to lodge in for the night. The servant suggested that they should go into the town, but this place was still in the occupation of the Jebusites; and although, from the relations which by this time had grown between the nations, there was no reason to apprehend any personal danger or molestation, the Levite preferred pushing on some miles farther to Gibeah, or to Ramah, which were in the sole occupation of Benjamin, to turning aside into the city of a stranger. Gibeah stood upon a low, conical, or rather round eminence, about five miles north by east from Jerusalem. By the time they got near this the sun went down, and the Levite concluded to turn

in there. As he had no acquaintance in the place, and there seems to have been no lodging-place or khan to which he could repair, he tarried, as the custom was, in the street, sure that some

GIBEAH.

one would soon invite him to his house. We do not think there is any charge against the men of Gibeah on *this* account merely, for no one could receive him till it was known that he wanted reception, and this was the proper mode of making his want known. The same practice still exists in the East under the like circumstances, and it is not long that any one has to wait before entertainment is offered to him. But in this vile place it is expressly stated that "no man invited him to his house," and he was left waiting in the street, until at last an old man, who was also of Mount Ephraim, and who very possibly recognized the Levite, saw the party as he returned from his work in the fields, and invited them to his humble dwelling.

It is a beautiful circumstance, that the exercise of hospitality was not, as we see, confined to the rich and great, but was a gratifying and honourable duty which even the labouring poor did not consider themselves exempt from discharging. That this old man had been labouring in the fields, would not indeed imply that he was in low circumstances, did not the fact of his not belonging to the place show that they were not his own grounds on which his labour was expended. It is to be noted, however, that the Levite told the old man that he wanted only lodging; he had everything required for the refreshment of the whole party : "There is straw and provender for our asses; and there is bread and wine also for me and for thine handmaid, and for the young man which is with thy servants." This shows that the Israelites did then, as the Orientals do now, take with them the provisions for themselves and their beasts that they require during a journey, replenishing their stores from time to time when they come to a town that can supply them. The "straw" was chopped straw, used in the East instead of hay, and the "provender" barley. This is carried in hair-bags, something like the mouth-bags of our horses, but of larger size. We must not neglect to observe the deferential courtesy of the language which this prosperous Levite uses towards the poor old labouring man. From this and other instances, such as the salutations exchanged between Boaz and his reapers in the book of Ruth, one cannot but entertain a most favourable impression of the polite and courteous manners of the Israelites in this remote age, which some regard as barbarous.

The gross neglect of the duties of hospitality must have given the Levite some misgiving as to the character of the place, seeing how highly these duties are estimated in the East, and seeing that his Levitical character gave him a more than common claim to kind and generous entertainment. The result justified his misgivings. A crowd of worthless fellows soon beset the place, with the most offensive intentions against the person of the stranger; and in the morning his wife lay dead upon the threshold, from the usage she had received at their hands.

The Levite said nothing. It was not a time for words, which were all too feeble to express the terrible thoughts that burned within him. He took up the dead body, and placing it on the ass, proceeded to his home. The crime which had been committed, and the state of that miserable place, seemed to him such, that only a great and signal act of public judgment could avert from the nation which owned such miscreants, a doom like that which, in old time, overwhelmed the Cities of the Plain. He therefore determined to demand the punishment of this awful crime after a fashion which was sanctioned by ancient custom, though startling even to the Israelites, from its infrequency or disuse. He divided the corpse into twelve pieces, and sent one piece to each of the tribes of Israel, the messengers being no doubt commissioned to give therewith a circumstantial account of the transaction. Shocking as this resource appears, it seems to have been in accordance with the notions of the time, as a resort in extreme cases for summoning the distinct tribes into united action, in the absence of any general authority for calling them forth. It is therefore, not without purpose, stated that at this time there was "no king, ruler, or chief magistrate in Israel; but every man did what was right in his own eyes." This, then, was, at such a time, the most stringent resource the Levite could adopt for calling them to avenge this wickedness in Israel. Judging from some parallel instances, it seems that this proceeding on his part laid them under an anathema, solemnly binding them, on pain of being themselves dealt with in the same manner, to avenge this dreadful and infamous deed. This was usually done with pieces of a bullock that had been sacrificed, or devoted with peculiar solemnities; and that the Levite used the dead body of the victim of this outrage, was calculated to deepen the horror and strengthen the obligation. It may be justly objected that, as a private man, the Levite had no right to lay the whole nation under the anathema—that so might it be done to them and theirs, unless they avenged the wrong. This right to summon them authoritatively could only belong to a king, a judge, and perhaps the high priest. We see Saul resorting to it in order to call the people to the relief of Jabesh-Gilead. "He took a yoke of oxen, and hewed them in pieces, saying, Whosoever cometh not forth after Saul and after Samuel, so shall it be done unto his oxen." (1 Sam. xi. 7.) A private person could not do this; but he could, and did, send or offer the pieces, and those who accepted them came under the obligation, and regarded themselves as solemnly devoted to carry it out. Burder, in his *Oriental Customs*, cites a somewhat apposite, or at least illustrative, custom from Lucian, who, speaking of the Scythians and Molossians, says, "When any one had received an injury, and had not the means of avenging himself, he sacrificed an ox, and cut it in pieces, which he caused to be dressed and publicly exposed. Then he spread out the skin of the victim, and sat upon it with his hands tied behind him. All who chose to take part in avenging the injury that had been done, took up a piece of the ox, and swore to supply and maintain for him—one, five horses; another, ten; others still more; some, infantry—each according to his strength and ability. They who had only their persons, engaged to march themselves. Now, an army composed of such soldiers, far from retreating or disbanding, was invincible, as it was engaged by oath."

THE FIRST TRIBAL WAR

Judges 20-21

IT behoves us to point out some strange irregularities in the behaviour of the tribes who undertook the avengement of the Levite's wrong, not only to show how ill the true working and obligations of their theocratical system were understood by the Israelites in this age, but to account for some results which surprise the reader of these chapters no less than they confounded the Israelites themselves.

A deep horror thrilled through all the tribes when the message reached them; and they declared that no such dreadful wickedness had been seen among the nation from the time they quitted Egypt to that day. From northernmost Dan to southernmost Beersheba, and in the region beyond the Jordan, the agitation was most intense. Then there was the hurried march of innumerable feet from all parts of the land to the place of concourse at Mizpeh. No less than four hundred thousand men of the strongest and bravest of all the tribes proceeded thither in arms, headed by their tribal chiefs. Here the Levite appeared in person, and related his cruel wrongs, referring the matter to their decision. That decision was prompt and earnest. All the people arose as one man, and declared that they would not return to their homes till this great iniquity was purged from Israel. Their first step was to appoint ten men out of every hundred among all the tribes to keep the camp supplied with victuals. The next was to send to the tribe of Benjamin to require them to deliver up, for judicial execution, the men in Gibeah who had wrought this guilt in Israel. Instead of doing this, or rather, instead of offering themselves to execute this judgment upon the men who had brought this disgrace upon their tribe, the men of Benjamin resolved to take up arms in defence of Gibeah against the united forces of all the other eleven tribes. Much as this astonishes, it is entirely in keeping with other actions of this fierce and turbulent tribe, whose character well sustained the prophetic description of it given by the dying Jacob, "Benjamin shall ravin as a wolf." (Gen. xlix. 27.) The number this tribe was able to bring into the field against the four hundred thousand of Israel did not exceed twenty-six thousand men, including seven hundred left-handed men, "who could sling stones at a hair and not miss."

On learning that the Benjamites were thus resolved to adopt the quarrel of Gibeah, the Israelites were highly exasperated, and pledged themselves by a solemn vow that none of them would give their daughters in marriage to any man of that tribe; which, in effect, amounted to a determination to extinguish the tribe altogether. They expected and hoped to destroy the greater number in the war; and this vow pursued those who might escape, making them aliens from the commonwealth of Israel.

The tribes then repaired to Shiloh—to which, we apprehend, they ought to have gone at first—to inquire, not, as they were bound to do, at the divine oracle, whether or not they should enter upon this war with Benjamin, which threatened the extinction of a tribe in Israel, but only what tribe should take the lead in the campaign. This shows, that in thus deciding upon war with Benjamin, without trying further means of conciliation, they acted much less from the result of a cool and deliberate conference upon the most effectual means of extirpating such shameful impieties from the commonwealth, than from the heat of resentment against the Benjamites, for daring to undertake the defence of the miscreants of Gibeah against the whole congregation of Israel. Had they given themselves time to think coolly upon the matter, they might have recollected that it was not permitted them to engage even in a war against strangers without consulting their Divine King through the high priest; much less could it be right for them to engage in a war against one of their own tribes, and to pursue it with such furious zeal. Although, therefore, they got an intimation that Judah was to take the lead—this being all they required to know—it must be well understood that their engagement in this war was entirely on their own responsibility, without any authority from the Lord, and in direct contravention of the prerogatives which he had specially reserved to himself. Nothing can be clearer than that they never once thought of consulting the divine oracle till the war had been fully resolved upon, and settled beyond recall by solemn pledges and oaths. The enterprise seemed to them so laudable, that they could not doubt of success, and the immense advantage of their numbers assured them of victory. They forgot that their own hands were not clean. They had got into such a state as to tolerate, if not approve, such establishments as that of Micah, afterwards adopted by a large division of one of their tribes. By this indifference they indicated the same want of proper sense of the speciality of their relation to their Divine King, as they showed throughout the present transaction; and it was important that they should be brought round by a sharp correction to a right understanding of their position. It was doubtless on this account, and to punish them for their presumption in thus undertaking the excision of a tribe without consulting the Lord's will in the matter, and without exhausting all pacific resources—and for making themselves both judges and executioners in what appeared to be God's cause, without His authority, direction, or consent—that they were allowed to sustain a most disastrous and disgraceful defeat in their first battle with Benjamin at Gibeah, into which place the force of the tribe had thrown itself, and from which it readily came forth to give the vast host of Israel battle. Of that host twenty-two thousand—a number not far from equal to the whole army of Benjamin—were left dead upon the field.

This result naturally filled them with consternation. It brought them to the tears and prayers with which it had been well for them to have commenced so deplorable an undertaking. They now began to consult God, not about a commander as before, but about the lawfulness of the war. Finding that the war itself was approved, they gathered confidence, and again went out against Benjamin; but with no better result than before, for they lost this second time no less than eighteen thousand men. If they had been as much as they ought to have been, in the habit of consulting the divine oracle, which was instituted for their guidance as a people, they must have seen that the approbation of the war gave no promise of success, and they would have

humbled themselves until that promise had been obtained. The full and *customary* answer, " Go up, for I will deliver them into thy hand," was not given : only, " Go up," without any promise as to the result. This alone ought to have awakened their apprehensions that something was still wrong, and to have caused them to inquire diligently wherein that wrong lay.

The second defeat produced the effect that was intended by it. It led them to consider wherein they had erred, and brought them to a proper sense of their relation to their Divine King, and of the obligations which that relation involved. From the particularity with which their regular course of proceeding is now described, it may be doubted whether they had previously appeared before God for the purpose of consulting Him in a proper *manner*, as they certainly had not in a proper *spirit*. It is now first plainly stated that they all went up into the house of God, where they not only fasted and wept until the evening, but prefaced their address to Him by the usual sacrifice of burnt and peace offerings. Then the high priest Phinehas, the grandson of Aaron—whose name helps to fix the time—stood before the ark to ask counsel of God, with the usual solemnity, in their name : "Shall I yet again go out to battle against the children of Benjamin, my brother, or shall I cease?" Under the circumstances, what a sad and touching emphasis is there in the term, "the children of Benjamin, *my brother;*" and what a heart-rending consciousness of the horror of this fraternal conflict it implies! The answer was now given freely, fully, and explicitly : " Go up, for to-morrow I will deliver them into thy hand." They are now, in fact, in a proper frame for victory; and this is incidentally evinced by the fact that the promise thereof, instead of leading them into wild presumption, induces them to renew their hostilities in a more cautious and orderly manner. The Benjamites were now made to pay dearly, not only for the lives of the forty thousand they had slain, but likewise for daring to take up arms in defence of the impious Gibeathites, while the fire consumed the city, and the sword devoured the lives of these rebellious miscreants. The whole tribe was, in fact, reduced to about six hundred desperate fugitives, who went and fortified themselves upon a barren rock, and would in all probability have perished there, to the utter extinction of the tribe, had not God inspired the Israelites with returning sentiments of pity towards that small and unfortunate remnant, and with remorse for having so nearly destroyed one of the twelve tribes out of Israel.

This result seemed, indeed, still unavoidable, by reason of the solemn curse which, in their rash and precipitate zeal, they had at the first pronounced upon any who should give a daughter in marriage to a Benjamite, while they had suffered their revenge to transport them so far as to destroy all the women of that miserable tribe. Thus, although they resolved to spare these six hundred men, it was seen that this could have but little effect in the ultimate preservation of the tribe, unless they could find means of supplying them with wives, by whom to raise up a new offspring. Some blame them for thinking themselves bound to keep such a vow, or for not applying to the Lord to excuse them from the obligation they had so unwisely incurred; but we must confess that we cannot regard with favour any alternative which would, on the one hand, lead them to think more lightly than they did of the solemn obligation of an oath once taken, or which, on the other, would tend to an encouragement of rash and fatal oaths, by enabling them to relieve themselves from the consequences. Besides, the only oaths that appear fairly entitled to be regarded as dispensable, are such as involve injurious consequences not reckoned upon or foreseen at the time the oath was taken; but this was by no means the case here: the oath, if it had any meaning at all, having been plainly taken *for the very purpose* of securing the result which was now deplored. Still there can be no doubt that, seeing they had gone too far in the heat of their wrath, their duty was to seek counsel of the Lord in the way which He had appointed; and we cannot doubt that some proper remedy would have been indicated. But instead of this, they proceeded in their old irregular way; and while lamenting that so much blood had been shed, they could think of no remedy but the shedding of more. An anathema had been laid upon all who should not join the crusade against Benjamin; and it being found that the inhabitants of Jabesh-Gilead had absented themselves, they must all be destroyed, in order that all the unmarried females found among them may be obtained for the Benjamites.

Yet these were not sufficient. Two hundred more were still wanting; and to secure these, the unprovided Benjamites were instructed to lie in wait and carry off the required number of brides for themselves from among the damsels of Shiloh, when they went forth, during one of the great festivals celebrated there, to solace themselves in the gardens. There are not in eastern towns places where assemblies can be held for such festivities. It is therefore usual to assemble in such pleasant spots as may be in the neighbourhood—in any small valley through which a stream flows—near some secluded fountain—in gardens or plantations. The women especially affect this mode of enjoyment, which agreeably diversifies their somewhat monotonous existence. A few years ago the ladies of Aleppo bribed an astrologer to predict a coming plague, for no other reason than that they might—as they knew to be usual in such cases—be sent out of the way into the suburban gardens.[1] The plot was in due time discovered, and the astrologer put to death; but the women had secured their enjoyment. That these festivities are held by the different sexes apart, explains the circumstance that there were no men present to oppose the Benjamites in carrying off their daughters and sisters. The feat was successfully executed; and when the men of Shiloh began to complain of this outrage, the elders of the congregation interposed with gentle counsels; and by intimating that it had been done at their suggestion, and by pointing out that in this way the tribe would be preserved without the oath being slighted—seeing that the brides had not been given by their fathers, but had been taken from them—they were prevailed upon to submit quietly to this wrong. Thus the poor remains of Benjamin were reinstated among the tribes; and one of the most remarkable and ominous transactions in the history of Israel was brought to a close.

WOMAN

As if to intimate that man should not take occasion from her part in the sad history of the

---

[1] In the East the private gardens are not connected with the houses in towns, but are apart in the suburbs, and are only occasionally visited.

Fall, to hold in light esteem the appointed companion of his life's journey, deeming her to be merely a

"Fair defect of nature,"

God has chosen to confer singular honours upon woman throughout the sacred Scriptures. They who disparage her capacities, and pour contempt upon her understanding; they who contemn her faithfulness and distrust her truth; they who make her man's household drudge, or the mere instrument of his pleasures or convenience—have no warrant in Scripture for so doing. Although we may not overlook the sad part which woman took in the fall of our race, yet that terrible damage—which was not, after all, wholly her work—may be held to have been fairly and fully counterbalanced by the part she had in bringing salvation. It was not without some such significance that the illustrious "Seed of the woman," who took upon Him "to bruise the serpent's head," was "born of a woman," and nourished from her breast.

But let us look at the women mentioned in Scripture, and observe how few of them are undistinguished by some useful quality or holy grace. Some are seen to have been endowed before men with supernatural knowledge, being favoured by the Spirit of God with the high gifts of prophecy: such were Miriam, Deborah, Huldah, and Anna. Others are noted for their sagacity and understanding, for which indeed they were proverbial: such as the wise woman of Tekoah, and she of Abel-Bethmaachah. Sarah lacked not strong capacities of faith; and strong was the faith of Rahab, of Samson's mother, and of that alien woman whose faith won from Christ a blessing which then belonged only to "the lost sheep of the house of Israel." Some have shown greater courage for the church, and manifested firmer resolution, than men have done. Did not Deborah encourage Barak to battle against the innumerable host and iron chariots of Jabin, and adventure her presence with him to the war, when, without her, he—the selected champion—was afraid to go? And who could be more resolved to jeopardize her life for God's people than the beautiful Esther, when she uttered and acted upon the memorable words, "If I perish, I perish?" Others are famous or memorable for various things: for attention to God's word—as the Virgin Mary, and as Lydia; for going far to seek knowledge—as the Queen

of the south to hear the wisdom of Solomon; for works of charity—as Dorcas; for works of pious zeal—as the women whose busy hands in spinning and needlework helped forward the labours of the tabernacle; for fervency in prayer—as Hannah; for patient waiting on God in daily fasting and prayer—as Anna; for the cordial entertainment of God's messengers for His sake—as the Shunammite woman, as Lydia, and as one of the gospel Marys; for the fear of God—as the midwives in Egypt; for courtesy to a mere stranger—as Rebekah; for humility and patience—as the aged Naomi; and for truthful and devoted affection—as the beloved Ruth. In Thessalonica, not only "devout Greeks," not only humble persons, but "chief women not a few," were among the first to receive the Gospel at the preaching of Paul and Silas; and among the learned of Athens, an Areopagite could not become a believer without a woman, Damaris, being joined with him. What is there, in fine, in which men have been renowned, wherein some women have not been remarkable? In wisdom, in faith, in charity, in love to the word, in regard for God's servants, in fervent affections, and in the desire of heavenly things—in all these there have been women who excelled. If men have suffered imprisonments, cruel persecutions, and bonds for Christ, women have done no less. When persecuting Saul made havoc of the church, not only men but women were torn from their homes and committed to prison; and his commission had equally injurious respect to the believers, "whether they were men or women." (Acts viii. 3; ix. 2.) And although we confine our illustrations chiefly to the Scripture itself, it is impossible, in mentioning this, not to call to mind the numerous illustrious women who, in a later age, were tortured, not accepting deliverance, that they might obtain a better resurrection, and who might say, with Anne Askew in the prison-house—

"I am not she that lyst
My anker to let fall
For every dryslynge myst;
My shippe's substancyal."

Nay, more than this, have not the female worthies of the Scripture often in many respects surpassed the men of their own day and generation? Who entertained Christ so much, so devotedly, and so often, as Martha and Mary? Who are in any instance said to have contributed to our Lord's necessities, but women? Who, of all the ordinary followers of Christ, took note of the place where He was buried, but women? Who went first to the sepulchre to anoint His body with sweet spices, but women? In Acts, xvi. 13, we read of a congregation of women to whom Paul preached, being gathered together at the accustomed place of prayer. They put a value on social devotion, while the men were strangers to the feeling.

Some might count it tedious, were we to mention all the notable things reported concerning women in the Holy Scriptures, and the excellent graces that were bestowed upon them. Yet we may not pass without a thought the knowledge which Priscilla shared with her husband in the ministry of the Gospel, which qualified her no less than him to instruct even the eloquent Apollos; nor Lois and Eunice, by whom the well beloved Timothy was trained up in the knowledge of the Holy Scriptures; nor Persis, "who laboured much in the Lord," as many other women did. (Phil. iv. 3.) But, not to dwell further on particular instances, it may be well worth our while to note one great matter that deserves to be mentioned to their praise, and to be kept in everlasting remembrance. We have read of men once held in high esteem, who became apostates—Demas, Alexander, Philetus, and others; but never, by name, in all the New Testament, of a woman who had once been reckoned among the saints. This is great honour. But not only have women been thus honoured with extraordinary gifts; they have been otherwise favoured with special marks of attention from the Lord. To whom but unto women did Christ first appear after His resurrection? Of what act did He ever so speak as to render it everlastingly memorable, save that woman's who poured upon his feet her alabaster box of precious ointment, and to whom He promised that, wherever in the whole world His Gospel should be preached, there should her work of faith be held in remembrance?

Nor do the honours rendered to women in the sacred Scriptures end here. One of the precious epistles of the beloved disciple is addressed to "the elect lady;" and in the Old Testament, two of the six unprophetical books that bear the name of individuals, present to us those of women—those of Ruth and Esther.

It is with the book of Ruth that we are now concerned. As this book appears to have been written for the purpose, principally, of tracing the genealogy of David to a source most honourable, and as it does contain a genealogy traced down to him, it must have been written during his reign, or soon after. Although it is expressly stated that the incidents took place "in the days when the judges ruled," this beautiful history does therefore connect itself as much with the period upon which we enter as with that through which we have passed. In one point of view, it is an appendix to the book of Judges; in another, it is an introduction to the history of the kings. With its interesting incidents we are thus enabled to commence this week. The simple and touching interest of the story, the beautiful and engaging rural scenery which it exhibits, the homely and honest manners which it describes, and the impressive and heartfelt piety which pervades the whole,—render it the most remarkable picture of ancient life and usages extant, and give us a far more complete idea of the real features of Hebrew life, in the early ages of the settlement of that people in Canaan, than we could otherwise possess. The young and the old read it with equally absorbed interest; and we have known strong and rough voices break down with emotion in reading aloud some of the passages that occur in the progress of the narrative.

The book of Ruth forms a link in the great chain of Messianic history. In the genealogy of our Lord by Matthew only three women are named, and it is a remarkable fact that these three are foreigners: Thamar the Canaanitess, Rahab of Jericho, and Ruth the Moabitess. Ruth is, in some respects, one of the most interesting female characters in the Bible. Brought up among idolaters, she yet, under most trying circumstances, renounces the false religion of her fathers, professes her faith in the true God, and manifests a submission to His will, and a devotedness to His service, that might well put many professing Christians to shame. Educated among a people notorious for their abandoned profligacy and indifference to the ties of nature, she yet exhibits a depth of affection and delicacy of moral feeling such as have been seldom equalled, and never surpassed. How can we account for this? A noble and generous heart was doubtless the foundation. But even a generous heart could never have emancipated itself from national corruption, or triumphed over the temptations by which Ruth was surrounded. I believe that her excellence was mainly owing, under God, to the training of her mother-in-law. Naomi was manifestly a woman of singular piety and strength of character. In the East, parents contract alliances for their children at a very early age—sometimes even in infancy. Naomi probably did so for her two sons. Her intended daughters-in-law would thus be for years under her care; and Ruth drank deeply of the fountain of divine truth providentially opened up to her. When Naomi was about to return to her country and her people, Ruth would not leave her. The earthly tie that bound her to Naomi and to Israel was broken, the husband of her youth was in the grave; yet she showed the influence and the power of sanctified instruction, for "she longed for the God and people of Israel with all the deepest earnestness of her nature, and joined herself to them with all the power of love."

P.

NAMES

Ruth 1:2

IT is worthy of remark that Bethlehem, which is connected with both the histories that form the appendix to the book of Judges, is also the scene of the history of Ruth, which is another appendix to that book, and seems to have anciently formed part of it. By means of these varied references to it, we are more familiar with the name, and perhaps better acquainted with the condition of Bethlehem, than of any other place mentioned in the early Scriptures. This knowledge is kept up—the place is kept before us by various subsequent historical intimations—until at last the heavenly host hail there the hour in which the Son of God becomes man within its walls.

In a time of severe famine, a man belonging to this place withdrew, with his wife and two sons, into the land of Moab for a subsistence. The names of all these persons are particularly given. The names of the father, Elimelech (*my God is king*), and of the mother, Naomi (*pleasant, happy*), indicate divine favour and worldly prosperity; and the names of the sons, Mahlon (*weakness, sickness*), Chilion (*consumption, decay*), imply the very reverse of health and comfort. Some old writers speculate curiously upon these names. Indeed, many of the Hebrew names are so remarkably appropriate to the persons who bear them, that it has been much questioned how this conformity was produced. Some have supposed that the names were changed, as circumstances arose to render the old names inappropriate. In proof of this, we are referred to this very book of Ruth, in which Naomi, in the sequel of the history, says, "Call me not

Naomi; call me Mara (bitter), for the Almighty hath dealt very bitterly with me." Yet this seems rather a mode in which she expressed the sense of her condition, than an intention or wish for an actual change of her name; and, in fact, there was no change, for she continued to be called Naomi. Instances of change of name do indeed occur; but these are such as to show that the practice was not common, the change being generally mentioned as a memorable circumstance, and as made by God Himself, or by some great public authority, mostly by a foreign king or conqueror, who imposes or confers upon the person a name proper to his own nation. Of the former kind is the change of Abram's name to Abraham, Sarai's to Sarah, Jacob's to Israel; and in the New Testament, of Simon to Cephas (in Greek, Peter);—and of the latter, the change of Joseph's name to Zaphnath-paaneah, of Daniel's to Belteshazzar, and of those of his companions Hananiah, Mishael, and Azariah, to Shadrach, Meshach, and Abed-nego. In all the latter class of changes, and in some of the former, the original name remains, notwithstanding the common name by which the person is known; and in the exceptional cases of even the first class of changes— those made by divine authority—the old and new names remain in concurrent use, save only in the case of Abraham and Sarah, in regard to which it is probable that the slightness of the oral change led to the exclusive adoption of the new name. There is no example of a change of name by private or paternal authority, and certainly not any of a man making such a change himself. Indeed, as names are intended to identify men, and to distinguish them from each other, all the use and purpose of proper names would be lost were they to be frequently altered. Such cases occur among ourselves, by the change of titles used as proper names. The rarity of this case prevents the inconvenience from being very sensibly felt; but the degree of inconvenience which is experienced when, for instance, a Gower becomes an Egerton, and then an Ellesmere, and has a public reputation under each of these names, may show what confusion would arise were such a practice common among any people.

We find in various instances, that the names by which people were known throughout their whole lives, were imposed at the time of birth, and were founded upon peculiarity of personal appearance—as Esau from his redness; upon some circumstance attending the birth—as in the case of Jacob; or upon some hope or expectation which the parents entertained, or upon some sentiment or idea that was then prominent in the paternal mind—as in the case of Cain, Seth, Noah, and the twelve founders of the tribes of Israel, not to mention later instances.

As to the question of appropriateness, it may appear that the point has been too much pressed by some writers. Most of the names of which we know the origin are appropriate to the *occasions* in which they originated; but not many of these, or of others, have any special appropriateness to the *character or career* of the men by whom they were borne. Some of the names are manifestly inappropriate to the history of the persons who bore them. Thus even the wise Solomon was mistaken in giving the name of Rehoboam (*an enlarger*) to his son; for that son, instead of *enlarging* the realm of the house of David, *reduced* it from the dominion over twelve tribes to two. So David gave the name of Absalom (*father of peace*, or, as some make it, *father's peace*) to the son who proved the greatest disturber of his peace and happiness. So also Jehu signifies *a constant man;* yet the king who bore it proved inconstant in his latter days, and "regarded not to walk in the law of the Lord God of Israel." (2 Kings x. 31.) Naomi felt her name to be inappropriate, as it certainly was during ten years of her life; and such is the course of human life, that there is no name, whether of pleasant or unpleasant import, which will not be suitable in some portion of any man's life, and unsuitable at another. Still there is a degree of appropriateness in many of the Scripture names considerably beyond what might be expected, and sufficient to justify surprise. Some go so far as to suppose that parents were often inspired to bestow upon their children names prophetically indicative of their future state and career. A pious and intelligent writer[1] remarks, on the very case before us, "Perhaps the names were respectively given by the suggestion of the Holy Spirit, to indicate the mournful contrast between the once flourishing condition of the hopeful pair, and the subsequent sore adversity and blighting desolation of the family." That this was sometimes the case we know. How far it was so in this particular case we know not; but it is quite

[1] Hughes's *Female Characters of Holy Writ*, ii. 26. 1846.

possible that both Chilion and Mahlon were such weakly children as to suggest a difficulty in rearing them, and to indicate the probability of that early death which actually befell both of them. In a learned American writer[1] we find a remark on the general subject which well deserves consideration. He is speaking with regard to the name of Gideon's aspiring son, Abimelech, which means "my father a king," and hints that the name may have prompted to the ambitious course he pursued, by suggesting reflections upon the import of the name. "The influence of names," he adds, "in the formation of character, is probably much greater than is usually imagined, and deserves the especial attention of parents in their bestowment. Children should be taught that the circumstance of their bearing the names of good men or women who have lived before them, constitutes an obligation upon them to imitate or perpetuate their virtues." This observation has peculiar force in America, where the people are prone to give the surnames of noted persons as first names to their children.

To the same effect an old writer[2] observes on the place before us: "And here note, in all their names, how significant they be, which the Hebrews did ever observe in naming their children. True it is, that good names have no virtue in them to make men better, nor names without significance to make any worse; yet, for reverence of our holy profession, let us give our children good names, significant and comely—not absurd, ridiculous, and impious, as some have done, out of the spirit of profaneness."

Christopher Ness makes substantially the same remark, adding, "Our very names should mind us of our duty." He pleasantly applies this view of the use of names to the case of Elimelech: "A good name (in its sense and signification) may be of great comfort to a man in an evil day. Thus it was to this man, whose name signified, *My God is king*. He might make a believing use thereof, pondering in his mind after this manner: Although there be a famine in the land of promise, whereby I am driven out of my native country, and constrained to dwell in idolatrous Moab, yet my God is king over all—over all persons, over all nations. He hath an uncontrollable sove-

[1] Professor Bush, in his *Notes on Judges*.
[2] Richard Bernard, "preacher of God's Word at Batcombe in Somersetshire," in his *Ruth's Recompense*. London, 1628.

reignty over all men and matters, and is not bound to give an account of any matter to any man.[1] 'Tis good for me to be where my God, who is my king, will have me to be. I am, wherever I am, evermore upon my Father's ground; for 'the earth is the Lord's, and the fulness thereof.' "[2]

Let us recollect that these names, which are to us abstract and unintelligible proper names, were by the Jewish people apprehended in their full meaning whenever used. This is rarely the case with us; for although most of the names we employ are significant, their significance lies hid in the foreign languages from which they are derived; and even if we use the very same names the Hebrews employed, they would not appear to us, unless specially instructed, as containing the same force and meaning which they had to them. We are disposed to regret the increasing disuse into which names consciously significant—at least to those who give and to those who receive them—have fallen. They are even treated with something like disrespect. We have lived to hear the use of one of the most touching and beautifully significant names of Scripture received, as a name merely—and merely from its unusual sound—with coarse merriment in one of the highest assemblies of our nation. Let the scorners refer to 1 Chron. iv. 9, 10, and "laugh" no more: "And JABEZ was more honourable than his brethren: and his mother called his name Jabez (sorrowful), saying, Because I bare him with sorrow. And Jabez called on the God of Israel, saying, Oh that Thou wouldest bless me indeed, and enlarge my coast, and that thine hand might be with me, and that Thou wouldest keep me from evil, that it may not grieve me! And God granted him that which he requested." This is, in fact, an illustration of the *use* which the Hebrews made of their significant names, and one precisely of the kind which is suggested by Ness, although he takes no account of this example. The reference in which the name originated we see clearly enough; but the interesting recognition of it in the last words of the prayer of Jabez escapes notice in a translation. In the original, the word *grieve* ("that it may not *grieve* me") is the verb from which his own name (sorrowful) is derived.

[1] Job 33:14.　　[2] Psalms 24:1.

HOME

Ruth 1:3-18

AT the end of ten years, of the four persons who went to the land of Moab to preserve their existence, one only remained alive, and that one was Naomi. They died amidst the plenty of Moab. They could but have died amid the dearth of Israel. The Jewish writers generally think that they did wrong in leaving their own country to go and live among idolaters. It was a privilege to dwell in the chosen land, and among the chosen people, under the ordinances of religion; one which was highly esteemed by the Israelites, and which in their estimation was not to be lightly abandoned. Was famine a sufficient reason for leaving it? If it were a sufficient reason for one, it was for another; and, therefore, under its full operation, the land would have been forsaken of its people. Observing that the law of the old covenant contained promises of unfailing subsistence to those who trusted in God, it is held that it would have been the more faithful part for them to remain, trusting to the Lord for their sustentation. The Jewish feeling on this subject is well expressed by the Psalmist: "Thou shalt dwell in the land, and verily thou shalt be fed." As it is, these persons went to avoid famine from the land of the Lord's inheritance, and in the land of their choice they found death, which the Jewish writers believe to have befallen them as a judgment. First the father died, and then the two sons, leaving Naomi alone; and yet not wholly alone, for these sons had espoused in the country two of the daughters of Moab, whose names were Orpah and Ruth. Some venture to suggest, that the judgment of premature death, without children, was inflicted upon them partly on account of these marriages, which are affirmed to have been unlawful under any circumstances; while others hold that the marrying of these Moabitish damsels, although not commendable, was not unlawful, in case they were proselytes, which there is little doubt that they both became. Intermarriages with the condemned nations of Canaan only, were forbidden by the law (Deut. vii. 3); and from the case before us, as well as from others, it appears not to have been at first considered to extend to other nations, unless as idolaters—though in a later age, when the people were few, the law was more stringently interpreted, and intermarriages with the Moabites and Ammonites were decreed to be as unlawful as with the women of any other nation. This is clearly seen in Ezra ix. 1, 2, and Neh. xiii. 23, 25, 26. It seems, indeed, that the two sons of Naomi carried the matter with a high hand. In respect of persons so young as they appear to have been, and entering into their first marriage, it is usually intimated that the father or the mother provided wives for them, as Hagar did for Ishmael; but here it is said that " they took them wives,"—a kind of phrase which usually occurs in a bad sense, as done without the concurrence of their parents, or not left so entirely to them as custom required. The inference is that they acted against the wishes of Naomi, who contemplated a return home with them, and their marriage in the land of their nativity with the daughters of their own people,—a matter which the Israelites justly deemed of great concern; whereas they seem to have thought it as well to establish themselves in a strange country, and to that end married in the land of Moab, which the lapse of years had rendered a home to them. Nine or ten years, which appear but a short period—too short to deaden the love of home and country in persons of advanced years —form the half of life, the more conscious half, to persons of twenty or thereabouts; and beyond that age marriage was rarely deferred among the Israelites. To one of that age, the ten last years of his life are by much the most important portion of his existence; and Moab rather than the land of Israel may very well have been regarded by these young men as their real home. Parents do not always apprehend the essential difference between their own ideas and those of their children in this respect. The offence of the sons of Naomi, if they offended at all, seems to have lain rather in this, than in their marriages considered in themselves. We are not, indeed, able to urge the fitness of these marriages from the fact that a pious man like Boaz afterwards became the husband of Ruth, which, it is alleged, he would not have done, had such marriages been wrong. Ruth had been married to an Israelite, and was no longer to be regarded as a Moabitess, but as one who had already been introduced into the house of Israel, and had thence acquired certain rights which did not belong to her in that condi-

tion, from which her first marriage had removed her. Boaz had not to regard her as a woman of Moab merely, but as the widow of a near relation, towards whom he had certain duties to discharge.

The death of her sons, however disastrous, enabled the widow to gratify her heart's longing to return home. To account for her being able to return, it is stated that she had heard that " the Lord had visited His people in giving them bread." It does not follow that the famine had lasted all the ten years. Ten successive years of famine, one is apt to suppose, might destroy any nation. Yet even this is not incredible. Herodotus[1] records a scarcity in Lydia that lasted eighteen years; and states that even then, the famine not abating, the king divided his people into two parts, and cast lots for one to tarry at home, and for the other to quit the country, himself retaining the command of those whose lot it was to stay. This fact is worth noticing, as pointing to emigration as an ancient resource against famine at home. Indeed, it is more ancient than this, as we find not only by the case before us, but by that of the patriarchal family going down into Egypt from the same cause. The natural tendency of such a measure to cause a country to be depopulated, was, in the instance mentioned by the Greek historian, sagaciously obviated by restricting the emigration to a moiety of the inhabitants.

Neither does the statement imply that, after the famine had ceased, ten years had elapsed before she heard of it. It is very true that intelligence travels with wonderful slowness in the East,—a slowness incredible to us, with our newspapers, railways, and telegraphs. Letter writing was then but little practised. Indeed, in all the Scripture history, so far as we have advanced, no instance of epistolary communication on any subject has occurred. Intelligence was principally conveyed by travellers. A person hearing that some one was going to, or would pass through, a certain place, would desire him to convey a message to a particular person residing there, with perhaps a further intimation that he was, when opportunity offered, to send the same communication on to persons in other places. Travellers were glad to be the bearers of such messages, for it gave them a kind of claim to the hospitable atten-

[1] *Clio*, 94.

tions and friendly offices of the persons to whom they were delivered, whose anxiety to learn something more of places and persons, by questioning the stranger, gave to him the pleasant consciousness that he was conferring a favour, not receiving one, in accepting their hospitable solicitudes. But the land of Moab, although not distant, being on the other side of the Dead Sea, and lying altogether out of the lines of route which the inhabitants of Southern Palestine might take to any place beyond, north, south, or east, would be very rarely visited by such travellers, and intelligence would reach it but slowly.

Nevertheless, we take not this resort; for the phraseology will very well imply that "she had heard" of this some time before, although now only, in consequence of the death of her sons, she was enabled to act upon the information she had received. The statement of the fact seems to be made, in order to account for the circumstance that, having now concluded to return home, the famine which had occasioned the departure of the family no longer offered any obstacle to her doing so, seeing that it had some time before ceased. Certain it is, that when she did return there were no signs of recent scarcity, but rather of such prosperity as would hardly have existed had the harvest then in progress been the first good harvest of the ten years.

It was the intention of Naomi to return alone. But, as friends and relations were wont to do, and as is still the custom in the East, her two daughters-in-law went part of the way with her to see her off. When at length the moment of parting came—when they kissed each other and wept together—they both declared that they could not return, but would go to the land of Israel with her. Like a wise woman, she declined to take advantage of the impulse of passionate regret, which seemed adverse to their temporal welfare, and which their cooler judgment might not sanction; and she urged them, by many strong arguments, to return to their parents, and leave her to pursue her bereaved course alone. Once more they wept, and Orpah being now prevailed upon, gave Naomi the farewell kiss. Ruth remained, and once more Naomi renewed her arguments with her. But poor Ruth realized, in her affectionate heart, a keen sense of her mother-in-law's forlorn condition. She knew that Naomi could not but feel most acutely how, when last she passed that way, she had been ac-companied by a worthy husband and two hopeful sons; now, she left them behind her in a foreign grave, and was returning alone—alone to her once prosperous but now desolate home. Ruth could not consent to abandon her under these circumstances. The reply is beautiful beyond expression, in the tenderness with which the firm purpose of an affectionate heart is uttered: "Entreat me not to leave thee, or to return from following after thee: for whither thou goest, I will go; and where thou lodgest, I will lodge: thy people shall be my people, and thy God my God. Where thou diest, will I die, and there will I be buried; the Lord do so to me, and more also, if aught but death part thee and me."

Surely the simple eloquence of the mouth that speaks out of the abundance of the heart, never found more beautiful and touching expression than in these words of this young widow.

When a famine visits a country, all classes are not affected at the same time or in the same degree. The rich can buy food, and can bring it from a distance. But the poor have little—sometimes nothing in store; and they feel an immediate pressure, and must beg or die. The family of Elimelech seems to have been in humble circumstances. The crops on his little mountain property failed. His yoke of oxen and few sheep had to be exchanged for bread. Then all was gone. Ruined and broken-hearted, he was forced to leave his country, and seek food among the prosperous Moabites. Landed property in Palestine is of very little value, except the possessor has the means of cultivating it; and as it was under Jewish law inalienable, strangers could not purchase it. A landed proprietor might thus be reduced to beggary, and in times of general distress might long remain so. Such seems to have been the case with the family of Elimelech, and they were therefore forced to remain in Moab. Even upon the return of Naomi and Ruth, though the family property was still theirs, they were completely destitute. Their property was valueless, because they did not possess the means of cultivating it. This will serve to explain the peculiar position of Naomi and Ruth on their arrival in Bethlehem.

P.

GLEANING SALUTATIONS

Ruth 2:1-4

IT was the commencement of the barley harvest when the two women came to Bethlehem. In that part of the country this is usually in the middle of April.[1] We are thus at once introduced into the most engaging scenes of the active season of agricultural labour. The fact suggested to Ruth, that she might contribute something to their mutual subsistence by going forth to glean. Naomi cheerfully consented to this, knowing that the law of Moses, and the usage founded on it, gave the poor a right to glean in the harvest fields: and *they* were poor indeed. This right of gleaning was one of the legal provisions for the poor of Israel; and as the landholders were not subject to money taxes for the support of the poor, this claim was liberally construed by them. Still, as its rude assertion by the poor as a right might subject the operations of the field to serious inconvenience, and occasion undue pressure upon particular fields, it appears that the proprietor retained the power of nominating the persons who were to glean after his reapers. In other words, the poor applied to the proprietors for permission to glean in their fields. Hence Ruth did not enter abruptly, and commence gleaning where she chose; but asked permission of the overseer, who very kindly and readily gave it. Some think this right of gleaning so absolute, that they incline to ascribe Ruth's demeanour to her being a foreigner, and hence not well acquainted with the nature of this right in Israel; but it is to be observed that Naomi herself sanctioned her impression that she was going to glean in the fields of him "in whose sight she should find grace;" and that, on Ruth's return, she ascribed the success of her daughter-in-law to the favour of the master of the field.

This Mosaic institution, founded upon the absence of any *regular* legal provision for the poor, no doubt gave rise to the popular notion as to the right of the poor, in this country also, to glean the fields after the harvest, which did formerly, and does still to a great extent, prevail in our rural districts. It is probable that, had no compulsory provision for the poor by rates been made, the right of gleaning would never have been questioned. But since then it *has* been

questioned in the courts of law; and the decision has been against it as a matter of right. A case, which has been regarded as settling the question, is reported in the law-books. It was a solemn judgment in the Court of Common Pleas, that no such right could be claimed at common law. Mr. Justice Gould dissented, quoting the passages in the Levitical law which bore on the subject,[1] together with a recognition of the custom or privilege in the Private Enclosure Act of Basingstoke parish. The other judges, however, were of opinion that it would be impolitic and dangerous to admit gleaning to be a right, and would, in fact, be prejudicial to the poor themselves, now provided for under various positive statutes. They also remarked, that the custom of gleaning was various in different places, and was in many places restricted to particular kinds of corn, and could not therefore be set up as a universal common law right; that it would be opening a tempting door to fraud and idleness, and had never been specifically recognized by any judicial determination.

Nevertheless, gleaning seems to be still regarded by the rural poor as one of their rights, and is generally exercised by consent of the farmer as to the persons. Some farmers, however, resist it, excluding the gleaners, and after the harvest raking the fields themselves. We have had occasion to witness the resentment, amounting to animosity, felt and expressed against the one farmer, in a rural district not more than twenty-five miles from London, who followed this practice.

It is said that not "the field," but "the *part* of the field," to which Ruth was providentially directed, belonged to Boaz, a near kinsman of Naomi's late husband. This is explained by what we have already had occasion to mention, that the lands of the respective proprietors are not separated by enclosures, but the whole cultivated in one unbroken field, the separate lots being distinguished only by landmarks and narrow trenches, seldom visible when the corn is grown up.

By and bye the master himself came to the field from Bethlehem. The salutations exchanged between him and his reapers strike us forcibly as beautiful indications of the pious and simple courtesy of a people brought up under the Law. The manner in which this impresses us, arises

---

[1] The first-fruits of the barley harvest were, as we know, presented at the passover, before which it was not lawful to begin the harvest. In Egypt the harvest was a little earlier than in Judea—in Phœnicia a little later; and in both countries they began cutting their barley as soon as the cuckoo was heard. Hence the comedian calls that bird the king of Egypt and Phœnicia (Aristoph. in *Avibus*). Even with us this bird is heard in April—sometimes as early as the 9th, but not usually until a fortnight later.

[1] Leviticus 19:9,10; 23:2; Deuteronomy 24:19.

much from the unhappy lack of similar usages among ourselves; for in the East such salutations, both between equals and between superiors and inferiors, are still common. Under the same cir-

RUTH GLEANING IN THE FIELD OF BOAZ

cumstances, a master in the same land would still say to his men, "Peace be to you;" and they would answer, "To thee be peace, and the mercy of God, and His blessing." It is to be regretted that we, whose law enjoins us to "be courteous," should suffer even Mohammedans to outdo us in this respect. These common courtesies, especially when clothed in the expression of a pious wish, are of more real importance than we are apt to suppose. They are, in fact, of more real importance to *us* than they would be to any people. The tendency of our civilisation—and it is a great evil among the many benefits this civilisation has produced—is to segregate the classes, and widen the distance between them; and it therefore the more behoves us to cultivate the amenities which may keep before the mind a consciousness of the fact, that there is a link between man and man in the brotherhood of a common nature and a common faith. It would do no harm. The servile demeanour of the poor in this country is hateful to every well ordered mind. It has grown out of circumstances which there has been

too little effort to resist; and we may go to the East to learn how the poor may be treated with courtesy, and be continually reminded, in every passing form of speech, of their natural and religious brotherhood, without being thereby encouraged to disrespect or insubordination, but with the effect of a cheerful and willing character being thereby imparted to their obedience.

Among the Moslems, the salutation as above given, is used by all classes, and is a sign of their brotherhood in religion, and their actual equality before God. It is therefore not used in the same form to those who are known to be of another religion. Whether this restriction existed among the Hebrews or not, there is no authority that informs us directly; but it is probable, from the nature of things, that it did. We find in the Mohammedan books, that the Jews of Arabia, in Mohammed's time, always used a different salutation to Moslems from that which was in use among themselves, often changing it into a malediction. Hence Mohammed directs, "When a Jew makes a salam to you, and he says *Al-sámo âlaica*,[1] then do you answer *O-âlaica*."[2] When a Moslem discovers that he has inadvertently given the salutation of peace to one not a Moslem, he usually revokes the salutation, saying, "Peace be on *us*, and on [all] the right worshippers of God." The giving of it by one Moslem to another is a duty, but one that may be omitted without sin, though the returning of another's salutation is absolutely obligatory. The chief rules respecting salutation, given by Mohammed, and usually followed by mödern Moslems, are:

[1] So near in sound to the real salutation of peace, *Al-salámo âlaica*, that it might pass by an unobservant ear for it; but *sam* means death, and the meaning is, "May you die."

[2] That is, "Be the same to you."

The person riding is to salute first him who is on foot; and he who passes by, the persons who are sitting down or standing still; and a small party, or one belonging to such a party, should give the salutation to a large party; and the young to the aged. It may be observed, that these rules are irrespective of any social difference between the persons. The Orientals have modes of indicating such differences; but not in the salutation of peace, which is the same for all. We have before us a book of the acts and sayings of Mohammed, as reported by his associates, from which one or two illustrations of his own views and practice, which regulate those of his followers, may be drawn: "A man asked his majesty [Mohammed], 'What quality is the best of a Musleman?' He said, 'Giving food to others, and returning the salutation of acquaintance or strangers.'" "Anas said: Verily his majesty passed by some boys, and made a salam to them." The khalif Ali reports that he heard Mohammed say, "There are six duties from one Musleman to another: To salute each other when they meet; to accept each other's invitations to dinner; to say, God have mercy upon you, after sneezing;[1] to visit the sick; to follow each other's biers when dead; and for one Musleman to wish for another what he wishes for himself." Jabir reports: "Verily, his highness passed by a party of women, and made a salam to them;" but on this the commentators add: "This practice was peculiar to his highness; for it is bad for a man to make a salam to a strange woman, or a woman to a strange man, unless it be an old woman." Abuhurairah reports that he heard Mohammed say, "You will not enter into paradise until you believe; and you will not complete your faith until you love one another; and that is shown

[1] This illustration has escaped the notice of those who have written on the antiquities of sneezing, and of the *universal* custom, not extinct among ourselves, of blessing the person who sneezes. The account of the subject given by Mohammed is copied, with some little alteration, from the rabbins, who state that "sneezing was a mortal sign even from the first man, until it was taken off by the special application of Jacob. From this, as a thankful acknowledgment, this salutation first began, and was afterwards continued by the expression *Tobim Chaiim*, or *vita bona*, by by-standers, upon all occasions of sneezing."— Buxtorff, *Lex. Chald.* It is in this, doubtless, that Mohammed gives his history of Adam's first sneeze. The custom also prevailed among the heathen, and is still found in the East. The subject is curiously illustrated in Brand's *Popular Antiquities*.

by making salam to friends and strangers." A Moslem generally accompanies the verbal salutation, whether as given or returned, by the very graceful motion of laying his right hand upon his breast; or else by touching his lips, and then his forehead or turban, by the same hand. This was not the custom of the Jews, though they had some equivalent motion; for Mohammed says, "That person is not of us who likens himself to another. Do not copy the Jews or Christians; *because a Jew's salam is making a sign with his fingers;* and that of a Christian with the palm of his hand."

The salutations recorded by Dr. Kitto are those which ordinarily pass between Mohammedans in the town and in the desert. Those, however, which one almost universally hears between peasants in the fields are different, and are identical with those used by Boaz and his reapers. I have heard and employed them a hundred times. On several occasions, when travelling during harvest, I have seen the master enter his field and salute his workers. *Ullah makum,* "God be with you," was the uniform address on approaching; and *Ullah yubarekek,* "God bless thee," the uniform response. In fact, the beautiful story of Boaz and Ruth is, in so far as the harvest scene is concerned, realized now in almost every harvest field in Palestine. The masters, the reapers, and the gleaners are there; the salutations are the same; the modes of eating, drinking, and sleeping are unchanged. One would almost think, in passing through the country at that season, that he had in some way been transported back to the time of the old prophets.

P.

HARVEST FARE

Ruth 2:5-14

THERE were no doubt some distinctions of costume and appearance between the Israelites and Moabites; and Ruth was too poor to have, as yet, rendered her habit wholly conformable to that of the women of the place. Then there was something about her that showed that she was not a woman of Israel; and it was probably this that drew the attention of Boaz towards her, and led him to inquire of his overseer who she was. The man informed him that she was "the Moabitish damsel who had come back with Naomi out of the country of Moab." The story, it seems, was well known in Bethlehem, and this information sufficed to apprise Boaz of the whole case. Being himself a good man, the goodness she had evinced in her conduct to her mother-in-law won upon his heart. He accosted her kindly, and desired her to avail herself of all the privileges of the harvest field; so that while she gleaned for her own benefit, she might partake of the refreshments and advantages of those who laboured for him. He begged she would keep to his grounds during the harvest, and not, in the hope of bettering herself on the one hand, or in the fear of presuming on the other, remove to the lands of any other person. And it will be observed how, in the absence of enclosures, he gives her the means of knowing his grounds, by telling her to adhere to the company in which she already finds herself, that of his own labourers, among whom she might rely upon being perfectly safe. We gather that the persons employed in the field were men servants, woman servants, and day labourers,— the women seemingly being chiefly employed in ministering to the wants of the men engaged in active toil, and in performing some of the lighter labours. One of the most important provisions of the harvest field was water, often necessarily brought from some distance, and placed so as to be kept cool. The labours of the hot harvest field could not be carried on without the occasional refreshment of a draught of water; and the importance attached to this is shown by the particular mention which Boaz makes of it in desiring Ruth, "When thou art athirst, go to the vessels and drink of that which the young men have drawn." This seems to be a special indulgence to a gleaner; at least it was one of which a young stranger, so diffident as Ruth, might dislike to avail herself without distinct permission.

EGYPTIAN HARVEST SCENE

In the tomb paintings of Egypt there are representations of harvest scenes which strikingly remind us of this. Among such analogies we perceive a provision of water in skins, hung against trees, or in jars upon stands, with the reapers drinking, and women, perhaps gleaners, applying to share the draught.

Overpowered by this unexpected kindness, poor

Ruth humbly acknowledged her deep sense of it, and her great surprise at it; on which Boaz told her that he knew her deeply interesting story, and that her generous self-denial could not but win for her the respect of all good men, and that it ensured her the protection and blessing of Him "*under whose wings she had come to trust*,"—a beautiful figure, derived, as some think, from the cherubim whose wings overshadowed the mercy seat; or, quite as probably, from the act of a parent bird in fostering and sheltering its callow brood underneath its wings. In the latter sense the idea is familiar in Scripture. So in the last address of Moses to the people: "As an eagle stirreth up her nest, fluttereth over her young, spreadeth abroad her wings, taketh them, beareth them on her wings, so the Lord alone did lead him."[1] And again, more emphatically, our Lord Himself says to Jerusalem: "O Jerusalem, Jerusalem, . . . how often would I have gathered thy children together, as a hen doth gather her brood under her wings, and ye would not!"[2]

Heart-touched by this short conversation, the good man continued still more kindly to attend to Ruth's comfort, and to show the interest he took in her welfare. It seems that there was a tent pitched in the field of labour for the more perfect refreshment of the reapers, particularly at the noontide meal and subsequent repose. This is what is called "the house,"—the word for house being often in Scripture applied to a tent. It was here, seemingly, that Boaz held this conversation with Ruth, for he goes on to say: "At meal-time come thou hither, and eat of the bread, and dip thy morsel in the vinegar." On this we have to remark, that "bread" is a general term for any kind of "provisions" which may have been prepared, and that it was probably not confined to bread. On the contrary, there appears to have been generally liberal diet prepared on such occasions. We know of the large store of various food provided even by the niggardly Nabal for his shearers; and it is not likely that the labour of the reapers would be less bountifully considered by the liberal Boaz. However, the chief meal in the midst of harvest labour seems to have been in the evening, at supper, after the labours of the day had closed; and this at noontide, after which labour was resumed, was a comparatively slight meal, such as we should call a lunch, as is still the case in the East. A full

[1] Deuteronomy 32:11,12.   [2] Luke 13:34.

meal at mid-day would have been little suited to the resumption of active labour. Indeed, this is implied in the fact, that when Boaz retired to rest on a subsequent night, it was "when he had eaten and drunk, and his heart was merry." So in Homer, although in his beautiful description of harvest labour, as depicted on the shield of Achilles, large provision is made for the reapers, it is for the supper at the close of the day, while refreshments of a lighter kind are provided for intermediate use. This picture is just such as the reader forms in his mind of the field of Boaz:—

"There, too, he form'd the likeness of a field
Crowded with corn, in which the reapers toil'd,
Each with a sharp-tooth'd sickle in his hand.
Along the furrow here, the harvest fell
In frequent handfuls : there, they bound the sheaves.
Three binders of the sheaves their sultry task
All plied industrious, and behind them boys
Attended, filling with the corn their arms,
And offering still their bundles to be bound.
Amid them, staff in hand, the master stood
Silent, exulting, while beneath an oak
Apart, his heralds busily prepared
The banquet, dressing a well-thriven ox
New slain, and the attendant maidens mix'd
Large supper for the hinds, of whitest flour."—*Iliad*, xviii.
(*Cowper*).

The "vinegar" has engaged some attention, from its being something much apart from our own usages. Some have questioned whether it was vinegar at all, rather supposing that it was some weak acid wine, such as the small table wine of France and Germany. We would rather take it to be proper "vinegar," which the Jewish writers describe as being used for its refrigerating qualities, by those who laboured hard in the heat of the sun. Such was the ancient opinion of its virtue in this respect; and Pliny describes it as being refreshing to the spirits, binding and bracing the nerves, and very sustaining and strengthening for labour. It is said to be still used in Italy in harvest time when the weather is hot. It seems that in that country they anciently used, and still use, instead of wine, vinegar mixed with a good deal of water, which they call household wine, to which it is said that if oil and bread be added it makes a cooling meal, good for labourers and travellers in the heat of the sun. The use of vinegar by reapers is alluded to by Theocritus in his tenth Idyl. This is supposed to be what the Targum means by pottage boiled in vinegar. We know also that the Romans

had an "embammia," or sauce made of vinegar, in which they dipped their food. We have ourselves a vinegar sauce, with herbs, to use with lamb, which is not improbably derived from the sauce used by the Jews with the paschal lamb, the same into which our Lord dipped the sop He gave to His betrayer. The "mint" which we commonly use may represent the "bitter herbs" used by the Hebrews at the passover; for the sauce which the law prescribed to be used with the paschal lamb, was probably not confined to that occasion. Here, in like manner, Ruth is directed to "dip her morsel in the vinegar."

At the refection itself, which followed soon, it is stated that "she sat beside the reapers." This is a point of more importance than the cursory reader might suppose. It has been imagined by many, from the analogy of modern eastern customs, that men and women among the ancient Israelites did not eat together; but this passage affords evidence to the contrary, and is, we apprehend, the only passage which clearly shows that they did. This is one among many indications which confirm us in the opinion we have long entertained, that the women among the Israelites enjoyed far more social freedom than is now allowed to them in Western Asia, and that we should often err in representing their condition too rigidly by comparisons drawn from the existing customs of the East. It may indeed be urged that the customs of the harvest field do not adequately illustrate, in this respect, common domestic usages. And to this we are unprovided with any satisfactory answer, as we do not recollect any other scriptural instance of the two sexes taking their meals together. What we mean to say is, that according to the present customs of the East, the incident, as here described, could not have occurred even in the harvest field.

Of this meal Boaz himself partook with his reapers; for it is said that "he reached her parched corn, and she did eat." Of this parched corn we may allow Dr. Robinson to speak, under date May 22, on the road from Gaza to Hebron: —"The crops of grain were good. In one field, as we approached Ruheibeh, nearly two hundred reapers and gleaners were at work; the latter being nearly as numerous as the former. A few were taking their refreshment, and offered us some of their parched corn. In the season of harvest the grains of wheat, not yet fully dry and hard, are roasted in a pan, or on an iron plate, and constitute a very palatable article of food: this is eaten along with bread, or instead of it. Indeed, the use of it is so common at this season among the labouring classes, that this parched wheat is sold in the markets. The Arabs are said to prefer it to rice; but this we did not find to be the case. The whole scene of the reapers, the gleaners, and their parched corn, gave us a lively representation of the story of Ruth and the ancient harvest-home in the fields of Boaz." He adds: "Of the vinegar mentioned in the same chapter we saw nothing."

There is another mode of parching corn in the East, very similar to that which still exists in the Western Islands of Scotland, where this mode is called *gradden*, from the Irish word *grad*, signifying quick. A woman, sitting down, takes a handful of corn, holding it by the stalks in the left hand, and then sets fire to the ears, which are presently in a flame: she has a stick in her right hand, which she manages very dexterously, beating off the grain at the very instant when the husk is quite burnt: and experience has taught the people this art to perfection. The corn may be so dressed, winnowed, ground, and baked within an hour after being reaped from the ground. This and other analogies between eastern usages and such as now or recently subsisted in the Highlands and Western Islands of Scotland, go some way to substantiate Mr. Urquhart's claim of an eastern origin for the ancestors of the inhabitants of these localities.

It is customary at the present day throughout Palestine, and especially in the mountain districts, for the inhabitants to leave their houses, and take up their abode during harvest in the fields, and on the threshing-floors. Each family usually erects a rude arbour of branches, or, where these cannot be obtained, an awning of canvas or hairweb is constructed, under which the labourers rest during the mid-day heat, and the children sleep at night. To this arbour or awning the name "house" is given.

A large water-bottle of skin or earthenware is universally found in the harvest field, and sometimes the water has to be brought from a great distance. I have also seen in Lebanon men and women sitting together at meal-time on such occasions; the latter always a little in the background, but still stretching out their hands and dipping their bread in the common dish of viands. In Mohammedan districts this never occurs.

P.

THRESHING

Ruth 2:17-3:2

THE book of Ruth is so rich in its indications of Oriental and ancient Hebrew customs, that, in dealing with them, we are—to use an *appropriate* figure—but as gleaners in the harvest field which it offers.

We are told that Ruth, having continued her gleaning until the evening, then "beat out what she had gleaned." This is contrary to our custom, for our gleaners carry home the corn with the straw. One reason for this may be, that the gleaners were more bountifully treated among the Hebrews, and were thus enabled to collect a quantity of corn greater than they could conveniently transport with the straw. This was certainly the case with Ruth; for her corn, when threshed out, formed no less than "about an ephah of barley," being not much less than a bushel. This produce of one woman's gleaning for one day would not be regarded with much satisfaction by our cultivators. Nor was it usual among the Hebrews; for the surprise of Naomi was excited when her daughter-in-law brought home the rich produce of her day's labour. But Ruth had been specially favoured through the delicate attention of Boaz, who had privately instructed the reapers to let fall some of the handfuls, and leave them on purpose that she might glean them, and to suffer her to glean even among the sheaves without rebuke. This custom of beating out the corn upon the harvest field still subsists in Palestine. Robinson remarks, in passing a harvest field near Gaza: "Several women were beating out with a stick handfuls of the grain which they seemed to have gleaned."

Corn, though more bulky in the straw, is with us more conveniently carried in that form; and one reason for threshing it out on the spot, doubtless arose from the facility which the dress of the eastern woman afforded for carrying away the corn when separated from the straw. It will have occurred to the reader to ask how Ruth could bear away nearly sixty pounds weight of corn. One of our own women could carry corn only in her apron, and she could not carry much of it so, lest the strings should break or be loosened. But the eastern woman has an unfailing resource in such cases in her veil. It was in this that Ruth, on a subsequent occasion, bore away a still larger quantity of corn that Boaz presented her with at the threshing-floor. This

EGYPTIAN VEILS

veil is, among poor women, made of cloth quite strong enough for such services, and coarse enough not to be damaged by them: for these, indeed, it is much used. Its amplitude, and its sufficiency for the purpose, as well as the manner of wearing it, may be seen from the engraving.

In the East corn is not stacked, as with us, and taken to be threshed as occasion requires. All but the last process of grinding the corn is performed at once, upon or close by the harvest field, and forms part of the proper labour of the harvest season. Thus we find that Boaz not only threshed his corn, but winnowed it immediately after it was reaped. In this state, ready for the mill, all corn is stored away in the East until it may be required for use.

Both the threshing and the winnowing are performed in the open air. This would be impossible with us, on account of the uncertainty of the weather. But the Syrian agriculturist has no thought of the weather at harvest time. He *knows* it will not rain, and therefore makes all his arrangements accordingly. Rain in the time of harvest was so much out of the course of nature, that when at that season thunder and rain came at the call of Samuel, it was recognized by all the people as a miraculous sign. (1 Sam. xii. 17, 18.) This gives a degree of certainty and regularity to the labours of harvest, which strangely contrasts with the anxiety, interruption, haste, and pressing labour which accompany that season in our more variable climes, where

the most arduous and unintermitting exertions are often necessary to secure the crop in some possibly brief interval of fine weather. Hence not only days, but often nights, of toil in harvest time. The eastern cultivator may also labour by night; yet it is not from haste or apprehension, but to avoid the oppressive heat of the day, or, in the case of winnowing, to take advantage of the evening breeze.

The threshing-floor is a clear and level space upon the ground, laid with a well beaten compost of clay and cow-dung. The small quantity of corn which rewards the industry of the gleaner may be beaten out with a staff; but the large produce of the harvest field is never thus dealt with in the East. It is either beaten out by the frequent treading of cattle, or forced out by some heavy implement being dragged over it. The former was the more ancient and common mode, and is often alluded to in Scripture. The sheaves being opened out upon the floor, the grain is trodden usually by oxen, arranged from three to five abreast, and driven in a circle, or indeed in any direction, over the floor.

It was one of the lesser laws of mercy, of which many are found in the books of Moses, that the oxen engaged in this labour should not be muzzled to prevent them from tasting the corn.[1] This freedom of the labouring animals is now the rule throughout the East; nor do we remember, in any instance in which the operation came under our own notice, to have seen them subject to any restraint in this respect. It is probable that the harvest of Boaz was threshed by oxen. But this is not certain, for we find

THRESHING BY TREADING OF ANIMALS

threshing instruments in use not far from Bethlehem in the time of David, to whom Araunah offers them for fuel, and the oxen by which they were drawn for sacrifice.[2] Their existence is

[1] Deuteronomy 25:4.   [2] 2 Samuel 24:22.

also implied in the expression which occurs in Scripture, "made them like the dust by threshing,"[1] which is a result not so much of the treading of cattle, as of the working of the

THRESHING BY THE DRAG

threshing implement, which cuts up the straw, and makes it fit for fodder. The ancient Hebrews seem to have possessed both of the implements now in use. One of them, represented in the annexed figure, is very much used in Syria. It is composed of two thick boards fastened together side by side, and bent upward in front, to prevent its course from being obstructed by accumulations of straw. The under part is furnished with rough stones, embedded in holes made for the purpose, and sometimes with iron spikes instead of stones. This is commonly drawn over the corn by oxen, a man or boy standing upon it to increase the weight.

THRESHING BY THE SLEDGE

The other consists of a frame, in which are fixed three rollers, armed with iron teeth, and

[1] 2 Kings 13:7.

surmounted by a seat, in which the driver sits—not so much for his own ease, as to add the advantage of his weight. It is drawn by two oxen, and breaks up the straw more effectually than the one first described, and is in other respects a better implement; but it is not now often seen in Palestine, though often enough in other parts of Syria, and very common in Egypt.

The winnowing was performed by throwing up the grain with a fork against the wind, by which the chaff and broken straw were dispersed, and the grain fell to the ground. The grain was afterwards passed through a sieve, to separate the morsels of earth and other impurities; and it then underwent a final purification, by being tossed up with wooden scoops, or short-handed shovels, such as we see figured in the monuments of Egypt.

WINNOWING CORN

How exactly the ancient agricultural customs of the book of Ruth are preserved to this day in Palestine, may be seen from the following extract from Robinson:—"The wheat harvest here in the mountains (or Hebron) had not yet (May 24) arrived; but they were threshing barley, adas or lentiles, and also vetches, called by the Arabs kersenna, which are raised chiefly for camels. The various parcels had apparently lain here for several days; the people would come with their cattle and work for two or three hours, and then go away. Some had three animals, some four; and once I saw two young cattle and a donkey driven round together.[1] In several of the floors they were now winnowing the grain by tossing it up against the wind with a fork.

"Here are needed no guards around the tent. The owners of the crops came every night and slept upon their threshing floors to guard them; and this we found to be uni-

[1] This conjunction, even in labour, of diverse animals, was forbidden by the law of Moses in ploughing, which prohibition must also have extended to threshing. The ox and ass are particularly mentioned, and the instance before us gives the practice against which the injunction was levelled. The unequal nature of the animals must have rendered the conjunction distressing to both, and the horns of the ox could not but have been of some annoyance to the ass.

versal in all the region of Gaza. We were here in the midst of scenes precisely like those of the book of Ruth, where Boaz winnowed barley, and laid himself down at night to guard the heap of corn."[1] The custom is by no means confined to the neighbourhood of Gaza. Throughout the East, the owner guards thus the precious produce of his fields at night while it is exposed—and that in person, like Boaz, unless he is a very great man indeed, or unless he has sons to perform the duty for him. Boaz had no sons; and although he had an overseer of the labours of the field, he watched his corn in person, that too great temptation to connive at depredation might not be placed in the way of persons whose interest was not altogether one with his own.

I remember, some years ago, when travelling on the Spanish side of the Pyrenees, being struck with the practice there of threshing corn by means of oxen. The sheaves were scattered on the ground, and the cattle were driven over them thus spread out, round and round in a circle. The preservation of an Oriental custom in this region of the West is very curious; and its introduction must be attributed to the Moors, who were masters in the country. Other signs of eastern life in the same neighbourhood I also witnessed, such as the shepherd leading his sheep.

S.

THE LEVIRATE LAW [2]

Ruth 3-4

ACCORDING to the custom described yesterday, Boaz went one night at the close of the harvest, and lay down at the end of the heap of corn which had been winnowed. When he was fast asleep, a woman came into the field, and approaching very softly, uncovered his feet, and lay down there. At midnight the man awoke, and was much startled to find some one lying at his feet; he then turned himself, and perceived that it was a woman.

The incident thus far has been well illustrated by Mrs. Postans:[3] "Natives of the East care little for sleeping accommodation, but rest where weariness overcomes them, lying on the ground. They are, however, careful to cover their feet, and to do this have a chudda, or sheet of coarse cloth, that they tuck under the feet, and drawing it up over the body, suffer it to cover the face and head. An Oriental seldom changes his position, and we are told that Boaz did so because 'he was afraid;' the covering of the feet, in ordinary cases, is consequently not disturbed. I have frequently observed the singular effect of this custom when riding out in a native city before dawn; figures with their feet so covered, lying like monumental effigies in the pathway, and in the open verandahs of the houses—a practice that at once explains the necessity for closing the city gates when it is dark, as we read was the case at Jericho, in Josh. ii. Neither men nor women alter their dress at night; and the labouring class, or travellers in a serai, where there are men, women, and children, rest together, the men with their feet covered, and the women wrapped in their veils or sarees."

Boaz soon found that the woman was Ruth. She had come thither at the suggestion of Naomi, who informed her that Boaz was the nearest kinsman of her deceased husband; and seeing that he had died childless, on him, according to the old patriarchal practice, adopted by the law of Moses, devolved the duty of making her his wife, in order that, if she had children, the eldest should be counted the legal heir of the deceased, so that his name might not be lost in Israel, nor his heritage pass into another family. This was a public duty which a man could not refuse to discharge without discredit; and it was of great importance to the woman, seeing that her place in the social system of the Hebrews, and all the consideration that belonged to motherhood, depended on it. We see an ancient instance of this in the anxiety which Tamar manifested that the conditions of this obligation should not be left unaccomplished. (Gen. xxxviii.) To Naomi it was of special importance; for if Ruth married thus, the first child to which she gave birth would be accounted as belonging to Naomi's deceased son—therefore her grandson; and she would thus be once more restored to her place as a mother in Israel.

This was the mode in which Ruth was to claim from Boaz the discharge of this solemn duty to the living and to the dead. The act is strange

[1] *Biblical Researches*, ii. 445, 446.
[2] This term is usually employed to designate the law which required the nearest relative to marry the widow of a man who had died childless.
[3] *Journal of Sacred Literature*, iv. 48.

and startling to us. It must be accounted for, partly by the customs already alluded to, partly by the simple manners of these ancient times, and much by the consideration of the difference of ideas as to modest demeanour in different ages and nations. Thus, for instance, the exposure of the face to public gaze, is at this day regarded as the height of infamy and immodesty by an Eastern woman, which yet with us is the common practice, and is consistent with the most perfect decorum. We can hardly suppose that so serious and godly a woman as Naomi would have given such counsel had there been anything, according to the views of the times, conventionally wrong in it, or calculated to offend the moral sense of the age. Had that been so, she must have been aware of the danger of disgusting such a man as Boaz, instead of ensuring his protection; and we think that *his* appreciation of at least the *motive* of the proceeding, must be regarded as stamping its true character, when he emphatically declared, "All the city of my people do know that thou art a virtuous woman." It shows, at all events, the perfect confidence which Naomi had in the virtue of Ruth, and in the honour of Boaz, whom indeed she regarded as already, in the eye of the law, the husband of her son's widow.

It seems to have been necessary that the woman, in this case, should claim from the kinsman the performance of this duty in a certain form, by saying to him, as Ruth does now, "Spread thy skirt over thine handmaid, for thou art a near kinsman." This, although essentially figurative, has some literal meaning in it; for, even to this day, it is customary among the Jews for a man to throw the skirt of his talith or prayer-veil over his spouse, and cover her head with it. We still think, however, that the *occasion* for making this demand was unusual, and to a certain degree indiscreet. This may be gathered from the anxiety which Boaz himself eventually expressed—while doing the utmost honour to her character and motives—that it should not be known a woman had been there. He must have feared that evil tongues might misconstrue, to his and her discredit, a proceeding far from evil when rightly understood. It is not unlikely that, when this matter had been first suggested by Naomi, Ruth, as a stranger, had shrunk from making this claim publicly in the harvest field, and that Naomi had, therefore, to spare her in that respect, devised this mode of

enabling her to do so in private, in which she would find less difficulty, seeing that Boaz had already won her confidence by his fatherly consideration for her. It may be that the desire to evade one difficulty, somewhat blinded this good woman to the danger that may have lurked in the other alternative.

Boaz cordially responded to the claim; but he informed Ruth that Naomi had laboured under a mistake. There was a kinsman nearer than himself on whom the right devolved. If, as was possible, that kinsman should decline to assume the obligation, then, said Boaz, "will I do the part of kinsman to thee, as the Lord liveth."

The next day he accordingly took the necessary measures for bringing the matter to a close. All the circumstances of the process are interesting and suggestive; but we must forbear to dwell upon more than one or two of them. In those days, and in the absence of lawyers and written documents, public business was, as we have before had occasion to observe, transacted in the gates of towns, both for convenience of attendance, and to ensure the presence of witnesses. The elders of the town seem to have been in the habit of repairing thither to transact such affairs in the early morning, when the people would be going forth to their business at the market, or in the fields. So Boaz went to the gate; and when the nearer kinsman passed by, he called him aside, and requested ten of the elders present to give particular attention, as witnesses, to the proceedings.

Knowing the man he had to deal with, Boaz began with the circumstances involved in the transaction, instead of with what was really its main feature. He apprised him that Naomi meant to sell for her present necessities such right as remained with her in the lands of her husband: the right of purchase, he added, belonged to the person he addressed as nearest of kin; but if he declined, Boaz himself stood next, and was ready to make the purchase. The man liked the land, and declared himself ready to do what was expected from him. But on being apprised that it was clogged with the condition of marrying the widow of Naomi's son, in order that the first-born might take the heritage of this land in the name of the deceased, the land lost all value in his eyes, and he declined, lest he should "mar his own inheritance." Some have thought from this that he was married and had children already, and disliked the increased burden and divided inheritance. We think otherwise; for the custom is understood to have been, that when the case was not that of a *brother's* widow, the next of kin to the deceased was relieved from the obligation of making her his wife if he already had

CITY GATE

children. It would therefore seem, that the man before us rather felt the objection to be, that his first-born son, with the uncertainty that there would be any other, would be counted the son and heir of a dead man.

In the law itself, the course directed to be taken was this:—When a man's brother refused to marry the widow, she was to go up to the gate and complain to the elders: "My husband's brother refuseth to raise up unto his brother a name in Israel." Then the elders were to call the man; and if he persisted in his refusal, the woman was to come forward and "loose his shoe from off his foot, and spit in his face," and was to say, "So shall it be done unto that man that will not build up his brother's house." [1] It would seem, however, that when the man was not a brother, the more ignominious part of this ceremony was omitted; for, in the case before us, the man took off his own shoe, and delivered it to Boaz, to signify that he transferred his right to him.

Except in a recent work,[2] which contains much

[1] Deuteronomy 25:5-10.
[2] Urquhart's *Pillars of Hercules*, i. 305. Lond. 1850.

notice of the Jews in a country (Barbary) where their simple ancient customs are perhaps better preserved than in many other parts, we have not seen any notice of the subsisting use of the shoe in connection with Jewish marriage ceremonies: "At a Jewish marriage, I was standing beside the bridegroom when the bride entered; and, as she crossed the threshold, *he stooped down and slipped off his shoe,* and struck her with the heel on the nape of the neck. I at once saw the interpretation of the passage in Scripture respecting the transfer of the shoe to another, in case the brother-in-law did not exercise his privilege. The slipper being taken off in-doors, or if not, left outside the apartment, is placed at the edge of the small carpets upon which you sit, and is at hand to administer correction, and is here used in sign of the obedience of the wife and the supremacy of the husband. The Highland custom is to strike for "good luck," as they say, the bride with an old slipper. Little do they suspect the meaning implied. The regalia of Morocco is enriched with a pair of embroidered slippers, which are, or used to be carried before the Sultan, as among us the sceptre or sword of state."

It is observed by Dr. Plumtree, that "The fact, not mentioned in the Old Testament, but preserved in the traditional genealogies of the House of David, that Boaz was himself the son of Rahab—of one who, by the law, suffered under a twofold taint, as an alien and a harlot (Matt. i. 5)—may explain the absence of any reluctance on his part, to contract marriage with one who, though a proselyte in faith, was an alien in blood, belonging to the races which, though not formally prohibited by the law of Moses, were considered by the stricter Judaism of later times, to be among those between whom and Israel there was to be neither giving nor taking in marriage. If we believe the book to have been written at a time when that aversion was gaining strength, we may even assume that the writer wrote with a conscious purpose, as desiring to teach what, at all events, he taught unconsciously, that the favour of God flows out beyond the visible limits within which it is more conspicuously manifested. Even then, in the midst of so much that seemed, and actually was, narrow and exclusive, there was a witness borne that God is no respecter of persons, but that in every nation he that feareth God and worketh righteousness, is accepted with Him."--*Bible Educator*, vol. iii., 258.

S.

RUTH'S RECOMPENSE

Ruth 4:13-22

UPON a monument which has already outlasted thrones and empires, and which will endure until there be a new heaven and a new earth—upon the front page of the New Testament, is inscribed the name of RUTH. Of her came David—of her came a long line of illustrious and good men—of her came Christ.

These were great honours. Little did this poor foreign woman think, when she left her native home to comfort the destitution of her mother-in-law—little did she suppose when she humbly sought leave of Boaz's servant to glean in his master's field—little, when she laboured homeward beneath the burden of her corn—what high distinctions awaited her. She was, by her marriage with Boaz, raised to perhaps the highest station which a woman in Israel could at that time attain, as the wife of one of the most prosperous and influential elders of Bethlehem. Henceforth nothing of comfort or honour was lacking to her ; and, although her husband probably died before her, for he seems to have been advanced in years, the station she occupied as the mother of his son—the heir of a twofold inheritance—gave her a consideration no less honourable and exalted than that which she had before enjoyed. But far above that was her interest in the great future, in which was given to *her* that part for which the women of Israel sighed, which was the object of their most intense desires, excited by the ancient prophecies, that from the seed of Abraham should come the bruiser of the serpent's head—HE in whom all the nations of the earth were to be blessed.

But there was a cause. That cause was the faith which God had enabled her, under most peculiar and trying circumstances, to exercise for His glory. To her was given the opportunity which, in the even tenor of their way, few women

in that age could find, of honouring God conspicuously by the greatness of her decision—by the marked manner in which she forsook her paternal gods for Him, and cast in her lot with His people. It was no mean sacrifice. One of a nature so affectionate as hers, could not but feel the rending of the human ties, interwoven with most of her past existence, which that decision involved. She did not the less feel the ties she left behind, because she preferred those that lay before. So far as the human abnegation of self is concerned, women have made as great sacrifices for husbands—for children—for parents. They did their duty. She made her sacrifices for her mother-in-law—a relation not usually of the highest or tenderest nature—not so exacting as the others upon the score of duty. No one could have blamed her had she, like Orpah, kissed her mother-in-law, and bidden her farewell. Many would have said that that was the right and proper decision for her to make. But Ruth thought not so ; she failed not in the trial. God upheld her heavy heart. The words passed—to be no more recalled, no more repented off—" Thy people shall be my people, and thy God, my God." There is more in this than simple regard for Naomi, though so mixed with it as to escape much of the attention to which it is entitled.

Ruth, brought up amid the low and limited ideas of the Godhead which idolatry presented, and knowing nothing better than the degrading worship of Chemosh, had learned from this Hebrew family the pure and grand conception of Jehovah's nature, attributes, and government, which He had disclosed to the chosen people ; and she had been privileged to observe most narrowly the effect of these views in the consistent conduct and beautiful life of this pious household. This won her heart ; she feared to have anything more to do with idols. This God should be hers—this privileged people hers, even unto death. That this is the right view of her conduct is shown by what Boaz said to her in the harvest field—which, indeed, evinces further that this is the impression concerning her which was generally entertained,—for Boaz knew her then only from the appreciation of her motives and feelings which was current in Bethlehem. " It hath fully been shown me," he said, " all that thou hast done to thy mother-in-law since the death of thine husband ; and how thou hast left thy father and thy mother, and the land of thy nativity, and art come to a people which thou knewest not heretofore. The Lord recompense thy work; and a full reward be given thee of the Lord God of Israel, under whose wings thou art come to trust."

Boaz knew—and we know better than Ruth herself did—that from the moment she had cast her world behind her back, and thrown herself in simple trust upon God, His blessing surrounded her and overshadowed her, and would not fail to be manifested in due time. Those that honour Him, He will honour; and as she had honoured Him by her faith, He was bound, by all His covenants of mercy, to honour her before men and angels. Boaz knew that godliness has the promise of this life, and of the life to come; he knew that they who truly fear God, and yield up anything for Him, are entitled to look for the recompense of reward, which in due time they shall receive to the full—double measure, and pressed down, and running over—if they faint not. Boaz knew all this when these words were uttered; but he did not then know the important part secured for himself in the providence of God, in being the instrument of blessing to her, and of sending down, through her, blessings to distant generations.

It is admitted that the blessings of the Old Testament have generally a more material character than there is any reason to expect, since the Gospel brought life and immortality—the blessings beyond the grave—into fuller light than had previously shone upon them. Yet God is one, and He has at all times taken pleasure in the prosperity of His servants, although He has retained the right to judge wherein the *true* prosperity of all His servants lies. He has fixed *our* eyes upon the treasures of heaven, and has taught us to garner up all our hopes there. Yet He has not shortened His own hand, nor precluded Himself from allowing His servants so much temporal prosperity as may be safely permitted to them, without danger to their great spiritual inheritance. If He give trouble, if He withhold prosperity, it is for our sakes; it is owing to the weakness of our hearts; it is because we cannot endure much prosperity without finding this world becoming too dear to us, and our desires less fervent for the treasures which He has laid up for those that fear Him. No doubt, if man, who is but dust, were able to bear worldly prosperity uninjured, it might be

otherwise; and if, indeed, there be those who, through His grace, are so strong in faith, so raised above the world, as to be able to bear an unbroken flow of temporal blessing, that may be their lot, and in fact is their lot, so far as their real welfare will allow. Indeed, the words of our Lord Himself respecting such as had left all to follow Him, furnish the best commentary and most striking parallel to the words which Boaz addressed to the woman who had, according to the light of her day, left all, that she might come to put her trust under Jehovah's wings: "Verily I say unto you, that there is no man that hath left house, or brethren, or sisters, or father, or mother, or wife, or children, or lands, for my sake, and the Gospel's, but he shall receive an hundred-fold now in this time, houses, and brethren, and sisters, and mothers, and children, and lands, with persecutions; and in the world to come, eternal life." (Mark x. 29, 30.) This is as ample a promise as any the Old Testament contains of earthly blessedness, for its language is "now, in this time," with the Gospel addition of far more distinct and still greater blessings for the world to come—the blessings of eternal life—than any which the Old Testament affords. This magnificent extension of the promise richly counterweighs the Gospel limitation of "with persecutions," as connected with blessing in this world. But, indeed, that also is part of the blessing; seeing that it pledges that God's fatherly care is to intermix the temporal benefits afforded to us with such trials as may be needful to hedge up our way, and to prevent the blessings of the life that now is from becoming too dear to us, and from leading us to forget that we are but strangers here, in the midst of all the enjoyments that may be afforded to us in this house of our pilgrimage.

TWO WIVES

1 Samuel 1:1-12

THE first chapter of the first book of Samuel is of peculiar interest, from the picture of domestic life which it offers; from its furnishing the only description in the Old Testament of the visit of a family to the place of ritual service at the yearly festivals; and from the glimpses which are afforded in it of the course of proceeding on such occasions at the holy place.

The opening of the chapter presents to us the singular spectacle of a man in a private station possessed of two wives. Not long since we had occasion to allude to this case, and to remark that, although a plurality of wives was not forbidden by the law of Moses, the possession of more than one was exceedingly rare, except among chiefs and princes, as is still the case in those eastern countries where the same permission exists. The popular feeling, even in the presence of such a permissive law is, and we have reason to suppose was, averse to the exercise of this privilege, except in particular cases. This is evinced by the notion of some old Jewish commentators on the case before us, that one of this man's wives was childless, as a punishment upon him for having taken more than one. This shows the tendency of Jewish opinion; and among the Jews at this day, polygamy is scarcely ever practised, even in those eastern countries where the public law offers no restriction. In this particular instance, however, it is likely that Elkanah had taken a second wife only because the first had given him no children. As to the modern Orientals, the country in which polygamy most prevails is Persia; but even there it is not common to find a man who has more than one wife. The extent to which public feeling is against it, especially among the women themselves, may be judged of from a curious native book, on *The Customs and Manners of the Women in Persia*.[1] In this we read—"That man is to be praised who confines himself to one wife; for if he takes two it is wrong, and he will certainly repent of his folly. Thus say the seven wise women:

> "'Be that man's life immersed in gloom
>   Who weds more wives than one:
> With one his cheeks retain their bloom,
>   His voice a cheerful tone;
> These speak his honest heart at rest,
> And he and she are always blest.
> But when with two he seeks for joy,
> Together they his soul annoy;
> With two no sunbeam of delight
> Can make his day of misery bright.'"

To this the translator adds in a note:—"The learned seven have here, as indeed on all occasions, meritoriously shown a proper regard for

[1] Translated by James Atkinson, Esq., for the Oriental Translation Fund, among whose publications it appears. London, 1832.

strictly moral conduct, and the happiness of domestic life. They very justly insist upon it, that a man ought not to be burdened with more than one wife at a time, being satisfied that the management of two is beyond his power, if not impossible." To this effect he quotes the sentiments of a widow, named Wali, as expressed in the old Eastern drama of "The Sultan:"—

> "Wretch! wouldst thou have another wedded slave?
>   Another! What, another! At thy peril
>   Presume to try th' experiment; wouldst thou not
>   For that unconscionable, foul desire,
>   Be linked to misery? Sleepless nights and days
>   Of endless torment,—still recurring sorrow
>   Would be thy lot. Two wives! O never, never.
>   Thou hast not power to please two rival queens;
>   Their tempers would destroy thee, sear thy brain;
>   Thou canst not, Sultan, manage more than one!
>   Even one may be beyond thy government."

To these Mr. Atkinson adds the short but decisive testimony of Mirza Abu Taleb Khan:—"*From what I know*, it is easier to live with two tigresses than with two wives."

All the discomfort which these popular Oriental notions on the subject allot to him who dares to take two wives, was realized in the fullest extent by Elkanah. It is in some degree the story of Jacob and his wives over again, though it would appear that the fortunate wife Peninnah, the one favoured with children, was more outrageous than Leah; while the childless one, Hannah, was certainly a more meek and pious woman than Rachel. As in that case, so also in this, the childless wife seems to have been the one whom the husband best loved. At least it is said, as if to point a contrast, that "he loved her," although the Lord had shut up her womb.

The man was a Levite, and hence it peculiarly behoved him to be heedful to all the requirements of the law. By the law it was obligatory only upon the adult males to visit the place of the Lord's house at the three yearly festivals. But it seems that pious persons took their wives and families with them. Thus Joseph took his wife Mary, and her son, the blessed Jesus, with him when he went up to Jerusalem at the passover. We account for that instance by observing that this was when our Lord was of the age of twelve years, and that at that age the obligation upon the males to attend the great festivals commenced. But from the case before us, we learn that whole families were taken to these holy solemnities; for Elkanah was accompanied not only by his two wives, but by the children of Peninnah—not only by the sons, but by the daughters. It seems that on these occasions, Peninnah was wont to make a special display of her ill-will towards, and contempt of Hannah, by reason of her having no children, and of her abortive prayers from year to year for that coveted blessing. From day to day poor Hannah was at home subject to these insults, and could then bear them better, because they were unwitnessed by others. But as they journeyed in company with their neighbours to Shiloh, and there consorted with them, the bitter sarcasms of Peninnah became more pointed, from her desire of mortifying and degrading her rival in the presence of others; and they were then, in such goodly company, the more keenly felt by her who was the object of them. She had reason; for in Israel childlessness was not only a privation, but a disgrace; and we may calculate that the most good-natured and considerate of the company, would scarcely suppress a smile at the cruel taunts which Peninnah delighted to shower upon Hannah's head. Sad was the contrast. There was the loquacious mother surrounded by her children—children afraid to manifest any of the kind attentions which their little hearts might prompt, towards one whom their mother hated; and there was Hannah by herself alone, destitute of all the little charities and kind solicitudes of motherhood, and possessed of no comfort but in God, and in the kind attentions of her husband's unalienable love, which, indeed, enfolded her like a mantle, though it availed little to protect her from the keen shafts of a woman's scurrilous tongue.

At these festivals, it was usual for those who possessed the means, to present some lawful animal as a peace-offering; and after it had been slain, and the priest had taken his portion —the breast and the right shoulder—the rest was returned to the offerer, with which he might feast his family and such friends as he invited to partake of it. On this occasion, Elkanah failed not to give Peninnah and her sons and daughters becoming portions; but he signalized his esteem for Hannah, and his desire to comfort her with some mark of distinguishing attention, by the truly Oriental mark of consideration, such as Joseph had in former times shown to Benjamin, of giving her "a worthy portion,"

which some think to have been a double portion, but others suppose to have been a choice and dainty part of the meat. Such marks of regard on the part of the husband gave new venom to the sting of Peninnah's cruel tongue, whereat Hannah's grief of heart was such, that she could not taste the dainties Elkanah's love provided. He, on his part, was greatly touched by her affliction, and sought to comfort her. "Hannah, why weepest thou? and why eatest thou not? and why is thy heart grieved? am I not better to thee than ten sons?" Some think from this that Peninnah had made him the father of ten sons. But it seems rather that the number is indefinitely used to express the thought, that the share she had in his affection—the assurance of his unalterable regard—ought to be as much a source of comfort to her as the possession of *many* children. There is, however, the more significance in this, if, as there is some reason to think, a woman who had given birth to ten sons was, as among the Arabians, deemed entitled to distinguished honours. In the Bedouin romance of *Antar* we read:—"Now it was a custom among the Arabs, that when a woman brought forth ten male children, she should be Moonejeba, that is, ennobled, and for her name to be published among the Arabs, and they used to say that such an one is ennobled."

Although sensible of her husband's affection, the heart of Hannah was too deeply wounded to receive all the comfort his words were designed to convey. She had one resource—the best resource for the people of God in all ages, and under all the troubles that afflict them. When the meal was over, she quietly withdrew, and went to the tabernacle, where, being in great "bitterness of soul," she "prayed unto the Lord, and wept sore." The prayer ended with a vow, that if the Lord would indeed remember her, and bless her with a man-child, that child should be "given unto the Lord all the days of his life, and there should no razor come upon his head." This means that he should be a Nazarite for life; and this is the only instance recorded of such life devotement, spontaneously imposed by the parent before the birth of the child. In the other instances, those of Samson and John the Baptist, the obligation was imposed by the will of God. Here, it will be observed, that any male child which might be born to her would, as a Levite, be already given to the Lord. But the period of the Levites' service did not begin till thirty years of age, and it was Hannah's meaning that he should be devoted to the Lord's service even from infancy, besides being under the vow of a Nazarite. It may further be noted, that a wife had no right to make a vow of this nature without the concurrence of her husband, or at least that, if made, he might disallow it if it met not his approval. We may, therefore, be sure that it had the after consent of Elkanah, without which it would have had no force. The law on this point may be seen in Num. xxx. 6-8.

It also well deserves our attention, that it is in this prayer of Hannah that God is, for the first time in Scripture, addressed as "the LORD OF HOSTS,"—a magnificent title, which describes Jehovah as the Creator and Master of the universe and its heavenly bodies, which are expressed in Scripture as "the hosts of heaven." The title, indeed, occurs in the early part of the chapter, but it is there the word of the historian, and therefore posterior in point of time to this use of it by Hannah. We may infer that it had before this come into use in designed opposition to the worship of the heavenly bodies, which had, in this age, under one name or another, become universally prevalent.

The birth-place of the prophet Samuel demands a passing notice. Elkanah, his father, is described as "a certain man of *Ramathaim-zophim*, of Mount Ephraim." In the nineteenth verse, however, of this chapter, the town is called *Ramah*. The English reader may see some difficulty here, but it is easily explained. *Ramah* signifies "a height;" and *Ramathaim* is the dual form, "two heights." The town was probably built on a double hill ; popularly it may have been called simply Ramah, and more definitely Ramathaim. There were many Ramahs in Palestine— cities set upon hills ; hence this one was distinguished by the additional appellative *Zophim*. The most natural explanation of the latter appears to be this : *Zuph* was one of Samuel's ancestors, who, having migrated from his house in Ephrata (1 Sam. i. 1, with 1 Chron. vi. 35), settled in a district which was thence called "the land of Zuph" (1 Sam. ix. 5). Ramah, or Ramathaim, was the chief town of the district, and was therefore called *Ramathaim-zophim*, that is, "Ramah of the Zuphites."

The site of Ramathaim is unknown. All the researches of recent geographers have failed in discovering it. The most probable view is, that it was situated in the tribe of Judah, near the confines of Benjamin, and not far distant from the sepulchre of Rachel. For fuller information on this interesting question of Biblical geography, the student may consult Kitto's *Cyclopædia of Biblical Literature*, third edition, under the article *Ramathaim-zophim*.

P.

A LOAN TO THE LORD

1 Samuel 1:13-28; 2:18-21

IN the time of Samson, the high priest seems to have been Eli, who probably also exercised the civic functions of judge, which, by the theocratical constitution of the state, naturally devolved upon the high priest, in the absence of the kind of dictatorship which "the judges," raised up from time to time, exercised. Some exception may be made in respect of such authority as may have been conceded to Samson in the tribes of Dan and Judah ; but from the death of that hero, we must regard Eli as exercising alone the authority which belonged to the office.

The last high priest whom the preceding history presents to us is Phinehas, the son of Eleazar, who was Aaron's eldest surviving son, and the succession to the high-priesthood seems to have been the inheritance of that line. But this Eli was descended from Aaron's youngest son, Ithamar. We have no intimation how the change took place. It was not from the failure of the line of Eleazar, for that line subsisted, and was, in the person of Zadok, restored to the priesthood in the time of Solomon. Josephus places three high priests between Phinehas and Eli—the same who are set down by the names of Abishua, Bukki, and Uzzi, in 1 Chron. vi. 50, 51 —where they are placed in the line of Eleazar, so that Eli must have been the first high priest of the line of Ithamar. It is possible that when Uzzi died, his son was too young to exercise the office of high priest ; and that as that office was too essential to the theocratical institutions to remain in abeyance, Eli, as the representative of the line of Ithamar, was appointed to the priesthood in his place. This is a circumstance that often happens in the regal successions of the East ; and we have no reason to suppose that this was a usurpation or an unwarranted intrusion into the high-priesthood on the part of Eli.

Now, when Hannah went to the tabernacle to pour out her grief before the Lord, Eli was sitting "upon a seat by a post of the temple of the Lord." The "temple" is here, of course, the tabernacle— the original word being applicable to any sacred structure appropriated to the service of Jehovah. Sometimes the temple itself, built after this time, is called a tabernacle in Scripture, as in Jer. x. 20. We do not understand that Eli's seat was by a post of the tabernacle itself; for while it may be questioned whether even the high priest had any right to sit there, it is certain that if he had been seated there, Hannah could not have approached near enough for him to mark the movements of her lips, as he did. It would therefore appear, that Eli had a seat by a post at the entrance of the court of the tabernacle, where, probably, he sat as high priest and judge, to give advice in matters of difficulty, and to hear and decide any causes that might be brought before him.

Now we learn that Hannah "spake in her heart; only her lips moved, but her voice was not heard." This is the first instance of muttered prayer *recorded* in Scripture. Prayer is almost always oral in the East, even in public; and that this was the case in Israel, at least at the holy place, is shown by the fact that Eli did not readily comprehend this proceeding of the afflicted woman, but hastened to the conclusion that she had taken too much wine at the feast—in fact, that she was drunken. He therefore rebuked her. It must have seemed to her a great aggravation of her affliction that every one, except her husband—that even the high priest of God— would misunderstand her, and that she must meet with misconstruction and reproof from the very quarter where she was best entitled to look for encouragement and support. She, however, humbly vindicated herself; and Eli, finding he had been mistaken in her, said, "Go in peace; and the God of Israel grant thee thy petition that thou hast asked of Him." She did go in peace. She was no more sad. Her faith sustained her. She was persuaded that her prayer had been accepted of God; and so it was. In due time she had a son, and she called him SAMUEL (asked of God), because she had asked him of God.

From that time Hannah went not up with the family to Shiloh at the festivals. She purposed not to go up until the child should be weaned, and "then she would bring him, that he might appear before the Lord, and there abide for ever." This would suggest a protracted age for weaning, if he was then to be of a fit age to be taken up and left at the tabernacle. In fact, weaning takes place much later in the East than with us. The Mohammedan law prohibits a woman from weaning her child before the expiration of two years from the period of its birth, unless with the consent of her husband. The Jewish commentators generally take the period, in this instance, to have been two years; and we know that the time was sometimes extended to three years or more. But even three years seems too early an age for the child to be taken from the mother, and left in the care of strangers at the tabernacle—especially, if we consider that his destination was to render some service there. There may therefore be something in the observation of an old writer,[1] that there was a three-fold weaning of children in old times: the first, from the mother's milk, when they were three years old; the second, from their tender age and the care of a nurse, when they were seven years of age; and the third, from childish ways, when they reached the age of twelve. We incline to the seven years, which is certainly not too early,—and twelve is perhaps too late; for Hannah, when she re-appeared at the tabernacle with the child, expected that Eli would speedily call to mind their previous interview,—an incident not sufficiently marked, one would think, however important to her, to be remembered after twelve years, by one who had, in the meanwhile, been in the habit of seeing numerous people under every variety of circumstance, from all parts of the land. However, we may not be too positive. Eli was an old man; and twelve years are but a short space to those who are advanced in life. Alas, our years shorten sadly, and pass with rapid wings, the more precious they become to us.

It is an interesting and touching picture to see that now glad mother appearing in the same place before Eli, leading her child by the hand up to the venerable man, who seemed as if he had not moved from that seat by the pillar of the Lord's house, during the time that had elapsed since she saw him there last. "Oh, my lord," she said, "I am the woman that stood by thee here, praying unto the Lord. For *this* child I prayed; and the Lord hath granted me the petition which I asked of Him. Therefore, also, have I lent him to the Lord; as long as he liveth shall he be lent unto the Lord."

[1] Comestor, *Historia Scholastica*, 1473, of which there is a French translation by Guyart, under the title *Les Livres Historiaulx de la Bible.* Paris, 1495.

After the event had been commemorated by proper offerings and sacrifices, and Hannah had given vent to her full heart in an exulting hymn, she returned home with her husband, leaving her child in the care of Eli. She did not, however, discontinue her maternal cares for him. She knew he was in safe hands; but her motherly heart made her watchful for him, and solicitous for his welfare. Now she was constant in her periodical visits to the tabernacle, and she witnessed with joy of heart the growth of her eldest son in person and heavenly grace, and in favour with God and man. "She made him a little coat, and brought it from year to year, when she came with her husband to the yearly sacrifice."

While her diligent fingers wrought that "little coat," how pleasantly her thoughts dwelt on the son who was to wear it! She hoped great things for him, as mothers do; but her highest aspirations for him could hardly reach that exalted pitch of real greatness in Israel which awaited him. The lad's immediate duty lay in rendering such little services as his age allowed about the person of the high priest; and, eventually, some of the lighter duties of the tabernacle. Old Eli became greatly attached to him; and he perhaps found, in the reverent affection and endearing ways of this little boy, some consolation under the grief and disappointment which the profligate career of his own sons occasioned. So impressed was he by the fine qualities of this child, so affected by the circumstances of his birth, and so gratified by the excellent conduct of the pious parents, that he bestowed upon them his solemn blessing, and prayed that they might have rich returns in kind for the child they had so faithfully and entirely *lent* to the Lord. And so it came to pass. Hannah had afterwards three sons and two daughters. This was large interest for her "loan." But the Lord is a very bountiful paymaster; and amidst all the fervid speculations which inflame the world, to lend to Him remains the best investment

which any one can make of aught that he possesses.

The "temple" (i. 9), or "house" (i. 24), or "tabernacle of the Lord," to which Hannah went up to worship, was

SHILOH

that sacred tent constructed by Moses in the wilderness, after the pattern or model shown him in a vision on Mount Sinai. It contained the ark of the covenant, the altar of incense, and other things specified. When the Israelites entered Canaan, the tabernacle was first set up at Gilgal, on the Plain of Jericho. It then appears to have been taken to the valley between Ebal and Gerizim (Josh. viii. 33), and probably to other places where the people encamped for a time. But after the conquest of the land, it was permanently fixed at Shiloh (Josh. xviii. 1), a city of Ephraim, situated among the hills, about half-way between Bethel and Shechem, and a little eastward of the great road. This city was probably selected because it was central; and in it the tabernacle and ark remained from the time of Joshua, during the ministry of the judges, down to the end of Eli's life—a period of more than three hundred years.

P.

There can be no doubt respecting the identity of Shiloh with the present *Seilun,* "on the north side of Bethel, on the east side of the highway that goeth up from Bethel to Shechem, and on the south of Lebonah." Dr. Stanley remarks, "That, had it not been for the preservation of its name, and for the extreme precision with which its situation is described in the book of Judges (xxi. 19), the spot could never have been identified; and, indeed, from the time of Jerome till the year 1838, its real site was completely forgotten, and its name was transferred to that commanding height of Gibeon (Neby Samwil), which a later age naturally conceived to be a more congenial spot for the sacred place, where, for so many centuries, was the tent which He had pitched among men—'Our living dread, who dwells in Silo, His dread sanctuary.'" (*Sinai and Palestine*, 229.) There are ruins in the place covering a *tell*, which forms a spur between two valleys. Under these may be traced much more ancient foundations. Also, indications remain of an open space hewn out of the rock, possibly the site of the tabernacle, which the Rabbis say consisted of low stone walls, with a tent drawn over them. In Jeremiah we read (vii. 12), " Go ye now unto my place, which was in Shiloh, where I set my name at the first, and see what I did to it for the wickedness of my people Israel." These words deeply affected my mind as I visited the ruins, and looked over the neighbourhood, presenting a picture of extreme desolation and disorder. Tradition points to rock-hewn tombs, where it says Eli and his sons were buried. Reference is made by Dr. Porter to this subject in the Daily Illustration for the Twenty-eighth Week—Seventh Day.

S.

THE PILLARS OF THE EARTH

1 Samuel 2:8

In Hannah's song of gladness and thanksgiving, we meet with one expression which is calculated to bring some readers to a pause :—

" The pillars of the earth are the Lord's,
And He hath set the world upon them."

There are many similar expressions in Scripture, which, however interpreted, certainly do not agree with that form and condition which is known, through the discoveries of modern science, to belong to the earth. The truth of this matter seems to be that, since the object of the sacred writers was not to teach natural science, they were left in all such matters to express themselves according to the prevalent notions of their time and country. Had they done otherwise, they would not have been intelligible without such explanations, and such elaborate circumvallations of every phrase with elucidatory matter, as would have confused the meaning of their utterances, and rendered them a weariness to the mind. Under the teachings of the Holy Spirit, they were led in all things to set forth the Lord as the creator, sustainer, and governor of the universe, but in other respects they expressed themselves according to the prevailing ideas of the times in which they lived ; and from their expressions, it is quite possible to collect what those ideas were, and even to detect

some variation in them in the progress of time ; and it is always interesting to trace the alterations of notions and usages which occur in the course of ages. It is, indeed, too much our habit to look upon the Bible without regard to the fact, that it covers a historical period of four thousand years, and, in composition, of two thousand. If we take the latter period only, and reflect upon the great differences of language, usage, and civilisation which have occurred in every known country within the nearly equal period since the birth of Christ, we may, from the analogy, reasonably expect to find very considerable variations in regard to external things, and the ideas of them, between the earlier and later books of Scripture. It is true, and it has often been said, that certain ideas and customs have a somewhat stereotyped character in the East. Nevertheless, certain changes must have arisen, and may be traced in the most fixed of nations ; and, while making large allowance for the alleged permanency of eastern ideas, we may surely concede for two thousand years in the East, as much change as for a fourth of that period in the West. Yet, it is probable that few read the Bible with the impression on their minds, that the manners and ideas of the later scriptural period may have been as different from those of the earlier, as our own manners and ideas are different from those which prevailed in the time of the Plantagenets.

The earth is usually represented by the sacred writers as a vast and widely extended body, environed on all sides by the ocean, and resting upon the waters. But the earlier idea presented to us in the book of Job, seems to represent the earth as sustained floating in the air—or rather, perhaps, in empty space—by an omnipotent and invisible power. It is difficult to see what other signification to affix to the text to which we refer,[1] " He stretcheth out the north over the empty place,[2] and hangeth the earth upon nothing,"—a much finer and truer idea than is to be found in the gross cosmographies of the remote East, in which sundry coarse material supports are provided for the earth. Take, for instance, the annexed view of the Hindu system of the universe.

The three, or as more minutely subdivided, the twenty-one worlds, of this system, are sustained by a tortoise, the symbol of strength and

[1] Job 26:7.　　[2] The void; Hebrew, TOHU.

conservative power, which itself rests upon the great serpent, the emblem of eternity, which embraces the whole within the circle formed by its body. These worlds form three grand

HINDU COSMICAL SYSTEM OF THE UNIVERSE

regions, each subdivided into seven spheres, zones, or countries, which are supposed to be arranged spirally, or in concentric circles. The upper region is composed of the seven *Swargas* or *Lokas*, which are, at the same time, the domiciles of the seven planets, and the residence of the gods. Below this is the earth, divided into seven isles, separated by different seas. Below, upon the back of the tortoise, is the lower region, or hell, in it seven *Patalas*. Three, sometimes four elephants, standing upon the tortoise, sustain the earth, and eight elephants standing upon the earth, uphold the heavens. Mount Meru is supposed to traverse and unite the three worlds; and it is upon its topmost summit, in the most elevated of the spheres, that we behold the radiated triangle—the symbol of the Yoni and of the creation.

The highly poetical and figurative language of the book of Job may, however, leave us in some doubt how far the notion there exhibited is to be regarded as the expression of a current theory or fixed opinion. It is, indeed, certain that the passages which disclose the other view are not only far more numerous, but much more distinct. So the Psalmist calls upon the Lord, "that stretched out the earth above the waters."[1] There are passages which appear to assign to the earth even a more substantial basis than the water. In Job, this notion may be detected:— "Where wast thou when I laid the foundations of the earth? declare, if thou hast understanding. Who hath laid the measures thereof, if thou

[1] Psalms 136:6.

knowest? or who hath stretched the line upon it? Whereupon are the foundations thereof fastened? or who hath laid the corner stone thereof?"[1] And so Isaiah: "Hath it not been told you from the beginning? have ye not understood from the foundations of the earth? It is He that sitteth upon the circle of the earth, and the inhabitants thereof are as grasshoppers; that stretcheth out the heavens as a curtain, and spreadeth them out as a tent to dwell in."[2] It is quite clear that in these passages the earth is compared to a building, whose foundations are deep and immovable. It is clearly under this idea, and with reference to a building, that Hannah speaks of "the pillars of the earth." To the same essential purport are the words of Solomon, who in Proverbs viii. 29, represents Divine Wisdom as saying, "When He appointed the foundations of the earth, then I was by Him;" and also those of Jeremiah,[3] "If heaven above can be measured, and the foundations of the earth searched out beneath, I will also cast off all the seed of Israel."

In such passages as these, the waters, on which the earth is supposed to rest, do not immediately appear. But the subsistence of this idea as to the lowermost waters is in all evinced by the fact that when the sacred writers describe some great convulsion of nature, such as an earthquake, they, in their accumulated images of terror, speak not only of the mountains being rent, and the foundations of the earth being shaken, but of the lower waters being disclosed by the riven earth. So the Psalmist: "The earth shook and trembled; the foundations also of the hills moved and were shaken. Then the channels of the waters were seen, and the foundations of the world were discovered."[4] Finally, the prophet Jonah is very clear for the opinion of the earth being above the waters; for, in expressing his condition when entombed in the body of the fish, he very poetically supposes that he had gone down to these lowermost waters, where the earth lay over his head. "I went down," he says, "to the bottoms of the mountains: the earth with her bars was about me for ever."[5] He was, as it were, shut down in the lower mass of waters by the floating earth, without the hope that he should ever rise again. In fact, it would seem that the popular

[1] Job 38:4-6.   [3] Jeremiah 31:37. [5] Jonah 2:6.
[2] Isaiah 40:21.   [4] Psalms 18:7,16.

cosmological ideas of the Jews bore considerable resemblance to that which still subsists among the Persians, who hold that the earth floats in the water like a melon[1] in a round pool. This was also not very dissimilar to the view of some of the old Gentile philosophers, and it was likewise entertained by the ancient Christians, by whom it was probably founded on the scriptural intimations. Under such views, it could not, of course, be supposed that there were any antipodes; and as only the upper surface, that above the water, was habitable, it follows that the inhabited parts of the earth were supposed to be of very limited extent, compared with the fact, which allows the entire land surface of the globular earth to be habitable. Even if the world had been supposed to be spherical, only the part of it rising out of the water could under this view be inhabited. The earth, under this system was no other than an extended level surface, excepting the inequalities occasioned by the mountains. The Israelites do not, however, appear to have supposed that it was round. In the Hebrew the earth is never called a ball, nor by any name corresponding to those employed by the Latins, *orbis* and *globus*: the word (*thebel*) rendered *orbis* in Latin versions of the Scripture, means simply the world as it exists, and in particular the habitable world. There are, on the other hand, passages which distinctly describe the earth as extended or stretched out upon the surface of the waters. Thus, in Isaiah xlii. 5: "He that created the heavens, and stretched them out; He *that spread forth the earth*, and that which cometh out of it." And, again, the Psalmist says: "Him that *stretched out the earth above the waters*."[2] In both these texts the word rendered "stretched" is the same, or rather from the same root, as that rendered in other places "firmament," or more properly "an expansion," as applied to the visible heavens above, showing the analogy of ideas under which the term is in both respects used. This upper firmament is regarded as a sort of dyke against the waters above, to prevent them from falling upon the earth; and so the lower expansion, the earth, keeps down the waters on which it lies, and prevents them from breaking forth and reducing the world to its ancient chaos.

[1] *Hindoùàny*, a species of Indian melon, otherwise called *kharboùzeh hindy*. See Chardin's *Description de la Perse*, iv. 448, and Langles' note. [2] Psalms 136:6.

It is doubtful whether any distinct figure was, under these impressions, assigned to the earth. Some have supposed that it is described as being square, seeing that God is said to gather His elect from "the four corners of the earth,"[1] or "from the four winds;"[2] and in the glorious prediction of the Messiah's dominion over all the world, it is said, "He shall have dominion also from sea to sea, and from the river to *the ends of the earth*."[3] We cannot, however, build much on this; but it is certain that the ancient heathen geographers supposed the length of the habitable earth to be greater than its breadth; and that its extent was greatest from east to west, and least from north to south.

It appears to me to be a singular and not very safe mode of interpretation, to construct a cosmogony, or system of natural philosophy, upon a series of poetic figures. Every passage quoted or referred to by Dr. Kitto in this day's reading is poetry. The poetry of Scripture, like all other poetry, takes its figures from external objects as they appear to the eye; and also from such creations of the imagination as may seem to the poetic genius to convey ideas of majesty and beauty. It is manifest that the sacred writers never intended these descriptions to be interpreted literally, or as embodying their views as inspired men on scientific subjects. A glance at the context in one or two of the passages will show this to any thoughtful reader, and will show how dangerous, I would almost say how absurd, it is to interpret the poetry of the Bible in such a manner. Thus, in Job xxxviii., after the words, "Where wast thou when I *laid the foundations of the earth?*" we have this other question, "Who *shut up the sea with doors . . . and set bars and doors?*" Will any man presume to say that in this latter passage the writer is setting forth "the prevalent notions of his time and country" regarding the manner in which the sea is confined? And yet this would be only carrying out the same hermeneutical principles. So again in Ps. xviii., if we interpret the words, "The earth shook and trembled; the foundations also of the hills moved and were shaken. Then the channels of the waters were seen, and the foundations of the world were discovered:"—if we interpret these words as conveying the ideas of the sacred writer regarding the physical structure of our globe, we must interpret the words which accompany them as conveying his real ideas regarding God: "There went up a smoke out of His nostrils, and fire out of His mouth devoured: coals were kindled by it," etc. So also in Jonah ii. 4-6. The figures employed by some of the greatest of our modern poets are as far removed from physical reality as those of the Old Testament writers. Would we be justified in saying that in these respects "they expressed themselves according to the prevailing ideas of the times?"

P.

[1] Revelation 7:1; 20:8. [2] Matthew 24:31. [3] Psalms 72:8.

TABERNACLE ABOMINATIONS

1 Samuel 2:12-17,22

THE sons of Eli were "men of Belial"—that is, men of profligate disposition and conduct—men who had no regard for their own character, or for the honour of God, whose commissioned servants they were. This ungodliness pervaded their demeanour, and their misconduct was by no means limited to the particular instances recorded. Yet these instances are so remarkable as to claim special attention.

The custom of sacrifice was, that *burnt-offerings* were wholly consumed by fire upon the altar, and that *sin-offerings* were eaten by the priests. But in the case of *peace-offerings*, the internal fat alone was consumed, first of all, upon the altar; then the priest had for his share the breast and the shoulder, after these had been waved before the Lord; and the remainder of the carcase was returned to the offerer, to be eaten by himself and his friends, or such as he invited. This was ample allowance for the priest, who had the whole of the sin-offerings, and some of the principal parts of the peace-offerings. But Eli's sons thought not so. Not satisfied with the breast and the shoulder of every victim, they begrudged the offerer the remainder. Properly their interest in the matter ceased as soon as they had received their allowance. But they pursued the remainder with greedy eyes; and at length they ventured to introduce the custom, while the meat was boiling for the offerer and his family—which was done in some part of the tabernacle, as afterwards of the temple—of sending a servant round "with a flesh-hook of three teeth in his hand." This trident, which no doubt had the prongs wide enough apart, the man thrust into the boiler, and claimed as the perquisite of the priest whatever the instrument brought up; and this could not but frequently make a serious reduction of the food with which the offerers were used to entertain their friends, and to extend their bounty to the needy.

Even this mean and ludicrous greediness did not long satisfy the sons of Eli. Finding that this exaction was submitted to by the people, they went yet further. After the breast and

shoulder had been given, but *before* the remainder had been put to boil, the servant came and demanded the raw meat, alleging that the priests did not want it boiled, but to roast. This might be one reason, although there were the breast and shoulder which they might roast if they liked; but the real reason probably was, that the three-pronged fork, striking somewhat at a venture, did not always afford such large or such choice portions as the avidity of the priests required. To secure this exaction, and to prevent all evasion, they made their demand even before the fat was offered upon the altar, which, as it belonged to the Lord, and the offering of it was a highly religious act, should have been, if only for the sake of decency, first of all performed. But knowing that the offerers could not withdraw till the Lord's portion had been presented, the demand was made before the fat was offered. The people could not but feel the gross indecorum of this proceeding; and the manner in which they met this new exaction was in all respects praiseworthy, and showed that the men who brought the offerings had religion more at heart, and were more concerned for the honour and glory of God, than were His own ministers. They implored these godless priests to allow the Lord's offerings to be first presented. "And then," said they, "take as much as thy soul desireth." The answer of Eli's sons to this becoming remonstrance and handsome offer was usually, "Nay, but thou shalt give it me now; and if not, I will take it by force."

What wonder that the people were disgusted at these proceedings, and that the result was, that they abstained from bringing their peace-offerings to the altar, seeing that their doing so subjected them to such insult and oppression, and produced circumstances so revolting to their religious feelings? "Wherefore," we are told, "the sin of the young men was very great before the Lord: for men abhorred the offering of the Lord."

This was their offence, and a very terrible one it was, amounting to a betrayal of the high trusts committed to their care. Nor was this all; for we are told that they behaved themselves most vilely towards "the women who assembled at the door of the tabernacle of the congregation." Who were these women? That is a question of greater interest at this day than the historical fact here connected with it. The question has indeed been much discussed. The most obvious and common-sense view, as suggested by this text alone, would seem to be, that they were women who went thither for worship, and who, not being admitted into the interior of the court, assembled in front of the entrance, the curtains of which being drawn aside on such occasions, allowed them a view of the interior, and of the solemn proceedings there. It has been thought, however, that there is some reference to a particular class of women, habitually attending at the tabernacle in discharge of some special duty or vocation. Some fancy that they came upon business which it belonged to women to do there, such as to wash and clean the rooms. But in that case they would be assembled, not "at the door of the tabernacle," but *within* it. And then we do not know that there were any rooms to wash and clean at the tabernacle, though there were at the temple; and, more than all, such offices, and many others (such as even the washing of clothes) usually performed by women in the West, are as usually discharged by men in the East, except in the apartments appropriated to the use of women. In this, as in a thousand instances, we arrive at erroneous conclusions by arguing from the analogy of our own customs, without proper inquiry whether those of the East may not be very different. Others imagine that the women came to sew and spin at the tabernacle; as if, because "the women that were wise-hearted did spin" at the original construction of the tabernacle, they did so always after. This is a curious instance of generalizing upon a particular passage of Scripture, having reference to a merely temporary and occasional matter. Some spinning and sewing might be necessary to renew the priestly vestures, but this was doubtless done at home, as indeed the original dresses and hangings of the tabernacle were, and probably in the families of the priests themselves. It is preposterous to suppose that the little spinning and sewing that might be necessary to keep the attire of the priests in order should be carried on at the door of the tabernacle. The Jewish interpreters usually understand, that the congregation of females was caused by the attendance of women who had recently given birth to children, and who came with their offerings of purification; and as these were attended by their female friends and relations, a few of these parties (and there must have been several every day) would collectively form a considerable crowd at the door of the tabernacle.

Upon the whole, we incline to regard the first mentioned and least special explanation as the most reasonable, admitting, however, that a certain proportion of the women may have been, and probably were, such frequent and regular attendants from devout feelings, that they became well known at the tabernacle—like the communicant of a church as distinguished from the general congregation—and might be pre-eminently distinguished as "the women who [habitually] assembled at the door of the congregation." To go beyond this, as some have done, and suppose that there was a body of devout women who had specially consecrated themselves to the service of the tabernacle, and to a holy life, in a state of celibacy, is more than we can find in the Bible, and seems to us a Romanist invention, wrought out of some incidental expressions, which admit and require a different interpretation; and this for the purpose of producing a show of Scripture authority for the practice of female ascetic devotement, to which both the spirit and the letter of the Old Testament and of the New are decidedly opposed, and which has been, and is, one of the resources wherein "the proud mind of the flesh" seeks nourishment.

A VOICE IN THE NIGHT

1 Samuel 3

SAMUEL was introduced to his prophetic office very early, and in a very remarkable manner.

It seems that old Eli attached him to his person, to render such little services to him as his condition rendered necessary; for, from extreme age, "his eyes began to wax dim, that he could not see." For this reason, apparently, it was that the lad slept at night within call of the high priest, retiring to his own rest after the old man had lain down, and all his little duties had been performed. It would appear, from the tone of the statement, that these circumstances took place within the enclosure of the tabernacle. This is not, indeed, distinctly stated; and the mention of the time of the tabernacle lamps going out may merely be a mark of time. We know that at a later period, under the temple, there were tenements within the enclosure for the priests and the Levites on duty. But these were for the accommodation of priests who performed their duties in rotation, and came for that purpose to the temple, generally leaving their families at home. Under the tabernacle, however, the priests were not so numerous as to allow of this arrangement, and they seem to have been all in attendance at the place of the tabernacle with their households. This, therefore, scarcely consisted with residence within the enclosure, where the constructions could hardly have been of the permanent nature required for constant habitation. We therefore suppose that the priests lived in the town, repairing to the tabernacle when the discharge of their duties required. But the Levites, who must have been too numerous to be all in attendance at once, and who, as we know, dwelt in dispersed towns of their own, might remain in lodges in or about the tabernacle enclosure during their term of service. While engaged in the discharge of a temporary service, men can and do dispense with the accommodations and domestic conveniences which are needful in their permanent abodes. Nor was the arrangement materially different in the temple, the accommodations being for those who were separated from their families, on temporary service, and not for such domestic establishments as they all possessed in their proper homes. Even the high priest was not in constant residence, that is, not in domestic residence, at the temple—much less, therefore, at the tabernacle. In the time of our Lord, it is distinctly stated that the high priest had his residence in the city. To compare ancient things with modern, and ecclesiastical with political office, it was the same with the high priests as with our chief ministers of state, who have their official residence in Downing Street, but have their private and domestic abodes elsewhere. Yet it has happened that a minister without family (as was the case with

Pitt) might reside altogether in Downing Street; and so might a high priest at the temple. And thus Eli, who was now an aged man, apparently a widower, with all his family grown up and settled in their own households, might, both from feeling and from convenience, incline to reside constantly at his humble official lodge, under the shadow of the tabernacle. The proper place of Samuel at night would have been among the attendant Levites; but on account of his personal services to the aged high priest, he rested not far from him. And that Eli was in the habit of requiring his services during the night, appears from the readiness of the lad in concluding that the voice which called him one night by name was that of Eli.

It has been thought by many that Samuel had some charge about the lamps of the tabernacle; for it is said, "Ere the lamp of God went out in the temple of the Lord, where the ark of God was, and Samuel was laid down to sleep." But this attendance on the lamps was a higher Levitical office than was likely to devolve upon a lad; and

THE GOLDEN CANDLESTICK

it appears to have been a mode of marking time merely, which had grown into use at the tabernacle. "The lamp" is, of course, the golden candlestick with its seven lamps. These were lighted every evening, and they burned until the morning, by which time some of them at least usually went out ; and if any remained burning, they were put out by the Levites when they came in the morning to attend to them. The Jewish writers, indeed, affirm that one of the lamps—the western one—was always kept burning day and night, being so well filled as to burn until the morning, and being then replenished instead of extinguished.

It was, then, in the dead of night, towards morning, but before any of the lamps had gone out, that the slumbers of the young Samuel were broken by a voice which pronounced his name. With prompt attention the lad started from his couch, and hastened to the bedside of his aged lord, who, as he supposed, had called him. This he did three times, for thus often was he called, and each time he supposed that Eli called him. The strangeness of this at length led the high priest to see something more than human in the circumstance ; and he directed the boy to go and lie down once more, and if again called, not to come to him, but say, " Speak, Lord, for thy servant heareth!" Samuel did as he was directed, and the divine voice then declared the terrible judgments which should speedily fall upon Eli and upon his house : upon his sons, because they had " made themselves vile ;" and upon him, because " he restrained them not."

As this is the first circumstance which throws light upon the character of one who was destined to become a great man in Israel, it behoves us to regard it well. Most lads of his age evince much eagerness in communicating anything surprising, with little regard to the pain it may be calculated to inflict. Samuel knew that he had been highly honoured by a special communication from God ; and he must have been too well instructed not to be aware of the extraordinary and important character of the distinction thus conferred upon him. Yet his young heart was not elated, nor was his tongue impatient to proclaim this honour which had come to him from God. The burden of a great doom had been imparted to him, and such secrets of high import it is hard for youth to bear undisclosed. But with Samuel there was one consideration that overruled every other. The secret concerned his venerable lord, who had been as a father to him, and it could not fail to afflict his spirit. Therefore, with a pious and generous discretion, far beyond his years, and altogether worthy of manhood, he pur-

posed to keep it all to himself. He lay quiet until the morning; and on arising from his rest, he proceeded about his ordinary business, as if nothing remarkable had happened.

Nevertheless, Eli perceiving that his youthful attendant had risen, but had not come to him as usual, suspected that something had transpired which he was afraid to communicate. He therefore called him, and solemnly charged him to hide nothing from him. Thus adjured, Samuel was constrained to make known all that had passed. And when Eli heard that dreadful sentence, every word of which must have fallen like molten lead upon his heart, the poor old man, so small in active daring, but so great in passive suffering, broke forth into no vain lamentations or complaints. " It is the Lord," he said, " let Him do what seemeth Him good !" For, as Bishop Hall well paraphrases the words, " Whatsoever seemeth good to Him, cannot but be good, howsoever it seems to me. Every man," he adds, " can open his hand to God while He blesses; but to expose ourselves willingly to the afflicting hand of our Maker, and to kneel to Him while He scourges us, is peculiar only to the faithful." This is a charitable judgment, and it commends itself to our esteem much better than the austere censures of those who accuse Eli of hypocrisy, because he took no means to correct the evil by which this doom had been brought down. This is a harsh judgment. He was old and dim-sighted now, and little suited for a task of paternal correction and theocratical reform, from which he had unhappily shrunk in the days of his strength and vigour. He found it easier to leave the matter in the Lord's hands, whether for judgment or for mercy. It was for judgment; for the Lord's justice required to be satisfied, and the honour of His institutions vindicated.

THE TIDINGS

1 Samuel 4:1-18

THE doom upon the house of Eli, for the enormities by which the Lord's service had been dishonoured, was not first denounced through Samuel, nor was this the first warning the high priest received. Before this, a prophet, whose name is not recorded, had been sent to declare the judgment of God upon such high offences. That this warning had been followed by no beneficial results—had not roused the old man to a more stringent exercise of that authority which belonged to the pontiff and the father—could not but give the more force to the denunciation delivered through Samuel; and the language of Eli on that occasion may have been as much the expression of hopeless incapacity as of pious resignation. The doom consisted in the deposition of the family from the high-priesthood—the sudden death of the offenders in one day—the impoverishment and premature deaths of the family—and the doing of a deed which should cause the ears of all that heard it to tingle. The event to which this last intimation has reference, has been differently understood; for there were two historical circumstances, to either of which the words would be awfully applicable: the one, the capture of the ark by the Philistines, with the death of Eli's guilty sons in battle, with his own death when the news came to Shiloh, together with that of his daughter-in-law in giving premature birth to a son; the other, that of the slaughter of the seventy priests at Nob by the order of Saul, at a later date, which nearly effected the extinction of Eli's house.

Without pretending to determine to which of these events this remarkable denunciation refers, the former of them is that which demands our present attention.

A war arose with the Philistines—from what immediate cause we know not—and the armies confronted each other in battle. In the first action the Israelites were beaten with the loss of four thousand men. This result was received by the "elders of Israel" in a right spirit, in so far as it was ascribed to the absence of that divine protection which would have rendered Israel victorious. But the inference was very mistaken, that if they had the ark of the covenant among them, they would be assured of the Lord's favouring presence therewith, and victory could not then fail to crown their arms. They no doubt remembered that the Israelites were formerly successful against their enemies when the ark was with their armies;[1] but they forgot that this was not simply because the ark was present, but because the Lord was with them. And now, instead of inquiring what

[1] Numbers 31:6; Joshua 6:6.

there was wrong in their faith or conduct which had drawn down the Lord's displeasure, and for which they ought to humble themselves before Him, they thought to settle the matter by a cheap ceremonial. "Much like hereunto," as an old commentator remarks,[1] "was the superstitious practice of the Papists, who in time of common calamities, as the pestilence and unseasonable weather, would go about in procession in the streets, with their pix and the host, as though there were vertue in such ceremonies to appease the wrath of God."

With truer faith—a faith rising gloriously above external symbols—David, in a later age, refused to allow the ark to be removed with him in his retreat from Jerusalem, but chose rather to leave it there in the hands of his enemies. The priests had even brought it forth without the city, when he directed them to "carry the ark of God back into the city: if I shall find favour in the eyes of the Lord, He will bring me again, and show me both it and his habitation. But if He thus say, I have no delight in thee; behold, here I am, let Him do to me as seemeth good unto Him."[2]

We must not, however, overlook in the measure now taken, the providence of God, by which both the guilty priests were thus drawn to their doom —to perish together in one day. The ark being removed, it was necessary that they should attend it to the scene of action; and there they fell, by the sword of the Philistines, in the day when the ark of God was taken. No such result, however, was anticipated when that symbol of God's presence, borne in solemn state, with the train of priests and Levites, was seen slowly advancing towards the camp. The host of Israel hailed it with exulting shouts, as if their triumph were now secure. Their enemies, on the other hand, regarded it with downcast hearts. In their gross materialism—scarcely more gross, however, than that of the Israelites themselves—they regarded the ark as the god of the Israelites, or at least as the symbol with which the presence of their God was inseparably connected; and, remembering the wonders which had been wrought by that God for this people in Egypt and in the wilderness, they were filled with dismay, and anticipated nothing but disaster and ruin. The impression made upon them, at this distant day,

[1] Willet, *Harmonie upon the First Book of Samuel*, 1614.
[2] 2 Samuel 25:25,26.

by those ancient miracles, shows how materially those manifestations of the Lord's presence with His people, and of the irresistible might which was exerted on their behalf, must have facilitated their original conquest of the land. The Philistines, however, while alarmed, did not lose all spirit. Though the impression made upon them was very deep, the inference they drew—but which we should scarcely have anticipated from the consternation they expressed—was that of brave men whom the desperateness of the emergency moved only to more heroic exertions. "Be strong, and quit yourselves like men, O ye Philistines, that ye be not servants to the Hebrews, as they have been to you." It was the Lord's appointment that they should conquer in this war, and therefore were they thus inspirited to accomplish the purposes of His will. They did conquer. Israel was defeated—the priests were slain—the ark was taken. Thus did the Lord rebuke the vain confidence of the Israelites, and the discredit they had done Him before the Philistines, by the sanction which their proceedings had given to the pagan delusion, that the presence of God was inseparably connected with aught made with hands. In proportion as men neglect or misapprehend the thing signified, they take to rendering exaggerated honours to the sign or symbol. The ark was becoming an idol, and therefore the ark was suffered to be taken captive by the unbelievers.

Still the ark was a sacred thing. It was the visible cynosure of a worship which was in its forms symbolical and ritual; and above it, in its place, the clouded radiance which indicated the divine presence visibly abode. Apart, therefore, from the false notions concerning it which had crept in, the loss of it might well be felt to be a national calamity. It was so considered. The right-minded might tremble at the thought of the dishonour brought upon the Lord's great name in the eyes of the heathen, who would not fail to consider that their own gods had at length triumphed over the great and dreadful JEHOVAH of the Israelites.

Many hearts waited with unusual anxiety the tidings from the battle. Among them was the blind old Eli, who caused his seat to be set by the wayside, that he might catch the first tidings that might come from the war; "for his heart trembled for the ark of God." His sons were there; but it was not for them his heart trembled—he trembled for the ark. He was not, however, the first to receive the tidings. It was spread through the town before he heard it; for every one was reluctant to impart it to him. But he heard the stir and the lamentations through the city, and asked what this meant. The messenger, a man of Benjamin (some Jews think it was Saul), a fugitive from the battle, with his clothes rent, and earth strewn upon his head, as the bearer of heavy tidings, then came before him. Eli's blindness spared him the sight of these ominous indications. But let us note what passed. "The man said to Eli, I am he that came out of the army, and I fled to-day out of the army. And he said, What is there done, my son? And the messenger answered and said, Israel is fled before the Philistines, and there hath been also a great slaughter among the people, and thy two sons also, Hophni and Phinehas, are dead, and THE ARK OF GOD IS TAKEN. And it came to pass, when he made mention of the ark of God, that he fell from his seat backward by the side of the gate, and his neck brake, and he died."

The manner in which this sad tale is told far excels anything of the kind which the wide range of literature can furnish. It is one of those traits of pure and simple grandeur in which the Scriptures are unequalled. The learned Madame Dacier compares these words, "Thy two sons, Hophni and Phinehas, are dead, and the ark of God is taken," with those of Antilochus, who brings to Achilles the tidings of the death of his friend Patroclus:

"Patroclus is no more. The Grecians fight
For his bare corse, and Hector hath his arms;"

and she quotes the gloss of Eustathius upon this passage of Homer. "This speech of Antilochus," says this critic, "may be cited as a model of emphatic brevity in announcing tidings so terrible, for in two verses it contains all that really can be told: the death of Patroclus—by whom he was slain—the combat around his corpse—and that his arms were in the hands of the enemy. The tragic poets of Greece have not always imitated this grand simplicity; and Euripides, in particular, has the fault of making long recitals on trifling occasions. But Homer only, in this, ought to be followed. In great distresses, nothing is more absurd than for a messenger to impart his tidings in long discourses and pathetic descriptions. He speaks without being understood, for those to whom he addresses himself have no time or heart to pay attention. The first word which enables them to apprehend the calamity is enough to them, and they are deaf to all besides." Now, this Homeric rule of fit brevity in messages of grief is still more strongly, and with more exquisite propriety, exemplified in the Scriptures, which abound in passages unapproachable even by Homer for significant brevity and sublime abruptness; and is particularly observable in those very cases in which, according to this sagacious canon of criticism, diffuse narration would have been inappropriate and unseemly. And notwithstanding that, in regard to such a book as the Bible, the literary beauties are of secondary importance, the secondary matters of the Bible surpass in interest the first matters of other things; and although we do not, as the Mohammedans with their Koran, point to the mere literary composition of the Bible as a standing miracle, and a sufficient evidence of divine authority, it is not the less advantageous and pleasurable to us to be able to show, that the book of God, though its various truths come to us through the necessarily imperfect channel of human language, surpasses in manner, as well as in matter, all other books.

It may be interesting to note the effect which the capture of the ark produced upon the city of Shiloh. It had remained there in the tabernacle for more than three hundred years. Though the disgraceful conduct of Eli's sons had tended largely to dull those feelings of reverence which the Israelites entertained for the holy sanctuary, and for the spot where it was stationed, yet still Shiloh was the most venerated place in the land. The crowds of worshippers which assembled there during the great annual feasts, the multitude of offerings presented, and the numbers of priests and Levites in constant attendance upon the sanctuary, must have made Shiloh prosperous, populous, and rich. But with the loss of the ark it lost all its prosperity. The tabernacle still remained there, the priests were in attendance, and offerings were presented. Even after the ark was restored by the Philistines, and after it was finally removed by king David to Jerusalem, the old sanctuary at Shiloh was still visited. But its glory was gone. The city rapidly declined. A curse fell upon it, because of the sins of its corrupt priesthood. So remarkable was its fall and its desolation, that, just before the captivity, the Lord uttered these words regarding it by the lips of Jeremiah : "But go ye now to my place which was in Shiloh, where I set my name at the first, and see what I did to it for the wickedness of my people Israel." (Jer. vii. 12).

For centuries Shiloh has been ruined and deserted.

The shattered walls of a mosque or church, the foundations of some houses, and a number of shapeless mounds of stones and rubbish scattered over a rocky hill side, are all that remain to mark the site of Shiloh. "An air of oppressive stillness hangs now over all the scene, and adds force to the reflection, that truly the 'oracles' so long consulted there are dumb; they had fulfilled their purpose and given place to a more sure word of prophecy."

P.

ICHABOD

1 Samuel 4:21

THE deep concern evinced at the loss of the symbol of Jehovah's presence, which constituted the highest distinction and most sacred treasure of Israel, is very affecting, and affords a most impressive and gratifying indication of the exalted and just views and feelings by which the hearts of some among the Israelites were animated. We have seen Eli fall to the ground and die, when he heard that the ark of God was taken; it being doubtful, as Bishop Hall quaintly remarks, whether his heart or his neck were first broken.

The same tidings wrought in the same family another death. The wife of one of the doomed priests, Phinehas, herself unnamed, although worthy of being held in lasting remembrance, was with child, and near to be delivered, when the doleful tidings of Israel's overthrow and the capture of God's ark came to Shiloh. Her husband's death—her father-in-law's death—the ruin of Israel—the capture of God's ark, threw her into such distress of mind, that her pains came suddenly upon her, and terminated her life. She appears to have been a woman of great tenderness of spirit, and of still greater piety. She felt deeply—how deeply, we may judge from the effects—the successive calamities that had taken place; but, like Eli himself, she felt most of all the one the messenger had last mentioned —the capture of the ark. Her father-in-law was dead. True; but his death was to be expected soon in the course of nature, and the loss could be repaired; for there would not be wanting a high priest in the house of God. Her husband lay dead on the battlefield, his priestly raiment defiled in dust and stained with blood. And his offence was rank : his sins, some of them, had not only been public wrongs, but private wrongs to her. Yet still, in the deep caverns of her womanly heart, there lingered much love to the husband of her youth, the father of her children; and the loss of him—his life quenched in blood—would, under any ordinary circumstances, have been a devouring grief. As it was, it no doubt hastened the time of her travail. Still it is clear from her dying words, that a concern for the interests of religion, occasioned by the loss of the ark, lay nearest to her soul. This was the master grief, in whose presence the others were dumb.

. The women around her bed sought to rouse her from her dying lethargy, by the most gladdening tidings a Hebrew woman could learn: "Fear not; for thou hast born a son!" "But," it is emphatically added, "she answered not, neither did she regard it." As her last moment came, however, she roused herself so far as to indicate the name the child was to bear—by that name making him a living memorial of her despairing grief. She called his name I-CHABOD—which means *without glory*—saying, "The glory is departed from Israel!" And with these words upon her lips, she died. That glory having departed, there was nothing of joy or hope for life to offer to her: it only remained for her to die.

This is a noble and refreshing example of deep concern, manifested even unto death, for the glory of God, and the well-being of His church. It is refreshing, because any experience of the sort has become rare in these latter days, in which the supreme anxiety of men is to get on, to do well in the world, to thrive; and concern for the glory of God is a subordinate and tempered feeling, calling forth very little of that burning ardour, that restlessness of zeal and labour, with which the matters belonging, more or less, to this life, are studied and pursued. No doubt there is abroad in the Christian world a certain kind of zeal for the glory of God. But how few are there in whom that zeal reigns paramount above all the interests that belong to earth—in whom that zeal is as a burning fire shut up in their bones, which makes them weary with forbearing— which allows them no rest so long as their Lord's great name is unglorified, or His cause does not prosper!

Look at this woman; and if an instance of real patriotism, of true public spirit, be wanted, behold it here! and let the just admiration which it excites, teach us that it is not proper, far less

is it godly, that the chief of our care should be given to the concernments of our private condition, or the affairs of our party, our sect, or our town. We have among us God's spiritual ark. Dangers often threaten it; clouds often obscure the lustre of its most fine gold; at times it seems as if it were going, as if it were gone, into the hands of the Philistines. Where is, then, " the exceeding great and bitter cry," such as arises when some great reverse of temporal fortune comes; when some plague reaps the life of the land; when some great ship, laden with souls, sinks into the deep; when one of our chief of men is smitten suddenly down in the noontide of his honours? Alas! we have a different standard for the measurement of the relative importance of these things, from that nameless woman of Israel, who, amid the most cruel death agonies to which the human frame is subject, and in the severest reverses we can be called to suffer, called her new-born son Ichabod, not for these things, but chiefly " because the ark of God was taken."

On this case it is well remarked by an old writer, whose subject led him naturally to it (it is part of a meditation for a woman expecting to be delivered): "She took no comfort in her deliverance, though she had a son, while the Church of God was not delivered. Oh that the same mind might be in me, that I might learn also to be more affected with the affairs of the Church! Alas, what is my danger to the universal danger; my travail to the travail of the Church? What comfort to me to have many children, unless I might see the good of God's chosen? What content have I in being delivered of my pains, unless God deliver Israel from all its troubles? What delight had Abraham in all his mercies while he was childless, or I in all my children, if the children of God be comfortless? Oh my God, bless me out of Zion, and thus let me be blessed as those are that fear the Lord; let me not only be a fruitful vine, but let me see the good of Jerusalem all my days. Let me not only see my children's children, but peace upon Israel." [1]

To which we may suitably add the words of a still earlier writer: " What cares she for a pos-

[1] *A Present to be given to Teeming Women by their Husbands and Friends.* By John Oliver, less than the least of all saints, London. At the Golden Bible on London Bridge, 1669.

terity which should want the ark? What cares she for a son come into the world of Israel, when God was gone from it? And how willingly doth she depart from them from whom God was departed! Not outward magnificence, not state, not wealth, not favour of the mighty, but the presence of God in His ordinances, was the glory of Israel; the subduing whereof is a greater judgment than destruction."[1]

DAGON

1 Samuel 5:1-5

THE history of the ark in the hands of the victorious Philistines offers several circumstances of striking and peculiar interest.

They had been permitted by the Lord thus far to triumph, for the accomplishment of His own high purposes. And it remained for Him now to vindicate the honour of His own great name, equally from the despair of the Israelites, and the profane exultation of the Philistines. The latter, indeed, by making it a triumph of their own god over the God of Israel, rendered it inevitable that He should move His terrible right arm to redeem His name from reproach. It was the custom among the ancient idolaters to place among the captives, and to bear along in triumph, the idols adored by their enemies, and eventually to deposit them in the temples of their own idols as memorials of their victory. The prophet Isaiah predicts that the gods of Babylon should thus be treated by Cyrus. Instead of using the direct language of prophecy or description, he represents himself as seeing in vision the heavy laden animals and wains moving slowly along, pressed down by the weight of the captured gods that were to be borne to the distant land of the conqueror: "Bel boweth down, Nebo croucheth; their images are laid upon the beasts and upon the cattle. Your burdens are packed up as a load to the weary beast. They crouch, they bow down together; they cannot rescue the burden; themselves into captivity are gone."[2] It is very probable that, in thus deriding the Babylonian idols for their inability to save them-

selves from captivity, he meant to glance back at the case before us, in which the ark of God came forth in triumph from captivity among the Philistines. Another prophet predicts that Ptolemy Euergetes should carry captive into Egypt the gods of the Syrians.[1] Jeremiah also foretold that Chemosh, the god of Moab, should be borne into captivity, to the shame and confusion of his worshippers.[2] There are several examples of this among the pagan writers.

Plutarch relates, that till the time of Marcellus the Romans had been content with really warlike trophies; but he first brought fine Grecian images and pictures of the gods to adorn his triumph on his return from Syracuse. This, he says, pleased the multitude; but thoughtful men were dissatisfied, doubting whether he had not brought upon them the malice and hate of the gods he thus pretended to make captive. He adds, the old men liked better the conduct of Fabius Maximus, who, when he took Tarentum, brought away indeed much gold and other useful things, but left the images of the gods standing in their places, observing, "Let us leave to the Tarentines the gods offended with them."

With these analogous cases before us, and with the result in view, we have no doubt that the ark was placed by the Philistines "in the house of Dagon," their god, at Ashdod, in order to give honour to their own idol, by exhibiting him as triumphant over Jehovah, although some have fancied that they placed the ark in this their sacred place, in order to render it honour, and even to adopt it as a god.

This people had reason to distrust the triumph of their idol when, next morning, they found it lying on the floor, prostrate before the ark of God. But it might be an accident; so they set it up in its place. The morning after, it was not only fallen, but broken. The language in which this is related is remarkable: "The head of Dagon, and both the palms of his hands, were cut off upon the threshold; *only the Dagon was left to him.*" This raises a question as to the form of this idol, and what was "the Dagon" which remained after the head and hands were separated, and which gave name to the whole image. *Dagon* means "corn" in Hebrew, whence some have thought that Dagon was the Philistine god of agriculture. There is nothing but the mere name to countenance this notion, and every other cir-

[1] Hall's *Contemplations*, Book xi., Cont. 7.
[2] Isaiah 46:1,2.
[1] Daniel 11:8.   [2] Jeremiah 48:7,13.

cumstance is against it. Then, again, *Dag* means "a fish;" whence, and from the incidents, it has been generally understood that the image was that of a kind of merman—the upper part human, with a fishy extremity. Certainly, the expression in the text, that "the Dagon" remained after the head and hands were broken off, is greatly in favour of this conclusion. This is the opinion of the Jewish writers, and it is supported by analogies. We know, in fact, that the neighbouring Phœnicians had an idol of this shape—essentially, indeed, the same, except that it bore a female form. This was called Derketo, otherwise Atergatis. The Babylonians had also a tradition, that in the beginning of their history, an extraordinary being, called Oannes, having the body of a fish, but the head, hands, feet, and voice of a man, emerged from the Erythrean Sea, appeared in Babylon, and taught the rude inhabitants the use of letters, arts, religion, law, and agriculture; that, after long intervals, other similar beings appeared, and communicated the same precious lore in detail, and that the last of these was called Odakon, the resemblance of which to Dagon is very clear. It is not difficult to recognize in these fables the distorted tradition of more civilized persons, who in ancient times came by sea or river, and taught useful arts to barbarous nations, by whom they were after death worshipped as gods. Having no memorials of the Philistines, no figure of their Dagon has been found; but representations of the corresponding Oannes or Odakon of the Babylonians, and Derketo of the Phœnicians, have been discovered, and answer to the general notion respecting the form this idol bore.[1]

BABYLONIAN REPRESENTATION OF DAGON AND DERKETO

One would suppose that this event would have convinced the Philistines of the impotency of the idol they worshipped. It seems, indeed, to have revived their former dread of the God of Israel; but it did not lessen their devotion to their own idolatry. Nay, rather, it engaged them in a new

[1] The cut is from a Babylonian engraved stone in the British Museum, and appears to represent both the Oannes, Odakon, or Dagon; and the Atergatis or Derketo, of the Babylonians and the Syrians.

form of superstition; for "therefore neither the priests of Dagon, nor any that come into Dagon's house, tread upon the threshold of Dagon's house in Ashdod unto this day." It may be doubtful whether this was in reverence of the threshold, since it had been touched by the superior parts of Dagon's image, or in detestation of it, as having been instrumental in this mutilation of the idol. Henceforth, however, they were careful not to tread upon it, but stepped or leaped over it; a custom which, it seems, continued not only to the latter days of Samuel, the author of this book, but down to the time of Zephaniah, who seems to allude to it: "In the same day will I punish all them that leap on [or *over*] the threshold."[1] It is curious that their very superstition led to the establishment of a custom which could not but serve as a standing memorial of the discomfiture of their idol in the presence of the ark of the Lord. Not unlike this usage in form, though different in principle, being simply a memorial of an event, and not a superstitious rite, is the ancient custom of the Jews in abstaining from the part, in the animals they use for food, corresponding to "the sinew that shrank" in the thigh of Jacob when the angel wrestled with him.[2]

Although this fact accounts for the reverence of the threshold among the Philistines, such a superstition was not peculiar to them. There are many traces of it with regard to other temples and among other nations. It comes before us, indeed, chiefly in the form of the votaries kneeling and kissing the threshold in adoration or reverence. But this implies the not treading on it; for votaries do not tread beneath their feet that which they thus venerate. The allusions to this in the Roman poets are well known. The early Christians adopted this custom of kissing the threshold, in regard to churches particularly venerated. It is indeed still in use among Roman Catholics; and old Christopher Ness remarks, "'Tis pity such reverencing of the thresholds of temples should be found as among Pagans, so among Papagans also, who kiss the threshold of St. Peter's Church at Rome to this day."

This ancient reverence for the threshold was not limited to temples. A sort of superstitious regard for the threshold generally may be detected among many nations. The threshold was

[1] Zephaniah 1:9.   [2] Genesis 32:32.

sacred to Vesta among the Romans, who held this deity in so much respect, that a bride, in entering for the first time the house of her husband, was not allowed to touch the threshold of the door;[1] and we learn from Tibullus,[2] that it was regarded as a very ill omen for a person to strike his foot against the threshold on quitting his house in the morning.

In the modern East, the indications of the same custom are abundant. The Persians, in particular, treat with great respect the thresholds of certain mosques, in which the remains of their holy men are deposited. They are usually covered with plates of silver; and to tread upon them is a crime not to be expiated but by severe penalties. Thus, immediately below the sixth distich, inscribed over the gate of the famous mausoleum at Kom, are the words: "Happy and glorious is the believer, who through reverence shall prostrate himself with his head *on the threshold of this gate*, in doing which he will imitate the sun and the moon." In fact, before they venture to cross such thresholds, they kneel down and kiss them; and in passing over, are most careful not to touch them with any part of their feet or their raiment. This feeling is in a measure extended to the palaces of kings, and in a lesser degree to the thresholds of private mansions. In writing to a prince, it is usual to say: "Let me make the dust of your threshold into *Surmeh* (collyrium) for my eyelids;" and Chardin relates, that in his time the threshold of the royal palace at Ispahan was one large stone of green porphyry, on which no one was allowed to tread.

Ashdod, to which the ark of the Lord was taken, was one of the five royal cities of Philistia. It stood on a low rounded hill, with the great fertile plain stretching out eastward from its base to the mountains of Judah; while on the west it looked over a broad belt of sandy downs to the bright waters of the Mediterranean. The temple of Dagon crowned the summit; and the worshippers of the "Fish-god"—emblem apparently of maritime wealth and prosperity—could see the wide and fair dominions of their deity. Ashdod was captured by the victorious Jews during the wars of the Maccabees, and the temple of Dagon laid in ruins. Though mentioned in New Testament history under its Greek name Azotus, it never recovered its prosperity; and now it is a mere village of mud hovels, without a trace of ancient greatness, save a few broken columns and hewn stones strewn among its terraced vineyards.

[1] Lucan, lib. ii., 359.   [2] Tibullus, lib. i., *Eleg.* iii.

It is worthy of note, with regard to the image of Dagon, that Layard, in his *Nineveh and its Remains*, describes a bas-relief from Khorsabad, in which a figure is represented in the sea, with the head of a man and the body of a fish. It is surrounded by a variety of marine animals. Layard supposes that the bas-relief represents the capture of the towns of Philistia, and especially Ashdod, by the Assyrian king Sargon; and if so, there can hardly be a doubt that the principal figure upon it is the fish-god Dagon.

P.

TELESMS

1 Samuel 6:1-5

THE men of Ashdod, although impressed by the discomfiture of their idol, were not thereby moved to any immediate action with respect to the ark of Israel. Their obdurate determination still to retain this glorious monument of their triumph, drew down upon them further judgments to constrain them to render to Jehovah the glory which was His due. Men are most keenly sensible of the evils which touch their skin and their flesh. They were therefore smitten with a painful and grievous disease, the nature of which is not well determined, but which is supposed to have been the hemorrhoids or piles, which seems to have been in many cases fatal. This they rightly ascribed to the wrath of the God whose ark they detained; but instead of seeing at once that their best course was to restore it to the Israelites, their reluctance to part with it induced them to try the experiment of removing it to another of their cities—to Gath, in the hope that as the judgment was confined to Ashdod and its neighbourhood, the indignation which had gone forth might be only against that particular place. The people of Gath seem to have placed it in the open fields; if, indeed, it had not been removed to the open ground of Ashdod immediately after the judgment on Dagon, as they might naturally after that apprehend special judgment upon any building in which it was contained. This inference is built upon the language of the text (in the original), that the ark "abode in *the field* of the Philistines seven months." The reason indeed is not conclusive, seeing that the word "field" may be understood generally of "land" or "country," and is here so understood by our translators. A probability in favour of that opinion is, that the next judgment was upon the fields—the produce of the ground being destroyed by immense swarms of field mice—if this were not indeed simultaneous with the "emerods," for by that grievous disease the men of Gath also were smitten, as soon as the ark of God arrived. This could not be borne; and the ark was removed to another town called Ekron. But the people there positively refused to receive it. Their language bore most emphatic testimony to the effect which had been produced: "They have brought about the ark of the God of Israel to us, to slay us and our people." This brought matters to a crisis: the "lords" or magistrates of the five cities constituting this state—as well those that had not been visited by the ark as those that had—came together in counsel to determine the course which was to be taken. The conclusion reluctantly reached was to send the ark back to the Israelites with all becoming observances, and not without such offerings as might, it was hoped, avert from themselves the wrath under which they so long had suffered. These were five golden mice, one for each of the Philistine cities; and five golden emerods, as symbolical of the afflictions they had endured, and in recognition that they came from Jehovah, and that He alone could remove them.

This offering, so remarkable in our view, but so familiar to the ideas of the ancients and of the modern Orientals, does in various points well merit more attention than our limits allow us to bestow upon it.

It appears to us that these articles are to be regarded not merely as votive or trespass offerings, but as *telesms* (talismans), specially formed under astrological calculations, to counteract the plagues with which they were visited, unless the effect were neutralized by the continued implacability of Israel's offended God; and we have little doubt that this course was suggested by the astrologers, who would not fail to be consulted on the occasion, as the best that, under the circumstances, could be adopted. The general reader can have little idea of the extent to which notions of this sort, founded on astronomical combinations, pervaded the ancient mind, and were prevalent even in Europe until a comparatively recent period. Indeed, they are not wholly extinct among ourselves even now. We are not

sure of being successful in making the principles and the practical jargon of this branch of "science, falsely so called," intelligible to the reader, rendered, as its peculiar terms must be, out of the Hebrew, Arabic, Greek, and Latin languages into our own.

It is, then, held that the forms of things here below correspond with the like forms of things above, and that the celestial forms have a ruling influence upon the sublunary. For example, the scorpion and the serpent in the heavens have an influence upon those on the earth. The wise, therefore, it is stated, carefully observing when a planet entered into any of these forms or signs, placed the planet on the horoscope, and engraved the form upon a stone; adding what else might be necessary to fit it for preservation or for destruction, according to the purpose of the operation. The *telesm*, thus rendered efficient for good or for evil, was then completed. A great authority on these subjects, Ali Ibn Rodoan, illustrates this by an anecdote of a Saracen's servant, who had been stung by a scorpion, but was instantly cured by his master with a telesm, which had the figure of a scorpion engraven on it. In explanation of this, the Saracen said that

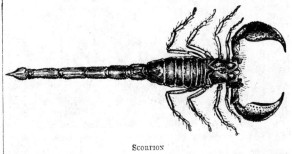

SCORPION

the figure was cut when the moon was in the sign Scorpio, and that the sign was in one of the four angles.

A man of note in this kind of lore was Apollonius Tyaneus, who was reported to have wrought such extraordinary effects by his skill in this branch of occult science, that there were not wanting among the enemies of Christianity, those who dared to compare the wonders wrought, or pretended to be wrought, by him, with the miracles of Christ Himself; and there were even those who gave the preference to the pagan philosopher, an enormity justly denounced by Eusebius of Pamphylia. But it is well to notice a few of the deeds of this man which bear upon the subject, and tend to illustrate the ideas concerning it which prevailed. His deeds were such, in truth, as in their day excited the doubt and perplexity of even orthodox believers, who, although they were unable to account for them, supposed that this wonderful man had, by means of his telesms, stilled the waves of the sea and the raging of the winds, and had protected countries from destructive vermin and the incursions of wild beasts. Take the following from an ancient author, cited by Joannes Antiochenus Melala, in the tenth book of his *Chronographia.* The original is in Greek, which may be thus translated: " In the reign of Domitian, flourished the most learned Apollonius Tyaneus, who won for himself a great name by travelling about and making telesms in all the places to which he came, for cities and for the countries to which they belonged. From Rome he went to Byzantium, and entering into that city (now more happily called Constantinople), he made there

CONSTANTINOPLE

also many telesms at the instance of the citizens, as that against the storks, that against the river Lycus, which passes through the middle of the city, that against the tortoises, that against the horses, and other strange things. Then, afterwards, leaving Byzantium, he went and did the like in other cities. From Tyanis he came into Syria, and so to Antioch the Great, where also he was requested by the chief men of the city to make such telesms as they had need of. And he made one against the north wind, and set it up in the east part of the city."

This author goes on, and describes at some length the charms of Apollonius against the gnats and scorpions; adding, moreover, that walking one day with the chief men of the town to observe the situation of the place, he came to a ruinous pillar, and on inquiring for what object it had been erected, was told that in the days of Caius Cæsar, when the city had been shaken by an earthquake, one Debboris, a talismanic philosopher, had set up this pillar as a telesm to protect the city in time to come. On the pillar he had fixed a brazen pectoral inscribed with certain words: but this had in process of time been consumed by lightning, and the citizens were now urgent with Apollonius to set up a new one. But the philosopher, fetching a deep sigh, refused to make any more telesms against earthquakes.

That which has most bearing upon the present case is the telesms against scorpions. It is related that Apollonius caused an image of a scorpion to be molten in brass, and set it up upon a small pillar in the midst of the city of Antioch, whereupon the scorpions vanished out of all the district.

Telesms of this kind are noticed as existing in various places. There was one at Hamah (the Hamath of Scripture), in Syria. In the midst of this town, says an Arabian geographer, there is a stone fixed in a wall, having upon it the figure of a scorpion; and when any one is bitten by one of these animals, he takes in clay the figure of this scorpion, and on applying it to the part affected, is immediately cured. It used to be reported, that in the lower part of the district in which Cairo is situated, the crocodiles were harmless, but in the upper part devoured the people. To provide against this, the wise men cast a crocodile in lead, and inscribing it with an Egyptian charm, buried it in the foundations of a temple. The crocodiles of the upper region then became as harmless as those of the lower. But when, at the command of the Sultan Achmet-ibn Tulon, the image was melted down, the crocodiles again became as injurious as of old. This superstition was not confined to the East. It is related by Gregory of Tours, that at the repair of an old bridge in Paris there were found the images of a serpent and a mouse in brass; and when they were taken away, the serpents and the mice came up in great numbers.

Travellers have speculated much upon the

possible object of the Serpentine Column (now broken) in the grand square (hippodrome) of Constantinople. It consists of the bodies of three intertwisted serpents, in hollow bronze. It formerly terminated at the top in three serpents' heads; but these have now disappeared, and it is related that when the victorious Mohammed the Second entered the city, either flushed with the excitement of triumph, or desirous of exhibiting his personal strength, he struck off one of the serpents' heads at a single blow. This curious work once belonged to the Persians, and was among the spoils taken from them at the battle of Platæa. It was even then supposed to have been very ancient, and could not well have been less than 3,000 years old. The result of our own inquiries on the spot, as to the existing notions concerning its original design, coincides with the intimations of old authors, that it was a telesm designed to protect from serpents the locality in which it might be found. It is known that there once existed in the same square an equestrian statue set up against the plague, the destruction of which was supposed to have left the city exposed to fearful periodical mortalities.[1]

Again, there is said to have been in the same city a talismanic ship of brass, set up against the dangers of the tempestuous sea. While it stood entire, the raging of that sea was repressed; but some parts having been (no one knew how) broken off and removed, the sea became again unruly and troubled. The cause of this being inquired into, the broken parts of the marvellous ship of brass were diligently sought out and put together, and once more the wind and the sea obeyed the mighty spell thus laid upon them. That it might be seen beyond question whether this were really the cause why vessels could not safely come into port, the broken parts were again removed, and forthwith all ships that touched upon the coast were driven back by the violence of the waves. This confirmed the opinion, that the injury to the brazen ship was the cause of the impeded navigation, and it was therefore most carefully repaired, to the great comfort of the city.[2]

[1] Leunelav. *Pandect. Hist. Turc.*, 130. Much more of this sort may be found in Mizald, *Cent. M.S.*, and Gaffarel, *Curiositez inouyes, sur la sculpture talismanique des Persans*, etc. Paris, 1629; chap. 6.

[2] Zonaræ, *Annales*, tom. iii., in *Anastasio*.

The results of these examples, and of many others which might be cited, illustrate the prevalence of the notion, that in case of any extraordinary plague, either of disease or of noxious creatures visiting a town or country, it was usual, by way of remedy, to erect an image or symbol of the evil, under the supposed influence of celestial configurations. That the Philistines meant something of this sort, is in the highest degree probable. Had the ark remained among themselves, these memorials would no doubt have been set up in the temple; but as it was to be sent away, there was no mode of suitable appropriation but by placing these things thereon.

As to the mice, Parcelsus thought that he had found the way in which they might be prepared with reference to such an object. He gives this recipe for purging a house of mice: "Make an iron mouse, under the conjunction of Saturn and Mars, in the house of ♃. Imprint upon its belly ALBAMATATOX, etc. Then place the telesm in the middle of the house, and the vermin will instantly leave the place." He furthermore declares, that if a live mouse be tied to this image, it will die immediately.[1]

With regard to the images of emerods, Maimonides, who lived in an age and country which entertained these old beliefs, supposes that they were so called, not from their external form, which indeed it would be difficult to give, but from a secret influence which resided in them, remedial against the malady.[2]

Again, the Philistine astrologers could not but have heard that *this* God had shown his Divine complacency in the brazen serpent set upon a pole in the wilderness. This they, with their notions, would regard as a telesm, constructed on some such principles as have been indicated; and as that image of a serpent was effectual against the plague of serpents, they might not unreasonably infer that similar images of their own inflictions might be equally effectual. Indeed, there have not been wanting persons to suggest that the whole of this set of ideas regarding telesms may have originated in a distorted view of this transaction.

[1] *Archidox. Mag.*, iii., 135.

[2] *More Nevochim*, Pt. i., ch. I.

THE ARK RESTORED

1 Samuel 6:7-21

WITH all their anxiety to repair the error they had committed, the Philistines had a lurking suspicion that, after all, there might be no real connection between the ark of the Lord and the inflictions under which they had been suffering. It might have been a " chance " that happened to them. The plan to which they resorted for making this matter clear, doubtless seemed to themselves very ingenious and conclusive, and was certainly so overruled in the providence of God as to confirm them in the conviction that all these things were the work of His hand.

First, they prepared a " new cart." The word rendered "cart" is the same which is translated by " waggon " at an earlier period, in the mention of the vehicles which the king of Egypt sent to assist in transporting the family of Israel from Canaan. It would seem that carts, at least as adapted to purposes of travel, were not then used in that country, seeing that the king would scarcely have sent conveyances that might have been obtained in Canaan, and since the sight of them convinced Jacob of the truth of the strange story told by his sons. The Israelites themselves brought carts into Palestine; for although the more sacred utensils, as the ark, the altars, the table of shew-bread, and the golden candlestick,

EGYPTIAN AGRICULTURAL CART

were borne on the shoulders of priests and Levites, six covered carts were prepared in the wilderness, and employed in the removal of the parts of the

tabernacle itself, each being drawn by two oxen.[1] In the pagan East, at the present day, wheel carriages or cars are still employed in the conveyance of the idols in sacred processions; but in *south-western* Asia carts are only used for the transport of agricultural produce. They are of rude construction, with solid wheels, and exceedingly like those represented in Egyptian paintings. Indeed, *all carts* so represented have the wheels solid, although all *chariots* have light wheels with spokes. We find that although the sacred arks of the Egyptians were usually borne on the shoulders of priests, carts were sometimes employed. As shown in the annexed engraving, these cars were little more than platforms mounted on small

EGYPTIAN SACRED CAR

wheels; and it is likely that the cart prepared by the Philistines for the ark, and subsequently that in which David first attempted to remove it to Jerusalem, were of the same kind. In the latter case, its construction will explain the anxiety of Uzzah lest it should be displaced when the cart was jolted by the oxen. (2 Sam. vi. 6.) Among the sculptures of the Assyrians we do not find any instance of sacred objects being borne on carts, although wheeled vehicles were in use among them; but there is one piece in which the images of the gods are borne on the shoulders of men. With these instances of mixed usage even among the Israelites, the Philistines may perhaps have been doubtful as to the right mode of conveying the ark; at least they would not have been aware that it was wrong to transport it in a cart. But we must recollect that they had actually seen it borne upon the shoulders of the Levites; and we therefore think they chose this mode, partly because they were reasonably afraid to carry it, and partly because this mode of conveyance was essential to the experiment they meant to try. They provided a *new* cart, in the proper feeling that this sacred object required a vehicle which had not previously been employed for meaner uses.

The experiment to be tried was this: To the

[1] Numbers 7:3-9; compare 4:4-15.

cart were attached two kine which had never yet been under the yoke, and which, therefore, were not likely to exhibit much docility in being thus first put to draught. These kine had also calves, which were shut up at home; and from the well known impatience of such animals in being separated from their young, it was certain that they would naturally be altogether disinclined to go away from the place where their calves remained. Then, again, the cows, thus unused to the service to which they were put, and indisposed for it, were not to be driven or guided: they were to be left entirely to their own impulses. If they took the direct course to the land of Israel, instead of turning back to their calves, or proceeding in any other direction, it was to be concluded that it was the hand of the God of Israel which had been so heavy upon the Philistines; but if not, they had been visited in the ordinary course of events: "it was a chance"—an entirely fortuitous set of circumstances. The Lord condescended to respond to an appeal which, from a people that knew Him, would have been unbecoming, although something essentially of the same nature had been tried by Gideon. The kine proceeded quietly along, lowing, indeed, at being separated from their calves, and thereby showing the restraint that was laid upon their nature. And more than this: they proceeded straight away from their young, taking no other road than the direct one to the nearest point of the land of Israel, followed by the Philistine lords, who, doubtless, beheld these things with great admiration.

The name of the first place to which the ark came by this road was Beth-shemesh. The people were at work in the fields, it being harvest time, when they caught the first sight of the approaching ark. Their delight and exultation at the return of that glory which had departed from Israel, may perhaps be imagined, but cannot well be described. Beth-shemesh, it may be observed, was a city of the priests, and some of them, with Levites, formed a part of the population. In such places the public grief for the loss of the ark can easily be supposed to have been of peculiar intensity. In the transports of their joy, the Bethshemites— or say the priests and Levites there—supposed that on an occasion so extraordinary they might allow themselves to dispense with the ordinary law regarding sacrifices, which forbade any to be offered save on the one altar in the court of the tabernacle. They therefore took down the ark from the cart, near a great stone, which might serve for an altar. The cart they broke up to serve for fuel, partly because there was no other so ready at hand, and partly in order that, since it had borne the ark, it might not afterwards be used for any less noble service. They then slew the kine which had drawn the cart, and offered them up upon the great stone for a burnt-offering. One who has studied the laws regulating sacrifices, perceives in this other irregularities besides the one just pointed out. By offering the sacrifice here, they necessarily dispensed with the sacred fire originally kindled from heaven; and, moreover, in holocausts, or sacrifices wholly consumed upon the altar, only the male animal could be used, though the female was allowed in peace-offerings, when parts only of the victims were consumed upon the altar. It may be conceived that the Bethshemites were led into this last irregularity—if they knew that it was such, and they ought to have known it—by their wish to prevent these kine from being thereafter engaged in any less sacred service. In the inspired narrative these facts are not, in themselves, imputed to the Bethshemites as a fault. But with a view to what subsequently occurred, they are important, as showing the beginnings of an encroaching and disorderly spirit, regardless of some of the plainest directions of the law, which being thus far, in tenderness to them, unrebuked, led to further encroachments, by which a terrible judgment was brought upon them. Many, from insufficient reference to these circumstances— from not considering how much had previously been overlooked,—are inclined to feel as if the punishment which fell upon them for a further and more audacious encroachment, was too sudden, and too severe; but we now see that it was to repress a growing evil, which might, if altogether unpunished, end in the entire subversion of the ritual service, which the wisdom of God had established as the fittest for this people. There is no knowing to what lengths the matter might have gone, if the next encroachment had been left without signal chastisement.

The offence was, that they *looked into the ark.* To do this it must have been handled very irreverently, and the lid with the cherubim removed. For this there was no possible occasion or excuse, but the merest and idlest curiosity; and a painful sight to a well regulated mind it must have been, to behold this sacred object, never approached even by the priests without the most profound reverence, and never but by them beheld unless enveloped with veils,[1] exposed in the open fields with the sacred cover removed, and a tumultuous rabble flocking from all quarters to view its mysteries exposed to the light of day. Even the Philistines had been less irreverent. They had not dared to open the ark, even to insert therein their golden offerings, but had placed them in a casket which they laid upon the top of the ark. This, it is expressly stated, the Bethshemites "took down;" and it is very possible that the intention of placing this casket in the ark supplied them with the excuse for removing the cover.

They were heavily punished. A large number of them were smitten dead upon the spot. There is some doubt about the number. In the authorized version we read: "He smote of the people fifty thousand and threescore and ten men." To this it is objected, that a place like Beth-shemesh, of no figure in history, and which Josephus calls a village, could hardly have had so many inhabitants altogether. But it must be remembered that the important news of the arrival of the ark would spread rapidly, and bring together in a very short time a large multitude from all the neighbouring places. There is, therefore, no real objection as to the presence of such a number of people as might sustain this loss. Still, one is willing to suppose there is some mistake in this high number; and the mode of expression in stating the number is so peculiar, as to suggest that it has been misunderstood. It is to be noted that Josephus and the Talmuds, with the same text before them, make the number to be seventy—the very number which is stated *above* fifty thousand. It is, therefore, reasonably conjectured that these authorities read not "fifty thousand," but "fifty of a thousand," which, by a kind of decimation of the number of offenders, whatever was the actual population, would make the whole number concerned not exceed 1,400, which seems so suitable a popula-

[1] The ark lay in the innermost sanctuary, only entered by the high priest once a year. In its removals the priests entered and covered it up, and only after this was done the Levites came in and bore it away. It was not lawful even for a Levite to touch it, on pain of death.

tion for such a place as Beth-shemesh, as may suggest that this transaction occurred before any considerable number of people had time to gather from the neighbouring parts. The supply of the particle *of* in such a case is not only admissible, but is often required by the construction of the Hebrew language. This often occurs in every version; and among other and very numerous instances the reader may refer to Ex. xix. 12; xxxvi. 8, 19, 34; Josh. x. 13; 2 Sam. xxiii. 24; 2 Kings xvii. 25.

I was never more deeply impressed with the simple, graphic truthfulness of the Scripture narrative, than on reading, first at Ekron and then at Bethshemesh, the story of the taking back of the ark. Ekron, now a miserable village, is situated on the southern slope of a low broad ridge, which separates the plain of Sharon from that of Philistia. At the foot of the ridge is Wady Surâr, a wide rich tract of meadow and corn field, lining the banks of a little torrent bed. And from the site of the old city the eye can follow the wady in its easy windings, up to the spot, some ten miles distant, where it contracts into a narrow glen, and disappears in the mountains of Judah. Just within the mouth of that glen, but hidden behind a projecting shoulder, lie the ruins of Bethshemesh. We read that the kine which drew the new cart "took the straight way to the way of Bethshemesh." The way lies straight up that valley. And we further read, that "they of Bethshemesh were reaping their wheat harvest *in the valley;* and they lifted up their eyes, and saw the ark:" they saw it in the distance as it came up through the mouth of the glen into their more confined mountain territory, and they "rejoiced to see it."

P.

ISRAEL AT MIZPEH

1 Samuel 7:1-6

AFTER the death of Eli and his sons, there was no one in Israel who stood before the people, with any claims to attention comparable to those of Samuel. His constant presence at the tabernacle had made the Israelites familiar with his person and history from childhood. The vision of the Lord with which he had even in early youth been favoured, followed by subsequent communications, which enabled him, "in the name of the Lord," to speak for warning, for reproof, for counsel, pointed him out as a commissioned prophet—a character rare before his time, but which afterwards became conspicuous and frequent in the history of Israel. After the account of that remarkable denunciation upon Eli and upon his house which we have already considered, the historian, before proceeding to the public transactions, carries forward the history of Samuel to the point where he means to take it up again, by the remark: "And Samuel grew; and the Lord was with him, and did let none of his words fall to the ground. And all Israel, from Dan even to Beersheba, knew that Samuel was established to be a prophet of the Lord." These words may indicate the nature of the influence which Samuel exerted during the twenty years following the subjugation of Israel by the Philistines. During this period, we cannot doubt that he continually lifted up his voice against the corruption of the times, and strove to rouse the people to a sense of the duty they owed to their country and their God. His exhortations were greatly needed. The abominations of the sons of Eli had corrupted the people, and brought discredit upon the worship of God. Under these cir-

apart to the charge of the ark; probably to keep things clean and orderly about it, to guard from intrusion the place where it lay, and to prevent it from being used or touched irreverently. It was thus that the ark remained for nearly a half century, until it was removed by David. It would seem, from Jer. vii. 12, 14; xxvi. 6, 9, that Shiloh, so long the seat of the ark and the tabernacle, had been destroyed by the Philistines, which may account for its not having been restored to that place; and may have tended in no small degree to increase the disorders of the times, by inducing much neglect of, and irregularity in, the performance of the ritual services and sacrifices.

During the same period, the Israelites seem to have submitted in hopeless despondency to the dominion of the Philistines. The numbers of that people were too small to allow them to think of occupying the country they had conquered; nor did they at any time evince much disposition to spread themselves inland. They were content with their position on and near the coast, and seem only to have attached a few border towns to their own territory: the rest—or, more properly speaking, the southern part of the land—they held simply in military subjection by means of garrisons established at different strong points in the country. The Israelites were, of course, made to defray the heavy expense of these garrisons; and this, with the tribute exacted by their uncircumcised masters, could not but form a heavy burden upon an agricultural people like the Israelites, and must have been a serious check upon their temporal prosperity, if it did not keep them in an impoverished condition.

KIRJATH-JEARIM

cumstances, idolatry had re-appeared and become prevalent, while the ark lay neglected by the nation at Kirjath-jearim, whither it had been removed from Beth-shemesh, and deposited in the house of a man named Abinadab, who probably was, as Josephus affirms, a Levite, though in that case he could only have been a sojourner at Kirjath-jearim, which was not a Levitical city. This man's son, Eleazar, was set

By the time that the twenty years had expired, the exhortations of Samuel, and probably some other righteous men, had brought the Israelites round to a better state of thought and feeling; and, convinced that their best course for returning to prosperity and health would be to place themselves under the guidance of a man so wise and holy as Samuel, he was formally recognized by them as their judge, although most of the essential functions of that office had already come insensibly into his hands, and been exercised by him.

The first act of Samuel as judge was to extirpate idolatry; and he hesitated not to promise the people, that at this cost God would not fail to deliver them from the yoke of the Philistines. He then called an assembly of the people at Mizpeh, on the borders of Judah and Benjamin (not the Mizpeh beyond the Jordan), to engage with him in a solemn act of prayer and humiliation before the Lord, as a suitable commencement of a new and more prosperous career. Mizpeh seems to have been chosen as a known place of concourse to the tribes on high national occasions. It was here that the tribes gathered together when the injured Levite called them to vengeance. (Judg. xx. 1.)

The ceremonies, being not at the tabernacle, and not under the regular ordinance of the law as administered by the priesthood, offer some peculiarities which may well be noticed. They fasted on that day, and began it by *drawing water and pouring it out before the Lord,* and said, "We have sinned against the Lord." We find no such ceremonial as this prescribed in the law, or exhibited in any former instance; yet it must have had a very distinct and intelligent signification to the people. Some have explained it by reference to the custom at the feast of tabernacles (in a later age), of drawing water from the pool of Siloam, and pouring it out before the Lord. But there is no trace of this custom in the law, or indeed in the Old Testament. It seems to have come into use after the captivity, and it was an act of rejoicing, not like this, of humiliation. There is an allusion to it in John vii. 36-38. It is related by Jerome as a tradition of the Jews, that, as in the water of jealousy, curses were cast into the water, by being written, and the writing being washed off into it, and that idolaters were tried by drinking of it. If any idolater denied the worship of idols, and tasted it, his lips became immediately so glued together that they could not be separated, and he thus became known, and was put to death. In answer to this, it is sufficient to remark, that the water was not drunk, but *poured out.* Some say it was a symbol of the

pouring out of their hearts in humiliation before the Lord, and of the atonement and expiation of their sins, which passed away as water, to be remembered no more. Others make this act a sign of their renunciation of idolatry, so that, as of water entirely poured out, nothing of it should remain. Josephus makes it a libation; but it does not appear that water was used by the Jews in their libations. Another opinion, enforced by some writers of good judgment, is, that the Israelites, to render the fasting more complete, and in evidence of its intensity, drew forth, and cast away from the wells and reservoirs, all the water to be found in the place. They might have been led to this by considering that the indiscretion of one person might neutralize the intended effect of this solemnity. But in case this were done, how did they get water to quench their thirst in the evening after the fast, and what were the fixed inhabitants likely to say to this exhaustion of their store of water? There is something wrong in all these *special* interpretations. We take this act to have been the sign and symbol, or rather confirmation, of an oath— a solemn vow. To pour out water on the ground, is in the East an ancient way of taking a solemn oath; the words and promises that had gone forth from their mouth being as "water spilt upon the ground, that cannot be gathered up again." Mr. Roberts well illustrates this by an anecdote from the Hindu mythology: "When the god Vishnu, in the disguise of a dwarf, requested the giant Maha-Ville (Bali) to grant him one step of his kingdom, the favour was conceded, and CONFIRMED by Maha-Ville pouring out water before the dwarf. But in that ancient work, the *Scanda Purana,* where the account is given of the marriage of the god Siva with Paravati, it is said of the father—He placed the hand of the goddess Paravati, genetrix of the world, in the hand of Parama Easuran (Siva), and *pouring out the water,* said, "I give her to thee with all my heart." This, therefore, was done in confirmation of the compact.

Nebi *Samwell,* or Samuel, is a conspicuous eminence, to the north of Jerusalem, which is sure to attract the traveller's attention, and it has been identified by Dr. Robinson, as Mizpeh. But Nebi Samwell, is more probably shown by Dr. Stanley to be the high place of Gibeon. The Hebrew word *Mizpeh* means *the Watch Tower:*—and the same meaning attaches to the Greek word *Scopus;*

and Scopus, as Dr. Stanley remarks, was another eminence to the north of the Holy City. Wherever Scopus was, there was Mizpeh.

Lieutenant Conder, of the Palestine Exploration Society, believes that he has identified the spot, and for it he gives several reasons. To the north of Jerusalem, on the road to Nablous, there is one particular elevation which corresponds with the description of Scopus as given by Josephus. "It is one of the peculiarities," says Lieut. Conder, "of the site of the capital, that it is entirely concealed until the last ridge has been reached, from which the road descends, and passes along to the Damascus gate. From this ridge the grey northern wall of the city is seen in its full extent, the great domes of the Holy Sepulchre and Jewish Synagogue, the Tower of David, and the Crescent of the Mosque lying low down on the sloping site, which makes Jerusalem appear as if in constant danger of sliding into the Kedron Valley; all these burst suddenly on the view, at the distance of about one and a half miles, and remind one forcibly

of the description by Josephus of that place, very properly called Scopus,—from which point 'a plain view might be taken of the great temple and the flourishing city.' Directly in front of the ridge is a plateau, averaging 300 yards in breadth, and extending 800 yards eastward. On the west the rough ground extends to the eminence above the tombs of the Judges."—*Quarterly Statement*, January 1874, 112.

At all events Mizpeh must have been within sight of the spot where Jerusalem was afterwards built. Hence, the solemn assembly held, at the time described in the above illustration, met in the vicinity of the place whither afterwards the tribes went up to keep holy festival in the Temple : and the drawing of water must have been performed at no great distance from the scene of the Feast of Tabernacles, when Jesus stood, and cried, on "the last day, that great day of the Feast,"—"If any man thirst, let him come unto me and drink."

S.

FEAST OF TABERNACLES

EBENEZER

1 Samuel 7:7-14

IT is easier to gain a battle than to retain in long subjection the nation by whom a battle has been lost. The Philistines, however potent in the field, seem to have been consciously weak for occupation, their small territory being but ill able to afford the number of warriors, constantly in arms, which was required to maintain permanent garrisons in a country much larger and far more populous

than their own. This feeling would make them more jealous and suspicious than a greater power would have been; and they would be led to exercise severer measures of repression and safeguard by the consciousness of wanting an overwhelming force, immediately available for the putting down of any overt act of revolt that might occur. The strong endures and tolerates much, in the consciousness that his power, whenever he chooses to put it forth, is sufficient to redress all that may have gone wrong. The weak is watchful to prevent or smother all that carries the possibility of danger, in order to avert a trial of strength, of the issue of which any doubt can be entertained. Of this class were the Philistines, who were under much alarm when they heard of the great assemblage of the tribes at Mizpeh; apprehending that such a gathering, under one so well known as Samuel, boded no good to their dominions, and might be intended to organize the nation's assertion of its own independence. They therefore, without waiting for precise information, hastened to advance in military force towards the place of assemblage. The Israelites had at the time no such immediate designs as were imputed to them, although they doubtless looked forward to eventual deliverance from the sway of their neighbours. They were greatly distressed when this news came to them, being wholly unprepared for action against the Philistines. Probably the actual impulse of the moment would have led them not to offer battle to their oppressors, but to tender submission to them. Now was the time, however, for Samuel to show himself equal to the exigency imposed upon him, and worthy of the leadership of the people, to which he had been appointed. It is true that he was a man of peace, whose habits and associations were far different from those of persons who have been "men of war from their youth." But his heart was full of patriotism and faith; and he shrank not from encouraging the people to stand up against the approaching host, nor from leading them himself to the battle.

The steps taken by him were, however, peculiar, and deserve attention. First, Samuel "took a sucking lamb, and offered it for a burnt-offering wholly unto the Lord." By this it is usually understood that he offered it entire, without taking off the skin, which was the perquisite of the priest, and without dividing the carcase into parts, as usual, and separating the head, the tail, the feet, and the internal fat. Samuel could not be unacquainted with the proper ceremonies, but there was probably no time for their exact observance. Samson's former case had now become his; the Philistines were upon him. At the first view there appear also other irregularities, equal seemingly to such as, before and after, drew down the divine displeasure. First, Samuel erected an altar for this sacrifice; although nothing is more distinct in the law, than that there were to be no offerings but at the great altar at the place of the tabernacle. Samuel did the same thing on other occasions, as did, at a later period, Elijah on Mount Carmel. It would also appear that Samuel himself, at this as at the other times, offered the sacrifice, although this was a function peculiar to the priesthood, and Samuel was only a Levite. This also is parallel to the case of Elijah. That they committed no offence, but rather did what was well-pleasing to God, appears from their sacrifices being most signally accepted. In the case of Elijah, this was shown by the descent of fire from heaven upon the sacrifice, which was consumed thereby; and this made that sacrifice less irregular than the offering of Samuel, for it was not lawful to offer sacrifice with any fire but that which was originally kindled from heaven, and which was preserved for the use of the great tabernacle altar. It is clear that Samuel's sacrifice must have been offered with common fire.

The difficulty is to reconcile the severe judgments denounced and inflicted for irregularities in the ritual service, with not only the complete impunity, but the direct sanction and approval, which attended the irregular actions of Samuel and other prophets with regard to the ritual observances. The point is of importance: for it is the action of the prophets from this time forward upon public affairs which gives to the history of the Jews much of its *peculiar* character; for which reason we mean to bestow especial attention upon their proceedings, without a clear apprehension of which the history itself can never be well understood.

It would appear, then, that the prophets, as men divinely authorized and inspired, were regarded as having a right to dispense with the strict requirements of the law on special and extraordinary occasions; and that, as prompted by the Spirit, it was lawful for them to do that which would have been most criminal in persons not so authorized, and would have brought down condign punishment upon them. And this authorized departure, when occasion demanded, from the strict requirements of the law, could not but operate beneficially upon the public mind. The rigid enforcement of every jot and tittle of the law, on ordinary occasions, might eventually, without the presence of a corrective and counteracting influence, have created a sort of idolatry for the mere letter of the law, and of every ritual detail, as in itself a divine thing. But the permitted departures therefrom by the prophets corrected this tendency, by directing attention more to the spiritual essence of those observances, teaching, as Samuel himself expressly declared on one occasion, that "to obey was better than sacrifice, and to hearken than the fat of lambs." The diligent reader of Scripture is aware that this upholding of the spirit above the mere letter of the ritual service was a peculiar function of the prophets, appearing with more and more distinctness as time advanced, until at last the prophets declared, with great plainness of speech, that the mere ritual service in all its parts, and the most sacred solemnities prescribed by the law, were, in the nakedness of their literal truth —apart from the spiritual influences which should be connected with them—not only unacceptable to the Lord, but abomination in His sight. Thus a most important part of the prophetic office was to maintain the spiritual character of the Hebrew worship, and to prevent the degeneracy of the people into such mere ritualism as they had fallen into at the time our Lord appeared. Indeed, it is important to notice, that this character of Judaism, as then existing, followed, and was no doubt in a great degree the effect of the long discontinuance of the prophetic office. Would not a man like Isaiah, for instance, have lifted up his voice day and night, against such a state of religion as prevailed in the time of our Saviour?

Still, these remarkable departures from the regular course of ritual observance were only resorted to when that course could not well be followed. It is clear that if, in the case before us, there was to be any sacrifice to seal the covenant which Israel had taken, it could only be then and there, as soon as it appeared that the Philistines were advancing. Besides, as it appears that Shiloh had been destroyed, it is doubtful whether the tabernacle and the altar, although preserved, had yet been set up elsewhere, or the regular service maintained. So, in the case of Elijah, a more regular sacrifice than that which he offered at Mount Carmel would have been impossible; for there was, in fact, no authorized altar of the Lord in the kingdom which was the scene of His labours and His mighty deeds. The temple and altar were afar off in the neighbouring kingdom of Judah.

Strengthened by these religious acts, the Israelites stood their ground when the Philistines appeared in battle array against them. They had only to stand still; for the Lord had put their enemies into such confusion by a tremendous thunderstorm, that they soon fled in dismay, and were pursued with great slaughter by the triumphant Israelites. The thunder was no doubt attended with lightning, which probably, as Josephus says, flashed in their faces, and struck their weapons out of their hands. He adds, also, that there was an earthquake, which caused great gaps in the earth, into which they fell. At the place where the pursuit ceased, and where it was seen that the Philistines were utterly beaten, and that Israel once more was free, Samuel set up a great stone, and called it Eben-ezer (the stone of help), saying, "Hitherto hath the Lord helped us." Now it is a memorable fact, which gave a touching emphasis to this memorial, that this was the very place where, twenty years before, the Israelites were defeated, and the ark of God was taken. The stone of help thus became a twofold monument.

It is interesting to note how, in most of their great struggles for their country and their liberty, God fought for His people. They were never left to the might of human arm or the wisdom of human tactics. These were not overlooked; but it was seen and felt that a supernatural power was at work directing and overruling all. The mightiest victories of Moses and Joshua, Barak and Gideon, Samuel and David, were owing to a direct forthputting of divine power. The God of Israel was emphatically the "God of battles."

The battle of Ebenezer must have been fought on, or very near, the spot where Joshua triumphed over the five confederate kings; and it is a remarkable fact, that in both cases the completeness of the victory was mainly the result of a terrific storm: "The Lord thundered on that day upon the Philistines, and discomfited them; and they were smitten before Israel" (compare Josh. x. 11; Judg. iv. 15; v. 20, 21).

P.

CORRUPTION OF JUSTICE

1 Samuel 7:15;8

It is remarkable how little is related of Samuel calculated to throw light upon his character and position during the twenty years in which he was the sole ruler of the Hebrew state. We hear more of him before he attains that high distinction, and more after he had been reluctantly constrained to resign much of his authority into other hands. Peace and prosperity are, however, seldom fruitful in materials for narrative; and the inference from the silence of the history is that the people enjoyed ease and security under his rule. It is related that his usual residence was at Ramah, his native place, whence he pro-

RAMAH

ceeded, in yearly circuit, to administer justice to the people, at Mizpeh, Gilgal, and Bethel, all of them places of sacred interest in the ancient history of the Israelites, and selected probably for that reason. We do not find that any writer has thought it needful to inquire why, if the object of Samuel was, as in the circuits of our own judges, to carry justice to the people, and to render it of more easy access to them, the circuit was confined to places so near to each other,—all, in fact, lying within the narrow limits of the small tribe of Benjamin. We should rather expect that, with that object in view, one of the towns would have been away in the north, another in the south, and the third in the country beyond the Jordan. We can only explain this by supposing that the territory of the southern tribes alone *practically* acknowledged Samuel's authority, or had any concern with the part of his history we have gone through. The northern and central tribes seem to have been little affected by the triumphs or defeats of the Philis-

tines, who do not appear to have ever manifested much solicitude to push their dominion to any distance from their own country. Supposing they had remained unaffected by these circumstances, their internal government must be conceived to have proceeded under the authority of their own tribal chiefs and elders, without any further reference to the government of Samuel, than to recognize it as a fact existing in the south, and as, perhaps, in conjunction with his prophetic character, giving him a claim to consideration in case he should have occasion to bring forward any matter affecting the general interests of all the tribes. The probability of this limitation of Samuel's practical authority to the southern tribes — we may say Judah, Benjamin, Dan, and Simeon— is confirmed by the fact, that when Samuel made his sons his assistants in the administration of justice, he did not send them north or east, but only south, fixing their stations at Beersheba, on the southernmost border of the land.

This appointment was made in the latter part of the period under our survey. It may be doubted whether Samuel acted wisely in making this appointment, especially if, as seems to have been understood, the nomination in his lifetime of his sons to fulfil the functions he had hitherto discharged alone, was an intimation that he meant them to be regarded as his successors in such government as he exercised. Nothing of the kind had ever been done before. No son had hitherto succeeded his father as judge; and Gideon, for one, had nobly declined to nominate any one of his sons as his successor. Besides, no judge had hitherto taken office but at the special appointment of God, or at the spontaneous call of the people. Whether his intentions were justly interpreted or not, his integrity of purpose is beyond all suspicion; and his proceedings, however mistaken, or biassed by fatherly partialities, could only have been founded on a sincere regard for the welfare of the people, and a deep anxiety to carry out the principles which had guided his own administration, and which he believed to be essential to the abiding prosperity of the nation. He might naturally suppose, that sons trained up by him, and introduced to office under his eye, would be better qualified than any other persons to carry out his views, and to walk in his steps. There might be others as well or better able to do this, and qualified to hold the reins of the state with even a firmer hand; but he could not know them so well, or trust them so fully; and thus, almost unconsciously, perhaps, he was led to give a kind of sanction to the hereditary principle of government, which was soon to be turned against himself.

It does not appear that this appointment was at first regarded with any discontent; and none can say what results might have ensued had the sons been like their father, and had their conduct given satisfaction to the people. But this was not the case; and Samuel is not blameworthy for not knowing his sons better, for the misconduct into which they fell was of a nature which could only have been developed by the possession of power. Uncertain, as they must have felt, of their tenure of office, and lamenting, as they probably did, that their father had, after such long possession of power, done so little to enlarge the patrimony of his family, they made haste to be rich; and in doing this, they fell into the temptation and the snare which ever attend the inordinate pursuit of worldly gain. The easiest way of doing this was to sell justice, and they sold it. "They took bribes and perverted justice." It is highly creditable to the law, and its administration among the Hebrews, that from this offence, so common throughout the ancient and modern East as scarcely to excite any of the abhorrence and indignation with which it is regarded among ourselves, their history is signally and memorably free, though it crept in at a later and more corrupt age, and is sometimes rebuked by the prophets. It must at this time have appeared specially heinous, as contrasted with the spotless administration of Samuel himself, who, in the grand address in which he laid down his power, could call upon the assembled people to avouch the cleanness of his hands. "Behold,

here I am: witness against me before the Lord, and before His anointed: whose ox have I taken? or whose ass have I taken? or whom have I defrauded? whom have I oppressed? or of whose hand have I received any bribe, to blind mine eyes therewith?" The loud and ready answer of that one-voiced multitude was, "Thou hast not defrauded us, nor oppressed us, neither hast thou taken aught of any man's hand."

The corruption of justice throughout the East impresses an emphatic value upon this testimony in behalf of Samuel, scarcely credible to us who regard the matter as scarcely ground for commendation in a judge, being points of ordinary and common duty which it would be gross dishonour to neglect; and although the administration of justice was, for the East, singularly pure among the Israelites, the fact that, although its corruption was deemed to be an offence and a wrong, in their judgments it was not a *disgraceful* offence or a *shameful* wrong, as with us, appears to be shown in the credit attached to exemption from it. Men are not held in distinguished honour for conduct which it would be ignominious *not* to exemplify.

Speaking of the administration of justice in Egypt, Mr. Lane says: "The rank of a plaintiff or defendant, or a bribe from either, often influences the decision of the judge. In general the Naib[1] and Mooftee[2] take bribes, and the Ckadee[3] receives from his Naib. On some occasions, particularly in long litigations, bribes are given by each party, and the decision is awarded in favour of him who pays highest. This frequently happens in difficult law-suits; and even in cases respecting which the law is perfectly clear, strict justice is not always administered; bribes and false testimony being employed by one of the parties. The shocking extent to which bribery, and suborning false witnesses, are carried on in Moslem courts of law, and among them in the tribunal of the Ckadee at Cairo, can scarcely be credited."[4] Matters are in this respect still worse, if possible, in the farther East. Mr. Roberts, illustrating Isa. v. 23 from Indian customs, says: "Not a man in a thousand will hesitate to give or receive a bribe, when there is the least chance of its being kept secret. Nearly all the situations which are at the disposal of the

[1] Deputy of the Judge.   [2] Chief Doctor of the Law.
[3] Chief judge—usually written *Cadi*.
[4] *Modern Egyptians*, i. 136.

native chiefs are acquired by *ki-cooly, i. e.,* 'the reward of the hand,' and yet there are numerous proverbs against this system." [1]

The corruption of justice in Oriental countries is proverbial, and it was never so fully and strikingly brought under the notice of Europeans in general, and of Englishmen in particular, as during the agitation of the Eastern question (1877). In connection with the foregoing remarks respecting the treatment of people accused of crime, it may not be inappropriate to observe, that the traveller in Syria in the present day is struck with what he sees of the state of prisoners. Within wretched rooms, with barred windows, may be discerned crowds of miserable beings committed for some offence against the law— no arrangements for health or cleanliness, no prison discipline, but only filth and idleness, and that which is calculated to make the bad worse. The heat, the stench, the misery, is frightful. The place of justice, or the court in which culprits real or accused are tried, is often still met with in the entrance gate of the Pasha's palace or castle. There you may notice a sort of divan, on which, covered with carpets, sits his highness, to administer what is called justice, but which often proves the greatest injustice. Samuel probably discharged his judicial office in the gates of Mizpeh, Gilgal, and Bethel.

As to Gilgal, it may be stated here that it stood about two miles from Jericho, enjoying "the shade and the streams of the noble forest," contiguous to that ancient city. "The ground of Gilgal was the first that was pronounced holy" after the taking of Canaan by the Israelites. "On its hill, during the long wars in the interior of Palestine, the Tabernacle remained, till it found its resting place in Shiloh. And in those sacred groves were celebrated, in later times, the solemn assemblies of Samuel and of Saul, and of David on his return from exile." (Stanley's *Sinai and Palestine*, 306.) Since this passage was written, Lieutenant Conder has explored the neighbourhood, and discovered a pool choked with soil and scattered stones, and also a cemetery of tombs, seemingly Arab. He found that the name *Birket Jiljulieh*, of which he had heard before, applies to the pool; and that south-east and east of this point, are a number of small mounds, seemingly artificial. They are said to be very ancient, and to belong to an ancient city, called "the City of Brass." The pool indicates an old supply of water, and this would favour the idea of *Birket Jiljulieh* being Gilgal; for water would be of immense value to the Israelites, when encamped there. (*Palestine Exploration Statements*, 1874, p. 37.)

S.

THE HOLINESS OF GOD

1 Samuel 6:20

WHEN the Lord visited with His awful judgment the men who trespassed in regard to the ark, the

men of Beth-shemesh cried, "Who is able to stand before this holy Lord God?" This judgment was therefore not without its fruit, since it impressed upon them a more lively conviction than they had been wont to entertain of the holiness of God. But it may be asked, What is this holiness? In the general notion of it, it is His moral perfection—that excellence or moral loveliness, in virtue of which all moral imperfection is removed from His nature. The holiness of the will of God is therefore that by which He invariably and necessarily chooses that which is morally good, and refuses that which is morally evil. This attribute implies, that no sinful inclination can be found in God—that it is abhorrent to His very nature. Hence He is said to be incapable of being tempted to evil;[1] and to be light, and without darkness[2]—that is, holy and without sin. It further implies, that He never chooses that which is deceitful and false, but only what is truly good—what His perfect intelligence recognizes to be such.

This attribute is, to our own apprehension, so essential to the mere idea of God—is in itself so obviously a perfection of the divine character— that we may at times be inclined to wonder at the frequency with which it is stated and enforced in the Scriptures. But the view of the divine character out of which this feeling arises, is itself the creation of those scriptural declarations on the subject; and the formation of this high conception of God is the use which they were designed to serve, and which we thus find that they have served.

It may also be remembered, that to the Hebrews the enforcement of this doctrine was of an importance which it is scarcely in our power to understand or appreciate fully. The surrounding heathen—indeed, all the heathen—had very different and inferior notions of the gods they worshipped. Holiness was not their attribute. They were very capable of sin; and the choice of good in preference to evil was not essential to their nature. They were above man in their essence and in their sovereign powers; but in character they were men, and not always good men. The popular mythologies of every nation ascribed to the gods acts which would have been vile even in men. There was no one attribute by which Jehovah was so pointedly distinguished from the gods of the nations as by this. Its

[1] *Oriental Illustrations*, p. 402.

[1] James 1:13.   [2] 1 John 1:5.

maintenance, its constant assertion, was therefore of the utmost importance among a people whose tendencies so often were to merge the worship of their own Lord in that of the neighbouring idols. This attribute set a great gulf between them, which could not be overpassed so long as its presence was constantly kept before the mind of the people. So long as they retained in remembrance the essential and distinctive holiness of God, so long as they did not allow themselves to think God was altogether such a one as themselves (Ps. l. 21), it was impossible for them to compare Him with other gods, still less could they prefer any of them to Him.

Such was the special use of this doctrine to the Israelites; but there was another and a more general use in it, of which we share the benefit with them. It is a check to sin, and an incitement to righteousness. It seems impossible for any one to realize a clear and distinct idea of the holiness of God—of the truth that sin, that whatever defiles, is abhorrent to His pure and holy nature—without hearing His voice crying to us, "Oh, do not that abominable thing which I hate!" When sin entices, and when temptation is near, we cannot doubt that He hates it, for He is holy; and if we are strongly impressed with a sense of His holiness, we can never be in doubt respecting the things which He, a holy God, must hate. It will then be impossible for us to sin but in the presence of an offended God, a crucified Saviour, a burning world, and a judgment to come.

This use of the holiness of God in promoting the holiness of those that love Him, is constantly enforced in Scripture. In the New Testament, no less than in the Old, that God is holy, is urged as a reason why we should be holy, that we may be like Him—that is, in a state of moral harmony with Him, and conformity to Him—in a state of fitness for His presence. Surely that attribute which, above all others, is proclaimed in the courts of heaven continually by the cherubim, and by saints made perfect in glory, is one of most exalted importance, and claims our most careful thought—not abstract thought, but thought evidenced in, and having a wholesome influence upon, all our conduct in the church and in the world. Indeed, we are told that "without holiness no man shall see the Lord." (Heb. xii. 14.) It is therefore of supreme importance for us to consider what this holiness —a reflection of God's holiness—is, seeing that it becomes so essential to our welfare. We apprehend, indeed, that without holiness not only will no one see God, but no one will have even *a real desire to see Him*. There are thousands who desire a place in heaven, not because they love God, not because they, being made partakers of His holiness, long for more perfect union with Him and conformity to Him, but because they dread hell, and know no other way of escaping from it but by going to heaven. But of such is not the kingdom of heaven. They would be as miserable in the immediate presence of ONE with whose holiness their souls have not been brought into unison, as they would be in hell. Let us believe that it is impossible for the soul of man to be happy with God, till it has become holy like Him.

Seeing, then, that to be holy is to be like Him, it behoves us to count holiness as our highest attainment and most glorious distinction; and instead of imitating the ignorant Bethshemites, in putting away the ark of God from us, because we cannot stand before His holiness, let us rather strive after this assimilation to Him, that we may be enabled to keep the ark among us. But for the fact that we are commanded to be holy as He is holy, it might seem presumption to aspire so high. It is a glorious privilege, and it becomes us to regard it as such, while it is not the less an indispensable duty. Here our ambition may have free scope; and our highest aspirings to a greater degree of that holiness which brings us nearer to God, by making us more and more like Him, meet no rebuke. To stand before a holy God in holiness like His, may indeed seem difficult to flesh and blood; but there is a way, a safe, a certain, and a pleasant way, known of those to whom Christ is revealed as a Redeemer, and to whom the Spirit has come as a Sanctifier. "Christ gave Himself for us, to redeem us from all iniquity, and purify unto Himself a peculiar people, zealous of good works," and the holiness of which they become possessed is *His*.

What the elements of this holiness in God are, has been pointed out. In man it consists in that blamelessness of feeling and conduct which at once constitutes and adorns the Christian character; and also in the habitual *abhorrence* of sin and love of goodness.[1] In this way the Christian becomes like God, and loves Him from similarity

[1] 1 John 3:7; Romans 6:18.

of disposition; and in return is loved by God, as a dutiful son who resembles his father is loved by him. Man is destined by God for holiness, and for the happiness which is invariably connected with it; and hence, when any one is admitted to the communion of saints, holiness becomes the great object of his pursuit. Without this, his admission into the Church, and his fellowship with the saints, would avail him nothing; indeed, his condemnation would be the greater on account of these privileges, for of him to whom much is given, much will be required. Holiness is, therefore, justly stated by theologians, to be at once the result and the evidence of conversion, or of repentance and regeneration. Let no one cherish vain delusions. He who is destitute of holiness, or who is remiss in the pursuit of it, has not been converted, has not repented, has not been born of the Spirit, and is still a child of wrath.

A CHARGE DEMANDED

1 Samuel 8:4-7

No nation, perhaps, can render so noble a testimony to the integrity and public spirit of its ruler, as when, in the conviction that he will do right, they call upon him to lay down his own power for the public good, and leave to him the organisation of the new government and the choice of the ruler who is to supersede him. This was what the elders of Israel did, when they appeared before Samuel one day at Ramah, and requested of him the establishment of a regal government. It does not appear to us that the solemnity of this great circumstance has been adequately apprehended. The demand was not the outcry of an ignorant and deluded rabble, but the grave and deliberate application of the *elders* of Israel—of those whose years or high standing in the nation gave to them the utmost weight and influence. It was not made from the mere impulse of the moment, but was the result of previous deliberation and conference; for the elders repaired to Ramah *for the purpose* of proposing the matter to the prophet; and beyond all doubt they had met together and considered the matter well before they took a step so decided.

It seems to us that the subject was set forth to Samuel in a manner marked by respect and delicate consideration. The elders were careful to show that their movement arose from no discontent with him. But they intimated that he was now advancing in years, and that his sons evinced no disposition to tread in his steps; by this implying, that had it been otherwise, they would have been content to let matters take their natural course, and to see his power consolidated in the hands of his sons, and inherited by them. But since this was not the case, they were anxious to avert the evils likely to ensue upon his demise, by having the secular government established on a permanent basis during his lifetime, and under the sanction of his authority.

It is true that they went so far as to limit his action in this great matter by declaring the form of government they desired to see established. They must have "a king to judge them," like the nations. It is far from unlikely that this preference for a regal government, at this time, was suggested by circumstances with which we are unacquainted. It is possible that there were already signs of movement against Israel among the Philistines on the west, and the Ammonites on the east, which suggested that they would soon be called upon to engage in a severe military contest, without their having any one before the public qualified by his position or prowess to take the command of their armies and lead them to battle. Samuel himself, besides being advanced in years, was a man of peaceful pursuits; and his sons had forfeited, or rather had not won, the respect and confidence of the people, while, as Levites, they were scarcely the class of persons to be looked to for the performance of such duties. We do not, indeed, lay too much stress on this sort of disqualification; for in those days there was no military profession, and almost every man was more or less qualified to wield the sword and the spear. Still, as the results of military conflicts were then often determined by the prowess and experience of individuals, it was a natural subject of anxiety that they saw no one with pre-eminent claims, from fitness or station, to be their leader in the conflicts that seemed to be at hand. They were then led to regard as enviable in this respect the condition of the neighbouring nations, each of which had a king who relieved his subjects from all anxiety in this matter, being naturally, as his chief office, the leader in war, and, from the necessities of his position, trained from his youth up in all martial exercises. To him belonged the consideration and decision of all matters of peace and war; and his people were spared the trouble of deliberation and decision. They had nothing to do but to obey his orders and follow him to battle.

It may also appear, from previous indications, that the Israelites craved to have an earthly sovereign, surrounded with the usual attributes of power and state, and representing to the eyes of those around them the power and dignity of the nation. Besides, the eastern mind is so essentially and pervadingly regal, that to be without a sovereign is scarcely an intelligible state of things to an Oriental; and they must have had occasion to feel that the absence of a king gave them an appearance of inferiority in the eyes of their neighbours, incapable of understanding or appreciating the special and glorious privileges of their position. The want of a royal head must often have been cast in their teeth by their neighbours, as a kind of stigma; and they would in course of time come to regard it as such themselves, and long to be in this point on a level with other nations. Even good men, able to appreciate the advantages of existing institutions, would eventually become weary of a peculiarity which the nations would obtusely persist in regarding as discreditable.

This principle, which has not been before urged as contributing to the explanation of this transaction, does not lack such confirmation as historical illustration can supply. We remember to have read some years ago in Harris's *Collection of Travels*, that when the English and Dutch were competing for power and influence in the East, the English, in order to damage their rivals, industriously circulated the dangerous secret, that the Dutch HAD NO KING. The Oriental mind was astonished and perplexed by the indication of a condition so utterly beyond the scope of its experience and comprehension, and the Dutch, alarmed for the effect of this slur upon their respectability, stoutly repelled the charge as an infamous calumny, affirming that they had a very great king, thus exalting for the nonce their stadtholder to that high rank.

The magnates of Israel—who are the parties we behold moving in this matter—may also have considered that, although a form of government

had been organised by Moses, in which the presence of a human king was not recognized, he had clearly contemplated the probability that a regal government might eventually be adopted, and had even laid down certain rules involving principles by which the conduct of their future king was to be guided. (Deut. xvii. 14-20.) This, it might be urged, was inconsistent with any absolute interdiction of the erection of the state into a temporal monarchy; and the time had now come, if ever, which the wise and farseeing lawgiver had contemplated.

Such seem to us the considerations by which the elders of Israel were influenced in the important step which was now taken by them. They were not satisfactory to Samuel, who, it is clear from the words in which the divine will was presently made known to him, deemed himself personally affronted by what he could not but view as a requisition to abdicate the authority which he had so long and efficiently exercised. There may have been something of human infirmity in his displeasure. As men grow older in the possession of power, it becomes dearer to them, and the more reluctant are they to part with it; and in this case Samuel could not but see that, whatever consideration he might retain, from the deference of the people and of the king, it would be rather a concession than a right, and that the most essential powers of the government would, and must, go into the hands of the new sovereign.

But, hurt and displeased as Samuel was, under this keen sense of a nation's ingratitude, he is not stated to have expressed any opinion till he felt authorized from the Lord to do so. His resource was that which has been the resource of the servants of God in all ages: " Samuel prayed unto the Lord." The answer to his prayer was not delayed. He was told to act as the people desired, but to do so under a strong and decided protest, that in this they had forsaken the wiser and happier course, and would involve themselves in greater troubles than those from which they sought to be freed. Samuel thought they had rejected him. But the Divine Voice directed him to a broader view of the question: " They have not rejected thee, but they have rejected ME, that *I* should not reign over them."

If the reader bears in mind the explanation which has been already given of the principles of the theocracy as established under the institutions of Moses,[1] he will be at no loss to see the reasons why the course which the people were bent upon, and which they were allowed under protest to follow, was regarded with disapprobation. Jehovah was their king; and from past experience they had no reason to suppose that, so long as they remained true to Him, He would fail to do all things well and prosperously for them. He would, as He had done, raise up from time to time faithful men, abundantly qualified for the public service, whether in peace or war. They, not knowing the hearts and qualities of untried men, might not see the man or men then qualified for such service. But HE knew, and in the appointed time and place would not fail to call out from among the thousands of Israel the man best suited for the work which was to be done.

It may be suspected that the Israelites had grown weary of a system of government which made their welfare entirely dependent upon their right conduct; and were partly led to desire this change, under some vague impression that a permanent government under a king would relieve them from some of this distinct responsibility for their conduct to an infallible authority which could not be mistaken, and against which they had no right to murmur; and they may have dimly fancied that their well-being might henceforth be more connected with the character of their government and the qualities of their king. But as the Lord did not mean to abandon the Israelites to their own devices, or to allow the great objects of His dealings with them to be frustrated, it became important that the principle of national responsibility to Him should be preserved under any form to which the government might be altered.

In the demand made by the Israelites, "Make us a king to judge us like all the nations," there was, as is stated in the answer to Samuel's prayer, a distinct rejection of God, because a rejection of His mode of government. It was one of the most signal acts of rebellion the nation had ever been guilty of, and all the more so in that it was not the act of an angry, excited mob, but the deliberate doing of the leaders of the people. The people, in fact, were becoming totally corrupted by their evil passions, and by contact with the surrounding heathen. They knew that the Lord had repeatedly, by a direct exercise of His omnipotent power, saved them from impending calamity, sometimes even from total extinction as a nation. They

[1] See Vol. 1, pp.355-357.

knew that His power was sufficient to meet any peril that might arise. But they felt that He was holy and just as well as powerful. They felt that His laws were strict, and that no violation of them would be tolerated among the people over whom He ruled. However much they appreciated and desired His protection and deliverance, still their evil nature led them to seek release from His holy and just rule. Then, they saw the nations on the borders of their country, though revelling in the grossest licentiousness, and unrestrained by any sense of propriety, enjoying some prosperity, and even victorious on the battle-field. Poor infatuated slaves of passion and sin, the Israelites now prayed Samuel to be governed like other nations. The folly and wickedness of Samuel's sons, and the increasing infirmities of the great judge himself, afforded them a plausible excuse for the demand. But, after all, it was only an excuse. The true source of the application lay deeper, and the eye of the Omniscient detected it. "They have not rejected thee," was the Lord's reply to Samuel; "but they have rejected me, that I should not reign over them."

P.

MONARCHICAL INSTITUTIONS

1 Samuel 8:9-22

GOD had promised to Abraham that kings should come from him;[1] and Jacob had foretold that the sceptre should not depart from Judah until Shiloh came.[2] Connecting this with the directions laid down in the law respecting the principles which should guide the nation in the appointment of a king, and those which were set down for the regulation of the king's conduct, the Israelites might reasonably have inferred, that it was the divine intention that a monarchial government should eventually be established among them. More than this; we apprehend that they were right in this conclusion, not only for the same reasons, but because it must from ancient times have been determined, that the ancestry of the Messiah should be illustrated and distinguished by royal rank in the house of David. But if this were the view of the Israelites, their course was to wait the appointed time, when God should see fit to establish a monarchy under such forms as might not have obscured, but illustrated, the great principles of the theocratical government, and with such restrictions as might have secured the rights and privileges of the chosen and peculiar people. The least they could have done was

[1] Genesis 17:6. [2] Genesis 49:10.

to apply reverentially to ascertain the Lord's will in the matter, by the means which He had appointed. Had they done so, they would probably have been told that the time for the accomplishment of their desires was not far off; that the man was already born who was destined to reign over them.

From the indications furnished, we may venture to think, that had the matter been left, as it should have been, entirely in the Lord's hands, the monarchical government would still have been established, and that David would have been the first king. How, we know not; but the crown was eventually secured to him through greater difficulties than needed to have occurred, had not the monarchy been prematurely established. It is easy to suppose, for instance, that in the one case, as in the other, he might have been brought into public notice by the overthrow of Goliath, which, from the feeling of the people in favour of monarchy, would probably have resulted in the offer of the crown to him; and as this would have been in accordance with the purposes of God, David would have become king under such circumstances, and with such conditions, as would have secured the true doctrine of the Hebrew government from being thrown into the shade.

It is said, indeed, by Hosea, xiii. 11, that the Lord "gave them a king in His anger." But this does not militate against the view we have taken; for it is quite true, as appears from the history, that in answer to their unreasonable and unbecoming demand, He did give them their first king in His anger—did concede the premature establishment of the regal government in His wrath. But it does not therefore follow that it would not ere long have been established with His favour, in the person of "the man after God's own heart."

The grievous error of the elders of Israel was, that instead of taking counsel of their Divine King, as they were bound to do, they made a peremptory demand in a matter with which, according to the principles of the constitution, they had no right to interfere. And there was another error, scarcely inferior to this,—namely, that instead of manifesting any anxiety to secure the liberties and invaluable public rights which they enjoyed under their present government, they wanted to have a king to rule them as the nations around were ruled. If this mean anything, it means, that in exchange for their present mild government, they were willing to subject themselves to the rule of a despotic sovereign, invested with absolute power over their substance and their lives. O foolish people and unwise! How wonderful it is that the Lord endured their perverse manners so long, not only in the wilderness, but in the promised land!

That there might be no misapprehension in this matter, the prophet, in the audience of the people, drew a graphic picture of the kind of government to which, in desiring to be governed like the nations, they wished to be subjected. There can be no question that in this picture the monarchical governments of the time and country are correctly represented; and, in fact, the details agree in every essential point with the existing despotisms of the East. "This will be the manner of the king that shall reign over you: he will take your sons, and appoint them for himself, for his chariots, and to be his horsemen; and some shall run before his chariots. And he will appoint him captains over thousands, and captains over fifties; and will set them to ear his ground, and to reap his harvest, and to make his instruments of war, and instruments of his chariots. And he will take your daughters to be confectionaries, and to be cooks, and to be bakers. And he will take your fields, and your vineyards, and your oliveyards, even the best of them, and give them to his servants. And he will take the tenth of your seed, and of your vineyards, and give to his officers, and to his servants. And he will take your men-servants, and your maid-servants, and your goodliest young men, and your asses, and put them to his work. And he will take the tenth of your sheep: and ye shall be his servants. And ye shall cry out in that day, because of your king which ye shall have chosen you; and the Lord will not hear you in that day."

The conditions of regal power thus described are, and always have been, so familiar to the Oriental mind, that we know not anything which gives to ourselves a stronger and more distinct idea of the immunities and peculiar privileges which the Israelites practically enjoyed, than the fact that the prophet knew the condition in which they lived to be so different from that which he described, as not to be without hope that the picture which he drew might have some effect in changing their purpose, especially when they were also aware that the course they were taking was not regarded with favour by their Divine King. In this reasonable expectation the prophet was disappointed. They had, it seems, counted the cost, and were willing to pay it; or rather, the love of change blinded their eyes, and they thought that the advantages which they imagined themselves to perceive in the kingly government, especially as to their standing among the nations, would more than counterbalance the disadvantages the prophet set before them. Their answer therefore was: "Nay; but we WILL have a king over us, that we also may be like all the nations: and that our king may judge us, and go out before us to fight our battles."

On this, Samuel sorrowfully dismissed them to their homes that he might have time to take the necessary measures for effecting this great change. But although the people thus, with criminal disregard of their rights as men, and their privileges as the Lord's peculiar people, declared their willingness to bend their necks to the yoke of regal despotism—instead of waiting until the Lord should arrange the matter for them in unison with their rights and His own laws—it was not the wish of the prophet to leave them to all the consequences of their infatuation. With wise and noble patriotism, it was henceforth his solicitude, while accomplishing their wishes, to save them as far as possible from the consequences they declared themselves willing to incur. And if, in the result, we find the Hebrew monarchy less absolute than it generally has been among eastern nations—if the people retained possession of more of their natural and social rights than in other eastern kingdoms—and if the strong exertion of kingly power was in after ages resented by them as a wrong, instead of being recognized as a just prerogative,—it is entirely owing to the sagacious care and forethought of Samuel, acting under divine direction, in securing from utter destruction at the outset, the liberties which the people so wilfully cast into the fire. In fact, the more deeply we contemplate the character of Samuel, the more its greatness grows upon us, and the more distinctly we recognize the most truly illustrious character in Hebrew history since Moses.

There is a sentiment running through the foregoing remarks of Dr. Kitto which seems to me to be not merely wrong in itself, but exceedingly dangerous in its theological and philosophical tendencies. One paragraph especially strikes me as appearing at least to embody grave error in regard to God's providence. Referring to the demand of the Israelites for a king, it is said, "From the indications furnished, we may venture to think, that *had the matter been left*, as it should have been, *entirely in the Lord's hands*, the monarchical government would still have been established, and that David would have been the first king. How, we know not, but the crown was eventually secured to him *through greater difficulties than needed to have occurred, had not the monarchy been prematurely established*." Then, again, in supposing a possible way of bringing this about, it is said, "*And as this would have been in accordance with the purposes of God*, David would have become king," etc.

These singular remarks seem to imply that the divine plan for the temporal government of the Jewish nation was deranged by human acts; or, in other words, that the Almighty had, in His infinite wisdom, laid down a definite course of action to be carried out in the after history of the Jewish nation, but that, by the premature demand for a king, this course was broken in upon, and that then a new and imperfect, or less perfect, arrangement had to be made by the divine Ruler. The same idea manifestly pervades the other sections of this day's reading.

It is an exceedingly delicate thing to speculate in any way on such a subject as this. The connection of the divine foreknowledge, involving as it must do, foreordination, with human action, the bearing of God's eternal decrees upon the freedom of man's will, and upon his responsibility for all his acts, is one of those profound problems which the creature, in his present state of imperfection, can never fully fathom. Yet there are general principles, certain and eternal, which must ever control and regulate our theories and speculations. These, in my opinion, have been here overlooked by Dr. Kitto.

It is a fundamental truth, that God, being omniscient—the present, the past, and the future being alike to Him—did foresee and foreknow all things that would take place: all physical changes in the universe; all actions, good or bad, voluntary or involuntary, in the whole history of mankind; and all thoughts and dispositions of the human mind. Nothing, therefore, did or could arise in human history new to Him, or unprovided for in the scheme of His providence. Again, it is a fundamental truth, that God is the Author and Supreme Ruler of the universe both of matter and mind. The laws which regulate it are His. They are under the control of His supreme and sovereign will, and they extend to and embrace within their sphere every event or change which takes place. Consequently nothing can ever arise, whether in the physical or spiritual world, whether as the result of material or moral convulsion, to derange the divine plan of government, or to call forth, as it were, a new arrangement of providential dealing. Further, it is a fundamental truth, that God, in the full and sovereign exercise of His infinite wisdom and power, so directs and controls the acts of free agents, as, on the one hand, not to coerce the nature of the agent so as to destroy or interfere with his accountability; and yet, on the other hand, infallibly to determine all things in accordance with His eternal purpose and decree. The way in which this is done we cannot explain. Like many another problem in the natural and spiritual world, it is beyond the limits of thought. But that it is done we know; and we further know, that it is done in a way consistent alike with the divine perfections and the moral constitution of the creature. Consequently, to speculate about what God would have done, or how He would have conducted His providential government, had man acted differently from what he did, is to speculate about an impossibility. To speak also of an act or event in the history of the past not having been left in God's hands, or having been *prematurely* brought about by human agency, seems to involve a limitation of divine power, and a virtual denial of God's absolute and universal government.

P.

TALLNESS

1 Samuel 9:2

IF, as we have ventured to infer from facts and circumstances, it was the divine plan that a monarchy should be established in Israel, and that it was in any case to be established in the person and family of David; and if, as we also suppose, this intermediate action of the people did not retard or hasten the accomplishment of that design for one hour, it follows that the king whom God gave in His anger had the function merely of filling up the interval to the time appointed for the son of Jesse to take the throne. Under these circumstances, it was necessary that the king to be appointed should, on the one hand, possess such qualities as would recommend him to the choice and admiration of the people; and that, on the other hand, his career should manifest such dispositions as would gradually alienate from him their respect and confidence, and lead them so to repent of the step they had taken, that they would acquiesce with pleasure in his dynasty being eventually set aside for that of David. This was precisely the case with Saul, the first king of Israel; and the view we have taken completely meets the doubt which some have ventured to express, whether the Lord did really concur in the appointment of Saul, seeing that He, to whom all hearts and dispositions are open, must have known from the first how unfit Saul was to reign. But the Scripture distinctly states, that the Lord did concur in the selection of this particular man; and, according to our view, the unfitness which his career at length developed, and which disqualified him from

establishing a permanent dynasty upon the throne of Israel, constituted, in conjunction with his *apparent* qualifications, his peculiar fitness.

This person was Saul, the son of Kish, a man of some consideration in the tribe of Benjamin, for he is described as "a mighty man of power," from which we must take the correct impression concerning this family; the humble designations which Saul himself afterwards applied to it being obviously such expressions of formal humility as Orientals are wont to use. Saul himself was "a choice young man, and a goodly. There was not among the children of Israel a goodlier person than he. From his shoulders and upward he was higher than any of the people," by which it would appear that he could not have been much less than seven feet high. Great stress is laid upon this, because this distinguished stature, with the impression of bodily prowess which it conveyed, helped much to recommend him to the choice of the people. When, after a long peace, there was no man of distinguished renown among them; and when in battle much less depended upon military skill than upon the bodily prowess of the chief in single combats, or in the partial actions with which most battles commenced,—it was natural enough that the people should take pride in the gigantic proportions of their leader, as calculated to strike terror into the enemy, and to inspire confidence into his followers; besides

GIGANTIC PROPORTIONS OF SOVEREIGN, FROM EGYPTIAN SCULPTURES

that, it was no mean advantage that the crest of the leader should, from his tallness, be seen from afar by his people. The prevalence of this feeling of regard for personal bulk and stature is seen in the sculptures of ancient Egypt, Assyria, and Persia, and even in the modern paintings of the last named nation, in which the sovereign is invested with gigantic proportions in comparison with the persons around him. Even Samuel, man of peace as he was, and, from his habits and character, necessarily more disposed than most of his contemporaries to regard the inner more than the outer man, was not free from the influence of this feeling. We might not be entitled to infer this from the mere fact of his recommending Saul to the attention of the people on the ground of his physical qualifications, as that might have been done in condescension to the known infirmity of the unreasoning populace; but we are enabled to see that he spoke from real feelings of admiration; for, in a case where his own judgment only was concerned, in the choice of a future king among Jesse's sons, he, if left to himself, would clearly have chosen the tallest and best looking. He no sooner saw the fine young man Eliab, than he internally pronounced: "Surely the Lord's anointed is before Him," which drew down upon him this rebuke; "Look not on his countenance, *or on the height of his stature*, because I have refused him: for the LORD seeth not as man seeth; for man looketh on the outward appearance, but the Lord looketh on the heart." (1 Sam. xvi. 6, 7.) In this, as we view it, there was an implied rebuke addressed to Samuel, not only as to this case, but for his former and grievously mistaken appreciation of Saul, on account of his being a head taller than any of the people. Even we want not experience of this in the involuntary respect with which tallness of stature and powerful physical endowments are regarded among ourselves by the uncultivated, and indeed by persons not wholly uncultivated, if we may judge from the not unfrequent sarcasms which we may meet with in the most "respectable" monthly, weekly, and daily publications upon the shortness, by yard measure, of some of the most eminent and highly gifted public men of this and a neighbouring country.

There is certainly, however, more of this appreciation of stature in ancient than in modern literature. It appears to have been usual with the ancient Orientals, as well as with the Greeks and Romans, to choose persons to the highest offices of the magistracy, whose personal appearance was superior to that of others; and this is what ancient writers often take notice of as a recommendation of them as princes. Herodotus, after recounting the numbers of men in the army of Xerxes, makes the remark, that among this vast host there was not one who appeared, by his comeliness and stature, more worthy than he to fill the throne.[1] The same writer also informs us that the Ethiopians deemed the man who was strongest and tallest of stature fittest to be their king.[2] In Virgil, Turnus is another Saul in the superiority of his person to others, whom he by a whole head overtops.[3] It is not surprising that, as Quintus Curtius[4] remarks, barbarians made part of the royal majesty consist in the outward form and goodly figure of their princes; but it does excite some surprise to hear a man so cultivated and refined as Pliny the Younger naming qualities of this sort among those which entitled his hero, Trajan, to the supreme rank to which he had been elevated.[5] There is a curious passage in Homer, where, in order to secure greater respect for Ulysses from the Phæacians, upon whose island he was cast,

> "Pallas o'er his head and shoulders broad,
> Diffusing grace celestial, his whole form
> Dilated, and to statelier height advanced,
> That worthier of all reverence he might seem
> To the Phæacians."—*Odyssey*, viii., 20, 24.

He had before been announced as—

> "A wanderer o'er the deep,
> But in his form majestic as a god."

This latter intimation lets us into the secret of the extraordinary estimation of stature in ancient times, among at least the Gentiles. They had a notion, that such persons came nearer to the deities, and looked more like them. So Diana is described in Ovid[6] as superior in stature to the nymphs and inferior goddesses by whom she is surrounded.

Something of this has passed away, but not all; and the time is probably not yet near, when in this respect man will see as the Lord seeth—looking less to the outward appearance, and more to the heart.

[1] *Polymnia*, ch. 187.   [2] *Thalia*, ch. 20.
[3] " Ipse catervis
Vertitur in mediis, et toto vertice supra est."—
                                        Æneid, xi., 682.
[4] Q. Curtius, lib. vi.   [5] *Panegyric. Trajani*, iv., 22.
[6] *Metam.*, iii., 181, 182

STRAYED ASSES

1 Samuel 9:3

THE circumstances of Saul's first interview with Samuel are very remarkable and interesting, not only in themselves, but from the indications of ancient usages which they afford.

The future king of Israel had hitherto known no other employment than what the charge of his father's estate, and particularly the superintendence of the cattle, afforded. This, however, was an occupation held in much esteem. It was regarded as the proper office of a son, and by no means implies the smallness of Kish's possessions, or the want of servants, by whom such duties might have been discharged. Men were in those days in the habit of thinking that the affairs were best looked after which they attended to themselves; and therefore persons of substance and consideration were in the habit of discharging in their own persons, or in the persons of their sons, duties which, in a more refined age, are entrusted to slaves or hired servants.

Among cattle in the East at all times, and especially before horses were in use for riding, asses were of very much importance. When, therefore, it was found one morning that some of Kish's asses were missing, Saul himself, accompanied by a servant, at once set out in search of them. If such an incident now happened in Palestine, it would be at once concluded that the animals had been stolen; and it speaks well for the state of society in the time of Samuel, that this suspicion never crossed the mind of Saul or of his father. It was simply concluded that the asses had strayed.

A long and weary chase they had after the asses—so long, that Saul, with a tender regard for his father, which impresses us with a favourable idea of his character, began to think of abandoning the pursuit, and returning home, lest Kish should, from such protracted absence, suppose that some evil had befallen his son.

By this time they were near the town in which Samuel resided. The servant mentioned this circumstance, and advised that he should be consulted before they abandoned the search. The terms in which the man described the prophet are remarkable enough: "Behold, there is in this city a man of God, and he is an honourable man; all that he saith cometh surely to pass: now let us go thither; peradventure he can show us the way that we should go." Considering that Saul belonged .to Benjamin, within the small territory of which tribe Samuel constantly abode, and to which his circuits were confined, it is somewhat surprising that Saul should need this information concerning Samuel; for it seems clear that the servant speaks under the impression that his master knew nothing of him. It shows, at least, that Saul had too much occupied himself with his father's business to take much heed to public affairs. It might, indeed, seem that there were few public matters to engage attention; and that the office of Samuel being to decide differences between man and man, Saul, having no such differences with his neighbours to decide, had no occasion to become acquainted with the person or character of Samuel. Even in our assize towns, how little is known or thought of the judges of assize, except by those who have causes before them for judgment! But one would have thought that the recent agitation for a king must have stirred all the tribes, and would have drawn general attention to Samuel, who was required to take so important a part in their transactions, and upon whose further movements in this important affair we should suppose that the attention of all Israel, or at least of the southern tribes, would with deep anxiety be fixed. Yet Saul seems to have been quite uninformed on these subjects, or to have had only some vague impression that the people wanted a king. And if it be said, that although he must have known Samuel as judge, he did not know him as prophet, it is answered, that it was not only as a judge, but as a prophet, that he had in this great matter been applied to by the people, and the result had shown that he had access to the secret oracles of God. The ignorance of Saul as to Samuel is further shown by the fact, which presently appears, that he was altogether unacquainted with his person, which we should have supposed to have been well known to almost every man in Benjamin. We cannot solve this further than by saying that it proves how little interest in public concerns had hitherto been taken by the man who was destined to become the first king of Israel.

The manner in which the servant brings Samuel to the notice of Saul is also very remarkable. The character he gives of the man of God is correct so far as it goes ; but one would scarcely gather from it that he is speaking of him who was the acknowledged ruler of the land. The practical conclusion also surprises us—that, seeing he was a man of God whose word failed not to come to pass, he was the person to be consulted respecting the lost asses. We may fancy that the servant and his master either entertained a very high sense of the importance of their asses, or a very low one of the prophetic office, but the former would scarcely have reached this conclusion, unless it had been notorious that Samuel had often been consulted respecting things lost or stolen. We may therefore infer, that at the commencement of the prophetic office in the person of Samuel, it was usual, in order to encourage confidence in their higher vaticinations, and to prevent that dangerous resort to heathenish divinations to which people are in such cases more than in any other addicted, for the prophets to afford counsel, when required, in certain matters of private concernment.

Saul was willing to follow the suggestion of his servant; but a difficulty occurred to him, which strikes those imperfectly informed of eastern customs somewhat strangely. Then, as now, in the East, it would have been the height of rudeness and indecorum for any one to present himself before a superior or equal, especially if he had any request to make, without some present, more or less, according to his degree,—not by any means as a fee or bribe, but in testimony of his homage, his respect, or his compliments. Of the numerous examples of this custom which have occurred in our reading, or have come under our own notice in the East, the one which has most impressed itself upon our mind, is that which Plutarch records of the Persian king Artaxerxes Mnemon. On one occasion a poor husbandman, seeing every one give the king a present of some sort or other, as he passed by them, but having nothing at hand that seemed proper to be given, ran to a stream that was near, and filling both his hands with water, came and offered it to the king, who was so gratified with the inventive spontaneity of this act of homage, that he ordered to be given to the man a thousand darics, and a cup of massive gold. This same " king of kings " always received with satisfaction the smallest and most trifling gifts which evinced the zeal and attention of the officers; and in a country where we have our-

selves bought six of the finest possible pomegranates for a penny, he evinced the utmost pleasure on receiving from a man named Romises the finest pomegranate his garden yielded. A present equally small would have enabled Saul to pay his respects to Samuel; but it was as impossible for him to appear empty handed as it would be for us to enter a gentleman's parlour with covered heads. He lamented that, owing to the length of the way they had been led, there was not a morsel left of the bread they had taken with them, clearly intimating that one of the small cakes or loaves into which eastern bread is made, would in his view have been a suitable offering. The servant informed him, however, that he had sixpence[1] in his pocket, which could be applied to this purpose. Here is another difference from our ideas. With us, to offer a small sum of money to a superior or a public man, or even to an equal, would be a gross affront. Even we might take a small matter—an orange, a flower, or a little book—with satisfaction and acknowledgment; but money—that must not be named. All this is different in the East, where a small coin is not less acceptable as a mark of respectful attention, than its value in any other shape. Travellers in the East might spare the solicitude they often evince to provide or select suitable presents for the persons to whom they have to show respect. Money is quite as acceptable as anything that money could buy. It is often more acceptable; and it is not uncommon for a stranger to be desired to retain his present, and give the value of it in money. This was the general practice of no less a personage than Futteh Ali Shah—not many years ago king of Persia—who, when the customary presents were offered to him, would often, in his later years, ask, " What may these things be worth ?" and on being told, would answer, " Keep them, and give me the money." Had there been any feeling in the mind of Saul that aught else would have been better than money as a present to the man of God, it would have been easy for him to spend his sixpence in the town for the purchase of something more suitable as an offering; but that this did not occur to him, shows that money had then, nominally as well as really, that universal fitness for all such purposes which it still possesses in the East, and which, indeed, it possesses really, but not nominally, in the West also.

[1] A quarter of a shekel—rather more than sixpence.

THE SEER

1 Samuel 9:9

THE further progress of the narration of Saul's visit to Samuel brings before us a very curious piece of information, which is introduced in the way of a parenthesis: "Beforetime in Israel, when a man went to enquire of God, thus he spake, Come, and let us go to the seer: for he that is now called a Prophet, was beforetime called a Seer." Some have argued from this, that the book was written at a later period than is commonly ascribed to it, since it refers to a custom of language existing in the time of Samuel, but extinct in the time of the writer. Others allege that these words might have been written by Samuel himself towards the close of his life, when he might with propriety notice that in his younger days, and quite down to the anointing of Saul, "when there was no open vision," and afterwards when there was scarcely any that had it but himself, he used to be called "the Seer;" but that in his latter days, when there were many that had the vision of prophecy, and schools of the prophets had been established, it was more common to call them "prophets." In this explanation it seems, however, to be overlooked, that the name Seer continued in use long after the death of Saul, and that with a pointed discrimination. Thus, down to the time of Solomon, we have Gad and Iddo the seers, while their contemporary Nathan is always called a prophet, never a seer. We therefore think there is more probability in the opinion that this verse is an explanation inserted by a later hand. There are many such explanations of archaic customs and names to be found in the early books of Scripture, and their introduction is usually ascribed to Ezra; and we would not willingly regard even these incidental illustrations, interwoven with the sacred text, as the work of any hand less than inspired, as Ezra's was. The distinction between seer and prophet is intelligible enough. The seer was one who "beheld things invisible to mortal sight," visions of God; and it is expressly said of Iddo, the last to whom the name of seer is given, that "he saw visions of God against Jeroboam," (2 Chron. ix. 29.) Elisha, though never called a seer, was no less so, when he beheld the chariots and horses of fire, that his servant saw not until his eyes were opened. Nor less a seer was Ezekiel, so eminent for his frequent and elaborate visions. In later times, however, the utterances of the prophets, and the visions on which these utterances were founded, embraced a wider scope into the future; and the *predictive* character of their disclosures becoming proportionally more prominent and signal, they came to be universally designated as "prophets,"—that is, in the primary sense, foretellers of things to come.

As Saul and his attendant went up the hill to the town, they met some maidens coming out to draw water, the wells in Palestine being usually outside the towns. Of them they inquired, "Is the seer here?" In reply to this a long recital was given; so unusually long for maidens to give to a simple question from a stranger, as to have suggested to some Rabbinical commentators, that the damsel who acted as spokeswoman was charmed by the personal graces of the tall traveller, and sought by this means to detain him and engage his attention. Her communication is interesting to us, whatever Saul may have thought of it. The purport of it was, that Samuel had come that day to the city, for there was to be "a sacrifice of the people to-day in the high place;" and if they made haste, they might come up with him before he got thither and sat down to eat with the people; for if not, they would scarcely be able to see him, and speak with him of their private matters for some time, if at all that day. The people would not, it was added, sit down to meat until Samuel came "to bless the sacrifice." That a feast was to be made of the sacrifice, implies that this was some holy festival occasion, upon which peace-offerings were sacrificed, and afterwards eaten by the people. With regard to the fact of sacrifice being offered in this manner under the sanction of the prophet, we shall add nothing here to what we have lately had occasion to state on that point; and as to the sacrificing in high places, we are content to observe, intending to look into this matter more fully hereafter, that the practice has here the sanction of Samuel's example. The blessing of the sacrifice must mean the asking of a blessing upon the food before the meal,—an old and universal practice among the Israelites, which we, as a nation, have but imperfectly adopted. This was done at every common meal, and much more at a solemn festival like this. The present, however, is the first *recorded* example of the custom. The Jewish commentators give us what they apprehend to have been the "blessing" used on such occasions as this: "Blessed be Thou, O Lord our God, the King of the world, who hath sanctified us by His commandments, and commanded us to eat the sacrifice."

With this information Saul hastened on, and on his way met Samuel himself. The prophet, though virtually the ruler of Israel, and about to preside at a high festival, was undistinguished— such were the simple manners of these ancient times—by his dress, or by the presence of attendants or disciples, from an ordinary townsman; and as such Saul addressed him, and inquired the way to the seer's house. Now, Samuel had previously received a divine intimation, which enabled him at once to recognize in the stranger the man whom the Lord had chosen to meet the demands of the people for a king, and to deliver them from the hand of their enemies. Having received this intimation, and being now conciliated by the noble carriage and ingenuous aspect of the man, the generous hearted prophet threw himself with cordiality and kindness into his interests, subject always to his higher duty to the supreme interests of the Hebrew commonwealth; and thus did he continue to feel, until, and even after, the career of Saul had developed the qualities which rendered him unfit to reign.

In answer to Saul's question, Samuel answered, "I am the seer," and proceeded to invite him to come to the feast, and to remain with him until the morrow; and to reconcile him to the delay, he assured Saul that the lost asses had been found; and now said the prophet, "On whom is all the desire of Israel? Is it not on thee, and on all thy father's house?" Little interest as Saul had taken in the matter, he could not misunderstand this. But he replied as one who, having no doubt that some person of high standing and character would be appointed king, did not suspect that Samuel could be in earnest in thus speaking to a man so obscure as himself.

Without any further explanation, Samuel conducted him to the feast. There, in the presence of the chief men of the town, he assigned to this travel-worn but noble-looking stranger the place of honour, which we know was the right-hand corner, and directed the cook to set before him the most distinguished portion of the meat. This was the shoulder; and it seems to have been,

under Samuel's direction, reserved for this purpose. We apprehend this was the right shoulder, which, as the due of the sacrificer, had been assigned to Samuel; and he had thus directed it to be prepared for his expected guest. We the rather think this, as we are aware of no distinction belonging to the left shoulder; whereas the assignment of the right shoulder, the priestly joint, to the stranger, was a most remarkable distinction and honour, well calculated to draw general attention to him, and, together with his stately figure, and the honourable place assigned him, to lead to the expectation of some remarkable disclosures respecting him.

No disclosures were then, however, made. The time was not come. Samuel took Saul home with him after the feast, which seems to have been held towards the close of the day; and, before retiring to rest, communed with him privately as they walked together upon the flat roof of the house.[1] The subject of this conversation is not stated; but from what took place the next morning, there can be little doubt that the prophet apprized him more fully of the high destinies that awaited him, and tried to impress upon him the true position which he would occupy in a state so peculiarly related to the Divine King as that of Israel. Doubtless that memorable night was a wakeful one to both of them; and in the morning Samuel called Saul very early to his journey, and walked forth with him some way on his homeward road. When they had got beyond the town, Samuel desired Saul to send his servant onward; and when they were alone, the prophet drew forth a vial of oil, and consecrated him to his future office, by pouring the contents upon his head. We shall have a future occasion of illustrating this old custom of anointing kings; and it suffices to remark here, that the oil could hardly have been the holy anointing oil of the tabernacle, first used in the consecration of Aaron to the high-priesthood; and that the vessel was not a horn, but a vial, which held but a small quantity, and was brittle. The Rabbis point out the analogy between this and the anointing of Jehu, and remark, superstitiously, that the reigns of Saul and Jehu, who were anointed from a vial, were (as they say) comparatively short; whereas those of David and Solomon, who were anointed from a horn, were long.

---

[1] Concerning such flat roofs, and their uses, see p. 472.

Having anointed Saul, Samuel kissed him. Subjects of rank were wont to kiss a new king in token of homage and subjection, just as among us the HAND of the sovereign is kissed now. There was no doubt something of this in the kiss

SAUL ANOINTED KING

of Samuel; but, under the peculiar circumstances, there must have been something more. It was also the kiss of congratulation upon the dignity to which he had been raised; and while it indicated the dignified respect of Samuel to the man appointed to reign over the house of Israel, it also testified his cheerful acquiescence in the appointment, and his willingness to hand over the government to him. There is nothing churlish or reserved in the conduct of Samuel under these trying circumstances. It is noble, generous, and open—in all respects worthy of the man "asked of God" before his birth as a blessing, and from the womb consecrated to the Lord under the holy sanction of a mother's vow. No man ever resigned the first power of the state into other hands with so much courtesy, tenderness, dignity, and grace. Samuel was truly a great man.

"Though, however, Samuel's personal greatness is thus apparent, it is no less clearly marked that his place is one not of *absolute* but of *relative* importance. Samuel's dignity as a judge and as a prophet is, as it were, the ante-chamber to David's kingdom. To prepare the way for David's monarchy, to select David while he kept his father's sheep, to anoint him with the holy oil, and to surround his throne and person with the halo of prophecy, was Samuel's great mission. And thus, when we view the history as a whole, the eye does not rest upon Samuel, and stop there, but is led on to the throne and person of David as typical of the kingdom and person of Christ. That throne, however, was Samuel's work, and so the book which contains the record of it was called by the name of Samuel, though he himself was dead when David began to reign. A curious incidental mark of this subordination of the ministry of Samuel to the central glory of David, may be seen in the fact that the books of Samuel are really a continuation of the book of Ruth; a book which derived its whole significance from its containing a history of David's ancestors, and closed with a genealogy of David, deduced from Pharez the son of Judah (Gen. xxxviii. 29). The sequel to this genealogy is the history of David's life and reign contained in the books of Samuel, which, consequently, contain no further genealogy of him, beyond the statement of the fact of his being the son of Jesse. Clearly, therefore, in the mind of the sacred historian, the personal history of Samuel was only a link to connect David with the patriarchs, just as the subsequent history connects David himself with our Lord Jesus Christ." (*Speaker's Commentary*, ii. 243.)

S.

A CONSTITUTIONAL KING

1 Samuel 10:17-25

IT was very important for the fair fame of Samuel that the nomination of a king should not seem to be determined by any partial favouritism on his part. It was necessary that respect should be secured for the new king, by his appointment being manifestly under the divine direction and control. In due time, therefore, the tribes were convened at Mizpeh for the choice of a king by lot. The same process sufficed for the detection of a criminal and for the choice of a king. Achan was convicted and Saul was chosen by precisely the same process:[1] tribes, families, and individuals, were successively taken by lot, until the right person was reached. In this case the tribe indicated was that of Benjamin, the family that of Matri, and the individual Saul the son of Kish. That individual feeling, from his previous conference with Samuel, assured of the result, was yet so little ambitious to undertake this trying though honourable office—so desirous to avoid the responsibilities it involved—so attached to the peaceful rural life he had hitherto led—that he withdrew himself from notice, and remained among the baggage away from the place of assemblage. He perhaps hoped that, if he were not forthcoming when inquired for, they would proceed with the lot for the election of some one else. But so solemn a decision was not to be thus trifled with. He was sought and found; and on his being produced to the people, Samuel pointed with pride to his noble stature, towering head and shoulders above all that assembled multitude. "See ye him," cried Samuel, "whom God hath chosen, that there is none like him among all the people!" The qualification to which Samuel directed attention was physically so evident, that the people responded to it by an enthusiastic shout of recognition, "Long live the king!"

But whatever good opinion Samuel himself may by this time have conceived of Saul, he remembered that this was not merely the election of a king, but the foundation of a monarchy, and that it was his duty to care not only for the present but future generations. He saw that the entire character of the monarchy would be determined by the steps which might now be taken; and that this was the time, or never, to subject the sovereign authority to such conditions, and place it on such a basis, as might prevent it from becoming a mere secular despotism, such as the neighbouring nations exhibited. On the first establishment of the monarchy—on the free election of a sovereign who had no natural claim whatever to the crown—it was possible to make conditions and to impose restrictions, to which any future king, royal by birth, and on whom the crown devolved by hereditary right,

[1] See Vol. 1, p. 491.

would not very willingly submit. There can be no doubt that the people, under the infatuation which now possessed them, would have put themselves under the monarchy without any conditions whatever; and it is entirely owing to the wise forethought of Samuel, acting under divine direction, that this great evil was averted, and that the kings of Israel did not become absolute and irresponsible masters of the lives and properties of their subjects. Some of the future kings, indeed, advanced far enough towards making themselves such; but they did so under such evident violation of the principles of the monarchy as established by Samuel, as always gave their subjects the right of protest and complaint, and even of resistance, as against an unlawful exercise of power.

Samuel then addressed the people, explaining to them "the manner of the kingdom," setting forth that the king was not to possess unlimited authority, and expounding the royal rights and privileges, and the limitations to which they were to be subject. Although institutions thus promulgated, in the presence of many witnesses, and accepted by all the parties concerned, were binding ordinances in an age before seals and writings were required to give validity to every transaction, Samuel neglected nothing which might give security to the people; and instead of setting up a stone as a witness, as would have been done in a somewhat earlier age, he committed the whole to writing, and laid up the manuscript "before the Lord"—from which we may suppose that he consigned it to the keeping of the priesthood, to be deposited with the most sacred muniments of the nation. Thus, under divine sanction, and amidst the despotisms of the East, arose the earliest example of a constitutional monarchy.

It may be regretted that we are not acquainted with the precise terms of the limitations and responsibilities under which the crown was accepted by the first Hebrew king. But the real conditions may, without much difficulty, be collected from the subsequent history itself, and from the writings of the prophets. It is also to be borne in mind, that the idea of such limitations did not originate with Samuel, although it devolved on him to give them practical effect, and probably to enforce them by new conditions. Moses himself had laid down the principles of the Hebrew monarchy, whenever it should be established; and whatever other conditions were added when the time came, there can be no doubt that these essential principles were included.

It had been foreseen that the day would come when the Israelites would insist on having a king. To resist this wish absolutely, might have tempted them into open rebellion against the authority which opposed the attainment of their desires; and having accomplished their object in distinct opposition to the declared will of God, and thrown themselves into rebellion against their Divine King, they would feel that they had cast themselves loose from the theocratical institution, and would no longer recognize their obligations to it, or submit to the restrictions it imposed. This would have been to ruin the entire object for which the nation had been established, preserved, and made a peculiar people. This could not be allowed. It was therefore provided, even from the time of Moses, that their wishes should be so met as to keep the management of the whole operation in the hands of the Lord's servants, and so guided as that the new government should, as far as possible, be interwoven with, and rendered subservient to, the great theocratical institutions.

As a clear view of this matter is essential to the correct understanding of many points in the history of the Hebrew monarchy, we shall devote a day to its consideration.[1]

The first interview between Samuel and Saul was at a town (probably Ramah) on the southern border of Benjamin, and not far distant from Rachel's sepulchre at Bethlehem. But Saul was elected king at Mizpeh. The name signifies "a place of look-out," or "a watch-tower." No less than seven Mizpehs are mentioned in Scripture: this, however, was doubtless Mizpeh of Benjamin, now called Neby Samwil, one of the most commanding spots around Jerusalem. After the capture of the ark by the Philistines, though the tabernacle still remained at Shiloh, it would seem that Mizpeh became the national sanctuary. There the people were assembled at the call of Samuel, and, after a solemn sacrifice, attacked and conquered the Philistines. There, again, the tribes were called together by the prophet, and Saul was chosen king. It is interesting to note also, that another solemn assemblage was held at, or close to, this same spot. The ancient city of Gibeon lay in the centre of a little plain, scarcely a mile north of Mizpeh; and it may, perhaps, have been on this commanding height, though called Gibeon because in its territory, that Solomon offered up his great sacrifice to the Lord, and received the gift of wisdom.   **P.**

[1] See Vol. 1, pp. 647-650.

SAUL AMONG THE PROPHETS

1 Samuel 10:11

It is well that this day we should seek some matter for profitable thought in the portion of Israel's history over which we have during the last week passed.

To some it has seemed strange that the Lord should, in yielding (so to speak) to the demand of the people for a king, have allowed a step which met not his approbation. The reason of this we have explained. But it may now be pointed out, that God does often thus act in His dealings with nations and individuals. He often grants when He is angry, and refuses when He is pleased. As illustrations of the former, we have seen that God granted Balaam leave to go to the land of Moab, but at his peril; and He granted quails to Israel in the wilderness, but it was in His wrath. So foolish are we and ignorant, that we often desire things that would be our bane, and often deprecate things which would prove our chiefest blessings. It therefore behoves us to prefer our supplications in reliance upon His perfect knowledge of what is best for us in every circumstance. Even our Saviour, in uttering a wish to His Father to be relieved, "if it were possible," consistently with the great object for which He came into the world, from the most appalling agony that earth ever witnessed—even He felt it needful to add a clause of limitation and dependence: "Nevertheless, not as I will, but as Thou wilt." And even His prayer was not granted. The cup did *not* pass from Him; but an angel was sent to comfort and sustain Him, and to enable Him to drink it even to the dregs. How much more, then, should we subject our suits to the same dependence—not in a form of words only, but in truth—upon the will and high judgment of God, knowing that His love may often be no less shown by a refusal than a compliance with our requests! "This is the confidence which we have in Him, that *if we ask anything according to His will*, He heareth us."[1] And if that which is asked be not according to His will, it is a fatherly favour and mercy in Him not to grant it. It is nevertheless true, that when the mind and heart have been brought under the influence of divine grace, a growing conformity

[1] 1 John 5:14.

to the will and purposes of God is produced, and a quick perception as to what it is fit to ask of Him is awakened, so that he who walks in the Spirit seldom errs in that which he asks; and his prayer is generally granted, because, being taught by the Spirit of God what to ask, he usually asks aright. Thus, "whatsoever we ask, we receive of Him, because we keep His commandments, and do that which is pleasing in His sight."[1] Many who do not enjoy any spiritual life, though they observe the decencies of prayer, and have even a conviction of its efficacy (for all who pray have not that conviction), and many who are yet in the infancy of their spiritual being, have not their petitions granted, not merely because they ask what might be injurious to them, but because they ask not from truly spiritual motives: "Ye ask, and receive not, because ye ask amiss, that ye may consume it upon your lusts."[2] This form of danger in prayer is connected with a lower stage of the inner life than that which leaves the petitioner merely open to mistake in his judgment as to what may be good for himself and others, and which requires the supplication to be accompanied by the conviction and the faith that, although the Father will not give His son a stone when he asks Him for bread, He will often refuse a stone when asked, that He may give bread instead. But if He be angry at our obduracy and self-will, He may give us the stone we seek, that by the disappointment of our expectations we may be punished, or brought to repentance, or learn better the wisdom and blessedness of living in complete dependence upon Him.

When Saul had parted from Samuel, and was on his way home, he fell in with "a company of prophets," with their instruments of music—persons belonging to one of those "schools," or "colleges," of the prophets which Samuel seems to have instituted, and which we shall have to notice fully hereafter. Then happened to Saul what Samuel had predicted to him before they separated: "The Spirit of the Lord will come upon thee, and thou shalt prophesy with them, and be turned into another man. And let it be, when these signs are come upon thee, that thou do as occasion serve thee." (1 Sam. x. 6, 7). It will occur to most readers, that although these words describe Saul as being turned into *another* man, they do not declare that he was turned into a *new* one; and although they have reference to

a lesser work of the Holy Spirit than His regenerating and sanctifying work, they are remarkably typical or adumbrative of that larger and greater work of God in the soul of man.

It is observable that this coming of the Spirit of God upon Saul, and turning him into another man, was properly his introduction to the kingdom, and constituted his fitness for it. It was the proper sequel to and completion of the operation commenced by his anointing, and by it he acquired all the fitness he ever possessed for the kingdom. In like manner, no one is fit for the kingdom of heaven until the Spirit of God has come upon him, and turned him not only into another, but into a new man, so that with him old things are passed away, and all things have become new. The change is greater than that of Saul; for having received this anointing from the Holy One, we become not only subjects of Christ's kingdom, but indeed "kings and priests unto God."

We see also that the lesser change wrought in the heart of Saul was the work of the Spirit of God. How much more, then, the great change by which man becomes a new creature, and the subject of a new kingdom; by which he passes from outer darkness into that inner light which shines through the realm where God abides, and which transfers the liberated soul, captivated so long, from the power of Satan unto God! All is the work of the Spirit. There is no other power in the universe than His that can make any real change in the least atom of the human heart. None else can furnish, nor any hand but His pour in, the wine and oil by which the soul's deadly wound is healed, and from which it receives new life, new perceptions, new emotions, new strength; so that they who lay sunk, lost and exanimate, in the valley of the shadow of death, are enabled to mount up with wings like eagles, to run and not be weary, to walk and not faint.

Saul, when this change had passed upon him, had new privileges which belonged not to him before. Till then Samuel had told him everything that should happen to him by the way, and every step that he should take. But at the point when the Spirit of God came upon him, when he was changed into another man, the prophet gave no further directions; he simply said, "Do as occasion serve thee, for God is with thee." When light had come to him from heaven, the lamp of the prophet was no longer needful to guide his steps; and if he followed that light in the simplicity of faith, it would guide him safely home. He who has God with him has a sufficient guardian, counsellor, and guide, and he may walk freely and fearlessly in his appointed path. But he must take care that God *is* with him; he must be sure that the light he follows *is* light from heaven. That light—the true light that lighteth every one that really enters the spiritual world—never led astray, or left in darkness, any that followed it. The only danger is, that the candles which men hold up should be taken for the light of God; but the children of the kingdom possess a Witness with their spirits which will not suffer them to make this mistake, if they but heed His testimony.

With regard to the change that was wrought in Saul, we apprehend that it was rather a civil than a sanctifying change. God gave him not that free and noble spirit that David prayed for and attained (Ps. li. 12), but only common gifts of princely parts—prudence, courage, and conduct. The change, however, although not the greatest, was very great, insomuch that it became thenceforth a common proverb among the people, "Is Saul also among the prophets?" when they beheld any rude person raised up and ranked among men of eminence far above his birth and breeding. Thus the people wondered at the change in Saul, whom they deemed more fit to feed his father's asses than to take part in the holy exercises of the prophets. But they knew not yet that this very man was to be their king.

It may be well to consider a little more minutely the character of Saul, in connection with that remarkable divine inspiration communicated to him after he was anointed. Up to that period he was a modest, retiring youth, attentive to his ordinary business, taking little if any interest in public affairs, and shrinking from, rather than courting, that notoriety to which his distinguished appearance might have justly entitled him. He seems, too, to have been as indifferent about religious as about political matters. The words of Samuel, which would have roused the ambition of most men, only produced in Saul a vague feeling of wonder. His sluggish spirit was in a great measure dead to feelings of religious enthusiasm and exalted patriotism. But Samuel, in anointing him, predicted a most remarkable change,—a change, however, to be effected, not by the rousing of any dormant energy, but by the infusion of a supernatural power: "The Spirit of the Lord shall come upon thee, and thou shalt prophesy

with them, *and shalt be turned into another man.*" This work of the Spirit must be carefully distinguished from His ordinary work in regeneration. Saul was to be made *another*, not a *new* man. The change effected was on the feelings and aspirations, not on the nature or heart; it was fitful and temporary, not permanent. The gift of the Spirit, in fact, was intended to inspire him (as it had inspired Samson before him), whenever necessity should require, with ambition to aim at, and courage to perform, the work of a king (chap. xi. 6); and, therefore, when he transgressed so heinously against God that David was anointed in his stead to rule over Israel, we are told that the Spirit of the Lord "departed from Saul," and "came upon David" (xvi. 13, 14).

Another phase of the character of this unfortunate man ought not to be overlooked. Naturally weak and passionate, his sudden elevation to supreme power completely overthrew his mental balance. There was promptness of action and dashing courage while the Spirit was upon him; but there was no steadfastness of purpose, there was no faith, and there was no truth. There was at the same time a rashness and a recklessness, which went far to alienate his best friends; and there was an impatience of delay, and a rebellion against all restraint, human or divine, which in the end deprived him of the presence of Samuel and of the favour of God. Under these painful circumstances, we are told that "an evil spirit from the Lord troubled him." Disappointed hopes and bitter hatred of a rival preyed upon his shattered intellect. His passions obtained at times so complete a mastery over reason, that he became mad. During long and lucid intervals, his better nature even then manifested itself; but the least excitement seems to have roused the demon within, and led him recklessly on to the wildest acts of revenge.

P.

THE LAW OF THE KINGDOM

If we turn to Deut. xvii. 14-20, we shall find certain principles stated, which were destined to form the standing law of the Hebrew monarchy.

It is first of all clearly laid down, that the nomination of the man who should be king was to be left to Jehovah Himself. The regular mode of ascertaining the Lord's will would have been by Urim and Thummim through the high priest; but the intimation could also be given through prophets, or by the sacred lot. Saul, David, and Jeroboam, all received the promise of the throne from prophets. Saul was further designated by the sacred lot, and David was elected by the elders of Israel to the throne, on the express ground that God had promised the kingdom to him. The same may be said of Jeroboam, whose elevation to the throne of the ten tribes must at least have been materially influenced by the fact of his previous nomination to the throne by the prophet Ahijah. These divine interpositions were well calculated to remind the kings of Him on whom they were dependent, and to whose appointment they were indebted for the throne. "As monarchs, called kings of kings, were accustomed to appoint sub-kings, or viceroys, in the several provinces of their dominions, so was the king of the Hebrews to be called to the throne by Jehovah, to receive the kingdom from Him, and in all respects to consider himself as His representative, viceroy, and vassal."[1] In fact, it seems to us that his position with respect to the Lord as Supreme King, bore much external resemblance to that which the Herodian kings of Judea bore to the Roman emperor. There can be no doubt that this point in the Hebrew constitution was fully and plainly expressed by Samuel when he showed to the people "the manner of the kingdom;" and in the sequel we shall find that the Lord Himself failed not to enforce on all occasions, by rewards and by punishments, the responsibility of the sovereigns to Him. The best and most prosperous kings were such as had the truest conception of this essential condition of their power.

It was further ordained that the king should be one of themselves—a native Israelite—not a foreigner, not one born such, even though a proselyte. The reasons for this restriction are obvious in a state so peculiarly constituted as that of the Hebrews, not only from the high estimation in which the descent from Abraham was held, but because all other nations were wholly given to idolatry. This, however, had respect only to free elections, and was by no means to be understood, as interpreted by Judas of Galilee,[2] and by the zealots, during the great war with the Romans, that the Hebrews were not to submit to those foreign powers to which, in the providence of God, they were from time to time subjected. On the contrary, Moses himself had predicted such events, and Jeremiah and Ezekiel had earnestly exhorted their countrymen to submit themselves quietly to the rule of the Chaldeans. As to proselytes, the lapse of

generations, and a Hebrew mother, did not render even them capable of reigning in Israel: they were not of the chosen people, nor "brethren" of the descendants of Abraham. To indicate this purity of descent, the name of the mother of a new king is often mentioned.[1] But this occurs only in the kingdom of Judah, where the law of Moses was held in higher respect than in the other kingdom. To be born of a foreign mother was not indeed an obstacle to the attainment of the throne, if the descent had been unbroken on the side of the father from one of the families of Israel. Rehoboam succeeded Solomon, although his mother was an Ammonitess;[2] but it may in this case be remembered that, so far as we know, he was the only son of the possessor of a thousand wives. The Idumeans counted among their ancestors Abraham and Isaac; but seeing that they came from Esau, not from Jacob, they were included within this proscription of the law; and although Herod the elder, who was an Idumean, was king of Judea, he never possessed the cordial sympathies of his subjects, and certainly never would have attained his monarchy, but by the irresistible will of the mightiest of conquerors.

Females are not *expressly* excluded from the throne; but their disqualification seems to be assumed. It appears never to have entered the mind of the Jewish lawgiver that they might be called to reign. The exclusion is, indeed, traced in the text by Jewish writers, from the constant use of the masculine noun in referring to the contingencies of sovereign power.[3] It is true that Deborah was judge in Israel, but she did not wear a diadem. Athaliah did; but that was by usurpation, in the teeth of the law, and from her the crown passed to the head of the rightful heir.[4] The same character, in a form somewhat mitigated, applies to the nine years' reign of Alexandra, wife of king Alexander Janneus, who, after his death, assumed the throne.[5] There can be no reason to question that the Hebrew theory of government, like that of other oriental nations, was unfavourable to the rule of females, although women did occasionally reign. This may be

[1] Jahn's *Biblische Archæologie*, B. i., sec. 25.
[2] Acts 5:37.

[1] 1 Kings 15:2,10; 22:42; 2 Kings 8:26; 12:1; 14:2; 15:2, 33; 18:2.
[2] 1 Kings 14:31; 2 Chronicles 12:13.
[3] Deuteronomy 17:15, et non pas *Reginam.*"—*Pastoret.*
[4] 2 Kings 11.
[5] Josephus, *Antiq.*, xiii., 16 p. 287.

traced even in the prophets: "As for my people," says Isaiah, "children are their oppressors, and women rule over them."[1] Those ancient times and distant nations wanted the experience furnished under our milder manners and more matured institutions—that a female reign may be as vigorous as that of any man, and not less prosperous and happy.

The Talmudists held the opinion that these were not the only disqualifications, but that various professions or trades precluded a man from becoming king in Israel. At the head of this list are physicians, who, say these sages, live too proudly, without fear of disease, and with hearts unhumbled before God, and are often guilty of the blood of their poor brethren, by refusing to them the succour of their skill.[2] We might be astonished to see the noblest of secular professions thus unfavourably estimated, and mixed up with some of the coarsest of the arts, did we not read, in the history of antiquity, that the profession of medicine was for the most part abandoned to slaves. Other disqualifying employments are those of butchers, barbers, bathmen, weavers, tanners, grooms, and camel-drivers. They apprehended, it seems, that an Israelite could not have exercised such employments without contracting low and ignoble sentiments; and it was believed that the remembrance of his former condition would cause him to be held in contempt by his subjects. The same professions equally debarred an Israelite from the high-priesthood. Other employments which, to our notions, are scarcely of higher consideration than these, did not disqualify a man from being king. Saul had the care of asses, and David of sheep; but the asses and the sheep were those of their fathers, in a country where pastoral employments were long held in high respect. The son of a slave, or even of a captive, was also by usage excluded from the throne. Most readers will remember that the priest-king Alexander Janneus was once pelted with citrons when he stood at the altar about to offer sacrifice, and reviled as the descendant of a captive, and therefore unfit to sacrifice. This charge, founded on a false report that his grandmother had been a captive in the time of Antiochus Epiphanes, Alexander

resented so highly that his wrath was scarcely appeased by the blood of six thousand Israelites, whom he slew in his rage.[1]

Certain exterior advantages—or rather the absence of certain bodily imperfections—seem also to have been regarded as essential to the possessor of the throne. We have seen, in the case of Saul, that his eminent stature materially contributed to his nomination and acceptance: and in the account of the appointment of David to the throne, the beauty of his person is emphatically indicated. The Scripture itself, as we have already seen, is far from sanctioning this class of ideas; and some of the most eminent men of ancient times were subject to infirmities: Moses had a stammering tongue; Jacob was lame; Isaac was blind; yet they were not the less chiefs of the chosen race, and men honoured of God.

Looking to the position which the Hebrew king occupied, it was of course impossible for him to possess the power of introducing any new object or mode of religious worship. The kings of other nations performed the functions of priests on great occasions; but although more than one Hebrew king evinced a disposition to assume this power, it was entirely unlawful, except the king were of the family of Aaron, as was the case with the Maccabæan or Asmonæan sovereigns, who, therefore, rightfully discharged the functions of the priesthood.

So far from being allowed to make any alteration in the religious worship of the people, the king was required, as the servant and minister of the Lord, to be watchful in all respects over its conservation, and to repress all tendency to change. He was to be the champion of the law against the encroachments of idolatry, and he was deeply responsible for any neglect of this high and solemn duty. He was required to be himself most strict in his observance of the law; and that he might be well acquainted with it, he was required to make a transcript of the authentic copy in the possession of the priests, and to "read therein all the days [2] of his life, that he

---

[1] Isaiah 3:12.

[2] This exclusion of the physicians is not stated in Maimonides' *Treatise upon the Kings*. But Maimonides was himself a physician.

[1] Josephus, p. 285.   See also *De Bell. Jud.*, i. 4, 3.

[2] It has been questioned whether the king was to copy the whole of the law entire, or only the abstract of it given in the book of Deuteronomy. The latter is the sense given in the Septuagint and the Vulgate, as well as by some Jewish commentators of authority; but the prevailing opinion among the Rabbis, and, we think, among Christian writers, is in favour of the whole law being understood. In

might learn to fear Jehovah his God, to keep all the words of the law, *that his heart be not lifted up above his brethren;*" that is, that he should be no arbitrary despot, whose only law is his own pleasure.

That his heart might not be lifted up in kingly pride, it was further directed, that he should eschew the pernicious luxury to which Oriental monarchs have in all ages been prone. An effectual check upon this was provided, and at the same time a powerful motive to oppressive exactions upon his subjects was taken away, by the interdiction of the accumulation of large treasures; neither was he to adopt that usual accompaniment of eastern state—a numerous harem. Besides the other and obvious disadvantages of such establishments, many of the women in such cases are always foreigners; and it was to be feared that the servant of God might be led to regard idolatry with favour through their influence. This actually happened in the case of Solomon.

Furthermore, as the object of preserving the Israelites as a separate people in Canaan was incompatible with views of extended empire, the king was forbidden to maintain large bodies of cavalry, which were in that age chiefly used in such undertakings. In fact, to strike at the root of the danger, the breeding and possession of horses may be said to have been discouraged. This could be no great hardship in Palestine, the mountainous character of which, together with the difficult passes which continually occur, renders, even to this day, the horse of less use and value there than in the neighbouring countries.

It will be seen that some of those wise regulations were more or less neglected by many of the kings; and it will also be seen that this neglect brought down upon themselves and their people the very dangers and evils which they were designed to avert.[1]

Schickard's learned work, *De Jure Reg. Hebræorum,* theor. v., p. 9 *et seq.*, ample details may be found from the Rabbinical writers, as to what was understood to be the manner in which this royal copy of the law was to be made, the characters, the pages, the lines, the dimensions, the divisions, the material of the volume, its covering, the preparation of the ink, the inscription of the name of Jehovah, the copying of the poetry contained in these sacred books, and various other matters.

[1] On the subject of this day's Reading, the following works have been looked into, and may be consulted with advantage by the reader : Schickard, *Jus Regium Hebræ-*

It is especially worthy of note here, that the words in which the Israelites demand a king are identical with those used in the prophetic picture in Deut. xvii. 14 : " When thou art come into the land which the Lord thy God giveth thee, and shalt possess it, and shalt dwell therein, and shalt say, *I will set a king over me, like as all the nations that are about me.*" Every change in events, however sudden and unexpected humanly speaking, was foreseen and provided for of God.

It is said that, immediately after Saul's election, "Samuel told the people *the manner* of the kingdom." The word translated " manner " signifies " law ;" and Samuel's discourse appears to have been a definite explanation of the place which the earthly monarchy held in relation to the theocracy,—the precise duties which the king owed to the heavenly King on the one hand, and to the people on the other. It will be observed that it is not "the law of the king" which was explained, but "the law of the kingdom," or rather of "the monarchy." In the Septuagint version the word is rendered "statute" ($\delta\iota\kappa\alpha\iota\omega\mu\alpha$) and in the Vulgate "law." Josephus takes a different view of it. He represents Sumuel's document as a prophetical statement of the evils that would result from kingly rule, and a protest against its establishment. The high probability is, that it was as Dr. Kitto has represented it. Samuel wrote it in a book, and deposited it where the sacred books were then kept—" before the Lord." No such book has come down to us. In all likelihood, it was just an expanded and authoritative comment on Deut. xvii. 15-20.

P.

THE KING AROUSED

1 Samuel 11:1-8

IN the choice of representatives for our own senate, it is remarkable that, in the majority of cases, the impulse of popular excitement, as manifested by the show of hands at the nomination, is not in accordance with the result of the election. We need not therefore be surprised to learn that, notwithstanding the enthusiasm with which the appearance of Saul had been hailed, there was so widespread a dissatisfaction at his appointment, that he was suffered to withdraw to his own house, and almost to return into private life. This had been the case, but that a few kindly disposed and faithful men attached themselves to his person, and remained with him; and these he seems to have been able to

orum e tenebris Rabbinicis erutum, Leipzig 1674 ; Jahn, *Biblische Archæologie,* Wien 1805 ; Pastoret, *Legislation des Hebreux,* Paris 1817 ; Salvador, *Histoire des Institutions de Moise et du Peuple Hebreux,* Paris 1828 ; Hullmann, *Staatsverfassung der Israeliten,* Leipzig 1834.

maintain, by means of the "presents" which some of the people brought in testimony of their homage and respect. But a very considerable proportion of the people—a large minority, if not a majority—said, "How shall this man save us?" And they despised him, and brought him no presents. The source of their discontent it is not difficult to trace to the obscurity of the person on whom the crown had fallen, with the absence of tried character and experience, which they thought themselves entitled to look for in an elected king; and something of it may have been due to the sheepish and unregal deportment of Saul in hiding himself "among the stuff," instead of meeting with manly dignity the call of God and the people.

It is emphatically remarked, that Saul "held his peace." *That* was kingly. He was content to bide his time. He knew that the state of affairs around must soon afford him an opportunity of acquiring the personal consideration he yet lacked; and he felt that any show of resentment and bald assertion of his authority till then, would only expose him to derision.

The opportunity he must have greatly desired was very soon afforded. The Ammonites on the east of the Jordan began to move. That people had ere this recovered the effects of the terrible overthrow they sustained in the time of Jephthah; and feeling their own strength, and beholding the apparent weakness of Israel, they judged the time to be favourable for the sharp avengement of that never-forgotten blow, and for the recovery of those territories east of the Jordan which they still regarded as rightfully their own, notwithstanding the ability with which, first by arguments and next by blows, Jephthah had of old disposed of their claim.

They appeared suddenly in great force before the town of Jabesh-gilead. The inhabitants were in no condition to make any effectual resistance, and therefore offered to surrender on terms. This the Ammonite king, whose name was Nahash, refused on any other conditions than that he should put out all their right eyes—not only that he might thereby disqualify them for the use of arms, but, avowedly, that the fact might remain as a brand of infamy upon the whole nation. Appalled by this barbarous stipulation, yet not seeing how to resist, they begged and obtained a truce of a week, at the expiry of which they would accept of these hard terms,

unless some relief in the meantime arrived. Some surprise has been felt that he who breathed nothing but disgrace and ruin against the Israelites, should have yielded to the people of Jabesh even this short respite, and have thus subjected himself to the risks of delay. But here we may avail ourselves of the probably accurate information of the Jewish historian,[1] that the besieged had already sent to implore the assistance of the two and a half tribes beyond the Jordan, and that none had dared to stir a hand for their relief. So, there being little likelihood that the ten tribes west of the river, who were at a still greater distance, and less immediately affected than the nearer tribes, could bring any aid in so short a time, Nahash might, in that confidence, and as a further manifestation of his scorn, the more easily grant the beleagured citizens the respite they required. But we may quite as well, or even better, suppose that Divine Providence thus far restrained his hands by a sort of infatuation, in order to give to the new monarch an opportunity of affording such signal proof of his capacity, decision, and military conduct, as might win for him the general admiration of his subjects, and secure his full possession of the royal power to which he had been appointed.

Saul had by this time returned to his old employment, which shows how little was the support or attention he received as king. It may be doubtful indeed if the "band of men," who had followed him in the first instance, had till now remained with him. The inattention to him is further indicated by the fact, that the persons who brought the tidings of this affair to Gibeah, did not seek him out as one who had any peculiar interest in the matter; and it was only when he came home from the field, following the herd, and *in answer to his inquiries*, when he witnessed the lamentations of the people, that he was apprised of the event. This news awoke all the patriot and the king within him. Like Samson aroused from slumber, he "shook his invincible locks," and stood up in the fulness of his strength. The time was come to *use*, in behalf of the people, the office to which he had been chosen, and to make that office a truth in their eyes, and in the eyes of their enemies. He did not hesitate one moment to call the people to arms, and that not with uncertain voice, but commandingly as their king, whose summons it

[1] Josephus, *Antiq.*, vi., 5. page 128.

was their duty to obey. He took a yoke of oxen, and hewing them in parts, sent the pieces by swift messengers through the country, to declare the event, and say, " Whosoever cometh not after Saul, and after Samuel, *so* shall it be done unto his oxen."

There has been occasion to refer to this custom in connection with the similar act of the Levite,[1] and it therefore need not detain us here. There are, however, so many points of interest in this summoning of the tribes, and so many questions have been raised as to some of the particulars, that it is well worth while to examine the circumstances with some attention. Most of the objections which have been felt or urged, turn upon the difficulty of imagining how all the recorded operations could have been accomplished within the time specified. The case may be thus stated. The besieged city of Jabesh-gilead was not much less than sixty miles from Gibeah, the place of Saul's residence, by direct distance, and considerably more if we take into account the mountainous character of the country, and the windings and turnings of the roads. Thus allowing that the seven days' respite had been granted to the besieged very early in the morning, the persons who brought the tidings could hardly have reached Gibeah till the evening of the next day. It was certainly the evening when Saul first heard the intelligence, as he was then bringing home his cattle from the field. There remained then but five days more to summon the tribes to arms, some of which were a hundred miles north from Gibeah, and as far south from Bezek,[2] the place appointed for the general rendezvous; where, nevertheless, upon a review of the whole army, there were found to be 330,000 effective men. From Bezek they had still about eight miles to Bethshan, where they were to cross the Jordan, and from that place, ten miles more to reach the camp of the Ammonites, which, considering the vastness of the army, and the mountainousness of Gilead, could hardly take less than one day more. If this be allowed, it will follow that Saul's summons must have reached the ten tribes, and these must have armed and assembled themselves under their respective standards within the short space of four days. We may even count it as

less; for the text expressly says that the forces assembled at Bezek in time to be reviewed by the king, which must have taken some considerable time; after which he had still his messengers to send to Jabesh-gilead with assurance of effectual relief by the next morning's dawn, before he could march from Bezek to their assistance. All these things being duly weighed, and the distance being considered from Gibeah, whence the message was despatched, to the remotest tribes north and south, and from those again to Bezek, the place to which they were to repair, in some cases by a march of a hundred or a hundred and fifty miles, through wildernesses, over craggy mountains, and along narrow and difficult defiles, it is very hard to understand— some insist that it is incredible—that it could have been performed in so short a space of time. For, allowing Saul's messengers to have travelled day and night, and with the utmost despatch, not less than a day and a half must be allowed them to reach the more distant tribes; so that they could have but two days and a half more to equip themselves, to provide themselves with victuals, to assemble under their chiefs, and to reach the place of rendezvous over roads so difficult and retarding. This transmission of messages, this raising of an army (and not simply calling into action troops standing ready for service), this march of that large army by difficult roads, this reviewing of it, the final advance to meet the enemy, and the complete and sudden victory within so short a time, far surpass anything we find in modern warfare. An experienced general, with all the modern advantages of intercommunication and travel, would not be able to get together an army of 20,000 or 30,000 men in as many weeks as Saul —a raw and inexperienced monarch and commander—took days only to raise a force of ten times the number, from ten different tribes, several of them at a serious distance. Such are the difficulties and objections; and we have stated them, because the answering them tomorrow will enable us to throw some light upon sundry matters involved in these considerations.

A further and preliminary objection we may dispose of now. Was it at all likely that a people who so contemned their king as to leave him to resume his pastoral avocations, should all at once, and " as one man," have obeyed his call, and flocked in such immense numbers to his

---

[1] See Vol. 1, pp. 572-575.

[2] Seventeen miles from Shechem, on the road to Bethshan on the Jordan.

standard? But the news which accompanied this summons, was surely likely to animate the hearts of a brave people, with the same indignation and zeal that it had kindled in the bosom of Saul; and if they were to move at all for the relief of their brethren, and to save Israel from the threatened disgrace, Saul, whatever they might think of him, was the only person authorized to lead them against the enemy. Besides, if a similar mandate formerly, even from a Levite, was not to be neglected or despised, much less could it be so when it came from their anointed king. It deserves notice, that the very name of Jabesh-gilead was enough to warn them of the peril of disobedience; for it was notorious that the people of that place had perished by the sword of Israel, for neglecting to appear in arms upon a similar but less authoritative summons, sent forth on that former occasion to which reference has been made.

THE CALL OF THE TRIBES

1 Samuel 11:1-8

THE difficulties which have been found in the first transaction, by which the new king won to himself honour in Israel, were stated yesterday; and we may now see what evidence can be afforded of the truthfulness of the scriptural account, and the feasibility of the transaction.

There being at this time no military profession among the Israelites—none who were, actually *soldiers*,—for the men were to be called from the flocks and the fields to march against their enemies,—the case has no parallel among ourselves, with whom anything like this would imply the necessity of some previous training of the raw levies to the use of their weapons, before they could be trusted to face the enemy in battle. This, however rapidly and imperfectly done, would necessarily consume considerable time. But it was not so among the Israelites. With them, as is still the case in most eastern nations, every man was familiar with the use of weapons from his youth, and was at all times ready and qualified to take his part in such martial operations as the simple tactics and rude discipline of that age required. Besides,

all the men between the ages of twenty and sixty were deemed liable to the call for military service, and were, in their several tribes, registered for it. There was no confusion when they were called out by a competent authority. A man had only to take down the weapons he possessed—and every one possessed some sort of weapon—and hasten to the place of rendezvous in his own tribe, where he put himself under the orders of the officers, who, in their various grades, were well known to him, being the chiefs of the tribes and families. The admirable order of encamping large bodies of men, and of marching them under their banners, which had been established in the wilderness, was no doubt retained for military purposes, and must have materially contributed to facilitate their movements and to prevent confusion.

All the men took the field at their own expense, providing their own food; for the cause was their own, and they looked for no pay, save the spoil of their enemies, beyond the acquisition of a national advantage, the redress of a general wrong, or the resistance of a public aggression. The difficulty of provisioning so large a host is therefore imaginary. Every man provisioned himself, taking with him a few days' supply of light and portable food—some bread, some cheese, some olives, some hard dates, some dried figs and rasins, and other matters of this description. If detained in the field longer than was expected, one man in ten was appointed to provide food for the rest, as was done when Israel was out to avenge the Levite.[1]

The difficulties presented by the state of the country in the way of the rapid passage of messengers, and the march of armies, are altogether imaginary, and founded upon the present neglected state of the same land. It is entirely forgotten by most persons, that the presence of unexampled facilities of communication throughout the country was ensured by the law respecting the cities of refuge, to which the innocent manslayer might flee from the pursuit of the avenger. Every facility for the flight of those who had taken away the life of another unawares, was to be provided. "The way was to be prepared,"[2] not only, as the Jewish writers explain, to those cities on either side Jordan, but to the forty-eight cities of the Levites, which were places of sanctuary; and if, as we have

[1] Judges 20:10.   [2] Deuteronomy 19:3.

reason to believe, the ways were "prepared" in the manner described by the old Jewish writers, there could have been no ancient country better provided with wide and commodious roads for messengers and travellers. All these roads, which, from the manner in which the cities were dispersed, must have intersected the country in all directions, were kept wide, level, dry, and plain, with convenient bridges over rivers, with posts, the indications on which, directing travellers from place to place, were so plainly written that those who ran might read;[1] and with every possible contrivance for rendering travelling as easy and expeditious as possible. It is not unlikely that traces of those ancient ways still exist in the well made roads which travellers sometimes fall in with in parts now forsaken, and which, in ignorance of these circumstances, they set down for Roman roads. The utmost care was bestowed on this matter by the local authorities, because it was deemed that the nearest town or village incurred the burden of blood-guiltiness, if, through any obstruction upon the road, the course of the fugitive manslayer were so retarded as to enable the avenger of blood (*goel*) to overtake him and wreak his vengeance upon him.

Although the use of swift camels (dromedaries) is difficult in the present state of the country, they might well be used on such roads as these; and in the absence of saddle-horses, which were not at this time in use, they might be, and doubtless were, employed on extraordinary occasions like this; and those of the right breed, trained for the saddle, travelling without baggage, and with only a single rider, have been known to go as much as two hundred miles in twenty-four hours. We may be sure that no available means of expediting the message were neglected; and if dromedaries were at all known in Palestine, as they were, and if the state of the roads allowed of their being used, as was the case, there can be no doubt that they were employed; and by these means the summons might be transmitted to the uttermost parts of the land in an incredibly shorter space of time than has been imagined.

Again, throughout the East there are trained runners who can for a long time accompany a horse at full speed, and who do habitually attend on foot the princes and great men when they ride out. There were doubtless such men in Israel, for in the next generation we find men employed to run before Absalom's chariot;[1] and how much this accomplishment of swift running was valued and cultivated, even among young men of station in Israel, for the sake of the swift transmission of intelligence in time of war, is seen in the case of Ahimaaz, the son of the high priest Zadok; of Cushi,[2] and of Asahel, king David's nephew, who was "light of foot as a wild roe."[3] It is quite likely that the message would be taken from town to town by such swift runners in turn, one after another, until it reached the utmost limits of the land.

There is yet another resource, which there is much reason to suppose was employed on this, as we know that it was on many other occasions. It is very possible that the alarm, or summons for a general armament, was conveyed by beacons, or fiery signals kindled upon the tops of the hills; so that when the human messengers arrived, they would find the people ready assembled in arms at the several towns of their tribes in which they were wont to congregate on such occasions. Such signals were particularly available in Canaan, by reason of the mountainous nature of the country, and by the absence of any plains of great extent in which no eminences occur. By this means the call to arms, transmitted from post to post, would reach the utmost bounds of the land in the course of a few hours. These beacons are often mentioned by the prophets,[4] and were in use not only among the Hebrews, but among all nations inhabiting hilly countries; and being easily perceived at a vast distance from each other, especially in the nighttime, and being moreover distinguished by some well known differences, according to the notice or order intended to be conveyed, were immediately answered by the sound of the trumpet in the valleys below. By such means not a city or village, whether in a low or high situation, but would in less than the space of one night be roused by the general alarm, and receive some intimation of its object, either from the nature of the signal, or from the difference in the sound of the trumpets. When, therefore, the signal was for a general armament, all men able to bear arms were bound to repair at once, with weapons and

---

[1] The Jews think there is an allusion to this custom in the phrase in Hab. 2:2, "Make it plain, that he may run that readeth it."

[1] 2 Samuel 15:1. [2] 2 Samuel 18:19-31. [3] 2 Samuel 2:18.
[4] Isaiah 5:26; 11:10; 13:2; 18:3; 30:17; 49:22; 42:10; Jeremiah 50:2; 51:27; Zechariah 9:16.

provisions, to their respective standards, where they put themselves under the orders of their tribal commanders, and were mustered by the chiefs or captains of hundreds, of thousands, and at last by the chief or prince of the tribe, after which they had only to await orders from the king or general-in-chief, as to when they were to commence their march, and to what point their course was to be directed.

It will thus be seen that the couriers, bearing the parts of the oxen, and charged with the urgent mandate of the king, had only to repair to the places known to be those where the several tribes usually assembled within their own territories, where they would find them under arms, ready to march, and awaiting the orders which they brought. This statement incidentally meets the puerile objection of some, that the two oxen must have been cut up into mince-meat, in order that a small portion might be sent to all the towns and villages of Israel; and we can see that if, as Josephus affirms, the legs only of the animals were thus employed, these would have sufficed. In confirmation of this view it may be observed, that the Levite separated the dead body of his concubine into twelve parts, one for each of the tribes of Israel. This was all that he felt to be necessary, and doubtless all that was required now; and assuredly for the same reason—that each portion was sent direct to the place which was recognized as the centre of union in each of the tribes.

It would seem, from the biblical narrative, that while the elders of Jabesh-gilead asked seven days' respite to send messengers "unto all the coasts of Israel," in reality they sent immediately and directly to Benjamin. It was natural they should do so, because they had doubtless heard of the election of Saul ; and, besides, they were closely related to the Benjamites. Saul himself may have sprung from one of the daughters of Jabesh (Judg. xx.) The ties of blood were felt ; and outraged family feeling may have served to awaken his spirit. It does seem a remarkable coincidence, that the relief of Jabesh should have been the first triumph of the young Benjamite warrior. The people of Jabesh never forgot their deliverance, and their debt of gratitude to Saul. When his headless trunk hung dishonoured on the walls of Bethshean, the men of Jabesh, at the risk of their lives, rescued and buried it ; and when the family of the fallen monarch was driven from home and country, they found an asylum among the fastnesses of Gilead.

P.

RELIEF OF JABESH—GILEAD

1 Samuel 11:9-15

THE objections which have been urged to the raising and bringing into action of so large an army in so short a time, have, we trust, been satisfactorily disposed of. But there remain other objections, as to the final movement and result which likewise deserve our attention.

The objections against the probability of the respite granted by the Ammonites to the besieged, have been also considered ; but it has, moreover, been urged as altogether unlikely that king Nahash would, during the interval of respite, keep so bad a look-out, as to remain wholly in ignorance of what was passing on the other side the Jordan, and to suffer his camp to be surprised and surrounded by Saul and his army, on the very morning of the day on which he expected the city to be delivered up to him. Surprising and uncommon, however, as this oversight may appear, we meet with similar instances of apparent neglect, not only in sacred and ancient history, but even among modern and warlike nations. It was the maxim of the greatest of modern generals, never to despise an enemy; and most of the failures of this kind have arisen from inattention to this principle. There is the remarkable instance of the French general Count Tallard, who, when he might easily have opposed the confederate army under Marlborough, and prevented them from passing the Rhine to come at him, yet suffered them to cross that rapid river unmolested ; alleging, that the more that came over, the more there would be to be killed or taken : the consequence of which egregious oversight was the total defeat of the French army at Hochstadt, the taking of their insolent general prisoner, with a prodigious number of other officers of distinction, and the preservation of the German empire from the impending danger. How much Nahash despised the Israelites, has already been indicated ; and supposing him apprised of their movements, the probability is that he would, under the influence of such feelings, keep his army in its cantonments till the enemy came up, without taking the trouble of meeting them, or of resisting their passage of the Jordan.

Considering the strange neglect of ancient

armies, and indeed of modern Oriental armies, in sending out scouts for intelligence, in maintaining advanced picquets, and in keeping strict watch —of which neglect we have many examples in Scripture—it does not appear to us by any means incredible, that the Ammonites were unapprised of these movements among the Israelites. But without taking advantage of this resource, and again supposing that they did know that the Israelites were bestirring themselves west of the Jordan, it is more probable, considering the shortness of the time, that they supposed all this movement was intended to resist their farther progress into Palestine, than that it was destined for the relief of the besieged. And further, whatever martial precautions they may have taken, yet several seemingly accidental circumstances, such as often occur in warfare, may, through the policy of the Hebrew monarch, have rendered them ineffectual, if not indeed contributory to that fatal security and indolence which their contempt of the enemy was calculated to induce. It is quite likely that Saul and some of the tribes might take advantage of their proximity to the place of rendezvous, to secure all the passes and defiles leading from the Jordan to the enemy's camp, and thereby intercept all intelligence of his approach from reaching them, and they would think themselves the more secure on that very account. It may also be suggested as far from improbable, that they may have been confirmed in their security by the very messengers whom Saul sent, the night before his arrival, to encourage the men of Jabesh, by informing them of his intention to be present for their relief the next morning; for, while they were bearing this cheering intelligence to the besieged, it is probable that they spread a contrary report through the enemy's camp, through which they passed, making them believe that Saul and the tribes on the other side the Jordan had not the power or the spirit to come to their relief. But that which appears most to have contributed to the fatal security of the Ammonites, was the subtle message sent out by the besieged, that having in vain implored the help of their brethren beyond the river, they had now no resource left but to march out the next morning, and cast themselves upon the mercy of the Ammonitish king. This news, once spread through the camp, could not fail to render the guards and sentinels still more remiss and negligent.

There was yet another stratagem so common in these early times, and still so characteristic of Eastern warfare, that Saul was not likely to neglect the advantage which it offered; for, from the nature of the country among the mountains of Gilead, it might be used with peculiar advantage, and with much assurance of success: this was to fetch a compass, instead of marching directly upon the enemy, and so fall upon them unawares, and from a quarter least suspected. This Saul might the more easily accomplish, as it appears that he marched his army in three divisions. It might be done under the guidance of the men of Jabesh, who originally brought the intelligence to Gibeah, and who, as belonging to this region, may be assumed to have been well acquainted with the situation of the enemy's camp, and with all the passes that led to it. Thus, by continuing the march all that night, and with as little noise as possible, the Hebrew army might with ease come upon the Ammonites, unperceived and unexpected, until its warlike outcries aroused them, perhaps out of a profound sleep, and the growing daylight disclosed the enemy on all sides of the camp, and ready to rush upon them in all their might. In the confusion which could not but ensue in the host of the besiegers, the people of Jabesh may be conceived to have made good their promise of "coming out" in the morning; not indeed to yield themselves up, but to fall upon the rear of the Ammonites, while their front and flanks were belaboured by Saul's three powerful corps.

With all these advantages, there is nothing hard to believe in the fact stated, that the Israelites gained so signal and easy a victory, and made so fearful a slaughter of their enemies. This dreadful execution lasted from morning, until the heat of the day compelled them to give over: by which time the survivors were so completely scattered, that two of them were not left together.

It is stated by Josephus, and is in itself probable enough, though not recorded in Scripture, that Saul, not content with this signal victory, and the complete deliverance of Jabesh-gilead, carried the war into the country of the Ammonites, which he laid waste, enriched his army with the spoil, and brought back his victorious troops safe to their homes, laden with glory and plunder. He adds that king Nahash was killed in the battle. However this may be, it is certain that the Ammonites were so humbled by this great overthrow, that we do not read of any further hostilities between them and the Israelites during the remainder of Saul's reign, nor indeed until the latter end of that of David, when Hanun, their newly crowned monarch, did, by an unheard-of affront offered to his ambassadors, provoke that warlike prince to use them with much greater severity.

The reader will recollect several instances of this favourite course among the Hebrews, of surprising the enemy by means of swift marches. In fact, it is the distinguishing feature of the first military operation on record—Abraham's pursuit and overthrow of the four invading kings. It was also by the very method in question, that Joshua won many signal victories over the combined forces of the Canaanites. There is, especially, that celebrated action against the five confederate kings, who had brought together their numerous forces against the Gibeonite allies of the Hebrews (Josh. x. 4, 5); and the still more remarkable victory which he gained, with a small flying army, over the king of Hazor, at the waters of Merom, although the Canaanitish force consisted of chariots, and horsemen, and foot, as numerous "as the sand of the sea-shore." (Josh. xi. 4). Against this formidable host he marched with the choice men of his troops, with such long and rapid strides, that he came unexpectedly upon them, and falling upon them, according to custom, in three or four distinct bodies, put them to a total rout, seized their camp, burned all their chariots, hamstrung their horses, and having totally dispersed them that escaped the sword, became, by that single action, master of a wide tract of country, and of a large number of cities, which it would doubtless have taken a long time to reduce by regular siege.

In reference to the identification of Jabesh Gilead, the following extract from Tristram's *Land of Israel* is appropriate and interesting:—" We crossed the Wady el Hemar (in the Jordan valley on the Gilead side), and in three hours more, another steep climb and steeper descent brought us to the Yâbis (Jabesh). This was a lovely valley, not inferior in its way to the magnificent forest scenery through which we had been winding. Straggling old olives, patches of barley, and rich pasture filled the glen, but no other trace of man, save old ruins, featureless and shapeless. On the southern brow we came to a knoll of indistinct ruins with no hewn stones distinguishable, which was called by our Kûrah man Er Maklub (the overthrown). Anxious to visit

the site of Jabesh Gilead, we inquired particularly for the *Ed Deir* of Dr. Robinson, but he did not know the name. Determined, however, to ascertain the site, we trusted to Robinson's description, of which we had a faint recollection; and fortunately, proceeding on the south side of the Wady, came upon an isolated round-topped hill, just such an one as is ordinarily seized upon for a Gilead village, whose top was strewn with ruins, much larger than those of Maklub, and with some broken columns among them. This was the spot conjecturally identified as Jabesh Gilead. It stands where Jabesh ought to do, and in full sight of Bethlehem. There were, however, no traces of walls, or of any important station."—P. 566.

S.

THE INAUGURATION

1 Samuel 12

IT must not escape our notice, that in his summons to the tribes, Saul called the people in the joint names of himself and Samuel: "Whosoever cometh not forth after Saul and after Samuel," etc. Was this use of Samuel's name authorized by the prophet? We incline to think that it was not. It is true that Samuel's residence was not so distant from that of Saul, that any very serious delay would have been occasioned by an actual application to Samuel. Yet, to such excited urgency as that by which Saul was impelled, the delay of a few hours would seem intolerable; and from what later events disclose of Saul's character, the probability is that he *assumed* the concurrence of Samuel as a matter of course, and acted accordingly. It was the fault of this man's temper—the ruinous fault, which caused his destruction—to have such proud reliance upon his own judgment, or rather upon his impulses, that he continually assumed the approbation and sanction of those whom he was bound to consult —whether it were the Lord, or whether it were Samuel. These were not only acts of great disrespect, involving the assumption of powers not committed to him, but they left him open to errors of conduct which might have been avoided, had he availed himself of the mature experience of Samuel, or had he sought counsel of God by the appointed means. In this case it is probable, therefore, that, without consulting the prophet, he coupled his name with his own; not only in seeming deference to Samuel, but as conscious that he had not yet himself been fully inaugurated as king, and as aware that many would come forward at the call of Samuel, who might not pay the same attention to his own, unsupported by the authority of the prophet. We cannot help thinking, from some expressions which occur in Samuel's farewell address to the people in laying down his power, that he had from this, or some such circumstance, gained some insight into the true character of Saul, and begun to discern the danger that might flow from it. Yet for the present he held his peace, not willing to damp the general satisfaction; fearing, perhaps, lest he might be premature in his judgment, and being anxious to take advantage of the enthusiasm which Saul's exploit had awakened, to secure the general recognition of his authority.

So strong now ran the tide of public opinion in Saul's favour, that the people hinted to Samuel (who had by this time joined the army) that those who had contemned the election of Saul should be brought to punishment. This motion was with prompt and graceful magnanimity put down by Saul himself, whose kingly style on *this* occasion became him well : " There shall not a man be put to death this day; for to-day the Lord hath wrought salvation in Israel."

Availing himself of the good disposition of the people, Samuel then proposed that they should go and " renew the kingdom at Gilgal,"—the old camping ground of the tribes, and the place where the twelve stones of memorial, taken out of the bed of the Jordan, were set up. This was probably, at this time, the nearest to them of the places where the Israelites were wont to assemble on great national occasions. Arrived at that place, Saul was there solemnly inaugurated and hailed as king, and the act was confirmed by peace-offering sacrifices. The rejoicing at this consummation was general, and no doubt sincere. In the midst of these exultations, Samuel arose to address the people, and every voice became mute that his might be heard. Then followed that great oration to which we have already had occasion to refer. He commenced by pointing out the completeness with which he had given effect to their wishes in setting a king over them, although avowedly in opposition to his better judgment: " And now, behold, the king walketh before you: and I am old and grey-headed; and, behold, my sons are with you: and I have walked before you from my childhood unto this day."

All the parties concerned were there: the king, in the fulness of his power; the people, triumphant in the apparent sanction to their judgment, which the late victory under their new king afforded; Samuel himself, too old to be expected much longer to exercise any control over the movements of the government; and his sons, of whom they were jealous, were there present like themselves, as subjects of Saul. In that audience he appealed to them to testify whether there had been aught in his administration to call for the change they had demanded. Having obtained their cordial recognition of the integrity of his government, he proceeded, in a rapid glance over the past history of the nation, to show that the government, as originally established, and as illustrated by the special interposition of the Divine King in raising up public servants equal to every emergency, had been quite adequate to the wants of the nation. In laying down the power which he had so long exercised for the benefit of his people, it became him not to let them go away with the impression that the performance of the official acts necessary to the establishment of the new government was to be taken as expressive of his satisfaction with their conduct. It was far otherwise. Their mode of acting was wickedness; it was sin, for which they would not fail to be deeply punished, unless they and their king continued to walk in the fear of the Lord, and remembered that their prime obedience was due to His commandments. " But if ye still do wickedly," he concluded, " ye shall be consumed, both ye and your king." To show that his words were in conformity with the will of God, Samuel lifted up his hand to heaven, and called for thunder and rain, which came in abundance, although such phenomena were never witnessed in Canaan at that season of the year, it being the time of wheat harvest. The people were quite satisfied of the supernatural character of this visitation; and the result was salutary, " for they feared the Lord and Samuel."

It has been questioned whether it was right in Samuel, or fair to Saul, to set forth a view of the case such as, if the former gained the attention to which he was entitled, was calculated to excite disaffection to the new government. Supposing his view right—as no doubt it was—was it good taste or sound judgment to advance it on this happy occasion ? But we must remember that Samuel, besides having been the governor of Israel, was still a prophet who lay under a solemn responsibility to make known the mind of God, without such prudential reservations as might influence the conduct of other men. The occasion, however awkward it might seem, was proper. It was the closing act of his administration; and in laying down his power in the presence of the assembled states, it surely became him to declare the principles of the divine government; to vindicate his own administration; to pronounce his view of the present condition of the nation; and give solemn cautions and warnings as to the future. He spoke only as he had always spoken; and he might now finally, and once for all, declare his mind freely, seeing that the authority of the king was now fully established, and the monarchy was to be taken as an accomplished fact—a fact accomplished through his own instrumentality. His object was, not to lead the Israelites to recall the step they had taken, but to ensure their good conduct and their proper subservience to Jehovah, as still not only their spiritual, but their political Lord, under the new institutions.

But although this view sufficiently vindicates Samuel, it is more than probable that his strong remonstrance was displeasing to Saul, coming, as it did, in the moment of his highest triumph, when his mind was powerfully excited by the perception of his exalted relation and important service to the state. It is, as already hinted, not unlikely that the discourse owed some of its touches to the perception Samuel had been already enabled to obtain of Saul's real character, which he had soon occasion to learn that he had too truly judged. Thus it is probable that the seeds of future disagreement between the king and the prophet were already sown, before the great assembly at Gilgal broke up.

ISRAEL DISARMED

1 Samuel 13:1-4, 19-22

THE narrative may have suggested to many that Saul was a young man at the time of his nomination to reign over Israel. Yet, on reflection, it must seem unlikely that the disadvantage of youth, and consequently of inexperience, should have been added to the other disqualifications for winning the confidence of the people under which he had laboured. In the course of hereditary succession, the occasional youth of the sovereign at the time of his accession is accepted as an inevitable consequence and necessity of that form of government; but in the first establishment of a dynasty—in the choice of a first king—we remember no instance of a young man being preferred. David was thirty years old when he began to reign, and had thus arrived at full maturity of years, and still greater maturity of character and experience. We are, therefore, not surprised when it transpires that Saul had already a son entering upon manhood, and fit to take a military command, and to act in it with valour and conduct. This son was JONATHAN—a worthy name—a name dear to every student of Scripture history. The possession of such a son at the commencement of his reign, implies that Saul could not well have been much less than forty years of age.

Although under the necessity of disbanding the army when the great service for which it was brought together had been accomplished, Saul was so well aware of the dangerous attention which this exploit and deliverance would awaken on the part of the remaining enemies of Israel, that he deemed it expedient to keep a small body of men under arms. There was need for his doing so on this account, that the Philistines in fact still retained, or had in the later years of Samuel's government acquired, possession of some posts in Israel, which they held by their garrisons at the time of Saul's anointing. In dismissing him from Ramah, Samuel had indicated that on his way home he would pass by a place where there was "a garrison of the Philistines." This being the case, the election of a king by the Israelites could not but have engaged the earnest attention of this people; and the military resources and decision evinced by that king in the splendid action against the Ammonites, must have made them feel that their own position in regard to the Israelites would not long remain unquestioned. In fact, the recent victory of Saul must have stimulated him to the purpose of gaining possession of these Philistine posts, and of confirming himself in the regards of the people, by ridding the country entirely of these inveterate enemies of Israel. Thus the parties stood watching each other—the Philistines

looking for some overt act, which might afford
them cause for bringing their full power into the
field; for, being already in possession of such
superiority over Israel as they desired, they had
nothing to fight for, until the Israelites should
manifest a purpose of shaking off their yoke.
That yoke was heavier than we should have conceived from anything that has transpired in the
history; for it appears eventually that the Philistines had gone so far as to disarm the population,
and had even removed the smiths; so that the
people had to take their agricultural implements
to the Philistine garrisons to be sharpened, that
is, to have the edge beaten out on the anvil.
They were not, as some imagine, compelled to go
to the Philistines by any direct order; but they
went because with them only smiths were to be
found. Hence, probably, they managed as well
as they could to make their tools work without
this resource, by the aid of the files which we are
told they possessed for common sharpenings.
The extent of this disarmament may appear from
the fact, that in the action which eventually
came on, no one of the Israelites had a sword or
spear save the king and his son Jonathan.

It may be, and has been, urged as an objection
to this statement, that it is scarcely credible that
a vast army of men should have taken the field
against the Ammonites not long before without
weapons; or that the Ammonites should have
been defeated by an unarmed multitude. But
this would equally apply to the ensuing engagement with the Philistines themselves, with reference to which this statement is expressly made.
They were not unarmed, although deprived of
those usual weapons of warfare and the means of
obtaining them which only a smith could provide.
There were bows, there were slings, there were
ox-goads, which had once been so efficient against
this very people in the days of Shamgar. In
fact, there were a hundred things which might
be turned into efficient weapons in the hands of
brave and resolute men, before the use of fire-
arms was known. The Benjamites—Saul's own
tribe—were, we know, especially expert in the
use of the sling; and it is far from unlikely that
the want of other customary weapons caused
this to be especially cultivated, which was
destined ere long, in the hands of David, to lay
the great champion of the Philistines low.

It has been ingeniously suggested that, seeing
that during and after the Mosaic, as well as the
Homeric period, spears and swords of "brass"—
that is, a mixture of copper and tin, very hard,
but also brittle—were in common use; and seeing
that the Hebrews, even to a late period of their
history, received their iron from abroad, the
object of the restriction imposed by the Philistines was to retain in their own hands at this
time the use of *iron* weapons, which gave an
indisputable advantage to those who exclusively
possessed them. By their position, they would
be enabled to realize this superiority; for, by
blocking up access to the maritime traffic on the
one hand, and to Egypt on the other, they could
keep iron from the use of the inland tribes near
their border—not permanently, for no advantage
of this nature can long remain exclusive, but undoubtedly for a considerable length of time.

Ancient history is not without analogous
examples of these restrictions. A like condition
was imposed upon the Romans by Porsenna, king
of the Etrusci, at a time and under circumstances
when it was far more difficult to be enforced.
In the covenant contracted with the Romans on
the expulsion of their kings, he made it a condition of peace with them that they should use
no iron *except in husbandry*.[1] The same policy
occurs again, indeed, in Scripture itself; for
Nebuchadnezzar was careful to remove "the
craftsmen and the *smiths*," the latter obviously
being taken away, that the poor people whom
he left behind might be in no condition to
rebel.

The force which, under these circumstances,
Saul deemed it expedient to retain in arms, did
not exceed three thousand men. This strikes us
as a large rather than a small number for him to
reserve as a sort of body-guard about his person.
The absence of a standing army—compensated
by the great facility of calling large bodies of the
people into prompt action—was adverse to the
keeping of any large number of men in arms;
and the *profession* of a soldier was confined to
the royal guards, who alone remained constantly
on duty. This body was of course composed of
picked men, and formed the efficient nucleus of
an army, when the militia (so to speak) were
called out. Their commander was thus the only
officer of rank on permanent service; and this
gave him such advantages, that the same person
was usually the general-in-chief of the whole
army (under the king) when the levies were

[1] Plin. *Hist. Nat.*, xxxi. 14.

raised. Of the three thousand, which Saul probably thought sufficient as an army of observation, till an opportunity should be found of striking a blow against the Philistines, he kept two thousand with him, and committed the other thousand to the charge of his son Jonathan, who was stationed in closer observation upon the Philistine post at Geba. The impetuous valour of this young man, stimulated by his keener, if not deeper, sense of the shame and dishonour which were cast on Israel by the presence of hostile strangers in the sacred land, precipitated matters to a crisis, sooner perhaps than the cooler judgment of Saul would have dictated. Although, however, startled one day to receive intelligence that his son had smitten and cut off the Philistine garrison at Geba, he saw that the time for observation was past, and that of action come. It will be noted that he did not attempt anything further with the force in hand. He saw that it was his duty not to waste time in petty actions; but, being assured that the intelligence of this affair would bring the whole force of the Philistines into the field, he once more summoned the tribes to his standard.

FOOLISHNESS

1 Samuel 13:13

LOOKING back to the interview between Saul and Samuel, after the first public transgression of the former, we cannot fail to be struck by the terms in which the prophet administers his rebuke: "Thou hast done *foolishly*: thou hast not kept the commandment of the Lord thy God, which He commanded thee."

Now it probably may strike many readers that "foolishness" is not exactly the term they would have employed in characterizing the character of the king. They would have thought of "presumption," of "self-will," of "distrust," and other like terms, but scarcely of "foolishness." But the prophet's word is the right one after all. It goes to the root of the matter. Saul *had* acted foolishly. And why? Because he had not obeyed the voice of the Lord his God. The prophet knew very well that there are many foolishnesses in the heart of man; but in his view, and in that of all the sacred writers, the lowest depth of human

foolishness—its most astonishing and incredible manifestation—was disobedience to the Lord's commandments. There are two kinds of fools prominently noticed in Scripture: the fool who denies there is any God—"The fool hath said in his heart, There is no God,"—a text which suggests the remark, that if he is a fool who says this "in his heart," a much greater fool is he who utters that foolish thought. This is one. There is another: the fool who does not obey God, though he does not deny His existence. And yet, after all, these are but one. If we probe the matter closely, we shall find that there is scarcely more than an impalpable film of real difference between the foolishness of the man who says in his heart there is no God, and that of the man who does not render Him obedience. One may as well believe there is no God, as not obey Him. Indeed, the man who does not render Him true and heartfelt obedience, has no such real, no such practical belief in His existence, as is of any use or value, or as will avail him aught at the last day. There are few, perhaps, who really believe all they suppose themselves to believe. There is none of us who distrusts the existence of God—not one who would not shudder at the thought of saying, even in his heart, that "there is no God." This is well. Granted that this is believed, what then? Devils also believe it, and are not saved: they only tremble. That which even devils believe without profit, will be of small advantage to us, if we believe it as devils do. Theirs is a cold and barren assent of the understanding—barren, or fruitful only in fears. If ours be no more, we believe just as the devils do. In religion, nothing is accounted real that is not vital. Men, no less than trees, are known by their fruits; and if a man's belief in the existence of God be a real and living thing, it will be manifested by the fruit of obedience. It is impossible for any one to realize a distinct, and therefore a vital, and because vital true, conviction "that God is, and that He is a rewarder of those that diligently seek Him," without the understanding, the will, and the active powers being brought into a condition of submission and obedience to His will. The reality of our conviction must be tested by the degree of our anxiety to ascertain the will of the Lord, by our patience in awaiting its disclosure, and by the entireness of our obedience to it.

The foolishness of the man who denies that

there is a God, is therefore more nearly allied than people are apt to think, to the foolishness of the man whose spirit is not in a state of obedience to His will.

To appreciate the intense foolishness of the disobedience of Saul, we should bear in mind the peculiar position in which the Lord stood to Israel. Whoever was king or judge, so long as the Mosaic constitution lasted, and so long as recognized means existed, whether by prophet, by priest, or by Urim and Thummim, of learning His will on every national matter, He was the real sovereign of Israel. Now there were few, if any, ancient monarchies, the sovereign of which did not exact implicit, unreasoning obedience to his mandates. These might be obviously preposterous or mischievous, yet they were to be obeyed. Now, if a human king—a fallible mortal—expected this; if the ideas of the East acknowledged his right to this degree of submission, how much more might the Divine King of Israel expect in everything the most ready and cheerful obedience? There was here nothing to connect those difficulties with the obedience which wise and conscientious men must often have felt in rendering submission to earthly kings. The Lord could not, like them, have any special objects or interests to promote. It was impossible for Him to have any other object in view than the essential welfare of His people. *That* might be true of many human kings, but they might err greatly in the measures taken to carry out their good intentions; and a well meaning monarch, by his blunders in execution, might do more serious mischief than one of evil purposes and dispositions. But the Israelites had, or ought to have had, under all circumstances, the conviction not only that the Lord's purposes towards them were good, but that His power of effecting these purposes was boundless, and that He could not err in the measures dictated by His infinite wisdom in giving them effect. There could be no ground for doubt, hesitation, or questioning, in regard to any of His counsels or mandates. They must be good, they could not be otherwise than best; and obedience became not only an imperative duty, but a most exalted and happy privilege, and distrust or disobedience beyond all conception "foolish." Hence the great stress which is laid on the necessity of implicit obedience to the Lord's commands, on the privileges of entire submission, and on the absurdity

and wickedness of disobedience. The most eminent men in Scripture are those who entered most into this spirit. Look at the obedience of Abraham, of Moses, of Joshua, of whom it is emphatically remarked: "As the Lord commanded Moses His servant, so did Moses command Joshua, and so did Joshua; *he left nothing undone of all that the Lord commanded Moses.*" (Josh. xi. 15.) Look also at David. Eminent as were his personal qualities among men, it was not these, but his disposition to place entire reliance upon the Lord, and to carry out the designs and true principles of the government, by the most implicit obedience to His declared will, that rendered David "the man after God's own heart." He, more perfectly than any in high place, before or after, realized in his public, and indeed in his private capacity, the true duty and real privilege of submission and obedience; and it was on account of this, more than with regard to his private character—which, with all his faults, was very lovely—that he was honoured with this high distinction. The difference between him and Saul was, that his heart was right—his public principle was right—though more than once, being still but dust, he fell into crime, and committed grievous mistakes; whereas Saul was wrong in public principle, wrong at heart, although his career was not altogether wanting in honourable actions, just sentiments, and heroic deeds.

But let us not think that obedience is less imperative now than it was under the old law. It is far more so; and disobedience on our part, active or passive, is still greater foolishness than it was in the time of king Saul. God has now evinced the unfathomable depth of His love towards us, by yielding up His own dear Son to die upon the cross for our redemption. In this we have the pledge, the complete assurance, that He who spared not His own Son, will not fail to bestow upon us freely all things that are for our good; that He will forbid nothing but what would harm us, and command nothing really hard or difficult—nothing but what we should ourselves most intensely desire, were our eyes wholly purged of earth, so as to see as He sees. Let us, therefore, with willing hearts obey all His commandments, and cheerfully submit to all His appointments. In the annihilation of self-will, and in the temper of implicit devotedness, let us, as to every duty, say, "Lord, what wilt Thou have me to do?" And as to every event: "Here am I; let Him do what seemeth Him good."

The Bible teaches very explicitly that the highest wisdom consists in rendering obedience to God's commands, and the greatest folly in transgressing them. One of the most striking of Solomon's proverbs was to this effect: "The fear of the Lord is the beginning of knowledge; but fools despise wisdom and instruction." In other proverbs he gives us the reason. He tell us its philosophy, as it were. Thus, in one place, "The fear of the Lord is to hate evil;" in another, "In the fear of the Lord is strong confidence; and His children shall have a place of refuge. The fear of the Lord is a fountain of life, to depart from the snares of death;" and in another, "By humility and the fear of the Lord are riches, honour, and life."

Is not this the religion of common sense and reason? Admitting that God exists; that He is the sole Creator and Ruler of all things; is it not the acme, the essence of sound, practical wisdom, to obey His laws, and thus to secure His love and fatherly care? And is it not the height of folly to dishonour and disobey Him, seeing we thus deliberately cast away from us the best and surest—nay, the only means of securing prosperity and happiness, either temporal or eternal? The words of the Lord to Moses are as fully applicable to us now as they were to the Israelites of old: "Behold, I have taught you statutes and judgments. . . . Keep, therefore, and do them; for this is your wisdom and your understanding."

P.

SAUL'S TRANSGRESSION

1 Samuel 13:4-15

When Saul "blew the trumpet throughout all the land, saying, Let the Hebrews hear," he had a right to expect that they would hear. The alacrity which had been evinced by the tribes in following him to the relief of Jabesh-gilead, evinced a degree of spirit and zeal on which he had reason to calculate. But he was mistaken. There was a *sentiment* in that affair which was wanting in this. Then, the transaction to which their attention was called was in the highest degree stimulating; and the people against whom they marched on that occasion were those whom they had more than once signally defeated in battle. But in the present case, the people generally were filled with terror when they heard that the Philistine garrison had been smitten. By the Philistines they had repeatedly been brought low in battle, and to them they had long

and often been under subjection. As a dog which has dared in a moment of irritation to snap at the hand of his master, cowers in terror or flees from the look of punishment—so cowered, so fled, the Israelites when they heard that Saul had drawn his sword against the Philistines. Many of the people fled for safety to the land beyond the Jordan, which river the Philistines had never yet crossed. Others abandoned their houses, and hurried off to the mountains and rocky wildernesses. Some resorted to the caverns in which certain parts of the country abound; some retired to the woods, and many even sought shelter in pits, that is, in the capacious cisterns prepared to hold rain-water for the use of the inhabitants, and which are often in a dry state, either from not having been filled in the last season of rain, or from the preserved waters having become exhausted. They may also have been subterranean granaries. In both the orifice was small, and might be easily closed. We have one instance of this in the cistern wherein the messengers sent to David from Jerusalem—when that city was in the power of Absalom—were hid from their pursuers by a friendly woman, who covered the mouth with corn, so that the existence of this refuge was unsuspected.

The rendezvous was at Gilgal, and to that place some men did repair, albeit with heavy hearts and misgiving spirits. In fact, the Philistines were already in the field with an immense army, the presence of which filled the Israelites with dismay; and even the more stout-hearted men who had come to Gilgal began gradually to steal away from the camp. The king beheld this with dismay, and it seemed to him that all would be lost unless he took some decided steps before he was altogether deserted. This he was precluded from doing by the absence of Samuel, who had promised to be there within seven days, and had intimated that nothing was to be done before he came and offered the proper sacrifices. As he could not but know that Samuel would be able to make known to him the will of the Divine King, whose viceroy he officially was, and as he had no reason to doubt that from that source counsels and aids equal to the greatest emergency would be provided, it was the duty of Saul to await patiently the arrival of the prophet; and although his men did leave him, it behoved him to evince the same noble and pious confidence which Gideon had manifested under the like circumstances, who was content that the Lord should have all the glory, by the inadequacy of the means employed, and who contentedly beheld his men go away from him by thousands, knowing that it was the same to the Lord to save by many or by few. He had his reward; and Saul would not have failed of his, had he profited by this great example. This was, in fact, a test of his obedience to the principles on which he had accepted the crown; and it was doubtless to render it such that Samuel had delayed his coming to the very close of the period he had appointed. Saul, however, looked at these matters merely in a human point of view. He looked at them as a king and a soldier, and not as " an Israelite indeed." It must not be concealed that he was a vainglorious man, covetous of military renown, and, from the exercise of autocratic power, impatient of restraint. There is reason to suspect that he was far more desirous that the power of his own arm, the success of his own combinations, should be evinced in this transaction, than the might of the Lord's right hand; and there is cause for more than a surmise that he was jealous that the Lord should possess, or too manifestly share, the glory of Israel's deliverance. That he was a patriot king, after a certain blind fashion of his own, cannot be denied; and as little can it be doubted that self was so mixed up with his patriotism, that Israel's deliverance would scarcely have been a joy to him—certainly not an unmingled joy—unless *he* had the whole credit of its accomplishment. This view of his temper, which is derived from the whole of his career, may well be brought forward now to illustrate his position under the present circumstances.

To the faithful servant of Jehovah, which Saul was officially required to be, this trial ought not to have been a hard one. It would not have been so to David, who was great in that very reliance upon Jehovah wherein Saul so signally failed. It must be admitted, however, that the trial *was* a hard one to flesh and blood. It was hence hard to Saul. But it was most important that he should be subjected to it. He was the first king, and his acts would form precedents for his successors. The very nature of the kingly authority in Israel depended upon his conduct. It was therefore essential that his way should be hedged about, and his steps determined, whether willingly or not, according to the conditions of the monarchy.

He was either to be forced into the proper position belonging to him, or, by refusing to fill it, to subject himself to the high penalties of disobedience. The people would then know that his measures were not to be taken as the precedents of the Hebrew regal constitution, seeing that they were employed in known contrariety to the will of Jehovah, as declared by prophet and by priest. Saul might have done well enough (for he had some fine heroic qualities) in a line of hereditary kings, under whom the principles of the government had been established; but he was unfit for the responsibilities attached to the founder of a kingdom, whose acts required to be weighed with regard to their influence on the political rights of unborn generations.

Samuel had promised to join the king in seven days. The seventh day had commenced, and he was not yet come. Seeing, probably, that many of his men had taken their departure over the night, and that not more than six hundred men remained to him, Saul determined not to lose another day in waiting for Samuel, who might not arrive till the evening. He himself offered the sacrifices; not only burnt-offerings, but peace-offerings. This was a twofold offence: it was not only disobedience to the word of the Lord, and the act of an independent king, but the mode of proceeding was in itself a crime. Among the nations, kings indeed offered sacrifice, combining the offices of priest and king, but it was not to be so in Israel. Priests only might offer sacrifice; the only exception being in the case of the prophets, who occasionally claimed that right for the honour of God, by whose Spirit they were moved. This, therefore, was another assumption of autocratic power, of a nature most offensive and dangerous under theocratical institutions. The priesthood formed the constitutional check, on behalf of Jehovah and the people, upon the power of the crown; and to assume the most important of their functions, was nothing less than with a high hand to cast down the barrier which the wisdom of God had reared up to secure the safety of the chosen people against the encroachments of regal ambition. It has been said, indeed, that Saul did not himself offer the sacrifice, but ordered a priest to do so. It has, however, all the appearance of a personal act, and the character of Saul suggests that he would be likely to take the opportunity of indicating his possession of the same functions as belonged to other kings. "Bring *hither* a burnt-offering *to me*, and peace-offerings; and he offered the burnt-offering." There even seems to us to be an emphasis in the last clause, the burnt-offerings being wholly consumed on the altar, and the holiest of all sacrifices—this, even this, he offered—leaving, perhaps, the peace-offerings to be offered by other hands.

Samuel came before the sacrifices were completed. He evinced the deepest concern and displeasure; and although received by the king with respect and attention, he plainly told the latter, that by this deplorable failure of obedience, by this utter forgetfulness of his true position, he had placed his crown and dynasty in peril.

HONEY AND BLOOD

1 Samuel 14

ABOUT seven miles north by east from Jerusalem, is a steep precipitous valley, extending east and west. North of this valley, which is called in 1 Sam. xiii. 23, " the passage of Michmash " (now Wady es-Suweinit), lay the Philistine host, which had established a garrison, or advanced post, upon the high promontory or angle formed by the intersection of another valley ending north and south. Upon the heights, about a mile on the southern side of the same passage of Michmash, stood Geba, from which Jonathan had lately expelled the Philistine garrison, and which Saul and Jonathan now occupied with not more than six hundred men. Michmash (now Mukhmas), which gave name to the passage, and where the Philistine outpost was stationed, and Geba (now Jeba), therefore, were separated by this valley, and were then, as now, in sight of each other. In this " passage," near the point where the other valley intersects it, are two hills of a conical, or rather spherical shape, having steep rocky sides, with small wadys running up behind each, so as almost to isolate them. One is on the side towards Jeba, and the other on the side towards Mukhmas. These are apparently the two mentioned in connection with the circumstances to which our attention is now directed, and which these particulars will better enable the reader to understand.[1]

We may be sure that the movements of the Philistine force, stationed on the height at Michmash, were watched with much attention and solicitude from Saul's headquarters at Geba. This attention may have been reciprocal. One morning an extraordinary commotion was discovered among the Philistines. Its nature could not well be discovered in the grey of the morning, and in the want of telescopes. It was clear there was a conflict of some kind going on; for the host gradually melted away, as if the men were beating down one another. What could it be? The Philistines had no enemies but the Israelites. Was it some broil among themselves, or had some of the garrison undertaken, without orders, a wild and desperate enterprise? When the latter thought crossed the mind of Saul, he hastened to muster his small army, or rather troop, to see if any were absent, and then he found that all were there except Jonathan and his armour-bearer; and knowing the chivalrous and daring character of his son, he had no doubt that his hand was in this affair. It was so, indeed. That heroic young prince, strong in the true old Gideonic faith—that, as he said, " There is no restraint to the Lord to save by many or by few "—had privately prevailed upon his armour-bearer to scale the rock, and penetrate to the Philistine garrison. Now it is stated, in conformity with the above description, that " between the passages by which Jonathan sought to go over to the Philistines' garrison, there was a sharp rock on the one side, and a sharp rock on the other side; and the name of the one was Bozez, and the name of the other Seneh. The fore-front of the one was situate northward over against Michmash, and the other southward over against Geba." It seems to us that Jonathan chose to

To prevent confusion, it is necessary to mention, that in 1 Samuel 13:15,16; 14:5, where we read Gibeah in the authorized version, the original has Geba, which is important as identifying it with the plain form which the Philistine garrison had been expelled. It is true that in 1 Samuel 14:16 the original itself has Gibeah; but as the same place, so repeatedly mentioned before as Geba, is evidently denoted, this must be taken as an error of transcription, the more easily accounted for by the fact that Gibeah, in Hebrew, is but the feminine of Geba, which has indeed, led some to suppose that the two names were applied to one place.—See *Bibliotheca Sacra, ii.* 508-602.

make the attempt here, by the hill Bozez, not only because of some facility afforded, but because the projection of the hill would conceal his advance till a good part of the ascent had been made.

When at length the two men were discovered by the sentinels scrambling up the rock, it was supposed that they were of those who had hid themselves in caverns, and who had no doubt come as deserters to the Philistines. This seems to us the obvious inference from the words, "Behold, the Hebrews come forth out of the holes where they had hid themselves." This was a reasonable conjecture; for, in fact, a little way farther down the valley there are caverns in the cliffs, particularly one great cavern, called Jaihah; and it was not to be imagined that two men could be coming with hostile intentions. This explains also why no attempt was made to hinder their ascent after they were discovered, but they were rather invited to come up. Had their hostile purpose been suspected, nothing could have been easier than to destroy them, by casting down stones or other missiles upon them. As soon as Jonathan and his armour-bearer had gained a footing upon the top of the cliff, their intentions were at once evinced. The scouts or sentinels were speedily struck down, and on the two heroes marched, destroying all who opposed them. By the time they had slain twenty men, the alarm spread to the garrison, and created a general panic and confusion. Those who had seen how the assailants got up were dead. It was not known how they had got there, nor that there were only two of them; and those who saw only two, would scarcely conceive that there were no more, but must have supposed that these two belonged to a larger number, perhaps to Saul's entire force, which had gained possession of the post; for where only two had ascended, it was clear that more could come. In their blind fury and fear they ran against each other, and slew all they met; while those who fled hastened to the main army, carrying their own terrors to it. Their tale, no doubt, conveyed the announcement that the strong post at Michmash, believed to be inaccessible, had been seized by a large force of the Hebrews, who were in close pursuit, and might soon be expected. And, in fact, the crests of the Hebrews soon appeared in sight; for Saul no sooner discovered the fact from Geba, than he put his force in motion to take advantage

of the panic that appeared to have been raised among the Philistines, his troop being at every step augmented by the fugitive Israelites, who, now that the tide had turned, flocked—such of them as were near enough—to his standard, as eager to join in the pursuit of an enemy already defeated by fear, as, yielding to cowardly impulses, they had formerly slunk appalled from the aspect of his strength. There is a curious statement, "that moreover the Hebrews that were with the Philistines before that time, which went up with them into the camp from the country round about, even they also turned to be with the Israelites that were with Saul and Jonathan." This shows that there were some Israelites with the Philistines, being, as we conceive, deserters, who had betaken themselves for safety and subsistence to them as the stronger party. This fact strengthens the probability we have ventured to suggest, that Jonathan and his armour-bearer were taken for deserters by the sentries who saw them scaling the cliffs.

The pursuit was hot and bloody, as it was likely to be under the circumstances; for the Hebrews had many ancient and recent wrongs to avenge, and they would not fail to exact retribution for their late fears.

Saul was so apprehensive lest any part of this great opportunity of effectually humbling the Philistines should be lost, that in the hearing of the troops, though not in that of Jonathan, who was not near at the moment, he laid an anathema upon any one who should taste food until the evening. The people, in consequence, were greatly distressed, being prevented from taking even such refreshments as offered in the way, however greatly needed. Jonathan, with one of the pursuing parties, was passing through a wood which so abounded with honey, that it dropped upon the ground. But no man ventured to touch it except Jonathan, who, being ignorant of his father's ban, put the end of his staff into a honeycomb, and raised it to his mouth. The fact is of some interest, as a perfectly incidental illustration of the phrase, so frequent with Moses, describing Canaan as "a land flowing with milk and honey." To ourselves, the fact of wild bees thus fixing their combs upon the trees in the woods to the extent here intimated, may seem somewhat strange, although the tendency of these insects to do this is shown by the frequency with which the swarms of our hive-bees alight upon trees.

Although we never kept bees in the country, nor did our immediate neighbours, we have had swarms repeatedly alight upon the trees of our garden, where they would probably have established themselves in some way, if not captured for the hive. We should like to have the experiment tried of letting them alone, to see how they would manage their own affairs. We very much doubt if bees were kept by the ancient Hebrews in hives. The woods, we apprehend, so abounded in the settlements of wild bees, that honey was too abundant and cheap to be worth private attention. It was the property of any one who gathered it; and as all who wanted it could not do that, doubtless many poor persons earned a subsistence by collecting it in the woods, and selling it in the towns at such a price as would pay them for this trouble. "Bees in the East," says Mr. Roberts, "are not, as in England, kept in hives; they are all in a wild state. The forests literally flow with honey. Large combs may be seen hanging in the trees as you pass along, full of honey. Hence this article is cheap and plentiful." It is true that this writer has a tropical country (India) in view; but the statement is applicable to many other countries in which bees and the materials for their wax and honey abound, as was the case in the land of Canaan. Probably, as population increased, and the soil became more densely occupied by men, the production of honey lessened, and then the bees were reared in hives. Hence, in the time of Christ, we read of "wild honey," implying that there was some *not* wild; but this distinction is not to be found in the Old Testament.

Another remarkable consequence flowed from this unwise restriction which Saul imposed. No sooner had the sun gone down, than the famishing people flew upon the spoil of cattle, and in the rage of their hunger hastily slew them, and began to eat, if not the raw flesh, as we apprehend, yet at least flesh so imperfectly exsanguinated, from improper slaughtering and imperfect dressing, that the law against the eating of meat with any blood remaining in it was visibly transgressed. The importance attached to this law by the Hebrews has always been most remarkable, and continues even to the present day, when a Jew will not touch meat that has been killed by a Christian, chiefly from the belief that the blood has not been properly discharged; and during a journey he will abstain from animal food alto-

gether, except when he comes to places where he can obtain that which has been killed by Jews, or has himself been so well instructed in the proper usages as to have obtained a licence to slay for his own use, in which case he can kill a fowl occasionally. These customs are well illustrated in the *Orphans of Lissau*, in which we find it stated that the Jews of Ramsgate formerly got all their meat from Canterbury, having among themselves no one qualified to kill in the proper manner.

When Jonathan's transgression in regard to the honey became known to Saul, he was for putting his son to death, according to the tenor of his vow. But this the more enlightened conscience of the people forbade. With generous enthusiasm they cried: "God forbid! As the Lord liveth, there shall not one hair of his head fall to the ground; for he hath wrought with God this day." These remarkable words should be meditated upon in connection with those addressed by Jonathan himself that morning to his armour-bearer: "It may be the Lord will work for us." The Lord did work for him; and truly he wrought with God. It was a great day for Israel; and from the beginning to the end, Jonathan was the hero of that day.

Jonathan is the leading character in this romantic episode of Jewish history. Only a few disconnected sketches of his life have been preserved; but these invest him with a singular, though somewhat melancholy interest. As Dean Stanley has said, he is one of the finest specimens of early Scripture characters. Unequalled for skill in the use of arms; daring even to recklessness on the battle-field; "swifter than the eagle, stronger than the lion;" Jonathan yet possessed a heart of the most exquisite tenderness. His devoted attachment to his father, amid all that waywardness of temper and wildness of passion, is without a parallel even in sacred biography. Then, too, his romantic friendship for David, and regard for his interests, under circumstances so strange and perplexing, evidence a mind at once of the deepest sensibility and highest honour. He appears to have possessed the rare faculty of inspiring all who came within the sphere of his influence, with confidence in his powers and love to his person. When setting out alone on that daring enterprise against the Philistines at Michmash, his armour-bearer never dreamt of questioning its prudence, or shrinking from his side. "Do all that is in thine heart," was his noble answer when consulted; "Behold, I am with thee according to thy heart." And when, by his father's rash vow, he was sentenced to death, the whole army, to a man, braved the tyrant's anger, and cried, "Shall Jonathan die? God forbid: as the Lord liveth, there shall not one hair of his head fall to the ground." But the most striking proof of his noble filial devotion was given in linking himself indissolubly with his father's fortunes, even after his own feelings had been outraged, and his life all but sacrificed, and after he had become fully aware that the mind of the nation and the favour of God had been estranged by the monarch's folly and crimes. With touching pathos David sang—

" Saul and Jonathan, beloved and kind, in life
   And in death they are not divided. . . .
   I am distressed for thee, Jonathan, my brother;
   Thou wast very kind to me.
   Stronger than the love of woman was thy love to me."
                        P.

THE PUBLIC ENEMY

1 Samuel 15

THERE is hardly any nation which has not had some especial public enemy—generally a near neighbour—which it was held to be a peculiar duty of patriotism to hate and to destroy. We need not name instances. It were difficult to find exceptions; and the reading and observation of every one will supply examples. Such sentiments between nations have generally their origin in bitter wars and ancient wrongs. Israel had many ordinary enemies, but the one marked out in this distinctive manner as *the* public enemy were the Amalekites. This people had some kinds of settlements in the Sinai Peninsula, and in the country south of Palestine and west of Edom; and being a people of semi-nomad habits, they appear to have been in the habit of wandering with their flocks over the intervening countries. With this location, they came much into collision with the Israelites during the forty years' wandering. They opposed the Israelites after they had crossed the Red Sea, on their march to Sinai. They opposed and repulsed them also when they advanced to enter the Promised Land on the south; and, besides these recorded instances, there was probably a succession of aggravating petty contests between them during the long intervening period of wandering, respecting which we have no account. It is not wonderful, therefore, that, according to ancient usage, the people of Israel solemnly doomed the Amalekites to utter destruction, whenever they should be able to wreak upon them all the fierce wrath which fired their hearts. This was, in fact, the same doom upon a nation which we have formerly seen inflicted upon a town, in the case of Jericho.

This doom was incurred by the Amalekites in presence of the miracles, and the manifest tokens of the divine presence which attended Israel's march of mystery through the wilderness. Such had been the unprovoked assaults of this people upon Israel in the time of their weakness, and such their acts of defiance of the Power by which they were seen to be protected, that the honour of His own great name, no less than His official guardianship of the chosen people, procured the Lord's sanction of this devotement. It had not yet been executed. The Amalekites still kept up their ancient hostility to the Israelites. They had not by repentance sought to avert the execution of the sentence which hung over their heads; on the contrary, they rather derided the impotent hatred which had so long left unexecuted the threatened doom. They had thus kept their sentence alive—had not suffered it to sleep by lapse of time. The silence of the Scripture—which is, from great conciseness, confined in all that relates to foreigners to great demonstrative results—conveys an aspect of harshness to the seeming revival of an old and forgotten quarrel, and the punishment of ancient crimes upon new generations. It is more than probable, and more natural, that the Amalekites themselves had never suffered this hostility to sleep, or their doom to be forgotten. That they were forward on every occasion that offered to join in any aggressive warfare against Israel, we know. It is also easily understood that they allowed little peace to the southern Israelites settled on their borders, or to those who travelled, or were out with the flocks. Observation upon the occasional meetings and intercourse of adverse races in the East, will also suggest, with all but the absolute certainty of written fact, that an Amalekite and Israelite seldom met without aggravating altercations. It seems to us as if we heard the Amalekite launching forth into such language as this: " Five hundred years ago ye doomed us to utter destruction; yet here we are. We are still alive; still we flourish under this terrible doom. Where is the great God of whom ye boast? His arm, it seems, is too short to reach unto us. We have not done aught to turn His fierce wrath aside. We have not bent the knee to you or to Him. We have done nothing to mollify you; rather, we hate you as much now as of old, and are as ready now as then to root you up. Think ye to appal by your curses the strong men your arms cannot subdue? We do defy you and your idle doom. Do it! do it!"

The time of long-suffering—in this case very protracted long-suffering—had at length passed, and the time of accomplished doom was come. It might have been executed by famine or pestilence; but although the Israelites might have ascribed this form of judgment to the proper source, the neighbouring nations would not; and therefore judgment of extermination was committed to the sword of Saul, who, as king, would at once be recognized as the authorized fulfiller of the ancient devotement.

Some years had passed, during which Saul had distinguished himself in the field by a series of successful operations against the hostile nations around, whom he taught to respect the power of Israel, though he did not bring them under subjection. It would appear, that in all these proceedings he acted much as an independent sovereign, without the required indications of his dependence upon the Divine King of Israel.

One trial more was to be afforded him—one more test of his obedience, before the sentence of exclusion against his dynasty was finally pronounced. He was commanded, through Samuel, to march against the Amalekites, and execute to the letter the ancient doom of devotement—of utter extermination—against them and theirs. If he had power to execute it—and power was given to him—whatever was spared became, according to the tenor of the old vow, as much " an accursed thing " as in the days of Jericho. Saul undertook the task; but he executed it entirely according to his own judgment of what was expedient and proper. He felt no objection as to any cruelty in the command, for he executed it fiercely upon all the people of the Amalekites who came within the scope of his expedition. He destroyed them utterly with the edge of the sword. But the king Agag, who fell into his hands, he spared, he being the very person most obnoxious to destruction, as being, officially at least, the chief offender; and this assuredly not from any sentiment of pity, but for the vainglory of possessing and displaying so illustrious

a captive. So of the spoil: whatever was worthless or immovable was destroyed; but the best and choicest of everything, especially of the flocks and herds, was spared. In this line of conduct, however otherwise interpreted, Saul assumed to himself such large discretion in the execution of a positive commandment, and so closely resembled some of his former acts,—he manifested so unequivocally the fixed bias of his mind towards autocratic power,—that his unfitness to become the founder of a line of theocratic kings could no longer be disputed, and his own doom was sealed.

The vainglorious character of Saul was further evinced in his homeward march, by his setting up a monument of his exploit at Carmel, thus appropriating to himself all the honour of the success,—a thing most offensive under the peculiar principles of the Hebrew government, and such as no future king ever ventured to do. Compare the spirit which this evinces with the constant and heartfelt dependence upon God, and the formal ascription of all honour and glory to Him, evinced in the Psalms and the history of David—a far greater conqueror than Saul.

Yet when Samuel came to join him at Gilgal, on his return, Saul had the confidence to meet him with the assurance that the task committed to him had been perfectly accomplished. "What meaneth then," asked Samuel, "this bleating of the sheep in mine ears, and the lowing of the oxen which I hear?" Without awaiting the answer, the prophet, who saw through the whole transaction, and had received his commission before he set out, proceeded to denounce his conduct, reminding him that, "when he was little in his own sight," he had by the Lord's free appointment been made head over all the tribes, and anointed king over Israel. Yet he had become exalted in his own esteem, and in this and other instances had forgotten his fealty to Jehovah, and acted in disobedience to His express commands. But Saul persisted that he *had* obeyed, seeing that, as he now insinuated, the spoil had only been reserved for sacrifice to Jehovah. This we take to have been a gross attempt to bribe the Lord, under a most offensive misconception of His nature and character, to acquiesce in the exemption he had made. For although stated as an original motive, it is palpably an after-thought, suggested by the stringency of

Samuel's rebuke. This is proved out of Saul's own mouth; for when the prophet met this subterfuge by the indignant and noble rebuke, "Hath the Lord as great delight in burnt-offerings and sacrifices as in obeying the voice of the Lord? Behold, to obey is better than sacrifice, and to hearken than the fat of rams," the king shifted his ground, and urged that the army would not consent to the destruction of the spoil —that is, would not forego the beneficial interest they had in the distribution of it, which is quite different from the reason previously given. But had it been a truth, it would, on the view taken by Samuel, have been no extenuation of the offence. The prophet then pronounced the irrevocable sentence, "Because thou hast rejected the word of the Lord, He hath also rejected thee from being king." This brought Saul down from

SAUL'S DETHRONEMENT FORETOLD

his high tone. He confessed that he had sinned, and without remonstrating against the sentence passed upon him—the justice of which his conscience probably admitted for the moment—he implored Samuel not to suffer the fact of their disagreement to appear, but to turn and take part with him in a public act of solemn worship. Samuel refused; and when the king took hold of his mantle to detain him, and it rent in his hand, the prophet, with great readiness, turned the incident into an illustration of his doom: "The Lord hath rent the kingdom from thee this day, and hath given it to a neighbour of thine that is better than thou." Satisfied, however, that he had discharged the painful duty committed to him—for it *was* painful, as he had much personal

feeling in favour of Saul—he did turn, and worshipped the Lord with him.

Samuel then felt that he had another stern duty to perform. When the Lord's sentence had passed, it was not for the future kings of Israel to think that they possessed a dispensing prerogative, and the neighbouring princes had to learn that there was in Israel a Power higher than the throne, to which even the kings were accountable. This had been far from the thought of king Agag. Since the king had spared him, he thought there was nothing more to fear; the bitterness of death had passed with him. So he intimated when he was brought before Samuel, who, as judge and commissioned prophet, took upon himself the stern and terrible duty of exacting the long stored vengeance for Israel which the king had wilfully neglected. Samuel answered, "As thy sword hath made women childless, so shall thy mother be childless among women." He was then stricken down and slain by the sword. The text would intimate that this was done by Samuel's own hand; and although it is rightly alleged that in Scripture men are often described as doing what they order to be done, it is not improbable—having due regard to the habits of the East, and to the notions of ancient times—that the common interpretation is the right one. Samuel might deem it an honour to execute with his own hand the full judgment which had been neglected by the man to whom the sword had been entrusted. If it be urged that this act is contrary to the idea of Samuel's character which his previous history has conveyed, the answer is, that mild natures like his are often, when thoroughly roused into high excitement, capable of stronger deeds than men of habitually harsher temper.

Samuel then repaired to his home, and he and Saul never met by agreement again. Saul was left alone from that time. His doom was FIXED; and he was left to work it out. Alas for him!

SAMUEL AT BETHLEHEM

1 Samuel 16:1-13

WHO was that "neighbour," better than he, who was destined to succeed Saul, and at whom

Samuel hinted in his rebuke? It does not appear that the prophet himself knew, at the time when his words were uttered. But he knew that another dynasty was to be provided, and that its founder would doubtless be a man after God's own heart, since he would be one not forced (so to speak) upon Him, not selected with regard to a temporary exigency, but chosen freely by Himself from among the thousands of Israel, as the man best suited, by the qualities of his mind and spirit, to be the father of a race of kings over His people.

It is a remarkable fact, that while Saul thus incurred the divine displeasure for the wilfulness of his conduct, there is no reason to question that his popularity was great with the people, and his power continually increasing. He had many qualities which the multitude admired; and even the very qualities which drew down the anger of the Divine King upon him, were not such as an Oriental people regard with much disfavour in their sovereign, or deem to be unbecoming the kingly character. It was while thus powerful and popular, his throne being sustained by the consummate military talents of his cousin Abner, and the continuance of his race being guaranteed by several noble sons, headed by Jonathan, whose fine qualities and pious temper opened large promise for the time to come, even to those who had sufficient discernment to regard the father's principles of government with displeasure: it was at such a time, in his pride of place, that the hand of the prophet, in the sentence which he declared, wrote "Ichabod" upon all that he had and all that he hoped for. The king knew that this was no vain word. He seemed to take it lightly at first; nevertheless, the iron entered into his very soul, rankling and cankering there. He brooded over this doom in his saturnine mind. He became irritable, suspicious, despairing, and occasionally fell into a gloom of mind bordering closely upon madness.

Samuel, on his part, was deeply concerned at what had passed. Let those who ascribe all this to the ill will of the prophet at Saul's not proving that subservient tool to him which he had calculated on finding—let them consider his manifest reluctance at every step which he was *constrained* to take. So, now, even after sentence had gone forth, " he mourned for Saul," and interceded urgently and perseveringly for him. So far from the act of deposition being his, it is clear that it was most grievous in his eyes; and that if he had been left to himself, nothing of the kind would have taken place. He liked *the man;* and although compelled to reprove *the king*, he would probably have been willing to let him run his course, looking forward to the succession of Jonathan as a sufficient remedy for the errors of his father's reign.

It is important to bear this in mind. Besides, not only was the deposition of Saul's dynasty not Samuel's act, but the appointment of a successor was against his inclination, and the choice of the person was far from being that which he would have made. Eventually, this state of his feeling even subjected him to a gentle rebuke from the Lord he served; and he was ordered to go to Bethlehem and anoint, for the throne of Israel, one of the sons of Jesse (descended from Boaz and Ruth), who would there be pointed out to him. Even then Samuel shrank from this task, which added all that was wanting to confirm the doom of Saul. He sought to shun the duty by expressing apprehensions for his safety, should Saul hear of the transaction. This was overruled, and the prophet went to Bethlehem. Yet he took such steps as appeared requisite to avert suspicion. He took a heifer with him to offer a sacrifice, for which there must have been some apparent ground not precisely stated. Some Jewish writers suppose that there had been a man slain in the neighbourhood, and that as it was not known by whom the crime had been committed, Samuel, to whom such a case would naturally be referred, went to sacrifice a heifer according to the law as laid down in Deut. xxi. To the feast which followed the sacrifice, and to which the offerer invited whom he pleased, Samuel called Jesse and his sons. These sons were eight in number; but the youngest, David, was considered by his father too insignificant to be included, and he therefore remained in the field, tending his father's sheep. When Jesse's sons passed before Samuel, he was struck by the noble presence of Eliab, the eldest, and at once concluded that the Lord's anointed was before him. For this he was rebuked, as formerly described; and, surprised at the absence of the expected indication from above, he asked Jesse whether he had any more children. Then it was that Jesse seemed first to remember that he had another son, and he answered, " There remaineth yet the youngest, and he keepeth the sheep."

David was then sent for, and no sooner did he appear than the word for which the prophet waited came: "Arise, anoint him, for this is he!" Samuel then did anoint him; and although this was done "in the presence of his brethren," it may be doubted if they understood the full purport of the act; for these brethren did not subsequently evince any recognition of his high destination; and it is little likely that Samuel, who anointed Saul secretly, when there was no direct danger to apprehend, should have anointed David avowedly for the kingdom in the presence of several persons, when there was much to be apprehended from the wrath of Saul. Had the real purport of the transaction been even in this extent public, it could scarcely, under the circumstances, have been kept from the knowledge of the king, at a time when, had a word been breathed to that effect, it had been death both to David and to Samuel. There were those at Saul's court who were well acquainted with David and his family, and David at length came to have at that court enemies not a few; yet no one seems to have been aware of the fact or significance of this anointing. The conviction that David was the man appointed to succeed him, seems to have gradually dawned upon the mind of Saul from circumstances, and to have been confirmed beyond question when David eventually fled to Samuel. At that time, the fact of this anointing may have become known to him; but then Samuel was on the borders of the grave; and David beyond his reach. It may be doubtful whether David himself clearly understood the purport of the act. It does not appear that Samuel declared its object, and prophets were anointed as well as kings. We rather think, however, that a young man of so quick apprehension could not but have understood what was meant by this proceeding; and we ascribe the apparent unconsciousness of the destinies awaiting him, which his earlier history exhibits, and his declared and often acknowledged loyalty to Saul, simply to that excellent disposition which enabled him to see that it ill became him to take any steps to hasten the purposes of God, but that it rather behoved him to pursue the even path of his duty, leaving Him whose choice had fallen upon him, to accomplish, in His own good time, the purposes of His will.

Now it is clear that, if this important matter had been left to Samuel, he would have taken no step at all towards carrying out the sentence he had been compelled to pronounce; and being at length obliged to do so, it is equally clear that, had it been left to himself, the choice would have fallen upon Eliab, not on David; and had the choice been left to Jesse, any one of his seven other sons would have been preferred to the youngest. It is altogether most evident that the designation of David to the kingdom was the immediate act of Providence, without the least intervention of human wisdom or contrivance.

DAVID

1 Samuel 16:12

PRIOR to his appearance on this occasion, nothing is distinctly stated of the history and character of David, who was destined to make so important a figure in the history of Israel. There are, however, as we go on, a few retrospective intimations regarding his youthful life; and he has himself left materials in his divine songs, from which some particulars may be gleaned, and some circumstances inferred.

In his person, he does not appear to have been of commanding stature, but he was eminently handsome. In a country and race, where exceptions to darkness of complexion are rare, this young man was distinguished by a fair and ruddy countenance; and as the beauty of his eyes is particularly noticed, they were probably blue or grey, as belongs to this complexion. In them the fire of genius shone, and from them beamed that enchanting expression of kindliness and generous warmth, by which the hearts of men and women were drawn to him as by a charm. Altogether, he was "goodly to look to." The eyes of men rested upon his engaging and happy countenance with pleasure, and withdrew from it with regret. The rare combination in him of all that was gentle, tender, and mild— with the most exalted enthusiasm, the most noble aspirations, the most generous sentiments, the most manly deportment, the most heroic daring, and the most invincible prowess—joined to his invariable consideration for others, his openheartedness, his humbleness, and the entire absence of all pretension in him, made men feel better when they looked upon him; and it exalted their hearts, to know that they were sharers of the nature which, under divine grace, became capable of such impressive development. He was known to be a man of God, and to be much in communion with Him; and this diffused an ineffable grace over his demeanour and conversation, to which, beyond question, much of the extraordinary influence he possessed over the minds and hearts of others must be ascribed.

To these personal qualities, David added all the accomplishments of his age and country. That age was not one of scholarship or books. Yet such scholarship as was valued among his countrymen he possessed; and the books that were found among them, he well knew. Above all, he had deeply studied such parts of the sacred Scripture as then existed. His writings continually evince his close acquaintance with it—his admiration of it—his intense appreciation of its value—his LOVE for it. This shows that he was truly under the influence of divine grace, and had been favoured with those teachings of the Divine Spirit, by which all true, that is, all vital spiritual knowledge is imparted—as is the case under a more perfect system, and with more ample materials and broader revelations. There has been but one Spirit from the beginning; and David was taught of Him. We know this, because he *loved* God's law, and rejoiced in it. It is easy to know that law, as it existed in his time, and as it exists in ours, externally, as a body of words—easy to admire it and value it. But for *love* to it, the Spirit's teachings were necessary; and David loved the law of God with an ardency of affection which puts to shame the cooler appreciation, often seen among us, of the more ample and demonstrated treasures of wisdom and knowledge which we possess. Now, love is a sign of grace; and undoubtedly David possessed in the highest degree that grace of which love is a sign. His psalms abound in such declarations as these: "O how I love thy law! it is my meditation all the day. Thy word have I hid in my heart, that I might not sin against Thee. I have rejoiced in the way of thy testimonies, as much as in all riches. Open Thou mine eyes, that I may behold wondrous things out of thy law. Thy statutes have been my song in the house of my pilgrimage. Thy word is a lamp unto my feet, and a light unto my path. Thy testimonies have I taken as my heritage for ever, for they are the rejoicing of

my heart. Thy word is very pure, therefore thy servant loveth it." Mark, that to love the law of God for *that* reason—to love it *because* it is pure —to love its purity—is an undoubted sign of the highest degree of grace.

His pursuits were pastoral, and the pastoral life has been regarded in all ages as favourable to poetry and music. David was a poet. The frequency with which rhythmical utterances, from all sorts of people, occur in the Scripture, shows that the poetical faculty existed largely among the Hebrews, and was much cultivated by them. The genius of their language, and the spirit of their institutions, were favourable to it, inasmuch as they drew out and cherished the higher sentiments, which find in verse their most congenial expression. Hence, throughout the Scripture, the higher moods of spiritual feeling— whether in man or woman, in king, or priest, or prophet, or warrior, or shepherd, or husbandman —fall naturally into high-toned verse. David was, in the highest sense of the word, a poet. He has left us elegies, odes, triumphal songs, descriptive pieces, and sacred lyrics, in which every chord of the human heart—every emotion of the soul—every aspiration of the spirit, is touched with a master hand. So deeply does he sound the depths of man's nature, so loftily does he soar to the gates of light, that no poet has ever lived whose ideas have become so much the common property of nations—none in whose beautiful words the hopes, the fears, the joys, the griefs, of the spiritual man have found such adequate expression. Manners, costumes, outer forms of life, for ever change; but the unchanging character of that which is really man, is by nothing more strikingly evinced than by the fact that for three thousand years, and in many different lands and languages, the words of David have given voice to the pious thoughts and devout feelings of millions; and are no less appropriate, at this day, in the mouth of the weaver at his loom, and the cordwainer at his stall, than they were of old to the men who sat beneath the fig-trees and the vines of Canaan. Most of David's poems that remain to us were probably composed after, through many trials, he had attained to greatness. Most of them have that plaintive tone which his adult experiences and trials were calculated to impart; but among them there are some which breathe the free air of the fields, and the cheerful fragrance of green pastures, and may well have been composed while he yet followed the sheep.

Poetry was in those ages more strictly allied to music than it is now. The poet was also a musician, and he sang to his instrument of music the verses which he composed. This we see constantly in the poems of Homer, no less than in the Bible. David was hence a musician as well as a poet. His instrument was a "harp," so called—not such as the ponderous instrument of that name with us, but a light and portable stringed instrument, more like a lyre, such as we see it figured in ancient sculptures and coins, which seems to have been in about as common use with the Hebrews as the violin with ourselves.

STRINGED INSTRUMENTS

With this instrument he solaced the hours spent in watching his flock. His skill therewith was even then notorious to all the neighbourhood, and became the means of his introduction to the court of Saul.

Not less had the youth been able to approve his prowess and dauntless courage in his pastoral pursuits. We must not draw our ideas of such pursuits from the exhibitions on Dresden china, nor from the descriptions of Western poets; we must not conceive of David merely as an innocent youth harping under the trees, while his flock fed quietly before him. The pastoral life was in those ages full of perils and hardships which we wot not of. A shepherd needed to be a man of powerful hand, firm nerve, and great presence of mind. If he went into distant pastures, he had to protect his sheep from the depredations of the Bedouin tribes. Sometimes—especially in being led over the mountains—a sheep or two, if not the whole flock, would get into difficulties, from which it required much agility and hardihood to rescue them. Sometimes the flock would be assailed by fierce beasts of prey,—lions, wolves, and bears,—with which the shepherd had to fight in defence of the sheep. It is set down by our Saviour as the character of the hireling shepherd, to flee when he saw the wolf coming, leaving his flock to its mercy. But the owner, the true shepherd, would rather lay down his life than abandon his sheep. This was the point of honour among shepherds.

Now, David was a true shepherd, and is known to have in his youth performed memorable exploits for the protection of his flock. One of his exploits of this nature he himself related to Saul, in order to show that he did not altogether lack that experience of deadly strife which the king supposed, when he offered to fight the gigantic Philistine: "Thy servant kept his father's sheep; and there came a lion and a bear, and took a lamb out of the flock; and I went out after him, and delivered it out of his mouth: and when he arose against me, I caught him by his beard (probably *mane*), and smote him, and slew him."

Even in relating this incident, David evinced the difference between him and Saul, which constituted his fitness and Saul's unfitness to reign in Israel. Saul wished to appropriate the credit of everything to himself; David habitually, and in all the sincerity of a truly religious spirit, referred everything to the will and providence of God. So on this occasion he adds, "The Lord who delivered me out of the paw of the lion, and out of the paw of the bear, will also deliver me out of the hand of this Philistine."

In this most engaging person, this pious man, this poet, this minstrel, this hero, this Israelite indeed, behold the anointed of the Lord, the man after God's own heart!

After Abraham and Moses, David stands out as the most prominent character in the Old Testament. It must therefore be both interesting and important to obtain as much information as possible regarding his early life and his early writings.

David's youth was passed as a shepherd—a mountain shepherd, amid the pastures of Bethlehem. His native city—or rather village, for in size it is now, and must ever

have been, but a village—his native city stands on a rugged ridge, which projects eastward from the crest of the mountain range, overlooking and overhanging the wild, desolate wilderness of Judea. The steep slopes beneath the village are carefully terraced, and covered, as of yore, with olives, vines, and fig-trees. Below the terraces are the little corn fields, where Ruth and Boaz met; and beyond these is the wilderness—white limestone hills, with yawning glens, and jagged cliffs, all naked and barren. Not a tree is there. Not a shrub can be seen. Away far beneath, over the frowning rocks of Engedi, the Dead Sea appears, lying like molten lead in the bottom of the deep valley.

It was among these rugged hills that David was keeping his father's sheep when God called him to the throne. Such a country and such an occupation fitted well to nurse a warrior. David and his companions were thorough mountaineers, accustomed from childhood to vigorous exercise, inured to fatigue, and to all changes of heat and cold by day and by night. From around Bethlehem wild ravines descend eastward to the Dead Sea, and westward to the Philistine plain. Up these, robber bands were, as they still are, wont to come at all seasons; and in them lions and bears lurked of old, as panthers and hyenas do now. These were the perpetual enemies of the shepherds of Bethlehem, who were thus trained to constant watchfulness, and prepared at a moment's notice to meet danger, and fight with every kind of antagonist. In that wilderness, under that training, David learned to use the sling with such effect; and "his mighty men," the chief of whom were Bethlehemites, learned the use of sword and spear. When pursued by Saul, David was at home in "the wilderness of Engedi." Its ravines, and caves, and mountain paths were all known to him; and he was able to baffle alike the soldiers and the spies of the king.

The writings of David bear no dates. But there is something in the thoughts, and the style, and the imagery, to guide us with tolerable certainty to the period of his life when some at least of his noble lyrics were composed. The twenty-third Psalm is surely the natural tribute of

praise rendered by an inspired shepherd to his God amid the wild hills of Judah. The opening verses of the nineteenth appear to have fallen from the lips of one accustomed to gaze on the glory of the starry skies during the wakeful night-watches. Other Psalms, though manifestly of a later date, show, in their allusions to wild beasts, how vivid was the memory of early dangers and struggles, (Ps. vii. 2; x. 9; xvii. 12; xxii. 13, 20, etc.) Many of them also, in what may be called the individuality of their character, being the free and full outpouring of the soul to God—the candid, unrestrained unfolding of joys and sorrows, hopes and fears, sins and struggles,—many of the Psalms thus bear the impress of a mind accustomed to solitude, alone with itself and with God. It is this which gives to the book of Psalms one of its peculiar charms. "The patriarchs speak as the fathers of the chosen race; the prophets speak as its representatives and its guides. But the Psalmist speaks as the mouthpiece of the individual soul—of the free, independent, solitary conscience of man everywhere."

P.

MUSIC

1 Samuel 16:15-23

JESSE the Bethlehemite was one day astonished, and perhaps alarmed, to receive a somewhat peremptory command from the king: "Send me David, thy son, who is with the sheep." What could the king know of his son? What did he want with him? If Jesse knew—and if any one knew, he was the most likely to know it—the true purport of the anointing which that son had received, his first thought must have been, that the fact had come to the knowledge of Saul, and that this summons to his presence boded no good to David. However, as they say in the East, to hear was to obey. It behoved that the young man should not appear before the king empty-handed; and his father therefore provided a suitable present, in testimony of homage and respect. It consisted of a live kid, a quantity of bread, and a skin of wine. This was carried by an ass; and it is a pleasant picture, to conceive the future king of Israel stepping lightly along behind the animal, with his shepherd's staff and scrip, and entertained as he went by the gambols of the kid. His light harp was no doubt slung to his back; and it is likely that he now and then rested under a tree, and solaced his soul with its music. His fearless temper would not allow him to look forward to the result of his journey with misgivings; or, if a doubt crossed his mind, he found sufficient rest in his confidence in God.

There was nothing really alarming when the facts became known.

When the king had leisure to reflect, the denunciation of Samuel sank deep into his soul. The more he thought of it, the more terrible that doom appeared. What, in comparison, mattered it to him, that he was still to reign, if the higher hope of leaving a race of kings to Israel was to be taken from him, from him who had sons well worthy to be kings? The Hebrew mind so linked itself to the future by the contemplation of posterity, that it is scarcely possible to us, with our looser attachment to the time beyond ourselves, to apprehend in all its intensity the deep distress of mind with which any Hebrew, and much more a king, regarded the prospect that there would be "no son of *his* succeeding." Besides, there was ground for anxiety respecting his own personal safety. From the lapse of time, it might be inferred that his doom was not, as regarded himself, to be immediately executed. But who knew what might come to pass when the threatened rival should appear? Was he in his lifetime to yield up his kingly power to that rival; or was his sun to go down suddenly in blood, to make room for him?

The mind of this prince, not in his best fortunes strong, gradually gave way beneath the terror of these thoughts, the certainty of his doom, and the uncertain shapes in which it appeared. He sank into a deep melancholy, which being regarded as a divine judgment, it is said that "an evil spirit from the Lord troubled him." "What more may be meant by this than that God, for Saul's hardened impenitence, withdrew his restraining and guiding grace, I cannot say," observes Dr. Delaney;[1] "this only I am sure of, that no man living needs a heavier chastisement from Almighty God, than the letting his own passions loose upon him. The consequence to the mind would, I apprehend, in that case, be much the same as it would be to the body, if the restraining pressure of the air were removed, and all the muscles, vessels, and

[1] *An Historical Account of the Life and Reign of David, King of Israel.* Lond. 1745.

humours left to the full freedom of their own powers and tendencies."

After many other remedies had no doubt been tried, it was suggested that something might yet be hoped from music, the power of which over the diseases of the mind was well understood in times of old. The king caught eagerly at this idea, and directed that the services of some accomplished minstrel should be secured. It would seem, that although music was much cultivated, the *profession* of the musician did not exist; for if it did, some one of professional fame would no doubt have been named. This was not done; but some one present remembered that he had not long since seen "a son of Jesse the Bethlehemite," whom he then mentioned by that designation, not only as one "skilful in playing," but also a youth of great abilities and acknowledged valour; nor was his handsome person forgotten, nor the still more important fact, that "the Lord was with him,"—a phrase denoting a religious man, whom the Lord seemed to have favourably distinguished in His providence and grace.

This was the cause which led Saul to summon David to his presence. The distance was not great, about ten miles; and the youth reached Gibeah the same day that he left his home. He delayed not to present himself before the king, who little thought, as he looked upon the comely youth who stood before him, that he beheld in him the unknown rival who haunted his repose, and the destined heir of his sceptre. It was, as we have stated, the faculty of David to win with unconscious ease the hearts of all who were brought within the sphere of his influence. Even the austere and troubled Saul was no exception. "He loved him greatly," and speedily sent back to Jesse the message: "Let David, I pray thee, stand before me, for he hath found favour in my sight." So David remained at court; and when one of Saul's fits came upon him, he took his harp and played before him, and gradually the king's spirit yielded to the sweet sounds which the master hand drew from the wires; and "he was refreshed, and was well, and the evil spirit departed from him."

This remarkable instance of the power of music over the mind, especially in soothing its perturbations and allaying its disorders, is in conformity with the experience of physicians, and with various intimations which may be found in ancient authors. So are those other scriptural instances, which evince the power of music over the moods of even the sanest minds, as in the case of Elisha, who called for the aid of a minstrel to bring his mind into the frame best suited to receive the impulses of the prophetic spirit. One would almost think that there was some power in ancient music, which has since been lost, or that there existed, amid the simple manners of ancient times, a susceptibility to the influence of sweet and solemn sounds, which has disappeared amid the multitudinous business and varied pursuits of modern existence. But, in truth, the wonderful effects so often described, resulted from the concurrence of masterly skill in the minstrel, with a peculiar sensibility to the influence of sweet sounds in the patient ; and that where this concurrence is found, it will still produce the same effect as of old, a few " modern instances " may be cited to show.

In the *Mémoires* of the French Royal Academy of Sciences for 1707, are recorded many accounts of diseases, which, having obstinately resisted the remedies prescribed by the most able of the faculty, at length yielded to the powerful impression of harmony. One of these is the case of a person who was seized with fever, which soon threw him into a very violent delirium, almost without any interval, accompanied by bitter cries, by tears, by terrors, and by an almost constant wakefulness. On the third day, a hint that fell from himself suggested the idea of trying the effect of music. Gradually, as the strain proceeded, his troubled visage relaxed into a most serene expression, his restless eyes became tranquil, his convulsions ceased, and the fever absolutely left him. It is true, that when the music was discontinued his symptoms returned ; but by frequent repetitions of the experiment, during which the delirium always ceased, the power of the disease was broken, and the habits of a sound mind re-established. Six days sufficed to accomplish the cure.

It is stated by Thuanus, that after the massacre of St. Bartholomew, the sleep of Charles the Ninth was wont to be disturbed by nightly horrors, and he could only be composed to rest by a symphony of singing boys.

At the first grand performance im commemoration of Handel at Westminster Abbey, Mr. Burton, a noted chorus singer, was immediately, upon the commencement of the overture of Esther, so violently agitated, that, after lying in a fainting fit for some time, he expired. At intervals he was able to speak ; and but a few minutes before he drew his last breath, he declared that it was the wonderfuld effect of the music which had operated so powerfully upon him. Dr. Halifax, then Bishop of Gloucester, was so greatly affected during one of the performances of the Messiah at this commemoration, that he greatly wished to quit the place, fearing that he should be entirely overcome.

More remarkable, as well as more truly parallel, is the case of Philip the Fifth of Spain, and the musician Farinelli, in the last century. The king was seized with a total dejection of spirits, which made him refuse to be shaved, and rendered him incapable of appearing in council, or of attending to any affairs. The queen, after all other methods had been essayed, thought of trying what might be effected by the influence of music, to which the king was known to be highly susceptible. We have no doubt that the experiment was suggested to her by this case of Saul and David. The celebrated musician Farinelli was invited to Spain ; and on his arrival, it was contrived that there should be a concert in a room adjoining the king's apartment, in which the artist should perform one of his most captivating songs. The king appeared at first surprised, then greatly moved ; and, at the end of the second air, he summoned the musician to his apartment, and, loading him with compliments and caresses, asked him how he could reward such talents, assuring him that he could refuse him nothing. Farinelli, previously tutored, answered, that he desired nothing but that his Majesty would permit his attendants to shave and dress him, and that he would endeavour to make his appearance in the council as usual. The king yielded, and from this time his disease gave way, and the musician had all the honour of the cure. By singing to his Majesty every evening, his favour increased to such a degree, that he came to be regarded as first minister, in which capacity he conducted himself with such propriety and discretion, that the proud Spanish nobles about the court, instead of envying his prosperity, honoured him with their esteem and confidence. This favour he did not forfeit under Philip's successor (Ferdinand VI.), who made him a knight of Calatrava, and employed him in political affairs.

"THE LORD LOOKETH ON THE HEART"

1 Samuel 16:7

THESE words, in the Lord's rebuke to Samuel at Bethlehem, are very full of solemn and encouraging matter to every one who will pause to meditate upon them. Knowing, feeling as we do, what the heart of man really is, the declaration that " the Lord looketh on the heart " might seem most appalling, and almost discouraging, were it not that our care and vigilance must be alarmingly and profitably quickened by the knowledge that there exists One " to whom all hearts are open, all desires known, and from whom no secrets are hid," who judges not as man, by inference and induction, but who sees at once the most latent operations of the whole machine of mind, every minute bias and propensity, every secret spring of inclination and action, which even escapes our own self-consciousness and penetration, and all the intricate and complicated mechanism which connects human motive with human action; and that all this He beholds in its real and undisguised essence, without any intervening mists of passion or prejudice, such as distract human judgments.

These things are very wonderful to us—it is very difficult to *realize* them—although the understanding is ready enough to assent passively to them. Yet, wonderful as all this is— difficult to be apprehended clearly—there is nothing more true, more real, in the commonest things around us, than that " all things are naked and open to the eyes of Him with whom we have to do " (Heb. iv. 13), and that in His great account all our thoughts and impulses, not less than all our actions, are written down. There is nothing hidden from Him. Even our actions are not measured by the aspect which they present before men, but by the intentions in which they originate; and these are far better known to Him than they can be to ourselves, without the aid of His Holy Spirit to seek and search them out. " Discerning of spirits " is a gift from God; discerning our own spirit is eminently His gift.

To deceive others as to the condition of our heart, and as to the motives of our actions, is not difficult; and still more easy—fatally easy— is it for us to deceive ourselves; but there is no deceiving Him who " looketh on the heart." It is, therefore, our most imperative and essential duty to look there ourselves, to examine ourselves whether we be in the faith, to pray for God's Holy Spirit—that Spirit who searcheth all things—to guide us in this inquiry; and to remember that the Scripture has put us on our guard against self-deceit, by telling us that " the heart is deceitful above all things;"[1] by warning us " to keep the heart with all diligence, for out of it are the issues of life;"[2] and that " he that trusteth in his own heart is a fool."[3]

Serious, and even awful, as is to a reflecting mind the thought that the most secret counsels of the heart—counsels often at the time secret even to ourselves—appear in broad daylight before the searching eye of " the Father of spirits," there is no reason why we should be so overwhelmed with this reflection, as not to remember that God, while He views our infirmities, is most compassionate and merciful; and although He cannot tolerate or endure the sins, even of thought, which are so abhorrent to the purity of His nature, He has, for our sakes, provided a most efficient remedy, a most safe resource, a most powerful means of purification.

With this consideration in view, there is not in all the Bible a truth more consolatory to the true Christian, than that which assures us that the hearts of all men are open to the Lord. If this were not the case, we must depend for all our happiness upon the judgment of man, who can look no farther than the outward appearance. How often, in the judgment of man, are our kindest and best intentions misconstrued, our purest motives questioned, and our best actions maligned! But this need not affect us greatly, we can yet be of good cheer. The soul, shrinking from the world's ungentleness, finds rest and comfort in the thought that our merciful Father has looked upon our heart, has seen all, knows all, and will be our witness, our advocate, our vindicator, in that day when the thoughts of all hearts shall be revealed; when that which has been spoken in darkness shall be heard in light; when that which has been spoken in the ear in closets shall be proclaimed upon the housetops; and when He who seeth in secret, shall reward

[1] Jeremiah 17:9.　[2] Proverbs 4:23.　[3] Proverbs 28:26.

us openly, for much in our hearts that man has misunderstood or despised.

The reflection that we ourselves have often been thus misunderstood and misrepresented, even in matters in which we know that our conscience is most void of offence towards God and towards man; the consideration that this has often arisen not from the uncharitableness of evil-minded or unfriendly men, not from intentional wrong or malignity of purpose, but merely from the want of caution and the proper use of such means as we do possess of understanding the character and purposes of each other; and the recollection that even so good and religious a man as Samuel, honoured with prophetic gifts, was grievously mistaken in his judgment from outward appearances, ought to make us careful to exercise towards others the forbearance and the candour which we claim for ourselves. "Judge not, that ye be not judged," is an awful sentence, which has a deeper and larger meaning than we usually assign to it as the words pass over our tongues. It teaches that, in the absence of all knowledge of the heart, in the necessity of being guided much, if not entirely, by the outward appearance, it is not only a moral obligation, but a Christian duty, to be kind and lenient in our judgment of the actions and motives of others, and in our appreciation of their characters. It may be doubtful whether, in fact, it does not forbid all judgment of *motives*, as a matter beyond the scope of our limited view, and which God alone can truly estimate. The maxim of the world is to trust no man till you have tried him; but the true rule of Christian conduct in this world is to distrust no man till you have tried him, that is, until his unworthiness has been evinced by conduct concerning which even human judgment cannot well be mistaken. Knowing what evil there is in the world, it is not, indeed, any part of our duty to commit the lives or welfare of ourselves or others into the hands of strangers, in the supposition that they will prove faithful, but in our dealings with others it is our duty to put the best possible construction upon all their actions; and our manifest incapacity of viewing the hearts of men, should restrain us from all curious speculation upon the characters of those with whom we have no concern. Could we even see their hearts as clearly as we observe their outward conduct, we should still be inexcusable in passing judgment upon our brethren:

our judgments may be as false as they are cruel and criminal. Like Jesse, nay, like Samuel, we may despise those whom God has not despised; we may condemn as reprobate and unconverted those to whom God will give the kingdom of heaven; and we may draw comparisons favourable to ourselves where "the Lord, who looketh upon the heart," may judge far otherwise. [1]

GOLIATH'S ARMOUR

1 Samuel 17:1-7

It would seem that Saul, while under the process of cure for his grievous malady, contracted great regard for David. "He loved him, and made him his armour-bearer,"—the latter being a mere honorary mark of consideration and attachment, at a time when there was no actual war.

By degrees the intervals of the king's phrenzy became more distant, and eventually he seemed to be altogether cured. The services of David being no longer required, he went home to his father, and resumed the care of the sheep. By this it would seem that Saul's affection towards his healer cooled as soon as the cure had been effected. The probability of this, most physicians can vouch from their own experience. Besides, it is likely that, from the peculiar nature of his complaint, Saul cared not to be continually reminded by the presence of his healer, of the sufferings he had gone through, and of paroxysms which it humbled his proud mind to think had made him an object of compassion in the eyes of his subjects. He therefore made no opposition to the application for his son's return home, which Jesse probably made when he found that David's services were no longer necessary.

An interval passed—how long we know not, but probably about two or three years—when we again behold David traversing the road from Bethlehem, nearly in the same condition as before. But his appearance is considerably altered. You would scarcely know him for the same person that you saw some three years ago. He was then a growing youth; but he has now attained to greater fulness of stature,

[1] See the Rev. Henry Thomson's *Davidica*. Lond. 1827.

and to more firmly knit limbs. Above all, his
beard has grown; and to those who, like us,
remove the beard as soon as it appears, the
great difference produced by the presence of
this appendage on the face of one who, a year

DIFFERENCE OF APPEARANCE FROM GROWTH OF THE BEARD

or two ago, was a beardless youth, is scarcely
conceivable. The ass, also, is more heavily laden
than it was formerly with Jesse's present for
Saul. It now bears an ephah of parched corn,
ten loaves, and ten cheeses. There is war with
the Philistines; the three eldest sons of Jesse
are with the camp; and the anxious father sends
the youngest to inquire after their welfare. The
corn and bread are for their use, and the cheeses
are a present for the colonel of their regiment.

When David came to the borders of the camp,
he left the provisions in charge of the servant
who accompanied him, and went to seek out his
brothers. He made his way through the host to
the standard of Judah, and soon found them.
He was conversing with them, when a general
stir and shudder through the camp drew his
attention to what was going on around him.
The two armies were drawn up fronting each
other, on opposite sides of the valley of Elah.
From the Philistine camp stalked forth a giant,
Goliath by name, whose stature, little short of
ten feet, inspired scarcely more terror than the
formidable weapons he bore, and the magnificent accoutrements, and seemingly impenetrable
armour, with which he was invested. The particulars may be worthy our attention: "There
went out a champion out of the camp of the
Philistines, whose height was six cubits and a
span. And he had a helmet of brass upon his
head, and he was armed with a coat of mail;
and the weight of the coat was five thousand
shekels of brass. And he had greaves of brass
upon his legs, and a target of brass between his

shoulders. And the staff of his spear was like a
weaver's beam; and his spear's head weighed six
hundred shekels of iron; and one bearing a shield
went before him." Taking into account the
enormous stature of this man, and his dreadful
clanking tramp under two hundredweight of
metal, it is scarcely wonderful that the very sight
of him filled the Israelites with terror, and that
no one was found ready to engage in the single
combat with him, which, with terrible shouts and
thundering voice, he invited, as a mode of settling
the contest between two nations.

Let us look more closely at his equipment, this
being the earliest particular description of warlike panoply which we meet with in the Bible.
But, first, a word of the Philistines, who have
now become a people of much interest in the
history of the Bible. Mr. Osburn seems, in his
Ancient Egypt, to have identified this people
among the foreign nations represented, in all the
peculiarities of person, arms, and costumes, in the
Egyptian sculptures. He says, "The personal
appearance of the Philistines differed very little
from that of the Egyptians, to whom they were
allied by blood. Like them, they are represented
to have been a tall, well-proportioned race, with
regular features, and complexion somewhat
lighter than in Egypt. Like the southern
Canaanites, they shaved the beard and whiskers.

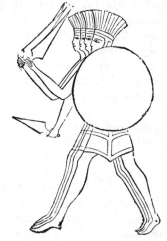

ANCIENT PHILISTINES, FROM EGYPTIAN SCULPTURES

Their arms and accoutrements very conspicuously
distinguished them from all other nations to the
east of Egypt. They wore a head-dress or helmet
of a peculiar, and far from inelegant, form. It
has the appearance of a row of feathers set in
a jewelled tiara or metal band, to which were

attached scales of the same material, for the defence of the back of the neck and the sides of the face."[1] The helmet of Goliath may have been probably of this sort, seeing that the race of giants to which he belonged had been for some generations settled among the Philistines. In that case we learn from the text that this curious helmet was of brass. The gigantic race was that of the Anakim, whose presence in and about Hebron terrified the spies

PHILISTINE HELMET

who explored the land in the time of Moses, and the remnant of which, on their defeat and expulsion, found refuge among the Philistines. It is not unlikely that they preserved the kind of armour and weapons in use in the quarter from which they came, and the more so as that would distinguish them from the ordinary Philistine warriors; and we find that people of gigantic stature are fond of adding a distinction of dress to that which their stature creates; their peculiar equipments concurring with their stature in drawing attention to them, and indeed, making their stature the more conspicuous. The marked manner in which this giant's equipments are mentioned, may strengthen the supposition that they were not such as the Philistines themselves wore. If this supposition be correct, the war costume of the Hittites probably was the same as that worn by the Anakim, at least before they went among the Philistines. This people, if Mr. Osburn has correctly identified them, used in war a helmet or skull-cap extending far down

HITTITE HELMETS OR SKULL-CAPS

the neck behind, and cut out high and square above the ear, so as to expose the bald place and long lock, which they deemed a personal ornament.[2] Sometimes a metal scale defended this

[1] Osburn's *Egypt*, pp. 137, 138.
[2] "They (the Hittites) had a hideously unsightly custom

part of the head. It was secured under the chin by a strong band or clasp-string, probably of metal like the helmet. The badges of distinction were one or two ostrich feathers, which were worn drooping.

Goliath's "coat of mail" was, like his helmet, of brass. The Philistines, as represented in the Egyptian sculptures, wore in war "a kind of corslet, quilted with leather or plates of metal, reaching only to the chest, and supported by shoulder-straps, leaving the shoulders and arms at full liberty."[1] The terms describing the giant's coat of mail, however, literally mean "har-

ASSYRIAN WARRIOR IN COAT OF SCALE ARMOUR

ness of scales," denoting a scaled coat of mail, consisting of small plates like scales. An excellent authority[2] thinks that it expresses armour in which the pieces of metal were sewed upon cloth, and not hinged into each other as in the kind of "tiled armour" which Ahab appears to have worn when the random arrow smote him between "the joints of his harness." This corresponds well to the *description* of the Philistine corslet, though we are unable to recognize the squamous arrangement of the pieces of metal in the figures of this or *any other people* represented in the Egyptian sculptures, except in the broad military girdle of one of the gods. This, however, shows the very ancient use of this species of armour, and recently this fact has been further attested by the discoveries at Nineveh. In these, the warriors who fought in chariots, and held the shield for the defence of the king, are generally seen in coats of scale armour, which descend either to the knees or to the ankles. A large number of the actual scales were discovered in the earliest palace of Nimrud. They are generally of iron, slightly embossed or raised in the

of shaving a square place just above the ear, leaving the hair on the side of the face and the whiskers, which hung down in a long plaited lock."—Osburn, p. 125.
[1] Osburn, p. 138.
[2] Col. C. H. Smith, in *Cyclop. of Bib. Literature*, art. Arms, Armour.

centre; and some are inlaid with copper. They were probably, Layard thinks, fastened to a shirt of felt or coarse linen.[1] Such is the armour always represented in the most ancient sculptures. At later periods other kinds were used, the scales were larger, and appear to have been fastened to bands of iron or copper.

Of the greaves, such as Goliath wore for the defence of his legs, there is no example among the Egyptian representations of their own and foreign warriors. Their form is, however, well known from other ancient sources. They consisted usually of a pair of shin-covers, of brass or strong leather, bound by thongs around the calves and above the ankles. The Assyrian sculptures represent greaves as being worn both by spearmen and slingers, and they appear to have been laced in front. "They were perhaps of leather," says Layard, " or like the boots of the Bœotians, of wood, or even of brass, as the greaves of Goliath." They are seen in the annexed figure of an Assyrian warrior, whose equipment seems to afford much resemblance to that of Goliath, except as to his coat of scale armour.[2]

ASSYRIAN SPEARMAN

The shield in use among the Philistines was large and circular, exactly resembling that of the Greeks in a later age. This, indeed, was the form of the shield among the Phœnicians; while we see shields square, oblong, and escutcheon-shaped among the inland natives of Canaan. The form of an Assyrian shield given above, is also quite similar to that of the Philistines. The Assyrians had other forms, but this is the most ancient. It was either of hide or of metal—perhaps, in some instances, of gold or silver. It was held by a handle fixed to the centre. Layard says : " The archers, whether fighting on foot or in chariots, were accompanied by shield-bearers, whose office it was to protect them from the shafts of the enemy. The king was always attended in his wars by this officer; and even in peace, one of his eunuchs usually carried a circular shield for his use. This shield-bearer was probably a person of high rank, as in Egypt. On

[1] *Nineveh and its Remains,* ii. 335.
[2] Layard, ii. 337.

some monuments of the later Assyrian period, he is represented carrying two shields, one in each hand." In a note this explorer refers to the instances in the *Iliad* of the same practice,[1] and also to this of Goliath, who had " one bearing his shield who went before him."

The "spear" of the Philistines and other people of Canaan was not such a long reed-like instrument as we find in use among the modern Arabs, and which has been accepted as the type of the oriental spear. It does not seem to have been quite five feet long, and might be also used as a javelin, like the spear of Saul.[2] It was like the Assyrian spear, except that it was shorter, the latter being fully equal to a man's height. The *iron* head of a spear from Nimrud is in the British Museum; and it is remarkable that this is the only part of Goliath's accoutrement that is said to have been of iron, though his sword was also doubtless of this metal. The shaft of the Assyrian spear was probably of some strong wood, as that of Goliath certainly was.

These facts may help the reader to some idea of the appearance which the giant presented to the host of Israel, as he strode forth in his panoply of burnished brass.

Goliath was not a Philistine. He was, as his name seems to imply, " a stranger." It would appear, from numerous detached passages and incidental references in the Bible, that the aboriginal inhabitants of Palestine, both east and west of the Jordan, were a race of giants, or at least of men above the ordinary stature. One tribe of them was called *Rephaim,* and had possessions in Bashan, where Og was the last of the race (Gen. xiv. 5 ; Deut. iii. 11). They had also a settlement near Jerusalem, and gave their name to the " Valley of Rephaim ; " and from them, in all probability, sprang Goliath, Sippai, and Lahmi (1 Chron. xx. 4, 5). Other tribes were called *Emim* (Gen. xiv. 5 ; Deut. ii. 10), *Anakim* (Num. xiii. 33), and *Zuzim* (Gen. xiv. 5 ; Deut. ii. 20), and are said to have been a people " great, and many, and tall." The Jewish spies, in their exaggerated report, stated : " There we saw the giants, the sons of Anak, which come of the giants ; and we were in our own sight as grasshoppers ; and so we were in their sight." This gigantic and warlike race of men was extirpated at an early period on the east of the Jordan, the last of them having been killed in the invasion of Moses ; but in the west they continued long to terrify the Hebrews, having found a home among the Philistines (2 Sam. xxi. 18-22).

The height of Goliath it is now impossible to fix with precision. The Hebrew text says he measured " six cubits and a span." But critics differ as to the length of the

[1] *Iliad,* viii. 319, 327.　　[2] 1 Samuel 19:9,10.

cubit. Probably the estimate of Thenius is nearest the truth. He makes the cubit nineteen inches and a fraction, and the span half a cubit. Hence Goliath's height would be about 124 inches, or ten feet four inches.

P.

THE COMBAT

1 Samuel 17:8-52

WE may be sure that it was not without burning indignation that David beheld the gigantic and proud pagan stand forth to defy the host of Israel, nor without astonishment and grief that he witnessed the consternation which his presence inspired. Judging by his own fearless spirit, he reckoned that some valiant man would stand forth, to repay him scorn for scorn, and blow for blow. But it was not so. None moved, except to tremble in dismay. Not even the valiant Saul, nor his daring son, durst undertake this adventure. David then learned that this scene had been repeated several days, and that the king had vainly sought to stimulate the courage of some bold man, by offering the hand of his daughter in marriage, and other advantages, to the man who should bring that vast champion low.

The son of Jesse felt the spirit of patriotism and heroic daring stirred within him; and he began to make such pointed inquiries, as drew down the ungracious sneers of his eldest brother—the tall and handsome Eliab. Regardless of this, he pursued his inquiries in such a manner, that the matter at last reached the ears of the king, who, willing in his despair to catch at what seemed little better than a straw, caused the young man to be brought before him. Taking into account the change wrought in his appearance by the lapse of time, and by the growth of his beard—as well as from his appearing in the guise of a shepherd, with the usual implements connected with that employment—it does not seem to us very surprising that the king did not know him again; besides, it is likely that Saul's memory had been somewhat impaired by his disease, while the constant variety and change of persons presented to the notice of a king would tend to reduce any slight recollection he might have, to a vague and dim impression that he had at a former period seen some person of whom this young man reminded him. Seeing this to be the case, David did not then attempt to make himself known, neither did he make any studied concealment, but left the disclosure to circumstances.

In the presence of the king, David spoke as one who was ready to undertake this enterprise, and who was assured that the victory in this strange combat would be his. The king was pleased with his spirit, but kindly pointed out that the antagonist with whom he proposed to wage mortal strife, was not only a man of gigantic proportions and enormous strength, but also a skilled man-at-arms, practised in war from his youth. David humbly related the story of the lion and the bear, which he had aforetime slain in defence of his flock. This he did not in vain ostentation of his own exploits, though in the East more self-praise of this sort is allowed than would be considered becoming among us; but to point out the source of his confidence: "The Lord who delivered me out of the paw of the lion, and out of the paw of the bear, He will deliver me out of the hand of this Philistine." Saul could not fail to be impressed by this; for his self-consciousness must have apprised him at that moment that *this* was the true heroic confidence for Israel, and that in which, more than any other duty, he was wofully deficient. This impression doubtless disposed him, without further demur, to consent to risk the lot of Israel upon the issue of a conflict between this young man and the enormous Philistine. He said at once, "Go, and the Lord be with thee." Nevertheless, he insisted that the heroic youth should be suitably equipped for the conflict in complete armour. But when thus arrayed, David felt himself embarrassed rather than strengthened by this heavy panoply; and, quickly casting it off, stood forth, light and agile, in his simple shepherd's dress. The weapon he chose was his own sling, much used by shepherds in repelling the assailants of their flocks, and in the use of which they often, like David, possessed extraordinary expertness. It was formerly used, and is still much employed, by husbandmen in driving away birds from the corn fields. It was, however, also largely employed in war; and, in skilled hands, delivered stones against the enemy with the force almost of a shot. Saul's own tribe of Benjamin was famous for its left-handed slingers, who could cast stones at a hair and not miss. Slings were also used in war by both the Egyptians and the Assyrians. Among the latter, the sling consisted of a double rope with a thong, probably of leather, to receive the stone; it was swung round the head. The slinger held a second stone in his left hand; and at his feet is frequently seen, in the sculptures, a heap of stones ready for use. The Persian slingers, also, as we learn from several passages in Xenophon, were very expert in casting unusually large stones, and could annoy their enemies when out of the reach of their darts or arrows. The sling of the ancient Egyptians, which was probably of the same sort as that of David, was a thong of leather or plaited string, broad at the middle, and having a loop at one end, by which it was fixed upon and held firmly by the hand; the other extremity terminated in a leash, which escaped from the fingers when the stone was thrown; and when used, the slinger whirled it two or three times round his head to steady it and to increase the impetus. Besides stones and arrows, the Greeks threw heavy leaden plummets from the sling. Some had a single or winged thunderbolt represented upon them; and others bore the name of the person to whom they belonged, or a word, as ΑΓΩΝΙΣ or ΔΕΞΑΙ, "Take this;" but simple pebbles, found on the sea-shore or in the brooks, were usually employed. The Egyptians used round stones for this purpose, which they carried in a

EGYPTIAN SLINGERS

small bag or scrip hanging from a belt over the shoulder. So David selected five smooth pebbles from the brook, and put them into his shepherd's bag.

The use of the sling was, however, rather despised by regular heavy armed troops; and Goliath opened his great eyes with disdain and astonishment when he beheld this light shepherd spring forward to confront him, armed only with his pastoral sling. The giant's pride was grievously affronted that this simple implement should be deemed adequate to a conflict with one so strong and so terribly arrayed: "Am I a dog," he roared, "that thou comest against *me* with staves?"[1] He then cursed the young man "by his gods," and poured forth insulting threats upon his head. "Come to me," he said, "and I will give thy flesh to the fowls of the air, and to the beasts of the field!" In the single combats of the East, even in those preceding and bringing on general actions, the opposed champions are still wont thus to kindle each other's wrath by mutual abuse, and the reader of Homer will recollect many examples of the same practice. These often extend to long addresses, and each party waits as patiently as he can till the other has done, without allowing himself to be provoked to cut short the harangue by force of arms. The staple of these harangues usually consists of boastings of the speaker's own exploits, with abuse of the opponent, and threats of what shall be done to him. In the present case, we seem to have only an abstract of Goliath's harangue; for it is not stated in what terms he cursed the son of Jesse by his gods. But David's speech is given in full, and it beautifully manifests the spirit by which he was animated, and which is evinced in all his subsequent career. He assumes nothing to himself; his trust is not in the might of his own arm; it is to the Lord he looks for victory; and it is to Him he beforehand ascribes all the glory which may flow from it. He said to the Philistine, "Thou comest to me with a sword, and with a spear, and with a shield; but I come to thee in the name of the Lord of hosts, the God of the armies of Israel, whom thou hast defied. This day will the Lord deliver thee into mine hand; and I will smite thee, and take thine head from thee; and I will give the carcases of the host of the Philistines this day unto the fowls of the air, and to the wild beasts of the earth, that all the earth may know that there is a God in Israel. And all this assembly shall know that the Lord saveth not

[1] By this it is probable that David had a staff in one hand, and that, not discerning the sling in his other hand, Goliath conceived that *this* was the intended weapon of conflict. Mrs. Postans states, that "the shepherds of the East always carry a staff, which they hold in the centre, the object of its use not being as a support, but to beat bushes and low brushwood into which flocks stray, and where snakes and other reptiles abound."—*Journal of Sacred Literature*, iv. 51.

with sword and spear; for the battle is the Lord's, and He will give you into our hands."

The giant then strode forth to meet the young Hebrew, who stood still; but, taking from his bag one of the stones, he fitted it to his sling, which he whirled around his head, and discharged with such force, and with so true an aim, that it smote the Philistine in almost the only exposed part of his person, the middle of his forehead, and crunched through the strong bone deep into his brain. His vast frame sank to the ground with a heavy crash, which cast terror into the hearts of the Philistines; while David, stepping lightly forward, drew the giant's own great sword from its sheath, and therewith separated his head from his body, and bore it triumphantly away. Taking

DAVID SLAYETH GOLIATH

advantage of the consternation into which the Philistines were cast by this downfall of their champion, the Israelites arose with a triumphant shout—the hearty utterance of which was in full proportion to their previous dismay—and pursued the Philistines, who fled before them, with such earnestness and zeal, that they gave not over the chase until the fugitives who escaped their swords had reached the very gates of their own towns.

A visit I made to the valley of Elah, some years ago, left an impression upon my mind which time can never efface. The scene of David's combat and Israel's triumph was before me in all its details. The valley—then called

Elah, from its "terebinths," but now *es-Sumpt*, from its "acacias"—is about a quarter of a mile wide, and has a gently undulating surface of cultivated ground. The ridges along each side rise steeply, though not precipitously, to a height of some five hundred feet. Through the centre of the valley winds a broad torrent bed, now dry, but filled with smooth white stones, and fringed with shrubberies of acacia. Half-way up the ridge, on the left bank, lie the grey ruins of Shocoh, where the Philistines had pitched their camp. Along the crown and side of the ridge opposite, less than a mile distant, were ranged the tents of Saul. The encampments were in full view of each other; and the warriors on both sides could send shouts of defiance across the intervening valley. Down the left bank strode the haughty Goliath, his brazen armour glittering in the sunbeams, and his deep voice sending a thrill of terror through the camp of Israel. Down the opposite bank David sped quickly, armed only with his sling and his shepherd's staff. Reaching the torrent bed before his assailant, he selected "five smooth stones," and put them in his scrip. Active as a gazelle, skilled in the use of his weapon, cool and collected as one accustomed to daily danger, and above all, strong in the faith of his God, David was no mean foe. In fact, the champions were not so unequally matched as is generally supposed. The hardy mountaineer who had courage to grapple with, and strength to rend by force of arm, a Syrian bear, had not very much to fear from the vast bulk and cumbrous panoply of the Philistine giant. The ease with which he was able to wield, and afterwards wear, Goliath's sword, showed that David possessed great muscular strength. The supernatural element in the victory must not be overlooked; but still full allowance must also be made for the skill, and courage, and prowess of David.

P.

Lieut. Conder has recently visited the valley of Elah, and he remarks, "There is a point with regard to the valley which has always been considered to require investigation on the spot. Saul camped in the Emek, ' broad or deep valley,' whilst between him and the Philistines was the *Gäi*, generally translated *ravine*. The valley is, however, of uniform breadth; nor does a gorge of any kind exist in its lower course, as the usual interpretation supposes; the derivation of the latter word is, however, according to Dean Stanley, from *Gih*, 'to break out; used of water bursting forth.' It may be very well applied, therefore, I should suggest, to the trench, or *ghor*, dug out by the winter torrent. This bed, some ten to twenty feet wide, with banks over ten feet high, would form a natural barrier between the hosts, and a formidable obstacle to the flight of the defeated. It was in this that David found the five smooth stones of the brook which, according to tradition, cried out, ' By us thou shalt defeat the giant.' The gleaming torrent bed, and the steep water-worn banks, consist of pebbles of every size, worn smooth by the great winter brook which has brought them from the hills." (*Report, Exploration Fund.* 1875. 193.)

S.

CLOUDED TRIUMPH

1 Samuel 17:53 - 18:12

DAVID has now at once become a public man. There is no more obscurity—no more sweet solitude of private life—no more feeding of sheep, for him. If we look to the deep depression into which the Israelites had fallen, so that the most daring spirits, under the stimulus of the highest rewards, had not ventured upon the enterprise which the son of Jesse so nobly and so piously achieved, we may form some notion of the admiration and gratitude with which this exploit was regarded, and the enthusiasm which it excited. It was the one great act by which some men are enabled, in one little hour—or even in the time of a passing thought—to illustrate and adorn their whole career, presenting to the public view one illustrious deed, the memory of which becomes in every mind inseparably connected with their name, and goes down with it to future ages. It was impossible for any Israelite thenceforward in David's lifetime to behold him, or in the ages to come to think of him, without remembering this great exploit, with its antecedents and its consequences. How naturally, even in David's old age, the remembrances of this rose freshly to the minds of the people: "The king delivered us out of the hand of the Philistines!"

Glorious spoil had the Israelites when they returned to the camp, from the abandoned tents of the Philistines. It was then that David was brought before the king, bearing the enormous head of Goliath in his hand. The king's words evince that he had not the slightest recollection of David. At the time Goliath fell, Saul had asked Abner, "Whose son is this youth?"—a natural question, seeing that in those days a man was more known by his father's name than by his own, as is still the case in Arabia, where a man is generally called *the son* of such a person. Thus David is quite as frequently, when spoken of by others, called "the son of Jesse" as by his proper name. Saul had a further interest in the inquiry, as he had promised that the conquerer of Goliath should become his son-in-law, and he would naturally wish to know something of the parentage of the youth on whom this honour had fallen. Abner was unable to answer the question;

for he, too, failed to recognize the son of Jesse, or very probably he had not been at Saul's court during David's previous residence there, his services being little needed in time of peace. It is now Abner who brings David before Saul, that he may answer the question for himself. Saul asked, "Whose son art thou, thou young man?" The answer is, "I am the son of thy servant Jesse the Bethlehemite." It strikes us that the form of expression implies that David felt that Saul would recognize him and his father by this description, thus corroborating the account of their previous connection. We may also note two things in this answer: that David does not give his own name, which was not indeed asked, his father's name being a sufficient designation; and that he does not say, "Thy servant is the son of Jesse," but, "I am the son of thy servant Jesse,"—the latter form expressing more profound homage, seeing that one to whom David owed filial respect and obedience, was himself thus described as the king's servant.

How Saul received this intimation we are not told. He was probably too much astonished to say anything, and kings conceive that their dignity requires them to be men of few words. He, however, intimated that David was to remain at court, and that from that day "he would let him go no more home to his father's house." It was at this interview that the young prince Jonathan found his heart drawn towards the son of Jesse, in whom, as the hero, he recognized the congenial spirit which he had overlooked in the minstrel. He soon made known his sentiments of deep admiration to the object of them, and the two young men soon entered into covenants of a friendship strong as death, which was in the highest degree honourable to both, and which, in the case of Jonathan, constitutes his chief claim to our admiration and regard. We read that Jonathan, to evince his regard and admiration, "stripped himself of the robe that was on him, and gave it to David." In the East, this mode of showing regard or approval is still very general. "I recollect," says Mrs. Postans, "a tiger-hunting party, held by Meer Alli Moorad in Upper Sindh, where that chief sat in a small tower with his personal friends to see the sport. A Sindhian behaved most valiantly, killing a tiger and her cubs; and the hero was brought up on the tower, when Meer Alli Moorad took from his neck a muslin scarf, and bestowed it on the man, who felt himself distinguished above all honour, and remunerated beyond all price." [1]

Thus far all was favourable to David; but on the homeward march from the camp, circumstances arose which first awakened in the mind of Saul that suspicion and dislike which never after left his mind, and which perhaps gave to him the first dim notion, that in Jesse's son he had at length found the long-threatened and long-dreaded inheritor of his throne.

As they went along, the damsels came out of their towns and villages to hail their deliverers with songs and music. And this was the burden of their song :—

> "Saul hath slain his thousands—
> David hath his ten thousands slain."

Saul was keen enough to see that this expressed the popular appreciation of their respective merits; and his morbid craving for the pre-eminence and for the sole glory in all things caused him to be deeply mortified at this preference of David's share of the exploit before his own. Perhaps, as since that time has been common, he held that all the honour won by subjects merely went to fill up the measure of his own renown. At all events he was greatly displeased. " They have ascribed unto David," said he, " ten thousands, and to me they have ascribed but thousands; and what can he have more but the kingdom !" These last were dangerous words, full of evil omen to David, as indicating a line of thought in the king's darkening mind, which was destined to spoil his own peace and that of David for many years. It is added that " Saul eyed [invidiously] David from that day and forward." Indeed, it was but the next day that these rankling thoughts brought back upon the king a strong paroxysm of his former disease. David, who was present, and whose experience detected the symptoms of the gathering cloud, seized his harp, and once more sought by its powerful strains to soothe the troubled mind. But at that moment the king, before the softening influence could be felt, launched from his hand the short spear or javelin which he bore as the symbol (equivalent to a sceptre) of regal power, at the son of Jesse, with the full purpose of pinning him to the wall. Had he succeeded, the act would have been ascribed to his madness, and he would have been more pitied than blamed. But he was not to enjoy the advantage of this

[1] *Journal of Sacred Literature*, iv. 51.

construction of his acts, for David shunned the stroke at the critical moment, and left his presence. This happened more than once, and Saul began to be terrified, thinking that his arm had become powerless, or that (as was true) the son of Jesse bore a divinely protected life. He began to be " afraid of David, *because the Lord was with him.*"

SNARES

1 Samuel 18:13-30

SAUL, under the first influence of good feeling towards David, had " set him over his men of war," by which it is understood that he made him captain of his guard, and this post he appears to have occupied at the time when the attempts were made upon his life. That this attempt should twice have failed when the object was so near, and when a hand so strong and skilful aimed the stroke, must have seemed to Saul a divine interposition in favour of Jesse's son. Such an interposition, it was natural to think, had some extraordinary object; and what object so likely as his designation to the kingdom ? When this impression arose, all the circumstances which Saul could recollect must have tended to confirm it; and it would be no satisfaction to him to find that the object of this preference over himself was in all respects worthy of it. By whatever means David's elevation was to be brought about, it was clear that it would not be attempted through any such disloyal acts or low intrigues as might give the king an advantage over him, and enable him to effect his destruction with a show of public justice; and as yet Saul's mind was not so steeled in wrong-doing, or so indifferent to public opinion, as openly to destroy, without apparent cause, and by his mere arbitrary act, a man who was daily growing into higher favour with the nation, which owed to him such essential benefits.

Alarmed to see the progress David was making in the affections of the notable persons at court, and that even his son Jonathan had become entirely subject to the fascination by which the son of Jesse gathered to him the hearts of men like summer fruits, Saul deemed it wise to remove him from this sphere of influence, by sending him into a sort of honourable exile. He was entrusted with the command of a thousand men, and sent upon the dangerous service of guarding the frontier, in the hope that his daring spirit would lead him into such hazardous enterprises as would soon accomplish his destruction by the sword of the Philistines. But this only afforded David better opportunities of showing that he possessed, not only the qualities of a champion, but the talents, the sagacity, and prudence of a military leader, while he was thus also enabled to gather that experience in war which availed him much in later years. Still further dismayed at the rapid growth of David's popularity with the people, Saul next thought of making him a prop to his family by uniting him to his eldest daughter, Merab. The hand of the king's daughter had been promised beforehand to the conqueror of Goliath; but Saul had conveniently forgotten this promise, and David had been too discreet to press for its fulfilment. Now the king proposed it as a new matter, and caused it to be intimated that such an alliance was not beyond his hopes, in case he proved himself worthy of it, by renewed exertions against the enemies of his country. The manner in which he received this intimation well deserves attention. He did not decline the honour proposed; both prudence and respect forbade that; but he was careful to make it appear that not only did he not claim or accept it as a matter of right, but that he disavowed all pretence to it on the score of merit. Such greatness as David possessed is but little conscious of its own deservings; and we have reason to suppose that David spoke with no less sincerity than prudence when he said, " Who am I? and what is my life, or my father's family in Israel, that I should be son-in-law to the king?"

By what increased exertions David showed his worthiness of this honour, and by what escapes from the perils into which his daring spirit threw him, he defeated the king's secondary, no longer primary, object of effecting his destruction, we do not learn; but we know that when the time for the fulfilment of the promise arrived, Saul shamefully violated his word, and bestowed his daughter upon another man. This harsh indignity and disappointment must have been deeply felt by David. Many men would have been exasperated by it into some act of outrage or some indiscreet expressions. Perhaps the act was designed to produce this effect, that advantage might be taken of David's indiscretion to effect his ruin. But from this snare he was delivered. It was well that it thus happened, and that his submission under injuries is so much more obvious than his resentments, as to have caused it to be questioned whether he might not well have manifested a little more of what is very *improperly* called "proper spirit." But it has been acutely remarked by an old writer, that retired students are not always the best judges of what best becomes a truly heroic spirit. We are glad that David's conduct took this direction; for had it been otherwise—had he, even under strong temptation, swerved from his loyalty to the right hand or to the left, much would have been made of it to the discredit of his rectitude in these latter days, when the whole of his conduct has been so searchingly and unsparingly investigated.

Some time after this—and it is a loss to us that the intervals of time are not distinctly marked—it came to the knowledge of Saul that his daughter Michal cherished a tender regard for David. It might have displeased him to hear that the heart of another of his children had gone over to one whom he had by this time learned to hate and to dread. But it happened to please him, as he hoped to be able to use her as an instrument for his destruction. We all know that in the East the husband is expected in some sort to *purchase* his bride, by a payment to her father. One who cannot pay this in money may do it by his services, as Jacob did, or by some exploit fixed by the father, as was done by Othniel. David had a clear claim to one of Saul's daughters; but this, as a matter of right, he did not urge; and his family was not in such circumstances as to afford such " gift and dowry" as a king had a right to expect when he bestowed a daughter. To meet this difficulty, the king was graciously content to accept some great exploit against the public enemy as a sufficient equivalent for his daughter's hand. Thus understood, what Saul required was not, as the difference of manners has led many to suppose it to be, a gratuitous task, the real object of which might have been, even at the first view, very obvious; but it was in appearance a generous and considerate mode of enabling the son of Jesse to contract this match on somewhat equal terms, by the acceptance of a service that he could render in lieu of payments beyond his power. For Saul to give his daughter without any consideration, would have been a slur upon her; and to accept her on such terms would have been, according to Eastern notions, dishonourable in David. It was, therefore, not without the appearance of generosity on the part of the king that he offered to accept a public service in lieu of a private benefit; and it was right that he should make that service bear some proportion, in hazard and difficulty, to the value he set upon his daughter. This, as we view it, was the aspect in which Saul intended the transaction to appear, and in which it probably did appear in the eyes of all but the few who were prepared to see through it the deeper design to compass the ruin of Jesse's son. Whether David himself was of the number is not clear—probably not, if we may judge from the alacrity with which he undertook the proposed enterprise; and if we consider that, to his heroic spirit there were few achievements which would seem difficult or dangerous.

This enterprise was, that he should, probably within a given time, destroy with his own hand a hundred of the Philistines, and bring to the king such proofs of their deaths as might assure him that they were Philistines and no others who had been slain. This demand, so much in unison with the spirit of the age, and of which we have a subsisting example in the scalps which the North American Indians take from their slaughtered enemies as trophies of their valour, was undertaken by David; and when the time expired, he appeared before the king with not only an hundred, but with two hundred such proofs of his prowess as the king had required. This was another great exploit, far more arduous, although less renowned than the overthrow of Goliath. It must, however, have attracted great attention at the time, and have conduced in no small degree to the public estimation in which David was held. Thus, whatever the hitherto concealed aversion of Saul devised for his destruction led only to his greater honour, and materially advanced the results which the king desired to avert. So shall it be with every one who blindly and foolishly endeavours to frustrate the counsels of God.

TERAPHIM

1 Samuel 19:1-17

DAVID was now still more conspicuously brought before the view of the people, and his consequence in their eyes was much enhanced by his alliance with the royal family. Aware of this, and perceiving that his underhand devices only tended to raise the son of Jesse to higher credit, and gave him opportunities of achieving greater distinction, the king's dislike ripened fast into mortal hatred. He also found that his daughter really loved her husband, and could not in any way be made instrumental in bringing his person into danger. These things goaded Saul on to infuriate rage. He began among his intimates to throw aside the mask which had hitherto veiled, however thinly, the motive of his proceedings; and he hinted that the removal of David, by any means, would be a service most acceptable to him. Providentially, he mentioned this to Jonathan among the rest. That faithful friend said nothing at the time, but went and apprised David of his danger, and directed him to a place of concealment; and he promised to lead Saul the next day in that direction, so that his friend might overhear what passed when he interceded with his father for him. He arranged this, probably, that in case the king broke forth into violence, or proved inexorable, David might be aware of it, and escape without incurring the danger of further personal communications.

In this conversation with his father, Jonathan took a strong and decided tone. He plainly told him that he was about to commit a great sin in thus seeking the destruction of a valuable public servant, who had rendered great services to the state, and all whose conduct towards him had been most true and loyal. " Wherefore, then," he said with vehemence, " wilt thou sin against innocent blood, by slaying David without a cause ?" The king—a man of impulses, and in whom the impulse to right feeling was not yet extinct—was moved by this earnest appeal, and he pledged himself by an oath to Jonathan, that he would no longer seek the life of Jesse's son.

David then left his concealment, and resumed his usual duties; and soon after he went again to the wars, and acquired still further renown, so that his praise was in the mouth of all the people. This was wormwood to Saul. His former malignity, suspicion, and hatred, all revived; and when David came back to court, his old paroxysms of madness returned with such violence, that the harp of David, who had now a place at the king's table as his son-in-law, had no longer the power over him it once possessed. He could no longer heed the voice of the charmer, charm he ever so wisely. One day his pent-up passion so overmastered him, that he again threw his javelin at David. With such force was it thrown, that it stuck into the wall and remained there, for David had evaded the stroke, and immediately withdrew from the king's presence. But now that he had committed himself by this act, Saul was determined to carry his purpose out; and he sent a guard to watch David's house all night to prevent his escape. We may guess that only the fear of alarming the town, and of rousing the populace to rescue their favourite hero, prevented him from directing them to break into the house, and to slay David there. It was so providentially ordered; for he was thus, at the suggestion of his wife, enabled to escape through a back window, by which she let him down.

David having thus escaped, the remaining anxiety of Michal was to protract the time as much as possible, that he might be far enough off before the pursuit commenced. She "took an image, and laid it in the bed, and put a pillow of goats' hair for a bolster, and covered it with a cloth." The object of this was to convey the impression, on a cursory view, that some one was lying in the bed. The "image" is, in the original, "teraphim." There is much difficulty about these teraphim. They are first mentioned as things that had been secreted by Rachel when her husband fled from Padanaram, and about which Laban made so much uproar when he overtook the fugitives. That they were held in superstitious regard, partaking of idolatry, is manifest; nevertheless, that they were not looked upon by those who used them as interfering with the worship of Jehovah, but were, on the contrary, regarded as being auxiliary to it, seems evident from their being found in families which professed to be true worshippers of the Lord. It seems to us that they were superstitious symbolical figures, which were supposed to bring peculiar blessings, and to secure peculiar protection—essentially the blessings and protection of

Jehovah—to the houses in which they were found, like, in some degree, the tutelary and household gods, the Penates and Lares of the Romans; or, as we take it, still more like the pictures of St. Nicholas or of the Virgin, which one sees in every Russian shop, before which a lamp is kept continually burning, and which every one who enters the place reverently salutes. Of their sinful character there can be no question, from their tendency to lead into more direct idolatry, and from the deficient appreciation which the use of them evinced of the spiritual worship which God, who is a Spirit, requires, and which is most acceptable in His sight. It was a form of worshipping God; but, being an unscriptural and dangerous form, it was evil in His eyes, and was, with the express commendation of God, put down, along with others forms of idolatry, by Josiah;[1] yet it is nowhere denounced and suppressed with the same rigour as the worship of Moloch or of Baal. It is observable that women were peculiarly addicted to the use of these teraphim. First, there was Rachel, who had them without the knowledge of her husband; and now here is Michal, who has a teraph, doubtless without the privity of David. That may have been easy in the case of Rachel, seeing the images appear to have been small, from the facility with which they were concealed; but this of Michal seems to have been as large as a human body; and it may be asked, Was it possible for David to have been ignorant of its existence in his house? It was very possible under the arrangement of Eastern habitations, which assigns a separate part of the house to the women; and particularly so in the case of David, who, as being now a high military commander, and especially as having married the king's daughter, doubtless dwelt in a large house, and showed to his wife all the consideration in these matters which a lady of her rank was entitled to expect.

There has been some difference of opinion as to the form of the teraphim. The passage before us would seem to intimate that it had the human shape, being intended, when lying in the bed, and covered with the bed-clothes, to be taken for David, ill in bed. This is not, however, conclusive, seeing that almost anything of sufficient bulk might be made to suggest that idea in a

[1] 2 Kings 23:24. where the word "images" is in the original "teraphim."

darkened room, and in the dim of the morning, so long as the head was not visible.

There is a very prevalent notion among the Jewish writers, that the teraphim were figures of brass, constructed under certain horoscopic and astrological aspects; and that a plate of gold being placed under the tongue, they were, on being invoked with ceremonies of divination, enabled to deliver oracles. To state this idea is to refute it.

The mention of a pillow of goat's hair in the present passage, leads Josephus astray into the odd fancy that Michal put in the bed the lungs of a goat recently killed, the palpitations of which would impart the motion caused by a man's breathing in bed. Then how was it with respect to the form of a man in bed, which the teraph must have presented? And how long do the lungs of a slain goat continue thus to palpitate? The thing is absurd. Nevertheless, we are not very sure that we understand this statement respecting "the pillow of goat's hair." The hair of a Syrian goat might form a good stuffing for a pillow-case; but how were the persons to be deceived to know that the pillow was filled with goat's hair? We incline to think that the pillow was of goat's skin, with the hair outside; and that such a pillow was then regarded as having a sanative property in some diseases; whence to see such a pillow in a bed would strengthen the illusion that a sick man lay there. Although this is a conjecture of our own, it seems to us more probable than the notion of some interpreters, that Michal made a kind of wig for the teraph with the goat's skin, to produce a passable resemblance to David's head.

———

A far better explanation of the original word translated *pillow* is given by Ewald. He suggests that it means a net of goat's hair, such as is used for protection from mosquitoes, the plague of the country. The word is only once employed, and from its etymology signifies what is *twisted* or *plaited*, and therefore may well refer to a net made of goat's hair. Covering the figure with a cloth alludes to the wide *beged* or plaid in which it is common to enwrap oneself. To suppose that Michal would take the image of a household god and employ it for that purpose is reasonable enough, and the suggestion of pillows being used for sanative ends is far-fetched and wide of the mark. Michal, we are told distinctly, "loved David" (1 Sam. xviii. 20). He was a handsome youth, and might well on that account, as well as by his valour and skill in music, inspire the affections of a Hebrew maid. This love was evidently

returned, and the union seems to have been so far a happy one. Probably had nothing occurred to separate the two, they might have lived on in peace, and spent a wedded life of singular prosperity, saving David from the sins and sorrows which followed. The effect of their separation on the character and destiny of both has scarcely obtained the attention it claims. It will be noticed by me again.

S.

———

THE SCHOOL OF THE PROPHETS

1 Samuel 19:18-24

DAVID had now to evade not merely the sudden paroxysms of Saul's wrath, but the fixed and avowed purpose of the latter to effect his destruction, in the face of the oath which had been made to Jonathan. Any step he might now take was of the utmost importance to David, and might be pregnant with ulterior consequences. He, therefore, wisely resolved to repair to Samuel at Ramah, to obtain the advantage of his counsels and experience. Whether there had been any intercourse between them during the years which had passed since the anointing of David, we do not learn. On account of the suspicious character of Saul, and the probability that too close an intercourse would have led him to suppose that some collusion existed between them, and that Samuel was preparing to bring the son of Jesse forward, as the worthier man destined to fill the throne, it is probable that there had been little, if any, communication between him and David. It was not needed. They knew enough of each other without it. David knew that Samuel had relinquished all part in public affairs, and was solely occupied in his religious duties as prophet, and in the superintendence and instruction of the college of religious young men, which he had established at the rural hamlet of Naioth, in the vicinity of Ramah. There they were instructed in sacred learning and religious exercises, and were led to cultivate, especially by psalmody and music, the devotional feelings which might fit them, when occasion called, to become the messengers of God and teachers of the people. Samuel, on his part, could not be ignorant of the public history of David; and we may conceive the interest with which he beheld the providence of God gradually leading this young man forward in his appointed path and to his destined station. The purposes of God were ripening every hour; and Samuel was content to wait, knowing well what the end must be.

David not only sought counsel of the prophet, but probably expected that with him he might find safety and protection. The school at Naioth formed a sanctuary which even Saul, he might think, would not be likely to invade. Besides, the presence of Samuel alone must surely be a sufficient protection from outrage. It is true, this step might confirm the suspicions of Saul as to his being the man whom Samuel had announced as the heir of his throne. Yet the movement would not be in itself conclusive, seeing that it was, doubtless, still the practice for every one who was in great perplexity, to repair to the venerable prophet for counsel and advice.

At Ramah David reported to Samuel all the particulars of Saul's conduct towards him; and on hearing this, the prophet took him to his college at Naioth, as if to put him into sanctuary there. At this place the son of Jesse remained some time before Saul learned where he was. These were, no doubt, happy days with him. Here he was in an atmosphere congenial to his best feelings, his highest tastes, and his holiest aspirations; and here his accomplishments, in sacred minstrelsy and song, had ample scope and exercise, enabling him to join heart and soul in their harmonious "prophesyings," and doubtless endearing him greatly to the good men who had their quiet dwelling there. There were probably moments when, feeling sick of the turmoils of public life, and tired of the suspicions and persecutions which followed him, he would have been content to abandon his high career for the peaceful and holy life he was now allowed to share. It may even be possible that such was his intention, and that he hoped this voluntary retirement would abate the suspicions of Saul, and mollify his hatred.

But it was not so to be. When Saul learned to what place David had retired, he sent a body of men to apprehend him. These men, however, no sooner came to the sacred place, and beheld the prophets engaged in their sacred exercises, led by the venerable Samuel, than their hearts were smitten. They felt that they dared not attempt any violence, and they stood contentedly, swelling by their voices the loud chorus of praise to God.

This occurred to two other sets of emissaries —three in all; and at last Saul determined to go himself, and execute on the spot the fell purposes of his will. So forth he went. On his approach to Ramah, he came to the great well of Sechu, and finding there a number of people who had come from the town for water, he inquired of them where Samuel and David then were. On hearing that they were at Naioth, he turned his steps in that direction; but he had proceeded only a little way, when the Spirit which had moved his messengers, fell upon him also—with this difference, that they had not thus been moved till they reached the presence of Samuel and his pupils; whereas Saul felt the Spirit come upon him while he was on the road, giving him, for the time, the heart of another man. This is very remarkable. The messengers, like Saul himself on a former occasion, may be supposed to have been influenced by a sympathy with what they saw and heard, when they came into the presence of the prophets; but now the heart of Saul is moved in the absence of all such associations, as if purposely to show that the change wrought in him was the immediate work of Him who holds the hearts of all men in His hand. It showed, also, that this power was not confined to place or persons, and that the prophesyings at Naioth were owing to no influence of example—to no intoxicating vapours, or to the temperature of the air, as was suspected of some of the heathen oracles of old.

Thus the king went on singing in high excitement the praises of God; and when he came to Naioth, and entered the presence of Samuel— between whom and himself an angry scene might have been expected but for this divine intervention—he cast off his weapons, and the outer robes which belonged to his rank, and stood among the sons of the prophets as one of themselves, taking his part in their holy chants. Thus disarrayed of all that marked the king or the warrior, Saul, when the "prophesyings" were ended, lay down exhausted or entranced all the remainder of that day, and all the ensuing night. It is said that "he lay down naked," which we have interpreted to mean, that he divested himself of his outer raiment, which from its looseness could be easily slipped off, and remained in his closer inner vesture and girdle. This is not the only instance in which the term "naked" is thus applied in Scripture. We have another in the order given to the prophet Isaiah to put off his sackcloth, and go "naked and barefoot" for three years. This was to denote, that the Egyptians and Æthiopians were to be carried away captives in the like guise by the Assyrians. It was not, however, the custom to strip captives altogether naked; but only to deprive them of good clothes and flowing vestures, and to give them others shorter and more sordid, that they might be the more fit for service. Apart from this, no one who reflects on the matter will imagine that the prophet literally remained three whole years without any covering, in a climate, the winter cold of which is much more severe than we are apt to think. The same use of the term "naked," may be recognized among other ancient nations. Thus Aurelius Victor relates, that those who were sent to summon L. C. Cincinnatus to assume the dictatorship, found him "naked," ploughing on the other side of the Tiber. This can hardly mean that he was entirely without clothing; and that it does merely signify that he wrought with no clothing but his inner garment, is intimated by Livy, who, in relating the same occurrence, says that, on being thus summoned, Cincinnatus called to his wife, Rucca, for his gown or toga, that he might appear fit to accompany them.

Indeed, we need not go far to look for illustrations of this limited signification of the word "naked;" for it is common enough with ourselves, especially among women, to say that one is "naked" who has not adequate clothing.

It will appear, then, that Saul's being naked consisted in his being without the outer robes which he usually wore in public; and this is the sense in which David was "naked" when he played on his harp before the ark of God.

The following comment of Keil on this remarkable narrative deserves the attention of the thoughtful student. "This miraculous seizure by the Spirit of God was repeated, . . . so that Saul was obliged to relinquish the attempt to seize David. This result, however, we cannot regard as the principal object of the whole occurrence, as Vatablus does when he says, 'The spirit of prophecy came upon Saul, that David might the more easily escape from his power.' Calvin's remarks go much deeper into the meaning : 'God,' he says, 'changed their (the messengers') thoughts and purpose, not only so that they failed to apprehend David according to the royal command, but so

that they actually became the companions of the prophets. And God effected this, that the fact itself might show how He holds the hearts of men in His hand and power, and turns and moves them according to His will.' Even this, however, does not bring out the full meaning of the miracle, and more especially fails to explain why the same thing should have happened to Saul in an intensified degree. Upon this point Calvin simply observes, that 'Saul ought indeed to have been strongly moved by these things, and to have discerned the impossibility of his accomplishing anything by fighting against the Lord ; but he was so hardened that he did not perceive the hand of God : for he hastened to Naioth himself, when he found that his servants mocked him ;' and in this proceeding on Saul's part he discovers a sign of his increasing hardness of heart. Saul and his messengers, the zealous performers of his will, ought no doubt to have learned, from what happened to them in the presence of the prophets, that God had the hearts of men in His power, and guided them at His will ; but they were also to be seized by the might of the Spirit of God, which worked in the prophets, and thus brought to the consciousness that Saul's raging against David was fighting against Jehovah and His Spirit, and so to be led to give up the evil thoughts of their heart. Saul was seized by this mighty influence of the Spirit of God in a more powerful manner than his servants were, both because he had most obstinately resisted the leadings of divine grace, and also in order that, if it were possible, his hard heart might be broken and subdued by the power of divine grace."[1]

P.

THE SLING AND STONE

1 Samuel 17

AMONG the events which have, during the past week, been considered, the combat of David with Goliath stands forward with special prominence ; and to some of the circumstances of that great deed, our attention may this day be profitably directed.

Although we do not, with some, think that "*these* things are an allegory," or that this great combat was a type of our Lord's victory over Satan, or even of man's combat with the enemy of his soul, it is impossible for the experienced Christian to read it without being reminded of eventful passages in his own spiritual history. There is no doubt some mysterious connection between even the external things of Scripture history, and the inner things of the spiritual life, which "the wise" are enabled, by the Spirit's

[1] *Commentary on the Books of Samuel.*

teaching, to discern, and which renders the seemingly least spiritual parts of holy writ richly nourishing to their souls.

The reader will remember the feeling with which the son of Jesse undertook this combat. It is with precisely the same feeling that we should advance to the contest with the enemy of our souls. He is far more powerful than we; and those who have not faith to oppose to him the invincible weapons of the Spirit of God, waver and tremble as he advances. But the experienced Christian, whose faith is unshaken, looks around him, and beholds with wonder so many of his brethren tremble before the defier of God's sacramental host. Their fear is unknown to him. He inquires with David, "What shall be done to the man that taketh away the reproach from Israel?" And the answer is, "The man who killeth him, the king will enrich with great riches,"—the "riches of the glory of His inheritance." "He that overcometh," the Lord says, "shall inherit all things, and I will be his God, and he shall be my son." [1] Faith in this promise, and the hope of attaining the reward, determine him to exertion. He heeds not the reproaches of the fearful brother who dares not resist the enemy; he will not listen to those who would persuade him that his strength is not equal to the enterprise; for he knows that the strength on which he relies is not his own, but that of the All-Strong—the Strengthener. Firmly, therefore, he advances to the conflict, exclaiming, "I come to thee in the name of the Lord of hosts, the God of Israel, whom thou hast defied."

This, and no other, is the spirit in which we must struggle with all the temptations of the world, the devil, and the flesh. "Not that we are sufficient of ourselves to think anything as of ourselves, but our sufficiency is of God." [2] With this sufficiency we can do everything required of us. "I can," says Paul, "do all things through Christ who strengtheneth me." [3] So can we. But we must remember, that from the moment we renounce His strength and rely upon our own, we are no longer to be compared to the commissioned servant of God, executing His purposes upon the evil and impious, but are rather like the simple unguarded youth that David would have been, had he acted on no other confidence than his own.

Although the weapons of our warfare are not

carnal, yet we must use such weapons as we have —such as we best know how to use. The power and courage which David possessed would have availed him little without his sling and his stone; and the powers of resistance which God has graciously consented to afford us, will be equally useless unless we apply them through the appointed means: these are prayer, watchfulness, resistance to sin, resolutions of holiness, and a frequent participation of the means of grace. The gifts of God avail us nothing without the disposition to use them; and this disposition is also His gift, which will not be refused to any that diligently seek it. So God gives the sun, the rain, the soil, the seed; but man must till the field and sow the ground, or else there will be no harvest. It is God that gives the increase; but Paul must plant and Apollos water. It is God who gives the talents; but man must put them out to the exchangers, or else Christ at His coming will not receive His own with usury. The grace of God is an invincible weapon; but we must employ it, or it will rust—it will no more fight our spiritual battle, than a sword will defend us while we delay to draw it, or than the stones of the brook could avail David while they only lay in the sling. Again, the sling and the stone would both have been useless, had not the Spirit of God guided the hand of David; and in like manner must the Christian be convinced that the means which are given to him of contending with sin, are only efficacious because "it is God that worketh in us to will and to do." [1] The assurance that all our strength is from above, and the determination actively to employ that strength, must go together: neither will effect anything without the other; but the two combined will, by the blessing of God, finally beat down Satan under our feet.

If there be any who, like Eliab, are not only afraid to engage in the contest themselves, but are ready to reproach us with "pride and naughtiness of heart," because we have determined to follow the Lord wholly, and to subject our conversation to a rule of severer holiness than they can bring themselves to bear—let us answer with David, "Is there not a cause?" There is every conceivable cause. "There is gratitude for love which eternity could never repay; there is love which eternity could never satisfy; and there is even private interest, which

[1] Revelation 21:7.　[2] 2 Corinthians 3:5.　[3] Philippians 4:13.

[1] Philippians 2:12,13.

is more effectually promoted by the service of God than by any other assignable means." [1]

There may, again, be some who, like Saul, will tell us that we are too weak to contend with all the difficulties which lie before us, and they will offer us, as Saul offered David his armour, a panoply of worldly precepts and maxims for the conduct of life, taken from their own experience, and adapted to persons like themselves; but which, not being founded on the strict and undeviating model of Christ's law, are no more fitted to our use, than the massive and cumbersome armour of Saul became the slender and unaccustomed David. Our answer must be "We cannot go with these." We "have not proved them;" and did we prove them, we should find them useless indeed. We must go in the might of the Lord, and in that alone; and in this we shall go forth conquering and to conquer the enemies of our peace, till we receive the end of our faith—the salvation of our souls.

THE FAREWELL

1 Samuel 20

In the remarkable turning of the heart of Saul —so full when he set out, of fell, and probably bloody purposes—and in the long entrancement in which he lay, several objects may be discerned: first, to magnify the power of the Lord over the hearts of men; then to protect Samuel and his college from the king's wrath, for we must not reckon too much upon his forbearance even towards the aged prophet, when we consider what was afterwards done to the priests at Nob for the shelter they gave to David; and lastly, his altered state of feeling was designed to frustrate all the king's designs, and to give the son of Jesse an opportunity of escaping to a safe distance before he became himself again.

David now saw clearly that his life at the royal court was ended, and that it only remained for him, thenceforth, to keep himself beyond the reach of Saul, and await in patience the progress of events. This was probably also the purport of the advice that he received from Samuel.

[1] Rev. H. Thompson's *Davidica*.

Yet he took advantage of the king's state to return to Gibeah, wasting, as some may deem, the precious time which might have served him well for his escape. But every generous heart will appreciate his motive in subjecting himself to this risk—it was to see once more his beloved Jonathan, the friend and brother of his soul, and to obtain his sanction to the step he was about to take. The interview between these two generous and high-minded young men is deeply interesting; and although there are longer speeches in the historical Scriptures, there is no *conversation*—with the natural changes of interlocution—reported at equal length. The object of David was to convince his friend of the reality of the danger he was in, and the necessity of his departure. This was opposed by Jonathan, partly from the love he bore to David, and from the pain he would feel in being for an indefinitely long period separated from him, and partly from the charity that thinketh no evil, rendering him reluctant to judge harshly of his father. He could not bring himself to believe that, after the oath which Saul had taken to make no attempt against David's life, he had any real intention to destroy him. He urged that he was in his father's confidence, and would surely have known had any such intention existed. The reader will do well to note the admirable delicacy of David's reply to this: "Thy father certainly knoweth that I have found grace in thine eyes, and he saith, *Let not Jonathan know this lest he be grieved;* but truly, as the Lord liveth, and as thy soul liveth, there is but a step between me and death." To avoid giving pain to Jonathan, he avoids expressing or implying that his father had any distrust of him, and gives it quite another turn, as if Saul conceals his designs upon David from his son only to spare his feelings.

Jonathan could not, however, be satisfied without further proof of his father's present state of feeling towards David. He probably hoped, from David's account, that whatever had been his intentions, a more effectual change had been wrought in him at Ramah than his friend supposed. To satisfy him, David agreed to defer his flight. It was arranged that he should visit his family at Bethlehem, and return in three days to his former place of concealment, near the stone of Ezel, where, by a concerted signal,

Jonathan was to apprise him of the result of his inquiry, it being uncertain but that he might be so watched, as to render another interview unsafe. The next day was the feast of the new moon, when the king was wont to entertain the high officers of his court; and David, as his son-in-law, and a high military officer, had a seat at his table. Saul knew that David had been seen at Gibeah, and concluded that the change which he had seen come over himself at Naioth, had led him to think that there was nothing more to fear. He therefore expected he would appear in his place at the feast; but his place remained empty. The king made no remark then, supposing that some accident prevented his attendance, and that he would doubtless be present the following day; for that day also was a feast for the proclamation of the new moon, according to its actual appearing; and the appearance being uncertain, sometimes in the evening, at noon, or at midnight, two days were observed as a feast in honour of the occasion. Still David was absent, and Saul asked Jonathan, with all the indifference he could assume, "Wherefore cometh not the son of Jesse to meat, neither yesterday nor to-day?" Jonathan answered, that he had asked for, and obtained, his permission to attend a family celebration at Bethlehem. On hearing this, the king could restrain himself no longer. Looking upon his son as one who was infatuated, by his love for David, into madly throwing away his own prospects and those of his house, he broke forth into violent and insulting abuse of him. To any Oriental, nothing is so grievously insulting as a reproach cast upon his mother; so Saul, to sting his son to the uttermost, spoke contemptuously of his mother, regardless of the fact that Jonathan's mother was his own wife: "Thou son of the perverse, rebellious woman," etc. There are some traces of this form of abuse, in principle, among the least refined portion of our own population; but in the East, no man is too high or too refined to be above it. Even a son will abuse his brother by casting contumely upon *his* mother, regardless of the fact that she is also his own mother, and whom, as such, he venerates and loves.[1] The mother herself is not held to be affronted in such cases, but the son who hears such words applied to her is insulted,

[1] So Antar to his uterine brother: "Thou base-born! thou son of a foul mother! thou didst instigate my master to beat me."—*Journal of Sacred Literature*, v. 25.

and is meant to be insulted, beyond expiation. Jonathan, however, remembered that the man who spoke was his father, and that the lot of his friend was in the balance; so he restrained himself, and the king went on to tell him that while the son of Jesse lived, the prospect of his own inheritance of the crown was nothing worth. This was the first time that Saul expressed that conviction, showing that the previous flight of David to Samuel had turned into certainty the suspicions he had before entertained. Even this did not move the firm friendship of Jonathan, who seems to have, before this, reached the conviction that David was indeed the man chosen of God to reign—according to the announcement of Samuel, which must have been known to him—and to have brought his mind to acquiesce in it, seeing that the man so chosen was one whom he loved as his own soul. It was in the recollection of this, among the other manifestations of his deep and self-sacrificing affection, that David, in a later day, characterized Jonathan's regard for him in the memorable words, "Thy love to me was wonderful, passing the love of women." So now, in this trying moment, Jonathan ventured to speak for his friend, urging justly that a man was to be judged by his acts and intentions, and that those of David were laudable and pure. "Wherefore," he asked, "shall he be slain? What hath he done?" The answer was from the javelin of the infuriated king, which this time he cast at his own son. He missed his aim; and his son, regardless of the insult and danger to himself, but seeing from this that his father was determined to slay David, arose from the table and went out "in fierce anger," leaving his food untasted.

Early the next morning he went out with his bow into the field, where David was concealed, attended by a boy, the words used to whom, in directing him to find the arrows which his master shot, as if at a mark, formed the signal previously agreed upon. The signal was that of danger. But the lad having been sent back to the town with the arrows, and there being no one in sight, the two friends could not refuse themselves the satisfaction of one more farewell interview. It is, and was, the custom, in approaching a sovereign or prince, to pause, and bow at regulated intervals. Xenophon ascribes the origin of the practice to Cyrus;[1] but it was of earlier date, although he

[1] *Cyropædia*, l. viii., c. 23.

may have first introduced it among the Persians. David thus testified the respect due to Jonathan's high station, in advancing to meet him; but when they came near, everything but their heart-brotherhood was forgotten: "They kissed one another, and wept one with another, until David exceeded." But time was precious, and delay dangerous; so, bidding each other hastily farewell, they separated, to have but one more interview in life.

DAVID AT NOB

1 Samuel 21

THE tabernacle was at this time at Nob. This place must have been in the immediate vicinity of Jerusalem, on the Mount of Olives, or a continuation of this ridge, a little north of its summit and north-east of the city; but no trace of it has yet been discovered. This may be taken to have been not more than five miles south from Gibeah. It was to this place that David repaired after his separation from Jonathan. As the Sabbath—or the sunset of Friday—had already commenced when he reached Nob, and as it was not lawful to travel on the Sabbath day, it seems to us that, seeing it was not safe for him to remain at Gibeah, and the little time which remained before the commencement of the Sabbath would preclude further travelling, he had concluded to go to Nob as a place of safety, till the termination of the holy day should enable him to resume his journey. At that place he would be safe, because, supposing his presence there were known, no one could travel thither after him on the Sabbath day, neither could any one who might be at Nob when he came, go to Gibeah to give intelligence of his arrival. It may be supposed, therefore, that David went to Nob first, because it was just at a sufficient distance for him to reach it before the commencement of the Sabbath; and this being the case, he would prefer it to other places equally within reach, not only from its being, as a sanctuary, a place of greater safety than any other, but from the natural desire, that the last Sabbath he was likely for some time to enjoy in the land, should be spent in that holy place, and among the servants of the Lord.

There seems ground for suspecting that, from the time of his parting with Jonathan—if not, indeed, from the time of his leaving Naioth—David had lost some of his trust in God. In contemplation of the implacable hatred with which he was pursued, and the dangers which beset all his movements, and in the face of the now publicly avowed intention to destroy him, his heart failed him, and he no longer rested secure in the confidence of the Lord's all-sufficient protection. He felt that his position was altered. Hitherto he had to meet, or rather to evade, what had been the private, unreasoning, and fluctuating antipathy of Saul. But *now*, the king no longer had any reserves or restraints; he had publicly denounced him as marked for slaughter; publicly declared his belief that he was a traitor who aimed at the crown, and with whom no terms were any longer to be kept. The fact that he had been anointed by Samuel was now publicly known—even the Philistines knew it; and David could not but feel that the public knowledge of that fact laid upon him heavy responsibilities, from which he had been before exempt; and that it was impossible now to hope for any reconciliation with a prince of Saul's temper, or to expect any safety while within his reach. He might have reflected that all these things did but tend to bring his claims and destination into public notice; that the pursuing hatred of the king was in fact but the means of working out the plan of the Lord's providence towards him; and that it offered no real ground of discouragement or fear to one who believed that He was well able to accomplish all the purposes of His will. His plain course had been "by patient continuance in well-doing," to put to shame the calumnies of malicious men; and, while taking all reasonable care for his own safety, to honour the Lord by the confidence which he evinced in the sufficiency of His protection. But it was not so. He began to look to the matter in its simply human points of view; and *then* he began to despair—to be afraid. He who had subdued the lion and the bear,—he who had stood up against the giant whose very presence had dismayed the armies of Israel,—he now at last quailed at the fear of Saul; and having lost his shield of faith, he became, like the shorn Samson, "weak as other men," and has left us a memorial of what the best of men may become when left to themselves.

This is the view we take of the transactions

now immediately before us. We have indeed met with elaborate and ingenious vindications of David's proceedings throughout, in which very learned and worthy men have laboured to show in what degree it is lawful to lie and to deceive —thereby compromising the sacred interests of truth and righteousness, in order to vindicate the character of Jesse's son. Now, the character of David is very dear to us, and he has ever been the object of our sympathy, our admiration, and our love. But truth is dearer still than even the character of David; and we must not consent to call evil good, and to put darkness for light, because the evil was David's, and the darkness David's. If we were to set about proving that all David did was right, and the best that could be done, we should not only contradict the Scripture, but have work enough upon our hands. Far be it from us to claim for him that which belongs to One only of all who ever walked the earth. Let us admit the errors and weaknesses

of David, as they occur, and our task grows easy, and his history becomes consistent and clear; but let us uphold him through good and evil, through "the sweet and the bitter," and we soon find ourselves "in wandering mazes lost," and our perceptions of the broad landmarks between truth and error very painfully disordered.

We regard David, then, as under a spiritual cloud from the time he left Jonathan, onward to a point which we shall indicate in the proper place. This cloud, we first trace distinctly in his declaration to Jonathan, that there was but "a step between him and death." Now there were as many steps between him and death then as at any other time; but an excessive fear had come upon him, which for the time made him forgetful of God, and urged him to seek his safety by any feasible means, whether right or wrong.

So, first he comes to Nob, with not only one lie, but with a whole nest of lies in his mouth—

TABLE OF SHEW-BREAD

the more heinous when we consider the place in which, and the person to whom, they were uttered, and when we recollect the danger into which they were calculated to bring that friendly and venerable person, and *did* bring him and his, even unto death; whereas, had he been sincere and candid, there can be little doubt that the high priest would have found means of discharging the duties of hospitality and assist-

ance, without any apparent compromise of his duty to his sovereign. As it was, David, aware that the priest would be astonished to see a person of his rank arrive alone—without the guard and attendants, with whom he had usually been seen at that place—prepared an ingenious tale to delude the pontiff. He told him that he was upon most urgent and private business for the king, citing the very words which, as he said, Saul had used in intrusting this secret mission to him; and his servants, he alleged, had been directed to meet him at a certain place. This, of course, left the high priest to understand, that whatever aid was rendered to him, would be advancing the king's service.

The unsuspecting high priest, whose name was Ahimelech, finding that David wanted bread, went so far as to give him some of that which had just been taken (at the commencement of the Sabbath day) from the table of the shew-bread in the tabernacle, when the new bread had been laid on, and which, in strictness, it was not lawful for any but the priests to eat. There was no other; and we might be surprised at this, did we not know that bread was prepared from day to day. On any other day bread might have been baked to meet any want that arose; but this could not be done on the Sabbath, and there was hence no bread to be had but the shew-bread, which would have sufficed for the use of the priests themselves on that day.

Having been furnished with bread, David intimated that in his haste he had left the court without a sword, and expressed a wish that one might be provided for him. He was told there was no sword but that of Goliath, which was wrapped up in a cloth, and laid up in the tabernacle. This David claimed, and it was given to him. This fact seems to prove, that in Israel swords were not worn even by military men when not on actual service or on a journey.

David was not the only person detained at Nob over the Sabbath day. There was also present one Doeg, a proselyte of Edom, high in the confidence of Saul, and holding the post of chief herdsman, that is, having the management of this branch of the king's property. He was arrested, by the arrival of the Sabbath, on his way to

Gibeah, and was not therefore aware of the recent occurrences, nor did he find any ground for question or interference. He knew, however, that David was in growing disfavour with his master, and he watched narrowly all that passed. David was well acquainted with the malignant temper

COSTUME OF HIGH PRIEST

of this man, and confessed afterwards, that while he was misleading the high priest, he was aware that the attention shown to him at Nob, would, through the presence of Doeg, bring them to ruin. "I knew it," he says, with bitter remorse, "I knew it that day when Doeg the Edomite was there, that he would surely tell Saul; I have occasioned the death of all the persons of thy father's house." Yes, it was no less. They did perish. When Saul was inquiring about David, and was lamenting that none would or could tell whither he had gone, Doeg related that he had seen him cherished by the priests at Nob, but he did not state the representations from David under which that assistance had been given. On hearing this, the king sent for all the priests, and

COSTUME OF A PRIEST

on their arrival vehemently accused Ahimelech of being in a conspiracy with David against him. The high priest repelled the charge with dignity and force, declaring that he was, at the time, utterly ignorant of there being any cause of complaint against him. But the king would not be convinced; and his dreadful words were, " Thou shalt surely die, Ahimelech, thou and all thy

father's house." And forthwith he ordered the guard to fall upon them, condescending to give a reason, " Because their hand also is with David, and because they knew when he fled, and did not show it to me." But for once he was not obeyed. No hand moved against the priests of the Lord. If the king had been wise, he would have seen from this the danger of proceeding with this horrid purpose. But he was *not* wise; he would not be instructed. In his obstinate ferocity he told Doeg to execute his purpose; and that person, assisted probably by his men, and not awed by the considerations which weighed upon the minds of native Israelites, turned upon them, and slew in that one day no fewer than " fourscore and five persons that did wear a linen ephod."

From that day Saul was a doomed and ruined man. The atrocious massacre filled every humane and religious mind with disgust and horror, while it made the priestly body throughout the whole land, and in all its departments, inveterately hostile, and led them to look towards the son of Jesse as the instrument of their security and vengeance. Abiathar, the son, and virtual successor, of the murdered high priest, escaped to David, and by his presence, possessing as he did the means of officially consulting the Lord, gave weight and dignity to his position, so that the public attention became more and more directed to him; while Saul declined daily in public estimation, and sunk more and more into the deepest glooms of horror and despair.

The site of Nob has at length been discovered. Gibeah, as is well known, stood upon a conical hill about three miles north of Jerusalem. A mile south of Gibeah is another conical hill. On its summit and sides are traces of a small but very ancient town. There are large cut stones, cisterns hewn in the rock, and old foundations. The name appears to be lost; but the site corresponds exactly to that of Nob, being south of Gibeah, not far distant from it, and commanding a view of Jerusalem, as indicated by Isaiah (x. 28).

It appears that, after the fall of Shiloh, the national sanctuary was set up at Nob. A colony of priests gathered round it. Eighty-five persons ministered there in white linen, and their families occupied the houses of the town. David's visit was a fatal one to them. Saul, in his fierce wrath, massacred them all, with one solitary exception. There is not in the whole scope of history a more wanton act of savage cruelty than this : " And Nob, the city of the priests, smote he with the edge of the sword, both men and women, children and sucklings, and oxen, and asses, and sheep, with the edge of the sword."

Though Gibeah and Nob were in full view of each other, there lay between them a deep rocky glen. In it doubtless took place that tender and romantic interview between David and Jonathan. I saw as I stood in it many a high rock and projecting cliff, behind which David might lie concealed while Jonathan shot the arrows, and gave the preconcerted signal which told him that he must leave for ever the court of Saul.

P.

The site of Nob is not yet clearly fixed by geographers. Lieutenant Conder, of the Palestine Exploration, has paid much attention to the subject, and he considers that *Nob* is identical with *Gibeon*. The high place of Gibeon is believed by Dr. Stanley to be the same as *Neby Samwell;* but *El Jib* has been also fixed upon, just by where the road from Jerusalem to the Mediterranean branches into two. Near that spot is a tank of considerable size, supposed by Dr. Robinson to be "the pool of Gibeon." The position of Gibeon being thus unsettled, the identification of Nob with Gibeon does not help us much. In Neby Samwell much is found to recommend Mr. Conder's opinion, though the union of the two names *Nob* and *Gibeon* in one place is not without serious difficulty. "The view from Nebi Samwell is splendid, and its steep sides form a picturesque detail, contrasting with the rounder outlines of the Judean and Benjamite summits." "In a report written last winter," says Mr. Conder, "I noticed the curious rock cut approach to the great Church (still standing on Mount Samwell, and built by the Crusaders), which we were inclined to attribute to crusading date ; it does not, however, show any very distinctive marks of date, and may very well be older. It is true that no permanent structure was erected at Nob ; but a flat court of some kind would be necessary for the outer enclosure ; and when we reflect on the discovery by Major Wilson, of a similar court-yard at Shiloh, it seems very probable that this cutting was originally intended for the accommodation of the tabernacle." This is plausible, but not conclusive, and the site of Nob remains an open question.— *Exploration Statement*, 1875, 34, 94.

S.

DAVID AT GATH

1 Samuel 21:10-15

THE step which David took on leaving Nob seems to us equally objectionable with his conduct there, and was equally the result of the unworthy fears which now oppressed his spirit. He WENT OVER TO THE PHILISTINES. He probably argued that there was no safety for him in the dominions of Saul, unless he assumed an attitude of self-defence, which would look like hostility and rebellion. He must therefore leave the country. But whither was he to go ? The neighbouring states were at peace with Saul, and would not probably provoke his anger by affording shelter to one whom he regarded as his enemy. The Philistines being at war with Israel, would not be likely to give him up. But he should also have considered what aspect the act would bear in the eyes of Israel on the one side, and of the Philistines on the other. The Israelites could not but view it as a desertion of their great general to the enemy, whose protection could only be secured by services *against* his own country. The Philistines, on their side, if they agreed to afford shelter to one who had done them so much harm, would expect him to employ his experience and talents for their advantage against Israel. In the desire to stand well with both, he could not maintain his position without a degree of double-dealing adverse to all truth and honour. It could not, therefore, be of God that this step was taken ; and it was thus a further manifestation of David's *distrust* of the sufficiency of the Lord's protection, confidence in which had been hitherto, and was to be hereafter, the crowning glory of his great career.

By the good providence of God, David was spared—through what seemed at first a situation of trial and danger—from his tremendous perils.

It must be confessed to have been a bold step, so far as human confidence is concerned, for him to put himself into the hands of those whom he had so often humiliated. But, on the other hand, he might reckon with confidence upon the protection which the Eastern people invariably extend, and the hospitality which they show, even to an enemy who claims shelter with them ; and there was room to think that the satisfaction of the Philistines, in seeing the Israelites deprived of their most renowned warrior, would preponderate over their resentment at the injuries he had inflicted upon their nation. In fact, it seems that Achish, the king of Gath, to which place he went, was, in the first instance, well enough disposed to receive him ; but presently strange and dangerous murmurs passed among the lords and princes. "Is not this David, the *king of the land?* Did they not sing to one another of him in dances, saying, Saul hath slain his thousands and David his ten thousands ?" By this we see how perfect the intelligence of the Philistines was, as to what passed among the Israelites. They knew of this special point in the songs of the Hebrew maidens; and they were even already aware of what had so recently transpired, as to his having been anointed as the future king of Israel. Even David was surprised to find them in possession of this fact. He saw at once that the treatment he might expect as one recognized as being destined, by his position, to become the public enemy of the Philistines, might be very different from that which would have been afforded him as a fugitive general. He was greatly dismayed. He probably saw that the countenance of the king himself changed at this intelligence. What was he to do? This we cannot answer, as we are not sufficiently acquainted with all the minute circumstances which might help to a right conclusion. We can, however, see that what David decided to do under the influence of instant apprehension, is not by any means entitled to our approbation. It was an *acted* untruth, and such untruths are not more innocent than oral ones. It would have become him much better, if he conceived himself in such great danger, to have prayed in his heart to the Lord, and then waited for the seemly and becoming means of deliverance which He would without doubt have opened for his imperilled servant. But "he feigned himself mad," or perhaps to fall into a fit of epilepsy, which was in ancient times regarded as a form of madness. This character he acted to such disgusting perfection, that the court had no doubt of the reality of his affliction. He not only "scrabbled upon the wall," but let his slaver fall down upon his beard. This last was convincing. Considering the regard in which the beard is held, the care taken of it, and the solicitude of the owner to protect it from insult and pollution, who could possibly doubt the abject and absolute madness of the man who thus defiled his own beard? On the other hand, a sort of respect for the persons thus afflicted, as if they were under some kind of supernatural influence, has always existed, and does now exist, in the East; so that David knew that his personal safety, and even his freedom, were guaranteed by the belief in his madness. Such was the case. The king was not, perhaps, sorry to be thus relieved from the difficulty which he saw to be gathering round the question. He therefore turned, in seeming, or real wrath, to his servants, rebuking them for admit-

ting a madman to his presence. "Lo, ye see the man is mad: wherefore have ye brought him to me? Have I need of madmen, that ye have brought this fellow to play the madman in my presence? Shall this fellow come into my house?" The Jewish writers think there was more emphasis than we are aware of in Achish's asking if *he* had need of madmen. They tell us that the king's wife and daughter were both mad, and that while David was simulating madness without, they were exhibiting the reality within, so that poor Achish might well think he had already quite enough of this.

We should like to be able to entertain the belief that the epileptic madness of David was real and not feigned. Some, in their anxiety to vindicate his character, have laboured hard to prove that this was the case. Both the Septuagint and the Vulgate versions intimate that it was real; and the curious in these matters know, that the question whether the madness of Hamlet was assumed or real, has not been more ably, earnestly, or ingeniously discussed, than the truth or simulation of David's madness. To us it seems, that the plain meaning of the text is, that the madness was assumed; but we are ready to admit, that were the text less explicit, we should see no improbability in a sudden attack of epilepsy under such circumstances. There is an anecdote which shows this in the life of St. Bernard. This renowned Abbot once went into Guienne, to the court of the anti-Pope, Analectus II., to set right some matters which in his judgment had gone wrong through the counsels of William X., Duke of Aquitaine and Count of Toulouse. Having celebrated mass, Bernard stood forth, with the host in his hands, and uttered a most terrible denunciation against the duke, who was present. He had no sooner ended, than the prince fell to the ground trembling and powerless. The soldiers lifted him up, but his countenance was altogether changed; he regarded no one, nor could any coherent words be drawn from him. He heaved forth profound sighs, and presently fell into epileptic convulsions, letting his saliva fall upon his beard. A striking instance this of the effects which strong terror may produce upon even resolute minds. It is the reality of that which David feigned.

David was a man of the most extraordinary coolness in danger. His presence of mind seems never to have deserted him under any circumstance. It was shown in his combat with Goliath; it was shown in cutting off the skirt of Saul's robe in the cave; and in taking the water bottle and spear from beside the very pillow of the sleeping king. But never was there a more striking example of it than the scene acted before Achish in Gath. It was a bold act to enter that city with the sword of Goliath at his side. Having done so, and being recognized, most men would have considered the case hopeless. But the resources of David's mind were equal to any emergency. He feigned madness, "probably suggested," as Stanley observes, "by the ecstacies of the prophetic schools; violent gestures, playing on the gates of the city, as on a drum or cymbal, letting the beard grow (untrimmed), and foaming at the mouth." Many of the dervishes in the East act in the same way at present, and are venerated as saints by an ignorant and superstitious people. I have heard it said that Akeil Aga, a notorious Arab sheikh still living, when seized and imprisoned by the governor of Acre, escaped as David did, pretending to be a madman.[1]

P.

"As regards Gath, it is only necessary to say that the requirements of the narrative seem fully met by the Jell et Safi site (by the Vale of Elah, where David fought Goliath of Gath), advocated by Dr. Porter, and which alone fits with the description of the *Onomasticon* (a geographical work by Eusebius). Gath, so placed, guards the entrance of the Valley of Elah into the plain, and is about six miles from the scene of the conflict."—*Palestine Exploration Statement*, 1875, 194. It is remarkable and admonitory that David should lose his confidence, and betake himself to such a mean device, in the immediate neighbourhood of the spot where God had given him so signal a proof of His presence and succour.

S.

DAVID IN THE WILDERNESS

1 Samuel 24-25

WITH the necessity of returning into the land which was ruled by the man who sought his life, David recovered his strength of character, and the resources which lay in his dependence upon the guidance and protection of God. He felt that it would not be wise for him to go into any town. He could not venture even to his native town of Bethlehem. But he was aware that about six miles south-west from that town there was a large natural cavern, called the cave of Adullam; and in this he determined to take shelter for the present, until his further course should be made plain to him. The cave was well suited for the

[1] See Stanley's *Jewish Church*, ii. 62.

purpose. The mouth of it can only be approached on foot, along the side of steep cliffs; and it runs in by a long, winding, narrow passage, with small chambers or cavities on each side. With reasonable vigilance, it was impossible that he could here be discovered or surprised by any pursuers.

He soon contrived to make his retreat known to his own family, the principal members of which came to him there. Among these were Abishai, the son of his beloved sister Zeruiah, and probably his brother Joab—both afterwards the valiant and devoted upholders of their uncle's cause. Zeruiah must have been one of the eldest of Jesse's children, for her renowned sons seem not to have been much, if anything, younger than her youngest brother. Nor did these alone come; for no sooner did it transpire that David was in the neighbourhood, than a number of daring men of various characters flocked to him. Many, especially his near relatives, went out of regard to his person; many, because by this early adhesion to one whose future had become known, they expected to advance their eventual interests; many, because their circumstances were so bad, that they could not but be bettered by placing themselves under so valiant and successful a leader; many, because they were so immersed in debt, that their best chance against being made bondmen by their creditors, must be found in joining the fugitive; and many, who were "bitter of soul" (as the original has it)—whether from private affliction or from dissatisfaction with the state of affairs under Saul—were naturally drawn towards one whose position served to render him the proper organ and representative of public discontents and private wrongs.

The adhesion of four hundred of such men seemed to point out to David the course he had to take. It was no longer necessary that he should skulk about privately, from one hiding place to another—from house to house, and from cave to cave. He was enabled to take a stand upon the defensive, and to assume such a position before the public eye as would engage the interest of the people in his person and movements, and prevent his claims, his services, and his wrongs from passing out of mind. It was not his purpose to set himself forth as a competitor for the crown—*that* his sworn friendship for Jonathan, no less than his determination to await the course of the Lord's providence, forbade. Still, as an oppressed man, in a public position, who had rendered great services to the state, and whose life was unjustly pursued, the notions of the East would account it just and laudable, that, while abstaining from any offensive acts against the government, and shunning rather than seeking occasions of collision, he should organize such a power around him, in a body of attached and hardy followers, as might ensure his safety, and even bring the royal oppressor to some conditions of peace. We constantly meet with this in Eastern history. It necessarily arises from the absence of adequate checks upon the extravagances of the royal power on the one hand, and from the want of a lawful outlet for the expression of public discontent on the other. With us, opposition to the government is a recognized part of the public system, and therefore safe to all parties. It is parliamentary, it is legal, it is oral. In the East it of necessity takes a more demonstrative shape—the shape of organized bands, of weapons of war, of military action. David became in fact the leader of the opposition in the reign of king Saul, without more personal animosity to the sovereign, or any more immediate design upon the crown—except that he knew it would in the course of time come to him—than any leader of our own parliamentary opposition may be supposed to entertain. It is true, that all the opposition leaders of the East have not been so forbearing as David in this respect. This was the peculiar merit of his faith, of his real loyalty to Saul, and of his fixed determination that his own conduct should afford no justification of the inveterate hatred with which the king sought his destruction.

David knew that when he took this position, Bethlehem was no longer a place of safety for his parents, while, on the other hand, he was unwilling to expose them, in their old age, to the hardships and anxieties of the life he was to lead. He therefore took them over the river, and left them in charge of the king of Moab. The Moabites seem for a long time to have kept up a friendly connection with the Israelites; and David being now known as one anointed to be hereafter king in Israel, the fact would not be forgotten in Moab, and was probably dwelt on with national gratification, that he was a descendant of Ruth the Moabitess. It may be asked why he did not stay there himself, and why he had not in the first instance gone thither, instead of to the Philistines? But it is probable that the king of Moab, although ready enough to render any service that he could without danger, was not at all willing to involve his people in a war by harbouring David. David, however, was commanded by "Gad the seer," of whom mention is now first made, to return into the land of Israel. This Gad, it is likely, was an esteemed member of Samuel's college of the prophets, and had probably joined David at the instance of the aged prophet, who was now very near the close of his days. Abiathar also, the son of the murdered high priest Ahimelech, had fled to him after the massacre at Nob. He was virtually the high priest, and the recognized official medium of ascertaining the will of the Lord. The presence of both the high priests and the seer with David must have given great importance to his movements and position in the eyes of the people; and he was by no means unmindful of the advantages he thus possessed, for he consulted the sacred oracle as to all his movements, and implicitly followed the indications it afforded.

Two hundred more like-minded men joined him after his return to the land of Judah; and it must have become a matter of much consideration to him, how to sustain and employ so large a body of men consistently with his purpose of not taking a hostile attitude towards the king, nor of giving the people any cause of complaint against him. He found the means of employing them chiefly, it seems, in protecting the cattle in the wild and open border country, into which the great sheepmasters sent their flocks for pasture, from the depredations of their marauding neighbours, such as the Arabs, the Amalekites, the Jebusites, the Hittites, and others. This species of service creates a claim for a kind of tribute from the wealthy persons thus so essentially benefited, in food and other necessaries, which is almost invariably most willingly, and even thankfully, rendered, and when not so, is enforced as a matter of right. This part of David's history affords an example of this in the case of Nabal of Carmel, whose insulting refusal to afford any supplies to David's troop, by which his flocks had been protected in the wilderness, had brought destruction upon his head, but for the prudent intervention of his wife Abigail, who, without apprising her husband, hastened to meet the incensed hero with a most acceptable offering of provisions, and mollified his wrath by her prudent and persuasive words, which, no less than her comeliness, so engaged his esteem that he eventually made her his wife, for her husband shortly died heart-stricken when he was made acquainted with the danger to which his churlishness had exposed him.

———————

Much attention has been paid of late, both by M. Gannau, Lieut. Conder, and Mr. T. Drake, to the wanderings of David, and the identification of sites mentioned in the history of them.

David appears to have confined himself within an area of about twenty miles, around his native city, Bethlehem : generally managing to put himself on one side of that city when Saul was pursuing him on the other. The first flight was from Gibeah of Benjamin, probably the present *Jeba*, in a plateau overlooking the great *Michmash* Valley, in the centre of the inheritance of the tribe. He rested at *Nob*, wherever that was, and then descended to the *Shephalah*, the Philistine plain, and took refuge at Gath, supposed to be identical with the white mound of *Tell el Safi*, commanding the Valley of *Elah*, where David fought with Goliath. From Gath he proceeded to the Cave of Adullam, once thought to be east of Bethlehem, in *Wady Khureitùn*, a spot pointed out to me on the opposite side of the beautiful vale on the edge of which I was riding from the pools of Solomon towards Jerusalem. Another theory has fixed the cave in another part of the district, at *Deir Dubban*, the Convent of Flies ; but M. Gannau (and Lieut. Conder follows him), thinks that, as the most famous scene of David's outlaw life was, according to Josephus, near the city of Adullam, the cave must be sought contiguous to the site of an ancient city. Lieut. Conder, working out a suggestion of the French geographer, fixes upon a place between Gath and Bethlehem, Ed el Meijè, or Ayd el Mieh. It is an ancient site of importance, with rock cut tombs, good water supply, and main roads from different sides. There is no great cavern there, like the traditional one, but several small caves are found, such as are at the present day inhabited by the Troglodite peasantry. Such caves are black with smoke, and large families live in them ; whilst neighbouring caves are used as granaries for corn or stables for cattle. Places of this kind, it is thought by Lieut. Conder, would be more likely resorts for bands of outlawed men than a very large subterranean chamber, with a damp and feverish atmosphere, requiring many lights to dispel the darkness, and infested with bats and scorpions. Though this identification is probable, it is not certain.

From Adullam, David crossed over to Moab, the country of Ruth, his ancestress. Thence he is said to have come into "the forest of Hareth" (1 Sam. xxii. 5), and afterwards he is represented as dwelling in the "wood," in the wilderness of Ziph. (1 Sam. xxiii. 16.) Lieut. Conder considers that neither "wood" nor "forest" is intended in these passages—that among the hills of Judea, about Bethlehem, in David's time, there were no woods or forests ; and that the Septuagent gives the true description in a word signifying the *new ground, or place*, a conclusion corroborated by Josephus, who speaks of "the *new place* belonging to Ziph."

(*Ant.* vi., xiii. 2.) *Tell Zif*, a conspicuous mound south-east of Hebron, with a quarry, and some Jewish tombs, is most likely the spot. A rock in the wilderness of Maon (1 Sam. xxiii. 25) was also David's abode, the present *Tell Ma'in*, according to Conder, at the head of a wady running down to the Dead Sea. Hence the chieftain went to Engedi, following the custom of the Bedouins, who, when the summer is over, leave the hills and descend to a sheltered plain. Engedi, on the shores of the Dead Sea, is well known ; and Carmel, where Nabal lived (not the Carmel of Samaria), seems to have been a spot about two miles from Maon, now in autumn time full of water, and surrounded by Arabs with their herds. The valleys still grow corn and maize ; there are also traces of wine-presses ; but pasture-land is most abundant, goats and sheep thriving on the scanty herbage. The hill of *Hachilah* is also on the list, definitely described as "on the south of" and before "Jeshimon." (1 Sam. xxiii. 19 ; xxvi. 1-3.) The site must have been north, or north-east of Ziph, where deep wadys run down to the desert. Mr. Conder thinks he can find it on a high hill where *Yekin* now stands.— *Exploration Fund Statements*, 1874, 25 ; 1875, 41, 145, 168.

S.

———————

THE BROTHERLY COVENANT

1 Samuel 23:16-18

IT is not to be supposed that, while in the wilderness, the sole care of David was the protection of other people's cattle. Such daring spirits as he commanded were not to be restricted to such narrow bounds. His fell purpose against Nabal —every soul belonging to whom he intended to destroy for the churlish words of their master— shows that he assumed the right of dealing in a very summary manner with his personal enemies, or those by whom he conceived himself to be wronged ; and it is likely that if Doeg, or any other obnoxious persons, had travelled their way, they would have been subjected to very rough treatment by this troop of outlaws.

Again, his expedition to the relief of Keilah, when besieged by the Philistines, shows that he was ever ready to employ his force against the public enemies of Israel—thus at once rendering a service acceptable to the people, and obtaining supplies for the use of his troop. The necessity of keeping them employed, and of procuring them a maintenance, without doubt occasioned other expeditions which are not recorded — sudden forays, when opportunity offered, into the territories of the various ancient enemies of Israel with whom there was no active war. This continually occurs under the like circumstances, and was the mode in which Jephthah, in a former age, employed his men, and acquired the experience and reputation which led to his being called to lead the armies of Israel. Of the expedition to relieve Keilah, which was the very first operation performed by David when his troop was organized, it may be remarked, that it must have been of signal service to his character; for, involving as it did the defeat of a Philistine force, its effect must have been to rectify in public estimation the error he had committed in going over to the Philistines.

The proceedings of David, and the position he had assumed, were regarded by Saul with alarm and unmitigated hatred. He probably thought that the present moderation of Jesse's son would last no longer than till his force should become strong enough to enable him to strike for the crown, by meeting the royal forces in arms. He might well judge, that if his cause were suffered to gather strength by time, the issue of a contest might be doubtful. It would not be difficult for David to render his troop fully equal to that which the crown kept in constant service, and the rest would depend on the result of a call upon the tribes, the success of which, for an expedition against a man so eminent and so popular as David, and whose cause was so strong in at least the great and powerful tribe of Judah, he might well have reason to doubt. The king, therefore, determined to hunt down and crush the son of Jesse with his household troops at once, without allowing him time to become more formidable.

From all that appears, David's men were eager for the fray, and were with great difficulty kept by their leader within the bounds he had prescribed to himself. His policy was to avoid, by all the means in his power, a rencontre with the royal forces. For this, his position among the mountains, cliffs, narrow ravines, and caverns of the rocky wilderness west of the Dead Sea, offered peculiar advantages—and many a weary chase did he lead king Saul through this wild region. Yet Saul was, from time to time, supplied with good information respecting David's movements, and once was, without knowing it, so close upon him,—had, in fact, so completely hemmed him in,—that he must have been taken, or driven into the armed conflict with the king

which he was so anxious to avoid, had not, most providentially, a messenger arrived at the moment to apprise Saul that the Philistines had invaded the land, which obliged him immediately to turn his steps to another quarter.

Jonathan was not present at any time with the force in pursuit of David. Under all the circumstances, it was best that he should be absent. His heart, however, yearned after his friend. This was not an age of epistolary communications; and letters as well as messages would have been dangerous. Having therefore heard that David was in the forest of Ziph, he resolved to pay him a secret visit from his own home at Gibeah, seemingly before Saul had commenced his personal pursuit of David. This was the last time the two friends met in this world; and the interview was of deep interest to both. The object of the generous prince was to "strengthen his hand in God," to encourage him in his faith and hope, and to prevent him by his friendly counsels from sinking into despair: "Fear not," he said, "for the hand of Saul my father shall not find thee." This was a faith as strong as David himself ever expressed, and stronger than even he was enabled always to maintain. More than this, he now avowed, without reserve, his clear knowledge that David was to be king; and—in his submission to what he knew to be the divine appointment, and in his intense admiration of his friend's high qualities —his most cheerful acquiescence in that arrangement. He even contemplated it with pleasure, looking forward to the many happy days they should spend together, when David should be king, and he next to him, his uncrowned equal. "Thou shalt be king over Israel, and I shall be next to thee: *and that also Saul my father knoweth.*" Alas for him! it was not so to be: and perhaps, upon the whole, it was well that it was not; for looking at what afterwards took place in regard to Jonathan's son—a son worthy of such a father, it may be feared that in the position which his imagination pictured as one of perfect happiness to his generous heart, difficulties which he saw not would have arisen to mar that picture which we now possess of the most perfect friendship the world ever witnessed. Yet who can tell but the presence of such an influence as that of Jonathan—the possession of such a refreshment to his spirit, as the perfect love of such a friend would have supplied—might have had such a salutary operation upon David's temper, that his great name would have come down to us without spot?

Before they parted, "they two made a covenant before the Lord." It was no doubt of the same purport as that previously taken, which was thus confirmed—amounting to this, that David should, not only while Jonathan lived, "show him the kindness of the Lord," but should do so by himself and his heirs to Jonathan's descendants for ever. This was not much for David to promise to one who gave up for him all that men most prize. But we must not forget, that if in this beautiful friendship Jonathan shines more than David, this was the necessary result of the great difference in their position. Jonathan could make actual sacrifices such as few men have ever made; but Jesse's son had nothing to give up that could be of any avail to Jonathan. Had their situations been reversed, there is no reason to suppose that David would have been less generous than the prince. But he could only promise; and promises seem but small coin to give in exchange for golden sacrifices.

These covenants of brotherhood are rather common in the East; they are for the most part, like this, contracted under a religious sanction, and are of a very binding nature. In China they are especially frequent; and that country, notwithstanding its remoteness, affords more materials for scriptural illustration than is usually imagined. We find repeated instances of such covenants in Chinese histories and fictions. Here is one from the *Rambles of the Emperor Ching-Tih*:—"'Your kindness,' said Yung to To Gaon, 'cannot be forgotten through the lapse of ages. I have ventured to form the desire to contract an alliance with you which death shall not be able to dissolve.' To Gaon was delighted with the proposal, on which they inquired each other's age. Gaon being twenty-eight, and Yung no more than twenty-three, the former received the honours due to the elder. After this they knelt, he on the left, and Yung on the right; and worshipped in the face of heaven, while the latter declared their engagement in the following terms: 'I here, Chou-Yung, and my senior kin, engage by oath to be devoted brothers. Though our surnames be not the same, we shall be to one another as if we were children of one mother. Our friendship is for no purpose of wickedness, nor for mutual aid in crime; but the resolute

intention of us both is to delight in justice, and not to give way to feelings of unrighteousness. We will encourage each other in what is good, and warn each other of what is evil; thereafter, should we find our way to the court, we shall together become pillars of the empire, that we may leave a fragrant memorial for the historian, and that our names be together magnified before the people. Should riches and honour hereafter fall to the lot of either of us, he shall share the glory with the other. If either be false to this agreement—may the gods mark him!'"

MAGNANIMITY

1 Samuel 24-26

WHEN Saul had repulsed the Philistines, he resumed his designs against David. The opportunity seemed favourable; for although, for various reasons, he may have hesitated to call out the national force, in addition to his bodyguard, expressly against David, it would be in his power to retain for this service a proportion of the men who had joined him in his march against the Philistines. Thus it is mentioned, that the force with which he returned to the pursuit of the fugitive band, amounted to no less than three thousand men.

The king obtained intelligence that David had meanwhile retreated into the wilderness of Engedi, and abode "among the rocks of the

THE BEDEN, OR MOUNTAIN GOAT

wild goats,"—that is, among the high rocks and precipices, in which these animals delight. This wilderness is everywhere of limestone formation, with a large mixture of chalk and flint. The surface is broken into conical hills and ridges, from two hundred to four hundred feet in height, and gradually sloping towards the Dead Sea. Some stunted shrubs are found in the highest part of this wilderness; farther down, occasionally a little grass is seen, and then, to a great extent, the aspect of the region is one of utter sterility and desolation. Here the *beden*, or mountain goat, still starts up on the approach of the traveller, and bounds along the face of the rock before him. On all sides the country is full of caverns, which might well serve as lurking-places for David and his men, as they do for outlaws at the present day.

One day, when closely pursued by Saul, David and his men lay in the innermost darkness of one of the largest of these caverns, when, to their great amazement, they beheld Saul enter there (his people remaining respectfully in the vale below), and compose himself to the usual short rest during the afternoon heat. Being between them and the light at the entrance of the cave, they could observe all the king's movements, while they were themselves screened from view by the inner darkness. Now, then, was the opportunity of vengeance for great wrongs,—of turning against Saul's own life the sword which he aimed at theirs—of ending by one stroke all these hardships and wanderings—and of removing what seemed the sole obstacle between David and his promised throne. So the men viewed it. As the king slept, they whispered eagerly to their leader: "Behold the day of which the Lord said to thee, I will deliver thine enemy into thy hand, that thou mayest do unto him as shall seem good unto thee." We read of no such promise, nor should we have known of it, had it not been thus incidentally mentioned. It did not indicate to David what he should do, when this opportunity was placed in his hands. It gave him the power of doing whatever his heart prompted; but *what* he did, would show what manner of a man he was. It was an occasion afforded him of vindicating the Lord's choice of him, by showing to all Israel his faith, his patience, his nobleness—by once more bringing forth the true greatness of his character, and proving his exemption from all vindictive feelings and all low ambition. So *he* viewed it. The Lord had delivered David's enemy into his hand, not that he might destroy him, but that he might forgive him. "The Lord forbid," he said,

"that I should do this thing unto my master, the Lord's anointed, to stretch forth my hand against him, seeing he is the anointed of the Lord." This rightness of feeling, so frequent in the history of David—this spontaneous, undeliberating truthfulness of expression and action, only possible to the man whose heart is essentially right, falls refreshingly upon the sense, like the gush of waters to one who plods thirstily along the dry and dusty ways of life.

To the comparatively coarse minds of his followers, the relinquishment of so signal an advantage must have seemed, and did seem, like madness; and it needed all the authority he had established over their rough natures, to compel their submission to his view of the case. Yet this conduct of David was not only true and noble in feeling, but, although he then thought not of that, it was politically wise. Indeed, that which is in feeling truest, is always wisest in the long run; and this is so clearly shown in the history of David, that some have perversely argued from it as if the spontaneous impulse of a generous and noble spirit were the result of sagacious political calculation. But the sole and simple maxim of David was, Do right, and leave the results to God; and that the results thus left to God were generally favourable to him, was not because of his political astuteness, but because his spirit, under divine enlightenment, generally led him the right way. Many men, while wishing to do right, often hesitate and deliberate as to what is right. But it was not so with David. He at once, as by an inspiration, saw what was right, good, and true; and without hesitating, but with all the confidence which experience gives, he committed himself to the instant impulse of that truthful spirit, which never, when heeded, led him wrong, and seldom suffered him to stray.

It is not the less true, that had David allowed the king to be slain under these circumstances, the result could not but have been most discouraging to himself. Would the people willingly have consigned the sceptre to the hands stained with the blood of Saul? Would not Jonathan himself have been stung into open war against the slayer of his father; and instead of submitting to the exaltation of his friend, would he not rather, with the approval and sympathy of all Israel, have stood up for his own rights? Besides, by this act, David would have set an example of disregard for the character and condition of the " Lord's anointed," which might have been turned most dangerously against himself when exalted to the throne.

But although, under the influence of the master-hand which held back the fierce outlaws, Saul was suffered to escape unscathed from that dangerous cave, David was willing to secure some evidence of the fact that Saul's life had been in his power. He therefore approached him softly as he slept, and cut off the skirts of his robe. No sooner, however, did Saul arise and leave the cavern, and his men begin to laugh at the ridiculous figure the sovereign presented in his skirtless robe, than David's heart smote him for the indignity he had been instrumental in inflicting on the royal person. Yielding to the impulse of the moment—which again was right, though it might have been in common calculation most dangerous—he went boldly forth to the entrance of the cave, and called to the king as he descended into the valley, " My lord the king !" Well did the king know that voice. A thunder-clap could not have struck him more. He looked up ; and David bowed himself very low, in becoming obeisance to his king. He spoke. In a few rapid and strong words, he told what had happened—he described the urgency he had resisted —he held up the skirt in proof how completely had been in his hand the life he spared— saying, " I have not sinned against thee ; yet thou huntest my life to take it. The Lord judge between me and thee ; and the Lord avenge me of thee : but mine hand shall not be upon thee." Behold, now that stern heart is melted. The hard wintry frosts thaw fast before the kindly warmth of this generous nature. Saul weeps ; the hot tears, the blessed tears, fall once more from those eyes, dry too long. " Thou art more righteous than I," he cried, in the agony of his self-conviction ; " for thou hast rewarded me good, whereas I have rewarded thee evil. . . . The Lord reward thee for the good that thou hast done unto me this day." Nor was this all. In the presence of the man whom he recognized as worthier than himself, his proud heart yielded for the moment to acknowledge him as destined to inherit his crown, and he humbled himself to ask of David to make him swear, that in the coming time he would spare Saul's family, and not doom it to extirpation. This request pain-

fully reminds us of the antiquity of the Eastern custom, which has subsisted to our own time, of a new ruler destroying all those of the previous family, whose claims might, by any possible circumstances, be brought into rivalry with his own.

Although relieved from the immediate pursuit of Saul, David was too well acquainted with his character to forego the safeguards which his present mode of life afforded. Nor had he miscalculated ; for, after an uncertain interval of time, during which occurred the affair with Nabal, we find the king again upon the track of David, in a different part of the wild region towards the Dead Sea. This relapse of Saul into his old inveteracy, this forgetfulness of that noble forbearance which had once so deeply impressed him, would have thrown many men—even rightminded men—off their guard of patience and moderation. It was a hard test, but David stood it. He lost not one jot of heart or hope, and would not consent that the wrong of Saul should make him wrong also. An opportunity was again afforded him of showing the invincible truth of his character, and his immeasurable superiority to the man who hunted his life through the mountains.

Having received from his scouts certain intelligence of Saul's movements, David went down one night to the place where the royal party had bivouacked, accompanied by two faithful friends, one of whom was his nephew, Abishai. They found the whole troop sunk in sleep—the king in the midst, with Abner and the men round about him. The position of the king was clearly marked in the dimness of the night to the visitants, by the spear stuck into the ground,—a practice by which the tent of the chief, or his place in the open air, is still marked among the Arabians. This precluded all mistake as to the person, and Abishai begged David's permission to pin Saul's body at once to the earth on which he lay. " I will not," he whispered, with ferocious significance, "smite him a second time." But David withheld his hand. There was, beside the spear at the king's head, a pitcher of water within his reach, from which he might drink, if he awoke athirst. These things—the pitcher and the spear—David was content to remove as proofs of his visit. When they had got to the top of a hill at some distance, David shouted to Abner by name, and taunted him for the lax watch he had kept over the king's safety, telling him to look for the spear and the pitcher which had stood at the king's head. David had not declared himself; and in the darkness and distance his person could not be recognized. But the king knew his voice, and called out, with returning admiration, "Is this thy voice, my son David?" By this David knew the frame of mind to which he had been brought, and remonstrated with equal force, but with even more tenderness and respect, than on the former occasion. He delicately supposed that all this persecution was owing to the malicious misrepresentations of others: he demanded to know what evil he had done, and appealed to the undoubted proofs he had given of his respect for the king's life and person. Saul was greatly impressed. Pride and hatred fled his heart for the time, and his confession of wrong-doing was most humble: "Behold, I have played the fool, and have erred exceedingly." He also promised that he would no more do him harm; and said, finally, "Blessed be thou, my son David: thou shalt both do great things, and also shalt still prevail."

His prophecy was true. How great the pity that the beams which now and then penetrated thus through the rents of his ruined spirit, had no abiding for light or warmth in the darkened chambers of his heart!

CUSH THE BENJAMITE

Psalm 7

IF we turn to the seventh Psalm, we find from the superscription [1] that it was composed or sung by David unto the Lord, "concerning the words of Cush the Benjamite." This person is not mentioned in the history, nor are his words recorded. But from the Psalm it may be collected that this man, having won the confidence and friendship of the unsuspecting David, used these only to entrap him into the power of Saul, whose then slumbering hostility he roused by misrepresenting David's motives and intentions to the king. There is indeed so much similarity

---

[1] The authority of the titles to the Psalms is a matter of some doubt, but there is no reason to distrust the one which the present Psalm bears.

between the words which David addressed to Saul in the last interview with him, under the circumstances recorded yesterday, and those of this Psalm, as to show that this sacred song belongs to that occasion. This Cush, then, was the person to whom he alluded as having by his treacherous malignity incited the king to this renewed pursuit. It may also not be difficult to collect that the purport of his unjust accusation was that David sought the life of the king, in order to clear his own way to the throne. Hence the special value of the opportunity of practically refuting this calumny which had been afforded to him. Seeing the frame of mind to which Saul had been thus brought, we shall not feel prepared for the step David next took—of going over again to the Philistines, in the apprehension that he should yet one day perish by the hand of Saul, unless we add the conduct of Cush the Benjamite to the influences which worked his mind up to this course. Indeed, this was the *primary* influence; for, in his words to Saul, he indicates it as a conclusion already for that reason formed: "If the Lord hath stirred thee up against me, let Him accept an offering; but if they be the children of men, cursed be they before the Lord; for *they have driven* me out this day from abiding in the inheritance of the Lord." It was therefore not so much the blind fury of Saul which led David to take this step, as the chilling effect upon a confiding spirit like his, of the feeling that his worst enemies contrived to worm their way into his confidence, and that he was betrayed and calumniated by those he trusted most. In the open violence of Saul there was something he could meet and understand; but throughout his career there was never anything that grieved his generous spirit, and crushed it down, so much as the treachery and ingratitude of those he loved and trusted. His own openheartedness rendered this exquisitely painful to him. Here he was all nerve; and it was here that he was most often wounded.

The case being as stated, it becomes deeply interesting to contemplate that full development of his feelings which the seventh Psalm affords. His sense of the wrong done to him is very keen, and his repudiation of the accusations brought against him becomingly warm and indignant. He did not feel it to be any part of his duty to rest under such imputations, without an attempt to clear his character. It is necessary that the character of the servant of God should, for his Master's honour, be free from even "the appearance of evil." His faith does not require him to lie passive under injurious imputations. He will do all that becomes him to clear his character, but he will not be over-anxious respecting the result, knowing that his character is in God's keeping, and that a great day of unclouding is coming, when his righteousness shall in these matters be made manifest to men and angels. Those clouds that hang darkly upon the horizon now, shall presently, when the sun arises, be lit up with unutterable glory; and that which seemed a spot in the face of heaven, become a radiance and a renown. It is under the influence of such feelings that David speaks: "O Lord my God, if I have done this, if there be iniquity in my hands; if I have rewarded evil to him that was at peace with me (yea, I have delivered him that without cause is mine enemy); let the enemy persecute my soul, and take it; yea, let him tread down my life upon the earth, and lay mine honour in the dust."

In express reference to the adversary by whom he had been thus wronged and betrayed, he says, "Behold, he travaileth with iniquity, and hath conceived mischief, and brought forth falsehood. He made a pit and digged it, and is fallen into the ditch which he made. His mischief shall return upon his own head, and his violent dealing upon his own pate." A close observation of the course of God's providence, as well as his acquaintance with the principles of Judaism, which led to the expectation of the demonstrated results of retributive justice in this life, assured David that this must happen; and it would appear that in some measure it had already happened in this particular case. In saying that Cush had fallen into the ditch which he had made, he seems to refer to some calamity which had befallen him, or to some disgrace which he had already incurred, in consequence of his treachery; but what that may have been, we cannot, in the absence of any record of facts, conjecture. Although the Gospel of Christ carries our views for the final adjustment of all things to the great day of decision, it is still often true in our own time, as of old, that righteousness is, even in this life, vindicated from injurious aspersions, and treachery and wrong-doing brought to shame.

The present effects of such conduct on the part of others—the calumnious treachery of some, and the violence of others—were, however, distressful and disheartening to David; and he could only find comfort in the assured conviction that the Lord could and would deliver him from the trials which made life a calamity to him, and vindicate his integrity by bringing his wicked persecutors to condign punishment. For this he with great earnestness supplicates: "O Lord my God, in Thee do I put my trust: save me from all them that persecute me, and deliver me. My defence is of God, who saveth the upright in heart. The Lord shall judge the people: judge *me*, O Lord, according to my righteousness, and according to my integrity that is in me." None knew better than David the fallen nature of man; none knew better than he—for, alas, he knew it experimentally —man's utter weakness when he ceases to lean upon the staff which God puts into his hand. But in this particular matter, in all his conduct towards Saul, he could assert his integrity, his entire freedom from all sinister and underhand designs; and it was his hope and belief that God would judge, though man did not, according to his righteousness.

Surrounded by enemies, slandered by the tongues of evil men, sickened by treachery, it was at times hard to wait the day of complete vindication. He was assured that the Lord could justify him before the people; he was confident that He would eventually do it. But the time was long, very long, to one to whom a good name was dear; and at intervals the thought could not be resisted, that perhaps God had forgotten to be gracious, or was at least too slow in assuming the robes of judgment. "Arise, O Lord, in Thine anger. Lift up Thyself because of the rage of mine enemies; and awake for me to the judgment that Thou hast commanded. So shall the congregation of the people compass Thee about: for *their sakes*, therefore, return Thou on high."

He is convinced of the ultimate establishment of righteousness; he is grieved lest the present triumph of wrong-doing and oppression of truthfulness should lead the people to distrust the great fact, that, "there is a God that ruleth in the earth." This he will not allow himself for one moment to doubt. That were a greater treachery against his Lord, than any which man had committed against David. No. "God judgeth the righteous, and is angry with the wicked every day. O let the wickedness of the wicked come to an end; but establish the just: for the righteous God trieth the reins and the heart."

The view which we are thus enabled, from his own words, to obtain of the state of David's mind at this trying period of his career, will enable us to contemplate with advantage the further steps of his progress.

A FALSE STEP

1 Samuel 27:1-7

DAVID was quite justified, from past experience, and from his perfect knowledge of the man, in reposing no confidence in the declarations and repentance of Saul. The king, it may be believed, had no intention to deceive him—doubtless he expressed what he felt at the time; but David knew that all the good impression which had been made would soon pass away, and that his heart would become all the more inveterate against him, for the humiliation in which he, so proud of spirit, had stood before the moral dignity of Jesse's son. It is in the nature of such hearts as his, to resent as wrongs the rebukes which their pride receives from men better than themselves. Angry in the recollection of what they deem a weakness, the persons who have witnessed their humiliation, and who oppress them by their real superiority, become more and more hateful in their eyes; and it is no longer to be borne, that the man capable of exercising this intolerable mastery over their spirits, should tread the same earth with them.

Allowing due weight to this consideration, we were never able to understand the step taken by David in going over once more to the Philistines, until we took into account the further influence exercised upon his most susceptible temper by the treachery of the man he had trusted. This was likely to make him feel, for the time, that he was continually in the power of spies and traitors, who might gain his confidence only to destroy him. How could he know but that the men who had hitherto been most faithful to him, and in whom he most trusted, might one day desert him to win the favour of a king, or betray him, at unawares, to his undoing? It was under the influence of such depressing feelings that he resolved to put an insurmountable barrier against the further pursuit of the king, by going over to his enemies. He did so: and the immediate result was such as he expected; for when Saul heard of this step taken by David, he abandoned all further designs against him. But although we can account for this step, we cannot justify it. Indeed, there was a certain consciousness in his own mind which prevented him from asking counsel of the Lord in this matter, as he had habitually done in affairs of much less importance. Instead of this, he reasoned the matter "in his heart," in his own heart, in this manner: "I shall now one day perish by the hand of Saul; there is nothing better for me than that I should speedily escape into the land of the Philistines." But instead of their being nothing better for him, there could really have been nothing worse for him; and had the Lord's pursuing mercy not followed His chosen servant, even in this his wandering from steadfast faith, and averted from him by His shielding hand the perils he brought upon himself by this step, there is no knowing what the result might have been. "The overlong continuance of a temptation may easily weary the best patience, and may attain that by protraction which it could never do by violence," says Bishop Hall. Knowing, therefore, what is in man, we do not wonder that David at length began to bend under his trial; but we do wonder that he went over to the Philistines under this influence. It was not only a fault—it was a mistake, which politicians say is worse than a fault. It is true that it was most effectual, as a human means, for safety from Saul—which was the immediate object in view. But it is lamentable that such a man as David should have made that the primary consideration in such a movement; and had not his naturally courageous spirit been for the time utterly prostrated by personal apprehensions, it is scarcely credible that the political error of the step should have escaped his penetration. That he had a latent misgiving as to its religious fitness, is shown by his refraining from seeking counsel of God. The considerations which belong to this matter have already passed under our notice, in contemplating his first lapse of the same kind; but so far as the political influences of the movement are in question, the present step was far more dangerous than the former, as in this instance he goes not alone, but takes with him a strong band of resolute and daring men; and it must be manifest that they would be received only in the expectation that they might be employed to the detriment of the Israelites—and this employment of them would have been a slur upon his name all the rest of his life, if it did not prevent or retard the recognition of him as king. In fact, so much was he eventually aware of this, that he was reduced to a series of low contrivances, and degrading falsehoods, to avert the natural consequences of the step he had taken.

Nevertheless, David entered the land of the Philistines in a far different attitude from that in which he had before appeared there. The inveterate hatred of Saul, now so well known, was his recommendation; and no distrust could be entertained of a man who fled for his life to the enemies of his country—exasperated by wrongs, and willing, it might be supposed, to avenge them. Won by these considerations, and by the assurance that this able leader and valiant troop were withdrawn from the defensive force of Israel, and added to the strength of the Philistines; David found a most friendly reception from the king of Gath, in whose presence he had some years before so egregiously played the madman. It is, indeed, not unlikely that Achish, acting upon the hint of the previous attempt of David to find refuge with him, had sent to offer him an asylum from the wrath of their common enemy; and there can be little doubt that, as Josephus suggests, David had at least taken care previously to ascertain the footing on which he would be received.

We may be sure that the redoubted son of Jesse, the slayer of Goliath, and the overcomer of so many Philistines, was beheld with great admiration at Gath. Some closet commentators, whose knowledge of life and man is rather a matter of excogitation than of experience, marvel that he did not find himself in personal danger among a people he had so much aggrieved—indeed, that he was not torn in pieces by the mob. But in reality there was no danger. Prowess is respected among a military people; and a great general, when he comes as a fugitive among them, is liked none the less for his skill and courage having been manifested at their expense. In fact, he is rather liked the better for it.

Nevertheless, David found himself in an embarrassing position at Gath. It must have been obviously difficult for him and his men to be living there among idolaters without giving or taking offence; and there was constant danger lest, with so many brave and reckless men moving about among their old enemies, some affray might arise on religious or national grounds, which might have a fatal and ruinous termination. Besides, they lived under constant observation; and the mere presence of so many strong and daring men, would of itself be likely to suggest the employment of them against the Israelites,—a result which David regarded with such dread and apprehension, as probably left him little of the repose he had expected to find among the Philistines. He therefore at length ventured to ask the king to assign to him some town in the land, where he might live apart with his men; and where, as seems to be adroitly implied, they might provide for themselves, and be no longer burdensome as guests in the royal city. This was a large and bold request. But it was met in an open and generous spirit; and David was at once raised almost to the dignity of an independent prince, by having the fortified town of Ziklag assigned to him, in such absolute and free possession, that it remained attached to the house of David ever after.

Understanding the wishes of Achish, and being also desirous to maintain and exercise his men, he led them, from time to time, in forays against the neighbouring nations. But these nations were friends of the Philistines; and as he wished it to be believed, and indeed positively affirmed, that these expeditions were against the Israelites, the troop made it their constant practice to put to death every living soul of the places they assaulted, that there might be none left to apprise the Philistines of the truth. The delight the king felt in the assurance that, by these alleged operations against Israel, David had made himself odious to his own people, and must therefore remain attached to his interests, clearly shows the nature of the danger he incurred by the step he had taken, and indicates the deplorable error into which he had fallen, seeing that he could only evade the consequences by bloodshed, by falsehood, and by making a dupe of the confiding protector by whom he had been treated so generously. Bishop Hall, who excuses the slaughter, on the ground that these people were of the doomed nations, whom the Israelites held a commission from God to extirpate, yet finds no excuse for this dealing with king Achish: "If Achish were a Philistine, yet he was David's friend, yea, his patron; and if he had been neither it had not become David to be false. The infirmities of God's children never appear but in their extremities. It is hard for the best man to say how far he will be tempted. If a man will put himself among Philistines, he cannot promise to come forth innocent."

> "Ah! what a tangled web we weave,
> When first we venture to deceive!"

To some it may probably appear strange that, of all the cities of Philistia, David should have twice selected Gath as an asylum. Gath had suffered most severely from him in former days; and there, if anywhere, he might naturally anticipate a cold reception, if not hidden treachery or open violence. The solution of the difficulty appears to be this, that Gath stood upon the borders of the Jewish territory, just at the foot of the mountains, while the other royal cities were far out upon the plain. David wished to be close to his own country, that he might watch the current of events, receive refugees, and return to his native mountains whenever a favourable opportunity should offer. He felt, besides, that he would be safer near the border; he would be more free to act, and less exposed to the espionage and lurking hostility of the Philistines. Even though Gath was upon the border he was too wise to remain long in it. He asked for and obtained a town for himself; and he got one just where it best suited him to dwell—on the southern confines of Philistia, and not far distant from Judah. Ziklag was, moreover, a frontier fortress from which raids and forays could be made at any moment upon the hereditary enemies of his country, the Amalekites.

A study of David's character and acts during the period in which he was outlawed, is calculated to leave a somewhat painful impression upon the mind. We cannot but feel that his sufferings and his wrongs were very great. Driven from a court to which he had been invited; outlawed by a monarch whose honour and whose kingdom he had saved by his valour; beset and betrayed by those in whom he trusted,—one's heart bleeds for the poor, houseless, persecuted wanderer, as he reads those words of deep pathos and thrilling power, in which he depicts his trials and sorrows. And yet there is another side to the picture. There are words and plans and acts recorded which nothing can excuse. There are displays of passion, and purposes of revenge, and deeds of cruelty and blood. There are unworthy schemes, and deceptions, and barefaced falsehoods. These are all recorded, honestly recorded by the sacred historian. They are never palliated. No attempt is made to excuse them. The life of David is written faithfully. His conduct is depicted truthfully. And in all this we have evidence, full and convincing, that the Spirit of God inspired the biographer. David is set before us as "a man after God's own heart;" but still a man—a man of fiery passions, of many and heinous sins, yet a man redeemed at length from sin's curse and passion's slavery by the almighty power of divine grace. David's character and life are best sketched by his own pen in the fifty-first Psalm. In the words of an eloquent living author: "David's life and history, as written for us in those Psalms of his, I consider to be the truest emblem ever given us of a man's moral progress and warfare here below. All earnest souls will ever discern in it the faithful struggle of an earnest human soul towards that which is good and best. Struggle often baffled—sore baffled—driven as into entire wreck; yet a struggle never ended, ever with tears, repentance, true unconquerable purpose, begun anew."[1]

P.

REINFORCEMENTS

1 Samuel 27:1-12; 1 Chronicles 12:1-22

AT Ziklag David's power received constant accessions. The position he now occupied, in a strong town on the frontier towards Judah, no longer a wandering exile, but a great lord, able to find rewarding employment for the swords of resolute men, and the hopes of whose great future began to loom distinctly in the horizon, caused his force to be greatly increased by additions from various quarters. In 1 Chron. xii. 1-22, a long list is given of persons of more or less consideration in their tribes, who, through disaffection to the government of Saul, made themselves voluntary exiles, and staked all their prospects on David's cause. The list opens with members of the tribe of Benjamin, "Saul's brethren," at which we might wonder, did we not recollect that the influence of Samuel had been very strong in that tribe, and that the seat of Saul's government being within its territory, it had probably been more annoyed than more distant tribes, by some of his unpopular acts. This body of Benjamites were "armed with bows, and could use both the right hand and the left in hurling stones, and shooting arrows out of a bow." They were therefore invaluable for breaking and discouraging an enemy's force before coming to close quarters.

During the reign of Saul, the tribes beyond the Jordan had taken a very independent part, and had gained great accessions of power and territory by wars waged on their own account

[1] Carlyle, *Hero-Worship*.

with the neighbouring nations. This, with their separation by the river from their brethren, and the greater separation effected by their pastoral habits, rendered very loose the connection between them and the agricultural tribes of the west, and it would seem that they acknowledged little, if any, subjection to Saul. Indeed, it may appear that there was something like a small harassing civil war between them and Saul; for a strong party of Gadites, who crossed the Jordan at the time of flood, and marched through the country to join David at Ziklag,[1] are described as having chased away the inhabitants of the river valley, on both banks, in their course. The names of their leaders are given, eleven in number, and they are described as "captains of the host: one of the least was over a hundred, and the greatest over a thousand, —not that they brought such numbers with them, but that they were such men as were, from their rank and military worth, entitled, when Israel was under arms, to act as centurions and chiliarchs in the army. That they were, notwithstanding, in considerable force, is shown by their exploit in the valley of the Jordan. It is said of these auxiliaries, that they "were men of war, fit for the battle, that could handle shield and buckler, whose faces were like the faces of lions, and were as swift as the roes upon the mountains." These were, then, trained and well armed soldiers, of the kind most valued in ancient warfare, being most formidable in close action.

Not long after there came over to him a large number of men, headed by persons of distinguished valour, from the tribes of Judah and Benjamin. As this large force appeared before him, David was somewhat suspicious of their intentions, perhaps owing to the presence of the Benjamites, who might naturally be supposed to be attached to Saul, who was of their own tribe. He therefore went out to them, not only as án act of civility, but to ascertain their intentions before they were admitted into the fortress. This anecdote, found in an obscure place,[2] is interesting, as everything is that illustrates David's position at this time, as the leader of a troop so variously composed, and so difficult to manage, except by the influence of personal regard and high military character. The words in which

David addressed the newly arrived force are striking, and well illustrate the kind of oratory by which he spoke to the hearts of men : "If ye be come peaceably unto me, to help me, mine heart shall be knit unto you ; but if ye be come to betray me to mine enemies, seeing there is no wrong in mine hands, the God of our fathers look thereon and rebuke it." These words awoke the enthusiasm of the strangers, whose sentiments found expression in the voice of their leader Amasai :[1] "Thine are we, David, and on thy side, thou son of Jesse. Peace, peace, be unto thee, and peace be to thine helpers; for thy God helpeth thee." They were then most gladly received—the leaders remaining in command of those whom they had brought over with them.

The king of Gath beheld these accessions to David's force with satisfaction, reckoning upon their services in the approaching campaign against Saul. This expectation he declared to David. After the recent impositions practised upon him, Achish had no reason to doubt that this intimation would be most acceptable to David, and it is clear that he meant it as a mark of his confidence rather than as an exaction. So David was obliged to receive it, after the pretences he had made ; and with seemingly cheerful acquiescence he said, "Surely thou shalt know what thy servant can do." Upon this Achish, in testimony of his satisfaction, appointed him "keeper of his head"— that is, captain of his body guard,—a post of high honour and confidence, but which further embarrassed David's position, by obliging him to be near the king in the approaching action, so that all his movements would be under the eye of his royal protector. Under this arrangement, it would seem that some Philistines were added to his force, who, with his own band, might act as the royal guard ; and the men thus added probably formed the Gittite (Gathite) troop under Ittai, which afterwards followed his fortunes, formed his own body guard, and remained most faithfully attached to him under all the changes of his career—a striking instance of his extraordinary power of attracting the hearts of even foreigners to himself.

How David might eventually have deported himself, it may be difficult to conjecture. It is

---

[1] Compare 1 Chronicles 12:8-22; 5:11, 18-22.
[2] 1 Chronicles 12:16-18.

[1] Perhaps the same as Amasa, son of David's sister Abigail—at a later period Absalom's general-in-chief, and designed by David to be his, but that he was slain by Joab.

hard to believe that he would really have fought against his own nation, and quite as hard to suppose that he would have betrayed the generous confidence which Achish reposed in him. It may be that he would have confined himself to the duty which his new office imposed, of defending the person of the Philistine king. God was pleased, however, to release him from the embarrassment which his own false step and his disingenuousness had occasioned, by awakening the jealousy and alarm of the Philistine princes, who were startled to behold the large body of Hebrews in the rear, under the orders of David, when the army was drawn up near Jezreel, and deemed it possible that there might be a secret understanding between Saul and his son-in-law, or at least that David might intend to purchase forgiveness by betraying the Philistines. An incident which occurred at this moment, and which we learn from 1 Chron. xii. 19, may have tended to confirm this suspicion. A troop of Manassites deserted from Saul, and went over to David, which might very well, in the eyes of the Philistines, look like a concerted movement to strengthen David, when, at some appointed signal, he should fall on the rear of the Philistines, while Saul contended with them in front. The chiefs of the other Philistine states, therefore, insisted that David's force should withdraw; and, notwithstanding the remonstrances of the confiding Achish, they absolutely refused to allow it to take any part in the action. Thus, happily relieved from a most difficult position, the son of Jesse marched his men slowly back to Ziklag.

THE WITCH OF ENDOR

1 Samuel 28

WITH the east alienated, with the south disaffected, compelled to witness from a distance the rising power and popularity of David, and the defection from himself of many noted men in person, and of many more in heart—Saul beheld, with a misgiving spirit, the storm of war approaching. The counsels of God, of which he had made so light in the day of his pride, he vainly seeks in the time of his distress. He craves a token for good, and none is vouchsafed to him.

His crimes now bear their fruit; and the burden of old sins presses heavily upon his soul. The blood of God's slaughtered priests cries not to heaven in vain—he gets no answer from the sacred oracle; Samuel had been contemned, and the prophets have no message of encouragement for him; precious gifts of God he had made light of, and now no heavenly visions point out the path he ought to take, or give assurance of victory. What resource has he left? Samuel is dead. Had he been living, stern and awful truths might have been expected from his lips: still Saul would have sought him, for any certainty was better than these terrible doubts. But was there indeed no access to *his* counsels? Were there not powers which might for one brief moment call him from his rest, to give the required answer, be it for good or evil? The general belief was that such powers did exist, and were held by those who possessed mysterious knowledge, and were versed in the practice of the diabolical arts. All these knowledges and arts, real or pretended, were sternly forbidden by the law, and the profession of them declared a capital offence. This law had been enforced by Saul, so that none of these wizards and necromancers were known to exist in the land. When, therefore, the king, repulsed from every lawful means of acquiring the knowledge he craved, thought of this secret and forbidden alternative, he yet feared that none could be found to gratify him. By diligent search, it was at length ascertained that there was a woman living in retirement at Endor, near Mount Tabor, who had eluded the search of Saul's officers, and was believed to possess these forbidden powers. To her he repaired, disguised, with two faithful servants. The pythoness at first refused to listen to the proposal, alleging her fear that it should come to the knowledge of the king. But Saul pledged himself by oath that no harm should befall her; and as it is not clear how this assurance from a stranger could be of any value to her, we cannot but think that from this she suspected who her visitor was. His distinguished stature also—impossible to be disguised, and notorious to every one in Israel, even to those who had never seen him—might alone have disclosed him to a less "cunning woman" than the witch of Endor. However, she was too sagacious to betray the discovery she had made. Satisfied, apparently, she asked whom she was to summon. We are not called upon to inquire what trick she meant to play upon the king, what art to practise; for the name of SAMUEL had scarcely passed the king's lips, when, to the amazement of the woman herself, Samuel himself appeared. It was not to be borne, that since Samuel was really to be permitted to appear, it should even seem to be at the command of this miserable woman; and thus, therefore, her incantations were anticipated. The apparition appeared at the demand of Saul, and not at the woman's invocation. This, with perhaps some indication from the spectre, confirmed her suspicion that the tall stranger was no other than the king; and she uttered a loud cry, and said, "Why hast thou deceived me? for thou art Saul." The king pacified her, and eagerly demanded what she saw. She answered that she beheld a great and venerable personage—like the gods, or judges and civil magistrates, to whom that title was sometimes given. It is thus that we understand her declaration that she saw "gods ascending out of the earth." Either this took place in her inner room, or the object had not yet become visible to Saul; for he asked, "What form is he of?" and she said, "An old man cometh up, and he is covered with a mantle." There could be no doubt that this was Samuel; and the king, looking closely at the place to which the woman's fixed regards were turned, discerned the figure she described condensing into visibility before him. It has been thought, and we once thought so, that the king did not see the shade, but merely judged it was Samuel from the woman's description; but on looking more closely at the text, it becomes more emphatic than at first appears. It is stated that "Saul perceived (knew, or assured himself) that it was Samuel *himself.*" This is not what the woman saw, but what Saul saw; and as the sacred writer gives us the authority of his own declaration for the fact that it was "Samuel himself" that Saul perceived, we do not feel at liberty to suppose that it was anything else—that it was a fiend or a confederate personating Samuel; or that there was in fact nothing—the woman only saying she saw this, and Saul taking her word for it. The narrator all along says it *was* Samuel, which is better authority for the fact than the assertion of the woman or the impression of Saul. The latter, indeed, forthwith bent himself low in humble obeisance, which he was not likely to have done unless he saw the figure visibly before him, and felt assured that it was Samuel. He might, indeed, be imposed upon, and without much difficulty, under the circumstances; but the historian says that he was not—that it was Samuel whom he saw, Samuel to whom he spoke, Samuel who spoke to him. All the circumstances agree with this, and are unaccountable on any other hypothesis; the woman had no time for collusive arrangements; the answer given by the apparition was true, was fulfilled to the letter, and was anything but such as the woman would be likely to have given by ventriloquism (as some suppose), or through a confederate, but was altogether such as Samuel would have been likely to deliver had he been alive. It foretold not only the defeat of the Israelites by the Philistines in the coming battle, but that Saul himself, and his sons (such of them as were present), should perish. It might by human sagacity be foreseen that the Philistines would be victorious; but it could not so certainly be predicted by human calculation that Saul would perish—he might, even if defeated, withdraw with part of his forces, to make another stand against the enemy; still less could it be predicted that of several persons, Saul and his sons, all would perish. The chances, on which alone an impostor could calculate, were altogether against it. It would have been entirely the interest of an impostor to predict success. Were success foretold, the prediction, if fulfilled, would bring her credit; if falsified, there would be none to bring her to account. But if the calamity predicted came not to pass, she would be sought out and punished as a deceiver.

One cannot help being affected by the words in which the unhappy king addressed the shade of Samuel: "God is departed from me, and answereth me no more, neither by prophets nor by dreams: therefore have I called thee, that thou mayest make known to me what I shall do." Neither had he been answered by Urim, as we have before learned, which was the more important, as the regular mode of obtaining an answer from God. Why does he not mention that? The omission is probably significant. It may fairly be supposed that he shrank from naming to Samuel that which could not but bring to mind his slaughter of the priests at Nob. The answer of Samuel was impressively terrible: "Wherefore dost thou ask of me, seeing the Lord hath departed from thee, and is become thine enemy? The Lord hath done as He spake by me, and hath rent the kingdom out of thy hand, and given it to thy neighbour, even to David. The Lord will deliver Israel with thee into the hand of the Philistines; and to-morrow shalt thou and thy sons be with me,"—that is, dead like him. Those expend their ingenuity very needlessly, who speculate whether this phrase were more proper in the mouth of Samuel, or of a demon, or of a confederate of the woman speaking in his name. The poet has interpreted them rightly—

> " And when shall sink
> In night to-morrow's day, thou and thy sons
> Shall be with me in death." [1]

These dreadful words laid Saul prostrate upon the ground as one void of life. Exhausted by long abstinence, "for he had eaten no bread all that day, nor all the night," and worn out by anxiety, this announcement, which left him without hope, and assured him that all was lost and his doom accomplished, laid him in the dust. Revived by the kind solicitude of the woman and his attendants, and prevailed upon to refresh exhausted nature with some food, the king departed ere the morning dawn, with a riven heart, but with composed and resolute demeanour —to meet his doom.

A knowledge of the topography of the district gives great additional vividness to the battle of Gilboa, and the story of Saul's visit to the witch of Endor.

About six miles north of Gilboa is a parallel range of nearly equal elevation, called "the hill of Moreh" (Judg. vii. 1). Between the two ranges lies the beautiful valley of Jezreel, a branch of the great plain of Esdraelon. At the western extremity of Gilboa stood the city of Jezreel, and about half a mile eastward, at the very base of the mountain, is the fountain of Jezreel, or "Harod." On the opposite side of the valley, near the western extremity of Moreh, is the town of Shunem; and about four miles northeast, behind Moreh, lies the village of Endor.

The Philistines were encamped at Shunem; and Saul took up a position on the lower slopes of Gilboa, at the fountain of Jezreel. From the brow of the hill Saul got a full view of the enemy, and he was struck with terror at their numbers and warlike array. The position he had chosen was a bad one. There is an easy descent from Shunem to the base of Gilboa, and here the Philistine chariots could bear down with tremendous force upon the Israelites. On the night before the battle Saul went to Endor. It was a long journey. Endor lay partly in the rear of the Philistines, and Saul was thus forced to make a considerable *detour* to the right. The distance from his camp could not be less than nine miles. A night march of

[1] *The Fall of Saul: A Sacred Epic Poem.* By John Gunning Seymer, M.A. London, 1836.

eighteen miles after a day's fast, and in a state of mind bordering on despair, exhausted Saul's physical strength, and rendered him wholly unfit for the command of an army at such a critical period. The result was, as might have been expected, the complete overthrow of Israel.

P.

THE WORTHIES

2 Samuel 23; 1 Chronicles 11

DAVID, on his return to Ziklag, was joined by seven more chiefs of Manasseh. They are called "captains of thousands;" and as they must have come over from the camp of Saul, they doubtless brought some of their men with them. This accession of force proved to be most opportune; for, on arriving at Ziklag, it was found that the place had been burned with fire, and that, together with all the portable substance, the women and the children had been carried away captive. It seemed that the Amalekites had taken advantage of David's absence to retaliate his ravages of their country by an attack upon Ziklag. There was none to resist them, and they had shed no blood—not, we apprehend, from any humane consideration, but simply because David's supposed detention in the camp permitted them to remove the women and the children alive; and when that was the case they were valuable property, to be retained or sold as slaves. David's two wives—for he now had two—were among the captives.

The men were outrageous when they beheld what had taken place, and were not sparing of reproaches against their general, for having left the place without defenders. There were even sinister murmurs about stoning him. Probably the presence of the Manassites, who had joined in the field and on the road, served him in good stead. They had lost nothing, and naturally would side with David against the murmurers. It seems to have been they who suggested the wisdom of a pursuit after the marauders, for it was clear that, being under no apprehension of David's return, they would make a leisurely retreat, especially when encumbered with so many women and children; and it appeared by the heat of the still smouldering ruins, and by the freshness of their camel-tracks, that the attack had been very recent, and they could not yet have got to any great distance. David himself had lost more than any one else; but his faith in God was not shaken, and his self-possession and decision under this calamity, and the present outbreak of his own men, are worthy of high commendation, and tended rapidly to restore confidence. "He encouraged himself in Jehovah his God;" and calling for Abiathar, desired him to consult the Lord by the sacred Urim, whether he should pursue the enemy or not. The answer was favourable, and he set out with extreme rapidity, coming upon them when they were encamped, encumbered with spoil, and enjoying themselves at their ease, supposing David, whom alone they had any reason to fear, to be afar off with the Philistine host. Thus surprised, they offered little resistance; but some of them betook themselves to their camels and escaped. Not only was every thing and person taken from Ziklag recovered safe, but all the rich spoil which the band had collected in a wide marauding excursion fell into the hands of the victors. This incident was likely to have created another misunderstanding, which was averted by the discretion of David. Many of the men having been from weariness unable to pursue the march, had been left on the way by the brook Besor; and it was suggested that these had no right to any of *this* spoil, but only to have their own property and families restored to them. But David decided that they should all share alike; and this henceforth became established as a law in the Hebrew army, and has been adopted into the practice of modern warfare. The policy of this regulation is obvious; for, were every man at liberty to retain what he could take, or were the spoil to be appropriated only by the actual combatants, there must be at least great discontent among those detained by garrison or other duties from the immediate scene of action.

A considerable portion of the spoil fell to the share of the commander; and this he, with his usual open-handed liberality, employed in sending presents to the elders of various towns and villages in Judah, and to all the places where he had received encouragement and support during his wanderings. This came to them with the message, "Behold a present for you of the spoil of the enemies of the Lord." The natural effect of his success, of his discreet liberality, and of the admiration in which he was held was, that men came over to him in great numbers. "At

that time," says the writer of First Chronicles (xii. 22), day by day there came to David to help him, until it was a great host, like the host of God."

It seems to have been while at Ziklag that David, in the lack of means of affording more substantial marks of his regard and admiration for valiant deeds, and proofs of attachment to his person, devised something that looks exceedingly like an order of knighthood, or, on a small scale, a legion of honour, which has scarcely received all the attention it deserves. Out of the general body of his followers, he organized a band of worthies or knights, answering very much, we suspect, to the three degrees in the Order of the Bath, in which we have Grand-Crosses, Knights-Commanders, and Companions. In David's band there were *three* chief heroes, *three* second in prowess, and *thirty* inferior to these—thirty-six in all. It is also very likely that they were distinguished from the general band, and the different degrees from each other, by insignia of honour. It is a great mistake to suppose, that the use of such insignia is a modern invention. The modern decorations, crosses, medals, and stars, are in principle but the revival of an ancient practice. It is known to have existed among the Romans, who had *phialæ* and *phaleræ* of honour—terms which have been supposed to signify bracelets and medals; but all opinion on the subject was only conjectural, previously to the discovery on the borders of the Rhine of a monumental bas-relief,

ROMAN BAS-RELIEF OF TRIBUNE, WITH MEDALS OF HONOUR

raised by the freedman of Marcus Cælius Lembo, tribune of the (XIIX) 18th Legion, who fell in the disastrous overthrow of Varus. This effigy is of three-quarter length, in a full suit of armour, with a laurel crown on the head, a Gallic twisted torque around the neck; and from the lion-headed shoulder-clasps of the cuirass hang two embossed bracelets, having beneath them a label with three points, from which are suspended five medals of honour; one large, on the pit of the stomach, representing a head of Medusa; and two on each side, one beneath the other—and all, as far as can be seen, charged with lions' faces and lions' heads in profile. This monument is now in the University of Bonn.[1]

The exploits which won for some of David's illustrious band their high distinction are recorded; but some of them seem to have been performed after David became king, showing that he kept up this body during his reign, probably by supplying vacancies as they occurred. This also accounts for our finding in the list such names as that of Benaiah, who, seeing that he was in the prime of life at the end of David's reign, could hardly have been one of the worthies before its commencement. The three chiefs who formed the first class, were Jashobeam the Hachmonite, Eleazar son of Dodo, and Shammah son of Agee. The first, according to one account,[2] lifted up his spear against 800 men, whom he slew at one time; but another account makes the number *three* hundred,[3]—a difference which some reconcile by supposing that he slew 800 men in one action and 300 in another. However interpreted, this exploit well entitled the valiant Jashobeam to his place as "chief among the captains." Eleazar was one of those three who, with David, maintained the ground against a Philistine force, when their people had retreated, and at length routed them; so that when the men returned for very shame, there was nothing for them to do but to divide the spoil of their enemies. On that occasion Eleazar "smote the Philistines till his hand was weary and clave unto his sword."[4] This seems to have occurred during the period when David acted as Saul's

general against the Philistines. So, seemingly, does the exploit of Shammah, who defended a field of barley against a troop of Philistines, and compelled them to retreat. These were the three men who formed the first class of David's worthies. The three next, who composed the second class, were renowned for a deed of truly chivalrous devotion to David—so that opposing hosts could not prevent them from fulfilling his slightest wish. When he was in the cave of Adullam, the Philistines had a garrison in Bethlehem; and he was unmindful of this circumstance when, suffering from thirst, and remembering the pleasantness of the water from the well of his native town, he expressed a longing for a draught thereof. The words had no sooner passed his lips than these three men took their departure, and going boldly through the Philistine host, drew water from the well, and brought it to their chief. Touched by this proof of hardihood and strong attachment, he refused to drink the draught so hardly won—"he poured it out before the Lord," declaring that he would not drink the blood of his men. Alexander did something like this, only not so striking, at Gerodosia.[1] A vessel of water was offered him when under extreme thirst, but he refused to take it, because he could not bear to drink it alone, and the small quantity could not be divided among all those who were about him.

The chief of this second class of three was Abishai, nephew of David and brother of Joab. He was celebrated for putting to rout three hundred adversaries; and this twofold distinction gave him the first place in this second rank of heroes. To this rank, probably at a later period, was Benaiah elevated, whose exploits were very remarkable. It is said that he "had done many acts;" and three of them are mentioned as examples of their quality: in fact, there is more recorded of this man than of any others. First, "he slew two lion-like men of Moab;" next, "he went down and slew a lion in the midst of a pit in time of snow." Why the snow is mentioned is not clear, though it had no doubt some connection with the exploit; perhaps its lying on the ground had caused the lion to fall into the pit. Josephus understands that the lion, having fallen into a pit where there was much snow, got covered with it, and there making a hideous roaring, Benaiah went down and slew him.[2] So

---

[1] Col. C. Hamilton Smith, Art. "Arms," "Armour," in *Cyclop. of Biblical Literature.*

[2] 2 Samuel 23:8.   [3] 1 Chronicles 11:11.

[4] This reminds one of the case of the Highland sergeant at Waterloo, whose basket-hilted sword had, after the battle, to be released from his hand by a blacksmith (Simpson's *Visit to Flanders in July* 1815); and of the incident in the life of the celebrated Colonel Gardiner, who, when lying severely wounded on the field of battle, to secure his gold from being plundered, placed it in his hand, which he smeared with his blood, to prevent his grasp relaxing in the event of his fainting from weakness. In the same way the hand of Eleazar may have been in a manner glued to his sword by his own blood.

[1] Quintus Curtius, *Hist.*, lib. vii. cap. 5.   [2] *Antiq.*, vii. 12, 4.

read, it seems no great exploit. It has been very much outdone of late by Mr. Cumming, though, to be sure, Benaiah had no gun. Altogether, the exploit would have been more signal, apparently, had the lion *not* been in the pit, although there may be something not altogether agreeable in such close quarters with a lion. Upon the whole, it is likely Bochart may be right in his notion, that Benaiah went into a *cave* for shelter from a snow-storm, and was there attacked by a lion, which had also sought shelter therein, and which he overcame and slew.

The third recorded exploit of this valiant man is in some respects comparable to David's combat with Goliath. The opponent was an Egyptian giant about eight feet high, and armed with a spear. But Benaiah went down against him with no weapon save his staff; and plucking the spear out of his hand, slew him with his own spear. The man distinguished by these romantic feats eventually became captain of David's guard—a post which he retained under Solomon.

Of the thirty who formed the third class, we possess only the names. Few of them are historically known; but we find in it, with a feeling of painful surprise, the name of *Uriah the Hittite*. That this man had been deemed worthy of this high honour, given only to the brave and the devoted, gives a still deeper dye to the crimson of David's sin against his life and honour.

In this list also occurs the name of Joab's armour-bearer, Naharai; and yet the name of Joab himself is not found in any of the classes. This is difficult to account for, except by supposing that his position was too eminent, as commander-in-chief, to need the distinction which the belonging to this order conferred on other men. Or, as this high place was of later acquirement, it may be that Joab was the unnamed *third* of the second trio of worthies.

THE SONG OF THE BOW

2 Samuel 1

THERE are two accounts of the death of Saul. One is that of the sacred historian himself, the other that of an Amalekite who brought the tidings to David. The former is of course the true account. According to both, the Israelites were put to flight by the Philistines in the battle of Gilboa. Saul and his three valiant sons (of whom Jonathan was one) disdaining to flee with them, were all slain upon the field. The regular narrative says, that being sorely wounded by an arrow, Saul begged his armour-bearer to run him through, that he might not fall alive into the power of the Philistines. The armour-bearer declined; whereupon the king took a sword, and cast himself upon it, dying, probably, with some such sentiments as the poet ascribes to him:—

" My kingdom from me rent, my children slain,
My army lost, myself from hope cast out,—
The seer hath spoken well. All is achieved.
David, thou art avenged."

It would seem that the Amalekite had, from a distance, witnessed this transaction, and approaching, took the royal insignia from the body. These were, the bracelet—in the East a most ancient,

ANCIENT BRACELETS

and still subsisting symbol of royalty—which we recognize in the ancient monuments of Egypt, Persia, and Assyria, and among the existing regalia of Persia, India, China, and other lands; also his crown, which, being worn in battle, was probably some kind of diademed helmet, such as we find in ancient monuments. It was, no doubt, a question with the man whether he should not make off with this precious spoil; but, on second thoughts, he fancied it would be better to take them to David, who, flattered by this recognition of his claims, would not fail to reward him beyond their intrinsic worth. To enhance his merits, he also determined to claim the credit of having, at Saul's request, slain him with his own hand. How could David fail to load with honours and wealth the hand which had laid his great enemy in the dust? Never was human sagacity more at fault. David was affected with most sincere grief at the tidings which the man brought; but he burned with indignation that an Amalekite should have dared to shed the blood of the Lord's anointed, whose life had heretofore been so precious in his eyes. After, therefore, reproaching the man for the deed, he commanded that he should be put to death,—a hard measure, scarcely justified by the higher standard of feeling which Christianity has introduced, but which was, without doubt, highly applauded in that day.

The touching and beautiful lamentation which David composed on receiving tidings of the death of Saul and Jonathan, remains to bear witness to his grief, and to that delicate susceptibility which made tears for a fallen rival natural to him, but which few are able to retain so freshly as he did amidst constant association with men of coarse natures and wild manners, such as had been his mates in the wilderness. Here is the song, in a somewhat more correct form than that of the authorized version :—

On thy heights, O Israel, is the Gazelle slain !
  How are the mighty fallen ! [1]

Tell it not in Gath, publish it not in the streets of Askelon,
  Lest the daughters of the Philistines rejoice,
  Lest the daughters of the uncircumcised triumph.

Hills of Gilboa, no dew, no rain, come on you, devoted
    fields,
  For there was stained the bow of the mighty,
  Saul's bow, never anointed with oil.

From the blood of the slain, from the fat of the mighty,
  The bow of Jonathan turned not aside,
  And the sword of Saul came not back empty.

Saul and Jonathan ! lovely and pleasant were ye in life,
  And in death ye were not divided.
  Swifter than eagles, stronger than lions, were they.

Daughters of Israel, weep ye for Saul :
  He arrayed you pleasantly in scarlet ;
  He put ornaments of gold on your apparel.
    How are the mighty fallen in the midst of the battle!
    O Jonathan, slain in thy high places!

O Jonathan, my brother, I am grieved for thee :
  Very pleasant wast thou to me—
  Wonderful was thy love, passing the love of woman,
    How are the mighty fallen,
    And the weapons of war perished.

In the authorized version, this noble elegy is introduced by a strange parenthesis: "And David lamented with this lamentation over Saul and

[1] The lines in *italics*, it will be readily seen, form the chorus.

over Jonathan his son (also he bade them teach the children of Judah *the use of* the bow; behold it is written in the book of Jasher)." The words, *the use of,* are interpolated, to give the sense that the clause refers to instruction in archery; and it must be admitted that this sense is given to it by divers Jewish and Christian commentators.

Without these words the clause stands, " He bade them teach the children of Judah the bow"— suggesting that this was the title given to the lamentation itself, from the repeated mention of the bow in it—an explanation quite conformable to the Hebrew practice in giving titles to their sacred songs, and which supplies to the parenthesis a close connection with, instead of an abrupt and harsh transition from, what precedes and follows.

It may well be asked, Had the men of Judah yet to learn the use of the bow ? It was the common weapon. The Hebraism for " bow" is like that for " bread." As the latter includes all food, so does the former include all weapons. The argument on which the current interpretation is founded is weak indeed—that because Saul and Jonathan fell before the arrows of the Philistines, therefore the children of Judah should be taught the use of the bow. But no deficiency in this weapon appears among the Judahites, and Saul and Jonathan themselves were excellent archers. In the elegy itself it is said, " The bow of Jonathan turned not back."

The coherence is quite spoiled by this interpretation. The author of the book brings in David as about to commence an epicedium on the death of Saul and Jonathan, and immediately breaks off with an utterly irrelevant order that the men of Judah should be taught to handle the bow. And why is it that for *this* we should be referred to the book of Jasher, which, from the quotation given from it here and in Josh. x., seems to have been rather a book of national songs than a military order book ?

That "The Bow" should be the title assigned to this lamentation, will not surprise those who look to the titles of some of the Psalms, such as "Hind of the Morning,"[1] the "Mute Dove among Strangers,"[2] the "Lilies,"[3] and others, having some kind of reference to the contents, besides others which denote the instruments whose music accompanied them. It is easy to see why this poem should bear the name of *Keseth*, or "The Bow." First, probably, because it was occasioned by the Philistine archers;[4] and also, it would seem, with special regard to the bow of Saul and that of Jonathan, both of which are emphatically noticed in this lament. And the allusion to the bow of Jonathan, which turned not back from the blood of the slain, could not but suggest to David another recollection of *that* bow, out of which, in a day tenderly remembered, was shot the arrow which was to be to him the signal of safety or of danger. At that time it was that the brotherly covenant was made, and that affection was expressed between the two which was greater than the love of woman. In fact, there is not one of the Psalms, the contents or occasion of which afford so much reason for the title it bears as this elegy does.

It is observable that the translation of the Septuagint, and of the older editions and manuscripts of the Vulgate, is quite conformable to this, and not to the now current interpretation. It is the same in Tyndale's translation, which forms the basis of the authorized version. In that we read: "And David sang this song of mourning over Saul and over Jonathan his son, and bade to teach the children of Israel the staves thereof."

[1] *Aijeleth Shahar*, Ps. xxii.
[2] *Jonath-elem-rechokim*, Ps. lvi.
[3] *Shoshannim*, xlv., lxix., lxxx., and in lx., the same in the singular—*Shushan*, the lily.
[4] 1 Samuel 31:3.

DAVID IN HEBRON

2 Samuel 2:1-7; 1 Samuel 31:11-13

THE death of Saul with his three eldest sons in the fatal battle of Gilboa, fully authorized David to advance his own claims without the reserve he had hitherto maintained. He was king by right. He had been anointed for the reversion, and he was now entitled to possession. By the same right under which Saul had held his crown, David was now entitled to claim it. Saul had been appointed on certain well understood conditions, which he had violated; and on certain principles, which he had contravened. The forfeiture of the succession of his descendants was the penalty, and that he had incurred. The Lord, therefore, acting on the right reserved from the first, and under which Saul had become king, declared that forfeiture, and nominated David to the succession, and had caused him to be anointed to it by His prophet. This was now known to all Israel; Saul's heir had acquiesced in it; and Saul himself had acknowledged the constitutional validity of this deposition, although he persecuted the individual on whose head the lapsed crown was to fall. It is useless to enter into any argument here with reference to the principles and practices of other monarchies. The Hebrew monarchy had a definite constitutional principle of its own, and it is by this that we must judge—that we must call a thing fit or unfit, right or wrong. According to that constitution, David was *de jure* king; nor was there ever any one by whom, or in whose favour, the *jus divinum* might with so much truth be urged. The hereditary principle had no application here. But allowing for a moment that it had—the true heir of the house of Saul was Mephibosheth, the son of Jonathan, who had expressly renounced all claims for himself and his heirs in favour of David.

Still it was not the object of the divine nomination to force an unacceptable king upon the chosen people. Even Saul had waited until his nomination had been confirmed by the choice of the nation. The claim was good as against any other candidate, but was not intended to be good for military or other compulsory enforcement upon the people. This was very well understood by David, who acted with commendable delicacy and discretion in the somewhat trying position in which he now found himself. He sought not to force himself into the vacant throne by his armed bands; but he presented himself to the choice of the people, clothed with the honour of the Lord's nomination, of which, by several years of conspicuous trials and triumphs, he had been enabled to show himself worthy.

The crisis was too important for a man like David to move in without taking counsel of God. His first question was, if he should now go into the land of Judah? and this being affirmatively answered, he asked, to what place? and Hebron was named. This ancient city of Abraham was the capital of the tribe of Judah, and the strongest and most important place within its limits. It was also one of the Levitical cities, and therefore strong in the interests of David, not only from the keener perception the priestly tribe would have of the validity of his nomination to the crown, but from their sympathy with the man whose cause, since the massacre at Nob, had become identified with their own.

To Hebron, accordingly, David marched his now considerable army, entering the town with the *élite* of his force, and stationing the rest with their families in the neighbouring villages and towns. He was here welcomed with joy by his own tribe, and with little delay the crown of Judah was tendered to him by the leaders of the tribe, and was accepted by him. They could not offer him more. They had no right to offer him the dominion over other tribes than their own. But that was no reason why they should delay to declare their own sentiments. The rank of Judah among the tribes—the pre-eminence belonging to it, which only Ephraim ventured to question—gave it a right to take the initiative; and there was reason to expect that it would be followed by the other tribes.

It seems to have been felt that very much would depend on securing the adhesion on the loosely attached tribes beyond the Jordan. David had reason to think his cause was popular there, by reason of the parties from Gad and Manasseh which had joined him, and remained attached to his person. An opportunity of gracefully inviting attention to his claims, was afforded by the men of Jabesh-gilead, which belonged to Manasseh.

After the battle of Gilboa, when the Philistines came to strip the slain, they found the bodies of Saul and his three sons. The head of Saul they cut off, that they might carry it about in triumph, a custom too general to need illustration, and which David himself had exemplified when he slew Goliath. The king's rich armour they removed, and sent to be hung up as a trophy in the temple of Ashtaroth. David in like manner had given the sword, and probably the armour, of Goliath, to be laid up before the Lord. This was a mode in which the ancients acknowledged that their victories were due to the gods they worshipped, or at least of presenting suitable offerings of thanksgiving for such victories. It was especially the custom of the Greeks and Romans—whose usages we know better than those of other nations— thus to adorn their temples. Virgil, who is scarcely greater as a poet than as an antiquary, describes it as an ancient custom of the Latins:

ROMAN MILITARY TROPHY

> " Around the posts hung helmets, darts, and spears,
>   And captive chariots, axes, shields, and bars,
>   And broken beaks of ships, the trophies of their wars."
>   *Dryden.* [1]

We have ourselves retained what is essentially the same custom, in hanging up in our churches the banners taken from the enemy. In fact, one who is careful to trace the analogies of customs and usages, does not expect to find many that are peculiar to any people.

The trunk of Saul, and the bodies of his sons, not being available as trophies, were gibbeted by way of insult and intimidation, on the walls of Bethshan—a place not far from the field of battle, towards the Jordan. To the Jews, whose law forbade such exposure of a dead body beyond the sunset of the first day, this dreadful spectacle was far more disgusting and horrible than it would, until recently, have been to us, whose roads and shores, and solitary places, have within the memory of living men been defiled with

---

[1] Multaque præterea sacris in postibus arma,
    Captivi pendent currus, curvæque secures,
    Et cristæ capitum, et portarum ingentia claustra,
    Spiculaque, clypeique, ereptaque rostra carinis.
                    Æn., vii. 183 *seq.*

corpses similarly exposed. It is possible that the Philistines, knowing how adverse this practice was to the customs of the Israelites, and how revolting it must seem to them, were all the more inclined to treat the body of Saul thus ignominiously.

Shocked as the Israelites were, none ventured to interfere save the men of Jabesh, whose grateful remembrance of their deliverance by Saul at the commencement of his reign, impelled them to undertake the bold and dangerous enterprise of rescuing the remains of their benefactor and his sons from this disgrace. They travelled at least ten miles, and having crossed the Jordan, stole away the bodies by night, in the face, as it were, of a hostile garrison. Returning the same night to Jabesh, they there burned the bodies, and having gathered up the bones, buried them under a tree, and mourned and fasted seven days for their fallen king. It was not the custom of the Jews to burn the dead, as among the Greeks and Romans. There must, therefore, have been some special reason for the men of Jabesh burning the remains of these princes. It was probably to prevent the possibility of the Philistines again maltreating the dead bodies, in case that, finding they had been taken away, they should search after them, and discover the place in which they had been deposited.

This act of devoted attachment was well calculated to impress the susceptible heart of David, especially as one of the corpses thus rescued from disgrace was that of his beloved Jonathan. He wished the men of Jabesh-gilead to feel, that although Saul had treated him as an enemy, and although he had reaped advantage from his death, such proofs of attachment to the fallen prince were not displeasing to him, but were entirely in unison with his own sentiments. He notified that the tribe of Judah had anointed him king, and intimated that, in case they also adhered to him, they might expect his special consideration and protection. This, as we take it, was the purport of his message: "Blessed be ye of the Lord, that ye have showed kindness to Saul your lord, and have buried him. Now may the Lord show you kindness and truth, and I also will requite your kindness. Therefore let your hands be strong, and be ye valiant; for though your master Saul is dead, yet the house of Judah have anointed me king over them."

This was a very kind and considerate message.

It must be admitted that, in sending it, David assumes a certain right to acknowledge officially a public service, and invites them to recognize his authority. Such a recognition on the part of persons who had evinced so much attachment to Saul, could not but have much weight with others. But what rendered it the more proper was, the probability that the Philistines might attempt to call them to account for the deed they had achieved; in which case he encourages them to hold out, in the assured expectation, notwithstanding his recent connection with the Philistines, that they should receive the same assistance and support from him as they had formerly received from Saul. If this promise be, as we apprehend, involved in the message of David to the men of Jabesh-gilead, it must have been full of significance to a wider audience than that to which it was addressed, as it assured the people that his duty to the nation was, in his view, superior to all considerations of recent obligation to the Philistines, and that he should, notwithstanding this, be ready to take arms against them if their conduct presented an adequate reason and provocation. Such an assurance could not, under the circumstances of the time, have been more openly expressed; and if taken in the sense we have defined, it could not but convey a most satisfactory intimation to the people, that he was not at all disposed to reign by mere sufferance of the Philistines, or as their tool or instrument,— a suspicion of which might naturally have been engendered by his late intercourse with them, his protection by them, his obligations to them, and the apparent willingness he had manifested to fight under their banners against his own people.

My first sight of Hebron was memorable. We entered from the north; shadows gathered denser and denser in the valleys, the hills stood out distinct against the sky, every tree and shrub on the near horizon was sharply defined, as if cut out of metal. Delicious were the gold and green after sundown, the light becoming paler and paler, every object in the distance dark, as in some of Millais' pictures. We looked out for the city on each turning of the path, on the ascent of every hill, but we looked for it in vain. I rode on silently mile after mile, getting into narrow pathways, rocky and uneven, now dry, now full of pools of water, then between rude walls and vineyard and garden fences. The sky was beautiful, the region was sacred, for we were approaching one of the oldest cities of the world —the famous burial place of Abraham and his family. For an hour we journeyed in the dim moonlight; but at length shadowy looking buildings and a gateway told us we were entering the precincts of a town. We passed through a portion of it, and issued from it again on the south side by a gate and pool (a square tank still full of water), where David hanged the murderers of Ishbosheth, his rivals.

HEBRON—LOWER POOLS

After a few minutes' groping and stumbling where we had dismounted, we picked our way through a field up to our encampment.

S.

THE TURNING POINT

THERE is a feature in God's providential dealings with His people, which is strikingly exemplified in that portion of David's history which has passed under our survey. It is this: Afflictions and trials are often allowed to accumulate, one after another, without rest or pause, for a certain time, until a point of such accumulated wretchedness is reached, that it seems as if the last point to which even human endurance can stretch— the utmost pitch to which even heavenly sustainments can uphold this earthly essence—has been attained, and that it needs but one atom more added to the agglomerated burden of these troubles, to break the spirit on which it has been piled up. Then, at what seems to us the last moment, He who knoweth our frame, and remembereth that we are but dust—He who will never suffer us to be tempted beyond what we are able to bear—appears as a deliverer. With His strong hand He lifts the burden from the shoulder, and casts it afar off; tenderly does He anoint and bind up the deep sores it has worn in the flesh, and pour in the oil and the wine; and graciously does He lead us forth into the fresh and green pastures, where we may lie down at ease under the warm sunshine of His countenance, till all the frightful past becomes as a half-remembered dream—a tale that is told.

In David's case the long misery of the first stage of his public career seems to have reached its culminating point when, on his return to Ziklag, he found his pleasant home burnt up with fire—his wives and children borne away into captivity, he knew not whither—surrounded by men who were the sharers in this calamity, and who, in the bitterness of their spirits, mutinied against their leader, and placed his very life in peril.

This was the trial. It was, as Joab said of another trial, many years after, the worst to him " of all the evil that had befallen him from his youth until now." This was a sign that relief was at hand. When things are at the worst, as the common proverb says, they must mend. And they mended with David from that hour. And this was not *because* things were then at the worst with him, but because, being at the worst, he fought that great fight of affliction well. "HE ENCOURAGED HIMSELF IN THE LORD HIS GOD ; " and he found that his encouragements in God exceeded beyond all measure his discouragements from man, although friends combined with enemies to discourage him then. From that moment when he believingly cast all his dependence upon the Lord his God only, whom he had found faithful in all His promises, and whose providence had never failed him in his deepest dangers—from that moment he was safe—from that moment he was prosperous. " God loves"— and this David well knew—says an old writer,[1] " to reserve His holy hand for a dead lift in behalf of His servants in covenant with Him, when there is a damp upon their hopes, and a death upon their helps."

Now that the time of change was come, all things went well with him, and his prosperity increased like a river, gathering strength and fulness in its course, until, long after, a great crime stayed its course, and overwhelmed him with tides of trouble and grief, compared with which the trials of his early days were light.

[1] Christopher Ness.

This Ziklag is laid in ashes; but no sooner is he left shelterless than God provides him a better city, even Hebron, a city of refuge, and most truly a refuge to him. Saul dies at this time to give him room. "Now doth David find the comfort," says Bishop Hall, "that his extremity sought in the Lord his God. Now are his clouds for a time passed over, and the sun breaks gloriously forth. David shall reign after his sufferings. So shall we, if we endure to the end, find a crown of righteousness, which the Lord, the righteous judge, shall give us at that day." With regard to his taking with him his companions to be the sharers of his better fortunes, while their mutiny was yet fresh and green, the same writer beautifully remarks, "Thus doth our heavenly Leader, whom David prefigured, take us to reign with Him, who have suffered with Him. Passing by our manifold infirmities, as if they had not been, He removeth us from the land of our banishment, and the ashes of our forlorn Ziklag, to the Hebron of our peace and glory."

Nor do these observations find application only to temporal prosperity. The same is observable in the higher matters of spiritual life. It is, perhaps, the general rule, that we are seldom admitted to the fulness of God's presence, and to the enjoyment of that peace which passeth all understanding, until we have gone through great throes of spirit, and groanings that cannot be uttered, in the conviction of our forlorn and miserable condition. It is then that the Comforter comes to reveal Christ to our hearts as a Redeemer and a Healer; and then, to us old things are passed away, and all things are become new. We are not healed, till we feel how desperately we have been wounded—not redeemed, till we know how utterly we have been enslaved—not saved, till we know how entirely we were lost.

And again, how often, in our spiritual course, have we seasons, sometimes long, of darkness and gloom of spirit, during which our Lord seems to hide His face from us, and to have forgotten to be gracious to us; and then, at the moment of most extreme despondency and discouragement, when the gloom is deepest, the agony most intense, and we gasp as in the throes of spiritual death—the cloud rolls away, the sun shines out upon us, and all the fair fields and gardens of our inner paradise again look green—the drooping flowers of the heart revive—and all that is not earthly in us exults in the enlivening rays.

These considerations are most proper to the history of David, for there is no human history in which those transitions are more distinctly marked; while his Psalms are full of passages which may be, and are, continually cited to illustrate these contrasted aspects of our spiritual condition.

THE FIRST BLOW

2 Samuel 2:12-32

It seems to us highly probable, that the whole of the tribes would have invited David to reign over them, had they been left to follow their own convictions and impulses. Even those most indifferent to his cause, would have shrunk from the responsibility of setting up a rival, and of thereby dividing the realm into two kingdoms, which must have been the result; for although they might assert the right of appointing over themselves another king than David, they had no right to interfere with the choice which Judah had made, or to say that David should not be its king. Besides, there was no motive for opposition to one who came before them under the highest sanctions known to their institutions. He was untried as a king; there was hence nothing on account of which complaints could be made against him; and nations are always disposed to hope more from an untried man than from one whose worst and whose best they know. But it was only as a king that David was not tried. As a public man, as a general, as one chosen of God, he was already well known and eminent; and what was thus known, must have led to the expectation that his reign would be beneficent and glorious.

The natural result which might have been expected to flow from these considerations was, however, prevented by Abner, the first cousin of Saul, and who had long been chief captain of his host. This man was held in high respect throughout Israel, and his influence with the tribes was very great. This he determined to exert in upholding the house of Saul; and he acted with a promptitude and decision which evince the great abilities for which he had credit, and which ensured his success. From what eventually transpires, it is indeed clear, as was but too natural under the circumstances, that views of personal ambition, and an unwillingness to sink into an inferior position to that which he had hitherto occupied, swayed him against his own convictions that David ought to reign, and that it was for the good of the country that he should do so. Besides, he was aware that there were great men about David, whose claims, by services and nearness of blood, upon his consideration, were greater than any he could produce; and seeing that David's character had not yet been tried by the possession of power, he may have doubted the safety of so eminent, and possibly dangerous, a member of Saul's family as himself.

Abner, not less than David, seems to have attached great importance to the adhesion of the tribes beyond the Jordan; and therefore he crossed into the land of Gilead with Ishbosheth, the only surviving son of Saul, and proclaimed him king at Mahanaim. This step was not miscalculated. The western tribes successively gave in their adhesion, and David was, for the present, shut out from the expectation of establishing his authority over the whole nation. It was adverse to his policy, and would in itself have been fruitless, to attempt to coerce the tribes to accept him; he was therefore content to await the course of the Lord's providence, assured that not one of the things which had been promised him would fail to be realized. There is no appearance that he sought to enter into any conflict with the house of Saul. This did indeed arise; but it seems to have arisen rather through some attempt of Abner upon the kingdom of Judah, than of David upon that of Ishbosheth. As a general rule, the military aggressor is he who marches an armed force towards the territory of the other; and we find that Abner concentrated a large force at Gibeon, close upon the frontier of Judah. This had a threatening aspect, whatever was its intention; and a corresponding force advanced from David, to observe its movements. It was under the command of Joab, whose valour, whose military capacity, and the rough energy of whose character, had already given him that power with David, which he managed to maintain during his reign. Two such forces could not long remain apart; nor could two men of such fiery spirits as

Abner and Joab long stand in presence of each other with folded hands. Very shortly, a proposal came from Abner, that twelve picked men on each side should fight the battle out for the rest. This had the show of a wish to avoid the needless effusion of brothers' blood, and was therefore a decency suitable to both parties at the commencement of such a conflict; although both sides must have been aware, from repeated experience, that nothing could in this way be conclusively settled. Twelve men stood forth on either side, out in the midst, between the two armies, and assailed each other with an inveteracy only known in civil conflicts. Each of the twelve on the opposite side seized his opponent by the beard, and the whole twenty-four fell to the ground, slain by contrary wounds. A pregnant instance this of the inconvenience of beards in warfare, and an apt illustration of the saying of Alexander, of whom it is related by Plutarch in his Apophthegms, that when all things seemed ready for action, his captains asked him whether he had anything else to command them? He answered, "Nothing, but that the Macedonians shave their beards." Parmenio expressed his wonder at this, when the monarch added: "Know you not, that in fight there is no better hold for the enemy than a beard?"

This result, as almost always happens in such cases, whatever be the original intention, brought on a general action, in which Abner's troop was, after a severe struggle, obliged to give way, and fled before that of Joab. Abner himself was pursued by Joab's swift-footed brother, Asahel, who, having formed the purpose of possessing the spoils of this great chief, suffered not himself to be diverted to any other object. Eventually, they were both far away from their companions, Abner fleeing and Asahel pursuing. Perceiving this, and knowing himself to be a far more powerful man than the light and agile pursuer, Abner begged him to desist from the pursuit, being anxious, as he said, that a brother's blood should not lie between him and Joab, which would create a deadly animosity, where only a generous rivalry in arms existed now. This reasoning was not likely to have much weight with one who believed himself a match for the other; for, had he not so believed, he would not have pursued him. Finding this to be the case, and that Asahel followed close upon his steps, Abner gave a backward thrust with the heel of his spear, which was sharpened in order to its being stuck into the ground when the army was in cantonments. There needed no second stroke; the brother of Joab had received his deathblow, and lay weltering in his gore upon the ground.

At length, as the evening approached, Abner, being joined by some Benjamites, no longer fled. He stood on a vantage-ground, upon the top of a hill, and made an earnest appeal to Joab's better feelings against further bloodshed. " Knowest thou not," he said, " that it will be bitterness in the latter end?"—a point he might well have considered before he provoked this disastrous conflict. Joab, however, felt the force of the appeal, and he forthwith recalled his men from the pursuit by sound of trumpet. Abner, on his part, afraid probably that Joab might change his mind when he knew that his brother had been killed, marched all the night, and rested not until he had passed the Jordan, and found himself once more at Mahanaim.

The combat of twelve on each side, at the pool of Gibeon, may call to mind many similar transactions in history. Such affairs are frequent in Arabian warfare. Roman history affords a familiar instance in the combat of the Horatii and Curiatii. Not less familiar *now* is the incident in Scottish history on which Scott founded his tale of *The Fair Maid of Perth*. We may adduce this in the version of a German traveller (Kohl), for the sake of his closing remark :—" In this year (1390) reigned in Scotland King Robert III., who, perceiving that the wild refractory clans would annihilate one another in their endless contentions, proposed to the two hostile clans, clan Chattan and clan Kay, that they should settle their differences in the following manner. They were each to select their doughtiest men, and appear with them upon the Inches of Perth. These were to fight together in the presence of the king and his court; the victors were to be declared to have been in the right, and the vanquished were to forget and forgive. Thirty chosen warriors, children of the Kays, and the same number of Chattans, came down. . . . . . . In the fight, the clan Chattan triumphed; all the children of the Kay were slain but one, who leaped into the river Tay, and fled to the hills. Although we have all read this narrative in *The Fair Maid of Perth*, yet we cannot abstain from thinking once more of the circumstances when upon the very spot,—especially if the Tschergisses

of the Caucasus, and the ancient Bible histories of the Philistines, Carmelites (?), and the other inhabitants of the mountains, occur to the memory, who agree altogether so remarkably in their manners,—and when we again discover in these clans, clan feuds and clan fightings, and that in a similitude so exact, that they coincide in almost the slightest particular."

The parley at the end of the day, between Abner and Joab, may remind one of that between Hector and Ajax in the seventh book of the *Iliad*. Hector had been the challenger at the commencement, and it is he who, like Abner, makes the motion for the cessation of the combat :

" Now let the combat cease. We shall not want
　More fair occasion ; on some future day
　We will not part till all-disposing heaven
　Shall give thee victory, or shall make her mine.
　But night hath fallen, and night must be obeyed."

Mahanaim was situated on the east of the Jordan, and not far distant from the city of Jabesh-Gilead. Abner had wisely selected this place as the seat of Ish-bosheth's kingdom. The people of Jabesh were closely allied by blood to the Benjamites ; and the first and greatest of Saul's victories had saved that city and the land from the savage cruelty of a merciless foe. That noble act was held in grateful remembrance ; and now Ish-bosheth found an asylum and a throne among the people whom his father had saved from disgrace and ruin.

The sudden advance of Abner to Gibeon is accounted for by the fact that Gibeon was one of the strongholds of Benjamin, and that tribe was still devoted to the fortunes of its own royal house. It was also near the frontier of Judah, and the skilful general could from it watch the operations of his dangerous enemy. " The pool," or tank, where the battle was fought, exists to this day. It is at the eastern base of the hill on which the city stood, and beside it stretches out a broad upland plain, the same on which Joshua first attacked the banded hosts of the five Canaanite kings. Sitting on the brink of that pool a few years ago, I read the tragic story with a deeper interest, and a fuller appreciation of the minute accuracy of the Bible narrative, than I had ever felt before.

P.

ABNER

2 Samuel 3:1-16

ABNER was the sole stay of the house of Saul; and although all Israel knew this, there was no man in Israel half so conscious of the fact as

Abner himself. He behaved accordingly. Ishbosheth, whom he had made king, and whose throne he, for his own purposes, sustained, was a good, easy, imbecile man; and Abner cared not though he should feel that he was nothing without him—that it was not because of his rights, but because he was sustained by Abner, that he reigned. This character of feebleness in a king is favourable to the pretensions of a great subject, in enabling him to fix upon himself the consideration and real influence which should belong to the crown. We have seen this in our own history; and we see it to-day in the great rajahs and nawaubs of the East. But the final result is damaging to the real strength of the crown; and it was so in the case of Ishbosheth.

The people could not behold the feeble character of Ishbosheth without contrasting it with the brilliant qualities of David, his firm and beneficent government, the success which crowned all his enterprises, and the attachment of his people to him. All this was detrimental to the cause of the house of Saul; nor less so the fact, that in the small conflicts which arose in the course of years between the two parties—for both avoided bringing the matter to the decision of any great engagement—the issue was usually favourable to David. Under these various influences, concurring with the doubt which must have haunted the minds of many, whether, in upholding the condemned house and refusing the son of Jesse, they did not incur the awful responsibility of setting themselves in opposition to the known purposes of God, it came to pass that the cause of Ishbosheth became weaker every day, while that of David daily gathered strength. Abner himself was too sagacious a man not to perceive this; indeed, the observations of every day must have made him feel it most acutely; and he could not but know that it would not much longer be in even his power to uphold the tottering throne which he alone supported. When things were in this state, it would want but little to bring about a revolution. We are continually committing mistakes in assigning great effects to small and inadequate causes. There is never any effect without an adequate cause, although the circumstance which brings the already existing causes into operation, and which is so often mistaken for the cause itself, may be of small or trifling importance, and only one of a hundred other circumstances which might equally have brought them into operation. The fuel is laid, and anything that has fire in it will equally serve to kindle it up; whether it be a lighted candle, a match, a rag, a bit of paper, or a straw—it matters little.

From the time that Abner perceived that it was impossible for him to carry on much longer the high game he was playing, he must often have turned over in his mind the possibility of going over to David, and of acquiring power with him by some signal service in his cause. Pride, some sense of honour, and a lingering wish to retain possession of a more independent power than he could hope for under such a king as David, and with such rivals as the sons of Zeruiah, restrained him for the present; but he was prepared, if occasion should offer, to take the lead in the national movement towards David, in preference to becoming the victim of it. Occasion enough for him soon did offer.

King Ishbosheth, feeble as he was, had something of manly and royal spirit in him; and when he heard that Abner had appropriated to himself a woman named Rizpah, who had been Saul's secondary wife, or "concubine," and had borne him children, he was shocked and indignant at what the usages of the East rendered an act of gross disrespect to himself and to the memory of his father, if it did not indicate the same disposition to establish a claim to royal power in his own person, which, in the next generation, Solomon detected in the application of Adonijah for leave to espouse the virgin concubine of his deceased father. Whether the charge were well founded or not, is not very clear; but the presumption of the king in daring to call *him* to account in such a matter, or even to hint disapprobation, threw Abner into a towering passion, and he swore a fierce oath to cast down the throne he had reared up. "So do God to Abner, and more also, except, as the Lord hath sworn to David, even so do I to him; to translate the kingdom from the house of Saul, and to set up the throne of David over Israel, and over Judah, from Dan to Beersheba." Abner is self-convicted by these words. He knew that the Lord had sworn to give the throne to David, and yet he had resisted—consciously resisted—to the best of his power, the fulfilment of that high decree. He now reaps his reward in this—that his return to what was really his duty, bears the aspect of treachery, meanness, and dishonour. It is well, however, to remember that what he did now was his duty, had always been his duty, and was not the less his duty because he had intermediately rebelled against it. But that rebellion placed him in this invidious position—that it now devolved upon him to undo his own work, whereas at the first it was in his power to subside into graceful and honourable acquiescence in a degree which, although distasteful to him, he could not and ought not to resist. Had he done this, his acknowledged abilities must have secured for him no second place among the worthies of David, and his end might have been very different.

It may occur to many readers that the rage of Abner was as much affected as real, and that he was not sorry that the poor king had given him a pretext for turning away from him. As it was, Ishbosheth answered not a word to this outburst of his haughty kinsman—he was so greatly terrified. Afterwards he probably reflected that Abner's interests were too visibly bound up with his own to allow him to execute his threats; and that he abstained from any immediately demonstrative action, must have confirmed him in this impression.

But Abner's were not idle words. He sent faithful messengers to David, to make terms for his assistance in bringing over the other tribes to his cause. The king of Judah was alive to the importance of this intimation, yet he manifested no unbecoming eagerness to seize the opportunity. He knew that the Lord's purposes regarding him were in visible process of accomplishment; and he who had waited so long in patient faith, could, if need were, afford to wait a little longer. He therefore made it an essential preliminary to all negotiation, that his wife Michal should be restored to him. There is no law in any state, and there was certainly none among the Hebrews, which allows a father to divorce his daughter from her husband, and give her in marriage to another. But this Saul had done, having given Michal in marriage to Phaltiel the son of Laish. David's claim to her therefore remained intact. She was his first love; and although he had now other wives, his heart yearned towards this one in the keen and fresh remembrance of early affection. He had also purchased her dearly at the risk of his life; and he might not be unwilling thus to bring to the

remembrance of the people his old exploits against the Philistines, and to evince at this time the value he set upon his connection with the house of Saul. It might be very important that it should now appear that the members and partisans of that house were not beyond the scope of his clemency and favour.

Abner used this demand as the means by which to accomplish his ulterior object. It was in itself so reasonable, that he made it known to Ishbosheth, who readily consented that Michal should be taken from Phaltiel, and that Abner himself, as her natural protector, should conduct her to David. There has been much idle talk about the cruelty of taking her away from a man with whom she had lived some years, and who, for all that appears, was a good husband, seeing that he followed her, weeping and lamenting, until he was compelled to desist by those who bore her from him. But this was the fruit of his own wrong, which a man always reaps in the long-run. He had coveted another man's wife, and had wrongfully possessed himself of her, knowing well that she belonged to another; and Phaltiel was not the first man nor the last, who has lamented to be deprived of that which did not belong to him. Michal was David's wife—she was his *purchased* possession. Scarcely a month passes in which our own law does not in the like case take the woman from the second husband, and assign her to the first—declare her living with the second to have been a state of adultery—and even subject her to punishment for having married a second husband while the first lived. In the present case, there is every reason to suppose that Michal had been reluctantly coerced into this marriage; and although Phaltiel lamented her departure, there is no indication that she felt any sorrow in going. It is more probable that she rejoiced to be called to the side of her true husband, saying, "I will go and return to my first husband, for then it was better with me than now." (Hos. ii. 7.)

It would appear that the marriage between David and Michal had been dissolved by royal authority, though not assented to by David; and in a country and at a time when such authority was supreme and absolute, Phaltiel might regard Michal as free to marry him, when the lady was bestowed by the gift of a royal father. At all events, they seem to have lived happily together for fourteen years. During that period, the love of Michal towards David most likely diminished, if it did not totally expire, exposed, as it must have been, to sinister influences on the part of Saul and his family, who, with the exception of Jonathan, disliked the young hero. After her father's death she went with her husband, and the remains of the royal family, to the east of Jordan, whence she was brought back to David by Abner, captain of the host. David seems to have reverted to her with the renewal of his old affection. " I will not see thy face except thou first bring Saul's daughter . . . . my wife Michal, whom I espoused to me for a hundred foreskins of the Philistines." If the rending asunder of Michal from Phaltiel was sad in one way, the reunion between her and her previous husband turned out in another way still more sad. It must have been, at least, with much diminished affection that she became his wife a second time ; and the presence of other wives, Abigail and Ahinoam, was not likely to fan into a bright flame the embers of a love at best nearly dying out. The circumcumstances, too, at Hebron, were unfavourable to her happiness, for there she found herself among the courtiers and soldiers of the new king, full of resentment and hatred to the memory of her father, and the interests of her kindred. Probably there would be some mutual disappointment in the pair so inauspiciously reunited. Both were changed. Michal had reached the age of thirty, when eastern women lose their charms ; David, the once handsome artless youth had been for years an experienced chieftain, full of cares and troubles, he was now king of a struggling state, which required the utmost skill and care in government, and domestic love in his heart might be giving way to other passions. A terrible rupture between the two soon took place, to be described hereafter. When David entered Jerusalem in triumph, he danced before the ark clad only in a thin linen ephod. (1 Chron. xv. 27.) Michal was shocked at what she saw, and construed her husband's conduct as both undignified and indecent. (2 Sam. vi. 20.) The outburst of the wife's indignation provoked the violent resentment of her husband, and the hot words between them, recorded by the faithful historian, separated for ever the unhappy couple, who, but for the troubles which led to their early violent divorce, might have been blessed with a far different destiny.—See Art. " David," in Smith's *Dictionary of the Bible.*

S.

BLOOD REVENGE

2 Samuel 3:17-39

IT may be easily conceived that the passage through the country of so great a man as Abner, on such a business as that of conducting Saul's daughter to the king of Judah, attracted very general attention, and necessarily excited much speculation. Abner, on his part, regarded it as affording him a suitable opportunity of opening his views to the tribe of Benjamin, in which the strength of Saul's family lay, aware that few would be found to stand up for the cause which was abandoned by those most nearly interested in its support. To the elders of that tribe, and of such other tribes as came in his way, he plainly said that the Lord had chosen David to be king, and that David was the man whom the exigencies of the time demanded. There appears to have been some movement of the neighbouring enemies of Israel at this time, which might impart a freshness and a present interest to his tardy admission, that it was through David the Lord had promised to deliver Israel from their adversaries. He confesses his knowledge that they had wished to have David for their king ; *he* chiefly had interposed to prevent it, but he now graciously consents that they should have the king they desired. " Ye sought for David in times past to be king over you—now, then, do it."

Abner had no reason to complain of his reception by David, who entertained him and his guard of twenty men in a most princely style. The result of the conference was highly satisfactory to Abner, who took his departure with the promise of gathering deputies from Israel, who should publicly acknowledge David for their king. This was certainly no more than he was able to perform. He had only to permit what he had hitherto striven to prevent, but what, he knew well, it would not be in his power much longer to hinder.

Joab had at this time been absent on a military expedition ; and as neither David nor Abner would desire his presence, it is likely that this visit of Abner had been timed accordingly. But Joab returned immediately after Abner had left. He was greatly moved when he heard of this visit. He feared for himself. He bore testimony to the influence which his abilities, age, and long experience had secured for Abner, by the dread he entertained of him. There can indeed be little doubt that Abner would have become the second man in David's enlarged kingdom, and commander of the armies of Israel. There is no reason to question that Joab really felt the apprehensions he expressed—that Abner was, after all, deceiving David, and only sought an opportunity of effecting his ruin. He hurried to the king, and with the roughness and freedom which their near relationship and their old companionship in trouble seemed in his eyes to warrant, he sharply rated him for his easiness, and affirmed that Abner could have no other object than to betray him. That such was his real belief, goes somewhat to relieve his next step of some portion of the blackness which belongs to it, when regarded merely as the effect of individual jealousy and apprehension. He sent to call Abner back, under the pretence that some important communication had been forgotten. Abner accordingly returned, and was met without the gate by Joab, who saluted him in a friendly manner, and taking him aside as if to speak privately with him, smote him suddenly with his sword under the fifth rib, so that he died.

This, he chose to allege,—and his brother Abishai upheld him in that view,—was done in his right of blood revenge for his brother Asahel, whom Abner had slain. The question is not whether this was the true reason, but whether the excuse was so sound and valid as to justify him in the eye of the law, so as to protect him from the legal consequences of this assassination; in short, whether public opinion would or would not bear him out in this excuse.

The law was, that when a man slew another by what we should call manslaughter or justifiable homicide, the nearest relative had a right to exact vengeance—to put him to death wherever he could find him. This was an old custom of the pastoral tribes, too deeply rooted to be abolished by the Mosaic law, but the manifest evils of which that law sought to neutralize, by providing certain cities throughout the country, within whose walls the manslayer was safe from the sword of the avenger, who was dealt with as a murderer if he slew him there, but was not called to account if he met with him and slew him anywhere beyond the verge of the asylum. The real question therefore is, whether Abner was responsible to Joab for the blood of Asahel, shed in self-defence, under the circumstances lately described, and sorely against the wish of Abner himself. It is urged, that it was most unreasonable that Abner should be held accountable for this. The unreasonableness may be granted. The question is not, what was reasonable, but what was the custom. The custom was, in its very essence, unreasonable; and the law had striven, as much as possible, to mitigate what it could not do away with altogether. The act of Abner was justifiable homicide; but it was precisely to such cases that the rule applied, not to those of murder, against the penalties of which

no sanctuary afforded protection. Besides, unless the right of avengement for blood did apply to such cases as this, whence the deep anxiety of Abner to avoid slaying Asahel? Those expressions used by him on that occasion have no meaning, unless they show his knowledge of the fact, that the death of his pursuer would establish a blood-feud between him and Joab. In further confirmation of this view of the case, it may be noted that the other brother, Abishai, who had no direct hand in this bloody and barbarous deed, yet adopted and maintained it on the same grounds, as an act of avengement for a brother's blood. It may be admitted that a case of this nature may have involved some doubt as to the application of the rule to it, and very likely it was not, in such cases, often enforced. But where any room for doubt existed, Joab and Abishai might interpret it in their own favour, as their justification for an act, the true motives of which durst not be alleged, and as a ground on which they might claim exemption from the punishment due to murder. That the case stood on this doubtful ground, which did not render it an imperative duty of the next of kin to exact retribution, when in his power to do so—which did not, as among the Arab tribes at this day, leave him disgraced if he neglected to avenge a brother's blood, seems probable from the fact, that Abner went so readily aside with Joab, which he would hardly have done, had he not supposed that his offence was one which might be, and had been, forgiven. It was in the assurance that public opinion, however shocked, would, upon the whole, sanction the deed when placed on this ground, that this reason was produced; and as it was highly important, even for the king, that it should appear as an act of private revenge, rather than of political jealousy (in which he might have seemed to be implicated), there was abundant reason why David should not, by subjecting Joab to punishment for murder, give to the act a different complexion. It is usually said that Joab was too powerful to be brought to justice. We do not know that his power had *already* become so great as this implies; and we cannot but think that David would have found means of subjecting him to disgrace or punishment, but for the considerations we have stated— that public opinion would allow the deed to stand on the ground upon which the brothers placed it; and that, in the existing state of affairs, it was as well that it should rest upon that footing, the reason alleged being well calculated to relieve the king from any suspicion of having connived at this mode of ridding himself of a powerful and dangerous rival.

In corroboration of this view—which is the one advanced by the sacred historian, and which, on that ground alone, we ought to prefer—we may look back to Gideon's slaying the captive kings, Zebah and Zalmunna, on the express ground that they had slain his brothers at Tabor, in the course of the recent engagement. He said, "They were my brethren, the sons of my mother. As the Lord liveth, if ye had saved them alive, I would not slay you." And as it had thus become a case of blood-revenge, he slew them with his own hand, after his eldest son, Jether, had shrunk from the task. If more confirmation be needed, we may refer to the existing practice of the Arab tribes, in the frequent engagements between whom, blood-revenge is exacted for every life taken, if the person who inflicted the mortal stroke is known. It is this which renders the combats between the tribes so protracted and so comparatively blood-less, as every one dreads to subject himself to the pursuing sword of the avenger. These considerations do not, of course, operate in engagements with foreigners; and in Israel, contests between the tribes had hitherto been too infrequent to bring the results of the common law of blood-revenge into the usages of general warfare. When the tribes became permanently divided into two realms, after Solomon, the right of private blood-revenge could not exist as between the subjects of the two kingdoms, though it doubtless still subsisted between the tribes of which these kingdoms were severally composed.

David, who did not share Joab's suspicions of Abner's sincerity, was deeply concerned at a crime which not only marred all the expectations he had conceived from that great chief's adhesion, but threatened to widen the breach more than ever. As well, therefore, from real concern at the untimely end of a man so illustrious, and natural horror of the deed, as from policy, he was anxious that it should appear how deeply he lamented the event. He ordered a general fast and mourning; and the body of the unhappy Abner was honoured with a public funeral, at which the king himself appeared as chief mourner, and followed the corpse with loud lamentations to the grave, where, amid his own tears and the tears of the people, he, as was natural to him under strong emotion, gave vent to his feelings in this poetical utterance:

"Should Abner die as a villain dies?
  Thy hands—not bound,
  Thy feet—not brought into fetters:
As one falls before the sons of wickedness, so didst thou fall."

To explain this, it should be observed that Hebron was a city of refuge. If one fled to such a city, he was subjected to a sort of trial to ascertain his claim to the right of sanctuary. If found to be a murderer, he was delivered up, bound hand and foot, to the avenger, to deal with him as he pleased. Although Abner had left the city of refuge, not thus delivered up as a murderer, but free, he had no sooner left its gates than he had met a murderer's doom from the hands of the avenger. The idea of the lamentation is founded upon Abner's being slain as soon as he had quitted a city of refuge—a most unusual circumstance to one not found guilty of murder, seeing that those entitled to protection were not sent away.

TREACHERY PUNISHED

2 Samuel 4

At the first view, the death of Abner may seem to have been disastrous to the cause of David; but it may be doubted whether it was not eventually an advantage to him. Abner had been the chief, if not the sole, obstacle to the union of the tribes under Jesse's son. His consent had already removed that obstacle, and his death did but the more effectually remove it. Besides, had he lived, he was likely to have claimed all the merit of David's exaltation, and it would have been difficult to recompense him in a manner adequate to his own sense of his deservings. The command of the army he must have had, and this was probably the first of his stipulations; and a man of his temper, and in his position, would have been likely to vaunt (like our Earl of Warwick, under Edward IV.), on any occasion of discontent, that he could make and unmake kings at his pleasure; and he might have wanted but little inducement, from pique or ambition, to make further trial to establish the reality of that pretension. The high position which must have been given to him, could not but excite discontent among the brave men who, in the cloudy and dark day, had cast in their lot with David, and would have exposed him to the bitter taunt which Joab, at a later day, ventured to utter; "Thou lovest thine enemies and hatest thy friends!" Upon the whole, it seems well for David's peace that Abner was removed at this time, however the mode of his removal may be abhorred.

When Ishbosheth heard of Abner's death, he gave up all for lost, not knowing that his death could not be more dangerous to the crown than his life would have been. The tribes were for the moment perplexed, less, it would seem, from any doubt as to the result, than because the conduct of their negotiation with David had been committed to Abner. They might also be under some doubt how to act with reference to Ishbosheth, who had been acknowledged as their king, and whose very feebleness of character prevented him from having any enemies, and rendered him an object of compassion. It is very probable that, unless some other strong man had risen up to maintain his cause, Ishbosheth would in a short time, when he came to comprehend the real state of the people's mind, have made a voluntary resignation to David. But while men were talking together about these things, the news spread rapidly through the land that Ishbosheth also was dead.

It was even so. At his own court his cause was despaired of, and men began to consider how to do best for themselves. Two officers of his guard, named Rechab and Baanah, formed the notion that their advancement under the future king would be essentially promoted by their sweeping from his path the feeble life which seemed to lie between him and his destined throne. They therefore conspired to slay their master. In the heat of the day, when the king and most of the persons about him were taking the repose customary in Eastern lands, they entered the palace as if to procure some corn from the royal stores; and, penetrating to the private apartment in which Ishbosheth slumbered, they smote off his head, and bore it away undiscovered, probably placing it in the bag among the corn they had pretended to require. They

posted away to Hebron with their prize, and presented the ghastly trophy of their crime to David, with the words, "Behold the head of Ishbosheth, the son of Saul, thine enemy, who sought thy life; and the Lord hath avenged my lord the king this day of Saul, and of his seed." These words were artfully concocted, to put David into a frame of mind favourable to their views. But it was in vain. The king was, for a moment, mute with horror and detestation. It was dreadful that men should thus continually seek to win his favour by crimes which his soul abhorred. He spoke at last, and terrible were his words: "As the Lord liveth, who hath redeemed my soul out of all adversity, when one told me, saying, Behold Saul is dead, thinking to have brought good tidings, I took hold of him and slew him in Ziklag; who thought that I would have given him a reward for his tidings. How much more when wicked men have slain a righteous person in his own house upon his bed? Shall I not therefore require his blood at your hands, and take you away from the earth?" He then immediately commanded them to be slain, and their hands and feet, the instruments and messengers of murder, to be cut off and hanged up over the pool in Hebron, as monuments of the condign punishment of such frightful treachery. The head of Ishbosheth was honourably deposited in the tomb which had been prepared for Abner.

We have quoted at length the words of David, that we may be enabled to invite the reader to observe how finely his indignation is painted in that hurry and impetuosity of language, which carries him directly to the execution of the Amalekite, without waiting to mention any of the circumstances which tended to alleviate his guilt; and yet he adds, as if he had mentioned them all at large, "How much more when wicked men have slain a righteous person!" etc. If he had put the Amalekite to death for merely saying that he had slain Saul, even at his own command, and when he despaired of his own life, how much more would he take signal vengeance of their united treachery and murder? The Amalekite might have some ground of vengeance against Saul, in respect of the destruction that king had wrought upon his nation; but what had they— the trusted servants of Ishbosheth, the appointed guardians of his life—what had they to allege against their master?

The conduct of David towards the murderers of one who was, at least officially, his chief public enemy, may well be compared with that of Alexander to the slayer of Darius, and contrasted with that of Antony to the assassins of Cicero. In the former case, when Darius found that Bessus was plotting against his life, he did his great enemy the credit of believing that the traitor would fail to win from the generous conqueror the approbation and reward he expected. Nor was he mistaken in this. Alexander sternly and terribly rebuked the assassin: "With what rage of a wild beast wast thou possest, that thou durst first bind and then murder a sovereign to whom thou wast under the highest obligations?" And, rejecting his attempted extenuation of his crime with abhorrence, gave him over to the torture and death of the cross. On the same principle it was that Cæsar put to death the murderers of Pompey; and that the Romans sent back the Faliscian schoolmaster under the lashes of his own scholars.

With all this, and especially with the conduct of David, contrasts the behaviour of a man of far meaner spirit, though of immortal name. Mark Antony caused Cicero to be most cruelly murdered, and commanded his head and right hand to be cut off and brought to him. When these melancholy memorials of that eloquent tongue and gifted intellect—able, one would think, to move the sternest enemy to tears—were laid before him, Antony beheld them with visible and avowed satisfaction, and even broke forth into peals of exulting laughter; and after he had fully satiated his indecent joy with the sight, he ordered the head to be placed upon the rostra of the Forum, to insult him yet more after his death.

The cutting off the murderers' hands and feet, is clearly intended as a real, though somewhat metaphorical, application of the *lex talionis*—the crimes which the hands or feet have committed, being punished by the excision of these members. It is remarkable that in our own law—that is, in the letter of it—such mutilation only remains as a punishment for offences against the majesty of the sovereign; the loss of the hand being ordained for striking within the limits of the king's court, or in the presence of his judicial representative. In the Book of Moses the *lex talionis*, "eye for eye, and tooth for tooth," is distinctly laid down; but we find no

examples of its literal enforcement, unless in the instance of Adonibezek,[1] and in the present case, in which it is executed upon the dead body, as superadded to capital punishment. We infer from this, that, as among the Arabs of the present day, mutilations were generally commuted for pecuniary fines, so much being the assigned value of an eye, so much of a tooth, and so on. In fact, there is no history of ancient times, nor any of the modern East, in which we read so little of mutilations as in the Bible. At the present day, mutilating punishments are frequent among Orientals; and are inflicted, according to no definite rule, upon those whose situation in life renders them subject to the immediate operations of arbitrary power. But in other cases, where the law is left to its regular action, the excision of the hand is usually for offences of the hand, as theft, forgery, etc. In some Mohammedan nations, as Persia, robbery and theft are punished with death, though the Moslem law directs only mutilation; and this law was formerly so much observed in Moslem countries, that, as the readers of the Thousand and One Nights will recollect, the loss of the hand was a permanent stain upon a man's character, as evincing that he had been punished for robbery or theft.

THE BLIND AND THE LAME

2 Samuel 5:1-10

DAVID had reigned seven years and a half in Hebron, as king of Judah only, when a large concourse from all the tribes repaired thither to offer him the crown. There is a list of the numbers in 1 Chron. xii., in which the remarkable fact appears, that the remote northern tribes, and the tribes beyond the Jordan, among whom Ishbosheth had reigned, sent the largest numbers to this great assembly. The two and half tribes beyond the river sent above a third of the whole number; and the two tribes of Zebulun and Asher nearly a fourth of the whole. This was natural, as the distant tribes could only be represented by the numbers they sent; whereas the nearer tribes might be regarded as present in their stationary population. This accounts for

[1] See Vol. 1, pp. 508-509.

the fact, that the number assigned to the tribe of Judah, in which the cause of David was really strongest, is but small compared with many of the other tribes.

It is interesting to notice the grounds on which the elders offered him the crown.

He possessed the general but requisite qualification of being one of themselves: "Behold, we are thy bone and thy flesh."

He had been in former times their leader, and had proved himself worthy to be their king: "In time past, when Saul was king, thou wast he that leddest out and broughtest in Israel."

But above all, the Lord had nominated him to the kingdom: "The Lord said to thee, Thou shalt feed my people Israel, and thou shalt be captain over Israel." They knew this seven years before, as well as they knew it at this time, and their acknowledgment was somewhat tardy. It is, however, satisfactory to find them so distinctly placing his nomination on this footing; and the acknowledgment of the constitutional validity of his claim to the throne is important.

David then "made a league with them in Hebron before the Lord." They had no intention of placing their rights at the disposal of the king. Certain conditions were agreed to on both sides, defining his rights and theirs; and where such conditions exist, the monarchy is constitutional, not absolute. The conditions were, doubtless, such as had been established by Samuel, forming something like a coronation oath—which all future kings seem to have taken at their accession, although the limitations it involved do not appear to have been very exactly observed by all of them—the tendency of all power in the East, however formally limited, being towards absolutism.

David was then anointed king over all Israel—this being the third anointing he had received.

The king soon found that Hebron, although a very suitable capital for a realm confined to the tribe of Judah, was too far south to be a proper metropolis for a kingdom which embraced all the tribes. Yet he was reluctant to remove to a distance from his own tribe, on which he could most entirely rely. He therefore fixed upon Jerusalem (then called Jebus), which lay close upon the northern border of the tribe, but within the territories of Benjamin. Even this was scarcely central enough for the capital of all the tribes; but it was naturally a strong situation,

and the best that could be selected with regard to the limitation in view, being far more accessible than Hebron to the northern and eastern tribes. We see something similar in Persia, where the political metropolis is of recent establishment, in a remote and unpleasant situation northward, while much finer sites, far larger towns, and old metropolitan cities, have been avoided—and this solely that the sovereign may be near his own tribe, and able to throw himself among his own people in time of peril. Considering, however, that this place was to become ere long the capital of a southern kingdom, it was no doubt the providence of God which directed the choice of a site suited to this ulterior destination.

But first, Jerusalem was to be won. It was still in the hands of the Jebusites—at least the upper and fortified part, comprising Mount Zion.

CASTLE OF ZION

In the lower part, or the town as distinguished from the citadel, the Jebusites and Israelites (chiefly of Benjamin) seem to have lived intermingled. The fortress was so strong, and had been so long retained in their possession, that the Jebusites regarded it as impregnable, and derided all attempts to take it. This view of the case is conveyed in two verses, which have engaged much curious speculation. "The inhabitants of the land spake unto David, saying, *Except thou take away the blind and the lame,* thou shalt not come in hither. . . . And David said on that

day, Whosoever getteth up to the gutter, and
smiteth the Jebusites, and *the lame and the
blind which are hated of David's soul*, the same
shall be chief and captain; wherefore they said,
The *lame and the blind shall not come into the
house*." The question is, What is meant by "the
blind and the lame?" A very common interpretation is, that these were actually blind and lame
persons to whom, in derision, the Jebusites gave
the defence of the walls, as quite sufficient to
protect them from the impotent assaults of David.
This seems to us to leave much unexplained.
Supposing the case so, why should David express
such hatred and abhorrence of the poor creatures
who were forced into this service? How does
the act of *taking away* apply to such persons, or
any persons? To kill them would have had a
more obvious meaning. And again, citadels are
not usually encumbered with useless hands; how,
then, came there to be such blind and lame
persons in the stronghold of the Jebusites?
Upon the whole, in the presence of these objections to the other interpretation, we incline to
accept that of the best Jewish commentators, who
hold that idols were intended—idols of *brass*,
they say. This explains all—David's abhorrence,
the taking of them away, and their presence in
the fortress. But why called "the blind and the
lame?" It is a fact that the sacred writers do,
in derision, apply these terms to idols, because
"they had eyes, but saw not; and feet, but walked
not."

The meaning then will be, that the Jebusites
relied so strongly upon the protection of their
consecrated images, that they defied David to
take the town until these should be removed—
that is, never. They probably brought them
forth, and placed them on the walls, for greater
confidence, declaring they should not again be
"brought into the house" of idols, so long as the
enemy remained before the walls.

But it may be asked, What were the images
in which so much faith was reposed by the
Jebusites? It may be possible to answer this
question.

The founders of ancient cities and fortresses
were wont to cause the astrologers to find out a
fortunate position of the heavens under which
the first stone might be laid. "The part of
Fortune," fixed by this first figure, was made the
"ascendant" of another. The first had respect
to the continuance or duration of the place, and

the second regarded its outward fortune and glory.
Under the influence of the latter configuration,
an image of brass was erected, *into* which this
fortune and genius of the city was to be drawn
and fixed by the powers of alleged occult arts.
When imbued with this secret power, the image
was set up in some eminent or retired place in
the city, and was looked upon by the inhabitants
as *embodying* the special power and protecting
influence, on which the destiny and welfare of
the place and its inhabitants depended.

Such ceremonies (observed for such objects) are
known to have taken place at the foundation of
Alexandria by Alexander the Great, at the foundation of Antioch by Antiochus, of Apamea by
Seleucus, as well as at the foundation of Rome,
and of Byzantium, afterwards Constantinople.

It would seem that these solemnities were not
completed without bloody rites. In the instance
of Antioch, and this was probably the case elsewhere, a virgin was offered in sacrifice. A statue
of this virgin was then set up, upon which the
new and secret name of the city was imposed,
and then sacrifice was offered to this image.

The substance of this practice was retained in
the East by both Moslems and Christians. The
foundation of the city was still laid under astrological calculations—its horoscope, however, was
not embodied in an idol, but in a talisman; and
the human sacrifices were discontinued. When
old Byzantium was revived under the name of
Constantinople, the statue of the Emperor was
set up, "holding in his right hand the fortune of
the city." A sacrifice was also offered, but not
one of blood, nor to the fortune of the city, but
"to God Himself."

These facts will remind the reader of the
Palladium of Troy. It is also related by Olym-
piodorus, that while Valerius was governor of
Thrace, under the Emperor Constantius, certain
silver images were buried under the border line,
between Thracia and Illyria, talismanically consecrated against the incursions of the barbarians.

Some curious examples of analogous practices
of comparatively modern date, occur in quarters
where we should least expect to find them. Thus,
at the instauration of Rome, in the time of Pope
Paul the Third, Gauricus drew the figure of the
heavens, while Vincentius Campanatius observed
the time by his astrolabe, and at the proper
moment cried out, "Ecce, adest hora, præcisa
decima sexta fere completa"—whereupon the

Cardinal Ennius Verulannus immediately laid the first stone.

The exploit proposed by David was accomplished by Joab, who seems to have found his way into the fortress through an aqueduct. Thus, the stronghold which had been so long coveted by the Israelites fell into the hands of Joab, and the latter became chief commander of the armies of all Israel, as he had previously been of Judah alone. The conquest was fortunate for him, as, but for it, it is by no means certain that in his present frame of mind David would have given this large command to Joab; on the contrary, it is very likely that he hoped to supersede the claim of that brave and devoted, but rude and unscrupulous, man.

The explanation here given of this difficult passage does not appear to me satisfactory, though it has been adopted by Luther and several others since his time. I believe the Hebrew words only require to be accurately translated in order to make the meaning plain. I would translate them thus:—And the Jebusite "spake to David, saying, Thou shalt not come up hither, for the blind and the lame will drive you back; meaning (or saying) that David would not (that is, could not) go up thither. But David captured the stronghold of Zion, which is the city of David. Then David said on that day, Whosoever defeats the Jebusite, let him smite in the water-course the lame and the blind, hated of David's soul. Wherefore they say (it has become a proverb), The blind and the lame shall not enter the house."

The whole passage may be thus explained:—It has always been customary in the East for the poor, the blind, and the lame to take up stations at the gates of towns and castles, so as to beg of the passers-by. A little colony of wretched lepers now occupies the Zion gate of Jerusalem, and beg most piteously of all who go in and out. The Jebusites, too confident in the fancied impregnable nature of their fortress, placed these poor blind and lame beggars upon their ramparts, and in bitter mockery said that they would be sufficient to drive back David's warriors. But David having captured the city itself, attacked the citadel with fresh vigour; and his fiery spirit being stung to madness by the taunts of the haughty and insulting Jebusites, he spake the words recorded above. The walls were scaled by Joab and his men, the blind and the lame were smitten, and the fortress taken. In memory of this remarkable incident, blind and lame persons were never afterwards permitted to enter the citadel of Zion. Hence the proverb.

Such appears to me to be a simple, natural, and satisfactory explanation of a difficult and much controverted passage. It would be out of place here to enter on those minute grammatical details by which the translation given above may be defended.

P.

About twelve years ago were discovered steps, hewn on the south-west side of Jerusalem, on the steep slope leading down to *Wady er Rahâbi.* Thirty-four of these were laid bare, and many more remained uncovered. These steps are considered by Mr. Tristram (*Land of Israel,* 189) to be the very *gutter* alluded to in 2 Sam. v. 8, "Whosoever getteth up the gutter and smiteth the Jebusites, he shall be chief and captain." On all other sides, the accumulation of subsequent ages have sloped the cliffs of the once impregnable fortress, so that David's "blind and lame" might easily mount them; and it is difficult, at first sight, to realize the native strength of the citadel of Zion, still more elevated, and, in the time of David, more precipitous than its sister Mount Moriah. Jebus was a fortified city when attacked by David, and these steps seem to have belonged to that period; and, if so, then by these rock-hewn footholds we are carried back, not only to the time of David, but to a period anterior, while the original city remained in the hands of an old Canaanitish tribe. They must be the most ancient relics to be found in the neighbourhood.

S.

THE ARK

2 Samuel 6; 1 Chronicles 15

DAVID having established himself at Jerusalem, was anxious that it should become the sacred city of all Israel, and as such the centre of real union to all the tribes, who would have to repair thither periodically at the great yearly festivals. David knew that the Lord had of old promised to indicate a city which He should choose "to put His name there;" and David might from circumstances infer, that this was the intended city, if, indeed, he had not already received some intimation to that effect. There can be no doubt that this was distinctly made known to him afterwards.

For the accomplishment of this object, it was necessary that the ark should be removed thither from Kirjath-jearim, where it had so long remained. David was careful to take measures that this removal should be accomplished with such high and solemn state as befitted the occasion, and as should mark his own sense of its importance. Thirty thousand men, chosen out of all Israel to represent the tribes, were present, together with numerous musicians, and David himself was there playing upon his harp. It seems surprising that, instead of the proper and ancient mode of removing the ark, by its being

borne on the shoulders of the Levites,[1] the same
mode was adopted as that followed in a former
day by the Philistines, who had not the same
means of correct information. It was placed on
a new cart, which was drawn by oxen. They
had not proceeded far, not farther than to
Nachon's threshing-floor, when the ark received
a jolt that endangered its fall; on which Uzzah,
in whose charge it had been, and still was during
its removal, hastily put forth his hand to steady
it, and immediately fell dead on the spot. This
seems a hard judgment upon him for a well
meant and natural movement. David himself
appears to have felt it to be such at the moment,
and till he had leisure to reflect upon it. He
was, indeed, so greatly distressed and alarmed,
that he for the time abandoned his intention, and
caused the ark to be deposited in the nearest
house, which happened to be that of Obed-edom

the Gittite—that is, of Gath; and the lately
exulting thousands dispersed themselves, sad and
downcast, to their homes.

We have already explained our impression[1] as
to the necessity there was that, for His own
honour, for the welfare of His people, and for the
integrity of the institutions He had committed to
them, the Lord should rigidly exact a proper and
ordained reverence for the sacred symbols. If
at all necessary, there was never an occasion in
which it could be more so than on this great
public solemnity; and at a time, moreover, when
the due ordinances of divine worship were about
to be re-established and enforced with greater
state and honour than had been known since the
twelve tribes, and their innumerable hosts, encamped around the tabernacle in the wilderness.
Now Uzzah, being a Levite, ought to have known
that it was altogether irregular, and against the

BURNT-OFFERING

ritual law, to remove the ark in this manner,
which the entire absence of carriage roads rendered peculiarly unbecoming. It is very likely
that the responsibility of this matter had been
left by the king to him; as, having been so long

[1] The Levites were not allowed to *touch* the ark; but
after the priests had covered it up, the Levites might carry
it by the staves. The priests could also, of course, carry
it, and did so at times, but it was not their regular duty.

in charge of the ark, he might naturally be
supposed to have made himself particularly
acquainted with the observances connected with
it. The priests and Levites had been long separated from the ark, and not having had charge of
it for two generations, might be supposed to have
less carefully acquainted themselves with what
belonged to the occasion. It is also probable that

[1] See Vol. 1, pp. 620-622.

they were not consulted, and did not know of the arrangements made by Uzzah, until they came with David to take part in the procession. There might then be a natural hesitation in objecting, even on the part of the few who knew or suspected the irregularity of the proceeding. We may, therefore, regard this irregularity as part of the error for which this man was punished—a very essential part of it too; for, had not this informality been allowed, the accident which followed could not have taken place.

There is reason to suspect that Uzzah had allowed his mind to regard the ark with undue familiarity during the years it had been in his charge in a private house, and was not suitably impressed with the reverence exacted by a symbol, with which the divine presence was so closely connected. From the example of one who had been so long in charge of it, this familiarity would

gather strength, if it were not at once and decisively checked, and if becoming reverence to the ark of the Lord were not enforced. Such familiarity he indicated by laying his hand upon the ark to steady it when the oxen stumbled. By the ritual ordinances, it was forbidden to the simple Levite to touch the ark under pain of death; and Uzzah was only a Levite. He either knew this, or he did not know it. If he did not know it, he was punishable for his ignorance of a restriction so important, and which belonged so directly to his official duties; if he did know it, he was punishable for his irreverent disobedience to so stringent an injunction.

But it may be urged, that the ark might have fallen if he had not steadied it. We think not so. He thought so; and it was another of his errors, to suppose that God was not able to protect and ensure from falling His own ark, before

PEACE-OFFERING

which Dagon had fallen. But supposing that it had been overturned, would not Uzzah have been as liable to punishment for suffering that, as for taking forbidden means to prevent it? Surely not. He might have been punishable for adopting a mode of conveyance which exposed the ark to such an accident, but not for omitting what he was forbidden to do, in order to prevent that accident.

This is not all that might be said to show that there was a painful necessity that this judgment should be inflicted. When the act, light as it seems, is considered in all its consequences, and when we reflect what an encouragement the impunity of this offence might have been to the introduction of other innovations, it is not to be wondered at that the Lord should manifest His displeasure at this offence, by inflicting the punishment He had denounced against it, thus discouraging any future attempts to make alterations in the theocratical institutions which He had established.

In time David came to view this matter in its proper light, and having, three months after, heard that the household of Obed-edom had been greatly blessed since the ark had been deposited with him, he was encouraged to resume his design. On this occasion everything was conducted in a proper manner—"None ought to carry the ark of God but the Levites," said David; "for them hath the Lord chosen to carry the ark of God, and to minister unto Him for ever." And so again, in directing the chief Levites to prepare themselves for this service, he said: "Because ye did it not at the first, the Lord our God made a breach upon us, for that we sought Him not after the due order." The marred solemnity of the former ceremonial was magnificently exceeded by this. The concourse was greater, the musicians in greater and better organized force, and the king himself, divested of his royal raiment, and wearing a linen ephod, such as the Levites wore, headed with his harp the sacred choir, accompanied by those movements of the body which are called "dancing" in the East.

The ark was placed in a tent which David had prepared to receive it, and burnt-offerings and peace-offerings were then largely offered, for the first time in Jerusalem. When these religious solemnities were performed, the king "blessed the people in the name of the Lord;" and then he himself superintended the distribution to the assembled thousands of the bountiful fare he had provided for them. Every one, man and woman, received "a loaf of bread, a good piece of flesh, and a flagon of wine." He then went home "to bless his own house also." But there a discordant element had found entrance. Saul's daughter Michal had witnessed the proceedings from a window; and when she saw that David had laid aside his royal state altogether, that he might take an active part in the proceedings, "she despised him in her heart."

In the East, women have not much the gift of concealing their sentiments; and Michal hid not hers. David kindled at her sarcasms; he detected the affected superiority of the "king's daughter," and the artificial exaltations of royalty in the words she uttered; and with grave and solemn warmth he said, "It was before the Lord, who chose me before thy father, and before all his house, to appoint me ruler over the people of the Lord, over Israel; therefore will I play before the Lord, and I will yet be more vile than thus, and will be base in my own sight." He thus plainly gave her to understand that it was possible she took too much upon her—that it was not to her, or to the influence of her house, that he owed his crown, but to the simple gift of Jehovah, whose he was, and whom he served. The sort of spirit evinced by Michal on this occasion was punished by her having no children, through whom, as it might have happened, the line of Saul would again attain to sovereign power. Whether this result is to be interpreted as a special judgment from God, or is to be referred to the displeasure which this unseemly altercation left on the mind of David, we are not informed.

It has been questioned why David provided a new tent for the ark at Jerusalem, when the old tabernacle (together with the altar of burnt-offerings) was not far off at Gibeon, and might easily have been brought to Jerusalem. It is conjectured that the once splendid hangings of the wilderness tent had become old and faded, and David hence deemed a new one more becoming. But it is incredible that the hangings of a tent, open to the air, had so long remained in use. They had perhaps been more than once renewed. It is, therefore, more probable that since David had now two high priests, neither of whom he could depose—the one Abiathar, who had been attached to his person from the commencement of his troubles, and the other Zadok, who had been set up by Saul, and who was really of the elder line—the king found it expedient to keep up the establishment at Gibeon, to afford the latter the opportunity of exercising his functions without interfering with the other, who superintended the new establishment at Jerusalem. This state of matters remained during all the reign of David. The king, probably, could not remove Zadok, had he been so minded, without displeasing the ten tribes, who had been accustomed to his ministrations. But he had probably no wish to do so, as we soon find Zadok very high in his favour and esteem.

———————

The readers of the authorized version may find some difficulty with the topography of this passage. It is said that David "arose *from Baale* of Judah, to bring up *from thence* the ark of God;" while in the next verse we read that "they brought it out of the house of Abinadab *that was in Gibeah.*" From 1 Chronicles xiii. 6, we learn that Baalah (or Baale) was another name for Kirjath-jearim, where the ark had been put when brought back by the Philistines (1 Sam. vii. 1). The town of Kirjath-jearim, or Baalah, stood upon the side of a hill; and it would appear, from a comparison of various passages, that upon the summit of the hill, just over the town, there was a small village or suburb called Gibeah (that is, "the hill"), in which was the house of Uzzah, where the ark had been placed.

The hill is very rocky, and the road from it to Jerusalem, over the bare crowns of mountains, is one of the most rugged in Palestine. No one who has passed along it will wonder at the oxen stumbling, and the ark being shaken.

P.

This is an appropriate place for considering the question—What is the true Scripture appropriation of the name of *Zion?*

In the book of Joshua (xviii. 28), we find Jerusalem included among the cities belonging to the tribe of Benjamin; and in the book of Judges (i. 21) it is said, "The children of Benjamin did not drive out the Jebusites that inhabited Jerusalem; but the Jebusites dwell with the children of Benjamin in Jerusalem." Also we read in Judges (i. 8), "Now the children of Judah had fought against Jerusalem, and had taken it, and smitten it with the edge of the sword, and set the city on fire;" and earlier, in Joshua (xv. 63), "As for the Jebusites, the inhabitants of Jerusalem, the children of Judah could not drive them out; but the Jebusites dwell with the children of Judah at Jerusalem." From these texts it is plain that, at the time referred to, Jerusalem was a twofold city; one part within the lot assigned to Benjamin, and the other part within the lot assigned to Judah; and as the lot of Benjamin was to the north, and the lot of Judah to the south, the position of the double city is determined accordingly. In 1 Chron. xi. 4-8, we are informed that, "David and all Israel went to Jerusalem, which is Jebus, where the Jebusites were the inhabitants of the land. And the inhabitants of Jebus said to David, Thou shalt not come hither. Nevertheless David took the castle of Zion, which is the city of David." "And David dwelt in the castle; therefore they called it the city of David. And he built the city round about, even from Millo round about; and Joab repaired the rest of the city." The part of Jerusalem taken by David, and which received his kingly name, was the fortified part—the citadel. In the partition of Palestine, the boundary line of Benjamin descended to the valley of Hinnom, and ran south of Jebus (Joshua xviii. 16), including, no doubt, the most important part of it, the citadel; but that would not positively determine its position, for it might, consistently with the direction of the boundary, have stood either where it is generally supposed, that is to say, on the modern Mount Zion, or on the part called Akra, to the north. Captain Warren takes this last view, and illustrates the relative position of the city of David, or Zion, the suburb or remainder of Jerusalem in the earliest time,

and the adjoining hill of Moriah, on which the temple was built by Solomon, by the following simple comparison:— "If we place three round shot close together, we have a rough model of Jerusalem in the time of Solomon; the shot to the north being Mount Zion, that to the south-east Moriah, and that to the south-west the remainder of Jerusalem." The *relative* position thus indicated seems quite correct. The castle of Zion, or city of David, stood to the north of the suburb afterwards incorporated within Jerusalem, and Moriah lay to the east; but, at present, I cannot satisfy myself as to whether the ancient castle and city occupied Akra, or the hill which bears the name of Zion. Be this as it may, this much is certain, that the original Zion was that part of Jerusalem in which stood the kingly fortress, where dwelt David and his family—where the ark found a resting-place after its removal from the house of Obed-edom—where the priests ministered—and where existed the royal sepulchre. It is the place intended in those historical and poetical passages which belong to the reign of the psalmist king. But as to later times, the application of the term is different. Though still used to designate the city of David in particular, as in Isaiah xxx. 19, and Micah iv. 8, it came to receive a wider signification. It was employed to denote the temple, or house of God—thus pointing to the sacred enclosure on Mount Moriah; perhaps, also, designedly suggesting the Church and people of the Most High, who there found their central place of worship, because it was the scene of the solemn national sacrifices (Ps. xcix. 2; cxxxii. 13; cxlvi. 10; Isa. viii. 18; Jer. viii. 19; Micah iv. 7). In the time of the Maccabees, Moriah had come to bear the name of Zion (1 Macc. iv. 37; v. 54.) All this shows a change in the use of the name since the time of the dedication of the temple, before which "Solomon assembled the elders of Israel, and all the heads of the tribes, the chief of the fathers of the children of Israel, unto King Solomon in Jerusalem, that they might bring up the ark of the covenant of the Lord out of the city of David, which is Zion" (1 Kings viii. 1). The name, from having meant that which was the core and heart of the Holy City in the days of David, came to mean that which was the core and heart of the Holy City in the days of his great son, and under the reign of after kings. By a further stretch of application the name of Zion was employed to denote Jerusalem as a whole (Ps. cxlix. 2; Isa. xxxiii. 14), a stretch of application very natural, similar to the use of the name of London as including the suburbs of Westminster, Lambeth, and Southwark.

S.

THE ENTRANCE SONG

Psalm 24

IT is universally admitted that the twenty-fourth Psalm was composed, and, as we now say, set to music, to be used on the occasion of the removal of the ark, and sung in the procession. The tenor of this noble canticle renders this purpose of it manifest; and a closer examination may enable us to understand it better, and to appreciate it more distinctly.

It will be seen that it is written to be chanted in responsive parts, with two choruses. To comprehend it fully, it should be understood that Jerusalem, as the city of God, was by the Jews regarded as a type of heaven. It so occurs in the Apocalypse, whence we have adopted it in our poetical and devotional aspirations. The court of the tabernacle was the scene of the Lord's more immediate residence—the tabernacle His palace, and the ark His throne. With this leading idea in the mind, the most cursory reader —if there be cursory readers of the Bible—cannot fail to be struck with the beauty and sublimity of this composition, and its exquisite suitableness to the occasion.

The chief musician, who was probably in this case the king himself, appears to have begun the sacred lay with a solemn and sonorous recital of these sentences:

> "The earth is the Lord's, and the fulness thereof;
> The world, and they that dwell therein.
> For He hath founded it upon the seas,
> And established it upon the floods."

The chorus of vocal music appears to have then taken up the song, and sung the same words in a more tuneful and elaborate harmony; and the instruments and the whole chorus of the people fell in with them, raising the mighty declaration to heaven. There is much reason to think that the people, or a large body of them, were qualified or instructed to take their part in this great ceremonial. The historical text says, "David, and *all the house of Israel, played before the Lord* upon all manner of instruments," etc.

We may presume that the chorus then divided, each singing in their turns, and both joining at the close:

> "For He hath founded it upon the seas,
> And established it upon the floods."

This part of the music may be supposed to have lasted until the procession reached the foot of Zion, or came in view of it, which, from the nature of the enclosed site, cannot be till one comes quite near to it. Then the king must be supposed to have stepped forth, and begun again, in a solemn and earnest tone:

> "Who shall ascend into the hill of the Lord?
> Or who shall stand in His holy place?"

To which the first chorus responds:

> "He that hath clean hands and a pure heart,
> Who hath not lifted up his soul unto vanity, nor sworn deceitfully."

And then the second chorus:

> "He shall receive the blessing from the Lord,
> And righteousness from the God of his salvation."

This part of the sacred song may, in like manner, be supposed to have lasted till they reached the gate of the city, when the king began again in this grand and exalted strain:

> "Lift up your heads, O ye gates,
> And be ye lifted up, ye everlasting doors,
> And the King of Glory[1] shall come in!"

repeated then, in the same way as before, by the general chorus.

The persons having charge of the gates on this high occasion ask:

> "Who is this King of Glory?"

To which the first chorus answers:

> "It is Jehovah, strong and mighty—
> Jehovah mighty in battle,"

which the second chorus then repeats in like manner as before, closing with the grand universal chorus:

> "He is the King of Glory! He is the King of Glory!"

We must now suppose the instruments to take up the same notes, and continue them to the entrance to the court of the tabernacle. There the king again begins:

> "Lift up your heads, O ye gates,
> And be ye lifted up, ye everlasting doors,
> That the King of Glory may come in!"

This is followed and answered as before—all closing, the instruments sounding, the chorus singing, the people shouting:

> "He is the King of Glory!"

"How others may think upon this point," says Dr. Delany, "I cannot say, nor pretend to describe; but for my own part, I have no notion of hearing, or of any man's ever having seen or heard, anything so great, so solemn, so celestial on this side the gates of heaven."

Christian preachers and poets have delighted to apply this noble psalm to our Lord's ascension; and in this application there is certainly much force and beauty. None has produced this application with more triumphant energy

[1] That is, "Glorious King."

than Young, whose *Night Thoughts* is, with all its faults, a wonderful poem, which will, we doubt not, in no long time recover more than all the popularity it once possessed. This is the passage which he who has read once forgets not soon:

> "In His blessed life
> I see the path, and in His death the price,
> And in His great ascent the proof supreme,
> Of immortality. And did He rise?
> Hear, O ye nations ! hear it, O ye dead !
> He rose ! He rose ! He burst the bars of death.
> Lift up your heads, ye everlasting gates !
> And give the King of Glory to come in.
> Who is the King of Glory ? He who left
> His throne of Glory for the pangs of death.
> Lift up your heads, ye everlasting gates !
> And give the King of Glory to come in.
> Who is the King of Glory ? He who slew
> The ravenous foe that gorged all human race.
> The King of Glory, He whose glory filled
> Heaven with amazement at His love to man,
> And with divine complacency beheld
> Powers most illumined " wildered in the theme.""

There is yet another application, and which, indeed, as Hengstenberg remarks, is not so much an application as a translation. The Psalmist addresses the gates of Zion, and commands them to open that the glorious King may enter in. What in the first instance was only a poetical figure, becomes within the spiritual domain a reality. What the *external* gates would have done, if they had been endued with reason, will in reality be performed by *hearts* which are capable of comprehending the majesty and glory of the approaching King. Here the doors and gates will in reality open. They will give to the King that wide and ready entrance, which once they gave to the world and to sin. Happy they who have heard the summons, and who have been enabled to open wide the portals of the heart, that the King of Glory may come in and take possession of it wholly, saying :

> "Welcome, great Guest ; this house, mine heart,
> Shall all be thine :
> I will resign
> Mine interest in every part :
> Only be pleased to use it as thine own
> For ever, and inhabit it alone."—*Quarles.*

Information was offered on pp. 691-693 and notice was taken of the schools of the prophets. It is interesting to trace a connection between that institute and the service of song described in the above illustration. The schools of the prophets paid attention to music and psalmody, and the subject has been fully investigated by Dr. Payne Smith, Dean of Canterbury, in his Bampton Lecture on *Prophecy a preparation for Christ.*

" At first," he says, " these young men probably dwelt in tents or booths on the open pasture land ; for the ways of life were still simple, and houses rare, and possessed only by those of higher rank. But as their numbers increased, and a regular constitution was given them, and a settled discipline, it is probable that their dwellings acquired more of a permanent character. In the text (1 Sam. xix. 19, 20,) they certainly appear as a regularly organized body : for we find ' Samuel standing as appointed over them.' Now, these words may only refer to that religious service of song and chant in which they were engaged when Saul's messengers arrived. If so, they would show that they had arrived at that stage when the service of God was conducted according to a dignified and impressive ceremonial. But the words more probably signify that Samuel ' was chief over them.' Not appointed by any one : that is not the meaning of the Hebrew. As a prophet of the highest rank, he was by the virtue of his office their chief. And thus the words suggest, what we should also gather from other things, that after the appointment of Saul to the kingdom, Samuel, for the remaining thirty years of his life, concentrated all his energies upon these schools. Hence the deep root they struck in Israel, and the vast effects they produced."

" The training of these young men was partly in reading and writing, the two sole foundations of all intellectual culture, and the two greatest steps that men can take forward on the road from barbarism to civilization. But it was partly also, as we have seen, in music, with which was joined probably singing, such as subsequently formed the great charm of the temple services, as established there by David, Nathan, and Gad, all three, I doubt not, trained by Samuel himself."

" In a coarse and violent age like that described in the book of Judges, music and poetry, which inevitably go together, exercise a powerful influence in civilizing men, and giving the softer arts, and the pleasures of a milder and more refined mode of life, value in their eyes. We now are subject to innumerable softening influences. It was not so then. Music, the song, the religious chant, the solemn dance at holy festivals, these were the chief, and well-nigh the sole civilizing elements of early times."

" It is certain from 1 Chron. ix. 22, that Samuel commenced that reorganization of the Levites which David completed. From 1 Chron. xxv. we learn that all the great singers and musicians, Heman, Asaph, Jeduthun, &c., were Levites, and that Heman was a Kohathite, like Samuel himself (1 Chron. vi. 22, 28, 33). From the part taken by Gad and Nathan in the arrangement of the temple service (2 Chron. xxix. 25), it is exceedingly probable that it was modelled upon the same plan as that originated by Samuel in the schools of the prophets : and when in the text Saul's messengers found ' the company of the prophets prophesying, and Samuel standing as appointed over them,' there can be little doubt that they were engaged in a religious service, consisting of music and singing, like that subsequently instituted by David for the tabernacle, and performed by a chorus of 288 trained voices (1 Chron.

xxv. 7). How impressive Samuel's service was we gather from the effect produced upon three successive sets of messengers sent by Saul, and subsequently upon Saul himself (1 Sam. xix. 20-24). From the last verse we learn that there were also solemn dances, in which Saul, clad only in a linen ephod, or tunic, such as David danced in before the ark (2 Sam. vi. 14, 20), took part so enthusiastically, that he finally fell down completely exhausted, and for many hours afterwards lay motionless." [1]

S.

COMMERCE AND ARTS

2 Samuel 5:11

IN the measures taken by David to render Jerusalem, his new conquest, a metropolis worthy of the importance of his kingdom, he became sensible of the deficiency of his subjects in the arts of construction and design. The position of the Israelites had not been favourable to the progress of such arts. Dwelling-houses, ready to their hands, they had acquired by conquest—sufficient to meet the wants of the first two or three generations; and those that were subsequently required were doubtless built after the same models. This was the case also with fortresses— the Israelites probably gaining possession of more than they found it necessary to maintain, and having certainly no occasion to build new ones. These were the only public buildings of which we read. In fact, there was never any people who had less need of public buildings than the Israelites, down to the time of David. They were precluded from having temples, like other nations, in almost every town, by the regulation which restricted the solemn ritual worship to one place. Palaces there could be none in the absence of any great princes, lords, and sovereigns, having power beyond the narrow limits of the several tribes. The power of the "judges" being merely personal, precluded them from building palaces for themselves; and the office being only occasional, the state would find no inducement to build grand residences for them. Besides, they were men of simple habits; and even the great chiefs of the tribes were eminent rather for their position than for their wealth—large possessions in land being prevented by the manner in which

[1] Payne Smith's *Prophecy a preparation of Christ.* 127-133.

the territory was divided among all the families of Israel. These circumstances, together with the simply agricultural habits of the population west of the Jordan, and the pastoral habits of that to the east, were highly unfavourable to any progress in the constructive arts; and we do not see any indications of advance in them, until some time after the monarchy had been established.

Thus it is that David found himself in danger of being stopped in his intended improvements by the inability of his subjects to carry out his designs. From this difficulty he was relieved by the establishment of a friendly intercourse with the Phœnicians of Tyre, which proved of great advantage to both parties. The Phœnicians excelled in the arts in which the Israelites were deficient; and a good understanding with their neighbours of the interior was very important to them. Their narrow slip of maritime territory, full of cities, and their preference for the more lucrative pursuits of commerce and manufacture, left them but little opportunity or inclination for agricultural pursuits; while the wants of their dense population rendered the corn, wine, and oil which the interior so abundantly afforded, a most important source of supply to them. In return for this, they could furnish the Hebrews with the various products of their large commerce, and the commodities of their own manufacture. The possession of so valuable a market for their surplus produce was no less important to the Israelites. This kind of intercourse had probably existed almost from the first, and it accounts for the remarkable fact, that the Phœnicians are the only neighbouring nation with whom the Israelites never had any war. The frequently depressed state of the country, and its repeated subjection to foreign powers, had probably prevented the adequate development of this interchange of advantages until the time of David, when the establishment of a powerful general government, and the enjoyment of continued peace (after the neighbouring nations had been reduced), gave a great impulse to the productive industry of the people, which was much stimulated by easy access to so excellent a market as Tyre—always ready and glad to take, at amply remunerating prices, whatever raw produce their neighbours could raise. This enabled the Israelites to possess themselves, in large abundance, of the various foreign commodities which abounded in the

Phœnician markets, while their diffusion through the land produced a marked change for the better in the attire, the arms and armour, the dwellings, the furniture, the domestic utensils, and probably the agricultural implements, of the Hebrews. Of this we find frequent indications in the later historical books of Scripture, and in the writings of the prophets. We call this a change for the better; for whatever may be said in favour of simple and rude habits, it will hardly at this day be disputed, that everything which stimulates the industry of the people, urges them to make two stalks of corn grow where but one grew before, and enlarges their social comfort by bringing

to them the products of other lands, and furnishing them with the appliances of human ingenuity and art, is a real advantage to them.

What was a convenience to the Hebrews, became in time a vital necessity to the Phœnicians, and always continued to be such. So late as the time of the apostles, we find the Phœnicians of Tyre and Sidon taking the most earnest and even humiliating means of overcoming some resentment that Herod Agrippa had conceived against them; and why? "Because their country was nourished by the king's country." (Acts xii. 20.) Their joy, indeed, was so exuberant at the restoration of a good understanding, so important for

SIDON

this reason to them, that, being heathens, they scarcely stopped short of rendering to him divine honours, for accepting which with complacency he was, in the righteous judgment of God, smitten with the terrible disease of which he died.

From this the reader will understand the anxiety which the Phœnician princes always showed to cultivate friendly relations with the Israelitish kings. It is not until David becomes king over all Israel that this is brought into prominent notice. While he was king only of Judah, his power was too limited to the south to offer much advantage to this people; but his authority is no sooner extended northward, than

a friendly mission of congratulation is sent to him by Hiram, king of Tyre. No doubt there had existed previous relations beteen the Phœnicians and the northern tribes; and we think we can trace the existence of such an intercourse with Saul in the fact that he, greatly to the disgust of the Israelites, gave to a son the name of Esh-baal (man of Baal), and to a grandson the name of Merib-baal (strife of Baal), which Baal was the chief god of the Phœnicians. The disgust of the people with these names may be conceived from the fact, that in order to avoid pronouncing the name of this idol, they ordinarily changed the first into Ishbosheth (*man of shame*), and the second into Mephibosheth (perhaps *mouth of shame*). These names might indeed open ground for more inquiry into the nature of Saul's religious sentiments, after his rupture with Samuel, than we can now enter into.

The messengers of King Hiram were well received by David, and when the former understood the nature of the difficulty the king of Israel laboured under in the prosecution of his improvements, he agreed to furnish cedar wood from Lebanon, which was highly valued as a timber for building, with an adequate supply of skilled artificers—masons and carpenters—under whose hands soon arose on Mount Zion a royal palace for the habitation of the king, being such as had not hitherto been seen in Israel. A similar arrangement, at a later period, in regard to the temple, will enable us to look more closely into the nature of this treaty.

Those who have explored and carefully examined the ruined cities of Palestine and Syria, must have been struck with the similarity in style and workmanship in the most ancient specimens of Jewish and Phœnician architecture. The walls of the Temple Court at Jerusalem, and of the Haram at Hebron, bear the closest possible resemblance to the ramparts of Gebal and of the Castle of Subeibeh at Banias, both of which were founded by the Phœnicians. The stones are of colossal magnitude, laid in uniform courses, and so hewn with grooves at the edges, that the surface of the masonry presents the appearance of raised panelling. That peculiar groove, which is generally known now as the *bevel*, is characteristic both of Jewish and Phœnician masonry.

This fact illustrates the statement that Hiram, king of Tyre, sent masons to David, who built him a palace at Jerusalem. The style of architecture thus introduced by the workmen of Tyre was subsequently adopted by the Jews in all their public buildings.

P.

THE PHILISTINE WARS

2 Samuel 5:17-25; 8:1

THE Philistines had kept themselves quiet so long as David was king of Judah alone, and found sufficient employment for his resources in upholding himself against the designs of Abner. But when he became king over all Israel—when he reigned without a rival, and all the resources of the nation were in such strong hands—they became alarmed. Still they moved not until after the success of his attempt to gain possession of Jerusalem. This they seemed to have interpreted as an indication of aggressive policy, not to be by them regarded with indifference, especially as it is highly probable that the dispossessed Jebusites were allies of theirs. Seeing that war would in no long time be inevitable, they deemed it best to take the initiative, and to march against Jerusalem at once, without, by longer delay, allowing the king to consolidate a power which would, as they supposed, be eventually employed for their destruction. Military men will say this was a wise policy, seeing that in war the offensive attitude has many advantages over a defensive one.

The Philistines then appeared in great force upon the high plain of Rephaim to the south, or rather south-west, of Mount Zion, where they encamped. David could not behold this sight unmoved, and he was deeply sensible of the importance of the occasion. It was a question with him whether to remain in Jerusalem, until the force of the tribes could be brought into operation, or at once to march out against the enemy. He inquired of the Lord by the usual means, and, being assured of victory, he went forth against the embattled host of the Philistines with all the confidence which such an intimation was calculated to awaken in the breast of a man of his unwavering faith. Apprised of this movement, the Philistines advanced to meet him, and were repulsed by David, who obtained possession of the images of their gods, which they left behind them, and which were committed by his orders to the flames. From this it would appear that these idols were of wood, and were probably attached to the standards, like the Roman eagles. By this, as well as by the expression of his abhorrence of the "blind and lame" idols of the Jebusites, David afforded sufficient evidence that he regarded hostility to idolatry as belonging to the functions of his office, being the only indication of practical hostility to the gods of the heathen, when not introduced for worship among the Israelites, that has hitherto appeared. The Philistines had dealt very differently with the ark—which they regarded as the God of the Israelites—having, as being themselves polytheists and idolators, no objection on principle to recognize it as a god. But, apart from the true Mosaic dislike to all idolatrous images, the step taken by David was one of great prudence, as it might be feared that the Israelites, from their deplorable propensity to adopt the worship of foreign idols, might themselves be ensnared by such dangerous trophies, if they were allowed to be preserved.

David called the name of the place where this transaction occurred *Baal-perazim*, "place of breaches," for the reason which is assigned—"God hath broken in upon mine enemies by my hand, like the breaking in of waters;"[1] or, as in 2 Sam. v. 20, "The Lord hath broken forth upon mine enemies before me, as the breach of waters;" or rather, perhaps, as this may be translated, "God hath broken or divided mine enemies as waters are broken." This is as fine an image, perhaps finer, than any in Homer. It is common for David to consider a host of enemies as a great flood or sea, ready to break in and overwhelm him with its waves. Thus: "The sorrows of death compassed me, the floods of ungodly men made me afraid;" "They came round about me daily like water, and compassed me together on every side;" "The floods are risen, O Lord; the floods have lifted up their voice; the floods lift up their waves."[2] But in the present instance, an army coming up in one vast body, broken in upon by a brave enemy, put to flight, and in their flight scattered into many broken parties, is finely compared to a vast flood or body of water broken or dispersed into many streams. Nothing is more common with Homer than to describe an army under the image of a flood of waters, wave impelling wave. Many instances of this might be quoted, but one will suffice :

> " As when the waves, by Zephyrus upheaved,
> Crowd fast towards some sounding shore, at first,
> On the broad bosom of the deep, their heads
> They curl on high, then breaking on the land,
> Thunder, and o'er the rocks that breast the flood,
> Borne turgid, scatter far the showery spray ;
> So moved the Greeks, successive, rank by rank,
> And phalanx after phalanx."—*Iliad*, iv. 78.

But Homer has nowhere painted, like David, the rout of an army under the image of a flood of waters, broken and dispersed by a storm.

Although repulsed, the Philistines were not discouraged. After an interval of uncertain duration, they reappeared in the plain of Rephaim, probably with increased force, for all David's language in reference to this incursion implies that their numbers were great. Once more the

[1] 1 Chronicles 14:11. [2] Psalms 18:4; 88:17; 93:3.

sacred oracle was consulted, and this time he was forbidden to go out and assail them in front; he was to fetch a compass, and to come out secretly behind them over against a certain mulberry plantation, which it would seem stood in the rear of the enemy's camp. He was to remain quiet till he heard " the sound of a going upon the tops of the mulberry trees "—a sound probably like the rush of a mighty host to battle—which was to be a signal to him that the Divine Power was moving forth to defeat and destroy his enemies ; and then he was to march out against them. It was, doubtless, to assure his faith that the Lord wrought for him, that this sensible token of the Divine assistance—which he was always ready to acknowledge—was graciously afforded to him.

The king followed these directions most implicitly. The enemy hearing, it would seem, the sound of a mighty army in their rear, which they might easily imagine to be more numerous and formidable than that led by David, which appeared at the very moment when that sound was heard, fell into panic and confusion, and were easily put to the rout. The victors pursued them hard for many long miles, even to the frontier of their own territory. From this the Philistines learned that they were not able to contend with the king of Israel single-handed, and however they might dread the increase of his power, they had no means of keeping it in check. They found that it would therefore be their wisest policy to remain quiet in future. But after a time David himself became the aggressor in his turn, by invading Philistia. That he was entirely successful we know ; but of the exact character of his success we are not told. He probably left them under tribute, retaining in his hands some frontier fortresses to hold them under control. The fortress called Metheg-Ammah, or Bridle of Ammah, is particularly named, the acquisition of it being probably the most important result of the expedition. This is explained in Chronicles, to denote " Gath and her towns."

The Valley of Rephaim is situated in the very centre of what became, in after times, the kingdom of Judah, and of what was in David's day the nucleus of the Jewish empire. It is an upland plain, oval shaped, about a mile long and half a mile broad, encompassed by the bare rocky crowns of the central range of Palestine, which do not rise, however, more than from fifty to a hundred feet above its surface. Being on the watershed, deep wild ravines run down from it eastward to the Jordan, and westward to the plain of Philistia. Up one of the latter, probably that now called Wady el-Werd, the Philistines marched, unseen by the Israelites, until they "spread themselves in the valley." David, by divine command, led his chosen troops round through the mountains, until he got into the ravines behind the Philistines. Then, when the Lord gave the signal, he fell upon them suddenly in the rear, cutting off their retreat, and driving them in terror and confusion among the fastnesses of the Judean hills. It was a daring act for the Philistines to leave their native plain and penetrate into the very heart of the mountain strongholds of their foes. But they probably thought that some of the Canaanite tribes which still occupied their old cities would join them; and they fully expected to be able, in case of reverse, to fall back upon their own country through the defiles by which they advanced.

P.

Before leaving this notice of the Philistine wars, it will be neither inappropriate nor uninteresting, to add some personal reminiscences of the country they inhabited, and some reference to their position and history in other parts of Holy Scripture. Half a day's journey, according to the slow travelling of the East, takes one from Gaza to Askelon, through beautiful wooded scenery much resembling the parks of England, bordered here and there by the sand, with which the husbandman battles in vain, and which threatens more and more devastation from year to

and beyond all that, historic memory goes back to the time when Askelon had its temple in honour of the Syrian mermaid, Venus, the female counterpart of the Scripture Dagon—and the sacred doves flocked round the shrines, whose representatives, if not descendants, may still be heard cooing among the figs, apricots, and citrons, round heaps of ruins. Another couple of hours and we reached Ashdod, now a village of mud huts—the Azotus of the New Testament, where Philip the Evangelist was found after the baptism of the Eunuch. Proceeding northward, you are soon at Ekron, on the border of Judah, now a poor village, without any remnant of antiquity except two good wells, once a city with a temple, dedicated to Baalzebub, lord of flies. As to Gath, its position is disputed and uncertain; but some identify it with Tell es Sâfieh (a hill conspicuous on the plain of Philistia, the Shephelah, or lowland of the Bible), from the top of which, even now exhibiting traces of ruins, the eye can range over the white downs of Gaza and Askelon, the olive groves of Ashdod, the gentle eminence of Ekron, the tower of Ramleh, and the dark-brown heights of Judea. The cities of Canaan were of great renown. Rumour, no doubt, exaggerated their extent and their strength; yet even Moses spoke of their being great, and fenced up to heaven (alluding to their position on great heights), and of their containing people great and tall, the children of the Anakims. The cities of Philistia were as distinguished as any in the neighbouring country. Gaza, Askelon, Gath, Ashdod, and Ekron, with their five lordships, might vie with Jericho, Ai, Gibeon, Makkedah, and Hazor. Gaza is, like Damascus, mentioned in the book of Genesis, even as it is, like Damascus, mentioned in the Acts of the Apostles. Before the call of Abraham, it was a border city of the Canaanites. The frequent Bible references to the city, the sieges it endured, the battles fought under or near its walls, and the probability of its having been the capital of Philistia, indicate its importance. If the reader will take the trouble to consult a concordance, he may perhaps be surprised to find what a large number of references there are to Philistia, its cities, and its inhabitants. As with regard to Egypt, so with regard to Philistia, we may say that its place in the Bible is suggestive of some great interest in its

ASKELON

year. Askelon reached, you wander through little valleys of dense verdure and foliage, and climb up gentle hills, which command prospects of the sea, and which are covered with huge masses of ruins. Walls and towers, as if overturned by an earthquake, point to the ravages of time and war, and bring up scenes of the Crusades, when Saracen and Christian there met in deadly fight;

history, and of practical lessons afforded by it for all ages. Very curious it is, that this narrow district, once inhabited by the neighbours and enemies of Israel, has given a name to the whole of the country, for "Palestrina" and "Philistia" are modern renderings of one ancient appellation. The "Palestina" of Isaiah, in our version, is in truth Philistia; and Philistia is, in fact, the name we now give, unwittingly, to the country of prophets and kings, of Christ and his apostles, when we call it Palestine. We follow the Greeks in transferring the name of the coast to the whole of the interior. The Philistines were not aborigines, but colonists. They were "wanderers," "strangers," as their name imports; now called Caphtorim, as if originally coming from the Cappadocia of Asia Minor; and now Cherethites, as if immediately landing from the shores of Crete. They occupied the region identified with their name in the days of Abraham and Isaac; and both those patriarchs entered into covenant relations with Abimelech, the Philistine king.

S.

THE THRONE ESTABLISHED

2 Samuel 7

DAVID, dwelling in the new, and for the age magnificent, palace built by the Phœnician craftsmen, was one day struck with compunction at the thought that the ark of God was much worse lodged than himself. It still remained within curtains, as in its wilderness state; and surely it was proper that it should by this time have a fixed abode. He mentioned this notion to Nathan, who, seeing that it redounded to the glory of God, at once expressed the warmest approbation of it. It is remarkable, that although, as the result shows, this was no more than his private opinion, he spoke with great confidence, as if in his capacity of a prophet: " Go, do all that is in thine heart, for the Lord is with thee." He had to learn, however, that even the obviousness of a thing to human conception did not excuse a prophet from the duty of consulting the Lord, before he declared an authoritative opinion. The very next night the word of the Lord came to him with a message for David. It was declared that his intention was commendable and highly pleasing to God. Yet, as he had been a man of war from his youth, and had shed much blood, it was not intended that he should build this temple; but the undertaking was to be reserved to glorify the peaceful reign of his successor. This is not, indeed, the reason assigned in the leading accounts; but it is mentioned by David in his dying address to the people,[1] and by Solomon at the dedication of the temple.[2] Nevertheless, the laudable zeal for the Lord's honour, in

<hr/>

[1] 1 Chronicles 28:3.   [2] 1 Kings 5:3.

which this conception originated, was highly approved, and received a rich reward in the promise of a succession to the throne in his house, and an eternal kingdom for his posterity. This promise referred, doubtless, in the first instance, to the temporal kingdom, but it also looked beyond to the spiritual reign of Christ; and from the value David set upon this promise, it is clear that he had some conception, not only of its immediate, but of its more extensive import. Indeed, the Jews have since then always believed that the Messiah was to come of the line of David. They believed it in the time of our Lord, and they believe it now. Even in its merely temporal acceptation, the promise was of the utmost importance to David. It assured him of the perpetuity of his dynasty in the occupancy of the throne of Israel. Saul had sinned, and had been cast out; but if David's children sinned, they were not to incur this penalty, but should receive the chastisement of children from a father's hand. Practically, then, all the succeeding kings of the line of David were chosen and appointed by the Divine King, and ascended the throne under the sanction involved in this covenant with their father, which is often referred to in later times, and which the kings strove, very properly, to keep before the minds of the people as the best security of their own power. But although the Lord, in order to show His favour to David, and to glorify the family from which His ANOINTED was to come, gave up, so to speak, the right of changing the *dynasty*, the imperial right of nominating the *individual* was reserved. The heir by primogeniture might in general succeed to the throne; but in case the Lord saw fit to indicate any other member of the family, the individual so nominated acquired the right to the throne. To show that this was to be the rule of the kingdom, the Lord thought it meet to exercise the right so reserved in the very first instance—Solomon, one of David's younger sons, being preferred to his elder brothers. But the principle having been in this case established, the succession was afterwards allowed to follow the usual course. This right of interference with what, according to our notions, would be the just claim of the first-born, had none of that harshness which to us it may seem to have. The law of primogeniture is by no means so rigid in Western Asia as it is in Europe; nor does the first-born hold any right, which the will of the father may not take away and assign to another son. Hence, although the first-born does commonly succeed, it is not unusual in Oriental history for the eldest to be passed over, and a younger but more able, or more favoured son, to be recognized as the heir. We have seen this instanced in our own time in countries no less important than Persia and Egypt. The father appears to have possessed this right—which, indeed, is in the East inherent in kingly power —under the Hebrew monarchy, except where the divine indication of a successor had been afforded. That indication the king was bound to enforce; and it is probable that the necessary subjection of any change in the order of the succession to the approval of the Divine King, was the reason why, although the abstract right of the sovereign to appoint any of his sons to the succession subsisted, it was more rarely exercised than in most other monarchies of the East.

The gracious promise thus given to David filled his heart with irrepressible joy and gratitude. "He went in and sat before the Lord," to give vent to his strong emotions. It was to the tabernacle, of course, that he went; and his "sitting," which to our notions may seem scarcely an adequately reverent posture, was no doubt that position between kneeling and sitting— kneeling first upon the ground, and then sitting back upon the heels — which in the East is counted a very respectful posture, and is in fact one of the attitudes of Mohammedan worship. The words are very beautiful; and we cannot refrain from citing a few of them, that mark the sentiments with which the heart of this good and pious king received a promise of so great interest and importance to him. "Who am I, O Lord God, and what is my house, that Thou hast brought me hitherto? And this was but a small thing in thy sight, O Lord God; but Thou hast spoken also of thy servant's house for a great while to come. . . . And what can David say more unto thee? for Thou, Lord God, knowest thy servant. . . . And now, O Lord God, the word that Thou hast spoken concerning thy servant and concerning his house, establish it for ever, and do as Thou hast said. . . . For Thou, O Lord of hosts, God of Israel, hast revealed to thy servant, saying, I will build

thee an house: therefore hath thy servant found in his heart to pray this prayer unto Thee. . . Therefore let it please Thee to bless the house of thy servant, that it may continue for ever before Thee; for Thou, O Lord God, hast spoken it; and with thy blessing let the house of thy servant be blessed for ever."

Dr. Delany says of this: "To my eye, the workings of a breast oppressed and overflowing with gratitude, are painted stronger in this prayer than I ever observed them in any other instance. It is easy to see that his heart was wholly possessed with a subject which he did not know how to quit, because he did not know how to do justice to the inestimable blessings poured down upon himself and promised to his posterity; much less to the infinite bounty of his Benefactor."

The key to the leading difficulties in the prophetical portion of this chapter is to be found in the fact that Solomon was a type of David's greater Son. The prophecy relates to Solomon, but mainly in its typical character, as foreshadowing the person and work of our Lord Jesus Christ. The prophetic words, while they began to be fulfilled in David's natural son, did not, and could not, find their full consummation in him. Another and a higher was manifestly looming up before the prophet's eye. Such expressions as these, "I will establish the throne of his kingdom *for ever;*" "thy house and thy kingdom shall be established *for ever;*" "thy throne shall be established *for ever;*"—point beyond the time of Solomon and of all earthly dynasties. An eternal duration of the reign of David's seed is indicated; and this cannot be explained away. Such a prediction could only find its fulfilment in one who lives and reigns for ever. The promise, therefore, must refer to the posterity of David, commencing with Solomon, the type, but closing and consummating with Christ, the great and glorious Antitype. So also there is something typical in the building of the house. The words, "He shall build *an house* for my name, and I will establish the throne of his kingdom for ever," appear to indicate that the house and kingdom should be in some sense alike eternal. And this idea is more clearly set forth in 1 Kings viii. 13; "I have surely built thee an house to dwell in, a settled place for thee to abide in *for ever.*" In its real or material sense, the temple was temporal; but in its typical sense, foreshadowing Christ's church, it was eternal. The temple built by Solomon was a type of that spiritual house of which Paul speaks: "In whom ye also are builded together for an habitation of God through the Spirit." (Eph. ii. 22).

P.

THE DECIMATION OF MOAB

2 Samuel 8:2

SEEING David had formerly been on such terms with the king of Moab, that he felt he could with confidence commit his parents to his care, we are somewhat unprepared to find him turning his hand against the Moabites, and treating them with great severity.

The Jewish writers imagine that the king of Moab had put the parents of David to death. But this is of no authority, being a mere conjecture devised to meet the exigencies of the case. No cause is stated. An occasion may have existed, or may not; for a real or ostensible *casus belli* is by no means so essential to Oriental warfare as it is in the West. Every sovereign is held to be justified in aggrandising his power at the expense of his neighbours, whenever a suitable opportunity offers, if he feels strong enough, and sees that they are weak enough to afford him a prospect of success. This was the rule on which all the neighbouring powers acted towards Israel; and there is no reason why we, with our later, our Western, and our Christian notions, should exact from Israel alone an adequate cause of war, sufficient, in our view, to warrant all its military enterprises. The silence of Scripture does not, however, prove that no justificatory cause existed. It is more than probable, that the relations of the tribes beyond the Jordan with their neighbours had become complicated, and needed the interposition of the sovereign power. If Dr. Delany is right in assigning to this period the eighty-third psalm, which is usually ascribed to the time of Jehoshaphat, there had been a confederacy of all the neighbouring nations to put down the rising power of Israel, which the king resented, and punished by assailing, one after another, all the states which belonged to this confederacy. Certain it is, that all the hostile powers which David reduced, even the Philistines, are named in the confederacy described in that psalm. The campaign against Moab is very concisely related, and in words which have excited much speculation: "He smote Moab, and measured them with a line, casting them down to the ground; even with two lines measured he to put to death, and with one full line to keep alive. So the Moabites became David's servants, and brought gifts."

There have been many translations of, and criticisms on, this text, with the view of finding an interpretation less harsh than that generally received, and which is conveyed in the authorized version, that David put to death a large proportion of his prisoners of war. We have repeatedly examined this text with much attention, and have always been led to conclude, that the real meaning of it is conveyed by our version, and that no new translation of it is needed. There may still be some question about the form in which this judgment was executed. Some think the line marked out the sections of the country whose inhabitants were to be destroyed; but others conceive that the prisoners of war were made to lie down, and that a line was extended so as to mark off about two-thirds of the whole mass, and that these were to be devoted to destruction, and the remainder spared. This was merely a rough substitution for counting them off, which probably their great numbers would have rendered a tedious and slow operation; but, that they might not suffer by the roughness of this mode of marking them out, the line was so drawn as palpably to make the proportion marked off to be spared by much the largest of the three parts—which is assuredly the meaning of the "full line to keep alive." Now, this is certainly a shocking transaction, as most of the usages of ancient warfare are, when we come to look on them closely, and as our own war usages will, we doubt not, appear when our posterity come to look upon them through a much shorter interval of time than has elapsed since the wars of David. The question is not, whether this conduct of David to the Moabites was shocking, barbarous, and cruel—seeing that this is true of all ancient warfare, and is, although in a less degree, true of even modern warfare, and in fact of all warfare —but it is, whether this conduct of his was conformable to the war usages of the time in which he lived, and of the people with whom he had to do? and whether this measure, which seems to us so terrible, was or was not shocking in the eyes of David's contemporaries? In reference to a case in which *all* the prisoners, except the female children, were destroyed by the express order of Moses himself,[1] we have shown that, unless the Israelites chose to wage war at a disadvantage, and with maimed hands, it was necessary that they should wage it on the prin-

[1] See Vol. 1, pp. 466-468.

ciples recognized by the nations with whom they were brought into conflict, and deal out to them the same measure which they received from them.

In the first wars, the conquerors gave no quarter at all, but destroyed all their enemies, without distinction of age or sex. Prisoners were also destroyed in the same manner. This was the ancient war law. But by the law of Moses, the Israelites were forbidden to enforce it except in aggravated cases, like the one to which reference has just been made, and except as regarded the devoted nations of Canaan. In process of time, men began to perceive that they might safely gratify the natural impulse to spare helpless women and children, and even secure an advantage in so doing, by retaining them for the discharge of servile offices, or selling them to those who had need of their services. At first, this degree of mercy was limited to women and female children, as it was considered that the boys might grow up to avenge their fathers, or at least to prove troublesome; but eventually the male children also were spared. It was to this point that men had come in the time of David, of Homer, and even of Moses. It had been probably the practice of Egypt to spare the male prisoners, owing to the great demand for servile labour in that country; and Moses, in enforcing it with respect to all but the devoted nations, probably went beyond the practice of Syria and Arabia, in which the old custom still prevailed. In expeditions against all nations but these last, the whole were to be spared, if they submitted without fighting, and consented to tribute. But in case they resisted and were taken in arms, the men so taken were to be put to death. Now, the Moabites were not of the devoted nations, and came therefore under the general law, as laid down by Moses, in conformity with the usages of the time. That law was certainly transgressed by David in the present case, but it was on the side of leniency, not of severity; and we are fully persuaded that it is for the very purpose of marking his humane consideration for the Moabites, contrary to all the rules of warfare in that age, that the fact is mentioned, which has been fastened upon by thoughtless persons as a proof of his harshness. There can be no doubt, we think, that every man among the Moabitish prisoners fully expected to be put to death; and that the exemption of a large section, or rather

more than a third, was received as an act of unparalleled grace and mercy on the part of David.

It may indeed be asked, Why, since he had made up his mind to save one-third of the prisoners, he might not as well have saved the whole? Nothing is easier than to ask, Why, if a person does one thing, he does not also do another? There is no end of such questions; for they may be applied to any case in which an alternative is possible. David intended his war to produce a certain result—to be effectual not only for the present, but with reference to future undertakings. This result, he thought, might not be compromised by his sparing a portion of the prisoners, but might be so to a serious extent if, by sparing the whole, the enemies he had yet to subdue were led to presume upon his leniency, and to expect from him a degree of forbearance which was not known in that age, and which they were not themselves in the habit of showing to those whom they overcame. The war usages of that part of the world were in ancient times notoriously barbarous, and retained their severity long after they had been considerably softened among other nations. Thus the Carthaginians, who were of Canaanitish origin, and retained the usages of Canaan, were reprobated for their severities to prisoners by the Romans, although the latter were themselves, according to our notions, by no means the most gentle of conquerors.

THE GREAT WAR

2 Samuel 8:3-13

ALL the enemies with whom David has been hitherto engaged, were of the small neighbouring nations, well known to us from the frequency with which their names occur in the sacred history. But we next find the king of Israel leading his forces against a more distant and formidable enemy than any against which his arms had been hitherto directed. The particulars given are few, and such as rather excite than satisfy our curiosity. The inferences deducible from the facts stated are, however, very important and interesting to those who like to explore the precious fragments of foreign history preserved in the amber of the sacred pages.

Hadadezer, king of Zobah—by which we are, perhaps, to understand the Zobathites, as no such place as Zobah is known—had established a great power in Syria, which extended into northern Mesopotamia, if indeed it did not originate there, and spread thence westward. This power was achieved apparently by the subjection of the various small states which lay between Lebanon and the Euphrates. It is questioned where the metropolitan seat of this power lay. The Syrian writers, followed by Christian commentators, say it was at Nisibis, beyond the Euphrates, while the Jews place it at Helbon, the modern Haleb or Aleppo. Damascus was comprehended in this realm, but was not its metropolitan seat. The object of this conquering and aggressive power must have been to push westward to the sea; and that being done, the south-west—forming the dominion of David—would not have been long left unmolested. Against this westward progress, were opposed the double chain of the Lebanon mountains, and the arms of Toi, king of Hamath. The city of Hamath, which gave name to this kingdom, still known by this name, was, in a later age, called by the Greeks Epiphania. It lay northward upon the river Orontes, about midway between Aleppo and Damascus; but the dominion extended southward through the great plain called the Hollow Syria (Cœlesyria), which lies between the ranges of Lebanon and Anti-Lebanon. Its southern frontier thus touched the northern frontier of the Hebrew dominion, the limit of which, in this direction, is often described as being at " the entrance of Hamath." Hence Israel and Hamath were neighbouring powers, though their capitals lay far apart; and they had a common interest in repressing the inroads of the king of Zobah. The name of Ṭoi, does not, indeed, occur till after David's expedition has been recorded; but from the nature of the case, they had probably acted together from the first; and as the king of Hamath's danger was more immediate than that of David, it is highly probable that the latter engaged in this war upon his representations. It must have been clear to David, that Hadadezer and himself must come eventually into conflict; and it could not but appear to him wiser to act at once, than to wait until the power of the king of Zobah should be strengthened by the acquisition of Hamath. In any case, he must

have seen that it was better policy to support Hamath, as interposed between him and this aggressive power, than to remain quiet until its territories impinged upon his own frontier.

The forces of Hadadezer consisted chiefly of chariots of war, which, however well suited to the warfare in which he had hitherto been engaged upon the high plains of Syria, were but ill suited for action in such mountainous territories as those of David and Toi. Hence the power of infantry—of which the Hebrew army entirely consisted—against chariots in such regions; and the good policy of the law which discouraged the use of horses, and therefore compelled the chosen people to rely upon the kind of force best suited to the nature of their country. On the other hand, this infantry was ill suited to conflict with chariots in the open plains; and as David was too experienced a general to throw away any advantages, it is probable that he sought, in his repeated engagements with this new kind of force, to meet them on ground unsuited to their operations. Matters eventually came to the decision of a great battle, in which Hadadezer was totally defeated, and his power for the time broken; and Damascus, with the other small states to the west of the great river, beholding in the event merely a change of masters, received without any visible repugnance the king of Israel as a conqueror. Thus were realized for the first time the ancient promises, that the dominion of Abraham's seed should extend to the Euphrates.

The troops of Hadadezer seem to have brought something like Assyrian magnificence from beyond the Euphrates. There were not only chariots and horses, but some of the troops had golden shields, which of course came into the hands of David. He found also valuable spoils of brass in some of the captured cities. All this, as well as the metallic spoils of his other wars, David appropriated, not to his own enrichment, but to the object he had most at heart, the future temple of the Lord. He was forbidden to build it himself, but there was nothing to prevent him from gathering materials for it; and this he did to such an extent—not only by the treasure he accumulated, but by leaving a plan of the building, and by organizing the sacred ministrations— that a careful consideration of the matter may leave it doubtful whether much more of the credit of the undertaking is not due to him than to Solomon.

To the same object were appropriated the

costly presents which king Toi sent by his own son Joram (for the greater honour), in acknowledgment of the essential services which had been rendered to him, amounting to little less than the preservation of his kingdom. These presents consisted of various articles in gold, silver, and brass—which last we find now continually mentioned along with the precious metals. Some kinds of it were probably little inferior in value to silver; and we know that, anciently, some qualities of brass were even more precious than gold. Thus, even under David, began that influx of precious metals which came to its height in the next reign. This must have wrought a great change in the land, where these metals had hitherto been scarce. This we may appreciate by the great changes which have been produced in Europe by the discovery of the South American mines, and the consequently great abundance of the precious metals, and by the results that are expected, and are already felt, from the recent discoveries of gold in California and Australia. We do not afterwards find any apparent scarcity of such metals in Palestine. We must consider that *all* the wealth acquired in these wars was not locked up for the future temple. David was not the man to take from his soldiers their fair share of the spoil. What he dedicated to the Lord, was such as accrued to him as king. This was a large share, no doubt—perhaps a tenth; besides which, there were probably certain articles of spoil which were in all cases considered to belong to the crown; and the men themselves certainly devoted a portion of what they obtained to the same object. Still a large proportion of the metallic spoil must have belonged to the soldiers, and soon passed from their hands into the general circulation of the country, thereby producing the effects at which we have hinted.

David was not unmindful of the law against the multiplication of horses in the hands of the king; and his clear military judgment could not but appreciate the reasons on which this prohibition was founded. He had now a large spoil of horses and chariots; but he caused the former to be destroyed, and burned the latter. He reserved a hundred of the chariots, with a proper number of horses; but as this was for state purposes, and not for use in war, the measure seems not to have deserved any blame, nor did it incur any.

At verse 3 we read, "David smote also Hadadezer, the son of Rehob, king of Zobah, as he went to recover (or establish) his border (or his power) at the river Euphrates." The question has been asked, Who is the subject of the last clause—David or Hadadezer? Grammatically it may be either, but the scope seems unquestionably to indicate David. Zobah was far to the west of the Euphrates. It appears to have been situated between Damascus and Hamath. In marching from Zobah to the Euphrates, Hadadezer would thus be going farther away from David's kingdom: how, therefore, could David have encountered him? If, on the other hand, we regard David as the subject, then the narrative is consistent. David marched toward the Euphrates to secure to its utmost limits that wide empire given to the seed of Abraham in covenant promise (Gen. xv. 18). Zobah lay on his line of march: and Hadadezer having opposed him, was attacked and conquered.

Zobah was evidently the name of a wide region, extending from the confines of Hamath and Damascus on the west, to the Euphrates on the east. It was also apparently the name of a city, the site of which has not yet been satisfactorily identified. It seems to me highly probable that it may be identical with the classic Emesa, now called Hums. The immense artificial mound at Hums, on which a famous temple formerly stood, shows that the site was of remote antiquity: its position, too, between Damascus and Hamath agrees with that assigned to Zobah both in the Bible and Assyrian inscriptions; while the splendid plain around the city, stretching from the banks of the Orontes in an unbroken expanse to the Euphrates, afforded the very best field in Syria for the evolutions of war-chariots.

It may be well to note that verses 13 and 14 are closely connected, containing a brief record of an expedition different from that mentioned in the preceding verses. The Hebrew word rendered Syrians in verse 13, is *Aram*, which, as is proved by many MSS., by the context, and by the parallel passage in 1 Chron. xviii. 12, 13, is a mistake of a copyist for *Edom*. The passage, therefore, will read thus: "And David got him a name when he returned from smiting Edom in the valley of Salt," etc. The valley of Salt was probably at or near the Salt hills of Usdum, at the southern end of the Dead Sea.

P.

HADAD

2 Samuel 8:14; 1 Chronicles 18:12-13
1 Kings 11:14-21

THE employment of the force of Israel in the north seemed to afford to the Edomites an opportunity of encroaching upon the south of the Hebrew territory. It is indeed very likely that they acted upon an understanding with the Syrians for the purpose of making a diversion in their favour. The superscription to Psalm lx. indicates that the main army of David was still occupied in the Syrian war, when Abishai was detached to oppose the Edomites. Certainly an expedition against them would not have been spontaneously undertaken at such a time; and nothing but the most urgent necessity for resisting very alarming aggressions, could have constrained the king thus to weaken an army engaged in the most important campaign of all his wars. The Edomites were therefore the aggressors, and by that aggression brought down upon their heads the ancient doom of eventual subjection to the house of Jacob. On the approach of Abishai, the Edomites retired before him into the valley of Salt, at the southern extremity of the Dead Sea; or it may be that he met them there in their march upon Israel. A most bloody battle was fought between the two armies; and the desperateness with which the Edomites contested the victory, may be judged from the fact that they left twelve thousand of their number slain upon the battle-field.

As soon as Joab was released from the Syrian campaign, he marched to this new scene of action, in order to settle the conquered country. He remained there six months, with the bulk of the Hebrew army. Joab's mode of settling the

PETRA

country was after the Oriental fashion—of making a desolation, and calling it peace. Having a keener thirst for blood than his brother, and his higher command making him more exasperated at the attempt of the Edomites, which might have endangered the large operations in the north, he seems to have considered that Abishai had but half accomplished his work. He caused the male Edomites to be hunted out and put to death, wherever they were found; and established Hebrew garrisons in the strongholds and principal towns of Edom. Many Edomites escaped, and of these no doubt the greater part returned when the fierceness of the storm had blown over; but the blow was so terrible that it was a hundred and fifty years before the nation recovered such strength as to be able to make any strenuous endeavour to shake off the Hebrew yoke. Thus Edom became subject to David. Hitherto Selah, called by the Greeks Petra, whose curious remains, entombed among the rocks, have been within the present century brought to light, and have engaged much attention, had been the chief seat of the Edomite power, as it seems to have been in the time of Moses; but now the population, driven from the heart of the country far a-field, concentrated in continually retiring upon the borders, and it is from this time that Teman on the east, and Bozrah on the north, of Edom's frontier, rise into importance.

In the account given in the First Book of Kings (xi. 14-21) of the enemies who disturbed the latter years of Solomon, there occurs a most interesting and suggestive anecdote respecting this transaction, which is not to be found in the leading narrative. The king of Edom seems to have been slain in the battle. He left a son, a child, named Hadad, for whose safety no apprehension appears to have been entertained until the terrible Joab came into the country, and gave signs of the tiger-like spirit by which he was at that time animated. Some faithful servants of the royal house then carried off their young master, and being joined by other fugitives on the road, went down into Egypt. The king of that country received the young prince with truly royal hospitality and consideration. He assigned to him and his followers a suitable provision: "He gave him a house, appointed him victuals, and gave him land;" and when Hadad grew up, he bestowed upon him the sister of his queen Tahpenes in marriage. By her he had a son, Genubath, who, as soon as he was old enough to be separated from his mother, was removed to the royal palace, where he was weaned by the queen, and brought up with the royal children. Of Genubath we hear nothing more; but Hadad himself will again come under our notice hereafter. The particulars given tantalize our curiosity, under the interest with which every historical fact respecting Egypt is now regarded. We are here brought to the very threshold of the haram of Pharaoh, but are not permitted to enter, and view the interior life of the Egyptian court. The attention with which Hadad was received, his marriage with an Egyptian princess, and the admission of his son into the royal family, remind us of facts in the histories of Joseph and Moses, and do not bear out the impression transmitted to us by the Greek writers, respecting the antipathy of the Egyptians to foreigners. The royal rank of Hadad, and the alliance which he had contracted with the court, afford special reasons for the consideration with which his child was treated. But on other grounds, it appears not to have been unusual in Egypt for strange children to be taken into the royal household, and brought up with the king's sons. It is related that the father of the great Sesostris ordered all the male children of Egypt who were born on the same

day with his son to be brought to him, and having appointed nurses and proper persons to take charge of them, he gave instructions that they should be educated and treated in every respect like the young prince; being persuaded that those who were his constant companions in childhood and youth, would prove his most faithful adherents and affectionate fellow-soldiers. They were abundantly furnished with everything needful: as they grew up they were by degrees inured to robust and manly exercises, and were even forbidden to taste any food till they had performed a course of 180 stadia, or nearly twenty-three Roman miles. By this severe training of the body, and by a corresponding cultivation of the mind, they were equally suited to execute and to command.[1]

It would in fact appear that the privilege of being brought up with the royal princes was by no means a privilege of royal luxury and self-indulgence, the discipline to which they were subjected being unusually strict. The duties of children have always been more severe in the East than among any European people; and to the present day a son, even when grown up to manhood, is not expected to sit in the presence of his father, without express permission. Those

EGYPTIAN PRINCES

of the Egyptian princes were still more austere. One of their offices was that of fan-bearers to the king; and they were also obliged to carry the monarch in his palanquin or chair of state. As fan-bearers, they stood by him while seated on his throne, or in processions to the temples; and in this capacity they followed his chariot on foot, as he celebrated his triumphant return from battle. The distinguishing mark of their princely rank was a badge dependent from the side of the

[1] Diodorus, i. 4.

head, intended seemingly to cover and enclose the lock of hair which was left in shaving the head, and which among the Egyptians was the sign of youth.

These facts may illustrate the nature of the privilege which Genubath probably shared with others, of being brought up with the sons of Pharaoh.

Eleven successive kings of *Syria* are said to have borne the name of Hadad. And in Genesis (xxxvi. 35), an Edomite sovereign is denominated in the same way. See also 1 Chron. i. 50. Like the word *Pharaoh* it appears to have been a title rather than a personal appellation. Joab's severity might possibly proceed beyond the orders of David, though as sovereign the latter would be held responsible; but in connection with the fact it may be observed, that the king did not often proceed to extremities in the treatment of vanquished foes, and in this case he might adopt a relentless policy according to the letter of the law in Deut. xx. 13. The Edomites seem to have been widely scattered through all the country on the southern borders of Judea. When it is said "they arose out of Midian, and came to Paran" (1 Kings xi. 18), we are led upon the track of the history of Moses, and the wanderings of the Israelites. He kept his father-in-law's flock in Midian; and in the wilderness of Paran the tribes encamped. Paran is a geographical name of wide application, and refers to a considerable part of the great plateau of the Sinaitic peninsula, called the Desert of *El Tih*, now the flattest, wildest, and most uninteresting district of the whole region.

S.

A DEAD DOG

2 Samuel 9:8

WHEN the son of Jonathan received the assurance of kindness and protection from David, he said, "What is thy servant, that thou shouldst look upon such a dead dog as I am?" This, according to Jewish notions and phraseology, is the strongest expression of humility and a sense of unworthiness, nay of vileness, that could be employed. On account of its various unclean habits, the dog was abhorred by the Hebrews, and became the type of all that was low, mean, and degraded; although, by reason of its usefulness, its presence was endured in certain capacities —chiefly in the care of flocks and in hunting. To be called a dog, was therefore the height of ignominious reproach and insult; and for a man

to call himself a dog, was the depth of humiliation and self-abasement. The reader will call to mind many instances of this, which it is therefore not needful to point out. Now, if such were the disesteem in which the living animal was held—if to be called "a dog" merely was so shocking—for one to be called, or to call himself, not only a dog, but a "dead dog," is the strongest devisable hyperbole of unworthiness and degradation; for in a dead dog the vileness of a corpse is added to the vileness of a dog.

And who is it that uses this expression? One who was by his birth a prince, of whom we know nothing but what is good; whose sentiments, whenever they appear, are just, generous, and pious; whose private character seems to have been blameless, and his public conduct without spot. Yet this man calls himself a "dead dog"—that is, the most unworthy of creatures, the vilest of wretches. The phrase, "I am a worm, and no man," is nothing to this. Allowing for the hyperbole, it may thus seem that Mephibosheth abased himself far more than he needed, and confessed himself to be that which he really was not.

This raises a question of wider meaning than the particular instance involves, and which concerns us very deeply. It touches upon one of the things that are foolishness to the wisdom of the world, and which its philosophy cannot apprehend, because they are spiritually discerned. The world sees men like Mephibosheth, not only "decent men," as they call them in Scotland, and "respectable men," as they are termed in England —men not only of stainless moral character, but men of distinguished piety, zealous in every work by which God may be glorified and mankind advantaged—men ready, if need be, to suffer the loss of all things, and to give their bodies to be burned for conscience' sake, and who, like Count Godomar, would "rather submit to be torn to pieces by wild beasts than knowingly or willingly commit any sin against God;"—the world sees this, and yet hears these very men speak of themselves in terms which seem to them applicable to only the vilest of criminals, the offscourings of the earth. This is a case which the world's philosophy has never yet been able to fathom. It sees but the alternative of either taking these men at their own valuation, and holding that whatever fair show they present, they really are what they say, and therefore unfit for the company of honest men—unfit to live upon the earth; or else, that they speak with a disgusting mock humility, in declaring themselves to be what they know that they are not; and there is, perhaps, a general suspicion in the world that these persons would not like to be really taken for such "dead dogs" as they declare themselves to be.

How does this matter really stand? The obligations of truth are superior to all others. A man must not consciously lie, even in God's cause, nor even to his own disparagement, nor to express his humility. He has no more right to utter untruths to his own disparagement than to his own praise. Truth is absolute. It is obligatory under all circumstances, and in all relations. There is nothing on earth or in heaven that can modify the obligation to observe it. Yet such is the tendency to think well of ourselves, that although it is counted ignominious and contemptible for a man to utter a falsehood, or even a truth, to magnify himself, it is not considered to be in the same degree dishonourable for him to speak in his own disparagement. Perhaps it might be so, were it supposed that he spoke the truth, or what he believed to be true; for so intense is the degree of self-love for which men give each other credit, that perhaps no man is ever believed to be sincere in whatever he says to his own disadvantage; and it is because nobody believes him—because it is concluded that he either deceives himself, or says what he knows to be untrue, that self-disparagement is not regarded dishonourable in the same degree as self-praise. Still it is the fact, that if self-disparagement be knowingly untrue, it is not less culpable than self-praise.

Yet Mephibosheth calls himself a "dead dog;" Agur avows himself "more foolish than any man;"[1] and Paul declares himself "the chief of sinners."[2] Nevertheless, Mephibosheth was a worthy man; and there were far more foolish men than Agur—far greater sinners than Paul. What then? did they lie? By no means. The man of tender and enlightened conscience knows that in God's sight the very heavens are not clean, and that He charged even His angels with folly. The more advanced he is in the spiritual life, the more clear is the perception which he realizes of the holiness of God, the more distinctly he feels how abhorrent all sin—of thought, word, or

[1] Proverbs 30:2.　　　[2] 1 Timothy 1:15.

action—must be to Him, and how it separates the soul from Him. He knows not the hearts of others, and he does not judge them. But he knows something of the evil of his own heart; he knows that he is to be judged according to his light—according to what he has, and not according to what he has not; and, judging by that measure, considering how much has been given to him, he knows, he feels, that a doubt, a misgiving, an evil thought, a carnal impulse, involves him —with his light, and with the proofs of God's love in Christ towards him which have been brought home to his heart—in far greater sin than belongs to the grosser offences of less instructed men. He reasons also, that if he, with eyes blinded by self-love, is able to see so much of the plague of his own heart, what must be the sight presented to the view of the pure and holy God, who sees far more defilement in the best of our duties, than we ever saw in the worst of our sins! What man of wakeful conscience is there, who, when he looks well to the requirements of God's holy law—when he meditates upon the essential holiness of the Divine character—when he considers his own neglected means and mercies—when he sees how the remaining depravities of his nature have defiled his holiest things—and knows how unthankful, how wayward, how rebellious, his heart has often been, is not compelled to smite upon his breast and cry out, "Behold, I am vile; what shall I answer Thee?" Ah, it is well for him that he is not required to answer. Through the cloud of sin and grief, he hears that voice which it is life to hear, "Son of man, be not afraid." This is He who has taken the burden not only of his cares, but of his sins. This is his Beloved; this is his Friend. All is well.

Every one acquainted with the East will see how thoroughly characteristic of eastern manners is Mephibosheth's address to David, under the circumstances in which he was placed. In ordinary conversation, nobles and princes call themselves "your slaves," and speak of themselves as unworthy even to sit at the feet of their visitors. A matter-of-fact Englishman scarcely knows what to make of the profound respect and honour shown him by men of rank in the East, and the terms of abject humility they employ in reference to themselves. This trait is especially observed when a man of position happens to be detected in an attempt to defraud or to wrong one, a circumstance by no means uncommon. I remember the governor of a district once saying to me, when I exposed his villany, "I am as a very swine before your highness. The language of the East is essentially hyperbolical. The people perfectly understand it to be so.

P.

The estimate formed of dogs in the East requires a little further illustration. They were not used by the people of Judea for hunting as with us—though they were employed in Idumea to guard the shepherd's flocks against jackals and wolves. They were, and are still employed, as scavengers in towns and villages, and may sometimes be seen flocking together in large numbers free from ownership and control. Though they were permitted of old "to eat of the crumbs that fell from the master's table," they were never domesticated as is the case in this country: nor do they seem to have contracted those personal attachments, if we may so call them, which distinguish these favourite animals in the Western world. "The dog went after them" (Tobit xi. 4), is a solitary instance in which the fidelity of dogs is noticed in early Jewish writings—we may be said to treat dogs—or at least some dogs—with respect, and we count them as friends; but no sentiment of the kind has ever existed among the Orientals. All allusions to dogs in the Bible are unfriendly and contemptuous; and on account of their habits, they are regarded in Syria and the neighbouring countries with aversion and disgust. It is curious to notice how the feeling shows itself. Dogs are avoided. They lie in the streets, and intercept the path of wayfarers, who, instead of driving them away, let them alone —and fetch a compass to avoid coming in contact with such despised creatures—yet the "live dog is better than the dead lion." And if even the lion be degraded by death, what must be the abhorrence felt for a dead dog? We saw the carcase of one flung out by the gate of Jerusalem as we entered, and thought of the words "without are dogs."

S.

MEPHIBOSHETH

2 Samuel 9

KNOWING, as we do know, that Jonathan had left a son, it is not without some misgiving that we have beheld him so long neglected by David, who owed so much to his father. We remember the brotherly covenant, and begin to be fearful that David has forgotten it. It has, however, been perhaps too hastily assumed that the king was aware of the existence of Jonathan's son. The probability seems to us to be that he did *not* know it.

Let us look into this matter somewhat more closely.

Mephibosheth was a child, five years of age, at the time of his father's death. At that time, it was at least six years since David had fled the court of Saul. At the birth of this son he was wandering about in the wilderness, and was not in the way of receiving information; and at any considerably later period, when the fact was no longer new, and was not brought under notice by any public transactions, no one would think of reporting to David the circumstance, but would suppose that it was already known to him.

When the intelligence came to Gibeah that the Philistines were victorious, and that Saul and Jonathan were slain, the nurse, supposing that the Philistines were close at hand, and that all belonging to Saul would be sought for and rooted out, hastened to flee with the young child, and as her speed was not equal to her fears, she seems to have carried him in her arms. In her extreme haste she either let him fall, or stumbled and fell with him, by which his feet were so badly injured, that he remained lame for life. He was taken for safety beyond the Jordan, and was brought up in the house of the generous and wealthy Machir, the son of Ammiel, at Lo-debar, in Gilead. There he remained, probably in such obscurity as left few aware of his existence; for it could not have consisted with the policy of Ishbosheth or Abner to bring him conspicuously into notice, and David could have had little opportunity of becoming acquainted with a fact, shrouded from view in a quarter so remote, and in the dominions of his rival. Besides, if David had ever heard of his existence, it had been by his rightful name of Merib-baal, and he would hardly recognize him under the altered name of Mephibosheth. This nickname was not at all a pleasant one for any man to be called by; but having got into use, it would be preferred by those anxious for his safety on the one hand, and by those whose interest it was to keep him out of mind on the other. When Ishbosheth was slain, and all Israel went over to David, Mephibosheth was about twelve years old, and there were obvious reasons why the friends who had taken charge of him should desire his existence to be forgotten. Thus Mephibosheth lived a quiet and peaceful life among his friends at Lo-debar; and when he grew to manhood, he married and had a son.

When David was well established on his throne, and all his enemies were subdued around him, he inquired one day of those about him, "Is there yet any left of the house of Saul, that I may show him kindness for Jonathan's sake?" This confirms the opinion we have advanced, that he did not *know* that Jonathan had a son living; and we think it shows that he did not even suspect such to be the case. Had it been so, and seeing that the inquiry arose out of his tender regard for the memory of his friend, he would surely rather have inquired whether Jonathan himself had any children remaining.

The obscurity in which Mephibosheth had been kept, is further shown by the fact that those of whom the king inquired were unable to give him the information he desired. They knew, however, of one Ziba, an old and trusted servant of Saul, now a prosperous man, with fifteen sons and twenty servants, and supposed that he could acquaint the king with that which he desired to know. This man was sent for. The king asked: "Is there yet any of the house of Saul, *that I may show the kindness of God unto him?*" Ziba then told him of Mephibosheth, and where he was to be found; on which the king forthwith sent messengers to bring him to Jerusalem. They were probably charged not to disclose the king's object; for when the lame youth appeared before the king, and prostrated himself in humble reverence, some trepidation seems to have been visible in his manner, as we may gather from the kind and assuring words which David addressed to one in whose countenance he probably found some traces of the friend he had loved so well. He called him by his name, and said to him, "Fear not: for I will surely show thee kindness for Jonathan thy father's sake." He then proceeded to state that he meant to restore him the private estate of Saul, for the maintenance of his household; but as for himself, he said, "Thou shalt eat bread at my table continually." Here was comfort, independence, and the highest honour the king could bestow, conferred with most paternal and kingly grace upon this afflicted man. What more could David do for one incapacitated by his infirmity for the employments of active life? and it was done not grudgingly nor with cold reserve, but with the heartfelt tenderness which made him desire to have always near him this living memorial of his lost friend. A less noble mind might have shrunk from thus keeping before the public eye, in connection with himself, the true heir of the house of Saul; especially as, though lame himself, Mephibosheth had a son who would eventually inherit whatever claims his father might be supposed to possess. But in the large heart of David there was found no room for such low suspicions and mean misgivings. God had promised to perpetuate the royal power in his house, —and what had he to fear? Mephibosheth was the son of his heart's friend,—what could he suspect?

It is to be observed that the estate now made over to Mephibosheth was assigned for cultivation to Ziba, who, with his sons and servants, was to devote himself to it, and was to retain one half of the produce in recompense for his expense and labour, paying the other moiety as rent to the owner of the land. The numerous landowners in Israel so generally cultivated their own grounds, that there is scarcely another instance which enables us to see on what terms farming was conducted. It was probably on some plan like this, which is indeed a very common one in the East. It is found to be in most soils a very equitable arrangement, especially when, as is usually the case, the landowner supplies the seed.

Mephibosheth was thus enabled to keep up a becoming establishment for his family in Jerusalem, while habitually taking his principal meals at the royal table, and associating with the king's sons, some of whom were nearly of his own age. As men do not, when at home, sit down at table with their wives and children in the East, this constant dining at court was a distinction unaccompanied by any of the domestic drawbacks it would bring to us.

THE SHAVEN AMBASSADORS

2 Samuel 10

THE reader will not have forgotten Nahash, king of the Ammonites, and his intended barbarities upon the men of Jabesh-gilead. This man had, however, been friendly to David in the time of his troubles. How, we know not; but the wilderness history of David must have had many more incidents than the few which have been recorded. When, therefore, he heard that Nahash was dead, and that his son Hanun had mounted the throne of Ammon, he sent an honourable embassage of condolence and congratulation. This is not the first instance of the mention of an embassy in Scripture, but it is the first for such a purpose. There was that of the king of Tyre to David on his accession to the throne of Israel; that which king Toi of Hamath sent to congratulate him on his victories; and earlier still, that sent by Moses to the king of Edom, and to other kings, to ask a passage for Israel through their territories; that sent by the king of Moab to Balaam; that of the Gibeonites to Joshua, pretending to have come from a far country; and that sent by Jephthah to the king of Ammon, remonstrating against his aggressions upon Israel. These instances illustrate nearly all the various occasions out of which embassies could arise. All of them, and indeed all ancient embassies, were what we call embassies extraordinary, that is, embassies sent on particular and extraordinary occasions; embassies in ordinary, or resident embassies at foreign courts, being altogether a modern European invention, not more than two hundred and fifty years old.

The rights of ambassadors, the peculiar privileges belonging to their office, as representing the power from whom they came, and as being still under its protection in a foreign land, were already, however, well understood. They were then, as now, invested with a sacred character, which protected them from any offensive action in a foreign land, whatever might be their conduct. They were not amenable in any respect to the king or laws of the country to which they went. If they gave cause of complaint, the king might refuse to receive them, or might send them away, or request the power from whom they came to recall them; but to subject them to molestation, or injury of any kind, was an affront as severely resented in ancient as in modern times. We may therefore conceive the indignation of David when he heard that his ambassadors—men of rank and station—had been treated with the most gross indignity by the king of Ammon, under the pretence that they had come to spy the nakedness of the land. The courtiers of Rabbah persuaded Hanun to believe this; and although we have no doubt that the suspicion was sincerely entertained, and may admit that it may have been in some measure justified by the recent subjugation of the neighbouring

and kindred nations, nothing can excuse or justify the insolent contempt with which the ambassadors were treated. They might have been sent away; but this was not enough for the Ammonites. They sent them not away till they had shaved off half their beards, and cut off the skirts of their robes, so as to leave half of their persons bare. The object was clearly to make them ridiculous and contemptible. To shave off one side of the beard only, was even more ignominious than to remove it altogether, although *that*, among the ancient and modern Eastern nations that cultivate the beard, was an offence not to be named without horror. It is very difficult for us to realize the intense appreciation of, and respect for, the beard, which is entertained among the Persians, Arabians, and other bearded nations. They treat their own beards with respect, suffering no defilement to come near them, and handling them with deliberate care. They bury with solicitude any stray hairs that come from the beard; and to lose it by accident were worse than the loss of the head itself, which would, in their esteem, become ridiculous and useless without this essential appendage. For any one else to touch a man's beard irreverently, to speak of it lightly, to cast a reproach upon it, were an offence never to be forgotten or forgiven; but to cut or remove it by violence or stealth, were an affront, a disgrace, a horror, which scarcely the heart's blood of the offender could expiate. All these notions respecting the beard doubtless had their origin in its being the grand mark of distinction between the male and the female face, whence it became the symbol of manly dignity and strength, and the want of it the sign of weakness and effeminacy. Conceive the ecstasies of mirthful derision which attended the progress of David's unfortunate ambassadors through the country in their way home, with half their faces shaven, and their garments cut far too short for decency or comfort. In smiling at the idea of the awkward figure these illustrious and worthy persons presented, one cannot help feeling indignant that it should be in the power of foolish men, by anything they can do, to render ridiculous and contemptible the persons of men entitled to veneration or respect. It *is* really in their power; for, let us say what we will, few of us would be able to repress a laugh at beholding even a great and good man in a ridiculous position; nor must we be too confident that we should have been able to keep our countenances, had the disfigured ambassadors presented themselves to our view. Truly, the sense of the ridiculous, which seems peculiar to man, is often a very great misfortune.

King David was well aware that his ambassadors would never again be able to face those who should once see them in this absurd and wretched plight. He therefore, with a tender consideration for their feelings, which they must have prized most highly, sent a messenger to meet them, releasing them from the duty of coming to the court, and permitting them to remain at the first town on this side the Jordan, at Jericho, until the growth of their beards should enable them again to appear in public.

Fully persuaded that David could not overlook this grievous insult, the Ammonites prepared for war. With the terrible result in view, it is well to note that David, although naturally quick tempered, was slow to move in this matter; or rather, the Ammonites were so prompt in taking the initiative, that they appeared in the field against him before he manifested any disposition to move. They were most entirely and most unprovokedly the aggressors in this war. Reposing in conscious power, the king's lion-like wrath was but slowly awakened; but when fairly aroused, it was irresistible and terrible.

There is a very noticeable circumstance that meets us here. The Ammonites, sensible that they were not able to encounter the might of David in their own strength, *hired* the aid of various Syrian princes; this being the first recorded example of mercenary warfare. Under the circumstances, these powers were probably but too willing to join the coalition; and it speaks much for the wealth and influence which the Ammonites had by this time attained, that they were able to organize this powerful confederacy, and to bear its expenses. The expense amounted to a thousand talents of silver, which would be of the present value of £360,000, but of far greater worth at that time, when silver seems to have borne a much higher value than it does now; but even at the present value, it would not be less than at the rate of eleven pounds for each of the chariots employed during the campaign. The writer of the book of Chronicles states the number of chariots at 32,000; and it has been thought that this may be an error of transcrip-

tion, as it is seen that the numbers of that book often differ from those of the books of Samuel and Kings, and are always in excess. One must be wrong, and in most cases the accounts in Chronicles are not preferred. In this case, however, there is no contradiction, as the numbers are not stated in Samuel. Such a force in chariots is certainly unparalleled. Yet the circumstances agree with it. The money is fairly proportioned to the number; and it is stated that the force of a large extent of country, in which chariot warfare prevailed, was engaged in this enterprise, and that the chariot forces of four kingdoms were brought together on this occasion.

David beheld not this confederacy with indifference. He called out the military force of Israel; and when he learned that the Syrians had marched to join the Ammonites, he despatched Joab to take charge of the war. This great commander decided to prevent the intended junction. With the flower of the army he went himself to meet the Syrians, and gave to Abishai the easier task of engaging the Ammonites, with the understanding that the one should help the other in case either were distressed by his opponents. The words of Joab to his brother, before they separated to their respective tasks, were altogether worthy of the commander of the armies of Israel, and appear to indicate that, with all his faults, and even crimes, he possessed more real piety, and truer theocratical views, than he has usually had credit for : "Be of good courage, and let us play the men for our people, and for the cities of our God; and the Lord do what seemeth Him good."

The result of an engagement undertaken in this spirit, could not be doubtful. The hired army of chariots soon gave way before the stedfast front of Joab's indomitable infantry; and when the Ammonites beheld this, and saw that Joab was coming to join his brother against them, they lost heart and fled. They shut themselves up in their strongholds, and laboured to incite the Syrians again to take the field. They probably urged that they had not obtained the worth of their money; and although the lesser princes seem to have declined any further action, the greatest of them, Hadadezer of Zobah, who had had a sufficient case of his own against the Israelites, was effectually roused, and collected forces from every available source for another struggle. Even his troops beyond the Euphrates were brought over for this service. This force, worthy to decide the fate of an empire, took the field under a renowned general named Shobach; and David deemed the occasion of sufficient importance for him to command in person. The result was as before. The Syrians were beaten, and the power of Hadadezer so entirely broken, that he no more appears in history. The Syrian tributary princes, who had been obliged to join him, made their own terms with David, and left the Ammonites to their own resources.

The word rendered "Syrians" in our version, is uniformly *Aram* in the Hebrew. Aram was the name given to a wide extent of country, embracing north-eastern Syria and Mesopotamia. That section of it which lay east of the Euphrates was called Aram-Naharaim; while the western portion was divided into a number of small principalities—Aram-Zobah, Aram-Maachah, Aram-Bethrechob, and Aram-Damascus. The greater part of Aram is a plain. clothed with rich pastures, and famous in ancient as well as modern times for its horses. The Bedawin of Northern Syria and Mesopotamia could, at any moment, bring into the field fifty thousand cavaliers. The level plains, too, were well adapted for war chariots. It ought not to be overlooked, however, that the Hebrew word rendered "chariots," both in this chapter and in the parallel passage in 1 Chron. xix., is a general term, properly signifying "riders," and may mean those riding in chariots, or on horses, or on camels. Camels have been always much used by the Arabs in warfare. Each animal carries two men, in special cases even three. They either fight from the back of the camel, or dismount and act as foot soldiers.

The numbers given in the parallel passages in Samuel and Chronicles are widely different. With our present information, it is impossible satisfactorily to harmonize them. It ought to be remembered, however, that the narratives are fragmentary; that the numbers, though diverse, are not necessarily contradictory; and that, were the full account before us, the whole might appear perfectly consistent.

P.

SIN AND SORROW

2 Samuel 11-12

THE Ammonites, who, although beaten, were not wholly reduced, having retired to their fortified towns, held out with much obstinacy. The next campaign against them was conducted by Joab, who, after ravaging the country, laid siege to the metropolitan city of Rabbah.

It was while the army was engaged in these distant operations that David fell into those deep sins, which have left a dark blot upon his name, that all his tears have not been able to expunge from the view of man, nor all his griefs to make man forget. It is indeed profitable that they should be held in remembrance, in their causes and results, that the sad fall of so distinguished a saint—a man so near to God—may teach us not to be high-minded, but fear.

The facts are so well known to every reader, that it will suffice to indicate them very briefly.

David, when walking upon the roof of his palace, after having risen from his afternoon rest, obtained a view of a beautiful woman, of whom he became most passionately enamoured. Her name was Bathsheba, and she was the wife of Uriah the Hittite, who, notwithstanding his Canaanitish origin, was one of the king's most distinguished officers, and a member of the illustrious band of "worthies." After gratifying his criminal passion, and finding that it would not be much longer possible to conceal a fact which would expose Bathsheba to the death punishment of an adulteress, David did not shrink from sending orders to Joab, so to expose her valiant husband in battle as to ensure his destruction by the sword of the Ammonites. Joab obeyed this order to the letter, and Uriah perished. Bathsheba was then free, and David barely suffered the days of her mourning to pass (probably a month) before he added her to the number of his wives.

Here is adultery; here is murder. O David, David, how art thou fallen! To our minds, there is nothing in all that man has written so terribly emphatic as the quiet sentence which the historian inserts at the end of his account of these sad transactions:

"BUT THE THING THAT DAVID HAD DONE, DISPLEASED THE LORD."

His high displeasure was made known to David by the prophet Nathan, in a parable of touching beauty, applied to the case with a degree of force, which at once brought conviction home to the heart of a man not hardened in guilt by a course of less heinous and unrepented sins, but who had plunged headlong into one great and complicated crime. The awful words, "THOU ART THE MAN," at once brought David to his knees. He confessed his guilt. He deplored it with many tears. He was pardoned; and God hid not His face from him for ever. But seeing that this deed, in a man so honoured, had "given great occasion to the enemies of the Lord to blaspheme," it became necessary that God should vindicate His own righteousness, by testifying, in the punishment of his servant, His abhorrence of that servant's sin. The sentence pronounced upon him— "Behold, I will raise up evil against thee out of thine own house,"—furnishes the key to David's future history and career, which was as unprosperous and troubled, as the earlier part of his reign had been happy and successful. There was in all things a great change, even in the man himself. Broken in spirit by the consciousness of how deeply he had sinned against God and against man; humbled in the eyes of his subjects, and his influence with them weakened by the knowledge of his crimes; and even his authority in his own household, and his claim to the reverence of his sons, relaxed by his loss of character,—David appears henceforth a much altered man. He is as one who goes down to the grave mourning. His active history is past —henceforth he is passive merely. All that was high, and firm, and noble in his character, goes out of view; and all that is weak, and low, and wayward, comes out in strong relief. Of the infirmities of his temper and character, there may have been previous indications, but they were but dimly discernible through the splendour of his worthier qualities; now that splendour has waxed pale—the most fine gold has grown dim, and the spots have become broad and distinct. The balance of his character is broken. Still he is pious; but even his piety takes an altered aspect. It is no longer buoyant, exulting, triumphant, glad; it is repressed, humble, patient, contrite, suffering. His trust in the Lord is not less than it had been, and that trust sustains him, and still gives dignity to his character and sentiments. But even that trust is different. He is still a son, but he is no longer a Joseph, rejoicing in his father's love, and delighting in the coat of many colours which that love has cast upon him; but rather a Reuben, pardoned, pitied, and forgiven, yet not unpunished, by the father whose honour he has defiled. Alas for him! The bird which once rose to heights unattained before by mortal wing, filling the air with its joyful songs, now lies with maimed wing upon the ground, pouring forth its doleful cries to God.

The change we have indicated furnishes the key to David's subsequent career; and unless it be borne in mind, the incidents of that career will not be thoroughly understood.

As this was a turning-point in the history of David, it would be interesting to know at what period of his life it occurred. The common computation places it in the twentieth year of his reign, and the fiftieth of his age. But David lived to the age of seventy, and reigned forty years; and as Solomon his son was not born till a year or two after these events, he must, according to that view, have been in the nineteenth or twentieth year of his age when he succeeded his father. The impression conveyed by the narrative of his accession, and particularly by his request to the Lord for wisdom on account of his extreme youth and inexperience, is, that he was not quite so old as this. We apprehend that, on the other had, the learned Lightfoot goes a little too far, in fixing the date to the twenty-sixth year of David's reign, and the fifty-sixth of his life. The middle, between these extremes, is probably nearer the truth; and David may, with sufficient probability, be supposed to have lived fifty-three years, and to have reigned twenty-three, when this base unrighteousness rent from his head the honour due to his grey hairs.

Of Bathsheba we would wish to know something more than appears in the narrative. She is said to have been the daughter of Eliam. A person of that name occurs in the list of the worthies—2 Sam. xxiii. 34—and is supposed by some to have been her father. This person was a son of Ahithophel, the famous counsellor of David; and his eventual defection from his cause, when Absalom raised the standard of rebellion, is fancied to have arisen from his disgust at this dishonour done to his granddaughter. It must be allowed, that the fact that this Eliam was of the same body to which Bathsheba's husband belonged—his companion in arms and honour—is much in favour of this supposition. In 1 Chron. iii. 5, the father of Bathsheba is called Ammiel, which is the same name as Eliam reversed. This form of the name leads Lightfoot to identify him with Ammiel of Lo-debar beyond the Jordan. In that case, Bathsheba was sister of that Machir, son of Ammiel of Lo-debar, in whose house Mephibosheth had been brought up, and who afterwards signalized his loyalty to David by the bountiful contributions which he furnished for the subsistence of the court, when the king sought refuge beyond the river.   (2 Sam. ix. 4; xvii. 27-29.)

TORTURES

2 Samuel 12:26-31

To bring the crime and punishment of David into one view, we omitted an intermediate circumstance of much interest.   It was stated, that at the time of David's twofold sin, Joab was engaged in reducing the metropolis of the Ammonites.   The siege must have been of some duration, for Bathsheba, who was not known to David till after it had been commenced, had borne him two children before it was taken.   The first of these, the child of their infamy, died soon after its birth, just subsequent to the rebuke from the prophet; the other, begotten and born in the days of his contrition, was Solomon.   This cannot well mark a shorter interval than two and a half or three years.

Soon after the birth of his son, David received a message from Joab, stating that he had taken the lower city of Rabbah, distinguished as the " city of waters," from its situation among the streams, and that as the upper city, or citadel, could not hold out much longer, the king had better come in person, with fresh troops, and secure the honour of closing the war.   This has the appearance, and probably the reality, of magnanimity on the part of Joab, in thus devolving the actual capture upon the king; but he also knew that David was somewhat covetous of military renown, and that it might not be prudent to awaken his jealousy by adding the glory of the conquest of Ammon to that which he had won as the conqueror of Edom; and it appears that sovereigns had not yet reached the refinement of appropriating the glory of the exploits performed by their generals in their absence.   The phrase is remarkable: " Lest I take the city, and it be called after my name."   This alludes to a custom which frequently occurs in ancient history, of giving a name to a city with regard to particular occasions, or changing it with reference to some extraordinary event. This we find instanced in the names of Alex-andria, Constantinople, and other places.   The same practice is prevalent in India, where such names as Ahmedabad, Hyderabad, and Arungabad, perpetuate the memory of the founder or conqueror.

The city of Rabbah was easily taken when David reached the camp.   The crown of the Ammonitish king was with all due form set upon his head, and the treasures of the city made public spoil. It would appear that, by causing himself to be crowned, David meant to assume the direct sovereignty of the Ammonites, which was not his usual policy, although the peculiar circumstances of this war seemed to call for and justify it.   This crown is stated to have been of gold enriched with jewels, and seems to have been the most splendid thing of the kind that had yet been seen by the Israelites.   It is said to have weighed a talent of gold.   This would be equal to 114 pounds; and as this seems to be too great a ponderosity for mortal head to bear, it has been suggested, that the worth of the crown was *equivalent* to, rather than that the crown was *equipollent* with, or contained, a talent of gold. We object to the former interpretation, chiefly for two reasons—that not gold, but silver, was the measure of value in the time of David, so that the mere value of anything in gold was not likely to be stated; and that the *value* of a talent in gold seems scarcely adequate for a crown of gold set with precious stones.   It would not have been more than £5,475, which will seem but a small sum when we recollect that (as we happen to know) our George IV. gave £10,000, being ten per cent on its value, for the mere making and temporary use of the crown used at his coronation —the crown being, immediately after the ceremony, returned to the jewellers.   If, therefore, we assume the weight only to be intended, we must conclude that it was used only for a short time on great state ceremonials.   Crowns are only so used in the East, or indeed anywhere else; and they are generally of such weight that they cannot long be borne without inconvenience. The " weight of a crown " is not only a figurative truth, but a material fact.   Sir Harford Jones Brydges, who had an opportunity of examining the Persian regalia at leisure, describes the crown of state as excessively heavy.   The same ambassador relates that, happening to look back, on quitting the audience chamber, he saw the king lifting his crown from his head, as if anxious to relieve himself from its oppressive weight. But the ponderous ancient crowns were not always even worn upon the head; they were sometimes suspended over it, or attached to the top of the throne. Several crowns, of great size and weight, thus used, are mentioned by Athenæus and by Pliny. Among them, one is described by the former writer as being composed of 10,000 pieces of gold, and placed on the throne of King Ptolemy. Benjamin of Tudela speaks of a crown of gold and gems suspended over the throne of the Emperor Commenes. Some of the Rabbins have a curious conceit, that the Ammonitish crown was kept in suspension by a loadstone, as if the loadstone attracted gold as well as iron.

The question respecting the crown is, however, of less interest than that regarding the treatment to which the Ammonites themselves were subjected. It is said, "He put them under saws, and under harrows of iron, and under axes of iron, and made them pass through the brick kiln." And it is added, that he did this, not only to the defenders of Rabbah, but "thus did he unto all the cities of the children of Ammon."

The common, and as it seems to us the true, interpretation of this is, that they were put to deaths of torture. We would very gladly, were it in our power, agree with Dantz,[1] who, followed by Delany, Chandler, and other writers, contends that David merely condemned his Ammonitish captives to severe bodily labours, to hewing and sawing wood, to burning of bricks, and to working in iron mines. But this interpretation has little real foundation. It does much violence to the Hebrew words, which it takes in an unusual and previously unimagined acceptation. Some of the alleged labours are also wholly unsuited to the age and country, or the people. Firewood, for instance, is so scarce in Palestine, that the people of so many cities could not have found employment as hewers and sawers of wood; and the only public want in this respect, that of the tabernacle and its altar, was already provided for by the services of the Gibeonites; while the people generally used stubble and dried dung for fuel. Then, for building, stone has always been more used than brick in Palestine, and it is therefore marvellous that the more laborious work of quarrying stone is not named, if penal labours were really intended; and as to iron

[1] In his Dissertation *De Mitigata Davidis in Ammonitas Crudelitate.*

mines, there is not the least evidence that any were ever worked in the territories over which David had sway.

Besides, if David thus dealt with the Ammonites, he would have been far less severe to them than the war law of the age authorized, and far less so than to the Moabites and Edomites, of whom a large proportion of the males in the one case, and all who could be caught in the other, were destroyed. And is this credible in regard to a people, the aggravations of whose conduct had been so much greater?

The practice of putting prisoners to death has lately been explained.[1] The only question therefore is, why the Ammonites should be handled with such peculiar severity? To ascertain this, the special circumstances of the war should be considered. Without going back to ancient enmities, it is to be noticed how flagrantly the Ammonites had, in the first instance, violated the law of nations, by their treatment of David's friendly ambassadors; how they had once and again striven to organize a coalition of the nations against him, and had even brought troops from the far-off regions beyond the Euphrates; and finally, how obstinately they had held out to the last extremity, which alone was, by the war laws of the age, a sufficient cause for putting them to death. A "vexatious defence" is to this day punishable upon an enemy both by military and by civil law.

Still, we incline to think that these causes alone would not have led the king of Israel to put the Ammonite captives to death with torture, for this was not a war custom of the Hebrews, whose legislation is remarkable beyond that of any other people for the absence of torturing punishments. We have, therefore, no doubt that these punishments were retaliatory for similar treatment of Jewish and other prisoners who had been taken by the Ammonites. It is like the case of Adonibezek, the mutilation of whom would have come down to us as a gratuitous barbarity, had it not accidentally transpired from the lips of the man himself, that *he* had been in the habit of so treating *his* prisoners. That case has a distinct bearing upon this, because it shows that the Hebrews were accustomed to deal out to their enemies the same measure which they received from them. And this was quite necessary, it being the only way

[1] See Vol. 1, pp. 753-754.

in which other nations could coerce such offenders into an adherence to the established usages of war. Although the fact is not stated (as it is incidentally, in the case of Adonibezek), that the present severity was retributive, the certainty that it was so is sufficiently indicated by sundry dispersed facts, which bring out the peculiarly savage character of this people. Look, for instance, at their refusal of any other terms than the loss of their right eyes to the men of Jabesh-gilead, who were inclined to surrender without resistance. This is quite of a piece with their treatment of David's ambassadors; and the character thus manifested they still show in a later age, when they are reproached by the prophet for ripping up the pregnant women of Israel, not in the heat of a storm, but deliberately, in order to lessen the number of the Israelites, and thus to enlarge their own borders. (Amos i. 13.)

Now, in transacting with an enemy of this description, it could not have appeared unjust to treat them according to their dealings with others. Severe that treatment was, no doubt, and was meant to be; but to call it more than this, is to confound the ancient with the modern law of nations, or with the law of nature itself. This severity has, however, always appeared as a stain upon the character of David, in the view of those who are unable to discern the arbitrary character of the law of nations, and who judge of it according to the comparatively mild war laws of modern times. We are not competent to pass judgment in this matter, until we have carefully considered whether, considering the times in which David lived, the character of the enemy, and the proof they had given of the atrocities to which their malignant disposition against the Israelites would have carried them had they been victorious, he was not justified by *the public opinion of his own time*, in his treatment of the Ammonites. Why, after all, should we judge this ancient Hebrew king by a different measure from that which we apply to the comparatively modern, and professedly more civilized Romans? We call Titus just and humane, and yet he, at Jerusalem, crucified his prisoners around the city until crosses enough could not be found for the bodies, nor places on which the crosses could stand. Thousands, also, were after the close of the war thrown to wild beasts, for the amusement of the people, and

thousands were compelled to slay each other in the amphitheatres. These "just" Romans were also wont, even to the days of Cæsar, to massacre their prisoners in cold blood, whenever they happened to survive the disgrace of the triumph; and they *very frequently* put to death the magistrates and citizens of conquered cities, *after* making them undergo a flagellation, the slow torture of which was probably greater in physical pain than that which the Hebrews on this peculiar and exceptional occasion inflicted. It may also not be inappropriate to remark, that, up to a recent period, throughout the continent of Europe, the sentiment of public justice was not satisfied with the simple death of robbers and other offenders, but they were broken alive upon the wheel.

THE WAGES OF SIN

2 Samuel 13

THE most nobly born of David's wives was Maacah. She was the daughter of Talmai, king of Geshur, whose territory bordered on that of eastern Manasseh. David had sought the hand of this princess soon after his accession to the throne of Judah in Hebron, when, probably, the connection was, on public grounds, of much importance to him. By this lady he had two children, a son named Absalom, and a daughter called Tamar, both of them remarkable for their beauty. With the beauty of Tamar the heart of her half-brother Amnon—David's eldest son, by Ahinoam of Jezreel—was deeply smitten. So hot was his passion, that he fell into great depression of spirits and pined away. The impossibility of any happy result from a love so unlawful, had doubtless much to do with his melancholy, though the obstacle thus created may not have seemed to him so insuperable as it does to us, knowing as he did that it was common in some of the neighbouring countries—in Egypt for instance—for princes to espouse their sisters, and remembering that the practice had the sanction of Abraham's example. Probably, therefore, the first cause of his melancholy was the difficulty of getting access to her without witnesses, living as she did in her father's haram. For although the regulation respecting the separation of women from intercourse with men was less strict in those times than it has since become, it was such, at least in the royal harem, as to preclude a half-brother from the chance of being alone in her company. Had that been possible, he would probably have urged her to concur with him in persuading their father to consent to their marriage, notwithstanding the legal objections to which it lay open. But this was impossible; and in that age epistolary correspondence was so little thought of, that even lovers do not seem to have found out the advantages of this mode of communication. Besides, it is very likely that Tamar could not read.

The cause of Amnon's trouble was discovered by his cousin Jonadab, a very subtle man, who pointed out a mode in which he might obtain an unrestrained interview with Tamar. It is remarkable that in disclosing his passion, Amnon called not Tamar his sister, but "my brother Absalom's sister." In the harems of the East, where there are many children by different mothers, the children of the same mother become knit in a peculiar manner to each other, and if any of them be females, they come under the special care and protection of their brother, who, as far as their special interests are concerned, and in all that affects their safety and honour, is more looked to than the father himself. We have had an instance of this in the vengeance taken by Simeon and Levi for the wrong done to their full sister Dinah.

Tamar added to the fame of her beauty that of being a maker of very nice cakes—no mean recommendation for even a princess in the East. So, in conformity with Jonadab's advice, Amnon put himself to bed, and pretended to be ill; and when his father paid him a visit, he begged, that in consideration of his delicate appetite, his sister Tamar [it is now "my sister"] might be allowed to come and make him a few cakes—there, in his presence, that he might receive them hot from her hand. This seemed to the king not unreasonable as the fancy of a sick man, knowing, as he did, the dainty quality of his daughter's cakes. So Tamar came, and prepared the cakes there in his presence, which she might easily do, according to more than one of the existing modes of baking cakes in the East; and, proud of her skill, and gratified by the compliment which his demand had paid to it, she took them to him. Greatly was she shocked to find that he not only refused

to eat, but pressed her to sin; and notwithstanding her abhorrence, her resistance, and her declared belief that David would not refuse to bestow her on him, he accomplished her ruin. It seems probable that he had been carried by the rage of his guilty passion beyond his first intention, and now that the wretched act was accomplished, all the terrible consequences—the sin, the danger—rushed upon his mind, and all his love was in one moment turned to hate of the innocent object, whose fatal beauty had been the instrument of drawing this sin upon his soul. He spurned her from his house, and she hurried through the streets in tears, with her robe rent and ashes upon her head, to the house of her brother Absalom. It is said that the rent robe was "of divers colours; for with such robes were the king's daughters that were virgins apparelled;" in which case her rending the robe which was the distinction of the king's virgin daughters, had a meaning beyond the mere ordinary significance of mourning. It also reminds us of the precious coat of many colours with which Jacob invested his favourite son; and the present instance enables us to discern that dresses of variegated patterns were still costly and distinctive, and had not yet come into general use. When Absalom saw this robe rent, he at once understood what had happened; and his manner of receiving it is conformable to the character this young man finally discloses, rather than that which might have been expected from his position and spirit. He told Tamar to rest quiet—to remember that Amnon was their brother, and not needlessly proclaim abroad his crime and her own dishonour. He took her, however, to his own house thenceforth, and there she remained secluded and desolate.

The king, when he heard of this thing, was "very wroth;" and yet he did nothing. He saw that he had begun to reap the harvest he had sown, and the evils threatened by the prophet were coming fast upon him. How could he, who had himself sinned so deeply, call his son to account for his misconduct? and with what an awful retort, drawn from the example he had set to his children, might not his rebuke be met? Being also passionately fond of his children, to a degree of infatuation which rendered him unable to punish their offences, or even to find fault with them, he was content to let the matter pass, the rather as Absalom, whose honour it touched so nearly, seemed to take no notice of it. Of him it is said that "he spoke not a word to Amnon, neither good nor bad." He "hated" him for the wrong he had done to his sister; but he was too proud to "speak good" to one who had brought this dishonour to him, and too wary to put Amnon on his guard by expressing the hatred he nourished in his heart. He intended to make his revenge effectual, and to use it for clearing his way to the throne. We cannot but think that he had already taken up the design upon the kingdom, which he eventually carried out; and that as Amnon was his elder brother, and the heir-apparent, he meant to use his private wrong as the excuse for removing so serious an obstacle from his path. But to this end it was necessary that the king as well as Amnon should be lulled into the conviction that he had no thoughts of revenge, and that the matter had gone from his mind. Yet two years passed before he felt it prudent to show any civility to Amnon; but then the occasion of holding a great sheep-shearing feast on his estate, eight miles off at Baal-hazor, enabled him to accomplish his object. He first invited the king with his court to attend, which his father declined, on the ground that he was not willing to subject him to so heavy an expense. This he expected: he was then able to intimate his wish, that since the king himself could not go, his eldest son Amnon might represent him, and with the other sons of the king grace the feast. Unwilling to mortify him, and hoping this might bring about a perfect reconcilement between the brothers, David consented, though not without some misgivings.

Great was the feast; and it was in the very height of the enjoyment, "when Amnon's heart was merry with wine," that Absalom gave the preconcerted order to his servants, who immediately assailed the heir of the kingdom, and slew him with many wounds. On this the other sons of the king hastened to their mules, and hurried in great affright to Jerusalem. Absalom also fled, but it was to his maternal grandfather, the king of Geshur, who was more likely to praise than to blame the deed he had committed.

We may note here, that this is the first undisputed mention of *mules* in Scripture—the instance in Genesis xxxvi. 24 being of doubtful interpretation. We here find them in use at the same time that horses also begin to be named among this people. It appears that in this age, while a few horses were kept for state, mules were employed for riding by persons of distinction, both in peace and war. The ass, however, continued to maintain a respectable position, and never wholly gave place either to the mule or the horse. At this time the taste seems to have been decidedly for mules. Eventually we find Absalom possessed of chariots drawn by horses, but he was mounted upon a mule in the great action which he fought with his father for the crown; and it transpires still later that the king himself had a mule known to be his—a mule of state, which he rode on high occasions.[1] The combination in the mule of the useful qualities of both the horse and the ass—its strength, activity, steadiness, and power of endurance—are characteristics of peculiar value in the East; and therefore, although the Jews were interdicted from the *breeding* of mules, they did not find it convenient to consider that the *use* of them was forbidden.

David's declining to attend Absalom's feast on account of the expense which would thus be occasioned to his son, is the first instance history offers of the ruinous cost of royal visits to those who are honoured with them. A comparatively modern instance of this has just met our view in a useful periodical.[2] It is stated that the decay of the Hoghton family is locally ascribed to the visit of king James I. to Hoghton Tower, near Blackburn, Lancashire—the following characteristic anecdote being cited in corroboration of the current opinion :—" During one of his hunting excursions, the king is said to have left his attendants for a short time, in order to examine a numerous herd of horned cattle, then grazing in what are now termed the Bullock Pastures, most of which had probably been provided for the occasion. A day or two afterward, being hunting in the same locality, he made inquiry respecting the cattle, and was told, in no good-humoured way, by a herdsman unacquainted with his person, that they were all gone to feast the beastly king and his gluttonous company. ' By my saul,' exclaimed the king, as he left the herdsman, ' then 'tis e'en time for me to gang too ;' and accordingly, on the following morning, he set out for Lathom House."

[1] 1 Kings 1:33.
[2] *Notes and Queries* for October 19, 1850.

Absalom's mother was a native of Geshur, a sister of the king. The position of the little principality of Geshur is clearly, though incidentally, indicated in Scripture. It lay within the kingdom of Bashan and province of Argob, and at the northern extremity of both. It was independent of Og; and the Israelites did not conquer it, though its people submitted so far as to pay tribute. This may account for the fact, that while Geshur was geographically within Bashan, politically it was reckoned to Aram. The region embraced a considerable portion of that wild labyrinth of rocks and ravines called Lejâh. The people appear to have been as wild as the country they inhabited ; and probably much of the reckless daring and unnatural rebellion of Absalom was owing to his maternal training. When an exile from his father's court and kingdom, on account of the murder of his half-brother, he found a home and an asylum with his kinsmen amid the fastnesses of Geshur. It is a remarkable fact that, to this day, the Lejâh forms the asylum for every outlaw in Syria.

P.

ABSALOM'S HAIR

2 Samuel 14

ABSALOM was David's favourite son. His remarkable beauty, his engaging manners, and the rank of his maternal connections, must have contributed to this. But it is also true that the peculiarly affectionate temperament of David rendered him incapable of fully enjoying life, without some special object on whom to bestow the *utmost* tenderness of his love. Hence we always find some one in the enjoyment of his special favour and regard throughout his whole career. It is now Absalom. Three long years the king endured his absence, and during that time his grief for the loss of Amnon was assuaged, and his horror in the remembrance of Absalom's crime became less keen. He longed to have the young man back, but on many grounds feared to call him home. Joab discerned the struggle in the king's mind ; and although he seems himself to have had no liking for Absalom, he devised the means of impressing upon the king, that he might gratify his own wishes without giving offence to public opinion, which he seems to have much dreaded. He employed a clever woman of Tekoah to appear as a mourner before the king, and tell him a fictitious tale of distress, well calculated to awaken in him the feelings of paternal affection towards his absent son. The application of the recital which she made was

less striking than that of Nathan's parable, but it ended by imploring David to "fetch home his banished." The king began to perceive that Joab was at the bottom of this matter, and glad to have the sanction, thus delicately conveyed, of that rough but influential soldier, he authorized him to go to Geshur and bring Absalom home.

If the reader looks through the chapter which records these transactions, he will perceive in this cautious mode of proceeding, in the manner of the woman, and in that of Joab himself, that the kingdom was, even in the hands of David, assuming much of the character of an Eastern despotism, notwithstanding the conditions on which the royal power was held in Israel. We are not, however, disposed to build so much on this as some have done. We see the king chiefly in his own court, and in the East the court is always despotic; that is, the king's power is absolute over all who take employment under him, while the people may be comparatively free, and their franchises respected. What a difference, accordingly, always appears between the intercourse of the king with his own courtiers and officers, and that with the great landowners and sheep-masters in the country! This distinction is not sufficiently attended to by European travellers, who, in their views of Eastern nations, are too much in the habit of estimating the condition of the kingdom from what they see of the state of the court. But it is quite possible that there may be a considerable degree of freedom among the people, while the sovereign is absolute and despotic in his court, and over all who come within the sphere of his personal influence. We do not, therefore, regard the absolutism which appears in the Hebrew court, during this and subsequent reigns, as at all implying that the substantial liberties of the people were in any way compromised.

But although Absalom was allowed to return to Jerusalem, two whole years passed before he was admitted to his father's presence; and, considering how deeply that father loved him, and that he had not beheld his face for three years, David is entitled to much credit for this self-restraint. That Absalom was not admitted into his presence was a sign well understood, far more significantly in the East than it would be even with us, that he was still under disgrace. It in fact compelled him to live as a private person, and to lead a retired life; for it would have been outrageously scandalous for him to appear in public, or to assume any state, until he had appeared at court. The courtiers were also constrained to avoid him, and he could not even obtain an interview with his cousin Joab, until by a rough stratagem—that of causing his barley field to be fired—he drew him to make complaint of a wrong; and, having thus got within reach of his ear, the young prince easily prevailed upon him to persuade the king to admit him to the royal presence.

In the chapter whose contents we have thus scanned, it is stated that: "In all Israel there was none so much to be praised as Absalom for his beauty; from the sole of his foot to the crown of his head there was no blemish in him. And when he polled his head (for it was at every year's end that he polled it; because the hair was heavy on him, therefore he polled it); he weighed the hair of his head at two hundred shekels after the king's weight." By this it would appear, that this vain young man let his hair grow as long as he could bear it without much inconvenience; and when it was cut, caused it to be weighed in evidence of its abundant growth. "From year to year"—implying, that he had his hair cut every year—does not convey the meaning of the original, which signifies that he cut it "from time to time"— occasionally; that is, as the text explains, when it became heavy, which may have been, and probably was, at longer intervals than a year. The fact would imply, that long and abundant hair was fashionable at this time; although, in a later age, we find it counted as an effeminacy in a man. There are passages in Solomon's Song which confirm this; and it is stated by Josephus, that the picked men who formed the body-guard of Solomon wore their hair in long flowing tresses, which they anointed and sprinkled with gold dust every morning. This loading of the hair with unguents and gold dust, may, perhaps, lessen the surprise that an unusually ample head of hair should be so heavy. Two hundred common shekels would be about 112 ounces troy; but less, if, as is usually supposed, "the king's shekel" was not so much as the common shekel. The use of this denomination clearly implies that there was *some* difference, and no one has supposed the difference to have been in favour of "the king's shekel." One great authority (Bochart) makes the weight not

to exceed three pounds two ounces; and even that is not the lowest estimate, for others bring it down to little more than two pounds. Some, indeed, by supposing one Hebrew letter to have been taken for another very like it,[1] reduce the weight to four shekels, or two ounces; but this weight is too little remarkable to have been mentioned with such distinction. The hair of men will grow as thick as that of women, and perhaps thicker; and if we may judge from the queues of the Chinese, which sometimes reach to the ground, it will grow as long; and such hair, if of proportionate bulk, must, one would think, weigh at least three or four pounds. Indeed, we have read the well known case of a lady whose hair reached the ground, and weighed, upon her head, and therefore without including the weight of the parts nearest the scalp, upwards of four pounds, which is close upon Bochart's weight for the hair of Absalom.

Some, as in the case of the Ammonitish crown, suppose value, not weight, to be meant. But, was the king's eldest son likely to sell his hair at all, even if there were any one disposed to give for it any sum worth *his* acceptance? And what use could it have been to any one that bought it? Hardly to make wigs of; for although wigs were known among the Egyptians, there is no probability that they were in use among the Jews; and to meet the suggestion, that persons might be employed to buy up hair for the use of the Egyptian barbers, it may suffice to remark, that such wigs as have been discovered seem to have been made of horse hair or goat's hair, like those worn by our barristers.

Great attention was paid by the Jews to the growth and appearance of the human hair. It was worn long and in large quantities, and, perhaps, the memory of Samson, and the reverence for Nazaritism helped to enhance its value. Baldness was disliked, and specific directions were laid down in reference to cutting and trimming the locks of the head, the whiskers, and the beard. (Lev. xix. 27; xxi. 5.) The Dervishes of the East still allow their hair to grow very long; and we have a lively recollection of certain shock-headed persons of this class whom we saw in Egypt and Syria.

In reference to Absalom, who was so eminently distinguished in this respect, it may be added, that there is a well known monument bearing his name in the valley of

[1] ר, which, as a numeral, stands for 200, for ד, which represents 4.

Jehoshaphat, under the wall of Jerusalem. The inner chamber is full of stones, and stones are piled up all round the building. This arises from the custom of pelting his grave, as a sign of the detestation in which his memory is held, on account of his unnatural rebellion. The custom is

VALLEY OF JEHOSHAPHAT

ancient, and Surius, in his *Le pieux Pelerin*, published in 1644, remarks, that Jews and Mohammedans taught their children to pelt the tomb, crying, "Here he is! Here he is! the wicked man, the murderer, the cruel, who made war against his father."

S.

THE SPILT WATER

2 Samuel 14:14

IN the wise woman of Tekoah's address to David, this beautiful and touching passage occurs: "For we must needs die, and are as water spilt upon the ground, which cannot be gathered up again." Joab could scarcely have found an advocate better suited than this woman to make the desired impression upon the king's mind. What could be better calculated to gain the attention of a poet like David than the beautiful images which she employs, and which are equal to any that he himself ever uttered? There is scarcely anything in all literature finer than the image we have quoted; and if we, with our comparatively dull intellects, are impressed at once by the exquisite beauty and pathos of this expression, how keenly must it have been appreciated by him, the great master of solemn

thought and poetical expression! We can conceive him starting on his throne when these words fall upon his ear, for he feels at once that no common woman is before him. She had previously used another image,—fine, indeed, and striking, but eclipsed by this. She had compared the prospective death of her only surviving son to the quenching of her last live coal: "They shall quench my coal that is left, and shall not leave to my husband neither name nor remainder upon the earth;" and now, again, death is compared to water, which, being once lost upon the ground, can be gathered up no more. The idea is, that there is no recovery of the life once lost, no return from the cold desolations of the grave. This idea is common in the Old Testament, though nowhere else expressed by the same image. It occurs, however, less frequently in the Psalms than might be expected, whereas the instances in the Book of Job are numerous, and some of them very striking. The following have considerable analogical, but not literal resemblance to the one which now engages our attention:—

"As the cloud is consumed and vanisheth away; so he that goeth down to the grave shall come up no more. He shall return no more to his house, neither shall his place know him any more." [1]

"Man dieth, and wasteth away; yea, man giveth up the ghost, and where is he? As the waters fail from the sea, and the flood decayeth and drieth up; so man lieth down and riseth not." [2]

"The eye also which saw him shall see him no more; neither shall his place any more behold him." [3]

The most striking of the analogous passages which occur in the writings of David himself, is in Psalm lxxviii. 39: "He remembered that they were but flesh; *a wind that passeth away and cometh not again.*"

Even this image is in Job: "O remember that my life is wind." [4]

Beautiful as these images are, appealing as they do to our sympathies and consciousness— *are they true?* That is, are they in conformity with the later revelation, in which no such passages as these are to be found, and in which the restoration of the body is distinctly declared?

[1] Job 7:9,10.   [3] Job 20:9.
[2] Job 14:10-12.   [4] Job 7:7.

Do they not rather express the obscurity of that earlier light, which, although it eventually grew on to the perfect day of the Gospel, was in many things obscure at the beginning, and although it faintly disclosed the immortality of the soul, is thought scarcely to have revealed the resurrection of the dead? If revealed, it is certainly revealed obscurely. The mere question, whether it be revealed at all or not, shows this. It was, therefore, probably one of those doctrines which were purposely left obscure until the fulness of time should come—until the risen Redeemer had become the first-fruits of them that slept. We think that this doctrine is to be found in several passages of the early books of the Old Testament Scriptures, which were not so understood by the Jews themselves, but which we are enabled so to understand by the later light of the Gospel—as in that word of the Lord to Moses, from which Christ Himself declares that this doctrine might be inferred. (Matt. xxii. 32). And in the more certain light of later prophecy, this comfortable doctrine, though not very distinctly declared, is so clearly *indicated*, that the Jews themselves, by the time our Lord appeared, believed nearly all that we believe in this great matter, although there were those by whom it was still denied. It was drawn from the completed canon of the Old Testament, though it was not, perhaps, a matter of ancient popular belief, like the immortality of the soul. The belief existed, and that belief must have been drawn from the Old Testament—it must have been a revelation; for there was no other source from which the Jews could derive a doctrine (seeing that it was a true doctrine) not held by any other people, not discoverable by the human understanding, and one at which philosophy curled its lip in proud disdain.

It may therefore be, that the woman of Tekoah meant what her words literally indicate, and expressed the popular belief of her time—that life returned not to the dead. But, blessed be God, it is not so. The very contrary to what she said is the fact. We must needs die, but are *not* as water spilt upon the ground, which cannot be gathered up again. It shall be gathered up:

> " Wherever slept one grain of human dust,
>   Essential organ of a human soul,
>   Wherever tossed, obedient to the call
>   Of God's omnipotence, it hurried on

> To meet its fellow-particles, revived,
>   Rebuilt, in union indestructible,
>   No atom of his spoils remained to Death."

Again:

> " Each particle of dust was claimed : the turf
>   For ages trod beneath the careless foot
>   Of men, rose organized in human form ;
>   The monumental stones were rolled away :
>   The doors of death were opened ; and in the dark
>   And loathsome vault, and silent charnel-house,
>   Moving, were heard the mouldered bones
>   That sought their proper place. Instinctive every soul
>   Flew to its clayey part : from grass-grown mould,
>   The nameless spirit took its ashes up."—*Pollok.*

Yet, in returning to the words of the woman of Tekoah, it must be confessed that such expressions being in their very essence poetical and figurative, must not be pressed too closely for matters of doctrine. They may prove the existence of a doctrine or belief, but not the absence of a doctrine or belief. They take the lower and obvious sense of facts as they appear, and go not into the higher sense of unseen and unexperienced things. Gray's "Elegy in a Country Churchyard" supplies a case very much in point. The poet certainly knew and believed in the immortality of the soul—he knew the doctrine of the resurrection of the body, and probably believed in it. Yet in his poem, the subject of which might seem naturally to suggest the production of these doctrines, there is not one word bearing the slightest reference to either ; and if, in a distant age, inferences as to the belief of the British people were drawn from that poem alone, it might, with as much probability as in the case before us, be inferred that they possessed no knowledge nor belief of either doctrine. But the fact is, that the poet had only to deal with the external and social aspects of his subject ; and although he knew that there were higher and remoter aspects, his manifest object did not require him to extend his view to them. In a great variety of phrases and images he illustrates the idea that man shall no more return to the relations he has filled, and the position he has occupied—shall never recover the very form of life which he has laid down.

Indeed, all Gray's images and illustrations, so much admired and so often quoted, are but expansions and variations of the words of Job: "He that goeth down to the grave shall come up no more. He shall return no more to his house, neither shall his place know him any more."

Here, on the words, " shall come up no more," an elaborate old commentator[1] remarks: "No! That is sad news indeed, to go down into the grave and come up no more. Are all the hopes of man shut up in the grave? And is there an utter end of him when this life ends? Shall he come up no more? . . . . What he saith, it is not a denial of a dying man's resurrection to life, but of his restitution to the same life, or to such life as he parted with at the grave's mouth. They who die a natural death do not live a natural life again; therefore he added in the next verse, *He shall return no more to his house.* He does not say absolutely, he shall return no more, but he shall return no more to his house : he shall have no more to do with this world, with worldly businesses or contentments, with the labours or comforts of the creature, or of his family; he shall return *no more to his house.*"

A portion of this fine old expositor's remarks upon the next clause, might persuade one that Gray had read his ponderous volumes, with which he might certainly have employed himself to much more advantage than by reading Crebillon's romances upon a sofa, which was *his* idea of supreme enjoyment. The words are, "*Neither shall his place know him any more;*" on which Caryl observes, "When a man lives and comes home to his house, his house (as it were) welcomes him home, and his place is glad to entertain him. As in the psalm the little hills are said to rejoice at the showers, so when a man comes home, his house and all he hath, have, as it were, a tongue to bid him welcome, and open arms to receive and embrace him; but when he dies, he shall return no more, and then his place shall know him (that is, receive him) no more."

Interest attaches to the place where this "wise woman" lived. Fortified by Rehoboam, it became the birth-place of the prophet Amos, who, as herdsman, performed his humble toils in that neighbourhood. Thus two religious teachers are associated with the place. Eusebius and Jerome describe it as twelve miles from Jerusalem, and six from Bethlehem, travelling southward; and the latter says, when living at Bethlehem, he had Tekoah constantly before his eyes. In the Middle Ages a Christian church was built there; but the town was sacked by Turks, in the

[1] Joseph Caryl, *Exposition, with Practical Observations on the Book of Job.* London, 1676. A work in two immense and closely printed folio volumes, of about 4,700 pages together, now very scarce.

year 1138, and a traveller, Mr. Tyrwhitt Drake, who visited it in 1873, describes it as follows:—"The ruins at this place are extensive but uninteresting. To the east are many excavated caves and cisterns, but the town itself is simply a heap of ruins, the stones of which are small and friable. A fine octagonal font, ornamented on four sides with crosses, and the double square, stands over a well mouth. It is cut in the hard pink marbly stone, known at Jerusalem as the *Hajr el Musallabeh,* from the fact of the finest quality being found in the neighbourhood of the Convent of the Cross (Dayr el Musallabeh)." Robinson's *Researches,* ii. 183 ; *Palestine Exploration Statements,* 1874, 27.

S.

FILIAL INGRATITUDE

2 Samuel 15:7; 16:14

WHEN Absalom had gained permission to appear at court, and consequently acquired the right to show himself in public, and mingle freely in society, he adopted a line of conduct which enables us, by the light of subsequent events, to see that he had already formed the design of depriving his father of his crown.

It may occur to many to ask, What motive he could have to take a step so premature? There is, at the first view, a want of adequate *motive*, seeing that he was the eldest living son of the king,[1] and as his father was now advanced in life, the lapse of a few years would, in the course of nature, place the crown upon his head. But if our previous statements have been understood, it must be clearly seen that under the Hebrew constitution, the fact of his being the eldest son by no means ensured the succession to him. No one had yet succeeded to the kingdom of Israel by right of primogeniture, and the principle of such succession was not, as yet, therefore, established by a single precedent. Besides, David could not have failed to make his sons clearly understand that, although the crown was assured to his family, the nomination of the individual was with the Lord; and they needed not him to teach them that in the absence of any such nomination, the power rested with himself of bequeathing the crown to any one of his sons he pleased. This alone was enough to make Absalom's pros-

[1] Chileab, the son of David by Abigail, was born before him, but he appears to have died ere this time, for nothing is reported of him but the fact of his birth.

pects in the future somewhat precarious. The divine nomination of another might, at any time, be interposed; and he had probably seen enough to feel that he was not to calculate too surely even upon his father's preference. He knew indeed, that he had no second place in his father's heart, but enough had passed to satisfy him that he held no high place in that father's judgment. More than this, it is our impression that David already knew that Solomon was, by the Lord's appointment, to be his successor on the throne. In the promise made to David through Nathan, it was clearly indicated that a son not yet born was to sit upon his throne; and when Solomon was born, he could not but understand that this applied to him. If he had any doubt of this, it must have been removed by his knowledge that the "Lord loved him," and had, through Nathan, bestowed upon him the new name of Jedidiah (beloved of the Lord). (2 Sam. xii. 24, 25.) It is even probable that he had long before the present time, if not from the first, received those more distinct intimations of the Lord's will in this matter, which he mentions in 1 Chron. xxviii. 5-7; but this alone could not but be enough to enable one so anxious as David was, to trace and act upon the divine indications. Besides, we learn from 1 Kings i. 17, that the king had pledged himself to Bathsheba, who must have been aware of all this, that her son should be his successor, or, in other words, that his choice should enforce these intimations, and that no impulses of affection or preference for any other son should induce him to contravene them. Whether this pledge had been already given, is not clear; but as Solomon was now about fourteen years of age, and as the intimations we have traced were long before afforded, it is likely that the pledge which was founded on them had not been so long delayed.

Now, if David had not yet made this designation of Solomon publicly known, enough may have transpired, or have been surmised, to lead Absalom to think his succession by right of primogeniture to be in danger, and to feel that the danger would increase by lapse of time; and thus we perceive that, to a man of Absalom's temper, there were motives for immediate action which do not at first sight appear.

Absalom did not, however, plunge at once into open rebellion. He began by assuming a semi-regal magnificence, to assert his rank as heir apparent. He procured for himself chariots and horses—then a new, and therefore striking, luxury in Israel—and appeared abroad in much state, with fifty outrunners. The dignity thus assumed, rendered the more persuasive the blandishments by which he strove to seduce from their allegiance the suitors who repaired from all parts of the land to Jerusalem, and gave emphasis to his seditious insinuations, and his promises of redressing all public wrongs. These people spread through the country, on their return home, glowing accounts of the inexpressible beauty of the king's son, his gracious condescension, his sympathy with the poor and the oppressed, and the advantages that might be expected from his reign. In the striking words of the sacred historian, "So Absalom stole the hearts of the men of Israel"—stole the hearts that belonged to his father.

When all appeared ripe for action, Absalom repaired to Hebron with 200 men, and after seizing that strong town — the metropolis of David's first kingdom—he caused himself to be proclaimed king, by sound of trumpet, in several parts of Israel at once. The king was confounded and dismayed at the suddenness of the outbreak, and apparently wide disaffection to his government and person which its extent implied. As news came to him that one place after another had proclaimed Absalom, he felt as if all were falling away from him, and that he could rely only upon the foreign guards, whom, under the names of Gittites, Cherethites, and Pelethites, he had in the course of years gathered around his person. With these he marched out of Jerusalem, purposing, if need were, to proceed to the country beyond the Jordan, and there collect his resources and watch the progress of events. From the people beyond the river he had received many proofs of attachment, and his wars had brought him much into connection with them, and had materially advanced their prosperity; and he thought that he might count on their fidelity. The geographical position was also well suited to his purpose; and the step seems to have been, under all the circumstances, the best that could have been taken.

Even in departing, the king received many proofs of attachment, which must have refreshed his heart. Some, indeed, might be supposed to serve his cause better by remaining at Jerusalem than by going with him. Among them was

Hushai, an esteemed friend, who was prevailed upon to return, for the express purpose of endeavouring to neutralize the counsels of Ahithophel, a crafty but most able man, who had been high in the councils of David, and whose defection seems to have disturbed him more than any single incident of this melancholy affair. Such faith had he in this man's sagacity, that he apprehended Absalom's chief power lay in the possession of such a counsellor; and hence his anxiety to prevent his advice from being followed. This perilous mission was undertaken by Hushai; and he performed it well.

The sympathy of the priestly body was also entirely with David. Both the high priests, Abiathar and Zadok, were not only prepared to go with him, but they caused the ark of the covenant to be brought out, to be borne away with the king. David was deeply affected at this sight; but he declined to avail himself of the advantage which the presence of the ark and of the high priests would have given to his cause. He directed them to take it back, and to remain themselves in the city. "Carry back the ark of God into the city," he said; "if I shall find favour in the eyes of the Lord, He will bring me again, and show me both it and His holy habitation."

It was, nevertheless, a hard thing thus to be compelled to wander forth in his old age from his beloved city, his pleasant home, and the place of the Lord's tabernacle; and to find himself thus forsaken by his own subjects, who owed so much to him, and by the friends in whom he had trusted; and all this at the instance and by the contrivance of the son whom he loved so well. No wonder that he departed as a mourner. "David went up by the ascent of Mount Olivet, and wept as he went up, and had his head covered; and he went barefoot: and all the people that was with him covered every man his head, and they went up, weeping as they went up." No more striking picture of a great man under adversity was ever drawn than these simple words portray. The conduct of David throughout—his goodness, resignation, and patience—is clearly evinced in all these trying scenes. This, as Dr. Chalmers observes, "marks strongly his subdued and right spirit; partly induced, we doubt not, by the humility of his own conscious transgressions. He fell, but it was the fall of the upright, and he rose again; submitting himself meekly, and in the meantime, to the will of God."

His patience had a further trial on the way. As he went on by the pass of Bahurim, one Shimei, a relation of Saul, cast stones and bitter curses at him, as one whom vengeance had at last overtaken, for all the evil he had done to the house of Saul. The indignation of Abishai was naturally roused at this; and with the instinctive impulse of the sons of Zeruiah towards blood, he begged David to let him go over and take off the venomous scoundrel's head. But David saw the hand of God even in this, and he refused. "Behold, my son seeketh my life; how much more now may this Benjamite do it? Let him alone, and let him curse, for the Lord hath bidden him. It may be that the Lord will look upon mine affliction, and that the Lord will requite me good for his cursing this day." This was the true spirit which makes chastisement profitable. David is always great in affliction. His soul is prospering largely amid these circumstances of mental trial and personal suffering.

So David pursued his sorrowful way until he reached the plains of Jericho and the banks of the Jordan, where he awaited such tidings as might direct his further course.

This graphic narrative exhibits the character of David in a new light. A total change has taken place. His old lion heart is completely subdued. In former days, the imminence of danger and the cry to arms would have only served to call into action his splendid military genius, and to rouse his warlike spirit. Now he seems paralysed by the first murmur of rebellion. He flies in terror even before the enemy appears. One feels inclined to pity his weakness rather than to admire his submission. He would have given way altogether to despair, had it not been for the encouraging words of his devoted followers. The first gleam of hope in his breast was kindled by the sudden appearance of Hushai the Archite.

What was it which produced a change so marked and so melancholy? The answer is not difficult. Conscience made a coward of him. David was a heart-broken man. His own great sin had crushed him to the dust, and had filled him with an overwhelming sense of shame. Those who in former times all but idolized him, now saw his weakness, and were, by a wily and plausible and fascinating prince, taught to despise him. The feuds that distracted his family, and the crimes that stained his hearth with blood, he probably regarded as the righteous judgments of Heaven upon himself; and Absalom's unnatural rebellion he perhaps looked upon as the natural result of his own indulgence of a wild youth, and neglect of due parental training. With a heart swelling with feelings of self-reproach, and deep sorrow, and fear for the kingdom, and affectionate solicitude for a misguided and ungrateful child, it is not strange that David, as he turned away from his home and his capital, "wept as he went up" the side of Olivet, and buried his face in his mantle.

Every stage and every incident of that mournful journey is detailed with great simplicity, and yet with graphic power. More than once I have followed David's footsteps, noting each well defined spot,—his station at "the farthest house" ("a place that was far off," ver. 17), on the brow of Moriah, where his body-guard and the people passed in mournful procession, and where Ittai the Gittite gave such a proof of his devotion; then the bridge over the Kidron; then the old "way of the wilderness" up the side of Olivet, where the priests bearing the ark overtook the king; then the summit of the mount where the faithful Hushai "came to meet him, with his coat rent, and earth upon his head;" then the place, "a little past the top," on the eastern declivity, where Ziba appeared with his present, and his deceitful story. The city was now hid from view, and the bleak wilderness of Judah in front, with the deep valley of the Jordan far below, and the blue range of Gilead away beyond. It did not need the reproaches and curses of Shimei to make the monarch fully conscious of his fallen fortunes, as he hastened on through the desert to seek an asylum amid the fastnesses of Gilead.

P.

TWO HANGINGS

2 Samuel 16:15 - 19:8

Soon after his father's departure, Absalom marched into Jerusalem, and took possession of the palace and the treasures of the crown. Absalom knew how relentless his own purposes were towards that father, whose love he possessed without measure; he knew how firm was his own resolve to reign. Yet he gave the people credit for not believing how black his own heart was—for supposing that there was yet in his breast some sense of filial duty, some gleams of filial tenderness. But, instead of being gratified that people thought better of him than he deserved, he was disturbed by it. He feared that, in contemplation of possible circumstances which might bring about a reconciliation between him and his father, and leave his supporters open to the resentment of David, many would be afraid to commit themselves to his cause. He was therefore ready to adopt any means, however atrocious, which might convince those inclined to support him, that they would never be compromised by any reconciliation between him and his greatly wronged father. The means sug-

gested by the Satanic "wisdom" of Ahithophel were most effectual, but most atrocious. It was, that Absalom should take public possession of the "concubines" whom David had left behind in charge of the palace: his *wives* he had probably taken with him. This counsel was followed; and the people were satisfied that this deed had rendered all reconcilement between David and his son impossible.

Absalom's next step was to attempt his father's destruction, in the conviction that his own throne would never be secure so long as he lived. The son had no relentings. He had knowingly subjected himself to the inevitable necessity of taking his father's life, and he only desired to learn how that object might be most effectually secured. A council was held on this question, and it is the first cabinet council to which history admits us. It was, doubtless, conducted in the same form as other royal councils; and from the instance before us, it appears that the members who had anything to suggest, or rather such as the king called upon for their opinion, described the course they thought best suited to the circumstances. The council at large then expressed its collective opinion upon the advice thus offered, and recommended that course to the king. It does not appear whether or not the king was regarded as bound to follow the advice so tendered; but it seems to have been generally followed—the king probably disliking to take the responsibility of acting on his individual opinion in opposition to the collective wisdom of his council. This "collective wisdom" is seldom other than the wisdom of one man, who devises the course of action, and induces the others to concur in his views. In this case the choice lay between the "wisdom" of Ahithophel and the wisdom of Hushai. The former sagaciously advised immediate action, before David should be able to collect his resources. Hushai was not a member of this council; but he had been well received by Absalom, whose greater treachery against his father made him give ready credence to the pretended treachery of his father's friend. It was at Absalom's suggestion that he was called in; and being informed of the course Ahithophel had advised, he saw at once the danger that this course threatened to David; and, in fulfilment of his mission to defeat this man's counsel, he advanced divers reasons against it, all tending to delay—reasons so specious, that the council with one voice declared his advice to be better than that of Ahithophel. Mortally offended at this disrespect to that sagacity which all Israel admired, and convinced, in his clear-sighted scope of "things before and after," that the cause of Absalom would be lost by the delay Hushai recommended, he saddled his ass, rode home to his house in Giloh, and having deliberately set his affairs in proper order, hanged himself. Ahithophel was probably not the first man who hanged himself, but he bears the unenviable distinction of being the first whose hanging himself is recorded; and society would have little reason to complain, if all who have since sentenced themselves to this doom were as worthy of it as this father of self-suspenders. Bishop Hall quaintly remarks of him, that though mad enough to hang himself, he was wise enough to set his house in order before he did it.

Hushai seems not to have been too sure that his counsel would be followed, for he sent trusty messengers to apprise David of what had passed, and advised him immediately to cross the river. This the king did, and went to reside at Mahanaim, where Ishbosheth had formerly reigned—a circumstance which probably dictated his choice of that place. Here he received abundant supplies of all necessaries for himself and his followers from three men, whose names are mentioned with honour in the sacred narrative. We are somewhat surprised to find that the first of these is Shobi, son of Nahash, king of Ammon, and therefore brother of Hanun, whose people had been dealt with so severely by David. Nothing is known with certainty of him; but it is by some reasonably enough conjectured, that he was believed to have disapproved of his brother's conduct, and had in consequence been made governor of Ammon by David, after the land had been subdued. The second was that Machir of Lo-debar, whom we have already had occasion to mention as the person who had acted as host and father to Mephibosheth, until David had taken notice of him, and as being by some considered the brother of Bathsheba. The third was the aged Barzillai of Gilead, in whose hearty adhesion to his king there is something peculiarly affecting. The catalogue of the commodities which these and other like-minded men supplied, at probably an all but ruinous expense to themselves, is curious, as showing the nature of the articles considered

in that age to be necessary for the comfort and subsistence of the king and his people : "Beds, and basons, and earthen vessels, and wheat, and barley, and flour, and parched corn, and beans, and lentiles, and parched pulse, and honey, and butter, and sheep, and cheese of kine." It will be perceived that in this pastoral land, unusual prominence is given to the produce of flocks and herds, and the agricultural produce is confined to prime necessaries. There is no mention here of wine, or oil, or raisins, or figs, or dates, or in fact of various articles which would have been very conspicuous in a list of commodities supplied in the countries west of the Jordan. Here in this pastoral region, where there was little commerce, the wealth of the people consisted chiefly in flocks and herds, and in the prime articles of food. Here brave and hardy men, attached to their family-chiefs, abounded, and were ready at the call of their leaders to gather around their king, who, although without treasure, thus found himself in a short time at the head of a considerable army.

Their services were speedily required, for Absalom soon crossed the Jordan also, his army being under the command of his cousin Amasa, a son of David's sister Abigail, who probably felt discontented at having been kept in the shade by the sons of Zeruiah, and hoped to exercise under Absalom the same authority which Joab wielded under, or rather over, David.

A battle, bloody and decisive, was now inevitable; and David, finding that the soldiers would not allow him to risk his own person in the engagement, divided his force into three brigades, severally under the command of Joab, Abishai, and Ittai (the commander of the foreign guards), the general command being with Joab. The battle was fought in what was called the Forest of Ephraim; and as it was not the Lord's purpose that *this* chastening should proceed any further, the cause of David triumphed. Absalom himself fled for his life upon his mule; but as he rode in unguarded haste through the wood, the long hair in which he so much gloried, caught in the low branches of an oak, and the escape of his mule from under him left him dangling in the air. When Joab got news of this, he hurried to the spot, and settled all further questions by sending three darts through the body of the guilty prince. This was contrary to the orders of David, who that morning, as the troops defiled before him at the gate of Mahanaim, had strictly enjoined the soldiers to respect the life of Absalom for his sake. There was probably a true regard for the king and kingdom in this act of Joab. He knew that Absalom could not with safety be suffered to live; and that it would be difficult to rid the state of so foul a member at any other time than now, when a just right to slay him had been earned in open battle.

THE DEATH OF ABSALOM.

This is by no means to be classed with Joab's assassinations. It had nothing in common with them. Nothing can be alleged against him in this matter but his disobedience to the king: but he, in his position, felt that he dared to disobey him for his own good; and that he was quite prepared to vindicate and maintain this deed. He did so; and when the king, in the bitterness of his grief, on receiving the tidings that his son was dead, bewailed him aloud in cries that go to one's heart, "O my son Absalom! my son, my son Absalom! would God I had died for thee, O Absalom, my son, my son!"—Joab went in to him, and reprimanded him in strong language for thus discouraging the men who had risked their lives in his cause, by making them feel as if they had committed a crime in delivering him from his enemies. David felt the force of this, and presented himself with a cheerful countenance to the people. But it is evident that for this act he abhorred Joab in his heart, even to his death-bed.

THE RESTORATION

2 Samuel 19:9-15, 41-43; 20

ABSALOM is dead. David is victorious. What more has the king to do but to cross the Jordan, march to Jerusalem, and take possession of his throne? This had been ill speed—it had been too abrupt. David is much to be commended for the delicacy with which he acted. Seeing that the defection of the people, and the preference of Absalom, had been so general among the tribes west of the Jordan, he feared even the appearance of forcing himself upon them, or seeming to recover possession of his throne as a conqueror. He therefore tarried beyond the river, waiting to be invited back. There was some delay in giving this invitation, perhaps because the king's wish and his motive in delaying to move westward were not at first understood. When these were understood, and the king seemed thus voluntarily to throw back the option into their hands, his delicacy was not so generally appreciated as it deserved. There was a strife of parties, and some seemed to be inclined to accept the option he appeared to offer, by declining to receive him; and it appears to us not unlikely that if any acceptable candidates had appeared, the division of the realm into two, if not into three kingdoms, might then have taken place. David's power was safe beyond the Jordan, and in any event he would have reigned there—and so far the promise to him would have been accomplished. But on this side the river, the seeds of disunion between the great tribe of Judah and the other tribes had already so far ripened, that they would scarcely have concurred in the choice of a new sovereign unconnected with the house of David, and thus the disruption, which after another reign took place, would then have been consummated. As it was, the strife of parties ended in the general, but scarcely unanimous, determination to recall David; and it is remarkable that the initiative was taken by the ten tribes, which, it is important to observe, are now, for the first time, called Israel, as distinct from Judah. But it is likely that, although it now first appears, this distinction had actually grown up while David reigned over Judah only, and Ishbosheth over the other tribes. Ishbosheth's kingdom must have had some name to distinguish it from that of Judah, and what so likely as that it should have been the name of Israel, at least among the populace? As each of the kings considered himself entitled to the sole dominion, they may have avoided the appearance of limiting their claim, by calling themselves respectively, king of Judah and of Israel; and the fact is, that in the history they are never so designated. But the populace, in every age and country, will have names for things, whether they be appropriate or not; and there can be no doubt that the people of Israel had a short and easy name, free from ceremonious circumlocution, for the realm of Ishbosheth.

When David became acquainted with the desire of the ten tribes to recall him, he felt himself in a new difficulty. It was a separate decision of the ten tribes, in which his own tribe of Judah had not concurred. Some may think that he might have *assumed* the fact of that tribe's attachment to him; but it seems to us that the facility with which Absalom had been hailed as king at Hebron, and been joined by such numbers as enabled him to move at once upon Jerusalem, might well justify David in suspecting that the procrastination of the Judahites arose from some disinclination to receive him. The step he did take is, however, of questionable discretion. There was great danger in adopting a course which might indicate to the other tribes that he took a separate interest in Judah; as it was too well remembered that he belonged to it, and that it had for some years been his separate kingdom. He, however, recognized their tribal interest in him by treating with them separately. He sent the two high priests to incite them to escort him home, and not to be the last in the general movement. They did so. Though the last to call him, they were the first to escort him; and when they sent to conduct him home, he at once moved forward, without waiting till the other and more distant tribes arrived to take part in this great public act. The dangerous impolicy of this is apparent. The least he could have done, was to wait until the other tribes arrived to concur in this procedure, aware, as he must have been, of the importance which all Orientals attach to such points of ceremony. But it is plain to us that, being aware that eventually the main interest of his house lay in Judah, he was determined to reign there at all hazards, whatever became of the rest of his kingdom.

The result that might he anticipated ensued. When the other tribes came to conduct the king home, they were affronted to find that they had been superseded, and that Judah alone had assumed the right and honour of bringing the king back. There then arose a hot contention between Israel and Judah. The former contended with reason, that as they "had ten parts in the king," and Judah but one, the latter had taken too much upon it in bringing the king back upon its own authority; in reply to which the Judahites used the argument, dangerous for David's house, but which his own part in the matter had distinctly sanctioned, that they had a right to act as they had done, because the king was peculiarly their own—"was near of kin to them." David must have smiled to witness this eager contention among the tribes, as to which had the best right to bring back the sovereign whom they had all concurred, but lately, in driving forth.

The argument of the Judahites was by no means calculated to conciliate the ten tribes; and there can be no doubt that the king himself incurred a share in the displeasure of the latter for the part he had taken in this matter, for it was certainly on his distinct invitation that the men of Judah had acted. Here, as Chalmers aptly describes it, "was a festerment that broke out at a future day." Even now, as he remarks, this feeling, on the part of Israel, "came to a formidable eruption." Among the watchers of events was one Sheba, the son of Bichri, who, perceiving the disgust of the ten tribes at the arrogance of the men of Judah, thought that the contention of these tribes for ten parts in David might easily be turned into a disavowal of any part in him. He therefore raised the seditious cry, "We have *no part* in David, neither have we inheritance in the son of Jesse: every man to his tents, O Israel." This cry, in the present state of feeling, acted like magic. Nearly all the men of Israel left the king to the Judahites, and he was by them escorted from the Jordan to Jerusalem.

Here was a perilous emergency. David had no hesitation in thinking that this outbreak was to be treated as rebellion. But whom was he to employ? Considering that this recall was like the commencement of a new reign, which vacated the warrant whereby all offices were previously held, he had offered to Amasa (the late commander of Absalom's forces) the lure of making him commander-in-chief, in place of Joab—a step which we cannot view with satisfaction, involving, as it did, the sacrifice of the long tried devotion of Joab and Abishai (who would not be likely to overlook this affront to his brother), and the disregard of the high services they had often and lately rendered to the king and the state, for the purpose of purchasing the allegiance of one who had but yesterday been in arms against him, and who had certainly not acquired much military reputation in the campaign. He was to have the rewards of Albemarle, without the services of Monk. The truth is, no doubt, that the king thought that he might thus, by a side blow, rid himself of the inconveniently overpowering influence of Joab, and relieve himself from the presence of the man who had slain Absalom, but whom he durst not ostensibly punish on *that* account. He was, however, greatly mistaken in his calculation, and much over-rated his own strength. Joab was not thus easily to be disposed of.

Amasa was, however, made commander-in-chief, and it was to him that David committed the charge of putting down Sheba's dangerous insurrection. He was ordered to collect the forces of Judah within three days, and appear with them at Jerusalem. The rapid Joab would hardly have required even three days for this service; but this time passed, and Amasa appeared not. The fact is significant. The men did not approve of the step which the king had taken, and were reluctant to follow this new leader, so that he could not get the required force together in the time assigned. This might have convinced David that he had again erred; and, himself sudden and quick in his military operations, and accustomed to the sharp, rapid, and decisive action of Joab, he could little brook this tardiness. Still, reluctant to call Joab again into service, yet aware of the danger of delay, he commissioned Abishai to put down this dangerous conspiracy. He only had been commissioned, but Joab went with him, and doubtless became the actual commander. They had got no farther than Gibeon, where they halted, when Amasa, with such forces as he had got together, overtook them. On his approach, Joab went to meet him, and so contrived that his sword should fall out of its sheath to the ground, as he drew near to him. Snatching it hastily up, without pausing to sheath it, in the polite zeal of his attention to Amasa, he took hold of his beard, to impress upon it the kiss of affectionate respect, saying, "Art thou in health, my brother?" and as the words passed his lips, and the beard was in his hand, he buried the naked sword in the body of Amasa, under the fifth rib. This was almost exactly as he had before dealt with Abner, and from almost entirely the same motives. This, however, is by much the more villanous act of the two, seeing that it stood more entirely on the ground of personal objects. In Abner's case he had the excuse, at least, of vengeance for a brother's blood, as well as of a real or pretended belief that Abner designed to betray David. But here there was nakedly nothing but the desire to fling a formidable rival from his path. One knows not whether most to be astonished at the atrocity or the hardihood of the deed. It was no less than the murder of a general at the head of his troops. But Joab knew his own influence. One near him cried, "He that favoureth Joab, and he that is for David, let him follow Joab." And such was the power of that name, and the wonderful ascendancy the owner of it had acquired over the troops, that the men of Amasa forthwith joined the others in following Joab in pursuit of Sheba. The advantage of this unexpected promptitude appears in the fact, that the rebel leader, being allowed no time to gather strength, shut himself up in the strong town of Abel Bethmaachah, where the people, to escape a siege, after some parley with Joab, cut off Sheba's head, and threw it to him over the wall.

Thus ended this dangerous commotion; and although the result was the establishment of David's power over all Israel, some damage had been sustained by all the parties concerned. The king himself had committed some serious political indiscretions, tending to establish an ill feeling between Israel and Judah; while the high-handed manner in which Joab had resumed his command had satisfied David that he could not be displaced, and must have materially deepened his now settled hatred of the high officer to whom he was obliged to entrust the military power of the state, while his horror at the murder of Amasa was not lessened by his inability to call the assassin to account, or by the consciousness that his own untoward proceedings had been the exciting cause of this frightful crime.

In going through these sad passages, the question continually recurs: How is it that we hear no more of David asking counsel of the Lord? The time was when the sacred oracle was consulted on matters of comparatively small importance; but since he became king over all Israel, we have had only one instance of his resort to this sure means of guidance, and that was at the beginning of his reign. We shall not be far wrong in ascribing to this neglect the serious mistakes into which he appears to have fallen.

INCIDENTS

2 Samuel 19:16-40

YESTERDAY we surveyed the political incidents connected with the restoration of David to his throne; and we proceed now to regard some remarkable lesser circumstances which are interwoven therewith in the sacred narrative.

A great surprise met David as soon as he had crossed the Jordan on his return. Who shall be the first to meet him—to proffer his allegiance and devotion—but that very Shimei who had so bitterly insulted him on his mournful retreat from Jerusalem! He fell at the king's feet, confessed his error, and pleaded for pardon on the ground of his contrition, and of his being the first of the tribe of Benjamin to come forward on this happy occasion. This was important; for he came at the head of a thousand men of the same tribe, all probably, like himself, warm partisans of the house of Saul, whom he seems to have induced to take part with him in this decided act of adhesion. An appeal thus made could not be resisted; and besides, David was, both from policy and inclination, in a forgiving temper, and felt that it would ill become him at such a time to avenge or remember former wrongs. He therefore rebuked the vengeful suggestion of Abishai, and pledged himself by oath to Shimei, that he should not die. It is to be regretted that our knowledge of later circumstances prevents us

from ranking this forbearance with acts of Christian forgiveness.

The good old chief Barzillai went to the Jordan with the king, and took leave of him when he was about to cross the river. David pressed him to proceed with him to Jerusalem, and remain there with him, that he might have the opportunity of manifesting his gratitude for the great and costly services he had rendered. But the prospect of a life at court had no charms for this great pastoral chief. There is something very touching in his words: " I am this day fourscore years old; and can I discern between good and evil? can thy servant taste what I eat or what I drink? can I hear any more the voice of singing men and singing women? wherefore, then, should thy servant be yet a burden to my lord the king?" He would, he said, go a little way beyond the Jordan with the king; but, he added, " Let thy servant, I pray thee, turn back again, that I may die in mine own city, and be buried by the grave of my father and my mother." This touch is affecting, and true to universal nature, but particularly to Oriental nature. The tendency of our civilisation is to put us above—or perhaps below —these things; and in so far as it does so, it makes us less wise than we think. We do not say,

"Perish the lore that deadens young desire;"

but we do say there is much in this modern atmosphere of ours which narrows life by deadening —or rather, by concentrating in the present— that imagination which, in younger and more vernal times, extended the vitality of existence into both the future and the past.

Among the first to meet the king at the Jordan was Ziba, " the servant of the house of Saul," with his fifteen sons and twenty servants. This person had good cause to come. On David's retreat from Jerusalem, he had met him with an acceptable supply of bread, wine, and summer fruits; and when the king inquired what had become of his master Mephibosheth, he said that he had remained at Jerusalem in the expectation that the turn of events might lift him up as the heir of the house of Saul. On hearing this, David, stung by such ingratitude, told Ziba he might have for himself the estate he had hitherto farmed for Mephibosheth. This was a hasty step; and one cannot but feel that a little delay and inquiry would have become David in regard to the son of Jonathan. At Jerusalem, Mephibosheth soon presented himself before the king, who asked him sternly why he had not gone with him. In reply, he touchingly alluded to his lameness. He had ordered an ass to be saddled, on which to follow the king; but Ziba had interfered, and had gone and slandered him to David. Although he did not himself mention it, his haggard and forlorn appearance bore witness to the fact, that during the king's absence he had passed his time as a mourner, and had not dressed his feet, nor trimmed his beard, nor washed his clothes. But, while he vindicated his character, and knew how the king had disposed of his property, he intimated his indifference to that part of the matter —"Do what is good in thine eyes. . . . What right have I yet to cry any more unto the king?" Reluctant to think that he had been too hasty; having a royal aversion to admit that he could err, and had been duped; and being, in his present humour of overlooking and pardoning everything, indisposed to the task of calling to account a man of such influence as Ziba, who had been forward in his cause, when many tried friends forsook him; the king's answer was something less than generous, and much less than kind to the son of Jonathan: "Why speakest thou any more of thy matters? I have said, thou and Ziba divide the land." The injustice of this is obvious. If he disbelieved Mephibosheth, it was unjust to Ziba to deprive him of the land, which had been the reward of his fidelity when his master forsook what seemed to be a falling cause: whereas, if he believed Mephibosheth, escape from punishment had been sufficient grace for Ziba. The matter is not, however, perhaps so bad as it looks. The king reverts to what he had said, which carries the mind back to his first arrangement, which was, that Mephibosheth should be proprietor, and Ziba his tenant, dividing the *produce* of the land with him. It may therefore be, that the king meant to be understood as restoring this arrangement; thus depriving Ziba of the advantage which his treachery acquired, without ejecting him from his tenancy under Mephibosheth. Even this would be hard enough for the son of Jonathan, to be thus still connected with a steward who had betrayed him. But the student of history knows that at a restoration the rules of right and wrong are seldom strictly carried out, and that the king having two parties to satisfy, feels obliged to act upon compromises, which give to all something less than their due. Nothing can, however, excuse the tart manner of David in answering Mephibosheth. If he was not then at leisure to attend to his representation, why decide the matter—and that to his disadvantage—before he had time to inquire fully into the case? The tone of the afflicted man's reply to this sharp answer, gives us reason to fear that the worst interpretation of David's decision may be the right one: "Yea, LET HIM TAKE ALL, forasmuch as my lord the king is come again in peace unto his own house." Oh noble heart! Let us fain hope that David was touched by this, and could once more say, "I am distressed for thee, my brother Jonathan."

The various incidents connected with the rebellion of Absalom, the return of the king, and the suppression of the outbreak under Sheba, show the increasing weakness of David. He appears almost incapable of judging for himself, or of conducting public affairs so as to secure peace and harmony in the kingdom. He appears also to have well nigh forgotten his allegiance to the God of Israel. Humiliated by a consciousness of guilt and sense of shame, harassed by open foes and domineering friends, he for a season forgot alike his dignity as a monarch, and his duty as the Lord's anointed. We do not read now of his asking counsel of God. Joab was at this period the master mind in Israel. His vast influence and commanding ability first saved the throne, and then saved the kingdom from being rent in twain. But his rough and rugged nature often grated harshly on the exquisitely tender sensibilities of David. David was afraid of Joab, and did not treat him well. He required his strong arm; he acknowledged the wisdom of his counsel; yet he tried all means, except that of open deposition, on which he would not venture, to displace him from his high office as commander-in-chief. It was a weak, almost cowardly, policy to attempt to supersede Joab by setting up a powerful rival. But Joab was equal to the emergency, and did not scruple to murder Amasa as he had murdered Abner. Joab knew well enough the king's feeling toward him—he saw through the duplicity of his master; yet there is one thing remarkable, almost unaccountable, considering the nature of the times and the character of the man—he never for a moment swerved from his allegiance. Unscrupulous in all besides; conscious of possessing almost paramount influence in the kingdom; of unequalled military skill; filled with towering ambition,—he nevertheless served David with undeviating fidelity. He did more; he never lost an opportunity of asserting, defending, and advancing his master's dignity as king of Israel.

P.

FAMINE AND PESTILENCE

2 Samuel 21:24

WHEN Saul was disclosing to his courtiers at Gibeah his suspicions against David, he used these remarkable words : " Hear now, ye Benjamites ; will the son of Jesse give every one of you fields, and vineyards, and make you captains of thousands and captains of hundreds?" (1 Sam. xxii. 7). That is—Whether they fancied that David would do for them what he had done, or meant to do ? But the question comes, Where did Saul get lands and vineyards to distribute among his servants ? Not by conquest from the neighbouring nations. The domains of the Amalekites were too distant, and it does not appear that he retained them in possession. At home all the lands were appropriated among the tribes and families of Israel, and could not be acquired even by purchase. This was the first reign in Israel, and there had been no treasons which could have placed at his disposal the forfeited estates of traitors. His own property does not seem to have been considerable ; and he could hardly yet have ventured to take the private estates of his subjects by force from them. There was only one available source that we can see ; and from what now transpires, it is likely that he availed himself of it. The Gibeonites having filched a covenant of peace and safety from Joshua, were, out of regard to the oath that had been taken, secured in the possession of their towns and lands, on condition of their discharging, by certain of their number, all the menial services of the tabernacle. It would seem that Saul viewed their possessions with a covetous eye, as affording him the means of rewarding his adherents, and of enriching his family ; and hence, on some pretence or other, or without any pretence, he slew large numbers of them, and, doubtless, seized their possessions. It is said that he did this "in his zeal for Israel and Judah ;" and this cannot be explained but on the supposition that the deed was done in order to give the tribes possession of the reserved territories of the Gibeonites. And there is no doubt this would be, as it was designed, a popular and acceptable act. From the first, the people murmured greatly at the covenant that had been entered into, mainly, it would seem, because they were thus deprived of the spoil of the Gibeonites, and of cities and lands situated in the most desirable part of the country. This feeling in all probability strengthened as the population of Israel increased, and land, especially in this quarter, acquired increased value. As one of the towns of this people was in Judah, and three in Benjamin, when they were destroyed out of their cities, none but persons of those tribes could pretend to any right to them ; and they, no doubt, originally had them, and in all probability willingly undertook the task of turning out the Gibeonites at the point of the sword. Thus Saul's zeal for Israel (Benjamin) and for Judah appears ; and thus also, by their complicity in this gross breach of ancient covenants with a now harmless and faithful people, who for many ages had been Israelites in faith and practice, they laid themselves open to punishment from Him who abhors iniquity and broken faith, and to whom the innocent blood cries not in vain. It would seem that Saul's own family must have been active in this cruel wrong, and must have had a good share of the spoil ; for we find them all, when reduced to a private station, much better off in their worldly circumstances than can else be accounted for, especially as Saul's own estate had gone with the crown, until assigned by David to Mephibosheth.

But the punishments of a just God for wrongdoing, whether in nations or individuals, though often delayed, come at last—often when, from lapse of time, the wrong-doers think that they are secure in the possession of their blood-stained gains, and that all danger is past. It was so in this case, if, as some suppose, the transactions which follow did not take place at an earlier period of David's reign, being set down here with other miscellaneous matters, as a sort of appendix, interposed before the account of the close of David's life.

There came a famine of three years' duration If the time be indicated by the place which the chapter occupies, David may reasonably have ascribed it at first to the recent commotions, during which the labours of the field had been neglected, or less sedulously pursued ; and probably the well stored granaries he had established throughout the country prevented the scarcity from being very severely felt during the first and second years. But when a third year brought matters to a famine point, David began to see something extraordinary in this succession of bad seasons, and, as became him, consulted the oracle of the Lord. He was answered, that it was because of the wrongs done by Saul to the Gibeonites. "Because of Saul and his bloody house"—a phrase which seems to show that the family of Saul was particularly active in this evil matter, and had stimulated him to it in expectation of the benefits they might derive from the spoil, seeing that three-fourths of the property of the Gibeonites lay in their tribe.

On hearing this, David applied to the remnant of the Gibeonites to learn what atonement would satisfy them for the cruel wrongs they had sustained. Their answer was vindictive—blood for blood—the blood of Saul's house. Not the price of blood—no silver or gold, would they accept. They would have life for life, as avengers of the blood of their own slain. The claim of blood-revenge holds good for any lapse of time, extends to new generations, and is never cleared till the representatives of the offenders—the next of kin —have paid the fatal price. We have seen that the law of Moses retained this ancient principle of rough natural justice, while striving to ameliorate some of its evils; but among these Gibeonites and the other persons of Canaanitish origin, the practice seems to have lost less of its original severity than among the Hebrews, and to have been as rigidly carried out as it is at this day among the Caucasian mountaineers, or among the Arabians, although the latter do more frequently accept the "price of blood" than the former. The answer of the Gibeonites implies their feeling that the Hebrew nation, as such, by its sympathy and concurrence with Saul, had sinned against them; and they seemed to regard it as an act of moderation on their part, that they waived their claim as against the nation, and restricted it to Saul in the persons of a few of his representatives. "We will have no silver nor gold of Saul, nor of his house; *neither for us shalt thou kill any man in Israel.* . . . . . The man that consumed us, and that devised against us, that we should be destroyed from remaining in any of the coasts of Israel, let seven men of his sons be delivered up to us, that we may hang them up before the Lord at Gibeah." The Gibeah which they proposed to make the scene of this tragedy was the very town in which Saul had held his residence, and which was no doubt chosen by them, to make this act the more monu-

mental. David dared not refuse their demand. He gave them seven of Saul's descendants. They were two sons of Saul by Rizpah, the same concubine respecting whom Abner had offended Ishbosheth, and five sons of Merab the daughter of Saul. David was determined to save Mephibosheth and his sons for Jonathan's sake; and it was probably out of respect to this feeling, that the Gibeonites did not insist upon the inclusion of these—the rightful heirs and representatives of Saul. One would think this fact a sufficient answer to those who venture to suspect that the whole matter was a contrivance between David and the priest to get rid of the remnant of the house of Saul, of whose remaining influence in the land the late commotion had made him apprehensive. If this were the case, how came he to cut off only unessential branches, and spare all those in the direct line of succession to the throne? In this point of view, Mephibosheth and his son Micah, and his four sons (perhaps already born), were those from whom there was most danger to be apprehended. Yet these were spared by preference, when there was actually an accusation of treason lying against Mephibosheth, which, however unfounded, might, if David had wished to get rid of him, have furnished, even without the intervention of the Gibeonites, a plausible ground for cutting him off. If the reader turn to 1 Chron. viii. 34, 35, he will find an enumeration of the descendants of Merib-baal or Mephibosheth, heirs of the house of Saul—exhibiting, perhaps, the most numerous descent from any one person of the age in which David lived.

If it be asked—and it has been asked—why vengeance was exacted rather for this slaughter of the Gibeonites, than for Saul's greater crime, the massacre of the priests at Nob? the answer is, that the people, and even the family of Saul, had no sympathy with or part in this latter tragedy, which none but an alien could be found to execute. But both the people and Saul's family had made themselves parties in the destruction of the unhappy Gibeonites, by their sympathy, their concurrence, their aid, and above all, as we must believe, by their accepting the fruits of the crime.

Yet, although this be the intelligible public ground on which the transaction rests, it is impossible to withhold our sympathy for these victims of a public crime in which it is probable that none of them had any direct part. They were hanged up at Gibeah; and the Gibeonites, contrary to the practice of the Hebrews themselves, left them upon the gibbets till their bodies should waste away. This was bad policy in them, to say the least, as it could only exasperate the Israelites, who, however, under the circumstances, dared not interfere between them and their allowed vengeance. But there was one whose true womanly, motherly heart would not allow her to quit her sons on this side the grave's brink. This was Rizpah, the mother of two of them. She fixed her abode upon the rock, under the shadow of these dangling, blackening corpses, and watched them with vigilance, and "suffered neither the birds of the air to rest upon them by day, nor the beasts of the field by night."

It seems to have been some time before this touching instance of maternal devotion came to the knowledge of David. When he heard of it, he felt himself bound to interfere to prevent the continuance of a scene so distressful, and so revolting to the feelings of the Israelites. He caused the remains to be removed; and, obtaining the bones of Saul and Jonathan from Jabeshgilead, had the whole deposited, with becoming respect and honour, in the sepulchre of the family at Zelah. The reader who recollects the strong desire of the Israelites, that their bones should rest with those of their kindred—as lately instanced in the case of Barzillai—will appreciate this mark of attention on the part of David, which must have been most gratifying to all Israel, and especially to the friends and connections of the house of Saul.

The last chapter of the Second Book of Samuel is the recital of a most destructive pestilence. It is scarcely correct to say, as is usually said, that this was on account of David causing his people to be numbered. That was the *immediate* cause; for the procedure, innocent and even laudable in itself, and such as had in former times been undertaken by divine command, originated in motives which the Lord condemned. But the *primary* and *real* cause is to be found in the verse which introduces the narrative, and which is almost invariably lost sight of in the common accounts of this transaction. It is, that "the anger of the Lord was kindled against Israel." Now the anger of the Lord could only be awakened by unfaithfulness and evil-doing; and that, whatever its precise nature, was the real cause of the calamity that followed, and relieves the case of the apparent harshness, of which so much has been said, of making the people suffer for the offence of their king.

On *this* account "the Lord moved David to number Israel." What? Did the Lord move David to offend, and then punish him for the offence? By no means. Let us turn to the parallel phrase in 1 Chron. xxi. 1: "Satan stood up against Israel, and incited David to number Israel." Now, if we carefully consider these texts together, we shall see the meaning to be, that for the sins of the people, the Lord permitted the great enemy of mankind to have an advantage which would not otherwise have been allowed him. Still David was under no compulsion to yield to the incitement; and that he so readily yielded, even when such a man as Joab could see the heinousness of the offence, and remonstrate against it, shows the evil state of his heart at that time. As usual with him—and indeed with most of us—calamity brought him to a sounder mind; and we cannot but sympathize in the piety and wisdom of his decision, when, the choice of punishments having been offered him through Gad the seer, he preferred three days' pestilence to three years of famine, or three months of defeat and loss before his enemies. "I am in a great strait," he said; "let us fall now into the hand of the Lord, for His mercies are great, and let me not fall into the hand of man."

The episode related in the books of Samuel and Chronicles, in connection with the pestilence, is too striking and instructive to be passed over in silence. There lived outside the eastern wall of the limited city of Jerusalem, on a spot overlooking the valley of the Kedron, and the Mount of Olives, a farmer belonging to the race of the Canaanites, a Jebusite in fact, one who belonged to the city before David captured it, and made it his royal seat. His name was Araunah, or Ornan; and he owned a threshing floor, where he and his sons were one day engaged in threshing corn just brought home from the harvest field. As David, with his attendants, all clothed in sackcloth, approached the place, "he lifted up his eyes, and saw the Angel of the Lord stand between the earth and the heaven, having a drawn sword in his hand, stretched out over Jerusalem. Then David and the elders of Israel fell on their faces. And David said unto God—Is it not I that commanded the people to be numbered? Even I it is that have sinned, and done evil indeed; but as for these sheep, what have they done? Let thine hand, I pray thee, O Lord my God, be on me, and on my father's house; but not on thy people that they should be plagued." David was then divinely commanded to set up an altar on Ornan's threshing floor. Ornan courteously offered at once the property to the king as a free gift for that sacred purpose; but the latter declined to offer to the Lord that which cost him nothing, and therefore said, "Thou shalt grant it me for the full price. So David gave Ornan six hundred shekels of gold by weight." The altar was immediately built, and burnt-offerings and peace-offerings were laid thereon. And the Lord "answered David from heaven by fire upon the altar of burnt-offering. And the Lord commanded the angel, and he put up his sword again into the sheath thereof." (1 Chron. xxi. 14-30.) The altar at once was invested with the most sacred sanction. The whole hill assumed, from the divine vision, the name of *Moriah*, the vision of Jehovah. The spot itself, in a few years, became the site of the altar of the temple, and therefore the centre of the national worship, with but slight interruption for more than a thousand years; and, according to some authorities, is still, preserved in the rocky platform and cave, regarded with almost idolatrous veneration, under the Mussulman "Dome of the Rock."

"It was the meeting of two ages. Araunah, as he yields that spot, is the last of the Canaanites—the last of that stern old race that we discern in any individual form and character. David, as he raises that altar, is the close harbinger of the reign of Solomon—the founder of a new institution which another was to complete. Long before, he had cherished the notion of a mighty temple which should supersede the temporary tent on Mount Zion. Two reasons were given for delay—one, that the ancient nomadic form of worship was not yet to be abandoned; the other, that David's wars unfitted him to be the founder of a seat of peaceful worship. But a solemn assurance was given, that his dynasty should last 'for ever' to continue the work. Such a founder, and the ancestor of such an immortal dynasty, was Solomon to be."—Stanley's *Jewish Church*, ii., 134-5.

THE LAST DAYS

1 Kings 1:1-11; 1 Chronicles 28-29

MEN get old at different ages: David was older at seventy than Moses at a hundred and twenty, and older than many persons are now at eighty and upwards. As the vital heat departed from his blood, it became manifest that his eventful life was drawing to its close. It is lamentable that the quiet of his departing days should have been disturbed by a new rebellion of another beloved son—not, in this instance, against his person and authority, but against his appointment in regard to the succession.

It was by this time well and generally known, that Solomon was the nominated successor. But Adonijah, the eldest surviving son of David, a very comely man, and much beloved by his father, formed the resolution of securing the crown for himself. He must have been double the age of Solomon; yet if David had lived until the latter had reached to fuller years, and become better known to the people, it is likely that Adonijah would have acquiesced; but, finding his father at the point of death when Solomon was scarcely out of his nonage, he seems to have indulged the hope, that by prompt and decisive measures he might secure the crown for himself. He felt strong in his riper years, in his right of primogeniture, in the absence of any evil design against his father, in the supposed good feeling of the people towards his claim, and in the support it had from many old servants of the state, who had been faithful to David in all his troubles. Among these were persons of no less weight than Joab, the commander of the army, and Abiathar, one of the high priests, who, indeed, are named as his chief abettors. His policy was to anticipate Solomon, by causing himself to be proclaimed king before his father's death. It was probably calculated that David was too far gone to interfere to any purpose, and that, when the thing was done, and in favour of a son he loved so well, he would acquiesce in it as a fact accomplished.

So Adonijah made a great sacrificial feast in the gardens outside Mount Zion, in which lay the fountain of En-rogel, and invited to it all the king's sons except Solomon, and all the king's servants and officers, except those known to be in the interest of his young rival. Among the latter are particularly named Zadok the high priest, Nathan the prophet, Benaiah the captain of the guard, and the "mighty men," or select band of "worthies," which we have had repeated occasion to mention. The necessity for such exceptions, of which he was himself aware, was ominous for the cause of Adonijah. Not to speak of the "worthies," the influence of Zadok in the church was at least equal to that of Abiathar; and although the name of Joab seems more than a counterbalance for that of Benaiah, yet its immediate value was probably less, as the body-guard, which the latter commanded, constituted the main part of the army always under arms, and, doubtless, the only part then present at the capital.

Intending to assume the honours of royalty, Adonijah proceeded to the feast in high state, with chariots and outrunners, like Absalom. He was hailed with enthusiasm as king by the assembled guests.

These proceedings had not passed unobserved. The friends of Solomon saw that no time was to be lost. Nathan, in particular, who had been the means of making known the Lord's will to David, felt that his office and character required him to interfere. Fearing to agitate the king too abruptly in his present feeble state, he went to Bathsheba, and induced her to go and break to him a matter that so nearly concerned the interest and even safety of her son. She accordingly went to the chamber of David, and "bowed, and did obeisance unto the king." Knowing that she had not come unbidden without some important cause, he inquired her errand —the etiquette which had by this time grown up at court requiring that she should not speak until the king had spoken. The manner of the thing was much the same as when Esther appeared before the king of "a hundred and seven and twenty provinces." Thus permitted to speak, Bathsheba performed a mother's part well. She repeated what she had learned, and reminded the king of his promise that Solomon should be king after himself. When she had finished, and before David could answer, the prophet Nathan was announced, as had been arranged between him and Bathsheba, and the latter then withdrew, but remained within call. Nathan confirmed Bathsheba's statement by a more particular recital of what was going on outside the city, and asked if it was done by his authority and with his concurrence. The greatness of the exigency roused the king to clear-minded and decisive action. His body was bowed down for death by age and feebleness; but his mind could go forth freely and vigorously into all the circumstances, and apprehend all that so great an occasion required. He desired Bathsheba to be called in; and at once, without any question or circumlocution, pledged himself by oath to see his original intentions carried out. His words were solemn and impressive: "As

Jehovah liveth, that hath redeemed my soul out of all distress, even as I sware unto thee by the Lord God of Israel, saying, Assuredly Solomon thy son shall reign after me, and he shall sit upon my throne in my stead; *even so will I certainly do this day.*"

Accordingly, she had no sooner departed gladdened by the assurance, than he sent for Zadok, Nathan, and Benaiah, and directed them at once to mount Solomon upon his own mule of state, and to escort him, with all the royal servants and

VALLEY OF GIHON

the guards, down to Gihon, which lay in the valley on the west side of the city, Adonijah's party being in the valley to the north-east. There Zadok was to anoint him king with the sacred oil from the tabernacle, and with a royal flourish of trumpets they were to proclaim, "Long live king Solomon." This was a most sagacious and effective movement, exactly suited to the circumstances, and shows, that while the king's natural strength was prostrated, his intellect remained quick and unclouded to the last.

All was done as the king had directed. The open march of so stately a procession, with the official sanction which the presence of the royal guards and the king's own mule conferred, together with the engaging youth of the prince, drew a large concourse with the train to Gihon, where the inauguration took place, as David had directed. The operation was so sudden, that the city had scarcely been aware of it till the procession returned, with Solomon as king. He was then hailed by the citizens with intense acclamation. "The people piped with pipes, and rejoiced with great joy, so that the earth rung with the sound of them." The joyful uproar in the city even reached the ears of the banqueters at En-rogel. They were not left long in doubt as to the purport of this joyous clamour; for Abiathar's son Jonathan came with a full account of the proceedings in the city and at Gihon. His first words must have filled them with dismay: "Our lord king David hath made Solomon king!" The transactions lost nothing in Jonathan's report, which he carried down to what followed the return of the coronation procession into the city. "Solomon sitteth on the throne of the kingdom. Moreover the king's servants came to bless [congratulate] our lord king David, saying, God make the name of Solomon greater than thy name, and his throne greater than thy throne." At this, according to Jonathan, the king bowed upon the bed and said, "Blessed be the Lord God of Israel, who hath given one to sit upon my throne this day, mine eyes even seeing it."

On hearing of this successful master-stroke, by which their fine plan was at once blown to pieces, the banqueters dispersed in dismay. Adonijah himself, in dread of Solomon's vengeance, hastened to the tabernacle, and put himself in sanctuary by taking hold of the horns of the altar, which he refused to quit unless Solomon should swear not to slay him. Solomon, who was now really and *de facto* king, David being but a dying ceremony, behaved himself in this initiatory act of power with a dignity and discretion beyond his years. He tacitly declined to take any oath, but said, "If he will show himself a worthy man, there shall not a hair of him fall to the earth; but if wickedness shall be found in him, he shall die." On this assurance Adonijah quitted his asylum, and "came and bowed himself to king Solomon," who coldly bade him "Go to thine house"—thus remanding him for the present to the retirement of private life. The Eastern mind is familiar with such transactions and contrasts, and does not pay much heed to them; but as Adonijah does not seem to have been a wicked man, or to have had any other design than the assertion of what he conceived to be his rights, in which he was supported by the oldest friends of his father, we must confess to some sympathy for

him, a man of little less than forty years old, standing in this position before his brother—a boy in comparison with him. Still, keeping hard to the principles of the Hebrew institutions, our *judgment* is with Solomon.

In the last two chapters of the First Book of Chronicles, there is an account (not given in the First Book of Kings) of a farewell address delivered by David in the presence of the assembled people and of Solomon. It was his last public appearance, and his last regal act. It took place, doubtless, between the events last noticed and his death. He had probably been so invigorated by the excitement which he had gone through, that he felt himself equal to this proceeding, which appears to have been in the presence of the people, and therefore in the open air, and not to a few in the privacy of his chamber. It may be added, that the appearance of a sick or dying man in the open air in that country is by no means so unusual or dangerous a proceeding as it would be in such a climate as ours. But David was past all danger, for he knew he was to die. This noble address, full of striking passages, has regard chiefly to Solomon's nomination by the Lord, from among all his sons, as the one to reign, and to build the temple. He describes his own exertions, and the liberal contributions of the people towards that object. For himself he took no credit—all he had was the Lord's and he had but given Him his own. He ended with an impressive prayer, and then called upon his audience to bless the Lord, which they did with bowed heads. There was then a great sacrifice—a thousand bullocks, and as many rams and lambs—to supply a feast for the people. It was on this occasion, seemingly, that Solomon, while his father yet lived, was, in the presence of the people assembled from all parts, anointed "a second time," in a more regular and formal manner. This mention of a *second* anointing in a narrative that does not record the first, and the description of the *first* in a narrative that takes no notice of the second, form an incidental corroboration of great value.

In several passages of his address, the dying king and father spoke directly to Solomon, in words worthy of his high character and illustrious name, showing that the lamp of his inner life—the life of his soul—burned up brightly before he expired. These are golden words: "And thou, Solomon, my son, know thou the

God of thy father, and serve Him with a perfect heart, and with a willing mind; for the Lord searcheth all hearts, and understandeth all the imaginations of the thoughts. If thou seek Him, He will be found of thee; but if thou forsake Him, He will cast thee off for ever." More nearly at the point of death, David had another and final interview with his son, in which he delivered to him another and more private charge, introduced with the remarkable words: " I go the way of all the earth ; be thou strong, therefore, and show thyself a man."

There was nothing now left for David to do but to die. So " he died, in a good old age, full of days, riches, and honour ; and Solomon his son reigned in his stead."

At the very close of his life, we notice a striking revival alike of David's early spirit and early piety. With a vigour and ability worthy of his best days, he put down the attempt to transfer the succession to Adonijah, although favoured by the great Joab himself. Every trace of weakness and fear had now disappeared. His trust was in God ; and fully conscious of pardon, acceptance, and divine guidance, he regarded not the opposition of one who had so long swayed the destinies of the empire. His " last words," too, show not only the full power and brilliance of his high poetic genius, but show also that the Spirit of God inspired him with thoughts purer, holier, and more sublime than those of earth.[1]

                                                        P.

THE REFUGE

1 Kings 2:5-6, 28-34

At the commencement of the period upon which we now enter, we behold that man of blood, Joab, when he saw cause to be apprehensive of his safety, fleeing to the tabernacle of God, and placing himself in sanctuary there by taking hold of the horns of the altar. This step, taken by him when there lay, in his judgment, but a step between him and death, raises some profitable suggestions in the mind. That altar was sanctified by the victims offered and the blood sprinkled upon it, typifying the atonement made for the sins of the world by the blood of the Lord Jesus Christ. Now, in the extremity of our spiritual distresses, as our only means of

[1] See 2 Samuel 23:1-7.

safety, pardon, and hope, what is there for us to do but that which Joab did?—what but to repair to this altar, grasp it with the strong hand of faith, and declare ourselves at length in refuge—that at length we have found the ransom of our souls, and that we have entered the sacred precincts within which the enemy, the accuser, has no power to enter, and whence his hand has no power to rend us? Christ is that refuge; and, beyond all men upon whom the sun shines happy are they who have taken sanctuary in Him. Nothing from without can harm, nothing affright them more. They rest secure in Him; and, enfolded in His protecting arms, the storms which trouble the life of man, and sprinkle grey hairs here and there upon him, often before he knows of it, affect him not, in his quiet rest, or they are heard merely as the muttering thunders of the distant horizon, which only enhance his sense of safety, and do not trouble his repose. The winds may blow bitter, and cold, and fierce around him; but the house of his hope is not shaken, for it is founded upon a rock.

> " Betake thee to thy Christ, then, and repose
>   Thyself, in all extremities, on those,
>   His everlasting arms,
>   Wherewith He girds the heavens, and upholds
>   The Pillars of the earth, and safely folds
>   His faithful flock from harms.
>   Cleave close to Him by faith, and let the bands
>   Of love tie thee in thy Redeemer's hands."—*Quarles.*

Yet there was a difference. The altar of the " worldly sanctuary " did not give its shelter to all who took hold of it in faith in the efficiency of its protection. There were exceptions. There were sins too great for it to shelter. A murderer might be torn from the altar to die, or might, as the case of Joab himself evinces, be slain even there. Here the parallel wholly fails. None, however guilty, has been cast forth from the refuge which the cross of Christ affords, as unworthy of its protection, nor did any ever perish at its foot. Nor have any ever been cast forth on account of their sins; for Christ came not to call the righteous, but sinners to repentance; and the heavier a man feels the burden of his sins, the dearer is the refuge, and the more will it be prized by him. The sinner who is destitute of faith, is not within the refuge; but no one who has fled to it need fear rejection on account of the lack of faith; for faith only—justifying faith —the faith which brings a troubled soul to the rights of sanctuary—only such faith, could have brought him where he is—to the foot of the cross.

Yet there is a mirage in the spiritual as in the natural atmosphere; and many appear to be safe within the refuge, who are indeed far away from it. Their hand may seem to grasp the very horns of the altar; but no drop of the blood of the atonement can be found upon their raiment. The world reigns still in their hearts, and its lusts and lucre fill their hands. And yet the self-deceivers know it not. They like quiet in an ideal refuge of their own creation; but its walls will not stand the day of decision, which is destined to burn up the hay, the straw, and the stubble of man's confidences, and shall try even the silver and gold by the sure test of fire. These are they who in the greatest, to man, of all coming days, shall claim a favourable recognition from the great King: "Lord, Lord, have we not taught in Thy name, in Thy name cast out devils, and in Thy name done many wonderful works?" but whose ears shall tingle even unto blood at the answer: "I NEVER KNEW YOU. Depart from Me."

In the East a shepherd does not *drive* his sheep, but *leads* them. He goes before them and they follow him. So it is in the spiritual kingdom. Men are not driven but "drawn" to their refuge in Christ. The world *drives*—but not to God. Joab was not drawn but driven to the altar, and therefore he found no refuge there. "It is the fashion of our foolish presumption," observes Bishop Hall on this case, "to look for protection where we have not cared to yield obedience. Even a Joab clings to God's altar in his extremity, which in his prosperity he regarded not. The worst men would be glad to make use of God's ordinances for their advantage. Necessity will drive the most profane and ·lawless man to God." But this is not the right spirit, that brings with it a claim, through grace, to refuge with Him. To establish that claim, it is not enough to feel that the world is a hard master, still less to seek to avoid the punishment which the world's law inflicts upon our sins. It is necessary that sin should be felt to be exceeding sinful, and known as the abominable thing which God hateth; it is requisite that the burden of sin should press heavy on the soul, and that the most burning desire to be rid of it should be felt —not because of its human penalties—not for the loss, the bonds, the stripes, the death, with

which man may visit it—but because it separates the soul from God, because He is angry with it every day, and because, unless atoned for, purged away, pardoned, blotted out, it will for ever exclude the soul from the blessedness of His presence, which is heaven here, and heaven hereafter.

It may seem hard that Joab, who had rendered more services to the state than any man in Israel, who was so successful in all his military undertakings, and who had been so faithful to David in all his troubles, should thus in his old age be called to account for his old sins, which were at the time passed over, which had, as it were, been expiated by subsequent services and employments of trust and honour,—hard that he should thus be called so late to pay blood for blood to Abner and to Amasa. No doubt he ought to have been punished; but whether by those whom he had served so well, and whether after so long an interval, may be questioned by some. It was justice. But was David (for it was he who enjoined this task on his son) the man to exact the severest extremity of avenging justice from Joab—was it for him to forget that he had himself made this very Joab the instrument of his murder of Uriah? Joab deserved to die; and at an earlier day we had been content to see him brought by the king to justice —and even at this late period, we do not much murmur to see him fall under the sword of the bloood-avenger of Abner or Amasa. But we like not the mode, the time, or the circumstances of this judgment; we like not that David should, on his death-bed, have laid the charge upon his son, "not to allow his hoar head to go down to the grave in peace." Let us learn from it, however, this lesson, that it is not in the power of any of our services or best deservings to buy off the penalty due to our ancient sins. It remains written in the great book of death against us. The pen is not ours—the power is not on earth—that can cancel that page, or blot out the handwriting which stands on high against us. But there is One that can do it— who, for our sakes, purchased at no mean price the right to do it. And He *will* do it, if, with true faith in His power, and with truly humbled hearts, we ask Him. He is ready—He is most willing—He only waits to be asked, to make these things be as though they had not been; to cancel all, the old and the new. Let us not grieve Him—let us not insult His blood-bought prerogative, by wasting our strength in the vain attempt to do for ourselves that which He alone is able to do for us.

JOAB AND ADONIJAH

1 Kings 2:13-25

THE execution of Joab, to some points of which we referred yesterday, grew out of, and was connected with, other matters, which may to-day engage our attention.

We have seen that David, on his death-bed, enjoined his youthful heir to put Joab to death; and we have stated the impression which this injunction, from a man on the borders of the grave, is calculated at the first view to make upon the mind. There has, indeed, been a disposition manifested to set aside the reason assigned by David himself, and to substitute others, such as his secret resentment for the slaughter of Absalom, joined to a politic desire to relieve the reign of the young king from the presence of a person so powerful, whose dangerous influence had been felt most oppressively by himself, and whose recent support of Adonijah rendered it doubtful whether Solomon could reckon upon his allegiance. It is impossible to deny that these considerations may have had weight in David's mind, unconsciously to himself. But if they were consciously entertained by him, there was no reason why he should not have stated them to Solomon; and we are, therefore, driven to the reasons he does give, as those which he deemed sufficient, not only to justify, but call for, this extreme and apparently harsh measure. In these, there is nothing of private vengeance, but everything rests on the basis of public duty. He refers to the foul murders of Abner and Amasa, whom Joab "slew, and shed the blood of war in peace, and put the blood of war upon his girdle that was about his loins, and in his shoes that were on his feet. Do therefore according to thy wisdom, and let not his hoar head go down to the grave in peace."

Now, it is very possible that we lose the force of this declaration, by estimating it according to the views and sentiments of our own later law

of mercy and forgiveness. The sentiment continually set forth in the Old Testament is, that innocent blood cries to God from the ground for vengeance; and that, if suffered to go unpunished, it brings down a curse and judgment upon the land. Let us look at some texts enforcing the view which both David and Solomon were bound to take of this matter. "If a man come presumptuously upon his neighbour to slay him with guile, thou shalt take him from mine altar, that he may die." [1] This exactly met the case of both the murders by Joab; and the neglect of a rule so plain, and so stringently stated, might well appear to be a perilous neglect of public duty. Again: "Ye shall take no satisfaction for the life of a murderer which is guilty of death: but he shall surely be put to death." [2] After a similar injunction in Deut. xix. 13, it is added, "Thine eye shall not pity him; but *thou shalt put away the guilt of innocent blood from Israel, that it may go well with thee.*" Look also to the case of Manasseh, whose punishment and captivity are mainly ascribed to "the innocent blood which he shed (for he filled Jerusalem with innocent blood), *which the Lord would not pardon.*" [3] That this point of view was, as it ought to be, present to the mind of David, and influenced his conduct, is very clear; for, at the very time of Abner's murder, he publicly implored that the judgment of this innocent blood might be averted from his house and kingdom, and that it might rest upon Joab and upon his house. (2 Sam. iii. 28, 29.) This, in fact, was formally reserving Joab for the future judgment which he then felt powerless to execute. Besides this, it must not be overlooked that the recent terrible judgment upon the land, on account of the long past destruction of the Gibeonites by Saul, was well calculated to enforce these views, and give great intensity to David's apprehensions of the consequences to the realm, of these crimson sins of Joab being much longer suffered to pass unpunished. The same event was likely to bring out, with strong and terrible force, the point of view constantly produced under the theocratical constitution, that mere lapse of time weakens nothing, strengthens nothing; and that before Him who is the same yesterday, and to-day, and for ever, and whose existence knows no morrow nor yesterday, the sin a generation old is as fresh as at the time of its committal,—even as the holy

[1] Exodus 21:14.   [2] Numbers 35:31.   [3] 2 Kings 24:4.

and blessed thought or aspiration which comes over the mind, or rises from the heart of any reader at the present moment, will be as fresh to His knowledge a thousand years hence as it is at this instant of time.

If this statement of the case be correct, and we are persuaded that it is, no excuse for David's conduct in this matter is required ; it was rather —under the views he was bound to entertain— not only blameless, but laudable, and entirely in accordance with his duty as a theocratical king and a father.

These remarks have had reference to David's injunction; and Solomon places its execution entirely on the same ground, although the immediate *occasion* was of another sort, and supplied a new ground of offence.

It will be remembered that Adonijah had been remanded by the young king, his brother, to private life. But it seems that after his first alarm had subsided, his hopes began to revive ; and it may be collected that his old and powerful supporters, Joab and Abiathar, encouraged his hopes. They seem, however, to have been closely watched, and the king knew much more of their projects than they at all suspected.

The first tangible matter, however, which occurred to afford Solomon an occasion of arresting their designs was of a remarkable nature, and it is difficult for us, trained up in a different class of ideas and associations, to grasp it in all its breadth.

While David lay in his last illness, the officious zeal of his attendants recommended that the most beautiful damsel in all Israel should be sought out, and that she, becoming his wife, should remain in constant attendance upon him to cheer and comfort him. This lot fell upon Abishag, the Shunammite, who at his death remained a virgin widow. Now, the indicative fact is neither more nor less than this, that Adonijah sought this lady for his wife. Fearing to make any direct application to the king, and being well aware of his mother's influence with him, he applied in the first instance to her. To one of more suspicious temper and of keener discernment than Bathsheba, some misgiving might have been awakened by the connection of ideas which he suffered to appear when introducing the subject : " Thou knowest that the kingdom was mine, and that all Israel set their faces on me, that I should reign over them ; howbeit the kingdom is turned

about, and is become my brother's ; "—and then, as if suddenly conscious that he was unwisely committing himself, he added,—" for it was his from the Lord." This was certainly a curious preamble to the request he came to make, and at least evinces his own consciousness of its high importance. The good natured Bathsheba, anxious to soothe his wounded pride, and to make what seemed to her a harmless atonement for the frustration of his hopes, in which she herself had been an instrument, noticed none of the latent and dangerous meanings involved in these things, but hastened to assure him of her readiness to undertake the mission he proposed. One might suppose that she would have been somewhat shocked at the grossness involved in the idea of a son espousing his father's widow,—the rather, as she was unaware of his real object, which would have rendered the matter more intelligible to her. But the truth obviously is, that strict as was the law of the Israelites respecting intermarriages—strict beyond the law of any nation —a great practical laxity had grown up in these matters, especially in high quarters, and above all at the royal court. Of this we have had some painful instances already in the family of David, even during his lifetime.

Nothing can more clearly show the large measure of formal and truly Oriental state which had by this time been introduced into the Hebrew court, than the ceremonious manner of the interview between the king and his mother. One would suppose that she might have made an application in private ; but, whether from choice or necessity, it was not so. She entered the hall in which the king sat on his throne ; and when he saw her, he arose, and advanced to meet her, bowed to her, and conducted her to a seat on his right hand. She said that she had a small request to make, and deprecated a refusal ; and he assured her that it should be granted whatever it might be. But he no sooner understood the nature of her application, than his countenance darkened. " Ask for him," he said, " the kingdom also ; for he is mine elder brother ; even for him, and for Abiathar the priest, and for Joab the son of Zeruiah." These words can mean nothing else than that he discerned in this application the first development of a further design upon the crown, concocted between these men, of which he had already some information, but of which this was the first tangible intimation on which he could act. And he did act—and that with an unhesitating promptitude, which justly shocks those who look not beyond the simple fact which appears in the face of the transaction. He sent Benaiah, the captain of the host, to put Adonijah to death wherever he might find him. It was when Joab heard of this that he fled to the altar— his doing which seems to us a sufficient indication of such conscious complicity with Adonijah in a further design as Solomon had detected. Unless he knew himself to be guilty, and supposed, from the execution of Adonijah, that all was known to the king, there was nothing in what had happened to lead him to conclude himself in danger. Whatever wrong or treason might be latent in Adonijah's application for Abishag, there was nothing, taking that matter by itself, to connect Joab with it; but his own act, and the words of the king, show that there was something more, within and beyond this, with which he was connected, and which involved him in the doom of Adonijah. The past offence of this prince had been overlooked. Solomon had pledged his royal word to respect his life so long as he should show himself a worthy man. That he was punished, therefore, proved that there was a new offence of the same nature; and it was Joab's part in this, not his share in the old offence, for which Adonijah himself had been pardoned, that supplied Solomon with the occasion of executing the injunctions of his father.

Some reader may still be at a loss to perceive how the application which was made by Adonijah, for leave to espouse the widow of his father, afforded the indication of ulterior pretensions which Solomon could so readily discern. It may therefore be proper to go back to the instance of Absalom's taking possession of his father's concubines at Jerusalem, and to the remarkable words of Nathan, in his rebuke to David: "I gave thy master's wives into thy bosom." Connecting these instances with the one before us, we may perceive that among the Jews, as in other Eastern and in various African nations, the harem of the preceding king was regarded as a sort of regalia appertaining to the crown, and so essentially the property of his successor, that the possession of it, or of any essential part of it, gave much strength to a claim that might otherwise be disputable. The usage is curious, and so

adverse to our own notions, that it is difficult thoroughly to understand it. But the existence of such a custom, and of the notions connected with it, is certain, and might be illustrated by instances which cannot here be produced.

If this explanation of these unpleasant transactions be correct, Solomon stands fully justified for the course taken by him towards Adonijah, Joab, and Abiathar; and Adonijah loses all claim to the degree of sympathy which may have been felt for him in regard to his previous attempt; for we have his own word for his knowledge of the fact that the appointment of Solomon was "from the Lord." Abiathar was declared by Solomon to be also worthy of death; but his life was spared in consideration of his sacred character, and his long companionship with David. But he was deposed from the honours and emoluments of the priesthood, and was directed to confine himself to his own private estate at Anathoth.

To a cursory reader of the closing scenes of David's life and the commencement of Solomon's reign, it might seem as if there really had been a "cold-blooded vengeance" enjoined and executed on "crimes long forgotten." A recent eloquent writer has said so. I cannot agree with him. It seems to me that for a long period David was guided in his acts by worldly policy rather than a strict sense of justice. He was more influenced by the fear of man, and a short-sighted desire to promote his own interests, than by the glory of God, and a regard for that holy law which He had revealed for the government of His people. Blood, "innocent blood," had been shed. The land was polluted by it. According to the theocratic principle, the guilt was chargeable against the land, and the punishment might at any moment be executed. "Ye shall take no satisfaction for the life of a murderer, which is guilty of death; but he shall be surely put to death. . . *So ye shall not pollute the land wherein ye are; for blood it defileth the land: and the land cannot be cleansed of the blood that is shed therein, but by the blood of him that shed it*" (Num. xxxv. 31-33).

At the close of his life, David was roused to a sense of his neglect of this imperious duty. The kingdom was in peril. Divine vengeance was impending over it. He was then too weak to carry out the law. He was at the point of death; but, as the representative of the Divine Lawgiver and Judge, he pronounced sentence upon the criminals, and charged his heir and successor to carry it out. In this there was no "cold-blooded revenge." There was strict, though somewhat tardy justice.

P.

SHIMEI

1 Kings 2:8-9; 36-46

JOAB was not the only man whom the dying charge of David recommended to the unfavourable notice of Solomon. Shimei was another. His words concerning this notorious person were: "Behold, thou hast with thee Shimei the son of Gera, a Benjamite of Bahurim, who cursed me with a grievous curse in the day when I went to Mahanaim: but he came down to meet me at Jordan, and I sware to him by the Lord, saying, I will not put thee to death with the sword. Now therefore hold him not guiltless; for thou art a wise man, and knowest what thou oughtest to do unto him; but his hoar head bring thou down to the grave with blood." Believing the meaning to be here correctly given, we reject the attempts which have been made to modify this translation in order to remove its apparent harshness. Taking it, therefore, as it stands, the sense appears to be this: David intends to warn Solomon against Shimei, as a dangerous subject, prone to break out into disaffection, and whose power of doing harm required that he should be carefully watched. He himself had, for reasons of policy, and in consideration of Shimei's meeting him with a large body of Benjamites at the Jordan, pardoned him for his gross and treasonable insults at Bahurim. He had pledged his oath for Shimei's safety. Solomon, however, was not bound to regard him as altogether expurgated from that crime; and, should he be detected in any new offence against the king, the latter was advised not to excuse and pardon him, as his father had done. We excuse David altogether from the attempt to palter with his oath, on which some found his justification. Those who say that the oath bound only David, but left his successor free to punish the crime he had sworn not to punish, forget that, in matters of grace and justice, the word of a king binds not only the individual monarch, but the crown. Were it otherwise, the beginning of a new reign would be equivalent to a revolution, and would be a reign of terror and dismay throughout the land. David was incapable of the miserable quibble here ascribed to him. Still, the law of Christian forgiveness was not in those times dis-

tinctly known; and we are unable to find, nor have we much reason to expect, this grace in the behaviour of those ancient kings—not even in David, still less in Solomon. It is a beautiful testimony to the spirit of Christianity, that those who have been brought up under its influence find much to distress them in transactions which would, at this very day, appear perfectly reasonable, just, and even laudable among Eastern nations. The difference is nowhere more emphatically announced than in the words of our Saviour: "Ye have heard that it hath been said by them of old time, Thou shalt love thy neighbour and hate thine enemy: but I say unto you, Love your enemies; bless them that curse you; do good to them that hate you; and pray for them that despitefully use you and persecute you." Since our Lord Himself announces this as a new doctrine, and declares that it did not exist in "old time"—had no practical operation—it would be in vain to look for its operation in the conduct of men belonging to those times. The greatest men were animated by the spirit of the age in which they lived, and belonged essentially to that age; and we might as well complain that they travelled from Dan to Beersheba upon the slow-footed ass rather than by the rapid rail, as that they were not in all things actuated by the spirit of a later revelation and a later time. We are therefore not anxious to show that there was nothing vindictive in this counsel of David to his son; but we do think that a prudential regard for the safety of that son's reign, in warning him against dangerous persons, was the predominant motive of his counsel, and the only motive of which he was himself conscious.

Under the like circumstances, a king in the situation of Solomon, in almost any country of Europe itself—excepting, perhaps, our own country, where "the liberty of the subject" cannot be interfered with—would have shut such a man as Shimei up in some fortress for life; or in the East, would have put out his eyes, or deprived him of his tongue, or both, or have subjected him to some other infliction to render him harmless; and in either part of the world, any prince who dealt with so suspicious a character not more harshly than Solomon, would be deemed to have acted leniently by him. He put him upon his parole, or rather made him a prisoner at large, assigning him for his residence, however, the largest and the most pleasant city in the land, even Jerusalem, in which many counted it a privilege to dwell. The brook Kidron was assigned him as a limit; and he was solemnly warned that, whenever he ventured beyond this limit, the penalty was death. This was necessary; for, to a man who was the object of political suspicion, freedom to go beyond the assigned limit whenever he liked, would quite have nullified the design of placing him under *surveillance* in the metropolis. He might as well have been left entirely at large. And it was equally necessary that the order should have been absolute and indiscriminate; for if *any* excuse were to be allowed, an excuse could easily be found or created whenever the man desired to be absent.

At all events, Shimei accepted the sentence, and was clearly thankful that the limitations were so lenient and reasonable, and the conditions so easy to observe. As it is clear that he did not consider himself hardly dealt with, and as he appears to have expected some harsher judgment, we, at this later day, and with no minute knowledge of all the facts, have scarcely the right to censure that conduct towards him, of which he found no reason to complain.

Under this limitation, Shimei abode three years at Jerusalem. At the end of that period two of his slaves ran away from him, and were perhaps encouraged to do so by the notion, that the restriction under which their master lay must prevent him from following them. They were mistaken; for Shimei no sooner heard that they had been seen at Gath, than he saddled his ass, and hastened thither to reclaim them. He returned with them to Jerusalem; but had no sooner arrived than he was summoned to appear before the king, who, after reminding him of his solemn engagement under oath never to quit Jerusalem upon pain of death, and reproaching him with wickedness "*which his heart was privy to*," gave the signal of death to Benaiah, now captain of the host in the place of Joab, who "went out, and fell upon him that he died."

Justifying, as we have done, the limitation imposed upon Shimei, we are bound to uphold also this stern judgment consequent upon its infraction. He had been fully warned of this result, and had accepted the condition. Had he refused, he would probably have been kept in close confinement; but since he accepted the terms of his punishment, he was allowed full

freedom within the assigned limits. The opportunity of leaving the city was allowed him, simply because he had pledged himself not to avail himself of it. Even so, however, we were formerly disposed. with Dr. Chalmers and others, to regard the transaction as "indigestible," at least in its closing points. We argued to ourselves that had Shimei been pursued, overtaken, and brought back, it would have been quite right to inflict the severest judgment upon him; but that, to say the least, it was a hard measure seeing that he had come back voluntarily, and had thereby evinced the absence of any sinister object, or of any intention to escape. But on closer reflection, it appeared that the restriction put upon him was meant to guard against, not so much escape (for if he escaped, how was he to be put to death?), as occasional absences, during which he might plot and conspire, and then return until matters should be ripe for his final disappearance. And as the king had imposed a simple and clear regulation, he was not bound to burden himself with a particular inquiry into the validity of all the excuses which might from time to time be produced for its infraction. How, for instance, in this very case, was the king to know that the slaves had not been sent away, on purpose to afford their master an excuse for visiting a most suspicious quarter?

Upon the whole, it seems to us that in this incident, as in many other austere circumstances of Scripture history, the apparent "difficulty" disappears, or becomes greatly attenuated, when *all* the circumstances are closely weighed, and when we contemplate the subject not exclusively from our own point of view, but from that of contemporaries, and in connection with influences —religious, political, and social—very different from our own, but which some degree of careful study may enable us to realize. The more this is done, the more "digestible" many of the hardest things of Scripture history will appear. One thing is certain, that there is not a word or hint in the sacred books to show that the conduct of David and Solomon to Joab, Shimei, Adonijah, or Abiathar, was regarded as other than perfectly right and just, if not laudable, by the people of the age and country in which David and Solomon lived. Indeed, we may be sure that Solomon was too sagacious to disfigure the commencement of his reign by acts abhorrent to the public opinion of his time. And if he had that sanction—as we are sure he had—we feel that, in matters not affecting any principle of God's ancient law, we have no right to stigmatize his conduct as unjust or barbarous, although, with our keener sense—with our Christian and occidental perceptions—of human obligations, we turn with relief from the grim severities of this blood-stained page.

THE WISDOM OF SOLOMON

1 Kings 3

As it appears eventually that Solomon did some foolish and some mistaken things, it becomes a matter of interest to know wherein lay that "wisdom" with which he is described as having been supernaturally endowed.

God giveth to him that hath. It was the previous possession of wisdom which qualified him for more. David distinctly recognizes his son as "a wise man;" and his wisdom is evinced by nothing more than his choice of wisdom beyond all other blessings, when the fruition of his wishes was in the vision at Gibeon offered to him. What he asked was "a wise and understanding heart,"—"wisdom to govern this great people;" and his choice was so much approved, that benefits which he had refrained from asking—wealth, power, length of days—were thrown in without his seeking. The terms of his request indicate the nature of the "wisdom" he required. That divine wisdom in spiritual things, that heart religion, which the Jews sometimes denoted by this name, is not intended. With that he was not pre-eminently gifted; not more gifted certainly than his father David—hardly so much gifted. The wisdom which he craved was that of which he had already enough to be able to appreciate the value of its increase—practical wisdom, sagacity, clearness of judgment and intellect in the administration of justice and in the conduct of public affairs, with an aptitude for the acquisition and use of the higher branches of philosophical knowledge, natural and moral, which constituted the learning of his age. In the latter he excelled the most famous men of his time. We are told that in the course of his career he found a sufficiency of learned leisure to compose three thousand proverbs, and songs a

thousand and five; and that he "spoke," or wrote, on all known species of plants, "from the cedar in Lebanon to the hyssop that springeth out of the wall," as well as on every branch of zoology,—"of beasts, of fowls, of creeping things, and of fishes." The loss of these works in natural history is greatly to be deplored. We are not, however, to suppose, that they were regular scientific descriptions and accounts of the various subjects, but such concise observations as we find interspersed among the existing writings ascribed to him, more frequently than in any other books in Scripture. The Jews have a notion, that a considerable portion of Solomon's observations of this kind is preserved in the works of Aristotle, to whom, according to them, his great pupil, Alexander, sent a copy of Solomon's writings, which he met with in the East.

Of his "Songs" we have a few interesting specimens in one of the Psalms—in the wonderful "Song of Songs," which perhaps rightly bears his name; besides which, the introductory chapters of the book of Proverbs, abound in poetry of the highest order. Of his "Proverbs" also, we have many specimens left; and these, with the book of Ecclesiastes (if it be rightly ascribed to him), contains such lessons of practical wisdom, and embody such profound observations on man's life and nature, as would alone account for the wide-spread reputation which this great king acquired.

It was, however, a monarch's sagacity in the administration of justice which was calculated to make the most marked impression upon the popular mind, and likely to be most generally talked about throughout the land. This quality also came more home to the personal concerns of his subjects than any other, and was for that reason alone the more carefully regarded. The administration of justice was in all ancient monarchies, as it is now in the East, a most important part of the royal duties and functions; and there is no quality more highly prized than that keen discernment in the royal judge which detects the clue of real evidence amidst conflicting testimony, or that ready tact which devises a test of truth where the evidence affords no clue to any grounds of decision. It was an instance of this kind which supplied to the watchful people the first evidence of the marvellous judicial sagacity with which their king was endowed.

The story is well known. Two mothers, one

of whom had lost her son, contend for the possession of the living child; and the king, having to
decide which of the two has the best claim to it,
detects the real mother by the emotion she
evinces when he orders the living child to be
divided, and half given to each, and by her
readiness to abandon her claim rather than see
the child perish before her eyes. We are not

The Wisdom of Solomon

aware of anything in Hebrew history that more
strongly evinces the despotism which had by this
time crept into the kingdom, than the fact that
the woman really believed this outrageous mandate would be executed. If a judge made such a
suggestion among us, he would be laughed to
scorn for so futile an experiment, which the most
ignorant woman in the land would know that he
was utterly unable to execute. The real terror
of the mother, at a judgment which she too well
knew *might* be executed, becomes, in this point
of view, doubly affecting.

In the East, at the present day, the people are
prone to exalt the civil wisdom of their kings by
nothing so much as their discernment and equity
in judgment. The reader of Eastern history or
tale will recollect numerous instances by which
the kings and judges resort to the most ingenious
devices for the discovery of the truth, not
demonstrable by direct evidence. Some of these
have a certain resemblance to that of Solomon.
The Hindus reverently preserve the memory of
some of their kings who have rendered themselves famous by the equity of their judgments.
One of the most celebrated of these was Maria-

diramen, among other instances of whose sagacity
the following is recorded:

A rich man had married two wives; the first
of whom, although ugly, had a great advantage
over the second, in that she had brought her
husband a son, while the other was childless.
But, as if to compensate for her sterility, the
second wife possessed such charms of person and
character, that she reigned supremely in the
heart of her husband. Provoked at this preference, the first wife concocted a plan of vengeance equally astounding for its diabolical
ingenuity and its savageness. She lavished
every external mark of maternal love and
tenderness upon the infant at her breast, and
let the neighbourhood know that this child
was now her only comfort, the centre of her
hopes, in the absence of that affection which
her husband denied her. As soon as she had
convinced the world that her heart was altogether wrapt up in her little son, she, one
night when the husband was away from home,
twisted the child's neck, and laid the corpse
beside the second wife, who lay asleep in her
bed. In the morning, pretending to seek for her
infant, she ran into the chamber of her rival, and
there finding the child dead, she fell upon the
ground, tore her hair, and gave vent to the most
frightful howls and lamentations. This brought
the neighbours together; and the other wife was
already condemned in their eyes; for it was clear
the child had been murdered, and it could not
cross their minds that any mother—and, least of
all, a mother so fond as this—should thus destroy
her own infant, whom she had held up as the
only comfort left to her in life. This, however,
was what the other urged in her defence—
dwelling upon the enmity which the mother
entertained against her, and maintaining that no
passion was so cruel and relentless as jealousy.

The case was brought before Mariadiramen;
and a day was appointed for each woman to plead
her cause. They did so, with that natural eloquence which passion usually inspires. The king,
unable to decide upon the statements before him,
pronounced this sentence: Let the woman who
is innocent, and who pretends that her rival is
culpable, move through this assembly in the
posture which he would show her. The posture
he indicated was one from which modesty would
shrink. But the mother of the child with much
vehemence declared that, in order to convince the

assembly that her rival was guilty, she would not only take this turn through the assembly once, but a hundred times if required. The other sorrowfully declined the test, declaring that, although innocent, she would sooner submit to the most cruel death than do what was then required of her. The mother of the child was about to reply; but the voice of the king stilled all other sounds. He pronounced her guilty, and her antagonist innocent. "A woman," he said, "whom the prospect of certain death cannot constrain to an unbecoming action, is incapable of so great a crime; but a female who, having lost all sense of womanly reserve, hesitates not at an immodest action, sufficiently declares herself to be capable of the blackest crimes." Confounded to find herself thus discovered, the mother of the child vindicated the penetration of the royal judge, by publicly acknowledging her crime.

The sagacity of Solomon was, however, more marked than this; for the evidence in the case brought before him was more equal, and the test more intelligent and more appropriate to the particular case. Solomon's was altogether a most wonderful decision; and its results were most important to him; for it evinced, in the judgment of the people, his fitness to fill worthily the high place to which he had been raised. Of this some doubt and misgiving appear to have been previously entertained, on account of his age—too young for experience, yet too old for a regency. But now all this was at an end. He had delivered a judgment which the most ripened experience could not surpass. "They saw that the wisdom of God was in him to do judgment;" and thenceforth they regarded him with the respect and veneration due to riper years.

Attention has of late been called, in two interesting works, Smith's *Dictionary of the Bible*, &c., (Art. "Solomon"), and the Manual of *Old Testament History*, 405, to the personal appearance of Solomon. Dr. Plumtree, the author of the article in the Dictionary, who is followed by the Editor of the Manual, observes, "We may rightly ask, what manner of man he was outwardly and inwardly, who, at the age of nineteen or twenty, was called to this glorious sovereignty? We have, it is true, no direct description in this case, as we have of the earlier kings. There are, however, materials for filling up the gap. The wonderful impression which Solomon made upon all who came near him, may well lead us to believe that with him, as with Saul and David, Absalom and Adonijah, as with most other favourite princes of Eastern peoples, there must have

been the fascination and the grace of a noble presence. Whatever higher mystic meaning may be latent in Psalm xlv., or the Song of Songs, we are all but compelled to think of them as having had, at least, a historical starting point. They tell us of one who was in the eyes of the men of his own time 'fairer than the children of men,' the face bright and ruddy as his father's (Cant. v. 10 ; 1 Sam. xvii. 42), bushy locks, dark as the raven's wing, yet not without a golden glow, the eyes soft as the eyes of doves, the 'countenance as Lebanon, excellent as the cedars, the chiefest among ten thousand, the altogether lovely.' (Cant. v. 9-16). Add to this all gifts of a noble, far reaching intellect, large and ready sympathies, a playful and genial humour, the lips full of grace, the soul anointed as with 'the oil of gladness,' (Psalm xlv.), and we may form some notion of what the king was like in the dawn of his golden prime."

As to Solomon's wisdom, it is remarked, "It does not appear that he possessed what now would be considered great proficiency in natural science, nor even such knowledge as Aristotle's, whose works on natural history the Rabbis pretend to have been derived from a copy of the writings of Solomon sent to him from the East by Alexander. Solomon's natural science, like that of Oriental philosophers in general, consisted rather in the observation of the more obvious facts in the common life and habits of God's creatures, with a special view to use them for the poetical illustration of moral lessons, and in this way we find such knowledge used, not only in the proverbs ascribed to him, but in many of the Psalms, and throughout the Book of Job."—*Manual of Old Testament History*, 406.

S.

PREPARATIONS

1 Kings 5; 2 Chronicles 2

It was one of the first cares of Solomon to discharge the obligation laid upon him before he was born—of building a temple to the Lord at Jerusalem. For this, David had made very large preparations; but there was still much to prepare, and the young king found it requisite to seek the assistance of the king of Tyre, as his father had formerly done. The king is still named Hiram; and as he is said to have been "ever a lover of David," he was no doubt the same person with whom David had carried on a friendly correspondence.

The correspondence between him and Solomon is given both in the books of Kings and Chronicles,—in the latter more fully than in the former, and with added points which we are thankful to have preserved. The correspondence is, to our view, very important and interesting. One particular must not pass unnoticed. It is said that "Solomon *sent to* Hiram, saying,"—thus implying that the message was orally conveyed; but of Hiram's reply, it is remarked—doubtless with designed emphasis—that he "*answered in writing*,"—showing that the epistolary application of the art of writing was still remarkable, and therefore recent. We have indeed but one earlier instance, which occurs in the case of the letter which David sent to Joab by the hand of Uriah.

Solomon's message was in every way creditable to him. Hiram was an idolater, a non-worshipper of Jehovah; and public men of more modern times would, in such a case, probably have thought it becoming to suppress their own special views, in which the person addressed might be supposed not to agree, and confine themselves to the strict matter of business. This was not the course which the wisest of men thought it became him to adopt. He bore testimony to the truth he knew, apprehending that it became him to uphold the Lord's honour under all circumstances,—not wishing to displease Hiram, but determined to pay no timid deference to heathen prejudices. He boldly asserted the very positions which a heathen was least of all likely to receive—the infinity of Jehovah, and His supreme dominion. "The house which I build is great, for *great* is our God above all gods. But who is able to build Him a house, seeing the heaven of heavens cannot contain Him?" The effect of this conscientious boldness in bearing testimony to the truth, was such as invariably follows the same line of conduct. Hiram was *not* displeased, but rather spoke reverently of this high God, and expressed his earnest desire to co-operate in so good a work. Indeed, his language is stronger than that of Solomon himself, and may suggest that this declaration had made a serious impression upon his mind, or at least had strengthened some convictions made during his former intercourse with David, in whose mind the glory of God was so active a principle of thought, speech, and action, that it seems impossible for one to have been a "lover of David," without being also, in some measure, a lover of David's God. In Hiram's answer, these remarkable words occur: "Because Jehovah hath loved His people, He hath made thee king over them." And again: "Blessed be Jehovah, God of Israel, *that made heaven and earth*." Here is a clear acknowledgment of

Jehovah as creator of the universe, of His government of the world, of His providence, and of the truth that by Him kings reign.

As in the case of David, what Solomon requires is assistance in art, and certain kinds of wood for building from the mountains of Lebanon. The payment was also, in like manner, to be in agricultural produce—corn, wine, and oil. Solomon does not want, as David did, carpenters and masons; so that there can be little doubt that David had retained in his employment, on various works, the men who had previously come to him from Tyre, and these had doubtless taught others. Indeed, there was probably great activity in building, particularly at Jerusalem, throughout the reign of David. In that city, the rapid increase of the population, from its being made the metropolis of the kingdom, must have created a constant demand for new buildings. There is a hint of this in Solomon's command to Shimei to fix his residence in Jerusalem. He does not tell him to rent a house, but tells him to *build* a house—assuming, apparently, that, under the circumstances, the two things were the same; that to tell him to fix his abode in Jerusalem involved the necessity of building a house; or, in other words, that no person could find a house to live in who did not build one for himself.

As Solomon had already established a close intercourse with Egypt, and had even espoused a daughter of the Egyptian king, he had also very probably secured the advantage of a supply of artisans from that country, so famous for old experience in the arts of construction. What Solomon wanted most was a master of the works, able to carry out the plans left by David; and it was for such a man that Solomon applied to Hiram. The account of the attainments required is curious, as showing the very diverse qualifications sought in one man, in an age wherein labour and skill were much less subdivided than they afterwards became. The qualifications, however, had respect to the furniture of the temple, and not to the construction of it; which raises the question, whether Solomon had otherwise provided for this part of the undertaking— say by obtaining an architect from Egypt; or whether, on the other hand, the qualifications required for this purpose are to be regarded as included among those of the skilful person sought from the king of Tyre. The latter seems probable, as the qualifications enumerated are nearly the same as those found in Bezaleel, who, however, not only excelled in the matters specified, but superintended the whole construction of the tabernacle. The selection of Hiram fell in this instance on a person who bore the same name as himself, and who had the advantage of being the son of a Hebrew woman of the tribe of Dan, though his father was a man of Tyre. It is probable that there were others at Tyre as well qualified as this person; but this man was chosen by king Hiram, on the supposition that his connection on the mother's side with the Israelites would render him more acceptable to them, as well as cause him to feel more interested in his undertaking.

What Solomon demanded was, "a man cunning (skilful) to work in gold, in silver, and in brass, and in iron, and in purple, and crimson, and blue, and that can skill to grave," etc. Josephus understood that Hiram was skilful in "*all kinds of works*," but in these particularly. And this is probable; for in the case of Bezaleel, after the enumeration of the like qualifications, it is added, that he was skilled "in all manner of workmanship."

Comparing this enumeration with that of Bezaleel's qualifications, we find some significant additions. Among the metals in which that person wrought, "iron" is not named, nor is there mention of anything composed of that metal in the works of the tabernacle. The mention of it here shows that iron had, through the intercourse of the Israelites with the maritime coast, come into considerable use. There is, indeed, no mention of iron in the account of the building of the temple; but where so much wood was used, much iron must have been employed in fastening the parts together, as well as in the tools of the workmen; and we are told, in fact, that David prepared "iron for things of iron," in large abundance. (1 Chron. xxii. 3; xxix. 2.)

Here, also, is the additional mention of colouring,—in fact, of the very dyes for which the Tyrians have been immemorially famous. There has been some dispute about the true nature of these colours. This seems to be set at rest by the discovery of the figures of two Tyrians in the tomb of Rameses Miamun, at Thebes, arrayed in dresses which exhibit the colours in question. It may be, indeed, imagined that we may not take these colours as determining the exact shade, but as furnishing the nearest approximation, which

the pigments of the Egyptian artists allowed. But we should think there is little doubt they could obtain the exact colour, if they desired it, although, with regard to the blue or purple, it may be doubted whether it was of as much use for a painting as it was for a dye. The dress itself is remarkable, as shown in the annexed figure, and is a valuable contribution to the costumes of the region to which Palestine belongs.

TYRIAN, FROM THE TOMB OF RAMESES MIAMUN, AT THEBES

The colours are purple and scarlet, and are so arranged that one half of the person is clothed with the one, and the other half with the other Both colours are extremely vivid, as the Greek and Latin writers represent them to have been. The scarlet part of the outer short mantle or cape has a pattern of large purple spots upon it, which appear to have been formed during the process of dyeing, either by sewing on patches of cloth of the shape of the spots, or by applying more earthy ground to protect the purple in these places from the reagent which turned the rest scarlet. The mantle and tunic are both edged with a deep gold lace; and the whole forms a gorgeous dress, agreeing well with the refinement and luxury which ancient writers ascribe to the Tyrians, and which are so vividly described by the prophet Ezekiel,—chap. xxvii. On comparing the colours with those given in Syme's edition of Werner's *Nomenclature of Colours*, we find the blue or purple to have a close resemblance to China blue, or perhaps a shade lighter, between that and azure blue. The red is a distinct scarlet red, deepening into vermilion. As far as appears, the only use of these colours in connection with the temple, was in the veils or curtains which covered the doors of entrance to the outer and the inner sanctuary. (2 Chron. iii. 14.) The material of these veils was dyed of these colours, and they were decorated with figures of cherubim, probably wrought in needlework. To this skill in dyes, in colours, in textile fabrics, in brassfounding, in smithery, in gold and silver work, Hiram added the knowledge of "carving," probably wood-carving and modelling; for the analogous qualification of Bezaleel was "carving of timber,"—of which kind of work there was much more in the temple than in the tabernacle.

Solomon says in his message to Hiram, "Thou knowest that there is not among us any that can skill to hew timber like unto the Sidonians." This is one of those incidental allusions which show the historical accuracy of the sacred writers even in the most minute points. Sidon stood on the shore of the Mediterranean, at the base of Lebanon. Its people were from the earliest times famous for their commercial enterprise. The fleets which they were obliged to build, gave them ample opportunity for exercising and increasing their skill in all kinds of timber work. From the forests of Lebanon their supplies were drawn; and thus they would know better than all others, both where the best timber was to be obtained, and how the immense trees could be felled and conveyed down the rugged mountain sides to the sea.

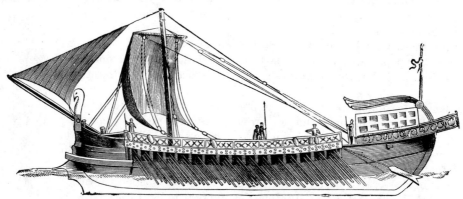

SHIP, FROM A PAINTING AT POMPEII

While the subjects of Hiram were asked to supply Solomon with skilled labour, he, on the other hand, promised in return what was equally acceptable to the Phœnicians—corn, wine, and oil. The Phœnicians were a nation of merchantmen. They had little time for agriculture. Their country, too, was limited in extent, and altogether inadequate to supply the wants of the numerous population of the great cities. Solomon knowing this, engaged not merely to supply ample provisions to Hiram's labourers in the mountains, but also to give a suitable present of the fruits of his rich kingdom to Hiram himself (2 Chron. ii. 10, with 1 Kings v. 10)

There is just one other point in the narrative requiring a note of explanation Hiram, the artist, who is represented as "filled with wisdom and understanding, and cunning to work all works in brass," is said in one place to be a "widow's son of the tribe of Naphtali" (1 Kings vii. 14), and in another to be "the son of a woman of the daughters of Dan" (2 Chron. ii. 14). Is there not a contradiction here? There would seem to be so, yet the explanation is easy. A section of the tribe of Dan seized upon and colonized a portion of old Sidonian territory on the north-eastern border of Naphtali. One of the daughters of Dan probably married a man of the neighbouring tribe of Naphtali, was left a widow, and then took for her second husband a Tyrian. Hiram was the fruit of the latter marriage; and his mother was both "a woman of the daughters of Dan," and a "widow of Naphtali." It is interesting to observe that one of the two skilled artists selected to construct the ark and tabernacle in the wilderness, was likewise of the tribe of Dan (Exod. xxxi. 6); Jewish tradition affirms that he was an ancestor of Hiram.

P.

Light is shed upon the preparations made for building the temple in recent explorations. In the wonderful discovery at the south-east angle of the temple wall, stones were found with letters or characters, apparently painted with a brush, a few red splashes being dropped in the operation. They are considered to be quarry marks made before the stones were placed *in situ*, and as indicating that the stones were dressed before leaving the quarry. There are no remains which tend to prove that the dressing of the stones occurred after being placed in their present position. (*Recovery of Jerusalem*, 139-144). The letters are pronounced to be Phœnician letters. This preparing of the stones ere they were removed from the quarry exactly accord with the biblical account, that "the house, when it was in building, was built of stone made ready before it was brought thither, so that there was neither hammer nor axe, nor any tool of iron heard in the house while it was in building (1 Kings vi. 7. Comp. Exod. xx. 25; Deut. xxvii. 5): and the Phœnician inscription corroborates the statement.

There are extensive stone quarries to the north of the holy city, just outside the Damascus gate; they have been recently visited and described by two intelligent travellers, Mr. Lewin and Canon Tristram. The former says, after mentioning that he entered by a hole just large enough to admit a person of moderate size, "We lit our tapers, but they were lost in such a vast expanse, and all that we could see was the bare frowning rock over our heads." "We reached at length the wall of the cavern in the eastern side, and were curious to see the mode in which the stone had been quarried. It appeared that the size of the stone was marked out, and then a groove to the requisite depth was cut by the chisel, and the stone was then broken off. In general the severance was tolerably even, but occasionally, from the inclination of the stratum, the stone was detached with an irregular inner surface, leaving a stump behind, and not preserving the cubic form intended for it."—*The Siege of Jerusalem*, 161.

Canon Tristram gives the following account:—"The quarries are not one vast cavern, but a succession of irregular hollowed chambers in labyrinthic disorder, with enormous shapeless pillars left here and there to support the roof; and the whole very much reminded us of a visit to the disused workings of an English coal mine, with the advantage that it was neither coal nor black." "In many places the very niches remained, out of which the great blocks had been hewn which form the temple wall. There lay on the ground in one corner a broken monolith, which had evidently split in process of removal, and had been left where it fell. The stone here is very soft, and must easily have been sawn whole. Like some other limestones, it hardens almost to marble on exposure. There are a few wells, generally dry, sunk probably for the use of workmen, and for the most part now filled up with rubbish. In one, however, we found good water."—*Land of Israel*, 187.

S.

CEDARS OF LEBANON

1 Kings 6:10; 2 Chronicles 2:8-9

TIMBER of various kinds was what Solomon chiefly required of king Hiram. That it was needful to procure timber from so distant a quarter, and that through the intervention of foreigners, shows that, although trees of various kinds, and especially such as bear fruit, may have been abundant in Palestine, those which afforded wood suited for building purposes were not much more common in the country than they are at present. As it is eventually said that Solomon made the cedar wood of Lebanon as abundant in Palestine "as the sycamores that are in the vale" (1 Kings x. 27), this shows that the sycamore was the native timber tree in common use. But the wood is coarse, and would not be much valued where anything better could be procured. Hence it was a sort of luxury to use cedar wood, which, although not the most desirable of timbers, is at least considerably better than sycamore; and, being brought with cost and trouble from a distance, would be the more valued on account of its comparatively high price. Thus it is said, in Isaiah ix. 10: "The sycamore trees are cut down, but we will change them into cedars;" which does not mean that

cedar trees were to be planted in lieu of sycamores, seeing that the cedar tree does not flourish in Palestine, but that the Israelites would soon be able to repair their losses, and rebuild in greater perfection. These cedar trees formed Solomon's chief requirement from Hiram.

The tree called the "cedar of Lebanon" is very well known in this country, where many specimens of it exist, having been originally propagated in the seventeenth century from seeds obtained from Lebanon. It is a wide-spreading tree, generally from fifty to eighty feet high, and where it stands singly, often covering, with its branches, a space the diameter of which is much greater than its height. The horizontal branches, when the tree is exposed on all sides, are very large in proportion to the trunk, being often equal in bulk to the stem of the fir or the chestnut—a circumstance alluded to by the prophet Ezekiel, in his magnificent description of this noble tree (chap. xxxi. 3-9.) These branches are disposed in horizontal layers or stages, the distance to which they extend diminishing as they approach the top, where they form a pyramidal head, broad in proportion to the height. The branchlets are disposed in a fanlike manner upon the branches, and the evergreen leaves lying thickly upon them in tufts, give sometimes to the whole the appearance of an almost unbroken field of dark green.

The cedar grove, which is regarded as the remnant of the forest which supplied the cedarwood to Solomon, or rather perhaps, as the principal existing site of these trees, lies far up among the higher mountains, at a spot which it takes above a day to reach from the coast at Tripoli. The grove is here found, not, as some have conceived, upon any of the summits of Lebanon, but at the foot of a lofty mountain, in what may be regarded as the arena of a vast amphitheatre, shut in on all sides by high mountains, which form part of the upper ridge of Lebanon. Here the trees stand upon five or six gentle elevations, occupying a spot of ground about three-fourths of a mile in circumference. They appear to be of several generations. Of the oldest there are few, perhaps not more than seven or eight; but besides these, there are forty or fifty good-sized, well looking trees, and a great number of smaller ones, with some small pines among them. The largest trunks are distinguishable by having the small branches at the top only, and by four, five, or seven trunks springing from one base. The trunks are quite dead, and exhibit externally a greyish tint. The branches of some are larger, and the foliage more abundant; but there are none whose leaves come so close to the ground as

CEDARS OF LEBANON

in the fine specimens in Kew gardens. These large and noble trees are known to be not above two centuries old; and as this shows the tree not to be of so slow growth as is commonly supposed, we find a satisfactory reason for the varying accounts of travellers as to the number of the largest specimens in Lebanon, during the last three hundred years over which accounts extend. The trees have meanwhile been growing, and their relative proportions have been undergoing constant change. It is usually stated that the number of the largest trees has rapidly declined. We are reminded that the number which Belon found in 1550 was twenty-eight, and that we afterwards successively hear of sixteen, then of twelve, now of seven. But it is probable the difference is more apparent than real, travellers not being agreed as to what they should regard as the largest trees—some counting more and some less, and the number of those reckoned as largest being smaller in proportion as the notions of travellers became more definite, and as their means of comparison increased. How little reliance is to be placed upon such estimates, where measurements are

not given, is shown by the fact that Maundrell reckons only sixteen large trees, while Le Bruyn, who travelled some years later, counted thirty-six, and he admits that it was as difficult to count them by the eye, as to count the stones at Stonehenge. The trees which were of secondary age three centuries ago, must by this time have so increased in bulk, as to be among those which Belon would now reckon among the largest, could he count them over again. There is no apparent cause of decrease; and in a place where the axe of the hewer never comes, there would naturally be a succession of large trees—as, without doubt, has actually been the case. The dimensions of the trees whose trunks are dead, and which must have attained the utmost size, afford the best standard for the full growth of the cedar of Lebanon; and the circumference of the largest and most remarkable of these is thirty-nine or forty feet a little above the ground. Now, we have found the means of calculating that the cedar increases in bulk at the rate of about $1\frac{1}{4}$ inch in one year, consequently this tree must have been 384 years in actual growing.[1] Then we must allow the time it took in gradually decaying after it had ceased in bulk, and the time it has stood in its present decayed condition; taking which into account, it cannot be too little, nor probably too much, to allow that from 500 to 600 years may have passed since it first sprang from the ground. This is a great length of time,—more, perhaps, than it is quite safe to allow to a soft-wooded tree, seeing that it gives the cedar an existence at least equal to that of the hard-wooded oak. In fact, the estimate may probably be in excess, from its being founded upon the growth of the tree in England, where, as an exotic, the growth is probably slower—or, in other words, the annual deposit of woody matter thinner—than in the region where the cedar is indigenous. It is

[1] This calculation is founded on the fact, that the cedar in the garden of the Manor-house at Enfield, known to have been planted in 1670, measured sixteen feet one inch in circumference in 1821, being 193 inches in 151 years, which is rather more than $1\frac{1}{4}$ inch in a year.

certainly the largest possible estimate; and therefore the more strongly shows the error of those who fancy that the older of these trees may be such as grew on this spot in the time of Solomon—nearly three thousand years ago. Indeed, although it is also fondly imagined that this is the very grove from which the king obtained his cedars, there can be no question that the supply was drawn from parts of the mountain more accessible to the coast, and from which all traces of the cedar have long since disappeared. The trees here, doubtless, owe their preservation, and the venerable age they have been suffered to attain, to the fact, that if they were cut down, no means could be found of transporting them to the sea. For the same reason, this grove must have been left unmolested from the most ancient times, although we cannot cherish the notion that any of the old patriarchal trees now found here, grew up under the same light that shone upon the throne of Solomon. The spot might, however, very well have furnished, even in that age, those grander specimens of the tree from which the sacred writers drew the conceptions which they have imparted to us of its magnificence.

It may be stated that some writers doubt whether the tree known as the cedar of Lebanon, be really the ERES of Scripture. The description in Ezekiel can, however, hardly apply to any other tree known in that region, and belonging to Lebanon; but it is possible that the name may have been extended to other trees of the same genus (*Pinus*), some of them with wood better suited for beams and planks than the cedar. In appearance, it is scarcely distinguishable from white deal, and it is scarcely of harder consistence; but it has a much finer scent than any kind of deal, and may possibly be more durable. It has been supposed by some, that the wood may in Lebanon be of a firmer texture than that afforded by the specimens in this country; but we have before us a small piece of the wood from Lebanon, which fully answers to this description. Some describe the wood as certainly of not greater value than deal—if indeed so valuable. Yet it is stated that a skilful carver of Warwick has in his rooms some specimens of furniture made from cedar of Lebanon, ornamented with carved work in flowers, leaves, etc., in the best taste, and in sharpness and colour so similar to box-wood, that any casual observer

would suppose it to be such. It seems to be established by recent research,[1] that receptacles made of cedar-wood are highly injurious to their contents, of almost every description, from a kind of resinous vapour which the wood emits, and which is condensed on the surface of the articles, and is difficult of removal; but this property, we apprehend, must tend to the preservation of the wood itself, and to its protection from the attacks of insects, and may, in fact, account for the estimation in which it was held for building purposes, and for ornamental wood-work.

Travellers err in supposing that there are no other cedars in Lebanon than those which are found at this place. Many other single specimens and clumps of cedars are to be met with among the mountains, but nowhere else have so many together, or such large and venerable specimens, been discovered. The tree is not even peculiar to Lebanon—it is found growing wild in the mountains of Amanus and Taurus; and it grows very freely in this country—specimens being now rather numerous, at least within twenty-five miles around London. It has considerable general resemblance to a yew, and is sometimes taken for it by the uninitiated. We are aware of one growing in the churchyard of a village in which we formerly resided, which the peasantry resolutely affirmed to be yew, but which is a real cedar of Lebanon. This specimen is above forty feet high, and about seven feet in girth; and as a servant of our own used to boast that it was planted by the hand of her father, it must have been of comparatively recent growth.

As the accounts given by writers regarding the quality of cedar-wood are so different and conflicting, I may be permitted to state my own experience of it. When in Damascus in 1856, I obtained a piece of a branch of one of the largest cedars of Lebanon, which had been broken off by a storm during the previous winter. The fragment was nearly five feet long, and about eighteen inches in diameter. In 1858 I brought it with me to England; and two years later, when it was thoroughly seasoned, I had a portion of it made into an ornamental piece of furniture. In appearance, the wood does not differ much from ordinary red pine. It is somewhat darker, and the veining better marked. It is also becoming darker by age. The wood is hard and close-grained. It takes a good polish, and the

[1] *On the Injurious Effects of Cedar-Wood Drawers on Objects of Natural History, etc.* By the Rev. Dr. John Fleming. Read before the Royal Physical Society of Edinburgh, 11th December, 1852.

carving remains, after six years' wear, perfectly sharp and firm. I can have no doubt of the durability of such wood, and of its high value for building purposes. It is much superior to any of the ordinary pines, as well as to any specimen of English-grown cedar I have ever seen.

It has now been ascertained—at least Mr. Tristram affirms it, and he ought to be an authority—that the cedar still exists on Lebanon to a far larger extent than has been generally believed. In addition to the sacred grove described by all travellers, cedar has been found near the village of Hadith, and also at the village of Duma, some ten miles to the south-west. Mr. Tristram says, "More interesting still is its existence in a far distant part of the mountains. In one of the glens to the north of Deir el Kamar, the ancient stronghold of the Druzes, up the course of the Nahr el Baruk, south-east of B'hamdun, near the village of Ain Zahalteh, are many scattered trees and small clumps." And he adds: "Probably a careful search among the *western* roots of the Lebanon would result in the discovery of many more relics of the primeval forest."[1]

P.

WOODCUTTERS

1 Kings 5:10-16; 2 Chronicles 2:10, 15-18

CEDAR was not the only timber which Solomon required from the forests of Lebanon. Firs are also named among the trees which Hiram supplied to Solomon. In Chronicles "almug trees" are added; but as this wood is in 1 Kings x. 11 described as being brought from distant parts by Hiram's ships in the famous voyage to Ophir, it is not credible that it was also found in Lebanon; for in that case it could not be said, as is said in Kings, that no such "algum trees" (so written in Kings) had been seen in Israel as those which the navy of Hiram brought. As the author of Chronicles does not name this among the products of this expedition, he was probably led to introduce it here (as he had occasion to mention the use to which the wood was applied), as it was equally with the cedars from Lebanon obtained through Hiram, without thinking it needful to specify the separate source from which it was derived. We mention this timber to obviate a seeming difficulty, which has perplexed many; but have no present intention to inquire into the nature of the almug tree.

We are more interested in inquiring into the system organized for the cutting and squaring of

[1] *Land of Israel*, p. 629.

the wood in the mountains, and the removal of it to Joppa.

Solomon allowed that none of his people were skilful to cut timber "like the Zidonians;" and it was therefore arranged that Hiram was to supply a certain number of workmen to direct the proceedings, and perform the more difficult parts of the work; for it is to be remembered, that all the timber was fully prepared and fitted for its final use on the spot, not only to facilitate the work at Jerusalem, but that no labour might be wasted in the transport of the superfluous parts. So small and busy a state as that of Tyre, could not, however, supply all the numerous hands required for the ruder labour, such as trimming the wood, and dragging it down through the defiles of the mountains to the coast. For this, Solomon undertook to find labourers. How were they to be found? David had, it seems, subdued all the remnants of the Canaanitish tribes, and at so late a period, when they were no longer dangerous, and national animosities had abated, he considered himself exempted from the obligation of extirpating them. He had therefore spared them, on the condition, not of reducing them to personal slavery, but of their being liable to be called out for service on any public works that might need their aid. They were now therefore numbered, and the adult males were found to amount to 153,600. Of these, 70,000 were made bearers of burdens, 80,000 hewers of wood, and 3,600 overseers of the others. A levy of 30,000 Israelites was also made for this service, and there were 300 Israelites as overseers of the whole work. They were not all employed at once, but in relays of one-third at a time, so that every man spent annually eight months at home and four in the mountains. This, and the great numbers employed, must have rendered the obligation less onerous than has been represented. These arrangements were continued for several years on a well organized plan. The wood prepared by these multitudes was taken down to the sea, there made up into large rafts, and floated down along the shore to Joppa, whereby the land carriage was reduced to about thirty miles to Jerusalem. To support these labourers, and to remunerate Hiram for the aid of his people, Solomon agreed to supply the king, year by year, with 20,000 measures of wheat, 20,000 baths of wine, and 20,000 baths of oil.

It may not be known, that operations somewhat of the same kind were going on, upon a smaller scale indeed, in Lebanon, during the time Syria was in possession of the Pasha of Egypt, who had great need of timber for various uses, and whose proceedings in procuring it seem to us to illustrate, in many particulars, those of Hiram and Solomon for the same purpose,—especially as to the manner in which labourers were obtained for the service, and the way in which they were supplied with food.

Most of the wood destined for Egypt was embarked at Scanderoon, and was of course obtained as near as might be from the mountains by which the bay is bordered. The timber chiefly procured was yellow oak, green oak, whitish-yellow pine or fir, beech, and linden. The last is the *largest*, but it is scarce; next to that the yellow oak, then the beech.[1] The oak of both kinds is straight-grained, like the American; the pine is very knotty and full of turpentine; the beech is of a good, close-grained quality, but not nearly so plentiful as the other two. In the year 1837, about 750 men were employed in the mountains, of whom 250 were occupied in cutting down the trees, and the rest, twice that number, in trimming and dressing the same; and to bring down these to the sea, required the labour of 1,200 men, with *practicable roads*, and with buffaloes and bullocks. If obtained from parts of the mountains remote from the coast, with difficult roads, and without the help of animals, the number required for the transport would of course be proportionally greater. We thus see the comparatively small number of Phœnician fellers, whose work would suffice to supply labour to the large levies of Solomon. By the Pasha's men about 60,000 trees were cut down, trimmed, and brought down to the coast in one year, besides about 5,000 abandoned on the road from the difficulty of transport. Of these, 40,000 were fit for shipbuilding purposes, and the remainder for house purposes. The wood was freighted for Alexandria in thirty-nine vessels, collectively of 14,120 tons burdens, besides eight or nine small craft of eighty or ninety tons each, which received cargoes of firewood.

From this statement, it is not difficult to dis-

[1] The following are the sizes of the different kinds :— *Yellow Oak*, 80 feet long by 18 to 20 inches square; *Green Oak*, 18 to 20 feet by 7 to 9 inches; *Beech*, 30 to 35 feet by 14 to 15 inches; *Pine*, 30 feet by 16 to 20 inches; *Linden*, 40 to 50 feet by 25 to 27 inches.

cover one of the reasons why the mountain forests of Syria have been a coveted possession to the rulers of Egypt, from the Pharaohs and Ptolemies down to the Moslem sultans and to Mehemet Ali. It also enables us to see the extent to which the nearer forests of Lebanon must have been denuded of their trees, to meet the large wants of a country so void of timber as Egypt.

But let us turn to the labourers employed in these operations. They were, like the labourers of Solomon, and probably of Hiram, pressed into the service. In this case they are, however, more oppressively, taken from the immediate neighbourhood, all the effective men being forced into the service, leaving an insufficient number to till the ground for their own maintenance. But grain was imported by the government (as by king Hiram from Palestine) from other parts of Syria and from Egypt, and issued to the men as a portion of their pay. This pay was nominally three piastres, or sevenpence farthing a day; but it came short of this fully one-third, by their being obliged to take a fixed portion in grain, without reference to their actual wants, and more than they required, at a fixed price, which was so enhanced in various ways, and under various pretences, as to be much higher than what grain could be procured for in the neighbourhood. It is very likely, the system being an old one, that Hiram dealt thus with the corn he obtained from Solomon, unless the interests of the Hebrew subjects employed were protected by the presence of the king's own officers.

The men employed, at the present day, in transporting the timber to the coast, receive each a pair and a half of bullocks, which are valued to them at from 700 to 1,000 piastres a pair, which sum they are debited with, and must make good in case of loss, accident, or death. The effect of this is, that when a man meets with such a misfortune before he has the means of repairing it—which he can rarely hope to do—he has no resource but flight.

The season for working the timber is eight months, from the middle of March till the middle of November. During the remaining four months, the people are left in a great measure to themselves; but, being winter months, they cannot turn them to much account, unless to prepare and sow a little land for the most pressing exigencies of their families; a few of them, however, who have trades, find some employment in the neighbouring villages. Independently of such resources, their yearly earnings may be thus stated:—The cutters get two and a half piastres a day, for 224 working days; amounting in all, after deducting twelve shillings for contingencies, to five pounds. The trimmers get three piastres a day, or about six pounds fourteen shillings for the whole term, which, after deducting sixteen shillings for contingencies, leaves about five pounds eighteen shillings. The transporters have three and a half piastres a day, making in all about seven pounds sixteen shillings; but from this must be deducted more than half for the keep of animals, leaving them less than four pounds—so that they remain in a worse condition than even the cutters, although their nominal wages are one third higher.

In regard to the last branch of employment, it seems to us likely that the arrangement was different in the time of Solomon; for, considering the great quantity of timber secured by the comparatively small number of men employed by the Egyptian government in 1837, it is difficult to account for the employment of such vast numbers in the earlier time, unless by supposing that the labour of men was employed instead of that of cattle, in dragging the timber down from the mountains to the shore.

———

THE CHOICE

1 Kings 3

GOD is a great teacher; and all the docile scholars of His school are richly rewarded by Him. Look back to the transaction between the Lord and Solomon at Gibeon for full proof of this.

The senses and judgment of the young king were locked up in sleep; he was in the state least of all suited to instruction, when the greatest lesson of his life was taught to him. But it matters little in what state the scholar is—how, for the time, or even habitually, dull or insensate—when He undertakes to be his instructor, who can enlighten both the organ and the object. None teaches like Him in mode or matter, and hence the blessedness and the advan-

tage connected with learning of Him. There is nothing good for us in all His treasures of wisdom and knowledge, which He is not most ready, with abounding fulness to impart. "If any of you lack wisdom," says James, "let him ask of God, that giveth to all men liberally, and upbraideth not, and it shall be given him." Solomon found the truth of this, and so shall every one find who makes the like experiment. The Lord is never displeased with large asking—so that it be proper asking; and His free bounty delights to surpass the largest requests and boldest hopes of the petitioner. And in this case He did not wait to be asked. He came to press His gifts upon the acceptance of David's son; asking him to make his choice of all the gifts His almightiness enabled Him to offer—or rather, of all that the man was capable of receiving. Whatever we may think of it—and practically we every day deny most of the things we profess to believe—God daily makes as large and liberal offers to us, ay, offers which are more liberal by far; and quite as surely will He bestow upon us what we ask, and much more, if that which we seek be well pleasing in His sight. Then

> "Come, let us put
> Up our requests to Him, whose will alone
> Limits His power of teaching; from whom none
> Returns unlearned, that hath once a will
> To be His scholar."—*Quarles.*

And well is it with those who, like the same writer, can say—

> "I am a scholar. The great Lord of love
> And life my tutor is; who from above,
> All that lack learning to His school invites."

Solomon had learned in His school, and had there received that enlightenment which enabled him at once to discern, even in sleep, the exact good that was fittest for him, and that he most wanted.

Solomon asked for wisdom; and enforced by many reasons his want of it, his own sense of his great need of it. The speech of the young king "pleased the Lord." And why? because it was in accordance with His will. It was Himself that enabled him, that "put it into his heart, to pray this prayer unto Him." He could not have done so, had not God given him the grace to do it. God loves and approves that which is His own, and both accepts and rewards that which is His own acting in us. "Thou wilt ordain peace for us," says the prophet; "for Thou hast wrought all our works in us." (Isa. xxvi. 12.)

Take twelve men from the streets—take them, if you like, from schools and colleges—take them even from the church doors—and propose to them the same question which God proposed to Solomon. Let them be assured that they shall have what they will from One who has full power to bestow it. How many of them, do you think, will say as Solomon said, "Give me wisdom?" We greatly doubt if there would be even one; but surely not more. This is just the last thing that people suppose themselves to be in need of. Probably there are not three of the twelve—perhaps not two—perhaps not one—who does not think himself every whit as wise as Solomon already, although he does not like to say it. It has not occurred to us in our life—not now scant of days, though, alas! scant in accomplished purposes—to have met with one man who avowed any lack of wisdom, or who, therefore, would have made the choice of Solomon, had that choice been offered to him.

As statistical information is deemed of peculiar value in this age, we may attempt to make "a return" of the mode in which our twelve men would distribute their choice.

Three at least would answer, "Give us wealth. In the land where our lot is cast, wealth is needed for comfort and usefulness. Yet we seek not our own luxury, but thy honour. That we may have wherewith to be bountiful to those that need,—that we may qualify our children for eminent service to Thee in high places,—that we may aid mission, and Bible, and church societies, to the utmost of the means bestowed upon us,—that we may subscribe handsomely to the new church, to the parsonage fund, to the fund for the increase of ministers, to the dispensary, to the schools, to the clothing club, to the soup kitchen,—to the thousand objects which demand our attention, and which we cannot neglect without discredit in the eyes of the minister and the gentry here." So some would answer, in meaning, if not in words; but alas for the widow's mite!

Perhaps three more would not speak so high. They would not call it wealth but competency, freedom from anxiety—securing them ability to attend upon the things of the Lord without distraction. Only secure them that, and they have nothing more or better to ask. For who can go on without distress of soul in this way—

troubled for the present and the future—with no security against want in one's old age, and with this continual struggle how to keep up the "appearances" which are so necessary in this evil world? Alas for the sparrows! alas for the lilies of the field!

There are, perhaps, three who covet power, honour, distinction, more than even wealth, which is but a coarser form of the same desire. In one shape or another—from an impatience of superiority—from the love of command—from the burning wish to come out from the general multitude, and to be admired and observed of men, and leave an unforgotten name—power is more generally desired than may at the first view appear, seeing that, although in this country, at least, it is a less ostensible and avowed pursuit than that of wealth, the latter is often sought in subordination to the former, and as a means to its attainment. Or there may be among the three, *one*—or less than one (for in statistics one is a divisible proportion)—who, fretted by his external impotency, which hampers him on every side, and prevents him from giving due effect to the large potencies within him, craves beyond all things such power as may enable him to accomplish his large designs, and render fruitful the bold and useful purposes of his will and hope.

There may be two, hardly more, who, on being asked such a question, would think length of days of more consequence than wealth, or competence, or power. They are those whom the tremor, the chill, the cough, the inner pain, the sense of declining strength, have impressed with alarm at the probable shortness of their lives; for, without such warning, length of days is seldom in these latter times an object of distinct solicitude; for

"All men think all men mortal but themselves,"

and every one silently assumes that his own life will be long. But among those who would make this choice, there may be a few who, standing free in their strength, yet, from the oppressive consciousness of the swift passage of their days—days so long in youth, so short in age—would passionately entreat for the lengthening out of life—time—time only to finish all their labours—time to work out and produce all their large conceptions, and finish all their beneficent undertakings. Such as these will also regard with something like dread, the breaking up of all their old and cherished habits and associations—their children, their friends, their books, their gardens, their trees. With much of this we can sympathize. But let them be of good cheer. Life, though short, is long enough. Even in its ordinary duration it wears out before it ends; and before that end there lies a gulf of "evil days," in which no pleasure is found. Desire has failed. The sources of life's enjoyments have been cut off. The sweet uses of life have passed away. Books, and trees, and gardens cease to interest. Plans and purposes that promised us the labour of three lives in one, fall unregretted from our stiffening fingers. And man becomes content to gather up his feet and die, hoping to join the friends who have dropped away one by one before him, and knowing that his children will come to him soon in that land to which he is going. Nor will the Christian's hope make him ashamed.

There is but one of our twelve left. What doth he ask? Let us trust that, among so many —we can scarcely hope there may be more— there is this one, at least, who has the heart to say, "Give me thyself; for all things are contained in Thee. Thou art wisdom; Thou art wealth; Thou art power; Thou art length of days; Thou art fulness."

"Give what Thou wilt, without Thee I am poor,
And with Thee rich, take what Thou wilt away."

GREAT STONES

1 Kings 5:17-18

It must not be allowed to escape our notice, that although the operations for obtaining timber are chiefly described, great hewn stones for the foundation of the temple were also, by the aid of Hiram's workmen, to be procured. It is distinctly stated, that "the king commanded, and they brought great stones, costly stones, and hewed stones, to lay the foundation of the house. And Solomon's builders and Hiram's builders did hew them, and the stone-squarers: so they prepared timber and stones to build the house." As to the descriptive epithets, we may combine them into "great costly hewn stones." If they were hewn and squared in Lebanon, and were of such size as the text leads us to suppose, they must have been costly enough by the time they reached Jeru-

salem, whatever the quality of the stone. It must be confessed, that it is not clear from this text that the stones did come from Lebanon; it may be understood to mean no more than that, wherever procured, they were wrought by Hiram's stone-masons, conjointly with those of Solomon. The transport of great "stones" from so great a distance, suggests the chief difficulty; but besides this, there could really be no need to go so far for them, as stone of the same quality as that of Lebanon might have been obtained much nearer home. In Lebanon, however, and not nearer, they might find large masses of stone which, in the course of time, had been loosened by earthquakes and frosts, and cast down into the valleys, and which needed only to be squared to be serviceable for the required use.

The stone of these regions is hard, calcareous, and whitish, sonorous like freestone, and disposed in strata variously inclined. This stone has nearly the same appearance throughout Syria and Palestine, where it is still used for building, and is perhaps that with which the temple was built, and which Josephus describes as "white stone." The previous squaring of the stones in the quarry, not only facilitated their removal to the place of building, but produced the remarkable result, that the house being "built of stone made ready before it was brought thither, there was neither hammer, nor axe, nor any tool of iron heard in the house while it was in building." (1 Kings vi. 7.)

The terms employed by the sacred historian will scarcely strike us in all their force, unless we bear in mind that stones of enormous size are known to have been employed in the ancient buildings of Syria. Thus, in the subbasement of the great temple of Baalbek, which is probably much more ancient than the now ruined Roman structure which rests upon it, there is one stone sixty-six feet in length by twelve in breadth and thickness, with others of not greatly inferior size; while in a neighbouring quarry, which tradition declares to be that from which Solomon obtained his "great stones," are stones of equal and greater dimensions, cut and ready for use, one of them being no less than seventy feet in length and fourteen in breadth, by fourteen feet five inches in thickness. This stone, therefore, contains 14,128 cubic feet, and would, if of Portland stone, weigh no less than 1,135 tons.

At Jerusalem, the immense size and obvious

antiquity of much of the stonework around the area which contains the mosque of Omar, and formerly contained the temple of the Lord, have led many to ascribe it to the age of Jewish mag-

MOSQUE OF OMAR

nificence,—some carrying it back to the time of Solomon, and others being content to refer it to the time of Herod the Great. This is found in the lower courses of masonry, and at the angles; the superstructure of the enclosing wall being of smaller and inferior masonry, comparatively modern, and doubtless of Saracenic workmanship. To these remains we incline to assign the higher antiquity, regarding them as relics—the only relics—of the original work of Solomon. The foundation walls, and the lower courses of masonry in the superstructure, so solidly constructed, and composed of stones so large, are seldom wholly destroyed or eradicated—especially when they belong not to a building, but to the enclosing wall of an area which seems to have remained the same in all ages, while the sacred fane within the area has itself been repeatedly renewed. Time makes little impression upon such work; and wilful destroyers, before the invention of gunpowder, found the task of demolition to this extent too laborious. They were content generally to destroy the more visible parts of such walls, which was also the more easy, from the upper parts being usually of smaller masonry; and by the time they had demolished all but the lowermost courses, they would find these concealed by the stones and rubbish cast down from above, which opposed a further obstacle to the progress of the work of destruction. They would thus

have destroyed all that appeared of the walls, that is, all down to the accumulations of rubbish: while, in fact, many of the lower courses of masonry, as well as the whole of the sub-structures, remained entirely underneath the ruins. On rebuilding the wall after the lapse of time, some of this *debris* must be cleared away, to extract from it the stones to be used in rebuilding the wall, and to get at the old work upon which to rear the new; and thus the lower courses of the old masonry, so long hidden beneath the rubbish, would be again brought to light. It is to be noted that, leaving out of view the obviously Saracenic, Crusading, and Turkish portions of the superstructnre, the architectural remains of earlier times at Jerusalem exhibit at least *three* distinct periods of construction. The latest of these must, it is historically evident, have belonged to the Emperor Hadrian's restoration of the city as a seat and home of Paganism—the Elia Capitolina of the second century. If there be any works to which those of Hadrian were appended, or in which they were reared, they must at the latest be those of Herod's reign; and if we trace a substratum sustaining the labour of *his* time, and if, further, these works are seen to be of a kind demanding the resources and the tranquillity of a long and prosperous era, and such as could not have been undertaken or carried on during centuries of foreign domination, of fiscal exactions, of precarious political existence, and of intestine commotion,—then shall we be almost compelled to go back to the earliest times of the monarchy as to our nearest landing-place.[1]

It is in this more ancient substratum that the largest stones are found. As we are only seeking for "great stones" *among* the ancient remains of Jerusalem, it is unnecessary to give any description of these remains, for which another occasion may be found. It will suffice simply to indicate some of these large stones, and to suggest that the fact of their being found in the most ancient masonry at Jerusalem, as evinced by their forming the lowermost portions of it, irresistibly takes back the mind to the great and costly hewn stones of Solomon; for to what other period anterior to the time of Herod can any works of this nature be assigned?

Along nearly the whole of the eastern side, upon the brow of the steep valley of Jehoshaphat,

[1] Trail's *Josephus*, i. xxxi.

courses of ancient masonry may be traced in almost a continuous line. In some places the courses scarcely appear above the soil, while in others they rise nearly to the height of the modern walls, especially at the angles and projecting towers, which were built to a greater height with great stones, and of such firm masonry as could not easily be destroyed. [1] The inequality may be in part accounted for by the irregularities of the ground, and the unequal accumulation of *debris*. At the north-east angle, for instance, several courses of ancient masonry form a corner tower, projecting slightly from the general face of the wall along a length of eighty-one feet.

SOUTH-EAST ANGLE OF WALL AT JERUSALEM

Many of the stones here measure from seventeen to nineteen feet in length, while a few exceed twenty-four feet. They vary from three to four feet in depth, and from five to eight in width. Speaking of this corner, a very competent observer, Mr. Tipping, [2] remarks, "A close scrutiny of the masonry of the two sides of this corner shows it to be (allowance being made for the ravages of time and war) of the highest order, immeasurably superior to the rude piling of Cyclopean blocks at Mycenæ and Tyrinthus; indeed, I consider it to be the finest specimen of mural masonry in the world. The joints are close, and the finishing of the bevelling and

[1] Hence the repeated allusion to "corner-stones" in Scripture. And as it was a great feat to elevate such huge stones to their places, the operation is described as being accompanied by "shoutings."

[2] Trail's *Josephus*, i. xlv.

facing is so clean and fine, that, when fresh from the hands of the builder, it must have produced the effect of gigantic *relievo* panelling. The material employed is a fine limestone, and is now clothed with that golden hue which a course of ages produces in southern climes."

But the south-east angle of the enclosing wall is perhaps the most imposing object in or near Jerusalem, consisting of enormous blocks of stone rising at the corner to the height of seventy feet. In the upper portions, however, the stones are so irregularly interlocated as to show that they belong to the restorations from old materials, upon the basis of the more ancient lower courses. At this place, and in the wall upon each face of this corner, in the three lower courses, stones are found measuring nearly thirty feet long, and of proportionate breadth and depth; and wherever such stones occur, at this and other spots, there is always observable more regularity than is found higher up—more of uniform intention—more indication of adequate means and leisurely construction.

In the western wall, about thirty-nine feet from the south-west corner, several huge stones jut out, as if, one is apt to think at the first sight, from the bursting of the wall by an earthquake. On closer inspection, it is seen that the three courses of these immense stones retain their original places. Their external surface is hewn to a regular curve; and, being fitted one upon another, they form the commencement or foot of an enormous arch, which once sprung from the western wall in a direction towards Mount Zion, across the valley which separated that mount from Mount Moriah. If the principle of the arch may be supposed to have been known at so early a period—and there is no evidence to prove that it was *not*—this may have belonged to the causeway by which the court went from Mount Zion to the temple, and which was an object of special admiration to the queen of Sheba. However, not to discuss this question, it suffices to say that the extreme width of the abutting stones is fifty-one feet. One of them is twenty-four feet six inches in length, and several of them exceed five feet in thickness.

About a hundred yards northward of the arch, we come to what is called the Jews' Wailing Place, where occur some specimens of the finest and best preserved masonry in this wall of enclosure. It derives its name from the fact,

.that the Jews have purchased permission to assemble here every Friday, in the precincts of these ancient stones, to recite a set form of prayers, and to bewail the ruin of "the holy and

JEWS' WAILING PLACE

beautiful house in which their fathers worshipped." At this spot we find five courses of bevelled stones, and over them three courses of smoothed-faced stones, little, if at all inferior in size. The lower courses of the masonry are beautifully fresh and polished in surface; others, either by time, or more probably by external injury, are much decayed.

The mode of transporting such large stones was no doubt the same as is shown in the Egyptian sculptures—on low-wheeled trucks drawn by oxen. On this point there is an interesting

EGYPTIAN MODE OF TRANSPORTING LARGE STONES

passage in Procopius, having reference to the building of the church of St. Mary (probably the present mosque el Aksa) at Jerusalem, by the Emperor Justinian. "They hewed rocks of immense size from the mountains; and, having carved them skilfully, carried them thence as follows:—First, they made carts of a size equal to the rocks, and placed a single stone in each cart, which was drawn by forty oxen, chosen by the emperor's order for their excellence. Then,

as it was impossible for the roads leading to the city to bear these great carts, they cut out to a considerable extent the mountains, and made a passage for them as they arrived."

There is no reason to suppose that the stones for building the temple were brought from a great distance, as extensive quarries exist in the neighbourhood, and signs remain of their having been anciently worked. (See additional illustration, See Vol. 1, pp. 801-805.

Josephus, in his *Antiquities*, tells us, "that the king laid the foundations of the temple very deep in the ground, and the materials were strong stones, and such as would resist the force of time; these were to unite themselves with the earth, and become a basis, and a sure foundation for that superstructure which was to be erected over it." (Book viii., c. iii. 2.) And again, "Solomon also built a wall, beginning at the bottom, which was encompassed by a deep valley; and, at the south side, he laid rocks together, and bound them one to another with lead, and included some of the inner parts, till it proceeded to a great height, and till both the largeness of the square edifice and its altitude were immense." (*Antiq.*, B. xv. cxi.3.) Josephus also speaks of the south front of the temple in his own time, after the rebuilding by Herod, "as deserving to be mentioned better than any other under the sun; for, while the valley was very deep, and its bottom could not be seen, if you looked from above into the depth, the further vastly high elevation of the cloister stood upon that height, insomuch that if any one looked down from the top of the battlements, or down both those altitudes, he would be giddy, while his sight could not reach to so immense a depth." (*Ibid.* 5.) I remember, when standing by the south-eastern angle of the Haram Wall, and admiring the stones, "polished after the similitude of a palace," I thought of the words of Josephus, and it seemed that he had greatly exaggerated the facts of the case, since the apparent height of the wall was not so immense as to make any one giddy who looked down from the top. But the recent discovery by the agents of the Palestine Exploration Fund, has removed all doubts respecting the description by Josephus. No result of the important enterprise is so astounding as this. The explorers sunk a deep shaft, at a short distance from the angle, having to contend with difficulties and dangers, minutely related in the *Recovery of Jerusalem*, Int. xv. From the point thus reached, they cut a gallery in the direction of the wall, where they came upon layers of enormous marble blocks, resembling those so long familiar to travellers at the top of the mound of earth at that spot. The excavation proves that, at an immense depth, under an accumulation of *debris*, we have the original base of the temple wall. The course of the shaft and gallery is well represented in the publications of the Exploration Society ; and it indicates the wonderful extent of the wall from top to bottom, an extent which justifies the language of Josephus, and strikingly illustrates the account in Holy Scripture of the magnitude of the temple. The final results of their vast labour was at the conclusion

ORIGINAL BASE OF TEMPLE WALL

of the excavation of the south-east angle of the sanctuary —a discovery of the lowest point at "a little over 125 feet below the present surface. This is the greatest depth of *debris* we have yet found." (*Recovery of Jerusalem*, 187.)

"In the course of the exploration ancient pottery was found ; amongst the rest six vase handles. Each of these handles bears impressed upon it a more or less well defined figure, resembling in some degree a bird, but believed to represent a winged sun or disc, probably the emblem of the sun-god, and possibly of royal power. On each handle, Phœnician letters appear above and below the wings ; and these, in two instances, have been interpreted by Dr. S. Birch, of the British Museum, and imply that the vessels were made for the royal use, or, at all events, in a royally privileged manufactory." (*Recovery*, 474.)

S.

THE TEMPLE

1 Kings 6-7; 2 Chronicles 3-4

As no two persons who have attempted to describe or depict the temple built by Solomon

have furnished the same idea of the building, it is obvious that the materials which we possess, although sufficiently clear in some of the details, either do not suffice for conveying a distinct notion of the building as a whole, or else that the true signification of the architectural terms employed has not been correctly apprehended. A new source of information has, however, of late years presented itself, in the particulars which have been afforded respecting the plan and arrangements of ancient Egyptian temples,—a careful consideration of which enabled us, many years ago, to suggest the obvious analogy between them and the temple of Solomon. This has since been confirmed by many other writers of high name, and has been the more forcibly impressed upon our own conviction by the repeated occasions we have found of reconsidering the subject. The idea of such a comparison being once established, it became less difficult to apprehend much that had formerly seemed incomprehensible, and so to realize something like a distinct idea of the sacred structure.

The building was a rectangle,—sixty cubits long in the clear from east to west, and twenty cubits wide from north to south. Some take the cubit at half a yard, and scarcely any estimate makes it more than twenty-one inches ; and, taking even the largest estimate, it must be admitted that these dimensions are but small in comparison with Christian churches and Mohammedan mosques. But these are intended to contain great numbers of worshippers ; whereas this, like the Egyptian and other ancient temples, also of small dimensions, was not constructed with a view to the accommodation of worshippers, who never entered the interior,—all public worship and sacrifices being performed, not in the temple, but towards it (as the residence of the Deity), in the enclosed court or courts in front of the sacred house. Viewed with reference to this special object, and keeping in mind this essential difference, a building becomes large which seems small and insufficient compared with modern sacred structures. The temple was simply twice as large as the tabernacle. Those who accuse the sacred writers of exaggeration may do well to reflect on this instance, in which an apparent difficulty, thus satisfactorily explained, is at the first view created, not by the largeness, but by the smallness of the dimensions given.

Small as the temple was, its proportions were noble and harmonious. The porch was ten cubits deep; so that the interior, or cella, was equal to a treble square; but one square was divided off for the inner sanctuary, so that the just geometrical proportion was thus established. This prevented the appearance of narrowness which would have been given to the interior, had its dimensions remained unbroken by the division into the inner and outer holy place; while any appearance of narrowness in the exterior view was obviated by the storeys of chambers for the use of the priests built against the sides. These storeys were three, each storey wider than the one above it, as the walls were made narrower or thinner as they ascended, by sets-off of half a cubit on each side, on which rested the ends of the flooring joists, to avoid *inserting* them in the walls of the sacred building itself. Thus, *externally*, the building had the appearance of a small church, with a nave and two side aisles. But this was not the appearance internally, seeing that the side buildings were not, like the aisles of a church, open to the interior. These additions at the sides must have materially enlarged the apparent bulk of the building in the external view, which has been much overlooked in the usual estimates of its dimensions. If, as Josephus affirms, the porch was higher than the rest of the building, the resemblance to a church must have been still greater, as this would give the tower in front, besides the nave and two side aisles. Nor is this a strange coincidence; such Christian churches as have not been modelled after Greek and Roman temples, having been framed after what was conceived to have been the plan of Solomon's temple.

Like the Egyptian temples, that of Solomon was composed of three principal parts. The porch, or pronaos, the depth of which was equal to half of its length. Next to this was a large apartment, designated the Sanctuary, or Holy Place,—forty cubits long by twenty wide. This was the *naos*. And lastly, beyond this lay the third or innermost chamber, a square of twenty cubits, called the Holy of Holies, answering to the *sekos* of Egyptian temples, where was placed the ark with its hovering cherubim, and where also the most sacred objects of their religion were placed by the Egyptians. The arrangements of the external buildings, with the different courts, also coincided with the arrangements of Egyptian temples, as described by Strabo, and as they are still to be seen in the existing remains of ancient temples in that country.

The Holy of Holies, or inner sanctuary, was divided from the rest of the temple by a partition of cedar, in the centre of which was a pair of folding-doors of olive wood, very richly carved with palm-trees, and open flowers, and cherubim, —the whole overlaid with gold. A like pair of folding-doors, of grander dimensions, also overlaid with gold, embossed in rich patterns of cherubim, and knops, and open flowers, formed the outer entrance. Both pairs of doors were furnished with massive pins of gold (not " hinges," which were not known), turning in holes made in the lintel and the threshold.[1] These were, in Egypt, often of metal; and some of bronze have been found, and exist in cabinets of antiquities. The door forming the entrance to the Most Holy Place was left open, and the space covered, as is usual in the East, by a magnificent veil or curtain. It may be asked, how the interior received light, seeing that the storeys of chambers occupied the sides? But these buildings did not reach the top, and in the upper part of the wall between the flat roof of the chambers and the top of the wall of the main building, was a row of narrow windows which lighted up the interior.

The floor of the temple was formed of planks of fir, covered with gold. The inside walls and the flat ceiling were lined with cedar beautifully carved, representing cherubim and palm-trees, clusters of foliage and open flowers, among which, as in Egypt, the lotus was conspicuous; and the whole interior was so overlaid with gold, that neither wood nor stone was anywhere to be seen, and nothing met the eye but pure gold, either plain, as in the floor, or richly chased, as on the walls, and, as some think, with precious stones in the representation of flowers, and other enrichments. This style of ornamentation is quite

[1] See Vol. 1, pp. 556-559.

Oriental, and certainly ancient. The examples of it which have come under our notice, show that precious stones may be applied with greater advantage than is usually supposed to internal decoration, and satisfy us that they might, with truly rich and beautiful effect, be employed in this instance in setting off the costly enchasement in gold. That precious stones were employed in the interior decoration appears from 2 Chron. iii. 6, which expressly states that Solomon "garnished the house with precious stones." And we know that David provided for the work, and his nobles contributed "all manner of precious stones." (1 Chron. xxix. 2-8.)

It seems that even the inside of the porch was lined with gold. This front part of the building was also enriched with two pillars of brass—one called Jachin, and the other Boaz—which, being cast entire, seem to have been regarded as master-pieces of Hiram's art. They exhibited the usual

GATE OF THE TEMPLE OF LUXOR

proportions of Egyptian columns, being five and a half diameters high. Their use has been dis-puted. Some think that they stood as detached ornaments in front of or in the porch, like the

two obelisks which we often see before Egyptian temples; while others suppose that they con-tributed to support the entablature of the porch.

FACADE OF TEMPLE AT DANDOUR

Their height and dimensions are favourable to this opinion, as are the analogies afforded by Egyptian buildings, in which two pillars are seen supporting the entablature of the pronaos, resembling the two pillars on which rested the porch of the Philistine temple which Samson overthrew.

It is not our intention to notice the furniture of the temple, which was the same in kind as that of the tabernacle. The ark was the same as that made in the wilderness; but over it Solomon constructed two colossal cherubim of gold, whose inner wings, outspread, touched each other over the ark, while the outer wings touched the opposite walls of the sacred chamber. In the large hall, or outer chamber, there were also seven golden candelabra instead of one; and besides the table of shew-bread, which was the only table in the tabernacle, there were here ten golden tables, with others of silver, on which were laid out above a hundred golden vases of various patterns, with the different utensils—the censers, spoons, snuffers, etc.—all of gold, used in the service of the temple.

While the interior of the temple was literally lined with gold, and all its ornaments and furniture were of that rich metal, brass prevailed in the court in front of it—the inner court, in which the priests performed their ministrations. Here was a wonderful specimen of the skill of Hiram, in the shape of the great "molten sea," resting on the backs of twelve oxen of brass—in the

SUPPOSED FORM OF THE LAVER

same manner as the *stone* fountain in the palace of the old Moorish kings of Granada rests upon the backs of lions. Here there were also ten other lavers of the same metal, ornamented most richly.

From this it will be seen that the importance of the temple of Solomon, which we have been led to regard as one of the wonders of the ancient world, consisted not in its size—which, as regards the principal building, has been greatly exceeded in every civilized country, and by a vast number of churches in our own—but in the elaborate, costly, and highly decorative character of its whole interior and furniture, and also in the number, extent, grandeur, and substantial masonry of its surrounding courts, chambers, walls, and towers. Indeed, it is not too much to pre-

sume that these outer constructions, forming the massive ring in which the costly gem of the temple was set, cost as much as the sacred building itself, immense as was the quantity of gold bestowed upon it.

The dimensions of the temple of Solomon may be summed up as follows:—The Most Holy Place was a cube, twenty cubits long, twenty wide, and twenty high. The Holy Place was of the same width and height, but double the length. The porch was also of the same width and height, but only half the length of the Most Holy Place. The chambers round the temple were five cubits wide internally on the ground floor; and the side walls being each two and a half cubits thick, the whole space thus occupied was ten cubits. Taking these together, the ground plan of the temple measures eighty cubits by forty. The walls were twenty cubits high, and the pitch of the roof apparently ten cubits more; making the full height of the building thirty cubits. These dimensions were exactly double those of the tabernacle. It appears, however, from 2 Chron. iii. 4, that over the porch there was a tower, 120 cubits in height, being three times that of the building.

The temple stood in an open court, which was surrounded by a wall of three courses of stones, and a row of cedar beams. The height is not stated; but the probability is, it was double that of the court of the tabernacle, ten cubits. It would seem that spacious outer courts, with porches or cloisters, were afterwards added, though there is no direct mention of them in the Old Testament. Courts and cloisters are mentioned in the New Testament, but they, of course, belonged to the temple of Herod.

P.

"A good deal of speculation has lately prevailed as to whether the temple was copied from an Egyptian or an Assyrian model. The former was in vogue thirty or fifty years ago, but, since Layard's discoveries, the latter has been the favourite theory. Now that we have got a correct restoration of the Tabernacle, we are able to assert that the Temple was not copied from either the one or the other. According to the Book of Exodus, the plan of the Tabernacle was Divinely revealed to Moses, and when it came to be superseded by a more permanent structure, it was copied literally in plan and arrangement, with this singular and marked distinction, that in the Temple every dimension of the Tabernacle was exactly doubled. Thus :—The Holy of Holies in the Tabernacle was a cube of 10 cubits, in the Temple of 20. The Holy Place in the Tabernacle was a double cube of 10, in the Temple of 20 cubits. The porch of the Tabernacle was 5 cubits by 10, of the Temple 10 by 20. The verandah of the Tabernacle was 5 cubits wide, the chambers that surrounded the Temple measured 10. But perhaps the most remarkable concidence is that the angle of the roof made the Tabernacle 15 cubits in height, and consequently the Temple was raised by a false roof, or upper chamber, till its height was 30 cubits. Unfortunately, the dimensions of the court of Solomon's house are not given in the Bible or Josephus. But with the knowledge of this duplication before us, we may safely assume that the dimensions of the court of the Tabernacle were doubled also, and that the court of Solomon's Temple was in reality 100 cubits wide by 200 east and west, a dimension that we shall afterwards find fully confirmed by subsequent statements."

" In order to give an idea of the dimensions of Solomon's Temple, I may mention that the building itself was, as nearly as may, of the size of the Church of St. Paul's, Covent Garden. If that building had a flat roof, and its interior was occupied by two chambers, surrounded by a range of cells on three sides, it would, mechanically, very nearly represent the most celebrated building in the world. Most of our London churches, such, for instance, as St. Martin's-in-the-Fields, are, both as to dimensions and lithic ornament, larger and more splendid than Solomon's Temple. The truth seems to be that it was built in the 'Bronze Age' of architecture, which, unlike what happened in archæology, preceded the great 'Stone Age.' Its magnificence consisted in the brazen pillars of its porch, its brazen seas and altars, its cedar pillars covered with gold, and generally in its richness and metallic splendour. Those employed to build it were smiths, not masons, and consequently any attempt to compare it with our modern buildings is absurd, and, I am afraid, every attempt to restore its features by drawing equally hopeless. No specimen of the brazen architecture of those days has been preserved, and no representation of it is known to exist. So we must, at least, wait a little before we can hope to realize the appearance of this celebrated building."—*Fergusson's Holy Sepulchre*, 78-82.

The precise situation of the Temple on the great plateau overlooking the valley which separates it from the Mount of Olives, is another interesting question. The ridge of the hill of Moriah, as it now appears, runs from the north-west angle, nearly in a straight line, south-east by south, until it reaches the triple gate in the south wall, and then falls away very steeply. The threshing floor of Araunah the Jebusite, which, we know, became the site of the Temple, would naturally be on the summit, not on the side or edge—the winnowing of corn, in the days of David, being effected by tossing it up in the air. This circumstance at once withdraws our idea of the Temple site from the corners of the plateau, where the native rock declines, and fixes it somewhere in the middle, where the native rock attains its highest elevation. Herod's Temple enclosure appears to have consisted of the enclosure of Solomon's Temple, the old palace and a piece added at the south-west

angle making the whole a square of about 900 feet wide. The altar of sacrifice is suggested by Captain Warren to have been where is now the dome of the rock, on the platform of the Sakrah, to the south-west. The wall standing at the Jews' Wailing Place is, probably, part of Solomon's enclosure wall ; so, also, is the south-east corner. The south-west corner is of the time of Herod, and the south-east angle may be considered a work of the kings of Judah.

The conclusion thus formed as to the position of the ancient Temple, and its precincts, is in accordance with an impression which I received when in Jerusalem, and which was emphatically expressed by the eminent Prussian antiquary, Dr. Rosen, as made on his own mind, namely, that the present area is not a piece of patch-work, arising from additions made in Christian times to what had existed in Jewish days, and for a different purpose than was contemplated at the first ; but is coincident, or nearly so, with the plateau, as constructed by Solomon, and somewhat altered by Herod for the accomplishment of one simple object, and according to one original idea. There is unity of design apparent in the area, inconsistent with the notion of half of it having been laid down after the other half, and for totally different purposes. Such a notion is entertained by Mr. Fergusson in connection with his theory about the site of our Lord's sepulchre, to which we shall have occasion to refer hereafter.

S.

GOLD

THROUGHOUT the history of Solomon, nothing is more striking than the vast quantities of gold and silver which were in his possession, and which he employed in his great undertakings. but the statement of the quantities of these precious metals left by David for the work of the temple, carries our astonishment to the utmost stretch, and creates some suspicion, either that the numbers have been corrupted in the course of transcription, or that we do not rightly understand them.

The *gold* delivered by David to Solomon for ornamenting the temple, and for the fabrication of its utensils, was the following. As king, he bestowed the savings of his reign, amounting to 100,000 talents, which, at 125 pounds troy (equal to 93 pounds 12 ounces avoirdupois), which is the usual calculation, amounted to 12,500,000 pounds. Besides this, he gave, as an individual, out of his private estate, 3,000 talents, which, at the same calculation, make 375,000 pounds. The nobles also contributed 5,000 talents and 10,000 drachms (equal to 52 pounds), which, at the above rate, amount to 625,052 pounds. This makes the entire amount of gold no less than 13,500,052 pounds troy.

This was of gold. The silver was in full proportion. David, as king, bestowed a million of talents, making 125,000,000 pounds troy; to which, as an individual, he added 7,000 talents, weighing 875,000 pounds. Besides this, the nobles gave 10,000 talents, weighing 1,250,000 pounds. This makes the whole quantity of silver 127,125,000 pounds.

Such are the quantities of gold and silver set apart by David alone to the service of the temple, without taking into account any appropriations to the same purpose by Solomon himself. The imagination faints in the attempt to apprehend such inconceivable amounts. But as values are better apprehended than quantities, let us turn these weights into values.

The 13,500,052 pounds of gold, taken at the present value of pure gold, four pounds sterling the ounce, would be equal in value to £648,002,496. The silver, at the present price of the unalloyed metal, which is five shillings the ounce, would be no less than £381,375,000;—making together £1,029,377,496 sterling. But that our national debt exists, and is only one-fourth less than this amount, the mere idea of such a sum would be inconceivable. Let us look at it closely. To accumulate such a sum during the thirty-three years of his reign over the united kingdom, would have required David and his nobles to lay by above £31,000,000 every year, an amount equal to the *entire annual revenue* of the greatest realms in Europe, excepting our own.

In a curious and rare book before us,[1] we meet with this remarkable passage with reference to the vastness of this amount: "I have read a pamphlet, printed about a year and a half before the peace of Utrecht was concluded, which (as it was said) was written by the command of Queen Anne's ministry, that the subjects might be convinced of the necessity of a peace with France; and among the powerful motives made use of in that pamphlet, one of the strongest was, that the nation was fifty millions of pounds sterling in debt, which the author affirmed was the eighth

[1] Published in 1722, under the title of "The State of the Greatest King, set forth in the Greatness of Solomon and the Glory of his Reign." By George Renold's, Professor of the Mathematics (at Bristol).

part of the value of the whole kingdom. If that be true, then there was much above three times the value of this kingdom laid out upon the temple of the Lord at Jerusalem, which was built by Solomon, which is much above the value of two of the best kingdoms in Europe."

The comparison thus suggested may be pursued upon the more exact materials we now possess. If the above statement be correct, the value of this kingdom, which probably means the value of the real property, has increased in a proportion scarcely less astonishing than that of the national debt. The debt which, at fifty millions, excited apprehension in Queen Anne's reign, is now £768,789,240, and has been more. But the property which, at the same time, was reckoned at four hundred millions (*i. e.* eight times fifty millions), is now about six times that amount—the estimated value, at twenty-five years' purchase, of the real property assessed under the property and income-tax being £2,382,112,425. Yet, of this immense sum, the money left by David for the temple would not be greatly less than one half (say five-twelfths). It would exceed eight years' purchase of all the costly tillage of this country, and equal eleven years of the annual value of the real property in Great Britain. It would be equal to eleven and a half years' value of all the leading manufactures of the realm, and to twenty years' value of all the exported produce and manufactures of the country. It would also absorb, for about the same period, all the public revenue of the United Kingdom. To state this, is surely sufficient to show that there must be some error either in the text, or in our apprehension of it. Some of our ingenious arithmetical readers may, if they please, carry out the calculations further, by reckoning how many waggons, how many ships, would be required to carry all this metal, —what would be its cubic contents,—what extent of surface would it pave with sovereigns, flat or set on edge?—for how many miles would it extend a golden line?—and whether it would not take a man a century of constant employment to count it out in sovereigns?

These estimates must be admitted to be simply impossible, after making allowance to the utmost extent for the opportunities which David possessed of acquiring wealth by his conquests of the neighbouring nations. The plunder of the richest country in the world, though regarded even in the East as most amazing, did not furnish Nadir Shah with a twentieth part of this amount; and it may be safely affirmed that the treasures of all the kings of all the world, do not even at a far distance approach it. It therefore becomes necessary to seek some explanation. This is not difficult to find. The numbers stated are found in the book of Chronicles, which was written after the Babylonish Captivity. Now, it is reasonable to suppose that the people, most of whom were born and bred in Chaldea, used the weights and measures of that country—of which we have, indeed, a singular proof in the fact, that the Persian and Chaldean gold coin called the *daric* is mentioned in the computation of the donations of the nobles, although the coin was assuredly unknown in David's time.[1] Then the value of the Babylonian talent was greatly less than that of the Hebrews; that of the talent of gold being £3,500, and of silver £218, 15s., which would reduce the entire amount to about six hundred millions. This, though an immense reduction, seems still to be far too large: and some therefore think the Syriac talent to be intended, which was but one-fifth of the Babylonian. This would bring it down to the comparatively reasonable, and not absolutely impossible, sum of £120,000,000. There is an independent corroboration of this in the fact that Josephus, whether by so reading in the original text as then extant, or by reducing the talents into talents of accompt, produces nearly the same result, by making the talents of gold not more than ten thousand, and of silver a hundred thousand. Even this sum seems far too large in comparison with anything known to our experience; but we have no determinate data on which it may be further reduced, without supposing a corruption of the text of Chronicles. This is possible, from the facility with which numbers are corrupted in the course of time, as is illustrated in the circumstance that the numbers of Chronicles repeatedly differ from those of the same account in the book of Kings, and are always in excess; which may be the case here also, where there is no parallel text in Kings to employ the means of comparison. It is certain that the details in Kings, so far as given, are favourable to a lower estimate. For instance, it is stated in 2 Chron. iii. 8, that the gold consumed in overlaying the interior of the temple

[1] It is that which is rendered " dram " in 1 Chronicles 29:7.

was 600 talents, which, by the usual computation of the Hebrew talent, would make £3,600,000. The remaining consumption of gold upon the utensils and furniture could scarcely have more than doubled this; and if all the other materials —the brass, iron, stone, and timber—with the expense of skill and labour in the construction, not only of the central building, but of all the courts, walls, gates, corridors and towers, added another similar sum, the whole expense, on what seems to us a liberal calculation, would not much exceed ten millions. This is of itself an enormous sum, only to be explained by the extraordinary consumption of precious metal. This estimate, based on what is the most tangible item afforded in the book of Kings, also happens to be in accordance with other particulars which are given to us of the wealth of Solomon, who was proverbially said to have made gold and silver as common as stones in Jerusalem. He appears to have had more opportunities of acquiring wealth than David; and yet, when the accounts transmitted to us are examined, the millions come before us in units, not in tens, in hundreds, or in thousands. The largest sums that came to him were from the distant three-year voyages to Ophir, from king Hiram, and from the queen of Sheba.

It is stated in 1 Kings x. 14, that the weight of gold that came to Solomon in one year (besides that by inland traffic), was 666 talents —equal to £3,996,000. This was probably the year in which the Ophir fleet returned from its three years' voyage with 450 talents of gold, equal to £2,700,000. Another three years' voyage produced 420 talents, equal to £2,520,000. These are comparatively moderate sums, especially when the expense of the ships, the mariners, and their victuals for three years comes to be deducted. The queen of Sheba, coming from a gold-producing country, made Solomon a present of 120 talents of gold, equal to £720,000. The same quantity Solomon obtained from Hiram —doubtless for an equivalent consideration; and his want of so small a quantity of gold, as if to complete his works in that metal, strongly corroborates the impression that the amount left by David could not be so large as is usually supposed. Let it always be remembered that the gold was only wanted for ornamental work, and not as money. It does not therefore represent the *cost* of the works, but the actual metal worked up in them. Gold was a valuable property, but was not money; it was not the representation of value, as a medium of exchange. And this fact—its not being used as money—accounts for the great quantities thus expended. Had gold been a circulating medium, the use of such immense quantities in this manner would have been foolish, if not impossible. Silver was the standard of value; and hence it is that, although ten times as much silver as gold was accumulated for the undertaking, we read of very little being used up in the works of the temple. It has perplexed some to guess what became of it. The answer is easy: it was used to pay the workmen, and to purchase materials. It is very likely that Solomon may have bought gold with silver.

The fact is, that we who regard gold as a circulating medium, err greatly in transferring our own ideas of value to its ancient applications. Not being the medium of exchange, it was not diffused in small portions throughout a country, but, like jewels and other valuables, was accumulated in large masses in the hands of princes and individuals, who, not regarding it as available for money, though it was money's worth, wrought it up in various forms for the ornaments of their palaces and temples—considering justly, that they might as well do this as store it up in unwrought masses in vaults and jars. Had it been possible then, as now, to employ gold profitably, or to render the possession of it a source of income, in the shape of interest, no such vast collections of gold as we meet with in ancient times would have been heard of.

Gold was found in Ophir, Sheba, Uphaz Parvaim, and Raamah. Sir J. G. Wilkinson says there were gold mines in Egypt (*Ancient Egypt*, iii. 227), and whatever may be said to the contrary, there is evidence that Arabia contained the most precious of metals (*Bible Educator*, iii. 189). "The ships of Tarshish" brought treasures from the East—probably gold among the rest. Gold must have been abundant in Jerusalem during the latter part of David's reign and the whole reign of his son Solomon. The spoils of conquered countries must have been large; Syrians, Moabites, Ammonites, Philistines, and Amalekites were all laid under contribution, and how much a vanquished people in those days might be able to yield appears from the shekels of gold paid by the Midianites in earlier days (Numbers xxxi. 52; Judges viii. 26). Golden shields were captured from Hadadezer, King of Zobah. We read of Toi, King of Hamath, sending to David vessels of gold

as presents (2 Samuel viii. 10). A curious illustration of the abundance of treasure of this kind amongst half barbaric people occurs in an account given by the *Daily News* of the spoil taken from the King of Ashantee. Six or seven Ashantees paid over to the government gold-taker "a long white cloth of native manufacture, filled with gold plates and figures, nuggets, bracelets, knobs, masks, bells, jawbones and fragments of skull, plaques, bosses,—all of the metal as pure as it can be, and of an endless variety of shape and size. Besides these, door ornaments and golden nails were thrown in, and a number of odds and ends that must have been wrenched off in the hurry of escape from the palace, and which now added quaintness to the rich handfuls that were poured into the balance."—*Bible Educator*, iii. 190.

To these illustrations of the sources whence gold was derived, may be added others respecting the uses to which it was applied. "The lavish use of the precious metals in ornamentation was a peculiar feature of early Oriental architecture. Polybius tells us that the royal palace at Ecbatana was not only coated with them internally, but had a roof composed of thin plinths of silver (*Polyb.*, x. 27, §10). The temple of Anäitas, at the same place, was similarly adorned. According to Herodotus, two of the seven walls which guarded the palace had battlements of these metals. And recent researches have given reason to believe that two stages of the great temple at Borsippa—now known as the Birs Nimrud, had respectively a gold and a silver coating."—*Speaker's Com.*, ii. 513; 1 Kings vi. 22.

S.

WORKING IN METAL

1 Kings 7:13-51

SOME have thought that the covering of the interior of Solomon's temple with gold was simply *gilding*, which, from the extraordinary ductility of gold, would have been a comparatively inexpensive operation. The only objection to this is, that it would have been too little expensive. It is expressly stated that six hundred talents, or 75,000 pounds troy, of gold were consumed in this overlaying, which shows that it was not laid on very thinly; indeed, any reader, whose taste lies in that direction, may calculate how thickly the gold was spread, for he knows the space required to be covered. The phrase in 1 Kings vi. 35, that "the gold was fitted upon the carved work," agrees also with overlaying better than with gilding. Besides, we have no right to lower the magnificent terms descriptive of decoration and wealth in the sacred narrative to this extent, bringing the whole down to a piece of gilding. The considerations advanced at the close of yesterday's illustration show that the economical use of the metal could have been no object.

Apart from this view of the case, we should have preferred the gilding to the overlaying,—at least in those parts in which the gold covered figures and ornaments carved in wood. The sharpness and delicacy of the carving would also have been certainly better seen through the gilding than through a layer of metal. It would seem that the art of chasing in simple gold was not practised upon any large scale, or was not judged expedient in this case. It was thought preferable to carve the wood, and to force the overlaid gold into the shape of the carvings,— the surface of the gold being probably touched up with graving tools to bring out the sharpness of the carving. Unless this had been the process, it would have been absurd to carve the wood at all, seeing that it was afterwards to be covered with gold. But that the carved wood was to form the base of the enchasement explains all; and although economy was not the object, the process was more economical than a surface enchasement in solid gold; and, if left hollow inside, the raised parts would have been more liable to injury than when backed, and the hollows filled by the wooden carvings behind. This was, perhaps, the principal object of these carvings.

Of the existence of the art of *overlaying* with gold, from the most ancient times, in Egypt, the most satisfactory evidence is furnished by the actual remains of overlaid work, which are by no means of infrequent occurrence. We might also point to the overlaying with gold in some of the works of the tabernacle, such as the ark and altar of incense, by the Israelites, immediately on their departure from Egypt. Among the examples of this work derived from that country, there is in the British Museum a small figure of the god Amun, in silver, having the head-dress and the lower part of the body represented by plates of gold laid over the silver. There is also, in the same collection, the finger of a mummy overlaid with silver. A few years ago, a mummy was

FIGURE OF THE GOD AMUN

found in the necropolis of Thebes, entirely wrapt in plates of gold. It was unfortunately broken up by the Arabs, on its discovery, for the sake of the metal; and the only remnant of it is a signet ring bearing the name of Pharaoh-Mœris. There are, likewise, in the Museum of the Louvre several small female figures in wood, of exquisitely beautiful workmanship, having the hair and parts of the dress represented by plates of gold or silver overlaid. In one of the tombs at Beni Hassan there is even found what appears to be a representation of the very operation of overlaying. We see a kind of press or chest,

EGYPTIAN OPERATION IN METALS

inscribed "the gold chest." The person engaged with it is called "the giver out of the gold." He hands out to the workmen bars of gold, or more probably thin slips of gold-latten, which they are fixing by strong manual pressure, without any apparent aid from tools, upon a block, bearing some general resemblance to an ark or sacred

EGYPTIAN OPERATION IN METALS

chest. The hieroglyphic inscription over their heads signifies "fixing," or "fastening on." It is very clear that the representation is that of overlaying with gold, though the details of the process cannot be clearly made out.

Much is said of the *casting* of metal by Hiram —particularly as regards the casting of the great brazen laver, with the oxen on which it rested, and of the two pillars, Jachin and Boaz. The former, at least, seems, as a work of art, to have been worthy of all the praise it drew forth, and clearly evinces the perfection to which this branch of metallurgy had been carried. The basin, and oxen on which it was to rest, were, we should suppose, cast separately. They were cast in the plain of the Jordan, between Succoth and Zarathan, for which, considering the distance, and the difficulty of the road for the subsequent conveyance of the work to Jerusalem, there must have been some potent reason, which is furnished by the fact that it was a "clay ground," and therefore suited to these extensive operations in the casting of metals.

There are paintings in one of the tombs at Thebes which throw light on this operation also. One group represents the blowing of the furnace, preparatory to melting the metal. A workman on each side of the fire is working the double bellows, an implement similar in principle to that now in use, but very different in construc-

EGYPTIAN OPERATION IN METALS

tion. It consisted of two boards, connected by a leathern collar. Each man stands with his feet on two such bellows, and holds in each hand a cord fastened to their upper boards. He works them with a seesaw motion, pressing down one of them with his foot, and at the same time inflating the other by raising the upper board with the opposite hand. They communicate with the fire by means of reeds coated with clay at the end next the fire. A third workman at the same time stirs the fire ; and behind them is a heap of fuel, and a vessel containing the metal to be fused. A second picture exhibits a further stage of the process. The metal is in a state of fusion, and the workmen have left the bellows, and are removing the crucible from the fire by means of two rods or thick wires, the ends of which are coated with clay. This mode of removing the crucible would require great caution and dexterity on the part of the workman, as was the case with all the operations of ancient art.

A third picture carries the operation still farther. It represents the rough exterior of a large mould of baked clay, with a row of many earthen funnels at the top of it, into all of which the molten metal was poured successively, for the purpose of diffusing it equally over the entire internal surface. Two workmen are depicted in the act of pouring metal into one of them. In founding large casts the metal is poured into many apertures by the Arab workmen at the

present day. The objection that, by this piecemeal application, a part would cool in the mould

EGYPTIAN OPERATION IN METALS

before the remainder could be introduced, is met by the operations of a third figure, who is emptying fuel, apparently charcoal, from a basket, for the purpose of kindling a fire around the mould,

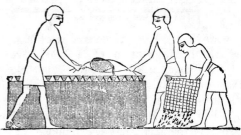

EGYPTIAN OPERATION IN METALS

in order to keep it at a high temperature for some time after it has received the metal. This process greatly improves both the delicacy and beauty of the cast, and the temper of the metal. It is used for bronze-castings in China, and is said to be one of the causes of their great superiority over those of European artists.

It is not said that any of the works in connection with the temple were of "beaten" gold, or other metal. Yet neither is it said that any were "cast," or founded, except the brazen sea, the lavers, and the pillars,—all of which were of brass. All the rest are said simply to have been "made ;" and probably all were beaten, those larger works only being cast. The golden candelabrum of the tabernacle was, we know, of beaten gold ; and no doubt the ten candelabra of Solomon were similarly constructed. Although this is not distinctly stated, it is, from the nature of things, almost as certain as if it were. Indeed, at a much later period, the ancients seem only to have resorted to casting when the work was too large to be conveniently executed by any other process. And that this common mode of operation was in use in the time of Solomon, in application to works that admitted of it, incidentally transpires in the statement, that the shields and targets subsequently made for this magnificent king were of "beaten gold." We conceive that, with the known exceptions, all the vessels and utensils of the temple were thus made; and, indeed, what was the overlaying of the interior of the temple but an application of beaten gold? Of this process there is also a representation in the same tomb at Beni Hassan which exhibits

EGYPTIAN OPERATION IN METALS

the overlaying. It represents a workman engaged in the fabrication of a brazen vessel, something like a crock. The process is the same as that in use at the present day,—the man places the material on an anvil, and shapes it with a hammer. It almost passes belief, however, but is the fact, that the hammer has no handle—the workman holding *in his hand* the piece of metal with which he operates. Mr. Osburn well remarks on this: "The jar occasioned to the nerves of the hand by this violent contact of metal with metal, without the interposition of a wooden handle or other deadening substance, would be intolerable to a modern workman, or, if he had resolution to persevere, would probably bring on tetanus. Long practice from an early age, had habituated the robust frames of the ancient mechanics to these rude concussions." We might also indicate the loss of power in the strokes by the absence of the lever which the handle furnishes. This matter seems so strange, that we have looked through copies of Egytian figures engaged in various arts, as we find them in different works, and have been unable to discover a handled hammer in any of them. Accompanying the hammerer are two figures engaged in the process of heating a piece of metal which they are manufacturing into some sort of utensil. The one blows up the charcoal fire with a blowpipe, while the other holds the metal to the flame. The application of beating to the fabrication of many delicate and elaborate works in gold, is shown abundantly in the Egyptian tombs. The tools employed seem to have been small pieces of metal, like chisels of various shapes, held in the hand, and struck

upon the gold to produce the required pattern. Notwithstanding that the lack of those mechanical means which modern workmen possess, rendered the tax upon the skill, precision, and patience of the individual workman very great, exceedingly beautiful works were completed by the goldsmiths of ancient Egypt, as some existing remains of them testify, and as is still more completely evinced by the elegant and richly ornamented vases represented in the tombs of the kings and elsewhere.

WINDOWS

1 Kings 6:4

"WINDOWS of narrow lights" are assigned to the temple in the text of the authorized version, while the margin affords the alternative of "windows broad *within* and narrow *without*, or *skewed and closed*." "Skewed" means "slanted;" so "a-skew," that is, aslant. None of these versions gives much information; and their variety only shows the obscurity of the original term. The one that seems most intelligible and distinct —" broad *within* and narrow *without*"—is only obtained by inserting the words in italics, which are supplied to complete the sense, the words being thus indicated as not existing in the original. Divested of these interpolations, the phrase would be, "windows broad and narrow," which certainly, if found in the original, which is not the case, would need something to make sense of it. This idea is, however, founded on the statement of Josephus with respect to Herod's temple, and is reasonable, by its intrinsic probability—this form of window being best calculated to radiate the light into the interior through thick walls, and hence it is very general in our own churches, as also in ancient sacred buildings; "partly," as an old writer observes, "for the strength's sake of the building, partly for devotion, which is much distracted by great and glaring windows,[1]—much like, it seems, they were to the windows of some of our ancient

[1] *Orbis Miraculum; or, The Temple of Solomon Pourtrayed by Scripture Light.* [No author's name on title, but the preface subscribed "Samuel Lee."] Folio. London, 1659.

British churches, as particularly that of Saint Paternus, now Llanbadern-vawre, in Cardiganshire, in Wales, or some of the more ancient Saxon churches in this land." We know nothing, however, positively of the form or position of the windows, except that they must have been high up—at least fifteen cubits above the pavement—because the "chambers" on the outside of the temple reached as high, if not higher. As to their shape, no more probable idea can be suggested than that they resembled some one of the kinds of windows found in ancient Egyptian buildings and representations, which in fact present such forms as answer to all the various conjectures which have been offered. We know that one of Solomon's later buildings—his palace, called "the house of the forest of Lebanon"—had three rows of square windows, in which light was opposite to light on the different sides of the building.

A curious question has been raised as to the way in which they were closed, so as to exclude birds and bats, and rain, while admitting the light. We know from experience that, in the East, bats will enter through windows affording any apertures that will admit them, and establish themselves, clustered to the ceilings of even inhabited rooms, through all the day time, only leaving the place at night in search of food; and,

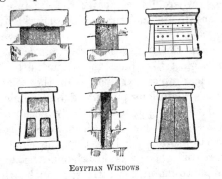

EGYPTIAN WINDOWS

whatever may have been the case with private dwellings, means must have been found of preventing such incidents in a structure so sacred.

The learned old author lately quoted, asked whether it might not be that glass was employed, "seeing the Phœnicians, the first inventors of it, were neighbours to the people of Israel, and gave great assistance to this glorious work. Besides, it is sufficiently known that the glassy sands of the river Belus were within the territories of the

tribe of Asher.[1] But whether the discovery was so ancient as the time of Solomon, I have not yet read." This information is now in part supplied. It would seem, however, that the manufacture was long in the hands of the Phœnicians, its

SAREPTA

principal seats being at Sidon and Sarepta,—and so long it was accounted a precious commodity and esteemed an article of luxury,—which may the rather lead to the supposition of its having been used in the temple, if at all known at this time to the Phœnicians. For a long time after it became known, glass was not in very common use. A modern author[2] infers this from the small number of the glass-houses ascribed, even so late as the time of Pliny, to the Phœnicians; and seems to assert that much use for it was not found. "While the mildness of the climate in all southern countries, as well as all over the East, rendered any other stoppage of windows unnecessary, except that of curtains or blinds, goblets of the precious metals or stones were preferred as drinking vessels." To the first statement we demur; for the winter cold is often severer in the countries in question than this writer assumes; and in summer, it is always desired to exclude the birds, bats, and many large and troublesome insects which abound in the East. But he is right in supposing that glass was not, even after it became known, generally used for the purpose;

[1] This alludes to the alleged accidental discovery of glass from the vitrification of the sands beside this river, by a fire kindled by some travellers.

[2] Heeren. *Researches*, vol. ii. p. 88.

nor is it at present, even where it might be obtained at no great expense.

Herodotus[1] states that the Ethiopians were wont to deposit their dead in sarcophagi hollowed out of masses of crystal, which is dug in abundance in their country, and which was so transparent that the bodies enclosed within were perfectly visible. Dr. Lee regards this as a datum for the antiquity of glass; but remarks, that there is no intimation to what earlier age its use may have extended. But he forgot that the Greek word ($\H{v}\alpha\lambda o\varsigma$), which is indeed used for glass, also means any transparent material, as crystal, various kinds of stones, and the like; and the statement of the mode in which it was obtained, shows that certainly it was not glass, whatever else it may have been. It was doubtless of much more ancient use than the time to which the statement refers, and might have been applicable to windows, if that use for it had been thought of. But from the manner in which it is mentioned by the historian, it seems to have been confined to Ethiopia, and to the use which he indicates.

Pursuing his inquiry after glass, Dr. Lee remembers "the Arabian story of the pyramids, recited by the learned Mr. Greaves, that the king which built the pyramids put in the westermost of them glass that might be bended, and not broken. This entire story is by him counted little less than a romance. Yet possibly there might be rocks in Ethiopia like those in Muscovia (Russia), mentioned by M. Fletcher in his history, whose scalings might be transparent and flexible, and not so fragile as our artificial glass, and which we use for ship lanthorns and other ends." This may have been talc or scaly mica, which, if then known, may have very well been used for windows in the absence of glass. The want of transparency would have been no objection, but rather a recommendation, for temples at least. Translucency was the only quality desired, and the lack of transparency would have availed to prevent irreverent persons from looking into the interior from the roofs of the collateral buildings. Still, we do not imagine that such substances were used, whatever be the value of Mr. Greaves' "Arabian story of the pyramids."

The earliest indication of real glass which can be found in ancient writers is that of Theo-

phrastus (320 B.C.), who, in his Greek work on Stones, speaks of it, but, as it seems to us, as a matter not within the range of his own observation and experience. "If glass be made, *as some affirm*, of the Uëlitis—a vitrifiable sand,—it owes its production to the extreme force of fire. The best is that in the making of which flints have also been used; for, besides that they melt and mix with the general mass, they have a peculiar excellency in the making of glass, insomuch that they give the differences in the clearness of the colour." Some of the editions of this author have "brass" for "flints," and are doubtless wrong. Sand was certainly the first ingredient ever used or thought of for the making of glass; and for many years there was no other sand used than that found clean washed on the banks or in the beds of rivers, and this from its use might very probably acquire the name of Uëlitis or "glass-sand." That the further improvement of using flint was so well known to this old author, implies a much remoter antiquity of the original invention.

In the Old Testament there is no explicit mention of glass. All our readers know that the "looking-*glasses*" of the women, mentioned in Exodus xxxviii. 8, were not of glass. It is clear that, like the other ancient mirrors, they were of polished metal—in this case of brass. So also where Job compares the expanse of the heavens to "a molten looking-glass." In both places the word "mirror" would have been better in the translation. We must not, however, neglect to request the reader's attention to the remarkable text where, in the relation of Joshua's victorious pursuit of his enemies, it is stated that he pursued them "even unto Zidon and Misrephoth-maim." (Josh. xi. 8.) Taken in connection with the fact, that the chief manufacture of glass was at Sidon, the name of Misrephoth-maim has attracted much attention. The versions vary in the translation of it. In the marginal reading of our Bibles, we have "burnings," or "salt-pits." One Latin version makes it to mean "burnings of water;" another has "the conflux of waters;" another, "the place of hot baths;" another, "the salt-pit waters." John Rogers' translation (1539) has "whotte waters," and the margin of the Bishops' Bible (1752) has "bryne or salt-pits;" but Tremellius translates it, "to the glass furnaces." The original words *literally* agree to the first trans-

<hr>

[1] *Thalia*, xxiv., confirmed by Strabo, *Geog.* xvii., and Diodorus, ii. 15; iii. 9.

lation, and the others are *interpretations* thereof. It has been well conjectured that we should take the words to mean, "burnings *by* water," not "of water;" and this a great Hebrew scholar (Gesenius) is inclined to understand of either lime-kilns or smelting furnaces situated near water. But there is no apparent reason why these should be near water; whereas, there is an obvious one in regard to glass furnaces, on account of the sand. Certain it is, that this alternative much engaged the fancy of the no less learned than valiant Sir Walter Raleigh, who thought that the passage might furnish ground for a good conjecture, that the glass sands of the river Belus were in demand for this use as early as the time of Joshua.[1] This is not impossible or incredible; and although it cannot be *proved* from the passage under consideration, the fact that glass is really of as ancient, or still more ancient, date, is proved from the monu-

EASTERN LATTICE WINDOW

ments of Egypt, in which the process of glass-blowing is represented in paintings whose date reaches up to the time of Joseph; and actual specimens are extant of glass ornaments manufactured about the time of the Exodus.

Our own opinion is, that the windows were filled with close lattice-work, which was probably in this instance gilded. This is still, in the East, the favourite mode of filling windows, even where

[1] *History of the World*, i. 2; vii. 3.

glass is in partial use, as being better suited to a warm climate; for it admits not only light, but air, and, as completely as glass, excludes bats and birds, and almost as effectually insects, for it is well known that few insects will pass through lattice or net-work, even where the interstices are much larger than their own bodies. Latticed windows are preferred also for this, that they allow persons within to view distinctly all that passes without, while no one on the outside can see the persons within. In winter the cold is excluded by curtains, or translucent coverings inside the lattice.

In confirmation of this it may be stated, that lattices are indicated in Scripture long before, and long after, this period. The mother of Sisera watched through "the lattice" for the return of her son;[1] Ahaziah "fell down through the lattice;[2] and the bridegroom in Solomon's Song "shows himself through the lattice."[3] But what is more to the purpose, the very passage which we noticed at the outset, with regard to the temple windows, may very well signify "windows with closed (fixed) bars," which is a very good indication of lattice work. The art of forming the patterns of such lattices is much studied in the East; and the Oriental craftsmen frequently produce really beautiful and most elaborately executed specimens of joinery in this department.

THE CHERUBIM

"THOU shalt not make unto thee any graven image, nor any likeness of anything that is in heaven above, or that is in the earth beneath, or that is in the waters under the earth."[4]

These were among the words which the voice of the Lord was heard to utter amid the thunderings and the lightnings of Mount Sinai; and which were afterwards engraven upon the tables of stone. Yet only five chapters farther on, the same voice commands Moses to "make two cherubim of gold on the two ends of the mercy-seat, and the cherubim shall stretch forth their wings on high, covering the mercy-seat (the ark) with

[1] Judges 5:28.
[2] 2 Kings 1:2.
[3] Song of Solomon 2:9.
[4] Exodus 20:4.

their wings, and their faces shall look one towards another; towards the mercy-seat shall the faces of the cherubim be."[1] Here were creatures having at least wings and faces, whatever their general form may have been. But it is remarkable that no description of their figures is given, in a document which minutely describes less essential particulars. The inference is, that the figure of the cherubim was, from the traditions of Eden, too well known to Moses and to the Israelites to require minute description; although it became of importance to define the place they were to occupy amid "the shadows of good things to come," which the tabernacle service embodied.

Solomon not only preserved the original cherubim, but, the most holy place in the temple being much larger than the corresponding portion of the tabernacle, he made two colossal cherubim, which were placed, one on each side of the ark, with expanded wings, so that two wings touched each other over the ark while the other two reached the opposite walls. Besides this, the figures of cherubim were multiplied in the golden enchasements which lined the temple. Not only so, but there were images of oxen supporting the brazen sea, and figures of lions designed upon the bases of the ten lavers in the court of the temple; while there were within, among the interior adornments of the fretted gold, figures of palm trees, lilies, and pomegranates.

Was the commandment transgressed by this? Certainly not as to the cherubim, seeing that the original introduction of this figure was by divine direction. As to the other figures introduced by Solomon, there has been difference of opinion. Josephus, and the Jews generally, seem to think that they were unlawful, and that they opened the way to that idolatry which eventually proved this king's ruin. But it does not seem likely that he would transgress a recognized prohibition in the construction of the very temple itself: and as it is stated that David left the pattern of everything to Solomon, it would appear that there was no harm in them, even in his zealous eyes, nor in those of the priests, who would not have failed to point out the error. We are not, in fact, to interpret these things by the rigid constructions of a later age, which refined upon the most simple ordinances, and carried them out to the utmost possibilities, far beyond their original intention. Even Mohammed, who en-

[1] Exodus 25:18-22.

forced the prohibition of pictures and sculptures with great rigidity, and declared that artists should be punished at the last day, by being required to infuse life into their paintings; and who said, "Every painter is in hell-fire; and God will appoint a person, at the day of resurrection, for every picture he has drawn, to punish him; and they will punish him in hell,"—even he added, "Then if you must make pictures, make them of trees and things without souls." And so the matter is understood by his followers, who object only to the representation of the human figure—and not always to that,—or to pictures designed to represent celestial or infernal intelligences. It appears that the intention of the divine prohibition was to obviate the remotest occasion of idolatry, by forbidding the representation of any object with the view of offering worship to it. This is rendered clear enough, by the significant words added to the prohibition: "Thou shalt not bow down thyself to them, nor serve them."

With regard to the objects besides the cherubim, they certainly were representations of things "in the earth beneath." If unlawful, therefore, it must be urged that they were not, like the cherubim, sanctioned by a divine command; and that, in introducing them into the sacred building, Solomon exceeded the pattern received from his father, and for which that father seems to advance some claim to a divine inspiration. Yet it is obvious that these objects could not be in the same degree liable to idolatrous abuse as the cherubim, which *had* the divine sanction, and which occupied the place of honour in the sacred structure. It has been urged, indeed, that these figures, being symbolical combinations, represented creatures not existing in heaven above, in the earth beneath, or in the water under the earth. It may be so; and yet, although such creatures might be non-existent taken as a whole, they were composed of parts which, separately, represented real existences. And this argument, if pressed, would go to sanction the dog-headed and hawk-headed idols of Egypt, seeing that they represented creatures existing only in separate parts; and, in fact, exhibited that very form of idolatry to which the Israelites, when fresh from Egypt, would be particularly prone.

But it is time to ask, What was the form of these cherubim?

In the first chapter of his prophecy, Ezekiel, a captive in Assyria, describes certain " living creatures " that he beheld in a vision. He does not say there that they were the temple cherubim; but they certainly were so, for in another vision, narrated in the tenth chapter, he is transported in the spirit to Jerusalem, and is set down in the precincts of the temple, then still standing. There he beheld, among other objects, *the same " living creatures,"* and the throne previously described, standing in the inner court. " Then," he adds, " the glory of the Lord (the Shekinah that rested above the cherubim in the inner sanctuary) departed from off the threshold of the house, and stood over the cherubim; and the cherubim lifted up their wings, and mounted up from the earth in my sight. . . . *This is the living creature that I saw* (in the former vision) *under the God of Israel by the river of Chebar;* and I KNEW THAT THEY WERE THE CHERUBIM." He then gives a description of them in conformity with his previous account, but somewhat less particular. It is clear that he did not at first recognize the temple cherubim in the living creatures he beheld in the first vision; but now, from the position of the same creatures in the temple, he knows that the figures he had previously seen were the cherubim. Let us therefore turn back to his description. There were four of them, and they all *" had the likeness of a man.* And every one had four faces, and every one had four wings. And their feet were straight feet; and the sole of their feet was like the sole of a calf's foot: and they sparkled like the colour of burnished brass. And they had the hands of a man under their wings on their four sides; and they four had their faces and their wings. Their wings were joined one to another; they turned not when they went, they went every one straight forward. As for the likeness of their faces, they four had the face of a man and the face of a lion on the right side; and they four had the face of an ox on the left side; they four also had the face of an eagle. Thus were their faces: and their wings were stretched upwards; two wings of every one were joined one to another, and two covered their bodies."

This information respecting the figures of the cherubim throws light upon what has seemed a difficulty to many—the introduction of the figures of oxen and lions in the temple court, as supporters of the brazen sea, and on the lavers. The heads of these animals being combined in one figure in the cherubim, Solomon might feel that there could be no impropriety in employing separately creatures composing that figure. They were therefore separate parts of the cherubic figure, and as such lawful, although representations of living objects. Solomon may have felt some scruple about using the entire compound figure anywhere but within the temple itself, and therefore thus embodied the parts separately. The connection between them and the cherubim, though not at the first view obvious to us, must have been clear to the Israelites; and this could not but tend to obviate that danger of idolatry which might have existed in the absence of any such connection.

This is not the only instance of the separation of the cherubim into their component parts; for there can be no question that, as the four " living creatures " of Ezekiel are identical with the cherubim, so are the " four beasts " which make so eminent a figure in John's apocalyptic vision. " Before the throne there was a sea of glass, like unto crystal: and in the midst of the throne, and round about the throne, were *four beasts*, full of eyes before and behind. And the first beast was like a lion, and the second beast like a calf, and the third beast had a face as a man, and the fourth beast was like a flying eagle. And the four beasts had each of them six wings about

WINGED HUMAN FIGURES FROM BABYLON, NINEVEH, &c.

him; and they were full of eyes within, and they rest not day and night, saying, Holy, holy, holy, Lord God Almighty, which was, and is, and is to come." Here we have a winged lion, a winged ox, a winged man, and a winged eagle. In the figure of the cherubim we have the four combined—that is all the difference. Yet not all; for each of these figures has *six* wings, whereas the cherubim have but four. We may reach the reason for this difference, by recollecting that of the four cherubic wings, two were for flying, and the other two for dress, forming a kind of screen or skirt for the lower part of the figure—as in Isaiah's *six*-winged seraphim (which were also essentially cherubic), "with twain he covered his face, with twain he covered his feet, and with twain he did fly." The two additional wings may therefore be meant to denote, that as the cherubim in this view are nearer the throne and the incumbent majesty than in the other, it was proper that their persons should be more completely veiled from the glance of that Holy One, in whose sight the heavens are not clean.

It will, no doubt, be recollected that figures more or less analogous to the cherubim have been found in Egypt, and among all the nations of south-western Asia—in Assyria, in Persia, and in Asia Minor. Some exhibit the same combination as in the temple cherubim; but we have also the separate parts of the same, just as they were separable even under the Hebrew symbolization. Symbols the cherubim assuredly were, and not representations; and the heathen figures doubtless belonged to the same system of symbolization, if they did not symbolize the same things,—which may partly have been the case, if all were founded on dim traditions, common to all the races of men, of the cherubim stationed to keep the way of man's lost paradise.

WINGED HUMAN FIGURES FROM BABYLON, NINEVEH, &c.

We are at once reminded of the winged human figures of Egypt, Babylon, Nineveh, and Persia, —of which the last were remarkable, as known to be representations of disembodied souls. In the next engraving, to the left, is a figure of the great Cyrus, winged, to show that he is no more of this world—a fact to which there will be occasion to refer. Opposite to it we place a figure, analogous in form, from the sculptures recently discovered at Nineveh. There are

WINGED PORTRAIT OF CYRUS, AND SCULPTURE FROM NINEVEH

others of the same kind, as elaborately carved in the wings and raiment, and all holding what appears like a fir cone in the right hand, and a sort of basket in the left. They are little distinguished from each other, except one, which, upon the winged body, exhibits the head of an

WINGED SPHINX AND BULL

eagle. The import of these Assyrian images has not yet been determined; but will probably prove to be the same as that of the Persian figures of the like kind. The Babylonian figure placed in the middle between two others on the first column of this page, has the same essential characteristics.

Still more does the figure of the cherubim bring to mind the human heads attached to the bodies of winged lions and oxen in the sculptures of the same countries and Assyria, as in the sphinx of Egypt—too well known to need description,—a like figure at Babylon, and the same combination of beast, bird, and man, at Persepolis. In this latter case the beast is a bull; so it is also in the Assyrian colossal figure lately brought to this country from Nineveh, in which it is remarkable that the ears of the human head are those of the bull. In another similar figure from the same quarter, the body is that of a lion instead of a bull. These figures may suggest the question, whether the bulls and lions of Solomon were not likewise winged, to indicate their connection with the cherubim, and to show that the images were symbolical. The latter figure (of the lion), which we introduce, is that,

WINGED LION FROM NINEVEH

the discovery of which excited a strong sensation among the natives, as recorded by Layard. It is in admirable preservation. The expression is calm, yet majestic. The cap has three horns,—a circumstance which seems to be especially worthy of notice, as pointing to an intended combination of the man, the lion, the bull, and (in the wing) the eagle.

In other instances, in the same countries, we have the heads, and sometimes the wings, of birds, generally eagles, attached to human bodies. This is frequent in Egypt; where, also, we find the rare example of a human head affixed to a bird's body. Of the eagle's head and wings attached to a human body, a remarkable example has been found at Nineveh; [1] and one very similar occurs in a Babylonian cylinder.

In other cases, the heads of birds, usually eagles, are mounted on the bodies of other animals; and, more rarely, the head of one animal upon the body of another. In all these combinations, any

[1] Layard, i. 125.

other creature than the four combined in the cherubic symbol scarcely ever appears. In none of them are the four combined in one figure, as in the cherubim; and in the highest combinations —as those in which man, beast, and bird are united—the combination is so far different, that separate parts are taken to make one body, and none have more than one head; whereas, in the cherubim, four *faces* (not necessarily *heads*) appeared upon one body. We apprehend the common representations err in giving the different heads, instead of merely different *faces*, to the cherubim, and also in bestowing upon them the lower limbs of oxen. It is clearly stated that the human figure predominated, and even hands are mentioned; but, lest it should be supposed

HUMAN HEADED BIRD FROM EGYPT, AND WINGED HUMAN FIGURE

that it had human feet also, it is added that the feet were like those of a calf. We infer that all the body was human, excepting the head, which had four faces, and excepting the feet, although the legs may have been human; the wings were partly a vesture, and partly instruments of motion.

DOCTRINE OF THE CHERUBIM

WE may be reasonably anxious to inquire into the meaning of the figures to which a place so eminent was assigned, first in the tabernacle, and afterwards in the temple. That they were representations of objects actually existing in the "heaven above," has been supposed by very few. They were, therefore, symbols; and the question is, What did they symbolize? On this question every conceivable variety of opinion has been entertained. By various expositors the cherubim are made to signify either the four covenants; or all the creatures; or the four cardinal virtues—justice, wisdom, fortitude, and temperance; or the four faculties in the soul—

rational, irascible, concupiscible, and conscience; or the four chief passions—joy, grief, hope, and fear; or the four great monarchies; or the four elements; or the four evangelists; an opinion, this last, which seems to have been entertained by those who assigned the symbols—the angel, the lion, the ox, and the eagle—usually in paintings connected respectively with Matthew, Mark, Luke, and John. We shall not waste upon these crudities the space which may be better given to more received opinions.

One of these is, that the cherubic figures were intended to symbolize the Divine Persons in the sacred Trinity,—the figure of the lion being associated with the human form, to indicate the promised incarnation. This opinion was warmly and ably maintained by the learned but fanciful Hutchinson, and by others who more or less leaned to his opinions,—such as Parkhurst, Bishop, Horne, Julius Bates, Romaine, and Cuming. It has not, however, stood the test of criticism, and has now few supporters. In the first place, it would have been in direct opposition—and that, too, under the sanction of divine authority—to the stringent prohibition of making any similitude of God—of aught designed to represent Him. "Take ye good heed to yourselves," said Moses to the people, "for ye saw no manner of similitude in the day the Lord spoke to you in Horeb out of the midst of the fire; lest ye corrupt yourselves, and make you a graven image, the similitude of any figure." It would surely be monstrous for this to be followed by an injunction to make a representation of the Trinity to be set in the most holy place. Besides, the Divine Presence—the Shekinah—is always spoken of as distinct and separate from the cherubim,—it "dwelt between the cherubim." So, in Ezekiel's vision, the four "living creatures," or cherubim, are "*under* the God of Israel;" and in Rev. v., the four *zoa*, "beasts," "living creatures," or cherubim, rendered thanks to Him that sat upon the throne; they, with the four-and-twenty elders, *fell down* before the Lamb, and sang this new song, "Thou wast slain, and hast redeemed us to God by thy blood." It is surely unnecessary to point out the incompatibility of these circumstances with this view of the cherubic symbol.

Another opinion, and indeed the general one at this day, is that which considers the cherubim to be holy angels, and the figures of them in the sanctuary to be symbolical representations of their nature and ministry. But how could angels, or any order of angels, say, as in the Revelation, that Christ had redeemed them to God by His blood? Let it be remembered, too, that the appearance of the "living creatures" in that vision is clearly distinguished from that of the angels. The number of the angels was ten thousand times ten thousand, and thousands of thousands, and they all stood around the *zoa*, or "living creatures"—which is incompatible with the latter being any order of angels. These considerations seem to compel us to withhold our assent to the ingenious arguments which have been produced in favour of a notion, which is at the best only a conjecture, and which its warmest supporters admit to be incapable of direct proof from Scripture. We need not state the arguments; for since, as the engineers say, no fortress is stronger than its weakest part, if these weak points clearly exist, the strength of all other arguments and illustrations must count for nothing. It is true that this opinion is very ancient, and probably may be traced up to its origin among the Jews themselves; and from them it may have been inherited by the Christian church. But it has been forgotten that this is almost the only opinion they would be likely to reach, in the want of that illumination of the hidden mysteries of revelation with which we have been favoured. Having that clearer light, we needlessly, and sometimes dangerously, limit ourselves, by carelessly adopting the narrow views which the Jews entertained of their own symbols and institutions.

It was shown lately that the cherubim of the tabernacle and temple were the same as those which Ezekiel saw, and which were seen in the apocalyptic vision. What is therefore declared of the last is equally applicable to all; and this being the last and the New Testament revelation on the subject, might be expected to furnish some further disclosure in regard to this mystery than had in old times been possessed. This appears to be furnished in their new song: "Thou art worthy to take the book, and to open the seals thereof: for Thou wast slain, and hast redeemed us to God by Thy blood, out of every kindred, and tongue, and people, and nation; and hast made us unto our God kings and priests: and we shall reign on the earth." Can this possibly be the language of angels,—especially when we hear the apostle's doctrine, "For verily He took not upon Him the nature of angels, but He took on Him the seed of Abraham," (Heb. ii. 16),—and when, moreover, in the context here, the angels are expressly distinguished from the four beasts? It can only be the language of human beings—of the multitude of the redeemed from among men, out of every nation,—not of any section of the church, nor of any class of its members, but of the great body of the believers in the atonement, throughout all ages, countries, and nations. In the immediate application of this symbol, it may be said that, when the high priest entered the most holy place of the tabernacle—*which he never did without the blood of atonement in his hand*—and looked upon the ark of the covenant with its cherubic appendages, with the Shekinah enthroned between, he beheld, in fact, but a miniature model of what he saw on a large scale without, when standing amidst the many thousands of Israel abiding in their tents. *Here* were the cherubic symbols resolved into their constituent multitudes; and over the host rested in calm majesty the pillar of cloud, the visible *external* token of the Divine Presence permanently residing among the tribes. And even this was, as our further light indicates, but a type of that which the Israelites could not see, and would not like to have seen—of multitudes redeemed to God, out of all nations, by the blood of atonement, forming the church of God, among whom He should dwell.

When this clue to the meaning of the symbol is once apprehended, a multitude of circumstances come to the recollection in confirmation of it. We recall the assurance of Ezekiel, that the human figure predominated in the cherubim, and that they possessed the hands of men. We may also call to mind that, although the etymology of *cherubim* is uncertain, the word *"living creature"* is often used as a noun of multitude, and is so translated in the English version; and as the living creatures and the cherubim are the same, this idea must be common to both. So "thy congregation," in Psalm lxviii. 10, is, in Hebrew, "thy living creature;" and 2 Sam. xxiii. 11, "a troop," is, in Hebrew, "the living creature." We may also observe that the presence of the cherubim is always more or less connected with the idea or practice of sacrifice and atonement. We see this constantly in the tabernacle and temple; we see it in the live coal (the efficient atoning

power of sacrifice) wherewith one of the seraphim (the same as cherubim) purified Isaiah's unclean lips; and we see it still more plainly in the Apocalypse.

We regret that space does not allow us to follow out this idea fully, to enforce it by further illustrations, and to vindicate it from possible objections. As regards the fitness of the strange, anomalous, and, it may almost be said monstrous, diversity of forms and faces of which the symbol was composed, to denote *men*—men standing in a covenant relation to God—men possessed of renewed spiritual life, and thus enjoying the divine favour,—we may reasonably conclude that this singular combination of forms represents some remarkable attributes in the character which the symbol adumbrates. Taking this view, it is asked by Professor Bush: "What, then, are the distinguishing traits in the character of the people of God which may be fitly represented by emblems so unique? How shall the hieroglyphic be read? The face of the ox reminds us of the qualities of the ox; and these, it is well known, are patient endurance, unwearied service, and meek submission to the yoke. What claim has he to the title of a man of God, who is not distinguished by these ox-like attributes? The lion is the proper symbol of undaunted courage, glowing zeal, triumph over enemies, united with innate nobleness and magnanimity of spirit. The man, as a symbol, we may well conceive as indicating intelligence, meditation, wisdom, sympathy, philanthropy, and every generous and tender emotion. And finally, in the eagle, we recognize the impersonation of an active, intelligent, fervent, soaring spirit, prompting the readiest and swiftest execution of the divine commands, and elevating the soul to the things that are above."[1] It must be confessed that the symbolization of qualities by animal representations is not congenial to the European taste in its present state of cultivation. It is, however, frequent in the Bible, and we must not forget how well it was calculated to impress the ancient and Oriental imagination. It

---

[1] *Notes on Exodus*, p. 100. New York, 1843. This writer takes substantially the same view we have stated as to the nature of the symbol—which has also been very ably advocated by Mr. George Smith, F.S.A., in his recent work (1850) on the *Doctrine of the Cherubim*. This interpretation is not, however, a new one, for we have traced it in several good old authors, English and foreign.

is merely a kind of embodied imagery, and all ancient literature—as well as all modern Eastern literature—is full of it. Even our austerer taste still tolerates this kind of impersonation in poetry, and the language of the least educated classes still avouches its former predominance, and its present convenience in giving expression to the ideas entertained of the physical, intellectual, and spiritual qualities of men. It is the language of simple nature, which is full of material imagery; and in this language God often speaks to men.

Dr. Layard, speaking of the Assyrian symbols (which he takes to be representations of the Deity), says: "I used to contemplate for hours these mysterious symbols, and muse over their intent and history. What more sublime images could have been borrowed from nature, by men who sought, unaided by the light of revealed religion, to embody their conceptions of the wisdom, power, and ubiquity of a Supreme Being? They could find no better type of wisdom and knowledge, than the head of the man; of strength, than the body of the lion; of ubiquity, than the wings of the bird."[1]

Dr. Kitto's theory regarding what he terms the "doctrine of the cherubim," does not appear to me to agree at all with the notices of these mysterious beings in the various parts of Scripture. The very first passage in the Bible in which they are mentioned, is fatal to the opinion that they were in any respect symbols of human beings. In Gen. iii. 24, *the cherubim* are abruptly introduced as the guardians of Paradise and of the Tree of Life, to prevent Adam and Eve, then the only human beings existing, from re-entering that place from which they had just been expelled. That the name is applied by Moses to some high angelic beings is evident; and that these were the more immediate attendants on the Divine Majesty, and ministers of His presence and judgment, is also evident. They were distinct from God, and not mere attributes of Godhead or emblems of those attributes; but they were still more decidedly distinct from man.

The cherubim which Moses was commanded to make and place upon the ark, were intended as representatives of these heavenly beings; and the same idea of their being the immediate attendants upon the Lord, is set forth in the frequently repeated formula: "He who *dwelleth between the cherubim*." So also in Ezekiel's sublime vision, the cherubim were seen forming the gorgeous chariot-throne of Jehovah, while their wings, sounding like thunder, heralded His approach (x. 5, 19, 20). The representations of John, in the book of Revelation, accord exactly with those of Ezekiel and Moses: "In the midst of the throne, and

[1] *Nineveh*, i. 70.

round about the throne, were four *living creatures*, full of eyes before and behind." They were the first to raise the anthem of praise to God (iv. 9), in which the whole host of heaven joined. They, too, as the immediate attendants upon the Lord, when with the four-and-twenty elders they present before Him the adorations of a ransomed world, are again the first to join in the new triumphant song of praise to the LAMB: "Thou art worthy to take the book, and to open the seals of it: for Thou wast slain, and didst redeem to God by thy blood, out of every tribe, and tongue, and people, and nation, and madest them a kingdom and priests, and they reign upon the earth" (v. 9, 10). The word *us*—"Thou didst redeem *us*"—which is found in the English version, and on which Dr. Kitto's whole argument is based, appears to be an interpolation, as it is not found in the best MSS. It is also especially worthy of note, that no ancient MS. has the word *us* (ἡμᾶς) in ver. 10; they all read "*them*" (αὐτούς). On the whole, therefore, it would appear that the *cherubim* mentioned by Moses, symbolized in the figures over the mercy-seat, and described in the sublime visions of Ezekiel and John, were glorious angelic beings in immediate contact with, and attendance upon, Jehovah. "Standing on the highest step of created life, and uniting in themselves the most perfect created life, they are," as Baehr says, "the most perfect revelation of God and the divine life."

P.

THE ROYAL MERCHANT

1 Kings 9:26-28

IT was probably by the exhaustion of the ample means left by his father, and the inadequacy of the ordinary sources of revenue to cover his vast expenses in sacred and regal building, as well as to sustain the great expense of his magnificent court and numerous household, that Solomon was led to turn his attention to commerce. His intimate connection with the Phœnicians could not but indicate to his sagacious mind, that commerce was the sole foundation of the extraordinary prosperity which that small nation had attained, and the great wealth which it possessed. He saw not why similar advantages might not accrue to himself from the like source. But his people had no knowledge of the sea, nor of shipbuilding; and he perceived that he could not act without the co-operation of Hiram. Now, Hiram was his very good friend; but aware of the commercial jealousy of the Phœnicians, he could not but see that he must not reckon upon their assistance, if his plans or his line of operations interfered with theirs, or unless he could propose to them advantages unattainable to them without his assistance. They monopolized the maritime traffic of the west—the coasts and isles of the Mediterranean—and of the nearer Atlantic shores. With this he had no wish to interfere. But he possessed the ports at the head of the Red Sea, which opened up to maritime enterprise the treasures of the rich south and east, to which they could have no access but through him. He was therefore in a condition to make with them what terms he judged equitable; and there can be no doubt that Hiram listened eagerly to proposals, which allowed him to participate in the advantages of this line of traffic, so full of promise, and which in no wise interfered with the commerce of his own people. Perhaps the Phœnician zeal may have been quickened by the knowledge that, although Solomon preferred their assistance as upon the whole the best and the safest course, he was not altogether dependent upon it. The Edomites, at this time subject to his crown, had been accustomed to navigate the Red Sea, and probably to some extent beyond; and although we know not that they ever reached the shores to which, under the experienced guidance of the Phœnician mariners, the fleets of Solomon penetrated, it is very probable that they might, with adequate encouragement, have been the instruments of his designs. Probably, it was mainly from policy, and from regard to the greater experience of the Phœnicians in long voyages, that the sage king of Israel was induced to prefer the co-operation of a people who had no territorial connection with the shores of the Red Sea. It may be, indeed, that we err in ascribing the credit of the plan to Solomon. It is quite possible that the Phœnicians were themselves the first to perceive how the possession of the Red Sea ports by their powerful ally might be turned to account for the benefit of both nations; and it may appear to some, that the idea was more likely to occur to an enterprising commercial people like them, than to a king who had no previous experience of shipping or commerce.

Be this as it may, the co-operation was readily entered upon, and presently the port of Ezion-geber resounded with the strokes and cries of the multitude of wrights, busy in building such ships as those with which the Phœnicians navigated the length of the Mediterranean to Tar-shish,[1] and which, although now having a very different destination, were still called "ships of Tarshish,"—just as our ships built for the Indian voyage are called "Indiamen." The interest which Solomon felt in the enterprise, may be judged of from the fact, that he went in person to Ezion-geber to hasten the preparations, and to witness the departure of the fleet—a sight at all times beautiful, and altogether new to the eyes of a Hebrew king.

It was three years, or, as we may understand it, the third year,[2] before the ships returned from a most prosperous voyage, laden with costly and rare commodities, and with objects, such as foreign beasts and birds, suited to gratify the philosophic zeal of the king in the study of nature. These were no doubt procured by his order; and it is not too large a stretch of conjecture to suppose, that he had been careful to send some like-minded man with the expedition, to secure such specimens in natural history as might appear worthy of the king's attention. The journal of the naturalist of this expedition would have been a most interesting and useful book to us; and no doubt king Solomon read it eagerly, and found in it rich materials for his own writings on animals and plants. At all events, so wise a king was little likely to leave to the rude appreciation and random judgment of mariners, the selection of the objects worthy of being presented to his notice. The things named are: gold and silver in vast quantities; various kinds of valuable timbers, especially that of the algum-tree (supposed to be the white sandal-wood); ivory; and various curious animals, instanced by monkeys and peacocks, probably as being the most remarkable, or as the most different from the forms of animal life with which the Israelites were previously acquainted. There is no mention of plants; and perhaps the skill was not possessed in that age of transporting living plants with safety from a great distance. Yet, considering the king's love for botany, there

[1] Supposed to be Tartessus in Spain.
[2] The Hebrews in popular computation reckoned parts of years and days as whole ones; so that, to apply this mode of reckoning, a ship of ours that sails for India in December 1849, and returns in January 1851—returning in the third year—may be said to have been absent three years, though actually little more than one year. So our Saviour is said to be three days in the tomb, though actually only one day and two nights,—from Friday evening to Sunday morning.

can be no doubt that his naturalist had instructions to bring the seeds of any plants that appeared worthy of attention from their use or beauty; and we may probably, therefore, refer to this reign the introduction of various plants into Palestine, which had not been known there in former times. It is a curious fact, that in the grounds hard by "the fountains of Solomon," near Bethlehem, which exhibit manifest traces of an ancient garden, and where the intimations of Josephus would lead us to suppose that Solomon had a rural retreat, are still to be found a number of plants self-sown from age to age, which do not exist in any other part of the Holy Land. This is indeed, in ecclesiastical tradition, the *Hortus Conclusus*—the "Enclosed Garden," to which there is an allusion in the "Song of Songs."

But whither went this fleet? When or where were these commodities obtained? The answer is to Ophir—at least this seems to have been the most distant point of the voyage, in the course of which these things were procured. And where was Ophir? *That* is a question —one of the *quæstiones vexatissimæ* of sacred

ELATH

geography, respecting which many volumes and treatises have been written. This is scarcely the place for the adequate discussion of such a question; but as the matter is one which often

comes under notice in some shape or other, we shall, to-morrow, endeavour to state various considerations which may assist the reader to some probable, if not certain, conclusions.

———

The Red Sea has been in all ages the main channel of communication between the Eastern and Western worlds. From the upper part of it two branches shoot out. One of them stretches north-west, and terminates at Suez, on the borders of the great oasis in the valley of the Nile. At its head stands Suez, now, as in classic times, the entrepôt for the commerce of India. The other cuts deeply into the wild and desolate mountains of Arabia, in a course due north. At its head stood, in former days, the ancient maritime cities of Elath and Ezion-geber, where the fleets of Solomon were constructed, and from whence the treasures they imported were conveyed up the valley of Arabah to Palestine. From the city of Elath this eastern arm of the Red Sea was called the Elanitic Gulf, as it is now called the Gulf of Akabah, from the fortress of that name, which occupies the site of Elath.

P.

———

In connection with what has just been said of the "fountains of Solomon," and as a further illustration of the improvements introduced by this famous Jewish monarch, I may refer to the aqueducts which were constructed during his reign. At a distance of two hours' journey from Jerusalem, the fountains or pools adverted to are situated—the upper pool 380 feet long; the middle pool 423; and the lower 582. They vary in breadth from 148 to 236 feet. They are plainly of ancient construction, and were intended to supply Jerusalem with water. To the place where I found them,— *Etham* it is called,—the king, according to Josephus, drove in the cool of the morning, dressed in white, sitting in a lofty chariot, attended by servants in purple livery, their hair powdered with gold dust. (*Antiq.*, viii. 7.) An aqueduct extended over the watershed at Bethlehem, "and then passed over the valley at Rachel's tomb, by an inverted stone syphon, which was first brought to notice by Mr. M'Neil, who made an examination of the water supply for the Syrian Improvement Committee." (*Recovery of Jerusalem*, 25.) The last trace of the aqueduct appears in the plain of Rephaim. Not far from the Jaffa gate, the aqueduct crossed the valley of

Hinnom, and perhaps flowed into a pool lately discovered on the high ground to the north-west of the citadel. Farther down the valley, below the south-eastern angle of the city wall, is the *Birket es Sultân*, or the pool of the Sultan ; and this has been identified by some with the waters of the lower pool, and Gihon, where Solomon was anointed and proclaimed. "So Zadok the priest, and Nathan the prophet, and Benaiah the son of Jehoiada, and the Cherethites, and the Pelethites went down, and caused Solomon to ride upon King David's mule, and brought him to Gihon. And they came up from thence rejoicing, so that the city rang again." (1 Kings i. 38, 45.) (See Smith's *Dictionary of the Bible*, art. "Gihon" and "Jerusalem.")

S.

OPHIR

1 Kings 9:28, 10:11

IF you take away the O from OPHIR there remains PHIR, or, if you like, PIR, which contains all that is essential of the name PERU. Or, still further, if you retain the O and place it at the end instead of the beginning of the word, you have PIRO—which is, we may say, the very same word as PERU. Moreover, Ophir was famous for its gold; so is Peru. What more do you require to prove that Ophir was Peru ? What more is needed to prove that America was discovered under the commission of Solomon and Hiram ; and not under that of Ferdinand and Isabella ?

Now, seriously, this argument, or something very like it, has been used to prove that Peru was the Ophir of Solomon ; and arguments of the same kind, and not stronger when strictly analysed, have been used in favour of places *physically* not so improbable. In this case, the physical improbability of the allocation makes us sensible of the absurdity of this process of argumentation ; but surely the *argument* is not less inconclusive when the *allocation* is less certainly improbable, if that argument is all that can be produced in its favour. Yet this sort of reasoning, as applied to more possible sites, forms the basis of two-thirds of all the attempts which have been made to identify the Ophir of Solomon.

It seems to us that the way to a correct, or rather to a proximate, solution of the difficulty, is to look to the practical results of the expedition, and deduce from the commodities it brought the countries it had visited. This process is obvious. There is scarcely a ship that comes into the port of London from a distant voyage, whose cargo does not indicate the quarter from which it comes, even though the diffusion of commodities and products, which has arisen from the intercourse of nations, renders the process less easy now than in former times, when products, animal or vegetable, were more confined to the countries in which they were indigenous. If the ship is laden with tea, we know it comes from China; if with sugar, from the West Indies; if with cotton, from North America : if with silver or gold, from South America, or Australia, or California ; if with figs, from the Levant; if with spices, from the Indian Sea ; and so on. Still, the conclusion may not be quite certain in every case, seeing that some of these commodities may, in small quantities, come from other quarters than those from which they are principally received,—and it is possible that the cargo may have been taken on board at some intermediate commercial port. But if we find curious animals on board for the Zoological Gardens, our conclusions are materially assisted ; for these have assigned habitats, and not being objects of commerce, they are almost invariably, even now, as they were in ancient times, brought direct from the countries to which they belong. If there be a hippopotamus, we conclude that the ship comes from the mouth of the Nile ; if a lion, a zebra, a gnu, or a koodoo, from the Cape ; if a tiger or zebu, from India : if a rein-deer, glutton, or white bear, from the Arctic Seas ; if a bison or racoon, from North America ; if a macaw, or humming-bird, or kinkajou, or llama, or armadillo, from South America ; if an orang-outang, a paradoxure, or a napu, from Borneo, Sumatra, or Java ; if a kangaroo or ornithorhyncus, from Australia ; if a babirousa, from the Molucca Isles ; and so of any others which inhabit definable localities.

Now, we must apply this to the case in hand.

A favourite opinion of late is, that Ophir was on the east coast of Arabia, in Oman, because the name of Ofor has been found there, and because it can be made out that gold was once yielded in that quarter. This makes the great voyage a mere creeping round the Arabian coast, and affords *only one* of the products, gold. Granting that gold was got here, where else, where farther, did the fleet go to get ivory, apes, peacocks, and algum wood, none of which were ever found in any part of Arabia?

Another hypothesis sends the fleet not eastward at all, but southward along the African shore. Now, certainly, had the fleet taken this direction, a very large proportion of the objects named—gold, apes, ivory—and even some kinds of spices, might have been obtained in the ports of Abyssinia. But in this quarter the peacocks or the algum-trees could not be found; and so long as any one creature or object is on board the fleet which cannot be ascribed to the assigned country, we are bound to seek another. The one or two things wanting, then, become the tests for ascertaining the true country—the more valuable, inasmuch as the scope of the inquiry becomes more limited and distinct; and the more important, according to the degree in which the object in question becomes more singular, distinct, and remarkable. For the purposes of this inquiry, it may be well to dismiss the algum-trees for the present, for two reasons: because the tree is of disputed identification, and because it cannot *with certainty* be affirmed that it was not a tree growing in Africa or Arabia. There is, then, nothing left but the peacock; and on this we must take our stand.

But, first, are we sure that the word in the Hebrew text, which is THUKYIM, does really denote peacocks? We think it certain. There is hardly any bird named in Scripture, respecting which there is more general agreement among interpreters; and there is some strong objection to every other bird which has been indicated. Then, what is the native country of the peacock? It is India; and it could have been found both wild and domesticated by navigators upon the coasts from Camboge to Ceylon; and, which is of great importance, the bird would, better than any of its congeners, or, indeed, than any other bird which has been suggested, bear a long voyage in such crowded ships as those of the ancients. Moreover, the name itself, THUKI [1]—which is evidently not Hebrew, but a foreign term imported along with the bird,[2]—has much analogy to the native name of the peacock, as found in those parts—which is in Malabaric, *togei*, in Sanscrit, *sikhi*. Now, we would not contend

[1] The final *im*, as above quoted, being the sign of the plural.

[2] Probably imitated from its note or cry; but we do not know, for *we* never *heard* it.

that this is the region of Ophir, but we do contend that the voyage to Ophir, wherever that lay, although it may not necessarily have been the remotest point of the voyage, must have extended to the place where peacocks were found; and we have indicated the *nearest* place where they might then be obtained, though not bound to do so, for peacocks might be found in remoter parts of India and its isles; we might even, if we liked, go as far as the peninsula of Malacca—the Aurea Chersonesus of the ancients, —where we find that the inhabitants to this day call their gold mines *ophirs*, and where, most certainly, *all* the products brought to Solomon might be found in rich abundance. But they might all likewise be found at the nearer point we have indicated; and therefore we prefer this, for the sake of the scrupulous reader who might shrink from the longer voyage. But, for our own part, we find no difficulty even in that; for it seems that an intercourse even with China was open not much later than, and possibly much before, the age of Solomon—articles of China manufacture, with legible Chinese characters upon them, being at this day found in the ancient tombs of Egypt.

But, adhering to the nearer parts of the Indian coast, we find that these would furnish all that was obtained. This includes even the algum-trees; for although we have declined to rely upon it, for the reasons stated, we consider that it has been satisfactorily shown by Dr. Royle[1] to have been the fragrant white sandal-wood,[2] so highly prized in the East, which is a native of the mountainous parts of the coast of Malabar, where large quantities are at this day cut for export to China, to different parts of India, and to the Persian and Arabian Gulfs.

We therefore think the fleet went so far as India, touching, perhaps, at Arabian and African ports on its way. This also agrees with the length of the voyage; for although, as we showed yesterday, the indication of time is not necessarily to be understood of *three* years, we think it could not have been much less in this case; for the time consumed is mentioned as something extraordinary, which would scarcely have been the case with anything less than two years, under the slow processes of ancient navigation.

Yet, as we have said, we do not contend that

[1] *Cyclop. of Biblical Literature*, art. "Algum."

[2] *Santalum album.*

Ophir was a place on the Indian coast. Nay more, we do not insist that it was ANY particular place. It seems to us that Heeren is quite right in his remark, that "Ophir, like the name of all other distant places or regions of antiquity—as Thule, Tartessus, and others—denotes no particular spot, but only a certain region or part of the world, such as the East or West Indies in modern geography. Hence Ophir was a general name for all the countries lying on the African, Arabian, or Indian Seas, so far as at that time known."

That Ophir was a definite, and, in ancient times, a well known country, no biblical geographer will now venture to deny. But its exact locality cannot, as I think, be ascertained from the nature of the several commodities imported in the fleets of Solomon. The fleets evidently made long voyages, touching at different ports, and bringing from each country such of its products as might minister to the luxury of the great Jewish monarch. Ophir was one of the chief points visited in this triennial cruise, and gold was its special product.

The position of Ophir is incidentally indicated by the sacred writers. The country took its name from the eleventh son of Joktan (Gen. x. 29); and it is said that the dwelling of the sons of Joktan was "from Mesha, as thou goest unto Sephar, a mountain of the East." Both these places were in Arabia, and hence it may be concluded that Ophir was also in Arabia. Several circumstances

known to have been gold-producing; and traces of the name Ophir are found in the *Aphar* or *Sapphara* of Ptolemy, and the modern *Zafar*.

P.

TADMOR

1 Kings 9:18

AMONG the cities built by Solomon was "Tadmor in the wilderness." All our readers know that this Tadmor was Palmyra, whose magnificent ruins still fill European travellers with wonder. We shall not describe these ruins, which belong to a much later age than that of Solomon; though it is possible that some of the substructions may belong to the more ancient city on that spot, of which he was the founder. We feel more interest in the inquiry, What could have been Solomon's object in establishing a city so important in this remote and inhospitable region? It is reasonable to suppose that he was influenced by a clear perception of the relations and circumstances, which could not but render a city in that quarter of great commercial importance —of such importance as it actually possessed, and to which its prosperity was wholly owing, in ages long posterior to that in which Solomon flourished. This object on Solomon's part is not clearly stated, but it is easily collected from a consideration of the facts, and from the comparison of some intimations which do transpire.

His commerce with Egypt, and his maritime traffic, evince the king's wakeful attention to his commercial advantages. As he possessed all the territory to the Euphrates, and held the

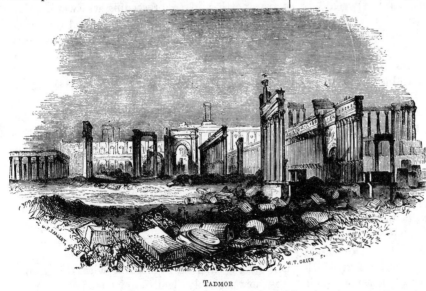

TADMOR

fortified towns which commanded the places of passage over that river, he possessed the means of entirely controlling the great caravan trade, which from ancient times existed between the

tend to confirm this view. It would appear that it was when the fleet visited Ophir, that the queen of Sheba heard of Solomon's greatness; and Sheba was a region of south-eastern Arabia. Besides, that part of Arabia is regions east of the Euphrates on the one hand, and the emporiums of Syria and Egypt on the other. The site of Tadmor is an oasis in the midst of an arid and sandy desert, being rendered such by the abundance of water. This circumstance compelled the caravans to pass in this direction—the water being essential for the refreshment of the cattle in the passage across the desert.

There can, therefore, be no doubt that this was an important watering-station for the great caravans, from the very earliest period, in which were transported, on long files of camels, the products of the East across the great Syrian desert. It could not but occur to the sagacious Hebrew king, that here was a most proper station for a commercial town. It was doubtless fortified, and adequately garrisoned; so that, while it enabled him to maintain the region in complete subjection, and to prevent the passage of the trade without his concurrence (which, indeed, would otherwise have been impossible, owing to the want of water), it put him in a position to give complete security to the caravans against the predatory Arab tribes, which formerly, as now, infested this region, and rendered the passage either positively dangerous, or purchasable only at a fearful sacrifice, which, as it must fall on the ultimate consumer, helped to render the products of this traffic exceedingly costly by the time they reached the shores of the Mediterranean. As Solomon held the fortress of Thapsacus at the place where the caravans crossed the Euphrates, he could afford an escort of troops thence to Tadmor, and thence again to the western coast, if required; and for this, as well as for the aid obtained at Tadmor, and for the advantages of its stores and khans, a toll might reasonably be required; and this would be cheerfully paid, as a return for actual benefits, and as a most gratifying exchange for the harassing, irregular, inordinate, and greedy exactions of the Arab tribes.

But we apprehend that Tadmor was more than this; that it became under Solomon what we know that it.was in later times, an actual emporium for the products of the East, at which the caravans did not merely rest on their journey, but where they terminated it, deposited their ladings, transacted their sales with the factors from the West, who then took charge of the commodities, and bore them away thence to the

Western markets at their leisure, or whither the dealers repaired to purchase such of those commodities as they required from the consignees. This is the usual mode in which the goods brought by distant caravans are disposed of in the East; almost always at some border town, and rarely at the ultimate market. More than this, we see little room to doubt that Solomon himself took up, by his agents, the greater part, if not the whole, of the goods thus brought into his territories, and kept them in his stores, eventually selling them at a profit to such of the Western merchants as required them. This would in fact amount to a monopoly of the Eastern trade. But such is the custom of Eastern kings, when they take any interest in commercial undertakings. And not only so, but these royal merchants are very much in the habit of taking such commodities from the caravans *at their own price*, which the seller dare not refuse to accept. This, however, has a *practical* limit, and it must especially have had it in the case of Solomon; for, had he oppressed the trade, by compelling the merchants to dispose of their goods at a price *essentially* less than they might have obtained in the ordinary course of business, the result might have been to direct the traffic into some other channel, which might have been found by crossing the Euphrates more to the north, and so proceeding westward. But this would have been an expensive and fatiguing course, not to be adopted without more serious cause than so prudent a king as Solomon would be likely to give.

That this, in substance, was the course taken by Solomon, seems to us to be proved by the fact, that it was really the policy on which he conducted his trade with Egypt; and also by the fact, that we read of "store cities" which he built; and as this is mentioned in connection with his building of Tadmor, it is obviously suggested that these towns were intended to be places for the deposit and sale of the products of this great Eastern land trade—so ancient, so important—and which now seems to have been chiefly in the hands of Solomon. Among other cities held by the king in connection with this trade, was very probably Baalbek (or Heliopolis), which may have been included among the "store cities" of Hamath, if it be not expressly named under the designation of Baalath (1 Kings ix. 18),—about which there is some difference of opinion.

It is a most important fact in evidence of the truth of the conjectures we have hazarded, that all our information respecting this place, under its name of Palmyra, transmitted through heathen writers, exhibits it as a city of merchants—the factors of the Eastern trade,—who sold to the Romans and others the valuable products and precious commodities of India and Arabia, and who were so enriched by the traffic, that the place was proverbial for its wealth and luxury, and for the expensive habits of its citizens.

The position of Palmyra suggests at once the history of its origin. The rich valley of the Euphrates, from the most remote age the seat of some of the greatest cities of the world, was separated from the commercial nations of Syria and Phœnicia by an arid desert 150 miles across. To traverse this with heavily laden caravans was extremely difficult. Water was absolutely necessary for the animals. About midway in the desert a copious stream, slightly sulphureous, bursts from the base of a long chalk range. It is the only fountain in a wide region. Solomon at once saw the immense advantages of its position, and founded beside it "Tadmor in the wilderness." Besides being a necessary watering and resting-place for caravans, it was important in other respects. Then, as now, the desert swarmed with roving tribes which lived by plunder. Caravans were constantly exposed to their attacks. No amount of watchfulness could save them. But these tribes required water for their flocks and herds. During the long summer drought the great fountain of Tadmor was almost their only source. By fortifying it, Solomon was able perfectly to control these tribes, and to command their allegiance. His caravans could thus pass in safety at all times ; and he was made practically the ruler of the whole desert of northern Syria.

It is worthy of note that Jews appear to have constituted a large and influential part of the population of Palmyra under the Roman rule ; and even so late as the twelfth century, Rabbi Benjamin of Tudela found there a colony of 4,000 of his brethren. The commercial depôt of Solomon, and the magnificent city of Zenobia, is now represented by a village of wretched huts, built within the court of the temple of the Sun. The massive platform on which the temple stands resembles that at Baalbec, and may probably have been founded by the great Jewish monarch.

P.

TRADE WITH EGYPT—THE HITTITES

1 Kings 10:28-29

IT is under Solomon that for the first time we read of a commercial intercourse with Egypt,

which perhaps, if fully investigated, might be found of more real importance than the seemingly larger commercial proceedings to which our attention has been given. These derive apparent magnitude from distance of place, and length of interval in time, which necessarily gave an extensive and massive character to each distinct operation ; while the intercourse which neighbouring nations may carry on with each other from week to week, or month to month, needs no such extensive organization, or imposing circumstances, and though smaller in each separate act, becomes in the aggregate of far greater consequence. To us, however, the contemplation of this branch of Solomon's traffic is scarcely of less interest than that with Ophir.

We are informed of the articles which Solomon imported from Egypt through his factors, but not of the commodities he gave in exchange. These, however, it is not difficult to discover, seeing that there are certain products of Palestine which were not produced, or not adequately produced, in Egypt, and which must in all times have found a welcome in the markets there. Of the staple productions of Palestine, corn was one that Egypt did not want ; but in regard to oil and wine the case was different.

The inhabitant of northern Europe can scarcely form any adequate conception of the important uses of oil in a warm climate, in which animal fat, or any solid substance capable of being melted by the natural temperature of the climate, cannot be used. It serves instead of butter, instead of lard, instead of tallow. This constantly appears in Scripture. Of all oils, that of the olive is most valued ; and the tree that afforded it did not flourish in Egypt, but was native to Palestine, and grew there to its utmost perfection, shooting even from the crevices of the rocks, where scarcely any soil appears. Hence, " oil out of the flinty rock " (Deut. xxxii. 13), was among the blessings of the land promised to the chosen people. So of wine. It is not true that the vine did not grow in Egypt, or that wine was not made there. This old notion is overturned by the evidence of the mural paintings. Yet the nature of the climate—as unfavourable to the vine from heat as our own climate is from cold—shows that it must there have been rather an object of amateur culture, than a natural and extensive production. The wine, also, although made in some limited degree, as formerly in this country,[1] was probably of inferior quality, and not greatly prized. But in Palestine the vine attained its perfection, affording excellent grapes, which yielded the finest wine. This wine was prized even by the Phœnicians, who had access to the vines of Lebanon. Much more, therefore, must it have been valued by the Egyptians; and these two commodities, olive oil and wine, alone must have afforded Solomon ample means of return for whatever articles he required of the Egyptians. Another commodity afforded by his kingdom in large abundance, and but scantily produced in Egypt, was honey. The frequent mention of this in Scripture is apt to perplex the reader, who forgets that *sugar* was unknown, and that honey was used for all the purposes to which sugar is applicable. Some have thought "that the sweet cane" mentioned in a later age, was the sugar-cane; but the *sweetness* of that was its *fragrance*,—"the fragrant reed"—*Calamus aromaticus.*

We are, however, at no loss respecting the commodities which the Hebrew king obtained from Egypt. They were horses, chariots, and linen yarn. There were probably many other articles; but these are named as the chief. The Egyptian breed of horses is shown by the paintings to have been exceedingly fine,—like a more powerful Arab, from which it was doubtless derived. Its somewhat heavier build than that of the Arabian breed well qualified it for chariots, in which it was chiefly employed. It was, therefore, as we gather, much in demand among the Syrian princes, who affected this kind of force; and, as it was impossible for horses to be brought from Egypt without passing through Solomon's territories, he availed himself of this circumstance to monopolize the trade, purchasing the Egyptian horses by his agents, and selling at a profit to the northern princes. The compact, light, and yet solid fabric of the Egyptian chariots, is seen also from the paintings. When we recollect that the use of springs was unknown, it is easily apprehended that the construction of these vehicles was a peculiarly difficult art. It is an interesting fact, that the price which Solomon gave for a horse and for a chariot is particularly stated, by which we find that the cost of a chariot was four times that of a horse. A horse cost 150

[1] There is evidence that wine was formerly made in Devonshire.

shekels, which, according to the lower or higher value assigned to the shekel (2s. 3⅜d. or 2s. 6d.), would be from £17, 2s. to £18, 15s.; while that of a chariot was 600 shekels, being from £68, 9s. to £75. It is to be remembered, however, that an Egyptian chariot usually had two horses, so that a chariot with a pair of horses would together cost about £112 of our money, at first hand. But we have no means of determining whether, with reference to the cost of commodities, this was of less or more value at that time than the same amount now; perhaps more, but probably not much more, considering the great quantities of the precious metals that seem to have been about this time in use.

It is said that in this way Solomon provided out of Egypt horses and chariots "for all the kings of the Hittites, and for the kings of Syria." Who were the kings of the Hittites? One would have supposed that these, being among the doomed nations in Palestine, had been rooted out or destroyed long ago. Indeed, the Hittites are expressly named in 1 Kings ix. 20, among the remnants of the Canaanitish nations whom Solomon held in bondage. Instead, therefore, of finding this people still subsisting in a state of separate regal independence among the Israelites, as some have imagined to be the case, it is more reasonable to conclude that the present Hittites were a branch of the same family, or even the descendants of those expelled from Palestine, settled among the Syrian nations beyond Lebanon, and perhaps not only there, but on the south-eastern frontier towards Arabia. There does not want some indication of the existence of this separate domain of the Hittites. In Judges i. 26, we read of a man of Bethel, formerly called Luz, who retired into "the country of the Hittites," and there built a town, which he called Luz, after his native place. Further, we read that Solomon had several Hittite women among his wives; and so late as the reign of Jehoram, we read of kings of the Hittites named with the king of Egypt as having probably been "hired" against the Syrians by the king of Israel.

HITTITE IN CIVIL COSTUME

(2 Kings vii. 6.) This connection, and the apprehension of it which the king of Syria enter-

tained, indicate that some branch of the Hittite family was then in a condition of power and independence. We may suppose that these are represented by the Egyptian figures, supposed to be Hittites; though their origin and appearance were doubtless the same as those of the old Hittites of southern Palestine. We have them represented in both civil and warlike attire. The complexion given to them by the Egyptian artists is, though dark, rather florid than sallow, with black hair, regular features, and a very prominent and somewhat hooked nose. The civil dress is a plain bright-coloured tunic, with a deep edging of lace or embroidery, gathered into a knot on the left shoulder, so as to leave the right arm at freedom. Under this was worn a kind of kilt or skirt, of similar colour and pattern, but reaching only to the knees. They shaved not only the beard and mustachios, but even the eyebrows, as did many other of the nations of Canaan; besides which, the Hittites had an almost peculiar custom of their own, of shaving a square place just above the ear, leaving the hair on the side of the face, and whiskers hanging down in a long plaited lock. This frightful custom, and other eccentric dealings of those nations with their hair, throw some light upon the injunctions to avoid such practices, which we find in the books of the law. If we want to know what is meant by "marring the corners of the beard," we have only to look at such pictures to be perfectly satisfied. [1]

We do not often touch on matters of costume. But there is a natural curiosity to know what sort of dress was worn among the nations so often mentioned in Scripture. The intimations on this subject which may be collected from Egyptian paintings and sculptures, are of singular interest, as being the only possible source of information on the subject. There is also a common character among these different attires, which leaves a general idea of the prevalent style and manner of dress in the times and lands of the Bible, of which that of the Israelites themselves probably partook, though it might differ in details.

It remains to notice the war dress of the Hittites. It consisted of a helmet skull-cap, extending down the neck, cut away high and square above the ear, so as to expose that bald

place, which they seem to have regarded as peculiarly charming. It was fastened by a strong band or cheek-string, probably, like the helmet, of metal. The badges of distinction were one or two ostrich feathers, worn drooping. They wore a kind of cape or short mantle, tied close in front, either by the two ends of the cloth, or by a cord with tassels at the end. Over this was the girdle, which was broad and thick, and hung down in front, with a long end, terminating in a ball and tassel. It was long enough to pass round the neck and across the breast, and thus formed a species of defensive armour, illustrative of the military use of the girdle so often mentioned in Scripture. The only weapon assigned to the Hittites by the Egyptian artists is the arrow.

HITTITE IN WAR COSTUME

This agrees with the intimation in our text,—the arrow being pre-eminently a weapon for chariot warfare.

Chariots and horses were not, however, brought from Egypt entirely as objects of merchandise. Solomon's tastes were too magnificent to allow him to be a mere instrument of the luxury or power of others, without retaining some portion thereof in his own hands. He established a new species of military force, strongly discouraged by the law of Moses, and from which all previous rulers of this people had abstained—that of chariots and horses. Of the former he had 1,400, and of the latter, 12,000. Apart even from the prohibition, this was an extreme and perilous extravagance for such a country as that over which this king reigned. The country was mountainous, and unsuited for cavalry. It was also a time of peace; and all the great victories of his father and other conquerors had been won in reliance upon the strength of the Lord's arm, without any such force, and in opposition to those who possessed it. David could triumphantly say, "Some trust in chariots, and some in horses; but we will remember the name of the Lord our God." Besides, such a number of horses and chariots was wholly disproportioned to so small a country; and it is likely that no act of royal extravagance was so unpopular among the people, under whose eyes

[1] See Leviticus 29:27; and compare Jeremiah 9:26; 25:21-23.
See also *Daily Bible Illustrations*, Vol. 1, pp. 679-682.

it was continually present. This kind of expenditure in the keeping of animals not for manifest use, is always more offensive to a people, and especially to an agricultural people, than any other form of expenditure, because it is a living expense. The people soon fall to reckoning that each horse consumes the food of so many persons, the produce of so much land; and when, to support such extravagance, they are oppressed with special burdens, the grievance becomes intolerable. We do not call to mind any deep popular complaint against the extravagance of a sovereign, which had not its origin in some such form of living expenditure—that is, in the really or apparently unprofitable maintenance of persons or animals—horses, servants, functionaries, soldiers, women. Indeed, a popular complaint against even a war, will, when examined, generally resolve itself into a discontent at the cost of maintaining the army—of so many consumers of food not employed in reproductive labour.

As to the ancient Oriental use of horses, the cavalry of the Assyrians seems to have been most imposing. Assyrian sculptures agree with the testimony of Habakkuk i. 8, that the horses were "swifter than leopards, and more fierce than the evening wolves;" whilst their riders, "clothed in blue, captains and rulers, all of them desirable young men" (Ezek. xxiii. 6), were armed with "the bright sword and glittering spear." (Nah. iii. 3.) Horses do not seem to have been introduced to Egypt in the earliest period of its history. No figure of a horse is found on the most ancient monuments. But, subsequently, horses were introduced; and graziers were employed in improving the breed (Wilkinson's *Ancient Egyptians*, Second Series, i. 20). There were horses in Egypt at the time of the Exodus; and allusions are made to them at a later date (2 Kings vii. 6; xviii. 24; Isaiah xxxvi. 8; Ezek. xvii. 15). The monuments exhibit private persons seated in chariots, paying visits to friends. The harness of the Assyrian horses was richly ornamented with bridles, tassels, bells, and bows; no doubt the Egyptians, in this respect, vied with other nations.

There is some obscurity in 1 Kings x. 28, "And Solomon had horses brought out of Egypt, and linen yarn: the king's merchants received the linen yarn at a price." There is no obvious connection between horses and linen yarn. Gesenius, and other distinguished Hebrew scholars, think the word translated linen yarn "really means a troop, or company." The Septuagint translators must have had before them a different reading altogether, as they translate the words "and from Tekoa." Hence some have thought that the Egyptians held a sort of horse fair in Tekoa, whither Hebrew dealers were sent by Solomon to make purchases.

S.

THE QUEEN OF SHEBA

1 Kings 10:1-10

THE time was when men travelled far in search of wisdom. They made long journeys and voyages,—they traversed seas, and deserts, and mountains, to visit the seats of learning, or the towns in which men famous for their knowledge abode. All ancient history, and comparatively modern Oriental history, is full of this. It may be traced even in what are called "the dark ages." But this seems now to be numbered among the things that have passed away. Yet it is not wholly so. The intercommunication of even distant nations is now so frequent and abundant, and the motives for it are so mixed, that the career of a seeker after knowledge does not stand out with that prominence which it did in old time. The differences of religion, also, have contributed to make such examples fewer in number. The ancient polytheists found little obstacle in seeking from each other such wisdom as they were respectively reputed to possess; for, although they knew their systems to be different, they did not regard those of each other as necessarily untrue or abominable. But in our times, the Christian seeks not wisdom from Moslems or idolaters,—nor do they seek it from him or from each other. Even within the range of the same religious persuasion, there are few nations which allow the existence anywhere of higher degrees of wisdom than may be found among themselves. But, more than all, the press, by rendering the best results of the wisdom and learning of all nations available *at home*, to all who understand the languages in which they are imparted—and without this, travel itself would be useless—has necessarily withdrawn the principal motive for travel in search of knowledge. Yet, where adequate motive does exist, instances of this ancient practice may still be found. There are biblical scholars—it is our privilege to know one—who have travelled far and often, to see and note for themselves the differences and agreements of those ancient copies of God's word which time has spared to us, and which lie dispersed among the nations, shut up in libraries, churches, and monasteries.

Without pressing this parallel—though it seems to us the most significant and interesting which modern times can furnish, while the high object places it far above all ancient instances of wisdom-seeking travel—we have to remark, that this was eminently the form which any ancient zeal for knowledge took, and that the earliest instances of it occur in the Scriptures.

They belong to the time we have now reached; for we are told that "there came of all people to hear the wisdom of Solomon, from all kings of the earth which had heard of his wisdom." In ordinary circumstances, the wisdom of a Jewish king would have been but little heard of beyond the immediately neighbouring nations; but the extended conquests of David—the large dominions of his son—the great and magnificent works and undertakings of that son—his extensive commerce by sea and land—his connection with the Phœnicians, who, of all people, were from their position best qualified to spread such intelligence far and wide—and even Solomon's too numerous matrimonial connections with foreign princesses—all contributed to spread his reputation abroad. In some cases, foreign princes themselves repaired to Jerusalem, to view his glorious and curious works of art, and to hear his sage utterances; others sent ambassadors to felicitate him, and to bring back all that they could gather of his wisdom. This concourse of foreign princes and nobles from all parts, with their magnificent retinues, and curious and costly offerings, must have given singular liveliness and splendour to Jerusalem during the reign of Solomon. It must have supplied continual matter of admiration and entertainment to the citizens, who could not but feel great contentment, and some feeling of human exultation, in the glory thus reflected upon them, from the greatness and wisdom of their sovereign.

The only visit of an illustrious pilgrim of knowledge which has been particularly recorded, is that of a woman, the queen of Sheba, who "heard of the fame of Solomon, concerning the name of the Lord, and came to Jerusalem with a very great train, with camels that bare spices, and very much gold, and precious stones." And whence came she? Probability unites with ecclesiastical history, and with the Jewish traditions and Mohammedan accounts, in pointing her out as queen of the Sabæan kingdom of Yemen, and Mariaba or Saba, as the seat of its government. This point is so well established by Bochart and others, that it may be received as

an ascertained fact. It is besides verified by the terms employed by our Saviour in alluding to this pilgrimage. He calls her the "Queen of the South," or *Yemen*, which is in Hebrew, as in

THE QUEEN OF SHEBA'S VISIT TO SOLOMON

Arabic, the proper word for *south*; and He speaks of her as having come "from the uttermost parts of the earth to hear the wisdom of Solomon," which exactly corresponds to the Joktanite kingdom of Sheba, Saba, or Sabæ, which is terminated only by the Indian Ocean, whose waters, blending with those of the Atlantic, divide Asia from Africa. It may be added, that all the precious commodities which the queen brought to Jerusalem, were such as the region thus assigned to her was in old time famous for producing. The Abyssinians, indeed, claim this illustrious queen for their sovereign, and trace to her their ancient kings,—which may suggest, what is on other grounds probable, that the country on both shores of the southern part of the Red Sea was at this time under one government.

It was what this queen heard of Solomon in her own land, that induced her to undertake this long and expensive journey. In all probability, nay, to a moral certainty, the Ophir fleet had, in its way, put into her ports, perhaps in both the outward and the homeward voyage, which gave her the opportunity of acquiring this information concerning the great king to whom that fleet belonged; and the successful result of the expedition must have confirmed the accounts she received of the wisdom of the prince by whom it had been planned.

At Jerusalem the queen was received with courtesy and attention by Solomon, who freely gave her all the required evidence of the wisdom which had been given to him. It is said she tried it with "hard questions," generally supposed by Jewish writers to have been of the nature of enigmas or riddles; and this is very likely, as the genius of the Orientals inclines them to test wisdom or cleverness by the solution of difficult matters. We have seen this in Samson's riddle, and more lately in Solomon's judgment. The reader may be entertained, if not interested, in seeing what kind of problems are conceived by the Orientals to have been submitted to the sagacity of Solomon. The Mohammedan legends on this subject are derived from those of the Jewish rabbis; and at least afford some idea of the notions entertained in the region from which the queen of Sheba came, of the kind of questions best suited to test the wisdom of a Solomon.

No name is given to the queen in Scripture. The Arabians call her Balkis. According to their accounts, the princess sent ambassadors with a letter to Solomon before she went herself. With them she sent five hundred youths dressed like maidens, and the same number of maidens like young men, with instructions that they were to behave accordingly in the presence of Solomon. She had also a thousand carpets prepared, wrought with gold and silver, a crown composed of the finest pearls and hyacinths, and many loads of musk, amber, and aloes, and other precious products of South Arabia. To these she added a closed casket, containing an unperforated pearl, a diamond intricately pierced, and a goblet of crystal. The letter thus referred to these things: "As a true prophet, thou wilt no doubt be able to distinguish the youths from the maidens; to divine the contents of the enclosed casket; to perforate the pearl; to thread the diamond; and to fill the goblet with water that hath not dropped from the clouds, nor gushed forth from the earth."

When they reached Jerusalem, Solomon told them the contents of the letter before they presented it, and made light of their mighty problems. He caused the slaves to wash themselves, and from the manner in which they applied the water, detected their sex. He directed a young and fiery horse to be ridden through the camp at the top of its speed, and on its return caused its copious perspiration to be collected in the goblet. The pearl he perforated by a stone occultly known to him. The threading of the diamond puzzled him for a moment, but at length he inserted a small worm, which wound its way through, leaving a silken thread behind it. Having done this, he dismissed the ambassadors, without accepting their presents.

This, and the reports her emissaries brought, determined the queen to visit Jerusalem in person. When she came, Solomon, who had heard a piece of scandal about her—no less than that she had cloven feet—first of all demonstrated his sagacity by the mode in which he tested this report. He caused her to be conducted over a crystal floor, below which was real water, with a quantity of fish swimming about. Balkis, who had never before seen a crystal floor, supposed there was water to be passed through, and therefore slightly lifted her robe, enabling the king to satisfy himself that she had a very neat foot, not at all cloven.

We should be glad to know how this idea of a crystal floor before the king's throne originated. In the Revelation of John (iv. 6), a "sea of glass, like unto crystal," is placed before the throne of God; and as the images of that glorious vision are necessarily combined from known objects, it may be that the tradition of a crystal floor before the throne of Solomon already existed, or that something of the kind was somewhere known to exist, or to have existed, as a piece of regal magnificence. If we could suppose that this circumstance had any foundation in fact, it might form a curious addition to the considerations which we have lately had occasion to advance respecting the origin of glass.

According to the Scripture narrative, the queen of Sheba found evidence of the wisdom of Solomon, not only in his words, but in his works. His magnificent palace, "the house of the forest of Lebanon;" the manner in which meat was provided for, and served at his table; the ordering of his courts and audiences, with his ministers and high officers standing according to their rank, in their gorgeous apparel; his cup-bearers, with their precious goblets; and above all, the viaduct whereby he crossed the valley which separated his palace from the temple of the Lord,—all these things were objects of special admiration to this foreign princess, and drew from her the striking declaration: "It was a true report that I heard in my own country of thy acts and thy wisdom. Howbeit, I believed not the words until I came, and mine eyes had seen it; and, behold, the half was not told me. Thy wisdom and prosperity exceedeth the fame which I heard." There is a general belief among the Jewish writers, that the queen was turned from her dumb idols to worship the living God, under the instructions of Solomon. There is nothing unlikely in this. Indeed, the words which connect "the name of the Lord" with the wisdom of Solomon, give much sanction to the opinion that the search for religious truth, the true "wisdom," was the main object of her journey—as do the words which closed her address to Solomon: "Happy are thy men, happy are these thy servants, which stand by and hear thy wisdom. Blessed be Jehovah thy God, which delighteth in thee to set thee on the throne of Israel; because Jehovah loved Israel for ever, therefore hath He made thee king, to do judgment and justice."

Among the magnificent sights in Jerusalem which filled the queen of Sheba with astonishment, was one which may require a word of explanation. It is the last mentioned: "His ascent by which he went up unto the house of the Lord." The palace of the king was built on Mount Zion, while the temple stood on the summit of Moriah. Between these two hills was a deep valley or ravine. Recent research has brought to light the remains of a colossal bridge which spanned this ravine, and connected the palace and the temple. It must have been one of the most splendid architectural works in the Holy City. The masonry is unquestionably Jewish, but of what period of Jewish rule, has not yet been satisfactorily ascertained. One of the stones in the fragment of the arch still remaining measures twenty-four feet in length, and another twenty. Calculating by the curve of the arch, and the distance from the temple wall to the rocky side of Mount Zion opposite, the bridge when complete would seem to have been composed of five arches, each about forty-one feet in span; and its elevation above the bottom of the ravine could scarcely have been less than a hundred feet.

The first definite mention of this bridge is in connection with the siege of Jerusalem by Pompey, twenty years before Herod ascended the throne. It was not, therefore, a work of Herod. It was built long before his day. There are no data, however, by which to connect it with the "ascent" of Solomon. The Hebrew word is correctly rendered "ascent," and it may either be by stairs or otherwise. The same ascent is apparently referred to in 1 Chron. xxvi. 16: "To Shuppim and Hosah the lot came forth westward, at the gate Shallecheth *by the causeway of the going up.*" The word translated "causeway" means a viaduct of any kind, and then a staircase. Would it not strike one, on reading the whole narratives, that some very

remarkable approach to the temple is referred to by the sacred writers; and that it was in some way appropriated to the use of the king? If such a bridge as that whose ruins are now seen, existed in Solomon's day, it would unquestionably make a profound impression on the mind of the queen of Sheba.

P.

THE KING'S CRIME

1 Kings 11:1-8

WE must not suffer our eyes to be so dazzled by the magnificence of Solomon's commercial operations, as to preclude ourselves from discerning the unsoundness of their principles, and the hollowness of the prosperity which they appeared to create. Although it may be, that no cause so directly contributes to the material prosperity of a nation as commerce—to ensure that result, the commerce must be national, not regal. It must be the effect of the natural development of the nation's resources, or of the direction given to its tastes and habits. It must be in the hands of the people, open to all who can command the needful capital, or possess the required commodities—and so diffusing by numerous channels throughout the land its enlivening influence. Without this, commerce can have no really beneficial existence; and although it may gild the head of the state, it can impart no quickening life to its frame.

Solomon, with all his wisdom, did not discern this. Though a wise man, he was an Oriental prince; and his sagacity failed to carry his views in this matter beyond the influences and circumstances belonging to his position. To seek *first* the prosperity of the people subject to his rule, and to wait for his own harvest of profit and renown, through and from their prosperity, was a reach of thought and patriotism to which even Solomon could not attain. An Oriental prince generally seeks *first,* as he did, his own glory and advantage, and the welfare of the people may or may not result from it. If it does—and it seldom does, and never does to the extent that it might under right principles—so much the better; it is a fortunate accident, forming no part of the design, which is nothing more or less than to fill the royal coffers, and to supply the mean of regal outlay. Nothing is clearer than that the commerce of Israel in all its lines, was, in the great reign of Solomon, a monopoly of the crown. In the maritime traffic this was absolute; and although it may be, that all the land trade was not in the hands of the king and his servants, and that dealers and chapmen were within certain limits tolerated, and allowed to send their camels in the royal caravans, it will appear that permission to do this could only be obtained at a cost, by the payment of dues, which went far to secure for the monopolist all the profits of individual enterprise. Besides, it has always been the rule in such cases, that all gooods, *except those imported by the crown*, are subject to heavy duties on entering the country; and this is a dead loss to the merchants, for they cannot find purchasers unless their goods come into the market at the same price as those which are not subject to any such charges and imposts.

One advantage may accrue to the people through such monopoly of trade in the hands of the crown; and this is, where the wants of the court are thus so far supplied as to render the ordinary source of revenue, the taxation of the people, more light than it would otherwise be. The Israelites did not reap this benefit from their wise king's undertakings. Either his traffic was such that, notwithstanding of its magnificence, or, perhaps, by reason of its magnificence, the expenses nearly or quite devoured the profits; or else the costliness of his buildings and improvements, and the splendour of his court, were so wholly out of proportion to his means and position—were so much more suited to the sovereign of a vast empire than to the ruler of a state small at the largest—as to render all his traffic and tributes from without unequal to his wants. Certain it is that the Israelites were never so exactingly and heavily taxed as during the latter part of his reign. The amount of this taxation might not, if stated, seem heavy to *us;* but almost any amount of taxation must at this time have appeared onerous to the Hebrews, who, during the reign of David, had seen the tributes of conquered kings far more than adequate to the moderate expenses of the government, and who, during the early part of Solomon's own reign, had beheld the expenditure of the state sustained from the treasures left by David, which were in the end exhausted, and from outer sources of revenue, which fell off as the king advanced in years. Solomon had to learn that taxation, really or relatively heavy,

unless for great public objects which touch the national heart, is incompatible with popularity. And this he did learn, from the deep discontent which his exactions occasioned throughout the land, and which was with difficulty, and only through the Lord's special purpose, restrained during his lifetime from that violent outbreak which, in the next reign, rent the kingdom in twain.

The discerning eye may detect other errors in the conduct of this wise man. Some of them are Oriental miscalculations—mispolicies — for which, in regard to the notions of his time and country, we may hold him excused. But others were of a different nature — scarlet sins, for which as a man, as a king in Israel, as one who knew the Lord and was His covenanted servant, no excuse is to be found.

He had a numerous harem—700 wives and 300 concubines, or wives of a lower order; a thousand in all. This was an enormity. In the simplest view, the sexes being nearly equal, it deprived 1,000 men of wives, that one man might have 999 more than he required. Still this was not strictly unlawful. Polygamy was not absolutely forbidden, although, with a view to the very danger into which Solomon fell, kings were forbidden to *multiply* wives unto themselves. From convenience, and from regard to economy, few men had more than one wife; and when these are the only considerations that keep a man from a form of indulgence which he holds to be lawful—whether in wives, in horses, in chariots, in servants, or in palaces—then the number he possesses becomes an index of his wealth and importance. It is a piece of state, his greatness is estimated by it. Hence, in the East, at the present day, the extent of a man's harem rises with his rank; and usually the king (unless he be a man of ostensibly ascetic profession, as is sometimes the case) considers it a sort of duty, a piece of necessary state, to have most of all—more than any of his subjects can afford to maintain. It is, therefore, often not so much with regard to sensual indulgence, as with reference to the consequence which the possession of a large harem imparts, that some Eastern kings are found to have establishments as great as that of Solomon. The king who reigned in Persia in the early part of this century, was reputed to possess wives and concubines scarcely less numerous than those of the Hebrew monarch. In fact, the analogy incidentally stated just now is substantially correct. The same consideration of state which leads a Western prince or noble to multiply horses, leads an Eastern prince to multiply wives—with often as little of personal consideration in the one case as in the other. We can conceive the possibility of an Eastern king feeling himself bound to maintain a hundred wives, who, so far as his own wishes are concerned, thinks he might be happier with one. This view of the case is one excuse that may be urged for Solomon; but how far it may have been really in his case available, it is impossible to tell. It is right, however, to put the best construction upon his motives that circumstances will allow; and certainly his manifest and even inordinate taste for regal state and magnificence, may be some encouragement to us in placing his harem on the same footing as his other great and stately establishments.

There is yet another excuse suggested by the fact, that the "wives"—that is, we suppose, the majority of them—were women of high rank, "princesses;" which may suggest that many of them were taken, as is still the usage in Persia, as virtual hostages for the good behaviour of their fathers—the lords or chieftains of the numerous small tribes and states subject to his sway, and which were for the most part ruled internally by their native chiefs under conditions of tribute.

But although the mere fact of possessing so many wives may be thus variously accounted for or extenuated in an Eastern king, nothing whatever can be urged in excuse of the woful fact, that "in his old age" he suffered his wives "to turn away his heart." Turn it away from what? From God, and from the simplicity of His faith and worship. His strong mind, like the strong body of Samson, lay besotted and enthralled in the lap of the "fair idolatresses" with whom he had filled his house from the nations around, and from whose blandishments he rose another man, shorn of his glory, shorn of his strength. He tolerated their corruptions and worships; this soon grew into active patronage and participation. Presently, upon the high hills, overlooking the temple of the Lord at Jerusalem, arose the shrines, the altars, and the images of Chemosh, of Molech, of the Ashtaroth, and the other gods of his wives; and the heart of every holy man fainted within him, to behold the son of David, himself so highly favoured of God, sanctioning, by his presence and active co-operation, the degrading worship of the grim, the bloody, and abominable idols of Moab, of Ammon, and of Sidon, in the very presence of that "holy and beautiful house," which in his younger days he had reared to the glory of the Lord.

"Various opinions have been held as to the extent and the true nature of Solomon's idolatry. Some (as Augustine) have regarded it as complete apostacy—an apostacy from which there could be no recovery ; others (as Ewald) have seen in it nothing but a wise toleration, rather praiseworthy than blameable, misrepresented and misunderstood by the religious zealots of the day. The truth seems to lie between these two extreme views. Solomon did not ever openly or wholly apostatize. He continued his attendance on the worship of Jehovah, and punctually made his offerings three times a year in the temple (1 Kings ix. 25). But his heart was not 'perfect' with God. Many causes had concurred to weaken the religious earnestness of his younger days—as the corrupting influence of wealth and luxury, the canker of sensualism, an increasing worldliness, leading him to adopt more and more a worldly policy, and perhaps a growing latitudinarianism, arising from contact with all the manifold forms of human opinion. His lapse into deadly sin was no doubt gradual. Partly from ostentation, partly from that sensualism which is the most common failing of Oriental monarchs, he established a harem on a grand and extraordinary scale ; he then admitted among his wives and concubines 'strange women,' i. e., foreigners, either from worldly policy, or for variety's sake ; he allowed himself to fall too much under seraglio influence ; his wives 'turned away his heart.' To gratify them he built magnificent temples to their false gods, temples which were the scene of rites cruel and impure ; he was not ashamed to build these temples right over against Jerusalem, as manifest rivals to 'the Temple.' He thus became the author of a syncretism, which sought to blend together the worship of Jehovah and the worship of idols—a syncretism which possessed fatal attractions for the Jewish nation. Finally, he appears himself to have frequented the idol temples (see verses 5 and 10) and to have taken part in those fearful impurities which constituted the worst horror of the idolatrous systems, thus practically apostatizing, though theoretically he never ceased to hold that Jehovah was the true God."—*Speaker's Commentary*, ii. 547.

S.

THE WISE FOOL

WE have seen many strange sights in our time— many horrible sights ; but none so strange, none so horrible, as that of a wise man making himself a fool. Solomon did that; and he was a wise man, even the wisest of men. If the deep sagacity of Solomon—if his keen discernment—if his strong reason—if his profound knowledge of human life and character—if even his intimate acquaintance with the law and counsels of the Lord—did not preserve his name from that stamp of "foolishness" which we find impressed upon so many of the great names and great acts of men, who is there that can hope to stand? Not one, as of himself; but there is without us and above us a Power that can exalt even the lowly to high things, and can sustain them in all true wisdom, so long as they rest upon it, instead of thinking that the light which shines upon their path and glorifies their way, shines out of themselves, and not into them. Solomon was wise: Solomon was foolish. Strange contrast and contradiction of terms! Yet it does not astonish. It may astonish angels, but not us. We are used to this kind of experience. We see it—the same in kind, if not in degree—every day; and that which would amaze us from any other point of view than that from which we look, becomes familiar to our thoughts. Look around. We see men who are foolish without being wise; but we see not one who is wise without being also foolish. It is "foolishness," and not wisdom, that "is bound in the heart of a child." Foolishness, which every man certainly has, is his nature; wisdom, if he has it, is a gift bestowed upon him—bestowed as freely upon him as it was upon Solomon. The wisdom does not suppress or drive out the foolishness, but is a weapon—it may be a staff, it may be a glittering sword—given into his hands to fight against it, to keep it under; a weapon to be used with daily and ever-watchful vigilance, and not to rest idly in the scabbard. This was king Solomon's fault. Having been victor in many a deadly fray, until victory became easy and habitual, he forgot that the enemy of his greatness and peace still lived—was not mortally wounded—did not even sleep. He suffered his weapon to rest until its keen edge was corroded —until it clung in rust to the scabbard, and could not be drawn forth.

If there be on earth one sight more sorrowful than that of wisdom become foolishness—or, rather, suffering foolishness to be victorious—it is that of the fall of an old man whose youth had been promising, and whose manhood beautiful

and glorious. Yet this was the case of Solomon, and the thought of it is enough to draw forth most bitter tears. The fall of an old tree, or of some noble old ruin, is beheld with some regret, but it occasions no rending of heart. It was their doom. Age ripened them but for their fall; and we wondered more that they stood so long, than that they fell so soon. But man is expected to ripen in moral and religious strength— to harden into rock-like fixedness as his age increases. He whom we have looked up to so long, —he whose words were wise as oracles, and from whose lips we had so long gathered wisdom,—he who had borne noble testimonies for the truth,— he who had laboured for the glory of God, who had withstood many storms of human passion and many temptations of human glory, and in whose capacious mind are garnered up the fruits of a life's knowledge and experience,—for such a man to fall from his high place, fills the most firm of heart with dread, and makes the moral universe tremble. It is altogether terrible. It is a calamity to mankind: it is more than that; it is a shame, a wrong, and a dishonour. The righteous hide their heads, and the perverse exult:—hell laughs.

There is yet something more: the grace of God is blasphemed. To see a man set forth as one specially gifted of God—as endowed with a surpassing measure of wisdom from above, to fit him to become a king and leader of men,—for HIM to fall, is, with the unthinking, an awful scandal upon the gifts of God. If he who ascribes heaven-given powers to the influence of demons, commits, as most suppose, the unpardonable sin against the Holy Ghost, of what sin, think you, is he guilty, who *gives occasion* to that blasphemy by his misconduct and his fall?

Yet amid this dreadful scene of wreck and ruin, something profitable to our own souls may be gathered up.

Let it teach us not to rely too implicitly upon any past attainments or present convictions. Let us never think that the time of danger to our souls is past, or that the great troubler of spirits is wholly discomfited, and despairs of all advantage over us. There is no time wherein we can be safe, while we carry this body of sin about us. "Youth is impetuous, mid age stubborn, old age weak,—ALL DANGEROUS." In the conviction of this ever present peril, and of the sleepless vigilance of the enemy, may we be led to look out of ourselves altogether for strength and sustainment. When we are strongest, it is best to be weak in ourselves; and when at our weakest, strong in Him in whom we can do all things. "If God uphold us not, we cannot stand; if God uphold us, we cannot fall." Then, why did He not uphold Solomon, that he might not fall? There can be but one answer,—Solomon did not want to be upheld. He thought he could stand alone—he relied upon his own strength—he trusted in his own heart; and we have Scripture and experience to tell us, that "he who trusteth in his own heart is a fool." He, in the pride of his intellectual wealth, was like the rich man in the parable with his material goods,—"Soul! thou hast much goods laid up for many years." It was at that moment, when the rich worldling had realized the conviction that he had need of nothing, that the word went forth against him: "Thou fool!" So, also, assuredly, was it then—when Solomon thought himself perfect in wisdom, that he was rich, and increased in goods, and that he had need of nothing—that the word went forth: "Thou fool!" and he became foolish indeed.

"So fallen! so lost! the light withdrawn
　　Which once he wore!
The glory from his grey hairs gone
　　For evermore!
Of all we loved and honoured, nought
　　Save power remains;
A fallen angel's pride of thought,
　　Still strong in chains.
All else is gone, from those great eyes
　　The soul has fled:
When faith is lost, and honour dies,
　　The man is dead.
Then pay the reverence of old days
　　To his dead fame;
Walk backward with averted gaze,
　　And hide the shame."—*Whittier.*

Did Solomon repent? Scripture says nothing positively; but it may be hoped that he did. If the book of Ecclesiastes be correctly ascribed to Solomon—and we are of those who think that it is—it is most natural to suppose that it exhibits his maturest convictions and experiences; and although there are no such direct expressions of repentance as we find in the Psalms of David—no such lamenting cries for sin—it may be considered that the framework of the book did not well admit them. But there is much in the warnings against the vanity and vexation of

spirit by which the wicked and profligate are deceived and tormented, to remind us of the sad and sorrowful experience which the history ascribes to the latter days of Solomon.

―――――

OUTER TROUBLES

1 Kings 11:21-25

THE sin of one so gifted and favoured as Solomon, required such punishment as should remain to all generations a monument of the Lord's displeasure. He was that servant who, knowing his Lord's will, and doing it not, required to be beaten with many stripes: and if judgment be required according to what a man hath, an awful severity of judgment was needed here; for to whom had more of light and knowledge been given than to Solomon? Yet, in judgment the Lord remembered mercy. Solomon had sinned; but David could not be forgotten, and to him a sure house had been promised. But for that, doubtless, the house of David had been, like that of Saul, utterly cast down. But this extremity of judgment, this utter degree of forfeiture, was not exacted. Still the house should reign—but reign only over one part of a divided realm; and even this mitigated doom was, with paternal tenderness in punishment, spared the aged king in person. It was announced to him, but was not to be executed while he lived; yet his last years were not suffered to pass without heavy troubles, which must have brought down his kingly pride very low.

Enemies, one after another appeared, who had in his early years been kept down by the memory of David's victories, and by the show of substantial strength which his own government presented. At length, however, they ventured to try its texture; and finding it more vulnerable than even they had suspected,—that there was nothing very terrible to resolute men in its showy greatness,—and having found that the king had really no power to make any effectual opposition to their assaults, far less to put them down, they were emboldened to take further measures, until some established their independence, while others offered the passive resistance of withholding their tributes, so that his power became shorn at the borders, and eventually shaken at home, where the discontinuance of many outer supplies of revenue, and probably the interruption of his various lines of trade— no longer in his undisputed possession—urged him, not to economy and retrenchment, but to make good the deficiency by the taxation of his native subjects.

The principal foreign disturbers of Solomon's repose were Hadad, prince of Edom, and Rezon, king of Damascene-Syria. Of Hadad, and his escape in childhood into Egypt, when his country was ravaged by Joab, we have already had occasion to speak.[1] When he reached riper years, the keen remembrance of his native land, his lost kingdom, and the slaughter of all his house, gathered strength within him; and all the ease and princely honour which he enjoyed in Egypt, availed not against the claims of ambition, vengeance, and patriotism. He dreamed of recovering the throne of his fathers; he dreamed of wresting the hard yoke of Jacob from Esau's neck; he dreamed of exacting stern vengeance for the blood of his kin and country; he dreamed of making to himself a name, like unto the names of the great ones that were upon the earth. These things he dreamed, and

"Dreams grow realities to earnest men."

And he was earnest. It was not without difficulty that he obtained leave of the Egyptian king, by whom he had been so generously entertained, to take his departure. It does not appear that he ventured fully to disclose his real objects —for which a reason may be found in the fact that this king was in amicable relations with Solomon, and the same, apparently, whose daughter had been espoused by the Hebrew monarch.

Proceeding to Edom, the attempts which Hadad made to recover his kingdom seem to have given considerable trouble to the Hebrew government; but the strong garrisons which David had left in the land, and which Solomon maintained there, prevented them from being successful. Seeing that his case was for the time hopeless in that quarter, Hadad, instead of returning to Egypt, determined to push his fortunes in another direction. He therefore went and joined himself to Rezon, who had already given considerable disturbance to Solomon's power in Syria.

This Rezon had held some post of honour

[1] See Vol. 1, pp. 756-759.

under that great Hadadezer, king of Zobah, whose overthrow formed one of the most renowned military acts of David's reign.[1] It seems that, on the defeat of the Syrian host, Rezon succeeded in drawing off the force under his command, and directed the power thus acquired to the advancement of his own ambitious views. At first the wilderness afforded its shelter to his troop, which there subsisted for a time by that wild life of predatory warfare, of which, in the like cases, there are many examples in Scripture, and which seems, indeed, to have been the usual resource of fugitive military chiefs of that age and region—on the borders of the Syrian and Arabian deserts. Gradually, however, he acquired a sort of fixed power over a portion of Syria nearest to the desert, and eventually established a kingdom, of which Damascus became the capital. All this could not have been effected without much loss and disadvantage to the Hebrew king — especially by interrupting his communication with Tadmor and the Euphrates, and by harassing, if not destroying, the important trade established on that line of route.

It was to this prince that Hadad carried his sword when he found that he could not employ it with any advantage in Edom. Hadad seems to have been a very engaging or very plausible person, for he was well received and won high favour wherever he went. Rezon gave to him and his followers a most encouraging reception, and afforded them assistance in establishing themselves in another and a neighbouring portion of Syria, where Hadad seems to have had ample opportunities of disturbing the peace of Solomon. Nor is this all: for when Rezon died, Hadad added his dominions to his own, and thus became the virtual founder of that important kingdom of Damascene-Syria, which we afterwards find in powerful and often successful warfare with the Israelites. Hadad was, on account of his success and his royal qualities, so much honoured by his successors, that Ben-hadad, "son of Hadad," became a common name among them, if, indeed, it was not made an official title, like that of Pharaoh in Egypt.

The reader must not expect to find all this in Scripture. The intimations which it contains respecting Hadad and Rezon, and, in particular, respecting the connection between them, are brief, and, seeing that they refer to historical

[1] See Vol. 1, pp. 754-756.

circumstances of no common interest, tantalizing. That which we have given is the most consistent and intelligible account we are able to collect from the statements in Scripture and in Josephus. These, so far as Hadad is concerned, afford glimpses of what would probably be a most instructive and interesting story, were all its particulars fully understood.

The fragments of history given in these verses I interpret somewhat differently from Dr. Kitto. I would not follow Josephus implicitly in his story of Hadad, because it does not appear consistent with other parts of his own history, or with other passages of Scripture. Damascus was the head of a powerful kingdom long before the days of Hadad the Edomite—so powerful, that when David defeated the king of Zobah, the Arameans of Damascus ventured to attack him ; and Josephus tells us that the leader of this attack was king Hadad, a man of great power, and whose posterity, he adds, reigned in Damascus for ten generations, each monarch, on ascending the throne, adopting the name Hadad (*Ant.*, vii. 5, 2 ; 2 Sam. viii. 3-6). But how is this to be reconciled with the statement in 1 Kings xi. 25, " He (*i. e.* Hadad) abhorred Israel and reigned over Syria ?" The word translated Syria is *Aram;* but several MSS. read *Edom*, and this reading is supported by the Septuagint. The two words resemble each other very closely in Hebrew ; and there is more than one case in which they have been confounded. Adopting the latter reading, the narrative is clear and consistent. Hadad having returned from Egypt to his native Edom, ruled there, and kept up a guerilla warfare against Solomon amid its mountain fastnesses.

Still another difficulty meets us. If the descendants of the first Hadad reigned in Damascus for ten generations, how can it be said of Rezon, that "he gathered men unto him, and became captain over a band ; and they went to Damascus, and dwelt therein, and reigned in Damascus ?" The meaning of this passage would appear to be simply this, that Rezon, with his band of freebooters, established himself within the kingdom of Damascus, became a skilful general, acquired great influence at court, and was, for a time, the main director of public affairs, though he never ascended the throne.

P.

THE RENT MANTLE

1 Kings 11:26-40

WAS there no priest, no prophet, to warn the besotted king of the evil of his ways, and of the danger that hung over him ? Gad the seer was, no doubt, long since dead, and Nathan the prophet could not well be alive ; but there could not have been wanting faithful and true men in Israel, whose hearts trembled for him, and the echoes of whose discontent and apprehension must have reached him, even in the curtained recesses of his harem. But we read not of any commissioned and authoritative warning to him, previous to that which denounced his doom, and the forfeiture of the largest and fairest portion of his realm. Perhaps there was no such anterior warning. When God has given to a man sufficient inner light to guide his path, He often does not deem the same measure of warning from without needful, as where light is more dim, and knowledge less perfect.

By what agency this awful message of judgment was conveyed to him we do not know ; nor is the manner in which the king received it clearly indicated. It must have been a terrible stroke to the kingly pride which he had by this time contracted. He had, no doubt, rested in the impression that, whatever else might happen to him, the royal domain of the house of David had been secured under the promise made to his father, and the possibility of a divided empire had probably never crossed his thoughts ; although, to us, such an event has been foreshadowed by significant antecedents in the latter part of David's reign. But now he finds himself doomed, like another Saul, to have ten-twelfths of his domain rent from his house and "given to his servant." Little as he was prepared for this stroke, there were probably thousands in Israel who looked for nothing less ; and both he and they must have waited with eager anxiety for some indication of the man on whom this high lot should fall.

They waited not long. In this case, as in that of David, the appointment came upon one of no high station nor influence. It was thus, therefore, a proof only the more signal of the favour of the Divine King. Apart from this, and the possession of certain engaging qualities which captivated the hearts of men, there was no resemblance between David and Jeroboam : that was his name. He was a young man of Ephraim, the son of a widow. He was a person of great capacity for public business—of high parts ; and as he is said to have been " a mighty man of valour," he must have had some opportunities of distinguishing himself. Solomon had marked the talents of this young man, and made him overseer of the persons of his own tribe who were engaged on the public works. And here we may note another grievance of the Israelites. It had been the boast of the early part of Solomon's reign that no Israelites—only foreigners—were employed in compulsory labour. That this had now ceased, and that Solomon had, like other Oriental despots, assumed the absolute right to such services from his subjects as he might need from them, is clear from this fact. That they were classed according to their tribes, with officers of the same tribes, evinces the nature of this service. Except where distinctly marked castes exist, voluntary service is never subject to such classification.

While thus employed in government service, Jeroboam was flaunting about one day in a fine new mantle, when he encountered a rough and venerable man, who, to his great consternation, rent the mantle from his shoulders, and tore it into pieces. He knew, however, that this was the prophet Ahijah,—the same, perhaps, who had conveyed the Lord's judgment to Solomon; and instead, therefore, of resisting this rough treatment of his cloak, he stood still to hear what it might mean. The pieces were twelve into which the prophet divided the robe. Two of them he reserved; but the other ten he presented to Jeroboam with the words—"Take these ten pieces; for thus saith the Lord, the God of Israel, Behold I will rend the kingdom out of the hand of Solomon, and will give ten tribes to thee."

It is uncertain whether or not it was intended that this fact should transpire. From the privacy sought by the prophet, it may be conceived that it was designed to be secret for the time. Jeroboam was, however, too much elated by his good fortune to keep it to himself. Hitherto the chief restraint upon the people had lain in the notion that the Lord had guaranteed the throne over all Israel to the house of David, and the most turbulent spirits had been kept under restraint by the fear of resisting the purposes of God. The intimation of this nomination, under divine authority, fell like a spark upon fuel. The important principle involved—freedom from a restriction which had become intolerable—at once raised the agent, in whose person it had been set forth, to the height of popularity among the tribes under the influence of the house of Joseph; and although he had been warned that no change was to take place until after the death of Solomon, he found himself driven, by the force of circumstances, if not by the promptings of his own ambition, into some immediate demonstrations. The movement was not attended with the result he expected; and, finding that he had become a marked man to Solomon, he deemed it prudent to evade the storm he had raised by retiring into Egypt, and there awaiting the progress of events. Egypt seems to have become, in this age, the common resort of political refugees. For the attention which Hadad received there, we can account by recollecting that he was a child and a prince, but the consideration with which Jeroboam was treated—seeing that the king of Egypt would not, if he could understand it, recognize the authority of the nomination he had received, and that in his eyes the young man was merely a rebel against his master—will not be very easily understood, without recollecting that the throne of Egypt was now occupied by a king of a family different from that with which Solomon had contracted affinity in his youth; and that the signs of declining power, which the Hebrew government had already evinced, had probably directed the attention of the Egyptian king before this period to the far-renowned treasures of the temple and palace as his future spoil. It thus became his policy to weaken the resources, and promote whatever might tend to lame the greatness, of a power which had of late become more formidable than a king of Egypt could regard with perfect satisfaction.

So Jeroboam remained in Egypt till the death of Solomon. During his stay he noted, with a curious eye, the institutions and strange worship of the country which had been the scene of ancient bondage to his people. It is to be feared that much which met his view, and which could only be abhorrent to a true Israelite, inspired him with no disgust, but on the contrary drew forth his admiration; that he saw much which he deemed worthy of imitation, and that he treasured up what appeared to him useful hints, which might be applied with advantage when his predicted destinies were fulfilled. But whatever was the immediate safety found in this Egyptian refuge, he lived to lament that his steps had not turned some other way. The visit was ruinous to him, by filling his mind with ideas wholly alien to the Hebrew constitution; and the attempt to work out these brought disaster upon his house, and dishonour upon his name.

REHOBOAM

1 Kings 11:43; 12:1

Only one son of Solomon appears in history, and it is generally supposed that he had no other. On this Hall quaintly observes: "Many a poor man hath an housefull of children by one wife, whereas this great king hath only one son by many housefulls of wives." And this one son was, as Ness remarks, "none of the wisest, but a silly child when at the age of forty years." It should seem to be in the course of nature, that sons brought up under the nurture of wise fathers should be themselves wise. But it is not always seen—perhaps not often seen—that wise fathers have wise sons. How is this? It may be that the wisdom of the son—the formation of his character—depends more on the mother than the father, and that a wise mother is even more essential than a wise father to the formation of a wise son. It is probably for this reason that the sacred historian is careful to record that Rehoboam's mother was an Ammonitess, and being such, was, we may presume, one of those women who seduced Solomon into idolatry; for the gods of the Ammonites are specified among those which he worshipped. As the mother of his only son, or at least of his heir, the influence of this lady, whose name was Naamah, must have been paramount in the harem; and with reference to the worship of her gods, no other woman could have had any influence comparable to hers; for we cannot suppose that Solomon would go into this Ammonitish idolatry in direct opposition to her wishes. At any rate, she could hardly have been a wise mother in the Hebrew point of view, if in any other.

The importance of a wise mother to the bringing up of a wise son, is not obscurely expressed more than once by Solomon himself. He had a wise father, and he gratefully acknowledges the advantages he derived from his instructions; but he gives praise to his mother also, whom he mentions with affectionate regard, as one to whose tender counsels he owed not less. "I was," he says, "my father's son, tender and only beloved in the sight of my mother;"[1] and in his book of Proverbs, he concludes with "the words of king Lemuel, the prophecy which his mother

[1] Proverbs 4:3.

taught him;" and from the specimen of her instruction there given, we can see that she was indeed a wise, a loving, and an experienced mother, however frail and fatal her conduct may at one time have been. Ah, with what emphasis could she pour into the heedful ears of her son the words, "Favour is deceitful, and beauty is vain; but a woman that feareth the Lord, she shall be praised!" She herself had that praise, and from her own son too, when, in mature life, he looked thankfully back upon the large benefit he owed to her early instructions. No; we may hear of foolish sons having wise fathers, and of foolish fathers having wise sons, but rarely of a wise son having had a foolish mother.[1]

That Solomon was conscious of the imbecile character of his son, there can be no doubt. It is impossible to resist the conviction, that he speaks in the book of Ecclesiastes[2] on this point, from the bitterness of his own misgivings: "I hated all my labour which I had taken under the sun; because I should leave it unto the man that shall be after me. And who knoweth whether he shall be a wise man or a fool? Yet shall he have rule over all my labour wherein I have laboured, and wherein I have showed myself wise under the sun."

Rehoboam's conduct was so childish and ignorant, and betrayed such utter unacquaintance with the spirit of the age and temper of the people, as to remind us of the Oriental princes called out of the harem to reign, with all their experience, even at a mature age, yet to be acquired. And this was very probably the case. The common reason for this is jealousy of his heir on the part of the reigning prince, whether of his ambition, or of his becoming so popular as to induce the people to call him to reign before his time. To prevent this, he is kept within the palace, beyond which little concerning him, besides the fact of his existence, is suffered to transpire. This had not been the policy of David, nor was it *generally* that of the Jewish kings. But Solomon might have been led to seclude his

[1] "Several young men who were associated in preparing for the Christian ministry, felt interested in ascertaining what proportion of their number had pious mothers. They were greatly surprised and delighted in finding that, out of 120 students, more than 100 had been blessed by a mother's prayers, and directed by a mother's counsels to the Saviour."—Arvine's *Anecdotes*, p. 553. New York.

[2] Ecclesiastes 2:18,19.

son, by the recollection of how much his own father had suffered by the conspiracy of two of his children. Or it may be that he did it from the desire of concealing the deficiencies of that son from the knowledge of the people. It is impossible to say whether the imbecility of Rehoboam was the cause or the effect of his being kept in the seraglio; but that he was shut up there, seems altogether probable. It is charitable to him to suppose, that his utter ignorance of public affairs and public principles, arose less from natural incapacity than from the privacy in which he lived. In confirmation of this conjecture as to the previous seclusion of Rehoboam, there is a passage in Ecclesiastes (iv. 14), describing a king as coming out of confinement to reign; which at least shows that the mind of the author was familiar with the practice. This, coupled with the fears of his son's foolishness hinted at in the same book, seems to evince that Solomon did not keep him in retirement from any interested motive, but merely to prevent any prejudice from being conceived against him before the time came for him to reign. We cannot question that in this seclusion, Solomon attempted to impart to his son such knowledge and instruction as his station required. But probably he gave up the attempt at length; for nothing discourages one more than the endeavour to fill a leaky vessel.

When the death of Solomon became known, the chiefs of the tribes assembled at Shechem, an ancient and venerated place of convocation, to which on that account, as well as from its central position, Rehoboam could not object, although he would doubtless have preferred that the assembly should have been held at Jerusalem, rather than in the chief town of a tribe so disaffected as that of Ephraim, and so notoriously adverse to the predominance which the tribe of Judah possessed through the rule of David's house. It will be remembered, that both Saul and David had received the crown under certain covenants with the people, and with certain limitations, which had been overlooked under the peculiar circumstances of Solomon's accession. To this neglect the people appear to have ascribed the despotic tendencies and oppressive exactions of Solomon's later government; and they felt that their consequent inability to lay to his charge the neglect or contravention of personal covenants, had deprived them of a powerful weapon of constitutional opposition, and had laid them comparatively helpless at the foot of his throne. They resolved that this mistake should not again occur; and that the new king must accept the throne under stipulations for redress of grievances, and of reigning in accordance with the principles of the old covenants. This course was perfectly constitutional. Even Rehoboam—high as were his notions of the royal prerogative and of his divine rights as the heir of David—had sense enough to see that it was such, and therefore proceeded with his court to Shechem, to accept the crown in the presence of the assembled states. So far, both parties acted guardedly; and although the place of meeting, and the sending for Jeroboam out of Egypt to take a leading part in the transactions, afford some indication of a foregone conclusion on the part of the tribes, it is impossible not to respect their determination to keep within the forms of the constitution, in resisting those marked tendencies to absolutism which the government had of late years manifested.

WHIPS AND SCORPIONS

1 Kings 12:1-24

IT strongly shows the fearlessness of Jeroboam's character, that he not only hastened from Egypt at the call of the malcontents, but appeared before the king at their head, as their representative and spokesman in demanding redress of grievances. The demand made seems in itself reasonable and just: "Thy father made our yoke grievous: now, therefore, ease thou somewhat the grievous servitude of thy father, and his heavy yoke that he put upon us, and we will serve thee." The manner in which it was put forward, however—in the person of Jeroboam, a known pretender to the crown, and lately a fugitive rebel—could not but have given it an aspect most offensive to the pride of the king. The presence of Jeroboam in fact supplies the threat, the alternative, the "or if not ——!" to which utterance was not given. It must be admitted that this thrusting forward of Jeroboam at the outset, and before the disposition of Rehoboam in regard to their claims had been ascertained, has much the aspect of an act of intimidation, and an uncalled for affront. We must therefore couple the manner of the demand with the words which contain it, in order to realize the entire force of the case as it presented itself to Rehoboam. It was a critical moment for him; it was a moment for prompt and decisive action, to which Saul or David would have been equal, but to the requirements of which the son of Solomon could not reach. Humanly speaking, and setting aside our knowledge that the result was foreordained, it is open to us to fancy how different that result might have been had the king been equal to the occasion. May we not suppose it likely that, if he had at once met the boldness of Jeroboam by the greater boldness of seizing him on the spot, and in a few strong and kindling words declared his hearty purpose to relax the burdens of the people and redress their grievances, he might have turned the tide in his own favour, and have roused the crowd to enthusiastic shouts of "Long live the king!"

To hesitate in such a crisis is ruin. Even a prompt refusal had been less dangerous than delay. But Rehoboam could not trust his own understanding. He asked three days for deliberation. Even consent after such delay would lose the generous aspect of spontaneous grace, and would have the appearance to the people of having been extorted from his fears. And it rendered refusal doubly ruinous. The indication of reluctance gave warning of the result that might be expected, and afforded time for the disaffected to mature their plans and preparations for revolt. We cannot doubt that these three days were among the busiest of Jeroboam's life.

The first impulse of Rehoboam was good. He sought the advice of the reverend councillors who had "stood before his father." Their council was excellent: unreserved and cheerful acquiescence in the wishes of the people—kind and gracious treatment of them now, in order to win them for ever. It is clear that this counsel did not suit the king's humour, or he would have acted upon it without seeking further. But it is manifest that he was in search of such advice as would afford a sort of sanction to the course he was most inclined to follow, and such as would bring in others to share the responsibility with him. He resorted to "the young men who had been brought up with him,"—those who had been

chosen for his associates, and who, judging from the fact of their having led the same kind of life as himself, were doubtless quite as inexperienced in state affairs. Their thought was all of royal rights and prerogatives; and their advice was, that he should give to the audacious varlets, who dared to exact conditions from their sovereign, such an answer as would teach them to know their master.

Accordingly, at the appointed time the king made his appearance before the assembled states of Israel; and, in a voice intended to be stern and awful, he stated their demand, and gave this answer, which reaches to the sublime of simpleness: "My little finger shall be thicker than my father's loins. For whereas my father put a heavy yoke upon you, I will put more to your yoke: my father chastised you with whips, but I will chastise you with scorpions." This is to say—if we are to explain the simile—that whereas his father had scourged them with simple whips, he would scourge them with twisted lashes armed with sharp and lacerating points; for to such the name of "scorpion" was given.

The almost insane fatuity of the man who could expect any good effect from an answer like this to an aggrieved and exasperated people, whom the mere fact of Jeroboam's presence must, to an ordinary understanding, have shown to be ripe for any ulterior consequences, can scarcely be explained but on the interpretation, that the king was subjected to judicial blindness, that wisdom and common sense had been withheld from him, in order that the doom which had already gone forth against the house of David might be accomplished.

The king's answer was received with indignation and scorn by the people, to whom it indeed supplied a cause and justification of the course to which they were already well inclined. They at once renounced their allegiance to the house of David,—casting it off, indeed, with mingled wrath and derision, as a worthless and abominable thing. Rehoboam could not, however, easily understand the extent of his misfortune, that a revolt could be so real and general—that it was indeed a fact accomplished, without its reality having been evinced by blows given and taken—was incomprehensible to him. Kingdoms are not usually broken up and divided in this quiet fashion; and the son of Solomon suffered himself to believe that he still reigned. There was clearly no disposition to subject him to ill treatment; he still remained at Shechem, in the very heart and headquarters of the revolted district; and he might, perhaps, have remained there for some time longer, cherishing his delusions, had he not taken it into his head to set the most obnoxious person in the land (if we may judge from analogy rather than from document)—one Adoram, the head tax-gatherer—to collect on that very spot the burdensome taxes which had brought things to such a pass. This was too much for the forbearance of the naturally turbulent Shechemites. They rose upon the unlucky comptroller of the taxes, and pelted him with stones till he died of the injuries he received. This very broad hint opened the king's eyes; and he lost no time in mounting his chariot, and driving off at full speed to Jerusalem, which he reached in safety.

Judah remained, as might be expected, faithful to the house of David; and, since the establishment of the royal court and the temple at Jerusalem, the interests of Benjamin had become so much intermixed with those of Judah, that it naturally, and almost inevitably, adhered to the same side. Thus, of the twelve tribes, only two held by the house of David, and these not the two of highest importance—for although the one was the greatest of the tribes, the other was the least. Among the revolted tribes were those beyond the Jordan; so that all that extensive region was lost, and with it the tributary nations in the eastern and north-eastern borders. But although lost to Judah, it is not probable that any of these, except Moab, were preserved to Israel. These tributaries had been falling away in the time even of Solomon, and were not likely to neglect taking advantage of the further weakening of the realm which this divison both occasioned and indicated. On the side of Judah, the only foreign possession that remained in some kind of dependence was Edom; but it may be doubted if this dependency added much to the strength of the kingdom, though it enabled the sovereigns of David's house, for some generations, to claim a dominion extending to the Red Sea, the ports of which must have become an unprofitable possession, now that another realm was interposed between this kingdom and the Phœnicians, if indeed this was not the case at an earlier period.

Rehoboam was not likely to abstain from some efforts to regain the important portion of his dominions which had thus been rent from him. He called out an army; and with the ready resources of an organized state at his command, the two tribes might have been at that time more than a match for the ten. But when the army was about to march, a prophet appeared, and, in the name of the Lord, forbade them to go forth to fight against "their brethren," seeing "this thing was from Him"—had been in conformity with His will and declared purpose. The king has received some compliments for his submission to the divine mandate on this occasion —when he stood in all his kingly pride, with his arms and banners, ready to march forth against the rebels, and make a stroke for the heritage of his house. We have no wish to take this credit from him. But it seems to us, that there was more necessity than virtue in his resignation. The words of the prophet were addressed not only to the king, but to the assembled warriors, and were imperative upon the latter—"Return every man to his house;" and, we are immediately told, "they hearkened therefore to the word of the Lord, and returned to depart." There is no reason to suppose that they would remain under arms after such a command, however much Rehoboam may have wished them to do so. They obeyed the prophet, and he could not but do the same.

The sinful luxuries of Solomon's reign prepared the way for the overthrow of the kingdom of Israel, and the folly of Rehoboam gave it the first fatal blow. The land was God's gift; the kingdom was established and sustained by God's power. But God's laws were to be the kingdom's laws, and its stability was conditional on those laws being kept. Solomon, giving rein to the wild passions of his nature, recklessly, and one would almost say systematically, violated the divine commands. "Thou shalt have no other gods before me," was the first and greatest of all the commands. But Solomon established an idolatrous worship in the very centre of the land. The licentious and cruel rights of Ashtaroth, and Molech, and Chemosh, were performed almost beneath the walls of the Lord's temple on Moriah. "He (the king) shall not multiply horses to himself," was another command. But Solomon's stables were on a style of regal magnificence. Forty thousand stalls of horses for his chariots were attached to the royal palace; and twelve thousand horsemen served as life-guards. "Neither shall he multiply wives unto himself, that his heart turn not away." Solomon "loved many strange women, women of the Moabites, Ammonites, Edomites, Zidonians, and Hittites. He had seven hundred wives, princesses, and three hundred concubines." His own heart was thus turned away from the true God. The morals of the court and of the nation were corrupted. Not only was the judgment of Heaven called down by a broken law ; but humanity was outraged, and robbed of its natural health and vigour. "Neither shall he greatly multiply to himself silver and gold." But "all king Solomon's drinking vessels were of gold, and all the vessels of the house of the forest of Lebanon were of pure gold : none were of silver ; it was nothing accounted of in the days of Solomon. . . . The king made silver to be in Jerusalem as stones." Humility in demeanour, moderation in living, justice in judgment, and leniency in rule, were strictly enjoined. But Solomon in his latter days became proud, luxurious, unjust, and tyrannical. The enormous expenses of his court compelled him to levy contributions which his people were ill able to bear. The foreign tribes and nations which had become tributary under the victorious reign of David were the first to rebel. Then the Israelites began to murmur ; and these murmurs were the preludes of that storm which convulsed the kingdom at the commencement of Rehoboam's reign. The whole after history of the disruption, the gradual decline of power and influence, the corruption of morals, and at times the almost total forgetfulness of God, were only the necessary developments of those pernicious principles and practices introduced by Solomon.

P.

THE SCHISM

1 Kings 12:24-33

JEROBOAM, being chosen king by the revolted tribes, soon found his throne not without anxious cares, nor his crown without a thorn.

Shechem he fortified and made his capital. But he soon perceived that Jerusalem, as the seat of the temple and of all ritual service, was the real metropolis of the whole nation, and would remain a centre of union to all the tribes, notwithstanding the political separation which had taken place. Thither, to the metropolis of the rival state, his subjects would repair at the yearly festivals, and convey their dues and offerings. This alone would give an immense superiority of dignity and prosperity to Judah ; and was it to be expected that the ten tribes, thus continually reminded of their separated state, and of the disadvantageous position in which it placed them, would be long content to remain in this condition of religious inferiority and separation ? Unless some means could be

found of counteracting this influence, and of rendering his kingdom independent, not only in government, but in ritual worship, was it not to be feared that the coincidence of a popular king and prosperous reign in Judah, with an unpopular king and unprosperous reign in Israel, might in some future, and perhaps not remote day, induce the ten tribes to return to their allegiance to the house of David?

Thus Jeroboam reasoned ; and the danger seemed to him so serious, that no means were to be neglected in order to avert it. It appeared clear to him, that no effectual remedy could be found but in such alterations of the law—or rather in a departure from so much of the ritual law as was based on the unity of the nation. This he determined to do, scrupling at nothing that might, in his judgment, tend to the establishment of his kingdom. We have no right to suppose that he reached this conclusion without hesitation ; but having once decided upon it as his only means of safety—having once committed himself to this policy, he carried it out with that unshrinking boldness which is indicated in most of his doings. He was perhaps the more stimulated to this, by observing that in Egypt the king himself was high priest, and exercised the priestly functions, with the supreme power in ecclesiastical matters. This seemed to him a covetable position to occupy, as he may have thought that the priesthood, as established in Israel, with an independent high priest, possessed a degree of power which might prove an inconvenient check upon that of the crown.

Under these views, Jeroboam concluded to establish two places of ritual worship, one in the north, and the other in the south of his kingdom—at Dan and Bethel—under the plausible excuse to his people, that Jerusalem was inconveniently distant for their visits at the annual festivals. In the absence of ark and cherubim, he set a golden calf or young bull at each place, as a symbolical figure consecrated to Jehovah, and not, as we may be apt to imagine, as an idolatrous representation of any other god. In this point of view, it might have seemed to him as lawful as the cherubim ; and indeed it may have been intended as a partial substitute for the compound cherubic figures of the temple and tabernacle. But the words that he employed in inviting the attention of his people to this image—being the same that

Aaron employed in the wilderness with regard to the golden calf—"This is thy God, O Israel, that brought thee out of the land of Egypt," show that he had that case in view, and knew, therefore, the history connected with it, and how severely that act had been condemned and punished. The views under which that symbol was adopted in the wilderness apply equally here, and it is not necessary to repeat what has been already stated in reference to it. It was not idolatry as regards the worship of strange gods, and hence it is not mentioned with such strong condemnation and burning resentment by the prophets, as the subsequent introduction of foreign gods under Ahab. But it was an infraction of the law, which forbade any representation or symbol of Jehovah. It was a degradation "to liken the glory of the invisible God to an ox that eateth grass;" and it was a step towards that direct idolatry against which the law so sedulously guarded. This applies to the representation merely; but in Jeroboam's case, there was added the sin of schism, brought in among a people intended to be religiously united beyond any other, and whose most important institutions were framed with reference to that object. We may give this man credit for believing, that he did not mean to go further with his innovations than might seem to him barely necessary to secure his object. It was probably his design merely to establish local shrines to Jehovah, with little alteration in the mode and circumstances of worship. But having begun in this evil way, he felt compelled to proceed further than he had contemplated, unless he would abandon his object altogether, and for this he was not prepared. As many of the Levitical cities were in his dominions, he calculated that priests and Levites enough would be found to conduct this worship, rather than abandon all they possessed in the world. In this, like other worldly calculations upon the weakness and corruption of human character, he was mistaken. The world was not quite so bad as he thought it, and men were a little better and more honest than he judged. The Levitical body repudiated the whole concern, and refused to lend it the prestige of their name and influence; and when, in resentment for this, Jeroboam forbade them to attend in their regular courses to discharge their duties at the temple of Jerusalem, they aban-

doned their cities, their fields, and pleasant homes, where they had been born and brought up, and shaking the dust of a polluted land from their feet, departed to the southern kingdom. The accession of so large a body of learned and religious men, and of the numerous right-minded and conscientious persons who followed them, added materially to the fixed population of Judah and Benjamin, and more to the moral strength and character of the southern kingdom, while it in the same degree weakened that of Jeroboam.

He was at first confounded by this movement, which affixed the stigma of inferiority to his position, and this at the instance of the recognized priesthood. He had to abandon his project, or to seek other priests out of the non-clerical tribes. But he found no persons of character willing to undertake the office; so that he had to ordain priests from "the lowest of the people,"—persons in such condition in life, that the emoluments of the office were an inducement, and the credit of even a degraded priesthood an honour to them. To keep them in countenance, at least at first, Jeroboam himself assumed the office of high priest, and as such officiated in the solemn ministrations when present at Dan or Bethel at the three yearly festivals.

Perhaps the most generally popular and best frequented of these festivals was that of autumn —the Feast of Tabernacles; being held at the close of the agricultural year, after the vintage came, when men were at leisure, and disposed to commemorative enjoyments.

The time of this festival was changed by Jeroboam to a month later,—a most unauthorized and high-handed innovation, for which it is difficult to account, except by supposing that he was at length led on to wish to widen the difference as much as possible. The distinction produced by a difference in the time of observing a great festival is very serious indeed, and may be partly illustrated by the less considerable difference, exhibited in the Holy Land at this day, between the time of observing Easter, and also (through the Gregorian reform of the calendar) of Christmas, by the Eastern and Western churches. It has at times occurred to us, that Jeroboam may have been partly influenced by the consideration, that the agricultural labours of the year were not nearly so soon over in some parts of his dominion as in the territory of Judah, and that hence he might in this also allege publice convenience as the ground of the alteration. It is at all events certain, that the harvest, ingathering, and vintage, are two, three, and even four weeks later in the northern parts of Israel, than in the southern parts of Judah.

We must not conceal from ourselves that there are many persons who, at the bottom of their hearts, will think that Jeroboam acted wisely in the course he took, and cannot see how he could have got over the serious difficulty in his path but by some such course as that which he adopted? How could he otherwise have managed? The answer is, he need not have managed at all. He had been appointed king under the divine sanction. He held his crown under the condition of obedience; and on that condition the continuance of the crown to his house was pledged to him. Nothing was wanted on his part but unreserved faith in that promise. If Jeroboam had possessed that faith he would have been free from any anxiety on the subject; he would have felt that it was safer to incur an apparent danger in pursuing the career of duty and right doing, than to seek exemption from it by unlawful doings and tortuous policy. The Lord had given him every reason to trust in the sufficiency of His protection, when He had compelled king Rehoboam to dismiss the forces with which he was prepared to fall upon him in his comparatively helpless condition. If it be asked, *how* he was to be secured from the danger which stood so distinctly before him, we can only answer, "We do not know." Nor had Jeroboam any need to know. God knew; and it was his clear course to do right, trusting all the rest to God.

Jeroboam was evidently a shrewd and clear-sighted worldly politician. The means he adopted to wean the people first from their loyalty to the throne, and then from their allegiance to God, were well fitted to accomplish his purposes. He stirred up the pride of his own powerful tribe of Ephraim, and he promised to all others immediate relief from intolerable exactions. Then he established a system of worship, professedly identical in principle with that of Jerusalem, though different in form. The form, too, was neither new, nor, judging from past history, unacceptable to the Israelites. One sanctuary was erected on the southern border of the new kingdom, beside the leading road to Jerusalem, evidently for the purpose of intercepting all worshippers proceeding southward. The other was set up at Dan on the northern border, beneath the shadow of the ancient shrine of Mount Baal-Hermon;

and would naturally attract around it those northern tribes which early showed an inclination to adopt alike the customs and the religion of their heathen neighbours.

P.

THE TWO PROPHETS

1 Kings 13

JEROBOAM'S offence was rank, and it suited not the honour of God that it should pass undenounced. It was denounced, and that in a truly remarkable manner.

Bethel, from its vicinage to Judah, seems to have engaged the particular attention of Jeroboam, though, in fact, his sacerdotal establishment there, so near to Jerusalem, was alone sufficient to apprise observant persons of the hollowness of his alleged object; for this place being but little to the north of Jerusalem, it was absurd to allege the inconvenient distance of the latter city as a ground for setting up his golden calf at Bethel.

On a day of high festival, Jeroboam himself, censer in hand, was officiating at the altar in Bethel, when a stranger, with the marks of recent travel upon him, stood forth, and in the name of the Lord prophesied against *the altar*, declaring that a time should come when a child named JOSIAH should be born to the house of David, who should burn on that very altar the bones of its dead priests. To accredit his word, the altar was on the instant rent, and the ashes scattered around. Without this sign, the prophecy of an event which did not take place for three hundred and fifty years, would have wanted authority with those who knew not the utterer; and therefore was it given.

Probably a prophecy against Jeroboam's own person, instead of against the insensate altar, would have touched him less nearly. But this showed that his policy would come to nought, and that the power he was establishing with so much solicitude would be utterly subverted, while the house of David would still subsist in its strength; for only so could a king of that house be able to do this upon an altar in this realm.

The king grasped the full meaning of this message, and it filled him with rage against the man who had dared to deliver it then and there. He stretched forth his hand to seize him; but the limb suddenly stiffened, and he could not draw it back again. The prodigy, which touched his bone and his flesh, humbled the king a little; and he implored the prophet to intercede with the Lord for him, that his arm might be restored. The man of God did so; and, at his supplication, vigour returned to the arm which had been raised against him. Grateful for this, Jeroboam said to the prophet, " Come home with me and refresh thyself; and I will give thee a reward." But he alleged that the command had been laid upon him to deliver his message and to return, not by the way he came, without making any stay, or eating bread, or drinking water, in that place. So he remounted his ass, and commenced his journey home.

He had come out of Judah; but who he was we are not told, and we must be content not to know. The Jewish commentators generally suppose that he was Iddo the seer, who is recorded in 2 Chron. ix. 29 to have had visions against Jeroboam. But as Iddo lived to write the history of Rehoboam's son Abijah, who died but little before Jeroboam,[1] the conjecture is only tenable on the improbable supposition that the incident, although recorded here, really happened near the very close of Jeroboam's reign. Shemaiah—the same whose mandate stayed the march of Rehoboam's army—has also been named; but the like objection applies here, as this prophet lived to write the history of Rehoboam, who died in the eighteenth year of Jeroboam.[2] But Jewish (that is, Rabbinical) authority is of no weight in a question of this description; it being indeed one of its rules to ascribe anonymous acts and sayings to persons whose names are known. The value of the identifications may be estimated from the fact that the " old prophet " is by some of the same authorities identified with Gershom the son of Moses, and by others with the Amaziah who was priest at Bethel in the time of the prophet Amos, 186 years later than the death of Jeroboam. The schismatical proceedings of Jeroboam certainly took place very early in his reign, and with these the sacred historian naturally connects this strong protest of the Lord by His prophet against them. With this all the circumstances agree; whereas, if Iddo were the prophet from Judah, the date of this incident

could not have been earlier than within the last two years of Jeroboam's reign of twenty-two years; or if Shemaiah, not earlier than the last five years of that reign.

The good man was plodding homeward with the satisfying consciousness of having becomingly discharged an important and perilous duty, when evil came upon him from a quarter he could little have expected.

There was in Bethel an old temporizing " prophet," of Balaam's cast, who, although he had sufficient regard for appearances to be absent from the king's sacrifice, allowed his sons to be there. From them he heard what had passed, and avouched the verity of the prophecy which the man of God had delivered. Yet, with this conviction on his mind, he formed the resolution of going after the stranger, to induce him to come back and accept the hospitalities of his house. We cannot allow him the excuse of thoughtless hospitality, which some have urged in his favour. As one having his own eyes opened, he must have felt that the stranger had alleged a true and valid reason for his departure; and he could not but know the imperative nature of the obligation under which that stranger acted. His determination to bring him back, must therefore have had some proportionate ulterior object, although we entirely acquit him of intending to involve the man of God in the disastrous consequences which ensued. He may have had a vague impression that his disobedience would not escape some kind of punishment; but had he been aware how awful and immediate that punishment would be, it is probable that he would have paused. It is our own impression that this man was one of the numerous class who

"Know the good, but still the ill pursue;"

and that his single but guileful object was to lay his king under an essential obligation, by making the man of God contradict himself in a matter which he alleged to be most binding and urgent upon him, and of thus reducing the moral weight and authority of the message he had delivered, and weakening its impression upon the minds of the people.

He soon overtook the home-bound prophet; and his invitation having received the same answer as that before given to the king, the profane old reprobate urged that he also was a prophet, and had received a counter-command from God to follow and bring him back. The

[1] 2 Chronicles 13:22.   [2] 2 Chronicles 12:15.

poor prophet was too guileless himself to suspect that any one of this venerable appearance could be daring enough to fabricate such a statement, and he therefore turned his ass's head, perhaps not unwillingly, back to Bethel.

It was while they sat at meat in the house of the Bethelite prophet, that a true word from God came to the latter, which, we are willing to believe, he received with real concern, and delivered with reluctance. It was, that inasmuch as the prophet from Judah had "disobeyed the word of the Lord," in coming back to the place where he had been forbidden to rest or to eat bread, "his carcass should not come unto the sepulchre of his fathers." This amounted to a declaration, that he should not reach his home either alive or dead; for if he did, he would of course come to the sepulchre of his fathers. We read of no accusation or reply on the part of the seduced prophet, or any excuse on the part of his seducer. The matter was too solemn for bandying words; and both understood very clearly where the guilt lay. The beguiled prophet, being himself in the direct receipt of divine intimations, had no right to act upon a contradiction to the mandate imparted to himself, on any less direct authority than that from which he had received it; and his easy credulity had brought discredit upon the high mission entrusted to him, and marred much of the good effect it might have produced upon the minds of the king and people. For this he must die, while the guiltier man incurs no punishment,—even as a soldier on high and responsible duty suffers death for offences which would scarcely incur blame at another time, and in other men. It is the unheeded responsibility, the breach of duty, rather than the act, which constitutes the crime.

As one doomed to death, but not knowing in what shape it was to come, the stranger set forth. Was he to be smitten with disease or lightning? Were robbers to set upon him and slay him? Were walls to fall down and crush his devoted head? Of a thousand deaths that lurk ambushed for the life of man, which was the one destined to smite him down? He knew not— perhaps he cared not; but he could scarcely guess that which really came to pass. A lion came forth against him and slew him; and the brute so acted, as to evince to all beholders that he also had a mission, and that his native instincts were under control. It is said that lions

like not to fall on man when they have other prey; it is also said, that an ass is choice food to a lion; and it is certain that a lion destroys to eat. Yet here the lion assails the man, and leaves the ass unmolested; and having inflicted the appointed death, the beast attempts not to devour or carry off the carcass, but leaves it in the road, and stands watching by, along with the trembling ass, as if to guard the corpse from other beasts, until witnesses should come to avouch what had been done, and to take away the body. Truly this was the finger of God. The old Bethelite thought it so, when he heard what had happened. He felt that it devolved on him to remove the body and give it sepulture. He went, therefore, and beheld the lion still keeping guard over the corpse; but the fierce creature suffered him to carry it away without molestation, and then slowly retired as one whose work was done.

The old Bethelite deposited the corpse in the grave he had prepared for himself; "and they mourned over him, saying, Alas, my brother!" Believing the prediction of the stranger to be certain of fulfilment, he directed his sons to bury his own corpse in the same grave; and the bones of the seducer and the seduced being thus intermingled in the tomb, it so happened, as the former probably intended, that his bones escaped, at the appointed time, the defilement to which they would otherwise have been subjected. The tomb of "the prophet that came out of Judah" was then recognized, and for his sake the contents were spared from dishonour.

THE DISGUISED PRINCESS

1 Kings 14:1-18

THIS quiet place, apart among the enclosing hills, is Shiloh. It was once the seat of the Lord's tabernacle, His altar, and His ark, and was then replete with holy activities and solemn sounds. But since these departed, it has been well nigh forsaken, and has relapsed into a silent village, or a small rural town. Yet still holy things are here—holy men, who have found here a sort of refuge from the wickedness of the time—a quiet retreat, favourable to sacred memories, and to the nourishment of holy thoughts. Among them is Ahijah, that old prophet, who rent the new cloak of Jeroboam, and promised him the larger share of the divided kingdom. He is now blind. Upon the outer world, made foul by man's abominations, he has closed his eyes, and he sees and lives by the light that shines within.

Now, observe that woman stealing down the street, and seeking the old prophet's house. By her guise she is of the peasantry, and she bears a basket. Yet her gait scarcely befits her garb; and the quick furtive glance she casts around under her coarse hood-veil, betrays some conscious concealment, some fear of recognition, some purpose she would not wish to have known.

This woman, mean as she seems, is the lady of the land; and although her basket contains but a few cakes and biscuits, and a little honey, she might, if she pleased, have filled it with precious and costly things. She is the wife of Jeroboam— so far as we know, his only wife—the mother of his heir; and, therefore, if he had a score of wives, the chief of them all. That heir, by name Abijah. is alarmingly ill; and, at the instance of Jeroboam, and impelled by motherly love, that royal lady has come all the way from Tirzah, in this disguise, that she may learn from the prophet what is to become of her son; and the things in her basket are gifts for the man of God, suited to the condition she has assumed. The disguise was thought necessary to conceal this visit from the people, and was assumed partly in the idle hope of obtaining, in the semblance of another, the desired answer, unmixed with the reproof and denunciation, which Jeroboam knew that his conduct had been calculated to draw down, from the prophet who had foretold his exaltation. He thus foolishly thought to cozen the Lord, through His prophet, out of an answer of peace, and slily to evade the judgment he feared might be connected with it; and he idly calculated that the prophet, whose view could extend into the future, hid in the counsels of God, could not see through a present matter wrapped up only in the thin cover of a woman's hood. "There was never," says Bishop Hall, "a wicked man who was not infatuate, and in nothing more than in those things wherein he hoped most to transcend the reach of others."

All this fine contrivance was blown to pieces the moment the wife of Jeroboam crossed Ahijah's threshold; for then she heard the voice of the blind prophet: "Come in, thou wife of Jeroboam; why feignest thou thyself to be another? for I am sent to thee with heavy tidings." He then broke forth in a strong tide of denunciation against Jeroboam, because he had sinned and made Israel to sin; and the voice which had proclaimed his rise from a low estate to royal power, now, with still stronger tone, proclaimed the downfall and ruin of his house—quenched in blood—its members to find tombs only in the bowels of beasts and birds. There was one exception—only one. The youth of whom she came to inquire—he only should come to his grave in peace, by dying of his present disease, because in him only was "found some good thing towards the Lord God of Israel in the house of Jeroboam."

Woful tidings these for a mother's heart; and scarcely, perhaps, intelligible to her stunned intellect. Here was the beginning of judgment upon Jeroboam, and upon her, because she was his—judgment in taking away the only well conditioned and worthy son; and judgment stored up in and for the ill conditioned ones who were suffered to remain. God, when it suits the purposes of His wisdom and His justice, can afflict no less by what He spares than by what He takes.

Yet there was mercy in this judgment; mercy, strange as it seems to say, to that amiable youth on whom the sentence of death was passed. It is so stated; and it is more intelligible than it seems. It was because there *was* some good thing found in him that he should die. Death was to be for him a reward, a blessing, a deliverance. He should die peaceably upon his bed; for him all Israel should mourn; for him many tears should be shed; and he should be brought with honour to his tomb. More than all, he would be taken from the evil that hung over his house; and the Lord's vindicatory justice would thus be spared the seeming harshness of bringing ruin upon a righteous king for his father's crimes. Alas! how little do we know the real objects of the various incidents of life and death—of mercy, of punishment, and of trial! In this case the motives were disclosed; and we are suffered to glance upon some of the great secrets of death, which form the trying mysteries of life. With this instance in view, we can find the parallels of lives, full of hope and promise, prematurely taken, and that in mercy, as we can judge, to those who depart. The heavenly Husbandman often gathers for His garner the fruit that early ripens, without suffering it to hang needlessly long, beaten by storms, upon the tree. Oh, how often, as many a grieved heart can tell, do the Lord's best beloved die betimes—taken from the evil to come,—while the unripe, the evil, the injurious, live long for mischief to themselves and others! Roses and lilies wither far sooner than thorns and thistles.

Doleful were the tidings the disguised princess had to bear back to the beautiful town of Tirzah. All remoter griefs were probably to her swallowed up in this—which rung continually in her ears in all her homeward way,—"When thy feet enter into the city the child shall die." It is heavy tidings to a mother that she must lose her well beloved son; but it is a grievous aggravation of her trouble that she might not see him before he died. They who were about him knew not that he was to die to-day, and therefore could not estimate the preciousness of his last hours, and the privilege of being then near him, and of receiving his embrace. *She* knew; but she might not be near, nor pour out upon her dying son the fulness of a mother's heart. Knowing that her son lay on his death-bed, her first impulse must have been to fly home to receive his dying kiss; but her second to linger by the way, as if to protract that dear life which must close the moment she entered the city. Never, surely, before or since, was a distressed mother so wofully torn between the antagonist impulses of her affection!

HIGH PLACES

1 Kings 14:22-24

IT seems that king Rehoboam, in Judah, profiting by the chastisement he had received, conducted himself reasonably well for three years, during which he employed himself vigorously in strengthening his kingdom, by collecting arms, and depositing them in a large number of cities which he fortified. "When Rehoboam had established his kingdom and strengthened himself, he forsook the law of the Lord, and all Israel with him." The iniquity into which the Judahites fell, is described as greater than had been in former times committed—perhaps not greater than individuals in authority had committed (Solomon for instance), but greater than any part of the nation had before concurred in. Indeed, from all that appears, the sin was for the time greater than that of Jeroboam; but there was this essential difference, that Jeroboam's sin was not repented of, and that of Rehoboam was. The form of this great offence is thus described: "They built them high places, and images, and groves, on every high hill and under every green tree." We remember the time when we used to be perplexed about these high places and groves. What is the harm in worshipping upon a high place or in a grove? Are they not, on the contrary, very proper places for worship? And, what is more to the purpose, did not the patriarchs worship upon high places and in groves? And the fact of their doing so is mentioned, certainly without blame, if not with approbation; while in later ages we find these practices severely condemned, and calling down divine punishments. The way to get at the cause of this, is to consider that things indifferent, or even good, in themselves, may become evil in the lapse of time, from the considerations that come to be associated with them. If a British consul or governor upon the African coast sets up the union jack over his house on Sundays, there may be no harm in that; but if the barbarous people around come to the conclusion that, since he does this on the day set apart to his worship, this flag is the white man's god, and begin to treat it with superstitious reverence, or assemble to render it worship, the practice of setting it up becomes a sin. But we need not travel out of Scripture for an illustration. What could be more dutiful and seemly than the feeling which led Moses to preserve in the tabernacle the brazen serpent, which had been lifted up in the wilderness for the healing of the nation? But when the people came to regard it with superstitious reverence, and manifested a disposition to render idolatrous honours thereto, it became an abomination, and as such was most properly destroyed by king Hezekiah.

Now we read in the book of Genesis, that Abraham, on entering the promised land, built an altar upon a mountain between Bethel and Hai. At Beersheba he planted a grove, and called there upon the name of the everlasting God. It was to a mountain (Moriah) that he was directed to go, there to offer up his son Isaac; and it was upon another mountain (in Gilead) that Jacob and Laban offered sacrifices before they parted in peace.[1] So far, therefore, as appears from the book of Genesis, there was no harm in worshipping in high places and in groves. But in a later age, when the Israelites had departed from Egypt, and approached the same land to take possession of it, we find something had arisen to cause high places and groves to be regarded with great disfavour. The people are strictly enjoined to cast down and destroy all those belonging to the Canaanites which they might find in the land.[2] It might be supposed that this was because *these* had been consecrated to the worship of idols; but that it did not involve any prohibition of high places and groves to the Israelites. But, first, the Israelites by the law of Moses could worship by sacrifice only at one place, that is, at the tabernacle altar; and therefore, because not anywhere else, certainly not in high places; and, further, it was expressly enjoined, that near this sole altar, no trees should be planted.[3] This last restriction is very remarkable. Apart from that, the limitation of the Israelites to one place of ritual worship would suggest a perfectly sufficient reason for the destruction of the Canaanitish [altars upon the] high places, and the demolition of the consecrated groves; for there would be a danger that the Israelites, in taking possession of the localities in which they were found, would retain their use as places of worship. But the intimation that even at the one altar any approximation to a grove was to be carefully avoided, compels us to look into the question a little further.

One great object of the Mosaic dispensation was to maintain, in the persons of the Israelites, a living testimony against the polytheism which had overspread the nations; and whatever might directly or indirectly tend to the worship of many gods, or to the associating of other gods of man's devising with the only real God Jehovah, the Creator of heaven and earth, was carefully guarded against and discouraged. When, in process of time, the high places and groves of primitive worship became consecrated to divers idols, the danger was, that, in adopting the use

[1] Genesis 12:7,8; 21:33; 22:2,4; 31:54.
[2] Exodus 34:13; Deuteronomy 7:5; 12:2,3.
[3] Deuteronomy 16:21.

of them, the Israelites should retain some lingering recollection of the god to whom they had been set apart; and this, gathering strength, would insensibly lead them into idolatry, and to the association of other gods with Jehovah.

Before the erection of temples, or before temples became general, groves and high places were the usual places of worship. Hence we do not find any order to the Israelites to destroy the *temples* of the Canaanites, for there were none to destroy. The order to demolish their groves and high places was, therefore, an order to destroy their places of worship, as well as their objects of worship, wherever found. This was important in an age when the entire tendency of the human mind was towards polytheism—the multiplication of gods; so that the demolition of a place of worship was equivalent to the demolition of an idol, and the setting up of one, in its ultimate results, almost equivalent to the setting up of an idol. The result dreaded and guarded against in these directions was the multiplication of gods; and how wisely this was ordered, and how imminent the danger was, is shown by the fact, that the very evil which the law sought by its interdiction to prevent, did arise from the neglect of that interdiction by Rehoboam and subsequent kings of Judah; so that, at the time when the nation was ripe for the overthrow which it sustained, Jeremiah could exclaim, "According to the number of thy cities are thy gods, O Judah!" (Jer. ii. 28).

But it may be asked, Was not the danger equally imminent at the time when the patriarchs worshipped in groves, and set up their altars upon high places? Perhaps not. There is no indication throughout the book of Genesis that the Canaanites had yet gone far, if at all, into the corruptions of polytheism, and it is expressly stated that *their* iniquity was "not yet full." Moral iniquity abounded; but that they had as yet gone into gross idolatry, is more than we know. The only hint we have respecting the religion of the land, sets before us one king (Melchizedek) who was a worshipper, not less than Abraham, of "the Most High God, Creator of heaven and earth." All mankind were at first His worshippers; and in the different places of their dispersion, the nations of men varied in the time and extent of their corruptions of original truth. The country out of which Abraham came, seems to have been much further gone in polytheistic error than that into which he entered. *There*, probably, nothing was found to point out the kind of danger which afterwards became connected with groves and high places; and if there had been something of the sort, the danger, which might be great to a nation composed of people of different habits of mind and varied depth of religious feeling, would be but small in the case of the single family of the faithful Abraham, abiding in one locality. The danger arose when the nation lay dispersed over a wider country,—and if high places and groves were at all tolerated, they would have many in simultaneous use in different parts of the land.

It is remarkable with what inveteracy the Israelites clung to the worship offered in high places. These were even tolerated by monarchs who exerted themselves to root out idolatry, and of whose zeal for the purity of the worship of Jehovah no doubt can be entertained. As they were not for this subjected to any such judgment as that denounced on Rehoboam, some peculiar enormity must have been found in his case. This is discovered in the connection of "images" with high places; for these must have been symbolic representations either of Jehovah or of strange gods—most likely the latter; whereas the others were merely sanctioned as places for the local worship of the Lord, and, so far as tolerated, did not present an immediately idolatrous aspect. This toleration of an acknowledged irregularity, the sacred historian indicates as the only blot upon the character of some truly right-minded kings, who certainly would not have allowed anything that seemed to them to savour of idolatry. It probably arose from the known indisposition of the people living at a distance from the temple, to be limited to the altar services at that spot, in which they could only at distant intervals participate; while their earnest wish to possess places for the chief ritual acts of their religion—sacrifices and offerings—near to their own homes, may have suggested the fear that, unless they were gratified in having in their own neighbourhood places of religious assemblage and of offerings to the Lord, they might be led to present their offerings to idols. Under its first aspect, the wish has the appearance of an excess of religious zeal—which, apart from its latent dangers, may account for the hesitation which the kings felt in putting down this abuse, and for their winking at an irregularity contrary to one of the first principles of the theocratic institutions. It is worthy of note, in corroboration of this view, that we hear no more of worship in high places and groves, after the establishment of synagogues in the towns afforded an adequate and ready vent to the craving of the people to localize their religion. They were then enabled to have near their homes so much of their religious observances as admitted, without danger, of being separated from the grand ritual solemnities for which the great common centre at Jerusalem was still preserved. Besides, the tendency to idolatry had then passed away, and perhaps groves and high places would then not have been refused had they been desired. But so it was, that the people craved to worship upon high places and in groves when it was really dangerous and seducing for them to do so, but ceased to care about them when the danger no longer existed.

It is sufficiently plain, that the things which "provoked the Lord to jealousy," in these instances, were the idolatries and immoralities practised by the people.

When we read in our version, "they also built them high places, and images and groves, on every high hill, and every green tree," we are led to ask, how could groves be "*built*," and how could they be, in any way, placed *under every* green tree. The original word, *ashērāh*, here used in the plural, means something fixed in the ground upright, and composed of wood which could be destroyed, and cut down and burnt. Whatever it was, a carved image of it was set up in the Temple by Manasseh, and destroyed by Josiah. (2 Kings xxi. 7; xxiii. 6.) The worship of *ashērāh* is found associated with that of Baal, like that of Astarte. (Judg. iii. 7; 1 Kings xviii. 19; xxi. 3; xxiii. 4.) It has been inferred by De Witte to be another name for Astarte. More likely, it was a wooden symbol of the goddess, in form resembling the sacred tree of the Assyrians, familiar to those who are acquainted with Assyrian antiquities. The *image* or pillar of *Matzēvāh*, which, previous to the word just noticed, occurs in the verse before us, in the plural, seems to have been some erection in stone in honour of the same deity. "The high places which are said to have been built, were probably small shrines or tabernacles, hung with bright coloured tapestry (Ezek. xvi. 16), like the sacred tent of the Catheginians (Diod. Sic., xx. 65)." The expression, "under every green tree," is explained as meaning "under all those remarkable trees which, standing singly about the land, were landmarks to their respective neighbourhoods, and places of resort to travellers, who gladly rested under their shade." (*Speaker's Commentary*, ii. 571; compare with vol. 1, 166 and 417.) Large trees are still objects of veneration in the East; and on the branches may be seen hung up a profusion of dirty rags.

With the idolatries thus betokened, were associated immoral practices—"And there were also Sodomites in the land; and they did according to all the abominations o the nations which the Lord cast out before the children." Nothing can be more revolting than the thought that immorality constituted the very *ritual*, the outward form, or "religion," of the old idolatry. In holy and blessed contrast with this, we have "pure and undefiled religion," as the ritual, the outward expression of Christianity, even this—"to visit the fatherless and widows in their affliction, and to keep himself unspotted from the world." (James i. 27.)

S.

THE EGYPTIAN INVASION

1 Kings 14:25-28; 2 Chronicles 12:2-12

OUR own house here, in this "wicked London," is safe, though defenceless, and with small protection of bolts and bars, because there is little in it to tempt the spoiler; whereas the great house of the old lady in Threadneedle Street is never deemed to be safe without a company of dreadful bearskin-capped grenadiers within its walls, because of the great riches it contains. Now, we should not be over glad to have all that gold down in our cellars, without the grenadiers also, to keep guard over it. What a perilous life it would be to have it, without adequate means of protecting it from the envious hands ready to clutch at it, and whose endeavours would be excited by our obviously defenceless condition!

This was the case of Rehoboam. The immense treasures in gold which the temple and palace contained—the accumulations of David and Solomon—were known far and wide, and were such as required a strong power to protect them from the neighbouring princes, who could not but calculate, from time to time, upon the glorious spoil which might be obtained by the rapid pillage of Jerusalem alone, even apart from any views of territorial aggrandisement. Such power Solomon had possessed; and grievously as the strength which Rehoboam inherited from him had been impaired, it was still sufficient, under the judicious measures which had in the early years of his reign been adopted for putting the country in a state of defence, to withstand any attempt of the small neighbouring states. Of these, the new kingdom was alone to be seriously dreaded; and the alienation had not yet become such as to render it probable that the ten tribes

would dare, even if Jerusalem were in their power, to pillage the temple of the Lord.

There was, however, in the distance a more powerful and dangerous enemy, not to be restrained by any such considerations, and who had for some time regarded with longing eyes the treasures of the sacred city. This was the king of Egypt. So long as Rehoboam continued in a right course, this powerful prince was restrained by the Lord from the measures he contemplated; but no sooner had the king, with his people, sinned against Jehovah, than the hands of the Egyptian monarch were loosened, and he proceeded to invade the land with a mighty host levied from the different African territories subject to his sceptre. This was the first time the Egyptians had appeared in the sacred land with hostile purposes against the Hebrews; and it is probable that so formidable a body of chariots, horsemen, and infantry had never before invaded the country. The appearance of this new enemy, whose power and resources they well knew, must have filled the Judahites with dread,—the rather, as their unfaithfulness had disentitled them to the right of looking to the Lord for His protection. Probably, in the first instance, the king placed some hope in the strong fortresses he had built towards the southern frontier; but these fell, one after another, before the might of the invaders,—and the Egyptians, having cleared the intervening country from obstruction, marched direct upon Jerusalem.

At this juncture, the same prophet Shemaiah, who had before interposed to prevent Rehoboam's army from marching against Jeroboam, again appeared, and delivered to the king and his princes the short but awfully emphatic message, "Thus saith the Lord, Ye have forsaken me; and therefore have I also left you in the hand of Shishak." At this they were conscience-stricken, and acted exactly as became them, and as was best suited to turn the Lord's anger aside. They admitted the justice of the punishment they had brought upon themselves, and they humbled themselves, and said, "The Lord is righteous," —an admission as brief and significant as the reproof.

This humiliation was graciously received in heaven; and it was intimated that for this they should be spared some portion of the ignominy they had incurred. This seems to have meant that their lives would be spared, and that the city would not be destroyed by the Egyptian host; yet they should for a time feel that these overbearing foreigners were their masters, that they might know the difference between the service of the Lord and that of strange princes.

It was probably as an act of submission to this doom that no defence of Jerusalem was attempted; and He in whose hand is the heart of kings so mollified the stern purposes of Shishak, that he was content with the spoils of the temple and the palace, without molesting the inhabitants, or damaging the city, or attempting to retain the country in subjection. Indeed, recollecting the prodigious quantities of precious metal lavished by Solomon on these buildings, this spoil must have been amply sufficient to fulfil the greedy expectations of the invaders, and satisfy the wishes of their nation. It has indeed been urged that no such spoil could have proved an adequate return for the cost of the expedition, and that it was unlikely that its objects should be gained by the plunder of a palace and a temple. But it may be answered, that, under ancient military arrangements, an

EGYPTIAN SOLDIERS.

army was a less costly instrument than—happily for the peace of the world—it has now become; and that the balance of profit and loss, in expeditions furnishing an immediate return of plunder and glory, was less nicely calculated in former times than it is now,—although, indeed, modern history has furnished examples, not few nor far between, of expeditions costing millions of money being employed upon objects not worth as many shillings. Besides, to allege that the plunder of a temple is not an adequate object of military action, is against the facts of history, and is to forget that riches equal to the wealth of a nation were often in ancient times lavished upon or treasured up in temples. The reader will call to mind the celebrated temple in Elymais of Persia—the rich treasures of which were the object of attention to two of the greatest of the Seleucidian kings of Syria, one of whom (Antiochus the Great) lost his life in a commotion created in the attempt to seize them; and whose son (Antiochus Epiphanes) was engaged in the same distant quarter, quelling the disturbances created by the actual plunder of the temple to recruit his exhausted finances, when he received the news respecting the Jewish successes over his officers, which made him hastily quit the place with horrid purposes of vengeance against the Jews, which he lived not to accomplish.

It may also be observed, that Shishak was not allowed to accomplish all the purposes of his expedition, as is clearly shown by the promise given on the repentance of the king and the princes. What that intention was, it is difficult to see. The fact that he did not march into the territory of the ten tribes, coupled with Jeroboam's previous sojourn in Egypt, and his favourable reception there, may suggest that the invader acted at the instance of Jeroboam, with the view of weakening the rival power, if not of adding the dominions of Rehoboam to those of the sovereign of the ten tribes, or of holding them as a dependency of his own Egypt. The subsequent impulse which led him, under divine influence, to alter his views, and to be content with the treasures of the palace and temple, may have originated in the consideration that it might not be good policy for Egypt to push its frontier in this direction—thus destroying politically the desert barrier which separated it from other nations,—and still less to reconstruct and render once more formidable the kingdom which had been weakened by separation into two; for although, perhaps, he might count on the subserviency of Jeroboam, he could not know but that his kingdom, reunited to that of Judah, might in no long time acquire such strength, and lapse into such hands, as might render its neighbourhood inconvenient to Egypt. In old times, as in our own, thinking politicians—and there *were* thinking politicians even in those days—must have seen the futility of basing political arrangements on personal considerations. Men die, and men change; but political action has permanent effects, which survive the men by whose hands it was wrought.

That the result was not unequal to the extent and importance of the expedition—that it was, in fact, regarded as a memorable event in Egypt —is shown by the circumstance that the successful results of the campaign are celebrated in a series of sculptures on the north external wall of the temple at Karnak. The king, as usual, presents his prisoners to the deity of the temple; and to each figure is attached an oval, indicating

the town or district which he represents; one of which is concluded to be Yooda Melchi, or "kingdom of Judah." It is not to be supposed that Rehoboam was actually carried captive to Egypt, but that the figure is a symbol of the king's triumph over him.

Whether the figure be a portrait or not, is uncertain; but as the Egyptian artists were used to make as near a likeness as they could of the objects which they intended to represent, it doubtless presents a general resemblance, if not of the king, of as much of the Jewish physiognomy and costume as it discloses. We introduce it, together with the head of Shishak himself.

JEWISH CAPTIVE FROM TEMPLE AT KARNAK

The preservation of this figure is a notable circumstance, especially as the picture is so much mutilated that nothing remains but three captives bound to a stake, which form, as usual, a sort of

EGYPTIAN PORTRAIT OF SHISHAK

title page at the beginning, and a portion of the triumphal procession at the end, which is so much mutilated that only the names of the captives are legible. This defaced condition of the monument is much to be deplored, as it might possibly have presented details, not only confirmatory but illustrative of the sacred narrative.

Solomon was at great pains to amass enormous wealth. He filled his capital with gold and silver. Wealth did him no good. On the contrary, it drew his mind from wisdom to folly—from God to licentiousness. It corrupted his court besides, and was, indirectly, the means of weaning the Israelites from their national faith. That which occasioned such grievous offence, afterwards occasioned a great national humiliation, and had it not been for the merciful interposition of Heaven, would have brought ruin upon Israel. Attracted apparently by the vast treasures stored up in Jerusalem, Shishak, king of Egypt, invaded the land, "and took away the treasures of the house of the Lord, and the treasures of the king's house; he even took away all; and he took away all the shields of gold which Solomon had made."

So it is often in this world. Great riches are only a great curse. Except where there is wisdom rightly to employ them, and grace to resist the temptations they entail, men are better without them. The prayer of Agur, the son of Jakeh, was probably the offspring of painful experiences: "Remove far from me vanity and lies; give me neither poverty nor riches; feed me with food convenient for me: lest I be full, and deny Thee, and say, Who is the Lord? or lest I be poor and steal, and take the name of my God in vain."

P.

Subsequent investigations show that the inscription above referred to as *Yooda Melchi*, or *Yudeh Malk*, cannot mean *Kingdom of Judah*, but probably signifies *Judah's King*, entered on the lists of Shishak's victories as a tributary prince.

Sheshenk, or Sheshonk, in the monuments at Karnak, is undoubtedly the Shishak of Kings and Chronicles. According to the Egyptian chronology, he ascended the throne about B.C. 980, and reigned twenty-one years. This synchronizes with the period of Rehoboam's reign, according to Bible chronology. The Karnak record gives a list of conquered countries, tribes, and cities; and amongst the identified names are cities of Judah, Levitical and Canaanite cities of Israel, and Arab tribes lying to the south of Palestine. The first class exactly correspond with 2 Chron. xii. 2-4—"He took all the fenced cities which pertained to Judah, and came to Jerusalem." The very names of Adoraim, Aijalon, and Shoco, fenced cities of Judah (2 Chron. xi. 7-10), and of Gibeon, Bethtappuah, Beth-lebaoth, Beth-anoth, and Azem, towns of less consequence, appear on the wall of the Karnak Temple.

As to Levitical and Canaanite cities, taken by Shishak, here the inscription both harmonizes with Scripture, and adds to its information. The Levites were ill affected towards Jeroboam, as we learn from 2 Chron. xi. 13, 14, and joined themselves to Rehoboam. "The Levites left their suburbs, and their possessions, and came to Judah and Jerusalem." It is in harmony with this to suppose, that other Levitical cities detached themselves from the kingdom of Israel, and united their interests with the older kingdom; and hence the Karnak inscription is consonant with Scripture, when it informs us that Levitical towns fell into the hands of the Egyptian monarch. The policy of Shishak was to strengthen Jeroboam, and to weaken Rehoboam. He therefore reduced Canaanite

cities, which we infer had, like some Levitical towns, transferred their allegiance from Samaria to Jerusalem.—*Bible Educator*, i. 106. See references there.

S.

ABIJAH

1 Kings 15:1-9; 2 Chronicles 13:1-20

IT is observable, that although Rehoboam had fewer wives than his father—*only* eighteen wives and sixty concubines—he had a far more numerous progeny; no less than twenty-eight sons and sixty daughters,—a somewhat singular disproportion of sexes. Even this comparatively moderate harem was opposed to the opinions and habits of his subjects; for the historian remarks that "he desired many wives," implying that so far he contravened the prohibition imposed by the law against a king "multiplying wives unto himself." Of all Rehoboam's wives, the one who had most influence with him was Maacah, who appears to have been a grand-daughter of Absalom by his daughter Tamar, who married one Uriel of the house of Saul. This special attachment to the mother induced Rehoboam to determine that her son Abijah (otherwise called Abijam) should be his successor; and the solicitude he is described as evincing in this matter, and the means he took to secure this object, seem to show that Abijah was not his eldest son. To obviate the competition of his brothers, and to prevent them from forming an interest in rivalry to his at the seat of power, Rehoboam took much the same course as Abraham took to secure the undisputed heritage to Isaac. He provided for them, and gave them employment in his lifetime, by making them governors of cities; thus dispersing them through his dominions for their own advantage, and at the same time preventing them from engaging in any combined operations to the detriment of the heir. This is an early scriptural example of the same kind of policy which has only within the present age been adopted in the courts of Persia and Turkey, where the princes were kept shut up in the harem till the death of their father, and then either imprisoned, killed, or incapacitated for public life (in Persia by blinding) when their brother mounted the throne. Now, at least in Persia, they are sent into the provinces, where they administer the civil and military local government for the king, collect the crown dues, and remit them to court, after deducting their own expenses and the provincial charges. These princes, in their lesser spheres, reflect the royal dignity, maintaining courts on the royal model, but on a smaller scale; administering justice like the king; and appearing, when required, with the military force to be raised within their districts. Doubtless the sons of Rehoboam performed the same functions in their respective districts; but the smallness of the territory over which so many princes were distributed, must have given a proportionately diminished scale to their establishments; and if they, as princes of the blood, affected, as is likely, more magnificence than ordinary governors, this must have rendered the task of supporting the courts of so many royal governors rather burdensome to the people. The crown also, probably found it unprofitable in the end; a large proportion of the public imposts being in such cases absorbed, before they reached the royal treasury, in the expenses of local government,—and the king being obliged to allow expenses for his sons, and to admit excuses on their behalf, which would not have been endured in an ordinary functionary.

The precautions of the king were, however, successful; and at his death the son he had designated succeeded to the throne without opposition. This young man, of the same name with Jeroboam's lost son, took up the cause of the house of David with the ardour natural to a lofty-minded youth just come to the throne. He purposed to himself to re-establish the dominion of his house over the ten tribes; and no priest or prophet interfered this time to discourage the undertaking. This was not now necessary, seeing that the kingdom of Israel was now fully equal to its own defence against Judah; and now, moreover, Jeroboam had forfeited all claim to the Lord's interference, and his house had indeed been sentenced to deprivation.

Abijah took the initiative, and marched into the territory of Jeroboam, at the head of a general military levy of his kingdom. Jeroboam was, however, too able and experienced a commander to be taken unprepared, and he met the king of Judah with a force that greatly outnumbered his own.

The circumstances of this first great action between the two kingdoms are very interesting, and well deserve careful consideration, from the light they cast upon the state of feeling with which the house of David at this time regarded the rival kingdom. This we are enabled to collect from the harangue which king Abijah addressed to the enemy opposed to him, before they came to blows, according to a custom which strikes us as somewhat strange, but of which there are numerous ancient examples. The staple of such harangues always has consisted, and always does consist in the East, of self-praise on the part of the orator, and dispraise and abuse of the enemy. Of this we find enough in the speech of Abijah, the tone of which seems to us not in all respects so gratifying as it has appeared to many.

The oration consists properly of two parts—political, and religious or theocratical. The political part is based entirely on the divine-right principle, which was certainly not sanctioned by the Hebrew constitution. Wholly overlooking the offence of Solomon, the judgment of Heaven, the divine appointment of Jeroboam, the constitutional conduct of the people, the aggravating folly of Rehoboam, and the Lord's recognition of the separation,—Abijah talks loftily of the rights of the house of David, and treats the tribes as unreasonable and causeless rebels,—servants who had turned against their master when they found their opportunity in the accession of the "young and tender-hearted" Rehoboam, and whom it behoved now, at his son's call, to return to their allegiance. The egregious foolishness of all this seems about equal to the imbecility which Rehoboam himself had manifested, and must have been heard with calm disdain by the veterans of Israel. This purely dynastic and party view of the great question, was such as a hot and not over-wise young prince of the house of David was likely to take, and is in itself perfectly intelligible. But we know that there was another side of the question which found no expression; and the reader may do well to supply for himself the answer which Jeroboam *could* have given if he had liked.

The remainder of Abijah's harangue was, however, in substance unanswerable, although one is not over-satisfied with the self-righteousness of its tone, its inordinate appreciation of ritual observances, and the absence of more spiritual grounds of confidence than it indicates. He animadverted on the measures, the corruptions, and arbitrary changes by which Jeroboam had endeavoured to secure his kingdom ; and, with not unbecoming pride, contrasted this disorder and profanity with the beautiful order in which, according to the law, and the regulations of

PRIESTS SOUNDING AN ALARM

David and Solomon, the worship of the Lord was conducted by the Levitical priesthood, in "the holy and beautiful house which the divine King honoured with the visible symbol of his inhabitance." "We keep the charge of Jehovah," he declared, "but ye have forsaken Him. And, behold, God Himself is with us for our captain, and His priests with sounding trumpets, to cry alarm against you. O children of Israel, fight not against Jehovah, the God of your fathers, for ye shall not prosper."

By the time he had finished, Abijah found, to his great amazement, that he was surrounded by the enemy; and that he had purchased the satisfaction of making a speech at the cost of allowing a large body of the enemy to move quietly round the hill, so as to take his force in the rear, while the main body still confronted him. This difficult and bold manœuvre had well nigh decided the action; for the Judahites raised a cry of dismay, and a serious panic would probably have followed, had not the priests at that moment sounded their silver trumpets, at which old and inspiriting signal, the more stout-hearted men raised a cry to the Lord for help, and rushed

upon the enemy, inspiring by their example the more timid and wavering. The embattled host of Israel could not withstand the force of this terrible shock. Their ranks were broken, they fled, and the slaughter inflicted upon them was most awful, and can only be explained by reference to the peculiar animosity and bloodiness of wars of kindred. Besides, the conquerors were in the enemy's country, and in numbers much the weaker party—too weak for mercy.[1]

Notwithstanding this decisive success, Abijah was too well advised, to pursue his original design of reducing the ten tribes, and was content to re-establish his authority over certain border towns and districts, which had originally belonged to Judah or Benjamin, but which Jeroboam had found means to include in his portion of the divided kingdom. This was but a poor result from the shedding of so much blood, and a miserable compensation for the increased alienation which must have ensued between the subjects of the two kingdoms, which still formed but one nation. All that can be said is, that much blood has often been shed with as little real advantage to the conquerors.

THE QUEEN

1 Kings 15:13

THE disproportion of daughters to sons which was noticeable in the case of Rehoboam, was

---

[1] A great commander of our day, Sir Charles Napier, on lately presenting new colours to the 22nd Foot, in India (Dregshai), delivered a remarkable speech, full of characteristic points, in which occurs the following : " Never can I forget the banks of the Fulailee, and the bloody bed of that river, where 2,000 of our men fought 35,000 enemies ! —where for three hours the musket and the bayonet encountered the sword and the shield in mortal combat ; for on that dreadful day no man spared a foe,—*we were* TOO WEAK FOR MERCY."—*The Times*, January 17, 1851.

counterbalanced in the case of Abijah by a preponderance of sons. Of these he had twenty-two, and of daughters sixteen. His wives were fourteen; and that the number was so much below that which constituted the harem of his father, shows an increasing deference to public opinion, which was undoubtedly unfavourable to this "multiplication of wives" by the kings, of which Solomon, or perhaps we may say David, had set the example. Even this number is named with the marked emphasis which implies disapprobation; and as nothing is said of the number of his son Asa's wives, and as it appears *he* had but one child, it is to be inferred that he so far respected the national feeling and the dignity of woman as to be content with the one wife, whose recorded name is Azubah. After that reign we hear no more of the numerous wives of the kings of Judah, so that this abuse appears to have been rectified; and in the other kingdom it does not seem to have had any existence, for we meet not there with any king who is known to have had more than one wife.

King Abijah reigned only three years; but his son Asa, who succeeded him, reigned forty-one years, and beheld the close of the reign of Jeroboam in Israel, and the commencement of that of Ahab, so that this one reign in the house of David covered the entire reigns of five, and part of the reigns of two, kings in Israel—seven in all, including four different families or dynasties.[1] The contrast is striking, and there can be no doubt that this long, and upon the whole prosperous and meritorious reign, while Israel was torn by internal factions and revolu-

tions, and stained with the blood of fallen princes, massacred by the successful competitors for the perilous crown, tended much to consolidate the strength of Judah, and to raise it to that equality with the rival kingdom, which might not in the first instance have appeared very probable when the great disproportion of territory is considered.

The mention of royal wives in connection with this reign may remind us of the remarkable fact, that it is while Asa is on the throne that the word translated QUEEN first occurs, as applied to one not a reigning sovereign, as the queen of Sheba appears to have been.

If the reader reflects a little, he will see that the practice of polgamy is incompatible with the existence of the rank of queen-consort. Where there are many wives, some of them of equal or nearly equal rank, how can any one of them be queen? Hence David, Solomon, Rehoboam, and Abijah, who had many wives, could have had "no queen," in the European sense of the word, which is that of female-king. So it is still in the polygamous courts of the East; and hence the court of the antepenultimate king of Persia, Futteh Ali Shah, was greatly perplexed when a British ambassador appeared with a letter from queen Charlotte, addressed to "the queen of Persia," and bearing presents for her. However, that the presents might not be lost for the want of a lady to receive them, and that the "king of kings," known to be the husband of many wives and the father of many children, might not appear to be destitute of that which the princes of Europe appeared to consider so necessary to him as a queen, the favourite lady of the day was instructed to represent this character, to receive the presents and the letter, which last was answered in her name.

The fact is, that there can be no queen-consort where there is more than one wife; and, in the East, when there is no more than one, she is not a queen—she has no recognized public position in the state—she is simply the *zan-i-shah*, "the king's wife,"—that is all. There is, however, in most cases, some one in the harem who, on one account or another, is recognized as the chief lady. This position is seldom fixed by the king's mere arbitrary will or personal liking, but is determined by circumstances which usage compels him to respect. Hence the *favourite*

---

[1] Jeroboam was on the throne of Israel when Asa succeeded to that of Judah. His son NADAB then became king; and in the second year of his reign was put to death, with all his father's house, by BAASHA of Issachar, who then mounted the throne, and reigned twenty-four years. He fixed his residence at Tirzah, and was succeeded by his son ELAH, who, in the second year of his reign, was murdered, with all his family, by ZIMRI. On hearing this, the army elected their general, OMRI, as king, and marched to Tirzah against Zimri, who had there assumed the crown. He made no resistance, but fled to the harem, which he set on fire, and perished in the flames. In the meantime, some of the people had made Tibni king; but this party was at length put down, and Omri was generally recognized as king. He built Samaria, which henceforth became the capital of Israel; and, after a reign of twelve years, left the throne to his son AHAB, whose reign fills a large portion of sacred history, and will require considerable attention from us.

wife or concubine is not always, or even generally, the chief lady. The circumstances which usually fix that position are either high birth, priority of marriage, or giving birth to the heir of the throne; and if these three conditions, or the first and the last, concur in the same person, the superiority over the others becomes clear and indisputable; and in any case, the fact of becoming mother of the future king overrides every other consideration, and renders the happy woman so privileged the chief lady, even though she be not a favourite wife.

Now, to apply this. It is likely that the individual among David's wives who was recognized as the chief lady was the mother of his eldest son, Amnon,—although, perhaps, Absalom's mother, by virtue of her high rank as the daughter of a king, asserted her claim to scarcely less consideration, and had a separate establishment of her own; and when, by the death of Amnon, her son became the heir, and these two claims were united in her person, her pre-eminence must have been beyond question or dispute. When Absalom was slain, she necessarily lost the maternal part of her pre-eminence, but retained that which her exalted birth conferred. So, when Solomon became the acknowledged heir to the crown, his mother became the chief lady of the harem,—though perhaps, at first, Haggith, the mother of Adonijah, who was really the elder son, may have put forth some pretensions to that enviable station. Amid these changes, arising from births and deaths of sons, the fixed position which her rank gave to king Talmai's daughter may have seemed not the least enviable, but for this—that she who was chief lady by virtue of her maternity, had to look forward to the still higher state which she might expect to enjoy when her son reached the throne.

Solomon had among his thousand wives one of the most exalted rank, this being no other than the king of Egypt's daughter. She was treated with great distinction, and had a separate palace for herself; and the only claim to be regarded as the chief wife that could at all interfere with hers, was that of the mother of Rehoboam, the heir to the throne. As, however, the rank is not one of public or official recognition, and as Pharoah's daughter had a separate establishment, there is no likelihood that their claims came into conflict.

There was in fact one whose claim to be chief lady, or "queen," was superior to either of theirs, and to which both could not but submit; and this was that of the MOTHER of the king. The chief *wife* claimed that distinction as mother of the future king; but the chief *lady* was the mother of the king himself. This is in conformity with the prevalent usage of the East, which assigns the first rank in every household, not to the wife of the master, but to his mother, to whom the wife merely becomes another daughter. Thus, so far as there was any woman who could be called "queen" in the time of Solomon, it was Bathsheba who enjoyed that distinction. We see a trace of this in the ceremonious respect with which she was received by her son, who rose to meet her, bowed himself to her, and caused a seat to be set for "the king's mother" on his right hand. It was this fact of being "the king's mother" which really constituted the distinction, making the nearest approach to the rank and dignity of a non-regnant queen in the countries of western Europe. [1]

So now we come to the remarkable fact by which these observations have been suggested. We have already had occasion to mention that Rehoboam's favourite wife was Maachah, the grand-daughter of Absalom. On the accession of her son Abijah, she of course became, as the "king's mother," the chief lady in the land, or "queen;" and it appears that she would have retained it under her grandson Asa, but for a cause which is thus stated: "And also concerning Maachah, the mother [grandmother] of Asa the king, he removed her from being queen, because she had made an idol in a grove." The rights which she enjoyed as the king's mother were not lessened, but rather strengthened, by her becoming the king's grandmother—the maternal head of the royal house. But she might lose the conventional

[1] We have obtained, from an unexpected quarter, an African illustration of the statements here advanced. A missionary in Old Calabar gives some curious instances of the power possessed by mothers in that country, and then adds: "The question has perhaps occurred to you, Seeing that women are so much undervalued in Old Calabar, how has that old lady Obuma so much influence?" and referring to the present Reading of the Daily Bible Illustrations as a satisfactory exposition of the chief points involved in the question, he proceeds to state that, "Here, as in the lands of the Bible, the king's *wives* may be and are of little importance in the country, while his *mother* occupies a very high place."—*United Presbyterian Missionary Record*, Aug. 1852.

pre-eminence and state rights (if any) which this position conferred upon her, by her misconduct; and doubtless Asa, by this decided act, intended to express, and was understood to express, in the strongest possible manner, his abomination of idolatry, and his determination to put it down. The rank of which she was thus deprived, would then devolve on the king's own mother.

The most striking analogy to this is found in the high rank, eminent privileges, and even political influence, to which the mother of the sovereign of the Turkish empire succeeds when her son ascends the throne. We hear little or nothing in Turkish history of any woman except the *validé sultan*, or empress-dowager—but of her often, and under various circumstances, which indicate her exalted position and high influence. It was much the same in ancient Persia, where the king's mother enjoyed a peculiar rank and title, corresponding to that of the validé sultan, and with privileges much higher than those of his wife. As the true distinction lay in being the king's mother, the mother of his father probably retained that name whenever—which the course of nature rendered unusual—she continued to enjoy the rank and privileges of the chief lady under her grandson, as in the case before us. It is, however, so common in Scripture for a grandmother to be called a mother, that perhaps even this explanation is scarcely necessary to account for Maachah being called the mother of king Asa.

THE CUSHITE INVASION

1 Chronicles 14:4-15

THE zeal of Asa against idolatry, and for the purity of Divine worship according to the law, has been already intimated. He extirpated whatever appeared to him to savour of idolatry, even to the extent of removing his grandmother from the dignity of "queen" on account of the encouragement she had given to idolatrous practices. In connection with the remarks we lately had occasion to offer respecting "high places," it is, however, worthy of special notice, that although it is said of Asa by one of the sacred historians, that "he took away the altars of the

strange gods, *and the high places*, and brake down the images, and cut down the groves,"[1] the other assures us, that "the high places were not removed," although "Asa's heart was perfect with the Lord all his days."[2] This apparent contradiction is obviated when we observe, that the high places he removed were those in which idols had been worshipped, whereas those consecrated to the Lord Himself were suffered to remain. The historian obviously notes this as a short-coming to be deplored, yet not as a wilful or doom-bringing sin.

In such care for the interests of religion, in promoting the temporal welfare of his people, in strengthening his kingdom by fortresses, and by organizing a large force liable to, and fitted for military service, and in repairing, so far as his means allowed, the shorn magnificence of the Lord's temple and his own palace, the first ten years of Asa's reign happily passed.

Then the clouds of an impending storm appeared in the south—from a quarter unexpected by us, but probably not so by the Judahites: "Zerah the Ethiopian" appeared with a countless host, in which a large proportion of Lubim, or Libyans, was included. To the less instructed reader of Scripture, this suggests the idea of an army of negroes; and they are led to think of the region south of Egypt, to which the name of Ethiopia properly belongs. But the better informed will be unable to see the possibility of such an army as that of Zerah marching through the length of Egypt from Ethiopia, as it must have done in order to reach Palestine, in the reign of such a prince as Osorkon I., who succeeded Shishak in the throne of that kingdom. And although the "Lubim" are undoubtedly the Libyans, he will hesitate to suppose that they could have crossed the breadth of Egypt for the purposes of an invasion, in which the king of that country took no interest. The passage of a large army through any country is a great calamity to that country, and not likely to be allowed for objects in which its king takes no part. Either Osorkon was willing, or was not, that the kingdom of Judah should sustain detriment by invasion. If he were willing, he, with the experience of Shishak's invasion before him, would be apt to consider that this was his own affair, not theirs—that, as the nearer neighbour, it was his right, and not theirs, to profit by the

[1] 2 Chronicles 14:3.   [2] 1 Kings 15:14.

spoliation and ruin of Judah; but if he were not willing — and there are various considerations which render it probable that he was not—it is scarcely credible that he would have consented, greatly to the detriment of his own people, to their passage through his territories; and the might of Egypt would in that reign surely have sufficed to prevent a passage from being forced, against the wish of the king through the land. In fact, it seems that little less than the previous conquest of Egypt must have taken place, before this vast invading force could have reached the land of Judah from the quarters usually indicated; and this, we know, was not the case.

All the difficulty seems to have been created by one of the commonest accidents of translation —that of rendering a large term by another, of more limited signification in the language into which the translation is made. In the original here, Zerah the Ethiopian is "Zerah the Cushite," —a name applicable to all the descendants of Cush, the son of Ham, and even to the inhabitants of the regions originally settled, but afterwards abandoned, by them. Now the name Cush is very rarely in Scripture applicable to the African Cush, or Ethiopia proper, but almost always to the Asiatic Cush, in Arabia. The original settlements of the great Cushite family can be traced at the head of the Persian Gulf, where the name Khusistan, or "land of Cush," still denotes an important district, anciently renowned by the classically softened name of Susiana. Thence, all along *the coast* of Arabia, down the eastern coast, and up the western, the course of the great settling migration of the Cushites may be traced, in the continued occurrence of the *names* of the great Cushite families, as denoting localities dispersed over the peninsula in the very track which, from the antecedent probabilities created by the physical constitution of the country—a vast wilderness belted by fertile mountains towards the coasts,—a progressive colonization would be likely to follow. Hence Arabia, or certain important parts of it, would be probably called Cush, not only as originally settled by Cushites, but as still the abode of many Cushite tribes, the distinct origin of some of which can, it appears, be recognized even at this day.

It may be shown by the internal evidence of most of the passages of Scripture in which the name of Cush occurs, that it was in Arabia; and

in fact this is evinced in the very passage under our consideration. It appears by the results that the invaders were a mixture of pastoral and settled tribes. They had tents and cattle—the latter in great numbers; and they had also chariots and towns. The pastoral herds inevitably fix them to Arabia, if only as confirming the improbability of their having passed through Egypt. Besides, one of their towns to which they fled, and where they attempted to make a stand, was Gerar in the southern wilderness, which fixes them to Arabia Petræa, and the parts about and between Egypt and Palestine. Many doubtless came from more distant parts of Arabia, for this "huge host" seems to have been a great gathering of Cushite and other tribes for this promising expedition, the prime movers of which were doubtless such of them as lay nearest to Palestine, who stimulated the remoter tribes to join them in this enterprise.

The Libyans were, we doubt not, such, and the descendants of such, as had been among Shishak's levies when he invaded the land some twenty-five years before, and who, finding here kindred tribes, and a country and modes of life congenial to their own habits, chose to be left behind, doubtless with the glad consent of Shishak, who thus got rid of them when their work was done, without the expense and trouble of restoring them to their own land. It is indeed very likely that the idea of the present expedition originated with this people—in their continual talk of the ease with which the country had been subdued in the time of Rehoboam, of the golden glories of Jerusalem, and of the rich pillage obtained there. We may fancy these rough fellows talking this matter over around their tent fires to greedy eared listeners. Deep, no doubt, were the retrospective murmurs at the king of Egypt, for refusing to give up the rich city to be sacked by the troops; or for allowing it to be redeemed by the treasures of the temple and palace, thus depriving the soldiers of the just reward of their toils. But so much the better now. What was not then taken was there still; and much had, no doubt, been added to repair that loss. Thus they would argue in their barbarous fashion, and stimulate those who heard them to the plunder and devastation of a country still in their view rich, and possessed, as they judged, of no strength to resist the force they could bring against it.

In the *Speaker's Commentary*, Zerah, the Ethiopian, is regarded as Usarken (Osorkon II.), the third king of Egypt after Shishak, a name appearing on the Egyptian monuments. The three main consonants in the two names are the same. Osorkon may have been an Ethiopian by birth. If this reading be correct, the result is important. " The defeat of Zerah is one of the most remarkable events in the history of the Jews. On no other occasion did they meet in the field and overcome the forces of either of the two great monarchies between which they were placed. It was seldom they ventured to resist except behind walls. Shishak, Sennacherib, Esarhadden, Nebuchadnezzar, Alexander, Ptolemy, were either unopposed or opposed in this way. On the other occasion on which they took the field—which was under Josiah against Necho—their boldness issued in a most disastrous defeat. (2 Chron. xxxv. 20-24.) Now, however, under Asa, they appear to have gained a complete and most glorious victory over the entire force of Egypt, or of Ethiopia wielding the power of Egypt. The results which follow are most striking. The southern power cannot rally from the blow, but rapidly declines, and for above three centuries makes no further effort in this direction." (*Speaker's Commentary*, iii. 310.) Perhaps in this passage the magnitude of the victory is overrated, as in the above illustration it is underrated. Something more than the defeat of the tribe of Cushite Arabs seems to be meant by smiting the cities round about Gerar—cities containing " very much spoil." As Gerar was on the borders of Egypt, and as Zerah's army, even according to Dr. Kitto, was connected with former Egyptian levies under Shisak, the victory, it is probable, affected the interests of Israel's ancient oppressors.

S.

THE CONTRAST

1 Kings 15:15-23; 2 Chronicles 16:7-10

THE conduct of Asa, on receiving tidings of the Cushite invasion, was in all respects most praiseworthy, and in perfect conformity with the principles of the theocratical constitution. It seems also to evince much sound judgment in a military point of view. Instead of waiting in Jerusalem the appearance of the invaders, after they had ravaged the country in the march to that city, it appeared to him better to spare his people this misery, by marching to the southern frontier, and giving battle to the enemy at one of the great passes into the country (that of Zephathah), where, and to guard which, his grandfather had built the strong fortress of Mareshah. The situation for posting his army, at this pass, was admirably chosen. But Asa, while doing the best that

circumstances allowed, and taking every advantage in his power, did not rely upon this, and was deeply conscious of his inability to resist the invaders in any strength of his own. His reliance was elsewhere, even in Him who, on taking the position of real Head of the Hebrew commonwealth, had pledged Himself to the defence and deliverance of His people. Viewed from the theocratical point of view, or indeed from any point of view, nothing can be finer than the prayer which Asa uttered before he fell to mortal conflict with the enemy: " Lord, it is nothing to Thee to help, whether with many, or with them that have no power. Help us, O Lord our God; for we rest on Thee, and in thy name go against this multitude. O Lord, Thou art our God; let not man prevail against Thee."

The Israelites never, from the commencement of their history, failed to be victorious in any battle undertaken in this spirit,—evincing that faith in Him, to which the Lord, by all His covenants, had bound Himself to respond. This was so much a matter of course, that the historian simply, but with a truly grand laconism under the circumstances, adds: "So the Lord smote the Cushites before Asa, and before Judah, and the Cushites fled." They were pursued with great slaughter to their encampments, and to their towns about Gerar; and the spoil with which the Judahites returned was prodigious, and being largely in sheep and camels, it must have made a material contribution to the substantial wealth of the country.

This victory, so signally the doing of the Lord, together with the encouragements given to the king by a prophet named Azariah, who came out to meet him on his return, greatly stimulated the king in his great work of religious reform and purification. A great festal sacrifice was held at Jerusalem, at which seven hundred oxen and seven thousand sheep were offered, and the assembled people then and there entered into a high and solemn covenant, " to seek the Lord their God with all their heart and with all their soul."

The result was peace and prosperity for many years. This was so signal and manifest, that after a time a tide of migration into this kingdom set in from the more troubled one of Israel, which excited the serious apprehension of Baasha, who was then upon the throne, and incited him to a bold measure for the purpose of preventing it, or holding it in check. He seized the town of Ramah, which lay within the territory of Judah, six miles from Jerusalem, on the way to Bethel, and began to turn it into a strong fortress. This audacious measure, which held out to Asa the prospect of having an able and resolute enemy master of a position of great strength within a short distance of his capital, filled with dismay the royal heart, which had not quailed before the hosts of Zerah. He lost that faith which had ennobled his past career, and betook himself to miserable diplomacies, no less impolitic than degrading.

The now important Syrian power seated at Damascus, was at this time under a treaty of peace with the kingdom of Israel, to which it was naturally, from its position, and had been before, and was afterwards, most hostile. Asa, knowing the really adverse temper of Syria towards Israel, thought it not unlikely that the king might be induced to break the existing treaty, and by appearing in the north, compel Baasha to abandon his designs in the south. He tried it, and succeeded: but he received this aid from Benhadad at a most costly sacrifice; for he sent all his silver and gold, whether in the form of money or of vessels, which he could make available, sparing neither the precious things of his own palace nor those of the temple. He reckoned, probably, that it was better to give up his treasure in this way, than to have it taken by force from him; while, if peace resulted from the sacrifice, he would be able to replace it with interest in a few years. For *this* part of his conduct, it is worthy of note, he was not blamed. The treasure which the ambassadors brought was doubtless more effectual than their arguments in prevailing upon Benhadad to accede to a course so dishonourable. He did accede, and sent an army against the north of Israel, which captured and plundered many important towns, and ravaged the whole land of Naphtali, and the country about the sea of Galilee. On hearing this, Baasha at once abandoned Ramah, and went to protect his own country; and the war between him and the Syrians being thus renewed, he found too much employment to resume his former design.

But, however successful it seemed in its immediate object, the thing that Asa had done displeased the Lord. Its offence was gross and accumulated. It betrayed a want of that reliance upon the Lord, which once, in a really more urgent strait, had won him so much honour; it was the tempting of another to do a dishonourable breach of faith; and it was the bringing of a heathen destroyer into that land which was still the Lord's heritage, though it belonged not to Judah, and upon that people who were still His, although they had strayed from Him. For this—but especially for his relying upon the king of Syria more than upon the King of Heaven— a prophet was sent to rebuke and threaten him. It was intimated that, for this, he had lost a great victory over the Syrians, which the Lord would have given to him, and that the remainder of his reign should be troubled with wars. The former intimation is worthy of notice, as being of that rare kind which indicates what *would* have occurred had a certain course *not* been taken. We understand it to mean, that Baasha would have called the Syrians to his aid, and that Asa would have been afforded a signal victory over them.

To be thus rebuked in the moment when his diplomatic stroke seemed to have fulfilled its purpose so well, was more than one so little used to contradiction could bear; and in his rage he sent the faithful prophet to prison—adding to his original fault the grievous sin of persecuting an inspired messenger of Jehovah. Here we have the melancholy spectacle of a prophet of God imprisoned, not by an idolatrous or notoriously wicked king, but by one who has hitherto borne a noble character, and whose heart was substantially right with God. Not so did David receive Nathan's more stern rebuke. This descendant of his does that, for only attempting to do which Jeroboam had his arm palsied. But, as Bishop Hall charitably remarks: "It were pity that the best man should be judged by each of his actions, and not by all; the course of our life must either allow or condemn us, not these sudden eruptions."

THE WAY OF HELP

2 Chronicles 14:11

"O Lord, Thou art our God, let not man prevail against Thee!" These were the words with which king Asa, full of faith, marched against the Cushite host. Great words they are, and they deserve to be well considered. Observe the root of the idea from which they spring. At the first view it might seem more obvious and natural to say, " Let not man prevail against *us ;* " but he says, " Let not man prevail against *Thee.*" This is a bold word. It assumes that the Lord's cause was so much identified with theirs, His honour so much involved in theirs in this matter, that man's triumph over them would be a triumph over Him—would compromise the glory of His great name even more than it would compromise theirs. If this notion rested not on strong foundations, it were egregious presumption ; but if it were well founded, it was faith. On what, then, was it founded ? We are left at no loss in this matter, for Asa himself declares the grounds of this strong, we may almost say daring, claim upon the Lord's assistance.

It was the conviction of his utter helplessness, and therefore of the absolute necessity of the Lord's deliverance, and of his knowledge that all the glory must therefore be His. " Lord, it is nothing with Thee to help, whether with many, or with them that have no power. Help us, O Lord our God." This is something. This goes a great way. It is indispensable that we should feel our own helplessness, in order to estimate at its true value the help that may be given to us. The claim to help is not with him who thinks that he has need of nothing, or only of a little help just to make out the " possible insufficiency of his own resources ;" but with him who feels that he has need of everything, that in himself he has no resources whatever—no works, no worthiness, no strength that may, so to speak, somewhat help the Lord to help him—that old delusion, that old snare, which has in all time kept so many souls from the help they might else have had from God. See that man drowning in the waters, and see that other coming forth from the shore with a strong stroke to save him ! See the vain efforts of the first to help himself ! He kicks, he struggles, he beats the waters, he rears aloft his arms, he will not be still. He thinks he is helping himself; but all the while he is only doing his utmost to aid his own submersion. If he would be but quiet, in the conviction of the utter impotency of all such attempts to save himself, he might float quietly upon the water until the deliverer came near. [1] He *is* near—he

grasps the sufferer by the hair—he holds his head above the wave—he propels him gently on towards the shore. Let not the thought of helping his helper cross his mind, or he is again undone. Let him lie still in the hands of his preserver, let him have faith in his power to save, and that strong arm shall bear him triumphantly through ; but if he yet struggles to help himself, and lifts himself up to catch convulsively at every floating straw, there is no help for him —down he goes.

Asa knew he was in himself helpless, and he knew where to seek an all-sufficient Helper, and he desired to know no more. In this he rested : " We rest on Thee." This resting on God was both a cause and an effect. That he was enabled so to rest with undisturbed mind on God, was one of the grounds on which he expected help— "*for* we rest on Thee;" and so far it was a cause. But the capacity of enjoying this rest, in leaning so entirely upon the Lord, was an inevitable effect of the previous convictions which he had reached of his own helplessness, and of the boundless sufficiency of his Helper. These things belong to the life of faith, and are essentially the same, whether they have regard to our defence against the innumerable ills that disturb or threaten our temporal repose, or to the spiritual enemies, within us and without us, that bring danger to our souls. In either case, perfect love to God, and perfect trust in Him, which trust is essential to love, give REST—cast out all fear and doubt. " He that feareth is not made perfect in love ;" and therefore he has not yet attained to perfect rest. To enjoy this rest, which is the result of perfect love and perfect faith, is a state of inconceivable blessedness, infinitely greater than that of those whom the multitude look up to with envy and admiration. It is the state of the man who can say, in the quaint language of an old poet :

" The God that made my heart is He alone
　　That of Himself both can and will
　　　Give rest unto my thoughts, and fill
　　Them full of all content and quietness ;
　　　That so I may possess
　　　　My soul in patience,
　　Until He find it time to call me hence.

---

[1] It is a fact, that if a man lie still with his arms below the water, he may float any length of time with his face above the water. Men are drowned by their blind struggles in the effort to save themselves.

In Thee, as in my centre, shall
The lines of all my longings fall.
To Thee, as to mine anchor, surely tied,
My ship shall safely ride.
On Thee, as on my bed
Of soft repose, I'll rest my weary head.

Thou, Thou alone, shalt be my whole desire;
I'll nothing else require
But Thee, or for thy sake.
In Thee I'll sleep secure; and, when I wake,
Thy glorious face shall satisfy
The longing of my looking eye.
I'll roll myself on Thee, as on my rock,
When threatening dangers mock."

School of the Heart.

A man who has realized these convictions, and who has attained that state of rest, of reliance, of perfect freedom from all anxiety and care, who is fully clad in the armour of God—his hands are fit for war and his fingers for fight— he goes forth conquering and to conquer all the enemies of his peace, as well those who lurk in the corners of his soul's dark cottage, as those that beset him round in his open walk, and prowl, and grin, and jabber about his path. He is fearless. Nothing can harm him; for he has that peace with him which all the world's armies could not wrest from him, which the world's terrors cannot disturb, which its foul breath cannot sully, and which the raging of its utmost storms can as little ruffle, as it can the "sea of glass" before the throne of God.

It was because Asa had attained to the state of "rest on God," by which all these privileges became his, that he could say, "In Thy name we go against this multitude." This was his might. In this might he went, and he overcame. And it was because, feeling his own weakness, and knowing where help was to be found, he relied upon that help and on no other, in going forth to oppose the Cushite host, that he was entitled and authorized to regard the cause as the Lord's own, and to say, "O Lord, Thou art our God; let no man prevail against THEE."

Israel was a type of the church of God, and of the child of God. The special instructions given by the Divine Ruler for the guidance, the preservation, and the defence of that nation are just such as God's people require most carefully to observe. Everything like self-trust and confidence was emphatically condemned. In all times of difficulty, of temptation, and of danger, the Israelites were strictly enjoined to appeal to and rely upon their God.

The divine promises covered all exigencies; and the divine power was equal to all emergencies. When the Israelites, helpless and hopeless, stood trembling on the shore of the Red Sea, and cried in despair, "Because there were no graves in Egypt, hast thou taken us away to die in the wilderness?" then Moses, by divine command, told them their duty: "Fear ye not, stand still, and see the salvation of the Lord." So it was in every stage of their after history. The Lord was their Guide, their Help, their Deliverer. And it was only when forsaking that heavenly Guide, and relying either on themselves, or upon the assistance of earthly allies,—it was then only that they experienced defeat and disaster. In regard to *faithful* Israel, whether in ancient or modern times, the words of the Lord by Isaiah have ever been, and must ever become, a cheering and glorious reality: "Fear not: for I have redeemed thee, I have called thee by thy name; thou art mine. When thou passest through the waters, I will be with thee; and through the rivers, they shall not overflow thee: when thou walkest through the fire, thou shalt not be burned; neither shall the flame kindle upon thee. *For I am the Lord thy God, the Holy One of Israel, thy Saviour.*"

P.

PHYSICIANS

1 Kings 15:23; 2 Chronicles 16:12

ASA was in his latter days afflicted with "a disease in his feet," which is generally supposed to have been the gout. Here, again, the king incurs some blame for having resorted to "the physicians," instead of relying upon God. We cannot suppose that he was blameworthy for taking proper means for his recovery, but he was for relying upon them instead of upon the Lord's blessing upon the means they employed. It was, therefore, a new manifestation of that lapse of faith to which he had unhappily become too prone. Much had been given to him—even large capacities of faith—and much more therefore was required from him than from men less favoured. It may have been something even worse. It is even probable that the "physicians" may have been foreigners and idolaters, whose practice consisted much in superstitious arts and idolatrous rites, instead of the priests, or rather Levites, in whose hands the medical practice of the Jews chiefly rested. In this case, his offence was the same *in kind* as that of the king of Israel (Jehoram) in the next generation, who sent to Baalzebub, the god of Ekron, respecting the disease with which he was afflicted, and who incurred thereby a dreadful rebuke for not having consulted the God of Israel. This shows that the cure, no less than the infliction, of disease, was among the Israelites regarded as the *immediate* act of God. It was usual to ascertain His will through the priests or prophets. It was also sought to propitiate Him by vows, by prayers, and by sacrifices. Under the same views as to the cause of the disease, the heathen resorted to their gods, and sought to win their favour or to pacify them, by various strange, superstitious, and often brutal rites. In any case, certainly, under such a state of things, to apply to a foreign physician was but an indirect mode of application to the god he served.

We shall take this opportunity of producing a few particulars respecting the state of medicine among the ancient Hebrews.

There have been some curious speculations among them as to the medical knowledge of Adam, founded on the idea that the knowledge of all creatures, implied in his bestowal of appropriate names upon them, must have comprised a knowledge of their medicinal properties and uses. The mere conjecture shows the extent to which animal substances were applied in the materia medica of the Hebrews. In this age, when more potent medicinal agents have been found, it is hard to conceive the extent to which the parts of animals were used, not only by the ancients, but, until a comparatively recent date, by the moderns. Indeed, most of the practices connected with the application of animal simples, which, where found in use among our peasantry, are cited (under such headings as "Folk-Lore") as rural superstitions, are often little else than remnants of ancient and legitimate medical practice.

The point is curious; and in proof of it we might quote largely from a work bearing the date of 1664, which sets forth the medicinal uses of most animals, citing ancient and medical authorities for most of the statements, including Jewish medical writers.[1] We wish our space allowed quotation from this book; but we can

[1] ΠΑΝΖΩΟΡΥΚΤΟΛΟΓΙΑ, sive *Panzoologicomineralogia;* or *a Compleat History of Animals and Minerals, containing the summe of all Authors, both Ancient and Modern, Galenicall and Chymicall, touching Animals, viz. Beasts, Birds, Fishes, Serpents, Insects, and Man, as to their Place, Meat, Temperature, Vertues, Use in Meat and Medicine, Description, Kinds, Generation, Sympathie, Diseases, Cures, Hurts, and Remedies, &c.* By Robert Lovell, St. C. C., Oxon. Φιλνθεολογιατρόνομος. Oxford, 1664.

give only a sample or two. The first article is "Ape,"—in which, among other things, we are told that "an ape eaten by a lion cureth his diseases"—a fact we most potently believe, having often noticed a lion to seem greatly refreshed after demolishing an ape. Under "Asse" we are told, among other delectable matter, that "a little of the water being drunke, of which the cow or asse hath drunke, doth effectually help the headach." "The dryed brain of an asse, being drunke daily in water and honey, helpeth the epilepsic in 30 daies." "The heart of a black male asse, being eaten with bread, helpeth the falling sicknesse." "The gall doth asswage the signes of abscesses." "The flesh helpeth against the paine of the backbone and hipps. The marrow anointed cureth the gout, and easeth the paine. The ashes of the hoofes burned help the falling sickness. The dung mixed with the yoke of an egge, and applied to the forehead, stoppeth the fluxe of blood, and, with a bull's gall, curleth the haire." Of the mouse it is said, "The flesh causeth oblivion. A mouse dissected and applied draweth out reeds, darts, and other things that stick in the flesh. Being eaten by children, when rosted, they dry up their spittle. The water in which they have been boiled helpeth against the quinsey. The ashes, with honey, used ten dayes, clear the eyes. The head, worne in a cloth, helpeth the headache and epilepsy. The liver, rosted in the new of the moon, trieth the epilepsie. The brain, being steeped in wine and applied to the forehead, helpeth the headache. The gall, with vinegar, dropped into the eare, bringeth out live creatures in the eare. The dung, given in any liquor, helpeth the cholic;" and is further stated to be good, as are other of its parts and products, for a variety of other uses, which must have rendered this little creature formerly of much more estimation in public opinion than it now is.

The first mention of physicians in Scripture is in the time of Joseph, and in connection with Egypt, which may be regarded as the western cradle of this and many other ancient sciences and arts. We refer to the physicians who embalmed Jacob, and who were, therefore, rather embalmers than physicians, whose profession is to cure the living, not to embalm the dead. Nevertheless, we know from other sources that the Egyptians had early made great progress in the study of medicine, and acquired high reputation; so that the aid of Egyptian physicians was much sought for, even in foreign lands. Indeed, it is far from unlikely that the physicians, whose skill Asa so unwisely relied on, were from Egypt. It was believed that they had a knowledge of materia medica more extensive than any other men by whom medical science was cultivated, and that in this their great strength lay. Indeed there is clear enough allusion to this in one of the prophets, who exclaims, "O virgin daughter of Egypt, in vain shalt thou use *many medicines*, for thou shalt not be cured." (Jer. xlvi. 11.)

No one can doubt that the Hebrews must have brought some considerable portion of this knowledge of medicine with them from Egypt. Their actual possession of it is strikingly manifested in the indication of the characters by which the priest was to recognize the leprosy, as well as of the sanitary measures to be taken, and the means of cure to be adopted. All this may be seen in Lev. xiii.; and it suffices to observe, that modern physicians,[1] who have given attention to the subject, have only found occasion to attest the exact accuracy of these indications. The knowledge thus possessed by and required from the priests, sufficiently proves that medicine was in all essential respects a sacred pursuit, and was, as such, in the hands of the Levitical priesthood, whose learned leisure and dispersion through the country, as well as their superior education, rendered them in these remote ages the best and fittest depositaries of medical science. Indeed, nothing is more certain than the essential identity among all ancient nations of the professions—religion, law, and medicine—which the progress of civilization has separated into three. Even in our country, the profession of the law still bears the outward and visible marks of its ancient connection with religion; and the time is not remote when every parish priest was expected to possess some acquaintance with medicine.

Among the Hebrews, leprosy, and all other diseases, were deemed to be the immediate effect of the omnipotence of God. They were sent for punishment or fatherly correction to those who had offended Him or incurred His rebuke; and they were cured when the sufferers had appeased Him by their contrition

[1] See, in particular, Dr. John Mason Good's *Study of Medicine.*

and their prayers, or when the object of their chastening had been accomplished. This theory of disease and cure among the Hebrews will, in its application, throw much light upon all the passages which more or less bear upon the subject.

As we shall, in the Illustrations of the New Testament, have to take up the further developments of a subject which is most prominently brought forward in that portion of divine revelation, we here limit our view, as much as possible, to the state of the matter before Christ. For the elucidation of this, there is a most remarkable passage in the Apocrypha, which has been much overlooked in the consideration of the question. It is in Ecclesiasticus; and as the apocryphal books are not now generally accessible, we give it entire below.[1]

It appears to us that this passage very exactly defines the position of the physician. It allows him honour, and gives due weight to his skill and the real use of the means he employs, but admirably refers all to God. The skill of the physician is His; the medicaments are His; and the cure is His. Even the skill of the physician is proportioned to the faculty he possesses of rendering God honour, by his knowledge and employment of the healing properties which He has imparted to various productions of the earth.

[1] "Honour a physician with the honour due unto him, for the uses which ye may have of him: for the Lord hath created him. For of the Most High cometh healing, and he shall receive honour of the king. The skill of the physician shall lift up his head [*i. e.*, raise him to honour]: and in the sight of great men he shall be in admiration. The Lord hath created medicines out of the earth; and he that is wise will not abhor them. Was not the water made sweet with wood, that the virtue thereof might be known? And He giveth men skill, that He might be honoured in His marvellous works. With such doth He heal [men], and taketh away their pains. Of such doth the apothecary make a confection; and of His works there is no end; and from Him is peace over all the earth. My son, in thy sickness be not negligent: but pray unto the Lord, and He will make thee whole. Leave off from sin, and order thine hands aright, and cleanse thine heart from all wickedness. Give a sweet savour, and a memorial of fine flour; and make a fat offering, as not being. Then give place to the physician, for the Lord hath created him: let him not go from thee, for thou hast need of him. There is a time when in their hands there is good success: for they shall also pray unto the Lord, that He would prosper that which they give for ease and remedy to prolong life. He that sinneth before his Maker, let him fall into the hands of the physician."—Ecclesiasticus 38:1-15.

In the last clause there is, however, something which would be regarded as a sarcasm on the profession if it were met with in a modern writing: "He that sinneth before his Maker, let him fall into the hands of the physician!"

OMRI

1 Kings 16:23-29

AHAB was on the throne of Israel when Asa died in Judah. He was the second king of his family. It is remarkable of his father Omri, that he was the first founder of a new dynasty, who did not come to the crown by a revolt against his sovereign, and the extermination of his house. It is true that he led the army against Zimri; but, in so doing, he appeared as the avenger of the king whom Zimri had murdered, and the usurper's reign of a week, if it can be called a reign, was too short to enable his family, if he had any, to establish any influence dangerous to Omri, or to render their extermination politically expedient. However, it came to pass that Omri attained to the throne with comparatively undefiled hands. He was even spared the blood of Zimri, that guilty man having burned the royal palace over his head in Tirzah, which had by this time become the capital.

This incident had the effect of removing the metropolis to a more central and desirable situation. Instead of rebuilding the consumed palace, Omri concluded to build not only a new palace, but a new town elsewhere. It is much to the credit of his judgment and taste, that he perceived the advantages which the hill of Samaria offered for the seat of a royal city. There is probably not a finer or more desirable situation in Palestine; and many travellers have expressed a conviction, that the spot was in most respects much preferable to the site of Jerusalem, although the special objects contemplated in the divine wisdom rendered it expedient that the ecclesiastical metropolis of the Hebrew nation should be established there.

The verdant valley which breaks through the mountains westward between Ebal and Gerizim, spreads out, often for three or four miles, into a broad circular basin, five or six miles in diameter,

and bounded on every side by beautiful mountains. From the rich plains of this glorious valley, enclosed by an amphitheatre of mountains, and near to the western side, rises a very high and steep hill, affording a position of impregnable strength, and of almost unapproachable loveliness. About midway up the ascent, the hill is surrounded by a narrow terrace of level ground, like a belt, below which the roots of the hill spread off more gradually into the valleys. This was the hill which belonged to one Shemer, and which Omri bought of him for about seven hundred pounds. Here he established the royal seat of his kingdom; and he had the good taste to call the new town not by his own name, but by that of the previous owner of the land, in the form of Shimron—better known to us in the softened shape of SAMARIA, which it assumed in the Greek language. We are not sure, however, that the credit of this graceful course is due to the spontaneous generosity of Omri. Considering how reluctant the Hebrews were to alienate any lands belonging to them, and that the kings had no power to compel such alienation, it is quite possible that Shemer could only be induced to part with the hill on the condition that his name at least should stand there as a memorial that it had once belonged to him. This, which occurs to us at the moment of writing, seems a very probable explanation of this remarkable fact, and is consonant to the known feelings of the Hebrew landholders. Without it, there does not after all appear any adequate reason why Omri should give the name of Shemer to a place which had become his by the payment of what was no doubt regarded as an adequate, if not liberal, compensation.

Of Omri it is said, that, *in the eyes of the Lord,* his conduct on the throne was worse than that of all the kings before him. The particulars are not directly stated in the history, further than that he carried out with vigour the fatal and ruinous policy of Jeroboam. But if we reflect upon the incidental facts and allusions connected with his name and proceedings, we may be able to obtain some clearer idea of his character and offences. If we refer to the prophecy of Micah (vi. 16), we find this remarkable statement,— "For the *statutes of Omri* are kept, and all the works of the house of Ahab. Taking this into connection with the character which the historian ascribes to him, we cannot doubt that "these statutes of Omri," which were but too well maintained by his successors, and observed by the subjects of his kingdom, were measures adopted for more completely isolating the people of Israel from the services of the house of the Lord at Jerusalem, and for perpetuating, perhaps increasing, their idolatrous practices. His indifference to the evils of idolatry at least, if not his desire to encourage it, as tending to render the separation between the two kingdoms more complete, is incidentally confirmed by the fact, that he brought about a marriage between Ahab, his son and heir, and Jezebel, the daughter of Ethbaal, king of Tyre.[1] The Tyrians were devoted to the worship of Baal; and the reigning family seem to have carried an ardour of proselytism into this worship not often witnessed in the ancient idolatries. Knowing this, and knowing, as he must have known, that the feeble character of his son would be sure to bring him entirely under the control and influence of a strongminded woman, especially as the kings of Israel confined themselves to one wife, we cannot acquit Omri of a culpable disregard of the duty of maintaining the interests of the true religion among his people, even if he had not the sagacity to foresee, nor the wickedness to design, the consequences which actually occurred from this connection.

The circumstance is historically interesting, as showing that it fell to the kings of Israel, and not to the descendants of David in Judah, to maintain the connection with Tyre which David and Solomon had established. The house of David, separated now by the kingdom of Israel from Tyre, had no longer any interest in maintaining a political connection with Tyre, though it did not forfeit nor relinquish the accustomed advantages of finding there, in common with Israel, a mart for its surplus agricultural produce. This interesting fact we learn from Ezekiel (xxvii. 17), where, speaking of Tyre, the prophet says: "Judah, and the land of Israel, they were thy merchants: they traded in thy market wheat of Minnith, and Pannag, and honey, and oil, and balm."

[1] In the text Ethbaal is called "king of the Zidonians;" but it appears from Josephus, that he was also king of Tyre. The dominion included both cities, and the people collectively are called "Zidonians" in Scripture. The territorial title in Scripture is "king of Tyre;" the Gentile title, "king of the Zidonians."

With Israel the connection gradually became more close, closer even than it had been in the time of Solomon. There was not, indeed, the same interest in commercial enterprises. But even a stronger tie of common interest had at this time grown up between the nations. The active, ambitious, and encroaching power which had arisen in Damascene-Syria could not be regarded without uneasiness even by Tyre, which must have felt an interest in sustaining, by its alliance, the kings of Israel in possession of that portion of northern territory, which alone separated its own dominion from so dangerous a neighbour. That neighbour was about this time very active, and had made alarming advances towards Phœnicia, by wresting from Omri a considerable portion of the intervening territory. The natural tendency of this was to draw the two courts of Tyre and Israel more closely to each other for mutual support—the friendship of each being desirable to the other: Omri needing the alliance of Tyre to strengthen himself against the encroachments of Syria; and Tyre clearly perceiving that to strengthen Israel, was a measure of defence for itself. We thus behold an adequate reason—in such human policy as was now alone considered in Israel—for the closer connection which was by this marriage sought between the two kingdoms, and which, in its remoter consequences, might be expected to place on the throne of Israel a king equally related in blood to both the royal houses. It was, we know, the duty of the king of Israel to entrust the defence of his kingdom and the safety of his people to the Lord, who had given that land to them, and who had promised to maintain them in it, so long as they walked worthy of the high vocation to which they had been called. But this was a pitch of duty to which these kings could not reach. It was too high for them. They could not attain unto it.

AHAB AND JEZEBEL

1 Kings 16:29-31

HITHERTO the Israelites had not cast off their allegiance to Jehovah, nor ceased to worship Him, although their worship was damaged by the presence of unworthy emblems, and degraded by maimed rights and an unlawful priesthood. But in the time of Ahab, and under the influence of Jezebel, although they did not formally and expressly renounce Jehovah, they did what was practically the same, by setting up other gods besides Him, and holding Him of no more account than them. Temples were built to them in the metropolis, altars were set up, sacrifices were offered, and bloody and abhorrent rites were performed by a numerous priesthood. There were nearly a thousand of these priests; and their frequent presence in the town, and their diligent attendance at the royal court, gave a new and strange aspect to the streets and palaces of Samaria. It is said that there were four hundred who ate their meat at Jezebel's table; which probably means that they were sustained in the precincts of the palace at her expense. It was clearly seen that this was the fashionable and court religion; whence it would naturally follow, that the mass of the worldly-minded would adopt it also, or at least give a divided attention to it. Had this been endured, the worship of Jehovah would still, doubtless, have been tolerated among those that followed the new religion; for polytheism was tolerant of other gods, and the worshippers of Baal or Ashtaroth would not, on principle, object to the worship of Jehovah, though for themselves they preferred Baal. Jehovah was in their view a God, but He was not *their* god; they were not His votaries, and He had no claim upon them. It was the sublime monotheism of Judaism that could not be tolerant of any other gods than Jehovah within the sacred land, and that asserted His claim to universal and exclusive worship. This gave voice to the prophets, who proclaimed throughout the land the abomination and futility of this new worship. They denounced the judgments of God upon Ahab and Jezebel, upon the worshippers of Baal, and upon the lands and cities which had been defiled by these detestable enormities; and by miracles, sometimes of judgment and sometimes of mercy, they avouched the divine authority by which they gave forth their utterances. This gave rise to fierce persecution against the worshippers of Jehovah, and especially against the prophets—faithfulness to the Lord God of Israel being by the court regarded as disaffection to the government and its measures. Or, otherwise, Jezebel was determined to maintain her own

idolatrous religion in Israel at all hazards; and if, as the prophets alleged, the worship of Baal and of Jehovah could not co-exist, and there could be no peace between their worshippers, then it necessarily became a contest for exclusive and paramount worship; and since either Jehovah or Baal must give place, the hard-willed queen determined that it should not be the god in whose worship she had been brought up. These considerations gave more intensity to her zeal in the establishment of her own worship, and in the suppression of that of Jehovah. Thus, between the smiles of the court upon those who came over to Baal, and the now active hostility evinced against the worshippers of the Lord, it ere long came to pass, that the whole nation was turned into a nest of idolators. So it seemed to man's eye: but the Lord had His hidden ones, even in this time of peril; and when the prophet deemed that he alone had kept the faith, it was made known to him that there were full seven thousand who had not bowed the knee to Baal. Only seven thousand among the millions of Israel! A small number, indeed, to him who counted the nation, but large to him who had deemed that nation lost in this iniquity. It was but a little flock, yet a flock worthy of the great Shepherd's care; and He did care for it.

Besides the difference in the ultimate object of worship, the worship of the golden calves had never appeared in an aspect so imposing as that now given to the service of Baal and Ashtaroth. This worship was raised up in some degree to a parallel with that of Jehovah at Jerusalem. The golden calves had been established in two provincial towns at the opposite extremities of the kingdom, without any temples, but simply with emblematic images and altars. But now the worship of Baal was centralized in the metropolis, where a temple, doubtless of considerable splendour, was erected, and ceremonial services were rendered by numerous bodies of priests. Samaria could now pride itself on being an ecclesiastical as well as regal metropolis, like Jerusalem; and doubtless many not over-wise persons reckoned that something the realm had hitherto wanted was now at last supplied.

And what manner of a man was he—this Ahab, son of Omri—who gave his royal countenance and sanction to all these doings? Excuse is sometimes made for him as not an essentially wicked, but only a weak man, overborne by the powerful will of a resolute woman. But

"All wickedness is weakness;"

and it is also true, that all weakness is wickedness, and most of all in a king. He to whose care the welfare of a nation has been entrusted has no right to be weak. The weakness ascribed to Ahab seems to us merely indolence of character—a love of ease, an indisposition to exertion, unless when thoroughly roused by some awakening stimulus. He was such a man as would rather allow what he feels to be wrong, for the sake of a quiet life, than take the trouble of asserting what he knows to be right. To shake off—to battle against — this sloth of temper, which made him the tool of others, and rendered him impotent for all good, was his duty as a man, and tenfold more his duty as a king; and to neglect that duty was wickedness, was ruin; and it ended, as all such neglect does, in bringing down upon him tenfold the trouble and disturbance of ease which he had striven to avoid. "Anything for an easy life," seems to have been Ahab's rule of conduct. But a king has no right to an easy life. It is hard work to be a king. Especially is it hard work in an Eastern country, where, on the person of the sovereign, are devolved many duties of decision, of judgment, and of action, which in Western countries he assigns to his advisers and ministers.

Jezebel was just the woman to manage such a man; and she soon found how to manage Ahab as she pleased, and to become in fact, through him, the regnant sovereign of Israel, while on him devolved the public responsibility of her acts. It was not by imperious temper, though she was imperious, nor by palpable domineering, that she managed this. No. She made herself necessary to him—necessary to his ease, his comfort, his pleasures. She worked for him; she planned for him; she decided for him. She saved him a world of trouble. She taught him to consider the strength of her will necessary to supply the weakness of his own—necessary to save him the labour of exertion and thought. Prompt in decision, ready in resource, quick in invention, ruthless in action,—she saw her way at once to the point at which she aimed, and would cut with a sharp stroke through knotty matters which the king shrunk from the labour of untying. She was thus often enabled to secure for her husband the object of his desires, which he himself hesitated to pursue, or despaired to obtain; and in accepting it from her hands, he cared not too nicely to inquire whether it were not stained with blood, or whether it heaped not upon his head coals of fire, which would one day consume him.

———

As the story of Samaria's origin is here recorded, and as mention is made of the sins by which it was polluted, it may not be out of place to add a brief note of its fate. The temple built by Jezebel, in honour of her national god Baal, probably stood on the summit of the hill. The worship of Baal was there set up in the very centre of the Holy Land. A grievous curse was thus entailed, not on the people merely, but upon the city. Hosea and Micah were specially commissioned to pronounce it; and they did so in language of terrible import: "Samaria shall become desolate; for she hath rebelled against her God." "I will make Samaria as an heap of the field, and as plantings of a vineyard; *and I will pour down the stones thereof into the valley,* and I will discover the foundations thereof." The fulfilment of this curse was long delayed. For a thousand years and more after the words were penned, the city continued to exist and to prosper. But the evil day came at last; and this fearful sentence was executed to the letter. The hill is now almost as bare as when Omri bought it of Shemer. A miserable village occupies a corner of the ancient site, and all the rest is desolate. On the summit, where Baal's temple was built, a group of lonely columns now stand in the midst of a corn field. Half way down the hill, a long range of naked shafts, without capital or pediment, extends from a shapeless heap of stones, probably the site of an old gateway, to the modern village. The hill sides are clothed with terraced vineyards, and the terrace walls are everywhere built up of the remains of the ancient city. Down at the southern base of the hill, also, are great heaps of hewn stones and fragments of columns, which, in the striking language of Micah, have been "poured down into the valley." The present state of Samaria, viewed in the light of past history, affords one of the most striking illustrations of the fulfilment of prophecy in all Palestine.

P.

———

BAAL

1 Kings 16:32

IT is in some respects to be regretted, that the information we possess regarding the system of idolatry which pervaded the region in which the chosen people were set down is very scanty. The intimations of the Bible are few and unconnected; and the more recent information supplied by the Greeks and Romans is generally superficial, and not always trustworthy; besides, it is always coloured, and sometimes distorted, by the ideas derived from their own idolatries.

From all that can be understood, the idolatry of South-Western Asia seems to resolve itself into the most gross and material form of Sabeism, or the worship of the heavenly bodies. This agrees with Scripture, which continually connects this idolatry, or rather identifies it, with the worship of the "host of heaven." The sun, the moon, some planets, and certain constellations, in their mutual relations, or in their relation to the earth, appear to have been the principal objects of adoration; and it is among these, mostly as personified under human figures and symbols, that we are to seek for the Baals, the Molechs, the Ashtaroths, and other idols named in the Scriptures.

The earth, with its phenomena and accidents, had also a part in the myths of this religious system. The different aspects and circumstances of different localities, invested with varying hues legends which in their bases were identical; while the impassioned nature of man, wrought upon by various influences, caused important differences, and even marked oppositions, to be presented, not only in the fables and symbols belonging to what were really the same idols, but even in the rites and ceremonies by which they were worshipped; and the excited imaginations of men, with the same essential objects before them, bore them away to the most opposite excesses Thus the worship which was in one place (as at Babylon) altogether voluptuous, in another exhibited the most ascetic discipline, and was full of deadly rigours and bloody rites.

We must not, however, go into all the breadth of this question, but confine our attention to the Phœnician Baal, which here mainly requires our notice. It seems that Baal or Bel is the generic term signifying *master, lord,* or *husband;* and, as such, is applied merely as a title of honour to different gods,—sometimes to the sun, sometimes to Jupiter, sometimes to another planet. Thus we have in Scripture Baalim (plural of Baal) for false gods collectively; and in one case the term Baal, in its substantive signification, is applied even to Jehovah himself.[1] When used by itself in Scripture as the name of an idol, it designates the chief god of the Tyrians and Zidonians. Sometimes it occurs in combination with other

[1] Hosea 2:16.

names, as Baalzebub, the *lord of flies*, which was worshipped at Ekron, among the Philistines;[1] but it is doubted whether this was the proper name, or one imposed in contempt by the Hebrews. If the former, it may be considered as a title of honour corresponding to the "fly-expelling Jove" of the Peloponnesus;[2] but if the latter, it is probably a Jewish nickname formed by an easy distortion of the sound of Baal-samen, the *lord of heaven*. The proneness of the Israelites to deal with obnoxious names in this manner, is much in favour of this latter conclusion. Under the name of Baal-Gad (lord of the troop), which occurs in Joshua xi. 17, as the name of a town which was probably the chief seat of the worship, the Syrians appear to have honoured the moon as presiding over sublunary bodies under the blind movements of chance, and consequently, as Fortune. Baal-zephon, from whom also another town was called,[3] was a name distinguishing the deity who had the north for his empire. The Moabites and the Ammonites adored Baal-peor, or Bel-phegor, by which name the generative or reproductive power of nature —still ultimately the sun—was worshipped with obscene rites and under indecent symbols. Sometimes we find the name of Baal united to that of a city in which he was worshipped, or simply as designating the chief idol of that city, as Baal-Beryth, the *lord of Beryth*,[4]—a city which is said to have been founded by the Phœnicians. There is also the name Baal-Thares, probably *lord of Tarsus*, found upon several medals of the Phœnicians.

But our immediate concern is with the Baal of the Phœnicians. This was undoubtedly the sun; and the name by which he was generally distinguished among the Phœnicians was Melkart, Melkrat, or Melchrat. This has been thought to mean "king of the city," *i. e.* of Tyre, or Zidon, though some make it denote "the strong king." To us, however, it seems to be a compound term, the meaning and sound of which may be drawn from the Hebrew words MELEK ERETZ, "king of the earth," which is an epithet sufficiently appropriate to the sun, as a type of the life-giving power in nature. With this Phœnician Melkart

[1] 2 Kings 1:2.   [2] Pausanias, v.; *Eliac.*, i. 14.
[3] Exodus 14:2.
[4] The classical Berytus, now Beirut. From Judges 8: 33, it appears that the worship of this idol had extended into the Sacred Land in the time of the Judges.

or Baal, the Greeks—according to their well known custom of identifying the gods of other nations with such of their own as they appeared most to resemble—identified their own Hercules, and called him the Hercules of Tyre. This was one of their worst identifications, as there appears but little analogy between the deified hero of that name and the supreme deity of the Phœnicians, unless, as we have oftener than once suspected, Hercules himself is but a type of the energies which the sun exercises, or was deemed to exercise upon the earth.

From such accounts as we possess, it appears that, from the earliest foundation of Tyre, Baal must have been the tutelary god of that city; and his worship had probably a still more ancient existence at Zidon. The worship gradually spread with the power of Tyre, until it not only prevailed throughout the Phœnician states, but was extended to its distant colonies. At Gades (Cadiz) the everlasting light was kept burning in his temple; and the Carthaginians, who inherited this worship from their Phœnician forefathers, continued for a long time to send to the parent city a tithe for the support of his temple.

Under the name of Melkart, or of the Tyrian Hercules, this idol was very famous throughout the West. The Egyptians claimed that he originally belonged to them—was one of the primeval gods of their country. This is likely enough, as Egypt seems to have been a great cradle of gods for all the near nations. The fact that this claim was asserted by the Egyptians is interesting, from its having awakened the special attention of Herodotus to this god, and induced him to make a journey to Tyre (about 456 B.C.) for the express purpose of seeking further information at the famous temple there dedicated to his service. What he there learned confirmed his previous information as to the remote antiquity of Melkart's worship. The priests affirmed the foundation of the temple to have been coëval with that of the city, which they said was founded 2,300 years before their time. In surveying the temple itself, his attention was attracted by various rich offerings which had been presented to it by votaries—particularly by one pillar all of gold, and another of emerald, which by night shone with amazing splendour.[1]

Some of the particulars furnished by this and other writers are of peculiar interest, presenting as they do such resemblances to the worship of the true God at Jerusalem, as may have induced the Israelites the less reluctantly to conform to the idolatry of their neighbours, when it was thus enforced upon them. No human sacrifices were offered to him, as there were to Molech; nor does the Scripture anywhere lay this charge to the worship of Baal. No swine were offered to him, although this was rather a common sacrifice to other idols. The fire was always kept burning upon his altar. His priests always officiated with naked feet; and kissing was among the acts of worship—a fact which the reader may find expressly mentioned in 1 Kings xix. 18: "All the knees which have not bowed unto Baal, and every mouth which hath not kissed him."

The figure, or rather figures, under which the Phœnicians themselves represented their Baal or Melkart, are now sufficiently ascertained from such of their coins as have been found in the lands they once occupied. They are rude, barbarous, and fantastic—reminding one of the idols of the New Zealanders. They are not, however, to be taken as specimens of Phœnician art. The artists of that time could probably have represented them better, had they been better to represent. But they are true likenesses of their gods; for it often happened that the images of

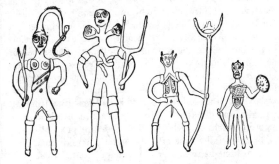

PHŒNICIAN AND CARTHAGINIAN FIGURES OF BAAL

idols preserved the very forms which belonged to them in ancient and barbarous times, although the worshippers had become comparatively civilised and skilled in arts, so that they could, had it been lawful, have fabricated much finer

[1] It has been suggested that this column may have been of pseudo-smaragdus, or bastard emerald. But these stones give no light at night. Larcher therefore inclines to think, with the authors of the *Universal History*, that if the historian was correctly informed, and his ingenuousness not imposed upon, the pillar may have been of stained glass lighted by lamps from within.

images, and much better representations of them. Use, and the veneration for antiquity, may have prevented the Phœnicians from perceiving, or rather from *feeling*, how outrageously absurd such figures were; but what had Israel become!—how had Israel fallen!—when such monstrosities as these were set up for Israel to worship, and for Israel to kiss!

The foregoing figures of Baal are from Phœnician and Carthaginian coins, and are all taken from Creuzer's *Symbolik*, where the authorities are given, and where other figures of the same sort may be found.

The worship of Baal would seem to have been universal among the ancient Canaanites. We find no less than thirteen geographical names in Palestine of which Baal forms a part. In each, there was doubtless a sanctuary of the god. We have *Kirjath-Baal* "city of Baal," Baal-gad, Baal-meon, Baal-zephon, etc. The highest mountain in the land was dedicated to this deity, and called *Baal-Hermon;* and amid the eternal snows on its summit, the writer discovered one of Baal's primeval high places and temples.

The Phœnicians studded the Mediterranean, and even the Atlantic, with their colonies; and wherever they went, they carried their national deity with them. Like the Hebrews, and indeed most Eastern nations, their personal names were largely compounded with that of their favourite deity; thus, for example, Hanni-*bal*, Hasdru-*bal*, Adher-*bal*, Mahar-*bal*, Mastana-*bal*, etc. Perhaps they may have introduced the worship of Baal into our own land, and left us as a relict of it those *Beltanes*, or *Bel*-fires, which at May eve or Midsummer light up so many of the hills. "In Ireland," says Macpherson, "*Beltein* is celebrated on the 21st of June, at the time of the solstice. There, as they make fires on the tops of the hills, every member of the family is made to pass through the fire, as they reckon this ceremony necessary to ensure good fortune through the succeeding year." It is also not unusual to drive the cattle through these fires, so as to keep them free from all contagion and disease. A singular custom prevails in some remote districts of Ireland. The fires are put out in all the houses on the first of May, and then rekindled by a live coal brought from a neighbouring Beltein.

P.

ELIJAH

1 Kings 17:1-3

God never yet wanted a man for any work which He had to be done. He to whom all hearts are open, and all desires known, and from whom no secrets are hid, never experiences the embarrassments common among the rulers of the earth in choosing the fittest agent for every task and every work. The world would be well governed if the great ones of the earth possessed the faculty of discovering, and the desire of employing, the best and fittest man in the land for every service. But this is what God does. The spirits of all the men of a whole people lie open as a book before Him; and the man wanted for His day and generation is at once singled out by Him, and called to his work. Such a man never fails to be found; for if the demand be extraordinary—such as the ordinary gifts and attainments of a nation are not likely to supply,—the man is appointed for his work from childhood, or even before his birth. He is born for it, trained to it; and, lo, at the appointed time—the time foreseen in the eternal counsels of Heaven—he is summoned to his task and he goes to it—he must go. Willingly or not, he must go. A force greater than all the modern enginery of the two worlds impels him; a weight greater than the crush of mountains lies upon him: he must go. What says the prophet, when craving peace, and weary of his task of confronting a stiff-necked generation, he purposed to abandon it? "Then I said, I will not make mention of Him, nor speak any more in His name. But His word was in mine heart as a burning fire shut up in my bones, and I was weary with forbearing, and I could not stay." (Jer. xx. 9.) Mark the tremendous force of these phrases, "a burning fire shut up in my bones," "weary with forbearing," "*could not* stay," as indicating the strong compulsions under which the prophets acted, whether they were prophets of utterances, or prophets of deeds.

So now, peculiar and hopeless as the exigency in Israel seemed, the Lord found a man fit for it —a man fitted beyond all others, by the force of his character, his grasp of faith, and his fearless spirit, to "stem the torrent of a *faithless* age." This man was Elijah the Tishbite; so called from Tishbe, a place in Gilead beyond the Jordan. He was one of the most extraordinary characters mentioned in the Bible. Great evils require great remedies; extraordinary diseases, extraordinary physicians; gigantic corruptions, gigantic reformers. And such was Elijah, who, in his gifts and qualities, assumes a figure scarcely human, from its gigantic proportions, and towers aloft like one of the sons of Anak among common men. He was such stuff as the heathen made their gods of; and had he appeared in a heathen country, he would have come down to us as scarcely less than a god, side by side, perchance, with Hercules, instead of being only something more than a prophet. There are two sorts of prophets: prophets of deeds, prophets of words. Of the latter the greatest is doubtless Isaiah; of the former, there has not been among men born of women any greater than Elijah. Moses might be named; but he stood alone. He was "mighty *both* in words and in deeds."

Elijah is introduced with remarkable and significant abruptness, as appearing before Ahab and declaring, "As the Lord God of Israel liveth, before whom I stand, there shall not be dew nor rain upon the earth these years, but according to my word." He did not say *why* this judgment came. It was sufficient to declare whence it came, for too well could Ahab's conscience supply the cause. The form of the message was also most extraordinary and unexampled. The lack of rain and dew implied the destruction or prevention of all vegetable growth, and therefore famine in the land; and this stay of the life-bestowing waters of heaven, was not to be withdrawn but when the prophet should give the word. The visitation came at his word, and only at his word would it be removed. Note also, that the denunciation has a very peculiar character—referring the judgment more to the prophet himself than is in such cases customary. Instead of the usual formula, "Thus saith the Lord," he swears by the Lord God of Israel, that no rain shall come but at his own word. In a matter like this, so godly a man as Elijah could not have departed so much from all precedent—could not have given so autocratic a character to his denunciation, had he not been especially ordered to do so. With what object? The object must be estimated from the result. It tended to fix the attention of the court and nation upon the person and character of the prophet; and such an example of zeal for the Lord, and daring boldness for His cause, could not but be most beneficial in its action upon an age so corrupt, unprincipled, and nerveless—an age so void as this seemed of champions for the truth, so destitute of that martyr-spirit which is the salt of life to a nation.

It was not likely that Elijah would stay long within reach of the royal clutches after he had delivered such a message. Here was a man who said that there should be no rain till *he* called for it. What so obvious, then, as to clap him into a dungeon, and feed him with the bread and water of affliction, till it were seen whether the timely rains came or not? If they did, he could be punished as a false prophet; if they did not, he might, being in their hands, be compelled to give the word which should bring rain to the thirsty earth. In any case, his movements and proceedings became matters of vast importance—of such importance, as no other form of the message could possibly have imparted to them. This personal importance, in connection with the result, was not of his own seeking. It gave him nought to glory in, nothing for pride to rest upon. It was a duty imposed upon him—a duty which exposed him to persecution and arrest—which made him a fugitive and a vagabond until the appointed day came round, the great day of vindication.

Meanwhile, it was necessary that he should remain in concealment; and therefore he was directed to withdraw from the haunts of men, and fix his abode away upon the solitary banks of the brook Cherith. Where was this brook? We do not know. It is not even known whether it was on the east or west of the Jordan. One would think it most probably on the east, as it would seem obvious to interpose the river between himself and the search of Ahab, especially as the prophet was a native of Gilead. However, there were towards the Jordan many secluded places even in the west; and Dr. Robinson suggests, that what is now called the Wady Kelt, formed by the union of many streams in the mountains bordering the plain of Jericho on the west, and issuing from a deep gorge in which it passes by that village and crosses the plain to the Jordan, may be the Cherith. This learned traveller rests this conjecture upon the analogy of name. The reader may be at some loss to see the analogy between Cherith and Kelt. But *r* and *l* are commutable letters, frequently exchanged for each other; and if the *l* in Kelt be exchanged for *r*, it becomes Kert, or with the softer sounds of the initial and final letters, Cherth. This seems to us hardly sufficient to make out the identity, as the situation of this brook seems less suitable for the purpose in view than many others that could be indicated.

Much attention has been given of late to the significancy of Scripture names, and the name of *Elijah* in connection with that of *Elisha* may well arrest our notice. *El* signifies God, and it is compounded with several other names : but a peculiar interest attaches to the two names now before us. The first name is written *Elijahu*, whenever it occurs in the first book of Kings, but in the second book it is found *Elijah*, as we use it. Elijahu is interpreted by some to mean *a mighty God is Jehovah*, understanding the syllable *El* in its original meaning of *a strong one*. Others attaching the same meaning to *El*, and adopting what may be called the original meaning of *Jah*, render the name *mighty is he who shall be*, that is, *almighty is the eternal*. A simpler explanation is *my God is Jehovah*, or *Jehovah is my God*. Thus Elijah carried, in his very name, a protest against the worship of Baal, to the overthrow of which his life was devoted ; and a confession of the one true God of Israel, whose glory he ever proclaimed. Perhaps his name suggested the shout at Carmel, *Jehovah, He is the God—Jehovah, He is the God*. It is supposed that *Elijah* might not be the prophet's birth-name, but a descriptive appellation given to him from the character of his mission and ministry ; as the name of Peter, *a rock*, was given by our Lord to His disciple Simon.

Elisha is a name signifying *God (is) salvation*, an idea harmonious with that of the former name, but presenting the Divine character under a distinct aspect. It betokens mercy, grace, deliverance,—divine blessings, beautifully illustrated in the life of Elijah's disciple and successor. The history of this wonderful messenger of the Lord to Israel contains a succession of facts unfolding the above ideas. He healed the unwholesome waters by casting in salt, and restored fruitfulness to a barren land (2 Kings ii. 19-22). He ordered a parched valley to be cut up into ditches, and caused them to be filled with water (Ibid., iii. 16, 17). He relieved the distress of a widow harassed by her husband's creditors through miraculously supplying her with an abundance of oil, which paid her debts (iv. 1-7) ; and raised to life the Shunnamite's child, who had died from sun-stroke in the harvest field (iv. 32-37). He fed the sons of the prophets with wild gourds ; and when poisonous plants were found in the cauldron, he cast in meal and rendered them harmless (iv. 38-42). He multiplied twenty loaves of barley, and ears in the husks, so as to satisfy a hundred men (42-44). He healed Naaman of his leprosy (v. 1-14). He comforted the poor man who had dropped his axe into the river by making the iron swim (vi. 1-7). He saved the servants of the King of Syria from being slain (14-23). He proclaimed plenty in the midst of famine (vii. 1-9). He saved from want the woman whose son he restored to life (viii. 1-6) ; and finally, after death, contact with his bones resuscitated a man who was flung into his grave (xiii. 20, 21). It is a wonderful life from beginning to end, suggesting many points of typical resemblance to Him, whose name is *Immanuel, " God with us "*—whose name is Jesus, for *He shall save His people from their sins*.

See on the whole subject Wilkinson's *Personal Names in the Bible*—particularly chap. v. and vi.

S.

THE RAVENS

1 Kings 17:4-6

ELIJAH, in his retreat by the brook Cherith, would have water enough so long as the lesser streams were not dried up. But how was he to be fed, seeing that the necessities of his seclusion would prevent him from seeking his subsistence? The Lord, who sent him thither, had also promised him food : " Behold, I have commanded *the ravens* to feed thee there." And accordingly it is stated that, during his stay by the brook Cherith, "the ravens brought him bread and

ELIJAH IS FED BY RAVENS

flesh in the morning, and bread and flesh in the evening." This is a very startling statement, particularly when the nature and habits of the bird are considered ; and it well deserves our attentive consideration.

The first objection is, that the raven was a legally unclean bird. But its uncleanness only consisted in its being itself unfit to be eaten; and it imparted no uncleanness to that which it carried, any more than Abigail's asses, although unclean animals in the same sense, imparted defilement to the bread and roast mutton which, with other comestibles, they carried as that bountiful lady's present to David.

At the outset it should be observed, that the statement in the text does not require us to suppose that the ravens with purpose and forethought brought victuals designedly for Elijah, and laid them before him, or presented them to him. This was not required for the object in view, and therefore was probably not done; for God does not work needless miracles. Yet it is hard to judge when or in what degree miracles are needless; and in this case the degree of miracle which might not have been necessary, so far as the mere subsistence of Elijah was concerned, may have been necessary to evince the miraculous nature of his subsistence, and to show that he was supported, not by a concatenation of fortunate accidents, but out of the special care and bounty of Him who will sooner root up the mountains, and rain bread from heaven, than suffer those who trust in Him to lack any good thing. Apart from this consideration, and supposing that the subsistence of Elijah was the only object sought, and that by the simplest and safest means, it may suffice to suppose that the place to which he had been directed to retreat, was the chosen resort of ravens, which had their nests among the trees that grew on the banks of the stream. That the ravens were *commanded* to feed him, implies no more than that constraint was laid upon them to become the unconscious instruments of the divine will; as in Amos ix. 3. "Though they be hid in the bottom of the sea, yet thence will I command the serpent, and he shall bite them." These brought home, morning and evening, to their nests, as much animal and vegetable food as sufficed not only for their own wants, but for those of Elijah, who secured what he required, and dressed it with the dry wood which abounds in such situations. The only objection to this is, that, except during the period of incubation, when the male brings food to the female, and subsequently, when both bring home food to the young until they are able to provide for themselves, ravens do not bring home food at all, but devour it on the spot where they find it. Well, we are content with this. Seeing that, with birds, the period of helplessness in the nest is proportioned to the duration of life—the longest lived having the longest infancy,—and seeing that the raven is one of the birds that live the longest, it is not likely that the periods of incubation and of rearing the young occupy together less than six months, which, and not a year, as some imagine, we take to be the period that the prophet spent by the brook Cherith.

But the natural food of the raven was that which, least of all, an Israelite obedient to the law could touch. He could not eat that which died of itself; yet this is generally the case with the carrion, which forms the proper diet of the raven. There is great weight in this objection Still, the food of the raven is not exclusively carrion. Among birds, there is none more omnivorous in its appetite. There is scarcely anything that comes amiss to it; and although its ordinary food be carrion, it does not scruple, especially in times of comparative scarcity, to attack ducks, chickens, and small quadrupeds, which its strong and powerful beak enables it to despatch with a few strokes. It even assaults young lambs and sickly sheep; but it does not, of course, carry them away. It does not even kill them, but pecks out their eyes, and leaves them to a miserable lingering death—a fact alluded to in Prov. xxx. 17. In addition to these, eggs, grains, grubs, reptiles, and shelled molluscs, are among the articles of its bill of fare.

This, at the first view, seems to remove much of the difficulty, and appears to offer an ample range among which Elijah might obtain food proper for him as an Israelite. But we are to remember that, although the raven may slay animals of some size, it *cannot* carry them entire to its nest—though it may do so with small animals and birds, such as chickens, rats, mice, and the like; yet such larger animals than these as it may be able to slay, it is obliged to rend, and carry portions to its nest, as neither its bill nor its claws are suited to the *carriage* of any heavy or bulky substance. Now, this presents greater difficulties than any which have been hitherto suggested. An Israelite was not only unable to eat that which died of itself, but that from which the blood was not perfectly discharged by a mode of killing suited to that purpose. Hence he could not eat that which was "torn of beasts," unless, *before* the animal so torn was dead, he could slay it in the proper manner. It is therefore difficult to see how the ravens could have brought any meat fit for Elijah to eat, if what they did provide was in accordance with their own instincts and habits. The meat would be a portion of some animal—a piece of flesh. But Elijah would have several questions to decide before he could eat it. Was it the flesh of an unclean animal, that is, of an animal unfit for food to an Israelite? Was it from an animal that had died of itself? Was it from one that the bird itself, or some other ravenous creature had destroyed? It was almost certain to come under one of these three disqualifications, and therefore it could not be eaten by the prophet. It was hardly possible for him to suppose that the meat brought by a raven was the flesh of a lawful animal, killed in a proper manner. Then, again, if small animals were brought entire, it could scarcely ever happen that they were of kinds fit for his food; and even if they were, they would in almost every case be dead, and therefore unlawful, as "torn of beasts," without the opportunity of killing them by the knife being furnished.

It is therefore impossible to suppose that the prophet was supplied from the ordinary resources and operations of the ravens. If we admit that ravens were the agents through which subsistence was given to him, we must hold their agency to have been miraculous in all its circumstances; and that suitable and adequate food was daily presented by miracle twice to the notice of the ravens, which they were impelled to bear away to Elijah's hiding-place, and to drop there. If so, where did they get it so regularly? Some say they stole it from Ahab's kitchen; others, that it was from the provision made by the good Obadiah for the persecuted prophets whom he hid by fifties in caves. Or again, Elijah, as a prophet, may have been enabled to discern what of all the matters brought to their common retreat by the ravens was suited to be his food. Or, further, it may be supposed, that under the circumstances, it was made lawful for him to eat whatever food he could obtain, or the ravens brought within his reach,—being instructed, like Peter in a later age, that what the Lord had cleansed had ceased to be "common or unclean."

We have made this statement on the hypothesis most generally received, that ravens are really intended. On this point there are warrantable differences of opinion, seeing that the word translated "ravens" may have other meanings. We must try to make this a little plainer. We beg even such of our readers as do not know Hebrew, to *look* closely at the words noted below,[1] and take notice of any differences they may find between them. They will see that there is no difference but in the little points above and below the words. These points express the vowel sounds, the letters themselves being only the

consonants. Originally, all Hebrew was written, as it still is very frequently, without these vowel marks, as is the case also in Arabic, and other Oriental languages. Men, when the Hebrew was a living tongue, supplied the vowels orally, in reading that which was written without them. Usage made this easy to those to whom Hebrew was a native tongue. The differences between words of like consonants was, of course, brought out by the interposed vowels, just as to the common consonants GRN the sense of *grain, green, groan,* or *grin,* is fixed by the vowels added. After the Hebrew text had for many ages remained without the vowel marks, or indeed without such marks being known, they were at length, in the seventh century after Christ, invented, and inserted throughout by the Jewish doctors, to fix the pronunciation, and with it the sense,—thus insuring uniformity of interpretation, as it was feared that diversities might otherwise arise, and the true transmitted signification might be in many cases lost, through the dispersions of the people and the neglect of the language. They *fixed* the vowels, which determined, as it were, whether in particular places the consonants GRN should mean *grain* or *green, groan* or *grin,*—bestowing thus a permanent written form on much which had hitherto rested in the memories of men, and had been distinguished only by oral usage. This was a great and noble work, and was for the most part executed with great integrity and sound judgment. But Christian scholars do not conceive that they are in every case bound to the decisions of the Masorites (as they are called); while some (fewer now than formerly) reject their authority altogether, and feel at liberty in every case to take the sense which agrees best with the context. This agreement, both parties allow, the present vowel points do not always afford; and the text before us is one of those on which that question is raised. Look at the Hebrew words again. The consonants of all are the same as of the word which means "raven," and may be made plural by the usual masculine termination *im.* But the vowels make these differences between them:— The first word (left to right) is *ārob,* a gad-fly; the others are *ărāb,* Arabian (Gentile—*Arabi,* an Arabian,—plural *Arbim,* Arabians); *ēreb,* the woof; *ĕrĕb,* evening; *orĕb,* raven. Now, the Masorites assigned the sense of "raven" to the word in this case, by affixing the points which it bears, in preference to any other sense. But this, perhaps, is the last of all the senses which would occur to any one reading the Bible without the points, and without a previous knowledge of this interpretation; while, recollecting that these vowel points were added in an age when the Hebrew mind had gone astray after prodigies, and after it had given birth to the monstrous creations of the Talmud, we might expect that in such a case as this the most marvellous interpretation would be adopted in preference to any of the others.

Going again over the list of alternatives, that of "Arabs," instead of "ravens," is probably the one that persons free from any previous bias would spontaneously select as the most probable. For ourselves, although we should not hesitate at the ravens, if quite sure that those birds are really intended, yet when the alternative is thus open, we rather incline to the Arabs,—influenced, perhaps, by such a knowledge of the habits and character of that people, as enables us to perceive their entire fitness to be the agents of this providential dispensation in favour of Elijah. To us nothing seems more likely than that encampments of Arabs—who still intrude their tents, at certain times of the year, upon the borders, or into the unappropriated pastures of settled countries,—would at this season of drought have been forced within reach of the brook Cherith; and, knowing the increasing scarcity of water, would have remained there as long as its stream afforded any to them, that is, as long as Elijah himself remained, which was until the stream was dried up. They were also, from their condition and habits of life, the very persons to whom the secret of his retreat might be most safely entrusted,—far more so than it would have been to any towns-people, subjects of Ahab, whom some conceive to have been the parties in question.[1] They were the least likely to know his person, or that he was sought after by the king; or, if they did know this, they were less than any other persons open to any inducements to betray him which the king could offer, or any fears he could awaken. Besides, when he had *once* eaten of their bread and meat, the great law of Arabian honour made him secure of con-

tinued support, and safe from betrayal. Nothing they could afterwards learn concerning him—no temptation that might afterwards be presented—could have any force against the solemn obligation which was thus incurred, and the breach of which would cover the tribe with scorn and shame for many generations. With these views, it seems to us that "I have commanded the *Arabs* to feed thee there," is, under all the circumstances, a more probable and natural interpretation than "I have commanded the *ravens* to feed thee there."

ZAREPHATH

1 Kings 17:7-16

FAITH is the great word to be written in the forefront of Elijah's history. He "was a man of like passions as we are,"—tempted as we are, open as we are to joy and pain; yet of him, of all men that have lived since "the father of the faithful," it was most eminently true that "he staggered not at the promises" or commands "of God through unbelief."

The chapter before us is full of faith—nothing but faith.

The waters of the brook Cherith began to fail. Now, in such a case, it is to be feared that they who read and we who write these words, should not have been perfectly at ease. The Arabs will go away when this water is done; then what shall we do for food? And even more than that, what shall we do for water? We should tremble to see the stream decreasing from day to day. What a sinking of the heart, when we wake one morning and note that the water-mark is lower than it was yesterday; and so, day by day, to see the stream of our life getting lower and lower, till at length there is but a narrow thread of water through the midst of the channel; and at last we are obliged to resort to the lessening pools, or to scoop hollows with our hands to collect the dribbling waters! It is such slow processes that try faith most of all. There are many having a faith strong enough for any sudden, great, and heroic deed, for one who can maintain his confidence unshaken in the midst of such slow trials as this.

---

[1] Some conceive there was a place in the neighbourhood called Oreb, and that the Orebim (according to the present vowels), who ministered to the wants of Elijah, were the inhabitants thereof.

This trial the faith of Elijah stood. Yet it may be, that now and then, in his solitary musings upon the ways of God, the thought may have occurred to him, that this one stream might have been spared for his sake. But there was faith even in such a doubt. Such an exemption of this stream, would, however, have brought crowds of people thither for water, and thus his retreat would have been discovered. In a time when water was everywhere sought for, the fact that it was to be found in the brook Cherith could not long have remained hidden from the people. Besides, God does not always exempt those whom He loves from their share in such visitations as these. "It is," says Bishop Hall, "no unusual thing with God, to suffer His own dear children to be inwrapped in the common calamities of offenders. He makes difference in the use and issue of their stripes, not in the infliction. The corn is cut down with the weeds, but to a better purpose."

We cannot doubt that Elijah awaited the gradual failure of his means with untroubled thoughts, believing that the Lord whom he served would in due time appear to make provision for his wants; and He did so—but not until the brook was actually "dried up." We may say that the Lord might have relieved his anxiety sooner. But he had probably no anxiety in the matter; and it very often happens that God does not appear for help until the last moment of our exigency, when to delay any longer were to let us perish. Not that He takes pleasure in our trials; but He cares above all things for our spiritual welfare, and therefore subjects us to such wholesome discipline as may help to build us up in the faith, and bring our souls nearer to Him. It is when help comes but at the last pinch, that we value it the more, and are proportionably more thankful to our helper.

The relief came in the very extraordinary shape of an order to proceed across the country to Zarephath, in the territory of Zidon, where a widow woman had been commanded to feed him. Strange it must have seemed, that he should be directed to go into that very region which had been, by its gods and by its Jezebel, the occasion of all Israel's troubles, and which, as appears by the sequel, had a common share in the calamity. Doubt might have asked, Why send him to such a country—subject to the same visitation; and why, out of all who dwelt there, to a poor widow,

who could have little means of providing for his subsistence? And if to a widow, why not rather to one of the thousands of widows in Israel? But the noble-hearted prophet knew that his course was not to reason and speculate, but to hear and obey. So he forthwith girded his hairy mantle closer to his body, and taking his staff in hand, set forth at a strong pace upon his journey.

When he approached Zarephath, he encountered a woman gathering sticks. He accosted her. He had drunk no water since he left the brook; and, devoured with keen thirst as he was, his first thought was naturally of water. "Fetch me, I pray thee, a little water," he said, "that I may drink." This was a great thing to ask in such a time of drought; but although the poor woman perceived from his appearance and accent that he was a Hebrew, and even gathered from his hairy mantle and leathern girdle that he was a prophet of the God of Israel, she was hastening to satisfy his want, when he called after her with the additional request, "Bring me a morsel of bread in thine hand." On this she spoke; for this thing was more than she could do: "As Jehovah thy God liveth, I have not a cake, but a handful of meal in a barrel, and a little oil in a cruse; and behold I am gathering two sticks; that I may go and dress it for me and my son, that we may eat it and die." Here note that, as among the Germans at this day, "two" is equivalent in Hebrew to "a few."

By this Elijah knew that he beheld the woman to whom he was sent. But how came *she* to know the Lord? That she was a worshipper of Him, as some have thought, is not likely, and betrays some ignorance of the extent to which the heathen were disposed to recognize the gods of other nations as gods, and powerful gods, but not as their gods. Besides, she says, "*thy* God," —an addition which she would not be likely to have made, had the Lord been her God also. The prophetic garb of Elijah pointed him out as not one of the votaries of Baal, but a worshipper of Jehovah, and, as such, it was a civility to mention his God; besides, she really had such notions of the Lord's power as inclined her to speak well of His name; and, moreover, it had probably reached this quarter, that the existing drought was owing to the wrath of the God of Israel against His people, which could not but raise a fear of offending Him, and a desire to mention His name with honour.

We see that the kindness of this poor woman shrunk from *this* test. Human kindness can scarcely rise to the pitch of giving the *last* morsel that is left, to serve as a meal for oneself and one's child, to another. The prophet hastened to reassure her: "Fear not; go and do as thou hast said: but make me thereof a little cake *first*, and bring it unto me, and *after* make for thee and for thy son: for thus saith the Lord God of Israel, the barrel of meal shall not waste, neither shall the cruse of oil fail, until the day that the Lord sendeth rain upon the earth." Now here was a demand upon the faith of this woman, from a foreign man and a foreign God, as large as any exacted from the great prophet himself. See how it stands. First, she was to make up her provisions for Elijah, trusting that, as he had said, more would then come miraculously to supply her own wants. What a trial! What would the "bird in the hand worth two in the bush" principle say to this? Who could have it in his heart to blame her, had she declined to run what was, under the circumstances, so hard a risk? Who would condemn her if she had discredited this stranger? How could she know but that, after he had eaten up her precious bread, he might laugh in her face? Besides, was not his very anxiety to be served first of all very suspicious? Looked it not as if he were determined, at all hazards, to secure a meal for himself; and could we call it unreasonable had she asked for the proof first—which could be given as well before as after—that it should be as he had said? But nothing of this occurred. She went and did as Elijah had told her, and found the result as he had promised. That barrel from which she had taken the prophet's dole never wanted meal, and the flask was never void of oil, during all the three years more that passed before the rains again watered the gasping earth. This was faith of the true sort—heroic sort—the faith that asks no questions. "Verily, I say unto you, I have not found so great faith, no, not in Israel."

THE DEAD CHILD

1 Kings 17:17-24

How Elijah employed himself all the time that he was at Zarephath we know not. If he had been in Israel, we might guess that he taught and governed the schools of the prophets. But he had nothing of this kind to occupy him at Zarephath; and it is clear that he kept himself as private as possible, as he must have been aware that Ahab sought him diligently; and if the king had known where he was, his influence at the court of Tyre was amply sufficient to cause the prophet to be given up. To the looker-on he might seem to be leading an idle life. But he whom the world calls idle is often "busied most" when he seems least occupied. To a holy man, meditation and prayer are an occupation, and make time pass swiftly. Then such a man as Elijah must have felt a generous pleasure in leading the comparatively untutored but open mind of this poor widow to true conceptions of the God of Israel, and the great designs of His grace and providence. Her son, also, could hardly escape his earnest solicitude; and we cannot doubt that he laboured much to educate his mind in all true knowledge.

He became interested in this lonely pair, whose lives he had been the means of preserving. He loved them. It was a grief of heart, a dreadful shock to him, to learn one day that the boy was dead—had died suddenly; and to discern, through the form which the grief of the mother took, that by some process of reasoning—or rather, perhaps, of unreasoning feeling, which it is difficult to follow with certainty—she ascribed this calamity to his presence. Consider that this boy was her only child, and that she was a widow, to estimate the extent of her loss and the agony of her spirit. To lose one of many in death, is a most awful and trying thing; how hard, then, to lose the one who stands alone, and besides whom there is no other to us! When we behold that a child so dear,

—"Like a flower crusht with a blast, is dead,
And ere full time hangs down his smiling head,"

how many sweet interests in life, how many hopes for the time to come, go down to the dust with him! The purest and most heart-felt enjoyment which life offers to a mother in the society of her little child, is cut off for ever. The hope, the mother's hope, of great and good things to come from this her son is lost for her. "The coal that was left," and which she had reckoned that time would raise to a cheerful flame to warm her home, and to preserve and illustrate the name and memory of his dead

father, is gone out—is quenched in darkness.
The arms which so often clung caressingly
around her, and whose future strength promised
to be a staff to her old age, are stiff in death.
The eyes which glistened so lovingly when she
came near, now know her not. The little tongue,
whose guileless prattle had made the long days
of her bereavement short, is now silent as that
of the "mute dove." Alas! alas! that it should
ever be a mother's lot to close in death the eyes
of one whose pious duty, if spared, should be in
future years to press down her own eyelids.
This is one of the great mysteries of life, to be
solved only thoroughly, only fully to our satisfaction, in that day when, passing ourselves the
gates of light, we behold all our lost ones gather
around our feet.

We marvel not that the poor widow of Zarephath, thus suddenly smitten, spoke in the bitterness of her spirit to Elijah: "What have I to do
with thee, O thou man of God? art thou come
to call my sin to remembrance, and to slay my
son?" This is manifestly founded on the notion,
prevalent in those days, that sickness and untimely death were special judgments from
Heaven; and it would appear that, the consciousness of sin, having been awakened in the
breast of this woman by the views of the divine
character which Elijah set before her, and by the
observation of the man of God's holy life and
conversation, she was led to suppose that the
God of Israel had probably, at the instance of
His prophet, taken this means of impressing her
with a sense of her unworthiness.

The imputation, however interpreted, upon one
who had really been the means of so long preserving her son's life, as well as her own, was
unjust to him, and perhaps had, under other
circumstances, kindled up his naturally warm
temper. As it was, her deep affliction left room
for no feeling but commiseration, which seems to
have been strong enough to make him feel disposed, for the moment, to question the Lord's
justice and mercy in bringing this deep affliction
upon one who had so befriended His servant.
These are among the occasions on which the best
and holiest of men often lose the soundness of
their judgment; and Elijah, although a wonderful man, was still a man of like passions as we
are. He said nothing before the woman. He
had not the heart to reprove her, in her grief,
for the harsh suspicion that he had been instru-

mental in bringing this misery upon her. The
bereaved, and not yet wholly chastened heart,
seeks some object on which to wreak its sense
of wrong. God Himself is the real object of this
feeling; but, dreading to smite the throne of
Heaven, the distressed soul seeks, and is glad to
find, some intermediate object of its indignation.
Elijah understood this, and made no attempt to
cast back the words which this poor childless
widow flung forth in the trouble of her spirit.
He forbore to tell her, that such words as these
showed her need of the affliction that had come
upon her. He simply asked her to give him
the child; and on receiving the corpse from her
bosom, where it lay, he bore it away to his own
little garret, and laid it down upon his bed.
There he gave free vent to his strong emotions.
Remember that the most marked characteristic
of Elijah was the strength of his will, the indomitable character of his faith. Our Lord says,
"The kingdom of heaven suffereth violence, and
the VIOLENT TAKE IT BY FORCE." Now, Elijah
was one of those who take the kingdom of
heaven by force—who storm its crystal walls in
unconquerable faith, and batter them with prayers
that will not be denied. To use fitly the com-
pulsive prayers of Elijah, it is needful to have
Elijah's faith, just as only one who wrestles till
break of day, as Jacob did, could dare to say, "I
WILL NOT let Thee go, except Thou bless me."
Behold this great man in his chamber, alone with
the corpse of that fair child. See how vehemently he strides up and down, gradually working himself up to the height of the great demand
which gleams before his thought. Hear him.
He ventures to expostulate; humbly indeed, but
with some soreness of feeling, natural enough—
only too natural—to one who began to think
that afflictions attended him wherever he went.
Trouble he could bear, so that it came upon
himself alone; but it was hard to feel that his
presence brought nothing but misery to those
who befriended him most. "O Lord, my God,"
he cried, "hast Thou also brought evil upon the
widow with whom I sojourn, by slaying her
son?" This thought was hard to bear. Again
he lashes himself up to his great purpose, which
had not crossed the mind of man since the
beginning of the world, only because no man
before had had the same degree of faith—the
faith to deem it possible that the dead might be
restored to life at man's urgent prayer. It is

done. His purpose is taken. The child may live. Nothing is too hard for the Lord. It is as easy for Him to give back life as to take it: and He will do this if asked with adequate faith. Elijah knew that men too often expect to move the mountains by such faith as suffices not to shake the mole-hills; and that because, from the insufficiency of the means, the hoped-for results do not follow, the power of faith is disparaged. But he felt the true mountain-moving faith heaving strong within him, and he gave it unrestrained vent. He threw himself upon the corpse, as if, in the vehement energy of his will, to force his own life into it; and he cried, with

ELIJAH RAISING THE WIDOW'S SON

mighty and resistless urgency, to God, to send back to this cold frame the breath He had taken.

Faith conquered. It was *adequate*, and therefore irresistible. The fleeing soul was arrested in mid-career, and sent back to its earthly house. The child revived; and we may conceive the deep emotion with which the forlorn widow received—far beyond all her hopes or thoughts —her living son from the hands of the prophet. The effect was salutary. It removed all lingering doubt in her heathen trained mind of the mission of the prophet, and of the truth of the great things he had so often told her. "Now *by this* I KNOW that thou art a man of God, and that the word of the Lord in thy mouth is truth."

In Dean Stanley's remarks on this romantic incident in the life of Elijah, is the following beautiful and suggestive

passage : "The Phœnician mother knew not what great destinies lay in the hand of that gaunt figure at the city gate, worn with travel, and famine, and drought: she obeyed only the natural instinct of humanity; she listened to his cry, as that of one who suffered as she was suffering; she saw in him only at most the prophet of a hostile tribe. But she saved in him the deliverer of herself and her son. There was a rebound of unexpected benefits, such as sometimes, even in the prose of common life, equals the poetic justice of an ideal world. It may be that this incident is the basis of the sacred blessing of the Prophet of prophets on those who, even by 'a cup of cold water,' 'receiving a prophet in the name of a prophet, shall receive a prophet's reward.' But he makes a more direct comment on the whole story, which brings out a loftier and more striking peculiarity : 'There were many widows in Israel in the days of Elijah, but to none of them was Elijah sent, save to Zarephath, a city of Zidon.' He whose life was to be employed in protesting against the false worship of Tyre and Zidon, was now to have his life preserved by one who was herself a slave of that false worship. It seems like a foretaste of Gospel times that this one gleam of gentler light should be shed over the beginning of his fierce and stormy course; that we should see the prophet of Israel and the woman of Zidon dwelling peaceably under the same roof, and sharing together the last remains of her scanty sustenance; she giving food and shelter to the enemy of her country's gods, and he creating and supporting the scanty faith of the good heathen. It was a prelude to the scene which, many generations later, took place near that very spot, when a greater than Elijah overstepped for once the limits of the Holy Land, and passed into the coasts of Tyre and Zidon, and met the Syro-Phœnician woman of the same accursed race, and blessed her faith, and told her that it should be even as she would. It is a likeness of the way in which distress and danger make strange bed-fellows—bring together those who are most unlike. The horrors of famine, the shadow of the death-bed, are the divine conciliators of the deadliest feuds."[1]

P.

THE REAPPEARANCE

1 Kings 18:1-20

ELIJAH had long concealed himself from the search of Ahab—not because he feared, but because the hour was not yet come. When the hour had come, and he was ordered not only to care no more for concealment, but to go and present himself before the king, he conferred not with flesh and blood, but girding up his loins, set forth upon the journey. Sad were the sights

[1] *Lectures on the Jewish Church*, ii. 298.

that met his eye. The land lay desolate before him. All was dry, and parched, and barren, and the face of the earth seemed to have been burnt up by the wrath of God. No trace of the products or the labours of the field was to be seen; cultivation had ceased; and the eye sought in vain the groups of those who were wont to till the ground, and gather in the harvest and the vintage. All seemed solitary. Men had no business to bring them abroad, and they remained at home musing in their cottages, or crouching about the market-places, which trade had by this time almost forsaken. Even the birds had abandoned the land which afforded no nourishment—except only the screaming fowl that fed on dead creatures, and they found no lack. Even the cattle had disappeared. The shepherd tending his sheep and goats was to be seen no longer; and the herds of neat cattle, which once enlivened the scene, had altogether disappeared, for there was no more pasture.

The calamity had reached such a pitch that the king himself had determined to explore the land in one direction, in search of green herbage for the royal cattle, while Obadiah, the governor of the palace, was, at the head of another party, to search in an opposite direction. This was to be sought at the brooks; for it was possible that in some a little moisture might still remain, and there some herbage was likely to be found,—likely, but not certainly, for such places form, in times of drought, the resort of wild herbivorous creatures, which seldom leave the places while any green thing remains. If, therefore, in the course of their researches, the king and his trusted servant did come to some slight traces of water—which is scarcely probable—the expectations raised by it must often have been disappointed.

This journey of the king in person in search of herbage, is a somewhat remarkable example of the simple manners of those ancient times. It is, however, the same among the emirs of Arabia, the chiefs of central Asia, and the kings of southern Africa, at the present time. None of these high personages (and some of them have great power) think it in any way below their dignity to lead an expedition in search of grass or water. The matter is indeed of so much importance, that it is regarded as a sort of official duty in them to conduct the search; and success in it contributes very materially to their popularity among their people, who are apt to ascribe the happy result in a great measure, if not wholly, to the "fortune" of their chief.

Obadiah, who led the other party, although an officer of high rank and trust in the court of Ahab, was known to be a sincere worshipper of Jehovah—one of the few whom neither fear nor favour had induced to bow the knee to Baal. Nay, further, it was now publicly known that, during the first heat of the persecution against the Lord's servants, he had secured the safety of no less than a hundred of his prophets,[1] by concealing them in caves, and there providing for their support at his own cost, until the storm had blown over. It is creditable to Ahab that he had for his most trusted servant such a man as this; and he must have been so much attached to him that even Jezebel had not ventured to remove him from near his person. It was the policy of that evil-minded but sagacious woman, not to rouse her husband to any exertion of strength by running counter to his known wishes and predilections; and she no doubt found her advantage in another way, from the concessions which this plan of action occasionally extorted from him.

Such a man as Obadiah could not but be acquainted with the person of Elijah. Yet so incredible did it seem, that he who had long remained in such concealment as that the emissaries of the king had been utterly unable to discover him, should now appear thus openly abroad in the high road to Samaria, hastening as it were, into the very jaws of the lion, that Obadiah could scarcely trust his own eyes when he beheld the hair-clad prophet advancing towards him. "Art thou my lord Elijah?" was the expression of his astonishment. The answer was laconic: "I am. Go and tell thy lord, Behold, Elijah is here." This raised the perplexity and apprehension of the good governor to the utmost. The prophet was so accustomed to render unquestioning obedience to the mandates he received, that he seems to have got into the habit of expecting the same from others whom he knew to be true and faithful men. The reply of Obadiah apprised him that he had made a mistake. This person explained how diligently Ahab had sought him through all lands to which he had access, and how intense was his anxiety and eagerness to gain possession

---

[1] Probably "sons of the prophets," or those under training in the schools of the prophets.

of his person. He could not believe that the king's intentions could be otherwise than intensely hostile towards one whom he regarded as the cause of all the misery that he and his people had suffered; and such being the case, he felt persuaded that the Lord would protect His servant, by withdrawing him from the face of his greatest enemy, whose rage would then be turned against Obadiah himself, as one who had deceived him. He prayed, therefore, to be excused from a task so dangerous.

The reply of Elijah convinced him that he fully intended to meet the king: and being satisfied of this, Obadiah reasoned no more about motives and consequences, but set forth in search of his master. It seems that he was not long in finding him; and soon the king and the prophet confronted each other face to face. "Art thou he that troubleth Israel?" was the salutation of the king. He was hardly prepared for the daring and faithful retort. "I have not troubled Israel; but thou, and thy father's house, in that ye have forsaken the commandments of the Lord, and thou hast followed Baalim." This stern rebuke led the poor king to feel that he had his master before him, and that the hairy mantle of the prophet was a symbol of greater power than the royal robe, and his staff an emblem of higher authority than his own sceptre. He quailed before the fearless prophet; and the same facility of temper which inclined him to evil when under the influence of Jezebel, swayed him to good in the presence of Elijah. We have heard of men whose whisper could quell the rage of the wildest horse, and bend him down to sudden tameness. Power of the like kind some men possess over other men. Elijah possessed it eminently; it was the gift of God; and such a man as Ahab was a proper subject for its influence.

Besides, Ahab seems to have had some capacities for right feeling when away from under the deadly influence of his wife; and whatever may have been his first purpose when he heard that Elijah awaited him, he had time to cool in the way to the place where he was. This, indeed, had probably been the object of the prophet in sending to him, instead of going with Obadiah, and so appearing abruptly before him.

Now, overawed by the words and demeanour of the great prophet, the king became anxious lest any untowardness on his part should obstruct that prospect of rain, the want of which was now so deeply felt in the sufferings of himself and his people, and which he believed could only be brought at the intercession of Elijah. He therefore consented, at his demand, to call together not only the four hundred and fifty "prophets" or priests of Baal, dispersed through the land, but the four hundred priests of the groves [rather of Ashtaroth] who ate at Jezebel's table—with a view to that trial of spiritual strength which the prophet proposed. The obvious fairness of the demand, the little there could be to apprehend from one man against a thousand, with some curiosity as to the result, together with the hope of rain, which the prophet probably held forth as the issue of the contest,—concurred to secure Ahab's compliance. It is indeed likely that more passed between the king and the prophet than has been recorded; and that the latter, as we have supposed, explained in general terms his object in making this demand. So it was, that Ahab consented, and sent forth the required summons. It is a significant fact, that although it was obeyed by the priests of Baal, the four hundred priests under the immediate influence of Jezebel were absent. In this we cannot fail to see her hand.

CARMEL

1 Kings 18:19-21

FORTY miles below Tyre, and little more than half that distance west of Nazareth, and forming the south-western boundary towards the sea of the plain of Esdraelon, extends for several miles the mountain ridge of Carmel, throwing out a bold promontory right into the sea. The beauty of Carmel is celebrated in Scripture; and even in this day of desolation it sustains its ancient praise. The enlivening atmosphere, the sides covered with perpetual verdure, the brow dark with woods, and the wide prospects around, combine to form a scene which he who has once beheld forgets no more. And this is saying much; for there are few travellers who do not forget as much of what they have seen, as most people do of the books they have read. The mountain is from a thousand to twelve hundred feet in height, and the views which it commands are very extensive. In front, the view extends to the distant horizon, over the dark blue water of the Mediterranean; behind stretches the great plain of Esdraelon, with the mountains of the Jordan and of Judea; below, on the right hand,

CARMEL

lies the city of Acre, lessened to a mere spec; while, in the far distance beyond, the eye rests upon the high summits of Lebanon.

The spot where "Israel was gathered together unto Carmel," the scene of the great transaction —"the Lord's controversy," which they came to witness—was doubtless the inner side of the mountain, where it gradually descends into the noble plain beneath. This declivity overlooks a vast extent of country on every side; and from the hills of Galilee and Samaria the consummating miracle might have been beheld by the more distant gazers; while, from the plain in front, the prophets of Baal, their useless altars, and their frantic movements, as well as the calm majesty of the avenging prophet, would have been as distinctly visible as if the whole had been brought to their feet. It was a most noble and fitting spot for one of the greatest transactions in the history of man; and which the imagination can so inadequately grasp in all the fulness of its grandeur, that we know not of any painter who has even attempted to portray it.

The great assembly gathered there together consisted of the priests of Baal, and some others, perhaps not very numerous, who were exclusively worshippers of that idol, and disavowed all knowledge of, or care for, Jehovah. There was also the court party surrounding the person of the king, who could not but know the claims which Jehovah had to their exclusive reverence, and who, perhaps, had not gone so far as absolutely to deny Him, but who practically ignored His existence and His claims, by giving all their attention and all their service to the fashionable idolatry. To them, this was but another form of the universal world-worship. The worship of Baal was favoured at court,—to follow it was the road to advancement and honour; therefore Baal was great, therefore Baalism was true. And to them it was true; for Mammon was the real object of their worship, and Baal to them was Mammon. Then there was the great crowd of people, who, while they worshipped Baal, had never formally renounced Jehovah, nor had ceased to regard themselves as His people, and heirs of the promises made to the fathers. Sometimes they worshipped Baal, sometimes Jehovah, as convenience or impulse dictated, —generally, perhaps, rendering their more public service to Baal, while Jehovah had the higher place in their private service, and in their thoughts, and hoping in their hearts that they might not be far wrong in serving *both*. This was *their* form of serving two masters, which so many of us do at this day in some form or other, although the idol we associate in our worship with Jehovah may bear some other name than Baal.

It was to this great multitude of time-servers that the prophet addressed himself. When he stood forth, and lifted up his hand as one about to speak, there was a dead silence among that great assembly; and in that thin air his strong and awful voice was heard afar. Those who expected a long harangue, full of sharp rebukes and vehement calls to repentance, were disappointed. Elijah was habitually a man of the fewest words; but these few words were always full of power, and produced more effect than the laboured discourses of the most "eloquent orators." He spoke from God, he spoke from the heart—from his own heart—to the hearts of others.

In the present case, his words were aimed not at the apostasy, but at the hesitancy of the people; not at their idolatry, but at their doubleness and indecision. Under the old dispensation, as under the new, nothing was more abhorrent to God than a profane neutrality in matters of vital moment—than the lukewarmness which admits not of decided opinions. He likes decision. He wishes something real. Be hot; be cold; be something. To be

"Everything by turns, and nothing long,"

is intolerable, is hateful, to Him. So now the prophet: "How long halt ye between two opinions? If Jehovah be God, follow Him; but if Baal, then follow him." In this was a boldness characteristic of this wonderful man. Instead of a tirade against Baal and his worshippers, here is a simple alternative of choice. His simple cry is, "Decide! decide!" But decision is the most difficult of all things to lukewarm and temporizing men. The demand to take a part at once and for all is the most cruel task that could be imposed upon them. This great audience shrunk from it. Dismay and astonishment held them mute. "They answered him not a word." Some say that they feared to pronounce for the Lord in the presence of the king and the priests of Baal. Some say that they feared to pronounce for Baal, in the presence of that prophet whom they believed to possess the means of bringing down to the parched earth the refreshing showers, which could alone fertilize its barren womb. But we venture to say —it is our humble opinion, that they were silent as careless men, shrinking from the trouble and responsibility of decision. It required something more than they had yet witnessed to rouse them out of the inertness into which they had fallen.

Let us observe that, although the essential meaning of the prophet is correctly enough conveyed in the phrase, "How long halt ye between two opinions?" this is rather an explanation than a literal rendering of the original, which to us has a significance that ought not to be lost. Literally, the words may be translated, "How long leap ye upon two branches?"—a most beautiful and poetical allusion to the restlessness of a bird, which remains not long in one posture, but is continually hopping from branch to branch. Somewhat less expressive, but still very significant, is the version which others extract from the original words: "How long limp ye upon two hams?"—alluding to the alternate movements of the body—now on one side, and then on the other—of a lame man in his walk.

No one who has spent such a day on the plain of Esdraelon, as I did twelve years ago, can ever forget its scenery and associations. A summary of the objects which

then came within sight will serve to show, what it is difficult for any one unacquainted with the Holy Land to understand, namely, the contiguity of interesting places, and the narrow limits within which a large number of them are comprised. After leaving Dothan, where Joseph was seen by his brethren afar off—where the Ishmeelites met them, and where the pit was into which he was thrown: —where also Elisha became surrounded by the chariots and horsemen of the Syrian king, and his servant's eyes were opened, to see the hill "full of horses and chariots of fire round about Elisha:"—we came to Jenin, just where a glen, to the south-west, opens upon the wide plain. Jenin was a Levitical city of Issachar, now numbering from 2,000 to 3,000 inhabitants. There we had the great battle field of Palestine before us, extending north about fifteen miles, from Jenin to the foot of the hill on which Nazareth stands. It is a vast undulated expanse; and, when we saw it in spring, it was green here and there with early corn. There Barak triumphed, and Josiah received his death wound; and, in numerous directions, the sites of stirring events could easily be identified. We dipped down from Jenin upon a sea of verdure, and, looking Jordanward to the east, we saw Mount Gilboa to the right. Our first excursion was to Zerin, the ancient Jezreel, where Ahab had his summer palace—his Windsor or Fontainbleau—standing on a low spur projecting from the Gilboa range into the wide plain. Sarcophagi, sculptured ornaments, and heaps of rubbish lie scattered about; we were not far off Naboth's vineyard, and as we saw miserable looking dogs prowling about, we thought of those that licked up the blood of Jezebel. Starting again eastward, in half an hour we reached the fountain of *Ain Jālūd*, at the northern base of Gilboa, with streams flowing from the spring where Gideon's men stooped down, and lapped the water; near which was afterwards heard the cry, "the sword of the Lord and of Gideon," to the discomfiture of the Midianitish host. It so happened that the day we were there the plain was spotted with the black tents of Arabs; and at the same time there hovered close by us swarms of locusts, reminding one of the double Scripture reference to the Midianites as like grasshoppers for multitude. In the forenoon, crossing the sultry plain, we saw a valley to the east running towards the Jordan, where stands *Beisân*, the ancient *Bethshean*, or *Scythopolis*, one of the Canaanite strongholds, whose inhabitants were in alliance with the Philistines; and where the armour of Saul was dedicated to Ashtaroth, and the corpses of his sons were hung against the walls. At noon, we rested in a pleasant pomegranate orchard, where the scarlet blossoms flashed like fire, in a village still called *Sôlam*, no doubt a perpetuation of the ancient Shunem. There, as we sat within encompassing hedges of prickly pears, we opened the book of Kings, and read the story of Elisha and the Shunammite woman:—and looking west, there rose the majestic ridge of Carmel. On the hot plain, we fancied the corn field reapers, where the child received the sun stroke, to receive life again through the prophet's intercession. We thought we saw the mother riding across to the opposite blue hill,—and the prophet coming to the house;—nor could we forget the great sacrifice on Carmel, and the rain storm Elijah watched, and his fleet race over the plain to the gates of Jezreel. After rest and refreshment, we walked over the shoulder of a hill behind Sôlem, and found ourselves at Nain, where our Lord raised the widow's son;—within three quarters of an hour's ride is Endor, where Saul met the witch. Opposite, in a northerly direction, is Mount Tabor, a green round hill, which may be reached in an hour. Proceeding from Nain along the plain, in the course of two or three hours, we attained the rim of the beautiful basin, where Nazareth lies among the northern hills.

S.

THE CONTEST

1 Kings 18:22-40

THE silence of the people at his appeal was no surprise to Elijah. He knew them and their state too well. He had calculated on it, and was prepared for it. He was prepared, by one grand demonstration, to force upon them the conviction of the impotency of their idol, and to compel them to acknowledge the supremacy of Jehovah. This was probably deemed by him to be necessary, before he could be justified in interceding for them, that they might have rain, with the God whom they as yet refused to acknowledge. What right had they to expect favours from Him whose authority they had disavowed, and whose greatness they had insulted? No; they must be brought to a more suitable state of mind before he could pray the Lord to open wide that hand, in which the seasonable rains had been so long shut up.

Elijah proposed a trial which should demonstrate to their senses the proportion between the claims of Jehovah and of Baal. He desired that two bullocks should be provided,—one for him, and one for the priests of Baal. These they were to lay out upon two altars for sacrifice, in the usual manner; but that, instead of applying fire to their offerings, each party should supplicate their God, and the God that answered by sending fire to consume the victim should be acknowledged as the Almighty Lord. To show that the human disadvantage was all on his side, the prophet touchingly alluded to the disproportion of their numbers: "I, even I only, remain a prophet of Jehovah; but Baal's prophets are four hundred and fifty men."

The proposal was altogether so fair and unobjectionable, that the people assented to it with entire approbation, and the Baalite priests, what-ever may have been their misgivings, could not with any credit refuse to abide by this ordeal. Indeed they would have done so with a bad grace, seeing that, as we have shown, their Baal was no other than the sun, whence it should have been very much in his line thus to supply them with the fire they wanted for his service. Remembering what we have read respecting the skill of the ancient heathen priests, in the arts of producing sudden combustion by their knowledge of pyrotechnics, one almost shudders at the danger of the trial proposed; for, if the priests had been able, by some secret arts or contrivances, to kindle the fire upon the altar, the result would have been deemed conclusive by the people in favour of Baal. But they either did not possess such arts, or, from the suddenness of their being called on for this trial, *off their own ground*, and watched by thousands of vigilant eyes, were unable to exercise them.

They, however, set to work with the reality or show of great courage and vigour. They built their altar, they laid on their wood, they slew the victim, and set it ready for the burning. They then commenced their sacred invocatory dances around the altar—first slow and solemn, then quicker, then with frantic energy, their numerous skirts flaunting in the air, and creating an artificial breeze. Then, as their blood waxed hot, and their enthusiasm was kindled, there arose from among them shrill cries, fit to pierce the heavens, of "Baal, hear us! Baal, hear us!" and presently, in the madness of their wildering excitement, they smote themselves with their knives, and the blood gushed out and streaked their persons with gore, presenting a most frightful spectacle to the eyes of unexcited observers. But still their oracle was dumb: no responsive fires came down from heaven in answer to their cries; and as the time advanced in their abortive efforts to rend the brazen heavens, the voice of the Lord's prophet was heard lashing them with sarcasms, which smote them with far keener cuts than the knives which, in their madness, they thrust into their flesh: "Cry aloud, for he is a god: either he is talking, or he is pursuing, or he is on a journey, or peradventure he sleepeth, and must be awaked." This is one of the few examples of ridicule to be found in the Scripture, and justifies the use of that somewhat dangerous weapon on proper occasions. The present occasion was pre-eminently proper, and the prophet's words must have had an awakening effect upon the minds of the people, coupled as they were with the wild doings of the priests, which might have been stimulating had they been less protracted, or had any result appeared. But the whole affair grew vapid by its long duration, and by its entirely abortive character. We have no doubt that the people were heartily weary of it, and had ceased to pay attention to their proceedings, long before the priests found it in their hearts to give over their attempts, and were constrained to confess that their god could not, or would not, move to vindicate his own honour.

The expectancy of the people had, however, a remaining object. It was yet to be seen whether or not the Lord would do that which Baal had failed to accomplish. But Elijah was in no hurry. He allowed them to occupy the greater part of the day in their vain endeavours, that their utter futility might be manifest to all the people. It was not until the regular time of evening sacrifice approached that the prophet arose for action. Then the relaxed attention of the people was once more wound up, and directed with eager interest to his proceedings. The murmur of voices all around became suddenly silent, and those who had sat down, or were lounging on the dry plain, stood up.

Some may think that Elijah might as well have gone over to the altar of the Baalites, where everything was ready, and call down, in the Lord's name, the fire which the priests had been unable to obtain from their idol. But he would have nothing to do with the unclean thing. He knew the place of an old altar there, which had been formerly used for the worship of Jehovah. It was in ruins, and had, as a high-place altar, been irregular; still, as consecrated to the Lord, it was better than one set up for Baal, and better than one altogether new. He repaired it, so that, when completed, it was composed of *twelve* large stones. *Ten* tribes only had a direct concern in this controversy; but the faithful prophet would not omit the opportunity of impressing upon the assembled people the essential unity of the nation, and the unity of their true worship. All being ready, the prophet directed that the altar, the victim, and the wood should be flooded with water, in such abundance that, as it flowed down, it quite filled a trench he had caused to be digged around to receive it. He multiplied difficulties, in order that the mira-

culous nature of the result might be rendered the more striking, in contrast with the vain efforts of Baal's votaries, of which the cold altar and the unconsumed victim stood there for a monument. It may be asked, How was the water thus copiously provided in a time of drought? Perhaps from the Kishon, which, towards the end of its course, is supplied from perennial springs in Carmel when the upper part (which is but the bed of a winter torrent) has become dry. Being so near the sea, these fountains may not have dried up from lack of rain. Or if these were exhausted, salt water would have served the purpose, and this could easily be obtained from the sea, which was not far off.

At the right moment of national sacrifice, the prophet approached the altar; and the simplicity of his proceedings—of his words and actions—appears in fine contrast with the demonstrative antics in which Baal's priests had consumed the day. He called upon "Jehovah, God of Abraham, Isaac, and Israel," to "let it be known this day that Thou art God in Israel, and that I am thy servant, and that I have done all these things at thy word. Hear me, O Lord, hear me, that this people may know that Thou art the Lord God, and that Thou hast turned their heart back again." The words had no sooner passed his lips than the fire of the Lord came visibly down with such devouring energy, that it consumed not only the victim, not only the wood, but the very stones of the altar, and licked up the water that was in the trench. It had been something—it had been enough—to have kindled the wood merely. The Baalite priests would have been glad of so much from *their* god; but here was something far more and greater, something to suggest to the people that it was only of the Lord's mercies that they, in their clustered thousands, were not also consumed. The effect was irresistible. Every knee smote the ground, every face sought the dust, and one universal cry rose to heaven: "The Lord, He is the God: the Lord, He is the God!"

In that moment of profound excitement, Elijah felt that the power of the sword was in his hands; and he shrunk not from exercising it. He called to the people to prevent the escape of the priests of Baal. They were accordingly seized by the people, and conducted to the river Kishon; and, at the suggestion of the prophet, they were put to death—the spot being chosen, probably that the stream might presently bear away to the sea the pollution of their blood. It does not appear that Ahab took any part in this matter. The appeal of Elijah was to the people. He called upon them to inflict, then and there, upon these ringleaders of the people in idolatry, the punishment which the law denounced, and such as would have been inflicted upon himself had the victory been on their side; and the king seems to have been too awe-stricken to interfere. From the character of Elijah, we have no doubt that he executed this act of blood heartily, and with entire satisfaction. It is not for us to vindicate him. The only question is, Was this in accordance with the law and with the spirit of the times? It certainly was. And Britons, not so much as fifty years ago, performed under their own laws, with perfect peace of mind, upon far less heinous offenders, the deadly executions which we now regard with horror. If, then, in looking back upon the last generation, we make allowance for this great change of law and sentiment within so short a time, we must needs make the same allowance in surveying the more remote, and less refined, age in which Elijah lived.

Recent research has discovered the scene of this, one of the most tragic events of Bible history. The spot is distinctly marked by the agreement of its physical features with the notices of the sacred narrative ; also by local tradition, and by its name, *el-Muhrakah,* "the sacrifice." It is about six hours' ride along the mountain ridge, east of the convent. It is on the eastern brow of Carmel, and commands a noble view of the vast plain of Esdraelon, away to Jezreel, and Shunem, and Tabor. On the south, the wooded tops of the hills of Samaria roll backward in graceful undulations to the horizon ; while on the north, over the picturesque range of Galilee, the pale blue cone of Hermon shoots up till its icy crown touches the clouds. Close to the base of Carmel, below el-Muhrakah, flows the Kishon, on whose banks Baal's prophets were massacred ; and just above it is a projecting peak, from which Elijah's servant saw the "little cloud, like a man's hand, rising out of the sea."

The scene of the sacrifice is a rocky platform, or terrace, encompassed by thickets of evergreens. Upon it are the ruins of a quadrangular structure of large hewn stones, evidently of remote antiquity, and doubtless marking the site of the Lord's altar. Near it, in a vault of ancient masonry, is a copious fountain, which may have supplied the water with which the sacrifice was deluged. "Sitting on that commanding height, on a bright spring evening, I felt persuaded I was upon the scene of Elijah's great sacrifice. Beside and under me were probably the very stones of which God's altar was built, and over which

played the heavenly flame. A few paces beneath me was the well from which the water was drawn, that the prophet's servants poured upon the altar. Around me were the thickets from which the wood was cut. Away at the foot of the mountain flowed the Kishon in its deep bed, which, on the eve of that day, ran red with the blood of Jehovah's enemies. There, stretching out before me, was the plain across which Ahab dashed in his chariot ; and yonder, on its eastern border, I saw the little villages which mark the sites and still bear the names of Jezreel and Shunem. Is it strange that when one thus visits the holy and historic places of Palestine, the grand events of Bible history should appear to be enacted over again, and should become living realities ?"[1]

P.

INCIDENTS

1 Kings 18:22-40

THE great theme of yesterday allowed us no pause for the illustration of its subordinate incidents ; but some of them are too remarkable to be passed over, and therefore we give this day to them.

The sign chosen to manifest the Lord's presence and power, namely the descent of fire upon the altar to consume the victim, must be allowed to have been in the highest degree appropriate, probably the most appropriate that could be suggested ; for it was an old and venerable form in which He had, in former times, manifested His presence and made known His favour. Perhaps it was so in respect of the sacrifice of Abel ; certainly it was so in the covenant sacrifice with Abraham,[2] and at the consecration of the tabernacle by Moses,[3] and at the dedication of the temple by Solomon.[4] The historical knowledge which the people possessed of the previous use of this symbol, rendered its adoption in the present instance peculiarly striking and appropriate.

But the idea itself, of such a trial of strength between Baal and Jehovah, is less obvious to us, and somewhat shocking. It was, however, familiar to the ancient mind. Judaism was the only religion that denied the existence of all other gods than the One it worshipped. Polytheism admitted the existence of the diverse

---

[1] *Giant Cities of Bashan,* p. 238.   [3] Leviticus 9:24.

[2] Genesis 15:17.   [4] 2 Chronicles 7:1.

gods worshipped among different nations. The only questions, therefore, that could arise among them, had reference to the comparative power and strength of the different gods, as—Whether the god we serve is greater or not than the god you serve ? This was sometimes tried by actual experiment, the result of which was usually held to be conclusive. Some reports of such contests have come down to us, and are usually of a nature that seems to us exceedingly whimsical. Such is that of the fire-worshipping Chaldeans, who believed their god to be superior to all others, and bore him in solemn embassage to various nations. The story runs that this fire-god baffled the power of the gods of gold, silver, brass, stone, wood, and of every other material, by melting their images out of all form, and by calcining them, or reducing them to ashes. The arrival of this conquering god in Egypt filled the priests of that country with dismay, till a cunning old priest of Canopus thought of a device for securing the victory to the god he served. The jars in which the Egyptians were wont to purify the water of the Nile, being perforated with imperceptible holes, he took one of them and stopped the holes with wax, and filling the jar with water, he fitted to the top the dog's head of Canopus. The unsuspecting Chaldeans, rendered confident by past victories, subjected this fresh idol to their fiery proof. But presently the heat melted the wax, and then a strange commotion in the fire was witnessed, as if it had got something it did not like. There was a hissing, a spitting, a fizzing, a fuming, and at length the fire went out, and the jar-god stood triumphant over the steaming embers. This story is in Rufinus. How far it may be true we cannot say. The form of the Canopic jars gives it the semblance of truth ; and it at least shows, that the idea of such contests for power among the gods was familiar to the ancient mind.

The cutting of the flesh by the excited priests of Baal, is not the only or first intimation of the existence of this practice among the nations of Canaan. The law expressly forbade the adoption of this practice. "Ye shall not make any cuttings in your flesh for the dead." (Lev. xix. 28.) This shows that it was chiefly used as an act of mourning, an act of deep and affectionate grief ; and to this effect are all the allusions to it in Scripture. But occasionally, as in the present instance, it was an act of strongly excited feeling —whether of love, of grief, or of devotion, and as such held to be acceptable to gods and men. This is easily intelligible to one who has had occasion to witness the strong demonstrative emotions of the East, where there seems to be a general impression that nothing is true that cannot be evinced to the senses. Cutting the flesh is therefore a common mode of demonstrating strong feeling in the pagan East ; and although the spirit of Islamism is less favourable to such displays than that of Paganism, it has not been able wholly to eradicate them, as will be obvious to one who has witnessed the furious gashes which the Persians inflict upon themselves in their frantic annual lamentations for Hossein, or the bloody smitings by which the young Turkish gallants seek to demonstrate the depth of their affection. There are also, as in the remoter East, devotees who seek to gain credit before men, and merit before God, by self-inflicted tortures. Such are often mentioned by the older travellers in Palestine, one of whom gives an illustrative figure, of which a copy has been already given in this work. [1] There are many notices of this custom in ancient writings, most of which show that, in the religious point of view, the gods were pacified and rendered propitious by human blood, on which was also founded the idea of human sacrifice. Herodotus relates, that when the Persian fleet (of Xerxes) was near ruin from a storm on the coast of Magnesia, the Magi, by making cuttings in their flesh, and by performing incantations to the wind, succeeded in allaying the storm—" or it may be," adds the sagacious old Greek, "that the storm subsided of its own accord." We are also told, that the priests of the Syrian goddess (who was nearly allied to Baal) were wont to cut and gash themselves with knives until the blood rushed out, when they carried her about in procession. The priests of Bellona, also, in their service to that sanguinary goddess, were accustomed to mingle their own blood with that of their sacrifices.

The question may occur, and has often been asked, Whether Elijah did not make himself a transgressor of the law by offering sacrifice to the Lord, which was the function of the priests ? This question may have been suggested in other instances, posterior to the enactment of the law by which this priestly function was limited, as in

[1] See Vol. 1, pp. 247-249.

the case of some of the judges, and Samuel, who, though a Levite, was not a priest.

But it is to be recollected that the priest, as a priest, was simply and solely a minister of the temple service; the prophets—through whom God gave His law, announced His purposes, inculcated truth, gave His specific commands, uttered His promises or His threatenings, and disclosed the future—were quite a distinct class of men. It is a remarkable fact, that the whole of the Hebrew Scripture, at least all that is didactic and prophetic, was, with the exception of the books of Ezra, Jeremiah, and Ezekiel, written by men who were not of the priestly order. Moses, Samuel, David, Solomon, Isaiah, and Daniel were not priests. Priests were indeed sometimes called to the prophetic office, as in the case of Jeremiah and Ezekiel; but it was evidently as to a new and additional office. The prophetic office was undoubtedly the higher of the two. It was special, and only men of extraordinary gifts and piety were called to it. Those endowed with it were sent directly from God, and were admitted into a near and most peculiar intimacy. God spoke to them, and showed to them the symbols of His ineffable glory. They were the great inspired teachers of the world; and while the priest could not as of right be a prophet, the prophet could, by virtue of his direct commission and his higher function, act as a priest. Hence it is, that we find Elijah here, and Samuel there, offering sacrifices. Before the Mosaic economy, the priest and prophet were the same. Upon the introduction of this economy, the priesthood became a distinct class; but the prophet lost none of his original official capacities.

Elijah's story affords a subject for thoughtful study. There is not one among the prophets, of whose outward life we know so much; of whom so many incidents are recorded, whose story is so graphically told, and around whose name there gathers such a dazzling halo of miracle and mystery. We see him, hear him, know him. His face and figure are familiar. Countenance, costume, attitude, are all portrayed, or suggested, as we think over the narrative of his life.

A dauntless courage comes out in his interview with Ahab—a poor man, an outcast, living on charity, in the world's eye a mere beggar, he meets the monarch without a dash of fear, and reproves him for breaking God's commandments and following Baal. The weak and the strong here changed places; moral principle triumphed over royal greatness; the servant of God triumphed over the vicegerent of the devil, and truth from heaven was seen to be mightier than armed and crowned lies, fresh from hell. On Carmel Elijah stands forth alone for the true God, the true religion, the true worship, before king and court, church and people, apostate and idolatrous; ready to stake all in the issue, like another, of kindred spirit, who stood up in the old hall of the bishop's palace at Worms, before princes and potentates, staking his religion and his life on the Bible. And when Ahaziah sent three troops of fifty soldiers each to the man of God, they were all nothing to him, for he felt that God was on his side, and calmly walked back with the messenger to the king's chamber, and repeated the unwelcome words which had aroused his majesty's indignation.

Yet was Elijah a man of like passions with ourselves. He quailed before the threat of Jezebel, and fled into the wilderness, and sat under a juniper tree and prayed that he might die. The man at Horeb and the man at Carmel do not appear the same; yet the one was identical with the other, reminding us how inconsistent and contradictory we appear at different periods of our lives. "What dost thou here?" was a startling enquiry for him; and so it is for us, when we place ourselves in questionable positions. His complaint of being left alone, indicated pride and rashness, impatience and presumption, such as linger often in the bosoms of the best of men. Perhaps it was to humble the prophet that the fire burned, and the wind rocked the mountain, and the earthquake shook the ground. Certainly it was to show God's glorious power, and to awaken confidence on the part of His servant, such confidence as springs from faith in Him.

S.

THE LITTLE CLOUD

1 Kings 18:41-46

ONE would think that Elijah was the king, and Ahab his subject. It is not Ahab who says to Elijah, but Elijah to Ahab: "Go, and he goeth; and, Come, and he cometh." So now the prophet tells the king to withdraw and refresh himself after the fatigues of the day; and Ahab, glad to be relieved, retires to eat and to drink. But Elijah's "meat was to do the will of Him that sent him, and to FINISH his work." He then went to the top of the mountain, and cast himself down upon the earth, with his face between his knees—thus remaining in earnest prayer. He then desired his servant to go to the top of the promontory, and look towards the sea. The man went, and returned to report that he observed nothing. Seven times the prophet bent down in prayer, and six times the servant returned without the report of coming rain. But the seventh time he announced, with quickened words, that he saw on the horizon a little cloud, not larger than a man's hand, arising out of the sea. On hearing this, the prophet sent the man to tell Ahab to betake himself to his chariot, and hasten home, *lest the rain should prevent him.* The king caught the precious meaning of this message. Never was the prospect of a journey being hindered by rain so gladly received by mortal man. He hastened to his chariot. It was full time. The heavens were already black with clouds; the wind arose; and presently the rain fell down in mighty streams. The king, meanwhile, was scouring the great plain of Esdraelon for Jezreel. But who is that strong man, with tightly girded loins, who flees swifter than the horses, and runs before the chariot of his king? It is Elijah. The great prophet chose, in this remarkable and characteristic way, to evince that, after all the great deeds he had done, after all the stern things he had spoken, he forgot not that Ahab was his sovereign; for the part he took was that of a servant, whose duty it is to run before the chariot of his master. It is seen by the Egyptian monuments that the princes and nobles of that country had attendants who ran before their chariots. Such vehicles are not now used in Egypt, or in western Asia; but in Persia it is at this day regarded as a piece of necessary state for the king and great nobles to have several men to run before and behind them as they ride out on horseback. This they do even when the rider puts his horse to a gallop; and, as a general rule, it is understood that a well-trained footman ought to remain untired fully as long, if not longer, than the horse ridden by the master. The men are of course trained to this arduous service; and it is astonishing to observe the apparent ease with which they keep their relative distance from the master's horse, in all its paces, even the most rapid. These men are called *shatirs;* and the reported feats of some of them would be incredible, were they not well authenticated. One is known to have accomplished about 120 miles in fourteen hours' unremitted running; and instead of getting praise for this, he was rather censured for not having accomplished the task in twelve hours.

These men are, like Elijah, tightly girded; so tightly, that to stoop were death, and to fall were to rise no more. There is near Ispahan a monument called the Shatir's Tower (*Meel e Shatir*), the story connected with which is, that a king of Persia promised his daughter in marriage to any one who would run before his horse all the way from Shiraz to Ispahan. One of the shatirs had so nearly accomplished the task as to gain the height on which the tower stands, and where the city comes full into view, when the monarch, alarmed lest he should be forced to fulfil his engagement, dropped his whip. The shatir, aware that, owing to the ligatures around his body, it would cost him his life to stoop, contrived to pick it up with his feet. This device having failed, the royal rider dropped his ring; the shatir then saw that his fate was decided, and exclaiming, "O king, you have broken your word, but I am true to the last!" he stooped, picked up the ring, and expired.

There is something remarkable in the sign by which the prophet knew that the rain was coming. A little cloud in the horizon would to us be of small significance; but it is not so in the East. The clearness of the sky renders the slightest appearance of the kind distinctly visible, and it is known to be a sign of an immediate storm with violent rain. Of several instances that might be mentioned, one of the most graphic is that given by Mr. Emerson in his *Letters from the Ægean.* He is at sea in a Greek vessel in the Levant. One morning, which had opened clear and beautiful, it was announced that a squall might be expected. No sign recognizable by European landsmen appeared; but on attention being properly directed, "a little black cloud" was seen on the verge of the horizon towards the south, which was every instant spreading rapidly over the face of the sky, and drawing nearer to the vessel. Orders were immediately given to strike sail, and to prepare the vessel for scudding before the hurricane. "But scarcely an instant had elapsed ere the squall was upon us, and all grew black around; the wind came rushing and crisping over the water, and in a moment the ship was running almost gunwale down, while the rain was dashing in torrents on the decks. As quick as thought the foresail was torn from the yards, and as the gust rushed through the rigging, the sheets and ropes were snapping and crackling with a fearful noise. The crew, however, accustomed to such sudden visitants, were not slow in reefing the

necessary sails, trimming the rigging, and bringing back the vessel to her proper course; and in
about a quarter of an hour, or even less, the
hurricane had all passed away; the sun burst
out again through the clouds that swept in its
impetuous train; the wind sunk to its former
gentleness, and all was once more at peace, with
the exception of the agitated sea, that continued
for the remainder of the day rough and billowy."

To this Mr. Emerson adds the interesting fact,
that it is mainly the dread of such sudden
borasques as the present, that compels almost
every vessel in the Levant to shorten sail at the
close of day, since in cloudy weather it would be
next to impossible, during the night, to discern
the cloud which announces the approach of the
tempest, in time to prepare for its reception; and
to a ship with all her canvas spread, the effect
might be terrific.

THE STILL SMALL VOICE

1 Kings 19

It is said that the hand of the Lord was upon
Elijah to bring him to Jezreel. He knew that
Jezebel was there. Her character was well
known to him; but he feared not to go where
duty called him, and to carry on and complete
the great work he had so signally commenced—
of bringing back the people to the faith of their
fathers—of keeping them firm in the choice they
had made—of strengthening the good impressions
they had received—and of maintaining the influence he had begun to establish over the mind
of the unstable king. These were great objects,
and it was not to be expected that such a man
as Elijah, whose conquering faith had never yet
known doubt or fear, would shrink from any
danger in order to realize them. His duty called
him to Jezreel, and to Jezreel he went.

All that has gone before, and all that we know
of his character, would naturally prepare us to
hear of his great doings there—in that very place
of Satan's seat—in purging out the unclean thing.
It was a great task; and of all the men that ever
lived, Elijah seemed the one best fitted for it, by
his extraordinary spiritual gifts, and by the convincing assurances which he had just received,
that the Lord was with him, would hear his

prayer, would hold his life precious, and would
afford him all the aid his work required. But
the expected history of great doings and great
reforms is a blank. Nothing was done. The
great Elijah—that strong-hearted man—failed
at the critical moment, fled from his post to save
his life when threatened by the wrath of Jezebel,
as soon as she heard that her prophets had been
slain. He who had experienced the sufficiency
of the Lord's protection from prince, prophets,
and people, now shrinks at last, at the crisis of
his highest duty, from the face of a woman,
whom his Master could, if He had seen fit, have
cut off in a moment. He fled; and, lacking their
great guide, and the prime leader in this auspicious
movement, the people became discouraged, and
the impression made upon the king's mind rapidly
cooled down, both relapsing into nearly their
former state. Truly in this did Elijah show
himself "a man subject to like passions as we
are." O Lord, what is man? O Lord, who shall
stand, when even thy Elijahs fail in their high
trust?

Those who vindicate Elijah for fleeing when
his life appeared in danger, forget that he was
not a private person, but a commissioned prophet,
set forth prominently before the eyes of men, as
the appointed corrector of his times and people.
He had a set post to occupy, a determined duty
to fulfil, in which his Master would certainly sustain him, and from which not even the fear of
certain death should have prompted him to flee.
Suppose, indeed, that he had been absolutely
certain that the Lord would not interfere, and
that to stay was death—how could he know but
that the Lord's cause might be better promoted,
and His great name more glorified, by his death
than by his life? From such a man as Elijah
we are entitled to make exactions of duty from
which commoner men might be excused. In
him, of all men, we are entitled to look for the
martyr-spirit; for if not in him, in whom of that
age was it to be looked for?

Still, in this deplorable lapse of faith, there is,
we suspect, some mystery that does not at first
sight appear; for so signal a failure of duty in a
man so eminent, is seldom without its antecedents
—is seldom other than the due effect of something that has gone before. Seeing how often
the declinations or lapses of great and good men
follow closely upon the moments of their highest
exaltation, there is reason to suspect that Elijah

had suffered his mind to be too much elevated, "exalted above measure," by the great deeds he had accomplished, and by the notion in his mind, that he alone, of all Israel, had maintained his faith untainted. It was therefore necessary that he should be humbled, by being allowed to feel his own weakness, and to know that of himself he was nothing. For this correction it was only necessary that the Lord's hand should for a moment be withdrawn from him, that for a little while he should be left to HIMSELF. The example is most instructive, as showing how timid and forlorn a creature even an Elijah may become, when but for a short time stripped, in correcting mercy, of all save his own strength.

The prophet, haunted by fears hitherto unknown to his stout heart, hastened to get into the neighbouring kingdom of Judah. Even there he was uneasy until he had reached Beersheba, the most distant inhabited place of that kingdom, towards the southern desert. Good Jehoshaphat then reigned in Judah, and one would think that the prophet might have deemed himself safe under his protection, even if he had openly declared himself. But with his shaken trust in God, he had lost much of his trust in man; and he seems to have recollected that Jehoshaphat was politically in close alliance with Ahab, and that his eldest son had espoused the like-minded daughter of that Jezebel, whose name had become a terror to him. He began to feel uneasy even in Beersheba. He therefore dismissed his servant, and set forth alone into the wilderness, whose wide but desolate bosom offered, as it seemed to him, the best security against detection and pursuit. Perhaps he had some reason to expect that he would find in this quarter, at the present time of the year, the friendly Arabs through whom the Lord had provided for his wants by the brook Cherith, and who would be glad to receive him into their tents. All day he travelled and found no refuge; and in the evening, worn out with fatigue, and consumed with hunger, he cast himself down under the shelter of one of the broom-trees,[1] which alone flourish in that wilderness. Here this lately strong-souled man lay hopeless, helpless, and despairing; and he who fled so anxiously from death, prayed for himself that he might die. "It is enough; O Lord God, take

[1] *Genista rœtam,* or Spanish broom, is allowed to be the tree (in Hebrew *rothem*) the name of which is translated "juniper" in the text.

away my life; for I am not better than my fathers." Strange contradiction! Here the man who was destined not to taste of death, flees from death on the one hand, and seeks it on the other! And who told him it was "enough?" God did not; He knew what was enough for Elijah to do and to suffer. It was not enough. God had more to teach him, and had more work for him to do. If the Lord had taken him at his word, and had also said it was "enough," Elijah's history would have wanted its crowning glory.

Hitherto the Lord had not manifested Himself to Elijah since he had left his high post. But He had not lost sight of His servant, and the time was come when it seemed to Him fit to evince so much care towards him as might prevent him from being consumed with over-much sorrow. From restless sleep, troubled with dreams and doubts, he was roused by the touch of an angel; and he beheld close by a cruse of water and a cake of bread just baken on the coals. After having partaken of this simple but grateful fare, he sunk into sounder sleep; and, as the morning rose, he was again awakened, and found the same provision made for him. In this food, prepared by angel hands, he found more than mortal nourishment; for the strength it imparted enabled him to travel without weariness, and to remain for no less than forty days without the need or wish for other food.

He was now in a better mind, yet not wholly corrected. Something more was needed to be taught him. His journey now assumed a definite object. He proposed to go among the mountains of Sinai, probably as being uninhabited, and as affording among their recesses many caverns in which he might rest without danger of detection. And although he was still astray from the path of strict duty, we make no question that he expected and hoped to build his heart up in holy thoughts among the scenes which the footsteps of the Lord had hallowed.

So he went to Horeb, and took up his quarters in a cave.[1] Here at last the word of the Lord

[1] In the Sinai mountains, where the ascent to the higher peak of Mount Sinai commences from a little plain which lies 1,200 or 1,300 feet above the lower valleys, is a low rude building containing the chapels of Elijah and Elisha. "Here was evidently once a small monastery; and the older travellers speak also of a chapel of the Virgin. In that of Elijah the monks show near the altar a hole just large enough for a man's body, which they say is the cave where

came to him once more. It came in the form of questioning rebuke. "What doest thou here, Elijah?" As much as to say, "What hast THOU, of all men, to do here? Thou, whose post in my service is among the haunts of men—to fight my battles against a perverse generation, and to strengthen the hearts of those who still encourage themselves in the Lord their God. What hast thou to do in this selfish, moaning solitude? With whom hast thou left those few sheep in the wilderness? What hast *thou* to do *here?*"

Elijah's answer is less candid, or rather more self-deceiving, than we could wish. He upholds his own zeal for the Lord; he believes himself to be the only true worshipper left; and therefore he seeks to preserve a life which had thus become so important, that forsaken truth might not be without a living witness. He was then directed to go forth and stand on the mount before the Lord. He obeyed; and as he stood, a great strong wind went by, that brake the rocks and rent the mountains. But the Lord was not in that wind; it was only His harbinger. Then an earthquake made the everlasting hills tremble beneath his feet; but the Lord was not there. Then a fire wrapt in flame the crests of the mountains; but the Lord was not in the fire. All these terrors were but His harbingers—the harbingers of a "still small voice." When the prophet heard that Voice, he knew it; and since he might not hide within the cavern, he wrapped his face in the folds of his mantle, and stood to receive the word of the Lord. The question was repeated. "What doest thou here, Elijah?" And

to this the same reply was given. The answer bade him return to the world, and do the Lord's work in it; with the assurance that, alone in the faith, as he thought himself, the Lord, who knew and numbered His hidden ones, had found in Israel "seven thousand knees the prophet dwelt in Horeb. Tapers are lighted and incense burnt in these chapels." (Robinson's *Researches*, i. 152.) This is a fair specimen of local tradition. Jewish writers are of opinion that the cave in which Elijah lodged, was the same with the cleft of the rock in which Moses was put when the Lord passed before him; but, were this the case, there had been no need that Elijah should go forth to stand upon the mount while the Lord passed by.

which have not bowed unto Baal, and every mouth which hath not kissed him." [1]

> " Back, then, complainer, loathe thy life no more,
> 　Nor deem thyself upon a desert shore,
> 　　Because the rocks the nearer prospect close.
> Yet in fallen Israel are there hearts and eyes
> That day by day in prayer like thine arise ;
> 　Thou knowest them not, but their Creator knows.
> Go, to the world return, nor fear to cast
> Thy bread upon the waters ; sure at last
> 　In joy to find it after many days.*—*Keble.*

And we also! Has it not often been so with us, that after we have been tossed by the rough winds, shaken by the earthquake, and scorched in many fires, the "still small voice" has come to us in the solitude of our chamber, in the night watches upon our beds, accusing us of neglected duty and broken faith, yet speaking comfort, and whispering encouragement and hope?

I can see no ground for the grave charge which Dr. Kitto here brings against the great prophet. Flight in times of danger is not always a sign of cowardice. It becomes the duty of God's servants to escape when to resist would be hopeless, and to remain, death. They were not taught to expect that a miracle of mercy would, in every case, relieve them from the necessary exercise of human prudence and foresight. Moses fled from Egypt, Paul from Damascus, and even our Lord Himself from the temple. There is nothing in the narrative to indicate that Elijah's flight was a cowardly escape from a dangerous duty, or that it was opposed to the divine will. On the contrary, the miraculous provision of food for him in the desert, and the words of the angel, "Arise and eat because the journey is too great for thee," appear to imply an approval of the journey. The question of the Lord, twice repeated, "What doest thou here, Elijah?" undoubtedly conveys a rebuke, but it is a rebuke not for the journey, which, so far as we can see, was a necessity, but for the prophet's despondency in the desert, and in the mountain cave. The fact that his great enemy had been permitted to triumph for a time appears to have shaken his personal trust in God, and to have overthrown all hope for the final triumph of God's cause in Israel. "What dost thou here, Elijah, faithless and despairing? There is work for thee, and success for thee still. The enemy seems to triumph now, but God's prophet and God's cause shall triumph in the end." The divine directions then given to Elijah on the mount of God, moulded the destinies of the two kingdoms for the next generation.

P.

---

[1] Literally, "kissed *to him*," suggesting that this act of homage consisted in kissing the hand to him—an ancient act of worship represented in sculptures.

BENHADAD

1 Kings 20:1-21

THE twentieth chapter of the First Book of Kings contains the history of two invasions of the kingdom of Ahab by Benhadad, king of Syria, and of his defeat on both occasions by the Israelites, under the special intervention of the Lord, who, grievously as He had been offended, still had pity for the seed of Abraham, would try them longer yet, and would not yet give them over to utter misery and ruin. He therefore, unasked, interfered by His prophets, and encouraged the king and people by exhortations and promises. We hear nothing of Baal in these transactions. Their holiday god was of no use to them in time of trouble; and Ahab himself had of late seen too many proofs of the Lord's power not to know that, whatever He promised, He was able to perform, and to follow, in a spirit of becoming submission, the instructions he received. Still, there is throughout the narrative a sort of cheerlessness, arising from the want of that spontaneous reference to the Lord, and thankfulness to Him, which plays like a sunbeam over the history of public transactions of equal, or even less moment, in the time of devout kings.

The chapter is deeply interesting for the picturesque indications it presents of ancient usages and sentiments, especially in regard to warlike matters, forming a remarkable instance of that consummate word-painting, of which we find in the sacred books the most perfect existing specimens.

The arrogance engendered in an ill regulated mind by the consciousness of irresistible power, is strikingly shown in the whole conduct of Benhadad, whose immense force was such as seemed to render the mere idea of opposition ridiculous. What might have been the case had Ahab been allowed time to call out and embody the resources of his kingdom, may be a matter of question: but it had been the policy of Benhadad to prevent this by marching direct upon Samaria, to strike at the head at once, without allowing his force to be detained by securing the towns and fortresses on his way. Nothing can be more insulting than the message he sent to the king of Israel when he came before Samaria: "Thy silver and thy gold is mine: thy wives also and thy children, even the goodliest, are mine." Many would have said, "Come and take them." Many would have answered, that they would first die among the ruins of Samaria. And, seeing the natural strength of the position, a spirited man might have calculated on holding out until the country had been roused against the invaders, or until relief had been obtained from some quarter—perhaps from the king of Judah, perhaps from the Phœnicians. But the answer was beyond measure tame and submissive, even to abjectness—furnishing another illustration of the yielding temper of this king to any kind of force put upon him from without. It is quite possible that another kind of force would have roused the same man to heroic daring and true kingly action. The answer was: "My lord, O king, according to thy saying, I am thine, and all that I have." Yet, notwithstanding the servile tone of this answer, it is probable, from what follows, that he understood the Syrian king to mean no more than that Ahab should hold all things of him under tribute. Encouraged to still more inordinate arrogance by this submissiveness, Benhadad sent afresh to declare, not only that his message was to be literally understood—that all was to be actually given up to him,—but that his officers should make a general search of the palace and the dwellings of the city, to take what they pleased, and to ascertain that nothing worth the having had been retained. The insolence of this is almost beyond precedent. Such treatment is the worst that could be expected for a city taken by storm; and even an unscrupulous Eastern conqueror would hardly demand it of a power which had yielded without fighting. It was worse in effect than the treatment to which Nadir Shah subjected Delhi, after the emperor Mohammed Shah had been defeated in a hard fought battle, and had rendered his personal submission. *Then* that not very scrupulous conqueror, while treating the emperor with distinction, and protecting the inhabitants from injury and insult, and while, in fact, all was in his hands, claimed, as a prize he had won, the wealth of the emperor, and a great proportion of that of his richest and most distinguished subjects. The whole of the jewels which had been collected by a long line of sovereigns, and all the contents of the imperial treasury, were made over by Mohammed Shah to the conqueror. The principal nobles, imitating the example of the monarch, gave up all the money and valuables which they possessed.[1] This exaction, after a great battle lost, severe as it seems, bears no comparison to Benhadad's demand upon those who had not struck a blow against him. He not only required as much as this, but demanded the persons of wives and children, and exacted a right of search equivalent to pillage, throughout the city of Samaria. Twenty-four hours were given to Ahab to consider this proposal. There is reason to think that he would have consented even to this, so abject had he become in spirit; but the elders of his council, whom he was obliged to consult, together with the general voice of the people, stimulated him to resist this insolence. Yielding to this counteracting force laid upon his facile temper, he replies with some spirit, though with less than became the occasion: "Tell my lord the king, All that thou didst send for at the first, I will do ; but this thing I may not do." This looks very much like an intimation that he would even in this have yielded, had not the public voice forbidden—

"Letting, I dare not; wait upon, I would,"—

as was often the case with this king. We do not like this renewed offer to consent to the first demand. Now, beholding the spirit and temper of the people, he might well have been stimulated to some more courageous course. But he was at this disadvantage, that he could not, as had been the custom of kings and judges in Israel, appeal to the Lord for protection and assistance. This had been their strength in weakness, and their victory in conflict. But in Ahab we do not expect this true Hebrew faith; and we fail to find in him even the mere human qualities of kingly greatness.

Tame as this reply seems to us, it affronted the pride of the great Benhadad, who sent back the thrasonical answer, that he would reduce Samaria to dust, which would then not suffice to give

handfuls to all the men of his numerous host. The answer of Ahab to this hectoring boast, was neat, noble, and significant: " Tell him, Let not him that girdeth on his harness, boast himself as he that putteth it off." This sensible and spirited answer, divested also of the former preamble— "Tell him," not, "tell my lord the king,"—goes some way to restore Ahab to our good opinion. It is clear that his spirit was now fairly up, and it would appear that his feelings were taking a right direction.

The scene now changes to the luxurious camp of Benhadad, where the king, though it was scarcely yet high noon, was, with his allied tributary princes (thirty-two in number), drinking in the pavilions; a remarkable touch of description at such a time, serving to convey a distinct idea of the habits of the leaders of this great army. It was when thus engaged that the king received Ahab's reproving answer. In human writing, it would be regarded as a noble stroke of literary art, that nothing is said of the Syrian king's feelings, his wrath, his indignation. He says nothing, his astonishment and rage are too big for words, and are intimated only in the effects, in the laconic military order given in a single word—"Set," or "Place,"—which we are obliged to paraphrase into several, in order to give it its probable meaning. "Set yourselves in array," or, in other words, invest the city. This absence of oral abuse or expressed anger, save as implied in the command to proceed to the instant punishment of the offender, is exceedingly fine. The celebrated instance—

"Off with his head !—So much for Buckingham,"

is exceeded by this in the proportion which exists between one word and eight. Benhadad meant much the same; but one word sufficed to express his feeling and his purpose.

The order was obeyed; and it was at this juncture that a prophet stood forth to promise victory, in the name of the Lord, against this great multitude, and to direct the course that should be taken. The king was all submission and acquiescence, for he saw no other help, and dreamed not of looking in this emergency to Baal. Thus instructed, two hundred and thirty-two young men, attendants on the princes of the provinces, or, as an old version (Rogers's) has it, of the "shrifes, (sheriffs) of the shires," went boldly out to the enemy, while seven thousand more, probably volunteers, followed at some distance behind, or,

---

[1] There was a massacre afterwards ; but this was only when the inhabitants had risen upon the Persian troops. The prisoners were also required to pay their arrears of tribute to the conqueror, which produced much suffering to the inhabitants ; but this was chiefly through the villany of the *native* agents, who, to enrich themselves, extorted from the people four or five times as much as they paid into the treasury of Nadir.

it is likely, remained at the gate ready to march out to support the others.

The Syrian king was still at his cups, when the watchmen reported that men were coming out of the city; on which, with quiet indifference, which seems characteristic of his arrogant temper, or might be the effect of his wine, he simply directed that they should be taken alive, whether they came for peace or for war. He probably wished to learn from them the state of the city and the intentions of Ahab; but the direction, given without any question as to their numbers, indicates the most sovereign, if not sottish, indifference to any force that Samaria could send forth. To take them alive was, however, much easier said than done. The young men had no mind to be taken. On the contrary, they smote right and left, and presently laid prostrate those who stood against them. This, with the sight of the seven thousand behind coming out of the gates to take part in the fray, struck the Syrian host with a sudden panic, and they fled with all their might, the arrogant king himself being not the hindmost, for he hastened away on a fleet horse.

This was the Lord's doing; but we do not hear of any thanksgivings and sacrifices offered to Him in gratitude for help to which they had so little claim.

———

THE GOD OF THE HILLS

1 Kings 20:22-23

WHEN the Syrians were beyond harm's reach, they began to speculate upon the causes of their extraordinary and most humbling discomfiture. As they saw no adequate human cause, they rightly referred the matter to the power of the God of Israel. Who the God of Israel was, they perhaps did not distinctly know; and, in fact, from the corrupt state of religion among the Israelites, it might be difficult to discover what god they worshipped. With this the Syrians probably did not much concern themselves. But their reasoning upon this conclusion is curious to us, although perfectly natural to them, who entertained the belief in the merely local power of particular deities: "Their gods are gods" [or "their god is a god"] "of the hills, therefore they

were stronger than we; but let us fight against them in the plain, and surely we shall be stronger than they."

Believing that the God of Israel was merely a national god like their own, and that, like theirs, His power was limited by local or other circumstances, it was easy for them to infer that He was a God of the hills and not of the valleys. Their impression in this matter may have arisen from the traditional knowledge, that this God had given His law to His people from Mount Sinai; that on a mountain had died their great lawgiver, and their first high pontiff. They must also have heard of the recent miraculous manifestation of His power upon Mount Carmel; and they saw that Canaan was a mountainous country, with all its chief cities seated upon hills. All these recollections may have had their foundation in the fact, that the parts of the country into which they had ventured were unsuited to chariots, in which their military force seems to have chiefly consisted; and in the conclusion, that if they kept more exclusively to the plains and valleys, a very different result might be expected.

In the parcelling out of the earth by paganism among national and territorial gods, and among gods who presided over the various forms, and powers, and qualities of nature, we find many gods of the mountains, and some, but not so many, of the valleys. At the present day the Hindoos have their gods of the hills, and also of the lower places. Thus Siva, Vishnu, and Murraga-Murte, are those of the high places; while Vyravar, Urruttera, and many demons are the deities of the lower regions. So in classical antiquity we meet with Collina, the goddess of hills, and Vallina, of valleys. We also hear of the god Montinus, and of a god Peninus, who had his name from a part of the Alps so called, where he was worshipped, and where also the goddess Penina was honoured. Even Jupiter had names from mountains, as Olympius, Capitolinus, etc.; and the "great universal Pan" is called "mountainous Pan" by Sophocles. Some have expressed surprise that the Syrians should have conceived their own god to be a god of the valleys—supposing this an admission of inferiority. We see not this; and as the greater part of their territory was level country, and the capital was seated in one of the finest plains in the world, they could scarcely, when they came to this mode of reasoning, and compared the difference between the two countries, arrive at any other conclusion. This was, however, a conclusion ruinous to them; for this attempt "to limit the Holy One of Israel," by making Him a mere God of mountains, rendered it necessary that He should vindicate His universal power and the honour of His own great name. This is, indeed, assigned by the prophet, who promised another and a crowning victory, as the reason for the Lord's further and decisive interposition in behalf of a people who had so little deserved His care.

The king had been forewarned of this second invasion, and was not now taken unprepared, though his utmost preparations bore no comparison to the Syrian power. This time, however, he concluded he would not be again shut up in Samaria, but that the contest should be in the open country. The Syrians, firm to their purpose, chose a route which led them through the plains and valleys—though this was necessarily circuitous—and would not be drawn among the hills, although the presence of the Israelites attending their march upon the hills tempted them to action. Six days this caution was maintained on both sides; but on the seventh day they came to blows, as it would seem, by the Israelites venturing down from the hills to give battle, undeterred by the chariots which were so formidable in the plains. On this occasion, we are told that the army of Israel appeared in comparison "like two little flocks of kids,"—a significant simile, flocks of goats being smaller than those of sheep; and they were not only flocks of goats, but of small (or young) goats or kids; and not only flocks of kids, but little flocks; and not only little flocks, but "two little flocks"—"two" being, as we have already explained, an epithet applied to a small number.

Again, through the might of the Lord, were the Israelites victorious. They fell upon the Syrians with great vigour, and slew large numbers of them. The rest fled, and sought shelter in Aphek, which they appear to have taken on their march. But even here many of them were crushed beneath a wall which fell upon them. The wall was probably cast down by an earthquake. Hither Benhadad himself came, and withdrew to an inner chamber to hide his sorrow and his shame. There was no chance of escape; nor, since the wall had fallen, was there any de-

fence for the city against the pursuers. The case was manifestly desperate; and there was no hope but in throwing himself upon the clemency of Ahab. Remembering how roughly the old theocratists had been wont to handle their captives, there might well have been room for a doubt even in this; but the servants of Benhadad assured him that they had heard the kings of Israel were merciful kings—which we take to mean that the present and some past kings of Israel had manifested so much sympathy for, and friendly feeling towards, foreign idolaters, that there was little probability of his being harshly treated.

Benhadad accordingly sent ambassadors to meet Ahab, for the purpose of begging his life—nothing more than life: but with injunctions to note the manner in which the application was received, and to frame their demeanour accordingly. Ambassadors charged with such a suit are wont to present themselves in a pitiful plight, in order to express their affliction, and to move compassion. In the present case the messengers not only clad themselves in sackcloth, but appeared with ropes about their necks. This, though probably an old custom of suppliants —intended to express that their fate lay in the hands of him before whom they appeared—is here for the first time mentioned in Scripture; but we see prisoners of war strung together by ropes around their necks in the sculptures of ancient Egypt and Persia. In the present and such like cases, it seems to express their entire helplessness and dependence upon the king's mercy. He might hang them up if he liked; and here were the ropes ready for him to do it with. Or it may be that, as we see captives were thus dealt with, they appeared tied together by the necks to show that they were prisoners of war.

The language of the ambassadors corresponded with their appearance. "Thy servant Benhadad saith, I pray thee, let me live,"—language in very edifying contrast with the former arrogance of this same Benhadad. But it has always been observed that the men most arrogant in prosperity, are in adversity the most abject and cast down. So it was now. The easy-tempered Ahab was moved to commiseration at this marked change of language and fortune in his greatest enemy; and yielding, as usual, to the impression of the moment, he said quickly, "Is he yet alive?

He is my brother." The men, keenly watching the impression made on his mind, caught eagerly at these words, and replied, "Thy brother Benhadad liveth." On this, he desired him to be called, and on his appearance took him up into his own chariot. Eventually he was restored to liberty on his own terms—namely, allowing the Israelites to have a quarter in which they might observe their own laws, customs, and worship in Damascus, and giving up the northern towns that had been formerly taken from Israel.

At the first view, one is rather favourably impressed with this clemency of Ahab towards the great enemy of his country. But as we afterwards perceive that it was visited with the divine displeasure, we are obliged to examine it more closely. We may then find that what might have been magnanimity becomes in reality a gross weakness; and that the generosity, which might entitle a man to praise if shown towards a private enemy, may become a crime in a king towards a public adversary. It corresponds to the case of Agag whom Saul spared, but whom Samuel slew. The Lord had appointed this man to "utter destruction;" and Ahab knew it. He was appointed to taste the utmost dregs of that calamity with which the Governor of the world so often punishes the pride of kings. He was to be taught to know, in avenging justice, the greatness of that God he had blasphemed; and the power of the state which he ruled was to be so broken as to render it incapable of giving further trouble to Israel. All these public duties Ahab had neglected, to gratify a private sentiment; and, doubtless, from a sympathy with idolatry, which it ill became a king of Israel to show. It was in this that he offended; and his offence was great. To view it rightly, we must look to the misery thereafter caused to Israel by the very power which he threw away this opportunity of rendering harmless; and with peculiar intensity must we regard the fact that, a few years after, Ahab met his death in battle with the very king whom he thus befriended, and under the orders of that king to his soldiers to aim their weapons exclusively against the life of the man who had spared his own.

Suppose that five-and-thirty years ago, when the great troubler of Europe was brought a prisoner to our shores, the Regent had (allowing him to have been in his power) behaved like Ahab in setting him free. No doubt, some sentimentalists would have applauded his "magnanimity" towards the greatest enemy his country had ever known. But Europe would have mourned his "weakness;" and his people would have execrated it, if, as is likely, instead of the longest peace known in their history, the thirty-five subsequent years had been marked with trouble, distress, confusion, warfare, rapine, and blood; and the Regent would doubtless have experienced from this "Themistocles" gratitude of the same quality as that which Ahab received from the Syrian king.

***

In connection with the "magnanimity of Ahab," it may be observed, that " his vanity was gratified at having so powerful a monarch, suitor for his life, at his hand. The feeling of brotherhood was even then existing among crowned heads, and on hearing that the King of Syria had escaped the destruction of his army, he thoughtlessly recognized the tie as still existing between them. "Is he yet alive ? He is my brother." Benhadad's servants were eagerly watching what Ahab would say, and quickly caught up this reassuring word, — repeating it, "thy brother Benhadad"—thus fastening him to this implied recognition of amity. Oriental laws of honour forbad the retraction of the pledge. By the Oriental laws of *dakheel*, still in force, any one is, at any time, entitled to put himself under the protection of another, be that other his friend, or his greatest enemy : and if the man applied to, does not at once reject him, if the slightest form of friendly speech pass between the two, the bond is complete, and must not be broken. If two enemies meet and exchange the *salam aleikum*, even by mistake, there is peace between them, and they will not fight. If a man be pursued by an enemy, or even be on the ground, he can save his life by calling out *dakheel*, unless there be blood between them (Layard's *Nineveh and Babylon*, 317, 318). "Benhadad's friends were on the watch to obtain for him *dakheel*, and the simple phrase, 'he is my brother,' though perhaps thoughtlessly uttered, having been accepted by them on his part, was sufficient to complete the bond, and secure the life of the captive." Professor Rawlinson, *Speaker's Commentary, in loco.—Bible Educator*, iii., 337.

S.

***

NABOTH'S VINEYARD

1 Kings 21-22

ALTHOUGH Samaria was the metropolis of his kingdom, Ahab had a palace at Jezreel, where he seems to have resided during part of the year. This palace was situated on the heights at the western extremity of Mount Gilboa. on the eastern borders of the plain of Esdraelon, and about twenty-five miles north of Samaria. It was the Windsor of Israel. It is a fine site for a town, and commands a wide and noble view, overlooking on the west the whole of the great plain to the long ridge of Carmel, and extending in the opposite direction down the broad low valley to Bethshean, and towards the mountains of Ajlun beyond the Jordan.

One day it struck Ahab, that the garden at this place would be greatly improved by an enlargement which would take in an adjoining vineyard. He therefore caused application to be made to the owner, whose name was Naboth, stating his wish to turn this vineyard into "a garden of herbs;" and, as became a king, offered him another vineyard in exchange for it, or any price that he might choose to ask for it. But Naboth, strong in his indefeasible right of property, declined—somewhat bluntly, it seems—to part with it at all, on any terms, on the ground that he could not, and would not, alienate a property which he had derived from his fathers, and which it behoved him to transmit to his descendants. In fact, Naboth seems to have regarded the proposal with a kind of religious horror, and did not mind letting the king see that he did so. There was ground for this in the peculiar tenure by which land was held in Israel. At the original occupation of Canaan, every family had a portion of land assigned it by lot, the size of which was proportioned to the number in the family.

These portions remained in the family, and could not legally be alienated but for a term of years, ending at the next jubilee year, when all lands that had been thus leased reverted to the original owners or to their heirs. We know that the observance of the sabbatic year had by this time fallen into disuse, and so, doubtless, had the jubilee year. Yet the solemnity of the distribution, and its unalterable character, coupled with its beneficent object, in securing to every family an indefeasible right to the land originally bestowed from the Lord Himself, who insisted on being regarded as the sovereign proprietor of the soil, must have fixed in the public mind a feeling of something like a religious duty in retaining possession of inherited property. The disuse, however, of the jubilee as a national institution, must have contributed to loosen the force of this obligation in the minds of weak or careless

persons; and it is likely that many sold their lands in perpetuity. It is true this would be illegal; but Britain is not the only country where possession constitutes nine points of the law; and few heirs probably would, at the jubilee year, stand forth to assert their claim to lands held by kings and other high personages. In this way, and by means of the estates of persons attainted of treason, which lapsed to the king, the crown was eventually enabled to acquire considerable landed property, which would have been impossible had due attention been paid to the law of Moses, by which the land was strictly tied up in private hands, in order that none should have too much, nor any too little. These practices, by which "field was added to field," are severely reprehended by the prophets, whose reprehension of them proves their existence.

It is creditable to Ahab, unless it may have have been the mere result of his passive character, that he, of himself, thought not of securing, by any tyrannous or violent act, the land which Naboth had so steadily refused to sell. But his own garden, in which he had hitherto taken much pleasure, lost all value and beauty in his eyes, since the nice plan he had framed for its improvement was baulked by the churlishness of his neighbour. We should not wonder if he decapitated with his staff half the flowers in his parterres, while this fit of ill humour was upon him. It gathered strength with indulgence, till at last he betook himself to his bed, and lay with his face to the wall, refusing to take any food. This pitiable display of childish fretfulness is something more than we should have expected, even from Ahab. No wonder such a man as this was a mere tool in the hands of his wife. It is not unlikely that, relying upon her power of action, and her fertility of resource, he indulged his ill humour on purpose to draw her attention to the matter, that she might learn, in answer to her inquiries, that which he was unwilling to carry to her spontaneously as a matter of complaint.

She came to him as soon as she heard of his strange behaviour, and soon learned the cause of his affliction; when she exclaimed, with indignant surprise, "Dost thou now govern the kingdom of Israel?" But she did not belie his confidence in her resources; for she immediately added, "Arise and eat bread, and let thine heart be merry, for *I will give thee the vineyard.*"

She!—how? Ahab did not care to inquire; he only knew she had said it, and would do it; and that was enough for him. He gave her authority to act as she pleased in the matter, by entrusting to her his signet, which gave her the power of issuing in his name whatever orders she liked. It will be remembered that in giving validity to documents, names were not in those days, nor are they now in the East, signed by the hand in writing, but impressed by a seal on which the name is engraved. Hence the importance which is attached to the signet throughout the sacred books.

Thus armed, Jezebel sent orders into the city, that two lawless men should be provided, who at a public assembly should stand up and accuse Naboth of cursing God and the king; and that they should forthwith proceed to execute judgment upon him. Dreading Jezebel's resentment, and having their consciences seared by corrupting idolatries, the elders of Jezreel obeyed this atrocious mandate; and soon Jezebel was enabled to come and tell her husband that she had accomplished her task; and that he might go down and take possession of the coveted vineyard, for the owner was stoned and dead. The estate of Naboth had lapsed to the crown by his execution on the charge of treason, or cursing the king; for which reason that charge had doubtless been added to the other, which was of itself capital. Instead of shrinking with horror from the deed, Ahab, now that it was done, accepted it with all its consequences, by hasting to take possession of his blood-stained acquisition, probably not without a secret, or even declared, admiration of his wife's decision of character and hardihood —qualities which inspire such souls as his with deep reverence.

But One whom Ahab had forgotten had noted all this; and when he went to the vineyard he found there—Elijah! and from his mouth received his doom—the overthrow and ruin of his house, and the terrific announcement that "where dogs licked the blood of Naboth, shall dogs lick thy blood, even thine."

Ahab was not, like his wife, hardened. These words struck him down, and humbled him completely. He rent his clothes; he assumed the habit of a mourner; he "fasted and lay in sackcloth and went softly." His misery was real, and the Lord had some compassion on him; for the destruction

of his house was deferred, that his eyes might be spared that doleful sight. But his personal doom was accomplished three years after, when he was slain in battle against Benhadad. His body was

THE DEATH OF AHAB

brought to Samaria; and when his chariot and armour were washed in the pool of Samaria, the dogs licked up the blood, as they had done that of Naboth at Jezreel.[1] His death was kingly, and became him better than his life. When mortally wounded, he directed his chariot to be quietly driven aside that he might have his wounds dressed; and then returned to the battle, supported in his chariot, until the evening, when he died.

Jezebel was a high-minded, proud, revengeful woman; as strong in will as she was imperious in temper, influencing her husband, who in natural endowments was of inferior mould, and prompting him to do, what without her, he would not have had nerve enough to accomplish. The parallel between her character and influence, and the character and influence of Lady Macbeth, is very obvious, and has been pointed out again and again. She was the evil star of her husband, and of Israel. Her marriage with Ahab turned the current of his kingdom's history. She brought with her the idolatries and superstitions of her native country, and her policy was to make Samaria like Phœnicia. (See Vol. 1, pp. 887-889). Her

[1] The words of Elijah, "*Where* dogs licked the blood of Naboth, shall dogs lick thy blood," were literally accomplished in his son, to whom his doom was in some sense transferred on his humiliation; and it was virtually thus accomplished in Ahab. The words may mean no more than that dogs should lick his blood, even as they had licked the blood of Naboth.

evil genius continued to trouble the people after her husband's death ; and her wild licence and magical fascination became proverbial. (2 Kings ix. 22). Her terrible decision comes out in the words, " As surely as thou art Elijah and I am Jezebel, so may God do to me, and more also, if by this time to-morrow I make not thy life as the life of one of them." (1 Kings xix. 2, Sept. Version). " Dost *thou* now govern the kingdom of Israel—*play the king*. Arise and eat bread, and let thine heart be merry, and *I* will give thee the vineyard of Naboth, the Jezreelite." (1 Kings xxi. 7, Sept. Version). There appears Lady Macbeth, and a still earlier personation of feminine pride and power, Clytemnestra. (See art. on "Jezebel" in Smith's *Bible Dictionary*).

S.

THE MANTLE

2 Kings 1; 1 Kings 19:15-21

AHAZIAH, who succeeded his father Ahab in the throne of Israel, did not reign more than two years. He was entirely under the influence of his mother, and sanctioned the idolatries she had introduced. His death was the result of a disaster that befell him, described as a fall through a lattice that was in his upper chamber—which would suggest that he fell through the open window into the court below. Some think that he fell through a sky-light on the top of his palace ; but there are no sky-lights to Eastern houses. The word rendered " lattice " may be a " rail,"—which may suggest that, in leaning against the rail, forming the inner fence of the house-top (the outer, towards the street, being usually a wall, and the inner, towards the interior court, a light rail of wood), it gave way, and he fell into the court below. Such accidents frequently occur in the East ; and the risk of such an occurrence taking place is constantly presented to the mind of one who walks on the house tops, until use begets insensibility to the danger.

The hurts which the king received in his fall

were serious enough to occasion doubts of his recovery; and he therefore, like one thoroughly imbued with idolatrous sentiments, sent messengers to the oracle of Baalzebub, the fly-god of Ekron,[1]

BAALZEBUB ON SILVER COIN OF ARADUS. to inquire if he should recover. They came back much sooner with

[1] This idol has been noticed already under Baal, 1 Kg. 16:32. See Vol. 1, (p. 890). Although Ekron was in the

an answer than he expected; for they had been encountered by a prophet, who sent them back with the doom that he should never more rise from his bed, seeing he had forgotten there was a God in Israel, and had sent to learn his fate from the paltry idol of Ekron. It is clear that his proper course would have been to send to a prophet of the Lord to inquire of him, if the proud stomach of a king of Israel could not brook the still more becoming course of sending to the temple of Jerusalem, to inquire of the Lord through the appointed agencies and regular ministers. To send to Baalzebub implied, or left it to the heathen to infer, that there was no God in Israel who could or would satisfy him, and was therefore a deep affront to Jehovah.

The men did not know who it was that had met them; but on their describing his dress and appearance—" a hairy man, girt with a girdle of leather about his loins,"—the king at once said, " It is Elijah the Tishbite." It is understood that the hairiness ascribed to the prophet is to be referred, not to his person, but his mantle —made of hair, which, with the girdle of leather, formed the cheap, durable, and humble attire of the prophets. Instead of having its proper effect upon Ahaziah's mind, this discovery only exasperated him ; and he forthwith sent an officer with fifty men to bring Elijah before him. What was his purpose we know not; but from his sending a troop of soldiers, and from the result that followed, it could not have been good. Very likely the king's design was to destroy him, unless he recalled the sentence he had pronounced; for by this time there had come to be a strong conviction throughout the land that whatever the prophet said *must* come to pass. The awful destruction by fire from heaven—that is, we suppose by lightning—at the word of Elijah, of the first two parties sent to apprehend him, must have tended powerfully to impress upon the nation the fact that the Lord still asserted His right to reign over them, and would be known to them in His protesting judgments, since they would not know Him in His mercies. Elijah's

territory of the Philistines—not in that of the Phœnicians —their idolatries seem to have been in most respects identical ; and it is remarkable that we find on a silver coin of Aradus (the Arvad of Scripture), which belonged to the Phœnicians, an insect figure, which may be presumed to have some reference to this idol.

cheerfully going with the third party, the leader of which approached him with humble entreaties, must have suggested that the door to those mercies was still open to all who becomingly approached it. This was practical preaching, of the kind that this people could most easily understand. The fearless prophet repeated in person to the king the words of rebuke and death that he had sent by the messengers; and the doomed king was too awe-struck, after what had passed, to make any attempt upon his life or liberty.

According to his prediction, Ahaziah died soon after, and, as he had no son, was succeeded by his brother Jehoram.

Elijah had now, and for some time before, a personal follower or attendant—one of those so well known in the East, and in ancient history, who are the disciples and followers of a holy or learned man, and who, although they may themselves be persons of some consideration in the world, feel glad and honoured in being allowed to discharge for their master the light servile duties which his habits of life require, but which they would feel it a degradation to render to any other man. This person was Elisha, the son of Shaphat, of Abel Meholah beyond the Jordan—a name scarcely less illustrious than that of Elijah. The latter had in Horeb received the command to anoint Hazael as king of Syria, and Jehu as king of Israel, and this Elisha to be prophet in his own room. The last of these offices only he performed in person, leaving the rest to his successor. This Elisha was the son of a substantial landowner, as appears by the fact that, although the prophet found him personally engaged in the field, he was ploughing with no less than twelve yoke of oxen. This is, no doubt, intentionally mentioned, for to this day in Syria a man's wealth is estimated by the number of ploughs which he works, or by the yokes or pairs of cattle he employs in drawing them. As Elijah passed, he, without any previous intimation, slipped his mantle from his shoulders and threw it over those of Elisha. This was a summons equivalent to that which our Saviour addressed to His disciples—" Leave all, and follow me!"—and it was more than this, for it implied that the person thus addressed was to succeed the man who called him. It was his investiture with his present heirship to, and the assurance of his future possession of, that very mantle. And to this day in the East, a reputed saint, when departing from life, indicates his successor by bequeathing to him his mantle, the symbol of his spiritual power; and although that mantle may be dirty, patched, tattered, or threadbare, it is deemed to be of higher price than the brocade robes of kings; and the older it is the more precious it becomes. Elisha well understood the sign, and appreciated the distinction conferred upon him at its true value, by leaving his home to follow the prophet, after he had given an extemporaneous feast to the field labourers, and to others who had come from the town, by slaying a yoke of the oxen, and burning the agricultural instruments to dress the meat.

He then took his departure with Elijah, who must have been much comforted by the company of such a friend and follower; and who was doubtless most thankful to the Lord for thus providing for him one much better fitted to be his helper than the " servant " he had left behind at Beersheba.

Until Elisha became distinguished on his own account, he was known as the " Elisha who poured water on the hands of Elijah." This was a servile office, and might be understood of any servant. The Easterns, in washing, never, if they can help it, dip their hands in water unless it be running water, as they abhor the idea of using in this form water which has been already soiled. To pour the water upon the hands from a vessel, requires the assistance of another; and this is usually the office of a servant, and the most frequent one he

EGYPTIAN BASIN AND EWER

has to render to his master—which makes the phrase, " who poured water upon the hands," appropriately descriptive of a personal attendant. Friends, neighbours, and fellow-travellers often, however, pour water on each other's hands in the absence of a servant, as it is exceedingly inconvenient to fill one hand repeatedly with water from a vessel held in the other, and which is laid frequently down to be taken up again. No one washes thus who can find any one willing to pour water on his hands. Indoors, a ewer and basin of tinned copper are commonly used. The water poured from the ewer upon the hands, falls into the basin held below them, which generally has a perforated false bottom through which the used water passes out of sight. The same kind of ewer and basin as are now in use, we find represented on the most ancient monuments of Egypt.

Elijah's mantle in the hand of Elisha became the instrument of dividing the waters of Jordan. The mantle was a cape of sheepskin. The latter having caught it from his ascending master, who rolled it up like a staff—so the original word (2 Kings ii. 8) signifies—would probably imitate him, and with it struck the waters, as Moses, with his rod, smote the Red Sea. A cycle of miracles gathers round the history of the first great Lawgiver and his successor Joshua; and another, like a brilliant halo, encircles the names of the first great prophet, and his disciple Elisha.

It has been acutely remarked, that as Elijah appears a true Bedouin, or child of the desert, dwelling in the clefts of Cherith, among the wild bushes of the wilderness, in the solitudes of Horeb, and on the summit of Mount Carmel, Elisha is at home in civilized life, taking up his abode in cities. He is found dwelling at Samaria and at Dothan. He has a house with doors and windows (2 Kings vi. 32; xiii. 17). He occupies the furnished bed chamber of the lady of Shunem; he is on friendly terms with the king of Israel, the Captain of the host, and the General of Damascus. "The touches of the narrative are very slight, but we can gather that his dress was the ordinary garment of an Israelite, the *beged*, probably similar in form to the long *abbeyeh* of the modern Syrians (2 Kings 11, 12); that his hair was worn trimmed behind [so as to be called baldheaded], in contrast to the disordered locks of Elijah, and that he used a walking staff, of the kind ordinarily carried by grave or aged citizens."—Smith's *Dictionary of the Bible*. Art. "Elijah" and "Elisha."

Further, it may be here noticed that in the same article from which these illustrations of Elisha's life are taken, there is this suggestive remark: "The ordinary meaning put upon the expression, 'a double portion of thy spirit,' is that Elisha possessed double the power of Elijah. This, though sanctioned by the renderings of the Vulgate and Luther, and adopted by a long series of commentators from St. Ephrem Syrus to pastor Krummacher, would appear not to be the real force of the words. The Hebrew words, literally 'a mouth of two,' a double mouthful, is the phrase employed in Deut. xxi. 17 to denote the amount of a father's goods which were the right and token of a first-born son. Thus the gift of 'the double portion' of Elijah's spirit was but the legitimate conclusion of the act of adoption which began with the casting of the mantle at

Abelmeholah years before."—"For a curious calculation by St. Peter Damianus that Elijah performed twelve miracles, and Elisha twenty-four."—See *Acta Sanctorum*, July 20; Smith's *Dictionary of the Bible*, i. 535.

S.

HEAVENWARD

2 Kings 2:1-15

IT is clear that a great day is come. The young men in the schools of the prophets at Gilgal, at Bethel, and at Jericho, are in unusual agitation. Elijah visits them all in succession. His manner is that day even more than commonly solemn, and his countenance and converse more heavenward; and all his demeanour seems to say, "Ye shall see my face no more." They fear to question their great master; but they venture to whisper to Elisha the inquiry, If he knows that his master and theirs was that day to be taken away? They seemed to want his confirmation of a fact of which they had received a Divine intimation, but feared to misapprehend. His answer was, "Yea, I know it. Hold ye your peace." Being aware of this, Elisha resolves not to quit his master that day, notwithstanding Elijah plainly declares a wish to proceed alone. Whether this were to try the depth of Elisha's affection and zeal, or in actual ignorance that others would be allowed to witness the approaching event, cannot be said; but it may be that he knew not that the matter had been revealed, not only to Elisha, but to the "sons of the prophets." But his faithful and devoted follower will not thus be dismissed. For once he ventures to decline obedience to one whose wish had hitherto been a law to him. He refuses to discontinue his attendance, with the gentle and respectful persistence of one who will not be dissuaded from seeing his friend yet further on his way.

They came to the Jordan, for even an Elijah must cross the Jordan before he passes from the world, though it be not by the gates of death. But, lo, a wonder!—the prophet takes his mantle, and smites therewith the stream, which then divides to let the friends pass. This, with what ensued, was witnessed by fifty of the sons of the prophets, who, though they durst not obtrude their presence, watched the doings of the friends from the distant hills. Here again was faith: but Elijah knew that seas, rivers, and mountains are no obstruction to him who, with stedfast feet, walks in the path of duty. It was because he was in that path, and because *he knew* that what he asked was in accordance with God's will, that his faith was met by miracles, which, apart from these conditions, it had been presumption in him to demand. Faith must have the word or promise of God on which to rest. It is in this we discern the difference between the sublime and effectual faith of the devout Elijah, and the insane pretensions of such men as William Hackett (afterwards hanged), who, in the reign of Elizabeth, had the hardihood to declare, that if all England prayed for rain, and he himself prayed against it, there would be dry weather. "Thou, Lord," he said, "hast the power, and I have the faith—therefore it shall be done!"

It was when they had passed the Jordan that the departing prophet asked his faithful disciple what last favour he desired of him. This was a trying question, which few would be able promptly to answer with entire satisfaction to their afterthoughts. But Elisha knew that of spiritual blessings too much could not be asked. He therefore said, "Let a double portion of thy spirit be upon me." His master confessed that this was a hard thing; but that it would be granted, if he took care to be present at the moment of separation. But what was that double portion of Elijah's spirit which his disciple desired? One would think that it expressed the possession of such qualities as should make him twice as great a prophet as his master. But it was not so; for although Elisha became a great prophet, and wrought miracles as great as those of Elijah, and in greater number, no one feels that he was greater as a prophet or as a man than his master—or so great. His meaning is explained by the fact, that the heir was entitled to a double portion of his father's goods; hence, in asking for the double portion of his master's spirit, Elisha meant to claim the heirship or succession to Elijah in his place as prophet in Israel. He had reason to suppose that it was meant for him; but he wished to be assured of this by some token which should be satisfactory to himself and others.

As they went on, conversing of high things, suddenly a whirlwind reft Elijah from his companion, and he was borne aloft like an exhalation, in a chariot with horses of fire, or glowing like fire, to heaven, followed by the cry of the forsaken disciple, as he rent his clothes, "My father, my

ELIJAH TAKEN UP INTO HEAVEN

father! the chariot of Israel, and the horsemen thereof!"—meaning, as is generally understood, that he regarded Israel as bereft of its strength, its chariot, and its horsemen, by the departure of this great prophet. He failed not, however, to take up the precious mantle which fell from Elijah as he rose; and he felt, in the beating of his own heart, the assurance that his prayer had been granted. And he knew it still more when he reached and smote the waters with the mantle. At first, it seems, there was no response; but when he repeated the stroke, with the words, "Where is the Lord God of Elijah?" the waters separated, and he passed over. The sons of the prophets noted this on their distant watch, and recognized by this sign their new master on whom rested the spirit of Elijah.

This is a strange transaction, and we cannot hope as yet to understand it fully. It seems to us, however, that it is but an isolated anticipation of that which shall happen collectively to the righteous that are alive on the earth at our Lord's second coming. "The dead in Christ shall rise first: then we which are alive and remain, shall be caught up together with them in the clouds, to meet the Lord in the air: and so shall we ever be with the Lord." (1 Thess. iv. 16, 17.) And "in that sudden strange transition," the body will undergo a change divesting it of its earthly essence, and bringing it into conformity with the glorified bodies of the saints raised from the dead,

For the same apostle, alluding in another place to the same great transaction, says: "The dead shall be raised incorruptible, and we [who are then alive] *shall be changed.* For this corruptible must put on incorruption, and this mortal immortality." And he had said before, "Behold, I show you a mystery: We shall not all sleep [die], but we shall all be changed." (1 Cor. xv. 51-53.) Then what hinders that this rapture of the living, and change in the act of rapture—change, because flesh and blood cannot inherit the kingdom of God, which is to take place on so large a scale on *that* great day—should be exemplified in one or two instances before—in this instance of Elijah, and in the earlier instance of Enoch?

Under this view, there is no more any objection to the departed Elijah having his place in heaven, seeing that his body must have undergone all that change which was needful to fit it for abiding in that place where nothing corruptible can exist. Not discerning this, the old schoolmen were of opinion, that Elijah was taken to some place—doubtless a pleasant place—prepared of old, as they supposed, for those pious spirits which awaited the coming of the Messiah, who should open paradise for them. Others have staggered at that text, John iii. 13, understanding it to allege that none ascended to heaven before Christ. Hence they imagine that Elijah was taken to "Abraham's bosom," which they conceive to be an intermediate state in the air—granting, however, that his garments were burned in the fire, and his body changed and made immortal. But is *that* really a staggering text? We think not. It is not usually supposed to refer to the ascension at all; but allowing it to have that reference, it could only mean that none of the *dead* should ascend to heaven before Christ, seeing that He was the first-fruits of *them that slept,* that is, that died. But Elijah did not die.

Elijah is supposed by the Jews to be frequently employed in missions to mankind, and as in some sense ubiquitous, being present in many places at one time. He is visible only to those deeply versed in the Cabbala, and is described as a venerable old man with a long beard. He is supposed to be always present at circumcisions, and there is a chair kept vacant for him. Those who are the special objects of his notice are highly favoured. "Happy," says one, "is he who hath beheld him in dreams, happy he who hath saluted him with peace, and to whom the saluta-

tion of peace hath been returned." One of the Jewish commentators, Abarbanel, has explained how Elijah became qualified for these missions. "He was carried away in a powerful wind, with a chariot and horses of fire, that his moisture might be exhaled and dried away. Thus he became light and swift, to appear in all places. He has no need of meat or drink, or of anything necessary to human life, because his body was transformed into a spiritual state, and he received a spiritual nature."

Elijah is unquestionably one of the grandest characters in Old Testament history. The sacred writers attempt no regular biography of the great prophet; and yet, by the vividness of their fragmentary notices, he is made to stand out before us with more distinctness than any other of their heroes. In person he was stalwart and commanding; his face, neck, chest, arms, and legs deeply bronzed by exposure to the sun and weather, and covered with hair. Trained amid the mountains of Gilead; from boyhood inured to toil and fatigue; roaming free with his semi-nomad brethren in the forests, and over the vast plains of Gilead and Moab—Elijah felt alike at home amid the fastnesses of Carmel, in the wilderness of Sinai, and bounding across the plain of Esdraelon by the side of Ahab's chariot. His only robe was the shaggy sheepskin mantle, such as is worn to this day by his countrymen; and it was bound round the waist, after the Arab style, by a leathern girdle. His language, like that of a modern Bedawy poet, was abrupt, pointed, and eloquent, occasionally seasoned with cutting irony. His movements were rapid, and his visits sudden and startling as those of an Arab of the desert. His courage, when in the way of duty, no danger, no human threats could daunt. His warnings aud rebukes were delivered with a boldness and daring unequalled even in sacred history. There must have been something most intensely thrilling in those sudden appearances of the prophet before the timid and startled monarch, when he charged him, "I have not troubled Israel; but thou, and thy father's house;" and when he pronounced his doom, and that of his wicked queen: "The dogs shall eat Jezebel by the wall of Jezreel. Him that' dieth of Ahab in the city the dogs shall eat; and him that dieth in the field shall the fowls of the air eat." Elijah, like Moses, and Paul, and Luther, and Knox, was a man of an age. He was specially raised up, and specially gifted for a great work. Christian tenderness and soft sentimentalism would not have suited the times in which he lived. The infamous Jezebel was ruling Israel with a high hand. Not content with overthrowing the national worship of Jehovah, she aimed at the total extermination of God's priests and people. With the ferocity of a wild beast she ever sought for blood, blood. It needed a man with the dauntless courage, and stern sense of justice, and enthusiastic devotion, and iron will, of Elijah to meet the fierce queen, to thwart her cruel designs, and to save the church of God.

P.

THE MOCKERS

2 Kings 2:19-25

ABOUT a mile and half north-west of Jericho, at the base of some low hillocks, thought by some to be mounds of rubbish, is the fountainhead of a stream, to which the place owes now, and must have formerly owed, its supply of water, and the irrigation of its fields. The water rises into an old ruinous basin, and flows off in a stream large enough to turn a mill. The principal stream runs towards the village, the rest of the water finding its way at random, in various channels, down the plain, which is here decked with a broad forest of the *nubk* and other thorny shrubs. The water is beautifully clear, and although slightly tepid at the fountainhead, is sweet and pleasant. Josephus, by whom it is mentioned, ascribes to it a peculiar efficacy in promoting vegetation, and declares that "it affords a sweeter nourishment than other waters." The fountain is now called by the Arabs Ain es-Sultan; but the Christians and Jews recognize it as Elisha's Fountain, and give it the prophet's name.

Formerly, and perhaps in consequence of the curse pronounced on the place by Joshua, the waters were wholly unfit for domestic purposes or for irrigation, by reason of their bitterness and unwholesomeness. But the evil was miraculously healed by Elisha, and the waters brought into their present wholesome state. Jericho was the first place he reached after he had crossed the Jordan; and it was probably the stupendous miracle by which he passed it that suggested to the people that he had power over the waters, and might remove the disadvantage which rendered scarcely habitable what would otherwise be a most pleasant place—there being perhaps no water available in dry weather but such as might be preserved in cisterns, or brought from the inconveniently distant Jordan. So a deputation of the inhabitants waited upon the prophet, respectfully drawing his attention to the case. He heard them, and desired them to bring him a *new* dish. In the original the word indicates a kind of dish used in cooking or serving up victuals—which may be remarked as of itself a suggestive indication that the waters were to be made drinkable. And it was *new*—the more to illustrate the intended miracle, by making it

evident that there was nothing in the vessel, or adhering to it from previous use, which possessed any curative power. He also told them to put salt into the vessel. So far from in any way contributing to the intended result, the salt might be supposed rather fitted to increase the evil—water charged with salt being unfit for use, and unfriendly to vegetable life. No people knew this better than the inhabitants, living, as they did, within ken of the Salt Sea; and being well acquainted, therefore, with the effects of salt in water. It was probably for this reason that the salt was chosen—that the effect might be seen to be produced not only without the intervention of an agency in any way contributing to the result, but in spite of the use of one naturally contrary to it. This was, therefore, what the Jews call a miracle within a miracle. Thus furnished, Elisha forthwith proceeded to the spring—attended, doubtless, by a large concourse of people; and there he cast in the salt, saying, in the fulness of faith, and in language well fitted to divert attention from himself as the agent, to the Lord as the author of the miracle: "Thus saith the Lord, I have healed these waters: there shall not be from thence any more death or barren land." And so it came to pass, to the great joy of the people, who could not but see the entirely miraculous nature of the transaction, not only in the agency employed, but in the fact that no human act could have had any *permanent* effect upon the water. The effect of whatever human resource or knowledge could have done, must have passed off before the day closed, as the water then in the basin and the channel became mixed with that which rose fresh from the spring. It is surely impossible for human art by any one act to produce an abiding effect upon running water.

Soon after this the prophet went to Bethel. This, it will be recollected, was a seat of the worship of one of Jeroboam's golden calves—the inhabitants of which were therefore, doubtless, very corrupt in their religious notions and services. The reception which the prophet met with confirms the impression. He was assailed by a rabble of young blackguards with cries of "Go up, thou baldhead! go up, thou baldhead!" And how did the prophet meet this rude assault, from what the reader takes from the narrative to have been a gang of unmannerly boys? He turned and *cursed* them—nothing less—cursed them in the name of the Lord; and forthwith came two she-bears—perhaps robbed of their whelps—and tore forty and two of them. We dare say there are few young readers, or indeed old ones, of this passage in the Bible, who do not think the prophet was terribly severe; and that, although the " children" deserved a good whipping or something of that sort for their impudence, it was going rather too far to punish them with death. But, in the first place, he did not do so. He " cursed them," and that not from personal resentment, but under a Divine impulse, without which, we will venture to say, no prophet ever dared to pronounce a curse. He cursed, and that was all. He did not punish. He left it to the Lord to determine and inflict the measure of punishment; and that the Lord judged the crime worthy of death, requires us to look more closely into its nature.

In the first place, we are to take the children not as mere thoughtless boys, scarcely knowing what they were about, but as young men acting from a strong animus against the prophet for his work's sake, and with a full intention to insult and discourage him at the commencement of his career. The Hebrew word here employed to describe them (*naarim*, singular *naar*), no doubt does denote even an infant, and a mere child; but also does as frequently denote grown-up lads, youths, and young men, and is often used, irrespective of age, in application to servants and soldiers. In fact, its use is more extensive than ours of the term " boy," though that is very wide, and more nearly corresponds to the Irish use of the same word " boy," or " gorsoon," or the French use of " garçon." We need only to point out a few passages to show this. The term is applied to Ishmael when he was about fourteen years old;[1] to Isaac when he was grown up to a young man;[2] to Shechem the son of Hamor, when of marriageable age, and probably not less than twenty years old;[3] to Joseph when he was seventeen;[4] to Gideon's son Jether, when old enough to be ordered to slay two kings;[5] to Solomon after he had become king;[6] to the four hundred Amalekites who escaped on camels;[7] to Elisha's servant Gehazi;[8] to the son of the prophets who anointed Jehu;[9] to the two hundred and thirty-two attendants of the princes of the provinces who went out against Benhadad;[1] to the soldiers of the Assyrian king;[2] and in other places too numerous to cite. In all these cases, though differently translated according to the apparent meaning of the sacred writer—by child, lad, young man, servant—the word is but one in the original, and is the same which is here employed to express " children."

But it will be said those designated here are not only children, "but little children." Even so; but in one of the instances just cited, Solomon calls himself "a *little* child" when he was certainly a young man; and we wish to point attention to the fact, which we have never seen noticed, that although those who come out against the prophet are called "little children," the "little" is dropped where the forty-two who are slain are mentioned. Even the word for " children " is then changed to another (*jeladim*, singular *jeled*); and although that word is of nearly synonymous use and application with the other,[3] the change, with the dropping of the word "little," is probably intended to mark the distinction. Wherever there is a mob of idle young men, there is sure to be a number of mischievous urchins, who shout and bawl, as they do, without knowing much of the matter. Although, therefore, there were no doubt little children among this rabble of young Bethelites, there is every reason to suppose that the forty-two *of them* who were destroyed were the oldest ones, the ringleaders of the set, who very well knew what they were about. It is worthy of note here, that the Jews have long considered a father responsible for the sins of his sons, while they are under thirteen years of age, after which they become accountable for themselves. There is a ceremony, wherein the father publicly in the congregation transfers to his son, when he attains that age, the responsibility he has hitherto borne for him. This notion is old. We trace it in John ix. 21, where the parents decline to answer for their son, on the ground that he has reached the age of personal responsibility, and can answer for

[1] 1 Kings 20:15.   [2] 2 Kings 19:6.
[3] Lamech applies it to the person he had slain, whom he also calls "a man" (Genesis 5:23). It is also applied to Joseph when seventeen years old (equally with the other term), Genesis 37:30, 42:22; to the "young men" who had been brought up with Rehoboam, who was forty years old (1 Kings 12:8,10); to Daniel and the pious youths his companions (Daniel 1:4,10,etc.)

[1] Genesis 21:16.   [4] Genesis 37:2.   [7] 1 Samuel 30:17.
[2] Genesis 22:12.   [5] Judges 8:20.   [8] 2 Kings 4:12.
[3] Genesis 34:19.   [6] 1 Kings 3:7.   [9] 2 Kings 9:4.

himself. If this idea was as old as the time of Elisha—and it probably was, though the age may then have been later—it supplies a fresh argument to show that the *youngest* of those destroyed was not under the age to which personal responsibility was fixed by the Jews themselves—the Bethelites among the rest.

Observe further, that these youths were not accidentally encountered: they did not happen to be at their sports outside the town where the prophet passed; but they "came out" of *malice prepense* "to meet" and insult him. Such a purpose against the prophet must have been the result of their ungodly training in that evil place, and must have had its root in the sneers and sarcasms which they had all their lives heard levelled at the name and acts of Elijah. Him, surrounded as he was with terrors, they would not have dared thus to insult and abuse; but from his comparatively meek and gentle successor, whom they had never hitherto seen in any position of authority, they thought there was nothing to apprehend, so that they could with impunity pour forth the blackness of their hearts upon him. They had heard that Elijah had been taken up to heaven, and they believed it; but instead of being suitably impressed by it, they regarded it as a fine new subject of derision—telling the disciple to "go up" after his master, and then they should be well rid of both. To this they added the ignominious term of "baldhead," which was one of great indignity with the Israelites—baldness being usually seen among them as the effect of the loathsome disease of leprosy. It was a term of contempt, equivalent to calling him a mean and unworthy fellow—a social outcast. In this sense it is still employed as a term of abuse in the farther East (India, etc.), and is often applied as such to men whose heads are well covered with hair. In western Asia, where men shave their heads, the term is not now known as one of reproach.

The offence, involving as it did a blasphemous insult cast upon one of the Lord's most signal acts, made a near approach to what in the New Testament is called the sin against the Holy Ghost. It became the Lord to vindicate His own honour among a people governed by sensible dispensations of judgment and of mercy; and it became Him to vindicate the character and authority of His anointed prophet at the outset of his high career.

WATERS

2 Kings 2:19

WHEN the elders of Jericho described to Elisha their distressed condition, they did so in the words, "Behold, the situation of this city is pleasant; but the water is naught, and the ground barren." The material facts, thus combined and contrasted, are very suggestive to the mind of spiritual conditions. Let us therefore examine these words more closely. The situation is pleasant; it appears to present everything that might render life happy and prosperous; but this great advantage is neutralized by the barrenness of the ground, where nothing will grow, where no fruit is brought forth to perfection; and, seeking the cause of this, we find it is because the water is naught. It is not that there is drought, the usual cause of sterility in the East; it is not that water is even scanty, it is abundant; but that the water is bad—such as, instead of sustaining, destroys the powers of vegetation.

Why, this becomes a very parable to us, touching, with painful force, upon the spiritual condition of many of us. The situation in which we stand is pleasant. What more could the Lord have done for us than He has done? While so many fair regions of the earth lie in spiritual darkness, the full and blessed light of God's truth shines upon our habitations. We have the written word of truth—we have the uttered word of truth; one of the first sounds that entered our infant ears was that name which is above every name, and in which all our hope is found; and not a day passes in which, under some form or other, we may not see or hear the words of salvation. What situation could be more pleasant, more favourable to our spiritual progress? Surely our city stands upon the delectable mountain, whence on any clear day we may have fair prospects of the goodly land that lies beyond the swelling of Jordan.

Yet, pleasant as all things seem, it is not well with us. "The ground is barren." The great Husbandman has ploughed it up, with which of His ploughs He would; for He has many ploughs for different soils. He has cast in the seed—carefully cast it in; and it is good seed, bursting with ripeness, and He has a right to expect large returns from it—if not sixty-fold, if not thirty-fold, at least ten. But nothing comes from it. The seed will not germinate—nothing will grow. Yet the ground is clean and sweet; for it has been under heavenly tillage, and the Sun of Righteousness has beamed warmly on it. What ails it, then? Something is wrong, or something wanting. It is the waters that are either bad or deficient. Who shall heal them? Only God; it is of no use to look to any one else. If they are bad, if they have been poisoned, and our souls rendered barren by bitter doctrine, read or heard, there is no cure till the handful of wholesome salt is cast in. If they are deficient through the starving poverty of our faith and love, there is no help but in the waters He will send, either in streams or showers, and which He will send if earnestly implored; for He is not a husbandman who forgets the soil He has tilled, or the seed He has planted.

> "See how this dry and thirsty land,
>   Mine heart, doth gaping, gasping stand,
> And, close below, opens towards heaven and Thee;
>   Thou fountain of felicity;
> Great Lord of living waters, water me."

If, then, He send not His rains, His streams in abundance, let Him send *enough* to refresh, to heal, and fertilize.

> "If not full showers of rain, yet Lord,
>   A little pearly dew afford.
> A little, if it come from Thee,
>   Will be of great avail to me."

Nothing but this water of divine grace and doctrine is wanting to make our "situation pleasant" altogether—to render this once barren ground a very land of Beulah.

> "O let thy love
> Distil in fructifying dews of grace,
> And then mine heart will be a pleasant place."

Such ideas and images derived from water are entirely scriptural. The remarkable and almost marvellous effects upon the parched lands, produced by the coming of water, whether of rains or streams, in the warm and dry regions of the earth, quickening into sudden verdure, beauty, and life, that which lay dead, dreary, and un-fruitful, suggest analogies to the influence of divine doctrine upon the soul, and of heavenly grace upon the heart, the singular beauty and appropriateness of which are scarcely appreciable in our moist climate, where the prime anxiety of our cultivators is not to obtain water, but to get rid of its superabundance. But to such as know

the East, such passages as these speak to the very heart:

"My doctrine shall drop as the rain, my speech shall distil as the dew; as the small rain upon the tender herb, and as the showers upon the grass." [1]

"He shall come down like rain on the mown grass; as showers that water the earth." [2]

"I will pour water upon him that is thirsty, and floods upon the dry ground: I will pour my Spirit upon thy seed, and my blessing upon thine offspring." [3]

"I will open rivers in high places, and fountains in the midst of the valleys: I will make the wilderness a pool of water, and the dry land springs of water." [4]

And then, not to quote more—for there is much—of the same purport are almost the last words of Scripture: "The Spirit and the bride say, Come. And let him that heareth say, Come. And let him that is athirst come. And whosoever will, let him take the water of life freely." [5]

I have seen an eastern river which always struck me as being one of the most beautiful emblems of Christian love. It springs from a riven rock high up in the wild ravine of Anti-Lebanon. It has cut its way through mountain ridges. It rushes with resistless force past projecting cliffs. It dashes down foaming rapids and over lofty pre-cipices. It never stops—never rests, until, having cleared

HERMON, FROM MEROMSEE

the last gorge, its abundant waters are led away by the hand of wisdom and industry, in a thousand channels, and

[1] Deuteronomy 32:2.   [3] Isaiah 44:3.   [5] Revelation 22:17.
[2] Psalms 72:6.   [4] Isaiah 41:18.

diffused far and wide over a vast plain, converting, in their course, a parched wilderness into a very paradise of verdure, richness, and beauty. That river is the Abana. And many a time, looking down from the heights of Hermon on its swift torrent, and out over the glorious fruits of its life-giving waters, I have re-echoed the words of the proud old Syrian general, "Are not Abana and Pharpar, rivers of Damascus, better than all the waters of Israel?"

Such is Christian love. It gushes forth from the flinty rock of the human heart riven by the finger of God. Its torrent is impetuous, resistless. It cuts its way through mountains of difficulty. It dashes past all opposition—over all obstacles of dangers. It never stops—never rests, until its pure copious stream is led by divine wisdom through a thousand channels of Christian philanthropy, and diffused over the broad surface of society, converting a moral waste into a paradise of joy.

P.

THE THREE KINGS

2 Kings 3:4-16

THE Moabites, rendered tributary—conquered by David, and remaining tributary to the kingdom of the ten tribes—took advantage of Ahab's troubles from the Syrians, in the latter years of his reign, to assert their independence. This they did by withholding their customary annual tribute. The relation of this circumstance brings out the curious fact that Mesha, king of Moab, was a sheep-master, and rendered unto the king of Israel a hundred thousand lambs, and a hundred thousand rams, with the wool. A strange proportion of rams; and it seems so unlikely that so large a number should be kept, that it has been supposed that wethers are intended. It claims notice, also, that the word translated "sheep-master" is in the original (*noked*), literally "*a marker;*" a name which came to denote a shepherd, because it was a pastoral duty to mark the sheep by some colour to distinguish them from others, and so to prevent the confusion that might arise from the accidental mingling of two flocks—a circumstance very likely to occur in lands destitute of enclosures; and also, more particularly to distinguish the animals of better breed or quality from others. But we find that the corresponding term denotes among the Arabs a species of sheep and goats, short-legged and deformed, but distinguished for the length of the wool; and it is also applied to the shepherd of a flock of sheep.

This custom of calling a man from the species of animal in which his trade lies, or from the commodity in which he deals, is common in the Hebrew and other Eastern languages. Nor is it unknown in our own common language; for, according to a writer of the present day,[1] this usage is common among our own street-folk, who call a man who deals in baked potatoes, "a baked 'tatur;" one who sells pickled whelks, "a pickled whelk;" and so on. As a tribute is always of the best of the land, and as "with the wool" is particularly mentioned, it is very probable that the sheep in question may have been of the same breed with the Arabian, to which the same name is given—distinguished for the quality of the wool. Some of our older versions render the designation sheep-master (so translated in our version), by "rich in sheep," and "a lord of sheep;" and there can be no doubt of the attention the king of Moab paid to this branch of industry and source of wealth, from the form which the tribute took. It is only highly civilized countries, possessing such active commerce as enables them rapidly to turn their products into money, that could pay tribute other than in kind; and in ancient history instances of tributes being otherwise rendered than in the principal products of the tributary country are comparatively rare. The Hebrews themselves usually rendered their tributes in precious metal; and this argues the relative wealth of their country—arising partly from the hoards of ancient kings, and partly from the facility they possessed of turning their produce into money in the Phœnician markets. But the Moabites, beyond almost any of the neighbouring nations, were cut off from the ordinary lines of traffic, and could have but little occupation or commerce except in cattle, for the pasturage and nourishment of which their country was well adapted. Much curious information might easily be presented with respect to ancient and even modern tributes in cattle. But it suffices to state that all our information is confirmatory of Pliny's statement, that in ancient times the only tribute was from the pastures. A curious instance is that of the Cappadocians, of whom Strabo relates that they used to deliver as tribute to the Persians, every year, fifteen hundred horses, two thousand mules, and five myriads of sheep, or fifty thousand.

[1] Mr. Henry Mayhew, in *London Labour and London Poor.*

The Moabite tribute seems very heavy, and doubtless was so felt by them while it lasted; but in the same degree was it valuable to the crown of Israel; and the internal taxation, to which resort must have been made to make up for this lapse of external revenue, would of course render the expedition eventually undertaken for the purpose of reducing the Moabites, highly popular in Israel. Yet this was not undertaken by Ahab; and his unwarlike son Ahaziah seems to have shrunk from the enterprise. It was left to his brother Jehoram, and it became one of the first objects of his reign. He easily prevailed upon Jehoshaphat of Judah to join him in the undertaking. His primary inducement seems to have been to assist in putting down a resistance to Jewish authority, which afforded an example dangerous to the dominion of Judah over the neighbouring country of Edom. Indeed, although the viceroy of Edom was compelled to bring his forces into the field in aid of Judah against Moab, there is much reason to suspect that the Edomites were nearly ripe for revolt, and were watching the turn of events to declare their own independence, if not to make common cause with Moab. It may be traced, we apprehend, in the narrative, that the king of Moab had expectations from them; and it is likely these expectations would not have been disappointed had any reverse attended the arms of the allies. The direct course into the land of Moab would have been to cross the Jordan somewhere above the estuary of the river; but instead of this, the Israelites marched down through Judah's territory, and, being joined by the forces of Jehoshaphat, proceeded round by the southern extremity of the Dead Sea, where, being joined by the auxiliaries of Edom, they entered Moab on the south. The course thus taken admits of various explanations. The fact that the Syrians were posted in Gilead, where they still held the stronghold of Ramoth, may have rendered it unadvisable to assail Moab on the north; but we are ourselves more inclined to ascribe it to the necessity which the king of Judah felt of holding the Edomites under close observation.

By the time the allies entered the land of Moab, they were nearly consumed for lack of water; and in this emergency good Jehoshaphat inquired if there were any "prophet of the Lord" within reach. In his own country, and among his own people, the designation of "a prophet"

would have sufficed; but mixed as he was with the Israelites, he felt the need of specifying that he desired the counsel of "a prophet of the Lord." On hearing that Elisha had followed the camp, he readily recognized the name and claims of the inheritor of Elijah's mantle, although his prophetic career had just commenced; and, at his suggestion, the three kings—sent for him? No, went down to him. Not at all abashed by the presence of three crowned kings, the prophet, albeit a mild mooded man, greeted Ahab's son with a rebuke as stern as Elijah himself could have administered. A soft answer turned away some of his wrath; and his heart softening towards Jehoshaphat, he consented to seek counsel of God. But Elisha, who always appears as more susceptible to external influences than his great Master, needed first to calm down the perturbations of his spirit, to bring his soul into a fit frame for receiving the intimations he sought from heaven, and to bear his spirit upon the wings of melodious sound into the harmonious company around that throne which no dissonance can approach. Nor was it for him alone. The kings, as they listened, could not but come also under this, the most spiritual of earthly influences, and be thereby prepared to receive in a right spirit the word they sought. As the minstrel with rapt ardour swept the strings, the Divine influence came down upon the prophet's mind, and the last note had scarcely died away when he spoke. His words were strange: "Make this valley full of ditches." This was to receive the water, which, as he said, should, without sign of wind or rain, speedily fill the valley. Unlikely as the thing seemed, the kings recognized the power of the Lord by following the directions of His prophet; and presently thousands of men were at work scooping out wide and deep trenches in the valley—trenches larger, it is probable, than their real need, though less capacious than their present thirst.

A most valuable discovery has lately been made in reference to this portion of sacred history. In 1868, a Moabite stone was found bearing inscriptions which have excited great interest, and tasked the learning of Oriental scholars. Into the story respecting the stone itself we cannot enter; but that portion of the record upon it, which relates to *Mesha*, the king of Moab, and what he did to the kings of Israel, certainly requires our attention. From the Second Book of Kings, chapter iii., we learn that Mesha was king of Moab—that after the death of Ahab the king of Moab rebelled against the king of Israel; and that Jehoram, the king of Israel, a descendant of Omri, in the days of Mesha, went to war with the Moabites and overcame them. Now the Moabite stone contains the following words, according to the translation of Dr. Ginsburg, revised by Canon Rawlinson:—"I am Mesha, the son of Chemosh-Gad, king of Moab, the Dibonite." "Omri was king of Israel, and he oppressed Moab many days, for (the god) Chemosh was angry with his land. His son (Omri's son) succeeded him, and he also said, 'I will oppress Moab.' 'In my days,' he said, 'let us go and I will see my desire on him, and his house;' and Israel said, 'I will destroy it with an everlasting destruction.' Now Omri took the land of Medeba and occupied it (he, and his son, and his son's son) forty years. But Chemosh had mercy on it in my days." "The king of Israel fortified Ataroth, and I assaulted the wall and took it, and killed all the warriors of the wall."

The probable date of the inscription is between B.C. 950 and 850, which includes the date of the history now before us in the Second Book of Kings. The *Mesha* of the inscription can be no other than the *Mesha* who rebelled against Israel. The Omri in both must be the same person. Here, then, we have manifest points of contact, and the inscription confirms the statement in Kings that "Moab revolted against Israel, after the days of Ahab;" and that a campaign against Moab was conducted by Omri's grandson. It confirms the fact of grievous oppression on the part of Israel, described in the Bible narrative, "exacting tribute to the extent of 100,000 lambs, and 100,000 rams with the wool." Of sixteen places mentioned in the inscription on the stone, as situated in Moab, all but three are found in the Bible occupying the same position. The *god Chemosh* in the inscription is the *god Chemosh* of the Bible, "the abomination of Moab." (1 Kings xi. 7.) "The 'pleasing' of Chemosh by the massacre of all the warriors who defended Ataroth, is in accordance with what Scripture tells us of the bloody character of the rites by which he was worshipped." (2 Kings iii. 27.) Neither the Bible narrative nor the narrative inscription gives the whole history of the relation between Israel and Moab. Each is fragmentary. The Bible tells us of the defeat of Moab by Israel under Jehoram. (2 Kings iii. 4, 27.) The inscription omits to mention that—this we might expect —but it gives us particulars not in the Bible with regard to the resistance of Moab and its victory over Israel. Scripture breaks off with the notice of Moab indignation, and there is nothing to contradict the assertion of Moab afterwards recovering independence. That independence, with the victories and achievements of Mesha, are boastfully celebrated in the writing upon this most valuable relic of antiquity.—*Bible Educator*, i. 124.

S.

THE BLOOD—LIKE WATER

2 Kings 3:22-23

LARGE as were the trenches which the eager allies digged to receive the promised water, they were filled to overflowing. To show more distinctly that it was from the Lord, the time was that of the morning sacrifice, which was offered towards the rising of the sun, and before all other sacrifices. At that moment the waters came from the way of Edom, and filled the ditches which had been digged in the bed of a winter torrent.

The distant Moabites, having no suspicion of the presence of water, and beholding a reddish tinge along the valley, jumped to the conclusion that the allies had fallen out, and fought together during the night, and that this was the blood of the battle. They probably thought that it was the king of Edom who had risen upon the Israelites, being aware that he was present only by constraint. Under this delusion, they hastened to plunder the camp, which they supposed to be forsaken, but found it full of living and refreshed men, whose swords soon made the visionary blood a truth.

A word respecting this water. The time of its coming, and all the circumstances, were framed to evince the miraculous nature of the supply, by the special and extraordinary putting forth of divine power. We are expressly told there was no rain. Neither was a new spring opened; for in that case the stream would have continued to run, and the trenches would have been unnecessary. The opening of a fountain, also, although a temporary advantage to the Israelites, would have been an enduring benefit to their enemies; and as the allies were not to remain there, and only sought present relief, to render the supply as temporary as the occasion made the miracle but the more illustrious, and the more distinctly showed that the waters were meant for them, and for them only. To send a sudden rush of waters just to fill the trenches at the precise moment, and then to cause it to cease, was as distinctly a supply on purpose for them as if the Lord had sent a host of angels, under the guise of water-carriers, to empty full skins of water into the trenches they had made. Nevertheless, the water must have been produced by some *means*, and one would like to know what took place at the spot from which the stream came. Perhaps something of the same nature that has been occasionally, but rarely, witnessed in different lands, and of which an instance occurred at no remote date in our own country. The journals of the time record that, on the 20th of September 1810, the inhabitants of the town of Lutton, in Bedfordshire, were surprised by a singular phenomenon. The common pond, situated in a rather elevated part of the town, which, as there had been no rain in the neighbourhood for some weeks, was gradually becoming shallower of water, suddenly filled, and ejected from its bottom all the filth and sediment. It continued flowing over and discharging a large quantity of water for some hours; but afterwards remained quiet as usual. It is added that the town's people were struck with considerable alarm at the circumstance, and apprehended that there would soon be intelligence of some distant earthquake, as it was recollected by some that a similar emission of water at this spot had taken place at the precise instant of the great earthquake at Lisbon, in 1755.

There are also some curious questions respecting the colour of the water. It is stated that it appeared to the Moabites as red as blood. As this appearance was presented when the morning sun shone upon it, the probability seems to be, that the colour was reflected from the redness of the horizon at the sun-rising. But it may be asked, How could the Moabites be deceived by so common a phenomenon, especially when the glaring sun and the crimson clouds around it must have instantly indicated the cause of this appearance? The answer is, that this would have been the case had they known there was any water in the valley; but they felt quite sure there was none; and as in the absence of water there could be no reflection from the skies, the reason they assigned was really the most probable that could be suggested under the circumstances. That this was the cause of the redness is the general sentiment of interpreters. We are of the same judgment, for this reason, among others, that any real redness in the water would have laid its wholesomeness open to doubt, and would have been felt as rendering the boon less valuable than the gift of pure limpid water would have been. Nevertheless, some have thought there may have been something in or on the water to impart to it a red appearance. The possibility of this is not to be denied; and were there not examples in nature of such redness in water, God might have imparted it supernaturally, for He is not limited to natural agencies, though He commonly works through them when they are available. And it may be argued, that an adequate motive for such

colour being given to the water is found in the fact, that the taking it for blood by the Moabites was the means, and was intended to be the means, of giving an immediate victory to the allies, according to the promise of Elisha.

Various instances of the redness of water have been recorded. The most famous instance is that of the river Leontes in Lebanon, which becomes red at a certain time of the year, from its stream then washing or passing over beds of colouring earths. This is, indeed, the common cause of the periodical redness of certain rivers. In the case of the Leontes, it was regarded by the Syrians and Phœnicians as an annual commemoration of the death of Adonis—the Tammuz of Scripture; and while it lasted, the mourning rites of Tammuz were celebrated, as alluded to in Ezek. viii. 14. Milton finely refers to this mythological fable:

"Thammuz came next behind,
Whose annual wound in Lebanon allured
The Syrian damsels to lament his fate
In amorous ditties all a summer's day;
While smooth Adonis from his native rock
Ran purple to the sea, supposed with blood
Of Thammuz yearly wounded."

It is related by Pliny, that the water of the lakes near Babylon was of a red colour during eleven days in summer. The water at the mouth of the river Plata has often been observed of a blood-red colour; and the French missionary Consag observed, in 1746, that the open sea near California was of a bluish-red colour. The same has been observed in the *Red* Sea; and from this some have been of late inclined to suppose its name was derived. In this case it was shown to be a jelly-like substance floating upon the surface of the water, and composed of a multitude of very small mollusca, each having a minute red spot in the centre, forming in the mass a bright body of red colour.

When observed in the sea, it is probably in most cases of this nature; but when in lakes or rivers, it seems as likely to be a vegetable product or deposit, as in the case of the lake supposed to have been turned into blood towards the close of the last century, near Strautsberg. When scientifically examined in January 1799, the colouring matter was found to be some vegetable substance. Professor Klaproth found that the colouring substance in another lake (near Lubotin in South Prussia), exhibited a chemical affinity to the colouring matter obtained from the indigo plant; and although the water appeared of a dark-red crimson colour, this was merely an optical illusion, occasioned by the refraction of the rays of light, the real colour being a pure blue.

PRINCIPLE OF HUMAN SACRIFICE

2 Kings 3:26-27

THE victory won by the allies was followed up with vigour and with severity, until at last the king of Moab was obliged to shut himself in his strong city of Kir-haraseth, which was soon invested by them. In the desperate state of his affairs, and feeling that it would be impossible for him to hold out long, the king of Moab made the bold attempt of forcing his way through the beleaguering force, at the head of a small body of seven hundred resolute men. That he chose to make the attempt upon the quarter which the king of Edom occupied, may have arisen either from the comparative weakness of this part, or from his having reason to suspect that the Edomites were not hearty in the cause for which they fought, and would, after some decent show of resistance, allow him to pass. He was, however, disappointed; for he was repelled by the Edomites, and driven back into the city.

This seemed to king Mesha the last of his human resources, and nothing was left for him but a solemn appeal to his gods for deliverance. The emergency was great. Not only the welfare, but the very existence of his house and nation, was at stake. He therefore conceived that the blood of bulls and goats would not suffice for the greatness of the occasion, which was such as to demand the most precious and costly offering known to Paganism—the life of a man; and that of no common man, but of him whose life was most precious to the king himself, and to the state—even the life of his own son, his eldest son, who was to succeed him on the throne.

This is the only positive example of human sacrifice recorded in Scripture, though there are frequent allusions to such sacrifices, as an abominable custom of idolatry, to which the Israelites were solemnly interdicted from conforming.

There can be no question here as to the possibly limited meaning of such phrases as "burning with fire," and "causing to pass through the fire." The young prince was clearly offered for a "burnt offering" upon the wall of the city, and in the sight of the allied besiegers, who were so horror-struck, that they raised the siege and departed.

Human sacrifice was very prevalent in ancient times. Various accounts of its origin have been given, but all are necessarily conjectural. It seems to us, that the practice grew out of the notion that whatever was most costly and precious must needs be most acceptable as an offering to the gods; and it being established that the life of animals was an acceptable offering, perverse ingenuity reasoned, that the life of the human creature—the noblest of creatures—and his lifeblood, the most precious on earth, must be still more acceptable to Heaven, still more valuable in the sight of the gods. This being the case, it further followed, that the more illustrious, the more pure or exalted, the person whose life was offered, the more proper still was the offering, and the more cogent its force in gratifying, soothing, or rendering propitious the stern powers that ruled the destinies of man. Hence the lives of the most pure, the most beautiful, the most high-born—children, virgins, and noble youths— were considered the most splendid and effectual sacrifices; although, in default of such, captives and slaves were offered, the life of the meanest human creature being of far more value than that of the noblest beast of the field. As to the precise object, it appears to us that in all, or nearly all, the cases fully known, these offerings were propitiatory at least, if not expiatory. Thus: a certain danger threatens the nation or family, or a certain calamity has been inflicted. Hence it is inferred that the gods are angry, and the evil cannot be averted, or will not cease, or prosperity will not return, until they are pacified. For this end nothing must be spared; the public good requires that at all costs the angry gods must be placated — rendered propitious. The priest is supposed to possess the means of knowing what will turn their wrath away; and if he names the son or daughter of the king himself as the needful victim, it becomes the duty of the latter not only to submit to the demand, but to acquiesce in it with all the marks of cheerful obedience, lest the manifestation of natural grief should neutralize the merit of the costly and powerful offering.

That these offerings were regarded as expiatory of sins which had brought down, or which threatened, the judgments of Heaven, is clearly indicated by Micah (vi. 7): "Shall I give my first born for my transgression, the fruit of my body for the sin of my soul?" And indeed this prophet, in the context, makes it distinctly a further development of the principle of expiatory animal sacrifice. His mention of the "first born," perhaps glances at the very case now before us; but, indeed, when the most precious life was sought, that of the first born, as in this case, and still more of an only child, as in the case of Iphigenia, would be regarded as the most precious.

Even the wrath of man, his wicked inventions, may redound to the glory of God, and illustrate the mysteries of His grace and providence; and it has been often to us a matter of solemn thought, that in this matter the heathen themselves, in doing this awful and forbidden thing—which God never exacted from any people, but which was abhorrent to Him—did yet bear witness to the great doctrine of the Atonement, and declare the need for it. Their consciences bore witness, that the blood of bulls and goats could not put away sin; they craved some higher, some more effectual expiation, and sought it in the life of man. They could go no higher. If they could, they would have done so; for still they must have felt unsatisfied: a more precious life than any they could offer was really needed for effectual expiation, and that life the Lord Himself provided when He gave His well-beloved Son to be offered up as an atonement for the sins of the world. Awfully affecting is the contemplation of the blind ways in which the ancient heathen unknowingly expressed their consciousness of the need there was for some greater and higher atonement than any they had to offer.

Having alluded to the case of Iphigenia, we feel constrained to return to it, as expressed in the tragedy of Æschylus, as it seems to embody the ancient ideas bearing on the subject. This sacrifice of the king's only daughter was declared by the priest to be the sole means of atoning for the offence, which the angry goddess avenged by storms and adverse winds, which prevented the Argive fleet from sailing. The sacrifice was thus expiatory. The manner in which this demand was received, powerfully suggests how the hearts of men were rent by the exactions which their "dark idolatries" imposed upon them, whatever aspect of fortitude and submission they might feel it becoming to put on when the deed was consummated.

> "The sons of Atreus, starting from their thrones,
>   Dash'd to the ground their sceptres, nor withheld
>   The bursting tears that dew'd their warrior cheeks;
>   And thus exclaiming spoke the elder king:
> "O heavy, fatal doom! to disobey!
>   O heavy, fatal doom! my child to slay—
>   My child! the idle treasure of my house!
>   Must I, her father, all bedabbled o'er
>   In streaming rivers of her virgin gore,
>   Stand by the altar with polluted hands?
>   O woe! woe! woe!
>   Where shall I turn me!'"

But at length—

> "——He bent his neck beneath the yoke
>   Of dire necessity, and champ'd the curb."

And then, when all was ready, the mailed chiefs who stood around

> "Heard in silence stern
>   Cries that called a father's name,
>   And set at nought prayers, cries, and tears,
>   And her sweet virgin life and blooming years."

Then followed a solemn prayer, during which the victim sinks to the ground in a swoon; and at length, on the word being given by the father, the priests lift her up,

> "And bear her to the altar dread,
>   Like a young fawn or mountain kid;
>   Then round her beauteous mouth to tie
>   Dumb sullen bands to stop her cry,
>   Lest aught of an unholy sound
>   Be heard to breathe those altars round,
>   Which on the monarch's house might cast a deadly spell."

PRACTICE OF HUMAN SACRIFICE

2 Kings 3:27

HAVING yesterday developed the principle of human sacrifice, we may to-day contemplate some ancient and modern instances in illustration of the practice.

Although, as we have seen, the practice was not unknown to the Greeks, and there are even examples of it among the Romans in the early period of their history, it was never so common among the classical ancients as among the Canaanites and other nations of Syria. On this point the testimony of ancient heathen and early Christian writers concurs with that of Scripture. It was indeed awfully common among the Carthaginians in North Africa; but they derived it from the same quarter, being a colony of the Phœnicians. Their customs in this matter are better known than those of the Phœnician and Syrian nations, and it is hence usual to carry back their usages to supply the details which the Scripture does not furnish. But one who has expressly written on the subject,[1] says they are not strictly applicable to the usages of the worship of the Molech of Scripture by human sacrifice, but are later developments of the primitive rites. Jewish Rabbis and Christian fathers concur, however, in this reference; and although the mode of operation may have been different in some particulars, the essential facts and principles of action are identical. It is with MOLECH that human sacrifices are usually connected in Scripture. "Causing children to pass through the fire to Molech," is frequently alluded to in Scripture; and some Jewish Rabbis, tender of the reputation of their ancient kings, to whom this practice is ascribed, started the ingenious notion that the ceremony was not one of sacrifice or death, but a sort of lustration or purification by fire, which, although idolatrous, and, indeed, an act of devotement to the idol, was not cruel, and inflicted no bodily harm. But this view of the matter is untenable in the face of the evidence we possess, and is not now usually entertained. When the Israelites fell into this practice, this passing "through the fire" took place in the valley of Hinnom, south of Jerusalem; and Jeremiah, speaking of what there took place, expressly says that the subjects of this operation were "burned in the fire."[2]

"Moloch, horrid king, besmeared with blood
Of human sacrifice, and parents' tears,"

was the same, doubtless, as the Kronos whom the Greeks identified with Saturn, and concerning whom we have the mythological fable of his devouring his own children. There is a difficulty in distinguishing him from Baal. Both names

are appellative—Baal being *lord*, and Molech *king*. Recent investigation seems to point to the conclusion that Baal represented the life-giving and cherishing, and Molech the life-destroying powers of the same god—the sun. In that aspect, the offering of human victims, to be consumed by fire, must have seemed highly appropriate.

Without further explanation or application, we proceed to sum up a few of a large body of facts and instances which we have been able to collect on this painful subject.

The Phœnicians and Carthaginians are reported to have had a yearly celebration, at which human sacrifices were offered in large numbers to their idol; and it is worthy of note that the Jews appear to have traced some analogy between the ceremonies of this day and those of their own great and solemn day of atonement—with the difference of human for animal victims. Victims were also offered on particular emergencies, as in the instance by which these remarks have been suggested. Princes and great men under severe calamities, used to offer their beloved children to the god. Private persons soon came to imitate the example of their princes; and thus in time the practice became general. Indeed, to such a height did this infatuation rise, that those who had no children of their own bought those of the poor, that they might not be deprived of the benefits they expected from such offerings. The original practice seems to have been to slay the victim, and then to place the body on the altar, to be consumed in the fire. Indeed, that they should be burned alive, as some suppose, would have been adverse to the analogy of sacrifice. Afterwards, a kind of burning fiery furnace was used; and, eventually, among the Carthaginians, the victims were—at least sometimes—cast into a large brazen statue of the god, made red hot. To drown the cries of the young victims, musicians were made to play on noisy instruments—particularly drums;[1] and the mothers made it a sort of merit to divest themselves of natural affection, or rather to restrain its manifestation. A tear rendered the sacrifice of no effect, and the one who shed it was deemed an enemy to the public peace. Tertullian, who was himself a native of Carthage, says that this inhuman custom was maintained there long after the

---

[1] Munter in his *Religion der Karthager;* also Movers, *Die Phönizier.*

[2] Jeremiah 7:31. See also Psalms 106:38; Ezekiel 16:20; 23:37, to show that these were real sacrifices by fire.

[1] Hence the place in the valley of Hinnom was called Tophet, from *Toph*, a drum.

Carthaginians had been subdued by the Romans. He affirms that children were sacrificed to this Molech, Kronos, or Saturn, down to the consulship of Tiberius, who, to put a stop to it, hanged the sacrificing priests on the tree that shaded their temple, as on so many crosses raised to expiate their crimes, of which the soldiers who assisted at the execution had been the witnesses.

There is a curious and painfully illustrative anecdote on this subject in Diodorus Siculus, who relates that, when Agathocles was going to besiege Carthage, the people, seeing the extremities to which they were reduced, ascribed their misfortunes to the anger of their god, in that they had latterly spared to offer to him in sacrifice children nobly born, and had fraudulently put him off with the children of slaves and foreigners. To make an atonement for this crime, two hundred children of the best families in Carthage were at once offered in sacrifice, and no less than three hundred of the citizens voluntarily sacrificed themselves—that is, they went into the fire without any compulsion.

Nor was the practice of human sacrifice confined to the East. It] was found among the British Druids, as well as with the Gauls and Germans. Prisoners taken in battle were thus disposed of as offerings to the god who had given the victory. The victim was chained with his back to an oak, and while music was played, and the people danced to the music, the officiating Druid smote the victim on the bowels, and professed to draw auguries of the future from the manner in which the blood flowed. On other occasions prisoners were consumed by hundreds in a wicker machine or cage, to which the sacrificial priest set fire. With such offerings the infernal powers were supposed to be well pleased; and it is likely that they were.

Among many of the nations of Africa, the custom has subsisted to our own time—with this difference, that, instead of sacrifice by fire, the blood of the victims (unless, as in Dahomey, kept to be made into black puddings) is poured out as an offering to the gods, the bodies being eaten by the people, partly as a religious act. The travellers of the sixteenth century relate that the sovereign of Guagua never entered upon a military expedition without a solemn sacrifice, in which he immolated a youth with his own hatchet; and afterwards four slaves, two by his own hand, and two by the aid of others

Snelgrave, in his *New Account of Some Parts of Guinea,* published in 1734, speaks of two cases of human sacrifice that came under his own notice in Old Calabar. On the occasion of the illness of the king Jabru, the priests prescribed, as an effectual means of cure, the sacrifice of a child six months old. Snelgrave saw the dead body of the child suspended from the branches of a tree, with a living cock, which had been tied to him for the completion of this horrid ceremony. This was in 1704. Nine years after, in his last voyage to this coast, visiting one of the chiefs, he saw a negro child fastened by the arms to a post driven into the ground; and observing the poor creature to be covered with flies and vermin, he inquired concerning him, and was told that he was a victim intended to be sacrificed the night following to the god Egbo, for the prosperity of the realm. The rough seaman could not endure this, and, his men being with him, he rescued the victim by little less than force of arms.

The same captain witnessed in Dahomey the very same practices of human immolation, but on a more extensive scale, which Commander Forbes,[1] in the present day, has horrified us by describing. This fact, not known to the late traveller, shows the inveteracy of such customs, especially such as comprise bloody rites. Commander Forbes declined to witness the actual immolation of the victims, and he and a companion were allowed to buy off three of the fourteen for a hundred dollars each; but both he and Snelgrave bear witness to the amazing coolness of the victims. "These sturdy men met the gaze of their persecutors with a firmness perfectly astonishing. Not a sigh was breathed. In all my life I never saw such coolness. It did not seem real; but soon proved frightfully so. One hellish monster placed his finger to the eyes of a victim who hung down his head; but finding no moisture, drew upon himself the ridicule of his fiendish coadjutors."

In Snelgrave's time, the immolation of no less than four hundred victims took place upon four small stages, about five feet above the ground. One stroke of a sabre separated the head from the body, amid the shouts of the assembly. The heads were placed on the scaffolds, and each body, after having lain on the ground until drained of blood, was carried forth by slaves to

[1] *Dahomey and the Dahomans.* By F. E. Forbes, Com. R. N. 1850.

a place beyond the camp. He was told by the interpreter that the heads were for the king, the bodies for the people (to eat), and the blood for the fetishes or gods. These larger instances of immolation seem to belong to the class in which numbers of slaves are killed, in order that they may attend, in the next world, upon some great person deceased. This savage custom was, in Old Calabar, from which some of the above facts are drawn, formally abolished by a law in February 1850, under the influence of the United Presbyterian missionaries; and the latest advices show this law to be well observed. Solitary sacrifices of expiation have, however, not been entirely put down. A recent instance is given of a certain town, called Ekrikok, being devoted to destruction for high treason. But it was allowed to redeem itself, partly by a fine, and partly *by one life* being offered in expiatory substitution for the whole, which was accomplished in the person of a new slave bought for the purpose. Mr. Waddell, the missionary, remonstrating on the subject with "Old Egbo Jack, the head of a great family," that personage asserted that "it was impossible the affair could be settled without a death, for Egbo law was the same as God's law to Calabar; and he pointedly asked me if it were better for all Ekrikok to die, or for one slave instead to die for all the town? I thought of the words of Caiaphas, and of the value of life as substitution and atonement for sin. A poor slave bought in the market for a few hundred coppers, by his death redeemed a town, for which many thousands of money would have availed nothing." [1]

If we go to America, we still find the same customs among the ancient inhabitants. The human sacrifices of the Mexicans were performed with peculiar atrocity, and on a dreadfully extensive scale. They never sacrificed fewer than forty or fifty at one time, and often a much larger number. The poor wretches were placed upon a terrace, and the immolation of each victim was performed by six of the priests' servants. Two held the victim's arms, two his legs, one his head, while the sixth ripped open his stomach, whence he tore the heart, and after holding it up to the sun, turned round and flung it in the face of the idol. The body was then cast down into the area of the building,[1] which was a cemetery or charnel house for such sacrifices, whose remains, thousands in number, might there be seen. On solemn occasions, it was the duty of the high priest to operate upon the victim; and the dexterity with which he discharged his butcherly office was a matter of great admiration to the people.

Many more instances of these abominations might be given; and we purposely abstain from noticing immolations in which the idea of an offering to the gods is not so obviously involved, such as those who are slain in order to be deposited in the tombs of kings and great men; as well as prisoners of war, slain by savages as an act of vengeful triumph, consummated by the bodies of the victims being devoured.

In reference to all this, there needs but one remark: "The dark places of the earth are full of the habitations of cruelty."

DEBTORS AND CREDITORS

2 Kings 4:1-7

AFTER these great public events, the course of the sacred history brings us into the midst of scenes of private trouble. The poor widow of one of the sons of the prophets, comes to Elisha to tell him her tale of sorrow. Her husband, though a good man and a servant of the Lord, had died, leaving some debt unpaid, and the harsh creditor was come upon her, claiming her only son as his slave, in discharge of his father's debt. The precise object of the woman in making this statement to the prophet, is not clear. She must have been aware that he had no means of defraying her debt from his own resources. She might think that he would apply to the king on her behalf, or that he would use the influence of his character and position with the creditor, to induce him to forego his claim. To both these courses there were objections, more likely to strike the mind of Elisha than that of the applicant. It was undesirable that he should compromise his independence, and the dignity of his

[1] *Missionary Record of the United Presbyterian Church,* Dec. 1852.

[1] There is a fearfully suggestive picture of this place and of the sacrifices in the *Histoire Générale des Voyages,* tom. xii., 4to edition.

office, by seeking favours of the king; and he would not like to use the influence which his character gave, to persuade the suitor to submit to a loss by foregoing a claim which might be harsh, but which was yet such as the law sanctioned. He preferred that the debt should be paid—but how? He asked the woman what she had left in the house; and she told him that there was nothing but a little oil. It is indeed remarkable, that poor people in Israel who are reduced to the last extremities, generally have a little oil left. So the woman of Zarephath had, besides a morsel of bread, nothing remaining but a small quantity of oil. Such facts, much better than any laboured statements and illustrations, show the very great and conspicuous importance of oil to this people. It seems to have been the most essential necessary of life next to bread. On learning this, the prophet told her to borrow as many vessels as she could, and to *fill them* out of the one containing this small portion of oil, and sell what she thus obtained to pay the debt, and to deliver her son from the danger. She did this; and the miraculous supply of oil ceased not while there remained one vessel to be filled.

The Jews have a notion that the husband of this woman was no other than Obadiah, the well known intendant of Ahab's household; and they suppose that the debt was incurred while he maintained the Lord's prophets in a cave. This, they say, he reckoned upon paying in time out of the proceeds of his office; but being soon deprived of that office, through the influence of Jezebel, he was reduced to poverty, and died without paying the debt. They even fancy that the harsh creditor was no other than king Jehoram himself. We need not say that there is no scriptural foundation for these conjectures, which seem to have been devised in order to supply a cogent reason for the divine interference, through Elisha, on this poor widow's behalf. But surely this is not needed; and the fact that her husband was known to Elisha, and was one of the sons of the prophets (which, by the bye, Obadiah was not), supplies a sufficient reason for the interest the prophet took in her sad case.

We wish, however, to direct attention to the law under which this sad emergency was produced. As with us, the property of one who died insolvent became chargeable for his debts; but the principle which operated in determining

what constituted property, was carried further than with us, and created all the real difference in the case. Children were regarded as the property of the father in a sense so absolute, that it was in his power to sell them to pay his debts. The law expressly provided, that in the case of poverty, a man might sell himself, and also his children.[1] It was by an extension of this permission, and in virtue of another law, which ordained that a thief, who had not wherewith to make restitution, should be sold,[2] that creditors were allowed to seize the children of their debtors in payment. The law made no express provision in the case; but we see by the passage now under consideration, and some others, that this usage was common among the Hebrews, and was recognized as having the force of law. There is a manifest allusion to it in Isaiah l. 1: "Which of my creditors is it to whom I have sold you? Behold, for your iniquities have ye sold yourselves." Our Lord himself uttered a parable respecting a creditor, who, having found a large sum due to him, commanded the debtor to be sold, with his wife, his children, and all that he had.[3] We thus see that the usage existed among the Hebrews, to the latest times of their commonwealth.

The custom was not peculiar to them. It was general in ancient times. The Romans, the Athenians, the nations of Asia, and divers other peoples, exercised the same right over their children, in this and most other respects, as did the Hebrews. The parents sold them in their poverty; and creditors seized the children of their debtors as freely as their cattle and movables. Romulus gave to a father every kind of power over his children; and that not only during their nonage, but throughout their lives, and to whatever dignity or power they might attain. He might imprison them, or flog them, or compel them to labour in his fields, or even kill them, or sell them for slaves. Numa Pompilius moderated the severity of this law by enacting, that when a man had married with the consent of his father, the latter no longer had power to sell him for a slave. Apart from this restriction, the practice of selling their children existed for a long time among the Romans. Eventually it was forbidden by the emperors Dioclesian and Maximian, that any

[1] Exodus 21:7; Leviticus 25:39. [2] Exodus 22:3.
[3] Matthew 18:25.

free persons should be reduced to slavery because of their debts. The paternal rights over children were originally exercised by the Athenians with the same rigour as by the Romans; but the severity of these customs was moderated by Solon. When Lucullus governed Roman Asia, he found the practice of the Asiatics in respect of the selling of children for payment of debt, and the eventual seizure of the parents themselves, when no children were left, to be such as appalled even his Roman mind; and he laboured to ameliorate the great evils which he witnessed.

In our own day, the absolute right of parents in the disposal of their children exists in the East, in all, or nearly all, its ancient force. In regard to selling them, which is the point under notice, it may suffice to refer to the practice of a Christian nation, the Georgians, who habitually sold both their sons and daughters, and who still do so, as far as they can, notwithstanding the laudable efforts of the Russian government to suppress this odious traffic. We have ourselves known children to be offered for sale by their parents, in the streets of a Mohammedan city, during a time of famine.

It will be seen that the two things—the sale of children by parents, and their seizure by creditors—merge into each other, as the right of the creditor in this matter accrues from the right of the father. There is no instance in any nation, of a creditor being empowered to seize children, where the father himself did not possess the right of selling them.

ELISHA'S STAFF

2 Kings 4:29

A DECEASED friend once told us that he never was able to find in any commentary, or to obtain from any minister whom he had consulted, an explanation that he could regard as satisfactory, of Elisha's design in sending his staff to be laid upon the face of the dead son of the friendly Shunammite. As the prophet went himself, why send his staff before? and as no effect resulted from the operation, what was his view—apparently a mistaken one—in sending it at all?

Attention being thus drawn to what seemed a matter not likely to have been overlooked by any commentator, we turned over a large number of volumes of all sizes, and ascertained with some surprise that our friend's information was correct. There is a dead silence on this point; and even Krummacher, who has written a whole volume on a part of the history of Elisha, has passed this over, though he, as well as others, does suggest reasons for the failure of the experiment.

Elisha evidently sent his staff by his servant with the expectation that it would be effectual to raise the dead. This was great faith in him—faith as strong almost as any that his great master exemplified; we say almost, for Elijah was the first to conceive the great thought that even the raising of the dead was not a thing too great for faith to ask. Elisha had that for a precedent; but he was the first to think that even his presence was not needful to this effect—that his faith might act thus mightily even at a distance, by the mere instrumentality of his staff, to indicate the power and influence from which it came. But why his *staff* in particular? One might think that the mantle of Elijah would more readily have occurred to his mind in connection with such a purpose and with such ideas. We should at once have understood that. It would have been a most intelligible sign.

Now, it may be possible to explain both why he did not send the mantle, and why he did send the staff. As to the former point, little explanation is needed; for, bearing in mind what has been already stated in regard to the value and importance of the prophetic mantle, every one can understand how he would not like to trust it out of his own possession; and, in point of fact, the Eastern inheritors of saintly mantles never do let them go out of their immediate charge on any account whatever, and scarcely, indeed, will they allow them to be separated from their persons. They even sleep in them.

To see why he did send his staff, we must consider that the prophetic staff was probably of some particular shape or materials, which indicated the authority and function of the person who bore it—being to him, in his degree, what a sceptre was to a king. In fact, ancient sceptres, as symbols of power, were only rods or staves. So, in Ezekiel xix. 11, we read of "strong rods for the sceptres of those that bear rule." Now, the authority of the owner of such an official or symbolical staff was, and even to this day is, considered to be as effectually delegated, for any object, to the person to whom it is entrusted, as it would be by a signet ring. Thus, when Captains Irby and Mangles left an Arab camp to proceed to Shobek, the sheikh Abu Rashid sent on with them an Arab bearing his own mace, to ensure for them the same reception as if he had himself been in their company.

In connection with this matter, we cannot fail to recollect the rod of Moses, which was the instrument of all his numerous miracles in Egypt, and in the wilderness, and which he was on all occasions enjoined to use. We remember also that the chiefs of the tribes had staves or rods as the symbol of their authority; and that the budding of Aaron's rod, when it was laid up along with theirs, became the sign of the peculiar powers with which he was invested. This rod was preserved for a standing memorial in the tabernacle. Even the magicians of Egypt had rods like that of Moses, which they used in the same manner, as signs of the thaumaturgic power with which they claimed to be endowed.

In India the *orou-mulle-pirambu* (*i. e.* cane with one knot) is believed to possess miraculous powers, whether in the hands of a magician or of a private person. It is about the size of the middle finger, and must have only one knot in its whole length. Mr. Roberts, in his *Oriental Illustrations*, produces the following native declarations on the subject: "A man bitten by a serpent will be assuredly cured, if the cane or rod be placed upon him: nay, should he be dead, it will restore him to life. 'Yes, sir, the man who has such a stick need neither fear serpents nor evil spirits.'" Mr. Roberts adds, "A native gentleman known to me, has the staff of his umbrella made of one of these rods; and great satisfaction and comfort he has in this, his constant companion. 'The sun cannot smite him by day, neither the moon by night; the serpents and wild beasts move off swiftly; and the evil spirits dare not come near to him.'"

Various reasons have been offered to explain why the application of the staff to the dead child did not produce the effect intended by the prophet. Some suppose that the fault was in his servant, Gehazi, who either did not follow the particular directions given him by his master, or lacked the proper faith, or was under the influence of wrong motives and feelings. All this is, however, purely conjectural, and has no foundation whatever in the sacred narrative. Others imagine that Elisha himself was not free from presumption in supposing that his staff alone would be a sufficient instrument for so great a miracle, even without his presence; and that for this reason his call upon the Lord was not in this form answered. Finally, some ascribe the failure to the mother's manifest want of faith in any result to be produced by the staff. To us the fact appears to be clearly this. Elisha did not at first mean to go himself to Shunem, and for that reason sent his staff to supply the lack of his own presence. If he had then intended to go himself, there would have been no need for sending his staff beforehand; and his haste to do so might afford an opportunity to the ungodly of throwing disparagement on the miracle, by saying that he did this because he apprehended the child would be "too dead," before he came himself, to be revived at all.

But after he had sent away the servant, his observation of the uneasiness of the mother, whom he now expected to go home satisfied, and her avowed determination not to leave him, which was a polite way of pressing him to go in person, induced him to alter his purpose, and, with the kindness natural to him, to forego his own engagements at Carmel, in order to satisfy

ELISHA RAISING THE SHUNAMMITE'S SON

her wishes by accompanying her to her forlorn home. It was probably in consequence of this change of plan that no response was made to the first claim of faith by means of the staff. *That* appeal was in fact superseded the moment he resolved to go in person—the Lord thus reserving for the personal intercession of His prophet the honour of this marvellous deed.

THE PROUD MIND OF THE FLESH

2 Kings 5:11-12

THE deeply interesting and suggestive anecdote of Naaman the Syrian, who came to Samaria to be cured of his leprosy, and was healed by bathing seven times in the Jordan at the command of Elisha, is one on which volumes might be, and actually have been, written.[1] It especially abounds with matter from which, by nearer or remoter analogy, instruction in things spiritual may be drawn; and seeing that, in its first aspect, it is no more than a simply told incident in the history of Elisha, we scarcely know any passage of holy writ of the same extent, which more remarkably bears out the declaration of the apostle, that "*all Scripture* is profitable for doctrine, for reproof, for instruction in righteousness." The history of Naaman is "profitable," not for one of these things separately, but for all of them.

The point of this narrative, to the consideration of which our mind is to-day most drawn, is Naaman's near failure of cure, by reason of his having settled in his own mind the mode in which it was to be done, and his scorn of the simple and naturally inadequate instrumentality prescribed by the prophet.

We, knowing much better than Naaman did, the character and claims of Elisha, are apt to be amazed at the petulance and pride of Naaman. Yet in fact there are few of us—are there any? —who have not manifested many times in the course of our career, as much, or more, resistance to the demands upon our faith, and to the exigencies appointed by God for the humiliation of "the proud mind of the flesh," than ever Naaman did, and often with far less reason. Let us rather admit, that the demand upon the faith of Naaman, and the extent to which he was required to bend down his natural reason, formed

[1] We have before us one old folio volume of about 900 pages, upon seven verses of this history.

somewhat of a severe exaction from one so raw and inexperienced in the things of God. Yet it is the common course of the Lord's dealings with those whom He brings under the operation of His healing grace. The course is paternal. As a father deals with his children, so deals He with us. He demands obedience, He exacts submission, He requires faith; and then, the mind being brought into the right state, He teaches, He leads, He heals. So His soldiers at their enlistment are subject to the same discipline as the world's soldiers. Obedience, discipline, is first of all exacted. This is the foundation of all things, and facilitates the education and training, which go to complete the good soldier for the spiritual no less than for the temporal warfare.

This fundamental requisite is generally enforced upon us in the same way as in the case of Naaman, by the Lord's refusing to be bound by the course of proceeding which seems to us best, and pursuing a course of His own, to which our unqualified submission is demanded. And often, in the course of our career, we are checked in the same manner, with rigorous claims upon our submission, until we are brought into the state of having no will of our own, but are content to be still in the Lord's hands, leaving Him to dispose of all things for us, and recognizing in all matters, and that readily and cheerfully, His way as the best. This refusal to be bound by our courses, is a right which the Lord exercises for our good, by bringing us into a state of affectionate and constant dependence upon Him in all things. Hence we are continually taken at unawares, with incidents which we did not expect, or could not calculate upon, but the right reception of which, or the contemplation of our constant liability to which, serves to hedge up our way when we become prone to wander, and to instruct as well in all the lessons of His school.

"I am a scholar : The great Lord of love
    And life my Master is, who from above,
    All that lack learning to his school invites."

And in that school it is as often by His discipline —by His rod as by His book—that He teaches us to profit.

It is only by the grafting of our will into His, that we can bear much fruit—any fruit; and no branch was ever yet grafted without being cut to the quick. In what He allows us, or in what He takes from us, in His dealings with us, or in His actions upon us through others, the same object is always kept in view, of teaching us our dependence upon Him; and it is well with us—very well, then *only* well—when our will so works with His, that in all we see, or hear, or enjoy, or suffer, we strive to realize for ourselves that which He strives to teach—to see His will, and to have no will but His.

This dependence upon Him, and this submission in all things to Him, is health to our souls and marrow to our bones; and therefore, for our profit, and because the Lord loves us, will He seek to bring us into this state by the dispensations of His providence and grace. He is a great King. He is our sovereign Master; and often the soul that shrinks most keenly from man's despotisms, submits the most cheerfully to hold all things, from the least even to the greatest, at the absolute disposal of Him whose imperial prerogatives are not only beyond dispute, but give that which man most needs, and which he can nowhere else find—REST for the soul amidst all life's perturbations.

We may, to a certain extent, take it for granted, that if we have well tilled our ground, we shall in due course have a sowing season; that if we have sown our seed, we shall in due time reap the crop; and that if we have carried it to our barns, we shall at leisure thresh out and eat the fruit of our labour. And so, generally, it comes to pass. Yet we still hold all at our Lord's prerogative; and by wet, by drought, by sunshine, and in a hundred other ways, He will teach us that He reigns; and He is not so tied by the means and husbandry we use, but that for our presumption, unbelief, or unthankfulness, He will use His prerogative in bringing all the labour of our hands to nought. We are thus taught to walk with awe and fear before our God, who is, when it so befits Him, A CONSUMING FIRE.

There remains, therefore, nothing for us but to shut up ourselves and ours, daily and nightly, in the ark of His protection; to rise up, to dress, to eat, to work, to converse, to lie down with a humble and thankful heart, not as slaves, nor yet as presumers, but as those who know that they are not their own; as those who, if their Lord should say, "Thy silver and thy gold are mine; thy wives also, and thy children, even the goodliest are mine," could answer, "My Lord, O King, according to thy saying, I am thine, and all that I have."

How narrowly should we look, how guardedly should we walk, and how soberly should we use every blessing, if we were under bond to surrender all to a creditor at an hour's warning, and were beholden only to his courtesy for the bread we eat! Even so, let us walk humbly before God, who is our Sovereign, and has our lives, our wealth, our persons at His command—in a moment to take all, if it so please Him, from us. Let us daily take all we have as lent one day more from His hand, and use His blessings humbly and purely, as though we used them not; and strive to realize the condition of that holy man, who, when asked over-night whether he would go to such a place on the morrow, made answer, "I thank God I have known no morrow these twenty years."

We cannot part company with Elisha, in these illustrations, as we are now about to do, without adverting to the close of his days, in comparison with his master's translation. Elijah ascended to heaven in a chariot of fire, an ocular proof being thus given of the existence of another world—a world, the home of holy men with God for ever. Elijah had tastes of its blessedness before he realized its perfect fruition. The gate was opened, the chariot was on its way, the convoy was coming, as the man—persecuted, reviled, and despised on earth—walked along on his journey to heaven. "And it came to pass as they still went on and talked, that behold there appeared a chariot of fire, and horses of fire, and parted them both asunder, and Elijah went up by a whirlwind into heaven." (2 Kings ii. 11.) The world retired, the prophet approached a divine home, nature's sounds died into silence, the valley of the Jordan disappeared, new scenes burst on his view, and he found himself in that presence, where there is fulness of joy, and at that right hand, where there are pleasures for evermore. Elisha saw the miracle; and we conceive, that if he exulted afterwards at finding the waters dried at the stroke of his master's rolled up mantle, and felt that a "double portion" of his spirit had fallen on himself, he also rejoiced in the consciousness of an inward moral strength, quite as much the gift of God, as the superhuman energy which cleaved the rushing flood.

Elisha's departure was different from Elijah's. A prophet to the last, with a king in his bedchamber, teaching him to shoot the arrows of the Lord's deliverance, seeking to infuse his own strong faith into the monarch's breast, wishing him to strike the darts on the floor, not thrice, but six times, as the token of a six-fold victory; he died full of years and honours, and then gave life to a buried man after he was dead himself. "And it came to pass, as they were burying a man, that behold they spied a band of men; and they cast the man into the sepulchre of Elisha, and when the man was let down and touched the bones of Elisha, he revived and stood up on his feet." (2 Kings xiii. 14, 21.)

We shall not be translated like Elijah, nor do signs and wonders like Elisha; but if we have their spiritual life, their faith, their courage, their love of God, and their good will to men, we shall find, as we feel the stroke of mortality, and experience the mystery of dissolution, and go through the valley and across the flood, that such are our supports, such the presence of the Lord God of Elijah, such the hope going before, and the rapture following after—that the stroke is repelled, and the pain is nothing —that there is moonlight in the valley, and that if the bed of the river be not dry, yet the pilgrim can ford the waters safely. And when we are gone, and are happy in heaven, we may leave behind us in what we have said and done, that through which God shall work, to give life to some spiritually dead, who perchance may pass by and touch our graves.

S.

NAAMAN

2 Kings 5

In the remarkable history of the visit of the Syrian general, Naaman, to seek the cure of his leprosy from the hands of Elisha, there are a few points that especially awaken our curiosity and interest; and it is to the consideration of these that we shall limit our claim upon the reader's attention. Some may be disposed to sympathize in the surprise and disappointment of the Syrian, that the prophet sent him away to wash in the Jordan, instead of coming out, and, after praying to the Lord, laying his hand upon him and healing him on the spot. When we allow ourselves to think, the expectation that he would do this appears highly reasonable, and the process indidicated exceedingly proper and becoming. Looking to the result, we know that important objects were gained by the course which the prophet took. On this topic we may not enter. But we desire to point out how exactly this course is conformable to the practice of resorting on all occasions to intermediate agencies, which distinguished the miracles of Elisha from those of Elijah, who simply *called* upon God for what he required; and which marked very prominently those of our Saviour, to whose mighty works those of Elisha bear considerable resemblance, both in their quality and number. Run over the list of these great acts, and observe how constantly this rule applies. When he wants to cross the Jordan, he smites the waters with Elijah's mantle. But it may be remarked that

he had, as would seem, simply *called* upon God previously, without the expected result; and it may be that it was this circumstance which gave him the habit of working through intermediate agencies, instead of by direct invocation. In curing the waters of Jericho, he makes use of salt; in multiplying the widow's oil, he works upon the basis of the oil she already possessed; in causing the iron axe to float, he casts a piece of wood into the water; to cure the poisoned pottage, he puts meal into the vessel; to the Shunammite's dead son he sends his staff; and now, to cure the leper, he sends him to wash in the Jordan. The same tendency of his mind towards the use of material instrumentalities and symbols is shown even on his death-bed, when predictions of future victories to Israel over the Syrians are founded upon the shooting of arrows out of the window by the hand of the king.

It has been asked, Why should Elisha refuse, in so decided a manner, the presents offered by the grateful Syrian, when he returned from the Jordan, cured of his inveterate malady? The reasons for his accepting them were stronger with him, as an Oriental, than they could be to us; for, as we have shown,[1] such presents were customary, and to decline them when offered is regarded as an incivility, if not an affront; and it was only the peculiar position in which he stood, and the high obligation he had conferred, which enabled Elisha to do so without offence. There must have been some special reason; for, on a subsequent occasion, we find him accepting, without hesitation, when in Damascus, the presents sent to him by the king of Syria. But the *onus* of the breach of etiquette lay on the side of Naaman himself. He ought to have presented his gifts in the first instance, before he had made his request; and to offer them after the request had been granted, divested them of their grace, by giving them the aspect of a poor return for one vast obligation conferred by the prophet. The omission was scarcely Naaman's fault, but arose from the peculiarity of the circumstances; seeing that he went first of all to the king of Israel, and was referred by him to Elisha in such a manner that the prophet already knew his errand, and was thus enabled to send directions to him the moment he appeared at the door, without giving him time to tender his presents. Offered now, they assumed a different

[1] See Vol. 1. pp. 639-640.

aspect, and Naaman had no longer any right to feel offended at their being refused; and, in fact, although pained, he was not offended. As the prophet might decline, without offence, presents thus offered, he wisely chose to do so. And why? "Doubtless," as an old writer remarks,[1] "the Lord would not that rewards coming from a novice (whose strength was small, though his wealth great), nor any bruite thereof among heathens (who must have heard of the fee as well as of the cure), should disparage and prejudice the grace and freedom of so miraculous a worke, as the conversion of a soule and the healing of a leper. And therefore he would have all such sinister constructions to be dasht. God's prophets never stand in such deep needs, that God must be dishonoured by their supply. God scorned to be thought to send for Naaman to possess his treasure or enrich His prophet."

But what are we to say respecting the new convert's request to be allowed to take two mule's burden of earth away with him? That he made this request at all, implies that he desired the prophet's sanction for the use to which he designed to put it, otherwise it would have been easy for him to secure what he wanted anywhere on his way home, without asking any one's leave. What, then, was that use? It may perhaps be gathered from his own words. He says that this miracle had convinced him that "there was no God in all the earth but in Israel;" and following his request are the words, "for thy servant will henceforth offer neither burnt-offering nor sacrifice unto other gods, but unto the Lord." It will here be observed that Naaman was converted, but not yet instructed. He believed in the power and greatness of the God who had healed him, but he still regarded Him as the God of Israel, whose power was, if not confined to that land, chiefly exercised there. He would therefore carry a portion of this land with him, that he might, as it were, have an Israel even in Damascus—believing that such worship as he could render would be more acceptable in connection with this sacred soil. Some think he intended to make an altar with it, as the altars of Israel were to be altars of

[1] *Naaman the Syrian, his Disease and his Cure.* By Daniel Rogers, B. in Divinity, and Minister of God's Word at Wethersf. in Essex. London. Printed by Th. Harper, for Philip Nevil, and to be sold at his Shop in Ivy Lane, at the Sign of the Gun. 1642.

earth. But Naaman was not likely to know this; and Israel did not actually offer the example of any such altars. Besides, local altars were discountenanced by the law, the sacrifices offered at the place of central worship being for and in behalf of all believers; and proselytes might worship God anywhere with most true worship, though only in one place by sacrifices. This, moreover, would have involved the grievous irregularity of the new convert performing a function reserved to the priests—that of offering sacrifice. If this had been his meaning, much harm might have ensued from Elisha's neglecting to correct the notions and purposes thus indicated. According to the principles of ancient Judaism, the practices here supposed are so exceedingly illegal and dangerous, and might have produced so much evil, that the prophet could hardly fail to have pointed out the mistake under which, in his sincere but uninstructed zeal, Naaman laboured; and as we do not hear that he did so, we apprehend that something less dangerous, and which might be conceded to the weakness of a novice, must be meant; and there are certainly existing Oriental usages, a reference to which may suggest less hazardous explanations. Naaman distinctly intimated his conviction that the land of Israel was a sacred soil, seeing that there alone the true God was to be found; and it was for this reason that he desired to possess a portion of its venerated dust. If, therefore, we look to the uses to which the Easterns apply the soil of places accounted holy, it is possible we may discover the right reason for Naaman's singular request. To Mohammedans the sacred soil is that of Mecca; and the man accounts himself happy who has in possession the smallest portion of it for use in his devotions. He carries it about his person in a small bag; and in his prayers he deposits this before him upon the ground in such a manner that, in his frequent prostrations, the head comes down upon this morsel of sacred soil, so that in some sort he may be said to worship thereon. May it not be that Naaman contemplated forming, with this larger portion of the soil of the sacred land, a spot on which he might offer up his devotions to the God of Israel?

Again, prayer, as among the ancient Jews, is always preceded by ablutions; and where water is scanty, earth may be used. May it not be that Naaman, in his compunction at having disparaged the waters of Israel in comparison with those of Damascus, now, since he had been healed by the waters of the Jordan, rushed into the other extreme, and conceived that no water but that of Israel could be fit for ceremonial ablution; and the water of Israel being unattainable in Damascus, it was quite possible for him to conceive that the earth might be used instead?

Then, again, the appreciation of sacred ground is so intense in the East, that there is a craving desire to be buried in it; and corpses are often carried to great distances for interment therein. When this is impracticable, the next object is to secure a portion of it, so that one may be buried representatively in sacred soil, by being laid upon some of it, or by having a pillow filled with it under his head, or even by having a small portion of it placed upon his person. The Jews at the present day partake strongly of this feeling. Such as possibly can, strive to go to Jerusalem to die and to be buried there. Those who cannot realize this, resort to the other expedients; but where the distance and consequent expense require it to be sparingly used, as in England, a very small quantity is made to suffice—as much as will lie upon a shilling being placed upon each eye.

With such diversified uses and applications of soil counted sacred, it is possible that Naaman had some other and less questionable object for his two mules' burden of earth than is usually ascribed to him: but these alternatives not being present to the minds of commentators, it was natural enough that they should have perceived no other object than that of making an altar.

The story of Naaman forms one of the most interesting episodes in sacred history. It is simple, graphic, and thoroughly Eastern in all its details. The raid upon Jewish territory, the capture of the little maid, her touching sympathy with her master even in captivity, the letter and presents to the king of Israel, the pomp and pride of the great man, his abrupt change both of manner and of faith, and his subsequent temporizing policy, are all characteristic of Eastern life. Naaman was no true convert to Judaism. He had experienced the omnipotent power of the God of Israel: he resolved henceforth to acknowledge Him as supreme God; but He would not go so far as to give up his rank, or to risk his worldly power by refusing to join with his sovereign in the worship of an idol. He was an intellectual convert, but his heart remained untouched by divine grace. Even his knowledge was yet very imperfect. His old superstitious feelings remain, though they have received a new object. He thinks Jehovah can only be worshipped aright on that soil over which He specially ruled. We are not informed whether he was ever fully instructed, or whether the germs of intellectual belief implanted in his mind were ever changed by the power of the Divine Spirit into saving faith. Elisha's answer to the plausible, but really humiliating, plea of Naaman throws no light on this point. "Go in peace," was, and is still in the East, the ordinary parting salutation. It neither approves nor disapproves of Naaman's pleas or plans. Naaman may in the end have been healed in soul as well as in body, through the instrumentality of his visit to the Lord's prophet; but of this the Scriptures give us no intimation.

P.

FAMINE

2 Kings 6:25-29

WE read of another siege of Samaria by the Syrians, in which they so well succeeded in cutting off all the supplies which the metropolis required from the country, that the utmost horrors of famine were ere long experienced in the crowded city. Not only were the vilest substances sold at an exorbitant price for human food, but an anecdote is related of two women, who contracted together each to contribute her child for their common subsistence. One of the women devoured her share of the other's boiled child, and then refused to give her own for the same purpose; and she who fulfilled her part of the contract disclosed the horrible fact, by appealing to the king against the other's injustice.

To show the extremities to which the people were reduced from scarcity of food, it is stated that "an ass's head was sold for fourscore pieces of silver, and the fourth part of a cab of dove's dung for five pieces of silver." If shekels be meant, the ass's head must have fetched nearly ten pounds of our money, and half a pint of "dove's dung" about twelve shillings and sixpence. As to the ass's head, it is to be remarked that the ass was forbidden food to the Israelites; but this would not restrain them, when mothers had come to eat their own children. The case even in this point is not without parallel. In modern warfare it not seldom happens that soldiers are driven to eat their own horses; and in Plutarch's life of Artaxerxes, an instance occurs of the Persian army being reduced to such distress, that they had to eat their beasts of burden; and even that kind of food became so scarce, that an ass's head would be sold for sixty silver drachmæ.

As to the "dove's dung," most people think that it was a kind of pulse, which has some resemblance to dove's dung, and is even now called by that name. It is preseved by being parched and dried, and is stored up for use chiefly upon long journeys. It is a sort of food which, from its quality of keeping as a dry pulse, would be likely to exist among the stores of a large city, and to acquire a high value when softer food had disappeared. To this interpretation we incline. Some, however, think that it means corn taken from the crops of pigeons; for the birds could go out into the open country, where food abounded, and would return with full crops to their cotes in the town. Others apprehend that it was really the dung of the bird; but suppose it was employed as manure for cucurbitaceous fruits, such as melons, for which it is now highly valued in the East. But we imagine, that people in such circumstances of famine are little solicitous about the culture of melons, or disposed to incur large expenditure for a future benefit. Men ravening for the food of the passing day, are not apt thus to occupy their attention or to expend their money. A few go so far as to suppose that it was not only dove's dung, but that it was actually bought to be eaten; and although we think the better explanation has been given, we would not pronounce this to be absolutely impossible, in the knowledge we possess of the extremities to which a starving people may be reduced. We are assured, on the authority of a highly credible historian,[1] that during the famine which afflicted Egypt in the year 1200, the poorer people in the city of Old Cairo "were driven to devour dogs, the carcases of animals and men, yea, even the dried excrements of both."

Than this, there is perhaps no description of a famine on record which supplies details more fitted to illustrate those which are given in the passage of Scripture now before us. We have ourselves been shut up with famine in an Eastern city, and know something of these awful matters; but nothing in our own experience, however distressing, will bear comparison with the details of the famine in Egypt, which the Arabian historian has furnished. After noticing the unclean and

[1] Abdallatif in his *History of Egypt*.

abominable food to which the people resorted in the extremity of their hunger, we are told that they at length went a step farther, and began to feed on young children, and it was not uncommon to surprise parties with children half boiled or roasted. At first this was treated by the authorities as a horrible crime, and those who were found thus occupied, as well as all who had eaten such food, were burnt alive. But it often happened, that when a miserable wretch, convicted of having eaten human flesh, had been thus burned, his carcass was found devoured the next morning. Indeed, these monsters ate of it the more willingly, because, being already roasted, it required no further preparation. When the poor people began to eat human flesh, the dismay and astonishment were so great, that these crimes became the general topic of conversation among the citizens; but afterwards they grew so accustomed to the fact, and even came so generally to conceive a taste for this horrible food, that persons of a better sort might be found who ate it with relish at their ordinary repasts, and even laid up a provision of it. They devised different modes of preparing it; and the use of it, being once introduced, rapidly spread through the provinces, so that there was no part of Egypt in which examples of this enormity might not be met with. It no longer created the least surprise; the horror which had been first experienced entirely subsided; and every one spoke of it, and heard it spoken of, as an indifferent and ordinary matter. There was at first no scarcity of this food. The streets were swarming with children of the poor, both of the tenderest years and also older, whose parents had died of the famine, and who had none left to take care of them; for the difficulty of procuring food prevented the friends and neighbours of those who died from taking charge of their children. The poorer people, men and women, lay in wait for these unfortunate children, hurried them of, and devoured them. They were seldom taken with the proofs of their crime. The guilty persons were surprised in this flagrant act but rarely, and only when they were not well on their guard. It was most commonly women who were taken; not that these were more guilty than men, but, as the historian supposes, because the women had less presence of mind than men, and could not flee with so much promptitude, or conceal themselves so well from search. In the course of a few days, thirty women were burnt at Misr (Cairo), not one of whom but confessed she had eaten of several children.

When these poor little vagrants became scarce, the wretched people, now accustomed to this resource for keeping themselves alive, infested the streets, seizing and bearing off such children of those who were less destitute, as appeared for a moment unguarded, or who had strayed, and even rending them with violence from the slaves and nurses in whose charge they appeared.

The historian assures us, that many women had related to him that persons had thrown themselves upon them, in order to snatch from them their infants, and that they were obliged to use all their efforts to preserve them. " Seeing," he says, " one day, a woman with a male child, just weaned, and very plump, I admired the child, and recommended her to take good care of it. On which she related to me, that while she was walking along the banks of the canal, a stout man had thrown himself upon her, and attempted to snatch away her infant; and that she had found no other way of protecting it but to throw herself upon the ground and hold it under her, till a cavalier, who happened to pass, forced the man to quit her. She added, that the villain snatched eagerly the opportunity to seize any limb of the child that protruded from under her, in order to devour it; and the child was ill a long time from the sprains and bruises it received from the contrary efforts of the ravisher and herself, the one to snatch the child, and the other to retain it."

There are other anecdotes too horrible to be transcribed here. But we may mention that in one case, a slave was playing in the dusk of the evening with a child newly weaned, belonging to a wealthy private citizen. While the infant was still at his side, a female beggar seized a moment when his eyes were turned from it to snatch up the child, and rent it, and began on the spot to devour its quivering flesh.

The government punished these enormities when they became known, long after the public had ceased to regard them with horror. Abdallatif says, that he one day beheld a woman wounded in the head, and dragged along through the market place. She had been arrested while eating a little child roasted, which had been seized with her. This incident made no stir in the market; but every one pursued his own business, without showing any marks of astonish-

ment or horror—a circumstance which occasioned the narrator more surprise than the crime itself. But, as he remarks, these were now among the things to which people were accustomed, and which had therefore no longer any power to astonish. Even adult persons were inveigled by the more reckless wretches, and murdered in order to be eaten. This was particularly the case with physicians, some of whom were called away as if to visit sick persons, and never returned, while some who did return reported the dangers they had escaped. The following incident acquired great notoriety, and was related by the commandant himself, who, in the painful circumstances in which he was placed, behaved with more firmness and discretion than king Jehoram. A woman came one day to seek his office. She was without the veil—a mark of strange disorder—and seemed overwhelmed with affright. She said she was a midwife, and had been called professionally to a certain family, where they had presented her with some *sickbadj* upon a plate, very well prepared, and seasoned with spices; that she observed that there was a good deal of meat in it of a different kind from that usually employed in making *sickbadj*, which had excited in her an extreme loathing; and having found means of drawing aside a little girl, so as to ask her what that meat was, the child said, " Such a woman, who was so fat, came to see us, and my father killed her. She is here in this place, cut into pieces, and hanged up." Upon this she had gone to the place, and had found there quantities of human flesh. The commandant, having received this declaration, sent with her persons who surprised the house, and arrested all they found there; but the master escaped, and afterwards managed to purchase his pardon.

Even the bodies of the recent dead were frequently devoured by the surviving relations. Nothing was more common than for those who indulged in this revolting practice, to allege that it was the body of their son, their husband, or some other near relative. An old woman was found eating the flesh of a male child, and she excused herself by saying that it was her daughter's son, and not the child of another, and that it was more fit the child should be eaten by her than by any other person.

We have given but a small selection from the illustrative facts which this single famine offers, and have no need to resort to the accounts of other Eastern famines, which present the same features, although seldom with the same intensity. Such things as the eating of children by their own parents occurred in the famines caused in Jerusalem by the siege of Nebuchadnezzar and the Romans. For the former we have the testimony of Ezekiel,[1] and for the latter that of Josephus, who furnishes details nearly, if not fully, as horrible as those we have supplied, all strikingly and emphatically fulfilling the words of Moses; "The tender and delicate woman among you, which would not adventure to set the sole of her foot upon the ground for delicateness and tenderness, her eye shall be evil toward the husband of her bosom, and toward her son, and toward her daughter; for she shall eat them for want of all things secretly in the siege and in the straitness, wherewith thine enemy shall distress thee in thy gates."[2]

THE WET CLOTH

2 Kings 8:7-15

THE Lord has won to Himself honour among the heathen. In Israel we have seen kings sending to consult heathen gods; among the heathen we behold a king sending to consult the God of Israel through his prophet. The great Benhadad lay on a sick-bed; and having heard that the famous prophet of Israel, who had healed his general, Naaman, was come to Damascus, he sent an officer of high rank named Hazael to ask him if he should recover from his disease. He arrived with the usual complimentary present; and it was in this instance such as became a great king, for no less than forty camels came laden with all the good things of Damascus. It is not, however, to be understood that each camel was burdened with as much as it could carry; for it is, and always has been, usual in the East—especially in gifts to or from kings—to render honour both to the giver and the receiver by distributing the articles among a number of human or animal bearers, greatly disproportionate to what they are able to carry—ten or more men, camels, or horses being employed to carry what would be

[1] Ezekiel 5:10. [2] Deuteronomy 28:53-57.

but a light burden for one. It is a piece of state; and as such has a parallel to the state custom among ourselves, of six or eight strong horses being employed to draw carriages which one or two might pull with ease.

Still the offering was royal; and we do not find that Elisha declined it, as he had formerly that of Naaman. The circumstances were altogether different. No cure, but only an oracular response, was sought; and the name of the Lord whom the prophet served would not be in any way dishonoured, but rather magnified, by his acceptance of the gifts thus rendered to him in the presence of the heathen. It served to mark the more signally in the eyes of the Damascenes their king's appreciation of the power and greatness of the God whose prophet Elisha was known to be, and the comparative disparagement which he cast upon his own idols. He had either sought the assistance of his own gods in vain, or thought it in vain to seek their assistance.

The interview between the prophet and the Syrian general is very remarkable, and it is of some importance to the character of Elisha that it should be rightly understood. The reader must refer to the account in the text, and then may consider the sense conveyed in the following account of it.

Hazael opened his mission thus: "Thy son Benhadad saith, Shall I recover of this disease?" Elisha promptly replied: "Go, say unto him, Thou mayest certainly recover." That is, the disease which laid him upon his bed was not mortal: he might certainly recover from it, and would recover if let alone. This was all that was required from the prophet, and he gave it. But he knew more, about which he was not consulted. He read the heart, the purposes, and the future life of the man who stood before him, and was willing to let him know it. So, after a pause, he added these words—addressed to Hazael himself, and not meant to be part of his response to the king: "Howbeit the Lord hath showed me that he shall surely die." Much misapprehension has arisen from regarding this as part of the response to be borne to the sick king, though the change of personal pronouns in the two sentences might alone suffice to show the difference: "Thou" in the first; "He" in the second. Having said this, the prophet looked stedfastly at Hazael, until the latter quailed beneath that searching gaze; and then the man of God turned his head aside and wept. Why wept he? Hazael himself respectfully asked that question. Elisha answered that he wept because he clearly saw the misery and desolation which this man would hereafter inflict upon Israel. On hearing this, the Syrian exclaimed, "But what is thy servant —a dog?—that he should do this great deed?" He was not offended, as the current version would seem to imply, or he would not have called it a *great* deed. But he asked, How could a person of comparatively low condition like himself have such high influence upon the fate of nations? The prophet answered that the Lord had disclosed to him that he should become king over Syria.

Hazael then returned to his master, and in reply to his anxious inquiries, delivered the message which the prophet intended for him, suppressing the intimation given to himself that he should really die. But the very next day it would seem that Hazael accomplished the purpose which he had probably long contemplated, and which the prophet had detected. He put his master to death, and in such a manner that the crime remained undiscovered, and the king was supposed to have died of his disease; and dying, so far as appears, childless, the wicked and unscrupulous general was enabled to secure the object of his ambition.

The mode in which this regicide was committed is very singular, and has been variously understood. It is said " He took a thick cloth, and dipped it in water, and spread it on his face, so that he died." We have interpreted this as Hazael's act, as is commonly done: but there is an ambiguity in the original which renders it really uncertain whether this was done by the king's order for the purpose of allaying his burning fever, and so as to *cause* his own death, or whether Hazael did it either violently, thereby smothering him, or by making what he knew would prove a fatal application, under pretence of affording relief. From the mere circumstances of preparation (supposing it Hazael's act), the latter seems to us to have been the case; and it consists entirely with his presumed object of destroying the king without leaving any marks of violence that might lead to detection.

What our translator calls " a thick cloth," seems to mean some part of the bed furniture— probably the thick quilted coverlet still in use. It is an Eastern practice in some cases of fever to wet the bedding, and then it is often done with good effect; while in other cases such an application would be dangerous, if not fatal. With reference to fevers of the former class, Bruce, speaking of the disorders common in the region of the Red Sea, says: " Violent fevers, called there *nedad*, make the principal figure in the fatal list, and generally terminate the third day in death. If the patient survive till the fifth day, he very often recovers, by drinking water only, and throwing a quantity of cold water upon him, even in his bed, where he is permitted to lie without any attempt to make him dry, or to change his bed, until another deluge adds to the first." We have ourselves received exactly this treatment, under the orders of a native physician, in a fever that seemed likely to be fatal; and we certainly recovered, though whether by reason of this treatment or in spite of it, we know not. Now, it may be supposed that Benhadad's fever was not of the sort to which such treatment can bring relief; but that Hazael recommended this mode of treatment with the knowledge that it was likely to be attended with fatal results; or else that the complaint *was* of this description, and was thus treated, and that Hazael took the opportunity of smothering or strangling the king, under the pretence of laying over him a coverlet fresh dipped in water. The coverlet used in the East, where blankets are unknown, being thickly quilted with wool or cotton, is of great weight when soaked in water; and it thus became the fittest instrument for such a purpose that could be found about an Eastern bed; while the use of wet bed clothes in fever would prevent any suspicion arising from the coverlet being found saturated with moisture.

It grieves us to find some right-minded men, such as Dr. Chalmers, assenting to the notion that Elisha put it into Hazael's mind to murder his master. But, in the first place, there is no positive evidence that he did murder him, or had any hand in producing his death; and, in the second place, and supposing that this crime *was* wrought by his hand, the tone of the narrative suggests that the prophet was rather intimating his knowledge of a purpose Hazael had already formed, than that he was suggesting anything new to his mind. All we can allow is, that Hazael was watching the turn of his master's disease, in the expectation that it would prove mortal, and that he would thus be spared the murder, but with a secret determination that his lord should never rise from that bed; and that the prophet's intimation that the king would recover, led him at once to execute his purpose, being now aware of the result of the disease.

———————

The thoughtful reader will observe something peculiar in the language of this narrative; and the peculiarity becomes greater when the Hebrew text is examined. In our English version of Elisha's reply to Hazael there is an apparent contradiction: "Go, say unto him, Thou mayest certainly recover; howbeit the Lord hath showed me that he shall surely die." If we adopt this translation, Dr. Kitto's interpretation of it is natural. But, in my opinion, the translation is somewhat strained. The conditional word "mayest" has no representative in Hebrew. The insertion of it is an unauthorized gloss. If we take the Hebrew text *as it stands*, we must translate it thus: "Go say, Thou wilt certainly not live: Jehovah showed me that he will surely die." The first clause of the sentence contains the prophet's reply to Benhadad's question, "Shall I recover of this disease?" The second clause is a statement made to Hazael himself, confirmatory of the former. The Masoretic critics, however, have so pointed the words in the text, that, as indicated in the *keri*, the negative particle is converted into a pronoun with a prefixed preposition, "to him:" "Go, say *to him*, Thou wilt certainly live." In addition to the authority of the Jewish critics, which is unquestionably high, this change is supported by the ancient versions, and by most modern commentators. I prefer the simple rendering of the passage as given in the original Hebrew text. It is in strict accordance with grammar and with the written text; and it requires no straining to bring it into harmony with fact. It has been said against it, that Hazael gave a directly opposite answer to Benhadad: "He told me, Thou wilt certainly live." I admit this: but I believe Hazael gave that answer because it suited his purpose better. To me it seems probable that Hazael's lie may have suggested the suppression of the negative in the previous passage.

There seems to me to be no ambiguity in the concluding verse of this narrative. Hazael is the chief actor in the drama. He is the natural, and indeed, according to the structure of the passage, the necessary subject of the verb: "He (that is Hazael) took the coverlet," etc. A deliberate murder was committed, and Hazael was the murderer. It was committed, too, in a way that is still known, and too often practised, in the East.

P.

———————

The present mentioned in the sacred narrative (2 Kings viii. 9), consisting of "every good thing of Damascus," so as to furnish loads for forty camels, must have been of great value. As we were approaching the city twelve years ago, on a beautiful spring noon, having crossed the long plain to the south, whence a distant view is obtained of the green oasis, amidst which rise the bright buildings of the old Syrian metropolis—we saw a train of laden camels passing the road with measured tread, which reminded us of this incident in Elisha's history. With it, of course, occurred the recollection of the words of Hazael to Elisha, "Why weepeth my lord?" and the answer, "Because I know the evil that thou wilt do unto the children of Israel: their strongholds wilt thou set on fire, and their young men wilt thou slay with the sword, and wilt dash their children, and rip up their women with child." Then follows the well known question as it stands in our version, "But what, is thy servant a dog, that he should do this thing?"—a question generally supposed to have arisen out of horror created by a prophecy of so much cruelty and suffering. It is often employed to illustrate men's ignorance of themselves, and how at one time they start back at the idea of certain things, which they afterwards accomplish without compunction. "But after all the dog did it," is the quaint comment of a preacher on this popular text. On our return from the East a different explanation came before us, which we are constrained to adopt, and we cannot do better than give it in the following passage,—" Here was a man who, but give him the power, would oppress and 'cut Israel short,' would 'thrash the land with thrashing instruments of iron,' and make them 'like the dust by thrashing,' as no former king of Syria had done; and that at a time when the prophet would be no longer alive to warn and to advise. At Hazael's request Elisha confesses the reason of his tears. But the prospect is one that has no sorrow for Hazael. How such a career presented itself to him may be inferred from his answer. His only doubt is the possibility of such good fortune of one so mean. 'But what is thy slave, dog that he is, that he should do this great thing?' To which Elisha replies, 'Jehovah hath showed me that thou wilt be king over Syria.'"—*Smith's Dictionary of the Bible*, art. "Elisha," Vol. i. 541.

It is added in a note, "The authorized version, by omitting, as usual, the definite article before dog, and by its punctuation of the sentence, completely misrepresents the very characteristic turn of the original, given above, and also differs from all the versions. In the Hebrew the word 'dog' has the force of *meanness*, in the authorized version, of *cruelty*." It certainly appears to me that Hazael, as a Syrian soldier, would be more struck with grateful surprise at the thought of having power to accomplish such bloody victories, than with painful compassion at the idea of sufferings so commonly inflicted by great conquerors.

In the *Speaker's Commentary* the passage is translated, "But what is thy servant, the dog, that he should do this great thing?" It is added, "he does not shrink from Elisha's words, or mean to say that he would be a dog, could he act so cruelly as Elisha predicts he will. On the contrary, Elisha's prediction has raised his hopes, and his only doubt is whether so much good fortune, 'this great thing' can be in store for one so mean." The Septuagint translates here "this *dead* dog," the exact phrase which occurs in 1 Sam. xxiv. 14; 2 Sam. ix. 8; xvi. 9. *Speaker's Com.*, iii. 39.

S.

THE DAY OF DOOM

2 Kings 9:1-29

THE two kings—Jehoram of Israel, and Ahaazih of Judah—are both at Jezreel. Jehoram had received a bad but not mortal wound in battle, attempting to recover Ramoth-gilead from the Syrians. So he has left the army in charge of his general, Jehu the son of Nimshi—the very same Jehu whom Elisha had long ago been commissioned by Elijah to anoint as king over Israel—while he goes home to be healed of his wounds, and when he is thus laid up, he is visited at Jezreel by his nephew of Judah.

At the camp is a very different scene. Jehu is sitting with the officers of the army, when he is called to see a stranger. It is one of the sons of the prophets, deputed by Elisha; and when he has Jehu alone, he takes out a flask of oil, and anoints him king in the name of the Lord, with a commission to execute the Lord's judgments upon the house of Ahab. When he had done this he fled, and Jehu returned to his company. This affair had not passed unnoticed, and the officers were curious to know what "this mad fellow"—one whom they must have seen from his appearance to be a son of the prophets—could possibly have wanted with their general. He told them that he was indeed a mad fellow, for he had anointed him king over Israel. On hearing this they rose as one man, and leading him to a place, at the top of an outer stair, in sight of the troops, they laid their rich robes for him to stand on, and proclaimed "Jehu is king."

Their readiness in throwing off their allegiance to Jehoram is something remarkable. But it was known that the house of Ahab was in the present generation doomed to extinction. This was a thing people were not likely to forget. It was known that Elisha, who had sent this man, was a commissioned prophet, authorized to declare the will of the Lord, who had reserved the right of appointing whom He saw fit to the kingdom. And it is probable that the military were dissatisfied with the rule of a house so completely under the influence of one bad woman, and the errors and crimes of which had first and last brought so much discredit upon the nation. Add to this, that in the absence of a fixed succession to a throne which so many aspiring adventurers

have already won, loyalty sits but lightly upon the soldiery; and they are very prone to vote a popular commander into the throne when it becomes vacant, or even to make it vacant for him.

Jehu evinced his fitness to rule by the promptitude with which he decided on his course of action. He determined to set out at once for Jezreel, and to be the first to declare to Jehoram that his reign had ended.

This relative position of the two parties in the action forms the foundation of perhaps the most striking, forcible, graphic, and yet concise description of a revolution in all literature. If it were not in the Bible—the literary beauties and excellences of which are to many swallowed up in its higher and holier claims—this is such a piece of writing as would be entered in "Readers," "Speakers," "Beauties," or "Elegant Extracts," as the most masterly record of a revolution to be found in all the world.

There was usually in ancient times a watch-tower over the royal residence, where a man was always stationed, night and day, to keep a good look-out in all directions, but especially in that direction from which any sort of tidings might be expected. What he beheld that he deemed of any consequence he declared below in the courts of the palace. The "Agamemnon" of Æschylus opens with the soliloquy of such a watchman:

> "For ever thus? O keep me not, ye gods,
> For ever thus, fixed on the lonely tower
> Of Atreus' palace, from whose height I gaze
> O'er-watched and weary, like a night-dog still
> Fixed to my post: meanwhile the rolling year
> Moves on, and I my wakeful vigils keep
> By the cold starlight sheen of spangled skies."

In the present case, the frequency of the reports from the seat of war, and the king's anxiety for intelligence, naturally kept the attention of the watchman much in that direction. At length he is heard to call out, "I see a company!" and then the king, in his anxiety for news, sends out a horseman to learn the tidings. Again the watchman reports that the horseman had reached the advancing party, but there was no sign of his return. Jehu had in fact ordered him to the rear. On this another was sent out, whom the watchman follows with his eyes, and then renders the same report as before; but by this time they had all come nearer; and the watchman was able to declare that, from the manner in which he drove, it was probably Jehu himself—" for he driveth *furiously*." Hence it is that the name of Jehu has become a by-word for a fast and reckless driver. Yet it is perhaps doubtful that it is so intended. Josephus seems to have read it in his copy of the Scripture that Jehu drove not "furiously" but "slowly;" and when we take into account that, in the period between the first appearance of the party, and that of its coming within such a distance as enabled the style of driving to be distinguished, sufficient time had elapsed for *two* successive journeys to him from the city, there may appear some probability in this interpretation.

On hearing that it was Jehu, the king ordered his chariot, and went forth himself to meet him and those who were with him. This he would hardly have done had he entertained any suspicion of the truth; but that the commander should have left the army without orders, seemed so strange a circumstance as to excite to the utmost his anxiety and interest. It might be supposed to imply either that the Israelites had been utterly beaten by the Syrians, or that the army had revolted against its commander, who had fled to court. To this, and not, as we apprehend, to any intimations of Jehu, are his words to be applied, when they meet, ominously in the plat of ground that had once belonged to Naboth: "Peace, Jehu!" which may be read as the ordinary salutation of peace in meeting; or, if read interrogatively, "Peace, Jehu?"—or, as given paraphrastically in most of the versions, "Is it peace?" or "Bring ye peace?" The salutation can indicate no more than the wish to know that he brought no evil tidings from the seat of war. The answer suggests that it *was* put interrogatively. That answer was: "What peace, so long as the whoredoms [idolatries] of thy mother Jezebel, and her witchcrafts, are so many?" From this it would appear that the fatal predominance of the influence of Jezebel in the reign of her son, as well as of her husband, was the chief ground of public discontent and reprehension; and the most ostensible fault of this king—the least bad of Ahab's house—was his passive submission to her influence. If there had been anything more flagrantly evil to allege against the king himself, it would most certainly have been thrown in his teeth on such an occasion as this. These words, which no one would have dared to utter who had not cast away the

scabbard of his drawn sword, disclosed all to the king. Coming as they did from the general of the forces, attended by the chief officers, their full meaning and awful significance became in a moment plain, and the unhappy king saw that the doom which had been so long impending over the house of Ahab had come down at last. He said to the king of Judah, who had gone with him in his separate chariot, "There is treachery, O Ahaziah;" and forthwith turned his horses for flight, as his only chance. But Jehu was not the man to leave his work unfinished. He drew his bow "with his full strength"—with all the strength which a man throws into the stroke upon which hang his fortunes. His aim was sure, and the winged mischief he sent forth found its rest in the heart of the king, who sank down dead in his chariot.

Jehu had been commissioned to execute the Lord's judgment upon the house of Ahab; and his relentless nature concurred with his own interest in giving the widest possible interpretation to his commission; while he was careful, in every fresh deed of blood, to declare himself the Lord's avenger, who did but execute the orders given to him. No doubt, he was the appointed minister of delayed judgment; but we cannot fail to see that he used that commission for the purpose of sweeping away from his path all those from whose vengeance or hate any disturbance might, even by remote construction, be apprehended to his future reign. At this moment he chose to recollect that the king of Judah was Ahab's grandson, and to suppose that he was included in his commission. This monarch had fled, and, in the pause which Jehoram's death had occasioned, had gained some distance; but Jehu sent his servants in pursuit of him, with orders to slay him. He fled swiftly, but was so closely followed as to receive a mortal wound. His chariot, however, bore him off, far westward of Jezreel, to Megiddo, below Mount Carmel. There he died; and was carried by his servants in a chariot to Jerusalem, where he was buried in the sepulchre of the kings.

Meanwhile, Jehu looked upon his bloody work with grim complacency, and directed the body of his slain master to be taken from the chariot, and thrown into the plat of ground. "Remember," he said to Bidkar, his chief captain, "Remember how that, when I and thou rode together after Ahab his father, the Lord laid this burden upon him: Surely I have seen yesterday the blood of Naboth, and the blood of his sons; and I will requite thee in this plat, saith the Lord. Now therefore take and cast him into the plat of ground, according to the word of the Lord."

This reminiscence completes the first act of this awful tragedy, in which, like the old Greek dramas—far less old than this—one reads of accomplished fate. To it we owe the knowledge of the fact, that the appointed executor of the doom was himself the witness of its being imposed. All is complete.

On one of the Assyrian obelisks, in the British Museum, belonging to the reign of Shalmanezer II., there is an account of wars in Syria during sixteen years. His adversary was *Binidri* of Damascus, whom cuneiform scholars generally identify with Benhadad II.; afterwards Binidri fought with *Khazail*, king of Damascus—beyond doubt, the Scripture Hazael. Their force is estimated at above 80,000. Amongst Binidri's allies, "Ahab of Jezreel," or Israel, is mentioned, who brought a contingent of 10,000 footmen and 2,000 chariots. Compare with this, 1 Kings xx., xxii.; 2 Kings v., vi., viii., x.

When Shalmanezer made a second and third attack, Benhadad had hard work to resist; and it appears from the inscription on the Assyrian obelisk, that Israel stood aloof, and afforded no assistance. In these particulars, the testimony accords with the Bible narrative; and an additional circumstance is mentioned, namely, that of assistance rendered by Ahab to Benhadad. (See *Bible Educator*, paper by Canon Rawlinson, i., 127.)

In conclusion, this same record makes another addition to our knowledge, for it mentions "Jehu, son of Omri" (successor and supposed descendant of the great builder of Jezreel), as paying to Shalmanezer tribute of gold and silver. There is a sculptured representation of the tribute payers. They are six in number, of whom the first prostrates himself at the feet of the king, while the rest bear in their hands various valuable products. Two Assyrian officers introduce these tribute bearers; one of them is apparently reading their names, and a list of their treasures. "We have here the earliest representation that has come down to us of persons belonging to the chosen race; and though, perhaps, the artist did not aim at much accuracy of costume or physiognomy, yet there must ever attach an interest to his delineation of the contemporaries of Jehu and Elisha." (*Bible Educator*, i. 128; Rawlinson's *Ancient Monarchies*, i. 105.)

S.

JEZEBEL'S END

2 Kings 9:30-37

WHAT would Jezebel be likely to do, when tidings of these doings reached her—when she saw that

her son was slain, that her power was gone, that the hour of doom was come, and the destroyer was at the palace gates? Did she hide herself in the sacred recesses of the harem, which even he would scarcely violate? Did she, like some pagan heroine, strike the dagger into her own bosom? Broke she forth into bitter wailings at the desolation of her house? None of these things did Jezebel; but what she did became her character. The Jezebel she had been, that Jezebel was she to the last.

She knew that her doom was sealed; but she determined to let it be seen that she feared not, mourned not; and to cast one bitter and burning word upon the head of the destroyer, such as should haunt and scorch him all his days. As, for this purpose, it was necessary to show herself, if but for a moment, instead of casting herself upon the floor and tearing her garments and her hair, she applied herself to her toilet, and arrayed herself carefully, even to the painting of her eyes, to make it evident that she appeared as a queen, and not as a suppliant or a mourner, as the neglect of her person would have implied. This was her motive, and not, as some in ignorance of Eastern manners have supposed, from any idea of making an impression, by the charms of her still splendid person, upon the stern heart of the avenger. This painting of the eyes, still a general custom of the female toilet in Western Asia, amounted to putting the face in dress; just as laying on patches, or applying colour to the cheeks, did formerly in this country. This custom, which the translators of the current version of the Bible did not understand, and which they therefore render into "painting the face," consists

PAINTED EYES

in tinging the eyelids with a dark colour, from a black metallic powder. In performing this operation the eye is closed, and a small ebony rod, smeared with the composition, is squeezed between the lids, so as to tinge their edges with the colour. This is considered to add greatly to the brilliancy and power of the eye, and to deepen the effect of the long black eyelashes of which the Easterns are excusably proud. The ancient Egyptians practised this long before the date of the present transaction. Figures of painted eyes appear in the monuments, and the implements used in the operation have been actually found in the tombs, with some of the composition remaining in the vessels. To a European the effect is at first unpleasant; and it used for a time to remind us of a chimney sweeper who had cleansed his face as well as he could, but had not succeeded in clearing the soot from his eyelids. But one soon comes round to Asiatic notions in such matters.

Thus prepared, Jezebel presented herself at the window or kiosk over the palace gate, when the noise of the chariot wheels announced the arrival of the new master. When he looked up, she returned his glance with a stare of defiance, and cried out—"Had Zimri peace, WHO SLEW HIS MASTER?" Jehu made no reply, but called out to the eunuchs, who appeared behind in attendance on her, to throw her out of the window. The slaves saw in him their future master; and the words had scarce passed his lips before she was hurled down in front of him, as he was entering the gates. He passed over her and entered the palace, the hoofs of his horses and his chariot wheels red with her blood, without pausing to see whether she was dead or alive. He took possession, and after a while sat down to refresh himself with meat and drink after that morning's bloody work. The coolness of this iron-hearted man is astonishing, but not without parallel. He probably ate with zest, and with as little saddened thought as a sportsman who has spent the morning in hunting unto death the wild deer. And why not? he would have asked. He had done a meritorious duty that day, and who had more right than he to eat and drink in the gladness of an easy conscience? It may be so. We had rather that he had accepted his task with reluctance, and had performed it with a leaning to mercy's side, than that he should have performed it with the tiger-like instincts and atrocious circumstances of one delighting in blood. But Jehu was perhaps the best man for the dreadful work in hand. Human sympathy and tender-heartedness are not the qualities one looks for in a public executioner, nor are they such as fit him for his dreadful task; and Jehu was an executioner.

In the midst of his good cheer, the new king chose to remember Jezebel, and said to those about him: "Go, see now this cursed woman, and bury her; for she is a king's daughter." Presently they returned with horror to inform him, that they found no more of her than the skull, the feet, and the palms of the hands. The street dogs had eaten the rest; and this was at the palace gates! Were there none at hand, even there, to scare away the vile brutes from the corpse of the woman before whom, yesterday, the nation trembled? We can hardly think but that there were some who looked on, and saw it all, but forbore to interfere,—whether from the brutal joy which low minds take in the abasement of the great,—or, which is as likely, because they feared to do aught which might bear the aspect of an interference between the savage king and his prey. That king heard the account, and declared that in this also a part of his task as doom-worker had been accomplished. "This," said he, "is the word of the Lord, which He spake by His servant Elijah the Tishbite, saying, In the portion of Jezreel shall dogs eat the flesh of Jezebel: and the carcass of Jezebel shall be as dung upon the face of the field in the portion of Jezreel; so that they shall not say, This is Jezebel."

SYRIAN STREET DOG

In illustration of this shocking end of the corpse of Jezebel, it remains to remark, that the more than half-wild street dogs of the East, living upon their own resources, and without owners, soon make a rapid clearance of the flesh of dead bodies left exposed, whether of human creatures or beasts. Among other instances it is recorded, that a number of Indian pilgrims were drowned by the sinking of a ferry-boat in which they were crossing a river. Two days after, a spectator relates: "On my approaching several of these sad vestiges of mortality, I perceived that the flesh had been completely devoured from the bones by the Pariah dogs, vultures, and other obscene animals. The only portion of the several corpses I noticed that remained entire and untouched, were the bottoms of the feet and insides of the hands; and this extraordinary circumstance immediately brought to my mind the remarkable passage recorded in the Second Book of Kings, relating to the death and ultimate fate of Jezebel, who was, as to her body, eaten of dogs, and nothing remained of her but the palms of her hands and the soles of her feet. The former narration may afford a corroborative proof of the rooted antipathy the dog has to prey upon the human hands and feet. Why such should be the case, remains a mystery."

HEADS

2 Kings 10

THE great body of Ahab's descendants, seventy in number, and many of them of very tender age, were at Samaria, "with the great men of the city who brought them up." This would suggest that the existing usage in Persia and some other Eastern countries, by which the king throws upon his nobles the cost of maintaining a numerous progeny, existed at this ancient date in Israel. In this case the king, as a great favour, gives one of his sons to some person whom he supposes able to bear the expense, to be brought up and educated according to his rank. The young prince soon becomes the cuckoo in the sparrow's nest—the little despot of the house—who must not be denied anything, or be in any way checked or controlled. The simple threat to complain to his father or to his mother, if any of his wishes are left ungratified, or any of his impulses checked, is quite sufficient to fill the house with terror, and to make all subservient to his will, however unreasonable. Hence, besides the great expense, the inconvenience and the subversion of domestic comfort are such, that the distinguished favour is received with little real gratitude—although it cannot be declined, and must be received with expressions of the profoundest thankfulness and devotion.

To the persons in charge of the young princes in Samaria, Jehu *wrote*—for we now begin to hear of written communications more frequently than of old—a curious epistle. He assumed their devotion to the house of Ahab, and told them that, since they had the resources of the capital at their disposal, they had better set up one of the likeliest of the princes as king, and uphold his cause by force of arms. There was a latent irony in this letter; for the writer must have known well the real state of the case, and how little reason there was to suppose that they would take up the cause of a fallen house, known to have been doomed of God. It so happened. The elders of Samaria, having conferred on the subject, sent in reply their unreserved submission to Jehu, declaring their readiness to obey his orders in all things. His orders were that they should send the heads of these seventy princes to Jezreel, and themselves appear there "to-morrow about this time." The great ones of Samaria shrunk not from this frightful test of their obedience. The heads were sent in baskets to Jezreel; and when Jehu left his palace in the morning, his sight was greeted by two piles of gory heads, heaped up on each side the gate. He gloated his eyes for a moment upon the appalling spectacle, and then, looking up with a bold front, he said to those around, in that voice of hard sarcasm which seems to have belonged to his character, "*Ye* be righteous : behold, *I* conspired against my master and slew him; but WHO SLEW ALL THESE ?" By which it seems that he concealed the orders to this effect that he had sent—desirous of making it appear that this had been the spontaneous act of the leading men of the metropolis, then present, in testimony of their adhesion to his cause. None of course dared then to contradict his account of the matter, although the truth eventually transpired.

This cutting off of heads in collective masses, and making them into heaps, is or has been frightfully common in the East; and an Oriental, familiar with blood and beheading from his cradle, would read this portion of Scripture with little, if any, of the disgust and horror, and certainly with none of the surprise, with which it inspires us. The commonness of this also in ancient times is demonstrated by the numbers of heads severed from bodies, which, under various circumstances, appear in the Egyptian and Assyrian monuments. Heads, in fact, have always in the East been regarded as the best trophies of victory.

Among various nations, the heads of enemies slain in battle, of robbers, and of persons put to death by the royal order (not in ordinary course of justice), are presented to the king, and afterwards exhibited at the palace gate. There used to be, and there still are, niches in the palace gate (Porte) at Constantinople for the reception of heads recently taken off; and they were formerly seldom empty, though at the present day rarely occupied. It used to be not unfrequent in Turkey and Persia to meet a Tartar (or king's messenger) bearing behind him a bundle containing the head—pickled if the distance were great—of some pasha or satrap, whom he had been sent to decapitate, and which he was bearing to his sovereign in proof that his orders had been executed well. This has respect to single heads, or to small numbers of men. But when the numbers are great—as after a battle, a massacre, or the rout of a band of robbers—the heads are, as in the present instance, heaped up pyramidally, faces outward, on each side of the palace gate; and the builder of this horrid pile, if a man of taste and fancy, usually reserves a

BAGHDAD

picturesque head, such as one with a fine long beard, to form the crown of his handiwork. Indeed, we have it on credible authority, that these men make little scruple of taking off the head of a bystander for the purpose, if they find not one in their stock equally becoming for the apex of the pile. Nothing in the East so much shocks a European as the frightful cheapness of human life, and, with it, of human heads. In Persia the king has not seldom been known to express his displeasure at a town or village by demanding from it a pyramid of heads of given dimensions. Sometimes the Eastern conquerors conceive the wish to form such piles of heads into permanent monuments of the transaction; and this is usually done by erecting pillars for the purpose of inlaying them with the heads of the slain. There are many of these monuments—some of long standing—in Turkey and Persia. The most recent of these known to ourselves, are two pillars on each side of the road outside one of the gates of Baghdad, erected above five-and-twenty years ago, and inlaid with the heads of two hundred Khezail Arabs who had been slain or captured in an engagement with the troops of the pasha.

Jehu soon after proceeded to Samaria, to take possession of the capital. On the way he met a gay and gallant party of princes from Judah, proceeding on a visit to the court of Israel, whom the tidings of the revolution had not reached, so rapid had been Jehu's movements. These, in his still unslacked thirst for blood, he ordered to be slain on the spot; and it is quite possible that, like the early Moslem conquerors, he sincerely thought that, while performing these and other atrocities, which were greatly beyond his commission, though under cover of it, he was doing God service, and that he suffered not himself to perceive that he was following to a still greater extent the ferocious instincts of his nature, or that sanguinary excitement under which he laboured, combined with an under-current of selfish policy, which taught him that, after such a beginning as he had made, the more complete the riddance he accomplished of all the adherents of the house of Ahab—whether from sympathy of principles or from alliance of blood—the more thoroughly the power of future reaction would be weakened. Jezebel's question—"Had Zimri peace, who slew his master?"—rang constantly in his ears; and he was answering it after his hard fashion, which seemed to say, "Zimri had no peace because he slew *only* his master: I slay more, that I may have peace." Hence, also, the massacre of the Baalites—whom he slew, assuredly not more from zeal for religion, than from the conviction that among them the most attached partisans of the fallen house were to be found—and whom he seduced into an avowal of their apostasy by pretending that he was himself inclined to favour the worship of Baal even more than Ahab had been. That it was possible for a large number of persons to be imposed upon by this pretence, after what Jehu had done, painfully evinces the extent of religious corruption in Israel. Something may, however, be allowed for the still imperfect knowledge of the transactions at Jezreel. News travelled but slowly in those days; and the men who had come over with the king to Samaria—his personal followers and guards—had perhaps been instructed not yet to disclose the full particulars of the great tragedy at Jezreel.

HEART READING

2 Kings 8:11

LET us to-day recur to the fact that, when Elisha looked stedfastly in the face of Hazael, and the latter perceived that the prophet was reading his heart, "*he was ashamed.*" "Ay," it will be said, "and there was good reason why he should be ashamed, for there was murder in his heart." That there was murder in his heart we do not quite know; but we do know that, whether this were so or not, there was great reason why he should be ashamed in the presence of one whom he believed to know his most secret thoughts. This we know; because we believe the man lives not, and never did live, who could stand such inspection without quailing before it. Is there one that reads this who can affirm that he could stand with unblenched cheek before the man whom he believed to be viewing his naked soul—divested of all the purple and fine linen which cover its littleness, its foulness, its deformities, its sores, from the view of the outer world? Is there one who could endure, without confusion of face, without a quivering frame, the keen dissection of his character, his conduct, his spirit, by even the most friendly hand in the world? Would he be content that any human eye should trace the tortuous meanderings of feeling in regard to any one matter in which he has ever been engaged—the unholy thought—the ungenerous imputation—the low suspicion—the doubt, the dislike, the coveteousness, the hate, the contention—the lust of the flesh, the lust of the eye, the pride of life—that more or less enter into and defile, with the prints of villanous hoofs, the fairest gardens of life?

We get on pretty well by ourselves,—indeed, far too well. If the conscience be tender enough to make us aware of the plague of our own heart, and to smite us with the sense of our sins and our shortcomings, we too generally find ourselves in a condition to deal gently with our own case. The act of self-accusation is soon followed by one of self-excusation; and in time the hand acquires good practice in trimming the obvious asperities and sharp angles of one's own character into roundness. Very soon

"Excuse
Comes prologue, and apology too prompt."

No man hateth his own flesh, but nourisheth and cherisheth it too well. Every person knows that no one will handle the sore places of his character so softly as he himself does—that no one will confine himself so much to the oil and the wine, or abstain so wholly from rough medicaments and harsh operations. This, he thinks, is knowing himself better—is a more careful balancing of all the circumstances of his case, than can be expected from others, or is possible to them. They will not, he thinks, take the same trouble to understand him so thoroughly, to allow for all his difficulties so unreservedly, to adjust the balance of his good and evil so nicely, as he himself does. It is partly for these reasons, and partly because he abhors that less friendly eyes than his own should look behind the outer veil he presents to the world, and because he would not that any should be privy to the great secret which lies between him and the world, that he shrinks from the too near inspection of his fellow-creatures.

In this we show how much more fear we have of man than of God. To us it is of infinitely less concernment, both for this world and for the world to come, what man thinks of us than what God thinks—what man knows than what God knows; yet while we shrink with such instinctive dread from the too near survey of a fellow-sinner, we manage to get on very quietly, with small trouble of mind, in the perfect knowledge that One who cannot be mistaken—who sees through all disguises, and from whom nothing can be for a moment hid, and who understands us far better than we ourselves know, or than our nearest friends or keenest enemies imagine—has a sleepless eye fixed with unceasing vigilance upon our hearts.

This keen susceptibility to the inspection and good opinion of man, and this comparative indifference to the constant survey of God, is a familiar thing, and strikes us little, because it is familiar; but it is nevertheless one of the strangest anomalies of our nature, and is beheld with astonishment and grief by the angels of God. In their view it is an inversion of the whole order of life and being. To them God is all—His inspection is all; and that different state of things, which gives more *practical* importance to the survey of a sinful fellow-creature like ourselves, must present a greater mystery than any of those deep problems in material or spiritual

nature, which men have vainly laboured for a thousand years to solve. To us it is plainer. Evil is, alas! more intelligible to man than to angels; and the good and the true is more intelligible to them than to us. It is sin which has cast a veil between our souls and God—a veil transparent to Him, but opaque to us. He sees us as clearly in our deformity as He did in our beauty; but we have ceased to see Him, or to see Him as He is. There was a day when man welcomed God's inspection, and rejoiced that

"God was ever present—ever felt."

But he had no sooner fallen, than the consciousness of God's presence became irksome to him, and he sought to hide himself from His sight. We do the same, and for the same reason; for we are our father's heirs. There is a bird of which we are told that it plunges its head into darkness, and because it no longer sees its pursuers, believes itself unseen by them. This was the very thing that Adam did when he hid himself among the trees of the garden, and it is the thing that we do daily. We do not *realize* the unseen. We live by sight, and not by faith.

How different would be our conversation and our walk, if we lived and moved in the ever-present consciousness that the unseen Eye was upon us and noted all our steps, and that the opinion of us, hereafter to be pronounced in the presence of the assembled universe, as the foundation of final and unchangeable judgment—fixing our lot for ever—shutting us up in despair, or opening all the golden doors of joy—is a matter of inconceivably more importance to us than all the world can think or say, can offer to us or deprive us of! Let us believe, that to walk and act from day to day with this as a vital consciousness about us—as a check to sin, an encouragement to faith, and a stimulus to duty—without any supreme anxiety but to walk so as to please God —is a most pleasant life, is the very antepast of heaven. There is no bondage in it. It is perfect freedom; and is happiness as complete as this world allows. It relieves us from many masters, and redeems from bondage to a thousand fears. O the blessedness of being freed from this slavish reference to erring man's judgment of our conduct and our motives, by being enabled to realize the presence, and to welcome the inspection, of One who, although He be of purer eyes than to endure iniquity, is incapable of harsh, unjust, or unkind judgment—who has become to us, in Christ

Jesus, a kind and loving Father, and who longs with deep yearnings of paternal affection to pour out upon us all the fulness of His everlasting love! It is impossible for any one to be truly happy until this great work—the reversal of the ordinary influences upon his life — has been wrought within him, making God first and man second in all his thoughts: until the great matter becomes God's judgment of us, and the small matter man's; until, in answer to all injurious thoughts and imputations, we can answer with Paul: "It is a very small thing for me to be judged of you or of man's judgment; He that judgeth me is the Lord. And *I serve the Lord Christ.*"

ATHALIAH

2 Kings 11:1; 2 Chronicles 22:10

JEZEBEL is dead; but her daughter Athaliah lives, and the mother's spirit yet haunts the earth in her.

Athaliah had been married to Jehoram, the eldest son of Jehoshaphat, the good king of Judah. We hear nothing more of her than the simple fact of this marriage, until the time to which we have come; but, considering the spirit she now evinces, and recollecting the nature of the influence which her mother had set her the example of exerting over first her own husband, and then her sons, we may not be far wrong in ascribing to this true daughter of Jezebel much of the evil which characterized the reign of her husband Jehoram, and her son Ahaziah. The former no sooner mounted the throne than he destroyed all his brothers,—a piece of Eastern state policy, indeed, but alien to the spirit of Judaism; and which her own later conduct enables us to attribute to her influence over her weak husband.

To that also may be ascribed the extent to which this king went into "the ways of the kings of Israel, like as did the house of Ahab." Indeed, this is all but expressly said; for as a cause for this, it is immediately added, "he had the daughter of Ahab to wife." So Ahab-like, indeed, was Jehoram's conduct, that it was only the Lord's regard for His covenant with David

which prevented the same doom from being denounced upon his house as had been denounced upon Ahab's. He was, however, not suffered to escape punishment. His realm was invaded by the Philistines and Arabians, he was bereft of all his treasures, and his wives and children were carried away captive. Athaliah only remained, and the youngest of his sons, Ahaziah. To crown all, his latter days were full of torture from a grievous disease, of which he prematurely died; and the people marked their sense of the ignominy of his reign by refusing his corpse a royal burial. No burnings of costly incense honoured his funeral; and, although his remains were not cast out from the city of David, he was denied a place in the sepulchre of the kings.

His son Ahaziah reigned but one year; and being as much under Athaliah's influence as his father had been, he followed the same course. It is expressly stated that "his mother was his counseller to do wickedly." The end of this unhappy prince we have already seen.

When the corpse of her son was brought to Jerusalem,—when she heard how horribly her mother, and how treacherously her brother had been slain,—that her son's kindred had been cut off at "the pit of the shearing-house," and that the worshippers of Baal had been immolated in Samaria,—she caught the strong contagion of blood-thirstiness from the report of these doings. She saw herself a stranger in a strange land, an alien by birth and by religion, without common sympathies between herself and the people among whom she occupied so high a place, and without support from the remaining members of the family to which she had become allied. All the strong ones were gone. What hindered that she should herself seize the dropped reigns of the government, and guide the fierce steeds of ruin which threatened to whirl her to destruction? Her son had been slain because he was the grandson of Ahab and Jezebel;—what had she, their daughter, to expect from the spirit which had gone abroad, and from the ulterior designs of Jehu, unless she entered upon a bold course of reaction, which might insure both her safety and her greatness? There have been those who deemed themselves compelled to leap into a throne to save themselves from utter ruin; and we would fain believe that this was the case with Athaliah.

But what of the house of David? Surely

that was not extinct? No; there were many who had a right to the throne—all of them young, children of Ahaziah, her own grand-children. These stood in her way; or, though impotent now, might live to become a terror to her. Such natures as hers are incapable of re-lentings or tenderness, or account the feelings of natural pity as weaknesses to be crushed down, when they stand in the way of selfish interests or daring hopes; so, though blood of her blood, the young princes perished. As mother of the king, she had great power, high influence, and many dependants, which rendered her, in default of a king, and of a capable heir to the throne, the most powerful person in the land. She was thus enabled to accomplish all her objects; and Judah beheld the strange sight of a woman, and that woman a foreigner, seated upon the throne of David. She lacked not ability for that place. The conception and the realization of this object by a woman, among a people to whom the osten-sible rule of females was unknown, show that her talents were great; but far greater was her wickedness, and had she been as eminent for virtues as she was for crimes, it would have been impossible for her long to maintain her footing in a station promised and covenanted to the house of David. With that house her connection had been extinguished by the very steps which she took, to

> "Wade through slaughter to a throne;"

and she stood in Judah as a princess of Tyre and of Israel—in the former capacity an upholder of Baal, and in the latter the representative and avenger of Ahab's slaughtered house. Under such auspices, idolatry became rampant in Judah; the very abominations which, with his strong and bloody hand, Jehu had put down in Israel, reappeared in the neighbouring realm, which had hitherto been comparatively free from these grosser idolatries. It would have seemed to a cursory observer, that nothing had been gained by the repression of idolatry in Israel; that the same thing existed still, the place only having been changed, just as the piece of wood which disappears for a moment under the water comes up again a little way off. No doubt the cause of the Baalite worship was strengthened by large accessions of fugitives, who stole away from Israel when the change of affairs in Judah offered them a prospect of that safety and

protection which they could no longer find in their own country.

It does not appear that Athaliah attempted to avenge on the priests of Jehovah the massacre which Jehu had made of the priests of Baal, or that the worship of the Lord was forbidden by her, or His worshippers persecuted. Had that been the case, the temple itself would probably have been applied to idolatrous uses. From this she abstained, partly, as we have already ex-plained, because idolatry was not adverse to the worship of different gods; and partly, because her sagacity must have shown her the danger of the attempt. The worship of Jehovah was therefore permitted to exist on sufferance. It was tolerated, while that of Baal was patronized and favoured. A temple had been erected to the Phœnician god in the holy city; and for its furniture and decoration, the Lord's house was stripped of its treasures and "dedicated things," —a fact which transpires incidentally in 2 Chron. xxiv. 7; and it is there ascribed, it is curious to observe, not to Athaliah herself, but to her sons. What sons? We thought they had all been destroyed. Certainly her sons by Jehoram had been lost in captivity; and her grandsons, the children of Ahaziah, had also perished. Some suggest that, after the death of her husband, she had married another man, and that these were her children by him. But this is untenable; because Ahaziah, who succeeded his father, had reigned but a year; and even supposing that she had married immediately on the death of Jehoram, and assuming that this sacrilege took place towards the close of her reign, the eldest of any children she might have had by a second marriage, could not have been more than six years old. It is not even said that the Baalite temple was built by her. It merely transpires that it was in existence at the time of her death. Putting all these circumstances together, it would appear that the erection of this temple was among the enormities committed at her suggestion in the time of Jehoram, and in which, particularly, the sons of Jehoram, brought up under the influence of such a mother, actively exerted themselves. We thus arrive at the fact, that it was not less for their own sins, than for the sins of their father and their mother, that these princes were sold into captivity, and heard of no more.

A CORONATION

2 Kings 11:4-16; 2 Chronicles 23:1-15

For all that appears in the narrative, the six years of Athaliah's reign were quiet and undisturbed; and she doubtless flattered herself that her throne was established, and that the people were contented with her government. But they were only silent: they only waited because they knew not what to do. They had no leader; and, what was more, they had no ostensible object to fix their attention; for there appeared not, nor was there supposed to exist, any claimant of the throne of David to rouse them to action.

At length, when the power of Athaliah seemed most secure, it began to be secretly whispered that a young scion of the royal house had escaped the massacre. And it was so. The youngest of the doomed—Jehoash by name—then a mere infant of a year old, was saved by his aunt Jehoshabeath, daughter of king Jehoram, and wife to the high priest Jehoiada, who privately introduced him and his nurse into the temple, where he was preserved and brought up in the chambers of the high priest. When the child was seven years old, Jehoiada considered the time was come to put an end to this unseemly usurpation, and to restore the true heir to the throne of his fathers. The present state of things, besides being a great public wrong, was a scandal to religion, not to be endured one moment longer than necessity compelled. The high priest took his measures with great prudence and skill. He communicated the fact, with his plans, to those on whom he could rely; and rejoiced to find a great readiness on all hands to enter into his views, and carry out his designs.

The Sabbath-day was chosen for the demonstration, because then there would be a great number of the people present, and still more, because he could then obtain a double force of priests and Levites; for at the change of the weekly turn of service, he would be enabled to detain those who were to go out, and add them to those who had come in for the service of the ensuing week. For these to enter the temple in arms, would have prematurely awakened suspicion. They were therefore furnished with the swords and spears which, as we now first learn, were deposited within the temple. Even the officers of Athaliah's guard, or at least some of them, had been gained over, and lent the important sanction of their presence to the proceedings. Indeed, we may presume that Jehoiada would hardly have taken this bold step, had he not previously ascertained that the troops were not hearty in the service of Athaliah, and were prepared to hail the restoration of the royal line with gladness. All being ready, and the Levites properly stationed to guard the person of the young king and the approaches to the temple, the people, when they assembled at the morning sacrifice, were astonished at this strange display of military armaments within the temple, wondering what it might mean. But while astonishment held them mute, the high priest appeared, conducting a fair boy to a stage under the pillar which formed the usual station of the kings when they came to the temple. He then, with a loud voice, proclaimed who he was, and proceeded to anoint him, and to place the crown-royal on his head, while the trumpets sounded, and the people hailed the act with loud acclamations of "Long live the king!"

The noise of this rapturous uproar in the temple reached the palace, and Athaliah hurried off to learn its cause. What she there beheld, revealed the truth to her at once. She rent her clothes, and shouted "Treason! treason!" But no voice responded to her cry: no friends gathered around her; no arm was lifted in her cause; and on a word from Jehoiada, she was hurried forth from the temple and put to death. Hers was the only blood shed in this well managed revolution, except that of Mattan, the high priest of Baal, who was slain at the altar when the people hastened to destroy the idol temple. It is rare that any revolution of such importance takes place so peacefully, and at so little cost of blood.

The kings of Judah generally succeeded each other with little, if any, ceremony, without even the anointing, the solemn inauguration of the founder of the dynasty being usually considered sufficient for his descendants. The only kings whose accession was attended with ceremonial observances were Saul, the first king; David, the first of his line; Solomon, who had an elder brother aspiring to the crown; and now Jehoash, in whose person the broken line was restored. By this it is seen that the coronation was rather an exceptional than a customary ceremony, resorted to only when peculiar circumstances seemed to require the solemn public recognition which it involved.

The ceremonies are more particularly described in this case than in any other, though still with great conciseness. "He brought forth the king's son, and put the crown upon him, and gave him the testimony: and they made him king, and anointed him; and they clapped their hands, and said, God save the king!"[1] Again, it is stated that "the king stood by a pillar, *as the manner was,* and the princes and the trumpeters by the king; and all the people of the land rejoiced, and blew with trumpets."

There is nothing in the law respecting the anointing of kings; it speaks only of high priests. But as Samuel anointed the first two kings, and as it was an ancient custom to anoint them, this came to be regarded as an essential part of the ceremony. Its antiquity is evinced by the monuments of Egypt, which exhibit this anointing of kings by priests. When this coronation did take place, the kings were usually, but not indispensably, anointed with the same "holy anointing oil," stored up in the temple, which was used in the anointing of the priests; but the Jewish rabbinical writers tell us there was this curious difference in the form of anointing, that the king was anointed in the form of a diadem encircling his head, to show that he was the head of the

EGYPTIAN MODE OF ANOINTING A KING

people; but the high priest was anointed in the form of a cross, one line drawn in the oil, running down his forehead, crossed by another line drawn between his eyebrows. The scrip-

[1] Rather "Long live the king;" or, more literally, "Live the king,"—answering exactly to the French "Vive le Roi."

tural expression, as well as the Egyptian monuments, would, however, rather suggest that the oil was poured out somewhat copiously upon the head. One who had been himself royally anointed, describes the oil with which Aaron was anointed, as running down his beard to his garments. (Ps. cxxxiii. 2.)

EASTERN CROWNS

After the king had been anointed, the officiating priest, or prophet, gave the king what the Jews called the kiss of majesty or greatness, but what we should call the kiss of homage. This was upon the forehead, or between the eyes. It is recorded that Samuel so kissed Saul; and although the act is not afterwards historically mentioned, it was probably retained, as there is a distinct allusion to it in Psalm ii. 12: "Kiss the Son, lest He be angry." The crown was then placed upon the king's head. This was probably a stiff cap or turban, enriched with gold and jewels, such as is still used in the East, and which was doubtless worn, as at present, only on occasions of high state.

The "testimony" was then, as in the case before us, put into the royal hands. This was the book of the law; and while the prince held it, he entered into a covenant with God, to observe and keep His commandments as set forth therein. Then he entered into an engagement upon oath with the people, to govern them with justice, and to violate none of their rights and privileges; while the people, on their part, took a kind of oath of allegiance, and promised faithful obedience to him. The trumpets then sounded, and the people hailed their king. The ceremonies of the day were not, however, complete until the new sovereign had been conducted in high state from the temple to the palace, and was put in actual possession of the kingdom by being placed upon the throne, where none but the king dared, it is said, to be seated on pain of death. But if a king were proclaimed when another was in actual possession of the throne, the guards of the new monarch, to supply this defect in the ceremonies, would place him upon some kind of eminence, so as to raise him above the rest of the people. Thus Jehu was acknowledged as king by his captains, when they extemporized a throne for him, by setting him at the head of the stairs, and spreading their clothes under his feet.

On such an occasion many sacrifices were offered, and a splendid feast was held, at which the nobles and high officers were entertained with great state and magnificence—in fact, a coronation feast. The poor also were liberally cared for, and there were few who were left unprovided with " a loaf of bread, a good piece of flesh, and a flagon of wine."

POSTHUMOUS JUDGMENT

2 Kings 12; 2 Chronicles 24

THE conduct of the high priest Jehoiada in respect to the restoration of David's line in the person of Jehoash, suggests to us that he was a man of energetic and resolute character. In this we are probably mistaken.

There are few men whose character can be safely estimated from an isolated fact. The greatness of the occasion, the importance of the responsibilities devolved upon them, and the vital character of the interests confided to their care, often impel men of no distinguished energy to some one great and decisive action; but the occasion over, they subside to the ordinary level of their character—and we may search their after-history in vain for deeds answerable to the greatness which the one grand act appeared to promise.

In the case of Jehoiada, however, a little attention to the chronology will enable the reader to perceive that he was a very aged man. He was a hundred years old when he placed the crown of Judah on the head of Jehoash, and he lived thirty years longer—dying at the great age of a hundred and thirty. As the period of human life had been reduced to its present rate before the time of David, this age must have been as remarkable in the time in which Jehoiada lived as it would be in our own. A man of such constitutional stamina as to live to the age of a hundred and thirty, may not be physically older at a hundred than an ordinary man at sixty or seventy; still, at such an age he had reached what is, even for him, the time of life at which men love quiet and seek repose, and when little of vigorous or energetic action is expected. Thus we may account for the fact that, during the remainder of his life—in part of which he held supreme power as regent for the young king—he exhibited a kind of passive character, enduring, for the sake probably of quiet, evils which he might have been expected to prevent or remove. The high places, for instance, were not abolished by him; and under him occurred a most gross misappropriation by the priests, to their own use, of the funds obtained from the people for the repair of the temple, which had fallen into a dilapidated condition. That the high priest had any part in this malversation is not to be imagined; but such vigilance might have been expected from him as would have rendered it impossible. It was the king himself who first moved in the matter, and authorized the collection of funds for this important work : and when, after some years, his attention was again directed to the subject, and he found that neither had the work been done, nor was the money which had been collected forthcoming, he was much and justly displeased; but it was arranged that in future the dues proper to this object, and the voluntary contributions of the people, should be put into a chest, with a hole in its lid, placed near the altar, and which was not to be opened but in the presence of the king's accountant. The money was then told out, and placed in bags, which seem to have been delivered sealed, a certain amount in each, to those trustworthy men to whom the charge of the work was confided. We see here a distinct indication of a practice still followed in the East, where large sums of money are concerned, as in the disbursements of the government, and in the taxes and tributes paid to the crown. The money is in such cases deposited in long narrow bags, each containing a certain sum, and carefully sealed with the official seal. As this is done under the authority of the government, by responsible public officers, the bag or purse passes current for the sum marked thereon, so long as the seal remains unbroken. The antiquity of this custom is attested by the monuments of Egypt, in which ambassadors from distant nations are represented as bringing their tribute in sealed bags to the king; and the same bags are deposited intact in the royal treasury. This custom is so well established in the Levant at the present day, that "a purse" has become the name for a certain amount of money thus made up—now usually about five pounds sterling. In the receipt and payment of large sums, this is a great and important public convenience, in countries where the transaction of large accounts by paper is but little used, and where, the currency being chiefly in silver, great trouble and much loss of time in counting loose money are thus spared. Bankers and merchants resort to the same expedient, when the seal of the firm can be regarded as a sufficient guarantee for the amount contained in the bag.

EGYPTIAN TRIBUTE STORED IN SEALED BAGS

The money thus raised in Judah sufficed to put the fabric of the temple into a state of thorough repair, but not enough remained to provide the sacred structure with vessels of gold and silver, for which a supplementary collection seems to have been made; for it appears, from 2 Chron. xxiv. 14, that even these wants were eventually supplied.

The high priest, who had rendered such essential services to the house of David, was at his death honoured with the high and singular privilege of being buried in the sepulchre of the kings. During his lifetime, and under the check of his presence and oversight, Jehoash reigned well. But he was no sooner dead than the nobles who retained a predilection for idolatrous practices, made their appearance at court, and so won upon the king by their obsequious attentions, that he was soon seduced from the service of the Lord, and was led first to tolerate, then to sanction, and at last to practise, idolatrous rites; and when at length he dared to introduce such rites

into the temple itself, and the high priest Zechariah, the son of Jehoiada, ventured to raise his voice against these abominations, the king, by a word or sign, gave him over to the rabble, who stoned him on the spot. This act of Jehoash —in slaying the son of his benefactor, his near relative, the friend and companion of his youth, regardless of the sanctity of his person and of the place in which he stood, and while he was in the discharge of a public duty—is altogether one of the most atrocious in the Hebrew annals. This Jewish martyr, did not, like the first Christian martyr, pray with his last breath, "Lay not this sin to their charge;" but in conformity with the severer spirit of the Jewish dispensation, his dying prayer was exactly the reverse—"The Lord look upon it, and require it."

And He did look upon it; He did require it. With that deed ended the peace and prosperity of Jehoash's reign. The Syrian king, Hazael, invaded the land,—the first time this power had appeared in the southern kingdom,—and threatened Jerusalem. The force was small,— much less than that which Jehoash had at his command; but the king and his large army sustained a most disgraceful defeat; and he then thought that he had no alternative but to buy off the Syrians by the sacrifice of the treasures and precious vessels of the temple, as well as of the accumulations in the royal treasury.

He seems to have been wounded, for it is stated that "they left him in sore diseases." But his bed screened him not from the popular indignation, insomuch that two of his servants, reckoning upon impunity, if not applause, from the people, murdered him upon his sick couch. That they were nearly right in this, is shown by the fact that his son Amaziah, who succeeded, dared not, until some time after, "when his kingdom was established," to call the murderers to account. Indeed, the nation gave its solemn posthumous judgment upon the demerits of this king's reign, by refusing his corpse a place in the sepulchres of the kings, although he was allowed a tomb with the city.

It was thus in Judah that public opinion expressed a final and unalterable verdict upon the worth of its kings; and, considering the importance which the Hebrews attached to sepulchral honours, the prospect of this posthumous judgment may have had more influence upon the conduct of the kings than we can readily comprehend. It is to be recollected that the sepulchres of the Jews, and their public cemeteries, were outside the towns, as is still the wholesome custom in all Eastern lands. Only kings were privileged to have their family sepulchre in a town, as at this day we see the sepulchre of the Osmanlee princes in Constantinople. The only exception is now in favour of individuals eminent for their sanctity; and the like exception was made in Judah, as we see by the case of Jehoiada, if not of Huldah the prophetess, whom the Jews believe to have been also interred in Jerusalem. For a king to be refused a place in the royal sepulchres was a great dishonour; and this was as far, generally, as the Hebrews cared to go in their judgment upon their dead princes. That which would have been a great honour to a subject, to find a grave in the city, was a sufficient disgrace to a king, unless his remains were also deposited in the sepulchre of his fathers. To exclude *him* from burial in the city altogether, would have been a frightful ignominy. The reader of the history of the kings will do well to note the differences as to the modes of their burial. It is always indicated, and that clearly, for the very purpose of intimating the final public judgment on the character of the deceased king. There was something like this in Egypt, —or, indeed, the very same practice. Every man was brought to a sort of trial after death; and if it were proved that the deceased had led an evil life, his memory was condemned, and he was deprived of the honours of sepulture. Even the sovereign himself was not exempt from this kind of public inquest after his death. At the present day the Jews retain a fragment of this custom, by interring evil characters ignominiously in a separate and neglected part of the burial ground. We are not without some trace of the ideas on which this custom is founded, seeing that not long ago, suicides were buried in the public roads, —and at the present day executed murderers are buried within the walls of their prison.

David, and most of his successors on the throne, were buried in the "city of David." The royal sepulchres were as well known as the royal palace. The destruction of the city by the Assyrians did not, and could not, obliterate them, for they were hewn in the rock, like all the tombs of great men in that age. Nehemiah incidentally describes their position (iii. 16). Josephus tells us that Solomon buried David with great pomp, and placed

immense treasures in his tomb. These remained undisturbed until Hyrcanus, when besieged by Antiochus, opened one chamber and took out three thousand talents to buy off the enemy. Herod the Great also plundered the tomb; and it is said that two of his guards were killed

THE GRAVE OF DAVID

by a flame that burst upon them when engaged in the sacrilegious act. We have a still later testimony to the preservation of the royal sepulchres, in the words of the apostle Peter regarding king David: "His sepulchre is with us unto this day" (Acts ii. 29). We hear no more of it until the twelfth century, when Rabbi Benjamin of Tudela relates a wonderful story of two labourers finding their way into it, and being driven back by a gust of wind that threw them lifeless on the ground.

On the southern brow of Zion, outside the modern walls, stands a little group of buildings distinguished from afar by a dome and high minaret. These, according to an old tradition, believed in by all sects in the Holy City, cover the sepulchre of David. As matters now stand, the tradition can neither be proved nor disproved. The Mohammedans esteem the spot one of their holiest shrines, and will neither examine it themselves, nor permit others to do so. The principal apartment is a Gothic chamber, evidently a Christian chapel of the crusading age. Tradition has filled it with "holy places," making it the scene of the Last Supper, of the meeting of the disciples with Christ after the resurrection, of the miracle of Pentecost, of the residence and death of the Virgin, and of the burial of Stephen. The crypt below it is the real Holy Place. A portion of it has been walled off and consecrated as a mosque mausoleum. So sacred is it esteemed, that no person is permitted to enter except the Sheikh who keeps it, and the members of his family. The so-called tomb of David is here, a large sarcophagus of rough stone, covered with gold-embroidered satin tapestry. The real sepulchre of the kings, if here at all, is in the cave beneath, to which a private door gives admission.

This is all that is now known of the royal tombs. Fuller information is greatly to be desired. Let it be hoped that the day is not far distant when this and the other shrines of Palestine shall be freely opened to Christians, Jews, and Mohammedans, who have a common interest in them. Were this effected, I have no doubt that archæological discoveries of the very highest importance would be the result.

P.

PETRA

2 Kings 14:1-20; 2 Chronicles 25

WHEN Amaziah felt himself in a position to put the murderers of his father Jehoash to death, it is mentioned to his praise that, out of regard to the law of Moses, he abstained from including their children in their doom. This intimates in a remarkable manner the previous prevalence of the contrary practice, and that Amaziah would have followed it, had not his attention been called to the prohibition in Deut. xxiv. 16. The custom of including the unoffending family in the doom of their parents was formerly prevalent throughout the East. Mohammedanism has checked, if not suppressed, it in Western Asia; but, in the pagan East, frightful examples of it still occur. In our own recent war with China, the late emperor, displeased at the ill result of Keshen's operations against us, issued a decree ordering that the unhappy general should "be cut asunder at the waist; and that those who officially attended him, whether small or great, *his relations and all who appertain to him,* and those who are arranging affairs with him, be all indiscriminately decapitated." In the same decree, another general, Paoutsung, is ordered to be put to a slow and ignominious death, by having his flesh cut bit by bit from his bones; and it is added, "Let his native place be made desolate for a hundred lee around, and let his relations be sentenced to the punishment of transportation."

Under a young king of warlike tastes, the kingdom was soon astir with military movements and preparations. Amaziah was anxious to ascertain the military resources at his command, and caused a general muster to be taken of all the males fit to bear arms, from twenty years old and upwards; and the number was found to be three hundred thousand. Some have thought this number incredible. But why so? It is expressly said to have-been the number of all who were fit to carry arms—that is, all the adult male population from twenty to sixty—such as it was usual in ancient warfare to call out on great occasions, all Orientals being more or less familiar with the use of arms. The numbers given in Scripture are only high with reference to modern European circumstances, in which warfare is a distinct profession, which can never as such be followed by proportions of the population so large as this. Having this in view, and recollecting that the present is expressly stated to be the number of those qualified to bear arms, it seems to us small rather than large; for as the number of such is generally about one-fourth of the population, it would make the entire population of the kingdom of Judah only one million two hundred thousand—which we take to be by far too little. Josephus, who copies these numbers, was aware of this inference from the number stated, and little suspected that it would ever be doubted on account of its largeness, and he therefore states, that this three hundred thousand was only a selection from the whole number fit to bear arms. This we do not believe; for not only is it contrary to the plain meaning of the text, but it is evident that Amaziah would tax the powers of his own kingdom to the utmost before he thought of hiring, as he did, one hundred thousand men out of Israel, for a hundred talents of silver. If he could have got more than three hundred thousand in his own kingdom, he would not have gone to this great expense for another hundred thousand.

The object he had in view was the reduction of the Edomites, who had in the time of his father shaken off the yoke of Judah. But when about to march, a prophet demanded, in the name of the Lord, that the mercenaries from the northern kingdom should be sent away, seeing that no success would be granted to an expedition in which they took part. Amaziah objected, naturally enough, that it was hard to throw away all the money he had expended to procure their assistance; but when the man of God answered, "The Lord is able to give thee much more than this," he submitted, and sent the army of Israel away—thus affording a splendid example of faith, which makes our hearts warm towards him, and which it is lamentable to find unsustained by the later incidents of his career. The Israelites, however, regarded it as a slur cast upon them, and were highly exasperated, as the inhabitants of the towns and villages were made to feel on their homeward march. The campaign against Edom was quite successful. Amaziah was victorious in a battle fought in the Valley of Salt, at the south end of the Dead Sea; and pursued his march to Selah, the metropolis of the Edomites, and acquired possession of it. This Selah was afterwards known to the Greeks as Petra (both names

looked down from the edge of some tall cliff into this or some other of the deep valleys of Edom, that put into the mind of the king of Judah the atrocious idea of inflicting upon the defeated Edomites a memorable punishment for their revolt, by casting them headlong down from the cliffs of their own mountains. No fewer than ten thousand were thus destroyed; and the king, whose head was plainly turned by the intoxication of success, doubtless thought he had in this done a great deed.

ROCK VALLEY IN THE VICINITY OF PETRA

By all the rules of ancient reasoning, Jewish or pagan, Amaziah should have considered that this victory over the Edomites demonstrated the impotence of their idols, and the greatness of Jehovah, to whose worship he should therefore have been the more attached— the rather as this victory had been promised to him by the prophet as the reward of his faith. But instead of this, the king, by a monstrous perversity of spirit, took a foolish and wicked fancy to the gods of a defeated people, and thereby forfeited the favour of Him to whom he owed all his greatness. Henceforth he acted as a man whose judgment had been taken from him.

He was admonished by a prophet, whom he repelled by the stern rebuke, " Who made thee of the king's counsel ? " and by the threat of punishment. So the prophet ceased with the fearless remark : " I know that God hath determined to destroy thee!"

meaning *a rock*), the same city which had been shut up for ages in a ravine of Mount Seir; and the recent restoration of which to our knowledge, with its singular remains, and the innumerable excavations, many of them with richly sculptured façades, which line the cliffs of this deep enclosed valley, has excited the wonder and admiration of the present generation. But all these things were the work of a later age than that of Amaziah; though certainly the valley was even then the metropolis of Edom, and many of the excavations were probably of as old or even older date. The place is mentioned in the prophets as " the strong city ; " and its inhabitants as " building their nests on high among the munitions of the rocks," —an expression which would suggest that the excavated caves in the cliffs were not originally designed for tombs, but for human habitations.

When a man stands upon the brink of a precipice, he usually feels a strong inclination to cast himself or others down. It was probably the experience of this strange sensation, when he

Exalted in his own esteem by his victory over Edom, Amaziah seems to have entertained the notion of reviving the obsolete claims of the house of David to reign over all Israel; and it may be that the long unbroken line of kings in Judah descended from David, gave them a great superiority in their own esteem, and in that of the nation, over the kings of the short and rapidly succeeding dynasties in Israel. The king of Israel must have been greatly surprised to receive a declaration of war, in the shape of a challenge from Amaziah, in the words, " Come, let us look one another in the face,"—words that have a friendly enough appearance, but which had a most unfriendly meaning. To this challenge the other returned a most significant and sarcastic answer in the shape of a parable : " The thistle that was in Lebanon sent to the cedar that was in Lebanon, saying, Give thy daughter to my son to wife : *and there passed by a wild beast that was in Lebanon, and trod down the thistle."* The sovereign contempt so neatly conveyed in this message, smote the proud spirit of Amaziah, and made him more eager for the conflict. So he marched ; and not long after was seen marching back—a prisoner in the hands of the victorious Israelites, whose king entered Jerusalem in triumph.

The conqueror did not, however, attempt to annex the territory, or any part of it, to his own. He was content to seize all he could readily lay hands on, not sparing the precious things of the temple. He then departed, leaving Amaziah on the throne, but not until he had cast down a large piece of the wall of the city as a memorial of his triumph. How could it be a memorial, when the breach was without doubt speedily built up again ? The reply is, that the freshness of the masonry, and the recollection of the people, from age to age, that *this* was the part of the wall which the king of Israel threw down, would for a long time render it a monument of the transaction ; for none but a conqueror could thus deal with the wall of a great city.

As this incident brings the history of Judah and of Israel into connection, we may here note that the conqueror in this case was Jehoash, son of Jehoahaz, son of Jehu. During the reigns of Jehu and his son, Israel had been brought very low by Hazael, king of Syria. But after that king's death, his realm became so weakened under his son Benhadad, that Jehoash was enabled to recover most of the advantages which had been lost by his predecessors, and to restore the kingdom to a comparatively prosperous condition. It was, however, left to his successor, Jeroboam II., not only to drive the Syrians from all their acquisitions beyond the Jordan, but actually to enter Damascus as a conqueror.

As for Amaziah, his folly, and the disgrace he had brought upon the holy city—more intolerable than its conquest by a foreigner—rendered him odious to his people. A conspiracy was formed against him, and he fled from Jerusalem to the fortress of Lachish ; but the conspirators sent after him, and slew him there.

———

Edom is described as a narrow slip of mountainous country, extending from the gulf of Akaba to the southern boundary of Moab. Its mountains consist of a range of porphyritic rock, forming the backbone of the region, above which is a mass of sandstone, of rich colouring and fantastic form. The country is very fertile, watered by streams, and adorned with trees and flowers. It abounds in corn fields and pasture lands. The colouring and outline of the rocks, in the well known Wády Músa, are said by a recent traveller, Mr. Palmer, to be very fine, but not so magnificent in effect as he expected. " The stone is all of a deep chocolate colour, but where the surface has been removed by more recent cutting or excavation, it is really magnificent—red, white, and yellow streaks, coming one upon another, and giving, in the sunlight, the effect of gorgeous watered silk. The excavations themselves are very curious, and many which we saw could never have been tombs, but must always have been used as dwellings ; we had not, however, leisure to do more than just glance at them then, as our time was fully occupied in keeping a sharp look-out after our new companions." Afterwards he describes several tombs excavated in the white limestone, and amongst them a few detached monolithic monuments, resembling that known as the tomb of Absalom at Jerusalem, but without the conical roof which distinguishes the latter.

The formation on the way to the *Sik,* he describes as mostly limestone, and less rich in colouring than the Wády Músa, but the quaint excavations are worth visiting. The principal are a temple with Corinthian columns, and two side aisles—a tomb with four pyramids on the top—and three tombs, cut out of the solid rock, like that mentioned above. A narrow passage is spanned by an archway, built high up, and now out of reach, anciently carrying an aqueduct. The gorge becomes narrower as the traveller advances, and half way down are small square cuttings, intended for tablets, and niches supposed to have once contained statues. The *Khazneh* surpasses the other tombs and temples. The façade is of a deep, but delicate rose colour, the uncut rock varies from every shade of red to chocolate. The façade, Mr. Palmer thinks, consists of a portico ; the four middle pillars support a pediment ; on the open is an ornament, in the shape of a lyre. There is also a cylindrical form surmounted by an urn. The pediment, divided into three portions, presents nine faces, each with a pilaster, on either side, and on them are draped female figures. Mr. Palmer takes them for the Nine Muses, and the lyre for the symbol of Apollo. "The mysterious excavation, then, is nothing but the *Musæcim* of Petra—not what the Turks would call an Antiquity House, but the philharmonic institution of the place." He then describes the amphitheatre, with its boxes and benches ; which have nothing to do with the artificial construction, but are parts of the rock left as they were in cutting out the theatre. In front of the amphitheatre are tombs. There are inscriptions in the neighbourhood, and not far off is a ravine containing an aqueduct upon an arch, called "Pharaoh's Daughter's Arch," and the ascent to the east is named "Pharaoh's Gardens." There are other somewhat similar remains in the district, and Mr. Palmer may well ask, "who that passes through this goodly but desolate land, and regards the vestiges of perished grandeur in these rock house cities, can recall, without emotion, the solemn words of prophecy —'Thy terribleness hath deceived thee, and the pride of thine heart, O thou that dwellest in the clefts of the rock, that holdest the height of the hill : though thou should make thy nest as high as the eagle, I will bring thee down from thence, saith the Lord. Also Edom shall be a desolation ; every one that goeth by shall be astonished, and shall hiss at all the plagues thereof.'" (Jerem. xlix. 16, 17.)—*The Desert of the Exodus*, by E. M. Palmer, ii. 437-454.

The ruins described bear signs of Greek and Roman architecture, and belong to a period subsequent to that of the kingdom of Israel ; but Selah was a stronghold in the days of Amaziah (2 Kings xiv. 7) ; and Eloth and Eziongeber were sea ports, captured by David, and used by Solomon for equipping his fleets. (1 Kings ix. 26.) Probably Edom rose to greater prosperity after the fall of the Israelitish kingdom than before, but of old it was a country of importance ; and its connection with Egypt seems shadowed forth by the name of Pharaoh given to some of the ruins.

S.

ENGINES OF WAR

2 Kings 14:21-22; 15:1-7; 2 Chronicles 26

THE facility with which Jerusalem had been taken in the time of Amaziah, seems to have made a strong impression upon the mind of his son Uzziah, and to have rendered him studious of means by which cities might be defended. The ordinary fortifications, in their strongest form, were applied to the walls of Jerusalem and other towns ; but beyond this, we now first in history or monument read of military engines for the defence of towns, mounted upon the walls. It is said of Uzziah : "He made in Jerusalem engines invented by cunning men, to be upon the towers and upon the bulwarks, to shoot arrows and great stones withal." And it is immediately added, that "his name spread far abroad." It may be asked, were these properly "inventions?" We have no doubt that it is so stated—that is to say, that the word does signify "invented;" and if inventions, they were new inventions, for to speak of old and well known

things as the invention of cunning men, would have been unusual and absurd. We therefore conclude that they were invented for Uzziah— he probably suggesting the desideratum, the object ; and the "cunning men" devising the means, under his encouragement and at his expense, of giving effect to his views. "It is not said that the inventors were Jews." No ; but as it is not said that they were not Jews, the inference is that they were, the rather, as the sacred historians usually record the fact, when any great or curious works are wrought by foreigners. There seems an unaccountable reluctance in these days to regard the Jews as inventors in any sense. But why not? They were at least as ingenious and competent as any other ancient people ; and they had such wants as lead to the inventions ascribed to them. Why should not the people so high in literature—of which their monuments are the most ancient in the world—be below other nations in capacity for the material arts? Here, eight hundred years before the Christian era, inventions are ascribed to them which must have wrought a most important revolution in ancient warfare ; and if we can establish no prior claim for another people, why should not the Jews be allowed whatever credit belongs to the invention? It cannot now be said that we lack materials for judging of the claims of others. We possess sculptures and paintings at Nineveh and in Egypt, ascending to a much higher date, and abounding in representations of the defence and attack of towns, without any trace of military engines of the sort here said to have been *invented* under Uzziah's auspices ; and until evidence can be produced of their earlier existence, we shall rest content with this testimony. It is indeed a remarkably corroborative fact, that Pliny assigns a Syrian origin to these inventions ; and in his view, as in ours, Palestine belonged to Syria. Such engines for throwing stones and darts, once invented, continued to be used in the siege and defence of cities down to the invention of artillery. The engines for throwing stones are known in military history by the name of balistæ, and those for casting darts, of catapultæ. They varied in power, like our cannon. Some of the balistæ used in sieges threw stones of *three hundred*, some of a hundred, some of fifty pounds weight, while those employed in the battle-field cast still smaller weights. The darts projected from the catapultæ varied in like manner from small beams to large arrows, and their range exceeded a quarter of a mile, or 450 yards. All these engines were constructed upon the principle of

BALISTA

the sling, the bow, or the spring; the last being an elastic bar, bent back by a screw, or a cable of sinews, with a trigger to set it free, and contrived either to impel darts by its stroke, or to cast stones from a kind of spoon formed towards the summit of its spring.

Josephus records, that engines of this sort were employed with tremendous effect in the siege of Jerusalem by the Romans. The defenders of the city had three hundred engines for projecting

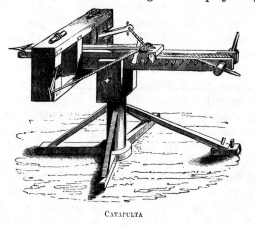

CATAPULTA

darts, and forty for casting stones, which they had taken from the Romans, and which practice taught them how to use. Among the engines employed by the Romans against the city, however, were some exceeding in power any they possessed. Some of them discharged a stone weighing a talent to the distance of two fur-

longs, and with such terrible force, that not only did it destroy the foremost men, but with unspent power rushed through their masses, sweeping away whole files of them in its course. The same historian, in describing the siege of Jotapata, where he commanded the defence, says, that the darts and stones were thrown from the engines with such power, that numbers of people were destroyed at once by them. The force of the stones, in particular, was such, that they broke down the battlements, and carried away the angles of the towers. He adds, that a man standing near him had his head knocked off by a stone cast from a machine nearly three furlongs distant.

This king Uzziah, wisely considering public security as the best foundation of public prosperity, put the country in a state of vigorous defence; and was enabled to hold a strong hand over the nations which had been the troublers of Judah. He repelled the Philistines and Arabians; he established his power over Edom, and fortified Elath, the port on the Red Sea; and, awed by his power, the Ammonites submitted to him. He organized his military force; and as men had been more ready at command than efficient weapons for their use, he laid up abundant stores of good weapons and shields in his arsenals. He also built strong castles on the frontier, as well as towers through the open country towards the desert, for the protection and refuge of those who were out with their flocks in distant pastures. "He loved husbandry;" and both by his example and encouragement, he promoted agriculture, planting, and the breeding of cattle.

These wise measures produced, under the Lord's blessing, a rapid return of prosperity to the country, which does not seem to have been materially injured by the great earthquake which happened in this reign,[1] and by which several cities in Israel also were swallowed up; indeed, the northern portion of Palestine, in the parallel of the Lake of Tiberias, usually suffers more than the south from such visitations.

Thus Uzziah became great, not by his own wisdom, but because he was a righteous man, and was therefore "marvellously helped till he was strong." But, alas! "when he was strong, his heart was lifted up to his destruction." He could not see why, to all his honours, that of exercising priestly functions should not be added,

[1] Amos 1:1; 4:11; Zechariah 14:5.

seeing how closely the regal and sacerdotal functions were connected in other nations. Accordingly, one day he went into the temple itself, which he could not lawfully enter, and attempted to offer the incense upon the golden altar. But he was followed by the high priest, and by eighty other priests, who resisted the sacrilege, who remonstrated with him, and warned him of the danger he incurred by this trespass. But the king was angry; and while he stood thus wrathful, with the censer in his hand, the priests perceived the undoubted signs of leprosy upon his person, and hastened to thrust him out as unclean, from that holy place. Yea, in his horror, shame, and confusion, he "himself hasted to go out." He was never again seen in public. He lived in seclusion as a leper, while his son Jotham administered the affairs of the kingdom.

Josephus says, that the earthquake which is noticed as having taken place in this reign, occurred at the moment of the king's trespass. He adds, that a rent was made in the temple, through which the sun shone upon Uzziah's face, and he was immediately struck with the leprosy. He also states, that outside the city, at the place called Eroge, half the mountain broke off from the west side, and rolled down four furlongs, and remained at the base of the cliffs on the eastern side of the ravine, so that the roads, as well as the king's gardens, were spoiled by this obstruction.

It is observable that, as a leper, Uzziah was not allowed, after death, a place in the sepulchre of the kings; but he was interred in the field which contained that sepulchre.

Uzziah was succeeded by Jotham.

In 2 Chronicles xxvii. 3, Jotham is described as having built much "in the wall of *Ophel.*" Other references are made to Ophel, as near the water gate (Neh. iii. 26), and as the residence of the Levites (Neh. xi. 21). Josephus also refers to Ophla—no doubt the same place—as near the Kedron valley. Ophel is a swelling declivity (as the name indicates), sloping off on the southern side of the Haram down into the valley of Hinnom, forming a spur or promontory between the Tyropœan and the valley of Jehoshaphat. Here Captain Warren has been at work, having sunk fifty shafts in search of a wall—such a wall as Jotham is said to have built. This has been done with complete success. The line of wall is ascertained to extend to a distance of 700 feet along the eastern ridge of Ophel. A tower has been discovered at a distance of 76 feet from the south-east angle. About 200 feet farther south it is believed

by Captain Warren another tower existed. A long break in the line of the wall is accounted for by supposing that the stones were taken away and used for building, such material being much in demand in the neighbourhood of Jerusalem. "The rock steps and caves which existed among the slopes of Ophel, are also fast becoming obliterated. The farmers find that these are the places where they have least trouble in blasting and quarrying the rock, and within the last few years many old features on the side of the old city have vanished; thus, year by year, the old Jerusalem will become more difficult to be understood."

S.

POLITICAL COMBINATIONS

2 Kings 15-16; 2 Chronicles 28

DURING the long reign of Uzziah in Judah, which lasted fifty-two years, no fewer than six kings sat upon the throne of Israel. He ascended the throne in the twenty-seventh year of Jeroboam II., the fourth king of the house of Jehu, who seems to have had the most prosperous reign that had for a long period been known in Israel. He extended the successes of his father against the Syrians, and ceased not until he had made himself master of Damascus and of Hamath. It is reasonably conjectured, that the weakness which had fallen upon this recently powerful kingdom may have been owing to the pressure, on the other side, of the great Assyrian power, which was already advancing westward, and soon appears historically upon the scene.

Of all the five kings after Jeroboam only one died upon his bed. The history sounds much like this: B murdered A, and reigned in his stead; C murdered B, and reigned in his stead; D murdered C, and reigned in his stead; E murdered D, and reigned in his stead. Jeroboam's son Zachariah was, in the very first year of his reign, publicly assassinated by Shallum, who mounted the throne, but only occupied it one little month, being then in his turn slain by Menahem, who of course ostensibly avenged the murder of Zachariah, but who, instead of seating the heir of Jehu's house upon the throne—and such doubtless existed—sat down in it himself. One locality refused to recognize him; but was treated by him with such ferocious barbarity, as effectually checked all further opposition. It was in this reign that the Assyrians, under Pul, first threatened the land of Israel. Menahem well knew his incapacity to cope with a power so formidable. He did not attempt it, but sent a thousand talents of silver to propitiate the invader, and induce him to forego his purpose. Pul, having other important work on hand, took the money, and turned aside for the present, allowing the kingdom a respite, during which Menahem died on his bed, leaving his throne to his son Pekahiah, who, lacking the military experience and fierce energy of his father, was unable to maintain his influence over the army, and was after two years assassinated by Pekah, the chief captain of the war chariots—a step on which he would hardly have ventured, but in the assurance that the army would sustain him in it.

It was in the reign of this Pekah that both Uzziah and his son Jotham died in Judah. In this reign, also, the Assyrians, under their new king, Tiglath-pileser, appeared once more with hostile purposes against Israel—purposes not so easily turned aside as those of Pul had been. If the Assyrians regarded Menahem as a tributary prince under their protection, the murder of his son, and the establishment of a new dynasty in the person of the usurper, without their concurrence, may well have supplied to them an ostensible *casus belli*, had any been wanted. But it is likely that this great conquering people did not condescend to allege any ground or pretext for their incursions. Tiglath-pileser seems to have desired not only the plunder of the country, but the *persons* of the people—to be sent for the replenishment of his own land, not peopled in proportion to its extent; his intention being to replace, by useful captives, the large drafts upon the industrious population, which his schemes of extensive conquest obliged him to make for military service. He seems, however, contrary to the expectations and fears of the nation, to have satisfied himself with sweeping away the tribes east of the Jordan, and with taking possession of all their wealth. His object does not appear to have been territorial acquisition; for he established no hold upon the land he had desolated, but, satiated with the rich plunder and the abundant slaves the East afforded, and perhaps called away from the prosecution of the enterprise by other objects, Pekah was left in undisturbed possession of the western territory.

About this time the kingdom of Damascus, under Rezin, again rises into temporary importance; and the king of Israel, as well as all the neighbouring potentates, all of whom have had occasion to feel their impotence singly against the power of Assyria, hasten to contribute their united help against the common enemy. Damascus was, by its geographical position, in the van of the great conflict; and the common support which it was agreed to render to it in this great emergency, accounts for the temporary importance it once more acquired. As for the Israelites, all their hopes of future safety rested upon the opposition which Damascus, thus supported, might be able to offer to the farther progress of the Assyrian arms. Judah, however, not having been hitherto molested by the Assyrians, prudently kept itself aloof from this great alliance; and it was this, probably, with other causes now unknown, which drew upon it the arms of Rezin and of Pekah, each of whom separately defeated Ahaz in battle, and inflicted great miseries upon the people. After his victories, Pekah marched off a great number of prisoners to Samaria; but, amid this history of bloodshed and war, it is pleasant to find that the Israelites were not forgetful of the ancient brotherly covenant between the tribes. Their hearts were smitten at the misery of their brethren, when the unhappy captives appeared under the walls of Samaria; and a prophet named Oded stood forth, and with the full sanction of public approbation and applause, forbade the king to hold them captive; and Pekah, finding that he expressed the feeling of the princes and people, consented, with good grace, to release them. They were tenderly treated by the Israelites; they were well fed; other clothes were given to replace those which the soldiers had rent from them; they were mounted on asses, and conducted carefully to Jericho, where they were delivered up to their countrymen. Such instances of amenities in ancient warfare engage our special sympathy and interest, from the extreme rarity of their occurrence; and they are valuable for the indications which they offer, of the warm under-current of true and humane feeling and sympathy which flowed beneath the hard and frozen surface of public strife.

The war, however, went on. The kings of Syria and Israel united their forces, with no less purpose than that of deposing the house of David altogether, and of setting up some obscure person, known only as "Tabeal's son," upon whose subserviency they could calculate.

This unwise menace united all parties in Jerusalem in a stout resistance; and, while the besiegers held possession of the open country, the siege was protracted, until matters became so urgent, that Ahaz ventured upon the desperate remedy of applying to the king of Assyria for deliverance. This application was accompanied with professions of homage, and with an offering of the gold and silver of the palace and the temple. Tiglath-pileser willingly accepted such handsome payment, for doing what he was ready to have done without pay. Marching down upon Damascus, he compelled its king to turn back and attend to his own affairs. Rezin was defeated and slain in battle, and the conqueror took possession of the extinguished kingdom.

Soon after, Ahaz proceeded to Damascus to pay his respects to the Assyrian conqueror, to whom he had in fact tendered his submission in the words, "I am thy servant and thy son," when he applied for aid. The payment of tribute was the price of protection; and the consequences of submission were made so heavy and galling, that although thus temporarily relieved, he was rather distressed than strengthened in the result; besides that, he incurred much odium by having thus voluntarily rendered himself tributary to Assyria, and subjected his people to the heavy exactions necessary for the payment of the tribute. He had moreover greatly failed, by manifesting so little reliance upon the divine protection, which had been promised him by the prophet Isaiah.

His visit to Damascus was also otherwise damaging to him. He saw there an elegant altar, and resolved to have one like it in the temple at Jerusalem, to be used for the regular services, while the old brazen altar was set aside for occasional use. The high priest Urijah did not resist this so far as he ought to have done. But when the king proceeded further, and sought to introduce more distinctly idolatrous observances, he appears to have been resisted; and then he shut up the temple altogether, and set up altars at every corner of Jerusalem, besides establishing high places for the worship of strange gods in every city. There seems, in fact, to have been no abomination of idolatry into which this infatuated king did not fall. He is even recorded "to have burned his children in the fire," in the fatal valley of Ben-Hinnom. He died at last, unlamented by the righteous, and his corpse was not allowed a place in the sepulchres of the kings.

Again the Assyrian inscriptions become available. They give a king, whose name is *Tiglat-pal-tsira*, reigning from 745 to 727 B.C. He relates a war against Syria—how he made Rezin, king of Damascus, and Menahem, king of Samaria, tributaries. He states that the next year, Rezin having rebelled, he, Tiglath-pilezer, marched into Syria, and defeated him, and put him to death. Next, he says, that he attacked Pekah, king of Samaria; that he returned to Damascus and deposed a son of Rezin, and received tribute from Tyre, Gaza, Ascalon, and Judah. In many points the Scripture history and the Assyrian record are perfectly coincident; but each refers to circumstances unnoticed by the other, yet both combined exhibit one harmonious narrative.

Nothing is said about the altar in this inscription, but a side light is thrown upon the subject by others. Assyrian monarchs, it appears, were accustomed to require subject countries to acknowledge the religion of the conquerors. This seems to have been the general practice of antiquity. The Assyrian king is described as setting up in new provinces, "the laws of Asshur," and "altars to the great gods." Portable altars were carried in royal expeditions, and these would furnish patterns for imitation. Ahaz, we find, visiting Tiglath-pilezer at Damascus, saw an altar, whose fashion and pattern, according to all the workmanship thereof, he sent to Urijah the high priest, requiring him to build one like it, and to set it up in the place of the brazen altar at Jerusalem. (2 Kings xvi. 10–15.) From the Scripture narrative, it does not appear that the altar he saw at Damascus was an Assyrian one. It might have been, for anything which appears to the contrary, a Damascene altar—one used in Syrian worship. But what we learn from the Assyrian inscriptions, leads us to infer that that altar was a portable one, such as were carried about by the Assyrian monarchs in their expeditions; and probably in the adoption of it, Ahaz intended to pay a compliment to the king to whom he had submitted as his suzerain. We have a picture of an Assyrian altar, with a circular top perforated by a hole, and supported on a solid triangular base, with a pillar at each angle, terminating at the bottom in what was like a clawed foot. Probably it was an altar of this kind which Ahaz ordered to be erected in the temple. (*Bible Educator*, i. 141.)

S.

TEMPTING THE LORD

Isaiah 7

THERE is one incident in the history of Ahaz which does not appear in the regular narrative, but which we find in the book of the prophet Isaiah.

When the tidings first came of the alliance into which the kings of Syria and Israel had entered against Judah, the heart of Ahaz was "moved, and the heart of his people, as the trees of the wood are moved with the wind." At this juncture the prophet received a command to go forth, with his son Shearjushub, to meet the king "at the end of the conduit of the upper pool, in the highway of the fuller's field."

What Ahaz was doing there is not stated; but as his being engaged in some matter evincing his apprehensions from the threatened invasion, would afford peculiar point and emphasis to the message with which the prophet was charged, we incline to concur in the conjecture, that he had gone out to see whether the fountain could not be stopped, or its waters diverted, so that it might not be used by the enemy, who would thus be prevented from carrying on a protracted siege. This is rendered the more probable by the fact, that this is recorded to have been done by his son Hezekiah, when threatened with a siege by the Assyrians, as well as in later sieges of the city,—especially during the crusades, whence it happened that the besiegers were much distressed for water, which does not appear to have been ever wanting to the inhabitants. In this case, Ahaz, who, like his grandfather Uzziah, appears to have been a man of an inventive turn of mind, must have the credit of devising a defensive resource, which was afterwards found of much importance.

On such an occasion the king would be attended by many of his counsellors; and, as a considerable concourse of people might be found at this place of waters, due publicity would be given to the prophetic utterance which was necessary to inspire the alarmed inhabitants of the city with confidence.

Arrived at this place, Isaiah exhorted the king to dismiss all alarm; to rely with confidence on the protection of Jehovah, who, through him, conveyed the assurance, that the confederacy to subvert the line of David in favour of Tabeal's son "shall not stand, neither shall it come to pass." It is clear, however, that the words of the prophet made no impression upon the king, who had, perhaps, already more than half made up his mind to the course he afterwards took. Perceiving this want of faith, the prophet continued with vehemence, "Ask thee a sign of the Lord thy God: ask it either in the depth, or in the height above!" Had he possessed the spirit of David, and of many of his nearer ancestors, Ahaz would have been greatly encouraged by the assurance which the prophet gave, and would have put entire confidence in it without further proof. But since he appeared wanting in this strength of faith, the Lord, in condescension to his infirmity, invited him to ask a sign of assurance, which, however miraculous, should be granted, to strengthen his feeble faith, and to satisfy him that the prophet spoke not without due authority from One well able to perform all that He promised. But Ahaz, with keen perception, saw in a moment that, by accepting such a sign, he would leave himself altogether without excuse before the public, in following the course to which his own judgment was already inclined. It would, he thought, take away his liberty of action, by compelling his judgment to go where his heart would not follow. He therefore declined the proposed sign, under an affectation of pious humility and deference to the law, which is no less curious than lamentable: "I will not ask; neither will I tempt the Lord." This has an apparent allusion to the text, Deut. vi. 16, "Thou shalt not tempt the Lord thy God."

Here the question arises, What is "tempting God?" This is an important question, and has not always been rightly understood. It seems to mean simply putting the power, the goodness, or the will of God, to an unauthorized and uncalled for *test*. A test implies, not faith, but mistrust. If one lays untold gold in the way of a servant, in order to test his honesty, this is not because that servant is trusted, but because he is mistrusted. If confidence in him were perfect, the test would not be needed. It is not possible, as some have thought, to tempt God by any degree of trust in Him, so that the occasion for that trust arises in *the path of duty*, and is not voluntarily and needlessly sought out for the purpose of a test. Take an instance. When Ezra was about to cross the desert with his caravan of Jews returning to Jerusalem, he was quite aware of the perils of the journey from the attacks of the Arabs, who would not be likely to permit so rich a caravan to pass through their wild territory with impunity. He might have had a guard of soldiers for the asking; but he was afraid to ask, lest he should dishonour the Lord in the eyes of the Persian king, to whom he had stated that the God he served was well able to defend His people. He dreaded lest this heathen king should construe such an application into distrust of that protection, in the sufficiency of which he had boasted, and that thus some dishonour might be reflected upon that high and holy name. He therefore committed himself and his party, in solemn prayer, to the Almighty, and then plunged fearlessly into the perils of the wilderness: and the Lord responded to this call upon Him,—for they all arrived safely at Jerusalem, without any molestation from "the liars in wait by the way." This was trust—not a test—not tempting. Ezra had a well grounded confidence in the Lord's protection: he had no wish to try it. He knew it already; and, being assured that he was in the path of duty, he felt that he might trust in it, and boldly rest upon it.

The case that most perfectly contrasts with this is that which our Lord's temptation supplies. Being upon the summit of a high tower, Satan tempted Him to cast Himself down needlessly, out of the path of duty, in order to test the promise—" He shall give His angels charge concerning thee: and in their hands they shall bear thee up, lest at any time thou dash thy foot against a stone." This had been a venturesome, foolhardy, and presumptuous test of God's promises, undertaken in a wagering spirit, and not growing out of any of the circumstances which the course of life presents; besides being a falsely literal application of those grandly hyperbolical expressions, by which the Lord strives to render intelligible the greatness of His love for and care over His people.

That the refusal of Ahaz did excite displeasure, is clear from the strong words of the prophet: "Hear ye now, O house of David: Is it a small thing for you to weary men; but will ye weary my God also?" The king had wearied or tried the patience of the prophet by seeming to question his commission,—that, however, was comparatively a small matter,—but now he must try the patience of God Himself, by refusing the tendered attestation. But he should not so escape his responsibility. A greater sign than any his heart could have devised was forced upon him. He refused to ask a sign; "Therefore the Lord Himself shall give you a sign. Behold, a virgin shall conceive and bear a son, and shall call his name Immanuel. Butter and

honey shall he eat, that he may know to refuse the evil, and to choose the good. For before the child shall know to refuse the evil and to choose the good the land that thou abhorrest shall be forsaken of both her kings."

On this remarkable passage much has been written and said, and various interpretations have been offered. That in its *ultimate* signification it has reference to Christ, cannot be doubted, for St. Matthew affirms it. But this could not well have been a sign to Ahaz, since its accomplishment did not take place in his time. It seems, therefore, that the prophet speaks of the birth of a child which should soon take place, of some one then a virgin, and that before the child so born should be of age to discern between good and evil, both the nations he dreaded—Israel and Syria—should cease to be kingdoms. As this could be known only to God, it would constitute a sign to the house of David of the truth of what He had affirmed by His prophet. But in delivering this prophecy, language was designedly employed which would also mark a more important event, and carry the mind of the hearers onward to the future birth of One who should more fully answer to all that is here said of the child to be born, and to whom the name IMMANUEL (God with us) should be more appropriately given. It had, we know, this effect; for the Jews ever after entertained the opinion, founded on this prophecy, that the expected Messiah would be born of a virgin. We have thus some reason to be thankful for the churlish obstinacy of Ahaz, since his refusal to ask a sign produced this splendid link in the chain of prophetic testimonies to the coming Saviour.

We may wrestle with God, like Jacob, in prayer for His blessing; but we may not wrestle with Him in a gladiatorial spirit,—to try, as it were, if He be indeed so strong as He tells us that He is.

To accept the sign which He offers, and to which He invites one, is not, as Ahaz foolishly alleged, to tempt Him. He would not offer it unless there were cause; and, under certain circumstances, to decline it when offered is an insult to Him. Had this been to tempt the Lord, then still more would this king's son, good Hezekiah, have tempted Him by asking a sign that his life would be spared. Yet this is not mentioned to *his* blame; and if he did in this somewhat err in the other extreme, the error may with probability be ascribed to his keen remembrance of the displeasure which his father's self-willed refusal of a sign excited.

THE ASSYRIANS

2 Kings 27-28; 2 Chronicles 32; Isaiah 36

A VERY important event in the history of the Hebrews is the withholding of their tribute from the Assyrians by the kings of both Israel and Judah. The king of Israel at this time was Hoshea, who slew his predecessor—" his friend," Josephus says—and reigned in his stead: while the throne of David was occupied by the pious Hezekiah, the son of Ahaz. This measure appears to have originated in the expectation of being sustained by Egypt, which had at length become alive to its own danger from the steady progress in empire of so great a power as Assyria, and seen the importance of encouraging the barrier kingdoms. It is clear that both received such assurances from Egypt, as gave them ground to expect that Pharaoh would afford them vigorous aid, in any difficulties that might arise from the assertion of their independence. It was so clearly his interest to do so, that the sincerity of his assurances cannot be doubted; and that he did not eventually fulfil the expectations he had raised, is accounted for by the peculiar circumstances of the country, which deprived the reigning king of the confidence of the army, and indisposed them to work out his objects. This had been foreseen by the contemporary prophets, who strongly discouraged all reliance upon the help of Egypt.

This stoppage of tribute soon brought the forces of the Assyrian king upon Israel. There was no help from Egypt, and the country was easily subdued; all, save Samaria, in which the king had shut himself up with the remnant of his forces, and where he held out for three years, vainly expecting the help from Egypt which never came. At length the city fell: Hoshea was sent off in chains to Nineveh; and the kingdom of the ten tribes ceased to exist. This was in the year 721 before Christ. According to the

policy followed by Eastern conquerors, with regard to the nations or provinces which they designed to incorporate with their own domains, Shalmaneser sent away beyond the Euphrates the flower of the conquered nation, comprising all those distinguished for their rank or wealth, or for their abilities or qualifications in useful arts. To replace these, new settlers were brought from the east; and being merely designed to keep the land in occupation, formed a much less numerous and valuable population than that which had been removed. This policy was further carried out by Esarhaddon, the grandson of Shalmaneser, who gleaned the remnant of native Israelites, and substituted an additional draft of foreigners. These strangers gradually combined with the dregs that remained of the Hebrews, and the population thus constituted took the name of Samaritans, from the city of Samaria. They were all originally idolaters; but believing in national or territorial deities, they thought it necessary to learn something respecting the God of the land into which they had come. The Assyrian king thought this a reasonable wish, and sent back from Assyria a Jewish priest to " teach them the manner of the God of the land." The result was, that they combined the worship of Jehovah with that of their native idols. But in time the idolatrous dross got purged out, and eventually the Samaritan system of belief and practice became as pure as that of the Jews, though less exact in some of its observances. In some respects it may have been purer, as the Samaritans would have nothing to do with the mass of oral traditions with which, before the birth of Christ, the Jewish system became disfigured and overladen.

The process of the Assyrians conquerors, as described by the sacred historians and the prophets, is remarkably corroborated by the Assyrian cuneiform inscriptions, as deciphered by Colonel Rawlinson; and it is not by any means unlikely that further research may bring to light accounts of the expeditions of the Assyrian kings in Palestine. We copy some sentences in corroboration. The king, in the first instances, is called Temen-bar, and all the inscriptions make the kings speak in the first person. The inscription begins with an invocation, which Rawlinson ingenuously confesses his inability to follow. He perceives, however, that first there is a list of gods: then the favour of all these deities, with Assarac at their head—the supreme god of heaven—is invoked for the protection of Assyria. The king then goes on to give his own titles and genealogy. He calls himself king of the nations who worship Husi and Assarac; king of Mesopotamia; son of Sardanapalus, the servant of Husi, the protector, who first introduced the worship of the gods among many peopled nations. Then the king proceeds to register the various military glories of his reign. "These campaigns," says Rawlinson,[1] "are almost all described in the same terms; the king of Assyria defeats the enemy in the field, subjugates the country, sacrifices to the gods, and then generally carries off the inhabitants, with their most valuable effects, into captivity in Assyria; replacing the people with colonists drawn from the nations immediately subject to him, and appointing his own officers and prefects to the charge of the colonists, and the administration of the new territory." "In the third year Ahuni, son of Hateni, rebelled against me. The country beyond the Euphrates he placed under the protection of the god Assarac, the Excellent, while he committed to the god Rimmon the country between the Euphrates and the Arteri. . . . Then I went out from the city of Nineveh, and crossing the Euphrates, I attacked and defeated Ahuni, the son of Hateni, in the city of Sitrat, which was situated upon the Euphrates, and which Ahuni had made one of his capitals. The rest of the country I brought under subjection; and Ahuni, the son of Hateni, with his gods and his chief priests, his horses, his sons, and his daughters, and all his men of war, I brought away to my country of Assyria."

The phrase frequently occurs, that in the places conquered "I raised altars to the immortal gods." Those who adopted the Assyrian religion seem to have been spared,—a curious analogy to the Moslem propagandism by the sword: "The cities which did not acknowledge the god Assarac, I brought under subjection." So again: "By the grace of Assarac, the great and powerful god, I fought with them and defeated them: twenty thousand five hundred of their men I slew, or carried into slavery; their leaders, their captains, and their men of war I put in chains." "I took the city of Arama, which was the capital of the country (Ararat), and I gave up to pillage

[1] *A Commentary on the Cuneiform Inscriptions of Babylonia and Assyria.* London, 1850.

one hundred of the dependent towns. I slew the wicked, and I carried off the treasures."

Egypt was by this time the principal object of attention to the Assyrians; and the king deemed it advisable to secure Tyre and other strong cities on the coast before dealing with Hezekiah. This occupied attention many years, for Tyre in particular made a most vigorous and protracted resistance; and meanwhile Shalmaneser died, and Sennacherib, his son, succeeded him. This king prosecuted the war with vigour and overwhelming force, and at length applied himself to the reduction of Hezekiah's fortresses. This prince was then really alarmed, having seen cause to abandon all hope from Egypt; and he therefore sent to Sennacherib, humbly acknowledging his fault, and offering to submit to any demand that might be made upon him. The Assyrian required as the price of his forbearance, three hundred talents of silver, and thirty of gold. This was a heavy sum for Judah to pay, and it was not raised without extreme difficulty. It obliged the king to take all the silver in the house of the Lord, all the treasure in the palace, and even to strip off all the gold with which the doors and pillars of the temple had been overlaid. Whether he was enabled thus to raise the entire sum, is not clear; but it is certain that, after Sennacherib had taken Ashdod, which was regarded as the key of Egypt, he changed his mind, and concluded that it would be unsafe to leave so doubtful a power as Judah unbroken in his rear. He therefore resumed his military operations against Judah; and, while engaged in reducing the fortified towns of Lachish and Libnah, sent two great officers—the chief of the eunuchs, and the chief cup-bearer, these being the offices which the names Rabsaris and Rabshakeh imply—with a large force, to demand the unconditional surrender of the king and the capital. In that case, they were to be left alone till Sennacherib returned from the conquest of Egypt, when he promised to transport them to a better land than their own. This is curious, as an indication that the application of this well known policy of Eastern conquerors was set forth as anything but disadvantageous to those brought under its operation. It shows also, that it was already notorious that the persons thus expatriated were well treated and much encouraged in the lands to which they were removed. There is, indeed, a marked distinction between the

language addressed to the rulers, and that intended for the citizens. Poor Hezekiah is abused
most vilely, and overwhelmed with scorn and
insult; while the material advantages to be
realized by submission are studiously placed
before the eyes of the people. The dignity of
independence, the pride of nationality, were of
small account in the eyes of these Assyrians.
The gasconading language of these commissioners, as recorded in the pages of Isaiah, well
marks the arrogant and boastful character of the
Assyrians, and is in remarkable conformity with
the tone of the inscriptions to which we have
already referred—as is also the religious tone
and pretension to a divine commission which is
advanced. The language used was indeed so
insulting and blasphemous, that Hezekiah conceived from it that the Lord Himself would hear
and revenge His own cause, and, encouraged by
the prophet, he gathered confidence from that
which seemed calculated to intimidate him.

He was, in fact, by this treatment brought
into the state of feeling proper to his condition,
which, if he had earlier realized it, would have
saved him from much distress and anxiety, and

teaching that he did not know—that a king,
walking as he had done, in the paths of
righteousness, and striving, as he had striven,
to advance the glory of God, was *entitled*,
under the peculiar covenants of the Hebrew
theocratical constitution, to expect, and even to
demand, the protection of the Divine King of
the land and people. No sooner, therefore, did
he realize the sufficiency of this—no sooner did
he cast himself in entire confidence upon the
Lord's protection—than his heart was cheered
by the promise of a great deliverance.

Dr. Kitto's account of the origin of the Samaritan nation,
though pretty generally adopted, is not entirely in accordance with the Scripture narrative. There is no historic
evidence that they were a mixed people, composed in part
of Assyrian colonists, and in part of the "dregs that remained of the Hebrews." The scriptural account of their
settlement altogether ignores any Jewish element. We
read that "the Lord was very angry with Israel, and
removed them out of His sight: there was none left but
the tribe of Judah alone. . . . So was Israel carried
away out of their own land to Assyria unto this day. And
the king of Assyria brought men from Babylon, and from
Cuthah, and from Avah, and from Hamath, and from
Sepharvaim, and placed them
in the cities of Samaria,
instead of the children of
Israel" (2 Kings xvii. 18, 23,
24). In their letter to the
king of Persia, given in Ezra
iv. 9-16, the Samaritans
describe themselves as "the
people whom the great Asnap-
per brought over and set in
the cities of Samaria." When
applying to the Jews also
for permission to join in building the temple, they plead,
not their Jewish origin, but
only the fact that they had
observed the Jewish ritual
"since the days of Esarhaddon,
which brought us up hither"
(Ezra iv. 2). They seem also
to have been, on their first
settlement, so utterly ignorant
of the simplest elements of
Jewish worship, that they
asked for a priest to instruct
them; thinking that the hard-

RUINS OF CÆSAREA IN PALESTINE

we should have been spared the display of that
vacillating indecision which forms the only drawback in the character of that righteous man and
excellent king. He certainly ought to have
known — and it was not for want of prophetic

ships and dangers they were exposed to in their new homes,
arose from their ignorance of the God of the land. Our
Lord upon two occasions distinctly rejects their claims to
Jewish origin. He tells His disciples to go not to Samaritans, but "to the lost sheep of the house of Israel" (Matt.
x. 5, 6). And to the woman of Samaria He says, "Ye

know not what ye worship : we know what we worship : for salvation is of the Jews " (John iv. 22).

The Samaritans being disowned by the Jews, erected a temple of their own on Mount Gerizim, about the year B.C. 420 ; and the city of Shechem, situated at the base of the mountain, then became their capital. During the reign of Vespasian, Shechem was rebuilt and called *Neapolis*, a name which still exists in the corrupted form Nâbulus. The modern history of the Samaritans is a mournful one—a long tale of oppression, persecution, and slaughter. They have been gradually wasting away for ages. In the twelfth century there was a large community in Cæsarea of Palestine. Only two centuries ago there were settlements in Cairo, Gaza, and Damascus. Now these are all gone. The whole nation is clustered together in Nâbulus, close beside their "Holy Mount ; " and their number does not exceed a hundred and fifty.

Dr. Kitto's prediction, "that further research may bring to light accounts of the expeditions of the Assyrian kings in Palestine," has been most remarkably fulfilled. Sargon Inscriptions from the ruins of Nineveh contain the following interesting and valuable statement : " Because Hezekiah, king of Judah," says the Assyrian monarch Sennacherib, " would not submit to my yoke, I came up against him, and by force of arms, and by the might of my power, I took forty-six of his strong fenced cities ; and of the smaller towns which were scattered about, I took and plundered a countless number. And from these places I captured and carried off, as spoil, 200,150 people, old and young, male and female, together with horses and mares, asses and camels, oxen and sheep, a countless multitude. And Hezekiah himself I shut up in Jerusalem, his capital city, like a bird and a cage, building towers round the city to hem him in, and raising banks of earth against the gates, so as to prevent escape. . . . Then upon this Hezekiah there fell the fear of the power of my arms, and he sent out to me the chiefs and elders of Jerusalem with thirty talents of gold, and eight hundred talents of silver, and divers treasures, a rich and immense booty. . . . All these things were brought to me at Nineveh, the seat of my government, Hezekiah having sent them by way of tribute, and as a token of submission to my power." [1]

P.

THE SIMOOM

2 Kings 19; 2 Chronicles 32; Isaiah 37

THE prophet Isaiah, in promising deliverance from the haughty Assyrian, clearly indicated the mode in which it would be effected. It was, that the Assyrian should hear a rumour which would be the means of compelling him to abandon his designs upon Judah, and that eventually

[1] Rawlinson's *Ancient Monarchies*, ii. 435.

he would return disappointed and unsuccessful to his own land, to perish there by the sword.

The rumour had already reached him by the time Rabshakeh joined him at Libnah. It was, that Tirhakah, the great king of Ethiopia, whose warlike exploits remain to this day recorded on the walls of a Theban temple, had undertaken the task to which the king then reigning in Lower Egypt was unequal; and in the determination not to allow the Assyrians a footing in that country, was moving down in great force against them. This made Sennacherib anxious to proceed to Egypt at once, without any longer delay in Judah ; and he was therefore highly exasperated at the ill success of Rabshakeh's threatening mission to Hezekiah, and not the less so as he had no leisure to punish his obduracy, and saw reason to conclude that the reduction of the strong fortresses would be a less easy matter than he had reckoned. He, however, sent a terrible letter to Hezekiah, threatening what he would do on his return, and full of even more awful blasphemies than those of his foul-mouthed commissioners, against the God in whom Hezekiah trusted, and deriding His power to save.

The king took the letter, and having read it, went at once to the house of the Lord, spread out the letter as it were before Him, and poured out his soul in earnest prayer. The answer was a strong denunciation of the pride and blasphemy of Sennacherib, the Lord's determination to bring him low being expressed in strong and decided language, and concluding with the remarkable words, " I know thy abode, and thy going out, and thy coming in, and thy rage against me. Because thy rage against me, and thy tumult, is come into mine ears, therefore will *I put my hook in thy nose*, and my bridle in thy lips, and I will turn thee back by the way by which thou camest." The mode of punishment thus indicated, is curiously illustrated by a bas-relief from Khorsabad, where captives are led before the king by a rope passed through the mouth and nose.[1]

What followed between this and the great judgment which came upon the Assyrian host, is not recorded in Scripture ; and we are left to collect it from other sources—as Herodotus, Josephus, and, in his citation, the Chaldean

[1] See illustration in Vol. 2, pp. 247-249.

historian Berosus. By all these accounts, Sennacherib did go to Egypt; and the Egyptian account, as preserved by Herodotus, is, that the king, Sethos, having prayed to his god, and been encouraged by a dream, resolved to march against the invaders with a body of artisans and shop-keepers, seeing the soldiery would not follow him. The night before the expected action, an army of mice invaded the Assyrian quarters, and gnawed asunder their bow strings and the thongs of their shields, whereby, being for the time disarmed, and thunderstruck by the prodigy, they retreated in confusion "by the way that they came,"—intimidated, perhaps, also by the rumour of Tirhakah's near approach, and by the dread of meeting him in this condition. The historian adds, that this current tradition was in his days attested by a statue of the king in the temple of Vulcan, bearing in his hand a mouse, with the inscription, "Whosoever looks at me, let him be pious."

One does not know what to make of this story. The omission of Tirhakah's name in it is suspicious; and it may be conjectured that the Assyrians were actually driven back by him, and that the rest is an appropriation to Egypt of a disjointed version of the judgment that afterwards actually befell the Assyrian host. But that the resemblance suggests such imitation, the story fits in well enough to the sequel, as it supplies or strengthens the motive for an abandonment of the design upon Egypt; whence, it would seem, the army returned through Judah, perhaps with the intention of resuming operations against Hezekiah. Accordingly, it is stated by Berosus, that it was on the return from the Egyptian war to Jerusalem, and in the first night of the siege, that the calamity befell the Assyrian which broke his strength. And this we take to be an important testimony, from an impartial authority, to settle the question *where* and when the doom that befell him took place. The prediction also in Isa. xxxvii. 33, that the king should not come *into* the city, nor exhibit any of the usual operations of siege before its walls, seems to become more emphatic when understood to imply that he should come *to* the city, but should not be allowed time to commence the usual proceedings.

The sequel is thus told: "Then the angel of the Lord went forth and smote in the camp of the Assyrians one hundred and fourscore and five thousand; and when they arose early in the morning, behold they were all dead corpses." How is this to be understood? Not, surely, as Dr. Johnson remarked, "that an angel went about with a sword in his hand, stabbing them one by one." Either some terrible known agency, such as that of the pestilence, or the hot poisonous wind, was employed, or some extraordinary and unknown operation took place. In either case the divine power is equally manifested; and assuredly nothing could be easier than for that power to extinguish so frail a thing as the life of man at a stroke. The tens of thousands were but an aggregate of individuals, whose breath was in their nostrils. Berosus says that it was a pestilence. It has been objected that no pestilence is so suddenly destructive. Yet we do read of instantaneously destructive pestilences in Scripture, as in the wilderness and at Bethshemesh; and it may be remarked, even of the natural pestilence, that under that disease death supervenes at a certain number of days (not more in any case than seven) from the commencement; and if, therefore, any number of men were smitten with it at one time, they would all die at the same period, or within a very few hours of each other. If this were the case here,

THE OVERTHROW OF SENNACHERIB

the Assyrians who died before Jerusalem may have been smitten with the pestilence before they left Egypt. But we do not think that it *was* the plague. The almost immediately mortal pestilence so often mentioned in Scripture, and known from other ancient authorities, was clearly not the plague: the symptoms described do not agree with those of the plague; and it is probably an extinct disease. It is not now known even in the East, though there is abundant evidence in history, tale, and song of its former existence. Of the glandular plague, the present prevailing epidemic of the East, there is no certain trace in history anterior to the third century even in Egypt.

Some have thought the powerful natural agent employed was the hot pestilential wind, or simoom, which is often represented as suddenly destroying travellers, and indeed whole caravans. The effects of this wind are felt most strongly in the heart of the great deserts, and with mitigated results the farther one recedes from them. It has become the fashion lately to deny those effects, or to set down the accounts we have received as gross exaggerations. But these denials are founded, with a manifest want of discrimination, on the accounts of travellers who did not pass through the quarters where this visitation is most severe; nor does it often occur in the most fatal form even in those districts, or else they would be quite impassible. The counter-evidence is wholly negative, and is not adequate to countervail the evidence of history, and of persons who know those regions well. The testimony of five men who tell us what they did see, is of more importance than that of fifty who tell us what they did not see. In this case, however, the fifty, traversing countries on the distant borders of the desert, did experience some slight inconvenience from a hot wind, and fancied this was the fell simoom of which they had heard, and that, after all, it was not so calamitous as had been reported. But experiences brought from the heart of the desert would be far more conclusive. Dr. Russell, in his *Natural History of Aleppo*, rightly distinguishes between the weak and strong simoom, calling the latter the "true simoom." This never reaches so far north as Aleppo, nor is it common in the desert between that city and Basrah on the Euphrates. It is in the great Arabian and African deserts of sand that the effects of the wind are strongest and most disastrous. Dr. Russell was careful to collect and compare the accounts given by the Arabs, and thus states the result: "They assert that its

progression is in separate and distinct currents, so that the caravan, which in its march sometimes spreads to a great breadth, suffers only partially in certain places of the line, while the intermediate parts remain untouched. That sometimes those only that are mounted on camels are affected, though most commonly such as are on foot, but that both never suffer alike. That lying flat on the ground till the blast passes over, is the best method of avoiding danger; but that the attack is sometimes so sudden as to leave no time for precaution. Its effects sometimes prove instantly fatal, the corpse being livid, or black, like that of a person blasted by lightning; at other times it produces putrid fevers, which become mortal in a few hours; and that very few of those who have been struck recover."

It is willingly granted, that in this strong manifestation the simoom does not naturally reach Palestine. But if this were the agency employed in the destruction of Sennacherib's host, it had been a small matter for the Lord to cause it to blow beyond its usual range upon that special mission of doom. It might be an objection to this agency, that such a wind would be destructive to others than the Assyrians. To this it is a sufficient answer to say, that the power of God could prevent it from hurting any but the destined victims. But to many this may not be satisfactory; and therefore we willingly point to the defined currents in which the wind moves, at a greater or lesser elevation from the ground, as containing an agency—a wheel within a wheel—which, under the divine guidance, might be made effectual for sparing whom He pleased, and for smiting whom He saw fit. Upon the whole, therefore, it seems probable, that the simoom was the agency by which this great judgment was brought to pass. It also appears that not all the Assyrians were slain. The king himself (reserved for future judgments), and many others, escaped; and these were doubtless such as lay beyond the borders of the current of pestilential air.

Canon Rawlinson says, relative to the destruction of the Assyrians, "The annals of Sennacherib, as might have been expected, omit it altogether, and represent the Assyrian monarch as engaged in a continuous series of successful campaigns, which seem to extend uninterruptedly from his third to his tenth year" (Rawlinson's *Ancient Monarchies*, ii. 168). Sennacherib did not die until seventeen years after the disaster described in Kings and Chronicles, and during that period, no doubt, greatly retrieved the fortunes of the empire. The statement in 2 Kings xix. 36, that after his return he "dwelt at Nineveh," conveys the idea of some long residence there. The story in the Book of Tobit is quite unfounded.

"The disguised form in which the story of the destruction reached Herodotus is curious and interesting. His informants were the priests of Memphis, who naturally enough twisted the circumstances to the glorification of their own caste and country. According to them, on the approach of Sennacherib, the priest-king Sethos was bewailing his danger in the great temple of Phtha, when he suddenly fell asleep, and saw in a vision the god himself draw near, and promise him a sure deliverance. Thus encouraged, he marched out to Pelusium, and encamped opposite his enemy; whereupon, during the night, silently and secretly, an innumerable multitude of field-mice spread themselves through the Assyrian host, and gnawed their quivers, bows, and shield-straps, so as to render them useless. Discovering this when morning broke, the Assyrians hastily fled, and the Egyptians pursuing, put a vast number to the sword. (Herod. ii. 141.) It will be observed that, while so much is changed, the following features of the history are kept:—1. The *promise* of deliverance, consequent upon a special appeal. 2. The coming of the deliverance *in the night*. 3. Its miraculous, or at least its *extraordinary* character. 4. Its *silence and secrecy*, which caused it to create no disturbance at the time; and, 5. Its discovery *when morning came*, and its immediate consequence, *flight*." (On the symbolical origin of the "mice" in the Egyptian story, see Rawlinson's *Herodotus*, Vol. I., p. 394, note 7.)

"The meaning seems to be, not that Sennacherib made no more expeditions at all, which would be untrue, for his annals show us that he warred in Armenia, Babylonia, Susiana, and Cilicia during his later years; but that he confined himself to his own part of Asia, and did not invade Palestine or threaten Jerusalem any more. Nineveh appears here unmistakably as the Assyrian capital. It has previously been mentioned, so far as the historical books are concerned, only in Genesis (x. 11, 12). No doubt it was a very ancient city, but it seems not to have become the seat of the Assyrian government till towards the close of the ninth century B.C. Sennacherib was the first king who made it his permanent residence. Previous monarchs held their court there only occasionally. Its great size and large population are marked in the description of Jonah (iii. 2, 3; iv. 11), whose visit probably fell about B.C. 760. The ruins opposite Mosul, which have always been regarded traditionally as marking the site, have been found in modern times to be the actual remains of the Assyrian town, which has never been built upon to any important extent. (For descriptions of ancient Nineveh, see *Ancient Monarchies*, Vol. I., pp. 310-327; and Smith's *Dictionary of the Bible*, Vol. II., pp. 553-555. Its actual extent is still a subject of controversy.")— *Speaker's Com.* iii. 113.

S.

THE DIAL OF AHAZ

2 Kings 20; Isaiah 38

IT must have been very soon after the ruin of Sennacherib's host, if not just before that event, and while the Assyrians were absent in Egypt, that Hezekiah fell sick of a disease which he knew to be mortal. The prospect of death at such a time was very grievous to this good king. The personal grounds are obvious; but there were also public grounds which might render the expectation of dissolution distressing even to one to whom death itself had no terrors. He had no son; for it is certain that Manasseh, who succeeded him, was not then born, for twenty years later he was but twelve years old; and the land had not yet begun to recover from the late ravages,—so that his death would have left the nation in a distracted condition, and would probably have exposed it to many new calamities.

He prayed, therefore, to be spared; and his prayer was granted, the prophet Isaiah being sent to tell him that fifteen years should be added to his life. To assure him that this recovery was indeed miraculous, not a chance, but a token of the Lord's special favour to him, and to give him due confidence in the promise, a token was given in the going backward of the sun's shadow, "ten degrees upon the dial of Ahaz."

This is the first time that we read in Scripture of any instrument for measuring time; and its connection with the name of Ahaz, is another instance of the ingenious tastes of that unhappy king. It is also the first mention of a dial in history. This may, however, like the tasteful altar which he saw and fancied at Damascus, have been a foreign curiosity, which, or the idea of which, he introduced, rather than an invention of his own, or one made under his auspices.

Indeed, it is a somewhat remarkable corroboration of the usual ascription of the art of dialling to the Chaldeans, that this first scriptural mention of the subject connects it with the name of a king, whose personal intercourse with the Assyrian neighbours of the Chaldeans at Damascus, and whose fondness for foreign novelties are equally notorious. In connection with this point of the case, it is further worthy of note, that the princes of Babylon sent to enquire of Hezekiah respecting the wonder that had been done in the land.

Strictly, however, we know not that this was a dial. The Hebrew language has no word for such an instrument. The word so translated means "steps," or "degrees,"—so that it reads "the steps" or "degrees of Ahaz." This has led many to suppose that this famous "dial" was no other than a kind of stair, framed and proportioned with such art, that the shadow upon the steps, or cast by the steps, expressed the time of the day and the course of the sun.

Among the opinions of the Jewish Rabbis on this subject, is that of Rabbi Elias Chomer, quoted with approbation by Grotius, that the dial of Ahaz was a concave hemisphere, in the midst of which was a globe, the shadow of which fell upon several lines engraved upon the concavity of the hemisphere, and which lines are said to have been twenty-eight in number.

This description corresponds nearly with that of the instrument which the Greeks knew by the name of *scapha*, or boat, and *hemisphairion*, or hemisphere, and the invention of which they ascribed to the Chaldeans, having been introduced to their knowledge by Anaximander, who travelled in Chaldea at the time of the captivity.

The difficulty in the present case is to understand what is meant by the *steps* or *degrees* of Ahaz. They may mean lines or figures on a dial-plate of any kind, or on a pavement; or they may signify a set of steps to the palace of Ahaz, or to a staircase which stood apart elsewhere. On the whole, however, the "steps of Ahaz" seem to have been some distinct contrivance constructed to mark the divisions of time, rather than any part of the house accidentally found to be serviceable for that purpose. The dial stood probably in one of the courts of the palace; for it must have been so placed, and of such dimensions, that the king, now convalescent but not perfectly recovered, could view the phenomenon from his chamber or pavilion. May it not have been situated in the "middle court," mentioned in 2 Kings xx. 4?

Although we do not conceive that we are bound to the literal signification of "steps," yet if it can be shown that a kind of stair, scientifically constructed, may be or has been used for the purpose indicated, we should be inclined to give it the preference. Now, this is actually the case, as a single glance at the annexed engraving will show. It represents a sort of dial in Hindustan, near Delhi, the construction of which would exceedingly well suit all the circumstances

GREAT WALL DIAL NEAR DELHI

recorded respecting the dial of Ahaz. It seems framed to answer the double purpose of an observatory and a dial. It is a rectangled triangular figure, whose hypothenuse is a staircase apparently parallel to the axis of the earth, and bisects a zone or coping of a wall, which wall connects the two terminating towers right and left. The coping itself is of a circular form, and accurately graduated to mark, by the shadow of the gnomon above, the sun's progress before and after noon; for when the sun is in the zenith he shines directly on the staircase, and the shadow falls upon the coping. A flat surface on the top of the staircase of the gnomon fitted the building for the purpose of an observatory.

As respects the miracle itself, the fact is clear that the shadow was made to recede ten degrees upon the dial. Of the way in which this was accomplished, nothing is said—nothing offered to our belief. We can see that there are several modes, all miraculous, in which it might be done. Various agencies may be suggested; and it may be that there was no agency at all, but that it was brought to pass directly by the simple operation of the divine will.

Some have supposed that, to produce this effect, the earth was made to retrograde upon its axis for a space corresponding to that marked by ten degrees upon the dial. This would certainly have produced the effect intended; but it would doubtless have produced something more. Such a reversal of the order of nature, and disturbance of the solar system, could hardly have happened without such results as would be remembered through the world to the end of time. Yet history records no such event; and its local character is indirectly recognized in the fact that the prince of Babylon sent to inquire respecting the wonder that had been done *in the land*. Besides, in the course of human conduct, it is not deemed wise "to leap over the house to unbar the little gate;" neither do we find that the Almighty is ever redundant in manifestations of power, but rather sparing—employing just so much power, and no more, as may be needful to produce the intended result. It is therefore not likely, judging from the analogy of the divine operations, that the earth would be sent backward in its course to produce an effect which might be accomplished by means as sufficient, and as truly miraculous, though with less derangement to those laws on which God has established the universe, and which He does not Himself disturb without a most adequate cause.[1]

In the case before us, the effect upon the shadow might have been produced by a miraculous deflection of the rays which fell upon the dial, so as to throw back the shadow to the extent required. This theory best agrees with the statement of the sacred writer, who speaks only of the retrogression of *the shadow*.

There are some who suppose that the phenomenon might be produced by the simple refraction of the rays, through the sudden interposition of a different medium. That such refraction takes place when rays of light pass through a denser medium, is a well known physical fact. The most striking illustration is perhaps found in the observation made, on the 27th of March 1703, by P. Romauld, prior of the cloister of Metz, that, owing to such refraction in the higher regions of the atmosphere, in connection with the appearance of a cloud, the shadow of his dial deviated an hour and a half.

However produced, the retrogression of the shadow upon the dial of Ahaz was certainly of a miraculous nature. Nothing less than this could have been satisfactory to Hezekiah as a sign; and nothing but a divine communication could have enabled the prophet to predict its occurrence at that time and place. Besides, the king was allowed to make his choice, whether the shadow should go backward or forward; and he avowedly chose what appeared to him the least possible to any power but that of God.

[1] See also Vol. 1, pp. 495-497.

The steps, or degrees, here mentioned, were probably, says Lieutenant Conder, "of the Chaldean scale, which is used by Ptolemy in the *Almagest*, for the account of the lunar eclipses observed at Babylon. Those degrees were 60 in the course of a diurnal revolution of the earth; and thus each one contained 24 of our minutes." "There can be little doubt, that our ordinary division of the day into 24 hours, and of the hour into 60 minutes, is also Chaldean."

"Before the discovery of the pendulum, accurate measurement of mean time was impossible. In the time of Charlemagne, a *clepsydra*, or water clock, was sent to that Emperor, by the Caliph Hasoun al Rashid. Our own King Alfred is said to have invented the use of graduated candles to measure the hours of the night. The Chaldee sun dial seems to have been introduced into Palestine by Ahaz; although the determination of the moment of noon, by the absence of shadow cast from a wall built north and south, was well known to all Eastern people, and appears to have been introduced into the structure of the court of Israel by King Solomon. The division of the sun dial of Ahaz was probably the Chaldean division into 60 degrees, each degree containing 80 semples of time." (*Bible Educator*, iii. 238.)

S.

JOSIAH

2 Kings 22-23; 2 Chronicles 34-35

IT is a dismal thing to see how often, in life and history, an ungodly son comes after a godly father. So Hezekiah, one of the most pious of the Jewish kings, was succeeded by Manasseh, undoubtedly the most impious who ever sat upon the throne of David. He was but a child of twelve years when his father died. Yet we may be sure that he had been well brought up, and fully instructed in the things of God; and as "the child is father of the man," it is probable that the influences to which he is subjected before he is twelve years old have the most abiding influence upon his character. The seed sown may seem to have been lost—rotted in the ground; yet after many years it may germinate, and grow, and bear much fruit. So it was with Manasseh, who, after a long period of wickedness without example in Judah, fell into captivity and trouble, and in his bondage remembered the holy lessons of his childhood; and, turning to God, was forgiven, restored to his country and his throne, and spent the rest of his life in repairing, as far as he was able, the evil he had done.

The history of the war that led to his captivity is not given. But the Assyrians had recovered strength, in the course of years, under Senna-cherib's successor, Esarhaddon, who eventually marched into Palestine, and sent away the remnant that still lingered upon the mountains of Israel, while his generals were despatched against Jerusalem. The city was taken, and Manasseh was sent away in chains to Babylon, then belonging to Assyria. He returned to his throne as a sworn tributary of Assyria. On the same terms, his son Amon, who followed rather the evil than the good example of his father, reigned; and subject to the same conditions, Amon's son, Josiah, mounted the throne at the early age of eight years.

Notwithstanding that difficulty of obtaining a good education upon a throne which appears to have been the ruin of his grandfather Manasseh, this prince was the best and most beloved of the kings who had sat upon this throne since David, and was approached by none in his zeal against idolatry and in his devotedness to the Lord. He extirpated every trace of idolatrous abominations, root and branch, throughout the country, —abolishing all the high places, which previous kings had spared, and which even high priests had tolerated. He extended his holy researches into the neighbouring territory—once of Israel ; and at Bethel performed the task which had been, more than three hundred years before, allotted to him by name. And here note, that this king, and Cyrus of Persia, are the only personages in Scripture predicted by name long before their birth. The accomplishment of the prophecy against the altar of Bethel, delivered in the time of Jeroboam, was in all respects complete. At once to defile that altar, and to inflict posthumous dishonour upon the leaders of the corrupt worship there celebrated, he caused their bones to be taken from the sepulchres and burned thereon. In this labour a noticeable incident occurred. Observing an inscription upon one of the tombs, but not being near enough to read it, he asked what it was, and was told by the people of the place : " It is the sepulchre of the man of God who came from Judah, and *proclaimed these things that thou hast done* against the altar of Bethel." Then he said, " Let him alone ; let no man move his bones." So they let his bones alone ; " and," as the historian fails not to observe, " with the bones of the prophet that came out of

Samaria ; " justifying the worldly sagacity of the astute old knave, in giving the order to his sons —" Lay my bones beside his bones,"—in the calculation that, besides the impossibility of distinguishing their remains after the lapse of so much time, all the contents of the sepulchre would be spared from defilement for the sake of the man of God. The notice taken of this inscription by the king would suggest that there were no inscriptions on the other sepulchres, and that it was not usual for the Jews to put any inscriptions upon their tombs,—nor, indeed, have any ancient tombs been found in Palestine with inscriptions upon them. This inscription was probably placed upon the tomb by the old prophet's order, for the very purpose which it now accomplished, by indicating the tomb as that of " the man of God."

The thorough search which was made in the temple for the removal of every relic of idolatry or superstition, which former kings had introduced, brought to light the autograph copy of the law written by Moses ; and, in opening it, the eye fell upon the passage, Deut. xxviii. 15-68, declaring the doom which awaited the nation if it fell into idolatry. Offered to the attention thus, in an old manuscript written by that holy and venerable hand, it made an extraordinary impression—which may, in part, although still imperfectly, be understood by one who has been privileged to examine some one of the most ancient manuscripts of the Scriptures now existing ; and whom the very oldness of the vellum, and the antique style of the writing, with the knowledge of the long ages through which its existence may be traced, seem to take back so much nearer to the time of the writer, and give a vividness to his impressions of ancient truth which no modern copy can impart. It is a curious feeling, which one must experience fully to appreciate. And if this be the case in respect of manuscripts which still fall far short of the time of the writers, how still more intense would it be in the presence of an autograph copy ! Suppose, for instance, we had the autograph of St. John's Gospel, and read on the last page the words : " This is the disciple that testifieth of these things, and wrote these things ; and we know that his testimony is true ; " would not this, written under his own hand, give an intensity to our conviction of the truth of his testimony, such as we had never before been able to realize in the perusal of the printed copies, or even of the most ancient manuscripts? It is a matter of feeling or impression, which some will understand, and which some hard intellects will not. To ourselves, the impression made upon the king's mind by the denunciations given under the hand of Moses, which he too well knew the nation had incurred, is very intelligible. His anxiety was so great, that—Jeremiah being doubtless absent at his home in Anathoth—the king sent at once to "Huldah the prophetess," to inquire whether this judgment would indeed be executed. The answer was, Yes; that the sentence had already gone forth, and would soon be executed; but that his eyes should be spared from beholding it. He was spared; for he died.

The death of Josiah took place in consequence of the resistance which he offered to the march of the Egyptian king, Pharaoh-Necho, through his territories, with an intention to take advantage of the waning of the Assyrian power, by wresting from it some of its acquisitions west of the Euphrates. This put Josiah into a serious difficulty. If he allowed this march without opposition, he would be looked upon by his Assyrian master as unfaithful to his duty, as his engagements certainly bound him to regard the military resources of his kingdom as available for Assyrian objects. To suffer the unmolested passage of the Egyptians, would be to take part with them against the Assyrians. It put him to deciding for the one power or the other; and he decided to adhere to his Assyrian allegiance, remembering how much the kingdom had formerly suffered for trusting to the Egyptians, and how strongly that trust had been denounced by the prophets.

The Egyptian king was sincerely desirous of avoiding a collision with Josiah, and sent to remonstrate against the opposition which he offered, urging that he had a divine commission, and that it would be perilous to interfere with him. Josiah, however, thought that his duty was clear, and persisted in opposing him by force of arms. He could doubtless see through Necho's pretence of being sent by God; yet it did leave so much impression upon him, and he had so much of misgiving, that he went disguised into the battle. He was defeated; and a commissioned arrow found him, and gave him a mortal wound. His end was much like that of Ahab;

and he was the only king of Judah who perished in battle. He died quickly of his wound; and his body was conveyed in his "second chariot" to Jerusalem for burial. All the nation mourned deeply for him; and the prophet Jeremiah gave expression to the universal grief in the funeral lamentation which he composed for one so greatly beloved, and so truly mourned.

Much cause was there for weeping; for with Josiah terminated the peace, the prosperity, and the piety of Judah. With him all the hopes of the nation perished; and after him nothing is to be found but idolatry and desolation.

The effect produced by finding the book of the law, as described in the sacred histories, goes far beyond the impression made by discovering an ancient MS., with the contents of which the reader had, by other means, become familiar. "When the king had heard the words of the book of the law he rent his clothes." (2 Kings xxii. 11.) So we are distinctly told, and this shows that something in the *contents* of the MS. struck him as altogether new. Not that he, and the people, were totally ignorant of the law of Moses. That is an impossible supposition. The existence and service of the temple—the institutes of the kingdom, the whole frame-work of Jewish society—precludes such an idea. At the same time, it seems plain that not only had the autograph of the Mosaic law been lost, but the knowledge of its contents, to some extent, had passed out of the king's recollection. The language of the Divine code had not been studied; ignorance of what it really was to a great extent prevailed, so that the discovery and reading of it "amounted almost to a new revelation." (Stanley's *Jewish Church*, ii. 499.) The book, "from its unexpected and welcome appearance, was to make his remembrance, like the composition of the perfume that is made by the art of the apothecary, sweet as honey in all mouths, and as music at a banquet of wine." (Ecclus. xlix. 1.) The result of reading, or hearing the words of the Divine lawgiver, was like what took place at the Reformation, when, though people knew something of the contents of the Bible, there was much they were unacquainted with. Mathesius tells us of Luther in the Augustinian library at Erfurt, that "when he was carefully viewing the books, one after another, to the end that he might know them that were good, he fell upon a Latin Bible, which he had never before seen in all his life. He marvelled greatly as he noted that more texts, or more Epistles and Gospels, were therein contained than were set forth and explained in the common postills (or homilies) and sermons preached in the churches." It would be unwarrantable to infer from that narrative that no Latin Bible could have been found before, or even that no German translation of it existed at the time; but it shows how possible it was, even for a priest, though familiar with Gospels and Epistles, and other parts of Scripture, to be ignorant of other portions not included in the church services. So in the days of Josiah, he and others might be acquainted with some things in the ancient law, and unacquainted with others ; and, therefore, it was natural for them to be startled when the whole was read in their hearing. " And the king went up into the house of the Lord, and all the men of Judah and all the inhabitants of Jerusalem with him, and the priests, and the prophets, and all the people, both small and great : and he read in their ears all the words of the book of the covenant which was found in the House of the Lord." (2 Kings xxiii. 2.)

Some have endeavoured to make it appear that no book of the law had been known before this—that what was now said to be found was in reality forged, or, at any rate, that a book of unknown date, and authorship, was now palmed upon the nation, as the original Sinaitic code. It has been remarked that the Jewish liturgies incorporated large parts of it as Romish liturgies included large parts of the Bible—that there might be living men who knew by heart what the law contained, even as modern Samaritans have been found with the whole five books of Moses preserved memoriter ; that surely some copies of the law must have remained in the schools of the prophets, and that quotations of the law were certainly contained in other sacred books then existent. "On the whole, it may be said that fraud or mistake might as easily have imposed a new Bible on the Christian world in the sixteenth century, as a new law on the Jews in the reign of Josiah." (*Speaker's Commentary*, iii. 126.)

S.

THREE KINGS

2 Kings 23:31-24:16; 2 Chronicles 36:1-10

It is recorded that, on the death of Josiah, " the people of the land " made his son Shallum king in preference to his elder brother Eliakim ; and, as usual, when there was any departure from the ordinary course of succession, he was anointed. It also claims to be noted that the same formula, as to the people nominating the king, occurs only after the previous king (as Amaziah and Amon) had come to a violent end, which may suggest, that when a king had been himself prevented from nominating a successor out of the number of his sons, the right devolved on the people of indicating the one that would be most acceptable to them. Their decision was usually in favour of the eldest son; but with the right of exercising the power, which belonged to the king himself, of passing him over if cause appeared.

It is further remarkable that Shallum *and all the kings after him*, changed their name on their accession—a custom which the practice of the Roman pontiffs has rendered familiar to us, but the occurrence of which, in the present instance, seems to indicate the increased intimacy of the Jews with the remoter East, where this practice appears to have had earlier prevalence. The royal name which Shallum took was Jehoahaz,[1] which, with the fact that the two kings who followed also took names beginning with *Jeho*, may suggest that names commencing with the sacred name of JEHOVAH had by this time come to be considered more dignified and fortunate than any others.

But the king of Egypt, on his return from his successful campaign against the Assyrians, paused to enforce the rights which his victory over Josiah had given. Displeased, probably, at the liberty which had been taken of appointing a king out of the ordinary course without any reference to him, or, which is more probable, wrought upon by the representations of the party of the eldest son, he sent to summon Jehoahaz to appear before him at Riblah, in the land of Hamath, one of the most important of his new acquisitions, and which he was busy in fortifying. The new king seems to have gone without personal constraint ; but on his arrival he was cast into chains by Necho, who presently sent him to Egypt, both as a trophy of his conquest, and to prevent him from giving any disturbance to his elder brother Eliakim, whom the Egyptian placed on the throne, by the name of Jehoiakim. As a token of homage, Necho required from the new king the moderate sum of a hundred talents of silver and one talent of gold. It seems to be mentioned as a grievance, that the king raised this sum by direct and immediate taxation, instead of paying it out of his own pocket; or, it may be that the kingdom had become so poor, that the levying of even this small sum was felt as a heavy burden by the people. But it may be noted, that the Orientals in general greatly exceed any Western nation in their aversion to taxes : and this is saying much.

Meanwhile a power was growing in the East, which was destined to exercise an important influence upon the destinies of Judah. The Babylonians had succeeded to the heritage of the Assyrian empire, and were not inclined to allow the Egyptians to retain possession of the

[1] Compare Jeremiah 22:11 with 2 Kings 23:30 and 2 Chronicles 36:1.

territories west of the Euphrates, which they had wrested from the enfeebled grasp of the Assyrians. Young Nebuchadnezzar, who was in command for his father Nabopolassar, came into collision with Necho, at Carchemish on the Euphrates, in the fourth year of Jehoiakim's reign, and gained over him so decisive a victory, as constrained him to abandon all his conquests, and retire to his own country. This event excited much sensation in Jerusalem. Jeremiah the prophet rejoiced in the defeat of Egypt, and foretold that the Chaldean would soon appear and take possession of Judah, and exhorted submission to his arms. The result could be but a change of masters; yet as the king of Egypt had shown himself the patron of his personal interests, Jehoiakim concluded that it would be best to adhere to him. This involved the necessity of resistance to Nebuchadnezzar, who had now become king of Babylon. The insanity of such opposition was somewhat disguised by the hope of assistance from the Egyptian king, whose interests were identified with his own; and Jeremiah was subject to much persecution, on the alleged ground that his declarations were calculated to discourage the troops.

The Babylonians at length appeared, and no help came from Egypt, Necho being now advanced in years, and apparently unwilling to provoke the Chaldeans to attack him in his own country. In reducing Judah, they seemed to assert their right to the heritage of the Assyrian power; and with that they would perhaps be satisfied, without attempting to invade a country which the Assyrians never had subdued. Deprived of this hope, Jehoiakim saw the uselessness of resistance, and therefore tendered an ungracious and reluctant submission to the Babylonians. In three years, however, he conceived new hopes of help from Egypt, where a new king (Psammis) had ascended the throne; and therefore, knowing that Nebuchadnezzar was employed elsewhere, he ventured to withhold his tribute. The Babylonian king was too much occupied to look after him for a good while; but in the meantime he sent a few regiments of Chaldeans to form the nucleus of a military force to be raised on the spot from among the Syrians, Moabites, and Ammonites, and to be employed in harassing the kingdom. In this warfare Jehoiakim was taken prisoner and sent to Nebuchadnezzar, who put him in chains, intending to send him to Babylon. It does not appear whether he gave effect to this intention. The probability is, that the captive king died before it could be executed; and to die among strangers and enemies was a dolorous fate for a Jewish prince. Jeremiah had foretold his doom: "They shall not lament for him, saying, Ah, lord! or, Ah, his glory! He shall be buried with the burial of an ass, drawn and cast forth beyond the gates of Jerusalem."

His son Coniah, who then mounted the throne, prefixed the sacred name to his own, and was called Jeconiah—which is also written Jehoiachin. In spite of the earnest remonstrances and strong denunciations of Jeremiah, he persevered in his father's fatal policy of resisting the Chaldeans. But Nebuchadnezzar soon arrived in person, and the siege of Jerusalem was pressed with vigour. Jeconiah held out for a little time, in the hope that the Egyptians would appear to raise the siege; but when constrained to abandon that hope, he saw the impolicy of exasperating the besieger by a protracted and desperate resistance, and determined to surrender while the hope of favourable terms might yet be entertained. He therefore came out, with *his mother* Nehushta, and chief officers, and placed himself at the disposal of Nebuchadnezzar. We must not neglect to point out that this marked mention of the king's mother is an incidental, but valuable, corroboration of the fact we have already had occasion to state, of the public importance of the queen-mother's position in the Hebrew monarchy.

Jeconiah was not mistaken in calculating that the city would be spared, and the state maintained, in consequence of his timely surrender; but if he also reckoned that the conqueror would confirm him in the kingdom as a tributary prince, he soon discovered his error. Nebuchadnezzar saw the impolicy of leaving on the throne the nominee of Egypt. He therefore set the now lustreless crown upon the head of Josiah's youngest son, Mattaniah, whose name he changed to Zedekiah, and sent away Jeconiah to Babylon, together with his mother, his harem, and his chief officers,—of which last, those, no doubt, were selected who were of the Egyptian party, and, as such, had shown themselves most eager opponents of Jeremiah. Jeconiah was at this time but eighteen years of age; and he survived in Babylon till long after the entire subversion of the kingdom over which he had so briefly ruled.

He seems to have been kept in some sort of confinement until the death of Nebuchadnezzar, but was liberated from restraint by his successor, and was treated with high distinction among the kings of subverted thrones, whose presence glorified the imperial court. By the numerous captives who were eventually removed to the east, he was doubtless looked up to as their natural prince—the sole relic of the house of David; and it is likely that his influence availed much to secure for them many of the advantages they enjoyed in the land of their captivity.

THE LAST REIGN

2 Kings 24:17-20; 25; 2 Chronicles 36

ALTHOUGH Nebuchadnezzar set up a king, he left him but little more than the shadow of a throne to sit on. All the treasures of the temple, as well as of the palace, were taken, and even the golden vessels that remained in the house of the Lord were cut up and sent away. The temple and palace had more than once before this been stripped of their treasures; but Nebuchadnezzar inflicted a severer weakening, from which recovery would be much more difficult. He sent away to Babylon, besides the deposed king and his courtiers, all the chief inhabitants of Jerusalem, to the number of ten thousand, with all "the mighty of the land," comprising seven thousand of the most able warriors, with a thousand of the best artisans. The Mordecai of Esther's history, and the future prophet Ezekiel, were among the captives. There are some remarkable points in the description of these captives. Those which, in the common version, appear as "the mighty of the land," are in the Eastern versions, "the great ones of the land," and in the Vulgate, "the judges of the land," but literally, in the original Hebrew, "the rams of the land,"—being, like many other epithets descriptive of the character and conditions of men, derived from animals. In this case, the leadership of the male animal, its strength, and its prominence in the flock or herd, rendered it a suitable epithet for nobles and leading men. Such terms, when they come into established use, suggest little idea of the animal

from which they are taken, but only of the quality designed to be expressed. It will be remembered by many of our readers, that Homer sometimes compares princes to rams.

The artisans are described in the authorized version as "craftsmen and smiths." The first of these terms, in the original, denotes a workman in general, whether in wood, stone, or metal. The second term is more obscure; and it is difficult to see what special trade it may be that is not included in the general term of craftsmen. The term means, strictly, one that shuts up—an encloser. From this, some think it means a mason, because he builds the enclosing walls and repairs the breaches of towns; while others declare in favour of locksmiths, from their securing of gates and doors. Others fancy that it denotes goldsmiths, whose art consisted chiefly in the manufacture of enclosing rings, and in enclosing precious stones in metal. In fact, the meaning has been sought in almost every art with which the idea of *enclosing* can be connected. Perhaps the great importance to kings, and to founders and fortifiers of cities, of masons, beyond all other trades, gives the highest degree of probability to the first of these interpretations, as it was more likely to acquire a designation distinct from the general term of "worker." It may be that the fortresses built by king Uzziah excited the admiration of Nebuchadnezzar, and made him especially desirous of possessing the masons capable of constructing such works. At all events, it is clear that Nebuchadnezzar had great need of skilful masons, engaged as he was in improving and enlarging his metropolis.

It is distinctly stated that Nebuchadnezzar took a solemn oath of Zedekiah to remain in honourable allegiance to the prince who had placed him on the throne; and this oath he kept so long as he had no temptation to break it. But temptation came, as usual, from the side of Egypt, which had now as king, Pharaoh-Hophra, the Apries of the Greek historians, whose active and enterprising character, with the success of his warlike enterprises, suggested that he would be able and willing to afford efficient aid against the Chaldeans. Jeremiah the prophet perceived his inclination, and warned the king of the consequences. But eventually, in the ninth year of his reign, after having entered into a secret compact with the Egyptian king, Zedekiah went into open revolt. This soon brought the king of Babylon, with a most powerful army, before Jerusalem; and a regular seige was commenced, by the building of forts and other military works outside the town to annoy the city, to cut off supplies from the country, and to prevent sallies. Eager longings were directed towards Egypt; and hope and exultation rose high within the city when it was known that the Egyptians were actually on the march for its relief. This compelled Nebuchadnezzar to raise the siege in order to meet this new enemy. It is uncertain whether a battle was fought or not. The impression seems to be that, on becoming acquainted with the force of the Chaldeans, the Egyptians declined to risk an action that was certain to be bloody, and probably disastrous, in behalf of the Jewish king; and therefore drew back to their own country, leaving Nebuchadnezzar to pursue his plans at leisure. So when the people of Jerusalem beheld the dust of an advancing army, and were prepared to hasten forth to greet their deliverers, they found, with bitter disappointment, that the Chaldeans had returned to resume the siege of the city. This interruption had, however, enabled the besieged to recruit their supplies, and so to sustain a more protracted siege than might otherwise have been practicable. This was important, as the military art was, even in the hands of the Chaldeans, so imperfect for the reduction of towns, that, in the case of a city so strong by

THE SIEGE OF JERUSALEM.

nature and art as Jerusalem, there was no effectual means of reduction but that of sitting down before the place until the people were starved into surrender; meantime, taking such opportunities as might offer of harassing the inhabitants. So, in this case, the walls being found impregnable, the siege was soon turned into a strict blockade. Eventually this produced the usual effects of extreme famine and mortality, and it became evident that the city could not hold out much longer. In fact, in the fourth month of the eleventh year of Zedekiah's reign, the Chaldeans succeeded in making a practicable breach in the first wall, which the besiegers had no heart to defend. But, during the ensuing night, the king, with his family and chief officers, fled, escaping apparently through some vaults that led into the king's garden, aided by the relaxed vigilance which the excitement of success produced in the Chaldean host. But his flight was soon discovered, and he was pursued, though not captured until he had reached the plain of Jericho. He was sent off by the captors to Nebuchadnezzar, who was then at Riblah, in the land of Hamath,—the very same place to which, twenty years before, Jehoahaz had been brought a prisoner to Pharaoh-Necho. Zedekiah could not expect mercy from Nebuchadnezzar, but perhaps did not anticipate the severity of judgment —worse than death—which was executed upon him. His two sons—who must have been of tender years, for their father was but thirty-two years of age—were slain before his eyes; and then his eyes were put out, as if, with fiendish ingenuity, to keep that harrowing spectacle for ever present to him, by rendering it the last sight his eyes beheld. In this condition he was sent off in chains to Babylon, and we hear of him no more, except that he remained in prison in the imperial city to the day of his death.

Not only the king of Babylon, but his chief commander Nebuzar-adan, seems to have been absent when the city was taken; and those left in command appear to have been in doubt how to deal with it, until orders came from the king. In the next month, Nebuzar-adan himself arrived with a commission to destroy everything, and leave the city a desert. Effectually did he discharge this commission. The temple and other buildings were set on fire; and what the fire had spared, and the strong walls of the city, on which fire could make no impression, were broken down by the soldiers. Eleven years previously, the Chaldeans had well cleared the temple of its gold and silver. What remained was now taken, together with all the utensils and ornaments of brass, and the two pillars, Jachin and Boaz, and the brazen sea with its bulls. It is remarkable that nothing is said of the ark, the most valuable and important of all the furniture of the temple. It could hardly escape the cupidity of the Chaldeans; and yet, had it been at Babylon when Cyrus gave back the spoils of the temple, it would doubtless have been restored. But this is not stated; and, in fact, it is known that there was no ark in the second temple. It seems to us likely that it was taken away; and it is possible that, if it were still in existence at the restoration, the Jews were afraid to point it out as belonging to them, lest the king should take the figures thereon to be idols which they worshipped. It might have been difficult to undeceive him in this; and they knew that a strong point in his sympathy for them consisted in their common abhorrence of idols—he being a worshipper of the sun, and of fire as its symbol. It may have been broken up, however, for more convenient transport to Babylon, being valuable to the conquerors only for the precious metal, as it could not, like the golden vessels, be applied to unconsecrated or idolatrous uses. The Jews have a tradition that the ark was hidden by the prophet Jeremiah, and that it will not be brought to light until their polity and ritual service are hereafter gloriously restored at Jerusalem.

In the Second Book of Kings, chap. xxv. 7, it is said that the Chaldees "slew the sons of Zedekiah before his eyes, and put out the eyes of Zedekiah, and bound him with fetters of brass, and carried him to Babylon." Blinding has ever been a favourite punishment in Eastern countries. The Philistines blinded Samson. The Persians blinded malefactors. Sargon represents himself, on one of his monuments, piercing with a spear the eyes of a prisoner. The usage prevailed in Persia, only of late have the Shahs relinquished the barbarous practice. The blinding of Zedekiah reconciled predictions apparently contradicting each other. Jeremiah said he should be carried to Babylon (Jer. xxxii. 5; xxxiv. 3). Ezekiel declared he should *not see* Babylon (Ez. xii. 13). Both were fulfilled—he was carried to the city, but did not behold it.

In 2 Kings xxv. 21, it is said, with reference to certain captives, that "the king of Babylon smote them and slew them at Riblah, in the land of Hamath." Such severities are illustrated by the Assyrian inscriptions, executed captives are reckoned by hundreds. According to Herodotus, 3,000 Babylonians were put to death by Darius Hystaspis. —*Speaker's Com.*, iii. 151.

S.

THE END

2 Chronicles 36:13-16

THE author of the books of Chronicles, approaching the close of his history, indulges us with some reflections on the causes of the catastrophe which he relates. This is unusual in Scripture history, where commonly the facts are recorded, and the reader is left to his own reflections, unless where a prophet, priest, or angel, appears to warn or to exhort. The case being so rare in which the scriptural historian appears as a commentator upon his own narrative, the instance before us claims special notice. The greatness of the event—the awfulness of the consummation—did, however, in this case call for the observations which are introduced. After describing the iniquities of the nation, especially in the latter years, and the obduracy of the king, who "stiffened his neck and hardened his heart from turning unto the Lord God of Israel," and after distinctly stating that even "*all* the chief of the priests and the people transgressed very much," he goes on to say, "And the Lord God of their fathers sent to them by His messengers, rising up betimes and sending; because He had compassion on His people, and on His dwelling-place: but they mocked the messengers of God, and despised His words, and misused His prophets, until the wrath of the Lord arose against His people, TILL THERE WAS NO REMEDY." These are awful words—"There was no remedy!" The word "remedy" is to be understood medicinally—"no healing," as the marginal reading indicates; and this renders it clear that the analogy in view is that of the physician who, as long as there is any hope of curing his patient of the disease under which he labours, bestows the utmost solicitude and attention, and leaves untried no means or resources which the art of healing offers. But he sees at length that the disease is incurable—that there is no remedy, no healing for it. There is no hope; and therefore, at length, after much reluctant delay, he abandons the case, and leaves the patient to die. The analogy is true and striking. But it may be made still more exact. The disease, we shall say, is not essentially mortal—not absolutely beyond the resources of medicinal skill. But the patient is obstinate; he neglects the regimen prescribed;

he refuses the medicines offered; and he loads the physician with insult and contumely, until even his meek and kind spirit is roused to anger, and he leaves the miserable man to perish of the disease which his obduracy has placed beyond all cure.

The judgment which now befell this people, terrible as it was, is less striking than the patience which had so long endured their perverseness—which had so long withheld the stroke that at last laid them low. Even as it was, the judgment came most gradually, with constant solicitations to repentance, and with warnings from day to day. The whole Jewish nation, both in Judah and Israel, had all along evinced a strong propensity to idolatrous abominations, which would be almost incredible, in the presence of the light with which they were favoured, did we not recollect the prevailing ideas of the times, and the condition of all the neighbouring nations, and consider the strong tendency of an exceptional system to be absorbed into those which are more prevalent, especially when the latter are more material, unspiritual, and demonstrative than the former. Still, we are scarcely able, in our blessed ignorance of idolatrous enticements, to appreciate the temptations to which the Hebrew people were exposed, and before which they fell, and which brought them into a state from which the jealous endeavours of good kings—the warnings, the invectives, entreaties, and threats of a long series of glorious prophets, specially commissioned by God—were ineffectual to rouse them so as to produce a real reformation.

It was for this the nation was carried away captive, and the holy city and its temple reduced to ruin. This calamity came gradually, and, as it were, piecemeal, leaving ample opportunity of repentance while God had not yet forgotten to be gracious. But they repented not. Gradual punishment produced no reform in the religion or morals of the people, for their morals also had become exceedingly corrupt; and the last king was no better than his predecessors, notwithstanding the more sharp and frequent warnings he received. Therefore the long suspended doom at length came down, and the land was given over to desolation, and the people to what must have seemed their extinction and utter ruin.

The mercy, the justice, and the wisdom of God, are all equally displayed in this event. His *mercy* appears in bringing this judgment so gradually— from less to greater, during the space of twenty-two years—so that most ample warning was given, and abundant opportunity of repentance was afforded to the nation, and it was shown that the successive threatenings denounced by the prophets were not vain words, but would assuredly be accomplished in their season.

That it was a most *just* punishment for their sins no one ever questioned, and the Jews have themselves constantly admitted it, even with tears. It was, in particular, a most righteous punishment of their idolatry, whereby they forsook God, and so provoked Him to forsake them, and to suffer their enemies to prevail over them, as Moses had long ago foretold in Lev. xxvi., where the *succession* of the divine judgments is most remarkably traced out. This is altogether a wonderful chapter, which should be read in connection with the closing portion of the books of Kings and Chronicles.

But the *wisdom* of God is also seen here. He did not mean utterly to cast off His people, and He therefore brought them under this great affliction, because, as had too plainly appeared, nothing less would suffice to purify them, and turn their hearts from the love of idols; for in the midst of wrath the Lord remembered mercy, and this was the end He had in view. In their captive and disconsolate state they had abundant time, and their grievous calamities gave them the disposition, to look narrowly into the past, and reflect upon the long course of iniquity and perverseness, which had brought upon them the heaviest judgments of God. Now, "their own wickedness corrected them, and their backslidings reproved them," and they failed not to "know and see that it was an evil thing and bitter that they had forsaken the Lord their God, and that His fear had not been in them." In the land of their captivity, the utterances of the prophets, declaiming on the highest authority against their profane and wicked practices, and foretelling all that had now so dismally come to pass, would still be sounding in their ears; and their abject and wretched condition—the known consequence of these sins—made those warnings sink deep into their hearts, and gave them an utter detestation of that which they thus learned to regard as the true cause of all their sufferings. This is no hypothesis. It is certain that after this captivity—and under occasional inducements, as strong as any to which they had ever been subjected in former times—there was never among them the least tendency to idolatry, but the most intense and vehement abhorrence of it, as the true cause of all their ancient miseries,—so deep and salutary was the impression made upon them by this great affliction, and so effectual the cure.

THE RESTORATION

Ezra 1-3

It had been foretold by the prophet Jeremiah that, at the expiration of seventy years—dating, it would seem, from the first expatriation under Jeconiah—the captive Jews should return to their own land; and before that, Isaiah had predicted that this should take place under an unborn king called Cyrus, of whom high things were spoken.

When the seventy years had expired, the Babylonian empire had ceased, and Cyrus the Persian had become master of the many realms of which it had been composed, as well as of the more eastern empire of the Medes and Persians. In the very first year of his imperial reign, this king issued a decree distinctly recognizing these prophecies, acknowledging the authority by which they were given, and his obligation to act upon them. He accordingly permitted such as wished, to return to their own country, and to rebuild the temple at Jerusalem; allowing them also to collect funds from such as chose to remain behind, and giving the promise of the royal protection and encouragement in the undertaking.

Accordingly, a large caravan was formed of the more devout and zealous Jews, *as they now begin to be called*, who were liberally supplied with treasure from the bounty of those who, preferring to remain in the east, felt the more induced to evince their less adventurous zeal by the liberality of their contributions. The king also caused to be made over to them the vessels which Nebuchadnezzar had taken from the temple. Their leader, who went with the appointment of governor of the colony, was the lineal representative of the house of David, being the grandson of Jeconiah, and is distinctly recognized by Cyrus as "the prince of Judah." He was born in Baby-

lon, and his name was Zerubbabel; but, as appears to have been usual with the great men of Judah during the captivity, he had another name—that of Sheshbazzar—by which he was known among the heathen.

We need not trace the history of the colony, which is in the main too plainly stated to require illustration; but there are a few points to which it will be desirable to refer.

The first question that probably occurs to every one who opens the book of Ezra is, How came Cyrus to be so well informed of the matters to which his proclamation refers, and to be so impressed with the power of Jehovah as to acknowledge that He was "the God of heaven," and that He owed to Him all the greatness to which he had attained? "Jehovah, God of heaven, hath given me all the kingdoms of the earth; and He hath charged me to build Him a house at Jerusalem, which is in Judah." Now, it is not difficult to trace the channel through which Cyrus *might*, and probably did, become acquainted with these matters. At his first coming to Babylon, he found the prophet Daniel there, as an old minister of state,—renowned throughout the empire for wisdom, faithfulness, and experience. How well he knew and respected his character is shown by the fact, that he not only continued him in office, but, on settling his newly acquired dominion, made him superintendent over all the provinces of the empire—an office which must have given him a degree of rank and power scarcely less, if at all less, than that of an Eastern vizier, or European first minister. This position was just the one which qualified him, at this important juncture of affairs, to be of most essential service to his people; and he himself informs us that his attention had been particularly drawn to the fact, that the seventy years of the captivity had expired. Nothing can therefore be more probable—indeed it is as probable as anything short of absolute certainty can be—that Daniel brought the prophecies of Isaiah concerning himself under the notice of the king; and as he could prove that these prophecies had been written long before Cyrus was born, and as it was seen that in them his victories were foretold, and the Lord declared Himself to be the giver of all his greatness, and claimed him as His "servant"—as one appointed and commissioned to do His pleasure,—Cyrus, as a candid man, possessed of higher notions of the

Godhead than mere idolators could realize, could not fail to acquiesce in the evidence thus presented before his mind; and it is likely that when this disclosure had made its proper impression, Daniel opened the prophecy of Jeremiah, and showed that the time for the restoration of Israel had come.

After so long an interval, very few of the original captives could be alive. The great body of the existing generation had been born and bred in Babylon, which was thus, in fact, their native country. As a body, they throve well there; and ceasing to take any interest, unless in certain localities, in the culture of the soil, that change of habits and pursuits took place among them which has ever since been maintained; and they probably followed nearly the same vocations in the ancient as they do in the modern Babylon, and other cities of our own country; and presented nearly the same aspect to the ancient Chaldeans as to the modern Britons, apart, however, from the special odium which they have incurred among Christians on our Lord's account. They became then traders, pedlars, money-changers, money-lenders, jewellers, and possibly dealers in old clothes. Upon the whole, they were so comfortable and satisfied with their position, that, although unshaken in their attachment to Judaism, they felt but little disposition to forego their realized advantages, and break up their homes, to encounter the perils of the wilderness, and to undergo the privations and trials to which a small settlement in a deserted country must expect to be exposed. The largest, the wealthiest, and the noblest portion of the nation, therefore, took no part in the movement, except by their sympathies, and by their bountiful contributions in furtherance of the object; and it has ever been the sentiment of the Jews, that the most illustrious part of their nation voluntarily remained in the land of their exile.

Those who did go were such as were animated by strong desires to behold and possess once more their fathers' land, and to restore the Lord's house in Jerusalem, and such as were least attached by prosperity and family ties to the land of their sojourning. That the great body of them were of the poorer sort, is shown, among other circumstances, by the fact, that although there were 42,360 Jews who returned, they had but 7,337

male and female servants among them; and still more by the circumstance, that the long and perilous journey across the desert was performed by the greater part of them on foot; that of those

THE RETURN FROM THE BABYLONIAN CAPTIVITY

who did ride, the far greater part were on asses, animals never now employed on such journeys; and that, indeed, the whole number of animals could scarcely have been sufficient for the women and children, even on a low computation. It is probable, however, that although those who had families took them, as they had no intention of returning, a very considerable portion of those who did go were unmarried; a fact which explains their readiness in contracting marriages, soon after their arrival, with the women of the neighbouring heathen. There were but 435 camels, the animals best suited for the journey, and not more than 736 horses. These, we suppose, were ridden by persons of condition, and the camels by their families. Of mules, then a more favourite animal than now, there were but 245, while the asses were 6,720; in all, little more than 8,000 animals, for nearly 50,000 persons, including servants.

Considering the circumstances of the returned exiles, and the constant opposition which they met with from the strangers who had intruded into the land, or who dwelt upon the borders, together with the time required for the collection of materials, it is clear that strong exertions were made by the pilgrims to forward the great work they had undertaken; for, by the fourteenth month after their return, they were enabled to lay the foundations of the temple. That was a great day for them, and the ceremony took place with as much of grandeur and solemnity as their means allowed. It is affecting to read, that while the younger men who had been born in a strange land, shouted with joy to behold the foundations of this goodly structure laid in the sacred city of their fathers, the older men, who had seen the first temple, " wept with a loud voice," so that it was impossible to distinguish the noise of the shouting from that of the weeping. What wept they for? Not certainly that the foundations were inferior in extent, or that there were marks of littleness in anything then before their eyes; but that they looked forward, and saw that there was not the least probability that the structure, the foundations of which were then laid—the effort of a small company of strangers in their own land—would ever make even the faintest approach in splendour and magnificence to the ancient building, on which the long savings of David and the wealth of Solomon had been lavishly expended. Some say that they lamented, rather, the absence of the five great things which glorified the first temple, but which were not to be found in the second,—the ark of the covenant, the sacred fire on the altar, the Urim and Thummim, the Shekinah or sacred symbol of the divine presence, and the spirit of prophecy. But the spirit of prophecy was not then extinct, seeing that Haggai and Zechariah prophesied; and as for the Shekinah and the sacred fire, they could not, until the completion of the building, know that these would be wanting. We think, therefore, that their mourning arose from the perception that the new temple, taken altogether, would be " as nothing in comparison with the first." So says Haggai (ii. 3, 7, 9), who was commissioned to comfort them by the assurance, that the deficiency of this temple in exterior glory should be abundantly compensated by the coming of the Messiah, whose presence should give to the second house a glory far greater than that which the first house could boast.

The fact that the *noise* of the weeping equalled that of the rejoicing shouts, strikes an English reader as something strange. It will remind him, however, of the frequent phrase, " He lifted up his voice and wept." The fact is, indeed, that the Orientals do at this day lift up their voices to some purpose when they weep. Silent tears, inaudible grief, are unknown,—loud lamentations and mournful cries, rather than tears, being regarded as the proper and comely expression of grief. In fact, the Scriptures throughout corroborate travelled experience, in showing that sorrow is not only more *demonstrative*, but is more commonly *expressed*, in the East than with us; so that not only women and children, but grown-up and full-bearded men, are prone to weep and lament, even under those common crosses and vexations which we should consider insufficient to warrant any *sensible* demonstration of grief.

EZRA

Ezra 7-10

ONE would hardly expect, from the zeal with which the work of rebuilding the temple was commenced, that nearly twenty years should have passed before it was completed. Various circumstances co-operated to produce this slowness. First, the opposition of the people around, and particularly of the Samaritans, who at the beginning wished to be allowed to take part in the great work, but finding themselves repelled somewhat roughly by the Jews, became the most inveterate opponents of the undertaking, and eventually succeeded in procuring an order for its suspension from the Persian government. The discouragements, indeed, were such, that the people began to regard them as a sign that the time for the restoration of the temple was not yet come, and that the commencement period of seventy years should be computed from the destruction of the former temple, and not from the first captivity under Jeconiah. Thus for some time the work was altogether abandoned, and the people employed themselves in building comfortable dwellings at Jerusalem for themselves. For thus building for themselves " ceiled houses," while the Lord's house lay waste and open, they were severely rebuked by the prophet Haggai, and they were at length stimulated to resume their labour, which an encouraging *firman* from the Persian court enabled them to bring to a successful close.

Few readers of Scripture history look to dates so much as they ought to do; and it will surprise many to learn the simple fact, that when Ezra made up his second great caravan of pilgrims for

Jerusalem, the new temple had been completed nearly sixty years, and it was nearly eighty years since the first caravan of pilgrims set out under Zerubbabel, who, with all that generation, had assuredly been long since dead.

Ezra was a learned man and a priest, and came not only with a plenary commission from the crown to rectify the disorders which had crept into this orphan state, but with an important auxiliary force of people and of treasure.

He found the religious and social disorders of the state to be such as required the exercise of all the powers vested in him; but there was a willing mind in the people, which rendered his task easier than it might else have been. Ezra may be regarded as the legist of the restoration; and the task which devolved upon him, and which he zealously executed, embraced nothing less than the re-organization of the nation according to the law of Moses and the institutes of David. All that belonged to the order of worship, to the rites and festivals, to the classification of families, to the levying of imposts, to the franchises of the Levitical tribe, to the administration of justice,—in a word, all the immense details, the complete re-establishment of the internal organization of the Mosaic state, belonged to the office he had undertaken, and must be viewed as the work of this man, whom the Jews have always regarded as a second Moses. The particulars of his proceedings are not supplied in the book which bears his name, except as respects his zealous labours in abolishing the intermarriages between the Jews and their pagan neighbours, into which dangerous offence even the nobles and the priests had to a large extent fallen, in apparent ignorance that they were trangressing the law. A curious effect resulted—that the young children spoke a mixed tongue, made up out of the languages of both parents; a case analogous to that which occurs at this day in the families of American missionaries in the Levant, where the children, picking up words all around them, will often make up their sentences with words from three or four different languages—English, Arabic, Greek, and Italian.

When the fact of these intermarriages was disclosed to Ezra, he rent his mantle and tore his hair, and sat at the temple gates, as one desolate and lost in grief. But, at the hour of evening sacrifice, he arose, and poured forth to the Lord, in the presence of the assembled citizens, a con-

fession on the part of the people, and a prayer on their behalf, well calculated to move the sternest heart. After this, all the people were summoned to Jerusalem; and, alarmed and convinced of the sin into which they had fallen, and the danger they had incurred, they voluntarily offered to leave the matter entirely in the hands of Ezra, promising to obey his orders. These were, that all their foreign wives should be straightway divorced: and zealous commissioners were sent through the country to see the order duly carried out.

There can be no question that such a wholesale divorce throughout the land is repugnant to our notions, and appears to us as awfully, if not needlessly, severe. But we are to recollect that Ezra was there to enforce and re-establish the law of Moses, and that he had to decide the matter, in view of the precedent which would thus be established for the generations to come. Such marriages seem to be forbidden by the law,[1] and were hence sacrilegious in the eyes of all true Israelites. There can be no doubt that such connections had in former times been one of the principal causes of the ruin of the two kingdoms and their dynasties, idolatry having generally found entrance into Israel by this road. In the present state of the people, the danger was still greater, and the evil less to be endured; and, if the practice were really to be stopped, and such marriages were to be discouraged, this was the time for the evil to be cut up by the root. We are not, however, bound to consider that, because this was done by Ezra, it was absolutely right. There may have been something in it of that over-straining of the law to which the Jews, after the captivity, became prone; and it may be that this example, under the authority of a personage so deservedly venerable as Ezra, tended to furnish a precedent for that readiness in divorcing their wives, for which the Jews were in our Lord's time notorious. It is clear to us that Moses only meant to interdict intermarriages with the devoted nations of Canaan; and, in extending the interdiction to *all* foreigners, a step was taken towards that rigorous interpretation of the law which began from this time to prevail, and which can only be explained by the aversion and profound dread with which idolatry was regarded by the Jewish people after the captivity.

[1] Exodus 34:16; Deuteronomy 7:3.

THE WALLS OF JERUSALEM

Nehemiah 1-5

THE decree of Cyrus in behalf of the Jews, had reference only to the building of the *temple*. But in the East it is so important that a town of any consequence should be surrounded by a wall, and in the case of the returned captives it was of such special importance, that they reasonably concluded that the permission to build a temple necessarily implied leave to surround with a wall the place where it stood. The presence of a temple such as they had been allowed to build raised the city to such a rank, that the absence of a wall would be most strange and anomalous; besides that, it was needful for the protection of the inhabitants, subject as they were to hostile annoyances from all their neighbours, who regarded with malignant hatred the prospect of the re-establishment of the Jews as a people in their own land. So much, indeed, were the inhabitants distressed, and so natural was it that they should conceive themselves free to take this measure for their own safety, that they began to rebuild the town wall as soon as the temple had been finished. This raised a clamorous opposition, especially from the Samaritans, the authorities in charge of whose local government sent a forcible representation on the subject to the Persian court, urging the danger to royal power on "this side the river" (Euphrates), of allowing this "rebellious city" to be fortified. This procured what they desired—authority to stop the work. The kings of Persia had been willing, when the case was fairly set before them, to allow all that had been literally allowed in the decree of Cyrus, which formed to the Jews their great charter in all the troubles to which they were subjected; but beyond this they would not go, when it appeared, from the records of the realm, that Jerusalem had once been the seat of mighty kings, and that the later sovereigns had constantly rebelled against their foreign masters. Thus, in all the favours granted by the Persian court, and all the renewals of the charter of Cyrus, permission to fortify the town by a wall is studiously withheld, though known to be greatly desired; and Jerusalem remained as a town whose growing prosperity was kept in check, and whose peace was continually endangered, by the want of a wall; and it still presented to the external view the aspect of a ruined and burnt city, surrounded by fragments of broken wall, and by vast accumulations of rubbish; for in the East people never clear away the *debris* of old ruins till they need to build again on the same foundations.

But, thirteen years after the arrival of Ezra, the house-tops of Jerusalem were crowded to witness the arrival of a new civil governor, whose high rank and power at court were evinced by the splendid escort of "captains of the army and horsemen" which attended him. It is the king's cup-bearer. "Only a cup-bearer!" Softly: this designation, which sounds so undignified to us, was one which inspired the citizens with the most lofty ideas of power and influence, and they felt that surely good days were come, since so great a man had deigned to take the government of their poor state, and since "the king of kings" had spared him from his side. This office is mentioned by ancient writers as one of the highest honour and influence in the great monarchies of the East, the fortunate possessor of which enjoyed great influence, from the peculiar facilities afforded him of access to the royal presence, and might aspire to the highest civil or even military employments without presumption. It was the same with the Assyrians, of which we have a scriptural instance; for that foul-mouthed Rabshakeh, who seems to have held the chief command under Sennacherib, was, as his name, or rather title, imports, "chief cup-bearer" to the king. At the Persian court, the expatriated natives of conquered states and their children might, equally with native Persians, aspire to the highest offices at the court or in the state; and this high place was, in the present instance, held by a pious Jew called Nehemiah, whose patriotic heart felt a deep interest in the welfare of "the city of his fathers' sepulchres." A Jew named Hanani, who had come back to the imperial city of Shushan, gave him a saddening account of the state of affairs at Jerusalem, dwelling particularly upon the disadvantages experienced from the still ruined condition of the wall. This afflicted Nehemiah greatly, and he conceived an absorbing wish to be the honoured instrument of repairing the desolations of Zion. He felt that, as he was the individual of the nation highest in place and influence, the service seemed to devolve upon him; and how could he know but that he had been so prospered and exalted—that he had been placed in this peculiar position—for this very end? The thing was not in itself too much for him to ask; but he could not conceal that there was much danger in asking. The king had been used to see him about his person, and his self-love might be offended at the wish of a servant so favoured to leave him for some years; and then, although *that* danger were escaped, and the king, in a moment of happy humour, might consent to let him go, with large powers as governor, might he not demur at the very point which was of most consequence—the rebuilding of the walls—seeing that this had, on grounds of public policy, been refused by many kings who had in other respects evinced a favourable disposition towards the Jews? In this perplexity and danger, Nehemiah did exactly the right thing: he cast the matter in earnest prayer upon the Lord, imploring him " to give him favour in the sight of this man."

Kings do not like the sight of unhappy faces. It looks like a disparagement of their greatness—an insinuation that they have not the power of conferring universal happiness;[1] and in the Persian court it was a capital crime to appear sad in the king's presence. Nehemiah knew this very well; but when he found that the lapse of time, day after day, afforded him no suitable opportunity of naming the matter to the king, he could not prevent some traces of his trouble from being visible in his countenance. This was noted by the royal eye; and the cupbearer had reason to tremble when the monarch asked, " Why is thy countenance sad, seeing thou art not sick?" " This is nothing else," he added, " but sorrow of heart." At these words, Nehemiah confesses that he was " very sore afraid." But he took courage to speak out: " Let the king live for ever. Why should not my countenance be sad, when the city, the place of my fathers' sepulchres, lieth waste, and the gates thereof are consumed with fire?" Then the king said, " For what dost thou make request?" This brought the matter to a truly critical point. " So," says this good Jew, " I prayed to the God of heaven," —a silent prayer, the aspiration of a moment,—

[1] So the existing president of the French Republic declines to grant an audience to Abd-el Kader till he shall have the power of making him happy. A right royal sentiment!—*April*, 1851.

the first of the kind recorded in Scripture, but not the first by many that the children of God had sent up on high. He then found his heart strengthened, and he asked for leave of absence, and to be sent to Jerusalem with full powers to build up its walls. This was granted, on his undertaking to return within an appointed time; and he set forth, furnished with such royal letters to the governors west of the Euphrates as were needful to facilitate his object, together with orders for the free supply of materials for the city wall, and for the palace which the governor intended to build for himself.

Nehemiah came with the title of Tirshatha—the same that had formerly been borne by Zerubbabel. The exact signification is doubtful; but it is supposed to come from the Persian *torsh*, "severe," and to signify something like " your severity," " your dreadness,"—reminding one of the " *dread* sovereign " of our forefathers.

When Nehemiah arrived, he did not at once make known the full extent of his commission—that he was the bearer of the long desired privilege of building the wall. But one moonlight night, the third after his arrival, he went out privately with a few attendants, and rode quite round the outside of the town, making a complete survey of the walls in their ruined state. The next day, however, when the chief persons attended his levee, he said to them, " Ye see the distress that we are in; how Jerusalem lieth waste, and the gates thereof are burned with fire: COME AND LET US BUILD UP THE WALL OF JERUSALEM, THAT WE BE NO MORE A REPROACH." We may easily imagine the thrill of surprise and joyful excitement which these words produced, and the zeal which they inspired. Nehemiah, all whose narrative is in the first person, proceeds to state: " Then I told them of the hand of my God which was good upon me, as also the king's words that he had spoken unto me. And they said, Let us rise up and build. So they strengthened their hands for this good work."

No time was lost. They went to the work with vigour; and men of all trades—every one, young or old, that could be of the slightest use, was engaged in this great service,—the governor and chief persons being always present to encourage them. The danger was great from their old enemies, whose animosity was excited to frenzy when they saw that the Jews were thus securing themselves against them. All kinds of scoffs and insults were showered upon the undertaking. A bitter sarcasm of Tobiah the Ammonite is recorded: "Even that which they build, if a fox go up he shall even break down their stone wall." At last, seeing the work proceeding so vigorously, they took counsel to put a stop to it by force of arms. This coming to the knowledge of Nehemiah, he took remarkable precautions for safety. Every one was kept on the alert—every workman was armed; and the governor, who had

NEHEMIAH ARMETH THE LABOURERS

put all his attendants and guard to the work, withdrew half of them to be constantly in arms beside the men who wrought on the wall. Nehemiah was ever present, with a trumpeter by his side, and the people were enjoined to hasten to him whenever the trumpet sounded. These vigilant precautions had the effect intended. The enemies knew their plot was discovered; and the great work was in a short time brought to a close. Nehemiah declares that, during the time the work was in progress, "Neither I, nor my brethren, nor my servants, nor the men of the guard which followed me, none of us put off our clothes, saving that every one put them off for washing." The whole work was completed in fifty-two days.

It might be supposed, from the precision with which the gates of Jerusalem are enumerated in Neh. iii. 1-32, that it would be easy to trace the exact direction of the wall built at that time;—and also from the existence of well known gates to the Holy City at the present day—that it would not be difficult to identify some of them with those mentioned by Nehemiah. But it is not so in either case.

It is uncertain whether all the gates of which we read in Nehemiah were in the external walls: some might be gates of the temple inside the outer boundaries. One thing seems obvious, as pointed out by Dr. Robinson (*Biblical Researches*, i. 472), that the list begins with the sheep gate; and proceeding northward, then runs westward, and so round the city back to the starting point. The position of some of them may be approximately fixed. The fountain gate would be near the pool of Siloam. Upon the northern side would be a gate towards the territory of Benjamin and Ephraim; and deriving an appellation from that circumstance. (Neh. xii. 39.) It might correspond with the site of the present Damascus gate. The Valley gate and the Dung gate are not indicated with any precision. Robinson thinks the Valley gate might correspond with the *Gennath* of Josephus. He also thinks the Dung gate must be looked for on the south side of the city. No writer has added anything of importance to what the American traveller has written on the subject.

There is still a Dung gate at Jerusalem. It was open and used some years ago, but is now closed, being in a neglected and filthy part of the city. I remember that when I saw it, there was an accumulation of rubbish in the neighbourhood, amidst wild and entangling growths of the prickly pear. Topographers do not identify the gate with that named by Nehemiah, yet, if Robinson's idea be correct, here may be the spot on which it stood. Yet against this it may be said, that though called by Englishmen, the *Dung gate*, it is by the inhabitants named *Bâb el Mughâribeh*, the gate of the Western Africans: and, moreover, it never was an entrance of any magnitude, as it only leads down to a village called *Siloam*. Josephus mentions a gate named *Bethso*, which corresponds in meaning with the Hebrew for Dung gate; but that stood south of *Hippicus* on the western brow of the Hill of Zion. Tradition reports that the modern St. Stephen's gate is the old Sheep gate, from its contiguity to the temple, whither sheep were driven for sacrifice; but that cannot be correct, as the city wall north of the temple was not erected until five centuries after the restoration under Nehemiah.

S.

ABUSES RECTIFIED

Nehemiah 5-13

NEHEMIAH'S office, as royal cup-bearer, was not only most honourable, but must have been highly lucrative. This is shown by the fact that he was able, probably without any serious detriment to his fortune, to gratify his own generous and patriotic feelings, by declining to receive the dues and supplies for his table to which he was entitled, and which former governors had received. He defrayed the whole expenses of his government out of his own private purse. This must have been at a great cost; for he not only maintained a large and liberal establishment, but entertained a hundred and fifty of the principal Jews frequently, if not daily, at his table; besides that on him devolved the expense of receiving and providing for the Jews who were continually coming into the city of their fathers from foreign parts. Some idea of his expenditure in victuals alone may be formed from his own statement: "Now that which was prepared for me daily, was one ox, and six choice sheep: also fowls were prepared for me; and once in ten days store of all sorts of wine. Yet for all this required not I the bread of the governor, because the bondage was heavy upon this people." This indicates a large expenditure, —heavy for a private purse, and probably equal to that of some of the later kings. But it reads small beside the greatness of Solomon; and the comparison might suggest some curious reflections as to the relative condition of the nation at the two periods. Solomon required for his household daily thirty oxen and a hundred sheep, "besides harts, and roebucks, and fallow deer, and fatted fowl."

Cares still more painful than those connected with the restoration of the wall soon engaged the attention of the Tirshatha. Usury, that great trade in money for which the Jews ever since the captivity have been notorious, was found to be in full vigour in Judah; and as there had been of late much scarcity, those who had any command of money reaped a rich harvest from the exigencies of their brethren. Some had sold or pledged the liberty of their children; others had mortgaged their fields, their vineyards, their houses—the heritage of their fathers; others had borrowed money at extortionate interest to pay the king's taxes. Thus, in various ways, the body of the people were ground to powder, and all their available possessions went to add riches to the rich.

The grievance became intolerable; and the wretched people, whose confidence in Nehemiah gained strength every day, ventured to bring their complaints before him. His anger, when he heard of these doings, was very great, and he felt the necessity of dealing with this great evil in the bulk. After having, therefore,

sharply rebuked the magistrates and chief persons for the sanction they had given to this disgraceful traffic, he convoked a general assembly of the people. He then set forth the wrong of this oppression in such forcible language, that no one ventured to answer him, or to gainsay his demand for the liberty of the enslaved Hebrews, the restoration of the heritages, the remission of the debts, and the foregoing of the enormous interest which had been exacted. They in fact promised to meet his views, and he made them confirm the promise with an oath. Perceiving, however, the visible, though undeclared, distaste of many to this proposal, Nehemiah significantly shook his lap, and said, "So God shake out every man from his house and from his labour that performeth not this promise, even thus be he shaken out and emptied." All the people said "Amen:" and it is gratifying to learn that every one of the persons who had subjected themselves to this censure performed his promise. The act of Nehemiah in shaking his lap, resembles that of Paul, who *shook his raiment*, and said, "Your blood be upon your own heads; I am clean." (Acts xviii. 6.) Significant acts of this kind are still very common in the East. By shaking his garment, or his lap, as if to clear it from dust, a person expresses his dissent from, or reprobation of, that which is done or asserted, and his disavowal of any responsibility in connection therewith. When performed inadvertently, in the presence of others, such acts are considered rude and ill omened, and the person who shakes his garment subjects himself to sharp reproof. In their quarrels, both men and women accompany the curses they liberally bestow on each other by the shaking of their robes, and by such expressions as, "Thus may it be with thee."

In the present day, Nehemiah's stringent measures would be regarded as an interference with the rights of property and of trade. But it is to be remembered that the Israelites were as a band of brothers, bound to assist each other freely in their distresses, and between whom such dealings as these were expressly forbidden. Usury in the abstract—that is, the trade in money—was not, as some suppose, forbidden by the law. Jews might lend money on interest to foreigners, but not to their fellow-Israelites, not only for the reason stated, but because this employment of money is mainly an exigency of commerce; and the Hebrews were intended to be, not a commercial, but an agricultural, people, each with his own landed heritage ; and among such there could be little real need for this traffic in money. So we see that it was when they got to dwell among foreigners that they took up this trade ; and they had now to be reminded that they were not to carry it on at the expense of their brethren.

Nehemiah gladly co-operated with Ezra, who still survived and acted as a great teacher of the law, in all his efforts for the instruction of the people, and the restoration of the Mosaic institutions. A large portion of the Book of Nehemiah is occupied with an account of the revival of the great and beautiful Feast of Tabernacles ; preceded, on this occasion, by the public reading of the law at the commencement of the ecclesiastical new year. This reading was, by the law, to take place at the commencement of every seventh year ; but the wholesome custom seems to have fallen into entire disuse, until thus revived. It was done with great solemnity, and with an earnest desire that the people should be really instructed. The fact was, however, that during the captivity the people had materially altered their language ; and although the pure old Hebrew was cultivated by and known to the learned, the mass of the people spoke the Chaldee dialect, which resembled the Hebrew pretty nearly, but was still so different from it as to render the old language only partially intelligible to those who knew the Chaldee merely. So was Chaldee unintelligible to those who knew only the Hebrew, of which we have a remarkable instance in the time of Hezekiah, when the Chaldean general Rabshakeh refused to deliver his insulting speech in Chaldee (which it would from this appear the nobles of Judah understood), but persisted in speaking in Hebrew, avowedly that the people, who crowded the walls, might understand what he said. Now the case is reversed ; and the people understand Chaldee, but cannot follow the Hebrew. And here also it may be noted, that the present handsome alphabetical character, in which Hebrew manuscripts are written and books printed, and which is probably more gratifying to the eye and more pleasant to a reader than any other alphabetical character in existence, was borrowed from the Chaldeans during the captivity, the old Hebrew character being far less handsome. This older character

was, however, retained by the Samaritans in their copies of the law; and it is hence known as the Samaritan character. Thus it curiously happened that the old people obtained a new written character, while the old form remained in possession of the new people.

It is clear that simply to read the books of the law in Hebrew would have been an unprofitable service ; and yet Ezra did not feel authorized to translate the lections off-hand into Chaldee : in fact, the Jews never have read the books in their public services in other than the sacred language. To meet this difficulty, Ezra, standing upon a raised platform of wood with several Levites, read the law out in pure Hebrew, which was translated, sentence by sentence, to the people by the Levites into the vernacular tongue. Some, indeed, deny that the Hebrew was at this time unintelligible to the people, and hence urge that the Levites did not *translate* what Ezra read, but made it intelligible by an explanation of all the difficult passages. It seems to us that, if the language of the people was then in such a state that not long after, as all admit, Chaldee became the vernacular tongue, that tongue must even at this time have been so much more familiar to them than pure old Biblical Hebrew, as to have rendered some verbal explanations of the latter indispensable, if the people were to be " made to understand" what Ezra read. Those who have looked to the case of languages in a state of transition, will feel assured that much of what was read could not be understood by the people, owing to differences of pronunciation, of vowels, and of termination, as well as from the occurrence of words and phrases which had gone out of colloquial use, and had been exchanged for Chaldean words and forms of speech ; and such will conceive that the Levites' labour of love consisted in repeating from different sides of the platform, to the people around, what Ezra read in Hebrew, with the substitution of the corresponding Chaldee for such words and expressions as they felt to be in that language not easy for the hearers to understand. Whether they besides gave any exposition of the text, is a different question. They may have done that also ; and it is not unlikely that they did, considering how ignorant of the law the people had become. The scene must altogether have been highly impressive and interesting,—the more so, as it seems to have become the model of the synagogue services.

That it made a salutary impression upon the minds of the people, is shown by the zeal and gladness of heart with which they forthwith applied themselves to the celebration of the long neglected Feast of Tabernacles; and once more the picturesque booths of green boughs appeared in their courts and upon their house-tops.

The public reading and explanation of the Holy Scriptures among the Jews are intimately connected with the *synagogue* services. It may, therefore, be interesting to add a note regarding the probable origin and history of synagogues.

Tradition has traced the origin of synagogues to the patriarchs, and affirms that they were commonly used as places of worship and public instruction during the whole existence of the nation under the judges, kings, and governors. Of this, however, there is no evidence. Scripture history affords no indication of any regularly constituted public service among the Jews, except that of the temple, down to the time of the Babylonish captivity. Then, when the temple was destroyed, and the temple-worship temporarily abolished, the Jews were accustomed to meet in the land of their exile for public prayer. Ezekiel appears to have frequently assembled the elders and people for instruction and worship in his house in Babylon (viii. 1; xx. 1; xxxiii. 31). Ezra observed the same custom of public assembly (viii. 15), and established it in Palestine after the return from captivity. The *Law* was probably read; and as most of the people had forgotten their ancient language, the Hebrew original was translated orally by persons appointed for that purpose. This is indicated in Neh. viii. 8: "So they read in the book, in the law of God, distinctly, *and gave the sense, and caused them to understand the reading.*"

It would seem that at first the Law, or Pentateuch, was the only portion of Scripture read in the synagogue; and it was divided into fifty-four *parshiyoth*, or "sections," so that the whole might be completed in a year. At the time of the persecutions of Antiochus Epiphanes, the reading of the Law was forbidden in the synagogues of Palestine; and then the second division of the sacred books, namely, *the Prophets*, was arranged in fifty-four lessons, and substituted for the *parshiyoth*. When freedom of worship was again established, the reading of the *Law* was resumed, while that of the *Prophets* was still retained; hence we find the statement in Acts xiii. 15: "And after the reading of the Law and the Prophets, the rulers of the synagogue sent unto them, saying, Ye men and brethren, if ye have any word of exhortation to the people, say on." And in the same chapter it is affirmed that the Scriptures were thus read in the synagogues of Jerusalem every Sabbath-day. Such public and systematic readings and explanations of the Law and the Prophets to the people in the synagogues, must have made Scripture doctrine and history familiar to the great body of the Jewish people. Wherever the Jews had a colony or community, they had one or more synagogues; and in these the Gospel was first preached by the apostles of our Lord. We find synagogues in Syria, Egypt, Asia Minor, and Greece; and these formed at once the commencement, and to some extent the models, for the first Christian churches in those countries.

P.

THE PERSIAN COURT

Esther 1-2

NEHEMIAH was not the only Jew who rose to high office at the Persian court. A still higher office than his—no less than that of prime minister—had, before him, and even before Ezra, been held by Mordecai. The deeply interesting story of the chain of providential circumstances by which this man was led to that eminent station, is recorded in the Book of Esther. A story so familiar in all its details to every reader, needs not to be recapitulated in order to connect the remarks we have to offer on some of its circumstances.

The king who figures in this history is called Ahasuerus, and it has been much disputed to which of the Persian kings the name is in this instance applied. It is generally agreed that the king who sent, first Ezra, and then Nehemiah, to Jerusalem, is Artaxerxes Longimanus; and although kings anterior to either have been named, the real alternative seems to lie between this king and his predecessor, Xerxes. We do not mean to enter into this question; but there is some force in the consideration that the character given of the king in Esther has few traits in common with that of Artaxerxes Longimanus, but has more points of agreement with that which the Greek historians assign to his father. "The king who scourged and fettered the sea, who beheaded his engineers because the elements destroyed their bridge over the Hellespont, who so ruthlessly slew the eldest son of Pythius because his father besought him to leave him as the sole support of his declining years, who dishonoured the remains of the valiant Leonidas, and who beguiled the shame of his defeat by such a course of sensuality that he publicly offered a reward for the invention of a new pleasure,—is just the despot to divorce his queen because she would not expose herself to the gaze of drunken revellers,—is just the despot to devote a whole people, his subjects, to indiscriminate massacre; and by way of preventing that evil, to restore them the right of self-defence, and thus to sanction their slaughtering thousands of his other subjects."[1]

The history opens with the account of a magnificent feast which the king gave, in the third year of his reign, to the princes and nobles of all parts of his empire, which lasted a hundred and eighty days,—followed by one of seven days to all the people of the metropolis, held in the court of the palace garden. The description of this feast, which is given fully, corresponds to the statements of ancient Persian luxury and magnificence which the Greek authors have sent down to us, and which they state to have been remarkably evinced in their banquets. Their sumptuousness in this respect, indeed, became proverbial. The vast numbers of persons entertained at their great feasts, as well as the long continuance of these feasts, are points noticed by ancient writers. The Persian kings are recorded to have often feasted as many as five thousand men at once, each time at the expense of two hundred talents. On the march to Greece, those who required to provide for the king and the companions of his table were ruined, though they tarried but a night; and this not more from the number to be entertained than from their luxurious and extravagant habits, which gave occasion to the sarcasm of Megacreon of Abdera, who called upon the people to bless the gods that it was not the custom of king Xerxes to take two meals in one day; for, had they been called upon to provide dinner as well as supper, they must either have fled at his approach, or have remained to be utterly ruined.[2]

The duration of this feast is, however, very extraordinary. It continued for half a year, as the Persian year consisted of 360 days. There are few examples of any festivals of such long duration. The apocryphal book of Judith records that Nabuchodonosor, the Assyrian, after his victory over Arphaxad, banqueted all his army, comprising a multitude of men out of various nations, a hundred and twenty days at Nineveh.[3] The most remarkable parallel instance of protracted and abundant feasting is that of a Gaul, named Ariamnes, who undertook to feast all the Gaulish nation for an entire year. And he per-

formed his promise; for he caused tents, each capable of containing 300 men, to be pitched at regular distances on all the principal roads, keeping in each of them boilers furnished with all kinds of meats in abundance, as well as vessels full of wine, and a great number of attendants to wait upon the guests and supply all their wants.[1] The occasion of Ahasuerus' great feast is not known. Some think it was to commemorate the dedication of Susa as one of the royal capitals. Those who identify the king with Xerxes, suppose that we have here the festivity in which the king sought, after his return, to drown in himself and others the keen sense of his disgrace. Perhaps the fact, that the feast was held in the third year of the king's reign, may receive an illustration from the custom of China, where the three years' mourning for the deceased king precludes any public festivity, but on the expiry of that period, the reigning monarch holds a great and sumptuous festival to celebrate his inauguration.

Some may be surprised to read of *queens*—first Vashti and then Esther—in the court of Persia. But this is in conformity with ancient history, from which we learn that the king had many wives, one of whom was chosen by him to fill the rank of queen, to whom all the others rendered the profoundest respect, amounting to something very like adoration, as to their mistress, and whose rank was, like that of the king, indicated by a purple band rayed with white, around the head. This was the usage also in some near countries; for we read that Monimia, the wife of Mithridates, was strangled with her own diadem.

One cannot but sympathise with poor queen Vashti, in her refusal to appear before the drunken king and his jovial compotators, especially when we consider the gross indecorum, according to Eastern notions, of a lady being, under any circumstances, constrained to appear before strangers. Great, however, as must have been her astonishment and indignation at such a demand, it could scarcely equal that which her refusal to obey, even to the most unreasonable extent, the summons of the king of kings must have inspired. That any one should dare to say nay to him, whose will was, in the strongest sense, law to all about him, was a

---

[1] Art. "Ahasuerus," in the *Cyclopædia of Biblical Literature*.

[2] *Herodotus*, vii. 118-120. [3] *Judith*, ii. 15.

[1] See Athenæus (iv. 13), whose book (*Deipnosophis*) is the great storehouse for facts relating to ancient festivity and good cheer.

thing of which it would have seemed treasonable to an ancient Persian even to dream; and here the refusal was sent back to the king in the presence of all the high lords of his realm. We have no doubt that this unheard-of and terrible audacity sobered them all most completely. We do not ourselves wonder, that when the king's high council, his "wise men," came to consider the matter, they decided that Vashti must have her diadem taken from her. They saw, also, that the question was one of near interest to themselves; for if it went abroad, as it was sure to do, that the queen had flatly refused to obey even the king of kings, what had they and the other princes of the land to expect in their own families from the example, if this high crime were not condignly punished? But one is amazed at the infantine simplicity of these famous sages, in recommending the issue of a royal decree, in all the languages of this great empire—"that every man should bear rule in his own house!" This is undoubtedly one of the most amusing things in all history. One cannot but imagine the inextinguishable burst of shrill merriment, which rung through every one of "the hundred and twenty-seven" provinces of the Persian empire, when this sage decree was promulgated.

All these strange matters did, however, but pave the way, in the mysteries of the Divine providence, for the advancement of a Jewish orphan maiden to a post which qualified her to be of high service to her people in a time of great peril. Her name was Hadassah (myrtle), or Esther; and she was worthy of that name, for it is recorded of her, that she was not only perfect in beauty, but that she "obtained favour in the sight of all them that looked upon her;" and it is beautifully noted, that when in the harem of the great king, she still forgot not the guide of her youth, her cousin and adopted father: "For Esther did the commandment of Mordecai, like as when she was brought up with him." She had been a good while in the harem before the purple circlet was placed on her fair brow; and it is affecting to read that her cousin, who might see her face no more after she had entered there, walked daily to and fro before the court of the harem, "to know how Esther did, and what would become of her." This he could do through the eunuchs who went in and out, and by whom also messages and kind inquiries could and did

pass between them. Yet it was not known that Esther was of Jewish parentage, as her cousin had, for some reason or other, desired her not to disclose the fact. This was no doubt providential, as it prevented Haman from being so much on his guard in his plot to destroy the Jews, as he would have been, had he been aware of the queen's connection with that people.

Twenty-two centuries have passed away since the splendid scenes in the Court of Persia were enacted, as described in the Book of Esther; but some years since, certain enterprising travellers in that country, discovered what appear to be the remains of the palace of Ahasuerus—lighting upon the bases of the columns, to which silken draperies from Oriental looms were attached in that monarch's day, in all their bravery. Mounds, fragments of marble, bricks, vases, little relics, and heaps of dust, are all that remain of Shushan the palace. Humiliating mementos are they of the pride, pomp, and pageantry of him who reigned "from India even to Ethiopia, over a hundred and seven and twenty provinces." With that wonderful capacity for restoration, exercised through the knowledge of comparative architecture, and by means of skill acquired in such investigations, forming a characteristic of modern times, Mr. Loftus, in 1852, examined the ruins; and Mr. Fergusson, following up the results with his extensive knowledge, identifies several portions according to the story in the Book of Esther! The results are described by Dr. Porter at the close of the following Illustration.

S.

PROVIDENCE

Esther 3-10

THE great man of the day in the Persian court was Haman, belonging to that nation, the Amalekites, the hereditary grudge and hatred between whom and the Jews the reader will remember. We the rather point to this circumstance, because it seems to us to supply the true explanation of the most important circumstances in the history. Thus, many explanations have been sought of Mordecai's reasons for refusing to this mighty lord the obeisance which others rendered, as he stalked forth from the presence of the king, and which was doubtless considered by all as due to his high station. That Haman was an Amalekite, seems to us a sufficient explanation. That a rigid and somewhat stiff-backed Jew should refuse the marks of reverend homage to one of that doomed and abominated race, is in the highest degree natural and probable. And, on the other hand, the same fact, if it does not adequately account for, relieves from absolute insanity, the determination of Haman to exterminate the whole nation for the affront of one individual. Had Mordecai been any other than a Jew, the favourite would doubtless have been content to wreak his vengeance upon the man whose quiet scorn provoked him so greatly; but to learn that this man belonged to the very nation which had vowed the extermination of Amalek, opened a wider scope to his vengeance. He could not but call to mind the wondrous passages of the ancient hatred between them, and which even the present demeanour of Mordecai showed to be inextinguishable; and he would then remember, that this hated and hating nation was, as it seemed, completely under his hand, being dispersed, as captives and tributary subjects, through the realm in which he had all but absolute rule. It is, under this view, explicable that the bold and murderous idea—which appeared to him a grand one, no doubt—should occur to him, of destroying the whole of this nation in one day. To attribute this determination *merely* to the personal slight from Mordecai, overlooking all these considerations, seems little less than puerile. It was simply the occasion, the exciting cause, the key that opened the gates to a sweeping flood of old hatreds and vengeances.

Haman had only to obtain the king's consent; and the light and careless way in which the monarch placed at his disposal the lives of tens of thousands of his industrious and useful subjects, is perhaps the most shocking example of Oriental despotism on record. If he had not been wilfully blind and besotted—and he was probably drunk,—the extravagant sum which Haman offered to pay in compensation for the loss to the royal revenue by their destruction, ought to have awakened his suspicion that Haman was not, as he pretended, seeking the public good, but the gratification of a private vengeance. If it were "not for the king's profit" to suffer this people to live, it was preposterous that the minister should pay so heavily from his own purse for the realization of a public benefit. But the truth no doubt is, that the king cared nothing about it; and even when at length he is brought to see Haman's real motives, which were transparent at the first, and he turns upon his

guilty favourite in a passion of "virtuous" indignation, his wrath is roused, not by his having been so nearly led into the perpetration of a tremendous crime, but by Haman having dared to contemplate the destruction of a race *to which the queen belonged*, and in whose doom she might, by the letter of the decree, have been involved.

The plot seemed perfect. Everything had been well considered and well devised. Swift messengers had been sent to all the provinces, directing the slaughter of all the Jews on a given day, and even the selection of an auspicious day by lot had not been overlooked. What was wanting? Nothing that human calculation could have provided. Yet when the Lord blew upon this grand contrivance, it became as the desert sand before the wind, and overwhelmed the contriver. Even in the choice of the day by lot, we can trace the movings of the Lord's hand, for the frustration of the design. The Persians have always been greatly addicted to the arts of divination; and even at the present day, all important movements of the court are regulated with regard to astrological calculations, and propitious and inauspicious days. In this case the lot was chosen; and it seems they cast the lot for one month after another, to determine in what month the execution should fall, and then for day after day, to fix the day of the determined month. Now we doubt not that it was the Lord's doing, for the confusion of Haman, and for the accomplishment of the secret designs of His providence, that the lot was made to fix the time to the remotest possible period to be within the year, so that the execution was delayed for almost a complete year, affording time not only for the subversion of the plot at court, but for the arrival of the messengers who were despatched with the countermanding decree. It is manifest, that if the interval had been anything shorter, these messengers could not have reached the remoter provinces of an empire which stretched from India to Ethiopia, in time to prevent the execution of the first decree. It was most probably the perception of this which induced the Jews, in their annual festival in commemoration of their deliverance from national extinction, to give so much prominence to this casting of lots, for they called it the Feast of Purim—that is, the Feast of Lots. To the instructed eye, the determination of the lot is thus seen in a double sense, where to Haman only one sense appeared.

Some reflection has been cast upon the Book of Esther, on the ground that the name of God does not once occur in it. That is true: and it *is* a remarkable fact. But God HIMSELF is there, though His NAME be absent. We trace Him at every step through this wonderful book, and everywhere behold the leadings of His providence. To name one instance among many,— What was it, or rather, Who was it, that kept the king's eyes from slumber, on a night big with the doom of the Hebrew nation? Who moved him to call for the chronicles of his reign, and not to summon the tale reciter or the minstrel to beguile his waking hours? Who moved the reader to open at that part which related to the service of Mordecai in disclosing a plot against the king's life? Who quickened the king's languid attention and interest, and stirred him to inquire what rewards had been bestowed upon the man to whose fidelity he owed his life and crown? Who timed this so, that this glow of kindly feeling towards Mordecai, and the determination right royally to acknowledge his unrequited services, occurred at the very moment that Haman had arrived at the palace to ask leave to hang this very Mordecai upon a gallows fifty cubits high, which he had caused already to be set up, in the assured conviction that the king would not refuse him so trifling a request, and little thinking that he himself was destined to swing high in air upon it? Lastly, Who ordered it so, that, coming with this errand in his mouth, he was only stopped from uttering it, by an order to hasten to confer upon this Mordecai, with his own hands, the highest distinctions the king could bestow upon the man he "delighted to honour?" God not in the Book of Esther! If not there, where is He? To our view, His glory —the glory of His goodness, in caring for, and shielding from harm, His afflicted church, shines through every page.

One of the most interesting discoveries of recent times, is that of the ruins of "Shushan the palace." They were laid bare by the excavations of Mr. Loftus, in the year 1852. The city of *Susa* was, from the time of Cyrus, the winter capital of the Persian kings; and the citadel or castle of Susa is called in Scripture "Shushan the palace." It is repeatedly mentioned in the later books of Scripture. It was here Daniel saw his great vision of the ram and goat (viii. 2 *seq.*). And it was the scene of one of the most touching and romantic episodes in Jewish history—the devotion and triumph of Esther. Mr. Fergusson has, with that rare architectural skill for which he has been long celebrated, not only formed a complete plan of the great building, but he has been able to localize the leading events of Esther's story.

The palace consisted of a central hall about 200 feet square, supported by thirty-six columns, sixty feet in height. Outside the hall were three porches, each 200 feet wide by 60 deep, and supported by 12 columns. These were the audience halls of the palace; the western being probably intended for morning, and the eastern for evening, ceremonials; while the northern formed the chief throne-room, as being most sheltered from the sun.

"From what we know of the buildings at Persepolis, we may assert that the 'king's gate,' where Mordecai sat (Esth. ii. 21), and where so many of the transactions in the book of Esther took place, was a square hall, measuring probably a little more than 100 feet each way, and with its roof supported by four pillars in the centre, and that this stood at the distance of about 150 to 200 feet from the front of the northern portico. We may also be tolerably certain that the inner court, where Esther appeared to implore the king's favour (v. 1), was the space between the northern portico and this square building, the outer court being the space between the 'king's gate' and the northern terrace wall. We may also predicate, with tolerable certainty, that the 'royal house' (i. 9), and the 'house of the women' (ii. 9, 11), were situated behind this great hall to the southward. . . .

"There seems also no reasonable doubt but that it was in front of one of the lateral porticos of this building, that king Ahasuerus 'made a feast unto all the people that were present in Shushan the palace, both unto small and great, seven days, in the *court of the garden of the king's palace;* where there were white, green, and blue hangings fastened with cords of fine linen and purple to silver rings and pillars of marble: the beds were of gold and silver upon a pavement of red, and blue, and white, and block marble' (Esth. i. 5, 6). From this it is evident that the feast took place, not in the interior of any hall, but out of doors, in tents erected in one of the courts of the palace, such as we may easily fancy existed in front of either the eastern or western porches of the great central building." [1]

[1] Smith's *Bible Dictionary*, s. v. *Shushan.*

P.